1 MONTH OF
FREE
READING

at

www.ForgottenBooks.com

By purchasing this book you are eligible for one month membership to ForgottenBooks.com, giving you unlimited access to our entire collection of over 1,000,000 titles via our web site and mobile apps.

To claim your free month visit:

www.forgottenbooks.com/free1114793

ISBN 978-0-331-37980-8
PIBN 11114793

LIBRARY BLOCK, MILWAUKEE.

Public Library on Second Floor.

SYSTEMATIC CATALOGUE

INV. 1898.

OF THE

PUBLIC LIBRARY,

OF THE

CITY OF MILWAUKEE,

WITH

ALPHABETICAL AUTHOR, TITLE AND SUBJECT INDEXES

1885

MILWAUKEE

PUBLISHED BY THE BOARD OF TRUSTEES OF THE LIBRARY

1885-86

J. H. YEWDALE & SONS, PRINTERS & ELECTROTYPERS, MILWAUKEE.

DIRECTIONS FOR USE.

1. When you want to find a book by a certain **author,** look in the author-index, where a short title of the book will be given, if it is in the library, with a number referring to the column of the main catalogue, in which a full entry occurs together with the call-number of the book. If the book sought is a novel or play, it will save time to turn at once to the fiction or drama-list in the main catalogue.

2. If you only know the **title** of the book you want, but not the author, turn to the title-list of fiction for novels, and to the title-list of drama for plays. If the book does not belong to either of these classes, the title itself will frequently indicate the class where it will be found ; if not, it may be entered in the author-index, printed in roman type.

> For instance, it might be difficult to guess in what class "American archives" have been placed, but a reference to the author-index under "American" will give you the number of the column where the series is entered.

3. If you want to find the resources of the library on a certain **subject,** turn to the class in the main catalogue, in which this subject belongs. Should you be in doubt about the class, the subject-index at the end of the catalogue will give you the number of the class in which to look.

> For instance, if you want to find what books there are in the library on Ventilation, it may not occur to you to look in "Building," but under "Ventilation", in the subject-index, you will find the class-number 697, and the class-numbers printed at the top of the page in the main catalogue will guide you at once to column 461, where such books are entered.

Remember, however, always to refer back to the general classes, of which the sub-class forms a division, in order to exhaust the resources of the library on a certain subject. General works often contain the most exhaustive treatises on their component parts.

> If you want all books on birds, for instance, you must first examine the class "Birds," then go back to the division "Vertebrates," then to the main class "Zoology in general", and finally see what there may be on birds in the comprehensive works on "Natural Science," with its general subdivisions of Collected works Dictionaries, Compends, Essays, etc.

4. If you want to refer to what has been written regarding a certain **person,** turn to the index to biographies, where you will find all the biographical treatises and essays contained in the library, arranged under the name of each individual.

5. Write the call-number, which is invariably printed in heavy type, just as it is given in the catalogue, punctuation marks and all. If the work should be in more than one volume, state, in addition to the call-number, the number of the volume you want.

> For instance, if you want of Smyth's "Lectures on modern history" the volume containing the "American war" (col. 1198), write it down thus **940:28 v2.**

6. If you cannot find your book anyway, consult the librarian.

CONTENTS.

(For subdivisions, see the catalogue.)

INTRODUCTION.

THIS catalogue comprises all the works at present contained in the Milwaukee Public Library, aggregating about 35,000 volumes, and divided among the several literary classes as follows : Bibliography and general works and magazines 3234, Philosophy 474, Religion and theology 1446, Sociology, including collective documents of national, state and municipal governments 5324, Philology 219, Natural sciences 1566, Applied science and useful arts 1393, Fine arts and amusements 699, Literature in general 3778, Prose fiction 7082, Reading for children 961, History 3168, Geography, description and travels 2275, Biography 2869 volumes. In the belief that, as a rule, the title-page of a book is its own best explanation, the entries have been made as full and accurate as possible, only omitting unimportant or redundant words, and occasionally supplying an explanatory word or phrase, indicated by being placed in [brackets]. Contents have been added in all cases where the character of a book seemed to require it, and a special effort has been made to record in their proper places the important contributions to the scientific and special series published by various governments, national and local. The same attention has been paid to works published under collective titles, each component part being entered in the class to which it belongs ; but no mention has been made of magazine articles, however important, since Dr. Poole's admirable "Index to periodical literature" furnishes an adequate clue to that class of publications.

The systematic method of arrangement was adopted mainly for two reasons : a personal conviction, strengthened by previous experience in this library, that the general public is better served by a catalogue of this kind than by one arranged on the plan of a dictionary, unless it be made extreme-ly full and minute in its details, and, secondly, the necessity of providing, in a rapidly increasing library, for a printed catalogue that may be added to, as new accessions make such an addition desirable, without necessitating a reprint of the work already done or destroying the unity of the catalogue as a whole. The latter problem can be solved in no other way than by the arrangement here presented, where the main catalogue is intended to be permanent, subsequent supplements being made on the same uniform plan and paged consecutively with the old part, while the author-index will be recast with each new edition so as to refer, in one single alphabet, to the entire catalogue. By this means, it is expected that at least 100,000 volumes can be conveniently included in this catalogue, without making the use of it so burdensome, as to require a reconstruction of the whole work. It is intended to issue temporary lists of new books added to the library at regular intervals of three months, until so large a number of titles shall have accumulated, as will render the preparation of a regular supplement necessary.

The catalogue consists of three principal divisions :

1. The alphabetical **index** of authors represented in the main division, which also includes the titles of all anonymous publications (except fictitious literature, for which special provision is made), together with a large number of striking or indefinite titles, not readily suggesting the class where these works belong. For the sake of convenience, the names of learned and economical societies, and the titles of all periodical publications, not included among the general periodicals in col. 36-42, have also been added to this index. All such title entries are distinguished by being printed in the regular roman type.

2. The main catalogue, arranged systematically and following the numerical order of the shelf classification as closely as the number and character of the books in the library would permit. As to the arrangement of the works in each ultimate subdivision, no fixed rule has been observed, but in each case such an arrangement employed as seemed best suited for convenient reference in that particular class. In general, an analytical order, commencing with books on the entire subject

in question, followed by those on special branches or topics, has been most frequently used, minor distinctions being sometimes indicated by a line of asterisks (* * *). In other cases, a chronological order has been preferred, being either a "subjective-chronological" arrangement according to the date of printing (as, for instance, in Chemistry, where the oldest publications are practically useless for modern requirements), or an "objective-chronological" arrangement according to the date or period of the matters treated, which has been largely employed in the division of History and Travels. An alphabetical arrangement based on the name of the subject has been followed principally in individual Biography, and the name forming the catchword in such cases spaced so as to be more readily perceived. Where no other arrangement seemed to offer any positive advantage, the strict alphabetical order of the authors' names has been made the guide. Wherever a sharp distinction between certain works for and against was apparent, as for instance in Roman-catholicism, the books have been arranged accordingly. Geographical divisions follow the order of the scheme of classification, even if there is no heading to indicate the fact.—Included in this division of the catalogue are title-indexes of dramatic literature and prose-fiction, and an index to subjects of biography, which contains references to special works, as well as to essays, in all classes of the library, even when the biographical feature is subordinate to a general estimate of the person in question.

3. The **synopsis of classification** and alphabetical **index of subjects**. The latter gives a clue to the number of the specific class or classes, in which books on each subject have been placed or will be placed as they are received, and forms an index to the catalogue, which will, in some measure, answer the same purpose as a dictionary catalogue with its cross-references.

MINOR POINTS OF ARRANGEMENT.

A special effort has been made to enter authors' names with as much fulness and detail, as possible. Pseudonyms have been replaced by the real name, when known, with the pseudonym following immediately after it, italicized and enclosed in parenthesis, and a reference made from the pseudonym at its proper place in the alphabetical indexes. Given names and parts of surnames omitted on the title-page have been supplied, and initials expanded into the full name. The vernacular form of the names of foreigners has been used exclusively, which seems to be the only safe rule to follow in the catalogue of what will ultimately become a cosmopolitan collection of books, care being taken to represent accurately any peculiar sounds expressed in a differentiation of symbols by means of diacritical marks, in those languages that make use of the roman alphabet. The names from other languages employing a special alphabet of their own, russian, greek, arabic, etc., have been transliterated in such a manner as to express, as nearly as practicable, the actual *sounds* of the original name. For this purpose, the consonants have been used with their usual power in english, but to the vowels must be given their continental pronunciation (*a* as in *father*, *e* as *a* in *ale*, *i* as in *machine*, *u* as in *pull*). In oriental names, the rules formulated for the use of the collaborators in the "Sacred books of the east" have been followed. Any inconsistency, however, that may be noticed in the method of transliterating a particular name is attributable to the impossibility of finding, among the resources of the library, the name expressed in its original characters.

Compound english names, as a rule, have been entered under the last, and names from other languages under the first component part, with a reference from the other part, when necessary. English names with the prefix *De* or *Van* appear under the prefix, as well as french names beginning with *Le, La, L', Du, Des;* but french and other names beginning with *de* or *d'*, german names beginning with *von, vom, von der, zu, im* or *auf,* dutch names beginning with *van, van der* or *ten,* swedish names beginning with *af,* etc., must be sought under the letter immediately following the prefix. *O'* and *M', Mc* or *Mac* have been put under their initial letters, the latter names invariably arranged as if spelled out in full. German names, in which the letters *ä, ae, ö, oe,* and *u, ue,* occur, have been arranged as if spelled with the ordinary letters, *a, o* and *u,* except in the beginning of a name, where they follow the order of *Ae, Oe* and *Ue.*

English noblemen have been put under their family name, generally with a reference from their title, but the nobility of other countries have been entered under their titles. All titles of honor, whether hereditary or personal, have been printed in italics, and the proper vernacular form of each

employed, instead of a frequently inaccurate or, at the best, merely approximately correct translation. Titles of sovereign princes, however, have been given in english. A list of the foreign titles
of nobility occuring in the catalogue will be found below, arranged under the english equivalent
most nearly corresponding to each.

The capitalization of words has been reduced to a definite system of uniformity for all languages
in accordance with the evident tendency of modern catalogue work. An extravagant use of capital
letters in a catalogue, where a great number of words must be capitalized under any circumstances,
confuses the eye, instead of aiding it, and makes them meaningless. Each language has a system
of its own, differing in important particulars from the usage of other languages, which makes it
impossible to conform with any existing standard, and the following simple rule has, therefore, been
adopted as the easiest solution of the difficulty. Capitals are to be used only in proper names and at
the beginning of a new sentence or book title ; but are discarded in english adjectives and generic
nouns derived from names, such as *french, spencerian, darwinism*, etc., (with the exception of indian
and other little known tribes), and in german and danish nouns, as well as in other instances of
merely local use. The result is a system of capitalization almost identical with the present french
and swedish usage. When a capital letter does occur in this catalogue, it has a definite meaning,
either denoting the individual name of a person, a country, and so forth, or the beginning of a title
of a book or its component parts, including a new or secondary title of the same book. In practice,
however, it is sometimes extremely difficult to determine from abstract principles whether to use or
not to use a capital, and there will be noticed occasionally apparent discrepancies, for which the
only existing excuse is contained in the words of the illustrious Gibbon: "I can feel, where I cannot explain, the motives of my choice."

In conformity with the recommendations of the American Library Association, the most common masculine christian name under each letter has been abbreviated by means of a colon after the
initial, and the size marks have been given in letters, instead of the usual 8°, 12°, etc., in order to
emphasize the fact, that size, in this catalogue, means, not a certain folding of the sheet, but merely
the height of the book within a certain limit. Full explanation of these symbols and abbreviations
will be found hereafter.

BOOK NUMBERS.

The shelf-numbers, which also from the call-numbers of the books, consist of two parts, a general class-number and a place-number for each work within a class, both together forming the individual book-mark for identification. The two parts of the number are separated by a *colon* (:) or a
plus (+), the latter signifying that the book is more than 23 centimeters high and, therefore, placed
among the books that are of more than average size, on the bottom shelf of each division. All the
volumes of the same work carry the same number, and when the catalogue shows that a certain
work is published in more than one volume, it is, therefore, necessary to give, in addition to the number of the work, also the number of the particular volume desired. When the place-number is
omitted and a letter put in its stead, or a letter occurs between the class- and place-number, it shows
that the book belongs to a collection in a separate part of the library or is subject to special restrictions. Thus **L** refers to the librarian's room, **M** to the magazine, D to the public document and **Pam**
to the pamphlet collection, **R** to the reference room, and **P** signifies that the book can be taken out
only by special permission from the librarian.

In conclusion, I wish to acknowledge the intelligent zeal and faithful devotion to her work of
the deputy librarian, Miss Theresa H. West, who has for a number of years been occupied with the
preparation of the material for this catalogue. The printing commenced in May 1885 and has pro-
ceeded without interruption to the present time, the new books added to the library in the meantime
being included as the printing progressed. The first Quarterly index of new accessions, embracing
the period from january to june 1886, will comprise all works which were received too late for insertion in their proper places in this catalogue. A few works that have been put into a nearly related
class, which was not printed, rather than omit them altogether from catalogue, will be repeated in
this list.

Milwaukee Public Library,
    in june 1886.

          KLAS AUGUST LINDERFELT,
                Librarian.

TITLES OF NOBILITY.

Baron; Baroness.

Báró ; Báróné (*hungarian*).
Baron ; Baronne (*french*).
Baron ; Baronessa (*russian*).
Baron ; Baronesse (*danish*).
Freiherr, Reichsfreiherr ; Freiherrin, Freiin (*german*).
Friherre ; Friherrinna (*swedish*).

Baronet; Lady.

Chevalier, Seigneur (*french*).
Edler, Ritter ; Edle (*german*).

Count; Countess.

Comes (*latin*).
Comte ; Comtesse (*french*).
Conde ; Condesa (*spanish*).
Conde ; Condessa (*portuguese*).
Conte ; Contessa (*italian*).
Graf ; Gräfin (*german*), Grafinia (*russian*).
Grefve ; Grefvinna (*swedish*).
Greve ; Grevinde (*danish*).
Gróf ; Grófné (*hungarian*).
Hrabia ; Hrabina (*polish*).

Duke ; Duchess.

Duca ; Duchessa (*italian*).

Duc ; Duchesse (*french*).
Duque ; Duquesa (*spanish*).
Duque ; Duqueza (*portuguese*).
Herzog ; Herzogin (*german*).

Marquess ; Marchioness.

Marchese ; Marchesa (*italian*).
Markgraf ; Markgräfin (*german*).
Marques ; Marquese (*spanish*).
Marquez ; Marqueza (*portuguese*).
Marquis ; Marquise (*french*).

Prince; Princess.

Fürst ; Fürstin (*german*).
Kniaz ; Kniaginia (*russian*).
Książe ; Księżna (*polish*).
Prince ; Princesse (*french*).
Principe ; Princesa (*spanish*), Princeza (*portuguese*), Principessa (*italian*).

Viscount; Viscountess.

Vicomte ; Vicomtesse (*french*).
Visconde ; Viscondessa (*portuguese*).
Visconte ; Viscontessa (*italian*).
Vizconde ; Vizcondesa (*spanish*).

ABBREVIATIONS.

Christian names:

A: = Augustus (*eng.*, *dutch*), August (*ger.*, *dan.*, *swed.*, *pol.*), Auguste (*fr.*), Augusto (*it.*, *sp.*, *port.*), Avgust (*russ.*), Ágoston (*hung.*), Augustin (*bohem.*)

B: = Benjamin ; Beniamino (*it.*)

C: = Charles (*eng.*, *fr.*), Carl (*ger.*, *dan.*, *swed.*), Carlo (*it.*), Carlos (*port.*), Cárlos (*sp.*)

D: = David ; Davide (*it.*)

E: = Edward (*eng.*), Eduard (*ger.*, *dutch*, *dan.*, *russ.*, *bohem.*), Edvard (*swed.*), Édouard (*fr.*), Eduardo (*it.*, *sp.*, *port.*), Edvárd (*hung.*)

F: = Frederick (*eng.*), Friedrich (*ger.*), Frederik (*dutch*, *dan.*), Fredrik (*swed.*), Frédéric (*fr.*), Federigo (*it.*), Federico (*sp.*), Frederico (*port.*), Fryderyk (*pol.*), Fridrik (*hung.*)

G: = George (*eng.*), Georg (*ger.*, *dutch*, *dan.*, *swed.*), Georges (*fr.*), Giorgio (*it.*), Georgii (*russ.*), György (*hung.*)

H: = Henry (*eng.*), Heinrich, Henrich (*ger.*), Hendrik (*dutch*, *dan.*), Henrik (*swed.*, *hung.*), Henri (*fr.*), Henrique (*port.*), Heinrikh (*russ.*), Henryk (*pol.*)

I: = Isaac (*eng.*, *fr.*), Isaak (*ger.*, *dutch*, *russ.*), Isak (*dan.*, *swed.*), Isacco (*it.*), Izak (*pol.*), Izsák (*hung.*), Izaak (*bohem.*).

J: = John (*eng.*), Johann (*ger.*), Johan (*dan.*, *swed.*), Jan (*dutch*, *pol.*, *bohem.*), Jean (*fr.*), Juan (*sp.*), João (*port.*), János (*hung.*).

K: = Karl (*ger.*, *dan.*, *swed.*, *russ.*), Karel (*dutch*, *bohem.*), Károly (*hung.*).

L: = Louis (*eng.*, *fr.*), Ludwig (*ger.*, *dan.*), Ludvig (*swed.*), Lodewijk (*dutch*), Luigi (*it.*), Luis (*sp.*), Luiz (*port.*), Ludovik (*russ.*), Ludwik (*pol.*), Lajos (*hung.*), Ludvík (*bohem.*)

M: = Mark (*eng.*, *russ.*), Marcus (*ger.*, *dan.*), Markus (*dutch*, *swed.*), Marc (*fr.*), Marco (*it.*), Márcos (*sp.*), Marcos (*port.*), Marek (*pol.*, *bohem.*), Márk (*hung.*).

N: = Nicholas (*eng.*), Nikolaus (*ger.*), Nikolaas (*dutch*), Niels (*dan.*), Niklas *or* Nils (*swed.*), Nicolas (*fr.*, *sp.*), Nicolò (*it.*), Nicoláo (*port.*), Nikolai (*russ.*), Nikołaj (*pol.*)

O: = Otho (*eng.*), Otto (*ger.*, *dutch*, *dan.*, *swed.*, *bohem.*), Othon (*fr.*), Ottone (*it.*), Oton (*sp.*), Othão (*port.*) Otton (*russ.*, *pol.*), Ottó (*hung.*).

P: = Peter (*eng.*, *ger.*, *swed.*), Pieter (*dutch*), Peder (*dan.*), Pierre (*fr.*), Pietro (*it.*), Pedro (*sp.*, *port.*), Piotr (*russ.*, *pol.*), Péter (*hung.*), Petr (*bohem.*)

R: = Richard (*eng.*, *ger.*, *dutch*, *dan.*, *fr.*, *bohem.*), Rikard (*swed.*), Riccardo (*it.*), Ricardo (*sp.*, *port.*), Ritchard (*russ.*), Rikárd (*hung.*)

S: = Samuel ; Samuele (*it.*).

T: = Thomas (*eng.*, *ger.*, *dutch*, *dan.*, *fr.*, *port.*), Tomas (*swed.*, *sp.*, *russ.*), Tommaso (*it.*), Tomasz (*pol.*), Tamás (*hung.*), Tomáš (*bohem.*)

U: = Ulrich (*ger.*, *bohem.*), Ulrik (*dutch*, *dan.*, *swed*, *hung.*), Ulrikh (*russ.*), Ulryk (*pol.*).

V: = Victor (*eng.*, *dutch*, *fr.*), Viktor (*ger.*, *dan.*, *swed.*, *bohem.*), Vittore *or* Vittorio (*it.*).

W: = William (*eng.*), Wilhelm (*ger.*, *dan.*, *swed.*, *pol.*), Willem (*dutch*.)

Book sizes :

(The last letter in the description of a book and denotes height only.)

Tt. (32mo)	up to 12½	centimeter, nearly 5 inches.		
T. (24mo)	" 15	"	" 6	"
S. (16mo)	" 17½	"	" 7	"
D. (12mo)	" 20	"	" 8	"
O. (8vo)	" 25	"	" 10	"
Q. (4to)	" 30	"	" 12	"
F. (Folio)	more than 30	"		

Other abbreviations :

a.d. — anno Domini.
abth. — abtheilung.
add. — added, additions, additional.
agr. — agriculture, agricultural.
amer. — american.
anon. — anonymous.
app. — appended, appendix.
arr. — arranged.
assoc. — association.
aufl. — auflage.
augm. — augmented.
ausg. — ausgabe.
b. c. — before Christ.
bearb. — bearbeitet, bearbeitung.
biogr. — biography, biographical.
cl. — class.
col. — column.
comp. — compiled, compiler.
cont. — continued, continuation, containing.
corr. — corrected, corrections.
corresp. — correspondence.
D — public docouments collection.
del. — delivered.
dep. — department.
dir. — direction.
ed. — edited, editor.
eds. — editors.
eng. — english.
engr. — engraved, engravings.
enl. — enlarged.
estab. — established.
eve. — evening.
explan. — explanations, explanatory.
explor. — exploration.
fortg. — fortgesetzt, fortgeführt.
forts. — fortsetzung.
geogr. — geography, geographical.
geol. — geological.
germ. — german.
hist. — history, historical.

hs. — handschrift.

hss. — handschriften.

ill. — illustrated, illustrations, illustrative.

impr. — improved, improvements.

incl. — included, inclusive.

introd. — introduction, introductory.

jahrh. — jahrhundert.

L — librarian's room.

lib. — library.

lsp. — lustspiel.

M — magazine collection.

misc. — miscellaneous.

ms. — manuscript.

mss. — manuscripts.

n. d. — no date.

n. t. — no title.

no. — number.

norw. — norwegian.

obl. — oblong.

obs. — observation, observatory.

p. — page.

P — special permit required for use.

Pam — pamphlet collection.

pref. — preface, prefatory, prefixed.

prep. — prepared.

pseud. — pseudonym.

pt. — part.

pts. — parts.

pub. — published, publisher, publication.

R — reference room.

rep. — report.

rev. — revised, revision.

sel. — selected.

ser. — series.

soc. — society.

sq. — square.

ssp. — schauspiel.

supp. — supplement, supplementary.

swed. — swedish.

T. p. w. — title page wanting.

th. — theil.

tr. — translated, translator, translation.

tsp. — trauerspiel.

übers. — übersetzt.

übertr. — übertragen.

umgearb. — umgearbeitet.

v. (in names) — von.

v. (otherwise) — volume.

verb. — verbessert.

verm. — vermehrt.

Other abbreviations, such as place of publication, states, months, etc., are in common use and readily understood.

INDEX OF AUTHORS

INCLUDING

Anonymous and Indefinite Titles.

INDEX OF AUTHORS.

Entries in small type refer to contents only.

Entries in small type refer to contents only.

Entries in small type refer to contents only.

Entries in small type refer to contents only.

Carpenter, H. Mother's and kindergartner's friend. 246.
Carpenter, J. E. [Drama.] 537.
Carpenter, J. E:, *ed.* Songs. 1029.
Carpenter, M. B. Mining code. 216.
Carpenter, P. P. Mollusks of western North America. 374.
Carpenter, R. L., *see* Livermore, A. A. 66.
Carpenter, S. C. Overland journey to India. 1192.
Carpenter, S. H. English analysis 274.
— English of the 14th century. 1021.
Carpenter, W: B: Human physiology. 398.
— Mental physiology. 51.
— Mesmerism, spiritualism. etc. 53.
— Physical and vital forces. 311.
—· Unconscious action of the brain *and* Epidemic delusions. 284.
Carpenter, W: H. [Fiction.] .692.
Carpenter, W: L. Energy in nature. 311.
Carpet-bagger, A. Recollections of the Carolinas. 1380.
Carr, A. C. [Fiction.] 692.
Carr, A. E. All the way round. 1190.
Carr, L. Mounds of the Mississippi valley. 349.
Carré, M. [Drama.] 537.
— *and* J. Barbier. [Drama.] 537.
— *and* L. Battu. [Drama.] 537.
Carriere, M. Aesthetik. 465.
— Kunst- und culturentwickelung. 471.
— P: Cornelius. 1430.
Carrington, H: B. Battles of the revolution. 1351.
Carrington, K. [Fiction.] 692.
Carrol, *Mrs.* S., *see* Centlivre, S. 537.
Carroll, H. Twelve americans. 1438.
Carroll, Lewis, *pseud., see* Dodgson, C: L. 715.
Carse, G: B. Florida. 1381.
Carter, E. Poems and essays. 1547.
— *and* C. Talbot. Letters. 1079.
Carter, N. H. Letters from Europe. 1207.
Carter, R. Summer cruise. 1369.
Carter, R. B. Eyesight. 400.
Carter, S. N. Drawing in black and white. 481.
Cartoons from Punch. 482.
Cartwright, D: W. Western wild animals. 505.
Cartwright, J. Mantegna and Francia. 1531.
Cartwright, T. Diary. 1456.
Carus, C: G. King of Saxony's journey. 1230.
Carus, J. V: Bibliotheca zoologica. 24.
Caruthers, W: A. [Fiction.] 692.
Carvalho, S. N. Incidents of Frémont's last expedition. 1397.
Carver, J. Travels in Wisconsin. 1343.
— Travels through North America. 1343.
Cary, A. [Fiction.] 692.
— Lyra. 1029.
Cary, H: Great civil war in England. 1223.
Cary, H: F. Lives of the poets. 1544.
Casey, E. [Fiction.] 692.
Cashel-Hoey, F. S., *see* Hoey, F. S. Cashel-.
Caspari, O: Urgeschichte der menschheit. 346.
Cass, L. France. 1257.
— Right of search, *see* Young, W: T. 1485.
Cassagnac, *see* Granier de Cassagnac.
Casseday, D. B. [Fiction.] 692.
Cassell's book of sports 498.
— book of in-door amusements. 499.
— history of the russo-turkish war. 1291.
— history of the war between France and Germany. E. Ollier. 1259.
— household guide. 444.

Cassell's natural history. 366.
— old and new Edinburgh. 1231.
— popular natural history. 366.
Cassin, J: Birds of California, *etc.* 383.
— [Zoological papers.] 371, 373.
Castelar y Rissoll, E. Byron. 1547.
— Old Rome and new Italy. 1267. .
Castelli, I. F: [Drama.] 537. .
Castle, C. [Fiction.] 692.
Castleman, A. L. Army of the Potomac. 1359.
Castlereagh, *Viscount, see* Stewart, R., *marquess of Londonderry.*
Castner, J. Militär-lexikon. 231.
Caswall, H: Martyr of the Pongas. 1456.
Caswell, A. Meteorological observations. 332.
Caswell, E: Poems. 1029.
Catherine II, *see* Yekaterina. 1478.
Catherwood, M. H. [Fiction.] 692.
Catholic world. 78.
Catlin, G: Breath of life. 409.
— Eight years travels in Europe. 1207.
— Last rambles among the indians. 1340.
— Life among the indians. 1340.
— North american indians. 1340.
Catlin, G: L. Among the biscayans. 1206.
Caunter, H. Romance of history: India. 1301.
Caustic, *Mrs., pseud.* [Fiction.] 692.
Cavalcaselle, G. B. *joint author, see* Crowe, J. A.
Cavallius, H., *see* Hyltén-Cavallius, G. O.
Cave, W: Antiquitates apostolicæ. 118.
— Biographia ecclesiastica. 1464.
Cavendish, *pseud., see* Jones, H:
Cavendish, *Lady* C. [Drama.] 537.
Cavendish, G: Cardinal Wolsey. 1495.
Caverly, R. B. Indian wars of New England. 1369.
— Life and labors of J: Eliot. 1369.
Caxton, Pisistratus, *pseud., see* Bulwer-Lytton, E: G: E. L.
Cazelles, E. Evolution-philosophy. 353.
Cazin, A. Heat. 314.
— Wärme. 314.
Ceba, A. Citizen of a republic. 163.
Cecil, *pseud., see* Tongue, C.
Cecil, R: Visit to the house of mourning. 101.
Celebrated musicians. 1533.
Celestin, F: J. Russland. 1278.
Cellini, B. Memoirs. 1531.
Censor, *pseud., see* Bunce, O. B.
Census reports of the U. S. 157.
Centennial exhibition at Philadelphia. 391.
Centlivre, S. [Drama.] 537.
Century, *N. Y.* Bryant memorial meeting. 1540.
Century of independence. J. R. Hussey. 165.
Centz, P. C., *pseud., see* Sage, B. J.
Cervantes-Saavedra, M. de. [Fiction.] 692.
— Wit and wisdom of Don Quixote. 1134.
Cesnola, *see* Di Cesnola, L: P.
Cetshwayo's dutchman. C. Vijn. 1328.
Chadbourne, P. A. Instinct. 57.
— Waste of labor in education. 241.
Chadwick, F. E. Training systems. 234.
Chadwick, H: Sports and pastimes of american boys. 499.
Chadwick, J: W. Bible of to-day. 84.
— Liberty and the church. 73.
Chadwick, W: De Foe. 1548.
Challen, J. Igdrasil. 1029.
Chalmers, A. [Fiction.] 692.
Chalmers, T: Adaptation of nature to the moral and intellectual condition of man. 81.

Crowe, E. E. History of France. 1251.
Crowe, J. A , *and* G. B. **Cavalcasalle.** History of painting in north Italy. 487.
— Raphael. 1532.
— Titian. 1532.
Crowest, F. Great tone-poets. 1533.
Crowfield, Christopher, *pseud., see* **Stowe,** H. E.
Crowquill, Alfred, *pseud., see* **Forrester,** A. H:
Cruden, A. Concordance. 85.
Cruikshank, G: Comic almanack. 1083.
Cruise of the Corwin. 1425.
Cruisings and adventures in Italy and Africa. 1319.
Crump, A. Pretensions of H: George. 197.
Crusenstolpe, M. J. [Fiction.] 707.
Cruttwell, C: T: Roman literature. 1134.
Cubas, A. Garcia, *see* **Garcia Cubas.**
Cubitt, G: Columbus. 1517.
Cudlip, A. [Fiction.] 707.
Cudmore, P. Irish republic. 1213.
Cudworth, R. Intellectual system of the universe. 49.
Cuffe, W: U. O., *earl of Desart.* [Fiction.] 707.
Culin, E. v., *see* **Von Culin,** E. 608.
Cullerne, E:, *joint author, see* **Edwards,** C. 546.
Culross, J. W: Carey. 1458.
Cumberland, *Earl of, see* **Clifford,** E:
Cumberland, R. [Drama.]. 542.
— Memoirs. 1548.
— Observer. 1057.
Cumming, C. F. Gordon-. At home in Fiji. 1421.
— Fire fountains. 1422.
— In the Hebrides. 1231.
— In the Himalayas. 1304.
— Lady's cruise in a french man-of-war. 1422.
— Via Cornwall to Egypt. 1321.
Cumming, J: God in history. 92.
— *Same.* 73.
— God in science. 92.
— Great consummation. 95.
— Last of the patriarchs. 1463.
— Moses right and Colenso wrong. 87.
— Prophetic studies. 88.
— Romanism. 127.
Cumming, R. G. Five years of a hunter's life. 1328.
Cumming, W: G. Wild men and wild beasts. 1303.
Cummings, J. W. [Fiction.] 707.
Cummings, W: H. Purcell. 1535.
Cummins, A. M. G: D: Cummins. 1451.
Cummins, G: D: Virginia Hale Hoffman. 1451.
Cummins, M. S. [Fiction.] 707.
Cundall, J. Holbein. 1530.
Cunningham, A. [Fiction.] 707.
— British painters and sculptors. 1528.
— Sir Joshua Reynolds. 466.
— Sir Walter Scott. 1552.
Cunningham, J: W: [Fiction.] 707.
Cunynghame, *Sir* A. T. My command in south Africa. 1328.
Cunzer, C: B. [Fiction.] 707.
Cupples, G: [Fiction.] 707.
Curiosities of the search-room. 213.
Curious schools. 249.
Curran, J: P. Speeches. 189.
Curran, W: H. J: P. Curran. 1511.
Currie, J. Common school education. 244.
Currier, E:, *ed.* Political text-book. 166.
Curteis, A. M. Macedonian empire. 1174.
— Roman empire. 1180.

Curtis, B: R., *ed.* Memoir. 1485.
Curtis, G. E. [Meteorol. observations.] 331.
Curtis, G: T. Daniel Webster. 1489.
— History of the constitution. 211.
— James Buchanan. 1466.
Curtis, G: W: [Fiction.] 707.
— Bryant. 1540.
— Hawthorne. 1050.
— Howadji in Syria. 1312.
— Lotus-eating. 1376.
— Potiphar papers. 1081.
— Wendell Phillips. 1488.
Curtis, L. [Fiction.] 707.
Curtius, E. History of Greece. 1173.
Curtius Rufus, Q. Alexander the great. 1480
Curwen, H: History of booksellers. 1545.
Curwen, S: Journal and letters. 1485.
Curzon, R. Armenia. 1309.
Cusack, M. F. Daniel O'Connell. 1493.
— Present case of Ireland. 172.
Cushing, C. Reminiscences of Spain. 1273.
— Social condition of woman. 1050.
— Treaty of Washington. 171.
Cushing, F. H. Zuñi fetiches. 1340.
Cushing, L. S. Law and practice of legislativ assemblies. 225.
— Parliamentary practice. 225.
Cushing, W: Index to North american review 35.
Custer, E. B. Boots and saddles. 1396.
Custine, A. *marquis* de. [Fiction.] 708.
— La Russie. 1277.
Cutter, C: A. Library catalogues. 1.
— Rules for a dictionary catalogue. 1.
Cutter, W: Israel Putnam. 1503.
Cutts, R: D. Field-work of triangulation. 41
— *and* C: A. **Young.** Astronomical and met orological observations. 308.
Cuvier, G: L. C. F: D. *baron.* Animal kingdo 366.
— Theory of the earth. 335.
Cypress, J., *jr., pseud., see* **Hawes,** W: P.
Cyprianus, T. C. Treatises. 99.
Cyrillus, *St.* Catechetical lectures. 109.
Czaykowski, M. [Fiction.] 708.

D., J. [Fiction.] 708.
Dach, S. Gedichte. 1105.
Dacier, M. Life of Monstrelet. 1201.
DaCosta, J. M. Medical diagnosis. 408.
— Strain and over action of the heart. 409.
Dacus, J. A. Great strikes in the U. S. 198.
Daddow, S: H., *and* B: **Bannan.** Coal, iron ar oil. 428.
Dagley, R: Ludicrous in art. 481.
— Takings. 1031.
Daguet, A. Confédération suisse. 1287.
Dahlgren, M. V. [Fiction.] 708.
— Memoir of J: A. Dahlgren. 1501.
— South Mountain magic. 55.
— South Sea sketches. 1414.
Dahlmann, F: C. Geschichte von Dännemar 1282.
Dahn, F: J. F. [Fiction.] 708.
— Geschichte der deutschen urzeit. 1238.
— Urgeschichte der germanischen und roma schen völker. 1200.
Daldorne, E. [Fiction.] 708.
Dale, F. [Drama.] 543.
— *joint author, see* **Simpson,** J. P. 600.
Dale, J. S. of, *pseud., see* **Stimson,** F: J: 864.

Entries in small type refer to contents only.

Entries in small type refer to contents only.

Dun, F. American farming and food. 430.
Duncan, H: [Fiction.] 720.
— Sacred philosophy of the seasons. 81.
Duncan, J. Entomology. 368.
Duncan, P: M. Heroes of science. 1520.
— Sea-shore. 284.
— ed. Cassell's natural history. 366.
Duncker, M. W. Geschichte des alterthums. 1165.
— History of antiquity. 1165.
— History of Greece. 1174.
— Preussische geschichte. 1244.
Duncombe, J: [Essays.] 1049.
Dundonald, Earl of. see Cochrane, T:
Dunger, H. Verdeutschungen entbehrlicher fremdwörter. 277.
Dunglison, R. Human health. 401.
— Medical lexicon. 391.
Dunham, S: A. Denmark, Sweden and Norway. 1281.
— Europe during the middle ages. 1199.
— Germanic empire. 1237.
— History of Poland. 1277.
— History of Spain and Portugal. 1269.
Dunlap, W: [Fiction.] 720.
Dunlop, J: History of fiction. 513.
— Memoirs of Spain. 1272.
Dunlop, M. A. Wallace-. Glass. 452.
Dunraven, Earl of, see Quin, Sir W. T: Wyndham-.
Dunster, H: P: Times of Richard II. 1221.
Düntzer, J: H: J. Charlotte v. Stein. 1559.
— Goethe. 1556.
— Lessings leben. 1558.
— Schiller. 1559.
Dunwoody, H. H. C. Rainfall. 331.
— Weather proverbs. 331.
Duplessis, G: Wonders of engraving. 488.
Dupré, A:, joint author, see Thudichum, J: L: W:
Dupré, J. V: Atlas of Milwaukee. 1394.
Durand, A. M. C. H. [Fiction.] 720.
Durandeau, E. [Drama.] 546.
Durbin, J: P. Observations in Europe. 1207.
— Observations in the east. 1308.
Durden, Dame, pseud. [Fiction.] 720.
Durfee, C: A. Index to Harper's monthly. 35.
— Poetical concordance. 1021.
Durham, Earl of, see Lambton, J: G:
Düringsfeld, I. freiin v. Reinsberg-. [Fiction.] 720.
— Aus der Schweiz. 1288.
— Aus Italien. 1266.
— and O. freiherr v. Reinsberg-Düringsfeld. Sprichwörter. 517.
Durrie, D. S. Bibliographia genealogica americana. 1566.
— History of Madison. 1395.
— joint author, see Davis, W. B.
Duruy, V: Histoire de France. 1249.
— Histoire des temps modernes. 1201.
— Histoire du moyen âge. 1199.
— History of Rome. 1176.
Dusch, J: J. Moralische briefe. 1109.
Dussaud, Mme. —. [Fiction.] 720.
Du Terreau, —, joint author, see Clarke, H. S. 538.
Dutheil, E. [Fiction.] 720.
Dutt, S. C. Historical studies. 1158.
— India, past and present. 1308.
Dutt, Toru. Ancient ballads and legends of Hindustan. 1032.

Dutton, C. E: High plateaus of Utah. 342.
— Physical geology of the Grand Cañon district. 338.
Duveyrier, A. H. J. baron, and E. R. de Bully. [Drama.] 546.
Duyckinck, E. A: Eminent men and women. 1428.
— Geschichte des krieges für die union. 1355.
— National portrait gallery. 1437.
— and G: L. Cyclopædia of american literature. 1006.
Dwight, B: W. Modern philology. 263.
Dwight, H: O. Turkish life in war time. 1293.
Dwight, J. S. Music. 1071.
Dwight, N. Signers of the declaration. 1482.
Dwight, T. Hartford convention. 181.
Dwight, T., jr. History of Connecticut. 1374.
— ed. Garibaldi. 1507.
— joint ed., see Darby, W:
Dyce and Forster collections. W: Maskell. 470.
Dyer, T: F. T. Domestic folk-lore. 261.
— Folk-lore of Shakespeare. 1046.
Dyer, T: H: History of the city of Rome. 1176.
— Imitative art. 465.
— Modern Europe. 1201.
— ed. Pompeii. 1269.
Dymon, J. Principles of morality. 60.
Dynamic electricity. 316.

E., A. L. O., see Tucker, C. M. 879.
Eads, J. B. Naval defences. 420.
Earl, G: W. Eastern seas. 1418.
Early, J. A. Last year of the war. 1359.
Early, M. A., pseud., see Fleming, M. A. 728.
Eassie, W: Cremation. 406.
— Sanitary arrangements for dwellings. 405.
Eastlake, Sir C: L. Household taste. 484.
Eastlake, E. lady. Five great painters. 1526.
— joint author, see Jameson, A.
Eastman, J. R. Solar parallax. 307.
Eastman, M. H. [Fiction.] 720.
Eaton, C. A. Rome in the 19th century. 1268.
Eaton, D. B. Civil service in Great Britain. 229.
— Spoils system. 228.
— Tenure of office. 228.
Eaton, D. C. Ferns of North America. 362.
— Ferns of the southwest. 362.
Eaton, J: Commissioner of education reports. 240.
— Needs of the bureau of education. 241.
— What has been done by the government in aid of education. 241.
Eberhard, A: G. [Auswahl.] 1108.
Eberhardt, J: A: Synonymisches handwörterbuch. 277.
Ebering, E., ed. Bibliographischer anzeiger für romanische sprachen. 23.
Ebers, G: M. [Fiction.] 720.
— Durch Gosen zum Sinai. 1314.
— Egypt. 1320.
Ebert, F: A. Bibliographisches lexikon. 14.
— Fritz Reuter. 1558.
Eberty, F. Geschichte des preussischen staats. 1243.
Ebner v. Eschenbach, M. freiin. [Fiction.] 721.
Ecce Deus. J. Parker. 94.
Ecce homo. J: R. Seeley. 94.
Echoes from mist-land. 1114.
Eck, E. Civil-prozess-ordnung. 228.
Eckardt, J. Aus dem Petersburger gesellschaft. 1279.
— Modern Russia. 1278.
— Russland vor und nach dem kriege. 1279.

Fawcett, H: Free trade and protection. 205.
— Political economy. 193.
Fawcett, M. G. Political economy. 193.
— Tales in political economy. 193.
Faxon's handbook to Saratoga, *etc.* 1342.
Fay, A. Music-study in Germany. 496.
Fay, T. S. Dreams and reveries. 1061.
Featherstone, J. L. [Drama.] 548.
Featherstonhaugh, G: W: Canoe voyage up the Minnay Sotor. 1386.
— Elevated country between Missouri and Red rivers. 340.
— Excursion through the slave states. 1377.
Federalist, The. 210.
Feiling, C. A., *joint tr., see* **Oxenford,** J: 819.
Feldborg, A. A., *comp.* Poems from the danish. 1144.
Felkin, R. W., *joint author. see* **Wilson,** C: T.
Fellows, H: P. Boating trips. 1369.
Fels, *pseud., see* **Bäuerle,** A. 673.
Fels, Egon. *pseud., see* **Herbert,** J. 755.
Felton, C. C. Familiar letters from Europe. 1208.
— Greece, ancient and modern. 1171.
— W: Eaton. 1438.
Fénelon. [Fiction.] 727.
— Ancient philosophers. 1445.
— Christian counsel. 103.
— Education of a daughter. 248.
— Reflections and meditations. 101.
— Spiritual letters. 103.
Fenn, C: Compendium of the funds. 156.
Fenn, G. M. [Fiction.] 727.
Fenn, *Sir* J:. *ed.* Paston letters. 1221.
Fenton, H. T., *joint author, see* **Cooper,** T: V.
Fenwick, T:, *and* T: **Baker.** Subterraneous surveying. 428.
Ferdinand ***. [Fiction.] 727.
Féréal, M. V. de, *pseud, see* **Suberwick,** *Mme.* 868.
Fergus historical series. 1387.
Ferguson, A. History of civil society. 151.
Ferguson, R. Works. 1032.
Ferguson, S: [Fiction.] 727.
Fergusson, J. Archaeology in India. 475.
— History of architecture. 473.
— Parthenon. 475.
— Temple of Diana. 475.
— Topography of Jerusalem. 1311.
— Tree and serpent worship. 138.
Fern, Fanny. *pseud., see* **Parton,** S. P.
Ferrall, J. S., *see* **Larson,** A. L.
Ferrel, W: Barometric hypsometry. 419.
— Discussion of tides. 304.
— Meteorological researches. 330.
— [Papers on physical geography.] 331.
— Ratio between diameter and circumference. 299.
Ferrier, D: Functions of the brain. 400.
Ferrier, S. E. [Fiction.] 727.
Ferrier de Tourettes, A. Belgium. 1286.
Ferris, *Mrs.* B: G. Mormons at home. 140.
Ferris, G: T. German composers. 1583.
— Great singers. 1534.
— Great violinists. 1533.
— Italian and french composers. 1533.
Ferry, B: Recollections of Pugin. 1529.
Ferry, Gabriel, *pseud. for* **Bellemarre,** E. L: G. de Ferry de. [Fiction.] 675.
— Vagabond life in Mexico. 1410.
Fetherstonhaugh, M. G. [Fiction.] 727.
Fetridge, W. P., *ed.* Harper's hand-book. 1204.
Feuchtwanger, L. Gems. 323.

Feudge, F. R. India. 1301.
Feuerbach, L: A. Essence of christianity. 91.
— Sämmtliche werke. 48.
Feuerbach, P. J. A. *ritter* v. Criminal trials. 223.
Feuillet, O. [Drama.] 548.
— [Fiction.] 727.
Féval, P. H: C. [Fiction.] 727.
— *joint author, see* **Bourgeois,** A. A. 526.
Fichte, I. H. J: G. Fichte. 1447.
Fichte, J: G. Characteristics of the present age. 48.
— Destination of man. 1108.
— Literarischer briefwechsel. 1123.
— Science of knowledge. 48.
— Science of rights. 60.
Ficklin, J. Algebra. 297.
Field, B: R. Medical thoughts of Shakespeare. 1046.
Field, D: D. International code. 209.
Field, G: Grammar of colouring. 485.
Field, H: M. Among the holy hills. 1313.
— From Egypt to Japan. 1190.
— From the lakes of Killarney to the Golden Horn. 1190.
— On the desert. 1314.
— Summer pictures. 1209.
Field, *Mrs.* H: M. Home sketches. 1259.
Field, K. [Drama.] 548.
— C: Albert Fechter. 1537.
Field, M. B. Memories of men and women. 1432.
Field, Michael. *pseud.* [Drama.] 548.
Fielding, H: [Drama.] 548.
— [Fiction.] 727.
Fields, A., *mrs.* J. T: [Fiction.] 727.
— How to help the poor. 235.
Fields, J. T: Biographical notes. 1540.
— Underbrush. 1061.
— Yesterdays with authors. 1007.
Fields, *Mrs.* J. T:, *see* **Fields,** A.
Fielt, C. [Fiction.] 727.
Figg, R. W. Where men only dare to go. 1360.
Figuier, G. L: Human race. 349.
— Mammalia. 384.
— Ocean world. 369.
— Primitive man. 346.
— Reptiles and birds. 381.
— Tomorrow of death. 84.
— Vegetable world. 357.
— World before the deluge. 343.
Fillmore, J: C. Pianoforte music. 496.
Financial reform almanack. 157.
Findlay, C. [Fiction.] 727.
Finlay, G: History of Greece. 1287.
Finley, J: P. Tornadoes. 331.
Finley, M. [Fiction.] 728.
Finotti, J. M. Bibliographia catholica. 22.
Firdausi. Epic of kings. 1148.
First century of the republic. 1348.
Fischel, E: English constitution. 162.
Fischer, E. K. B. Geschichte der neuern philosophie. 46.
— Spinoza. 1448.
Fischer, F: E. Verbandlehre. 410.
Fischer, G: Krankheiten des halses. 411.
Fischer, H. Verletzungen durch kriegswaffen. 410.
Fischer, J: H: L. [Fiction.] 728.
— Schlachtengemälde. 1190.
Fischer, K: Deutschland's öffentliche meinung. 123.
— Politik und diplomatie im reformations-zeitalter. 1202.
— Volks-gesundheitspflege. 405.

Numbers refer to columns in the main catalogue.

Numbers refer to columns in the main catalogue.

Entries in small type refer to contents only.

Entries in small type refer to contents only.

Gilder, W: H. Ice-pack and tundra. 1426.
— Schwatka's search. 1425.
Gildersleeve, B. L. [Philological essays]. 245.
Giles, C. Who was Jesus Christ ? 93.
Giles, E. A. [Fiction.] 735.
Giles, H: Christain thought on life. 101.
— Human life in Shakespeare. 1046.
— Illustrations of genius. 1062.
Giles, H. A., *ed.* Gems of chinese literature. 1148.
Gilfillan, G: Martyrs of the scottish covenant. 123.
— Modern literature and literary men. 1007.
— Poets and poetry of the Bible. 1146.
Gilfillan, J. The sabbath. 115.
Gill, T. Scientific libraries. 1.
Gill, T. N: Bibliography of fishes. 25.
— Families of fishes. 380.
— Families of mammals. 384.
— Families of mollusks. 374.
— Insectivorous mammals. 386.
— [Papers on fishes.] 380.
— *and* E. Coues. Bibliography of north amer. mammals. 25.
Gill, W: F. Poe. 1542.
Gill, W: J: River of golden sand. 1299.
Gillespie, T: [Fiction.] 735.
Gillet, R. H. Federal government. 227.
Gillett, E. H. J: Huss. 1460.
— Presbyterian church in the U. S. 128.
Gilliat, E. [Fiction.] 735.
Gillies, J: Whitefield. 1459.
Gilliss, J. M. Astronomical observations. 308.
— Chile. 1417.
— Magnetical and meteorol. observations. 317.
— Naval astronomical expedition. 296.
— Solar eclipse, july 18, 1860. 309.
— Total eclipse. 1858. 308.
Gillmore, P. Great thirst land. 1329.
— Hostile Africa. 1329.
— Prairie and forest. 505.
Gillmore, Q. A. Limes, cements and mortars. 460.
— Siege of Ft. Pulaski. 420.
Gillow, J. Bibliographical dictionary of english catholics. 1442.
Gilly, W: S. Felix Neff. 1461.
Gilman, A. History of the american people. 1345.
— Kings, queens and barbarians. 1159.
— Tales of the pathfinders. 1349.
Gilman, B. I. Operations in relative number. 44.
Gilman, C. [Fiction.] 735.
— Poetry of travelling in the United States. 1365.
Gilman, D. C. James Monroe. 1466.
Gilmor, H. Four years in the saddle. 1360.
Gilmore, J. R. Down in Tennessee. 1378.
— James A. Garfield. 1467.
Gilmour, J. Among the mongols. 1299.
Gindely, A. Dreissigjähriger krieg. 1238.
— Thirty years' war. 1238.
Ginx's baby. E: Jenkins. 1082.
Giraldus de Barri *Cambrensis*. Historical works. 1211.
Girard, C: Fresh water fishes of North America. 380.
— [Papers on fishes.] 371, 372.
— *joint author, see* Baird, S. F.
Girardin, D. [Drama.] 551.
— [Fiction.] 735.
Girault, A. N. Vie de Washington. 1465.
Giseke, H: L: R. [Fiction.] 735.

Gladden, W. Christian league of Connecticut. 105.
— Working people and their employers. 197.
Gladstone, J: H. Michael Faraday. 1521.
Gladstone, W: E. Bulgarian horrors, *etc.* 192.
— "Ecce Homo". 93.
— Gleanings of past years. 191.
— Hellenic factor in eastern problem. 192.
— Homer. 1137.
— Homer and the Homeric age. 1137.
— Montenegro. 189.
— Rome. 192.
— Vatican decrees. 192.
Glasbrenner, A. [Fiction.] 735.
— Neuer Reinecke Fuchs. 1116.
— Die verkehrte welt. 1116.
Glasenapp, C: F: R: Wagner. 1536.
Glaser, A. [Fiction.] 735.
Glaubrecht, J. [Fiction.] 735.
Glaubrecht, Otto, *pseud., see* Oeser, R. L: 819.
Glazier, W. American cities. 1364.
— Battles for the union. 1357.
— Heroes of three wars. 1499.
— Three years in the federal cavalry. 1360.
Gleanings from natural history. 285.
Gleed, C: S. From river to sea. 1399.
Gleich, F: [Fiction.] 735.
Gleig, G: Primitive church. 117.
Gleig, G: R. [Fiction.] 735.
— Battle of Waterloo. 1257.
— Essays. 1062.
— History of the Bible. 84.
— Der leichte dragoner. 1504.
— Sir T: Munro. 1505.
Gleim, J: W: L: Anthologie. 1109.
— Lessing, Wieland, Heinse. 1555.
Glengall, *Earl of, see* Butler, R: 533.
Glenn, S: Tornado near Huron, Dak. 331.
Gliddon, G: R., *joint author, see* Nott, J. C.
Glogau, B. [Fiction.] 735.
Glück, E. Romancero. 1116.
Glümer, C. v. [Fiction.] 735.
Glynn, J. Construction of cranes. 415.
— Power of water. 426.
Gneist, R. Englisches verwaltungsrecht. 162.
— Self-government. 162.
Goadby, E. England of Shakespeare. 1233.
Goadby, H: Vegetable and animal physiology. 345.
Gobat, S: Life and work. 1456.
— Residence in Abyssinia. 1323.
Gobrecht, J. C., *ed.* National home at Dayton. 235.
Göckingk, L. F: G. v. Anthologie. 1109.
— Episteln. 1106.
Gödeke, K: Grundrisz zur geschichte der deutschen dichtung. 1104.
Godfrey, *Mrs.* G. W. [Fiction.] 736.
Godin, Amélie, *pseud., see* Linz, A. 789.
Godkin, E. L. Office-holding aristocracy. 228.
Godkin, G. S. Victor Emmanuel. 1477.
Gödsche, H. O. F: [Fiction.] 736.
Godwin, P. Bryant. 1539.
— Cyclopædia of biography. 1428.
— History of France. 1252.
— Organization. 1071.
— Political essays. 184.
Godwin, W: [Fiction.] 736.
Goethe, J: W. v., *see* Göthe, J: W. v.
Goetschy, G. [Drama.] 551.
Gogol, N: V. [Fiction.] 736.

Entries in small type refer to contents only.

Grove, W: R.—*Continued.*
— Correlation of physical forces. 311.
Grube, A: W: Biographische miniaturbilder. 1430.
— Heroes of history and legend. 1199.
— *ed.* Charakterbilder. 1151.
— - Geographische charakter-bilder. 1183.
Gruber, F. J. [Fiction.] 740.
Gruber, Ludwig, *pseud., see* Anzengruber, L. 666.
Grün, Anastasius, *pseud., see* Auersperg, A. A., *graf* v.
Grund, F. J. Position of Europe. 161.
Grundy, S. [Drama.] 554.
Grüner, L: E. Manufacture of steel. 455.
Gryphius, A. Werke. 1105.
Guarasci, C. Coast defense. 420.
Guard, T: Christianity and the age. 72.
Guardian. 1049.
Gubitz, F: W: Lachender ernst. 1125.
Gudrun. 1113, 1114.
Guénot, C., *abbé.* [Fiction.] 740.
Guérin, E. de. Journal. 1561.
— Letters. 1130.
Guermante, C. [Fiction.] 740.
Guernsey, A. H. Emerson. 1447.
— *and* H: M. Alden. Harper's history of the rebellion. 1354.
— *and* I. P. Davis. Health at home. 401.
Guernsey, L. E. [Fiction.] 740.
— Jenny and the birds. 382.
— Jenny and the insects. 376.
Guerrazzi, F. D. [Fiction.] 740.
Guest, E. English rhythms. 276.
Guest, M. J. History of England. 1216.
Guhl, A: Schule und heer. 231.
Guhl, E., *and* W: Koner. Leben der griechen und römer. 1171.
— - Life of the greeks and romans. 1171.
Guhrauer, G. E:, *joint author, see* Danzel, T. W:
— *see also* Mackie, J. M. 1447.
Guiccioli, T. G. *contessa, see* Boissy, T. G.
Guide to selecting plays. 498.
Guides for science teaching. 283.
Guild, R. A. James Manning. 1453.
— Librarian's manual. 13.
Guillemin, A. V: Comets. 303.
— The heavens. 301.
— The sun. 304.
— Wonders of the moon. 304.
Guillemot, J. [Drama.] 554.
Guirey, G: [Fiction.] 740.
Guischard, W. K. [Fiction.] 740.
Guise, *Mrs.* F. [Fiction.] 740.
Guizot, F. P: G. Actual state of christianity. 119.
— Character and influence of Washington. 1465.
— Charlemagne and the Carlovingians. 1252.
— Civilization in Europe. 151.
— Corneille. 1561.
— English revolution. 1222.
— Essence of christianity. 98.
— Francis I and the 16th century. 1253.
— History of civilization. 151.
— History of England. 1216.
— History of France. 1250.
— Memoirs. 1496.
— Monk. 1493.
— Monk and Washington. 1499.
— Oliver Cromwell. 1222.
— Origin of representative government. 160.
— Outlines of history of France. 1250.

Guizot, F. P: G.—*Continued.*
— Richard Cromwell. 1222.
— St. Louis and the 13th century. 1252.
— Shakespeare and his times. 1045.
— *and* H. de Witt. History of France. 1250.
Guizot, H., *see* Witt, H. de.
Guizot, P., *see* Witt, P. de.
Gulielmus *Malmesburiensis.* Chronicle of the kings of England. 1220.
Güll, F: Kinderheimath in liedern. 1116.
Gumpert, T. v., *see* Schober, T. v.
Günderode, K. v., *and* E. v. Arnim. Correspondence. 1124.
Gundling, J. [Fiction.] 740.
— Aus Frankreich. 1260.
Gunning, W: D. Life-history of our planet. 335.
Gunnison, J: W. The mormons. 140.
Günther, A. C: L: G. Study of fishes. 380.
Günther, J: C. [Gedichte.] 1116.
— Gedichte. 1105.
Gurney, E. Power of sound. 493.
— Wagner and Wagnerism. 468.
Gurney, J. J: Habitual exercise of love to God. 100.
Gurney, R. Natural religion. 72.
Gurowski, A. *comte* de. America and Europe. 164.
— Diary. 1360.
— Russia as it is. 1278.
Gurteen, S. H. Charity organization. 235.
Guseck, Bernd v., *pseud., see* Berneck, C: G. v. 676.
Gushington, Angelina, *pseud., see* Cooke, C. W. R.
Gusserow, A. Neubildungen des uterus. 411.
Gustaf III, *king of Sweden.* [Drama.] 554.
Gustafson, A. Foundation of death. 66.
Gustafson, Z. Genevieve Ward. 1537.
Gustafsson, R: A. [Fiction.] 740.
Gustav vom See, *pseud., see* Struensee, G. K: O: v. 868.
Guthrie, F: First book of knowledge. 284.
Guthrie, F. A. [Fiction.] 741.
Guthrie, T: The gospel in Ezekiel. 109.
— The parables. 90.
Guthrie, W: Christian's great interest. 100.
Guttmann, O. Aesthetic physical culture. 515.
— Gymnastics of the voice. 400.
Guttmann, P. Physical diagnosis. 408.
Gutzkow, K: F. [Drama.] 554.
— [Fiction.] 741.
— Börne's leben. 1555.
— Briefe aus Paris. 1261.
— Gesammelte werke, b. 1. 1116.
— Oeffentliche charaktere. 1432.
— Philosophie der that und des ereignisses. 1149.
Gutzlaff, C: F: A: Chinese history. 1297.
— Voyages along the coast of China. 1298.
Guyon, J. M. Method of prayer. 103.
— Way to God. 103.
Guyot, A. H: Creation. 80.
— Directions for meteorological observations. 331.
— Earth and man. 323.
Guyot, Y. Social economy. 193.
Gwilt, J. Encyclopædia of architecture. 473.
Gwinner, W: Schopenhauer's leben. 1447.
— Schopenhauer und seine freunde. 1447.
Gwynfryn, *pseud., see* Miller, O. T.
Gwynne, T. [Fiction.] 741.
Gyllembourg-Ehrensvärd, T. K. [Fiction.] 741.
Gymnastics without a teacher. 404.

Entries in small type refer to contents only.

Entries in small type refer to contents only.

Entries in small type refer to contents only.

Entries in small type refer to contents only.

Numbers refer to columns in the main catalogue.

Hosmer, G: W. People and politics. 160.
Hosmer, J. K. [Fiction.] 762.
— The color-guard. 1360.
— German literature 1101.
— Samuel Adams. 1484.
— *Same.* 1384.
Hosmer, W: H: C. Poetical works. 1034.
Hospitalier, E. Modern applications of electricity. 316.
Hotten, J: C. Thackeray. 1553.
— *ed.* Original lists of emigrants. 1566.
— *joint author, see* Sadler, L. R.
Houdin, R. J: E. Memoirs. 1538.
Hough, F. B. Forestry. 438.
— Periodical phenomena in plants and animals. 332.
— Report on forestry. 439.
Hough, G. W. Velocity of the electric current. 315.
Houghton, *Lord. see* Milnes, R: M.
Houghton, G: Niagara. 1084.
Houghton, R. C. Women of the orient. 152.
Houghton, W. R. American politics. 165.
House, E: H. Japanese episodes. 1330.
House documents and reports. 175.
House manager. 444.
Household amusements. 499.
Household conveniences. 445.
Household economy. 445.
Household narrative of current events. 1162.
Household words. C: Dickens, *ed.* 1090.
Housman, R. F. Robert Housman. 1456.
Houssaye, A. Life in Paris. 1262.
— Men and women of the 18th century. 1431.
— Philosophers and actresses. 1432.
Houwald, C. E. *freiherr* v. Leuchtthurm. 1108.
Hovelacque, A. Science of language. 263.
Hovey, H. C. Celebrated american caverns. 327.
Hovgaard, A. Nordenskiöld's voyage. 1426.
How, T: Y. Vindication of the protestant episcopal church. 128.
How a penny became £1000. 198.
How to make up. 498.
Howard, B. W. [Fiction.] 762.
— One year abroad. 1247.
Howard, E: [Fiction.] 762.
Howard, H: Lectures on painting. 485.
Howard, H:, *earl of Surrey.* Poetical works. 1034.
Howard, J: Experiences and opinions. 405.
Howard, J. B., *joint author, see* Pitman, B:
Howard, L. O. Chalcididæ. 379.
Howard, O. O. Nez Percé Joseph. 1440.
Howe, E. W. [Fiction.] 762.
Howe, H: American mechanics. 1524.
— Historical collections of Virginia. 1379.
Howe, J. Burdett. [Drama.] 559.
Howe, J: B. Common sense, mathematics and metaphysics of money. 200.
— Monetary and industrial fallacies. 200.
— Mono-metalism and bi-metalism. 200.
— Political economy in the use of money. 200.
Howe, Joseph W. Winter homes for invalids. 333.
Howe, Julia W. Later lyrics. 1034.
— Margaret Fuller. 1540.
— Trip to Cuba. 1413.
Howe, M. [Fiction.] 762.
Howe, M. A. [Fiction.] 762.
Howe, M. A. De W. Physical theory of development. 98.
Howe, W. W. Pasha papers. 1095.
Howel, J. Epistolæ Ho-Elianæ. 1077.

Howell, E. E. Geology of Utah, Nevada, *etc.* 342.
Howell, G: Conflicts of capital and labour. 199.
Howell, J: [Fiction.] 762.
Howell, J. L. [Fiction.] 762.
Howell, J: W. Electric light by incandescence. 316.
Howells, W: D. [Drama.] 559.
— [Fiction.] 762.
— Italian journeys. 1267.
— Poems. 1034.
— Rutherford B. Hayes. 1467.
— Three villages. 1065.
— Tuscan cities. 1268.
— Venetian life. 1268.
— *ed.* Little girl among the old masters. 481.
Howgate, H: W. Polar colonization. 1422.
Howison, G: H. Analytic geometry. 300.
Howison, R. R. History of Virginia. 1379.
Howitt, A. M., *see* Watts, A. M.
Howitt, M. [Fiction.] 763.
— Ballads. 1034.
— History of the U. S. 1347.
— Songs of animal life. 1025.
— With the birds. 1025.
— With the flowers. 1025.
— *ed.* Pictorial calendar. 1065.
Howitt, W: [Fiction.] 763.
— German student life. 250.
— History of the supernatural. 54.
— Homes and haunts of British poets. 1233.
— Land, labor and gold. 1420.
— Rural life of England. 1065.
— Visits to remarkable places. 1233.
— *and* M. Literature of northern Europe. 1141.
Howson, J: S., *joint author, see* Conybeare, W: J:
Hoy, P. R. Cold-blooded vertebrates of Wisconsin. 379.
— Fish of Wisconsin. 433.
— Lepidoptera of Wisconsin. 378.
— Woods of Wisconsin. 433.
Hoyer, E., *joint author, see* Brelow, G.
Hoyle, American. W: B. Dick. 500.
Hoyt, J. K., *and* A. L. Ward. Cyclopædia of practical quotations. 517.
Hoyt, J: W. Report on education. 240.
— University progress. 247.
Hoyt, R. Sketches of life and landscape. 1034.
Hozier, H: M. Seven weeks' war. 1239.
Hubbard, F: H. Opium habit and alcoholism. 410.
Hubbard, F. M. W: Richardson Davie. 1438.
Hubbard, H. P. Newspaper directory. 33.
Hubbard, J: N. Red Jacket. 1410.
Hubbard, L. L. Woods and lakes of Maine. 1370.
Huber, J. N. Kirchlich-politische wirksamkeit des jesuiten-ordens. 119.
Huber, V: A. Pope and council. 114.
Huber-Liebenau, T. v. Kunstgewerbe. 388.
— Verfall des zunfthumes. 388.
Hubert, L: F. Ausgewählte erzählungen. 1109.
Hübner, J. A. *freiherr* v. Sixtus V. 1462.
Hübner, O: Geographisch-statistische tabellen. 155.
Huc, E. R. Christianity in China. 116.
— Through Tartary, Thibet and China. 1299.
— Through the Chinese empire. 1299.
Hudson, E. H. History of the jews in Rome. 1169.
Hudson, F: Journalism in the U. S. 1006.
Hudson, H: N. Lectures on Shakespeare. 1045.
— Studies in Wordsworth. 1021.
Hudson, M. [Fiction.] 763.
— Alice and Phœbe Cary. 1540.

Entries in small type refer to contents only.

Hutchinson, E. Music of the Bible. 86.
Hutchinson, E. M. Songs and lyrics. 1034.
Hutchinson, H. Thought-symbolism. 274.
Hutchinson, Louisa. In tents in the Transvaal. 1329.
Hutchinson, Lucy. Col. Hutchinson. 1505.
Hutchinson, T: Diary and letters. 1487.
— History of Massachusetts. 1371.
— Witchcraft delusion of 1692. 54.
Hüter, C: Septikämische und pyämische fieber. 410.
— Tracheotomie. 411.
Huth, A. H: H: T: Buckle. 1546.
Hutton, B. Castles and their heroes. 1229.
— Tales of the saracens. 1308.
Hutton, J. James and Philip Van Arteveld. 1285.
Hutton, L., joint author, see Waters, C. E.
Hutton, R: H. Sir Walter Scott. 1552.
Huxley, T: H: Administrative nihilism. 354.
— American addresses. 286.
— Anatomy of invertebrated animals. 373.
— - of vertebrated animals. 379.
— Crayfish. 375.
— Critiques and addresses. 286.
— Hume. 1447.
— Introductory. 281.
— Lay sermons. 286.
— Man's place in nature. 351.
— More criticisms on Darwin. 354.
— Origin of species. 354.
— Physiography. 325.
— Science and culture. 286.
— Yeast. 284.
— and W: J. Youmans. Physiology and hygiene. 399.
Hyatt, A. Hydroids, corals, etc. 283.
— Mollusks. 283.
— Pebbles. 283.
— Sponges. 283.
— Worms and crustacea. 283.
Hyde, A. M. Washington. 1465.
Hyde, E: earl of Clarendon. Life and correspondence. 1491, 1492.
— Rebellion and civil wars in England. 1223.
Hyde, E. W. Skew arches. 413.
Hyltén-Cavallius, G. O., joint author, see Stephens, G:
Hymns of the ages. 104.
Hyndman, H: M. Socialism in England. 203.

Ibsen, H: [Drama.] 559.
Ideville, H: comte d'. Marshall Bugeaud. 1507.
Iffland, A: W: [Drama.] 560.
Ihering, R. v. Struggle for law. 208.
Ihne, W: Early Rome. 1178.
— History of Rome. 1178.
Ilanor, see Sigmund v. Ilanor.
Illustrations of the history of art. 472.
Illustrirte mannsperson. 1125.
Im Thurn, see Thurn, E. F. im.
Imbert de Saint Amand, A. L. baron. Madame de Girardin. 1560.
Immermann, K: L. [Drama.] 560.
— [Fiction.] 765.
In the polar regions. 325.
In the temperate regions. 325.
In the tropics. J. W. Fabens. 1413.
Inchbald, E. [Drama.] 560.
— [Fiction.] 765.
Index society publications. 21.
Induction coils. 325.
Ingelow, J. [Fiction.] 765.

Ingelow, J.—Continued.
— [Poetical works.] 1034.
Ingersleben, E. v. [Fiction.] 766.
Ingersoll, C: J. Second war between the U. S. and Great Britain. 1352.
Ingersoll, E. [Fiction.] 766.
— Birds'-nesting. 358.
— Country cousins. 367.
— Crest of the continent. 1401.
— Friends worth knowing. 367.
— Knocking round the Rockies. 1401.
— Old ocean. 328.
— Oyster industry. 444.
Ingersoll, L. D. History of the war department. 233.
— ed. Explorations in Africa. 1317.
Ingham, Col. Frederic. pseud., see Hale, E: E.
Ingle, E: Local institutions of Virginia. 1334.
— Parish institutions of Maryland. 1334.
Inglis, H: D: [Fiction.] 766.
Inglis, J. Nepaul frontier. 1304.
Ingoldsby, Thomas. pseud., see Barham, R: H.
Ingraham, E: D. Capture of Washington. 1352.
Ingraham, J. H. Pillar of fire. 106.
Ingraham, S. R: Mrs. M. Prior. 1453.
Ingram, J: H. Claimants to royalty. 1468.
— Haunted homes. 1230.
— Edgar Allan Poe. 1542.
— Memoir of Poe. 1017.
Ingulphus. Chronicles of the abbey of Croyland. 1220.
Innes, T: Ancient inhabitants of Scotland. 1213.
Intelligencer. 1049.
Inter-oceanic canal and Monroe doctrine. 171.
Iowa state board of health reports. 397.
Irby, A. P., joint author, see Sebright, G. M. lady.
Ireland, A. Book-lover's enchiridion. 509.
— Emerson. 1447.
Ireland, J: Hogarth illustrated. 488.
Ireland, J. N. Mrs. Duff. 1537.
Irish eloquence. 189.
Irons, W. J. The national church. 72.
Irvine, W: see Washington, G: 1080.
Irving, F. B. [Fiction.] 766.
Irving, J., comp. Book of scotsmen. 1444.
Irving, J: T. [Fiction.] 766.
Irving, P: M. Life and letters of W. Irving. 1541.
— Same. 1014.
Irving, R. D. Copper-bearing rocks of Lake Superior. 339.
— Same. [Summary.] 338.
Irving, T. Conquest of Florida. 1349.
Irving, W. [Fiction.] 766.
— Astoria. 1403.
— Bonneville's adventures. 1397.
— Christmas in England. 1095.
— Columbus. 1517, 1518.
— Crayon miscellany. 1095.
— Goldsmith. 1549.
— History of New York. 1084.
— Mahomet and his successors. 1463.
— Norsemen. 1050.
— Sketch book. 1095.
— Spanish papers. 1095.
— Washington. 1465.
— Works. 1014.
Irvingiana. 1541.
Irwin, E: [Drama.] 560.
Isaacsohn, S. Preussisches beamtenthum. 228.
Isaiah, tr. by R. Lowth. 88.

Numbers refer to columns in the main catalogue.

Entries in small type refer to contents only.

Entries in small type refer to contents only.

Numbers refer to columns in the main catalogue.

Entries in small type refer to contents only.

Entries in small type refer to contents only.

Entries in small type refer to contents only.

Entries in small type refer to contents only.

Mathiot, G: Electrotyping operations. 453.
Mathison, F: v. Anthologie. 1108.
Mathison, G: Religion of China. 133.
Matsell, G: W. Rogue's lexicon. 273.
Matson, N. Pioneers of Illinois. 1387.
Matthæus Paris, (eng. Matthew Paris). English
    history. 1221.
Matthews, C., comp. Hiawatha. 144.
Matthews, J. B. [Fiction.] 799.
— French dramatists. 1128.
— Home library. 510.
— Theatres of Paris. 498.
— comp. Poems of american patriotism. 1024.
— and H: C. Bunner. [Fiction.] 799.
Matthews, Wash. Hidatsa indians. 1342.
— Navajo silversmiths. 1340.
— Navajo weavers. 1340.
Matthews, W:, joint author, see Perkins, F: B. 1.
Matthison, A. [Drama.] 570.
Mätzner, E: English grammar. 275.
Maudsley, H: Body and mind. 53.
— Body and will. 57.
— Physiology and pathology of mind. 52.
— Physiology of mind. 52.
— Responsibility in mental disease. 53.
Maundevile, Sir J: Voiage and travaile. 1193.
Maupas, C. É. de. The coup d'état. 1258.
Maurer, G: L: v. Dorfverfassung in Deutsch-
    land. 213.
— Markenverfassung in Deutschland. 213.
— Städteverfassung in Deutschland. 213.
Maurer, K. Island. 1282.
— Isländische volkssagen. 142.
Maurice, F:, ed. F: Denison Maurice. 1456.
Maurice, J: F: D. Morality and divinity. 73.
— Religions of the world. 133.
— Social morality. 65.
Maurice, Jacques, pseud., see Morris, J. W.
Maurice, Walter, pseud., see Besant, W.
Mauris, M., marchese di Calenzano. French men
    of letters. 1560.
Maury, J: S. Principles of eloquence. 515.
Maury, L: F. A., joint author, see Quérard,
    J. M. 19.
Maury, M. F. Physical geography. 325.
— Physical geography of the sea. 328.
Maverick, A:, joint author, see Briggs, C: F.
Mavor, W: Universal history. 1153.
Maxton, J: Engineering drawing. 483.
Maxwell, C. [Fiction.] 799.
Maxwell, J. C. Electricity and magnetism. 315.
— Matter and motion. 311.
— Theory of heat. 315.
Maxwell, J: S. The czar, his court and people.
    1210.
Maxwell, M. E. [Fiction.] 799.
Maxwell, P. [Fiction.] 801.
Maxwell, W: H. [Fiction.] 801.
Maxwell, Sir W: Stirling-. Don John of Austria.
    1202.
May, A. Swedish grammar. 278.
May, C. Poems. 1036.
May, G. Bibliography of electricity. 24.
May, Sophie, pseud., see Clarke, R. S. 696.
May, Sir T: E. Constitutional history of Eng-
    land. 162.
— Democracy in Europe. 164.
Mayer, A. M. Sound. 313.
— ed. Sport with gun and rod. 503.
— and C: Barnard. Light. 314.
Mayer, B. Mexican history and archæology.
    1409.

Mayer, B.—Continued.
— Mexico. 1408.
Mayer, C: Media of exchange. 201.
— Mercantile manual. 450.
Mayer, J. R. Celestial dynamics. 311.
— Forces of inorganic nature. 311.
— Mechanical equivalent of heat. 311.
Mayer, K: F: H. Ludwig Uhland. 1559.
Mayers, C: G: Mendota. 1036.
Mayhew, A:, and S. Edwards. [Drama.] 570
Mayhew, A: H. and H: [Fiction.] 801.
Mayhew, E:, and G. Smith. [Drama.] 570.
Mayhew, H: [Drama.] 570.
-- Boyhood of Luther. 1460.
— German life and manners. 1247.
— London characters. 1236.
— London labour and London poor. 1236.
— Peasant-boy philosopher. 1521.
— Wonders of science. 1521.
— Young Benjamin Franklin. 1486.
Mayhew, I. Popular education. 239.
Maynard, C. J. Taxidermy. 358.
Maynard, F., ed. Zouave before Sebastopo
    1276.
Mayo, A. D. National aid to education. 242.
— Symbols of the capital. 1376.
Mayo, I. F. [Fiction.] 801.
Mayo, W: S. [Fiction.] 801.
Mayr, G: Gesetzmässigkeit im gesellschaft
    leben. 155.
Mayrhofer, C: Sterilität. 411.
Mazade, C: de. Cavour. 1497.
Mazarin, Duchesse de, see Saint Évremon
    1129.
Mead, E. D. Philosophy of Carlyle. 47.
Mead, P: B. American grape culture. 438.
Meade, G: G. Lake survey. 419.
Meade, L. T., see Smith, E. T. 856.
Meade, W: Old churches of Virginia. 126.
Meadow, A. [Drama.] 570.
Meadows, K. Heads of the people. 1085.
Mearns, A. Bitter cry of outcast London. 20
Mears, D. O. Jubilee sabbath of Piedmo
    church. 110.
Mears, J: W. Bible in the work-shop. 64.
— Heroes of Bohemia. 1460.
Mechanic's magazine. 390.
Meddlhammer, J: B. v. [Drama.] 570.
Mediæval tales. 515.
Medical and surgical history of the war of th
    rebellion. 393.
Meding, J: F. M. O. [Fiction.] 801.
— Memoiren. 1558.
Medley, G: W. England under free trade. 205.
— Reciprocity craze. 205.
Medwin, T: Conversations with Byron. 154
Meech, L. W. Intensity of the heat and light
    the sun. 325.
Meek, F. B. Palæontology. 343.
— [Palæontological papers.] 314.
— and F: V. Hayden. Palæontology of th
    upper Missouri. 344.
Megerle, U., see Abraham a S. Clara.
Mehring, F. Deutsche socialdemokratie. 20
Meier, E:, tr. Morgenländische anthologie. 114
— - Sakuntala. 1148.
Meigs, J. F. Sanitary care of children. 404.
Meikle, J. Solitude sweetened. 101.
Meilhac, H:, and L: Halévy. [Drama.] 570.
Meinhold, I. W: [Drama.] 571.
Meinhold, J: W: [Fiction.] 801.
Meissner, A. [Fiction.] 801.

Entries in small type refer to contents only.

Entries in small type refer to contents only.

Montor, A. F. de, *see* **Artaud de Montor.**
Moodie, S. Roughing it in the bush. 1407.
Moody, W: G. Land and labor in the U. S. 198.
Moon, G: W. Dean's english. 271.
Moore, Annie, *and* L. D. **Nichols.** Overhead.
 301.
Moore, Arthur, *joint author, see* **Hancock,** W:
 555.
Moore, C: H. Elementary practice in delinea-
 tion. 481.
Moore, C. J. Sensible etiquette. 262.
Moore, E: [Drama.] 573.
Moore, F. Women of the war. 1500.
— *ed.* American eloquence. 181.
— — Anecdotes of the war. 1356.
— — Diary of the revolution. 1351.
— — Patriot preachers of the revolution. 108.
— — Rebellion record. 1355.
— — Songs and ballads of the revolution. 1024.
Moore, F. F. [Fiction.] 806.
Moore, G: Power of the soul. 52.
— Use of the body. 52.
Moore, H. N. Gen. Anthony Wayne. 1503.
Moore, J: Society and manners in France,
 Switzerland and Germany. 1206.
— — in Italy. 1266.
Moore, J., *jr.* Outlying Europe. 1205.
Moore, J. B. Governors of New Plymouth. 1481.
— *joint author, see* **Farmer,** J:
Moore, J. S. Pre-glacial man. 347.
Moore, R. Universal assistant. 387.
Moore, T: Epicurean. 806.
— History of Ireland. 1211.
— Irish gentleman in search of a religion. 126.
— Letters to James Power. 1552.
— Life of Byron. 1547.
— Life of R: B. Sheridan. 1553.
— Memoirs, journal and correspondence. 1552.
— [Poetical works.] 1037.
Moore's handbook of Canada. 1407.
Morais, H: S. Eminent israelites. 1432.
Moran, C: Money. 201.
Mordecai, A. Military report. 232.
More, H. [Drama.] 573.
— [Fiction.] 806.
— Letters to Z. Macaulay. 1080.
— Works. 1016.
More, M. Mendip annals. 1512.
More, R. J. Under the Balkans. 1294.
More, *Sir* T: Selection from his works. 1097.
Moreau, L. I. E. L., P. **Siraudin** *and* A. C. L.
 Delacour. [Drama.] 573.
Morehouse, C. B. Kindergarten. 246.
Morehouse, G: R., *joint author, see* **Mitchell,** S:
 W.
Morell, J. D. Speculative philosophy of Europe.
 47.
Morey, W: C. Roman law. 224.
Morfill, W: R. Russia. 1278.
— Slavonic literature. 1145.
Morfit, C., *joint author, see* **Booth,** J. C.
Morford, H: Sprees and splashes. 1085.
Morgan, A. Shakespearean myth. 1048.
— Some Shakespearean commentators. 1048.
Morgan, H. H. Topical Shakesperiana. 1045.
Morgan, J: H., *and* J: T. **Barber.** Aurora bore-
 alis. 330.
Morgan, L. H: Ancient society. 152.
— Houses and house-life of amer. aborigines. 1342.
— League of the Iroquois. 1341.
— Systems of consanguinity and affinity. 350.

Morgan, N. D. [Fiction.] 807.
Morgan, S. *lady.* [Drama.] 573.
— [Fiction.] 807.
— Autobiography. 1552.
— Salvator Rosa. 1532.
— *joint author, see* **Morgan,** *Sir* T: C. 807.
Morgan, *Sir* T: C. *and Lady* S. [Fiction.] 807.
Morgan, W: F. Christ's espousal of the lost. 93.
Morgans, W: Mining torts. 430.
Morice, F. D. Pindar. 1140.
Morier, J. [Fiction.] 807.
Morier, R. B. D. Agrarian legislation of Prussia. 203.
Mörike, E: [Fiction.] 807.
Morin, A. Histoire politique de la Suisse. 1287.
Morin, A. J. Fundamental ideas of mechanics.
 312.
Morison, J. C. Gibbon. 1549.
— Macaulay. 1551.
Morley, F: Michigan and its resources. 1389.
Morley, H: [Fiction.] 807.
— English literature. 1004.
— — in the reign of Victoria. 1005.
— Palissy, the potter. 1562.
— *ed.* King and commons. 1024.
Morley, J: Burke. 1491.
— Richard Cobden. 1492.
— Diderot. 1560.
— Diderot and the encyclopædists. 1561.
— Rousseau. 1562.
— Voltaire. 1448.
Morley, S. [Fiction.] 807.
Morning, Richard, *pseud., see* **Zeising,** A. 901.
Morrell, B: Four voyages. 1190.
Morrill, P. Atmospheric electricity. 331.
Morris, B. F., *comp.* Memorial to Abraham
 Lincoln. 1467.
Morris, C: D. [Philological essays.] 266.
Morris, E: Farming for boys. 430.
— How to get a farm. 429.
Morris, E: E. Age of Anne. 1225.
Morris, F. O. British birds. 382.
— Dogs and their doings. 441.
— Nests and eggs of british birds. 382.
Morris, G. Correspondence and miscellaneous
 papers. 1487.
Morris, G: S. British thought and thinkers.
 1446.
— Kant's Critique of pure reason. 49.
Morris, J: G. Lepidoptera. 378.
Morris, James W. K. N. Pepper. 1085.
Morris, J: W. Andrew Fuller. 1458.
Morris, Peter, *pseud., see* **Lockhart,** J: G.
Morris, R: English accidence. 275.
— English grammar. 275.
— *and* H: C. **Bowen.** English grammar exer-
 cises. 275.
Morris, W: Earthly paradise. 1037.
— Hopes and fears for art. 469.
— Sigurd the Volsung. 1037.
Morris, W: G. Report on Alaska. 1404.
Morris, W: O. French revolution. 1257.
Morrison, M. J., *comp.* Songs and rhymes for
 the little ones. 1025.
Morrison, R: J. Grammar of astrology. 54.
Morse, C. F. [Fiction.] 807.
Morse, E: S. First book of zoology. 369.
Morse, J. Amer. universal geography. 1182.
Morse, J: T., *jr.* Alexander Hamilton. 1486.
— Famous trials. 222.
— John Adams. 1465.
— John Quincy Adams. 1466.
— Thomas Jefferson. 1465.

Müller, W:, *1794–1827*. Griechen l eder. 1118.
Müller, W: Kaiser Wilhelm. 1474.
— Political history. 1203.
— Politische geschichte. 1203.
Müller, W: (*Frater Jocundus*). Schabiade. 1118.
Müller, W: [Konrad Hermann]. Mittelhoch-
　　deutsches wörterbuch. 276.
Müller *von der Werra*, F: K. Buch der lieder.
　　1118.
Müller *von Halle*, K: Albrecht v. Haller. 1444.
— Buch der pflanzenwelt. 358.
Müller *von Königswinter*, W. [Fiction.] 809.
— Johann von Werth. 1118.
Mullinger, J. B. Schools of Charles the great.
　　243.
— *joint author, see* Gardiner, S: R.
Müllner, A. [Dramen.] 1108.
Munby, A. J. Dorothy. 1037.
Münch, E. Geschichte von Portugal. 1272.
Münch-Bellinghausen, E. F. J. *freiherr* v.
　　[Drama.] 577.
Mund, E. D., *pseud., see* Pechammer, E. v. 823.
Mundt, C. [Fiction.] 809.
Mundt, T. [Fiction.] 811.
— Italienische zustände. 1267.
Munger, T. T. Freedom of faith. 110.
Munro-Butler-Johnstone, H. A., *see* Johnstone.
Münter, B. Conversion and death of Struensee.
　　1498.
Munter, Jeremias, *pseud., see* Fornell, B. E:
　　729.
Murdoch, J. E: Patriotism. 1097.
— Plea for spoken language. 515.
— The stage. 498.
Murdock, D: [Fiction.] 812.
Mure, W: Language and literature of ancient
　　Greece. 1136.
Murfree, M. N. [Fiction.] 812.
Murger, H: [Fiction.] 812.
Murphy, A. [Drama.] 577.
— Life and genius of S: Johnson. 1015.
Murphy, *Lady* B. E. M. A. Down the Rhine.
　　1248.
— *Same.* 1206.
Murphy, J. Travels in Portugal. 1274.
Murphy, J. J: Habit and intelligence. 345.
Murphy, J: M. Rambles in north-western Ame-
　　rica. 1399.
— Sporting adventures in the far west. 505.
Murray, A. M. Letters from the U. S. 1344.
Murray, A. S. Greek sculpture. 479.
— Manual of mythology. 185.
Murray, C: A: [Fiction.] 812.
Murray, D: C. [Fiction.] 812.
Murray, E. C. G. [Fiction.] 812.
— Doine. 143.
— Russians of today. 1278.
Murray, G., *joint author, see* Hipkins, H. T.
Murray, H. British America. 1405.
— *and others.* British India. 1302.
— - Encyclopædia of geography. 1181.
Murray, J. A. H., *ed.* English dictionary. 272.
Murray, N: Letters to J: Hughes. 127.
— Men and things. 1208.
— Preachers and preaching. 105.
Murray, R. Marine engines. 417.
Murray, T: C. Origin and growth of the psalms.
　　1146.
Murray, W: [Drama.] 577.
Murray, W: H. [Drama.] 577.

Murray, W: H: H. Adventures in the wilder-
　　ness. 1376.
Musäus, J: K: A: [Fiction.] 812.
— Ausgewählte werke. 1108.
— Deutsche volksmährchen. 1108.
— Legends of Number Nip. 141.
Muskerry, W: [Drama.] 577.
Musset, L: C: Alfred de. [Drama.] 577.
Musset, Paul E. de. [Fiction.] 812.
— Alfred de Musset. 1562.
— *Same.* 1560.
Mützelburg, A. [Fiction.] 812.
Muzzey, A. B. Men of the revolution. 1438.
My cave life in Vicksburg. A lady. 1360.
My opinions and Betsy Bobbett's. M. Holley. 1084.
Myers, F: W: H: Wordsworth. 1554.
Myers, J. F. Industrial training for girls. 240.
Myers, P. V. Remains of lost empires. 1297.
Mylius, Otfried, *pseud., see* Müller, K: 809.

N., B. The jesuits. 119.
Naaké, J: T. Slavonic fairy tales. 142.
Nachtseiten der gesellschaft. 222.
Nack, J. [Drama.] 577.
Nadaillac, *Marquis* de. Pre-historic America.
　　318.
Nadal, E. S. Essays. 1070.
— London social life. 1235.
Napier, C: O. G. Lakes and rivers. 284.
Napier, H. D. F. Shores of the Mediterranean.
　　1193.
Napier, H: E: Florentine history. 1264.
Napier, M. Selection from [his] correspondence.
　　1080.
Napier, *Sir* W: F. P. War in the Peninsula. 1272.
Napoléon I. Correspondence. 1130.
— Letters and despatches. 1130.
— Table talk and opinions. 1130.
Napoléon III. Julius Cæsar. 1508.
Napoleon gallery. 1476.
Napoleonic ideas. 161.
Napp, R:, *and others.* Argentine Republic. 1416.
Nares, E: [Fiction.] 813.
— *joint author, see* Tytler, A. F.
Nares, *Sir* G: S. Voyage to the Polar sea. 1425.
Nares, R. Glossary to Shakespeare. 273.
Narrey, C: [Drama.] 577.
Näs, A. *and* J. [Fiction.] 813.
Nasby, Petroleum V., *pseud., see* Locke, D: R.
Nash, W. Two years in Oregon. 1404.
Nasmyth, J. Autobiography. 1525.
Nason, E., *and* T: Russell. Henry Wilson. 1489.
National almanac. 156.
National board of health reports. 394.
Natur. 290.
Natural history of enthusiasm. I: Taylor. 92.
Natural history rambles. 284.
Naturalist's library. 367.
Nature. 290.
Nau, C. Mary Stewart. 1471.
Naubert, C. B. E. [Fiction.] 813.
Naumann, E. W: R. Zukunftsmusik. 493.
Nautical almanac. 302.
Naval astronomical expedition. 296.
Naval encyclopædia. 234.
Naville, J. E. Heavenly Father. 80.
— Modern physics. 311.
Navy in the civil war. 1357.
Naylor, F. H. History of Germany. 1239.
Neal, A. B.. *see* Haven, A. 749.
Neal, D. History of the puritans. 129.

Entries in small type refer to contents only.

Entries in small type refer to contents only.

Numbers refer to columns in the main-catalogue.

Entries in small type refer to contents only.

Phelps, Austin. English style in public discourse. 515.
— Men and books. 105.
— My portfolio. 77.
Phelps, E. S. [Fiction.] 824.
— [Poetical works.] 1038.
— Beyond the gates. 106.
— Gates ajar. 106.
— What to wear. 106.
Phelps, H. P. Players of a century. 498.
Phelps, J. W. Force electrically exhibted. 285.
Phelps, W: F. Teacher's hand-book. 244.
Phelps's travellers' guide through the United States. 1363.
Philadelphia and its environs. 1377.
Philbrick, E: S. American sanitary engineering. 405.
Philip, R. George Whitefield. 1459.
— The Hannahs. 100.
— The Lydias. 100.
Philippi, K: F. Geschichte der Vereinigten Freistaaten. 1347.
— Geschichte von St. Domingo. 1413.
Philippson, M. Friedrich II. 1480.
— Heinrich IV von Frankreich. 1429.
— Philipp. II. 1429.
— Westeuropa im zeitalter von Philipp II. 1202.
— Zeitalter Ludwigs XIV. , 1254.
Philleo, C. W. [Fiction.] 825.
Phillimore, C. M. Fra Angelico. 1531.
Phillmore, L. Sir Christopher Wren. 1529.
Phillips, *Mrs.* A. [Drama.] 581.
Phillips, C: Curran. 1511.
— Speeches. 189.
Phillips, D: Christmas Evans. 1458.
Phillips, E. C. Havelock and Clyde. 1504.
Phillips, F: [Drama.] 581.
Phillips, G: S. [Fiction.] 825.
— Wordsworth. 1554.
Phillips, J. A. Ore deposits. 323.
Phillips, L. [Drama.] 581.
Phillips, L. B. Dictionary of biographical reference. 1427.
Phillips, S: [Fiction.] 825.
Phillips, Watts. [Drama.] 581.
Phillips, Wendell. Scholar in a republic. 1072.
— Speeches, lectures and letters. 1071.
Philobiblos, *pseud., see* **Ireland,** A.
Philochristus. E. A. **Abbott.** 104.
Phin, J: Cements and glue. 445.
Phipps, A. J. [Drama.] 582.
Phipps, C. H:, *marquis of Normanby.* Year of revolution. 1258.
Phipps, R. W. Preserving and replanting forests. 439.
Phipson, E. Animal-lore of Shakspeare's time. 1046.
Phisterer, F: Statistical record of U. S. armies. 233.
Phœnix, John, *pseud., see* **Derby,** G: H.
Phusin, Kata, *pseud., see* **Ruskin,** J:
Piassetskii, P. Russian travellers in Mongolia and China. 1299.
Piatt, J: J. Poems. 1038.
Piatt, L. K. Bell Smith abroad. 1261.
Piatt, S. M. Irish garland. 1038.
Piazzi, A. [Fiction.] 825.
Picard, L. B. [Drama.] 582.
Pichler, C. [Drama.] 582.
— [Fiction.] 825.
— Anthologie. 1109.
— Denkwürdigkeiten. 1558.

Pichler, C.—*Continued.*
— Gedichte. 1118.
— Idyllen. 1118.
Pichler, L., *see* **Zeller,** L. 901.
Pickering, C: Gliddon mummy case, 1167.
— Races of man. 350.
Pickering, E. [Fiction.] 825.
Pickering, E: C. Physical manipulation. 310.
Pickering, O., *and* C: W. **Upham.** Timothy Pickering. 1503.
Picton, J. A. Oliver Cromwell. 1469.
Pictorial battles of the civil war. 1354.
Pictorial gallery of arts: Fine arts. 472.
— Useful arts. 387.
Pictures of heroes. 1430.
Pictures of travel in far-off lands: Central America. 1411.
— South America. 1415.
Picturesque America. W: C. **Bryant,** *ed.* 1363.
Picturesque Europe. 1203.
Picturesque world. L. **Colange,** *ed.* 1183.
Pidgeon, D. Old-world questions. 1369.
Pidgin, C: F. Bureau of statistics of labor of Massachusetts. 199.
Pidoux, H., *joint author, see* **Trousseau,** A.
Pierantoni, G. [Fiction.] 825.
Pierce, E: L. Charles Sumner. 1489.
Pierce, G. A. Dickens dictionary. 1048.
Pierpont, J: Airs of Palestine. 1038.
Pierrepont, E: Fifth avenue to Alaska. 1405.
Pierron, E., *and* A. **Laferrière.** [Drama.] 582.
Pierson, H. W: In the brush. 1453.
— Jefferson at Monticello. 1465.
Pierson, N. G. Münzfrage. 202.
Pietsch, L: Aus welt und kunst. 1127.
Pietzker, M. A., *tr.* From peasant to prince. 1498.
Pigault-Lebrun, G. C: A. [Fiction.] 825.
Piggot, J: Persia. 1306.
Pike, G. D. Singing campaign. 495.
Pike, J: G. Guide for young disciples. 103.
Pike, Z. M. Expeditions to the sources of the Mississippi. 1397.
Pilgrim, J. [Drama.] 582.
Pilkington, M. Dictionary of painters. 1525.
Pilling, J. C. Catalogue of linguistic mss. 1340.
Pilon, F: [Drama.] 582.
Pilon, M. R. Demonetization. 201.
Pilpay, *see* **Bidpai.** 1148.
Pinard, A. Ferdinand de Lesseps. 1444.
Pindaros. Odes. 1140.
Pine, Cuyler, *pseud., see* **Peck,** E. 823.
Pinkerton, J: Collection of voyages and travels. 1187.
Pinney, S. U., *comp.* Reports. 226.
Pinto, *see* **Serpa-Pinto.**
Pinzer, *Frau* v., *see* **Binzer,** E. v. 678.
Piozzi, H. L. Autobiography, letters and literary remains. 1552.
Pipitz, F. E. [Fiction.] 825.
Pirkis, C. L. [Fiction.] 825.
Pise, C: C. [Fiction.] 825.
— Letters to Ada. 127.
Pisko, F: J. Licht und farbe. 314.
Pitawall, Ernst, *pseud., see* **Dedenroth,** E. H. 709.
Pitha, F. *freiherr* v. Verletzungen und krankheiten der extremitäten. 412.
— *and* C. A. Th. **Billroth,** *eds.* Handbuch der chirurgie. 410.
Pitman, B:, *and* J. B. **Howard.** Phonographic dictionary. 448.

Entries in small type refer to contents only

Entries in small type refer to contents only.

Entries in small type refer to contents only.

Sainte Beuve, C: A: Celebrated women. 1560.
— Mme. Desbordes-Valmore. 1561.
— Monday-chats. 1129.
— Théophile Gautier. 1590.
Saintine, J. X. Boniface, *called.* [Fiction.] 842.
Saintsbury, G: W. Dryden. 1549.
— French literature. 1127.
Sala, G: A: [Fiction.] 842.
— America revisited. 1367.
— Breakfast in bed. 1098.
— Due north. 1279.
— Due south. 1267.
— Living London. 1098.
— Looking at life. 1098.
— Paris herself again. 1261.
Salice-Contessa, *see* **Contessa**.
Salis-Seewis, J: G. *freiherr* v. Gedichte. 1106.
— Gedichte. 1108.
Salisbury, *Marquis* of. Speeches. 1494.
Salisbury, A. Normal instruction in Wis. 243.
— Wis. teachers' association. 243.
Salkeld, J. [Fiction.] 842.
— Classical antiquities. 1170.
Sallustius Crispus, C. [Works.] 1178.
Salm-Salm, A. *prinzessin* v. Ten years of my
life. 1480.
Salmon, G: Analytic geometry. 300.
— Conic sections. 300.
— Higher plane curves. 300.
Salomon, L: Deutsche national-literatur. 1103.
Saltus, E. E. Balzac. 1561.
Samarow, Gregor, *pseud., see* **Meding**, J: F.
M. O.
Sampleton, Samuel, *pseud., see* **Monti**, L:
Samson, G: W. Art criticism. 467.
Samuels, A. F. [Fiction.] 842.
Samue.son, J. Roumania. 1292.
Sanborn, A. L., *and* J. R. Berryman. Supp.
to Revised statutes of Wis. 220.
Sanborn, F. B. Thoreau. 1542.
— *ed.* Emerson. 1447.
— - John Brown. 1484.
Sanborn, K., *ed.* Wit of women. 1083.
Sancroft, W: New whole duty of man. 103.
Sand, George, *pseud., see* **Dudevant**, A. L. A.
716.
Sandeau, L. S. J. [Fiction.] 842.
— *and* A. Decourcelle, *see* **Clarke**, C. 538.
Sander, F. Lexikon der pädagogik. 240.
Sanders, D. Ergänzungswörterbuch. 276.
— Hauptschwierigkeiten. 276.
Sandham, E. [Fiction.] 842.
Sandras de Courtilz, G., *see* **Courtilz de San-
dras**. 703.
Sandwith, H. Belagerung von Kars. 1291.
Sands, R. C: [Fiction.] 842.
— Writings. 1017.
Sangster, M. E. [Fiction.] 842.
Sanitarian. 397.
Sanitary care and treatment of children. 404.
Sanitary commission. 235.
Sanitary engineer. 390.
Sankey, C: Spartan and theban supremacies.
1174.
Sankey, D:, *joint author, see* **Bliss**, P. P.
Sansom, J. Lower Canada. 1407.
Sanson, H:, *ed.* Memoirs of the Sansons. 1511.
— Mysterien vom schaffot. 1511.
Santa Barbara. All about. 1403.
Santarem, M. F. *visconde* de. Americus Ves-
pucius. 1518.

Saphir, M. G. Schriften. 1125.
Sarcey, F. [Fiction.] 842.
Sardou, V., *see* **Amcotts**, V. 520.
Sargent, C: S. Forests of North America. 439.
Sargent, E. Planchette. 56.
— *ed.* [Drama.] 591.
— - [Fiction.] 842.
— - Arctic adventure. 1423.
— - Harper's cyclopædia of poetry. 1022.
Sargent, G: E. [Fiction.] 842.
— Stories of old England. 1227.
— *joint author, see* **Walshe**, E. H. 886.
Sargent, J: Henry Martyn. 1456.
Sargent, L. M. [Fiction.] 842.
— Dealings with the dead. 1072.
Sargent, M. E., *ed.* Radical club of Boston. 1073.
Sargent, N. Public men and events. 1353.
Sargent, W. Major André. 1504.
Sarpi, P: History of the council of Trent. 122.
Sartoris, A. [Fiction.] 842.
Sartorius, G: F: C. *freiherr von Waltershausen.*
Hanseatischer bund. 1245.
Saturday review. 512.
Sauer, K: M. [Fiction.] 843.
— Italienische litteratur. 1131.
Saulcy, L: F. J. de. Journey round the Dead
sea. 1312.
Saunders, F: About woman. 65.
— Great metropolis. 1235.
— Pastime papers. 1098.
— Salad for the social. 1098.
— Salad for the solitary. 1098.
Saunders, J: [Fiction.] 843.
Saunders, K., *see* **Cooper**, K. 703.
Saunders, W: Insects injurious to fruit. 436.
— Soils and products of Florida. 1381.
Saunders, W:, *of England.* Through the light
continent. 1367.
Saussure, H: de. American wasps. 379.
Sauzade, John S., *pseud., see* **Payn**, J.
Sauzay, A. Wonders of glass-making. 452.
Savage, James, *of the Lond. inst.* The librar-
ian. 16.
Savage, James, *pres. of Mass. hist. soc.* Genea-
logical dictionary of New England. 1566.
Savage, J: [Drama.] 591.
— '98 and '48. 1212.
— Our living representative men. 1483.
— [Poetical works.] 1039.
Savage, J:, *D. D.* Letters of the antients. 1133.
Savage, M. J. [Fiction.] 843.
— Belief in God. 92.
— Beliefs about the Bible. 85.
— Beliefs about man. 95.
— Christianity the science of manhood. 99.
— Man, woman and child. 64.
— Modern sphinx. 1073.
— Morals of evolution. 62.
— Religion of evolution. 77.
Savage, M. W. [Fiction.] 843.
Savage, W. H. Intellectual basis of faith. 92.
Savarin, *see* **Brillat-Savarin**, A.
Saville, J: F. [Drama.] 591.
Savin, Una, *pseud., see* **Hepworth**, *Mrs.* G: H.
754.
Saxby, *Mrs.* Breakers ahead. 1197.
Saxe, J: G. [Poetical works.] 1039.
Say, J: B Political economy. 195.
Say, T: Entomology. 376.
Sayce, A. H: Ancient empires of the east. 1165.
— Fresh light from ancient monuments. 1165.

Entries in small type refer to contents only.

Simpson, J. P.—*Continued.*
— *and* H. C. Merivale. [Drama.] 600.
— *and* C: Wray. [Drama.] 600.
— *joint author, see* Yates, E. 613.
Simpson, M. C. M. [Fiction.] 855.
Simpson, T: Discoveries on the north coast of America. 1424.
Simrock, K: J. Deutsche mythologie. 136.
— *ed.* Deutsche sprichwörter. 1125.
— - Rheinsagen. 1114.
— *tr.* Edda. 1142.
— - Heldenbuch. 1113.
— - Heliand. 1113.
Sims, J. M. Story of my life. 1523.
Simson, W. History of the gipsies. 1295.
Sinclair, C. [Fiction.] 855.
— Hill and valley. 1233.
— Scotland and the scotch. 1231.
Sinclair, *Sir* J: Statistical account of Scotland. 1213.
Sinding, P. C. History of Scandinavia. 1281.
Sinnett, A. P. Esoteric buddhism. 52.
— Occult world. 44.
Siogvolk, P., *pseud., see* Mathews, A. 799.
Siraudin, P. [Drama.] 600.
— *joint author, see* Clairville. 538.
— - *see* Moreau, L. I. E. L. 573.
Sismondi, J: C: L. Simonde de, *see* Simonde.
Sister Augustine. 1460.
Sitgreaves, L. Expedition down the Zuñi and Colorado. 1399.
Sivewright, J., *joint author, see* Preece, W: H:
Six hundred dollars a year. 445.
Sjöberg, E. Gedichte. 1143.
Skeat, W. W: Concise etymological dictionary. 272.
— Etymological dictionary. 272.
Skelton, J:, *of England.* Poetical works. 1040.
Skelton, J: (*Shirley*). [Fiction.] 855.
— Essays in history and biography. 1161.
Sketches of the west. 1390.
Sketchley, Arthur, *pseud., see* Rose, E: 590.
Skinner, G. M. Sermons. 111.
Skinner, T: Journey overland to India. 1308.
Slack, H: J. Marvels of pond-life. 356.
Slagg, J: Free trade and tariffs. 205.
Slater, J:, *joint author, see* Smith, T. R.
Slater, J. H. Library manual. 13.
Slick, Jonathan, *pseud.* [Fiction.] 855.
Slick, Sam, *pseud., see* Haliburton, T: C.
Slocum, C: E. History of the Slocums. 1566.
Slosson, A. T. China hunters club. 481.
Small books on great subjects. 1087.
Smalley, E. V. Northern Pacific railroad. 258.
Smart, A. Germs, dust and disease. 408.
Smart, H. [Fiction.] 855.
Smart, J. H. High school question. 241.
Smedley, E: Venetian history. 1264.
Smedley, F. E. [Fiction.] 855.
Smee, A. Miscellaneous writings. 1522.
Smellie, W: Philosophy of natural history. 370.
Smet, P: J: de. Western missions and missionaries. 115.
Smidt, H: [Fiction.] 855.
Smiles, S: Brief biographies. 1431.
— Character. 62.
— Duty. 62.
— George Stephenson. 1526.
— Industrial biography. 1524.
— Life of a scotch naturalist. 1521.
— Men of invention and industry. 1523.

Smiles, S:—*Continued.*
— Robert Dick. 1521.
— Self-help. 62.
— Successful merchant. 1515.
— Thrift. 62.
— *ed.* James Nasmyth. 1525.
Smiles, S:, *jr.* Round the world. 1191.
Smiley, C: W. Principal lakes of the U. S. 1365.
— Principal rivers of the U. S. 1365.
— Work of the U. S. fish commission. 444.
Smith, Abigail. Correspondence. 1079.
Smith, Adam. Moral sentiments. 62.
— Wealth of nations. 195.
Smith, Albert. [Drama.] 600.
— [Fiction.] 855.
— Story of Mont Blanc. 1288.
Smith, Alex. [Fiction.] 855.
— Dreamthorp. 1073.
— [Poetical works.] 1040.
— Summer in Skye. 1231.
Smith, A. H. Ma-ka-tai-me-she-kia-kiak. 1040.
Smith, A. T. Rural schools. 242.
Smith, B: G., *joint author, see* Tomes, R.
Smith, Bell. *pseud., see* Piatt, L. K.
Smith, C: H. Bill Arp's peace papers. 1086.
Smith, C: Hamilton. Natural history of the human species. 351.
Smith, C: J: Synonyms and antonyms. 274.
— Synonyms discriminated. 274.
Smith, D, M., *ed.* Round the world. 1191.
Smith, E: Foods. 445.
— Health. 402.
Smith, Edwin. Transit of Venus. 310.
Smith, Eli. Researches in Armenia. 1307.
Smith, E. A. Myths of the Iroquois. 1340.
Smith, E. L., *joint author, see* McCray, F. T. 792.
Smith, E. R. Araucanians. 1417.
Smith, E. T. [Fiction.] 856.
Smith, G., *joint author, see* Mayhew, E: 570.
Smith, G: Assyria. 1170.
— Assyrian discoveries. 1310.
— Babylonia. 1170.
— Chaldean account of Genesis. 139.
Smith, Goldwin. Cowper. 1548.
— Does the Bible sanction american slavery ? 170.
— False hopes. 204.
— Lectures and essays. 1073.
— Lectures on modern history. 1161.
— Letter to a whig. 167.
— Political destiny of Canada. 189.
— Slave-owner and the turk. 189.
— Speeches on reform. 186.
— Three english statesmen. 1400.
Smith, G: B. Famous ambassadors. 1481.
— John Bright. 1491.
— Poets and novelists. 1008.
— Shelley. 1553.
— Sir Robert Peel. 1493.
— Victor Hugo. 1561.
Smith, G. W. Painting, spanish and french. 487.
Smith, Hannah. [Fiction.] 856.
Smith, Horace, (*Paul Chatfield*). [Fiction.] 856.
— Gaieties and gravities. 1098.
— Tin trumpet. 1086.
— *and* J. Rejected addresses. 1040.
Smith, H. H. Brazil, the Amazons and the coast. 1416.
Smith, H: I. Education. 239.
Smith, H: P., *ed.* Glossary of terms and phrases. 273.

Sommerfeldt, H. A. Construction of ships. 462.
Sommers, W: [Fiction.] 857.
Sonntag, A: Terrestrial magnetism in Mexico. 318.
Sohrel, L. Bottom of the sea. 329.
Sophoklês. Tragedies. 600.
Sorignet, A. Sacred cosmogony. 82.
Sorrel, W: J. [Drama.] 601.
— *joint author, see* **French,** S. 550.
Sötbeer, G: A. Die fünf milliarden. 196.
Soubron, W: O: Souvenir. 1120.
Soule, C: C. Lawyers' reference manual. 207.
Soulé, F., J: H. **Gihon** *and* J. **Nisbet.** Annals of San Francisco. 1402.
Soule, R: English synonymes. 274.
Soulié, M. F: [Fiction.] 857.
Soutar, R. [Drama.] 601.
— *joint author, see* **Claridge,** C. J. 538.
South Kensington museum. Catalogue of books on art. 26.
— Handbooks. 281.
Southall, J. C. Epoch of the mammoth. 347.
— Recent origin of man. 347.
Southard, S. L. Mystery of godliness. 111.
Southerne, T: [Drama.] 601.
Southey, C. A. [Fiction.] 857.
Southey; C: C., *ed.* Life and correspondence of Robert Southey. 1553.
Southey, R. Chronicle of the Cid. 1271.
— The doctor. 1073.
— Early naval history of England. 1228.
— Life of Nelson. 1505.
— Life of Wesley. 1459.
— Life of William Cowper. 1548.
— Peninsular war. 1272.
— Poetical works. 1040.
— *and* C. A. Correspondence. 1080.
— *and* C: C. Life of dr. Bell. 1456.
Southgate, H. Visit to Mesopotamia. 1309.
Southworth, A. S. Winfield Scott Hancock. 1501.
Souvestre, E. [Fiction.] 857.
Sozinskey, T: S. Infantile unfoldment. 352.
Spalding, J. W. Japan expedition. 1191.
Spalding, M. J. Miscellanea. 1073.
— Protestant reformation. 121.
Spalding, T: A. Elizabethan demonology. 54.
Spalding, W: Italy. 1261.
Spamer, J: G. C. F. O: Goethe. 1444.
— Männer eigener kraft 1435.
— Merkwürdige kinder. 1436.
— Schiller. 1444.
— *ed.* Deutsche dichter, denker und wissensfürsten. 1444.
— — Wohlthäter der menschheit. 1431.
Spangenberg, L: Fatigue of metals. 458.
Sparhawk, F. C. [Fiction.] 857.
Sparks, J. Benedict Arnold. 1437.
— Benjamin Franklin. 1486.
— *Same.* 183.
— Charles Lee. 1438.
— Count Pulaski. 1438.
— Ethan Allen. 1437.
— Father Marquette. 1438.
— Gouverneur Morris. 1487.
— John Ledyard. 1438.
— John Ribault. 1438.
— LaSalle. 1438.
— Washington. 1465.
— *Same.* 188.
— *ed.* Correspondence of the revolution. 1351.
— — Library of american biography. 1437.
Sparrowgrass papers. F: S. **Cozzens.** 1084.

Späth, C. [Fiction.] 857.
Spaulding, M. C. Statistics of the U. S. 157.
Speaker's commentary, The, *see* **Cook,** F: C:, *etc.* 85.
Spear, S: T. Law of extradition. 209.
Specht, G: J. Topographical surveying. 418.
Speckter, O:, *illustrator, see* **Hey,** W: 1126.
Spectator. 1049.
Speeches of british statesmen. 189.
Speke, J: H. Source of the Nile. 1325.
Speling reform asosiashun papers. 270.
Spence, J. M. Land of Bolivar. 1418.
Spencer, A. Andersonville. 1361.
Spencer, C: C. Art of playing the piano fort 496.
— Treatise on music. 490.
Spencer, Edmund. Sketches of Germany. 124
Spencer, E: Thomas F. Bayard. 1484.
Spencer, E. A., *comp.* Digest of laws of Wi consin. 219.
Spencer, G:, *and* W. **James.** [Drama.] 601.
Spencer, H. Ceremonial institutions. 48.
— Data of ethics. 48.
— Education. 240.
— Essays. 1073.
— First principles. 43.
— Illustrations of universal progress. 1074.
— Man versus the state. 160.
— Principles of biology. 48.
— Principles of morality. 48.
— Principles of psychology. 48.
— Principles of sociology. 48.
— Recent discussions. , 1074.
— Social statics. 145.
— Study of sociology. 145.
— System of synthetic philosophy. 48.
— *ed.* Descriptive sociology. 145.
Spencer, J. A. Geschichte der Vereinigten Sta ten. 1345.
— *and* B. J: **Lossing.** History of the U. S. 134
Spencer, W: G: Inventional geometry. 298.
Spender, E. [Fiction.] 857.
Spender, L., *mrs.* J: K. [Fiction.] 857.
Spenser, E: [Poetical works.] 1040.
— Spenser for children. 1026.
Sperry, H. T. Country love. 1040.
Speyer, O: Cavour. 1429.
— Tasso. 1430.
Spielhagen, F: [Fiction.] 857.
— Theorie und technik des romans. 513.
Spiers, A., *and* G. **Surenne.** French and engli dictionary. 1126.
Spiller v. Hauenschild, R: G:, *see* **Hauenschil**
Spindler, C: [Drama.] 601.
— [Fiction.] 859.
Spinnstube. P. F: W: **Oertel,** *ed.* 1126.
Spinoza, B. de. Chief works. 50.
Spirit of the times. 501.
Spiritual progress. 103.
Spiritual voices from the middle ages. 102.
Spitta, J. A: P. Johann S. Bach. 1534.
Spofford, A. R. Binding of books. 1.
— Library bibliography. 1.
— Parliamentary rules. 225.
— Periodical literature. 1.
— *ed.* American almanac. 156.
Spofford, H. E. [Fiction.] 860.
— Art decoration. 484.
— Poems. 1040.
— Servant girl question. 448.
Spofford, J. Gazetteer of Massachusetts. 13
Spon, E., *joint ed., see* **Byrne,** O.

Numbers refer to columns in the main catalogue.

Entries in small type refer to contents only.

Strutt, J. Sports and pastimes of the people of England. 261.
Struve, G. Weltgeschichte. 1153.
Stuart, C: B. Naval dry docks of the United States. 424.
Stuart, E. [Fiction.] 868.
Stuart, G. Society in Europe. 152.
Stuart, I: W. Jonathan Trumbull, sen. 1489.
Stuart, J., and N: Revett. Antiquities of Athens. 1172.
Stuart, J. M. Free trade in Tuscany. 205.
Stuart, M. Interpretation of prophecy. 85.
Stuart, R. Cyclopædia of architecture. 473.
Stuart, V. Egypt after the war. 1321.
Stubbs, W: Constitutional history of England. 161.
— Early Plantagenets. 1221.
— ed. Select charters. 162.
Stübel, A., joint anthor, see Reiss, W.
Student's concordance to the revised New testament. 89.
Students' songs. 495.
Studer, J. H. Columbus, Ohio. 1387.
Studley, M. J. What our girls ought to know. 404.
Stürenberg, H: Wehrpflicht und erziehung. 231.
Sturgis, J. R. [Drama.] 602.
— [Fiction.] 868.
Sturm, C. C. Being and attributes of God. 102.
Sturm, J. K: R. Buch für meine kinder. 1128.
— Neues fabelbuch. 1128.
Sturtevant, J. M. Economics. 196.
Sturz, H. P: Beste schriften. 1108.
Stwin, Adam, pseud., see Richardson, J. 834.
Suberwick, Mme. —. [Fiction.] 868.
Suckley, G: Genus salmo. 380.
Sue, M. J., called Eugène. [Fiction.] 868.
Sue-Sand, Alexander, fils, pseud., see Hamley, E: B. 745.
Suetonius Tranquillus, C.' Twelve Cæsars. 1480.
Sugenheim, S: Aufhebung der leibeigenschaft. 170.
Sulivan, R. [Drama.] 602.
Sullivan, J: T. Interoceanic communication. 424.
Sullivan, W: Public men of the revolution. 1482.
Sullivant, W. S. Mosses and liverworts. 364.
Sully, J. Illusions. 53.
— Psychology. 58.
Sully, M. duc de. Memoirs. 1253.
Sumner, C: Eulogy on Abraham Lincoln. 1467.
— Letters. 1489.
— Orations and speeches. 187.
— Works. 187.
Sumner, J: B. Apostolical preaching. 105.
— Four sermons. 106.
Sumner, W: G. Andrew Jackson. 1466.
— Problems in political economy. 196.
— Protection in the U. S. 206.
— What social classes owe to each other. 196.
— and others. Bibliogr. of political economy. 195.
Supernatural religion. J: Muir. 92.
Supersac, L. [Drama.] 602.
Surenne, G., joint author, see Spiers, A.
Surrebutter, John, esq., pseud., see Anstey, J:
Surrey, Earl of, see Howard, H:
Suter, W: E. [Drama.] 602.
Sutherland, A. Knights of Malta. 1201.
Sutherland, D: From Gibraltar to Constantinople. 1293.
Sutro-Schücking, K. [Fiction.] 869.

Suttières, S. de, see Sarcy de Suttières, F.
Sutton, F. Volumetric analysis. 321.
Svetchin, A. S. Writings. 1146.
Swan, J. G. Haidah indians. 1342.
— Indians at Cape Flattery. 1342.
— Northwest coast. 1404.
Swank, J. M. Iron and steel production of the United States. 453.
Swayne, G: C. Herodotus. 1138.
Swedenborg, E. Works. 131, 132.
Sweet, H: History of anglo-saxon poetry. 1019.
Sweet, O. P. Amusement directory. 1364.
Sweeting, R. D. R. Experiences of J: Howard. 405.
Sweetser, M. F. Allston. 1527.
— Claude Lorraine. 1530.
— Dürer. 1530.
— Fra Angelico. 1531.
— Guido Reni. 1532.
— Landseer. 1529.
— Leonardo da Vinci. 1532.
— Michael Angelo. 1532.
— Murillo. 1532.
— Raphael. 1532.
— Rembrandt. 1530.
— Sir Joshua Reynolds. 1529.
— Titian. 1532.
— Turner. 1529.
— What the people read. 510.
— see Hodder, E. Cities of the world. 1184.
Swetchine, see Svetchin.
Swezey, G. D. Plants of Wisconsin. 363.
Swift, A: M. [Fiction.] 869.
Swift, F., and M. R. Clark. Skaters' text-book. 502.
Swift, J. [Fiction.] 869.
— Gulliver's travels. 1083.
— Intelligencer. 1049.
— Poetical works. 1041.
— Works. 1019.
Swinburne, A. C: [Drama.] 603.
— [Poetical works.] 1041.
— Study of Shakespeare. 1045.
Swindell, J: G: Well-digging. 426.
Swing, D: Club essays. 1074.
— Great presbyterian conflict. 129.
— Motives of life. 112.
— Truths for to-day. 112.
Swinton, W: Campaigns of the army of the Potomac. 1357.
— Rambles among words. 271.
— Twelve decisive battles of the war. 1357.
Swisshelm, J. G. Half a century. 1542.
Sybel, H: K: L. v. French revolution. 1255.
— History of the crusades. 1200.
Sydow, C. v. [Fiction.] 869.
Sylva, Carmen, pseud., see Elisabeth of Rumania. 724.
Sylvanus, pseud., see Colton, R.
Sylvin, E: Jules Ferry. 1444.
Symington, A. J. Bryant. 1540.
— Hints to our boys. 63.
— Samuel Lover. 1551.
— Thomas Moore. 1552.
— William Wordsworth. 1554.
Symonds, J: A. Greek poets. 1137.
— Italian by-ways. 1131.
— Renaissance in Italy :
— 1. Age of the despots. 1263.
— 2. The revival of learning. 1263.
— 3. The fine arts. 472.
— 4, 5. Italian literature. 1131.

Numbers refer to columns in the main catalogue.

Entries in small type refer to contents only.

Entries in small type refer to contents only.

Entries in small type refer to contents only.

Entries in small type refer to contents only.

CLASSIFIED CATALOGUE

WITH

Title Indexes of Drama and Fiction.

I. BIBLIOLOGY AND UNCLASSIFIED WORKS.

1. Libraries.

1. Library science and history.

Jewett C: Coffin. Notices of public libraries in the U. S. of America ; printed by order of congress as an app. to the 4th annual report of the board of regents of the Smithsonian institution. Wash. 1851. O.   **L**

United States. *Bureau of education.* Public libraries in the U. S. of America ; their history, condition and management. [Ed. by S: R. **Warren** and S. N. **Clark**.] Wash. 1876. 3 v. O.   **L**

Contents. V. 1. [*Historical essays*.]. **Editors.** Introd.—**Scudder,** H. E. Public libraries a hundred years ago.—**Editors.** School and asylum libraries; College libraries.—**Librarian,** A, J: S. **Sumer,** *and* editors. Theological libraries in the U. S.—**Griswold,** S. B. Law libraries.—**Billings,** J. S. Medical libraries in the U. S.—**Gill,** T. Scientific libraries in the U. S.—**Editors.** Libraries in prisons and reformatories.—**Perkins,** F: B., *and* W: **Matthews.** Professorships of books and reading.—**Editors.** Libraries of the general government ; Copyright, distribution, exchanges and duties.—**Homes,** H: A. State and territorial libraries.—**Homes,** H: A., W. I. **Fletcher** *and* editors. Historical societies in the U. S.—**Perkins,** F: B. Young men's mercantile libraries.—**Brainerd,** C. Young men's christian associations.—**Quincy,** J. P. Free libraries. **2.** [*Management and Cataloguing*]. **Fletcher,** W: I. Public libraries in manufacturing communities ; Public libraries and the young.—**Perkins,** F: B. How to make town libraries successful.—**Winsor,** J. Reading in popular libraries.—**Frieze,** H. S. Art museums and their connection with public libraries.—**Editors.** Free town libraries.—**Todd,** W. C. Free reading rooms.—**Winsor,** J. Library buildings.—**Poole,** W: F: The organization and management of public libraries.—**Robinson,** O. H. College library administration.—**Cutter,** C: A. Library catalogues—**Dewey,** M., S. B. **Noyes,** J. **Schwartz,** J: J. **Bailey.** Catalogues and cataloguing—**Robinson,** O. H. On indexing periodical and miscellaneous literature.—**Spofford,** A. R. Binding and preservation of books ; Periodical literature and society publications ; Works of reference for libraries.—**Winsor,** J. Library memoranda.—**Robinson,** O. H. Titles of books.—**Perkins,** F: B. Book indexes.—**Spofford,** A. R. Library bibliography.—**Cutter,** C: A. Rules for a printed dictionary catalogue. **3.** [*Reports and statistics*.] **Editors.** Library reports and statistics.—Public libraries of ten principal cities.—**Editors.** General statistics of all public libraries in the U.S.

Cowtan, Robert. Memories of the British museum. Lond. 1872. O.   **L**

Edwards, E: Lives of the founders of the British museum ; with notices of its chief augmentors and other benefactors, 1570—1870. Lond. 1870. O.   **L**

— Free town libraries, their formation, management and history in Britain, France, Germany and America, together with brief notices of book-collectors, and of the respective places of deposit of their surviving collections. Lond. 1869. O.   **L**

Edwards, E:—*Continued.*
— Libraries and founders of libraries. Lond. 1865. O.   **L**

— Memoirs of libraries, including a handbook of library economy. Lond. 1859. 2 v. O.   **L**

Wynne, James. Private libraries of New York. N. Y. 1860. O.   **L**

*   *   *

Columbia·college, *N. Y. School of library economy.* Circular of information, 1884. D.   **L**

Blackburn, C : F. Hints on catalogue titles and on index entries, with a rough vocabulary of terms and abbreviations, chiefly from catalogues, and some passages from journeying among books. Lond. 1884. Q.   **L**

Boston athenæum. How to get books ; with an explanation of the new way of marking books, by C. A. Cutter. Bost. 1882. O.   **L**
— *Same.*   **R**

Boston public library. Handbook for readers, with regulations. 5th ed. 1877. Bost. 1877. Tt.   **L**
— *Same.* New ed. Bost. 1879. S.   **L**
— *Same.* New ed. Bost. 1883. S.   **L**

Cutter, C : Ammi. Rules for a printed dictionary catalogue. (Public libraries in the U. S. ; special report of the bureau of education, pt. 2.) Wash. 1876. O.   **R**
— *Same. In* U. S. Special report on libraries, v. 2.

Dewey, Melvil. A classification and subject index for cataloguing. and arranging the books and pamphlets of a library. Amherst, Mass. 1876. O.   **L**
— *Same* [as adapted to the Buffalo young men's asso. lib'y].   **L R**

Edmands, J : New system of classification and scheme for numbering books, applied to the Mercantile library of Philadelphia. Repr. from the bulletin of the library. Phila. 1883. Q.   **L**

Green, S: Swett. Library aids. Rev. and enl. ed., with references from Poole's Index and a chapter on Books and articles on reading from Foster's Libraries and readers. N. Y. 1883. T.   **L**
— *Same.*   **R**

Jewett, C: Coffin. Smithsonian report on the construction of catalogues of libraries and their publication by means of separate stereotype titles, with rules and examples. 2d ed. Wash. 1853. O.   **L**

Perkins, F: Beecher. A rational classification of literature for shelving and cataloguing books in a library; with alphabetical index. San Francisco. 1881. O. *With* Dewey, M. Classification and subject index.   **L**
— *Same.*   **R**
— *Same.* Rev. ed. San Francisco. 1882. O.   **L**
— San Francisco cataloguing for public libraries; a manual of the system used in the San Francisco free public library. San Francisco. 1884. O.   **L**
Petzholdt. Julius. Katechismus der bibliothekenlehre ; anleitung zur einrichtung und verwaltung von bibliotheken. 3te aufl. Leipz. 1877. S.   **L**
Smith, Lloyd Pearsall. On the classification of books ; a paper read before the American library association, may 1882. Bost. 1882. O.   **L**

2. Associations and Periodicals.

American library association. Papers and proceedings of the 4th general meeting held at Washington, feb. 9, 10, and Baltimore, feb. 11, 1881. Bost. 1881. O.   **L**
Note. Proceedings of other meetings are found in various volumes of the Library journal.
— The library journal ; v. 1-9. N. Y. 1877-84. 9 v. Q.   **L**
Library-association of the United Kingdom. Transactions and proceedings of the conference of librarians held in London, 1877. Ed. by the secretaries of the conference, E. B. Nicholson and H: R. Tedder. Lond. 1878. Q.   **L**
— Transactions and proceedings of the 1st—3d annual meetings. held at Oxford, oct. 1-3. 1878. at Manchester, sept. 23-25, 1879, at Edinburgh, oct. 5-7, 1880, ed. by the secretaries. Lond. 1879—81. 3 v. Q.   **L**
— Monthly notes; v. 1-4. Lond. 1880—83. 4 v. in 2. O.   **L**
— The library chronicle ; a journal of librarianship and bibliography; v. 1. Lond. 1884. Q.   **L**
Centralblatt für bibliothekswesen ; herausg. unter ständiger mitwirkung zahlreicher fachgenossen des in- und auslandes, von O. Hartwig und K. Schulz. 1er jahrg. Leipz. 1884. O.   **L**

3. Reports.

Albany. Young men's association for mutual improvement. 50th and 51st annual reports of the officers. 1883, 1884.   **L**
— 50th anniversary and exercises; semi-centennial celebration at the Leland opera house on wednesday eve., dec. 12, 1883. O.   **L**
Astor library of the city of New York. 25th-28th, 30th–33d annual reports. Albany. 1874-82. O.   **L**
Baltimore. Mercantile library association. 34th annual report of the board of directors. Balt. 1874. O.   **L**
Birmingham, *England*. Free libraries committee. 17th and 18th, 20th and 21st annual reports. 1878 and 1879, 1881 and 1882. Birm. [1880], 1883. O.   **L**
Boston public library. 2, 3, 5, 10, 12—20,22—32d annual reports of the board of trustees. Bost. 1854—84. O.   **L**
Bridgeport public library. 2d annual report, july 1, 1883. Bridgep. 1883. O.   **L**

Brookline, *Mass.* **Public library.** 25th-27th annual reports. Brookline. 1882—84. O. **L**
Brooklyn library. 26th annual report of the board of directors ; presented march 27, 1884. Brooklyn. 1884. O.   **L**
Buffalo. Young men's association. 36th, 38th-48th annual reports of the executive committee and the record of the proceedings of the annual meetings, feb. 26, 1872—feb. 25, 1884. Also, the 7th, 9th—19th annual reports of the real estate commissioners of the association. Buffalo. 1872—84. O.   **L**
Chicago public library. 1st—5th, 7th—12th annual reports of the board of directors, june 1873—june 1884. Chicago. 1873—84. O.   **L**
Cincinnati. Public library. 6th, 13th, 16th, 17th annual reports of the librarian and treasurer, june 1873—june 1884. Cin. 1873—84. O.   **L**
— **Young men's mercantile library association.** 42d, 47th, 49th annual reports of the board of directors, 1876, 1881, 1883. Cin. 1877—84. O.   **L**
Cleveland. Public school library. 12th, 14th, 15th annual reports of the board of managers and librarian. Cleveland, 1880, 1882, 1883. O.   **L**
Columbia college library, *N. Y.* 1st annual report of the chief librarian, may 31, 1884. N. Y. 1884. O.   **L**
Handsworth, *Eng.*, public library. Report of committee for year end. march 25, 1884. **L**
Hartford library association. 42d—44th, 46th annual reports of the executive committee, june 1, 1880—june 1, 1884. Hartford, 1880—84. O.   **L**
Haverhill, *Mass.*, **public library.** 5th annual report for the year ending dec. 31, 1879. Haverhill. 1880. O.   **L**
Iowa state library, *Des Moines.* Reports of the state librarian for the years 1878 and 1879, 1880 and 1881, and biennial report july 1, 1883. Des Moines. 1879—83. O.   **L**
Lawrence, *Mass.* **Free public library.** 7th—10th, 12th, 13th annual reports of the board of trustees and librarian. Lawrence, 1879 -85. O.   **L**
Lowell, *Mass.* **City library.** Annual reports of the directors, 1879—1881. 1883. Lowell, 1880—84. O.   **L**
Lynn, *Mass.* **Public library.** 17th—21st annual reports of the trustees. Lynn. 1880—84. O. **L**
Madison, *Wis.* Free library and reading room. 4th annual report of the board of directors, year ending july 1, 1879. Madison, 1879. O.   **L**
Manchester, *N. H.* **City library.** 26th—31st annual reports of the trustees, 1879—1884. Manchester. 1880—85. O.   **L**
Michigan. State library, *Lansing.* Report of the state librarian for 1881 and 1882. Lansing. 1882. O.   **L**
Milwaukee. Public library. 2d—7th annual reports of the board of trustees, oct. 1879—oct. 1884. Milw. 1879—84. O.   **L**
Note. The first annual report for the period elapsing between the time of the actual transfer of the library of the Young men's association to the city, and september 30th 1878, has never been printed.
Mitchell library, *Glasgow.* Report, 1883. Glasgow, 1884. O.   **L**
New Haven young men's institute. Book lists and annual reports, 1879, 1880, 1882.   **L**

New York. General society of mechanics and tradesmen. 97th and 99th annual report, prepared by the finance committee, 1883 and 1885. N. Y. 1883, 1885. O.   L
— **Mercantile library association.** 53d to 63d annual reports of the board of direction, may 1873—april 1884. N. Y. 1874—84. O.   L
New York state library, *Albany.* Annual reports of the trustees; 39th, 62—64th. Albany. 1858, 1880—82. O.   L
Newburyport, *Mass.,* **public library.** 25th, 26th and 28th annual reports of the directors. Newburyport, 1881—84. O.   L
— Dedicatory exercises of the Simpson annex to the public library building of the city of Newburyport on the eve. of april 28, 1882. Newburyport, 1882. O.   L
Newton, *Mass.,* **free library.** Annual reports of the trustees, 1878—1883. Bost. 1879—84. O. L
Peabody institute, *Baltimore.* 12th annual report of the provost to the trustees, june 1, 1879. Balt. 1879. O.   L
Philadelphia. Mercantile library company. 60th—62d annual reports, jan. 1883—1885. Phila. 1883—85. O.   L
Pittsburgh library association. 32d annual report for 1879.   L
Providence public library. 1st—6th annual reports of the librarian, for the year ending feb. 3, 1879 to the year ending dec. 31, 1883. Providence. 1879—84. O.   L
Rotherham, *Eng.,* **Free public library of** the borough of. 1st—3d annual reports of the committee. Rotherham. 1881—[83]. O. L
St. Louis mercantile library association. Annual reports 1876, 1884, 1885. St. Louis. 1877-85. O.   L
— **Public school library.** Annual reports 1876— 1883. St. Louis. 1878—84. O.   L
San Francisco free public library. 3d—5th reports of the board of trustees for the years ending june 30, 1881—june 30th, 1883. San Francisco. 1881—83. O.   L
— **Mercantile library association.** 25th—29th, 32d annual reports of the president, treasurer and librarian, 1877–1881, 1884. San Francisco. 1878—82, 1885. O.   L
Swansea, Borough of. **Public library and gallery of art committee.** 7th—9th annual reports, 1880-'1—1882-'83. Swansea, 1881—83. O.   L
Taunton, *Mass.* **Public library.** 11th—18th annual reports of the trustees, 1876—1883. Taunton. 1877—83. O.   L
Toledo, *O.* **Public library.** 6th--10th annual reports of the trustees for the years ending dec. 31, 1879—dec. 31, 1883. Toledo. 1880 —83. O.   L
Toronto, *Ont.* **Mechanics' institute.** 49th—51st annual reports, with abstracts of the annual meetings, 1880—1882. Toronto. 1880 —82. O.   L
— **Public library.** 1st annual report, 1883–'84. Toronto. 1885. O.   L
Uxbridge, *Mass.,* **free public library.** 8th annual report of the board of trustees. Uxbridge. 1883. O.   L
Willard library, *Evansville, Ind.* Papers relating to [its] establishment. Evansville. 1877. O.   L
Wilmington institute. 23d—27th annual reports of the president, treasurer and executive committee, 1880—1884. Wilmington, Del. 1880—84. O.   L

Woburn, *Mass.* **Library committee.** 22d—28th annual reports for the years ending feb. 28, 1879—march 1, 1885. Woburn *and* Bost. 1879—85. O.   L
Worcester, *Mass.* **Free public library.** 19th— 24th annual reports for the years ending nov. 30, 1878—nov. 30, 1883. Worcester. [1879]—1884. O.   L
— Rules, regulations and documents. Worcester. 1881. O.   L

4. Catalogues.

Public libraries.

Amherst college library. Catalogue. Amherst. 1855. O.   L
Astor library, *New York.* Catalogue or Alphabetical index of the Astor library; in 2 pts. Pt. 1: Authors and books. N. Y. 1857-1861. 4 v. Q.   L
Bloomington, *Ill.,* **library association.** A list of books, as found in the library on jan. 1st 1868. Bloomington, 1868. O.   L
Boston athenæum. Catalogue of the library, 1807—1871. Bost. 1874—82. 5 v. O.   R
— — Additions, 2d ser.; nos. 6—162, mar. 15, 1878—feb. 7, 1885.   L
     Note. Nos. 19—20, 39—40, 59—60, 79—80, 98—100, 137—140 and 160 contain indexes to the nos. issued during the preceeding year.
Boston public library. Bulletins, showing titles of books added, with bibliographical notes etc.; nos. 4, 6, 8, 10—18, 21—27, 29—45, 47—50, 53, 57, 59—70.   L
— Catalogue of the american portion of the library of the rev. T: Prince; with a memoir and list of his publications by W: H. Whitmore. Bost. 1868. D.   L
— Periodicals in the central library, as currently received in the periodical reading room and kept bound in the shelves of the Lower hall and Bates hall. 2d ed., april 1873.   L
— *Bates hall.* Index catalogue of books in the Bates hall. 2d ed. Bost. 1865. Q.   L
— — *Same.* 1st supplement. Bost. 1866. Q.   L
— *Lower hall.* A catalogue of books in the classes of history, biography and travel, including the histories of literature, art, sects etc., politics, geography, voyages, sketches and manners and customs, together with notes for readers under subject references. 2d or consolidated ed. Bost. 1873. Q.   R
— — Catalogue of books in foreign languages. 3d ed., may 1881. Bost. 1881. Q.   L
— — Class list for works in the arts and sciences, including theology, medicine, law, philosophy, moral, mental and social, education, religious and devotional books, ecclesiastical history and missions, domestic and rural economy, recreative arts, trades etc. 2d ed., sept. 1871. Q.   L
— — Catalogue of the works in arts and sciences, supplementary list, may 1881; containing books added between 1871 and 1881, with references to books in the Bates hall. Bost. 1881. Q.   L
— — Class list for english prose fiction, incl. translations and juvenile books, with notes for readers, intended to point out for parallel reading the historical sources of works of fiction. 6th ed., april 1877. Bost. 1877. Q.   L
— — *Same.*   R

Boston public library. *Lower hall—Continued.*
— - Class list for poetry, the drama, rhetoric, elocution, collections, periodicals and miscellaneous works. 1st ed., july 1870.   **L**
— - *Same.*   **R**
— - Index catalogue of a portion of the library arranged in the Lower hall. Bost. 1859. O.   **L**
British museum. A list of the books of reference in the reading room. [Lond.] 1859. O.   **L**
Brookline public library. Catalogue ; supplement, 1873—1881. Compiled by the librarian. Brookline, Mass. 1881. O.   **L**
Brooklyn library. Analytical and classed catalogue; authors, titles, subjects and classes. Brooklyn. 1878—80. F.   **L**
— Bulletin of new books ; no. 5—19, aug. 1872—march 1884.   **L**
Buffalo young men's association. Books for young readers; a classified catalogue. Buffalo. 1881. D.   **L**
— Catalogue of the library. Buffalo. 1871. Q.   **L**
— *Same.* 1st supplement, 1872. Q.   **L**
— Catalogue of the library; in 2 pts. Pt. 1: Catalogue of authors; pt. 2: Classified catalogue. Buffalo. 1848. O.   **L**
California state library. Bibliotheca Californiæ; a descriptive catalogue. Vol. 2: General library, by Ambrose P. Dietz. Sacramento. 1871. O.   **L**
Chicago public library. Finding lists. 3d ed. Chicago. 1876. O.   **L**
— - *Same.* 5th ed. Chicago. 1880. O.   **L**
— - *Same.* 1st supp., april 1881. Chicago. 1881. O.   **L**
— - *Same.* 6th ed., pt. 1, 2. Chicago. 1884. O.   **L**
—**Young men's association.** Catalogue of the library, together with the charter, rules, regulations etc. of the association. Chicago. 1859. O.   **L**
— - Catalogue of the books belonging to the Young men's association of the city of Chicago. V. 1, containing the titles added from the foundation of the library to april 1st 1865, together with an alphabetical index to the whole, compiled by J: M. Horton, librarian. Chicago. 1865. O.   **L**
Cincinnati public library. Catalogue. Cincinnati. 1871. Q.   **L**
— - Catalogue of books in english, french and german, belonging to the class of prose fiction. Cinc. 1876. Q.   **L**
— - Catalogue of the dramas and dramatic poems. Cinc. 1879. Q.   **L**
— - Bulletin of books in the various departments of literature and science, added during the years 1878—1884. Cinc. 1878—84. 7 v. Q.   **L**
— **Young men's mercantile library association.** Catalogue of the books. Cinc. 1869. O.   **L**
Cleveland public library. Bulletins, nos. 1—3: Catalogue of books added to the circulating department 1880—1883. Cleveland. 1880—84. O. and Q.   **L**
— Catalogue of fiction in the public school library; rev. and cor. to jan. 1, 1882. Cleveland. 1882. O.   **L**
— Classified catalogue: Fiction. Cleveland. 1877. O.   **L**
— Subject catalogue of the books in the reference department; alphabetically arranged. Cleveland. 1883. Q.   **L**
Concord, *Mass.,* **free public library.** Catalogue. 1875. Concord. 1875. O.   **L**

Cornell university, *Ithaca, N. Y.* The library of Cornell university ; v. 1, no. 1—11. Ithaca. 1882—85. Q.   **L**
Edinburgh. Faculty of advocates. Catalogue of the printed books in the library of the Faculty of advocates. Edin. 1867—79. 7 v. Q.   **R**
Evansville public library. Catalogue, 1876. Evansville, Ind. 1876. O.   **L**
Franklin institute, *Syracuse, N. Y.* Catalogue. Syracuse. 1857. O.   **L**
Grand Rapids public school library. Classified lists; published by the board of education, oct. 1878. Grand Rapids. 1878. O.   **L**
— *Same.* Supplement, no. 1. Grand Rapids. 1879. O.   **L**
Hamilton and Gore mechanical institute. Catalogue of the library, july 1, 1878; founded feb. 27, 1839, incorp. by act of parliament may 30, 1849. [Offered for sale april 14, 1882.] Hamilton, Ont. 1878. O.   **L**
Hartford library association. Bulletin; ed. by C. M. Hewins, librarian, issued quarterly; v. 1—6. Hartford. 1878—84. O.   **L**
— **Young men's institute.** Catalogue of the books in the library. Hartford. 1839. O.   **L**
— - Catalogue of the library and reading room. Hartford. 1844. O.   **L**
Harvard university bulletin, ed. by Justin Winsor ; nos. 5—30, june 1877—jan. 1885. Cambridge. 1879—85. 3 v. Q.   **L**
Note. Title page of v. 1 reads : Library of Harvard univ. Bulletin of more important accessions, with bibliographical additions.
Illinois state library. Catalogue; 1880. Springfield. 1880. O.   **L**
Indiana state library. Catalogue for 1865; comp. and arr. by B. F. Foster, state librarian. Indianapolis. 1865. O.   **L**
Indianapolis public library. Catalogue; pt. 1: A—E. Indianapolis. 1883. O.   **L**
Long Island historical society. List of recent additions to the library; an app. to the report of the directors presented may 10, 1881. Brooklyn. 1881. O.   **L**
Maryland institute. Catalogue of books in the library of the Maryland institute for the promotion of the mechanic arts; classified and alphabetically arranged by titles. Balt. 1865. O.   **L**
Massachusetts historical society. Catalogue of the library. Bost. 1859, 1860. 2 v. O.   **L**
Milwaukee public library. Catalogue of the books belonging to the Milwaukee public library jan. 1, 1881. Pt. 1: Catalogue of the Y. M. A. 1877; pt. 2: Supplementary catalogue of additions from jan. 1878 to jan. 1881. Milw. 1881. O.   **L**
— - Katalog der bücher in deutscher sprache welche in der öffentlichen bibliothek der stadt Milwaukee zu finden sind ; inhaltlich geordnet, nebst alphabetischem verzeichniss der verfasser. Milw. 1882. Q.   **L**
— - Additions ; nos. 1—38, apr. 30, 1881—jan. 30, 1885.   **L**
— - Katalog der deutschen leih-bibliothek von Holzapfel und Eskuche [incorporated with the public library]. Milw. *n. d.* O.   **L**
— **Public school teachers' library.** Catalogue. Milw. [1879]. D.   **L**
— - Classified catalogue, alphabetically arr. according to names of authors; compiled un-

der the direction of W : E. Anderson. Milw. 1884. D.   **L**

— **South side literary and library association.** First catalogue of the south side library, together with the act of incorporation, names of original subscribers, rules and regulations, list of first and present officers, report of treasurer, etc. Milw. 1869. O. **L**

— **Verein Germania.** Catalog der bibliothek. Milw. 1879. T.   **L**

— **Young men's association.** Constitution, list of officers, by-laws of the library and reading room, and catalogue of the library. Milw. 1848. D.   **L**

— — Charter, rules and regulations of the association and board of directors, with a catalogue of the library. Milw. 1852. D. · **L**

— — Charter, rules and regulations of the association and board of directors, with a catalogue of the library and list of the members. Milw. 1855. D.   **L**

— — *Same.* Supplementary catalogue, with annual report, may 1857. D.   **L**

— — *Same.* 2d supplementary catalogue, with annual report to may 1859. D.   **L**

— — Catalogue of the library. Milw. 1861. O. **L**

— — *Same.* 1st supp. Milw. 1863. O.   **L**

— — *Same.* 2d supp. Milw. 1865. O.   **L**

— — Catalogue of the library, together with the annual reports, rules, etc. Milw. 1868.   **L**

— — Catalogue of books belonging to the library 1877; comp. by W: Ward Wight. [Milw. 1877.] O.   **L**

Minneapolis athenæum. Catalogue of the library. Minneapolis. 1877. O.   **L**

Morrisson library, *Richmond, Ind.* Catalogue, dec. 1876. Richmond. 1876. O.   **L**

— Supplementary catalogue, jan. 1879 to jan. 1881.   **L**

— List of books added from jan. 1881 to jan. 1883.   **L**

Newton, *Mass.,* free library. Class catalogue. Bost. 1880. O.   **L**

— Class bulletin. 1881.   **L**

New York apprentices' library. Catalogue of the apprentices' library, estab. and supported by the General society of mechanics and· tradesmen of the city of New York; in 3 pts. Pt. 1, Classified index; pt. 2, Catalogue of titles and subjects; pt. 3, Catalogue of authors, with a supplement of additions and omissions, and a special catalogue of prose fiction and juvenile literature. Compiled by J. Schwartz, jr., librarian. N. Y. 1874. Q.   **L**

— — Supplement to the catalogue of 1874; a consolidated classified bulletin of all the additions from march 1874 to dec. 1881. N. Y. 1881. Q.   **L**

— **Mercantile library association.** Systematic catalogue, with a general index and one of dramatic pieces, with an app. containing the constitution and the rules and regulations of the association. N. Y. 1837. O.   **L**

— — Catalogue. N. Y. 1850. O.   **L**

— — Catalogue of the books. N. Y. 1866. O. **L**

— *Same.* Supp.; accessions march 1866 to oct. 1869. N. Y. 1869. O.   **L**

— — *Same.* 2d supp.; accessions oct. 1869 to april 1872. N. Y. 1872. O.   **L**

— — Bulletins, nos. 4–6, april 1883—oct. 1884.   **L**

New York state library. Catalogue, jan. 1, 1850. Albany. 1850. O.   **L**

— Catalogue: Maps, manuscript, engravings coins, etc., 1856. Albany. 1857. O.   **L**

— Catalogue of the books on·bibliography, typography and engraving. Albany. 1858. O.   **L**

— *General library.* Catalogue, 1855. Albany. 1855. O.   **L**

— — *Same.* 1st supp., 1861. Albany. 1861. O.   **L**

— — Subject-index, 1872. Albany. 1872. O. **L**

— — *Same.* 1st supp., 1872–1882. Albany. 1882. O.   **L**

— *Law library.* Catalogue. Albany. 1856. O.   **L**

— — *Same.* 1st supp., 1865. Albany. 1865. O. **L**

Peoria public library. Reference list of books in the english language, belonging to the classes of fiction and juveniles; prepared by F: J. Soldan. Peoria, Ill. 1882. Q. **L**

— The library news; a journal for the friends of good reading. Peoria. 1882. O.   **L**

Philadelphia. Library company. A catalogue of the books belonging to the Library company of Phila.; prefixed, a short account of the institution, the charter, laws and regulations. Phila. 1835. 2 v. O. **L**

— — *Same.* V. 3; containing the titles added from 1835 to 1856, with an alphabetical index to the whole. Phila. 1856. O.   **L**

— — Bulletin, new series ; nos. 1–6, 8–14, july 1878–jan. 1885.   **L**

— **Mercantile library company.** Catalogue of books added 1856—1860 ; with an alphabetical list of novels. Phila. 1860. O.   **L**

— — Catalogue of books in closed cases on the north gallery ; arr. by subjects. Phila. 1878. O.   **L**

— — Finding list for novels. Phila. 1878. O. **L**

— — Bulletin ; v. 1, nos. 1—10, oct. 1882—jan. 1885.   **L**

Poughkeepsie public school library. Catalogue, jan. 1858. Poughkeepsie. 1858. O.   **L**

Providence public library. Finding list. Providence. 1880. Q.   **L**

— *Same.* 1st. supp., 1882. Providence. 1882. Q. **L**

Queensland. Parliament. Analytical and classified catalogue of the parliament of Queensland, by D. O'Donovan. Brisbane. 1883. Q.   **L**

St. Louis public school library. Catalogue, classified and alphabetical, of the books ; including also the collections of the St. Louis academy of science and St. Louis law school. Prepared, under direction of the board of managers, by Jno. Jay Bailey, librarian. St. Louis. 1870. Q.   **L**

— — Bulletin ; nos. 1—28, jan. 1879—dec. 1883. **L**

San Francisco free public library. Catalogue no. 2, nov. 1880 ; short titles. San Francisco. [1880]. O.   **L**

— *Same,* no. 3, june 1882 ; short titles. San Francisco. [1882]. O.   **L**

— Monthly bulletin ; v. 1, nos. 1—3, 5—7, 9—11, aug. 15, 1881—july 15, 1882.   **L**

Seymour library, *Auburn, N. Y.* Finding lists. Auburn, N. Y., 1878. O.   **L**

Springfield, *Ohio,* **public library.** Catalogue and classified list. Springfield. 1882. O.   **L**

Taunton, *Mass.,* **public library.** Catalogue ; together with classified index, revised rules and regulations, etc. Taunton. 1878. O. **L**

Taunton public library—*Continued.*
— *Same*, 1st supp. Taunton, 1878. O.　　L
— *Same*, 2d supp. Taunton, 1884. O.　　L
Tennessee state library. Catalogue of the general and law library; prepared by order of the judges of the supreme court. Nashville. 1871. O.　　L
Toronto public library. Catalogue of the circulating library, july 1, 1884. Toronto. [1884]. D.　　L
United States. Library of congress. Additions since nov. 1, 1860, with omissions from the last general catalogue, dec. 1, 1861. Wash. 1862. O.　　L
— - Catalogue of additions from dec. 1, 1865 to dec. 1, 1866. Wash. 1866. O.　　L
— - Catalogue of publications of societies and of periodical works belonging to the Smithsonian institution jan. 1, 1866, [and] deposited in the library of congress. *In* Smithsonian misc.　　**506 : R4v9**
— **Bureau of navigation** Catalogue of the nautical almanac library. Wash. 1883. O.　　L
— **Patent office.** Catalogue of the library. Wash. 1878. Q.　　L
— - Catalogue of additions to the library from may 1, 1878 to may 1, 1883. Wash. 1883. Q.　　L
— **Surgeon general's office.** Index catalogue of the library; v. 1-5. Wash. 1880-82. 5 v. Q.　　L

Contents. V. 1. A—Berlinski. 2. Berlioz—Cholas. 3. Cholecyanin—Dzoudi. 4. E—Fizes. 5. Flaccus —Hearth.

— **War department.** Alphabetical catalogue of the library ; authors and subjects. Wash. 1882. Q.　　L
— **Home for disabled volunteer soldiers**, *Northwestern branch.* Catalogue of the library. National Home. 1875. O.　　L
— - *Same*, 1882. National Home. 1882. O.　　L
Uxbridge free public library. A classed catalogue ; authors, titles, subjects and classes, based on the Dui or Amherst scheme of classification. Uxbridge, Mass. 1881. O. L
Winchester, *Mass.*, **town library.** Class- and author lists. *n. t.* [Winchester. 1879]. Q.　　L
— *Same.* 1st supp. *n. t.* [Winchester. 1882]. Q.　　L

Wisconsin state historical society. Catalogue of the library ; prepared by Daniel S. and Isabel Durrie. Madison. 1873-81. 5 v. O.　　L

Contents. V. 1. A—L. 2. M—Z. 3. 1st supp. 1873-1875. 4. 2d supp. 1875-1878. 5. 3d supp. 1878-1881.

Wisconsin state library. Catalogue, in 3 pts., [by] W: Dudley, state librarian. Madison. 1852. O.　　L
— Catalogue, 1872. Madison. 1872. O.　　L
Woburn, *Mass.*, **public library.** Class lists. Bost. *n. d.* Q.　　L
— Bulletin of accessions for the year ending march 1, 1880. Woburn. [1880]. Q.　　L
— *Same*, for the year ending march 1, 1881. Woburn. 1881. Q.　　L

Worcester free public library. Catalogue of the circulating department, and of a portion of the books belonging to the intermediate department. Worcester, Mass. 1884. O.　　L
— Additions ; nos. 1-77, nov. 1, 1878—mar. 14, 1885.　　L

Private libraries.

Lundstedt, Bernhard. Katalog öfver Finspongs bibliotek. Stockholm. 1883. O.　　L
Beckford, W : The Hamilton palace libraries ; catalogue of the first portion of the Beckford library, removed from Hamilton palace. Sold at auction june 30, 1882.　　L
Béhague, Octave *comte* de. Catalogue des livres rares et précieux composant [sa] bibliothèque. Paris. 1880. O.　　L
Bouton, J. W. Catalogue of a magnificent private library, the property of a gentleman of New York, who has taken up his residence abroad. N. Y. 1868. O.　　L
Campbell, Archibald. Catalogue of the library of the late Archibald Campbell of Germantown. [Sold may 21-25, 1883]. Phila. 1883. Q.　　L
Cooke, Joseph J. Catalogue of the library of the late Joseph J. Cooke, of Providence, R. I. [Sold march 13-15, 1883]. N. Y. 1883. O. L
Farnum, Alexander. Catalogue of the library of Alexander Farnum of Providence, R. I. [Sold nov. 18-20, 1884.] N. Y. 1884. O. L
Ganay, C : Alexandre *marquis* de. Catalogue d'un choix de livres rares et précieux, manuscrits et imprimés, composant [son] cabinet. Paris. 1881. O.　　L
Harris, Caleb Fiske. Catalogue of the second portion of the library of the late C. Fiske Harris of Providence, R. I. [Sold april 1884]. Providence. 1884. Q.　　L
Harrison library, Catalogue of the, with addenda. [Sold feb. 18-20, 1884]. N. Y. 1884. O.　　L
Murphy, H : C. Catalogue of [his] library ; consisting almost wholly of americana or books relating to America. N. Y. 1884. O.　　L
Perkins, H : The Perkins library ; a catalogue of the library formed by [him] at the beginning of the present century. [Lond. 1873]. Q.　　L
Sabin, Joseph. Catalogue of the library collected by Amos Dean, principally with reference to his History of man as unfolded in his civilization. Sale. N. Y. 1868. O.　　L
Spencer, C :, *3d earl of Sunderland.* Bibliotheca sunderlandiana ; sale catalogue of the truly important and very extensive library of printed books, known as the Sunderland or Blenheim library, comprising a remarkable collection of the greek and roman classic writers in first, early and rare editions, a large series of early printed Bibles and Testaments in various languages, a few ancient and important mss. Lond. 1881, 1882. 4 pts. in 1 v. O.　　L
Stevens, H : Bibliotheca geographica et historica, or A catalogue of nine days sale of rare and valuable ancient and modern books, maps, charts, manuscripts, autograph letters, et cetera, illustrative of historical geography and geographical history, general and local annals, biography, genealogy, statistics, ecclesiastical history, poetry, prose and miscellaneous books, very many relating to North and South America and others to Europe, Asia, Africa, Australia and Oceanica ; collected, used and described, with an introd. on the progress of geography and notes and annotatiunculæ

Stevens, H :—*Continued.*
on sundry subjects, with an essay upon the Stevens system of photobibliography ; pt. 1. Lond. 1872. O.   **L**
— Catalogue of my english library. Lond. 1853. S.   **L**
— Stevens historical collections : Catalogue of the first portion of the extensive and varied collections of rare books and manuscripts, relating chiefly to the history and literature of America ; comprising the great collections of voyages and travels of De Bry, in latin and german, Hulsius, Thevenot, Purchas and Hakluyt, with early separate voyages of the dutch, english and french navigators, early american history and literature, Burns' autograph poems, black-letter and other english and american ballads, Chaucer's works, 1532, highly important collections of mss. relating to sir Francis Drake, the colony of Georgia, New England and Virginia, including 18 of the earliest autograph letters of Washington, and H : Stevens's Franklin collection. Lond. 1881. O.   **L**

Thomson, P : G. Bibliotheca carsoniana ; catalogue of a magnificent private library, the property of a gentleman of Cincinnati, especially rich in works on the fine arts, galleries of engravings, dramatic literature, bibliography, manuscripts on vellum, xylography, early printing, etc. Cinc. [1880.] O.   **L**

2. Bibliography and authorship.

1. Books about books.

(*See also* Literary periodicals, class 805, *and* Courses of reading, class 807.)

Blades, W : The enemies of books. 3d ed. Lond. 1881. O.   **L**
Burton, J : Hill. The book-hunter etc., with notes by R: Grant White. N. Y. 1863. S.   **L**
Dibdin, T : Frognall. Bibliomania, or Book-madness; a bibliographical romance illustrated with cuts. A new and imp. ed., to which are added preliminary observations and a supp. including a key to the assumed characters in the drama. Lond. 1876. O.   **L**
Lang, Andrew. The library, with a chapter on modern english illustrated books by Austin Dobson. [Art at home ser.] Lond. 1881. D.   **L**
Petzholdt, Julius. Chronologische übersicht von bibliographischen systemen. Dresden. 1860. D.   **L**
Slater, J. Herbert. The library manual, a guide to the formation of a library, and the valuation of rare and standard books. Lond. [1883]. O.   **L**

* * *

British museum. *Library.* Hand-list of bibliographies, classified catalogues and indexes placed in the reading-room of the British museum for reference. Lond. 1881. O.   **L**
Guild, Reuben Aldridge. The librarian's manual; a treatise on bibliography, comprising a select and descriptive list of bibliographical works, to which are added sketches of publick libraries. Ill. N. Y. 1858. O.   **L**
Petzholdt, Julius. Bibliotheca bibliographica; kritisches verzeichniss der das gesammtgebiet der bibliographie betreffenden litteratur des in- und auslandes, in systematischer ordnung; mit alphabetischem namen- und sachregister. Leipz. 1866. O.   **L**
Vallée, Léon. Bibliographie des bibliographies. 1e pte: Catalogue des bibliographies générales et particulières par ordre alphabétique d'auteurs, avec indication complète du titre, des lieu et date de publication, du format, etc.; 2e pte: Répertoire des mêmes bibliographies par ordre alphabétique des matières. Paris. 1883. O.   **L**

Bibliographer, The; a journal of book-lore; v. 1-6. Lond. 1882-84. Q.   **L**
Neuer anzeiger für bibliographie und bibliothekwissenschaft; herausg. unter verantwortlicher redaction von Julius Petzholdt. Jahrg. 1881-1884. Dresden. 1881-84. 4 v. O.   **L**
Le livre; revue du monde littéraire, archives des écrits de ce temps: Bibliographie moderne. 4e et 5e année. Paris. 1883-84. 2 v. Q. **L**
— Bibliographie rétrospective. 4e et 5e année. Paris. 1883-84. 2 v. Q.   **L**

2. General bibliographies.

Appletons' library manual; containing a catalogue raisonné of upwards of 12,000 of the most important works in every department of knowledge in all modern languages. Pt. 1: Subjects alphabetically arranged; pt. 2: Biography, classics, miscellaneous and index to pt. 1. N. Y. 1847. O.   **L**
Brunet, Jacques C: Manuel du libraire et de l'amateur de livres; contenant, un nouveau dictionnaire bibliographique, une table en forme de catalogue raisonné. 5e éd. Paris. 1860-65. 6 v. O.   **L**
Deschamps, P: C: Ernest, and P: Gustave Brunet. Manuel du libraire et de l'amatuer de livres; supplement contenant 1, un complément du dictionnaire bibliographique de J. Ch. Brunet, 2, la table raisonnée des articles. Paris. 1878, 1880. 2 v. in 1. O.   **L**
Deschamps, P: C: Ernest. Dictionnaire de géographie ancienne et moderne à l'usage de libraire et de l'amateur de livres, par un bibliophile. Paris. 1870. O.   **L**
Ebert, F: Adolph. Allgemeines bibliographisches lexikon. Leipz. 1821, 1830. 2 v. Q.   **L**

Contents. V. 1. A-L. 2. M-Z.

Georgi, Theophilus. Allgemeines europäisches bücher-lexicon, in welchem nach ordnung des dictionarii die allermeisten autores oder gattungen von büchern zu finden [sind], welche....noch vor dem anfange des 16. seculi bis 1789....sind geschrieben und gedrucket worden....anfänglich von

Georgi, Theophilus—*Continued.*
dem autore nur zur privat-notitz zusammengetragen, nummehro aber auf vieler instandiges verlangen zum druck befördert und in 4 theile abgetheilet. Leipz. 1742. F.   **L**
— *Same.* 5er theil; in welchem die frantzösischen auctores und bücher von allen disciplinen, so von dem 16. seculo an bis auf gegenwärtige zeit geschrieben und gedrucket worden sind, in alphabetischer ordnung zu finden [sind]. *Also* Supp. 1–3 [1739–1757]. Leipz. 1750-58. F.   **L**
Perkins, F: Beecher, *ed.* The best reading; hints on the selection of books, on the formation of libraries, public and private, on courses of reading, etc., with a classified bibliography for easy reference. 4th rev. and enl. ed., continued to aug. 1876, with the add. of select list of the best french, german, spanish and italian literature. N. Y. 1877. D.   **L**
Jones, Lynds E., *ed.* The best reading, 2d ser.: A priced and classified bibliography, for easy reference, of the more important english and american publications for the five years ending dec. 31, 1881. N. Y. 1882. D.   **L**
Putnam's library companion; a quarterly summary giving priced and classified list of the english and american publications, with the add. of brief analysis or characterizations of the more important books; a quarterly continuation of the best reading; v. 1–5. N. Y. 1878-82. 5 v. O.   **L**
Clarke, Robert, *and co.* A general catalogue of choice books for the library; comprising a selection of the best books by ancient and modern authors in all departments of literature, science and art; classified and priced. Cinc. 1880. D.   **L**
Leypoldt, F:, *and* Lynds E. Jones. The books of all time; a guide for the purchase of books. N. Y. 1882. T.   **L**
Hewins, Caroline Maria. Books for the young; a guide for parents and chidren. N. Y. 1883. Tt.   **L**
— *Same.* 2d ed. with add. N. Y. 1884. Tt.   **L**
Note. Continued in the Literary news.
Theden, Dietrich. Führer durch die jugendliteratur; grundsätze zur beurtheilung der deutschen jugendliteratur, winke für gründung, einrichtung und fortführung einschlägiger bibliotheken,und verzeichniss empfehlenswerther schriften, für eltern, erzieher und bibliothekare; mit einem vorwort von J. Chr. Gottlob Schumann. Hamb. 1883. O.   **L**
Frankfurt *a. M.* Lehrerverein; *Jugendschriften-kommission:* Ratgeber für eltern, lehrer und bibliothekvorstände bei der auswahl von jugendschriften. Frankfurt a. M. [1884]. O.   **L**

3. Special countries.

American.

Trübner, N: Bibliographical guide to american literature; a classed list of books publ. in the U. S. of America during the last forty years, with bibliographical introd., notes and an alphabetical index. Lond. 1856. O.   **L**

Roorbach, Orville A. Bibliotheca americana; catalogue of american publications, incl. reprints and original works from 1820–1852 incl., together with a list of periodicals published in the U. S. N. Y. 1852. O.   **L**
— *Same.* Supplement, oct. 1852 to may 1855. N. Y. 1855. O.   **L**
— *Same.* Addenda, may 1855 to march 1858. N. Y. 1858. O.   **L**
Kelly, James. The american catalogue of books, original and reprints, published in the U. S., from jan. 1861 to jan. 1871, with date of publication, size, price and publisher's name, [v. 1.] supp. containing pamphlets, sermons and addresses on the civil war in the U. S., 1861–1866, [v. 1 and 2] and names of learned societies and literary associations, with a list of their publications, 1861–1870, N. Y. 1866, 1871. 2 v. O.   **L**
Leypoldt, F:, *and* Lynds E. Jones. The american catalogue of books in print and for sale, incl. reprints and importations, july 1, 1876 ; under the direction of F : Leypoldt, comp. by Lynds E. Jones. [V. 1 :] Author and title entries ; [v. 2 :] Subject entries. N. Y. 1880, 1881. 2 v. Q.   **L**
— *Same.* Supp., july 1, 1876 to july 1, 1884. N. Y. 1885. Q.   **L**
Leypoldt, F:, *ed.* Annual reference list of books recorded in the Publishers' weekly from july 1, 1876 to june 30, 1884 ; with additional titles, corrections, changes of price and publisher, etc. N. Y. 1877-84. O.   **L**
Publishers' trade list annual, The ; embracing the latest catalogues supplied by the publishers, preceded by an order list, a classified summary and alphabetical reference list of books recorded in the Publishers' weekly, with additional titles, corrections, changes of price and publisher. 1873, 1875, 1877-1884. N. Y. 1873-84. 10 v. Q.   **L**
American publishers' circular and literary gazette; v. 1, sept. 1, 1855—v. 8, dec. 1, 1862; New series, v. 1, nos. 1-6. N. Y. 1855-63. 8 v. Q.   **L**
— *Same.* Octavo series; v. 1—18 [G. W. Childs, ed.] Phila. 1863-1872. 18 v. in 15. O.   **L**
Note. V. 2-18 are entitled "American literary gazette and publishers' circular." Jan. 18, 1872 the journal became the property of F: Leypoldt of N. Y. and has since been published as the Publishers' weekly, which see.
Publishers' weekly, The, american book-trade journal, with which is incorporated the American literary gazette and publishers. circular, estab. in 1852. N. Y. 1872-84. 26 v. O.   **L**
Note. V. 1—5 are called "The publishers' and stationers' weekly trade circular," and v. 6-12 "The publishers' weekly ; a journal devoted to the interests of the book and stationery trade."

English.

Collier, J: Payne. A bibliographical and critical account of the rarest books in the english language, alphabetically arranged, which during the last fifty years have come under [his] observation. N. Y. 1866. 4 v. O.   **L**
Walpole, Horace, *4th earl of Orford.* A catalogue of the royal and noble authors of England, with the list of their works. New ed. Edinb. 1792. 2 v. S.   **L**
Savage, James. The librarian, Lond. 1808, 1800. 3 v. O.   **L**

Watt, Robert. Bibliotheca britannica, or A general index to british and foreign literature; in 2 pts : authors and subjects. Edinb. 1824. 4 v. in 8. Q.   **L**
Contents. V. 1. Authors: A—H. 2. I—Z. 3. Subjects: A—H. 4. I—Z.

Lowndes, W: T: The bibliographer's manual of english literature ; containing an account of rare, curious and useful books published in, or relating to Great Britain and Ireland, from the invention of printing, with bibliographical and critical notices, collations of rarer articles and the prices at which they have been sold in the present century. New ed., rev. and enl. by H : G : Bohn. Lond. 1857–64. 6 v. D.   **L**
Note. V. 6 contains Appendix ; an account of books issued by literary and scientific societies and printing clubs, books printed at private presses, privately printed series, and the principal literary and scientific serials, comp. by H: G. Bohn.

Hazlitt, W: Carew. Hand-book to the popular, poetical and dramatic literature of Great Britain, from the invention of printing to the restoration. Lond. 1867. O.   **L**
— Collections and notes, 1867–1876. Lond. 1876. O.   **L**
— Second series of bibliographical collections and notes on early english literature, 1474–1700. Lond. 1882. O.   **L**

Bent, Robert. London catalogue of books, with their sizes, prices and publishers, containing the books published in London, and those altered in size or price since 1814 to dec. 1834. Lond. 1835. O.   **L**

Low, Sampson. The english catalogue of books ; an alphabetical list of works published in the United Kingdom and of the principal works published in America, with dates of publication, indication of size, price, ed. and publisher's name; 1835–1880. Lond. 1864–82. 3 v. O.   **L**
Contents. V. 1. 1835–1863. 2. 1863–1871. 3. 1872–1880.
— Index to the english catalogue of books pub. during [v. 1.] 1837–1857, [v. 2.] 1856–1875, [v. 3.] 1874–1880. Lond. 1858–84. 3 v. O. **L**
Note. The title-page of v. 1 reads : Index to the British catalogue, &c.
— The english [annual] catalogue of books, containing a complete list of all books pub. in Great Britain and Ireland in 1872[–1884], with their sizes, prices, and publishers' names, also of the principal books pub. in the U. S. of America, with the add. of an index to subjects ; a continuation of the London and British catalogues. Lond. 1873–85. O.   **L**

Whitaker, Joseph. The reference catalogue of current literature, containing the full titles of books now in print and on sale, with the prices at which they may be obtained of all booksellers, and an index [containing upwards of 53,000 references] ; 1874, 1875, 1877, 1880, 1885. Lond. 1874–85. 5 v. O. **L**
Note. The v. for 1877 contains also a list of the most familiar pen names.

Publishers' circular, The, and general record of british and foreign literature ; containing a complete alphabetical list of all new works pub. in Great Britain, and every work of interest pub. abroad; v. 43–46. Lond. 1880–84. 5 v. O.   **L**

Bookseller, The ; a newspaper of british and foreign literature, with which is incorporated Bent's literary advertiser, estab. in 1802; pub. monthly. Lond. 1880–84. 5 v. O.   **L**

German.

Maltzahn, Wendelin v. Deutscher bücherschatz des sechzehnten, siebenzehnten und achtzehnten, bis um die mitte des neunzehnten jahrhunderts, gesammelt und mit bibliographischen erläuterungen herausg. Jena. 1875. O.   **L**

Völcker, G: Register zu Wendelin v. Maltzahn's Deutschen bücherschatz des 16ten, 17ten und 18ten bis um die mitte des 19ten jahrhunderts. Frankfurt a. M. 1882. O. *With* **Maltzahn,** W. v. Deutscher bücherschatz.   **L**

Kayser, Christian Gottlob. Index locupletissimus librorum ; vollständiges bücher-lexicon, enthaltend alle von 1750 bis zu ende des jahres [1882] in Deutschland und in den angrenzenden ländern gedruckten bücher, in alphabetischer übersicht aller autoren, der. anonymen sowohl als der pseudonymen, und einer genauen angabe der kupfer und karten der auflagen und ausgaben, der formate, der druckorte, der jahrzahlen, der verleger und der preise. Leipz. 1834–83. 22 v. Q.   **L**
Contents. V. 1–6. 1750–1832. 7, 8. 1833–1840. 9, 10. 1841–1846. 11, 12. 1847–1852, bearb. von Ernst A. Zuchold. 13, 14. 1853–1858, bearb. von Gustav W: Wuttig. 15, 16. 1859–1864, bearb. von G. W: Wuttig. 17, 18. 1865–1870, bearb. von G. W: Wuttig und R: Haupt. 19, 20. 1871–1876, bearb. von R: Haupt. 21, 22. 1877–1882, bearb. von R: Haupt.
— Sachregister zum Kayser'schen Bücher-lexicon, [b. 1–6]. Leipz. 1838. Q.   **L**

Ersch, J: S: Handbuch der deutschen literatur seit der mitte des 18ten jahrhunderts bis auf die neueste zeit, systematisch bearb. und mit den nöthigen registern versehen. Neue, mit verschiedenen mitarbeitern besorgte ausg. Leipz. 1822–40. 4 v. Q.   **L**
Contents. V. 1.—1te abth. Literatur der philologie, philosophie und pädagogik, bearb. von Ernst Gottfried Adolph Böckel.—2te abth. Literatur der theologie, bearb. von E. G. A. Böckel. 2.—1te abth. Literatur der jurisprudenz und politik mit einschluss der cameral-wissenschaften; neue ausg. bearb. von J. Christian Koppe.—2te abth. Literatur der schönen künste; neue fortgesetzte ausg., bearb. von J: K: A: Rese und Christian Anton Geissler. 3. 1ste abth. Literatur der medicin, bearb. von F: A: B: Puchelt.—2te abth. Literatur der mathematik, natur- und gewerbs-kunde, mit einbegriff der kriegs-kunst und anderer künste, ausser den schönen, bearb. von Franz W: Schweigger-Seidel. 4. 1ste abth. Geschichte und deren hülfswissenschaften.—2te abth. Literatur der vermischten schriften; neue fortgesetzte ausg. bearb. von Christian Anton Geissler.
— Literatur der philologie ,philosophie und pädagogik seit der mitte des 18ten jahrh. bis auf die neueste zeit ; systematisch bearb. und mit den nöthigen registern versehen. Neue fortg. ausg. von Ernst Gottfried Adolph Böckel; aus der neuen ausg. des Handbuebs der deutschen literatur besonders abgedruckt. Leipz. 1822. O.   **L**
— Bibliographisches handbuch der philosophischen literatur der deutschen, von der mitte des 18ten jahrh. bis auf die neueste zeit ; in systematischer ordnung bearb. und mit den nöthigen registern versehen von Christi n Anton Geissler. 3te aufl. Leipz. 1850. Oa   **L**

Gödeke, K: Grundrisz zur geschichte der deutschen dichtung, aus den quellen. Hannover *and* Dresden. 1859–84. 4 v. in 5. O. **830. 1 : L5**
Note. Contains an exhaustive bibliography of the subject, from the earliest time to 1830.

Othmer, Gustav. Vademecum des sortimenters; zusammenstellung der wissenswürdigsten erscheinungen auf dem gebiete der gesammelten werke und schönen literatur, vorzugsweise der deutschen, von anbeginn bis zur gegenwart. nebst genauer angabe der preise und verleger, sowie kurzen biographischen und bibliographischen notizen. 3te aufl.; mit einem vorworte von Leo Meyer. Hannover. 1878. D. **L**

— — Nachtrag zur 3. auflage, umfassend die jahre 1878-1884, bearbeitet von C: Georg und Leopold Ost. Hannover. 1884. D. **L**

Verzeichniss der bücher, landkarten etc., welche vom januar [1878] bis dezember 1884 neu erschienen oder neu aufgelegt worden sind, mit angabe der seitenzahl, der verleger, der preise, literarischen nachweisungen und einer wissenschaftlichen übersicht. Herausg. und verlegt von der J. C. Hinrichs'schen buchhandlung in Leipzig. Leipz. 1878-84. 14 v. in 13. D. **L**

Baldamus, E:, *ed.* Hinrichs' repertorium über die nach den halbjährlichen verzeichnissen 1876-1880 erschienenen bücher, landkarten etc.; mit einem sachregister. Leipz. 1882. D. **L**

Russell, Adolph, *ed.* Buch- und kunst-katalog: gesammt-verlags-katalog des deutschen buchhandels; ein bild deutscher geistesarbeit und cultur, vollständig bis ende 1880. Münster i. W. 1881. 13 v. in 9. Q. **L**
Contents. V. **1.** *Deutsches reich.* Aachen-Bensheim. **2.** Berlin. **3.** Bernburg-Düsseldorf. **4.** Ebersbach-Gütersloh. **5.** Habelschwerdt-H u s u m. **6.** Jauer-Leer. **7.** Leipzig. **8.** Leisnig-Nürnberg. **9.** Oberglogau-Striegau. **10.** Stuttgart. **11.** Suhl-Zwickau. **12.** *Not yet published.* **13.** *Oesterreich-Ungarn.* Wien. **14.** Schweitz.

Börsenblatt für den deutschen buchhandel und die mit ihm verwandten geschäftszweige, redigirt von Julius Krauss; märz 1880— dez. 1884. Leipz. [1880—84]. 13 v. Q. **L**

French.

Ventouillac, L. T. The french librarian, or Literary guide; pointing out the best works of the principal writers of France, in every branch of literature, with criticisms, personal anecdotes and bibliographical notices, preceded by a sketch of the progress of french literature. Lond. 1829. O. **L**

Quérard, Joseph Marie. La France littéraire, ou Dictionnaire bibliographique des savants, historiens et gens de lettres de la France, ainsi que des littérateurs étrangers qui ont écrit en français, plus particulièrement pendant les 18e et 19e siècles. Paris. 1827-39. 10 v. O. **L**

—, C: Léopold **Louandre,** L: Félix **Bourquelot** and L: Ferdinand Alfred **Maury.** La littérature française contemporaine, 1827-[1849], continuation de la France littéraire; dictionnaire bibliographique renfermant : 1o, par ordre alphabétique de noms d'auteurs l'indication chronologique des ouvrages français et étrangers publiés en France, et celle des ouvrages français publiés à l'étranger ; 2o, une table des livres anonymes et polyonymes ; 3o, une table générale méthodique ; le tout accompagné de biographies et de notes historiques et littéraires. Paris. 1842-57. 6 v. O. **L**
Note. The titles of v. 1 and 6 vary somewhat from the above.

Lorenz, O: H: Catalogue général de la librairie française depuis 1840. Paris 1867-80. 8 v. O. **L**
Contents. V. **1-4.** 1840-65. **5,6.** 1866-75. **7,8.** Table des matières 1840-75.
Note. Title-page of v. 1-4 reads: Catalogue général de la librairie française pendant 25 ans, 1840-65.

— Catalogue annuel de la librairie française pour 1876. Paris. 1877. O. **L**

— Catalogue mensuel de la librairie française, 1877-83. Paris. [1878-84.] 7 v. O. **L**

Swedish.

Linnström, Hjalmar. Svenskt boklexikon, åren 1830-65. Stockholm. 1883, 1884. 2 v. Q. **L**

Broberg, C. Svensk bok-katalog för åren 1866-75. [*Anon.*] Stockholm. [1878]. O. **L**

Årskatalog för svenska bokhandeln : nominalkatalog ; systematisk katalog. 1876, 1877, 1879-1883. Stockholm. 1877-84. O. **L**

Norwegian and Danish.

Nyerup, Rasmus, *and* Jens E. **Kraft.** Almindeligt litteraturlexicon for Danmark, Norge og Island, eller Fortegnelse over danske, norske og islandske, saavel aldde som nu levende, forfattere med anförelse af deres vigtigste levnets-omstandigheder og liste over deres skrifter. Kjöbenhavn. 1820. O. **L**

Halvorsen, J. B. Norsk forfatter-lexikon, 1814-1880 ; og grundlag af J. E. Krafts og Chr. Langes "Norsk forfatter-lexikon, 1814-1856" samlet, redigeret og udgivet. Kristiania. 1881-84. O. **L**
Note. Published only to the art. Bugge.

Erslew, T: Hansen. Almindeligt forfatter-lexicon for kongeriget Danmark med tilhörende bilande fra 1814 til 1840, eller Fortegnelse over de sammesteds födte forfattere og forfatterinder, som levede ved begyndelsen af året 1814, eller siden ere födte, med anförelse af deres vigtigste levnets-omständigheder og af deres trykte arbejder ; samt over de i hertugdömmerne og i udlandet födte forfattere, som i bemeldte tiderum have opholdt sig i Danmark og der udgivet skrifter. Kjöbenhavn. 1843-53. 3 v. O. **L**

— — Supplement, indtil udgangen af året 1853. Kjöbenhavn. 1858-68. 3 v. O. **L**

Fabricius, F: Dansk bogfortegnelse for årene 1841-58. Kjöbenhavn. 1861. Q. **L**

Vahl, Johannes. Dansk bogfortegnelse for 1859 -68. Kjöbenhavn. 1871. Q. **L**

— *Same.* 1869-80. Kjöbenhavn. 1882. Q. **L**

Dutch.

Meulen, R. van der. Brinkman's catalogus der boeken-, plaat- en kaartwerken die gedurende de jaren 1850-1882 in Nederland zijn uitgegeven of herdrukt ; in alphabetische volgorde gerangschikt, met vermelding van den naam des uitgevers of eigenaars, het jaar van uitgave, het getal deelen, de platen en kaarten, het formaat en den prijs. Amsterdam. [1884.] O. **L**
Note. Published only to the art. Levensboek.

4. Special subjects and Indexes.

(For indexes of periodicals, see below, class 51.)

Collections.

Harvard university library. Bibliographical contributions, ed. by Justin Winsor, librarian. No. 1-6, 8-15, 18. Cambridge. 1879–84. Q.   **L**

Contents. **1. Holden, E: S.** Index-catalogue of books and memoirs on the transits of Mercury. [To be found only in Harvard university bulletins, v. 1: 209.] **2. Winsor, J.** Shakespeare's poems ; a bibliography of the earlier editions. **3. Norton, C: E.** List of the principal books relating to the life and works of Michelangelo, with notes. **4. Winsor, J.** Pietas et gratulatio; an inquiry into the authorship of the several pieces. **5.** List of apparatus available for scientific researches involving accurate measurements and contained in different american laboratories. **6.** The collection of books and autographs bequeathed to Harvard college library by the hon. C: Sumner. **7.** [Not yet publ.] **8.** Calendar of of the Arthur Lee mss. in the library of Harvard university. **9. Goodale, G: L.** The floras of different countries. **10. Winsor, J.** Halliwelliana; a bibliography of the publications of James Orchard Halliwell-Phillipps. **11. Scudder, S: H.** The entomological libraries of the U. S. **12.** List of the publications of Harvard university and its officers; 1870—1880. **13. Scudder, S: H.** A bibliography of fossil insects. **14. Tillinghast, W: H.** Notes on the historical hydrography of the Handkerchief Shoal in the Bahamas. **15. Whitney, J. D.** List of american authors in geology and palæontology. **16. Bliss, R:** Classified index to the maps in Petermann's geographische mittheilungen, 1855–1881. **17.** [Not yet publ.] **18. Winsor, J.** The bibliography of Ptolemy's geography.

Index Society. [Publications.] Lond. 1879–84. 11 v. O.   **L**

Contents. **1878. No. 1.** What is an index? a few notes on indexes and indexers; by H: B. Wheatley. **2.** An index of the names of the royalists whose estates were confiscated during the commonwealth, with a reprint of the three confiscation acts of 1651 and 1652, from Scobell's "Collection of acts and ordinances of general use from the 3d of nov. 1640 to the 17th of sept. 1856", comp. by Mabel G. W. Peacock. **3.** Index of municipal offices, comp. from the appendixes to the 1st report of the commissioners appointed to inquire into the municipal corporations in England and Wales, 1835, with an historical introd. by G. Laurence Gomme. **1879. 4.** 1st annual report, to which are added four appendixes: I. Index to books and papers on marriage between near kin, by Alfred H. Huth; II. Index of the styles and titles of English sovereigns by Walter De Gray Birch; III. Index of Portraits in the "European magazine," "London magazine" and "Register of the times", by E. Solly; IV. Index of obituary notices for 1878. **5.** An index of hereditary english, scottish and irish titles of honour, comp. by E: Solly. **1880. 7.** 2d annual report and appendixes: I. Index of portraits in the "British gallery of portraits", Jerdan's "Portrait gallery", Knight's "Gallery of portraits" and "Lodge's po t ai s"; II. Index of abridgments of patents; IIIr Index of obituary notices for 1879. **8.** Guide to the literature of botany; being a classified selection of botanical works, including nearly 6000 titles not given in Pritzel's Thesaurus, by B: Daydon Jackson. **1881. 9.** Index of obituary notices for 1880. **10.** An index to Norfolk topography by Walter Rye. **1882. 11.** Vegetable technology; a contribution towards a bibliography of economic botany with a comprehensive subject index, by B: Daydon Jackson, founded upon the collections of G: James Symons. **12.** 'Index of obituary notices for 1881. **1883. 13.** Index to english speaking students who have graduated at Leyden university, by E: Peacock. **14.** Index of obituary notices for 1882.

Providence public library. Monthly reference lists, ed. by W. E. Foster; 1881–1884. Providence and N. Y. 1881–84. 4 v. O.

                                    L

— *Same.*   **R**

Note. Continued in the Literary news.

Müller, J: Die wissenschaftlichen vereine und gesellschaften Deutschlands im 19ten jahrhundert ; bibliographie ihrer veröffentlichungen seit ihrer begründung bis auf die gegenwart. 1te–4te lief. Berlin. 1883, 1884. Q.   **L**

Theology.

Briggs, C: A: A catalogue of books of reference on biblical study.   *in* **220 : 15**

Hurst, J: Fletcher. Bibliotheca theologica ; a select and classified bibliography of theology and g n l religious literature. N. Y. 1883. O.e era   **L**

Clark, Robert, *and co.* Catalogue of theological and religious books, alphabetically arranged by subject and author; comprising a large collection of the best works, both new and old, american and foreign, in the various departments of theological literature. Cinc. [1879]. O. *With their* Bibliotheca americana, 1878.   **L**

Wolf's theologisches vademecum ; alphabetische und systematische zusammenstellung der neueren und besseren literatur-erscheinungen auf dem gebiete der theologie. [Leipz. 1881]. D.   **L**

Spurgeon, C: Haddon. Commenting and commentaries ; lectures addressed to the students of the pastor's college, Metropolitan Tabernacle, with a list of the best biblical commentaries and expositions, also a lecture on eccentric preachers, with a complete list of all of Spurgeon's sermons, with the scripture texts used. N. Y. 1876. D. **L**

Alger, W: Rounseville. A critical history of the doctrine of a future life ; with a complete bibliography of the subject. Phila. 1864. O.   **218 : 1**

Arnott,—.Bibliotheca diabolica ; a choice selection of the most valuable books relating to the devil, his origin, greatness and influence, comprising the most important works on the devil, satan, demons, hell, hell-torments, magic, witchcraft, sorcery, divination, superstitions, angels, ghosts, etc., with some curious volumes on dreams and astrology; in two parts, pro and con, serious and humorous, chronologically arranged, with notes, quotations and proverbs and a copious index. Ill. [*Anon.*] N. Y. 1870. Q.   **L**

Finotti, Joseph M. Bibliographia catholica americana ; a list of works written by catholic authors and published in the U. S. Pt. 1: 1784–1820. N. Y. 1872. O.   **L**

Dexter, H: Martyn. Collections toward a bibliography of congregationalism. *In his* Congregationalism of the last 300 years.   **285+3**

Bixby, J. T. The study of the non-christian religions. *In* Unitarian rev., v. 17, p. 126–149.   **M**

Sociology and philosophy.

Cossa, L: Guide to the study of political economy. Tr. from the 2d italian ed. with a preface by W. Stanley Jevons. Lond. 1880. D.   **330 : 13**

Society for political education. Political economy and political science ; a priced and classified list of books recommended for general reading, and as an introd. to special

study, on the following subjects : political
economy, finance, taxation, relations of
labor and capital, wages, coöperation, land-
tenure, free trade and protection, commerce and trade, social science, communism, socialism, political science, civil service, minority representation, the constitution of the U. S., etc.; comp. by W. G.
Sumner, D: A. Wells. W. E. Foster, R. L.
Dugdale and G. H. Putnam. (Economic
tracts, no. 2.) N. Y. 1881. D.   **L**

Foster, W: E. The literature of civil service reform in the U. S.; publ. by the Young
men's political club. Providence. 1881.
O.   **L**

Clarke, Robert, *and co.* Catalogue of american
and british works on political economy,
finance and kindred subjects ; with an index of subjects. Cinc. 1879. O. *With
their* Bibliotheca americana, 1878.   **L**

Wolf's juristisches vademecum ; eine alphabetisch und systematisch geordnete handbi-
bliothek von allen brauchbaren werken,etc.
älterer bis neuester zeit, auf dem gesammt-
gebiete der rechts- und staats-wissenschaf-
ten. 2te völlig umgearb. und erweiterte
aufl.; mit materienregister. Leipz. 1883.
D.   **L**

Spencer, Herbert. Political institutions. N. Y.
1882. O.   **192 : 7 v7 pt 2**
Note. Contains, on p. 678-686, list of "Titles of
works referred to."

Wolf's philosophisch-pädagogisches vademecum ; alphabetische und systematische zusammenstellung der neueren und besseren
literaturerscheinungen auf dem g i
der philosophie, pädagogik und d̶e̶s̶ a̶t̶e̶
schauungs-unterrichts aller länder. [Leipz.
1882]. D.   **L**

Larned, J. N. List of works on charity and
kindred subjects, p. 249-254 of   **361 : 2**

Gustafson, Axel. The foundation of death ; a
study of the drink question.   **178 : 7**
Note. Contains, on p. 499-562, a bibliography of the
subject.

Philology.

Wolf's linguistisches vademecum ; eine alphabetisch und systematisch geordnete hand-
bibliothek ausgewählter werke und abhandlungen auf dem gebiete der lingui-
stik. 1 : Orientalia, Americana etc., mit
materienregister. [Leipz. 1883.] D.   **L**

Trübner *and co.* Catalogue of dictionaries and
grammars of the principal languages and
dialects of the world. 2d ed. enl. and rev.
with alphabetical index ; a guide for students and booksellers. Lond. 1882. O. **L**

Müldener, F: A: W:, *ed.* Bibliotheca philologi-
ca, oder Geordnete übersicht aller auf dem
gebiete der classischen alterthumswissenschaft wie der älteren und neueren sprach-
wissenschaft in Deutschland und dem aus-
land neu erschienenen bücher. Göttingen.
1876-82. 9 v. in 5. O.   **L**

Ebering, Emil, *ed.* Bibliographischer anzeiger
für romanische sprachen﹜und literaturen.
Leipz. 1883, 1884. O.   **L**

Möbius, Theodor. Catalogus librorum islandicorum et norvegicorum ætatis mediæ, edi-
torum, versorum, illustratorum. Skáldatal
sive Poetarum recensus Eddæ upsaliensis.
Lipsiæ. 1856. O.   **L**

Möbius, Theodor.— *Continued.*
— Verzeichniss der auf dem gebiete der altnor-
dischen, altisländischen und altnorwegi-
schen, sprache und literatur, von 1855 bis
1879 erschienen schriften. Leipz. 1880. O.
With his Catalogus librorum islandicorum
et norvegicorum.   **L**

Natural science.

Engelmann, W: Bibliotheca historico-naturalis:
Verzeichniss der bücher über naturgeschichte welche in Deutschland, Scandina-
vien, Holland, England, Frankreich, Italien und Spanien in den jahren 1700-1846
erschienen sind ; mit einem namen- und
sachregister. Leipz. 1846. O.   **L**

— *Same.* Supplement-band : Bibliotheca zoologica ; verzeichniss der schriften über zoologie, welche in den periodischen werken
enthalten und vom jahre 1846-1860 selbst-
ständig erschienen sind, mit einschluss der
allgemein-naturgeschichtlichen, periodischen und palæontologischen schriften;
bearb. von J. Victor Carus. Leipz. 1861.
2 v. O.   **L**

Metzger, Adolph, *ed.* Bibliotheca historico-
naturalis, physico-chemica et mathematica,
oder Systematisch geordnet übersicht der
in Deutschland und dem auslande auf dem
gebiete der gesammten naturwissenschaften und der mathemathik neu erschienenen
bücher. Göttingen. 1874-83. 10 v. in 5.
O.   **L**

Royal society of London. Catalogue of scientific papers; v. 1-6, 1800-63, v. 7, 8, 1864-73.
Lond. 1867-79. 8 v. Q.   **L**

May, G:, *comp.* A bibliography of electricity
and magnetism, 1860 to 1883 ; with special
reference to electro-technics. Index by
O. Salle. Lond. 1884. D.   **L**

Waitz, Theodor. Anthropologie der naturvölker. 2te aufl. Leipz. 1860-77. 6 v. O. **572:1**
Note. V. 1. p. xvii-xxxii. 2. p. xvii-xxiv. 3. p.
xix-xxxii. 6. p. xviii-xxii contain "Literatur" of
the subject.

Balfour, Francis M. A treatise on comparative
embryology. Lond. 1881. 2 v. O.   **576:1**
Note. Contains a bibliography of the subject, a
portion at the end of each volume, in v. 1. p. i-xxii,
in v. 2. p. i-xxii.

Pritzel, G: A: Thesaurus literaturæ botanicæ
omnium gentium, inde a rerum botani-
carum initiis ad nostra usque tempora ;
quindecim millia operum recensens. Ed.
nov. ref. Lipsiæ. 1872. Q.   **L**

Jackson, B: Daydon. Guide to the literature of
botany ; being a classified selection of
botanical works, including nearly 6000
titles not given in Fritzel's Thesaurus.
(Index society pub., no. 8). Lond. 1881.
O.   **L**

— Vegetable technology; a contribution towards
a bibliography of economic botany, with
a comprehensive subject index ; founded
upon the collections of G: James Symons.
(Index society pub., no. 11). Lond. 1882.
O.   **L**

Agassiz, L: J: Rudolph. Bibliographia zoolo-
giæ et geologiæ ; a general catalogue of
all books, tracts and memoirs on zoology
and geology; corr. enl. and ed. by H. E.
Strickland and sir W: Jardine. [Ray
society.] Lond. 1848-54. 4 v. O.   **L**

Magnin, Antoine. The bacteria. Tr. by G: M. Sternberg. Bost. 1880. O.   **593 : 2**
Note. Contains, on p. 191–222, a bibliography of the subject.

Gill, Theodore N: Bibliography of the fishes of the Pacific coast of the U. S. to the end of 1879. *In* Smithsonian misc.   **506 : R4 v23**

Giebel, Christoph Gottfried. Thesaurus ornithologiæ ; repertorium der gesammten ornithologischen literatur und nomenclatur sämmtlicher gattungen und arten der vögel, nebst synonymen und geographischer verbreitung. Leipz. 1872–77. 3 v. O. L

Coues, Elliott. American ornithological bibliography. Pt. 1: Faunal publications relating to North America. *In his* Birds of the Colorado valley; U.S. geol. survey, Hayden, misc. publ., no. 11.   **557.5 : D**
— *Same.* Pt. 2: Faunal publications, relating to Central and South America, and the West Indies. *In* U. S. geol. survey of the terr., Hayden; Bulletin, v. 5.   **557.5 : D**
— *Same.* Pt. 3: Systematic bibliography of the whole of America. *In* U. S. geol. survey of the terr., Hayden; Bulletin, v. 5.   **557.5: D**

Gill, Theodore, *and* Elliott **Coues.** Material for a bibliography of north american mammals. *In* Coues, E., *and* J. A. **Allen.** Monographs of north amer. rodentia; app. B.   *in* **557.5: D**

Allen, Joel Asaph. Preliminary list of works and papers relating to the mammalian orders cete and sirenia. *In* U. S. geol. survey of the terr., Hayden; Bulletin, v. 6.   **557.5: D**

Practical arts.

Wolf's medicinisches vademecum; alphabetisch-systematische zusammenstellung von neuen und renommirten erscheinungen der literatur des in- und auslandes auf dem gebiete der heilwissenschaft und thierheilkunde; mit register der systeme und schlagwörter. 3te verm. und verb. aufl. [Leipz.] 1883. D. L

Clarke, Robert, *and co.* Bibliotheca medica; a catalogue of american and british books, periodicals, transactions etc. relating to medicine, surgery, dentistry, pharmacy, chemistry, and kindred subjects, classified by subjects with an index by authors. 3d ed. Cinc. 1879. D. L
— Catalogue of books on engineering, mechanics, mining, manufactures and trades. Cinc. 1878. D. *With* Bibliotheca medica. L
— List of recent books on agriculture, botany, horticulture, etc. Cinc. 1877. D. *With* Bibliotheca medica. L

Jeffries, B: Joy. Color-blindness; its dangers and its detection. Bost. 1879. D.   **616:10**
Note. Contains, on p. 291–308, a bibliography of the subject.

Pitha, Franz *freiherr* v., *and* Christian Albert Theodor **Billroth,** *eds.* Handbuch der allgemeinen und speciellen chirurgie. Erlangen. 1865–82. 13 v. in 12. O.   **617: 6**
Contents. see under Useful arts, Medicine.—Each treatise included contains a special bibliography of its subject.

Bigmore, E. C., *and* C. W. H. **Wyman,** *comp.* A bibliography of printing, with notes and illustrations, v. 1, 2. Lond. 1880, 1884. 2 v. O.   L
Contents. v. 1. A—L. 2. M—S.

Rockwell, Julius Ensign. Bibliography of short-hand works in the english language. (U. S. Bureau of education ; Circulars of information, no. 2, 1884.)   **370: D**

Fine arts.

South Kensington museum. *Science and art department of the committee of council on education.* The first proofs of the universal catalogue of books on art, compiled for the use of the national art library and the schools of art in the United Kingdom. Lond. 1870, 1877. 3 v. O.   L

Vinet, Ernest. Bibliographie méthodique et raisonnée des beaux-arts, esthétique et histoire de l'art, archéologie, architecture, sculpture, peinture, gravure, arts industriels, etc., accompagnée de tables alphabétiques et analytiques; publiée sous les auspices du ministère de l'instruction publique, des cultes et des beaux-arts. [Complément du Manuel du libraire et de l'amateur de livres.] Pt. 1, 2. Paris. 1874, 1877. O.   L
Note. All published up to the author's death, and not continued.

Clarke, Robert, *and co.* Catalogue of works on the fine arts. Pt. 1: General art, painting, sculpture, engravings, ceramics, descriptive, historical and biographical ; pt. 2 : Practical drawing, painting, carving, engraving and photography. Cinc. 1879. D. *With their* Bibliotheca medica.   L

Hoe, Robert, *jr.* Bibliography of engraving. *In* **Maberly,** J. The print collector.   **769+P3**

Literature.

Harrison, J. E. Myths of the Odyssey in art and literature. Lond. 1882. O.   **292:4**
Note. Pages 215–219 contain App. of authorities.

Ireland, Alexander. Ralph Waldo Emerson. his life, genius and writings ; a biographical sketch. 2d ed. Lond. 1882. D.   **921.1: 3**
Note. Contains, on p. 334–337, "Articles on Emerson in english and american periodicals."

Shepherd, R: Herne. The bibliography of Carlyle ; a bibliographical list, arranged in chronological order, of the published writings in prose and verse of T: Carlyle, 1820 to 1881. Lond. [1881]. D.   L
— The bibliography of Dickens; a bibliographical list, arranged in chronological order, of the published writings in prose and verse of C: Dickens, 1834 to 1880. Lond. [1880]. D.   L
— The bibliography of Ruskin; a bibliographical list, arranged in chronological order, of the published writings in prose and verse of J: Ruskin, from 1834 to the present time, oct. 1878. N. Y. 1878. D.   L

Hay, D: Ramsay. A catalogue raisonné of the works of D. R. Hay, with critical remarks by various authors. Edinb. 1849. O.   L

Hirzel, Salomon. Verzeichniss einer Goethe-bibliothek, mit nachträgen und fortsetzung herausg. von L: Hirzel. Leipz. 1884. D.   L

Wyman, W. H. Bibliography of the Bacon-Shakespeare controversy, with notes and extracts. Cinc. 1884. O.　　**L**

Parton, James. Life of Voltaire. Bost. 1881. 2 v. O.　　　　**921.4:3**
Note. Contains, at the end of v. 1. pp. 615–639, "A list of publications relating to Voltaire and to his works" and "A list of the works of Voltaire".

Bowen, H: Courthope, *comp.* Descriptive catalogue of historical novels and tales, for the use of school libraries and teachers of history ; enl. from the list in the Journal of education, march 1882. Lond. 1882. O.　**L**

Leypoldt, F: A reading diary of modern fiction ; containing a representative list of the novels of the 19th century, preceded by suggestive remarks on novels and novel reading. N. Y. 1881. T.　　　　**L**

Whitney, James Lyman. A modern Proteus, or A list of books published under more than one title. N. Y. 1884. S.　　　　**L**

History and Geography.

Adams, C: Kendall. A manual of historical literature ; comprising brief descriptions of the most important histories in english, french and german, together with practical suggestions as to methods and courses of historical study, for the use of students, general readers and collectors of books. N. Y. 1882. D.　　　　　**L**

Short, J: T. Historical reference lists for the use of students in the Ohio state university. Columbus, O. 1882. D.　　　　**L**

Müldener, F: A: W:, *and* E. **Ehrenfeuchter,** *eds.* Bibliotheca historica, oder Systematisch geordnete übersicht der in Deutschland und dem auslande auf dem gebiete der gesammten geschichte neu erschienenen bücher. Göttingen. 1874–82. 9 v. in 5.　**L**

Gardiner, S: Rawson, *and* James Bass **Mullinger.** Introduction to the study of english history. Lond. 1881. O.　　**942 : 13**
Note. Pages 207–404 contain a bibliography.

Allen, W: Francis. The reader's guide to english history, [and supplement.] Bost. 1882. *obl.* T.　　　　　　**L**
Contents of supplement: Ancient history; Modern history of Europe; American history.

Franklin, Alfred L: A: Les sources de l'histoire de France ; notices bibliographiques et analytiques des inventaires et des recueils de documents relatifs à l'histoire de France. Paris. 1877. O.　　　　**L**

Solberg, L: Thorvald. A bibliography of the important books in the english language relating to the scandinavian countries. *In* **Horn,** F. W. Literature of the scandinavian north.　　　　　　**898 : 5**

Lanman, C: Foreign bibliography of Japan. *in* **920.5 : 3**

Griffis, W: Eliot. Corea ; the hermit nation. N. Y. 1882. O.　　　　**915.1 : 19**
Note. Contains, on p. xi–xvii, a bibliography of the subject.

Lansdell, H: Through Siberia. Ill. and maps. 3d ed. Bost. 1882. O.　　**915.7 : 8**
Note. Contains, on p. 772–778, a "Bibliography of Siberia and list of works referred to."

Rich, Obadiah. A catalogue of books relating principally to America, arranged under the years in which they were printed. Lond. 1832. O.　　　　**L**

Rich, Obadiah.—*Continued.*
— Bibliotheca americana nova, or A catalogue of books in various languages, relating to America, printed since 1700. Lond. 1835, 1846. O.　　　　**L**

Clarke, Robert, *and co.* Bibliotheca americana, 1878; catalogue of a collection of books and pamphlets relating to America, with a descriptive list of Robert Clarke and co.'s historical publications. Cinc. 1878. O.　**L**
— *Same,* supp. 1879. Cinc. 1879. O. *With* Bibliotheca americana, 1878.　　　　**L**
— *Same.* 1883. Cinc. 1883. O.　　　　**L**

Watson, Paul Barron. Bibliography of the precolumbian discoveries of America. *In* Lib. journal, v. 6, pp. 227–244.　　　　**L**

Charlevoix, P: François Xavier de. History and general description of New France. Tr. with notes by J: Gilmary Shea. N. Y. 1866. 6 v. Q.　　　　**970 : P 2**
Note. V. 1 contains, p. 67–96, Critical list of authors consulted.

Griffin, Appleton P. C. The discovery of the Mississippi ; a bibliographical account, with a fac-simile of the map of L: Joliet, 1674. App., a note on the Joliet map by B. F. De Costa, with a sketch of Joutel's maps. Repr. from the Magazine of american history, march and april 1883. N. Y. 1883. F.　　　　　　**L**

Winsor, Justin. The reader's handbook of the american revolution, 1761–1783. Bost. 1880. S.　　　　　　**L**

Campbell. C: A. Bibliography of major André. *In* Mag. of am. hist., v. 8, pp. 61–72.　**M**

Bartlett, J: Russell. Bibliography of Rhode Island ; a catalogue of books and other publications relating to the state, with notes, historical, biographical and critical. Providence. 1864. Q.　　　　**L**

Thomson, P: G. Bibliography of the state of Ohio; catalogue of the books and pamphlets relating to the history of the state, with collations and bibliographical and critical notes, together with the prices at which many of the books have been sold at the principal public and private sales since 1860, and a complete index by subjects. Cinc. 1880. Q.　　　　**L**

Bancroft, Hubert Howe. History of the Pacific states of North America: California, v. 1. San Francisco. 1884. O.　**975.8+4 v1**
Note. Contains, on p. xxv–lxxxviii, list of authorities quoted.
— *Same:* Northwest coast, v. 1. San Francisco. 1884. O.　　　　**975.8+5 v1**
Note. Contains, on p. xvii–xxxiii, list of authorities quoted.
— *Same:* Mexico, v. 1. San Francisco. 1883. O.　　　　　**977+12 v1**
Note. Contains, on p. xxi–cxii, list of authorities quoted.
— *Same:* North mexican states, v. 1. San Francisco. 1883. O.　　**977+13 v1**
Note. Contains, on p. xix–xlviii, list of authorities quoted.
— *Same:* Central America, v. 1. San Francisco. 1883. O.　　　　**978+2 v1**
Note. Contains, on p. xxv–lxxii, list of authorities quoted.

* * *

Griswold, W: Maccrillis. An index to articles relating to history, biography, literature, society and travel, contained in collections of essays, etc. (Q. P. index, no. 13.) Bangor. 1883. O.　　　　**L**

5. Publishers' and booksellers' catalogues.

Dingman, J: H. Directory of booksellers, stationers, news dealers and music dealers, and a list of libraries in the U. S. and Canada, nov. 1, 1870. N. Y. 1870. O. **L**

Harper *and brothers.* Descriptive list of their publications, with trade-list prices. N. Y. 1881-84. 3 v. O **L**

Holt, H:, *and co.* Descriptive catalogue of books issued, june 1882. N. Y. 1882. S. **L**

Steiger, E. Führer durch E. Steiger's lager deutscher bücher. N. Y. 1875. D. **L**

Bohn, H: G: A catalogue of books. Lond. 1841. O. **L**

— Catalogue of a very select collection of books, english and foreign, offered at prices affixed. Lond. 1831. O. **L**

Dowding, J. General catalogue of his stock of second-hand books for 1829...... Lond. 1829. D. **L**

Dulau *and co.*, London. Catalogue of french books offered for sale. Lond. *n. d.* D. **L**

Howell, E: Catalogue of books in almost every department of ancient and modern literature. Liverpool. 1878. O. **L**

Paterson, W: Catalogue of a selection of books in various classes of literature from [his] stock. Added, a valuable collection of musical works. Edinb. 1881. D. **L**

Quaritch, Bernard. A general catalogue of books. Lond. 1874. O. **L**
— *Same.* Supp., 1875-1877. Lond. 1877. O. **L**
— *Same.* 1880. Lond. 1880. O. **L**
— *Same.* 1880-1883, pt. 1-7. Lond. 1880-83. O. **L**

Simmons, G: Descriptive catalogue of rare and valuable books, pamphlets etc. embracing american and foreign standard works in every department of literature, colonial and state records and U. S. government publications. Wash. 1878. O. **L**

Smith, Alfred Russell. A catalogue of rare, curious and valuable old books on sale. Lond. 1882. D. **L**

Note. A large number of other publishers' and booksellers' catalogues will be found in the librarian's room, arranged in pamphlet cases.

6. Anonyms and pseudonyms.

Weller, Emil. Die maskirte literatur der älteren und neueren sprachen. 1 : Index pseudonymorum ; wörterbuch der pseudonymen oder verzeichniss aller autoren · die sich falscher namen bedienten. Leipz. 1856. O. **L**

— *Same,* 2 : Die falschen und fingirten druckorte; repertorium der seit erfindung der buchdruckerkunst unter falscher firma erschienenen deutschen, lateinischen und französischen schriften. Leipz. 1864. 2 v. in 1. O. **L**

— Nachträge zum Index pseudonymorum. Leipz. 1857. O. *and*

— Neue nachträge zum Index pseudonymorum und zu den Falschen und fingirten druck-

orten. Leipz. 1862. O. *Both bound with his* Index pseudonymorum. **L**

Franklin, Alfred L : A : Dictionnaire des noms, surnoms et pseudonymes latins de l'histoire littéraire du moyen âge, 1100 à 1530. Paris. 1875. O. **L**

Haynes, J : E : Pseudonyms of authors, including anonyms and initialisms. N. Y. 1882. O. **L**

Halkett, S :, *and* J : **Laing**. A dictionary of the anonymous and pseudonymous literature of Great Britain, including the works of foreigners written in, or tr. into the english language; v. 1. [A-E] ; v. 2. [F-N]. Edinb. 1882, 1883. Q. **L**

Thomas, Ralph. (*Olphar Hamst*). Handbook for fictitious names ; a guide to authors, chiefly in the lighter literature of the 19th century, who have written under assumed names, and to literary forgers, impostors, plagiarists and imitators. Lond. 1868. O. **L**

— Aggravating ladies ; a list of works published under the pseudonym of "A lady", with preliminary suggestions on the art of describing books bibliographically. Lond. 1880. D. **L**

Quérard, Joseph Marie. Les supercheries littéraires dévoilées ; galerie des ecrivains français de toute l'Europe qui se sont déguisés sous des anagrammes, des astéronymes, des cryptonymes, des initialismes, des noms littéraires, des pseudonymes facétieux ou bizarres, etc. 2e éd. aug. par G. Brunet et P: Jannet. Paris. 1869, 1870. 3 v. O. **L**
Note. V. 3 contains also Pseudonymes latins.

Barbier, Antoine Alexandre. Dictionnaire des ouvrages anonymes. 3e éd. rev. et aug. par Olivier Barbier, René et Paul Billard. Suite de la 2e éd. des Supercheries littéraires dévoilées par J. M. Quérard, publiée par Gustave Brunet et P: Jannet ; Avec une table générale des noms réels des écrivains anonymes et pseudonymes cités dans les deux ouvrages. Paris. 1872-79. 4 v. O. **L**
Note. V. 4 contains also Anonymes latins. The Table générale des noms réels etc., mentioned in the title, is not published.

Joliet, C : Les pseudonymes du jour. Nouvelle éd. Paris. 1884. D. **L**

Melzi, Gaetano *conte.* Dizionario di opere anonime e pseudonime di scrittori italiani o come che sia aventi all' Italia. Milano. 1848-59. 3 v. Q. **L**

Collin, E:, *comp.* Anonymer og pseudonymer i den danske, norske og islandske literatur samt i fremmede literaturer, forsåvidt disse omhandle nordiske forhold, fra de äldste tider indtil året 1860. Kjöbenhavn 1869. Q. **L**

Doorninck, J. I. van. Bibliotheek van nederlandsche anonymen en pseudonymen. 's Gravenhage [1867]. Q. **L**

Montagne, V. A. de la. Vlaamsche pseudoniemen; bibliographische opzoekingen. Roeselare. 1884. O. **L**

3. General cyclopedias.

American.

Family encyclopedia, The, of useful knowledge and general literature ; containing about 4000 articles upon scientific and popular subjects, designed for instruction and amusement, by J: Lauris Blake. Ill. N. Y. 1846. O.   R

Encyclopædia americana ; a popular dictionary of arts. sciences, literature, history, politics and biography ; a new ed. including a copious collection of original articles on american biography, on the basis of the 7th ed. of the german Conversations-lexicon, ed. by Francis Lieber. assisted by E : Wigglesworth [and T : Gamaliel Bradford]. Phila. 1849. 14 v. O.   R

Iconographic encyclopædia of science, literature and art, systematically arranged by J: G. Hick. Trans. from the german, with add.. and ed. by Spencer F. Baird. In 4 v. [Plates 2 v.] N. Y. 1857. 6 v. Q.   R
Contents. V. **1.** Mathematics.—Astronomy.—Physics.—Meteorology.—Chemistry.—Mineralogy.—Geognosy and Geology. **2.** Botany.—Zoology.—Anthropology.—Surgery. **3.** Geography and planography.—History and ethnology.—Military sciences.—Naval sciences. **4.** Architecture.—Mythology.—The fine arts.—Technology.

New american cyclopædia, The ; a popular dictionary of general knowledge, ed. by G: Ripley and C: A. Dana. N. Y. 1859–63. 16 v. Q.   R

American cyclopædia, The ; a popular dictionary of general knowledge. ed. by G: Ripley and C : A. Dana. N. Y. 1873–79. 16 v. Q.   R
— *Same.* A general and analytical index, by T. J. Conant. assisted by his daughter Blandina Conant. N. Y. 1879. Q.   R

American annual cyclopædia, The, and register of important events ; embracing political. civil, military and social affairs, pub. lic documents, biography, statistics, commerce. finance. literature, science, agricultural ture and mechanical industry. [1st ser.] 1861–1875. N. Y. 1863–1877. 15 v. O.   R
— *Same.* General index. N. Y. 1876. O.   R

Appletons' annual cyclopædia and register of important events ; embracing political, civil, military and social affairs, public documents, biography, statistics, commerce, finance, literature, science, agriculture and mechanical industry. New ser. v. 1–8. 1876–1883. N. Y. 1877–84. 8 v. Q.   R
Note. V. 8 contains a general index to the new series.

Johnson's new universal cyclopædia ; a scientific and popular treasury of useful knowledge. ill. with maps, plans and eng.; F: A. P. Barnard and Arnold Guyot, editors-in-chief. N. Y. 1875-78. 4 v. Q.   R

People's cyclopædia, The, of universal knowledge, with numerous appendixes invaluable for reference in all departments of industrial life, the whole brought down to 1884; with the pronunciation and orthography conformed to Webster's Unabridged dictionary, by W. H. DePuy. Ill. N. Y. [1884]. 3 v. Q.   R
Contents. v. **1.** A–E. **2.** F–P. **3.** P–Z. Appendixes.

Zells' popular encyclopædia ; a universal dictionary of english language, science. literature and art, by L. Colange. Ill. Phila. 1870. 2 v. Q.   R

Stoddart's encyclopædia americana ; a dictionary of arts, sciences and general literature, and companion to the Encyclopædia britannica, 9th ed., and to all other encyclopædias. Ill. v. 1, 2. Phila. 1883, 1884. 2 v. Q.   R
Note. Title page of v. 2 reads "Supplement to Encyclopædia britannica, 9th ed., a dictionary of arts, sciences and general literature."

Young folks' cyclopædia, The, of common things, by J: D. Champlin. Ill. N. Y. 1879. O.   R
— *Same.* Persons and places, by J: D. Champlin. Ill. N. Y. 1881. O.   R

British.

Cyclopædia, The, or Universal dictionary of arts, sciences and literature by Abraham Rees. with the assistance eminent professional gentlemen. Ill. In 39 [45] vols. Lond. 1819, 1820. 45 v. Q.   R
Note. The last 6 vols. contain plates.

Penny cyclopædia, The, of the society for the diffusion of useful knowledge. Lond. 1833–46. 29 v. in 16. Q.   R
— *Same.* V. 2–6. Lond. 1834–36. 5 v. Q.   R

Popular encyclopedia, The ; a general dictionary of arts, sciences, literature, biography, history and political economy. Repr. from the amer. ed. of the Conversations-lexikon. with cor. and add. [and] with dissertations on The rise and progress of literature by sir D. K. Sandford, on The progress of science by T: Thomson. and on The progress of the fine arts by Allan Cunningham. Glasgow. [1849, 1850]. 7 v. O.   R

English cyclopædia, The ; a new dictionary of universal knowledge, conducted by C: Knight. Lond. 1854–68. 20 v. Q.   R
Contents. Pt. **1.** Biography, 5 v. **2.** Geography, 3 v. (v. 4 missing). **3.** Natural history, 4 v. **4.** Arts and sciences, 8 v.

Chambers's encyclopædia : a dictionary of universal knowledge for the people, [ed. by Andrew Findlater.] Ill. Phila. 1861. 10 v. Q.   R
— *American additions.* N. Y. 1880. 4 v. O.   R

Chambers's information for the people, ed. by W : and Robert Chambers. 5th ed. Edin. 1880. 2 v. Q.   R
— *Same.* 1st amer. ed., v. 2. Phila. 1847. Q.   R

Dictionary, A, of science, literature and art ; comprising the definitions and derivations of the scientific terms in general use, together with the history and descriptions of the scientific principles of nearly every branch of human knowledge. New ed., ed. by W: T: Brande and G: W: Cox. Lond. 1867. 3 v. O.   R

Encyclopædia britannica, The, or Dictionary of arts, sciences and general literature. 8th ed., [and Index]. Edinh. 1853–60. 23 v. Q. R
— *Same.* 9th ed., v. 1–17. N. Y. 1878–84. 17 v. Q. R
Note. To the art. Ormuzd incl.

German.

Bilder-atlas ; ikonographische encyklopädie der wissenschaften und künste ; ein ergänzungswerk zu jedem conversations-lexikon. 2te aufl. bearb. von K : Gustav von Berneck und anderen. 500 tafeln in 8 b ; erläuternder text in 2 b. Leipz. 1875. 10 v. Q. **R**

Brockhaus' Conversations-lexikon. 12te aufl. Leipz. 1875–79. 15 v. O. **R**

Deutsch-amerikanisches conversations-lexikon ; mit spezieller rücksicht auf das bedürfniss der in Amerika lebenden deutschen, mit benutzung aller deutschen, amerikanischen, englischen und französischen quellen und unter mitwirkung vieler hervorragenden deutschen schriftsteller Amerika's bearb. von A. J. B. Schem. N. Y. 1869–74. 11 v. O. **R**

Meyer, Joseph. Hand-lexikon des allgemeinen wissens, mit technologischen und wissenschaftlichen abbildungen und vielen karten der astronomie, geographie, geognosie, statistik und geschichte. 8te umgearb. und verm. aufl. Leipz. 1883. 2 v. D. **R**

4. General periodicals.

1. Directories.

Hubbard, Harlan Page. Newspaper and bank directory of the world, with gazetteer and atlas combined. New Haven. 1882. 2 v. O. **L**

— Right-hand record and newspaper directory ; complete list of all american newspapers, and all the leading newspapers of the world. New Haven. 1880. O. **L**

Alden, Edwin, *and bro.* American newspaper catalogue, including lists of all newspapers and magazines published in the U.S. and the Canadas ; together with the population of the cities, towns, counties and states in which they are published, their politics, class or denomination, size and estimated circulation ; also special lists of religious, agricultural, the various class publications, and of all newspapers published in foreign languages, and a list of all newspapers and magazines in the U. S. and the Canadas by counties. Cinc. 1883. Q. **L**

Rowell, G: P., *and co.* American newspaper directory, containing accurate lists of all the newspapers and periodicals published in the U. S., territories, and the dominion of Canada, together with a description of the towns and cities in which they are published. 16th annual ed. N. Y. 1884. O. **L**

Steiger, Ernst. The periodical literature of the U. S. of America ; with index and appendices. N. Y. 1873. Q. **L**

London catalogue, The, of periodicals, newspapers and transactions of various societies, with a list of metropolitan printing societies and clubs for 1881. 40th annual ed. Lond. 1881. O. **L**

2. Indexes.

Poole, W: F: An index to periodical literature. N. Y. 1853. O. **L**

— An index to periodical literature. 3d ed. brought down to jan. 1882, with the assistance as associate ed. of W: I. Fletcher and the coöperation of the American library association and the Library association of the United Kingdom. Bost. 1882. O. **L**

— *Same.* **M**

Fletcher, W: I., *ed.* Co-operative index to leading periodicals. (Supp. to the Library journal). 1883, 1884. N. Y. 1884, 1885. O.

Griswold, W: Maccrillis. General-autor- und sachregister zu zeitschriften, meist historischen inhalts, und zwar : Die historische zeitschrift, Unsere zeit, Das historische taschenbuch. (Q. P. indexes no. 9.) Bangor, Me. 1882. O. **L**

— The Q. P. index annual for 1881–84. (Q. P. indexes. 7, 12, 15, 17.) Bangor. 1882–85. 4 v. O. **L**

Contents. **1881.** Atlantic, Century, Eclectic, Harper's, International review, Lippincott's, Living age, Nation, Popular science. **1882.** American, Art-amateur, Atlantic, Californian, Century, Deutsche rundschau, Eclectic, Education, Harper's, Independent, International review, Lippincott's, Living age, Longman's, Magazine of art, Nation, New-Englander, North american review, Our continent, Penn, Potter's, Unitarian review. **1883.** *Same as for 1882* (except Californian, Education, Living age, Penn, Potter's) *but with addition of* Catholic world, English illustrated, Macmillan's, Magazine of amer. history, Manhattan, Modern age, Nord und süd, Overland, Popular science, Princeton review, Republic, United service, Westermann's monatshefte, Wheelman, U. S. Consular *and* Education reports. **1884.** *Same as for 1882* (exc. International rev.) *with add. of* Auf der höhe, Belgravia, Choice liter., Current, Deutsche litteraturztg, Education, Every other saturday, Foreign eclectic, Gentleman's mag., Grenzboten, Jährbuch für gesetzgebung, Mag. für litteratur, Preussische jahrbücher, Revue de Belgique, Russische revue, Scandinavia, Schorer's familienblätter, Unsere zeit, Vom fels zum meer, Weck.

— Index to the leading british reviews and magazines for 1882, 1883 and 1884. Bangor, Me. 1885. O. **L**

Contents. Blackwood's mag., Contemporary rev., Cornhill mag., Contemporary rev., Fraser's mag., Edinburgh rev., Fortnightly rev., Gentleman's mag., Good words, Macmillan's mag., Nineteenth century, Quarterly rev., Scottish rev., Temple bar, Westminster rev.

* * *

Atlantic monthly, The. Index. v. 1–38, 1857–76 : Index of articles ; Index of authors. Bost. 1877. O. **L**

— A supplementary index, v. 1–38, and 39–46, by W: M. Griswold. [Q. P. indexes, no. 2]. Bangor, Me. 1880. O. **L**

Contemporary review, The. A general index to the Contemporary review [v. 1–41], the Fortnightly review and the Nineteenth century by W: M. Griswold. (Q. P. indexes, no. 11.) Bangor, Me. 1882. O. **L**

Deutsche rundschau. Autoren- und sach-register, b. 1-29. von W: M. Griswold. (Q. P. indexes, no. 8.) Bangor, Me. 1882. O.   **L**

— Generalregister, 1-10 jahrg., b. 1-40; nebst systematisher übersicht der hauptartikel. Berlin. 1885. Q.   **L**

Eclectic magazine, The. A general index to v. 1-96, by W: M. Griswold. [Q. P. indexes, no. 5.] Bangor, Me. 1881. O.   **L**

Every saturday. A general index to v. 1-12, by W: M. Griswold. *With his* General index to the Eclectic magazine.   **L**

Fortnightly review, The. A general index, [v. 1-37], by W: M. Griswold. *With his* General index to the Contemporary review.   **L**

Harper's new monthly magazine. Index, alphabetical, analytical and classified. v. 1-60 incl., from june 1850 to june 1880; compiled by C: A. Durfee. N. Y. 1881. Q.   **L**

International review, The. A general index, v. 1-9, 1874-80, by W: M. Griswold. [Q. P. indexes, no. 3]. Bangor, Me. [1880]. O. **L**

Lippincott's magazine. A general index to the first series, v. 1-26, by W: M. Griswold. [Q. P. indexes, no. 4.] Bangor, Me. 1881. **L**

Littell's living age. General index to v. 37-148, by W: M. Griswold. *With his* General index to the Eclectic magazine.   **L**

— A complete index by E: Roth, v. 1, comprising contents of the first hundred vols. Phila. 1883, 1884. O.   **L**

    Note. Pts.1—6 only published, containing : Biography, A—H: Noad.

Nation, The. A general index, v. 1-30, july 1865—sept. 1880, by W: M. Griswold. [Q. P. indexes, no. 1.] Bost. 1880. O.   **L**

Nineteenth century, The. A general index, [v. 1-11], by W: M. Griswold. *With his* General index to the Contemporary review.   **L**

North american review. Index, v. 1-125, 1815-77 : Index of subjects ; index of writers, by W: Cushing. Cambridge. 1878. O.   **L**

— General index, v. 92-134, 1861-1882, by W: M. Griswold. (Q. P. indexes, no. 10.) Bangor, Me. 1882. O.   **L**

Nouvelle revue, La. Table alfabétique générale, v. 1-21, by W: M. Griswold. *With his* Table alfabétique générale de la Revue des deux mondes.   **L**

Revue des deux mondes. Table alfabétique générale des matières et des noms des auteurs, contenus dans les tomes 193-268, et 1-21 de la Nouvelle revue, par W: M. Griswold. (Q. P. indexes, no. 14.) Bangor. 1883. O.   **L**

Scribner's monthly. Index, v. 1-20. N. Y. 1881. 2 v. O.   **L**

— A general index, [v. 1-22], by W: M. Griswold. [Q. P. indexes, no. 6.] Bangor, Me. 1881. O.   **L**

Westermann's illustrirte deutsche monatshefte. Vollständiges inhalts-verzeichniss; autorenregister, sachregister and illustrationsverzeichniss des ersten bis fünfzigsten bandes. Braunschweig, 1883. O.   **L**

3. Special languages.

English.

Albany argus, *weekly.* Dec. 29, 1832—jan. 2. 1836. Albany, N. Y. F.   **M**

All the year round; a weekly journal, conducted by C: Dickens. V. 5, 6, 18-21, 29-33, 35, 46-54. Lond. 1861-84. Q.   **M**

American, The ; a national weekly journal of politics, literature, science, art and finance. V. 2-8, apr. 16, 1881—oct. 13, 1884. Phila 1881-84. F.   **R M**
    Note. Title-page of v. 7, 8 reads "journal of literature, science, the arts and public affairs."

American whig review, The. V. 9-16, jan. 1849-dec. 1852. N. Y. 1849-52. O.   **M**
    Note. Title-page of v. 9, 10 reads "The American review ; a whig journal devoted to politics and literature." *Discontinued.*

Appletons' journal of literature, science and art. V. 1-26, apr. 1869—dec. 1881. N. Y. 1869-81. Q.   **M**
    Note. Title-page of v. 16-20 reads "a monthly journal of popular literature," and of v. 21-26, "a magazine of general literature." *Discontinued.*

Argosy, The ; a magazine. V. 1-4, dec. 1865-nov. 1867. Lond. 1866, 1867. O.   **M**

Atlantic monthly, The ; a magazine of literature, science, art and politics. V. 1-11, 13-16, 18-26, 31, 32, 34-54, nov. 1857-dec. 1884. Bost. 1858-84. O.   **M**
    Note. Title-page of v. 1-15 omits "science."

Blackwood's Edinburgh magazine. V. 1-60, 63-105, 112, 113, 115, 117, 119-136, apr. 1817-dec. 1884. Edinb. 1817-46 ; N. Y. (Am. ed., v. 26-99) 1848-84. O.   **M**

British quarterly review, The. V. 54, 57, 58, 63-80, july 1871—oct. 1884. N. Y. (Am. reprint) 1871-83 ; Lond. 1884.   **M**

Century, The, illustrated monthly magazine. V. 1-6, nov. 1881—oct. 1884. N. Y. 1882-84. O.   **M**
    Note.· Successor to "Scribners" and also numbered consecutively with it, being v. 23-28.

— *Same.* [Circulating copy]. V. 1-6. N. Y. 1882-84. O.   **52 : 223-228**

Chambers's journal of popular literature, science and arts, conducted by W: and Robert Chambers. V. 17-26, 31-36, 39, 40, 42-44, 50, jan. 1852—june 1873. Edin. 1852-73. O.   **M**
    Note. Title-page up to v. 21 reads "Chambers's Edinburgh journal."

Contemporary review, The. V. 1-6, 33-45, feb. 1866—dec. 1884. Lond. 1866-84. O.   **M**

Continent, The ; a weekly illustrated magazine, conducted by Albion W. Tourgee. V. 1-6, feb. 1882—aug. 1884. Phila. v. 1-3, N. Y. v. 4-6. F. *and* Q.   **M**
    Note. V. 1 was called "Our continent." Eight numbers only of v. 6 were publ. when the magazine was discontinued.

Continental monthly, The ; devoted to literature and national policy. V. 1-6, jan. 1862-dec. 1864. N. Y. 1862-64. O.   **M**
    Discontinued.

Cornhill magazine, The. V. 1-19, 28, 29, 43-49, jan. 1860—Dec. 1884. Lond. 1860-84. O.   **M**

Current, The ; the weekly literary, news and family journal of our time. V. 1, dec. 23, 1883—june 28, 1884. Chicago. 1884. F.   **M**

Democratic review. V. 22-31, jan. 1848—dec. 1852. N. Y. 1848-52. O. **M**
Note. Title-page of V. 22-29 reads " The United States magazine and democratic review, ed. by T: Prentice Kettell." *Discontinued.*

Diplomatic review, books 1—7. Sheffield *and* Lond. 1855—81. F., Q., O. **M**
Contents. Book 1. v. 1-2, oct. 13, 1855—aug. 9, 1856; pub. as the [Sheffield] Free press. **2.** v. 3-6, aug. 16, 1856—dec. 1858. **3.** v. 7-13, 1859-65. **4.** v. 14-18, 1866-70. **5.** v. 19-21, 1871-73. **6.** v. 22-25, 1874—jan. 1877. **7.** Supplementary vol., 1825-81.

Dublin review, The. V. 88-95, july 1878—oct. 1884. Dublin. 1878-84. O.

Eclectic magazine, The, of foreign literature, science and art; W. H. Bidwell, ed. and prop. V. 59-75, 81-84, 88-103, may 1863—dec. 1884. N. Y. 1865-84. O. **M**
Note. v. 64 commences a new series, numbered separately.

English illustrated magazine, The. V. 1, oct. 1883—sept. 1884. Lond. 1884. O. **M**

Edinburgh review, The, or Critical journal. V. 1-50, 52, 54-59, 87-92, 95-160, oct. 1802—oct. 1884. Edinb. 1803-34, 1881-84, O.; N. Y. [Am. reprint] 1848-83. Q. **M**

Every saturday; a journal of choice reading selected from foreign current literature. V. 4, 5, 7, july 1867—june 1869. Bost. 1867-69. Q. **M**
Discontinued.

Fortnightly review, The, ed. by T. H. S. Escott. V. 31, 35-41, jan. 1879—dec. 1884. Lond. 1879-84. O. **M**
Note. V. 31-37 ed. by J: Morley.

Fraser's magazine for town and country. V. 76-80, 103-106, july 1867—oct. 1882. Lond. 1867-82. O. **M**
Discontinued.

Galaxy, The; a magazine of entertaining literature. V. 3-7, 15-24, jan. 1867—dec. 1877. N. Y. 1867-77. O. **M**
Note. Title-page of v. 3-7 reads "an illustrated magazine" etc. *Discontinued.*

Good words, ed. by Norman Macleod. V. 6-8, jan. 1865—dec. 1867. Lond. 1865-67. O. **M**

Graphic, The; an illustrated weekly newspaper. V. 29, 30, jan.—dec. 1884. Lond. F. **RM**

Greenbank's periodical library; containing a republication of new and standard works. V. 1-3. Phila. 1833-35. D. **M**
Discontinued.

Harper's new monthly magazine. V. 1-69, june 1850—nov. 1884. N. Y. 1850-84. O. **M**
— *Same.* [Circulating copy]. V. 5-7, 14, 15, 18-20, 23-25, 27, 37, 42-55, 62-69. N. Y. 1852-84. O. **52 : 5-69**

Harper's weekly; a journal of civilization. V. 1-28, jan. 1857—dec. 1884. N. Y. 1857-84. F. **RM**

Harper's young people. V. 1-5, nov. 1879—oct. 1884. N. Y. 1880-84. Q. **M**

Hesperian, The; a monthly miscellany of g n-eral literature, original and select, ed. by W: D. Gallagher. V. 2, nov. 1838—apr. 1839. Columbus, O. 1839. O. **M**
Discontinued.

Hours at home; a popular monthly of instruction and recreation, ed. by J. M. Sherwood. V. 3-9, may 1866—oct. 1869. N. Y. 1866-69. O. **M**
Note. Title-page of v. 3-6 reads "a popular monthly devoted to religious and useful literature". V. 9 drops the editor's name. *Discontinued.*

Illustrated London news, The. V. 1-85, may 1842—dec. 1884. Lond. 1842-84. F. **RM**

International monthly magazine, The, of literature, science and art. V. 2-5, dec. 1850—apr. 1852. N. Y. 1851, 1852. O. **M**
Discontinued.

International review. V. 1-14, jan. 1874—june 1883. N. Y. 1874-83. O. **M**
Discontinued.

Knickerbocker, The, or New York monthly magazine. V. 34-66, july 1849—oct. 1865. N. Y. 1849-65. O. **M**
Note. V. 60 adds "of literature, art, politics and society" to the title. Title-page of v. 61, 62 reads "The Knickerbocker monthly; a national magazine of literature, art, politics and society, ed. by Kinahan Cornwallis." Title-page of v. 63-65 reads "The american monthly Knickerbocker; devoted to literature, science and politics, ed. by J. Holmes Agnew." V. 66 became "The fœderal american" and was discontinued after four numbers were publ.

Land we love, The; a monthly magazine devoted to literature, military history and agriculture. V. 1-5, may 1866—oct. 1868. Charlotte, N. C. 1866-68. O. **M**
Discontinued.

Lippincott's magazine of popular literature and science. V. 6-34, july 1870—dec. 1884. Phila. 1870-84. O. **M**

Littell's living age, conducted by E. Littell. V. 1-9, 18, 20-31, 40-103, 116, 119-163, apr. 1844—dec. 1884. Bost. 1844-84. O. **M**

[London, *Eng.*]. The Times. Oct. 1878—dec. 1879. Lond. 1878-9. F. **M**

London society; an illustrated magazine of light and amusing literature for the hours of relaxation. V. 13-16, 34-46, jan. 1868—dec. 1884. Lond. 1868-84. O. **M**

Longman's magazine. V. 1-4, nov. 1882—oct. 1884. Lond. 1883, 1884. O. **M**

Macmillan's magazine. V. 36-50, may 1877—oct. 1884. Lond. 1877-84. O. **M**

[Madison] Wisconsin democrat, *weekly.* Oct. 18, 1842—feb. 1843. Madison. 1842-3. F. **M**

[—] Wisconsin enquirer, *weekly.* Nov. 8, 1838—june 15, 1842. Madison. 1838-42. F. **M**

[—] Wisconsin patriot, *weekly.* Sept. 23, 1884—june 1859. Madison. 1854-9. F. **M**

[—] Wisconsin daily patriot. April 1860—dec. 1862. Madison. 1860-2. F. **M**

Manhattan, The; an illustrated literary magazine. V. 1-4, jan. 1883—sept. 1884. N. Y. 1883, 1884. O. **M**
Discontinued.

Milwaukee sentinel, *weekly.* June 27, 1837—june 1841; sept. 23, 1843—march 1844. Milw. 1837-44. F. **M**
— journal, *weekly.* Aug. 27, 1841—feb. 16, 1842. Milw. 1841-2. F. **M**
— courier, *weekly.* March 27, 1841—dec. 13, 1843. Milw. 1841-3. F. **M**
— daily sentinel. Dec. 30, 1844—jan. 1, 1846. Milw. 1844-6. F. **M**
— daily gazette. Jan. 5—feb. 14, 1846. Milw. 1846. F. **M**
[—] Daily sentinel and gazette. Feb. 16, 1846—may 9, 1848. Milw. 1846-8. F. **M**
— weekly sentinel and gazette. May 24, 1848—june 5, 1850. Milw. 1848-50. F. **M**
— daily news. Feb. 15, 1855—dec. 1880. Milw. 1855-80. F. **M**
— weekly news. Jan. 1864—dec. 1878. Milw. 1864-78. F. **M**

Milwaukee—*Continued.*
[—] **Daily people's press.** Aug. 16—dec. 14, 1860. Milw. 1860. F.   **M**
[—] **Daily life,** *weekly.* Jan.—dec. 1864. Milw. 1864. F.   **M**
[—] **Daily wisconsin.** July 1863—dec. 1866. Milw. 1863-6. F.   **M**
[—] **Banner und volksfreund.** Sept. 1863—dec. 1866. Milw. 1863-6. F.   **M**
— **herold,** *weekly.* Sept. 19, 1863—sept. 1866. Milw. 1863-6. F.   **M**
— **see-bote,** *daily.* Sept. 24, 1863—dec. 1866. Milw. 1863-6. F.   **M**
— **journal of commerce,** *weekly.* Nov. 17, 1866—dec. 1873. Milw. 1866-73. F.   **M**
[—] **Daily commercial times.** Jan. 1875—dec. 1877. Milw. 1875-7. F.   **M**
— **daily sentinel.** July 4, 1864—dec. 1866; jan. 1879—may 20, 1882. Milw. 1864-82. F.   **M**
[—] **Daily republican and news.** Jan.3, 1881— may 20, 1882. Milw. 1881-2. F.   **M**
[—] **Daily republican-sentinel.** May 22—dec. 1882. Milw. 1882. F.   **M**
— **sentinel.** Jan. 1883—march 1885. Milw. 1883-5. F.   **M**
[—] **Daily journal.** Nov. 16, 1882—dec. 1884. Milw. 1882-4. F.   **M**
Minerva, The. V. 3, apr.—sept. 1825. *T. p. w.* [N. Y. 1825.]   **M**
  Note. Contains also "The New York literary gazette and Phi beta kappa repository" v. 1, no. 1-5.
Modern age, The. V. 1-3, jan. 1883—june 1884. Buffalo, N. Y. 1883, 1884. O.   **M**
  Discontinued.
Monograph, The; a serial collection of indexed essays. V. 1, no. 1-50. Bangor, Me. 1881-83. O. **M**
Nation, The; a weekly journal devoted to politics, literature, science and art. V. 2-39, jan. 1866—dec. 1884. N.Y. 1866-84. Q. **RM**
National quarterly review, The, ed. by E : I. Sears. V. 5-9, 11-19, 26, 27, 30, 32-41, june 1862—oct. 1880. N. Y. 1862-80. O.   **M**
  Note. In v. 35-37 the editor's name is changed to D: A. Gorton, in v. 38-40 the name of C: H. Woodman is added, and v. 41 is ed. by the latter alone. *Discontinued.*
New Englander, The, ed. by G: P. Fisher, Timothy Dwight and W: L. Kingsley. V. 21-28. New Haven. 1862-69. O.   **M**
  Note. No editor's name given on title-page of v. 21-24.
New York herald. Nov. 9, 1860—jan. 1, 1862; dec. 1862—dec. 1866. N. Y. 1860-6. F.   **M**
Nineteenth century, The; a monthly review ed. by James Knowles. V. 1-16, march 1877—dec. 1884 Lond. 1877-84. O.   **M**
North american review, The. V. 66-73, 75-109, 116-119, 127-139, jan. 1848—dec. 1884. N. Y. 1848-84. O.   **M**
North british review, The. V. 1-53, may 1844— jan. 1871. Edinb. 1844-71. O.   **M**
  Discontinued.
Old and new. V. 3, 4, 6, 8-11, jan. 1871—may 1875. Bost. 1871-75. O.   **M**
  Discontinued.
Outing and the wheelman; an illustrated monthly magazine of recreation. V. 1-4, oct. 1882—sept. 1884. Bost. 1882-84. Q.   **M**
  Note. V. 1, 2 are called: "The wheelman; an illustrated magazine of cycling literature and news."
Overland monthly, The, devoted to the development of the country. 1st ser., v. 8-11 ; 2d

ser., v. 1-4, jan. 1872—dec. 1873, jan. 1883— dec. 1884. San Francisco, 1872-84. O.   **M**
Penn monthly, The; devoted to literature, science, art and politics. V. 6-14, jan. 1875—july 1882. Phila. 1875-82. O.   **M**
  Discontinued.
Princeton review, The. V. 26, 28, and new ser., v. 5-14, jan. 1854—oct. 1856, jan. 1880—dec. 1884. N. Y. 1854-84. O.   **M**
  Note. V. 26, 28 have title-page, reading "The biblical repertory and Princeton review." *Discontinued.*
Punch. V. 86, 87, jan.—dec. 1884. Lond. 1884. Q.   **RM**
Putnam's monthly magazine of american literature, science and art. V. 1-14, 16, jan. 1853—nov. 1870. N. Y. 1853-70. O.   **M**
  Note. Title-page of v. 10 reads: "Emerson's magazine and Putnam's monthly, vol. 5." V. 11-16 form a new series of which the title is "Putnam's magazine; original papers on literature, science, art and national interests." *Discontinued.*
Quarterly review, The. V. 1-99, 101-120, 122-126, 128-130, 134, 135, 137-139, 141-158, feb. 1809 —oct. 1884. Lond. 1809-52, 1881-84. O.; N. Y. (Am. reprint) 1852-80. Q.   **M**
St. Nicholas; an illustrated magazine for young folks, conducted by Mary Mapes Dodge. V. 1-11, nov. 1873—oct. 1884. O.   **M**
  Note. Title-page of v. 1-8, pt. 1, reads: "St. Nicholas; Scribner's illustrated magazine for girls and boys, etc."
— *Same.* [Circulating copy.] V. 5-11. N. Y. 1877-84. O.   **52 : 305-311**
Saturday magazine, The ; a journal of choice reading selected from foreign literature. V. 1-3, dec. 1878—jan. 1880. Bost. 1879-80. Q.   **M**
  Discontinued.
Scribner's monthly; an illustrated magazine for the people, conducted by J.G. Holland. V. 1-22, nov. 1870—oct. 1881. N.Y. 1871-81. O.   **M**
  Note. Succeeded by "The century", which see.
— *Same.* [Circulating copy.] V. 9, 10, 12, 20-22. N. Y. 1875-81. O.   **52 : 209-222**
Southern literary messenger, The ; devoted to every department of literature and the fine arts. V. 15, 16, jan. 1849—dec. 1850. Richmond. 1849, 1850. Q.   **M**
  Discontinued.
Temple bar: a London magazine for town and country readers. V. 2-26, 30, 35, 36, 38-41, 43-72, apr. 1861—dec. 1884. Lond. 1861-84. O.   **M**
Vicksburg daily whig. Jan.—dec. 1839. Vicksburg. Miss. 1839. F.   **M**
Westminster review, The. V. 58-92, 96-100, 102, 103, 105-122, july 1852—oct. 1884. N. Y. (Am. ed.) 1852-83. Q. ; Lond. 1884. O.   **M**
Wide awake. V. 1-19, july 1875—nov. 1884. Bost. [1875]-1884. 19 v. Q.   **M**
— *Same.* [Circulating copy].   **52 : 401-419**
Youth's cabinet, The ; a repository of gems for the mind and heart, Francis C. Woodworth, ed. Ill. N. Y. 1846. O.   **M**

German.

Deutsche rundschau, herausg. von Julius Rodenberg. V. 1-41, oct. 1874—dec. 1884. Berlin. 1874-84. O.   **M**
Gartenlaube, Die ; illustrirtes familienblatt. V. 29-32, jan. 1881—dec. 1884. Leipz. 1881-84. F.   **M**

Illustrirte zeitung; wöchentliche nachrichten über alle ereignisse, zustände und persönlichkeiten der gegenwart, über tagesgeschichte, öffentliches und gesellschaftliches leben, wissenschaft und kunst, handel und industrie, musik, theater und mode. V. 82, 83, jan.—dec. 1884. Leipz. 1884. F. **M**

Im neuen reich; wochenschrift für das leben des deutschen volkes in staat, wissenschaft und kunst, herausg. von W: Lang. V. 16-22, july 1878—dec. 1881. Berlin. 1878-81. O. **M**

Note. Konrad Reichard ed. of v. 16. *Discontinued.*

Milwaukee freidenker; zeitschrift für freies menschenthum. V. 1-5, 10-13, apr. 1872—dec. 1884. Milw. 1872-84. F. **RM**

Note. The title, since jan. 1, 1875 is "Freidenker; freiheit, bildung und wohlstand für alle."

Nord und süd; eine deutsche monatsschrift, herausg. von Paul Lindau. V. 1-32, april 1877—march 1885. Etched portraits. Berlin and Breslau. 1877-85. O. **M**

Salon, Der, für literatur, kunst und gesellschaft, herausg. von Franz Hirsch. V. 28-34, jan. 1879—dec. 1884. Leipz. 1879-84. O. **M**

Ueber land und meer; allgemeine illustrirte zeitung. V. 49-52, oct. 1882—sept. 1884. Stuttgart. 1882-84. F. **RM**

Um die welt; Keppler und Schwarzmann's illustrirte zeitung. V. 1-3, sept. 1881—march 1883. N. Y. 1882-83. F. **RM**

Unsere zeit; deutsche revue der gegenwart. V. 1-46, jan. 1857—dec. 1884. Leipz. 1857-84. O. **M**

Note. Title-page of v. 1-9 reads "Jahrbuch zum Conversations-lexikon", of v. 10-27 adds "Monatsschrift zum Conversations-lexikon" to present title.

Vierteljährliches magazin der modernen literatur. V. 21-25, 28-31, 33, 35, 36, jan. 1881—jan. 1885. Milw. 1881-85. O. **M**

Vom fels zum meer; Spemann's illustrirte zeitschrift für das deutsche haus. V. 1-6. oct. 1881—sept. 1884. Stuttgart. 1881-84. O. **M**

Westermann's illustrirte deutsche monatshefte, herausg. von F: Spielhagen; ein familienbuch für das gesammte geistige leben der gegenwart. V. 45-56, oct. 1878—sept. 1884. Braunschweig. 1879-84. Q. **M**

French.

L'écho de la France; revue étrangère de science et de littérature. V. 1-5, Montreal. 1865-68. O. **M**

Revue des deux mondes. V. [195-198, 255-278], jan.—aug. 1871, jan. 1881—dec. 1884. Paris. 1871-84. O. **M**

Note. The numbering on the title-page of the vols. is as follows: 2de période, tome 91-94; 3e période, tome 43-66.

Revue internationale sous la direction de M. Angelo de Gubernatis. V. 1-3, dec. 25, 1883—sept. 10, 1884. Florence, 1884. O. **M**

II. PHILOSOPHY.

1. In general.

1. Comprehensive works.

Horwicz, Adolf. Wesen und aufgabe der philosophie, ihre bedeutung für die gegenwart
und ihre ansichten für die zukunft. *In*
Deutsche zeit- und streit-fragen.
304 : 15 v5

Grassmann, Robert. Die wissenschaftslehre,
oder philosophie. Stettin. 1875. O. **100:1**
Contents. 1. T. Die denklehre.—2. T. Die wissens-
lehre. 3. T. Die erkenntnisslehre. (1es buch: Die
bewusstseinslehre; 2es buch: Die bildungslehre; 3es
buch: Die geisteslehre; 4es buch: Das staatswissen.)
4. T. Die weisheitslehre. (1es buch: Die vertiefungs-
lehre; 2es buch: Die offenbarungslehre; 3es buch:
Die heilslehre; 4es buch: Das gotteswissen.)

Voltaire, François Marie Arouet de. A philosophical dictionary. From the french, with
add. notes, both critical and argumenta-
tive. Bost. 1856. 2 v. in 1. O. **103+1**

2. Essays.

Bowen, Francis. Philosophical essays. *In his*
Gleanings. **824.1 : 6**
Contents, see under English literature, Essays.

Cornwallis, C. F. Philosophical inquiries and
philosoph. experiences by a pariah. [*Anon.*]
In Small books on great subjects.
829.2 : 48 v1

Dana, Alexander H. Ethical and physiological
inquiries, chiefly relative to subjects of
popular interest. N. Y. 1862. D. **104:9**
Contents. Races of men.—Compensations of life.—
Identity. — Necessity. — Authorship. — Influence of
great men. — Lawyers. — Hereditary character.—
Sensuality.—Health.—Narcotic stimulants.—External
religion. — Inequality in the condition of men. —
Wisdom of the ancients. — Theology.—War.—Seminaries of learning.—Reason and faith.—The supernatural.—Fear of death.—Character as determined
by corporeal organism.—Self-renovation.—Government and laws.—Science of medicine.—Diet.—Population.—Probation of life. — Neuromathy.—Inspiration.—Nemesis.

De Quincey, T: Essays on the philosophical
writers. *In* 824.2 : 29
Contents, see under English literature, Essays.

Hedge, F: H: Atheism in philosophy, and other
essays. Bost. 1884. D. **104:8**
Contents. Epicurus.—Arthur Schopenhauer's philosophy.—Critique of pessimism as taught by Eduard
v. Hartmann.—Life and character of Augustine.—
Gottfried W: v. Leibniz.—Immanuel Kant.—Irony.—
The philosophy of fetichism.—Genius.—The lords of
life.

Hume, D: Essays and treatises on various subjects ; with a brief sketch of the author's
life and writings. Added, dialogues concerning natural religion. Bost. *n. d.* Q.
104:1
Contents. My own life.—Letter from Adam Smith
to W: Strahan.—Inquiry concerning human understanding.—Dissertation on the passions.—An inquiry
concerning the principles of morals.—A dialogue.—
The natural history of religion.—Essays on suicide.—
Dialogues concerning natural religion.

McCosh, James. Philosophie series ; no. 1-7.
N. Y. 1882-84. 2 v. D. **104:7**
Contents. (V. 1.) **1.** Criteria of diverse kinds of
truth, a treatise on applied logic. **2.** Energy, sufficient and final cause. **3.** Development, what it can
do and what it cannot do. **4.** Certitude, providence
and prayer. (V. 2.) **5.** Locke's theory of knowledge,
with a notice of Berkeley. **6.** Agnosticism of Hume
and Huxley, with a notice of the scottish school. **7.**
A criticism of the critical philosophy.

Mill, J: Stuart. [Philosophical essays.] *In his*
Dissertations and discussions. **824.2 : 70**
Contents, see under English literature, Essays.

Peirce, C: S., *ed.* Studies in logic by members
of the Johns Hopkins university. Bost.
1883. D. **160:9**
Contents. **Marquand, A.** The logic of the epicu-
reans; A machine for producing syllogistic variations.—**Franklin, C. L.** On the algebra of logic.—
Mitchell, O. H. On a new algebra of logic.—**Gilman, B. I.** Operations in relative number with
application to the theory of probabilities.—**Peirce,
C: S.** A theory of probable inference.

Porter, Noah. Science and sentiment ; with other
papers, chiefly philosophical. N. Y. 1882.
D. **104:5**
Contents. Science and sentiment.—The science of
nature versus the science of man.—What we mean
by christian philosophy.—The autobiography of J:
Stuart Mill.—J: Stuart Mill as a philosopher, *and as* a
theologian.—Prof. Tyndall's last deliverance.—Physiological metaphysics.—Force, law and design.—Prof.
Huxley's exposition of Hume's philosophy. — The
newest atheism.—Herbert Spencer's theory of sociology.—The Kantian centennial.—The collapse of
faith.

Prometheus in Atlantis ; a prophecy of the extinction of the christian civilization. N. Y.
1867. D. **104:2**

St. John, H:, *viscount Bolingbroke.* Letters or
essays addressed to Alex. Pope. *In his*
Works. **820.2:18 v3,4**
Contents. Concerning the nature, extent and reality
of human knowledge.—On the folly and presumption
of philosophers.—On the rise and progress of monotheism.—Concerning authority in matters of religion.

Sinnett, A. P. The occult world. Bost. 1882. D.
104:6
Contents. Occultism and its adepts.—The Theoso-
phical society of N. Y.—Recent occult phenomena.
—Teachings of occult philosophy.

Stewart, Dugald. Philosophical essays ; with
add., ed. by sir W: Hamilton. Edinb.
1877. O. **191+8 v5**
Contents. Preliminary dissertation: Some errors
relative to the philosophy of mind corrected; Some
objections relative thereto obviated.—Pt. 1. *Essays
of a metaphysical import:* On Locke's account of the
sources of human knowledge and its influence on the

doctrines of some of his successors; On the idealism of Berkeley; On the influence of Locke's authority upon the philosophical systems which p   il d in France during the latter part of the 18th century; On the metaphysical theories of Hartley, Priestly and Darwin; On the tendency of some late philological speculations.—Pt. 2. *Essays relative to matters of taste:* On the beautiful; On the sublime; On taste; On the culture of certain intellectual habits connected with the first elements of taste.

Warren, S: The intellectual and moral development of the present age. New ed. Edinb. 1854. D.   **104:3**

Wright, Chauncey. Philosophical discussions; with a biographical sketch of the author by C: Eliot Norton. N. Y. 1877. O.   **104:4**

Contents. Biographical sketch.—A physical theory of the universe.—Natural theology as a positive science. — The philosophy of Herbert Spencer. — Limits of natural selection.—The genesis of species. —Evolution by natural selection.—Evolution of self-consciousness.—The conflict of studies.—The uses and origin of the arrangements of leaves in plants — McCosh on intuitions. — Mansel's reply to Mill. — Lewes's Problems of life and mind. — McCosh on Tyndall.—Speculative dynamics.—Books relating to the theory of evolution.—German darwinism.—A fragment on cause and effect.—John Stuart Mill; a commemorative notice.—Index.

3. History.

Bautain, L: Eugène Marie. An epitome of the history of philosophy; the work adopted by the university of France for instruction in the colleges and high schools. Tr. from the french, with add. and a continuation of the history from the time of Reid to the present day, by C. S. Henry. [Harper's family lib.] N. Y. 1846. 2 v. S.   **109:4**

Lefèvre, André. Philosophy, historical and critical; with an introd. by A. H. Keane. Lond. 1879. D.   **109:5**

Lange, F: Albert. History of materialism and criticism of its present importance. Authorized tr. by Ernest Chester Thomas. Bost. 1877–81. 3 v. O.   **146:1**

Contents. V. 1. Materialism in antiquity.—The period of transition.—The 17th century. 2. The 18th century.—Modern philosophy. 3. The natural sciences.—Man and the soul.—Morality and religion.

Lewes, G: H: The biographical history of philosophy, from its origin in Greece down to the present day. Library ed. enl. and rev. N. Y. 1866. 2 v. O.   **109:1**

Owen, J: Evenings with the skeptics, or Free discussion on free thinkers. Lond. 1881. 2 v. O.   **109:3**

Contents. V. 1. Pre-christian skepticism. 2. Christian skepticism.

Schwegler, Albert F: K: Franz. A history of philosophy in epitome. Tr. from the original german by Julius H. Seelye. 5th ed. N. Y. 1866. D.   **109:2**

Stewart, Dugald. Dissertation exhibiting the progress of metaphysical, ethical and political philosophy since the revival of letters in Europe; with add. now first publ., ed. by sir W: Hamilton. 2d ed., imp. Edinb. 1877. O.   **191+8 v1**

Ueberweg, F: History of philosophy, from Thales to the present time. Tr. from the 4th german ed. by G: S. Morris. with add. by Noah Porter, [and] a pref. by the eds. of the Philosophical and theological libr. [H. B. Smith and Ph. Schaff]. N. Y. [1873]. 2 v. O.   **109+6**

Contents. V. 1. Ancient and mediæval philosophy.

2. Modern philosophy; with add. by the tr., an app. on english and american phil. by Noah Porter, and an app. on italian phil. by Vincenzo Botta.

4. Ancient philosophies.

Antoninus, Marcus Aurelius. Thoughts. Tr. by G: Long. 2d ed., rev. and cor. Lond. 1875. D.   **188:1**

Grote, G: Plato, and the other companions of Sokrates. 3d ed. Lond. 1875. 3 v. O.   **184+1**

Platon, (*lat.* Plato). Works; a new and literal version, chiefly from the text of Stallbaum. Lond. 1854. 6 v. D.   **184:2**

Contents. V. 1. Apology of Socrates. — Crito. — Phædo. — Gorgias. — Protagoras. — Phædrus. — Theætetus.—Euthyphron.—Lysis. Tr. by H. Cary. 2. The republic.—Timæus.—Critias. Tr. by G. H. Davis. 3. Meno.—Euthydemus.—The sophist.—The statesman.—Cratylus. — Parmenides. — The banquet. Tr. by G: Burges. 4. Philebus.—Charmides.—Laches.—Menexenus.—Hippias major.—Hippias minor.—Ion.—First Alcibiades. — Second Alcibiades. — Theages. — The rivals. — Hipparchus. — Minos. — Clitopho. — The epistles. Tr. by G: Burges. 5. The laws. Tr. by G: Burges. 6. The doubtful works, with lives of Plato by Diogenes Laertius, Hesychius and Olympiodorus, introductions to his doctrines by Alcinous and Albinus, the notes of T: Gray, and a general index to the whole work. Tr. by G: Burges.

— A day in Athens with Socrates; translations from the Protagoras and the Republic of Plato. N. Y. 1883. S.   **184:3**

Weygoldt, G. P. Die philosophie der stoa nach ihrem wesen und ihren schicksalen; für weitere kreise dargestellt. [Die grossen philosophen des alterthums.] Leipz. 1883. D.   **188:2**

Cornwallis, C. F. A brief view of greek philosophy, to the coming of Christ. *In* Small books on great subjects.   **829.2 : 48 v2**

5. Modern philosophies.

Cousin, Victor. Course of the history of modern philosophy. Tr. by O. W. Wight. N. Y. 1866. 2 v. O.   **190:2**

Dean, Amos. Elements of philosophy in modern Europe. *In his* History of civilization.   **309:5 v6**

Eucken, Rudolph. The fundamental concepts of modern philosophic thought, critically and historically considered. Tr. by M. Stuart Phelps, with add. and cor. by the author and an introd. by Noah Porter. N. Y. 1880. D.   **190:3**

Fischer, Ernst Kuno Berthold. Geschichte der neuern philosophie. München *and* Heidelb. 1867–80. 7 v. in 8. O.   **190:1**

Contents. V. 1. Allgemeine einleitung.—Descartes' leben, schriften und lehre. 1. *Theil 1, Anhang.* René Descartes' hauptschriften zur grundlegung seiner philosophie. 1. *Theil 2.* Fortbildung der lehre Descartes'.—Spinoza. 2. Leibniz und seine schule. 3. Kant's vernunftkritik und deren entstehung. 4. Kant's System der reinen vernunft auf grund der vernunftkritik. 5. Fichte und seine vorgänger. 6. Friedrich Wilhelm Joseph Schelling.

— *Same.* V. 3–5. München. 1882–84. 3 v. O.   **190:1**

Contents. Same as above. V. 3, 4. 3te neu bearb. aufl. 5. 2te verm. und rev. aufl.

Herbert, T: Martin. The realistic assumptions of modern science examined. Lond. 1879. O.   **142:2**

Morell, J. D. An historical and critical view of the speculative philosophy of Europe in the 19th century. N. Y. 1858. O. **190+4**

Rosmini-Serbati, Antonio. A short sketch of modern philosophies, and of his own system ; witn a few words of introd. by father Lockhart. Lond. 1882. D. **190:5**

English.

Frothingham, Octavius Brooks. Transcendentalism in New England ; a history. N. Y. 1876. O. **191:1**

Concord summer school of philosophy. Concord lectures on philosophy ; comprising outlines of all the lectures in 1882, with an historical sketch ; coll. and arr. by Raymond L. Bridgman. rev. by the several lecturers and approved by the faculty. Cambridge, Mass. [1883]. O. **191+7**

Emerson, Ralph Waldo. [Philosophical writings]. *In his* Complete works. **820.1:8**
Contents, see under English literature. Collected works.

*   *   *

Stephen, Leslie. History of english thought in the 18th century. 2d ed. N. Y. 1881. 2 v. O. **192:8**

Bacon, Francis. *baron Verulam and viscount St. Albans.* [Philosophical writings.] *In his* Works. **820.2:2**
Contents, see under English literature. Collected works.

Fowler, T: Bacon. [Eng. philosophers.] N. Y. 1881. D. **192:3**

Mead, Edwin Doak. The philosophy of Carlyle. Bost. 1881. D. **191:2**

Monck, W: H. S. Sir W: Hamilton. [Eng. philosophers.] N. Y. 1881. D. **191:5**

Veitch, J: Hamilton. [Phil. classics for eng. readers.] Phila. 1882. D. **191:6**

Mill, J: Stuart. An examination of sir W: Hamilton's philosophy, and of the principal philosophical questions discussed in his writings. Bost. 1865. 2 v. O. **191:3**

Mansel, H: Longueville. The philosophy of the conditioned ; comprising some remarks on sir W: Hamilton's philosophy and on mr. J: S. Mill's examination of that philosophy. Lond. 1866. O. **191:4**

Masson, D: Recent british philosophy ; a review, with criticisms ; incl. some comments on mr. Mill's answer to sir W: Hamilton. N. Y. 1866. D. **192:6**

Bower, G. S. D: Hartley and James Mill. [Eng. philosophers.] N. Y. 1881. D. **192:2**

Hobbes, T: [Philosophical writings.] *In his* English works. **820.2:12**
Contents, see under English literature. Collected works.

Locke, J: Works. Lond. *n. d.* 2 v. D. **192:4**
Contents. V. 1, 2. Philosophical works, with a preliminary essay and notes by J. A. St. John. V. 1. Preliminary discourse by the ed.—On the conduct of the understanding.—An essay concerning the human understanding, book 1-2. V. 2. *Same.* Book 3-4.—Controversy with the bishop of Worcester. — An examination of P. Malebranche's opinion of seeing all things in God, with remarks upon some of mr. Norris's books.—Elements of natural philosophy.— Some thoughts concerning reading and study for a gentleman.

Mivart, St. G: Nature and thought ; an introduction to a natural philosophy. Lond. 1882. O. **192:10**

Fowler, T: Shaftesbury and Hutcheson. [Eng. philosophers.] N. Y. 1883. O. **192:9**

Farrer, James A. Adam Smith, 1723—1790. [Eng. philosophers.] N. Y. 1881. D. **192:5**

Spencer, Herbert. [A system of synthetic philosophy.] N. Y. 1873-82. D. **192:7**
Contents. Pt. 1. First principles of a new system of philosophy : The knowable ; The unknowable. Pt. 2, 3. The principles of biology : V. 1. The data of biology: The inductions of biology; The evolution of life; V. 2. Morphological development; Physiological development; Laws of multiplication; Appendices. Pt. 4, 5. The principles of psychology : V. 1. The data of psychology: The inductions of psychology; General synthesis; Physical synthesis; App.; V. 2. Special analysis; General analysis; Corollaries. Pt. 6, 7. [8 unpubl.]. The principles of sociology : V. 1. The data of sociology; The inductions of sociology; The domestic relations; V. 2. Ceremonial institutions; Political institutions. Pt. 9. [10 unpubl.]. The principles of morality : V. 1. The data of ethics.

Birks, T: Rawson. Modern physical fatalism and the doctrine of evolution ; an examination of mr. H. Spencer's First principles. Lond. 1876. D. **192:1**

Stewart, Dugald. Collected works, ed. by sir W: Hamilton. Edinb. 1877. 11 v. O. **191+8**
Contents. V. 1. Progress of metaphysical, ethical and political philosophy. 2-4. Elements of the philosophy of the human mind. 5. Philosophical essays. 6, 7. The philosophy of the active and moral powers of man. 8, 9. Lectures on political economy. 10. Biographical memoirs of Adam Smith, W: Robertson, T: Reid.—Veitch, J. A memoir of Dugald Stewart with selections from his correspondence. 11. Translations of the passages in foreign languages contained in the collected works.—General index.

German.

Heine, H: Zur geschichte der religion und philosophie in Deutschland. *In his* Sämmtliche werke. **830 : 139 v5**

Gostwick, Joseph. German culture and christianity ; their controversy in 1770—1880. Lond. 1882. O. **211 : 21**

Hall, Granville Stanley. [Essays on german philosophy]. *In his* Aspects of german culture. **824.1 : 39**
Contents, see under English literature. Essays.

Feuerbach, L: Andreas. Sämmtliche werke. Leipz. 1846-76. 10 v. in 8. O. **193:1**
Contents. V. 1. Erläuterung und ergänzungen zum Wesen des christenthums. 2. Philosophische kritiken und grundsätze. 3. Gedanken über tod und unsterblichkeit. 4. Geschichte der neuern philosophie von Bacon v. Verulam bis Benedict Spinoza. 5. Darstellung, entwicklung und kritik der Leibnitz'schen philosophie. 6. Pierre Bayle; ein beitrag zur geschichte der philosophie und menschheit. 7. Das Wesen des christenthums. 8. Vorlesungen über das wesen der religion, nebst zusätzen und anmerkungen. 9. Theogonie nach den quellen des classischen, hebräischen und christlichen alterthums. 10. Gottheit, freiheit und unsterblichkeit vom standpunkte der anthropologie.

Fichte, J: Gottlieb. The characteristics of the present age. Tr. from the german by W: Smith. Lond. 1847. D. **142:5**

— The science of knowledge. Tr. from the german by A. E. Kroeger. Phila. 1868. D. **141:1**

Everett, C: Carroll. Fichte's Science of knowledge ; a critical exposition. (German phil. classics.) Chicago. 1884. S. **142:6**

Hartmann, K: Robert E: v. Philosophy of the unconscious ; speculative results according to the inductive method of physical science.

Authorized tr. by W: Chatterton Coupland.
N. Y, 1884. 3 v. O.   **193:8**
Vaihinger, Hans. Hartmann, Dühring und
Lange; zur geschichte der deutschen phi-
losophie im 19ten jahrhundert; ein kriti-
scher essay. Iserlohn. 1876. O.   **193:9**
Pfleiderer, Edmund. Der moderne pessimismus.
In Deutsche zeit- und streit-fragen.
                                    304 : 15 v4
Gätschenberger, Stephan. Nihilismus, pessim-
ismus und weltschmerz; geschrieben aus
anlass der enthüllung eines monuments
für den grafen Szechenyi in Pest. *In* Deut-
sehe zeit- und streit-fragen. **304 : 15 v10**
Sommer, Hugo. Die religion des pessimismus.
In Deutsche zeit- und streit-fragen.
                                    304 : 15 v13
Caird, E: Hegel. [Philos. classics for eng. read-
ers.] Phila. 1883. D.   **193:4**
Kant, Immanuel. Critique of pure reason. Tr.
from the german by J. M. D. Meiklejohn.
Lond. 1866. D.   **142:1**
Morris, G: S. Kant's Critique of pure reason; a
critical exposition. [German philosoph.
classics.] Chicago. 1882. S.   **142:4**
Watson, J: Kant and his english critics; a com-
parison of critical and empirical philosophy.
N. Y. 1881. O.   **142+3**
Seth, Andrew. The development from Kant to
Hegel, with chapters on the philosophy of
religion. (Pub. by the Hibbert trustees.)
Lond. 1882. O.   **193:5**
Schlegel, K: W: F: v. The philosophy of life
and philosophy of language, in a course of
lectures. Tr. from the german by A. J. W.
Morrison. N. Y. 1848. D.   **193:3**
Watson, J: Schelling's transcendental idealism;
a critical exposition. [German philosoph.
classics.] Chicago. 1882. S.   **141:2**
Schopenhauer, Arthur. Sämmtliche werke;
herausg. von Julius Frauenstädt. 2te aufl.
Leipz. 1877. 6 v. O.   **193:4**
Contents. V. **1**. Einleitung des herausg. — Arthur
Schopenhauer, ein lebensbild von dem herausg. —
Schriften zur erkenntnisslehre. **2, 3**. Die Welt als
wille und vorstellung. **4**. Naturphilosophie und
ethik : Ueber den willen in der natur. — Die beiden
grundprobleme der ethik. **5, 6**. Parerga und parali-
pomena, kleine philosophische schriften : I. Vom
idealen und realen. — Zur geschichte der philosophie.
— Die universitäts-philosophie. — Die absichtlichkeit
im schicksale der einzelnen. — Das geistersehen. —
Aphorismen zur lebensweisheit. — II. Philosophie
und ihre methode. — Logik und dialektik. — Der in-
tellekt. — Das ding an sich und die erscheinung. —

Pantheismus. — Philosophie und wissenschaft der
natur. — Farbenlehre. — Ethik. — Rechtslehre und
politik. — Unzerstörbarkeit durch den tod. — Nich-
tigkeit des daseins. — Vom leiden der welt. — Ueber
den selbstmord. — Die bejahung und verneinung des
willens zum leben. — Religion. — Sanskrit-literatur.
— Archäologische betrachtungen. — Mythologische
betrachtungen. — Metaphysik des schönen und ästhetik. — Urtheil, kritik, beifall und ruhm. — Gelehr-
samkeit und gelehrte. — Selbstdenken. — Schriftstel-
lerei und stil. — Lesen und bücher. — Sprache und
worte. — Psychologische bemerkungen. — Ueber die
weiber. — Ueber erziehung. — Zur physiognomik. —
Ueber lärm und geräusch. — Gleichnisse, parabeln
und fabeln. — Verse.
— The world as will and idea. From the german
by R. B. Haldane and J: Kemp. [In 3 v.]
V. 1. Bost. 1883. O.   **193:7**
Spinoza, Baruch de. Chief works. Tr. from the
latin, with an introd. by R. H. M. Elwes.
[Bohn's phil. lib.] Lond. 1883. 2 v. O.
                                    193:6
Contents. V. **1**. Introd. — Tractatus theologico-
politicus. — Tractatus politicus. **2**. De intellectus
emendatione. — Ethica. — Correspondence.
Kalischer, Alfred Christian. Benedikt (Baruch)
von Spinoza's stellung zum judenthum und
christenthum; als beitrag zur lösung der
judenfrage beleuchtet. *In* Deutsche zeit-
und streit-fragen.   **304 : 15 v13**

French and Italian.

Comte, A: Positive philosophy. Tr. by Harriet
Martineau. 3d ed. N. Y. 1858. O.   **194:2**
Lewes, G: H: Comte's Philosophy of the sciences;
an exposition of the principles of the Cours
de philosophie positive of A: Comte. Lond.
1853. D.   **194:1**
Mill, J: Stuart. The positive philosophy of
A: Comte. Bost. 1866. D.   **194:3**
Cousin, V: Lectures on the true, the beautiful
and the good; increased by an app. on
french art. Tr., with the approbation of
Cousin, by O. W. Wight. N. Y. 1857. O.
                                    194:4
Helvetius, Claude Adrian. A treatise on man,
his intellectual faculties and his education;
a posthumous work. Tr. from the french,
with add. notes, by W. Hooper. Lond. 1777.
2 v. O.   **194:5**
Steffens, H: Pascal und die philosophisch-ge-
schichtliche bedeutung seiner ansichten.
In his Nachgelassene schriften.   **898.2 : 1**
Flint, Robert. Vico. (Phil. classics.) Phila. 1884.
D.   **195:1**

2. Metaphysics.

Blavatsky, *Mme.* H. P. Isis unveiled; a master-
key to the mysteries of ancient and modern
science and theology. 2d ed. N. Y. 1877.
2 v. O.   **110+4**
Büchner, F: C: Christian L: Force and matter;
empirico-philosophical studies intelligibly
rendered. With an add. introd. expressly
written for the eng. ed. by L: Büchner, ed.
by J: F: Collingwood. 2d eng., completed
from the 10th german ed. Lond. 1870. D.
                                    113 : 1
Cudworth, Ralph. The true intellectual system
of the universe, wherein all the reason and
philosophy of atheism is confuted, and its

impossibility demonstrated.—A treatise on
immutable morality; with a discourse concerning the true notion of the Lord's supper. and two sermons on I John ii : 3, 4
and I Cor. xv : 27. 1st am. ed. with referenees to the several quotations in the Intellectual system, and an account of the life
and writings of the author by T: Birch.
Andover. 1837. 2 v. O.   **110 : 1**
Fiske, J: Outlines of cosmic philosophy, based
on the doctrine of evolution, with criticisms
on the positive philosophy. Bost. 1878. 2
v. O.   **113 : 2**
— *Same.* Vol. 2. Bost. 1875. O.   **113 : 2**

Hamilton, *Sir* W: Lectures on metaphysics; ed. by H: Longueville Mansel and J: Veitch. Bost. 1859. O.   **110 : 2**

Harris, James. Philosophical arrangements. Lond. 1775. O.   **112 : 1**

Lotze, Hermann. Metaphysic, in three books; ontology, cosmology and psychology. Eng. tr. ed. by Bernard Bosanquet. [System of philosophy, pt. 2.] (Clarendon press ser.) N. Y. 1884. O.   **110 : 5**

— Outlines of metaphysic; dictated portions of [his] lectures. Tr. and ed. by G: T. Ladd. Bost. 1884. D.   **110 : 7**

Paine, Martyn. Physiology of the soul and instinct as distinguished from materialism; with supplementary demonstrations of the divine communication of the narratives of the creation and the flood. N. Y. 1872. O.   **111+1**

Pressensé, Edmond Marcellin Déhault de. A study of origins, or The problems of knowledge of being and of duty. Tr. by Annie Harwood Holmden. Lond. 1883. D.   **110 : 3**

Schasler, Max. Ueber materialistische und idealistische weltanschauung. *In* Deutsche zeit- und streit-fragen.   **304 : 15 v8**

Shields, C: W. The order of the sciences, an essay on the philosophical classification and organization of human knowledge. N. Y.   **112 : 2**

Sinnett, A. P. Esoteric buddhism. Bost. 1884. D.   **110 : 6**

Spencer, Herbert. The classification of the sciences [and other philosophical essays]. *in* 824.2 : 81-83
Contents, see under English literature, Essays.

White, Hugh. Cosmogenia, or The philosophy of the world. Watertown, N. Y. 1830. O.   **113 : 3**

3. Mental morphology and hygiene.

1. Mind and body.

(See also Physiology, class 612.)

Bain, Alexander. Mind and body; the theories of their relation. (Intern. scientific ser.) N. Y. 1874. D.   **131 : 1**

— Common errors on the mind. *In his* Practical essays.   **824.2 : 91**

Barlow, J: The connection between physiology and intellectual philosophy. — On man's power over himself to prevent or control insanity. *In* Small books on great subjects.   **829.2 : 48 v1**

Bastian, H: Charlton. The brain as an organ of mind. Ill. N. Y. 1880. D.   **131 : 2**

Brodie, *Sir* B: Mind and matter, or Psychological inquiries, in a series of essays intended to illustrate the mutual relations of the physical organization of the mental faculties. With add. notes by an amer. ed. N. Y. 1873. D.   **131 : 3**

Brown-Séquard, C: E: Dual character of the brain. *In* Smithsonian misc.   **506 : R4 v15**

Calderwood, H: The relations of mind and brain. Lond. 1879. O.   **131 : 4**

Carpenter, W: B: Principles of mental physiology, with their applications to the training and discipline of the mind and the study of its morbid conditions. N. Y. 1878. D.   **131 : 5**

Elam, C: A physicians problems. Bost. 1869. D.   **130 : 7**
Contents. Natural heritage.—On degenerations in man.—On moral and criminal epidemics.—Body v. mind.—Illusions and hallucinations.—On somnambulism.—Revery and abstraction.

Goltz, Bogumil. Diagnosen, signalements und verdicte für exacte menschenkenntniss. [Feigenblätter, 2.] Berlin. *n. d.* D.   **130 : 1**

— Das menschen-dasein in seinen weltewigen zügen und zeichen. Berlin. 1868. 2 v. in 1. D.   **130 : 2**
Contents. V. 1. Der mensch und das menschliche leben.—Natur.—Die sittliche welt. 2. Die welt des geistes.—Die religion.—Die welt im staate.

Goltz, Bogumil.—*Continued.*

— Typen der geschellschaft; ein complimentirbuch ohne complimente. 4te aufl. Berlin. 1867. 2 v. in 1. S.   **130 : 3**

— Zur physiognomie und characteristik des volkes. [Exacte menschenkenntniss, b. 2.] Berlin, 1859. S.   **130 : 4**

Holmes, Oliver Wendell. Mechanism in thought and morals; an address delivered before the Phi beta kappa society of Harvard university, june 29, 1870, with notes and afterthoughts. Bost. 1871. D.   **131 : 6**

Laycock, T: Mind and brain, or The correlations of consciousness and organization systematically investigated and applied to philosophy, mental science and practice; with a preliminary dissertation on method and ill. of the text. 2d ed. N. Y. 1869. 2 v. D.   **131 : 7**

Luys, J. The brain and its functions. (Internat. scientific ser.) N. Y. 1882. D.   **131 : 11**

Maudsley, H: The physiology and pathology of mind. 2d ed., rev. Lond. 1868. O.   **131 : 8**

— The physiology of mind; the 1st pt. of a 3d ed. rev. and enl. and in great part rewritten of The physiology and pathology of mind. N. Y. 1878. D.   **131 : 9**

Moore, G: The power of the soul over the body, considered in relation to health and morals. N. Y. 1847. D.   **130 : 5**

— The use of the body in relation to the mind. N. Y. 1847. D.   **130 : 6**

Morselli, H: Suicide; an essay on comparative moral statistics. The original expressly rev. and abr. by the author for the english version. (Intern. scientific ser.) N. Y. 1882. D.   **131 : 13**

O'Dea, James J. Suicide; studies on its philosophy, causes and prevention. N. Y. 1882. D.   **131 : 12**

Tuke, Daniel Hack. Illustrations of the influence of the mind upon the body in health and disease, designed to elucidate the action of the imagination. Phila. 1872. O.   **131 : 10**

2. Mental derangements.

Brierre de Boismont, Alexandre Jacques François. Hallucinations, or The rational history of apparitions, visions, dreams, ecstasy, magnetism and somnambulism. 1st amer. ed. Phila. 1853. O. **132+1**

Buckham, T. R. Insanity considered in its medico-legal relations ; a treatise. Phila. 1883. O. **132 : 9**

Bucknill, J : C: Notes on asylums for the insane in America. Lond. 1876. D. **132 : 11**

Corning, J. Leonard. Brain exhaustion ; with some preliminary considerations on cerebral dynamics. N. Y. 1884. D. **132 : 10**

Hammond, W: Alexander. A treatise on insanity in its medical relations. N. Y. 1883. O. **132 : 8**

Kirchner, F: Der zweck des daseins, im hinblick auf die mehrung des selbstmordes. *In* Deutsche zeit- und streit-fragen. **304 : 15 v11**

Maudsley, H: Responsibility in mental disease. (Intern. scientific ser.) N. Y. 1875. D. **132 : 2**

— Body and mind : an inquiry into their connection and mutual influence, specially in reference to mental disorders. An enl. and rev. ed., to which are added psychological essays. N. Y. 1882. D. **132 : 7**

Contents. Lectures. Body and mind : On the physical condition of mental function in health ; On certain forms of degeneracy of mind, their causation, and their relations to other disorders of the nervous system ; On the relations of morbid bodily states to disordered mental functions : Conscience and organization. *Essays.* Hamlet.—Emanuel Swedenborg.—The theory of vitality.—The limits of philosophical inquiry.

Rush, B: Medical inquiries and observations upon the diseases of the mind. 2d ed. Phila. 1818. O. **132 : 3**

Seguin, E: Idiocy, and its treatment by the physiological method. N. Y. 1866. O. **132+15**

Storer, Horatio Robinson. The causation, course and treatment of reflex insanity in women. Bost. 1871. D. **132 : 4**

Sully, James. Illusions ; a psychological study. (Intern. scientific ser.) N. Y. 1881. D. **132 : 6**

Tuke, Daniel Hack. Chapters in the history of the insane in the British Isles. Ill. Lond. 1882. O. **132 : 13**

— Insanity in ancient and modern life, with chapters on its prevention. Lond. 1878. D. **132 : 12**

Upham, T: Cogswell. Outlines of imperfect and disordered mental action. N. Y. 1868. S. **132 : 14**

Winslow, Forbes Benignus. On obscure diseases of the brain and disorders of the mind ; their incipient symptoms, pathology, diagnosis, treatment and prophylaxis. Lond. 1860. O. **132 : 5**

3. Magic, witchcraft, etc.

Amort, Eusebius, *jr.* Biblische und profane wunderthäter. *In* Deutsche zeit- und streitfragen. **304 : 15 v9**

Conway, Moncure Daniel. Demonology and devil-lore. Ill. N. Y. 1879. 2 v. O. **133 : 3**

Ennemoser, Joseph. The history of magic. Tr. from the german by W: Howitt. Added, an app. of the most remarkable and best authenticated stories of apparitions, dreams, second sight, somnambulism, predictions, divination, witchcraft, vampires, fairies, table-turning and spirit-rapping, selected by Mary Howitt. Lond. 1854. 2 v. D. **133 : 4**

Hall, F : T. The pedigree of the devil. Ill. Lond. 1883. O. **133 : 20**

Hertz, W: Der werwolf ; beitrag zur sagengeschichte. Stuttgart. 1862. O. **133 : 1**

Howitt, W: The history of the supernatural in all ages and nations and in all churches, christian and pagan, demonstrating a universal faith. Phila. 1863. 2 v. D. **133 : 6**

Lee, F: G:, *ed.* Glimpses of the supernatural ; facts, records and traditions relating to dreams, omens, miraculous occurrences, apparitions, wraiths, warnings, second sight, witchcraft, necromancy, etc. 2 v. in 1. N. Y. 1875. D. **133 : 8**

Lenormant, François. Chaldean magic ; its origin and development. With considerable add. by the author and notes by the ed., tr. from the french. Lond. 1878. O. **133 : 24**

Lilly, W: An introd. to astrology, with numerous emendations, adapted to the improved state of the science in the present day.— A grammar of astrology and tables for calculating nativities by Zadkiel, [R: J. Morrison]. Lond. 1852. D. **133 : 9**

Radcliffe, J : Netten. Fiends, ghosts and sprites ; including an account of the origin and nature of belief in the supernatural. Lond. 1854. D. **133 : 10**

Rydberg, Abraham Viktor. The magic of the middle ages. Tr. from the swedish by A: Hjalmar Edgren. N. Y. 1879. D. **133 : 11**

Schele de Vere, Maximilian. Modern magic. N. Y. 1873. D. **133 : 22**

Scott, *Sir* Walter. Letters on demonology and witchcraft, addressed to J. G. Lockhart. N. Y. 1845. S. **133 : 13**

Spalding, T: Alfred. Elizabethan demonology ; an essay in illustration of the belief in the existence of devils and the powers possessed by them, as it was generally held during the period of the reformation and the times immediately succeeding ; with special reference to Shakspere and his works. Lond. 1880. D. **133 : 14**

Taylor, I: Fanaticism ; by the author of "Natural history of enthusiasm". N. Y. 1834. O. **133 : 16**

Yardley, E: The supernatural in romantic fiction. Lond. 1880. D. **133 : 15**

Special countries.

Hutchinson, T: The witchcraft delusion of 1692 ; from an unpub. ms., an early draft of his History of Massachusetts in the Mass. archives, with notes by W: F: Poole. Bost. 1870. O. **133+7**

Drake, S: Gardner. The witchcraft delusion in New England ; its rise, progress and termination, as exhibited by dr. Cotton Mather in The wonders of the invisible world, and by mr. Robert Calef in More wonders of the invisible world. With a

preface, introd. and notes. [Large paper ed. no. 18]. Roxbury, Mass. 3 v, in 2. Q.
133 : R21

Upham, C: Wentworth. Salem witchcraft; with an account of Salem village and a history of opinions on witchcraft and kindred subjects. Bost. 1867. 2 v. in 4. O. 133 : R26

— Lectures on witchcraft ; comprising a history of the delusion in Salem, in 1692. Bost. 1831. S. 133 : 27

Beard, G: Miller. The Salem witchcraft excitement of 1692 and its practical application to our own time. N. Y. 1882. S. 133 : 18

Dahlgren, Madeleine, *born* Vinton, *formerly mrs. Goddard*. South mountain magic ; a narrative. Bost. 1882. D. 133 : 19

Gomme, G: Laurence, *ed.* The gentleman's magazine library ; being a classified collection of the chief contents of the Gentleman's magazine from 1731 to 1868: Popular superstitions. Lond. 1884. O. 133+25

Grant, Anne, *born* Macvicar. Essays on the superstitions of the highlanders of Scotland. Added, Translations from the gaelic, and letters connected with those formerly published. Lond. 1811. 2 v. in 1. D. 133 : 5

Sharpe, C: Kirkpatrick. A historical account of the belief in witchcraft in Scotland. Lond. 1884. D. 133 : 28

Soldan, W: Gottlieb. Geschichte der hexenprozesse ; neu bearb. von H: Heppe. Stuttgart. 1880. 2 v. O. 133 : 23

Wächter, Oskar. Vehmgerichte und hexenprozesse in Deutschland ; nach den quellen dargestellt. Stuttgart. [1882]. D. 133 : 17

Nippold, F: W: Franz. Die gegenwärtige wiederbelebung des hexenglaubens ; mit einem literarisch - kritischen anhang über die quellen und bearbeitungen der hexenprozesse. *In* Deutsche zeit- und streitfragen. 304 : 15 v4

Mannhardt, W: Die praktischen folgen des aberglaubens, mit besonderer berücksichtigung der provinz Preussen. *In* Deutsche zeit- und streitfragen. 304 : 15 v7

Scherr, Johannes. Die gekreuzigte, oder Das passionsspiel von Wildisbuch. St. Gallen. 1860. D. 133 : 2

4. Spiritualism.

Babbitt, Edwin D. Health manual devoted to healing by means of nature's higher forces, incl. "The health guide", rev. and impr. N. Y. 1880. D. 133 : 111

— The principles of light and color ; including among other things the harmonic laws of the universe, the etherio-atomic philosophy of force, chromo chemistry, chromo therapeutics and the general philosophy of the fine forces, together with numerous discoveries and practical applications. Ill. N. Y. 1878. O. 133+112

— Religion, as revealed by the material and spiritual universe. N. Y. [1881]. D. 133 : 113

Beecher, C: Spiritual manifestations. Bost. 1879. D. 133 : 101

Carpenter, W: B: Mesmerism, spiritualism, etc., historically and scientifically considered ;

two lectures delivered at the London institution, with preface and app. N. Y. 1877. D. 133 : 102

Davis, Andrew Jackson. The principles of nature, her divine revelations, and a voice to mankind ; in 3 parts. Lond. 1847. 2 v. O. 133+103

Fairfield, Francis Gerry. Ten years with spiritual mediums ; an inquiry concerning the etiology of certain phenomena called spiritual. N. Y. 1875. D. 133 : 104

Gasparin, Agénor Étienne *comte* de. Science vs. modern spiritualism ; a treatise on turning tables, the supernatural in general, and spirits. Tr. from the french by E. W. Robert ; with an introd. by Robert Baird. N. Y. 1857. 2 v. D. 133 : 105

Hammond, W: Alexander. Spiritualism and allied causes and conditions of nervous derangement. Ill. N. Y. 1876. D. 133 : 106

Kirchner, F: Der spiritismus, die narrheit unseres zeitalters. *In* Deutsche zeit- und streit-fragen. 304 : 15 v12

Mitchell, T: Key to ghostism ; science and art. unlock its mysteries. N. Y. 1880. D. 133 : 107

Owen, Robert Dale. Footfalls on the boundary of another world, with narrative illustrations. Phila. 1850. D. 133 : 109

— The debatable land between this world and the next, with illustrative narrations. N. Y. 1872. D. 133 : 108

Sargent, Epes. Planchette, or The despair of science ; a full account of modern spiritualism, its phenomena, and the various theories regarding it, with a survey of french spiritsm. [*Anon.*] Bost. 1869. S. 133 : 12

Zöllner, J: C: F: Transcendental physics ; an account of experimental investigations from [his] scientific treatises. Tr. from the german, with pref. and app. by C. Carleton Massey. 2d ed. Bost. 1881. D. 133 : 110

5. Dreams.

Cobbe, Frances Power. Dreams, as illustrations of unconscious cerebration. *With her* Darwinism in morals. *in* 824.3 : 107

Leland, C: Godfrey, *ed.* The poetry and mystery of dreams. Phila. 1856. D. 135 : 1

Seafield, Frank. The literature and curiosities of dreams ; a common place book of speculations concerning the mystery of dreams and visions, records of curious and well-authenticated dreams, and notes on the various modes of interpretation adopted in ancient and modern times ; in 2 v. V. 1. Lond. 1865. D. 135 : 2

6. Phrenology, temperaments, etc.

Burton, Robert. The anatomy of melancholy ; what it is, with all the kinds, causes, symptoms, prognostics and several cures of it, in three partitions, with their several sections, members and subsections, philosophically, medically, historically opened and cut up, by Democritus junior, with a satirical preface, conducing to the following discourse. New ed., cor. and enriched by translations of the numerous classical extracts, by Democritus minor. Bost. 1859. 3 v. D. **137 : 2**

Combe, G: The constitution of man considered in relation to external objects. N. Y. 1860. S. **139 : 1**

Drayton, H: S., *and* James **McNeill**. Brain and mind, or Mental science, considered in accordance with the principles of phrenology and in relation to modern physiology. N. Y. 1880. D. **139 : 2**

Fowler, Orrin Squire. Self-culture, and perfection of character, including the management of youth. N. Y. 1847. D. **139 : 3**

Goltz, Bogumil. Zur charakteristik und naturgeschichte der frauen. 5te aufl. Berlin. [1874]. S. **136 : 1**

Lavater, J: Caspar. Essays on physiognomy; for the promotion of the knowledge and the love of mankind. Written in the german language, and tr. into english by T: Holcroft. 2d ed. Ill. To which are added 100 physiognomical rules, a posthumous work by mr. Lavater, and memoirs of the life of the author compiled principally from the life of Lavater, written by his son-in-law G. Gessner. Lond. 1804. 4 v. O. **138+P1**

Spurzheim, J: F: Kaspar. Phrenology, or The doctrine of the mental phenomena. 3d amer. ed. Bost. 1834. 2 v. O. **139 : 4**

Theophrastus. Characters; illustrated by physionomical [*sic*] sketches [by F. Howell]. Bost. 1831. D. **137 : 1**

4. Psychology.

Abercrombie, J: Inquiries concerning the intellectual powers and the investigation of truth. [Harpers' family lib.] N. Y. 1847. S. **150 : 1**

Bain, Alexander. The senses and the intellect. 2d ed. Lond. 1864. O. **150 : 14**
— The emotions and the will. 2d ed. Lond. 1865. O. **150+13**

Bascom, J: The science of mind. N. Y. 1881. D. **150 : 2**

Brown, T: Lectures on the philosophy of the human mind ; with a memoir of the author by D: Welsh. 7th ed. Edinb. 1833. O. **150 : 3**

Chadbourne, Paul Ansel. Instinct ; its office in the animal kingdom and its relation to the higher powers in man. (Lowell lectures, 1871.) N. Y. 1883. O. **158 : 1**

Edwards, Jonathan. A careful and strict inquiry into the modern prevailing notions of that freedom of the will, which is supposed to be essential to moral agency, virtue and vice, reward and punishment, praise and blame. N. Y. 1858. O. **159+1**

Hazard, Rowland Gibson. Man a creative first cause ; two discourses delivered at Concord, Mass., july 1882. Bost. 1883. D. **150 : 15**

Lewes, G: H: Problems of life and mind. Bost. 1874, 1875. 2 v. O. **150 : 4**
Contents. 1st ser. The foundations of a creed. V. 1. Introd.: pt. 1, The method of science and its application to metaphysics; pt. 2, The rules of philosophizing.—Psychological principles.—Problem 1, The limitations of knowledge. 2. Problem 2, The principles of certitude.—Problem 3, From the known to the unknown.—Problem 4, Matter and force.—Problem 5, Force and cause.—Problem 6, The absolute in the correlations of feeling and motion.
— *Same.* 3d series. Bost. 1879. O. **150 : 4 v3**
Contents. Problem 1. The study of psychology, its object, scope and method.

McCosh, James. The emotions. N. Y. 1880. D. **157 : 1**

Maudsley, H: Body and will ; an essay concerning will in its metaphysical, physiological and pathological aspects. N. Y. 1884 [1883]. O. **159 : 2**

Mill, James. Analysis of the phenomena of the human mind. A new ed. with notes, illustrative and critical, by Alexander Bain, Andrew Findlater and G: Grote. Ed. with add. notes by J: Stuart Mill. Lond. 1869. 2 v. O. **150 : 5**

Porter, Noah. The human intellect ; with an introduction upon psychology and the soul. 2d ed. N. Y. 1869. O. **150+6**
— The elements of intellectual science ; a manual for schools and colleges, abridged from the "Human intellect." N. Y. [1871]. O. **150 : 7**

Rauch, F: A: Psychology, or A view of the human soul, incl. anthropology. 2d ed., rev. and impr. *T. p. w.* [New York. 1841.] D. **150 : 8**

Ribot, Théodule. Diseases of memory ; an essay in positive psychology. From the french by W: Huntington Smith. (Intern. scientific ser.) N. Y. 1882. D. **154 : 1**
— *Same.* N. Y. [1883.] O. **154+1**

Silberstein, Adolph. Love's strategy ; studies on the art of winning and retaining love. From the german. Chicago. 1884. S. **157 : 2**

Steffens, H: Ueber die wissenschaftliche behandlung der psychologie. *In his* Nachgelassene schriften. **898.2 : 1**

Stewart, Dugald. Elements of the philosophy of the human mind. With add., ed. by sir W: Hamilton. Edinb. 1877. 3 v. O. **191+8 v 2-4**

Storrs, R: Salter. The constitution of the human soul ; six lectures delivered at the Brooklyn institute. [Graham lectures.] N. Y. 1857. O. **150+10**

Taine, Hippolyte Adolphe. On intelligence. Tr. from the french by T. D. Haye, and rev. with add., by the author. N. Y. 1879. 2 v. D. **150 : 11**

Sully, James. Outlines of psychology, with special reference to the theory of education. Lond. 1884. O. **150+16**

Walter, Johnston Estep. The perception of space and matter. Bost. 1879. O. **152 : 1**

Whately, R: Introductory lessons on mind. Bost. 1859. D. **150 : 12**
Note. For works on the instinct of animals, see Zoology, class 590.

5. Logic.

Bain, Alexander. Logic; deductive and inductive. New and rev. ed. N. Y. 1874. D. **160 : 1**

Hamilton, *Sir* W: Lectures on logic; ed. by H: L. Mansel and J: Veitch. Bost. 1860. O. **160+2**

Hedge, Levi. Elements of logick, or A summary of the general principles and different modes of reasoning. 2d ed. Bost. 1818. D. **160 : 8**

Jevons, W: Stanley. The principles of science; a treatise on logic and scientific method. N. Y. 1874. O. **160 : 3**

— Logic. (Science primers.) Ill. N. Y. 1878. S. **160 : 4**

Lotze, Hermann. Logic, in three books: Of thought, of investigation and of knowledge. Eng. tr. ed. by Bernard Bosanquet. [System of philosophy, pt. 1.] (Clarendon press ser.) N. Y. 1884. O. **160 : 11**

McCosh, James. The laws of discursive thought; being a text-book of formal logic. N. Y. 1870. D. **160 : 5**

Mill, J: Stuart. A system of logic, ratiocinative and inductive; a connected view of the principles of evidence and the methods of scientific investigation. 8th ed. N. Y. 1874. O. **160+7**

Sidgwick, Alfred. Fallacies; a view of logic from the practical side. (Intern. scientific ser.) N. Y. 1884. D. **160 : 10**

Watts, I: Logic, or The right use of reason. in the enquiry after truth; with a variety of rules to guard against error, in the affairs of religion and human life, as well as in the sciences. Lond. 1822. S. **160 : 6**

6. Ethics.

1. In general.

Abercrombie, J: The philosophy of the moral feelings. [Harpers' family lib.] N. Y. 1889. S. **171 : 1**

· — *Same.* 1840. **171 : 1**'

Adams, W: The elements of christian science; a treatise upon moral philosophy and practice. Phila. 1850. O. **170 : 2**

Aikin, J: Letters from a father to his son, on various topics, relative to literature and the conduct of life. Phila. 1794. D. **170 : 27**

Bain, Alexander. Moral science; a compendium of ethics. N. Y. 1869. D. **171 : 2**

— On the study of character, including an estimate of phrenology. Lond. 1861. O. **171 : 3**

Barthélemy, J: Jacques. A treatise on morals. *in* **B 4351**

Beattie, James. Elements of moral science. Edinb. 1790. 2 v. O. **171 : 3**

Beta, *originally* Bettziech, H: Die geheimmittel- und unsittlichkeits-industrie in der tagespresse. *In* Deutsche zeit- und streit-fragen. **304 : 15 v1**

Blackie, J: Stuart. Four phases of morals; Socrates, Aristotle, christianity, utilitarianism. N. Y. [1878]. O. **171 : 4**

Bucke, R: Maurice. Man's moral nature; an essay. N. Y. 1879. O. **171 : 5**

Burgh, James. The dignity of human nature, or A brief account of the certain and established means for attaining the true end of our existence; in 4 books: 1. Of prudence; 2. Of knowledge; 3. Of virtue; 4. Of revealed religion. By J. B. Lond. 1754. O. **170 : 4**

Chapone, Hester. Letters on the improvement of the mind; addressed to a lady. Bost. 1822. T. **170 : 5**

Choice pleasures for youth; recommended in a series of letters from a father to his son. Rev. by the eds. N. Y. 1854. T. **175 : 1**

Cook, Joseph. Conscience, with preludes on current events. (Boston Monday lectures.) Bost 1879. D. **171 : 6**

Dodd, W: The beauties of history, or Pictures of virtue and vice drawn from examples of men eminent for their virtues, or infamous for their vices, selected for the instruction and entertainment of youth. 4th ed. Lond. 1803. D. **170 : 25**

Dymon, Jonathan. Essays on the principles of morality, and on the private and political rights and obligations of mankind; with a pref. by G: Bush. N. Y. 1847. O. **170 : 6**

Emerson, Ralph Waldo. The conduct of life. Bost. 1860. S. **171 : 7**

Contents. Fate.—Power.—Wealth.—Culture.—Behavior.—Worship.—Considerations by the way.—Beauty.—Illusions.

— *Same.* New and rev. ed. Bost. 1885. D. **171 : 7**

— *Same.* *In his* Works. **820.1 : 8 v6**

Epiktêtos (*lat.* Epictetus). Epictetus his morals, with Simplicius his comment; made english from the greek by G: Stanhope. 4th ed., with the life of Epictetus from monsieur ─Boilieau (*sic*). Lond. 1721. D. **171 : 8**

Fichte, J: Gottlieb. The science of rights. Tr. from the german by A. E. Kroeger. Phila. 1869. D. **170 : 7**

Fowler, T: Progressive morality; an essay in ethics. Lond. 1884. D. **171 : 19**

Fuller, Osgood E. Ideals of life, or Wisdom of the ages; a series of wholesome practical topics, on which are presented the best things from more than two hundred great thinkers and actors of all times. Detroit. 1881. O. **170+26**

Goltz, Bogumil. Die weltklugheit und die lebensweisheit, mit ihren correspondirenden studien. Berlin. 1869. 2 v. in 1. S. **170 : 1**

Gregory, J: A father's legacy to his daughters. *With* Chapone, H. Letters. *in* **170 : 5**

Hartmann, K: Robert E: v. Phänomenologie des sittlichen bewusstseins; prolegomena zu jeder künftigen ethik. Berlin. 1879. O. **171+18**

Hickok, Laurens Perseus. A system of moral science. 3d ed. N. Y. 1861. D. **170 : 8**

Holland, Josiah Gilbert, (*Timothy Titcomb*). Gold-foil. hammered from popular proverbs by Timothy Titcomb. N. Y. *n. d.* D. 170 : 9
Contents. An exordial essay.—The infallible book.—Patience.—Perfect liberty.—Trust and what comes of it.—The ideal Christ.—Providence.—Does sensuality pay?—The way to grow old.—Almsgiving.—The love of what is ours.—The power of circumstances.—Anvils and hammers.—Every man has his place.—Indolence and industry.—The sins of our neighbors.—The canonization of the vicious.—Social classification. — The preservation of character. — Vices of imagination.—Questions above reason.—Public and private life.—Home.—Learning and wisdom.—Receiving and doing.—The secret of popularity.—The Lord's business.—The great mystery.

James, J: Angell. The christian father's present to his children. N. Y. 1853. S. 170 : 10

Janet, Paul. Elements of morals ; with special application of the moral law to the duties of the individual and of society and the state. Tr. by mrs. C. R. Corson. N. Y. [1884]. D. 170 : 36
— The theory of morals. N. Y. 1883. O. 171 : 17

Kirchner, F: Der mangel eines allgemeinen moralprincips in unserer zeit. *In* Deutsche zeit- und streit-fragen. 304 : 15 v6

Kradofler, J. Die altchristliche moral und der moderne zeitgeist. *In* Deutsche zeit- und streit-fragen. 304 : 15 v2

La Bruyère, J: de. The "characters" of Jean de La Bruyère, newly rendered into english by H: van Laun. with an introd., a biographical memoir and notes. Ill. N. Y. ·1885 [1884]. O. 170 : 35

La Rochefoucauld, François, *duc* de, *prince* de *Marsillac.* Reflections, or Sentences and moral maxims. Tr. from the ed. of 1678 and 1827 with introd., notes and some account of the author and his times by J. W. Willis Bund and J. Hain Friswell. [Bayard ser.] Lond. 1871. T. 170 : 24
— *Same.* Newly tr. from the french, with introd. and notes. Added, Moral senteuces and maxims of Stanislas, king of Poland. N. Y. 1853. D. 170 : 24

Mackintosh, *Sir* James. A general view of the progress of ethical philosophy, chiefly during the 17th and 18th centuries. Phila. 1832. O. 170+11

Mallock, W: Hurrell. Is life worth living ? N. Y. 1880. D. 170 : 22

Nott, Eliphalet. Counsels to young men on the formation of character, and the principles which lead to success and happiness in life ; addresses, principally delivered at the anniversary commencements in Union college. [Harpers' family lib.] N. Y. 1840. S. 170 : 12

Paley, W: The principles of moral and political philosophy. *T. p. w.* O. 170 : 29

Patterson, J: Stahl. Conflict in nature and life ; a study of antagonism of things, for the elucidation of the problem of good and evil and the reconciliation of optimism and pessimism. [*Anon.*] N. Y. 1883. D. 170 : 31
— Reforms ; their difficulties and possibilities, by the author of "Conflict in nature and life." [*Anon.*] N. Y. 1884. D. 170 : 34

Pennington, *Lady* S. A mother's advice to her absent daughters, with an additional letter on the management and education of infant children. *With* **Chapone,** H. Letters on the improvement of the mind. *in* 170 : 5

Read, Hollis. The foot-prints of Satan, or The devil in history ; the counterpart of "God in history". N. Y. 1873. O. 170 : 13

Ruskin, J: The crown of wild olive ; three lectures on work, traffic and war. N. Y. 1878. O. 170 : 14
— Precious thoughts, moral and religious, gathered from the works of J: Ruskin by mrs. L. C. Tuthill. N. Y. 1883. D. 170 : 33

Savage, Minot Judson. The morals of evolution. Bost. 1880. D. 171 : 9
Contents. Is life worth living.—Morality and religion in the past.—The origin of goodness.—Nature of goodness.— Sense of obligation.— Selfishness and sacrifice.—Relativity of duty.—Real and conventional virtues and vices.—Morals and knowledge.—Rights and duties in matters of opinion.—Moral sanctions.—Morality and religion in the future.

Seneca, Lucius Annæus. Morals, by way of abstract. Added, a discourse, under the title of An after-thought, by sir Roger L'Estrange. Phila. 1857. T. 171 : 10

Seume, J: Gottfried. Kurzes pflichten- und sittenbuch für landleute. *In his* Schriften. 830 : 147 v8

Sewall, Frank. The new ethics, or The moral law of use. N. Y. 1881. O. 171 : 14

Sewell, W: Christian morals. Flemington, N. J. 1844. O. *In* The churchman's library. 204 : 16

Simcox, Edith. Natural law ; an essay in ethics. 2d ed. [Eng and foreign phil. library.] Lond. 1878. O. 171 : 15

Smiles, S: Character. N. Y. *n. d.* D. 170 : 30
Contents. Influence of character.—Home power.—Companionship.—Example.—Work.—Courage. — Self-control.—Duty.—Truthfulness.—Temper.—Manner.—Companionship of books.—Companionship in marriage.—Discipline of experience.
— Duty ; with illustrations of courage, patience and endurance. N. Y. 1881. D. 170 : 16
Contents. Duty, conscience. — Duty in action. — Honesty, truth.— Men who cannot be bought.—Courage, endurance.—Endurance to the end; Savonarola.—The sailor.—The soldier.—Heroism in well doing.—Sympathy.—Philanthropy.—Heroism in missions.—Kindness to animals.—Humanity to horses ; E. F. Flower.—Responsibility.—The last.
— Self-help ; with illustrations of character, conduct and perseverance. N. Y. 1877. D. 170 : 15
Contents. Self-help, national and individual. — Leaders of industry ; inventors and producers.—Three great potters : Palissy, Böttgher, Wedgwood.—Application and perseverance.—Helps and opportunities ; scientific pursuits.—Workers in art.—Industry and the peerage.—Energy and courage.—Men of business.—Money, its use and abuse.—Self-culture, facilities and difficulties.—Example, models.—Character, the true gentleman.
— *Same.* N. Y. 1882. Q. 170+15
— Thrift. N. Y. 1876. D. 170 : 17
Contents. Industry.—Habits of thrift.—Improvidence. — Means of saving. — Examples of thrift.—Methods of economy.— Life assurance.— Savings banks.—Little things.—Masters and men.—The Crossleys.—Living above the means.—Great debtors.—Riches and charity.—Healthy homes.—Art of living.

Smith, Adam. The theory of the moral sentiments, or An essay towards an analysis of the principles by which men naturally judge concerning the conduct and character, first of their neighbors and afterwards of themselves. Added, a dissertation on the origin of languages. N. Y. 1822. 2 v. in 1. O. 171 : 11

Sprague, W: Buell. Letters on practical subjects to a daughter. 2d ed. N. Y. 1831. D. 170 : 18

Stephen, Leslie. The science of ethics. N. Y. 1882. O.   171 : 16

Stewart, Dugald. The outlines of moral philosophy. *In his* Collected works. 191+8 v2, 6, 8

— The philosophy of the active and moral powers of man ; with add., ed. by sir W: Hamilton. Edinb. 1877. 2 v. O. 191+8 v6, 7

Symington, Andrew James. Hints to our boys ; with an introd. by Lyman Abbott. N. Y. [1884]. S.   170 : 32

Thompson, Joseph Parrish. Young men admonished, in a series of lectures. N. Y. 1848. D.   170 : 19

Wayland, Francis. The elements of moral science. Bost. 1848. D.   170 : 20

— Elements of moral science, abridged and adapted to schools and academies. Bost. 1836. S.   170 : 28

— The limitations of human responsibility. 2d ed. N. Y. 1838. S.   171 : 13

Whewell, W: The elements of morality, including polity. N. Y. 1847. 2 v. D. 170 : 21

2. Special relations.

The state.

Bentham, Jeremy. An introduction to the principles of morals and legislation. New ed., cor. by the author. Lond. 1823. 2 v. O.   172 : 2

Lieber, Francis. Manual of political ethics, designed chiefly for the use of colleges and students at law. 2d ed. rev., ed. by Theodore D. Woolsey. Phila. 1876. 2 v. O.   172 : 1

Pfleiderer, Edmund. Kosmopolitismus und patriotismus. *In* Deutsche zeit- und streitfragen.   304 : 15 v3

Warner, Susan. American female patriotism ; a prize essay by Elizabeth Wetherell. N. Y. 1852. Tt.   172 : 3

The family.

Abbott, J: Stevens Cabot. The mother at home, or The principles of maternal duty, familiarly illustrated. N. Y. *n. d.* T.   173 : 14

Evans, Robert Wilson. The rectory of Valehead, or The edifice of a holy home. 2d amer. ed. N. Y. 1860. S.   173 : 3

Friswell, James Hain. The better self ; essays for home-life. Phila. *n. d.* D.   173 : 15

Jackson, Helen Maria, *born* Hunt, (*H. H.*) Bits of talk about home matters, by H. H. Bost. 1873. T.   173 : 16

James, J: Angell. The family monitor ; or A help to domestic happiness. Concord, N. H. 1832. T.   173 : 4

Keddie, Henrietta. Sweet counsel ; a book for girls. Lond. 1866. S.   173 : 5

Larned, Augusta. Talks with girls. N. Y. *n. d.* D.   173 : 6

Mothers in council. N. Y. 1884. S.   173 : 17

Osgood, S: The hearth-stone ; thoughts upon home-life in our cities. 6th ed. enl. and ill. N. Y. 1860. D.   173 : 7

Phelps, Almira. *born* Hart. *afterward mrs.* J: Lincoln. Christian households. App. con-

taining the history of "The church home and infirmary of Baltimore." 2d ed. N. Y. 1860. S.   173 : 8

Savage, Minot Judson. Man, woman and child. Bost. 1884. D.   173 : 18

Sherwood, Mary Elizabeth Wilson. (*M. E. W. S.*) Amenities of home. [Appleton's home books.] N. Y. 1881. D.   173 : 2

Sigourney, Lydia Howard, *born* Huntley. Letters to mothers. 2d ed. N. Y. 1839. D. 173 : 9

Stowe, Harriet Elizabeth, *born* Beecher. House and home papers by Christopher Crowfield. Bost. 1865. S.   173 : 10

Tomes, Robert. The bazar book of the household. [*Anon.*] N. Y. 1875. S.   173 : 1

Ware, J: Fothergill Waterhouse. Home life ; what it is and what it needs. Bost. 1867. D.   173 : 11

Yonge, Charlotte Maria. Womankind. Leipz. 1878. 2 v. in 1. S.   173 : 12

Young wife's book, The ; a manual of moral, religious and domestic duties. Phila. 1843. T.   173 : 13

Business.

Adams, W: H: Davenport. The secret of success, or How to get on in the world ; with some remarks upon true and false success and the art of making the best use of life. Amer. ed., ed. by P. G. H. N. Y. 1879. D.   174 : 1

Contents. Time and its uses.—Aims in life.—A steady purpose.—The three p's, punctuality, prudence, perseverance.—Business habits.—Business men and business notes.—The race and the athlete.—Self help.—Reasonable service and true success.

Boardman, H: A: The Bible in the counting-house ; a course of lectures to merchants. Phila. 1853. D.   174 : 2

Crafts, Wilbur F. Successful men of to-day, and what they say of success ; based on facts and opinions gathered by letters and personal interviews from five hundred prominent men, and on many more published sketches. N. Y. [1883]. D.   174 : 5

Hillard, G: Stillman. Dangers and duties of the mercantile profession ; an address delivered before the Mercantile library association, at its 30th anniversary, nov. 13, 1850. Bost. 1850. S.   174 : 3

Mears, J: W. The Bible in the workshop, or Christianity the friend of labor. N. Y. 1857. D.   174 : 4

The sexes.

Cobbe, Frances Power. The duties of women ; a course of lectures. Bost. 1881. D.   176 : 3

Cook, Joseph. Marriage, with preludes on current events. (Bost. Monday lectures.) Bost. 1879. D.   176 : 4

Cook, N. F. Satan in society, by a physician. [*Anon.*] St. Louis. 1877. D.   176 : 8

Dixon, W: Hepworth. Spiritual wives. Leipz. 1868. 2 v. in 1. S.   176 : 5

Madan, Martin. Thelyphthora, or A treatise on female ruin in its causes, effects, consequences, prevention and remedy, considered on the basis of the divine law ; ...with many other incidental matters, particularly including an examination of the

principles and tendency of stat. 26, Geo. II
c. 33, commonly called the marriage act.
Lond. 1780, 1781. 3 v. O.   **176 : P7**
Michelet, Jules. Love (L'amour). From the
french, tr. from the 4th Paris ed. by J. W.
Palmer. N. Y. 1867. D.   **176 : 2**
— Woman (La femme). From the french, tr. by
J. W. Palmer. N. Y. 1860. D.   **176 : 1**
— *Same, ger.* Die Frau. Uebers. von F: Spiel-
hagen. Leipz. 1860. S.   **176 : 1**
Saunders, F: About woman, love and marriage.
N. Y. 1874. D.   **176 : 6**

Society.

Chapin, Edwin Hubbell. Humanity in the city.
N. Y. [1854]. D.   **177 : 11**
Ellis, Sarah Stickney. Prevention better than
cure, or The moral wants of the world we
live in. N. Y. 1847. D.   **177 : 2**
Goltz, Bogumil. Eine umgangs - philosophie.
[Feigenblätter, 3.] Berlin. *n. d.* D. **177 : 1**
Hale, E: Everett. How to do it. Bost. 1881. S.
.   **x 177 : 12**
Holland, Josiah Gilbert, (*Timothy Titcomb*). Let-
ters to the Joneses, by Timothy Titcomb.
8th ed. N. Y. 1863. D.   **177 : 3**
Lecky, W: E: Hartpole. History of european
morals from Augustus to Charlemagne. 3d
ed. rev. N. Y. 1877. 2 v. D.   **177 : 4**
Kleinwächter, F: Zur philosophie der mode.
In Deutsche zeit- und streit-fragen.
        304 : 15 v9
Maurice, J: F: Dennison. Social morality ; 21
lectures delivered in the university of
Cambridge. 2d ed. Lond. 1872. D. **177 : 5**
Noah, Mordecai Manuel. Gleanings from a
gathered harvest. N. Y. 1847. S. **177 : 6**
Opie, Amelia. Illustrations of lying, in all its
branches. Hartford. 1827. D.   **177 : 7**
Peabody, Andrew Preston. Conversation ; its
faults and its graces. New ed. Bost. 1882.
        177 : 13
Richards, Cornelia Haven Bradley. Springs of
action. N. Y. 1863. D.   **177 : 8**
Stanhope, Philip Dormer, *4th earl of Chesterfield.*
The elements of a polite education ; carefully selected from [his] letters to his son,
by G: Gregory. New ed. Lond. [1800(?)]
D.   **177 : 9**
Talmage, T: De Witt. The abominations of
modern society. N. Y. 1872. D.   **177 : 10**
Uhlhorn, Gerhard. Christian charity in the
ancient church. From 'the german, with
the author's sanction. N. Y. 1883. O.
        177 : 14

x denotes books specially adapted for children.

Temperance.

Cook, Joseph. The new house and its battle-
ment, or The .relations of the temperance
reform to civil liberty. *In his* Occident.
        824.1 : 112
Goltz, Bogumil. Das kneipen und die kneip-
genies. Berlin. *n. d.* T.   **178 : 1**
Gustafson, Axel. The foundation of death ; a
study of the drink question. Bost. 1884.
D.   **178 : 7**
Lammers, A: Bekämpfung der trunksucht. *In*
Deutsche zeit- und streit-fragen.
        304 : 15 v10
— Umwandlung der schenken ; erläuterung der
vorschläge der schenken-commission des
Deutschen vereins gegen den missbrauch
geistiger getränke. *In* Deutsche zeit- und
streit-fragen.   **304 : 15 v13**
Livermore, Abiel Abbot. Anti-tobacco ; *also*
A lecture on tobacco, by Russell Lant **Car-**
penter ; *also* On the use of tobacco, by G.
F. **Witter.** Bost. 1883. S.   **178 : 6**
Macnish, Robert. The anatomy of drunkenness.
From the 5th Glasgow ed. N. Y. 1835. D.
        178 : 3
Parton, James. Smoking and drinking. [New
ed.] Bost. 1882. S.   **178 : 2**
Reade. A. Arthur, *ed.* Study and stimulants, or
The use of intoxicants and narcotics in re-
lation to intellectual life as illustrated by
personal communications on the subject
from men of letters and of science. Rev.,
with add. Manchester. 1883. D.   **178 : 5**
Select temperance tracts. N. Y. *n. d.* D.
        178 : 4

Miscellaneous.

Dexter, H: Martyn. Street thoughts. Ill.
Bost. 1859. S.   **179 : 1**
Nicholson, E: Byron. The rights of an animal ;
a new essay in ethics. With a reprint of
part of J: **Lawrence's** chapters "On the
rights of beasts," "On the' philosophy of
sports," and "On the animal question."
Lond. 1879. D.   **179 : 2**
Schasler, Max. Ueber moderne denkmalswuth.
In Deutsche zeit- und streit-fragen.
        304 : 15 v7
Spurgeon, C: Haddon. John Ploughman's pic-
tures, or More of his plain talk for plain
people. Phila. 1881. D.   **179 : 3**
Systematic beneficence ; three prize essays.
The great reform, by Abel **Stevens** ; The
great question, by Lorenzo **White** ; Prop-
erty consecrated, by B: St. James **Fry.**
N. Y. 1856. S.   **179 : 4**

Note. For Ethics in general, see also Business manuals, class 658.

Ancient and Modern philosophies.
Classes 180-199.

See Philosophy in general, col. 46.

III. THEOLOGY.

1. In general.

1. Philosophy and education.

Hartmann, K: E: Robert v. Die religion des geistes. Berlin. 1882. O. **201 : 2**

Müller, F: Max. Lectures on the science of religion, with a paper on buddhist nihilism, and a translation of the Dhammapada or "Path of virtue." N. Y. 1872. D. **201 : 1**

Graue, G. Der mangel an theologen und der wissenschaftliche werth des theologischen studiums. *In* Deutsche zeit- und streitfragen. **304 : 15 v5**

2. Cyclopedias and dictionaries.

McClintock, J:, and James **Strong**. Cyclopædia of biblical, theological and ecclesiastical literature. N. Y. 1879–84. 11 v. O. **203 : R1**
Contents. V. 1. A. B. 2. C. D. 3. E-G. 4. H-J. 5. K-Me. 6. Me-Neo. 7. New-Pes. 8. Pet-Re. 9. Rh-St. 10. Su-Z. 11. Supp., A-Cn.

Buck, C: A theological dictionary, containing definitions of all religious terms, a comprehensive view of every article in the system of divinity, an impartial account of all the principal denominations, which have subsisted in the religious world from the birth of Christ to the present day, together with an accurate statement of the most remarkable transactions and events recorded in ecclesiastical history. Scott's 2d amer. from the latest London ed., with extensive add. and improvements. Phila. 1823. O. **203 : R2**

Brewer, Ebenezer Cobham. A dictionary of miracles; imitative, realistic and dogmatic. Ill. Phila. 1884. D. **203 : R3**

Holtzmann, H: Julius, and R. **Zöpffel**. Lexikon für theologie und kirchenwesen; lehre, bräuche, feste, sekten und orden der christlichen kirche, das wichtigste aus den übrigen religionsgemeinschaften. Leipz. 1882. D. **203 : R4**

3. History of theology.

(For ecclesiastical history, see class 270–279.)

Child, Lydia Maria. The progress of religious ideas, through successive ages. N. Y. 1855. 3 v. O. **209 : 1**

Dorner, I: A: History of protestant theology, particularly in Germany, viewed according to its fundamental movements and in connection with the religious, moral and intellectual life. Tr. by G: Robson and Sophia Taylor. Edinb. 1871. O. **209 : 3**

Tiele, C. P. Outlines of the history of religion to the spread of the universal religions. Tr. from the dutch by J. Estlin Carpenter. 2d ed. [Eng. and foreign phil. library.] Lond. 1880. O. **209 : 2**

4. Collected works.

Arminius (*dutch* **Hermanz**). Jacobus. Works tr. from the latin, in 3 v.; 1st and 2d by James Nichols, 3d, with a sketch of the life of the author, by W. R. Bagnall. Auburn. 1853. 3 v. O. **200 : 1**
Contents, see Catalogue of the Boston athenæum, v. 1, p. 139.

Barrow, I: Works, being all his english works. 5th ed. Lond. 1741. 3 v. in 2. F. **23 : R**
Contents. V. 1. Sermons.—Exposition of the Lord's prayer, the creed, etc.—Treatise of the pope's supremacy. 2. Sermons and expositions upon all the articles in the apostles' creed. 3. Sermons.

Bunyan, J: Works; being several discourses upon various divine subjects. 6th ed. containing several pieces not to be found in any former ed. Edinb. 1771. 1 v. in 2. F. **23 : R**

Calvin, J: The institution of christian religion, written in latine, tr. into english according to the author's last ed., with sundry tables to finde the principall matters intreated of in the booke, and also the declaration of places of scripture therein expounded, by T: Norton. Whereunto there are newly add., in the margin of the booke, notes containing in brief the substance of the matter handled in ech section. Lond. 1611. Q. **23 : R**

Channing, W: Ellery. [Religious writings.] *In* his Works. **820.1 : 2**
Contents, see under English literature, Collected works.

Chillingworth, W: Works, containing his book entitl'd The religion of protestants, a safe way to salvation; together with his nine sermons preached before the king or upon eminent occasions, his letter to mr. Lewgar concerning the church of Rome's being the guide of faith and judge of controversies, his nine additional discourses and an answer to some passages in Rushworth's dialogues, concerning traditions. 7th ed. compared with all the editions now extant and made more correct than any of the former. In this ed. are two letters never before printed. Lond. 1719. F. **23 : R**

Cranmer, T: Miscellaneous writings and letters ; ed. for the Parker society by J: Edmund Cox. Cambridge. 1846. Q. **200+2**
Contents, see Catalogue of the Boston athenæum, v. 1, p. 696.

Dick, T: Works. 4 v. in 1. Hartford. 1847. D.
200 : 3
Contents. V. 1. On the improvement of society by the diffusion of knowledge. 2. The philosophy of a future state. 3. The philosophy of religion. 4. The christian philosopher.

Doane, G: Washington. Life and . writings ; containing his poetical works, sermons and miscellaneous writings ; with a memoir by his son, W: Croswell Doane. N. Y. 1860-61. 4 v. O. **200+4**
Contents. V. 1. Memoir, by W: Croswell Doane.—Songs by the way. 2. Episcopal writings, comprising his charges, conventional, missionary and visitation sermons. 3. Parochial sermons [at St. Mary's parish, Burlington.] 4. Educational writings and orations.

Fuller, Andrew. The principal works and remains ; with a new memoir of his life by his son, A. G. Fuller. Lond. 1852. D.
200 : 5
Contents. Memoir.—The gospel its own witness.—The calvinistic and socinian systems examined and compared as to their moral tendency.—Three letters.

Henry, Matthew. Complete works, his unfinished commentary excepted ; a collection of all his treatises, sermons and tracts as published by himself and a memoir of his life; in 2 v. V. 2. Edinb. 1853. O.
200 : 18

Hooker, R: Works, with an account of his life and death by I: Walton ; arr. by J: Keble. 3d amer. from last Oxford ed. ; with a general index, to which is appended a complete index of the texts of scripture, prepared expressly for this ed. N. Y. 1860. 2 v. O. **200+6**
Contents. V. 1. Ed's pref.—Walton's dedication to bishop Morley.—Pref. to the 1st ed. of the life of Hooker.—Life.—App.—Spencer's pref. to the reader.—Pref. to the books of the laws of ecclesiastical polity.—Of the laws of ecclesiastical polity, books 1-4.—Hooker's dedication to archbp. Whitgift.—Of the laws of ecclesiastical polity, book 5. 2. App. to book 5.—Of the laws of ecclesiastical polity, books 6-8.—Sermons.—Travers' supplication to the council.—Hooker's answer.—Sermons.—Jackson's dedication.—Sermons.—Index.

Hughes, J: Complete works, comprising his sermons, letters, lectures, speeches, etc. ; carefully compiled and ed. from the best sources by Lawrence Kehoe. N. Y. 1864. 2 v. O. **200 : 7**
Contents. V. 1. Pt. 1. Biog. sketch.—Obsequies, etc.—On catholic emancipation.—The school question. Pt. 2. Life and times of Pius VII.—Letters.—The school question, *continued.*—Influence of christianity upon civilization.— Pt. 3. The school question, *continued.* Pt. 4. Influence of christianity on social servitude.—N. Y. catholic church debt assoc.—Introd. to mr. Livingstone's book on "Imputation."—The mixture of civil and ecclesiastical power in the middle ages.—Moral causes which have produced the evil spirit of the times.—Alleged burning of Bibles.—Sermon on the jubilee.—Latest invention. Pt. 5. Importance of a christian basis for the science of political economy.—Eulogy on bp. Fenwick.—Causes of the irish famine of 1847. - Christianity the only source of moral, social and political regeneration.—"Kirwan."—Letters on the catholic church.—"Kirwan" unmasked. 2. Life and times, by J. R. Bailey.—The temporal power of the pope.—Lectures : The church and the world since the election of Pius IX : The decline of protestantism and its causes ; Present condition and prospects of the catholic church in the U. S. ; Life and times of O'Connell ; Relation between the civil and religious duty of the catholic citizen ; St. Patrick.—Sermons.—Letters.—The church property controversy.—Miscellaneous.—App.

Jackson, G: A. Apostolic fathers and apologists of the 2d century. (Early christian lit. primers, no. 1.) N. Y. 1879. S. **200 : 19**
Contents. Introd.—The earlier patristic writings.—**The apostolic fathers**: Clement of Rome, sketch, Epistle to the Corinthians, Clementine literature ; Ignatius, sketch and Epistle to Romans, Ephesians and Polycarp: Polycarp, sketch and Epistle to Philippians ; Barnabas, sketch and epistle.—**Associated authors**: Hermas, sketch and the Shepherd ; Papias, sketch and fragments. — **The apologists**: Introd. sketch ; Notice and Epistle to Diognetus ; Justin, sketch, First apology and Synopsis of dialogue with Trypho: Author of Muratonian fragment and the Fragment: Melito, sketch and Fragment ; Athenagoras, sketch, chapters from Mission about christians, and Final argument on the resurrection.

— The fathers of the 3d century. (Early christian lit. primers, no. 2.) N. Y. 1881. S.
200 : 20
— The post-nicene greek fathers. (Early christian lit. primers, no. 3.) N. Y. 1883. S.
200 : 21
— The post-nicene latin fathers. (Early christian lit. primers, no. 4.) N. Y. 1884. S.
200 : 22

Justinus *martyr.* The works, now extant, of S. Justin the martyr, tr. with notes and indices. [Library of the fathers, no. 40.] Oxford. 1861. O. **200 : 8**

Laud, W: A relation of the conference between W: Laud and Fisher the jesuite, by the command of king James, with an answer to such exceptions as A. C. takes against it. Lond. 1639. O. **23 : R**

Leighton, Robert. Works; prefixed, a life of the anchor. Lond. 1860. O. **200+9**
Contents. Life, by James Aikman.—A practical commentary on the first epistle of Peter.—Expository lectures on Psalm xxxix, Isaiah vi, Romans vii.—Charges, *etc.*, to the clergy of the diocese of Dunblane. — Letters. — Eighteen sermons.—Ten sermons, from the author's manuscripts.—Theological lectures —Exhortations to the students upon their return to the university after vacation.—Exhortations to candidates for the degree of M. A. in the university of Edinburgh.—Valedictory oration.—A defence of moderate episcopacy.—Meditations, critical and practical, on Psalms iv, xxii, and cxxx.—Sermon to the clergy, from 2 Cor. v: 20.—Letters.

Leslie, C: Theological works. Lond. 1721. 2 v. F. **23 : R**
Contents, see Catalogue of the Boston athenæum, v. 3, p. 1714.

Milton, J: Prose works. Phila. 1859. 2 v. O.
200+10
Contents. V. 1. Of reformation touching church discipline in England.—Of prelatical episcopacy.—The reason of church government urged against prelaty.—Animadversions upon the remonstrant's defence against Smectymnuus.—An apology for Smectymnuus.—Of education.—Areopagitica.—Doctrine and discipline of divorce.—Judgment of Martin Bucer concerning divorce.—Tetrachordon.—Colasterion.—The tenure of kings and magistrates.—Observations on Ormond's peace.—Eikonoclastes. 2. Defence of the people of England.—Treatise of civil power in ecclesiastical causes.—Letter to a friend concerning the ruptures of the commonwealth.—Present means and brief delineation of a free commonwealth.—The ready and easy way to establish a free commonwealth.—Brief notes upon a sermon, titled "The fear of God and the king," by M. Griffith.—History of Britain. — Of true religion, heresy, schism, toleration.—History of Moscovia.—Declaration for the election of John III, king of Poland.—Letters of state.—Manifesto of the lord protector against the spaniards.—Second defence of the people of England.—Familiar epistles.

Nevins, W: Select remains, with a memoir. N. Y. 1836. D. **200 : 11**

Porteus, Beilby, *bp. of London.* Works; with his life by Robert Hodgson. New ed. Lond. 1811. 6 v. O.   **200 : 12**
Contents. V. 1. Life, by R. **Hodgson.** 2, 3. Sermons. **4, 5.** Lectures. **6.** Tracts.

Scott, T: Theological works, pub. at different times and now coll. into vols. Buckingham. 1805-8. 5 v. O.   **200 : 13**
Contents. V. 1. The force of truth.—Fifteen Sermons. 2. Sermons. 3. Funeral sermons.—Missionary sermons—Rights of God.—Answer to T. Paine.—Civil government, and the duties of subjects. 4. Repentance.—Warrant and nature of faith in Christ.—Growth in grace. — Hints for the consideration of patients in hospitals.—Detached papers.—Family prayers. 5. Essays on the most important subjects in religion.

Taylor, Jeremy. Whole works; with an essay, biographical and critical. Lond. 1853. 3 v. O.   **200+14**
Contents. V. 1. **Rogers,** H: Essay on [his] genius and writings.—Funeral sermon, by G. Rust.—Christian consolations.—The life of Christ.—Contemplations of the state of man.—The rule and exercises of holy living.—The rule and exercises of holy dying.—Sermons. 2. Sermon.—On the sacred order and offices of episcopacy.—An apology for authorized and set forms of liturgy.—Theologia eklektiké, or A discourse on the liberty of prophesying.—The doctrine and practice of repentance.—Deus justificatus.—On the real presence of Christ in the holy sacrament.—Dissuasive from popery.—Letters. 3. Chrisis teleiótiké, a discourse of confirmation—A discourse on the nature, offices and measures of friendship.—Ductor dubitantium, or The rule of conscience.—Clerus Domini.—Rules and advices to the clergy of the diocese of Down and Connor.—The golden grove.—The psalter of David.—A collection of offices.—The worthy communicant.

Tertullianus, Quintus Septimius Florens. Apologetic and practical treatises. Tr. by C. Dodgson. 2d ed. [Library of the fathers, no. 10.] Oxford. 1854. O.   **200 : 17**

Tillotson, J: Works; containing 254 sermons and discourses on several occasions, together with the rule of faith. prayers composed for his own use, a discourse to his servants before the sacrament, and a form of prayer composed by him for the use of king William. Lond. 1757. 12 v. D.   **200 : 15**

Tyndale, W: An answer to sir Thomas More's dialogue, The supper of the Lord after the true meaning of John vi and 1 Cor. xi, and W: Tracy's testament expounded; ed. for the Parker society by H: Walter. Cambridge. 1850. O.   **200 : 16**

Wycliffe, J: Writings. Lond. *n. d.* D. **204 : 43**
Contents. Account of his life.—Specimens of his trans. of the bible.—His confession concerning the sacrament of the Lord's supper.—The poor caitif.—How the office of curates is ordained of God.—Of feigned contemplative life.—On prayer.—A short rule of life.—Wicklift's wicket.—Note on the doctrine of transubstantiation.—Twelve lettings of prayer.—Antichrist's labour to destroy holy writ.—Trialogues.—Opinions of the papacy.—Sermons.

5. Essays and miscellanies.

Burlingame, E: Livermore, *ed.* Current discussion; a collection from the chief english essays on questions of the time, v. 2 : Questions of belief. N. Y. 1878. D. **204 : 12**
Contents. **Harrison,** F: The soul and future life.—A modern symposium. 1. The soul and future life, by R. H. Hutton, T: H: Huxley, lord Blachford, Roden Noel, lord Selborne, W. R. Greg, Baldwin Brown, W. G. Ward.—A modern symposium. 2. The influence upon morality of a decline in religious belief, by sir James Stephen, lord Selborne, James

Martineau, F: Harrison, dean of St. Paul's, duke of Argyll, prof. Clifford, W. G. Ward, T: H: Huxley, R: H. Hutton.—**Lewes,** G: H: The course of modern thought.—**Hughes,** T: The condition and prospects of the church of England.—**Mallock,** W: H. Is life worth living?

Christ and modern thought; with a preliminary lecture on the methods of meeting modern unbelief by Joseph **Cook.** (Boston Monday lectures, 1880–81). Bost. 1881. D. **204 : 15**
Contents. Preliminary lecture.—**Clark,** T: M. The seen and the unseen.—**Robinson,** E. G. Moral law in its relation to physical science and to popular religion.—**Guard,** T: Christianity and the mental activity of the age.—**Hopkins,** M: The place of conscience.— **McCosh,** J. Development; what it can do and what it cannot do.—**Crosby,** H. A calm view of the temperance question.—**Crooks,** G: R. Old and new theologies.—**Dike,** S: W. Facts as to divorce in New England.—**Thomas,** J. B. Significance of the historic element in scripture.—**Smith,** J: C. The theistic basis of evolution.

Churchman's library, The; a series of publications, original and from the english press, issued in monthly numbers. Flemington. N. J. 1844. O.   **204 : 16**
Contents. **Massingberd,** F. C. A history of the english reformation.—**Gresley,** W. Church Clavering, or The schoolmaster.—**Sewell,** W. Christian morals.—**Teale,** W. H. The life of Lucius Cary, viscount Falkland.

Coan, Titus Munson, *ed.* Questions of belief. (Topics of the time, no. 5). N. Y. 1883. D.   **204 : 50**
Contents. **Lee,** V. The responsibilities of unbelief.—**Cobbe,** F. P. Agnostic morality.—**Gurney,** E. Natural religion.—**Stephen,** L. The suppression of poisonous opinions.—**Schuckburgh,** E. S. Modern miracles.

Conflicts of the age, The. N. Y. 1881. O.   **204+45**
Contents. An advertisement for a new religion, by an evolutionist.—The confession of an agnostic, by an agnostic.—What morality have we left? by a new-light moralist.—Review of the fight, by a Yankee farmer.

Essays and reviews. Leipz. 1862. S. **204 : 19**
Contents. **Temple,** F: The education of the world.—**Williams,** R. Bunsen's biblical researches.—**Powell,** B. On the study of evidences of christianity.—**Wilson,** H: B. Séances historiques de Génève: The national church.—**Goodwin,** C. W. On the mosaic cosmogony.—**Pattison,** M: Tendencies of religious thought in England, 1688–1750.—**Jowett,** B: On the interpretation of scripture.—Note on Bunsen's biblical researches.

Hedge, F: H:, *ed.* Recent inquiries in theology, by eminent english churchmen; being "Essays and reviews". 2d amer. from 2d London ed., with an app. [*and*] introd. Bost. 1861. D.   **204 : 20**
Contents, see **Essays** and reviews.

Goulburn, E: Meyrick, *and others.* Replies to "Essays and reviews"; with a pref. by the lord bishop of Oxford, and letters from the Radcliffe observer and the reader in geology in the university of Oxford. N. Y. 1862. D.   **204 : 47**
Contents. **Goulburn,** E. M. The education of the world.—**Rose,** H. J. Bunsen's criticism and dr. Williams.—**Heurtley,** C. A. Miracles.—**Irons,** W. J. The idea of the national church.—**Rorison,** G. The creative week.—**Haddan,** A. W. Rationalism.—**Wordsworth,** C. On the interpretation of scripture.—Letters from R. Main and J: Phillips.

Thomson, W:, *ed.* Aids to faith; a series of theological essays, by several writers, a reply to "Essays and reviews". N. Y. 1862. D.   **204 : 3**
Contents. **Mansel,** H: L. On miracles as evidences of christianity.—**Fitzgerald,** W: On the study of the evidences of christianity.—**McCaul,** A. Prophecy.—**Cook,** F: C: Ideology and subscription.

—**McCaul**, A. The mosaic record of creation.—**Rawlinson**, G: On the genuineness and authenticity of the Pentateuch.—**Browne**, E: H. Inspiration.—**Thomson**, W: The death of Christ.—**Ellicott**, C: J: Scripture and its interpretation.

Freedom and fellowship in religion; a collection of essays and addresses, ed. by a committee of the Free religious association. Bost. 1875. S.   204 : 22
Contents. **Frothingham**, O. B. Introductory; The religious outlook.—**Wasson**, D: A. The nature of religion.—**Longfellow**, S: The unity and universality of the religious ideas. — **Johnson**, S: Freedom in religion.—**Weiss**, J: Religion and science.—**Potter**, W: J. Christianity and its definitions.—**Abbot**, F. E. The genius of christianity and free religion.—**Frothingham**, O. B. The soul of protestantism.—**Chadwick**, J: W. Liberty and the church in America.—**Higginson**, T: W. The word philanthropy.—**Cheney**, E. D. Religion as a social force.—Voices from the free platform.

Lectures to young men; delivered before the Young men's christian assoc. in Exeter hall, London, from nov. 21, 1848, to feb. 6, 1849. Lond. [1849]. S.   204 : 27
Contents. **MacNeile**, Hugh. The characteristics of romanism and protestantism.—**Cumming**, J. God in history.—**Bickersteth**, Robert. The bearing of commerce upon the spread of christianity.—**Brock**, W: The common origin of the human race.—**Stowell**, Hugh. Modern infidel philosophy. — **James**, J: **Angell**. Spiritual religion the surest preservative from infidelity.—**Archer**, T: The characteristics of the middle ages.—**Arthur**, W: The french revolution of 1848.—**Noel**, Baptist W. The church and the world.—**Raffles**, T: Internal evidence of the divine inspiration of the scriptures.—**Martin**, S: Cardinal Wolsey.—**Binney**, T: Sir T: Fowell Buxton.

Manning, H: E:, *ed.* Essays on religion and literature, by various writers. Lond. 1865. O.   204 : 29
Contents. Inaugural discourse of cardinal Wiseman.—**Manning**, H: E: On the subjects proper to the Academia.—**Rock**, D. The action of the church upon art and civilisation.—**Hoey**, J. C. On the birthplace of St. Patrick.—**Oakeley**, F: The position of a catholic minority in a non-catholic country.—**Laing**, F. H: On bishop Colenso's objections to the veracity of holy scripture.—**Wiseman**, N. P. S. The truth of supposed legends and fables.—**Lucas**, E: Christianity in relation to civil society.

Selections from the writings of the reformers and fathers of the church of England. New ed.; no. 1-5. Lond. 1836-39. S.   204 : 35
Contents. 1. Extracts from Tyndal's prologues to the five books of Moses. 2. Cranmer's preface to the Bible; The sum and content of holy scripture; The first homily, or A fruitful exhortation to the reading and knowledge of holy scripture. 3. On the creed by archbp. Cranmer. 4. A discourse on the Lord's prayer. 5. On prayer.

Tracts for priests and people by various writers. Bost. 1862. D.   204 : 39
Contents. **Hughes**, T: Religio laici.—**Maurice**, J: F: D. The mote and the beam.—**Garden**, F. The atonement as a fact and as a theory.—**Davis**, J. L. The signs of the kingdom of heaven.—On terms of communion: **P.**, C. K. The boundaries of the church; **Langley**, J. N. The message of the church.—**Ludlow**, J. M. A dialogue on doubt.—**Maurice**, J: F: D. Morality and divinity.—**Ludlow**, J. M. Two lay dialogues: On laws of nature and the faith therein; On positive philosophy.

Tracts for the times, by members of the university of Oxford. N. Y. 1839, 1840. 2 v. O.   204 : 40
Contents, see Catalogue of the Boston athenæum, v. 5, p. 2999.

Goode, W: The divine rule of faith and practice, or A defence of the catholic doctrine that holy scripture has been since the times of the apostles the sole divine rule of faith and practice to the church, against the dangerous errors of the authors of the Tracts for the times and the romanists, as particularly that the rule of faith is "made up of scripture and tradition together", etc.; in which also the doctrines of the apostolical succession, the eucharistic sacrifice, etc., are fully discussed. Phila. 1842. O.   238+1

* * *

Adler, Felix. Creed and deed; a series of discourses. N. Y. 1877. D.   204 : 1
Contents. Immortality.—Religion.—The new ideal. —The priest of the ideal.—The form of the new ideal. —The religious conservatism of women.—Our consolations.—Spinoza.—The founder of christianity.— The anniversary discourse.—Appendix; The evolution of hebrew religion; Reformed judaism I. II. III.

Aguilar, Grace. Essays and miscellanies; choice cullings from [her] mss., sel. by her mother Sarah Aguilar. Phila. 1853. D.   204 : 2

Arnold, Matthew. St. Paul and protestantism; with an essay on puritanism and the church of England. N. Y. 1883. D.
                    204 : 51
— Last essays on church and religion. *With his* St. Paul and protestantism.   204 : 51
Contents. A psychological parallel.—Bishop Butler and the church of England.—A last word on the burials bill.

Bale, J: Select works; containing the examinations of lord Cobham, W: Thorpe and Anne Askewe, and the Image of both churches; ed. for the Parker society by H: Christmas. Cambridge. 1849. O. 204 : 4

Barnes, Albert. Miscellaneous essays and reviews. N. Y. 1855. 2 v. D.   204 : 5
Contents. V. 1. The analogy of religion, by Joseph Butler.—The christian ministry, by C: Bridges.—The works of lord Bacon.—How can the sinner be made to feel his guilt.—Episcopacy tested by scripture, by H: U. Onderdonk.—Scriptural argument on the episcopal controversy.—The position of the evangelical party in the episcopal church. 2. The ancient commerce of western Asia.—The relation of theology to preaching.—The position of the christian scholar. —The progress and tendency of science.—The desire of reputation.—The choice of a profession.—Practical preaching.—The literature and science of our country.—The law of paradise.—Thoughts on theology.

Beecher, H: Ward. 595 pulpit pungencies, with a table of contents. [*Anon.*] N. Y. 1866. D.   204 : 6
— Life thoughts, gathered from [his] extemporaneous discourses, by one of his congregation. 30th thous. Bost. 1858. D.   204 : 7
— New star papers, or Views and experiences of religious subjects. N. Y. 1859. D.   204 : 8
— Royal truths. Bost. 1866. D.   204 : 9

Browne, *Sir* T: Religio medici, Hydriotaphia and the Letter to a friend; with introd. and notes by J. W. Willis Bund. [Bayard ser.] Lond. 1877. T.   204 : 10
— Religio medici. A facsimile of the 1st ed. pub. in 1642; with an introd. by W. A. Greenhill. Lond. 1883. D.   204 : R10

Brownson, Orestes A: Essays and reviews; chiefly on theology, politics and socialism. N. Y. 1858. D.   204 : 11
Contents. Pref.—The church against no-church.— The episcopal observer versus the church.—Thornwell's answer to dr. Lynch, april and oct. 1848.— Protestantism ends in transcendentalism. — Protestantism in a nutshell.—Authority and liberty.— Political constitutions.—War and loyalty. — The higher law.—Catholicity necessary to sustain popular liberty.—Legitimacy and revolutionism.—Native americanism.—Labor and association.—Socialism and the church.

Brute, Walter, *and others*. Writings and examinations of Brute, Thorpe, Cobham, Hilton and others, with The lantern of light, written about A. D. 1400. Lond. *n. d.* D. *With* **Wycliffe**, J: Writings. **204 : 43**

Bushnell, Horace. Building eras in religion. *In his* Literary varieties. **824.1 : 16 v3**
Contents, see under English literature, Essays.

Chalmers, T: Miscellanies; embracing reviews, essays and addresses. N. Y. 1859. O. **204+14**
Contents. Memoir.—Sermon, by J: Bruce.—Example of our Saviour in the establishment of charitable institutions.—Necessity of uniting prayer with performance for the success of missions.—Influence of parochial institutions.—Consistency of legal and voluntary principles.—System of parochial schools in Scotland.—Technical nomenclature of theology.—Efficacy of moravian missions.—Style and subjects of the pulpit.—Difference between spoken and written language.—Remarks on Cuvier's Theory of the earth.—On a proposed modification of the law of patronage.—On the abolition of colonial slavery.—Introductory essays: to The imitation of Christ; to Treatises on the life, walk and triumph of faith; to The christian remembrancer; to The christian's great interest; to The grace and duty of being spiritually minded; to The call to the unconverted; to The christian's daily walk in holy security in peace; to Tracts by T: Scott; to Private thoughts on religion and a christian life; to The reign of grace; to Serious reflections on time and eternity; to The christian's defence against infidelity; to The living temple; to Select letters of W: Romaine; to A treatise on the faith and influence of the gospel.—Distinction, both in principle and effect, between a legal charity for the relief of indigence and for the relief of disease.—An historical and critical view of the speculative philosophy of Europe in the 19th century by J. D. Morell.—Political economy of a famine.

Clarke, James Freeman. Events and epochs in religious history; being the substance of a course of 12 lectures, del. in the Lowell institute, Bost. 1880. Bost. 1881. O. **204 : 44**
Contents. The catacombs.—The buddhist monks of central Asia.—Christian monks and monastic life.—Augustine, Anselm, Bernard, and their times.—Jeanne D'Arc.—Savonarola and the renaissance.—Luther and the reformation.—Loyola and the jesuits.—The mystics in all religions.—George Fox and the quakers.—The huguenots.—J: Wesley and his times.—Index.

Cobbe, Frances Power. [Essays on religion.] *With her* Darwinism in morals. **824.2 : 107**
Contents, see under English literature, Essays.

Cox, S: Hanson. Interviews, memorable and useful, from diary and memory reproduced. N. Y. 1853. D. **204 : 17**
Contents. With rev. dr. Chalmers.—With rev. dr. Emmons.— With two pseudo-apostles. — With a fashionable lady at Calais, France. Preceded by reflections miscellaneous.

De Quincey, T: Theological essays and other papers. New and rev. ed. Bost. 1860. 2 v. D. **204 : 18**
Contents. V. 1. Christianity as an organ of political movement.—Protestantism.—On the supposed scriptural expression for eternity.—On Hume's argument against miracles. — Casuistry. — Greece under the romans. 2. Secession from the church of Scotland.—Toilette of the hebrew lady.— Milton.— Judas Iscariot. — Charlemagne. — Modern Greece. — Lord Carlisle on Pope.

Dodge, Mary Abigail, (*Gail Hamilton*). Stumbling blocks. Bost. 1864. D. **204 : 48**
Contents. The outs and the ins.—The fitness of things.—Ordinances.—Church-sittings.—A view from the pews.—Prayer-meetings.—The proof of your love.—Controversies.—Amusements.— God's way.— The law of Christ.—Praying.—Forgiveness.—Error.—Words without knowledge.

Fisher, George Park. Discussions in history and theology. N. Y. 1880. O. **204 : 21**
Contents. The massacre of St. Bartholomew.—The influence of the old roman spirit and religion on latin christianity.—The temporal kingdom of the popes.—The council of Constance and the council of the Vatican.—The office of the pope and how he is chosen.—The relation of protestantism and of romanism to modern civilization. — The relation of the church of England to the other protestant bodies.—The philosophy of Jonathan Edwards.—Channing as a philosopher and theologian.—The system of dr. N. W. Taylor in its connection with prior New England theology.—The augustinian and the federal doctrines of original sin. — A sketch of the history of the doctrine of future punishment.—Rationalism.—The unreasonableness of atheism.—The apostle Paul.—The four gospels; a review of "Supernatural religion."

Froude, James Anthony. [Essays on theological subjects.] *In his* Short studies. **824.2 : 42**
Contents, see under English literature, Essays.

Gladstone, W: Ewart. Ecclesiastical essays. *In his* Gleanings of past years. **329.2 : 9 v5-7**

Hall, Robert. Miscellaneous works and remains; with a memoir of his life by Olinthus Gregory, and a critical estimate of his character and writings by J: Foster. Lond. 1853. D. **204 : 23**
Contents. Memoir. — Observations on mr. Hall's character as a preacher. — Christianity consistent with a love of freedom.—An apology for the freedom of the press.—Review of the apology for the freedom of the press.—Modern infidelity considered.—Reflections on war.—The sentiments proper to the present crisis.—The advantages of knowledge to the lower classes.—A sermon on the death of the princess Charlotte of Wales. — Reviews: Foster's essays; Custance on the constitution; Zeal without innovation; Gisborne's sermons; Gregory's letters; Belsham's memoirs of Lindsey.—General index.

Hill, Rowland. Thoughts on religious subjects. Lond. 1835. S. **204 : 24**

Hopkins, M: Strength and beauty; discussions for young men. N. Y. [1874]. D. **204 : 25**
Contents. Strength and beauty.—Receiving and giving.—The manifoldness of man.—Nothing to be lost.—God's method of social unity.—Enlargement.—The Bible and pantheism.—On liberality in religious belief.—Zeal.—Spirit, soul and body. —Choice and service.—Life.—The body the temple of God.—Perfect love.—Faith, philosophy and reason.—Self-denial.—The circular and the onward movement.—Higher and lower good.—The one exception.

Jackson, W: Remains; with a brief sketch of his life and character by W: M. Jackson. N. Y. 1846. O. **204+26**

King, T: Starr. [Religious essays.] *With his* Patriotism. **824.1 : 50**
Contents, see under English literature, Essays.

Luther, Martin. Table-talk; tr. and ed. by W: Hazlitt. New ed., to which is added the life of Martin Luther by Alexander Chalmers, with add. from Michelet and Audin. Lond. 1857. D. **204 : 28**

Middleton, Conyers. Posthumous works. Lond. 1753. Q. *With* **Brown**, J: Dissertation on poetry and music. *in* **23 : R**

Mill, J: Stuart. Three essays on religion. N. Y. 1874. O. **204 : 30**
Contents. Nature.—Utility of religion.—Theism.

Norton, James. [Essays on religious subjects.] *In his* Australian essays. **824.2 : 76**
Contents, see under English literature, Essays.

Nott, Eliphalet. Miscellaneous works; with an app. Schenectady. 1810. O. **204 : 31**

Pascal, Blaise. Pensées, précédées de sa vie par mme. Perier, suivies d'un choix des pensées de Nicole et son Traité de la paix avec les hommes. Paris. 1850. D. **204 : 32**

Pascal, Blaise.—*Continued.*
— Thoughts, letters and opuscules. Tr. from the french by O. W. Wight, with introd. notices, and notes from all the commentators. N. Y. 1859. D.   **204 : 32**

Rogers, H: Reason and faith, and other miscellanies. Bost. 1853. O.   **204 : 33**
Contents. Life and writings of T: Fuller.—Andrew Marvel.—Luther's correspondence and character.—Genius and writings of Pascal.—Sacred eloquence: the british pulpit.—The vanity and glory of literature — Right of private judgment. — Reason and faith; their claims and conflicts.

Phelps, Austin. My portfolio ; a collection of essays. N. Y. 1882. D.   **204 : 49**
Contents. A pastor of the last generation.—The rights of believers in ancient creeds.—The biblical doctrine of revolution. — The puritan theory of amusements.—The christian theory of amusements. — Is card-playing a christian amusement ?—The question of sunday cars.—Woman-suffrage as judged by the working of negro-suffrage.—Reform in the political status of women.—The length of sermons.—The calvinistic theory of preaching.—The theology of the "Marble faun.".—The debt of the nation to New England.—Ought the pulpit to ignore spiritualism ? — How shall the pulpit treat spiritualism ? — Foreign and home missions, as seen by candidates for the ministry.—Foreign missions, their range of appeal for missionaries limited. — Congregationalists and presbyterians: a plea for union; methods of union.—The preaching of Albert Barnes.—A vacation with dr. Bushnell.—Prayer viewed in the light of christian consciousness. — Intercessory prayer.—Hints auxiliary to faith in prayer.—The vision of Christ.—The cross in the door.—The premature closing of a life's work.—What do we know of the heavenly life ?

Rutherford, S: Joshua redivivus, or 352 religious letters, divided into three parts. Added, the author's testimony to the covenanted work of reformation, between 1688 and 1649, and also his dying words, containing several advices to ministers and near relations. 13th ed. Edinb. 1809. D. **204 : R34**

Savage, Minot Judson. The religion of evolution. Bost 1877. D.   **204 : 46**

Shedd, W: Greenough Thayer. Theological essays. N. Y. 1877. D.   **204 : 36**
Contents. The method and influence of theological studies.—The nature and influence of the historic spirit.—The idea of evolution defined and applied to history.—The doctrine of original sin.—The atonement a satisfaction for the ethical nature of both God and man.—Symbols and congregationalism.—Clerical education.

Taylor, I: Logic in theology and other essays. Lond. 1859. S.   **204 : 37**
Contents. Logic in theology.—The state of unitarianism in England. — Nilus. — Paula. — Theodosius. — Julian.—Without controversy.

Thompson, Joseph Parrish. Stray meditations, or Voices of the heart in joy and in sorrow. N. Y. 1852. D.   **204 : 38**

Vinet, Alexandre Rodolphe. Montaigne ; The endless study, and other miscellanies. Tr.

with an introd. and notes by Robert Turnbull. N. Y. 1850. D.   **204 : 41**

Whately, R: Thoughts and apophthegms. Phila. 1856. D.   **204 : 42**

6. Periodicals.

American presbyterian and theological review, The, ed. by H: B. Smith and J. M. Sherwood ; v. 13-18, jan. 1864—dec. 1869. N. Y. 1864-69. O.   **205 : M**
Note. The original name of the magazine was "The presbyterian quarterly review", vol. 18 again changes to "American presbyterian review."

American quarterly church review and ecclesiastical register, The ; v. 14-21, apr. 1861—jan. 1870. N. Y. 1861-70. O.   **205 : M**

Bibliotheca sacra and biblical repository, ed. by Edwards A. Park and S: H. Taylor ; v. 18-26. Andover. 1861-69. O.   **205 : M**
Note. Title-page drops "and biblical repository" after v. 21.

Brownson's quarterly review ; v. 18-21. Bost. 1861-64. O.   **205 : M**

Catholic world, The ; a monthly eclectic magazine of general literature and science ; v. 1-16, 20, 21, 23-28, apr. 1865—march 1879. N. Y. 1865-79. O.   **205 : M**

Christian examiner, The ; v. 1-51, 54-87, jan. 1824 - dec. 1869. Bost. 1824-65, N. Y. 1866-69. O.   **205 : M**
Note. V. 1-5 adds "and theological review", v. 6-35 "and general review", v. 36-62 "and religious miscellany" to the present title.

Evergreen, The, or Church offering for all seasons ; a repository of religious, literary and entertaining knowledge for the christian family ; v. 5, 6, jan. 1848—dec. 1849. N. Y. 1848-49. Q.   **205 : M**

Literary and theological review, The, conducted by Leonard Woods, jr.; v. 1-6. N. Y. 1834-39. O.   **205 : M**
Note. V. 5, 6 conducted by C: D. Pigeon.

Methodist quarterly review, ed. by D. D. Whedon ; v. 21-29. N. Y. 1861-69. O.   **205 : M**

Radical, The ; Sidney H. Morse and Joseph B. Marvin eds. and props. ; v. 4-6, july 1868—oct. 1869. Bost. 1868-69. O.   **205 : M**

Religious magazine, The, and monthly review, ed. by J : H. Morrison ; v. 49, 50, jan.—dec. 1873. Bost. 1873. O.   **205 : M**
Note. Changed to "The unitarian review and religious magazine."

Unitarian review, The, and religious magazine ; v. 1-22, march 1874—dec. 1884. Bost. 1874-84. O.   **205 : M**
Note. V. 1 ed. by C: Lowe, v. 2 by H: W. Foote, v. 3, 4 by J : H. Morison and H : H. Barber, after which no editor's name is given.

2. Natural theology.

1. In general.

Brougham, H: *baron Brougham and Vaux.* A discourse of natural theology, showing the nature of the evidence and the advantages of the study. Phila. 1835. D.   **210 : 1**

Bushnell, Horace. Nature and the supernatural,

as together constituting the one system of God. N. Y. 1858. O.   **210 : 2**

Cobbe, Frances Power. The peak in Darien, with some other inquiries touching concerns of the soul and body ; an octave of essays. Bost. 1882. D.   **211 : 15**

Cocker, B: Franklin. The theistic conception of

the world ; an essay in opposition to certain tendencies of modern thought. N. Y. 1875. O. **210 : 3**

Crabbe, G: An outline of a system of natural theology. Lond. 1840. O. **210+4**

Harris, J: Pre-adamite earth ; contributions to theological science. Bost. 1850. D. **210 : 5**

Hedge, F: H: Reason in religion. Bost. 1866. D. **210 : 6**

Nordhoff, C: God and the future life ; the reasonableness of christianity. N. Y. 1883. S. **210 : 11**

Paley, W: Natural theology, with illustrative notes etc., by H: lord Brougham, and sir C: Bell. Ill. Added, preliminary observations and notes. N. Y. 1845. 2 v. S. **210 : 7**

— *Same.* N. Y. 1824. T. **210 : 7**

— Natural theology, or Evidences of the essence and attributes of the deity, collected from the appearances of nature. New ed. Hartford. 1847. D. **210 : 7**

Tucker, Abraham. The light of nature pursued. From the 2d London ed., rev. and cor.; together with some account of the life of the author by sir H. P. St. J: Mildmay. Cambridge. 1831. 2 v. O. **210 : 8**

Seeley, J: Robert. Natural religion, by the author of "Ecce homo". Bost. 1882. S. **210 : 9**

Wilson, W: D. The foundations of religious belief; the methods of natural theology vindicated against modern objections. (The bishop Paddock lectures, 1883.) N. Y. 1883. D. **210 : 10**

2. Theism and atheism.

(See also Philosophy, col. 43-50.)

Blackie, J: Stuart. The natural history of atheism. N. Y. 1878. D. **211 : 1**
Contents. Presumptions.—Theism, its reasonable ground.—Atheism, its varieties and common root.—Polytheism.—Buddhism.—The atheism of reaction; Modern english atheists and agnostics; Martineau and Tyndall.

Cairns, J: Unbelief in the 18th century as contrasted with its earlier and later history. (Cunningham lectures for 1880.) N. Y. 1881. D. **211 : 2**

Faber, G: Stanley. The difficulties of infidelity. N. Y. 1829. D. **211 : 4**

Fisher, G: Park. Faith and rationalism, with short supplementary essays on related topics. N. Y. 1879. D. **211 : 3**

Frohschammer, Jakob. Das neue wissen und der neue glaube ; mit besonderer berücksichtigung von D. F. Strauss' neuester schrift "Der alte und der neue glaube". Leipz. 1873. D. **211 : 10**

Froude, James Anthony. The nemesis of faith. Chicago. 1879. D. **211 : 18**

Holbach, Paul H: Thiry *baron* d'. The system of nature, or Laws of the moral and physical world. A new and impr. ed., with notes by Diderot ; tr. for the first time, by H. D. Robinson. Bost. 1853. 2 v. in 1. O. **211+13**

Hurst, J: F. History of rationalism ; embracing a survey of the present state of protestant theology, with app. of literature. N. Y. 1865. O. **211 : 5**

Lecky, W: E: Hartpole. History of the rise and influence of the spirit of rationalism in Europe. Rev. ed. N. Y. 1875, 1876. 2 v. D. **211 : 6**

Martineau, James. Modern materialism, its attitude toward theology ; comprising two papers reprinted from the Contemporary review, and being a continuation of the argument of "Religion as affected by modern materialism." N. Y. 1876. S. **211 : 7**

Naville, Jules Ernest. The heavenly father ; lectures on modern atheism. Tr. from the french by H: Downton. Bost. 1867. D. **211 : 8**

Nelson, D: The cause and cure of infidelity ; with an account of the author's conversion. N. Y. 1837. D. **211 : 9**

Paine, T: The age of reason ; an investigation of true and fabulous theology. *T. p. w.* D. **211 : 14**

Parker, Theodore. Sermons of theism, atheism and the popular theology. 3d ed. Bost. 1861. D. **211 : 10**

Pearson, T: Infidelity ; its aspects, causes and agencies. People's ed., with a pref. by J. Jordan. Lond. [185-]. S. **211 : 11**

Strauss, D: F: The old faith and the new ; a confession. Authorized tr. from the 6th ed. by Mathilde Blind ; amer. ed., 2 v. in 1, the tr. rev. and partly re-written and preceded by an amer. version of the author's prefatory post-script. N. Y. *n. d.* D. **211 : 19**

Volney, Constantin François Chasseboeuf *comte* de. The ruins, or Meditation on the revolutions of empires. Added, the law of nature, a short biography by count Dara, and the controversy between dr. Priestly and Volney. N. Y. 1858. T. **211 : 12**

Wilson, J: G. Atheism and theism. Phila. 1883. S. **211 : 17**

Yorke, J. F. Notes on evolution and christianity. N. Y. 1883. D. **211 : 16**

3. Creation.

Campbell, S. M. The story of creation. N. Y. [1880]. D. **213 : 1**

Chapin, James H. The creation and the early developments of society. N. Y. [1880.] D. **213 : 2**

Dawson, J: W: The origin of the world according to revelation and science. N. Y. 1877. D. **213 : 3**

Guyot, Arnold H: Creation, or The biblical cosmogony. N. Y. 1884. D. **213 : 5**

Warington, G: The week of creation, or The cosmogony of Genesis considered in its relation to modern science. Lond. 1870. D. **213 : 4**

4. Providence.

Buckland, W: Geology and mineralogy as exhibiting the power, wisdom and goodness of God ; with add. by prof. Owen. prof. Phillips, Robert Brown. 4th ed. by Francis T. Buckland. [Bridgewater treatises.] Lond. 1869, 1870. 2 v. D. **214 : 6**
Contents. V. 1. Text. 2. Plates.

Chalmers, T: On the power, wisdom and goodness of God, as manifested in the adaptation of external nature to the moral and intellectual condition of man; with the author's last corr. Prefixed, a biographical preface by J: Cumming. [Bridgewater treatises.] Lond. 1853. D. **214 : 1**

Bell, *Sir* C: The hand; its mechanism and vital endowments as evincing design and illustrating the power, wisdom and goodness of God. Preceded by an account of the author's discoveries in the nervous system. 8th ed. [Bridgewater treatises.] Lond. 1882. D. **214 : 4**

Kidd, J: On the adaptation of external nature to the physical condition of man; principally with reference to the supply of his wants and the exercise of his intellectual faculties. [Bridgewater treatises.] Lond. 1852. D. **214 : 2**

Kirby, W: On the power, wisdom and goodness of God as manifested in the creation of animals, and in their history, habits and instincts. New ed. with notes by T. Rymer Jones. [Bridgewater treatises.] Lond. 1852, 1853. 2 v. D. **214 : 7**

Prout, W: Chemistry, meteorology, and the function of digestion, considered with reference to natural theology. 4th ed. by J. W. Griffith. [Bridgewater treatises.] Lond. 1855. D. **214 : 8**

Roget, P: M: Animal and vegetable physiology, considered with reference to natural theology. 4th ed. with add. and emendations. [Bridgewater treatises.] Lond. 1867. 2 v. D. **214 : 5**

Whewell, W: Astronomy and general physics, considered with reference to natural theology. [Bridgewater treatises.] Lond. 1852. D. **214 : 3**

Duncan, H: Sacred philosophy of the seasons; illustrating the perfections of God in the phenomena of the year, with important add. and some modifications to adapt it to amer. readers, by F. W. P. Greenwood. Bost. 1839. 4 v. D. **214 : 9**

Bledsoe, Albert Taylor. A theodicy or vindication of the divine glory as manifested in the constitution and government of the moral world. 6th ed. N. Y. 1856. O. **216+1**

McCosh, James. The method of the divine government, physical and moral. 4th ed. N. Y. 1865. O. **214+10**

Mather, Cotton. The christian philosopher; a collection of the best discoveries in nature, with religious improvements. Lond. 1721. D. **214 : 11**

Watts, I: A guide to prayer, or A free and rational account of the gift, grace and spirit of prayer, with plain directions how every christian may attain them; with a pref. by Robert Forbes. New ed. Aberdeen. 1854. Tt. **217 : 1**

5. Religion and science.

Campbell, G: J: Douglass, *8th duke of Argyll.* The reign of law. 5th ed. Lond. 1867. O. **215 : 1**

Cooke, Josiah Parsons, *jr.* Religion and chemistry, or Proofs of God's plan in the atmosphere and its elements; ten lectures del. at the Brooklyn institute, Brooklyn N. Y., on the Graham foundation. 2d ed. N. Y. 1865. O. **215 : 3**

Crofton, Denis. Genesis and geology, or An investigation into the reconciliation of the modern doctrines of geology with the declarations of scripture; with an introd. by E. Hitchcock. Bost. 1853. S. **215 : 4**

Dawson, J: W: Nature and the Bible; a course of lectures delivered in New York in dec. 1874 on the Morse foundation of the Union theological seminary. N. Y. 1875. D. **215 : 5**

Draper, J: W: History of the conflict between religion and science. 8th ed. (Intern. scientific ser.) N. Y. 1876. D. **215 : 6**

Drummond, H: The natural law in the spiritual world. N. Y. 1884. D. **215 : 19**

Fiske, J:, Evolution and religion. *In his* Excursions of an evolutionist. **824.1 : 107**

Gray, Asa. Natural science and religion; two lectures delivered to the theological school of Yale college. N. Y. 1880. O. **215 : 7**

Hitchcock, E: The religion of geology and its connected sciences. Bost. 1852. D. **215 : 8**

Lang, H: Die religion im zeitalter Darwins. *In* Deutsche zeit- und streit-fragen. **304 : 15 v2**

LeConte, Joseph. Religion and science; a series of sunday lectures on the relation of natural and revealed religion, or the truths revealed in nature and scripture. N. Y. 1874. D. **215 : 2**

Miller, Hugh. The testimony of the rocks, or Geology in its bearings on the two theologies, natural and revealed; with memorials of the death and character of the author. Bost. 1858. D. **215 : 9**

Mitchel, Ormsby MacKnight. The astronomy of the Bible; with a biographical sketch. N. Y. 1863. D. **215 : 10**

Molloy, Gerald. Geology and revelation, or The ancient history of the earth considered in the light of geological facts and revealed religion; with an introd. to the amer. ed. and a chapter on cosmogony, by permission, from the Manual of geology by J. D. Dana. Ill. N. Y. 1873. D. **215 : 17**

Smith, J: Pye. The relation between the holy scriptures and some parts of geological science. From the 4th London ed., greatly enl. Phila. 1850. O. **215 : 11**

Smyth, Newman. Old faiths in new light. N. Y. 1879. D. **215 : 18**

Sorignet, *L'abbé* A. Sacred cosmogony, or Primitive revelation demonstrated by the harmony of the facts of the mosaic history of the creation, with the principles of general science. Tr. from the french. St. Louis. 1862. O. **215 : 16**

Tefft, B: F. Evolution and christianity, or An answer to the development infidelity of modern times; with an introd. letter by bishop Simpson. Port. Bost. 1885. D. **215 : 20**

Temple, F: The relations between religion and science; eight lectures preached before the univ. of Oxford, in 1884. [Bampton lectures for 1884.] N. Y. 1884. D. **215 : 21**

White, Andrew Dickson. The warfare of science. N. Y. 1877. D.   **215 : 12**

Wiseman, N: Patrice Stephen (?). Galileo and the roman inquisition ; a defense of the catholic church from the charge of having persecuted Galileo for his philosophical opinions. From the Dublin review, with an introd. by an amer. catholic [James F. Meline]. 2d ed. [*Anon.*] Cinc. 1859. D.   **215 : 13**

— Twelve lectures on the connection between science and revealed religion, del. in Rome. 3d ed. Balt. 1852. 2 v. S.   **215 : 14**
Contents. v. 1. On the comparative study of languages.—On the natural history of the human race.—On the natural sciences. 2. On early history. —On archæology.—On oriental literature.

Wythe, Joseph H. The agreement of science and revelation. Phila. 1872. D.   **215 : 15**

6. Future life.

(*See also* Doctrinal theology, Future state ; col. 96.)

Alger, W: Rounseville. A critical history of the doctrine of a future life ; with a complete bibliography of the subject. Phila. 1864. O.   **218 : 1**

Blackwell, Antoinette Brown. The physical basis of immortality. N. Y. 1876. D.   **218 : 2**

Figuier, Guillaume L: The to-morrow of death, or The future life according to science. Tr. from the french by S. R. Crocker. Bost. 1872. S.   **218 : 3**

Fiske, J: The destiny of man viewed in the light of his origin. Bost. 1884. S.   **218 : 8**

— The unseen world.   *in* **824.1 : 32**

Kirk, Hyland C. The possibility of not dying ; a speculation. N. Y. 1883. S.   **218 : 7**

Tait, P: Guthrie, *and* Balfour Stewart. The unseen universe, or Physical speculations on a future state. [*Anon.*] N. Y. 1875. D.   **218 : 4**

Taylor, I: Physical theory of another life. N. Y. 1853. D.   **218 : 5**

Timbs, J: Mysteries of life, death and futurity. *In his* Things not generally known.   **829.2 : 64 v11**
Contents, see under English literature, Miscellany.

Weiss, J: The immortal life. Bost. 1880. D.   **218 : 6**

3. The Bible.

1. In general.

Biblia sacra vulgatæ editionis, Sixti v. pont. max. jussu recognita, et Clementis VIII. auctoritate edita, distincta versiculis indicéque epistolarum et evangeliorum aucta. Lugduni. 1675. F.   **23 : R**

Holy bible, The ; containing the Old and New testaments tr. out of the original tongues, and with the former translations diligently compared and revised, with Canne's marginal notes and references, together with the apocrypha, to which are added an index, an alphabetical table of all the names in the old and new testaments, with their significations, also tables of scripture weights, measures and coins. Cooperstown. 1845. O.   **220.2 : R1**

Holy bible, The ; containing the Old and New testaments tr. out of the original tongues ; being the version set forth a. d. 1611, compared with the most ancient authorities and revised [New testament in 1881, Old testament in 1885]. Printed for the universities of Oxford and Cambridge. Oxford. 1885. O.   **220.2 : 3**

Biblia pauperum, conteynynge thirty and eight wode cuttes illvstrating the liif, parablis and miraclis offe oure blessid Lord and Saviour Jhesus Crist, with the proper descrypciouns therof extracted fro the originall texte offe Iohn Wiclif, somtyme rector of Lutterworth. Preface by Arthur Penrhyn Stanley. N. Y. 1885. O.   **220.2 : R2**

Grimm, Willibald. Die Lutherbibel und ihre textesrevision ; vortrag im studentischen Gustav-Adolf-verein zu Jena gehalten. *In* Deutsche zeit- und streit-fragen.   **304 : 15 v3**

Briggs, C: A: Biblical study ; its principles, methods and history, together with a catalogue of books of reference. N. Y. 1883. O.   **220 : 15**

Chadwick, J: W. The Bible of to-day ; a course of lectures. N. Y. 1878. D.   **220 : 1**

Clark, S: A collection of the promises of scripture, or The christian's inheritance. N. Y. n. d. Tt.   **220.8 : 1**

Darby, J: Nelson. Synopsis of the books of the Bible. Lond. 1857. 3 v. D.   **220 : 2**
Contents. v. 1. Genesis—II Chronicles. 2. Ezra—Malachi. 3. Matthew—John.

Gleig, G: Robert. The history of the Bible. N. Y. 1846. 2 v. S.   **220 : 3**

Headley, Joel Tyler. Sacred scenes and characters. N. Y. 1851. D.   **220 : 4**

Horne, T: Hartwell. Introduction to the critical study and knowledge of the holy scriptures. N. Y. 1864. 2 v. Q.   **220+5**

Ladd, G: Trumbull. The doctrine of sacred scripture ; a critical, historical and dogmatic inquiry into the origin and nature of the Old and New testaments. N. Y. 1883. 2 v. O.   **220 : 14**

Liber librorum, its structure, limitations and purpose ; a friendly communication to a reluctant sceptic. N. Y. 1867. S.   **220 : 6**

Mahan, Milo. Palmoni, or The numerals of scripture a proof of inspiration ; a free inquiry. N. Y. 1863. O.   **220 : 7**

Merle d'Aubigné, J: H: The authority of God, or The true barrier against romish and infidel aggression ; four discourses, with an introd. written for this ed. Author's complete ed. N. Y. 1851. D.   **220 : 8**

Newton, T: Dissertations on the prophecies which have remarkably been fulfilled, and at this time are fulfilling in the world. A new ed. Lond. 1820. 2 v. O,   **220 : 9**

Savage, Minot Judson. Beliefs about the Bible. Bost. 1883. D.   **220 : 16**

Stuart, Moses. Hints on the interpretation of prophecy. Andover. 1842. D.   **220 : 10**

Testimony of eminent witnesses for the Bible; compiled for the special benefit of young men. N. Y. 1866. S.   **220 : 11**

Wordsworth, Christopher. On the inspiration of holy scripture, or On the canon of the Old and New testament, and on the Apocrypha; twelve lectures del. before the university of Cambridge. Phila. 1854. O.
                                        220 : 12

Whitaker, W: A disputation on holy scripture against the papists, especially Bellarmine and Stapleton. Tr. and ed. for the Parker society by W: Fitzgerald. Cambridge. 1849. O.   **220 : 13**

Concordances and commentaries.

Cruden, Alexander. A complete concordance to the holy scriptures of the Old and New testament, or A dictionary and alphabetical index to the bible, in 2 pts.: 1. The appellative or common words, 2. The proper names ; to which is add. a concordance to the books called Apocrypha, the whole digested in an easy and regular method which, together with the various significations and other improvements now added renders it more useful than any book of the kind hitherto published. From the 10th London ed., rev. and corr.; added, an original life of the author. N. Y. 1860. O.
                                        220.4 : R1

Warner, Susan. The law and the testimony. N. Y. 1853. O.   **220.4+2**

Young, Robert. Analytical concordance to the Bible, on an entirely new plan, cont. every word in alphabetical order, arr. under its hebrew or greek original, with the literal meaning of each and its pronunciation ; exhibiting about 311,000 references, marking 30,000 various readings in the New testament, with the latest information on biblical geography and antiquities, etc.; designed for the simplest reader of the english Bible. Rev. and authorized ed. N. Y. 1881. Q.   **220.4 : R3**

Cook, F: C:, *ed.* The holy bible according to the authorized version, a. d. 1611, with an explanatory and critical commentary and a revision of the trans. by bishops and other clergy of the anglican church. N. Y. [1871-81]. 10 v. O.   **220.5 : R1**
  Contents. V. 1. Genesis. — Exodus. — Leviticus. — Numbers. — Deuteronomy. **2.** Joshua. — Judges. — Ruth. — Samuel, I, II. — Kings, I. **3.** Kings, II. — Chronicles, I, II. — Ezra. — Nehemiah. — Esther. **4.** Job.—Psalms.—Proverbs.—Ecclesiastes.—The song of Solomon. **5.** Isaiah.—Jeremiah.—Lamentations. **6.** Ezekiel, Daniel and minor prophets. **7.** St. Matthew. —St. Mark.—St. Luke. **8.** St. John.—The acts. **9.** Romans-Philemon. **10.** Hebrews-Revelation.

Menochio (*lat.* Menochius), Giovanni Stefano. Brevis explicatio sensus literalis totius s. scripturæ ex optimis quibusque auctoribus per epitomen collecta. Coloniæ Agripp. 1680. 2 v. F.   **23 : R**

Dictionaries and cyclopedias.

Calmet, Augustin. Dictionary of the holy bible, as pub. by C: Taylor, with the fragments incorporated, the whole condensed and arranged in alphabetical order. 21st ed., rev. with large add. by E: Robinson. Ill. and maps. Bost. 1860. Q.   **220.6 : R1**

Kitto, J:, *ed.* The cyclopædia of biblical literature. Ill. by maps and engr. 11th ed. N. Y. 1864. 2 v. O.   **220.6 : R2**

Smith, W: Dictionary of the Bible ; comprising its antiquities, biography, geography and natural history, rev. and ed. by H. B. Hackett with the coöperation of Ezra Abbot. Bost. 1879. 4 v. O.   **220.6 : R3**
  Contents. V. 1. A—Gennesaret, Land of. 2. Gennesaret, Sea of—Market. 3. Marriage—Regem. 4. Regem-Melech—Zuzims.

— *and* S: **Cheetham.** A dictionary of christian antiquities ; a continuation of "The dictionary of the Bible". Ill. Hartford. 1880. 2 v. D.   **220.6 : R4**

Antiquities and history.

Burder, S: Oriental customs applied to the illustration of the sacred scriptures. 5th ed. Lond. 1851. D.   **220.7 : 1**

— Oriental literature, applied to the illustration of the sacred scriptures ; especially with reference to antiquities, traditions, and manners, collected from the most celebrated writers and travellers, ancient and modern, designed as a sequel to Oriental customs. Lond. 1822. 2 v. O.   **220.7 : 2**

Hutchinson, Enoch. Music of the Bible, or Explanatory notes upon those passages in the sacred scriptures which relate to music, incl. a brief view of hebrew poetry. Bost. 1864. O.   **220.7+3**

Palmer, Henrietta Lee. Home-life in the Bible ; ed. by J: Williamson Palmer. Ill. Bost. 1881. Q.   **220.7+4**

Trimmer, Sarah. Sacred history selected from the scriptures, with annotations and reflections particularly calculated to facilitate the study of the holy scriptures in schools and families. 3d ed. Lond. 1796. 6 v. S.   **220.8 : 2**

Merrill, G: E. The story of the manuscripts. Bost. [1881]. D.   **220.9 : 1**

2. Old testament.

Biblia hebraica secundum editiones J: Leusden, J: Simonis aliorunque, imprimis Everardi van der Hooght, recensuit, sectionum propheticarum recensum et explicationem, clavemque masorethicam et rabbinicam addidit A: Hahn. Ed. ster. C. Tauchnitzii quartum recognita et emend. Lipsiæ. 1872. O.   **221.1 : 1**

Leabhraiche an t-seann tiomnaidh air an tarruing o'n cheud chanain chum gaelic albannaich; ann an ceithir earrannaibh. Dun-Eidin. 1773, 1778. 2 v. in 1. O.   **23 : R**

Roberts, Alexander. Old testament revision ; a handbook for english readers. N. Y. 1883. S.   **221 : b**

Smith, W: Robertson. The Old testament in the jewish church ; twelve lectures on biblical criticism. N. Y. 1881. D. **221 : 1**

Watts, Robert. The newer criticism and the analogy of the faith ; a reply to lectures by W. Robertson Smith on the Old testament in the jewish church. 3d ed. Edinb. 1882. D.   221 : 4

Walworth, Clarence. The gentle skeptic, or Essays and conversations of a country justice on the authenticity and truthfulness of the Old testament records ; ed. by C. Walworth. N. Y. 1863. D.   221 : 2

Wette, W: Martin Leberecht de. A critical and historical introduction to the canonical scriptures of the Old testament. From the german, tr. and enl. by Theodore Parker. 4th ed. N. Y. 1864. 2 v. O.   221+3

Orton, Job. An exposition of the Old testament, with devotional and practical reflections for the use of families ; pub. from the author's mss. by Robert Gentleman. 1st amer. from the 2d Lond. ed. Charlestown. 1805, 1806. 6 v. O.   221.5 : 1

Historical books.

Gibson, J: Monro. The ages before Moses ; a series of lectures on the book of Genesis. N. Y. [1879]. D.   222 : 2

Davies, T: A. Genesis disclosed ; being the discovery of a stupendous error which changes the entire nature of the account of the creation of mankind ; also showing a divine law plainly laid down, proving the error that all men have descended from Adam and Eve. N. Y. 1874..D.   222 : 4

Mackintosh, C. H. Notes on the book of Genesis. [*Anon.*] 4th ed. Lond. [1861]. S.   222.5 : 1

— Notes on the book of Exodus. [*Anon.*] 2d ed. Lond. [1859]. S.   222.5 : 2

— Notes on the book of Leviticus. [*Anon.*] Lond. [1860]. S.   222.5 : 3

Colenso, J: W: The Pentateuch and book of Joshua critically examined. Lond. 1863, 1865. 5 v. O.   222.5 : 4
Contents.—V. 1, [5th ed. rev.] The Pentateuch examined as a historical narrative. 2. The age and authorship of the Pentateuch considered. 3. The book of Deuteronomy. 4. The first eleven chapters of Genesis. 5. The book of Genesis analysed and separated, and the ages of its writers determined.

Cumming, J: Moses right and bishop Colenso wrong ; popular lectures on the Pentateuch. N. Y. 1863. D.   222 : 1

Mahan, Milo. The spiritual point of view, or The glass reversed ; an answer to bishop Colenso. N. Y. 1863. O.   222 : 3

Poetical books.

Luther, Martin. A commentary on the psalms, called psalms of degrees ; in which, among many other subjects, the scriptural doctrine respecting the divinely instituted and honorable estate of matrimony is explained and defended, in opposition to the popish errors of monastic seclusion and enforced celibacy. Prefixed, an historical account of the monastic life, particularly of the monasteries of England. Lond. 1819. O.   223.5 : 1

Vincent, Marvin Richardson. Gates into the psalm-country. N. Y. 1883. D.   223.8 : 1

Prophetical books.

Smith, W: Robertson. The prophets of Israel and their place in history to the close of the 8th century ; eight lectures. N. Y. 1882. D.   224 : 3

Isaiah ; a new tr. with a preliminary dissertation and notes critical, philological and explanatory by Robert Lowth. 2d ed. Lond. 1779. Q.   224.2 : R1

Arnold, Matthew. Isaiah of Jerusalem. *In* **Coan**, T. M. Topics of the time.   820.5 : 21

Cowles, H: Jeremiah and his Lamentations, with notes critical, explanatory and practical, designed for both pastors and people. N. Y. 1869. D.   224.5 : 1

Cumming, J: Prophetic studies, or Lectures on the book of Daniel. Lond. [185-]. S.   224 : 1

Seiss, Joseph A: Voices from Babylon, or The records of Daniel the prophet. Phila. [1879]. D.   224 : 2

3. New testament.

Greek. **Novum testamentum** graecum ; ad exemplar Roberti Stephani accuratissime ed. cura P. Wilson. Phila. 1833. D.   225.1 : 1

—**Harris**, J: Rendel. New testament autographs. (Supp. to the American journal of philology, no. 12.) Balt. [1882]. O.   225.1 : 2

Eng. **New testament**, The, of our Lord and Saviour Jesus Christ. Tr. out of the greek, being the version set forth a. d. 1611, compared with the most ancient authorities and rev. a. d. 1881. Oxford. 1881. O.   225.2 : R1

— *Same.* With the readings and renderings preferred by the american committee of revision, incorporated into the text by Roswell D. Hitchcock. N. Y. 1881. D.   225.2 : 2

—**Trench**, R: Chenevix. On the authorized version of the New testament, in connection with some recent proposals for its revision. N. Y. 1858. D.   225.2 : 3

— — *Same.* N. Y. 1873. O. *In* **Lightfoot**, J. B., *and others.* The revision of the english version.   225.2 : 4

—**Lightfoot**, Joseph Barber, *and others.* The revision of the english version of the New testament; with an introd. by Philip Schaff. N. Y. 1873. O.   225.2 : 4
Contents. **Schaff**, Philip. Introduction on the revision of the english bible.—**Lightfoot**, Joseph Barber. On a fresh revision of the english New testament. 2d. ed. rev.—**Trench**, Richard Chenevix. On the authorized version of the New testament, in connection with some recent proposals for its revision. —**Ellicott**, C: J: Considerations on the english version of the New testament.

—**Roberts**, Alexander. Companion to the revised version of the New testament explaining the reasons for the changes made on the authorized version ; with supp. by a member of the amer. committee of revision. N. Y. [1881]. S.   225.2 : 5

—**Schaff**, Philip. A companion to the greek Testament and the english version; with facsimile ill. of mss. and standard editions of the New testament. N. Y. 1883. D.   225 : 1

French. **Nouveau testament,** Le, de notre Seigneur Jésus Christ ; revu sur les originaux par D: Martin. N. Y. 1859. S.   **225.3 : 1**

Swed. **Nya testamentet,** Det, af wår Härre och Frälsare Jesus Christus. N. Y. 1866. S.   **225.3 : 2**

Hindu. **New** testament, The, of our Lord and Saviour Jesus Christ. Tr. from the original greek into the Hinduwee language. [Lond.] 1860. O.   **225.3 : 3**

Chinese. [Portion of the New testament in chinese.] *T. p. w.*   **225.3 : 4**

*   *   *

Student's concordance, The, to the revised version, 1881, of the New testament of our Lord and Saviour Jesus Christ, compiled upon an original plan showing the changes in all words referred to, with appendices of the chief authorised words and passages omitted in the revision, and of new and disused words, a table of the genealogy of the english New testament, etc. N. Y. 1882. O.   **225.4 : R1**

Reuss, E: W: Eugen. History of the sacred scriptures of the New testament. Tr. from the 5th rev. and enl. german ed. with bibliographical add. by E: L. Houghton. Bost. 1884. 2 v. O.   **225.9 : 1**

Leland, T: A dissertation on the principles of human eloquence ; with particular regard to the style and composition of the New testament, in which the observations on this subject by the lord bishop of Gloucester, in his discourse on the doctrine of grace, are distinctly considered, being the substance of several lectures read in the oratory school of Trinity college, Dublin. Lond. 1764. Q. *With* **Brown,** J: Dissertation on poetry and music.   **23 : R**

Toy, Crawford Howell. Quotation in the New testament. N. Y. 1884. O.   **225+2**

Gospels and Acts.

Heiss, Michael. The four gospels examined and vindicated on catholic principles. Milw. 1863. O.   **226 : 1**

Alford, H: How to study the New testament; the gospels, the Acts of the apostles. Lond. 1865. D.   **226.8 : 1**

Clark, G: W. A new harmony of the four gospels in english, according to the common version; arr. with explanatory notes, brief descriptions of customs, words, names, sketch of prominent harmonies, and valuable tables, designed for popular use, and specially adapted to sabbath-schools; with an introd. by T. J. Conant. N. Y. 1870. D.   **226.4 : 1**

Robinson, E: A harmony of the four gospels in english, according to the common version; newly arr. with explan. notes. Bost. 1846. D.   **226.4 : 2**

Barnes, Albert. Notes, explanatory and practical, on the gospels, designed for sunday-school teachers and bible classes. 25th ed., rev. and corr., with an index, chronological table, table of weights, etc. N. Y. 1865. 2 v. D.   **226.5 : 1**

— Notes explanatory and practical on the Acts of the apostles, designed for bible classes and sunday schools. 20th ed. N. Y. 1865. D.   **226.5 : 2**

Trench, R: Chenevix. Notes on the miracles of our Lord. 2d amer. ed. N. Y. 1862. O.   **226.5+3**

— Notes on the parables of our Lord. 2d. amer. ed. N. Y. 1864. O.   **226.5+4**

Guthrie, T: The parables, read in the light of the present day. Lond. 1866. D. **226.8 : 2**

— *Same.* N. Y. 1866. D.   **226.8 : 2**

Stanley, E: Geoffrey Smith, *14th earl of Derby.* Conversations on the parables of the New testament, for the use of children. From the 5th Lond. ed. Phila. 1844. S.   **226.8 : 4**

Gospel of Matthew, The, in chinese, with explanatory notes by W: Dean. Hongkong. 1848. Q.   **226.3 : R1**

Trench, R: Chenevix. The star of the wise men ; a commentary on the second chapter of Matthew. N. Y. 1851. S.   **226.5 : 5**

Epistles and Apocalypse.

Paley, W: Horæ paulinæ. N. Y. 1824. T.   **227.4 : 1**

St. Paul's epistle to the Romans ; newly tr. and explained from a missionary point of view by J. W. Colenso. N. Y. 1863. O. **227.2 : 1**

Chalmers, T: Lectures on the epistle of Paul the apostle to the Romans. 7th thous. N. Y. 1859. O.   **227.5+8**

Barnes, Albert. Notes, explanatory and practical on the epistle to the Romans; designed for bible classes and sunday schools. 9th ed. N. Y. 1864. D.   **227.5 : 1**

— Notes, explanatory and practical, on the first epistle of Paul to the Corinthians. N. Y. 1864. D.   **227.5 : 2**

— Notes, explanatory and practical, on the second epistle to the Corinthians and the epistle to the Galatians. N. Y. 1864. D.   **227.5 : 3**

— Notes, explanatory and practical, on the epistles of Paul to the Ephesians, Philippians and Colossians. N. Y. 1864. D.   **227.5 : 4**

— Notes, explanatory and practical, on the epistles of Paul to the Thessalonians, to Timothy, to Titus and to Philemon. N. Y. 1864. D.   **227.5 : 5**

— Notes, explanatory and practical, on the epistle to the Hebrews. N. Y. 1865. D.   **227.5 : 6**

— Notes, explanatory and practical, on the general epistles of James, Peter, John and Jude. N. Y. 1865. D.   **227.5 : 7**

Cowles, H: The shorter epistles, viz. of Paul to the Galatians, Ephesians, Philippians, Colossians, Thessalonians, Timothy, Titus and Philemon ; also of James, Peter and Jude. [App.: Canon Farrar's doctrine of "Eternal hope"]. N. Y. 1879. D.   **227.5 : 10**

Weller (*latin* Wellerus), Hieronymus. Hieronymi Vuelleri theologiæ doctoris in epistolas d. Pavli ad Philippenses et Thessalonicenses [et Philemonem] annotationes piæ, breues et eruditæ ; antea in lvcem non editae. Noribergæ. 1561. S.   **23 : R**

Weller, H.—*Continued.*
— Hieronymi VVelleri theologiæ doctoris in epistolam diui Pauli ad Ephesios enarrationes piae, breues et eruditæ. Noribergæ. [15]59. S. *With the preceding.* 23 : **R**

Barnes, Albert. Notes, explanatory and practical, on the book of Revelation. N. Y. 1864. D. **228.5 : 1**

Trench, R: Chenevix. Commentary on the epistles to the seven churches in Asia, Revelation ii, iii. N. Y. 1864. D. **228.5 : 2**

4. Apocrypha.

Book of Enoch the prophet, The ; an apocryphal production supposed for ages to have been lost, but discovered at the close of the last century in Abyssinia ; now first tr. from an ethiopic ms. in the Bodleian library by R: Laurence. 3d ed. rev. and enl. Oxford. 1838. O. **229 : 1**

Hone, W: The apocryphal new testament, being all the gospels, epistles and other pieces now extant, attributed in the first four centuries to Jesus Christ, his apostles and their companions, and not included in the New testament by its compilers. Tr. and now first coll. into 1 vol., with pref. and tables and various notes and references. From the last Lond. ed. Bost. 1832. D. **229 : 2**

Contents, see Catalogue of the Boston athenæum, v. 1, p. 115, *art.* Apocryphal gospels.

Book of Adam and Eve, The, also called The conflict of Adam and Eve with Satan ; a book of the early eastern church. Tr. from the ethiopic with notes from the Kufale, Talmud, Midrashim, and other eastern works by S[olomon] C[æsar] Malan. Lond. 1882. O. **229 : 4**

Teaching of the twelve apostles, recently discovered and pub. by Philotheos Bryennios, metropolitan of Nicomedia ; ed. with a trans., introd. and notes by Roswell D. Hitchcock and Francis Brown. N. Y. 1884. O. **229+3**

4. Doctrinal theology.

Calfhill, James. An answer to John Martiall's Treatise of the cross ; ed. for the Parker society by R: Gibbings. Cambridge. 1846. D. **230 : 1**

Doddridge, Philip. A course of lectures on the principal subjects in pneumatology, ethics and divinity, with references to the most considerable authors on each subject. 2d ed. Lond. 1776. Q. **230 : R9**

Eliot, W: Greenleaf. Discourses on the doctrines of christianity. 15th thous. Bost. 1866. D. **230 : 2**

Feuerbach, L: The essence of christianity. Tr. from the 2d german ed. by Marian Evans. 2d ed. [Eng. and foreign phil. lib.] Lond. 1881. O. **230 : 7**

Greg, W: Rathbone. The creed of christendom, its foundations contrasted with its superstructure, with a new introd. 7th ed. [Eng. and foreign phil. lib.] Lond. 1880. 2 v. O. **230 : 8**

Martensen, Hans Lassen. Christian dogmatics ; a compendium of the doctrines of christianity. Tr. from the german by W: Urwick. Edinb. 1871. O. **230+11**

Parker, Theodore. A discourse of matters pertaining to religion. 4th ed. Bost. 1856. D. **230 : 3**

Peabody, Andrew Preston. Lectures on christian doctrine. New ed., with an introd. lecture on the scriptures. Bost. 1858. D. **230 : 4**

Pearson, J: An exposition of the creed ; with an app. containing the original greek and latin creeds ; rev. by W. S. Dobson. N. Y. 1865. O. **230+5**

Ridgley, T: A body of divinity ; wherein the doctrines of the christian religion are explained and defended, being the substance of several lectures on the assembly's larger catechism. 2d ed., corr. Lond. 1734. 2 v. F. **23 : R**

Smyth, Newman. The orthodox theology of today. New ed. N. Y. 1883. D. **230 : 10**

Taylor, I: Natural history of enthusiasm. [*Anon.*] Bost. 1830. S. **230 : 6**

God and Supernaturalism.

Cumming, J: God in history, *and* God in science. N. Y. 1855. D. **231 : 8**

Diman, Jeremiah Lewis. The theistic argument as affected by modern theories ; a course of lectures del. at the Lowell institute in Boston. Bost. 1881. D. **231 : 3**

Manning, H: E: The temporal mission of the Holy Ghost, or Reason and revelation. N. Y. 1866. D. **231 : 1**

Miller, J: Fetich in theology, or Doctrinalism twin to ritualism. N. Y. 1874. D. **231 : 2**

Muir, J: Supernatural religion ; an inquiry into the reality of divine revelation, in [3] v. V. 1 and 2, 5th ed. [*Anon.*] Lond. 1875, 1877. 3 v. O. **231 : 4**

Mulford, Elisha. The republic of God ; an institute of theology. 5th ed. Bost. 1882. O. **231 : 6**

Savage, Minot Judson. Belief in God ; examination of some fundamental theistic problems, [*also*] An address on the intellectual basis of faith by W. H. **Savage.** Bost. 1881. D. **231 : 7**

Sherlock, T: The use and intent of prophecy in the several ages of the world ; in six discourses del. at the Temple church in april and may 1724. Dublin. 1849. D. **231 : 5**

Whately, R: A view of the scripture revelations respecting good and evil angels. 2d ed. Phila. 1856. D. **235 : 1**

*   *   *

Cropp, Johannes. Lessings streit mit hauptpastor [J: Melchior] Goeze. *In* Deutsche zeit- und streit-fragen. **304 : 15 v10**

Christ and the Trinity.

Athanasius, *St.* Select treatises of S. Athanasius. archbishop of Alexandria, in controversy with the arians, tr. with notes and indices. [Library of the fathers, 8, 19.] Oxford. 1853, 1854. 2 v. O.   232 : 1

Barrett, B: Franklin. Letters on the divine trinity, addressed to H: Ward Beecher. 2d ed. N. Y. 1860. D.   232 : 3

Calvin, J: Christ the end of the law; the preface to the Geneva bible of 1550, now first rendered into english by T: Weedon. Lond. 1850. O.   232 : 4

Christ, his nature and work; a series of discourses. N. Y. 1878. D.   232 : 5
   Contents. **Crosby,** H. God ever active in Christ.—**Bellows,** H: W. The sacrificial element in christianity.—**Foss,** C. D. The four gospels: their differences and their essence.—**Morgan,** W: F. Christ's espousal of the lost.—**Anderson,** T: D. Christ's sanction to the authority of revelation.—**Armitage,** T: Jesus; his self-introspection.—**Newton,** R. H. Christ's law of co-operation.—**Washburn,** E: A. The life of Christ, the proof of his divine revelation.—**Giles,** C. Who was Jesus Christ?—**Rogers,** E. P. The magnetism of the cross.—**Robinson,** C: S. A live coal from the altar.—**Bevan,** L. D. The witness of Jesus to himself, as seen in some contradictory phenomena of his life and character.—**Chapin,** E. H. The conditions of religious life.

Examination, An, of canon Liddon's Bampton lectures on the divinity of our Lord and Saviour Jesus Christ, by a clergyman of the church of England. Bost. 1872. D.   232 : 2

Farrar, F: W: The life of Christ. N. Y. [1874]. 2 v. O.   232 : 19

Fleetwood, J: The life of our Lord and Saviour Jesus Christ; cont. a full and accurate history from his taking upon himself our nature to his crucifixion, resurrection and ascension, together with the lives, transactions and sufferings of his holy evangelists, apostles, and other primitive martyrs, *also* A history of the jews; to which is added a continuation of the history of the jews to the present time by W: Patton. Ill. Bost. 1860. O.   232 : 20

Frothingham, Octavius Brooks. The cradle of the Christ; a study in primitive christianity. N. Y. 1877. D.   232 : 7

Fry, Caroline. Christ our example. 2d ed. N. Y. 1834 S.   232 : 6

Furness, W: H: Thoughts on the life and character of Jesus of Nazareth. Bost. 1859. D.   232 : 21

Geikie, Cunningham. The life and words of Christ. Rev. ed. N. Y. 1884. 2 v. D.   232 : 29

Gladstone, W: Ewart. "Ecce homo." Lond. 1868. D.   232 : 8

Harris, J: The great teacher; characteristics of our Lord's ministry. 16th amer. from the 10th Lond. rev. ed.; with an introd. essay by Heman Humphrey. Bost. 1859. D.   232 : 9

Horsley, S: Letters from the archdeacon of Saint Albans, in reply to dr. Priestley; with an app. containing short strictures on dr. Priestley's letters, by an unknown hand. Lond. 1784. O.   232 : 10

Hughes, T: The manliness of Christ. Bost. 1880. D.   232 : 11

Lang, H: Das leben Jesu und die kirche der zukunft. *In* Deutsche zeit- und streitfragen.   304 : 15 v1

Life of Christ, The, in the words of the evangelists; a complete harmony of the gospel history of our Saviour, for the use of young persons. Ill. N. Y. *n. d.* D.   232 : 23

Mozoomdar, Protap Chundar. The oriental Christ. Bost. 1883. O.   232 : 28

Parker, Joseph. Ecce Deus; essays on the life and doctrine of Jesus Christ; with controversial notes on "Ecce homo." [*Anon.*] Bost. 1867. S.   232 : 12

Parsons, Theophilus. Deus homo: God-man. Chicago. 1867. D.   232 : 13

Patrick, Symon. The glorious epiphany, with the devout christian's love to it. Lond. 1678. D.   232 : 26'

Pressensé, Edmond Marcellin Déhault de. Jesus Christ; his times, life and work. Tr. from the french by Annie Harwood. 4th ed. Lond. 1871. D.   232 : 27

Rabbi Jeshua; an eastern story. [*Anon.*] N. Y. 1881. D.   232 : 14

Renan, Joseph Ernest. The life of Jesus. Tr. from the original french by C. Edwin Wilbour. [Origins of christianity, 1.] N. Y. 1864. D.   232 : 24

Schaff, Philip. The person of Christ, the miracle of history; with a reply to Strauss and Renan, and a collection of testimonies of unbelievers. Bost. [1871]. S.   232 : 15

Seeley, J: Robert. Ecce homo; a survey of the life and work of Jesus Christ. [*Anon.*] Bost. 1867. S.   232 : 16

Strauss, D: F: Das leben Jesu, für das deutsche volk bearbeitet. 3e aufl. Leipz. 1874. O.   232+22

— *Same, eng.* The life of Jesus, critically examined. Tr. from the 4th german ed. by Marian Evans. N. Y. 1860. 2 v. O.   232 : 22

Tulloch, J: The Christ of the gospels and the Christ of modern criticism; lectures on M. Renan's Vie de Jésus. Lond. 1864. D.   232 : 17

Turnbull, Robert. Christ in history. New and rev. ed. Bost. 1860. D.   232 : 18

Veuillot, L: François. The life of our Lord Jesus Christ. Tr. into english by Anthony Farley, from the 7th french ed. N. Y. 1875. D.   232 : 25

Man.

Beecher, E: The conflict of ages, or The great debate on the moral relations of God and man. 5th ed. Bost. 1854. D.   233 : 1

Boston, T: Human nature in its fourfold state, of primitive integrity, entire depravation, begun recovery, and consummate happiness or misery, subsisting in the parents of mankind in paradise, the unregenerate, all mankind in the future state. A new ed.; prefixed, a recommendation by Michael Boston, the author's grandson. Falkirk. 1787. D.   233 : 2

Dewey, Orville. The problem of human destiny, or The end of providence in the world and man. 2d ed. N. Y. 1864. O.   233 : 3

Harris, J: Man primeval, or The constitution and primitive condition of the human being ; a contribution to theological science. Bost. 1852. D. **233 : 4**

Smith, Theyre Townsend. Man's responsibility in reference to his religious belief explained and examined. [Hulsean lectures. 1839.] Lond. 1840. O. **233 : 5**

Savage, Minot Judson. Beliefs about man. Bost. 1882. D. **233 : 6**

Wesley, J:, *and others.* Christian correspondence ; a collection of letters written by the late J: Wesley and several methodist preachers in connection with him to the late mrs. Eliza Bennis, with her answers ; chiefly explaining and enforcing the doctrine of sanctification ; now first pub. from the originals. Phila. 1809. S. **233 : 7**

Salvation.

Barnes, Albert. The way of salvation ; a sermon, del. at Morristown, N. J., feb. 8, 1829. 7th ed. Together with mr. Barnes' defence of the sermon, read before the synod of Philadelphia, at Lancaster, oct. 29, 1830, and his " Defence " before the second presbytery of Philadelphia, in reply to the charges of G: Junkin. N. Y. 1836. D. **234 : 2**

Blood, B: The philosophy of justice between God and man ; being an attempt to show from a candid examination of the scripture and the power of entities, that the existing philosophy of religion, both calvinistic and arminian, is opposed to the Bible and to reason. N. Y. 1851. D. **234 : 3**

Bushnell, Horace. Christ and his salvation ; in sermons variously related thereto. 3d ed. N. Y. 1865. D. **234 : 4**

— Forgiveness and law, grounded in principles interpreted by human analogies. N. Y. 1874. D. **234 : 5**

— The vicarious sacrifice, grounded in principles of universal obligation. N. Y. 1866. O. **234 : 6**

Edwards, Jonathan. The history of redemption, comprising a summary of the history of the jews up to the destruction of Jerusalem. Lond. 1831. T. **234 : 1**

Goode, Francis. The better covenant practically considered from Hebrews viii: 6, 10–12, with supp. on Philippians ii: 12, 13 ; with a pref. and table of contents by Herman Hooker. From the 2d Lond. ed. Phila. 1836. D. **234 : 7**

McIlvaine, C: Petit. Justification by faith ; a charge delivered before the clergy of the protestant episcopal church in the diocese of Ohio, sept. 13, 1839 ; with app. Columbus. 1840. S. **234 : 8**

Death and resurrection.

Cumming, J: The great consummation ; the millennial rest, or The world as it will be. 2d series. N. Y. 1864. D. **236 : 1**

Miller, W: Evidence from scripture and history of the second coming of Christ about the year 1843 ; exhibited in a course of lectures. Bost. 1840. S. **236 : 2**

Norton, James. [On eternity and resurrection.] *In his* Australian essays. **824.2 : 76**

Seiss, Joseph A: The last times and the great consummation ; an earnest discussion of momentous themes. 8th ed. Phila. 1864. D. **236 : 3**

Shimeall, R: C. Age of the world, as founded on the sacred records, historic and prophetic ; and the "Signs of the times", viewed in the aspect of premonitions of the speedy establishment on the earth of the millennial state, by the second personal, pre-millennial advent of Christ ; with an introd. essay, vindicating the claims of sacred chronology against the cavils of the atheist, antiquarian and infidel. N. Y. 1842. D. **236 : 4**

West, Gilbert. Observations on the history and evidences of the resurrection of Jesus Christ. N. Y. 1830. D. *With* **Leslie,** C: Method with the deists. **239 : 17**

Future state.

(See also Future life, col. 83.)

Beecher, E: History of opinions on the scriptural doctrine of retribution. N. Y. 1878. D. **237 : 1**

Branks, W: Life in heaven ; there, faith is changed into sight and hope is passed into blissful fruition. [*Anon.*] Bost. 1865. S. **237 : 4**

— Tabor's teachings, or The veil lifted ; a glimpse of Christ's glory and intercourse with his people forever. [*Anon.*] Edinb. 1865. S. **237 : 5**

Farrar, F: W: Eternal hope ; five sermons preached in Westminster abbey, nov. and dec. 1877. N. Y. 1878. D. **237 : 2**

Goodwin, T: A. The mode of man's immortality, or The when, where and how of the future life. N. Y. 1874. D. **237 : 3**

Mant, R: The happiness of the blessed, considered as to the particulars of their state, their recognition of each other in that state, its difference of degrees. Added, Musings on the church and her services. Phila. 1833. D. **237 : 6**

Sears, Edmund Hamilton. Athanasia, or Foregleams of immortality. 8th ed. Bost. 1867. D. **237 : 7**

Sherlock, W: A discourse concerning the happiness of good men and the punishment of the wicked in the next world. 6th ed. Glasgow. 1744. S. **237 : 8**

Smith, Uriah. The state of the dead and the destiny of the wicked. Battle Creek. 1878. D. **237 : 9**

Thompson, Hugh Miller. Eternal penalty ; nine essays from "The northwestern church". Chicago. 1865. D. **237 : 10**

Townsend, Luther Tracy. Lost forever. Bost. 1875. D. **237 : 11**

Watts, Isaac. The world to come, or Discourse on the joys or sorrows of departed souls at death, and the glory or terror of the resurrection. New ed., with port. of the author. Bungay. 1813. O. **237 : 12**

Note. See also several works, included in religious fiction, class 249.

Apologetics.

Alexander, Archibald, *ed.* The evidences of christianity. Phila. [1831]. 2 v. in 1. T.   **239 : 9**
<small>Contents. v. 1. **Alexander,** A. Preliminary discourse on the evidences of christianity, with a short account of the treatises which these vols. contain. —**Watson,** R: An apology for christianity.—**Watson,** R: An apology for the Bible.—**Jenyns,** Soame. View of the internal evidence of the christian religion.—**Leslie,** C: Short and easy method with the deists. 2. **Paley,** W: View of the evidences of christianity.</small>

Apologia, oder Verantwortung des christlichen concordi-buchs [herausg. von Timotheus Kirchner, Nicolaus Selneccer und Martinus Chemnitz]. Dresden. 1584. Q.   **23 : R**

Armstrong, G: D. The theology of christian experience ; designed as an exposition of the "common faith" of the church of God. N. Y. 1858. D.   **239 : 1**

Arnold, Matthew. Literature and dogma ; an essay toward a better apprehension of the Bible. Bost. 1874. D.   **239 : 3**

— God and the Bible ; a review of objections to "Literature and dogma." N. Y. 1875. D.   **239 : 2**

Barnes, Albert. Inquiries and suggestions in regard to the foundation of faith in the word of God. Phila. 1859. D.   **239 : 4**

— Lectures on the evidences of christianity in the 19th century, del. in the Mercer st. church, N. Y., jan. 21 to feb. 21, 1867, on the Ely foundation of the Union theological seminary. N. Y. 1868. D.   **239 : 5**

Butler, Joseph. The analogy of religion, natural and revealed, to the constitution and course of nature. Added, two brief dissertations : 1. On personal identity ; 2. On the nature of virtue, with an account of the character and writings of the author by S: Halifax. N. Y. *n. d.* O.   **239 : 6**

Christlieb, Theodor. Modern doubt and christian belief ; a series of apologetic lectures addressed to earnest seekers after truth. Tr., with the author's sanction, chiefly by H. U. Weitbrecht, and ed. by T. L. Kingsbury. N. Y. 1874. O.   **239 : 7**

Clark, T: March. Primary truths of religion. N. Y. 1869. D.   **239 : 8**

Fisher, G: Park. Essays on the supernatural origin of christianity, with special reference to the theories of Renan, Strauss and the Tübingen school. N. Y. 1866. O.   **239 : 10**

Fuller, Andrew. The gospel its own witness, or The holy nature and divine harmony of the christian religion, contrasted with the immorality and absurdity of deism. New Haven. 1801. S.   **239 : 11**

Gregory, Olinthus. Letters to a friend, on the evidences, doctrines and duties of the christian religion. From the 4th Lond. ed. rev. and slightly abridged. N. Y. *n. d.* D.   **239 : 12**

Groot (*lat.* Grotius), Hugo de. The truth of the christian religion ; in 6 books, corr. and ill. with notes by mr. [J:] Le Clerc [Johannes Clericus] ; to which is added a 7th book, concerning this question : What christian church we ought to join ourselves to ? by the said mr. Le Clerc. 11th

ed. with add., particularly one whole book of mr. Le Clerc's against indifference of what religion a man is of. Done into english by J: Clarke. Lond. 1800. D.   **239 : 13**

Guizot, François P: Guillaume. Meditations on the essence of christianity, and on the religious questions of the day. Tr. from the french, under the superintendence of the author. N. Y. 1865. D.   **239 : 14**
<small>Contents. Preface.—Natural problems. — Christian dogmas.—The supernatural.—The limits of science.—Revelation.—The inspiration of the scriptures.—God according to the Bible.—Jesus Christ according to the gospel.—Note.</small>

Keith, Alexander. Demonstration of the truth of the christian religion. *T. p. w.* [Edinb. 1838.] D.   **239 : 15**

— Evidence of the truth of the christian religion, derived from the literal fulfilment of prophecy ; particularly as ill. by the history of the jews, and by the discoveries of recent travellers. From the 6th Edinb. ed. N. Y. 1832. D.   **239 : 16**

Leslie, C: A short and easy method with the deists, wherein the certainty of the christian religion is demonstrated by infallible proof, from four rules, which are incompatible with any imposture that ever yet has been, or can possibly be ; in a letter to a friend, with a letter from the author to a deist, upon his conversion by reading his book. N. Y. 1830. D.   **239 : 17**

McCosh, James. Christianity and positivism ; a series of lectures to the times on natural theology and apologetics. del. in New York, jan. 16 to march 20, 1871, on the Ely foundation of the Union theological seminary. N. Y. 1871. D.   **239 : 18**

McIlvaine, C: Pettit. The evidences of christianity in their external division, exhibited in a course of lectures del. in Clinton hall in the winter of 1831-2, under the appointment of the university of the city of New York. N. Y. 1832. O.   **239 : 19**

Mansel, H: Longueville. The limits of religious thought examined in eight lectures del. before the university of Oxford in the year 1858, on the Bampton foundation. 1st amer. ed., with the notes tr. Bost. 1866. D.   **239 : 20**

Martineau, James. Studies of christianity, or Timely thoughts for religious thinkers ; a series of papers, ed. by W: R. Alger. Bost. 1866. D.   **239 : 21**

Paley, W: Evidences of christianity ; with a life of the author. N. Y. 1824. T.   **239 : 22**

Porteus, Beilby. A summary of the principal evidences for the truth and divine origin of the christian revelation, designed chiefly for the use of young persons. N. Y. 1850. Tt.   **239 : 23**

Potter, Alonzo, *ed.* Lectures on the evidences of christianity, del. by clergymen of the protestant episcopal church, in the fall and winter of 1853-4 ; with an introd. essay by Alonzo Potter. Phila. 1855. O.   **239 : 24**
<small>Contents. **Potter,** Alonzo, Introduction: Apologetics.—**Littlejohn,** Abram N. The philosophy of religion.—**Harwood,** Edwin. Philosophical scepticism.—**Mason,** C: On miracles.—**Potter,** Alonzo. Immutability of natural laws.—**Howe,** M. A. De W. Physical theory of development. — **Atkinson,** T: Ecclesiastical development.—**Fuller,** S: Rationalistic development.—**Kerfoot,** J: B. The inspiration</small>

of the holy scriptures.—**Butler**, C: M. Analogies between God's world and word.—**Minnegerode**, C: Relation of the objective and subjective factors in revelation.—**Burgess**, G: The modern necromancy no argument against the gospel.—**Vinton**, Francis. Socialism.—**Vinton**, A. H. Science and revelation.—**Hopkins**, J: H: Historical evidences of christianity.—**Bedell**, Gregory T. Internal evidences of christianity.—Extract from bishop Potter's address to the diocese of Penn., may 1854.

Rogers, H: The eclipse of faith, or A visit to a religious sceptic. 7th ed. [*Anon.*] Bost. 1858. D.   **239 : 33**

Newman, Francis W: The reply to "The eclipse of faith," together with his chapter on "The moral perfection of Jesus," repr. from the 3d ed. of "Phases of faith." *In* **Rogers**, H: Defence of The eclipse of faith.   **239 : 25**

Rogers, H: A defence of "The eclipse of faith," by its author ; being a rejoinder to professor Newman's Reply. Bost. 1856. D.   **239 : 25**

Savage, Minot Judson. Christianity the science of manhood ; a book for questioners. 3d ed. Bost. 1875. D.   **239 : 26**

Savage, W. H. An address on the intellectual basis of faith. *With* **Savage**, M. J. Belief in God.   **231 : 7**

Sewell, W: Popular evidences of christianity. Lond. 1843. S.   **239 : 27**

Taylor, I: Lectures on spiritual christianity. N. Y. 1841. D.   **239 : 28**

Tupper, Martin Farquhar. Probabilities ; an aid to faith. N. Y. 1848. D.   **239 : 29**

Watson, R: An apology for the Bible, in a series of letters addressed to T: Paine, author of a book entitled The age of reason ; part 2, being an investigation of true and fabulous theology. 3d ed. Lond. 1796. S.   **239 : 30**

Watts, I: A rational defence of the gospel ; with a pref. by A. Alexander. N. Y. 1831. D.   **239 : 31**

Whately, R: Historic doubts relative to Napoleon Buonaparte, and historic certainties respecting the early history of America. N. Y. 1860. S.   **239 : 32**

5. Practical and devotional theology.

1. Practical.

Didactic.

Apostolic fathers. Genuine epistles of the apostolic fathers, St. Clement, St. Polycarp, St. Ignatius, St. Barnabas ; the shepherd of Hermas and the martyrdoms of St. Ignatius and St. Polycarp, written by those who were present at their sufferings ; being, together with the holy scriptures of the New testament, a complete collection of the most primitive antiquity for about 150 years after Christ. Tr. by William, archbishop of Canterbury, with prelim. discourses relating to the several treatises here put together by the same author, arr. by W. Adams ; added, biographical notices of the lives of St. Clement, St. Polycarp, St. Ignatius and St. Barnabas, abridged from Cave's Lives of the primitive fathers, from a late London ed. Hartford. 1836. O.   **241 : 5**

Adams, *Mrs.* —. Daily duties inculcated in a series of letters, addressed to the wife of a clergyman. Bost. 1835. S.   **241 : 1**

Clark, Alexander. Workday christianity, or The gospel in the trades ; with an introd. note by W: Cullen Bryant. Phila. 1871. D.   **241 : 2**

Constantin, Léon, *and* P: **Fournier.** Nouveau traité des devoirs du chrétien envers Dieu, [*Anon.*] ; chaque chapitre et chaque article suivis de traits historiques analogues aux vérités qui y sont traitées, par F. P. B. 26 me éd. Montréal. 1861. S.   **241 : 16**

Cyprianus, Thascius Cæcilius. The treatises of St. Cæcilius Cyprian, bishop of Carthage and martyr, tr. with notes and indices. [Library of the fathers, no. 3]. Oxford. 1846. O.   **241 : 3**

Edwards, Jonathan. A treatise on the religious affections. Lond. *n. d.* T.   **241 : 4**

Gurney, Joseph J: Essay on the habitual exercise of love to God, considered as a preparation for heaven. N. Y. [1842]. S.   **241 : 6**

Guthrie, W: The christian's great interest, or The trial of a saving interest in Christ, and and the way to attain it ; with an introd. essay by T: Chalmers. Phila. 1840. S.   **241 : 7**

Harris, J: Mammon, or Covetousness the sin of the christian church. Bost. 1836. D.   **241 : 8**

James, J: Angell. The christian professor addressed in a series of counsels and cautions to the members of christian churches. 2d ed. N. Y. 1838. S.   **241 : 9**

Mason, J: A treatise on self knowledge ; showing the nature and benefit of that important science and the way to attain it, intermixed with various reflections and observations on human nature. 4th ed. with notes. N. Y. 1824. S.   **241 : 10**

Philip, Robert. The Hannahs, or Maternal influence on sons. N. Y. 1841. S.   **241 : 11**

— The Lydias, or The development of female character. [The lady's closet library.] 4th ed. Lond. 1840. S.   **241 : 12**

Spring, Gardiner. The contrast between good and bad men, ill. by the biography and truths of the Bible. N. Y. 1855. 2 v. D.   **922.6 : 17**

Spurgeon, C: Haddon. Illustrations and meditations, or Flowers from a puritan's garden, distilled and dispensed by C. H. Spurgeon. N. Y. [1883]. D.   **241 : 17**

Wilberforce, W: A practical view of the prevailing religious system of professed christians in the higher and middle classes in this country, contrasted with the real christianity. 10th ed. Lond. 1811. O.   **241 : 14**

Meditative.

Beauties of sacred literature ; a compendium of christian doctrine, faith and practice, sel. from various authors, ed. by a lay member of the protestant episcopal church. N. Y. 1864. D. **242 : 1**

Beveridge, W: Private thoughts upon religion and a christian life. N. Y. 1857. 2 v. S. **242 : 2**

Cecil, R: A friendly visit to the house of mourning, with app. N. Y. 1831. Tt. **242 : 3**

Coleridge, S: Taylor. Aids to reflection ; with a preliminary essay by James Marsh. From the 4th London ed. with the author's last corr., ed. by H: Nelson Coleridge. Burlington. 1840. O. **242 : 4**

Collier, Robert Laird. Meditations on the essence of christianity. Bost. 1876. D. **242 : 5**

Doddridge, Philip. Thoughts on sacramental occasions ; with an introd. by James W. Alexander. Phila. 1858. S. **242 : 7**

Fénelon, François de Salignac de la Mothe. Reflections and meditations selected from [his] writings ; with a memoir of his life by J. K. G. Hassard, and an introd. by T: S. Preston. N. Y. 1865. D. **242 : 8**

Fuller, T: Good thoughts in bad times, and other papers. Bost. 1863. D. **242 : 9**
Contents. Good thoughts in bad times. — Good thoughts in worse times.—Mixt contemplations in better times.—The cause and cure of a wounded conscience.—Conclusion.

Giles, H: Christian thought on life ; in a series of discourses. 2d ed. Bost. 1851. D. **242 : 10**

Greenwell, Dora. The patience of hope, by the author of "A present heaven"; with an introd. by J: G. Whittier. Bost. 1864. D. **242 : 11**

— Two friends, by the author of "The patience of hope" and "A present heaven". Bost. 1863. D. **242 : 12**

Hervey, James. Meditations and contemplations ; prefixed, the life of the author. Bost. 1857. D. **242 : 13**

Hinton, James. The mystery of pain ; a book for the sorrowful. N. Y. 1872. S. **242 : 14**

Homar, *hermit.* Consolation from Homar, an hermit of the east. Added, a soliloquy by W: Smith. Newport, R. I. 1789. S. **242 : 6**

Juliana, *Mother.* Sixteen revelations of divine love made to a devout servant of our Lord, called Mother Juliana, an anchorete of Norwich, who lived in the days of king Edward III. Bost. 1864. D. **242 : 15**

Kelly, Denis. Self inspection. Lond. 1845. S. **242 : 16**

Meikle, James. Solitude sweetened, or Miscellaneous meditations on various religious subjects, written in distant parts of the world. N. Y. 1849. D. **242 : 23**

Molinos, Miguel. Golden thoughts from The spiritual guide of Miguel Molinos, the quietist ; with a pref. by J. H: Shorthouse. N. Y. 1883. D. **242 : 25**

Mountford, W: Euthanasy, or Happy talk toward the end of life. 4th ed., with add. Bost. 1852. D. **242 : 24**

Parkman, Francis, *ed.* An offering of sympathy to the afflicted, especially to bereaved parents. New ed., rev. with add. by F: A. Farley. N. Y. 1863. D. **242 : 17**

Sewell, Elizabeth Missing. Passing thoughts on religion. N. Y. 1865. S. **242 : 18**

Spiritual voices from the middle ages ; consisting of a selection of abstracts from the writings of the fathers adapted for the hour of meditation, and concluding with a biographical notice of their lives. Lond. 1865. S. **242 : 19**

Sturm, Christoph Christian. Reflections on the being and attributes of God, and on his works, both in nature and providence, for every day in the year. Originally compiled in german ; corr., tr., methodized and greatly enl. by Adam Clarke. Lond. 1854. 2 v. D. **242 : 20**

Taylor, I: Saturday evening, by the author of Natural history of enthusiasm. N. Y. 1832. D. **242 : 21**

Zschokke, J: H: Daniel. Meditations on death and eternity. Tr. from the german by Fredrica Rowan. Bost. 1863. D. **242 : 22**

Hortatory.

Abbott, J: Stevens Cabot. Practical christianity ; a treatise specially designed for young men. N. Y. 1862. S. **243 : 8**

Alleine, Joseph. An alarm to unconverted sinners, in a serious treatise on conversion ; rev. and abridged. N. Y. [1834]. S. **243 : 2**

Baxter, R: A call to the unconverted to turn and live. N. Y. 1853. S. **243 : 3**

Doddridge, Philip. Rise and progress of religion in the soul. Liverpool. *n. d.* Tt. **243 : 4**

Eliot, W: Greenleaf. Lectures to young men. 4th ed. Bost. 1854. D. **243 : 5**

Faber, F: W: Growth in holiness, or The progress of the spiritual life. With the approbation of J: N. Neumann. 8th amer. ed. Balt. 1866. D. **243 : 6**

Fletcher, Maria Jane, *born* Jewsbury. Letters to the young. Bost. 1835. D. **243 : 10**

Fuller, T: The holy and profane states ; with some account of the author and his writings. Bost. 1864. S. **243 : 7**

Hahn-Hahn, Ida Marie Louise Sophie Friederike Gustave *gräfin.* Aus Jerusalem. Mainz. 1851. S. **243 : 1**

James, J: Angell. Pastoral addresses, chiefly on the subject of christian duty. N. Y. 1852. S. **243 : 9**

Joceline, Elizabeth. The mother's legacie to her unborne childe ; repr. from the ed. of 1625, with a biographical and historical introd. Edinb. 1853. T. **243 : 11**

Lacordaire, J: Baptiste H: Dominique *abbé.* Letters to young men ; a complement to his life by the count de Montalembert. Tr. by James Trenor. Lond. 1865. O. **243 : 12**

Law, W: A serious call to a devout and holy life, adapted to the state and condition of all orders of christians. New ed., to which is added the life of the author. Thetford. 1809. O. **243 : 13**

Pike, J: Godfrey. A guide for young disciples of the holy Saviour in their way to immortality; forming a sequel to "Persuasives to early piety". Abridged. N. Y. *n. d.* S.
243 : 23

Sancroft, W: The new whole duty of man, containing the faith as well as practice of a christian; made easy for the practice of the present age, as the old Whole duty of man was designed for those unhappy times in which it was written; and supplying the articles of the christian faith which are wanting in that book, tho' essentially necessary to salvation. Necessary for all families and authorized by the king's most excellent majesty; with devotions proper for several occasions, also a help to reading the scriptures. Lond. 1798. O. 243 : 14

Spiritual progress, or Instructions in the divine life of the soul, intended for such as are desirous to count all things but loss that they may win Christ. Pt. 1, ed. by James W. Metcalf. N. Y. 1855. D. 243 : 15

Contents. Christian counsel, by Fénelon.—Spiritual letters, by Fénelon. — Method of prayer, by mad. Guyon.—Concise view of the way to God, by mad. Guyon.—Spiritual maxims, by père la Combe.

Sprague, W: Buell. Lectures to young people; with an introd. address by S: Miller. 3d amer. ed. N. Y. 1835. D. 243 : 16

Spring, Gardiner. Fragments from the study of a pastor; v. 1. N. Y. 1839. D. 243 : 17

Thomas à Kempis, [Hæmmerlein, *lat.* Malleolus]. The imitation of Christ. Rendered into english from the original latin by J: Payne; with an introd. essay by T: Chalmers, ed. by Howard Malcolm. A new improved ed., with a life of the author by C. Ullmann. Bost. 1859. D. 243 : 18

Tweedie, W: King. Home; a book for the family circle. Springfield, Mass. 1869. D.
243 : 19

— Man and his money; its use and abuse. Lond. 1855. D. 243 : 20

Upham, T: Cogswell. Religious maxims having a connection with the doctrines and practice of holiness. 2d ed. with add. Phila. 1854. S. 243 : 21

Williams, Roger. Experiments of spiritual life and health, and their preservatives, in which the weakest child of God may get assurance of his spiritual life and blessednesse, and the strongest may finde proportionable discoveries of his christian growth and the means of it. Lond. printed in the second month 1652; repr. Providence, 1863. O. 243 : 22

2. Devotional.

Ritual.

Butterworth, Hezekiah. The story of the notable prayers of christian history. Bost. [1880]. D. 244 : 1

Paley, W: Clergyman's companion in visiting the sick; containing, Rules for visiting the sick, The office for the visitation of the sick, The communion of the sick, Occasional prayers for the sick, Offices of public and private baptism. *With his* Horæ paulinæ. 227.4 : 1

Porter, J: The churchman's family prayer book, compiled from the most approved ancient and modern formularies. Prefixed, an essay on the nature and obligations of family religion by T: Best. Lond. [1856]. O. 244 : 2

Homilies. Certaine sermons or homilies appointed to be read in churches in the time of queen Elizabeth. Lond. 1640. Q. 23 : R

Hymnology.

Belcher, Joseph. Historical sketches of hymns, their writers, and their influence. Phila. 1859. D. 245 : 1

Havergal, W: H: A history of the old hundredth psalm tune with specimens; with a pref. note by J. M. Wainwright. N. Y. 1854. O. 245+2

Hymns of the ages; selections from Lyra catholica, germanica apostolica, and other sources; with an introd. by F. D. Huntington. 1st-3d ser. Bost. 1865. 3 v. D.
245 : 3

Kurssati, F., *ed.* Pagérintos giesmjû-knygos, kuriosè brangiáusios sénos in naûjos giesmès surassytos Diewui ant Garbês ir prúsû karalistêje ésantiemsiems lietûwininkams ant dûssiû issgánimo podraûg su maldûknygomis, kuriosè ne tiktày sénos, bet ir naûjos máldos ràndamos yrà. Iss naûjo pérweizdêtos. Königsberg. 1865. S.
245 : 7

Palmer, *Sir* Roundell, *earl of Selborne, ed.* The book of praise, from the best english hymn-writers. Cambridge. 1864. S.
245 : 4

Tupper, Martin Farquhar. A hymn for all nations, 1851. Tr. into 30 languages, upwards of 50 versions; the music composed expressly by S. Sebastian Wesley. Lond. 1851. O. 245 : 5

White, R: Grant. National hymns, how they are written and how they are not written; a lyric and national study for the times. N. Y. 1861. O. 245 : 6

Zabúr aur git Khudá ki' ibádat ke liye. Iláhábád [Allahabad]. 1872. S. 245 : 8

Worship.

Bickersteth, E: H: Sabbath evenings at home, or The christian life ill. by scripture images. Lond. 1855. T. 247 : 1

Bogatsky, C: H: v. Golden treasury for the children of God. Lond. 1850. Tt. 248 : 1

Prime, S: Irenæus. Five years of prayer, with the answers. N. Y. 1864. D. 247 : 2

Zittel, Emil. Der protestantische gottesdienst in unserer zeit. *In* Deutsche zeit- und streit-fragen. 304 : 15 v4

3. Religious fiction and anecdote.

Abbott, Edwin Abbott. Philochristus; memoirs of a disciple of the Lord. [*Anon.*] 2d ed. Bost. 1876. S. 249 : 10

— Onesimus; memoirs of a disciple of St. Paul, by the author of Philochristus. Bost. 1882. S. 249 : 9

Abbott, Jacob. The young christian, or A familiar illustration of the principles of christian duty. N. Y. 1833. D.   **249 : 2**

— The way to do good, or The christian character mature ; sequel to The young christian and Corner-stone. Bost. 1836. D.   **249 : 1**

Adams, W: Sacred allegories. Leipz. 1864. S.   **x249 : 14**

   Contents. Memoir of the author.—The shadow of the cross.—The distant hills.—The old man's home.—The king's messengers.

Bunyan, J: The pilgrim's progress from this world to that which is to come ; containing his authenticated third part, "The travels of the ungodly," collated for the first time with the early ed. and the phraseology of all his works, with ill. notes by T: Scott ; containing also an essay on the life and writings of Bunyan by Josiah Conder. Phila. 1847. O.   **249 : 3**

— The pilgrim's progress from this world to that which is to come ; with a memoir and notes by G: Offor. Ill. N. Y. [1883]. O.   **249 : 3**

Cheever, G: Barrell. Lectures on the Pilgrim's progress, and on the life and times of John Bunyan. 8th ed. N. Y. 1849. D.   **249 : 4**

Clarke, James Freeman. The legend of Thomas Didymus, the jewish sceptic. Bost. 1881. D.   **249 : 19**

Gladden, Washington. The christian league of Connecticut. N. Y. [1883]. D.   **249 : 13**

   x denotes books specially adapted for children.

Hackett, Horatio Balch. Christian memorials of the war, or Scenes and incidents, illustrative of religious faith and principle, patriotism and bravery in our army, with historical notes. Bost. 1864. D.   **249 : 5**

Ingraham, Joseph Holt. The pillar of fire. *T. p. w.* D.   **249 : 20**

Island of life, The ; an allegory by a clergyman. New ed. Bost. 1853. D.   **249 : 6**

Monod, Adolphe. Lucilla, or The reading of the Bible. Tr. from the french. New ed. Lond. [1883]. D.   **249 : 16**

Oliphant, Margaret O., *born* Wilson. A little pilgrim. Rep. from Macmillan's magazine. Bost. 1882. S.   **249 : 11**

— Old lady Mary ; a story of the seen and the unseen. [*Anon.*] Bost. 1884. S.   **249 : 17**

Phelps, Elizabeth Stuart. Beyond the gates. Bost. 1883. D.   **249 : 12**

— The gates ajar. *T. p. w.* S.   **249 : 21**

Sheepfold and common, The, or The evangelical rambler. N. Y. 1859. D.   **249 : 7**

Thisted, Waldemar Adolph, (*M. Rowel, Emanuel St. Hermidad, Herodion, Hortulanus*). Letters from hell. Given in english by L. W. J. S., with a preface by G: Macdonald. [*Anon.*] Lond. 1885. D.   **249 : 18**

Wallace, Lewis. Ben-Hur ; a tale of the Christ. N. Y. 1880. S.   **W 301**

Warner, Susan. The word ; walks from Eden. N. Y. 1866. S.   **249 : 8**

Wilberforce, S: The prophet's guard. N. Y. 1846. T.   **249 : 15**

6.   Pastoral theology.

1.   Homiletics.

Baxter, R: The reformed pastor ; showing the nature of the pastoral work, abridged by T: Rutherford. N. Y. 1821. T.   **251 : 1**

Gresley, W: Ecclesiastes anglicanus ; a treatise on preaching, as adopted to a church of England congregation, in a series of letters to a young clergyman. 1st amer. from the 2d eng. ed., with supp. notes, coll. and arr. by B: I. Haight. N. Y. 1843. D.   **251 : 2**

Hall, J: God's word through preaching ; the Lyman Beecher lectures before the theological department of Yale college, 4th ser. N. Y. 1875. D.   **251 : 3**

Murray, Nicholas, (*Kirwan.*) Preachers and preaching. N. Y. 1860. D.   **251 : 4**

Parker, Joseph. Ad clerum ; advices to a young preacher. Bost. 1871. D.   **251 : 5**

Phelps, Austin. Men and books, or Studies in homiletics ; lectures introductory to the theory of preaching. N. Y. 1882. D.   **251 : 10**

Plumer, W: Swan. Hints and helps in pastoral theology. N. Y. 1874. D.   **251 : 6**

Spring, Gardiner. The power of the pulpit, or Thoughts addressed to christian ministers and those who hear them. N. Y. 1848. O.   **251 : 7**

Sumner, J: Bird. Apostolical preaching considered in an examination of St. Paul's epistles. 1st amer. ed. N. Y. 1830. D.   **251 : 8**

— Four sermons on subjects relating to the christian ministry ; and preached on different occasions. *In his* Apostolical preaching.   **251 : 8**

Tyng, Stephen Higginson. The office and duty of a christian pastor. N. Y. 1874. D. **251 : 9**

2.   Sermons.

Fish, H: Clay. History and repository of pulpit eloquence, deceased divines. The masterpieces of Bossuet, Bourdaloue.... etc., with discourses from Chrysostom, Basil....and others among the Fathers, and from Wickliffe, Luther....etc., of the reformers, also sixty other celebrated sermons from as many eminent divines in the greek and latin, english, german, irish, french, scottish, american and welsh churches, a large number of which have now, for the first time, been tr.; the whole arr. in their proper order, and accompanied with historical sketches of preaching in the different countries represented, and biographical and critical notices of the several preachers and their discourses. N. Y. 1857. 2 v. O.   **252+26**

   Contents. V. 1. The greek and latin pulpit: Tertullian; Cyprian; Athanasius; Cyril; Gregory Nazianzen; Basil, the great; Chrysostom; Augustine.—

Fish, H: Clay.—*Continued.*

The english pulpit: J: Wickliffe; Hugh Latimer; J: Jewell; J: Donne; Joseph Hall; T: Adams; W: Chillingworth; R: Baxter; J: Bunyan; J: Howe; J: Tillotson; I: Barrow; Robert South; B: Keach; Francis Atterbury; J: Wesley; G: Whitfield; Robert Robinson; Robert Hall; W: Jay; J: Foster; R: Watson.—The german pulpit: Luther; Melanchthon; Spener; Zollikofer; Herder; Reinhard; Scheiermacher; Harms; Theremin.—The irish pulpit: Jeremy Taylor; Walter Blake Kirwan; Alexander Carson; C: Wolfe. 2. The french pulpit: Calvin; Bossuet; Bourdaloue; Flechier; La Rue; Fénélon; Abbadie; Superville; Massillon; Saurin; Vinet.—The scottish pulpit: J: Knox; Ralph Erskine; J: M'Laurin; Robert Walker; Hugh Blair; J: Logan; T: M'Crie; T: Chalmers; E: Irving.—The american pulpit: T: Hooker; Cotton Mather; Jonathan Edwards; S: Davies; J: Livingston; W: White; J: Léland; Jonathan Maxcy; E: D. Griffin; J: M. Mason; W: Staughton; Gregory T. Bedell; Stephen Olin; J: Summerfield; Bela B. Edwards; Albert B. Dod.—The welsh pulpit: D: Charles; Christmas Evans; J: Elias.

— Pulpit eloquence of the 19th century, supplementary to the History and repository of pulpit eloquence, deceased divines, and containing discourses of eminent living ministers in Europe and America, with sketches biographical and descriptive; with an introd. essay by Edwards A. Park. N. Y. 1857. O.   252 : 27

Contents. The german pulpit: F: A: G. Tholuck; Julius Müller; C: A. Harless; C: Immanuel Nitzsch; Rudolf Stier; F: W: Krummacher; W. Hoffmann; Emil W. Krummacher; Philip Schaff.—The french pulpit: J. H. Merle D'Aubigné; S. R. L. Gaussen; Cæsar Malan; Adolphe Monod; J. H. Grandpierre; Athanase Coquerel; W: Monod; J. J. Audebez.—The american pulpit: W: R. Williams; Albert Barnes; Robert J. Breckenridge; J: McClintock; M: Hopkins; G: W. Bethune; Alonzo Potter; F: D. Huntington; R: Fuller; T: H. Skinner; Eliphalet Nott; J: P. Durbin; Lyman Beecher; James Romeyn; C: Pettit McIlvaine; Francis Wayland; G: F. Pierce; R: S. Storrs, *jr.*—The english pulpit: H: Melvill; J: A. James; Baptist W. Noel; Jabez Bunting; Hugh McNeill; T: Binney; W: Arthur; C: H. Spurgeon.—The scotch pulpit: T: Guthrie; Alexander Duff; J: Caird; J: McFarlane; J: Cumming; James Buchanan; Robert S. Candlish; James Hamilton.—The irish pulpit: H: Cooke; R: Whately; Alexander King; Robert Irving.—The welsh pulpit: W: Roberts; W: Rees; T: Aubrey.

English pulpit, The; collection of sermons by the most eminent living divines of England. N. Y. 1854. O.   252+25

Contents. Jabez Bunting.—C. J. Bloomfield.—James Parsons.—F. J. Jobson.—T. Raffles.—James Hamilton.—Daniel Moore.—J: A. James.—Jabez Burns.—J. E. Beaumont.—E: Parsons.—Joseph Wolff.—D. E. Ford.—W: Atherton.—Isaiah Birt.—W: Jay.—C: Bradley.—W. M. Bunting.—R. W. Hamilton.—J. Bennett.—James Bromley.—H: Melvill.—Robert Newton.—Alex. Fletcher.—Timothy East.—James Sherman.—J. Belcher.—B. W. Noel.—J: Cumming.—Robert Young.—T. Adkins.—Timothy Gibson.

Scotch sermons, 1880. N. Y. 1881. D. 252 : 50

Contents. 23 sermons by J: Caird; J. Cunningham; D. J. Ferguson; W: Knight; W. Mackintosh; W. L. M'Farlan; Allan Menzies; T. Nicoll; T. Rain; A. Semple; J. Stevenson; Patrick Stevenson; R. H. Story.

Thornton, J: Wingate, *ed.* The pulpit of the american revolution, or The political sermons of the period of 1776; with a historical introd., notes and ill. Bost. 1860. D.   252 : 64

Contents. Historical introd.—Dr. Mayhew's sermon of jan. 30, 1750.—Dr. Chauncy's thanksgiving sermon on the repeal of the stamp act, 1766.—Mr. Cooke's election sermon, 1770.—Mr. Gordon's thanksgiving sermon, 1774.— Dr. Langdon's election sermon at Watertown, 1775.—Mr. West's election sermon, 1776.—Mr. Payson's election sermon, 1778.—Mr. Howard's election sermon, 1780.—Dr. Stile's election sermon, 1783.

Moore, Frank, *ed.* The patriot preachers of the american revolution, with biographical sketches. N. Y. 1862. D.   252 : 75

Contents. Jonathan Mayhew; The snare broken.—S: Langdon; Government corrupted by vice.—Jacob Duche; The duty of standing fast in our spiritual and temporal liberties.—W: Smith; Present situation of american affairs.—J: Joachim Zubly; The law of liberty.—J: Hurt; The love of country.—W: Gordon; The separation of the jewish tribes.—Nathaniel Whitaker; An antidote against toryism.—Oliver Hart; Dancing exploded.—S: Stillman; Sermon before the council and house of representatives of the state of Mass. Bay.—D: Tappan; Sermon occasioned by the ratification of peace between Great Britain and the U. S.—J: Rodgers; The divine goodness displayed in the american revolution.—G: Duffield; Sermon on the restoration of peace.

* * *

Alford, H: Meditations in advent, on creation and providence. Lond. 1865. S.   252 : 1

Augustinus Aurelius, *St.* Seventeen short treatises of S. Augustine, bishop of Hippo, tr. with notes and indices. [Library of the fathers, no. 22.] Oxford. 1847. O.   252 : 2

Baker, Francis Aloysius (*originally* Asbury). Sermons; with a memoir of his life by A. F. Hewit. 2d ed. N. Y. 1866. O.   252 : 3

Beecher, H: Ward. Freedom and war; discourses on topics suggested by the times. Bost. 1863. D.   252 : 4

— Lecture-room talks; a series of familiar discourses on themes of general christian experience. N. Y. 1870. D.   252 : 5

Bethune, A. N. Lectures upon historical portions of the Old testament. N. Y. 1857. D.   252 : 6

Beveridge, W: Twenty-six sermons on various subjects, selected from [his] works. [Society for promoting christian knowledge.] Lond. 1850. O.   252 : 7

Blair, Hugh. Sermons; prefixed, the life and character of the author by James Finlayson. Complete in 1 v. N. Y. 1859. O.   252+8

Boston, T: The crook in the lot, or A display of the sovereignty and wisdom of God in the afflictions of men, and the christian's deportment under them. Phila. 1839. S.   252 : 9

Boyd, Andrew Kennedy Hutchinson. Counsel and comfort spoken from a city pulpit. Bost. 1864. D.   252 : 10

— The graver thoughts of a country parson. Bost. 1863. D.   252 : 11

Brace, C: Loring. Short sermons to news boys; with a history of the formation of the News boys' lodging house. N. Y. 1866. D.   252 : 12

Bullinger, H: The decades. Tr. by H. I. 1st and 2nd decades, ed. for the Parker society by T: Harding. Cambridge. 1849. O.   252 : 13

Butler, Clement Moore. St. Paul in Rome; lectures del. in the legation of the U. S. of America in Rome. Phila. 1865. D. 252 : 14

Chalmers, T: Sermons and discourses; now completed by the introd. of his posthumous sermons. N. Y. 1858. 2 v. O.   252+15

Chrysostomus, J:, *St.* The homilies of S. John Chrysostom, archbishop of Constantinople, on the epistles of St. Paul, the apostle, to Timothy, Titus and Philemon; tr. with notes and indices. [Library of the fathers, no. 12.] Cambridge. 1853. O.   252 : 16

Churchill, C: Sermons on the Lord's prayer. *In his* Works. 820.2 : 6 v4
Collier, Robert Laird. Every-day subjects in sunday sermons. Bost. 1870. D. 252 : 17
Collyer, Robert. The life that now is; sermons. Bost. 1871. S. 252 : 18
— Nature and life; sermons. Bost. 1867. S. 252 : 19
Coxe, Arthur Cleveland. Sermons on doctrine and duty. 2d ed. Phila. 1856. D. 252 : 76
Cyrillus *Hierosolymitanus*. The catechetical lectures of S. Cyril of Jerusalem, tr. with notes and indices. [Library of the fathers, no. 2.] Oxford. 1845. O. 252 : 20
Davies, S: Sermons on important subjects. Bost. 1810. O. 252 : 21
Drummond, James. Thoughts for the christian life; with an introd. by J. G. Holland. N. Y. 1864. D. 252 : 22
Dudley, J: Langford. Tides and tendencies of religious thought. Phila. 1873. D. 252 : 23
— [Sermons. Milw. 1870-72.] O. 252 : 24
Frothingham, Octavius Brooks. The rising and the setting faith, and other discourses. N. Y. 1878. D. 252 : 28
Contents. The mission of the radical preacher.—The rising and the setting faith.—The unbelief of the believers.—Why does the popular religion prevail?—Formal religion and life.—The sectarian spirit. The dogma of hell.—The higher sentiments. — Attitudes of unbelief.—The office of prayer. — The american gentleman.—The american lady.
— Visions of the future, and other discourses. N. Y. 1879. O. 252 : 29
Contents. Life as test of creed.—The inspiration of scripture.—Morals and religion.—Religion and immortality. — The consolations of rationalism. — The demand of the age on religion. — The demand of religion on the age.—The practical value of belief in God.—The real God.—The popular religion.—The new song.—Visions of the future.
Goulburn, E: Meyrick. Thoughts on personal religion; a treatise on the christian life in its two chief elements, devotion and practice. 4th amer. ed.; with a prefatory note by G: H. Houghton. N. Y. 1866. S. 252 : 30
Guthrie, T: The gospel in Ezekiel, ill. in a series of discourses. N. Y. 1859. D. 252 : 31
Hitchcock, E: Religious lectures on peculiar phenomena in the four seasons : 1. The resurrections of spring; 2. The triumphal arch of summer; 3. The euthanasia of autumn; 4. The coronation of winter; del. to the students in Amherst college in 1845 —1849. 3d ed. Bost. 1853. D. 252 : 32
Hobart, J: H:, *bp. of New York.* Posthumous works, with a memoir of his life by W: Berrian. N. Y. 1832, 1833. 3 v. O. 252 : 33
Contents. V. 1. Berrian, W: Memoir. 2, 3. Sermons.
Hopkins, M: Teachings and counsels; twenty baccalaureate sermons, with a discourse on president Garfield. N. Y. 1884. D. 252 : 88
Huntington, F: Dan. Sermons for the people. 3d ed. Bost. 1856. D. 252 : 34
Kingsley, C: Discipline, and other sermons. (Works, v. 27). Lond. 1881. D. 252 : 83
— The good news of God; sermons. (Works, v. 24). Lond. 1881. D. 252 : 80
— The gospel of the Pentateuch; a set of p is sermons, *and* David; five sermons. (Works, v. 25). Lond. 1878. D. 252 : 81

Kingsley, C:—*Continued.*
— Sermons for the times. (Works, v. 23). Lond. 1880. D. 252 : 79
— *Same.* N. Y. 1858. D. 252 : 79
— Sermons on national subjects. (Works, v. 22). Lond. 1880. D. 252 : 78
— Village sermons, *and* Town and country sermons. New ed. (Works, v. 21). Lond. 1882. D. 252 : 77
— The water of life, and other sermons. (Works, v. 26). Lond. 1879. D. 252 : 82
— Westminster sermons, with a preface. [Works, v. 28]. Lond. 1882. D. 252 : 84
Leighton, Robert. Eighteen sermons, first pub. in Glasgow in 1692 at the desire of his friends, from his papers written with his own hand, and now reprinted; wherein all obvious errors of the press are amended, some notes added for the sake of the common reader, and an account of his life prefixed; with an app. cont. explications of the disputed points of justification, assurance, etc., and an index of the most material things. Lond. 1745. O. 252 : 36
Luther, Martin. A selection of [his] most celebrated sermons, never before pub. in the U. S.; prefixed, a biographical history of his life. Phila. 1831. D. 252 : 37
MacDonald, G: Unspoken sermons. N. Y. 1871. D. 252 : 38
Manning, H: E: The fourfold sovereignty of God. Lond. 1871. D. 252 : 39
— The four great evils of the day. Lond. 1871. D. 252 : 40
Contents. The revolt of the intellect against God.— The revolt of the will against God.—The revolt of society from God.—The spirit of antichrist.
Martineau, James. Endeavors after the christian life; a volume of discourses. Bost. 1844. D. 252 : 41
Massillon, J: Baptiste. Sermons; prefixed, the life of the author. Selected and tr. by W: Dickson. 3d ed. Lond. 1803. 3 v. D. 252 : 42
Mears, D. O. The jubilee sabbath of Piedmont church; two discourses, del. june 5, 1881. Worcester, 1881. Q. 252 : R74
Monod, Adolphe F: Théodore. Les adieux d'Adolphe Monod; parting words to his friends and the church, oct. 1855 to march 1856. Tr. from the 5th Paris ed. N. Y. 1873. D. 252 : 43
Munger, Theodore T. The freedom of faith. Bost. 1883. D. 252 : 85
Sermons with a prefatory essay, "The new theology".
Paley, W: Sermons on several subjects [and] Sermons on several occasions. N. Y. 1824. T. 252 : 44
Parker, Theodore. Ten sermons of religion. 2d ed. Bost. 1861. D. 252 : 45
Peabody, Andrew Preston. Christian belief and life. Bost. 1875. D. 252 : 46
Potter, Alonzo. Discourses, charges, pastoral letters, etc. Phila. 1858. D. 252 : 47
Powers, Horatio Nelson. Through the year; thoughts relating to the seasons of nature and the church. Bost. 1875. D. 252 : 48
Pusey, E: Bouverie. Parochial sermons. 2d ed. from the 3d Oxford ed. Phila. 1865. D. 252 : 49

Seabury, S: Discourses on several subjects. Hudson. 1815. 2 v. O.   252 : 51

Sewall, Frank. The pillow of stones; divine allegories in their spiritual meaning. Phila. 1876. D.   252 : 53

Sheldon, H: O. The itinerant minister, his work and his reward ; a sermon preached before the bishops and ministers of the Delaware conference, at its first session, sept. 24, 1856· Pub. by request. 4th ed. Cinc. 1860. O.   252 : 54

— Divine providence, or Fore-knowledge and the influence of motives consistent with free agency and God's government of events ; a sermon. Cinc. 1860. O. *With his* The itinerant minister.   252 : 54

— God is love ; a sermon on divine benevolence, preached in the universalist church, Calvert st., Baltimore, sept. 25, 1842. 8th ed. Cinc. 1860. O. *With his* The itinerant minister.   252 : 54

Skinner, G. M. Sermons, doctrinal and practical ; incl. a series of discourses upon the decalogue. Phila. 1871. D.   252 : 55

Smith, Sydney. Sermons. *In his* Works.   820.2+19

Smyth, Newman. The reality of faith. N. Y. 1884. D.   252 : 56

Southard, S: Lewis. The mystery of godliness. N. Y. 1848. O.   252+56

Spring, Gardiner. Pulpit ministrations, or Sabbath readings ; a series of discourses on christian doctrine and duty. N. Y. 1864. 2 v. O.   252+57

Spurgeon, C: Haddon. Sermons, 1st—7th ser ; with introd. and biograph. sketch by E. L. Magoon. N. Y. 1859-1862. 7 v. D.   252 : 58

Stanley, Arthur Penrhyn. Sermons preached before his royal highness, the prince of Wales, during his tour in the east in the spring of 1862, with notices of some of the localities visited. N. Y. 1863. D. 252 : 59

— Sermons on special occasions, preached at Westminster abbey. [Frank. sq. lib.] N. Y. 1882. Q.   252+72

— *Same.* Westminster sermons. N. Y. 1882. D.   252 : 72

Staples, Nahor A: Way, truth and life ; sermons, with a sketch of his life by J: W. Chadwick. Bost. 1870. S.   252 : 60

Sterne, Lawrence. Sermons. *In his* Works.   820.2 : 20 v3, 4

Sumner, J: Bird. The world lost by sin ; a sermon. *In his* Apostolical preaching.   251 : 8

Swing, D: Motives of life. 2d ed. Chicago. 1879. S.   252 : 61

Contents. Intellectual progress.—Home.—A good name.—The pursuit of happiness.—Benevolence.—Religion.

— Truths for to-day. Chicago. 1874, 1876. 2 v. D.   252 : 62

Tholuck, F: A: Gotttreu. Light from the cross ; sermons on the passion of our Lord. Tr. from the german. Phila. 1858. D.   252 : 63

Thompson, Joseph Parrish. The early witnesses, or Piety and preaching of the middle ages. N. Y. 1857. T.   252 : 73

Trench, R: Chenevix. The fitness of holy scripture for unfolding the spiritual life of men, ii.: Christ the desire of all nations, or The unconscious prophecies of heathendom ; the Hulsean lectures for 1845 and 1846. From 2d Lond. ed. rev. by the author. Phila. 1860. D.   252 : 65

— Sermons preached before the university of Cambridge. N. Y. 1857. D.   252 : 66

Tyler, W: Seymour. A discourse commemorative of hon. S: Williston, del. in the Payson church at Easthampton, sept. 13, 1874 and also in the college church at Amherst, sept. 20. Springfield. 1874. O.   252+87

Vinet, Alexandre Rodolphe. Gospel studies ; with an introd. by Robert Baird. N. Y. 1849. D.   252 : 67

Walker, James. Sermons preached in the chapel of Harvard college. Bost. 1861. D.   252 : 68

Whately, R: Essays, first series, on some of the peculiarities of the christian religion. 7th ed. rev. Lond. 1856. O.   252 : 69

Whewell, W: On the foundations of morals ; four sermons preached before the university of Cambridge, nov. 1837 ; with add. discourses and essays. Andover. 1839. S.   252 : 70

Whitehouse, H: J: The sepulchre in the garden ; preached at the funeral of mrs. Helen Anderson Carter in the church of the holy communion, Chicago, march 28, 1862. N. Y. 1862. O.   252+86

Wiseman, N: Patrice Stephen. The sermons, lectures and speeches del. during his tour in Ireland in aug. and sept. 1858, with his lecture del. in London on the "Impressions" of his tour ; rev. by his eminence, with a connecting narrative. Bost. 1859. D.   252 : 71

7. Institutions and Missions.

1. Institutions in general.

Stanley, Arthur Penrhyn. Christian institutions ; essays on ecclesiastical subjects. N. Y. 1881. D.   260 : 1

Contents. Baptism.—The eucharist.—Absolution.—Ecclesiastical vestments.—The basilica.—The clergy. —The pope.—The litany.—The roman catacombs.— The creed of the early christians.—The Lord's prayer.

—The council and creed of Constantinople.—The ten commandments.—Addenda.—Index.

Thayer, W: Makepeace. A book for the times, spots in our feasts of charity ; an exposure of the delinquencies of christian professors in regard to the ordinances of religion, and other agencies for doing good ; with an introd. by Jacob Ide. Bost. 1854. D.   260 : 2

2. The church.

(*See also* Christian sects, col. 125.)

Barrett, B: Franklin. The golden reed ; or The true measure of a true church. N. Y. 1855. D.   **261 : 1**

Baumgarten, Michael. Anti-Kliefoth, oder Die gefährlichste reichsfeindschaft an einem beispiel aufgezeigt. *In* Deutsche zeit- und streit-fragen.   **304 : 15 v3**

— Der kampf um das reichscivilstandsgesetz in der deutschen protestantischen kirche. *In* Deutsche zeit- und streit-fragen.   **304 : 15 v5**

— Der protestantismus als politisches princip im deutschen reich. *In* Deutsche zeit- und streit-fragen.   **304 : 15 v1**

Bunsen, Christian C: Josias *freiherr* v. Signs of the times ; letters to Ernst Moritz Arndt on the dangers to religious liberty in the present state of the world. Tr. from the german by Susanna Winkworth. N. Y. 1856. D.   **261 : 2**

Deutsches kaiserwort, Ein. *In* Deutsche zeit- und streit-fragen.   **304 : 15 v7**

Fry, Caroline. The listener in Oxford. [*Anon.*] 2d ed. Lond. 1840. S.   **261 : 3**

Geffcken, H: Church and state ; their relations historically developed. Tr. and ed. with the assistance of the author by E: Fairfax Taylor. Lond. 1877. 2 v. O.   **261+15**

Lathrop, Joseph. Christ's warning to the churches ; with an app. on the apostolical succession, [and] with an introd. notice by J. M. Wainwright. N. Y. 1844. S.   **261 : 5**

Manning, H: E: The reunion of christendom ; a pastoral letter to the clergy, etc. N. Y. 1866. O.   **261 : 6**

— The Vatican decrees in their bearing on civil allegiance. 2d ed. Lond. 1875. O.   **261 : 7**

Pusey, E: Bouverie. The church of England a portion of Christ's one holy catholic church and a means of restoring visible unity ; an eirenicon in a letter to the author of "The christian year." N. Y. 1866. D.   **261 : 8**

Note. For reply see **Newman,** J: H: Letter, no. 282+14.

Putnam, Ellen T. H. Where is the city ? 2d ed. [*Anon.*] Bost. 1868. S.   **261 : 4**

Sclater, W: The original draught of the primitive church. New ed. carefully corr., with the quotations from the fathers, etc., given at length. Oxford. 1850. D.   **261 : 9**

Stone, J: Kent. The invitation heeded ; reasons for a return to catholic unity. 2d ed. N. Y. 1870. D.   **261 : 10**

Stow, Baron. First things, or The development of church life. Bost. 1859. S.   **261 : 11**

Taylor, I: Spiritual despotism, by the author of Natural history of enthusiasm. N. Y. 1835. D.   **261 : 12**

Tuttle, I: H. Our brethren in every city ; brief sketches of european and eastern churches. N. Y. 1855. S.   **261 : 13**

Wasserschleben, F: W: A: Hermann. Das landesherrliche kirchenregiment. *In* Deutsche zeit- und streit-fragen.   **304 : 15 v1**

Whately, R: A general view of the rise, progress and corruptions of christianity ; with a sketch of the life of the author, and a catalogue of his writings. N. Y. 1860. D.   **261 : 14**

Ecclesiastical polity.

Coleridge, S: Taylor. On the constitution of church and state. *In his* Complete works.   **820.2 : 7 v6**

Ewer, F. C. Catholicity in its relationship to protestantism and romanism ; six conferences del. at Newark, N. J., at the request of leading laymen of that city. N. Y. 1878. D.   **262 : 1**

Hobart, J: H: An apology for apostolic order and its advocates, in a series of letters addressed to J: M. Mason. 2d ed. with notes and an index. N. Y. 1844. D.   **262 : 2**

Holtzendorff, Franz v. Der priester-cölibat. *In* Deutsche zeit- und streit-fragen.   **304 : 15 v4**

Hooker, R: Laws of ecclesiastical polity. *In his* Works.   **200+6**

Huber, Victor Aimé, (*Janus*). The pope and the council, by Janus. Authorized tr. from the german. Bost. 1870. D.   **262 : 3**

Kenrick, Francis Patrick. The primacy of the apostolic see, and the authority of general councils vindicated, in a series of letters addressed to J. H. Hopkins. Phila. 1838. D.   **262 : 4**

Ladd, G: Trumbull. Principle of church polity, illustrated by an analysis of modern congregationalism, and applied to certain important practical questions in the government of christian churches ; Southworth lectures, del. at Andover theological seminary in 1879—1881. N. Y. 1882. O.   **262 : 10**

Lea, H: C: An historical sketch of sacerdotal celibacy in the christian church. 2d ed. enl. Bost. 1884. O.   **262+11**

Maistre, Joseph Marie *comte* de. The pope considered in his relations to the church, temporal sovereignties, separated churches, and the cause of civilization. Tr. by Æneas McD. Dawson. Lond. 1850. D.   **262 : 5**

Mason, J: Mitchell. Essays on episcopacy, and the Apology for apostolic order and its advocates, reviewed ; ed. by Ebenezer Mason. N. Y. 1844. D.   **262 : 6**

Perceval, Arthur Philip. An apology for the doctrine of apostolical succession, with an app. on the english orders. N. Y. 1840. S.   **262 : 7**

Schulte, J: F: *ritter* v. Ueber kirchenstrafen. *In* Deutsche zeit- und streit-fragen.   **304 : 15 v1**

Stillingfleet, E: A defence of the discourse concerning the idolatry practised in the church of Rome, in answer to a book entituled Catholicks no idolaters. The two first parts. Lond. 1676. S.   **262 : R8**

Weninger, François Xavier. On the apostolical and infallible authority of the pope, when teaching the faithful, and on his relation to a general council. 2d ed. N. Y. 1869. D.   **262 : 9**

3. The sabbath.

Andrews, J. N. History of the sabbath, and the first day of the week. 2d ed. Battle Creek, Mich. 1873. D.   **263 : 1**

Bacon, Leonard Woolsey, *and* G: Blagden **Bacon.** The sabbath question, sunday observance and sunday laws ; a sermon and two speeches by Leonard W. Bacon ; six sermons on the sabbath question, by the late G: Blagden Bacon.. N. Y. 1882. S.
263 : 4

Gilfillan, James. The sabbath viewed in the light of reason, revelation and history, with sketches of its literature. N. Y. 1862. D.
263 : 2

Lammers, A: Sonntagsfeier in Deutschland. *In* Deutsche zeit- und streit-fragen.
364 : 15 v11

Littlejohn, W. H. The constitutional amendment, or The sunday, the sabbath, the change and restitution ; a discussion between W. H. Littlejohn, seventh-day adventist, and the ed. of the Christian statesman. Battle Creek. 1873. D.   263 : 3

4. Baptism.

Adams, W: Mercy to babes ; a plea for the christian baptism of infants, addressed to those who doubt and to those who deny the validity of that practice, upon the grounds of the doctrine of baptism, and the eternal sense of holy writ, and of the domestic, social and religious nature of man. N. Y. 1847. D.   264 : 1

Gale, J: Reflections on mr. [W:] Wall's History of infant baptism. [*Anon.*] *T. p. w.* [Lond. 1711.] D.   264 : 2

Woods, Leonard. Lectures on infant baptism. 2d ed. Andover. 1829. D.   264 : 3

5. Missions.

In general.

Harris, J: The great commission, or The christian church constituted and charged to convey the gospel to the world ; with an introd. essay by W: R. Williams. 8th thous. Bost. 1858. D.   266 : 2

Holmes, J: Historical sketches of the missions of the united brethren for propagating the gospel among the heathen, from their commencement to the present time. Dublin. 1818. O.   266 : 3

Marshall, T. W. M. Christian missions ; their agents, and their results. N. Y. 1864. 2 v. O.   266 : 7

Newcomb, Harvey. A cyclopedia of missions ; containing a comprehensive view of missionary operations throughout the world, with geographical descriptions, and accounts of the social, moral and religious condition of the people. 2d rev. ed. with the latest corr. N. Y. 1860. O.   266+8

Thompson, A: C. Moravian missions ; twelve lectures. N. Y. 1882. D.   266 : 11

Warneck, Gustav. Modern missions and culture ; their mutual relations. Tr. from the german by T: Smith. Edinb. 1883. D.
266 : 12

Home.

Beecher, Lyman. A plea for the west. 3d ed. Cinc. 1836. T.   266 : 1

Smet, P: J: de. Western missions and missionaries ; a series of letters. N. Y. 1863. D.
266 : 10

Kip, W: Ingraham. A few days at Nashotah. Albany. 1849. O.   266 : 5

— The early jesuit missions in North America. N. Y. 1848. D.   266 : 4

Loskiel, G: H: History of the mission of the united brethren among the indians in North America, in 3 parts. Tr. from the german by Christian Ignatius La Trobe. Lond. 1794. O.   266 : 6

Shea, J: Gilmary. History of the catholic missions among the indian tribes of the U. S., 1529—1854. N. Y. 1854. D.   266 : 9

Foreign.

Dean, W: The China mission ; embracing a history of the various missions of all denominations among the chinese. with biographical sketches of deceased missionaries. N. Y. 1859. D.   266 : 1

Huc, Evariste Régis *abbé.* Christianity in China, Tartary and Thibet. N. Y. 1857. 2 v. D.
267 : 2

Contents. V. 1. From the apostleship of St. Thomas to the discovery of the Cape of Good Hope. 2. From the discovery of the Cape of Good Hope to the establishment of the Mantchoo-Tartar dynasty in China.

Kesson, J: The cross and the dragon, or The fortunes of christianity in China ; with notices of the christian missions and missionaries, and some account of the chinese secret societies. Lond. 1854. D.   267 : 3

Siam and Laos, as seen by our american missionaries. Map and ill. Phila. [1884]. D.
267 : 6

Young, Robert. Modern missions, their trials and triumphs ; with introd. by James H. Wilson. 1st amer. ed., rev. and enl. N. Y. [1883]. D.   267 : 4

Note. Modern protestant missions in India, Burmah, Japan, China, south Africa, western Africa, central Africa, Madagascar, eastern and central Polynesia, Melanesia.

— Light in the lands of darkness ; a record of missionary labor among greenlanders, eskimos, patagonians, etc.; with introd. by the earl of Shaftesbury. Ill. N.-Y. 1884. D.   267 : 5

Adventures of a missionary, or Rivers of water in a dry place ; an account of the introduction of the gospel of Jesus into south Africa and of mr. Moffat's missionary travels and labors. Ill. N. Y. *n. d.* S.
x 267 : 7

Sunday schools and revivals.

Tyng, Stephen Higginson. Forty years experience in sunday schools. N. Y. 1860. S.
268 : 1

Sprague, W: Buell. Lectures on revivals of religion ; with an introd. essay by Leonard Woods, also an app. consisting of letters from drs. Alexander, Wayland [*and others*]. 2d ed. with add. letters. N. Y. 1883. D.
269 : 1

Clark, Rufus Wheelwright. The work of God in Great Britain under messrs. Moody and Sankey, 1873 to 1875 ; with biographical sketches. N. Y. 1875. D.   269 : 2

Schramm, K: Rudolph. Das heer der seligmacher, oder Die heils-armee in England. *In* Deutsche zeit- und streit-fragen.
304 : 15 v12

x denotes books specially adapted for children.

8. Ecclesiastical history.

(See also general and special history classes.)

1. In general.

Abbott, J: Stevens Cabot. The history of christianity ; consisting of the life and teachings of Jesus of Nazareth, the adventures of Paul and the apostles, and the most interesting events in the progress of christianity from the earliest period to the present time. Bost. [1881]. D.   **270 : 1**

Allen, Joseph H: Christian history in its three great periods: 1. Early christianity ; 2. The middle age ; 3. Modern phases. Bost. 1883. 3 v. S.   **270 : 20**

Alzog, J: Manual of universal church history. Tr. with add. from the 9th and last german ed. by F. J. Pabisch and T: S. Byrne ; with 3 chronological tables and 3 ecclesiastico-geographical maps. Cinc. 1874. 3 v. O.   **270+2**

Döllinger, J: Joseph Ignaz v. A history of the church. Tr. from the german by E: Cox. Lond. 1840–42. 4 v. O.   **270 : 3**

Gieseler, J: C: L: A text book of church history. Tr. from the 4th rev. german ed.; new amer. ed., rev. and ed. by H: B. Smith. N. Y. 1857–80. 5 v. O.   **270 : 22**
Contents. V. 1. A. d. 1—726. 2. A. d. 726—1305. 3. A. d. 1305—1517.—Index to the 3 vols. 4. A. d. 1517—1648. 5. From the reformation to the present time, completed by Mary F. **Robinson.**

Milner, Joseph. The history of the church of Christ ; with add. and corr. by I: Milner. From the last Lond. ed. Phila. 1835. 2 v. O.   **270 : 11**

Mosheim, J: Lorenz v. An ecclesiastical history, ancient and modern, from the birth of Christ to the beginning of the 18th century, in which the rise, progress and variations of church power are considered in their connexion with the state of learning and philosophy, and the political history of Europe during that period. Tr. from the original latin, and ill. with notes, chronological tables and an appendix by Archibald Maclaine. Continued to the year 1826 by C: Coote, and furnished with a dissertation on the state of the primitive church by G: **Gleig.** Cinc. 1859. Q.   **270+4**

Neander, J: A: W: (*jewish name* Mendel). General history of the christian religion and church. From the german ; tr. from the 2d ed. and imp. ed. by Joseph Torrey. 6th–11th amer. ed. Bost. 1853–81. 6 v. O.   **270+5**

Palmer, W: Ecclesiastical history from the earliest period to the present time ; with a pref. and notes by an amer. ed. 5th ed., with a series of questions, adapting the work for parochial instruction. N. Y. 1844. D.   **270 : 6**

Schaff, Philip. History of the christian church. New ed., rev. and enl. N. Y. 1882, 1883. 3 v. O.   **270+14**
Contents. V. 1. Apostolic christianity. 2. Ante-nicene christianity, a. d. 100—325. 3. Nicene and post-nicene christianity, a. d. 311—600. *To be continued.*

Spalding, Martin J: [Essays on ecclesiastical history]. *In his* Miscellanies.   **824.1+75**
Contents, see under English literature, Essays.

* * *

Cave, W: Antiquitates apostolicæ, or The history of the lives, acts and martyrdoms of the holy apostles of our Saviour, and the two evangelists, SS. Mark and Luke, to which is added an introductory discourse concerning the three great dispensations of the church, patriarchal, mosaical and evangelical ; being a continuation of Antiquitates christianæ, or The life and death of the holy Jesus. 5th ed. rev., with add. Lond. 1684. F.   **23 : R**

Coquerel, Athanase Josué, *fils.* First historical transformations of christianity. From the french, by E. P. Evans. Bost. 1867. D.   **270 : 7**

Fisher, G: Park. The beginnings of christianity, with a view of the state of the roman world at the birth of Christ. N. Y. *n. d.* O.   **270 : 23**

Döllinger, J: Joseph Ignatz v. The first age of christianity and the church. Tr. by H: Nutcombe Oxenham. 3d ed. Lond. 1877. 2 v. D.   **270 : 24**

Farrar, F: W: The early days of christianity. N. Y. [1882]. O.   **270 : 18**

Milman, H: Hart. The history of christianity from the birth of Christ to the abolition of paganism in the roman empire. N. Y. 1881. 3 v. in 2. D.   **270 : 21**

Pressensé, Edmond Marcellin Déhault de. The early years of christianity; a comprehensive history of the first three centuries of the christian church. Tr. by Annie Harwood-Holmden. Lond. 1879, 1880. 4 v. D.   **270 : 25**
Contents. V. 1. The apostolic age. 2. The martyrs and apologists. 3. Heresy and christian doctrine. 4. Life and practice in the early church.

Schaff, Philip. History of the apostolic church ; with a general introd. to church history. Tr. by E: D. Yeomans. N. Y. 1864. O.   **270+12**

— History of the christian church, from the birth of Christ to the reign of Constantine, a. d. 1—311. 2d ed. N. Y. 1864. O.   **270+13**

Eusebius Pamphili *Cæsariensis.* Ecclesiastical history [to a. d. 324]. Tr. from the greek by C. F. Cruse ; with notes sel. from the ed. of Valesius. Lond. 1865. D.   **270 : 8**

Socrates *Scholasticus.* Ecclesiastical history ; comprising a history of the church, in seven books, from the accession of Constantine, a. d. 305, to the 38th year of Theodosius II, including a period of 140 years. Tr. from the greek ; with some account of the author and notes sel. from Valesius. Lond. 1853. D.   **270 : 19**

Taylor, I: Ancient christianity, and the doctrines of the Oxford tracts. Phila. 1840. D.   **270 : 15**

Uhlhorn, Gerhard. The conflict of christianity with heathenism. Ed. and tr. with the author's sanction from the 3d germ. ed. b, Egbert C. Smyth and C. J. H. Ropes. N Y. 1879. O.   **270 : 1**

Waddington, G: A history of the church, from the earliest ages to the reformation. [Library of useful knowledge.] Lond. [188-]. O.   **270 : 17**

Guizot, François P: Guillaume. Meditations on the actual state of christianity and on the attacks which are now being made upon it. Tr. under the superintendence of the author. N. Y. [1866]. D.   **270 : 9**
Contents. Preface.—The awakening of christianity in France in the 19th century.—Spiritualism.—Rationalism. — Positivism. — Pantheism. — Materialism. — Skepticism.—Impiety, recklessness and perplexity.

Lawrence, Eugene. Historical studies. N. Y. 1876. O.   **270 : 10**
Contents. The bishops of Rome.—Leo and Luther.—Loyola and the jesuits.—Ecumenical councils.—The vaudois.—The huguenots.—The church of Jerusalem.—Dominic and the inquisition.—The conquest of Ireland.—The greek church.

Newman, J: H: [Sketches of ecclesiastical history.] *In his* Historical sketches.
                            824.2 : 75
Contents, see under English literature, Essays.

2. Religious orders.

Taaffe, J: The history of the holy, military sovereign order of St. John of Jerusalem; or knights hospitallers, knights templars, knights of Rhodes, knights of Malta. Lond. 1852. 4 v. in 2. O.   **271 : 1**

Townsend, G: Fyler. The sea-kings of the Mediterranean. 2d ed. Lond. [1872]. D.
                            271 : 7

Montalembert, C: Forbes de Tryon, *comte* de. The monks of the west, from St. Benedict to St. Bernard. Authorised tr.; v. 1–3, 6, 7. Edinb. 1861-79. 5 v. O.   **271+3**

N., B. The jesuits; their foundation and history. N. Y. 1879. 2 v. D.   **271 : 5**

Orliac, Mme. J. M. S. (*J. M. S. Daurignac.*) History of the society of Jesus, from its foundation to the present time. Tr. from the french of J. M. S. Daurignac by James Clements. Cinc. 1865. 2 v. D.   **271 : 2**

Steinmetz, Andrew. History of the jesuits, from the foundation of their society to its suppression by pope Clement XIV; their missions throughout the world; their educational system and literature; with their revival and present state. Lond. 1848. 3 v. O.   **271 : 6**

Taylor, I: Loyola and jesuitism in its rudiments. N. Y. 1851. D.   **271 : 4**

Huber, Johannes Nepomuk. Die kirchlich-politische wirksamkeit des jesuiten-ordens. *In* Deutsche zeit- und streit-fragen.
                            304 : 15 v2
Note. "The best that has been written on the subject are the chapters concerning the jesuits in Ranke's work on the roman popes" [282:19 english, 904:36 v37-39 german].—*M'Clintock and Strong*.

3. Persecutions and Doctrines.

Foxe, J: Acts and monuments. New and complete ed., with a preliminary dissertation

by G: Townsend, ed. by Stephen Reed Cattley. Lond. 1837-41. 8 v. O.   **272+6**
Note. A facsimile of the first titlepage reads: Actes and monuments of these latter and perillous dayes, touching matters of the church; wherein are comprehended and described the great persecutions and horrible troubles that haue been wrought and practised by the romishe prelates, speciallye in this realme of England and Scotlande, from the year of our Lord a thousande unto the tyme now present, *etc.*

Llorente, J: Antonio. The history of the inquisition of Spain from the time of its establishment to the reign of Ferdinand VII; composed from the original documents of the archives of the supreme council and from those of subordinate tribunals of the holy office, abridged and tr. from the original works. Lond. 1826. O.   **272 : 7**

Rule, W: Harris. History of the inquisition from its establishment in the 12th century to its extinction in the 19th. Lond. 1874. 2 v. O.
                            272 : 4

Simonde de Sismondi, J: C: Léonard. History of the crusades against the albigenses in the 13th century. From the french, with an introd. essay by the translator. Lond. 1826. O.   **272 : 1**
— *Same.* 1st amer. ed., with an introd. Bost. 1833. D.   **272 : 1**

Tonna, Charlotte Elizabeth, (*Charlotte Elizabeth*). War with the saints: Count Raymond of Toulouse and the crusade against the albigenses under pope Innocent III, by Charlotte Elizabeth. Ill. ed. N. Y. 1864. S.   **272 : 5**

Browning, W: Shipton. A history of the huguenots. New ed., continued to the present time. Phila. 1845. O.   **272+3**

Weiss, C: History of the french protestant refugees, from the revocation of the edict of Nantes to our own days. Tr. from the french by H: W: Herbert; with an amer. app. by a descendant of the huguenots. N. Y. 1854. 2 v. D.   **272 : 2**
Note. For the huguenots, see also French ecclesiastical history, cl. 274.4, col.   .

*   *   *

Shedd, W: Greenough Thayer. A history of christian doctrine. 3d ed. N. Y. 1865. 2 v. O.   **273+2**

Dort, Synod of. Articles of the synod of Dort and its rejection of errors; with the history of events which made way for that synod as pub. by the States-general and the documents confirming its decisions. Tr. from the latin with notes, remarks and references by T: Scott. Utica. 1831. D.   **273 : 1**

4. Europe.

Dean, Amos. Religions of Europe: Celtic; Scandinavian; Roman catholic; Greek church; Protestantism. *In his* History of civilization.   **309 : 5 v5**

Merivale, C: The conversion of the northern nations; the Boyle lectures for 1865, del. at the chapel royal, Whitehall. N. Y. 1866. O.   **274 : 3**

Maclear, G: F: The slavs. [Conversion of the west; pub. by the society for promoting christian knowledge.] Map. Lond. 1879. S.   **274 : 2**

*   *   *

Mills, C: The history of the crusades for the possession of the Holy Land. Phila. 1844. O.   274+1

Edgar, J: G: The crusades and the crusaders, or Stories of the struggle for the holy sepulchre. Lond. *n. d.* D.   x 274 : 10

Gray, G: Zabriskie. The children's crusade ; an episode of the 13th century. [4th ed.] Bost. 1882. D.   274 : 9
Note. For the crusades see also General european history, cl. 940.

* * *

Milman, H: Hart. History of latin christianity, including that of the popes to the pontificate of Nicolas V. N. Y. 1860–62. 8 v. D.
                                                     274 : R4
Contents. V. 1. Introd.—A. d. 67-556.—Christian jurisprudence. **2.** Western monasticism.—A. d. 590-839. **3.** A. d. 844-1095. **4.** A. d. 1094-1200. **5.** A. d. 1199-1264. **6.** A. d. 1226-1313. **7.** A. d. 1313-1433. **8.** A. d. 1435-1454.—Survey.—Belief of latin christianity.—Latin letters.—Christian latin poetry.—History.—Christian letters in the new languages of Europe.—Christian architecture.—Christian sculpture.—Christian painting.—Index.

— *Same.* N. Y. 1881. 8 v. in 4. D.   274 : 4

Reuter, Hermann. Geschichte der religiösen aufklärung im mittelalter. Berlin. 1875. 2 v. O.   274 : 17

Poole, Reginald Lane. Illustrations of the history of medieval thought in the departments of theology and ecclesiastical politics. (Pub. for the Hibbert trustees.) Lond. 1884. O.   274 : 19

Hardwick, C: A history of the christian church ; middle age. New ed. by W. Stubbs. Maps. Lond. 1883. D.   274 : 15

— A history of the christian church during the reformation. New ed. by W. Stubbs. Lond. 1883. D.   274 : 16

Fisher, G: Park. The reformation. New ed. N. Y. 1883. O.   274 : 14

Hurst, J: Fletcher. A short history of the reformation. Ill., map and port. N. Y. 1884. D.   274 : 18

Merle d'Aubigné, J: H: History of the great reformation of the 16th century in Germany, Switzerland etc. 9th ed. N. Y. 1843–46. 4 v. D.   274 : 6

— History of the reformation in Europe in the time of Calvin. N. Y. 1864–79. 8 v. D.
                                                     274 : 5
Contents. V. I, 2. Geneva and France. **3.** France, Switzerland, Geneva. **4.** England, Geneva, France, Germany and Italy. **5.** England, Geneva, Ferrara. **6.** Scotland, Switzerland, Geneva. Tr. by W: L. B. Cates. **7.** Geneva, Denmark, Sweden, Norway, Hungary, Poland, Bohemia, the Netherlands. Tr. by W: L. B. Cates. **8.** Hungary, Poland, Bohemia, Netherlands, Geneva, Denmark, Sweden, Norway. Tr. by W: L. B. Cates.

Scott, J: Luther and the lutheran reformation. N. Y. 1848. 2 v. S.   274 : 7

Spalding, Martin J: The history of the protestant reformation in Germany and Switzerland, and in England, Ireland, Scotland, the Netherlands, France and northern Europe ; in a series of essays, reviewing D'Aubigné, Menzel, Hallam, bishop Short, Prescott, Ranké, Fryxell and others. Louisville. 1860. 2 v. O.   274 : 8

Creighton, Mandell. A history of the papacy during the period of the reformation. Bost. 1882. 2 v. O.   274 : 11

Beard, C: The reformation of the 16th century in its relation to modern thought and knowledge ; lectures del. at Oxford and in London in april, may and june, 1883. (The Hibbert lectures, 1883). Lond. 1883. O.
                                                     274 : 12

Sarpi, P:, *or* Fra Paolo. The history of the council of Trent; containing 8 books in which besides the ordinary acts of the council are declared many notable occurrences which happened in christendom during the space of 40 years and more, and particularly the practices of the court of Rome, to hinder the reformation of their errours and to maintain their greatness. Written in italian and faithfully tr. into english by sir Nathaniel Brent, whereunto is added the life of the learned author and the history of the inquisition. Lond. 1676. F.   23 : R

Lea, H: C: Studies in church history. Phila. 1883. O.   274 : 13
Contents. The rise of the temporal power.—Benefit of clergy.—Excommunication.—The early church and slavery.

Great Britain.

Beda *or* **Bede,** *Venerabilis.* The venerable Bede's ecclesiastical history of England, also the Anglo-saxon chronicle ; with illustrative notes, a map of anglo-saxon England, and a general index ; ed. by J. A. Giles. 3d ed. Lond. 1859. D.   274.2 : 1

Fuller, T: The church history of Britain, from the birth of Jesus Christ until 1648. New ed., with the author's corr. Lond. 1837. 3 v. O.   274.2 : 10

Herford, Brooke. The story of religion in England ; a book for young folk. 2d ed. Chicago. 1880. D.   x 274.2 : 5

Burnet, Gilbert. The history of the reformation of the church of England, with an index ; rev. and corr. with add. notes and a preface calculated to remove certain difficulties attending the perusal of this important history, by E. Nares. N. Y. 1843. 3 v. O.
                                                     274.2 : 2

Cobbett, W: The history of the protestant reformation in England and Ireland ; showing how that event has impoverished the main body of the people in those countries, etc., in a series of letters addressed to all sensible and just englishmen. Added, three letters by the same author never before publ. in the U. S. N. Y. [185–]. 2 v. in 1. S.   274.2 : 3

Geikie, Cunningham. The english reformation ; how it came about, and why we should uphold it. N. Y. 1879. D.   274.2 : 4

Massingberd, Francis C: The english reformation. Flemington, N. J. 1844. O. *In* The churchman's library.   204 : 16

Robinson, Hastings, *ed.* The Zürich letters, [a. d. 1558–79] comprising the correspondence of several english bishops and others, with some of the helvetian reformers, during the early part of the reign of queen Elizabeth. Tr. from authenticated copies of the autographs preserved in the archives of Zürich. and ed. for the Parker society. Cambridge. 1842. O.   274.2 : 7 v1

x denotes books specially adapted for children.

Robinson, Hastings, *ed.—Continued.*
— *Same.* Second series, [1558-1602]. Cambridge. 1845. O.   **274**.2 : 7 v2
— Original letters relative to the english reformation written during the reigns of king Henry VIII, king Edward VI, and queen Mary ; chiefly from the archives of Zürich. Tr. from the authenticated copies of the autographs, and ed. for the Parker society. Cambridge. 1846, 1847. 2 v. O.   **274**.2 : 8
Stoughton, J: History of religion in England from the opening of the long parliament to the end of the 18th century. New rev. ed. Lond. 1881. 6 v. D.   **274**.2 : 9
Contents. v. 1. The church of the civil wars. 2. Of the commonwealth. **3, 4.** Of the restoration. **5.** Of the revolution. **6.** Of the Georgian era.
Newman, J: H: Lectures on the present position of catholics in England ; addressed to the brothers of the Oratory. 3d ed. Dublin. 1857. D.   **274**.2 : 6
Gilfillan, G: The martyrs, heroes and bards of the scottish covenant. N. Y. 1858. S.   **274**.1 : 1

Germany.

Ranke, Franz Leopold v. History of the reformation in Germany. 2d ed. Tr. by Sarah Austin. Lond. 1845–47. 3 v. O.   **274**.3 : 3
Note. The original german work will be found in his collected works, 904 : 36 v1-6.
Fisher, K: Deutschland's öffentliche meinung im reformationszeitalter und in der gegenwart. *In* Deutsche zeit- und streit-fragen.
    304 : 15 v3
Nippold, F: W: Franz. Religion und kirchenpolitik Friedrich's des grossen ; vortrag im Berner grossrathssal am 3. märz 1879. *In* Deutsche zeit- und streit-fragen.
    304 : 15 v8
Kleinschmidt, Arthur. Die säcularisation von 1803. *In* Deutsche zeit- und streit-fragen.
    304 : 15 v7
Nippold, F: W: Franz. Ursprung, umfang, hemmnisse und aussichten der altkatholischen bewegung ; vortrag im Berner grossrathssaale am 7. januar 1873 gehalten und mit literarischen anmerkungen vermehrt. *In* Deutsche zeit- und streit-fragen.
    304 : 15 v2
Menzel, Wolfgang. Geschichte der neuesten jesuitenumtriebe in Deutschland, 1870 — 1872. Stuttg. 1873. O.   **274**.3 : 1
Schaff, Philip. Germany ; its universities, theology and religion ; with sketches of Neander, Tholuck, Olshausen, Hengstenberg, Twesten, Nitzsch, Muller, Ullmann, Rothe, Dorner, Lange, Ebrard, Wichern and other distinguished german divines of the age. Phila. 1857. D.   **274**.3 : 4
History of the protestant church in Hungary from the beginning of the reformation to 1850 ; with special reference to Transylvania. Tr. by J. Craig, with an introd. by J. H. Merle d' Aubigné. Bost. 1854. D.   **274**.3 : 2

France.

Marsh-Caldwell, Anne Caldwell. History of the protestant reformation in France. Phila. 1851. 2 v. D.   **274**.4 : 2

Baird, H: Martyn. History of the rise of the huguenots of France. N. Y. 1879. 2 v. O.   **274**.4 : 1
Note. See also Persecutions, cl. 272, col. 119.

Italy.

Kip, W: Ingraham. The catacombs of Rome as illustrating the church of the first three centuries. N. Y. 1854. D.   **274**.5 : 2
Baird, Robert. Sketches of protestantism in Italy, past and present ; including a notice of the origin, history and present state of the waldenses. Bost. 1845. D.   **274**.5 : 1
Merivale, C: The conversion of the roman empire ; the Boyle lectures for 1864, del. at the chapel royal, Whitehall. N. Y. 1865. O.   **274**.5 : 3
Renan, Joseph Ernest. English conferences : Rome and christianity ; Marcus Aurelius. Tr. by Clara Erskine Clement. Bost. 1880. D.   **274**.5 : 4

Other countries.

Butler, Clement Moore. The reformation in Sweden ; its rise, progress and crisis, and its triumph under Charles IX. N. Y. [1883]. D.   **274**.8 : 1
Scott, J: Calvin and the swiss reformation. Lond. 1833. S.   **274**.9 : 1

5. America.

Waylen, E: Ecclesiastical reminiscences of the U. S. N. Y. 1846. O.   **277**.1 : 1
Hunter, Joseph. Collections concerning the church or congregation of protestant separatists formed at Scrooby in north Nottinghamshire, in the time of king James I: the founders of New Plymouth, the parent-colony of New England. Lond. 1854. O.   **277**.2 : 1
Mather, Cotton. Magnalia Christi americana, or The ecclesiastical history of New England, from its first planting in the year 1620, unto the year of our Lord 1698, in 7 books ; with an introd. and occasional notes by T: Robbins and tr. of the hebrew, greek and latin quotations by Lucius F. Robinson. Added, a memoir of Cotton Mather by S: G. Drake ; also, a comprehensive index by another hand. Hartford. 1855. 2 v. O.   **277**.2+2
Contents. Book **1.** Antiquities; a narrative of memorable passages rel. to the settlement of these plantations.—Bostonian Ebenezer; some historical remarks on the state of Boston. **2.** Ecclesiarum clypei: the lives of the governours and the names of the magistrates. **3.** Polybius; lives of many divines of New Eng. that have been shields unto the churches of New Eng. **4.** Sal gentium; history of Harvard college. **5.** Acts and monuments; the faith and the order in the churches of New Eng. **6.** Thamaturgus; remarkables of the divine providence among the people of New Eng. **7.** Ecclesiarum prælia; the afflictive disturbances which the churches of New Eng. have suffered.—Appendix, Decennium luctuorum; remarkables of a long war with indian salvages.
Uhden, Hermann F. The New England theocracy ; a history of the congregationalists in New England to the revivals of 1740, with a preface by dr. Neander. Tr. from the 2d german ed. by H. C. Conant. Bost. 1859. D.   **277**.2 : 3

Young, Alexander. Chronicles of the pilgrim fathers of the colony of Plymouth, from 1602 to 1625 ; now first coll. from original records and contemporaneous printed documents, and ill. with notes. 2d ed. Bost. 1844. O.   **277.2 : 4**

Cheever, G: Barrell. The journal of the pilgrims at Plymouth, in New England, in 1620, repr. from the original vol. with historical and local ill. of providences, principles and persons. N. Y. 1848. D.   **277.2 : 5**

Dexter, H: Martyn. As to Roger Williams and his "banishment" from the Massachusetts plantation, with a few further words concerning the baptists, the quakers, and religious liberty ; a monograph. Bost. 1876. O.   **277.2 : 6**

Disosway, Gabriel P. The earliest churches of New York and its vicinity. N. Y. 1865. O.   **277.3 : 1**

Meade, W: Old churches, ministers and families of Virginia. Phila.1861. 2 v. O. **277.4+1**

9. Christian sects.

Schaff, Philip. The creeds of christendom, with a history and critical notes. [Bibliotheca symbolica ecclesiæ universalis.] N. Y. 1877, 1878. 3 v. O.   **280+1**
Contents. V. 1. The history of creeds. 2. Greek and latin creeds, with translations. 3. The evangelical protestant creeds, with translations.

Bossuet, Jacques Bénigne. History of the variations of the protestant churches. Tr. from the last french ed. N. Y. *n. d.* 2 v. O.   **280 : 3**

Cornwallis, C. F. Christian sects in the 19th century. *In* Small books on great subjects.   **829.2 : 48 v3**

American christian record, The ; containing the history, confession of faith, and statistics of each religious denomination in the U. S. and Europe ; a list of all clergymen with their post office addresses, etc. N. Y. 1860. D.   **280 : 2**

Oriental.

Grant, Asahel. The nestorians, or The lost tribes ; containing evidence of their identity, an account of their manners, customs, and ceremonies, together with sketches of travel in ancient Assyria, Armenia, Media and Mesopotamia, and ill. of scripture prophecy. N. Y. 1845. D.   **281 : 1**

Stanley, Arthur Penrhyn. Lectures on the history of the eastern church ; with an introd. on the study of ecclesiastical history. From the 2d Lond. ed. rev. N. Y. 1862. **281+2**

Roman catholic.

~ *(See also* cl. 261-262, col. 113.)

Darras, *Abbé* Joseph Epiphane. A general history of the catholic church, from the commencement of the christian era until the present time. 1st amer. from the last french ed.; with an introd. and notes by M. J. Spalding. N. Y. 1865-67. 4 v. Q.   **282+5**

Ranke, Franz Leopold v. The history of the popes, their church and state in the 16th and 17th centuries. Tr. from the last ed. of the german by Walter Keating Kelly. Phila. 1844. O.   **282 : 19**
Note. The original german work will be found in his collected works, 904 : 36 v 37-39.

Haupt, C: Die begründung der päpstlichen macht diesseits der Alpen. *In* Deutsche zeit- und streit-fragen.   **304 : 15 v10**

Heyer, Franz. Canossa und Venedig ; festschrift zur Canossa-feier. *In* Deutsche zeit- und streit-fragen.   **304 : 15 v5**

Frächsel, .G. Der katholicismus seit der reformation. *In* Deutsche zeit- und streit-fragen.   **304 : 15 v4**

Trede, Theodor. Die Propaganda fide in Rom ; ihre geschichte und bedeutung. *In* Deutsche zeit- und streit-fragen.   **304 : 15 v13**

Schulte, J: F: *ritter v.* Die neueren katholischen orden und congregationen, besonders in Deutschland, statistisch, canonistisch, publicistisch· beleuchtet. *In* Deutsche zeit- und streit-fragen.   **304 : 15 v1**

Dehn, Paul. Die katholischen gesellen-vereine in Deutschland. *In* Deutsche zeit- und streitfragen.   **304 : 15 v11**

*   *   *

Bossuet, Jacques Bénigne. An exposition of the doctrine of the catholic church in matters of controversie. Done into eng. from the 5th ed. in french: 2d ed. more correct. Lond. 1686. T.   **282 : 1**

Butler, C: The book of the roman catholic church ; in a series of letters addressed to Robt. Southey, on his Book of the church. Lond. 1825: O.   **282 : 2**

Hecker, I: T: Aspirations of nature. 3d ed. N. Y. 1859. D.   **282 : 7**

— Questions of the soul. N. Y. 1855. D. **282 : 8**

Ives, Levi Silliman. The trials of a mind in its progress to catholicism ; a letter to his old friends. 27th thous. Bost. 1855. D.   **282 : 9**

Milner, J: The end of religious controversy. in a friendly correspondence between a religious society of protestants and a roman catholic divine ; in 3 parts: pt. 1, On the rule of faith or the method of finding out the true religion ; pt. 2, On characteristics of the true church ; pt. 3, On rectifying mistakes concerning the catholic church ; addressed to the rt. rev. dr. Burgess, in answer to his lordship's protestant catechism. Added, the author's postscript. N. Y. 1865. D.   **282 : 10**

Moore, T: Travels of an irish gentleman in search of a religion ; with notes and illustrations. Balt. *n. d.* D.   **282 : 11**

Newman, J: H: A letter to the rev. E. B. Pusey, on his recent Eirenicon. N. Y. 1866. O.   **282+14**
Note. Dr. Pusey's Eirenicon, referred to, is no. 261: 8.

Pascal, Blaise. Provincial letters. A new tr. with historical introd. and notes by T: M'Crie. preceded by a life of Pascal. a critical essay, and a bibliographical notice; ed. by O. W. Wight. N. Y. 1859. D.
282 : 15

Pise, C: Constantine. Letters to Ada, from her brother-in-law. [*Anon.*] N. Y. 1834. S.
282 : 16

Spalding, Martin J: Influence of catholicity on civil liberty. *In his* Miscellanies.
824.1+75

Valdegamas, J: Francisco Maria de la Salud Donoso Cortés *marques* de. Essay on catholicism, liberalism and socialism. considered in their fundamental principles. From the original spanish; prefixed, a sketch of the life and works of the author from the italian of G. E. de Castro. Tr. by Madeleine Vinton Goddard [Dahlgren]. Phila. 1862. D.
282 : 3

Weninger, Francis Xavier. Photographic views, or Religious and moral truths reflected in the universe. 5th ed. N. Y. 1877. O.
282 : 17

Wiseman, N: Patrice Stephen. Lectures on the principal doctrines and practices of the catholic church ; del. at St. Mary's, Moorfield's, during the lent of 1836. 6th amer. ed. Balt. 1865. D.
282 : 18

＊   ＊   ＊

Bluntschli, J: Caspar. Rom und die deutschen: 1. Römische weltherrschaft und deutsche freiheit ; 2. Der jesuitenorden und das deutsche reich. *In* Deutsche zeit- und streit-fragen.
304 : 15 v1

Cumming, J: Lectures on romanism ; illustrations and refutations of the errors of romanism and tractarianism. Bost. 1854. D.
282 : 4

Faber, G: Stanley. The difficulties of romanism. Phila. 1829. O. ·
282 : 6

Gladstone, W: Ewart. The Vatican decrees, and other essays on the roman church. *In his* Rome.
329.2 : 12

Hesse, F: Hermann. Der felsen Petri kein felsen. *In* Deutsche zeit- und streit-fragen.
304 : 15 v3

Murray, N: (*Kirwan*). Letters to the right rev. J: Hughes ; revised and enl. by Kirwan. N. Y. 1855. D.
282 : 12

Nevins, W: Thoughts on popery. N. Y. [1836]. T.
282 : 13

Schulte, J: Roman catholicism, old and new, from the standpoint of the infallibility doctrine. N. Y. 1877. D.
282 : 20

Protestant episcopal.

(*See also* cl. 261-262, col. 113.)

Staunton, W: A dictionary of the church; an exposition of terms, phrases, and subjects, connected with the external order, sacraments, worship and usages of the protestant episcopal church, with an especial reference to the church in the U. S. 2d ed. rev., corr. and enl. Phila. 1840. O. 283 : 10

Hawks, Francis Lister, *and* W: Stevens Perry, *eds.* Documentary history of the protestant episcopal church in the U. S. of America, containing numerous hitherto unpubl. documents concerning the church in Connecticut. N. Y. 1863, 1864. 2 v. O. 283 : 12

Clergy list, The, for 1884 ; containing alphabetical list of the clergy in England and Wales, · list of the clergy of the episcopal church in Scotland, *etc.* Lond. 1884. O. 283 : R13

Works on episcopacy ; v. 2. N. Y. 1881. D.
283 : 1

Contents. Bowden, J: Second series of letters to dr. Miller.—Cooke, J: E. Essay on the invalidity of presbyterian ordination.—Onderdonk, H: U. Episcopacy tested by scripture.

Burnet, Gilbert. An exposition of the thirty-nine articles of the church of England ; with app., containing the Augsburg confession, creed of pope Pius IV, etc.; rev. and corr., with notes and add. references by James R. Page. N. Y. 1864. O. 283+2

Chapman, G: T: Sermons upon the ministry, worship and doctrines of the protestant episcopal church. 2d ed. Burlington. 1832.
283 : 3

Colton, Calvin. Thoughts on the religious state of the country ; with reasons for preferring episcopacy. N. Y. 1836. D. 283 : 4

Fowler, Andrew. An exposition of the articles of religion of the protestant episcopal church in the U. S. of America. Added, some useful extracts. Charleston. 1840. D. 283 : 5

How, T: Yardley. A vindication of the protestant episcopal church, in a series of letters addressed to the rev. S: Miller, in reply to his late writings on the christian ministry, and to the charges contained in his life of the rev. dr. Rodgers ; with prelim. remarks. N. Y. 1816. O. 283 : 6

Jewel, J: Works, 3d portion ; containing Apologia ecclesiæ anglicanæ ; an apology of the church of England, [and] The defence of the apology, parts 1-3 ; ed. for the Parker society by J: Ayre. Cambridge. 1848. Q. 283 : 7

Kip, W: Ingraham. The church of the apostles. N. Y. 1877. D. 283 : 8

— Double witness of the church. 2d ed. N. Y. 1844. D. 283 : 9

Presbyterian.

Spottiswoode, J: History of the church of Scotland, beginning the year of our Lord 203, and continued to the end of the reign of king James VI ; with biographical sketch and notes by M. Russell. Edinb. 1851. 3 v. O. 284 : 3

Webster, R: A history of the presbyterian church in America, from its origin until the year 1760, with biographical sketches of its early ministers. With a memoir of the author by C. Van Rensselaer and an historical introd. by W: Blackwood. Phila. 1858. D. 284+6

Gillett, Ezra Hall. History of the presbyterian church in the U. S. of America. Phila. [1864]. 2 v. D. 284 : 1

Smith, Joseph. Old Redstone, or Historical sketches of western presbyterianism, its early ministers, its perilous times and its first records. Phila. 1854. O. 284 : 2

Patton, Francis L., *vs.* D: **Swing**. The world's ed. of the great presbyterian conflict, Patton vs. Swing, both sides of the question. Portraits, etc. Chicago. 1874. O. **284 : 4**

Peet, Stephen. History of the presbyterian and congregational churches and ministers in Wisconsin, incl. an account of the organization of the convention, and the plan of union. Milw. 1851. T. **284 : 5**

Puritan.

Neal, Daniel. The history of the puritans or protestant nonconformists, from the reformation in 1517 to the revolution in 1688; comprising an account of their principles, their attempts for a farther reformation in the church, their sufferings, and the lives and characters of their most considerable divines. Repr. from the text of dr. Toulmin's ed., with his life of the author and account of his writings; rev., corr. and enl. with add. notes by J: O. Choules. Portraits. N. Y. 1844, 1848. 2 v. O. **285+1**

Coit, T: Winthrop. Puritanism, or A churchman's defence against its aspersions, by an appeal to its own history. N. Y. 1845. D. **285 : 2**

Goodwin, J: A. The puritan conspiracy against the pilgrim fathers and the congregational church, 1624. Bost. 1883. O. **285+4**

Congregational.

Dexter, H: Martyn. Congregationalism of the last 300 years, as seen in its literature, with special reference to certain recondite, neglected or disputed passages; 12 lectures del. on the Southworth foundation in the theological seminary at Andover, Mass., 1876–79; with bibliographical app. N. Y. 1880. O. **285+3**

Baptist.

Benedict, D: A general history of the baptist denomination in America, and other parts of the world. 10th thous. N. Y. 1860. O. **286+1**

Cox, Francis A:, *and* J. **Hoby**. The baptists in America; a narrative of the deputation from the baptist union in England to the U. S. and Canada. Lond. 1836. D. **286 : 2**

Methodist.

Stevens, Abel. The history of the religious movement of the 18th century called methodism, considered in its different denominational forms, and its relation to british and american protestantism. N. Y. [1868]. 3 v. D. **287 : 2**
Contents. V. **1.** From the origin of methodism to the death of Whitefield. **2.** From the death of Whitefield to the death of Wesley. **3.** From the death of Wesley to the centenary jubilee of methodism.

— The centenary of american methodism; a sketch of its history, theology, practical system and success; with a statement of the plan of the centenary celebration of 1866 by J: M'Clintock. N. Y. 1866. D. **287 : 1**

Stevens, Abel.—*Continued.*
— History of the methodist episcopal church in the U. S. of America. N. Y. 1864. 2 v. D. **287 : 3**

Jobson, F: J. America and american methodism; with prefatory letters by T: B. Sargent and J: Hannah. Ill. N. Y. 1857. D. **287 : 5**

Brownlow, W: G. The great iron wheel examined, or its false spokes extracted, and an exhibition of elder Graves, its builder, in a series of chapters. Nashville. 1856. D. **287 : 4**

Unitarian.

Woods, Leonard. Letters to unitarians, occasioned by the sermon of W: E. Channing at the ordination of J. Sparks. Andover. 1820. O. **288 : 1**

Quaker.

Barclay, Robert. An apology for the true christian divinity, being an explanation and vindication of the principles and doctrines of the people called quakers, written in latin and english. Phila. *n. d.* D. **289.2 : 5**

Greer, Sarah, *Mrs.* J: R. Quakerism, or The story of my life, by a lady who for forty years was a member of the society of friends. Phila. 1852. D. **289.2 : 2**

Janney, S: M. History of the religious society of friends, from its rise to 1828. Phila. 1861–70. 4 v. D. **289.2 : 1**

Penn, W: Primitive christianity revived in the faith and practice of the people called quakers; written in testimony to the present dispensation of God through them to the world, that prejudices may be removed, the simple informed, the well-inclined encouraged and the truth and its innocent friends rightly represented. Dublin. 1702. T. **289.2 : 3**

— No cross, no crown; a discourse showing the nature and discipline of the holy cross of Christ, and that the denial of self and daily bearing of Christ's cross is the alone way to the rest and kingdom of God. Added, the living and dying testimonies of many persons of fame and learning, both of ancient and modern times, in favour of this treatise. Phila. 1879. D. **289.2 : 4**

Friends, Society of. Rules of discipline of the yearly meeting of men and women friends, held in Philadelphia. Phila. 1877. D. **289.2 : 6**

Adventist.

Smith, Uriah. Thoughts, critical and practical, on the book of Daniel. Battle Creek, Mich. 1873. D. **289 : 4**

— *Same.* 2d ed. rev. and enl. Battle Creek, Mich. 1881. D. **289 : 4**

— Thoughts, critical and practical, on the book of Revelation. 2d ed. Battle Creek, Mich. 1875. D. **289 : 5**

— *Same.* 3d ed. rev. and enl. Battle Creek, Mich. 1881. D. **289 : 5**

Smith, Uriah.—*Continued.*
— The United States in the light of prophecy, or
An exposition of Revel. xiii, 11-17. Battle
Creek. 1872. S.   **289 : 6**
— *Same.*   3d ed. Battle Creek. 1876. S.   **289 : 6**
White, Ellen G. The spirit of prophecy: The
great controversy between Christ and his
angels, and Satan and his angels. Battle
Creek, Mich. 1870-78. 3 v. D.   **289 : 9**
White, James. Life incidents in connection
with the great advent movement, as ill. by
the three angels of Revel. xiv. V. 1. Bat-
tle Creek. 1868. D.   **289 : 7**

Swedenborgian.

Swedenborg, Emanuel. The Swedenborg
library, ed. by B. F. Barrett. Phila. [1875-
1881.] 12 v. T.   **289.1 : 17**
  Contents. V. 1. Death, resurrection and the judgment. 2. Heaven. 3. Freedom, rationality and
catholicity. 4. Divine providence and its laws. 5.
Charity, faith and works. 6. Freewill, repentance,
reformation and regeneration. 7. Holy scripture
and the key to its spiritual sense. 8. Creation, in-
carnation, redemption, and the divine trinity 9.
Marriage and the sexes in both worlds. 10. The
author's memorabilia. 11. The heavenly doctrine of
the Lord. 12. Swedenborg; with a compendium of
his teachings.
— Angelic philosophy of the divine love and wisdom. From the original latin as ed. by J.
F. I. Tafel, tr. by R. Norman Foster.
Phila. 1868. O.   **289.1 : 4**
— Angelic wisdom concerning the divine love
and the divine wisdom. Tr. from the latin,
originally pub. at Amsterdam 1763 ; from
the last Lond. ed. Phila. *n. d.* O.
       289.1 : 4
— Angelic wisdom concerning the divine providence. Tr. from the latin, originally pub.
at Amsterdam 1764 ; from the last Lond.
ed. N. Y. 1857. O.   **289.1+5**
— The apocalypse explained according to the
spiritual sense ; in which are revealed the
arcana which are there predicted, and
have been hitherto deeply concealed. From
a latin posthumous work. 1st amer. ed.
N. Y. 1846, 1847. 5 v. O.   **289.1+1**
— The apocalypse revealed, wherein are disclosed the arcana there foretold, which
have heretofore remained concealed. Tr.
from the latin ; new ed. rev. and corr. N.
Y. 1859. 2 v. O.   **289.1+2**
— Arcana cœlestia ; The heavenly arcana, contained in the holy scriptures or word of
the Lord, unfolded, beginning with the
book of Genesis ; together with wonderful
things seen in the world of spirits and in
the heaven of angels. Tr. from the latin.
N. Y. 1853-57. 10 v. O.   **289.1+7**
— Conjugial love and its chaste delights, also
Adulterous love and its sinful pleasures ;
a tr. of his "Delitiæ sapientiæ de amore
conjugali, post quas sequuntur voluptates
insaniæ de amore scortatorio ; Amstelo-
dami, 1768. N. Y. 1856. O.   **289.1 : 3**
— The four leading doctrines of the new church,
signified by the new Jerusalem in the
Revelation ; being those concerning the
Lord, the sacred scripture, faith and life.
N. Y. 1857. O.   **289.1+6**
— Heaven and its wonders, the world of spirits
and hell, from things heard and seen.

Swedenborg, E.—*Continued.*
From the latin, originally pub. at London
in 1758, tr. by S: Noble of London. N. Y.
1859. D.   **289.1 : 10**
— The true christian religion ; containing the
universal theology of the new church, foretold by the Lord in Daniel, vii : 13, 14, and
in the Apocalypse, xxi : 1, 2. Tr. from the
latin. N. Y. 1858. O.   **289.1 : 8**
— Miscellaneous theological works. N. Y. 1857.
O.   **289.1+9**
  Contents. The new Jerusalem and its heavenly
doctrine.—A brief exposition of the doctrines of the
new church.—Nature of the intercourse between the
soul and the body.—On the white horse mentioned in
the Apocalypse, chap. xix.—App. to treatise on the
white horse.—On the earths in the universe.—The
last judgment.—Continuation concerning the last
judgment.
— Compendium of [his] theological writings. N.
Y. 1875. O.   **289.1 : 11**
  Contents. Concerning God.—Creation.—Man.—The
fall of man.—The doctrine of the Lord.—The holy
spirit.—The divine trinity.—The sacred scriptures.—
Signification of the various terms and subjects in the
word.—The ten commandments.—Faith.—Charity and
good works.—Free will.—Repentance, reformation
and regeneration.—Imputation.—The church.—The
first or most ancient church.—The second or ancient
church.—The third or israelitish church.—The fourth
or first christian church.—The second coming of the
Lord.—The fifth or new christian church.—Baptism.
—The holy supper.—The priesthood.—Marriage.—
Divine providence.—The human soul.—Influx, and
intercourse between the soul and the body.—The
eternal world.—The intermediate state or world of
spirits.—Heaven.—Hell.—The last judgment.—The
earths in the universe.—Miscell. extracts.—Index.

New church essays on science. philosophy and
religion, incl. literature and the arts, by
new church writers in America and
Europe. Bost. 1854. O.   **289.1+13**
Bush, G: New church miscellanies, or Essays,
ecclesiastical, doctrinal and ethical. N. Y.
1855. D.   **289.1 : 12**
  Contents. The priesthood and the kingship.—
Preaching.—The ministry.—The New Jerusalem magazine and the new church ministry.—New church
organization and government.—A trained and professional clergy.—The party of order, and the party
of liberty.—Aphorisms on slavery and abolition.—
Pseudo-spiritualism.—Sleep.—The new church system
referable solely to a divine origin.—Swedenborg and
Paul.
Mercer, L. P. The Bible ; its true character and
spiritual meaning. Chicago. 1879. D.
      289.1 : 16
Silver, Abiel. The holy word in its own defence,
addressed to bishop Colenso and all other
earnest seekers after truth. N. Y. 1863. O.
      289.1 : 14
— Lectures on the symbolic character of the
sacred scriptures. N. Y. 1863. O.
      289.1 : 15

Other sects.

Braasch, A. H. Ist ein zusammenwirken der
verschiedenen richtungen innerhalb der
evangelisch-protestantischen kirche möglich ? *In* Deutsche zeit- und streit-fragen.
      304 : 15 v7
Schmidt, Paul W: Was trennt "die beiden
richtungen" in der evangelischen kirche ?
ein beitrag zur schätzung der kirchlichen
gegensätze. *In* Deutsche zeit- und streit-
fragen.   **304 : 15 v9**
Schmidt, Paul V: Gewalt oder geist ? ein fest-
liches bedenken über die zukunft von
Luthers kirche. *In* Deutsche zeit- und
streit-fragen.   **304 : 15 v12**

Strobel, Philip A.   The salzburgers and their descendants ; history of a colony of german lutheran protestants, who emigrated to Georgia in 1734 and settled at Ebenezer, 25 miles above the city of Savannah.   Balt. 1855. D.   289 : 10

Wycliffe, J: An apology for Lollard doctrines, attributed to Wicliffe ; now first printed from a ms. in the library of Trinity college, Dublin, with an introd. and notes of James Henthorn Todd. [Camden soc., no. 20].   Lond. 1842. O.   289 : 8

10. Non-christian religions and Folk-lore.

1. General mythology.

Faiths of the world, The ; a concise history of the great religious systems of the world. [St. Giles' lectures]. Edinb. 1882. D.
291 : 23
Contents. Caird, J: Religions of India; Vedic period, brahmanism; buddhism. — Matheson, G: Religion of China, confucianism.—Milne, J: Religion of Persia, Zoroaster and the Zend-avesta.— Dodds, J. Religion of ancient Egypt.—Milligan, W: Religion of ancient Greece.—MacGregor, J. Religion of ancient Rome.—Burns, G: S. Teutonic and scandinavian religions. — Lang, J: M. Ancient religions of Central America. — Taylor, M. C. Judaism.—Lees, J. C. Mohammedanism.—Flint, R. Christianity in relation to other religions.

Clarke, James Freeman. Ten great religions ; an essay in comparative theology. Bost. 1878, 1883. 2 v. D.   291 : 4
Contents. V. 1. Introd.—Ethnic and catholic religions.—Confucius and the chinese, or The prose of Asia.—Brahmanism.—Buddhism, or The protestantism of the east.—Zoroaster and the Zend-avesta.— The gods of Egypt.—The gods of Greece.—The religion of Rome.—The teutonic and scandinavian religion.—The jewish religion.—Mohammed and islam.— The ten religions and christianity. 2. A comparison of all religions.

Cook, F: C: The origins of religion and language, considered in five essays. Lond. 1884. O.   291 : 28
Contents. On the Rig Veda, specially on its religious system.—On the persian cuneiform inscriptions and the Zend avesta.—On the Gâthâs of Zoroaster.— On languages, ancient and modern.—On egyptian, compared with semitic, aryan and turanian words.

Döllinger, J: Joseph Ignaz v. The gentile and the jew in the courts of the temple of Christ ; an introd. to the history of christianity. From the german by N. Darnell. Lond. 1862. 2 v. O.   291 : 1

Kuenen, Abraham. National religion and universal religions. (Hibbert lectures, 1882). N. Y. 1882. D.   291 : 15

Maurice, J: F: Denison. The religions of the world and their relations to christianity. From the 3d rev. Lond. ed. Bost. 1854. D.
291 : 7

Moffat, James C. A comparative history of religions. N. Y. 1875. 2 v. D.   291 : 8

Müller, F: Max. Essays on the science of religion. *In his* Chips.   824.2 : 74 v1
Contents, see under English literature, Essays.

— Essays on mythology, traditions and customs. *In his* Chips.   824.2:74 v2
Contents, see under English literature, Essays.

Rawlinson, G: The religions of the ancient world, including Egypt, Assyria and Babylonia, Persia, India, Phœnicia, Etruria, Greece, Rome. N. Y. 1883. D.   290 : 5

Tiele, C. P. Comparative history of the egyptian and mesopotamian religions ; Egypt, Babel - Assur, Yemen, Harran, Phœnicia, Israel. Tr. from the dutch, with the co-

operation of the author by James Ballingal. [Trübner's oriental ser.] Lond. 1882. O.   291:27
Contents. V. 1. History of the egyptian religion.

*   *   *

Adams, W: H: Davenport. Curiosities of superstition and sketches of some unrevealed religions. Lond. 1882. D.   291 : 20

Bunce, J: Thackeray. Fairy tales, their origin and meaning, with some account of dwellers in fairyland. Lond. 1878. D.
291 : 13

Burkhardt, C. B. Fairy tales and legends of many nations, selected, newly told and tr. Ill. N. Y. *n. d.* D.   291 : 14

Clodd, E: The childhood of religions ; embracing a simple account of the birth and growth of myths and legends. N. Y. 1878. D.   291 : 5

Conway, Moncure Daniel. The wandering jew. N. Y. 1881. D.   291 : 10

Cox, *Sir* G: W: Introduction to the science of comparative mythology and folk lore. N. Y. 1881. D.   291 : 9

— The mythology of the aryan nations. New and rev. ed. Lond. 1882. O.   291 : 19

Creuzer, G: F: Symbolik und mythologie der alten völker, besonders der griechen. 3te verb. ausg. [Ill.] Leipz. 1836-42. 4 v. O.
291 : 21

Fiske, J: Myths and myth-makers ; old tales and superstitions, interpreted by comparative mythology. Bost. 1873. D. 291 : 22
Contents. The origins of folk-lore.—The descent of fire. — Werewolves and swan-maidens. — Light and darkness.—Myths of the barbaric world.—Juventus mundi.—The primeval ghost-world.—Index.

Folkard, R:, *jr.* Plant lore, legends and lyrics ; embracing the myths, traditions, superstitions and folk-lore of the plant kingdom. Lond. 1884. O.   293.1+33

Gould, Sabine Baring-. Curious myths of the middle ages. Bost. 1867. D.   291 : 26
Contents. The wandering jew.—Prester John.—The divining rod.— The seven sleepers of Ephesus. — William Tell.—The dog Gellert.—Tailed men.—Antichrist and pope Joan.—The man in the moon.—The mountain of Venus.—Fatality of numbers.—The terrestrial paradise.

Heine, H: Elementargeister und dämonen. *In his* Sämmtliche werke.   830 : 139 v7
Contents. Elementargeister.—Der doktor Faust.— Die götter im exil.—Die göttin Diana.

Keightley, T: The fairy mythology, illustrative of the romance and superstition of various countries. New ed. rev. and enl. Lond. 1878. D.   291 : 6

Keary, C: Francis. Outlines of primitive belief among the indo-european races. N. Y. 1882. O.   291 : 17

Knight, R: Payne. An inquiry into the symbol-
ical language of ancient art and mythology.
Privately printed 1818, repr. and repub. by
E. H. Barker. Lond. 1836. O.   290 : 2
Lang, Andrew. Custom and myth. Ill. N. Y.
1885 [1884]. D.   291 : 25
Moncrieff, Robert Hope.(*Ascott R. Hope*). Stories
of long ago, retold by Ascott R. Hope. Ill.
Lond. 1881. D.   291 : 12
Contents. The abbot and the emperor.—Havelock.
—The quarrelsome couple.—The fatal treasure.—Sir
Lauval.—The merchant among rogues.—The emperor
Jovinian.—The wise men of Gotham.—The lime-kiln.
—The boor and the bird.—The talismans.—The dog of
Montargis.—The fool of the family.—Eustace.—A tale
of the tournament.—The anchorite and the angel.—
The physician against his will. — The rings. — The
thieves.—The two friends.— The braggart knight.—
The knight and his greyhound.
Pabke, Marie, *and* Margaret J. Pitman (*Margery
Deane*), *eds.* Wonder-world stories from
the chinese, french, german, hebrew, hin-
dostanee, hungarian, irish, italian, japan-
ese, russian, swedish and turkish, coll. and
tr. by Marie Pabke and Margery Deane.
N. Y. 1877. D.   291 : 11
Peschel, Oscar Ferdinand. Der ursprung und
die verbreitung einiger geographischer
mythen im mittelalter. *In his* Abhand-
lungen.   910 : 2 v1
— Ueber den mann im monde. *In the same.*
    910 : 2 v2
Vignoli, Tito. Myth and science ; an essay.
(Intern. scientific ser.) N. Y. 1882. D.
    291 : 16
Westropp, Hodder M., *and* C: Staniland Wake.
Ancient symbol worship ; influence of the
phallic idea on religions of antiquity ; with
an introd., add. notes and an app. by
Alexander Wilder. N. Y. 1874. O.
    291+P18

*   *   *

Bulfinch, T: The age of fable, or Beauties of
mythology. Bost. 1865. D.   291 : 3
Cox, *Sir* G: W: A manual of mythology, in the
form of question and answer. N. Y. [1868].
S.   290 : 3
Göll, Hermann. Illustrirte mythologie ; götter-
sagen und kultusformen der hellenen,
römer, ägypter, inder, perser und ger-
manen, nebst zusammenstellung der ge-
bräuchlichsten symbole und allegorischen
bilder, für freunde des alterthums, inshe-
sondere für die reifere jugend. 4te aufl.
Leipz. 1879. O.   290 : 1
Murray, Alexander S. Manual of mythology ;
greek, roman, norse and old german,
hindoo and egyptian mythology. 2d ed.
re-written and enl. Ill. N. Y. 1874. D.
    290 : 4

2. Greek and roman mythology.

Cox, *Sir* G: W: Tales of ancient greece. New
ed. Lond. 1880. S.   292 : 8
Harrison, J. E. Myths of the Odyssey in art
and literature. Lond. 1882. O.   292 : 4
Kingsley, C: The heroes, or Greek fairy tales
for my children. Ill. [Works, v. 7]. Lond.
1879. D.   x 292 : 9
— *Same.* N. Y. 1880. D.   x 292 : 9

Larned, Augusta. Old tales retold from grecian
mythology in talks around the fire. Ill.
N. Y. [1876]. D.   x 292 : 6
Niebuhr, Barthold G: Greek hero-stories. Tr.
by B: Hoppin. Ill. N. Y. 1879. D.
    x 292 : 10
Ruskin, J: The queen of the air ; a study of
the greek myths of cloud and storm. N. Y.
1878. D.   292 : 3
Scull, Sarah Amelia. Greek mythology syste-
matized. Phila. [1880]. D.   292 : 5
Seemann, O: The mythology of Greece and
Rome, with special reference to its use in
art. From the german, ed. by G. H.
Bianchi. Ill. N. Y. 1881. S.   292 : 2
Smith, S: Francis, *ed.* Myths and heroes, or
The childhood of the world. Bost. [1873].
D.   x 292 : 7
Welcker, F: Gottlieb. Griechische götterlehre.
Göttingen. 1857-63. 3 v. O.   292 : 1

3. Norse and teutonic mythology.

Grimm, Jacob L: C: Teutonic mythology. Tr.
from the 4th ed. with notes and app. by
James Steven Stallybrass. Lond. 1882.
3 v. O.   293 : 11
Simrock, K: Joseph. Handbuch der deutschen
mythologie, mit einschluss der nordischen.
5te aufl. Bonn. 1878. O.   293 : 3
Thorpe, B: Northern mythology, comprising
the principal popular traditions and superstitious of Scandinavia, North Germany
and the Netherlands ; compiled from original and other sources. Lond. 1851. 3 v. O.
    293 : 12
Holtzmann, Adolf. Deutsche mythologie ; vorlesungen, herausg. von Alfred Holder.
Leipz. 1874. O.   293 : 2
Carlyle, T: Scandinavian mythology. *In his*
On heroes and hero-worship.   824.2 : 22
Anderson, Rasmus B. Norse mythology, or
The religion of our forefathers, containing
all the myths of the Eddas, systematized
and interpreted, with an introd., vocabulary and index. 2d ed. Chicago. 1876. D.
    293 : 1
— *ed. and tr.* The younger Edda, also called
Snorre's Edda, or the prose Edda ; an eng-
lish version of the foreword, the fooling of
Gylfe, the afterword to Brage's talk and
the important passages in the Poetical
diction (Skáldskaparmál), with an introd.,
notes, vocabulary and index. Chicago.
1880. D.   293 : 4
Baldwin, James. The story of Siegfried. Ill.
N. Y. 1882. D.   293 : 10
Jones, Julia Clinton. Valhalla, the myths of
Norseland ; a saga in 12 parts. N. Y. 1880.
D.   293 : 5
Keary, Annie *and* E. The heroes of Asgard ;
tales from scandinavian mythology. Ill.,
new ed. Lond. 1880. S.   293.1 : 11
Keyser, Jakob Rudolf. The religion of the
northmen. Tr. by Barclay Pennock. N.
Y. 1854. D.   293 : 6
Larned, Augusta. Tales from the norse grand-
mother, the elder Edda. N. Y. 1881. D.
    293 : 7
Mabie, Hamilton Wright. Norse stories retold
from the Eddas. Bost. 1882. S.   293 : 9

x denotes books specially adapted for children.

Mallet, Paul H: Northern antiquities. 948 : 1
Note. For full title, see under Scandinavian history.
Smith, J. Moyr, *ed.* Tales of old Thulê. Phila. 1879. D.   293.1 : 30
Contents. Rashycoat.—Rollo and the magic sword.—Jack and the fairy princess.—The brownie in the pantry.—Prince Corallu.—The trial of the suitors.—The sandals of Hermod.—The golden glove.
Steffens, H: Ueber die einwirkung des christenthums auf die nordische mythologie. *In his* Nachgelassene schriften.   898.2 : 1
Wägner, W: Asgard and the gods; tales and traditions of our northern ancestors told for boys and girls, adapted by M. W. Macdowall and ed. by W. S. W. Anson. Ill. Phila. 1880. O.   x 293 : 8

4. Brahmanism and buddhism.

Müller, F: Max, *ed.* Sacred books of the east.
—The Upanishads, pt. 1, 2. Tr. by. F: Max Müller. [Sacred books of the east. v. 1, 15.] Oxford. 1879, 1884. 2 v. O.   294 : 1
— The sacred laws of the âryas as taught in the schools of Âpastamba, Gautama, Vâsishtha and Baudhâyana; pt. 1, 2. Tr. by G: Bühler. [Sacred books of the east. v. 2, 14.] Oxford. 1879, 1882. 2 v. O.   294 : 2
— The institutes of Vishnu. Tr. by Julius Jolly. [Sacred books of the east, v. 7.] Oxford. 1880. O.   294 : 3
— The Bhagavadgîtâ with the Sanatsugâtiya and the Anugîtâ. Tr. by Kâashinâth Trimbak Telang. [Sacred books of the east, v. 8]. Oxford. 1882. O.   294 : 4
— The Dhammmapada, a collection of verses; being one of the canonical books of the buddhists. Tr. from pâli by F. Max Müller. [Sacred books of the east, v. 10, pt. 1]. Oxford. 1881. O.   294 : 5
— The Sutta-nipâta, a collection of discourses; being one of the canonical books of the buddhists, Tr. from pâli by V. Fausböll. [Sacred books of the east, v. 10, pt. 2]. Oxford. 1881. O.   294 : 5
— Buddhist Suttas. Tr. from pâli by T. W. Rhys Davids. [Sacred books of the east, v. 11]. Oxford. 1881. O.   294 : 6
— The Satapatha-Brâhmana according to the text of the Mâdhyandina school; pt. 1. Tr. by Julius Eggeling. [Sacred books of the east, v. 12]. Oxford. 1882. O.   294 : 7
— Vinaya texts. Tr. from the pâli by T. W. Rhys Davids and Hermann Oldenberg; pts. 1, 2. [Sacred books of the east, v. 13, 17]. Oxford. 1881, 1882. 2 v. O.   294 : 8
— The Fo-sho-hing-tsan-king; a life of Buddha by Asvaghosha Bodhisattva. Tr. from sanskrit into chinese by Dharmaraksha, a. d. 420, and from chinese into english by S: Beal. [Sacred books of the east, v. 19]. Oxford. 1883. O.   294 : 15
— Saddharma-pundarika, or The lotus of the true law. Tr. by H. Kern. [Sacred books of the east, v. 22]. Oxford. 1884. O.   294 : 22
Mahabharata, The, of Krishna Dwaipayana Vyasa, translated into english prose. Pub. and distributed chiefly gratis by Protap

x denotes books specially adapted for children.

Chundra Roy. [Vol. 1]. Calcutta. 1884. O.   294 : 25
Note. Continued in monthly parts.
Vedântasâra, The. A manual of hindu pantheism; the Vedântasâra, tr., with copious annotations, by major G. A. Jacob. Lond. 1881. O.   294 : 14

* * *

Barth, A: The religions of India. Authorized tr. by J. Wood. Lond. 1882. O.   294 : 11
Bose, Ram Chandra. Brahmoism, or History of reformed hinduism from its origin in 1830 under rajah Mohun Roy to the present time; with a particular account of babu Keshub Chunder Sen's connection with the movement. N. Y. 1884. D.   294 : 24
— Hindu philosophy, popularly explained; the orthodox systems. N. Y. 1884. D. 294 : 26
Davids, T: W: Rhys. Lectures on the origin and growth of religion, as ill. by some points in the history of indian buddhism. (Hibbert lectures, 1881). N. Y. 1882. O.   294+12
— Buddhism; a sketch of the life and teachings of Guatama, the buddha. [Non-christian religious systems.] Lond. *n. d.* S. 294 : 16
Gangooly, Joguth Chunder, *baptized* Philip. Life and religion of the hindoos, with a sketch of my life and experience. Bost. 1860. D.   294 : 17
Grimm, E: Die lehre über Buddha und das dogma von Jesus Christ; vortrag in märz 1876 zu Hamburg gehalten. *In* Deutsche zeit-und streit-fragen.   304 : 15 v6
Hönes, Christian. Die reformbewegung des Brahmosomadsch in Indien, als schranke des missionswesens; vortrag gehalten im feb. 1877 zu Basel. *In* Deutsche zeit- und streit-fragen.   304 : 15 v6
Johnson, S: Oriental religions, and their relation to universal religion: India. Bost. 1873. O.   294 : 18
Lillie, Arthur. Buddha and early buddhism. N. Y. [1882]. O.   294 : 13
— The popular life of Buddha; containing an answer to the Hibbert lectures of 1881, [by T. W. R. Davids]. Ill. Lond. 1883. D.   294 : 27
Müller, F: Max. Lectures on the origin and growth of religion, as ill. by the religions of India; del. in the chapter house, Westminster abbey, in april, may and june 1878. [Hibbert lectures, 1878]. N. Y. 1879. D.   294 : 10
— Buddhist nihilism; with a tr. of the Dhammapada, or Path of virtue. *With his* Science of religion.   *in* 201 : 1
— India; what can it teach us? a course of lectures del. before the university of Cambridge; with an introd. and notes by Alex. Wilder. N. Y. [1883]. D.   294 : 21
Oldenberg, Hermann. Buddha; his life, his doctrine, his order. Tr. from the german by W: Hoey. Lond. 1882. O.   294 : 23
Williams, Monier. Hinduism. [Non-christian religious systems]. Lond. 1878. S. 294 : 19
Fergusson, James. Tree and serpent worship, or Illustrations of mythology and art in India from the topes at Sanchi and Amravati. Lond. 1868. F.   299 : R15

5. Chinese religions.

Müller, F: Max, *ed.* The sacred books of China: The texts of confucianism. Tr. by James Legge. [Sacred books of the east, v. 3, 16]. Oxford. 1879, 1882. 2 v. O.   **299 : 1**

Edkins, Joseph. Religion in China; containing a brief account of the three religions of the chinese, with observations on the prospects of christian conversion amongst that people. 2d ed. [Eng. and foreign phil. library.] Lond. 1878. O.   **299 : 5**

Johnson, S: Oriental religions and their relation to universal religion: China. Bost. 1878. O.   **299 : 2**

Legge, James. The chinese classics, tr. into english, with prelim. essays and explanatory notes. Reproduced for general readers from the author's work containing the original text, etc. V. 1: The life and teachings of Confucius. 5th ed. Lond. 1877. O.   **299 : 3**

— — V. 2: The life and works of Mencius, with essays and notes. Phila. 1875. D.   **299 : 11**

— The religions of China; confucianism and tãoism described and compared with christianity. N. Y. 1881. D.   **299 : 4**

6. Parseeism.

Müller, F: Max, *ed.* Sacred books of the east.
— The Zend-avesta. Tr. by James Darmesteter. [Sacred books of the east, v. 4, 23]. Oxford. 1880, 1883. 2 v. O.   **295 : 1**

— Pahlavi texts. Tr. by E. W. West. [Sacred books of the east, v. 5, 18]. Oxford. 1880. 2 v. O.   **295 : 2**

Johnson, S: Oriental religions, and their relation to universal religion: Persia. With an introd. by O. B. Frothingham. Bost. 1885 [1884]. O.   **295 : 3**

7. Egyptian and chaldean religions.

Renouf, P: LePage. The origin and growth of religion, as ill. by the religion of ancient Egypt. (Hibbert lectures for 1879). N. Y. 1880. D.   **299 : 8**

Smith, G: The chaldean account of Genesis; containing the description of the creation, the fall of man, the deluge, the tower of Babel, the times of the patriarchs and Nimrod, babylonian fables and legends of the gods from the cuneiform inscriptions. Ill. N. Y. 1876. O.   **299+7**

8. Judaism.

(See also Jewish history, cl. 933.)

Nikelsburger, Jacob. Koul Jacob in defence of the jewish religion; containing the arguments of C. F. Frey, one of the committee of London society for the conversion of the jews, and answers thereto. N. Y. 1816. O.   **296 : 1**

Schleiden, Matthias Jacob. The sciences among the jews before and during the middle ages. Tr. from the 4th german ed. Balt. 1883. S.   **296 : 4**

Stanley, Arthur Penrhyn. Lectures on the history of the jewish church. Maps and plans. N. Y. 1864-82. 3 v. O.   **296+2**
Contents. v. 1. Abraham to Samuel. 2. From Samuel to the captivity. 3. From the captivity to the christian era.

Talmud, The; selections from the contents of that ancient book, its commentaries, teachings, poetry, and legends; also brief sketches of the men who made and commented upon it. Tr. from the original by H. Polano. Diagr. Phila. [1884]. D.   **296 : 5**

Statistics of the jews of the U. S., comp. under the authority of the board of delegates of amer. israelites and the union of amer. hebrew congregations. Phila. 1880. O.   **296 : Pam**

9. Mohammedanism.

Koran, The, commonly called the Alcoran of Mohammed. Tr. into english immediately from the original arabic, with explanatory notes, taken from the most approved commentators, [and] a preliminary discourse, by G: Sale. 5th ed., with a memoir of the transl. and with various readings and ill. notes from Savary's version of the Koran. Phila. 1856. O.   **297+1**

Müller, F: Max. *ed.* The Qur'ân. Tr. by E. H. Palmer. [Sacred books of the east, v. 6, 9]. Oxford. 1880. 2 v. O.   **297 : 2**

Poole, Stanley Lane-. Studies in a mosque. Lond. 1883. O.   **297 : 5**
Contents. The arabs before islam.—Mohammed.—Islam.—The Koran.—An eastern reformation.—The brotherhood of purity.—The persian miracle play.

Stephens, W: R: Wood. Christianity and islam; the Bible and the Koran, four lectures. N. Y. 1877. D.   **297 : 3**

Stobart, James W: Hampson. Islam and its founder. [Non-christian religious systems]. Lond. [1878]. S.   **297 : 4**

Görgens, E. P. Der islam und die moderne kultur; ein beitrag zur lösung der orientalischen frage. *In* Deutsche zeit- und streitfragen.   **304 : 15 v8**

10. Mormonism.

Smith, Joseph, *jr.* The book of Mormon; repr. from the 3d amer. ed., carefully rev. by the translator. N. Y. *n. d.* D.   **298 : 4**

Busch, Moritz. Die mormonen; ihr prophet, ihr staat und ihr glaube. Leipz. 1855. S.   **298 : 1**

Ferris, *Mrs.* B: G. The mormons at home; with some incidents of travel from Missouri to California, 1852-3, in a series of letters. N. Y. 1856. D.   **298 : 2**

Gunnison, J: W. The mormons, or latter-day saints, in the valley of the Great Salt Lake; a history of their rise, progress, peculiar doctrines, present condition and prospects, derived from personal observation, during a residence among them. Phila. 1853. D.   **298 : 3**

11. American indian religions.

(See also North-american indians, cl. 970.1.)

Bache, R: Meade. American wonderland. Phila. 1871. D.   **299 : 10**

Brinton, Daniel Garrison. American hero-myths ; a study in the native religions of the western continent. Phila. 1882. O.
299 : 13
— The myths of the new world ; a treatise on the symbolism and mythology of the red race of america. 2d ed. rev. N. Y. 1876. D.
291 : 2
Dorman, Rushton M. The origin of primitive superstitions and their development into the worship of spirits and the doctrine of spiritual agency among the aborigines of America. Ill. Phila. 1881. O.   299+6
Emerson, Ellen Russell. Indian myths, or Legends, traditions, and symbols of the aborigines of America. Plates and diagr. Bost. 1884. O.   291 : 24
Réville, Albert. The native religions of Mexico and Peru. Tr. by Philip H. Wicksteed. (Hibbert lectures, 1884). N. Y. 1884. D.
299 : 14

12. Folk-lore.

(See also General literature, Romance, cl. 813.)

Scotch and irish.

Old celtic romances. Tr. from the gaelic by P. W. Joyce. Lond. 1879. D.   293.1 : 13
Croker, T: Crofton. Fairy legends and traditions of the south of Ireland. New and complete ed. by T: Wright. Ill. Lond. *n. d.* D.   293.1 : 6
Kennedy, Patrick, T: Crofton Croker *and others.* Legends and fairy tales of Ireland. N. Y. 1880. D.   293.1 : 7
Rodenberg, Julius. Die irische märchenlehre. *In his* Harfe von Erin.   896 : 1

English and welsh.

Bowker, James. Goblin tales of Lancashire. [Ill. lib. of fairy tales]. Lond. *n. d.* D.
293.1 : 21
Sikes, W: Wirt. British goblins ; welsh folk-lore, fairy mythology, legends and traditions. Ill. 2d ed. Lond. 1881. D.
293.1 : 24
Rodenberg, Julius. Kymric Mabinogion, walisische kindermärchen. *In his* Ein herbst in Wales.   914.2 : 4

German.

Grimm, Jakob L: K: *and* W: K: Deutsche sagen. 2te aufl. Berlin. 1865, 1866. 2 v. S.
293.1 : 2
Hertz, W: Deutsche sage in Elsass. Stuttg. 1872. O.   293.1 : 3
Lauder, Toofie. Legends and tales of the Harz mountains. Lond. 1881. D.   293.1 : 4
Musäus, J: K: A: Deutsche volksmährchen ; mit der biographie and portr. des verf. V. 1, 4. Hildbgh. 1842. S. *in* 830 : 24, 27
— Legends of Number Nip. [Tr.] by Mark Lemon. Ill. Lond. 1864. D.   293.1 : 12
Contents. Introd.—The gnome king and the princess of Silesia.—The gnome and the tailor.—The gnome and his debtor.—Number Nip and the glass-seller.—The headless rogue.
Steffens, H: Mährchen and sagen aus dem Riesengebirge. *In his* Gebirgs-sagen.
S 4802

Italian and spanish.

Tuscan fairy tales taken down from the mouths of the people. Ill. Lond. *n. d.* D.
x 293.1 : 25
Middlemore, *Mrs.* S. G. C. Round a posada fire ; spanish legends. Ill. Bost. 1883. D.
293.1 : 27
Webster, Wentworth. Basque legends, coll. chiefly in the Labourd ; with an essay on the basque language by M. Julien Vinson, with app. Basque poetry. Lond. 1879. O.
293.1 : 8

Scandinavian.

Asbjörnsen, P: Christian. Auswahl norwegischer volksmärchen und waldgeistersagen. Aus dem norw. übers. von H. Denhardt. Leipz. 1881. D.   293.1 : 1
— *Same, eng.* Round the yule log ; norwegian folk and fairy tales. Tr. by H. L. Brækstad, with an introd. by Edmund W. Gosse. Lond. 1881. O.   293.1 : 5
Cappel, Emily S., *ed.* Old norse sagas. (Ill. lib. of fairy tales.) Lond. *n. d.* D.
Contents. Aslog.—Frithiof the bold and fair Ingeborg.—Ragnar Lodbrok.—King Gram.—King Helge and Rolf Kraki.—The battle of Brawalla.—Sigurd the dragon-slayer.—Wayland Smith.—Helgi.—Hamlet.
Stephens, G:, *and* Gunnar Olof Hyltén-Cavallius. Old norse fairy tales, gathered from the swedish folk. [Tr. by Albert Alberg.] (Ill. lib. of fairy tales.) Lond. *n. d.* D.
293.1 : 20
Contents. The princess Singorra (from Skåne).—The boy and the king's daughter (from Småland).—The three dogs (from West Gotland).—The boy and the giant (from Upland).—The cow-herd boy (from Småland).—The boy who stole the giant's treasure (from Upland).—The land of youth (from Småland).—Three old fays (from Småland). — Pinkel (from Småland). — The golden horse, the lunar lantern, and the maiden in the enchanted castle, (from Upland).
Thorpe, B:, *ed.* Yule-tide stories ; a collection of scandinavian and north-german popular tales and traditions, from the swedish, danish and german. Lond. 1880. D.
293.1 : 10
Steffens, H: Ueber sagen und mährchen aus Dänemark. *In his* Gebirgs-sagen.
S 4802
Arnason, Jón, *comp.* Icelandic legends. Tr. by G: E. J. Powell and Eirikr Magnússon. 2d ser., with notes and an introd. essay. Lond. 1866. D.   293.1 : 15
Maurer, Konrad. Isländische volkssagen der gegenwart ; vorwiegend nach mundlicher überlieferung gesammelt und verdeutscht. Leipz. 1860. O.   293.1+28

Slavonic.

Naaké, J: T. Slavonic fairy tales ; coll. and tr. from the russian, polish, servian and bohemian. Ill. Lond. 1874. D. 293.1 : 9
Ralston, W. R. S. Russian folk-tales. N. Y. 1880. D.   293.1 : 16
Mijatovics, Elodie Lawton, *Mme.* Csedomille. Serbian folk-lore ; popular tales sel. and tr. ; ed. with an introd. Lond. 1874. O.
293.1 : 22

x denotes books specially adapted to children.

Murray, Eustace Clare Grenville. (*Trois Etoiles*). Doine, or The national songs and legends of Roumania. Lond. 1854. D.   **293.1 : 32**

Asiatic.

Day, Lal Behari. Folk-tales of Bengal. N. Y. 1883. D.   **293.1 : 23**

Gréey, E: The golden lotus, and other legends of Japan. Bost. 1883 [1882]. D.   **293.1 : 14**

Griffis, W: Elliot. Japanese fairy world ; stories from the wonder-lore of Japan. Ill. Schenectady, N. Y. 1880. S.   x **293.1 : 26**

Sagas from the far east, or Kalmouk and mongolian traditionary tales, with historical pref. and explanatory notes by the author of "Patrañas" etc. Lond. 1873. D.   **299 : 12**

Tibetan tales. Tr. from the Kah-gyur by F. Anton v. Schiefner, and done into english from the german, with an introd. by W. R. S. Ralston. Bost. 1882. O.   **294 : 20**

African.

Theal, G: McCall. Kaffir folk-lore, or A selection from the traditional tales current among the people living on the eastern border of the Cape Colony, with copious explanatory notes. Lond. [1882]. O.   **293.1 : 18**

American.

Schoolcraft, H: Rowe. Algic researches, comprising inquiries respecting the mental

x denotes books specially adapted for children.

characteristics of the north american indians ; 1st ser.: Indian tales and legends. N. Y. 1839. 2 v. D.   **299 : 9**

Contents. v. 1. General considerations.—Preliminary observations on the tales.—Ojeeg Annung, or The summer-maker. — The celestial sisters. — Tau-Wau-Chee-Hezkaw, or The white feather.—Peboan and Seegwun.—The red lover.—Iamo, or The undying head.— Mon-Dau-Min, or The origin of indian corn.—Peeta Kway, or The tempest.—Manabozho.— Bokwewa, or The humpback.—Iena, or The magic bundle.—Sheem, or The forsaken boy.—Paup-Puk-Keewiss.—Iadilla, or The origin of the robin.—The enchanted moccasins.—The broken wing.—The three cranberries. — Paradise opened to the indians; Pontiac's tale. **2.** The red swan.—Aggo Dah Guada, or The man with his leg tied up.—Iosco, or A visit to the sun and moon.—The two Jeebi.—Pah-Ha-undoo-tah, or The red head.—Leelinau, or The lost daughter. —Puk Wudj Ininee, a fairy tale.—Mishosha, or The marician of the lakes.—The Weendigoes.—The racoon and crawfish, a fable.—La Poudre, or The storm fool. —Git-chee-gauzinee, or The trance.—Wassamo, or The fireplume. — Osseo, or The son of the evening star.—Kwasind, or The fearfully strong man.—Mud-jee Monedo and Minno Monedo.—The pigeonhawk and tortoise, a fable.—The charmed arrow.—Addik Kum Maig, or The origin of the whitefish.—Owasso and Wayoond, or The manito foiled.—Shawondasee. —The linnet and eagle, a fable.—The moose and woodpecker, or Manabozho in distress, — Weeng.— Iagoo.—The grave light, or Adventures of a warrior's soul.—Pauguk.—The vine and oak, an allegory.

— The myth of Hiawatha and other oral legends, mythologie and allegoric, of the north american-indians. Phila. 1856. S.   **293.1 : 31**

Matthews, Cornelius, *comp.* Hiawatha, and other legends of the wigwams of the red american indians. Lond. *n. d.* D.   **293.1 : 17**

Leland, C: Godfrey. The Algonquin legends of New England, or Myths and folk-lore of the Micmac, Passamaquoddy and Penobscot tribes. Ill. Bost. 1884. D.   **293.1 : 29**

IV. SOCIOLOGY.

1. In general.

1. Cyclopedias and general treatises.

Lalor, J: Joseph, *ed.* Cyclopædia of political science, political economy and of the political history of the U. S., by the best american and european writers. Chicago. 1881–84. 3 v. Q.   **303+1**
— *Same.*   **303 : R1**
Rotteck, C: Wenceslaus Rodecker v., *and* C: Theodor **Welcker**. Das staats - lexikon ; encyklopädie der sämmtlichen staatswissenschaften für alle stände ; in verbindung mit vielen angesehensten publicisten Deutschlands. Neue durchaus verb. und verm. aufl., redigirt von Hermann v. Rotteck und C: Welcker. Altona. 1845. 12 v. O.   **303 : 2**
Mohl, Robert v. Encyklopädie der staatswissenschaften. 2te umgearb. aufl. Tübingen. 1872. O.   **303 : 4**
Baumbach, K: Staats-lexikon ; handbuch für jeden staatsbürger zur kenntnis des öffentlichen rechts und des staatslebens aller länder, insbesondere des deutschen reichs. Leipz. 1882. D.   **303 : R5**

* * *

Calvert, G: H: Introduction to social science ; a discourse in three parts. N. Y. 1856. D.   **300 : 1**
Carey, H: C: Principles of social science. 1858. 3 v. O.   **300 : 2**
Michelet, Jules. The people. Tr. by G. H. Smith. N. Y. 1846. D.   **300 : 7**
Rogers, James E. Thorold. Social economy. Rev. for am. readers. [Putnam's handy-book ser.] N. Y. 1874. D.   **300 : 9**
Spencer, Herbert. Social statics, or The conditions essential to human happiness specified, and the first of them developed. N. Y. 1877. D.   **300 : 4**
— The study of sociology. (Intern. scientific ser.) N. Y. 1876. D.   **300 : 5**
— *ed.* Descriptive sociology, or Groups of sociological facts, classified and arr. by Herbert Spencer, compiled and abstracted by D: Duncan, R: Scheppig and James Collier. 8 pts. N. Y. 1873–83. F.   **R**
Contents. **Division 1,** *Uncivilized societies:* pt. 1, *a.* Types of lowest races, negritto races and malayo-polynesian races, by D: Duncan; pt. 2, *a.* African races, by D: Duncan; pt. 3, *a.* Asiatic races, by D: Duncan; pt. 4, *a.* North and south american races, by D: Duncan.—**Divison 2,** *Civilized societies, extinct or decayed:* pt. 1, *b.* Ancient mexicans, central americans, chibchas, and ancient peruvians, by R: Scheppig; pt. 2, *b.* Hebrews and phœnicians, by R: Scheppig. — **Division 3,** *Civilized societies, recent or still flourishing:* pt. 1, *c.* English, by James Collier.

Ward, Lester Frank. Dynamic sociology, or Applied social science, as based upon statical sociology and the less complex sciences. N. Y. 1883. 2 v. D.   **300 : 8**
Wright, R. J. Principia, or Basis of social science ; a survey of the subject from the moral and theological, yet liberal and progressive standpoint. Phila. 1875. O.   **300 : 6**

2. Essays and miscellany.

Braun, K: Aus der mappe eines deutschen reichsbürgers ; kultur-bilder und studien. Hannover. 1874. 3 v. O.   **304 : 2**
Contents. V. 1. I. An den grenzen des deutschen reichos: Dreimal in Nancy.—Der notar von Metz.—Bei mijnherr und seinem nachbar.—Auf dem Memeler leuchtthurm. II. Das deutsche reich sonst und jetzt, 1667 und 1867. III. Die wahlprüfungen und die constituirung des häuses. 2. I. Am deutschen herd: Briefe über die deutsche küche.—Nachwort zu schutz und trutz.—Etwas über den deutschen wein.—Etwas über deutsche vornamen. II. Volkswirthschaftliche streifzüge auf dem gebiete des rechts und der gesetzgebung: Das rechts-institut der vaterschaftsklage, kulturhistorisch und volkswirthschaftlich beleuchtet.—Das zwangs-cölibat der mittellosen in Deutschland.—Nachschrift von 1873.—Zinstaxen, wucherstrafen und schuldhaft. 3. I. Centrifugale gewalten: Dr. Johann Jacoby in Königsberg.—Bischoff von Ketteler in Mainz. II. Kulturgeschichtliche versuche: Die wirthschafts- und die rechts-kultur.—Zur physiologie des eigenthums und des erbrechts.—Zur geschichte der staats- und gemeinde-steuern.—Zur geschichte des deutschen waldes.—Zur geschichte des Rheingauer markwaldes.
Coan, Titus Munson, *ed.* Social problems. (Topics of the time, no. 1). N. Y. 1883. S.   **304 : 9**
Contents. **Giffen,** R. World-crowding.—Europe in straits.—**Paris,** J. de. Secret societies in France.—**Flanagan,** J. W. Home rule, socialism and secession.—**Labouchere,** H: A democrat on the coming democracy.—**Herbert,** A. A politician in trouble about his soul.—**Laveleye,** E. de. The european terror.—The nationalization of the land.
Cobden, R: Political writings ; with an introd. essay by sir L: Mallet. Lond. 1878. D.   **304 : 12**
Contents. Introd.—England, Ireland and America.—Russia, 1836.—1793 and 1853 in three letters.—A letter to H: Ashworth.—How wars are got up in India.—What next—and next ?—The three panics.
Goltz, Bogumil. Die bildung und die gebildeten ; eine beleuchtung der modernen zustände. 2te aufl. Berlin. 1867. S.   **304 : 1**
Greg, W: Rathbone. Rocks ahead, or The warnings of Cassandra. Bost. 1875. D.   **304 : 5**

Harrison, Jonathan Baxter. Certain dangerous tendencies in american life, and other papers. Bost. 1880. D.	**304 : 4**

Contents. Certain dangerous tendencies in american life.—The nationals, their origin and their aims.—Three typical workingmen.—Workingmen's wives.—The career of a capitalist.—Study of a New England factory town.—Preaching.—Sincere demagogy.

Holtzendorff, Joachim W: Franz Philipp v., *ed.* Deutsche zeit- und streit-fragen; flugschriften zur kenntniss der gegenwart. Berlin. 1873–84. 13 v. O.	**304 : 15**

Note. V. 1–5 were ed. jointly with W: Oncken, v. 6–13 with A: Kluckhohn, A: Lammers, Jürgen Bona Meyer, and Paul V: Schmidt.

Contents. V. 1. **Lang**, H: Das leben Jesu und die kirche der zukunft.—**Roscher**, W: Betrachtungen über die währungsfrage der deutschen münzreform.—**Perrot**, F. F. Deutsche eisenbahnpolitik.—**Schulte**, J: F: *ritter* v. Die neueren katholischen orden und congregationen, besonders in Deutschland.—**Stahl**, F: W: Die arbeiterfrage sonst und jetzt.—**Bluntschli**, J: C. Rom und die deutschen.—**Baumgarten**, M. Der protestantismus als politisches princip im deutschen reich.—**Mähly**, J. Der roman des XIX. jahrhunderts.—**Beta**, H: Die geheimmittel- und unsittlichkeits-industrie in der tagespresse.—**Zachariä**, H: A. Das moderne schöffengericht.—**Beck**, F. A. Das grundübel in der modernen jugendbildung.—**Schulte**, J: F: V. Ueber kirchenstrafen.—**Thaer**, K: W: A. Ueber ländliche arbeiter-wohnungen.—**Wasserschleben**, F: W: A: H. Das landesherrliche kirchen-regiment.

2. **Oncken**, A: Die Wiener weltausstellung, 1873.—**Meyer**, J. B. Die fortbildungsschule in unserer zeit.—**Jannasch**, R. Der musterschutz und die gewerbepolitik des deutschen reiches.—**Nippold**, F: W: F. Ursprung, umfang, hemmnisse und ansichten der altkatholischen bewegung.—**Oncken**, W: Das deutsche reich in 1872, I.—**Huber**, J. N. Die kirchlich-politische wirksamkeit des jesuiten-ordens.—**Schmoller**, G. Die entwicklung und die krisis der deutschen weberei im 19. jahrhundert.—**Eck**, E. Die neue deutsche civilprozess-ordnung.—**Oncken**, W: Das deutsche reich in 1872, II.—**Kradolfer**, J. Die altchristliche moral und der moderne zeitgeist.—**Landgraf**, J. Die sicherung des arbeits-vertrages.—**Lang**, H: Die religion im zeitalter Darwins.—**Beta**, H: Die dichtkunst der börse.

3. **Soetbeer**, G: A. Die fünf milliarden.—**Hesse**, F: H. Der felsen Petri kein felsen.—**Gierke**, O: F: Das alte und das neue deutsche reich.—**Pfleiderer**, E. Kosmopolitismus und patriotismus.—**Perrot**, F. F. Die reform des zollverein-tarifes.—**Neumann-Spallart**, F. X. *ritter* v. Die theuerung der lebensmittel.—**Bezold**, E. Das versicherungswesen.—**Grimm**, W. Die Lutherbibel und ihre textesrevision.—**Gareis**, C: Die börse und die gründungen, nebst vorschlägen zur reform des börsenrechts und der actiengesetzgehung.—**Baumgarten**, M. Anti-Klieroth, oder Die gefährlichste reichsfeindschaft.—**Hess**, R: Die forstliche unterrichtsfrage.—**Gallenkamp**, E. Die reform der höheren lehranstalten, insbesondere der realschulen.—**Cohn**, G. Streitfragen der eisenbahnpolitik.—**Fischer**, K: Deutschland's öffentliche meinung in reformationszeitalter und in der gegenwart.—**Lammers**, A: Die Bremer landwirthschafts-ausstellung im juni 1874.—**Meyer**, J. B. Deutsche universitäts-entwicklung.

4. **Laas**, E. Gymnasium und realschule. — **Hirsch**, A: Ueber die verhütung und bekämpfung der volkskrankheiten.—**Laspeyres**, E. Die katheder-socialisten und statistischen congresse. — **Kleinwächter**, F: Zur reform der handwerkerverfassung.—**Pfleiderer**, E. Der moderne pessimismus.—**Oppenheim**, H: B. Die hülfs- und versicherungskassen der arbeitenden klassen.—**Nippold**, F: W: F. Die gegenwärtige wiederbelebung des hexenglaubens.—**Schröder**, R: Das eheliche güterrecht Deutschlands.—**Bar**, K: L: v. Das deutsche reichsgericht.—**Beta**, H: Wohl- und übelthäter in unseren grossstädten.—**Zittel**, E. Der protestantische gottesdienst in unserer zeit.—**Holtzendorff**, F. v. Der priester-cölibat.—**Trächsel**, G. Der katholicismus seit der reformation.

5. **Gareis**, C: Irrlehren über den cultur-kampf.—**Jannasch**, R. Die volks-bibliotheken, ihre aufgabe und ihre organisation.—**Graue**, G. Der mangel an theologen.—**Vogel**, A: Einige aussprüche des landbaues auf steuer- und zollentlastung. — **Lammers**, A: Der moorrauch und seine cultur-mission.—**Wittmeyer**, L. Ueber die leichenverbrennung.—**Schneider**, J: P. Die ungedeckte banknote und die alternativ-währung.—**Laspeyres**, E. Das alter der deutschen professoren.—**Baumgarten**, M. Der kampf um das reichscivilstandsgesetz in der deutschen protestantischen kirche.—**Jagemann**, E. v. Die stellung der niederdeutschen in Belgien.—**Cohn**, G. Ueber die vertheuerung des lebensunterhaltes in der gegenwart.—**Horwicz**, A. Wesen und aufgabe der philosophie. — **Kirchner**, F: Zur reform des religions-unterrichts.—**Heyer**, F. Canossa und Venedig.

6. **Kaufmann**, G: Der kampf der französischen und deutschen schulorganisation.—**Naumann**, E. W: R. Zukunftsmusik und die musik der zukunft.—**Charikles**, *pseud.* Türkische skizzen.—**Baron**, J. Angriffe auf das erbrecht.—**Fischer**, K: Volksgesundheitspflege und schule.—**Hönes**, C. Die reformbewegung der Brahmosamdasch in Indien.—**Schneider**, J: P. Zur währungsfrage.—**Grimm**, E: Die lehre über Buddha und das dogma von Jésus Christus.—**Conrad**, J. Ueber das steigen der lebensansprüche.—**Kirchner**, F: Der mangel eines allgemeinen moralprinzips in unserer zeit.—**Wernich**, A: Ueber ausbreitung und bedeutung der neuen cultur-bestrebungen in Japan.—**Heinz**, —. Kanäle und stammelbhecken.—**Wagner**, A. Unsere münzreform.—**Scheel**, H. V. Eigenthum und erbrecht.

7. **Mannhardt**, W: Die praktischen folgen des aberglaubens.—**Genée**, R. Das deutsche theater und die reform-frage.—**Dannehl**, G. Die verfälschung des bieres.—**Osenbrüggen**, E: Eine metamorphose im deutschen strafrecht.—**Schasler**, M. Ueber moderne denkmalswuth.—**Braasch**, A. H. Ist ein zusammenwirken der verschiedenen richtungen innerhalb der evangelisch-protestantischen kirche möglich?—**Hergenhahn**, T. Das antragsrecht im deutschen strafrecht.—**Heinze**, T. Ueber die fremdwörter im deutschen.—**Kleinschmidt**, A. Die säcularisation von 1803.—**Cohn**, G. Was ist socialismus?—**Keferstein**, H. Die volksschule als erziehungsschule.—**Meyer**, J. B. Fichte, Lassalle und der socialismus.—Ein deutsches kaiserwort.

8. **Schasler**, M. Materialistische und idealistische weltanschauung. — **Oetker**, F: Ueber erziehungsanstalten für verwahrloste kinder.—**Stürenburg**, H: Wehrpflicht und erziehung.—**Kayser**, P. Der zeugnisszwang in strafverfahren in geschichtlicher entwickelung.—**Kleinwächter**, F: Zur frage des naturwissenschaftlichen unterrichts.—**Görgens**, E. P: Der islam und die moderne cultur.—**Malaroe**, A. de. Die schul - sparkassen. — **Huber-Liebenau**, T. v. Ueber den verfall des zunftthumes.—**Schröer**, K: J. Die deutschen in Oesterreich-Ungarn.—**Grause**, G. Darwinismus und sittlichkeit.—**Nippold**, F: W: F. Religion und kirchenpolitik Friedrichs des grossen.—**Meyer**, J. B. Die simultanschule.

9. **Kleinwächter**, F: Zur philosophie der mode.—**Schönhof**, J. Ueber die volkswirthschaftlichen fragen in den Vereinigten Staaten.—**Schwerin**, L: Die zulassung der frauen zur ausübung des ärztlichen berufes.—**Schmidt**, P. W: Was trennt "die beiden richtungen" in der evangelischen kirche?—**Hartung**, H. Der check- und giro-verkehr der deutschen reichsbank.—**Keferstein**, H. Die pädagogik der kirche.—**Huber-Liebenau**, T. v. Ueber das kunstgewerbe der alten und neuen zeit.—**Stammler**, C: Das römische recht in Deutschland.—**Amort**, E. *fr.* Biblische und profane wunderthäter.—**Gantier**, V: Das heutige Belgien.—**Milner**, E. Schwäbische kolonisten in Ungarn.—**Paul**, H: Zur orthographischen frage.—**Liliencron**, R. *freiherr* v. Ueber den chorgesang in der evangelischen kirche.

10. **Delsa**, L. Beiträge zur steuer-reform.—**Engel**, E. Aus dem pflanzerstaate Zulia.—**Meyer**, J. Der handfertigkeits-unterricht und die schule.—**Lammers**, A: Bekämpfung der trunksucht.—**Brentano**, L: J. Der arbeiter-versicherungszwang, seine voraussetzungen und seine folgen. — **Gutschenberger**, S. Nihilismus, pessimismus und schmerz.—**Haupt**, C: Die begründung der päpstlichen macht diesseits der Alpen.—**Hergenhahn**, T. Königthum und verfassung. — **Cropp**, J. Lessings streit mit hauptpastor Goeze.—**Schönhof**, J. Deutsche urtheile über Amerika.—**Lammers**, A: Handbildung und hausfleiss.—**Heitz**, E. Ursachen und tragweite der nordamerikanischen konkurrenz mit der west-europäischen landwirthschaft.—**Guhl**, A: Schule und heer.

11. **Holtzendorff**, F. v.   J. C. Bluntschli und seine verdienste um die staatswissenschaften. — **Pierson**, N. G.   Die münzfrage. — **Marggraff**, H. Moderne stadtbäder. — **Stehlich**, F: Die sprache in ihrer beziehung zum nationalcharakter. — **Lammers**, A: Sonntagsfeier in Deutschland. — **Kirchner**, F: Der zweck des daseins im hinblick auf die mehrung des selbstmordes. — **Geyer**, H: Ueber die den unrecht angeklagten oder verurtheilten gebührende entschädigung. — **Dehn**, P. Die katholischen gesellenvereine in Deutschland. — **Keferstein**, H. Die verantwortlichkeit der schule nach seiten der gesundheitlichen volksinteressen. — **Förster**, E. Mittelalter oder renaissance. — **Lammers**, A: Die unternehmung im sparkassen-geschäft. — **Löher**, F. v. Das neue Italien. — **Platter**, J. Die pflichten des besitzes.

12. **Portig**, G. Die nationale bedeutung des kunstgewerbes. — **Schramm**, K: R. Das heer der seligmacher. — **Schasler**, M. Ueber dramatische musik und das kunstwerk der zukunft, 1. abth. — **Bücher**, K: Die arbeiterfrage im kaufmannsstande. — **Siebeck**, H. Ueber wesen und zweck des wissenschaftlichen studiums. — **Löcher**, H: Die schulüberbürdungsfrage sachlich beleuchtet. — **Laas**, E. Zur frauenfrage. — **Schmeidler**, J. Die religiöse anschauung F. Fröbel's. — **Kirchner**, F: Der spiritismus, die narrheit unseres zeitalters. — **Schmidt**, P. Gewalt oder geist? — **Hirschberg**, E. Die selbsthilfe des arbeiterstandes als grundlage seiner versicherung. — **Schasler**, M. Ueber dramatische musik und das kunstwerk der zukunft, 2te abth. — **Paul**, E. Egypten in handelspolitischer hinsicht.

13. **Kalischer**, A. C. Spinoza's stellung zum judenthum und christenthum. — **Lammers**, A: Umwandlung der schenken. — **Meyer**, K: W. Die pflege des idealen auf unseren höheren schulen. — **Meyer**, J. B. Luther als schulbefreier. — **Bunsen**, T. v. Die Donau. — **Sommer**, H. Die religion des pessimismus. — **Janssen**, C. W. Holländische kolonial-politik. — **Trede**, T. Die propaganda fide in Rom. — **Keferstein**, H. Zur frage des prüfungswesens. — **Minckwitz**, J. Die entwicklung eines neuen dramatischen styls in Deutschland. — **Fuld**, L: Die entwicklung der moralstatistik. — **Lammers**, M. Deutsche lehrerinnen im auslande. — **Francke**, W: Die nachfolge in Braunschweig als frage des rechts. — **Gareis**, C: Der sklavenhandel, das völkerrecht und das deutsche recht.

Jevons, W: Stanley.   Methods of social reform, and other papers.   Lond. 1883. O.

304 : 10

Contents.   Amusements of the people. — The rationale of free public libraries. — The use and abuse of museums. — "Cram." — Trades societies, their objects and policy. — On industrial partnerships. — Married women in factories. — Manchester statistical society. — British association. — Cruelty to animals. — On the United Kingdom alliance and its prospects of success. — Experimental legislation and the drink tariff. — On the analogy between the post office, telegraphs, and other systems of conveyance of the United Kingdom, as regards government control. — The post office telegraphs and their financial results. — Postal notes, money orders and bank cheques. — A state parcel post. — The railways and the state.

Kingsley, C: Sanitary and social lectures and essays.   [Works, v. 18.]   Lond. 1880. D.

304 : 8

Contents.   Woman's work in a country parish. — The science of health. — The two breaths. — Thrift. — Nausicaa in London, or the lower education of women. — The air-mothers. — The tree of knowledge. — Great cities and their influence for good and evil. — Heroism. — The massacre of the innocents. — "A mad world, my masters."

Lassalle, Ferdinand.   Sämmtliche reden und schriften ; herausg. von G: Hotschick. 1ste aufl.   N. Y. [1882], 1883. 3 v. D.   304 : 11

Contents.   V. 1. Einführung in Ferdinand Lassalle's sozial-politische schriften. — Offenes antwortschreiben. — Ueber verfassungswesen. — Die feste, die presse und der Frankfurter abgeordnetentag. — Arbeiterlesebuch. — Macht und recht. — Arbeiterprogramm. — Offener brief von Rodbertus. — An die arbeiter Berlins. — Zur arbeiterfrage. — Stenogr. bericht über die strafgerichtlichen verhandlungen. — Die wissenschaft und die arbeiter. — Das Lassalle'sche kriminalprozess. **2.** Die indirekte steuer und die lage der arbeitenden klasse. — Der hochverraths-prozess. — Die agitation des Allgem. deutschen arbeiter-vereins und das versprechen des königs von Preussen. — Herr Bastiat-Schulze von Delitzsch. — Vertheidigungsrede wider die anklage der verleitung zum kassettendiebstahl. — Assisenrede. **3.** Prozess gegen Ferd. Lassalle zu Düsseldorf am 27 juni 1864. — Gotthold Ephraim Lessing vom kulturhistorischen standpunkt. — Der italienische krieg von 1859 und die aufgabe Preussens. — Herr Julian Schmidt, d. literarhistoriker, mit setzer-scholien von Ferd. Lassalle. — Franz von Sickingen, eine historische tragödie. — Das system der erworbenen rechte.

Lieber, Francis.   Miscellaneous writings.   Phila. 1881. 2 v.   O.   304 : 7

Contents.   V. 1. Introd. by the ed. — Biog. discourse by M. B. Thayer. *Reminiscences:* Of the historian Niebuhr. — Of the battle of Waterloo. — *Academic discourses:* Inaugural in Columbia, S. C., 1835. — First constituents of civilization, 1845. — Character of the gentleman, 1846. — On continued self-education, 1851. — History and uses of athenæums, 1856. — Inaugural in Columbia college, N. Y., 1858. — The teacher of politics, 1859. — Alexander V. Humboldt I., 1859, II., 1869. — *Essays:* Washington and Napoleon. — Vocal sounds of Laura Bridgman. — On the study of foreign languages. **2.** Introd. by prof. J. C. Bluntschli, of Heidelberg, on Lieber's service to political science and international law. — Contributions to constitutional law. — Contributions to military law. — Contributions to international law. — Contributions to political science. — Essays on educational policy. — Bibliographical list of the writings of Francis Lieber. — Index.

Mill, J: Stuart.   [Political essays].   *In his* Dissertations and discussions.   824.2 : 70

Contents, see under English literature, Essays.

Miller, Hugh.   Political and social essays.

in 824.2 : 71

Contents, see under English literature, Essays.

Nordau, Max Simon.   Die conventionellen lügen der kulturmenschheit.   Chicago. 1884. D.

304 : 13

— *Same, eng.*   The conventional lies of our civilization.   From the german.   Chicago. 1884. D.   304 : 13

Ruskin, J: Fors clavigera ; letters to the workmen and laborers of Great Britain.   N. Y. 1881-84. 3 v. D.   304 : 14

— Fors clavigera ; letters to the workmen and laborers of Great Britain.   New ser. N. Y. 1883, 1884. D.   304 : 14

Contents.   Ashestiel. — Dust of gold. — Lost jewels.

Treitschke, H: v.   Historische und politische aufsätze.   4te aufl.   Leipz. 1871. 3 v. O.

304 : 3

Contents.   V. 1. *Charaktere:* Milton. — Lessing. — H: v. Kleist. — Fichte und die nationale idee. — Hans v. Gagern. — K: A: v. Wangenheim. — L: Uhland. — Lord Byron und der radicalismus. — F. C. Dahlmann. — O: Ludwig. — F: Hebbel. — K: Mathy. **2.** *Die einheitsbestrebungen zertheilter völker:* Das deutsche ordensland Preussen. — Bundesstaat und einheitsstaat. — Cavour. — Die republik der Vereinigten Niederlande. **3.** *Freiheit und königthum:* Die freiheit. — Frankreichs staatsleben und der bonapartismus. — Parteien und fractionen. — Das constitutionelle königthum in Deutschland.

White, Andrew Dickson.   The message of the 19th century to the 20th ; an address del. before the class of 1853, in the chapel of Yale college, june 26, 1883.   New Haven. 1883. O.   304 : Pam

3. History of culture.

Buckle, H: T: History of civilization in England.   From the 2d London ed., to which is added an alphabetical index.   N. Y. 1859. 2 v. O.   309+3

Note. The author only finished the introd. on civilization in general.

Dean, Amos. The history of civilization. Albany. 1868-69. 7 v. O.   **309 : 5**
Contents. V. 1. Life of Amos Dean.—Introd.—Ethnography. — Elements of humanity.—Mongols, Tartars. — Chaldæa. — Assyria. — Babylonia. — Medo-Persia.—Egypt.—Arabia.— Palestine.—Phœnicia and Syria.—Asia Minor. 2. Greece: Description and history; Industry; Religion: Element of society; Government; Philosophy; Art. 3. Rome: Immediate sources of its history and civilization; Industry; Religion; Government; Society; Philosophy; Art.—Index to v. 1-3. 4. Modern or european civilization.—Europe: History; Industry.—Index. 5. Europe: Religion: Celtic; Scandinavian; Roman catholic; Greek church; Protestantism. — Europe: Government; British constitution. — Index. 6. European society.—Elements of philosophy in modern Europe. —Index. 7. European art: Architecture; Sculpture; Painting; Music; Poetry; Eloquence; The drama; Military art.—Index.

Draper, J: W: History of the intellectual development of Europe. Rev. .ed. N. Y. 1876. 2 v. D.   **309 : 6**

Factors of civilization, real and assumed, considered in their relation to vice, misery, happiness, unhappiness and progress ; the factors considered, theological, governmental, politico-economical ; in 3 v. V. 1, 2. Atlanta. 1882-83. 2 v. O.   **309 : 24**

Ferguson, Adam. An essay on the history of civil society. 5th ed. Lond. 1782. O.   **309 : 7**

Geiger, Lazarus. Contributions to the history of the development of the human race ; lectures and dissertations. Tr. from the 2d german ed. by D: Asher. (Eng. and for. phil. lib.) Bost. 1880. O.   **309 : 8**

Guizot, François P: Guillaume. General history of civilization in Europe, from the fall of the roman empire to the french revolution. 8th amer. from the 2d eng. ed., with occasional notes by C. S. Henry. N. Y. 1856. D.   **309 : 10**
— The history of civilization from the fall of the roman empire to the french revolution. Tr. by W: Hazlitt. N. Y. 1860. 4 v. D.   **309 : 9**

Hellwald, F: v. Culturgeschichte in ihrer natürlichen entwickelung bis zur gegenwart. 2te aufl. Augsburg. 1876, 1877. 2 v. O.   **309 : 1**

Hittell, J: S. A brief history of culture. N. Y. 1875. D.   **309 : 11**

Kolb, G: F: Culturgeschichte der menschheit mit besonderer berücksichtigung von regierungsform, politik, religion, freiheits. und wohlstandsentwicklung der völker ; eine allgemeine weltgeschichte nach den bedürfnissen der jetzteit. 2te umgearb. aufl. Leipz. 1872, 1873. 2 v. O.   **309 : 23**

Laurent, François. Études sur l'histoire de l'humanité. 2e éd., corr. Paris. 1879. 18 v. O.   **309 : 22**
Contents. V. 1. L'orient. 2. La Grèce. 3. Rome. 4. Le christianisme. 5. Les barbares et le catholicisme. 6. La papauté et l'empire. 7. La féodalité et l'église. 8. La réforme. 9. Les guerres de religion. 10. Les nationalités. 11. La politique royale. 12. La philosophie du 17e siècle et le christianisme. 13, 14. La revolution française. 15. L'empire. 16. La réaction religieuse. 17. La religion de l'avenir. 18. La philosophie de l'histoire.

Magoon, Elijah Lyman. Westward empire, or The great drama of human progress. N. Y. 1856. D.   **309 : 12**

Mitchell, Arthur. The past in the present ; what is civilization ? N. Y. 1881. O.   **309 : 13**

Morgan, Lewis H: Ancient society, or Researches in the lines of human progress from savagery through barbarism to civilization. N. Y. 1878. O.   **309 : 14**

Reade, W: Winwood. The martyrdom of man. N. Y. 1874. D.   **309 : 17**

Stuart, Gilbert. A view of society in Europe, in its progress from rudeness to refinement, or Inquiries concerning the history of law, government and manners. Edinb. 1792. O.   **309 : 15**

Tylor, E: Burnett. Primitive culture ; researches into the development of mythology, philosophy, religion, language, art and custom. 2d amer. ed. N. Y. 1877. 2 v. O. **309 : 16**

* * *

Adams, G: Burton. Mediæval civilization. (History primers.) N. Y. 1883. T. **309 : 21**

Brace, C: Loring. Gesta Christi, or A history of humane progress under christianity. N. Y. 1882. O.   **309 : 19**

Balmès, Jaime Luciano. European civilization ; protestantism and catholicity compared. Balt. 1858. O.   **309+4**

Burckhardt, Jacob. The civilization of the period of the renaissance in Italy. Authorized tr. by S. G. C. Middlemore. Lond. 1878. 2 v. O.   **309 : 18**

Scherr, Johannes. Deutsche kultur- und sittengeschichte. 7te aufl. Leipz. 1879. O.   **309 : 2**

Wessely, J. E. Deutschlands lehrjahre ; kulturgeschichtliche bilder. Stuttgart. [1883]. 2 v. D.   **309 : 20**
Contents. V. 1. Familienleben.—Buntes aus der aussenwelt. 2. Weltliche berufsarten.

4. The woman question.

Child, Lydia Maria. Brief history of the condition of women, in various ages and nations. Rev. and corr. by the author. 5th ed. N. Y. 1854. 2 v. S.   **307 : 2**

Schweiger-Lerchenfeld, Amand v. Woman in all lands ; her domestic, social and intellectual condition, interspersed with strange scenes, customs, romances, etc. From the german by A. S. Meyrick. N. Y. [1881]. Q.   **307+12**

Scherr, Johannes. Geschichte der deutschen frauenwelt. 3te aufl. Leipz. 1873. D.   **307 : 15**

Aguilar, Grace. The women of Israel. N. Y. 1860. 2 v. D.   **307 : 20**

Jessup, H: Harris. The women of the arabs, with a chapter for children ; ed. by C. S. Robinson and I: Riley. N. Y. [1873]. D.   **307 : 19**

Houghton, Ross C. Women of the orient ; an account of the religious, intellectual and social condition of women in Japan, China, India, Egypt, Syria and Turkey. Cinc. [1877]. D.   **307 : 14**

Graves, *Mrs.* A. J. Woman in America ; an examination into the moral and intellectual condition of american female society. N. Y. 1844. S.   **307 : 8**

Stanton, Elizabeth Cady. Susan B. **Anthony** *and* Matilda Joslyn **Gage**, *eds.* History of woman suffrage. Ill. N. Y. 1881, 1882. 2 v. O.   **307+13**

Robinson, Harriet H. Massachusetts in the woman suffrage movement; a general, political, legal and legislative history from 1774 to 1881. Bost. 1881. S. **307:18**

Stanton, Theodore, ed. The woman question in Europe; a series of original essays; with an introd. by Frances Power Cobbe. N. Y. 1884. O. **307+28**

* * *

Adams, W: H: Davenport. Woman's work and worth in girlhood, maidenhood and wifehood; illustrations of woman's character, duties, rights, position. influence, responsibilities and opportunities, with hints on self-culture and chapters on the higher education and employment of women. Lond. 1880. D. **307:1**

Ballou, Maturin M. Notable thoughts about women; a literary mosaic. Bost. 1882. D. **307:24**

Belloc, Bessie Rayner, born Parkes. Essays on woman's work. 2d ed. Lond. 1866. S. **307:11**

Church, Ella Rodman. Money-making for ladies. N. Y. 1882. S. **307:21**

Craik, Dinah Maria. born Mulock. A woman's thoughts about women. N. Y. 1861. D. **307:3**
Contents. Something to do. — Self-dependence. — Female professions. — Female handicrafts. — Female servants.—The mistress of a family.—Female friendships. — Gossip. — Women of the world.—Happy and unhappy women.—Lost women.—Growing old.

— Same. Leipz. 1860. S. **307:3**

Dall, Caroline Healey. The college, the market and the court, or Woman's relation to education, labor and law. Bost. 1867. O. **307:4**

— Woman's rights under the law; in 3 lectures del. in Boston, jan. 1861. Bost. 1861. D. **307:5**

Diaz, Abby Morton. A domestic problem; work and culture in the household. Bost. 1875. D. **307:6**

Dix, Morgan. Lectures on the calling of a christian woman and her training to fulfill it; del. during the season of lent, 1883. N. Y. 1883. S. **307:22**
Contents. The place of woman in this world.—The degradation of woman by paganism and her restoration by christianity. — The education of woman for her work.—The sins of woman against her vocation. —Divorce.—A mission for women.

Blake, Lillie Devereux. Woman's place to-day; four lectures in reply to lenten lectures on "Woman", by the rev. morgan Dix. N. Y. [1883]. S. **307:23**

Dodge, Mary Abigail, (Gail Hamilton). A new atmosphere. Bost. 1865. D. **307:7**

Héricourt, Jenny d'. A woman's philosophy of woman, or Woman affranchised; an answer to Michelet, Proudhon, Girardin, Legouvé, Comte, and other modern innovators. Tr. from the last Paris ed. N. Y. 1864. D. **307:9**

Heywood, E. H. Uncivil liberty; an essay to show the injustice and impolicy of ruling woman without her consent. Princeton, Mass. 1874. O. **307:29**

Higginson, T: Wentworth. Common-sense about women. Bost. [1881]. D. **307:17**

Jameson, Anna, born Murphy. "Woman's mission" and woman's position. In her Memoirs and essays. **824.2:57**

Laas, Ernst. Zur frauenfrage. In Deutsche zeit- und streit-fragen. **304:15 v12**

Livermore, Mary Ashton. What shall we do with our daughters? Bost. 1883. S. **307:26**
Contents. Changed conditions of woman's life. — Physical education.—Need of practical training.—Industrial and technical training.—Moral and religious training.—Superfluous women.

Manson, G: J. Work for women. (Putnam's handy-book ser.) N. Y. 1883. S. **307:25**

Mill, J: Stuart. The subjection of women. With his On liberty. **324:9**

Ossoli, Sarah Margaret, born Fuller, marchesa d'. Woman in the 19th century and kindred papers relating to the sphere, condition and duties of women; ed. by her brother Arthur B. Fuller. New ed., with an introd. by Horace Greeley. Bost. 1862. D. **307:19**
Contents. Pt. 1. Woman in the 19th century. Pt. 2. Miscellanies; Aglauron and Laurie; Wrongs and duties of am. women; George Sand; Consuelo; Jenny Lind, the "Consuelo" of George Sand; Caroline; Ever-growing lives; Household nobleness; "Glumdalclitches"; "Ellen, or forgive and forget"; "Courrier des Etats Unis"; Books of travel; Review of mrs. Jameson's essays; Woman's influence over the insane; Pocahontas; Children's books; Woman in poverty; The irish character; Educate men and women as souls. Pt. 3. Extracts from journals and letters. Pt. 4. Memorials.

Penny, Mrs. S. J. The afternoon of unmarried life. [Anon.] N. Y. 1859. D. **307:27**

Ruskin, J: Letters and advice to young girls and young ladies on dress, education, marriage, their sphere, influence, women's work, women's rights, etc. N. Y. 1879. D. **307:30**

— Pearls for young ladies; from the later works of John Ruskin, including letters and advice on education, dress, marriage, influence, work, rights, etc.; coll. and arr. by mrs. Louisa C. Tuthill. N. Y. 1881. D. **307:31**

Stowe, Harriet Elizabeth, born Beecher. The woman question. In her Chimney corner. **829.1:33**

2. Statistics.

1. Population.

Behm, E:, and Hermann Wagner, eds. Die bevölkerung der erde; jährliche übersicht über neue arealberechnungen, gebietsveränderungen, zählungen und schätzungen der bevölkerung auf der gesammten erdoberfläche, [b.] 6. Karten. Gotha. 1880. Q. In Petermann's mitteilungen, Ergänzungsb. 14. **905.1:M**

— Same, [b.] 7. Gotha. 1882. Q. In the same, 15. **905.1:M**

Malthus, T: Robert. An essay on the principle of population, or A view of its past and present effects on human happiness, with an inquiry into our prospects respecting the future removal or mitigation of the evils which it occasions. 8th ed. Lond. 1878. O.   **312 : 2**

Mayr, G: Die gesetzmässigkeit im gesellschaftsleben; statistische studien. München. 1877. S.   **311 : 1**

Zacharias, O: Die bevölkerungs-frage in ihrer beziehung zu den socialen nothständen der gegenwart. 3te aufl. Hirschberg. i. Schl. 1880. O.   **312 : 3**

Fuld, L: Die entwicklung der moral-statistik. *In* Deutsche zeit- und streit-fragen.
    304 : 15 v13

2. General statistics.

Mulhall, Michael G. Mulhall's dictionary of statistics. Lond. 1884. D.   **310 : R18**

Kolb, G: F: Handbuch der vergleichenden statistik der völkerzustands- und staatenkunde, für den allgemeinen praktischen gebrauch. 8te aufl. Leipz. 1879. O.
    310 : 1

— The condition of nations, social and political; with complete comparative tables of universal statistics. Tr., ed. and collated to 1880, by mrs. Brewer; with original notes and information by Edwin W. Streeter. Lond. [1880]. Q.   **310+2**

Wilson, Alexander Johnstone. The resources of modern countries; essays towards an estimate of the economic position of nations and british trade prospects. Reprinted, with emendations and add. from Fraser's magazine. Lond. 1878. 2 v. O.
    310 : 8

Schem, Alexander Jakob B., *ed.* Statistics of the world; containing area, form of government, head of government, population, expenses, debt, paper money, standing army, navy, merchant vessels, imports, exports, chief produce, coins and their value in the U. S. mint, liquid and grain measures, weights and linear measures, capitals and principal cities, population of cities, of all countries, and side tables showing the principal creeds of the world, statistics of christianity, religious statistics of Europe, religious statistics of the U. S., the railroads of the world, the railroads of the U. S., postal statistics of the world, telegraphs of the world, the presidents of the U. S., presidential elections from 1788 to 1872, centennial statistics of the population of Europe and the U. S. in 1786, 1876 and 2000. 4th rev. ed. Boston. 1876. O.   **310 : R15**

Hübner, O: Geographisch-statistische tabellen aller länder der erde. Jahrg. 1884, vollständig umgearb. und bedeutend erweitert von Fr. v. Juraschek. Frankfort a. M. 1884. Tt.   **310 : R17**

Mulhall, Michael G. The progress of the world in arts, agriculture, commerce, manufactures, instruction, railways and public wealth, since the beginning of the 19th century. Lond. 1880. D.   **310 : 9**

Mulhall, Michael G.—*Continued.*
— Balance-sheet of the world for ten years, 1870–1880. Lond. 1881. O.   **310 : 10**

Seaman, Ezra C. Essays on the progress of nations in productive industry, civilization, population and wealth; illustrated by statistics of mining, agriculture, manufactures, commerce, banking, revenues, internal improvements, emigration, mortality and population. N. Y. 1846. O.
    310 : 11

Blake, W: P. The production of the precious metals, or statistical notices of the principal gold and silver producing regions of the world; with a chapter upon the unification of gold and silver coinage. N. Y. 1869. O.   **310+3**

Fenn, C: Compendium of the english and foreign funds, debts and revenues of all nations; together with statistics relating to state finance and liabilities, imports, exports, population, area, railway guarantees, municipal finance and indebtedness, and all descriptions of government securities held and dealt in by investors at home and abroad; the regulations of the stock exchange, etc. 12th ed. re-written, with an app. bringing the work down to february 1876, by Robert Lucas Nash. Lond. [1876.] O.   **310 : 4**

Körösi, Joseph, *ed.* Bulletin annuel des finances des grandes villes; 4e année, 1880. Pub. sur le vœu de la commission permanente du Congrès international de statistique, aux frais de la ville de Budapest. Budapest. 1882. O.   **310 : Pam**
Contents. Paris, Berlin, Vienna, St. Petersburg, Warsaw, Budapest, Turin, Copenhagen, Munich, Bordeaux, Washington, Stockholm, Lille, Prague, Leipsic, Trieste, Venice, Cologne, Königsberg, Frankfort o. M., Bologna, Christiania, Stuttgart, Riga.

Year-books.

Almanach de Gotha; annuaire généalogique. diplomatique et statistique, 1870, 1871, 1874, 1882–84. Gotha. 6 v. T.   **310 : 13**

Statesman's year-book, The; statistical and historical annual of the states of the civilized world; 1877, 1879–85. Lond. 1877–85. 7 v. D.   **310 : 7**
Note. Edited by F: Martin through 1882, by J. Scott Keltie since.

American almanac, The, and repository of useful knowledge for 1830–1861. Bost. 1839–61. 32 v. in 17. D.   **310 : 5**

National almanac and annual record for 1863, 1864. Phil. 1863, 1864. 2 v. D.   **310 : 14**

Spofford, Ainsworth Rand, *ed.* American almanac and treasury of facts, statistical, financial and political, 1879–1885. N. Y. 1879–85. 7 v. D.   **310 : 6**

Hunt's merchant's magazine year-book; 1871. N. Y. 1871. O.   **310 : 12**

Whitaker, Joseph. An almanack for 1884, 1885; containing an account of the astronomical and other phenomena, a large amount of information respecting the government, finances, population, commerce, and general statistics of the british empire throughout the world, with some notice of other countries, etc. Lond. [1884–85.] 2 v. D.   **310 : 16**

3. Special countries.

Europe.

McCulloch, J: Ramsay, *and others.* A statistical account of the british empire ; exhibiting its extent, physical capacities, population, industry and civil and religious institutions. 2d ed., corr. and enl. Lond. 1839. 2 v. O.   314 : 2

Financial reform assoc. The financial reform almanack ; a vade mecum for fiscal reformers, free traders, politicians, public speakers and writers, and the public generally, containing elaborately - tabulated statistical information; 1878, 1881—1883. Lond. 1881-83. Q.   314+1

Paris *city. Direction de l'administration générale.*
Bulletin de statistique municipale ; publié par les ordres de M. le préfet de la Seine. 12e-15e année, 1876-1879. Paris. 1876-79. 3 v. Q.   314 : D
— — Bulletin récapitulatif de statistique municipale, 1876, 1878. Paris. 1877, 1879. Q. *With the above.*   314 : D
  Contents. Topographie et météorologie.—Population.—Variétés.
— *Service de la statistique municipale de la préfecture de la Seine.* Annuaire statistique de la ville de Paris ; 2e année, 1881. Ill. Paris. 1882. Q.   314 : D

Sidenbladh, Per Elis. Statistics [of Sweden]. (Swedish catalogue, International exhibition, 1876, Phila., pt. 1). [Phila. 1876]. O.   314+3

America.

Spaulding, M. C. Handbook of statistics of the U. S. ; a record of administrations and events, from the organization of the U. S. government to the present time. N. Y. 1874. D.   317 : 55

United States. *Census office.* 7th census of the U. S., 1850, embracing a statistical view of each of the states and territories, arranged by counties, towns, etc. J. D. B. De Bow, supt. Wash. 1850. F.   *in* 317 : D
— — *Same.* Mortality statistics, embracing the cause of death, the age and sex, color and condition, the nativity, the season of decease, the duration of illness, the occupation of the persons reported to have died in the 12 months preceding the 1st of june [1850], with sundry comparative and ill. tables, by J. D. B. De Bow, supt. (U. S. 33d cong. 2 sess. House ex. doc. no. 98.) Wash. 1855. O.   *in* 317 : D
— — [8th census, 1860]. Agriculture; Manufactures ; Population ; Statistics, including mortality, property, etc., of the U. S. in 1860, comp. from the original returns of the 8th census under the dir. of the sec. of the interior by Joseph C. G. Kennedy. Wash. 1864-66. 4 v. Q.   *in* 317 : D
— — 9th census, 1870. Wash. 1872. 3 v. Q.
                                        in 317 : D
  Contents. V. 1. Population. 2. Vital statistics. 3. Industry and wealth.
— — 10th census, 1880. Wash. 1883, 1884. 6 v. Q.
                                            317 : D
  Contents. V. 1. **Walker,** F. A. *and* H: **Gannett.** Introd.; general discussion of the movements of population, 1790 to 1880.—General population tables.

United States. *Census office.—Continued.*
  —Population by race, sex and nativity.—Population by ages specified and select.—Areas, dwellings and families.—Foreign parentage.—Statistics of the population of Alaska.—Tables of occupations.—Miscellaneous statistics: Newspapers and periodicals; Public schools; Illiteray; Defective, defendant and delinquent classes. **2.** Walker, F. A. Remarks on the statistics of manufactures.—General statistics: tabular statements.—Hollerith, H. Power used in manufactures.—Wright, C. D. The factory system. —Fitch, C: H. Manufactures of interchangeable mechanism.—Fitch, C: H. Hardware, cutlery and edge-tools.—**Swank,** J. M. Iron and steel production.—**Wyckoff,** W: C. Silk manufacture.—Atkinson, E: Cotton manufacture.—**Bond,** G: W: Woolen manufacture.—**Rowland,** W: L. Chemical products and salt.—**Weeks,** J. D. Glass manufacture. **3. Walker,** F. A. Remarks on the statistics of agriculture.—General statistics: tabular statements.—Brewer, W: H. Cereal production.—**Neftel,** Knight. Flour-milling.—**Killebrew,** J. B. Tobacco culture.—**Dodge,** J. R. Manufacture and movement of tobacco.—Gordon, C. Meat production.—**4. Shuman,** A. E. Statistics of railroads.—**Purdy,** T: C. Steam navigation.—Purdy, T: C. Canals.—**Shuman,** A. E. Telegraphs and telephones.—**Lines,** R. B. Postal telegraphs. **5. Hilgard,** E. W. General discussion of cotton production. — Cotton production in the Mississippi valley and southwestern states: Hilgard, E. W. Louisiana, Mississippi; **Stafford,** J. M. Tennessee and Kentucky; **Loughridge,** R. H. Missouri, Arkansas, Texas, Indian territory. **6.** Cotton production in the eastern Gulf, Atlantic and Pacific states: Smith, E. A. Alabama, Florida; **Loughridge,** R. H. Georgia; **Hammond,** H. North Carolina; **Kerr,** W. C. North Carolina, Virginia.—App. **Hilgard,** E. W. California; Notes on Utah, Arizona and New Mexico. **8. North,** S. N. D. History and present condition of the newspaper and periodical press of the U. S. with a catalogue of the publications of the present year.—**Petroff,** I. Report on the population, industries and resources of Alaska.—**Elliott,** H: W. Report on the seal islands of Alaska.—**Hall.** H: Report on the ship-building industry of the U. S.
— — *Same.* [Special monographs.] The oyster-industry by Ernest **Ingersoll.** Wash. 1881. Q.   *in* 317 : D
— — *Same.* Report on cotton production in the Indian Territory, with a brief description of the agricultural features of a portion of the country by R. H. **Loughridge.** Wash. 1884. Q.   *in* 317 : D
— — *Same.* Compendium of the 10th census, june 1, 1880, compiled pursuant to an act of congress, approved aug. 7, 1882. Wash. 1883. 2 v. O.   *in* 317 : D

Massachusetts *state. Secretary.* 22d [—32d, 34th, 37th, 39th, 40th] report to the legislature, relating to the registry and return of births, marriages and deaths in the commonwealth for 1863—1873, 1875, 1878, 1880, 1881. Bost. 1865-82. 15 v. O.
                                        in 317 : D
— — **Wright,** Carroll D. The census of Massachusetts, 1880 ; compiled by authority of the legislature from the returns of the 10th census of the U. S. Bost. 1883. O.
                                        in 317 : D
  Note. Gives statistics for cities and towns, which are not furnished by the U. S. census. except in the general aggregate for counties and states.

New York *state.* Census for 1855; taken in pursuance of art. 3, of the constitution of the state and of ch. 64, of the laws of 1855, prepared from the original returns, under the dir. of Joel T. Headley. sec. of state. by Franklin B. Hough. Albany. 1857. F.   317 : R53

Porter, Robert P., H: **Gannett** *and* W: P. **Jones.** The west [of the U. S.] from the census of 1880, a history of the industrial, commercial, social and political development of the states and territories of the west, from 1800 to 1880. Chicago. 1882. O.   **317+1**

Wisconsin *state.* Census, taken june 1855, 1865 and 1875. *In* Secretary of state reports *with* Governor's message for 1856, 1866 and 1876.   *in* **328.15 : D**

— Population as shown by the federal census for 1880, comp. by the sec. of state. Madison. 1881. O.   **317 : Pam**

Hittell, J: S. The Alta California almanac and and book of facts, 1875-76. San Francisco. S.   **317 : 51**

Tribune almanac and political register, 1857-61, 1863-68, 1870-75. N. Y. 2 v. D.   **317 : 52**

Hunt, J: Warren, *comp.* The Wisconsin almanac and annual register, 1857, no. 2. Milw. [1857]. D.   **317 : 56**

Empire of Brazil, The, at the universal exhibition of 1876 in Philadelphia. Rio de Janeiro. 1876. O.   **318+1**

3. Political science.

1. In general.

Amos, Sheldon. The science of politics. (Intern. scientific ser.) N. Y. 1883. D.   **320 : 12**
Contents. Nature and limits of the science of politics.—Political terms.—Political reasoning.—The geographical area of modern politics.—The primary elements of political life and action.—Constitutions.—Local government.—The government of dependencies.—Foreign relations.—The province of government.—Revolutions in states.—Right and wrong in politics.

Bagehot, Walter. Physics and politics, or Thoughts on the application of the principles of "natural selection" and "inheritance" to political society. (Intern. scientific ser.) N. Y. 1876. D.   **320 : 1**

Bentham, Jeremy. A fragment on government, or A comment on the commentaries; an examination of what is delivered on the subject of government in general, in the introd. to sir W: Blackstone's Commentaries; with a pref. in which is given a critique on the work at large. 2d ed. enl. Lond. 1823. O.   **320 : 2**

Bisset, Andrew. Is there a science of government ? *In his* Essays.   **904 : 13**

Brougham, H: *lord.* Political philosophy; pt. 1, Principles of government; Monarchical government; pt. 2, Of aristocracy; Aristocratic government; pt. 3, Of democracy; Mixed monarchy. 3d ed. Lond. 1853. 3 v. O.   **320 : 3**

Cooper, P: Ideas for a good government; in addresses, letters and articles on a strictly national currency, tariff and civil service. N. Y. 1883. O.   **320+17**

Crane, W:, *and* Bernard **Moses.** Politics; an introd. to the study of comparative constitutional law. N. Y. 1884. D.   **320 : 16**

Elyot, *Sir* T: The boke of the gouernour; ed. from the 1st ed. of 1531 by H: Herbert Stephen Croft. Lond. 1883. 2 v. O.   **320 : 15**

Freeman, E: A: Comparative politics ; six lectures read before the Royal institution in jan. and feb. 1873, *with* The unity of history, the Rede lecture read before the university of Cambridge, may 29, 1872. Lond. 1873. O.   **320 : 11**

Gareis, C: Irrlehren über den cultur-kampf. *In* Deutsche zeit- und streit-fragen.   **304 : 15 v5**

Grassmann, Robert. Das staatswissen. *In his* Wissenschaftslehre.   **100 : 1**

Helps, *Sir* Arthur. Thoughts upon government. Bost. 1872. O.   **320 : 4**

Hildreth, R: Theory of politics ; an inquiry into the foundations of governments, and the causes and progress of political revolutions. N. Y. 1853. D.   **320 : 5**

Hosmer, G: Washington. The people and politics, or The structure of the states and the significance and relation of political forms. Bost. 1883. O.   **320 : 14**

Mill, J: Stuart. Considerations on representative government. N. Y. 1867. D.   **320 : 6**

Paine, T: Rights of man. *In his* Political works.   **329.1 : 13**
— *Same, ger.* Die rechte des menschen. Phila. 1859. D.   **320 : 8**

Rousseau, J: Jacques. A treatise on the social compact, or The principles of politic law. *With his* Dissertation on political economy. *in* **330 : 19**
— *Same, ger.* Der gesellschaftsvertrag. Leipz. 1854. T.   **320 : 9**

Sidney, Algernon. Discourses on government ; added, an account of the author's life and a copious index. N. Y. 1805. 3 v. O.   **320 : 10**

Spencer, Herbert. The man versus the state. Repr. from the Popular science monthly, with a postscript. N. Y. 1884. O. **320+18**
Contents. The new toryism.—The coming slavery.—The sins of legislators.—The great political superstition.

Urquhart, D: The effect of the misuse of familiar words on the character of men and the fate of nations. Lond 1856. S.   **320 : 13**

Woolsey, Theodore Dwight. Political science, or The state, theoretically and practically considered. N. Y. [1877]. 2 v. O. **320+7**

2. Feudalism and monarchy.

Secrétan, É: Essai sur la féodalité ; introduction au droit féodal du pays de Vaud. Lausanne. 1858. O.   **322 : 1**

Roth, Paul. Geschichte des beneficialwesens von den ältesten zeiten bis ins zehnte jahrhundert. Erlangen. 1850. O.   **322 : 2**

Guizot, François P: Guillaume. History of the origin of representative government. in Europe. Tr. by Andrew R. Scoble. Lond. 1852. D.   **323 : 2**

Johnson, S. M. Free government in England and America ; containing, the great charter, the petition of right, the bill of rights, the federal constitution. N. Y. 1884. O.   **323+3**

Thierry, Jacques N: Augustin. The primitive meaning and extent of the title king. *In his* Hist. essays. , 904+37

Napoléon III, Louis Napoléon Bonaparte, *emperor of the french.* Napoleonic ideas: Des idées Napoléoniennes, Brussels, 1839. Tr. by James A. Dorr. N. Y. 1859. D. 323.4:1

Grund, Francis J. Thoughts and reflections on the present position of Europe, and its probable consequences to the U. S. Phila. 1860. D. 323:1

Gierke, O: F: Das alte und das neue deutsche reich; vortrag gehalten zu Breslau am 7. december 1873. *In* Deutsche zeit- und streit-fragen. 304:15 v3

Hergenhahn, Theodor. Königthum und verfassung. *In* Deutsche zeit- und streit-fragen. 304:15 v10

England.

Dean, Amos. The british constitution. Chicago. 1883. S. 323.2:17

Freeman, E: A: The growth of the english constitution from the earliest times. Leipz. 1872. S. 323.2:12

De Lolme, J: L: The constitution of England, or An account of the english government, in which it is compared both with the republican form of government and the other monarchies of Europe. 5th ed. Dublin. 1785. D. 323.2:13

— The rise and progress of the english constitution; with an historical and legal introd. and notes by A. J. Stephens. Lond. 1838. 2 v. O. 323.2:31

Creasy, *Sir* E: Shepherd. The rise and progress of the english constitution. Rev.. with add. N. Y. 1883. D. 323.2:18

Langmead, T: Pitt Taswell-. English constitutional history from the teutonic conquest to the present time. 2d ed., rev. with add. Bost. 1881. O. 323.2:4

Palgrave, Francis. The rise and progress of the english commonwealth: Anglo-saxon period; containing the anglo-saxon policy and the institutions arising out of laws and usages which prevailed before the conquest. Lond. 1832. 2 v. Q. 323.2:R29

Millar, J: An historical view of the english government, from the settlement of the saxons in Britain to the accession of the house of Stewart. Dublin. 1789. O. 323.2:14

Brodie, G: A constitutional history of the british empire from the accession of Charles I to the restoration; with an introd. tracing the progress of society and of the constitution from the feudal times to the opening of the history, and including a particular examination of mr. Hume's statements relative to the character of the english government. New ed. Lond. 1866. 3 v. O. 323.2:28

Stubbs, W: The constitutional history of England in its origin and development, [to the death of Richard III]. 2d ed. Lond. 1875–78. 3 v. D. 323.2:3

Hallam, H: The constitutional history of England, from the accession of Henry VII to the death of George II. N. Y. 1877. 3 v. D. 323.2:1

May, T: Erskine. The constitutional history of England since the accession of George III, 1760–1860. Bost. 1864. 2 v. D. 323.2:2

Russell, J:, *1st earl Russell.* An essay on the history of the english government and constitution from the reign of Henry VII to the present time. 2d ed. enl. Lond. 1823. O. 323.2:26

Yonge, C: Duke. The constitutional history of England from 1760 to 1860. Lond. 1882. O. 323.2:5

— *Same.* (Frank. sq. lib.) N. Y. 1882. Q. 323.2+5

Amos, Sheldon. Fifty years of the english constitution, 1830–1880. Bost. 1880. D. 323.2:10

Smith, Philip Vernon. History of english institutions. · 2d ed. [Histor. handbooks.] Lond. 1876. S. 323.2:22

Bagehot, Walter. The english constitution, and other political essays. N. Y. 1877. D. 323.2:11

Contents. The english constitution.—The character of lord Brougham.—The character of sir Robert Peel.

St. John, H:, *viscount Bolingbroke.* A dissertation upon parties. *In his* Works. 820.2:18 v2

Stubbs, W:, *ed.* Select charters and other illustrations of english constitutional history to the reign of Edward I. 4th ed. Oxford. 1881. D. 323.2:20

Cox, Homersham. The institutions of the english government, an account of the constitution, powers and procedure of its legislative, judicial and administrative departments, with references to ancient and modern authorities. Lond. 1863. O. 323.2:23

Ewald, Alexander C: The crown and its advisers, or Queen, ministers, lords and commons. Edinb. 1870. D. 323.2:21

De Fonblanque, Albany, *jr.* How we are governed; a handbook of the constitution, government, laws and power of Great Britain. 14th ed., rev. to the present date by Smalman Smith. Lond. [1879.] D. 323.2:16

Fischel, E: The english constitution. Tr. from the 2d german ed. by R: Jenery Shee. Lond. 1863. O. 323.2:27

Gneist, Rudolph. Das englische verwaltungsrecht mit einschluss des heeres, der gerichte und der kirche; geschichtlich und systematisch. 2te völlig umgearb. aufl. Berlin. 1867. 2 v. O. 323.2:24

Contents. V. 1. Geschichte des englischen verwaltungsrechts. 2. Das heutige englische verwaltungsrecht.

— Selfgovernment, communal-verfassung und verwaltungs-gerichte in England. 3te umgearb. aufl. Berlin 1871. O. 323.2:25

Traill, H. D. Central government. (The english citizen series.) Lond. 1881. D. 323.2:15

Creasy, *Sir* E: The imperial and colonial constitutions of the britanic empire, including indian institutions. Lond. 1872. O. 323.2:30

Cotton, J. S., *and* E. J. **Payne.** Colonies and dependencies: pt. 1, India, by J. S. Cotton; pt. 2, The colonies, by E. J. Payne. (English citizen ser.) N. Y. 1883. D. 323.2:19

Cox, Homersham. Antient parliamentary elections ; a history showing how parliaments were constituted and representatives of the people elected in antient times. Lond. 1868. O.   **324 : 11**

Hare, T: The election of representatives, parliamentary and municipal ; a treatise. 3d ed., with pref., app. and other add. Phila. 1867. D.   **323.2 : 6**

Sterne, Simon. On representative government and personal representation ; based in part upon T: Hare's treatise, entitled The election of representatives, parliamentary and municipal. Phila. 1871. D.   **323.2 : 7**

Hayward, Abraham. The british parliament ; its history and eloquence. *In his* Selected essays.   **824.2 : 46 v2**

Jennings, G: H: An anecdotal history of the british parliament from the earliest periods to the present time, with notices of eminent parliamentary men and examples of their oratory ; comp. from authentic sources. N. Y. 1881. O.   **323.2 : 8**

Charges against the lord viscount Palmerston ; proceedings on the motion of T: Chisholm Anstey, in the house of commons, wed. feb. 23, 1848. [Lond]. 1848. O. **323.2 : 32**

3. Republican institutions.

Camp, G: Sidney. Democracy. [Harper's family library.] N. Y. 1845. S.   **324 : 3**

Ceba, Ansaldo. The citizen of a republic ; what are his rights, his duties, and privileges, and what should be his education. Tr. and ed. by C. Edwards Lester. N. Y. 1845. D. **324 : 4**

Eliot, S: History of liberty: pt. 1, The ancient romans, in 2 v.; pt. 2, The early christians, in 2 v. Bost. 1853. 4 v. O.   **324 : 5**

Fate of republics. Bost. 1880. D.   **324 : 6**
  Contents. Pt. 1. *Extinct republics, ancient date:* Israelitish commonwealth; Grecian republics; Carthage; Rome.—Pt. 2. *Extinct republics, medieval and modern date:* Lombard communes; Genoa; Venice; Amalfi; Free cities of Germany; Iceland; Republic of the United Provinces; French republic of 1792-1804.—Pt. 3. Existing republics, exclusive of the United States; European republics, San Marino, Andorra, Switzerland, France; American republics, Mexico, Central America, South America, Hayti, San Domingo.—Pt. 4. United States of America.

Mann, H: Ancient and mediæval republics ; a review of their institutions, and the causes of their decline and fall. N. Y. [1879]. O. **324 : 7**
  Contents. The hebrew commonwealth.—The phœnicians.—Carthage.—Origin and formation of the hellenic states.—The institutions of Solon.—The imperial democracy of Athens.—Zenith and decline of Greece.—The roman commonwealth.—Roman jurisprudence.—The roman senate.—The roman armies. —Rome, from the decemvirate to the empire.—Imperial Rome from Augustus to Vespasian.—The age of the Antonines.—Rise of christianity.—Decline of the roman empire.—The emperors assume the diadem.—The decline and extinction of paganism.—Fall of the western empire.—A new italian nation formed. —Rise of the papal power.—The lombard communes. —The commonwealth of Florence. — Rise of the Medici. — Origin and growth of the venetian oligarchy. — Venetian jurisprudence. — The bank of Venice.—Venetian council of ten.—Decline and fall of Venice.

Freeman, E: A: History of federal government from the foundation of the achaian

Freeman, E: A:—*Continued.*
  league to the disruption of the United States. Lond. 1863. O.   **324 : 1**
  Contents. V. 1. General introd.—History of the greek federation. (*All published*).

— Presidential government. *In his* Historical essays.   **904 : 9 v1**

— *Same. In his* Select hist. essays.   **904 : 10**

Lieber, Francis. On civil liberty and self-government. Phila. 1853. 2 v. D.   **324 : 2**

May, *Sir* T: Erskine. Democracy in Europe ; a history. N. Y. 1878. O.   **324 : 8**

Mill, J: Stuart. On liberty. N. Y. 1877. O.
                                                  324 : 9

Monroe, James. The people the sovereigns ; a comparison of the government of the U. S. with those of the republics which have existed before, with the causes of their decadence and fall ; ed. by S: L. Gouverneur. Phila. 1867. D.   **324 : 10**

Rosenthal, L: America and France ; the influence of the U. S. on France·in the 18th century. N. Y. 1882. D.   **329.3 : 1**

Michelet, Jules. France before Europe. Tr. from the french. Bost. 1871. D. **327.3 : 1**
  Note. Reflections on the franco-prussian war of 1870-1.

United States.

Alden, Joseph. The science of government in connection with american institutions. New ed. N. Y. *n. d.* D.   **324.1 : 36**

Brownson, Orestes A: The american republic, its constitution, tendencies and destiny. N. Y. 1866. O.   **324.1 : 13**

Draper, J: W: Thoughts on the future civil policy of America. N. Y. 1865. O.
                                                324.1+6

Goodrich, C: B. The science of government, as exhibited in the institutions of the U. S. of America. (Lowell lectures.) Bost. 1853. O.   **324.1 : 7**

Gurowski, Adam *comte* de. America and Europe. N. Y. 1857. D.   **324.1 : 18**

Hopkins, J: H: The american citizen, his rights and duties, according to the spirit of the constitution of the U. S. N. Y. 1857. D.
                                                324.1 : 19

Nordhoff, C: Politics for young americans. N. Y. 1875. D.   **x 324.1 : 23**

Sage, Bernard J., (*P. C. Centz.*) The republic of republics, or American federal liberty, by P. C. Centz, barrister. 4th ed. Bost. 1881. O.   **324.1 : 4**

Schaff, Philip. America; a sketch of the political, social and religious character of the U. S. of North America, in 2 lectures. Tr. from the german. N. Y. 1855. D.
                                                324.1 : 24

Tocqueville, Alexis C: H: Clérel de. Democracy in America, tr. by H: Reeve, with an original preface and notes by J: C. Spencer. 4th ed., rev. and corr. from the 8th Paris ed. N. Y. 1843. 2 v. O.   **324.1 : 3**

— Democracy in America. Tr. by H: Reeve, ed. with notes, the tr. rev. and in great part re-written and the additions made to the recent Paris editions now first tr. by Francis Bowen. 7th ed. Bost. 1882. 2 v. O.
                                                324.1 : 41

---

x denotes books specially adapted to children.

Holst, Hermann v. The constitutional and political history of the U. S. Tr. from the g m n by J: J. Lalor and Alfred B. Mason. Chicago. 1877–81. 3 v. O.
324.1+1
Contents. v. 1. 1750–1833, State sovereignty and slavery. 2. 1828–1846, Jackson's administration.—Annexation of Texas. 3. 1846–1850, Annexation of Texas.—Compromise of 1850.

Porter, Luther H: Outlines of the constitutional history of the U. S. N. Y. 1883. D.
324.1 : 39

Reemelin, C: A critical review of american politics. Cinc. 1881. O. 324.1 : 34

Van Buren, Martin. Inquiry into the origin and course of political parties in the U. S.; ed. by his sons. N. Y. 1867. O. 324.1 : 28

McClellan, R. Guy. Republicanism in America; a history of the colonial and republican governments of the U. S. of America from 1607 to 1869. Added, constitutions, proclamations, platforms, resolutions, decisions of courts, laws, messages, addresses, speeches, debates, letters, election returns and statistics, also, a brief history of all the existing republics in the world. Ill. Phil. 1872. O. 324.1 : 40

Cooper, T: V., *and* Hector T. Fenton. American polities, non-partisan, from the beginning to date; embodying a history of the political parties, with their views and records on all important questions, great speeches on all great issues, the text of all existing political laws, a tabulated history of american politics, comprising tables of every kind, elections from the beginning to date, presidential, state, senatorial, congressional, etc.; tabulated financial history of all national and confederate debts, congressional appointments, tariffs, taxes, interest laws, etc. Parliamentary practice from Jefferson's manual with complete references, U. S. constitution, articles of confederation, declaration, etc. Also a complete federal blue book, with all the federal offices, their duties, locations, salaries and an accurate statement of the influences by which they are obtained. Chicago. [1882.] O. 324.1 : R35

Houghton, Walter R. History of american polities, non-partisan, embracing a history of the federal government and of political parties in the colonies and U. S. from 1607 to 1882. Ill. Indianapolis 1883. O.
324.1 : 38

Young, Andrew W. The american statesman; a political history, exhibiting the origin, nature and practical operation of constitutional government in the U. S.; the rise and progress of parties and the views of distinguished statesmen on questions of foreign and domestic policy; with an app. containing explanatory notes, political essays, statistical information and other useful matter. N. Y. 1861. O. 324.1 : 32
— *Same.* Rev. and enl. by G: T. Ferris. Milw. [1878.] O. 324.1+33

Hussey, J. R., *comp.* The century of independence ; embracing a collection, from official sources, of the most important documents and statistics connected with the political history of America; also a chronological record of the principal events, from its discovery to the present time, with biograph. and historical sketches. [*Anon.*] Chicago. 1876. D. 324.1 : 7

Currier, E:, *ed.* The political text-book; containing the declaration of independence, with the lives of the signers, the constitution of the U. S.; the inaugural addresses and first annual messages of all the presidents from Washington to Tyler, the farewell addresses of G: Washington and Andrew Jackson, together with an app. containing a variety of useful tables, etc. [*Anon.*] Cooperstown. 1844. D. 324.1 : 30

Williams, Edwin, *comp.* The addresses and messages of the presidents of the U. S., inaugural, annual and special, from 1789 to 1846; with a memoir of each of the presidents, and a history of their administrations; also the constitution of the U. S., and a selection of important documents and statistical information; comp. from official sources. N. Y. 1846, 1848. 2 v. O.
324.1+27

Cluskey, Michael W. The political text-book, or encyclopædia; containing everything necessary for the reference of the politicians and statesmen of the U. S. 9th ed. Phila. 1860. O. 324.1+29

Greely, Horace, *and* J: F. Cleveland, *comp.* A political text-book for 1860; comprising a brief view of presidential nominations and elections, including all the national platforms ever yet adopted; also a history of the struggle respecting slavery in the territories, and of the action of congress as to the freedom of the public lands, with the most notable speeches and letters of Lincoln, Douglas, Bell, Cass, Seward, Everett, Breckenridge, H. V. Johnson, etc., touching the questions of the day, and returns of all presidential elections since 1836. N. Y. 1860. O. 324.1+31

Blanchard, Rufus. Rise and fall of political parties in the U. S. Chicago. 1884. O.
324.1 : 44

Brucker, Joseph. Die zwei hauptparteien in den Vereinigten Staaten, ihre geschichte und ihre lehre; eine historisch-kritische darstellung. Milw. 1880. O. 324.1 : 5
— *Same, eng.* The chief political parties of the U. S., their history and teachings; a historical sketch. Milw. 1880. O. 324.1 : 5

Flower, Frank A. History of the republican party; embracing its origin, growth and mission, with appendices of statistics and information. Portr. and ill. Springfield, Ill. 1884. O. 324.1 : 48

Stanwood, E: A history of presidential elections. Bost. 1884. D. 324.1 : 49

* * *

Adams, Herbert B., *ed.* Johns Hopkins university studies in historical and political science, v. 1: Local institutions. Balt. 1883. O. 904+32 v1
Contents. v. 1. **Freeman,** E: A: An introd. to amer. institutional history. — **Adams,** H. B. The germanic origin of New England towns; Saxon tithing-men in Amer.; Norman constables in Amer.; Village communities of Cape Ann and Salem. — **Shaw,** Albert. Local gov. in Illinois.—**Gould,** E. R. L. Local gov. in Penna.—**Bemis,** E: W. Local gov. in Mich. and the northwest.—**Ingle,** E: Parish institutions of Maryland.—**Johnson,** J: Old Maryland manors, with the records of a court leet and a

Adams, Herbert B., ed.—Continued.
court baron.—**Johnston,** Alex. The genesis of a New England state. Connecticut.—**Ramage,** B. J. Local gov. and free schools in South Carolina.
— Same. V. 2, 3: Institutions and economics. Balt. 1884–85. O.   **904+32 v2,3**
Contents. V. 2. **Macy,** Jesse. Institutional beginnings in a western state [Iowa].—**Channing,** E: Town and county gov. in the english colonies of North Amer.—**Johnson,** J: Rudimentary society among boys.—**Shinn,** C: Howard. Land laws [i. e. Usages and customs) of mining districts. **3. Ingle,** E: Local institutions of Virginia.—**Wilhelm,** Lewis W. Local institutions of Maryland.

Cobbett, W: Porcupine's works; containing various writings and selections exhibiting a faithful picture of the U. S. of America, of their governments, laws, politics and resources, of the characters of their presidents, governors, legislators, magistrates and military men, and of the customs, manners, morals, religion, virtues and vices of the people; comprising also a complete series of historical documents and remarks from the end of the war in 1783 to the election of president in march 1801. Lond. 1801. 12 v. O.   **324.1 : 42**
Note. For contents, see Catalogue of the Boston athenæum, v. 1, p. 611.

Wolcott, Oliver. Memoirs of the administrations of G: Washington and J: Adams; ed. by G: Gibbs. N. Y. 1846. 2 v. O. **324.1+8**

Benton, T: Hart. Thirty years' view, or A history of the working of the american government for thirty years, from 1820 to 1850; chiefly taken from the congress debates, the private papers of gen. Jackson, and the speeches of ex-senator Benton, with his actual view of men and affairs; with historical notes and ill. and some notices of eminent deceased cotemporaries, by a senator of thirty years. [Anon.] N. Y. 1854. 2 v. O.   **324.1+11**

Julian, G: W. Political recollections, 1840 to 1872. Chic. 1884 [1883]. D.   **324.1 : 43**

Helper, Hinton Rowan. The impending crisis of the south; how to meet it. N. Y. 1860. D.   **324.1 : 16**

Mr. Buchanan's administration on the eve of the rebellion. N. Y. 1866. O.   **324.1+9**

Gasparin, Agénor Étienne comte de. The uprising of a great people; the U. S. in 1861. From the french by Mary L. Booth. 3d ed. N. Y. 1861. D.   **324.1 : 15**

— America before Europe; principles and interests. Tr. by Mary L. Booth. N. Y. 1862. D.   . **324.1 : 14**

Smith, Goldwin. A letter to a whig member of the Southern independence association. Bost. 1864. D.   **324.1 : 25**

Bright, J: Speeches on the american question; with an introd. by Frank Moore. Bost. 1865. D.   **324.1 : 12**

Raymond, H: Jarvis. History of the administration of president Lincoln, incl. his speeches, letters, addresses, proclamations and messages; with a prelim. sketch of his life. N. Y. 1864. D.   **324.1 : 10**

Stephens, Alexander Hamilton. A constitutional view of the late war between the states, its causes, character, conduct and results; presented in a series of colloquies at Liberty hall. Phila. [1868, 1870]. 2 v. O. **324.1+2**

Royall, W: L. A reply to "A fool's errand, by one of the fools". 3d ed. containing mr. Royall's rejoinder to mr. Tourgee's letter of answer in the New York tribune. N. Y. 1881. D.   **324.1 : 46**

Hinsdale, Burton A. The republican text-book for the campaign of 1880; a full history of gen. James A. Garfield's public life, with other political information. N. Y. 1880. O.
                                363+2

McPherson, E: A handbook of politics for 1882, 1884; a record of important political action, legislative, executive and judicial, national and state from july 1, 1880 to july 31, [1884]. Wash. 1882, 1884. 2 v. O.   **324.1+21**

*   *   *

Willis, Anson. Our rulers and our rights, or Outlines of the U. S. government, its origin, branches, departments, institutions, officers and modes of operation. Ill. Phila. 1869. D.   **324.1 : 26**

Ford, Worthington Chauncey. The american citizen's manual: part 1, Governments, national, state and local, the electorate, the civil service; pt. 2, The functions of governments, state and federal. (Questions of the day). N. Y. 1882, 1883. 2 v. D.
                                324.1 : 37

McKnight, D: A. The electoral system of the U. S.; a critical and historical exposition of its fundamental principles in the constitution, and of the acts and proceedings enforcing it. Phila. 1878. O.   **324.1 : 20**

Franchise reform league. Franchise reform; how local self-government, civil service reform and the political independence of citizens may be established upon a permanent basis; brief extracts from "The elective franchise in the U. S." by D. C. McMillan. [N. Y.] n. d. D.   **324.1 : 45**

Quincy, Josiah Phillips. The protection of majorities, or Considerations relating to electoral reform.   in **824.1 : 68**

Lockwood, H: C. The abolition of the presidency. N. Y. 1884. O.   **324.1 : 47**

4. Colonies and Emigration.

Raynal, Guillaume T: François, abbé. A philosophical and political history of the settlements … in the East and West Indies. Tr. by J. Justamond. Lond. 1777. 5 v. O.
                                382+3

Janssen, C. W. Holländische kolonial-politik in Ost-Indien; eine skizze. In Deutsche zeit- und streit-fragen.   **304 : 15 v13**

Seward, G: Chinese immigration, in its social and economical aspects. N. Y. 1881. D.
                                325 : 1

Jones, Evan R. The emigrant's friend; containing information and advice for persons intending to emigrate to the U. S. Rev. ed. Map. Lond. 1881. D.   **325 : 2**

United States. Immigration. **Young, E:** Special report on immigration, accompanying information for immigrants relative to the prices and rentals of land, the staple products, facilities of access to market, cost of farm stock, kind of labor in demand in the western and southern states.

United States. *Immigration.—Continued.*
Appended, tables showing the average weekly wages paid in the several states and sections for factory, mechanical and farm labor, the cost of provisions, groceries, dry goods and house rent in the various manuf. districts of the country in 1869-70. Wash. 1872. O. *in* **325 : D**
— — Annual reports on immigration. *See* Congressional documents. *in* **328. 1 : D**
Note. Forms part of the report on commerce and navigation by the bureau of statistics of the treas. dep't.

Wisconsin. *Board of immigration.* Annual report for 1880. *In* Assembly journal, 1881. *in* **328. 15 : D**
— — Annual report for 1881 and 1882. Milw. 1882-83. O. *in* **325 : Pam**
Note. For other reports on immigration, see Governor's message and accompanying doc's, *in* 328.15 : D.
— — Wisconsin, what it offers the immigrant ; an official report. Map. Milw. 1879. O. **325 : Pam**
— *Same, germ.* Wisconsin ; ein bericht über bevölkerung, boden, klima, handel und die industriellen verhältnisse dieses staates im nordwesten der nordamerikanischen union. 6te, 7te, 9te aufl. Milw. 1879-83. O. **325 : Pam**
— *Same, swed.* Wisconsin ; statens fördelar för invandraren ; dess befolkning, jordmån, klimat, handel och industri. Milw. 1881; Chicago. 1883. O. **325 : Pam**

5. Slavery.

Barnes, Albert. An inquiry into the scriptural views of slavery. Phila. 1857. D. **326 : 1**
Blake, W. O. History of slavery and the slave trade, ancient and modern, and of the political history of slavery in the U. S. *T. p. w.* [Columbus, Ohio. 1857 ?] O. **326+2**
Cairnes, J: Elliot. The slave power ; its character, career and probable designs ; an attempt to explain the real issues involved in the american contest. N. Y. 1862. O. **326+3**
Carey, H: C: The slave trade, domestic and foreign ; why it exists and how it may be extinguished. Phila. 1853. D. **326 : 4**
Chambers, W: American slavery and colour. Lond. 1857. O. **326 : 5**
Child, Lydia Maria. An appeal in favor of that class of americans called africans. N. Y. 1836. D. **326 : 6**
Clarke, James Freeman. Anti-slavery days ; a sketch of the struggle which ended in the abolition of slavery in the U. S. N. Y. 1884. D. **326 : 19**
Clarkson, T: The history of the rise, progress, and accomplishment of the abolition of the african slave-trade by the british parliament. Lond. 1808. 2 v. O. **326 : 7**
Cochin, P: Suzanne Augustin. The results of slavery. Tr. by Mary L. Booth. Bost. 1863. D. **326 : 9**
— The results of emancipation. Tr. by Mary L. Booth. Bost. 1863. D. **326 : 8**
Engel, Franz. Aus dem pflanzerstaate Zulia ; kulturgeschichtliche streiflichter aus der

gegenwart. *In* Deutsche zeit- und streitfragen. **304 : 15 v10**
Fortune, T. T: Black and white ; land, labor and politics in the south. N. Y. 1884. S. **326 : 23**
Fuller, R:, *and* Francis **Wayland.** Domestic slavery considered as a divine institution ; in a correspondence. Rev. and corr. by the authors. N. Y. 1845. S. **326 : 10**
Gareis, C: Der sklavenhandel, das völkerrecht und das deutsche recht. *In* Deutsche zeit- und streit-fragen. **304 : 15 v13**
Hopkins, J: H: A scriptural, ecclesiastical and historical view of slavery, from the days of the patriarch Abraham to the 19th century, addressed to the right rev. Alonzo Potter. N. Y. [1864]. D. **326 : 11**
Jay, W: Inquiry into the character and tendency of the american colonization and american anti-slavery societies. 6th ed. N. Y. 1838. D. **326 : 22**
Miscegenation ; the theory of the blending of the races applied to the american white man and negro. N. Y. 1864. D. **326 : 21**
Owen, Robert Dale. The wrong of slavery, the right of emancipation and the future of the african race in the U. S. Phila. 1864. D. **326 : 12**
Poole, W: F: Anti-slavery opinions before the year 1800 ; read before the Cincinnati literary club nov. 16, 1872. Appended, a facsimile reprint of dr. G: Buchanan's oration on the moral and political evil of slavery, del. at a public meeting of the Maryland society for promoting the abolition of slavery, Balt. july 4, 1791. Cinc. 1873. O. **326 : 13**
Seabury, S: American slavery distinguished from the slavery of english theorists, and justified by the law of nature. N. Y. 1861. D. **326 : 14**
Smith, Goldwin. Does the Bible sanction american slavery ? Cambridge. 1864. D. **326 : 15**
Smith, W: A. Lectures on the philosophy and practice of slavery, as exhibited in the institution of domestic slavery in the U. S. ; with the duties of masters to slaves; ed. by T: O. Summers. Nashville. 1857. D. **326 : 16**
Stowe, Harriet Elizabeth, *born* Beecher. A key to Uncle Tom's cabin ; presenting the original facts and documents upon which the story is founded, together with corroborative statements verifying the truth of the work. Leipz. 1853. 2 v. S. **326 : 24**
Sugenheim, S: Geschichte der aufhebung der leibeigenschaft und hörigkeit in Europa bis um die mitte des neunzehnten jahrhunderts. St. Petersburg. 1861. O. **326 : 20**
Wallon, H: Alexandre. Histoire de l'esclavage dans l'antiquité. 2e éd. Paris. 1879. 3 v. O. **326 : 18**
Williams, G: W. History of the negro race in America from 1619 to 1880 ; negroes as slaves, as soldiers and as citizens ; together with a preliminary consideration of the unity of the human family, an historical sketch of Africa and an account of the negro governments of Sierra Leone and Liberia. N. Y. 1882, 1883. 2 v. O. **326 : 17**

6. Foreign and domestic relations.

United States.

United States. The diplomatic correspondence of the U. S. of America from 10th sept. 1783 to march 4, 1789 ; being the letters of the presidents of congress, the secretary for foreign affairs, american ministers at foreign courts, foreign ministers near congress, reports of committees of congress and reports of the secretary for foreign affairs on various letters and communications, together with letters from individuals on public affairs. Pub. under the direction of the sec. of state from the original mss. in the dept. of state, conformably to an act of congress approved may 5, 1832. Wash. 1833, 1834. 7 v. O.   *in* **327.1 : D**

— [Papers on foreign relations, transmitted by the sec. of state to congress, with the president's message]. *In* Congressional documents.   *in* **328.1 : D**

— *Congress.* Treaties and conventions concluded between the U. S. of America and other powers since july 4, 1776 ; with notes showing what treaties or parts of treaties have been abrogated and decisions thereupon. (U. S. 41st cong. 3 sess. Sen. ex. doc. no. 36). Wash. 1871. O.   *in* **327.1 : D**
Note. Other treaties will be found in the U. S. statutes at large, in 343.1 : D.

— — Documents relative to central american affairs and the enlistment question. Wash. 1856. O.   *in* **327.1 : D**

— *Secretary of state.* French spoliations ; report relative to the papers on file in the dep. of state touching the unsettled claims of citizens of the U. S. against France for spoliations prior to july 31, 1801. (U. S. 48th cong. 1 sess. Sen. ex. doc. no. 205). Wash. 1884. O.   *in* **327.1 : D**

Kettell, T: Prentice. Southern wealth and northern profits, as exhibited in statistical facts and official figures ; showing the necessity of union to the future prosperity and welfare of the republic. N. Y. 1860. O.   **327.1+2**

Bemis, G: Hasty recognition of rebel belligerency, and our right to complain of it. Bost. [1865]. O.   **327.1 : 1**

Cushing, Caleb. The treaty of Washington [relating to the " Alabama claims," signed may 8, 1871] ; its negotiation, execution and the discussions relating thereto. N. Y. 1873. O.   **327.1 : 3**

Nordhoff, C: The cotton states in the spring and summer of 1875. N. Y. 1876. O.   **327.1+6**

Tourgée, Albion Winegar. An appeal to Cæsar. N. Y. 1884. S.   **327.1 : 7**

Jackson, Helen Maria, *born* Fiske, *formerly Mrs.* Hunt, (*H. H.*). A century of dishonor ; a sketch of the U. S. government's dealings with some of the indian tribes. N. Y. 1881. D.   **327.1 : 4**

Inter-oceanic canal, The, and the Monroe doctrine. N. Y. 1880. D.   **327.1 : 5**

Great Britain.

Sergeant, Lewis. England's policy, its traditions and problems. Edinburgh. 1881. O.   **327.2+11**

Whitelocke, Whitelock *or* Whitlock, *Sir* Bulstrode. A journal of the swedish embassy in the years 1653 and 1654, impartially written. First pub. from the original ms. by C: Morton ; new ed., rev. by H: Reeve. Lond. 1855. 2 v. O.   **327.2 : 8**

Oliphant, Laurence. Narrative of the earl of Elgin's mission to China and Japan in 1857-1859. N. Y. 1860. O.   **327.2+2**

Campbell, G: Douglass, *8th duke of Argyll.* The eastern question from the treaty of Paris 1856 to the treaty of Berlin 1878, and to the second Afghan war. Lond. [1879.] 2 v. O.   **327.2 : 1**

Gladstone, W: Ewart. Essays on the eastern question. *In his* Gleanings of past years.   **329.2 : 9 v4**

Keay, J. Seymour. Spoiling the egyptians ; a tale of shame told from the british Blue books. N. Y. 1882. D.   **327.2 : 7**

Peter *the hermit. pseud.* The brigands in Egypt ; solution of the international crisis, letters to an englishman. Tr. from the french. Lond. 1882.   **327.2 : Pam**

Cusack, Mary Frances, (*The nun of Kenmare*). The present case of Ireland plainly stated ; a plea for my people and my race. N. Y. 1881. D.   **327.2 : 3**

Russell, C: .New views on Ireland, or Irish land ; grievances, remedies. 2d ed. Lond. 1880. D.   **327.2 : 4**

O'Brien, R: Barry. Fifty years of concessions to Ireland, 1831—1881 ; in 2 v. V. 1. Lond. [1883]. O.   **327.2 : 12**

Great Britain. *Commissions on laws of naturalization and allegiance.* Report of the royal commissioners for inquiring into the laws of naturalization and allegiance, together with an app. containing an account of british and foreign laws, and of the diplomatic correspondence which has passed on the subject, reports from foreign states and other papers. Lond. 1869. F. **327.2 : R5**

— *Commissioners on neutrality laws.* Report of the neutrality laws commissioners, together with an app. containing reports from foreign states and other documents. Lond. 1868. F.   **327.2 : R6**

Diplomatic review pamphlets. 3 v. in 2. *v. p. and d.* O.   **327.2+9**

Contents. V. 1. **Monteith,** R. Reasons for investigation into charges against Lord Palmerston, 1840; Dangers to England of austrian subjugation, 1859.— **Urquhart,** D: The turkish bath with a view to its introduction into the british dominions, 1856; Fragments of ante-historic times, 1858.—**Fischel,** E: The duke of Coburg's pamphlet on Russia, 1859.—Palmerston unmasked, 1860; The frontier of the Rhine and the meeting at Baden-Baden.—**Marx,** Fs. The Pacific and the Amoor, 1856-1861; Mr. Kinglake's book on the Crimea, 1863.—**Rolland,** S. E. Growth of russian power contingent on the decay of the british constitution, 1858; Speech at the reception of deputies from Circassia, 1862; How is the queen's government to be carried on ? 1866.—**Montagu,** Lord R. Sucession to the crown of Denmark, 1861.— **Crawshay,** G: The treaty of London, 1864.—**Denbigh,** Earl of. Speech on Candia, 1867.—**Urquhart,** D: Mémoire sur les relations de la Russie et de l'Europe, 1870.—Mouvement populaire en Bavière, 1870.—Les procédures pour la guerre à l'appui de l'adresse à l'assemblée nationale de la France, 1872.— La nécessité pou l'Europe de revenir au droit des gens, 1872.—L'appel au pape dans l'age de fer, 1873.—Importance of the pontifical canons, 1873.— **Defourny,** P: G. *abbé.* The canonical doctrine of obedience, 1873. **2. Cargill,** W. Examen de la ligue Prussienne, 1840.—**Crawshay,** G: The immediate cause of the indian mutiny, 1857; The catastrophe of the East India company, 1858; Proselytism destructive of christianity and incompatible with political dominion, 1858.—**Dunlop, A. M.** Afghan papers; a speech, 1861.—**Smith,** Alphin. The defences of England, 1862.—Expedition of the Chesapeake to Circassia, 1864.—**Stanley of Alderley,** *Baron.* The Malay peninsula, 1876; Religious persecutions in Russia, 1877.   **3.** Transactions of political associations, chiefly reports on the foreign affairs committees, 1843–1877.

Urquhart, D: [Pamphlets.] 3 v. in 2. London. *v. d.* O.   **327.2+10**
 Contents. V. 1. Pt. 1. *Constitutional and international.* Newcastle committee: Limitation of the supply of grain; Constitutional remedies, evidence of mr. Urquhart before the above committee.—The queen and the premier; a statement of their struggle and its results. 2d ed. 1857.—The four wars of the french revolution examined judicially in order to demonstrate that they would have been impossible without the suppression of the functions of the privy council.—**Stapleton, A. G.** A day with one of the committees.—Politeness an element of power, letter to mr. Stapleton.—Pt. 2. *England defenceless since the declaration of Paris.* The invasion of England.—The right of search: in what it consists; how the british empire exists by it; that it has been surrendered up, with an introd. on lord Derby's part therein.—Answer to mr. Cobden on the assimilation of war and peace, also analysis of the correspondence with the U. S., showing the declaration of Paris to have been violated by England and France.—Sparing private property in war at sea; two letters to mr. Gregory on his motion of march 2d, 1866.—The days of England not "numbered"; reply to sir Archibald Alison by Caritas.—Naval power suppressed by the maritime states; Crimean war.   **2.** Pt. 1. *India.* The Edinburgh review and the afghan war; letters re-printed from the Morning herald.—The rebellion of India: Mr. Disraeli's speech reviewed; Illegality of the acts abolishing native customs and their consequences; The wondrous plate of India: the sradaha, the keystone of the brahminical, buddhistic and arian religions as illustrative of the dogma and duty of adoption among the princes and people of India.—The abyssinian war; the contingency of failure, dec. 1867.—Pt. 2. *Russia and Turkey.* A fragment of the history of Servia.—The Suez canal in 1853; a chapter extracted from the stereotyped plates of the progress of Russia in the west, north and south.—The story of the war by collated passages from the Times and Morning herald correspondents and the evidence before the Sebastopol committee.—The secret of Russia in the Caspian and Euxine, the circassian war as affecting the insurrection in Poland.   **3.** *The Vatican council of 1870.* Conscience in respect to public affairs; a correspondence.—Appeal of a protestant to the pope to restore the law of nations; reply to six questions on the business for the announced sixth lateran council.—Effect on the world of the restoration of the canon law, a vindication of the catholic church against a priest.—Fragments on politeness.—Le patriarche Hassoun: Le schisme arménien dans ses rapports avec le concile œcuménique et les décrets synodaux sur la guerre, avec les documents.

7. Legislative annals.

United States.

Congress. List of congressional documents from the 20th to the 46th cong. incl. (Dep't of the interior.) Wash. 1882. O.   **L**
 Note. A list of U. S. documents from the 1st to the 37th cong. incl. will be found in the Index to the catalogue of books in Bates hall of the Boston public library, and from the 1st to 45th cong. incl. in the catalogue of the Boston athenæum, vol. 5, p. 3054–3109. Both catalogues give complete contents up to and incl. the 14th cong., 1816–17, after which time the publications of each cong. were furnished with a separate index.

— **Ordway,** Albert. General index of the journals of congress from the 1st to [16th] congress incl.; a synoptical subject-index of

U. S. Congress.—*Continued.*
the proceedings of congress on all public business from 1789 to [1821]; with references to the debates, documents and statutes connected therewith. Wash. 1880 –83. 2 v. Q.   *in* **328.1 : D**
 Note. An alphabetical index to all papers of public interest from the 18th to the 35th cong., 1829–1859, will be found in the Index to the Catalogue of books in Bates hall of the Boston public library, p. 815–842, and for the 36th and 37th cong. 1859—1862, in the 1st supplement to the same, p. 647—654. Indexes to special sets are recorded in the proper place below. A chronological list and full analytical index to all government publications up to march 1881, prepared by authority of congress under the direction of B: Perley Poore, is now reported to be ready for the printer.

— History of congress; exhibiting a classification of the proceedings of the senate and the house of representatives from march 4, 1789, to march 3, 1793, embracing the first term of the administration of general Washington. Phila. 1843. O.   **328.1 : 2**

— Constitution of the U. S. of America, with the amendments thereto; added Jefferson's Manual of parliamentary practice, the standing rules and orders for conducting business in the house of representatives and senate of the U. S., and Barclay's digest. Wash. 1874. O. *in* **328.1 : D**

— Journals of the american congress, from 1774 to 1788. Wash. 1823. 4 v. O. *in* **328.1 : D**

— The debates and proceedings in the congress of the U. S.; with an app. containing important state papers and public documents and all laws of a public nature, with a copious index; 1st cong.—1st sess. 18th cong. Wash. 1834–56. 42 v. O. *in* **328.1 : D**

— Register of debates in congress; comprising the leading debates and incidents, together with an app. containing important state papers and public documents and the laws enacted during the session, with a copious index; 2d sess. 18th cong.—1st sess. 25th cong. Wash. 1825–1837. 14 v. in 29. O.
          in **328.1 : D**

— The congressional globe; containing sketches of the debates and proceedings of the 1st sess. of the 23d—2d sess. of the 42d congress. Wash. 1834–1873. 80 v. Q.
          in **328.1 : D**
 Note. The following volumes are missing: 24th cong., 1 and 2 sess.—25th cong., 1, 2 and 3 sess.—26th cong., 1 sess.—27th cong., 2 and 3 sess.—29th cong., 1 sess.—App. to 29th cong., 2 sess.—32d cong., 2 sess.—38th cong., 1 sess.—40th cong., 1 sess.

— Congressional record; containing the proceedings and debates of the 1st sess. of the 43d—1st sess. of the 48th cong. Wash. 1874–1884. 68 v. Q.   *in* **328.1 : D**

— **Benton, T: Hart.** Abridgment of the debates of congress, from 1789–1856; from Gale's and Seaton's Annals of congress, from their Register of debates, and from the official reported debates by J: C. Rives. N. Y. 1857. 16 v. O.   **328.1 : R1**

— American state papers: Documents, legislative and executive, of the congress of the U. S. from the first session of the first congress, commencing march 3, 1789; selected and ed. by the secretary of the senate and the clerk of the house of representatives. Wash. 1833–1861. 38 v. F.   *in* **328.1 : D**
 Contents. Class 1. *Foreign relations.* To end of 35th cong., march 3, 1859. 6 v.   **2.** *Indian affairs.* To

U. S. Congress.—*Continued.*

end of 19th cong., march 3, 1827. 2 v. **3.** *Finance.* To end of first sess., 20th cong., may 26, 1828. 5 v. **4.** *Commerce and navigation.* To end of 17th cong. march 3, 1823. 2 v. **5.** *Military affairs.* To end of 2d sess., 25th cong., march 1, 1838. 7 v. **6.** *Naval affairs.* To end of 1st sess., 24th cong., june 15, 1836. 4 v. **7.** *Post office dept.* To end of 22d cong., march 3, 1833. 1 v. **8.** *Public lands.* To end of 24th cong., march 3, 1837. 8 v. **9.** *Claims.* To end of 17th cong., march 3, 1823. 1 v. **10.** *Miscellaneous.* To end of 17th cong., march 3, 1823. 2 v.

Note. Each vol. is provided with a minute index.

— **Niles'** weekly register; containing political, historical, geographical, scientific, astronomical, statistical and biographical documents, essays and facts, together with notices of the arts and manufactures and a record of the events of the times. Balt. 1812–1848. 73 v.   **RM**

Note. From 1811—aug. 1814 called the "Weekly register;" from sept. 1837—dec. 1848 called Niles national register.

— **Congressional** directory, comp. for the use of cong. by B: Perley Poore. 44th cong. 2d sess; 46th cong. 1st sess.; 47th cong. 1st. sess.; 48th cong. 1st and 2d sess. Wash. 1876–84. O.   *in* **328.1 : D**

— **Senate.** Journal, 23d cong. 1st sess., 1833–34 [to 48th cong. 1st sess., 1883–84]. Wash. 1834– 84. O.   *in* **328.1 : D**

— — Public documents, 23d cong., 1833–34 [to 29th cong. 2d sess., 1846–47]. Wash. 1834–47. O.   *in* **328.1 : D**

— — Reports of committees, 30th cong. 1st sess., 1847–48 [to 47th cong. 2d sess., 1882–83]. Wash. 1848–83. O.   *in* **328.1 : D**

— — Executive documents, 30th cong. 1st sess., 1847–48 [to 47th cong. 2d session, 1882–83]. Wash. 1848–83. O.   *in* **328.1 : D**

— — Miscellaneous documents, 30th cong. 1st sess., 1847–48 [to 47th cong. 2d session, 1882–83]. Wash. 1848–83. O.   *in* **328.1 : D**

— **House of representatives.** Journal, 23d cong. 1st sess., 1833–34 [to 48th cong. 1st sess., 1888–84]. Wash. 1883–84. O.   *in* **328.1 : D**

— — Reports of committees, 23d cong. 1st sess., 1833–34 [to 47th cong. 2d sess., 1882–83]. Wash. 1834–83. O.   *in* **328.1 : D**

— — *Same.* Consolidated index, 26th to 40th cong. incl. [1839–1869], prep. under the dir. of E: McPherson. Wash. 1869. O.   *in* **328.1 : D**

— — [Executive] Documents, 23d cong. 1st. sess., 1833–34 [to 29th cong. 2d sess., 1846–47]. Wash. 1834–47. O.   *in* **328.1 : D**

— — Executive documents, 30th cong. 1st sess., 1847–48 [to 47th cong. 2d sess., 1882–83]. Wash. 1848–83. O.   *in* **328.1 : D**

— — *Same.* Consolidated index, 26th to 40th cong. incl. [1839–1869], prep. under the dir. of E: McPherson. Wash. 1879. O.   *in* **328.1 : D**

— — Miscellaneous documents, 30th cong. 1st sess., 1847–48 [to 47th cong. 2d sess., 1882–83]. Wash. 1848–83. O.   *in* **328.1 : D**

— — Reports of the court of claims, 34th cong. 1st sess., 1855–56 [to 37th cong. 3d sess., 1862–63; being nos. 1–296]. Wash. 1856–63. O.   *in* **328.1 : D**

Note. The several series of Senate and House documents, specified above, comprise what is known as the "set of congressional doc's". Each volume of each series contains an index to the entire series of a session.—A number of volumes previous to the 29th congress, 1845, are missing, but only a few after that date. Many special government publications

U. S. Congress.—*Continued.*

will be found in this catalogue entered in such classes, as are indicated by their subjects.

The executive documents (since 1862, of the house; before that time, sometimes of the senate, sometimes of the house, sometimes in both) contain, among other matter, the annual reports of the following permanently established departments and bureaus:

Agricultural dep't (estab. in 1847 as a branch of the patent office, from which it was separated in 1862), *containing reports of*
  Commissioner of agriculture,
  Botanist,
  Bureau of animal industry,
    "   forestry,
    "   chemistry,
    "   entomology,
    "   statistics.

Civil service commission (estab. in 1883).

Department of justice, *under the charge of the* Attorney-general.

District of Columbia, Commissioners.

Fish commission (estab. in 1871).

Interior dep't (estab. in 1849), *transmits reports of*
  Secretary of the interior,
  Bureau of education (estab. in 1867),
  Census office.
  Entomological commission (estab. in 1877, transferred in 1881 to the Agricultural dep.),
  General land office (estab. in 1812 as subordinate to the Treasury dep.),
  Geological survey (estab. in 1879 by the consolidation of the Survey of the territories, Survey of the Rocky mountain region, Survey west of the 100th meridian, etc.),
  Indian affairs, Office of, (estab. in 1832 as subordinate to the War dep.), *including* Commissioner, Board *and* Inspector of Indian schools.
  Patent office (estab. in 1849),
  Pension office (estab. in 1833 as subordinate to the War dep.),
  U. S. national museum *and*
  Bureau of ethnology (included under the management of the Smithsonian institution),
  Architect of the capitol,
  Commissioner of railroads (estab. in 1878 *under the name of* Auditor of r. r. accounts),
  Columbia institution for the deaf and dumb (estab. in 1857).
  Government hospital for the insane (estab. in 1855),
  Freedmen's hospital and asylum,
  Columbia hospital for women (estab. in 1866),
  U. S. inspector of gas-meters.
  Sup't of Hot Springs reservation,
  Sup't of Yellowstone national park,
  Utah commission.

National board of health (estab. in 1879, as subordinate to the Sec. of the treasury.)

Navy dep't (estab. in 1798), *transmits reports of*
  Secretary of the navy,
  Admiral of the navy,
  Advisory board, Naval,
  Arctic expeditions,
  Bureau of construction and repairs,
    "   equipment and recruiting,
    "   medicine and surgery,
    "   navigation,
    "   ordnance,
    "   provisions and clothing,
    "   steam engineering,
    "   yards and docks,
  Chief signal officer of the navy,
  Detailed movements of vessels,
  Estimates and pay,
  Hydrographic office (*a division of the Bureau of navigation*),
  Light-house board,
  Marine corps, Commandant of,
  Nautical almanac office (*a division of the Bureau of navigation*),
  Naval academy at Annapolis,
  Naval observatory,
  Navy-yards,
  Revenue marine.

Post-office dep't (estab. in 1789), *transmits reports of*
  Postmaster-general,
  First assistant postm.-gen. (*post-offices*),
  Second assistant postm.-gen. (*mail service*),
  Third assistant postm.-gen. (*accounts and supplies*),
  Auditor of the treasury for the p.-o. dep't,
  Chief post-office inspector,
  Foreign mail service,

U. S. Congress.—*Continued.*
　Postal money order system,
　Railway mail service,
　Topographer of the p.-o. dep't.
President of the U. S., *messages.*
Smithsonian institution, *annual rep. only.*
State dep't (estab. in 1789). The sec. of state makes
　　no annual report, but transmits with the presi-
　　dent's message papers on
　Foreign relations (*known also as* Diplomatic corre-
　　spondence),
　Commercial relations *and*
　　Consular reports.
Treasury dep't (estab. in 1776), *transmits reports of*
　Secretary of the treasury (*usually known as*
　　Finance report),
　Auditors of the treasury, 1st to 6th,
　Commissioner of customs (estab. in 1849),
　Commissioner of internal revenue (estab. in 1862),
　Commissioner of mining statistics (estab. in 1866,
　　abolished in 1876),
　Comptroller, 1st and 2d,
　Comptroller of the currency (*national banks,* estab.
　　in 1863),
　Register of the treasury,
　Treasurer of the U. S.,
　Bureau of engraving and printing,
　Bureau of the mint (*including* Production of gold
　　and silver),
　Bureau of statistics (*Commerce and navigation*),
　Coast and geodetic survey (reorgan. in 1843),
　Light-house board,
　Life-saving service (reorgan. in 1878),
　Marine-hospital service,
　Revenue-marine (*succeeded in 1884 by the* Bureau of
　　navigation),
　Steamboat inspection office,
　Supervising architect (estab. in 1853),
　Liabilities to Indian tribes,
　National board of health (estab. in 1879).
War dep't (estab. in 1789), *transmits reports of*
　Secretary of war,
　Adjutant-general,
　Chief of engineers, with appendices,
　Chief of ordnance,
　Chief signal officer of the army,
　Commissary-general of subsistence,
　General of the army (and department officers),
　Inspector-general of the army,
　Judge-advocate-general,
　Military academy at West Point,
　Paymaster-general,
　Provost-marshal-general (estab. 1863, abolished 1866),
　Quartermaster-general,
　Soldiers' home, Commissioners of.
　State, war and navy dep't building, Engineer of,
　Surgeon-general.
　—The government year is usually the fiscal year,
　july-june, and july 1883—june 1884 is the
　report for 1884. The report for any one year will be
　found by a reference to the index of the executive
　documents for the session of congress, *commencing
　during the year in question.*

U. S.—*Special states.*

New York *colony.* Journal of the legislative
　council of the colony of New York ; began
　the 9th day of april, 1691, and ended the 3d
　of april, 1775. Albany. 1861. 2 v. F.
　　　　　　　　　　　　　　328.13 : R1
Illinois *state.* Reports made to the general as-
　sembly at its 25th [-31st biennial] session,
　1867 [-1879]. Springfield. 1867-79. 23 v. O.
　　　　　　　　　　　　　　in **328.15 : D**
　Contain, in add. to committee and special reports,
　the following annual or biennial reports of officers
　and institutions;
　Adjutant-general, 1869—1878.
　Attorney-general, 1873—1878.
　Auditor of public accounts, 1865—1878.
　Canal commissioners, 1870—1878.
　Governor's messages, 1867—1879.
　Ill. and Michigan canal, Trustees, 1865—1869, (*trans-
　　ferred to canal* Commissioners).
　Ill. asylum for feeble-minded children, 1871—1878.
　Ill. charitable eye and ear infirmary, 1873—1878.
　Ill. central hospital for the insane, 1865—1878.
　Ill. eastern hospital for the insane, 1877—1878.

Illinois *state.—Continued.*
　Ill. industrial university, 1867—1872.
　Ill. institution for idiots and imbeciles, 1865—1868.
　Ill. institution for the education of the blind, 1865—
　　1878.
　Ill. institution for the education of the deaf and
　　dumb, 1865—1878.
　Ill. northern hospital for the insane, 1870—1878.
　Ill. soldiers' orphans' home, 1867—1878.
　Ill. southern hospital for the insane, 1873—1878.
　Ill. state hospital for the insane, *see* Ill. central
　　hosp.
　Ill. state penitentiary (northern), 1865—1878.
　Ill. state reform school for juvenile delinquents,
　　1871—1878.
　Insurance department, 1869—1878.
　Railroad and warehouse commissioners, 1871—1874.
　Secretary of state, 1872—1878.
　Southern Ill. normal university, 1873—1878.
　Southern Ill. penitentiary, 1877—1878.
　State board of agriculture, 1871—1872.
　State board of centennial managers, 1876.
　State board of health, 1877—1878.
　State commissioners of public charities, 1869—1878.
　State entomologist, 1870—1872.
　State house commissioners, 1867—1878.
　State normal university, 1875—1876.
　State treasurer, 1865—1878.
　Superintendent of public instruction, 1865—1872.
Michigan *state. Executive dep's.* Joint docu-
　ments for 1871[-1880]. Lansing. 1872-81.
　28 v. O.　　　　　　　　　　　　*in* **328.15 : D**
　Contain annual or biennial reports of the follow-
　ing officers and institutions:
　Adjutant-general, 1872—1880.
　Attorney-general, 1871—1880.
　Auditor-general, 1871—1880.
　Board of commissioners [for the building] of the
　　eastern asylum for the insane, 1875—1879.
　Board of fund commissioners, 1877—1878.
　Board of state auditors, 1871—1880.
　Board of state [house] building commissioners,
　　1871—1879.
　Board of state commissioners for the general
　　supervision of the charitable, penal, pauper and
　　reformatory institutions, 1871—1880.
　Building commissioners of the state house of cor-
　　rection, 1876.
　Commissioner of insurance, 1873—1880.
　Commissioner of railroads, 1872—1877, 1879—1880, *and*
　　Compilation of reports for 1871, by the Auditor
　　general.
　Commissioner of the state land office, 1871—1880.
　County superintendents of the poor, Abstract of
　　annual rep., 1871—1880.
　Eastern Mich. asylum for the insane, 1878—1880.
　Governor, messages, estimates, and pardons, 1871-
　　1881.
　Immigration commissioners, 1871—1872.
　Insane, deaf, dumb, and blind in Mich., Abstract of
　　statistics relating to, 1873—1880.
　Inspectors of the state prison, 1871—1880.
　Mich. asylum for the insane, 1871—1880.
　Mich. institution for educating the deaf and dumb,
　　and the blind, 1871—1880.
　Mich. reform school for girls, 1880.
　Quartermaster-general, 1871—1880.
　Sheriffs, Abstract of rep. relative to jails in Mich.,
　　1873—1880.
　State board of corrections and charities, *see* Board
　　of state commissioners, *etc.*
　State board of equalization, 1871, 1876.
　State commissioners and superintendent of fisher-
　　ies, 1873—1880.
　State house of correction and reformatory, 1877—
　　1880.
　State inspector of illuminating oils, 1877—1880.
　State librarian, 1871—1880.
　State military board, 1871—1874.
　State public school for dependent children, 1874-
　　1880.
　State salt inspector, 1880.
　State treasurer, 1871—1880.
　Superintendent of public instruction, (*incl.* Uni-
　　versity of Mich., State normal school, State pub-
　　lic school, State reform school, State agricultural
　　college, and other colleges in the state), 1871—1880.
　Superintendent of the St. Mary's Falls ship canal,
　　1871—1880.
　Swamp land state road commissioners, (*succeeded in
　　1875 by the* State swamp land commissioner) 1871-
　　1880.

Wisconsin *territory. Legislative assembly.* Journal of the council of the first [to fifth] legislative assembly. Belmont, Platteville and Madison. 1836–48. O.   *in* **328.15 : D**

— — Journal of the house of representatives of the first [to fifth] legislative assembly. Belmont, Green Bay, Mineral Point, Southport [Kenosha] and Madison. 1836–48. O.
          in **328.15 : D**
Note. For the number and duration of sessions, see note to session laws, in class 343.15.

— *State. Legislature.* In senate ; journal of proceedings of the [first to] thirty-sixth annual session, [1848–]1883. Madison. 1848–83. O.   *in* **328.15 : D**

— — In assembly ; journal of proceeedings of the [first to] thirty-sixth annual session, [1848–]1883. Madison. 1848–83. O.
          in **328.15 : D**

— — *Executive departments.* Governor's message [to the annual sessions of the legislature] and accompanying documents, [1848—] 1883. Madison. 1848–83. 47 v. O.
          in **328.15 : D**
Note. During 1848—1852 pub. as an appendix to the assembly journal. The accompanying documents include annual reports of the following state officers and institutions, the report for any given year being found with the documents of the session for the succeeding year:
Adjutant-general, [1–23, 26–30], 1852–1875, 1878–1882.
Attorney-general, I, 1853.
Bank comptroller, 1–17, 1853–1869, (*afterwards incl. in rep. of* State treasurer).
Board of public works for the improvement of the Fox and Wisconsin rivers, 1–5, 1848–1852.
Board of regents of normal schools, [1–4, 6–25], 1857–1861, 1863–1882.
Board of regents of the university of Wisconsin, 1–35, 1848–1882.
Board of trustees of the Northern hospital for the insane, 1–8, 1873–1880, (*for later reports, see* State board of supervison.)
Board of trustees of the Wisconsin institute for the education of the deaf and dumb, 1–29, 1852–1880, (*for later reports, see* State board of supervision.)
Board of trustees of the Wisconsin institution for the education of the blind, 1–31, 1850–1882, (*for later reports, see* State board of supervision.)
Board of trustees of the Wisconsin state hospital for the insane, 1–21, 1860–1880, (*for later reports, see* State board of supervision.)
Building commissioners of the Northern hospital for the insane, 1–2, 1871–1872.
Commissioner of emigration, 1–2, 1852–1853.
Commissioner of immigration, 1–5, 1871–1875.
Commissioner of insurance, 1–13, 1870–1882, (*previously incl. in rep. of* Secretary of state .
Commissioners for building the Wisconsin state hospital for the insane, 1–3, 1857–1859.
Commissioners of fisheries, 1–9, 1874–1882.
Commissioners of public printing, [1–9], 1874–1882. (*with rep. of* Secretary of state).
Commissioners of school and university lands, *changed in* 1878 *to* Commissioners of public lands, 1–33, 1850–1882.
Commissioners of the Wisconsin state lunatic asylum, 1, 1854.
Commissioners on a house of refuge for juvenile delinquents, 1–4, 1857–1860.
Directors and warden of the State prison, *see* State prison commissioner.
Geological survey, James G. Percival, 1853–55.
— E: Daniels, 1857–1858.
— James Hall, 1860.
— J: Murrish, 1871.
— T. C. Chamberlain, 1874–1879.
Managers of the state reform school, *changed in* 1871 *to* Managers of the Wisconsin industrial school for boys, 1–21, 1860–1880, (*for later reports, see* State board of supervision).
Milwaukee county insane asylum, 1–3, 1880–1882.
Quartermaster-general, 1862–1865, 1882 (*intervening years included in rep. of* Adjutant-gen.)
Railroad commissioner, 1–9, 1874–1882.
Secretary of state, [1–35], 1848–1882.

Wisconsin *state.—Continued.*
State agricultural society, Executive committee, 1–3, 1856–1858.
State board of charities and reform, 1–12, 1871–1882.
State board of health, 1–7, 1876–1882.
State board of supervision of Wisconsin charitable, reformatory and penal institutions, 1–2, 1881–1882.
State geologist, *see* Geological survey.
State historical society, 1–5, 1854–1859.
State prison commissioner, *changed in* 1874 *to* Directors and Warden of the state prison, 1–29, 1852–1880, (*for later reports. see* State board of supervision).
State superintendent of public instruction, 1–34, 1849–1882.
State supervisor of inspectors of illuminating oils, 2–3, 1881–1882.
State treasurer, [1–35], 1848–1882.
Surgeon-general, 1862–1865.
Trustees of the soldiers' orphans' home, 1–16, 1866–1881.

— — *Legislature.* Manual for the use of the assembly of the state of Wis. for 1853. Madison. 1853. O.   *in* **328.15 : D**

— — A manual of customs, precedents and forms in use in the assembly of Wis. ; together with the rules, the apportionment and other lists and tables for reference, 1859— 1861. Madison. 1859–61. 3 v. O.
          in **328.15 : D**
Note. Comp. by L. H. D. Crane; 1860 and 1861 are called the 2d and 3d annual ed.

— — The legislative manual of the state of Wis. ; comprising Jefferson's manual, the rules, forms and laws for the regulation of business, also lists and tables for reference, 1862—1878. Madison. 1862–78. 17 v. D.
          in **328.15 : D**
Note. From 1867, the constitutions of the U. S. and of Wis. are added.—Called the 1st–17th annual ed.; 1862–66 comp. by the chief clerks of the senate and assembly, 1867–71 by the sec. of state, from that time under the dir. of the sec. of state, 1872–74 by A. J. Turner, 1875–78 by R. M. Bashford.

— — The blue book of the state of Wisconsin, 1879—1883. Madison. 1879–83. 5 v. D.
          in **328.15 : D**
Note. The v. for 1879 adds to title: "containing the constitutions of the U. S. and of the state, Jefferson's manual, rules and orders of the senate and assembly, and annals of the legislature; also, statistical tables and history of state institutions".—Called the 18th–22d annual ed.; comp. under the dir. of the sec. of state, 1879 by D. H. Pulcifer, 1880 by J. A. Truesdell, 1881–83 by J. E. Heg.

— — The blue book of the state of Wis. ; comprising the constitutions of the U. S. and of the state, Jefferson's manual, forms and laws for the regulation of business ; also lists and tables for reference, etc. Under dir. of Ernst G. Timme, sec. of state, James E. Heg, comp. 23d v., 1885. Madison. 1885. O.
          in **328.15 : D**

Iowa *state. General assembly.* Legislative documents submitted to the 18th gen. assembly, convened jan. 12, 1880. Des Moines. 1880. 4 v. O.   *in* **328.15 : D**
Contains the following reports for 1878 and 1879:
Adjutant-general.
Auditor of state.
Board of capitol commissioners, 5th.
Board of railroad commissioners, 1st, 2d.
Central station of the Iowa weather service, 1st.
Iowa college for the blind, 14th.
Iowa hospital for the insane at Independence, 4th.
Iowa hospital for the insane at Mt. Pleasant, 10th.
Iowa institution for the education of the deaf and dumb, 13th.
Iowa reform school, 6th.
Iowa soldiers' orphans' home, 7th.
Iowa state agricultural college and farm, 8th.
Iowa state asylum for feeble-minded children, 2d.
Register of state land office.
Secretary of state, in relation to criminal returns.

Iowa *state.—Continued.*
State fish commission, 3d.
State historical society, 12th.
State librarian.
State normal school, 2d.
Superintendent of public instruction.
Treasurer of state.
Warden of Iowa state penitentiary.
Warden of additional penitentiary.

8. Political works, essays, speeches, etc.

United States.

Johnston, Alexander, *ed.* Representative american orations ; to illustrate american political history, with introd. and notes. N. Y. 1884. 3 v. S.   **329.1 : 47**

Moore, Frank, *ed.* American eloquence ; a collection of speeches and addresses by the most eminent orators of America, with biog. sketches and ill. notes. Ill. N. Y. 1864. 2 v. O.   **329.1+32**
Contents. V. 1. J. Otis.—P. Henry.—R: H: Lee.— W: H: Drayton.—J. Warren.—J. Wilson.—W: Livingston.—F. Ames.—J: Rutledge.—J. Madison.—J: Jay.— E. Randolph.—A. Hamilton.—J: Hancock.—J: Adams.—G: Washington.—E. Boudinot.—J: Dickinson.—J: Witherspoon.—D: Ramsay.—S: Adams.—J. Quincy, *jr.*—B: Rush.—R. R. Livingston.—H. H. Brackenridge.—C: Pinckney.—L. Martin.—O. Ellsworth.—C. Gore.—Red Jacket.—U. Tracy.—H: Lee.— G. Morris.—R. G. Harper.—T: A. Emmet.—G: R. Minot.—H. G. Otis.—De W. Clinton. **2.** J: Marshall. —H. King.—J. A. Bayard.—W: Pinkney.—A. Gallatin. —J. Hillhouse.—J: Randolph.—W: B. Giles.—E: Livingston.—S: Dexter.—J: Q. Adams.—H: Clay.—T. Burges.—W: Hunter.—Tecumseh.—D. Webster.—J: Story.—W: Wirt.—J: C. Calhoun.—J: Sergeant.—W: Gaston.—R. Y. Hayne.—S. S. Prentiss.

Whitman, C. W. American orators and oratory ; biographical sketches of the representative men of America, together with gems of eloquence upon the leading questions that have occupied public attention from the foundation of the republic to the present time ; with an introd. by Frank Gilbert. Ill. Chicago. 1884. O.
                      329.1+46

Niles, Hezekiah. Principles and acts of the revolution in America, or An attempt to collect and preserve some of the speeches, orations and proceedings, with sketches and remarks on men and things, and other fugitive or neglected pieces belonging to the revolutionary period in the U. S., which happily terminated in the establishment of their liberties, with a view to represent the feelings that prevailed in the "times that tried men's souls," to excite a love of freedom and lead the people to vigilance as the condition on which it is granted. Balt. 1822. O.   **329.1 : 42**

Maclay, W: Sketches of debate in the first senate of the U. S., in 1789-90-91 ; ed. by G: W. Harris. Harrisburg. *n. d.* O.
                      329.1 : 25

Adams, H:, *ed.* Documents relating to New-England federalism, 1800-1815. Bost. 1877. O.   **329.1 : 21**

Dwight, Theodore. History of the Hartford convention ; with a review of the policy of the U. S. government, which led to the war of 1812. N. Y. 1833. O.   **329.1 : 27**

Safford, W: H. The Blennerhasset papers, embodying the private journal of Harman Blennerhasset, and the hitherto unpublished correspondence of Burr, Alston, Comfort Tyler, Devereaux, Dayton, Adair, Miro, Emmett, Theodosia Burr Alston, mrs. Blennerhasset, and others, their contemporaries ; developing the purposes and aims of those engaged in the attempted Wilkinson and Burr revolution ; embracing also the first account of the "Spanish association of Kentucky", and a memoir of Blennerhasset. Cinc. 1864. O. **329.1+33**

Smith, W: H:, *ed.* St. Clair papers ; life and public services of Arthur St. Clair, with his correspondence and other papers arr. and annotated. Cinc. 1882. 2 v. O.
                      329.1 : 40

Lincoln, Abraham, *and* **Stephen Arnold Douglas.** Political debates in the celebrated campaign of 1858 in Illinois ; including the preceding speeches of each at Chicago, Springfield, etc.; also the two great speeches of mr. Lincoln in Ohio in 1859, as p p d by the reporters of each party and repeat the times of their delivery. Columbus. 1860. O.   **329.1+30**

* * *

Adams, J: Works, with a life of the author, notes and illustrations by his grandson, C: Francis Adams. Bost. 1850-56. 10 v. O.
                      329.1+1
Contents. V. 1. Life. **2.** Diary with passages from an autobiography.—Notes of debates in the continental congress in 1775-76.—Autobiography.—App. **3.** Autobiography, *continued.*—Diary.—Notes of a debate in the senate of the U. S.—Essays and controversial papers of the revolution. **4.** *Same, continued.* —Works on government. **5.** *Same, continued.*—App. **6.** *Same, continued.* **7-8.** Official letters, messages and public papers. **9.** *Same, continued.*—Correspondence. **10.** *Same, continued.*—App.—Indexes. *For expanded contents see* Catalogue of the Boston atheneum. V. 1, p. 13.

Adams, J: Quincy. The jubilee of the constitution ; a discourse del. at the request of the New York historical society in New York, 30th april 1839, the 50th anniversary of the inauguration of G: Washington. N. Y. 1839. O.   **329.1 : 22**

Ames, Fisher. Works, with a selection from his speeches and correspondence ; ed. by his son, Seth Ames. Bost. 1854. 2 v. O.
                      329.1+2
Contents. V. 1. Memoir, by J. T. **Kirkland.**—Letters. **2.** *Speeches.* On biennial elections.—On Madison's commercial resolutions.—On the british treaty. —*Political essays.* Lucius Junius Brutus.—Camillus.— Laocoon.—Falkland.—Observer.—Sketches of the state of Europe.—Phocion.—The new romans.—Russia.—Foreign politics.—No revolutionist.—Equality.— History is philosophy teaching by example.—Balance of Europe.—Political review.—Monitor.—The republican.—Sketch of the character of Alexander Hamilton.—Reflections on the war in Europe.—Character of Brutus.—Prospect of a new coalition against France.—The combined powers in France.—The successes of Bonaparte.—Dangerous power of France.— Non-intercourse act.—Lessons from history.—British alliance.—Duration of french despotism.—Dangers of american liberty.—Review of a pamphlet on the state of the british constitution.—*Miscellaneous essays.* School book.—Hercules.—Hints and conjectures concerning the institutions of Lycurgus.—American literature.

Calhoun, J: Caldwell. Works, [ed. by R: K. Cralle]. N. Y. 1853-79. 6 v. O. **329.1 : 3**
Contents. V. 1. A disquisition on government.—A discourse on the constitution and government of the U. S. **2-4.** Speeches in the house of representatives and in the senate of the U. S. **5, 6.** Reports and public letters.

Choate, Rufus. Works, with a memoir of his life by S: Gilman **Brown.** Bost. 1862. 2 v. O.   **329.1+5**
Contents. V. 1. Memoir.—Lectures and addresses. 2. Speeches in the senate of the U. S.—Miscellaneous speeches.—App.   Horæ Thucydidianæ.—1r. from Tacitus.—Index.

Clay, H: Life, correspondence and speeches, ed. by Calvin Colton. N. Y. 1857. 6 v. O.   **329.1 : 6**
Contents. V. 1-3. Colton, Calvin. Life and times. 4. Correspondence. 5, 6. Speeches.

Coe, Joseph, *ed.* The true american. Concord. 1840, 1841. 2 v. D.   **329.1 : 20**
Contents. [V. 1.] Inaugural addresses, together with the first annual addresses and messages of all the presidents of the U. S. from 1789 to 1839; the declaration of independence and constitution of the United States, with the signer's names, also the farewell addresses of Washington and Jackson, an address to the young men of the country, etc. 2. Portraits of Washington, Adams and Jefferson, with a sketch of their lives and political characters, together with all their messages except those in v. 1, Jackson's proclamation and nullification message. An address to young men and people of America, etc.

Cooper, James Fenimore. A letter to his countrymen. N. Y. 1834. O.   **329.1 : 23**

Davis, H: Winter. Speeches and addresses del. in the congress of the U. S., and on several public occasions; preceded by a sketch of his life, public services and character, an oration by J. A. J. Cresswell; with notes introductory and explanatory. N. Y. 1867. O.   **329.1+24**
Contents, see Catalogue of the Boston athenæum, v. 2, p. 744.

Dix, J: Adams. Speeches and occasional addresses. N. Y. 1864. 2 v. O.   **329.1 : 26**
Contents. V. 1. *Speeches in the senate.* The Oregon question.—French spoliations.—The warehouse system.—Lieut.-gen. of the army.—The three million bill.—The war with Mexico.—Minister to the papal states.—California claims.—The Yucatan bill.—A territorial government in Oregon.—Governments in the territories.—Trade with Canada.—Territories acquired from Mexico. 2. *Speeches in the senate.* The pilot laws.—On Dixon H. Lewis.—Memorials of officers in Mexico.—*Addresses and reports.* African colonization.—Opinion on two questions of alienism.—Education of teachers.—Report on the military system.—Geological report.—Progress of science.—Apportionment of members of congress.—Rural life and embellishments.—Growth of New York city.—Agriculture of New York.—War with Tripoli.—The rebellion in Louisiana.—Proclamation to the people of New York.

Franklin, B: Works, containing several political and historical tracts not incl. in any former ed., and many letters, official and private, not hitherto pub.; with notes and a life of the author, by Jared Sparks. Bost. 1840. 10 v. O.   **329.1+7**
Contents. V. 1. Autobiography.—Continuation, by Jared Sparks. 2. Essays on religious and moral subjects.—Essays on politics, commerce, and political economy. 3. 4. Essays and tracts, historical and political, before the american revolution. 5. Political papers during and after the american revolution.—Letters and papers on electricity. 6. Letters and papers on philosophical subjects. 7. *Correspondence.* Pt. 1: Private letters to the time of the author's first mission to England, 1725-57.—Pt. 2: Letters, private and official, from the time of the author's first mission to England to the beginning of the american revol., 1757-75. 8. *Same continued.*—Pt. 3: Letters, private and official, from the beginning of the revolution to the end of the author's mission to France, 1775-85.—App.: Fragment of Polybius on the athenian government; Memoir of sir J: Dalrymple. 9. Correspondence, pt. 3, *continued.*—Journal of the negotiation of the treaty of peace. 10. Correspondence, pt. 3, *continued.*—Pt. 4: Private let-

ters from the termination of the author's mission to France to the end of his life, 1785-90.—Supp.—Indexes.—Chronological list of the author's writings.

Gallatin, Albert. Writings, ed. by H: Adams. Phila. 1879. 3 v. O.   **329.1+8**
Contents. V. 1, 2. Letters, etc. 3. Speech in the house of representatives of Penn. touching the validity of elections in the four western counties of the state in 1794.—Sketch of the finances of the U. S.—Introd. to the collection of laws, treaties and other documents having operation and respect to the public lands.—Considerations on the currency and banking system of the U. S.—Suggestions on the banks and currency of the several U. S. in reference principally to the suspension of specie payments.—The Oregon question—Peace with Mexico.—*App.:* The Gallatin genealogy.—Indexes.

Garfield, James Abram. Works; ed. by Burke A. Hinsdale. Bost. 1882, 1883. 2 v. O.   **329.1 : 41**
Contents. V. 1. Pref.—Confiscation of the property of rebels.—Enrolling and calling out the national forces.—The sale of surplus gold.—Free commerce between the states.—Cabinet officers in congress.—The constitutional amendment abolishing slavery.—Suffrage and safety.—Restoration of the southern states.—American shipping.—The national bureau of education.—The jurisdiction of military commissions.—The public debt and specie payments.—The memory of Abraham Lincoln.—The tariff bill of 1866.—National politics.—Reconstruction.—College education.—The currency.—Strewing flowers on the graves of union soldiers.—Taxation of U. S. bonds.—Mr. Stevens and the five-twenty bonds.—Indian affairs.—Commissioner Wells's report.—Political issues of 1868.—The reduction of the army.—The Smithsonian institution.—The medical and surgical history of the rebellion.—Strengthening the public credit.—The 9th census.—The canvass in Ohio.—Civil service reform.—The tariff bill of 1870.—Currency and the banks.—Joshua R. Giddings.—Political issues of 1870.—American agriculture.—Gen. G: H. Thomas.—The right to originate revenue bills.—The Ku-klux act.—The Ohio campaign of 1871.—The 14th amendment and representation.—App.: Letter to gen. Rosecrans; Letter to Chase; Remarks on gen. Rosecrans. 2. Public expenditures; their increase and diminution.—National aid to education—8: F. B. Morse.—The presidential campaign of 1872.—The future of the republic; its dangers and its hopes.—The Northwest territory; settlement of the Western Reserve.—Chief justice Chase and prof. Agassiz. Revenues and expenditures.—Appropriations for the fiscal year ending june 30, 1875.—Effects of the rebellion on southern life insurance contracts.—Currency and the public faith—Census.—Amnesty.—The currency conflict.—The diplomatic and consular service.—H: H. Starkweather.—Almeda A. Booth.—The Hawaiian islands.—The Geneva award.—Phases of the silver question.—The democratic party and the government.—J: Winthrop and 8: Adams.—Congress and presidential elections.—Counting the electoral vote.—The Florida returns in the election of 1876.—The Louisana returns in the election of 1876.—A century of congress.—Proposed repeal of the resumption law.—The new scheme of american finance.—Oliver P. Morton.—Lincoln and emancipation.—The army and the public peace.—The wood tariff bill.—The Halifax award.—The press.—Honest money.—Suspension and resumption of specie payments.—Joseph Henry.—Gustave Schleicher.—The sugar tariff.—Revolution in congress.—The national elections protected by national authority.—Congressional nullification.—The revived doctrine of state sovereignty.—Obedience to law the first duty of congress.—The appointment of special deputy marshals.—National appropriations and misappropriations.—The democratic party and public opinion.—Zachariah Chandler.—Nomination for J: Sherman.—Letter accepting the nomination for the presidency.—Inaugural address.—Index.

Godwin, Parke. Political essays. N. Y. 1856. D.   **329.1 : 28**
Contents. Our parties and politics.—The vestiges of despotism.—Our foreign influence and policy.—Annexation.—"America for the americans."—Should we fear the pope.—The great question.—Northern or southern, which?—Kansas must be free.

Hamilton, Alexander. Works, comprising his correspondence, and his political and official writings, exclusive of the Federalist, civil and military. Pub. from the original mss. deposited in the dep't of state, by order of the joint library committee of congress; ed. by J: Church Hamilton. N. Y. 1850, 1851. 7 v. O.   **329.1 : 9**
For contents, see v. 7, p. 855, *or* Catalogue of the Boston athenæum. v. 2, p. 1823.

Jefferson, T: Writings; his autobiography, correspondence, reports, messages, addresses and other writings, official and private. Pub. by the order of the joint committee of congress on the library, from the original mss. deposited in the dep't of state; with explanatory notes, tables of contents, a copious index to each vol. and a general index to the whole; by the ed., H. A. Washington. Wash. 1853, 1854. 9 v. O.   **329.1+10**
Contents. V. 1. *Book 1.* Autobiography and app.—*Book 2, Correspondence.* Pt. 1: Letters written before his mission to Europe, 1773—1783. **2.** Pt. 2: Letters written while in Europe, 1785—1790. **3-6.** Pt. 3: Letters written after his return to the U. S. down to the time of his death, 1790—1826. **7.** *Same, continued.* —*Book 3, Official papers.* Pt. 1. Reports and opinions while secretary of state. **8.** Pt. 2: Inaugural addresses and messages.—Pt. 3: Replies to public addresses.—Pt. 4: Indian addresses.—*Book 4, Miscellaneous.* Pt. 1: Notes on Virginia.—Pt. 2: Biographical sketches of distinguished men.—Pt. 3: The batture at New Orleans. **9.** Pt. 4: Parliamentary manual.—Pt. 5: The anas.—Pt. 6: Miscellaneous papers.

Johnson, Andrew. Speeches; with a biog. introd. by Frank Moore. Bost. 1865. D.   **329.1 : 29**
Contents. Biog. introd.—Speech to the colored men of Nashville, Tenn.—Speech at Washington, april 3d 1865.—Speech at his inauguration as president.—On the veto-power.—On the homestead bill.—On the constitutionality and rightfulness of secession.—On the state of the union.—Reply to senator Lane of Oregon.—Speech at Cincinnati, Ohio, june 20, 1861.—On the war for the union.—On the proposed expulsion of Jesse D. Bright.—Appeal to the people of Tennessee.—Inaugural address.—Joint resolution proposing amendments to the constitution of the U. S.—Reply to the Illinois delegation, april 18, 1865.—Reply to the british ambassador.—Speech to the diplomatic corps.—Address to loyal southerners.—Speech to the Indiana delegation.

Leggett, W: A collection of [his] political writings, selected and arr. with a pref. by Theodore Sedgwick. N. Y. 1840. 2 v. D.   **329.1 : 11**

Lyon, Nathaniel. Last political writings, with a sketch of his life and military services. N. Y. 1861. D.   **329.1 : 31**

Madison, James. Letters and other writings. Published by order of congress. Phila. 1865. 4 v. O.   **329.1+12**
Contents, see Boston athenæum catalogue, v. 3, p. 1832.

Paine, T: Political works, now first coll., and to which are added several pieces never before pub. in England; and an app. containing [his] trial at Guildhall. Portr. Lond. [1844]. D.   **329.1 : 13**
Contents. Common sense.—Address to the quakers.—The american crisis.—Public good.—Letter to the abbé Raynal.—Letter to gen. Washington.—Letter from gen. Washington.—Dissertations on government, the affairs of the bank and paper money.—Prospects on the Rubicon.—Rights of man.—Letter to the addressers, on the late proclamation.—Dissertation of first principles of government.—Agrarian justice opposed to agrarian law, and agrarian monopoly.—The decline and fall of the english system of finance.—Letter to G: Washington on the late treaty between Great Britain and the U. S.—Memorial to mr. Monroe.—Letters to the citizens of the U.

8. after an absence of fifteen years.—Miscellaneous letters and essays on various subjects. App: Whole proceedings of trial.

Parker, Theodore. Speeches, addresses and occasional sermons. Bost. 1861. 3 v. O.   **329.1 : 44**
Contents. V. 1. The relation of Jesus to his age and the ages.—The true idea of a christian church.—A sermon of war.—A speech delivered at the anti-war meeting in Faneuil hall feb. 4, 1847.—A sermon of the mexican war.—A sermon of the perishing classes in Boston.—A sermon of merchants.—A sermon of the dangerous classes in society.—A sermon of poverty.—A sermon of the moral condition of Boston. **2.** A sermon of the spiritual condition of Boston.—Some thoughts on the most christian use of the sunday.—A sermon of immortal life.—The public education of the people.—The political destination of America and the signs of the times.—A discourse occasioned by the death of J: Quincy Adams.—A speech at a meeting of the American anti-slavery society, to celebrate the abolition of slavery by the french republic.—A speech at Faneuil hall before the New England anti-slavery convention, 1848.—Some thoughts on the free-soil party and the election of general Taylor. **3.** A speech at a meeting of the citizens of Boston in Faneuil hall, to consider the speech of mr. Webster.—A speech at the New England anti-slavery convention in Boston, 1850.—A discourse occasioned by the death of the late president Taylor.—The function and place of conscience, in relation to the laws of men.—The state of the nation.—The chief sins of the people.—The three chief safeguards of society.—The position and duties of the american scholar.

— Additional speeches, addresses and occasional sermons. Bost. 1859. 2 v. D.   **329.1 : 45**
Contents. V. 1. Speech at the ministerial conference in Boston, 1851.—The Boston kidnapping.—The aspect of freedom in America.—Discourse occasioned by the death of Daniel Webster.—The Nebraska question.—Address on the condition of America. **2.** Some thoughts on the progress of America.—The new crime against humanity.—The law of God and the statutes of men.—A sermon of the dangers which threaten the rights of man in America.—Some account of my ministry.—A sermon of the public function of woman.—A sermon of old age.

Seward, W: H: Works, ed. by G: F. Baker. New ed. N. Y. 1853 [v. 1-3]. Bost. 1884 [v. 4, 5]. 5 v. O.   **329.1+15**
Contents. V. 1. Biographical memoir.—Speeches in the senate of New York.—Speeches in the senate of the U. S.—Debates in the senate of the U. S.—Forensic arguments. **2.** Notes on New York.—State papers.—Official correspondence.—Pardon papers. **3.** Orations and discourses.—Occasional speeches and addresses.—Executive speeches.—Political speeches.—General correspondence.—Letters from Europe.—Speeches in the senate of the U. S. **4.** Memoir, biographical and historical.—Orations and addresses.—Biography of De Witt Clinton.—Political speeches.—Speeches in the senate of the U. S.—App.—Index.— **5.** Diplomatic history of the war for the union.

Sherman, J: Selected speeches and reports on finance and taxation, from 1859 to 1878. N. Y. 1879. O.   **329.1+34**

Smith, Gerrit. Speeches in congress. N. Y. 1855. D.   **329.1 : 35**
Contents. To the voters of the counties of Oswego and Madison.—On the reference of the president's message.—Answer to the question of mr. Wright of Pennsylvania.—On the resolution of thanks to capt. Ingraham.—Resolutions on the public lands.—On war.—On the distribution of seeds by the government.—On the homestead bill.—Letter explaining *same.*—On the bill to aid the territory of Minnesota in constructing a railroad for military, postal and for other purposes.—On the second deficiency bill.—Temperance.—On the Nebraska bill.—On the Meade claims.—Against limiting grants of land to white persons.—On polygamy.—On the Pacific railroad.—On the abolition of the postal system.—On supplying the city of Washington with water.—On the Mexican treaty and "Monroe doctrine."—Letter announcing his purpose to resign his seat in congress.—Second speech on the R: W. Meade.—For the Oswego harbor.

—Letter to senator Hamlin on the reciprocity treaty.
—On postage bill.—In favor of prohibiting all traffic
in intoxicating drinks in Washington.—Against providing intoxicating drinks for the navy.—In favor of
indemnifying mr. Riddle and mr. Peabody.—In favor
of custom-houses at Buffalo and Oswego. — Final
letter to his constituents.—Letter to F: Douglass.—
Letter to hon. H. C. Goodwin.

Sumner, C: Works. Bost. 1875—1883. 15 v. D.
          329.1 : 16

Contents. V. 1-12. *See* Catalogue of the Brooklyn
library, p. 1024-1026. **13.** Cheap ocean postage.—The
late hon. Thaddeus Stevens, remarks on his death.—
Claims of citizens in the rebel states.—Tribute to
hon. James Hinds.—Powers of congress to prohibit
inequality, caste, and oligarchy of the skin.—Claims
on England, individual and national. — Locality in
appointment to office.—National affairs at home and
abroad.— The question of caste.— Currency.— Colored physicians.—The late hon. W: Pitt Fessenden,
remarks on his death.—Cuban belligerency.—Admission of Virginia to representation in congress.—
Financial reconstruction and specie payments.—Major-general Nathaniel Greene.— Personal record on
reconstruction with colored suffrage.—Admission of
Mississippi to representation in congress.—The first
colored senator.—Consideration of treaties in open
senate.—Eligibility to the senate: question of inhab-
itancy.—Ratification of the fifteenth amendment.—
Admission of Georgia to representation in congress.
—Income tax.—More work to be done.—Education.—
No exclusion of retired army officers from civil office.
—Arctic expeditions.—One cent postage, with abolition of franking.—Chinese indemnity fund.—Tax on
books. — Naturalization laws; no discrimination on
account of color. **14.** The republican party; its
past and future work.—The duel between France and
Germany, with its lesson to civilization.—The patriot
dead at Arlington.—Naboth's vineyard.—New year's
day.—Italian unity.— Response to a toast.—Duty of
the young colored lawyer.— Charity to France or
Germany?—Colored schools in Washington. — Hon.
J: Corode, speech on his death.—Italian unity again.
—Violations of international law, and usurpations of
war powers.—Personal relations with the president
and secretary of state.—The Ku-klux-klan.—Our duty
against wrong.—Power of the senate to imprison
recusant witnesses. — The haytian medal.— Equality
of rights in public schools.—Peace and the republic
for France.—The great fire at Chicago, and our duty.
—Rights and duties of our colored fellow-citizens.—
One term for presidents.—The best portraits in engraving.—Equality before the law protected by national statute. **15.** The house of representatives,
its proper number.— Reform and purity in government. — Parliamentary law on the appointment of
special committees of the senate.—Books on the free
list. — The Nasby letters.— Advice to the colored
people.—Diplomatic agents of the U. S. not to accept
gifts from foreign powers.— Preservation of the park
at Washington.— Hours of labor.—Arbitration as a
substitute for war.—Republicanism vs. Grantism.—
Interest and duty of colored citizens in the present-
ial election.—Letter to speaker Blaine.—Retrospect
and promise.— F: Douglass and president Grant.—
Greeley or Grant?—No names of battles with fellow-
citizens on the army register, or the regimental colors of the U. S.—Tribute to Horace Greeley.—Relief
of Boston.—The late hon. Garrett Davis, remarks on
his death.—Equality in civil rights.—Equal rights of
colored fellow-citizens in normal schools.—The president of Hayti and mr. Sumner.—International arbitration.—A common-school system irrespective of
color.—Boston, its proper boundaries.—Yellow fever
at Memphis and Shreveport.—The case of the Virginius.—The supplementary civil-rights bill again.—
Our pilgrim forefathers.—Supplementary civil-rights
bill; the last appeal.

— Orations and speeches. Bost. 1850. 2 v. D.
          329.1 : 36

Contents. V. 1. The true grandeur of nations.—
The scholar, the jurist, the artist, the philanthropist.
—White slavery in the Barbary states.—Fame and
glory.—The law of human progress. **2.** The war
system of the commonwealth of nations.— Speech
against the admission of Texas as a slave state.—
Speech on the anti-slavery duties of the whig party.
—Letter to hon. Robert C. Winthrop on the declaration of war against Mexico.—Speech against the
mexican war.—Argument before the supreme court
of Mass. against the validity of enlistments in the

Mass. regiment of volunteers for the mexican war.
—Speech calling for the withdrawal of the american
troops from Mexico. — Speech before the Boston
prison discipline society.—Speech for political action
against the slave power and extension of slavery.—
Speech for union among men of all parties against
the slave power and the extension of slavery.—Speech
for the Buffalo platform and candidates.—Letter on
parties and the importance of a free-soil organization.—Remarks on calling the free-soil state convention of Mass. to order, 1849.—Address to the people of
Mass. explaining and vindicating the free-soil movement. — Argument against the constitutionality of
separate colored schools.—Report on the law school
of Harvard university.—Speech on our present anti-
slavery duties.—Three tributes of friendship: Joseph
Story; J: Pickering; H: Wheaton.

Train, G: Francis. Union speeches del. in England during the [civil] war. Phila. 1862.
O.   **329.1 : 37**

Ward, Elijah. Speeches on commercial, financial and other subjects. N. Y. 1877. O.
          329.1+38

Contents. A ship-canal connecting the Atlantic and
Pacific oceans.—A just bankrupt law.—Our commercial relations with the british north american provinces.—The tariff and the true principles of taxation.
—The treaty with the Hawaiian islands.—Our commercial relations with Canada.—The financial condition
of the nation.—The financial problem.—The distribution of the Geneva award.—Nationality of the democratic party.—The true policy of the government as
to the conduct of the war.—The best policy toward
the southern states.—The shipping act relating to
merchant seamen.—A coinage dept. at the assay
office in New York.—The questions of the times.—
A free canal policy.

Washington, G: Writings; his correspondence,
addresses, messages, and other papers,
official and private, selected and publ.
from the original mss., with a life of the
author, by Jared **Sparks.** N. Y. 1848-1852.
12 v. O.   **329.1 : 17**

Contents. V. 1. Life, by J. Sparks. **2.** *Pt. 1:* Official letters relating to the french war and private
letters before the american revol., march 1754 to may
1775. **3.** *Pt. 2:* Correspondence and miscellaneous
papers relating to the american revol., june 1775 to
july 1776. **4.** July 1776 to july 1777. **5.** July 1777 to
july 1778. **6.** July 1778 to march 1780. **7.** March
1780 to april 1781. **8.** April 1781 to dec. 1783. **9.** *Pt.
3:* Private letters from the time Washington resign-
ed his commission as commander-in-chief of the
army to that of his inauguration as president of the
U. S., dec. 1783 to april 1789. **10.** *Pt. 4:* Letters,
official and private, from the beginning of his presidency to the end of his life, may 1789 to nov. 1794.
11. Nov. 1794 to dec. 1799. **12.** *Pt. 5:* Speeches
and messages to congress, proclamations and addresses.—App.—Indexes.

Webster, Daniel. Works. 7th ed. Bost. 1853. 6
v. O.   **329.1+18**

Contents. V. 1. Biographical memoir, by E: Everett. — Speeches on various public occasions. **2.**
Speeches on various public occasions. **3, 4.** Speeches
in the convention to amend the constitution of
Mass.—Speeches in congress. **5.** Speeches in congress.—Legal arguments and speeches to the jury.
6. Legal arguments and speeches to the jury.—Diplomatic and official papers.—Miscellaneous letters.

— Diplomatic and official papers, while secretary
of state. N. Y. 1848. O.   **329.1+39**

Woodbury, Levi. Writings, political, judicial
and literary; now first sel. and arr. Bost.
1852. 3 v. O.   **329.1+19**

Contents. V. 1. Biograph. notice.—Speeches.—Reports. — Gubernatorial message, speeches, and
reports on state topics.—Occasional letters and
speeches on important topics.—App. 2. Judicial.
3. Literary.

Great Britain.

Adams, C: Kendall. *ed.* Representative british
orations, with introd. and explanatory
notes. N. Y. 1884. 3 v. S.   **329.2 : 21**

Speeches of eminent British statesmen during the thirty-nine years' peace. Lond. 1855, 1857. 2 v. S.   **329**.2:20

Contents. V. **1.** *From the closing of the war to the passing of the reform bill.* **Jenkinson,** C. C. C., *earl of Liverpool.* On moving an address to the prince regent on the treaties of 1815.—**Lambton,** J: G., *earl of Durham.* Against the alien bill of 1818.—**Romilly,** *Sir* S: In support of a petition againt a clause introduced by the lords into the alien act of 1818.—**Mackintosh,** *Sir* J. On moving for a committe to inquire into the state of the criminal law.—**Stewart,** R., *viscount Castlereagh.* On introducing the celebrated six acts against seditious meetings.—**Russell,** J: *lord.* On proposing the consideration of the state of the representation of the people in parliament.—**Huskisson,** W: On the motion of mr. Ellice for a select committee on the silk trade.—**Canning,** G: On moving the consideration of the king's message on the relations subsisting between Great Britain and Portugal.—**Wellesley,** A., *duke of Wellington.* On moving the second reading of a bill for the relief of the roman catholics.—**Grey,** C., *2d earl.* On moving the second reading of the reform bill for England and Wales. **2.** *From the passing of the reform bill to the commencement of the russian war.* **Macaulay,** T: B. *baron.* On the repeal of the union with Ireland.— **Stanley,** E: G., *14th earl of Derby.* On the emancipation of the slaves.—**Brougham,** H; *baron.* Immediate emancipation of the negro apprentices.—**Spencer,** J: C: *3d earl.* On the renewal of the bank charter.—**O'Connell,** D. On justice to Ireland.— **Sheil,** R: L. On irish municipal reform.—**Villiers,** C: P. On the corn laws.—**Lamb,** W: *viscount Melbourne.* On the penny postage bill.—**Robinson,** F: J: *1st earl of Ripon.* On the penny postage bill.— **Peel,** *Sir* R. On the repeal of the corn laws.— **Temple,** H: J: *3d viscount Palmerston.* On the affairs of Greece.—**Copley,** J: S., *baron Lyndhurst.* On the war with Russia.

Celebrated speeches of Chatham, Burke and Erskine; added, the argument of mr. Mackintosh in the case of Peltier; sel. by a member of the Phila. bar. Phila. 1860. O.   **329**.2:6

Burlingame, E: Livingstone, *ed.* Current discussion; a collection from the chief english essays on questions of the time. Vol. 1: International politics. N. Y. 1878. D.
     329.2:4

Contents. **Forbes,** A. The russians, the turks and the bulgarians.—**Canning,** *Sir* S., *viscount Stratford de Redcliffe.* Turkey.—**Gladstone,** W: E. Montenegro.—**Smith,** G. The political destiny of Canada.— **Blackie,** J: S. Prussia in the 19th century.—**Dicey,** E: The future of Egypt.—**Smith,** G. The slaveowner and the turk.—**Owen,** S. J. The stability of the british empire in India.—**Freeman,** E: A: The relation of the english people to the russo-turkish war.

Irish eloquence; the speeches of the celebrated Irish orators Philips, Curran and Grattan; added, appeal of Robert Emmet at the close of his trial for high treason; sel. by a member of the bar. Bost. 1857. O.
     329.2:17

*   *   *

Brougham, H: *lord.* Speeches on social and political subjects, with historical introd. Lond. 1857. 2 v. D.   **329**.2:1

Contents. V. **1.** Military flogging.—Queen Caroline.—Libel on the Durham clergy.—Army estimates.—Holy alliance.—Education.—Law in Ireland.—Imprisonment for debt.—Bed chamber question.—Wellington speeches. **2.** Commerce and manufactures.—Liverpool election.—Liverpool mechanics institute.—The slave trade.—Case of rev. J: Smith.—Negro slavery.—The slave trade.—Emancipation of negro apprentices.—Eastern slave trade.— Present state of the law.—Local courts. — Parliamentary reform.—Poor laws.

Burke, Edmund. Works. Rev. ed. Bost. 1865–67. 12 v. D.   **329**.2:2

Contents. V. **1.** Advertisement to the reader prefixed to the first octavo edition.—Advertisement to the second octavo ed.— A vindication of natural society.—A philosophical inquiry into the origin of our ideas of the sublime and beautiful, with an introductory discourse concerning taste.—A short account of a late short administration.—Observations on a late publication intituled The present state of the nation.—Thoughts on the cause of the present discontents. **2.** Speech on american taxation.— Speeches on arrival at Bristol and at the conclusion of the poll.—Speech on moving resolutions for conciliation with America.—Letter to the sheriffs of Bristol on the affairs of America.—Letters to two gentlemen of Bristol on the bills depending in parliament relative to the trade of Ireland.—Speech on presenting to the house of commons a plan for the better security of the independence of parliament, and the economical reformation of the civil and other establishments.—Speech at Bristol previous to the election.—Speech at Bristol on declining the poll.—Speech on mr. Fox's East India bill.—A representation to his majesty. **3.** Speech on the nabob of Arcott's debts.—Substance of speech on the army estimates.—Reflections on the revolution in France. **4.** Letter to a member of the national assembly, in answer to some objections to his book on french affairs.—Appeal from the new to the old whigs.— Letter to a peer of Ireland on the penal laws against irish catholics.—Letter to sir Hercules Langrishe on the subject of the roman catholics of Ireland.— Hints for a memorial to be delivered to monsieur de M. M.—Thoughts on french affairs.—Heads for consideration on the present state of affairs.—Remarks on the policy of the allies with respect to France; with an appendix. **5.** Observations on the conduct of the minority.—Preface to the address of M. Brissot to his constituents; with an appendix.—Letter to W: Elliot, occasioned by a speech made in the house of lords, etc.—Thoughts and details on scarcity.—Letter to a noble lord on the attacks made upon him and his pension.—Three letters to a member of parliament on the proposals for peace with the regicide directory of France. **6.** Fourth letter on the proposals for peace with the regicide directory of France, with preliminary correspondence.—Letter to the empress of Russia.—Letter to sir C: Bingham on the irish absentee tax.—Letter to the hon. C: James Fox, on the american war.—Letter, addresses to the king, and the british colonists in N. am. in relation to the measures of government in the am. contest, and a proposed secession of the opposition from parliament.—Letter in relation to a bill for the relief of the roman catholics of Ireland.—Two letters in vindication of his parliamentary conduct relative to the affairs of Ireland, 1780.—Letters and reflections on the executions of the rioters in 1780.— Letter to H: Dundas; with a sketch of a negro code, 1792. — Letter on the subject of parliamentary reform.—Fragments of a tract relative to the laws against popery in Ireland.—Letter on the subject of catholic emancipation.—Letters to sir H. Langrishe on the catholic question.—Letter to R: Burke on the protestant ascendancy in Ireland.—Letter on the affairs of Ireland, 1797. **7.** Fragments and notes of speeches in parliament: On acts of uniformity; On the bill for the relief of protestant dissenters; Bill to repeal and alter certain acts respecting religious opinions on petition of the unitarians; Speech relative to the Middlesex election; On a bill for shortening the duration of parliament; On the state of the representation of the commons in parliament; On powers of juries in prosecutions for libels, with letter on the same; On a bill for the repeal of the marriage act; On the dormant claims of the church; Hints for an essay on the drama.—An essay towards the abridgment of English history. **8.** Ninth and eleventh reports of the select committee of the house of commons on the affairs of India: Articles of charge of high crimes and misdemeanors against Warren Hastings; articles 1-6. **9.** *Same;* articles 7-22.—Speeches in the impeachment of Warren Hastings: speech in opening the impeachment, first and second days. **10.** *Same;* third and fourth days.— Speech on sixth article of charge. **11.** Report from committee appointed to inspect the lords' journals in relation to their proceedings on trial of Warren Hastings, also vindication of same.—Speeches in impeachment of Warren Hastings, *continued.*—Speech in general reply, first to fourth day. **12.** *Same;* fifth through ninth day.—General table of contents.— Index.

Burke, Edmund.—*Continued.*
— Works, with a memoir, in 3 v. V. 2, 3. N. Y. 1837, 1846. O.   **329.2 : 3**
    Contents. Same as above beginning with Appeal from the new to the old whigs, *in* v. 3.

Canning, G: Select speeches, with a prelim. biographical sketch and an app. of extracts from his writings and speeches, ed. by Robert Walsh. Phila. 1853. O.
                                        329.2+5
    Contents. The sardinian treaty.—On mr. Tierney's motion respecting peace with France.—The expedition to Copenhagen.—Conduct of the duke of York.— Expedition to the Scheldt.—Vote of credit bill.—On the report of the bullion committee.—The war with America.— Embassy to Lisbon.— Vote of thanks to the marquis of Hastings.— The state of the nation, 1819.—Roman catholic disability removal bill.—Parliamentary reform.—Negotiations relative to Spain.— The abolition of slavery.—Amelioration of the condition of the slave population.—State of slavery.— The king's message, 1826. — Election and dinner speeches.

Cobbett, W: Letters to the right hon. lord Hawkesbury, and to the right hon. Henry Addington, on the peace with Buonaparté, to which is added an app., containing a collection, now greatly enl., of all the conventions, treaties, speeches and other documents, connected with the subject. 2d ed. Lond. 1802. O.   **329.2+7**
— Manchester lectures, in support of his fourteen reform propositions ; del. in the Minor theatre in that town, on the last six days of 1831. Subjoined, a letter to mr. O'Connell, on his speech, made in Dublin on the 4th of jan. 1832, against the proposition for the establishing of poor-laws in Ireland. Lond. 1832. D.   **329.2 : 8**

Gladstone, W: Ewart. Gleanings of past years ; 1843—1879. N. Y. [1878—1879]. 7 v. S.
                                        329.2 : 9
    Contents. V. 1. *The throne and the prince consort.* The cabinet and the constitution. Death of the prince consort.—Life of the prince consort.—The county franchise, and mr. Lowe thereon.—Last words on the county franchise.—Postscriptum on the county franchise.—Kin beyond sea. 2. *Personal and literary.* —Blanco White.— Giacomo Leopardi.—Tennyson.— Wedgwood.— Bishop Patteson.—Macaulay.—Memoir of Norman Macleod. 3. *Historical and speculative.* The theses of Erastus and the scottish church establishment.—On "Ecce homo".—Courses of religious thought.—The influence of authority in matters of opinion. — Rejoinder on authority in matters of opinion.—16th century arraigned before the 19th. 4. *Foreign.* Letters to the earl of Aberdeen, on the state prosecutions of the neapolitan government.— An examination of the official reply of the neapolitan government.—Farini on the states of the church.— Germany, France and England, 1870.—The hellenic factor in the eastern problem.— Montenegro.— Aggression on Egypt and freedom in the east. 5. *Ec-*

Gladstone, W: Ewart.—*Continued.*
    clesiastical. Present aspect of the church, 1843. — Ward's ideal of a christian church, 1844.—Remarks on the royal supremacy, 1850. 6. *Ecclesiastical.* On the functions of laymen in the church. — The bill for divorce, 1857.—The church of England and ritualism, 1874–5. — Italy and her church. 7. *Miscellaneous.* Inaugural address on the work of universities, 1860.— Place of ancient Greece in the providential order.— A chapter of autobiography, 1868.—The law of probable evidence and its application to conduct.—The evangelical movement, its parentage, progress and issue.

— Bulgarian horrors and Russia in Turkistan, with other tracts. Leipz. 1876. S.
                                        329.2 : 10
    Contents. Bulgarian horrors and the question of the east.—Russian policy and deeds in Turkistan.— Speech at Blackheath, sept. 9th 1876. — Life and speeches of the prince consort: court of queen Victoria.—Italy and her church.

— The hellenic factor in the eastern problem, with other tracts. Leipz. 1877. ·S.
                                        329.2 : 11
    Contents. The hellenic factor in the eastern problem.—The life of lord Macaulay.—Life of the prince consort.—Two letters to the earl of Aberdeen on the state prosecutions of the neapolitan government.— An examination of the official reply of the neapolitan government.

— Rome and the newest fashions in religion ; three tracts: The Vatican decrees ; Vaticanism ; Speeches of the pope. Leipz. 1875. S.
                                        329.2 : 12
— The Vatican decrees in their bearing on civil allegiance ; a political expostulation. Added, A history of the Vatican council, together with the latin and english text of the papal syllabus, and the Vatican decrees, by Philip Schaff. N. Y. 1875. O.
                                        329.2 : 13

Horseley, S: Speeches in parliament. Dundee. 1813. O.   **329.2 : 14**
Macaulay, T: Babington, *baron Macaulay.* Speeches. N. Y. 1853. 2 v. D. **329.2 : 15**
O'Connell, Daniel. Select speeches, ed., with historical notices, by his son, J: O'Connell. 2d ser. Dublin. 1865. D.   **329.2 : 16**
Russell, J:, *1st earl Russell.* Recollections and suggestions, 1813—1873. Bost. 1873. O.
                                        329.2 : 18
Sheil, R: Lalor. Speeches, with memoir by T. MacNevin. *T. p. w.* [Dublin. 1862]. D.
                                        329.2 : 19
Spencer, Herbert. Political essays.
                        in **824.2 : 81-83**
    Contents, see under English literature, Essays.
Temple, *Sir* W: [Political writings]. *In his* Works.   **820.2 : 23 v1,2**
    Contents, see under English literature, Collected works.

4. Political economy.

1. In general.

About, Edmond François Valentin. Handbook of social economy, or The worker's A. B. C. Tr. from the last french ed. N. Y. 1873. D.
                                        330 : 46
Adler, A. Leitfaden der volkswirthschaftslehre zum gebrauche an höheren fach-lehranstalten und zum selbstunterricht. Leipz. 1880. O.   **330 : 40**

Bastiat, F: Essays on political economy. 4th people's ed. Lond. [1875]. S.   **330 : 8**
    Contents. Capital and interest.— That which is seen, and that which is not seen.— Government.— What is money ?—The law.

Blanqui, Jérôme Adolphe. History of political economy in Europe. Tr. from the 4th french ed. by Emily J. Leonard ; with a pref. by D: A. Wells. N. Y. 1880. O.
                                        330+9

Bowen, Francis. American political economy; incl. strictures on the management of the currency and the finances since 1861, with a chart showing the fluctuations in the price of gold. N. Y. [1870]. O.   330 : 10

Cairnes, J: Elliot. The character and logical method of political economy. N. Y. 1875. D.   330 : 11

Carey, H: C: The past, the present, and the future. Phila. 1848. O.   330 : 12

— Miscellaneous works. Phila. 1865. O.   330 : 23

Contents. The harmony of interests, agricultural, manufacturing and commercial.— Money.— Letters to the president on the foreign and domestic policy of the union, and its effects, as exhibited in the condition of the people and the state.—Financial crises; their causes and effects.—The french and american tariffs compared in a series of letters addressed to M. Michel Chevalier.—The way to outdo England without fighting her; letters to the hon. Schuyler Colfax, on the paper, the iron, the farmer's, the railroad, and the currency questions.—The resources of the union. —The public debt, local and national; how to provide for its discharge while lessening the burthen of taxation.—Contraction or expansion? repudiation or resumption?—National bank amendment bill.—British free trade, how it affects the agriculture and the foreign commerce of the union.— Protection of home labor and home productions necessary to the prosperity of the american farmer.

Cohn, Gustav. Ueber die vertheuerung des lebensunterhaltes in der gegenwart. *In* Deutsche zeit- und streit-fragen.
   304 : 15 v5

Conrad, Johannes. Ueber das steigen der lebensansprüche; vortrag gehalten am 24 feb. 1877 zum besten des Frauenvereins zu Halle a. Saale. *In* Deutsche zeit- und streit-fragen.   304 : 15 v6

Contzen, H: National-ökonomie; ein hand-und lehrbuch für alle stände. Leipz. 1878. O.   330 : 41

Cossa, L: Guide to the study of political economy. Tr. from the 2d italian ed., with a pref. by W: Stanley Jevons. Lond. 1880. D.   330 : 13

De Quincey, T: The logic of political economy, and other papers. Bost. 1859. D.   330 : 14

Contents. The logic of political economy.—Life of Milton.— The suliotes.— The fatal marksman.—The incognito, or Count Fitz-hum.—The dice.—The king of Hayti.

Dickinson, Anna Elizabeth. A paying investment. Bost. 1876. D.   330 : 31

Dühring, Eugen K: Kritische geschichte der nationalökonomie und des socialismus. Berlin. 1871. O.   330 : 42

Ely, R: T. The past and present of political economy. (Johns Hopkins university studies). Balt. 1884. O.   *in* 904+32 v2

Fawcett, H: Manual of political economy. 5th ed., rev. and enl. Lond. 1876. D.   330 : 5

Fawcett, Millicent Garrett. Political economy for beginners. 5th ed., rev. and enl. Lond. 1880. D.   x 330 : 25

— Tales in political economy. Lond. 1874. D.   x 330 : 26

Contents. The Srimats.—The shipwrecked sailors.— Isle Pleasant.—The islanders' experience of foreign trade.

George, H: Social problems. N. Y. 1883. D.   330 : 35

Guyot, Yves. Principles of social economy. Tr. from the french by C. H. d'Eyncourt Lippington. Lond. 1884. O.   330 : 50

Hanson, W: The fallacies in "Progress and poverty," in H: Dunning Macleod's "Economics," and in "Social problems;" with The ethics of protection and free trade, and the industrial problem considered à priori. N. Y. 1884. D.   330 : 49

Heitz, E. Ursachen und tragweite der nord-amerikanischen konkurrenz mit der west-europäischen landwirthschaft. *In* Deutsche zeit- und streit-fragen.   304 : 15 v10

Jevons, W: Stanley. Political economy. (Science primers). N. Y. 1878. S.   330 : 15

Károly, Akin. The dilemmas of labour and education. Lond. 1884. D.   330 : 51

Contents. Introd.—The dilemmas of labour.—Critical examination of "Progress and poverty."—Brief philosophy of rent.— The dilemma of education.— The literary artizan.

Laspeyres, Etienne. Die kathedersocialisten und die statistischen congresse; gedanken zur begründung einer nationalökonomischen statistik und einer statistischen nationalökonomie. *In* Deutsche zeit- und streit-fragen.   304 : 15 v4

Laveleye, Émile de. The elements of political economy. Tr. by Alfred W. Pollard; with an introd. and supplementary chapter by F. W. Taussig. N. Y. 1884. D.   330 : 36

Macleod, H: Dunning. The elements of economies; in 2 v. V. 1. Lond. 1881. D. 330 : 6

Mallock, W: Hurrell. Property and progress, or A brief inquiry into contemporary social agitation in England. N. Y. 1884. D.
   330 : 43

Contents. "Progress and poverty".—Socialism in England.—The statistics of agitation.

Mason, Alfred B., *and* J: Joseph Lalor. The primer of political economy, in 16 definitions and 40 propositions. Chicago. 1882. S.   x 330 : 24

Mill, J: Stuart. Principles of political economy, with some of their applications to social philosophy. People's ed. Lond. 1873. D.   330 : 7

— Principles of political economy, abridged; with critical, bibliographical and explanatory notes, and a sketch of the history of political economy by J. Laurence Laughlin; a text-book for colleges. Maps and diagrams. N. Y. 1884. O.   330 : 48

Mongredien, A: Wealth-creation; with introd. by Simon Sterne. N. Y. [1883]. D.
   330 : 30

Neumann-Spallart, Franz Xaver *ritter* v. Die theuerung der lebensmittel. *In* Deutsche zeit- und streit-fragen.   304 : 15 v3

Owen, Robert. The book of the new moral world; containing the rational system of society, founded on demonstrated facts, developing the constitution and laws of human nature and society. Lond. 1836. O.   330 : 16

Perry, Arthur Latham. Elements of political economy. N. Y. 1866. O.   330 : 17

— Introduction to political economy. N. Y. 1880. D.   330 : 27

Platter, Julius. Die pflichten des besitzes; rede geh. im rathhaus-saale zu Zürich am 18. jan. 1882. *In* Deutsche zeit- und streit-fragen.   304 : 15 v11

Potter, Alonzo. Political economy ; its objects, uses and principles, considered with reference to the condition of the american people. With a summary for the use of students. [Harper's family library]. N. Y. 1844. S.   **330 : 18**

Ricardo, D: Works ; with a notice of the life and writings of the author by J. R. McCulloch. Lond. 1852. O.   **330 : 33**

Contents. Life.— Principles of political economy and taxation.—High price of bullion a proof of the depreciation of bank notes.—Reply to mr. Bosanquet's practical observations on the report of the bullion committee.—Essay on the influence of a low price of corn on the profits of stock.—Proposals for an economical and secure currency, with observations on the profits of the bank of England.—On protection to agriculture.—Plan for the establishment of a national bank.—Essay on the funding system.—Observations on parliamentary reform.—Speech on voting by ballot.—Index.

Roscher, W: G! F: Principles of political economy. From the 13th, 1877, german ed.; with additional chapters furnished by the author for this 1st eng. and amer. ed. on paper money, international trade, and the protective system, and a prelim. essay on the historical method in political economy, from the french, by L. **Wolowski.** The whole tr. by J: J. Lalor. Chicago. 1878. 2 v. O.   **330+2**

Rousseau, J: Jacques. A dissertation on political economy. 1st amer. ed. Albany. 1797. D.   **330 : 19**

Ruskin, J: Unto this last ; four essays on the first principles of political economy. N. Y. 1866. D.   **330 : 20**

Contents. The roots of honor. — The veins of wealth.—Qui judicatis terram.—Ad valorem.

— Munera pulveris ; six essays on the elements of political economy. N. Y. 1882. D.   **330 : 47**

Say, J: Baptiste. A treatise on political economy, or The production, distribution and consumption of wealth. Tr. from the 4th ed. of the french by C. R. Prinsep, with notes ; new amer. ed. containing a tr. of the introd. and add. notes by Clement C. Biddle. Phila. 1863. O.   **330 : 3**

Schönhof, Jacob. Ueber die volkswirthschaftlichen fragen in den Vereinigten Staaten ; ein vortrag gehalten vor dem gesellig-wissenschaftlichen verein in New York. *In* Deutsche zeit- und streit-fragen.   **304 : 15 v9**

Smith, Adam. An inquiry into the nature and causes of the wealth of nations ; ed. by James E. Thorold Rogers. Oxford. 1869. 2 v. O.   **330 : 1**

Society for political education. Economic tracts ; no. 1-12, 15. N. Y. 1881—1884. 3 v. D.   **330 : 21**

Contents. V. 1. No. 1. **Atkinson,** E: What is a bank ? what service does a bank perform ? 2. Political economy and political science (bibliography), comp. by W. G. Sumner; D: A. Wells, W: E. Foster, R: L. Dugdale, and G. H. Putnam. 3. Subjects and questions pertaining to political economy, constitutional law, the theory and administration of government, and current politics. 4. Usury laws, their nature, expediency, and influence; opinions of Jeremy Bentham and John Calvin, with review of the existing situation and recent experience of the U. S., by R: H. Dana, jr., D: A. Wells, and others. 2. No. 5. **Courtois,** A. Political economy in one lesson; a lecture before the Polytechnic assoc. of Paris; tr. from the Journal des économistes, by W. C. Ford. 6. **White,** H. Money and its substitutes: an essay prepared for v. 2 of the Cyclopædia of political science by J: J. Lalor. 7. **White,** A. D. Paper-money inflation in France; how it came, what it brought, and how it ended. 8. **Whitridge,** F: W. Caucus system; an essay prepared for v. 1 of the Cyclopædia of political science, etc. 9. **Canfield,** J. H. Taxation; a plain talk for plain people. 10. **Bowker,** R: R. Work and wealth; a summary of economics. 11. **Green,** G: W. Repudiation. 12. **Shepard,** E: M. The work of a social teacher; a memorial of R: L. Dugdale. 15. **Richardson,** H. W. The standard dollar.

Soetbeer, G: Adolph. Die fünf milliarden ; betrachtungen über die folgen der grossen kriegsentschädigung für die wirthschaftsverhältnisse Frankreichs und Deutschlands. *In* Deutsche zeit- und streit-fragen.   **304 : 15 v3**

Stewart, Dugald. Lectures on' political economy, now first pub.; ed. by sir W: Hamilton. Edinb. 1877. 2 v. O.   **191+8 v8, 9**

Contents. V. 1. Introd: On the objects and province of political economy.—Pt. 1. Of political economy proper; Of population; Of national wealth. 2. *Same continued:* Of the poor, their maintenance; Of the education of the lower orders.—Pt. 2. Of politics proper, or Theory of government.

Sturtevant, Julian M. Economics, or The science of wealth. N. Y. 1878. D.   **330 : 22**

Sumner, W: Graham. Problems in political economy. N. Y. 1884. S.   **330 : 44**

— What social classes owe to each other. N. Y. 1883. S.   **330 : 32**

Thompson, Robert Ellis. Elements of political economy, with special reference to the industrial history of nations. Phila. 1882. D.   **330 : 28**

Walker, Amasa. The science of wealth ; a manual of political economy embracing the laws of trade, currency and finance. 7th ed. rev. Bost. 1874. O.   **330 : 4**

Walker, Francis Amasa. Political economy. (Amer. scientific ser.) N. Y. 1883. D.   **330 : 29**

Wilson, W. D. First principles of political economy with reference to statesmanship and the progress of civilization. Phila. 1879. D.   **330 : 45**

England.

Ochenkowski, W. v. Englands wirthschaftliche entwickelung im ausgange des mittelalters. Jena. 1879. O.   **330 : 39**

Rogers, James E. Thorold. A history of agriculture and prices in England from 1259 to 1793, compiled entirely from original and contemporary records. Oxford, 1866—1882. 4 v. O.   **330 : 34**

Contents. V. 1, 2. 1259-1400. **3, 4.** 1401-1582.

Tooke, T: A history of prices and of the state of the circulation from 1793 to [1856] ; preceded by a brief sketch of the state of the corn trade in the last two centuries. Lond. 1838-1857. 6 v. in 4. O.   **330 : R37**

Contents. V. 1. Introd.—To 1813. **2.** To 1838. **3.** 1838, 1839. **4.** 1839-1847.—With a general view of the currency question and remarks on the operation of the act, 7 and 8 Vict. C. 32. **5, 6. Tooke,** T: *and* W: **Newmarch.** 1848-1856.—Index to the 6 vols., in v. 6.

2. Capital and labor.

Barnard, C: Co-operation as a business. N. Y. 1881. S.   **331 : 3**

Blaikie, W: Garden. Heads and hands in the world of labour. Lond. 1865. D.   **331 : 7**

Brassey, *Sir* T: On work and wages. (Lib. of popular information.) N. Y. 1883. S.
331 : 23

Brentano, L: Joseph, *called* Lujo. Der arbeiterversicherungszwang, seine voraussetzungen und seine folgen. *In* Deutsche zeit- und streit-fragen.
304 : 15 v10

Bücher, K: Die arbeiterfrage im kaufmannsstande. *In* Deutsche zeit- und streit-fragen.
304 : 15v12

Cook, Joseph. Labor, with preludes on current events. (Boston Monday lectures.) Bost. 1880. D.
331 : 8

Crump, Arthur. An exposure of the pretensions of mr. H: George, as set forth in his book "Progress and poverty." 2d ed. Lond. 1884. O.
331+31

George, H: Progress and poverty; an inquiry into the cause of industrial depressions and of increase of want with increase of wealth ; the remedy. N. Y. 1880. D.
331 : 4

— *Same.* N. Y. 1881. D.
331 : 4

Gladden, Washington. Working people and their employers. Bost. 1876. D.
331 : 10

Granier de Cassagnac, Adolphe Bernard. History of the working and burgher classes. Tr. by B: E. Green. Phila. 1871. O.
331 : 11

Hawley, F: B. Capital and population; a study of the economic effects of their relations to each other. N. Y. 1882. D.
331 : 19

Hirschberg, Ernst. Die selbsthilfe des arbeiterstandes, als grundlage seiner versicherung. *In* Deutsche zeit- und streit-fragen.
304 : 15 v12

Jervis, J: Bloomfield. The question of labor and capital. N. Y. 1877. D.
331 : 6

Kellogg, E: A new monetary system ; the only means of securing the respective rights of labor and property, and of protecting the public from financial revulsions. Rev. from his work on "Labor and other capital," with numerous additions, ed. by Mary Kellogg Putnam. N. Y. 1861. D.
331 : 21

— *Same.* Labor and capital ; a new monetary system *etc.* Prefixed, a biog. sketch of the author ed. by his daughter, Mary Kellogg Putnam. N. Y. 1883. S.
331 : 21

Knight, C: Knowledge is power ; a view of the productive forces of modern society and the results of labour, capital and skill. Rev. and ed., with additions, by D: A. Wells. Bost. 1856. D.
331 : 12

Landgraf, Joseph. Die sicherung des arbeitsvertrages ; eine juridisch - ökonomische studie. *In* Deutsche zeit- und streit-fragen.
304 : 15 v2

Larned, Josephus Nelson. Talks about labor, and concerning the evolution of justice between the laborers and the capitalists. N. Y. 1876. D.
331 : 13

Lieber, Francis. Essays on property and labor, as connected with natural law and the constitution of society. [Harper's family library.] N. Y. 1847. S.
331 : 1

Ruskin, J: Time and tide by Weare and Tyne ; 25 letters to a working man of Sunderland on the laws of work. N. Y. 1883. D.
331 : 28

Rylance, J. H. Lectures on social questions : competition, communism, coöperation, and the relation of christianity to socialism. N. Y. 1880. D.
331 : 14

Scudder, Moses L., *jr.* The labor-value fallacy. Chic. 1884. D.
331 : 27

Stahl, F: W: Die arbeiterfrage sonst und jetzt. *In* Deutsche zeit- und streit-fragen.
304 : 15 v1

Thompson, Joseph Parrish. The workman, his false and his true friends. N. Y. [1879]. S.
331 : 15

Waterhouse, Sylvester. The advantages of educated labor in Missouri ; a lecture del. at Washington university, april 26, 1872. St. Louis. 1872. O.
331 : Pam

Weeden, W: Babcock. The social law of labor. Bost. 1882. D.
331 : 18

Wright, Carroll D. The relation of political economy to the labor question. Bost. 1882. S.
331 : 20

* * *

Peirce, Melusina Fay. Co - operative housekeeping ; how not to do it and how to do it ; a study in sociology. Bost. 1884. T.
331 : 24

* * *

Eggleston, G: Cary. How to make a living ; suggestions upon the art of making, saving and using money. N. Y. [1875]. S.
331 : 16

How a penny became a thousand pounds, by the author of "Life doubled by the economy of time." 33d thous. Lond. [1858]. D.
331 : 17

Special countries.

Dacus, J. A. Annals of the great strikes in the U. S.; a reliable history and graphic description of the causes and thrilling events of the labor strikes and riots of 1877. Ill. Chicago. 1877. D.
331 : 9

Moody, W: Godwin. Land and labor in the U. S. N. Y. 1883. D.
331 : 22

Massachusetts *state. Bureau of statistics of labor.* 5th—10th, 12th—14th annual report, 1874—1879, 1881—1883. Bost. 1874-83. 9 v. O.
331+32

Principal contents. **1874.** Education and employment of young persons and children, with digest of laws.—Relative to professional men.—Sanitary condition of working people.—Compar. rates of wages and hours of labor in Mass. and foreign countries.—Textile fabric manufactories in Mass., and digest of laws.—Prices of provisions etc. in Mass. and Europe. — Savings banks. **1875.** Education of working children.—Special effects of certain forms of employment upon female health.—Factory legislation.—Condition of workingmen's families.—Coöperation. **1876.** Wage receivers. — Salary receivers. — App. History of the bureau, and of labor legislation in Mass. **1877.** Industrial arbitration and conciliation in England and Mass.—Coöperation in Mass.—Motive power of Mass., or The labor of the sun.—The afflicted classes: blind, deaf, dumb, idiotic and insane. — Pauperism and crime.—Means of escape in case of fire. **1878.** Compar. condition of mnfrs. and labor, 1875 and 1877.—Education and labor of the young; half-time system.—Growth of Mass. mnfrs.—Relative importance of private establishments and corporations in mnfg. industries.—Conjugal condition, nativities and ages of married women and mothers.—Nativities, ages and illiteracy of farmers, farmlaborers, skilled workmen in mnfrs. and mech. industries, and unskilled laborers. **1879.** Convict labor.—Wages and prices, 1860, 1872 and 1878.—Testimony of workingmen.—Hours of labor.—Statistics of drunkenness and liquor selling under prohibitory and license legislation, 1874 and 1877. **1881.** In-

Massachusetts *state.—Continued.*
dustrial arbitration and conciliation.—Statistics of drunkenness and liquor-selling, 1870—1879.—Uniform hours of labor.—Influence of intemperance upon crime. **1882.** The canadian french in N. E.—Citizenship.—Fall River, Lowell and Lawrence.—Wages, prices and profits. **1883.** Employers' liability for personal injuries to their employees.—Time and wages.—Profits and earnings.—Early factory labor in N. E.

— — **Pidgin,** C: F. History of the bureau of statistics of labor of Mass., and of labor legislation in that state from 1833 to 1876 ; prep. for the bureau, as a contribution to the Centennial exhibition at Phila. in 1876. Bost. 1876. O.   **331+33**

— — **Wright,** Carroll D. Industrial conciliation and arbitration ; comp. from the material in the possession of the ... bureau ... by direction of the Mass. legisl. Bost. 1881. O.   *in* **331+33**

— — **Wright,** C. D. Uniform hours of labor, from the 12th annual report. Bost. 1881. O.   *in* **331+33**

— — **Wadlin,** Horace G. Labor laws of the Commonwealth of Mass.; comp. from the public statutes. Bost. 1882. O.   *in* **331+33**

— — **Weeks,** Joseph D. Industrial conciliation and arbitration in New York, Ohio and Pennsylvania. From the 12th annual report of the Mass. bureau of statistics of labor, with comments by Carroll D. Wright, chief. Bost. 1881. O.   *with* **331+26**

Illinois *state. Bureau of labor statistics.* 1st [and 2d] biennial report, for the years ending jan. 12, 1881 [and dec. 31, 1882]. Springfield. 1881, 1883. O.   **331+34**
Principal contents. Population. — Coal production.—Manufactures.—Lead mines.—Public indebtedness.—Prison and convict labor.—Strikes in Chicago and vicinity.—Wages, rents and cost of living.—Strikes; their evils and remedies.—Labor laws of Ill.

Wisconsin *state. Bureau of labor statistics.* First biennial report, 1883—1884, [by] Frank A. Flower, commissioner. Madison. 1884. O.   **331 : 30**
Principal contents. Labor bureaus. — Public penal and reformatory institutions.—Apprentices, Industrial education, etc. — Trades and labor unions. — Strikes.—Child labor, Compulsory education, etc.—Statistics of mnfrs.—Products of the soil; Railroad employes, etc.—Wages and cost of living.—Rep. on the Pullman investigation.

Commissioners of the state bureaus of labor statistics. Report on the industrial, social and economic conditions of Pullman. Illinois. *n. p.* 1884. O.   **331 : Pam**

* * *

Acland, Arthur H. Dyke. *and* B: **Jones.** Workingmen co-operators, what they have done and what they are doing ; an account of the artisans' co-operative movement in Great Britain. with information how to promote it. Map. N. Y. 1884. S. **331 : 29**

Holyoake, G: Jacob. The history of co-operation in England. its literature and its advocates. V. 1 : The pioneer period, 1812—1844. Phila. 1875. V. 2 : The constructive period, 1845—1878. 2d ed. Lond. 1879. D.   **331 : 2**

Howell, G: The conflicts of capital and labour, historically and economically considered ; a history and review of the trade unions of Great Britain, showing their origin, progress, constitution and objects in their

political, social, economical and industrial aspects. Lond. 1878. D.   **331 : 5**

Rogers, James E. Thorold. Six centuries of work and wages; the history of english labor. N. Y. 1884 O.   **331+25**

Weeks, Joseph D. Report on the practical operation of arbitration and conciliation in the settlement of differences between employers and employees in England. Harrisburg. 1879. O.   **331+26**

3. Banks and money.

Bagehot, Walter. Some articles on the depreciation of silver and on topics connected with it. Lond. 1877. O.   **332 : 3**

Bolles, Albert S. Practical banking. N. Y. 1884. O.   **332+39**

Chevalier, Michel. On the probable fall in the value of gold ; the commercial and social consequences which may ensue, and the measures which it invites. Tr. from the french, with pref. by R: Cobden. N. Y. 1859. O.   **332+4**

Gilbart, James W: A practical treatise on banking. 3d amer. ed. Phila. 1855. O. **332 : 6**

Hamilton, Rowland. Money and value ; an inquiry into the means and ends of economic production, with an app. on the depreciation of silver and indian currency. Lond. 1878. O.   **332 : 1**

Howe, J: B. The political economy of Great Britain, the U. S. and France, in the use of money ; a new science of production and exchange. Bost. 1878. O.   **332 : 7**

— The common sense, the mathematics and the metaphysics of money. Bost. 1881. D.   **332 : 20**

— Monetary and industrial fallacies ; a dialogue. [*Anon.*] Bost. 1878. O.   **332 : 21**

— Mono-metalism and bi-metalism, or The science of monetary values. Bost. 1879. S.   **332 : 22**

Jevons, W: Stanley. Investigations in currency and finance ; ed., with introd. by H. S. Foxwell. N. Y. 1884. O.   **332 : 36**

— Money and the mechanism of exchange. (Intern. scientific ser.) N. Y. 1875. D.   **332 : 8**

Kardorff-Wabnitz, *Baron* W: v. The gold standard ; its causes, its effects and its future. From the german. Phila. 1880. O.   **332 : 9**

Knies, C: Das geld ; darlegung der grundlehren von dem gelde, mit einer vorerörterung über das kapital und die übertragung der nutzungen. (Geld und credit ; 1ste abth.) Berlin. 1873. O.   **332 : 31**

— Der credit. [Geld und credit ; 2te abth.] Berlin. 1876, 1879. 2 v. O.   **332 : 32**

— Weltgeld und weltmünzen. Berlin. 1874. O.   **332 : 33**

McAdam, Graham. An alphabet in finance ; a simple statement of permanent principles and their application to questions of the day, with an introd. by R. R. Bowker. N. Y. 1881. S.   **332 : 26**

Marx, K: Das kapital ; kritik der politischen ökonomie. 1ster bd., buch 1 : Der produktions-process des kapitals. Hamburg. 1883. O.   **332 : 34**

Mayer, C: The media of exchange and credit. Milw. 1883. O. **332 : Pam**

Moran, C: Money. N. Y. 1863. D. **332 : 12**

Newcomb, Simon. The abc of finance, or The money and labor questions familiarly explained to common people in short and easy lessons. [Half-hour series.] N. Y. [1877]. Tt. **332 : 24**

Patterson, Robert Hogarth. The new golden age and influence of the precious metals upon the world. Edinb. 1882. 2 v. O. **332 : 37**

Percy, H. C. Our cashier's scrap-book ; bank notes new and old for general circulation ; a portfolio of bank anecdotes and incidents, queer, curious, odd, ludicrous, touching, poetry by and about bankers, "capital" items, conversations with customers and facts and statistics of general interest about banks accumulated from all the world during a personal experience of ten years behind a bank counter. Ill. N. Y. 1879. D. **332 : 28**

Pilon, Mt. R. What is demonetization of gold and silver ? N. Y. [1875]. O. **332 : 30**

Poor, H: Varnum. Resumption and the silver question ; embracing a sketch of the coinage and the legal-tender currencies of the U. S. and other nations ; a handbook for the times. 2d ed. N. Y. 1878. D. **332 : 13**

Price, Bonamy. Currency and banking. N. Y. 1876. D. **332 : 14**

Scudder, Moses L., jr. Congested prices. Chicago. 1883. D. **332 : 27**

Tucker, G: The theory of money and banks investigated. Bost. 1839. D. **332 : 16**

Walker, Francis Amasa. Money. N. Y. 1878. O. **332 : 17**

Walker, J. H. A few facts and suggestions on money, trade and banking. Bost. 1882 [1881]. D. **332 : 23**

Wells, D: Amasa. Robinson Crusoe's money, or The remarkable financial fortunes and misfortunes of a remote island community. Ill. N. Y. 1876. O. **332 : 18**

Special countries.

Weeden, W: B. Indian money, as a factor in New England civilization, (Johns Hopkins university studies). Balt. 1884. O. *in* **904+32 v2**

Michels, Ivan C. Current gold and silver coins of all nations together with their weights, fineness and intrinsic value, reduced to the standard of the U. S.; also, history of official coinage of the U. S. mint from 1792 to 1880. Ill. Phila. 1880. Q. **332 : R25**

Linderman, H: R. Money and legal tender in the U. S. N. Y. 1878. D. **332 : 11**

Knox, J: Jay. United States notes ; a history of the various issues of paper money by the government of the U. S.; with an app. containing the recent decision of the supreme court of the U. S. and the dissenting opinion upon the legal tender question. Ill. N. Y. 1884. O. **332+35**

Upton, J. K. Money in politics ; with an introd. by E: Atkinson. Bost. [1884]. D. **332 : 38**

Scudder, Moses L., jr. National banking ; a discussion of the merits of the present sys-

tem. [Economic monographs, no. 12]. N. Y. 1879. D. **332 : 29**

Richardson, H. W. The national banks. [Harper's half-hour ser.] N. Y. 1880. T. **332 : 15**

Gibbons, J. S. The banks of New York, their dealers, the clearing house, and the panic of 1857, with a financial chart. Ill. N. Y. 1859. D. **332 : 5**

Johnston, J: An address on banking in Wisconsin ; del. at the convention of the American bankers' asso., held at Saratoga. aug. 11-13, 1880. *n. p. or d.* **332 : Pam**

Homans, I. Smith, *ed.* The merchants' and bankers' almanac for 1869. N. Y. [1869]. O. **332+19**

* * *

Bagehot, Walter. Lombard street ; a description of the money market. N. Y. 1873. D. **332 : 2**

* * *

Beta, *originally* Bettziech, H: Die dichtkunst der börse. *In* Deutsche zeit- und streitfragen. **304 : 15 v2**

Hartung, H. Der check- und giro-verkehr der deutschen reichsbank. *In* Deutsche zeit- und streit-fragen. **304 : 15 v9**

Lammers, A: Die unternehmung im sparcassengeschäft. *In* Deutsche zeit- und streitfragen. **304 : 15 v11**

Malarce, Augustin de. Die schul-sparkassen ; deutsche ausgabe. *In* Deutsche zeit- und streit-fragen. **304 : 15 v8**

Pierson, N. G. Die münzfrage. *In* Deutsche zeit- und streit-fragen. **304 : 15 v11**

Roscher, W: G: F: Betrachtungen über die währungsfrage der deutschen münzreform. *In* Deutsche zeit- und streit-fragen. **304 : 15 v1**

Schneider, J: Philipp. Die ungedeckte banknote und die alternativ - währung. *In* Deutsche zeit- und streit-fragen. **304 : 15 v5**

— Zur währungsfrage ; eine entgegnung auf das buch des herrn dr. Theodore Hertzka "Währung und handel." *In* Deutsche zeit- und streit-fragen. **304 : 15 v6**

Wagner, Adolph. Unsere münzreform. *In* Deutsche zeit- und streit-fragen. **304 : 15 v6**

4. Land, stocks and credit.

Walker, Francis Amasa. Land and its rent. Bost. 1883. S. **333 : 3**

Campbell, G: Douglass, *8th duke of Argyll, and* H: George. Property in land, a passage at arms. N. Y. 1884. D. **333 : 6**
Contents. **Campbell,** G: D., *duke of Argyll.* The prophet of San Francisco.—**George,** H: The reduction to iniquity.

United States. *General land office.* Annual reports of the commissioner, *etc. See* Congressional documents. *in* **328.1 : D**
Note. Subordinate to the Dep't of the interior.— For land laws and decisions, see cl. 343.1.

Adams, Herbert B. Maryland's influence upon land cessions to the U. S.; with minor papers on G: Washington's interest in western lands, the Potomac company, and a national university. (Johns Hopkins university studies). Balt. 1885. O. *in* **904+32 v3**

Ross, Denman W. The early history of land-holding among the germans. Lond. 1883. O. **333+7**
Contents. Theory.—Sources of information.—Notes and references.—Literature of the subject.—Index.

Cobden club. Systems of land tenure in various countries ; a series of essays published under the sanction of the Cobden club, ed. by J. W. Probyn. New ed. rev. and cor. Lond. [1881]. D. **333 : 4**
Contents. **Longfield, H. M.** The tenure of land in Ireland.—**Brodrick, G: C.** The law and custom of primogeniture.—**Hoskyns, C. W.** The land laws of England.—**Campbell,** *Sir* G: The tenure of land in India.—**Leslie, T. E. C.** The land system of France.—**Fancher, J.** The russian agrarian legislation of 1861.—**Morier, R. B. D.** The agrarian legislation of Prussia during the present century ; also a report on the tenure of land in the grand duchy of Hesse.—**Laveleye, E. de.** The land system of Belgium and Holland.—**Fisher, C. M.** Farm land and land laws of the U. S.

Brodrick, G: C: English land and english landlords ; an inquiry into the origin and character of the english land system, with proposals for its reform ; with an index. (Cobden club.) Lond. 1881. O. **333 : 5**

George, H: The irish land question, what involves, and how alone it can be settled ; an appeal to the land leagues. N. Y. 1881. D. **333 : 1**

Fowler, W: Worthington. Ten years in Wall street, or Revelations of inside life and experience on 'change . . . Ill. Hartford. 1870. O. **333 : 2**

Gareis, C: Die börse und die gründungen, nebst vorschlägen zur reform des börsenrechts und der actiengesetzgebung. *In* Deutsche zeit- und streit-fragen. **304 : 15 v3**

Wirth, Max W: Gottlob. Geschichte der handelskrisen. Frankfurt a. M. 1858. O. **334 : 1**

5. Socialism and communism.

Baron, Julius. Angriffe auf das erbrecht ; mit einer nachschrift über die social-democratischen wahlen. *In* Deutsche zeit- und streit-fragen. **304 : 15 v6**

Cohn, Gustav. Was ist socialismus ? *In* Deutsche zeit- und streit-fragen. **304 : 15 v7**

Contzen, H: Die sociale frage, ihre geschichte und ihre bedeutung in der gegenwart ; eine volkswirthschaftliche skizze. Leipz. 1871. O. **335 : 7**

Democracy in the old world and the new, by the author of "The Suez canal, the eastern question and Abyssinia," "Egypt, India and the colonies," etc. Lond. 1884 D. **335 : 16**

Elementary system, An, of socialism, theoretical and practical, by a disciple of H: George. Oxford. 1884. D. **335 : 15**

Ely, R: T. French and german socialism in modern times. N. Y. 1883. S. **335 : 4**
— Recent american socialism. (Johns Hopkins university studies). Balt. 1885. O. *in* **904+32 v3**

Gronlund, Laurence. The co - operative commonwealth in its outlines ; an exposition of modern socialism. Bost. 1884. D. **335 : 10**

Hyndman, H: M. The historical basis of socialism in England. Lond. 1883. O. **335 : 17**

Kaufmann, M. Socialism ; its nature, its dangers and its remedies considered. Founded on the german work "Kapitalismus und socialismus," by A. E. F. Schäffle. Lond. 1874. D. **335 : 2**

Laveleye, Émile de. The socialism of to-day. Tr. into english by Goddard H. Orpen ; together with an account of socialism in England, by the translator. Lond. *n. d.* D. **335 : 14**

Mallock, W: Hurrell. Social equality ; a short study in a missing science. N. Y. 1882. D. **335 : 3**

Mehring, Franz. Die deutsche socialdemokratie, ihre geschichte und ihre lehre ; eine historisch-kritische darstellung. 2te verb. und verm. aufl. Bremen. 1878. O. **335 : 8**

Meyer, Jürgen Bona. Fichte, Lassalle und der socialismus. *In* Deutsche zeit- und streit-fragen. **304 : 15 v7**

Rae, J: Contemporary socialism. N. Y. 1884. D. **335 : 11**

Schäffle, Albert Eberhard F: Die quintessenz des socialismus. 6te aufl. Gotha. 1878. O. **335 : 6**
— Kapitalismus und. socialismus. *See* Kaufmann, M. Socialism. **335 : 2**

Schmoller, Gustav. Ueber einige grundfragen des rechts und der volkswirthschaft ; ein offenes sendschreiben an herrn prof. dr. H: v. Treitschke. 2te aufl. Jena. 1875. O. **335+13**

Shaw, Albert. Icaria ; a chapter in the history of communism. N. Y. 1884. S. **335 : 12**

Smith, Goldwin. False hopes, or Fallacies, socialistic and semi-socialistic. briefly answered ; an address. N. Y. 1883. D. **335 : 5**

Treitschke, H: Gotthard v. Der socialismus und seine gönner ; nebst einem sendschreiben an Gustav Schmoller. Berlin. 1875. O. **335 : 9**

Woolsey, Theodore Dwight. Communism and socialism in their history and theory ; a sketch. N. Y. 1880. D. **335 : 1**

6. Public funds and taxation.

Bolles, Albert S. The financial history of the U. S., from 1774 to 1860. N. Y. 1879, 1883. 2 v. O. **336+1**

Adams, H: Carter. Taxation in the U. S., 1789-1816. (Johns Hopkins university studies). Balt. 1884. O. *in* **904+32 v2**

Gibbons, J. S. The public debt of the U. S.; its organization, its liquidation ; administration of the treasury ; the financial system. N. Y. 1867. D. **336 : 2**

Vuitry, Adolphe. Études sur le régime financier de la France avant la révolution de 1789. Paris. 1878-1883. 3 v. O. **336+3**
Contents. [V. 1.] Les impôts romains dans la Gaule du 5e au 10e siècle.—Le régime financier de la monarchie féodale aux 11e, 12e et 13e siècles. [2, 3.] Nouvelle série. Philippe le bel et ses trois fils, 1285-1328.—Les trois premiers Valois, 1328-1380.

Paris *city.* Compte général des recettes et dépenses de la ville de Paris pour l'exercice 1876, clos le 31 mars 1877. Paris. 1877. Q. *in* **336 : D**
— - Budget de l'exercice 1878[-1882]. Paris. 1877-82. 5 v. Q. *in* **336 : D**

Delsa, L. Beiträge zur steuer-reform. *In* Deutsche zeit- und streit-fragen.
304 : 15 v10
Vogel, A: Einige aussprüche des landbaues auf steuer-und zollentlastung. *In* Deutsche zeit- und streit-fragen.   304 : 15 v5

7. Protection and free trade.

Arago, Dominique François J: Ueber die systeme des schutzes und der handelsfreiheit. *In his* Sämmtliche werke.   500 : 3 v6
Ashworth, H: Recollections of R: Cobden, and the anti-corn-law league. Lond. [1879]. D.
337 : 17
Bastiat, F: Essays on political economy. Tr. from the Paris ed. of 1863. Chicago. 1869. D.   337 : 1
Contents. Sophisms of protection, 1st and 2d ser.—Spoliation and law.—Capital and interest.
— *Same.* [2d ed.] Sophisms of the protectionists. [Amer. free trade league.] N. Y. 1872. D.
337 : 1
Byles, *Sir* J: Barnard. Sophisms of free-trade and popular political economy, examined by a barrister. 1st amer. from the 9th eng. ed. Phila. 1872. D.   337 : 2
Cobden club. [Publications.] Lond. 1871–80. 2 v. D.   337 : 3
Contents. [V. 1.] **Duff**, G. On the teachings of Richard Cobden, 1871.—Correspondence relative to the budgets of various countries, ed. by J. W. Probyn, 1877.—**Stuart**, J. M. The history of free trade in Tuscany, 1876.—**Mongredien**, A: Free trade and english commerce, 1879.—**Mallet**, L. Reciprocity, a letter, 1879. [2.] **Medley**, G: W. England under free trade; The reciprocity craze.—**Chamberlain**, J. The french treaty and reciprocity.—**Cross**, J. K. Imports, exports and the french treaty.—**Slagg**, J: Free trade and tariffs.—**Mongredien**, A: Pleas for protection examined; The western farmer of America. [App. **Hinton**, J: W. Reply to last essay.]
Cox, S: Sullivan. Free land and free trade; the lessons of the english corn laws applied to the U. S. N. Y. 1880. D.   337 : 4
Donnell, E. J. Slavery and "protection"; an historical review and appeal to the workshop and the farm. N. Y. 1882. O.   337 : 14
— The true issue; industrial depression and political corruption caused by tariff monopolies; reform demanded in the interest of manufacturers, farmers and working-men. (Questions of the day, no. 16.) N. Y. 1884. D.   337 : 19
Fawcett, H: Free trade and protection; an inquiry into the causes which have retarded the general adoption of free trade since its introduction into England. Lond. 1878. D.
337 : 5
Grosvenor, W: Mason. Does protection protect? an examination of the effect of different forms of tariff upon american industry. N. Y. 1871. O.   337+10
Mongredien, A: History of the free trade movement in England. [Library of popular information.] N. Y. 1881. S.   337 : 6
— *Same.* Lond. [1881]. S.   337 : 6
Perrot, Franz Fürchtegott. Die reform des zollvereinstarifes. *In* Deutsche zeit- und streit-fragen.   304 : 15 v3
Porter, Robert P. Protection and free-trade to-day at home and abroad, in field and workshop. Bost. 1884. S.   337 : 20

Rathbone, W: Protection and communism; a consideration of the effects of the american tariff upon wages. (Questions of the day, no. 15). N. Y. 1884. D.   337 : 18
Redington, Lyman W. Free trade vs. protection; a lecture del. in the unitarian church, Milwaukee, Wis., july 7, 1871. Milw. 1871. O.   337 : Pam
Roberts, Ellis H. Government revenue, especially the american system; an argument for industrial freedom against the fallacies of free trade. Bost. 1884. D.   337 : 16
Schönhof, Jacob. The destructive influence of the tariff upon manufacture and commerce; and the figures and facts relating thereto. N. Y. 1883. D.   337 : 12
— Wages and trade, in the manufacturing industries in America and in Europe; with an introd. by R. R. Bowker. N. Y. 1884. D.   337 : 15
Steiger, E., *and co.* On the removal of the duty on books. [*Anon.*] N. Y. 1882. D.
337 : Pam
Sumner, W: Graham. Lectures on the history of protection in the U. S., del. before the International free - trade alliance. Reprinted from "The new century." N. Y. 1877. O.   337 : 7
Taussig, Frank W. Protection to young industries as applied in the U. S.; a study in economic history. Cambridge. 1883. D.
337 : 11
— The history of the present tariff, 1860—1883. (Questions of the day, no. 19.) N. Y. 1885. D.   337 : 22
Villiers, C: Pelham. Free trade speeches, with a political memoir; ed. by a member of the Cobden club. Lond. 1883. 2 v. O.
337 : 21
Wells, D: Ames. Free trade essential to future national prosperity and development; a lecture, feb. 8th 1882, before the Young men's democratic club and the Brooklyn revenue reform club of Brooklyn. N. Y. 1882. D.   337 : 13
— How congress and the public deal with a great revenue and industrial problem [the sugar industry]. N. Y. 1880. O.
337 : Pam
— A primer of tariff reform. (Cobden club publications). Lond. 1885. D.   337 : 3
Wilson, Alexander Johnstone. Reciprocity, bimetallism and land-tenure reform. Lond. 1880. O.   337 : 8
Wise, Bernhard Ringrose. Facts and fallacies of modern protection; the Oxford Cobden prize essay for 1878. Lond. 1879. D.
337 : 9

* * *

United States. *Tariff.* **Young**, E: Special repo on the [history of the] customs-tariff legislation of the U. S., with appendices. (U. S. 42d cong. 2 sess. House ex. doc. no. 109). Wash. 1872. O.   *in* 337 : D
— — Report of the tariff commission, appointed under act of congress approved may 15, 1882. (U. S. 47th cong. 2d sess. House mis. doc. no. 6). Wash. 1882. 2 v. O.
in 337 : D
— — The existing tariff on imports into the U. S. etc. and the free list, together with com-

United States. *Tariff.—Continued.*
parative tables of present and past tariffs, and other statistics relating thereto ; prepared by the com. on finance, U. S. sen. (U. S. 48th cong. 1st sess. Sen. rep. no. 12). Wash. 1884. O.   *in* **337 : D**
— - **Evans,** C: H., *comp.* Duties [received] from 1867 to 1883, *etc. See his* Imports and duties.   *in* **380.1 : D**

8. Pauperism.

(See also Charitable institutions. cl. 361.)

Beta, *originally* Bettziech, H: Wohl- und übelthäter in unseren grossstädten. *In* Deutsche zeit- und streit-fragen.   **304 : 15 v4**
Dugdale, R: L. "The Jukes"; a study in crime, pauperism, disease and heredity, also further studies of criminals; with an introd. by Elisha Harris. 3d ed., rev. N. Y. 1877. D.   **339 : 1**

Campbell, Helen. The problem of the poor ; a record of quiet work in unquiet places. N. Y. 1882. S.   **339 : 3**
Kay, Joseph. The social condition and education of the people of England. N. Y. 1863. D.   **339 : 2**
Long, James Edmond. The hopeful cry of outcast London. Lond. 1884. D.   **339 : 8**
Mearns, Andrew. The bitter cry of outcast London ; an inquiry into the condition of the abject poor. [*Anon.*] Bost. 1884. O.   **339 : 4**
Nicholls, *Sir* G: A history of the english poor law, in connexion with the legislation and other circumstances affecting the condition of the people. Lond. 1854. 2 v. O. **339 : 5**
— A history of the scotch poor law, in connexion with the condition of the people. Lond. 1856. O.   **339 : 6**
— A history of the irish poor law, in connexion with the condition of the people. Lond. 1856. O.   **339 : 7**

5. Jurisprudence.

1. In general.

Soule, C: C. The lawyer's reference manual of law-books and citations. Bost. 1883. O.   **340 : R13**
Burrill, Alexander M. A law dictionary and glossary ; containing full definitions of the principal terms of the common and civil law, together with tr. and explanations of the various technical phrases in different languages, occurring in the ancient and modern reports and standard treatises, embracing also all the principal common and civil law maxims ; compiled on the basis of Spelman's glossary and adapted to the jurisprudence of the United States with copious ill., critical and historical. 2d ed. N. Y. 1859. 2 v. O.   **340 : R1**
Tayler, T: The law glossary ; a selection of the greek, latin, saxon, french, norman and italian sentences, phrases and maxims found in the leading english and amer. reports and elementary works, with hist. and explan. notes, alphabetically arr. and tr. into eng. for the use of members of the legal profession, law students etc. 9th ed., rev., corr. and enl. by a member of the N. Y. bar. N. Y. 1877. O.   **340 : R2**

* * *

Abbott, B: Vaughan. Judge and jury; a popular explanation of leading topics in the law of the land. N. Y. 1880. D. **340 : 10**
— The travelling law school and famous trials ; first lessons in government and law. (Business boys' lib. no. 2) Bost. [1884]. S.   **x 340 : 18**
Amos, Sheldon. The science of law. (Intern. scientific ser.) N. Y. 1880. D.   **340 : 12**
Bascom, J: The lawyer and the lawyer's questions ; a baccalaureate discourse preached in Assembly hall, university of Wisconsin, june 18, 1882. Milw. 1882. O.   **340 : Pam**

Essays in anglo-saxon law. Bost. 1876. O.   **340 : 15**
Contents. **Adams,** H: The anglo-saxon courts of law.—**Lodge,** H: C. The anglo-saxon land-law.—**Young,** E. The anglo-saxon family law.—**Laughlin,** J. L. The anglo-saxon legal procedure.—App. Select cases in anglo-saxon law.—Index.
Forsyth, W: The history of lawyers, ancient and modern. Ill. N. Y. 1875. O. **340 : 19**
Heard, Franklin Fiske. Oddities of the law. Bost. 1881. D.   **340 : 8**
Hoar, G: F. The function of the amer. lawyer in the founding of states ; an address del. before the graduating class at the 57th anniversary of the Yale law school, june 28, 1881. New Haven. 1881. O. **340 : Pam**
Holland, T: Erskine. The elements of jurisprudence. Oxford. 1880. O.   **340 : 3**
Ihering, Rudolph v. The struggle for law. Tr. from the 5th german ed. by J: J. Lalor. Chicago. 1879. D.   **340 : 7**
Maine, *Sir* H: James Sumner. Ancient law, its connection with the early history of society, and its relation to modern ideas ; with an introd. by Theodore W. Dwight. 1st amer. ed. N. Y. 1871. D.   **340 : 4**
— Dissertations on early law and custom ; chiefly sel. from lectures del. at Oxford. N. Y. 1883. O.   **340 : 14**
— Lectures on the early history of institutions. 3d ed. Lond. 1880. O.   **340 : 16**
— Village-communities in the east and west ; six lectures del. at Oxford. Lond. 1871. O.   **340 : 5**
Contents. The east and the study of jurisprudence.—The sources of indian law.—The western village community.—The eastern village community.—The process of feudalisation.—The early history of price and rent.—Appendices.—Index.
Montesquieu, C: de Secondat, *baron* de la Brède et de. Complete works. Tr. from the french ; in 4 v. V. 2-4. Lond. 1777. O.   **340 : 6**
Contents. V. **1** missing. **2.** The spirit of laws, book 20-31. **3.** Grandeur and decline of the roman empire.—Dialogue between Sylla and Eucrates.—Per-

x denotes books specially adapted for children.

Montesquieu, C: de.—*Continued.*
sian letters. **4.** Familiar letters. — Miscellaneous pieces.—Defense, analysis, explanations and index of The spirit of laws.
— The spirit of laws. Tr. from the french by T: Nugent. 4th ed. rev., with add. Lond. 1766. 2 v. O.   **340 : 9**
Wilson, *Sir* Roland Knyvet. History of modern english law. [Hist. handbooks]. Lond. 1875. S.   **340 : 17**

*   *   *

Livingston, J: Livingston's law register ; a guide for every man of business and handbook of useful information. N. Y. 1854. O.   **340 : 20**
State bar association of Wisconsin. Report of the proceedings of the meeting for [its] organization, held at Madison, jan. 9, 1878. Madison. 1881. O. *bound with*
— Report of the proceedings of the annual meeting held at Madison, june 14–16, 1881 ; with app. containing biographical sketches of the life and character of deceased members of the bench and bar of Wis., and also an alphabetical catalogue of Wis. attorneys, resident, non-resident and deceased ; comp. by Moses M. Strong. Madison. 1883. O.   **340 : 21**

2. International law.

Bar, K: L: v. International law ; private and criminal. Tr. with notes. by G. R. Gillespie. Bost. 1883. O.   **341 : 11**
Field, D: Dudley. Outlines of an international code. 2d ed. N. Y. 1876. O.   **341+4**
Gallaudet, E: Miner. A manual of international law. N. Y. 1879. D.   **341 : 5**
Hall, W: E: International law. Oxford. 1880. O.   **341 : 6**
Halleck, H: Wager. Elements of international law. Phila. 1878. O.   **341 : 7**
Hartmann, K: Robert E: v. Princip und zukunft des völkerrechts. *In his* Gesammelte studien.   **834+19**
Mackintosh, *Sir* James. A discourse on the law of nature and of nations. *In his* Miscell. works.   **904+28**
Vattel, Emmerie de. The law of nations, or Principles of the law of nature, applied to the conduct and affairs of nations and sovereigns ; from the french. From the new ed. by Joseph Chitty, with add. notes and references by E: D. Ingraham. Phila. 1879. O.   **341 : 3**
Woolsey, Theodore Dwight. Introduction to the study of international law, designed as an aid in teaching and in historical studies. [1st ed.] Bost. 1860. D.   **341 : 1**
— *Same.* 5th ed. N. Y. 1879. O.   **341 : 2**
Spear, S: Thayer. The law of extradition, international and inter state ; with an app. containing the extradition treaties and laws of the U. S., several sections of the english extradition act of 1870, and extradition regulations and forms. Albany. 1879. O.   **341+8**
Lawrence, W: Beach. Visitation and search, or An historical sketch of the british claim to exercise a maritime police over the vessels of all nations, in peace as well as in war,

with an inquiry into the expediency of terminating the 8th article of the Ashburton treaty. Bost. 1858. O.   **341+9**
Reade, C: The eighth commandment ; [international copyright]. Bost. 1860. D.   **341 : 10**
Putnam, G: Haven. International copyright considered in some of its relations to ethics and political economy ; an address del. jan. 29, 1879, before the New York free-trade club. [Economic monographs, no. 15.] N. Y. 1879. D.   **341 : 12**

3. Constitutional law.

United States.

United States. The federal and state constitutions, colonial charters, and other organic laws of the U. S.; comp. under an order of the U. S. senate by B: Perley Poore. Wash. 1877. 2 v. F.   *in* **342.1 : D**
Fallows, S:, *ed.* The constitutions of the U. S. and of the state of Wisconsin ; with questions adapted to the use of common schools. Madison. 1871. D.   **342.1 : 10**
Duer, W: Alexander. Lectures on the constitutional jurisprudence of the U. S., delivered annually in Columbia college. [Harper's family library]. N. Y. 1845. S.   **342.1 : 7**
Federalist, The, on the new constitution, written in the year 1788, by mr. Hamilton, mr. Madison and mr. Jay ; with an app. containing the letters of Pacificus and Helvidius on the proclamation of neutrality of 1793, also the original articles of confederation, and the constitution of the U. S., with the amendments made thereto. A new ed., the numbers written by mr. Madison corr. by himself. Hallowell. 1837. O.   **342.1 : 11**
Fœderalist, The ; a collection of essays, written in favor of the new constitution, as agreed upon by the fœderal convention sept. 17, 1787. Repr. from the original text, with an introd. and notes, by H: B. Dawson. V. 1. N. Y. 1864. O.   **342.1 : 22**
Fisher, Sidney G: The trial of the constitution. Phila. 1862. O.   **342.1+8**
Hickey, W:, *ed.* The constitution of the U. S. of America, with an alphabetical analysis ; the declaration of independence, the articles of confederation ; the prominent political acts of ·G: Washington ; electoral votes for all the presidents and vice-presidents, the high authorities and civil officers of government, from march 4, 1789 to march 3, 1847 ; chronological narrative of the several states, and other matter, with a descriptive account of the state papers, public documents, and other sources of statistical information at the seat of government. 7th ed. Phila. 1854. D.   **342.1 : 9**
Lessons of a century for the 4th of july 1876 ; prevention is better than cure. *n. p. or d.*   **342.1 : Pam**
    Note. Contains a series of criticisms on the U. S. constitution.
Marshall, J: Writings upon the federal constitution. Bost. 1839. O.   **342.1+15**
Paschal, G: W. The constitution of the U. S. defined and carefully annotated ; with an app., supp. and index thereto. Wash. 1878. O.   **342.1+3**

Story, Joseph. Commentaries on the constitution of the U. S.; with a preliminary review of the constitutional history of the colonies and states before the adoption of the constitution. 4th ed., with notes and add. by by T: M. Cooley. Bost. 1873. O. **342.1+4**

* * *

Poole, W: F: The ordinance of 1787, and dr. Manasseh Cutler as an agent in its formation. Cambridge, Mass. 1876. O.
 342.1 : Pam

Scott, Eben Greenough. The development of constitutional liberty in the english colonies of America. N. Y. 1882. O. **342.1 : 18**

Sterne, Simon. Constitutional history and political development of the U. S. N. Y. [1882]. D. **342.1 : 19**

Bancroft, G: History of the formation of the constitution of the U. S. of America. N. Y. 1882. 2 v. O. **342.1 : 21**

Curtis, G: Ticknor. History of the origin, formation and adoption of the constitution of the U. S.; with notices of the principal framers. N. Y. 1854. 2 v. O. **342.1+2**

Towle, Nathaniel Carter. A history and analysis of the constitution of the U. S.; with a full account of the confederations which preceded it, of the debates and acts of the convention which formed it, of the judicial decisions which have construed it; with papers and tables illustrative of the action of the government and the people under it. Bost. 1860. D. **- 342.1 : 16**

Elliot, Jonathan, ed. The debates, resolutions, and other proceedings in convention on the adoption of the federal constitution, as recommended by the general convention at Philadelphia, 17 sept. 1787; with the yeas and nays on the decision of the main question. Wash. 1827-30. 4 v. O. **342.1 : 5**
Contents. V. 1. Massachusetts and New York. **2.** Virginia. **3.** North Carolina and Pennsylvania. **4.** Journal and debates of the federal convention at Philadelphia, may 14–sept. 17, 1787, with the constitution illustrated by the opinions of twenty successive congresses, and a digest of decisions in the courts of the union.

— The debates in the several states conventions on the adoption of the federal constitution, as recommended by the general convention at Philadelphia in 1787; together with the journal of the federal convention, Luther Martin's letter, Yates's minutes, congressional opinions, Virginia and Kentucky resolutions of '98–'99, and other illustrations. of the constitution. 2d ed. with considerable add., coll. and rev. from contemporary publications. Pub. under the sanction of congress. Phila. 1876. 5 v. O. **342.1+6**
Contents. V. 1. Journal of the federal convention.—Martin's letter.—Yates's minutes. **2.** Massachusetts.—Connecticut.—New Hampshire. — New York.—Pennsylvania.—Maryland. **3.** Virginia. **4.** North Carolina.—South Carolina.—Virginia and Kentucky. **5.** Supp. Madison papers, containing debates on the confederation and contitution.

Yates, Robert. Secret proceedings and debates of the convention assembled at Philadelphia in 1787 for the purpose of forming the constitution of the U. S. of America, incl. "The genuine information," laid before the legislature of Maryland by Luther Martin; also other historical documents relative to the federal compact of the north amer. union. Cinc. [1838]. D. **342.1 : 13**

Chittenden, L. E. Report of the debates and proceedings in the secret sessions of the conference convention for proposing amendments to the constitution of the U. S., held at Washington, feb. 1861. N. Y. 1864. O. **342.1+14**

Hurd, J: C. Theory of our national existence, as shown by the action of the government of the U. S. since 1861. Bost. 1881. O.
 342.1 : 12

Giaque, Florien. The election and naturalization laws of the U. S.; a compilation of all constitutional provisions and laws of the U. S. relating to elections, the elective franchise, to citizenship and the naturalization of aliens, with notes of decisions. Cinc. 1880. O. **342.1 : 17**

U. S. — Special states.

Massachusetts state. Official report of the debates and proceedings in the state convention, assembled may 4, 1853, to revise and amend the constitution of the commonwealth of Massachusetts. Bost. 1853. 3 v. O. **342.12+401**

New York state. Report of the debates and proceedings of the convention for the revision of the constitution of the state of New York, 1846; reported by W: G. Bishop and W: H. Attree. Albany. 1846. O.
 342.13+101

Ohio state. Reports of the debates and proceedings of the convention for the revision of the constitution of the state of Ohio, 1850-51; J. V. Smith, official reporter to the convention. Columbus. 1851. 2 v. O.
 342.15 : 1

Wisconsin state. Journal of the convention to form a constitution for the state of Wisconsin; begun and held at Madison oct. 5, 1846. Madison. 1847. O. **342.15+301**

— Journal of the convention to form a constitution for the state of Wisconsin, with a sketch of the debates, begun and held at Madison, dec. 15, 1847. Madison. 1848. O.
 342.15+302

— The constitution of the state of Wisconsin, adopted in convention at Madison on the 16th day of dec. 1846, together with the act of congress and the act of the legislature in relation to the formation of a state government in Wisconsin. Pub. by order of the convention. Madison. 1846. D.
 342.15 : 307

Wright, A. O. An analysis of the constitution of the state of Wisconsin, designed for the use of teachers, advanced classes in schools and citizens generally. Madison. 1873. D.
 342.15 : 305

Other countries.

Roelker, Bernard. The constitution of France, monarchical and republican, together with brief historical remarks relating to their origin and the late Orleans dynasty. Bost. 1848. D. **342.3 : 1**

Thierry, Jacques N: Augustin. The formation and progress of the tiers état or third estate in France. Tr. from the french by Francis B. Wells. Lond. 1859. 2 v. in 1. D.
 342.3 : 2

Kaiser, Simon. Französische verfassungsgeschichte von 1789-1852, in ihrer historischen aufeinanderfolge und systemati-
schen entwickelung dargestellt. Leipz.
1852. O.   **342.3 : 4**

Waitz, G: Deutsche verfassungsgeschichte.
Berlin. 1874–84. 8 v. O.   **342.3+3**
Contents. V. 1. Die verfassung des deutschen
volkes in ältester zeit. 3te aufl. **2-4.** Die verfassung des fränkischen reichs. **5-8.** Die deutsche
reichsverfassung von der mitte des neunten bis
zur mitte des zwölften jahrhunderts.

Maurer, G : L : v. Geschichte der markenverfassung in Deutschland. Erlangen. 1856.
O.   **342.3 : 7**

— Geschichte der dorfverfassung in Deutschland.
Erlangen. 1865. 2 v. in 1. O.   **342.3 : 6**

— Geschichte der städteverfassung in Deutschland. Erlangen. 1869-1871. 4 v. O. **342.3 : 5**

Hegel, C : Geschichte der städteverfassung von
Italien ; seit der zeit der römischen herrschaft bis zum ausgang des 12ten jahrhun-
derts. Leipz. 1847. 2 v. O.   **342.3 : 8**
Note. For English constitutional history, see class
323. 2, col. 161–163: there being no written constitution in that country.

4. Statute and common law.

Woolsey, Theodore Dwight. Essay on divorce
and divorce legislation, with special reference to the U. S. N. Y. 1869. D.   **343 : 1**

— Divorce and divorce legislation, especially in
the U. S. 2d ed. rev. N. Y. 1882. D. **343 : 3**

Cowley, C : Famous divorces of all ages.
Lowell, Mass. 1878. D.   **343 : 2**

Schröder, R: Das eheliche güterrecht Deutschlands in vergangenheit, gegenwart und
zukunft. In Deutsche zeit- und streit-fra-
gen.   **304 : 15 v4**

Scheel, Hans v. Eigenthum und erbrecht. In
Deutsche zeit- und streit-fragen.
                                            304 : 15 v6

Curiosities of the search-room ; a collection of
serious and whimsical wills. (Frank. sq.
lib.) N. Y. 1884. Q.   **343+5**

Taylor, Alfred Swaine. A manual of medical
jurisprudence. 8th amer. ed. from the 10th
Lond. ed., containing the author's latest
notes, ed. with add. notes and references
by J: J. Reese. Ill. Phila. 1880. O. **343+6**

Wharton, Francis, and Moreton Stillé. A treatise on medical jurisprudence ; the medical
part rev. and corr. with numerous add. by
Alfred Stillé. 2d ed. rev. ed. [Incomplete].
Phila. 1860. O.   **343+7**

Löbner, Arthur. Lexikon des handels- und
gewerberechts für den kaufmann und
gewerbtreibenden. Leipz. 1882. D.
                                            343.3 : R1

Townsend, Calvin. A compendium of commercial law, analytically and topically arr.
with copious citations of legal authorities,
for the use of business colleges and universities, students of law and members of the
bar. N. Y. n. d. O.   **343 : 4**

Parsons, Theophilus. Laws of business for all
the states of the union and the dominion of
Canada ; with forms and directions for all
transactions, and abstracts of the laws of
all the states on various topics. Enl. and
imp. Hartford. 1884. O.   **343.1+11**

Peters, Nils. En analytisk framställning af
amerikansk lag om kontrakt ; utgifven till
gagn för skandinaverna i Amerika. Milw.
1884. D.   **343.1 : 12**

United States.

United States. Congress. Statutes at large, and
treaties, postal conventions and executive
proclamations. V. 1–17. Bost. 1845-75 ;
v. 18–22, Wash. 1875-83. 22 v. in 24. Q.
                                            in **343.1 : D**
Contents. V. **1-5.** Public laws, 1789–1845. **6.** Private
laws, 1789–1845. **7.** Indian treaties, 1789–1845. **8.**
Foreign treaties, 1789–1845. — General index. **9.** 1845
—1851. **10.** 1851—1855. **11.** 1855—1859. **12.** 1859—1863.
13. 1863—1865. **14.** 1865—1867. **15.** 1867—1869. **16.** 1869
—1871. **17.** 1871—1873. **18.** Pt. 1 and 2, see below. Pt.
3: 1873—1875. **19.** 1875—1877. **20.** 1877—1879. **21.** 1879
—1881. **22.** 1881—1883. V. 1-8 ed. by R: Peters, 9-10
by G: Minot, 11 by G: Minot and G: P. Sanger, 12-17
by G: P. Sanger, 18-22 under the dir. of the sec. of
state.

— — Revised statutes passed at the first session of
the 43d cong., 1873-74 ; embracing the statutes of the U. S., general and permanent
in their nature, in force on dec. 1, 1873, as
rev. and consolidated by commissioners appointed under an act of cong., and as reprinted with amendments under authority
of an act of cong. approved march 2, 1877.
2d ed. Wash. 1878. Q.   **343.1 : D**
Note. Originally pub. as V. 18, pt. 1 of the Stat-
utes-at-large.

— — Revised statutes relating to the District of
Columbia and post roads, passed at the
first session of the 43d cong., 1873-74 ; together with the public treaties in force on
dec. 1, 1873. Wash. 1875. Q.   **343.1 : D**
Note. Originally pub. as V. 18, pt. 2 of the Statutes-
at-large.

— A synoptical index to the laws and treaties of
the U. S. of America, from march 4, 1789
to march 3, 1851, with reference to the ed.
of the laws pub. by Bioren and Duane, and
to the statutes at large pub. by Little,
Brown & co. under the authority of cong.
Bost. 1852. Q.   **343.1 : D**

Gordon, T: F. A digest of the laws of the U. S.,
incl. an abstract of the judicial decisions
relating to the constitutional and statutory
law; with notes, explanatory and historical.
Phila. 1827. O.   **343.1 : 2**

Kent, James. Commentaries on american law.
12th ed. by O. W. Holmes, jr. Bost. 1873.
4 v. O.   **343.1 : R1**

Lewis, Francis A. Law relating to stocks, bonds
and other securities in the U. S. Phila.
1881. O.   **343.1+8**

United States. Public domain. Donaldson, T:
The public domain ; its history with statistics, with references to the national domain, colonization, acquirement of territory, the survey, administration and
several methods of sale and disposition of
the public domain of the U. S., with sketch
of the legislative history of the land states
and territories, and references to the land
system of the colonies, and also that of
several foreign governments. Prepared
under dir. of the Public land commission,
Committee on codification, and giving the
result of the several land laws to june 30,
1880 ; rev. july 16, 1881. Maps. (U. S. 46th
cong. 3d sess. House ex. doc. no. 47, pt. 4).
Wash. 1881. O.   in **343.1 : D**

United States. *Public domain.—Continued.*

— — General public acts of cong. respecting the sale and disposition of the public lands, with instructions issued from time to time by the sec. of the treas. and com'r of the gen. land office, and official opinions of the attorney-gen. on questions arising under the land laws. Prepared and printed by order of the sen. Wash. 1838. 2 v. O.

in **343.1 : D**

Contents. V. 1. Laws to the close of the 2d sess. of the 25th cong. 2. Instructions and opinions to aug. 17, 1838.

— — [Britton, Alexander T., *comp.*] The existing laws of the U. S. of a general and permanent character, and relating to the survey and disposition of the public domain dec. 1, 1880 ; embracing references to previous legislation, and citations of decisions from the federal and the state courts and from the executive officers of the U. S. Prepared under the direction of the Public land commission, Committee on codification. (U. S. 46th cong. 3 sess. House ex. doc. no. 47, pt. 1). Wash. 1881. O.

in **343.1 : D**

— — *Same,* with supp. embracing the laws of like character passed at the 3d sess. of the 46th, and 1st sess. of the 47th cong., and a digest of late decisions under the land laws, in continuation of the "Citation of decisions" of the Land commission [in pt. 2], prepared under the dir. of the Commissioner of the general land office. (U. S. 47th coug. 2 sess. House mis. doc. no. 45, pt. 1). Wash. 1884. O. *in* **343.1 : D**

— — [Britton, Alexander T., *comp.*] Laws of the U. S. of a local or temporary character, and exhibiting the entire legislation of cong. upon which the public land titles in each state and territory have depended, dec. 1, 1880 ; embracing also a digest of all indian treaties affecting the titles to public lands, an abstract of the authority for and the boundaries of the existing military reservations, and a table of judicial and executive decisions affecting the various subjects arising under the public land system. Prepared unter the dir. of the Public land commission, Committee on codification. (U. S. 46th cong. 3 sess. House ex. doc. no. 47, pt. 2, 3). Wash. 1881. 2 v. in 1. O. *in* **343.1 : D**

— — *Same,* with supp. embracing the laws of like character passed at the 3d sess. of the 46th, and 1st sess. of the 47th cong. 2 sess. House mis. doc. no. 45, pt., 2 3). Wash. 1884. 2 v. O. *in* **343.1 : D**

— — Public land laws ; an exhaustive compilation of the laws, rulings, decisions and late acts of congress with reference to the agricultural, mining and other lands of the U. S., with the instructions of the commissioner of the general land office regarding the same ; comp. from official sources. Sioux City. 1879. O. **343.1 : 4**

— *Congress.* An act to provide internal revenue to support the government, to pay interest on the public debt and for other purposes, passed june 30, 1864. *n. t.* O. **343.1 : 5**

— — *Same.* as amended by the act of march 3d, 1865 ; incl. sections relating to the collec-

United States. *Public domain.—Continued.*

tion of internal revenue, from other acts. *n. t.* O. **343.1 : 6**

— — Laws of the U. S. relating to internal revenue comprising the act of june 30, 1864, as amended by subsequent acts incl. the act of march 26, 1867. Wash. 1867. O.

343.1 : 7

Tax-payer's manual, The ; containing the acts of congress imposing direct and excise taxes, with complete marginal references and an analytical index, showing all the items of taxation, the mode of proceeding and the duties of the officers, with an explan. pref. N. Y. 1862. O. **343.1 : 9**

Redfield, Amasa Angell, *comp.* A hand-book of the U. S. tax law, approved july 1, 1862, with all the amendments to march 4, 1863 ; comprising the decisions of the commissioner of internal revenue, together with copious notes and explanations, for the use of tax-payers of every class and the officers of the revenue of all the states and territories. From official sources. N. Y. 1863. D. **343.1 : 10**

Carpenter, M. B. Mining code ; a compilation of all the existing mining, water, preemption and homestead laws of the U. S. and the state of Colorado, mining decisions of the courts and dep't of the interior, articles of incorporation and by-laws for mining companies, comments, forms, etc. 2d ed. Denver. 1879. O. **343.1 : 3**

U. S.—Special states.

Smucker, S: M., *ed.* The blue laws of Connecticut ; a collection of the earliest statutes and judicial proceedings of that colony, being an exhibition of the rigorous morals and legislation of the puritans ; with an introd. Phila. 1861. D. **343.12 : 501**

Trumbull, J. Hammond. The true-blue laws of Connecticut and New Haven and the false blue laws invented by the rev. S: Peters ; added, specimens of the laws and judicial proceedings of other colonies, and some blue laws of England in the reign of James I. Hartford, Conn. 1876. D. **343.12 : 502**

Boston *city.* Ordinances, and rules and orders of the city of Boston ; together with a digest of the general and special statutes of the Massachusetts legislature relating to the city. Pub. by order of the city council. Bost. 1876. O. **343.12 : 402**

New York *city.* Ordinances of the mayor, aldermen and commonalty, rev. 1859 by D. T. Valentine. Adopted by the common council and pub. by their authority. N. Y. 1859. O. **343.13 : 1**

Chicago *city.* Charter, 1867. Chicago. 1867. O. **343.15 : Pam**

Michigan *territory.* Laws, condensed, arranged and passed by the fifth legislative council ; together with the declaration of independence, the constitution of the U. S., the ordinance of 1787, and the acts of congress relative to said territory. Pub. by authority. Detroit. 1833. O. *in* **343.15 : D**

— *state. Legislature.* The compiled laws of the state of Mich., comp. and arr. under an act of the legisl. approved jan. 25, 1871,

Michigan *state.* *Legislature.—Continued.*
[by] James S. Dewey. Lansing. 1872. 2 v.
O.   *in* **343.15 : D**
— — General acts, and joint and concurrent resolutions, passed at the regular session of
1871, with app. Lansing. 1871. O.
                                             in **343.15 : D**
— — Acts, passed at the extra session of 1872, with
app. Lansing. 1872. O.   *in* **343.15 : D**
— — General acts, aud joint and concurrent resolutions, passed at the reg. session of 1873,
with app. Lansing. 1873. O. *in* **343.15 : D**
— — General [and local] acts, and joint and concurrent resolutions, passed at the extra
session of 1874, with app. Lausing. 1874.
O.   *in* **343.15 : D**
— — Public acts, and joint and concurrent resolutions passed at the regular session of
1875 [1877, 1879, 1881], with app. Lansing.
1875–81. 4 v. O.   *in* **343.15 : D**
— — Index to the general laws, enacted by the
legislature 1872—1881, and to sections and
chapters of the compiled laws amended or
repealed. Prep. and pub. under the supervision of the sec. of state. Lansing. 1881.
O. *With* Public acts for 1881.
                                             in **343.15 : D**
— — Public [and local] acts, and joint and concurrent resolutions, passed at the extra
session of 1882, with app. Lansing. 1882.
O.   *in* **343.15 : D**
— — Laws of the state, relating to highways and
bridges, with blank forms. Lansing. 1881.
O.   *bound with*
— — Laws of the state, rel. to drainage, with
blank forms. Lansing. 1881. O. *bound with*
— — Fish and game laws ; laws rel. to the protec-
tion of fish and of game, comp. in aug.
1881.   *bound with*
— — The liquor laws ; laws rel. to the manufac-
ture and sale of malt, spirituous, or intox-
icating liquors, comp. in aug. 1881.
                                             in **343.15 : D**
Wisconsin *territory.* *Legislative assembly.*
Acts passed at the 1st [2d and special] session, 1836-1838. [Reprinted] Madison. 1867.
O.   *in* **343.15 : D**
Contains the laws passed at the
  1st leg. 1st sess., oct. 25—dec. 9, 1836. Belmont, 1836.
    2d   "   nov. 6, 1837—jan. 20, 1838., *pub. with*
    special sess., june 11—25, 1838. Burlington,
    Ia., 1838.
— — Statutes of the territory of Wisconsin, passed
by the legislative assembly thereof, at a
session commencing in nov. 1838, and at
an adjourned session, commencing in jan.
1839. Pub. by authority of the leg. assembly. Albany. 1839. O.   *in* **343.15 : D**
Note. Contains also the general laws, passed at the
  2d leg. 1st sess. nov. 26 —dec. 22, 1838, *and*
    2d   "   jan. 21—march 11, 1839.
    The local acts of both sessions were pub-
    lished together and printed in Milwaukee,
    1839; but this volume is not in the library.
— — Laws passed by the [second to fifth] legislative assemblies. 1839 –1848. Milw. *and* Madison. 1840-48. 3 v. O.   *in* **343.15 : D**
Contains the following laws bound in 3 v. :
  2d leg. 3d sess. dec. 2, 1839—jan. 13. 1840. Milw. 1840.
    special sess. aug. 3—14, 1840, *interspersed with*
  3d leg. 1st sess. dec. 7, 1840—feb. 19, 1841; with app.
    [cont. Supreme court decisions, 1839—40].
    Mad. 1841.
    An act to provide for the gov. of the several
    towns in this terr., and for the revision of
    county gov. Mad. 1841.

Wisconsin *territory.— Continued.*
    2d sess. dec. 6, 1841 – feb. 19, 1842: with app.
      [cont. supreme court reports, 1841]. Mad.
      1842.
  4th leg. 1st sess. dec. 5, 1842—march 26. 1843, and
      march 27—apr. 17, 1843. Mad. 1843.
    2d sess. dec. 4, 1843—jan. 31, 1844. Mad. 1844,
      with Supreme court reports, 1842 and 1843,
      rep. by T. P. Burnett.
    3d sess. jan. 6—feb. 24, 1845. Mad. 1845.
      4th   "   jan. 5—feb. 3, 1846. Mad. 1846.
  5th leg. 1st sess. jan. 4—feb. 11, 1847. Mad. 1847.
    special sess. oct. 18—27. 1847. Mad. 1847.
    2d sess. feb. 7—march 13, 1848. Mad. 1848.
Wisconsin *state.* *Legislature.* Laws, together
with the joint resolutions and memorials
passed at the first session, commencing
june 1, and ending aug. 31, [1848]. Mad.
1848. D.   *in* **343.15 : D**
— — Acts and resolves passed in 1849. together
with memorials to congress. Mad. 1849. O.
                                             in **343.15 : D**
Note. From this time to 1883, the sessions were annual and opened on the 2d wednesday in jan.; after
1883, biennial.
— — The revised statutes of the state of Wisconsin, passed at the 2d session of the
legisl., commencing jan. 10, 1849 ; prefixed,
the declaration of independence and the
constitutions of the U. S. and the state of
Wis.; with app. containing certain acts
required to be pub. therewith. Southport
[Kenosha]. 1849. Q.   *in* **343.15 : D**
— — Acts and resolves passed in 1850[-1852], together with memorials to congress. Madison *and* Kenosha. 1850-52. 3 v. O.
                                             in **343.15 : D**
— — Supp. to the Revised statutes of the state of
Wis., containing all the general laws and
amendments enacted since the revision of
the statutes up to the present date, being,
with the Revised statutes, a complete transcript of all gen. laws now in force in this
state. Compiled from the official records
[by] C. Latham **Sholes**]. Kenosha. 1852. O.
With Laws for 1852.   *in* **343.15 : D**
— — General acts, passed in 1853[-1858], together
with memorials and resolutions. Madison.
1853-58. 6 v. O.   *in* **343.15 : D**
Note. The laws enacted during the special sessions,
june 6—july 13, 1853 *and* sept. 3—oct. 14, 1856, are pub.
with the laws of the regular sessions of the resp.
years.
— — Private and local acts, passed in 1853[-1858].
Madison. 1853-58. O.   *in* **343.15 : D**
Note. Each year is bound with the general acts of
the same year.
— — The revised statutes of the state of Wisconsin, passed at the annual session of the
legislature commencing jan. 13, 1858, and
approved may 17, 1858 ; prefixed, the declaration of independence and the constitutions of the U. S. and the state of Wis.;
with app. containing certain acts required
to be pub. therewith. Chicago. 1858. Q.
                                             in **343.15 : D**
— — General laws, passed in 1859[-1868], together
with joint resolutions and memorials.
Madison 1859-68. 10 v. O.   *in* **343.15 : D**
— — Private and local laws, passed in 1859[-1868].
Madison. 1859-68. O.   *in* **343.15 : D**
Note. Each year is bound with the general laws of
the same year.
— — A digest of the laws of Wisconsin from 1858
to 1868 incl.; added an app., giving a list
of all the laws and provisions of the con-

Wisconsin *state. Legislature.—Continued.*

stitution passed upon by the supreme court ; comp. by E. A. **Spencer.** Madison. 1868. O.   *in* **343.15 : D**

– – General laws, passed in 1869[–1871], together with joint resolutions and memorials. Madison. 1869-71. 3 v. O.   *in* **343.15 : D**

– – Private and local laws, passed in 1869[–1871]. Madison, 1869-71. O.   *in* **343.15 : D**

Note. Each year is bound with the general laws of the same year.

– – The revised statutes of the state of Wisconsin, as altered and amended by subsequent legislation ; together with the unrepealed statutes of a general nature, passed from the time of the revision of 1858 to the close of the legislature of 1871, arr. in the same manner as the statutes for 1858. with references showing the time of the enactment of each section, and also references to judicial decisions in relation to and explanatory of the statutes, prepared and arr. by D: **Taylor.** St. Louis. 1871. 2 v. Q.   *in* **343.15 : D**

– – General laws passed in 1872, together with joint resolutions and memorials. Madison. 1872. O.   *bound with*

– – Private and local laws passed in 1872. Madison. 1872. O.   *in* **343.15 : D**

– – A synoptical index of the general and private and local laws of Wisconsin from the organization of the territory to 1873 incl. [comp. by Roger C. **Spooner**]. Madison. 1873. O.   *in* **343.15 : D**

– – The laws of Wisconsin, together with joint resolutions and memorials, passed in 1873 [–1878]. Madison. 1873-78. 6 v. O.   *in* **343.15 : D**

– – A bill to revise the general statutes, prepared and reported to the legislature of 1878 by the revisers appointed pursuant to ch. 203, laws of 1875, and acts amendatory thereof. Madison. 1878. Q.   *in* **343.15 : D**

– – Report and explanatory notes of the revisers of the statutes, accompanying the bill to revise the general laws of Wis., submitted to the leg. of 1878. Madison. 1878. O.   *in* **343.15 : D**

– – Revised statutes of the state of Wisconsin, passed at the extra session of the legislature, commencing june 4, 1878, and approved june 7, 1878 ; prefixed, the constitution of the U. S. and the state of Wis., with app. containing certain acts of congress required to be pub. therein. Madison. 1878. Q.   *in* **343.15 : D**

– – *Same.*   **343.15 : R301**

Note. The laws passed at the extra session, in addition to the rev. statutes, are pub. at the end of the laws enacted at the regular session of 1878.

– – The laws of Wisconsin, passed at the annual session of 1879 [–1882]; together with joint resolutions and memorials. Madison. 1879-82. 4 v. O.   *in* **343.15 : D**

– – The laws of Wisconsin, passed at the biennial session of 1883, together with joint resolutions and memorials. Madison. 1883. 2 v. O.   *in* **343.15 : D**

Contents. V. 1. Laws, except city charters. 2. Laws relating to city charters and their amendments.

– – Index to the session laws of the state of Wisconsin, enacted by the legisl. during 1879— 1883, with reference to sections or chapters

Wisconsin *state. Legislature.—Continued.*

of the Revised statutes altered, amended or repealed ; prep. and pub. under the supervision of the sec. of state. Madison. 1883. O.   *With* Laws of 1883, v. 1. *in* **343.15 : D**

– – Supp. to the Revised statutes of the state of Wisconsin 1878 ; containing the general laws from 1878 to 1883, with the revisers' notes to the statutes of 1878, and notes to cases construing and applying these and similar statutes by the supreme court of Wis. and the courts of other states. Comp. and annotated by A. L. **Sanborn** and J. R. **Berryman.** Chicago. 1883. O.   **343.15 : R301**

Wisconsin. *Laws on special subjects.* [Laws providing for town and county government]. *See* Session laws for 1840-41.

– – Laws of Wis. relating to the organization and gov. of towns and the powers and duties of town officers, with practical forms, by E. M. **Haines.** Madison. 1858. O.   *in* **343.15 : D**

– – *Same,* by J: C. **Spooner** and E. E. **Bryant.** Madison. 1869. O.   *in* **343.15 : D**

– – *Same,* by J: C. **Spooner** and Hiram **Hayes.** Madison. 1879. O.   *in* **343.15 : D**

– – The assessment laws of the state, with forms and instructions ; rev. by Ll. **Breese,** sec. of state. Madison. 1872. O.   *in* **343.15 : D**

– – Compilation of the assessment laws of the state, with forms and instructions ; rev. by P: **Doyle,** sec. of state.   *in* **343.15 : D**

– – Election laws of the state, with extracts from the constitution ; together with forms and instructions for the use of clerks, inspectors, etc. Prepared under the dir. of D: W. **Jones,** sec. of state, by J: W. **Hunt.** Madison. 1857. O.   *in* **343.15 : D**

– – Election and registry laws of the state, with forms and instructions for the use of county and town officers; rev. by P: **Doyle,** sec. of state. Madison. 1876. O.   *bound with*

– – The registry and election laws, *etc.,* comp. by Hans B. **Warner,** sec. of state, 1878 and 1879. Madison. 1878-79. 2 v. in 1. O.   *in* **343.15 : D**

– – Compilation of the U. S. laws, state laws, decisions, messages and correspondence, relating to the swamp and overflowed land fund of the state of Wisconsin. Pub. by authority, 1882. Madison. 1882. O.   *in* **343.15 : D**

Milwaukee *city.* Charter and ordinances and amendatory acts ; together with a list of officers, and rules and regulations of the common council. Milw. 1853.   **343.15 : D350**

– Charter and ordinances, with the constitution of the state and acts of the legislature relating to the city, incl. a list of officers, and the rules and regulations of the common council, dec. 5, 1856. Milw. 1857. O.   **343.15 : D351**

– – Acts of the legislature of 1857, amendatory and otherwise, relating to the city of Milwaukee. Milw. 1857. O.   **343.15 : D352**

– – Amendments to the charter, approved march 27th 1858. Milw. 1858. O.   *in* **343.15 : D532**

– – [Acts of the legislature of 1859, relating to Milw.] *n. t.* O.   *in* **343.15 : D352**

Milwaukee *city.—Continued.*
— - The proposed new city charter. Milw. 1868.
O.   **343.15 : D353**
— - Acts of the legislature, relating to the city
of Milwaukee, a. d. 1871. Milw. 1871. O.
                                            in **343.15 : D353**
— - *Same*, a. d. 1872. *n. p.*   *in* **343.15 : D353**
— - The charter of the city of Milwaukee [codi-
fied and amended up to 1873]. [Milw.
1873]. O.   *in* **343.15 : D353**
— - An act to revise, consolidate and amend the
charter of the city of Milwaukee and the
several acts amendatory thereof, approved
march 10, 1874. Madison. 1874. O.
                                            in **343.15 : D353**
— The charter and ordinances of the city of
Milwaukee, with an app. [containing special laws and ordinances]. Milw. 1875. O.
                                                      343.15 : D353
— - Amendments, passed by the legislature, 1875–
1878.   *in* **343.15 : D353**
Note. For further amendments, see Wisconsin
session laws, in 343.15 : D
— Acts of the legislature of Wis., in relation to
supplying the city with pure and wholesome water ; acts of the legislature and an
ordinance of the city, authorizing the issue
of bonds for the construction of water
works in said city ; and statistics of taxation and municipal indebtedness. Milw.
1872. O. *With* City documents, 1872–73.
                                               in **351.15 : D**
— *Board of aldermen.* Rules, 1865. Milw. 1865.
D.   **347 : Pam**
— - Rules for the government of the board of
aldermen, adopted a. d. 1872. Milw. 1872.
D.   **347 : Pam**
— *Board of councilors.* Rules for the govern-
ment of the board of councilors, adopted
a. d. 1872-3. Milw. 1873. D.   **347 : Pam**
— *Fire dep't.* Rules and regulations for the gov-
ernment of the fire dep. and sup't of the
fire alarm telegraph, adopted by the chief
engineer and joint committee on fire dep.
Milw. 1870. S.   **343.15 : 361**

Great Britain.

Blackstone, *Sir* W: Commentaries on the laws
of England, in 4 books ; with notes sel.
from the eds. of Archbold, Christian, Coleridge, Chitty, Stewart, Kerr and others,
baron Field's analysis, and add. notes and
a life of the author by G: Sharswood ; in
2 v. V. 1. Phila. 1864. O.   **343.2+2**
— *Same.* Phila. 1880. 2 v. O.   **343.2 : R1**
Great Britain. *Commissioners on the public
records.* Ancient laws and institutes of
England ; comprising laws enacted under
the anglo-saxon kings from Æthelbirht to
Cnut, with an english trans. of the saxon,
the laws called Edward the confessor's,
the laws of William the conqueror and
those ascribed to Henry I, also Monumenta
ecclesiastica anglicana from the 7th to the
10th century and the ancient latin version
of the anglo-saxon laws with a compendious glossary, etc. Lond. 1840. 2 v. Q.
                                                      343.2+3
Dalton, Michael. Officium vice-comitum ; the
office and authority of sheriffs, gathered
out of the statutes and books of the common laws of this kingdom, to which is
added an app... Lond. 1682. F.   **23 : R**

5. Criminal law.

American social science association. Three
papers on crime. Bost. 1883. O.   **345 : 11**
Contents. Colby, James F. Disfranchisement for
crime.—Hill, Edwin. A plan for extinguishing crime.
—Hill, Hamilton Andrews. Punishment for certain
crimes.
Livingstone, E: Complete works on criminal
jurisprudence ; consisting of systems of
penal law for the state of Louisiana and for
the U. S. of America ; with the introd. reports to the same. Prefixed, an introd. by
Salmon P. Chase. N. Y. 1873. 2 v. O.
                                                      345.1+1
Redfield, H. V. Homicide, north and south ; a
comparative view of crime against the person in several parts of the U. S. Phila. 1880.
D.   **345.1 : 2**
Bovee, Marvin H. Reasons for abolishing capi-
tal punishment. Chicago. 1873. D. **345 : 7**
Cheever, G: Barrell. Punishment by death ; its
authority and expediency. N. Y. 1855. D.
                                                      345 : 8
Whately, R: Remarks on transportation, and
on a recent defence of the system ; in a 2d
letter to earl Grey. Lond. 1834. O.
                                                      345.2 : 1
Geyer, A: Ueber die den unrecht angeklagten
oder verurtheilten gebührende entschädigung. *In* Deutsche zeit- und streit-fragen.
                                                   304 : 15 v11
Kayser, Paul. Der zeugnisszwang im strafver-
fahren, in geschichtlicher entwickelung.
In Deutsche zeit- und streit-fragen.
                                                    304 : 15 v8
Hergenhahn, Theodor. Das antragsrecht im
deutschen strafrecht. *In* Deutsche zeit-
und streit-fragen.   **304 : 15 v7**
Osenbrüggen, E: Eine metamorphose im deutschen strafrecht. *In* Deutsche zeit- und
streit-fragen.   **304 : 15 v7**

Criminal trials.

Demme, W: L: Das buch der verbrechen ; das
interessanteste aus den 90 heften meiner
annalen der deutschen und ausländischen
criminalrechtspflege ; ein volksbuch in 4
b. V. 2-4. Leipz. 1851. D.   **345 : 1**
— Das buch der verbrechen ; das interessanteste
aus älterer, neuerer und neuester zeit der
länder dies- und jenseits des Oceans ; ein
volksbuch. Neue folge. Leipz. 1852. 4 v.
D.   **345 : 2**
Grieb, Christian F: *ed.* Dunkle thaten der civilisirten menschheit mit providenziellen
lichtblicken ; für leser aller stände. Stuttg.
1850. 6 v. T.   **345 : 3**
Löffler, K: Unschuldig verurtheilt ; entschlei-
erte geheimnisse aus den hallen der justiz.
2te aufl. N. Y. 1874. O   **345 : 4**
Morse, J: Torrey, *jr.* Famous trials. Bost. 1874.
O.   **345 : 9**
Contents. The Tichborne claimant.—Troppmann.—
Prince Pierre Bonaparte.—Mrs. Wharton.—The me-
teor.—Mrs. Fair.
Nachtseiten der gesellschaft ; eine gallerie merk-
würdiger verbrechen und rechtsfälle. 2te
serie. Leipz. 1848. 8 v. D.   **345 : 6**
Sikes, W: Wirt. Studies of assassination. Lond.
1881. D.   **345 : 10**
Contents. Catherine de Medici.—William of Orange.
The gunpowder plot. — Charlotte Corday. - Abraham
Lincoln.—Alexander II. of Russia.

Chandler, Peleg Whitman. American criminal trials. Bost. 1844. 2 v. D.   **345.1:3**
Contents. V. 1. Anne Hutchinson.—The quakers.—Salem witchcraft. — T: Maule. — J: P: Zenger.—N. Y. negro plot.—Leisler's rebellion.—Col. Bayard's treason.—The crew of the Pitt packet.—The Boston massacre. V. 2. Bathsheba Spooner and others. — Col. Henley. — Major André. — Joshua H. Smith. — The Rhode Island judges. — John Hauer and others. — App.—Notes.

United States. *Senate.* Trial of Andrew Johnson, pres. of the U. S., before the senate of the U. S. on impeachment by the house of representatives for high crimes and misdemeanors ; pub. by order of the senate. Wash. 1868. 3 v. O.   **345.1:D**
Contents. V. 1. Preliminaries. — Opening arguments. — Evidence. 2. Arguments and final vote. 3. Opinions and app.

— — Proceedings in the trial of W: W. Belknap, late sec. of war on the articles of impeachment exhibited by the house of representatives. (Congressional record, vol. 4, pt. 7.) Wash. 1876. Q.   *in* **328.1:D**

Wisconsin. *Senate.* Trial of impeachment of Levi Hubbell, judge of the second judicial circuit, by the senate of the state of Wisconsin, june 1853 ; reported by T. C. Leland, Madison. 1853. O.   *in* **345.15:D**

— — Journal of the court for the trial of impeachment, state of Wis. vs. Levi Hubbell. Madison. 1853. O. *With the above.*
    in **345.15:D**

State trials. A complete collection of state-trials and proceedings for high-treason and other crimes and misdemeanours ; the 4th ed., commencing with the 11th year of the reign of king Richard II and ending with the 16th year of the reign of king George III [1388—1749] ; with two alphabetical tables to the whole. Prefixed, a new preface by Francis Hargrave. Lond 1776-81. 11 v. F.   **-345.2:R6**

Browne, G. Latham. Narratives of state trials in the 19th century, 1st period : From the union with Ireland to the death of George IV, 1801—1830. Bost. 1882. 2 v. D.
    345.2:2

Society for the diffusion of useful knowledge. Library of entertaining knowledge : Criminal trials. Lond. 1832, 1835. 2 v. S.
    345.2:3
Contents. V. 1. Sir N: Throckmorton. — Duke of Norfolk.—Dr. W: Parry.—Earl of Essex. — Sir Walter Raleigh. 2. The gunpowder plot.

Amos, Andrew. The great oyer of poisoning ; the trial of the earl of Somerset for the poisoning of sir T: Overbury in the tower of London, and various matters connected therewith, from contemporary mss. Lond. 1846. O.   **345.2:5**

Griffiths, Arthur. The chronicles of Newgate. New ed. Ill. N. Y. 1884. O.   **345.2:4**

Feuerbach, Paul J: Anselm, *ritter* v. Narratives of remarkable criminal trials. Tr. from the german by lady Duff Gordon. N. Y. 1855. S.
    345.3:1
Contents. J: Paul Forster.—The Antonini family.—Francis Riembauer.—The unknown murderer.—Anna Maria Zwanziger. — James Thalreuter. — The Kleinschrot family.—J: G: Sörgel.—G: Wachs.—G: Rauschmaier. — Andrew Bichel. — J: Holzinger. — Caspar Frisch.—L: Steiner.

6. Maritime and martial law.

Amos, Sheldon. Political and legal remedies for war. N. Y. 1880. D.   **346:1**

Leavenworth, Jesse H., *late col. 2d Col. vol.* Judge advocate general's report and endorsements thereon in [his] case. Milw. 1881. O.   **346:Pam**

Bowles, T: Gibson. Maritime warfare. Lond. 1878. O.   **346:5**

Jacobsen, F: J. Laws of the sea, with reference to maritime commerce, during peace and war. From the german, Altona 1815, by W: Frick. Balt. 1818. O.   **346:2**

Johnstone, H. A. Munro-Butler-. Handbook of maritime rights, and the declaration of Paris considered. Lond. 1876. D.   **346:4**

Ward, Robert. A treatise of the relative rights and duties of belligerent and neutral powers in maritime affairs, in which the principles of armed neutralities and the opinions of Hubner and Schlegel are fully discussed. Repr. from the original ed., with a pref. by lord Stanley of Alderley, and an app. Lond. 1875. O.   **346:6**

Exquemelin, Alexandre Olivier. The history of the buccaneers of America ; containing detailed accounts of those bold and daring freebooters, chiefly along the Spanish main, in the West Indies, and in the great south sea, succeeding the civil wars in England. New ed. with some introd. notices of piracies on the coast of New England to the year 1724. Bost. [1851]. O.   **346:3**

7. Civil and canon law.

Arnold, W. T. The roman system of provincial administration to the accession of Constantine the great ; the Arnold prize essay for 1879. Lond. 1879. D.   **347:12**

Hadley, James. Introduction to roman law ; in twelve academical lectures. N. Y. 1881. D.
    347:6

Mackenzie, T:, *lord Mackenzie.* Studies in roman law, with comparative views of the laws of France, England and Scotland ; ed. by J: Kirkpatrick. 5th ed., rev. Edinb. 1880. O.
    347:9

Morey, W: C. Outline of roman law ; comprising its historical and general principles. N. Y. 1884. O.   **347:10**

Stammler, C: Das römische recht in Deutschland. *In* Deutsche zeit- und streitfragen.
    304:15 v9

France. Code Napoléon ; *avec* Répertoire alphabétique et raisonné pour l'éd. seule officielle dans le grand-duché de Wurzbourg. *n. p. or d.* O.   **347:4**
Note. Contains also a german transl., "Napoleons gesetzbuch".

Fulton, J: The law of marriage ; containing the hebrew law, the roman law, the law of the New testament, and the canon law of the universal church concerning the impediments of marriage and the dissolution of the marriage bond ; digested and arr. with notes and scholia. N. Y. 1883. D.
    347:7

Parliamentary law.

Bain, Alexander. Procedure of deliberative bodies. *In his* Practical essays. **824.2 : 91**

Cushing, Luther Stearns. Lex parlamentaria americana ; elements of the law and practice of legislative assemblies in the U. S. of America. 9th ed. Bost. 1874. O.
    347 : R1

—- Manual of parliamentary practice ; rules of proceeding and debate in deliberative assemblies, rev. by Edmund L. Cushing. Bost. 1880. T.
    347 : 2

Fish, G: T. American manual of parliamentary law, or Common law of deliberative assemblies, systematically arr. for the use of the parliamentarian and the novice. N. Y. 1880. S.
    347 : 3

Robert, H: M. Pocket manual of rules of order for deliberative assemblies : pt. 1, Rules of order ; a compendium of parliamentary law, based upon the rules and practice of congress ; pt. 2, Organization and conduct of business, a simple explanation of the methods of organizing and conducting the business of societies, conventions and other deliberative assemblies. Chicago. 1883. S.
    347 : 8

— The parliamentary guide ; a simple explanation of the methods of organizing and conducting the business of societies, conventions and other deliberative assemblies, incl. the various motions and a table of rules relating to motions, containing answers to 200 questions in parliamentary practice, from the Pocket manual of rules of order. Chicago. 1877. T.
    347 : 5

Spofford, Ainsworth Rand. A practical manual of parliamentary rules ; comp. for the ready reference of societies, conventions, public meetings, and deliberative and legislative assemblies. Chicago. 1884. S.
    347 : 11

8. Administrative law.

Zachariä, H: Albert. Das moderne schöffengericht. *In* Deutsche zeit- und streit-fragen.
    304 : 15 v1

Bar, K: L: v. Das deutsche reichsgericht. *In* Deutsche zeit- und streit-fragen.
    304 : 15 v4

American law register, The ; v. 13–15, nov. 1864–oct. 1867. Phila. 1864–67. O. **305.4 : M**

Wisconsin legal news ; v. 1–6, sept. 1878–july 1884. Milw. 1878–84. F. **305.4 : RM**

Wisconsin. *Supreme court.* Decisions, july term 1839 and aug. term 1840. (App. to Session laws, 1840–1).
    in **343.15 : D**

— - Cases decided at july term 1841, rep. by T. P. **Burnett.** (App. to session laws, 1841–2).
    in **343.15 : D**

— - Reports for 1842 and 1843, rep. by T. P. **Burnett.** Madison. 1844. O. *With* Session laws, 1843–4.
    in **343.15 : D**

Note. All of the above are reprinted in 1 Pinney.

— - Reports of cases argued and determined [1849–1852], by D: H. **Chandler.** Milw. 1850–54. 4 v. in 3. O.
    in **348.15 : D**

Note. Reprinted in 2 and 3 Pinney.

— - Reports of cases argued and determined [1839–1852] ; with tables of the cases and

Wisconsin. *Supreme court.—Continued.*
principal matters, and the rules of the several courts in force since 1838, by S. U. **Pinney.** Chicago. 1873–76. 3 v. O.
    in **348.15 : D**

Note. A pref. in v. 1 gives a sketch of the leading events of the early political and judicial history of Wisconsin.

— - Reports of cases argued and determined [1853–dec. 16, 1884] ; with tables of the cases and principal matters, [reported by] Abram D. **Smith** (v. 1–11), Philip L. **Spooner** (v. 12–15), O. M. **Conover** (v. 16–58 ; 55–58 prep. and ed. by F: K. Conover), F: K. **Conover** (v. 59–61). Chicago. 1868–85. 61 v. in 60. O.
    in **348.15 : D**

Note. Known as "The Wisconsin reports." V. 1–22 are a republication by the state of the original reports, with notes to v. 3 and 5 by Luther S. Dixon, and to v. 1, 2, 4 and 6–20 by W: F. Vilas and Edwin E. Bryant; v. 8 and 9 being bound as one. V. 16, though bearing the name of Conover as official rep., was actually prepared by S. U. Pinney.

— - A digest of Wisconsin reports [1839–1879] ; comprising all the published decisions of the supreme court of Wisconsin with references to the statutes, by James **Simmons.** Albany. 1874–79. 3 v. O.
    in **348.15 : D**

Contents. V. 1. To 1868, Burnett's, Chandler's and 20 vols. of Wisconsin reports. **2.** Pinney's reports, v. 1, and Wisconsin reports, v. 21–31. **3.** Pinney's reports, v. 2, 3, and Wisconsin reports, v. 32–43.

— - - Index-digest of the Wisconsin reports, embracing all the decisions of the supreme court of Wisconsin [1839–1882], by Merritt **Starr.** Chicago. 1883. O.
    in **348.15 : D**

9. Forms of practice.

Manual of the revised statutes of the state of New York, or A complete series of all the practical forms or precedents required by the revised statutes ; with appropriate directions, explanations and referenees to cases adjudged in the courts of said state and in the supreme court of the U. S., and designed for the use of professional men, officers, civil and military, and other citizens of said state ; in 5 parts. Prep. and comp. by a counsellor at law. Glen's Falls. 1831. O.
    349 : 3

Wisconsin. Rules of practice for the district court of the U. S. for the district of Wisconsin. Milw. 1848. O.
    349 : 1

— The code of procedure of the state, passed by the legisl. approved oct. 11, 1856, arr. and printed under the superintendence of J. C. Hopkins. Madison. 1856. O. *in* **349 : D**

— The code of procedure of the state, as passed by the legisl. in 1856 and amended in 1856 and 1857 ; pub. by dir. of D: W. Jones, sec. of state, with corr. and index by J : W. Hunt, asst. sec. Madison. 1857. O.
    in **349 : D**

— The code of procedure of the state, as passed by the legisl. in 1856 and amended in 1857–59, with app. containing the rules of the supreme and circuit courts, the time of holding the terms of court in the various circuits and of the U. S. district court, also a complete index. Comp. by Walter S. Carter. Milw. 1859. O. *in* **349 : D**

McMullen, Joseph F. The new Wisconsin form book ; a compendium of legal and practi-

McMullen, Joseph F.—*Continued.*
cal forms, incl. of probate practice, with principles of law adapted to the statutes of Wisconsin ; added, complete official forms and instructions under the recent

patent, bounty and homestead acts. 4th ed., rev. and enl. Milw. 1880. O. **349 : R2**

Eck, Ernst. Die neue deutsche civil-prozessordnung. *In* Deutsche zeit- und streitfragen.   **304 : 15 v2**

6. Administration.

1. In general.

Gillett, Ransom H. The federal government ; its officers and their duties. N. Y. 1871. D.   **350.1 : 2**

Lamphere, G: N. The U. S. government ; its organization and practical workings, including the declaration of independence, the constitution of the U. S., and a description of the three grand divisions of the government, namely the legislative, executive and judicial departments, their powers and duties, with the number, title and compensation of all persons employed in each, together with many interesting facts and histories. Phila. 1880. O.   **350.1 : 1**

United States. Official register of the U. S., containing a list of officers and employees in the civil, military and naval service, together with a list of ships and vessels belonging to the U. S., 1831, 1835, 1839, 1843, 1847, 1849, 1851, 1853, 1855, 1857, 1859, 1861, 1863, 1865, 1867, 1871, 1873, 1875, 1877, 1879, 1881, 1883. Wash. 1831–84. 26 v. D. and Q.   *in* **350.1 : D**
Note. Frequently designated as the "Blue book of the U. S."; the title sometimes reads "Biennial register, etc."
For reports of officers and bureaus of the national and state governments, *see* Legislative annals, class 328, col. 173–181.

Black book, The, or Corruption unmasked ; an account of places, pensions and sinecures, the revenues of the clergy and landed aristocracy, the salaries and emoluments in courts of justice and the police dep't, the expenditure of the civil list, the amount and application of the droits of the crown and admiralty, the robbery of charitable foundations, the profits of the bank of England, arising from the issue of its notes, balances of public money, management of the borough debt, and other sources of emolument, the debt, revenue and influence of the East India company, the state of the finances, debt and sinking fund. Added, correct lists of both houses of parliament from 1819 to 1828, showing their family connections, parliamentary influence, the places and pensions held by themselves or relations ; with a supp. and app., the whole forming an exposition of the cost, influence, patronage and corruption of the borough government. New ed. Lond. 1828. 2 v. O.   **350.2 : 1**

Haas, Claude P: Marie. Administration de la France ; histoire et mécanisme des grands pouvoirs de l'état, fonctions publiques, conditions d'admission et d'avancement dans toutes les carrières, priviléges et immunités. 2e éd. Paris. 1861. 4 v. O.   **350.3 : 1**

Isaacsohn, S. Geschichte des preussischen beamtenthums vom anfang des 15. jahrhunderts bis auf die gegenwart. Berlin. 1874, 1878. 2 v. O.   **350.3 : 2**

Oesfeld, Max v. Preussen in staatsrechtlicher, kameralistischer und staatswirthschaftlicher beziehung ; ein populäres hand- und hülfslehrbuch der inneren staatsverfassungs- und verwaltungs-kunde überhaupt ; zunächst für den preussischen staatsbürger, insbesondere aber für diejenigen welche sich dem staatsverwaltungs- und justiz-dienste widmen. 2te durchaus neu umgearb. und verm. aufl. Breslau. 1870, 1871. 2 v. O.   **350.3 : 3**
Note. For the administration of the English government, see also class 323.2, col. 162–163; and of the U. S., class 324.1, col. 164–168.

2. Civil service.

Foster, W: E. The literature of civil service reform in the U. S. [Young men's political club of Rhode Island.] Providence. 1881. O.   **351.1 : 1**
— The civil service reform movement. Bost. 1881. D.   **351.1 : 2**

Civil-service reform association. Publications, no. 1–5, 7. N. Y. 1881–82. D.   **351.1 : 5**
Contents. **1.** Purposes of the assoc. **2.** The beginning of the spoils system in the national gov., 1829–30; repr. from Parton's Life of Jackson. **3. Eaton,** Dorman B. The spoils system and civil-service reform in the custom-house and post office at N. Y. custom-house. **4. Brown,** Willard. Civil-service reform in the N. Y. custom-house. **5. Eaton,** Dorman B. The term and tenure of office; 2d ed. abr. **7. Godkin,** E. L. The danger of an office-holding aristocracy.
— *Same:* Daniel Webster and the spoils system ; an extract from sen. Bayard's oration at Dartmouth college, june 1882. N. Y. 1882. D.   *in* **351.1 : 5**

National civil-service reform league. Proceedings at the annual meeting held at Newport, R. I., aug. 2, 1882, with the address of the pres., hon. G: W: Curtis. N. Y. 1882. O.   **363 : Pam**
— Report on the expediency of asking candidates for public office their views of civil service reform ; with the resolutions adopted by the exec. com. june 22, 1882. N. Y. 1882. O.   **363 : Pam**
— An address to the reverend clergy of all denominations in the U. S. N. Y. 1883. O.   **363 : Pam**
— The progress of reform, an address del. at the annual meeting by G: W: Curtis. N. Y. 1883. O.   **363 : Pam**

Milwaukee civil service reform assoc. Annual meeting, may 3, 1883. [Milw. 1883]. O.   **363 : Pam**
— *Same.* May 7, 1884. [Milw. 1884]. O.   **363 : Pam**

Eaton, Dorman B. Civil service in Great Britain ; history of abuses and reforms, and their bearing upon american politics. N. Y. 1880. O.   **351.2 : 1**
— *Same.* (Frank. sq. lib.) N. Y. 1881. Q.
     351.2+1
Bain, Alexander. The civil service examinations. *In his* Practical essays.   824.2 : 91
Copp, H: N., *ed.* U. S. salary list and civil service law, rules and regulations, with specimen examination questions in the custom house, post office and classified departmental service. Wash. 1883. O.   **351.1 : 4**
United States. *Civil service commission.* 1st, 2d annual reports. Wash. 1884, 1885. O.
     in **351.1 : D**
— *Same.*   **351.1 : 6**
Kerr, R. W. History of the government printing office at Washington, D. C., with a brief record of the public printing for a century, 1789—1881. Ill. Lancaster. Pa. 1881. O.
     351.1+3
Baker, Lafayette C. History of the U. S. secret service. Phila. 1867. O.   **354.1 : 1**

Municipal governments.

New York *city.* Manual of the corporation of the city of New York, 1863 [by] D. T. Valentine.   *in* **351.13 : D**
— — *Same.* 1868, by Joseph Shannon.
     in **351.13 : D**
Albany, *city, N. Y. Police commissioners.* Annual report, 1874–75. Albany. 1876. O.
     354.1 : D
Philadelphia *city. Controller.* 29th annual report, exhibiting the receipts and expenditures of the city, 1882. Phila. 1883. O.
     in **352.13 : D**
St. Louis *city.* The mayor's message and accompanying documents to the city council at its may session 1870[–1872, nov. 1872, may and nov. 1873 and 1874, nov. 1875 and 1876 ; *and* to the municipal assembly at its 2d special april session 1877, and at its called session 1879]. St. Louis. 1870–79. 12 v. O.   **350.14 : D**
   Contains reports of the following officers and institutions : Board of health.—Board of public improvements. — City auditor.— City collector.— City comptroller.— City counselor.—City engineer. — City marshall.—City treasurer.—Fire dep't.—Harbor master.— Inspector of boilers. — Inspector of weights and measures.—Police commissioners.—St. Louis house of refuge. — Superintendent, city workhouse. — Water commissioners.
Chicago *city.* Annual reports of the various officers for the fiscal year, ending dec. 31, 1882. Chicago. 1883. O.   *in* **351.15 : D**
   Contents. Mayor's message.—Dep't of finance.— Dep't of public works.—Dep't of health, 1881 and 1882.—Fire dep't.—Police dep't.—House of correction.—Public library.—School dep't.
Detroit *city. Controller.* Report of the receipts and expenditures of the corporation for the fiscal year ending june 30, 1881[–1883]. Detroit. 1881–83. 3 v. O.   *in* **352.15 : D**
Milwaukee *city. Common council.* Proceedings and ordinances for the year ending april 1873 [–1884]. Milw. 1873–84. 12 v. O.
     in **351.15 : D**
— *Municipal officers.* Report of the city comptroller ; exhibiting the receipts, expenditures and financial condition of the city for the year ending march 4, 1854 [to the

Milwaukee *city. Municipal officers.—Continued.* year ending march 26, 1858]. Milw. 1854–58. O. *and* Q.   *in* **351.15 : D**
— – Report of the city attorney, city comptroller and joint committee on railroads of the city of Milw., on the amt. of bonds issued to aid in the construction of the several railroads, the securities held by the city and the coupons past due and unpaid to nov. 1, 1859. Milw. 1859. O. *in* **351.15 : D**
— – City documents ; mayor's addresses to the common council, and annual reports [of city departments], 1861–2 —1883. Milw. 1862–84. 23 v. O.   *in* **351.15 : D**
   Contains reports of the following officers and institutions :
   Board of health, apr. 1868–dec. 1877; (continued by the Commissioner of health).
   Board of public works, march 1872–dec. 1883.
   Board of water commissioners, april 1871–dec. 1874, (continued in rep. of the Board of public works).
   Chief engineer of the fire dep't, march 1869–1870, april 1872–dec. 1883.
   Chief of police, april 1868–march 1870, april 1872–march 1875, april 1881–march 1884.
   City attorney, march 1868–1870.
   City controller, march 1861–dec. 1883.
   City engineer, incl. in rep. of Board of public works.
   Commissioner of health, rep. 1878–1879, monthly statements, 1880–1883.
   ater works, report by E. S. Chesbrough, oct. 28, W1868.
   – report of board of experts on the trial of duty and capacity of the pumping engines, may 1875.—
   —*See* Board of water com'rs.
San Francisco *city.* Municipal reports for the fiscal year 1878–79, ending june 30, 1879 ; pub. by order of the board of supervisors. San Franc. 1879. O.   *in* **351.15 : D**
   Contains the following reports : Assessor.—Auditor. — Board of health. — City cemetery. — City police.—City hall commissioners. — City and county attorney. — City and county surveyor. — Clerk of justices' court. — Common schools. — Coroner. — County clerk.—County recorder.—Fire department. — Free public library. — Gas inspector. — House of correction. — Home for care of the inebriate. — Industrial school.—License collector.—Park commissioners. — Pound keeper. — Public administrator. — Registrar of voters. — Sheriff. — Superintendent of public streets.—Tax collector.—Treasurer.
France : Département de la Seine. *Conseil général.* Procès-verbaux, 1871–1876. Paris. 1872–76. 12 v. O.   **351.3 : D**
   Contents. Sessions ordinaires de 1872–1876, sessions extraordinaires d'avril-mai 1872, de juin 1874, et de juillet 1876, et session complémentaire de déc. 1872.— The proceedings for 1875 and 1876 are pub. in 2 pts., of which the 1st contains : Mémoires de M. le préfet de la Seine et de M. le préfet de police.
— *Direction de l'administration général.* Rapport sur le service des aliénés, pendant 1876, 1877. Paris. 1877–78. Q.   **351.3 : D**
— – Rapport présenté au nom de l'inspection départementale par l'inspecteur principal [sur le] service des enfants assistés, pour 1877, 1878. Paris. 1878–79. Q.
     351.3 : D
Paris *city. Direction des travaux.* Notes de l'inspecteur général des ponts et chaussées à l'appui de budget de l'exercice 1878. Paris. 1877. Q.   *in* **351.3 : D**

3. The army.

General works.

(*See also* Military engineering, cl. 623.)

Upton, Emory. The armies of Asia and Europe ; embracing official reports on the armies of

Japan, China, India, Persia, Italy, Russia, Austria, Germany, France and England, accompanied by letters descriptive of a journey from Japan to the Caucasus. N. Y. 1878. O.   355 : 6

Wraxall, *Sir* F: C: Lascelles. Handbook to the naval and military resources of the principal european nations. Lond. 1856. O.
355 : 8

Scott, H: Lee. Military dictionary ; comprising technical definitions, information on raising and keeping troops, actual service, incl. makeshifts and improved material, and law, government regulation and administration relating to land forces. N. Y. 1861. O.   355 : R1

Wilhelm, T: Military dictionary and gazetteer ; comprising ancient and modern military technical terms, historical accounts of all north amer. indians, as well as ancient war like tribes ; also notices of battles from the earliest period to present time, with explan. of terms used in heraldry and the offices thereof, [and] an app. containing the articles of war, etc. Rev. ed. Ill. Phil. 1881. O.   355 : R2

Castner, Julius. Militär-lexikon ; heerwesen und marine aller länder mit besonderer berücksichtigung des deutschen reichs, waffen und festungswesen, taktik und verwaltung. Leipz. 1882. D.   355 : R9

Stürenburg, H: Wehrpflicht und erziehung. *In* Deutsche zeit- und streit-fragen.
304 : 15 v8

Guhl, A: Schule und heer. *In* Deutsche zeit- und streit-fragen.   304 : 15 v10

Halleck, H: Wager. Elements of military art and science, or Course of instruction in strategy, fortification, tactics of battles, etc., embracing the duties of staff, infantry, cavalry, artillery and engineers, adapted to the use of volunteers and militia. 2d ed., with critical notes on the mexican and crimean wars. N. Y. 1861. O.   355 : 2

Jomini, Antoine H: *baron* de. The art of war. New ed., with app. and maps ; tr. from the french by G. H. Mendell and W. P. Craighill. Phila. 1862. D.   355 : 3

Machiavelli, Niccolò. The art of war. Added, Hints relative to warfare by a gentleman of the state of New York. Albany. 1815. O.   355 : 4

Szabad, Emeric. Modern war ; its theory and practice illustrated from celebrated campaigns and battles. Maps and diagrams. N. Y. 1863. D.   355 : 5

United States. *War department.* Revised regulations for the army of the U. S. 1861, with index. Phila. 1862. O.   *in* 355.1 : D

Viele, Egbert L. Hand-book for active service ; containing practical instructions in campaign duties for the use of volunteers. N. Y. 1861. D.   355 : 7

Mahan, Dennis H. An elementary treatise on advanced-guard, out-post and detachment service of troops, and the manner of posting and handling them in the presence of an enemy ; with a historical sketch of the rise and progress of tactics, etc., intended as a supp. to the system of tactics adopted for the military service of the U. S, and

especially for the use of officers of militia and volunteers. New ed. Plates. N. Y. 1861. D.   355 : 11

Scott, Winfield. Infantry tactics, or Rules for the exercise and manœuvers of the U. S. infantry. New ed. N. Y. 1861. 3 v. T.
356 : 2
Contents. V. 1. Schools of the soldier and company. 2. School of the battalion and instruction for light infantry or rifle. 3. Evolutions of the line.

United States. *War department.* Cavalry tactics. Phila. 1862. V. 2, 3. T.
in 357.1 : D
Contents. V. 2. School of the trooper, of the platoon and of the squadron, mounted. 3. Evolutions of a regiment.

Instruction for field artillery, prepared by a board of artillery officers. Phila. 1861. O.
358 : 1

United States. *Military commission to Europe in 1855 and 1856.* Report of G: B. McClellan [of the cavalry]. Ill. Wash. 1857. Q.   *in* 355 : D
Contents. Operations in the Crimea. — European engineer troops. — French, austrian, prussian and sardinian infantry.—Russian army.—Prussian, austrian, french, english and sardinian cavalry.—U. S. cavalry.—Regulations and instructions for the field service of cavalry, in time of war, for the U. S. army.—Index.

— — Report of Alfred **Mordecai,** of the ordnance department. Ill. Wash. 1861. Q.
in 355 : D
Contents. List of books, drawings, etc., obtained.—Military organization of Russia, Prussia, Austria, France and Great Britain.—Ordnance at the siege of Sebastopol.—Rep. of the french minister of war to the emperor on the administrative arrangements for the war in the east.—Arsenals of construction.—Field cannon.—Cannon of large caliber. — Garrison artillery.—Field artillery. — Shrapnell shells.— Fuzes for common shells.—Small arms. — Schön, J. Rifled infantry arms ; a brief description of the modern system of small arms as adopted in the various european armies. 2d ed. rev. and augm: Dresden, 1855. Tr. from the german by J. Gorgas.

— — Report on the art of war in Europe, by R: **Delafield,** maj. of the corps of engineers, from notes and observations. Maps and ill. Wash. 1861. Q.   *in* 355 : D
Contents. Introd. — Rifle balls. — Breech - loading small arms.—Gun-carriages and casemates. — Fortifications in the Crimea.—Field hospitals and ambulances.—Subsistence.— Mess furniture. — Transports for troops and supplies.—Jacobi mines at Sebastopol, Cronstadt, etc.— New method of firing mines by electricity. — Harbor defences: Cherbourg ; Naval depot at Toulon ; English system ; Sardinian naval depot at Genoa ; Austrian system ; Prussian system. —Floating batteries sheathed with wrought iron.— Theory and practice of modern system of fortification.—Stables and barracks for cavalry.—Artillery stables.—Infantry barracks.—Military hospitals.

Boguslawski, Albert v. Tactical deductions from the war of 1870–71. Tr. from the german by Lumley Graham. 3d ed. Lond. 1874. O.   355.3 : 1

United States. *Corps of engineers, U. S. army.* Report upon the practice in Europe with the heavy Armstrong, Woolwich and Krupp rifled guns, submitted by the board of engineers for fortifications, Z. B. Tower, pres. Ill. (Prof. papers no. 25.) Wash. 1883. Q.   *in* 358 : D

U. S. army and navy journal, The, and gazette of the regular and volunteer forces ; v. 18–21, aug. 1880—july 1884. N. Y. 1880–84. F.
305.5 : RM

Army history.

(For the history of campaigns, see class History.)

Lacombe, Paul. Arms and armour in antiquity and the middle ages, also a descriptive notice of modern weapons. Tr. from the french. with a pref., notes and one add. chapter on arms and armour in England. [Ill. lib. of wonders]. N. Y. 1876. D.
355 : 1

Burton, R: Francis. The book of the sword. Ill. Lond. 1884. Q. 355+P10
Note. Contains, on p. xxiii-xxxi, List of authorities.

Hamersly, T: H. S., *comp.* Complete regular army register of the U. S. for one hundred years, 1779-1879, together with the volunteer general staff during the war with Mexico, and a register of all appointments by the pres. of the U. S. in the volunteer service during the rebellion, with the official military record of each officer. Also, a military history of the department of war, and of each staff department of the army, with various tables relating to the army and other important military information, comp. from the official records. Wash. 1880. O. 355.1 : R1

Ingersoll, Lurton Dunham. A history of the war department of the U. S.; with biographical sketches of the secretaries. Wash. 1879. O. 355.1 : 2

United States. *Secretary of war.* Annual reports. *See* Congressional documents.
in 328.1 : D

Phisterer, F: Statistical record of the armies of the U. S. (Campaigns of the civil war, supp. vol.) N. Y. 1883. D. 355.1 : 4

O'Brien, T: M., *and* Oliver Diefendorf. General orders of the war department, embracing the years 1861-1863 ; adapted specially for the use of the army and navy of the U. S.; chronologically arr., with index. N. Y. 1864. 2 v. O. 355.1+5

Wisconsin. *Adjutant general.* Annual report, with reports from the quartermaster general and surgeon general for the year ending dec. 30, 1865. Madison. 1866. O.
in 355.15 : D
Note. A 2d ed., including "a reprint of so much of the adj.-gen.'s reports for 1863 and 1864 as pertains to the regimental history, for the purpose of giving a connected narrative of each organization during the entire term of service."

Cooke, Philip St. G: Scenes and adventures in the army, or Romance of military life. Phila. 1859. D. 357.1 : 2

Rodenbough, Theo. F., *ed.* From everglade to cañon with the second dragoons, 2d U. S. cavalry ; an authentic account of service in Florida, Mexico, Virginia and the indian country, incl. the personal recollections of prominent officers. App., containing orders, reports and correspondence, military records, etc., 1836–1875. Ill. N. Y. 1875. O. 357.1+3

Damon, Herbert C. History of the Milwaukee light guard, organized july 16, 1855. Milw. 1875. O. 356+3

Adams, W: H: Davenport. Famous regiments of the british army ; their origin and services. Ill. London. *n. d.* D. 355.2 : 1

Hering, F: Erinnerungen eines legionärs, oder Nachrichten von den zügen der deutschen legion des königs von England in England, Irland, Dänemark, der Pyrenäischen halbinsel, Malta, Sicilien und Italien. [*Anon.*] Hannover. 1826. O. 355.2 : 2

4. The navy.

Naval encyclopædia ; comprising a dictionary of nautical words and phrases, biographical notices and records of naval officers, special articles on naval art and science, written expressly for this work by officers and others of recognized authority in the branches treated of by them, with descriptions of the principal naval stations and seaports of the world. Phila. 1881. Q.
359 : R1

Busk, Hans. The navies of the world ; their present state and future capabilities. Ill. Lond. 1859. D. 359 : 2

Chadwick, F. E. Report on the training systems for the navy and merchant marine of England and on the naval training system of France, made to the bureau of equipment and recruiting, U. S. navy dep., sept. 1879. (U. S. 46th cong. 2d sess., Senate ex. doc. 52). Wash. 1880. O. 359 : D

Soley, James Russell. Report on foreign systems of naval education. (U. S. 46th cong., 2d sess., Senate ex. doc. 51.) Wash. 1880. O. 359 : D

Hamersly, T: H. S. General register of the U. S. navy and marine corps, arr. in alphabetical order, 1782-1882 ; containing the names of all officers of the navy, commissioned, warranted and appointed, incl. volunteer officers who have entered the service since the establishment of the navy dep. in 1798, showing the dates of their original entry, of their progressive rank and in what manner they left the service, if not now in it, with a sketch of the navy from 1775-1798 and a list of all midshipmen and cadet engineers at the naval academy since its establishment, etc. Comp. from the original ms. records of the navy dept. Wash. 1882. O. 359.1 : R3

United States. *Secretary of the navy.* Annual reports. *See* Congressional documents.
in 328.1 : D
— *Navy department.* Papers and discussions on ships, guns and armor ; reprinted from various sources. (Naval prof. papers, no. 15). Wash. 1883. O. *in* 359 : D

Osbon, B. S., *comp.* Handbook of the U. S. navy ; a compilation of all the principal events in the history of every vessel of the U. S. navy from april 1861 to may 1864. N. Y. 1864. D. 359.1 : 1

Jewell, J. Grey. Among our sailors ; with an app., containing extracts from the laws and consular regulations governing the U. S. merchant service. N. Y. 1874. D. 359.1 : 2

Kelley, J. D. Jerrold. The question of ships ; the navy and the merchant marine. N. Y. 1884. D. 359.1 : 4

Adams, W: H: Davenport. Famous ships of the british navy ; stories of enterprise and daring. London. 1878. D. 359.2 : 1

Elwes, Alfred. Ocean and her rulers ; a narrative of the nations which have from the

Elwes, Alfred.—*Continued.*
earliest ages held dominion over the sea,
comprising a brief history of navigation

from the remotest period to the present
time. New and rev. ed., ill. Lond. 1878.
D.   359 : 5

7.   Associations and institutions.

1.   Charitable.

(See also Pauperism, col. 207.)

Fields, Annie, *Mrs.* James T. How to help the
poor. Bost. 1883. S.   361 : 4
Gurteen, S. Humphreys. A handbook of charity
organization. Buffalo. 1882. O.   361 : 2
Lowell, Josephine Shaw. Public relief and private charity. (Questions of the day, no.
13.) N. Y. 1884. O.   361 : 8
State charities aid assoc. Hand-book for hospitals. N. Y. 1883. D.   361 : 3
Jameson, Anna, *born* Murphy. Sisters of charity,
catholic and protestant. Bost. 1857. D.
                                         362 : 1
— The communion of labor ; a second lecture on
the social employments of women. *With
her* Sisters of charity.   *in* 362 : 1
U. S. sanitary commission, The ; a sketch of its
purposes and its work, comp. from documents and private papers. Pub. by permission. Bost. 1863. D.   361 : 5
Boynton, C: B. (?) History of the great western
sanitary fair. [*Anon.*] Cinc. [1864]. O.
                                         361 : 6
American association of the red cross. History
of the red cross ; the treaty of Geneva and
its adoption by the U. S. Wash. 1883. O.
                                         361 : 7
Gobrecht, J. C., *ed.* History of the National
·home for disabled volunteer soldiers ; with
a complete guide-book to the central home
at Dayton, Ohio, written and comp. by a
veteran of the home. Dayton. 1875. D.
                                         361 : 1
National home for disabled volunteer soldiers.
Northwestern branch. Annual report of the
governor and treasurer for 1876 [-1884].
National home, near Milw. 1877-85. O.
                                      361 : Pam
National conference of charities and corrections. Proceedings of the 10th annual
conference, held at Louisville, Ky., sept.
24-30, 1883 ; ed. by A. O. Wright, sec.
Madison. 1884. O.   361+9
Industrial aid society for the prevention of
pauperism. 47th annual report, oct. 1882.
Cambridge, Mass. 1882. O.   361 : Pam
Willard asylum for the insane. 6th annual re-
port of the trustees for 1874, transmitted to
the legislature [of N. Y.] jan. 14, 1875.
Albany. 1875. O.   361 : Pam
Wisconsin humane society for the prevention
of cruelty. [Laws, objects, members,
history, etc.] Milw. 1880. O.   361 : Pam
Milwaukee *county.* Department reports : City
poor office ; County farm and alms house ;
County hospital, 1883-1884. Milw. 1884-
85. O.   361 : Pam
Milwaukee home for the friendless. 1st [-14th]
annual report, 1868 [-1881]. Milw. 1868-82.
O.   361 : Pam
Ladies' bible and benevolent assoc. of Milwaukee. 2d annual report for 1869. 361 : Pam

Deutsche gesellschaft von Milwaukee. 1er
[-4er] jahresbericht, 13. juni 1880— 30. sept.
1884. [Milw.] 1881-84. O.   361 : Pam
Note. For reports on public charitable, reformatory and penal institutions, see Legislative annals,
cl. 328, col. 176-181, and Municipal governments, cl.
351, col. 229-230.

2.   Reformatories and prisons.

Oetker, F: Ueber erziehungs-anstalten für verwahrloste kinder. *In* Deutsche zeit- und
streit-fragen.   304 : 15 v8
Hill, Micaiah, *and* Caroline Frances Cornwallis.
Two prize essays on juvenile delinquency.
Lond. 1853. D.   364 : 1
Wines, Enoch Cobb. The state of prisons and
of child-saving institutions in the civilized
world. Cambridge. 1880. O.   365 : 4
Hartmann, K: Robert E: v. Das gefängniss der
zukunft. *In his* Gesammelte studien.
                                         834+19
International penitentiary congress. Prisons
and reformatories at home and abroad ;
being the transactions of the International
penitentiary congress held in London, july
3-13, 1872, incl. official documents, discussions and papers presented to the congress;
ed., at the request of the international committee, by Edwin Pears. Lond. 1872. O.
                                         365+3
National prison association. Transactions of
the 3d national prison reform congress,
held at St. Louis, Mo., may 13-16, 1874 ;
being the 3d annual report of the National
prison association of the U. S., ed. by E. C.
Wines. N. Y. 1874. O.   365+1
Prison association of New York. 26th, 31st
annual report of the executive committee ;
with accompanying documents for 1870,
1875. Albany. 1871-76. O.   365+2
Note. An app. to the report for 1870 contains
papers and proceedings of the National congress on
penitentiary and reformatory discipline, held in
Cincinnati, O., oct. 12-18. 1870.
Milwaukee *county. House of correction.* Annual
report, 1879—1881, 1883. Milw. 1880-84. O.
                                         365 : Pam
Milwaukee industrial school. An act authorizing industrial schools, together with the
articles and by-laws and officers and committees of the [above]. Milw. 1875. D.
                                         364 : Pam
— 1st annual report of the [above], organized
april 7, 1875. Milw. 1877. O.   364 : Pam
Note. Succeeded by the following institution.
Wisconsin industrial school for girls. 3d[-6th]
annual report of the board of managers,
1879 [-sept. 30, 1881]. Milw. *and* Madison.
1879-82.   364 : Pam
Michigan. Annual report of the inspectors of
the state prison, 1878. Lansing. 1879. O.
                                         365+5
Note. For other reports on this, and similar institutions in other states, see Legislative annals, cl.
328, col. 176-181.

3. Secret societies.

Macoy, Robert. General history, cyclopædia and dictionary of freemasonry ; containing an account of the rise and progress of freemasonry and its kindred associations, ancient and modern, also definitions of the technical terms used by the fraternity. Ill. N. Y. 1870. O. **366 : 1**

Chase, G: W., *ed.* Digest of masonic law ; a complete code of regulations, decisions and opinions upon questions of masonic jurisprudence. 3d ed. N. Y. 1864. D. **366 : 2**

Adams, J: Quincy. Letters on the masonic institution. Bost. 1847. O. **366 : 4**

Huntington, P. C. The true history regarding alleged connection of the order of ancient, free and accepted masons with the abduction of W: Morgan in western New York in 1826 ; with contemporary history, comp. from documents and records. Chicago. 1880. D. **366 : 5**

Weisse, J: A. The obelisk and free masonry according to the discoveries of Belzoni and commander Gorringe ; also egyptian symbols compared with those discovered in american mounds. Ill. N. Y. 1880. O. **366 : 3**

Jennings, Hargrave. The rosicrucians, their rites and mysteries ; with chapters on the ancient fire and serpent-worshippers and explanations of the monuments and talismans of the primeval philosophers. 2d ed., rev., corr. and enl. Ill. Lond. 1879. D. **366 : 6**

4. Insurance.

Champness, W: Swain. An insurance dictionary ; a practical explanation of the technical, medical, legal and scientific terms commonly used in the transaction of life, fire, marine and other classes of insurance business. Lond. 1879. D. **368 : 1**

Walford, Cornelius. The insurance cyclopædia; a dictionary of the definition of terms used in connexion with the theory and practice of insurance in all its branches ; a biographical summary of the lives of all those who have contributed to the development and improvement of the theory and practice of insurance, whether as author, manager, actuary, secretary, agency superintendent or otherwise ; a bibliographical repertory of all works written upon the subject of insurance and its associated sciences ; an historical treasury of events and circumstances connected with the origin and progress of insurance, including a history of all known offices of insurance founded in Great Britain from the beginning, and also containing a detailed account of the rise and progress of insurance in Europe and America. V. 1–5. Lond. 1871–78. 5 v. O. **368 : R2**

Note. All published up to the present time, and containing Abacus *to* Hand-in-hand fire and life ins. co.

Bezold, Ernst. Das versicherungswesen. *In* Deutsche zeit- und streit-fragen. **304 : 15 v3**

Oppenheim, H: Bernhard. Die hülfs- und versicherungskassen der arbeitenden klassen. *In* Deutsche zeit- und streit-fragen. **304 : 15 v4**

Franklin fire insurance company of Philadelphia. Semi-centennial celebration june 25, 1879. Phil. 1879. O. **368.1 : 1**

Milwaukee mechanics' mutual insurance co. 25th anniversary ; 25th annual report and historical retrospect. Milw. 1877. O. **368.1 : Pam**

— *Same, in german.* **368.1 : Pam**

Note. For reports of the Wisconsin and other state commissioners of insurance, see Legislative documents, cl. 328.1, col. 179–180.

5. Miscellaneous.

Ludlow, J: Malcolm. Woman's work in the church ; historical notes on deaconesses and sisterhoods. Lond. 1866. S. **362+2**

American bible society. 61st annual report, presented may 10, 1877 ; with an app. containing a list of auxiliary societies and their officers, *etc.* N. Y. 1877. O. **362 : Pam**

Milwaukee young men's christian assoc. 5th annual report, oct. 1881. Milw. 1881. O. **362 : Pam**

Nordhoff, C: The communistic societies of the U. S., from personal visit and observation; incl. detailed accounts of the Economists, Zoarites, Shakers, the Amana, Oneida, Bethel, Aurora, Icarian, and other existing societies, their religious creeds, social practices, numbers, industries and present condition. Ill. N. Y. 1875. O. **363+1**

Early english text society. English gilds ; the original ordinances of more than one hundred early english gilds, together with ye olde usages of ye cite of Winchestre, the ordinances of Worcester, the office of the mayor of Bristol and the costomary of the manor of Tettenhall-Regis from original mss. of the 14th and 15th centuries. Ed., with notes, by Toulmin **Smith,** with an introd. and glossary by his daughter, Lucy Toulmin Smith, and a preliminary essay, in 5 parts, On the history and development of gilds by Lujo **Brentano.** Lond. 1870. O. **360 : 1**

Trant, W: Trade unions; their origin and objects, influence and efficacy. Lond. 1884. S. **367 : 1**

Cobden club. Reports of proceedings, 1873—1875. Lond. 1873–75. S. **369 : 1**

Society of the army of the Cumberland. Report of the first meeting, held at Cincinnati, feb. 1868. Cinc. 1868. O. **369 : 2**

— 14th reunion, Milwaukee, Wis., 1882. Cinc. 1883. O. **369+2**

Military order of the loyal legion of the U. S. The constitution and by-laws. Phila. 1881. O. **369 : Pam**

Wells, J: G., (*Gracchus Americanus*). The grange; a study in the science of society, practically illustrated in events in current history. N. Y. 1874. D. **369 : 4**

Note. Also attributed to T: Shepard Goodwin.

Milwaukee merchants' association. .7th annual banquet at the Plankinton house, thursday june 5, 1884. Ill. Milw. 1884. Q. **369+5**

United States. *Life-saving service.* Annual reports, 1876—1883. Wash. 1876–83. 8 v. O. *in* **369 : D**

8. Education.

1. In general.

Edmands, J: Reading notes on education. *In* Phila. Mercantile library; Bulletin, v. 1, p. 194–200. **L**

Bain, Alexander. Education as a science. (Intern· scientific ser.) N. Y. 1879. D. **370 : 6**

Craik, H: The state in its relation to education. (Eng. citizen ser.) N. Y. 1884. D. **370 : 22**

Everett, E: Orations and speeches [on educational subjects]. *in* **825.1+2**
Contents, see under English Literature, Essays.

— Importance of practical education and useful knowledge; a sel. from his orations and other discourses. N. Y. 1847. D.
370 : 8

Hecker, J: The scientific basis of education, demonstrated by an analysis of the temperaments and of phrenological facts, in connection with mental phenomena and the office of the holy spirit in the processes of the mind ; in a series of letters to the dep. of public instruction in N. Y. 2d ed. N. Y. 1868. O. **370 : 10**

Kaufmann, G: Der kampf der französischen und deutschen schulorganization, und seine neueste phase in Elsass-Lothringen. *In* Deutsche zeit- und streit-fragen. **304 :15 v6**

Keferstein, Horst. Die verantwortlichkeit der schule nach seiten der gesundheitlichen volksinteressen ; ein beitrag zur frage der entlastung unserer jugend. *In* Deutsche zeit- und streit-fragen. **304 :15 v11**

Lacher, H: Die schul-überbürdungsfrage sachlich beleuchtet. *In* Deutsche zeit- und streit-fragen. **304:15 v12**

Mayhew, Ira. Popular education ; for the use of parents and teachers and for young persons of both sexes. N. Y. 1850. D.
370 : 11

Pestalozzi, J: H: Sämmtliche werke ; gesichtet, vervollständigt und mit erläuternden einleitungen versehen von L. W. Seyffarth. Neue ausg. Brandenburg. 1869–73. 18 v. in 17. S. **370 : 1**
Contents, see Deutscher katalog, p. 14.

Richter, J: Paul F: Levana, or The doctrine of education. Tr. from the german. Bost. 1863. D. **370 : 12**

Rousseau, J: Jacques. Émile, or Concerning education ; extracts containing the principal elements of pedagogy found in the first three books ; with an introd. and notes by Jules Steeg. Tr. by Eleanor Worthington. Bost. 1885 [1884]. D.
370 : 25

— *Same, ger.* Emil, oder Ueber die erziehung. Deutsch von K. Grosse. 3e aufl. Leipz. 1854. 3 v. T. **370 : 2**

Seguin, E. On education. Milw. 1880. O.
370 : 15

Smith, H: I. Education : pt. 1, History of education ; pt. 2, A plan of culture and instruction, based on christian principles, and designed to aid in the right education of youth, physically, intellectually and morally. N. Y. 1845. S. **370 : 5**

Spencer, Herbert. Education ; intellectual, moral and physical. N. Y. 1865. D. **370 : 7**

Watts, I: Improvement of the mind. School ed., with Denman's questions. N. Y. 1850. S.
370 : 18

Cyclopedias and statistics.

Kiddle, H:, *and* Alexander Jakob **Schem,** *eds.* The cyclopædia of education ; a dictionary of information for the use of teachers. school officers, parents and others. N. Y. 1877. Q. **370 : R3**

— The year-book of education ; annual supp. to the Cyclopædia of education, 1878, 1879. N. Y. 1878–79. 2 v. Q. **370 : R4**

Sander, Ferdinand. Lexikon der pädagogik ; encyklopädisches handbuch, enthaltend das ganze des unterrichts- und erziehungswesens, deutsche und ausländische schuleinrichtungen, biographien, fachlitteratur, etc. Leipz. 1884. D. **370 : R23**

Barnard, H: National education in Europe ; an account of the organization, administration, instruction and statistics of public schools of different grades in the principal states. 2d ed. Hartford. 1854. O. **370 : 13**

Hoyt, J: W. Report on education. [Paris universal exposition, 1867 ; Reports of the U. S. commissioners.] Wash. 1870. O. **370+14**

United States. *Bureau of education.* Report of the commissioner of education made to the secretary of the interior, 1870–1883. Wash. 1872-84. 13 v. O. **370 : D**
Contents of accompanying papers. **1870.** General condition of the colored schools under the supervision of the freedmen's bureau, July 1, 1870.—General condition of education among the indians.—**Peabody,** E. P. Kindergarten culture.—Hebrew education.— Progress of education in the Argentine Republic.— Educational progress in England.—Education in Bengal, India.—Austria, education of the working class. —Education in Australia.— Education in Ecuador.— **Warren,** C: Medical education in the U. S.—Normal schools. — Educational conventions. — An american university.—Society, crime and criminals.—**Day,** H. N. The chinese migration. — School supervision.— German schools and teaching german.—The relations of education and labor.—Illiteracy in the U. S.—General school statistics of the U. S. **1871.** General conditions of education among the indians. — Educational conventions and institutes.— National schools of science.—Education of the blind.—Education of the deaf and dumb.—Annual review of education in foreign countries.—Education in foreign countries aided by american efforts. — Educational methods in Germany. — Progress of education for women. — Cooper union. — **Hinton,** L: J. Education of artisans.— **Peabody,** E. P. The objects of the kindergarten.— **Tourjee,** E. F. Musical education in common schools. —Relation of education to insanity.—**Fiske,** A. S. The relations of education to crime in New England.— **Noah,** J. J. The press as an educator. — Statistical tables relating to education in the U. S. **1872.** **Lyons,** C. J. Education in the Hawaiian Islands. — The value of common school education to common labor.—**Jarvis,** E: The value of common school education to common labor.—**Mansfield,** E: D. The relation between crime and education.—The relation between education and pauperism.—**Anderson,** M. B. Suggestions respecting art-training in american colleges. **1873.** **Thompson,** C. O. Art-education.— **Gallaudet,** E. M. On the instruction of deaf mutes. —**Myers,** J. F. Industrial training for girls. — *Note.* Papers of this character were henceforth pub. in a separate series, called Circulars of information.

United States. *Bureau of education.—Continued.*

— - Circulars of information of the bureau of education, 1871—1884. Wash. 1871–84. O.

                                      370 : D

Contents. **1871.** Report on systems of public instruction in Sweden and Norway.—Methods of school discipline.—Compulsory education. **1872.** German and other foreign universities. — Reports on the systems of public instruction in Greece, the Argentine Republic, Chili and Ecuador, with statistics of Portugal and Japan, and an official report on technical education in Italy.—An inquiry concerning the vital statistics of college graduates.— Distribution of college students in 1870–1871. — Facts of vital statistics in the U. S., with tables and diagrams.—The relation of education to labor. — Education in the British West Indies.—The kindergarten.—American education at the international exposition to be held at Vienna in 1873. **1873.** Historical summary and reports on the systems of public instruction in Spain, Bolivia, Uruguay and Portugal.—Schools in British India.—Account of college commencements for the summer of 1873 in Maine, New Hampshire, Vermont, Massachusetts, Rhode Island, Connecticut, New York, New Jersey and Pennsylvania.—List of publications by members of certain college faculties and learned societies in the U. S., 1867–1872.— Account of college commencements during 1873 in the western and southern states. **1874.** Proceedings of the department of superintendence of the National educational association.— Drawing in public schools : Present relation of art to education in the U. S. — History of secondary instruction in Germany. **1875.** Proceedings of the department of superintendence of the National educational association at Wash. D. C., jan. 27, 28, 1875. — Education in Japan.— An account of the systems of public instruction in Belgium, Russia. Turkey, Servia and Egypt.—Chadbourne, P. A. Waste of labor in the work of education. — Suggestions respecting the educational exhibit at the international centennial exhibition, 1876.—Statement relating to reformatory, charitable and industrial schools for the young. —Constitutional provisions in regard to education in the several states of the american union. — Schedule for the preparation of students' work for the centennial exhibition. **1876.** Public libraries in the U. S. of America ; their history, condition and management, [O: L]. **1877.** Education in China. **1878.** Training of teachers in Germany.— Elementary education in London. **1879.** Training schools for nurses.—Papers of the National educational association: Hitz, J:, Popular education in Switzerland ; Wines, E. C., Popular education in France ; Apgar, E. A., Technical education ; Pollock, L., Kindergarten training ; Orr, G. J., Education in the south ; Harris, W: T., Education and the 10th census ; Eaton, J:, The needs of the U. S. bureau of education ; Smith, W., Technical education and industrial drawing ; Eaton, J:, What has been done by the national government in aid of education ; Loring, G: B., American education ; Smart, J. H., The high school question ; Gregory, J. M., Collegiate degrees ; Orton, E:, The military system in state colleges. — Jarvis, E: The value of common school education to common labor. —Training schools of cookery.—American education as described by the french commission to the international exhibition of 1876. **1880.** College libraries as aids to instruction.—Proceedings of the National educational assoc.; Butterfield, L. A., Bell's system of visible speech ; Randall, C. D., Education of dependent children ; Smart, J. H., Best system of schools for a state ; Olin, R. A., Juvet's time globe ; Philbrick, J. D., Technical education in its relations to elementary schools ; Pollock, L., The value of kindergarten training to primary school teachers ; Philbrick, J. D., Technological museums ; Harris, W: T., The 10th census from an educational point of view; Ruffner, W. H., Congress and the education of the people : Outline of the school systems of the various states. — Legal rights of children. — Rural school architecture.—English rural schools. — Clarke, F. W. A report on the teaching of chemistry and physics in the U. S.—The spelling reform.—Vacation colonies for sickly school children.—The indian school at Carlisle barracks.—Progress of western education in China and Siam. **1881.** Peale, R: F: Construction of library buildings.— White, E. E. The relation of education to industry, *and* Technical education in american schools.— Proceedings of the National educational assoc., 1881 : McMillan, A:. Uniformity of school statistics ; Wickersham, J. P., Weak places in our systems of public instruction ; Thompson, C.

O., The conservation of pedagogic energy : Hough, F. B., Our schools and our forests ; Eaton, J:, Museums illustrative of education ; Patterson, J. W., Education in the state.—Education in France.—Sexton, S: Causes of deafness among school children.—Calhoun, A. W. The effects of student life upon the eyesight. **1882.** The inception, organization and management of training schools for nurses. — Proceedings of the national educational assoc.: Billings, J: S., Information necessary to determine the merits of the heating and ventilating of a school building ; Smart, C:, The chemical examination of air as applied to questions of ventilation ; Jones, H. S., Obstacles in the way of better primary education ; Hall, G. S., Chairs of pedagogy in our higher institutions of learning ; Mayo, A. D., Remarks on national aid to education ; Hawkins, D. A., National aid to education from a northern standpoint ; Curry, J. L. M., Remarks on national aid to education ; Jackson, S., Education in Alaska ; Gregory, J: M., Some fundamental inquiries concerning the common school studies ; Harris, W: T., How to improve the qualifications of teachers.—The university of Bonn.—Leland, C: G. Industrial art in schools.—Maternal schools in France.—Technical instruction in France.—Warren, C: Answers to inquiries of the U. S. bureau of education, its work and history.— Fifty years of freedom in Belgium. — Education in Malta. — 3d international geographical congress at Venice in 1881.—Illiteracy and crime in France.—School savings banks.—Education in Sheffield.—Wickersham, J. P., Education and crime.—National pedagogic congress of Spain.— Mühlberg, F.,Natural science in secondary schools.— Vessiot. A. Instruction in morals and civil government. — Hough, F. B. Planting trees in school grounds. **1883.** Legal provisions respecting the examination and licensing of teachers.—Coeducation of the sexes in the public schools of the U. S.—Proceedings of the National educational assoc.; Bickmore, A. S., Natural history in public schools; Harris, W: T., The educational lessons of the census; Haygood, A. G., If universal suffrage, then universal education; Lawrence, W:, Constitutionality of national aid to education; Northrop, B. G., S. C. Armstrong *and* A. C. Fletcher, Respecting indian education.—Smith, L. A. Recent school law decisions. **1884.** Meeting of the International prison congress at Rome, in oct. 1884.—Rockwell, J. E. The teaching, practice and literature of shorthand.—Warren, C: Illiteracy in the U. S. in 1870 and 1880.—Curry, J. L. M. National aid to education.—Proceedings of the National educational association : Holcombe, J: W., Supervision of public schools; Haworth, J. M., R. H. Pratt *and* S. C. Armstrong, Indian education ; Peaslee, J. B., *and* B. G. Northrop, Arbor day in the public schools: Harris, W: T., Recess; Ellis, S. A., No recess: Higbee, E. E., How a state superintendent can best advance popular education; Dickinson, J. W., National aid for the support of public schools; Bingham, R., Educational status and needs of the new south; Legislation respecting national aid to education, proposed by the Interstate educational convention; Northrop, B. G., The new bill for the national aid to public schools; Ordway, J: M., Industrial education; Marble, A. P., Public instruction in industrial pursuits; Angell, G: T., The new order of mercy, or Crime and its prevention; Jeffries, B. J., Education of the normal color sense; Luckey, G: J., Supplementary reading; Edwards, C: G., *and* J. O. Wilson, Reading.—Suggestions respecting the educational exhibit at the World's industrial and cotton centennial exposition.—Rural schools : progress in the past, means of improvement in the future.— Wead, C: K. Aims and methods of the teaching of physics.

Periodicals.

American journal of education, The, ed. by H: Barnard ; v. 1-7, july 1856—dec. 1859. Hartford. 1856-59. O.   **305.7 : M**

Education, an international magazine, bimonthly ; T: W. Bicknell, conductor ; v. 1-4, sept. 1880—july 1884. Bost. 1881-84. O.   **305.7 : M**

School monthly, The ; pub. by the Milwaukee teachers' association ; v. 1, 2. Milw. 1867-69. 2 v. O.   **305.7 : M**

Wisconsin journal of education; organ of the State teachers' association and of the dep't of public instruction; E: Searing and J: B. Pradt, eds.; v. 6. Madison. 1876. O.
305.7 : M

History.

Paroz, Jules. Histoire universelle de la pédagogie; renfermant les systèmes d'éducation et les méthodes d'enseignement des temps anciens et modernes, les biographies de tous les pédagogues célèbres, le développement progressif de l'école depuis le moyen âge jusqu, à nos jours, la comparaison et la caractéristique des pédagogies anglaise, allemande et française, etc., dédiée aux élèves des écoles normales, aux instituteurs, aux chefs d'institution et aux autorités scolaires. Paris. 1883. D.
370 : 20

Schmidt, K: Geschichte der pädagogik, dargestellt in weltgeschichtlicher entwicklung und im organischen zusammenhange mit dem culturleben der völker. 3te vielfach verm. und verb. aufl. Cöthen. 1873—76. 4 v. O.
370 : 21
Contents. V. 1. Die geschichte der pädagogik in der vorchristlichen zeit. 2. Die geschichte der pädagogik von Christus bis zur reformation. 3. Die geschichte der pädagogik von Luther bis Pestalozzi. 4. Die geschichte der pädagogik von Pestalozzi bis zur gegenwart.

Mahaffy, J: Peytland. Old greek education. [Education library]. N. Y. 1882. S.
370 : 17

Kingsley, C: Alexandria and her schools. *In his* Historical lectures.
904 : 23

Mullinger, James Bass. The schools of Charles the great, and the restoration of education in the 9th century. Lond. 1877. O.
370 : 19

Adams, C: Francis. The new departure in the common schools of Quincy, and other papers on educational topics. Bost. 1879. O.
370 : 9
Contents. The public library and the public schools. —Fiction in public libraries, and educational catalogues.—The new departure in the common schools of Quincy.

Schuricht, Herrmann. Geschichte der deutschen schulbestrebungen in Amerika. Leipz. 1884. O.
370 : 24

Whitford, W: Clarke. Historical sketch of education in Wisconsin. Madison. 1876. O.
379 : 1

Salisbury, Albert. Historical sketch of normal instruction in Wisconsin, 1846—1876. Madison. 1876. O. *With* Whitford, W: C., Education in Wisconsin.
379 : 1

— History of the Wisconsin teachers' association from 1853 to 1878. *With* Whitford, W: C. Education in Wisconsin.
379 : 1

Timbs, J: School-days of eminent men. N. Y. 1864. D.
370 : 16

2. Teachers and methods.

Alcott, W: Alexander. The confessions of a school-master. *T. p. w.* [Andover. 1839.] S.
371 : 6

Beck, Ferdinand Anton. Das grundübel in der modernen jugendbildung mit vorzüglicher berücksichtigung des gymnasialunter-

richts; reformvorschläge eines schulmannes. *In* Deutsche zeit- und streitfragen.
304 : 15 v1

Browning, Oscar. An introd. to the history of educational theories. [Education library, ed by Philip Magnus]. N. Y. 1882. S.
371 : 13

Calderwood, H: On teaching; its ends and means. N. Y. 1875. S.
371 : 1

Currie, James. The principles and practice of common school education. Cinc. 1884. O.
371 : 20

Emerson, G: Barrett. The schoolmaster; the proper character, studies and duties of the teacher, with the best methods for the gov. and instruction of common schools, and the principles on which school houses should be built, arr., warmed and ventilated. N. Y. 1842. D. *With* Potter, A. The school.
371 : 3

Genlis, Stéphanie Félicité Ducrest de St. Aubin, *comtesse* de. Lessons of a governess to her pupils, or Journal of the method adopted by [her] in the education of the children of M. d'Orleans, first prince of the bloodroyal; published by herself. Tr. from the french. Dublin. 1793. 2 v. D.
371 : 12

Hinsdale, Burton A. Schools and studies. Bost. 1884. D.
371 : 18

Keferstein, Horst. Zur frage des prüfungswesens. *In* Deutsche zeit- und streit-fragen.
304 : 15 v13

Lammers, Mathilde. Deutsche lehrerinnen im auslande. *In* Deutsche zeit- und streitfragen.
304 : 15 v13

Page, D: Perkins. Theory and practice of teaching, or The motives and methods of good school-keeping. Added, a biographical sketch of the author. 90th ed. N. Y. 1873. D.
371 : 2

Papers for the teacher; repub. from Barnard's American journal of education; 1st and 2d ser. N. Y. 1860. 2 v. O.
371 : 11
Contents. 1st ser. **Russell**, W:, Intellectual education.—**Hill**, T:, True order of studies.—**Thayer**, G. F., Letters to a young teacher.—Catechism on methods of teaching, from the german of Diesterweg, Honcamp, Hintz, Abbenrode.—**Burgess**, G:, Religious instruction in public schools.—**Huntington**. F. D., Unconscious tuition.—Questions for the examination of a school.—Topics for discussion in a teacher's meeting. 2d ser. Object teaching and oral lessons on social science and common things, with various illustrations of the principles and practice of primary education, as adopted in the model and training schools of Great Britain.

Payne, Joseph. Lectures on the science and art of education, with other lectures and essays; ed. by his son, Joseph Frank Payne, with an introd. by R. H. Quick. Bost. 1883. O.
371 : 14

Peabody, Elizabeth Palmer. Record of mr. Alcott's school, exemplifying the principles and methods of moral culture. 3d ed. rev. Bost. 1874. D.
371 : 7

Phelps, W: F. The teacher's hand-book for the institute and class room. N. Y. *n. d.* D.
371 : 16

Potter, Alonzo. The school; its objects, relations and uses, with a sketch of the education most needed in the U. S., the present state of common schools, the best means of improving them, and the consequent duties of parents, trustees, inspectors, etc. N. Y. 1842. D.
371 : 3

Pycroft, James. On school education, designed to assist parents in choosing and cooperating with instructors for their sons. Oxford. 1843. D.   **371 : 4**

Quick, Robert Herbert. Essays on educational reformers. Syracuse. 1882. D.   **371 : 15**
Contents. Schools of the jesuits. — Asham, Montaigne, Ratich, Milton.—Comenius. — Locke. — Rousseau's Émile. — Basedow and the philanthropin. — Pestalozzi. — Jacotot. — Herbert Spencer. —Thoughts and suggestions about teaching children.—Some remarks about moral and religious education.

Sewell, Elizabeth Missing. Principles of education, drawn from nature and revelation, and applied to female education in the upper classes. 2 v. in 1. N. Y. 1866. D.   **371 : 5**

Tate, T: The philosophy of education, or The principles and practice of teaching ; with an introd. by Francis W. Parker. 1st amer. from the 3d Lond. ed. (School bulletin publications.) Syracuse, N. Y. 1884. S.   **371 : 17**

Hall, G. Stanley, ed. Pedagogical library, v. 1 : Methods of teaching history, by G. Diesterweg, Herbert B. Adams, C. K. Adams, J: W. Burgess, E. Emerton, W. F. Allen and T: W. Higginson. Bost. 1883. D.   **371 : 19 v1**

Milwaukee city. Public schools. Syllabus of lessons in civil government ; for the use of teachers. Milw. 1882. O.   **371 : Pam**
— - Syllabus of the course of study in geography ; for the use of teachers. Milw. 1881. O.   **371 : Pam**

Binner, Paul. History of the education of the deaf and dumb. n. t. [Milw. 1881.] S.   **371 : 8**

Lamson, Mary Swift. Life and education of Laura Dewey Bridgman, the deaf, dumb and blind girl. Bost. 1881. D.   **371 : 10**

Cobb, Lyman. The evil tendencies of corporal punishment as a means of moral discipline in families and schools, examined and discussed ; in 2 parts : pt. 1, Objections to the use of the rod ; pt. 2, Substitutes for, and preventives of, the use of the rod. With app., containing letters from distinguished individuals, extracts from reports, resolutions, proceedings of educational conventions, etc. in different parts of our country on the subject of corporal punishment. N. Y. 1847. O.   **371 : 9**

3. Grades of education.

Elementary.

Arey, Mrs. H. E. G. Home and school training. Phila. 1884. S.   **372 : 5**

Burton, Warren. Helps to education in the homes of our country. Bost. 1863. D.   **372 : 4**

Dodge, Mary Abigail, (Gail Hamilton). Our common-school system, by Gail Hamilton. Bost. [1880]. D.   **372 : 1**

Keferstein, Horst. Die volksschule als erziehungsschule. In Deutsche zeit- und streit-fragen.   **304 : 15 v7**

Lammers, A: Hand-bildung und hausfleiss. In Deutsche zeit- und streit-fragen.   **304 : 15 v10**

Meyer, Johannes. Der handfertigkeits-unterricht und die schule, mit besonderer berücksichtigung der bestrebungen des rittmeisters [Adolf] Clauson-Kaas ; eine sozial-pädagogische studie. In Deutsche zeit- und streit-fragen.   **304 : 15 v10**

Peaslee, J: B. Moral and literary training in public schools. [Boston. 1881]. O.   **371 : Pam**

Taylor, J. Orville. The district school. N. Y. 1834. D.   **372 : 3**

Stetson, C: B. Technical education ; what it is and what american public schools should teach ; an essay based on an examination of the methods and results of technical education in Europe, as shown by official reports. Bost. 1874. D.   **372 : 2**

Gréard, Octave, inspecteur général de l'instruction publique. L'instruction primaire à Paris et dans le département de le Seine en 1875 ; mémoire adressé à M. le préfet de la Seine. Paris. 1877. O.   **372 : 6**

Kindergartens.

Hailmann, W: N. Erziehungs-grundsätze für schule und haus ; vorträge, gehalten unter den auspizien des Milwaukee kindergarten-vereins. [Milw.] n. d. D.   **372.1 : 6**
— Four lectures on early child-culture. Milw. 1880. D.   **372.1 : 1**
Contents. Laws of childhood.—The soul of Fröbel's gifts. — The specific use of the kindergarten. — The kindergarten ; a school for mothers.

Mann, Mary, Mrs. Horace, and Elizabeth Palmer Peabody. Moral culture of infancy and kindergarten guide, with music for the plays. Bost. 1864. D.   **372.1 : 2**

Morehouse, C. B. The kindergarten, its aims, methods and results ; a practical explanation of the system of Fröbel. N. Y. 1880. D.   **372.1 : 3**

Schmeidler, Johannes. Die religiösen anschauungen F: Fröbels. In Deutsche zeit- und streit-fragen.   **304 : 15 v12**

Shirreff, Emily. Essays and lectures on the kindergarten ; principles of Fröbel's system and their bearing on the higher education of women, schools, family and industrial life ; with app. by Elizabeth P. Peabody. N. Y. 1883. D.   **372.1 : 9**

*   *
*

Carpenter, Harvey. The mother's and kindergartner's friend. Bost. 1884. D.   **372.1 : 11**

Dörflinger, C:, ed. Herzblättchens spielwinkel ; eine gabe für die kleinsten, den müttern gewidmet von C. Dörflinger, unter mitwirkung von tante Therese, tante Auguste, tante Martha, tante Lina und dem "Aquariumonkel." Milw. 1881. O.   **372.1 : 5**

Fröbel, F: Mother-play, and nursery songs. Ill. With notes to mothers. Bost. [1878]. Q.   **372.1+P4**

Hailmann, W: N. Primary helps ; no. 1 of a new series of kindergarten manuals. Ill. (School bulletin publ.) Syracuse. 1882. O.   **372.1 : 8**

Köhler, A: Die bewegungsspiele des kindergartens ; nebst einem anhange von ball-, kugel- und bauliedern. 6te aufl. Weimar. 1878. O.   **372.1+10**

Noa, Henrietta. Plays for the kindergarten, as introduced in the gymnastic exercises of Mary institute, St. Louis, Mo. Bost. *n. d.* D.   **372.1 : 7**

Higher.

Bain, Alexander. The university ideal, past and present. *In his* Practical essays.
824.2 : 91
Bird, C: Higher education in Germany and England; a brief practical account of the organization and curriculum of the german higher schools, with critical remarks and suggestions with reference to those of England. Lond. 1884. S.   **373 : 3**
Gallenkamp, W: Die reform der höheren lehranstalten insbesondere der realschulen; ein beitrag zu den vorarbeiten für das unterrichtsgesetz. *In* Deutsche zeit- und streit-fragen.   **304 : 15 v3**
Hoyt, J: W. Address on university progress, del. before the National teachers' assoc. at Trenton, N. J., aug. 20, 1869. N. Y. 1870. O.   **373+1**
Huxley, T: H: Universities, actual and ideal. *With his* Science and culture.   **504 : 24**
Johnston, W: Preston. The work of the university in America; an address before the South Carolina college on commencement day, june 25, 1884. Columbia. 1884. O.
373 : Pam
— The university, its dangers and the remedies; an address at commencement exercises of the university of Texas, june 14, 1884. Austin. 1884. O.   **373 : Pam**
Laspeyres, Etienne. Das alter der deutschen professoren; ein beitrag zur universitätsstatistik und universitätspolitik. *In* Deutsche zeit- und streit-fragen.   **304 : 15 v5**
Leighton, R. F., *ed.* Harvard examination papers, coll. and arr. 7th ed. Bost. 1880. D.
373 : 2
Meyer, Jürgen Bona. Deutsche universitätsentwicklung; vorzeit, gegenwart und zukunft. *In* Deutsche zeit- und streit-fragen.
304 : 15 v3
— Die fortbildungsschule in unserer zeit. *In* Deutsche zeit- und streit-fragen.
304 : 15 v2
Meyer, K: Waldemar. Die pflege des idealen auf unseren höheren schulen; brief an einen arzt mit voraufgehender debatte. *In* Deutsche zeit- und streit-fragen.   **304 : 15 v13**

Classical and real.

Adams, C: Francis. *jr.* A college fetich; address del. before the Harvard chapter of the fraternity of the Phi beta kappa in Sander's theatre, Cambridge, june 28, 1883. Bost. 1883. O.   **375 : 3**
Bain, Alexander. The classical controversy. *In his* Practical essays.   **824.2 : 91**
Bowen, Francis. Classical and utilitarian studies. *In his* Gleanings.   **824.1 : 6**
Dick, T: On the improvement of society by the diffusion of knowledge, or An illust. of the advantages which would result from a more general dissemination of rational and scientific information among all ranks. Ill. [Harper's family lib.] N. Y. 1844. S.
375 : 2

Huxley, T: H: Science and culture. *in* **504 : 24**
— Scientific education. *In his* Lay sermons.
504 : 11
Laas, Ernst. Gymnasium und realschule; alte fragen mit rücksicht auf das bevorstehende preussische unterrichtsgesetz historisch und kritisch von neuem beleuchtet. *In* Deutsche zeit- und streit-fragen.
304 : 15 v4
Shedd, W: Greenough Thayer. Scientific and popular education. *In his* Literary essays.
824.1 : 73
Youmans, Edward Livingstone, *ed.* Modern culture, its true aims and requirements; a series of addresses and arguments on the claims of scientific education by profs. Tyndall, Daubeny, Henfrey, Huxley, Paget, Whewell, Faraday, Draper, Masson, De Morgan, Owen, drs. Hodgson, Carpenter, Hooker, Acland, Forbes, Grove, Herbert Spencer, sir John Herschel, sir Charles Lyell, dr. Seguin, etc. Lond. 1867. D.
375 : 1

4. Self-education.

(*See also* Courses of reading, class 807.)

Atkinson, W: P. On the right use of books; a lecture. Bost. 1880. S.   **374 : 3**
Bain, Alexander. The art of study. *In his* Practical essays.   **824.2 : 91**
Blackie, J: Stuart. On self-culture, intellectual, physical and moral; a vade mecum for young men and students. N. Y. *n. d.* S.
374 : 1
Clarke, James Freeman. Self-culture, physical, intellectual, moral and spiritual; a course of lectures. 2d ed. Bost. 1880. D.   **374 : 2**

5. Female education.

Clarke, E: Hammond. Sex in education, or A fair chance for the girls. Bost. 1873. S.
376 : 1
Comfort, G: F. *and* Anna Manning. Woman's education and woman's health; chiefly in reply to "Sex in education". Syracuse. 1874. D.   **376 : 6**
Brackett, Anna Callender, *ed.* The education of american girls considered in a series of essays. N. Y. 1874. D.   **376 : 2**
Contents. **Brackett,** A. C. Education of american girls.—**Cheney,** E. D. A mother's thought.—**Dall,** C. H. The other side.—**Stone,** L. H. Effects of mental growth.—**Beedy,** M. E. Girls and women in England and America.—**Jacobi,** M. P. Mental action and physical health.—**Hamlin,** S. D. Michigan university.—**Nutting,** M. O. Mount Holyoke seminary.—**Johnston,** A. A. F. Oberlin college.—**Avery,** A. C. Vassar college.—**Antioch college.**—**Rood,** *Mrs.* O. N. Letter from a german woman.—**Brackett,** A. C. Review of "Sex in education."—App.
Fénelon, François de Salignac de la Mothe. The education of a daughter. Tr. from the french. Added, Fenelon's epistle, Character of Antiope, etc. 2d ed. Balt. 1852. S.
376 : 3
More, Hannah. Strictures of the modern system of female education. *In her* Works.
820.2 : 28 v1
Phelps, Almira, *born* Hart, *afterward Mrs.* Lincoln. Hours with my pupils, or Educational addresses, etc.; the young lady's guide,

and parent's and teacher's assistant. N. Y. 1859. D.   **376 : 4**

Sigourney, Lydia Howard. Letters to my pupils ; with narrative and biographical studies. 2d ed. Lond. 1852. D.   **376 : 5**

6. Religious and secular education.

Beecher, Catharine Esther. Religious training of children in the school, the family and the church. N. Y. 1864. D.   **377 : 1**

Bushnell, Horace. Christian nurture. N. Y. 1864. D.   **377 : 2**

Bible, The, in the public schools ; arguments in the case of J : D. Minor et al. versus the board of education of the city of Cincinnati et al. [in the] superior court of Cincinnati, with the opinions and decision of the court. Cinc. 1870. O.   **377+3**

Domestic portraiture, or The successful application of religious principle in the education of a family, exemplified in the memoirs of three of the deceased children of the rev. Legh Richmond ; with introd. remarks on christian education by E: Bickersteth. N. Y. 1852. D.   **377 : 5**

Clark, Rufus Wheelwright. The question of the hour ; the bible and the school fund. Bost. 1870. S.   **377 : 4**

Keferstein, Horst. Die pädagogik der kirche. *In* Deutsche zeit- und streit-fragen.   **304 : 15 v9**

Kirchner, F: Zur reform der religions-unterrichts. *In* Deutsche zeit- und streit-fragen.   **304 : 15 v5**

Meyer, Jürgen Bona. Luther als schulbefreier. *In* Deutsche zeit- und streit-fragen..   **304 : 15 v13**

— Die simultanschulfrage. *In* Deutsche zeit- und streit-fragen.   **304 : 15 v8**

7. Schools and colleges.

Curious schools ; by various authors. Bost. 1881. D.   **378 : 12**
Contents. Cadet life at West Point.—Perkins' institution and Mass. school for the blind.—Boston whittling schools.—Philadelphia school of reform.—About some sewing schools.—A chinese mission school.—The flower school at Corlear's Hook.—Lady Betty's cooking school.—The bad boys of France.—The children's hour; a novel art school.—At a day nursery.—Some indian schools.—The training schoolship Minnesota.

Porter, Noah. The american colleges and the american public. New ed., with afterthoughts on college and school education. N. Y. 1878. D.   **378 : 1**

Richardson, C: F., *and* H: A. **Clark**, *eds.* The college book. Bost. 1878. O.   **378 : 16**

Thwing, C: F. American colleges ; their students and work. 2d ed., rev. and enl. N. Y. 1883. S.   **378 : 15**

Collection, A, of college words and customs. Cambridge. 1851. D.   **378 : 6**

Osgood, S: Student life ; letters and recollections for a young friend. N. Y. 1861. D.   **378 : 2**

Hitchcock, E: Reminiscences of Amherst college, historical, scientific, biographical and autobiographical ; also of other and wider life experiences. Plates and a geol. map. Northampton, Mass. 1863. D.   **378 : 3**

King, Moses. Harvard and its surroundings. 6th ed. Ill. Cambridge. 1884. D.   **378 : 17**

Belden, Ezekiel. Porter. Sketches of Yale college, with numerous anecdotes by a member of that institution. [*Anon.*] Ill. N. Y. 1843. S.   **378 : 14**

Bagg, Lyman Hotchkiss. Four years at Yale, by a graduate of '69· [*Anon.*] New Haven. 1871. D.   **378 : 4**

Butterfield, Consul Willshire. History of the university of Wisconsin, from its first organization to 1879 ; with biographical sketches of its chancellors, presidents and professors. Madison, Wis. 1879. O.   **378 : 5**

Hazeltine, Mayo W. British and american education ; the universities of the two countries compared. N. Y. 1880. T.   **378 : 7**

Turton, T: Thoughts on the admission of persons without regard to their religious opinions to certain degrees in the universities of England. 2d ed. corr. and enl. Cambridge. 1835. O.   **378 : 9**

Everett, W: On the Cam ; lectures on the university of Cambridge. Cambridge. 1865. D.   **378 : 8**

Banks, G: Nugent. Cambridge trifles, or splutterings from an undergraduate pen, by the author of "A day of my life at Eton." [*Anon.*] N.Y. 1881. S.   **378 : 13**

Hart, James Morgan. German universities ; a narrative of personal experience together with recent statistical information, practical suggestions and a comparison of the german, english and american systems of higher education. N. Y. 1874. D.   **378 : 10**

Howitt, W: (*Dr. Cornelius*). The student-life of Germany, from the unpub. ms. of Dr. Cornelius, containing nearly forty of the most famous student songs. Phila. 1842. O.   **378 : 11**

Statistisches jahrbuch der höheren schulen Deutschlands, Luxemburgs und der Schweiz ; neue folge von Mushacks Schulkalender, 2ter teil. Nach amtlichen quellen bearb. 4ter jahrg. Leipz. 1883. S.   **378 : 18**

Deutscher universitäts-kalender, 25ste ausg ; sommer-semester 1884, herausg. von F. Ascherson. 2ter t.: Die universitäten im deutschen reich, in der Schweiz, den russischen Ostseeprovinzen und Oesterreich-Ungarn. Berlin. 1884. T.   **378 : 19**

8. Reports.

National educational association. The addresses and journal of proceedings, session of 1876 in Baltimore, Maryland. Salem, Ohio. 1876. O.   **379 : 6**

Business educator's assoc. of America. Proceedings of the 6th convention, held at Rochester, N. Y. july 17–24, 1884. Trenton, N. J. 1885. O.   **379 : Pam**

Western literary institute and college of professional teachers. Transactions of the 4th annual meeting, held in Cincinnati oct. 1834. Cinc. 1835. O.   **379 : 9**

Rhode Island *state. Board of education.* 11th annual report, with the 36th annual report of the commissioner of public schools, jan. 1881. Providence. 1881. O.   **379 : 16**

Massachusetts *state.* *Board of education.* The Mass. system of common schools ; an enl. and rev. ed. of the 10th annual report of the first sec. of the board. Bost. 1849. O.
      379+19

— — 13th [15th—38th, 40th, 42d—46th] annual report, together with annual report of the sec., 1849, 1851—1874, 1876, 1878—1882. Bost. 1850-83. 32 v. O.   **379+19**

Worcester county free institute of industrial science. 13th annual catalogue, with the plan of instruction, 1883. Worcester. 1883. O.   **379 : Pam**

Connecticut *state.* *Board of education.* Annual report, presented to the general assembly, january session 1881, together with the annual report of the sec. of the board. New Haven. 1881. O.   **379 : 12**

New York *state.* 25th [and 27th] annual reports of the superintendent of public instruction. Albany. 1879, 1881. 2 v. O.   **379 : 13**

Cooper union for the advancement of science and art. Charter, trust deed and by-laws ; with the letter of P: Cooper accompanying the trust deed. N. Y. 1868. O.   **379 : Pam**

Albany *city, N. Y. Board of public instruction.* 7th [8th, 10th, 14th] annual report to the common council, 1872-3 [—1879-80.] Albany. 1873-80. O.   **379 : Pam**

— *High school.* Merit roll for the year ending june 28, 1882, and report of committees. Albany. 1882. O.   **379 : Pam**

Albany female academy, founded 1814. Catalogue and circular, 1881-82. Albany. 1882. D.   **379 : Pam**

Cornell university. Register, 1883-4 and 1884-5 Ithaca, N. Y. [1883, 1884]. D.   **379 : Pam**

Pennsylvania *state.* *Sup't of common schools.* 24th annual report for the year ending june 2, 1857. Harrisburg. 1858. O.   **379 : 8**

Philadelphia *city. Board of public education, 1st school district of Pennsylvania.* 1st annual report of the sup't of public schools of the city of Philadelphia for 1883. Phila. 1884. O.   **379+18**

Johns Hopkins university, *Baltimore.* 7th [and 9th] annual report of the pres., 1882, 1884. Balt. 1882-84. O.   **379:Pam**

Note. The rep. for 1882 contains a review of the work of the university since its opening in 1876, and a "Bibliographia hopkinsiensis, 1876-82".

— Register, 1883-4, 1884-5. Balt. 1884-85. O.   **379 : Pam**

— Circulars, v. 1—3, dec. 1879—sept. 1884. Balt. 1879-84. Q.   **379+11**

St. Louis *city. Board of directors of the public schools.* 26th annual report, for the year ending aug. 1, 1880. St. Louis. 1881. O.   **379 : 15**

Washington university. 25th anniversary, april 22, 1882. St. Louis. [1882]. O.   **379 : Pam**

Arkansas *state. Sup't of public instruction.* Biennial report for the school years 1879 and 1880. Little Rock. 1880. O.   **379 : 14**

Ohio *state. Commissioner of common schools.* 25th annual report to the general assembly, for the school year ending aug. 31, 1878. Columbus, 1879. O.   **379+17**

Cincinnati *city. Common schools.* 52d—55th

annual reports, 1881—1884. Cinc. 1882—84. 2 v. O.   **379+5**

Dayton *city, O. Board of education.* Annual report, 1878-9, 1880-1, 1881-2. Dayton. 1880-83. O.   **379 : Pam**

Indiana *state. Sup't of public instruction.* 28th report, being the 10th biennial report and for the years ending aug. 31, 1879 and aug. 31, 1880. Indianapolis. 1880. O.   **379 : 7**

Indianapolis *city. Public schools.* Manual of the public schools ; rules and regulations of the board of school commissioners of the public schools and the public library. 1881-82. Indianapolis. 1881. T.   **379 : 10**

Illinois industrial university. 11th report of the board of trustees for the two years ending sept. 30, 1882. Springfield. 1882. O.
      379+20

Note. For other reports, see Reports made to the general assembly of Ill., *in* 328.15 : D, col. 178.

Chicago *city. Board of education.* 8th annual report for 1861. Chic. 1862. O.   **379 : Pam**

Michigan *state. Sup't of public instruction.* Historical sketches of education in Michigan. *In* 44th annual rep., *with* Joint doc's, 1880, v. 1.   *in* **328.15 : D**

Wisconsin *state. Sup't of public instruction.* Annual reports, 1850-1882. *In* Governor's message and accompanying documents.
      in **328.15 : D**

— *University.* Catalogue of the officers and students, 1852-3—1864-5. *In* Reports of the regents, *with* Governor's message for 1854-1866.   *in* **328.15 : D**

— — Catalogue for 1879-80, 1881-82—1884-85. Madison. 1879-84. O.   **379 : Pam**

— — General catalogue of the officers and graduates from its organization in 1849 to 1883. Madison. 1883. O.   **379 : Pam**

Note. For reports of the Board of regents, see Governor's message and accomp. doc., in 328.15: D, col. 179.

— *State normal school, River Falls.* Catalogues. 1875-1879. [River Falls]. *n. d.* 3 v. O.
      379 : 4

Note. For reports of the normal school regents, see Governor's message and accomp. doc., in 328.15:D, col. 179.

Milwaukee *city. Board of school commissioners.* Annual reports, 1860-1—1883. Milw. 1861-84. 24 v. in 14. O.   **379 : 3**

— — Proceedings, 1875—1880. *n. t.* [Milw.] O.
      379 : R2

— — Annual reports of the standing committees, together with the annual address of the pres. of the board, submitted may 4, 1875. Milw. 1875. O.   **379 : Pam**

— — Rules and regulations, together with the provisions of the city charter relating to the public schools. Milw. 1875. O.
      379 : Pam

Markham academy, *Milwaukee.* Catalogue, 1881-82. Milw. 1882. O.   **379 : Pam**

Marquette college, *Milwaukee.* The 4th annual catalogue of the officers and students, 1884-85. Milw. 1885. O.   **379 : Pam**

Milwaukee college. Catalogue of the officers and students, 1884-85. Milw. 1885. O.
      379 : Pam

Spencerian business college, *Milwaukee.* Circular. *n. p. or d.*   **379 : Pam**

Wisconsin phonological institute for deaf mutes, *Milwaukee.* 1st[-3d] annual report

Wisconsin phonological institute for deaf mutes, *Milwaukee.—Continued.*
of the board of trustees, for 1878[-80]. Milw. 1879–81. O.   **379 : Pam**
— The articulate method to teach deaf mutes to speak, ed. by D. C. Luening. Milw. 1879. O.   **379 : Pam**

Madison *city. Board of education.* Annual report for 1880, 1881. Madison, Wis. 1881-82. O.   **379 : Pam**
Beloit college, *Wis.* Catalogue ; its officers, students and alumni. 1879-80—1884–85. Beloit. 1879–84. O.   **379 : Pam**

9. Commerce and communication.

1. In general.

Farrer, T: H. The state in its relation to trade. [Citizen series.] N. Y. 1883. D.   **380 : 4**

Hunt, Freeman. The library of commerce, practical, theoretical and historical ; v. 1. N. Y. 1845. D.   **380 : 1**
Contents. A sketch of the commercial intercourse of the world with China.—**Platt**, J. C. History of the british corn laws, with add. by the amer. ed.—**Mackay**, C: Memoirs of commercial delusions, embracing historical sketches of the Mississippi scheme and the South-sea bubble.

Bourne, H. R. Fox. The romance of trade. Lond. *n. d.* D.   **380 : 3**

McCulloch, J: Ramsay. A dictionary, practical, theoretical and historical, of commerce and commercial navigation ; ed. by H: Vethake, with an app. containing the new tariff of 1846, together with the tariff of 1842, reduced to ad valorem rates as far as practicable ; also the sub-treasury, warehousing and the canadian transit bills of 1846 ; the new british tariff as amended by the passage of the corn law and sugar duties ; with a table of all foreign gold and silver coin reduced to federal currency, etc. Phila. 1847. 2 v. O.   **380 : R6**

Waterson, W: A cyclopædia of commerce, mercantile law, finance, commercial geography and navigation. New ed. containing the present tariff and an essay on commerce, pub. by the society for promoting useful knowledge. Lond. 1847. O.   **380 : R7**

United States. *State dep't.* Reports from the consuls of the U. S. on the commerce and manufactures of their consular districts ; no. 1–48, oct. 1880—dec. 1884. Wash. 1881–85. 14 v. O.   *in* **380 : D**
— *Same.* Contents and index to no. 1-26. Wash. 1883. O.   **380 : D**
Note. The following numbers contain reports of importance on special subjects: **12.** Cotton goods trade of the world, and the share of the U. S. therein. **23.** Cotton and woollen mills of Europe. **25½.** Cereals of Europe, India and Algeria. **29.** Glass manufactures of Europe. **37.** Petroleum and kerosene oil in foreign countries. **41½.** Fruit culture in the several countries. **43.** Credit systems of the several countries. **48.** Agricultural machinery of the several countries.

— *Commerce.* Andrews, Israel D. Report on the trade and commerce of the british north american colonies, and upon the trade of the great lakes and rivers, [1850 and 1851] ; also notices of the internal improvements in each state, of the gulf of Mexico and straits of Florida, and a paper on the cotton crop of the U. S. Maps. Wash. 1854. 2 v. O.   *in* **380.1 : D**

United States. *Commerce.—Continued.*
— — Statistics of the foreign and domestic commerce of the U. S.; embracing a historical review and analysis of foreign commerce from the beginning of the gov., the present internal commerce between the Mississippi and Atlantic states, the overland trade and communications with the Pacific states, the productions and exchanges of the gold and silver districts, the commerce of the Pacific coast, and the internal relations of the northern frontier of the U. S.; communicated by the sec. of the treas. in answer to a resol. of the sen. march 12, 1863. Map. Wash. 1864. O.   *in* **380.1 : D**

— — Nimmo, Joseph, *jr.* Report on the internal commerce of the U. S. for 1876, 1879, 1881, 1882. Maps. Wash. 1877–84. O.   *in* **381.1 : D**
Note. Contain statistics and discussions of questions relating to commerce, manufactures, transportation, railroads and their relations to the government, descriptions of chief commercial centers, etc.

— — Annual reports on the commerce and navigation of the U. S. *See* Congressional doc.   *in* **328.1 : D**

— — Annual reports on the commercial relations of the U. S. to foreign nations. *See the same.*   *in* **328.1 : D**

— — Evans, C: H., *comp.* Imports [and] duties from 1867 to 1883 ; a compilation of foreign commodities imported and entered for consumption in the U. S., showing the quantities, values, rates of duty, amt. of duty received, the average cost, and duties reduced to an equivalent ad valorem rate, summaries of the values and duties of the principal class or g oups, also values and duties received and rexpense at each customs district and port of delivery ; with schedules of the articles, quantities and values admitted free of duty ... during the fiscal years ending june 30, 1867 to 1883 incl. From the annual reports of commerce and navigation. Wash. 1884. O.   *bound with*

— — Evans, C: H., *comp.* Exports, domestic and foreign. from the american colonies to Great Britain from 1697 to 1789 incl. *and* Exports, domestic, from the U. S. to all countries from 1789 to 1883 incl. Comp. and collated from official papers. U. S. 48th cong. 1 sess. House mis. doc., no. 49). Wash. 1884. O.   *in* **380.1 : D**

Commercial convention, held in Detroit july 11th–14th, 1865. Proceedings. 1865. O.   **381.1 : 1**

National board of trade. Proceedings of 2d and 3d annual meetings. Bost. 1870, 1871. 2 v. O.   **381.1 : 2**

New York produce exchange. Report for 1879, with the charter, by-laws, and the several trade rules adopted by the exchange, and a list of its members; *also* The report of the statistician of the exchange, with accompanying tables. N. Y. 1880. O.
381.1 : 3

Milwaukee. *Board of trade.* Annual report of the commerce, manufactures, banking business and railroad system of the city of Milwaukee, for 1856· Prep. by Andrew J. Aikens, sec. Map. Milw. 1857. O.
381.1 : 4

— *Chamber of commerce.* [1st—] 3d annual statement of the trade, commerce and general business of the city of Milwaukee for 1858 —1860. Reported by L. L. Crounse, sec. Milw. 1859–61. O.
381.1 : 4

— — 5th [and 6th] annual statement of the trade and commerce of Milwaukee for the year ending dec. 31, 1862 [and 1863]. Reported by James B. Kellogg, sec. Milw. 1863, 1864. O.
381.1 : 4

— — 7th [8th, 11th, 13th—27th] annual report of the trade and commerce of Milwaukee for the year ending dec. 31, 1864 [1865, 1868, 1870—1884]. Comp. by W: J. Langson, sec. Maps. Milw. 1865–85. O.
381.1 : 4

— — Act of incorporation, and rules and by-laws, as amended march 24, 1877. Milw. 1877. O.
381.1 : 4

*   *   *

Pope, C:, *ed.* The yearly journal of trade, 1856. Lond. 1856. O.
380+2
Contents. Matters as to laws of customs, excise and stamps.—Treaties and conventions with foreign powers.—Tariffs of the United Kingdom, british possessions abroad and of foreign countries.— Countervailing and inland duties.—Duties of lights, buoys, pilotage, etc.—Postoffice laws and rates.— Dangers of the seas.—Proclamations, orders in council and government boards. — Railways. — Electric telegraphs.—Parliamentary speeches and papers.— Reports of law cases.—Tr. of foreign documents.— Statistics. — Proceedings of scientific and learned societies. — Geographical sketches and recent discoveries.—Commercial usages and port charges.— Exchanges, moneys, weights and measures.—Descriptions of articles of merchandise and of improved methods of cultivating and bringing the same to market.—State of the markets and fresh channels of commerce. — Correspondence, home, colonial and foreign.

Public, The; a journal of finance, commercial interests and political science; v. 14–24, july 1878—dec. 1883. N. Y. 1878–83. F.
305 : RM

Hunt's merchants' magazine and commercial review, conducted by Freeman Hunt; v. 1–7, 18–62, july 1839—dec. 1869. N. Y. 1839–69. O.
305.8 : M
Note. Title-page of v. 1–7 omits "Hunt's". From v. 38 title-page reads "established by Freeman Hunt in 1839" instead of "conducted". V. 44 drops "Hunt's" and is ed. by I. Smith Homan and W: B. Dana. V. 46 –62 ed. by Dana alone.

Commercial and financial chronicle, The, and Hunt's merchant's magazine; a weekly newspaper, representing the industrial and commercial interests of the United States; v. 38, 39. N. Y. 1884. F.
305.8 : M

2. Foreign trade.

Heyd, W: Geschichte des levantehandels im mittelalter. Stuttgart. 1879. 2 v. O.
382 : 2

Raynal, Guillaume T: François. *abbé.* A philosophical and political history of the settlements and trade of the europeans in the East and West Indies. Tr. from the french by J. Justamond; 3d ed. rev. and corr. with maps and index. Lond. 1777. 5 v. O.
382 : 3

Wells, D: Amasa. Our merchant marine; how it rose, increased, became great, declined and decayed, with an inquiry into the conditions essential to its resuscitation and future prosperity. [Questions of the day, no. 3]. N. Y. 1882. D.
382.1 : 1

Staunton, *Sir* G: T: Miscellaneous notices relating to China, and our commercial intercourse with that country, incl. a few transl. from the chinese language. 2d ed., enl. in 1822, and accompanied in 1850 by introd. observ. on the events which have affected our chinese commerce during that interval. Lond. 1822-50. O.
382.2 : 1

Scrivenor, Harry. History of the iron trade, from the earliest records to the present period. New ed. Lond. 1854. O.
382 : 1

3. Post and telegraphs.

(See also Telegraphy, cl. 654.)

Rees, James. Foot-prints of a letter carrier, or A history of the world's correspondence; containing biographies, tales, sketches, incidents and statistics connected with postal history. Phila. 1866. D.
383 : 1

United States. *Postmaster-general.* Annual reports. *See* Congressional documents.
in 328.1 : D

United States official postal guide; rev. and pub. monthly by authority of the post office dep't. 2d ser., v. 4–6. Bost. 1882-84. D.
305.8 : M
Contents. An alphabetical list of all the post offices in the U. S. with county and state.—A list by states.— A list by states and counties.—Lists of money-order offices, domestic and international.—Rates of postage. —Synopsis of postal laws, orders and rulings of the department.—Information about all postal matters.— General regulations respecting foreign mails.

Plum, W: Rattle. The military telegraph during the civil war in the U. S., with an exposition of ancient and modern means of communication, and of the federal and confederate cipher systems; also a running account of the war between the states. Ill., portraits and maps. Chicago. 1882. 2 v. O.
384.1 : 1

4. Transportation.

(See also Engineering, cl. 625, 626.)

Tanner, H: S. A description of the canals and railroads of the U. S., comprehending notices of all the works of internal improvement throughout the several states. N. Y. 1840. O.
385.1+2

United States. *Census office.* Tenth census, 1880, v. 4: Report on the agencies of transportation in the U. S., incl. the statistics of railroads, steam navigation, canals, telegraphs and telephones. Ill. Wash. 1888. Q.
in 317 : D
Contents. **Shuman,** Armin E. Statistical report of the railroads in the U. S.: General review of traffic and fiscal operations; Statistics of the same; Physical

United States. *Census office.—Continued.*
characteristics ; Statistics of *the same* ; App.; Index.—**Purdy,** T. C. Report on steam navigation in the U. S.; History of steam navigation; U. S. interests; Statistical tables ; Tonnage tables ; Index.—**Purdy,** T. C. Report on the canals of the U. S.: History of operating canals; History of abandoned canals; Index.—**Shuman,** Armin E. Report on the statistics of telegraphs and telephones in the U. S.; Index.—**Lines,** Robert B. Report on the postal telegraph service in foreign countries; Index.—Addendum: Note on express companies.—General index.
— *Congress.* Report of the select committee on transportation - routes to the seaboard ; with app. and evidence. Maps. (U. S. 43d cong. 1 sess. Sen. rep. 307). Wash. 1874. 2 v. O.   *in* **380.1 : D**
Illinois *state. Railroad and warehouse commission.* 8th annual report for the year ending nov. 30, 1878 ; with app. Springfield. 1879. O.   *in* **385.15 : D**
— — 12th annual report ; railroads for the year ending june 30, 1882, grain inspection, oct. 31, 1882. Springfield. 1883. O.
                              in **385.15 : D**
Note. For other reports, see Reports made to the general assembly of Ill., *in* 328.15: D, col. 178.

By land: railroads.

Cohn, Gustav. Streitfragen der eisenbahnpolitik. *In* Deutsche zeit- and streit-fragen.
                              304 : 15 v3
Perrot, Franz Fürchtegott. Deutsche eisenbahnpolitik. *In* Deutsche zeit- und streit-fragen.   **304 : 15 v1**
Wisconsin *state. Railroad commissioner.* Taxation of railroads and railroad securities : report of a committee to a convention of railroad commissioners, held at Saratoga Springs, june 10, 1879, together with a summary of laws in relation to railroad taxation in force in the various states of the Union, as well as foreign countries. Madison. 1880. O.   **385 : 5**
Lardner, Dionysius. Railway economy ; a treatise on the new art of transport, its management, prospects and relations, commercial, financial and social, with an exposition of the practical results of the railways in operation in the United Kingdom, on the continent and in America. N. Y. 1850. D.
                              385 : 1
Jervis, J: Bloomfield. Railway property ; a treatise on the construction and management of railways, designed to afford useful knowledge in a popular style to the holders of this class of property, as well as to railway managers, officers and agents. N. Y. 1861. D.   **385 : 2**
Kennedy, W: Sloane. Wonders and curiosities of the railway, or Stories of the locomotive in every land. Ill. Chicago. 1884. D.
                              385 : 4
Minot, Robert S. Railway travel in Europe and America ; with 25 tables of recent and novel statistics of journeys, speeds, fares etc., for travellers and others. Bost. 1882. O.   **385 : 3**
Poor, H: Varnum. Manual of the railroads of the U. S. for 1880, showing their mileage, stocks, bonds, cost, traffic, earnings, expenses and organizations, with a sketch of their rise, progress, influence, etc., together with app., containing a full analysis of the

Poor, H: Varnum.—*Continued.*
debts of the U. S. and of the several states. N. Y. 1880. O.   **385.1 : R1**
— Manual of the railroads of the United States for 1884 ; showing their route and mileage, stocks, bonds, debts, cost, traffic, earnings, expenses and dividends, their organizations, directors, officers etc. N. Y. 1884. O.
                              385.1 : R1
Atkinson, E: The railroads of the U. S.; a potent factor in the politics of that country and of Great Britain. Bost. 1881. O.
                              385.1 : 4
Smalley, Eugene V. History of the Northern Pacific railroad. Ill. and map. N. Y. 1883. O.   **385.1 : 3**
Chemins de fer de l'Europe centrale. [Map.] Paris. 1857. D.   **385.3 : 2**
Ewbank da Camara, J. Chemins de fer de la province de St. Paul, Brésil ; données techniques et statistiques, publié par ordre du gouvernement. Rio de Janeiro. 1875. O.
                              385.3 : 1

                    * * *

Milwaukee and Mississippi railroad co. Acts incorporating the Milwaukee, Waukesha and Mississippi River R. R. Co., together with a report of the committee relating to a plan of operations, adopted by the board of directors may 19, 1849. Milw. 1849. O.
bound with
— 1st—11th annual report of the directors to the stockholders, together with the reports of the sec., treas. and sup't. Milw. 1850-60. O.   **385.1 : 5**
Milwaukee and Prairie du Chien railway co. Documents relating to [its] organization. N. Y. 1861. O.   *in* **385.1 : 5**
Chicago, Milwaukee and St. Paul railway co. 1st [-3d, 5th-13th, 15th-21st] annual report ; june 13, 1863 — dec. 31, 1884. Maps. N. Y. *and* Milw. 1865-85. O.   **385.1 : 6**
Note. "Chicago" was added to the corporate name in 1874.
Wisconsin central railroad co. 1st annual report, to dec. 31, 1878. Milw. 1879. O.
                              385.1 : 7
— President's statement to the stockholders, [and] Plan for the re-organization, submitted to the bondholders by vote of the stockholders, at their annual meeting, may 29, 1879. Milw. 1879. O.   **385.1 : 7**
— 2d annual report, to dec. 31, 1879. Milw. 1880. O.   **385.1 : 7**
— Report to J: A. Stewart and Edwin H. Abbot, trustees in possession, upon its management and operation from jan. 4, 1879 [to dec. 31, 1881], by C: L. Colby, agent of the trustees. Milw. 1880-82. O.   **385.1 : 7**
Note. For reports of the Wisconsin and other state railroad commissioners, see Legislative annals, cl. 328.1, col. 178–180.

By water: canals, etc.

Preble, G: H: A chronological history of the origin and development of steam navigation, 1543 to 1882. Phila. 1883. O. **387 : 1**
Heinz, —. Kanäle und sammelbecken. *In* Deutsche zeit- und streit-fragen. **304 : 15 v6**
Note. For reports on the Fox and Wisconsin river improvement, the Sault St. Mary ship canal, and the Illinois and Hennépin canal, see Legislative documents, cl. 328.1, col. 177–179.

New York *state. Canal board.* Report of the commissioners invited, july 10, 1877, to consider and report on the subject of tolls upon the canals, having reference to the subject of revenues, and also to increasing the commerce of the canals. Albany. 1878. O.
386 : Pam

Waterhouse, Sylvester. A memorial to congress to secure an adequate appropriation for a prompt and thorough improvement of the Mississippi river; with an app. [on the value of river transportation]. St. Louis. 1877. D.   387 : 2

5.   Weights and measures.

Colin, Alfred. The universal metric system; prepared especially for candidates for schools of science, engineers and others. N. Y. 1879. D.   389 : 1

Mc Vicar, Malcom. The metric system of weights and measures, combining many new and practical improvements in arrangement, notation and applications, prepared for Robinson's progressive arithmetics. (Robinson's mathematical ser.) N. Y. [1867]. D.   389 : 2

Barnard, F: A: Porter, *and* H. Tresca. Report upon the comparison of an iron meter forwarded to France by the gov. of the U. S. of America [with the original platina standard in possession of the Conservatoire impérial des arts et métiers]. *In* U. S. coast survey rep. 1867.   *in* 622 : D

Totten, C: A. L. A challenge to the metric system, and an earnest word with the english-speaking peoples on their ancient weights and measures. *In his* An important question in metrology.   916.2+36

Hilgard, Julius E. A statement concerning the relation of the lawful standards of measure of the U. S. to those of Great Britain and France. *In* U. S. coast survey rep. 1876.
in 622 : D

— Comparison of american and british standard yards. *In the same*, 1877.   *in* 622 : D

— On the length of a nautical mile. *In the same*, 1881.   *in* 622 : D

Woolhouse, W. S. B. Measures, weights and moneys of all nations, and an analysis of the christian, hebrew and mahometan calendars. 6th ed., rev. and enl. [Weale's ser.] Lond. 1881. D.   389 : 3

10.   Customs and costumes.

1.   General and ancient.

Farrer, James A. Primitive manners and customs. N. Y. 1879. D.   390 : 2

McLennan, J: Ferguson. Studies in ancient history; comprising a reprint of Primitive marriage, an inquiry into the origin of the form of capture in marriage ceremonies. Lond. 1876. D.   390 : 3

Lacroix, Paul, (*Le bibliophile Jacob*). Manners, customs and dress during the middle ages and during the renaissance period. Ill. Lond. 1876. Q.   392 : R1
Contents. Condition of persons and lands. — Privileges and rights, feudal and municipal. — Private life in the castles, the towns and the rural districts. — Food and cookery. — Hunting. — Games and pastimes. — Commerce. — Guilds and trade corporations. — Taxes, money and finance. — Laws and the administration of justice. — Secret tribunals. — Punishments. — Jews. — Gipsies, tramps, beggars and cours des miracles. — Ceremonials. — Costumes.

Wood, E: J. The wedding day in all ages and countries. N. Y. 1869. D.   390 : 5

Sharman, Julian. A cursory history of swearing. Lond. 1884. O.   390 : 9

Sabine, Lorenzo. Notes on duels and duelling, alphabetically arr., with a prelim. historical essay. Bost. 1855. D.   390 : 4

Truman, B: C. The field of honor; a complete and comprehensive history of duelling in all countries, incl. the judicial duel of Europe, the private duel of the civilized world and specific descriptions of all the noted hostile meetings in Europe and America. N. Y. 1884. D.   390 : 8

* * *

Kretschmer, Albert, *and* C: Rohrbach. The costumes of all nations from the earliest times to the 19th century; exhibiting the dresses and habits of all classes, regal,

ecclesiastical, noble, military, judicial and civil. Lond. 1882. F.   390 : R6

Racinet, A: Le costume historique; 500 planches, 300 en couleurs, or et argent, 200 en camaïeu, avec des notices explicatives et une étude historique. Paris. 1880-85. O.
390 : R1

Smith, J. Moyr, *ed.* Ancient greek female costume illustrated, with explan. letter-press and descriptive passages from the works of Homer, Hesiod, Herodotus, Aeschylus, Euripides, Aristophanes, Theocritus, Xenophon, Lucian and other greek authors. Lond. 1882. D.   391 : 1

Schild, Marie, *ed.* Old english costumes; an epitome of ladies' costumes from the 1st to the 19th century. Lond. *n. d.* Q.   390 : 7

2.   Modern.

Depping, Guillaume. Evening entertainments; comprising delineations of the manners and customs of various nations. New ed. enl. Phila. 1833. D.   393 : 1

Goodrich, S: Griswold, (*Peter Parley*). Manners and customs of the principal nations of the globe. [Youth's library of history.] Bost. [1844]. S.   x 393 : 6

Belloc, Bessie Rayner, *born* Parkes. Peoples of the world. Ill. Lond. *n. d.* D.   x 393 : 7

Remarkable people, [the arab, the jew, the egyptian]. Lond. [1846]. T.   393 : 3

Hervey, T: Kibble. The book of christmas; descriptive of the customs, ceremonies, traditions, superstitions, fun, feeling and festivities of the christmas season. N. Y. 1845. D.   393 : 2

x denotes books specially adapted for children.

Dyer, T: Firminger Thistleton. Domestic folk-lore. N. Y. [1881]. S.   **393 : 4**
Flower, W: H: Fashion in deformity, as ill. in the customs of barbarous and civilized races. [Nature ser.] N. Y. 1881. S.   **393 : 5**
Hunt, *Mrs.* Alfred W. Our grandmothers' gowns ; with 24 hand-colored ill. drawn by G: R. Halkett. Lond. *n. d.* D.   **393 : P9**

Great Britain.

Brand J: Observations on the popular antiqui-ties of Great Britain ; chiefly illustrating the origin of our vulgar and provincial customs, ceremonies and superstitions. Arr., rev. and enl. by sir H: Ellis ; new ed., with further add. Lond. 1877. 3 v. D.   **394 : 1**
Brookes, J: Manners and customs of the eng-lish nation, from the invasion of Julius Cæsar to the present time. Lond. [1860]. D.   **394 : 2**
Strutt, Joseph. The sports and pastimes of the people of England, incl. the rural and domestic recreations, may-games, mum-meries, shows, processions, pageants and pompous spectacles, from the earliest period to the present time. Ill. With a copious index by W: Hone. Lond. 1867. O.   **394 : 4**
Armytage, Fenella Fitzhardinge, *born* Berkeley. Old court customs and modern court rule. Lond. 1883. O.   **394 : 5**
Hindley, C: Tavern anecdotes and sayings, incl. the origin of signs, and reminiscences connected with taverns, coffee-houses, clubs, etc. (The wanderer's lib.) Lond. 1881. D.   **394 : 3**
Sadler, L. R., (*Jacob Larwood*), *and* J: Camden Hotten. The history of signboards, from the earliest times to the present day. 8th ed. Ill. Lond. 1875. D.   **393 : 8**
Gomme, G: Laurence, *ed.* The gentleman's ma-gazine library ; a classified collection of the chief contents of the Gentleman's ma-gazine from 1731 to 1868: Manners and customs. Lond. 1883. O.   **394 : 6**

3. Etiquette.

(See also Business manuals, cl. 658.)

Thornwell, Emily. The lady's guide to perfect gentility in manners, dress and conversa-tion, in the family, in company, at the piano-forte, the table, in the street, and in gentlemen's society, also a useful instructor in letter writing, toilet preparations, fancy needlework, millinery, dressmaking, care of the wardrobe, the hair, teeth, hands, lips, complexion, etc. N. Y. 1856. D.   **393.1 : 6**
Habits of good society, The ; a handbook for ladies and gentlemen ; with thoughts, hints and anecdotes concerning social observan-ces, nice points of taste and good manners, and the art of making one's self agreeable, the whole interspersed with humorous il-lustrations of social predicaments, remarks on the history and changes of fashion and the differences of english and continental etiquette. N. Y. 1870. D.   **393.1 : 1**
Moore, Clara Jessup, *Mrs.* Bloomfield H., (*Mrs. Henrietta Oxnard Ward*). Sensible etiquette of the best society, customs, manners, mor-als and home culture. Compiled from the best authorities by Mrs. H. O. Ward. 8th rev. ed. Phila. [1878]. D.   **393.1 : 4**
Lounger in society, *pseud.* Social etiquette and home culture ; the glass of fashion ; uni-versal hand-book of social etiquette and home culture for ladies and gentlemen ; with copious and practical hints upon the manners and ceremonies of every relation in life, at home, in society, and at court ; interspersed with numerous anecdotes. (Frank. sq. lib.) N. Y. 1881. Q.   **393.1+2**
Longstreet, Abby Buchanan. Social etiquette of New York. New enl. ed. [*Anon.*] N. Y. 1881. S.   **393.1 : 3**
Bunce, Oliver Bell, (*Censor*). Don't ; a manual of mistakes and improprieties more or less prevalent in conduct and speech. N. Y. [1883]. T.   **393.1 : 5**
Mentor, *pseud.* Never ; a hand-book for the uninitiated and inexperienced aspirants to refined society's giddy heights and glitter-ing attainments. N. Y. [1884]. T.   **393.1 : 7**
Osmun, T: Embley, (*Alfred Ayres*). The mentor; a little book for the guidance of such men and boys, as would appear to advantage in the society of persons of the better sort. N. Y. 1884. S.   **393.1 : 9**
Sherwood, *Mrs.* J : Manners and social usages. Ill. N. Y. 1884. S.   **393.1 : 8**
Milwaukee society blue book and family direc-tory, 1884–85. Milw. [1885]. D.   **393.1 : 10**

V. PHILOLOGY.

1. General linguistics.

1. Science of language.

Cook, F: C: On languages, ancient and modern, *and* On egyptian compared with semitic, aryan and turanian words. *In his* Origins of religion and language. **291 : 28**

Dwight, B: Woodbridge. Modern philology; its discoveries, history and influence. N. Y. 1877. 2 v. O. **400 : 7**
Contents. 1st series. 3d ed. Maps, tabular views and index.—Historical sketch of the indo-european languages.—History of modern philology.—Science of etymology. 2d series. Comparative phonology.—Comparative english etymology.

Hovelacque, Abel. The science of language; linguistics, philology, etymology. Tr. by A. H. Keane. [Lib. of contemporary science.] Lond. 1877. D. **400 : 6**

Humboldt, K: W: *freiherr* v. Sprach-philosophische werke; herausg. und erklärt von H. Steinthal. Berlin. 1884. Q. **400+8**
Contents. Notiz über die mss.—Allgemeine einleitung.—Der styl Humboldts.—Drei akademische abhandlungen: Ueber das vergleichende sprachstudium; Ueber das entstehen der grammatischen formen; Ueber die aufgabe des geschichtschreibers.—Ueber die verschiedenheit des menschlichen sprachbaues.

Johnson, Alexander Bryan. A treatise on language, or The relation which words bear to things; in 4 parts. N. Y. 1836. O. **400 : 4**

— The meaning of words analysed into words and unverbal things, and unverbal things classified into intellections, sensations and emotions. N. Y. 1854. D. **401 : 1**

Lieber, Francis. On the study of foreign languages. *In his* Miscell. writings. **304 : 7 v1**

Marcel, Claude. The study of languages brought back to its true principles, or The art of thinking in a foreign language. N. Y. 1869. D. **407 : 1**

Müller, F: Max. Essays on the science of language. *In his* Chips. **824.2 : 74 v4**
Contents, see under English literature, Essays.

Peile, J: Philology. (Literature primers.) N. Y. 1878. S. **400 : 5**

Smith, Adam. On the origin of languages. *In his* Theory of the moral sentiments. **171 : 11**

Stehlich, F: Die sprache in ihrer beziehung zum nationalcharakter. *In* Deutsche zeit- und streit-fragen. **304 : 15 v11**

Whitney, W: Dwight. Language and the study of language; twelve lectures on the principles of linguistic science. 5th ed. N. Y. n. d. D. **400 : 1**

Whitney, W: Dwight.—*Continued.*
— The life and growth of language; an outline of linguistic science. (Intern. scientific ser.) N. Y. 1878. D. **400 : 2**

* * *

Schleyer, J: Martin. Volapük; die weltsprache für alle gebildete der ganzen erde. Sigmaringen. 1880. D. **408 : 1**

2. Texts, essays, periodicals and transactions.

Anecdota oxoniensia; texts, documents and extracts, chiefly from mss. in the Bodleian and other Oxford libraries. Oxford. 1881-85. Q. **418 : 1**
Contents. **1. Classical series.** V. 1, pt. 1: The english mss. of the Nicomachean ethics, described in relation to Bekker's mss., and other sources by J. A. Stewart; pt. 2: Nonius Marcellus De compendiosa doctrina, Harleian ms. 2719, collated by J. H. Onions; pt. 3: Aristotle's Physics, book 7, a transcript of the Paris ms. 1859, collated with the Paris mss. 1861 and 2033, and a ms. in the Bodleian library, with an introd. account of these mss., by R: Shute; pt. 4: Bentley's Plautine emendations from his copy of Gronovius, by E. A. Sonnenschein; pt. 5: Collatio cod. Harleiani 2610, Ovidii Metamorphoseon i, ii, iii: 1-622.—Epigrammata latina xxiv ex codicibus Bodleianis et Sangallensibus—Glossae in Apollinarem Sidonium ex codice Digbeiano 172. Ed. Robinson Ellis. **2. Semitic series.** V. 1, pt. 1: Commentary on Ezra and Nehemiah by rabbi Saadiah, ed. from the mss. in the Bodleian library by H: J: Mathews. **3. Aryan series.** Buddhist texts from Japan; pt. 1: Vagrakkhedika. The diamond cutter, ed. by F: Max Müller; pt. 2: Sukhâvatî-vyûha, description of Sukhâvatî, the land of bliss, ed. by F. Max Müller and Bunyiu Nanjio, with two app., 1, Text and translation of Sanghavarman's chinese version of the poetical portions of the Sukhâvatî-vyûha, 2, Sanskrit text of the smaller Sukhâvatî-vyûha; pt. 3: The ancient palm-leaves containing the Pragñâ-pâramitâ-hridaya-sûtra and the Ushnîsha-vigaya-dhâranî, ed. by F. Max Müller and Bunyiu Nanjio, with an app. by G. Bühler [being Palaeographical remarks on the Horiuzi palm-leaf mss. **4. Mediaeval and modern series.** Sinonoma Bartholomei, a glossary from a 14th-century ms. in the library of Pembroke college, Oxford, ed. by J. L. G. Mowat; pt. 2: The Saltair na rann, a collection of early middle irish poems, ed. from ms. Rawl. B. 502 in the Bodleian library by Whitley Stokes.

Sears, Barnas, Bela Bates **Edwards** *and* Cornelius Conway **Felton,** *eds.* Classical studies; essays on ancient literature and art, with the biography and correspondence of eminent philologists. Bost. 1843. D. **404 : 1**
Contents. Introd.—**Sears,** B. Schools of german philology.—**Tegnér,** E. Study of greek literature.—**Jacobs,** C. F: W: The study of classical antiquity; The wealth of the greeks in works of plastic art.—Philological correspondence. — **Edwards,** B. B.

School of philology in Holland.—**Jacobs**, C. F: W: Superiority of the greek language in the use of its dialects.—**Hand**, F. G. History of the origin and progress of the latin language.—**Jacobs**, C. F: W: Education of the moral sentiment among the ancient greeks.—Notes.

American journal of philology, The; ed. by Basil L. Gildersleeve ; v. 1–4. Balt. 1880–83. 4 v. O.   **405 : M**

American philological association. Transactions, 1869–1883. Hartford. 1871–81 ; Cambridge. 1882–84. 14 v. in 5. O.   **406+P1**

Contents. V. **1. Hadley**, J. On the nature and theory of the greek accent.—**Whitney**, W: D. On the nature and designation of the accent in sanskrit.—**Goodwin**, W. W. On the aorist subj. and future ind. with *hopōs* and *ou mē*. — **Trumbull**, J. Hammond. On the best method of studying the north american languages.—**Haldeman**, S: S. On the german vernacular of Pennsylvania.—**Whitney**, W: D. On the present condition of the question as to the origin of language.—**Lounsbury**, T. R. On certain forms of the english verb which were used in the 16th and 17th centuries.—**Trumbull**, J. Hammond. On some mistaken notions of Algonkin grammar, and on mistranslations of words from Eliot's Bible, etc.—**VanName**, A. Contributions to creole grammar.—Proceedings, preliminary meeting, N. Y. 1868 ; 1st annual session, Poughkeepsie, 1869; 2d annual session, Rochester, 1870.

2. Evans, E. W. Studies in cymric philology.—**Allen**, F. D. On the so-called attic second declension.—**Whitney**, W: D. Strictures on the views of A: Schleicher respecting the nature of language and kindred subjects.—**Hadley**, J. On english vowel quantity in the 13th century and in the 19th.—**March**, F. A. Anglo-saxon and early english pronounciation.—**Bristed**, C. A. Some notes on Ellis's early english pronounciation.—**Trumbull**, J. Hammond. On Algonkin names for man.—**Greenough**, J. B. On some forms of conditional sentences in latin, greek and sanskrit.—Proceedings, 3d annual session, New Haven, 1871.

3. Evans, E. W. Studies in cymric philology.—**Trumbull**, J. Hammond. Words derived from indian languages of North America.—**Hadley**, J. On the byzantine greek pronounciation of the 10th century, as ill. by a ms. in the Bodleian library.—**Stevens**, W. A. On the substantive use of the greek participle.—**Bristed**, C. A. Erroneous and doubtful uses of the word *such*.—**Hartt**, C. F. Notes on the lingoa geral, or modern tupi of the amazonas.—**Whitney**, W: D. On material and form in language. — **March**, F. A. Is there an anglo-saxon language? ; On some irregular verbs in anglo-saxon.—**Trumbull**, J. Hammond. Notes on forty versions of the Lord's Prayer in Algonkin languages.—Proceedings, 4th annual session, Providence, 1872.

4. Allen, F. D. The epic forms of [greek] verbs in *aō*.—**Evans**, E. W. Studies in cymric philology.—**Hadley**, J. On Koch's treatment of the celtic element in english.—**Haldeman**, S. S. On the pronounciation of latin, as presented in several recent grammars.—**Packard**, L. R. On some points in the life of Thucydides.—**Goodwin**, W. W. On the classification of conditional sentences in greek syntax.—**March**, F. A. Recent discussions of Grimm's law.—**Lull**, E. P. Vocabulary of the language of the indians of San Blas and Caledonia Bay, Darien.—Proceedings, 5th annual session, Easton, 1873.

5. Tyler, W. S. On the prepositions in the homeric poems.—**Harkness**, A. On the formation of the tenses for completed action in the latin finite verb.—**Haldeman**, S. S. On an english vowel-mutation, present in *cag, keg*.—**Packard**, L. R. On a passage in Homer's Odyssey, x: 81–86.—**Trumbull**, J. Hammond. On numerals in american indian languages, and the indian mode of counting.—**Sewall**, J. B. On the distinction between the subjunctive and optative modes in greek conditional sentences.—**Morris**, C: D. On the age of Xenophon at the time of the Anabasis.—**Whitney**, W: D. *Physei* or *Thesei*; natural or conventional ?—Proceedings, 6th annual session, Hartford, 1874.

6. Harkness, A. On the formation of the tenses for completed action in the latin finite verb, 2d paper.—**Haldeman**, S. S. On an english consonant-mutation, present in *proof, prove*.—**Carter**, F. On Begemann's views as to the weak preterit of the

germanic verbs.—**Morris**, C: D. On some forms of greek conditional sentences.—**Williams**, A. On verb-reduplication as a means for expressing completed action.—**Sherman**, L. A. A grammatical analysis of the old english poem "The owl and the nightingale."—Proceedings, 7th annual session, Newport, 1875.

7. Gildersleeve, B. L. On [the greek] *et* with the future ind. and *ean* with subj. in the tragic poets.—**Packard**, L. R. On Grote's theory of the construction of the Iliad.—**Humphreys**, M. W. On negative commands in greek.—**Toy**, C. H. On hebrew verb-etymology. — **Whitney**, W: D. A botanico-philological problem.—**Goodwin**, W. W. On *shall* and *should* in protasis. and their greek equivalents. — **Humphreys**, M. W. On certain influences of accent in latin iambic trimeters.—**Trumbull**, J. H. On the Algonkin verb.—**Haldeman**, S. S. On a supposed mutation between *l* and *u*.—Proceedings, 8th annual session, N. Y., 1876.

8. Packard, L. R. Notes on certain passages in the Phaedo and Gorgias of Plato.—**Toy**, C. H. On the nominal basis of the hebrew verb.—**Allen**, F. D. On a certain, apparently pleonastic, use of [the greek] *hōs*.—**Whitney**, W: D. On the relation of surd and sonant.—**Holden**, E. S. On the Vocabularies of children under two years of age.—**Goodwin**, W. W. On the text and interpretation of certain passages in the Agamemnon of Aeschylus.—**Stickney**, A. On the single case-form in italian. — **Carter**, F. On Willmann's theory of the authorship of the Nibelungenlied.—**Sihler**, E. G. On Herodotus's and Aeschylus's accounts of the battle of Salamis.—**Whitney**, W: D. On the principle of economy as a phonetic force.—**Carter**, F. On the Kürenberg hypothesis.—**March**, F. A. On dissimilated gemination. — Proceedings, 9th annual session, Balt., 1877.

9. Gildersleeve, B. L. Contributions to the history of the articular infinitive. — **Toy**, C. H. The Yoruban language.—**Humphreys**, M. W. Influence of accent in latin dactylic hexameters. — **Sachs**, J. Observations on Plato's Cratylus.— **Seymour**, T. D. On the composition of the Cynegeticus of Xenophon. —**Humphreys**, M. W. Elision, especially in greek.—Proceedings, 10th annual session, Saratoga, 1878.

10. Toy, C. H. Modal development of the semitic verb. — **Humphreys**, M. W. On the nature of caesura; On certain effects of elision.—**Cook**, A. S. Studies in the Heliand.—**Harkness**, A. On the development of the latin subj. in principal clauses.—**D'Ooge**, M. L. The original recension of the De corona.—**Peck**, T. The authorship of the Dialogus de oratoribus.—**Seymour**, T. D. On the date of the Prometheus of Aeschylus.—Proceedings, 11th annual session, Newport, 1879.

11. Humphreys, M. W. A contribution to infantile linguistic.—**Toy**, C. H. The hebrew verb-termination *un*.—**Packard**, L. R. The beginning of a written literature in Greece.—**Hall**, I. H. The declension of the definite article in the cypriote inscriptions.—**Sachs**, J. Observations on Lucian.—**Sihler**, E. G. Virgil and Plato.—**Allen**, W. F. The battle of Mons Graupius.—**Whitney**, W. D. On inconsistency in views of language.—**Edgren**, A. H. The kindred germanic words of german and english, exhibited with reference to their consonant relations.—Proceedings, 12th annual session, Phila., 1880.

12. Whitney, W: D. On mixture in language.—**Toy**, C. H. The home of the primitive semitic race. — **March**, F. A. Report of the committee on the reform of english spelling.—**Wells**, B. W. History of the *a*-vowel, from old germanic to modern english.—**Seymour**, T. D. The use of the aorist participle in greek.—**Sihler**, E. G. The use of abstract verbal nouns in *-sis* in Thucydides.—Proceedings, 13th annual session, Cleveland, 1881.

13. Hall, I. H. The greek New testament as pub. in America.—**Merriam**, A. C. Alien intrusion between article and noun in greek.—**Peck**, T. Notes on latin quantity.—**Owen**, W. B. Influence of the latin syntax in the anglo-saxon gospels.—**Wells**, B: W. The ablaut in english.—**Whitney**, W: D. The indo-european case system.— Proceedings, 14th annual session, Cambridge, 1882.

14. Merriam, A: C. The Cæsareum and the worship of Augustus at Alexandria.—**Whitney**, W: D. The varieties of predication.—**Smith**, C: F. On southernisms.—**Wells**, B: W. The development of the ablaut in germanic.— Proceedings, 15th annual session, Middletown, 1883.

3. Comparative philology.

Bopp, Franz. A comparative grammar of the the sanskrit, zend, greek, latin, lithuanian, gothic, german and sclavonic languages. Tr. from the german by E: B. Eastwick. Lond. 1862. 3 v. O. **415 : 2**

Harris, James. Hermes, or A philosophical inquiry concerning universal grammar. 4th ed., rev. and corr. Lond. 1786. O. **415 : 1**

McCurdy, James F: Aryo-semitic speech ; a study in linguistic archæology. Andover. 1881. O. **410+1**

Phonology and orthography.

Bell, Alexander Melville. Visible speech ; the science of universal alphabetics · or self-interpreting physiological letters for the writing of all languages in one alphabet. Ill. by tables, diagrams and examples. Inaugural ed. Lond. 1867. Q. **414+1**

— Sounds and their relations ; a complete manual of universal alphabetics, illustrated by means of visible speech and exhibiting the pronunciation of english in various styles, and of other languages and dialects. Phila. 1881. O. **414 : 2**

Ellis, Alexander J: The alphabet of nature, or Contributions toward a more accurate analysis and symbolization of spoken sounds, with some account of the principal phonetical · alphabets hitherto proposed. Originally pub. in the Phonotypic journal, june 1844—june 1845. Lond. 1845. O. **400 : 3**

Lieber, Francis. The vocal sounds of Laura Bridgman, compared with the elements of phonetic languages. *In* Smithsonian contributions. **506 : R3 v2**

— *Same. In his* Miscellaneous writings. **304 : 7**

Taylor, I: The alphabet ; an account of the origin and development of letters. Lond. 1883. 2 v. O. **411+1**

Silvestre, Joseph Balthazar. Universal palæography, or Fac-similes of writings of all nations and periods, copied from the most celebrated and authentic mss. in the libraries and archives of France, Italy, Germany and England ; accompanied by an historical descriptive text and introd. by Champollion-Figeac and Aimé Champollion, *fils.* Tr. from the french and ed. with corr. and notes by sir F: Madden. Lond. 1850. 2 v. Q. **419+1**

2. Comparative dictionaries.

1. Ancient languages.

Ainsworth, Robert. An abridgement of Ainsworth's dictionary, english and latin, for the use of schools, by T: Morell, carefully corr. and imp. from the last London Q. ed. by J: Carey. Phila. 1818. O. **413 : R23**

Riddle, Joseph Esmond, *and* T: Kerchever Arnold. A copious and critical english-latin lexicon, founded on the german-latin dictionary of C: Ernest Georges. 1st amer. ed., carefully rev. and containing a dictionary of proper names, by C: Anthon. N. Y. 1860. Q. **413 : R5**

Andrews, Ethan Allen. Latin-english lexicon, founded on the latin-german lexicon of W: Freund. New ed., enl. and partly rev. N. Y. 1877. Q. **413 : R6**

Liddell, H: G:, *and* Robert Scott. A greek-english lexicon, based on the german work of Francis Passow, with corr. and add., and the insertion, in alphabetical order, of the proper names occurring in the principal greek authors by H: Drisler. N. Y. 1856. Q. **413 : R7**

Buxtorf, J: Lexicon hebraicum et chaldaicum ; complectens voces omnimodas quæ in sacris bibliis extant ; exemplorum biblicorum copia. et locorum difficilium ex hebræorum commentariis explicatione, auctum et illustratum. Accesserunt, Lexicon breve rabbinico-pilosophicum, et index latinus. Ed. nova. Glasguæ. 1824. O. **413 : R8**

2. Modern languages.

Grieb, Christian F: Englisch-deutsches und deutsch-englisches wörterbuch, mit einer tabellarischen übersicht der von den neueren englischen orthoepisten verschieden ausgesprochenen wörter und einem anhange. enthaltend eine geschichte der englischen sprache, erklärung der aussprache mit dazu gehörigen tabellen, leseübungen nach verschiedenen aussprachen, eine übersicht der unregelmässigen zeitwörter und eine zusammenstellung der im buche selbst fehlenden amerikanismen, von J. C. Oehlschläger. 1er band : Englisch-deutsch ; 2er band : Deutsch-englisch. Phila. 1857. 2 v. Q. **413 : R1**

Calisch, I. M. New complete dictionary of the english and dutch languages in two parts, [English-dutch and Dutch-english]. Tiel. 1875. 2 v. O. **413 : R9**

Spiers, Alexandre, *and* Gabriel Surenne. French and english pronouncing dictionary, newly composed from the french dictionaries of the French academy, Laveaux, Boiste, Bescherelle, Landais etc., and from the english dictionaries of Johnson, Webster, Worcester, Richardson etc.; followed by a vocabulary of the names of places and persons, mythological and classical, ancient and modern. by A. Spiers. Carefully rev., corr. and enl... by G. P. Quackenbos. N. Y. 1878. O. **413 : R2**

Nouveau dictionnaire de poche, français-allemand et allemand - français, enrichi des mots nouveaux généralement reçus dans les deux langues, des tables des verbes irréguliers, des nouvelles mesures et des poids et monnaies de l'empire français. 4e éd., rev., corr. et augm. Leipz. 1808. T. **413 : R22**

Villatte, Césaire. Parisismen ; alphabetisch geordnete sammlung der eigenartigen ausdrucksweisen des Pariser argot; ein supplement zu allen franz.-deutschen wörterbüchern. Berlin. 1884. D. **413 : 25**

Baretti, Giuseppe. A new dictionary of the italian and english languages, based upon that of Baretti, and containing among other add. and imp. numerous neologisms relating to the art and sciences ; a variety of idiomatic and popular phrases ; the inflections of irregular verbs and the anomalous plurals of substantives ; the augmentatives, diminutives and degrees of comparison ; and a copious list of geographical and proper names, both ancient and modern. Compiled by J: Davenport and Guilielmo Comelati. Lond. [1854]. 2 v. O. **413 : R3**
Contents. V. 1. Italian and english. 2. English and Italian.

Velazquez de la Cadena, Mariano. A pronouncing dictionary of the spanish and english languages, composed from the spanish dictionaries of the Spanish academy, Terreros and Salvá, upon the basis of Seoane's ed. of Neuman and Baretti, and from the english dictionaries of Webster, Worcester and Walker, with the add. of more than 8000 words, idioms and familiar phrases, the irregularities of all the verbs and a grammatical synopsis of both languages. In 2 pts : 1, Spanish-english ; 2, English-spanish. N. Y. 1856. Q. **413 : R4**

Ponce de Leon, Néstor. Diccionario tecnológico inglés-español y español-inglés, de los términos y frases usados en las ciencias aplicadas, artes industriales, bellas artes, mecánica, maquinaria, minas, metalurgia, agricultura, comercio, navegacion, manufacturas, arquitectura, ingenieria civil y militar, marina, arte militar, ferro-carriles, telégrafos, etc. N. Y. 1883-84. Q.
413 : R20
Contents. V. 1. Inglés-español ; A—M.

Elwes, Alfred. A dictionary of the portuguese language, in two parts : 1, Portuguese-english ; 2, English-portuguese ; incl. a large number of technical terms used in mining, engineering, etc., with the proper accents and the gender of every noun. [Weales ser.] Lond. 1884. D. **413 : 15**

Valdez, J: Fernandes. A portuguese and english pronouncing dictionary, newly composed from the best dictionaries of both languages ; containing a great number of terms connected with all the sciences and arts, short sentences and expressions ill. such acceptations as present any difficulty, many idiotisms and familiar phrases, and followed by vocabularies of the names of places and persons. 2d ed. Rio de Janeiro. 1879. 2 v. S. **413 : R10**

Öman, V: Emanuel. Svensk-engelsk handordbok. Stockholm. [1881]. D. **413 : R11**

Nilsson, Lars Gabriel, *and others.* Engelsk-svensk ordbok, med Walkers uttalsbeteckning. Stockholm. 1875. D. **413 : R12**
Note. A-E and T-W by L. G. Nilsson; F and L-N by Per F: Widmark; G-K and R, S by A. Z. Collin ; O-Q by H. N. Almkvist ; X-Z by I. T. Ruus.

Larsen, Anton Laurentius. Dansk-norsk-engelsk ordbog. Kjöbenhavn. 1880. S. **413 : R14**
Note. A rev. and enl. ed. of the Danish-english dictionary of J. S. Ferrall and T. G. Repp.

Rosing, Svend. Engelsk-dansk ordbog. Köbenhavn. 1883. S. **413 : R13**

New pocket dictionary of the english and russian languages. Leipz. 1874. 2 v. in 1. T.
413 : R16

Jordan, J. P. Vollständiges taschen-wörterbuch der polnischen und deutschen sprache. Leipz. 1880. 2 v. in 1. T. **413 : R17**

Technologisches wörterbuch, Deutsch-englisch-französisch ; gewerbe-, civil- und militär-baukunst, artillerie, maschinenbau, eisenbahnwesen, strassen- und wasserbau, schiffbau und schifffahrt, berg- und hüttenwesen, mathematik, physik, chemie, mineralogie u. a. m. umfassend, bearb. von E. Althans und anderen, und herausg. von C: v. Albert, mit einem vorwort von K: Karmarsch. 3te aufl. Wiesbaden. 1874-78. 3 v. Q. **413 : R21**

Veitelle, I. de. Mercantile dictionary ; a complete vocabulary of the technicalities of commercial correspondence, names of articles of trade and marine terms in english, spanish and french, with geographical names, business letters and tables of the abbreviations in common use in the three languages. N. Y. 1864. D. **413 : 24**

3. English language.

1. In general.

Marsh, G: Perkins. Lectures on the english language ; 1st ser. 4th ed., rev. and enl. N. Y. [1861.] O. **420 : 2**
-- The origin and history of the english language, and of the early literature it embodies. N. Y. 1882. O. **420 : 6**

Schele de Vere, Maximilian. Studies in english, or Glimpses of the inner life of our language. N. Y. 1867. D. **420 : 7**

Shepherd, H: E. The history of the english language, from the teutonic invasion of Britain to the close of the georgian era. New ed., rev. N. Y. 1880. D. **420 : 3**

Weisse, J: A. Origin, progress and destiny of the english language and literature. N. Y. 1879. O. **420+4**

Storm, J: Englische philologie ; anleitung zum wissenschaftlichen studium der englischen sprache, vom verfasser für das deutsche publikum bearb. 1: Die lebende sprache. Heilbronn. 1881. O. **420 : 1**

Hodgson, W: B. Errors in the use of english. Amer. rev. ed. N. Y. 1882. D. **420 : 5**

2. Orthography and orthoepy.

Speling reform asoshiashun. Buletinz from 1877 to 1880 ; prepärd and publisht under thi öspisez ov thi asoshiashun'z publicashun comiti, viz: F. A. March, ov Easton,

Pa.; O. C. Blackmer, ov Chicago, Ills.; and Melvil Dui, ov Boston, Mass. Colected, complited and baund bai T. R. Vicroi, coresponding secreteri and trezhurer. St. Luis, Mo. 1881. T.   **421 : 3**

Fonetic ticher ; v. 1–3. St. Luis. 1880–82. Q.
421+6

Bigelow, Marshall T. Punctuation and other typographical matters for the use of printers, authors. teachers and scholars. 2d ed. Bost. 1881. S.   **421 : 1**

Butterfield, Consul Willshire. A system of punctuation for the use of schools. Madison. [1878]. D.   **421 : 2**

Fallows, S: Handbook of abbreviations and contractions, current, classical and mediæval, also of secret, benevolent and other organizations, legal works of the U. S. and Great Britain, and of the railroads of the amer. continent. Chicago. 1883. S. **421 : 5**

Osmun, T: Embley, *(Alfred Ayres).* The orthoëpist ; a pronouncing manual containing about 3.500 words, incl. a considerable number of the names of foreign authors, artists, etc., that are often mispronounced, by Alfred Ayres. N. Y. 1880. S.   **421 : 4**

3. Etymology.

Alford, H: The queen's english ; a manual of idiom and usage. 6th ed. Lond. 1882. S.
422 : 10

Moon, G: Washington. The dean's english ; a criticism on the dean of Canterbury's essays on The queen's english. 4th ed. N. Y. [1865]. S.   **422 : 2**

Mathews, W: Words ; their use and abuse. 7th thous. Chic. 1877. D.   **422 : 1**

— *Same.* New ed., rev. and enl. Chic. 1884. D.
422 : 1

Palmer, Abram Smythe. Folk-etymology ; a dictionary of verbal corruptions or words perverted in form or meaning by false derivation or mistaken analogy. N. Y. 1883. O.   **422 : 8**

Swinton, W: Rambles among words; their poetry, history and wisdom. N. Y. 1859. D.   **422 : 3**

Trench, R: Chenevix. English, past and present ; eight lectures. 6th ed., rev. N. Y. 1868. S.   **422 : 4**

— On the study of words ; lectures addressed originally to the pupils of the diocesan training-school, Winchester. N. Y. 1878. D.   **422 : 5**

Wedgwood, Hensleigh. Contested etymologies in the dictionary of W. W. Skeat. Lond. 1882. D.   **422 : 9**

White, R: Grant. Words and their uses, past and present ; a study of the english language. 3d ed., rev. and corr. Bost. 1880. D.   **422 : 6**

— Every-day english ; a sequel to Words and their uses. Bost. 1880. D.   **422 : 7**

Haldeman, S: Stehman. Affixes in their origin and application. exhibiting the etymologic structure of english words. New ed. Phila. 1884. D.   **422 : 11**

Gomme, G: Laurence, *ed.* The Gentleman's magazine library ; a classified collection of the chief contents of the Gentleman's

magazine from 1731 to 1868 : Dialect, proverbs and word-lore. Lond. 1884. O.
427 : 3

4. Dictionaries.

Johnson, S: Dictionary of the english language ; with Walker's pronounciation. *T. p. w.* [Lond. 1856.] O.   **423 : R1**

Ogilvie, J: The imperial dictionary of the english language ; a complete encyclopædic lexicon, literary, scientific and technological. New ed, rev. and augm., ed. by C: Annandale. Ill. London. 1883. 4 v. Q.
423 : R7

Philological society, The. A new english dictionary on historical principles ; founded mainly on the materials collected by the Philological society, ed. by James A. H. **Murray,** with the assistance of many scholars and men of science. Pt. 1 : A–Ant. Oxford. 1884. F.   **423 : R12**

Richardson, C: A new dictionary of the english language, combining explanation with etymology, and ill. by quotations from the best authorities ; the words, with those of the same family in german, dutch and swedish, or in italian, french and spanish, are traced to their origin ; the explanations are deduced from the primitive meaning through the various usages ; the quotations are arr. chronol. from the earliest period to the beginning of the present century. Lond. 1875. 2 v. Q.   **423 : R2**
Note. Each vol. contains a supplement of a later date than the body of the work.

Skeat, Walter W: An etymological dictionary of the english language. N. Y. 1882. O.
423 : R5

— A concise etymological dictionary of the english language. N. Y. 1882. D.   **423 : 6**

Stormonth, James. A dictionary of the english language, pronouncing, etymological and explanatory ; embracing scientific and other terms, numerous familiar terms, and a copious selection of old english words. The pronounciation rev. by P. H. Phelp. N. Y. 1885. Q.   **423 : R14**

Webster, Noah. An american dictionary of the english language ; intended to exhibit the origin. affinities and primary signification of english words, as far as they have been ascertained, the genuine orthography and pronounciation of words, according to general usage, or to just principles of analogy, accurate and discriminating definitions, with numerous authorities and ill. Prefixed, an introd. dissertation on the origin, history and connection of the languages of western Asia and of Europe, and a concise grammar of the english language. N. Y. 1828. 2 v. Q. **423 : R13**

— An american dictionary of the english language ; thoroughly rev. and greatly enl. and imp. by Chauncey A. Goodrich and Noah Porter ; with an app. of useful tables. Added, a supp. of nearly 5,000 new words, with their definitions, etc., also, a new pronouncing biographical dictionary, containing nearly 10,000 names of noted persons in ancient and modern times, giving their nationality, their occupation and the dates of their birth and death. Springfield, Mass. 1880. Q.   **423 : R3**

Contents. Pref. to the new enl. and ill. ed.—Pref. to the rev. ed. of 1847.—Pref. to the ed. of 1828.—Memoir of Noah Webster.—Brief history of the english language.—Key to the pronunciation.—Principles of pronunciation.—Orthography.—Abbreviations and explanations.—Dictionary of the english language.—Supplement.—Metric system.—**App.** Pref.—Explanatory and pronouncing vocabulary of the names of noted fictitious persons, places, etc.—Pronouncing vocabulary of scripture proper names.—Pronouncing vocabulary of greek and latin proper names.—Vocabulary of modern geographical names.—Pronouncing biographical dictionary.—Pronouncing vocabulary of common english christian names, with their derivation, signification, etc.—Quotations, words, phrases, proverbs, etc. from the greek, the latin and modern foreign languages.—Abbreviations and contractions used in writing and printing.—Arbitrary signs used in writing and printing.—A classified selection of pictorial illustrations.

Worcester, Joseph Emerson. A dictionary of the english language ; with supp. containing over 12,500 new words and entries, and a vocabulary of synonymes in general use. Phila. 1881. Q.   **423 : R4**

Contents. Principles of pronunciation.—Orthography.—English grammar.—Origin, formation and etymology of the english language.—Archaisms, provincialisms and americanisms.—History of english lexicography.—Catalogue of english dictionaries, glossaries, encyclopædias, etc.—List of the principal scientific works used in the preparation of this dictionary.—Abbreviations and signs.—Dictionary of the english language.—**App.** Pronunciation of greek and latin proper names.—Pronunciation of scripture proper names.—Pronunciation of modern geographical names.—Pronunciation of the names of distinguished men of modern times.—Abbreviations used in writing and printing.—Signs used in writing and printing.—A collection of words, phrases and quotations from the greek, latin, french, italian and spanish languages.—Supplement.

*   *   *

Coleridge, Herbert. A glossarial index to the printed english literature of the 13th century. Lond. 1859. O.   **423 : 9**

Halliwell-Phillipps, James Orchard. A dictionary of archaic and provincial words, obsolete phrases, proverbs and ancient customs from the 14th century. 10th ed. Lond. 1881. 2 v. O.   **423 : R11**

Nares, Robert. A glossary or collection of words, phrases, names and allusions to customs, proverbs etc., which have been thought to require illustration in the works of english authors, particularly Shakespeare and his contemporaries. New ed. with considerable add. of both words and examples by James O. Halliwell and T: Wright. Lond. 1882. 2 v. O.   **423 : R10**

Smith, H: Percy, *ed.* Glossary of terms and phrases. N. Y. 1883. O.   **423 : R8**

Dialects.

Bartlett, J: Russell. Dictionary of americanisms; a glossary of words and phrases usually regarded as peculiar to the U. S. 4th ed. enl. Bost. 1877. O.   **427 : 1**

Fallows, S: Handbook of briticisms, americanisms, colloquial and provincial words and phrases. Chic. 1883. T.   **427 : 2**

Matsell, G: W. Vocabulum, or The rogue's lexicon ; comp. from the most authentic sources. N. Y. *n. d.* D.   **427 : 4**

5. Synonyms.

Crabb, G: English synonymes explained in alphabetical order, with copious ill. and examples drawn from the best writers ; added, an index to the words. New ed., with add. and corr. N. Y. 1880. O.   **424 : 1**

Jermyn, James. Book of english epithets, literal and figurative, with elementary remarks and minute references to abundant authorities. Lond. 1849. Q.   **424+3**

Roget, P: M: Thesaurus of english words and phrases, classified and arr. so as to facilitate the expression of ideas and assist in literary composition. New ed., enl. and imp. from the author's notes, and with a full index by J: L: Roget. N. Y. 1883. D.   **424 : R2**

— *Same.* Lond. 1879. O.   **424 : 2**

Smith, C: J: Synonyms and antonyms, or Kindred words and their opposites, collected and contrasted. Lond. 1881. D.   **424 : 4**

— Synonyms discriminated ; a dictionary of synonymous words in the english language, ill. with quotations from standard writers. New ed. with the author's latest corr. and add., ed. by H. Percy Smith. London. 1882. O.   **424 : R5**

Soule, R: A dictionary of english synonymes and synonymous or parallel expressions, designed as a practical guide to aptness and variety of phraseology. Boston. 1882. D.   **424 : 6**

6. Grammar.

Hutchinson, H. Thought-symbolism and grammatic illusions ; a treatise on the nature, purpose and material of speech and a demonstration of the unreality, the useless complexity and the evil effects of orthodox grammatic rules in general. Lond. 1884.   **425 : 12**

Brown, Goold. The grammar of english grammars with an introd., historical and critical, the whole methodically arr. and amply ill. with forms of correcting and of parsing, improprieties for correction, examples for parsing, questions for examination, exercises for writing, observations for the advanced student, decisions and proofs for the settlement of disputed points, occasional strictures and defences, an exhibition of the different methods of analysis and a key to the oral exercises ; added, four appendixes pertaining separately to the four parts of grammar. 10th ed., rev. Index by S: U. Berrian. N. Y. 1882. Q.   **425 : R9**

Carpenter, Stephen Haskens. The elements of english analysis ill. by a new system of diagrams. [Madison.] 1878. S.   **425 : 3**

Cobbett, W: A grammar of the english language in a series of letters intended for the use of schools and of young persons in general, but more especially for the use of soldiers, sailors, apprentices and ploughboys. Added, six lessons intended to prevent statesmen from using false grammar and from writing in an awkward manner. Notes by Robert Waters. *In* **Waters,** R. How to get on in the world. **923.23 : 4**

Mätzner, E: An english grammar, methodical, analytical and historical ; with a treatise on the orthography, prosody, inflections and syntax of the english tongue and numerous authorities, cited in order of historical development. Tr. from the german, with the sanction of the author, by Clair James Grece. Lond. 1874. 3 v. O. **425 : 2**

Morris, R: Historical outlines of english accidence ; comprising chapters on the history and development of the language and on word-formation. Lond. 1885. S. **425 : 11**

— English grammar. (Literature primers). N. Y. 1878. S. **425 : 4**

— and H: Courthope **Bowen.** English grammar exercises. (Literature primers). N. Y. 1878. S. **425 : 5**

Nesbitt, M. L. Grammar-land, or Grammar in fun for the children of Schoolroomshire. 3d ed. Ill. Lond. 1877. S. x **425 : 7**

Osmun, T: Embley, (*Alfred Ayres*). The verbalist ; a manual devoted to brief discussions of the right and wrong use of words, and to some other matters of interest to those who would speak and write with propriety, by Alfred Ayres. N. Y. 1882 [1881]. S. **425 : 6**

Quackenbos, G: Payne. First lessons in composition, in which the principles of the art are developed in connection with the principles of grammar ; embracing full directions on the subject of punctuation, with exercises. 164th thousand. N. Y. 1862. D. **425 : 8**

Whitney, W: Dwight. Essentials of english grammar, for the use of schools. Bost. 1880. D. **425 : 1**

Carolino, P: English as she is spoke ; a jest in sober earnest. with an introd. by James Millington. N. Y. [1883]. T. **469 : 1**

— "Her seconds part" ; English as she is spoke, or A jest in sober earnest, with an introd. by J. Millington. N. Y. 1883. T. **469 : 1 v2**

x denotes books specially adapted for children.

English as she is wrote ; showing curious ways in which the english language may be made to convey ideas or obscure them ; a companion to "English as she is spoke." N. Y. 1884 [1883]. T. **425 : 10**

7. Prosody.

Everett, Erastus. A system of english versification ; containing rules for the structure of the different kinds of verse, ill. by numerous examples from the best poets. N. Y. 1848. D. **426 : 2**

Guest, Edwin. A history of english rhythms. Lond. 1838. 2 v. O. **426 : 1**

Lanier, Sidney. The science of english verse. N. Y. 1880. O. **426 : 3**

Hood, Tom. The rhymester, or The rules of rhyme ; a guide to english versification, with a dictionary of rhymes, an examination of classical measures, and comments upon burlesque, comic verse and songwriting, ed. with add. by Arthur Penn [*pseud. for* J. B. Matthews]. N. Y. 1882. S. **426 : 4**

Walker, J. The rhyming dictionary of the english language; in which the whole language is arr. according to its terminations, with an introd. to the various uses of the work and an index of allowable rhymes, with authorities for their usage from our best poets. Rev. and enl. by J. Longmuir. New ed. Lond. n. d. D. **426 : 5**

8. Anglo-saxon language.

Corson, Hiram. Hand-book of anglo-saxon and early english. N. Y. 1871. D. **429 : 2**

Klipstein, L: F. A grammar of the anglo-saxon language. Rev. and enl. ed. N. Y. 1849. D. **429 : 3**

Hart, James Morgan. A syllabus of anglo-saxon literature ; adapted from Bernhard Ten Brink's Geschichte der englischen litteratur. Cinc. 1881. O. **429+1**

4. Foreign languages.

1. German.

Grimm, Jakob L: K: Geschichte der deutschen sprache. 3te aufl. Leipz. 1868. 2 v. in 1. O. **430 : 1**

— and W: K: Grimm. Deutsches wörterbuch, [fortgesetzt von Moritz Heyne, Rudolf Hildebrand, Matthias Lexer und K: Weigand]. Portr. Leipz. 1854–85. 7 v. in 8. Q. **434 : R4**

Contents. V. 1. A-B. 2. B-D. 3. E-Forsche. 4. 1ste abth.. abgeschlossen von K: Weigand u. R. Hildebrand. Forschel-G. 4, 2e abth., bearb. von R. Hildebrand, K: Weigand u. M. Heyne. H-J. 5, bearb. von R. Hildebrand. K. 6, bearb. von M. Heyne. L-M. 7, bearb. von M. Lexer. N-. *In course of publication.*

Hoffmann, W:, *ed.* Wörterbuch der deutschen sprache, wie sie in der allgemeinen literatur, der poesie, den wissenschaften, künsten, gewerben, dem handelsverkehr, staats- und gerichtswesen, etc., gebräuchlich ist. Leipz. 1871. 3 v. O. **433 : R1**

Sanders, Daniel. Ergänzungswörterbuch der deutschen sprache ; eine vervollständigung und erweiterung aller bisher erschienenen deutschsprachlichen wörterbücher, einschliesslich des Grimm'schen ; mit belegen von Luther bis auf die neueste gegenwart. Berlin. 1884. Q. **434 : R5**

Müller, W: Mittelhochdeutsches wörterbuch ; mit benutzung des nachlasses von G: F: Benecke. Leipz. 1854–63. 3 v. in 4. O. **433 : R2**

Contents. V. 1. A-L. 2, pt. 1, bearb. von F: Zarncke, M-R ; pt. 2, bearb. von W: Müller, S. 3. T-Z.

Sanders, Daniel. Wörterbuch der hauptschwierigkeiten in der deutschen sprache. Grosse ausg.; 13te verm. aufl. Berlin. 1882. O. **433 : 3**

Paul, Hermann. Zur orthographischen frage. *In* Deutsche zeit- und streit-fragen. **304 : 15 v9**

Regeln und wörterverzeichnis für die deutsche orthographie ; auf grundlage der von R. v. Raumer verfassten vorlage. Milw. 1876. O. 431 : 2

Duden, Konrad. Vollständiges orthographisches wörterbuch für die schule ; nach den amtlichen regeln der neuen orthographie. Leipz. 1882. O. 431 : 1

Frehse, F: Wörterbuch zu Fritz Reuters Sämmtlichen werken. N. Y. 1869. D.
in **R 951 v14**

Eberhardt, J: A: Synonymisches handwörterbuch der deutschen sprache, für alle, welche sich in dieser sprache richtig ausdrücken wollen. 12te ausg. durchgängig umgearb., verm. und verb. von F: Rückert ; mit bezeichnung der wörter in englischer, französischer, italienischer und russischer sprache und den zu diesen sprachen gehörenden indicis von A. Asher und A: Boltz, nebst einer vergleichenden darstellung der deutschen vor- und nachsilben, mit erläuternder beziehung auf die englische, französische, italienische und russische sprache, von A: Boltz. Leipz. [1851]. S. 434 : 1

Schlessing, A. Deutscher wörterschatz, oder Der passende ausdruck ; praktisches hilfs- und nachschlagebuch in allen verlegenheiten der schriftlichen und mündlichen darstellung, für gebildete aller stände und ausländer, welche einer correcten wiedergabe ihrer gedanken in deutscher sprache sich befleissigen ; mit einem den gebrauch erleichternden hilfswörterbuch. Stuttg. 1881. O. 434 : 2

Dunger, Hermann. Wörterbuch von verdeutschungen entbehrlicher fremdwörter, mit besonderer berücksichtigung der von dem generalstabe im postwesen und in der reichsgesetzgebung angenommenen verdeutschungen ; mit einer einleitenden abhandlung über fremdwörter und sprachreinigung. Leipz. 1882. O. 434 : 3

Heinze, Theodor. Ueber die fremdwörter im deutschen. *In* Deutsche zeit- und streitfragen. 304 : 15 v7

Whitney, W: Dwight. A compendious german grammar. 5th ed. rev. N. Y. *n. d.* D. 435 : 2

Laue, Adolphus H. The german substantive, its gender and declension ; an aid for all students of the german language. New Haven. 1880. D. 435 : 1

2. French.

Fasquelle, L: A new method of learning the french language ; embracing both the analytic and synthetic modes of instruction, on the plan of Woodbury's method with the german. Rev. N. Y. *n. d.* D. 445 : 3
— *Same.* Key. N. Y. *n. d.* D. 445 : 4

Bugard, B. F. A new treatise on french pronunciation, or A series of rules, by which every person acquainted with the english language may readily ascertain the french pronunciation of all words, even of those which do not belong to the french language. Phila. 1833. D. 441 : 1

Perrin, J: Entertaining and instructive exercises with the rules of the french syntax.

9th ed., rev. and corr. agreeably to the author's grammar by mr. Tocquot. N. Y. 1802. S. 445 : 1

Larousse, P: La lexicologie des écoles : Cours complet de langue française et de style, divisé en trois années et rédigé sur un plan entièrement neuf. 2e année. 5e éd. Paris. *n. d.* S. 445 : 2

Livre des petits enfants, Le ; ou Recueil de récits mis à la portée du premier âge, avec vocabulaire. Nouvelle éd. amér. N. Y. 1853. S. 448 : 1

3. Other languages.

E u r o p e a n .

Otté, Emily C. How to learn d a n i s h, dano-norwegian ; a manual for students of danish, dano-norwegian, based upon the ollendorffian system of teaching languages and adapted for self-instruction. 2d ed. Lond. 1884. D. 498.3 : 3

Ahn, F: A new practical grammar of the d u t c h language, with dialogues and readings in prose and verse. 3d ed. Lond. 1878. D. 439 : 2

Fisk, B: Franklin. A grammar of the g r e e k language. 25th ed. Bost. 1845. D. 485 : 3

Goodrich, Chauncey Allen. Elements of g r e e k grammar, used in Yale college, heretofore pub. as the grammar of Caspar F: Hachenberg. 6th ed. Hartford. 1833. D. 485 : 1

Fontana, G. B. An elementary grammar of the i t a l i a n language, progressively arr. for the use of schools and colleges. N. Y. 1882. D. 455 : 1

Marcellus, Nonius. De proprietate sermonis. Additus est [Fabius] **Fulgentius Planciades,** De prisco sermone. Ex recensione et cum notis Josiæ Mercerii, ad ed. parisiensem anni 1614 quam fidelissime repræsentati ; accedit notitia literaria. Lipsiæ. 1826. S. 474 : R1

D'Orsey, Alexander James Donald. A practical grammar of p o r t u g u e s e and english ; exhibiting in a series of exercises in double translation, the idiomatic structure of both languages as now written and spoken. 3d ed. Lond. 1868. D. 469 : 2

Riola, H: How to learn r u s s i a n ; a manual for students of russian, based upon the ollendorffian system of teaching languages and adapted for self-instruction ; with a pref. by W. R. S. Ralston. 2d rev. ed. Lond. 1883. D. 497 : 1

— A graduated russian reader; with a vocabulary of all the russian words contained in it. Lond. 1879. D. 497 : 2

Josse, A: L: A grammar of the s p a n i s h language, with practical exercises. Rev., amended, imp. and enl. by F: Sales. 3d amer. ed. Boston. 1827. D. 465 : 1

Knapp, W: Ireland. A grammar of the modern spanish language, as now written and spoken in the capital of Spain. Bost. 1882. D. 465 : 2

May, Alfred. A practical grammar of the s w e d- i s h language, with reading and writing exercises. Lond. 1850. D. 498.1 : 1

Asiatic.

Whitney, W: Dwight. Indische grammatik, umfassend die klassische sprache und die älteren dialecte. Aus dem englischen übers. von H: Zimmer. Leipz. 1879. O. **494 : 1**

American.

Gibbs, G: Instruction for research relative to the ethnology and philology of America. Wash. 1863. O. *In* Smithsonian misc.
         506 : R4 v7
— Dictionary of the Chinook jargon or trade language of Oregon. Wash. 1863. O. *In* Smithsonian misc. **506 : R4 v7**

Riggs, Stephen R., *ed.* Grammar and dictionary of the Dakota language ; coll. by the members of the Dakota mission. Wash. 1852. Q. *In* Smithsonian contributions.
         506 : R3 v4
Collins, C. R. Languages of the different tribes of indians inhabiting the terr. of Utah. *In* Simpson, J. H. Report of exploration.
         in **917.5 : D**
Bowen, T. J. A grammar and dictionary of the Yoruba language, with an introd. description of the country and people of Yoruba. Map. Wash. 1858. Q. *In* Smithsonian contributions. **506 : R3 v10**
 Note. For other american languages, see Northamerican indians, cl. 970.1.

VI. NATURAL SCIENCE.

1. In general.

1. Comprehensive and collected works.

Arago, Dominique François J: Sämmtliche werke; mit einer einleitung von Alexander v. Humboldt. Deutsche original-ausg., herausg. von W. G. Hankel. Leipz. 1854–65. 16 v. D. **500 : 3**
Contents, see Deutscher katalog, p. 15.

Campbell, G: Douglas, *8th duke of Argyll.* The unity of nature. N. Y. 1884. O. **501+4**

Chambers, W: *and* Robert, *eds.* Introduction to the sciences; for use in schools and for private instruction. New ed. (Chambers's educational course.) Edinb. 1838. D. **500 : 8**
Contents, see Deutscher katalog, p. 20.

Göthe, J: Wolfgang v. Naturwissenschaftliche schriften. *In his* Sämmtliche werke. **830 : 137 v32–34**

Humboldt, F: H: Alexander *freiherr* v. Kosmos; entwurf einer physischen weltbeschreibung, mit einer biographischen einleitung von Bernhard von Cotta. Stuttg. 1874. 4 v. S. **500 : 4**
— *Same, eng.* Cosmos; a sketch of a physical description of the universe. Tr. from the german by E. C. Otté. Lond. 1849, 1858. 5 v. D. **500 : 4**

Reichenbach, O. Einige gedanken eines nichtgelehrten bei lesung des Kosmos. Phila. 1857. D. **500 : 5**

Huxley, T: H: Introductory. (Science primers.) N. Y. 1880. S. **500 : 7**

Plinius Secundus, Caius. Natural history. Tr. with copious notes and ill. by J: Bostock and H. T. Riley. Lond. 1855–57. 6 v. D. **500 : 6**

Somerville, Mary. On the connection of the physical sciences. N. Y. 1854. S. **500 : 10**

Stallo, J: Bernhard. Concepts and theories of modern physics. (Intern. scientific ser.) N. Y. 1882. D. **501 : 3**

Voltaire, François Marie Arouet de. The elements of sir I: Newton's philosophy. Tr. from the french, rev. and corr. by J: Hanna, with explication of some words in alphabetical order. Lond. 1738. D. **501 : 1**

Johnston, Alexander Keith. The physical atlas of natural phenomena. New and enl. ed. Edinb. 1856. F. **500 : R12**

South Kensington museum. Handbook to the special loan collection of scientific apparatus, 1876. Lond. [1876]. D. **500 : 11**
Contents. Introd.—**Maxwell,** James Clerk. General considerations respecting scientific apparatus.— **Smith,** H: J: Stephen. Arithmetical instruments; Geometrical instruments and models.—**Clifford,** W: Kingdon. Instruments used in measurement; Instruments illustrating kinematics, statics and dynamics.—Molecular physics: **Guthrie,** F: General considerations.—**Maxwell,** James Clerk. Instruments connected with fluids.—**Stone,** W. H. Acoustical instruments.—Light: **Spottiswoode,** W: Optical instruments; **Abney,** W. de W. Photographic printing processes.—**Tait,** P: Guthrie. Instruments employ d in heat investigations.—**Foster,** G: Carey. Magnetic apparatus; Electrical instruments.— **Lockyer,** Joseph Norman. Astronomical instruments.—**Goodeve,** J. M. Applied mechanics.— **McLeod,** Herbert. Chemical apparatus and products.—**Scott,** Robert H. Meteorological instruments.—Geographical instruments and maps: **Markham,** Clements R. Instruments used for geographical purposes; Geographical maps: Arctic maps; **Davis,** J: E: Antarctic maps; **Markham,** Clements R. Maps of India.—**Geikie,** Archibald. Geology.— **Smyth,** Warington Wilkinson. Apparatus used in mining.—**Maskelyne,** Nevil Story. Crystallography and mineralogy.—**Huxley,** T: H: Instruments employed in biological research.—**Sorby,** H: Clifton. Microscopes.

2. Dictionaries and cyclopedias.

(See also Useful arts, Dictionaries, cl. 603.)

Buchanan, W. M. The dictionary of science and technical terms used in philosophy, literature, professions, commerce, arts and trades; with supp., ed. by James A. Smith. Lond. 1884. D. **503 : R4**

Rodwell, G: Farrer, *ed.* A dictionary of science; comprising astronomy, chemistry, dynamics, electricity, heat, hydrodynamics, hydrostatics, light, magnetism, mechanics, meteorology, pneumatics, sound and statics; preceded by an essay on the history of the physical sciences. Ill. Phila. 1873. O. **503 : R1**

Rossiter, W: An ill. dictionary of scientific terms. (Putnam's series of ill. dictionaries.) N. Y. [1878]. D. **503 : 2**

Wylde, James, *ed.* The circle of the sciences; a cyclopædia of experimental, chemical, mathematical and mechanical philosophy, and natural history. Lond. *n. d.* 1 v. in 2. Q. **503 : R3**

3. Compends and education.

Kleinwächter, F: Zur frage des naturwissenschaftlichen unterrichtes. *In* Deutsche zeit- und streit-fragen. **304 : 15 v8**

Siebeck, H. Ueber wesen und zweck des wissenschaftlichen studiums; rede gehalten

am jahresfeste der universität Basel. *In* Deutsche zeit- und streit-fragen.
304 : 15 v12

Bernstein, Aaron. Naturwissenscaftliche volks-bücher. 4te aufl. Berlin. 1880. 21 v. in 6. S. **500 : 1**
Contents, see Deutscher katalog, p. 16.

— — Neue folge. Berlin. [1881.] 3 v. in 1. D.
500 : 2
Contents, see Deutscher katalog, p. 16.

Boston society of natural history. Guides for science teaching; no. 1-7, 12. Bost. 1878-83. S. **507 : 2**
Contents. V. 1, no. 1-5. **Hyatt,** A. About pebbles.—**Goodale,** G: L. Concerning a few common plants.—**Hyatt,** A. Commercial and other sponges.—**Agassiz,** E. C. A first lesson in natural history.—**Hyatt,** A. Common hydroids, corals and echinoderms. 2, no. 6, 7. **Hyatt,** A. The oyster, clam and other common mollusks.—**Hyatt,** A. Worms and crustacea. 3, no. 12. **Crosby,** W: O. Common minerals and rocks.

Masius, Hermann, *ed.* Die gesammten naturwissenschaften ; für das verständniss weiterer kreise und auf wissenschaftlicher grundlage bearb. von Dippel, Gottlieb, Gurlt, Klein, Mädler, Masius, Moll, Nauck, Nöggerath, Overzier, Quenstedt, Reclam, Reis, Romberg, Zech, eingeleitet von Hermann Masius. 3te aufl. Essen. 1873-77. 3 v. O. **502+1**
Contents, see Deutscher katalog, p. 16.

Pouchet, Félix Archimède. The universe, or The infinitely great and the infinitely little. 6th ed. Ill. N. Y. 1882. O. **502 : 6**

Schödler, F: Das buch der natur; die lehren der physik, astronomie, chemie, mineralogie, geologie, botanik, zoologie und physiologie umfassend ; allen freunden der naturwissenschaft gewidmet. 20ste aufl. Ill. Braunschweig. 1875. 2 v. O. **502 : 2**
Contents, see Deutscher katalog, p. 16.

— *Same, eng.* The book of nature ; an elementary introd. to the sciences of physics, astronomy, chemistry, mineralogy, geology, botany, zoology and physiology. 1st amer. ed. with glossary and other add., from the 2d eng. ed., tr. from the 6th german ed. by H: Medlock. Ill. Phila. 1853. O. **502 : 2**

Society for the diffusion of useful knowledge. Library of useful knowledge : [natural philosophy]. **504 : 4**
Contents. V. 1. (1) **Brougham,** H: *lord.* A discourse of the objects, advantages and pleasures of science. London. 1827. O.—(2) **Brougham,** H: *lord.* Hydrostatics.—(3) **Millington,**—. Hydraulics.—(4) **Lardner,** D. Pneumatics.—(5) **Ogg,**—. Heat.—(8) **Brewster,** *Sir* D: Optics. 2, (9) **Pritchard,** A. (?) Optical instruments. 4. (7) **Bell,** *Sir* C. Animal mechanics.

Wells, D: Ames. Science popularly explained. (J: Cassell's educational course.) *T. p. w.* [Lond. 1856]. O. **502 : 3**

Wesley, J: A survey of the wisdom of God in the creation, or A compendium of natural philosophy ; containing an abridgement of The contemplation of nature by mr. Bonnet, also, an extract from mr. Denten's Inquiry into the origin of the discoveries attributed to the ancients. 3d amer. ed. rev. and enl. with notes by B. Mayo. N. Y. 1823. 2 v. O. **502 : 5**

Champlin, J: Denison, *jr.* The child's catechism of common things. N. Y. 1880. S. **x 502 : 4**

Boys' and girls' book of science. Ill. Lond. 1881. O. **x 504 : 28**

Guthrie, F: The first book of knowledge. N. Y. 1882. S. **x 504 : 37**

Joyce, Jeremiah. Scientific dialogues for the instruction and entertainment of young people, in which the first principles of natural and experimental philosophy are fully explained and ill. New ed., with questions for examination and other add. by W: Pinnock. Rev. and completed to the present state of knowledge, with an additional chapter on recent discoveries, by J. W. Griffith. Lond. 1859. D. **504 : 43**

Natural history rambles :
— **Ansted,** D: T: In search of minerals. Lond. 1880. S. **504 : 29**
— **Cooke,** M. C. Ponds and ditches. Lond. 1880. S. **504 : 30**
— — The woodlands. Lond. 1880. S. **504 : 31**
— **Duncan,** P: Martin. The sea-shore. Lond. 1880. S. **504 : 32**
— **Napier,** C: Ottley Groom. Lakes and rivers. Lond. 1879. S. **504 : 33**
— **Taylor,** J: E: Mountain and moor. Lond. 1879. S. **504 : 34**
— — Underground. Lond. 1879. S. **504 : 35**
— **Wood,** J: G: Lane and field. Lond. [1879]. S. **504 : 36**

Simple lessons for home use, chiefly intended for elementary schools. N. Y. 1879. S. **x 504 : 26**
Contents. **Miller,** *Mrs.* F. Our bodily life: How and why we breathe.—**Bevan,** G. P. Food.—**Mann,** R. J. Drink.—**Buckminster,** J. C. Cookery.—**Clarke,** *Mrs.* B. Plain needle-work.—**Pope,** J. J. Clothine.—**Miller,** *Mrs.* F. Air and ventilation; The sicknesses that spread.—**Mann,** R. J. The weather.—**Proctor,** R. A. Astronomy.—**Morris,** F. O. Birds.—**Henslow,** G. Flowers.—**Crallan,** T. E. Money.

4. Essays and miscellany.

Brown, Robert, *ed.* Science for all. Lond. [1880-1881]. 5 v. Q. **504+27**
Note. A collection of essays, by various authors, on acoustics, aërostatics, agriculture, anthropology, astronomy, botany, chemistry, electricity, entomology, geology, meteorology, military science, mineralogy, optics, ornithology, palæontology, physical geography, general physics, physiology, photography and general zoology. V. 5 contains a general index, which see for contents of the work.

Estes, Dana, *ed.* Half hour recreations in popular science; 1st ser. Bost. 1874. O. **504 : 5 v1**
Contents. **Proctor,** R: A. Strange discoveries respecting the aurora; Recent solar researches.—**Kent,** W. S. Measuring the brightness of the sun.—**Virchow,** R. The cranial affinities of man and the ape.—**Schellen,** T. J. H. Spectrum analysis explained and its uses to science illustrated; Spectrum analysis discoveries; Nebulae, comets, meteoric showers, and the revelations of the spectroscope regarding them.—**Dana,** J. D. Corals and coral islands.—**Carpenter,** W: B. Unconscious action of the brain; Epidemic delusions.—The Tiber exploration.—**Winchell,** A. The geology of the stars.—**Huxley,** T: H: On yeast.—**Tice,** J: H. The relations between matter and force.—**Tylor,** E: B. The stone age, past and present.—**Richardson,** B: W. Theory of a nervous ether.—**Cumming,** *Sir* A. R. Gordon-. Toads in the hole.—**Hunt,** T: S. The origin of metalliferous deposits.—Rotundity of the earth.—**Richardson,** B: W. The phenomena of sleep.—**Jeffry,** G: Animal life at great depths in the sea.—**Barry,** H. Russian metallurgical works.—**Hunt,** R. Coal as a reservoir of power.—**Meade,** H. Hot springs of New Zealand.—**Clifford,** W: K. Atoms.—**Dove,** H: W: The circulation of the waters on the surface of the earth.—What is actinism ?

x denotes books specially adapted for children.

Estes, Dana, *ed.—Continued.*
— Half hour recreations in popul science ; 2d
    series. Bost. [1879]. O.   ar **504 : 5 v2**
    Contents. **Tyndall**, J: On transmission of sound
    by the atmosphere. — **Kent**, W. S. Gigantic cuttle-
    fish.—**Braun**, A. The glacial epoch of our globe.—
    Stewart, B. The sun and the earth.—**Phelps**, J. W.
    Force electrically exhibited.—Weighing the earth in a
    coal-pit.—The influence of violet light on the growth
    of animals and plants.—**Geikie**, J. The ice age in
    Britain.—Perception of the lowest animals.—**Chase**,
    H: S. Causes of the degeneracy of the teeth.—The
    great pyramid of Egypt. — Photography. — **Kny**, L.
    Plant life in the sea. — The illumination of beacons
    and buoys.—**Garbit**, F. J. The telephone ; The pho-
    nograph.—**Proctor**, R: A. The use and abuse of food;
    Ozone.—**Williamson**, W. C. The succession of life
    on the earth.—**Roscoe**, H: E. What the earth is com-
    posed of.— **Proctor**, R: A. Dew. — **Lovering**, J. On
    sympathetic vibrations as exhibited in ordinary ma-
    chinery. — **Gray**, A. Notes on tree growth. — **Prit-
    chard**, H. B. Science and war. — **Hitchcock**, C. H.
    Existence of glacial action upon the summit of Mt.
    Washington.—**Proctor**, R: A. The levelling power of
    rain.

Proctor, R: Anthony, *ed.* Nature studies. N. Y.
    1883. D.   **504 : 45**
    Contents. **Proctor**, R: A. C: R. Darwin : Newton
    and Darwin.—**Clodd**, E: Dreams.—**Allen**, G. Honey
    ants.—**Wilson**, A. Colors of animals.—**Allen**, G.
    A winter weed.—**Wilson**, A. A poisonous lizard. —
    Foster, T: Birds with teeth. — **Proctor**, R: A. The
    Fiji islands. — **Allen**, G. Hyacinth bulbs. — **Wilson**,
    A. Our unbidden guests. — **Allen**, G. The first daffo-
    dil.—**Proctor**, R: A. Strange sea monsters. — **Allen**,
    G. The origin of buttercups. — **Wilson**, A. Found
    links. — **Proctor**, R: A. Intelligence in animals.—
    Allen, G. Our ancestors ; The beetle's view of life ;
    What is a grape?—**Wilson**, A. Germs of disease and
    death. — **Proctor**, R: A.   A wonderful discovery ;
    Brain troubles ; Thought-reading.—**Allen**, G. Monks-
    hood.

Brewster, *Sir* D: Letters on natural magic ;
    with chapters on the being and faculties
    of man and additional phenomena of na-
    tural magic, by J. A. Smith. New ed. ill.
    Lond. 1883. D.   **504 : 42**

Buckland, Francis Trevelyan. Curiosities of
    natural history. N. Y. 1859, 1860 ; Lond.
    1882. 3 v.   **504 : 1**
    Contents. 1st ser. A hunt in a horse pond.—Rats.—
    The cobra di capello.—Fish and fishing.—My monkey
    Jacko. 2d ser. A geological auction. — The game-
    keeper's museum. — In memoriam. — A hunt on the
    sea-shore. 3d ser. *Reprint of numerous short contri-
    butions to periodicals.*

— Log-book of a fisherman and zoologist. Ill.
    Lond. 1875. O.   **504 : 2**

Buckley, Arabella Burton. The fairy-land of
    science. Ill. N. Y. 1879. D.   x **504 : 3**

Cooke, Josiah Parsons. Scientific culture, and
    other essays. N. Y. 1881. D.   **507 : 1**
    Contents. Scientific culture.—The nobility of know-
    ledge.—The elementary teaching of physical science.
    —The radiometer. — Memoir of T: Graham. — Memoir
    of W: Hallowes Miller.

Fraser, Robert W: The seaside naturalist ; out-
    door studies in marine zoology and botany
    and maritime geology. Lond. [1868]. S.
        504 : 22

Gleanings of sacred philosophy from natural
    history and the works of creation. Lond.
    1855. S.   **504 : 25**
    Contents. Reason and instinct. — Wonders of the
    insect world.—Revelations in astronomy.—Rambles of
    a naturalist. — Thoughts from nature. — Affection in
    the lower animals. — Phenomena of the seasons. —
    Adaptation in birds of prey.—Associations of nature.

Helmholtz, Hermann L: Ferdinand. Popular
    lectures on scientific subjects ; [1st and]

2d ser. Tr. by E. Atkinson, with an introd.
    by J. Tyndall. N. Y. 1873, 1881. D.
        504 : 6
    Contents. 1st ser. On the relation of natural
    science to science in general, tr. by H. W. Eve. — On
    Goethe's scientific researches, tr. by H. W. Eve. — On
    the physiological causes of harmony in music, tr. by
    A. J. Ellis. — Ice and glaciers. — On the interaction of
    natural forces, tr. by J: Tyndall. — The recent pro-
    gress of the theory of vision, tr. by dr. Pye-Smith.—
    On the conservation of force. — On the aim and pro-
    gress of physical science, tr. by W. Flight. 2d ser.
    Gustav Magnus. — On the origin and significance of
    geometrical axioms. — On the relation of optics to
    painting. — On the origin of the planetary system. —
    On thought in medicine. — On academic freedom in
    german universities.

Herschel, *Sir* J: F: W: Familiar lectures on
    scientific subjects. N. Y. 1872. D.   **504 : 7**
    Contents. Preface. — About volcanoes and earth-
    quakes. — The sun. — On comets. — The weather and
    weather prophets.—Celestial measurings and weigh-
    ings.—On light. — On sensorial vision. — The yard, the
    pendulum, and the metre. — On atoms, a dialogue. —
    On the origin of force.—On the absorption of light by
    coloured media, viewed in connection with the undu-
    latory theory.—On the estimation of skill in target-
    shooting.

Hunt, Robert. The poetry of science, or Studies
    of the physical phenomena of nature. 3d
    ed. rev. and enl. Lond. 1854. D.   **504 : 8**

Huxley, T: H: American addresses, with a
    lecture on the study of biology. N. Y. 1877.
    D.   **504 : 9**
    Contents. Three lectures on evolution.—An address
    on the occasion of the opening of the Johns Hopkins
    university.—Lecture on the study of biology.

— Critiques and addresses. N. Y. 1873. D.
        504 : 10
    Contents. Administrative nihilism. — The school
    boards ; what they can do and what they may do. —
    On medical education.—Yeast. — On the formation of
    coal.—On coral and coral reefs.—On the methods and
    results of ethnology.—On some fixed points in british
    ethnology.—Palæontology and the doctrine of evolu-
    tion. — Mr. Darwin's critics. — The genealogy of ani-
    mals.—Bishop Berkeley on the Metaphysics of sensa-
    tion.

— Lay sermons, addresses and reviews. N. Y.
    1878. D.   **504 : 11**
    Contents. On the advisableness of improving na-
    tural knowledge. — Emancipation, black and white. —
    A liberal education and where to find it. — Scientific
    education.—On the educational value of the natural
    history sciences. — On the study of zoology. — On the
    physical basis of life.—The scientific aspects of positi-
    vism. — On a piece of chalk. — Geological contem-
    poraneity and persistent types of life. — Geological
    reform. — The origin of species. — Criticisms on the
    same. — On Descartes' "Discourse concerning the
    method of using one's reason rightly and of seeking
    scientific truth".—Spontaneous generation.

— Science and culture, and other essays. N. Y.
    1882. D.   **504 : 24**
    Contents. Science and culture.—Universities, actual
    and ideal. — Technical education. — Elementary in-
    struction in physiology. — Joseph Priestly. — On the
    method of Zadig. — On the border territory between
    the animal and vegetable kingdoms. — On certain er-
    rors respecting the structure of the heart, attributed
    to Aristotle.—On the hypothesis that animals are au-
    tomata, and its history. — On sensation and the unity
    of structure of the sensiferous organs.—Evolution in
    biology. — The coming of age of the "Origin of
    species". — The connection of the biological sciences
    with medicine.

Kingsley, C: Scientific lectures and essays.
    [Works, v. 19.] Lond. 1880. D.   **504 : 39**
    Contents. Town geology: The soil of the field; The
    pebbles in the street; The stones in the wall; The
    coal in the fire; The lime in the mortar; The slates on
    the roof. — On bio-geology.—The study of natural
    history. — Superstition. — Science. — Thoughts in a
    gravel-pit. — How to study natural history. — The
    natural theology of the future.

Lardner, Dionysius. Popular lectures on science and art. N. Y. 1846. 2 v. O.
                                                504+12
Contents. V. 1. The plurality of worlds.—The sun.—Eclipses.—The aurora borealis.—Electricity.—The minor planets.—Weather almanacs.—Halley's comet.—The atmosphere.—The new planets.—The tides.—Light.—The major planets.—Reflection of light.—Prospects of steam-navigation.—The barometer.—The moon.—Heat.—The Atlantic steam question.—Galvanism.—The moon and the weather.—Periodic comets.—Radiation of heat.—Meteoric stones and shooting stars.—Lunar influences.—Physical constitution of comets.—Thunder-storms.—The latitudes and longitudes.—Theory of colors.—The visible stars.—Waterspouts and whirlwinds. **2.** Matter and its physical properties.—Elasticity of air.—Effects of lightning.—Popular fallacies.—Protection from lightning.—Magnetism.—Electro-magnetism.—The thermometer.—Atmospheric electricity.—Evaporation.—Conduction of heat.—Relation of heat and light.—Action and reaction.—Composition and resolution of force.—Center of gravity.—The lever and wheel-work.—The pulley.—The inclined plane, wedge and screw.—Ebullition.—Combustion.—How to observe the heavens.—The stellar universe.—The steam engine.

Lubbock, *Sir* J: Chapters in popular natural history. Ill. N. Y. 1884. S.   **504 : 46**
Contents. Ants, bees and wasps.—The colors of animals.—Flowers and insects.—Plants and insects.—Fruits and seeds.

Masius, Hermann. Studies from nature. Tr. by C: Boner. Ill. Lond. 1855. D.
                                                504 : 13
Contents. The forest trees of northern Germany.—Sketches of character-birds.—The frog.—The fox.—The cray-fish and lobster.—Notes.

Mudie, Robert. A popular guide to the observation of nature, or Hints of inducement to the study of natural productions and appearances in their connexions and relations. N. Y. 1844. S.   **x 504 : 41**

Nichols, James R. Fireside science ; a series of popular scientific essays upon subjects connected with every-day life. N. Y. 1872. D.
                                                504 : 14
Contents. The origin and nature of springs.—Chemistry of a hen's egg.—Rebreathed air.—Chemistry of a cigar.—Chemistry of a pint of kerosene.—The lost arts.—The human hair.—Michael Faraday.—Chemistry of a lump of sugar.—Farm experiments at Lakeside.—What shall we use for water-pipes.—The clothing we wear.—The relations of water to agriculture.—The skin and bathing.—Diamonds and diamond cutting.—Among the coal miners.—Chemistry of the human body.—About quicksilver.—Experiments with air furnaces.—Farm pencillings at Lakeside.—Reminiscences of an experimenter.—Infectious germs.—The food of plants.

Peirce, B: Ideality in the physical sciences. Bost. 1881. D.   **504 : 15**

Proctor, R: Anthony. Light science for leisure hours ; a series of familiar essays on scientific subjects, natural phenomena, etc. N. Y. 1871. D.   **504 : 16**
Contents. Strange discoveries respecting the aurora.—The earth a magnet.—Our chief timepiece losing time.—Encke, the astronomer.—Venus on the sun's face.—Recent solar researches.—Government aid to science.—American aims for british science.—The secret of the north pole.—Is the gulf stream a myth?—Floods in Switzerland.—A great tidal wave.—Deep sea dredgings.—The tunnel through Mont Cenis.—Tornadoes.—Vesuvius.—The earthquake in Peru.—The greatest sea-wave ever known.—The usefulness of earthquakes.—The forcing power of rain.—A shower of snow crystals.—Long shots.—Influence of marriage on the death rate.—The topographical survey of India.—A ship attacked by a sword-fish.—The safety lamp.—The dust we have to breathe.—Photographic ghosts.—The Oxford and Cambridge rowing styles.—Betting on horse races, or The state of the odds.—Squaring the circle.—A new theory of Achilles's shield.

x denotes books specially adapted for children.

Proctor, R: Anthony.—*Continued.*
— Familiar science studies. N. Y. 1882. **504 : 38**
Contents. Notes on infinity.—Science and religion.—A menacing comet.—Meteoric dust.—Biela's comet and meteors.—Movements of Jupiter's cloud-masses.—The origin of the week.—Problem of the great pyramid.—Pyramids of Ghizeh.—Sun-spots and financial panics.—Cold and wet.—Our winters.—About lotteries.—Betting on races.—A gambling superstition.—The fifteen puzzle.—Etna.—Weather forecasts.—Some strangely fulfilled dreams.—Suspended animation.

Schele de Vere, Maximilian. Stray leaves from the book of nature. N. Y. 1855. D.
                                                504 : 17
Contents. Only a pebble.—Nature in motion.—The ocean and its life.—A chat about plants.—Younger years of a plant.—Later years of a plant.—Plant-mummies.—Unknown tongues.—A trip to the moon.

— Wonders of the deep ; a companion to Stray leaves from the book of nature. N. Y. 1870. D.   **504 : 18**

Timbs, J: Curiosities of science. 2 v. *In his* Things not generally known.
                                                829.2 : 64 v3,4
Contents, see under English literature, Miscellany.

— Notable things of our own time. *In the same.*
                                                829.2 : 64 v7
Contents, see as above.

Tyndall, J: Essays on the use and limit of the imagination in science. Lond. 1870. O.
                                                504 : 19
— Fragments of science ; a series of detached essays, addresses and reviews. 5th ed. N. Y. 1883. D.   **504 : 20**
Contents. The optical condition of the atmosphere in its bearings on putrefaction and infection.—The constitution of nature.—Radiation.—On radiant heat in relation to the colour and chemical constitution of bodies.—New chemical reactions produced by light.—On dust and disease.—Voyage to Algeria to observe the eclipse.—Niagara.—Life and letters of Faraday.—The Copley medalists, 1870, 1871.—Elementary magnetism.—Death by lightning.—Science and the "spirits."—Introd., embracing reflections on materialism.—Reflections on prayer and natural law.—Miracles and special providences.—Scientific materialism.—Scientific use of the imagination.—Vitality.—On prayer as a form of physical energy.—The Belfast address.—Apology for the Belfast address.—Crystals and molecular force.—Letter from the Times, nov. 9, 1874.

Wainwright, S: Scientific sophisms ; a review of current theories concerning atoms, apes and men. N. Y. 1883. D.   **504 : 44**

Williams, W. Mattieu. Science in short chapters. N. Y. [1883]. D.   **504 : 40**

Winchell, Alexander. Sparks from a geologist's hammer. Chicago. 1881. D.
                                                504 : 23

World of wonders, A ; or Marvels in animate and inanimate nature. N. Y. 1881. O.
                                                504 : 21

5. History.

Whewell, W: History of the inductive sciences from the earliest to the present time. 3d ed. with add. N. Y. 1869. 2 v. O.   **509 : 1**
Contents. V. 1. Greek school philosophy, with reference to physical science.—Physical sciences in ancient Greece.—Greek astronomy.—Physical science in the middle ages.—Formal astronomy after the stationary period.—*The mechanical sciences.* Mechanics, including fluid mechanics.—Physical astronomy.—Add. to the 3d ed. **2.** *The secondary mechanical sciences.* Acoustics.—Optics, formal and physical.—Thermotics and atomology.—*The mechanico-chemical sciences.* Electricity.—Magnetism.—Galvanism, or

voltaic electricity. — *The analytical science:* Chemistry. — *The analytico-classificatory science:* Mineralogy. — *Classificatory sciences:* Systematic botany and zoology. — *Organical sciences:* Physiology and comparative anatomy. — *The palætiological sciences:* Geology. — Add. to the 3d ed.

Buckley, Arabella Burton. A short history of natural science and of the progress of discovery from the time of the greeks to the present day, for the use of schools and young persons. Ill. N. Y. 1876. D.
                               509 : 3

Routledge, Robert. A popular history of science. [Ill.] Lond. 1881. O.   **509 : 2**

Lacroix, Paul. Science and literature in the middle ages and at the period of the renaissance. Lond. 1878. Q.   **509 : R4**
Contents. Universities, schools, students. — Philosophic sciences. — Mathematical sciences. — Natural sciences. — Medical sciences. — Chemistry and alchemy. — The occult sciences. — Popular beliefs. — Geographical science. — Heraldic science. — Proverbs. — Languages. — Romances. — Popular songs. — National poetry. — Chronicles, histories, memoirs. — The drama. — Civil and religious oratory.

Historical society of science. [Publications:] A collection of letters illustrative of the progress of science in England, from the reign of Elizabeth to that of Charles II, ed. by James Orchard Halliwell-Phillipps. Lond. 1841. O.   **509 : 5**

Lubbock, *Sir* J: Fifty years of science ; addresses delivered at York to the British assoc., aug. 1881. N. Y. 1882. O.   **509 : 6**

Annual of scientific discovery, The, or Yearbook of facts in science and art, exhibiting the most important discoveries and improvements in mechanics, useful arts, natural philosophy, chemistry, astronomy, meteorology, zoology, botany, mineralogy, geology, geography, antiquities, together with a list of recent scientific publications, a classified list of patents, obituaries of eminent scientific men, an index of important papers in scientific journals, reports, etc.; 1850—1871. Bost. 1850-1875. 21 v. D.   **505 : 1**
Note. 1850-51. ed. by D: A. Wells and G: Bliss, *jr.*; 1852-1865, by D: A. Wells; 1866-1869, by S: Kneeland; 1870, by J: Trowbridge, S: Kneeland and W. R. Nichols; 1871, by J: Trowbridge, W. R. Nichols and C. R. Cross.

Baird, Spencer Fullerton, *ed.* Annual record of science and industry ; 1873—1878. N. Y. 1872-79. 8 v. D.   **505 : 2**

— *sec.* Annual report of the board of regents of the Smithsonian institution for 1880—1882. Wash. 1881-84. O.   **506 : R5**
Note. The "General appendix" contains a continuation of the "Annual record" in the dep'ts of astronomy, geology, meteorology, physics, chemistry, mineralogy, botany, zoology and anthropology.

Science record, The ; a compendium of scientific progress and discovery ; ed. by Alfred E. Beach ; 1874. Ill. N. Y. 1874. D.   **505 : 3**

Fleischer, R:, *ed.* Vierteljahresberichte über die gesammten wissenschaften und künste, über handel, landwirthschaft, industrie und erfindungen ; unter mitwirkung von hervorragenden gelehrten und fachmännern herausg. von R: Fleischer, 1882. 1882. 3 v. O.   **505+9**

— Zeitschrift für die gebildete welt über das gesammte wissen unserer zeit und über alle wichtigen . berufszweige ; unter mitwirkung von hervorragenden gelehrten

und fachmännern herausg. Braunschweig. 1883, 1884. 5 v. O.   **505+10**
Note. Partly continued in the Deutsche revue.

6. Periodicals.

American journal of science, The ; eds. James D. and E. S. Dana, and B. Silliman ; v. 1-8, 51-62, 78-98, 121-127. New Haven. [1819-84]. O.   **505 : M**
Note. Title-page of v. 1 reads "The american journal of science, more especially of mineralogy, geology, and the other branches of natural history, including also agriculture, and the ornamental as well as useful arts. Conducted by B. Silliman." The second series, beginning with v. 51 adds James D. Dana as ed. and succeeding vols. give varying names of associate editors.

American naturalist, The ; an ill. magazine of natural history, ed. by A. S. Packard, jr.; v. 1-3, 10-18, mar. 1867—june 1884. Salem. 1868-70 ; Bost. 1876, 1877 ; Phila. 1878-84. O.   **505 : M**
Note. Title-page of v. 1-3 reads "a popular magazine of natural history." From v. 12, E: D. Cope is added as ed.

Journal of the Franklin institute of the state of Pennsylvania ; devoted to the mechanic arts, manufactures, general science and the recording of american and other patent inventions, ed. by T: P. Jones ; v. 5-23. Phila. 1828-37. O.   **505: M**

Natur, Die ; zeitung zur verbreitung naturwissenschaftlicher kenntniss und naturschauung für leser aller stände, organ des Deutschen Humboldt-vereins ; begründet unter herausgabe von O: Ule und K: Müller von Halle, herausg. von K: Müller von Halle ; v. 29-33, jan. 1880 — dec. 1884. Ill. Halle. 1880-84. F.   **505 : M**

Nature ; a weekly illustrated journal of science ; v. 1-30, nov. 1869 — oct. 1884. Lond. 1870-84. Q.   **505 : M**

Popular science monthly, The ; conducted by E. L. and W. J. Youmans ; v. 1-25, may 1872 — oct. 1884. N. Y. 1872-84. O. **505 : M**
Note. V. 1-10, ed. by E. L. Youmans only.

— **Supplement ;** v. 1-4, no. 1-21. N. Y. 1877-79. 3 v. O.   **505 : M**
Note. One number only of v. 5 was pub., being no. 21.

Science ; an illustrated journal, pub. weekly ; v. 1-4, feb. 1883 — dec. 1884. Bost. 1883-84. O.   **505 : M**

7. Societies.

Becker, Bernard H: Scientific London. Lond. 1874. D.   **506 : 201**

Deleuze, Joseph Philippe François. History and description of the Royal museum of natural history, pub. by order of the administration of that establishment. Plans and views. Paris. 1823. O.   **506 : 7**

Stockholm. *Kongliga svenska vetenskaps-akademien.* Der königl. schwedischen akademie der wissenschaften abhandlungen aus der naturlehre, haushaltungskunst und mechanik auf das jahr 1750. Aus dem schwedischen übersetzt von Abraham Gotthelf Kästner. V. 12. Hamburg. 1754. D.
                                 506 : 1

Smithsonian institution. Catalogue of publications, 1846—1882, by W: J. Rhees.   **506 : R2**

Smithsonian institution.—*Continued.*
— [1st—36th] Annual report of the board of regents. Wash. 1853–1883. 28 v. O.   **506:R5**
Note. For contents see **Rhees, W: J.** Catalogue of publications of the S. I. [506: R2]. The following reports are only in the regular set of congressional documents, viz.: 1st, 1846, in Sen. exec. doc. v. 3, no. 211, 29th cong. 1 sess.—2d, 1847, in Sen. misc., no. 23, 30th cong. 1 sess.—3d, 1848, in House misc. no. 48, 30th cong. 2 sess.—4th, 1849, in House misc. v. 2, no. 50, 31st cong. 1 sess.—5th, 1850, in Sen. misc. v. 1, no. 1, 32d cong. special sess.— 6th, 1851, in Sen. misc. no. 8, 32d cong. 1 sess.—7th, 1852, in Sen. misc. no. 53, 32d cong. 2 sess. —16th, 1861, in Sen. misc. no. 77, 37th cong. 2 sess.

— Contributions to knowledge ; v. 1–25. Wash. 1848–85.   25 v. Q.   **506:R3**
Note. For contents see **Rhees, W: J.** Catalogue of publications of the Smithsonian institution [506:R2]. The different papers are entered in their proper classes in this catalogue, and are also noted in the author index.
— Miscellaneous collections ; v. 1–27. Wash. 1862–83.   27 v. O.   **506:R4**
Note. For contents see **Rhees, W: J.** Catalogue of publications of the Smithsonian institution [506: R2]. The important papers are entered in their proper classes in this catalogue, and are also noted in the author index.

United States national museum, *Washington, D. C.* Proceedings, v. 1, 1878 ; v. 2, 1879. Wash. 1879, 1880. *In* Smithsonian misc., v. 19.   **506:R4 v19**
— *Same.* V. 3, 1880 ; v. 4, 1881. Wash. 1881, 1882. *In the same,* v. 22.   **506:R4 v22**

Philosophical society, *Washington, D. C.* Bulletin ; v. 1–3, march 1871—june 1880. Wash. 1874–80. *In* Smithsonian misc., v. 20.   **506:R4 v20**
— *Same.* V. 4, 5, oct. 1880—dec. 1882. Wash. 1881, 1883. *In the same,* v. 25.   **506:R4 v25**

New York state university. 3d, 6th–11th, 20th–31st annual reports of the state cabinet of natural history. Albany. 1850–74. 10 v. O.   **506:R8**

Academy of natural sciences of Philadelphia. Report on [its] condition on moving into its new edifice, made to the contributors to its building-fund, april 28, 1876, by W. S. W. Ruschenberger. Phila. 1876. O.   **506:Pam**

Wisconsin academy of sciences, arts and letters. Transactions ; v. 1–4. Madison. 1872–79.   **506:R9**
Contents. V. 1. Chapin, A. L. The relation of capital and labor.—Armitage, W: E. The german sunday.—Caverno, C: Social science and woman suffrage.—Hastings, S. D. The common jail system of the country.—Hoy, P. R. Deep water fauna of Lake Michigan.—Lapham, I. A. On the classification of plants.—Hoy, P. R. Insects injurious to agriculture; aphides.— Knapp, J. G. Conifere of the Rocky mountains and their adaptation to the soil and climate of Wisconsin.—Eaton, J. H. Report on the geology of the region about Devil's Lake.— Irving, R. On the age of the quartzites, schists and conglomerates of Sauk county.—Chamberlin, T. C. Suggestions as to a basis for the gradation of the vertebrata.— Knapp, J. G. Ancient lakes of Wisconsin.— Wright, A. O. On the rainy well at Waterloo, Wis.—Davies, J: E. On potentials, and their application in physical science. — Sherman, W. H. The production of sulphide of mercury by a new process, and its use in photography.—Allen, W: F. The rural population of England as classified in the Domesday book.—Feuling, J: B. On the place of the indian languages in the study of philology.
2. Carpenter, S. H. The metaphysical basis of science.—Holland, F. M. Vexed questions in ethics.—Carpenter, S. H. The philosophy of evolution.—Steele, G. M. Population and sustenance. — Holland, F. M. Records of marriages.—Smith, J: Y. Effect of the duty on imports on the value of gold.—

Hoyt, J: W. Requisites to a reform of the civil service of the U. S.—Hoy, P. R. Natural history as a branch of elementary education.—Irving, R. On some points in the geology of northern Wisconsin.—Hoy, P. R. Some peculiarities of the fauna of Racine.— Eaton, J. H. Relation of the sandstones, conglomerates and limestones of Baraboo valley to each other and to the azoic quartzites.—Daniells, W. W. Notes on the absorption of arsenic by the human liver.—Chamberlin, T. C. Some evidences bearing upon the method of the upheaval of the quartzites of Sauk and Columbia counties; On fluctuations in level of the quartzites of Sauk and Columbia counties.—Irving, R. On a hand specimen showing the exact junction of the primordial sandstones and huronian schists ; On the occurrence of gold and silver in minute quantities in quartz from Clark county.—Nicodemus, W. J. L. On the Wisconsin River improvement.—Nader, J: On the strength of materials as applied to engineering. —Nicodemus, W, J. L. Railway gauges.—Feuling, J. B. The etymology of *church.*—Nicodemus, W. J. L. History of the science of hydraulics.—Butler, J. D. The naming of America.—Allen, W: F. The rural classes in England in the 13th century ; Ranks and classes among the anglo-saxons.
3. Irving, R. Kaolin in Wisconsin. — Lapham, I. A. Oconomowoc and other small lakes of Wisconsin.—Hoy, P. R. Fish culture.—Sweet, E. T. Notes on the geology of northern Wisconsin.—Kumlien, T. The rapid disappearance of Wisconsin wild flowers. —Nicodemus, W. J. L. The ancient civilization of America.—Hoy, P. R. Extent of the Wisconsin fisheries.—Nader, J: Leveling with the barometer.—Sweet, E. T. On kerosene oil.—Nader, J: The improvement of the mouth of the Mississippi river.—Hoy, P. R. The catocalæ of Racine county.—Butler, J. D. Copper-tools found in the state of Wisconsin. — Report of committee on exploration of indian mounds in the vicinity of Madison.—Lapham, I. A. Embryonic development the same in plants as in animals. — Feuling, J. B. Studies in comparative grammar.—Allen, W: F. U. S. sovereignty, whence derived and where vested.—Hoyt, J. W. The formal commendation of government officials.—Holland, F. M. Industrial education.—Caverno, C: The people and the railroads.—Holland, F. M. The boa-constrictor of politics.—Hoyt, J. W. The revolutionary movement among women.—Holland, F. M. Were the stoics utilitarians?—Hubbel, H. P. An examination of S. H. Carpenter's theory of evolution.—Davies, J: E. Recent progress in theoretical physics.
4. Allen, W: F. Peasant communities in France. —Caverno, C: The abolition of the jury system.—Allen, W: F. The origin of the freeholders. — Mason, R. Z. The duty of the state in its treatment of the deaf and dumb, the blind, the idiotic, the crippled and deformed, and the insane.—Payne, A. Art as education.—Stuart, J. R. The harmonic method in greek art.—Sawyer, W. C. Letters an embarrassment to literature.—Simmons, H. M. Mr. Spencer's social anatomy.—Elmendorf, J. J. Nature and freedom.—Birge, E: A. Notes on cladocera.—Day, F. N. On the fauna of the Niagara and upper silurian rocks as exhibited in Milwaukee county, Wisconsin, and in counties contiguous thereto.—Andrews, E. Discoveries illustrating the literature and religion of the mound builders.—Hoy, P. R. How did the aborigines of this country fabricate copper implements?—Oldenhage, H. Remarks on the descent of animals.—Hoy, P. R. Why are there no upper incisors in the ruminantia?—King, C: I. Boiler explosions.—Jewell, J. S. Mind in the lower animals.—De Hart, J. N. The antiquities and platycnemism of the mound builders of Wisconsin.—Chamberlin, T. C. On the extent and significance of the Wisconsin Kettle moraine.—McMurphy, J. G. Rotation as a factor of motion.—Davies, J. E. Recent progress in theoretical physics : pt. 2, Magnetic rotatory polarization of light.

Wisconsin natural history society. Deutscher naturhistorischer verein von Wisconsin: Geschichtlicher überblick, statuten, *etc. n. t.* [Milw. 1866.] O.   **506:Pam**
— General-versammlung des naturhist. ver. von Wis., gehalten am 12 jan. 1868. *n. t.*   **506:Pam**
— Bericht für 1871[-1874]. Milw. 1872–75.   **506:Pam**

Wisconsin natural history society.—*Continued.*
— Vorträge, gehalten in der general-versammlung des naturhistorischen vereins. [Milw. 1874–76].   **506 : Pam**
Contents. **Brendecke,** F: Gedächtniss-rede auf P: Engelmann, 24 mai 1874.—**Breinig,** F: Ueber den einfluss der naturwissenschaften auf die moderne medizin. 14 märz 1875.—**Brendecke,** F: Ueber vorübergehende lichterscheinungen, nach eigenen beobachtungen, 14 märz 1875.—**Oldenhage,** H. H. Geologische beweise für das hohe alter des menschengeschlechts.
— Jahres - bericht für 1876 — 1881 [with app.]. Milw. 1876–81. O.   **506 : Pam**
'*Contents of app.* **1877-8. Bartlett,** Edwin N. On aspergillus. — **Brendecke,** F: Ueber die verwendung von bleiröhren für wasserleitung.—**Oldenhage,** H. H. Die abstammungs-lehre. **1878-9. Greiner,** Franz A. Die wilder Nord-Amerika's. **1879-80.** Ulrici, Emil. Das leben auf dem prairie. **1880-1. Baldauf,** Joseph. Amerika die alte welt.—Ulrici, Emil. Darwins entwickelungstheorie. — **Mann,** C: L. Die wandertaube.—**Dorner,** H. Das leben der eskimos, nach mittheilungen von Franz Melms, mitglied der schwatka-expedition, erzählt.
Milwaukee public museum. 2d annual report of the board of trustees, oct. 1, 1884. Milw. 1884. O.   **506 : Pam**
— Ward museum fund ; final report of the committee on subscriptions, jan. 1885. Milw. 1885. O.   **506 : Pam**
Royal society of Canada. Proceedings and transactions for 1882–83, 1884 ; v. 1, 2. Ill. Montreal. 1883, 1885. Q.   **61 : R**
Contents. V. 1. Proceedings, 1882, 1883. *Transactions,* 1882, 1883. **Section 1:** LeMoine, J. M. Nos quatre historiens modernes : Bibaud, Garneau, Ferland, Faillon. — **Faucher de St. Maurice,** N . Discours d'inauguration.—**Marchand,** F. G. Quelques scènes d'une comedie inédite, Les faux brillants. — **Tanguay,** Cyprien. Familles canadiennes. — **Sulte,** B: Les interprètes du temps de Champlain.—**LeMay,** Pamphile. Le bien pour le mal ; poésie.—**Chauveau,** P. J. O. Étude sur les commencement de la poésie française au Canada.—**Casgrain,** H. R. Notre passé littéraire et nos deux historiens.—**Fréchette,** L: H. Vive la France ; poésie.—**Verreau,** Hospice. Notice sur les fondateurs de Montréal.— **Le Moine,** J. M. Les archives du Canada.—**Foucher de St. Maurice,** N. Louis Turcotte.— **Tanguay,** C. Étude sur les noms.—**Fréchette,** L: H. Notre histoire, à la mémoire de F. X. Garneau ; poésie.— **Sulte,** B: Les premiers seigneurs du Canada.—**Marchand,** F. G. Un bonheur en attire un autre ; comédie. **Section 2:** **Wilson,** Daniel. Inaugural address.—**Todd,** Alpheus. On the establishment of free public libraries in Canada. — **Reade,** J: Language and conquest ; a retrospect and a forecast.—**Wilson,** Daniel. Pre-aryan amér. man. —**Bourinot,** J: G: Some old forts by the sea.—**Lesperance,** J: The literature of french Canada. — **Murray,** J. Clark. A problem of visual perception ; The nomenclature of the laws of association ; and addition to the logical square of opposition. **Section 3:** Hunt, T. Sterry. The relations of the natural sciences.—**Carpmael,** C: On the law of facility of error.— **Cherriman,** J. B. On an application of a special determinant ; The motion of a chain on a fixed plane curve; Note on the bishop's move in chess.—**MacGregor,** J. G. On the measurement of the resistance of electrolytes. — **Chapman,** E. J. Note on molecular contraction in natural sulphids.— **Deville,** E. Symmetrical investigation of the curvatures of surfaces.—**MacFarlane,** T: Note on zinc-sulphid ; On the reduction of sulphate of soda by carbon.— **MacGregor,** J. G. On some experiments, showing that the electromotive force in polarization is independent of the difference of potential of the electrodes. **Chapman,** E. J. Note on spectroscopic scales ; On cryptomorphism in its relation to classification and mineral types.—**Deville,** E. Sur la mesure des distances terrestres par des observations astronomiques. —**Haanel,** E. On the application of hydriodic acid as a blowpipe reagent. — **Dupuis,** N. F. On a mechanical means of making a sidereal clock show mean time.—**Harrington,** B. J. On some minerals, new to Canada.—Reports on the transits of Venus, dec. 6, 1882.—**MacGregor,** J. G. On the transition resistance to the electric current. **Section 4:** **Selwyn,** A. R. C. On the Quebec group in geology.—**Dawson,** Sir J. W. On the cretaceous and tertiary floras of British Columbia and the North West territories.—**Saunders,** W. On the importance of economising and preserving our forests. — **Dawson,** G. M. On a general section from the Laurentian axis to the Rocky mountains.— **Macoun,** J: Notes on the distribution of northern, southern and saline plants in Canada. — **Bell,** Robert. Notes on the birds of Hudson's bay.— **Murray,** Alex. On the glaciation of Newfoundland. — **Saunders,** W. On the introduction and dissemination of noxious insects. — **Whiteaves,** J. F. On the lower cretaceous rocks of British Columbia.— **Matthew,** G. F. Illustrations of the fauna of the St. John group.— **Whiteaves,** J. F. On some supposed annelid tracks from the Gaspé sandstones. — **Chapman,** E. J. On the classification of crinoids.—**Selwyn,** A. R. C. On the geology of Lake Superior.— **Saunders,** W. On the influence of sex upon the hybrids among fruits.— **Macoun,** J: On the flora of the Gaspé peninsula.— **Gilpin,** E., *jr.* On the folding of the carboniferous strata in the maritime provinces of Canada. — **Dawson,** G. M. On the triassic of the Rocky mountains and British Columbia.—**Matthew,** G. F. On a method of distinguishing lacustrine from marine deposits.— **Macoun,** J: Notes on canadian polypetalæ.— **Bell,** Robert. Causes of the fertility of the land in the canadian north west.—**Laflamme,** J. C. K. Note sur la géologie du lac St. Jean. — **Hunt,** T. Sterry. The geological history of serpentines, incl. notes on precambrian rocks : A historical account of the taconic question in geology, with a discussion of the relations of the taconian series to the older crystalline and to the cambrian rocks. pt. 1.—**Matthew,** G. F. Illustrations of the fauna of the St. John group, supp.—Notes and abstracts of papers.

2. Proceedings, 1884.—*Transactions,* 1884. **Section 1:** **Cazes,** Paul de. Deux points d'histoire: 1, Quatrième voyage de Jacques Cartier; 2, Expédition du marquis de La Roche.—**Tanguay,** C. Étude sur une famille canadienne: De Catalogne.—**Legendre,** Napoléon. La province de Québec et la langue française: Les races indigènes de l'Amérique devant l'histoire.—**Sulte,** B: Pontrincourt en Acadie, 1604-1623.—**Casgrain,** H. R. Les 40 dernières années: Le Canada depuis l'union de 1841, par J: C: Dent; étude critique. — **Verreau,** H. Les commencements de l'église du Canada.—**Marmette,** Joseph. Une promenade dans Paris; impressions et souvenirs.—**Le Moine,** J. M. Les aborigènes d'Amérique; leurs rites mortuaires.—**Chauveau,** P. J. O. Le sacré-cœur; poème.—**Fréchette,** L: H. Au bord de la Creuse; poème.—**L'Espagne:** Trois épisodes de la conquête; poèmes.—**Marchand,** F. G. Les travers du siècle; poème. **Section 2:** **Reade,** J: The making of Canada; The literary faculty of the native races of America.— **Lesperance,** J: The poets of Canada.—**Bryce,** G: A plea for a canadian Camden society.—**Wilson,** Daniel. The Huron-Iroquois of Canada: a typical race of amer. aborigines. **Section 3:** **Hunt,** T. Sterry. The origin of crystalline rocks.—**MacGregor,** J. G. On the density and thermal expansion of solutions of copper sulphate.—**Haanel,** E. Blowpipe reactions on plaster of paris tablets.—**Baillairge,** C. A particular case of hydraulic-ram or water-hammer.— **Laflamme,** J. C. K. Notes sur un fait météorologique particulier à Québec.—**Hamel,** T. E. Essai sur la constitution atomique de la matière. **Section 4:** **Dawson,** Sir J. W. On some relations of geological work in Canada and the old world. — **Gilpin,** Edwin. Notes on the manganese ores of Nova Scotia. — **Lawson,** G: Revision of the canadian ranunculaceæ.—**Bailey,** L. W. On geological contacts and ancient rocks in southern and central New Brunswick.—**Matthew,** G. F. Illustrations of the fauna of the St. John group, continued: On the corocoryphena, with further remarks on paradoxides. —**Hunt,** T. Sterry. A historical account of the taconic question in geology, *etc.*, pt. 2.—**Chapman,** E. J. On some deposits of titaniferous iron ore in the counties of Haliburton and Hastings, Ont.; On mimetism in inorganic nature.—**Macoun,** J., *and* T. J. W. Burgess. Canadian filicineæ.—**Laflamme,** J.C.K. Notes sur certains dépôts aurifères de la Beauce; Notes sur un gisement d'émeraude au Saguenay.— **Saunders,** W. Notes on the occurrence of certain butterflies in Canada.—**Whiteaves,** J. F. Note on a decapod crustacean from the upper cretaceous of Highwood river; Description of a new species of ammonite from the cretaceous rocks of Fort St. John, on the Peace river.—Abstracts: **Bell,** Robert. The geology and economic minerals of Hudson Bay and northern Canada; **Selwyn,** A. R. C. Notes on observations, 1883, on the geology of the north shore of Lake Superior.

8. Scientific travels.

Bates, H: Walter. The naturalist on the river Amazons; a record of adventures, habits of animals, sketches of brazilian and indian life and aspects of nature under the equator during eleven years of travel. 4th ed. Ill. Lond. 1875. D.   **508 : 4**

Darwin, C: Robert. Journal of researches into the natural history and geology of the countries visited during the voyage of h. m. s. Beagle, under the command of capt. Fitz Roy. N. Y. 1846. 2 v. in 1. S.   **508 : 5**
— *Same.* New ed. N. Y. 1876. D. *T. p. w.*   **508 : 5**
— What mr. Darwin saw in his voyage round the world in the ship Beagle. Ill. and maps. N. Y. 1880 [1879]. O.   **x 508 : 6**

Humboldt, F: H: Alexander *freiherr* v. Reise in die äquinoctial-gegenden des neuen continents. In deutscher bearb. von Hermann Hauff. Stuttg. 1874. 4 v. in 2. S.   **508 : 1**
— *Same, eng.* Personal narrative of travels to the equinoctial regions of America during 1799—1804, by Alexander v. Humboldt and Aimé Bonpland. Written in french, tr. and ed. by Thomasina Ross. Lond. 1870. 3 v. D.   **508 : 1**

Macgillivray, W: The travels and researches of Alexander v. Humboldt; a condensed narrative of his journeys in the equinoctial regions of America, and in asiatic Russia; together with analyses of his more import-

x denotes books specially adapted for children.

ant investigations. Map of the Orinoco and ill. [Harper's family lib.] N. Y. 1843. S.   **508 : 7**

Ratzel, F: Wandertage eines naturforschers. Leipz. 1873. 2 t. in 1 b. D.   **508 : 2**
Contents. **1.** Zoologische briefe vom Mittelmeer. — Briefe aus Süditalien. **2.** Schilderungen aus Siebenbürgen und den Alpen.

Thomson, *Sir* C: Wyville. The voyage of the "Challenger": The Atlantic; a preliminary account of the general results of the exploring voyage of h. m. s. Challenger during 1873 and the early part of 1876. N. Y. 1878. 2 v. O.   **508 : 9**

Wagner, Moriz F: Naturwissenschaftliche reisen im tropischen Amerika, ausgeführt auf veranlassung und mit unterstützung weiland s. m. des königs Maximilian II von Bayern. Stuttg. 1870. O.   **508 : 3**

United States. The naval astronomical expedition to the southern hemisphere, 1849–52, lieut. J[ames] M[elville] **Gilliss** supt.; v. 1, 2, 3, 6 (*all published*). Maps and ill. Wash. 1855–56. Q.   *in* **508 : D**
Contents. V. **1. Gilliss**, J. M. Chile. **2. Macrae**, Archibald. Report of journeys across the Andes and Pampas of the Argentine provinces. — **Smith**, J. Lawrence. Minerals and mineral waters of Chile.— **Ewbank**, T: A description of the indian antiquities brought from Chile and Peru by the exped.—Zoology. —Botany: **Gray**, Asa. List of dried plants; **Brackenridge**, W: D. List of living plants and seeds. — Paleontology: **Wyman**, Jeffries. Fossil mammals; **Conrad**, T. A. Fossil shells. **3. Gilliss**, J. M. Observations to determine the solar parallax; incl. origin and operations of the exped. **6. Gilliss**, J. M. Magnetical and meteorological observations.

2. Mathematics.

(For Kinematics, see under Physics, cl. 531.)

1. In general.

Davies, C:, *and* W: G. **Peck**. Mathematical dictionary and cyclopedia of mathematical science, comprising definitions of all the terms employed in mathematics, an analysis of each branch, and of the whole as forming a single science. N. Y. 1875. O.   **510 : R1**

Campin, Francis. A treatise on mathematics, as applied to the constructive arts; illustrating the various processes of mathematical investigation by means of arithmetical equations and practical examples; also the methods of analysing principles and deducing rules and formulæ, applicable to the requirements of practice. 2d ed. rev. and enl. by the author. [Weale's ser.] Lond. 1882. D.   **510 : 3**

Davies, C: Practical mathematics, with drawing and mensuration, applied to the mechanic arts. N. Y. 1873. D.   **510 : 4**

Berkeley, G: [Mathematical writings]. *In his* Works.   **820.2 : 3 v2**
Contents, see under English literature, Collected works.

Halliwell-Phillipps, James Orchard, *ed.* Rara mathematica, or A collection of treatises on the mathematics and subjects connected

with them, from ancient unedited mss. 2d ed. Lond. 1841. O.   **510 : 2**
Contents. Johannis de Sacro-Bosco. Tractatus de arte numerandi. — A method used in England in the 15th century for taking the altitude of a steeple or inaccessible object.—A treatise on the numeration of algorism.—A treatise on the properties and qualities of glasses for optical purposes, according to the making, polishing and grinding of them, by W: Bourne.—Johannis Robyns De cometis commentaria. — Two tables, one shewing the time of high water at London bridge; and the other, the duration of moonlight, from a ms. of the thirteenth century. — Treatise on the mensuration of heights and distances. — An account table for the use of merchants. — Alexandri de Villa Dei Carmen de algorismo. — Prefatio Danielis de Merley ad librum De naturis superiorum et inferiorum.—Proposals for some inventions in the mechanical arts.—The preface to a calendar or almanac for the year 1430. —Johannis Norfolk In artem progressionis summula.—App.

American journal of mathematics, pure and applied; ed. in chief J. J. Sylvester, pub. under the auspices of the Johns Hopkins university; v. 1-6. Balt. 1873-84. O.   **505.1 : RM**

2. Arithmetic.

Fish, Daniel W. The complete arithmetic; oral and written. (Robinson's shorter course.) N. Y. [1874]. D.   **511 : 5**
— Robinson's progressive practical arithmetic; containing the theory of numbers, in con-

Fish, Daniel W.—*Continued.*
nection with concise analytic and synthetic methods of solution, and designed as a complete text-book on this science for common schools and academies. N. Y. [1877]. D.   **511 : 6**

— *ed.* The progressive higher arithmetic for schools, academies, and mercantile colleges ; forming a complete treatise on arithmetical science and its commercial and business applications. (Robinson's mathematical series). N. Y. [1875]. D.   **511 : 7**

Olney, E: The elements of arithmetic for intermediate, grammar, and common schools ; in which the analytical processes, known as mental arithmetic, are assimilated and incorporated with the more mechanical and formal processes, called written arithmetic. N. Y. 1879. D.   **511 : 8**

— A practical arithmetic for intermediate, grammar, and common schools. N. Y. [1879]. . D.   **511 : 9**

— The science of arithmetic for high schools, normal schools, preparatory departments to colleges, and academies. N. Y. 1881. D.   **511 : 10**

Parke, Uriah. Lectures on the philosophy of arithmetic and the adaptation of that science to the business purposes of life, with numerous problems, curious and useful, solved by various modes, with explanations designed to make the study and application of arithmetic pleasant and profitable to such as have not the aid of a teacher, as well as to exercise advanced classes in schools. 2d ed. rev. Phila. 1849. O.   **511 : 3**

Groesbeck, J: The Crittenden commercial arithmetic and business manual ; designed for use in counting-houses, academies, and commercial colleges. Rev. ed. Phila. 1883. D.   **511 : 11**

Grier, W: The mechanic's calculator ; comprehending principles, rules and tables in the various departments of mathematics and mechanics, useful to millwrights, engineers and artisans in general. From the 5th Glasgow ed. Phila. 1839. D.   **511 : 4**

Hoare, C: The slide-rule, and how to use it ; containing full, easy and simple instructions to perform all business calculations with unexampled rapidity and accuracy. [Weale's ser.] Lond. 1875. D.   **511 : 1**

Hodgson, F: T., *comp.* The mechanics' slide rule, and how to use it ; a compilation of explanations, rules and instructions suitable for mechanics and others interested in the industrial arts. (Work manuals, no. 2). N. Y. 1881. D.   **511 : 2**

3. Algebra.

Davies, C: Elements of algebra ; on the basis of [P: L: Marie] Bourdon, embracing Sturm's and Horner's theorems. Rev. and re-written. N. Y. 1876. O.   **512 : 4**

Ficklin, Joseph. The complete algebra, designed for use in schools, academies, and colleges. (Robinson's shorter course.) N. Y. *n. d.* D.   **512 : 5**

Olney, E: The complete algebra for high schools, preparatory schools, and academies. New ed. N. Y. *n. d.* D.   **512 : 6**

— A university algebra ; comprising : 1, A compendious, yet complete and thorough, course in elementary algebra, and 2, An advanced course in algebra, sufficiently extended to meet the wants of our universities, colleges, and schools of science. N. Y. 1882. O.   **512 : 7**

Ray, Joseph. Elements of algebra for colleges, schools, and private students ; ed. by Del. Kemper. Cinc. [1875]. D.   **512 : 8**

Schuyler, Aaron. A complete algebra for schools and colleges. Cinc. *n. d.* D.   **512 : 9**

Vose, G: Leonard. A graphic method of solving certain algebraic problems. [Van Nostrand's science ser.] N. Y. 1875. T.   **512 : 1**

Schott, C: Anthony. Solution of normal equations by indirect elimination. *In* U. S. coast survey rep. 1855.   *in* **622 : D**

Burnside, W: Snow, *and* Arthur W: Panton. The theory of equations ; with an introd. to the theory of binary algebraic forms. (Dublin university press ser.) Dublin. 1881. O.   **512 : 3**

Cain, W: Symbolic algebra, or The algebra of algebraic numbers ; together with critical notes on the methods of reasoning employed in geometry. [Van Nostrand's science ser.] N. Y. 1884. T.   **512 : 2**

4. Geometry and trigonometry.

Argand, J: Robert. Imaginary quantities ; their geometrical interpretation. Tr. from the french by A. S. Hardy. [Van Nostrand's science ser.] N. Y. 1881. T.   **513 : 1**

Spencer, W: G: Inventional geometry ; a series of problems intended to familarize the pupil with geometrical conceptions and to exercise his inventive faculty ; with a pref. note by Herbert Spencer. (Science primers.) N. Y. 1877. S.   **513 : 3**

Schuyler, Aaron. Elements of geometry, with exercises for students, and an introd. to modern geometry. Cinc. *n. d.* D.   **513 : 6**

Robinson, Horatio Nelson. Elements of geometry, plane and spherical, with numerous practical problems ; rewritten by I: F. Quinby. N. Y. [1860]. O.   **513 : 5**

Playfair, J: Elements of geometry ; containing the first six books of Euclid, with a supp. on the quadrature of the circle and the geometry of solids ; added, elements of plane and spherical trigonometry. N. Y. 1833. O.   **513 : 2**

Tappan, Eli T. Treatise on geometry and trigonometry, for colleges, schools and private students. Written for the mathematical cóurse of Joseph Ray. Cinc. *n. d.* O.   **513 : 7**

Loomis, Elias. Elements of geometry, conic sections and plane trigonometry. Rev. ed., with app. N. Y. 1884. D.   **513 : 4**

Robinson, Horatio Nelson. Elements of plane and spherical trigonometry, with numerous practical problems. N. Y. 1874. O.   **514 : 7**

Schott, C: Anthony. Method of closing a circuit of triangulation under certain given conditions. *In* U. S. coast survey rep. 1875.   *in* 622 : D

Alvord, B: The tangencies of circles and of spheres. Ill. Wash. 1856. Q. *In* Smithsonian contributions.   506 : R3 v8

Ferrel, W: Converging series, expressing the ratio between the diameter and circumference of a circle. Wash. 1871. Q. *In* Smithsonian contributions.   506 : R3 v18

Barlow, P: Tables of squares, cubes, square roots, cube roots, reciprocals of all integer numbers up to 10,000. Ster. ed. examined and corr. Lond. 1856. O.   514 : 1

Callet, J: François. Tables portatives de logarithmes ; contenant les logarithmes des nombres depuis 1 jusqu'à 108,000 ; les logarithmes des sinus et tangentes, de seconde en seconde pour les cinq premiers degrés, de dix en dix secondes pour tous les degrés du quart de cercle, et, suivant la nouvelle division centésimale, de dix-millième en dix-millième ; précédées d'un discours préliminaire sur l'explication, l'usage et la sommation des logarithmes et sur leur application à l'astronomie, à la navigation, à la géométrie-pratique et aux calculs d'intérêts, suivies de nouvelles tables plus approchées, et de plusieurs autres utiles à la recherche de longitudes en mer, etc. Paris. 1795 [1855]. O.   514 : R3

Law, H: Mathematical tables for trigonometrical, astronomical and nautical calculations ; prefixed, a treatise on logarithms. New and rev. ed. [Weale's ser.] Lond. 1884. D.   514 : 6

Pocket logarithms to four places of decimals, including logarithms of numbers and logarithmic sines and tangents to single minutes, to which is added a table of natural sines, tangents and cotangents. [Van Nostrand's science ser.] N. Y. 1883. S.
                                                514 : 4

Vega, G: *freiherr* v. Thesaurus logarithmorum completus, ex arithmetica logarithmica et ex trigonometria artificiali Adriani Vlacci collectus, plurimis erroribus purgatus, in novem ordinem redactus et, prima post centesimam logarithmorum chiliade, partibus quibusdam proportionalibus differentiarum, logarithmis sinuum, cosinuum, tangentium et cotangentium pro primis ac postremis duobus quadrantis gradibus ad singula minuta secunda, formulis nonnullis' trigonometricis, Wolframii denique tabula logarithmorum naturalium locupletatus. Lipsiæ. 1794. F.
                                                514 : R2
— Logarithmisch - trigonometrisches handbuch.

Neue ausg. bearb. von C. Bremiker ; 64e aufl. von F. Tietjen. Berlin. 1880. O.
                                                514+5

Lee, T: J. A collection of the tables and formulæ useful in surveying, geodesy and practical astronomy, incl. elements for the projection of maps ; prep. for the use of the corps of topographical engineers. 2d ed. with add. (Papers relating to the duties of the corps, no. 3). Wash. 1853. O.
                                            in 514 : D

5. Analytic geometry and Calculus.

Davies, C: Elements of analytical geometry, embracing the equations of the point, the straight line, the conic sections, and surfaces of the first and second order. Rev. ed. N. Y. 1870. O.   516 : 3

Loomis, Elias. The elements of analytical geometry. Rev. ed. N. Y. 1884. D.
                                                516 : 4

Howison, G: H. A treatise on analytic geometry, especially as applied to the properties of conics ; incl. the modern methods of abridged notation. Written for the mathematical course of Joseph Ray. Cinc. [1869]. O.   516 : 5

Salmon, G: A treatise on conic sections ; containing an account of some of the most important algebraic and geometrical methods. 6th ed. Lond. 1879. O.   515 : 1

— A treatise on the higher plane curves ; intended as a sequel to A treatise on conic sections. 3d ed. Dublin. 1879. O.   516 : 1

— A treatise on the analytic geometry of three dimensions. 4th ed. Dublin. 1882. O.
                                                516 : 2

Clark, James G. Elements of the infinitesimal calculus, with numerous examples and applications to analysis and geometry. Cinc. *n. d.* O.   517 : 3

Loomis, Elias. Elements of the differential and integral calculus. Rev. ed. N. Y. 1884. D.   517 : 4

— *Same.* With his Elements of anal. geom.
                                                516 : 4

Williamson, B: An elementary treatise on the differential calculus ; containing the theory of plane curves, with numerous examples. 5th ed., rev. and enl. N. Y. 1884. D.
                                                517 : 1

— An elementary treatise on the integral calculus ; containing applications to plane curves and surfaces, with numerous examples. 4th ed., rev. and enl. N. Y. 1884. D.
                                                517 : 2

Hardy, Arthur Sherburne. Elements of quaternions. Bost. 1881. O.   518 : 1

3. Astronomy.

1. In general.

Gretschel, H: Lexikon der astronomie ; das gesamte der himmelskunde, mit berücksichtigung der astronomischen instrumente, der zeitrechnung und der hervorragendsten astronomen. Ill. Leipz. 1882. D.
                                                520 : R20

Arago, Dominique François J: Populäre astronomie. *In his* Sämmtliche werke.
                                            500 : 3 v11-14

Champlin, J: Denison, *jr.* Young folks' astronomy. Ill. N. Y. 1881. S.   x 520 : 17

Flammarion, Camille. The wonders of the heavens. From the french by Mrs. Nor-

x denotes books specially adapted for children.

man Lockyer. [Ill. lib. of wonders.] N. Y.
1874. D.   **520 : 3**
Guillemin, Amédée V: The heavens ; an ill.
handbook of popular astronomy, ed. by J.
Norman Lockyer and rev. by R: A. Proctor.
7th ed. N. Y. 1878. O.   **520 : 4**
Leitch, W: God's glory in the heavens. 3d ed.
Lond. 1866. S.   **520 : 15**
Lockyer, Joseph Norman. Astronomy. (Science
primers.) Ill. N. Y. 1879. S.   **520 : 5**
Mädler, J: H: v. Geschichte der himmelskunde
von der ältesten bis auf die neueste zeit.
Braunschweig. 1873. 2 v. O.   **520+1**
Mitchel, Ormsby McKnight. Popular astrono-
my ; a concise elementary treatise on the
suns, planets, satellites and comets. N. Y.
1876. D.   **520 : 7**
Moore, Annie, *and* Laura D. **Nichols.** Overhead,
or What Harry and Nelly discovered in
the heavens. Ill. Bost. 1878. D. **x 520 : 19**
Mudie, Robert. Lessons in astronomy. *T. p. w.*
[Lond. 1842.] S.   **520 : 14**
Newcomb, Simon. Popular astronomy. Ill. N.
Y. 1878. O.   **520 : 8**
— *and* E: Singleton **Holden.** Astronomy for
general readers. 2d ed., rev. (Amer. science ser.) N. Y. 1880. O.   **520 : 9**
Rollwyn, J. A. S. Astronomy simplified for
general reading, with numerous new explanations and discoveries in spectrum
analysis, etc. Lond. 1875. O.   **520 : 13**
Whewell, W: Astronomy and general physics,
considered with reference to natural theology. [Bridgewater treatises]. Lond.
1852. D.   **214 : 3**
Zech, Paul. Himmel und erde ; gemeinfassliche
beschreibung des weltalls. 2te aufl. München. 1878. S.   **520 : 2**
Loomis, Elias. The recent progress of astronomy, especially in the U. S. 3d ed., mostly
rewritten and enl. N. Y. 1856. D. **520 : 6**
Nichol, J: Pringle. Thoughts on some important points relating to the system of the
world. 1st amer. ed. rev. Bost. 1848. D.
                                         520 : 16
Proctor, R: Anthony. Essays on astronomy ; a
series of papers on planets and meteors,
the sun and sun-surrounding space, stars
and star-cloudlets, and a dissertation on
the approaching transits of Venus, preceded by a sketch of the life and work of
sir J: Herschel. Lond. 1872. O.
                                         520 : 10
Contents. Sir J: Herschel.—Sir J: Herschel as a
theorist in astronomy.—The study of astronomy.—
The planet Mars.—Saturn's rings.—Deceptive figures.
—The planet Saturn.—The november shooting stars.—
Gauging the november meteor-stream.—Meteors and
shooting stars.—The zodiacal light.—The solar corona
and the zodiacal light. — Further remarks on the
corona.—Note on Oudemann's theory of the coronal
radiations.—Note on the corona.—On the shallow-
ness of the real solar atmosphere.—Theoretical considerations respecting the corona.—The sun's journey through space. — Coloured suns. — News from
Sirius.— Equal-surface projections of the globe.—A
novel way of studying the stars.—Distribution of the
nebulæ.—A new theory of the milky way.—On the
resolvability of star-groups, regarded as a test of
distance.—A proposal for a series of systematic surveys of the star depths.
— Myths and marvels of astronomy. N. Y. 1877.
O.   **520 : 11**
Contents. Astrology. — The religion of the great
pyramid.—The mystery of the pyramids.—Sweden-

x denotes books specially adapted for children.

Proctor, R: Anthony.—*Continued.*
borg's visions of other worlds.—Other worlds and
other universes. — Suns in flames. — The rings of
Saturn.—Comets as portents.—The lunar hoax.—On
some astronomical paradoxes.—On some astronomical myths.—The origin of the constellation-figures.
— The poetry of astronomy ; a series of familiar
essays on the heavenly bodies, regarded
less in their strictly scientific aspect than
as suggesting thoughts respecting infinities of time and space, of variety, of vitality and of development. Phila. 1881. D.
                                         520 : 12
Contents. The age of the sun and earth.—The sun
in his glory.—When the sea was young.—Is the moon
dead ?— The moon's myriad small craters.—A new
crater in the moon.—A fiery world.—The planet of
war.—Living in dread and terror.—A ring of worlds.
—Earth-born meteorites. — The architecture of the
universe.
— Mysteries of time and space. N. Y. 1883. D.
                                         520 : 18
Contents. Newton and Darwin.—The vistas of the
past.—The birth of the moon.—Birth and death of
worlds.—The sun as a perpetual machine.—The sun's
corona.—The sun's long streamers.—Meteoric astronomy.—Comets.—Cometic mysteries.—Dangers from
comets.—The world's end.—The menacing comet.—
Jupiter's satellites. — Terrestrial magnetism. — The
star-depths. — Transits of Venus. — Star-clouds and
star-mist.—Herbert Spencer's philosophy.—A survey
of the northern heavens.—Star unto star.

2. The firmament.

Powalky, C. R. A new reduction of La Caille's
observations, made at the Cape of Good
Hope and at Paris between 1749 and 1757,
and given in his Astronomiæ fundamenta,
together with a comparison of the results
with the Bradley - Bessel Fundamenta ;
also a catalogue of the places of 150 stars
south of declination —30° for the epochs of
1750 and 1830. *In* U. S. coast survey rep.
1882.   *in* **622 : D**
Hilgard, Julius E. A catalogue of stars for
observations of latitude. *In* U. S. coast
survey rep. 1876.   *in* **622 : D**
Davidson, G: Azimuth and apparent altitude
of Polaris. *In* U. S. coast survey rep. 1870.
                                       in **622 : D**
Safford, T. H. Catalogue of the mean declination of 2,018 stars between 0 h. to 2 h., and
12 h. to 24 h. right ascension, and 10° and
70° of north declination, for jan. 1, 1875.
(U. S. geogr. surveys west of 100th mer.,
Wheeler). Wash. 1879. Q.   *in* **557.5 : D**
United States. *Bureau of navigation.* Apparent right ascensions of additional time-
stars 1881-1884, with mean places for 1884.0;
a supp. to the American ephemeris and
nautical almanac for 1884. (U. S. 47th cong.
1 sess. House misc. doc. no. 60). Wash.
1882. Q.   *in* **523 : D**
Davidson, G: Field catalogue of 1,278 time and
circumpolar stars ; mean places for 1885.0.
In U. S. coast survey rep. 1883. *in* **622 : D**
American ephemeris, The, and nautical almanac for 1886. (U. S. 47th cong. 2 sess.
House misc. doc., v. 7). Wash. 1883. Q.
                                       in **528 : D**
Proctor, R: Anthony. A star atlas for students
and observers, showing 6,000 stars and
1,500 double stars, nebulæ, etc., in 12 maps
on the equidistant projection, with index
maps on the stereographic projection. 4th
ed. Lond. 1877. F.   **524 : R1**

Proctor, R: Anthony.—*Continued.*
— Easy star lessons. N. Y. 1882. D.   **524 : 2**
— The expanse of heaven ; a series of essays on
the wonders of the firmament. N. Y. 1874.
D.   **523 : 7**
Contents. A dream that was not all a dream.—The
sun. — The queen of night. — The evening star. —
The ruddy planet.—Life in the ruddy planet.—The
prince of planets. — Jupiter's family of moons.—
The ring-girdled planet.—Newton and the law of the
universe.—The discovery of two giant planets.—The
lost comet.—Visitants from the star depths.—Whence
come the comets.—The comet families of the giant
planets.—The earth's journey through showers.—
How the planets grew.—Our daily light.—The flight
of light.—A cluster of suns.—Worlds ruled by coloured suns.—Worlds lit by coloured suns.—The king
of suns.—Four orders of suns.—The depths of space.
—Chatting the star depths.—The star depths astir
with life.—The drifting stars.—The milky way.
— Our place among infinities ; a series of essays
contrasting our little abode in space and
time with the infinities around us ; added,
essays on the Jewish sabbath and astrology.
N. Y. 1876. D.   **523 : 4**
Contents. Past and future of the earth.—Seeming
wastes in nature. — New theory of life in other
worlds.—A missing comet.—The lost comet and its
meteor train.—Jupiter.— Saturn and its system.—A
giant sun.—The star depths.—Star gauging.—Saturn
and the sabbath of the jews. — Thoughts on astrology.
— Flowers of the sky. Ill. N. Y. [1880]. S.
    523 : 3
Guillemin, Amédée Victor. The world of
comets. Tr. and ed. by James Glaisher.
Ill. Lond. 1877. Q.   **523 : 9**
Holden, E: Singleton. Index catalogue of books
and memoirs relating to nebulæ, clusters,
etc. Wash. 1877. O. *In* Smithsonian misc.
    506 : R4 v14

3. Solar system.

Alexander, Stephen. Statement and exposition
of certain harmonies of the solar system.
Ill. Wash. 1875. Q. *In* Smithsonian contributions.   **506 : R3 v21**
Newcomb, Simon. On the general integrals of
planetary motion. Wash. 1874. Q. *In*
Smithsonian contributions.   **506 : R3 v21**
Barnard, Jonathan Gilbert. Problems of rotary
motion presented by the gyroscope, the
precession of the equinoxes and the pendulum. Ill. Wash. 1872. Q. *In* Smithsonian contributions.   **506 : R3 v19**
— On the internal structure of the earth, considered as affecting the phenomena of precession and nutation; supplementary to
Problems of rotary motion. Ill. Wash.
1877. Q. *In* Smithsonian contributions.
    506 : R3 v23
Runkle, J: D. New tables for determining the
values of the coefficients in the perturbative
function of planetary motion, which de-
pend upon the ratio of the mean distances.
Wash. 1856. Q. *In* Smithsonian contributions.   **506 : R3 v9**
— Asteroid supplement to New tables for determining the values of $b_k^{(i)}$ and its derivatives. Wash. 1857. Q. *In* Smithsonian
contributions.   **506 : R3 v9**
Stockwell, J: N. Secular variations of the
elements of the orbits of the eight principal planets, Mercury, Venus, the Earth,
Mars, Jupiter, Saturn, Uranus and Nep-

tune, with tables of the same ; together
with the obliquity of the ecliptic and the
precession of the equinoxes in both longitude and right ascension. Wash. 1872. Q.
In Smithsonian contributions.
    506 : R3 v18
Guillemin, Amédée V: The sun. From the
french by A. L. Phipson. [Ill. lib. of
wonders]. N. Y. 1875. D.   **523 : 1**
Proctor, R: Anthony. The sun ; ruler, fire, light,
and life of the planetary system. 2d ed.
Ill. Lond. 1872. D.   **523 : 5**
Young, C: A: The sun. (Intern. scientific ser.)
N. Y. 1881. D.   **523 : 6**
Walker, Sears Cook. Researches relative to
the planet Neptune ; and Ephemerides of
Neptune, 1846–1852. Wash. 1848-53. Q. *In*
Smithsonian contributions. **506 : R3 v2,3**
Newcomb, Simon. An investigation of the orbit
of Neptune, with general tables of its
motion. Wash. 1866. Q. *In* Smithsonian
contributions.   **506 : R3 v15**
— An investigation of the orbit of Uranus, with
general tables of its motion. Wash. 1873.
Q. *In* Smithsonian contributions.
    506 : R3 v19

The Earth and Moon.

Guillemin, Amédée V: The wonders of the
moon. Tr. from the french by miss M. G.
Mesd. ed. with add. by Maria Mitchell.
[Ill. lib. of wonders]. N. Y. 1873. D.
    523 : 2
Schott, C: Anthony. Tidal observations in the
arctic seas by Elisha Kent Kane, made
during the second Grinnell expedition in
search of sir John Franklin, in 1853-5, at
Van Rensselaer harbor ; reduced and dis-
cussed. Ill. Wash. 1860. Q. *In* Smithsonian contributions.   **506 : R3 v13**
Ferrel, W: Discussion of tides in Boston harbor.
In U. S. coast survey rep. 1868. *in* **622 : D**
— On the moon's mass, as deduced from [the
above] discussion. *In the same*, 1870.
    in **622 : D**
— Report of meteorological effects on tides. *In
the same*, 1871.   *in* **622 : D**
— Discussions of tides in New York harbor. *In
the same*, 1875.   *in* **622 : D**
— Discussion of tides in Penobscot Bay, Me. *In
the same*, 1878.   *in* **622 : D**
— Discussion of the tides of the Pacific coast of
the U. S. *In the same*, 1882.   *in* **622 : D**
— Report on the harmonic analysis of the tides
at Sandy Hook. *In the same*, 1883.
    in **622 : D**
Schott, C: Anthony. Determination of time by
means of the transit instrument. *In* U. S.
coast survey rep. 1866, 1868.   *in* **622 : D**
— *Same*. Rev. and ill. *In the same*, 1880.
    in **622 : D**
— Determination of longitude by means of the
electric telegraph. Ill. *In the same*, 1880.
    in **622 : D**
— Determination of latitude by means of the
zenith telescope. *In the same*, 1866.
    in **622 : D**
— *Same*. Rev. and ill. *In the same*, 1880.
    in **622 : D**

Schott, C: Anthony.—*Continued.*
— Determination of the astronomical azimuth of a direction. *In* U. S. coast survey rep. 1866, 1868.   *in* **622 : D**
— *Same.* Rev. and ill. *In the same*, 1880.
                                     in **622 : D**
United States. *Coast survey.* Formulæ, tables and example for the geodetic computation of latitudes, longitudes and azimuth of trigonometrical points. *In* Report, 1860.
                                     in **622 : D**
— - Formulæ and factors for the computation of geodetic latitudes, longitudes and azimuths. *In the same*, 1875.   *in* **622 : D**
Peirce, B: Report upon the determination of the longitude of America and Europe from the solar eclipse of july 28, 1851. *In* U. S. coast survey rep. 1861.   *in* **622 : D**
— Reports on determining longitudes from the occultations of the Pleiades. *In the same*, 1861, 1863, 1865.   *in* **622 : D**
Walker, Sears Cook. Reports on longitude computations. *In* U. S. coast survey rep. 1866.
                                     in **622 : D**
Gould, B: Apthorp. On the longitude between America and Europe, from signals through the Atlantic cable; [with history of previous attempts at the determination of transatlantic longitude]. *In* U. S. coast survey rep. 1867.   *in* **622 : D**
— On the trans-atlantic longitude, as determined by the coast survey expedition of 1866; a report to the sup't of the U. S. coast survey. Ill. Wash. 1869. Q. *In* Smithsonian contributions.   **506 : R3 v16**
Hilgard, Julius E. Transatlantic longitudes; final report on the determination of 1872, with a review of previous determinations. *In* U. S. coast survey rep. 1874. *in* **622 : D**
Schott, C: Anthony. Report on the results of the longitudes determined up to the present time by means of the electric telegraph; together with their preliminary adjustment by the method of least squares. *In* U. S. coast survey rep. 1880.   *in* **622 : D**
— Results of the measure of an arc of the meridian of 3°23′, between Nantucket and Farmington, Me. *In* U. S. coast survey rep. 1868.   *in* **622 : D**
— The Pamplico-Chesapeake arc of the meridian, and its combination with the Nantucket and the Peruvian arcs, for a determination of the figure of the earth from american measures. *In the same*, 1877.   *in* **622 : D**
— Results of the transcontinental line of geodetic spirit-leveling near the parallel of 39°, executed by Andrew Braid. Pt. 1: From Sandy Hook, N. J., to St. Louis, Mo. *In* U. S. coast survey rep. 1882.   *in* **622 : D**
Kampf, F., *and* J: H. **Clark.** Report upon the determination of the astronomical coördinates of the primary stations at Cheyenne, Wyo., and Colorado Springs, Colo., made during 1872 and 1873. (U. S. geogr. surveys west of 100th mer., Wheeler). Wash. 1874. Q.   *in* **557.5 : D**
— - *and others.* Reports upon the astronomical determinations at main stations occupied in 1872, 1873 and 1874. Ill. (U. S. geogr. surveys west of 100th mer., Wheeler. Report, v. 2). Wash. 1877. Q.   *in* **557.5 : D**
Contents. Ogden, Utah, 1873-4.—Beaver, Utah, 1872.

—Pioche. Nev., 1872. — Gunnison, Utah, 1872.—Green River, Wyo., 1873.—Winnemucca, Nev., 1873.—Virginia City, Nev., 1873. —Georgetown, Colo., 1873.—Hughes, Colo., 1873.—Labran, Colo., 1873.—Trinidad, Colo., 1873. —Fort Union. N. Mex., 1873.—Santa Fé, N. Mex., 1873. —Bozeman, Mont., 1873.—Las Vegas, N. Mex., 1874.— Cimarron, N. Mex., 1874.—Sidney Barracks, Neb., 1874. —Julesburg, Colo., 1874.—North Platte, Neb., 1874. — Descriptive rep. on station at Salt Lake City, 1873. — Description of observatory and site at Ogden.—Description of personal-equation instr.—List of geograph. positions.

4. Practical astronomy, navigation, etc.

Loomis, Elias. An introduction to practical astronomy, with a collection of astronomical tables. N. Y. 1855. O.   **522+1**
Olmsted, Denison. An introduction to astronomy, designed as a text book for the students of Yale college. 2d ed. N. Y. 1841. O.   **522 : 2**
Ward, *The hon. mrs.* M. The telescope; a familiar sketch, combining a special notice of objects coming within the range of a small telescope, with a detail of the most interesting discoveries which have been made with the assistance of powerful telescopes, concerning the phenomena of the heavenly bodies. 3d ed. Ill. Lond. 1869. D.   **522 : 3**
Draper, H: On the construction of a silvered glass telescope 15½ inches in aperture, and its use in celestial photography. Ill. Wash. 1864. Q. *In* Smithsonian contributions.
                                     506 : R3 v14
Comer, G: N. Navigation simplified; a manual of instruction in navigation as practised at sea, adapted to the wants of the sailor, containing all the tables, explanations and illustrations necessary for the easy understanding and use of the practical branches of navigation and nautical astronomy; with numerous examples, worked out by the American ephemeris and nautical almanac, for several years ahead. N. Y. 1868. O.   **527+2**
Greenwood, James. The sailor's sea book; a rudimentary treatise on navigation: pt. 1, How to keep the log and work it off; pt. 2, On finding the latitude and longitude. Added, the deviation and error of the compass, great circle sailing, the international commercial code of signals, the rule of the road at sea, rocket and mortar apparatus for saving life, the law of storms, and a brief dictionary of sea terms. New rev. and enl. ed. by W. H. Rosser. Ill. [Weale's ser.] Lond. 1879. D.   **527 : 1**

* * *

Amerikanischer turner-kalender, 1880—1882. Milw. 1880-82. D.   **528 : 1**
Freidenker-almanach, 1879—1882. Milw. 1879-82. 4 v. D.   **528 : 2**

5. Observations.

Peirce, C: Sanders. On the theory of errors of observations. *In* U. S. coast survey rep. 1870.   *in* **622 : D**
Hilgard, Julius E. On the use of the zenith telescope for the observations of time. *In* U. S. coast survey rep. 1869.   *in* **622 : D**

Gilliss, James Melville. An account of the total solar eclipse of july 18, 1860, as observed near Steilacoom, Wash. terr. *In* U. S. coast survey rep. 1860.   *in* **622 : D**

United States. *Coast survey.* Reports of observations of the eclipse of the sun, aug. 7, 1869, made by parties of the survey. Maps and ill. *In* Report 1869.   *in* **622 : D**

— Reports of observations upon the total solar eclipse of dec. 22, 1870. *In* Report 1870, 1871.   *in* **622 : D**

Davidson, G: The total solar eclipse of jan. 11, 1880, observed at mount Santa Lucia, Cal. Ill. *In* U. S. coast survey rep. 1882.
                                    in **622 : D**

National academy of sciences. Memoir: Report of the eclipse expedition to Caroline Island, may 1883. Ill. [Wash. 1883]. Q.
                                    in **525 : D**

                    * * *

Proctor, R: Anthony. Transits of Venus ; a popular account of past and coming transits, from the first observed by Horrocks, a. d. 1639, to the transit of a. d. 2012. Ill. Lond. 1874. D.   **523 : 8**

Schott, C: Anthony. Transit of Venus, 1769 ; results of observations for determining positions occupied in lower California [by

Chappe d'Auteroche], and at Philadelphia [by Rittenhouse]. *In* U. S. coast survey rep. 1874.   *in* **622 : D**

Newcomb, Simon, *ed.* Observations of the transit of Venus, dec. 8–9, 1874, made and reduced under the dir. of the commission created by congress. Ill. (U. S. 46th congress, 1 sess. Senate ex. doc. no. 31.) Wash. 1880. Q.   *in* **525 : D**

Davidson, G: Report of the transit of Venus expedition to Japan, 1874. *In* U. S. coast survey rep. 1875.   *in* **622 : D**

Smith, Edwin. Report on the transit of Venus expedition to Chatham island, 1874. *In* U. S. coast survey rep. 1875.   *in* **622 : D**

United States. *Congress.* Instructions for observing the transit of Venus, dec. 6, 1882, prepared by the commission authorized by congress, and printed for the use of the observing parties by authority of the sec. of the navy. Maps. Wash. 1882. F.
                                    in **525 : D**

— *Coast survey.* Observations of the transit of Venus of dec. 6, 1882. *In* Report 1883.
                                    in **622 : D**

— - Reports on observations of the transit of Mercury, may 6, 1878. *In* Report 1878.
                                    in **622 : D**

4. Physics.

1. In general.

Lommel, Eugen Cornelius Joseph. Lexikon der physik und meteorologie in volksthümlicher darstellung. Ill. Leipz. 1882. D.
                                    530 : R23

Charleton, Walter. Physiologia Epicuro-Gassendo-Charltoniana, or A fabrick of science natural upon the hypothesis of atoms, founded by Epicurus, repaired by Petrus Gassendus, augmented by Walter Charleton. 1st pt. Lond. 1654. Q.   **23 : R**

Rutherford, T: A system of natural philosophy; a course of lectures in mechanics, optics, hydrostatics and astronomy, which are read in St. John's college, Cambridge. Cambridge. 1748. 2 v. Q.   **530 : R9**

Enfield, W: Institutes of natural philosophy, theoretical and practical, with some corrections, change in the order of the branches and the addition of an app. to the astronomical part, selected from mr. Ewing's Practical astronomy by S: Webber. 4th amer. ed., with improvements. Bost. 1824. Q.   **530 : R8**

Euler, Leonhard. Letters on different subjects in natural philosophy addressed to a german princess ; with notes and a life of Euler by D: Brewster, [and] containing a glossary of scientific terms, with add. notes by J: Griscom. N. Y. 1846. 2 v. S.
                                    530 : 5

Bird, Golding. Elements of natural philosophy ; an experimental introd. to the study of the physical sciences. From the 3d Lond. ed. Ill. Phila. 1848. D.   **530 : 3**

Hunt, Robert. Elementary physics ; an introd. to the study of natural philosophy. Lond. 1855. D. [*T. p. w.*]   **530 : 6**

Paris, J: Ayrton. Philosophy in sport made science in earnest ; an attempt to implant in the young mind the first principles of natural philosophy by the aid of the popular toys and sports of youth. [*Anon.*] N. Y. 1855. S.   **530 : 7**

Tomlinson, C: Introd. to the study of natural philosophy, for the use of beginners. 9th ed. [Weale's ser.] Lond. 1874. D.
                                    530 : 14

Arnott, Neil. Elements of physics, or natural philosophy. 7th ed., ed. by Alexander Bain and Alfred Swaine Taylor. N. Y. 1877. D.   **530 : 2**

Stewart, Balfour. Physics. (Science primers.) Ill. N. Y. 1879. S.   **530 : 13**

Privat-Deschanel, A: Elementary treatise on natural philosophy. Tr. and ed., with add., by J. D. Everett. Ill. N. Y. 1878. O.
                                    530 : 18

Ganot, Adolphe. Natural philosophy for general readers and young persons. Tr. and ed. from Ganot's Cours élémentaire de physique, with the author's sanction, by E. Atkinson. 2d ed. N. Y. 1876. D.   **530 : 4**

— Elementary treatise on physics, experimental and applied, for the use of colleges, and schools. Tr. and ed. from Ganot's Éléments de physique, with the author's sanction, by E. Atkinson. 11th ed., rev. and enl. Ill. N. Y. 1883. O.   **530 : 20**

Pickering, E: C. Elements of physical manipulation. 2d ed. N. Y. 1875, 1876. 2 v. O.
                                    530+17

Youmans, E: Livingstone, *ed.* The correlation and conservation of forces ; a series of expositions, with an introd. and brief bio-

graphical notices of the chief promoters of the new views. N. Y. 1876. D.   **530 : 15**
Contents. **Grove, W: R.** The correlation of physical forces.—**Helmholtz, H. L: F.** The interaction of natural forces.—**Mayer, J. R.** The forces of inorganic nature; Celestial dynamics; The mechanical equivalent of heat.—**Liebig, J. v.** The connection and equivalence of forces.—**Carpenter, W: B:** The correlation of the physical and vital forces.

Grove, W: Robert. The correlation of physical forces. 3d ed. Lond. 1855. O.   **530 : 24**

Saigey, Émile. The unity of natural phenomena; a popular introd. to the study of the forces of nature. From the french; with an introd. and notes by T: Freeman Moses. [Science for the people.] Bost. 1873. D.   **530 : 11**

Krebs, G: Die erhaltung der energie als grundlage der neuern physik. München. 1877. S.   **530 : 10**

Stewart, Balfour. The conservation of energy; with an app. treating of the vital and mental applications of the doctrine. (Intern. scientific ser.) N. Y. 1877. D.   **530 : 12**

Carpenter, W: Lant. Energy in nature; being, with some additions, the substance of a course of six lectures upon the forces of nature and their natural relations, del. under the auspices of the Gilchrist educational trust, in the autumn of 1881. Ill. N. Y. 1883. D.   **530 : 21**

Naville, Jules Ernest. Modern physics; studies historical and philosophical. From the french by H: Downton. N. Y. 1884. D.   **530 : 22**

* * *.

Abbott, Jacob. Science for the young: Force. Ill. N. Y. 1873. D.   **x 530 : 19**

Hooker, Worthington. The child's book of nature, for the use of families and schools, intended to aid mothers and teachers in training children in the observation of nature; in 3 pts. Pt. 3: Air, water, heat, light, etc. N. Y. 1881. S.   **x 530 : 16**

2. Mechanics.

Clifford, W: Kingdon. Elements of dynamic; an introd. to the study of motion and rest in solid and fluid bodies; pt. 1: Kinematic. Lond. 1878. D.   **531 : 18**

Minchin, G: M. Uniplanar kinematics of solids and fluids, with applications to the distribution and flow of electricity. Oxford. 1882. D.   **531 : 22**

Tait, P: Guthrie, *and* **W: J: Steele.** A treatise on dynamics of a particle, with numerous examples. 5th ed., rev. Lond. 1882. D.   **531 : 20**

Routh, E: J: The elementary part of a system of rigid bodies; pt. 1 of a treatise on the whole subject, with numerous examples. 4th ed., rev. and enl. Lond. 1882. O.   **531 : 19**

Maxwell, James Clerk. Matter and motion. [Van Nostrand's science ser.] N. Y. 1878. T.   **531 : 10**

Craig, T: Elements of the mathematical theory of fluid motion: On the motion of a solid in a fluid, and the vibrations of liquid spheroids. [Van Nostrand's science ser.] N. Y. 1879. T.   **531 : 7**

x denotes books specially adapted for children.

Craig, T:—*Continued.*
— — Wave and vortex motion. [Van Nostrand's science ser.] N. Y. 1879. T.   **531 : 8**

Minchin, G: M. A treatise on statics, with applications to physics; v. 1: Equilibrium of coplanar forces. 3d ed., corr. and enl. Oxford. 1884. O.   **531 : 21**

Laplace, P: Simon *marquis* de. A treatise on analytical mechanics; being the first book of the Mécanique céleste. Tr. and elucidated with explanatory notes by J: Toplis. Nottingham. 1814. O.   **531 : 3**

Bartlett, W: H. C. Elements of analytical mechanics. 3d ed., rev. and corr. N. Y. 1855. O.   **531+14**

Farrar, J: An elementary treatise on mechanics; comprehending the doctrine of equilibrium and motion as applied to solids and fluids, chiefly compiled and designed for the use of students of the university of Cambridge, New Eng. 2d ed., rev. and corr. Bost. 1834. O.   **531+16**

Morin, Arthur Jules. Fundamental ideas of mechanics and experimental data. Rev., tr. and reduced to english units of measure by Joseph Bennett. N. Y. 1860. O.   **531+15**

Kater, H:, *and* **Dionysius Lardner.** A treatise on mechanics. (Amer. lib. of useful knowledge, v. 2). Bost. 1831. D.   **531 : 2**
— *Same.* (Bost. soc. for the diffusion of useful knowledge). Bost. 1831. D.   **531 : 2**

Peirce, C: Sanders. On the flexure of pendulum supports.— On the deduction of the ellipticity of the earth from pendulum experiments.— On a method of observing the coincidence of vibrations of two pendulums. — On the value of gravity at Paris. *In* U. S. coast survey rep. 1881.   *in* **622 : D**
— Measurements of gravity at initial stations in America and Europe. Pt. 1 : [Methods employed and main results]. *In the same,* 1876.   *in* **622 : D**
— Determinations of gravity at Allegheny, Edensburgh and York, Pa., in 1879 and 1880. *In the same,* 1883.   *in* **622 : D**

Trowbridge, W. P. Investigation of the laws of motion governing the descent of the weight and line in deep-sea soundings. *In* U. S. coast survey rep. 1858.   *in* **622 : D**

Renwick, James. Applications of the science of mechanics to practical purposes. N. Y. 1840. S.   **513 : 6**

Moseley, H: Illustrations of mechanics. Rev. by James Renwick. Ill. N. Y. 1844. S.   **531 : 4**
— The mechanical principles of engineering and architecture. 2d amer. from 2d Lond. ed., with add. by D. H. Mahan. N. Y. 1866. D.   **531 : R17**

Byrne, Oliver. The essential elements of practical mechanics, based on the principle of work; designed for engineering students. 2d ed. Lond. 1872. D.   **531 : 1**

Nystrom, J: W: A new treatise on the elements of mechanics, establishing strict precision in the meaning of dynamical terms; accompanied with an app. on duodenal arithmetic and metrology. N. Y. 1877. O.   **531+5**

Tomlinson, C: Rudimentary mechanics ; a concise exposition of the general principles of mechanical science and their applications. 12th ed. [Weale's ser.] Lond. 1878. D.
531 : 12

Baker, T: The principles and practice of statics and dynamics, with those of liquids and gases. 3d ed., rev. and corr. by E: Nugent. [Weale's ser.] Lond. 1875. D.   531 : 13

Stahl, Albert W: Transmission of power by wire rope. [Van Nostrand's science ser.] N. Y. 1877. T.   531 : 11

3. Hydrostatics and Pneumatics.

Pfaff, F: Das wasser. (Deutsche originalausg.) 2te aufl. München. 1878. S.   532 : 1

Tomlinson, C: Pneumatics, for the use of beginners. 3d ed. enl. [Weale's ser.] Lond. 1866. D.   533 : 3

Hartley, Walter Noel. Air and its relations to life ; being, with some add., the substance of a course of lectures del. in the summer of 1874, at the Royal institution of Great Britain. N. Y. 1875. D.   533 : 1

Plympton, G: W., *comp.* The aneroid barometer, its construction and use ; compiled from several sources. [Van Nostrand's science ser.] N. Y. 1878. T.   533 : 2
Note. For works on the barometer, see Meteorology, cl. 552, and also hypsometry in Topographica engineering, cl. 622.

Zahner, Robert. The transmission of power by compressed air. [Van Nostrand's science ser.] N. Y. 1878. T.   533 : 4

Marion, Fulgence. Wonderful balloon ascents, or The conquest of the skies ; a history of balloons and balloon voyages. From the french. [Ill. lib. of wonders.] N. Y. 1874.   533 : 5

4. Acoustics.

Radau, Rodolphe. Die lehre vom schall ; gemeinfassliche darstellung der akustik. 2te aufl. München. 1875. S.   534 : 1

— Wonders of acoustics, or The phenomena of sound. From the french, the english rev. by Robert Ball. [Ill. lib. of wonders.] N. Y. 1872. D.   534 : 4

Tyndall, J: Sound. 3d ed. rev. and enl. N. Y. 1877. D.   534 : 2

Mayer, Alfred Marshall. Sound ; a series of experiments in the phenomena of sound. (Experimental science ser. for beginners.) N. Y. 1878. D.   534 : 3

Smith, T. Roger. Acoustics in relation to architecture and building ; the laws of sound as applied to the arrangement of buildings. New ed. ill., with index. [Weale's ser.] Lond. [1861]. D.   534 : 5

5. Optics.

Farrar, J: An experimental treatise on optics ; comprehending the leading principles of the science and an explanation of the more important and curious optical instruments and optical phenomena ; the 3d part of a course of natural philosophy, compiled for

the use of the students of the university at Cambridge, New Eng. Cambridge. 1826. O.   535+13

Abbott, Jacob. Science for the young: Light. N. Y. [1871]. D.   x 535 : 12

Lommel, Eugen. The nature of light, with a general account of physical optics. Ill. (Intern. scientific ser.) N. Y. 1876. D.   535 : 3

Marion, Fulgence. The wonders of optics. Tr. from the french and ed. by C: W. Quin. [Ill. lib. of wonders]. N. Y. 1875. D.
535 : 11

Mayer, Alfred Marshall, *and* C: Barnard. Light ; a series of simple, entertaining and inexpensive experiments in the phenomena of light for the use of students of every age. (Experimental science ser. for beginners.) N. Y. 1877. D.   535 : 4

Pisko, F: Joseph. Licht und farbe ; eine gemeinfassliche darstellung der optik. 2te aufl. München. 1876. S.   535 : 1

Tait, P: Guthrie. Light. Edinb. 1884. D.
535 : 15

Tyndall, J: Light and electricity ; notes of two courses of lectures before the Royal institution of Great Britain. N. Y. 1871. D.
535 : 6

— Lectures on light, del. in the U. S. in 1872-73 ; with an app. N. Y. 1873. D.   535 : 5

Lockyer, Joseph Norman. The spectroscope and its applications. (Nature ser.) Ill. Lond. 1873. D.   535 : 9

Nolan, T: The telescope ; the principles involved in the construction of refracting and reflecting telescopes. [Van Nostrand's science ser.] N. Y. 1881. T.   535 : 10

Le Conte, Joseph. Sight ; an exposition of the principles of monocular and binocular vision. Ill. (Intern. scientific ser.) N. Y. 1881. D.   535 : 2

Bezold, W: v. The theory of color in its relation to art and art industry. Tr. from the german by S. R. Köhler ; with an introd. and notes by E: C. Pickering. Authorized amer. ed., rev. and enl. by the author. Ill. Bost. 1876. O.   535 : 7

Rood, Ogden N. Modern chromatics, with applications to art and industry. Ill. (Intern. scientific ser.) N. Y. 1879. D.   535 : 8

6. Heat.

Abbott, Jacob. Science for the young : Heat. N. Y. [1871]. D.   x 536 : 8

Faraday, Michael. A course of six lectures on the chemical history of a candle ; added, a lecture on platinum, del. before a juvenile auditory at the Royal institution of Great Britain, during the christmas holidays of 1860-1. Ed. by W: Crookes. Ill. N. Y. 1861. S.   x 536 : 9

Cazin, Achille. Die wärme. Nach dem französischen deutsch bearbeitet ; herausg. durch Philipp Carl. 2te aufl. München. 1877. D.
536 : 1

— The phenomena and laws of heat. Tr. and ed. by Elihu Rich. [Ill. library of wonders]. N. Y. 1874. D.   536 : 2

x denotes books specially adapted for children,

Maxwell, James Clerk. Theory of heat. New ed. N. Y. 1875. S.   **536 : 5**

Tyndall, J: On radiation ; the Rede lecture, del. in the senate-house, before the univ. of Cambridge, Eng., may 16, 1865. N. Y. 1868. D.   **536 : 4**

— Heat as a mode of motion. From the 4th eng. ed. N. Y. 1877. D.   **536 : 3**

Siemens, *Sir* C: W: On the conservation of solar energy ; a collection of papers and discussions. Ill. Lond. 1883. O.   **536 : 10**

Williams, C: Wye. On heat in its relations to water and steam ; embracing new views of vaporization, condensation and explosions. From the 2d Lond. ed. Phila. 1867. O.   **536+6**

Ledoux, C: Ice-making machines ; the theory of the action of the various forms of cold-producing, or so-called ice machines, machines à froid. Tr. from the french. N. Y. 1879. T.   **536 : 7**

Gamgee, J: On artificial refrigeration. Ill. *In* U. S. fish com. report, v. 5.   *in* **639 : D**

7. Electricity and magnetism.

Thompson, Silvanus P. Elementary lessons in electricity and magnetism. Lond. 1884. S.   **537 : 21**

Gordon, J. E. H. A physical treatise on electricity and magnetism. N. Y. 1880. 2 v. O.   **537+9**

Maxwell, James Clerk. Treatise on electricity and magnetism. 2d ed. Oxford. 1881. 2 v. O.   **537 : 10**

Carl, Philipp. Die elektrischen naturkräfte ; der magnetismus, die elektricität und der galvanische strom, mit ihren hauptsächlichsten anwendungen, gemeinfasslich dargestellt. 2te aufl. München. 1878. S. **537 : 1**

Baille, J: Baptiste. Wonders of electricity. Tr. from the french, ed. with numerous add. by J: W. Armstrong. [Ill. lib. of wonders.] N. Y. 1872. D.   **537 : 2**

Harris, *Sir* W: Snow. Rudimentary treatise on galvanism and the general principles of animal and voltaic electricity. New ed. rev., with considerable add., by Robert Sabine. Ill. [Weale's ser.] Lond. 1869. D.   **537 : 5**

— Rudimentary electricity ; showing the general principles of electrical science and the purposes to which it has been applied. 7th ed. with add., incl. extracts from the Cavendish papers, and a general index. [Weale's ser.] Lond. 1875. D.   **537 : 6**

Tyndall, J: Lessons in electricity at the Royal institution, 1875-6. N. Y. 1877. D. **537 : 7**

Fonvielle, Wilfrid de. Thunder and lightning. Tr. from the french and ed. by T. L. Phipson. [Ill. lib. of wonders.] N. Y. 1875. D.   **537 : 4**

Secchi, Angelo. Researches on electrical rheometry. Ill. Wash. 1852. Q. *In* Smithsonian contributions.   **506 : R3 v3**

Hough, G. W. Velocity of the electric current over telegraph wire ; read before the Albany institute june 1869. Albany, N. Y. 1869. O.   **537 : Pam**

Induction coils ; how made and how used. Reprinted from the 8th eng. ed. [Van Nostrand's science ser.] N. Y. 1881. T.   **537 : 8**

Du Moncel, Theodore Achille L: *comte*. The telephone, the microphone and the phonograph. Authorized tr., with add. and corr. by the author. Ill. N. Y. 1879. D. **537 : 3**

— Electro-magnets ; the determination of the elements of their construction, tr. from the 2d ed. Reprinted from Van Nostrand's magazine. [Van Nostrand's science ser.] N. Y. 1883. T.   **537 : 12**

—— *and* W: H: Preece. Incandescent electric lights, with particular reference to the Edison lamps at the Paris exhibition. Rep. with add. and new ill. from Van Nostrand's magazine. [Van Nostrand's science ser.] N. Y. 1882. T.   **537 : 11**

Contains also "The economy of the electric light by incandescence," by J: W. **Howell**, and "Steadiness of the electric current," both rep. from Van Nostrand's magazine.

Prescott, G: B. The speaking telephone, electric light, and other recent electric inventions. Ill. N. Y. 1879. O.   **537+13**

Greer, H:, *ed.* Recent wonders in electricity, electric lighting, magnetism, telegraphy, etc.; articles by dr. Siemens, count Du Moncel and prof. Thomson. N. Y. [1883]. O.   **537+16**

Fiske, Bradley A. Electricity in theory and practice, or The elements of electrical engineering. Ill. N. Y. 1883. O.   **537 : 17**

Hospitalier, E. The modern applications of electricity. Tr. and enl. by Julius Maier. 2d ed. rev., with add. Ill. N. Y. 1883. 2 v. O.   **537 : 14**

Contents. V. 1. Electric generators.—Electric light. 2. Telephone. — Various applications. — Electrical transmission of energy.

Thompson, Silvanus P. Dynamo-electric machinery ; lectures, reprinted from the Journal of the society of arts, with an introd. by Frank L. Pope. [Van Nostrand's science ser.] N. Y. 1883. T.   **537 : 15**

— Recent progress in dynamo-electric machines ; a supplement to "Dynamo-electric machinery." Reprinted from the Journal of the society of arts. Ill. [Van Nostrand's science ser.] N. Y. 1884. T.   **537 : 20**

Dynamic electricity ; its modern use and measurement, chiefly in its application to electric lighting and telegraphy, incl., 1, Some points in electric lighting, by J: **Hopkinson** ; 2, On the measurement of electricity for commercial purposes, by James N. **Shoolbred** ; 3, Electric light arithmetic, by R. E. **Day**. Ill. [Van Nostrand's science ser.] N. Y. 1884. T.   **537 : 19**

Gore, G: The art of electro-metallurgy, incl. all known processes of electro deposition. 2d ed. N. Y. 1884. S.   **537 : 18**

Magnetism.

Harris, *Sir* W: Snow. Rudimentary magnetism, a concise exposition of the general principles of magnetical science and the purposes to which it has been applied. 3d ed., rev. and enl. by H: M. Noad. Ill. [Weale's ser.] Lond. 1875. D.   **538 : 1**

United States. *Navy dep't.* Magnetism ; its general principles and special application to ships and compasses. Ill. (Naval prof. papers, no. 13.) Wash. 1883. O. *in* **538 : D**

Lyons, T. H. The magnetism of iron and steel ships; an explanation of the various ways in which it affects the compass. (U. S. naval prof. papers, no. 17.) Wash. 1884. O.
in **538 : D**

Rogers, Fairman. The magnetism of iron vessels, with a short treatise on terrestrial magnetism. [Van Nostrand's science ser.] N. Y. 1877. T.   **538 : 2**

Locke, J: Observations on terrestrial magnetism. Wash. 1852. Q. *In* Smithsonian contributions.   **506 : R3 v3**

Harkness, W: Observations on terrestrial magnetism and on the deviations of the compasses of the U. S. iron clad Monadnock, during her cruise from Phila. to St. Francisco in 1865-6. Ill. Wash. 1872. Q. *In* Smithsonian contributions.   **506 : R3 v18**

Gilliss, James Melville. Magnetical and meteorological observations made at Washington, under orders of the sec. of the navy, dated aug. 13, 1838, [1838-1842]. Wash. 1845. O.   *in* **538 : D**

— Magnetical and meteorological observations, 1849-1852. (U. S. astron. exped. rep., v. 6). Wash. 1856. Q.   *in* **508 : D**
Contents. Introd.—Magnetical observ. at Santiago de Chile, 1849–52.—Results of the calculations of the horizontal force in Chile.—Results of observ. for the magnetic inclination in Chile.—**Bache**, A. D. Magnetic term-day observ. at Washington, D. C., and in California, 1851–55.— **Gerling**, C. L. Corresponding changes of the diurnal magnetic declination observed at Marburg, Hesse.—Meteorological observations at Santiago de Chile from nov. 17, 1849 to sept. 14, 1852.

Bache, Alexander Dallas. Records and results of a magnetic survey of Pennsylvania and parts of adjacent states in 1840-41, with some additional records and results of 1834-35, 1843 and 1866, and a map. Wash. 1863. Q. *In* Smithsonian contributions.
506 : R3 v13

— Observations at the magnetic and meteorological observatory at the Girard college, Phila., made under [his] dir. and with funds supplied by members of the American philosophical society and by the Topographical bureau of the U. S. (U. S. 28th cong. 2 sess. Sen. ex. doc. no. 97). Wash. 1847. 3 v. O.   *in* **538 : D**
Contents. Preface.—Observations from june 1840 to june 1845.—Means of the observations, 1840–1845.

— Discussion of the magnetic and meteorological observations made at the Girard college observatory, Philadelphia, 1840-45. Pt. 1: Investigation of the eleven year period in the amplitude of the solar-diurnal variation, and of the disturbances of the magnetic declination. Ill. Wash. 1859. Q. *In* Smithsonian contributions, v. 11.
506 : R3 v11

— *Same.* Pt. 2: Investigation of the solar-diurnal variation of the magnetic declination and its annual inequality. Ill. Wash. 1862. Q. *In the same*, v. 13. **506 : R3 v13**

— *Same.* Pt. 3: Investigation of the influence of the moon on the magnetic declination. Ill. Wash. 1862. Q. *In the same*, v. 13.
506 : R3 v13

— *Same.* Pt. 4-6: Horizontal force: Investigation of the eleven or ten year period, and of the disturbances of the horizontal component of the magnetic force; Investigation of the solar-diurnal variation and of the annual inequality of the horizontal com-

Bache, Alexander Dallas.—*Continued.*
ponent of the magnetic force; Investigation of the influence of the moon on the magnetic horizontal force. Ill. Wash. 1862. Q. *In* Smithsonian contributions, v. 13.
506 : R3 v13

— *Same.* Pt. 7-9: Vertical force: Investigation of the eleven-year period, and of the disturbances of the vertical component of the magnetic force, and app. on the magnetic effect of the aurora borealis; Investigation of the solar-diurnal variation, and of the annual inequality of the vertical component of the magnetic force; Investigation of the influence of the moon on the magnetic vertical force, inclination and total force. Ill. Wash. 1864. Q. *In the same*, v. 14.   **506 : R3 v14**

— *Same.* Pt. 10-12: Dip and total force: Analysis of the disturbances of the dip and total force; Solar-diurnal variation and annual inequality of the inclination and total force; Discussion of the magnetic inclination, inclination and intensity, between 1841 and 1845. Ill. Wash. 1865. Q. *In the same*, v. 14.   **506 : R3 v14**
Note. These discussions are also published in the annual reports of the U. S. coast survey, class 622: D, viz: Pt. 1 in 1859; pt. 2, 3 in 1860; pt. 4–6 in 1862; pt. 7-9 in 1863; pt. 10–12 in 1864.

— *Same.* General index to the whole series. *In* U. S. coast survey rep. 1864.   *in* **622 : D**

Sonntag, A: Observations on terrestrial magnetism in Mexico, conducted under the direction of baron von Müller; with notes and illustrations of an examination of the volcano Popocatepetl and its vicinity. Ill. Wash. 1860. Q. *In* Smithsonian contributions.   **506 : R3 v11**

Schott, C: Anthony. Magnetical observations in the Arctic seas by Elisha Kent Kane, made during the second Grinnell expedition in search of sir John Franklin, in 1853-5, at Van Rensselaer harbor and other points on the west coast of Greenland; reduced and discussed. Ill. Wash. 1859. Q. *In* Smithsonian contributions. **506 : R3 v10**

— Secular variation in the magnetic declination on the Atlantic and part of the Gulf coast of the U. S. *In* U. S. coast survey rep. 1855.
in **622 : D**

— Discussion of the secular variation of the magnetic inclination in the northeastern states. *In the same*, 1856.   *in* **622 : D**

— Secular change of the magnetic declination and inclination on the western coast of the U. S. *In the same*, 1856.   *in* **622 : D**

— Latest results of the discussion of the secular change of the magnetic declination, accompanied by tables, showing the declination for every 10th year from the date of the earliest reliable observation, for 26 stations on the Atlantic, Gulf and Pacific coasts of the U. S. *In the same*, 1859.
in **622 : D**

— New discussion of the distribution of the magnetic declination, with charts of the isogonic curves for 1860. *In the same*, 1861.
in **622 : D**

— On the secular change of magnetic declination in the U. S. and other parts of North America; new discussion. [2d ed.] *In the same*, 1874.   *in* **622 : D**

Schott, C: Anthony.—*Continued.*
— On the secular variation of the magnetic declination in the U. S., and at some foreign stations. 4th ed., june 1881. Ill. *In* U. S. coast survey rep. 1879.   *in* 622 : D
— *Same.* 5th ed. enl., nov. 1882. Ill. *In the same,* 1882.   *in* 622 : D
— Discussion of the secular change of the magnetic intensity, horizontal and total, on the Atlantic, Gulf and Pacific coasts of the U. S. *In the same,* 1861.   *in* 622 : D
— New investigation of the secular changes in the declination, the dip and the intensity of the magnetic force at Washington. D. C. *In the same,* 1870.   *in* 622 : D
— Results of observations of terrestrial magnetism at Key West, Fla., made between 1860 and 1866 under the dir. of W. P. Trowbridge and S. Walker; discussed and reported. *In the same,* 1874.   *in* 622 : D
— Account and results of magnetic observations made at the U. S. polar station Ooglaamie, Point Barrow, Alaska, lieut. P. H: Ray commanding post; pts. 1-3. Map and ill. *In the same,* 1883.   *in* 622 : D
— Terrestrial magnetism; collection of results for declination, dip and intensity, from observations made by the U. S. coast and geodetic survey between 1833 and july 1882. *In the same,* 1881.   *in* 622 : D

Hilgard, Julius E., and H. W. Blair. Records and results of magnetic observations, made at the charge of the "Bache fund" of the National academy of sciences, from 1871 to 1876. *In* U. S. coast survey rep. 1882.   *in* 622 : D

Bache, Alexander Dallas, and Julius E. Hilgard. On the general distribution of terrestrial magnetism in the U. S., from observations made in the coast survey and others. *In* U. S. coast survey rep. 1856, 1858, 1860.   *in* 622 : D

Hilgard, Julius E. Chart of the magnetic declination in the U. S. for 1875. *In* U. S. coast survey rep. 1876.   *in* 622 : D

Schott, C: Anthony. Distribution of the magnetic declination in the U. S. at the epoch jan. 1885, with isogonic charts. *In* U. S. coast survey rep. 1882.   *in* 622 : D
— Terrestrial magnetism; notes on magnetical observations by means of portable instruments. *In the same,* 1872.   *in* 622 : D
— *Same.* Reprinted, with add. *In the same,* 1875.   *in* 622 : D
— *Same.* Directions for magnetic observations with portable instruments. 3d enl. ed. with 4 plates. *In the same,* 1881.   *in* 622 : D

5. Chemistry and Mineralogy.

1. In general.

Watts, H: A dictionary of chemistry and the allied branches of other sciences. Lond. 1872-81. 8 v. in 9. ().   **540 : R1**
Contents. V. 1. A—Cong. 2. Conh—G. 3. H—M. 4. N—P. 5. Q—Z. 6. 1st suppl. 7. 2d suppl. 8, in 2 pts. 3d suppl.

Landolt, H., and R: Börnstein. Physikalisch-chemische tabellen. Berlin. 1883. Q.   **540+14**

Clarke, Frank Wrigglesworth. The constants of nature, pt. 1 : Specific gravities, boiling and melting points, and chemical formulæ. Wash. 1873. O. *In* Smithsonian misc., v. 12.   **506 : R4 v12**
— *Same,* pt. 1, 1st suppl.: Specific gravities, boiling points and melting points. Wash. 1876. O. *In the same,* v. 14.   **506 : R4 v14**
— *Same,* pt. 2 : A table of specific heats for solids and liquids. Wash. 1876. O. *In the same,* v. 14.   **506 : R4 v14**
— *Same,* pt. 3 : Tables of expansion by heat for solids and liquids. Wash. 1876. O. *In the same,* v. 14.   **506 : R4 v14**

Becker, G: F. *Same,* pt. 4 : Atomic weight determinations ; a digest of the investigations pub. since 1814. Wash. 1880. O. *In the same,* v. 27.   **506 : R4 v27**

Clarke, F. W. *Same,* pt. 5 : A recalculation of the atomic weights. Wash. 1882. O. *In the same,* v. 27.   **506 : R4 v27**

Booth, James C., and Campbell Morfit. Recent improvements in the chemical arts. Wash. 1852. O. *In* Smithsonian misc.   **506 : R4 v2**

Kane, Robert. Elements of chemistry, incl. the most recent discoveries and applications of the science to medicine and pharmacy, and to the arts. An amer. ed. with add. and corr., and arr. for the use of the universities, colleges, academies and medical schools of the U. S. by J: W: Draper. N. Y. 1846. O.   **540 : 4**

Prout, W: Chemistry, meteorology, and the function of digestion, considered with reference to natural theology. 4th ed. by J. W. Griffith. [Bridgewater treatises]. Lond. 1855. D.   **214 : 8**

Johnston, James Finlay Weir. The chemistry of common life. 9th ed. Ill. N. Y. 1859. 2 v. D.   **540 : 6**

Bloxam, C: Loudon. Chemistry, inorganic and organic, with experiments. Phila. 1872. O.   **540 : 2**

Miller, W: Allen. Elements of chemistry, theoretical and practical : pt. 1, Chemical physics ; pt. 2, Inorganic chemistry. Corr. from the 4th Lond. ed. N. Y. 1875, 1877. 2 v. O.   **540+15**

Fownes, G: Rudimentary chemistry, for the use of beginners ; with an app. on the application of chemistry to agriculture. [Weale's ser.] Lond. 1877. D.   **540 : 5**

Cooke, Josiah Parsons, jr. Elements of chemical physics. 3d ed. Bost. 1877. O.   **540+10**
— The new chemistry. (Intern. scientific ser.) N. Y. 1878. D.   **540 : 3**

Youmans, E: Livingstone. A class-book of chemistry on the basis of the new system. Re-written and rev. Ill. N. Y. 1878. D.   **540 : 8**

Roscoe, H: Enfield. Chemistry. (Science primers.) Ill. N. Y. 1879. S.   **540 : 7**

Foye, James C. Chemical problems, with brief statements of the principles involved. [Van Nostrand's science ser.] N. Y. 1883. T.
540 : 9

Watts, H: Manual of chemistry, physical and inorganic. Ill. Phil. 1884. D. 540 : 11

Wurtz, C: Adolphe. Elements of modern chemistry. 2d amer. ed., rev. and enl.; tr. and ed. with the approbation of the author from the 5th french ed., by W: H. Greene. Ill. Phila. 1884. O. 540 : 12

Roscoe, H: Enfield, and C: Schorlemmer. A treatise on chemistry. Ill. and a portr. of Dalton. N. Y. 1883, 1884. 3 v. in 5. O.
540+13
Contents. V. 1. The non-metallic elements. 2 [in 2 pts.]. Metals. 3 [in 2 pts.]. The chemistry of the hydrocarbons and their derivatives, or Organic chemistry.

Thorpe, T: E: A manual of inorganic chemistry. New ed., index. (Putnam's advanced science ser.) N. Y. n. d. 2 v. D. 546 : 1
Contents. V. 1. The non-metals. 2. The metals.

Gibbs, Wolcott, and F: A: Genth. Researches on the ammonia cobalt bases. Ill. Wash. 1856. Q. In Smithsonian contributions.
506 : R3 v9

Schützenberger, Paul. On fermentation. (Intern. scientific ser.) Ill. N. Y. 1876. D.
547 : 1

* * *

American chemical journal, ed. by Ira Remsen; v. 1-5. Balt. 1879-84. O. 505.4 : M
Note. V. 1-3 "ed. with the aid of other chemists at home and abroad."

Boston journal of chemistry, The, and popular science review ; devoted to the science of home-life, the arts, agriculture and medicine, ed. by James R. Nichols ; v. 7-10. 13-18. Bost. 1873—1884. F. 505.4 : RM
Note. Title-page of v. 17 changes to "The popular science news and Boston journal of chemistry," etc.

2. Theoretical chemistry.

Wurtz, C: Adolphe. The atomic theory. Tr. by E. Cleminshaw. (Intern. scientific ser.) N. Y. 1881. D. 541 : 1

Cooke, Josiah Parsons. Principles of chemical philosophy. Rev. ed. Bost. 1882. O.
541 : 2

Remsen, Ira. Principles of theoretical chemistry, with special reference to the constitution of chemical compounds. 2d ed., rev. and enl. Phila. 1883. O. 541 : 3

3. Analysis.

Berzelius, Friherre Jöns Jakob af. The use of the blowpipe in chemistry and mineralogy. Tr. from the 4th ed. by J. D. Whitney. Bost. 1845. O. 542 : 1

Wöhler, F: Hand-book of mineral analysis; ed. by H: B. Nason. Phila. 1871. D. 543 : 2

Sutton, Francis. A systematic hand-book of volumetric analysis, or The quantitative estimation of chemical substances by measure, applied to liquids, solids and gases ; adapted to the requirements of pure chemical research, pathological chemistry, pharmacy, metallurgy, manufacturing

chemistry, photography, etc., and for the valuation of substances used in commerce, agriculture and the arts. 3d ed. Phila. 1876. O. 545 : 1

Blyth, Alexander Wynter. A manual of practical chemistry ; the analysis of foods and the detection of poisons. Ill. Lond. 1879. D. 543 : 1

Austin, G. L. Water-analysis ; a hand-book for water-drinkers. Bost. 1883 [1882]. T.
543 : 3

Fresenius, C: Remigius. Manual of qualitative chemical analysis. Tr. into the new system and newly rev. by S. W. Johnson. 3d ed., ill. N. Y. 1883. O. 544+5

Dragendorff, G: Plant analysis, qualitative and quantitative. From the german by H: G. Greenish. N. Y. 1884. O. 543 : 4

Roscoe, H: Enfield. Spectrum analysis ; six lectures del. in 1868 before the Society of apothecaries of London. Ill. N. Y. 1869. O. 544 : 3

Schellen, T: Joseph H: Spectrum analysis in its application to terrestrial substances, and the physical constitution of the heavenly bodies familiarly explained. Tr. from the 2d enl. and rev. german ed. by Jane and Caroline Lassell ; ed., with notes, by W: Huggins. Ill., portr.. and Ångström's and Kirchhoff's maps. N. Y. 1872. O.
544+4

Zech, Paul. Das spektrum und die spektralanalyse. München. 1875. S. 544 : 1

Lockyer, Joseph Norman. Studies in spectrum analysis. (Intern. scientific ser.) N. Y. 1878. D. 544 : 2

4. Mineralogy.

Ruskin, J: The ethics of the dust ; ten lectures to little housewives on the elements of crystallisation. N. Y. 1866. D. 548 : 1

Hunt, T. Sterry. The origin of crystalline rocks. In Transactions of the royal soc. of Canada. 61 : R

Egleston, T: Catalogue of minerals, with their formulas, etc. Wash. 1863. O. In Smithsonian misc. 506 : R4 v7

Kobell, Franz v. Mineralogy simplified ; a short method of determining and classifying minerals, by means of simple chemical experiments in the dry and wet way. Tr. from the german ; with an introd. to blowpipe analysis and other add. by H: Erni. Phila. 1867. D. 549 : 2

Ramsay, Alexander. The rudiments of mineralogy ; a concise view of the general properties of minerals. 2d ed. [Weale's ser.] Lond. 1874. D. 549 : 5

Collins, J. H. Mineralogy. (Putnam's adv. science ser.) Ill. N. Y. n. d. 2 v. D.
549 : 17
Contents. V. 1. General principles of mineralogy. 2. Systematic and descriptive mineralogy.

Dana, James Dwight. Manual of mineralogy and lithology ; containing the elements of the science of minerals and rocks, for the use of the practical mineralogist and geologist, and for instruction in schools and colleges. 3d ed. Ill. N. Y. 1878. D. 549 : 1

— and G: Jarvis Brush. A system of mineralogy : Descriptive mineralogy, comprising

the most recent discoveries. 5th ed., re-written, enl. and ill.; 10th sub-ed. with 3 appendices and corr. N. Y. 1883. O.
549+14
Contents. Main work as above, 1868.—**Brush,** G: J. App. 1, 1868—1872.—**Dana,** E: S. App. 2. 1872—1875; App. 3, 1875—1882.

Zirkel, Ferdinand. Microscopical petrography, [of rocks from the country along the 40th parallel]. Ill. (U. S. geol. expl. 40th par., King; Report, v. 6.) Wash. 1876. Q.
in **557.5 : D**

Bauerman, Hilary. Text-book of descriptive mineralogy. [Text-books of science.] N. Y. 1884. S.
549 : 19

Phillips, J. Arthur. Treatise on ore deposits. Ill. Lond. 1884. O.
549+18

Jones, W: The treasures of the earth, or Mines, minerals and metals. Ill. London. *n. d.* D.
549 : 3

Orton, James. Underground treasures, how and where to find them ; a key for the ready de-termination of all the useful minerals with-in the U. S. Ill. Hartford. 1872. S.
549 : 4

Thorpe, T: E:, *ed.* Coal ; its history and uses. Lond. 1878. O.
549 : 9
Contents. **Green,** A. H. The geology of coal.—**Miall,** L: C. Coal plants; Animals of the coal mea-sures.—**Thorpe,** T: E: The chemistry of coal.—**Rücker,** A. W. Coal as a source of warmth ; Coal as a source of power.—**Marshall,** J. The coal question.

Lesley, J: P: Manual of coal and its topogra-phy. Ill. Phila. 1856. D.
549 : 10

Taylor, R: Cowling. Statistics of coal, incl. mineral bituminous substances employed in arts and manufactures, with their geo-graphical, geological and commercial distri-bution, and amount, production and con-sumption on the american continent, with incidental statistics of the iron manufac-ture. 2d ed. rev. and brought down to 1854 by S. S. Haldeman. Phila. 1855. O.
549+11

Feuchtwanger, Lewis. A popular treatise on gems in reference to their scientific value ; a guide for the teacher of natural sciences,

the lapidary, jeweller and amateur ; toge-ther with a description of the elements of mineralogy and all ornamental and archi-tectural materials. Ill. 3d ed. N. Y. 1867. D.
549 : 8

King, C: W: The natural history of gems or semi-precious stones. London. 1870. D.
549 : 12

— The natural history of precious stones and the precious metals. Lond. 1870. D. **549 : 13**

Dieulafait, L: Diamonds and precious stones ; a popular account of gems, containing their history, their distinctive properties and a description of the most famous gems, gem cutting and engraving, and the artificial production of real and counterfeit gems. Tr. from the french by Fanchon Sanford. [Ill. lib. of wonders]. N. Y. 1874. D.
549 : 6

Emanuel, Harry. Diamonds and precious stones ; their history, value and distin-guishing characteristics, with simple tests for their identification. 2d ed., with a new table of the present value of diamonds. N. Y. 1873. D. **549 : 7**

Streeter, Edwin W. The great diamonds of the world ; their history and romance, col-lected from official, private and other sources during many years of correspond-ence and inquiry. The ms. of the "Koh-i-nûr" graciously read and approved by her majesty the queen, the accounts of the "Pitt" and "Eugenie" rev. by her ma-jesty the empress Eugénie. Ed. and anno-tated by Joseph Hatton and A. H. Keane. Lond. [1882]. O. **549 : 15**
— *Same.* (Frank. sq. lib.) N. Y. 1882. Q.
549+15

Hamlin, A: C. Leisure hours among the gems. Bost. 1884. D. **549 : 20**

Beck, Lewis Caleb. Mineralogy of New York ; comprising detailed descriptions of the minerals hitherto found in the state, and notices of their uses in the arts and agri-culture. Ill. Albany. 1842. Q. *In* Natural history of N. Y., pt. 3. **557.3 : R1**

Geology, Class 550.
See after Physical geography.

6. Physical geography.
(See also Geography, cl. 910-919.)

1. In general.

Bucke, C: On the beauties, harmonies and sub-limities of nature, with notes, comment-aries and ill., sel. and rev. by W: P. Page. N. Y. 1846. S. **551 : 5**

Ewbank, T: The world a workshop, or The physical relationship of man to the earth. N. Y. 1855. D. **551 : 24**

Geikie, Archibald. Physical geography. (Sci-enee primers.) Ill. N. Y. 1880. S. **551 : 7**

Grimes, J. Stanley. Geognomy, creation of the continents b ocean currents ; an advanced system of physical geology and geography. Phila. 1885. D. **551 : 31**

Guyot, Arnold. The earth and man ; lectures on comparative physical geography in its

relation to the history of mankind. Tr. from the french by C. C. Felton. Bost. 1849. D. **551 : 8**

Higgins, W. Mullinger. The earth, its physical condition and most remarkable pheno-mena. N. Y. 1842. S. **551 : 18**

Humboldt, F: H: Alexander *freiherr* v. Ansich-ten der natur, mit wissenschaftlichen er-läuterungen. Stuttg. 1874. 2 pts. in 1 v. S.
551 : 1

— *Same, eng.* Aspects of nature in different lands and different climates, with scientific elucidations. Tr. by mrs. Sabine. Phila. 1850. D. **551 : 1**

— *Same.* Views of nature, or Contemplations on the sublime phenomena of creation, with scientific illustrations. Tr. from the german

by E. C. Otté and H. G. Bohn. Lond. 1870.
D.   **551 : 1**
Huxley, T: H: Physiography; an introd. to the
study of nature. 2d ed. ill. N. Y. 1878. D.
                         551 : 11
Klein, Hermann J., *and* O: W: **Thomé**. God's
glorious creation, or The mighty marvels
of earth, sea and sky ; the earth's place in
the universal plan, wonders of the water,
wonders of the land, wonders of the atmosphere. Tr. from the german by J. Minshull. Ill. Lond. [1884]. O.   **551+33**
— - The creator's wonders in living nature, or
Marvels of life in the animal and vegetable kingdoms ; organic life in all parts of
the world on land and in the ocean. Tr.
from the german by J. Minshull. Ill.
Lond. [1885]. O.   **551+34**
Lorenz v. **Liburnau**, Josef Roman *ritter*. Wald,
klima und wasser. München. 1878. S.
                         551 : 2
Marsh, G; Perkins. The earth as modified by
human action ; a new ed. of Man and
nature. New and rev. ed. N. Y. 1877. O.
                         551 : 13
Maury, Matthew Fontaine. Physical geography;
rev. by Mytton Maury. Ill. and maps. N.
Y. 1883. Q.   **551+28**
Meech, L. W. On the relative intensity of the
heat and light of the sun upon different
latitudes of the earth. Ill. Wash. 1856. Q.
In Smithsonian contributions. **506 : R3 v9**
Peschel, Oscar Ferdinand. Zur mathematischen
und physischen geographie. *In his* Abhandlungen zur erd- und völkerkunde.
                       910 : 2 v2
Somerville, Mary. Physical geography. 2d
amer. ed., with add. and a glossary prepared for this ed. Phila. 1850. D.
                         551 : 14
Tugnot de Lanoye, Ferdinand. The sublime
in nature; compiled from the descriptions
of travellers and celebrated writers. [Ill.
lib. of wonders.] N. Y. 1875. D. **551 : 12**

* * *

Adams, C: The earth and its wonders, in a series
of familiar sketches. Cinc. [1870]. S.
                       x 551 : 17
Abbott, Jacob. Science for the young : Water
and land. Ill. N. Y. 1872.   **x 551 : 4**
Bell, N. R. E. (*N. D'Anvers*). Forms of land
and water ; an ill. geographical reader, by
N. D'Anvers. (Science ladders, no. 1). N.
Y. 1882. S.   **x 551 : 20**
Garden, The, the woods and the fields, or The
teachings of nature as seasons change. N.
Y. 1882. D.   **x 551 : 21**
In the temperate regions, or Nature and natural
history in the temperate zones ; with anec-
dotes and stories of adventure and travel.
N. Y. 1882. S.   **x 551 : 23**
In the polar regions, or Nature and natural his-
tory in the frozen zone; with anecdotes and
stories of adventure and travel. N. Y. 1882.
S.   **x 551 : 22**
Kirby, Mary *and* Elizabeth. The world at home,
or Pictures and scenes from far-off lands.
Lond. 1880. O.   **x 551 : 32**
Vulliet, Adam. Esquisse d'une nouvelle géographie physique, destinée à intéresser la

x denotes books specially adapted for children.

jeunesse à l'étude de cette science par la
description d'animaux, de minéraux, de
plantes utiles, etc. Afrique, Amérique,
Océanie. 4e éd. rev. et aug. Paris. 1869. D.
                         551 : 19

Special localities.

Gannett, H: A dictionary of altitudes in the U.
S. (U. S. geol. survey, Powell; Bulletin,
no. 5.) Wash. 1884. O.   *in* **551 : D**
— Lists of elevations, principally in that portion
of the U. S. west of the Mississippi river.
4th ed. Map. (U. S. geol. survey of the terr.,
Hayden ; Miscel. pub. no. 1.) Wash. 1877.
O.   *in* **557.5 : D**
— *Same.* Additional lists, 1879. *In the same;*
Bulletin, v. 5.   *in* **557.5 : D**
Agassiz, L: J: Rudolph, *and others.* Lake
Superior; its physical character, vegetation and animals, compared with those of
other and similar regions ; with a narrative
of the tour by J. Elliott Cabot and contributions by other scientific gentlemen. Ill.
Bost. 1850. O.   **551 : R30**
Ellet, C:, *jr.* Contributions to the physical geography of the U. S. ; pt. 1 : Of the physical
geography of the Mississippi valley, with
suggestions for the improvement of navigation of the Ohio and other rivers. Ill.
Wash. 1850. Q. *In* Smithsonian contributions.   **506 : R3 v2**
Powell, John Wesley. Reports on the lands of
the arid region of the U. S., with a more
detailed account of Utah. 2d ed. Maps.
(U. S. geograph. and geol. survey of the
Rocky mountain region, J. W. Powell, geol.
-in-charge.) Wash. 1879. Q.   *in* **557.5 : D**

Special products.

Drude, Oscar. Die florenreiche der erde ; darstellung der gegenwärtigen verbreitungs-
verhältnisse der pflanzen, ein beitrag zur
vergleichenden erdkunde. Karten. Gotha.
1884. Q. *In* Petermann's mitteilungen,
Ergänzungsb. 16.   **905.1 : M**
Fischer, Theobald. Die dattelpalme ; ihre geographische verbreitung und culturhistori-
sche bedeutung. Karte. Gotha. 1881. Q.
In Petermann's mitteilungen, Ergänzungsb. 14.   **905.1 : M**
Schumann, C: Kritische untersuchungen über
die zimtländer ; ein beitrag zur geschichte
der geographie und des handels. Karte.
Gotha. 1883. *In* Petermann's mitteilungen,
Ergänzungsb. 16.   **905.1 : M**

Map construction.

(See also Topographical engineering, cl. 622.)

Peirce, C: Sanders. A quincuncial projection
of the sphere. *In* U. S. coast survey rep.
1877.   *in* **622 : D**
Schott, C: Anthony. A comparison of the comparative value of the polyconic projection,
used on the coast and geodetic survey,
with some other projections. Ill. *In the
same.* 1880.   *in* **622 : D**
Hunt, E. B., *and* C: A. **Schott**. Tables for projecting maps, with notes on map projec-
tions. *In the same*, 1853.   *in* **622 : D**

Hilgard, Julius E. Tables for projecting maps of large extent. *In* U. S. coast survey rep. 1856. *in* 622 : D
— *Same. In the same,* 1859. *in* 622 : D
Projection tables for a map of North America. *In the same,* 1865. *in* 622 : D

2. Land.

Reclus, J: Jacques Élisée. The earth ; a descriptive history of the phenomena of the life of the globe. Tr. by B. B. Woodward and ed. by H: Woodward. Ill. N. Y. 1873. O. 551.1+1

Hartwig, G: The subterranean world. Maps and ill. 3d ed. Lond. 1875. O. 551 : 10

— The tropical world ; aspects of man and nature in the equatorial regions of the globe. New ed., ill. Lond. 1873. O. 551 : 9

Wallace, Alfred Russel. Tropical nature, and other essays. Lond. 1878. O. 551 : 26
Contents. The climate and physical aspects of the equatorial zone.— Equatorial vegetation.— Animal life in the tropical forests.—Humming-birds, as illustrating the luxuriance of tropical nature. — The colours of animals and sexual selection.—The colours of plants and the origin of the colour-sense.—By-paths in the domain of biology.—The distribution of animals as indicating geographical changes.

Wagner, Moriz F: Beiträge zur naturgeschichte des hochlandes Armenien. *In his* Reise nach dem Ararat. 915.6 : 5

Mountains and volcanoes.

Reclus, J: Jacques Elisée. The history of a mountain. Tr. from the french by Bertha Ness and J: Lillie. Ill. Lond. 1881. D. 553 : 2

Pfaff, Alexius Burkhard Immanuel F: Die naturkräfte in den Alpen, oder Physikalische geographie des Alpengebirges. München. 1877. S. 551 : 3

Viollet-le-Duc, Eugène Emmanuel. Mont Blanc ; a treatise on its geodesical and geological constitution, its transformations and the ancient and recent state of its glaciers. Tr. by B. Bucknall. Ill. Lond. 1877. O. 551 : 29

Berndt, Gustav. Das Val d'Anniviers und das Bassin de Sierre ; ein beitrag zur physikalischen geographie und ethnographie der Walliser Alpen. Karte. Gotha. 1882. Q. *In* Petermann's mitteilungen, Ergänzungsb. 15. 905.1 : M

Rivoli, J. Die Serra da Estrella ; versuch einer physikalisch-geographischen beschreibung dieser gebirgsgruppe, mit specieller berücksichtigung ihrer forstlichen verhältnisse. Karte. Gotha. 1880. Q. *In* Petermann's mitteilungen, Ergänzungsb. 14. 905.1 : M

Dall, W: Healey. Report on Mount St. Elias, Mount Fairweather, and some of the adjacent mountains. *In* U. S. coast survey rep. 1875. *in* 622 : D

Hovey, Horace Carter. Celebrated american caverns, especially Mammoth, Wyandot and Luray ; together with historical, scientihe and descriptive notices of caves and grottoes in other lands. Cinc. 1882. O. 551 : 25

Pfaff, Alexius Burkhard Immanuel F: Die

vulkanischen erscheinungen. Deutsche originalausg. München. 1871. S. 553 : 1

Judd, J: W. Volcanoes ; what they are and what they teach. (Intern. scientific ser.) N. Y. 1881. D. 553 : 4

3. Water.

Tissandier, Gaston. The wonders of water. From the french ; ed., with numerous add. by Schele de Vere. [Ill. lib. of wonders.] N. Y. 1874. D. 551 : 15

Tyndall, J: The forms of water in clouds and rivers, ice and glaciers. Ill. (Intern. scientihe ser.) N. Y. 1876. D. 551 : 16

Whittlesey, C: On fluctuations of level in the north american lakes. Ill. Wash. 1860. Q. *In* Smithsonian contributions. 506 : R3 v12

Holley, G: W. The falls of Niagara ; with supplementary chapters on other famous cataracts of the world. Ill. N. Y. 1883. O. 551 : 27

The ocean.

(For animal life, *see* Zoology, cl. 590.)

Gosse, Philip H: The ocean. Phila. 1856. D. 551.2 : 1

Hartwig, G: The sea and its living wonders ; a popular account of the marvels of the deep and of the progress of maritime discovery from the earliest ages to the present time. Ill. New ed. Lond. 1881. O. 551.2 : 11

Ingersoll, Ernest. Old ocean. Ill. Boston. [1883.] S. 551.2 : 12

Jones, W: The broad, broad ocean, and some of its inhabitants. New ed. ill. Lond. *n. d.* D. 551.2 : 2

Jordan, W: Leighton. The ocean ; its tides and currents, and their causes. Lond. 1873. O. 551.2 : 13

Kirby, Mary *and* Elizabeth. The sea and its wonders ; a companion volume to "The world at home." [Ill.] Lond. 1878. O. x 551.2 : 3

Maury, Matthew Fontaine. The physical geography of the sea. New ed. N. Y. 1856. O. 551.2+6

Michelet, Jules. The sea. From the french. N. Y. 1861. D. 551.2 : 5

Reclus, J: Jacques Élisée. The ocean, atmosphere and life ; the second series of a descriptive history of the life of the globe. Ill. N. Y. 1874. O. 551.2+7

Schleiden, Matthias Jacob. Das meer. 2te aufl. Gera. 1878. O. 551.2+4

Davis, C: H: The law of deposit of the flood tide ; its dynamical action and office. Wash. 1852. Q. *In* Smithsonian contributions. 506 : R3 v3

Mitchell, H: Physical hydrography of the gulf of Maine. *In* U. S. coast survey rep. 1879. *in* 622 : D

— Notes concerning alleged changes in the relative elevations of land and sea [on the coast of Maine]. *In the same,* 1877. *in* 622 : D

x denotes books specially adapted for children.

Mohn, H: Die norwegische Nordmeer-expedition ; resultate der lothungen und tiefsee-temperatur-beobachtungen. Karten. Gotha. 1880. Q. *In* Petermann's mitteilungen, Ergänzungsb. 14.   **905.1 : M**

Dall, W: Healey. Report on the currents and temperatures of Bering Sea and the adjacent waters. Ill. *In* U. S. coast survey rep. 1880.   *in* **622 : D**

— Harbors of Alaska, and the tides and currents in their vicinity. *In the same,* 1872.   *in* **622 : D**

— Report of geograph. and hydrograph. explorations of the coast of Alaska. *In the same,* 1872.   *in* **622 : D**

Sonrel, L. The bottom of the sea. Tr. and ed. by Elihu Rich. [Ill. lib. of wonders.] N. Y. 1875. D.   **551.2 : 8**

Pourtalès, L: François de. List of publications relating to the deep-sea investigations, carried on in the vicinity of the coasts of the U. S. under the auspices of the coast survey. *In* U. S. coast survey rep. 1876.   *in* **622 : D**

— The Gulf Stream ; characteristics of the Atlantic sea-bottom off the coast of the U. S. *In the same,* 1869.   *in* **622 : D**

Agassiz, L: J: Rudolph. Report upon deep-sea dredgings in the Gulf Stream. *In* U. S. coast survey rep. 1869.   *in* **622 : D**

Thomson, Sir C: Wyville. The depths of the sea ; an account of the general results of the dredging cruises of h. m. ss. "Porcupine" and "Lightning", during the summers of 1868—1870, under the scientific direction of dr. Carpenter, J. Gwyn Jeffreys and Wyville Thomson. • Ill. and maps. N. Y. 1873. O.   **551.2 : 10**

Dana, James Dwight. On coral reefs and islands ; from the author's exploring expedition report on geology, with add. N. Y. 1853. O.   **551 : 6**

Agassiz, L: J: Rudolph. Report on the examination of the Florida reefs, keys, and coast. *In* U. S. coast survey rep. 1851.   *in* **622 : D**

— *Same.* Repr. in rep. for 1866.   *in* **622 : D**

Hunt, E. B. On the origin, growth, substructure and chronology of the Florida reef. *In the same,* 1862.   *in* **622 : D**

Simmonds, P. L. The commercial products of the sea, or Marine contributions to food, industry and art. Ill. N. Y. 1879. D.   **639 : 3**

Note. For discussions of the tides, see Astronomy, cl. 521, col. 304.

4. The atmosphere.

Flammarion, Camille. The atmosphere ; ed. by James Glaisher. Ill. N. Y. 1874. Q.   **552+3**

Hartwig, G: L: The aerial world ; a popular account of the phenomena and life of the atmosphere. Ill. N. Y. 1875. O.   **552 : 2**

Lommel, Eugen Cornelius Joseph. Wind und wetter ; gemeinfassliche darstellung der meteorologie. München. 1873.   **552 : 1**

Loomis, Elias. A treatise on meteorology ; with a collection of meteorological tables. N. Y. 1868. O.   **552+5**

Zürcher, F:, *and* Élie **Margollé.** Meteors, aerolites, storms and atmospheric phenomena.

From the french by W: Lackland. [Ill. lib. of wonders.] N. Y. 1876. D.   **552 : 6**

Ruskin, J: The storm cloud of the 19th century ; two lectures delivered at the London institution, feb. 4th and 11th 1884. N. Y. 1884. D.   **552 : 9**

Coffin, James H: The orbit and phenomena of a meteoric fire-ball seen july 20, 1860. Ill. Wash. 1869. Q. *In* Smithsonian contributions.   **506 : R3 v16**

Olmsted, Denison. On the recent secular period of the aurora borealis. Ill. Wash. 1856. Q. *In* Smithsonian contributions.   **506 : R3 v8**

Morgan, J: H., *and* J: T. **Barber.** An account of the aurora borealis seen near Cambridge, oct. 24th 1847 ; together with those of sept. 21st 1846, and march 19th 1847, seen at the Cambridge observatory. With 12 col'd eng. Cambridge. [1848]. Q.   **552+7**

Coffin, James H: Psychrometrical table for determining the elastic force of aqueous vapor, and the relative humidity of the atmosphere, from indications of the wet and the dry-bulb thermometer Fahrenheit. Wash. 1856. O. *In* Smithsonian misc.   **506 : R4 v1**

— The winds of the globe or The laws of atmospheric circulation over the surface of the earth ; the tables completed, on the author's decease, and maps drawn by Selden Jennings Coffin, with a discussion and analysis of the tables and charts by Alex. Wœikof. Ill. Wash. 1875. Q. *In* Smithsonian contributions.   **506 : R3 v20**

— The winds of the northern hemisphere. Ill. Wash. 1853. Q. *In* Smithsonian contributions.   **506 : R3 v6**

Schreiber, Paul. Die bedeutung der windrosen für theoretische und practische fragen der meteorologie und klimatologie bei dem heutigen zustand der wissenschaft, dargelegt durch die aus 15jähr. beobachtungen in Leipzig sich ergebenden beispiele. Ill. Gotha. 1881. Q. *In* Petermann's mitteilungen, Ergänzungsb. 15.   **905.1 : M**

Davis, W: Morris. Whirlwinds, cyclones and tornadoes. Ill. Bost. 1884. T.   **552 : 8**

Loomis, Elias. On certain storms in Europe and America, dec. 1836. Ill. Wash. 1860. Q. *In* Smithsonian contributions.   **506 : R3 v11**

Chappelsmith, J: Account of a tornado near New Harmony, Ind., april 30, 1852, with a map of the track, etc. Wash. 1855. Q. *In* Smithsonian contributions.   **506 : R3 v7**

Daniells, W. W. The Wisconsin tornadoes of may 23, 1878. Ill. *In* University of Wisconsin, Annual rep. of regents, 1878, *with* Governors message for 1879.   *in* **328.15 : D**

Ferrel, W: Meteorological researches for the use of the Coast pilot. Pt. 1: On the mechanics and general motions of the atmosphere. *In* U. S. coast survey rep. 1875.   *in* **622 : D**

— *Same.* Pt. 2: On cyclones, tornadoes and waterspouts. *In the same,* 1878.   *in* **622 : D**

— *Same.* Pt. 3: Barometric hypsometry and reduction of the barometer to sea-level. *In the same,* 1881.   *in* **622 : D**

Williamson, Robert S. Meteorology in its connection with hypsometry.— Practical tables in meteorology. *In his* On the use of the barometer. *in* 622 : D
Note. For barometric hypsometry, see also cl. 622.

United States. *Signal service.* Professional papers, prepared under the dir. of W. B. Hazen, chief signal officer of the army ; nos. 2, 4, 6, 8, 9, 11–13, 15, 16. Ill. Wash. 1881–85. Q. *in* 552 : D
Contents. No. 2. **Greely**, A. W. Isothermal lines of the U. S., 1871—1880. 4. **Finley**, J: P. Tornadoes of may 29 and 30, 1879, in Kansas, Neb., Missouri and Iowa. Ill. 6. **Hazen**, H: A. The reduction of air-pressure to sea-level, at elevated stations west of the Mississippi river. 8. **Ferrel**, W: The motions of fluids and solids on the earth's surface ; repr. with notes by Frank Waldo. 9. **Dunwoody**, H. H. C. Charts and tables showing geographical distribution of rainfall in the U. S. 11. **Sherman**, Orray Tart. Meteorol. and physical observations on the east coast of british America. 12. **Ferrel**, W: Popular essays on the movements of the atmosphere. 13. **Ferrel**, W: Temperature of the atmosphere and earth's surface. 15. **Langley**, S. P. Researches on solar heat and its absorption by the earth's atmosphere ; a report of the Mt. Whitney expedition. Ill. 16. **Finley**, J: P. Tornado studies for 1884. Maps.

— — Notes, prepared under the dir. of W. B. Hazen, chief signal officer of the army ; nos. 1, 3, 4, 6—20. Ill. Wash. 1882-85. O. *in* 552 : D
Contents. No. 1. **Bailey**, W: O. Report on the Michigan forest fires of 1881. 3. **Allen**, James. To foretell frost. 4. **Upton**, Winslow. The use of the spectroscope in meteorological observations. 5. **Hazen**, H: A. Report on wind velocities at the lake Crib and at Chicago. 7. **Hazen**, H: A. Variation of rainfall west of the Mississippi river. 8. **Waldo**, Frank. The study of meteorology in the higher schools of Germany, Switzerland and Austria. 9. **Dunwoody**, H. H. C. Weather proverbs. 10. **Garlington**, Ernest A. Report on Lady Franklin Bay expedition of 1883. 11. **Ward**, F: K. The elements of the heliograph. 12. **Finley**, J: P. The special characteristics of tornadoes ; with practical directions for the protection of life and property. 13. **Curtis**, G. E. The relations between northers and magnetic disturbances at Havana, Cuba. 14. supp. to no. 10. **Lamar**, W. H., jr., *and* Frank W. **Ellis**. Physical observations during the Lady Franklin Bay expedition of 1883. 15. **Hazen**, H: A. Danger lines and river floods of 1882. 16. **Curtis**, G. E. The effect of wind currents on rain-fall. 17. **Morrill**, Park. A first rep. upon observations of atmospheric electricity at Baltimore, Md. 18. **McAdie**, Alexander. The aurora in its relations to meteorology. 19. **Glenn**, S: W. Report on the tornado of aug. 28, 1884, near Huron, Dak. 20. **Hazen**, H: A. Thunder-storms of may 1884.

Meteorological observations.

(*See also* Astronomical observ. cl. 525, col. 307–308, *and* Magnetical obs., cl. 538, col. 317.)

United States. *Signal service.* Circular: The practical use of meteorological reports and weather-maps Wash. 1871. O. *in* 552 : D

Guyot, Arnold H: Directions for meteorological observations and the registry of periodical phenomena. Ill. Wash. 1860. O. *In* Smithsonian misc. 506 : R4 v1
— Tables, meteorological and physical. 3d ed., rev. and enl. Wash. 1859. O. *In* Smithsonian misc. 506 : R4 v1

United States. *Signal service.* Daily bulletin of weather reports, taken at 7.35 a. m., 4.35 p. m. and 11 p. m., Washington mean time ; with the synopsis, probabilities and facts for the month of nov. 1872. Wash. 1873. Q. *in* 552.1 : D

Cleaveland, Parker. Results of meteorological observations made at Brunswick, Maine,

between 1807 and 1859 ; reduced and discussed by C: A. Schott. Ill. Wash. 1867. Q. *In* Smithsonian contributions.
506 : R3 v16

Hildreth, S: Prescott. Results of meteorological observations made at Marietta, Ohio, between 1826 and 1859 incl. Added, results of obs. taken at Marietta by Joseph **Wood**, between 1817 and 1823. Reduced and discussed by C: A. Schott. Ill. Wash. 1867. Q. *In* Smithsonian contributions.
506 : R3 v16

Caswell, Alexis. Meteorological observations made at Providence, R. I., extending from dec. 1831 to may 1860. Wash. 1860. Q. *In* Smithsonian contributions. 506 : R3 v12
— Results of meteorological observations, made at Providence, R. I., extending over a period of 45 years, from dec. 1831 to dec. 1876. Wash. 1882. Q. *In* Smithsonian contributions. 506 : R3 v24

Smith, Nathan D. Meteorological observations made near Washington, Arkansas, from 1840 to 1859 incl. Wash. 1860. Q. *In* Smithsonian contributions. 506 : R3 v12

Espy, James P. 2d and 3d report on meteorology to the secretary of the navy. Maps and diag. Wash. 1850. Q. *in* 552.1 : D
— 4th meteorological report. Maps and diag. Wash. 1857. Q. (U. S. 34th cong. 3 sess. Sen. ex. doc. no. 65.) *in* 552.1 : D

United States. *Commissioner of patents.* Results of meteorological observations, made under the dir. of the U. S. patent office and the Smithsonian institution, from 1854 to 1859 incl.; v. 2, pt. 1. Wash. 1864. Q. (U. S. 36th cong., 1 sess. House exec. doc. no. 55). *in* 552.1 : D
Contents. **Hough**, Franklin B. Observations upon periodical phenomena in plants and animals from 1851 to 1859, with tables of the dates of opening and closing of lakes, rivers, harbors, etc.—**Coffin**, J. H. Observations relative to storms in 1859, reduced and arr.

Schott, C: Anthony. Meteorological observations in the Arctic seas by Elisha Kent Kane, made during the second Grinnell expedition in search of sir John Franklin in 1853–5, at Van Rensselaer harbor, and other points on the west coast of Greenland ; reduced and discussed. Ill. Wash. 1859. Q. *In* Smithsonian contributions. 506 : R3 v11
— Meteorological observations in the Arctic seas by sir Francis Leopold McClintock, made on board the Arctic searching yacht Fox, in Baffin bay and Prince Regent's inlet, in 1857–9 ; reduced and discussed. Map and ill. Wash. 1862. Q. *In* Smithsonian contributions. 506 : R3 v13

United States. *Navy dep't.* Scientific results of the U. S. Arctic expedition, str. Polaris, C. F. Hall commanding. V. 1 : Physical observations, by Emil **Bessels**. Map. Wash. 1876. Q. *in* 552.1 : D

Bryant, C: Meteorological register, Alaska territory, winter of 1870–71. *In* U. S. coast survey rep. 1871. *in* 622 : D

Gannett, H: Meteorological observations during 1872, in Utah, Idaho and Montana. (U. S. geol. survey of the terr., Hayden ; Miscel. pub., no. 2.) Wash. 1873. O. *in* 557.5 : D

Chittenden, G: B. Meteorological observations made during 1873 and the early part of

1874, in Colorado and Montana territories. (U. S. geol. survey of the terr., Hayden; Miscel. pub., no. 6.) Wash. 1874. O.
in 557.5 : D

Wisconsin. *State university.* Meteorological observations, from jan. 1869 to oct. 1878, by W. W. Daniells. *In* Annual reports of the regents, *with* Governor's message for 1870—1879. in 328.15 : D

— -*Washburn observatory.* Summary of meteorol. observ. taken at Madison, Wis., during 1853—1883. *In* Wisconsin agric. exper. station, 1st annual rep. 630 : 21

Schott, C: Anthony. Tables and results of the precipitation, in rain and snow, in the U. S. and at some stations in adjacent parts of North Amer., and in Central and South Amer.; coll. by the Smithsonian inst., and discussed, under the dir. of Joseph Henry, sec. Ill. and charts. Wash. 1872. Q. *In* Smithsonian contributions. 506 : R3 v18

— *Same.* Tables and results of the precipitation, in rain and snow, in the U. S. and at some stations in adjacent parts of North America; coll. by the Smithsonian inst., and discussed, under the dir. of Joseph Henry and Spencer F. Baird, sec's. 2d ed. Plates and charts. Wash. 1881. Q. *In* Smithsonian contributions. 506 : R3 v24

— Tables, distribution and variations of the atmospheric temperature in the U. S. and some adjacent parts of Amer. Maps and ill. Wash. 1876. Q. *In* Smithsonian contributions. 506 : R3 v21

5. Medical climatology.

Howe, Joseph W. Winter homes for invalids; an account of the various localities in Europe and America suitable for consumptives and other invalids during the winter months, with special reference to the climatic variations at each place and their influence on disease. N. Y. 1875. D.
552.2 : 4

Walton, G: E. The mineral springs of the U. S. and Canada, with analyses and notes of the prominent spas of Europe and a list of seaside resorts. N. Y. 1873. D. 552.2 : 5

Cook, M: The wilderness cure. N. Y. 1881. D.
552.2 : 2

Denison, C: Rocky mountain health resorts; an analytical study of high altitudes in relation to the arrest of chronic pulmonary disease. Bost. 1880. O. 552.2 : 3

Benjamin, S: Green Wheeler. The Atlantic islands, as resorts of health and pleasure. Ill. N. Y. 1878. O. 552.2 : 1

Gibbes, Robert W. Cuba for invalids. N. Y. 1860. D. 552.2 : 7

Bennet, James H: Winter and spring on the shores of the Mediterranean, or The Genoese Rivieras, Italy, Spain, Corfu, Greece, the Archipelago, Constantinople, Corsica, Sicily, Sardinia, Malta, Algeria, Tunis, Smyrna, Asia Minor, with Biarritz and Arcachon as winter climates. 5th ed. Lond. 1875. D. 552.2 : 6

Hlawaček, E: A guide to the mineral waters of Karlsbad, its walks and drives. 2d ed. Karlsbad. *n. d.* S. 552.2 : 9

Diruf, Oscar, *sen.* Kissingen und seine heilquellen; vorzugsweise zum gebrauche für curgäste bearb. 2te aufl., mit einem stadtplane und einer karte der umgegend Kissingens. Kissingen. 1873. D. 552.2 : 10

Wever, Gustav. Der klimatische und molkenkurort Badenweiler, mit seinen umgebungen, topographisch, historisch und medicinisch dargestellt; mit einem plane der römischen bäder, einem panorama der alpenkette und einer karte der umgegend. 4te umgearb. aufl. Badenweiler. 1873. S.
552.2 : 11

— Chronik der vogtei Badenweiler; ein beitrag zur entwicklungsgeschichte des kurorts Badenweiler. Badenweiler. 1869. S.
552.2 : 12

Hull, Edmund P. C. The european in India, or Anglo-indians' vade-mecum; a handbook of information for those proceeding to or residing in the East Indies, relating to outfits, routes, time for departure, indian climate and seasons, housekeeping, servants, etc., also an account of anglo-indian social customs and native character. 3d ed. with add. Lond. 1878. D.
552.2 : 8

Mair, R. S. A medical guide for anglo-indians; a compendium of advice to europeans in India... *With* Hull, E. C. P. The european in India. 552.2 : 8

7. Geology and Paleontology.

1. General geology.

(*See also* Religion and science, cl. 215, col. 81.)

Agassiz, L: J: Rudolph. Geological sketches. [1st and] 2d series. Bost. 1876, 1877. 2 v. D. 550 : 3
Contents. 1st ser. America the old world.—The silurian beach.—The fern forests of the carboniferous period.—Mountains and their origin.—The growth of continents.—The geological middle age.—The tertiary age and its characteristic animals.—The formation of glaciers.—Internal structure and progression of glaciers.—External appearance of glaciers. 2d ser. Glacial period.—The parallel roads of Glen Roy in Scotland.—Ice-period in America.—Glacial phenomena in Maine.—Physical history of the valley of the Amazons.

Agassiz, L: J: Rudolph.—*Continued.*

— *Same.* 2d series. Bost. 1876. D. 550 : 3 v2

Bakewell, Robert. An introd. to geology; intended to convey a practical knowledge of the science, and comprising the most important recent discoveries, with explanations of the facts and phenomena which serve to confirm or invalidate various geological theories. 3d amer. from 5th Lond. ed., ed. with an app. by B. Silliman. New Haven. 1839. O. 550 : 7

Buckland, W: Geology and mineralogy as exhibiting the power, wisdom and goodness of God; with add. by prof. Owen, prof.

Phillips, Robert Brown. 4th ed. by Francis T. Buckland. Lond. 1869, 1870. 2 v. D.   **214 : 6**
Contents. V. 1. Text. 2. Plates.

Campbell, G: Douglas, *8th duke of Argyll.* Continuity and catastrophes in geology; an address to the Edinburgh geological society on its 50th anniv., nov. 1, 1883. Edinb. 1883. O.   **553 : 6**

Croll, James. Climate and time in their geological relations; a theory of secular changes of the earth's climate. N. Y. 1875. D.   **550 : 9**

Cuvier, G: Léopold Chrétien Frédéric Dagobert *baron.* Essay on the theory of the earth; with geological ill. by prof. Jameson. 5th ed., tr. from the french, with numerous add. by the author and translator. Edinb. 1827. O.   **550 : 10**

Dana, James Dwight. The geological story briefly told; an introd. to geology for the general reader and for beginners in the science. Ill. N. Y. 1878. D.   **550 : 4**

— Manual of geology; treating of the principles of the science with special reference to american geological history. 2d ed. Ill. N. Y. 1876. O.   **550 : 5**

Dawson, J: W: The story of the earth and man. N. Y. 1877. D.   **550 : 6**

De la Beche, *Sir* H: T: How to observe geology. 2d ed. Ill. Lond. 1836. D.   **550 : 8**

Donnelly, Ignatius. Ragnarok; the age of fire and gravel. N. Y. 1883 [1882]. D.   **553 : 5**

Geikie, Archibald. Geological sketches at home and abroad. N. Y. 1882. D.   **550 : 26**

Geikie, James. The great ice age and its relation to the antiquity of man. Maps and ill. N. Y. 1877. D.   **550 : 13**

Gunning, W: D. Life-history of our planet. Ill. N. Y. 1879. O.   **550 : 14**

Hitchcock, E: Outline of the geology of the globe, and of the U. S. in particular, with two geol. maps and sketches of characteristic amer. fossils. 2d ed. Bost. 1854. O.   **550 : 25**

— Illustration of surface geology. Ill. Wash. 1857. Q. *In* Smithsonian contributions.   **506 : R3 v9**
Contents. On surface geology, especially that of Connecticut valley. — On the erosions of the earth's surface, especially of rivers. — Traces of ancient glaciers in Massachusetts and Vermont.

Kingsley, C: Madame How and lady Why, or First lessons in earth lore for children. Ill. [Works, v. 13.] London. 1880. D.   **x 550 : 24**

— Town geology. N. Y. 1873. D.   **550 : 15**
— *Same.*   *in* **504 : 39**

Le Conte, Joseph. Elements of geology; a textbook for colleges and for the general reader. N. Y. 1879. O.   **550 : 27**

Lee, C: Alfred. The elements of geology for popular use; containing a description of the geological formations and mineral resources of the U. S. N. Y. 1846. S.   **550 : 16**

Lyell, *Sir* C: A manual of elementary geology, or The ancient changes of the earth and its inhabitants as ill. by geological monuments. Repr. from the 6th ed., enl. Ill. N. Y. 1858. O.   **550 : 2**

x denotes books specially adapted for children,

Lyell, *Sir* C:—*Continued.*
— Principles of geology, or The modern changes of the earth and its inhabitants, considered as illustrative of geology. 11th and rev. ed. Maps and ill. N. Y. 1876. 2 v. O.   **550+1**

Marcou, Jules, *and others.* [Geological pamphlets].   **550 : 31**
Contents. Barrande, J. On the primordial fauna and the taconic system, with add. notes by J. Marcou. —Marcou, J. Notes on the cretaceous and carboniferous rocks of Texas; Reply to the criticisms of James D. Dana, including Dana's two articles with a letter of L: Agassiz; American geology; Observations on the terms "Pénéen," "Permian" and "Dyas"; Letter to J. Barrande on the taconic rocks of Vermont and Canada: The taconic and lower silurian rocks of Vermont and Canada.—Mass. museum of comparative zoology. Annual report. 1862.—Marcou, J. Les roches du Jura: Résumé explicatif d'une carte géologique des Etats-Unis et des provinces anglaises de l'Amérique du Nord; Esquisse d'une classification des chaînes de montagnes d'une partie de l'Amérique du Nord: Dyas et trias ou le nouveau grès rouge en Europe, dans l'Amérique du Nord et dans l'Inde. — Barrande, J. Documents anciens et nouveaux sur la faune primordiale et le système taconique en Amérique.—Marcou, J. Notes pour servir a une description géologique des Montagnes Rocheuses. — Gaudin, C: T., *and* P. Delaharpe. Flore fossile des environs de Lausanne.

Miller, Hugh. The foot-prints of the creator, or The asterolepis of Stromness. From the 3d Lond. ed., with a memoir by L: Agassiz. Bost. 1850. D.   **550 : 18**

— The old red sandstone, or New walks with an old friend. Ill., new and enl. ed. Bost. *n. d.* D.   **550 : 19**

— Rambles of a geologist, or 10,000 miles over the fossiliferous deposits of Scotland. *With his* Cruise of the Betsey.   *in* **554.1 : 1**

— Sketch book of popular geology: Popular geology; a series of lectures read before the Philosophical institution of Edinb., with descriptive sketches from a geologist's portfolio. With an introductory résumé of the progress of geological science within the last two years by mrs. Miller. Bost. 1859. D.   **550 : 20**

— The testimony of the rocks, or Geology in its bearings on the two theologies, natural and revealed; with memorials on the death and character of the author. Bost. 1858. D.   **215 : 9**

— A series of geological papers read before the Royal physical society of Edinb. *With his* Old red sandstone.   *in* **550 : 19**
Contents. Geological evidences in favor of revealed religion.—The ancient Grauwacke rocks of Scotland. —Red sandstone, marble and quartz deposits of Assynt.—The corals of the oolitic system. — The fossilliferous deposits of Scotland.

Nicols, Arthur. Geological history; chapters from the physical history of the earth. N. Y. 1880. D.   **550 : 21**

Ruschenberger, W: S. W. [Geology.] *In his* Elements of natural hist.   **590 : 11 v2**

Ruskin, J: Deucalion; collected studies of the lapse of waves and life of stones; pts. 1—4. N. Y. 1875, 1877. 2 v. D.   **550 : 30**

Senft, Ferdinand. Fels und erdboden; lehre von der entstehung und natur des erdbodens. München. 1876. S.   **550 : 12**

Shaler, Nathaniel Southgate, *and* W: Morris Davis. Illustrations of the earth's surface: Glaciers. Bost. 1881. F.   **553 : R3**

Tate, Ralph. Rudimentary treatise on geology, partly based on maj.-gen. Portlock's Rudi-

ments of geology: pt. 1, Physical geology, 3d ed.; pt. 2, Historical geology, 2d ed. Ill. [Weale's ser.] Lond. 1879, 1875. 2 v. D.
550 : 22

Taylor, J: E: Geological stories ; a series of autobiographies in chronological order. Ill. 4th ed. Lond. 1879. D.   **550 : 23**

Winchell, Alexander. Sketches of creation ; a popular view of some of the grand conclusions of the sciences in reference to the history of matter and life, together with a statement of the intimations of science respecting the primordial condition and the ultimate destiny of the earth and the solar system. Ill. N. Y. [1870]. D.
550 : 32

— World - life. or Comparative geology. Ill. Chic. 1883. D.   **550 : 28**

— Geological excursions, or The rudiments of geology for young learners. Ill. Chicago. 1884. D.   **x 550 : 29**

Zittel, K: Alfred. Aus der urzeit ; bilder aus der schöpfungsgeschichte. 2te aufl. München. 1875. S.   **550 : 11**

(For classes 551–553, see Physical geography, col. 323.)

2. Local geology.

Europe, Asia, Australia.

Geikie, James. Prehistoric Europe ; a geological sketch. Maps and ill. Lond. 1881. O.
554+1

Miller, Hugh. The cruise of the Betsey, or A summer ramble among the fossiliferous deposits of the Hebrides. Bost. 1860. D.
554.1 : 1

Mantell, Gideon Algernon. Geological excursions round the Isle of Wight and along the adjacent coast of Dorsetshire, illustrative of the most interesting geological phenomena and organic remains. 3d ed. Lond. 1854. D.   **554.2 : 1**

Bayberger, Franz. Der lnngletscher von Kufstein bis Haag ; ein beitrag zur kenntniss der südbayerischen hochebene. Karte und ill. Gotha. 1882. Q. *In* Petermann's mitteilungen, Ergänzungsb. 15.   **905.1 : M**

Pumpelly, Raphael. Geological researches in China, Mongolia and Japan, during 1862—1865. Maps and ill. Wash. 1866. Q. *In* Smithsonian contributions.   **506 : R3 v15**

Lendenfeld, R. v. Der Tasman-gletscher und seine umgebung. Karten und ill. Gotha. 1884. Q. *In* Petermann's mitteilungen, Ergänzungsb. 16.   **905.1 : M**

North America.

Macfarlane, James. The geologist's traveling hand-book ; an american geological railway guide, giving the geological formation at every railway station, with notes on interesting places on the routes and a description of each of the formations. N. Y. 1879. O.   **557 : 1**

Dawson, J: W: Acadian geology ; the geological structure, organic remains and mineral resources of Nova Scotia, New Brunswick

x denotes books specially adapted for children.

and Prince Edward Island. 3d ed., with map, ill. and supp. Lond. 1878. O.
557.6+1

Marcou, Jules. Geology of North America, with two reports on the prairies of Arkansas and Texas, the Rocky mountains of New Mexico, and the Sierra Nevada of California, originally made for the U. S. government. Zürich. 1858. Q.   **557 : R2**

United States geological survey. 1st–3d annual reports of the director. Wash. 1880–83. 3 v. in 2. Q.   *in* **557.1 : D**

Contents. V. 1. **King,** Clarence. 1st annual report, with map showing geographical divisions. 2. **Powell,** J: W. 2d annual report.—**Dutton,** C. E. The physical geology of the Grand Cañon district.—**Gilbert,** G. K. Contributions to the history of Lake Bonneville.—**Emmons,** S. F. Abstract of report on geology and mining industry of Leadville, Lake co. Colo.—**Becker,** G: F. A summary of the geology of the Comstock lode and the Washoe district.—**King,** C. Production of the precious metals in the U. S.—**Gilbert,** G. K. A new method of measuring heights by means of the barometer. 3. **Powell,** J: W. Report of the director. — Administrative reports. — **Marsh,** O. C. Birds with teeth—**Irving,** R. D. The copper-bearing rocks of Lake Superior.—**Russell,** I. C. Sketch of the geological history of Lake Lahontan.—**Hague,** A. Abstract of the report on the geology of the Eureka district, Nev.—**Chamberlin,** T: C. Preliminary paper on the terminal moraine of the second glacial epoch.—**White,** C. A. A review of the non-marine fossil mollusca of North America.

New York *state.* Communication from the governor, relative to the geological survey of the state. *n. t.* [Albany. 1838]. O.
557.3 : D

— Natural history of New York. Ill. N. Y. 1842–79. 24 v. Q.   **557.3 : R1**

Contents. Pt. 1. **Seward,** W: H: Introd.—**De-Kay,** J. E. Zoology. 5 v. 2. **Torrey,** J. Botany. 2 v. 3. **Beck,** L. C. Mineralogy. 4. **Mather,** W: Williams, Ebenezer **Emmons,** Lardner **Vanuxem** and James **Hall.** Geology. 4 v. 5. **Emmons,** E. Agriculture. 5 v. 6. **Hall,** J. Paleontology. 7 v.— Those works belonging to other classes than geology, have been entered in their proper places in this catalogue.

Shaler, Nathaniel Southgate. The phosphate beds of South Carolina. *In* U. S. coast survey rep. 1870.   *in* **622 : D**

Little, G: Report on the blue clay of the Mississippi river. *In* U. S. coast survey rep. 1880.   *in* **622 : D**

United States. *Exploration of the Red River of La., 1852.* Geology and palæontology. Ill. *In* Marcy, R. B. Report.
in **917.4 : D**

Contents. **Hitchcock,** E: Notes upon the specimens of rocks and minerals collected.—**Shumard,** G: G. Remarks upon the general geology of the country traversed.—**Shumard,** B: F. Description of the species of carboniferous and cretaceous fossils collected.

Hilgard, Eugene Waldemar. On the geology of lower Louisiana and the salt deposit on Petite Anse island. Ill. Wash. 1872. Q. *In* Smithsonian contributions.
506 : R3 v23

Arkansas *state.* First report of a geological reconnoissance of the northern counties of Arkansas, made during 1857 and 1858 by D: Dale Owen, assisted by W: Elderhorst, E: T. Cox. Little Rock. 1858. Q.
557.4 : D

Whittlesey, C: On the fresh-water glacial drift of the northwestern states. Map and ill. Wash. 1866. Q. *In* Smithsonian contributions.   **506 : R3 v15**

Ohio *state.* 2d annual report on the geological survey of the state of Ohio, by W: W. **Mather.** Columbus. 1838. O. **557.5 : R**

Illinois *state.* Economical geology of Illinois ; reprinted from the original reports of the geological survey, with add. and emendations by Amos H: **Worthen.** Springfield. 1882. 3 v. O. **557.5 : R**

— Geological survey of Illinois ; v. 6. [Boston]. 1875. O. **557.5 : R**

Contents. **Worthen,** Amos H:, *and others.* Geology. — **St. John,** Orestes Hawley, *and others.* Palæontology.

Jackson, C: T., *U. S. geologist.* Report on the geological and mineral survey of the mineral lands of the U. S. in the state of Michigan, made under the authority of an act of congress approved march 1, 1847. Maps and ill. (U. S. 31st cong. 1 sess. Sen. ex. doc. no. 1, pt. 3). Wash. 1849. O. *in* **328.1 : D**

Foster, J: Wells, *and* Josiah Dwight **Whitney.** Report on the geology and topography of a portion of the Lake Superior land district in the state of Michigan. Wash. 1850, 1851. Text, 2 v.; Maps, 1 v. O. **557.5 : R**

Contents. V. 1. Copper lands. 2. The iron region, with the general geology.

Michigan *state.* Geological survey ; publ. by authority of the legislature, under the dir. of the Board of geological survey. N. Y. 1873—1881. 4 v. and atlas. F. **557.5 : R**

Contents. V. 1. *Upper peninsula,* 1869—1873, with an atlas of maps: Pt. 1, **Brooks,** T: Benton. Iron-bearing rocks, economic; pt. 2, **Pumpelly,** Raphael. Copper-bearing rocks; pt. 3, **Rominger,** C: Palæozoic rocks. 2. **Brooks,** T: B. Appendices to v. 1, pt. 1. 3. *Lower peninsula,* 1873—1876, with a geol. map: **Rominger,** C: Pt. 1, Geology: pt. 2, Palæontology: Corals. 4. *Upper peninsula,* 1878—1880, with a geol. map: **Rominger,** C: Pt. 1, Marquette iron region: pt. 2, Menominee iron region.

Irving, Ronald Duer. The copper - bearing rocks of Lake Superior. (U. S. geol. survey, Monographs, v. 5.) Wash. 1883. Q. *in* **557.1 : D**

Wisconsin *state.* Report on the geological survey of the state, by James **Hall,** on general geology and palæontology, and J. D. **Whitney,** on the upper Mississippi lead region. V. 1. [Albany ?] 1862. Q. **557.5 : R2**

Note. This vol. was the only one pub.— Earlier reports of various dates will be found in the set of Wis. state documents.

— Geology of Wisconsin : Survey of 1873—1879 ; accompanied by an atlas of maps. Ill. Madison. 1877-83. 4 v. Q., and atl. F. **557.5 : R3**

Contents. V. 1. *Pt. 1.* **Chamberlin,** T: Chrowder. General geology. *Pt. 2, Natural history.* **Salisbury,** R. D., *comp.* Chemical analyses. — **Irving,** Roland Duer. Minerals; Lithology.—**Whitfield,** Robert P. List of fossils.—**Swezey,** G. D. Catalogue of the phænogamous and vascular cryptogamous plants.—**Bundy,** W. F. Partial list of fungi, with descriptions of new species; Crustacean fauna, with descriptions of little known species of cambarus.—**Hoy,** P. R. Catalogue of lepidoptera: Catalogue of the cold-blooded vertebrates.—**Strong,** Moses. List of mammals. — **King,** F. H. Economic relations of Wisconsin birds. *Pt. 3, Economic geology.* **Irving,** R. D. Iron ores.—**Strong,** Moses. Lead and zinc ores.—**Chamberlin,** T. C. Economic suggestions as to copper, silver and other ores; Building material; Soils and subsoils; Artesian wells. 2. Historical; annual reports 1873-1875. — **Chamberlin,** T. C. Geology of eastern Wis.—**Irving,** R. D. Geology of central Wis.—**Strong,** Moses. Geology and topography of the lead region. 3. **Irving,** R. D. General geology of the Lake Superior region.—**Pumpelly,**

Raphael. Lithology of the keweenawan or copper-bearing system.—**Irving,** R. D. Geology of the eastern Lake Superior district.—**Wright,** C: E. Huronian series west of Penokee Gap.—**Sweet,** Edmund Theodore. Geology of the western Lake Superior district.—**Strong,** Moses, *ed. by* T. C. Chamberlin. Geology of the upper St. Croix district. — **Brooks,** T: Benton. Geology of the Menominee region; with microscopical investigations of huronian rocks from the iron region of Lake Superior, by Arthur Wichmann.—**Wright,** C: E. Geology of the Menominee iron region: economic resources, lithology, and westerly and southerly extension. **4. Strong,** Moses. Geology of the Mississippi region north of the Wisconsin river.—**Wooster,** L. C. Geology of the lower St. Croix district.—**Whitfield,** R. P. Paleontology.—**Chamberlin,** T. C. Ore deposits of southwestern Wis.—The quartzites of Barron and Chippewa counties, comp. from notes.—**King,** F. H. Geology of the upper Flambeau valley.—**Irving,** R. D., *and* C: R: **Vanhise.** Crystalline rocks of the Wisconsin valley.—**Clark,** A. C., *ed. by* T. C. Chamberlin. Superficial geology of the upper Wisconsin valley.—**Davies,** J: Eugene. Character and methods of the geodetic survey. [5.] Atlas of maps.

Featherstonhaugh, G: W:, *U. S. geologist.* Geological report of an examination made in 1834, of the elevated country between the Missouri and Red rivers. Map. Wash. 1835. D. *in* **557.5 : D**

Ludlow, W: Report of a reconnaissance of the Black Hills of Dakota, made in the summer of 1874. Maps and ill. (Engineer dep't, U. S. army.) Wash. 1875. Q. *in* **557.5 : D**

Contents. General report. — **Winchell,** Newton Horace. Geological report: with app.: Botany, List of elevations.—**Grinnell,** G: Bird. Paleontological report; Zoological report.—**Whitfield,** R. P. Descriptions of new fossils.

— Report of a reconnaissance from Carroll, Montana territory, on the upper Missouri, to the Yellowstone national park and return, $m_a d_e$ in the summer of 1875. Maps and ill. (Engineer dep't, U. S. army.) Wash. 1876. Q. *in* **557.5 : D**

Contents. General report. — **Grinnell,** G: Bird. Zoölogical report.—**Dana,** E: Salisbury, *and* G: Bird **Grinnell.** Geological report. — **Whitfield,** R. P. Description of new fossils.

United States. *Pacific r. r. surveys.* [Geological reports of routes explored.] Ill. *In* Reports of the surveys. *in* **625 : D**

Contents. **Schiel,** James. Routes near the 38th and 41st parallels [in v. 2].—**Blake,** W: Phipps. Route near 32d parallel [in v. 2].—**Blake,** W: P., *and* Jules **Marcou.** Route near the 35th parallel [in v. 3].—**Blake,** W: P. Routes in California, to connect with the routes near the 35th and 32d par.; with app. containing paleontological papers by various authors [in v. 5].—**Newberry,** J: Strong. Route from the Sacramento valley to the Columbia river [in v. 6].—**Antisell,** T: Routes from San Francisco bay to Los Angeles, Cal., west of the Coast Range, and from the Pimas villages to the Rio Grande.

United States. *Geological and geographical survey of the territories,* Ferdinand Vandeveer **Hayden,** *U. S. geol. in charge.* Catalogue of the publications [of the survey]. 3d ed. rev. to dec. 31, 1878. Wash. 1879. O. *in* **557.5 : D**

— — Annual reports of progress, 1st-12th, 1867-1878. Maps and ill. Wash. 1872-83. 11 v. O. *in* **557.5 : D**

Contents. 1. Nebraska. 2. Wyoming. 3. Colorado and New Mexico. 4. Wyoming and portions of contiguous territories. 5. Montana and portions of contiguous terr. 6. Portions of Montana, Idaho, Wyoming and Utah. 7. Colorado. 8-10. Colorado and portions of adjacent terr. 11. Idaho and Wyoming. 12. Wyoming and Idaho, pt. 1: Geology, paleontology and zoology; pt. 2: Yellowstone national park; geology, thermal springs; topography. — For full contents of the various volumes, see Catalogue of publications.

United States. *Geological and geographical survey of the territories.—Continued.*
– – Geological and geographical atlas of Colorado and portions of adjacent territory, corrected to date. [N. Y.] 1881. F.
in 557.5 : D
– – Bulletins ; v. 1–6, 1874–1882. Maps and ill. Wash. 1875–82. 6 v. O. *in* 557.5 : D
Note. The principal papers have been entered in their proper places, in this catalogue. For full contents, see Catalogue of the publications of the survey.
– – Miscellaneous publications, nos. 1–12. Wash. 1873–80. 12 v. in 7. O. *in* 557.5 : D
Contents. 1. **Gannett, H:** Lists of elevations. 2. **Gannett, H:** Meteorol. observations. 3. **Coues, E.** Birds of the northwest. 4. **Porter, T: C.,** *and* J: M. **Coulter.** Flora of Colorado. 5. **Jackson, W. H.** Descriptive catalogue of photographs. 6. **Chittenden,** G: B. Meteorol. observations. 7. **Matthews,** W. Hidatsa indians. 8. **Coues, E.** Fur-bearing animals. 9. **Jackson, W. H.** Descriptive catalogue of photographs of indians. 10. **White,** C. A., *and* H. A. **Nicholson.** Bibliogr. of north amer. paleontology. 11. **Coues, E.** Birds of the Colorado valley. 12. **Allen, J. A.** North amer. pinnipeds.—These works have been entered separately in their proper places, in this catalogue.
– – Reports, v. 1–3, 5–12. Ill. Wash. 1873–84. Q.
in 557.5 : D
Contents. V. 1. **Leidy, J.** Fossil vertebrates. 2. **Cope,** E. D. Vertebrata of the cretaceous formations. 3. **Cope,** E. D. Tertiary vertebrata, book 1. 4. *Not pub.* 5. **Thomas, C.** Acrididæ of North America. 6, 7, 8. **Lesquereux, L.** Fossil flora of the western territories. 9. **Meek,** F. B. Invertebrate cretaceous and tertiary fossils. 10. **Packard,** A. S., *jr.* Geometrid moths of the U. S. 11. **Coues, E.,** *and* J. A. **Allen.** North amer. rodentia. 12. **Leidy, J.** Fresh-water rhizopods of North Amer.—These works have been entered separately in their proper places, in this catalogue.

United States. *Geological exploration of the fortieth parallel,* Clarence **King,** *geol.-in-charge.* Reports, v. 1–7. Maps and ill. (Professional papers of the engineer dep't, U. S. army, no. 18). Wash. 1870–80. 7 v. Q.
in 557.5 : D
Contents. V. 1. **King,** Clarence. Systematic geology; with atlas. 2. **Hague,** Arnold, *and* 8: Franklin **Emmons.** Descriptive geology. 3. **Hague,** J. D. Mining industry. 4. **Meek,** F. B., J. **Hall** *and* R. P. **Whitfield.** Paleontology. – **Ridgway,** R. Ornithology. 5. **Watson,** S., *and others.* Botany. 6. **Zirkel,** F. Microscopical petrography. 7. **Marsh,** O. C. Odontornithes. – Those works belonging to other classes than geology, have been entered separately in their proper places, in this catalogue.
– – Geological and topographical atlas, accompanying the [above] report. [N. Y.]. F.
in 557.5 : D
– – Atlas accompanying v. 3 [of above report], on mining industry. N. Y. [1870].
in 557.5 : D

United States. *Geographical and geological explorations and surveys west of the 100th meridian,* G: M. **Wheeler** *in charge.* Annual reports, with topographical atlas sheets, 1876—1879. Wash. 1876–80. 4 v. and 4 portf. O.
in 557.5 : D
Note. Earlier reports will be found in app. to Report of the chief of engineers, U. S. army, for the various years during which the exped. was carried on.
– – [Preliminary and progress reports.] Wash. 1872–75. 3 v. Q. *in* 557.5 : D
Contents. Prelim. rep. upon a reconnaissance through southern and southeastern Nevada, made in 1869 by G: M. Wheeler and D. W. Lockwood. – Prelim. rep. concerning explor. and surveys, principally in Nevada and Arizona, by G: M. Wheeler, 1871.—Progress rep. upon explor. and surveys west of the 100th mer. in 1872, by G: M. Wheeler.

United States. *Geographical and geological survey west of 100th mer.—Continued.*
– – [Miscellaneous reports and publications]. Wash. *v. d.* 1 v. O.; 2 v. Q. *in* 557.5 : D
Contents. **White,** C: Abiathar. Prelim. rep. upon invertebrate fossils, coll. by the exped. of 1871, 1872 and 1873; with descript. of new species. Pub. dec. 1874. – **Cope,** E: Drinker. Systematic catalogue of vertebrata of the eocene of New Mexico, coll. in 1874. Pub. april 1875. – **Yarrow,** H. C. Rep. upon ornithological specimens coll. in 1871, 1872 and 1873. Pub. 1874. – **Watson,** Sereno, *and* J. T. **Rothrock.** Catalogue of plants coll. in 1871, 1872 and 1873, with descript. of new species. Pub. 1874. – **Kampf,** F., *and* J. H. **Clark.** Astronomical report. Pub. 1874. – **Safford,** T. H. Catalogue of mean declinations of stars, jan. 1, 1875. Pub. 1879.
– – [Final] reports, in 7 v., accompanied by one topograph. and one geol. atlas; v. 2–6. Wash. 1875–78. 5 v. Q. *in* 557.5 : D
Contents. V. 2. Astronomy and Barometric hypsometry. 3. Geology. 4. Paleontology. 5. Zoology. 6. Botany.—These works have been entered separately in their proper places, in this catalogue.
– – Geology of portions of California, Nevada, Utah, Colorado, New Mexico and Arizona, examined in 1871—1873. Ill. (Report, v. 3.) Wash. 1875. Q. *in* 557.5 : D
Contents. **Gilbert,** Grove K: Geol. of portions of Nevada, Utah, California and Arizona.—**Marvine,** Archibald Robertson. Geol. of route from St. George, Utah, to Gila river, Ariz.—**Howell,** Edwin Eugene. Geol. of portions of Utah, Nevada, Arizona and New Mexico.—**Stevenson,** J: James. Geol. of a portion of Colorado.—**Gilbert,** G. K: Geol. of portions of New Mexico and Arizona.—**Loew,** Oscar. Investigations upon mineralogical and agricultural conditions, observed in portions of Colorado, New Mexico and Arizona.

Newberry, J: Strong. Geology of the Colorado river of the west. Ill. *In* Ives, J. C. Report of exploration, 1857–8. *in* 917.5 : D
– – Geological report of the exploring expedition from Santa Fé, New Mexico, to the junction of the Grand and Green rivers of the great Colorado of the west, in 1859, under command of capt. J. N. **Macomb.** Ill. (Engineer dep't, U. S. army.) Wash. 1876. Q. *in* 557.5 : D

Hall, James. Letter, containing observations on the geology and palæontology of the country traversed by [Stansbury's] exped. [to the Great Salt Lake], and notes upon some of the fossils collected. Ill. *In* Report. 1855. *in* 917.5 : D

Dutton, Clarence E: Report on the geology of the high plateaus of Utah. Ill. and atlas. (U. S. geograph. and geol. survey of the Rocky mountain region, J. W. Powell in charge.) Wash. 1880. 2 v. Q. and F.
in 557.5 : D

Gilbert, Grove K: Report on the geology of the Henry mountains. Ill. (U. S. geograph. and geol. survey of the Rocky mountain region, J. W. Powell, geologist-in-charge.) Wash. 1877. Q. *in* 557.5 : D

Becker, G: F. Geology of the Comstock lode and the Washoe district; with atlas. Ill. (U. S. geol. survey, King; Monographs, v. 3). Wash. 1882. Q. *in* 557.1 : D

Blake, W: P. Observations on the physical geography and geology of the coast of California, from Bodega bay to San Diego. Maps. *In* U. S. coast survey rep. 1855.
in 622 : D

Hall, James. Nature of the geological formations occupying the portion of Oregon and

north California included in a geographical survey under the dir. of capt. Frémont, 1843–44, *and* Description of organic remains collected. Ill. *In* **Frémont**, J. C. Report.
in **917.5 : D**

Blake, Theodore A. Geology of Alaska. *In* **Davidson**, G: Report, *in* U. S. coast survey rep. 1867.   **622 : D**

3. Paleontology.

General and vegetable.

Figuier, Guillaume L: The world before the deluge ; newly ed. and rev. by H. W. Bristow. Ill. N. Y. 1872. D.   **560 : 2**

Mantell, Gideon Algernon. The medals of creation, or First lessons in geology and the study of organic remains. 2d ed., rewritten. Lond. *n. d.* 2 v. D.   **560 : 3**
Contents. V. **1.** Fossil vegetables, zoophytes, echinoderms and molluscs. **2.** Fossil cephalopoda, crustacea, insects, fishes, reptiles, birds and mammalia.—Notes of geological excursions.

Hall, James. Palæontology of New York. Ill. Albany. 1847—79. 5 v. in 7. Q.   *In* Natural hist. of N. Y., pt. 6.   **557.3 : R1**
Contents. V. **1.** Organic remains of the lower division of the N. Y. system, or lower silurian rocks of Europe; with plates. **2.** Organic remains of the lower middle division of the N. Y. system, or middle silurian rocks of Europe; with plates. **3.** Organic remains of the lower Heidelberg group and the Oriskany sandstone, 1855–9: pt. 1, Text; pt. 2, Plates. **4.** Fossil brachiopoda of the upper Heidelberg, Hamilton, Portage and Chemung groups, 1862–6; with plates. **5.** Gasteropoda, pteropoda and cephalopoda of [the same] groups: pt. 1, Text; pt. 2, Plates.

— Geological survey of Wisconsin: Descriptions of new species of fossils from the investigations of the survey. *With* Governor's message, 1861.   *in* **328.15 : D**

United States. *Pacific r. r. surveys.* [Paleontological papers.] Ill. *In* Report of the surveys, v. 5.   *in* **625 : D**
Contents. V. **1.** Organic remains of the lower fishes.—**Conrad**, Timothy Abbott. Descriptions of fossil shells.—**Bailey**, J. W. Structure of a fossil plant.—**Schaeffer**, G: C. Structure of fossil wood.—*Note.* Other paleontol. papers will be found with the various reports on geology, which see.

Cope, E: Drinker, *and* C: A. **White**. Paleontological papers [relating to the territories of the U. S.] *In* U. S. geol. survey of the terr., Hayden ; Bulletin, v. 3, 4, 5, 6.
in **557.5 : D**

Meek, Fielding Bradford. Palæontology [of the country along the 40th parallel]. Ill. (U. S. geol. expl. 40th par., King ; Report, v. 4). Wash. 1877. Q.   *in* **557.5 : D**

Hall, James, *and* Robert P. **Whitfield**. Palæontology [of the country along the 40th parallel]. Ill. (U. S. geol. expl. 40th par., King ; Report, v. 4). Wash. 1877. Q.
in **557.5 : D**

Lesquereux, Leo. Contributions to the fossil flora of the western territories: pt. 1, The cretaceous flora ; pt. 2, The tertiary flora ; pt. 3, The cretaceous and tertiary floras. Ill. (U. S. geol. survey of the terr., Hayden ; Report, v. 6–8.) Wash. 1878–83. 3 v. Q.   *in* **557.5 : D**

Invertebrates.

White, C: Abiathar, *and* H. Alleyne **Nicholson**. Bibliography of north american inverte-

White, C: Abiathar, *etc.—Continued.*
brate paleontology, incl. the West Indies and Greenland. (U. S. geol. survey of the terr., Hayden ; Miscel. pub., no. 10). Wash. 1878. O.   *in* **557.5 : D**

— *Same.* Supp. [to 1879]. *In the same ;* Bulletin, v. 5.   *in* **557.5 : D**

Conrad, Timothy Abbot. Check list of the invertebrate fossils of North America ; eocene and oligocene. Wash. 1866. O. *In* Smithsonian misc.   **506 : R4 v7**

Meek, Fielding Bradford. Check list of the invertebrate fossils of North America ; miocene, cretaceous and jurassic. Wash. 1864. O. *In* Smithsonian misc.   **506 : R4 v7**

— A report on the invertebrate cretaceous and tertiary fossils of the upper Missouri country. Ill. (U. S. geol. survey of the terr., Hayden ; Report, v. 9). Wash. 1876. Q.
in **557.5 : D**

— *and* Ferdinand Vandeveer **Hayden**. Palæontology of the upper Missouri ; a report upon collections made principally by the expeditions under command of G. K. Warren, in 1855–6. Invertebrates ; pt. 1. Ill. Wash. 1865. Q. *In* Smithsonian contributions.   **506 : R3 v14**

White, C: Abiathar. Report upon the invertebrate fossils collected in portions of Nevada, Utah, Colorado, New Mexico and Arizona, by parties of the expeditions of 1871–1874. Ill. (U. S. geograph. surveys west of 100th mer., Wheeler ; Report, v. 4, pt. 1). Wash. 1877. Q.   *in* **557.5 : D**

Scudder, S: Hubbard. An account of some insects of unusual interest from the tertiary rocks of Colorado and Wyoming. *In* U. S. geol. survey of the terr., Hayden ; Bulletin, v. 4.   *in* **557.5 : D**

Vertebrates.

Cope, E: Drinker. The relations of the horizons of extinct vertebrata of Europe and North America. *In* U. S. geol. survey of the terr., Hayden ; Bulletin, v. 5.   *in* **557.5 : D**

Leidy, Joseph. The ancient fauna of Nebraska, or A description of remains of extinct mammalia and chelonia, from the Mauvaises Terres of Nebraska. Ill. Wash. 1853. Q. *In* Smithsonian contributions.   **506 : R3 v6**

— Contributions to the extinct vertebrate fauna of the western territories. Ill. (U. S. geol. survey of the terr., Hayden ; Report, v. 1.) Wash. 1873. Q.   *in* **557.5 : D**

Cope, E: Drinker. Report upon the extinct vertebrata, obtained in New Mexico by parties of the expedition of 1874. Ill. (U. S. geograph. surveys west of 100th mer., Wheeler; Report, v. 4, pt. 2). Wash. 1877. Q.
in **557.5 : D**

— Review of the vertebrata of the cretaceous period, found west of the Mississippi river. *In* U. S. geol. survey of the terr., Hayden ; Bulletin, v. 1.   *in* **557.5 : D**

— The vertebrata of the cretaceous formations of the west. Ill. (U. S. geol. survey of the terr., Hayden ; Report, v. 2.) Wash. 1875. Q.   *in* **557.5 : D**

— The vertebrata of the tertiary formations of the west, book 1. Ill. (U. S. geol. survey of

the terr., Hayden ; Report, v. 3.) Wash. 1883. Q.   ;*in* **557.5 : D**
Gibbes, Robert Wilson. A memoir on mosasaurus and the three allied genera: holcodus, conosaurus and amphorosteus. Ill. Wash. 1850. Q. *In* Smithsonian contributions.
506 : R3 v2
Leidy, Joseph. Cretaceous reptiles of the U. S. Ill. Wash. 1865. Q. *In* Smithsonian contributions.   **506 : R3 v14**
Marsh, Othniel C: Odontornithes ; a monograph

on the extinct toothed birds of North America. Ill. (U. S. geol. expl. 40th par., King; Report, v. 7.) Wash. 1880. Q.
in **557.5 : D**
Leidy, Joseph. A memoir on the extinct sloth tribe of North America. Ill. Wash. 1855. Q. *In* Smithsonian contributions.
506 : R3 v7
— Memoir upon the extinct species of american ox. Ill. Wash. 1852. Q. *In* Smithsonian contributions.   **506 : R3 v5**

8. Biology and Anthropology.

(*For* Physiology, *see under* Medicine, class 612.)

1. General biology.

Agassiz, L: J: Rudolph. Contributions to the natural history of the U. S. of America. Ill. Bost. 1857–62. 4 v. Q.   **570 : R1**
Contents. V. 1. Essay on classification. — North american testudinata. 2. Embryology of the turtle. 3. Acalephs in general.—Ctenophore. 4. Discophore.—Hydroidæ.—Homologies of the radiata.
Beale, Lionel Smith. Protoplasm, or Matter and life ; with some remarks on the Confession of Strauss. 3d ed. Lond. 1874. D.
570 : 3
Child, Gilbert W. Essays on physiological subjects. 2d ed. with add. Lond. 1869. D.
570 : 16
Contents. Marriages of consanguinity.—Recent researches on the production of the lowest forms of animal life.— On the production of organisms in closed vessels.—Some aspects of the theory of evolution. — Physiological experiments. — Physiological psychology.
Clark, H: James. Mind in nature, or The origin of life and the mode of development of animals. Ill. N. Y. 1865. O.   **570+4**
Coues, Elliott. Biogen ; a speculation on the origin and nature of life. 2d ed. Bost. 1884. T.   **570 : 15**
Goadby, H: A text-book of vegetable and animal physiology ; designed for the use of schools, seminaries and colleges in the U. S. Ill. N. Y. 1859. O.   **570 : 5**
Lardner, Dionysius. Hand-book of animal physics. 2d ed. with corr. Ill. [Weale's ser.] Lond. 1873. D.   **570 : 6**
Letourneau, C: Biology. Tr. by W: Maccall. [Lib. of contemporary science.] Ill. Lond. 1878. D.   **570 : 7**
Lewes, G: H: Studies in animal life. N. Y. 1860. D.   **570 : 13**
M'Alpine, D. *and* Archibald N. Biological atlas ; a guide to the practical study of plants and animals, adapted to the requirements of the London university, science and art department, and for use in schools and colleges ; with text, containing arrangement and explanation, equivalent terms, glossary and classification. Ill. Edinb. 1880. Q.   **570 : R2**
Murphy, Joseph J: Habit and intelligence in their connexion with the laws of matter and force ; a series of scientific essays. Lond. 1869. 2 v. O.   **570 : 8**
Papillon, Fernand. Nature and life ; facts and doctrines relating to the constitution of

matter, the new dynamics and the philosophy of nature. Tr. from the 2d french ed. by A. R. Macdonough. N. Y. 1875. D.
570 : 9
Semper, K: Animal life, as affected by the natural conditions of existence. (Intern. scientific ser.) N. Y. 1881. D.   **570 : 10**
Stevenson, Sarah Hackett. Boys and girls in biology, or Simple studies of the lower forms of life, based upon the latest lectures of T. H. Huxley and pub. by his permission. Ill. N. Y. 1875. D.   **x 570 : 12**
Wright, R. W. Life ; its true genesis. N. Y. 1880. D.   **570 : 14**
Biological society, *Washington, D. C.* Proceedings ; with the addresses read on the occasion of the Darwin memorial meeting, may 12, 1882 ; v. 1, nov. 1880—may 1882. Wash. 1882. *In* Smithsonian misc. **506 : R4 v25**
Anthropological society, *Washington, D. C.* Transactions ; v. 1, feb. 1879 — jan. 1882. Wash. 1882. *In* Smithsonian misc.
506 : R4 v25

2. Prehistoric archeology.

Baldwin, J: Denison. Pre-historic nations, or Inquiries concerning some of the great peoples and civilizations of antiquity, and their probable relation to a still older civilization of the ethiopians or cushites of Arabia. N. Y. 1869. D.   **571 : 38**
Caspari, O: Die urgeschichte der menschheit, mit rücksicht auf die natürliebe entwickelung des frühesten geisterlebens. 2te aufl. Leipz. 1877. 2 v. O.   **571 : 27**
Campbell, G: Douglas, *8th duke of Argyll.* Primeval man ; an examination of some recent speculations. N. Y. 1869. S.   **571 : 3**
Clodd, E: The childhood of the world ; a simple account of man in early times. N. Y. 1879. D.   **571 : 4**
Donnelly, Ignatius. Atlantis ; the antediluvian world. Ill. N. Y. 1882. D.   **571 : 1**
Figuier, Guillaume L: Primitive man. New ed. Ill. Lond. 1876. O.   **571 : 8**
Joly, N: Man before metals. (Intern. scientific ser.) N. Y. 1883. D.   **571 : 32**
Fiske, J: [Archeological essays]. *In his* Excursions of an evolutionist.   **824.1 : 107**
Contents, see under English literature, Essays.
_____
x denotes books specially adapted for children.

Keary, C: F., *ed.* The dawn of history; an introd. to pre-historic study. N. Y. *n. d.* D. 571 : 9

Lesley, J: P: Man's origin and destiny, sketched from the platform of the sciences in a course of lectures del. before the Lowell institute in Boston, in the winter of 1865–6. Phila. 1868. D. 571 : 10

Lubbock, *Sir* J: The origin of civilization and the primitive condition of man; mental and social condition of savages. N. Y. 1874. D. 571 : 11

— Pre-historic times, as illustrated by ancient remains, and the manners and customs of modern savages. N. Y. 1872. O. 571+12

Maclean, J. P. A manual of the antiquity of man. 8th ed. Cinc. 1879. D. 571 : 13

Moore, Joseph Scott. Pre-glacial man and geological chronology for 3,000,000 of years before 1800 a. d. 2d ed. with addenda, and diagram of the eccentricity of the earth's orbit for 4,000,000 of years. Dublin. 1869. O. 571 : 14

Nicols, Arthur. The puzzle of life, and how it has been put together; a short history of the formation of the earth with its vegetable and animal life from the earliest times, incl. an account of pre-historic man, his weapons, tools and works. Ill. 3d ed. Lond. 1878. D. x 571 : 28

Perkins, F: Beecher. Pre-historic man; two lectures: 1, the facts, 2, the conclusions; an outline of pre-historic archæology, intended as a syllabus of two lectures on the subject. San Francisco. 1883. O. 571 : Pam

Rau, C: Pre-historic fishing in Europe and North America. Plate and ill. Wash. 1884. Q. *In* Smithsonian contributions. 506 : R3 v25

Southall, James C. The recent origin of man, as illustrated by geology and the modern science of prehistoric archæology. Ill. Phila.-1875. O. 571+16

— The epoch of the mammoth and the apparition of man upon the earth. Ill. Phila. 1878. D. 571 : 15

Tylor, E: Burnett. Researches into the early history of mankind and the development of civilization. N. Y. 1878. O. 571 : 17

Wilson, Daniel. Prehistoric man; researches into the origin of civilization in the old and the new world. 3d ed., rev. and enl. Ill. Lond. 1876. 2 v. O. 571 : 18

Winchell, Alexander. Preadamites, or A demonstration of the existence of men before Adam; together with a study of their condition, antiquity, racial affinities and progressive dispersion over the earth. Charts and ill. Chicago. 1880. O. 571 : 19

Europe.

Ratzel, F: Vorgeschichte des europäischen menschen. München. 1874. S. 571 : 2

Dawkins, W: Boyd. Cave hunting; researches on the evidence of caves respecting the early inhabitants of Europe. Ill. Lond. 1874. O. 571 : 5

— Early man in Britain and his place in the tertiary period. Ill. Lond. 1880. O. 571+6

x denotes books specially adapted for children.

Evans, J: The ancient stone implements, weapons and ornaments of Great Britain. N. Y. 1872. O. 571+7

Nilsson, Sven. The primitive inhabitants of Scandinavia; an essay on comparative ethnography, and a contribution to the history of the development of mankind, containing a description of the implements, dwellings, tombs and mode of living of the savages in the north of Europe during the stone age. 3d ed., rev. by the author and tr. from his own ms.; ed. with an introd. by sir J: Lubbock. Lond. 1868. O. 571 : 36

Désor, E: Les palafittes, ou Constructions lacustres du lac de Neuchâtel. Ill. Paris. 1865. O. 571 : 29

America.

Rau, C: The archæological collection of the U. S. national musium, in charge of the Smithsonian institution, Washington, D. C. Ill. Wash. 1876. Q. *In* Smithsonian contributions. 506 : R3 v22

Nadaillac, *Marquis* de. Pre-historic America. Tr. by N. D'Anvers [*pseud. for* H. R. E. Bell]; ed by W: H. Dall. Ill. N. Y. 1884. 571+37

Wilson, Daniel. Pre-aryan american man. *In* Transactions of the Royal soc. of Canada, v. 1. 61 : R

Baldwin, J: Denison. Ancient America, in notes on american archæology. Ill. N. Y. 1878. D. 571 : 20

Short, J: T. The north americans of antiquity; their origin, migrations and type of civilization considered. N. Y. 1880. O. 571 : 25

Foster, J: Wells. Pre-historic races of the U. S. of America. 4th ed. Chicago. 1878. O. 571 : 23

Squier, Ephraim G: Antiquities of the state of New York; being the results of extensive original surveys and explorations, with a supp. on the antiquities of the west. Ill. Buffalo. 1851. O. 571 : 26

— Aboriginal monuments of the state of New York; comprising the results of original surveys and explorations, with an illustrative app. Ill. Wash. 1850. Q. *In* Smithsonian contributions. 505 : R3 v2

Priest, Josiah. American antiquities and discoveries in the west; an exhibition of the evidence that an ancient population of partially civilized nations, differing entirely from those of the present indians, peopled America many centuries before its discovery by Columbus, and inquiries into their origin; with a copious description of many of their stupendous works, now in ruins, with conjectures concerning what may have become of them, compiled from travels, authentic sources and the researches of antiquarian societies. 2d ed., rev. Albany. 1833. O. 571 : P34

Squier, Ephraim G:, *and* Edwin Hamilton Davis. Ancient monuments of the Mississippi valley; comprising the results of extensive original surveys and explorations. Ill. Wash. 1848. Q. *In* Smithsonian contributions. 506 : R3 v1

Conant, A. J. Foot-prints of vanished races in the Mississippi valley ; an account of some of the monuments and relics of pre-historic races scattered over its surface, with suggestions as to their origin and uses. St. Louis. 1879. O.   **571+21**

Whittlesey, C: Descriptions of ancient works in Ohio. Ill. Wash. 1851. Q. *In* Smithsonian contributions.   **506 : R3 v3**

Force, M. F. Some early notices of the indians of Ohio. Cinc. 1879. O.   **571 : 22**

— To what race did the mound builders belong. *With the above.*   **571 : 22**

MacLean, J. P. The mound builders ; an account of a remarkable people that once inhabited the valleys of the Ohio and Mississippi ; together with an investigation into the archaeology of Butler co., O. Ill. Cinc. 1879. O.   **571 : 24**

Carr, Lucien. The mounds of the Mississippi valley, historically considered. (Kentucky geol. survey.) Cinc. 1883. Q.   **571+35**

Jones, Joseph. Exploration of the aboriginal remains of Tennessee. Ill. Wash. 1876. Q. *In* Smithsonian contributions.   **506 : R3 v22**

St. Louis academy of science. Contributions to the archæology of Missouri by the archæological section of the academy. Pt. 1: Pottery. Plates and Maps. Salem, Mass. 1880. F.   **571 : R31**

Contents. Potter, W. B. Archæological remains in south-eastern Missouri. — Evers, E: The ancient pottery of south-eastern Missouri.

Lapham, Increase Allen. The antiquities of Wisconsin, as surveyed and described by [him], on behalf of the American antiquarian society. Ill. (Smithsonian contributions to knowledge.) Wash. 1855. Q.   **571 : R30**

— *Same. In* Smithsonian contributions.   **506 : R3 v7**

Whittlesey, C: Ancient mining on the shores of Lake Superior. Map and ill. Wash. 1863. Q. *In* Smithsonian contributions.   **506 : R3 v13**

Schumacher, Paul. Researches in the kjökkenmöddings and graves of a former population of the coast of Oregon ; and of Santa Barbara Islands and adjacent mainland. Ill. *In* U. S. geol. survey of the terr., Hayden ; Bulletin, v. 3.   *in* **557.5 : D**

Dall, W: Healey. On the remains of later prehistoric man obtained from caves in the Catherina archipelago, Alaska territory, and especially from the caves of the Aleutian islands. Ill. Wash. 1878. Q. *In* Smithsonian contributions.   **506 : R3 v22**

Bransford, J: F. Archæological researches in Nicaragua. Plates and ill. Wash. 1881. Q. *In* Smithsonian contributions.   **506 : R3 v25**

Cope, E: Drinker. On the contents of a bone cave in the island of Anguilla, West Indies. Plates. Wash. 1883. Q. *In* Smithsonian contributions.   **506 : R3 v25**

3. Ethnology.

Figuier, Guillaume L: The human race. Ill. N. Y. 1873. O.   **572 : 5**

Goltz, Bogumil. Der mensch und die leute ; zur charakteristik der barbarischen und der civilisirten nationen. Berlin. 1858. D.   **572 : 2**

Contents, see Deutscher katalog, p. 17.

Kriegk, G: L: Die völkerstämme und ihre zweige ; nach den neuesten ergebnissen der ethnographie. 5te aufl. bearb. von F: v. Hellwald. Frankfurt a. M. 1883. O.   **572 : 16**

Morgan, Lewis H: Systems of consanguinity and affinity of the human family. Ill. Wash. 1869. Q. *In* Smithsonian contributions.   **506 : R3 v17**

Nott, Josiah Clark, *and* G: Robins Gliddon. Types of mankind, or Ethnological researches, based upon the ancient monuments, paintings, sculptures and crania of races, and upon their natural, geographical, philological and biblical history, ill. by selections from the inedited papers of S: G: Morton and by additional contributions from L: Agassiz, W. Usher and H. S. Patterson. Phila. 1854. Q.   **572 : R8**

— *Same.* 10th ed. Phila. 1871. O.   **572+7**

Peschel, Oscar Ferdinand. The races of man and their geographical distribution. From the german. N. Y. 1876. D.   **572 : 13**

Pickering, C: The races of man, and their geographical distribution. New ed.; prefixed, an analytical synopsis of the natural history of man by J: C: **Hall**. Lond. 1851. D.   **572 : 6**

Quatrefages de Bréau, J: L: Armand de. The human species. (Intern. scientific ser.) N. Y. 1879. D.   **572 : 9**

Sharpe, W: The cause of color among races, and the evolution of physical beauty. New ed., rev. N. Y. 1881. S.   **572 : 10**

Waitz, Theodor. Anthropologie der naturvölker. 2te aufl. mit zusätzen des verf. vermehrt und herausg. von G. Gerland. Leipz. 1860–77.. 6 v. O.   **572 : 1**

Contents, see Deutscher katalog, p. 17.

— Introduction to anthropology ; ed., with numerous add. by the author, from the 1st vol. of "Anthropologie der naturvölker", by J. F: Collingwood. [Anthropological society of London publ.] Lond. 1863. O.   **572 : 3**

Wood, J: G: The natural history of man ; an account of the manners and customs of the uncivilized races of men : Australia, New Zealand, Polynesia, America, Asia and ancient Europe. Ill. Lond. 1870. Q.   **572+4**

     * * *

Brace, C: Loring. The races of the old world ; a manual of ethnology. N. Y. 1864. O.   **572 : 11**

Stein, F. v. Die russischen kosakenheere ; nach dem werke des obersten Choroschchin und andern quellen. Karte. Gotha. 1883. Q. *In* Petermann's mitteilungen, Ergänzungsb. 16.   **905.1 : M**

Pauw, Cornelis *or* Corneille de. Recherches philosophiques sur les américains, ou Mémoires interressants pour servir à l'histoire de l'espèce humaine. Nouvelle éd., augm. d'une dissertation critique par Dom Pernety, et de la défense de l'auteur des Recherches contre cette dissertation. Berlin. 1771. 3 v. S.   **572 : 14**

Berlin. *Königliche museen : Ethnologische abtheilung.* The north-west coast of America ; results of recent ethnological researches, from the collections of the Royal museums at Berlin, pub. by the directors of the ethnological dep't. Tr. from the germ. Ill. Lond. *n. d.* F.   **572 : R15**

— - *Same.* Amerika's nordwest-küste ; neueste ergebnisse ethnologischer reisen. Neue folge. Ill. Berlin. 1884. F.   **572 : R15 v2**

Thurn, Everard F. im. Among the indians of Guiana ; sketches, chiefly anthropologic, from the interior of British Guiana. Map and ill. Lond. 1883. O.   **918.8 : 2**

Blumentritt, Ferdinand. Versuch einer ethnographie der Philippinen ; nebst anhang : Die maritimen entdeckungen der spanier im archipel der Philippinen. Karte. Gotha. 1882. Q. *In* Petermann's mitteilungen, Ergänzungsb. 15.   **905.1 : M**

Fornander, Abraham. An account of the polynesian race, its origin and migrations, and the ancient history of the hawaiian people to the times of Kamehameha I. [Engl. and foreign phil. lib.] Lond. 1878. 2 v. D.   **572 : 12**

Note. Numerous treatises on anthropology, with full bibliographies of new publications, have appeared in the annual reports of the Smithsonian Institution, for which see class 506, col. 291.
Works on the ethnology of the american indians will be found in History, class 970.1.

4. Natural history of man.

Home, H:, *lord Kames.* Sketches of the history of man. Dublin. 1775. 4 v. in 2. S.   **573 : 1**

Huxley, T: H: Evidence as to man's place in nature. N. Y. 1876. D.   **573 : 2**

Quatrefages de Bréau, J: L: Armand de. The natural history of man ; a course of elementary lectures. Tr. from the french by Eliza A. Youmans, with an app. [Pop. science lib.] N. Y. 1875. D.   **573 : 3**

Smith, C: Hamilton. The natural history of the human species ; its typical forms, primæval distribution, filiations and migrations. Ill. Lond. 1859. S.   **573 : 4**

Topinard, Paul. Anthropology ; with pref. by Paul Broca. Tr. by Robert T. H. Bartley. Ill. [Lib. of contemp. sci.] Lond. 1878. D.   **573 : 5**

Tylor, E: Burnett. Anthropology ; an introduction to the study of man and civilization. Ill. N. Y. 1881. D.   **573 : 6**

Vogt, C: Lectures on man ; his place in creation and in the history of the earth ; ed. by James Hunt. Lond. 1864. O.   **573 : 7**

Beddoe, J: [Anthropological pamphlets.] *With his* Stature and bulk of man.   **573 : 10**

Being: On the head-forms of the west of England. — On the anthropology of Lancashire. — On the anthropology of Gloucestershire.—The kelts of Ireland.—On the physical characteristics of the inhabitants of Bretagne.—On the headform of the danes.— On the aborigines of central Queensland.—On the physical characteristics of the jewish race.—On the supposed increasing prevalence of dark hair in England. — On anthropological colour phenomena in Belgium and elsewhere.—Anniversary address.

Gould, B: Apthorp. Investigations in the military and anthropological statistics of american soldiers. N. Y. 1869. Q.   **573+8**

Anthropometry and growth.

Roberts, C: A manual of anthropometry, or A guide to the physical examination and measurement of the human body ; containing a systematic table of measurements, an anthropometrical chart or register, and instructions for taking measurements on a uniform plan. Ill. Lond. 1878. O.   **573 : 9**

Pagliani, L: Lo sviluppo umano per età, sesso, condizione sociale ed etnica, studiato nel peso, statura, circonferenza toracica, capacità vitale e forza muscolare. Milano. 1879. O.   **573 : 11**

Chervin, Arthur. Sur l'anthropométrie ; trois brochures addressées par M. Pagliani [à la Société d'anthropologie de Paris]. Paris. 1878. O.   *in* **573 : 11**

British association. *Anthropometric committee.* 4th and final reports. [1881, 1883].   *in* **573 : 11**

Beddoe, J: On the stature and bulk of man in the British Isles. Repr. from v. 3 of the Memoirs of the Anthropological society of London. Lond. 1870. O.   **573 : 10**

Bowditch, H: Pickering. The growth of children. Bost. 1877. O.   **573+12**

— *Same*, a supplementary investigation ; with suggestions in regard to methods of research. Bost. 1879. O.   *in* **573+12**

— The relation between growth and disease ; extracted from the transactions of the American medical assoc., 1881. Phila. 1881. O.   *in* **573+12**

Evetzky, Etienne. On the growth of children during the first year, and on the nutritive conditions of early childhood.   *in* **573+12**

Peckham, G: W. The growth of children ; reprint from the 6th annual report of the State board of health of Wisconsin.   *in* **573+12**

Sozinskey, T: S. Physical aspects of infantile unfoldment.   *in* **573+12**

Roberts, C: The physical requirements of factory children ; from the Journal of the statistical society.   *in* **573+12**

Hitchcock, E: A report of twenty years experience in the department of physical education and hygiene in Amherst college, to the board of trustees, june 27, 1881. Amherst, Mass. 1881. O.   *in* **573+12**

5. Evolution and darwinism.

Agassiz, L: J: Rudolph. Methods of study in natural history. Bost. 1874. D.   **575 : 5**

Allen, C: Grant. The evolutionist at large. Lond. 1881. D.   **575 : 6**

Bateman, F: Darwinism tested by language ; with a pref. by E: Meyrick Goulburn. Lond. 1877. D.   **575 : 7**

Bergen, Joseph Y., *jr. and* Fanny D. The development theory ; a brief statement for general readers. Ill. Bost. 1884. S.   **575 : 34**

Bouverie-Pusey, Sidney E: Bouverie. Permanence and evolution ; an inquiry into the supposed mutability of animal types. Lond. 1882. D.   **575 : 29**

Büchner, F: C: Christian L: Man in the past, present and future ; a popular account of the results of recent scientific research as regards the origin, position and prospects of the human race. From the german by W. S. Dallas. Lond. 1872. O.   **575 : 8**

Cazelles, Émile. Outline of the evolution-philosophy. Tr. from the french by O. B. Frothingham ; with an app. by E. L. Youmans. [Pop. science lib.] N. Y. 1875. D.   **575 : 28**

Chambers, Robert. Vestiges of the natural history of creation. *T. p. w.* [Cinc. 1858.] D.   **575 : 9**

— Explanations ; a sequel to Vestiges of the natural history of creation, by the author of that work. N. Y. 1846. O.   **575 : 10**

Darwin, C: Robert. On the origin of species by means of natural selection, or The preservation of favored races in the struggle for life. New ed. from the 6th Lond. ed., with add. and corr. N. Y. 1877. D.   **575 : 12**

— The descent of man, and selection in relation to sex. New ed. *T. p. w.* [N. Y.] D.   **575 : 11**

— The variation of animals and plants under domestication. 2d ed. rev. Ill. N. Y. 1876. 2 v. D.   **575 : 13**

— Darwinism stated by Darwin himself ; characteristic passages from the writings of C: Darwin, selected and arr. by Nathan Sheppard. N. Y. 1884. D.   **575 : 31**

Fiske, J: Darwinism.   *in* **824.1 : 31**

Graue, G. Darwinismus und sittlichkeit. *In* Deutsche zeit- und streit-fragen.   **304 : 15 v8**

Gray, Asa. Darwiniana ; essays and reviews pertaining to darwinism. N. Y. 1876. O.   **575 : 15**

Häckel, Ernst H: Natürliche schöpfungsgeschichte ; gemeinverständliche wissenschaftliche vorträge über die entwickelungslehre im allgemeinen und diejenige von Darwin, Goethe und Lamarck im besonderen. 7te aufl. Berlin. 1879. O.   **575 : 2**

— *Same, eng.* The history of creation, or The development of the earth and its inhabitants by the action of natural causes ; a popular exposition of the doctrine of evolution in general and that of Darwin, Goethe, and Lamarck in particular. From the german, the trans. rev. by E. Ray Lankester. N. Y. 1876. 2 v. D.   **575 : 2**

— Anthropogenie, oder Entwickelungsgeschichte des menschen ; gemeinverständliche wissenschaftliche vorträge über die grundzüge der menschlichen keimes- und stammes-geschichte. 3te aufl. Leipz. 1877. O.   **575 : 1**

— *Same, eng.* The evolution of man ; a popular exposition of the principal points of human ontogeny and phylogeny. [Ill.] Lond. 1879. 2 v. D.   **575 : 1**

— Freedom in science and teaching. From the german, with a prefatory note by T: H: Huxley. N. Y. 1879. D.   **575 : 4**

Hartmann, C. E. R. Darwinismus und thierproduktion. München. 1876. S.   **575 : 3**

Hartmann, K: Robert E: v. Ernst Häckel als

Hartmann, K: Robert E: v.—*Continued.* vorkämpfer der abstammungslehre in Deutschland. *In his* Gesammelte studien.   **834+19**

— Wahrheit und irrthum im darwinismus ; eine kritische darstellung der organischen entwickelungstheorie. Berlin. 1875. O.   **575+33**

Hodge, C: What is darwinism ? N. Y. 1874. D.   **575 : 16**

Huxley, T: H: More criticisms on Darwin, *and* Administrative nihilism. N. Y. 1873. D.   **575 : 17**

— On the origin of species, or The causes of the phenomena of organic nature ; a course of six lectures to working men. N. Y. 1877. D.   **575 : 18**

— [Essays on darwinism]. *See in* col. 286.

Mivart, St. G: On the genesis of species. Lond. 1871. D.   **575 : 20**

— Lessons from nature, as manifested in mind and matter. Lond. 1876. O.   **575 : 19**

Müller, Fritz. Facts and arguments for Darwin, with add. by the author. Tr. from the german by W. S. Dallas. Ill. Lond. 1869. D.   **575 : 21**

Romanes, G: J: Scientific evidences of organic evolution. (Nature ser.) N. Y. 1883. D.   **575 : 27**

Schmid, Rudolf. The theories of Darwin and their relation to philosophy, religion and morality. From the german by G: A. Zimmermann, with an introd. by the duke of Argyll. Chicago. 1883 [1882.] D.   **575 : 25**

Schmidt, E: Oskar. The doctrine of descent and darwinism. Ill. (Intern. scientific ser.) N. Y. 1876. D.   **575 : 22**

Wallace, Alfred Russel. Contributions to the theory of natural selection ; a series of essays. 2d ed., with corr. and add. N. Y. 1871. D.   **575 : 23**

Weismann, A: Studies in the theory of descent ; with notes and add. by the author. Tr. and ed., with notes, by Raphael Meldola, with a pref. notice by C: Darwin. Ill. Lond. 1882. 2 v. O.   **575 : 37**

Wilson, Andrew. Chapters on evolution ; a popular history of darwinism and allied theories of development. N. Y. 1882. O.   **575 : 26**

Winchell, Alexander. The doctrine of evolution ; its data, its principles, its speculations and its theistic bearings. N. Y. 1874. D.   **575 : 24**

Heredity.

Brooks, W: K. The law of heredity ; a study of the cause of variation and the origin of living organisms. Balt. 1883. D. **575 : 30**

Cooke, Joseph. Heredity ; with preludes on current events. Bost. 1879. D.   **575 : 35**

Contents. Lectures. Heredity.— Hereditary descent in ancient Greece.—Maudsley on hereditary descent.—Necessary beliefs inherent in the plan of the soul. — Darwin's theory of pangenesis. — Darwin on the origin of conscience. — What causes unlikeness in organisms ?— Lotze on the union of soul and body. — The twofold identity of parent and offspring. — Seven principal laws of heredity.—The descent of bad traits and good. *Preludes.* Schools for the american indian. — The future of american poetry.—An american-anglican alliance.—Is death disembodiment ?—Schöberlein on immortality.—Financial heresies in the U. S. — Agricultural colonization of the unemployed.—Skepticism in colleges.—The Elberfeld plan of poor-relief.—The lesser and the greater eastern question.

Galton, Francis. English men of science ; their nature and nurture. [Pop. science lib.] N. Y. 1875. D.   **575 : 14**

— Hereditary genius ; an inquiry into its laws and consequences. New and rev. ed. with an amer. pref. N. Y. 1884. O.   **575 : 32**

Ribot, Théodule. Heredity ; a psychological study of its phenomena, laws, causes and consequences. From the french. Lond. 1875. D.   **575 : 36**

6. Embryology.

Balfour, Francis Maitland. A treatise on comparative embryology. Lond. 1880. 2 v. O.   **576+1**

Bastian, H: Charlton. The beginnings of life ; some account of the nature, modes of origin and transformations of lower organisms. Ill. N. Y. 1872. 2 v. D.   **577 : 1**

Horst, R. A contribution to our knowledge of the development of the oyster, Ostrea edulis. Tr. by J: A. Ryder. *In* U. S. fish com. bulletin, v. 2.   *in* **639 : D**

Ryder, J: A. The microscopic sexual characteristics of the american, portuguese, and common edible oyster of Europe compared. *In* U. S. fish com. bulletin, v. 2.   *in* **639 : D**

— The metamorphosis and post-larval stages of development of the oyster. *In* U. S. fish com. report, v. 10.   *in* **639 : D**

— A contribution to the development and morphology of the lophobranchiates, (Hippocampus antiquorum, the sea-horse). Ill. *In* U. S. fish com. bulletin, v. 1.   *in* **639 : D**

Syrski, Dr. —. Lecture on the organs of reproduction and the fecundation of fishes, and especially of eels. Ill. *In* U. S. fish com. report, v. 3.   *in* **639 : D**

Jacoby, L. The eel question. Tr. by Herman Jacobson. *In* U. S. fish com. report, v. 7.   *in* **639 : D**

Goode, G: Brown. Notes on the life-history of the eel, chiefly derived from a study of recent european authorities. Ill. *In* U. S. fish com. bulletin, v. 10.   *in* **639 : D**

Ryder, J: A. Observations on the absorption of the yelk, the food, feeding, and development of embryo fishes. *In* U. S. fish com. bulletin, v. 2.   *in* **639 : D**

— Development of the silver gar, Belone longirostris, with observations on the genesis of the blood in embryo fishes and a comparison of fish ova with those of other vertebrates. Ill. *In* U. S. fish com. bulletin, v. 1.   *in* **639 : D**

— Development of the spanish mackerel, Cybium maculatum. Ill. *In* U. S. fish com. bulletin, v. 1.   *in* **639 : D**

— A contribution to the embryography of osseous fishes, with special reference to the development of the cod, Gadus morrhua. Ill. *In* U. S. fish com. report, v. 10.   *in* **639 : D**

7. Microscopy.

Beale, Lionel Smith. How to work with a microscope. 5th ed. Ill. Lond. 1880. O.   **578 : 1**

Frey, H: The microscope and microscopical technology ; a text-book for physicians and students. Tr. and ed. by G: R. Cutter. 2d ed. Ill. N. Y. 1880. O.   **578+2**

Gosse, Philip H: Evenings at the microscope, or Researches among the minuter organs and forms of animal life. N. Y. 1860. O.   **578 : 3**

Hogg, Jabez. The microscope, its history, construction and application ; a familiar introd. to the use of the instrument and the study of microscopical science. 6th ed. Lond. 1867. D.   **578 : 4**

Lankester, Edwin. Half-hours with the microscope ; a popular guide to the use of the microscope as a means of amusement and instruction. 14th ed. with chapter on the polariscope by F. Kitton. Ill. Lond. 1878. S.   **578 : 14**

Manton, Walter P. Beginnings with the microscope ; a working handbook, containing simple instructions in the art and method of using the microscope and preparing objects for examination. Ill. Bost. 1884. S.   **578 : 17**

Merkel, F: Das mikroscop und seine anwendung. München. 1875. S.   **578 : 6**

Somerville, Mary. On molecular and microscopic science. Ill. Lond. 1869. 2 v. D.   **578 : 5**

Ward, The hon. mrs. M. The microscope, or Descriptions of various objects of especial interest and beauty adapted for microscopic observation, with directions for the arrangement of a microscope and the collection and mounting of objects. Ill. 5th ed. Lond. 1880. D.   **578 : 12**

Wythe, Joseph H. The microscopist ; a manual of microscopy and compendium of the microscopic sciences, micro-mineralogy, micro-chemistry, biology, histology and practical medicine. 4th ed., enl. and ill. Phila. 1880. O.   **578 : 7**

Wood, J: G: Common objects of the microscope. Ill. Lond. n. d. S.   **578 : 9**

Clarke, Louisa Lane. Objects for the microscope ; a popular description of the most instructive and beautiful subjects for exhibition. 6th ed., ill. Lond. 1880. D.   **578 : 10**

Slack, H: J. Marvels of pond-life, or A year's microscopic recreations among the polyps, infusoria, rotifers, water-bears and polyzoa. 4th ed. Ill. Lond. 1880. D.   **578 : 11**

Leidy, Joseph. A flora and fauna within living animals. Ill. Wash. 1853. Q. *In* Smithsonian contributions.   **506 : R3 v5**

Herrick, Sophie Bledsoe. The wonders of plant-life under the microscope. N. Y. 1883. D.   **578 : 16**

Cooke, M. C. Fungi ; their nature and uses ; ed. by M. J. Berkeley. (Intern. scientific ser.) N. Y. 1875. D.   **578 : 8**

— Rust, smut, mildew and mould ; an introd. to the study of microscopic fungi. 4th ed. rev. and enl. Ill. Lond. 1878. S.   **578 : 13**

Tyndall, J: Essays on the floating matter of the air in relation to putrefaction and infection. N. Y. 1882. D.   **578 : 15**
Contents. Dust and disease. — Optical deportment of the atmosphere in relation to putrefaction and infection.—Further researches on the deportment and vitality of putrefactive organisms. — Fermentation and its bearings on surgery and medicine. — Spontaneous generation.—App.

Bailey, Jacob Whitman. Microscopical examination of soundings, made by the U. S. coast survey off the Atlantic coast of the U. S. Ill. Wash. 1851. Q. *In* Smithsonian contributions.   **506 : R3 v2**

— Microscopical observations made in South Carolina, Georgia and Florida. Ill. Wash. 1851. Q. *In* Smithsonian contributions.   **506 : R3 v2**

— Notes on new species and localities of microscopical organisms. Ill. Wash. 1854. Q. *In* Smithsonian contributions.   **506 : R3 v7**

8. Collectors' manuals.

Baird, Spencer Fullerton, *and others.* Directions for collecting, preserving and transporting specimens of natural history. Ill. Wash. 1859. O. *In* Smithsonian misc.   **506 : R4 v2**

Bailey, W. Whitman. The botanical collector's handbook. (Naturalists' handy ser.) Salem. 1881. D.   **579 : 1**

Manton, Walter P. Field botany ; handbook for the collector, containing instructions for gathering and preserving plants and the formation of the herbarium. Bost. 1882. T.   **579 : 2**

Maynard, C. J. Manual of taxidermy ; complete guide in collecting and preserving birds and mammals. Ill. Bost. 1883. D.   **579 : 5**

Manton, Walter P. Taxidermy without a teacher ; a complete manual of instruction for preparing and preserving birds and animals, with a chapter on hunting and hygiene, instructions for collecting and preserving eggs and insects, and a number of receipts. Ill. South Framingham. 1876. T.   **579 : 8**

— Insects, how to catch and how to prepare them for the cabinet ; a manual of instruction for the field naturalist. Ill. Bost. 1881. S.   **579 : 7**

Packard, Alpheus Spring, *jr.* Directions for collecting and preserving insects. Ill. Wash. 1873. O. *In* Smithsonian misc.   **506 : R4 v11**

Coues, Elliott. Field ornithology ; comprising a manual of instruction for procuring, preparing and preserving birds, and a check list of north american birds. Salem. 1874. O.   **579 : 4**

Ingersoll, Ernest. Birds'-nesting ; a handbook of instruction in gathering and preserving the nests and eggs of birds for the purposes of study. Salem. 1882. D.   **579 : 3**

9. Botany.

1. In general.

(For the distribution of plants over the earth, *see* Physical geography, cl. 551, col. 326.)

Allen, C: Grant. Flowers, and their pedigrees. Lond. 1883. D.   **580 : 25**
Contents. Introd.—The daisy's pedigree. — The romance of a wayside weed.—Strawberries.—Cleavers. The origin of wheat. — A mountain tulip. — A family history.—Cuckoo-pint.

Baily, W: L. Trees, plants and flowers, where and how they grow ; a familiar history of the vegetable kingdom. Ill. Phila. 1878. D. *With his* Our own birds.   **598 : 4**

Bessey, C: E. Botany for high schools and colleges. (Amer. science ser.) N. Y. 1880. O.   **580 : 21**

Comstock, J: L. The young botanist ; a treatise on the science, prepared for the use of persons just commencing the study of plants. 5th ed. N. Y. 1854. S.   **580 : 20**

Figuier, Guillaume L: The vegetable world ; a history of plants with their structure and peculiar properties. Adapted, with a glossary of botanical terms. Ill. Lond. [1882]. D.   **580 : 18**

Gray, Asa. School and field book of botany ; consisting of "Lessons in botany" and "Field, forest and garden botany" bound in one vol. N. Y. 1880. O.   **580 : 6**

Henderson, P: · Hand-book of plants. N. Y. 1881. O.   **580 : R8**
A dictionary of all the leading ornamental or useful plants, with brief instructions for propagation and culture; followed by a glossary of botanical and technical terms, together with general horticultural terms and practices.

Hooker, *Sir* Joseph Dalton. Botany. (Science primers.) Ill. 3d ed. rev. N. Y. 1878. S.   **580 : 22**

Kellerman, W. A. The elements of botany ; embracing organography, histology, vegetable physiology, systematic botany and economic botany, arr. for school use or for independent study, *also* A complete glossary of botanical terms. Ill. Phila. [1884]. D.   **580 : 26**

Kny, Leopold. Plant life in the sea. *In* Estes, D. Half hour recr. in pop. sci., 2d ser.   **504 : 5 v2**

Marion, Fulgence. The wonders of vegetation. From the french ; ed. with numerous add. by Sebele de Vere. [Ill. lib. of wonders.] N. Y. 1874. O.   **580 : 11**

Müller *von Halle*, K: Das buch der pflanzenwelt, eine botanische reise um die welt ; versuch einer kosmischen botanik, den gebildeten aller stände und allen freunden der natur gewidmet. 2te aufl. Leipz. 1869. O.   **580 : 1**

Prantl, K: An elementary text-book of botany. Tr. from the german, the tr. rev. by S. H. Vines. Ill. Phila. 1880. O.   **580 : 10**

Rhind, W: A history of the vegetable kingdom ; embracing comprehensive descriptions of the plants most interesting from their uses to man and the lower animals, their application in the arts, manufact-

ures, medicine and domestic economy, and from their beauty or peculiarities, together with the physiology, geographical distribution and classification of plants. Rev. ed. with supp. Ill. Lond. 1868. O.
580 : R9

Ruschenberger, W: S. W. [Botany]. *In his* Elements of natural hist.   **590 : 11 v2**

Ruskin, J: Proserpina ; studies of wayside flowers, while the air was yet pure among the Alps and in Scotland and England, which my father knew. V. 1. N. Y. 1879. D.,
580 : 28

Schleiden, Matthias Jacob. Poetry of the vegetable world ; a popular exposition of the science of botany and its relations to man. 1st amer. from the Lond. ed. of Henfrey, ed. by Alphonso Wood. Ill. Cinc. 1853. D.   **580 : 12**

Smith, J: Domestic botany ; exposition of the structure and classification of plants and their uses for food, clothing, medicine and manufacturing purposes. Ill. Lond. 1883. D.   **580 : 24**

Step, E: Plant-life ; popular p p s on the phenomena of botany. Illa N. Y. 1883. D.   **580 : 23**

Wallace, Alfred Russel. [Insular floras]. *In his* Island life.   *in* **590 : 7**

*   *   *

Bell, H. R. E. (*N. D'Anvers.*) Vegetable life ; an ill. natural history reader. (Science ladders, no. 3). N. Y. 1882. S.   **x 581 : 11**

— Flowerless plants. (Science ladders, no. 4). N. Y. 1884. S.   **x 580 : 27**

Fuller, Jane Jay. Uncle John's flower-gatherers ; a companion for the woods and fields. N. Y. *n. d.* S.   **x 580 : 16**

Gray, Asa. Botany for young people : [Pt. 1,] How plants grow ; a simple introd. to structural botany, with a popular flora or an arrangement and description of common plants, both wild and cultivated. Ill. N. Y. 1880. D.   **x 580 : 7 v1**

— - Pt. 2, How plants behave ; how they move, climb, employ insects to work for them, etc. N. Y. 1875. D.   **x 580 : 7 v2**

Masters, Maxwell T. Botany for beginners ; an introd. to the study of plants. Lond. [1872]. D.   **x 580 : 17**

Hooker, Worthington. The child's book of nature, for the use of families and schools ; intended to aid mothers and teachers in training children in the observation of nature ; in 3 pts. Pt. 1 : Plants. N. Y. 1880. S.   **x 580 : 15**

Youmans, Eliza A. The first book of botany, designed to cultivate the observing powers of children. New ed., ill. N. Y. 1872. D.   **580 : 13**

Nomenclature and legends.

Ulrich, W: Internationales wörterbuch der pflanzennamen in lateinischer, deutscher, englischer und französischer sprache ; zum gebrauche für botaniker, insbesondere für handelsgärtner, landwirthe, forstbeflissene und pharmaceuten. Leipz. 1872. O.
580 : 29

_____

x denotes books specially adapted for children.

Miller, W: A dictionary of english names of plants applied, in England and among english-speaking people, to cultivated and wild plants, trees and shrubs. In 2 pts.; english-latin and latin-english. Lond. 1884. O.   **580+30**

Alcock, Randal H. Botanical names for english readers. Lond. 1884. O.   **580 : 31**

Folkard, R:, *jr.* Plant lore, legends and lyrics ; embracing the myths, traditions, superstitions and folk-lore of the plant kingdom. Lond. 1884. O.   **293.1+33**

2.   Structural and physiological botany.

M'Alpine, D. The botanical atlas ; a guide to the practical study of plants, containing representatives of the leading forms of plant life,with explanatory letterpress. N. Y. 1883. 2 v. F.   **581 : R9**
Contents. [V. 1.] Phanerogams. [2.] Cryptogams.

Hamilton, G. Elements of vegetable and animal physiology, in two parts ; ed. by D. M. Reese. N. Y. 1855. D.   **581 : 10**

Thomé, O: W: Pflanzenbau und pflanzenleben. München. 1874. O.   **581 : 12**

Sachs, Julius. Text-book of botany, morphological and physiological. Tr. and annotated by Alfrew W. Bennett and W. T. Thistleton Dyer. [Ill.] Oxford. 1875. O.   **581+1**

Gray, Asa. Introd. to structural and systematic botany, and vegetable physiology. 5th and rev. ed. of The botanical text-book. Ill. N. Y. 1878. O.   **580 : 2**

— Lessons in botany and vegetable physiology. Added, a glossary or dictionary of botanical terms. N. Y. 1880. O.   **580 : 4**

— *Same. With his* Manual of the botany of the northern U. S.   **580 : 3**

— *Same. In his* School and field book of botany.
580 : 6

Darwin, C: Robert. Insectivorous plants. Ill. N. Y. 1875. D.   **581 : 4**

— The different forms of flowers on plants of the same species. Ill. N. Y. 1877. D. **581 : 5**

— The effects of cross and self fertilisation in the vegetable kingdom. N. Y. 1877. D.
581 : 6

— The various contrivances by which orchids are fertilised by insects. 2d ed. rev., ill. N. Y. 1877. D.   **581 : 7**

Kerner, Anton Joseph. Flowers and their unbidden guests ; with a pref. letter by C: Darwin, the tr. rev. and ed. by W. Ogle. Ill. Lond. 1878. O.   **581 : 8**

Müller, Hermann. The fertilisation of flowers. Tr. and ed. by D'Arcy W. Thompson ; with a pref. by C: Darwin. Ill. Lond. 1883. O.   **581 : 13**

Darwin, C: Robert. The movements and habits of climbing plants. 2d ed., rev. and ill. N. Y. 1876. D.   **581 : 3**

— *and* Francis **Darwin**. The power of movement in plants. Ill. N. Y. 1881. D. **581 : 2**

Allen, C: Grant. The colours of flowers, as ill. in british flora. Ill. (Nature ser.) Lond. 1882. D.   **581 : 14**

Hough, Franklin B. Dates of foliation or leafing of plants; Dates of blossoming of plants; Dates of ripening of fruits; Dates of defoliation or fall of leaf in plants; 1851-59. *In* Meteorological observations of U. S. patent office, v. 2.   *in* 552.1 : D

3. Systematic botany,

General and local.

LeMaout, J: Emmanuel Marie, *and* Joseph **Decaisne.** A general system of botany, descriptive and analytical; in two parts: Pt. 1, Outlines of organography, anatomy and physiology; pt. 2, Descriptions and illustrations of the orders. Tr. from the original by Mrs. Hooker, the orders arr. after the method followed in the universities and schools of Great Britain, its colonies, America and India; with add., an app. on the natural method, and a synopsis of the orders by J. D. Hooker. Ill. Lond. 1876. Q.   582+1

Torrey, J: Observations on the Batis maritima of Linnæus. Ill. Wash. 1853. Q. *In* Smithsonian contributions.   506 : R3 v6

— On the Darlingtonia californica, a new pitcher plant from northern California. Ill. Wash. 1853. Q. *In* Smithsonian contributions.   506 : R3 v6

Loudon, J: Claudius. Encyclopædia of plants; comprising the specific character, description, culture, history, application in the arts, and every other desirable particular, respecting all the plants indigenous to, cultivated in, or introduced into Britain. New ed. corr. to the present time by Mrs. Loudon [and others]. Lond. 1855. O.   584 : R1

— An enclyclopædia of trees and shrubs, being the Arboretum et fruticetum britannicum abridged; containing the hardy trees and shrubs of Britain, native and foreign, scientifically and popularly described, with their propagation, culture and uses in the arts. Abridged from the large ed. in 8 v. and adapted for the use of nursery men, gardeners and foresters. Lond. 1853. O.   584 : R2

Griffith, R. Eglesfield. Plants collected in Syria and Palestine by the U. S. exped. under lieut. Lynch, 1848. *In* Lynch, W: F. Report.   *in* 915.6 : D

Watson, Sereno. Bibliographical index to north american botany, or Citations of authorities for all the recorded indigenous and naturalized species of the flora of North America; with a chronological arrangement of the synonymy. Pt. 1: Polypetalæ. Wash. 1878. O. *In* Smithsonian misc.   506 : R4 v15

Darlington, W: American weeds and useful plants; a 2d and ill. ed. of Agricultural botany; an enumeration and description of useful plants and weeds which merit the notice or require the attention of amer. agriculturists. Rev. with add. by G: Thurber. N. Y. 1865. D.   587 : 3

Gray, Asa. Field, forest and garden botany; a simple introd. to the common plants of the U. S. east of the Mississippi, both wild

Gray, Asa.—*Continued.* and cultivated. N. Y. 1880. O. *In his* School and field book of botany.   580 : 6

— A manual of the botany of the northern U. S., from New England to Wisconsin and south to Ohio and Pennsylvania incl.; the mosses and liverworts by W: S. Sullivant; arr. according to the natural system, with an introd.. containing a reduction of the genera to the Linnæan artificial classes and orders, outlines of the elements of botany, a glossary, etc. Bost. 1848. O.   580 : 5

— *Same.* 5th ed. 20 plates. N. Y. 1880. O. *With his* Lessons in botany.   580 : 3

Lesquereux, Leo, *and* T: P. **James.** Manual of the mosses of North America; with plates, illustrating the genera. Bost. 1884. O.   587 : 9

Kellerman, W. A. Plant analysis; a classified list of the wild flowers of the northern U. S., with keys for analysis and identification; *also,* a complete glossary of botanical terms. Ill. Phila. [1884]. D.   587 : 6

Chapman, Alpha W. Flora of the southern U. S.; containing an abridged description of the flowering plants and ferns of Tennessee, North and South Carolina, Georgia, Alabama, Mississippi and Florida, arr. according to the natural system; the ferns by Daniel C. Eaton. 2d ed. N. Y. 1883. O.   587 : 7

Goodale, G: L. Wild flowers of America. With fifty colored plates from original drawings by I: Sprague. Bost. 1882. Q.   587 : R2

Vasey, G: The grasses of the U. S.; a synopsis of the tribes and genera, with descriptions of the genera and a list of the species. (U. S. Dep. of agr.; Special rep. no. 63). Wash. 1883. O.   *in* 630 : D

— The agricultural grasses of the U. S. Ill. Wash. 1884. O. *In* U. S. dep. of agr.; [special rep., v. 11].   *in* 630 : D

Eaton, Daniel Cady. The ferns of North America; colored figures and descriptions, with synonymy and geographical distribution, of the ferns, including the ophioglossaceæ, of the U. S. of America and the british north american possessions. The drawings by J. H. Emerton and C. E. Faxon. Salem. 1879, 1880. 2 v. Q.   587 : R1

— Ferns of the southwest; an account of the ferns which have been collected in so much of the territory of the U. S. of Amer. as is west of the 105th degree of w. longitude and south of the 40th degree of n. latitude. *In* U. S. geograph. surveys west of the 100th mer., Wheeler; Report, v. 6.   *in* 557.5 : D

Macoun, J., *and* T. J. W. **Burgess.** Canadian filicineæ. *In* Transactions of the Royal society of Canada, v. 2.   61 : R

Harvey, W: H: Nereis boreali-americana, or Contributions to a history of the marine algæ of North America, pt. 1: Melanospermeæ. Ill. Wash. 1852. Q. *In* Smithsonian contributions, v. 3.   506 : R3 v3

— *Same,* pt. 2: Rhodospermeæ. Ill. Wash. 1853. Q. *In the same,* v. 5.   506 : R3 v5

— *Same,* pt. 3: Chlorospermeæ. Ill. Wash. 1858. Q. *In the same,* v. 10.   506 : R3 v10

Farlow, W: Gilson. List of the marine algæ of the U. S. *In* U. S. fish com. report. v. 3.   *in* 639 : D

Farlow, W: Gilson.—*Continued.*
— The marine algæ of New England; with bibliography. Ill. *In* U. S. fish com. report, v. 7. *in* **639 : D**
Wood, Horatio **C.,** *jr.* A contribution to the history of the fresh water algæ of North America. Ill. Wash. 1872. Q. *In* Smithsonian contributions. **506 : R3 v19**
Marsh, Lester F. Marsh and aquatic plants of the northern U. S. *In* U. S. fish com. bulletin, v. 3. *in* **639 : D**
Lawson, G: Revision of the canadian ranunculaceæ. *In* Transactions of the Royal society of Canada, v. 2. **61 : R**
Baldwin, H: The orchids of New England; a popular monograph. [Ill.] N. Y. 1884. O. **587+8**
Torrey, J: A flora of the state of New York; comprising full descriptions of all the indigenous and naturalized plants hitherto discovered in the state, with remarks on their economical and medicinal properties. Ill. Albany. 1843. 2 v. Q. *In* Natural hist. of N. Y., pt. 2. **557.3 : R1**
Note. Supplementary articles on the flora of N. Y. appear in the annual reports of the N. Y. state museum of natural history, *in* 506 : D.
Tatnall, E: Catalogue of the phenogamous and filicoid plants of Newcastle county, Delaware, arr. according to the natural system, as recently rev. by A. Gray and others, with the synonyms of modern authors. Pub. by the Wilmington institute. Wilmington, Del. 1860. O. **587 : 5**
Torrey, J: Description of plants collected during the exploring exped. of the Red river of La. 1852. Ill. *In* Marcy, R. B. Report. *in* **917.4 : D**
Swezey, G. D. Catalogue of the phænogamous and vascular cryptogamous plants of Wisconsin. *In* Geology of Wis. **557.5 : R3 v1**
Bundy, W. F. Partial list of fungi of Wisconsin, with descriptions of new species. *In* the same. **557.5 : R3 v1**
Chickering, J. W. Catalogue of phænogamous and vascular cryptogamous plants collected during 1873 and 1874 in Dakota and Montana, along the 49th parallel, by Elliott Coues and G: M. Dawson. *In* U. S. geol. survey of the terr., Hayden; Bulletin, v. 4. *in* **557.5 : D**
United States. *Pacific r. r. surveys.* Botany of the route near the 47th and 49th parrallel. Ill. *In* Report of the surveys, v. 1, pt. 2. *in* **625 : D**
Contents. **Cooper,** James Graham. Report upon the botany of the route. — **Gray,** Asa. Catalogue of plants collected east of the Rocky mountains. — **Cooper,** J. G. Catalogue of plants collected in Washington terr.
— — Botany of the routes on the 41st par., and near the 38th and 39th par. Ill. Report of the surveys, v. 2. *in* **625 : D**
Contents. **Torrey,** J:, *and* Asa **Gray.** Report on the botany of the expeditions.
— — Botany of the route near the 32d par. Ill. *In* Report of the surveys, v. 2. *in* **625 : D**
Contents. **Torrey,** J:, *and* Asa **Gray.** Report on the botany of the exped.
— — Botany of the route near the 35th par. Ill. *In* Report of the surveys, v. 4. *in* **625 : D**
Contents. **Bigelow,** J. M. General description of the botanical character of the country; Forest trees.

United States. *Pacific r. r. surveys.*—*Continued.*
— **Engelmann,** G:, *and* J. M. **Bigelow.** Cactaceæ.— **Torrey,** J: Descriptions of the general botanical collections, (Compositæ, plantaginaceæ, orabanchaceæ, scrophulariaceæ and bignonia, by Asa **Gray).**—**Sullivant,** W. S. Mosses and liverworts.
— — Botany of the explorations in California for routes to connect with the routes near the 35th and 32d par. Ill. *In* Report of the surveys, v. 5. *in* **625 : D**
Contents. **Torrey,** J: Descriptions of plants collected along the route by W: P. Blake, and at the mouth of the Gila by major Thomas and lieut. Du Barry.—**Durand,** E., *and* T. C. **Hilgard.** Description of plants collected upon the expedition.
— — Botany of the route from the Sacramento valley to the Columbia river. Ill. *In* Report of the surveys, v. 6. *in* **625 : D**
Contents. **Newberry,** J: Strong. Geographical botany; Description of the forest trees of northern California and Oregon.—General catalogue of the plants collected: **Gray,** Asa, J: **Torrey** and J: S. **Newberry,** Exogenous plants: **Torrey,** J:, Endogenous plants; **Sullivant,** W. S., Mosses and liverworts; **Tuckerman,** E:, Lichens.
— — Botany of the routes from San Francisco bay to Los Angeles, Cal., west of the Coast Range, and from the Pimas villages to the Rio Grande, near the 32d par. Ill. *In* Report of the surveys, v. 7. *in* **625 : D**
Contents. **Torrey,** J: List and description of plants collected.—**Antisell,** T: Synoptical tables of botanical localities.
Gray, Asa. Plantæ wrightianæ texano-neomexicanæ, pt. 1. Ill. Wash. 1852. Q. *In* Smithsonian contributions, v. 3. **506 : R3 v3**
— *Same,* pt. 2. Ill. Wash. 1853. Q. *In the same,* v. 5. **506 : R3 v5**
Torrey, J: [Description of new genera and species of plants, collected during col. Emory's military reconnoissance from Ft. Leavenworth to San Diego, in 1846-7]. Ill. *In* Emory, J. W. Report. *in* **917.5 : D**
Contains also **Engelmann,** G: Notes on cactaceæ, *and* **Abert,** J. W. List of plants.
United States. *Mexican boundary survey.* Botany of the boundary. Ill. *In* **Emory,** W. H. Report of the survey, v. 2, pt. 1. *in* **917.7 : D**
Contents. **Parry,** C. C. Introd.; geographical distribution and botanical features. — **Torrey,** J: Botany [in general]. — **Engelmann,** G: Cactaceæ of the boundary.
Torrey, J: Botany [of the explor. exped. down the Zuñi and Colorado rivers, 1851]. Ill. *In* Sitgreaves, L. Report. *in* **917.5 : D**
Porter, T: C., *and* J: M. **Coulter.** Synopsis of the flora of Colorado. (U. S. geol. survey of the terr., Hayden; Miscel. pub., no. 4.) Wash. 1874. O. *in* **557.5 : D**
Brandegee, T. S. The flora of southwestern Colorado. *In the same;* Bulletin, v. 2. *in* **557.5 : D**
Gray, Asa, *and* J: **Torrey.** Botany [of the Colorado river of the west]. *In* Ives, J. C. Report of exped. *in* **917.5 : D**
Note. All the orders preceding verbenaceæ were elaborated by Gray, the remainder by Torrey; except cactaceæ and euphorbiaceæ by G: **Engelmann,** and gramineæ by G: **Thurber.**
Torrey, J: Botany [of Stansbury's exped. to the Great Salt Lake]. Ill. *In* Report, 1855. *in* **917.5 : D**
Watson, Sereno, *assisted by* Daniel C. **Eaton** *and others.* Botany [of the country long the 40th parallel]. Map and ill. (U. S. geol.

expl. 40th par., King ; Report, v. 5.) Wash. 1871. Q. *in* **557.5 : D**

Contents. General report.—Catalogue of the known plants of Nevada and Utah, with descriptions of such phænogamous genera and species as do not occur east of the Mississippi. (Cactaceæ by G: Engelmann; compositæ by Daniel C. Eaton ; polemoniaceæ and erigoneæ by Asa Gray; naïadaceæ by J. W. Robbins; carices by Stephen T. Olney; filices by Daniel C. Eaton ; musci by T: P. James ; lichenes by E: Tuckerman.) —Additions.—App. Synopses of genera.—Index.

Rothrock, J. T. Reports upon the botanical collections made in portions of Nevada, Utah, California, Colorado, New Mexico and Arizona, during 1871—1875. Ill. (U. S. geogr. surveys west of 100th mer., Wheeler ; Report, v. 6). Wash. 1878. Q. *in* **557.5 : D**

Contents. Notes on Colorado. — Notes on New Mexico. — Notes on economic botany. — Catalogue of plants collected in Nevada, Utah, Colorado, New Mexico and Arizona, with descriptions of those not contained in Gray's Manual of the northern U. S. and v. 5 of Geological exploration of the 40th parallel. (Leguminosæ by Sereno **Watson** ; cacteæ, asclepiadeæ, gentianeæ, cuscuteæ, euphorbiaceæ, cupuliferæ, loranthaceæ, coniferæ, amaryllideæ, junceæ by G: **Engelmann**; polemoniaceæ, borraginaceæ, scrophularineæ, labiatæ, polygonaceæ by T: C. **Porter**; salix by M. S. **Bebb**; carex by W: **Boott**; gramineæ by G: **Vasey**; ferns of the southwest by Daniel C. **Eaton**; musci by T: P. **James**; hepaticæ by C. F. **Austin**; lichenes by E:

Tuckerman.—App.: California collection 1875 ; Index ; Plates.

Gray, Asa, *and* Joseph D. **Hooker**. The vegetation of the Rocky mountain region, and a comparison with that of other parts of the world. *In* U. S. geol. survey of the terr., Hayden ; Bulletin, v. 6.

　　　　　　　　　　　　　　in **557.5 : D**

Torrey, J: Catalogue of plants collected by lieut. Frémont in his expedition to the Rocky mountains, 1842. *In* Frémont, J. C. Report. *in* **917.5 : D**

— Plantæ frémontianæ, or Descriptions of plants collected by J. C. Frémont in California. Ill. Wash. 1853. Q. *In* Smithsonian contributions. **506 : R3 v6**

— *and* J: C: **Frémont**. Descriptions of some new genera and species of plants, collected in capt. Frémont's exploring exped. to Oregon and north California in 1843-44. Ill. *In* Frémont, J. C. Report *in* **917.5 : D**

Kellogg, Albert. Botany of Alaska. *In* Davidson, G: Report, *in* U. S. coast survey rep. 1867. **622 : D**

Eggers, H: Franz Alexander *freiherr* v. The flora of the St. Croix and the Virgin Islands. Wash. 1879. O. *In* Smithsonian misc. **506 : R4 v23**

10.　Zoology.

1.　In general.

Scudder, Samuel Hubbard. Nomenclator zoologicus ; an alphabetical list of all generic names that have been employed by naturalists for recent and fossil animals, from the earliest times to the close of the year 1879. Wash. 1882. O. **590 : 57**

Contents. Pt. 1. Supplemental list of genera in zoology; list of generic names employed in zoology and paleontology to the close of the year 1879, chiefly supplemental to those catalogued by Agassiz and Marschall, or indexed in the Zoological record. Pt. 2. Complete list of generic names employed in zoology and paleontology to the close of the year 1879, as contained in the Nomenclators of Agassiz, Marschall and Scudder, and in the Zoological record.

Abbott, C: Conrad. A naturalist's rambles about home. N. Y. 1884. D. **590 : 54**

Agassiz, L: J: Rudolph, *and* A: Addison **Gould**. Principles of zoology ; touching the structure, development, distribution and natural arrangement of the races of animals, living and extinct. Pt. 1: Comparative physiology. Bost. 1848. D. **590 : 8**

Atkinson, J. C. Sketches in natural history ; with an essay on reason and instinct. N. Y. [1884]. D. **590 : 55**

Brehm, Alfred Edmund. Brehm's thierleben. Grosse ausg., 2te aufl. Leipz. 1876–78. 10 v. Q. **590+1**

Contents. V. **1-3. Brehm**, A. E. Die säugethiere. **4-6.** Die vögel. **7, 8.** Die kriechthiere, lurche und fische. **9, 10.** Taschenberg, Ernst L: Die insekten, tausendfüssler und spinnen.—Schmidt, E: Oskar. Die niederen thiere.

— 170 chromotafeln zu Brehms thierleben, unter leitung der zoologen dr. Girtanner, prof. dr. Klunzinger, prof. dr. O. Schmidt, und prof. dr. Taschenberg. nach dem leben ausgeführt vom maler Olof Winkler. Leipz. 1883, 1884. Q. **590 : R18**

Cassell's popular natural history. Ill. Lond. n. d. 4 v. Q. **590+2**

Contents. V. **1.** Mammalia: Four-handed animals.—Wing-handed an.—Insect-eating an.—Rodents or gnawing an.—Flesh-eating an. **2.** *Same, continued.*—Thick-skinned an.—Ruminating an.—Toothless an.—Pouch-bearing an.—Aquatic mammals or cetacea. **3.** Birds. **4.** Reptiles, fishes, insects, worms, crustaceans, molluscs, sea-stars, echinoderms, corallines, corals and animalcules.

Cuvier, G: Léopold Chrétien F: Dagobert *baron*. The animal kingdom arr. after its organization ; forming a natural history of animals, and an introd. to comparative anatomy. Tr. and adapted to the present state of science : the mammalia, birds and reptiles by E: Blyth ; the fishes and radiata by Robert Mudie ; the molluscous animals by G: Johnston ; the articulated animals by J. O. Westwood. New ed. with add. by W. B. Carpenter and J. O. Westwood. Ill. Lond. 1851. O. **590 : 9**

Duncan, P: Martin, *ed.* Cassell's natural history. Ill. Lond. 1883, 1884. 6 v. Q. **590+59**

Contents. V. **1.** Duncan, P: M. Apes and monkeys.—**Murie**, J., *and* P: M. Duncan. Lemurs.—**Dallas**, W. S. Chiroptera; Insectivora. **2.** **Parker**, W. K. *and* T. J. The land carnivora.—**Murie**, J: The aquatic or marine carnivora: Cetacea; Sirenia.—Dawkins, W: B. Proboscidea; Hyracoidea.—Dawkins, W: B., *H.* W. **Oakley** *and* A. H. **Garrod**. Ungulata. **3.** Garrod, A. H. Ungulata: Ruminantia.—**Dallas**, W. S. Rodentia.—Duncan, P: M. Edentata; Marsupialia.—**Sharpe**, R. B. Aves. **4.** Sharpe, R. B. Aves, *continued.*—Duncan, P: M. Reptilia; Amphibia. **5.** Seeley, H. G. Pisces.—Duncan, P: M. Invertebrata, introd.—**Woodward**, H: Mollusca; Tunicata.—**Crane**, A. Molluscoida. Brachiopoda and Bryozoa.—Dallas, W. S. Insecta, introd.—Bates, H. W. Coleoptera.—Dallas, W. S. Hymenoptera. **6.** Dallas, W. S. Hymenoptera, *concluded;* Neuroptera.—Kirby, W. F. Lepidoptera.—Dallas, W. S. Diptera; Aphaniptera; Rhynchota; Orthoptera; Thysanura; Myriopoda; Arachnida. —

Woodward, H: Crustacea. —**Duncan,** P: M.
Vernes.—**Carpenter,** P. H. Echinodermata.—**Duncan,** P: M. Zoophyta.—**Sollas,** W. J. Spongiæ.—
Jones, T. R. Rhizopoda.— **Duncan,** P: M. Infusoria.

Goldsmith, Oliver. A history of the earth and
animated nature. Portr. and ill. Edinb.
1837. O.   **590 : 45**

Gosse, Philip H: The romance of natural history. 1st ser., 12th ed.; 2d ser., 6th ed.
Lond. 1881. 2 v. D.   **590 : 41**

Gould, A: Addison, *ed.* The naturalist's library;
containing scientific and popular descriptions of man, quadrupeds, birds, fishes,
reptiles and insects, compiled from the
works of Cuvier, Griffith, Richardson,
Geoffrey, Lacépède, Buffon, Goldsmith.
Shaw, Montague, Wilson, Lewis and
Clarke. Audubon and other writers on
natural history, arr. according to the
classification of Stark. Ill. Bost. 1856. O.
    590+3

Hamerton, Philip Gilbert. Chapters on animals. Ill. Bost. 1877. D.   **590 : 16**

Harbison, M. Elements of zoology for schools
and science classes. (Putnam's elem. science ser.) N. Y. *n. d.* S.   **590 : 56**

Ingersoll, Ernest. Friends worth knowing;
glimpses of american natural history. N.
Y. 1881. S.   **590 : 17**
Contents. In a snailery.—First-comers.—Wild mice.
—An ornithological lecture.—Our winter birds.—The
buffalo and his fate.—The song-sparrow.—Civilizing
influences.—How animals get home.—A midsummer
prince.—Bank-swallows.

— Country cousins ; short studies in the natural
history of the U. S. Ill. N. Y. 1884. O.
    590+53

Jardine, Sir W:, *ed.* The naturalist's library.
Edinb. 1843. 40 v. S.   **590 : 58**
Contents. V. **1-13.** *Mammalia.* **Smith,** C: Hamilton. Introd. — Memoir of Dru Drury. **1. Jardine,**
Sir W: Monkeys.—Memoir of Buffon. **2. Jardine,**
Sir W: The feline.—Memoir of Cuvier. **3, 4. Jardine,** *Sir* W: Ruminantia.—Memoir of Camper. —
Memoir of J: Hunter. **5. Jardine,** *Sir* W: Pachydermes.—Memoir of sir Hans Sloane. **6. Hamilton,**
Robert. Ordinary cetacea or whales.—Memoir of
Lacépède. **7. Macgillivray,** W: British quadrupeds.—Memoir of Ulysses Aldrovandi. **8. Hamilton,**
Robert. Amphibious carnivora, including the walrus
and seal, also of the amphibious cetacea.—Memoir
of M. François Peron. **9, 10. Smith,** C: Hamilton.
Dogs.—Memoir of Pallas.—Memoir of Don Felix
d'Azara. **11. Waterhouse,** G. R. Marsupialia. —
Memoir of J: Barclay. **12. Smith,** C: Hamilton.
Horses.—Memoir of Gesner.
14-27. *Ornithology.* **1, 2. Jardine,** *Sir* W: Humming-birds.—Memoir of Linnæus.—Memoir of Pennant. **3. Jardine,** *Sir* W: Gallinaceous birds, pt. 1.
—Memoir of Aristotle. **4. Jardine,** *Sir* W: Gallinaceous birds, pt. 2: Game-birds.—Memoir of sir T:
Stamford Raffles. **5. Selby,** Prideaux J: Gallinaceous birds, pt. 3: Pigeons. — Memoir of Pliny. **6.
Selby,** Prideaux J: Parrots.—Memoir of T: Bewick.
7, 8. Swainson, W: Birds of western Africa. —
Memoir of Bruce.—Memoir of Le Vaillant. **9. Jardine,** *Sir* W: Birds of Great Britain and Ireland,
pt. 1: Birds of prey.—Memoir of sir Robert Sibbald.
10. Swainson, W: Flycatchers.—Memoir of baron
Haller. **11. Jardine,** *Sir* W: Birds of Great Britain
and Ireland, pt. 2: Incessores.—Memoir of W: Smellie.
12. Jardine, *Sir* W: Birds of Great Britain and Ireland, pt. 3: Rasores and grallatores.—Memoir of dr.
J: Walker. **13. Jardine,** *Sir* W: Nectariniadæ or
sun-birds.—Memoir of Francis Willughby. **14. Jardine,** *Sir* W: Birds of Great Britain and Ireland,
pt. 4: Natatores.—Memoir of Alex. Wilson.
28-33. *Ichthyology.* **1. Jardine,** *Sir* W: The perch
family.—Memoir of sir Joseph Banks. **2. Bushnan,**
J. S. Nature, structure and economical uses of
fishes. — Memoir of Hippolito Salviani. **3. Schomburgk,** Robert Hermann. Fishes of Guiana, pt. 1.—
Memoir of R. H. Schomburgk. **4. Hamilton,** Robert.

British fishes, pt. 1.—Memoir of Rondelet. **5. Schomburgk,** Robert Hermann. Fishes of Guiana, pt. 2.
— Memoir of Burckhardt. **6. Hamilton,** Robert.
British fishes, pt. 2.—Memoir of Humboldt.
34-40. *Entomology.* **1. Duncan,** James. Introd.
to entomology.—Memoir of Swammerdam.—Memoir
of De Geer. **2. Duncan,** James. Beetles.—Memoir
of Ray. **3. Duncan,** James. British butterflies.—
Memoir of Werner. **4. Duncan,** James. British
moths, sphinxes, etc. — Memoir of Maria Sibilla
Merian. **5. Duncan,** James. Foreign butterflies.—
Memoir of Lamarck. **6. Bees.**— Memoir of Huber.
7. Duncan, James. Exotic moths. — Memoir of
Latreille.

Kingsley, J: Sterling, *ed.* The standard natural
history ; v. 1, 2, 5. Ill. Bost. 1884, 1885.
3 v. Q.   **590 : P15**
Contents. V. **1.** Packard, A. S., Introd. — Lower
invertebrates by S: F. Clarke, J. W. Fewkes. R.
Hitchcock, A. Hyatt. D. S. Kellicott, J. S. Kingsley,
W. N. Lockington, C: S. Minot, A. S. Packard. **2.**
Crustacea and insects, by E. A. Birge, J. H. Comstock,
G: Dimmock, H: Edwards, C. H. Fernald, L. O. Howard, J. S. Kingsley, A. S. Packard, C. V. Riley, P. R.
Uhler, S. W. Williston. **5.** Mammals, by E. Coues, T.
Gill, J. S. Kingsley, W. N. Lockington, S: Lockwood,
G: Macloskie, W: B. Scott, R. R. Wright.

Kirby, W: On the power, wisdom and goodness
of God as manifested in the creation of
animals, and in their history, habits and
instincts. New ed. with notes by T: Rymer
Jones. [Bridgewater treatises]. Lond.
1852, 1853. 2 v. D.   **214 : 7**

Martin, F. Natural history. Tr. from the 34th
germ. ed. by Sarah A. Myers. 1st and 2d
ser. N. Y. 1861, 1862. 2 v. D.   **590 : 10**

Orton, James. Comparative zoology; structural
and systematic. [Rev. by E: A. Birge.]
N. Y. 1883. O.   **590 : 47**

Oswald, Felix Leopold. Zoological sketches ;
a contribution to the out door study of
natural history. Ill. Phila. 1883 [1882]. O.
    590 : 43

Packard, Alpheus Spring, *jr.* Zoology for high
schools and colleges. (Amer. science ser.)
2d ed. rev. N. Y. 1880. O.   **590 : 5**

Ruschenberger, W: S. W. Elements of natural
history, embracing zoology, botany and
geology, for schools, colleges and families.
Phila. 1850. 2 v. D.   **590 : 11**
Contents. V. **1.** Vertebrate animals. **2.** Invertebrate animals.—Botany.—Geology.

Shaw, G: Zoological lectures, delivered at the
Royal institution in 1806, 1807. Lond. 1809.
2 v. O.   **590 : 51**

Tenney, Sanborn. Natural history ; a manual
of zoology for schools, colleges and the
general reader. Ill. N. Y. 1865. D.
    590 : 12

Wallace, Alfred Russel. The geographical distribution of animals ; with a study of the
relations of living and extinct faunas, as
elucidating the past changes of the earth's
surface. Maps and ill. N. Y. 1876. 2 v. O.
    590+6

— Island life, or The phenomena and causes of
insular faunas and floras, including a revision and attempted solution of the problem of geological climates. N. Y. 1881. O.
    590 : 7

Wood, J: G: Popular natural history. Ill. Phila.
n. d. O.   **590 : 13**

— Sketches and anecdotes of animal life. Ill.
Lond. *n. d.* S.   **590 : 34**

— Animal traits and characteristics, or Sketches
and anecdotes of animal life, 2d ser. New
ed., ill. Lond. *n. d.* S.   **590 : 35**

Wood, J: G:—*Continued.*
— The common objects of the country. Lond.
n. d. S.   **590 : 32**
— Homes without hands; a description of the
habitations of animals, classed according
to their principle of construction. New
ed., ill. Lond. 1880. O.   **590 : 38**
Goode, G: Brown. Classification of the collection to represent the animal resources of
the U. S.; a list of substances derived from
the animal kingdom, with synopsis of the
useful and injurious animals, and a classification of the methods of capture and utilization. Wash. 1876. O. *In* Smithsonian
misc.   **506 : R4 v13**

* * *

Anderson, W: Treasury of the animal world
for the young. Lond. n. d. S. **x 590 : 40**
Harris, Amanda B. Dooryard folks, *and* A win-
ter garden. Ill. Bost. [1883]. D.
     x 590 : 48
Jackson, T: Stories about animals. 4th ed.
, Lond. n. d. O.   **x 590 : 30**
Kirby, Mary *and* Elizabeth. Things in the for-
est. Lond. 1879. S.   **x 590 : 44**
Maskell, *Mrs.* A. E. Anderson-. Four feet,
wings and fins. Ill. Bost. [1879]. D.
     x 590 : 29
Morse, E: S. First book of zoölogy. Lond.
1880. D.   **x 590 : 42**
Peabody, Selim H. Cecil's books of natural
history: Pt. 1, Beasts; pt. 2, Birds; pt. 3,
Insects. Ill. Phila. [1879]. D. **x 590 : 31**
Wood, J: G: The boy's own book of natural
history. Lond. [1880]. D. **x 590 : 37**

Animal life of the sea.

(See also Physical geogr., cl. 551.2, col. 328.)

Damon, W: E. Ocean wonders; a companion
for the seaside. Ill. N. Y. 1879. D.
     590 : 26
Figuier, Guillaume L: The ocean world; a
description of the sea and some of its inhabitants. From the french. New ed. rev.
by E. Perceval Wright. Ill. Lond. [1872].
D.   **590 : 39**
Gosse, Philip H: A year at the shore. Ill. Lond.
1865. D.   **590 : 27**
Kingsley, C: Glaucus, or The wonders of the
shore. Bost. 1855. S.   **590 : 28**
— *Same.* Ill. [Works, v. 5.] Lond. 1881. D.
     590 : 28
Martens, J. B. Life in the sea. Tr. by Herman
Jacobson. *In* U. S. fish com. bulletin, v.
2.   *in* **639 : D**
Verrill, A. E. Notice of the remarkable marine
fauna occupying the outer banks of the
southern coast of New England, and of
some additions to the fauna of Vineyard
Sound. *In* U. S. fish com. report, v. 10.
     in **639 : D**
Wood, J: G: Common objects of the sea-shore,
incl. hints for an aquarium. Lond. n. d. S.
     590 : 33
— The fresh and salt-water aquarium. Ill. Lond.
[1869]. S.   **590 : 36**

· **x** denotes books specially adapted for children. ·

Instinct and reason.

Brougham, H: *lord.* Dialogues on instinct, with
analytical view of the researches on fossil
osteology. Lond. 1844. S. **590 : 14**
Lindsay, W. Lauder. Mind in the lower animals, in health and disease. N. Y. 1880.
2 v. O.   **590+20**
Contents. V. 1. Mind in health. 2. Mind in disease.
Menault, Ernest. The intelligence of animals,
with illustrative anecdotes. From the
french. [Ill. lib. of wonders.] N. Y. 1875.
D.   **590 : 21**
Romanes, G: J: Animal intelligence. (Intern.
scientific ser.) N. Y. 1883. D. **590 : 46**
— Mental evolution in animals; with a post-
humous essay on instinct by C: **Darwin**.
N. Y. 1884. D.   **590 : 50**
Watson, J: Selby. The reasoning power of
animals. 2d ed. Lond. 1870. D. **590 : 23**
Wood, J: G: Man and beast here and hereafter,
ill. by more than 300 original anecdotes.
N. Y. 1875. O.   **590 : 25**

Animal structure.

(See also special classes below.)

M'Alpine, D. Zoölogical atlas, incl. comparative anatomy; with practical directions
and explanatory text, for the use of students. N. Y. 1884. 2 v. F. **590 : R52**
 Contents. [V. 1.] Vertebrata. [2.] Invertebrata.
Agassiz, L: J: Rudolph. The structure of animal life; six lectures del. at the Brooklyn
academy of music in jan. and feb. 1862. 3d
ed. N. Y. 1874. O.   **590 : 49**
Jones, T: Rymer. General outline of the organization of the animal kingdom and manual
of comparative anatomy. 4th ed. ill.
Lond. 1871. O.   **590 : 4**
Chauveau, A. The comparative anatomy of the
domesticated animals. 2d ed. rev. and
enl. with the co-operation of S. Arloing.
Tr. and ed. by G: Fleming. N. Y. 1884.
O.   **591+4**
Mivart, St. G: Lessons in elementary anatomy.
New. ed. Lond. 1877. S. **591 : 2**
Smellie, W: The philosophy of natural history;
with an introd. and various add. and alter-
ations, intended to adapt it to the present
state of knowledge by J: Ware. Bost. 1843.
D.   **590 : 19**
Ware, J: The philosophy of natural history.
Prepared on the plan, and retaining portions of the work of W: Smellie. Bost.
1863. D.   **590 : 22**
Dean, J: Gray substance of the medulla oblon-
gata and trapezium. Ill. Wash. 1864. Q.
In Smithsonian contributions.
     506 : R3 v16
Marey, Étienne Jules. Animal mechanism; a
treatise on terrestrial and aërial locomotion. Ill. (Intern. scientific ser.) N. Y.
1879. D.   **591 : 1**
Pettigrew, J. Bell. Animal locomotion, or Walking, swimming and flying, with a dissertation on aëronautics. Ill. (Intern. scientific ser.) N. Y. 1874. D. **591 : 3**
Schufeldt, R. W. Osteology of Speotyto cunicu-
laria var. hypogæa, [and] of Eremophila

Schufeldt, R. W.—*Continued.*
    alpestris. Ill. *In* U. S. geol. survey of the
    terr., Hayden ; Bulletin, v. 6. *in* 557.5 : D
— Osteology of the north american tetraonidæ,
    [and] of Lanius ludovicianus excubitorides.
    Ill. *In the same.* *in* 557.5 : D

2. Special localities.

White, Gilbert. The natural history of Sel-
    borne ; with add. notes by J. G. Wood.
    Ill. Lond. 1860. S. 590 : 24
Hough, Franklin B. Dates of first appearance
    of birds and other animals. *In* Meteoro-
    logical observations of U. S. patent office,
    v. 2. *in* 552.1 : D
DeKay, James E. Zoology of New York, or
    The New York fauna ; comprising detailed
    descriptions of all the animals hitherto
    observed within the state, with brief notices
    of those occasionally found near its bord-
    ers. Ill. Albany. 1842–1844. 5 v. Q. *In*
    Natural hist. of N. Y., pt. 1.
  557.3 : R1
    Contents. [V. 1.] Pt. 1. Mammalia. [2.] Pt. 2. Birds.
    [3.] Pt. 3. Reptiles.—Pt. 4. Fishes. [4.] Plates to pts.
    3, 4. [5.] Pt. 5. Mollusca.—Pt. 6. Crustacea.
United States. *Exploration of the Red river of
    La., 1852.* Zoology. Ill. *In* Marcy, R.
    B. Report. *in* 917.4 : D
    Contents. Marcy, Randolph B. Mammals.—Baird,
    Spencer F., *and* C: Girard. Reptiles; Fishes.—
    Adams, C. B., *and* G: G. Shumard. Shells.—
    Girard, C: Orthopterous insects; Arachnidians;
    Myriapods.
Lapham, Increase Allen. A systematic cata-
    logue of the animals of Wisconsin. *In* 4th
    annual rep. of the Regents of the univ. of
    Wis., *with* Governor's message, 1852.
  in 328.15 : D
Coues, Elliott. Commentary on the zoological
    results of [Lewis and Clarke's] expedition.
    In U. S. geol. survey of the terr., Hayden ;
    Bulletin, v. 1. *in* 557.5 : D
United States. *Pacific r. r. surveys.* General
    report upon the zoology of the several
    Pacific railroad routes. Ill. Wash. 1857-
    58. *In* Report of the surveys, v. 8–10.
  in 625 : D
    Contents. V. 8. Baird, Spencer F. Mammals.
    Mammals. 9. Baird, S. F., J: Cassin *and* G: N.
    Lawrence. Pt. 2. Birds. 10. Baird, S. F. Pt. 3.
    Reptiles.—Girard, C: Pt. 4. Fishes.
— - Zoolog. report of the route near the 47th
    and 49th parallel. Ill. *In* Report of the
    surveys, v. 1, pt. 2. *in* 625 : D
    Contents. Cooper, James Graham, G: Suckley
    and G: Gibbs. Mammals.—Cooper, J. G. Land
    birds.—Suckley, G: Water birds.—Cooper, J. G.
    Reptiles.—Suckley, G: Fishes.—LeConte, J: T.
    Insects [coleoptera].—Cooper, W: Mollusca.—
    Cooper, J. G. Crustacea.
— - Zoolog. report of the routes near the 38th
    and 39th par., and near the 41st par. Ill.
    In Report of the surveys, v. 10. *in* 625 : D
    Contents. Baird, S. F. Mammals; Birds; Reptiles.
    —Girard, C: Fishes.—LeConte, J: L. Insects.
— - Zoolog. report of the route near the 35th
    Par. Ill. *In* Report of the surveys, v. 4,
    10. *in* 625 : D
    Contents. V. 4. Kennedy, C. B. R. Field notes
    and explanations. 10. Kennedy, C. B. R. Mam-
    mals; Birds.—Baird, S. F. Reptiles.—Girard, C:
    Fishes.
— - Zoolog. report of the route near the 32d
    par., from the Rio Grande to the Pimas.

United States. *Pacific r. r. surveys.—Continued.*
    villages. Ill. *In* Report of the surveys, v.
    10. *in* 625 : D
    Contents. Heermann, A. L. Birds.—Hallowell,
    E: Reptiles.
— - Zoolog. report of the explor. in California
    for routes to connect with those near the
    35th and 32d par. Ill. *In* Report of the sur-
    veys, v. 10. *in* 625 : D
    Contents. Hallowell, E: Reptiles.—Heermann,
    A. L. Birds.—Baird, S. F. Mammals.—Girard, C:
    Fishes.
— - Zoolog. report of the explor. from the
    Sacramento valley to the Columbia river.
    Ill. *In* Report of the surveys, v. 6, 10.
  in 625 : D
    Contents. V. 6. Girard, C: Fishes.—Newberry,
    J: S. Mammals; Birds.—Binney, W. G. Land
    shells. 10. Baird, S. F. Reptiles.
United States. *Mexican boundary survey.* Zo-
    ology of the boundary. Ill. *In* Emory, W.
    H. Report of the survey, v. 2, pt. 2.
  in 917.7 : D
    Contents. Baird, Spencer F. Mammals ; Birds;
    Reptiles.—Girard, C: Fishes.
Woodhouse, S. W. Report on the natural history
    of the country passed over by the exploring
    expedition under the command of L. Sit-
    greaves [down the Zuñi and Colorado
    rivers], during 1851. Ill. *In* Sitgreaves, L.
    Report. *in* 917.5 : D
    Contents. Woodhouse, S. W. Mammals and Birds.
    —Hallowell, E: Reptiles. — Baird, Spencer F.,
    and C: Girard. Fishes. — Torrey, J: Botany.
United States. *Stansbury's expedition to the
    Great Salt Lake.* Ill. *In* Report, 1855.
  in 917.5 : D
    Contents. Baird, Spencer F. Quadrupeds and
    Birds.—Baird, S. F., *and* C: Girard. Reptiles, incl.
    a monographic essay on the genus phrynosoma. —
    Haldeman, S. S. Insects.
Yarrow, H. C., *and others.* Reports upon the
    zoological collections obtained from por-
    tions of Nevada, Utah, California, Colo-
    rado, New Mexico and Arizona during
    1871—1874. Ill. (U. S. geograph. surveys
    west of 100th mer., Wheeler ; Report. v. 5).
    Wash. 1875. Q. *in* 557.5 : D
    Contents. Yarrow, H. C. Introd.; Notes upon
    geograph. distribution and variation with regard to
    the zoology of the western U. S., as relates more
    particularly to mammals and birds.—Coues, Elliott,
    and H. C. Yarrow. Rep. upon the collections of
    mammals.—Henshaw, H. W. Rep. upon the orni-
    thological collections. — Yarrow, H. C. Rep. upon
    the collections of batrachians and reptiles. — Coues,
    Elliott. Synopsis of the reptiles and batrachians of
    Arizona, with critical and field notes and an exten-
    sive synonymy. — Cope, E: D., *and* H. C. Yarrow.
    Rep. upon the collections of fishes.—Cresson, E. T.
    Rep. upon the collections of hymenoptera ; with list
    of formicidæ, by E: Norton. — Mead, Theodore L.
    Rep. upon the collections of diurnal lepidoptera, with
    notes upon all species known to inhabit Colorado ;
    and a list of all species collected, by W. H. Edwards.—
    Stretch, R: H. Report upon new species of zygeni-
    dæ and bombycidæ.—Osten-Sacken, C: R. *baron* v.
    Rep. upon the collection of diptera, 1873. — Ulke, H:
    Rep. upon the collections of coleoptera. — Uhler,
    Philip R. Rep. upon the collections of hemiptera. —
    Thomas, Cyrus. Rep. upon the collections of or-
    thoptera.—Hagen, H. A. Rep. upon the collections
    of neuroptera and pseudo-neuroptera.—Yarrow, H.
    C. Rep. upon the collections of terrestrial and fluvi-
    atile mollusca.—Verrill, A. E. Rep. upon the collec-
    tions of fresh-water leeches.

Harford, W. G. W. Zoology of Alaska. *In*
    Davidson, G: Report, *in* U. S. coast survey
    rep. 1867. 622 : D
Kumlien, L: Contributions to the natural his-
    tory of arctic America, made in connection

with the Howgate polar expedition 1877-'78. *In* Smithsonian misc.   **506 : R4 v23**

Contents. **Kumlien, L:** Ethnology, mammals and birds. — **Bean, T. H.** Fishes. — **Verrill, A. E.** Annelides, molluscoids and radiates.—**Dall, W: H.** Mollusks. — Insects: **Edwards, W. C.** Diurnal lepidoptera; **Scudder, S. H.**, *and others.* Hymenoptera, nocturnal lepidoptera, diptera, coleoptera, neuroptera and arachnida.—**Gray, Asa.** Plants. — **Tuckerman, E.** Lichens.—**Farlow, W. G.** Algæ.

United States. *Naval astronomical expedition.* Zoology of Chile. Ill. *In* Report of exped., v. 2   *in* **508 : D**

Contents. **Baird, Spencer F.** Mammals.—**Cassin, J:** Birds.—**Girard, C:** Reptiles; Fishes; Crustacea.—**Gould, A: A.** Shells.

Streets, T. Hale. Contributions to the natural history of the Hawaiian and Fanning Islands and Lower California; made in connection with the U. S. north Pacific surveying exped. 1873-75. Wash. 1877. O. *In* Smithsonian misc.   **506 : R4 v13**

Contents. Ornithology. — Herpetology. — Ichthyology: Fishes of upper and Lower California; of the Hawaiian Islands; of the Fanning Islands; from the Samoan Islands.—Crustacea.—Botany.

Kidder, J. H. Contributions to the natural history of Kerguelen Island, made in connection with the american transit-of-Venus expedition, 1874-5. 2 pts. Wash. 1876. O. *In* Smithsonian misc.   **506 : R4 v13**

Contents. Pt. 1. Ornithology, ed. by Elliott Coues. 2. Oology.—Botany.—Geology.—Mammals.—Fish.—Mollusks.—Insects.—Crustaceans.—Annelids.—Echinoderms.—Anthozoa.—App.—Study of Chionis minor, with reference to its structure and systematic position.

2. Invertebrates.

Huxley, T: H: A manual of the anatomy of invertebrated animals. N. Y. 1878. D.   **592 : 2**

Buckley, Arabella Burton. Life and her children; glimpses of animal life from the amœba to the insects. Ill. N. Y. 1881. D.   **x 592 : 1**

Stimpson, W: Synopsis of the marine invertebrata of Grand Manan, or the region round the mouth of the bay of Fundy, New Brunswick. Ill. Wash. 1853. Q. *In* Smithsonian contributions.   **506 : R3 v6**

Verrill, A. E. The invertebrate animals of Vineyard Sound [in New England], with an account of the physical characters of the region. Ill. *In* U. S. fish com. report, v. 1.   *in* **639 : D**

Smith, Sidney I. Sketch of the invertebrate fauna of Lake Superior. *In* U. S. fish com. report, v. 2.   *in* **639 : D**

Beneden, P: Joseph van. Animal parasites and messmates. (Intern. scientific ser.) Ill. N. Y. 1876. D.   **592 : 3**

Protozoa, Radiata, Vermes.

(See also Microscopy, cl. 578, col. 356.)

Ryder, J: A. The protozoa and protophytes, considered as the primary,† or indirect source of the food of fishes. *In* U. S. fish com. bulletin, v. 1.   *in* **639 : D**

Magnin, Antoine. The bacteria. Tr. by G: M. Sternberg. Bost. 1880. O.   **593 : 2**

Agassiz, Elizabeth Cary, (*Actœa*). A first lesson in natural history. 2d ed. Bost. 1859. D.   **593 : 1**

Bell, H. R. E. (*N. D'Anvers*). Lowest forms of water animals; an ill. natural history reader, by N. D'Anvers. (Science ladders, no. 5.) N. Y. 1882. S.   **x 593 : 3**

Leidy, Joseph. Fresh-water rhizopods of North America [with bibliography of the subject]. Ill. (U. S. geol. survey of the terr., Hayden; Report, v. 12.) Wash. 1879. Q. *in* **557.5 : D**

Clark, H: James. Lucernariæ and their allies; a memoir on the anatomy and physiology of Haliclystus auricula and other lucernarians, with a discussion of their relations to other acalephæ, to beroids and polypi. Ill. Wash. 1878. Q. *In* Smithsonian contributions.   **506 : R3 v23**

Dall, W: Healey. Index to the names which have been applied to the subdivisions of the class brachiopoda, excluding the rudistes, previous to the year 1877. Wash. 1877. O.   **506 : R4 v13**

Verrill, A. E. Synopsis of the north american fresh-water leeches. *In* U. S. fish com. report, v. 2.   *in* **639 : D**

Darwin, C: Robert. The formation of vegetable mould through the action of worms, with observations of their habits. N. Y. 1882 [1881]. D.   **595 : 14**

Webster, H. E., *and* **James E. Benedict.** The annelida chætopoda from Provincetown and Wellfleet, Mass. Ill. *In* U. S. fish com. report, v. 9.   *in* **639 : D**

Mollusks.

Gill, Theodore N: Arrangement of families of mollusks. Wash. 1871. O. *In* Smithsonian misc.   **506 : R4 v10**

Carpenter, Philip P. The mollusks of western North America; embracing the 2d report made to the British assoc. on this subject, with other papers, reprinted with a general index. Ill. Wash. 1872. O. *In* Smithsonian misc.   **506 : R4 v10**

Bell, H. R. E., (*N. D'Anvers*). Lowly mantle- and armor-wearers; an ill. natural-history reader by N. D'Anvers. (Science ladders, no. 6.) N. Y. 1884. S.   **x̄ 594 : 5**

Binney, W: Greene. Bibliography of north american conchology to 1860: American authors. Wash. 1863. O. *In* Smithsonian misc.   **506 : R4 v5**

— *Same:* Foreign authors. Wash. 1864. O. *In* Smithsonian misc.   **506 : R4 v9**

Note. Is more than a bibliography, since it contains a full index of the various species described in each work.

Tryon, G: Washington, *jr.* Structural and systematic conchology; an introd. to the study of the mollusca. Col'd ill. Phila. 1882-84. 3 v. O.   **594 : P6**

Woodward, S: P. A manual of the mollusca; a treatise of recent and fossil shells. 2d ed., with an app. of recent and fossil conchological discoveries to the present time. Ill. Lond. 1868. D.   **594 : 4**

Wood, J: G: The common shells of the sea-shore. Ill. Lond. 1865. S.   **594 : 3**

Turton, W: Manual of the land and fresh-water shells of the british islands, with figures

x denotes books specially adapted for children.

of each of the kinds. New ed. with add.
by J: E: Gray. Lond. 1857. D.   **594 : 2**

Lea, I:, *and others*. Check lists of the shells of
North America, prepared for the Smith-
sonian institution. Wash. 1860. O. *In*
Smithsonian misc.   **506 : R4 v2**

Binney, W: Greene, *and* T: **Bland**. Land and
fresh water shells of North America, pt. 1.
Ill. Wash. 1869. O. *In* Smithsonian misc.
v. 8.   **506 : R4 v8**

— (*alone*). *Same*, pt. 2, 3. Ill. Wash. 1865. O.
In the same, v. 7.   **506 : R4 v7**

Tryon, G: Washington, *jr*. Land and fresh-water shells of North America, pt. 4. Ill.
Wash. 1873. O. *In* Smithsonian misc.
    506 : R4 v16

Stimpson, W: Researches upon the hydrobiinæ
and allied forms. Ill. Wash. 1865. O. *In*
Smithsonian misc.   **506 : R4 v7**

Prime, Temple. Monogram of american corbi-
culadæ, recent and fossil. Ill. Wash. 1865.
O. *In* Smithsonian misc.   **506 : R4 v7**

Verrill, A. E. The cephalopods of the north-
eastern coast of America. Ill. *In* U. S. fish
com. report, v. 7.   *in* **639 : D**

Note. For works on the oyster, see class 639.

Crustacea, Arachnida.

Huxley, T: H: The crayfish ; an introduction to
the study of zoology. Ill. (Intern. scientific ser.) N. Y. 1880. D.   **595 : 11**

Smith, Sidney I. The crustacea of the fresh
waters of the U. S. *In* U. S. fish com. report, v. 2.   *in* **639 : D**

Bundy, W. F. Crustacean fauna of Wisconsin,
with descriptions of little known species of
cambarus. *In* Geology of Wis.
    557.5 : R3 v1

Wilson, Edmund B. Pycnogonida of New England and adjacent waters. *In* U. S. fish
com. report, v. 6.   *in* **639 : D**

Harger, Oscar. The marine isopoda of New
England and adjacent waters. *In* U. S.
fish com. report, v. 6.   *in* **639 : D**

Smith, Sidney I. Decapod crustacea of the Al-
batross dredgings off the coast of the U. S.
in 1883. Ill. *In* U. S. fish com. report, v.
10.   *in* **639 : D**

Keyserling, Eugen W: Theodor *graf*. Die spinnen Amerikas : Laterigradæ. Nürnberg.
1880. Q.   **595+20**

Thorell, Tord Tamerlan Theodor. Descriptions
of the araneæ, coll. in Colorado in 1875 by
A. S. Packard, jr. *In* U. S. geol. survey of
the terr., Hayden ; Bulletin, v. 3.
    in **557.5 : D**

Peckham, G: W. *and* Elizabeth, *born* Gifford.
Descriptions of new or little known spiders
of the family attidæ from various parts of
the U. S. of North America. *n. t. p.* Milw.
1883. O.   **595 : 21**

Insects in general.

Cowan, Frank. Curious facts in the history of
insects, including spiders and scorpions ;
a complete collection of the legends, superstitions, beliefs and ominous signs connected with insects, together with their uses in
medicine, art and as food, with a summary
of their remarkable injuries and appearances. Phila. 1865. D.   **595 : 10**

Lubbock, *Sir* J: On the origin and metamorphoses of insects. (Nature ser.) 2d ed., ill.
Lond. 1874. D.   **595 : 7**

Agassiz, L: J: Rudolph. The classification of
insects from embryological data. Ill. Wash.
1850. Q. *In* Smithsonian contributions.
    506 : R3 v2

Packard, Alpheus Spring, *jr*. Guide to the
study of insects, and a treatise on those injurious and beneficial to crops ; for the use
of colleges, farm schools and agriculturists.
6th ed. N. Y. 1878. O.   **595+2**

Graber, Vitus. Die insekten. München. 1877.
2 v. S.   **595 : 1**

Le Baron, W: Outlines of entomology. Ill. *In*
8d an. rep. of the state entomologist of Ill.
1872.   *in* **328.15 : D**

McCook, H: Christopher. Tenants of an old
farm ; leaves from the note-book of a naturalist. Ill. N. Y. 1885 [1884]. D.   **595 : 23**

Rennie, James. The natural history of insects.
Ill. N. Y. 1843, 1846. 2 v. S.   **595 : 4**

Ballard, Julia P. Insect lives, or Born in prison.
Cinc. 1879. D.   **x 595 : 16**

Church, Ella Rodman. Flyers and crawlers, or
Talks about insects. Phila. [1884]. S.
    595 : 22

Guernsey, L. E. Jenny and the insects. [*Anon*.]
Phila. [1857]. S.   **x 595 : 17**

Kirby, Mary *and* Elizabeth. Sketches of insect
life. Lond. *n. d.* S.   **x 595 : 18**

Wood, J: G: Insects at home ; a popular account of british insects, their structure,
habits and transformations. Ill. Lond.
1876. O.   **595 : 6**

— Insects abroad ; a popular account of foreign
insects, their structure, habits and transformations. Ill. Lond. 1874. O.   **595 : 5**

American entomology.

Say, T: Complete writings on the entomology
of North America ; ed. by J: L. LeConte,
with a memoir of the author by G: Ord.
N. Y. 1859. 2 v. O.   **595+3**

Contents. v. 1. Pref.—Memoir.— Amer. entomology, v. 1-3, 1824-28.—Explanation of terms used in
entomol. — Description of some new species of
hymenopterous insects, 1823.—Descr. of insects belonging to the order neuroptera, coll. by the expedition under the command of Stephen H. Long, 1823.—
[Descr. of insects coll. on] Long's 2d expedition to
the source of St. Peter's river, etc., 1824.—Descr. of
north amer. curculionides, 1831. — New species of
north amer. insects, found by Joseph Barabino,
chiefly in La., 1832.—Descr. of new species of hetero-
pterous hemiptera of North Amer., 1831. — Correspondence relative to the insect that destroys the
cotton plant.— Note on capt. LeConte's paper on
New coleopterous insects of North Amer., pub. in
the first vols. of the Annals of the Lyceum of natural
hist. of N. Y., 1827.—Descr. of some new species of
hymenoptera of the U. S., 1828. — Descr. of new
amer. species of the genera buprestis, trachys and
elater, 1825. — Add. and corr. — Index. — Plates. 2.
Pref.—Descr. of several new species of north amer.
insects, 1817.—Some account of the insect known as
hessian fly, and of a parasitic insect that feeds on it,
1817.—Descr. of the thysanouræ of the U. S., 1821.—
An account of the arachnides of the U. S., 1821.—
Descr. of the myriapode of the U. S., 1821.—On a
south amer. species of oestrus, which inhabits the
human body, 1822.—Descr. of dipterous insects of the
U. S., 1823.—Descr. of coleopterous insects, coll. in
the expedition to the Rocky mountains under the
command of major Long, 1823-25.— Descr. of new
hemipterous insects, coll. in the same exped., 1825.—

x denotes books specially adapted for children.

Descr. of new species of hister and hololepta, inhabiting the U. S., 1825.—Descr. of new species of coleopterous insects, inhabiting the U. S., 1825–26.—Descr.
of north amer. dipterous insects, 1829–30.—Descr. of
new north amer. hemipterous insects, belonging to
the 1st family of the section homoptera of Latreille,
1830–31.—Descr. of new north amer. neuropterous
insects, and observ. on some already described, 1839.
—A monograph of north amer. insects of the genus
cicindela, 1818.—Descr. of insects of the families of
carabici and hydrocanthari of Latreille, inhabiting
North America., 1823.—Descr. of new north amer.
insects, aud observ. on some already described, 1834–
36.—Descr. of new north amer. coleopterous insects,
and observ. on some already described, 1835.—Descr.
of new ,north amer. hymenoptera, and observ. on
some already described, 1836–37.—Add. and corr.—
Index.

Hagen, Herrmann A: Synopsis of the described
neuroptera of North America ; with a list
of the south american species. Wash. 1861.
O. *In* Smithsonian misc.   **506 : R4 v4**

Scudder, S: Hubbard. Catalogue of the orthoptera of North America, described previous to 1867. Wash. 1868. O. *In* Smithsonian misc.   **506 : R4 v8**

Thomas, Cyrus. Synopsis of the acrididæ of
North America. Ill. (U. S. geol. survey
of the terr., Hayden ; Report, v. 5.) Wash.
1873. Q.   *in* **557.5 : D**

Uhler, Philip R. List of hemiptera of the region
west of the Mississippi river. *In* U. S. geol.
survey of the terr., Hayden ; Bulletin, v. 1.
                                in **557.5 : D**

— Report on the insects collected during the explorations [in the territories of U. S.] of
1875, incl. monographs on the families
cydnidæ and saldæ, and the hemiptera
collected by A. S. Packard, jr. Ill. *In* U.
S. geol. survey of the terr., Hayden ; Bulletin, v. 3.   *in* **557.5 : D**

Riley, C: V., and J. Monell. Notes on the aphi-
didæ of the U. S., with descriptions of
speeies occurring west of the Mississippi.
In U. S. geol. survey of the terr., Hayden ;
Bulletin, v. 5.   *in* **557.5 : D**

Le Conte, J: L. Classification [and description
of families] of the coleoptera of North
America, pt. 1. Ill. Wash. 1862. O. *In*
Smithsonian misc., v. 3.   **506 : R4 v3**

— *Same,* pt. 2. Wash. 1873. O. *In the same,* v.
11.   **506 : R4 v11**

— *and* G: H. **Horn.** Classification of the coleoptera of North America, [pt. 3]. Wash.
1883. O. *In the same,* v. 26. **506 : R4 v26**

— *(alone).* List of the coleoptera of North America, pt. 1. Wash. 1866. O. *In* Smithsonian misc., v. 6.   **506 : R4 v6**

— New species of north american coleoptera, pt.
1. Wash. 1863. O. *In the same.* **506 : R4 v6**

— *Same,* pt. 2. Wash. 1873. O. *In the same,* v.
11.   **506 : R4 v11**

— The coleoptera of Kansas and eastern New
Mexico. Ill. Wash. 1859. Q. *In* Smithsonian contributions.   **506 : R3 v11**

— The coleoptera of the region of the
Rocky mountains, pt. 1. *In* U. S. geol.
survey of the terr., Hayden ; Bulletin, v. 4.
                                in **557.5 : D**

— *Same,* pt. 2. *In the same,* v. 5. *in* **557.5 : D**

Osten - Sacken, C: Robert Romanoff *baron* v.
Catalogue of the described diptera of North
America. Wash. 1859. O. *In* Smithson-
ian misc., v. 3.   **506 : R4 v3**

— *Same,* 2d ed. Wash. 1878. O. *In the same,* v.
16.   **506 : R4 v16**

Loew, Hermann. Monographs of the diptera of
North America, ed., with add., by R. Osten-
Sacken ; pts. 1, 2. Ill. Wash. 1862, 1864.
O. *In* Smithsonian misc., v. 6.
                                506 : R4 v6

— The diptera of North America, pt. 3. Ill.
Wash. 1873. O. *In the same,* v. 11.
                                506 : R4 v11

Osten - Sacken, C: Robert Romanoff *baron* v.
Monographs of the diptera of North America, pt. 4. Ill. Wash. 1869. O. *In* Smithsonian misc.   **506 : R4 v8**

— Western diptera ; descriptions of new genera
and species of diptera from the region west
of the Mississippi, and especially from California. *In* U. S. geol. survey of the terr.,
Hayden ; Bulletin, v. 3.   *in* **557.5 : D**

Morris, J: G. Catalogue of the described lepidoptera of North America. Wash. 1860. O.
In Smithsonian misc.   **506 : R4 v3**

— Synopsis of the described lepidotera of North
America, pt. 1: Diurnal and crepuscular
lepidoptera. Ill. Wash. 1862. O. *In* Smithsonian misc.   **506 : R4 v4**

Hoy, Philo R. Catalogue of lepidoptera of
Wisconsin. *In* Geology of Wis.
                                557.5 : R3 v1

Scudder, S: Hubbard. Butterflies, their structure, changes and life-histories, with special
reference to american forms ; an application of the "doctrine of descent" to the
study of butterflies ; with an app. of practical instructions. [Ill.] N. Y. 1881. O.
                                595 : 13

Edwards, W: H: The butterflies of North America. Bost. 1879–84. 2 v. Q.   **595 : R24**

— Synopsis of north american butterflies. Bost.
1879. Q. *In his* Butterflies of North America.   **595 : R24 v1**

— List of species of the diurnal lepidoptera of
America, north of Mexico. Bost. 1884. Q.
In his Butterflies of North America.
                                595 : R24 v2

Grote, A: R. Descriptions of noctuidæ, chiefly
from California. *In* U. S. geol. survey of
the terr., Hayden ; Bulletin, v. 4.
                                in **557.5 : D**

— Preliminary list of the north american species
of agrotis, with descriptions. *In* U. S.
geol. survey of the terr., Hayden ; Bulletin,
v. 6.   *in* **557.5 : D**

— Preliminary studies on the north american
pyralidæ, pt. 1. *In* U. S. geol. survey of
the terr., Hayden ; Bulletin, v. 4.
                                in **557.5 : D**

— North american moths, with a preliminary
catalogue of the species of hadena and
polia. *In* U. S. geol. survey of the terr.,
Hayden ; Bulletin, v. 6.   *in* **557.5 : D**

— New moths. *In the same.*   *in* **557.5 : D**

Packard, Alpheus Spring, jr. A monograph of
the geometrid moths or phalænidæ of the
U. S. Ill. (U. S. geol. survey of the terr.,
Hayden ; Report, v. 10). Wash. 1876. Q.
                                in **557.5 : D**

Chambers, V. T. Index to the described
tineina of the U. S. and Canada. *In* U. S.
geol. survey of the terr., Hayden ; Bulletin, v. 4.   *in* **557.5 : D**

— Food-plants of tineina. *In the same.*
                                in **557.5 : D**

— Descriptions of new tineina from Texas, and

others from more northern localities. *In* U. S. geol. survey of the terr., Hayden; Bulletin, v. 4.　*in* 557.5 : D

Howard, L. O. Descriptions of north american chalcididæ, from the collections of the U. S. dep. of agr. and of dr. C. V. Riley; with biological notes. 1st paper; together with a list of the described north amer. species of the family. (U. S. dep. of agr., Bureau of entomol.; Bulletin, no. 5). Wash. 1885.
　in 632 : D

Lubbock, *Sir* J: Ants, bees and wasps; a record of observations on the habits of the social hymenoptera. (Intern. scientific ser.) N. Y. 1882. D.　595 : 19

Saussure, H: de. Synopsis of american wasps: Solitary wasps. Ill. Wash. 1875. O. *In* Smithsonian misc.　506 : R4 v14

McCook, H: Christopher. The natural history of the agricultural ant of Texas; a monograph of the habits, architecture and structure of Pogonomyrinex barbatus. Phila. 1880. O.　595 : 12

— The honey ants of the Garden of the Gods, and the occident ants of the american plains. Ill. Phila. 1882 [1881]. O.
　595 : 15

American entomologist, The; an illustrated magazine of popular and practical entomology; ed. by C: V. Riley. N. Y. 1880. O.　505.9 : M

Note. For injurious insects, see class 632. For bees and silkworms in their economic aspects, see class 638.

3. Vertebrates.

Huxley, T: H: A manual of the anatomy of vertebrated animals. N. Y. 1878. D.
　596 : 2

Müller, Adolf *and* K: Wohnungen, leben und eigenthümlichkeiten in der höheren thierwelt. Leipz. 1869. O.　596 : 1

Buckley, Arabella Burton. Winners in life's race, or The great backboned family. N. Y. 1883 [1882]. D.　596 : 6

Harting, James Edmund. British animals extinct within historic times, with some account of british wild cattle. Ill. Bost. 1880. O.　596 : 8

Jordan, D: Starr. Manual of the vertebrates of the northern U. S., incl. the district east of the Mississippi river and north of North Carolina and Tennessee, exclusive of marine species. Chicago. 1876. D. 596 : 3

— *and* Balfour H. **Van Vleck.** A popular key to the birds, reptiles, batrachians and fishes of the northern U. S., east of the Mississippi river. Appleton, Wis. 1874. T.
　596 : 5

Jones, Joseph. Researches, chemical and physiological, concerning certain american vertebrata. Ill. Wash. 1856. O. *In* Smithsonian contributions.　506 : R3 v8

Hoy, Philo R. Catalogue of the cold-blooded vertebrates of Wisconsin. *In* Geology of Wisconsin.　557.5 : R3 v1

Note. For the economic treatment of domestic animals, see under Agriculture, class 696.

Fishes.

Gill, Theodore N: Arrangement of the families

of fishes, or classes pisces, marsipobranchii and leptocardii. Wash. 1872. O. *In* Smithsonian misc.　506 : R4 v11

Günther, Albert C: L: Gotthilf. An introduction to the study of fishes. [Ill.] Edinb. 1880. O.　597+1

Jordan, D: Starr. Contributions to north american ichthyology, pts. 1, 2. Ill. Wash. 1877. O. *In* Smithsonian misc.　506 : R4 v13

Contents. Pt. 1. Review of Rafinesque's memoirs on north amer. fishes. 2. Notes on cottidæ, etheostomatidæ, percidæ, centrarchidæ, aphredoderidæ, dorosomatidæ and cyprinidæ, with revisions of the genera and descriptions of new or little known species.—Synopsis of the siluridæ of the fresh waters of North America.

— *and* Alembert Winthrop **Brayton.** Contributions to north amer. ichthyology, pt. 3. Wash. 1878. O. *In* Smithsonian misc.
　506 : R4 v23

Contents. **Jordan, D: S.,** *and* A. W. **Brayton.** On the distribution of the fishes of the Alleghany region of South Carolina, Georgia and Tennessee; with descriptions of new or little known species.—**Jordan, D: S.** A synopsis of the family catostomidæ; with bibliography.

— *and* C: H. **Gilbert.** Synopsis of the fishes of North America. [Bulletin of the U. S. national museum, no. 16]. Wash. 1883. O.　597+3

— — *Same. In* Smithsonian misc. 506 : R4 v24

— — Descriptions of 19 new species of fishes from the bay of Panama. *In* U. S. fish com. bulletin, v. 1.　*in* 639 : D

— — Review of the siluroid fishes found on the Pacific coast of tropical America, with descriptions of new species. *In* U. S. fish com. bulletin, v. 2.　*in* 639 : D

Gill, Theodore N: Catalogue of the fishes of the east coast of North America; with bibliography. *In* U. S. fish com. report, v. 1.
　in 639 : D

— *Same.* Wash. 1875. O. *In* Smithsonian misc., v. 14.　506 : R4 v14

Goode, G: Brown. Catalogue of the fishes of the Bermudas. Wash. 1876. O. *In* Smithsonian misc.　506 : R4 v13

— Materials for a history of the sword-fish. Ill. *In* U. S. fish com. report, v. 8.　*in* 639 : D

— The carangoid fishes of the U. S. *In* U. S. fish com. bulletin, v. 1.　*in* 639 : D

Gill, Theodore N: Natural and economical history of the gourami, Osphromenus goramy. *In* U. S. fish com. report, v. 2.　*in* 639 : D

Suckley, G: Monograph of the genus salmo, [1861]. *In* U. S. fish com. report, v. 2.
　in 639 : D

United States. *Fish commission.* [Memoirs upon some of the important fishes of the U. S.] *In* Report of the com., v. 1, 5, 9. 10.
　in 639 : D

Contents. V. 1. **Baird,** Spencer F. The scup, *Stenotomus argyrops;* The blue fish. *Pomatomus saltatrix.* 5. **Goode,** G. Brown. The natural and economical history of the amer. menhaden, *Brevoortia;* ill. 9. **Goode,** G. Brown. J. W. Collins *and others.* Materials for a history of the mackerel fishery, ill. 10. **Collins,** J. W. History of the tile-fish, *Lopholatilus chamæleonticeps,* ill.

Jordan, D: Starr. A catalogue of the fishes of the fresh waters of North America. *In* U. S. geol. survey of the terr., Hayden; Bulletin, v. 4.　*in* 557.5 : D

Girard, C: Contributions to the natural history of the fresh water fishes of North America:

A monograph of the cottoids. Ill. Wash. 1851. Q. *In* Smithsonian contributions.
      506 : R3 v3

Milner, James W. Notes on the grayling of North America. *In* U. S. fish com. report, v. 2.   *in* **639 : D**

Hay, O. P. On a collection of fishes from the lower Mississippi valley. *In* U. S. fish com. bulletin, v. 2.   *in* **639 : D**

Note. For artificial fish-culture and allied branches of industry, see under Fishing, cl. 639.

Amphibians and reptiles.

Cope, E: Drinker. Check-list of north amer. batrachia and reptilia; with a systematic list of the higher groups and an essay on geographical distribution. based on the specimens contained in the U. S. national museum. Wash. 1875. O. *In* Smithsonian misc.   **506 : R4 v13**

Mivart, St. G: The common frog. (Nature ser.) Ill. Lond. 1874. D.   **597.1 : 1**

Wyman, Jeffries. Anatomy of the nervous system of Rana pipiens. Ill. Wash. 1853. Q. *In* Smithsonian contributions.
      506 : R3 v5

Figuier, Guillaume L: Reptiles. *In his* Reptiles and birds.   **598 : 18**

Baird, Spencer Fullerton, *and* C: Girard. Catalogue of north american reptiles in the museum of the Smithsonian institution, pt. 1 : Serpents. Wash. 1853. O. *In* Smithsonian misc.   **506 : R4 v2**

Mitchell, S: Weir. Researches upon the venom of the rattlesnake ; with an investigation of the anatomy and physiology of the organs concerned. Ill. Wash. 1860. Q. *In* Smithsonian contributions.   **506 : R3 v12**

— *and* G: R. **Morehouse.** Researches on the anatomy and physiology of respiration in the chelonia. Ill. Wash. 1863. Q. *In* Smithsonian contributions. **506 : R3 v13**

Coues, Elliott, *and* H. C. **Yarrow.** Notes on the herpetology of Dakota and Montana. *In* U. S. geol. survey of the terr., Hayden ; Bulletin, v. 4.   *in* **557.5 : D**

Birds.

Giebel, Christoph Gottfried. Nomenclator sämmtlicher gattungen und arten der vögel, nebst synonymen und geographischer verbreitung [to 1876 incl.] *In his* Thesaurus ornithologiæ.   **16 : L**

Baird, Spencer Fullerton. Arrangement of families of birds, adopted provisionally by the Smithsonian inst. Wash. 1866. O. *In* Smithsonian misc.   **506 : R4 v8**

Buckland, Francis Trevelyan, W: C: **Linnæus Martin,** W: **Kidd,** *and others.* Birds and bird-life. Lond. *n. d.* S.   **598 : 6**

Figuier, Guillaume L: Reptiles and birds ; a popular account of their various orders, with a description of the habits and economy of the most interesting. From the french ; new ed., ed. by Parker Gillmore. Lond. [1882]. D.   **598 : 18**

Harting, James Edmund. Sketches of bird-life from twenty years' observations of their habits. Lond. 1883. O.   **598 : 22**

Church, Ella Rodman. Birds and their ways. Ill. Phila. [1884]. S.   **x 598 : 23**

Kirby, Mary *and* Elizabeth. Stories about birds of land and water. Ill. 4th ed. Lond. *n. d.* O.   **x 598 : 14**

Wood, J: G: My feathered friends. Ill. Lond. *n. d.* D.   **598 : 16**

Guernsey, Lucy Ellen. Jenny and the birds. [*Anon.*] Phila. [1860]. S.   **x 598 : 17**

Bechstein, J: Matthäus. Cage and chamber birds ; their natural history, habits, food, diseases, management and modes of capture. Tr. from the german ; with considerable add. on structure, migration and economy, compiled from various sources by H. G. Adams, incorporating the whole of Sweet's British warblers. Ill. Lond. 1853. D.   **598 : 5**

— Chamber and cage birds ; their management, habits, diseases, breeding and methods of taking them. Tr. from the last german ed. of dr. Bechstein's Chamber birds, by W. E. Shuckard. Rev. and partly re-written, and the points of show birds described by G: J. Barneby. Lond. *n. d.* D. **598 : 5**

Mudie, Robert. The feathered tribes of the British Islands. 4th ed., rev. by W. C. L. Martin. Ill. Lond. 1854. 2 v. S. **598 : 10**

Morris, Francis Orpen. A history of british birds. Lond. 1866-68. 6 v. Q. **598 : R1**

— A natural history of the nests and eggs of british birds. Lond. 1867. 3 v. Q.
    598 : R2

Stannard, H: Outdoor common birds ; their habits and general characteristics. Ill. Lond. *n. d.* D.   **598 : 11**

Ruskin, J: Love's meinie ; lectures on greek and english birds, given before the university of Oxford. N. Y. 1873. D. **598 : 25**

Lloyd, Llewellyn. The game birds and wild fowl of Sweden and Norway ; with an account of the seals and salt-water fishes of those countries. 2d ed., ill. Lond. 1867. Q.   **598 : R3**

Coues, Elliott. Check-list of north american birds. 2d ed., rev. to date, and entirely re-written under the dir. of the author ; with a dictionary of the etymology, orthography and orthoëpy of the scientific names, the concordance of previous lists, and a catalogue of his ornithological publications. Bost. 1882. O. **598 : R19**

— Key to north american birds ; containing a concise account of every species of living and fossil bird, at present known, from the continent north of the Mexican and U. S. boundary. Ill. Salem. 1872. Q.
    598 : 13

— *Same,* including Greenland. 2d ed. revised to date and entirely rewritten ; with which are incorporated General ornithology ; an outline of the structure and classification of birds,—and Field ornithology ; a manual of collecting, preparing and preserving birds. Ill. Bost. 1884. **598 : R13**

Contents. Historical preface.—Pt. 1. Field ornithology. — Pt. 2. General ornithology. — Pt. 3. Systematic synopsis of north american birds. — Pt. 4. Systematic synopsis of the fossil birds of North America.—Index.

x denotes books specially adapted for children.

Baird, Spencer Fullerton. Catalogue of north-american birds, chiefly in the museum of the Smithsonian institution. Wash. 1859. O. *In* Smithsonian misc.   **506 : R4 v2**

— Review of birds in the Smithsonian museum of the Smithsonian inst., pt. 1: North and middle America. Ill. Wash. 1864–66. O. *In* Smithsonian misc.   **506 : R4 v12**

Audubon, J: James. The birds of America; from drawings made in the U. S. and their territories. N. Y. [1870]. 8 v. Q.   **598 : R15**

Wilson, Alexander, *and* C: Lucien Jules Laurent **Bonaparte**, *prince de Canino.* American ornithology, or The natural history of the birds of the U. S. The illustrative notes and life of Wilson by sir W: Jardine. Lond. *n. d.* 3 v. O.   **598 : P21**

Gentry, T: G. Nests and eggs of birds of the U. S. Ill. Phila. [1884]. Q.   **598 : R24**

Brewer, T: Mayo. North american oölogy; pt. 1: Raptores and fissirostres. Ill. Wash. 1857. Q. *In* Smithsonian contributions.   **506 : R3 v11**

Dixon, C: Rural bird life; essays on ornithology, with instructions for preserving objects relating to that science. Pref. by Elliott Coues. Ill. Bost. [1880]. O.   **598 : 9**

Baily, W: L. Our own birds; a familiar natural history of the birds of the U. S.; rev. and ed. by E: D. Cope. Phila. 1878. D.   **598 : 4**

Cassin, J: Illustrations of the birds of California, Texas, Oregon, British and Russian America; intended to contain descriptions and figures of all north american birds, not given by former american authors, and a synopsis of north american ornithology, 1853–55. Phila. 1856. O.   **598+7**

Ridgway, Robert. Monograph of the genus leucosticte Swains., or gray-crowned purple finches. *In* U. S. geol. survey of the terr., Hayden; Bulletin, v. 1.   *in* **557.5 : D**

— Outlines of a natural arrangement of the falconidæ. *In the same,* v. 1.   *in* **557.5 : D**

— Studies of the amer. falconidæ. *In the same,* v. 1, 2.   *in* **557.5 : D**

— Studies of the american herodiones. *In the same,* v. 4.   *in* **557.5 : D**

Elliot, Daniel Giraud. A classification and synopsis of the trochilidæ. Ill. Wash. 1879. Q. *In* Smithsonian contributions.   **506 : R3 v23**

— List of described species of humming birds. Wash. 1879. O. *In* Smithsonian misc.   **506 : R4 v16**

Stearns, Winfrid A. New England bird life; a manual of New England ornithology; rev. and ed. from the ms. by Elliott Coues. Bost. 1881, 1883. 2 v. O.   **598 : 12**
Contents. V. 1. Oscines. 2. Non-oscine passeres, birds of prey, game and water-birds.

King, F. H. Economic relations of our birds. Ill. *In* Geology of Wis.   **557.5 : R3 v1**

Gibbs, Morris. Annotated list of the birds of Michigan. *In* U. S. geol. survey of the terr., Hayden; Bulletin, v. 5.   *in* **557.5 : D**

Ridgway, Robert. Ornithology [of the country along the 40th parallel.] (U. S. geol. expl.

40th par., King; Report, v. 4.) Wash. 1877. Q.   *in* **557.5 : D**

Coues, Elliott. Birds of the northwest; a handbook of the ornithology of the regions drained by the Missouri river and its tributaries. (U. S. geol. survey of the terr., Hayden; Miscel. pub., no. 3.) Wash. 1874. O.   *in* **557.5 : D**

— Birds of the Colorado valley; a repository of scientific and popular information concerning north american ornithology, pt. 1: Passeres to laniidæ. Bibliographical app. and ill. (U. S. geol. survey of the terr., Hayden; Miscel. pub., no. 11.) Wash. 1878. O.   *in* **557.5 : D**

— Field notes of birds observed in Dakota and Montana along the 49th parallel during 1873 and 1874. *In* U. S. geol. survey of the terr., Hayden; Bulletin, v. 4. *in* **557.5 : D**

McChesney, C: E. Notes on the birds of Fort Sisseton, Dakota. *In* U. S. geol. survey of the terr., Hayden; Bulletin, v. 5.
   in **557.5 : D**

Sennett, G: B. Notes on the ornithology of the lower Rio Grande of Texas, from observations made during 1877; ed., with annot., by Elliott Coues. *In* U. S. geol. survey of the terr., Hayden; Bulletin, v. 4.
   in **557.5 : D**

— Same. Observ. made during 1878. *In the same.*   *in* **557.5 : D**

Hoffman, W. J. Annotated list of the birds of Nevada. *In* U. S. geol. survey of the terr., Hayden; Bulletin, v. 6.   *in* **557.5 : D**

Lawrence, G: N. Birds of southwestern Mexico, collected by Francis E. Sumichrast. Wash. 1875. O. *In* Smithsonian misc.   **506 : R4 v13**

Nelson, E. W. Birds of Bering Sea and the Arctic ocean. Ill. *In* Cruise of the revenue str. Corwin.   *in* **919.8 : D**

Mammals.

Gill, Theodore N: Arrangement of the families of mammals, with analytical tables. Wash. 1872. O. *In* Smithsonian misc.   **506 : R4 v11**

Allen, Joel Asaph. The geographical distribution of the mammalia, considered in relation to the principal ontological regions of the earth, and the laws that govern the distribution of animal life. *In* U. S. geol. survey of the terr., Hayden; Bulletin, v. 4.   *in* **557.5 : D**

Mivart, St. G: The cat; an introduction to the study of backboned animals. especially mammals. Ill. N. Y. 1881. O.   **599 : 3**

Rennie, James. Natural history of quadrupeds. Ill. [*Anon.*] N. Y. 1847. S.   **599 : 4**

Figuier, Guillaume L: Mammalia; their various forms and habits popularly ill. by typical species. Adapted by E. Perceval Wright. Ill. Lond. [1875]. D.   **599 : 7**

Reid, Mayne, *and others.* Stories about animals. N. Y. *n. d.* D.   **x 599 : 10**

Miller, Olive Thorne, (*Gwynfryn*). Friends in fur and feathers, by Gwynfryn. Ill. 7th ed. Lond. 1882. D.   **x 599 : 6**

x denotes books specially adapted for children.

Miller, Lydia Falconer, *Mrs.* Hugh. Stories of the dog and his cousins, the wolf, the jackal and the hyæna. Lond. [1877.] S.
                      x 599 : 9
— Stories of the cat and her cousins, the lion, the tiger and the leopard. Lond. 1880. S.
                      x 599 : 8
Baker, Harriet Newell, *born* Woods, (*Mrs. Madeline Leslie*). Georgey's menagerie : the lion. Bost. *n. d.* T.   **x 599 : 11**
Andersson, C: J: The lion and the elephant ; ed. by L. Lloyd. Lond. 1873. O.   **599 : 5**
Rennie, James. Natural history : The elephant as he exists in a wild state, and as he has been made subservient in peace and in war to the purposes of man. [*Anon.*] N. Y. 1844. S.   **599 : 2**
Audubon, J: James, *and* J: **Bachman.** The quadrupeds of North America. Ill. N. Y. 1849. 3 v. Q.   **599 : R1**
Strong, Moses. List of mammals of Wisconsin. *In* Geology of Wis.   **557.5 : R3 v1**
McChesney, C: E. Notes on the mammals of Fort Sisseton, Dakota. *In* U. S. geol. survey of the terr., Hayden ; Bulletin, v. 4.
                    in **557.5 : D**
Coues, Elliott, *and* Joel Asaph **Allen.** Monographs of north american rodentia. Ill. (U. S. geol. survey of the terr., Report, v. 11). Wash. 1877. Q. *in* **557.5 : D**
   Contents. **Coues,** E. Muridæ.—**Allen,** J. A. Leporidæ; Hystricidæ; Lagomyidæ; Castoroididæ; Castoridæ.—**Coues,** E. Zapodiæ; Saccomyidæ; Haplodontidæ; Geomyidæ.—**Allen,** J. A. Sciuridæ; Synoptical list of the fossil rodentia of North Amer.—**Gill,** Theodore, *and* E. **Coues.** Material for a bibliography of north amer. mammals.—Index.
Coues, Elliott. Abstracts of results of study of the genera geomys and thomomys ; with the cranial and dental characters of geomyidæ. *In* **Powell,** J. W. Report of the exploration of the Colorado river of the west.   *in* **917.5 : D**

   x denotes books specially adapted for children.

Trouessart, E. L. Revision of the genus sciurus ; tr., with notes, by Elliott Coues. *In* U. S. geol. survey of the terr., Hayden ; Bulletin, v. 6.   *in* **557.5 : D**
Allen, Joel Asaph. Synonymatic list of the american sciuri or arboreal squirrels. *In* U. S. geol. survey of the terr., Hayden ; Bulletin, v. 4.   *in* **557.5 : D**
Gill, Theodore N: Synopsis of insectivorous mammals. *In* U. S. geol. survey of the terr., Hayden ; Bulletin, v. 1. *in* **557.5 : D**
Coues, Elliott. Precursory notes on american insectivorous mammals, with descriptions of new species. *In* U. S. geol. survey of the terr., Hayden ; Bulletin, v. 3.
                    in **557.5 : D**
Allen, Hermann. Monographs of the bats of North America. Ill. Wash. 1864. O. *In* Smithsonian misc.   **506 : R4 v7**
Allen, Joel Asaph. History of north american pinnipeds ; a monograph of the walruses, sea-lions, sea-bears and seals of North America. (U. S. geol. survey of the terr., Hayden ; Miscel. pub., no. 12.) Wash. 1880. O.   *in* **557.5 : D**
— On the coatis, genus nasua, Storr. *In* U. S. geol. survey of the terr., Hayden ; Bulletin, v. 5.   *in* **557.5 : D**
Coues, Elliott. Fur-bearing animals ; a monograph of north amer. mustelidæ, in which an account of the wolverene, the martens or sables, the ermine, the mink and various other kinds of weasels, several species of skunks, the badger, the land and sea otters, and numerous exotic allies of these animals, is contributed to the History of north amer. mammals. Ill. (U. S. geol. survey of the terr., Hayden ; Miscel. pub., no. 8.) Wash. 1877. O.   *in* **557.5 : D**
Allen, Joel Asaph. On the species of the genus bassaris. *In* U. S. geol. survey of the terr., Hayden ; Bulletin, v. 5.   *in* **557.5 : D**
   Note. For works on the natural history of man, see class 573, col. 351.

VII. USEFUL ARTS.

1. In general.

1. General works and history.

(See also Natural science, cl. 500-509, col. 281-290.)

Potter, Alonzo. The principles of science, applied to the domestic and mechanic arts and to manufactures and agriculture ; with reflections on the progress of the arts and their influence on national welfare. Rev. ed. N. Y. 1847. D. **602 : 1**

Bigelow, Jacob. The useful arts, considered in connexion with the applications of science. N. Y. 1847. 2 v. D. **602 : 2**

Hazen, E: Popular technology, or Professions and trades. Ill. N. Y. 1846. 2 v. S. **604 : 2**

— The panorama of professions and trades, or Every man's book. Ill. Phila. 1841. D. **604 : 3**

Goodrich, S: Griswold, (*Peter Parley*). The book of trades, arts and professions, relative to food, clothing, shelter, travelling and ornament, for the use of the young, by Peter Parley. Lond. *n. d.* S. **x 604 : 4**

Moore, R. The universal assistant and complete mechanic ; containing over one million industrial facts, calculations, receipts, processes, trade secrets, rules, business forms, legal items, etc., in every occupation from the household to the manufactory. N. Y. 1880. D. **602 : 3**

Courtney, W. S. The farmers' and mechanics' manual, with many valuable tables for machinists, manufacturers, merchants, builders, engineers, masons, painters, plumbers, gardeners, accountants, etc. Rev. and enl. by G: Waring, jr. N. Y. 1880. D. **602 : 4**

* * *

Pictorial gallery of arts, The ; v. 1 : Useful arts. Lond. *n. d.* F. **609 : R5**
Note. V. 2 contains Fine arts.

Beckmann, J: A history of inventions, discoveries and origins. Tr. from the german by W: Johnston. 4th ed., rev. and enl. by W: Francis and J. W. Griffith. Lond. 1846. 2 v. D. **609 : 1**

Bakewell, F: C. Great facts ; a popular history and description of the most remarkable inventions during the present century. Ill. N. Y. 1860. D. **800 : 2**

Buch der erfindungen, gewerbe und industrien ; rundschau auf allen gebieten der gewerblichen arbeit, herausg. in verbindung mit

x denotes books specially adapted for children.

C. Birnbaum, C. Böttger, K. Gayer, Fr. Kohl, Fr. Luckenbacher, R. Ludwig, Oskar Mothes, dr. Regis, K. de Roth, Julius Zöllner und anderen. 6te aufl. Leipz. 1872-74. 6 v. O. **600+1**
Contents, see Deutscher katalog, p. 16.

Timbs, J: Wonderful inventions ; from the mariner's compass to the electric telegraph cable. Ill. Lond. [1876]. D. **609 : 2**

— *Same.* New ed., rev. and corr., with add. bringing down the subjects to the present time. Lond. 1882. D. **609 : 3**

Routledge, Robert. Discoveries and inventions of the 19th century. 5th ed. Ill. Lond. 1881. D. **609 : 4**
Contents. Introd.—Steam engines.—Iron.—Tools.—Railways.—Steam navigation.—Ships of war.—Fire-arms.—Torpedoes.—The Suez canal.—Sand.—Iron bridges.—Printing machines.—Hydraulic power.—Pneumatic dispatch.—Rock boring.—Light.—The spectroscope.—Sight.—Electricity.—The electric telegraph.—Light houses.—Photography.—Printing processes.—Recording instruments.—Aquaria.—Gold and diamonds.—New metals.—India-rubber and gutta-percha.—Anæsthetics.—Explosives.—Mineral combustibles.—Coal-gas.—Coal-tar colours.—The greatest discovery of the age.
Note. For annual records of inventions and industrial progress, see Natural science, cl. 505, col. 289.

Biedermann, F: K: Die erziehung zur arbeit ; eine forderung des lebens an die schule. 2te völlig umgearb. aufl. Leipz. 1883. O. **607 : 1**

Portig, Gustav. Die nationale bedeutung des kunstgewerbes. *In* Deutsche zeit- und streit-fragen. **304 : 15 v12**

Huber-Liebenau, Theodor v. Ueber das kunstgewerbe der alten und neuen zeit. *In* Deutsche zeit- und streit-fragen. **304 : 15 v9**

— Ueber den verfall des zunftthumes und dessen ersatz im deutschen gewerbewesen. *In* Deutsche zeit- und streit-fragen. **304 : 15 v8**

Kleinwächter, F: Zur reform der handwerksverfassung. *In* Deutsche zeit- und streit-fragen. **304 : 15 v4**

2. Dictionaries and cyclopedias.

Weale, J: A dictionary of terms used in architecture, building, engineering, mining, metallurgy, archæology, the fine arts, etc., with explanatory observations on various subjects connected with applied science and art ; ed. with add., by Robert Hunt. 5th ed., rev. and corr. [Weale's ser.] Lond. 1876. D. **603 : 10**

Ure, Andrew. A dictionary of arts, manufactures and mines; containing a clear exposition of their principles and practice. Repr. from the last corr. and enl. english ed. N. Y. 1856. 2 v. D.   **603 : 2**

— Dictionary of arts, manufactures and mines; containing a clear exposition of their principles and practice, [ed.] by Robert Hunt, assisted by F. W. Rudler and others. 7th ed. Ill. Lond. 1878. 4 v. O.   **603 : R1**
     Contents. V. 1. A–C. 2. D–I. 3. J–Z. 4. Supplement.

Spons' encyclopædia of the industrial arts, manufactures and commercial products; ed. by C: G. Warnford **Lock.** Lond. 1879–80. 5 v. Q.   **603 : R12**

Brelow, G., O: **Dammer** *and* Egbert **Hoyer.** Technologisches lexikon für gewerbtreibende und industrielle. Ill. Leipz. 1883. 2 v. D.   **603 : R13**
     Contents. **1. Dammer,** O: Chemische technologie. **2. Brelow,** G., *and* E. **Hoyer.** Mechanische technologie und maschinenkunde.

Appleton's dictionary of machines, mechanics, engine-work and engineering. Ill. N. Y. 1852. 2 v. Q.   **603 : R3**

Appletons' cyclopædia of applied mechanics; a dictionary of mechanical engineering and the mechanical arts, ill. with nearly 5000 engravings, ed. by Park Benjamin. N. Y. 1880. 2 v. Q.   **603 : R4**

Knight, E: H. American mechanical dictionary; a description of tools, instruments, machines, processes and engineering, history of inventions, general technological vocabulary and digest of mechanical appliances in science and the arts. Ill. N. Y. 1877. 3 v. Q.   **603 : R5**

— Knight's new mechanical dictionary; a description of tools, instruments, machines, processes and engineering, with indexical references to technical journals, 1876—1880. Ill. Bost. 1884. Q.   **603 : R6**

Knight, Cameron. The mechanician; a treatise on the construction and manipulation of tools, for the use and instruction of young engineers and scientific amateurs, comprising the arts of blacksmithing and forging, the construction and manufacture of hand tools, and the various methods of using and grinding them, the construction of machine tools and how to work them, machine fitting and erection, description of hand and machine processes, turning and screw cutting, principles of constructing and details of making and erecting steam engines, and the various details of setting out work incidental to the mechanical engineer's and machinist's art. Ill. 2d ed. Lond. 1879. O.   **603 : R11**

Cooley, Arnold James. Cyclopædia of practical receipts and collateral information in the arts, manufactures, professions and trades, incl. medicine, pharmacy, and domestic economy. 6th ed., rev. and partly rewritten by R: V. Tuson. Ill. N. Y. 1880. 2 v. O.   **603 : R8**

Dick, W: B. Encyclopædia of practical receipts and processes; containing over 6,400 receipts, embracing thorough information, in plain language, applicable to almost every possible industrial and domestic requirement. 3d ed. N. Y. 1880. O.
     603 : R7

3. Periodicals, societies and exhibitions.

Mechanic's magazine; v. 1, 2, 4—15, 17—27, aug. 1823—apr. 1836. Lond. 1823-36. O.
     605.2 : M

Appletons' mechanics' magazine and engineers' journal; ed. by Julius W. Adams; v. 1—3, jan. 1851—dec. 1853. Ill. N. Y. 1852-54. O. *and* Q.   **605.2 : M**
     Note. V. 3 ed. by T: Drew Stetson.

Greenough's american polytechnic journal; a new monthly periodical of science, mechanic arts and engineering; conducted by J. J. Greenough [and] C: G. Page; v. 3, 4. 1854. N. Y. [1854]. O.   **605 : M**

Scientific american; an illustrated journal of art, science and mechanics; v. 8, 10—39, 42—51, 53—65, sept. 1852—dec. 1884. N. Y. [1852-84]. F.   **605.2 : RM**
     Note. V. 15—65 are called New series, v. 1—51.

Scientific american supplement; v. 1—18, jan. 1876—dec. 1884. N. Y. 1876-84. F.
     605.2 : RM

Sanitary engineer, The; a journal of civil and military engineering, and public and private hygiene, conducted by H: C. Meyer; v. 7—10, dec. 1882—nov. 1884. N. Y. 1882-84. F.   **605.1 : RM**

Van Nostrand's eclectic engineering magazine; v. 1—3, jan. 1869—dec. 1884. N. Y. 1869-84. O.   **605.2 : M**
     Note. From v. 21 "eclectic" is dropped from the title.

Association of engineering societies. Journal; v. 3, no. 12, oct. 1884. N. Y. 1884. O.
     605.2 : Pam

Amateur work, illustrated; ed. by the author of "Every man his own mechanic" [F. Y.]; v. 1—3. Ill. Lond. *n. d.* 3 v. Q.
     605+6

     *   *   *

Society of arts, manufactures and commerce. Lectures on the results of the [international] exhibition [in London, 1852], delivered at the suggestion of prince Albert. Lond. 1852. D.   **606 : 2**
     Contents. **Whewell,** W: The general bearing of the great exhibition on the progress of art and science.—**De la Beche,** *Sir* H: T. Mining, quarrying and metallurgical processes and products.—**Owen,** R: On the raw materials from the animal kingdom.—**Bell,** J. Chemical and pharmaceutical processes and products.—**Playfair,** L. On the chemical principles involved in the manufactures of the exhibition, as indicating the necessity of industrial instruction.—**Lindley,** J: On substances used as food.—**Solly,** E: The vegetable substances used in the arts and manufactures in relation to commerce generally.—**Willis,** R. On machines and tools for working in metal, wood and other materials.—**Glaisher,** J. Philosophical instruments and processes.—**Hensman,** H: On civil engineering and machinery generally.—**Royle,** J. F. The arts and manufactures of India.—**Washington,** J: On the progress of naval architecture, as indicating the necessity for scientific education, and for the classification of ships and of steam-engines; also on life-boats.

Greeley, Horace, *ed.* Art and industry, as represented in the exhibition at the Crystal palace, New York, 1853-4; showing the progress and state of the various useful and esthetic pursuits. From the New York tribune. N. Y. 1853. D.   **606 : 1**

Oncken, A: Die Wiener weltausstellung 1873. *In* Deutsche zeit- und streit-fragen.
     304 : 15 v2

United States. *Centennial commission.* International exhibition, 1876 ; Official catalogue. Phila. 1876. O.　*in* 606 : D

— — *Same.* Department of art. 3d ed. Phila 1876. D.　*in* 606 : D

— — Reports and awards, ed. by Francis A. Walker. Phila. 1878. 6 v. O.　*in* 606 : D

United States centennial exhibition. Norwegian special catalogue for the international exhibition at Philadelphia, 1876. Christiania. 1876. O.　*in* 606 : D

Milwaukee's industrial exposition and grand union dairy fair of 1882, with introd. sketches of the foundation and development of the Cream city, her commercial and industrial resources, future prospects, etc. Milw. 1883. O.　606 : Pam

San Francisco, Mechanics' institute. Report of the 18th, 19th industrial exhibition held at the Mechanics' pavilion from the 11th of sept. to the 13th of oct. 1883, [and] 5th of aug. to 6th of sept. 1884. San Francisco. 1884, 1885. O.　606.8 : 1

4. Patents.

Jannasch, R. Der musterschutz und die gewerbepolitik des deutschen reiches ; gekrönte preisschrift. *In* Deutsche zeit- und streit-fragen.　304 : 15 v2

United States. *Patent office.* List of patents for inventions and designs issued by the U. S. from 1790 to 1847, with the patent laws and notes of decisions of the courts of the U. S. for the same period ; comp. and pub. under the dir. of Edmund Burke. Wash. 1847. O.　608 : D

— — Annual report of the commissioner of patents, 1847—1883. Wash. 1848-84. 67 v. O. *and* Q.　608 : D
Note. The vols. up to and including 1871 contain also specifications and drawings, which, since that time, have been published in the Official gazette.

— — Official gazette of the U. S. patent office ; v. 1—29, 1872—1884. Wash. 1875-84. 29 v. Q.　608 : D

— — Subject-matter index of patents for inventions, brevets d'invention, granted in France from 1791 to 1876 incl. Tr., comp. and pub. under authority of the commissioner of patents. Wash. 1883. Q. 608 : D

2. Medicine and Surgery.

1. In general.

Dunglison, Robley. Medical lexicon ; a dictionary of medical science, containing an explanation of the various subjects and terms of anatomy, physiology, pathology, hygiene, therapeutics, medical chemistry, pharmacology, pharmacy, surgery, obstetrics, medical jurisprudence and dentistry, notices of climate and of mineral waters, formulæ for officinal, empirical and dietetic preparations, with the accentuation and etymology of the terms and the french and other synonyms. New ed., enl. and rev. by R: J. Dunglison. Phila. 1874. O.　610 : R1

Thomas, Joseph. A comprehensive medical dictionary ; containing the pronunciation, etymology and signification of the terms made use of in medicine and the kindred sciences. App., comprising a complete list of all the more important articles of the materia medica, arranged according to their medicinal properties, also an explanation of the latin terms and phrases occurring in anatomy, pharmacy, etc., together with the necessary directions for writing latin prescriptions, etc. Phila. 1874. O.　610 : 18

Quain, R:, ed. A dictionary of medicine, including general pathology, general therapeutics, hygiene and the diseases peculiar to women and children, by various writers. N. Y. 1883. O.　610 : R2

Hippokrates, and Claudius Galenus. The writings of Hippocrates and Galen, epitomized from the original latin, tr. by J: Redman Coxe. Phila. 1846. O.　610+4

Holmes, Oliver Wendell. Border lines of knowledge in some provinces of medical science ;

Holmes, Oliver Wendell.—*Continued.* an introductory lecture del. before the medical class of Harvard university, nov. 6, 1861. Bost. 1862. D.　610 : 5

— Currents and counter-currents in medical science ; with other addresses and essays. Bost. 1861. D.　610 : 6
Contents. Currents and counter-currents in medical science. — Homœopathy and its kindred delusions.—Some more recent views on homœopathy.— Puerperal fever as a private pestilence.—The position and prospects of the medical student.—Mechanism of vital actions.—Valedictory address.

— Medical essays, 1842-1882. Bost. 1883. D.　610 : 13
Contents. Homœopathy and its kindred delusions. —The contagiousness of puerperal fever.—Currents and counter-currents in medical science.—Borderlines of knowledge in some provinces of medical science.—Scholastic and bedside teaching.—The medical profession in Massachusetts.—The young practitioner. — Medical libraries. — Some of my early teachers.

Eddy, Mary Baker Glover. Science and health ; with a key to the scriptures. 6th ed., rev. Bost. 1883. 2 v. D.　610 : 16

*　*　*

Fort, G: F. Medical economy during the middle ages ; a contribution to the history of european morals, from the time of the roman empire to the close of the 14th century. N. Y. 1883. O.　610+14

History and education.

Hecker, Justus F: C: The epidemics of the middle ages. From the german, tr. by B. G. Babington. 3d ed. completed by the author's treatise on Child-pilgrimages. Lond. 1859. O.　610 : 15

De Foe, Daniel. History of the plague of London. *In his* Novels and misc. works.
                                              820.2 : 8 v5

Keating, J. M. A history of the yellow fever : The yellow fever epidemic of 1878, in Memphis, Tenn.; embracing a complete list of the dead, the names of the doctors and nurses employed, names of all who contributed money or means, and the names and history of the Howards, together with other data, and lists of the dead elsewhere. Memphis, Tenn. 1879. Q.
                                              614+29

United States. *Army.* Statistical report on the sickness and mortality, comp. from the records of the surgeon-general's office, from jan. 1839 to jan. 1855 ; prepared by R: H. Coolidge. Wash. 1856. Q.   *in* **610 : D**

— *Same.* From jan. 1855 to jan. 1860. Wash. 1860. Q.   *in* **610 : D**

— *Surgeon general.* The medical and surgical history of the war of the rebellion, 1861—1865 ; prepared, in accordance with acts of congress, under the dir. of surgeon gen. Joseph K. Barnes. Wash. 1870–83. 3 pts. in 5 v. F.   *in* **610 : D**
   Contents. Pt. 1, v. 1. Medical history, prep. by Joseph Janvier **Woodward**; v. 2. Surgical history, prep. by G: A. **Otis**. Pt. 2, v. 1. Medical hist., prep. by J: J. **Woodward**; v. 2. Surgical hist., prep. by G: A. **Otis**. Pt. 3, v. 1, *not pub.*; v. 2. Surgical hist., prep. by G: A. **Otis** and D. L. **Huntington.**

— *Provost-marshal-general's bureau.* Statistics, medical and anthropological, derived from records of the examination for military service in the armies of the U. S. during the l_{ate} war of the rebellion, of over a million recruits, drafted men, substitutes and enrolled men, compiled, under the dir. of the sec. of war, by J. H. **Baxter.** Wash. 1875. 2 v. F.   *in* **610 : D**

— *War dep't.* A report on barracks and hospitals, with descriptions of military posts. Ill. (Surgeon-general's off. Circular no. 4). Wash. 1870. Q.   *in* **610 : D**

— — A report on the hygiene of the U. S. army, with descriptions of military posts. Maps and ill. (Surgeon-general's off. Circular no. 8). Wash. 1875. Q.   *in* **610 : D**

Herdegen, Robert. Bilder aus der geschichte des ärztlichen standes ; ein für laien bestimmter vortrag, gehalten im Vereine Germania zu Milwaukee am 24. jan. 1884. Milw. 1884. O.   **610+17**

Green, S: Abbott. History of medicine in Massachusetts ; a centennial address, del. before the Mass. medical society at Cambridge, june 7, 1881. Bost. 1881. O.
                                              610+10

Hardwicke, Herbert Junius. Medical education and practice in all parts of the world. Phila. 1880. O.   **607.1 : 1**

Illinois state board of health. Medical education and the regulation of the practice of medicine in the U. S. and Canada. 2d ed., rev. and corr. to march 1, 1884. Chicago. 1884. O.   **607.1+4**

Bischoff, Theodor L: W: v. Das studium und die ausübung der medicin durch frauen. München. 1872. O.   **607.1 : 2**

Schwerin, L: Die zulassung der frauen zur ausübung des ärztlichen berufes. *In* Deutsche zeit- und streit-fragen.   **304 : 15 v9**

Thompson, W. G. Training schools for nurses ; with notes on 22 schools. N. Y. 1883. T.
                                              607.1 : 3

Flint, Austin. Medical ethics and etiquette ; the code of ethics adopted by the American medical association, with commentaries. N. Y. 1883. D.   **610 : 12**

Boards of health.

United States. *National board of health.* [1st–4th] annual report, 1879–1882. Ill. Wash. 1879–83. 4 v. O.   *in* **606.1 : D**
   Contents of app., being reports and papers:
   1879. Organization.—Havana yellow-fever commission.—**Remsen**, Ira. Organic matter in the air.—**Diehl**, C. Lewis. Deteriorations, adulterations and substitutions of drugs.—**Law**, James. Diseases of domestic animals; **Verdi**, Tullio S. Cattle disease in relation to the health of man, and in political economy.—**Waring**, G: E., *jr.* Gauging of sewers.—Schedule of questions for sanitary surveys.—Sanitary survey of Memphis, Tenn.—**Bailhache**, P. H. Hygiene of the mercantile marine, with recommendations.—**Harris**, E. Malignant diphtheria in northern Vermont.—Ports and cities of the Atlantic coast and Gulf of Mexico.—Sanitary regulations, quarantines, etc.
   1880. Havana yellow fever commission.—**Remsen**, Ira. Organic matter in the air, *continued.*—**Sternberg**, G: M. Disinfectants.—**Smart**, C: Deteriorations and adulterations of food and drugs.—**Waring**, G: E., *jr.* Gauging of public sewers, *continued.*—**Wood**, H. C., *and* H: F. **Formad.** Effect of inoculating the lower animals with diphtheritic exudation.—**Sternberg**, G: M. Microscopical examination of suspended particles found in the atmosphere. —**Woodward**, J. J. Pathological histology of yellow fever.—**Abbe**, Cleveland. Climate and diseases. — Sanitary survey of Memphis, Tenn. — **Smart**, C: Water-supply of New Orleans and Mobile. —**Chancellor**, C. N. Sanitary survey of selected portions of Baltimore, Md.—Rep. of committee on the nomenclature of diseases and on vital statistics.—**Brown**, Harvey E. Quarantine on the southern coast; extract. — **Bemiss**, S. M. Sanitary work in New Orleans.—**Mitchell**, R. W. Mississippi river inspection service.
   1881. **Wood**, H. C., *and* H. F. **Formad.** Diphtheria.—**Sternberg**, G: M. Experimental investigations relating to the etiology of the malarial fevers. — **Remsen**, Ira. Carbonic oxide as a source of danger to health in apartments heated by cast-iron furnaces or stoves.—**Hering**, Rudolph. Results of an examination made in 1880 of several sewerage works in Europe: with bibliography.—**Pumpelly**, Raphael, *and* G: A. **Smyth.** The relation of soils to health: Filtering capacity of soils, pt. 1.—Quarantine at Newport, R. I.: Ship Island station; Sapello station.—**Bemiss**, S. M. Yellow fever at Key West, Fla.—**Reilly**, F. W. Mississippi river inspection service.—**Chaillé**, Stanford E. Inspection service at New Orleans.—Conference on small-pox.
   1882. **Wood**, H. C., *and* H. F. **Formad.** Memoir on the relations of diphtheria to septic diseases.—**Waring**, G: E., *jr.*, E. S. **Philbrick**, *and* E. W. **Bowditch.** On the siphonage of traps.—**Bowditch**, E. W. Sanitary condition of summer resorts.—**Mallet**, J. W. Results of an investigation as to the chemical methods in use for the determination of organic matter in potable water: with a suppt. report by C: **Smart.** — **Billings**, J: S. The registration of vital statistics.—Reports of sup'ts of Ship Island refuge station; Sapelo refuge station; Mississippi river inspection service; New Orleans inspection service. —**Smith**, Stephen. The maritime sanitary service of the U. S., and the relations of national and state authorities.—Inspection of immigrants.—**Pumpelly**, Raphael, *and* G: A. **Smyth.** Filtering capacity of soils, pt. 2.

Massachusetts *state.* *Board of health.* 1st—11th annual report, june 1869—june 1879. Ill. Bost. 1870–79. 11 v. in 9. O. **606.1 : D101**
   Contain, beside the general reports of the board on important topics relating to public and private health, the following reports of special investigations:
   Meat supply, etc.: Derby, G: Slaughtering for

the Boston market (1870); Slaughtering, bone-boiling and fat-melting (1872).—**Merriam**, J. N. Report of the Butchers' slaughtering and melting assoc. (1879); The Brighton abattoir (1874, 1875). — **Folsom**, C: F. Our meat-supply and public health (1875).—**Hoadley**, J: C. The transportation of live-stock (1875).—Report of the evidence, etc., before the state board of health, in the case of the city of Cambridge vs. Niles bros. [for polluting water-supply by slaughtering operations] (1879).

Food and drink: Nichols, A. H. On the use of milk from cows affected with foot-and-mouth disease (1871).—**Nichols**, A. H., and J. F. **Babcock**. The adulteration of milk (1873).—**Hill**, H: B. The adulterations and impurities of food (1872, 1873).—**Oliver**, H. K. Character of substances used for flavoring articles of food and drink (1873).—**Derby**, G: The food of the people of Mass. (1873).—**Nichols**, W: R. The filtration of potable water (1878).

Public health, hygiene, etc. Report on the sale of poisons (1870). — **Derby**, G: The prevention of disease (1870).—**Derby**, G:, and F. W. **Draper**. H₂ealth of minors employed in factories (1871).—**Nichols**, A. H. The effects on health of the use of sewing-machines, moved by foot-power (1872). — **Draper**, F. W. Arsenic in certain green colors (1872); The homes for the poor in our cities (1873).—**Bowditch**, H: I. Houses for the people (1871).—**Plunkett**, Mrs. T. F. Some farm-houses, and some mistaken ways of living in them (1874).—**Adams**, J. F. A. The health of the farmers of Mass. (1874); Cremation and burial, an examination of their relative advantages (1875).—**Jarvis**, E: Political economy of health (1874). — **Boardman**, W. E. The value of health to the state (1875). — **Bowditch**, H: I. Sanitary hints (1876). — **Ames**, A., jr. The work of local boards of health (1874). — **Draper**, F. W. Registration of prevalent diseases (1876).—**Folsom**, C: F. Registration of deaths and diseases (1877). — **Jarvis**, E: Infant mortality (1873). — **Bowditch**, H: I. Some of the causes or antecedents of consumption (1873); Preventive medicine and the physician of the future (1874); Inebriate asylums or hospitals (1875); The use and abuse of intoxicating liquors, correspondence and analysis (1871, 1872). — **Oliver**, F. E. The use and abuse of opium (1872).—**Aldrich**, P. E. Beer-shops and prohibitory laws (1873).—**Derby**, G: Hospitals (1874).—**Adams**, J. F. A. Cottage hospitals (1878).—**Jeffries**, B. Joy. Dangers from color blindness (1878).—**Bowditch**, H. P. The growth of children (1877, 1879).—**Hitchcock**, E: Physical education in Amherst college (1879).

Air, ventilation, etc.: **Derby**, G: Air and some of its impurities (1871).—**Nichols**, W: R. Composition of the air of the ground atmosphere (1875).—**Cowles**, E. A contribution to the study of ventilation (1874). —**Martin**, A. C. Ventilation of school houses (1871). —**Winsor**, F. School hygiene (1874).—**Lincoln**, D. F. Sanitation of public schools in Mass. (1878).—**Fisher**; T. W. Ventilation of railroad cars, with chemical analyses of the air in cars by W: R. Nichols (1875).—**Winsor**, F. Coal-gas from heating-apparatus (1879).

Water supply, sewerage, etc.: **Derby**, G: Mill-dams and other water obstructions, effect on health (1872).—**Derby**, G:, and W: R. **Nichols**. Poisoning by lead pipe (1871); Pollution of Mystic-Pond water (1871); Sewerage, sewage, the pollution of streams, the water-supply of towns (1873).—**Nichols**, W: R. On the present condition of certain rivers of Mass., together with considerations touching the water-supply of towns (1874).—**Boardman**, W. E. On the use of zinced or galvanized iron for the storage or conveyance of drinking-water (1874).—**French**, H. F. Drainage for health (1873).—**Clarke**, E. C. Common defects in house-drains (1879).—**Kirkwood**, J. P. The pollution of rivers, with general observations on water-supplies and sewerage (1876).—**Winsor**, F. The water-supply, drainage and sewerage of Mass. from the sanitary point of view (1876).—**Folsom**, C: F. The disposal of sewage (1876, 1877); Pollution of streams (1877); Surface-drainage of the metropolitan district [of Boston] (1876). — **Philbrick**, E. S. Defects in house-drainage and their remedies (1876). — **Bowditch**, H: I. Convalescent homes and the sewage question (1871).—Drainage and health; sewerage and the pollution of streams, incl. the draught of a law (1878).

Diseases, insanity, etc.: **Nichols**, A. H. Report on an outbreak of intestinal disorder, attributable to the contamination of drinking-water by means of impure ice (1876).—**Johnson**, A. H. Scarlet fever (1878).—**White**, J: C. Vegetable parasites, and

Massachusets state. Board of health.—*Continued.*
the diseases caused by their growth upon man (1878). [Each year contains also reports on the health of towns; epidemics of small-pox, diphtheria, typhoid fever, cerebro-spinal meningitis, etc., in various localities, and by different authors].—**Folsom**, C: F. Disease of the mind (1871).—**Jarvis**, E: Proper provision for the insane (1872).—**Clouston**, T. S. Hospital homes for the insane (1879).

— — *Same.* General index, vols. 1–11, by Francis H. Brown. *In* 11th report, 1879.
606.1 : D101 v11

— - Summary of seven years' work ; prep. by W. R. Richardson. Bost. 1876. O.
in 606.1 : D101

— *Board of health, lunacy and charity.* 1st, 2d, 4th annual report, 1879, 1880, 1882–3 ; suppl., containing the report and papers on public health. Ill. Bost. 1881–83. 3 v. O.
606.1 : D102

Contents. **1879**. General report.—The pollution of streams: Westfield and Merrimac rivers; **Nichols**, W: R. Pollution by sulphuric acid.—**Billings**, F. S. Trichinæ in relation to the public health.—**Richards**, Ellen H. The adulterations of some staple groceries. **Wood**, E: S. The water-supply of Cambridge.—**Nichols**, W: R. Observations on Fresh Pond, Cambridge; On the examination of Mystic water, with remarks on Frankland's method of water analysis.—**Farlow**, W. G. On some impurities of drinking-water, caused by vegetable growths.—**Bowditch**, Ernest W. The drainage of summer hotels and country boarding-houses. — **Clarke**, Eliot C. Suggestions on sewerage. — Health of towns. **1880**. General rep.—**Hoyt**, W. E. The pollution of streams. —**Clarke**, Eliot C. The separate system of sewerage.—**Adams**, J. F. Alleyne. Intermittent fever in Mass.—**Bowditch**, Ernest W. Schoolhouse sanitation.—Health of towns: **Adams**, J. F. A., Epidemic in Adams; **Bowditch**, E. W. Sanitary condition of Holyoake; **Adams**, Z. B. Neglect of vaccination.—Index. **1882-83**. General rep.—**Sharples**, S. P. The adulteration of food [with bibliography].—**Jeffries**, B. Joy. Our eyes and our industries.—Leprosy in its relations to public health [with bibliography].—Reports of water boards.—The sewerage of Nahant.—Index.
Note. There was no health supp. published with the 3d report for 1881.

Illinois state. Board of health. 1st annual report, [june 12, 1877–dec. 31] 1878. Springfield. 1879. O. *With* Reports made to the general assembly. 1879, v. 4. *in* 328.15 : D

Wisconsin state. Board of health. 1st–7th annual report, 1876–1882. Madison. 1876–83. O. 606.1 : 103

— *Same.* 3d–7th rep. *With* Governor's message, 1879–1883. *in* 328.15 : D

Principal contents, aside from the general reports of the board, extracts from special correspondents and reports of local boards, etc.:

Food and drink: Selden, O. G. Foods and domestic beverages (1876).—**Chamberlin**, T. C. The adulteration of foods (1879).—**Wenzel**, H: P. Diseased meat, and its relation to health (1880).

Public health, hygiene, etc.: **Hobbins**, Joseph. Registration of vital statistics (1876).—**Davies**, J: E. The value of vital statistics (1877).—**Bintliff**, James. Homes for the people (1879).—**Favill**, G: Mental hygiene (1876).—**Strong**, H: P. Village sanitary work (1877); General hygienic knowledge a necessity for the people (1880).—**Hageman**, J. W. Recreation as a sanitary agent (1880).—**Lynde**, Mrs. W: P. Hints on hygienic education (1881).—**Bingham**, Helen M. Hygienic clubs for women (1881).—**Hoegh**, Knut. Hints concerning infantile hygiene and dietetics (1882).—**Chittenden**, T: W. Nostrums (1882). —**Bartlett**, Edwin W. Color blindness (1881). — **Witter**, G. F. Tobacco and its effects (1881). — **Peckham**, G: W. The growth of children (1881, 1882).—**Anderson**, R. B. The influence of reading upon health (1878).

Air, ventilation, etc.: **Witter**, G. F. Ground air in its relations to health (1879).—**Bintliff**, James. Ventilation of public buildings and dwelling houses (1876, 1877); Inspection of public buildings (1877, 1878, 1879). — **Reeve**, J. T. Our public schools in their

relations to the health of pupils (1879).—**Chittenden,
T: W.** School buildings (1878); Our school houses
1879); School hygiene, and what the teacher can do
to promote it (1880).—**Reeve, J. T.** Kerosene (1880).
    Water-supply, sewerage, etc.: Witter, G. F.
Water and the water-supply of Wis. (1877, 1878). —
Chittenden, T: W. Water and the water-supply of
the state (1877); An investigation of the drinking
water of a city (1878).—**Reeve, J. T.** Land drainage
and obstructions to water courses (1878).—The Aurora-
ville marshes (1882).—**Marks,** Solon. Sewerage and
drainage (1876).—The sewer of Waupun prison (1882).
—**Henry, W. A.** A simple earth closet (1882).
    Diseases, insanity, etc.: Wight, O. W. The
management of contagious diseases in the city of
Milwaukee (1880).—**Hubbell, S. B.** The influence of
unsanitary surroundings and habits (1882).—**Griffin,
E. L.** Small-pox and its prophylaxis (1876, 1877);
Scarlet fever, its nature and means of prevention
(1877); Diphtheria, its relation to filth causes (1878);
Disinfectants and their special application (1877).—
Marks, Solon. Hydrophobia (1877); The prevention
of typhoid fever (1878).—**Schweichler, A. J.** Typhoid
fever at Port Washington (1879).—**Kempster,** Walter.
Some of the preventable causes of insanity (1878).

Milwaukee *city. Board of health.* 1st–11th an-
    nual report, comprising remarks on sani-
    tary requirements, with returns of deaths,
    births and marriages, april 1866—dec. 1877.
    Milw. 1867–78. O. *In* City documents.
                                            351.15 : D
— *Commissioner of health,* [O. W. Wight.] 1st,
    2nd annual report, jan. 1879, 1880. Milw.
    1879, 1880. *In* City documents. **351.15 : D**
    Principal contents. **1879.** Laws regulating the
    health dep.—Sewers, sewage and sewer-gas.—The wa-
    ter-supply of Milw.—Sanitation of public schools of
    Milw.—The meat supply of Milw.—Brief discussions of
    diseases,ice, garbage, adulterations of food and drink,
    etc.—Mortuary and meteorological tables. **1880.**
    The plague as the type of diseases that may be con-
    trolled by cleanliness and isolation.—Sanitary legis-
    lation as the basis of sanitary administration.—The
    milk supply of Milw.— Premature death in Milw.—
    History of the river nuisance. — Sanitation of public
    institutions.—Public baths. — Mortuary and meteoro-
    logical tables.
— — Monthly statements [and meteorological
    tables], jan. 1880–dec. 1884. *In* City docu-
    ments.   **351.15 : D**
Iowa *state. Board of health.* 1st biennial report
    for the fiscal period ending sept. 30. 1881.
    Des Moines. 1882. O.   **606.1 : D105**
    Principal contents. Secretary's rep. — **Dickinson,**
    W. H. Water supply and its relation to health and
    disease.—**Andrews,** L. F. Glanders in men and do-
    mestic animals.—**Farquharson,** R. J. Adulteration
    of food.—**Loring,** James L. Sewerage, drainage and
    disposal of excreta.

Periodicals and societies.

Journal of comparative medicine and surgery,
    The ; a quarterly journal of the anatomy,
    pathology and therapeutics of the lower
    animals, W: A. Conklin and W: H: Porter,
    eds.; v. 1–5. N. Y. 1881–84. O.   **605.1 : M**
    Note. Title-page of v. 1 reads "The archives of com-
    parative medicine and surgery."
Hall's journal of health ; ed. by W. .W. Hall ;
    v. 6—16. N. Y. 1859–67. O.   **605.1 : M**
Sanitarian, The ; a monthly magazine devoted
    to the preservation of health, mental and
    physical culture ; A. N. Bell, ed.; v. 10–13,
    jan. 1882—dec. 1884. N. Y. 1882–84. O. *and* Q.
                                            605.1 : M
New York state homœopathic medical society.
    Transactions ; v. 7, 8. Albany. 1869, 1870.
    2 v. O.   **606 : 1+2**
Wisconsin state medical society. Transac-
    tions ; v. 3–14, 1869–1880. Janesville [v.

3]. Milw. [v. 4]. St. Paul [v. 5]. Milw. [v.
    6–14]. 3 v. O.   **606.1+1**
Homœopathic medical society of the state of
    Wisconsin. Transactions, 13th[-20th] an-
    nual session, 1877–1884. Chicago, Milw.
    and Grand Rapids. 1877–84. O.   **606.1 : 4**
    Note. Includes also the transactions of the semi-
    annual sessions for 1881, 1882 and 1883.
Toner, Josiah Meredith. Address before the
    Rocky Mountain medical association, june
    6, 1877 ; containing some observations on
    the geological age of the world, the appear-
    ance of animal life upon the globe, the
    antiquity of man, and the archæological
    remains of extinct races found on the
    american continent, with views of the
    origin and practice of medicine among
    uncivilized races, more especially the north
    american indians. App. a synopsis of the
    previous addresses and also biographies of
    the members of the association. Wash.
    1877. D.   **606.1 : 3**
    Note. A general index to medical literature, incl.
    reports, transactions and periodicals, will be found
    in the Index catalogue of the library of the Surgeon-
    general's office at Washington (L); of which 5 vols.,
    comprising A—Hearth, have been pub. so far.

2. Anatomy and physiology.

Draper, J: C. A text-book on anatomy, physi-
    ology and hygiene, for the use of schools
    and families. Ill. N. Y. 1866. O.   **611+2**
Bale, G. G. P. The elements of the anatomy
    and physiology of man ; a text-book for
    students and schools. Students' ed. Lond.
    1879. O.   **611 : 4**

Anatomy.

(For Comparative anatomy, *see* cl. 591, col. 370.)

Jeançon, J. A. Atlas of human anatomy ; con-
    taining 197 large plates, taken from the
    original designs from nature by drs. Oester-
    reicher and Erdl and many other of the
    greatest anatomists of modern times, with
    explanatory text. Cinc. [1879–80]. 2 v. F.
    and Q.   **611 : R1**
Gray, H: Anatomy, descriptive and surgical ;
    with an introd. on general anatomy and
    development by T. Holmes, ed. by T. Pick-
    ering Pick. New amer. from the 10th eng.
    ed.; added, Landmarks, medical and sur-
    gical, by Luther **Holden,** with add. by W:
    W. Keen. Phila. 1883. O.   **611+5**
Kölliker, Albert. Manual of human microscopi-
    cal anatomy. Tr. by G: Busk and T: Hux-
    ley, ed. with notes and add. by J. DaCosta.
    Ill. Phila. 1854. O.   **611+6**
Kollmann, J: Mechanik des menschlichen
    körpers. München. 1874. S.   **611 : 9**
Richardson, Tobias G. Elements of human
    anatomy ; general, descriptive and practi-
    cal. 2d ed., rev. and ill. Phila. 1867. O.
                                        611+3

Physiology.

(See also Biology, cl. 570–578; *and for* Mental physiology,
    see cl. 131, col. 51.)

Carpenter, W: B: Principles of human physi-
    ology, with their chief applications to

psychology, pathology, therapeutics, hygiene and forensic medicine. New amer. from the last Lond. ed., ed. with add. by Francis Gurney Smith. Ill. Phila. 1862. O.
    612+1

Flint, Austin. A text-book of human physiology; designed for the use of practitioners and students of medicine. Ill. N. Y. 1876. O.
    612+2

Foster, Michael. A text-book of physiology. 4th ed., rev., with ill. Lond. 1884. O.
    612+42

— Physiology. (Science primers.) Ill. N. Y. 1874. S.
    612 : 27

Hermann, Ludimar. Elements of human physiology. Tr. and ed. from the 6th ed. by Arthur Gamgee. 2d ed., in great part recast and enl. Lond. 1878. O.   **612 : 43**

Huxley, T: H: *and* W: Jay **Youmans**. The elements of physiology and hygiene; a textbook for educational institutions. Rev. ed. Ill. N. Y. 1878. D.   **612 : 35**

Martin, H. Newell. The human body; an account of its structure and activities, and the conditions of its healthy working. (Amer. scientific ser.) N. Y. 1881. O.
    612 : 4

LePileur, A. Wonders of the human body. From the french. [Ill. lib. of wonders.] N. Y. 1873. D.   **612 : 18**

Roget, P: M: Animal and vegetable physiology, considered with reference to natural theology. 4th ed. with add. and emendations. [Bridgewater treatises.] Lond. 1867. 2 v. D.   **214 : 5**

Rosenthal, Isidor. General physiology of muscles and nerves. (Intern. scientific ser.) Ill. N. Y. 1881. D.   **612 : 5**

Jäger, Gustav. Die menschliche arbeitskraft. München. 1878. S.   **612 : 9**

Bell, *Sir* C: The hand; its mechanism and vital endowments as evincing design and illustrating the power, wisdom and goodness of God. Preceded by an account of the author's discoveries in the nervous system. 8th ed. [Bridgewater treatises.] Lond. 1882. D.   **214 : 4**

Smith, Southwood. The philosophy of health, or An exposition of the physical and mental constitution of man, with a view to the promotion of human longevity and happiness; v. 2. 5th ed. Lond. 1851. T.
    612 : 19

Wilkinson, James J: Garth. The human body and its connection with man, ill. by the principal organs. Phila. 1851. D.   **612 : 20**

Griscom, J: H. Animal mechanism and physiology; an exposition of the structure and functions of the human system, designed for the use of families and schools. Ill. N. Y. 1839. S.   **612 : 28**

Beecher, Catharine Elizabeth. Physiology and calisthenics for schools and families. N. Y. 1856. S.   **612 : 6**

Blaisdell, Albert F. Physiology for the young; Our bodies, or How we live; an elementary text-book of physiology and hygiene for use in the common schools, with special reference to the effects of stimulants and narcotics on the human system. Ill. Bost. 1885. D.   **x 612 : 41**

Allen, Chilion B. *and* Mary A. The man wonderful in the house beautiful; an allegory teaching the principles of physiology and hygiene and the effects of stimulants and narcotics, for home reading, also adapted as a reader for high schools and as a text-book for grammar, intermediate and district schools. Ill. N. Y. 1884. D. **612 : 40**

Ferrier, D. The functions of the brain. Ill. N. Y. 1876. O.   **612 : 12**
    Note. For physiology of the mind, see cl. 131, col. 51.

Ranke, Johannes. Das blut; eine physiologische skizze. München. 1878. S.   **612 : 14**

Willis, Robert. William Harvey; a history of the discovery of the circulation of the blood. Portr. Lond. 1878. O.   **612 : 36**

Lewes, G: H: The physiology of common life. N. Y. 1860. 2 v. D.   **612 : 15**

Moleschott, Jacob. Physiologie der nahrungsmittel; ein handbuch der diätetik. 2te aufl. Giessen. 1859. O.   **612 : 13**

Macé, J: The servants of the stomach. N. Y. 1868. D.   **x 612 : 16**

— The history of a mouthful of bread, and its effect on the organization of men and animals. Tr. from the 8th french ed. by mrs. Albert Gatty. 1st amer. ed. repr. from the above, carefully rev. and compared with the 17th french ed. N. Y. 1868. D.
    x 612 : 30

Bernstein, Julius. The five senses of man. Ill. (Intern. scientific ser.) N. Y. 1876. D.
    612 : 22

Taylor, C: Fayette. Sensation and pain; lecture delivered before the N. Y. academy of sciences march 21, 1881, one of the public course for 1880–81. N. Y. 1881. S.
    612 : 33

Carter, Robert Brundenell. Eyesight, good and bad; a treatise on the exercise and preservation of vision. Ill. Phila. 1880. D.
    612 : 23

Darwin, C: Robert. The expression of the emotions in man and animals. Ill. N. Y. 1873. D.   **612 : 24**

Meyer, G: Herman v. The organs of speech and their application in the formation of articulate sounds. (Intern. scientific ser.) N. Y. 1884 [1883]. D.   **612 : 37**

Elsberg, L: The throat and its functions in swallowing, breathing and production of the voice. N. Y. 1880. D.   **612 : 34**

Holmes, Gordon. The science of voice production and voice preservation, for the use of speakers and singers. N. Y. 1880. D.
    612 : 25

— A treatise on vocal physiology and hygiene, with especial reference to the cultivation and preservation of the voice. Phila. 1880. D.   **612 : 26**

Browne, Lennox, *and* Emil **Behnke**. Voice, song and speech; a practical guide for singers and speakers, from the combined view of the vocal surgeon and the voice trainer. Ill. N. Y. 1883. O.   **612+38**

Guttmann, Oskar. Gymnastics of the voice; a system of correct breathing in singing and speaking, based upon physiological laws; a practical guide in the training and use of the singing and speaking voice, de-

    x denotes books specially adapted for children.

signed for schools and for self-instruction. Ill. Albany. 1884. D.   **612 : 39**

Youmans, E: Livingstone. Observations on the scientific study of human nature ; a lecture del. before the London college of preceptors. N. Y. 1867. J.   **612 : 21**

Hooker, Worthington. The child's book of nature, for the use of families and schools, intended to aid mothers and teachers in training children in the observation of nature ; in 3 pts. Pt. 2: Animals. N. Y. 1881. S.   **x 612 : 31**

Shepherd, *Mrs.* E. R. For girls ; a special physiology, being a supp. to the study of general physiology. N. Y. 1882. D. **612 : 32**

Cowan, J: The science of a new life. N. Y. [1869]. O.   **618 : 1**

3. Hygiene.

Buck, Albert H., *ed.* A treatise on hygiene and public health. N. Y. 1879. 2 v. O. **613+2**

Baird, James. The management of health ; a manual of home and personal hygiene, being practical hints on air, light, ventilation, exercise, diet, clothing, rest, sleep, and mental discipline, bathing and therapeutics. [Weale's ser.] London. [1867]. D.   **613 : 55**

Beecher, Catherine Esther. Letters to the people on health and happiness. N. Y. 1856. S.   **613 : 6**

Bellows, Albert Jones. How not to be sick ; a sequel to "Philosophy of eating." N. Y. 1869. D.   **613 : 7**

Blaikie, W: How to get strong, and how to stay so. N. Y. 1879. D.   **613 : 8**

Brown, J: Health ; five lay sermons to working people. N. Y. 1865. S.   **613 : 9**

Corfield, W. H. Health. N. Y. 1880. D.
                613 : 13

Cornaro, L: Discourses on a sober and temperate life ; wherein is demonstrated by his own example, the method of preserving health to extreme old age. Tr. from the italian original. New ed. Added, Physic of the golden age ; a fragment. Middletown, N. J. 1836. T.   **613 : 14**

Davis, Andrew Jackson. The harbinger of health ; containing medical prescriptions for the human body and mind. N. Y. 1862. D.   **613 : 15**

Dunglison, Robley. Human health, or The influence of atmosphere and locality, change of air and climate, seasons, food, clothing, bathing and mineral springs, exercises, etc., on healthy man. New ed. Phila. 1844. O.   **613 : 17**

Fothergill, J. Milner. The maintenance of health ; a medical work for lay readers. N. Y. 1875. D.   **613 : 18**

Guernsey, Alfred H., *and* Irenæus Prime **Davis.** Health at home. (Appletons' home books). N. Y. 1884. D.   **613 : 64**

Hall, W: W. Health and disease. *T. p. w.* [N. Y. 1866]. D.   **613 : 19**

— How to live long, or Health maxims, physical, mental and moral. N. Y. 1875. D.
                613 : 20

Hartshorne, H: Our homes. (Amer. health primers.) Phila. 1880. T.   **613 : 38**

x denotes books specially adapted for children.

Hinton, James. Health and its conditions. N. Y. 1871. D.   **613 : 21**

— *ed.* Physiology for practical use ; with an introd. by E: L. Youmans. N. Y. 1874. D.
                613 : 22

Kirk, J: Papers on health ; 1st–9th series. Glasgow. 1884, 1885. 9 v. T. **613 : 69**
Note. Detailed contents of the entire series will be found at the back of each volume.

Lankester, E. Ray. On comparative longevity in man and the lower animals. Lond. 1870. D.   **613 : 62**

Niemeyer, Paul. Gesundheitslehre des menschlichen körpers. München. 1876. S.
                613 : 5

— Aerztliche sprechstunden; gesundheitslehre für jedermann. Jena. [1878–82]. 10 v. D.
                613 : 46 v1-10

—*Same*; zeitschrift für naturgemässe gesundheits- und krankenpflege, organ des Hygienischen vereins zu Berlin. 2te folge, 1–5 b., des ganzen werkes 11–15 b. Jena. [1882–85]. 5 v. D.   **613 : 46 v11-15**

Oswald, Felix Leopold. Physical education, or The health laws of nature. N. Y. 1882. D.
                613 : 30

Parkes, Edmund Alexander. A manual of practical hygiene, ed. by F. S. B. François de Chaumont. 5th ed. Lond. 1878. O.
                613+1

Richardson, Joseph G. Long life and how to reach it. (Amer. health primers.) Phil. 1879. T.   **613 : 42**

Smith, E: Health ; a handbook for households and schools. N. Y. 1875. D.   **613 : 28**

Ticknor, Caleb. The philosophy of living, or The way to enjoy life and its comforts. N. Y. 1844. S.   **613 : 29**

Tomes, Robert. The bazar book of health. [*Anon.*] N. Y. 1873. S.   **613 : 49**

Wilson, G: Health and healthy homes; a guide to domestic hygiene, with notes and add. by J. G. Richardson. Phila. 1880. D.
                613 : 31

Wilson, J: Health and health resorts. Phila. [1880]. S.   **613 : 32**

* * *

Wilson, James C. The summer and its diseases. (Amer. health primers.) Phila. 1879. T.
                613 : 44

Osgood, Hamilton. Winter and its dangers. (Amer. health primers.) Phila. 1879. T.
                613 : 40

Youmans, E: Livingstone. Alcohol and the constitution of man ; a popular scientific account of the chemical history and properties of alcohol and its leading effects upon the healthy human constitution. Ill. by a colored chemical chart. [*Chart missing.*] N. Y. 1854. D.   **613 : 33**

Packard, J: H. Sea-air and sea-bathing. (Amer. health primers.) Phila. 1880. T. **613 : 41**

Wurm, W. Das wasser als hausfreund in gesunden und kranken tagen ; ein familienbuch. [Ill.] Stuttgart. [1882]. D. **613 : 56**

Urquhart, D: The turkish bath. Lond. 1856. O.   *in* **327.2+9 v1**

Pleasonton, A: James. The influence of the blue ray of the sunlight and of the blue colour of the sky in developing animal and vegetable life, in arresting disease and in

restoring health in acute and chronic disorders to human and domestic animals, as
ill. by the experiments of gen. A. J.
Pleasonton and others, between 1861 and
1876 ; addressed to the Phila. society for
promoting agriculture. Phila. 1876. O.
                                    613+27

Special organs.

Heart, The, and its function. (Health primers.)
N. Y. 1881. T.   **613 : 39**
Nervous system, The. (Health primers.) N. Y.
1882. T.   **613 : 59**
Clarke, E: Hammond. The building of a brain.
Bost. 1874. S.   **613 : 11**
Wood, Horatio C. Brain-work and overwork.
(Amer. health primers.) Phila. 1880. T.
                                    613 : 45
Granville, J. Mortimer. Common mind-troubles.
Salem. 1879. S.   **613 : 51**
— The secret of a clear head. Salem. 1879. S.
                                    613 : 52
— The secret of a good memory. Bost. 1881. S.
                                    613 : 53
— Sleep and sleeplessness. Bost. 1881. S.
                                    613 : 54
Hall, W: W. Sleep, or The hygiene of the night.
Bost. 1879. D.   **613 : 57**
White, J. W. The mouth and the teeth. (Amer.
health primers.) Phila. 1879. T. **613 : 43**
Holbrook, Arthur. Practical information about
the teeth ; a book for the people. Milw.
1879. S.   **613 : 23**
Cohen, J. Solis. The throat and the voice.
(Amer. health primers.) Phila. 1879. T.
                                    613 : 36
Harlan, G: C. Eyesight and how to care for it.
(Amer. health primers.) Phila. 1879. T.
                                    613 : 37
Burnett, C: H. Hearing and how to keep it.
(Amer. health primers.) Phila. 1879. T.
                                    613 : 35
Browning, J: How to use our eyes, and how to
preserve them by the aid of spectacles.
Ill. Lond. 1883. D.   **613 : 68**
Bulkley, Lucius Duncan. The skin in health
and disease. (Amer. health primers.)
Phila. 1880. T.   **613 : 34**

Men, women and children.

(*See also* Female education, class 376, col. 248.)

Ordronaux, J: Hints on health in armies, for
the use of volunteer officers. 2d ed., with
add. N. Y. 1863. S.   **613 : 26**
Lewis, Dio *or* Dioclesian. In a nutshell; suggestions to american college students. N. Y.
1883. D.   **613 : 61**
Wilder, Burt Green. Health notes for students.
N. Y. 1883. T.   **613 : 63**
Ames, Azel. Sex in industry; a plea for the
working-girl. Bost. 1875. S.   **613 : 4**
Lewis, Dio *or* Dioclesian. Our girls. N. Y. 1871.
D.   **613 : 25**
  Contents. Introd.—Girls' boots and shoes.—How
  girls should walk.—The language of dress.—Description of dress.—Outrages upon the body.—Woman tor-
  tures her body.—Stocking supporters. — Large *vs.*
  small women.—Idleness among girls.—Idleness is
  fashionable.—Work is for the poor.—Employments
  for women.—False tests of gentility.—A short sermon
  about matrimony.—Piano music.—Study of french.—

Lewis, Dio *or* Dioclesian.—*Continued.*
  Dancing. — The theatre. — Sympathy between the
  stomach and the soul.—About the treatment of diseases.—Sunshine and health.—A word about baths.—
  Home gymnasium.—What you should eat.—What you
  should drink.—Additional health thoughts.—Amusements for girls.—True education for girls.—Heroic
  women.
— Five-minute chats with young women and certain other parties. N. Y. 1874. D.
                                    613 : 24
Studley, Mary J. What our girls ought to know.
N. Y. 1882. D.   **613 : 60**
Duffey, *Mrs.* E. B. What women should know;
a woman's book about women, containing
practical information for wives and mothers. Phila. [1873]. D.   **613 : 16**
Alcott, W: Alexander. The young mother, or
Management of children in regard to
health. 2d ed. Bost. 1836. D.   **613 : 3**
Chavasse, Pye H: The physical training of
children; with a prelim. dissertation by F.
H. Getchel. Phila. 1885. O.   **613 : 10**
Thomas Wilson sanitarium of Baltimore. The
sanitary care and treatment of children and
their diseases; a series of five essays. Bost.
1881. O.   **614 : 9**
  Contents. **Anderson,** E. G. How can children in a
  city be kept healthy.—**Busey,** S: C. The mortality of
  young children; its causes and prevention.—**Jacobi,**
  A. On the improvement of the condition of poor and
  sick children.—**Meigs,** J. F. Observations upon the
  sanitary care and treatment of children and their
  diseases. **Smith,** J. L. Causes of the great mortality of young children in cities during the summer
  season, and the hygienic measures required for prevention.

Gymnastics.

Grohe, E: Kurzgefasste geschichte der leibes-
übungen. Milw. 1877. D.   **613 : Pam**
Maclaren, Archibald. A system of physical
education, theoretical and practical. Oxford. 1869. S.   **613 : 58**
Lewis, Dio *or* Dioclesian. The new gymnastics
for men, women and children ; with a tr. of
prof. Kloss's Dumb-bell instructor and
prof. Schriber's Pangymnastikon. Ill. Bost.
1862. D.   **613 : 48**
Hunt, Lucy B. Handbook of light gymnastics.
Bost. 1882 [1881]. T.   **613 : 50**
Hartelius, Truls J: Home gymnastics for the
preservation and restoration of health for
children and young and old people of both
sexes ; with a short method of acquiring
the art of swimming. Tr. and adapted
from the swedish original, by special permission of the author, by C[oncordia]
Löfving. Ill. Lond. [1881]. D.   **613 : 47**
Gymnastics without a teacher. Ill. N. Y. 1882.
D.   **613 : 67**
Blaikie, W: Sound bodies for our boys and
girls. Ill. N. Y. 1884 [1883]. S.   **613 : 65**
Safford, Mary J., *and* Mary E. Allen. Health
and strength for girls. Bost. [1884]. S.
                                    x 613 : 66

4. Public health.

Bowditch, H: Ingersoll. Public hygiene in
America; the centennial discourse del.
before the International medical congress,

x denotes books specially adapted for children.

Phila., sept. 1876, with extracts from correspondence from various states, together with a digest of amer. sanitary law by H: G. Pickering. Bost. 1877. D. **614:2**

American public health assoc. Papers and reports, v. 4, 5, 7, presented at the meetings in 1877–1878, 1879, 1881, with abstract record of proceedings. Bost. 1878–1883. 3 v. O. **614+21**
Note. Each vol. contains a minute index.

Wight, Orlando Williams. Maxims of public health. N. Y. 1884. S. **614:27**

Wilson, G: A handbook of hygiene and sanitary science. 4th ed. enl. and rev. Phila. 1880. D. **614:13**

Sweeting, R. D. R. Essay on the experiences and opinions of J: Howard on the preservation and improvement of the health of the inmates of schools, prisons, workhouses, hospitals and other public institutions, as far as health is affected by structural arrangements relating to supplies of air and water, drainage, etc.; to which was awarded the Statistical society's Howard medal and prize in nov. 1883. Lond. 1884. O. **614:28**

Fischer, K: Volks-gesundheitspflege und schule. *In* Deutsche zeit- und streit-fragen.
       304:15 v6

Marggraff, Hugo. Moderne stadtbäder. Ill. *In* Deutsche zeit- und streit-fragen.
       304:15 v11

Hirsch, A: Ueber die verhütung und bekämpfung der volkskrankheiten, mit specieller beziehung auf die cholera. *In* Deutsche zeit- und streit-fragen. **304:15 v4**

Denton, J. Bailey. Sanitary engineering; a series of lectures given before the school of military engineering at Chatham, 1876. Lond. 1877. O. **614:R26**
Contents. Air.—Water.—The dwelling.—The town and the village.—The disposal of sewage.

Kingsley, C: Sanitary essays. *in* **304:8**

Edwards, Joseph F. Malaria; what it means and how avoided. Phila. 1881. S. **614:15**

Billings, Frank S. The relation of animal diseases to the public health, and their prevention. N. Y. 1884. O. **614+24**

Corfield, W. H. Water and water supply. [Van Nostrand's science ser.] N. Y. 1875. T.
       614:6

— Dwelling houses; their sanitary construction and arrangements. [Van Nostrand's science ser.] N. Y. 1880. T. **614:4**

Eassie, W: Sanitary arrangements for dwellings; intended for the use of officers of health, architects, builders and householders. Lond. 1874. D. **614:8**

Gerhard, W: Paul. House drainage and sanitary plumbing. [Van Nostrand's science ser.] N. Y. 1882. T. **614:20**

Philbrick, E: S. American sanitary engineering. N. Y. 1881. O. **614+10**

Varona, Adolfo de. Sewer gases; their nature and origin, and how to protect our dwellings. 2d ed., rev. and enl. [Van Nostrand's science ser.] N. Y. 1882. T.
       614:19

Waring, G: Edwin, *jr.* The sanitary drainage of houses and towns. N. Y. 1876. D.
       614:18

— The sanitary condition of city and country

dwelling houses. [Van Nostrand's science ser.] N. Y. 1877. T. **614:12**

Teale, T: Pridgin. Dangers to health; a pictorial guide to domestic sanitary defects. 4th ed. N. Y. 1883. O. **614:22**

Brown, G: Preston. Sewer-gas and its dangers; with an exposition of common defects in house drainage and practical information relating to their remedy. Chicago. 1881. D. **614:3**

Adams, Julius W. Sewers and drains for populous districts, with rules and formulæ for the determination of their dimensions under all circumstances. Ill. N. Y. 1880. O. **614+1**

Corfield, W. H. Sewerage and sewage utilization. [Van Nostrand's science ser.] N. Y. 1875. T. **615:5**

— A digest of facts relating to the treatment and utilization of sewage. 2d ed., rev. and enl. Lond. 1871. O. **614:17**

Robinson, H: Sewage disposal. Lond. 1880. D. **614:11**

Humber, W: The rationale of the sewage question. *In his* Record of the progress of engineering, 1865. **620:R19**

— History of the drainage and sewage of London. *In his* Record of the progress of engineering, 1865. **620:R19**

London. Main drainage of the metropolis; report to the metropolitan board of works, presented by messrs. Bidder, Hawksley and Bazalgette, in accordance with a resolution of the board, dated 23d nov. 1857. Lond. 1858. F. **614:R25**

France: *Département de la Seine. Préfecture.* Assainissement de la Seine; épuration et utilisation des eaux d'égout. Rapports. Maps. Paris. 1876–78. O. *in* **614:D**
Contents. Avant-projet d'un canal d'irrigation à l'aide des eaux d'égout de Paris entre Clichy et la partie nordest de la forêt de Saint-Germain.— Rapport des ingenieurs de la ville de Paris.—Rapport de la première sous-commission de la commission d'études, chargée d'étudier les procédés de culture horticole à l'aide des eaux d'égout.—Rapport de la 3e sous-commission, chargée d'étudier l'influence exercée dans la presqu'île de Gennevilliers par l'irrigation en eau d'égout sur la valeur vénale et locative des terres de culture.

Waring, G: Edwin, *jr.* Suggestions for the sanitary drainage of Washington city. Wash. 1880. O. *In* Smithsonian misc.
       506:R4 v26

Sepulture.

Wickes, Stephen. Sepulture; its history, methods and sanitary requisites. Phila. 1883. O.
       614+23

Eassie, W: Cremation of the dead; its history and bearings upon public health. Ill. Lond. 1875. O. **614:7**

Bermingham, E: J. The disposal of the dead; a plea for cremation. N. Y. 1881. D.
       614:14

Wittmeyer, L. Ueber die leichenverbrennung. *In* Deutsche zeit- und streit- fragen.
       304:15 v5

5. Materia medica and therapeutics.

Hedges, H: T. A polyglot index of all the principal articles in the materia medica, in latin, english, french, german, swedish and norwegian-danish, with separate indexes referring to all and with tr. and full explanation in each language of equivalents of metric weights and measures, of incompatible medicines, of the heroic medicines and dose of each, and of poisons and their antidotes, besides other useful information for the pharmacist and the physician. Chicago. 1884. Q. **615 : R5**

Pharmacopœia, The, of the U. S. of America. 6th decennial rev. N. Y. 1882. O.
615 : R2

Wood, G: B., *and* Franklin **Bache.** The dispensatory of the U. S. of America. 15th ed. rearranged, thoroughly rev. and largely rewritten by H. C. Wood, Joseph P. Remington and S: P. Sadtler. Phila. 1883. O.
615 : R4

Attfield, J: Chemistry, general, medical and pharmaceutical, incl. the chemistry of the U. S. pharmacopœia; a manual on the general principles of the science and their applications in medicine and pharmacy. 10th ed. specially rev. by the author for America. Phila. 1883. O. **615 : 16**

Maisch, J: M. A manual of organic materia medica; a guide to materia medica of the vegetable and animal kingdoms, for the use of students, druggists, pharmacists and physicians. Ill. Phila. 1882. O. **615 : 10**

Stillé, Alfred. Therapeutics and materia medica; a systematic treatise on the action and uses of medicinal agents, incl. their description and history. 4th ed. rev. and enl. Phila. 1874. 2 v. O. **615+7**

Trousseau, Armand, *and* H. **Pidoux.** Treatise on therapeutics. Tr. by D. F. Lincoln from french. 9th ed. rev. and enl. with the assistance of Constantine Paul. N. Y. 1880. 3 v. O. **615+8**

Kidd, Joseph. The laws of therapeutics, or The science and art of medicine. 2d ed. Lond. 1881. D. **615 : 9**

Tichborne, C: R. C., *and* Prosser **James.** The mineral waters of Europe; incl. a short description of artificial mineral waters. Lond. 1883. D. **615 : 3**

Taylor, Alfred Swaine. On poisons, in relation to medical jurisprudence and medicine. 3d ed. Lond. 1875. D. **615 : 1**

Graham, Douglas. A practical treatise on massage; its history, mode of application and effect, indications, contra-indications, with results in over 1,400 cases. N. Y. 1884. O. **615 : 6**

Homœopathy.

Hahnemann, S: Organon der heilkunst. 6te aufl. mit abdruck der vorreden und wichtigsten varianten der fünf bis jetzt erschienenen auflagen, neuen bemerkungen und einem anbange aus Samuel Hahnemann's schriften herausg. von Arthur Lutze. Coethen. 1865. O. **615+11**

Burt, W. H. Characteristic materia medica. 2d ed. N. Y. 1873. D. **615 : 12**

Hughes, R: A manual of pharmaco-dynamics. 2d ed., with alphabetical index. N. Y. 1868. D. **615 : 14**

Sherman, Lewis. Therapeutics and materia me-

dica, for the use of families and physicians. Milw. 1878. D. **615 : 15**

Laurie, Joseph. The homœopathic domestic medicine; ed. and rev., with numerous important add. and the introduction of the new remedies and a repertory, by Robert J. McClatchey. 4th amer. ed. N. Y. 1872. O. **615+13**

6. Pathology, Theory and practice.

(For insanity and other mental derangements, *see* class 132, col. 53.)

Tanner, T: Hawkes. An index of diseases and their treatment. Phila. 1867. O. **616+33**

Darwin, Erasmus. Zoonomia, or The laws of organic life. 3d ed. corr. Lond. 1801. 4 v. O. **616 : 26**

Walker, Alexander. Pathology, founded on the natural system of anatomy and physiology; a philosophical sketch in which the natural classification of diseases and the distinction between morbid and curative symptoms, afforded by pain or its absence, are pointed out, as well as the errors of homœopathy and other hypotheses. N. Y. 1842. D. **616 : 12**

Aitken, W: Outlines of the science and practice of medicine. Lond. 1874. D. **616 : 29**

Bartholow, Roberts. A treatise on the practice of medicine, for the use of students and practitioners. N. Y. 1880. O. **616+30**

DaCosta, Jacob M. Medical diagnosis, with special reference to practical medicine; a guide to the knowledge and discrimination of diseases. Ill. 5th ed. rev. Phila. 1881. O. **616+31**

Guttmann, Paul. A handbook of physical diagnosis; comprising the throat, thorax and abdomen. Tr. from the 3d german ed. by Alex. Napier. N. Y. 1880. O. **616+32**

Beale, Lionel Smith. On slight ailments; their nature and treatment. 2d ed. enl. and ill. Phila. 1882. O. **616+17**

Richardson, B: Ward. Diseases of modern life. N. Y. 1876. D. **616 : 24**

Black, G. V. The formation of poisons by micro-organisms; a biological study of the germ theory of disease. Phila. 1884. D.
616 : 27

Smart, Andrew. Germs, dust and disease; two chapters in our life history. Edinb. [1884]. D. **616 : 38**

Edwards, Joseph F. Dyspepsia; how to avoid it. Phila. 1881. S. **616 : 6**

Chapman, J: Diarrhœa and cholera; their origin, proximate cause and cure through the agency of the nervous system, by means of ice. Repr., with add., from the Medical times and gazette of july 29, 1865. Phila. 1866. D. **616 : 4**

Collins, G. T. The cholera; a familiar treatise on the history, causes, symptoms and treatment with the most effective remedies, and proper mode of their administration without the aid of a physician, the whole in language free from medical terms especially adapted for the use of the public generally, also containing a history of the epidemics of the middle ages. N. Y. 1866. D. **616 : 5**

Catlin, G: The breath of life, or Malrespiration and its effects upon the enjoyments and life of man N. Y. 1864. O. **616 : 28**

Wagner, Clinton. Habitual mouth-breathing; its causes, effects and treatment. N. Y. 1881. S. **616 : 13**

Hall, W: W. Bronchitis and kindred diseases. 10th ed. N. Y. 1865. D. **616 : 7**

James, Prosser. Sore throat; its nature, varieties and treatment. incl. the connection between affections of the throat and other diseases. 4th ed. enl. Ill. [Hand-book series]. Phila. 1883. D. **616 : 18**

Lewis, Dio *or* Dioclesian. Weak lungs and how to make them strong, or Diseases of the organs of the chest, with their home treatment by the movement cure. Ill. Bost. 1863. D. **616 : 9**

Bennet, James H: On the treatment of pulmonary consumption by hygiene, climate and medicine. App. on the sanitaria of the U. S., Switzerland, and the Balearic Islands. 3d ed. Phila. 1879. O. **616 : 36**

Bartlett, Elisha. The history, diagnosis and treatment of the fevers of the U. S. 3d ed., rev. Phila. 1852. O. **616 : 35**

Wood, Horatio C., *jr*. Fever; a study in morbid and normal physiology. Ill. Wash. 1878. Q. *In* Smithsonian contributions. **506 : R3 v23**

— Study of the nature and mechanism of fever. Wash. 1875. O. *In* Smithsonian misc. **506 : R4 v15**

Gamgee, J: Yellow fever, a nautical disease; its origin and prevention. N. Y. 1879. O. **616 : 22**

Barker, Fordyce. The puerperal diseases; clinical lectures delivered at Bellevue hospital. 4th ed. N. Y. 1878. O. **618 : 2**

Both, C: Small-pox; the predisposing conditions and their preventives, with a scientific exposition of vaccination. 2d ed. Bost. 1872. D. **616 : 37**

Neumann, Isidor. Hand-book of skin diseases. Tr. from the 2d german ed. with notes. Ill. N. Y. 1879. O. **616+34**

Beard, G: Miller. A practical treatise on nervous exhaustion, neurasthenia; its symptoms, nature, sequences, treatment. 2d rev. ed. N. Y. 1880. O. **616 : 3**

— American nervousness, its causes and consequences; a supplement to Nervous exhaustion, neurasthenia. N. Y. 1881. D. **616 : 2**

Corning, J. Leonard. Brain-rest. N. Y. 1883. S. **616 : 20**

Mitchell, S: Weir. Fat and blood; an essay on the treatment of certain forms of neurasthenia and hysteria. 3d ed., rev.. with add. Phila. 1884. D. **616 : 25**

DaCosta, Jacob M. On strain and over action of the heart. Ill. Wash. 1874. O. *In* Smithsonian misc. **506 : R4 v15**

Bateman, F. On aphasia or loss of speech, and the localisation of the faculty of articulate language. Lond. 1870. O. **616 : 1**

Potter, S: O. L. Speech and its defects, considered physiologically, pathologically, historically and remedially. Lea prize thesis of Jefferson college, pub. by permission of the faculty. Phila. 1882. D. **616 : 16**

Kitto, J: The lost senses; deafness and blindness. N. Y. 1852. D. **616 : 8**

Jeffries, B: Joy. Color-blindness; its dangers and its detection. Bost. 1879. D. **616 : 10**

Roberts, C: The detection of colour-blindness and imperfect eyesight by the methods of dr. Snellen, dr. Daae and prof. Holmgren, with a table of coloured Berlin wools and a sheet of test-types. Arr. for the anthropometric committee of the British association for the promotion of science. Lond. 1881. O. **616 : R11**

Woodward, Joseph Janvier. On the structure of cancerous tumors, and the mode in which adjacent parts are invaded. Ill. Wash. 1872. O. *In* Smithsonian misc. **506 : R4 v15**

Kane, H. H. Opium-smoking in America and China; study of its prevalence and effects, immediate and remote, on the individual and the nation. N. Y. 1882. S. **616 : 23**

Hubbard, F: Heman. The opium habit and alcoholism; a treatise on the habits of opium and its compounds — alchohol, chloral hydrate, chloroform, bromide potassium and cannabis indica; incl. their therapeutical indications, with suggestions for treating various painful complications. N. Y. [1881]. D. **616 : 15**

Dulles, C: W. What to do first in accidents and emergencies; manual explaining the treatment of surgical and other injuries in the absence of the physician. 2d ed. Phila. 1883. S. **616 : 19**

Esmarch, Johannes F: A: Early aid in injuries and accidents. From the german by h. r. h. princess Christian. Phila. 1883. D. **616 : 21**

7. Surgery and Dentistry.

Erichsen, J: Eric. The science and art of surgery; a treatise on surgical injuries, diseases and operations. New ed. enl. and rev. Ill. Phila. 1873. O. **617+2**

Pitha, Franz *freiherr* v., *and* Christian Albert Theodor Billroth, *eds*. Handbuch der allgemeinen und speciellen chirurgie, mit einschluss der topographischen anatomie, operations- und verbandlehre. Ill. Erlangen. 1865–82. 13 v. in 12. O. **617 : 6**

Contents. [V. 1.] *1er band, 1e abth*. **Haeser**, H. Historische entwicklung der chirurgie und des chirurgischen standes.—**Weber**, O: Die gewebserkrankungen im allgemeinen und ihre rückwirkung auf den gesammtorganismus. [2.] *1er band, 2e abth.*, *1es heft*. **Hueter**, C: Die septikämischen und pyämischen fieber.—**Volkmann**, R: Erysipelas, rosé, rothlauf.—**Heine**, C: *ritter* v. Der hospitalbrand, wunddiphtheritis.—**Rose**, Edmund. Delirium tremens und delirium traumaticum; Ueber den starrkrampf.—**Reder**, Albert. Hundswuth, lyssa, rabies canina, hydrophobia.—**Korányi**, F: Der milzbrand.—**Sigmund** v. Ilanor, C: Syphilis und venerische geschwärsformen.—**Duchek**, Adalbert. Scorbut, scharbock.—**Billroth**, Theodor. Scrophulose und tuberculose. [3.] *1er band, 2e abth.*, *2es heft*. **Billroth**, Theodor. Verletzungen der weichtheile.—**Fischer**, Hermann. Verletzungen durch kriegswaffen, allgemeine kriegschirurgie.—**Thiersch**, C: Die feineren anatomischen veränderungen nach Verwundung der weichtheile.—**Nussbaum**, J: Nepomuk v. Anästhetica.—**Billroth**, Theodor. Allgemeine instrumenten- und operationslehre.—**Fischer**, F: Ernst. Allgemeine verbandlehre. [4.] *2er band, 1e abth*. **Lücke**, Albert. Die lehre von den geschwülsten in anatomischer und klinischer beziehung. [5.] *2er band, 2e* abth., 1es heft. **Weber,** O: Krankheiten der haut, des zellgewebes, der lymph- und blutgefässe, der nerven.—**Volkmann,** R: Verletzungen und krankheiten der bewegungsorgane. [6.] *2er band, 2e abth., 2es heft.* **Schede, Max.** Allgemeines über amputationen, exarticulationen und künstliche glieder [7.] **Lossen,** W: Allgemeines über resectionen. *3er band, 1e abth., 1es heft.* **Bergmann,** Ernst v. Die lehre von den kopfverletzungen.—**Heineke,** W. Chirurgische krankheiten des kopfes.—**Tröltsch,** Anton F: *reichsfreiherr* v. Die krankheiten des ohres. —**Weber,** O: Verletzungen und chirurgische krankheiten des gesichts. [8.] *3er band, 1e abth., 2es heft.* **Fischer,** G: Die krankheiten des halses: Topographische anatomie: angeborene krankheiten; unterbindungen; verletzungen. — **König,** Franz. Die krankheiten des unteren theiles des schlundes und der speiseröhre. — **Hueter,** C: Tracheotomie und laryngotomie. — **Lücke,** Albert. Krankheiten der schilddrüse.—**Stoerk,** K: Laryngoscopie und rhinoscopie. [9.] *3er band, 2e abth., 1es heft.* **Lorinser,** F: W: Die verletzungen und krankheiten der wirbelsäule.—**Billroth,** Theodor. Die verletzungen und krankheiten der brust.—**Nussbaum,** J: Nepomuk v. Die verletzungen des unterleibes.—**Heineke,** W. Entzündungen, anschwellungen und geschwülste des unterleibes. — **Schmidt,** Benno. Die unterleibsbrüche.—**Uhde,** K: W: F: Chirurgische behandlung innerer einklemmungen.—**Esmarch,** J: F: A: Die krankheiten des mastdarmes und des afters. [10.] *3er band, 2e abth., 2es heft.* **Dittel,** Leopold *ritter* v. Die stricturen der harnröhre. — **Kocher,** Theodor. Verletzungen und krankheiten des hodens und seiner hüllen, des nebenhodens, samenstrangs und der samenblasen.—**Podrazki,** Josef. Die krankheiten des penis und der prostata.—**Socin,** A: Krankheiten der prostata. [11.] *4er band, 1e abth., 1es heft.* **Chrobak,** Rudolf. Allgemeine gynäkologie.—**Mayrhofer,** C: Sterilität, entwicklungsfehler und entzündungen des uterus.—**Fritsch, H:** Die lageveränderungen der gebärmutter.—**Gusserow,** A. Neubildungen des uterus.—**Bandl,** L: Die krankheiten der tuben, der ligamente, des beckenperitonäum und des beckenzellgewebes. [12.] *4er band, 1e abth., 2es heft.* **Olshausen,** Robert. Die krankheiten der ovarien.—**Breisky,** A: Die krankheiten der vagina.

—**Hildebrandt,** H. Die krankheiten der äussern weiblichen genitalien.—**Winckel,** Franz K: L: W: Die krankheiten der weiblichen harnröhre und blase. [13.] *4er band, 2e abth.* **Pitha,** Franz *freiherr* v. Verletzungen und krankheiten der extremitäten.

Hamilton, Frank Hastings. A practical treatise on fractures and dislocations. 5th ed., rev. and imp. Ill. Phila. 1875. O.   **617+4**

Poulet, Alfred. A treatise on foreign bodies in surgical practice. N. Y. 1880. 2 v. O.
    617+3

Shakespeare, E: O. Nature of reparatory inflammation in arteries after ligature, acupressure and torsion. Ill. Wash. 1879. O. *In* Smithsonian misc.   **506 : R4 v16**

Adams, W: Subcutaneous surgery; its principles and its recent extension in practice. Wash. 1877. O. *In* Smithsonian misc.
    506 : R4 v15

Keen, W: W. On the surgical complications and sequels of the continued fevers; with a bibliography of works on diseases of the joints, bones, larynx, the eye, gangrene, hæmatoma, phlegmasia, etc. Ill. Wash. 1876. O. *In* Smithsonian misc.
    506 : R4 v15

Macleod, G: H. B. Notes on the surgery of the war of the Crimea; with remarks on the treatment of gunshot wounds. Phila. 1862. D.   **617 : 1**

Harris, Chapin A. The principles and practice of dentistry; including anatomy, physiology, pathology, therapeutics, dental surgery and mechanism. Rev. and ed. by Philip H. Austen. Ill. Phila. 1879. O.   **617+5**

3. Engineering.

1. In general.

Cresy, E: An encyclopædia of civil engineering, historical, theoretical and practical. Ill. Lond. 1847. O.   **620 : R16**

Spons' dictionary of engineering, civil, mechanical and naval, with technical terms in french, german, italian and spanish; ed. by Oliver **Byrne** and Ernest **Spon.** Lond. 1869-74. 8 div. in 6 v. Q.   **620 : R17**

— *Same.* Supplement, ed. by Ernest **Spon.** Lond. 1879-81. 3 v.   **620 : R17**

Law, H: The rudiments of civil engineering; incl. a treatise on hydraulic engineering by G: R. **Burnell.** 6th ed. rev., with large add. on recent practice in civil engineering by D. Kinnear **Clark.** [Weale's ser.] Lond. 1881. D.   **620 : 1**

Stevenson, D: Sketch of the civil engineering of North America. 2d ed. [Weale's ser.] Lond. 1859. D.   **620 : 2**

Mahan, Dennis Hart. An elementary course of civil engineering for the use of cadets of the U. S. military academy. 6th ed., enl. N. Y. 1857. O.   **620+22**

Fairbairn, W: Useful information for engineers; 1st-3d ser. Lond. 1860, 1866. 3 v. D.   **620 : 15**

Contents. 1st ser. On the necessity of incorporating with the practice of the mechanical and industrial arts a knowledge of practical science.—On the construction of boilers.—On boiler explosions.—On steam.—On steam and steam boilers.—On the consumption of fuel and the prevention of smoke.—On the economy of fuel, concentration of heat, and prevention of smoke.—Metallic constructions: on iron ship-building. App. 1-7. 2d ser. On the resistance of cylindrical wrought iron vessels to collapse. —On the resistance of glass globes and cylinders to collapse from external pressure, and on the tensile and compressive strength of various kinds of glass. —On the tensile strength of wrought iron at various temperatures.—On the comparative value of various kinds of stone.— On popular education. — On the machinery employed in agriculture.—On the rise of civil and mechanical engineering and its progress to the present century.—On the progress of civil and mechanical engineering during the present century. —On the construction of iron ships. — On the construction of iron vessels exceeding three hundred feet in length.—On wrought iron tubular cranes.— On the properties of steam, its management and application. 3d ser. On the applied sciences.—On the present state of progress in science and art.— On labour, its influences and achievements.—On literary and scientific institutions.—On first principles and the thickness of the earth's crust.—Iron and its appliances.—On the comparative merits of the machinery of the Paris universal exhibition, 1855.—On the machinery department of the international exhibition of 1862.—On the construction of iron roofs.— Circular roofs.—On insulation and other properties of submarine telegraph cables.—On the mechanical properties of the Atlantic cable.—Experiments to determine the effect of impact, vibratory action, and long-continued changes of load on wrought-iron girders.—On some of the causes of the failure of deep-sea cables.

Humber, W: A record of the progress of modern engineering, 1865; comprising civil, mechanical, marine, hydraulic, railway, bridge and other engineering works, with essays and reviews. Lond. 1866. F.

620 : **R19**

Contents. Biog. sketch of J: Robinson M'Clean.—Address.—Construction of harbours, ports and breakwaters.—Improved system of fortification.—Granite and iron forts.—The rationale of railway rolling stock.—The rationale of the sewage question.—History of the drainage and sewage of London.—Thames embankment.

United States. *Chief of engineers, U. S. army.* Annual report to the secretary of war, 1867—1884. Wash. 1867-84. 21 v. in 38. O.

620 : 20

Note. Reserved duplicates of these reports, and reports from 1863 to 1866, are contained in the full set of congressional documents, class 328.1.

— - Index to river and harbor improvements, 1866-79.   *see in* 627 : 3

American society of civil engineers. Transactions ; v. 13, sept. and oct. 1884. N. Y. 1884. O.   606.2 : **Pam**

Campin, Francis. Materials and construction, a theoretical and practical treatise on the strains, designing and erection of works of construction. [Weale's ser.] Lond. 1881. D.   620 : 3

Allan, W. Theory of arches. [Van Nostrand's science ser.] N. Y. 1874. T.   620 : 5

Woodbury, Daniel P. Treatise on the various elements of stability in the well-proportioned arch, with numerous tables of the ultimate and actual thrust. (Engineer dept., U. S. army. Papers on practical engin., no. 7.) N. Y. 1858. D.   *in* 620 : **D**

Cain, W: A practical theory of voussoir arches. [Van Nostrand's science ser.] N. Y. 1874. T.   620 : 6

— Voussoir arches applied to stone bridges, tunnels, domes and groined arches. [Van Nostrand's science ser.] N. Y. 1879. D.

620 : 7

— Theory of solid and braced elastic arches ; applied to arch bridges and roofs in iron, wood, concrete or other material. Graphical analysis. [Van Nostrand's science ser.] N. Y. 1879. T.   620 : 8

Hyde, E. W. Skew arches; advantages and disadvantages of different methods of construction. [Van Nostrand's science ser.] N. Y. 1875. T.   620 : 9

Jacob, Arthur. Practical designing of retaining walls. [Van Nostrand's science ser.] N. Y. 1873. T.   620 : 10

Tate, James S. Surcharged and different forms of retaining walls. [Van Nostrand's science ser.] N. Y. 1873. T.   620 : 12

Wiggins, J: The practice of embanking lands from the sea, treated as a means of profitable employment for capital; with examples and particulars of actual embankments, and also practical remarks on the repair of old sea-walls. New ed.; with notes by Robert Mallet. [Weale's ser.] Lond. [1867]. D.   620 : 13

McMaster, J: Bach. High masonry dams. [Van Nostrand's science ser.] N. Y. 1876. T.   620 : 11

Baker, B: The actual lateral pressure of earthwork. [Van Nostrand's science ser.] N. Y. 1881. T.   620 : 21

Campin, Francis. A treatise on the application of iron to the construction of bridges, girders, roofs and other works, showing the

principles upon which such structures are designed and their practical application, especially arranged for the use of students and practical mechanics, all mathematical formulæ and symbols being excluded. Ill. 2d ed. rev. and corr. [Weale's ser.] Lond. 1876. D.   620 : 14

Armstrong, Robert. Chimneys for furnaces, fire-places, and steam boilers. [Van Nostrand's science ser.] N. Y. 1873. T.

620 : 4

Claudel, J. Formules, tables et renseignements pratiques; aide-mémoire des ingénieurs, des architects, etc. 4e éd. Paris. 1857. O.

620 : **R18**

Haswell, C: H. Engineers' and mechanics' pocket-book; containing weights and measures, rules of arithmetic, weights of materials, latitude and longitude, cables and anchors, specific gravities, squares, cubes and roots, etc.; mensuration of surfaces and solids, trigonometry, mechanics, friction, aërostatics, hydraulics and hydrodynamics, dynamics, gravitation, animal strength, wind mills, strength of materials, limes, mortars, cements, etc., wheels, heat, water, gunnery, sewers, combustion, steam and the steam-engine, construction of vessels, miscellaneous illustrations, dimensions of steamers, mills, etc., orthography of technical words and terms. 43d ed., rev. and enl. N. Y. 1883. S.   629 : 4

Heather, J: Fry. Mathematical instruments, their construction, adjustment, testing and use. Enl. ed., for the most part entirely re-written. [Weale's ser.] London. 1877. 3 v. D.   629 : 3

Contents. V. 1. Drawing and measuring instruments, incl.: 1, Instruments employed in geometrical drawing and in the measurement of maps and plans; 2, Instruments used for accurate measurement, and for arithmetical computations. 2. Optical instruments, incl. more especially telescopes, microscopes and apparatus for producing copies of maps and plans by photography. 3. Surveying and astronomical instruments, incl.: 1, Instruments used for determining the geometrical features of a portion of ground; 2, Instruments used in astronomical observations.

2. Mechanical engineering.

Baker, T: The elements of mechanism and machine tools; with remarks on tools and machinery by James Nasmyth. Ill. 6th ed. [Weale's ser.] Lond. 1878. D.

621 : 25

Bale, M. Powis. Steam and machinery management ; a guide to the arrangement and economical management of machinery, with hints on construction and selection. [Weale's ser.] Lond. 1884. D.   621 : 40

Campin, Francis. A practical treatise on mechanical engineering ; comprising metallurgy, moulding, casting, forging, tools, workshop machinery, mechanical manipulation, manufacture of the steam engine, etc., with an app. on the analysis of iron and iron ores. Added, Observations on the construction of steam-boilers, remarks upon furnaces used for smoke prevention, and on explosions, by Robert Armstrong, rev., with notes, by J: Bourne ; Rules for calculating the change wheels for screws on a turning lathe and for a wheel-cutting

Campin, Francis.—*Continued.*
   machine, by J. **La Nicca**: The management of steel, including forging, hardening, tempering, annealing, shrinking, expansion and the case-hardening of iron, by G: **Ede**. Phila. 1864. O.   **621 : 1**
— A practical treatise on mechanical engineering; comprising metallurgy, moulding, casting, forging, tools, workshop machinery, mechanical manipulation. manufacture of the steam-engine, etc. Ill. [Weale's ser.] Lond. 1881. D.   **621 : 2**
— Details of machinery; comprising instructions for the execution of various works in iron, in the fitting shop, foundry and boiler-yard, arr. expressly for the use of draughtsmen, students and foremen engineers. [Weale's ser.] Lond. 1883. D.   **621 : 31**
Rose, Joshua. The complete practical machinist; embracing lathe work, vise work, drills and drilling, taps and dies, hardening and tempering, the making and use of tools, etc. Ill. 7th ed. rev. Phila. 1881. O.   **621 : 3**
Tomkins, E: Principles of machine construction; being an application of geometrical drawing for the representation of machinery; ed. by H: Evers. (Putnam's advanced science ser.) N. Y. [1878]. 2 v. D. *and* Q.   **621+4**
   Contents. v. 1. Text. 2. Plates.
Watson, Egbert P. The modern practice of american machinists and engineers; incl. the construction, application and use of drills, lathe tools, cutters for boring cylinders, and hollow work generally, with the most economical speed for the same, the results verified by actual practice at the lathe, the vise, and on the floor; together with workshop management, economy of manufacture, the steam-engine, boilers, gears, belting, etc. Ill. Phila. 1880. D.   **621 : 6**
Winton, J: G. Modern workshop practice, as applied to marine, land and locomotive engines, floating docks, dredging machines, bridges, ship building, cranes, etc. 3d ed. [Weale's ser.] Lond. 1878. D.   **621 : 27**
Glynn, Joseph. A treatise on the construction of cranes and other hoisting machinery. 6th ed. Ill. [Weale's ser.] Lond. 1880. D.   **621 : 22**
Armour, James. Power in motion; horse power, wheel gearing, driving bands, and angular forces. 2d ed. Ill. [Weale's ser.] Lond. 1875. D.   **621 : 26**
Roos, J. D. C. de. Linkages; the different forms and uses of articulated links. Tr. from Revue universelle des mines. [Van Nostrand's science ser.] N. Y. 1879. T.   **621 : 21**
Robinson, S. W. A practical treatise on the teeth of wheels, with the theory of the use of Robinson's ondontograph. [Van Nostrand's science ser.] N. Y. 1876. T.   **621 : 23**
Francis, James B. On the strength of cast-iron pillars, with tables for the use of engineers and builders. Extracted from the proceedings of the American academy of arts and sciences. N. Y. 1865. O.   **621+32**

Williams, C: Wye. Fuel; its combustion and economy; an abridgment of [his] A treatise on the combustion of coal and the prevention of smoke, with add. on recent practice in the combustion and economy of fuel, coal, coke, wood, peat, petroleum, etc., by D. Kinnear Clark. Ill. 2d ed. rev. [Weale's ser.] Lond. 1880. D.   **621 : 20**
Roper, Stephen. Questions and answers for engineers. 3d ed. Phila. [1880]. T.   **621 : 30**
Lukin, James. The young mechanic; containing directions for the use of all kinds of tools, and for the construction of steam engines and mechanical models, incl. the art of turning in wood and metal. From the english ed. with corr. N. Y. 1881. D.   **x 621 : 28**
— Amongst machines; a description of various mechanical appliances used in the manufacture of wood, metal and other substances; a book for boys. Ill. N. Y. *n. d.* D.   **x 621 : 29**

Steam and gas engines.
   (*See also under* Physics, Heat, cl. 536, col. 314.)

Schroot, A. Der dampf; eine darstellung des zeitalters der dampfmaschine. Stuttgart. [1884]. D.   **621 : 41**
Eddy, H: T. Thermodynamics. [Van Nostrand's science ser.] N. Y. 1879. T.   **621 : 44**
Thurston, Robert H: A history of the growth of the steam-engine. (Intern. scientific ser.) N. Y. 1878. D.   **621 : 18**
Isherwood, B: F. Experimental researches in steam engineering. Phila. 1863, 1865. 2 v. F.   **621 : R35**
Baker, T: The mathematical theory of the steam engine, with rules at length and examples worked out for the use of practical men. 6th ed. rev. by J. R. Young. [Weale's ser.] Lond. 1875. D.   **621 : 7**
Clark, Daniel Kinnear. An elementary treatise on steam and the steam-engine, stationary and portable, being an extension of the elementary treatise on steam of J: Sewell. Ill. 2d ed. rev. [Weale's ser.] London. 1879. D.   **621 : 9**
Lardner, Dionysius. The steam engine, for the use of beginners. 13th ed. [Weale's ser.] Lond. 1876. D.   **621 : 12**
Northcott, W. H: The theory and action of the steam engine; for practical men. 3d ed. Lond. *n. d.* O.   **621 : 39**
Nystrom, J: W: A new treatise on steam engineering, physical properties of permanent gases and of different kinds of vapor. Phila. 1876. O.   **621+15**
Rankine, W: J: Macquorn. A manual of the steam engine and other prime movers. Ill. 5th ed. rev. Lond. 1870. D.   **621 : 34**
Mallet, A. Compound engines. Tr. from the french. [Van Nostrand's science ser.] N. Y. 1874. T.   **621 : 13**
Turnbull, J:, jr. A short treatise on the compound steam engine, with a new method of finding the relative areas of the two

x denotes books specially adapted for children.

cylinders. Ill. [Van Nostrand's science ser.] N. Y. 1874. T.   **621 : 19**

Le Van, W: Barnet. The steam-engine indicator and its use ; a guide to practical working engineers for greater economy and the better working of steam-engines. [Van Nostrand's science ser.] N. Y. 1884. S.   **621 : 42**

Porter, C: T. A treatise on the Richards steam-engine indicator, and the development and application of force in the steam-engine. 3d ed. rev. and enl. Lond. n. d. O.   **621 : 33**

Burgh, N. P. The slide valve practically considered ; with an app., bringing the information down to the present time. 11th ed. Lond. 1884. D.   **621 : 43**

Pochet, Léon. Steam-injectors ; their theory and use. Tr. from the french. [Van Nostrand's science ser.] N. Y. 1877. T.   **621 : 16**

Armstrong, Robert. A rudimentary treatise on steam boilers ; their construction and practical management, with app. 3d ed. Lond. 1857. D.   **621 : 5**

— *Same.* The construction and management of steam boilers ; with an app. by Robert Mallet. 8th ed. Ill. [Weale's ser.] Lond. 1878. D.   **621 : 5**

Rowan, F. J. On boiler incrustation and corrosion. [Van Nostrand's science ser.] N. Y. 1876. T.   **621 : 17**

Colburn, Zerah. Steam boiler explosions. [Van Nostrand's science ser.] N. Y. 1873. T.   **621 : 10**

Buel, R: H. Safety valves. [Van Nostrand's science ser.] N. Y. 1875. T.ª   **621 : 8**

Dempsey, G. Drysdale. A rudimentary treatise on the locomotive engine, comprising an historical sketch and description of the locomotive engine, with large add., treating of the modern locomotive, by D. Kinnear **Clark.** [Weale's ser.] Lond. 1879. D.   **621 : 11**

Recent locomotives ; illustrations with descriptions and specifications and details of recent american and european locomotives. Reprinted from the Railroad gazette. N. Y. 1883. F.   **621 : R38**

Forney, Matthias N. Catechism of the locomotive. 27th thousand. N. Y. 1883. D.   **621 : 37**

Murray, Robert. A treatise on marine engines and steam vessels ; together with practical remarks on the screw and propelling power, as used in the royal and merchant navy. 7th ed., rev. and augm. with a glossary of technical terms and their equivalents in french, german and spanish. [Weale's ser.] Lond. 1878. D.   **621 : 14**

Clerk, Dugald. The theory of the gas engine. [Van Nostrand's science ser.] N. Y. 1882. T.   **621 : 36**

2. Surveying.

Talbot, B. The compleat art of land-measuring, or A guide to practical surveying ; teaching an exact method of measuring and mapping of lands, woods, waters, etc., by the catoptric sextant, and of casting up the same by the pen, together with directions for levelling in order to convey water either in pipes or canals. Added, an app., containing a new theory of the catoptric sextant and its use in taking heights and distances independent of trigonometry, also instructions for measuring standing timber, with several tables. 2d ed., ill. Lond. 1784. O.   **622 : 3**

Schuyler, Aaron. Surveying and navigation, with a preliminary treatise on trigonometry and mensuration. (Ray's mathematical series). Cinc. n. d. O.   **622 : 6**

Baker, T: Rudimentary treatise on land and engineering surveying, with all the modern improvements, for students and practical use. New ed., rev. and corr. by E: Nugent. [Weale's ser.] Lond. 1879. D.   **622 : 1**

Carpenter, Frank De Yeaux. Geographical surveying ; its uses, methods and results. (Geological commission of Brazil, C: F: Hartt, chief). [Van Nostrand's science ser.] N. Y. 1878. T.   **622 : 2**

Topographical surveying. [Van Nostrand's science ser.] Ill. N. Y. 1884. T.   **622 : 4**

Contents. **Specht,** G: J. Topographical surveying.—**Hardy,** A. S. New methods in topographical surveying.—**McMaster,** J: B. Geometry of position applied to surveying.—**Walling,** H: F. Co-ordinate surveying.

Cutts, R: D. Field-work of triangulation. 3d enl. ed. *In* U. S. coast survey rep. 1882.   **622 : D**

Harrison, A. M. On the plane-table and its use in topographical surveying. *In* U. S. coast survey rep. 1865.   *in* **622 : D**

Hergesheimer, Edwin. A treatise on the plane-table and its use in topographical surveying. Ill. *In the same,* 1880.   *in* **622 : D**

Boutelle, C. O. On the construction of observing tripods and scaffolds. *In* U. S. coast survey rep. 1882.   *in* **622 : D**

Hergesheimer, Edwin. Report on the preparation of standard topographical drawings. Ill. *In* U. S. coast survey rep. 1879, 1883.   *in* **622 : D**

Winslow, Arthur. Stadia surveying : the theory of stadia measurements ; [with] tables of horizontal distances and differences of level for the reduction of stadia field observations. [Van Nostrand's science ser.] N. Y. 1884. T.   **622 : 5**

Schott, C: Anthony. Observations of atmospheric refraction. *In* U. S. coast survey rep. 1876.   *in* **622 : D**

Contents. 1. Comparison of the methods of determining heights by means of leveling, vertical angles and barometric measures, from observations at Bodega Head and Ross Mountain, Cal., by G: Davidson. 2. Determination of several heights by the spirit-level, and measures of refraction by zenith-distances ; also observations of the barometer, at Ragged Mountain, Me., 1874, by F. W. Perkins. 3. Determination of the coefficient of refraction from zenith-distances observed in northern Georgia by C. O. Boutelle and F. P. Webber in 1873-74. and adjustment of differences of heights by application of the method of least squares. 4. Hypsometric formula based upon thermodynamic principles.

— Results of observations for atmospheric refraction on the line Mount Diablo to Martinez, Cal., in connection with hypsometric measures by spirit-level, the vertical circle and the barometer, made in march and april 1880, by G: Davidson. *In the same,* 1883.   *in* **622 : D**

Williamson, Robert S. On the use of the barometer on surveys and reconnaissances:
pt. 1, Meteorology in its connection with
hypsometry; pt. 2, Barometric hypsometry. Maps and ill. (Prof. papers of the
corps of engineers, U. S. army, no. 15). N.
Y. 1868. Q.   *in* **622 : D**

— *Same.* App.: Practical tables in meterology
and hypsometry. N. Y. 1868. Q.
in **622 : D**

Contents. 1. Reduction of the english barometer to
the freezing point.—2. To facilitate the reduction to
level.—3. Giving the force of vapor, relative humidity and temperature of the dew-point from psycho-
metrical observations.— 4. For computing differences of altitude from barometric observations.

Marshall, W: M. Results in barometric hypsometry, obtained during 1871-1875; with
tables of barometrically determined altitudes. Ill. (U. S. geogr. surveys west of
100th mer., Wheeler; Report, v. 2). Wash.
1877. Q.   *in* **557.5 : D**

Ferrel, W: Barometric hypsometry, and reduction of the barometer to sea-level. *In* U.
S. coast survey rep. 1881.   *in* **622 : D**

United States. *Coast and geodetic survey.* Annual report of the superintendent, 1848-
1883. Wash. 1848-84. 35 v. O. (1848-51),
and Q.   *in* **622 : D**

Note. The official title was the "U. S. coast survey"
until July 1878, when the service was extended so as
to embrace the whole country, and the title changed
as above.—All scientific papers of permanent value,
printed previously to 1852, were republished in the
report for 1866, thus making the quarto series practically complete.

— — Consolidated index to the annual reports,
1844-53, by E. B. **Hunt.** *In* Report 1854.
in **622 : D**

— — *Same.* 1854-63, by F. F. **Nes.** *In* Report
1864.   *in* **622 : D**

— — General index of professional and scientific
papers contained in the reports, from 1851
to 1870. *In* Report 1871.   *in* **622 : D**

— — General index of scientific papers, methods
and results contained in the appendices of
the annual reports, from 1845 to 1880 incl.,
by C. H. **Sinclair.** *In* Report 1881.
in **622 : D**

Note. Arranged under the following heads: Geodesy.—Hypsometry.—Surveying.—Physical hydrography.—Terrestrial magnetism.—Drawing, engraving and electrotyping.—Astronomy.—Mathematics.—
Miscellaneous.

— — Descriptive catalogue of publications relating to the coast and geodetic survey, and
to standard measures; comp. by E: **Good-
fellow.** *In* Report 1883.   *in* **622 : D**

— *Lake survey.* Report of the survey of the
north and northwest lakes by capt. G: G.
Meade, being part of the Report of the
chief topographical engineers accompanying annual report of the sec. of war, 1860.
Detroit. 1861. O.   *in* **622 : D**

Note. Contains geographical positions, meteorol.
observations, etc. Other reports will be found in
the annual reports of the sec. of war, in Congressional documents, class 328.1.

— — Report upon the primary triangulation by
C. B. Comstock, aided by the assistants on
the survey. Ill. (Prof. papers of the corps
of engineers, U. S. army, no. 24.) Wash.
1882. Q.   *in* **622 : D**

Contents. Historical account of the survey, may
1841 to July 1881.—Standards of length, bases and
base-apparatus.— Primary triangulation. — Astronomical determinations. — Principal results of the
geodetic work.—App.

3. Fortification.

Viollet-le-Duc, Eugène Emmanuel. Annals of
a fortress. Tr. by B: Bucknall. Bost. 1876.
O.   **623 : 1**

Mahan, Dennis H. A treatise on field fortification, containing instructions on the
methods of laying out, constructing, de-
fending, and attacking intrenchments,
with the general outlines also of the arrangement, the attack and defence of permanent fortifications. 3d ed. rev. and enl.
N. Y. 1861. S.   **623 : D**

United States. *Corps of engineers, U. S. A.*
The fortications of to-day.—Fire against
models of coast batteries and parados.—
Horizontal and curved fire in defense of
coasts. Tr. under the dir. of the Board of
engineers for fortifications, J: Newton,
pres. Ill. Wash. 1883. Q.   *in* **623 : D**

Note. The first article constitutes chapters 1 and 2
of Festungen und taktik des festungskrieges in der
gegenwart, by A. v. **Bonin**; the 2d and 3d art.
originally appeared in Giornale di artigliera e genio
for 1881.

Totten, J. G. Report addressed to the hon.
Jefferson Davis, sec. of war, on the effects
of firing with heavy ordnance from case-
ment embrasures, and also the effects of
firing against the same embrasures with
various kinds of missiles; in 1852, '53, '54
and '55 at West Point, N. Y. (Papers on
practical engineering, no. 6.) Wash. 1857.
O.   *in* **623 : D**

Maguire, E: Professional notes. Ill. (Engineer
dep., U. S. army.) Wash. 1884. O.
in **623 : D**

Contents. Perforation of armored walls.—Remaining velocity.—Vienna electrical exposition, 1883.

Gillmore, Q. A. Official report of the siege and
reduction of Fort Pulaski, Ga., feb., march
and april, 1862. Ill. (Papers on practical
engineering, no. 8.) N. Y. 1862. O.
in **623 : D**

Barnard, J: G. A report on the defenses of
Washington, to the chief of engineers, U.
S. army. (Professional papers, no. 20.)
Wash. 1871. Q.   *in* **623 : D**

Eads, James B. System of naval defences; report to the hon. Gideon Welles, sec. of the
navy, feb. 22, 1868. Ill. N. Y. 1868. Q.
623+2

Guarasci, Cæsar. Studies on coast defense,
applied to the gulf of Spezia. Tr. by G:
McC. Derby. Ill. (Engineer dep., U. S.
army.) Wash. 1884. O.   *in* **623 : D**

4. Bridge and road construction.

Bridges.

Haupt, Herman. General theory of bridge construction; containing demonstrations of
the principles of the art and their application to practice, furnishing the means of
calculating the strains upon the chords,
ties, braces, counter-braces and other parts
of a bridge or frame of any description,
with practical ill. N. Y. 1856. O.   **624+9**

Whipple, S. Bridge-building; the author's original work, pub. in 1847, with an app. containing corr., add. and explanations suggested by subsequent experience. Annexed

an original article on the doctrine of central forces. Albany, 1869. D.   **624 : 8**

Bender, C: Practical treatise on the properties of continuous bridges. [Van Nostrand's science ser.] N. Y. 1876. T.   **624 : 1**

Merriman, Mansfield. Theory and calculations of continuous bridges. [Van Nostrand's science ser.] N. Y. 1876. T.   **624 : 6**

Cain, W: Maximum stresses in framed bridges. [Van Nostrand's science ser.] N. Y. 1878. T.   **624 : 3**

Merrill, W: E. Iron truss bridges for railroads; methods of calculating strains, with a comparison of the most prominent truss bridges, and new formulas for bridge computations, also the economical angles for struts and ties. N. Y. 1870. F.   **624 : R10**

Robinson, S. W. Strength of wrought-iron bridge members. [Van Nostrand's science ser.] N. Y. 1882. T.   **624 : 12**

Dempsey, G. Drysdale. Tubular and other iron girder bridges, particularly describing the Britannia and Conway tubular bridges, with a sketch of iron bridges and illustrations of the application of malleable iron to the art of bridge-building. Ill. Lond. 1850. D.   **624 : 14**

Bland, W: The principles of construction in arches, piers, buttresses, etc.; a series of experimental essays, made with a view to their being useful to the practical builder. 4th ed. Ill. [Weale's ser.] Lond. 1875. D.   **624 : 7**

McMaster, J: Bach. Bridge and tunnel centres. [Van Nostrand's science ser.] N. Y. 1875. T.   **624 : 5**

Bender, C: Proportions of pins used in bridges. [Van Nostrand's science ser.] N. Y. 1873. T.   **624 : 2**

Hildenbrand, W: Cable-making for suspension bridges; with special reference to the cables of the East River bridge. [Van Nostrand's science ser.] N. Y. 1877. T.   **624 : 4**

Warren, Gouverneur K. Report on bridging the Mississippi river between Saint Paul, Minn., and Saint Louis, Mo.; being app. x 3 of the annual report of the chief of engineers for 1878. Wash. 1878. O.   **624+11**

— *Same.* (U. S. 45th cong. 2 sess. Sen. ex. doc. no. 69.) Wash. 1878. O.   *in* **624 : D**

Conant, W: C., *and* Montgomery **Schuyler**. The Brooklyn bridge: A history of the bridge, by W: C. Conant; The bridge as a monument, by Montgomery Schuyler; with an account of the opening exercises, may 24, 1883. (Frank. sq. lib.) N. Y. 1883. Q.   **624+13**

Roads.

Law, H:, *and* Daniel Kinnear **Clark**. The construction of roads and streets. in 2 parts: [Pt.] 1, The art of constructing common roads, by H: Law, rev. and condensed by D. K. Clark; [Pt.] 2, Recent practice in the construction of roads and streets, incl. pavements of stone, wood and asphalte, by D. K. Clark. Ill. [Weale's ser.] Lond. 1877. D.   **625 : 6**

Railways.

Stephenson, *Sir* Rowland MacDonald. Elementary and practical instructions on the science of railway construction. 5th ed. rev. and considerably augm. by E: Nugent. Ill. [Weale's ser.] Lond. 1874. D.   **625 : 7**

Adams, C: Francis, *jr.* Railroads; their origin and problems. N. Y. 1878. D.   **625 : 2**

— Notes on railroad accidents. N. Y. 1879. D.   **625 : 1**

Colburn, Zerah, *and* Alexander L. **Holley**. The permanent way and coal-burning locomotive boilers of european railways; with a comparison of the working economy of european and american lines, and the principles upon which improvement must proceed. Ill. N. Y. 1858. F.   **625 : R3**

Holley, Alexander L. American and european railway practice in the economical generation of steam, incl. the materials and construction of coal-burning boilers, combustion, the variable blast, vaporization, circulation, superheating, supplying and heating feed-water, etc., and the adoption of wood and coke-burning engines to coal-burning; and in permanent way, incl. roadbed, sleepers, rails, joint fastenings, street-railways, etc. Ill. N. Y. 1861. F.   **625 : R4**

Robinson, S. W. Railroad economics, or Notes with comments, from a tour over Ohio railways under the hon. H. Sabine, commissioner of railroads and telegraphs. [Van Nostrand's science ser.] N. Y. 1882. T.   **625 : 2**

Berlepsch, Herman Alexander [v.] Die Gotthardbahn; beschreibendes und geschichtliches. Karten. Gotha. 1881. Q. *In* Petermann's mitteilungen, Ergänzungsb. 14.   **905.1 : M**

Contents. Geologisches, gnostisches, mineralogisches. — Klimatisches. — Hydrographisches. — Pflanzendecke. — Geographisch-statistisches. — Historisches. — Finanzielles. — Bau. — Nachschrift: Geschäftsbericht von Juni 1881.

United States. *Secretary of war.* Report, communicating the several Pacific railroad explorations. Wash. 1855. 2 v. and maps. O.   *in* **625 : D**

— *Pacific railroad surveys.* Reports of explorations and surveys to ascertain the most practicable and economical route for a railroad from the Mississippi river to the Pacific ocean, made under the dir. of the sec. of war in 1853-54. Ill. Wash. 1855-59. 11 v. in 12.   *in* **625 : D**

Contents. V. **1.** Report of the sec. of war.—Humphreys, A. A., *and* G. K. **Warren**. Examination of the reports of explorations in 1853-4, and of the explorations made previous to that time which have a bearing upon the subject. — **McClellan**, G: B. Memoranda on railways.—**Stevens**, I. I. Explorations for a route near the 47th and 49th parallel of north latitude, from St. Paul to Puget Sound. V. 1, supp. *Same. Supplementary report:* General rep., with map and ill.—Botanical rep., ill.—Zoological rep., ill.—App. **2. Beckwith**, E. G. Explor. by J. W. Gunnison, near the 38th and 39th parallel of n. lat., from the mouth of the Kansas river, Mo., to the Sevier lake, in the great basin; ill. — **Beckwith**, E. G. Explor. on the 41st par. of n. lat.—Geological rep. of the country explored under the 38th and 41st par., ill.—Botany of the [two preceding] expeditions, ill.—**Lander**, F: W. Synopsis of a report of the reconnaissance of a r. r. route from Puget Sound via the South Pass to the Mississippi river.—Pope, J: Explor. near the 32d parallel of n. lat., from the Red River to the Rio Grande; Botany of the exped., ill; Geology of the route, ill.—Parke, J: G. Explor. for that portion near the 32d par. of n. lat., lying between Doña Ana, on the Rio Grande, and Pimas villages, on the Gila.—Emory, W. H. Extract from a rep. of a military reconnaissance, made in 1846-7. 3. Whipple, A. W. Extract from prelim. report.—Whipple, A. W., and J. C. Ives. Explor. near the 35th par. of n. lat., from the Mississippi river to the Pacific ocean, ill. Pt. 1, Itinerary; pt. 2, Topographical features and character of the country; pt. 3, The indian tribes; pt. 4, Geology. 4. Same, pt. 5, Botany; pt. 6, Zoology, introd.; Appendices [physical observations]. 5. Williamson, R. S. Explor. in California for routes to connect with the routes near the 35th and 32d par. of n. lat., ill. Pt. I, Report; pt. 2, Geological rep.; pt. 3, Botanical rep.; (pt. 4, Zoological rep., in v. 10); App. [distances, altitudes, etc.] 6. Abbot, H: L. Explor. from the Sacramento valley to the Columbia river, made by R. S. Williamson and H: L. Abbot, ill. Introd.; Pt. 1, General rep.; pt. 2, Geological rep.; pt. 3, Botanical rep.; pt. 4, Zoological rep.; App. (physical observations). 7. Parke, J: G., and Albert H. Campbell. Explor. from San Francisco bay to Los Angeles, Cal., west of the Coast Range, and from the Pimas villages on the Gila to the Rio Grande, near the 32d par. of n. lat., ill. Pt. 1, General rep.; pt. 2, Geological rep.; pt. 3, Botanical rep.; App. (meteorol. observ., etc.)—Humphreys, A. A. Conclusion of the official review of the reports upon explor. and surveys for railroad routes from the Mississippi river to the Pacific ocean. 8, 9. General report upon the zoology of the several Pacific railroad routes, pt. 1, 2. 10. Same, pt. 3, 4. —Zoological portions of the reports of E. G. Beckwith, A. W. Whipple, J: G. Parke, R. S. Williamson, and H: L. Abbot. 11. Warren, G. K. Memoir upon the material used and methods employed in compiling the general map to ill. the [above] reports.— Topographical maps, profiles and sketches.

Note. The scientific works have been entered separately in their proper places, in this catalogue.

5. Canals and harbors.

Barnard, J: G. Report on the North Sea canal of Holland, and on the improvement of navigation from Rotterdam to the sea, to the chief of engineers, U. S. army. Maps and ill. (Prof. papers of the corps of engineers, U. S. army, no. 22.) Wash. 1872. Q.   in 626 : D

Fitzgerald, Percy. The great canal at Suez; its political, engineering and financial history, with an account of the struggles of its projector Ferdinand de Lesseps. Lond. 1876. 2 v. O.   626 : 1

United States. Navy department. Report on interoceanic canals and railroads between the Atlantic and Pacific oceans, by C: H. Davis. Maps. Wash. 1867. O. in 626 : D

— - Reports of explorations and surveys to ascertain the practicability of a ship canal between the Atlantic and Pacific oceans, by way of the isthmus of Tehuantepec, by Robert W. Shufeldt. Maps and ill. Wash. 1872. Q.   in 626 : D
Contents. Shufeldt, R. W. Report.—Fuertes, A., chief civil engineer. Report, with app. on natural history.—Farquhar, Norman H. Report on hydrographic surveys on the Atlantic coast.—Hopkins, Alfred. Report on hydrogr. surveys on the Pacific coast.—Spear, J: G. Report on the geology, mineralogy, natural history, inhabitants and agriculture of the isthmus.—Beaumont, Horatio N. Report on the sanitary condition and climatic influences of the Coatzacoalcos river, Mexico.

— - Same, through Nicaragua, 1872-73, [by Alexander F. Crossman, Chester Hatfield and E: P. Lull]. Maps. Wash. 1874. Q.   in 626 : D
Contents. Hatfield, C. Report on surveys.—Lull,

United States. Navy department.—Continued.
E: P. Report.—Menocal, A. G., chief civil engineer. Report, with estimates.—Journals.—Bransford, J: F. Rep. on health, climate, food-productions, etc.— Cope, E: D. Reptiles.—Tryon, G: W., jr. Shells. —Endlich, F: M. Lithological and geognostic specimens.—Reed, A. V. Six months' observations of weather, etc.—Nourse, J. E. Brief historical memoir of interoceanic communication across the great isthmus, especially of the plans for a ship-canal across Nicaragua.

— - Same, by the way of the isthmus of Darien, by T: Oliver Selfridge. Maps and ill. Wash. 1874. Q.   in 626 : D
Contents. Selfridge, T: O. Reports, 1870, 1871, 1873. —Lull, E: P. Hydrographic operations, 1870, 1871.— Carson, J. Petigru. Geological rep. on the Darien route and Nercalagua river, bay of San Blas; Barometrical rep., 1870.—Bowditch, E. W. Geological formation of the Sassardi and Morti, and San Blas routes, 1870.—Maack, G. A. Geology and natural hist. of the isthmuses of Choca, of Darien, and of Panama, 1872.—Barker, G. F. Analysis of specimens of coal from the isthmus of Darien.—Mosman, A. T. Astronomical observations, 1870.—Blake, F. P., jr. Astronomical observations, 1871.—Simon, W. J., and Alfred Griffith. Sanitary condition of the Darien expedition.—Fussell, Linnæus. Medical report.— Collins, F: Winds and currents of the Pacific ocean, and sailing routes to and from Cupica bay.

— - Reports of explorations and surveys for the location of interoceanic ship-canals through the isthmus of Panama, and by the valley of the river Napipi by U. S. naval expeditions 1879. Maps and plans. Wash. 1879. Q.   in 626 : D
Contents. Lull, E: P. Report on Panama expedition.—Collins, F: Report on Napipi expedition.

— - Report of historical and technical information relating to the problem of interoceanic communication by way of the american isthmus, by J: T. Sullivan. Maps and ill. Wash. 1883. Q.   in 626 : D
Contains reviews and discussions of canal routes surveyed, canals and ship railways proposed, and a bibliography of works having reference to the subject.

Turnbull, W: Reports on the construction of the piers of the aqueduct of the Alexandria canal across the Potomac river at Georgetown, D. C., 1835—1840. Maps and ill. (Engineer dep't, U. S. army.) Wash. 1873. Q.   in 626 : D

Chandler, W: History of the St. Mary's Falls ship canal; showing the early efforts which were made to secure its construction, with a record of the business of the canal from its opening until the present time, together with the improvements made and in process of construction. Map. Lansing. 1878. O. In Michigan, Joint doc's, 1877, v. 3.
                                 in 328.15 : D

Bunsen, Theodor v. Die Donau. In Deutsche zeit- und streit-fragen.   304 : 15 v13

Stuart, C: B. The naval dry docks of the U. S. Ill. N. Y. 1852. F.   627 : R2

United States. Chief of engineers, U. S. army. Analytical and topical index to the reports of the chief of engineers and the officers of the corps of engineers, U. S. A., upon works and surveys for river and harbor improvement, 1866—1879; comp. under the direction of maj. H: M. Robert by L: Y. Schermerhorn, S: O. L. Potter and others. Wash. 1881. O.   627 : 3

— Coast survey. A table of depths for the harbors on the coasts of the U. S. In Report 1883.
                                 in 622 : D

Graham, James D. Annual report on the harbor improvements of lakes Michigan and St. Clair for 1855 and 1856. (U. S. 34th cong. 3 sess. Sen. ex. doc. no. 16). Wash. 1856. O. *in* 627 : D
— *Same*, 1857. (U. S. 35th cong. 1 sess. House ex. doc. no. 23). Wash. 1857. O. *in* 627 : D

Mitchell, H: Report concerning recent observations at South Pass bar, Mississippi river. *In* U. S. coast survey rep. 1875. *in* 622 : D

Corthell, E. L. A history of the jetties at the mouth of the Mississippi river. 2d ed. N. Y. 1881. O. 627+1

Williamson, Robert S., *and* W: H. **Heuer.** Report upon the removal of Blossom Rock in San Francisco harbor, Cal., 1870. Ill. (Engineer dep't, U. S. army). Wash. 1871. Q. *in* 627 : D

6. Hydraulic engineering.

Aubuisson de Voisins, J: Francois d'. Treatise on hydraulics for the use of engineers. Tr. from the french and adapted to the english units of measure by Joseph Bennett. Bost. 1852. O. 628 : R21

Downing, S: The elements of practical hydraulics for the use of students in engineering. 2d ed. rev. and enl. Lond. 1861. O. 628 : 19

Beardmore, Nathaniel. Manual of hydrology; containing : 1, Hydraulic and other tables ; 2, Rivers, flow of water, springs, wells and percolation ; 3, Tides, estuaries and tidal rivers ; 4, Rainfall and evaporation. Lond. 1862. O. 628 : R24

Box, T: Practical hydraulics ; a series of rules and tables for the use of engineers. 2d ed. Lond. 1870. D. 628 : 17

Neville, J: Hydraulic tables, coefficients and formulæ for finding the discharge of water from orifices, notches, weirs, pipes and rivers. 3d ed. with add., consisting of new formulæ for the discharge from tidal and flood sluices and syphons, general information on rainfall, catchment basins, drainage, sewerage, water supply for towns and mill power. Lond. 1875. D. 628 : R20

Flynn, P. J. Hydraulic tables for the calculation of the discharge through sewers, pipes and conduits, based on Kutter's formulas. [Van Nostrand's science ser.] N. Y. 1883. T. 628 : 35

Francis, James B. Lowell hydraulic experiments ; a selection from experiments on hydraulic motors, on the flow of water over weirs, in open canals of uniform rectangular section and through submerged orifices and diverging tubes. Made at Lowell, Mass. 2d ed., rev. and enl. N. Y. 1868. F. 628 : R26

Humphreys, Andrew Atkinson, *and* H: L. **Abbot.** Report upon the physics and hydraulics of the Mississippi river, upon the protection of the alluvial region against overflow, and upon the deepening of the mouths ; based upon surveys and investigations made under the acts of congress directing the topographical and hydrographical survey of the delta of the Mississippi river, with such investigations as

Humphreys, A. A., *and* H: L. **Abbot.**—*Continued.* might lead to determine the most practicable plan for securing it from inundation, and the best mode of deepening the channels at the mouth of the river. Submitted to the bureau of topographical engineers, war dep't, 1861. Wash. 1867. O. *in* 628 : D
— *Same.* Reprinted, with additions. Maps and ill. (Prof. papers of the corps of engineers, U. S. army, no. 13.) Wash. 1876. Q. *in* 628 : D

Glynn, Joseph. Rudimentary treatise on the power of water, as applied to drive flour mills, and to give motion to turbines and other hydrostatic engines. 6th ed., with add. and corr. Ill. [Weale's ser.] Lond. 1879. D. 628 : 7

Trowbridge, W: Petit. Turbine wheels ; on the inapplicability of the theoretical investigations of the turbine wheel, as given by Rankine, Weisbach, Bresse and others, to the modern constructions introduced by Boyden and Francis. [Van Nostrand's science ser.] N. Y. 1879. T. 628 : 39

Swindell, J: G: Rudimentary treatise on well-digging, boring and pump-work. 7th ed., rev. by G. R. Burnell. Ill. [Weale's ser.] Lond. 1877. D. 628 : 14

Ewbank, T: A descriptive and historical account of hydraulic and other machines for raising water, ancient and modern ; with observations on various subjects connected with the mechanic arts, incl. the progressive development of the steam engine,... in 5 books, ill. 4th ed., rev. and corr.; added, a supp. N. Y. 1850. O. 628 : 1

Hughes, S: A treatise on water works for the supply of cities and towns ; with a description of the principal g ologic l formations of England, as influencinga supplies of water, details of engines and pumping machinery for raising water, and descriptions of works which have been executed for procuring water from wells, rivers, springs and drainage areas. Lond. 1859. D. 628 : 9
— *Same.* A treatise on water works for the supply of cities and towns, with a description of the principal geological formations as influencing supplies of water. New ed., rev. and enl. [Weale's ser.] Lond. 1875. D. 628 : 9

Humber, W: A treatise on the water supply of cities and towns ; with numerous specifications of existing water works. Ill. Lond. 1876. F. 628 : R30

Jacob, Arthur. The designing and construction of storage reservoirs. [Van Nostrand's science ser.] N. Y. 1873. T. 628 : 10

Kirkwood, James P. Report on the filtration of river waters for the supply of cities, as practised in Europe, made to the board of water commissioners of the city of St. Louis. N. Y. 1869. Q. 628 : R25
— *ed.* Collection of reports, condensed, and opinions of chemists in regard to the use of lead pipe in the distribution of water for the supply of cities. N. Y. 1859. O. 628 : 18

Folkard, C: Watson. Potable water, and the relative efficiency of different methods of detecting impurities. [Van Nostrand's science ser.] N. Y. 1882. T.   **628 : 33**

Note. Relates to the contamination of city water supplies.

Bell, T: J. History of the water supply of the world, arranged in a comprehensive form from eminent authorities ; containing a description of the various methods of water supply, pollution and purification of waters and sanitary effects, with analyses of potable waters, also geology and water strata of Hamilton county, Ohio, statistics of the Ohio river proposed water supply of Cincinnati, together with a number of valuable tables and diagrams. Cinc. 1882. O.   **628 : 37**

London *city. Water supply.* Minutes of evidence taken before the select committee of the metropolis water supply bill and the Chelsea waterworks bill. 1851, 1852. 2 v. Lond. 1851, 1852.   **628 : R34**

Paris *city. Water, sewage.* Documents relatifs aux eaux de Paris. Paris. 1861. D.   **628 : 36**

Bradlee, Nathaniel P. History of the introduction of pure water into the city of Boston, with a description of its Cochituate waterworks. Ill. by maps and plans. Compiled by a member of the water board. Bost. 1868. Q.   **628 : R22**

Fitzgerald, Desmond. History of the Boston waterworks from 1868 to 1876 ; a supp. to a "History of the introduction of pure water into the city of Boston." Bost. 1876. Q.   **628 : R23**

Schramke, G. T. Description of the New York Croton acqueduct in english, german and french. Ill. 2d ed. N. Y. 1855. F.   **628 : R31**

Brooklyn *city, N. Y.* Documents and plans submitted by the water committee to the common council of the city of Brooklyn for 1854. Brooklyn. 1854. Q.   **628 : R28**

— The Brooklyn waterworks and sewers ; a descriptive memoir. Ill. N. Y. 1867. F.   **628 : R29**

Albany *city, N. Y. Water commissioners.* Report to the common council, transmitting the rep. of the sup't of the water works, of the resident engineer for the additional supply, and the engineer in charge of the new pumping works, for 1876. Ill. Albany. 1877. O.   **628 : Pam**

Note. For reports on the Milwaukee waterworks, see Municipal documents, cl. 351.1, col. 230.

Wells, Walter. The water-power of Maine. Augusta. 1869. O.   **628+27**

— *Same.*   **628 : R27**

Hearding, W: Hellins. Practical notes on hydrographic and mining surveys, with ill. Milw. 1872. O.   **628 : 8**

7. Mining engineering.

Burgoyne, *Sir* J: A treatise on the blasting and quarrying of stone for building and other purposes ; with the constituents and analysis of granite, slate, limestone and sandstone. Added, some remarks on the blowing up of bridges. New ed. [Weale's ser.] Lond. 1874. D.   **628 : 4**

Davies, D. C. A treatise on metalliferous minerals and mining. Lond. 1880. D.   **628 : 6**

Fenwick, T:, *and* T: **Baker.** Subterraneous surveying, with and without the magnetic needle. New ed. [Weale's ser.] Lond. 1877. D.   **628 : 15**

Lintern, W: The mineral surveyor and valuer's complete guide ; comprising a treatise on improved mining surveying, with new traverse tables and descriptions of improved instruments, also an exposition of the correct principles of laying out and valuing home and foreign iron and coal mineral properties. Ill. [Weale's ser.] Lond. 1877. D.   **628 : 12**

— Magnetic surveying, and angular surveying ; with records of the peculiarities of needle disturbances, compiled from the results of carefully made experiments. [Weale's ser.] Lond. 1881. D.   **628 : 11**

Smyth, Warington Wilkinson. A rudimentary treatise on coal and coal mining. 5th ed., rev. and enl. [Weale's ser.] Lond. 1880. D.   **628 : 13**

Atkinson, J: J. A practical treatise on gases met with in coal mines. [Van Nostrand's science ser.] N. Y. 1875. T.   **628 : 3**

— A practical treatise on friction of air in mines. [Van Nostrand's science ser.] N. Y. 1875. T.   **628 : 2**

Fairley, W. The ventilation of coal mines. [Van Nostrand's science ser.] N. Y. 1882. T.   **628 : 32**

Daddow, S. Harris, *and* B: **Bannan.** Coal, iron and oil, or The practical american miner ; a work on our mines and mineral resources and a text-book or guide to their economical development... Ill. Pottsville, Pa. 1866. O.   **628+5**

Wright, W: The oil regions of Pennsylvania ; showing where petroleum is found, how it is obtained and at what cost, with hints for whom it may concern. N. Y. 1865. D.   **628 : 16**

Michigan *state. Commissioner of mineral statistics.* First annual report for 1877—8 and previous years. Ill. Marquette. 1879. O.   *in* **628 : D**

— — Annual report for 1880[—1882]. Maps and ill. Lansing. 1881-83. 3 v. O.   *in* **628 : D**

United States. *Commissioner of mining statistics.* Statistics of mines and mining in the states and territories west of the Rocky mountains ; reports for 1867—1875. Ill. Wash. 1867-77. 10 v. O.   *in* **628 : D**

Note. The first three rep. are styled "Mineral resources of the states, etc." Reports for 1867, 1868, by J. Ross Browne, are preliminary to the remaining rep., made by Rossiter W. Raymond and called 1st—8th annual reports. The 4th, 6th and 8th of these we have only in the full set of congressional documents, being respectively the following nos. of the House exec. doc.: 42d cong. 2 sess. no. 211; 43d cong. 1 sess. no. 141; 44th cong. 1 sess. no. 159.

Hague, James Duncan. Mining industry [of the country along the 40th parallel] ; with geological contributions by Clarence King. Maps and ill. (U. S. geol. expl. 40th par., King ; Report, v. 3.) Wash. 1870. Q.   *in* **557.5 : D**

Contents. **King,** C. Mining districts; The Comstock lode.—**Hague,** J. D. The Comstock mines; Treatment of the Comstock ores.—**Hague,** Arnold. Chemistry of the Washoe process.—**Hague,** J. D. Central and eastern Nevada.—**King,** C. The Green river coal basin.— **Hague**, J. D. Colorado; Gold mining in Colorado; Silver mining in Colorado.— Index.

Lakes, Arthur. Profile map of Engineer mountain, Mineral Point mountain, Animas Forks and surrounding region. with general description of mines ; history and geology of the San Juan. Golden. [1882]. O.   **628 : 38**

Morgans, W: Manual of mining tools ; comprising observations on the materials from, and processes by which they are manufactured, their special uses, applications, qualities and efficiency. Ill. by an atlas, drawn to scale. [Weale's ser.] Lond. 1871. 2 v. D. *and* Q.   **629 : 2**

4. Agriculture.

1. In general.

Washington, G: Letters on agriculture, to Arthur Young and sir J: Sinclair, with statistical tables and remarks by T: Jefferson, R: Peters and other gentlemen, on the economy and management of farms in the U. S., ed. by Franklin Knight. Wash. 1847. Q.   **630 : R15**

Loudon, J: Claudius. An encyclopædia of agriculture ; comprising the theory and practice of the valuation, transfer, laying out, improvement and management of landed property, and the cultivation and economy of the animal and vegetable productions of agriculture ; incl. all the latest improvements, a general history of agriculture in all countries, a statistical view of its present state, with suggestions for its future progress in the British Isles, and supp. bringing down the work to 1844. 5th ed. ill. Lond. 1857. O.   **630 : R2**

Colman, H: European agriculture and rural economy, from personal observation. Bost. 1846, 1848. 2 v. O.   **630+4**

Lammers, A: Die Bremer landwirthschaftsausstellung in juni 1874. *In* Deutsche zeit- und streit-fragen.   **304 : 15 v3**

Emmons, Ebenezer. Agriculture of New York ; comprising an account of the classification, composition and distribution of the soils and rocks, and the natural waters of the different geological formations, together with a condensed view of the climate and the agricultural productions of the state. Ill. Albany. 1846–54. 5 v. Q. *In* Natural hist. of N. Y., pt. 5.   **557.3 : R1**

Norton, J: Pitkin. Elements of scientific agriculture, or The connection between science and the art of practical farming ; prize essay of the New York state agricultural society. 4th ed. Albany. 1853. D.   **630 : 13**

Emerson, Gouverneur. The american farmer's encyclopædia ; embracing all the recent discoveries in agricultural chemistry and the use of mineral, vegetable and animal manures, with descriptions and figures of amer. insects injurious to vegetation. On the basis of Johnson's Farmer's encyclopædia. Ill. N. Y. 1860. O.   **630 : 7**

Coulter, *Miss* —. Our farm of four acres, and the money we made by it. From the 12th Lond. ed.; with an introd. by P: B. Mead. N. Y. 1860. D.   **630 : 10**

Morris, E: How to get a farm and how to find one ; showing that homesteads may be had by those desirous of securing them, with the pu lic law on the subject of free homes and suggestions from practical farmers, with numerous successful experiences of others, who, though beginning with little or nothing, have become the owners of ample farms, by the author of "Ten acres enough." N. Y. 1864. D.   **630 : 12**

Martineau, Harriet. Our farm of two acres. N. Y. 1865. S.   **630 : 9**

Mitchell, Donald Grant. Rural studies, with hints for country places. [*Anon.*] N. Y. 1867. D.   **630 : 11**
Contents. An old-style farm.—Advice for Lackland. —Way-side hints.— Laying out of grounds.— Mr. Urban and a country house.

Roosevelt, Robert Barnwell. Five acres too much ; a truthful elucidation of the attractions of the country and a careful consideration of the question of profit and loss, as involved in amateur farming, with much valuable advice and instruction to those about purchasing large or small places in the rural districts. N. Y. 1869. D.   **630 : 14**

Beecher, H: Ward. Pleasant talk about fruits, flowers and farming. New ed. with add. matter from recent writings, pub. and unpub. N. Y. 1874. D.   **630 : 5**

Hamm, W: v. Die naturkräfte in ihrer anwendung auf die landwirthschaft. München 1876. S.   **630 : 1**

Allen, R: L. New american farm book ; rev. and enl. by Lewis F. Allen. N. Y. 1879. D.   **630 : 3**

Lupton, N. T. The elementary principles of scientific agriculture. N. Y. 1880. S.   **630 : 8**

Donaldson, J: Suburban farming ; a treatise on the laying out and cultivating of farms adapted to the produce of milk, butter and cheese, eggs, poultry and pigs, with considerable add., illustrating the more modern practice, by Robert Scott Burn. 2d ed. Ill. [Weale's ser.] Lond. 1881. D.   **630 : 6**

Dun, Finlay. American farming and food. Lond. 1881. D.   **630 : 16**

Morris, E: Farming for boys ; what they have done, and what others may do, in the cultivation of farm and garden ; how to begin, how to proceed, and what to aim at. Ill. Bost. [1881]. D.   **x 630 : 17**

Ludloff, K. Die ursachen des wohlstands und der verarmung der völker. Milw. 1882. O.   **630 : 18**

Henderson, P: Garden and farm topics. N. Y. 1884. D.   **630 : 19**

x denotes books specially adapted for children.

Periodicals and reports.

United States. *Census office.* Tenth census, 1880, v. 3: Report on the productions of agriculture, as returned june 1, 1880. Maps and ill. Wash. 1883. Q.   *in* 317 : **D**
Contents. **Walker,** Francis A. Remarks on the statistics of agr.—General statistics: tabular statements.—**Brewer,** W: H. Cereal production of the U. S. [incl. cost, methods, varieties, history of agr., etc.].—**Neftel,** Knight. Flour-milling processes.—**Killebrew,** J. B. Culture and curing of tobacco in the U. S.; with report on the chemistry of amer. tobaccos by Gideon E. **Moore.—Dodge,** J. R. Statistics of mfrs. of tobacco, and of its commercial distribution, exportation and prices.—**Gordon,** Clarence. Cattle, sheep and swine [incl. Pasture and forage plants by W: H. Brewer].—General index.

— — Tenth census, 1880, v. 5, 6: Report on cotton production in the U. S., also embracing agricultural and physico-geographical descriptions of the several cotton states and of California ; Eugene W. **Hilgard,** special agent in charge. Maps and ill. Wash. 1884. 2 v. Q.   *in* 317 : **D**
Contents. V. **1. Hilgard,** E. W. General discussion of the cotton production of the U. S., embracing the cotton-seed oil industry, methods and utility of soil investigation, and tables of cotton fiber measurements.—Pt. 1. Mississippi valley and southwestern states: Hilgard, E. W., Louisiana, Mississippi; **Safford,**James M., Tennessee, Kentucky; **Loughridge,** R. H., Missouri, Arkansas, Texas, Indian Territory. 2. Pt. 2. Eastern Gulf, Atlantic and Pacific states: **Smith,** Eugene Allen, Alabama, Florida; Loughridge, R. H., Georgia; **Hammond,** Harry, South Carolina; **Kerr,** W. C., North Carolina, Virginia.—App. **Hilgard,** E. W. Physical and ag'l features of California, with a discussion of the present and future of cotton production in the state; also, remarks on cotton culture in New Mexico, Utah, Arizona and Mexico.—General index.

— *Dep't of agriculture.* Reports of the commissioner of agriculture, 1849—1884. Wash. 1850-84. 35 v. O.   *in* 630 : **D**
Note. Up to and incl. 1861, the reports were pub. as a part of the patent office reports, and under the dir. of the commissioner of patents. The office of Com'r of agr. was created the year following.

— — General index of the agricultural reports of the patent office for the 25 years, 1837—1861 ; and of the department of agriculture for 15 years, from 1862 to 1876. Wash. 1879. O.   *in* 630 : **D**

— — Special reports ; no. 1-65. Wash. 1877-83. 10 v. O.   *in* 630 : **D**
Note. Contain principally monthly reports on crops, etc., with a few monographs, which have been entered in their proper place, in this catalogue.

— — [Special reports, v. 11]. Wash. 1883-85. O.   *in* 630 : **D**
Contents. Area and products of cereals grown in 1879, as returned by the census of 1880.—**Baker,** F. P. Prelim. rep. on the forestry of the Mississippi valley; *and* **Furnas,** Robert W. Tree planting on the plains.—Proceedings of a national convention of cattle breeders and others, called in Chicago, nov. 15-16, 1883, to consider the subject of contagious diseases of domestic animals.—**Waterhouse,** S. Report on jute culture, and the importance of the industry.—**Vasey,** G: The agricultural grasses of the U. S., ill., *and* **Richardson,** Clifford. The chemical composition of amer. grasses.—**Rapley,** E. E. The soils and products of southwestern Louisiana, incl. the parishes of St. Landry, La Fayette, Vermillion, St. Martin's, Iberia and St. Mary's.—**Welch,** A. S. Rep. on the organization and management of 7 agr. schools in Germany, Belgium and England.—A directory of dep's, boards, soc's, colleges and other organizations in the interest of agriculture, horticulture, stock-raising, dairying, bee-keeping, fish-culture and kindred industries, april 1885.—**Dodge,** J. R. A rep. of exhibits, ill. agricultural statistics at the World's ind. and cotton expos. at New Orleans, La., diagr.

United States. *Dep't of agriculture.—Continued.*
— — Miscellaneous ; Special report, no. 1—7. Wash. 1883-85. O.   *in* 630 : **D**
Contents. 1. **Loring,** G: B. Address before the American forestry congress, St. Paul, Minn., aug. 8, 1883.—2. Proceedings of a convention of agriculturists, held at the dep. of agr., jan. 23-29, 1883; 2d convention.—3. **Hurt,** A. B. Mississippi; its climate, soil, productions and agr'l capabilities.—4. **Boardman,** S: L. The climate, soil, physical resources and agr'l capabilities of the state of Maine; with special ref. to the occupation of its new lands.—5. The proper value and management of gov. timber lands and the distribution of north amer. forest trees; papers read at the U. S. dep. of agr., may 7-8, 1884.—6. **Loring,** G: B. Address at the National convention of cattle-breeders, Chicago, Ill., nov. 13, 1884; also the rep. of the veterinary inspectors in N. Y.—7. **Nesbit,** D. M. Tide marshes of the U. S.; with contributions from U. S. coast survey, S: L. Boardman, Eldridge Morse and others.

— — *Bureau of statistics.* Report, no. 1-18, oct. 1883—may 1885. Wash. 1883-85. O.
    in 630 : **D**
Note. Contain monthly rep. on condition and yield of crops in this country, Mexico, Europe, India, etc., condition of farm animals, and freight rates of transportation companies.

— — *Division of chemistry.* Bulletin, no. 1-4. Wash. 1883-84. O.   *in* 630 : **D**
Contents. 1. **Richardson,** Clifford. An investigation of the composition of amer. wheat and corn.—2. **Wiley,** H. W. Diffusion; its application to sugar-cane, and record of experiments with sorghum in 1883.—3. **Wiley,** H. W. The northern sugar industry; a record of its progress during the season of 1883. Maps and ill.—4. **Richardson,** C. An invest. of the composition of amer. wheat and corn; 2d rep.

Massachusetts *state.* Board of agriculture. 3d [4th, 15th, 16th, 22d, 23d, 25th] annual report of the secretary [C: L. Flint]; with app. containing reports of committees appointed to visit the county exhibitions, and returns of the finances of the agricultural societies for 1855, 1856, 1867, 1868, 1874, 1875, 1877. [2d series]. Ill. Bost. 1856-78. 7 v. O.
    606.3+D6

— — General index of the 25 annual reports of the sec. of the Mass. board of agr., 1853—1877. Bost. 1878. O. *In* Rep. for 1877.
    606.3+D6 v25

— — 28th[-30th] annual report of the secretary [J: E. Russell], with the returns of the finances of the agricultural societies for 1880—1882. Bost. 1881-83. 3 v. O.
    606.3+D6

American institute of the city of New York. Annual report for 1867-68. Albany. 1868. O.   **606.3+1**

• **New York state** agricultural society. Transactions, with an abstract of the proceedings of the county agricultural societies. 1867, v. 27. Albany. 1869. 2 v. O.
    606.3+2

Illinois state agricultural society. Transactions, with the proceedings of the county societies and kindred associations ; v. 1-4. Springfield. 1855-61. 4 v. O.   **606.3 : 5**

Michigan *state.* Board of agriculture. 9th[-19th] annual report of the secretary for 1870 [—1880]. Lansing. 1870-80. 11 v. in 10. O.
    606.3 : D13

— *Secretary of state.* 1st [and 2d] annual rep. of the cereal products of the state of Mich. 1876-7[—1877-8]. Lansing. 1877-78. 2 v. O.
    606.3 : D14

Michigan. *Secretary of state.—Continued.*
— - 1st[-3d] annual rep. relating to farms and farm products, 1878-9[—1880-1]. Maps. Lansing. 1880-82. 3 v. O. **606.3 : D14**
Michigan state pomological society. 6th[-9th] annual report of the secretary, 1876 [-1879]. Lansing. 1877-80. 4 v. O. **606.3 : D15**
— - Index to vol. 1 to 9 incl. *In* Rep. for 1880. **606.3 : D**
— - horticultural society. 10th [and 11th] annual report of the secretary, 1880, [1881]. Lansing. 1881-82. 2 v. O. **606.3 : D15**
Wisconsin state agricultural society. Transactions; v. 1-22, 1851 — 1884. Madison. 1852-84. O. **606.3 : 7**
Note. V. 4 covers the period 1854-57; v. 5, 1858-59; v. 7, 1861-68; all the rest one year each.—These vols. contain annual reports, records of proceedings, reports on the annual exhibitions, meteorological observations, reports on experiments at the university farm, and a large number of papers and discussions on topics, more or less intimately connected with husbandry in all its branches (for which see the contents of each vol.), the following being the principal special articles:
1852. Lapham, I. A. Fauna and flora of Wis.: Mammals; Birds; Reptiles; Fishes; Mollusks; Fossils in the rocks; Plants.—**Hoy,** P. R. Notes on the woods of Wis. **1853. Lapham,** I. A. The grasses of Wis., ill. **1855. Lapham,** I. A. The forest trees of Wis., ill. **1859. Hale,** T. J. Additions to the flora of Wisconsin. **1860. Daniels,** E: Building stones and marbles.—**Hale,** T. J. Additions to the flora of Wis.—Industrial resources and condition of counties, map. **1861-8. Hoyt,** J. W. Glimpses of western Europe: Report on the International exhibition of 1862 [at London]; Through continental Europe: Report on the Universal exposition of 1867 [at Paris]. **1869. Hoyt,** J. W. Agr'l schools in all countries. **1870. Willard,** X. A. Amer. butter factories and butter manufacture, ill.—**Riley,** C: V. The Colorado potato bug, ill.—Industrial reports of counties. **1871. Murrish,** J: Report on the geological survey. **1872-3. Parkinson,** J. B. Production and consumption, demand and supply.—**Palmer,** Alfred. Fish culture.—**Murrish,** J: Geological survey of the mineral regions. **1873-4. Flagg,** W. C. Republican democracy.—**Anderson,** M. Currency, taxation, transportation.—**Cheney,** Rufus. The importance of manufacturing.—**Lapham,** I. A. Geological survey, its relation to agriculture.—**Graham,** Alex. Labor.—**Carpenter,** S. H. Industrial education.—**Hoy,** P. R. Fish of Wis.—**Green,** Seth. Fish culture.—**Carpenter,** S. D. Production and consumption; transportation, population and taxation. **1874-5. Newton,** W. H. Peat, a cheap fuel in the near future. — **Sterling,** J: W. Protection from lightning.—**Field,** W. W. Interest on money; a high rate ruinous to productive industry.—**Phillips,** Wendell. Currency. — **Bascom,** J: Dress. — **Dennett,** Fannie B. The proper advancement of woman. —**Smith,** G: B. Monopolies in their relation to the industrial interests of the country. **1875-6. Myers,** Sidney. Finance. — **Orledge,** W: The farmer in politics.—**Benton,** E. H. Our agricultural rag-baby [currency].—**Steele,** G: M. Gold as a standard of value.—**Leland,** E. B. A consideration of the inter-convertible-note scheme.—**Carpenter,** S. D. Dollars and sense.—**Tenney,** H. A. Original creation of the soil, etc.—**Skavlem,** H. E. Self-culture.—**Field,** Jennie M. The ministry of toil. **1876-7. Bascom,** J: Conditions of progress in the agricultural classes. —**Lewis,** *Mrs.* H. M. Remarkable trees and plants. —**Allen,** W: F. Agriculture in the middle ages.— **Evarts,** W: M. Centennial address: What the age owes to America.—**Atwood,** D: The centennial exhibition of 1876. **1877-8. Welch,** W: Fish culture. —**Steele,** G: M. Taxation.—**Daniells,** W. W. Health in farmers' homes.—**Vincent,** H. Mental faculties of domestic animals. — **Bascom,** J: The common school.—**Stewart,** E. W. Cattle feeding: Fresh meat shipment to Europe.—Wisconsin and her governors. —Progress of industrial education.—**Johnston,** J: Currency. **1878-9. Whitford,** W. C. Education of work.—**Rice,** J: A. Mexico, the great west of the near future. — **Lockett,** S. H. The valleys of the Nile and Mississippi.—**Brewer,** W: H. Government and agriculture.—**Vilas,** W: F. The american sol-

dier. **1879-80. Gordon,** G: E. Taxation.—**Smith,** G: B. An historical address before Wis. pioneers.— Fish farming. **1880-1. Arnold,** A. A. Transportation from the northwest to the sea-coast.—**Westcott,** O. S. Economy of practical entomology.— **Babbitt,** Clinton. Railroads and the people.—**Carpenter,** A. V. H. Uses and abuses of railways.— **Case,** F. W. Entomological notes. **1881-2. Tanner,** C. Highways in Belgium and the U. S. **1883. Anderson,** Matt. Tariff, its effect upon agriculture. —**Naber,** Hiram. Protection.—**Merrill,** S. T. Economy and savings institutions. — **King,** F. H. The industrial relations of our birds.—**Broughton,** A. Industrial education.—**Goodale,** S. L. Remarks on the physiology of breeding. **1884.** *Same continued.* **Willard,** *Mrs.* F. P. Insectivorous plants.—**Crosby,** Howard. The dangerous classes.
Wisconsin fruit growers' assoc., (*now* Wisconsin state horticultural society.) Transactions, 1853—1859. *In* Wisconsin state agricultural society's trans., v. 4-6. **606.3 : 7**
Wisconsin state horticultural society. Transactions; v. 1-14, 1864—1884. Madison. 1871-84. O. **606.3 : 8**
Note. Transactions for 1864—1869 are in Wisconsin state agricultural society's trans. (606.3 : 7) v. 7, 8; from 1871, they are pub. separately and the vols. for each year numbered from 1 up.—The vols. for 1883 and 1884 are also bound with the reports of the state agricultural soc. for the corresponding year.
Northern Wisconsin agricultural and mechanical association. Transactions, incl. reports of conventions, etc.; v. 7, 8. Madison. 1880, 1881. 2 v. O. **606.3 : 9**
Wisconsin dairymen's association. [2d-]9th annual report of proceedings, annual address of the pres't, and essays relating to the dairy interests; [v. 5-9 comp. by D. W. Curtis, sec.]. Fort Atkinson *and* Madison. 1874-81. O. **606.3 : D10**
— 11th [and 12th] annual report, comp. by D. W. Curtis, sec.; 1883, 1884. Madison. 1883, 1884. O. *With* Wisconsin state agricultural society; Transactions. **606.3 : 7 v21,22**
Wisconsin. *State university.* Experiments in amber cane and the ensilage of fodders at the experimental farm, 1881, 1882. Madison. 1882-83. O. **630 : 20**
— — *Agricultural experiment station.* 1st annual report for 1888. Madison. 1884. O. **630 : 21**
— — *Same.* Bulletins, no. 1, 3-6, aug. 1883-july 1885. Madison. 1883-85. O. **630:22**
Iowa state agricultural society. Report of the board of directors, 1881. Des Moines. 1882. O. **606.3 : D11**
Contains also Proceedings of the 8th annual meeting of the Iowa state improved stock-breeders' asso., held at Iowa City, dec. 13-15, 1881.
Iowa state horticultural society. Transactions for 1881, being proceedings of the 16th annual meeting jan. 17-20, 1882; together with the proceedings of the Eastern Ia. hort. soc.; also of Western Ia. hort. soc., and other local societies for 1881. Des Moines. 1882. O. **606.3 : D12**
Kansas *state. Board of agriculture.* Centennial ed. of the 4th annual report, 1875. comp. from the original report by the state board of centennial managers.... Ill. [Topeka]. 1876. O. **606.3+3**
— — 1st and 4th biennial report to the legislature of the state of Kansas, 1877-8, 1883-4, containing statistical exhibits, descriptive statements, etc.... Topeka. 1878, 1885. O. **606.3+4**
— — Quarterly report for the quarter ending

sept. 30, 1880 [-sept. 30, 1881]. Topeka. 1880-81.   **606.3 : Pam**
Monthly journal of agriculture, The ; containing the best current productions in promotion of agricultural improvement. incl. the choicest prize essays issued in Europe and America, with original contributions from eminent farmers and statesmen ; v. 1, 2. N. Y. 1846, 1847. O.   **605.3 : M**
Wisconsin farmer, The, and northwestern cultivator ; a monthly journal devoted to agriculture, horticulture, mechanics and rural economy, D. J. Powers and E. W. Skinner, eds. Madison. 1856, 1857. Q.   **605.3 : M**
Country gentleman, The ; v. 20-31. Albany. 1862-66. F.   **605.3 : RM**
American agriculturist, The ; for the farm, garden and household ; v. 42, 43. N. Y. 1883, 1884. F.   **605.3 : M**

2. Soil and preparation.

Chaptal, J: Antoine, *comte de Chanteloup.* Chymistry applied to agriculture ; with a prelim. chapter on the organization, structure, etc., of plants by sir Humphrey Davy ; an essay on the use of lime as manure by M. Puvis, with introd. obs. to the same by James Renwick. Tr. and ed. by W: P. Page. N. Y. 1839. S.   **631 : 2**
Boussingault, J: Baptiste. Rural economy, in its relations with chemistry, physics and meteorology, or Chemistry applied to agriculture. Tr., with an introd. and notes, by G: Law. N. Y. 1845. D.   **631 : 1**
Johnston, James F. W. Lectures on the applications of chemistry and geology to agriculture ; with an app., containing suggestions for experiments in practical agriculture. N. Y. 1847. D.   **631 : 3**
Liebig, Justus *freiherr* v. Principles of agricultural chemistry, with special reference to the latest researches made in England. N. Y. 1855. D.   **631 : 7**
— Letters on modern agriculture ; ed. by J: Blyth. N. Y. 1859. O.   **631 : 5**
— The natural laws of husbandry ; ed. by J: Blyth. N. Y. 1863. O.   **631 : 6**
Johnson, S: W: How crops feed ; a treatise on the atmosphere and the soil, as related to the nutrition of agricultural plants. Ill. N. Y. [1870]. D.   **631 : 4**
Waring, G: Edwin, *jr.* Draining for profit and draining for health. Ill. N. Y. [1867]. D. **631 : 8**
Scott, J: Draining and embanking ; a practical treatise embodying the most recent experience in the application of improved methods. (Farm engineering text-books, no. 1). [Weale's ser.] Lond. 1888. D. **631 : 9**
— Irrigation and water-supply ; a practical treatise on water-meadows, sewage irrigation and warping, the construction of wells, ponds and reservoirs, and raising water by machinery for agricultural and domestic purposes. (Farm engineering text-books, no. 2). [Weale's ser.] Lond. 1888. D. **631 : 10**
— Farm roads, fences and gates ; a practical treatise on the roads, tramways and water-

Scott, J:—*Continued.*
ways of the farm, the principles of enclosures and the different kinds of fences, gates and stiles. (Farm engineering textbooks, no. 3). [Weale's ser.] Lond. 1883. D.   **631 : 11**
— Farm buildings ; a practical treatise on the buildings necessary for various kinds of farms, their arrangement and construction, with plans and estimates. (Farm engineering text-books, no. 4). [Weale's ser.] Lond. 1884. D.   **631 : 12**
— Barn implements and machines, a practical treatise on the application of power to the operations of agriculture, and on various machines used in the threshing barn, in the stock-yard and in the dairy, etc. (Farm engineering text-books, no. 5). [Weale's ser.] Lond. 1884. D.   **631 : 13**
— Field implements and machines ; a practical treatise on the varieties now in use, with principles and details of construction, their points of excellence and management. (Farm engineering text-books, no. 6). [Weale's ser.] Lond. 1884. D.   **631 : 14**
— Agricultural surveying ; a practical treatise on land surveying, levelling and setting-out, and on measuring and estimating quantities, weights and values of materials, produce, stock, etc. (Farm engineering text-books, no. 7). [Weale's ser.] Lond. 1884. D.   **631 : 15**
Lammers, A: Der moorrauch und seine culturmission. *In* Deutsche zeit- und streitfragen.   **304 : 15 v5**

3. Pests and hindrances.

Harris, Thaddeus W: A treatise on some of the insects injurious to vegetation. New ed. enlg. and imp., with add. from the author's mss. and original notes ; ed. by C: L. Flint. Ill. Bost. 1863. O.   **632 : 2**
Saunders, W: Insects injurious to fruit. Phila. 1883. O.   **632 : 4**
Quin, C: W., *ed.* Garden receipts. [Weale's ser.] Lond. 1882. D.   **632 : 3**
Emmons, Ebenezer. The more common and injurious insects of the state of New York. *In* Natural hist. of N. Y., pt. 5, v. 5. **557.3 : R1**
Le Baron, W:, *state entomologist.* 1st-3d annual report on noxious insects. Ill. *In* Reports to the gen. assembly of Illinois, 1871, 1873. *in* **328.15 : D**
Comstock, J. H: Report upon cotton insects ; prepared under the dir. of the com'r of agr. Ill. [U. S. dep. of agr.] Wash. 1879. O.   *in* **632 : D**
Contents. Pt. 1. The cotton-worm, Aletia argillacea. — Pt. 2. The boll-worm, Heliothis armigera.—Pt. 3. Trelease, W: Nectar; what it is, and some of its uses.—App.
United States. *Entomological commission* (C: V. Riley, A. S. Packard, jr., *and* Cyrus Thomas). First annual report for 1877, relating to the Rocky mountain locust and the best methods of preventing its injuries and of guarding against its invasions ; [with bibliography on the locusts of America]. Maps and ill. Wash. 1878. O. (U. S. geol. survey of the terr., Hayden). *in* **632 : D**

United States. *Entomological commission.—Continued.*

— — Second report for 1878 and 1879, relating to the Rocky mountain locust and the western cricket, and treating of the best means of subduing the locust in its permanent breeding grounds, with a view of preventing its migrations into the more fertile portions of the trans-Mississippi country; [with bibliography on the destructive locusts of Europe, Asia and Africa, by B: Pickman Mann]. Maps and ill. Wash. 1880. O. (U. S. dep. of the interior).

in 632 : D

— — Third report [for 1880-82], relating to the Rocky mountain locust, the western cricket, the army worm, canker worms, and the hessian fly; together with descriptions of larvæ of injurious forest insects, studies on the embryological development of the locust and of other insects, and on the systematic position of the orthoptera in relation to other orders of insects. Maps and ill. Wash. 1883. O. (U. S. dep. of agr.)

in 632 : D

— — Bulletin, no. 1-7. Ill. Wash. 1877-79. O.

in 632 : D

Contents. 1. Destruction of the young or unfledged locusts.—2. On the natural history of the Rocky mountain locust.—3. **Riley,** C: V. The cotton worm.—4. **Packard,** A. S., *jr.* The hessian fly.—5. **Thomas,** C: The chinch-bug.—6. **Riley,** C: V. General index and supplement to the nine reports on the insects of Missouri.—7. **Packard,** A. S., *jr.* Insects injurious to forest and shade trees.

— *Dep't of agr.; Division of entomology,* [C: V. Riley, entomologist]. Bulletin, no. 1-6. Wash. 1883-85. O. *in 632 : D*

Contents. 1. Rep. of experiments, chiefly with kerosene, upon the insects injuriously affecting the orange tree and the cotton plant.—2. Rep. on the Rocky mountain locust, and the chinch-bug; together with extracts from the corresp. of the division on miscel. insects.—3. Rep. of observations and exper. in the practical work of the division. Plates.—4. *Same;* together with extracts from corresp. on miscel. insects.—5. **Howard,** L. O. Descriptions of north amer. chalcididæ; 1st paper.—6. The imported elm leaf-beetle (*Galeruca xanthomelæna* Schrank); its habits and natural history, and means of counteracting its injuries. Ill.

Note. The annual report of the entomologist, and other articles on agricultural pests, will be found in the annual reports of the Com'r of agriculture, *in 630: D.*

Coues, Elliott. On the present status of Passer domesticus [the english sparrow] in America, with special reference to the western states and territories. *In* U. S. geol. survey of the terr., Hayden; Bulletin, v. 5. *in 557.5 : D*

4. Crops and fruits.

Johnson, S: W: How crops grow; a treatise on the chemical composition, structure and life of the plant, for all students of agriculture. Ill. and tables of analyses. N. Y. [1868]. D. **633 : 2**

Masters, Maxwell T. Plant life on the farm. N. Y. 1885 [1884]. D. **633 : 6**

Thurber, G:, *ed.* Silos and ensilage; the preservation of fodder corn and other green fodder crops, bringing together the most recent information from various sources. Ill. N. Y. 1881. D. **633 : 4**

Bailey, J: M. The book of ensilage, or The new dispensation for farmers; experience with ensilage at "Winning farm"... Billerica, Mass. 1880. O. **633+5**

Steele, J: The hay and straw measurer; new tables for the use of auctioneers, valuers, farmers, hay and straw dealers, etc., showing the weight of hay and straw, etc., in round or oblong stacks; the price of commodities by the stone, score, cwt. and ton; and how to measure timber, the contents of tanks or reservoirs, etc.; forming a complete calculator and ready reckoner, especially adapted to persons connected with agriculture. 3d ed. enl. [Weale's ser.] Lond. 1881. D. **633 : 3**

Hewett, Robert, *jr.* Coffee; its history, cultivation and uses. Ill. and map. N. Y. 1872. O. **633 : 1**

Fruits.

Downing, Andrew Jackson. The fruits and fruit trees of America, or The culture, propagation and management, in the garden and orchard, of fruit trees generally, with descriptions of all the finest varieties of fruit, native and foreign, cultivated in this country; rev. and corr. by C: Downing. N. Y. 1860. D. **634 : 2**

Baker, C: R. Practical and scientific fruit culture. Ill. Bost. 1866. O. **634 : 1**

Warder, J: A. American pomology: apples. Ill. N. Y. [1867]. D. **634 : 8**

Baltet, C: The art of gr f ing and budding. Tr. from the french. a Ill. [Weale's ser.] Lond. 1882. D. **634 : 9**

Fuller, Andrew S. The small fruit culturist. Ill. N. Y. 1879. D. **634 : 3**

Roe, E: Payson. Success with small fruits. Ill. N. Y. 1880. O. **634+7**

Haraszthy, A. Grape culture, wines and wine-making; with notes upon agriculture and horticulture. Ill. N. Y. 1862. O. **634+4**

Mead, P: B. An elementary treatise on american grape culture and wine-making. Ill. N. Y. 1867. O. **634+6**

Husmann, G: American grape growing and wine-making, with contributions from well-known grape growers, giving a wide range of experience. Ill. N. Y. 1880. D. **634 : 5**

5. Forestry.

Hess, R: Die forstliche unterrichtsfrage. *In* Deutsche zeit- und streit-fragen. **304 : 15 v3**

Brown, J: Croumbie. Forestry in Norway; with notices of the physical geography of the country. Edinb. 1884. D. **633.1 : 7**

Hough, Franklin B. Elements of forestry, designed to afford information concerning the planting and care of forest trees for ornament or profit, and giving suggestions for the creation and care of woodlands, with a view of securing the greatest benefit for the longest time; particularly adapted to the wants and conditions of the U. S. Cinc. 1882. D. **633.1 : 1**

American journal of forestry, The; devoted to the interests of forest tree planting, the formation and care of woodlands and

ornamental planting generally, and to the various economies therein concerned, ed. by Franklin B. Hough; v. 1, sept. 1882—oct. 1883. Cinc. 1882-3. O.   **605.3 : M**
Note. Discontinued after the first vol.

Fuller, Andrew S. Practical forestry; a treatise on the propagation, planting and cultivation, with a description and the botanical and popular names of all the indigenous trees of the U. S., both evergreen and deciduous, with notes on a large number of the most valuable exotic species. Ill. N. Y. 1884. D.   **633.1 : 5**

Egleston, Nathaniel H. Hand-book of tree-planting, or Why to plant, where to plant, what to plant, how to plant. N. Y. 1884. D.   **633.1 : 4**

Phipps, R. W. Report on the necessity of preserving and replanting forests; compiled at the instance of the government of Ontario. Toronto. 1883. O.   **633.1+3**

Peaslee, J: B. Trees and tree-planting; with exercises and directions for the celebration of arbor day; preface by Warren Higley. Cinc. 1884. O.   **633.1 : 6**

Lapham, Increase Allen, J. G. **Knapp,** *and* Hans Crocker. Report on the disastrous effects of the destruction of forest trees, now going on so rapidly in the state of Wisconsin. Madison. 1867. O.   **633.1 : 2**

United States. *Census office.* Tenth census, 1880, v. 9 : Report on the forests of North America, exclusive of Mexico, by C: S. Sargent. Maps. Wash. 1884. Q. *and* Atlas, F.
in **317 : D**
Contents. Pt. 1. The forest trees of North Amer., excl. of Mexico: General remarks; Catalogue, with remarks upon their synonymy, bibliographical history, distribution, economic value and uses; Index. —Pt. 2. The woods of the U. S.: Prelim. remarks; Specific gravity and ash; Fuel value; Strength; Comparative values; Tanning values; Tables of, 1, specific gravity, ash and weight per cubic foot of dry specimens, 2, actual fuel value, 3, 4, behavior under transverse strain, 5, behavior under compression.—Pt. 3. The forests of the U. S. in their economic aspects: General remarks; The lumber industry; Fuel; Forest fires; North Atlantic division; South Atlantic division; Southern central division; Northern central division; Western division.—General index.

Hough, Franklin B. [1st–3d] Report upon forestry, prepared under the direction of the commissioner of agriculture. Wash. 1878–82. 3 v. O.   *in* **633.1 : D**

Ohio state forestry assoc. Proceedings, at its meeting in Columbus, march 28, 1884 ; together with a report upon the forest condition of Ohio, ill. by charts by the forestry division of the U. S. dep. of agr. Columbus. 1884. O.   **633.1 : Pam**
Note. A list of books and articles on trees and forests will be found in the Bulletin of the Boston public library, no. 48, jan. 1879.

6. Gardening.

Perring, W. Lexikon für gartenbau und blumenzucht; handbuch für gärtner und gartenliebhaber über alle zweige des gärtnerischen betriebs, mit besonderer berücksichtigung von topfpflanzenkultur, obst- und gemüsebau. Leipz. 1882. D.   **635 : R7**

Loudon, J: Claudius. The horticulturist, or An attempt to teach the science and practice of the culture and management of the kitchen, fruit and forcing garden to those who have had no previous knowledge or practice in these departments of gardening. New ed. Ill. Lond. 1860. O.
635 : 3

Henderson, P: Gardening for pleasure; a guide to the amateur in the fruit, vegetable and flower garden, with full directions for the greenhouse, conservatory and window-garden. Ill. N. Y. 1879. D.   **635 : 1**

— Gardening for profit; a guide to the successful cultivation of the market and family garden. New enl. ed. Ill. N. Y. 1880. D.
635 : 2

Hobday, E. Cottage gardening, or Flowers, fruits and vegetables for small gardens. [Weale's ser.] Lond. 1882. D.   **635 : 4**

Burr, Fearing, *jr.* Garden vegetables, and how to cultivate them. Bost. 1866. D.
635.2 : 2

Shaw, C. W., *comp.* The kitchen and market garden, by contributors to "The garden." [Weale's ser.] Lond. 1882. D.   **635.2 : 3**

Warner, Anna B. Three little spades. N. Y. 1875. S.   **x 635 : 5**

— Blue flag and cloth of gold. Ill. N. Y. 1880 [1879]. S.   **x 635 : 6**

Flower culture.

Sheehan, James. Your plants; plain and practical directions for the treatment of tender and hardy plants in the house and in the garden. N. Y. 1885 [1884]. D.   **635.1 : 10**

Church, Ella Rodman. The home garden. (Appletons' home books.) N. Y. 1881. D.
635.1 : 1

Henderson, P: Practical floriculture; a guide to the successful cultivation of florists' plants for the amateur and professional florist. New and enl. ed. Ill. N. Y. [1874]. D.   **635.1 : 5**

Loudon, Jane Webb. Gardening for ladies and companion to the flower garden. 1st amer. from the 3d Lond. ed., ed. by A. J. Downing. N. Y. 1847. D.   **635.1 : 2**

Rand, E: Sprague, *jr.* Flowers for the parlor and garden. Ill. Bost. 1863. D. **635.1 : 4**

Williams, B: S: Choice stove and greenhouse flowering plants, comprising descriptions of upwards of 1,100 species and varieties, accompanied by instructions for their cultivation and mode of management. 2d ed. enl., ill. and rev. Lond. 1873. D. **635.1 : 6**

— Choice stove and greenhouse ornamental leaved plants, comprising descriptions of upwards of 800 species and varieties, accompanied by instructions for their cultivation and mode of management. Ill. Lond. 1870. D.   **635.1 : 7**

Williams, H: T., *ed.* Window gardening; devoted specially to the culture of flowers and ornamental plants, for in-door use and parlor decoration. 4th ed. N. Y. 1872. D.
635.1 : 8

Rand, E: Sprague. Bulbs; a treatise on hardy and tender bulbs and tubers. Bost. 1873. D.   **635.1 : 3**

Parsons, S. B. The rose; its history, poetry, culture and classification. N. Y. 1847. Q.
635.1+9

x denotes books specially adapted for children.

Robinson, J: Ferns in their homes and ours. [Ill.] Salem. 1878. D. **716 : 1**

7. Domesticated animals.

Jackson, T: Our dumb companions, or Conversations about dogs, horses, donkeys and cats. 6th ed. Lond. [1879]. O. **636 : 1**

Gautier, Théophile. My household of pets. Tr. by Susan Coolidge. Bost. 1882. S. **636 : 2**
Contents. Old times.—The white dynasty.— The black dynasty.—Our dogs.—Chameleons, lizards and magpies.—Horses.

Wood, J: G: Petland revisited. Ill. N. Y. 1884. D. **636 : 4**

Stables, W. Gordon. Cats ; their points and classification ; with chapters on feline ailments and their remedies, how to train, etc. Ill. N. Y. 1884. D. **636.5 : 3**

Youatt, W: The dog ; ed. with add. by E. J. Lewis. Ill. Phila. *n. d.* O. **636.4 : 2**

Dog life ; narratives, exhibiting instinct, intelligence, fidelity, sympathy, attachment and sorrow. Ill. after Landseer. N. Y. *n. d.* D. **636.4 : 1**

Morris, Francis Orpen. Dogs and their doings. N. Y. 1872. O. **x 636.4 : 3**

Williams, C: Dogs and their ways ; ill. by numerous anecdotes compiled from authentic sources. Ill. Lond. *n. d.* D. **636.4 : 4**

— Anecdotes of dogs. Ill. Lond. [1869]. S. **636.4 : 5**

Jennings, Robert. The horse and his diseases ; embracing his history and varieties, breeding and management and vices, with the diseases to which he is subject and the remedies best adapted to their cure. Added, Rarey's method of taming horses, and the law of warranty as applicable to the purchase and sale of the animal. Ill. Phila. [1860]. D. **636.1 : 1**

Every horse owner's cyclopedia ; the anatomy and physiology of the horse, general characteristics, the points of the horse, with directions how to choose him, the principles of breeding, and the best kind to breed from, the treatment of the brood mare and foal, raising and breaking the colt, stables and stable management, riding, driving, etc.—Diseases and how to cure them ; the principal medicines and the doses in which they can be safely administered, accidents, fractures and the operations necessary in each case, shoeing, etc., by J. H. Walsh.—The american trotting horse, and suggestions on the breeding and training of trotters, by Ellwood Harvey.— The turf and trotting horse of America, by J: Elderkin. Ill. Phila. [1871] D. **636.1 : 2**

Woodruff, Hiram. The trotting horse of America ; how to train and drive him, with reminiscences of the trotting turf ; ed. by C: J. Foster, incl. an introd. notice by G: Wilkes, and a biograph. sketch by the ed. N. Y. 1868. D. **636.1 : 3**

Clarke, W: H. Horses' teeth ; a treatise on their mode of development, anatomy, microscopy, pathology and dentistry, compared with the teeth of many other land and

marine animals, both living and extinct, with a vocabulary and copious extracts from the works of odontologists and veterinarians. 2d ed., rev. N. Y. *n. d.* D. **636.1 : 4**

Marsh, G: Perkins. The camel, his organization, habits and uses, considered with reference to his introd. into the U. S. Bost. 1856. D. **636.5 : 1**

Ewart, J: Meat production ; a manual for producers, distributors and consumers of butchers' meat ; a treatise on means of increasing its home production, also, comprehensively treating of the breeding, rearing, fattening, carcass-weight and slaughtering of meat-yielding live stock, indications of the quality, means of preserving, curing, and cooking of the meat, etc. [Weale's ser.] Lond. 1878. D. **636 : 3**

United States. *Dep't of agriculture.* Report on the diseases of cattle in the U. S. Ill. Wash. 1871. Q. *in* **636 : D**

— — Investigation of diseases of swine, and infectious and contagious diseases incident to other classes of domesticated animals. Ill. (U. S. dep. of agr. Special rep., no. 12). Wash. 1879. O. *in* **630 : D**

— — Contagious diseases of domesticated animals ; continuation of investigation. Ill. (U. S. dep. of agr. Special rep., no. 22). Wash. 1 80. *in* **630 : D**

— — Contagious diseases of domesticated animals ; continuation of investigation. Ill. (U. S. dep. of agr. Special rep., no. 34). Wash. 1881. O. *in* **630 : D**

— — Contagious diseases of domesticated animals ; investigations by dep. of agr., 1883-1884. Ill. Wash. 1884. O. *in* **636 : D**

— — *Bureau of animal industry.* First annual report for 1884. Ill. Wash. 1885. O. *in* **636 : D**

Beale, Stephen. Profitable poultry keeping ; ed. with add. by Mason C. Weld. Ill. N. Y. [1884]. D. **636.3 : 2**

Wright, Lewis. The practical poultry keeper ; a complete and standard guide to the management of poultry, whether for domestic use, the markets or exhibition. 5th ed. N. Y. *n. d.* D. **636.3 : 1**

— *Same.* 8th ed. N. Y. *n. d.* D. **636.3 : 1**

— The practical pigeon keeper. Ill. Lond. *n. d.* D. **636.5 : 2**

Root, L. C. Quinby's new bee-keeping ; the mysteries of bee-keeping explained, combining the results of 50 years' experience with the latest discoveries and inventions, and presenting the most approved methods, forming a complete guide to successful bee-culture. Ill. N. Y. 1879. D. **638 : 1**

Harris, W. H. The honey-bee, its nature, homes and products. Lond. [1884]. D. **638 : 2**

8. Fishing industry.

Starbuck, Alexander. History of the american whale fishery, from its earliest inception to 1876. Ill. *In* U. S. fish com. report, v. 4. *in* **639 : D**

United States. *Commission of fish and fisheries.*
Report of the commissioner [Spencer F.
Baird], pt. 1-10. Maps and ill. Wash.
1873-84. 10 v. O.   **639 : D**
Contents. V. 1, for 1871-2, contains: Report on the
condition of the sea fisheries of the south coast of
New England; v. 2-10, for 1872-1884, contain: Inquiry
into the decrease of the food-fishes *and* The propagation of food-fishes in the waters of the U. S.; the
following papers being appendices:
V. 1. **Verrill,** A. E. Invertebrate animals of
Vineyard Sound.—**Gill,** T. Catalogue of the fishes
of the east coast of North America. 2. **Milner,**
James W. The fisheries of the great lakes, and the
species of coregonus or whitefish.—**Stone,** Livingstone, C: G. **Atkins,** *and others.* The salmon and the
trout.—**Milner,** James W., *and others.* The shad and
alewife.—**Haime,** Jules, *and others.* History, theory
and practice of fish-culture in Europe and the U. S.
—**Atkins,** C: G., *and others.* Obstructions to the
upward movement in streams and the remedy.—
Natural history.— Miscel. papers. — Bibliography of
reports of fishery commissions. 3. Sea fisheries
[of Europe and Amer.], principally herring, and the
fishes and invertebrates used as food.—The river-
fisheries.—Fish-culture relating more especially to
species of cyprinidæ, or carps.— The restoration of
the inland fisheries: **Peyrer,** C: Fisheries and fish-
ery-laws in Austria and of the world in general.—
Natural history. 4. **Starbuck,** Alex. Hist. of the
amer. whale-fishery. — The inland fisheries. — The
propagation of food-fishes, carp, shad and salmon.
5. **Goode,** G: Brown. A history of the menhaden;
with an account of the agricultural uses of fishes,
by W. O. **Atwater.**—**Dambeck,** K: Geographical
distribution of the gadidæ or the cod family, in its
relation to fisheries and commerce.— **Sars,** G. O.,
and others. Norwegian cod fisheries.—**Yhlen,** G. v.
Swedish sea fisheries.—The propagation of food-
fishes.—Miscellaneous.—**Gamgee,** J: On artificial
refrigeration. 6. **Dyrenforth,** Robert G. List and
abstract of patents issued in U. S., Canada and Great
Britain up to 1878, relat. to fisheries.—**Anderssen,**
Joakim, *and A.* **Feddersen.** Fishery expositions.—
Wallem, F: M. Report on the amer. sea fisheries.
—**Widegren,** Hjalmar, *and* Axel W: **Ljungman.**
Swedish sea fisheries.—Deep-sea research: Norwegian exped. of 1878; Baltic and German ocean.—Natural hist. of marine animals.—Propagation of food-
fishes: General considerations; Application, herring,
carp, cod, salmon.—Miscell. 7. Natural hist.—The
sea fisheries: Herring, etc.—Deep-sea research: The
German seas; Rep. of dredging exped.—Propagation of food-fishes: General consid.; Special applications.—Miscell. 8. **Goode,** G: Brown. First decade
of the U. S. fish com.—Deep-sea research: Description of apparatus.—The sea fisheries: Europe, and
Davis' Strait.—Economic research.—Natural hist.;

United States. *Fish commission.—Continued.*
The sword-fish; **Earll,** E: The spanish mackerel,
ill.; **Miescher-Rüsch,** F. Contributions to the biology of the Rhine salmon.—Propagation of food-
fishes: General consid.; Special applications, whitefish, salmon, trout, carp.—**Möbius,** K:, **Félix Fraiche**
and others. The oyster and oyster-culture.—Miscell.:
Patents. 9. General app.: Stmr. Fish Hawk; Patents.—The fisheries: Hist. of the mackerel fishery;
European and amer. fisheries.— Natural hist. and
biological research; food of fishes, etc.—Propagation of food-fishes. 10. General app.: Reps. on
work of the com.: Lakes and rivers of
the U. S.—The fisheries: Whale fisheries; Fishery
board of Scotland; Tile-fish.—Natural hist. and biological research: **Collins,** J. W., Sea birds used as a
bait for codfish; **Bean,** T. H., Fishes collected;
Decapod crustacea; **Hensen,** V., Eggs of fish in
the Baltic; Embryography of osseous fishes; **Blake,**
W. P., Report upon the principal aquariums abroad
in 1873; Marine fauna off the coast of New England.—
Bouchon-Brandely, G., *and others.* The oyster
and oyster-culture.— Propagation of food fishes.—
Miscell.

— — Bulletins, v. 1-3, 1881—1883. Wash. 1882-83.
3 v. O.   *in* **639 : D**
Note. The most important scientific papers in the
publications of the U. S. fish com. have been entered
in their proper places, in this catalogue.

Smiley, C: W. List of papers relating to the
work of the U. S. fish commission from its
organization in 1871 to july 1, 1883, and
pub. under the direction of the U. S. fish
com., the National museum, and the Tenth
census ; together with a topical synopsis of
the titles. *In* U. S. fish com. bulletin, v. 3.
                                      in **639 : D**

— A list of the published reports of the commissioners appointed by authority of the
various states of the U. S. [1857-1883]. *In*
the same.   *in* **639 : D**

Ingersoll, Ernest. Report on the oyster indus-
try of the U. S. Ill. Wash. 1881. Q. *In*
U. S. 10th census, 1880.   *in* **317 : D**
Contents. Descriptive and statistical reports.—The
natural history of the oyster.—Glossary of terms.—
General summary.

Winslow, Francis. Report on the oyster beds
of the James river, Va., and of Tangier
and Pocomoke sounds, Md. and Va. Maps
and ill. *In* U. S. coast survey rep. 1881.
                                      in **622 : D**

5. Domestic economy.

1. In general.

Babcock, Emma Whitcomb. Household hints.
(Appletons' home books). N. Y. 1881. D.
                                      640 : 1
Beecher, Catherine Esther. A treatise on domestic economy, for the use of young
ladies at home and at school. Rev. ed.
with add. N. Y. 1848. D.   **640 : 3**
— *and* Harriet Elizabeth **Stowe,** *born* Beecher.
Principles of domestic science, as applied
to the duties and pleasures of home. *T.
p. w.* [N. Y.] D.   **640 : 2**
Blakeslee, Mary N., (*Mary Blake*). Twenty-six
hours a day, by Mary Blake. Bost. [1883].
D.   **640 : 1**b
Browne, Phillis. What girls can do ; a book for
mothers and daughters. 2d ed. Lond. *n.
d.* D.   **640 : 4**

Campbell, Helen. The easiest way in housekeeping and cooking ; adapted to domestic
use or study in classes. N. Y. 1881. S.
                                      640 : 5
Cassell's household guide to every department
of practical life ; a complete encyclopædia
of domestic and social economy. New rev.
ed. N. Y. *n. d.* 4 v. Q.   **640+16**
Cobbett, W: Cottage economy; containing information relative to the brewing of beer,
making of bread, keeping of cows, pigs,
bees, ewes, goats, poultry and rabbits....
Added, The poor man's friend, or A defence of the rights of those who do the
work and fight the battles. Hartford. 1854.
S.   **640 : 6**
Coleman, W: Werner, *ed.* Die hausfrau, gattin
und mutter. Milw. *n. d.* O.   **640 : 19**
House manager, The ; a guide to housekeeping
practical cookery, pickling and preserv

ing, household work, dairy management, the table and dessert, cellarage of wines, home - brewing and wine - making, the boudoir and dressing-room, travelling, stable economy, gardening operations etc., by an old housekeeper. [Weale's ser.] Lond. 1878. D.   640 : 7

Household conveniences; being the experience of many practical writers. N. Y. 1884. D.   640 : 18

Household economy; a manual for use in schools, published under the direction of the Kitchen garden assoc. N. Y. 1882. D.   640 : 13

Huntington, Emily. Little lessons for little housekeepers; a series of lessons given at the Wilson's industrial school. New and enl. ed. N. Y. [1879]. S.   x 640 : 11

Kitchen garden assoc., *N. Y.* Advanced lessons in kitchen garden, with songs and occupations. N. Y. 1883. S.   x 640 : 14

Power, *Mrs.* S. D. Anna Maria's housekeeping. Bost. [1884]. S.   640 : 17

Richards, Ellen H. The chemistry of cooking and cleaning; a manual for housekeepers. Bost. 1882. S.   640 : 10

Six hundred dollars a year; a wife's effort at low living under high prices. Bost. 1867. S.   640 : 8

Youmans, E: Livingstone. The hand-book of household science; a popular account of heat, light, air, aliment and cleansing in their scientific principles and domestic applications. Ill. N. Y. 1864. D.   640 : 9

*   *   *

Phin, J: The preparation and use of cements and glue. (Work manuals, no. 1.) N. Y. 1881. D.   640 : 12

Leavitt, T: H. Facts about peat as an article of fuel; with remarks upon its origin and composition, the localities in which it is found, the methods of preparation and manufacture and the various uses to which it is applicable, together with many other matters of practical and scientific interest. Added, a chapter on the utilization of coal dust with peat, for the production of an excellent fuel at moderate cost, specially adapted for steam service. 3d ed., rev. and enl. Bost. 1867. D.   644 : 1

Siemens, *Sir* C: W: Fuel; to which is appended the value of artificial fuels as compared with coal, by J: Wormald. [Van Nostrand's science ser.] N. Y. 1874. T. 644 : 2

2. Food and cookery.

Ranke, Johannes. Die ernährung des menschen. München. 1876. S.   643 : 1

Smith, E: Foods. (Intern. scientific ser.) N. Y. 1878. D.   643 : 6

Letheby, H: On food; its varieties, chemical composition, nutritive value, comparative digestibility, physiological functions and uses, preparation, culinary treatment, preservation, adulteration, etc.; the substance of four Cantor lectures, del. before the Society for the encouragement of arts, manufactures and commerce, in jan. feb. 1868. 2d ed. enl. and imp. Lond. 1872. D.   643 : 5

Atwater, W. O. Report of progress of investigations of the chemical composition and economic values of the fish and invertebrates used as food. *In* U. S. fish com. report, v. 8.   *in* 639 : D

Lankester, Edwin. Vegetable substances used for the food of man. [*Anon.*] N. Y. 1846. S.   643 : 7

Hoskins, T: H. What we eat; an account of the most common adulterations of food and drink, with simple tests by which many of them may be detected. Bost. 1861. D.   643 : 3

Bell, James. The analysis and adulteration of food: pt. 1, Tea, coffee, sugar, etc.; pt. 2, Milk, butter, cheese, cereal foods, prepared starches, etc. [South Kensington museum art handbooks.] Lond. 1883. 2 v. D.   643 : 9

Bellows, Albert Jones. The philosophy of eating. 12th ed. rev. and enl. Bost. 1881. D.   643 : 8

Brillat-Savarin, Anthelme. The handbook of dining, or Corpulency and leanness scientifically considered; comprising the art of dining on correct principles consistent with easy digestion, the avoidance of corpulency and the cure of leanness, together with special remarks on these subjects. Tr. by L. F. Simpson. N. Y. 1865. D.   643 : 2

Oyster epicure, The; a collation of authorities on the gastronomy and dietetics of the oyster. N. Y. [1883]. S.   643 : 12

T., N. T. Bread-making. [Putnam's handy book ser.] Ill. N. Y. 1884. S.   641 : 9

Cook-books.

Dodds, Susanna W. Health in the household, or Hygienic cookery. N. Y. 1884 [1883]. D.   641 : 10

Kirkland, *Miss* E. S. Dora's housekeeping. Chicago. 1878. S.   x 641 : 7

— Six little cooks, or Aunt Jane's cooking class. Chicago. 1881. S.   x 641 : 6

Lincoln, *Mrs.* D. A. Mrs. Lincoln's Boston cook-book; what to do and what not to do in cooking. Ill. Bost. 1884. D.   641 : 3

Miller, Elizabeth S. In the kitchen. [New rev. ed., with index.] N. Y. 1883. O.   641 : 11

Milwaukee cook book and business directory. [Milw. 1881]. D.   641 : 12

Parloa, Maria. New cook book; a guide to marketing and cooking. Ill. Bost. 1881. D.   641 : 1

Smith, Mary Stuart, *comp.* Virginia cookery-book. (Frank. sq. lib.) N. Y. 1884. Q.   641+8

Terhune, Mary Virginia, *born* Hawes, (*Marion Harland*). Common sense in the household; a manual of practical housewifery. N. Y. 1881. D.   641 : 2

— The cottage kitchen; a collection of practical and inexpensive receipts. (Common-sense in the household ser.) N. Y. 1883. D.   641 : 13

Wiel, Josef. Diätetisches koch-buch, mit besonderer rücksicht auf den tisch für magenkranke. Nach der in Deutschland erschienen 4ten aufl. bearb. von K: Kron. Milw. 1878. O.   641 : 5

x denotes books specially adapted for children.

3. Dress, Servants, Nursing.

Doran, J: Habits and men ; with remnants of record touching the makers of both. N. Y. 1865. D.   **646 : 6**
Contents. Between you and me.—Man and manners, and a story with a moral to it.—Adonis at home and abroad.—Remnants of stage dresses.—Three acts and an epilogue.—The tiring bower of queens.—"La mode" in her birth place.—Hats.—Wigs and their wearers. — Beards and their bearers. — Swords. — Gloves, b—s and buttons. — Stockings.— Masks and faces. — Puppets for grown gentlemen. — Touching tailors: Why did the tailors choose St. William for their patron ? The tailors measured by the poets; Sir J: Hawkwood, the heroic tailor; G: Dörfling, the martial tailor; Admiral Hobson, the naval tailor; J: Stow, the antiquarian tailor; J: Speed, the antiquarian tailor; S: Pepys, the official tailor; R: Ryan, the theatrical tailor; Paul Whitehead, the poet tailor; Mems. of "Merchant tailors".—Chapters on beaux: The beaux of the olden time; Beau Fielding; Beau Nash; The prince de Ligne; Beau Brummell. — Doctors ready dressed.—Odd fashions.

Church, Ella Rodman. The home needle. (Appletons' home books.) N. Y. 1882. D.   **646 : 5**

Dewing, *Mrs.* T. W., *born* Oakey. Beauty in dress. N. Y. 1881. S.   **646 : 1**

Oliphant, Margaret O., *born* Wilson. Dress. (Art at home ser.) Phila. *n. d.* D. **646 : 2**

Phelps, Elizabeth Stuart. What to wear ? Bost. 1873. D.   **646 : 3**

Power, *Mrs.* S. D. The ugly-girl papers, or Hints for the toilet. Rep. from "Harper's bazar". [*Anon.*] N. Y. 1875. S.   **646 : 4**

* * *

Spofford, Harriet Elizabeth, *born* Prescott. The servant girl question. Bost. 1881. T.   **647 : 1**

* * *

Ellis, E: What every mother should know. Phila. 1881. S.   **649 : 1**

Hopkinson, *Mrs.* C. A. Hints for the nursery, or The young mother's guide. Bost. 1863. D.   **649 : 2**

Nightingale, Florence. Notes on nursing ; what it is and what it is not. N. Y. 1860. D.   **649 : 3**

Lückes, Eva C. E. Lectures on general nursing ; del. to the probationers of the London hospital training school for nurses. Lond. 1884. D.   **649 : 4**

6. Communication and Commerce.

1. Communication.

Writing.

Astle, T: The origin and progress of writing, as well hieroglyphic as elementary ; ill. by engr.taken from marbles,mss. and charters, ancient and modern, also some account of the origin and progress of printing. Lond. 1876. F.   **651 : R1**

Fauvel-Gouraud, Francis. Practical cosmography; a system of writing and printing all the principal languages, with their exact pronunciation, by means of an original, universal phonetic alphabet, based upon philological principles and representing analogically all the component elements of the human voice, as they occur in different tongues and dialects, and applicable to daily use in all the branches of business and learning ; with specimens of the Lord's prayer in 100 languages. Prefixed, a general introd. elucidating the origin and progress of language, writing, stenography, phonography, etc. N. Y. 1850. O.   **653+1**

Anderson, T: His₁o₁₁ of shorthand ; with a review of its present condition and prospects in Europe and America. Lond. 1882. D.   **653 : 4**

Rockwell, Julius Ensign. The teaching, practice and literature of shorthand. (U. S. Bureau of education ; Circulars of information). Wash. 1884. O.   **653 : 7**
Contents. Systems.—In foreign countries.—In the U. S.—Bibliography of works in the english language.—Shorthand alphabets [1602—1882].

Cross, J. G: Eclectic short-hand ; writing by principles instead of arbitrary signs for general use und verbatim reporting. 5th thousand. [4th ed.] Chicago. 1883. D.   **653 : 2**

Graham, Andrew J. The hand-book of standard or American phonography ; in 5 parts. N. Y. *n. d.* D.   **653 : 6**

Longley, Elias. The american phonographic dictionary ; exhibiting the correct and actual shorthand forms for all the useful words of the english language, and, in add., many foreign terms ; also the best shorthand forms for 2000 geographical names, and as many family, personal and noted fictitious names. Cinc. 1882. D.   **653 : 3**

Pitman, B:, *and* Jerome B. **Howard.** The phonographic dictionary ; containing the reporting outlines for upward of 30,000 words, embracing every useful word in the language and a large number of proper and geographical names, legal, scientific and technical terms, etc. Cinc. 1883. D.   **653 : 5**

Telegraphy.

(*See also under* Physics, Electricity, cl. 537, col. 315.)

Briggs, C: F., *and* A: **Maverick.** The story of the telegraph and a history of the great Atlantic cable ; a record of the inception, progress and final success of that undertaking, a general history of land and oceanic telegraphs, descriptions of telegraphic apparatus and biographical sketches of the principal persons connected with the great work. Ill. N. Y. 1858. D.   **654 : 2**

Sabine, Robert. The history and progress of the electric telegraph, with descriptions of some of the apparatus. 3d ed., with add. [Weale's ser.] Lond. 1872. D.   **654 : 5**

Preece, W: H:, *and* J. **Sivewright.** Telegraphy. [Text-books of sciences]. N. Y. 1876. D.   **654 : 4**

Loring, A. E. A handbook of the electro-magnetic telegraph. [Van Nostrand's science ser.] N. Y. 1878. T.   **654 : 3**

Lockwood, T: D. Electricity, magnetism and electric telegraphy ; a practical guide and hand-book of general information for electrical students. operators and inspectors. Ill. N. Y. 1883. O.   **654+8**

Bond, R. Handbook of the telegraph ; a manual of telegraphy, telegraph clerks' remembrancer and guide to candidates for employment in the telegraph service. 4th ed., rev.; app., questions on magnetism, electricity and practical telegraphy for the use of students. by W. McGregor. Ill. [Weale's ser.] Lond. 1873. D.   **654 : 1**

Printing.

Humphreys, H: Noel. A history of the art of printing from its invention to its widespread development in the middle of the 18th century, preceded by a short account of the origin of the alphabet and the successive methods of recording events and multiplying ms. books before the invention of printing. Ill. Lond. 1867. F.   **655 : R7**

— Masterpieces of the early printers and engravers ; a series of facsimiles from rare and curious books, remarkable for illustrative devices, beautiful borders, decorative initials, printers' marks, elaborate title-pages, etc. Lond. 1870. F.   **655 : R8**

Hawkins, Rush C. Titles of the first books from the earliest presses established in different cities, towns and monasteries in Europe, before the end of the 15th century, with brief notes upon their printers ; ill. with reproductions of early types and first impr. of the printing press. N. Y. 1884. Q.   **23 : L**

Pearson, Emily C. Gutenberg, and the art of printing. 3d ed. Bost. [1880]. D.   **655 : 2**

Hessels, J: H: Gutenberg ; was he the inventor of printing ? an historical investigation embodying a criticism on dr. Van der Linde's "Gutenberg." Lond. 1882. O.   **655+P4**

Linde, A. van der. The Haarlem legend of the invention of printing by Lourens Janszoon Coster, critically examined. From the dutch by J. H. Hessels, with an introd. and a classified list of the Costerian incunabula. Lond. 1871. O.   **655+3**

Adams, T: F. Typographia ; a brief sketch of the origin, rise and progress of the typographic art, with practical directions for conducting every dep. in an office. Phila. 1837. S.

Hart, M. C. The amateur printer, or Typesetting at home ; complete instructor for the amateur in all the details of the printer's art, with explan. engr. N. Y. [1883]. S.   **655 : 6**

Bruce's, G:, *son and co.* Specimens of printing-types made at Bruce's N. Y. type foundry. N. Y. 1882. Q.   **655 : R5**

Putnam, G: Haven. Authors and publishers ; a manual of suggestions for beginners in literature. [*Anon.*] N. Y. 1883. O.   **655+9**

2. Commerce and transportation.

(*See also* Commerce and communication, cl. 380-389, col. 253-260.)

Navigation.

(*See also* cl. 527, col. 306.)

Brady, W: The kedge-anchor, or Young sailor's assistant ; appertaining to the practical evolutions of modern seamanship, rigging, knotting, splicing, blocks, purchases, running-rigging and other miscellaneous matters, applicable to ships of war and others. Ill. 3d ed. imp. and enl. N. Y. 1848. O.   **656+1**

Hunter, Theodore, *and* Jarvis **Patten.** Port charges and requirements on vessels in various ports of the world ; with tables of moneys, weights and measures of all nations and a telegraphic codex for masters, owners and ship brokers. N. Y. 1879. Q.   **656 : R2**

  Contents. Pt. 1. United States and Dominion of Canada. 2. Mexico, South America, Europe, Asia, Africa, Australia, East and West Indies, and the islands of the Pacific and Atlantic oceans.

Adams, W: H: Davenport. Light houses and light ships ; a descriptive and historical account of their mode of construction and organization. New ed., rev. Lond. 1878. D.   **656 : 3**

Russell, W: Clark. Sailors' language ; a collection of sea-terms and their definitions. Lond. 1883. D.   **656 : 4**

Book-keeping and business-manuals.

Haddon, James. Commercial book-keeping and phraseology in four languages. 15th ed. [Weale's ser.] Lond. 1879. D.   **657 : 1**

Mayer, C: Mercantile manual ; a compendium of the history and methods of trade. Milw. 1880. O.   **658 : 4**

Monsanto, H. M. Manual of commercial correspondence in french. N. Y. 1881. D.   **658 : 5**

Hamilton, Robert. An introduction to merchandise ; containing the theory and practice of arithmetic, algebra, with the doctrine of annuities, and commerce, incl. treatises on monies, weights, measures, exchanges, and book-keeping, with an app. containing tables of logarithms, compound interest and annuities, an explanation of commercial terms and answers ; the whole newly modelled by Elias Johnston. Edinb. 1820. O.   **658 : 3**

Beale, C: E. *and* M. R. **Gately,** *eds.* Universal educator ; an educational cyclopædia and business guide. 9th ed. rev. Bost. [1883]. Q.   **658+8**

Berg, Albert Ellery. The universal self-instructor and manual of general reference, incl.

many valuable vocabularies and carefully compiled tables. Ill. N. Y. 1883. Q.
658+11

Gaskell, G. A. Gaskell's compendium of forms, educational, social, legal and commercial; embracing a complete self-teaching course in penmanship and book-keeping, and aid to english composition. Also, a manual of agriculture and mechanics, with a complete guide to parliamentary practice; rules of order for deliberative assemblies, organization and conduct of business, etc. Ill. St. Louis. 1881. Q.   **658+7**

Hill, T: E. Hill's manual of social and business forms; a guide to correct writing, showing how to express written thought pl inl, rapidly, elegantly and correctly. Chicago. 1883. Q.   **658+9**

McCabe, James D. The national encyclopædia of business and social forms; embracing the art of writing well, how to express

written thought in a correct and elegant manner, an explanatory treatise on book-keeping, a practical guide to the preparation of business and legal documents, carefully prepared tables of reference, parliamentary laws, the laws of etiquette and good society, the art of making home happy, valuable household receipts; the art of writing poetry, with choice selections from the best authors. Ill. Chic. n. d. O.
658+10

Robinson, Nugent, *comp.* Collier's cyclopedia of commercial and social information, and treasury of useful and entertaining knowledge. N. Y. 1882. Q.   **658+6**

Epeneter, G: Franz. Table to find the exact contents of barrels, cistern tubs and all kinds of other round tubs for the use of brewers, coopers, kettle and tub manufacturers, government gaugers, etc. Milw. 1874. O.   **658 : 2**

7· Industrial arts.

1. Chemical technology.

Bolley, Pompejus Alexander. Manual of technical analysis; a guide for the testing and valuation of the various natural and artificial substances employed in the arts and in domestic economy, founded upon [his] Handbuch der technisch-chemischen untersuchungen, by B: H. Paul. Lond. 1857. D.   **660 : 1**

Kentish, T: The pyrotechnist's treasury, or Complete art of making fire works. Lond. 1878. D.   **662 : 1**

Berthelot, Marcellin P: Eugène. Explosive materials; a series of lectures delivered before the Collége de France, Paris. Added, a short historical sketch of gunpowder, tr. from the german of K: Braun by J: P. Wisser; and a bibliography of works on explosives. [Van Nostrand's science ser.] N. Y. 1883. T.   **662 : 2**

Eissler, Manuel. The modern high explosives, nitro-glycerine and dynamite; their manufacture, their use and their application to mining and military engineering; pyroxine or gun-cotton, the fulminates, picrates and chlorates, also the chemistry and analysis of the elementary bodies which enter into the manufacture of the principal nitro-compounds. N. Y. 1884. O. **662+3**

Hare, Robert. Memoir on the explosiveness of niter, with a view to elucidate its agency in the tremendous explosion of july 1845, in New York. Wash. 1850. Q. *In* Smithsonian contributions.   **506 : R3 v2**

Y-Worth, W. A new art of making wines, brandy and other spirits compliant to the late act of parliament, concerning distillation.... Lond. 1691. S.   **663 : 1**

Thudichum, J: L: W:, *and* A: Dupré. A treatise on the origin, nature and varieties of wine;

a complete manual of viticulture and œnology. [Ill.] Lond. 1872. O.   **663 : 2**
Note. For viniculture and wine-making, see also cl. 634, col.   .

Dannehl, Gustav. Die verfälschung des bieres; ein wort an das reichskanzler-amt. *In* Deutsche zeit- und streit-fragen.
304 : 15 v7

Antisell, T: The manufacture of photogenic or hydro-carbon oils from coal and other bituminous substances, capable of supplying burning fluids. N. Y. 1859. O. **665+1**

United States. *Census office.* Tenth census, 1880, v. 10: Report on the production, technology and uses of petroleum and its products, by S. F. **Peckham.**—Report on the manufacture of coke, by Joseph D. **Weeks.**—Report on the building stones of the U. S., and statistics of the quarry industry for 1880. Ill. Wash. 1884. Q.
in **317 : D**

Hughes, S: The construction of gas-works and the manufacture and distribution of coal gas. 6th ed. re-written and much enl. by W: Richards. [Weale's ser.] Lond. 1880. D.   **665 : 2**

Nesbitt, Alexander. Glass. Ill. (South Kensington art handbooks.) Lond. *n. d.* D. **666 : 1**

Sauzay, Alexandre. Wonders of glass-making in all ages. [Ill. lib. of wonders.] N. Y. 1875. D.   **666 : 2**

Dunlop, Madeline A. Wallace-. Glass in the old world. Lond. *n. d.* O.   **666 : 3**

Haigh, James, *tr.* The dier's [*sic*] assistant in the art of dying wool and woolen goods, extracted from the philosophical and chymical works of those most eminent authors Ferguson, Dufay, Hellot, Geoffery, Colbert and that reputable french dier M. de Julienne. Tr. from the french, with add. and practical experiments. Poughkeepsie. 1813. D.   **667 : 1**

Lieber, Oscar M. The assayer's guide, or Practical directions to assayers, miners and smelters for the tests and assays, by heat and by wet processes, of the ores of all the principal metals, of gold and silver coins, and alloys, and of coal. Phila. 1880. D.   668 : 1

Overman, F: A treatise on metallurgy, comprising mining and general and particular metallurgical operations, with a description of charcoal, coke and anthracite furnaces, blast machines, hot blast, forge hammers, rolling mills, etc. Ill. 2d ed. N. Y. 1854. O.   669+3

Lamborn, Robert H. The metallurgy of copper; an introd. to the methods of seeking, mining, and assaying copper, and manufacturing its alloys. 6th ed. [Weale's ser.] Lond. 1875. D.   669 : 1

— The metallurgy of silver and lead, a description of their ores, their assay and treatment, and valuable constituents. 6th ed. [Weale's ser.] Lond. 1878. D.   669 : 2

Watt, Alexander. Electro-metallurgy, practically treated. 7th ed., enl. and rev. [Weale's ser.] Lond. 1880. D.   669 : 4

Mathiot, G: Report on the electrotyping operations of the coast survey. In U. S. coast survey rep. 1851.   in 622 : D

— Same. Repr. in rep. for 1866.   in 622 : D

Note, For other art. on this subject, see General index in the rep. for 1854 and 1864.

2. Manufactures.

Bishop, J. Leander. A history of american manufactures from 1608 to 1860 ; exhibiting the origin and growth of the principal mechanic arts and manufactures from the earliest colonial period to the adoption of the constitution ; and comprising annals of the industry of the U. S. in machinery, manufactures and useful arts, with a notice of the important inventions, tariffs, and the results of each decennial census, with an app. containing statistics of the principal manufacturing centres, and descriptions of remarkable manufactories at the present time. 3d ed. Phila. 1868. 3 v. O.   670+1

United States. Census office. Tenth census, 1880, v. 2 : Report on the manufactures of the U. S., june 1, 1880. Maps and ill. Wash. 1888. Q.   in 317 : D

Contents. Walker, Francis A. Remarks on the statistics of mfrs.—General statistics; tabular statements. — Hollerith, Herman. Statistics of power used in mfrs.—Wright, Carroll D. The factory system of the U. S.—Fitch, C: H. Mnfs. of interchangeable mechanism, compiled, under the dir. of W. P. Trowbridge: Fire-arms; Ammunition; Sewing machines ; Locomotives and railroad machinery; Watches; Clocks; Ag'l implements. — Fitch, C: H. Manufacture of hardware, cutlery and edge-tools, also saws and files, comp. under the dir. of W. P. Trowbridge.—Swank, James M. Statistics of the iron and steel production of the U. S: Pt. 1, Statistics: pt. 2, History.—Wyckoff, W: C. Silk mfg. industry of the U. S.—Atkinson, E: Cotton mfrs. of the U. S.—Bond, G: W: Wool manufacture in all its branches.—Rowland, W: L. Manufacture of chemical products and salts.—Weeks, Joseph D. Manufacture of glass [incl. processes, products and history].—General index.

Ure, Andrew. The philosophy of manufactures, or An exposition of the scientific, moral and commercial economy of the factory system of Great Britain. 3d ed., continued in its details to the present time. Lond. 1861. D.   677 : 1

Noyce, Elisha. The boy's own book of the manufactures and industries of the world. Ill. Lond. [1881]. D.   x 670 : 2

Metals.

Pollen, J: Hungerford. Gold and silversmiths' work. Ill. [South Kensington art handbooks]. Lond. n. d. D.   671 : 3

Gee, G: E. The goldsmith's handbook ; containing full instructions for the alloying and working of gold, including the art of alloying, melting, reducing, colouring, colleeting, and refining ; the processes of manipulation, recovery of waste, chemical and physical properties of gold ; with a new system of mixing its alloys, solders, enamels, and other useful rules and recipes. 2d ed. enl. [Weale's ser.] Lond. 1881. D.   671 : 1

— The silversmith's handbook ; containing full instructions for the alloying and working of silver, incl. the different modes of refining and melting the metal ; its solders, the preparation of imitation alloys, methods of manipulation, prevention of waste, instructions for improving and finishing the surface of the work, together with other useful information and memoranda. [Weale's ser.] Lond. 1877. D.   671 : 2

— The hall-marking of jewellery, practically considered ; comprising an account of all the different assay towns of the United Kingdom, with the stamps at present employed, also the laws relating to the standards and hall-marks at the various assay offices, and a variety of practical suggestions concerning the mixing of standard alloys, and other useful information. [Weale's ser.] Lond. 1882. D.   671 : 7

Graham, Walter. The brass-founder's manual ; instructions for modelling, pattern-making, moulding, alloying, turning, filing, burnishing, bronzing, etc., containing copious receipts and tables, and notes of prime costs and estimates 5th ed. Ill. [Weale's ser.] Lond. 1879. D.   671 : 5

Warn, Reuben H: The sheet metal worker's instructor for zinc, sheet iron, copper and tin plate workers and others ; containing a selection of geometrical problems, also practical and simple rules for describing the various patterns required in the different branches of the above trades. Added, an app. containing instructions for boilermaking, mensuration of surfaces and solids, rules for calculating the weights of different figures of iron and steel, tables of the weights of iron, steel, etc. Ill. Phila. 1880. O.   671+4

Crane, W. J. E. The sheet metal worker's guide; a hand-book for tinsmiths, coppersmiths, zincworkers, etc.; comprising numerous

x denotes books specially adapted for children.

geometrical diagrams and working patterns with descriptive text. [Weale's ser.] Lond. 1883. D. **671 : 6**

Courtney, J: The boiler-maker's ready reckoner; with examples of practical geometry and templating, for the use of platers, smiths and riveters. Rev. and ed. by D. Kinnear Clark. 2d ed. rev. with add. [Weale's ser.] Lond. 1885 [1884]. D. **671 : 8**

Bauerman, H. A treatise on the metallurgy of iron, containing outlines of the history of iron manufacture, methods of assay, and analyses of iron ores, processes of manufacture of iron and steel, etc. 4th ed., rev. and enl. Ill. [Weale's ser.] Lond. 1874. D. **672 : 1**

Armour, James. Iron and heat, beams, pillars and iron smelting: exhibiting in simple form the principles concerned in the construction of iron beams, pillars and bridge girders and the action of heat in the smelting furnace. Ill. 2d ed. rev. [Weale's ser.] Lond. 1874. D. **672 : 2**

Overman, F: The manufacture of iron in all its various branches; incl. a description of wood-cutting, coal-digging, and the burning of charcoal and coke, the digging and roasting of iron ore, the building and management of blast furnaces, working by charcoal, coke, or anthracite, the refining of iron and the conversion of the crude into wrought iron by charcoal forges and puddling furnaces, also a description of forge hammers, rolling mills, blast machines, hot blast, etc. Added, an essay on the manufacture of steel. 3d ed. rev. Ill. Phila. 1854. O. **672+4**

Truran, W: The iron manufacture of Great Britain, theoretically and practically considered; incl. descriptive details of the ores, fuels and fluxes employed, the preliminary operation of calcination, the blast, refining and puddling furnaces, engines and machinery, and the various processes in union. 2d ed., rev. by J. Arthur Phillips and W: Dorman. N. Y. 1867. Q. **672+5**

Ede, G: The management of steel. 4th ed. rev. and enl. N. Y. 1867. D. **672 : 6**

Gruner, L: Emmanuel. The manufacture of steel. Tr. from the french by Lenox Smith, with an app. on the Bessemer process in the U. S. by the translator. Ill. N. Y. 1872. O. **672+3**

United States. *Congress*. Report of the U. S. board appointed to test iron, steel and other metals. Ill. Wash. [1878—]1881. 2 v. O. *in* **672 : D**

Contents. V. 1. Rep. of the committee on chain-cables, malleable iron, reheating and rerolling wrought iron; giving the result of experiments on the strength of wrought iron in bars and in chains, the effect of different degrees of reduction in rolling, of reheating, rerolling and hammering, and a comparison of chemical causes with physical results, proving strains for chain-cables, the correct form for test-pieces, and miscellaneous investigations into the physical properties of rolled wrought iron; with index. — Blair, Andrew A. Methods used in the analysis of iron and steel, copper, and the alloys of copper, zinc and tin. App.: Selected papers on the metallic alloys; with bibliography and index. **2.** Rep. on a preliminary investigation of the properties of the copper-zinc alloys, made under the dir. of the com. on metallic alloys, Robert H. Thurston chair-

man, in the mechanical laboratory of the Stevens institute of technology. — Records of tests of [the same]. — Rep. on the strength of iron girders and columns, made under the dir. of the com. on girders and columns, W: Sooy Smith chairman.—Results of tests and analyses of steels, made under the dir. of the com. on chemical research, Alex. L. Holley chairman.—Rep. on the tests of quality of steels for tools, made under the dir. of the com. on tool steels, D: Smith chairman. — App. **Tresca**, H: E: Memoir on the planing of metals; tr. from the french by C. F. Kroeh.

Other manufactures.

Dobson, E: A rudimentary treatise on the manufacture of bricks and tiles; containing an outline of the principles of brick-making, rev. and corr. by C: Tomlinson. 6th ed., with add. by Robert Mallet. Ill. [Weale's ser.] Lond. 1877. D. **673 : 1**

Wedgwood, C. R. The history of the tea-cup; with a descriptive account of the potter's art. Lond. *n. d.* S. **673 : 2**

Lukin, James. The lathe and its uses, or Instruction in the art of turning wood and metal; incl. a description of the most modern appliances for the ornamentation of plane and curved surfaces, an entirely novel form of lathe for eccentric and rose-engine turning, a lathe and planing machine combined, and other valuable matter relating to the art. 3d ed. with add. chapters and index. [*Anon.*] Lond. 1871. O. **674 : 1**

Davis, C: T: The manufacture of leather; a description of all the processes for the tanning, tawing, currying, finishing and dyeing of every kind of leather, incl. the various raw materials and the methods for determining their values, the tools, machines and all details of importance connected with an intelligent and profitable prosecution of the art, with special reference to the best american practice. Added, complete lists of all american patents for materials, processes, tools and machines for tanning, currying, etc. Phila. 1885. O. **675+1**

Smith, J. E. A. A history of paper, its genesis and its revelations; origin and manufacture, utility and commercial value of an indispensable staple of the commercial world. Holyoke, Mass. 1882. O. **676+1**

Rock, Daniel. Textile fabrics. Ill. [South Kensington museum art hand-books]. Lond. 1876. D. **677 : 2**

Ashenhurst, T: R. Design in textile fabrics. (Manuals of technology). N. Y. 1883. S. **677 : 3**

Schmoller, Gustav. Die entwicklung und die krisis der deutschen weberei im 19 jahrhundert; vortrag gehalten im zweigverein des Deutschen gewerbmuseums in Magdeburg. *In* Deutsche zeit- und streit-fragen. **304 : 15 v2**

Coxon, Herbert. Oriental carpets, how they are made and conveyed to Europe; with a narrative of a journey to the east in search of them. Lond. 1884. O. **677 : 4**

Ure, Andrew. The cotton manufacture of Great Britain investigated and ill., with an introd.

view of its comparative state in foreign countries. Added, a supp. completing the statistical and manufacturing information to the present time by P. L. Simmonds. Lond. 1861. 2 v. D.　　**678 : 1**

3. Mechanic trades.

Partington, C: F: The mechanic's library, or book of trades; comprehending a series of distinct treatises and practical guides, on architecture, carpentery, joinery, brick-laying, plastering, masonry, brickmaking, painting, glazing, plumbing, clock and watch - making, coach-making, printing, engraving, and shipbuilding. Ill. Lond. n. d. O.　　**680 : 1**

Boys' book of trades, and the tools used in them. Lond. [1879]. O.　　**x 680 : 2**

Beckett, Sir Edmund, formerly Edmund Beck-ett **Denison.** A rudimentary treatise on clocks, watches and bells. 6th ed., rev. and enl. [Weale's ser.] Lond. 1874. D.　　**681 : 1**

Engler, Edmund A. Time-keeping in London; repr. for distribution by the observatory of Washington university, St. Louis, from the Popular science monthly, dec. 1882, jan. 1883. N. Y. 1883. O. With his Time-keeping in Paris.　　in **681+2**

— Time-keeping in Paris; repr. for distribution by the observatory of Washington uni-versity, St. Louis, from the Popular science monthly, jan. 1882. St. Louis. 1882. O.　　**681+2**

Crane, W. J. E. The smithy and forge; a rudi-mentary treatise, incl. construction in the farrier's art, with a chapter on coach-smithing. Ill. [Weale's ser.] Lond. 1883. D.　　**682 : 1**

Hobbs, A. C. Locks and safes: The construction of locks, compiled from [his] papers, and ed. by C: Tomlinson; to which is added a description of J. Beverly Fenby's patent locks, and a note upon iron safes by Robert Mallet. Lond. [1868]. D.　　**683 : 1**

Greener, W. W. The gun and its development; with notes on shooting. Ill. Lond. [1881]. O.　　**683+3**

— Modern breech-loaders, sporting and military. Ill. [2d ed.] Lond. n. d. D.　　**683 : 2**

DuBois, H. P. Historical essay on the art of book binding. N. Y. 1883. D.　　**686 : 1**

Lukin, James. Toy making for amateurs; being instructions for the home construc-tion of simple wooden toys, and of others that are moved or driven by weights, clockwork, steam, electricity, etc. Ill. Lond. 1882. D.　　**688 : 1**

4. Building.

(See also Architecture, cl. 720–729.)

Clarke, Theodore M. Building superintendence. Ill., plans and diagrams. Bost. 1883. O.　　**690 : 8**

x denotes books specially adapted for children.

Allen, C: Bruce. Cottage building, or Hints for improving the dwellings of the work-ing classes and the labouring poor; with notes and add. by J: Weale and other authors. 9th ed., rev. and enl. [Weale's ser.] Lond. 1880. D.　　**690 : 1**

Brooks, S. H. Rudimentary treatise on the erection of dwelling-houses; ill. by a per-spective view, plans, elevations and sec-tions of a pair of semi-detached villas, with the specifications, quantities and esti-mates, and every requisite detail, in sequence, for their construction and finish-ing. New ed., with add. [Weale's ser.] Lond. 1877. D.　　**690 : 2**

Dobson, E: Rudiments of the art of building, in 5 sections: General principles of con-struction; materials used in building; strength of materials; use of materials; working drawings, specifications and esti-mates. Ill. 11th ed. [Weale's ser.] Lond. 1881. D.　　**690 : 3**

Oakey, Alexander F. Building a home. (Apple-tons' home books). N. Y. 1881. D.　　**690 : 4**

Plummer, P: W. The carpenters' and builders' guide; a hand-book for workmen, also a manual of reference for contractors, build-ers, etc. Portland. 1879. D.　　**690 : 5**

Christy, Wyvill J. A practical treatise on the joints made and used by builders in the construction of various kinds of engineer-ing and architectural works, with especial reference to those wrought by artificers in erecting and finishing habitable structures. [Weale's ser.] Lond. 1882. D.　　**690 : 6**

Tarn, E. Wyndham. An elementary treatise on the construction of roofs of wood and iron, deduced chiefly from the works of Robison, Tredgold and Humber. Ill. [Weale's ser.] Lond. 1882. D.　　**690 : 7**

Materials.

Barlow, P: A treatise on the strength of mater-ials, with rules for application in archi-tecture and the construction of suspension bridges, railways, etc., and an app. on the power of locomotive engines and the effect of inclined planes and gradients. New ed. revised by his sons P. W. Barlow and W. H. Barlow; added, a summary of experi-ments by Eaton Hodgkinson, W: Fairbairn and D: Kirkaldy; an essay with ill., on the effect produced by passing weights over elastic bars, by Robert Willis; he whole arr. and ed. by W: Humber. Lond. 1867. O.　　**691 : 8**

Kent, W: The strength of materials. [Van Nostrand's science ser.] N. Y. 1879. T.　　**691 : 5**

Allan, W. Strength of beams under transverse loads. [Van Nostrand's science ser.] N. Y. 1875. T.　　**691 : 1**

Spangenberg, L: The fatigue of metals under repeated strains, with various tables of results of experiments. [From the german, with a pref. by S. H. Shreve. [Van Nos-trand's science ser.] N. Y. 1876. T.　　**691 : 6**

Fairbairn, W: On the application of cast and wrought iron to building purposes. N. Y. 1854. O. **691+2**

United States. *Census office.* Report on the building stones of the U. S., and statistics of the quarry industry for 1880. Ill. *In* Tenth census, v. 10. *in* **317 : D**

Contents. **Hawes,** G: W. Introduction.—**Merrill,** G. P. Microscopic structure.—**Dewey,** F. P. Chemical examination.—**Sperr,** F. W. Quarry methods.—Statistics of building stones.—Descriptions of quarries and quarry regions: **Shaler,** N. S. General rep. on Rhode Island, Mass., Maine; Details regarding quarries, by states. [Wisconsin by Allan D. **Conover.]**—Stone construction in cities.—**Julien,** Alexis A. The durability of building stones in New York city and vicinity.—App.: Exportation, importation, *etc.*—Index.

Horton, R: The complete measurer; setting forth the measurement of boards, glass, etc., unequal-sided, square-sided, octagonal-sided, round timber and stone and standing timber, with just allowances for the bark on the respective species of trees and proper deductions for the waste in hewing trees, etc., with other essential instruction to timber growers, merchants, surveyors, architects, stone masons and others. 3d ed., with add. [Weale's ser.] Lond. 1876. D. **691 : 4**

Laslett, T: Timber and timber trees, native and foreign. Lond. 1875. D. **691 : 7**

Grandy, R: E. The timber importer's, timber merchant's and builder's guide. 2d ed., rev. [Weale's ser.] Lond. 1875. D. **691 : 3**

Richardson, W: The timber merchant's, sawmiller's and importer's freight-book and assistant; comprising rules, tables and memoranda relating to the timber trade; with a chapter on speeds of saw-mill machinery, etc., by M. Powis Bale, and a London price list for timber and deal sawing. [Weale's ser.] Lond. 1884. D. **691 : 9**

Plans and specifications.

Reed, S. B. House-plans for everybody, for village and country residences costing from $250 to $8,000, incl. full descriptions and estimates in detail of materials, labor and cost. Ill. N. Y. 1879. D. **692 : 2**

Beaton, Alfred C: Quantities and measurements; how to calculate and take them, in bricklayers', masons', plasterers', plumbers', painters', paperhangers', gilders', smiths', carpenters', and joiners' work; with rules for abstracting, hints for preparing a bill of quantities and rules for all work in the building trade. 5th ed., rev. and enl. [Weale's ser.] Lond. 1878. D. **692 : 1**

Blenkarn, J: Practical specifications of works executed in architecture, civil and mechanical engineering, and in road-making and sewering; added, a series of practically useful agreements and reports. Lond. 1865. O. **692 : R4**

Richardson, T. A. The art of architectural modelling in paper. Ill. [Weale's ser.] Lond. 1859. D. **692 : 3**

Masonry.

Walker, F. Brickwork; a practical treatise, embodying the general and higher principles of bricklaying, cutting and setting, with the application of geometry to roof-tiling, remarks on the different kinds of pointing, a description of the materials used by the bricklayer and a series of problems in applied geometry. [Weale's ser.] Lond. 1885 [1884]. D. **693 : 9**

Hammond, Adam. The rudiments of practical bricklaying. 3d ed., ill. [Weale's ser.] Lond. 1879. D. **693 : 5**

Dobson, E: The rudiments of masonry and stone cutting, exhibiting the principles of masonic projection and their application to the construction of curved wingwalls and domes, oblique bridges, and roman and gothic vaulting. 9th ed., with an app. on the causes of decay, and the preservation of stone. Ill. [Weale's ser.] Lond. 1878. D. **693 : 3**

— Foundations and concrete works; containing a synopsis of the principal cases of foundation work, with the usual mode of treatment, and practical remarks on the footings, planking, sand, concrete, béton, pile-driving, caissons and cofferdams. 4th ed., rev. by G: Dodd. [Weale's ser.] Lond. 1876. D. **693 : 2**

Gaudard, Jules. Foundations. Tr. from the french by L. F. Vernon Harcourt. [Van Nostrand's ser.] N. Y. 1879. T. **693 : 4**

Burnell, G: R. Rudimentary treatise on limes, cements, mastics, plastering, etc. 11th ed., with app. [Weale's ser.] Lond. 1878. S. **693 : 1**

Gillmore, Quincy A. Treatise on limes, hydraulic cements and mortars, containing reports of numerous experiments conducted in New York city during 1858–1861. U. S. engineer dep't. [Papers on practical engineering, no. 9.] N. Y. 1864. O. . **693 : D**

Austin, James G. Treatise on the preparation, combination and application of calcareous and hydraulic limes and cements; compiled and arr. from the best authorities and from the practical experience of the compiler; added, many useful recipes for various scientific, mercantile and domestic purposes. Lond. 1862. D. **693 : 6**

Reid, H: Treatise on the manufacture of Portland cement; added, a tr. of A. Lipowitz's work, describing a new method of manufacturing that cement by W. F. Reid. Lond. 1868. O. **693+7**

Faija, H: Portland cement for users. 2d ed., corr. [Weale's ser.] Lond. 1884. D. **693 : 8**

Carpentry.

Tredgold, T: Elementary principles of carpentry, chiefly composed from [his] standard work, with add., alterations and corr. from the works of the most recent authorities, and a treatise on joinery, containing a detailed account of the various operations

Tredgold, T:—*Continued.*
of the joiner, ed. by E. Wyndham Tarn. 3d
ed. Ill. [Weale's ser.] Lond. 1880. D.
                                 694 : 4
— *Same.* Atlas. Lond. 1880. Q.   **694+4**

Bell, W: E. Carpentry made easy, or The science and art of framing on a new and improved system, with specific instructions
for building balloon frames, barn frames,
mill frames, warehouses, church spires,
etc., comprising also a system of bridge
building ; with bills, estimates of cost, and
valuable tables. 2d ed., enl. and imp.
Phila. 1881. Q.   **694+1**

Hatfield, R. G. The american house-carpenter ;
a treatise upon architecture, cornices and
mouldings, framing doors, windows and
stairs, together with the most important
principles of practical geometry. 2d ed.
Ill. N. Y. 1845. O.   **694 : 2**

Robison, J:, F. Price, and T: Tredgold. A
treatise on the construction of roofs as
regards carpentry and joinery, deduced
from [their] works. [Weale's ser.] Lond.
[1859]. D.   **694 : 3**

Collings, G: A practical treatise on hand-rail-
ing, showing new and simple methods for
finding the pitch of the plank, drawing the
moulds, bevelling, jointing up and squaring the wreath. Ill. [Weale's ser.] Lond.
1882. D.   **694 : 7**

Y., F. Every man his own mechanic ; a guide
to every description of constructive and
decorative work that may be done by the
amateur artisan, at home and in the colonies, in 3 pts : 1, Household carpentry and
joinery ; 2, Ornamental and constructive
carpentry ; 3, Household building art and
practice. Lond. [1881]. O.   **694 : 6**

Wood-working tools and how to use them ; a
manual. Bost. 1881. D.   **694 : 8**

Boy's workshop, A ; with plans and designs for
in-door and out-door work by a boy and
his friends ; with an introd. by H: Randall
Waite. Ill. Bost. [1884]. S.   **x 694 : 9**

*Plumbing, ventilation and
heating.*

(*See also* Public health, cl. 614, col 404-406.)

Buchan, W: Paton. Plumbing ; a text-book to
the practice of the art or craft of the
plumber, with supp. chapters upon house
drainage, embodying the latest improvements. 2d ed. rev. and enl. Ill. [Weale's
ser.] Lond. 1880. D.   **696 : 1**

Butler, W. F. Ventilation of buildings. [Van
Nostrand's science ser.] N. Y. 1873. T.
                                   697 : 1

Rafter, G: W. Mechanics of ventilation. [Van
Nostrand's science ser.] N. Y. 1878. T.
                                   697 : 2

Tomlinson, C: A rudimentary treatise on warming and ventilation ; a concise exposition
of the general principles of the art of
warming and ventilating domestic and
public buildings, mines, lighthouses, ships,

etc. 8th ed. with index. [Weale's ser.]
Lond. 1878. D.   **697 : 3**

Briggs, H: Steam-heating ; an exposition of the
american practice of warming buildings by
steam. [Van Nostrand's science ser.] N.
Y. 1883. T.   **697 : 4**

Power, D. G. A treatise on heating, ventilation
and imperfect combustion ; smoke, its
formation and prevention. Milw. 1877. O.
                             697 : Pam

Painting, etc.

Cook, Clarence. "What shall we do with our
walls ?" N. Y. 1881. O.   **698+1**

Davidson, Ellis A. A practical manual of house-
painting, graining, marbling and sign-
writing ; containing full information of
the processes of house-painting in oil and
distemper, the formation of letters and
practice of sign-writing, the principles of
decorative art, a course of elementary
drawing for house-painters, writers, etc.,
and a collection of useful receipts. Ill. 3d
ed., rev. [Weale's ser.] Lond. 1880. D.
                                 698 : 2

Masury, J: W. House-painting, carriage-paint-
ing and graining. N. Y. 1881. D. **698 : 3**

Hints for painters, decorators and paper-hang-
ers ; selection of useful rules, data, memoranda, methods and suggestions for house,
ship and furniture painting, paper-hang-
ing, gilding, color-mixing and other matters, useful and instructive to painters and
decorators. Prepared, with special reference to the wants of amateurs, by an old
hand. (Work manuals, no. 3). N. Y. 1882.
D.   **698 : 4**

Rossiter, E. K., and F. A. Wright. Modern
house-painting ; containing 20 colored litho-
graphs, exhibiting the use of color in exterior and interior house-painting, and embracing examples of simple and elaborate
work in plain, graded and parti-colors ;
also the treatment of old styles of houses,
together with full descriptive letter-press,
covering the preparation, use and application of colors, with special directions applicable to each example. N. Y. 1882. O.
                                 698+5

Ship-building.

Hall, H: Report on the ship-building industry
of the U. S. Ill. *In* U. S. tenth census,
1880, v. 8.   *in* **317 : D**
Contents. Fishing-vessels. — Merchant sailing vessels.—Shipbuilding on the ocean coasts.—Steam vessels.—Iron vessels.—Canal-boats.—U. S. navy-yards.
—Ship-building timber.—Statistics of ship-building.

Sommerfeldt, Hakon A. The elementary and
practical principles of the construction of
ships for ocean and river service. [Weale's
ser.] Lond. 1861. D.   **699 : 3**
— *Same.* Atlas. Lond. 1861. F.   **699+P3**

Kipping, Robert. Rudimentary treatise on masting, mast-making and rigging of ships ;
also tables of spars, rigging, blocks, chain,
wire and hemp ropes etc., relating to every

Kipping, Robert.—*Continued.*
class of vessels, together with an app. of
dimensions of masts and yards of the royal
navy of Great Britain and Ireland. Ill. 14th
ed. [Weale's ser.] Lond. 1877. D. **699 : 1**
— Sails and sailmaking, with draughting and the
center effort of the sails ; also, weights and
sizes of ropes, masting, rigging and sails
of steam vessels, etc. Ill. 11th ed., enl.
[Weale's ser.] Lond. 1880. D. **699 : 2**

United States. *Navy dep't.* Papers and discussions on experiments with steel ; reprinted
from various sources. (Naval prof. papers,
no. 14.) Wash. 1883. O. *in* **699 : D**
— - Papers and discussions on engines, boilers
and torpedo boats ; repr. from the Transactions of the institution of naval architeets, vols. 1882 and 1883. Ill. (Naval prof.
papers, no. 16.) Wash. 1884. O. *in* **699 : D**

Cotsell, G: A treatise on ships' anchors. Ill.
[Weale's ser.] Lond. 1856. D. **699 : 4**

Kingston, W: H. G. The boy's own book of
boats ; with complete instructions how to
make sailing models. New ed. rev., with
add., incl. an account of the present condition of the british navy. Lond. *n. d.* D.
x 699 : 5

_____

x denotes books specially adapted for children.

VIII. FINE ARTS.

1. In general.

1. Aesthetics.

Alison, Archibald. Essays on the nature and principles of taste. 2d amer. ed. Hartford. 1821. O.   **701 : 18**

Allen, C: Grant. The colour-sense, its origin and development ; an essay in comparative psychology. [Eng. and foreign phil. lib.] Bost. 1879. O.   **701 : 2**

— Physiological æsthetics. N. Y. 1877. D.   **701 : 3**

Allston, Washington. Lectures on art, and poems ; ed. by R: H: Dana. N. Y. 1850. D.   **701 : 4**
Contents. Pref., by the ed. — Lectures on art. — Aphorisms. — The hypochondriac. — Poems.

Bascom, J: Æsthetics, or The science of beauty. Bost. 1862. D.   **701 : 5**

Burke, Edmund. A philosophical inquiry into the origin of our ideas of the sublime and beautiful, with an introd. discourse concerning taste. *In his* Works.   **329.2 : 2 v1**

— *Same.* Adapted to popular use by Abraham Mills. N. Y. *n. d.* D.   **701 : 19**

Carriere, Moriz. Aesthetik ; die idee des schönen und ihre verwirklichung im leben und in der kunst. 2te aufl. Leipz. 1873. 2 v. O.   **701 : 1**

Cousin, V: Lectures on the true, the beautiful and the good ; increased by an app. on french art. Tr. by O. W. Wight. N. Y. 1857. O.   **194 : 4**

Day, H: Noble. The science of æsthetics, or The nature, kinds, laws and uses of beauty. New Haven. 1872. D.   **701 : 6**

Dyer, T: H: On imitative art, its principles and progress ; with preliminary remarks on beauty, sublimity and taste. Lond. 1882. O.   **701 : 22**

Göthe, J: Wolfgang v. Zur kunst. *In his* Werke.   **830 : 137 v30**

Grillparzer, Franz. Aesthetische studien. *In his* Sämmtliche werke.   **832 : 35 v9**

Hartmann, K: Robert E: v. Aesthetische studien. *In his* Gesammelte studien.   **834+19**

Home, H:, *lord Kames.* Elements of criticism, with the author's last corr. and add. 1st amer. from 7th London ed. Bost. 1796. 2 v. O.   **701 : 7**

— *Same.* 3d amer. from 8th London ed. N. Y. 1819. 2 v. O.   **701 : 7**

Lemcke, K: H: Gottlieb. Populäre ästhetik. 3te verm. und verb. aufl. Ill. Leipz. 1870. O.   **701 : 26**

Lessing, J: Gotthold Ephraim. Selected prose works. Tr. from the german by E. C. Beasley and Helen Zimmern, ed. by E: Bell. Lond. 1879. D.   **701 : 8**
Contents. Introd. — Synopsis of the contents of Laokoon. — Laokoon. — How the ancients represented death. — Dramatic notes.

— Laokoon, oder Ueber die grenzen der malerei und poesie. *In his* Ausgewählte werke.   **830 : 140 v5**

— Wie die alten den tod gebildet. *In the same.*   **830 : 140 v4**

Longinus, Dionysius Cassius. On the sublime. Tr. from the greek, with notes and observations, and some account of the life, writings and character of the author, by W: Smith. 4th ed., corr Lond. 1770. D.   **701 : 20**

Oakey, Alexander F. The art of life and the life of art. (Frank sq. lib.) N. Y. 1884. Q.   **701+25**

Reynolds, *Sir* Joshua. Literary works. Prefixed, a memoir of the author, with remarks on his professional character, illustrative of his principles and practice, by H: W: Beechy. New ed. Lond. 1855. 2 v. D.   **701 : 10**
Contents V. 1. Introd. — Memoir. — Discourses. **2.** Discourses. — The idler: no 76. False criticisms on painting; no. 79. The grand style of painting; no. 82. The true idea of beauty. — Journey to Flanders and Holland. — The art of painting by C: A. du Fresnoy; tr. into eng. verse by W: Mason, with annotations by Reynolds. — Parallel between poetry and painting. — Epistle to Mr. Jervas, with Fresnoy's Art of painting, tr. by mr. Dryden. — Chronological list of painters, with short characters and an account of their respective births and deaths. — Alphabetical list of painters. — General index.

— **Cunningham**, Allen. The life and writings of sir Joshua Reynolds. Portrait. 1st amer. ed. N. Y. 1860. D.   **701 : 9**

Ruskin, J: Lectures on art, delivered before the university of Oxford, in Hilary term 1870. N. Y. 1878. D.   **701 : 12**
Contents. Inaugural. — The relation of art to religion. — The relation of art to morals. — The relation of art to use. — Line. — Light. — Colour.

— The eagle's nest ; ten lectures on the relation of natural science to art, given before the university of Oxford in lent term 1872. N. Y. 1883. D.   **701 : 24**

— Modern painters, by a graduate of Oxford. N. Y. 1876. 5 v. D.   **701 : 13**
Contents. V. 1. General principles. — Truth. **2.** Of ideas of beauty. **3.** Of many things. **4.** Of mountain beauty. **5.** Of leaf beauty. — Of cloud beauty. — Of ideas of relation: Of invention formal; Of invention spiritual.

Ruskin, J:—*Continued.*

— *Same.* Modern painters, by a graduate of Oxford. [With fac-simile reproductions of the plates in the original english ed.] N. Y. 1878–9. 5 v. Q.   **701 : R21**

— *Same.* V. 2, "Of ideas of beauty" and "Of the imaginative faculty." Rearr. and rev. by the author. N. Y. 1883. D.
    701 : 13 v2

— *Same.* V. 3, pt. 4. 1st amer. ed. N. Y. 1859. D.   **701 : 13 v3**
Contents. Of many things.

— Frondes agrestes ; readings in "Modern painters" chosen at her pleasure by the author's friend, the younger lady of the Thwaite, Coniston. N. Y. 1883. D.
    701 : 23

— Pre-Raphaelitism, by the author of Modern painters. N. Y. 1860. O.   **701 : 14**

— Art culture ; a handbook of art technicalities and criticisms, selected from [his] works, and arr. and supp. by W. H. Platt for the use of schools and colleges, with a new glossary of art terms, and an alphabetical and chronological list of artists. N. Y. 1877. D.   **701 : 11**

Samson, G: Whitefield. Elements of art criticism ; comprising a treatise on the principles of man's nature as addressed by art, together with a historic survey of the methods of art execution in the departments of drawing, sculpture, architecture, painting, landscape gardening and the decorative arts, designed as a text-book for schools and colleges and as a handbook for amateurs and artists. Phila. 1876. O.   **701 : 15**

Schiller, J: Christoph v. Kleine ästhetische schriften. *In his* Sämmtliche werke.
    830 : 143 v11,12

— *Same.*   *in* **830 : 144 v17,18**
Contents, see under German literature, Collected works.

Schlegel, K: W: F: v. Æsthetic ... works.
    in **804 : 4**
Contents. Description of paintings in Paris and the Netherlands, in 1802–4.—Principles of gothic architecture.—Modern german paintings.—On the limits of the beautiful.

Stewart, Dugald. Essays relative to taste. *In his* Philosoph. essays.   **191+8 v5**
Contents, see col. 45.

Taine, Hippolyte Adolphe. Lectures on art. Tr. by J: Durand. N. Y. 1875. 2 v. O.
    701 : 16
Contents. V. 1. The philosophy of art.—The ideal in art. 2. The philosophy of art in Italy.—The philosophy of art in the Netherlands.—The philosophy of art in Greece.

Véron, Eugène. Aesthetics. Tr. by W. H. Armstrong. [Lib. of contemp. science.] Lond. 1879. D.   **701 : 17**

Winckelmann, J: Joachim. Werke. Einzig rechtmässige original-ausgabe. Stuttgart. 1847. 2 v. O.   **700+1**
Contents. V. 1. Winckelmann's biographie.—Winckelmann's Vorrede zur Geschichte der kunst des alterthums.—Winckelmann's Vorrede zu den anmerkungen über die Geschichte der kunst des alterthums.—Geschichte der kunst des alterthums.—Von der kunst der zeichnung der alten völker. 2. Gedanken über die nachahmung der griechischen werke in der malerei und bildhauer-kunst, nebst sendschreiben und erläuterung.—Kleinere aufsätze über gegenstande der alten kunst.—Anmerkung über die baukunst der alten.—Schriften über die herculanischen entdeckungen.—Abhandlung von der Fähigkeit der empfindung des schönen in der kunst, und

dem unterricht in derselben.—Versuch einer allegorie, besonders für die kunst. — Nachlass, fragmente und zusätze.—Freundschaftliche briefe.—Uebersicht und erklärung der kupfer zu Winckelmann's werken.

2. Dictionaries and cyclopedias.

Müller, Hermann Alexander. Lexikon der bildenden künste ; technik und geschichte der baukunst, plastik, malerei und der vervielfältigenden künste ; künstler, kunststätten, kunstwerke, etc. Ill. Leipz. 1883. D.   **703 : R4**

Fairholt, F: W: A dictionary of terms in art. Ill. Lond. *n. d.* D.   **703 : 3**

Mollett, J: W. An illustrated dictionary of words used in art and archæology ; explaining terms frequently used in works on architecture, arms, bronzes, christian art, color, costume, decoration, devices, emblems, heraldry, lace, personal ornaments, pottery, painting, sculpture, etc. Bost. 1882. O.   **703 : R2**

Waters, Clara Erskine, *formerly mrs.* Clement. A handbook of legendary and mythological art. Ill. 10th ed. N. Y. 1876. D.   **703 : 1**

3. Essays and miscellany.

Cheney, Ednah Dean. Gleanings in the fields of art. Bost. 1881. O.   **704 : 2**
Contents. Art.—Greek art.—Early christian art.—Byzantine art.—Restoration of art in Italy.—Michael Angelo.—The poems of Michael Angelo.—Spanish art.—French art.—Albert Dürer.—Old german art.—American art.—English art.—D: Scott.—Contemporaneous art.

Coan, Titus Munson, *ed.* Art and literature. (Topics of the time, no. 6.) N. Y. 1883. D.   **704 : 12**
Contents. **Blackie, J: S.** The philosophy of the beautiful.—**Traill, H. D.** Hellenism in South Kensington: A dialogue; Plato and Landor.—**Poole, S. Lane.** The beginning of art.—The ancient, medieval and modern stage.—**Wedmore, F:** The impressionists.—**Gurney, E.** Wagner and Wagnerism.

Conway, Moncure Daniel. Travels in South Kensington ; with notes on decorative art and architecture in England. N. Y. 1882. O.   **704 : 9**

Fairholt, F: W: Rambles of an archæologist among old books and in old places ; papers on art in relation to archæology, painting, art decoration and art manufacture. Lond. 1871. O.   **704+P1**
Contents. Rambles of an archæologist among old books and in old places.— Grotesque design, as exhibited in ornamental and industrial art. — Facts about finger-rings.—Ancient brooches and dress fastenings.—Albert Dürer; his works, his compatriots, and his times.

Freeman, James E. Gatherings from an artist's portfolio. N. Y. 1877. S.   **704 : 13**

— Gatherings from an artist's portfolio in Rome. Bost. 1883. D.   **704 : 10**

Fuseli, H: Life and writings ; the former written and the latter ed. by J: Knowles. Lond. 1831. 3 v. O.   **704 : 19**
Contents. V. 1. **Knowles, J:** The life of H: Fuseli. 2. Ancient art.—Art of the moderns.—Invention.—Composition, expression.—Chiaroscuro.—On design.—Colour, in fresco painting.—Colour, oil painting.—The method of fixing a standard and defining the proportions of the human frame with directions to the student in copying the life. 3. On the prevailing method of treating the history of painting, with observations on the picture of Leonardo da Vinci of

"The last supper."—On the present state of the art and the causes which check its progress.—Aphorisms, chiefly relative to the fine arts.—A history of art in the schools of Italy.

Hamerton, Philip Gilbert. Thoughts about art. New ed.. rev., with notes and an introd. Bost. 1878. D.   **704 : 3**

Contents. That certain artists should write on art. —Painting from nature.—Painting from memoranda. —The relation between photography and painting.— Word-painting and colour-painting.—Transcendent-alism in painting.—The law of progress in art.— Artists in fiction.— Picture buying.—Fame. — Art criticism.—Analysis and synthesis in painting.—The reaction from pre-Raphaelitelsm.—The artistic spirit. —The place of landscape-painting amongst the fine arts.—The housing of national art treasures.—On the artistic observation of nature.—Proudhon as a writer on art.—Two art philosophers.—Leslie.—Picture-dealers.—Thorwaldsen. — The philosophy of etching. —Amateur painters.—Can science help art ?—Picture frames.—Autographic art.

Hamilton, Walter. The æsthetic movement in England. 3d ed. Lond. 1882. O. **704 : 14**

Hunt, W: M. Talks on art ; [1st and] 2d ser., comp. by Helen M. Knowlton. Bost. 1883. 2 v. O.   **704 : R7**

Morris, W: Hopes and fears for art. · Bost. 1882. S.   **704 : 8**

Nichols, G: Ward. Art education applied to industry. Ill. N. Y. 1877. O. **707 : 1**

Palgrave, Francis Turner. Essays on art. N. Y. 1867. D.   **704 : 4**

Contents. The Royal academy,1863-1865.—Mulready. —Dyce and W: Hunt. — Hippolyte Flandrin. — Herbert's Delivery of the law.—Recent works by Holman Hunt.—Exhibition of F. Madox Brown.—G: Cruik-shank.—Japanese art.—Sensational art.—Poetry and prose in art.—Lost treasures.—Behnes the sculptor. —Thorvaldsen's life and works.—The Farnese marbles.— On the position of sculpture in England.— Sculpture and painting.—Triquetl's " Marmor home-ricum."—The Albert cross and english monumental sculpture.—Thackeray in the abbey.—New Paris.

Ruskin, J: Mornings in Florence : simple studies of christian art for english travellers. N. Y. 1877. D.   **704 : 18**

Contents. Santa Croce. — Before the Soldan.—The strait gate.—The golden gate.—The vaulted book.— The shepherd's tower.

— The political economy of art ; the substance, with add., of two lectures delivered at Manchester, july 10 and 13, 1857. N. Y. 1878. D.   **704 : 17**

— The two paths ; lectures on art and its application to decoration and manufacture, delivered in 1858-9. Plates and cuts. N. Y. 1883. D.   **704 : 16**

*   *   *

Kemble, Marion, *ed.* Art recreations ; a guide to decorative art. [New ed.] Ill. Bost. [1884]. D.   **704 : 15**

Leland, C: Godfrey. The minor arts. (Art at home ser.) Lond. 1880. D. **704 : 11**

Contents. Leather work. — Porcelain or vitreous painting. — Designing and transferring patterns.— Wood - carving. — Stencilling. — Modelling. — Mosaic work.—Repoussé work and silver chasing. — Minor manufactures.—Useful recipes.

Urbino, Lavinia Buoncore, W: Day *and others.* Art recreations ; with valuable receipts for preparing materials. Ill. Bost. 1861. D. **704 : 6**

Contents. Drawing.— Oil painting.— Crayon drawing.—Grecian painting.—Painting in water colors.— Theorem painting.—Photograph painting.—Oriental painting.—Painting on glass.—Papier maché.—Leather work. — Taxidermy. — Wax work. — Plaster work.— Moss work.—Sea weed.—Hair work.—Feather flowers.— Cone work.—Shell work.—Wild tamarind seed

work.—Imitation pearl work for embroidery.—Paper flowers.—Potichomanie. — Transparencies.—Leaf impressions.—To dry botanical specimens for preservation.—The aquarium.—Miscellaneous receipts.

Parrish, E: The phantom bouquet ; a popular treatise on the art of skeletonizing leaves and seed-vessels and adapting them to embellish the home of taste. Phila. 1864. D.   **704 : 5**

4. Periodicals, societies and galleries.

American art review, The ; a journal devoted to the practice, theory, history and arch-æology of art ; v. 1, 2. Bost. 1880, 1881. Q.   **705 : RM**

Art amateur, The ; a monthly journal devoted to the cultivation of art in the household, ed. and pub. by Montague Marks ; v. 1-12, june 1879—may 1885. N. Y. [1880–85]. F.   **705 : RM**

Art journal, The ; v. 29-36, jan. 1877— dec. 1884. N. Y. 1877-85. Q. ,   **705 : RM**

Magazine of art, The ; v. 1-7, dec. 1877—nov. 1884. Lond. 1878-84. Q.   **705 : RM**

Portfolio, The ; an artistic periodical, ed. by Philip Gilbert Hamerton ; v. 12-15, jan. 1881—dec. 1884. Lond. 1881-85. Q.   **705 : RM**

Köhler, Sylvester R., *comp.* The U. S. art directory and year-book ; a chronicle of events in the art world, and a guide for all interested in the progress of art in America. [Ill.] N. Y. 1884. O.   **705+9**

New England manufacturers' and mechanics' institute. Art year-book, 1884 ; american art. Ill. Bost. 1884. Q.   **705 : R1**

*   *   *

Di Cesnola, L: Palma, *ed.* The metropolitan museum of art. Ill. N. Y. 1882. F.   **708 : R3**

Milwaukee museum of fine arts for the state of Wis. Articles of association and by-laws, 1882. Milw. D.   **706 : Pam**

Maskell, W: Handbook of the Dyce and Forster collections in the South Kensington museum. [*Anon.*] Engr. and facsimiles. [South Kensington museum art handbooks.] Lond. [1880]. D.   **708 : 2**

Gower, *Lord* **Ronald C:,** *ed.* The great historic galleries of England, [1st and 2d series]. Lond. 1881, 1882. 2 v. F.   **708 : R4**

Contents. V. 1. **Raphael,** Madonna with the palm tree.—**Van Dyck,** Thomas Howard, earl of Arun-del. — **Reynolds,** Caroline, countess of Carlisle.— **Holbein,** Christina of Denmark. — **Murillo,** The Virgin.— **Greuze,** Innocence. — **Gerbier,** Maria, infanta of Spain.—**Gainsborough,** The housemaid.—**Meissonier,** The halt.—**Carracci,** Annibale, The three Maries.—**Rembrandt,** Portrait of a lady. — **Delaroche,** Richelieu on the Rhône.— **Raphael,** Madonna of the Bridgwater gallery.—**Hals,** A cavalier.—**Mieris,** The musicians.—**Mabuse,** Adoration of the magi.— **Holbein,** Thomas Howard, duke of Norfolk.—**Reynolds,** The duchess of Devonshire.— **Rubens,** A daughter of Rubens.—**Janet,** School of, Mary, queen of Scots.— After **Raphael,** Madonna with the diadem.—**Murillo,** St. Justa: St. Rufina. 2. **Teniers,** Soldiers smoking. — **Hobbema,** The water mill.—Miniatures.—**Meissonier,** Punchinello. —**Reynolds,** Nelly O'Brien.—Miniatures.—**Metsu,** Lady reading a letter.—**Van Dyck,** Portrait of a gentleman.—Miniatures.—**Van Dyck** (?), Charles I.— **Cuyp,** Herdsman and cows.—**Holbein,** Miniatures. —**Ter Borch,** Officer writing orders.—**Hals,** Admiral de Ruijter.—Miniatures.—**Steen,** A village fête.—

Reynolds, George Howard, lord Morpeth. — Hilliard, N:, Miniatures. — DeHooch, An interior. — Greuze. Girl with doves. — Miniatures. — Gainsborough, The blue boy.—The Stuart miniatures.

Amsterdam, *Rijks museum*. Beschrijving der schilderijen ; met fac simile der naamteekens. 6de druk. Amsterdam. 1876. D.　708 : 6

Dresden gallery, Gems of the ; comprising the most famous and popular works in the Dresden collection, reproduced in heliotype from the best engr. with notices of the works and the artists. Bost. 1883. Q.　708 : R5

5. History of art.

Bell, N. R. E., (*N. D'Anvers*). Elementary history of art ; an introd. to ancient and modern architecture, sculpture, painting, music ; with a pref. by T. Roger Smith. Ill. N. Y. 1875. D.　709 : 7

Braun, Julius. Geschichte der kunst in ihrem entwicklungsgang durch alle völker der alten welt hindurch, auf dem boden der ortskunde nachgewiesen. 2te aufl. mit einem vorwort von Franz Reber. Wiesbaden. 1873. 2 v. O.　709 : 1

Carriere, Moriz. Die kunst im zusammenhang der culturentwickelung und die ideale der menschheit. 3te aufl. Leipz. 1877. 5 v. O.　709 : 2
　Contents. V, I. Die anfänge der cultur und das orientalische alterthum. 2. Hellas und Rom. 3. Das mittelalter. 4. Renaissance und reformation in bildung, kunst und literatur. 5. Das weltalter des geistes im aufgange.

Dean, Amos. European art. *In his* History of civilization.　309 : 5 v7

DeForest, Julia B. A short history of art. Ill. N. Y. [1881]. O.　709 : 17

General view of the fine arts, A, critical and historical ; with an introd. by D: Huntington. N. Y. 1851. D.　709 : 10

Lossing, Benson J: Outline of the history of the fine arts ; a view of the rise, progress and influence of the arts among different nations, ancient and modern, with notices of the character and works of many celebrated artists. Ill. N. Y. 1845. S.　709 : 13

Lübke, W: History of art. Tr. by F. E. Bunnètt. 3d ed. Lond. 1874. 2 v. Q.　709 : R3
— Outlines of the history of art. A new trans. from the 7th german ed., ed. by Clarence Cook. Ill. N. Y. 1884. 2 v. O.　709 : 25

Redgrave, Gilbert R., ed. Outlines of historic ornament. Tr. from the germ. Ill. N. Y. 1884. D.　709 : 24

Schnaase, C: Geschichte der bildenden künste. 2te verb. und verm. aufl. Ill. Düsseldorf. 1866–79. 8 v. in 7. O.　709+23
　Contents. V. 1. Die völker des orients ; unter mitwirkung des verf. bearb. von C: v. Lützow. 2. Griechen und römer; unter mitw. des verf. bearb. von C: Friederichs. 3. Altchristliche, byzantinische, muhammedanische, karonlingische kunst; bearb. vom verf. unter mithülfe von J. Rudolf Rahn. 4. Die romänische kunst; bearb. vom verf. unter mith. von Alwin Schultz und W: Lübke. 5. Entstehung und ausbildung des gothischen styls; bearb. vom verf. unter mith. von Alfred Woltmann. 6. Die spätzeit des mittelalters bis zur blüthe der Eyck'schen schule; bearb. vom verf. 7. Das mittelalter Italiens und die grenzgebiete der aberländischen kunst; bearb. vom verf. unter mith. von E: Dobbert. 8. Geschichte der bildenden künste im 15ten jahrhundert; unter mitw. von O. Eisenmann, herausg. von W: Lübke.—Lübke, W: Biographische skizze C: Schnaase's, mit port.

Winckelmann, J: Joachim. Geschichte der kunst des alterthums. *In his* Werke.　700+1 v1
— *Same, eng.* The history of ancient art. Tr. from the german by G. H: Lodge, with a life of Winckelmann by the ed. Bost. 1849, 1850. 2 v. Q.　709+6

Reber, Franz v. History of ancient art, rev. by the author. Tr. and augm. by Joseph Thacher Clarke. N. Y. 1882. O.　709 : 14

Creuzer, F: Zur archäologie, oder Zur geschichte und erklärung der alten kunst ; abhandlungen, besorgt von Julius Kayser. Leipz. 1846. 3 v. O.　709 : 19
— Die historische kunst der griechen in ihrer entstehung und fortbildung. 2te verb. und verm. ausg., besorgt von Julius Kayser. Leipz. 1845. O.　709 : 20

Perrot, G:, *and* C: **Chipiez.** A history of art in ancient Egypt. From the french, tr. and ed. by Walter Armstrong. Lond. 1883 [1882]. 2 v. Q.　709+P16
— History of art in Chaldæa and Assyria. From the french, tr. and ed. by Walter Armstrong. N. Y. 1884. 2 v. Q.　709+22

Lacroix, Paul (*Le bibliophile Jacob*). The arts in the middle ages and at the period of the renaissance. Lond. 1875. Q.　709 : R12
　Contents. Furniture: household and ecclesiastical. —Tapestry.—Ceramic art.—Arms and armour.—Carriages and saddlery.—Gold and silver work.—Horology.—Musical instruments.—Playing cards. — Glass-painting.—Fresco-painting.—Painting on wood, canvas, etc. — Engraving. — Sculpture. — Architecture.— Parchment and paper.—Manuscripts.—Miniatures in manuscript.—Book-binding.—Printing.

Lübke, W: Ecclesiastical art in Germany during the middle ages. Tr. from the 5th german ed. with app. by L. A. Wheatley. 4th ed. Ill. Edinb. 1877. O.　709+4

Baxter, *Mrs.* Lucy E., (*Leader Scott*). The renaissance of art in Italy ; an illustrated sketch by Leader Scott. Lond. 1883. Q. 709 : R18

Symonds, J: Addington. Renaissance in Italy : The fine arts. N. Y. 1879. O.　709 : 5

Jarves, James Jackson. A glimpse at the art of Japan. N. Y. 1876. D.　709 : 11

Benjamin, S: Green Wheeler. Art in America ; a critical and historical sketch. Ill. N. Y. 1880. O.　709+8

Farrar, C: S: History of sculpture and painting ; topical lessons with specific references to valuable books. Milw. 1879. O.　709 : 9
— Art topics ; history of sculpture, painting and architecture with specific reference to most of the standard works on art. N. Y. 1884. O.　709 : 9
　Note. This is the 2d ed. of the previous work.

Pictorial gallery of arts, The. V. 2 : Fine arts. Lond. *n. d.* F　609 : R5
　Note. V. 1 contains Useful arts.

Seroux d'Agincourt, J: Baptiste L: G: History of art by its monuments, from its decline in the 4th century to its restoration in the 16th. Tr. from the french ; in 3335 subjects on 328 plates. Lond. 1847. 3 v. in 1. F.　709 : R21

Seemann, E. A., *ed.* Illustrations of the history of art. Authorized amer. ed., pub. under the direction of S. R. Koehler. Bost. 1879. 5 v. obl. Q.　709 : R15
　Contents. [Pt. 1.] Architecture, sculpture and the industrial arts among the nations of antiquity. [Pt. 2.] Architecture and sculpture of the early christian,

romanesque and gothic periods.—Architecture and ornamentation of the mohammedan nations. [Pt. 3.] Architecture and sculpture of the renaissance period and of modern times. [Pt. 4.] The industrial arts among the oriental nations and the nations of Europe, from the middle ages down to modern times. [Pt. 5.] The history of painting from the time of the egyptians to the close of the 18th century.—A series

of ill. arranged chronologically and forming an atlas to be used in connection with any work on the history of art.

Springer, Anton. Text-book to the Illustrations of the history of art. Tr. from the german by Margaret Hicks Volkmann. [*Anon.*] Bost. 1883. O.   **709 : R15**

2. Architecture and Landscape gardening.

(*See also* Building, cl. 690-698, col. 458-464.)

1. In general.

Audsley, W: James *and* G: Ashdown. Popular dictionary of architecture and the allied arts ; work of reference for the architect, builder, sculptor, decorative artist and general student, with numerous ill. from all styles of architecture, from the egyptian to the renaissance. V. 1-3. Lond. 1881-82. Q.   **720 : R1**
Contents. V. 1. A-Aque. 2. Aqui-Bapt. 3. Bar-Buttery.

Gwilt, Joseph. An encyclopædia of architecture, historical, theoretical and practical ; rev., with alterations and add. by Wyatt Papworth. Ill. New ed. Lond. 1876. O.   **720 : R16**

Stuart, Robert. Cyclopædia of architecture, historical, descriptive, topographical, decorative, theoretical and mechanical, alphabetically arr., familiarly explained. and adapted to the comprehension of workmen, etc. 2 v. in 1. N. Y. 1854. O.   **720 : R2**

Parker, J: H: A glossary of terms used in grecian, roman, italian and gothic architecture. 4th ed. enl. Oxford. 1845. 2 v. O.   **720 : R15**
— A companion to the 4th ed. of A glossary of terms used in grecian... architecture ; containing 400 additional examples, a chronological table and a general index. Oxford. 1846. O.   **720 : R15 v3**
— A concise glossary of terms, used in grecian, roman, italian and gothic architecture. 4th ed. rev. Oxford. 1875. S.   **720 : 6**

Seemann, E. A. The styles of architecture ; ill. of the history of architecture from the ancient to the modern times. Leipz. 1883. F.   **720 : 14**

Fergusson, James. A history of architecture in all countries, from the earliest times to the present day. 2d ed. Ill. Lond. 1873-76. 4 v. O.   **720 : R3**
Contents. V. 1. Introd.—Pt. 1. Ancient architecture.—Pt. 2. Christian architecture. 2. Christian architecture, *continued.*—Pt. 3. Saracenic and ancient american architecture. 3. Indian and Eastern architecture. 4. Modern styles of architecture.
— *Same.* N. Y. 1883. 2 v. Q.   **720+3**

Freeman, E: A: Historical and architectural sketches, chiefly italian. Ill. Lond. 1876. D.   **729 : 1**
Contents. The venetian march.—Ravenna and her sisters.—Central Italy.—Rome.—Southern Italy.—Lombardy.—The burgundian march.

Lefèvre, André. Wonders of architecture. Tr. from the french ; added, a chapter on english architecture by R. Donald. [Ill. lib. of wonders.] N. Y. 1875. D.   **720 : 4**

Rosengarten, Albert. A handbook of architectural styles. Tr. from the german by W. Collett-Sandars. Ill. Lond. 1878. O.   **720 : 13**

Rudimentary architecture for the use of beginners and students : The orders and their æsthetic principles, by W: H: Leeds.—The styles of various countries and periods, by T. Talbot Bury. — Design as deducible from nature, by E: Lacy Garbett. Ill. [Weale's ser.] Lond. 1874. D.   **720 : 5**

Ruskin, J: The seven lamps of architecture. Ill. N. Y. 1877. D.   **720 : 7**
Contents. Introd. — Sacrifice. — Truth. — Power. — Beauty.—Life.—Memory.—Obedience.
— *Same.* [With fac simile reproductions of the plates in the original english ed.] N. Y. 1880. O.   **720 : R8**
— Lectures on architecture and painting, delivered at Edinb. in nov. 1853. Ill. N. Y. 1877. D.   **720 : 12**
— An inquiry into some of the conditions at present [affecting the study of architecture in our schools ; read at the ordinary general meeting of the Royal institute of british architects, may 15, 1865. N. Y. 1877. D. *In his* Lectures on architecture and painting.   **720 : 12**
— The poetry of architecture, cottage, villa, etc. Added, Suggestions on works of art by "Kata Phusin," conjectured nom-de-plume of J: Ruskin. Ill. N. Y. 1880. D.   **720 : 17**

Bishop, H: Halsall. Pictorial architecture of the British Isles. 2d ed. rev. and enl. Lond. 1884. obl. O.   **729 : R4**

Tuthill, Louisa Caroline. History of architecture from the earliest times, its present condition in Europe and the U. S., with a biography of eminent architects and a glossary of architectural terms. Ill. Phila. 1848. O.   **720+9**

Viollet-le-Duc, Eugène Emmanuel. Discourses on architecture. [Vol. 1] tr. with an introductory essay by H: Van Brunt ; [vol. 2] tr. by B: Bucknall. Bost. 1875. 1881. 2 v. Q.   **720+10**
Contents. V. 1. Translator's introd.—What is barbarism ?—What is art ?—What are the relations of art to civilization ?—What are the social conditions most favorable to the development of art ?— Primitive methods of construction as practised in greek architecture.—Comparison between the architecture of the greeks and romans. — The architecture of the romans.—The methods to be followed in the study of architecture.— The basilicas of the romans.— The domestic architecture of the ancients.—The decline of ancient architecture.— Style and composition.— The origins of byzantine architecture.— The architecture of the west since the establishment of christianity.—The principle of western architecture in the middle ages.—The causes of the decline of architecture.—Some of the principles of architectural composition.—The renaissance in the west and especially

in France.—The principles and information necessary to architects.—The architecture of the 19th century.—Method. 2. [*Title page reads:* Lectures on architecture, vol. 2.] The construction of buildings.—On the teaching of architecture.—General observations on the external and internal ornamentation of buildings.—On monumental sculpture. — Domestic architecture.—The state of architecture in Europe.

Wightwick, G: Hints to young architects, comprising advice to those, who, while yet at school, are destined to the profession, to such as, having passed their pupilage, are about to travel, and to those who, having completed their education, are about to practise ; together with a model specification involving a great variety of instructive and suggestive matter. A new ed. rev. and enl., comprising treatises on the principles of construction and design by G. Huskisson Guillaume. [Weale's ser.] Lond. 1880. D.   **720 : 11**

Tuthill, W: B., *ed.* Interiors and interior details : fifty-two large quarto plates, comprising a large number of original designs of halls, staircases, parlors, libraries, dining rooms, etc., with an introd., description of plates, and notes on wood finish. by W: B. Tuthill. N. Y. 1882. F.   **721 : R2**
"Together with special designs for low-cost, medium and elaborate wood mantels, sideboards, furniture, wood ceilings, doors, door and window trims, wainscots, bank, office and store fittings, in perspective, elevation and detail, making a valuable series of suggestions for architects and architectural designers, and a large collection of interior details suited to the requirements of carpenters, builders and mechanics, reproduced from the drawings of prominent architects of New York, Boston, Chicago and other cities."—*Title-page.*

American architect, The, and building news ; v. 9–16, jan. 1881—dec. 1884. Bost. 1881-85. F.   **705.2 : RM**

2. Ancient and medieval.

Parker, J: H: The architectural history of the city of Rome ; abridged from The archæology of Rome, for the use of students. Lond. 1881. D.   **722 : 1**

Fergusson, James. The Parthenon ; an essay on the mode by which light was introduced into greek and roman temples. Lond. 1883. Q.   **722+3**

— The temple of Diana at Ephesus, with especial reference to mr. Wood's discoveries of its remains ; extracted from the Transact. of the Royal institute of british architects. Lond. 1883. Q.   **722+4**

— Archæology in India, with especial reference to the works of babu Rajendralala Mitra. Lond. 1884. O.   **722 : 5**

Smith, T. Roger, *and* J: **Slater.** Architecture, classic and early christian. (Ill. handbooks of art history.) Lond. 1882. D.   **722 : 2**

Scott, *Sir* G: Gilbert. Lectures on the rise and development of mediæval architecture, delivered at the Royal academy. Ill. Lond. 1879. 2 v. O.   **723 : 8**

Norton, C: Eliot. Historical studies of church-building in the middle ages ; Venice, Siena, Florence. N. Y. 1880. O.   **723 : 4**

Paley, F: Apthorpe. A manual of gothic architecture. Ill. Lond. 1846. D.   **723 : 5**

Parker, J: H: An introduction to the study of gothic architecture. 5th ed. Oxford. 1877. S.   **724 : 1**

— A B C of gothic architecture. 2d ed. London. 1882. T.   **723 : 7**

Smith, T. Roger. Architecture, gothic and renaissance. (Text books of art education.) N. Y. 1880. D.   **723 : 6**

Pugin, A: Northmore Welby. The true principles of pointed or christian architecture, set forth in 2 lectures delivered at St. Maries, Oscott. Lond. 1853. Q.   **723 : R1**

— An apology for the revival of christian architecture in England. Lond. 1843. Q. *With his* True principles of pointed or christian architecture.   *in* **723 : R1**

Ruskin, J: The stones of Venice. Ill. N. Y. 1878. 3 v. D.   **723 : 3**
Contents. V. I. The foundations. 2. The sea-stories : 1st or byzantine period ; 2d or gothic period ; app. 3. The fall ; 3d or renaissance period ; app.

— *Same.* [With facsimile reproductions of the plates in the original english ed.] N. Y. 1880. 3 v. O.   **723 : R2**

Hunnewell, James F. The historical monuments of France. Ill. Bost. 1884. O.   **729+3**

3. Church, school and library.

Scott, *Sir* G: Gilbert. An essay on the history of english church architecture, prior to the separation of England from the roman obedience. Ill. Lond. 1881. F. **729 : R2**

Bonney, T. J., *ed.* Cathedral churches of England and Wales, descriptive, historical, pictorial. Ill. N. Y. 1884. O.   **726 : R4**

Buckler, J: Chessell *and* C. A. A history of the architecture of the abbey church of St. Alban, with especial reference to the norman structure. Lond. 1847. O.   **726+1**

Neale, J: Mason. Ecclesiological notes on the Isle of Man, Ross, Sutherland and the Orkneys, or A summer pilgrimage to S. Manghold and S. Magnus. Lond. 1848. S.   **726 : 3**

Gardner, Eugene C. Common sense in church building. Ill. N. Y. 1880. S.   **726 : 2**

Barnard, H: School architecture, or Contributions to the improvement of school houses in the U. S. N. Y. 1848. D.   **727 : 1**
Note. For school house architecture, see also Reports and circulars of the U. S. bureau of education, col. 240.

Poole, W: F: Remarks on library construction ; appended, an examination of J. L. Smith-meyer's pamphlet, Suggestions on library architecture, amer. and foreign. Chicago. 1884. O.   **725 : Pam**
Note. For the author's Construction of library buildings, see U. S. Bureau of education, Circulars of information, no. 1, 1881, in 370 : D, *or* Amer. library assoc. Proceedings, 1881.

4. Domestic and rural.

Viollet-le-Duc, Eugène Emmanuel. The habitations of man in all ages. Tr. by B: Bucknall. Ill. Bost. 1876. O.   **728 : 9**

— The story of a house. Tr. from the french by G: M. Towle. Ill. Bost. 1874. O. **728 : 10**

Bunce, Oliver Bell. My house ; an ideal. N. Y. 1884. S.   **728 : 14**

Gardner, Eugene C. Illustrated homes ; a series of papers describing real houses and real people. Ill. Bost. 1875. S.   **728 : 6**

— The house that Jill built, after Jack's had proved a failure ; a book on home architecture. (Our continent lib.) N. Y. 1882. S.   **728 : 12**

Palliser's model homes ; showing a variety of designs for model dwellings, also farm-barn and ·hennery, stable and carriage house, school house, masonic association building, bank and library, town hall and three churches ; together with miscellaneous matter. Bridgeport, Conn. [1878]. O.   **728+7**

Vaux, Calvert. Villas and cottages ; a series of designs prepared for execution in the U. S. Ill. N. Y. 1857. O.   **728 : 8**

Loudon, J: Claudius. An encyclopædia of cottage, farm and villa architecture and furniture ; containing numerous designs for dwellings from the villa to the cottage and the farm, incl. farm houses, farmeries and other agricultural buildings, country inns, public houses and parochial schools with the requisite fittings up, fixtures and furniture and appropriate offices, gardens and garden scenery ; each design accompanied by analytical and critical remarks. New ed., ed. by mrs. Loudon. Ill. Lond. 1869. O.   **728 : R1**

Lakey, C: D. Village and country houses, or Cheap homes for all classes, comprising 84 pages of designs. N. Y. 1875. F. **728 : R2**

Young, W: Town and country mansions, and suburban houses ; with notes on the sanitary and artistic construction of houses. Lond. 1879. F.   **728 : R3**

Downing, Andrew Jackson. Cottage residences, or A series of designs for rural cottages and cottage villas, and their gardens and grounds, adapted to North America. Pt. 1. 3d ed. N. Y. 1847. O.   **728+5**

— The architecture of country houses ; incl. designs for cottages, farm-houses and villas, with remarks on interiors, furniture and the best modes of warming and ventilation. Ill. N. Y. 1854. O.   **728 : 4**

Wheeler, Gervase. Rural homes, or Sketches of houses suited to american country life, with original plans, designs, etc. Auburn. 1853. D.   **728 : 13**

Woodward, G: E. *and* F. W. Country homes. N. Y. 1865. D.   **728 : 11**

Thaer, Konrad Albrecht W: Ueber ländliche arbeiter-wohnungen. *In* Deutsche zeit- und streit-fragen.   **304 : 15 v1**

5. Landscape gardening.

Downing, Andrew Jackson. Rural essays ; ed., with a memoir of the author, by G: W: Curtis, and a letter to his friends by Fredrika Bremer. N. Y. 1853. O.   **710 : 1**

Contents. Memoirs.—Letter from miss Bremer.—Horticulture.—Landscape gardening.—Rural architecture.—Trees.—Agriculture.—Fruit.—Letters from England.

Maitland, Fowler. Building estates ; a rudimentary treatise on the development, sale, purchase and general management of building land, incl. the formation of streets and sewers and the requirements of sanitary authorities. Plans and ill. [Weale's ser.] Lond. 1883. D.   **712 : 3**

Oakey, Alexander F. Home grounds. (Appletons' home books). N. Y. 1881. D. **712 : 1**

Kemp, E: How to lay out a garden ; intended as a general guide in choosing, forming or improving an estate, from a quarter of an acre to a hundred acres in extent, with reference to both design and execution. From the 2d Lond. ed. enl. 2d ed. N. Y. 1875. D.   **710 : 2**

Long, Elias A. Ornamental gardening for americans ; a treatise on beautifying homes, rural districts, towns, and cemeteries. Ill. N. Y. 1885 [1884]. D.   **710 : 3**

Scott, Frank J. The art of beautifying suburban home grounds of small extent ; with descriptions of the beautiful and hardy trees and shrubs grown in the U. S. Ill. N. Y. 1873. O.   **712+2**

New York *city. Commissioners of Central park.* 11th annual report, 1867. Maps and ill. N. Y. 1868. O.   **711 : P1**

Chapman, Silas. The Forest Home cemetery, Milwaukee, Wis., with a map of the grounds. Milw. 1871. S.   **719 : 1**

Northcote, James Spencer. The roman catacombs, or Some account of the burial-places of the early christians in Rome. Phila. 1859. S.   **719 : 2**

3. Sculpture, Keramics, etc.

1. Sculpture.

Flaxman, J: Lectures on sculpture as delivered before the Royal academy ; with an introd. lecture and two addresses to the Royal academy on the death of T: Banks, in 1805, and of Antonio Canova, in 1822, and an address on the death of Flaxman by sir R: Westmacott. Ill. New ed. Lond. 1865. D.   **731 : 1**

Ruskin, J: Aratra Pentelici ; six lectures on the elements of sculpture given before the university of Oxford in michaelmas term. 1870. N. Y. 1878. D.   **730 : 4**

Lübke, W: History of sculpture from the earliest ages to the present time. Tr. by F. E. Bunnett. Ill. Lond. 1872. 2 v. Q.   **730 : R1**

Shedd, Julia A. Famous sculptors and sculpture ; ill., with heliotypes from many famous works of sculpture. Bost. 1881. D.   **730 : 3**

Viardot, L: Wonders of sculpture. 2d ed. [Ill. lib. of wonders.] N. Y. 1873. D. **730 : 2**

Mitchell, Lucy M. A history of ancient sculpture. Ill. N. Y. 1883. Q.   **733 : R5**

Redford, G: A manual of sculpture, egyptian-assyrian-greek-roman. Ill., with a map of ancient Greece and a chronological list of ancient sculptors and their works. Lond. 1882. D.   **732 : 1**

Overbeck, Johannes. Geschichte der griechischen plastik für künstler und kunstfreunde. 2te verb. aufl. Ill. Leipz. 1869-70. 2 v. in 1. O.   **733+1**

— Griechische kunstmythologie ; v. 2, 3. Ill. Leipz. 1871-78. 2 v. O.   **733+2**

Contents. V. **1.** *Not pub.* **2.** Besonderer theil. v. **1**: Zeus. **3.** Besonderer theil, v. **2**: Hera.—Poseidon.—Demeter und Kora.

— Atlas der griechischen kunstmythologie ; lief. 1-4. Leipz. 1872-78. 4 pts. Portf.   **733 : R2**

Contents. Pt. **1.** Zeus. **2.** Zeus, *continued.*—Hera. **3.** Hera, *continued.* — Poseidon. **4.** Demeter und Kora.

Murray, Alexander S. A history of greek sculpture from the earliest times down to the age of Pheidias. Ill. Lond. 1880. O.   **733+P3**

Perry, Walter Copland. Greek and roman sculpture ; a popular introd. to the study of greek and roman sculpture. Ill. Lond. 1882. O.   **733 : P4**

Perkins, C: C. Historical hand-book of italian sculpture. N. Y. 1883. O.   **735 : 2**

Clark, W: J. Great american sculptures. 12 steel engr., india proofs. Phila. 1878. F.   **735 : R1**

Contents. Introd., ancient and modern sculpture.—American sculptors.—Powers and Greenough.—Crawford and Randolph Rogers.—W: Wetmore Story.—Roberts, Bailly. Harnisch and Rush.—Brown, Ward, Palmer, Connelly and Mozier. —Gould, Simmons, Bartholomew and Akers.—Harriet Hosmer and other female sculptors.

2. Carving and Numismatics.

Maskell, W: Ivories, ancient and mediæval. Ill. [South Kensington art museum handbooks.] Lond. *n. d.* D.   **736 : 1**

King, C: W: The handbook of engraved gems. Ill. Lond. 1866. D.   **736 : 2**

Prime, W: Cowper, *ed.* Coins, medals and seals, ancient and modern, ill. and described with a sketch of the history of coins and coinage, instructions for young collectors, tables of comparative rarity, price lists of english and american coins, medals, tokens, etc. N. Y. 1861. O.   **737 : 2**

Humphreys, H: Noel. Ancient coins and medals ; an historical sketch of the origin and progress of coining money in Greece and her colonies, its progress with the extension of the roman empire and its decline with the fall of that power. Ill. by facsimile examples in actual relief and in the metals of the respective coins. Lond. 1850. O.   **737 : R3**

Thorburn, W. Stewart. A guide to the coins of Great Britain and Ireland, in gold, silver, and copper, from the earliest period to the present time, with their value. Ill. Lond. 1884. O.   **737 : 4**

Remedi, Angelo. Catalogo delle monete romane consolari ed imperiali, delle zecche italiane medicevali e moderne e delle medaglie, componenti la collezione del Angelo Remedi di Sarzana, di cui la vendita al pubblico incanto avrà luogo in Milano nelle salle dell' impresa, corso Vittorio Emanule, 37,

per cura Giulio Sambon, mercoledi 7 gennajo, 1885. Milano. 1885. O.   **737 : 5**

Ancona, Amilcare. Catalogo delle monete romane consolari ed imperiali, monete bizantine, e delle zecche italiane mediœvali e moderne, componenti la collezione del Amilcare Ancona, di cui la vendita al pubblico incanto avrà luogo in Milano nelle salle dell' impresa, corso Vittorio Emanuele, n. 37, per cura Giulio Sambon, giovedi 8 gennajo 1885. Milano. 1884. O.   *With*

Remedi, A. Catalogo.   **737 : 5**

3 Pottery and bronzes.

Hancock, E. Campbell. The amateur pottery and glass painter ; with directions for gilding, chasing, burnishing, bronzing and groundlaying. Ill. With an app. repr. by the special permission of the dept. of science and art, South Kensington. Lond. *n. d.* D.   **738 : 5**

McLaughlin, M. Louise. Pottery decoration under the glaze. Cinc. 1880. D.   **738 : 14**

— China painting ; a practical manual for the use of amateurs in the decoration of hard porcelain. Cinc. 1882. D.   **738 : 13**

— Suggestions to china-painters. Cinc. 1884. D.   **738 : 19**

Lockwood, M. Smith. Hand-book of ceramic art. N. Y. 1878. S.   **738 : 7**

Janvier, C. A. Practical keramics for students. N. Y. 1880. O.   **738 : 6**

Bohn, H: G: A guide to the knowledge of pottery, porcelain and other objects of vertu ; comprising an ill. catalogue of the Bernal collection of works of art, with the prices at which they were sold by auction and the names of the present possessors. Added, an introductory essay on pottery and porcelain, and an engraved list of marks and monograms. Ill. Lond. 1857. D.   **738 : 2**

Jacquemart, Albert. History of the ceramic art ; a descriptive and philosophical study of the pottery of all ages and all nations. Tr. by mrs. Bury Palliser. 2d ed. Ill., marks and monograms. Lond. 1877. Q.   **738 : R23**

Prime, W: Cowper. Pottery and porcelain of all times and nations, with tables of factory and artists' marks for the use of collectors. Ill. N. Y. 1878. O.   **738+8**

Westropp, Hodder M. Handbook of pottery and porcelain, or History of those arts from the earliest period. Ill. Lond. 1880. D.   **738 : 9**

Birch, S: History of ancient pottery, egyptian, assyrian, greek, etruscan and roman. New and rev. ed. Ill. Lond. 1873. O.   **738+P11**

Beckwith, Arthur. Majolica and fayence ; italian, sicilian, majorcan, hispano-moresque and persian. Ill. N. Y. 1877. D.   **738 : 1**

Fortnum, C. Drury E. Majolica. [South Kensington art museum handbooks.] Lond. [187-.] D.   **738 : 4**

Jewitt, Llewellynn. The ceramic art of Great Britain. New ed., rev. Ill. Lond. *n. d.* Q.   **738 : R20**

Gasnault, Paul, *and* E: Garnier. French pottery. Ill. and marks. [South Kensington museum art handbooks.] Lond. 1884. D. 738 : 22

Audsley, G: Ashdown, *and* James L. Bowes. Keramic art of Japan. Ill. Lond. 1881. Q. 738 : R12

Slosson, Annie T. The china hunters club, by the youngest member. [*Anon.*] N. Y. 1878. D. 738 : 3

Wheatley, H: B., *and* Philip H: Delamotte. Art work in earthenware. (Handbooks of practical art.) Lond. 1882. O. 738+15

— Art work in porcelain. (Handbooks of practical art.) N. Y. 1883. O. 738+16

— Art work in gold and silver : mediæval.

Wheatley, H: B., *and* P. H: Delamotte.—*Continued.*
(Handbooks of practical art.) Lond. 1882. O. 738+17

— Art work in gold and silver : modern. (Handbooks of practical art.) N. Y. 1882. O. 738+18

Maskell, Alfred. Russian art and art objects in Russia ; a handbook to the reproductions of goldsmiths' work and art treasures from that country in the South Kensington museum. [South Kensington museum art handbooks.] Lond. 1884. D. 738 : 21

Fortnum, C. Drury E. Bronzes. Ill. [South Kensington museum art handbooks.] Lond. *n. d.* D. 738 : 10

4. Drawing and Design.

1. General and freehand drawing.

Hamerton, Philip Gilbert. The graphic arts ; treatise on the varieties of drawing, painting and engraving, in comparison with each other and with nature. Bost. 1882. D. 700 : 2

Walker, W: Handbook of drawing. Ill. 1st amer. ed. N. Y. 1880. D. 740 : 3

Carter, Susan N. Drawing in black and white ; charcoal, pencil, crayon and pen-and-ink. (Putnam's art handbooks, no. 8.) Ill. N. Y. 1882. S. 740 : 4

Moore, C: H. Examples for elementary practice in delineation, designed for the use of schools and isolated beginners. Bost. 1884 [1883]. Q. 741 : R4

Ruskin, J: The elements of drawing ; in three letters to beginners. Ill. N. Y. 1876. D. 740 : 1

— The laws of Fésole ; a familiar treatise on the elementary principles and practice of drawing and painting as determined by the tuscan masters, arr. for the use of schools. V. 1. N. Y. 1879. D. 740 : 5

Viollet-le-Duc, Eugène Emmanuel. Learning to draw, or The story of a young designer. Tr. from the french by Virginia Champlin. Ill. N. Y. 1881. D. x 740 : 2

Howells, W: Dean, *ed.* A little girl among the old masters ; with introd. and comment. Bost. 1884 [1883]. T. 741 : 3

Goethe gallery, The ; from the original drawings of W: v. Kaulbach, with explanatory text. Bost. 1881. Q. 749 : R1

Caricature.

Parton, James. Caricature and other comic art in all times and many lands. Ill. N. Y. 1877. O. 741+1

Dagley, R: Miscellaneous observations on the ludicrous in art. *With his* Takings. *in* 821.2 : 82

Worth, T: Plutarch restored ; an anachronatic metempsychosis, illustrating the illustrations of Greece and Rome. N. Y. 1862. O. 741 : R2

———
x denotes books specially adapted for children.

Leech, J: Pictures of life and character from the collection of mr. Punch. Ill. N. Y. 1884. T. 741 : 5

Half a century of english history, pictorially presented in a series of cartoons from the collection of mr. Punch. N. Y. 1884. D. 741 : 6

2. Perspective and figure drawing.

Davies, C: A treatise on shades and shadows, and linear perspective. 2d ed. Phila. 1840. O. 742+1

Pozzo, *Fra* Andrea. Rules and examples of perspective, proper for painters and architeets, etc., in english and latin ; containing a most easy and expeditious method to delineate in perspective all designs relating to architecture, after a new manner, wholly free from the confusion of occult lines, by that great master thereof, Andrea Pozzo, soc. Js. Engraved in 105 ample folio plates and adorned with 200 initial letters to the explanatory discourses ; printed from copper-plates on ye best paper by John Sturt. Done into english from the original printed at Rome in 1693 in latin and italian, by mr. John James of Greenwich. Lond. 1707. F. 23 : R

Pyne, G: Perspective for beginners ; adapted to young students and amateurs in architecture, painting, etc. 12th ed., ill. [Weale's ser.] Lond. 1879. D. 742 : 2

Ruskin, J: The elements of perspective, arr. for the use of schools and intended to be read in connection with the first three books of Euclid. N. Y. 1873. D. 742 : 3

Weigall, C: H. The art of figure drawing ; containing practical instructions for a course of study in this branch of art ; ed. by Susan N. Carter. (Putnam's art handbooks, no. 4). N. Y. 1879. S. 743 : 1

Rimmer, W: Art anatomy. 81 plates. Bost. 1884. Portf. 743 : R3

Fletcher, Robert. Human proportion in art and anthropometry ; lecture delivered at the National museum, Washington. Ill. Cambridge. 1883. O. 743+2

Metz, Conrad Martin. Studies for drawing the human figure; groups of figures and historical compositions. Phila. *n. d.* obl. F.   **743 : R4**

3. Mathematical drawing.

Appleton's cyclopædia of drawing; designed as a text-book for the mechanic, architect, engineer and surveyor, comprising geometrical projection, mechanical, architectural and topographical drawing, perspective and isometry; ed. by W. E. Worthen. N. Y. 1870. O.   **744 : R4**

Minifie, W: A text-book of geometrical drawing ; abridged from the octavo ed. for the use of schools, in which the definitions and rules of geometry are familiarly explained, the practical problems are arr. from the most simple to the more complex, and in their description technicalities are avoided as much as possible, with an introd. to isometrical drawing and an essay on linear perspective and shadows. Ill. 6th ed., rev. and enl. N. Y. 1875. D.   **744 : 3**

Rose, Joshua. Mechanical drawing self-taught; comprising instructions in the selection and preparation of drawing instruments, elementary instr. in practical mechanical drawing, together with examples in simple geometry and elementary mechanism, incl. screw threads, gear wheels, mechanical motions, engines and boilers. Ill. Phila. 1883. O.   **744+5**

Johnson, W: The practical draughtsman's book of industrial design ; forming a complete course of mechanical, engineering and architectural drawing, founded upon the "Nouveau cours raisonné de dessin industriel," of Mm. Armengaud ainé, Armengaud jeune, and Amouroux, civil engineers, Paris ; containing add. plates as examples of the most useful and generally employed mechanism of the day. 3d ed. rev. with the french measures converted into english. Lond. 1869. O.   **744 : R1**

Maxton, J: The workman's manual of engineering drawing. 4th ed. rev. [Weale's ser.] Lond. 1880. D.   **744 : 2**

Tuthill, W: B. Practical lessons in architectural drawing, or How to make the working drawings and write the specifications for buildings. N. Y. 1881. O.   **744+6**

4. Ornamental design.

Audsley, W: James *and* G: Ashdown. Outlines of ornament in the leading styles, selected from executed ancient and modern works ; book of reference for the architect, sculptor, decorative artist and practical painter. N. Y. 1882. F.   **745 : R3**

Jones, Owen. The grammar of ornament; ill. by examples from various styles of ornament. 112 plates. Lond. 1868. F. **745 : R2**

Loftie, W. J. A plea for art in the house, with special reference to the economy of collecting works of art and the importance of taste in education and morals. [Art at home ser.] Phila. *n. d.* D.   **748 : 3**

Falke, Jacob v. Art in the house ; historical, critical and æsthetical studies on the decoration and furnishing of the dwelling. Authorized am. ed., tr. from the 3d german ed., ed. with notes by C: C. Perkins. Bost. 1879. Q.   **745 : R1**

Church, Ella Rodman. How to furnish a home. (Appletons' home books.) N. Y. 1881. D.   **748 : 7**

Dewing, M. R., *mrs.* T. W., *born* Oakey. Beauty in the household. N. Y. 1882. S.   **748 : 5**

Facey, James W: Elementary decoration ; a guide to the simpler forms of every day art, as applied to the interior and exterior decoration of dwelling houses, etc. Ill. [Weale's ser.]   **745 : 5**

Edis, Robert W. Decoration and furniture of town houses; a series of Cantor lectures del. before the Society of arts, 1880. amplified and enl. Ill. Lond. 1881. O. **748 : 10**

Cooper, H. J. The art of furnishing on rational and æsthetic principles. N. Y. 1881. S.   **748 : 9**

Cook, Clarence. The house beautiful ; essays on beds and tables, stools and candlesticks. Ill. [N. Y.] 1881. O.   **748+8**

Garrett, Rhoda *and* Agnes. Suggestions for house decoration in painting, woodwork and furniture. [Art at home ser.] Phila. *n. d.* D.   **748 : 2**

Eastlake, *Sir* C: Lock. Hints on household taste in furniture, upholstery and other details ; ed., with notes, by C: C. Perkins. 1st amer. ed. Bost. 1872. O.   **748 : 1**

Spofford, Harriet Elizabeth, *born* Prescott. Art decoration applied to furniture. Ill. N. Y. [1877]. O.   **745+4**

Jacquemart, Albert. A history of furniture. Tr. from the french, ed. by mrs. Bury Palliser. Ill. Lond. 1878. Q.   **748 : R17**

Pollen, J: Hungerford. Ancient and modern furniture and woodwork. (South Kensington museum art handbooks). Lond. *n. d.* D.   **745 : 6**

Orrinsmith, Lucy. The drawing-room ; its decorations and furniture. [Art at home ser.] Lond. 1878. D.   **748 : 15**

Loftie, *Mrs.* M. J. The dining-room. [Art at home ser.] Lond. 1878. D.   **748 : 14**

Barker, Mary Anne *lady, now mrs.* F: Napier Broome. The bedroom and the boudoir. [Art at home ser.] Lond. 1878. D. **748 : 13**

Rees, Janet E. Ruutz-. Home decoration ; art needlework and embroidery, painting on silk, satin and velvet, panel painting and wood carving, with numerous designs, mainly by G: Gibson. (Appletons' home books.) N. Y. 1881. D.   **748 : 4**

Harrison, Constance Cary, *mrs.* Burton H. Woman's handiwork in modern homes. Ill. [N. Y.] 1881. O.   **748 : 11**
Contents. Embroidery. — Brush and pigment.— Modern homes.

Higgin, L. Handbook of embroidery; ed. by lady Marian Alford. (Royal school of art needlework). Lond. 1880. D.   **748 : 12**

Champeaux, Alfred de. Tapestry. Ill. [South Kensington museum art handbooks]. Lond. *n. d.* D.   **747 : 1**

Smith, J. Moyr. Album of decorative figures. Lond. 1882. F.   **748 : R6**

Dresser, Christopher. Japan, its architecture, art and art manufactures. Lond. 1882. O.
    748+16

Prang's standard alphabets; a collection of alphabets in the best ancient and modern styles, designs for titles, colored initials, borders, compass topographical signs, the state arms of the union, etc., especially adapted for the use of sign painters, engravers, illuminàtors, architects and civil engineers. Bost. 1878. obl. D. **745 : R7**

5. Painting.

1. Materials and methods.

Blanc, A: Alexandre Philippe C: The grammar of painting and engraving. Tr. from the french, of Blanc's Grammaire des arts du dessin, by Kate Newell Doggett. Ill. N. Y. 1874. O. **750+2**

Field, G: A grammar of colouring, applied to decorative painting and the arts. New ed., enl. and adapted to the use of the ornamental painter and designer, with additional sections on painting in sepia, water-colours and oils, and with the history and characteristics of the various styles of ornament, by Ellis A. Davidson. [Weale's ser.] Lond. 1877. D. **752 : 1**

Couture, T: Conversations on art methods; methode et entrétiens d'atélier. Tr. from the french by S. E. Stewart, with an introd. by Robert Swain Gifford. N. Y. 1879. O.
    751 : 1

Howard, H: A course of lectures on painting delivered at the Royal academy of fine arts ; ed., with a memoir of the author, by Frank Howard. Lond. 1848. D. **750 : 5**

Armitage, E: Lectures on painting; delivered to the students of the Royal academy. N. Y. 1883. O. **751 : 12**

 Contents. Ancient costumes.—Byzantine and romanesque art.—On the painters of the 18th century.—David and his school.—On the modern schools of Europe.—On drawing.—Color.—On decorative painting.—On finish.—On the choice of a subject.—On the composition of decorative and historical pictures.—Composition of incident pictures.

Ellis, Tristram J. Sketching from nature; handbook for students and amateurs. [Art at home ser.] Ill. N. Y. 1883. D.
    751 : 11

Rowbotham, T: The art of sketching from nature ; rev. by Susan N. Carter. Ill. (Putnam's art hand-books, no. 1.) N. Y. [1878]. S. **751 : 5**

Williams, W. The art of landscape painting in oil colors ; ed. by Susan N. Carter. (Putnam's art hand-books, no. 2.) N. Y. 1881. S. **751 : 6**

Duffield, *Mrs.* W: The art of flower painting. Ill. From the 12th Lond. ed.; ed. by Susan N. Carter. (Putnam's art hand-books, no. 3.) N. Y. 1882. S. **751 : 7**

Hatton, T: Hints for sketching in water-color from nature. (Putnam's art hand-books, no. 7.) N. Y. 1882. S. **751 : 10**

Penley, Aaron. A system of water-color painting ; complete exposition of the present advanced state of the art, as exhibited in the works of the modern water-color school. (Putnam's art hand-books, no. 5.) N. Y. 1879. S. **751 : 8**

Warren, H: Artistic treatise on the human figure ; containing hints on proportion, color and composition. 4th ed. (Putnam's art hand-books, no. 6.) N. Y. 1881. S.
    751 : 9

Merrifield, Mary Philadelphia. The art of fresco painting, as practised by the old italian and spanish masters ; with a prelim. inquiry into the nature of the colours used in fresco painting, with observations and notes. Lond. 1846. O. **751 : 3**

Gessert, M. A. Rudimentary treatise on the art of painting on glass or glass staining, comprising directions for preparing the pigments and fluxes, for laying them upon the glass, and for firing or burning in the colours. From the german. Added, an app. on the art of enamelling, etc. 4th ed. [Weale's ser.] Lond. 1878. D. **751 : 2**

Fromberg, Emanuel Otto. Rudimentary essay on the art of painting on glass. From the german. 4th ed. [Weale's ser.] Lond. 1878. D. *in* **751 : 2**

Winston, C: An inquiry into the difference of style, observable in ancient glass paintings, especially in England ; also Hints on glass painting. 2d ed. Oxford. 1867. 2 v. O.
    751+P4

2. History of painting.

General.

Dodge, Pickering. Painting ; its rise and progress from the earliest times to [1846] ; with sketches of the lives and works of many of the eminent artists of ancient and modern times and a brief notice of the principal public galleries of art in Europe. [*Anon.*] Bost. 1846. D. **750 : 6**

Heaton, Mary Margaret, *born* Keymer, *mrs.* C: A concise history of painting. Ill. Lond. 1873. D. **750 : 4**

Radcliffe, Anna G. Schools and masters of painting ; with an app. on the principal galleries of Europe. Ill. N. Y. 1879. O.
    750 : 7

Waters, Clara Erskine, *formerly mrs.* Clement. An outline history of painting for young people and students ; with complete indexes. Ill. N. Y. 1883. O. **750 : 8**

Woltmann, Alfred, *and* K: Wörmann. History of ancient, early christian, and mediæval painting. From the german, tr. and ed. by Sidney Colvin. Ill. N. Y. 1880. O.
    750 : R1

Viardot, L: Wonders of european art. [Ill. lib. of wonders.] N. Y. 1874. D. **750 : 3**

Flemish and dutch schools.

Kugler, Franz Theodor. Handbook of painting: The german, flemish and dutch schools, based on the handbook of Kugler, remodelled by prof. Waagen. New ed., revised and in part re-written by J. A. Crowe. Ill. Lond. 1874. 2 v. O.   **753 : P2**

Buxton, Harry J. Wilmot, *and* E: J. **Poynter.** German, flemish and dutch painting. (Ill. text-books of art.) Lond. 1881. D.   **753 : 1**

Förster, Ernst. Mittelalter oder renaissance? [C:] G[ottfried] Pfannschmidt und Anselm Feuerbach. *In* Deutsche zeit- und streitfragen.   **304 : 15 v11**

French and spanish.

Smith, Gerard W. Painting, spanish and french. (Ill. handbooks of art history). Lond. 1884. D.   **754 : 2**

Bacon, H: Parisian art and artists. Bost. 1883 [1882]. D.   **754 : 1**

Washburn, Emelyn W. The spanish masters ; an outline of the history of painting in Spain. Ill. N. Y. 1884. O.   **756 : 4**

Italian.

Kugler, Franz Theodor. Handbook of painting: The italian schools, based on the handbook of Kugler, originally edited by sir C: L. Eastlake. 4th edition rev. and re-modelled, from the latest researches, by lady Eastlake. Ill. Lond. 1874. 2 v. O.   **755 : P6**

Viardot, L: Wonders of italian art. [Ill. lib. of wonders.] N. Y. 1875. D.   **755 : 12**

Jarves, James Jackson. Art studies : The old masters of Italy ; painting. N. Y. 1861. O.   **755 : 5**

Poynter, E: J., *and* Percy R. **Head.** Classic and italian painting. (Text-boks of art education). Lond. 1880. D.   **755 : 7**

Crowe, Joseph Archer, *and* Giovanni Battista **Cavalcaselle.** A history of painting in north Italy, Venice, Padua, Verona, Ferrara, Milan, Friuli, Brescia, from the 14th to the 16th century ; drawn up from fresh materials after recent researches in the archives of Italy, and from personal inspection of the works of art scattered throughout Europe. Ill. Lond. 1871. 2 v. O.   **755 : 8**

Jameson, Anna, *born* Murphy, *and Lady* Elizabeth **Eastlake,** *born* Rigby. The history of our Lord, as exemplified in works of art, with that of his types, St. John the baptist and others, persons of the Old and New testament. 2d ed. Lond. 1865. 2 v. O.   **755 : 1**

— Legends of the madonna, as represented in the fine arts. Corr. and enl. ed. Bost. 1877. T.   **755 : 2**

— Sacred and legendary art, as represented in the fine arts. Bost. 1865. 2 v. T.   **755 : 4**

   Contents. v. **1.** Legends of the angels and archangels, the evangelists, the apostles, the doctors of the church and St. Mary Magdalene. **2.** The patron saints, the martyrs, the early bishops, the hermits, and the warrior saints of christendom.

— Legends of the monastic orders, as represented in the fine arts ; forming the second series of Sacred and legendary art. Corr. and enl. ed. Bost. 1865. T.   **755 : 3**

Emeric-David, Toussaint Bernard. A series of studies, designed and engraved after five paintings by Raphael, with historical and critical notes ; the work dedicated to Ferdinand VII, king of Spain, by the chevalier F. Bonnemaison. Amer. ed., reproduced by the heliotype process. Bost. 1881. Q.   **755 : R11**

Titian gallery, The ; a series of 24 of the most renowned works of Titian, reproduced in heliotype, with a sketch of the life and works of the artist. Bost. 1883. Q.   **755 : R9**

Toschi's engravings from frescoes by Correggio and Parmegiano, reproduced by the heliotype process. Bost. 1883. Q.   **755 : R10**

English and american.

Buxton, Harry J. Wilmot-. English painters ; with a chapter on american painters by S. R. Koehler. Lond. 1883. D.   **756 : 2**

Ruskin, J: The art of England ; lectures given in Oxford. N. Y. 1883. D.   **756 : 3**

Ireland, J: Hogarth illustrated. Ill. Lond. 1884. Q.   **756 : P6**

Engravings from Landseer, reproduced in heliotype, with a sketch of the life and works of the artist. Bost. 1882. Q.   **756 : R5**

Ware, W: Lectures on the works and genius of Washington Allston. Bost. 1852. D.   **756 : 1**

Champney, Lizzie, *born* Williams. John Angelo at the water-color exhibition. Ill. Bost. [1883]. O.   **x 759+1**

   x denotes books specially adapted for children.

6. Engraving and Photography.

1. Engraving.

Maberly, J. The print collector ; an introd. to the knowledge necessary for forming a collection of ancient prints, with an app. containing Fielding's treatise on the practice of engraving. Ed. with notes, an account of contemporary etching and etchers, and a bibliography of engraving, by Robert Hoe, *jr.* N. Y. 1880. O.   **760+P3**

Baker, W: S. The origin and antiquity of engraving ; with some remarks on the utility and pleasures of prints. Heliotype ill. Bost. 1875. Q.   **760 : R1**

Duplessis *or* **Gratet-Duplessis,** G: The wonders of engraving. [Ill. lib. of wonders.] N. Y. 1876. D.   **760 : 2**

Pettit, James S. Modern reproductive graphic processes. [Van Nostrand's science ser.] N. Y. 1884. T.   **760 : 4**

Ruskin, J: Ariadne florentina ; six lectures on wood and metal engraving, with app., given before the university of Oxford, in michaelmas term 1872. Plates. N. Y. 1880. D.   **760 : 5**

Chatto, W: Andrew. A treatise on wood engraving, historical and practical. Ill. New ed. with an add. chapter by H: G. Bohn. Lond. [1861]. Q.   **761 : R1**

Woodberry, G: E. A history of wood-engraving. N. Y. 1883 [1882]. O.   **761 : P2**

Linton, W. James. The history of wood-engraving in America. Ill· Bost. 1883. Q.   **761 : R3**

Hergesheimer, E. The pantograph ; its use in engraving. *In* U. S. coast survey rep. 1867.   *in* **622 : D**

Hamerton, Philip Gilbert. Etching and etchers. Ill. Bost. 1878. O.   **767+1**

Lalanne, François Antoine Maxime. Treatise on etching. Authorized amer. ed., from 2d french ed. by S. R. Koehler ; with introd. and notes by the tr. Bost. 1880. O.   **767 : R2**

Jackson, Mason. The pictorial press ; its origin and progress. Ill. Lond. 1885. O. **761 : 4**

2. Photography.

Abney, W: de Wiveleslie. A treatise on photography. 2d ed. [Text-books of science.] Lond. 1883. S.   **770 : 2**

Bigelow, L. G. Artistic photography, and how to attain it. Phila. 1876. O.   **770 : R4**

Lea, Mathew Carey. A manual of photography; intended as a text-book for beginners and a book of reference for advanced photographers. 2d ed., rev. and enl. Phila. 1871. O.   **770+5**

Price, Lake. A manual of photographic manipulation, treating of the practice of the art and its various applications to nature. 2d ed. Lond. 1868. D.   **770 : 10**

Thomas, R: Wheeler. The modern practice of photography. Phila. 1868. O.   **770 : 6**

Tissandier, Gaston. A history and handbook of photography. Tr. from the french, ed. by J. Thomson. 2d and rev. ed., with an app. by H: Fox Talbot. Ill. Lond. 1878. D.   **770 : 9**

Towler, J: The silver sunbeam ; a practical and theoretical text-book on sun drawing and photographic printing, comprehending all the wet and dry processes at present known with collodion, albumen, gelatine, wax, resin and silver, as also heliographic engraving, photolithography, photozincography, microphotography, celestial photography, photography in natural colors, solar camera work, tinting and coloring of photographs, printing in various colors, the carbon process, the card picture, the cabinet picture, the vignette and stereography. 9th ed., enl., imp. and ill., and containing matter written by Blanquart Everard, *and others.* N. Y. 1879. D.   **770 : 7**

Vogel, Hermann. The chemistry of light and photography. Ill. (Intern. scientific ser.) N. Y. 1875. D.   **770 : 1**

— Photographers' pocket reference - book and dictionary ; an alphabetically arranged collection of practically important hints on the construction of the gallery, selection and trial of lenses and chemicals, approved formulæ for the different photographic processes, tables of weights and measures, rules for avoiding failure, etc., for photographers and amateurs. Tr. from the german, by E: F. Moelling. Phila. 1873. D.   **770 : 8**

Tapley, D. J. Amateur photography ; a practical instructor. Ill. N. Y. 1884. D.   **770 : 12**

Wallace, Ellerslie, *jr.* The amateur photographer ; a manual of photographic manipulation, intended especially for beginners and amateurs, with suggestions as to the choice of apparatus and of processes. Phila. [1884]. D.   **770 : 11**

Ayres, G: B. How to paint photographs in water colors and in oil, how to work in crayon, make the chromo-photograph, retouch negatives, and instructions in ceramic painting ; a practical hand-book designed for the use of students and photographers, containing directions for brush work in all kinds of photo - portraiture. N. Y. 1883. D.   **770 : 3**

7. Music.

1. General and collected works,

including criticism.

Grove, Sir G:, ed. A dictionary of music and musicians, 1450–1880, by eminent writers, english and foreign ; in 4 v. Lond. 1879– 1883. V. 1–3. O.   **780 : R1**
Contents. V. 1. A—Impromptu. 2. Improperia— Plain song. 3. Planché—Sumer is icumen in.

Riemann, Hugo. Musik-lexikon ; theorie und geschichte der musik, die tonkünstler alter und neuer zeit mit angabe ihrer werke, nebst einer vollständigen instrumentenkunde. Leipz. 1882. D.   **780 : R14**

Spencer, C: Child. A rudimentary and practical treatise on music. 2 v. in 1. 8th ed. [Weale's ser.] Lond. 1875. D.   **780 : 7**

Hullah, J: Pyke. Music in the house. (Art at home ser.) Lond. 1878. D.   **780 : 5**

Upton, G: P. Woman in music ; an essay. Ill. Bost. 1880. D.   **780 : 9**

Engel, C: An introduction to the study of national music ; comprising researches into popular songs, traditions and customs. Lond. 1866. O.   **780 : 26**

Chorley, H: Fothergill. The national music of the world ; ed. by H: G. Hewlett. Lond. 1880. D.   **780 : 8**

Brown, J: A dissertation on the rise, union and

power, the progressions, separations and corruptions of poetry and music. Prefixed, The cure of Saul, a sacred ode. Lond. 1763. Q.   23 : R

Berlioz, L: Hector. Gesammelte schriften; übers. und herausg. von R: Pohl. Leipz. 1877. 4 v. in 3. D.   780 : 24
Contents. V. 1. À travers chants: musikalische studien, huldigungen, einfälle und kritiken. 2, 3. Orchester-abende; musikalische novellen und genrebilder. 4. Musikalische grotesken; humoristische feuilletons.

Hauptmann, Moritz. Opuscula ; vermischte aufsätze. Leipz. 1874. D.   780 : 22
Contents. Klang. — Temperatur. — Der dreiklang und seine intervalle.—Dreiklang mit der pythagoraischen terz.—Zum quintenverbot.—Zur auflösung des dominantseptimenaccordes durch erweiterung der septime zur octav. — Einige regeln zur richtigen beantwortung des fugenthemas.—Das hexachord.— Authentisch und plagaisch. — Contrapunct. — Metrum. — Zur metrik. — Ueber die recitative in J. S. Bach's Matthäus-pass'on.—Kunstvollendung.—Form in der kunst.—Ironie der kunst.—Männlich und weiblich.—Egoismus.—Mechanik.—Die sinne.

Haweis, Hugh Reginald. My musical memories. N. Y. 1884. D.   780 : 16

Schumann, Robert. Music and musicians ; essays on criticisms. Tr., ed. and annotated by Fanny Raymond Ritter. Portr. N. Y. 1880. D.   781 : 5

Wagner, W: R: Gesammelte schriften und dichtungen. Leipz. 1871–73. 8 v. O.
    780 : 20
Contents. V. 1. Einleitung.— Autobiographische skizze bis 1842.—Das liebesverbot.—Rienzi, der letzte der tribunen.—Ein deutscher musiker in Paris: Ein pilgerfahrt zu Beethoven; Ein ende in Paris; Ein glücklicher abend; Ueber deutsches musikwesen; Der virtuos und der künstler; Der künstler uud die öffentlichkeit; Rossini's Stabat mater. — Ueber die ouvertüre.—Der freischütz in Paris. — Bericht über eine neue Pariser oper.—Der fliegende holländer. 2. Tannhäuser. — Bericht über die heimbringung der sterblichen überreste Karl Maria v. Weber's aus London nach Dresden.—Bericht über die aufführung der neunten symphonie von Beethoven im jahre 1846.— Lohengrin.—Die Nibelungen; weltgeschichte aus der sage. — Der Nibelungen-mythus als entwurf zu einem drama. — Siegfried's tod. — Trinkspruch im gedenktage des 300-jährigen bestehens der Königlichen musikalischen kapelle in Dresden. — Entwurf zur organisation eines deutschen nationaltheaters für das königreich Sachsen. 3. Die kunst und die revolution.—Das kunstwerk der zukunft.—Wieland der schmiedt, als drama entworfen. — Kunst und klima.—Oper und drama: 1er t., Die oper und das wesen der musik. 4. Oper und drama: 2ter t., Das schauspiel und das wesen der dramatischen dichtkunst; 3ter t., Dichtkunst und tonkunst im drama der zukunft.—Ueber mittheilung an meine freunde. 5. Ueber die Goethestiftung.—Ein theater in Zürich. —Ueber musikalische kritik.—Das judenthum in der musik.—Erinnerungen an Spontini. — Nachruf an L. Spohr und chordirektor W. Fischer.—Glück's ouverture zu Iphigenia in Aulis. — Ueber die aufführung des Tannhäuser.—Bemerkungen zur aufführung der oper Der fliegende holländer. — Programmatische erläuterungen.—Ueber Franz Liszt's symphonische dichtungen.—Das Rheingold. 6. Der Ring des Nibelungen; bühnenfestspiel.—Epilogischer bericht über die umstände und schicksale, welche die ausführung des bühnenfestspieles Der ring des Nibelungen, bis zur veröffentlichung der dichtung desselben, begleiteten. 7. Tristan und Isolde. — Ein brief Hector Berlioz.—Zukunftsmusik.—Bericht über die aufführung des Tannhäuser in Paris.—Die meistersinger von Nürnberg.—Das Wiener Hof-operntheater. 8. Dem königlichen freunde.—Ueber staat und religion. —Deutsche kunst und deutsche politik.—Bericht an seine majestät den könig Ludwig II von Bayern über eine in München zu errichtende deutsche musikschule. —Meine erinnerungen an Ludwig Schnorr von Carolsfeld.—Zur widmung der zweiten auflage von Oper und drama.—Censuren.—Ueber das dirigiren.—Drei gedichte. 9. An das deutsche heer von Paris, jan. 1871.—Eine kapitulation.—Erinnerung

Wagner, W: R:—*Continued.*
an Auber.—Beethoven.—Ueber die bestimmung der oper.—Ueber schauspieler und sänger.—Zum vortrag der neunten symphonie Beethoven's.—Sendschreiben und kleinere aufsätze.—Bayreuth.—Inhaltsübersicht der Gesammelten schriften und dichtungen.—Sechs architektonische pläne zu dem bühnenfestspielhause.

— Art life and theories ; selected from his writings and tr. by E: L. Burlingame, with a catalogue of Wagner's published works ; and drawings of the Bayreuth opera house. (Amateur ser.) N. Y. 1875. D.   781 : 8
Contents. Introd.—Autobiography.—The love-veto; the story of the first performance of an opera.—A pilgrimage to Beethoven.—An end in Paris.—Der freischütz in Paris.—The music of the future.—An account of the production of Tannhäuser in Paris.— The purpose of the opera.—Musical criticism.—The legend of the Nibelungen.—The opera-house at Bayreuth.—Catalogue of Wagner's published works.— Index.

— Beethoven ; with a supp. from the philosophical works of Arthur Schopenhauer. Tr. by E: Dannreuther. Lond. 1880. D.
    781 : 6

Grove, *Sir* G: Beethoven's nine symphonies ; analytical essays, with an introd. by the author and a pref. by G: Henschel. Bost. 1884. S.   781 : 15

Keynote, The ; a weekly review devoted to music and the drama, ed. by F: Archer ; v. 1–4. N. Y. 1883. F.   705.8 : M

Milwaukee school of music, J: C. Fillmore, dir. Catalogue, 1884-5. Milw. [1885]. D.
    780 : Pam

2. History.

Ambros, A: W: Geschichte der musik ; mit zahlreichen notenbeispielen und musikbeilagen. 2te unveränderte aufl. Leipz. 1880 —1882. 5 v. O.   780 : 23
Contents. V. 1. Die ersten anfänge der tonkunst.— Die musik der antiken welt: Die völker der vorhellenischen cultur; Die völker der antik-klassischen cultur. 2. Die ersten zeiten der neuen christlichen welt und kunst.—Die entwickelung des mehrstimmigen gesanges. 3. Die zeit der niederländer.—Die musik in Deutschland und England.—Die italiänische musik des 15. jahrhunderts. 4. Palestrina.—Die zeit des Palestrinastyles.—Der monodische styl in Italien.— Die musikreform und der kampf gegen den contrapunkt.—Die zeit des überganges.—Die zeit der ersten dramatischen musikwerke.—Claudio di Montiverde. —Theoretiker und lehrer.—Die italienischen organisten. 5. Kade, O; ed. Auserwählte tonwerke der berühmten meister des 15. und 16. jahrhunderts.

Bell, N. R. E., (*N. D'Anvers*). Elementary history of music by N. D'Anvers. New ed. by Owen J. Dullea. Lond. 1882. D.   780 : 25

Burney, C: A general history of music from the earliest ages to the present period. 2d ed. Lond. 1789. 4 v. Q.   780 : R13

— The present state of music in France and Italy, or The journal of a tour through those countries, undertaken to collect materials for a general history of music. 2d ed., corr. Lond. 1773. O.   780 : R2

— The present state of music in Germany, the Netherlands and United Provinces, or The journal of a tour through those countries, undertaken to collect materials for a general history of music. 2d ed., corr. Lond. 1775. 2 v. O.   780 : R3

Busby, T: A general history of music from the earliest times to the present ; comprising the lives of eminent composers and musical

writers, the whole accompanied with notes and observations, critical and illustrative. Lond. 1819. 2 v. O.   780 : 27
Chappell, W: The history of music ; art and science. V. 1 : From the earliest records to the fall of the roman empire, with explanations of ancient systems of music, musical instruments and of the true physiological basis for the science of music, whether ancient or modern. Lond. [1874]. O.   780 : 18
Dommer, Arrey v. Handbuch der musikgeschichte von den ersten anfängen bis zum tode Beethoven's, in gemeinfasslicher darstellung. 2te verb. aufl. Leipz. 1880. O.   780 : 17
Hawkins, Sir J: A general history of the science and practice of music. Lond. 1776. 5 v. Q.   780 : R28
— Same. Supplementary volume of portraits. Lond. 1883. Q.   780 : R28 v6
Hogarth, G: Musical history, biography and criticism. N. Y. 1848. O.   780 : 21
Hunt, H: G: Bonavia. A concise history of music from the commencement of the christian era to the present time, for the use of students. New ed., rev. N. Y. [1878]. D.   780 : 6
Langhans, W: Die musikgeschichte in zwölf vorträgen. 2te wesentlich verm. aufl. Leipz. 1879. O.   780 : 15
Ritter, F: L: History of music ; in the form of lectures. 1st and 2d series. Bost. 1876. 2 v. S.   780 : 10
— Music in England. N. Y. 1883. D.   780 : 11
— Music in America. N. Y. 1883. D.   780 : 12
Riemann, Hugo. Studien zur geschichte der notenschrift. Leipz. 1878. O.   780 : 19

3. Theory of music.

Gardiner, W: The music of nature, or An attempt to prove that what is passionate and pleasing in the art of singing, speaking and performing upon musical instruments, is derived from the sounds of the animated world. Ill. Bost. 1838. O.   781 : 7
Gurney, Edmund. The power of sound. Lond. 1880. Q.   781+2
Hand, Ferdinand Gotthelf. Aesthetics of musical art, or The beautiful in music. Tr. from the german by Walter E. Lawson. Book 1st. 2d ed. Lond. 1880. D.   781 : 21
Hanslick, E: Vom musikalisch schönen ; ein beitrag zur revision der ästhetik der tonkunst. 6te verm. und verb. aufl. Leipz. 1881. D.   781 : 14
Helmholtz, Hermann L: Ferdinand. On the physiological causes of harmony in music. Tr. by A. J. Ellis. In his Popular lectures. 780 : 6 v1
Mathews, W: Smith Babcock. How to understand music ; a concise course in musical intelligence and taste. Added, a pronouncing dictionary and condensed encyclopedia of musical terms and information. Chicago. 1880. O.   781+3
Naumann, Emil W: Robert. Zukunftsmusik und die musik der zukunft ; ein vortrag gehalten am 6 jan. 1877 im Wissenschaftlichen verein zu Berlin. In Deutsche zeit- und streit-fragen.   304 : 15 v6

Piutti, C: Regeln und erläuterungen zum studium der musik-theorie ; für seinen unterricht herausg. Leipz. 1883. O.   781 : 17
Pole, W: The philosophy of music ; the substance of a course of lectures delivered at the Royal institution of Great Britain, in feb. and march 1877. [Eng. and foreign phil. lib.] Bost. 1879. O.   781 : 4
Riemann, Hugo. Musikalische logik ; hauptzüge der physiologischen und psychologischen begründung unseres musik-systems. Als Dissertation unter dem titel "Ueber das musikalische hören." Leipz. [1874]. S.   781 : 11
— Musikalische syntaxis ; grundriss einer harmonischen satzbildungslehre. Leipz. 1877. O.   781 : 12
— Skizze einer neuen methode der harmonielehre. Leipz. 1880. O.   781 : 10
— Neue schule der melodik ; entwurf einer lehre des contrapunkts nach einer gänzlich neuen methode. Hamburg. 1883. O.   781 : 9
— Die hülfsmittel der modulation ; studie. Cassel. 1875. O.   781 : 13
— Der ausdruck in der musik. (Sammlung musikalischer vorträge, no. 50.) Leipz. 1883. O.   781+16
— Die natur der harmonik. (Sammlung musikalischer vorträge, no. 40.) Leipz. 1882. O.   781+16
Schubart, Christian F: Daniel. Ideen zu einer ästhetik der tonkunst. In his Gesammelte schriften.   830 : 146 v5
Taylor, Sedley. The science of music, or The physical basis of musical harmony. [Pop. science lib.] N. Y. 1873. D.   781 : 1
Westphal, Rudolf G: Hermann. Allgemeine theorie der musikalischen rythmik seit J. S. Bach, auf grundlage der antiken und unter bezugnahme auf ihren historischen anschluss an die mittelalterliche, mit besonderer berücksichtigung von Bach's Fugen und Beethoven's Sonaten. Leipz. 1880. O.   781 : 18
— Die musik des griechischen alterthumes ; nach den alten quellen neu bearb. Leipz. 1883. O.   781 : 19

4. Dramatic, church and vocal music.

Clément, Félix, and P: Larousse. Dictionnaire des opéras, dictionnaire lyrique ; contenant l'analyse et la nomenclature de tous les opéras et opéras-comiques représentés en France et à l'étranger depuis l'origine de ce genre d'ouvrages jusqu'à nos jours. complété par des supplements périodiques, maintenant à cet ouvrage un caractère d'actualité. Paris. [1869]. O.   782 : R5
    Includes [1er] Supplément, contenant les ouvrages représentés en France et à l'étranger pendant le cours de l'impression du Dictionnaire lyrique, and 2e-4e supplément, contenant les ouvrages représentés en France et à l'étranger pendant les années 1869-1880, ainsi que des notices complémentaires pour les années précédentes.
Carleton, Fanny E., (Notelrac). Operas ; their writers and their plots, by "Notelrac." Phila. 1882. S.   782 : 2
Hogarth, G: Memoirs of the musical drama. Lond. 1838. 2 v. O.   782 : 4

Wolzogen und Neuhaus, Hans Paul *freiherr* v. Thematischer leitfaden durch die musik zu R: Wagner's festspiel Der ring der Nibelungen. 4te verb. und verm. aufl. Leipz. 1878. D.   782 : 3

Lindau, H: Gustav Paul. Nüchterne briefe aus Bayreuth. 10te aufl. Breslau. [1881]. D.
782 : 1

Schasler, Max. Ueber dramatische musik und das kunst-werk der zukunft ; ein beitrag zur ästhetik der musik. *In* Deutsche zeit- und streit-fragen.   304 : 15 v12
Contents. 1ste abth. Ist die musik eines dramatischen ausdrucks fähig?—2te abth. Die moderne oper und R: Wagner's musik-drama.

Maretzek, Max. Crotchets and quavers, or Revelations of an opera manager in America. N. Y. 1855. D.   782 : 6

Mason, Lowell. Musical letters from abroad ; including detailed accounts of the Birmingham, Norwich and Düsseldorf musical festivals of 1852. N. Y. 1854. D.
783 : 1

Robinson, C: Seymour, *ed.* Laudes domini ; a selection of spiritual songs, ancient and modern. N. Y. [1884]. O.   783 : 2

Bliss, Philip P., *and* Ira D: Sankey. Gospel hymns and sacred songs, as used by them in gospel meetings. Cinc. *n. d.* O.
783 : 4

Liliencron, Rochus *freiherr* v. Ueber den chorgesang in der evangelischen kirche. *In* Deutsche zeit- und streit-fragen.
304 : 15 v9

Krehbiel, H. E. Notes on the cultivation of choral music and the Oratorio society of New York. N. Y. 1884. D.   784 : 5

Johnson, Helen Kendrick. Our familiar songs and those who made them ; more than 300 standard songs of the english speaking race, arr. with piano accompaniment and p c d d by sketches of the writers and histories of the songs. N. Y. 1881. Q.
784 : R1

McCaskey, J. P., *ed.* Franklin square song collection ; songs and hymns for schools and and homes, nursery and fireside ; [no. 1, 2]. N. Y. 1881, [1884]. 2 v. O.   784 : 2

Hills, W: H., *comp.* Students' songs ; comprising the newest and most popular college songs, as now sung at Harvard, Yale, Columbia, Cornell, Dartmouth, Amherst, Vassar [and other colleges]. Cambridge. [1883]. Q.   784+3

Alexander, Frances, *tr.* Roadside songs of Tuscany ; ed. by J: Ruskin. Ill. N. Y. 1884. 3 v. O.   784+4
Contents. Pt. 1. The story of Lucia, with author's and ed.'s preface. Pt. 2. The ballad of Santa Zita. 3. Ballad of the madonna and the rich man.—The story of Paolina.—Notes on the priest's office by the ed.

Pike, Gustavus D. The singing campaign for ten thousand pounds, or The jubilee singers

in Great Britain ; with an app. containing slave songs. Rev. ed. N. Y. 1875. D.
789 : 1

5. Instrumental music.

Engel, C: Musical instruments. Ill. [South Kensington museum art hand-books.] Lond. *n. d.* D.   785 : 2

Stainer, J: The music of the Bible, with account of the development of modern musical instruments from ancient types. Lond. *n. d.* D.   785 : 1

Viard-Louis, Jenny. Music and the piano. Tr. from the french by mrs. Warington Smyth. Lond. 1884. D.   786 : 7

Rimbault, E: Francis. The pianoforte, its origin, progress and construction ; with some account of instruments of the same class which preceded it, viz. the clavichord, the virginal, the spinet, the harpsichord, etc. Added, A selection of interesting specimens of music composed for keyed-stringed instruments by Blitheman, Byrd, Bull, Frescobaldi, Dumont, Chambonnières, Lully, Purcell, Muffat, Couperin, Kuhnau, Scarlatti, Seb. Bach, Mattheson, Handel, C. P. Emanuel Bach, etc. Lond. 1860. F.
786 : R8

Fillmore, J: Comfort. Pianoforte music ; its history, with biographical sketches and critical estimates of its greatest masters. Chicago. 1883. D.   786 : 5

Kullak, Adolph. Die ästhetik des klavierspiels. 2te umgearb. aufl., herausg. von Hans Bischoff. Berlin. 1876. D.   786 : 6

Schmitt, Hans. Das pedal des clavieres ; seine beziehung zum clavierspiel und unterricht, zur composition und akustik ; vier vorlesungen gehalten am Wiener Conservatorium der musik. Wien. 1880. O.   781 : 20

Spencer, C: Child. The rudiments of the art of playing the pianoforte, with numerous exercises and lessons written and selected from the best masters. [Weale's ser.] Lond. 1875. D.   786 : 2

Taylor, Franklin. Primer of pianoforte playing, with numerous examples. (Science primers.) N. Y. 1878. S.   786 : 3

Fay, Amy. Music-study in Germany ; from [her] home correspondence, ed. by the author of "Co-operative housekeeping." Chicago. 1881. D.   786 : 1

Dickson, W. E. Practical organ-building. 2d ed. rev., with add. [Weale's ser.] Lond. 1882. D.   786 : 4

Hart, G: The violin ; its famous makers and their imitators. Ill. Lond. 1880. D.
787 : 1

— The violin and its music, with several engraved portraits on steel of eminent violinists, whose style, both in playing and in composition, may be regarded as representative. Lond. 1881. O.   787+P2

8. Amusements.

1. Entertainments.

Frost, T: The old showmen and the old London fairs. New ed. [The wanderer's lib.] Lond. 1881. D.   791 : 3

— Circus life and circus celebrities. New ed. [The wanderer's lib.] Lond. 1881. D.
791 : 1

— The lives of the conjurors. New ed. [The wanderer's lib.] Lond. 1881. D. 791 : 2

Blitz, Antonio. Fifty years in the magic circle ; an account of the author's professional life, his wonderful tricks and feats, with laughable incidents and adventures as a magician, necromancer and ventriloquist. Hartford. 1871. D.   791 : 4

Hoffmann, L: Modern magic; a practical treatise on the art of conjuring. Ill. 4th ed. Lond. 1882. D.   791 : 5

Frickell, G. Magic no mystery ; conjuring tricks with cards, balls and dice, magic writing, performing animals, by the author of "The secret out"; ed. by W. H. Cremer, jr. Lond. 1876. D.   791 : 6

Hermon, Harry. Hellerism, second-sight mystery, supernatural vision or second-sight. what is it ? a mystery ; a complete manual for teaching this peculiar art. Bost. 1884. S.   791 : 9

Frost, Sarah Annie. The book of tableaux and shadow pantomimes ; containing a choice collection of tableaux vivants or living pictures, embracing moving tableaux, charades in tableaux, Mother Goose tableaux and fairy-tale tableaux, together with directions for arranging the stage, costuming the characters and forming appropriate groups. Added, a number of shadow acts and pantomimes, with complete stage instructions. N. Y. [1869]. S.   791 : 7

Pollard, Josephine. Artistic tableaux ; with picturesque diagrams and descriptions of costumes. Arr. of diagrams by Walter Satterlee. N. Y. 1884. T.   791 : 8

Holt, Ardern. Fancy dresses described ; or What to wear at fancy balls. 4th ed. Lond. *n. d.* O.   791 : 10

Theater.

(*See also* Drama, cl. 812.)

Coquelin, Benoit Constant. The actor and his art. Tr. from the french by Abby Langdon Alger. Bost. 1881. S.   792 : 1

Fitzgerald, Percy. The world behind the scenes. [The wanderer's lib.] Lond. 1881. D.   792 : 3

Cook, Dutton. A book of the play ; studies and ill. of histrionic story, life and character. 2d ed. Lond. 1876. 2 v. D.   792 : 7

Doran, J: Wilberforce. Their majesties' servants ; annals of the english stage from Thomas Betterton to Edmund Kean; actors, authors, audiences. N. Y. 1865. 2 v. O.   792 : 2

Contents. V. 1. Prologue.—The decline and fall of the players.—The "boy actresses" and the "young ladies."—The gentlemen of the king's company.—T: Betterton.—"Exeunt" and "enter."— Elizabeth Barry.—" Their first appearance on this stage."—The dramatic poets.—Noble, gentile and humble authors.—Professional authoresses.—The audiences of the 17th century.—A seven years' rivalry.—The united and disunited companies.— Union, strength, prosperity.—Competition and what came of it.—The progress of James Quin and decline of Barton Booth.—Barton Booth.—Mrs. Oldfield.— From the death of Anne Oldfield to that of Wilks.—Robert Wilks.—Enter, Garrick.— Garrick, Quin, Mrs. Porter.—Rivalry; and enter, Spranger Barry.— The old Dublin theatre.— Garrick and Quin; Garrick and Barry.—The audiences of 1700–1750.—Exit, James Quin.—England and Scotland. 2. Margaret Woffington.—Colley Cibber.—England and Ireland.—Ryan, Rich, O'Brien.—Susanna Maria Cibber.—Reappearance of Spranger

Barry. — Retirement of mrs. Pritchard. — The last years of Garrick and Barry.—D: Garrick.— Spranger and Anne Barry.—Kitty Clive, Woodward, Shuter.—S: Foote.—Supplemental catalogue of new plays from the retirement of Garrick to the end of the 18th century.—Of authors, and particularly of condemned authors.—The audiences of the last half of the 18th century.—C: Macklin.—A bevy of ladies, but chiefly mrs. Bellamy, miss Farren, mrs. Abington, and "Perdita."—A group of gentlemen.—J: Henderson.—Sarah Siddons.—J: Kemble.—G: F: Cooke.—Master Betty.—Stage costume and stage tricks.—Prologue, epilogue, dedications and benefits. — Old stagers departing.—New ideas, new theatres, new authors, and the new actors.—Edmund Kean.

Fitzgerald, Percy. A new history of the english stage from the restoration to the liberty of the theatres, in connection with the patent houses, from original papers in the lord chamberlain's office, the state paper office, and other sources. Lond. 1882. 2 v. O.   792 : 11

Williams, Michael. Some London theatres, past and present. Lond. 1883. D.   792 : 10

Contents. The story of old Sadler's Wells.—Something about old Highbury barn.—The drama in Norton Folgate.—The drama in Portman-market.—Three lyceums.

Matthews, James Brander. The theatres of Paris. Ill. N. Y. 1880. D.   792 : 5

Phelps, H. P. Players of a century ; a record of the Albany stage, incl. notices of prominent actors who have appeared in America. Albany. 1880. D.   792 : 8

Ludlow, N. M. Dramatic life as I found it ; a record of personal experience, with an account of the rise and progress of the drama in the west and south, with anecdotes and biographical sketches of the principal actors and actresses who have at times appeared upon the stage in the Mississippi valley. St. Louis. 1880. O.   792 : 4

Murdoch, James E: The stage, or Recollections of actors and acting from an experience of fifty years ; a series of dramatic sketches, with an app. Phila. 1880. D.   792 : 6

Pollock, Walter Herries, *and lady* Pollock. Amateur theatricals. (Art at home ser.) Lond. 1879. D.   792.1 : 1

How to make up ; a practical guide to the art of "making-up" for amateurs, etc., by Haresfoot and Rouge. N. Y. 1877. D.   792.1 : 2

Guide to selecting plays, or Manager's companion: complete description of 1,500 pieces, showing number of characters, acts and scenes, the class of play,.costumes, time of representation, an account of the dramatis personæ, the plot or advice connected with each, arr. to the requirements of any company. N. Y. 1881. D.   792 : 9

2. Home amusements in general.

Sherwood, Mary Elizabeth Wilson. Home amusements. (Appletons' home books.) N. Y. 1881. D.   790 : 1

Cassell's book of sports and pastimes. Ill. Lond. [1882]. O.   790 : 2

Newell, W: Wells, *ed.* Games and songs of american children, collected and compared. N. Y. 1883. O.   790 : 5

Pardon, G: F: (*Rawdon Crawley.*) The book of manly games for boys ; a practical guide to the indoor and outdoor amusements of all seasons, by Captain Crawley. Lond. [1869]. D.   **790 : 3**

Beard, Daniel C. What to do, and how to do it; the american boy's handy book. N. Y. 1882. D.   **x 790 : 4**

Chadwick, H: The sports and pastimes of american boys; a guide and text-book of games of the play-ground, the parlor and the field, adapted especially for american youth. Ill. N. Y. [1884]. O.   **x 790 : 6**

3. In-door amusements.

Rees, Janet E. Ruutz-. Home occupations. (Appletons' home books). N. Y. 1883 [1882]. D.   **793 : 13**

Household amusements and enjoyments; comprising acting charades, burlesques, conundrums, enigmas, rebuses, and a number of new puzzles in endless variety. Lond. 1866. T.   **793 : 15**

Bellew, Frank. The art of amusing; a collection of graceful arts, merry games, odd tricks, curious puzzles and new charades, together with suggestions for private theatricals, tableaux and all sorts of parlor and family amusements; a volume intended to amuse everybody and enable all to amuse everybody else, thus bringing about as near an approximation to the millenium as can be conveniently attained in the compass of one small volume. Ill. N. Y. 1867. S.   **793 : 1**

— The art of amusing; a collection of graceful arts, games, tricks, puzzles and charades, intended to amuse everybody and enable all to amuse everybody else. Ill. Lond. n. d. D.   **793 : 7**

Bellew, Clara, ed. The merry circle; a book of new, graceful and intellectual games and amusements. Lond. n. d. D.   **793 : 6**

Cassell's book of in-door amusements, card games and fireside fun. 2d ed. Ill. Lond. [1882]. O.   **793 : 4**

Elliott, Alfred. Within-doors; a book of games and pastimes for the drawing-room, with a chapter on feathered pets. Lond. 1872. D.   **793 : 11**

Hoffmann, L: Parlor amusements and evening party entertainments. Ill. Lond. n. d. D.   **793 : 12**

— Same. Drawing-room amusements. Lond. n. d. D.   **793 : 12**

Frickell, G. Hanky panky; a book of conjuring tricks, by the author of "The secret out." New ed. by W. H. Cremer, jr. Lond. 1875. D.   **793 : 8**

— The magician's own book, by the author of of "The secret out," etc.; ed. by W. H. Cremer, jr. Lond. n. d. D.   **793 : 9**

— The secret out; or, 1,000 tricks in drawing-room or white magic with an endless variety of entertaining experiments. [Anon.]; ed. by W. H. Cremer, jr. Ill. Lond. n. d. D.   **793 : 10**

Rubin, Theodor A. Sphinx americana; räthsel. Milw. 1878. D.   **793 : Pam**

Bursill, H: Hand shadows to be thrown upon the wall; consisting of novel and amusing figures formed by the hand, from original designs. 2 ser. in 1 v. N. Y. n. d. O.   **x 793 : 5**

Campbell, Helen. The american girl's home book of work and play. Ill. N. Y. 1883. D.   **x 793 : 17**

Landells, E. and Alice. The girl's own toy-maker and book of recreation. 12th thous. Ill. N. Y. n. d. S.   **x 793 : 14**

Dick, W: Brisbane. The american Hoyle, or Gentleman's hand-book of games; containing all the games played in the U. S., with rules, descriptions and technicalities, adapted to the american methods of playing, by Trumps. Appended, A treatise on the doctrine of chances. 13th ed. rev. N. Y. 1883. D.   **793 : 16**

Chess and checkers.

Forbes, Duncan. The history of chess, from the time of the early invention of the game in India, till the period of its establishment in western and central Europe. Lond. 1860. O.   **794+8**

Chess handbook, The; teaching the rudiments of the game and giving an analysis of all the recognized openings, exemplified by appropriate games actually played by Morphy, Harrwitz, Anderssen, Staunton, Paulsen, Montgomery, Meek and many others, by an amateur. [Based on Staunton, H. Chess-player's handbook.] Phila. 1859. S.   **794 : 3**

Gossip, G. H. D. The chess-player's manual; containing the laws of the game according to the revised code laid down by the British chess association in 1862. 2d ed. Lond. 1888. O.   **794+7**

Cook, W: Synopsis of the chess openings; a tabulated analysis. 3d ed. with add. and emendations. Lond. 1882. O.   **794 : 6**

Staunton, Howard. The chess tournament; a collection of the games played at this celebrated assemblage, ill. by diagrams and notes, critical and explanatory. Lond. 1852. D.   **794 : 5**

Fiske, Daniel Willard. The book of the first american chess congress; containing the proceedings of that celebrated assemblage, held in N. Y. in 1857, with the papers read in its sessions, the games played in the grand tournament and the stratagems entered in the problem tournay, together with sketches of the history of chess in the old and new worlds. N. Y. 1859. D.   **794 : 2**

Lange, Max. Paul Morphy; a sketch from the chess world. Tr. by permission, with add. notes and games by Ernest Falkbeer. Lond. 1860. D.   **794 : 4**

Dubuque chess journal; v. 8, jan.-dec. 1875. [Dubuque. 1875]. D.   **705.9 : M**
T. p. w.

Goold, Joseph. The game of draughts; problems, critical positions and games, containing sections by dr. Brown, messrs. Drinkwater, Fred. Allen, F. Dunne, Kear, Robertson, Gourlay, Hedley, Smith, Leggett, Gilbert, Richards, Whitney and Wyllie, with special contributions from messrs. McCall, Parker, Willie Gardner, Ritchie, etc., selections from the works of the best authors and composers, and notes on the positions. Lond. 1884. S.   **795 : 9**

Card games.

Drayson, A. W. The art of practical whist ; a series of letters descriptive of every part of the game, and best method of becoming a skilful player, embodying the rules adopted by he Arlington and Portland clubs. Londt *and* N. Y. 1880. D.　**795 : 1**

Hayward, Abraham. Whist and whist-players. *In his* Selected essays.　**824.2 : 46 v2**

Jones, H:, (*Cavendish*). The laws and principles of whist stated and explained, and its practice illustrated on an original system, by means of hands played completely through, by Cavendish. 14th ed. Lond. 1884. S.　**795 : 7**

— Card essays, Clay's decisions, and Card-table talk by Cavendish. Amer. ed. with index. (Leisure hour ser.) N. Y. 1880. S.　**795 : 2**

Pembridge, *pseud.* Whist or bumblepuppy ? ten lectures addressed to children. From the 2d Lond. ed. Bost. 1883. S.　**795 : 5**

Pettes, G: W: American or standard whist, by G. W. P. Bost. 1880. D.　**795 : 3**

Pole, W: The theory of the modern scientific game of whist. 11th ed. Lond. 1879. S.　**795 : 4**

— The philosophy of whist ; an essay on the scientific and intellectual aspects of the modern game, in 2 pts : pt. 1, The philosophy of whist play ; pt. 2, The philosophy of whist probabilities. . 3d ed. Lond. 1884. S.　**795 : 8**

Proctor, R: Anthony. How to play whist ; with the laws and etiquette of whist, whist-whittlings, and forty fully - annotated games ; by "Five of clubs". (Knowledge library). Lond. 1885. D.　**795 : 10**

— *Same.* N. Y. 1885. S.　**795 : 10**

Walker, Arthur Campbell-. The correct card, or How to play at whist ; a whist catechism. N. Y. 1876. S.　**795 : 11**

Linderfelt, Klas A: The game of preference or swedish whist ; with a bibliography of english whist. Milw. 1885. S.　**795 : 12**

Dick, W: Brisbane, *ed.* Games of patience, or Solitaire with cards ; containing 44 games. Ill. N. Y. 1883. D.　**795 : 6**

4. Out-door sports.

Depping, Guillaume. Wonders of bodily strength and skill in all ages and all countries. Tr. and enl. from the french by C: Russell. [Ill. lib. of wonders.] N. Y. 1873. D.　**796 : 4**

Spirit of the times ; a chronicle of the turf, field sports, aquatics, agriculture and the stage ; v. 107, 108, feb. 1884—jan. 1885. N. Y. —85. F.　**705.9 : RM**

Blaine, Delabere Pritchett. An encyclopædia of rural sports, or Complete account. historical, practical and descriptive, of hunting, shooting, fishing, racing, etc. New ed., rev. and corr. Lond. 1858. O.　**796 : R1**

Walsh, J: H:, (*Stonehenge*). British rural sports ; comprising shooting, hunting, coursing, fishing, hawking, racing, boating and pedestrianism, with all rural games and amusements, by Stonehenge. 15th ed., ill. re-ed. with add. by the "Field" staff. · Lond. [1881]. O.　**796 : R13**

Appleton's summer book.　**829.1+1** *Contents, see under* English literature, Miscellany.

Elliott, Alfred. Out-of-doors ; a handbook of games for the play ground. Lond. 1872. D.　**796 : 11**

Miller, T: The boy's summer book ; descriptive of the season, scenery, rural life and country amusements. Ill. N. Y. 1880. S.　**796 : 7**

Gould, J: M. Hints for camping and walking : How to camp out. N. Y. 1880. S.　**796 : 9**

Pratt, C: E. The american bicycler ; a manual for the observer, the learner and the expert. Ill. Bost. 1879. S.　**796 : 3**

Thompson, Maurice. The witchery of archery ; a complete manual of archery, with many chapters of adventures by field and flood, with an app. containing practical directions for the manufacture and use of archery implements. New ed., with a chapter on english archery practice. Ill. N. Y. 1879. S.　**796 : 5**

Taylor, James. Curling ; the ancient scottish game. Ill. Edinb. 1884. O.　**796 : 17**

Swift, Frank, *and* Marvin R. Clark. The skater's text-book. N. Y. [1868]. D.　**796 : 12**

Greenwood, James. Wild sports of the world ; a boy's book of natural history and adventure. Ill. Lond. 1862. O.　**796 : 10**

Lloyd, Llewellyn. Field sports of the north of Europe ; comprised in a personal narrative of a residence in Sweden and Norway in 1827-28. 2d ed., with add. Lond. 1831. 2 v. O.　**796 : 14**

Gerstäcker, F: Wild sports in the far west. Tr. from the german. Phila. 1881. D.　**796 : 16**

Sears, G: W. (*Nessmuk*). Woodcraft. (Forest and stream ser.) Ill. N. Y. [1884]. S.　**796 : 15**

Northrup, A. Judd. 'Sconset cottage life ; a summer on Nantucket Island. N. Y. 1881. S.　**796 : 8**

Boating.

Boats, The, of the world ; depicted and described by one of the craft. Lond. *n. d.* O.　**x 797 : 2**

Prescott, C: E. The sailing-boat and its management. N. Y. 1883. T.　**797 : 3**

Maclaren, Archibald. Training in theory and practice. 2d enl. ed. with ill. Lond. 1874. S.　**797 : 1**

Horsemanship.

(*See also* Domestic animals, class 636.1, col. 441.)

Saddle-horse, The ; complete guide for riding and training. N. Y. 1881. D.　**798 : 2**

Anderson, E: L. Modern horsemanship ; a new method of teaching riding and training by means of pic u s from the life. Ill. Edinb. 1884. O. t re　**798 : 6**

Karr, Elizabeth. The american horsewoman. Ill. Bost. 1884. D.　**798 : 5**

x denotes books specially adapted for children.

Melville, G: J: Whyte-. Riding recollections. Leipz. 1879. S.   **798 : 1**

Waring, G: Edwin, *jr.* Whip and spur. Bost. 1875. T.   **798 : 3**
Contents. Vix.—Ruby.—Wettstein.—Campaigning with Max.—How I got my overcoat.—Two scouts.—In the gloaming.—Fox-hunting in England.

— Waring's horse stories. reprinted from "Whip and spur": no. 1, Vix ; no. 2, Ruby. Bost. 1883. S.   **798 : 4**

General field sports.

Hallock, C: The sportsman's gazetteer and general guide ; the game animals, birds and fishes of North America, their habits, and various methods of capture ; also instructions in shooting, fishing, taxidermy, woodcraft, etc., together with a glossary. Rev., enl. and brought down to date by the author. Ill., maps and portrait. N. Y., 1883. D.   **799 : 7**

Cross, D. W. Fifty years with gun and rod ; incl. tables showing the velocity, distance, penetration or effect of shot, calculated by Leonard Case, gun trials by the Chicago field, how and where to "hold," etc. Cleveland, O. 1880. D.   **799 : 6**

Mayer, Alfred Marshall, *ed.* Sport with gun and rod in american woods and waters. Ill. N. Y. [1883]. 2 v. Q.   **799 : R8**

Jefferies, R: The amateur poacher, by the author of "The gamekeeper at home" and "Wild life in a southern country." Bost. 1879. D.   **799 : 5**

Herbert, H: W: Frank Forester's fugitive sporting sketches ; miscellaneous articles upon sport and sporting, originally pub. in the early american magazines and periodicals, ed., with a memoir of Herbert and numerous explanatory notes, by Will Wildwood [F: Eugene Pond]. Westfield, Wis. 1879. O.   **799 : 1**
Contents. Memoir.—The game of North America.—Among the mountains.—A blaze at Barnegat.—The american bittern.—The death of the stag.—The red fox.—A trip to Chateau Richer, or Snipe shooting on the St. Lawrence.—Spring snipe.—Domestication of game-birds.

Northrup, A. Judd. Camps and tramps in the Adirondacks, and grayling fishing in northern Michigan ; a record of summer vacations in the wilderness. Syracuse, N. Y. 1880. S.   **799 : 2**

Davies, G. Christopher. The Swan and her crew, or The adventures of three young naturalists and sportsmen on the broads and rivers of Norfolk. 4th ed. with postscript and ill. Lond. [1880]. D.   **799 : 4**

Fishing.

Prouty, Lorenzo. Fish ; their habits and haunts and the methods of catching them, together with fishing as a recreation. Bost. 1883. O.   **799.1 : 8**

Roosevelt, Robert Barnwell. The game fish of the northern states and british provinces ; with an account of the salmon and sea-trout fishing of Canada and New Brunswick, together with simple directions for tying artificial flies, etc. N. Y. 1862. D.   **799.1 : 3**

— *Same.* N. Y. 1865. D.   **799.1 : 3**

Roosevelt, Robert Barnwell.—*Continued.*
— Superior fishing, or The striped bass, trout and black bass of the northern states ; embracing full directions for dressing artificial flies with the feathers of american birds, an account of a sporting visit to Lake Superior, etc. N. Y. 1865. D.   **799.1 : 4**

Stevens, C: Woodbury. Fly-fishing in Maine lakes, or Camp-life in the wilderness. [New ed.] Bost. 1881. Ill. Sq. D.   **799.1 : 7**

Walton, I: The complete angler, or The contemplative man's recreation, and Instructions how to angle for a trout or grayling in a clear stream, by C: Cotton ; with copious notes, for the most part original, a bibliographical preface, giving an account of fishing and fishing-books from the earliest antiquity to the time of Walton, and a notice of Cotton and his writings by the amer. ed. Added, an app. incl. ill. ballads, music, papers on amer. fishing and a catalogue of books on angling, also general index. N. Y. 1847. D.   **799.1 : 6**

Cotton, C: The complete angler, or The contemplative man's recreation, pt. 2: Instructions how to angle for a trout or grayling in a clear stream. N. Y. 1847. D. *In* **Walton,** I: The complete angler.   **799.1 : 6**

Davy, *Sir* Humphrey. Salmonia, or Days of fly-fishing, in a series of conversations ; with some account of the habits of fishes belonging to the genus salmo, by an angler. 1st amer. from the 2d Lond. ed. Phila. 1832. S.   **799.1 : 5**

Blakey, Robert, (*Palmer Hackle*). Hints on angling, with suggestions for angling excursions in France and Belgium ; app., some brief notices of the english, scottish and irish waters. Lond. 1846. O.   **799.1 : 1**

Newland, H: Garrett. Forest scenes in Norway and Sweden. *T. p. w.* S.   **799.1 : 2**

Hunting, shooting and trapping.

Riesenthal, O. v. Jagd-lexikon ; handbuch für jäger und jagdfreunde, mit besonderer berücksichtigung der naturgeschichte und hege des wildes. Ill. Leipz. 1882. D.   **799.2 : R10**

Lewis, Elisha J. The american sportsman, containing hints to sportsmen, notes on shooting, and the habits of the game birds and wild fowl of America. New rev. ed. Ill. Phil. 1885 [1884]. O.   **799 : 9**

Barber, E: C. The crack shot, or Young rifleman's complete guide ; a treatise on the use of the rifle, with rudimentary and finishing lessons, incl. a full description of the latest improved breech-loading weapons, ill. with numerous engr., rules and regulations for target practice, directions for hunting game found in the U. S. and british provinces, etc. N. Y. 1868. S.   **799.3 : 1**

Adams, W: H: Davenport. Scenes with the hunter and trapper in many lands. [*Anon.*] Ill. Lond. 1884. D.   **799.2 : 11**

Batty, Joseph H. How to hunt and trap, together with chapters upon outfits, guns, etc., abounding in information generally for sportsmen. N. Y. 1882. D.   **799 : 3**

Newhouse, S., *and others.* The trapper's guide; a manual of instructions for capturing all kinds of fur-bearing animals and curing their skins, with observations on the fur trade, hints on life in the woods and narratives of trapping and hunting excursions. 2d ed., ed. by J. H. Noyes and T. L. Pitt. Ill. Wallingford, Ct. 1867. O.   **639 : 2**

Gibson, W: Hamilton. Camp-life in the woods; and the tricks of trapping and trap-making. Ill. by the author. [New ed.] N. Y. 1881. D.   **639 : 4**

Cartwright, D: W. Natural history of western wild animals, and guide for hunters, trappers and sportsmen... 2d ed., written by Mary F. Bailey. Toledo. 1875. D.   **639 : 1**

Gillmore, Parker. Prairie and forest; a description of the game of North America, with personal adventures in their pursuit. N. Y. 1874. D.   **799.2 : 4**

Herbert, H: W: Frank Forester's field sports of the U. S. and british provinces of North America. N. Y. 1849. 2 v. O.   **799.2 : 5**

Murphy, J: Mortimer. Sporting adventures in the far west. Ill. N. Y. 1880. D.   **799.2 : 6**

Shakespear, H: The wild sports of India, with remarks on the breeding and rearing of horses and the formation of light, irregular cavalry. Bost. 1860. D.   **799.2 : 7**

Jefferies, R: The game keeper at home; sketches of natural history and rural life. 3d ed. Bost. 1879. D.   **799.2 : 3**

Tongue, Cornelius, (Cecil). Records of the chase and memoirs of celebrated sportsmen, ill. some of the usages of olden times and comparing them with prevailing customs, together with an introd. to most of the fashionable hunting countries, and comments by Cecil. Lond. 1854. S.   **799.2 : 2**

Carlton, J: W: (Craven). Recreations in shooting; with some account of the game of the British Islands. Lond. 1846. S. *T. p. w.*   **799.2 : 1**

Adams, W: H: Davenport. The forest, the jungle and the prairie, or Tales of adventure and enterprise in pursuit of wild animals. Ill. Lond. 1882. S.   **799.2 : 9**

Gérard, Cécile Jules Basile. Life and adventures; comprising his ten years' campaigns among the lions of northern Africa. Lond. [1856]. S.   **799.2 : 8**

IX. LITERATURE.

1. In general.

1. Dictionaries.

Bornhak, G. Lexikon der allgemeinen litteraturgeschichte; die nationallitteratur der ausserdeutschen völker aller zeiten in geschichtlichen übersichten und biographien, zugleich lexikon der poetik. Leipz. 1882. D.   **803 : R4**

Brewer, Ebenezer Cobham. Reader's hand-book of allusions, references, plots and stories; with 2 app. Phila. 1880. O.   **803 : R2**

— Dictionary of phrase and fable, giving the derivation. source or origin of common phrases, allusions and words that have a .tale to tell. 9th ed. Phila. *n. d.* O.   **803 : R1**

Edwards, Eliezer. Words, facts and phrases; a dictionary of curious, quaint and out-of-the-way matters. Phila. [1881]. O.   **803 : R3**

Wheeler, W: Adolphus. Who wrote it? an index to the authorship of the more noted works in ancient and modern literature; ed. by C: G. Wheeler. Bost. 1881. D.   **803 : R7**

— *and* **C: G.** Familiar allusions; handbook of miscellaneous information, incl. the names of celebrated statues, paintings, palaces, country-seats, ruins, churches, ships, streets, clubs, natural curiosities, and the like. Bost. 1882. D.   **803 : R5**

Ripley, G:, *and* Bayard Taylor, *eds.* Hand-book of literature and the fine arts; comprising complete and accurate definitions of all terms employed in belles-lettres, philosophy, theology, law, mythology, painting, music, sculpture, architecture and all kindred arts. (Putnam's home cyclopædia). N. Y. 1852. D.   **803 : 6**

2. Essays on literature.

Albee, J: Literary art; conversation between a poet, painter and philosopher. N. Y. 1881. S.   **801 : 1**

Beloe, W: Anecdotes of literature and scarce books. Lond. 1807. 2 v. D.   **804 : 6**

Dowden, E: Studies in literature, 1789—1877. Lond. 1878. O.   **804 : 1**
Contents. The french revolution and literature.—The transcendental movement and literature.—The scientific movement and literature.—The prose works of Wordsworth.—Walter Savage Landor.—Mr. Tennyson and mr. Browning.—George Eliot.—Lammenais.—Edgar Quinet.—On some french writers of verse, 1830—1877.—The poetry of Victor Hugo.—The poetry of democracy; Walt Whitman.

Gosse, Edmund W: Studies in the literature of northern Europe. Lond. 1879. D.   **804 : 2**
Contents. Norway: Norwegian poetry since 1814; Henrik Ibsen; The Lofoden islands. — Sweden: Runeberg.—Denmark: The danish national theatre; Four danish poets.—Germany: Walter von der Vogelweide.—Holland: A dutch poetess of the 17th century; Vondel and Milton; The Oera Linda book.—App.

Schlegel, K: W: F: v. Æsthetic and miscellaneous works. Tr. from the german by E. J. Millington. Lond. 1849. D.   **804 : 4**
Contents. Pref.—Description of paintings in Paris and the Netherlands. in 1802–4.—Principles of gothic architecture.—Contributions to the study of romantic poetry and genius.—Modern german paintings.—Romantic fictions of the middle ages: Lother and Maller.—Miscell. essays.—On the limits of the beautiful.—On the language and the philosophy of the indians.

Shepard, W: The literary life. N. Y. 1882–84 [1883]. 3 v. S.   **804 : 5**
Contents. V. 1. *Authors and authorship:* The literary life; The chances of literature; Concerning rejected mss.; The rewards of literature; Literature as a staff; Literature as a crutch; Some literary confessions; First appearance in print; Literary heroes and hero worship; Some successful books; The seamy side of letters; Literary society; The consolation of literature. 2. *Pen pictures of modern authors:* Carlyle; G: Eliot; Ruskin; J: H: Newman; Tennyson; Emerson; Bryant; Longfellow and Whittier; Lowell and Holmes; Hawthorne; Whitman; Bayard Taylor; Swinburne and Oscar Wilde; The Brownings; Dickens; Thackeray; Some younger writers. 3. *Pen pictures of the earlier Victorian authors.* Literary London in 1835; E: Bulwer, lord Lytton; B: Disraeli, lord Beaconsfield; T: Babington Macaulay; Charlotte Bronte; Washington Irving; Edgar Allan Poe; Harriet Martineau.

Tuckerman, H: Theodore. Characteristics of literature; illustrated by the genius of distinguished writers. 2d ser. Phila. 1851. D.   **804 : 3 v2**
Contents. The novelist, Manzoni.— The censor, Steele.—The naturalist, Humboldt.—The correspondent, Mme. de Sévigné. – The philologist, Horne Tooke.—The magazine writer, Wilson.—The dramatist, Talfourd.—The traveller, Beckford.—The critic, Hazlitt.—The orator, Everett.—The reformer, Godwin.

3. General literary history.

Botta, Anne C. Lynch. Hand-book of universal literature. 24th ed. Bost. 1891. D.   **809 : 5**

— *Same.* Hand-book of universal literature, from the best and latest authorities. New ed. rev. and brought down to 1885. Bost. 1885 [1884]. O.   **809 : 5**

Scherr, Johannes. Allgemeine geschichte der literatur; ein handbuch in 2 b. 5te aufl. Stuttg. 1875. 2 v. in 1. O.   **809+1**

Scherr, Johannes.—*Continued.*
— Bildersaal der weltliteratur. 3te neu bearb.
und stark verm. aufl. Stuttg. [1884]. Q.
809+10
Contents. V. 1. Das morgenland: China; Japan;
Indien; Hebräerland; Arabien; Persien; Türkei.—
Hellas und Rom.—Die romanischen länder: Frankreich; Italien; Spanien und Portugal, Rumänien.—
2. Die germanischen länder: Deutschland. *In course
of publication.*

Schlegel, K: W: F: v. Lectures on the history
of literature, ancient and modern. From
the german. Phila. 1818. 2 v. O. 809:4

Berington, Joseph. The literary history of the
middle ages ; comprehending an account
of the state of learning from the close of
the reign of Augustus to its revival in the
15th century. Lond. 1846. D. 809:2

Hallam, H: Introduction to the literature of
Europe in the 15th, 16th and 17th centuries.
N. Y. 1842. 2 v. O. 809+3

Hettner, Hermann. Literaturgeschichte des
18ten jahrhunderts. Braunschweig. 1879–
81. 3 pts. in 6 v. O. 809:9
Contents. 1er t. Die englische literatur von 1660–
1770, 4te aufl. 2er t. Die französische literatur im
18ten jahrhundert, 4te aufl. 3er t. [in 4 vols.] Die
deutsche literatur im 18ten jahrhundert, 3te aufl.

Brandes, G: Die hauptströmungen der literatur des neunzehnten jahrhunderts ; vorlesungen gehalten an der Kopenhagener
universität. Uebers. und eingeleitet von
Adolf Strodtmann. Berlin. 1872–83. 5 v. D.
809:6
Contents. V. 1. Die emigrantenliteratur.—Die romantische schule in Deutschland. 2. Die romantische schule in Deutschland, *fortsetzung.* 3. Die
reaktion in Frankreich. 4. Der naturalismus in
England. 5. Die romantische schule in Frankreich.

Reusch, F: H: Der Index der verbotenen bücher ; ein beitrag zur kirchen- und literaturgeschichte ; 1er band. Bonn. 1883. O.
809+8

Brinton, Daniel G. Aboriginal american authors and their productions, especially
those in the native languages ; a chapter
in the history of literature. Phila. 1883. O.
809:7

4. Books and reading.

Ireland, Alexander, (*Philobiblos*). The book-
lover's enchiridion ; thoughts on the solace
and companionship of books, selected and
chronologically arr. by Philobiblos. Amer.
ed., rev. and enl. Phila. 1888. S. 807:15

Langford, J: Alfred. Praise of books, as
said and sung by english authors, selected,
with a preliminary essay on books. Lond.
n. d. S. 807:7

Willmott, Robert Aris. Pleasures, objects and
advantages of literature. New ed. Lond.
1857. S. 807:8

Discourses on the objects and uses of science
and literature. N. Y. 1843. S. 807:2
Contents. Potter, A. Preliminary observations on
reading.—Brougham, H: lord. A discourse on the
objects, advantages and pleasures of science.—Potter, A. The pleasures and advantages of literature
and moral science.—Sedgwick, A. A discourse on
classical, metaphysical, moral and natural studies.—
Verplanck, G. C. On the importance of scientific
knowledge to the manufacturer and practical mechanic; The influence of moral causes upon opinion,
science and literature.

Foster, W: E. Libraries and readers. N. Y.
1883. S. 807:12
Contents. Some hints on right reading.—Correction
of aimless reading.—The specializing of reading, for
general readers.—"Current literature" and "Standard literature".—Securing the interest of a community.—What may be done at home.—How to use a
library.—Books and articles on reading.

Green, S: Swett, *comp.* Libraries and schools.
N. Y. 1883. S. 807:13
Contents. Adams, C: F., jr. The public library
and the public schools.—Green, S: S. The relation
of the public library to the public schools; Libraries
as educational institutions.—Metcalf, R. C. The
public library as auxiliary to the public schools.—
Foster, W: E. The relation of libraries to the school
system; A plan of systematic training on reading at
school.

* * *

Abbott, Lyman, *ed.* Hints for home reading ;
a series of chapters on books and their use.
N. Y. 1880. D. 807:1
Contents. Sweetser, M. F. What the people read.
—Warner, C: D. Why young people read trash.—
Perkins, F: B. What to read; Plans for reading.
—Hamlin, C. Plans of reading.—Beecher, H: W.
Plans of reading.—Mable, H. W. The art of reading.—Hale, E: E. The choice of books.—Cook, J.
How to make dull boys read; How to preserve the
results of reading.—Abbott, L. Hints for people
that do not read.—A symposium by many contributors.—Putnam, G: P. Suggestions for household
libraries.—Priced lists of suggested selections of 500,
1,000 and 2,000 volumes of the most desirable and important books.

Baldwin, James. The book-lover ; a guide to
the best reading. Chic. 1885 [1884]. S.
807:18

Carlyle, T: On the choice of books. 5th ed.,
with a new life of the author. Lond. 1878.
S. 807:9

Kent, James. A course of reading for the use
of the members of the Mercantile library
association. N. Y. 1840. D. 807:10

Matthews, James Brander, (*Arthur Penn*). The
home library. (Appletons' home books.)
Ill. N. Y. 1883. D. 807:17

Porter, Noah. Books and reading, or What
books shall I read and how shall I read
them ? 4th ed. with an index. N. Y. 1875.
D. 807:3

— *Same.* With an app. containing a select catalogue of books. [New ed.] N. Y. 1881. O.
807:4

Potter, Alonzo. Handbook for readers and
students ; intended as a help to individuals,
associations, school-districts and seminaries of learning in the selection of works for
reading, investigation or professional
study. 4th ed. N. Y. 1847. S. 807:5

Pryde, D: The highways of literature, or What
to read and how to read. N. Y. [1883]. D.
807:16

Pycroft, James. A course of english reading ;
adapted to every taste and capacity, with
anecdotes of men of genius, with add. by
J. G. Coggswell. N. Y. 1845. D. 807:6

Thwing, C: F. The reading of books ; its pleasures, profits and perils. Bost. 1883. S.
807:14
Contains chapters on: The advantage of reading;
Biography; History; Travel; Fiction; Historical
fiction; Poetry; Religious books; Books of literature;
Language, philosophy, science and the fine arts;
Books for children; Forming a library. An app. contains a selected list of books for reading and study,
classified under subjects.

Van Dyke, J: C: Books and how to use them; some hints to readers and students. N. Y. 1883. D.   **807 : 11**

5. Literary periodicals.

American bookseller, The; v. 7, 8, 13–16. N. Y. 1879–84. Q.   **805 : LM**

Appletons' literary bulletin, v. 1–3, dec. 1881—dec. 1884. *n. t.* N. Y. F.   **805 : LM**

Bookbuyer, The; a summary of american and foreign literature; v. 1, 2. N. Y. 1867–69. 2 v. O.   **805 : LM**
— Same. New series, v. 1, 2. N. Y. 1878–80. O.   **805 : LM**
— Same. New series, v. 1, feb. 1884—jan. 1885. N. Y. [1884, 5]. O.   **805 : LM**

Criterion, The; literary and critical journal; v. 1, and 2 nos. of v. 2, nov. 3, 1855—may 10, 1856. N. Y. 1856. F.   **805 : LM**

Critic, The; a fortnightly review of literature, the fine arts, music and the drama; v. 1–5. N. Y. 1881–1884. 5 v. Q.   **805 : LM**
   Note. V. 4, 5 are called "The critic and Good literature," and form v. 1, 2 of a new series.

Dial, The; a monthly review and index of current literature; v. 1–5, may 1880—april 1885. Chicago. 1881–85. Q.   **805 : LM**

Literary era, The; a monthly repository of literary and miscellaneous information for home reading; v. 1, 2, jan. 1883—dec. 1884. Phila. 1883–4. O.   **805 : LM**

Literary news, The; a monthly journal of current literature. New series, v. 1–5, jan. 1880—dec. 1884. N. Y. 1880–84. Q.   **805 : LM**

Literary world, The; a gazette for authors, readers and publishers, v. 1–3, 6–8. N. Y. 1847–51. Q.   **805 : LM**
   Note. The first 12 numbers were issued under the editorship of E. A. Duyckinck; from no. 13–87 C: F. Hoffman was ed., and with no. 88 Duyckinck again assumed the editorship. Title-page of vol. 3 reads "a journal of society, literature and art," of v. 6–8 "a journal of science, literature and art." (V. 8 contains also v. 4. of the Literary american, jan.-may 1850).

Literary world, The; a fortnightly review of current literature; v. 9–15. Bost. 1878–84. Q.   **805 : LM**

Academy, The; a weekly review of literature, science and art; v. 17–26, jan. 1880–dec. 1884. Lond. 1880–84. Q.   **805 : LM**

Athenæum, The; a journal of literature, science, the fine arts, music and the drama; v. 74–81, jan. 1881–dec. 1884. Lond. 1881–84. Q.   **805 : LM**

Notes and queries; a medium of intercommunication for literary men, general readers, etc.; 6th ser., v. 3–10, jan. 1881–dec. 1884. Lond. 1881–84. D.   **805 : LM**

Saturday review, The, of politics, literature, science and art; v. 49–58, jan. 1880–dec. 1884. Lond. 1880–84. Q.   **805 : LM**

Deutsche litteraturzeitung, herausg. von Max Rödiger; v. 1–5, oct. 1880–dec. 1884. Q.   **805 : LM**

Literarischer merkur; mittheilungen aus dem geistigen leben der gegenwart und nachrichten für bücherfreunde über erschienene neuigkeiten des in- und auslandes, v. 2–4. *n. t.* [Berlin. 1882–84]. O.   **805 : LM**

2. General literary classes.

1. Poetry.

Criticism.

Montgomery, James. Lectures on general literature, poetry, etc., delivered at the Royal institution in 1830 and 1831. N. Y. 1843. S.   **811.2 : 2**

Shairp, J: Campbell. Aspects of poetry; lectures delivered at Oxford. Oxford. 1881. O.   **811.2 : 3**

Browning, Elizabeth, *born* Barrett. Essays on the greek christian poets and the english poets. N. Y. 1863. S.   **811.2 : 1**

Collections.

Bulfinch, T: *ed.* Poetry of the age of fable. Bost. *n. d.* S.   **811 : 1**

Dobson, W: T. The classic poets; their lives and their times, with the epics epitomized. Lond. 1879. D.   **811 : 3**
   Contents. Homer's Iliad.—The lay of the Nibelungen.—Cid Campeador.—Dante's Divina comedia.—Ariosto's Orlando furioso.—Camoen's Lusiad.—Tasso's Jerusalem delivered.—Spenser's Fairy queen.—Milton's Paradise lost.—Milton's Paradise regained.

Church, Alfred J: Stories of the old world. (Classics for children). Bost. 1884. D.   **x 811 : 9**
   Contents. The story of the Argo.—The story of Thebes.—The story of Troy.—The adventures of Ulysses.—The adventures of Æneas.

Longfellow, H: Wadsworth. The poets and poetry of Europe; with introd. and biograph. notices. N. Y. 1855. O.   **811+P4**
— *ed.* Poems of places. Bost. 1877–79. 31 v. T.   **811 : 5**
   Contents. V. 1–4. England and Wales. 6–8. Scotland, Ireland, Norway and Sweden. 9, 10. France and Savoy. 11–13. Italy. 14, 15. Spain, Portugal, Belgium and Holland. 16. Switzerland and Austria. 17, 18. Germany. 19. Greece and Turkey. 20. Russia. 21–23. Asia. 24. Africa. 25–30. America. 31. Oceanica.

Clarke, James Freeman *and* Lilian. Exotics; attempts to domesticate them by J. F. C. and L. C. Bost. 1875. T.   **811 : 2**

Hunt, N. Clemmons, *comp.* The poetry of other lands; a collection of translations into english verse of the poetry of other languages, ancient and modern. Phila. [1883]. O.   **811 : 8**

Mountains, The; a collection of poems. Bost. 1876. T.   **811 : 6**

x denotes books specially adapted for children.

Walpole, *The rev.* Robert. The garland of flowers; composed of translations, chiefly original, from the spanish, italian, greek, latin, etc. N. Y. 1806. O. **811 : 7**

Symonds, J: Addington, *tr. and ed.* Wine, women and song; mediæval latin student songs now first tr. into eng. verse, with an essay. Lond. 1884. S. **811 : 10**

2. Drama.

(See also Dramatic music, cl. 782, col. 494; *and* Theater, cl. 792, col. 497.)*

History and criticism.

Schlegel, A: W: v. A course of lectures on dramatic art and literature. Tr. by J: Black; rev., according to the last german ed., by A. J. W. Morrison. Lond. 1846. D. **812.1 : 2**

Freytag, Gustav. Die technik des dramas. 4te verb. aufl. Leipz. 1881. O. **812.1 : 3**

Hase, K: A: Miracle plays and sacred dramas; a historical survey. Tr. from the german by A. W. Jackson and ed. by W. W. Jackson. Bost. 1880. O. **812.1 : 1**

Blackburn, H: The Oberammergau passion play: Art in the mountains; the story of the passion play. Ill., with app. for information of travellers. Lond. 1880. O. **812.2 : 1**

Collections.

See Class-list of drama.

*   *   *

Note. A complete class-list of dramatic literature will be found after class 819, col. 519.

3. Romance.

History and criticism.

Dunlop, J: The history of fiction; a critical account of the most celebrated works of prose fiction, from the earliest greek romances to the novels of the present age. 3d ed. Lond. 1845. O. **813.1+1**

Mitchell, Donald Grant, *(Ik Marvel).* About old story tellers; of how and when they lived, and what stories they told. N. Y. 1876. D. **813 : 1**

Besant, Walter, *and* H: James. The art of fiction. Bost. 1884. S. **813.2 : 2**

Spielhagen, F: Beiträge zur theorie und technik des romans. Leipz. 1883. D. **813.2 : 3**

Bryce, Carroll. A lost function in romance. N. Y. 1883. D. **813.2 : 1**

Mähly, Jakob. Der roman des 19. jahrhunderts. *In* Deutsche zeit- und streit-fragen. **304 : 15 v1**

Collections.

Hearn, Lafcadio, *ed.* Stray leaves from strange literature; stories reconstructed from the Anvari-soheili, Baitál Pachisi, Mahabharata, Pautchatantra, Gulistan, Talmud, Kalevala, etc. Bost. 1884. S. **810 : 1**

Wägner, W: Epics and romances of the middle ages; adapted from the work of W: Wägner, by M. W. Macdowall and ed. by W. S. W. Anson. Lond. 1883. O. **813 : 6**

Contents. Pt. 1. *The Amelung and kindred legends.* Langobardian legends: Alboin and Rosamund; King Rother; Ortnit.—The Amelungs: Hugdieterich and Wolfdieterich; King Samson; Dietwart. — Dieterich of Bern. Pt. 2. *The Nibelung and kindred legends.* The Nibelung hero. — The Nibelung's woe. — The Hegeling legend.—Beowulf. Pt. 3. *The Carolingian legends.* The children of Haymon; Roland; William of Orange.—The legends of king Arthur and the holy grail: Titurel; Percival; Lohengrin; Tristram and Isold.—Tannhäuser.

Cox, *Sir* G: W:, *and* Eustace Hinton Jones. Popular romances of the middle ages. 1st amer. from the 2d english ed. N. Y. 1880. O. **813 : 2**

Contents. King Arthur and his knights.—Merlin.—Sir Tristram.—Bevis of Hamtoun.—Guy of Warwick.—Havelock.—Beowulf.—Roland.—Olger the dane.—The story of the Volsungs.—The Nibelung story.—Walter of Aquitaine. — The story of Hugdietrich and Hildeburg. — The Gudrun lay. — The story of Frithjof and Ingeborg. — Grettir the strong.—Gunnlaug and the fair Hilda.—Burnt Njal.

Bulfinch, T: Legends of Charlemagne, or Romance of the middle ages. Bost. [1862]. D. **813 : 14**

— The age of chivalry, or Legends of king Arthur and the knights of the round table. Bost. 1858. S. **813 : 13**

— *Same.* Bost. n. d. D. **813 : 13**

— *Same.* The age of chivalry, or Legends of king Arthur; "King Arthur and his knights," "The Mabinogeon," "The crusades," "Robin Hood." New, enl. and rev. ed., ed. by E: E. Hale. Bost. [1884.]. O. **813 : 12**

Malory, *Sir* T: Morte d'Arthur; sir Thomas Malory's book of king Arthur and of his noble knights of the round table. The original ed. of Caxton, rev. for modern use, with an introd. by sir E: Strachey. Lond. 1876. D. **813 : 7**

— The boy's king Arthur; sir Thomas Malory's history of king Arthur and his knights of the round table, ed. for boys by Sidney Lanier. Ill. N. Y. 1880. O. **x 813 : 8**

Hanson, C: H: Stories of the days of king Arthur. Ill. N. Y. 1882. D. **x 813 : 9**

Contents. Merlin the wizard.—How Arthur got his crown, his queen and the Round Table.—The deeds and death of Balin. — The adventures of the hart, the hound and the lady.—The evil devices of Morgan le Fay. — The adventures of the three knights and the three damsels.—Lancelot du Lake.—Sir Gawaine and the green knight. — Sir Beaumain's quest. — Sir Tristam.—Geraint and Enid. — Sir Ewaine and the adventure of the fountain. — The tournament of Lonazep.—The end of the history of the round table and the passing of Arthur.

Boy's Mabinogion; the earliest welsh tales of king Arthur in the famous Red book of Hergest, ed. for boys, with an introd. by Sidney Lanier. Ill. N. Y. 1881. O. **x 813 : 4**

Gibb, J: Gudrun and other stories from the epics of the middle ages. Ill. Lond. 1881. D. **813 : 3**

Contents. Gudrun.—Hilda.—Wild Hagen.—Beowulf.—The death of Roland.—Walter and Hildegund.—Concluding chapter.

Baldwin, James. The story of Roland. Ill. N. Y. 1883. D. **x 813 : 10**

Moncrieff, Robert Hope, *(Ascott R. Hope).* The

x denotes books specially adapted for children.

old tales of chivalry, re-told by Ascott R. Hope. Ill. Lond. *n. d.* S.   **x 813 : 5**

Contents. Introd.—The knight of the lion.—Huon's task.—The dragon of Rhodes.—The rescue of the queen.—Roland and Oliver.—Florice and Blanche-flower.—The ransom.—The son of Amadis.—The knight and the abbot.—Steel Heart.—The demon knight.—The challenge.

Gesta romanorum ; the ancient moral tales of the old story-tellers. Lond. *n. d.* D.   **813 : 11**

Mediæval tales ; with an introd. by H: Morley. Lond. 1884. D.   **813 : 15**

Contents. Turpin's history of Charles the great and Orlando. — Ballad romance touching the days of Charlemagne and of the Cid Campeador, with the ballad of count Alarcos.—Tales from the Gesta ro-manorum.—A discourse of the most famous dr. J: Faustus.

*   *   *

Note. A complete class-list of prose fiction will be found after class 819, and immediately after the class-list of dramas.

4. Rhetoric and Oratory.

The art.

Bardeen, C. W. A system of rhetoric. N. Y. 1884. D.   **815.2 : 18**

Becker, K: Ferdinand. Der deutsche stil ; neu bearb. von O: Lyon. 3te aufl. Leipz. 1884. O.   **815.2 : 20**

Bell, Alexander Melville. The faults of speech ; a self-corrector and teacher's manual. Salem. 1880. S.   **815.2 : 1**

Blair, Hugh. Lectures on rhetoric and belles lettres ; with a memoir of the author's life. Added, copious questions and an analysis of each lecture. Phila. 1858. O.   **815.2 : 2**

Delaumosne, *Abbé.* The art of oratory ; system of Delsarte. From the french by Frances A. Shaw. Albany. 1882. D.   **815.2 : 11**

Guttmann, Oskar. Aesthetic physical culture ; a self-instructor for all cultured circles, and especially for oratorical and dramatic artists. Ill. Albany. 1884. O.   **815.2 : 16**

Hill, Adams Sherman. The principles of rhe-toric, and their application ; with an app. comprising general rules for punctuation. N. Y. 1878. D.   **815.2 : 3**

Legouvé, Gabriel Baptiste Ernest Wilfrid. The art of reading. Tr. and ill. with copious notes, mainly biographical, by E: Roth. Phila. 1879. D.   **815.2 : 4**

Mathews, W: Oratory and orators. Chicago. 1879. D.   **815.2 : 5**

Maury, J: Siffrein. The principles of eloquence; with an introd. etc., by A. Potter. [School dist. lib.] N. Y. 1842. S.   **815.2 : 12**

Murdoch, James E. A plea for spoken lan-guage ; an essay upon comparative elocu-tion. Cinc. [1883]. D.   **815.2 : 15**

Nichol, J: English composition. (Literature primers.) N. Y. 1879. S.   **815.2 : 6**

Phelps, Austin. English style in public dis-course, with special reference to the usages of the pulpit. N. Y. 1883. D.   **815.2 : 13**

Pittenger, W: Extempore speech ; how to ac-quire and practice it. Phila. 1883. D.   **815.2 : 14**

x denotes books specially adapted for children.

Quintilianus, Marcus Fabius. Institutes of ora-tory, or Education of an orator ; in 12 books, literally tr. with notes by J: Selby Watson. Lond. 1856. 2 v. D.   **815.2 : 7**

Rush, James. The philosophy of the human voice ; embracing its physiological history, together with a system of principles by which criticism in the art of elocution may be rendered intelligible, and instruction definite and comprehensive. Added, a brief analysis of song and recitative. 4th ed. enl. Phila. 1855. O.   **815.2+8**

Sheridan, T: Lectures on the art of reading. Lond. 1775. 2 v. O.   **815.2 : 19**

Contents. V. 1. The art of reading prose. 2. The art of reading poetry.

Shoemaker, J. W. Practical elocution ; for use in colleges and schools and by private stu-dents. Phila. 1883. D.   **815.2 : 17**

Theremin, L: F: Franz. Eloquence a virtue, or Outlines of a systematic rhetoric. Tr. from the german by W: G. T. Shedd, with an introd. essay. Rev. ed. Andover. 1882. D.   **815.2 : 10**

Whately, R: Elements of rhetoric ; comprising an analysis of the laws of moral evidence and of persuasion, with rules for argumen-tative composition and elocution. New ed. rev. by the author. Bost. 1860. D.   **815.2 : 9**

Benedix, Roderich. Der mündliche vortrag ; ein lehrbuch für schulen und zum selbstun-terricht. [1ster t.] 4te, [2ter und 3ter t.] 3te durchgesehene aufl. Leipz. 1873-77. O.   **815.2 : 21**

Contents. Die reine und deutliche aussprache des hoch-deutschen. — Die richtige betonung und die rythmik der deutschen sprache.—Die schönheit des vortrags, (declamationslehre).

Selections.

Manchester, Harriet E. What to read and where to find it ; a list of over 200 good selections for reading and recitation, with directions where to look for the same. Buffalo. 1880. S.   **815 : 1**

Baker, G: M., *ed.* The reading-club and handy speaker ; serious, humorous, pathetic, patriotic and dramatic selections in prose and poetry, for readings and recitations ; no. 1-14. Bost. [1874-85]. 14 v. S.   **815 : 4**

Coates, H: T., *ed.* The comprehensive speaker ; designed for the use of schools, academies, lyceums, etc., carefully selected from the best authors with notes. Phila. *n. d.* D.   **815 : 2**

Dickens, C: J: Huffam. The Dickens reader ; character readings from the stories of Dickens ; sel., adapted and arr. by Nathan Sheppard. (Frank. sq. lib.) N. Y. 1882. Q.   **815+3**

Shoemaker, J. W., *ed.* The elocutionist's an-nual, comprising new and popular read-ings, recitations, declamations, dialogues, tableaux, etc. Phila. 1881-84. 12 v. D.   **815 : 5**

5. Quotations.

Bartlett, J: A collection of familiar quotations, with complete indices of authors and sub-jects. 3d ed., with supp. Cambridge. 1858. D.   **819 : 16**

Bartlett, J:—*Continued.*
— Familiar quotations ; an attempt to trace to their sources passages and phrases in common use. 7th ed. Bost. 1878. D.   **819 : 17**
— *Same.* 8th ed., enl. Bost. 1882. D.
                     819 : R18
Hoyt, J. K., *and* Anna L. **Ward.** Cyclopaedia of practical quotations, english and latin ; with app. containing proverbs from the latin and modern foreign languages, law and ecclesiastical terms and significations, dates and nationality of quoted authors, etc., with indexes. N. Y. 1882 [1881]. O.
                     819 : R19
Handy book, The, of quotations, or Who wrote it ? A dictionary of common poetical quotations in the english language. N. Y. 1881. S.   **829.3 : 1**
Elmes, James, *ed.* Classic quotations ; a thought-book of the wise spirits of all ages and all countries, fit for all men and all hours. N. Y. 1863. S.   **819 : 3**
Edwards, Tryon. The world's laconics, or The best thoughts of the best authors in prose and poetry ; with an introd. by W: B. Sprague. N. Y. 1856. D.   **819 : 4**
Watson, J: T., *comp.* Poetical quotations, or Elegant extracts on every subject. Phila. 1865. D.   **819 : 23**
Bohn, H: G: A dictionary of quotations from the english poets. Lond. 1881. O. **829.3 : 2**

6. Proverbs and Fables.

Trench, R: Chenevix. On the lessons in proverbs ; the substance of lectures delivered to young men's societies at Portsmouth and elsewhere. From the 2d Lond. ed. rev. and enl. N. Y. 1859. D.   **819 : 21**
Düringsfeld, Ida *and* O: *freiherr* v. **Reinsberg-.** Sprichwörter der germanischen und romanischen sprachen, vergleichend zusammengestellt. Leipz. 1872. 2 v. O. **819+22**
Bohn, H: G: A polyglot of foreign proverbs ; comprising french, italian, german, dutch, spanish, portuguese and danish, with english translations and a general index. Lond. 1857. D.   **819 : 1**
Select proverbs of all nations ; pastimes, holidays and customs of olden times, wise sayings and maxims of the ancient fathers and the economy of human life, by an ancient bramin. Dayton, O. 1854. D.   **819 : 20**
Long, J. Eastern proverbs and emblems, illustrating old truths. [Eng. and foreign phil. lib.] Lond. 1881. O.   **819 : 13**
Bussey, G: Moir. Fables, original and selected ; with an introd. dissertation on the history of fable, comprising biograph. notices of eminent fabulists. N. Y. 1865. O. **819 : 12**
Bourne, W: Oland. Gems from fableland ; a collection of fables illustrated by facts. N. Y. 1853. D.   **819 : 11**

7. Anecdotes and Miscellany.

Bent, S: Arthur. Short sayings of great men, with historical and explanatory notes. Bost. 1882. O.   **819 : 15**
Byerley, T:, *and* Joseph Clinton **Robertson.** The Percy anecdotes. Rev. ed., added a

collection of american anecdotes, original and select. [*Anon.*] N. Y. 1863. 2 v. in 1. O.   **819+10**
Hoes, —, *and* — **Way.** Anecdotical olio ; a collection of literary, moral, religious and miscellaneous anecdotes. N. Y. 1858. O.
                     819 : 5
Kirkland, Frazar. Cyclopædia of commercial and business anecdotes ; interesting reminiscences and facts, remarkable traits and humors and notable sayings, dealings, experiences and witticisms of merchants, traders, bankers, mercantile celebrities, millionaires, bargain makers, etc., in all ages, designed to exhibit the piquancies and pleasantries of trade, commerce and general business pursuits. Ill. N. Y. 1864. 2 v. O.   **819+6**
— *Same*, v. 2. N. Y. 1865. O.   **819+6 v2**
Bigelow, L. J. Bench and bar ; a complete digest of the wit, humor, asperities and amenities of the law. New ed. enl. Portr. and ill. N. Y. 1871. O.   **829 : 1**
Browne, Irving. Law and lawyers in literature. Bost. 1883. D.   **829.1 : 53**
Edwards, C: Pleasantries about courts and lawyers of the state of New York. N. Y. 1867. O.   **829.1 : 56**
Jeaffreson, J: Cordy. A book about lawyers. 2 v. in 1. N. Y. 1867. D.   **829.2 : 18**
   Contents. Houses and householders.—Loves of the lawyers.—Money.—Costume and toilet.—Music.— Amateur theatricals.—Legal education.—Mirth.—At home.—In court.—In society.
Purves, D. Laing. Law and lawyers ; curious facts and characteristic sketches. [*Anon.*] Phila. *n. d.* S.   **829.2 : 46**

         *   *   *

Cox, S: Sullivan. Why we laugh. (Frank. sq. lib.) N. Y. 1883. Q.   **818+1**
Knight, C: Half hours with the best authors, selected and arr., with short biograph. and and critical notes. N. Y. 1856. 4 v. O.
                     819 : 7
Disraeli, I: Curiosities of literature ; with a view of the life and writings of the author, by his son. Bost. 1859. 4 v. S.   **819 : 2**
   Contents, see Catalogue of the Boston athenæum, pt. 2, p. 788.
Pell, Robert Cruger. Milledulcia ; a thousand pleasant things, selected from notes and queries. [*Anon.*] N. Y. 1860. D. **819 : 9**
Goodrich, S: Griswold. Peter Parley's merry stories, or Fact, fancy and fiction ; a collection of very merry stories, anecdotes, etc., by the renowned Peter Parley. N. Y. [1869]. D.   **819 : 14**
Lowell, Anna Cabot, *born* Jackson, *mrs.* C: Russell, *ed.* Seed-grain for thought and discussion. Bost. 1856. 2 v. D.   **819 : 8**
   Contents. V. 1. Pt. 1. Holy living. Pt. 2. Man's connection with the infinite.—Faith and reason, man's interpreters.—Instinct and emotion guides.— Two worlds.—Man a doer and a receiver.—The whole character on one level.—Development of the moral sense. Pt. 3. Happiness.—Life.—Man's highest relations.—Virtues and duties. 2. Pt. 3, *continued.* The cure of faults. — Temptations and duties. Pt. 4. Relations to the body ; personal.—Relations to other men : society.—Conversation and manners.—Friendship.— Home life.— Love.—Plain living and high thinking.—Work. Pt. 5. Circumstances.—Every part of the nature of use.—Culture of every part.—Various gifts and various characters.—Life earnest for all.—Different eras and careers.

3. Class-list of drama.

(For history, *see* col. 513; for the opera, *see* cl. 782, col. 494; for the stage, *see* cl. 792, col. 497-498).

1. Authors.

Note. In the following, **Lacy** refers to Lacy's Acting plays, v. 1-100, and **French's** to French's continuation of the same collection, v. 101-122.

A. S. S.: farce in 1 act. *In* Lacy. 812 : 1 **v10**
A'Beckett, Gilbert Abbott. The assignation, or What will my wife say ; a drama in 2 acts. *In* French's. 812 : 1 **v120**
— Glitter ; original comedy in 2 acts. *In* Lacy. 812 : 1 **v83**
— In the clouds ; a glimpse of Utopia ; fairy extravaganza. *In* Lacy. 812 : 1 **v100**
— The last of the legends, or The baron, the bride and the battery ; a psychological extravaganza. *In* Lacy. 812 : 1 **v99**
— Lending a hand ; a farce in 1 act. *In* Lacy. 812 : 1 **v69**
— The man with the carpet bag ; a farce in 1 act. 812 : 1 **v68**
— The siamese twins ; a farce in 1 act. *In* Lacy. 812 : 1 **v79**
— The turned head ; farce in 1 act. *In* Lacy. 812 : 1 **v67**
Addison, H: R. Locked in with a lady ; a sketch from life. *In* Lacy. 812 : 1 **v11**
— 117 Arundel street, Strand ; a farce in 1 act. *In* Lacy. 812 : 1 **v48**
— Sophia's supper ; farce in 1 act. *In* Lacy. 812 : 1 **v16**
Addison, Joseph. Cato ; tragedy in 5 acts. *In his* Poetical works. 821.2 : 18
— *Same. In* British drama. 822.2 : 1 **v1**
— *Same. In* Lacy. 812 : 1 **v99**
— The drummer, or The haunted house ; comedy in 5 acts. *In his* Poetical works. 821.2 : 18
— *Same. In* British drama. 822.2 : 1 **v2**
Aeschylus, *see* **Aischylos.**
After the party ; comedy in 1 act. *In* Lacy. 812 : 1 **v93**
Aikin, G: L. Uncle Tom's cabin ; a drama of real life in 3 acts, adapted from mrs. Beecher Stowe's celebrated novel. *In* Lacy. 812 : 1 **v12**
Aikin, L. Alfred. Ahmed. *In* Follen, E. L. Home dramas. 822.1 : 9
— The cobbler. *In the same.* 822.1 : 9
— Master and slave. *In the same.* 822.1 : 9
— The sword. *In the same.* 822.1 : 9
Aischylos, (*latin* Æschylus). [Tragedies.] Tr. by R. Potter. N. Y. *n. d.* S. 882 : 1
  Contents. Essay on the grecian drama.—Prometheus chained.—The supplicants.—The seven chiefs against Thebes.—Agamemnon.—The choephorae.—The furies.—The persians.
Albery, James. Two roses ; an original comedy in 2 acts. *In* French's. 812 : 1 **v118**
Albini, *pseud., see* **Meddlhammer,** J: Baptist v.

Alger, Horatio, *jr., and* O. Augusta **Cheney.** Seeking his fortune, and other dialogues. Bost. 1875. S. 822.1 : 1
Allen, James, *joint author, see* **Dilley,** Joseph J.
Allingham, J: Till. Fortune's frolic ; farce in 2 acts. *In* British drama. 822.2 : 1 **v1**
— *Same. In* Lacy. 812 : 1 **v60**
— The weathercock ; a farce. *In* Lacy. 812 : 1 **v71**
Almar, G: The charcoal-burner, or The dropping well of Knaresborough ; a drama in 2 acts. *In* Lacy. 812 : 1 **v71**
— Crossing the line, or Crowded houses ; a farce in 2 acts. *In* Lacy. 812 : 1 **v35**
— The fire raiser ; melo-drama in 2 acts. *In* Lacy. 812 : 1 **v84**
— The knights of St. John, or The fire banner ; a melo-drama in 2 acts. *In* Lacy. 812 : 1 **v56**
— Oliver Twist, or The parish boy's progress ; a drama in 3 acts, adapted from the novel by C: Dickens. *In* Lacy. 812 : 1 **v33**
— The robber of the Rhine ; melo-drama in 2 acts. *In* Lacy. 812 : 1 **v87**
— The rover's bride, or The bittern's swamp ; a romantic drama in 2 acts. *In* French's. 812 : 1 **v119**
— The wife of seven husbands, a legend of Pedlar's Acre ; a melo-drama in 3 acts. *In* Lacy. 812 : 1 **v74**
Amcotts, Vincent. Adonis vanquished ; comedy in 2 acts, adapted from "Le dégel" [by V. Sardou]. *In* Lacy. 812 : 1 **v75**
Amherst, J. A. The battle of Waterloo ; grand military drama in 3 acts. *In* Lacy. 812 : 1 **v98**
— Ireland as it was ; drama in 2 acts. *In* Lacy. 812 : 1 **v81**
— Napoleon Bonaparte's invasion of Russia, or The conflagration of Moscow ; military and equestrian spectacle in 3 acts. *In* Lacy. 812 : 1 **v13**
Andersen, Hans Christian. Dramatische schriften und gedichte. Leipz. *n. d.* S. 898.3 : 1
  Contents. Raphaella; trag. in 5 aufz.—Agnete und der meermann; dramatisches gedicht in 2 abtb.—Der mulatte; romantisches drama in 5 acten.—Die glücksblume; mährchen-komödie in 2 aufz.—Ahasverus; dramatisches gedicht in 4 abth.—Gedichte.
Anderson, James. Cloud and sunshine, or Love's revenge ; original drama in 4 acts. *In* Lacy. 812 : 1 **v87**
Angus, J. Keith. By this token ; an original comedietta. *In* French's. 812 : 1 **v122**
— Send thirty stamps ; an original farce. *In* French's. 812 : 1 **v122**

Arbuthnot, *Capt.* —. L'africaine, or The bell of Madagascar ; a burlesque in 1 act. *In* Lacy. **812 : 1 v67**

Archer, T: The inundation, or The miser of the hill fort ; a drama in 3 acts. *In* Lacy. **812 : 1 v45**

— Marguerite's colours, or Passing the frontier ; a comic drama in 2 acts, adapted from the french. *In* Lacy. **812 : 1 v47**

— The three red men, or The brothers of Bluthhaupt ; a romantic drama in 3 acts. *In* Lacy. **812 : 1 v41**

— *and* J: Cargill Brough. An eligible situation ; an eccentricity. *In* Scott, C. W. Drawing-room plays. **822.2 : 14**

Aristophanês. Die vögel ; übersetzt von J: W. v. Goethe. *In* Göthe, J: W. v. Werke. *in* **830 : 137 v22**

Arnim, L: Achim v. Halle und Jerusalem ; studentenspiel und pilgerabenteuer. Berlin. 1853. Q. **832 : 101**

Arnold, H: T:, (*Henry T. Arden*). The belle of the barley-mow, or The wooer, the waitress and the willian. *In* Lacy. **812 : 1 v78**

— Princess Charming, or The bard, the baron, the beauty, the buffer and the bogey. *In* Lacy. **812 : 1 v76**

Arnold, K: Der goldene boden, oder Bureau und boutique ; lustsp. in 2 acten. *n. t.* D. **832 : 3**

Arnold, W. H. The woodman's hut, or The burning forest ; a melo-drama in 2 acts. *In* Lacy. **812 : 1 v36**

Arnould, A:, *joint author, see* Simon, Joseph Philippe.

Auffenberg, Josef *freiherr* v. Sämmtliche werke. Wiesbaden. 1855. 22 v. S. **832 : 4**
Contents. V. 1. Pizarro. — Die spartaner. — Der schwärze Fritz. 2. Die Bartholomäus-nacht. — Die flibustier. 3. Wallace.—Die syracuser. 4. Die vorschau.—König Erich. 5. Das opfer des Themistocles.—Die verbannten, 6. Die schwestern von Amiens.—Fergus Mac Ivor. 7. Das nordlicht von Kasan.—Der schwur des richters. — Der prophet von Florenz.—8. Ludwig der eilfte in Peronne.—Das böse haus.—Der löwe von Kurdistan. 9. *Alhambra, 1. t.:* Boabdil in Kordova.—Abenhamet und Alfaïma. 10. *Alhambra, 2. t.:* Die gründung von Santa Fé. 11-14. *Alhambra, 3. t.:* Die eroberung von Granada. 15. Der renegat von Granada. 16. Berthold, der Zähringer.—Die raketen des teufels. 17. Die hexe von Pultawa.—Das nordlicht von Karlsruhe.—Cäsar Morbel's testament.—Denkschrift des Holofernus Spontenknabel. 18. Die furie von Toledo ; roman. 19. Humoristische pilgerfahrt nach Granada und Kordova in 1832. 20. Polyanthea ; gedichte. 21. Skanderbeg. 22. Timur in Tauris.

— Der flibustier, oder Die eroberung von Panama ; ein romantisches trauerspiel in 4 akten. Bamberg. 1819. D. **832 : 5**

Augier, Guillaume V: Émile. Good for evil or A wife's trial ; a domestic lesson in 2 acts, adapted from the french. *In* Lacy. **812 : 1 v43**

Austin, Alfred. Savonarola ; a tragedy. Lond. 1881. D. **822.2 : 43**

Ayres, Arthur, *and* Paul Blake. His own guest ; a comedy in 3 acts. *In* French's. **812 : 1 v120**

Aytoun, W: Edmondstoune. Firmilian ; a "spasmodic" tragedy by T. Percy Jones. N. Y. 1854. **822.2 : 14**

B., A. The girls of the period. *In* Scott, C. W. Drawing-room plays. **822.2 : 4**

Babo, Joseph Marius. Dagobert, king of the franks ; a tragedy in 5 acts. *In* Thompson, B: German theatre. **832 : 96 v4**

Babo, Ioseph Marius.—*Continued.*
— Otto of Wittelsbach, or The choleric count ; a tragedy in 5 acts. *In the same.* **832 : 96 v4**

Baddeley, G. C. The end of the tether, or A legend of the patent office ; an original drama in 2 acts. *In* Lacy. **812 : 1 v74**

Baillie, Joanna. Miscellaneous plays. Lond. 1805. O. **822.2 : 16**
Contents. Rayner.—The country inn.—Constantine Paleologus, or The last of the Cæsars.

— A series of plays in which it is attempted to delineate the stronger passions of the mind, each passion being the subject of a tragedy and a comedy ; v. 2, 3. Lond. 1802, 1812. 2 v. O. **822.2 : 15**
Contents. v. 2. The election. — Ethwald. — The second marriage. 3. Orra.—The dream.—The siege.—The beacon.—The family legend.

Baker, G: M. A baker's dozen ; original humorous dialogues. Bost. *n. d.* S. **822.1 : 19**
Contents. The thief of time. — The hypochondriac.—A public benefactor.—The runaways.— Ignorance is bliss.—The rival politicians.—Coals of fire.—Santa Claus' frolics.—A stitch in time saves nine.—The red chignon.—Using the weed.—A love of a bonnet.—A precious pickle.

— The drawing-room stage ; a series of original dramas, comedies, farces and entertainments for amateur theatricals and school exhibitions. Ill. Bost. 1873. D. **822.1 : 1**
Contents. My brother's keeper.—The revolt of the bees.—A tender attachment.—Among the breakers.—Gentlemen of the jury.—The seven ages.—The Boston dip.—The duchess of Dublin.

— Handy dramas for amateur actors ; new pieces for home, school and public entertainment. Ill. Bost. 1877. S. **822.1 : 4**
Contents. The flower of the family.—A mysterious disappearance.—Above the clouds.—Shall our mothers vote ?—Paddle your own canoe. — One hundred years ago. — The little brown jug.—Seeing the elephant.

— The mimic stage ; a series of dramas, comedies, burlesques and farces for public exhibitions and private theatricals. Bost. 1875. D. **822.1 : 2**
Contents. Down by the sea.—A close shave.—Capuletta. — The great elixir.—The man with the demijohn.—An original idea.—My uncle the captain.—No cure, no pay.—Humors of the strike.—Bread on the waters.

— The social stage ; original dramas, comedies, burlesques and entertainments for home recreation, schools and public exhibitions. Bost. 1875. D. **822.1 : 6**
Contents. The last loaf.—Too late for the train.—A grecian bend.—Snow-bound.—Bonbons.—Lightheart's pilgrimage.—The wars of the roses.—Thirty minutes for refreshments.—A little more cider.—New brooms sweep clean.

Banim, J: Damon and Pythias ; play in 5 acts. *In* Sargent, E. Mod. stand. drama. **822.2 : 2 v5**

— The sergeant's wife ; drama in 2 acts, taken from the author's tales of the O'Hara family. *In* Lacy. **812 : 1 v23**

Barber, James. The memoirs of the devil, or The mystic bell of Ronquerolles ; an eccentric drama in 3 acts. *In* French's. **812 : 1 v116**

— The weaver of Lyons, or The three conscripts ; a farce in 1 act. *In* French's. **812 : 1 v110**

Barbier, Paul Jules, *joint author, see* Carré, Michel.

Barefaced impostors ; a farce in 1 act. *In* Lacy.
812 : 1 v70

Barnett, C. Z. A christmas carol, or The miser's warning ; adapted from C: Dickens. *In* Lacy. 812 : 1 v94

— Midnight, the thirteenth chime, or Old St. Paul's ; a melo-drama in 3 acts. *In* French's. 812 : 1 v101

Barnett, Morris. The bold dragoons ; an original comic drama in 2 acts. *In* Lacy.
812 : 1 v9

— Lilian Gervais ; a drama in 3 acts. *In* Lacy.
812 : 1 v31

— Married unmarried ; drama in 2 acts. *In* Lacy. 812 : 1 v14

— Monsieur Jacques ; a musical piece. *In* Lacy.
812 : 1 v28

— Sarah the creole, or A snake in the grass ; a drama in 5 acts. *In* Lacy. 812 : 1 v31

— *and* B. Out on the loose ; a farce in 1 act. *In* Lacy. 812 : 1 v2

Barrière, Théodore, *and* H: de Kock. The old house on the bridge of Notre Dame ; a drama in 3 acts, adapted from the french. *In* Lacy. 812 : 1 v50

— *and* É: Plouvier. The angel of midnight ; a legend of terror in 3 acts, adapted from the french by W. E. Suter and T. H. Lacy. *In* Lacy. 812 : 1 v51

Barrymore, W: El Hyder, the chief of the Ghaut mountains ; a grand eastern melodramatic spectacle in 2 acts. *In* Lacy.
812 : 1 v6

— The secret ; a farce in 1 act, adapted from the french. *In* Lacy. 812 : 1 v48

— Wallace, the hero of Scotland ; a romantic historical drama in 3 acts. *In* Lacy.
812 : 1 v73

Battu, Léon, *joint author, see* Carré, Michel.

Bauernfeld, E: v. [Anthologie.] *in* 928.3 : 1

— Ernst und humor ; lustsp. in 4 aufz. n. t. D.
832 : 6

— Der literarische salon ; lustsp. in 3 aufz. n. t. D. 832 : 7

— Der musicus von Augsburg ; lustsp. in 2 aufz. n. t. D. 832 : 8

Bayly, T: Haynes. Comfortable service ; an original farce in 1 act. *In* Lacy.
812 : 1 v1

— The daughter ; a drama in 1 act. *In* Lacy.
812 : 1 v1

— How do you manage ? farce in 1 act. *In* Lacy.
812 : 1 v1

— Perfection, or The lady of Munster ; comedy in 1 act. *In* Lacy. 812 : 1 v13

— The Spitalfields weaver ; comic drama in 1 act, adapted from the french. *In* Lacy.
812 : 1 v21

— The swiss cottage, or Why don't she marry ? vaudeville in 1 act. *In* Lacy. 812 : 1 v1

Beaumarchais, P: Augustin Caron *called* de. The barber of Seville ; opera in 2 acts, adapted by Mr. Fawcett. *In* Lacy.
812 : 1 v89

Beaumont, Francis, *and* James Fletcher. Works ; the text formed from a new collation of the early editions, with notes and a biographical memoir by Alexander Dyce. Lond. 1843. 11 v. O. 822.2 : 8

Contents. V. 1. Biographical memoir, dedication, etc.—Commendatory poems.— The woman-hater.—Thierry and Theodoret.—Philaster.—The maid's tragedy. **2.** The faithful shepherdess.—The knight of

Beaumont, F., *and* J. Fletcher.—*Continued.*
the burning pestle.—A king and no king.—Cupid's revenge.—The masque of the Inner Temple and Grays Inn.—Four plays in one. **3.** The scornful lady.— The coxcomb.— The captain.— The honest man's fortune.—The little french lawyer. **4.** Wit at several weapons.—Wit without money.—The faithful friends.—The widow.—The custom of the country. **5.** Bonduca.—The knight of Malta.—Valentinian.— The laws of Candy. — The queen of Corinth. **6.** The loyal subject.—The mad lover.—The false one.— The double marriage. — The humorous lieutenant. **7.** Women pleased. — The woman's prize. — The chances.— Monsieur Thomas.—The island princess. **8.** The pilgrim.—The wild-goose-chase.—The prophetess. —The sea voyage. —The spanish curate. **9.** Beggar's bush.—Love's cure.—The maid in the mill.— A wife for a month. — Rule a wife and have a wife. **10.** The fair maid of the inn.—The noble gentleman. —The elder brother. — The nice valour. — The bloody brother. **11.** The lovers' progress. — The night walker. — Love's pilgrimage. — The two noble kinsmen.—Poems by Beaumont.—Poems by Fletcher.— Index to notes.

— — The chances ; comedy in 5 acts, altered by the duke of Buckingham. *In* British drama. 822.2 : 1 v2

— — Rule a wife and have a wife. *In the same.*
822.2 : 1 v2

— *See also* Knowles, J. S. The bridal.

Beauvoir, E: Roger de, *pseud., see* Bully, E: Roger de.

Beazley, S: Is he jealous ? a farce in 1 act. *In* French's. 812 : 1 v117

— The lottery ticket, or The lawyer's clerk ; a farce in 1 act. *In* Lacy. 812 : 1 v68

Beazley, S:, *jr.* The boarding house, or Five hours at Brighton ; a musical farce in 2 acts. *In* French's. 812 : 1 v121

Becher, Martin. A crimeless criminal ; a farce. *In* French's. 812 : 1 v101

— In possession ; farce in 1 act. *In* Lacy.
812 : 1 v95

— No. 6 Duke street ; farce. *In* Lacy. 812 : 1 v93

— Painless dentistry ; a farce. *In* French's.
812 : 1 v106

— A poetic proposal ; farce in 1 act. *In* Lacy.
812 : 1 v96

Bellingham, H:, *and* — Best. Prince Camaralzaman, or The fairie's revenge ; a new and original fairy extravaganza. *In* Lacy.
812 : 1 v67

— — Princess Primrose and the four pretty princes ; burlesque extravaganza. *In* Lacy.
812 : 1 v68

Benedix, Julius Roderich. Gesammelte dramatische werke ; v. 12. Leipz. 1860. D.
832 : 9

Contents. Ohne pass.—Junker Otto.—Die stiefmutter.—Nein.—Das dienstmädchen.—Die grossmutter.

Bernard, W: Bayle. The balance of comfort ; petite comedy in 1 act. *In* Lacy.
812 : 1 v17

— The dumb belle ; comedietta in 1 act, with alterations and add. *In* Lacy. 812 : 1 v23

— The evil genius ; an original comedy in 3 acts. *In* Lacy. 812 : 1 v26

— The farmer's story ; a domestic drama in 3 acts. *In* Lacy. 812 : 1 v44

— The four sisters ; farce in 1 act. *In* Lacy.
812 : 1 v23

— The happiest man alive ; petite comedy in 1 act. *In* Lacy. 812 : 1 v19

— A life's trial ; an original drama in 3 acts. *In* Lacy. 812 : 1 v30

— Lucille, or The story of the heart ; a drama in 3 acts. *In* Lacy. 812 : 1 v28

Bernard, W: Bayle.—*Continued.*
— The man about town ; a farce in 1 act. *In* French's. 812 : 1 v118
— The man of two lives ! new romantic play in 3 acts and a p ologu ; founded on Les misérables of V:rHugo.e *In* Lacy. 812 : 1 v85
— Marie Ducange ; an original domestic drama in 3 acts. *In* Lacy. 812 : 1 v32
— The middy ashore ; a farce in 1 act. *In* Lacy. 812 : 1 v48
— The mummy ; a farce in 1 act. *In* Lacy. 812 : 1 v53
— The nervous man and the man of nerve ; farce in 2 acts. *In* **Sargent**, E. Mod. stand. drama. 822.2 : 2 v5
— *Same. In* Lacy. 812 : 1 v39
— The passing cloud ; romantic drama in 2 acts. 812 : 1 v1
— Platonic attachments ; an original farce in 1 act. *In* Lacy. 812 : 1 v2
— A practical man ; farce in 1 act. *In* Lacy. 812 : 1 v1
— St. Mary's eve, or A Solway story ; an original domestic drama in 2 acts. *In* Lacy. 812 : 1 v33
— A splendid investment ; an original farce in 1 act. *In* Lacy. 812 : 1 v30
— A storm in a tea cup ; comedietta in 1 act. *In* Lacy. 812 : 1 v14
— The tide of time ; an original comedy in 3 acts. *In* Lacy. 812 : 1 v38
Berrie, E. Captain Smith ; farce in 1 act. *In* Lacy. 812 : 1 v89
Besant, Walter, *and* James Rice. Philanthropy ; an original comedy in 3 acts. *In* French's. 812 : 1 v112
— Ready-money ; a drama in 4 acts. *In* French's. 812 : 1 v104
Best, —, *joint author, see* **Bellingham**, H:
Bickerstaff, I: The hypocrite ; comedy in 5 acts. *In* British drama. 822.2 : 1 v1
— *Same. In* Lacy. 812 : 1 v76
— Lionel and Clarissa, or A school for fathers ; comic opera in 3 acts. *In* British drama. 822.2 : 1 v2
— Love in a village ; comic opera in 3 acts. *In the same.* 822.2 : 1 v2
— The padlock ; comic opera in 2 acts. *In the same.* 822.2 : 1 v1
— The recruiting sergeant ; musical entertainment in 1 act. *In the same.* 822.2 : 1 v1
Biez, Jacques de. The first love-letter. *In* Plays for private acting. 812 : 2
Bilkins, Taylor. A christmas pantomime ; original farcical extravaganza. *In* Lacy. 812 : 1 v95
— In three volumes ; original farce in 1 act. *In* Lacy. 812 : 1 v91
Birch-Pfeiffer, Charlotte. Ulrich Zwingli's tod ; historisches trauerspiel in 5 aufz. Schw. Hall. n. d. D. 832 : 10
Blake, Paul, *joint author, see* **Ayres**, Arthur.
Blake, T: G. Lonely man of the ocean, or The night before the bridal ; drama in 3 acts. *In* Lacy. 812 : 1 v16
— Our old house at home ; domestic drama in 2 acts. *In* Lacy. 812 : 1 v25
— A spanking legacy, or The corsican vendetta ; a farce in 1 act. *In* Lacy. 812 : 1 v6

Blanchard, E: Laman. The artful dodge ; a farce in 1 act. *In* Lacy. 812 : 1 v42
— Harlequin Hudibras, or Old dame Durden and the droll days of the merry monarch ; a new, grand, poetical, historical, operatical, dramatical, anachronismatical, tragical, pastoral christmas pantomime. *In* Lacy. 812 : 1 v9
— An induction, *and* The three temptations ; a masque for the moderns, novel, allegorical, musical and spectacular. *In* Scott, C. W. Drawing room plays. 822.2 : 14
— Pork chops, or A dream at home ; a farcical extravaganza in 1 act. *In* Lacy. 812 : 1 v45
Blum, K:, *tr.* Neue theaterspiele, zunächst für die königliche schaubühne zu Berlin bearbeitet. Berlin. 1830. 1 v. in 2. D. 832 : 11
  Contents. V. 1. **Scribe**, A. E. Der schönste tag des lebens.—**Scribe**, A. E. Die nachtwandlerin. 2. Ein abend vor dem Potsdamer thore.—Riquet, der haarbüschel, nach Brazier.
Bodmer, J: Jakob. Gottsched ; ein trauerspiel in versen, oder Der parodirte Cato. *In* **Kürschner,** J. Deutsche national-literatur. 830 : 152 v42
Boker, G: H: Plays and poems. Bost. 1856. 2 v. D. 822.1 : 7
  Contents. V. 1. Calaynos ; a tragedy. — Anne Boleyn ; a tragedy.—Leonor de Guzman.—Francesca da Rimini. 2. The betrothal.—The widow's marriage.—Poems.—Songs.—Sonnets.
Bolton, C: Caught in a line, or The unrivalled Blondin ; a pièce de circonstance in 1 scene. *In* Lacy. 812 : 1 v54
Börnstein, C: Hugo. Ein ungarkönig ; historisches drama in 4 akten. Pesth. 1847. D. 832 : 50
Boucicault, Dion. The Colleen Bawn, or The brides of Garryowen ; a domestic drama in 3 acts. *In* Lacy. 812 : 1 v63
— Jessie Brown, or The relief of Lucknow ; a drama in 3 acts. *In* Lacy. 812 : 1 v38
— London assurance ; a comedy in 5 acts. *In* Lacy. 812 : 1 v34
— The octoroon, or Life in Louisiana ; a play in 4 acts. *In* Lacy. 812 : 1 v65
— The prima donna ; a comedy in 2 acts. *In* Lacy. 812 : 1 v8
— The queen of spades ; a drama in 2 acts, adapted from "La dame de pique" [by Scribe.] *In* Lacy. 812 : 1 v24
Bourgeois, A: Anicet, *and* Ferdinand Dugué. The pirates of the savannah, or The tiger hunter of the p i i s ; romantic drama in 3 acts, adapted by W: Suter. *In* Lacy. 812 : 1 v51
— *and* Philippe François Pinel Dumanoir. The black doctor ; drama in 5 acts. Tr. from "Le docteur noir" by I. V. Bridgeman. *In* Lacy. 812 : 1 v23
— *and* Paul H: Corentin Féval. The duke's daughter, or The hunchback of Paris ; a drama in 3 acts and a prologue, dramatized from Paul Féval's "Le petit parisien" as "Le bossu." Adapted for the english stage. *In* Lacy. 812 : 1 v57
Bourget, Ernest, *joint author, see* Dennery, Adolphe Philippe.
Brachvogel, Albert Emil. Narcisse the vagrant ; a tragedy in five acts, adapted from the german by James Schönberg. *In* French's. 812 : 1 v107

Brawe, Joachim W: v.   Brutus; ein trauerspiel in 5 aufz.   *in* **830 : 152 v72**

Bridgeman, I: V.   A good run for it; farce in 1 act. *In* Lacy.   **812 : 1 v14**

— I've eaten my friend; farce in 1 act. *In* Lacy.   **812 : 1 v5**

— Matrimonial—a gentleman, etc., for further particulars apply at ——; an entirely original farce in 1 act. *In* Lacy.   **812 : 1 v7**

— *Same. In the same.*   **812 : 1 v37**

— The rifle and how to use it; an original farce in 1 act. *In* Lacy.   **812 : 1 v42**

— Where's your wife; an entirely original farce. *In* Lacy.   **812 : 1 v60**

Bridgman, Cunningham V.   Shipmates; an original comedy drama in 3 acts. *In* Lacy.   **812 : 1 v102**

Brigands of Calabria, The; a romantic drama in 1 act. *In* Lacy.   **812 : 1 v65**

Bright, *Mrs.* A: Not false but fickle; comedy drama in 1 act. *In* French's. **812 : 1 v116**

— "Noblesse oblige"; a comedy drama in a prologue and 3 acts. *In* French's.   **812 : 1 v116**

Brinckmann, H.   Johann von Leyden, könig der wiedertäufer zu Münster; schausp. in 5 aufz. Münster. 1855. D.   **832 : 12**

British drama, The; a collection of the most esteemed tragedies, comedies, operas and farces in the english language. Phila. 1854. 2 v. O.   **822.2 : 1**

Contents. V. 1. Lillo, G: Fatal curiosity.—Garrick, D: The guardian; The lying valet.—Murphy, A. The grecian daughter.—Macklin, C: The man of the world.—Murphy, A. The apprentice.—Rowe, N: Jane Shore.—Colman, G: Ways and means.—Coffey, C: The devil to pay.—Rowe, N: The fair penitent.—Centlivre, S. A bold stroke for a wife.—O'Hara, K. Midas.—Home, J: Douglas.—Farquhar, G: The inconstant.—Foote, S: The mayor of Garratt.—Browne, J: Barbarossa.—Bickerstaff, I: The recruiting sergeant.—Jackman, I: Hero and Leander.—Southerne, T: Isabella, or The fatal marriage.—Dibdin, C: The quaker.—Brooke, F. M. Rosina.—Otway, T: Venice preserved.—Centlivre, S. The wonder.—Murphy, A. Three weeks after marriage.—Addison, J. Cato.—Allingham, J: T. Fortune's frolic.—Bickerstaff, I: The padlock.—Young, E. The revenge.—Sheridan, R: B. The rivals.—Colman, G: The deuce is in him.—Brooke, H: Gustavus Vasa.—Goldsmith, O. She stoops to conquer.—Garrick, D: Bon ton.—Otway, T: The orphan.—Massinger, P. A new way to pay old debts.—Cobb, J. The doctor and the apothecary.—Moore, E: The gamester.—Hoadly, B: The suspicious husband.—O'Hara, K. Tom Thumb, the great.—Moore, H. Percy.—Cowley, H. P. The belle's stratagem.—Sheridan, R: B. The critic.—Southerne, T: Oroonoko.—Garrick, D: The country girl; The irish widow.—Lillo, G: Arden of Feversham.—Colman, G: The jealous wife.—Gay, J: The beggar's opera.—Lillo, G: George Barnwell.—Bickerstaff, I: The hypocrite.—Fielding, H: The mock doctor.—Congreve, W: The mourning bride. —Garrick, D:, *and* G: Colman. The clandestine marriage.—Foote, S: The liar.—Thomson, J. Tancred and Sigismunda.—Farquhar, G: The beaux's stratagem.

2. Bickerstaff, I: Lionel and Clarissa.—Hill, A. Zara.—Cumberland, R: The west-indian.—Townley, J. High life below stairs.—Rowe, N: Tamerlane.—Pilon, F: He would be a soldier.—Garrick, D: Miss in her teens.—Philips, A. The distressed mother.—Steele, *Sir* R: The tender husband.—Cowley, H.P. Who's the dupe?—Kotzebue, A: F: F. v. Pizarro.—Jonson, B. Every man in his humour.—Bickerstaff, I: Love in a village.—Jackman, I: All the world's a stage.—Lee, N. Alexander the great.—Murphy, A. The way to keep him.—Sheridan, R: B. The duenna.—Cibber, C. Ximena.—Beaumont, F., *and* J. Fletcher. Rule a wife and have a wife.—Macklin, C: Love à la mode.—Whitehead, W. The roman father.—Congreve, W: Love

for love.—Beaumont, F., *and* J. Fletcher. The chances. — Fielding, H: The intriguing chambermaid.—Dryden, J: All for love.—Vanbrugh, *Sir* J: The city wives' confederacy.—Foote, S: The lame lover.—Jones, H: The earl of Essex.—Cumberland, R: The brothers.—Cibber, C. The careless husband.—Milton, J: Comus.—Murphy, A. The orphan of China.—Vanbrugh, *Sir* J:, *and* C. Cibber. The provoked husband.—Colman, G: Inkle and Yarico.—Miller, J. Mahomet, the impostor.—Addison, J. The drummer.—Farquhar, G: The recruiting officer.—Cobb, J. The first floor.—Hughes, J: The siege of Damascus.—Vanbrugh, *Sir* J: The provoked wife.—Hill, A. Alzira.—Sheridan, R: B. The school for scandal.

Brooke, Francis Moore.   Rosina; an opera in 2 acts. *In* British drama.   **822.2 : 1 v1**

Brooke, H: Gustavus Vasa, or The deliverer of his country; an historical tragedy in 5 acts. *In* British drama.   **822.2 : 1 v1**

Brookes, Sheridan.   Calypso, queen of Ogygia; an original burlesque in 1 act. *In* Lacy.   **812 : 1 v67**

Brooks, C: Shirley.   Anything for a change; petite comedy in 1 act. *In* Lacy.   **812 : 1 v4**

— The creole, or Love's fetters; drama in 3 acts. *In* Lacy.   **812 : 1 v1**

— The exposition; a scandinavian sketch containing as much irrelevant matter as possible in 1 act. *In* Lacy.   **812 : 1 v3**

— The guardian angel; farce in 1 act. *In* Lacy.   **812 : 1 v5**

— *joint author, see* **Oxenford,** J:

Brough, J: Cargill, *joint author, see* **Archer,** T:

Brough, Robert B.   Alfred the great, or The minstrel king; an historical extravaganza. *In* Lacy.   **812 : 1 v43**

— Crinoline; an original farce in 1 act. *In* Lacy.   **812 : 1 v29**

— The doge of Duralto, or The enchanted eyes; extravaganza. *In* Lacy.   **812 : 1 v88**

— Kensington gardens, or Quite a ladies' man; comedy in 2 acts, adapted from the french. *In* Lacy.   **812 : 1 v88**

— Masaniello, or The fish 'oman of Naples; a fish tale in 1 act. *In* Lacy.   **812 : 1 v32**

— Medea, or The best of mothers with a brute of a husband; a burlesque in 1 act. *In* Lacy.   **812 : 1 v27**

— The moustache movement; farce in 1 act. *In* Lacy.   **812 : 1 v14**

— The overland journey to Constantinople as undertaken by lord Bateman, with interesting particulars of the fair Sophia; extravaganza in 2 acts. *In* Lacy.   **812 : 1 v15**

— The twelve labours of Hercules; a comedy in 2 acts. *In* Lacy.   **812 : 1 v6**

— *and* Sutherland Edwards.   Mephistopheles, or An ambassador from below; an extravaganza in 1 act. *In* Lacy. **812 : 1 v25**

Brough, W: Apartments; visitors to the exhibition may be accommodated, etc.; a piece of extravagance to suit the times in 1 act. *In* Lacy.   **812 : 1 v4**

— Bona fide travellers, a point of law arising out of the new beer bill; farce.   **812 : 1 v16**

— The caliph of Bagdad; original oriental, operatic extravaganza. *In* Lacy.   **812 : 1 v79**

— A comical countess; a farce in 1 act. *In* Lacy.   **812 : 1 v52**

Brough, W:—*Continued.*

— Conrad and Medora, or Harlequin corsair and the little fairy at the bottom of the well ; a new christmas burlesque and pantomime, founded upon the ballet of "Le corsaire". *In* Lacy.　　　　　　　812 : 1 v29

— Dinorah under difficulties ; piece of extravagance in 1 act. *In* Lacy.　812 : 1 v81

— Endymion, or The naughty boy who cried for the moon ; classical, mythological extravaganza in 1 act. *In* Lacy. 812 : 1 v49

— Ernani, or The horn of a dilemma ; a new and original burlesque extravaganza. *In* Lacy.　　　　　　　812 : 1 v67

— The field of the cloth of gold ; original, grand historical extravaganza. *In* Lacy.　　　　　　　812 : 1 v80

— The gnome king and the good fairy of the silver mine ; original extravaganza. *In* Lacy.　　　　　　　812 : 1 v86

— Hercules and Omphale, or The power of love; an original classical extravaganza. *In* Lacy.　　　　　　　812 : 1 v64

— A house out of windows ; a farce in 1 act. *In* Lacy.　　　　　　　812 : 1 v8

— How to make home happy ; comic drama in 1 act. *In* Lacy.　　　812 : 1 v13

— Joan of Arc ; new and original historical burlesque. *In* Lacy.　　　812 : 1 v86

— Kind to a fault ; original comedy in 2 acts. *In* Lacy.　　　　　　812 : 1 v78

— King Arthur, or The days and knights of the round table ; a new and original christmas extravaganza in 1 act. *In* Lacy.　　　　　　　812 : 1 v61

— Lalla Rookh, or The princess, the peri and the troubadour ; a burlesque and pantomime in 1 act. *In* Lacy.　　812 : 1 v34

— Number one, round the corner ; farce in 1 act. *In* Lacy.　　　　　812 : 1 v14

— Papillionetta, or The prince, the butterfly and the beetle ; an original, burlesque extravaganza. *In* Lacy.　　812 : 1 v68

— Perdita, or The royal milkmaid, being the legend upon which Shakespeare is supposed to have founded his Winter's tale ; a new and original burlesque. *In* Lacy.　　　　　　　812 : 1 v28

— Perseus and Andromeda, or The maid and the monster ; a classical extravaganza. *In* Lacy.　　　　　　　812 : 1 v53

— A phenomenon in a smock frock ; a comic drama in 1 act. *In* Lacy.　812 : 1 v9

— Prince Amabel, or The fairy roses ; an original fairy extravaganza. *In* Lacy.　　　　　　　812 : 1 v55

— Pygmalion, or The statue fair ; original burlesque. *In* Lacy.　812 : 1 v75

— Rasselas, prince of Abyssinia, or The happy valley ; an extravaganza. *In* Lacy.　　　　　　　812 : 1 v57

— The sylphide ; new and original extravaganza in 1 act. *In* Lacy.　812 : 1 v76

— Trying it on ; farce in 1 act. *In* Lacy.　　　　　　　812 : 1 v11

— *and* Andrew Halliday. The actor's retreat ; an extravaganza in 1 act and in prose. *In* Lacy.　　　　　　　812 : 1 v63

— — An april fool ; a farce in 1 act. *In* Lacy.　　　　　　　812 : 1 v62

— — The area belle ; an original farce in 1 act. *In* Lacy.　　　　812 : 1 v62

Brough, W:, *and* **A. Halliday.**—*Continued.*

— — The census ; a farce in 1 act. *In* Lacy.　　　　　　　812 : 1 v50

— — The Colleen Bawn settled at last ; a farcical extravaganza in 1 act. *In* Lacy.　　　　　　　812 : 1 v55

— — Doing Banting ; an apropos farce in 1 act. *In* Lacy.　　　812 : 1 v64

— — Going to the dogs ; an entirely original farce in 1 act. *In* Lacy.　　812 : 1 v65

— — Medborough election ; a new and original farce in 1 act. *In* Lacy.　812 : 1 v67

— — My heart's in the highlands ; a farce in 1 act. *In* Lacy.　　　812 : 1 v51

— — The pretty horsebreaker ; an apropos sketch in 1 act. *In* Lacy.　812 : 1 v51

— — A shilling day at the great exhibition ; a farce in 1 act. *In* Lacy.　812 : 1 v55

— — Upstairs and downstairs, or The great percentage question ; a farce in 1 act. *In* Lacy.　　　　　　812 : 1 v66

— — Valentine ; a compliment of the season in 1 act. *In* Lacy.　　812 : 1 v57

Brougham, J: Flies in the web ; an original comedy in 3 acts. *In* Lacy.　812 : 1 v69

— The irish emigrant ; comic drama in 1 act. *In* Lacy.　　　　812 : 1 v82

— The lottery of life ; a story of New York ; an original, local drama in 5 acts. *In* French's.　　　　　　812 : 1 v105

— Playing with fire ; an original comedy in 5 acts. *In* Lacy.　　812 : 1 v66

— A recollection of O'Flannigan and the fairies ; an extravaganza in 1 act. *In* Lacy.　　　　　　812 : 1 v26

Broughton, F: W. Ruth's romance ; a summer evening's sketch. *In* French's.　　　　　　812 : 1 v116

— Sunshine ; an original comedy in 1 act. *In* French's.　　　812 : 1 v121

— Withered leaves ; a comedietta in 1 act. *In* French's.　　812 : 1 v115

— *and* Walter Browne. Once again ; an original comedietta in 1 act. *In* French's.　　　　　812 : 1 v122

Brown, J: Barbarossa ; tragedy in 5 acts. *In* British drama.　　822.2 : 1 v1

— *Same. In* French's.　　812 : 1 v109

Browne, E. J. A lucky sixpence ; farce in 1 act. *In* French's.　　812 : 1 v103

Browne, Walter, *joint author, see* **Broughton, F: W.**

Browning, Robert. Strafford ; a tragedy ; with notes and a preface by Emily H. Hickey and an introd. by S: R. Gardiner. Lond. 1884. D.　　　　　822.2 : 48

Brueys, D: Augustin de. The village lawyer ; a farce in 1 act, adapted by mr. Lyons from "L'avocat Patelin". *In* Lacy.　　　　　　　812 : 1 v43

Bruton, James. Bathing ; a farce in 1 act. *In* French's.　　　812 : 1 v108

— Cut for partners ; a laughable farce in 1 act. *In* French's.　812 : 1 v112

Buckingham, Leicester. Don't lend your umbrella ; a comic drama in 2 acts. *In* Lacy.　　　　　　　812 : 1 v30

— Faces in the fire ; a comedy in 3 acts. *In* Lacy.　　　　812 : 1 v65

— Harlequin novelty and the princess who lost her heart ; a new and original burlesque pantomime in 1 act. *In* Lacy. 812 : 1 v34

Buckingham, Leicester.—*Continued.*
— Love's martyr; a drama in 4 acts, preceded
by a prologue. *In* Lacy.   812 : 1 v70
— Lucrezia Borgia at home and all abroad; a
new and original burlesque in 1 act. *In*
Lacy.   812 : 1 v45
— The merry widow; a comedy in 2 acts. *In*
Lacy.   812 : 1 v58
— Silken fetters; a comedy in 3 acts. *In* Lacy.
        812 : 1 v61
— The silver lining; a comedy in 3 acts. *In*
Lacy.   812 : 1 v62
— Take that girl away! comic drama in 2 acts.
In Lacy.   812 : 1 v18
— Virginius, or The trials of a fond papa; a bur-
lesque in 1 act. *In* Lacy.   812 : 1 v42
— William Tell; a telling version of an old tell
tale; an original burlesque. *In* Lacy.
        812 : 1 v32
— *and* A. **Harris.** Jeannette's wedding; an
operetta in 1 act. *In* Lacy.   812 : 1 v32
Buckstone, J: Baldwin. Agnes de Vere, or The
wife's revenge; a drama in 3 acts. *In*
French's.   812 : 1 v106
— The bear hunters, or The fatal ravine; a melo-
drama in 2 acts. *In* Lacy.   812 : 1 v31
— The breach of promise, or Second thoughts
are best; comedy in 2 acts. Bost. *n. d.* S.
With **Talfourd,** T: N. Ion.   822.2 : 3
— A dead shot; a farce in 1 act. *In* Lacy.
        812 : 1 v34
— Good for nothing; comic drama in 1 act. *In*
Lacy.   812 : 1 v17
— The happiest day of my life; farce in 2 acts.
In Lacy.   812 : 1 v80
— John Jones; farce in 1 act. *In* Lacy.
        812 : 1 v25
— Josephine, the child of the regiment, or The
fortune of war; musical comedy in 2 acts.
In Lacy.   812 : 1 v25
— The king of the Alps; a romantic drama in
3 acts.   812 : 1 v6
— A kiss in the dark; a farce in 1 act. *In* Lacy.
        812 : 1 v6
— The life and death of Jack Shepherd; drama
in 4 acts, adapted from Harrison Ains-
worth's popular romance. *In* Lacy.
        812 : 1 v23
— The lottery ticket, or The lawyer's clerk; a
farce in 1 act. Bost. *n. d.* S. *With* Tal-
fourd, T: N. Ion.   822.2 : 3
— Luke the labourer, or The lost son; a domes-
tic drama in 2 acts. *In* Lacy. 812 : 1 v69
— The maid with the milking pail; comic drama
in 1 act. *In* Lacy.   812 : 1 v10
— Mischief-making; farce in 1 act. *In* Lacy.
        812 : 1 v79
— Peter Bell, or The murderers of Massiac; a
melodrama in 3 acts. *In* French's.
        812 : 1 v110
— Popping the question; farce in 1 act. *In*
Lacy.   812 : 1 v87
— *Same. With* **Talfourd,** T: N. Ion. 822.2 : 3
— Presumptive evidence, or Murder will out;
domestic drama in 2 acts. *In* Lacy.
        812 : 1 v82
— A rough diamond; comic drama in 1 act. *In*
Lacy   812 : 1 v17
— The snapping turtles, or Matrimonial mas-
querading; a duologue in 1 act. *In* Lacy.
        812 : 1 v69

Buckstone, J: Baldwin.—*Continued.*
— The two queens; petite comedy in 1 act. *In*
Lacy.   812 : 1 v1
Bully, E: Roger de, *joint author, see* **Duveyrier,**
Anne Honoré Joseph *baron.*
Bulwer-Lytton, E: G: Earle Lytton, *1st baron
Lytton.* Dramatic works. Leipz. 1860. 2
v. in 1. S.   822.2 : 17
Contents. V. 1. Richelieu, or The conspiracy.—
Money. 2. The duchess de La Valliere.—The lady of
Lyons.—Not so bad as we seem.
— Die herzogin de la Vallière; ein drama in 5
akten. Aus dem englischen von G: N:
Bärmann. Stuttg. 1840. T.   822.2 : 18
— The lady of Lyons, or Love and pride; a play
in 5 acts. *In* French's.   812 : 1 v116
— *Same, germ.* Die lyoneserin, oder Hoffart und
liebe; ein lustspiel in 5 abth. Aus dem
englischen von G: N: Bärmann. Stuttg.
1840. T.   822.2 : 19
— Money; a comedy in 5 acts. *In* French's.
        812 : 1 v119
— Richelieu, or The conspiracy; a play in 5 acts.
In French's.   812 : 1 v117
Bunn, Alfred. My neighbor's wife; farce in 1
act. *In* Lacy.   812 : 1 v18
— *joint author, see* **Dibdin,** T:
Burnand, Francis Cowley. Acis and Galatea,
or The nimble nymph and the terrible
troglodyte; an extravaganza. *In* Lacy.
        812 : 1 v58
— Alonzo the brave, or Faust and the fair Imogene; a tragical, comical, demoniacal and
what-ever-you-like-to-call-it burlesque,
uniting in its construction the romantic
pathos of the well-known ballad, "Alonzo
and Imogene," with the thrilling horrors
of Goethe's Faust. *In* Lacy. 812 : 1 v58
— Black-eyed Susan, or The little Bill that was
taken up; original burlesque. *In* Lacy.
        812 : 1 v77
— Cupid and Psyche, or Beautiful as a butterfly;
a new and original extravaganza. *In* Lacy.
        812 : 1 v64
— Deadman's Point, or The lighthouse on the
Carn Ruth; drama in 4 acts and 2 tableaux.
In Lacy.   812 : 1 v92
— The Deal boatman; a serio-comic drama in 2
acts. *In* Lacy.   812 : 1 v60
— Deerfoot; a farce in 1 act. *In* Lacy.
        812 : 1 v53
— Dido, the celebrated widow; a new and orig-
inal extravaganza. *In* Lacy. 812 : 1 v44
— Fair Rosamond, or The maze, the maid and
the monarch! an entirely new, but histor-
ically true version of the ancient strange
story. *In* Lacy.   812 : 1 v55
— Faust and Marguerite; an entirely new orig-
inal travestie in 1 act. *In* Lacy.
        812 : 1 v63
— Helen, or Taken from the greek; burlesque in
3 scenes; a companion picture to "Paris."
In Lacy.   812 : 1 v77
— "Humbug!" comedy in 2 acts. *In* Lacy.
        812 : 1 v79
— In for a holiday; an original farce in 1 act.
In Lacy.   812 : 1 v26
— Ixion, or The man at the wheel; an original
extravaganza. *In* Lacy.   812 : 1 v60
— King of the Merrows, or The prince and the
piper; a fairy extravaganza, from an orig-
inal plot by J. Palgrave Simpson. *In* Lacy.
        812 : 1 v53

Burnand, Francis Cowley.—*Continued.*
— Lord Lovel and lady Nancy Bell, or The bounding brigand of the Bakumboilum ; a thrillingly interesting and tragically startling burlesque. *In* Lacy.   812 : 1 v30
— Madame Berliot's ball, or The chalet in the valley ; a comic drama in 2 acts, 5 scenes and 6 tableaux. *In* Lacy.   812 : 1 v61
— Mary Turner, or The wicious willin and wictorious wirtue! entirely new and original burlesque in 1 act. *In* Lacy.   812 : 1 v78
— Paris, or Vive Lemprière ; original burlesque. *In* Lacy.   812 : 1 v84
— Patient Penelope, or The return of Ulysses ; a burlesque in 1 act. *In* Lacy.   812 : 1 v61
— Pirithoüs, the son of Ixion ; a new and original extravaganza. *In* Lacy.   812 : 1 v65
— Robin Hood, or The forester's fate! extravaganza. *In* Lacy.   812 : 1 v57
— Romance under difficulties ; an original farce in 1 act. *In* Lacy.   812 : 1 v26
— Rumplestiltskin, or The woman at the wheel ; an extravaganza in 1 act. *In* Lacy.   812 : 1 v62
— Snowdrop, or The seven mannikins and the magic mirror ; an entirely new and original, burlesque extravaganza. *In* Lacy.   812 : 1 v64
— Ulysses, or The iron-clad warrior and the little tug of war ; an entirely original burlesque. *In* Lacy.   812 : 1 v66
— Venus and Adonis, or The two rivals and the small boar ; being a full, true and particular account, adapted to the requirements of the present age, of an ancient mythological piece of scandal. *In* Lacy.   812 : 1 v62
— Villikins and his Dinah ; a tragico-comico burlesque in 1 act. *In* Lacy.   812 : 1 v54
— The white cat, or Prince Lardi-Dardi and the radiant Rosetta ; fairy burlesque extravaganza. *In* Lacy.   812 : 1 v90
— The white fawn, or The loves of prince Buttercup and the princess Daisy ; entirely new spectacular extravaganza. *In* Lacy.   812 : 1 v79
— Windsor castle ; an original opera burlesque. *In* Lacy.   812 : 1 v67
— *joint author, see* **Morton, J: M.,** *also* **Williams, Montagu.**
Burton, W: Evans. Ellen Wareham, or The wife of two husbands ; a domestic drama in 2 acts. *In* Lacy.   812 : 1 v34
Butler, R:, *2d earl of Glengall.* The irish tutor, or New lights ; a farce in 1 act, adapted from the french. *In* Lacy.   812 : 1 v36
Byron, G: Gordon Noel, *6th baron Byron.* Dramas, in 2 v.; v. 1. Lond. 1837. Tt.   822.2 : 20
Contents. Manfred.—Marino Faliero.—Heaven and earth.—Sardanapalus.
— Manfred ; a choral tragedy in 3 acts. *In* Lacy.   812 : 1 v60
— Sardanapalus, king of Assyria ; tragedy in 5 acts, adapted for representation by C: Kean. *In* Lacy.   812 : 1 v11
— Werner, or The inheritance ; a tragedy in 5 acts. *In* Lacy.   812 : 1 v70
— *see also his* Poetical works.   821.2 : 59
Byron, H: James. Aladdin, or The wonderful scamp ; an original extravaganza in 1 act. *In* Lacy.   812 : 1 v50

Byron, H: James.—*Continued.*
— Ali Baba, or The thirty-nine thieves, in accordance with the author's habit of taking one off ; a burlesque extravaganza in 1 act. *In* Lacy.   812 : 1 v59
— The babes in the wood and the good little fairy birds ; a burlesque extravaganza in 1 act. *In* Lacy.   812 : 1 v41
— Beautiful Haidee, or The sea nymph and the Sallee rovers ; a new and original, whimsical extravaganza, founded on the poem of Don Juan, the ballad of lord Bateman and the legend of Lurline. *In* Lacy.   812 : 1 v58
— Blow for blow ; an original drama in a prologue and 3 acts. *In* French's.   812 : 1 v101
— Blue Beard ! from a new point of hue ; a burlesque extravaganza. *In* Lacy.   812 : 1 v49
— Bow bells ; an original comic drama in 3 acts. *In* French's.   812 : 1 v117
— The bride of Abydos, or The prince, the pirate and the pearl ; an original, oriental burlesque extravaganza. *In* Lacy.   812 : 1 v36
— Camaralzaman and the fair Badoura, or The bad djinn and the good spirit ; extravaganza. *In* Lacy.   812 : 1 v94
— Cinderella, or The lover, the lackey and the little glass slipper ; a fairy, burlesque extravaganza. *In* Lacy.   812 : 1 v49
— The corsican "bothers," or The troublesome twins ; original burlesque extravaganza, founded on a famous romantic drama. *In* Lacy.   812 : 1 v88
— Courtship, or The three caskets ; a comedy in 3 acts. *In* French's.   812 : 1 v120
— Cyril's success ; original comedy in 5 acts. *In* Lacy.   812 : 1 v89
— Daisy Farm ; an original drama in 4 acts. *In* French's.   812 : 1 v115
— 1863, or The sensations of the past season, with a shameful revelation of lady Somebody's secret ; a comical conglomerate absurdity in 1 act. *In* Lacy.   812 : 1 v61
— The enchanted wood, or The three transformed princes ; a fairy extravaganza. *In* Lacy.   812 : 1 v99
— Esmeralda, or The "sensation" goat ; a new and original burlesque extravaganza in 1 act. *In* Lacy.   812 : 1 v52
— Eurydice, or Little Orpheus and his lute ; grand burlesque extravaganza. *In* Lacy.   812 : 1 v92
— Fine feathers ; an original modern drama in 3 acts and a prologue. *In* French's.   812 : 1 v120
— Fra Diavolo, or The beauty and the brigands ; a burlesque burletta. *In* Lacy.   812 : 1 v35
— Der freischütz, or The bill ! the belle !! and the bullet !!! original burlesque. *In* Lacy.   812 : 1 v81
— The Garibaldi "excursionists"; an apropos sketch in 1 act. *In* Lacy.   812 : 1 v48
— George de Barnwell ; a burlesque pantomime opening. *In* Lacy.   812 : 1 v57
— Giselle, or The sirens of the Lotus lake ; a fanciful, musical legend. *In* Lacy.   812 : 1 v93

Byron, H: James.—*Continued.*
— The "grin" bushes, or The "Mrs." Brown of the "Missis"sippi ; a burlesque extrava-ganza in 1 act, founded on the famous Adelphi drama of "The green bushes." *In* Lacy.   **812 : 1 v64**
— Hundred thousand pounds ; original comedy in 3 acts. *In* Lacy.   **812 : 1 v77**
— Ill-treated Il trovatore, or The mother, the maiden and the musicianer ; a new burles-que extravaganza. *In* Lacy.   **812 : 1 v58**
— Ivanhoe, in accordance with the spirit of the times ; an extravaganza. *In* Lacy.
                                        812 : 1 v59
— Jack the giant-killer, or Harlequin, king Arthur and ye knights of ye round table ; a burlesque extravaganza, preceding a mirthful, magical, comical christmas pan-tomime. *In* Lacy.   **812 : 1 v43**
— Lady Belle Belle, or Fortunio and his seven magic men ; a christmas fairy tale in 1 act. *In* Lacy.   **812 : 1 v61**
— La ! Sonnambula ! or The supper, the sleeper and the merry swiss boy ; an original, operatic, burlesque extravaganza. *In* Lacy.   **812 : 1 v66**
— The Lancashire lass, or Tempted, tried and true ; a domestic melodrama in a prologue and 4 acts. *In* Lacy.   **812 : 1 v115**
— Little don Giovanni ; a burlesque. *In* Lacy.
                                        812 : 1 v72
— Lord Bateman, or The proud young porter and the fair Sophia ; burlesque founded on the loving ballad of "Lord Bateman." *In* Lacy.   **812 : 1 v87**
— Lucia di Lammermoor, or The laird, the lady and the lover ; a new original, operatic, burlesque extravaganza, founded on Doni-zetti's popular opera and consequently very unlike the romance. *In* Lacy. **812 : 1 v72**
— Lucretia Borgia, M. D., or La grande doc-tresse ; original burlesque extravaganza, founded on a famous opera. *In* Lacy.
                                        812 : 1 v87
— The maid and the magpie, or The fatal spoon ! a burlesque burletta founded on the opera of "La gazza ladra". *In* Lacy. **812 : 1 v37**
— Married in haste ; an original comedy in 4 acts. *In* French's.   **812 : 1 v115**
— Mazeppa ; a burlesque extravaganza in 1 act. *In* Lacy.   **812 : 1 v46**
— Mazourka, or The stick, the Pole and the Tartar ; a burlesque extravaganza in 1 act ; founded on a famous french ballet en-titled "Le diable à quatre". *In* Lacy.
                                        812 : 1 v63
— Miss Eily O'Connor ; a new and original bur-lesque extravaganza, founded on the great sensation drama of the "Colleen Bawn". *In* Lacy.   **812 : 1 v53**
— The motto, I am "all there"; a new and orig-inal burlesque founded on the Lyceum drama of the "Duke's motto". *In* Lacy.
                                        812 : 1 v59
— Not such a fool as he looks ; an original ec-centric comedy in 3 acts. *In* French's.
                                        812 : 1 v120
— The nymph of the Lurleyburg, or The knight and the naiads ; a spectacular extrava-ganza. *In* Lacy.   **812 : 1 v43**
— Old sailors ; original comedy in 3 acts. *In* French's.   **812 : 1 v116**

Byron, H: James.—*Continued.*
— Old soldiers ; an original comedy in 3 acts. *In* French's.   **812 : 1 v113**
— The old story ; an original comedy in 2 acts. *In* Lacy.   **812 : 1 v51**
— The orange tree and the humble bee, or The little princess who was lost at sea ; new extravaganza. *In* Lacy.   **812 : 1 v93**
— Orpheus and Eurydice, or The young gentle-man who charmed the rocks ; a comical, classical love tale in 1 act. *In* Lacy.
                                        812 : 1 v61
— "Our boys"; an original modern comedy. *In* French's.   **812 : 1 v116**
— Pan ; an original classical pastoral. *In* Lacy.
                                        812 : 1 v66
— Pandora's box ; a mythological extravaganza in 1 act. *In* Lacy.   **812 : 1 v76**
— Partners for life ; an original comedy in 3 acts. *In* French's.   **812 : 1 v108**
— The pilgrim of love ; a fairy romance in 1 act. *In* Lacy.   **812 : 1 v45**
— Princess Spring-Time, or The envoy who stole the king's daughter ; an original fairy ex-travaganza, founded on a story by the comtess d'Anois. *In* Lacy.   **812 : 1 v64**
— The prompter's box ; a story of the footlights and the fireside ; an original domestic drama in 4 acts. *In* French's.
                                        812 : 1 v120
— Robert Macaire, or The roadside inn turned inside out ; original burlesque extrava-ganza. *In* Lacy.   **812 : 1 v93**
— Robinson Crusoe, or Harlequin Friday and the king of the Caribee Islands ; a grotesque pantomime opening. *In* Lacy. **812 : 1 v49**
— Timothy to the rescue ; an original farce in 1 act. *In* Lacy.   **812 : 1 v63**
— £20 a year—all found, or Out of a situation, re-fusing twenty ; an apropos sketch with a moral for servants and mistresses. *In* French's.   **812 : 1 v116**
— "Uncle"; a new and original farcical piece in 3 acts. *In* French's.   **812 : 1 v120**
— The very latest edition of the Lady of Lyons ; a new burlesque extravaganza in 1 act. *In* Lacy.   **812 : 1 v34**
— War to the knife ; an original comedy in 3 acts. *In* Lacy.   **812 : 1 v67**
— Weak woman ; a new and original comedy in 3 acts. *In* French's.   **812 : 1 v112**
— William Tell, with a vengeance, or The pet, the patriot and the pippin ; grand, new and original burlesque. *In* Lacy.
                                        812 : 1 v78
— Wrinkles, a tale of time ; an original comedy. *In* French's.   **812 : 1 v115**
— *joint author, see* **Talfourd**, Francis.

Cæsar, the watch dog of the castle ; a romantic drama in 2 acts. *In* Lacy.   **812 : 1 v79**
Calcraft, J: W: The bride of Lammermoor ; a drama in 4 acts, adapted from sir Walter Scott's celebrated romance. *In* Lacy.
                                        812 : 1 v28
Calderon de la Barca, P: Schauspiele. Aus dem spanischen übers. von Adolf Martin. Leipz. 1844.   3 v. S.   **862 : 1**

Calvert, G: H: Comedies. Bost. 1856. O.
812.1 : 8
Contents. The will and the way.—Like unto like.

Campbell, A. L. Demon of the desert, or The murderer's sacrifice ; a melodramatic spectacle in 2 acts. *In* French's. 812 : 1 v110

Campbell, A. L. V. Tom Bowling ; a nautical drama in 2 acts. *In* French's. 812 : 1 v107

Campbell, Bartley. Little Sunshine ; play in 5 acts. *In* French's. 812 : 1 v110

Cantab, The ; a farce in 1 act. *In* Lacy.
812 : 1 v50

Carey, H: Chrononhotonthologos ; the most tragical tragedy that ever was tragedized by any company of tragedians, in 1 act. *In* Lacy. 812 : 1 v82

Carpenter, J. E. Love and honour, or Soldiers at home—heroes abroad ; an original domestic drama in 3 acts. *In* French's.
812 : 1 v107

Carré, Michel. Faust and Marguerite ; romantic drama in 3 acts. Tr. from the french by W: Robertson. *In* Lacy. 812 : 1 v15

— *and* Jules Barbier. Jeannette's wedding day ; musical farce in 1 act, adapted from "Les noces de Jeannette". *In* Lacy. 812 : 1 v72

— *and* Léon Battu. Love by lantern light ; operetta in 1 act, adapted from "Le mariage aux lanternes." *In* Lacy. 812 : 1 v73

Carrol, *Mrs.* S., *see* Centlivre, S.

Castelli, Ignaz F: D'schwoagarin ; a kumödigschbül a so z'åmagsödzd wia s' in Estaraich röd'n doan. *n. t.* D. 832 : 13

Cavendish, *Lady* Clara. The woman of the world ; a drama in 2 acts, adapted from the popular tale of that name. *In* Lacy.
812 : 1 v38

Centlivre, Susannah, *born* Freeman, *formerly mrs.* Fox *and mrs.* Carrol. A bold stroke for a wife. *In* British drama. 822.2 : 1 v1

— The busy body ; comedy in 3 acts. *In* Lacy.
812 : 1 v28

— The wonder ; a comedy in 5 acts. *In* British drama. 822.2 : 1 v1

— *Same. In* Lacy. 812 : 1 v25

Chapman, Westmacott, *joint author, see* Hay, F:

Cheltnam, C: Smith. Christmas eve in a watchhouse ; farcical sketch in 1 act. *In* Lacy.
812 : 1 v90

— Deborah, or The jewish maiden's wrong ; a drama in 3 acts. *In* Lacy. 812 : 1 v63

— Dinner for nothing ; an original farce in 1 act. *In* Lacy. 812 : 1 v67

— Edendale ; original drama in 3 acts. *In* Lacy.
812 : 1 v84

— A fairy's father ; an original dramatic sketch in 1 act. *In* Lacy. 812 : 1 v54

— Fireside diplomacy ; a comedietta in 1 act. *In* Scott, C. W. Drawing-room plays.
822.2 : 14

— Leatherlungos the great, how he storm'd, reign'd and mizzled ; entirely new and original extravaganza. *In* Lacy.
812 : 1 v96

— A lesson in love ; a comedy in three acts. *In* Lacy. 812 : 1 v64

— A little madcap ; a comic drama in 1 act. *In* French's. 812 : 1 v114

— A lucky escape ! a comic drama in 1 act, from the french. *In* Lacy. 812 : 1 v52

Cheltnam, C: Smith.—*Continued.*
— The matchmaker ; a farcical comedy in 2 acts. *In* Lacy. 812 : 1 v93

— Mrs. Green's snug little business ; an original farce in 1 act. *In* Lacy. 812 : 1 v65

— More precious than gold ; a comedy in 3 acts. *In* Lacy. 812 : 1 v51

— The shadow of a crime ; drama in 3 acts. *In* Lacy. 812 : 1 v86

— Slowtop's engagements ; a farce in 1 act, from the french. *In* Lacy. 812 : 1 v53

— The ticket-of-leave man's wife, or Six years after ; a new and original drama in 3 acts ; a continuation of Tom Taylor's drama of The ticket-of-leave man. *In* Lacy.
812 : 1 v69

Cheney, O. Augusta, *joint author, see* Alger, Horatio, *jr.*

Cherry and Fair Star, or The children of Cyprus ; a grand asiatic, melodramatic romance in 2 acts. *In* Lacy. 812 : 1 v6

Chesterfield Thinskin ; farce in 1 act. *In* Lacy.
812 : 1v12

Church, Florence, *born* Marryat, *and Sir* C: L. Young. Miss Chester ; drama in 3 acts. *In* French's. 812 : 1 v104

Churchill, Frank. Taking by storm ; a coloured sketch in 1 act. *In* Lacy. 812 : 1 v6

Cibber, Colley. The careless husband ; comedy in 5 acts. *In* British drama. 822.2 : 1 v2

— She wou'd and she wou'd not ; comedy in 5 acts. *In* Lacy. 812 : 1 v22

— Ximena, or The heroic daughter ; tragedy in 5 acts. *In* British drama. 822.2 : 1 v2

Clairville, L: François Nicolaie *called, and* Paul Siraudin *and* V: Koning. La fille de madame Angot ; an opera bouffe in 3 acts, adapted from the french by Carry Nelson. Music by C: Lecocq. *In* French's.
812 : 1 v103

— *joint author, see* Dennery, Adolphe Philippe.

Claridge, C. J., *and* Robert Soutar. The fast coach ; an original farce in 1 act. *In* French's. 812 : 1 v102

Clarke, Campbell. Awaking ; a drama in 1 act, altered and adapted from the french of Sandeau and Decourcelle. *In* Lacy.
812 : 1 v98

Clarke, H. Saville. Hugger-mugger ; a farce in 1 act. *In* French's. 812 : 1 v102

— *and* — Du Terreau. Love wins ; an original comedy in 3 acts. *In* French's.
812 : 1 v105

Clément, René, *joint author, see* Dennery, Adolphe Philippe.

Clements, Arthur. The telephone ; a farce in 1 act. *In* French's. 812 : 1 v112

— The two blinds ; an operetta. Music by Offenbach. *In* French's. 812 : 1 v102

— Two photographs ; an entirely new and original comedietta in 1 act. *In* French's.
812 : 1 v122

— Two to one, or The irish footman ; farce in 1 act. *In* Lacy. 812 : 1 v98

— *and* F: Hay. Cracked heads ; a burlesque. *In* French's. 812 : 1 v108

Clifton, Lewis, *joint author, see* Dilley, Joseph J.

Cobb, James. The doctor and the apothecary ; musical entertainment in 2 acts. *In* British drama. 822.2 : 1 v1

Cobb, James.—*Continued.*
— The first floor ; farce in 2 acts. *In* British drama.   **822.2 : 1 v2**
— *Same. In* Lacy.   **812 : 1 v86**
Coffey, C: The devil to pay, or The wives metamorphosed ; ballad farce. *In* British drama.
                                      822.2 : 1 v1
Coleridge, S: Taylor. [Dramatic writings]. *In his* Works.   **820.2 : 7 v7**
  Contents, see under English literature, Collected works.
Collier, W: Kate Kearney, or The fairy of the lakes ; a musical romance in 2 acts. *In* French's.   **812 : 1 v120**
Colman, G: The deuce is in him ; farce in 2 acts. *In* British drama.   **822.2 : 1 v1**
— The jealous wife ; comedy in 5 acts. *In the same.*   **822.2 : 1 v1**
— *Same. In* Lacy.   **812 : 1 v25**
— The manager in distress ; a prelude. *In* Lacy.   **812 : 1 v94**
— *and* D: **Garrick.** The clandestine marriage ; comedy in 5 acts. *In* Lacy. **812 : 1 v92**
— — *Same. In* British drama.   **822.2 : 1 v1**
— — *Same. In* Sargent, E. Mod. stand. drama.   **822.2 : 2 v5**
Colman, G:, *the younger.* Blue devils ; comic drama in 1 act.   **812 : 1 v87**
— The heir at law ; comedy in 5 acts. *In* Lacy.   **812 : 1 v24**
— Inkle and Yarico ; musical drama in 3 acts. *In* Lacy.   **812 : 1 v95**
— *Same. In* British drama.   **822.2 : 1 v2**
— The iron chest ; play in 3 acts. *In* Sargent, E. Mod. stand. drama.   **822.2 : 2 v6**
— *Same. In* Lacy.   **812 : 1 v39**
— John Bull, or The englishman's fireside ; a comedy in 3 acts. *In* Lacy.   **812 : 1 v42**
— Love laughs at locksmiths ; musical farce in 2 acts. *In* Lacy.   **812 : 1 v94**
— The poor gentleman ; a comedy in 3 acts. *In* Lacy.   **812 : 1 v39**
— The review, or The wags of Windsor ; a musical farce in 1 act. *In* Lacy. **812 : 1 v61**
— Sylvester Daggerwood ; a farce in 1 act. *In* French's.   **812 : 1 v111**
— Ways and means ; comedy in 3 acts. *In* British drama.   **822.2 : 1 v1**
— X. Y. Z.; farce in 2 acts. *In* Lacy. **812 : 1 v80**
Colomb, —, *Col. R. A.* The cast king of Granada ; historical extravaganza. *In* French's.   **812 : 1 v103**
— Davenport Done, or An april fool ; a comedietta in 1 act. *In* Lacy.   **812 : 1 v74**
— Hamlet improved, or Mr. Mendall's attempt to ameliorate that tragedy. *In* French's.   **812 : 1 v115**
Coming woman, The, or The spirit of seventy-six ; a prophetic drama. *In* French's.   **812 : 1 v112**
Congreve, W: Dramatic works. *With* **Wycherley,** W:, *and others.*   **822.2+10**
  Contents. Commendatory verses.—The old bachelor.—The double dealer.—Love for love.—The mourning bride.—The way of the world.—The judgment of Paris.—Semele.
— Love for love ; comedy in 5 acts. *In* British drama.   **822.2 : 1 v2**
— The mourning bride. *In the same.*
                                      822.2 : 1 v1
Conquest, G:, *and* Paul **Meritt.** Hand and glove, or Page 13 of the black book ; a drama in 3 acts. *In* French's.   **812:1 v109**

Conquest, G:, *and* Paul **Meritt.**—*Continued.*
— — Seven sins, or Passion's paradise ; a drama in 4 acts. *In* French's.   **812:1 v109**
— — Velvet and rags ; a spanish romance of the present day ; prologue and 3 acts. *In* French's.   **812:1 v112**
— *and* H: **Pettitt.** Neck or nothing ; a new and original drama in 3 acts. *In* French's.   **812:1 v113**
— — The sole survivor, or A tale of the Goodwin sands. *In* French's.   **812:1 v113**
Conrad, Robert T. Jack Cade, the captain of the commons ; tragedy in 4 acts, with an historical introd. *In* Lacy.   **812:1 v83**
Cooper, F: Fox. Hercules, king of clubs ; farce in 1 act. *In* Lacy.   **812:1 v89**
Cooper, James. Oor Geordie, or The horrid barbarian ; a farce in 1 act. *In* French's.   **812:1 v107**
Cornwall, Barry, *pseud., see* Proctor, Bryan Waller.
Court of lions, The, or Granada taken and done for ; an historical burlesque in 1 act. *In* Lacy.   **812:1 v70**
Courtney, J: Aged forty ; an original petite comedy in 1 act. *In* Lacy.   **812:1 v59**
— Deeds, not words ; a drama in 2 acts. *In* French's.   **812:1 v105**
— Double faced people ; a comedy in 3 acts. *In* Lacy.   **812:1 v31**
— Eustache Baudin ; drama in 3 acts. *In* Lacy.   **812:1 v15**
— Old Joe and young Joe ; a comic drama in 2 acts. *In* Lacy.   **812:1 v49**
— The soldier's progress, or The horrors of war ; a pictorial drama in 4 pts., ill. of the series of plates issued under the patronage of the Peace society. *In* Lacy.   **812:1 v1**
— Time tries all ; an original drama in 2 acts. *In* Lacy.   **812:1 v1**
— The two Polts ; an original farce in 1 act. *In* Lacy.   **812:1 v45**
— A wicked wife ; a drama in 1 act. *In* Lacy.   **812:1 v30**
— *joint author, see* Lacy, T: Hailes.
Cowley, Hannah, *born* Parkhouse. The belle's stratagem ; comedy in 5 acts. *In* British drama.   **822.2:1 v1**
— *Same. In* Lacy.   **812:1 v12**
— A bold stroke for a husband ; a comedy in 5 acts. *In* French's.   **812:1 v116**
— Who's the dupe ; farce in 2 acts. *In* British drama.   **822.2:1 v2**
Coyne, Joseph Stirling. Angel or devil ; a drama in 1 act. *In* Lacy.   **812:1 v29**
— Binks the bagman ; a farce in 1 act. *In* Lacy.   **812:1 v7**
— Black sheep ; an original comedy in 3 acts. *In* Lacy.   **812:1 v51**
— Box and Cox, married and settled ? an original farce in 1 act. *In* Lacy. **812:1 v8**
— Buckstone at home, or The manager and his friends ; an original domestic and dramatic apropos sketch. *In* Lacy. **812:1 v58**
— Catching a mermaid ; an amphibious piece of extravagance in 1 act. *In* Lacy.
                                      812:1 v24
— Dark doings in the cupboard by Knotting'em brothers ; a farce in 1 act. *In* Lacy.
                                      812:1 v64

Coyne, Joseph Stirling.—*Continued.*
— Duck hunting ; an original farce in 1 act. *In* Lacy.   812 : 1 v56
— A duel in the dark ; an original farce in 1 act. *In* Lacy.   812 : 1 v6
— Everybody's friend ; an original comedy in 3 acts. *In* Lacy.   812 : 1 v40
— Fraud and its victims ; a drama in 4 acts, preceded by a prologue. *In* Lacy. 812 : 1 v29
— The home wreck ; drama in 3 acts, suggested by Tennyson's poem of "Enoch Arden"; completed by J. Denis Coyne. *In* Lacy.   812 : 1 v85
— The hope of the family ; comedy in 3 acts. *In* Lacy.   812 : 1 v13
— Leo the terrible ; an entirely new and original Æsopian burlesque in 1 act. *In* Lacy.   812 : 1 v9
— The little rebel ; a farce in 1 act. *In* Lacy.   812 : 1 v50
— The love-knot ; a comedy in 3 acts. *In* Lacy.   812 : 1 v35
— The man of many friends ; comedy in 3 acts. *In* Lacy.   812 : 1 v23
— My wife's daughter, or Volunteer service ; a comedy in 2 acts. New ed. with alterations and corr. *In* Lacy.   812 : 1 v2
— Nothing venture, nothing have ; a comic drama in 2 acts. *In* Lacy.   812 : 1 v48
— The old chateau, or A night of peril. *In* Lacy.   812 : 1 v15
— Our clerks, or No. 3, Fig Tree Court, Temple ; an original farce in 1 act. *In* Lacy.   812 : 1 v6
— The pets of the parterre, or Love in a garden ; a romantic comedietta in 1 act. *In* Lacy.   812 : 1 v48
— The philosopher's stone ; an entirely new and original satirical and politico-economical whitsun morality, extremely serious and very comical. *In* Lacy.   812 : 1 v1
— Prince Dorus, or The romance of the nose, of which the most striking feature is borrowed from the countess d'Aulnois ; an aerial, florial and conchological fairy tale. *In* Lacy.   812 : 1 v3
— Samuel in search of himself ; a farce in 1 act. *In* Lacy.   812 : 1 v36
— Satanas and the spirit of beauty ; a romantic legendary spectacle in 2 acts. *In* Lacy.   812 : 1 v39
— The secret agent ; comedy, partly from the german, in 2 acts. *In* Lacy.   812 : 1 v18
— Separate maintenance ; farce in 1 act. *In* Lacy.   812 : 1 v94
— The signal ; a drama in 3 acts. *In* French's.   812 : 1 v110
— Sir Roger de Coverley, or The widow and her wooers ; a new and original drama in 3 acts. *In* Lacy.   812 : 1 v4
— A terrible secret ; a farce in 1 act. *In* Lacy.   812 : 1 v53
— That affair at Finchley ; a comic sketch in 1 act. *In* Lacy.   812 : 1 v52
— "To parents and guardians ! at Jubilee house establishment young gentleman are—etc."; comic drama in 1 act. *In* Lacy.   812 : 1 v13
— An unprotected female ; a farce in 1 act. *In* French's.   812 : 1 v111
— Urgent private affairs ; farce in 1 act. *In* Lacy.   812 : 1 v24

Coyne, Joseph Stirling.—*Continued.*
— Wanted 1000 spirited young milliners for the gold diggings ! a farce in 1 act. *In* Lacy.   812 : 1 v8
— The water witches ; an original farce in 1 act. *In* Lacy.   812 : 1 v41
— What will they say at Brompton ; a comedietta in 1 act. *In* Lacy.   812 : 1 v34
— Willikind and hys Dinah ; a pathetic and heart-rending tragedy in 3 sad scenes. *In* Lacy.   812 : 1 v14
— Wittikind and his brothers, or The seven swan princes and the fair Melusine ; an original fairy tale in 2 acts. *In* Lacy.   812 : 1 v6
— The woman in red ; drama in a prologue and three acts, adapted and altered from the french piece of "La tireuse des cartes". *In* Lacy.   812 : 1 v92
— The woman of the world ; comedy in 3 acts. *In* Lacy.   812 : 1 v81
Craven, H. T. Bowl'd out, or A bit of brummagem ; a farce in 1 act. *In* Lacy.   812 : 1 v47
— The chemistry corner ; an original domestic drama in 2 acts. *In* Lacy.   812 : 1 v50
— Coals of fire ; comedy drama in 3 acts. *In* Lacy.   812 : 1 v94
— Done brown ; farce in 1 act. *In* Lacy.   812 : 1 v81
— Meg's diversion ; a drama in 2 acts. *In* Lacy.   812 : 1 v73
— Milky white ; original serio-comic drama in 2 acts. *In* Lacy.   812 : 1 v85
— Miriam's crime ; a drama in 3 acts. *In* Lacy.   812 : 1 v60
— My daughter's debut ; a musical comedy in 1 act. The music composed and arr. by S. Nelson. *In* French's.   812 : 1 v113
— My preserver ; a petite comedy in 1 act. *In* Lacy.   812 : 1 v57
— One Tree Hill ; an original drama in 2 acts. *In* Lacy.   812 : 1 v66
— Our Nelly ; a domestic drama in 2 acts. *In* French's.   812 : 1 v108
— The post-boy ; an original drama in 1 act. *In* Lacy.   812 : 1 v48
— Unlucky friday ; drama in 1 act. Tr. and adapted from the french. *In* Lacy.   812 : 1 v76
— The village nightingale ; a burletta in 1 act. *In* French's.   812 : 1 v108
Cronegk, J: F: v. Olint und Sophronia ; ein trauerspiel. *In* **Kürschner,** J. Deutsche national-litteratur.   830 : 152 v72
Cros, C: A journey to * * *. *In* Plays for private acting.   812 : 2
Crown diamonds, The ; opera in 3 acts. Music by Auber. *In* Lacy.   812 : 1 v78
Culin, Everett, *see* **Von Culin,** Everett.
Cullerne, E:, *joint author, see* **Edwardes,** Conway.
Cumberland, R: The brothers ; a comedy in 5 acts. *In* British drama.   822.2 : 1 v2
— The jew ; comedy in 5 acts. *In* Lacy.   812 : 1 v84
— The west indian ; comedy in 5 acts. *In* British drama.   822.2 : 1 v2
— The wheel of fortune ; a comedy in 5 acts. *In* French's.   812 : 1 v104
Curious case, A ; comic drama in 2 acts. *In* Lacy.   812 : 1 v12

Dale, Felix. He's a lunatic; farce in 1 act. *In* Lacy. 812 : 1 v78
— Six months ago; comedietta in 1 act. *In* Lacy. 812 : 1 v77
— *joint author, see* Simpson, J. Palgrave.
Daly, Augustin. Leah, the forsaken; play in 5 acts. *In* Lacy. 812 : 1 v97
— Under the gaslight, or Life and love in these times; original drama of american life in 4 acts. *In* Lacy. 812 : 1 v81
Daly, J: Broken toys; drama in 2 acts. *In* Lacy. 812 : 1 v14
— Married daughters and young husbands; comic drama in 2 acts. *In* Lacy. 812 : 1 v20
Dance, C: Delicate ground, or Paris in 1793; comic drama in 1 act. *In* Lacy. 812 : 1 v18
— A dream of the future; comedy in 3 acts. *In* Lacy. 812 : 1 v21
— Marriage a lottery; a comedy in 2 acts. *In* Lacy. 812 : 1 v36
— A morning call; comedietta in 1 act. *In* Lacy. 812 : 1 v22
— Pleasant dreams; farce in 1 act. *In* Lacy. 812 : 1 v80
— The stock exchange, or The green business; a comic drama in 1 act. *In* Lacy. 812 : 1 v36
— The times; drama in 3 acts. *In* Lacy. 812 : 1 v11
— The victor vanquished; a comedy in 1 act. *In* Lacy. 812 : 1 v36
— Who speaks first? petite comedy in 1 act. *In* Lacy. 812 : 1 v23
— A wonderful woman; comic drama in 2 acts. *In* Lacy. 812 : 1 v18
— *joint author, see* Planché, James Robinson.
Dance, G: Lucky stars, or The cobbler of Cripplegate; burletta in 1 act. *In* Lacy. 812 : 1 v94
— Petticoat government; interlude farce in 1 act. *In* Lacy. 812 : 1 v23
Danvers, H. A comic scene, inculcating and entitled a conjugal lesson; in 1 act. *In* Lacy. 812 : 1 v27
— A fascinating individual, or Too agreeable by half; a farce in 1 act. *In* Lacy. 812 : 1 v27
Daryl, Sidney, *pseud., see* Straight, Douglas.
Daveau, Illion. The plague of my life; a farce in 1 act. *In* French's. 812 : 1 v104
David, J. H. Nummer 23, oder 9, 12, 47; lokalvaudeville in 1 aufz. 2te aufl. Hamburg. 1854. T. 832 : 14
Deinhardstein, J: L: Gesammelte dramatische werke. Leipz. 1848-57. 6 v. S. 832 : 16
Contents. V. 1. Liebe und liebelei.—Der egoist. 2. Brautstand und ehestand.—Das diamantene kreuz.—Modestus. 3. Verwandlungen der liebe.—Zwei tage aus dem leben eines fürsten. 4. Erzherzog Maximilian's brautzug.—Stradella.—Irrthum und liebe. 5. Fürst und dichter.—Die rothe schleife.—Florette.—Der wittwer.—Der gast. 6. Hans Sachs.—Die verschleierte dame.—Die gönnerschaften.—Das bild der Danäe. 7. Boccaccio.—Mädchenlist.—Pigault-Lebrun.—Garrick in Bristol.
— Theater von dr. Römer. Wien. 1837-41. 3 v. D. 832 : 15
Contents. V. 1. Stradella.—Liebe und liebeley.—Brautstand und ehestand. 2. Die gönnerschaften, nach Scribe.—Liebes-intriguen, nach einer idee des Fabre d'Eglantin. — Die seltene liebschaft, nach Fagan. 3. Leichtsinn und seine folgen, nach Alexandre Dumas.—Louise von Lignerolles, nach Dinaux und Legouvé.

Delacour, Alfred Charlemagne Latigue *called, joint author, see* Moreau, Eugène.
Delavigne, J: François Casimir. The monastery of St. Just; a play in 3 acts, adapted from the french by J: Oxenford. *In* Lacy. 812 : 1 v63
— Louis XI; an historical drama in 3 acts, adapted by W. R. Markwell. *In* Lacy. 812 : 1 v9
Dennery, Adolphe Philippe, *and* Ernest Bourget. London bridge 150 years ago, or The old mint; a romantic drama in 5 acts, adapted and re-written from "Les chevaliers du brouillard" by the author of "Our future king," *etc. In* Lacy. 812 : 1 v102
— *and* L: François Nicolaie *called* Clairville. My wife's diary; farce in 1 act. Tr. and adapted from "Les mémoires de deux jeunes mariées" by W: Robertson. *In* Lacy. 812 : 1 v18
— *and* René Clément. Noémie; drama in 2 acts. Tr. and adapted by W: Robertson. *In* Lacy. 812 : 1 v23
— *and* Ferdinand Dugué. Cartouche, the french robber; drama in 3 acts. Tr. and adapted from the french by W. R. Waldron. *In* Lacy. 812 : 1 v76
— — Sea of ice, or The prayer of the wrecked and the gold-seeker of Mexico; romantic drama in 5 acts. *In* Lacy. 812 : 1 v13
— *and* M: J: L: Fournier *called* Marc-Fournier. Belphegor, or Woman's constancy; a drama in 3 acts. Tr. and adapted from the french by C: Webb. *In* French's. 812 : 1 v103
— *joint author, see* Dumanoir, Philippe François Pinel.
De Pass, E. A. Debt; original farcical comedy in 2 acts. *In* Lacy. 812 : 1 v100
— Under false colours; an original comedietta in 1 act. *In* French's. 812 : 1 v111
Derley, J., *joint author, see* Nuitter, C: L: E. T.
Devrient, E: Dramatische und dramaturgische schriften. Leipz. 1846. 3 v. S. 832 : 17
Contents. V. 1. Das graue männlein.—Die gunst des augenblicks.—Hans Heiling. 2. Die verirrungen.—Der fabrikant.—Die kirmess. 3. Treue liebe.—Wer bin ich?—Der zigeuner.
Dibdin, C: The quaker; a comic opera in 2 acts. *In* British drama. 822.2 : 1 v1
— *Same. In* Lacy. 812 : 1 v86
— The waterman, or The first of august; ballad opera. *In* Lacy. 812 : 1 v23
Dibdin, T: Harlequin and Mother Goose, or The golden egg; a comic pantomime. *In* Lacy. 812 : 1 v54
— Ivanhoe, or The jew's daughter; romantic melodrama in 3 acts. *In* Lacy. 812 : 1 v92
— The lady of the lake; a romantic drama in 3 acts, adapted from the poem of sir Walter Scott. *In* Lacy. 812 : 1 v33
— The two Gregories, or Where did the money come from? a musical farce in 1 act. *In* Lacy. 812 : 1 v70
— Novelty fair, or Hints for 1851; an exceedingly premature and thoroughly apropos revue. *In* Lacy. 812 : 1 v1
— *and* Alfred Bunn. Kenilworth; drama in 2 acts, from Walter Scott. *In* Lacy. 812 : 1 v98

Dickens, C: J: Huffam. Plays and poems, with a few miscellanies in prose, now first collected ; ed., prefaced and annotated by R: Herne Shepherd. Lond. 1885. 2 v. O.
822.2 : 49
Contents. V. 1. Introductory monograph by the ed. on C: Dickens as dramatist, actor and poet.—The strange gentleman.—The village coquettes.—Is she his wife? or Something singular.—The lamplighter; a farce.—The lamplighter's story. 2. Mr. Nightingale's diary. — Sketches of young gentlemen. — Sketches of young couples.—Poems.—Miscellanies in prose: Sunday under three heads; Threatening letter to T: Hood from an ancient gentleman; Preface to J: Overs's "Evenings of a working man"; To be read at dusk; On Fechter's acting.—App., the bibliography of Dickens.—Index.

Dilley, Joseph J. Auld acquaintance ; a comedy drama in 1 act. *In* French's. 812 : 1 v113
— A highland fling ; a farce. *In* French's.
812 : 1 v114
— The sleeping hare ; comedy in 2 acts. *In* Lacy. 812 : 1 v76
— *and* James Allen. Chiselling ; a farce in 1 act. *In* French's. 812 : 1 v109
— *and* Lewis Clifton. Summoned to court ; a farce. *In* French's. 812 : 1 v119
— — Tom Pinch ; domestic comedy in 3 acts, adapted from C: Dickens' Martin Chuzzlewit., *In* French's. 812 : 1 v121

Dillon, C: The mysteries of Paris ; a drama in 3 acts. *In* French's. 812 : 1 v116

Dimond, W: The bride of Abydos ; from lord Byron's poem ; a romantic drama in 3 acts. *In* Lacy. 812 : 1 v70
— The broken sword, or The torrent of the valley ; melodrama in 2 acts, adapted from the french. *In* Lacy. 812 : 1 v85
— Brother and sister ; a comic operatic drama in 1 act. *In* Lacy. 812 : 1 v46
— The foundling of the forest ; a play in 3 acts. *In* Lacy. 812 : 1 v2
— The hunter of the Alps ; drama in 1 act. *In* Lacy. 812 : 1 v91
— The lady and the devil ; comic drama in 1 act. *In* Lacy. 812 : 1 v90
— Stage struck, or The loves of Augustus Portarlington and Celestina Beverley ; farce in 1 act. *In* Lacy. 812 : 1 v10

Dinaux, Prosper, *pseud., see* Goubaux, Prosper Parfait.

Dixon, Bernard H., *and* Arthur Wood. Behind a mask ; comedy in 3 acts. *In* Lacy.
812 : 1 v97

Dog, The, of Montargis, or The forest of Bondy; a melodrama in 2 acts, adapted from the french. *In* Lacy. 812 : 1 v43

"Dolly" ; a comic opera in 1 act. The music by Adolphe Adam. *In* Lacy. 812 : 1 v49

Douglass, J: T. A chapter of accidents ; farce in 1 act. *In* Lacy. 812 : 1 v96

Droz, Antoine Gustave. The cardinal's illness. *In* Plays for private acting. 812 : 2
— The registered letter. *In the same.* 812 : 2

Dryden, J: All for love, or The world well lost; a tragedy in 5 acts. *In* British drama.
822.2 : 1 v2

Dubourg, A: W. Sympathy ; comedietta in 1 act. *In* Lacy. 812 : 1 v96
— Twenty minutes under an umbrella ; comic interlude. *In* French's. 812 : 1 v106
— *joint author, see* Taylor, Tom.

Dugué, Ferdinand, *joint author, see* Bourgeois, A: Anicet, *also* Dennery, Adolphe Philippe.

Dumanoir, Philippe François *Pinel, and* Adolphe Philippe Dennery. Don Cæsar de Bazan ; a drama in 3 acts. Tr. and adapted from the french by G. A. A'Beckett and M: Lemon. *In* Lacy. 812 : 1 v12
— *joint author, see* Bourgeois, A: Anicet.

Dumas, Alexandre Davy. The chevalier of the Maison-Rouge, or The days of terror ; a romantic drama in 3 acts, adapted from the french by Colin Hazlewood. *In* Lacy.
812 : 1 v42
— Childhood's dreams ; a comedy in 1 act, freely adapted from "L'invitation à la valse," by sir C: L. Young. *In* French's.
812 : 1 v118
— Les frères corses, or The corsican brothers ; dramatic romance in 3 acts and 5 tableaux, adapted from the romance by M. E. Grangé and X. de Montépin. *In* Lacy. 812 : 1 v6
— The ladies of Saint-Cyr, or The run-a-way husbands ; comedy in 3 acts. *In* Lacy.
812 : 1 v84
— The lady of Belleisle, or A night in the Bastille ; a drama in 3 acts, adapted by J. M. Gully. *In* Lacy. 812 : 1 v91
— *joint author, see* Gaillardet, T. F:

Dumas, Alexandre, *fils.* The lady of the camellias ; a tragic drama in 4 acts, freely adapted from the "Dame aux camélias." *In* Lacy. 812 : 1 v27

Durandeau, Émile. Sergeant Bridell's letter. *In* Plays for private acting. 812 : 2

Du Terreau, —, *joint author, see* Clarke, H. Saville.

Duveyrier, Anne Honoré Joseph *baron,* (Mélesville), *and* E: Roger de Bully, (Roger de Beauvoir). The chevalier de St. George ; drama in 3 acts, from the french. *In* Lacy.
812 : 1 v25
— *joint author, see* Scribe, Augustin Eugène.

Edgeworth, Maria. Dumb Andy. *In* Follen, E. L. Home dramas. 822.1 : 9
— The grinding organ. *In the same.* 822.1 : 9
— The knapsack. *In her* Novels and tales, v. 2.
E 402
— Love and law ; a drama in 3 acts. *In the same,* v. 8. E 408
— Old Poz.. *In* Follen, E. L. Home dramas.
822.1 : 9
— The rose, thistle and shamrock ; a drama in 3 acts. *In her* Novels and tales, v. 8. E 408

Edwardes, Conway. Anne Boleyn ; original, historical, burlesque extravaganza. *In* Lacy. 812 : 1 v97
— Board and residence ; farce in 1 act. *In* Lacy.
812 : 1 v89
— Heroes ; an original comedy in 3 acts. *In* French's. 812 : 1 v111
— Linda di Chamouni, or The blighted flower ; original, operatic burlesque extravaganza. *In* Lacy. 812 : 1 v87
— Our pet ; an original comedy in 3 acts. *In* French's. 812 : 1 v105
— *and* E: Cullerne. Dreadfully alarming ; farce in 1 act. *In* Lacy. 812 : 1 v95

Edwards, Sutherland, *joint author, see* Brough, Robert B., *also* Mayhew, A:

35

Ellis, G: Harlequin Cherry and Fair Star, or The green bird, the dancing waters and the singing tree! a new and original, grand, comic, christmas pantomime. *In* Lacy. **812 : 1 v9**

Ellis, W. "Our relatives"; an original domestic comedietta in 1 act. *In* French's. **812 : 1 v117**

Emden, W. S. The head of the family; a comedietta in 1 act, from "Le moulin à paroles," [by Gabriel de Lurieu, *known as* J. Gabriel, *and* C: Désiré Dupeuty.] *In* Lacy. **812 : 1 v44**

— Love's labyrinth; comedietta in 1 act. *In* Lacy. **812 : 1 v70**

Emson, Frank E. Bumble's courtship; from Dickens' Oliver Twist. *In* Lacy. **812 : 1 v99**

Euripidês. Iphigenie in Aulis, übers. von J: C. F: v. Schiller, *in his* Sämmtliche werke. **830 : 143 v3**

— Medea; tragedy. Rendered into english from the greek by G: B. Goodwin. Milw. 1878. D. **882 : 2**

— Scenen aus den Phönizierinnen, übers. von J: C. F: v. Schiller, *in his* Sämmtliche werke. **830 : 143 v3**

Fabre d'Eglantin, Philippe François Nazaire. Liebes-intriguen; lustsp. in 3 aufz. [Uebers. von J: L: Deinhardstein.] *in* **832 : 15 v2**

Fagan, Christophe Barthélemy. The rendezvous; a farce in 1 act, adapted from the french by R: Ayton. *In* Lacy. **812 : 1 v43**

— Die seltene liebschaft; lustsp. in 1 aufz. [Uebers. von J: L: Deinhardstein.] *in* **832 : 15 v2**

Falconer, Edmund. Chrystabelle, or The rose without a thorn; an extravaganza. *In* Lacy. **812 : 1 v49**

— Does he love me? comedy in 3 acts. *In* Lacy. **812 : 1 v100**

— Eileen Oge, or Dark's the hour before the dawn; a drama in 4 acts. *In* French's. **812 : 1 v107**

— Extremes, or The men of the day; a comedy in 3 acts. *In* Lacy. **812 : 1 v42**

— The family secret; a comedy in 3 acts. *In* Lacy. **812 : 1 v47**

— The husband of an hour; an original drama in two periods. *In* Lacy. **812 : 1 v31**

— Next of kin; an original, comic drama in 2 acts. *In* Lacy. **812 : 1 v46**

— Too much for good nature! a farce in 1 act. *In* Lacy. **812 : 1 v42**

Farnie, H. B. The soul of honor; romantic drama in prologue and 5 acts, adapted from the french. *In* French's. **812 : 1 v104**

Farquhar, G: Dramatic works. *With* **Wycherley, W:,** *and others,* Dramatic works. **822.2+10**

Contents. Love and a bottle.—The constant couple. —Sir Harry Wildair.—The inconstant.—The twin rivals.—The recruiting officer.—The beaux stratagem.

— Dramatische werke, deutsch bearbeitet und mit einem vorworte von Siegmund Frankenberg. Leipz. 1839. S. **822.2 : 11**

Contents. Das beständige ehepaar.—Stutzerlist.

— The beaux stratagem; comedy in 5 acts. *In* British drama. **822.2 : 1 v1**

— The inconstant, or The way to win him; comedy in 5 acts. *In the same.* **822.2 : 1 v1**

— The recruiting officer; comedy in 5 acts. *In the same.* **822.2 : 1 v2**

Farrell, J: The dumb maid of Genoa, or The bandit merchant; a melodrama. *In* Lacy. **812 : 1 v29**

Farren, Percy. The field of forty footsteps; drama in 3 acts. *In* Lacy. **812 : 1 v16**

Fast train, A! High pressure!! Express!!! a short trip. *In* Lacy. **812 : 1 v10**

Featherstone, J. L. Mademoiselle Squallino; a farce in 1 act. *In* French's. **812 : 1 v121**

Feuillet, Octave. Honour before wealth, or The romance of a poor young man; drama in 4 acts, adapted from the french by Pierrepont Edwards and Lester Wallack, with further alterations by T: H. Lacy. *In* Lacy. **812 : 1 v80**

Féval, Paul, *joint author, see* **Bourgeois, A: A.**

Field, Kate. Extremes meet; a comedietta. *In* French's. **812 : 1 v111**

Field, Michael, *pseud.* Calirrhoë, [*and*] Fair Rosamond. N. Y. 1884. D. **822.2 : 47**

Fielding, H: The miser; a comedy in 3 acts. *In* French's. **812 : 1 v103**

— The mock doctor; farce in 2 acts. *In* British drama. **822.2 : 1 v1**

Fifteen years of labour lost, or The youth who never saw a woman; a farce in 1 act, from the french. *In* Lacy. **812 : 1 v26**

First night, The; comic drama in 1 act. *In* Lacy. **812 : 1 v13**

Fisher, D: Music hath charms; a comedy in 1 act. *In* Lacy. **812 : 1 v63**

Fitzball, E: Azael the prodigal; a grand romantic spectacle in 3 acts. *In* Lacy. **812 : 1 v56**

— The children of the castle; a drama in 3 acts. *In* Lacy. **812 : 1 v35**

— Christmas eve, or The duel in the snow; an original domestic drama in 3 acts. *In* Lacy. **812 : 1 v45**

— Esmeralda, or The deformed of Notre Dame; drama in 3 acts, founded on V: Hugo's novel of "Notre Dame." *In* Lacy. **812 : 1 v18**

— False colours, or The free trader; a nautical drama in 2 acts. *In* French's. **812 : 1 v110**

— The floating beacon, or The wild woman of the wreck; a melodrama in 2 acts. *In* Lacy. **812 : 1 v75**

— The flying dutchman, or The phantom ship; a nautical drama in 3 acts. *In* Lacy. **812:1 v71**

— Hans von Stein, or The robber knight; a melodrama in 2 acts. *In* French's. **812 : 1 v104**

— Home again, or The lieutenant's daughter; a domestic drama in 3 acts. *In* French's. **812 : 1 v111**

— The Inchcape bell; nautical drama in 2 acts. *In* Lacy. **812 : 1 v79**

— The inn-keeper of Abbeville, or The ostler and the robber; drama in 2 acts. *In* Lacy. **812 : 1 v90**

— Joan of Arc, or The maid of Orleans; a melodrama in 3 acts. *In* French's. **812 : 1 v103**

— Jonathan Bradford, or The murder at the road-side inn; a melodrama in 2 acts. *In* Lacy. **812 : 1 v55**

— The miller of Derwent Water; drama in 3 acts. *In* Lacy. **812 : 1 v12**

Fitzball, E:—*Continued.*
— The momentous question ; an original domestic drama in 2 acts. *In* Lacy. 812 : 1 v30
— The note forger ; a melodrama in 2 acts. *In* French's. 812 : 1 v115
— Pierette, or The village rivals ; a comic operetta in 1 act. *In* Lacy. 812 : 1 v36
— Robin Hood, or The merry outlaws of Sherwood Forest ; a dramatic equestrian spectacle in 3 acts. *In* Lacy. 812 : 1 v48
— The siege of Rochelle ; original opera in 2 acts. *In* Lacy. 812 : 1 v95
— Tom Cringle, or Mat of the iron hand ; a nautical drama in 2 acts. *In* Lacy. 812 : 1 v41

Fitzgerald, Percy. Proverbs and comediettas, written for private representation. Lond. 1869. D. 822.2 : 37
Contents. Amateur acting. — Scratch the russian and you will find the tartar.— A sheet of blotting paper.—It is the last straw that breaks the camel's back.—The William Simpson.— The family Shakspeare.—A burnt child dreads the fire.—Man proposes —she disposes.
— The William Simpson ; a comedietta in 1 act. *In* French's. 812 : 1 v101

Fletcher, James, *joint author, see* **Beaumont,** Francis.

Foglar, Adolf. Walter von Kastelen ; trauerspiel in 5 aufz. *n. t.* D. 832 : 19

Foglar, L: Der blaustrumpf ; lustsp. in 4 aufz. *n. t.* D. 832 : 20

Follen, Eliza Lee, *born* Cabot, *ed.* Home dramas for young people. Bost. 1859. D. 822.1 : 9
Contents. Olive merchants of Bagdat.—**Aiken,** L. Alfred.—The sword.—Ahmed the cobbler.—**Edgeworth,** M. Old Poz.—**Jameson,** A. Much coin, much care.—The little gleaner.—**Pulsky,** Mrs. The sleeper awakened.—**Edgeworth,** M. Dumb Andy; The grinding organ.—**Stowe,** H. B. Extracts from Christian slave.—Honesty is the best policy.—*Charade,* Partington.—*Charade,* Blue Beard.—*Charade,* Patriot. — Historical acting charades.—**Aikin,** L. Master and slave.

Foote, S: The lame lover ; farce in 3 acts. *In* British drama. 822.2 : 1 v2
— The liar ; comedy in 2 acts, altered and adapted by C: Matthews. *In* Lacy. 812 : 1 v74
— *Same. In* British drama. 822.2 : 1 v1
— The mayor of Garratt ; farce in 2 acts. *In* British drama. 822.2 : 1 v1
— *Same. In* Lacy. 812 : 1 v72

Foote, W. S. Bitter cold, a tale of two christmas eves ; a drama in 2 acts. *In* French's. 812 : 1 v115

Ford, J: Dramatic works ; with an introd. and explanatory notes by H: Weber ; v. 2. Lond. 1811. O. 822.2 : 9
Contents. V. 2. *joint author, see.* — The fancies, chaste and noble. — The lady's trial. — The sun's darling.—The witch of Edmonton.—Glossarial index.

Fournier, L: P: Narcisse. Comedy and tragedy ; comedy from the french, tr. by W: Robson. *In* Lacy. 812 : 1 v25

Fournier, M: J: L:, *joint author, see* **Dennery,** Adolphe Philippe.

Fox, Mrs. S., *see* **Centlivre, S.**

Frank, Gustav *ritter* v., (*Dr. Franck*). Autorsqualen ; lustsp. in 1 aufz. *n. t.* D. 832 : 21
— Der bräutigam von Haiti ; lustsp. in 5 aufz. und in alexandrinern. *n. t.* D. 832 : 22
— Der gascogner in Paris ; lustsp. in 1 akt. *n. t.* D. 832 : 23

Frank, Gustav *ritter* v.—*Continued.*
— Die sylvesternacht ; drama in 1 aufz. *n. t.* D. 832 : 24
— Der telegraph ; lustsp. in 1 aufz. *n. t.* D. 832 : 25
— Worcester, oder Geist und narrheit ; lustsp. in 2 aufz. *n. t.* D. 832 : 26

French, S: Acting plays. *See* Lacy, T: H.

French, Sidney, *and* W: J. **Sorrell.** A friend in need ; an original comedy in 2 acts. *In* Lacy. 812 : 1 v46

Freytag, Gustav. Dramatische werke. Leipz. 1881. 2 v. in 1. D. 832 : 95
Contents. Die brautfahrt, oder Kunz von der Rosen ; lustsp. in 5 acten.—Der gelehrte ; trsp. in 1 act. —Die valentine ; ssp. in 5 acten. — Graf Waldemar ; ssp. in 5 acten.—Die journalisten ; lsp. in 4 acten. — Die Fabier ; trsp. in 5 acten.

Fröbel, Julius. Die republikaner ; ein historisches drama in 5 acten. Leipz. 1848. S. 832 : 27

Gaillardet, Théodore F:, *and* Alexandre **Dumas.** The tower of Nesle, or The chamber of death ; a romantic drama in 3 acts, [adapted from the french] by G. Alnar. *In* Lacy. 812 : 1 v91

Gambold, J: The martyrdom of Ignatius ; tragedy written in 1740. Annexed, the life of Ignatius, drawn from authentic accounts and from the epistles written from Smyrna and Troas in his way to Rome. Lond. 1773. D. 822.2 : 21

Gardner, Herbert. After dinner ; a farce in 1 act. *In* French's. 812 : 1 v122
— Cousin Zachary ; a comedietta in 1 act. *In* French's. 812 : 1 v122
— He that will not when he may ; an original proverb in 1 act. *In* French's. 812 : 1 v122
— A night on Snowdon ; a farce in 1 act. *In* French's. 812 : 1 v122
— Time will tell ; an original comedy in 3 acts. *In* French's. 812 : 1 v122

Garrick, D: Bon ton, or High life above stairs ; farce in 2 acts. *In* British drama. 822.2 : 1 v1
— The country girl ; comedy in 5 acts ; altered from Wycherley. *In the same.* 822.2 : 1 v1
— *Same. In* French's. 812 : 1 v101
— The guardian ; a comedy in 2 acts. *In* British drama. 822.2 : 1 v1
— The irish widow ; farce in 2 acts. *In the same.* 822.2 : 1 v1
— The lying valet ; a farce in 2 acts. *In the same.* 822.2 : 1 v1
— Miss in her teens ; farce in 2 acts. *In the same.* 822.2 : 1 v2

Gärschen, Egbert: Die Medicäer, oder Die verschwörung der Pazzi ; historisches trsp. in 5 aufz. Würzburg. 1844. D. 832 : 28

Gastineau, Octave. Lelia. *In* Plays for private acting. 812 : 2

Gay, J: Acis and Galatea ; a opera arranged and adapted for stage representation from the serenata of Handel ; the poetry, with the exception of the introductory scene, by Gay. *In* Lacy. 812 : 1 v11
— *Same. In his* Poetical works. 821.2 : 93 v2
— The beggar's opera ; opera in 3 acts. *In* British drama. 822.2 : 1 v1
— *Same. In* Lacy. 812 : 1 v21

Gerstenberg, H: W: v. Ugolino ; eine tragödie. *In* **Kürschner, J.** Deutsche national-litteratur.   830 : 152 v48

Giacommetti, Paolo. Marie Antoinette, queen of France ; historical drama in 5 acts, with a prologue. From the italian tragedy written for madame Ristori, adapted and arranged by Harry Forrest. *In* Lacy.   812 : 1 v83

Gifford, J. Wear. Supper for two, or The wolf and the lamb ; a farce. *In* French's.   812 : 1 v122

Gilbert, W: Schwenck. Broken hearts ; an entirely original fairy play in 3 acts. *In* French's.   812 : 1 v118

— Creatures of impulse ; musical fairy tale. *In* Lacy.   812 : 1 v91

— Dan'l Druce, blacksmith ; a new and original drama in 3 acts. *In* French's.   812 : 1 v118

— Engaged ; an entirely original farcical comedy in 3 acts. *In* French's.   812 : 1 v117

— The gentleman in black ; original musical legend in 2 acts. Music composed by F: Clay. *In* Lacy.   812 : 1 v88

— A medical man ; a comedietta. *In* Scott, C. W. Drawing-room plays.   822.2 : 14

— An old score ; an original comedy drama in 3 acts. *In* French's.   812 : 1 v108

— On guard ; entirely original comedy in 3 acts. *In* Lacy.   812 : 1 v98

— The palace of truth ; fairy comedy in 3 acts. *In* Lacy.   812 : 1 v89

— The princess ; whimsical allegory, being a respectful perversion of mr. Tennyson's poem. *In* Lacy.   812 : 1 v87

— Pygmalion and Galatea ; an entirely original, mythological comedy in 3 acts. *In* French's.   812 : 1 v103

— Randall's thumb ; original comedy in 3 acts. *In* Lacy.   812 : 1 v91

— Sweethearts ; an original dramatic contrast in 2 acts. *In* French's.   812 : 1 v111

— Tom Cobb, or Fortune's toy ; an entirely original farcical comedy in 3 acts. *In* French's.   812 : 1 v117

— The wedding march, "Le chapeau de paille d'Italie"; an eccentricity in 3 acts. *In* French's.   812 : 1 v114

Girardin, Delphine, *born* Gay. The clockmaker's hat ; farce in 1 act, adapted from "Le chapeau d'un horologer". *In* Lacy.   812 : 1 v18

— *see also* Lewes, G: H: Sunshine through the clouds.

Glengall, *Earl of, see* Butler, R:

Godiva, or Ye ladye of Coventrie and ye exyle fayrie ; a burlesque historic fancy in 1 act. *In* Lacy.   812 : 1 v4

Goelschy, Gustave. The professor of elocution. *In* Plays for private acting.   812 : 2

Goldsmith, Oliver. The good-natured man ; a comedy in 5 acts. *In* French's.   812 : 1 v109

— *Same. In his* Works.   820.2 : 10 v1

— *Same. In his* Works.   820.2 : 30 v2

— She stoops to conquer ; comedy in 5 acts. *In* British drama.   822.2 : 1 v1

— *Same. In* Lacy.   812 : 1 v25

— *Same. In his* Works.   820.2 : 10 v1

— *Same. In his* Works.   820.2 : 30 v2

Gomes, J: Baptista. Ignez de Castro ; trauerspiel in 5 aufz. Nach der siebenten verbesserten auflage der portugiesischen urschrift übersetzt von Alexander Wittich ; mit geschichtlicher einleitung und einer vergleichenden kritik der verschiedenen Ignez-tragödien. Leipz. 1841. S.   862 : 2

Good night, signor Pantaloon ; a comic opera in 1 act, adapted from the french. *In* Lacy.   812 : 1 v73

Gordon, Lionel Smith. Keeper of the seals ; a comedietta in 1 act. *In* French's.   812 : 1 v104

Gordon, Walter. Dearest mamma ! comedietta in 1 act. *In* Lacy.   812 : 1 v46

— Duchess or nothing ; a comedietta in 1 act. *In* Lacy.   812 : 1 v47

— Home for a holiday ; a comedietta in 1 act. *In* Lacy.   812 : 1 v49

— My wife's relations ; a comedietta in 1 act. *In* Lacy.   812 : 1 v56

— An odd lot ; a farce in 1 act. *In* Lacy.   812 : 1 v62

— Old Trusty ; a comic drama in 1 act. *In* Lacy.   812 : 1 v50

— Through fire and water ; original comic drama in 2 acts. *In* Lacy.   812 : 1 v86

Gore, Catherine Grace Francis. The maid of Croissey, or Theresa's vow ; drama in 2 acts. N. Y. *n. d.* S. *With* Talfourd, T: N. Ion.   822.2 : 3

Gorostiza, Manuel E: de. Nachsicht für alle ; originalkomödie in 5 acten, übers. von Hedwig Wolf. *In* Laube, H: Dramatische werke.   832 : 59 v13

Göthe, J: Wolfgang v. Faust ; a dramatic poem. Tr. into english prose with notes, etc., by A. Hayward. New ed. Bost. 1854. D.   832 : 30

— *Same.* From the german by J: Anster ; with an introd. by H: Morley. [Morley's universal library.] Lond. 1883. D.   832 : 97

— *Same* ; a tragedy. Tr. in the original metres by Bayard Taylor. Bost. 1878. 2 v. D.   832 : 31

— *Same*, or The fate of Margaret ; romantic play in 5 acts, adapted from the poem of Goethe by W: B. Bernard. *In* Lacy.   812 : 1 v83

— Stella ; a drama in 5 acts. *In* Thompson, B: German theatre.   832 : 96 v6

— *See also his* Sämmtliche werke.   830 : R136
Werke.   830 : 137
Werke.   830 : 152 v87, 88, 93
Works.   830 : 151

Gott, H: The wizard of the moor ; melodrama in 3 acts. *In* Lacy.   812 : 1 v82

Gottsched, J: Christoph. Cato ; ein trauerspiel. *In* **Kürschner, J.** Deutsche nationallitteratur.   830 : 152 v42

Gottsched, Luise Adelgunde Victorine. Das testament ; ein deutsches lustspiel in 5 aufz. *In* **Kürschner, J.** Deutsche nationallitteratur.   830 : 152 v42

Goubaux, Prosper Parfait, (*Prosper Dinaux*,) *and* Gabriel J: Baptiste Ernest Wilfred Legouvé. Infatuation ; a drama in 4 acts, adapted from the french, Louise de Lignerolles. *In* French's.   812 : 1 v116

— *Same.* Louise de Lignerolles ; tragic drama in 5 acts, adapted from the french. *In* Lacy.   812 : 1 v14

Gowing, W: The state prisoner ; a drama in 1 act. *In* French's. 812 : 1 v101

Gozlan, Léon. Eva ; drama in 5 aufz., bearb. von K: G. T. Winkler. *n. t.* S. 832 : 86

Gozzi, C: Turandot, prinzessin von China ; ein tragikomisches mährchen, übers. von F: v. Schiller. *In* Schiller, J: C. F: v. Sämmtliche werke. 830 : 143 v6

— *Same. In* Schiller, J: C. F: v. Sämmtliche werke. 830 : 144 v9

Grabbe, Christian Dietrich. Sämmtliche werke und handschriftlicher nachlass. Erste kritische gesammt-ausgabe, herausg. und erläutert von Oskar Blumenthal. Detmold. 1874. 4 v. D. 832 : 22
Contents. V. 1. Herzog Theodor von Gothland.— Nannette und Maria.—Scherz, satire, ironie und tiefere bedeutung. 2. Don Juan und Faust.—Die Hohenstaufen, 1. theil: Kaiser Friedrich Barbarossa; 2. theil: Kaiser Heinrich der sechste. 3. Napoleon, oder Die hundert tage.—Marius und Sulla.—Hannibal. — Die Hermannsschlacht. 4. Aschenbrödel. — Der Cid.—Fragmente.—Ueber die Shakspearo-manie. —Das theater zu Düsseldorf.—Recensionen über einzelne aufführungen.—Theaterkritiken aus dem Düsseldorfer tageblatt. — Kleinere aufsätze. — Aus Grabbe's briefwechsel.

Grangé, P: Eugène **Basté** *called, and* Xavier Aymon de **Montépin.** The syren of Paris ; a romantic drama in 2 acts, adapted from the french by W: E. Suter. *In* Lacy. 812 : 1 v52

— *and* Lambert **Thiboust.** The idiot of the mountain ; a drama in 3 acts, adapted from the french by W: E. Suter. *In* Lacy. 812 : 1 v54

Green, Frank W. Cherry and Fairstar, or The pretty green bird and the fairies of the dancing waters ; a new burlesque extravaganza. *In* French's. 812 : 1 v101

Greene, Robert. Dramatic and poetical works, with memoirs of the author and notes by the rev. Alexander Dyce. Lond. 1861. O. 822.2+5
Contents. Robert Greene and his writings.—Greene's prose works.—Orlando furioso.—A looking-glass for London and England.—Friar Bacon and friar Bungay. —Specimen of the famous histoire of fryer Bacon.— James IV.—Alphonsus, king of Arragon.—George-a-Greene, the pinner of Wakefield.—Specimen of the history of George-a-Greene.—Poems.

Griepenkerl, Wolfgang Robert. Die girondisten ; trauersp. in 5 aufz. Bremen. 1852. D. 832 : 33

— Maximilian Robespierre ; trauersp. in 5 aufz. Bremen. 1851. D. 832 : 34

Grillparzer, Franz. Sämmtliche werke. Stuttg. 1874. 10 v. in 6. D. 832 : 35
Contents. V. 1. Gedichte. 2. Die ahnfrau.—Sappho. 3. Das goldene vliess ; 1. t.: Der gastfreund ; 2. t.: Die Argonauten ; 3. t.: Medea. 4. König Ottokar's glück und ende.—Ein treuer diener seines herrn. 5. Des meeres und der liebe wellen.—Der traum, ein leben.—Melusina.—Hannibal. 6. Weh dem, der lügt. —Libussa.—Esther. 7. Ein bruderzwist in Habsburg. —Die jüdin von Toledo. 8. Das kloster bei Sendomir. —Der arme spielmann.—Ein erlebniss.—Erinnerungen an Beethoven.—Studien zum spanischen theater. —Zur philosophie und religion. 9. Politische studien. — Aesthetische studien. 10. Selbstbiographie.— Reise-erinnerungen an Rom und Neapel.—Tagebuch aus dem jahre 1836, Paris und London.—Beiträge zur selbstbiographie.

Grosette, H. W. Raymond and Agnes, or The bleeding nun of Lindenberg ; a melodrama in 2 acts. *In* Lacy. 812 : 1 v43

Grosse, Julius. Cola di Rienzi ; trauerspiel in 5 aufz. und einem nachspiel. Leipz. 1851. S. 832 : 36

Grundy, Sydney. A little change ; farce in 1 scene. *In* Lacy. 812 : 1 v95

Gryphius, Andreas. Absurda comica, oder Herr Peter Squentz ; schimpff-spiel. *In* Kürschner, J. Deutsche national-litteratur. 830 : 152 v29

— Cardenio und Celinde, oder Unglückliche verliebte ; trauerspiel. *In the same.* 830 : 152 v29

— Die geliebte dornrose ; schertz-spiel. *In the same.* 830 : 152 v29

— Horribilicribrifax ; schertz-spiel. *In the same.* 830 : 152 v29

— Leo Arminius ; trauerspiel. *In the same.* 830 : 152 v29

Guillemot, Jules. The unlucky star. *In* Plays for private acting. 812 : 2

Gustaf III, *king of Sweden.* Schauspiele von könig Gustaf III. von Schweden. Aus dem schwedischen übers. von K: Eichel. Leipz. 1884. S. 898.1 : 1
Contents. Helmfelt, schauspiel in 5 aufz.—Gustaf Adolf und Ebba Brahe, schauspiel in 3 aufz.—Gustaf Wasa, schauspiel in 3 aufz.—Siri Brahe, schauspiel in 3 aufz.

Gutzkow, K: Ferdinand. Dramatische werke. 3te aufl. Leipz. 1850. 9 v. in 13. S. 832 : 37
Contents. V. 1. *Abth. 1:* Richard Savage. *Abth. 2:* Werner. 2. *Abth. 1:* Patkul. *Abth. 2:* Die schule der reichen. 3. *Abth. 1:* Ein weisses blatt. 4. Pugatscheff.—Das urbild des Tartüffe. 5. *Abth. 1:* Der dreizehnte November. 6. Wullenweber. 7. *Abth. 1:* Liesli. *Abth. 2:* Der königsleutenant. 8. *Abth. 1:* Ottfried.—Fremdes glück. *Abth. 2:* Lenz und söhne. 9. *Abth. 1:* Lorber und myrthe.

Hackländer, F: W: Werke. 1e gesammt-ausg. ; v. 15. Stuttg. 1855. S. 832 : 38
Contents. Der geheime agent.—Magnetische kuren. —Schuldig!

— Werke ; v. 27. Stuttg. 1860. S. 832 : 39
Contents. Zur ruhe setzen. — Monsieur de Blé.— Unten im hause.

Hagen, Ernst A: Der oberst und der matrose ; trauerspiel in 5 aufz. *n. t.* S. 832 : 40

Haines, J: T: Alice Gray, the suspected one, or The moral brand ; domestic drama in 3 acts. *In* Lacy. 812 : 1 v44

— The idiot witness, or A tale of blood ; a melodrama in 2 acts. *In* Lacy. 812 : 1 v46

— My Poll and my partner Joe ; a nautical drama in 3 acts. *In* Lacy. 812 : 1 v71

— The ocean of life, or Every inch a sailor ; a nautical drama in 3 acts. *In* Lacy. 812 : 1 v69

— Ruth, or The lass that loves a sailor ; a nautical and domestic drama in 3 acts. *In* Lacy. 812 : 1 v44

— The wizard of the wave, or The ship of the avenger ; a legendary, nautical drama in 3 acts. *In* Lacy. 812 : 1 v46

— The yew tree ruins, or The wreck, the miser and the mines ; a domestic drama in 3 acts. *In* Lacy. 812 : 1 v74

Halévy, L:, *joint author, see* Meilhac, H:

Halford, J. Faust and Marguerite, or The devil's draught ; a grand operatic extravaganza ; a "free and easy" adaptation of Goethe's Faust. *In* Lacy. 812 : 1 v73

Halliday, Andrew. Checkmate ; farcical comedy in 2 acts. *In* Lacy. 812 : 1 v85

— Daddy Gray ; original drama in 3 acts. *In* Lacy. 812 : 1 v85

Halliday, Andrew.—*Continued.*
— The loving cup ; serio-comic drama in 2 acts. *In* Lacy. **812 : 1 v85**
— Romeo and Juliet travestie, or The cup of cold poison ; a burlesque in 1 act. *In* Lacy. **812 : 1 v43**
— *and* F: **Lawrance.** Kenilworth, or Ye queene, ye earle and ye maydenne ; a comic operatic extravaganza in 1 act, rev. and re-written by A. Halliday. *In* Lacy. **812 : 1 v38**
— *joint author, see* **Brough,** W:

Halm, Friedrich, *pseud., see* **Münch-Bellinghausen,** E. F. J. *freiherr* v.

Hancock, W: John Smith ; a farce in 1 act. *In* Lacy. **812 : 1 v53**
— Stolen — £20 reward ! a farce in 1 act. *In* Lacy. **812 : 1 v61**
— *and* Arthur **Moore.** Mr. Scroggins, or Change of name ; farce in 1 act. *In* Lacy. **812 : 1 v77**

Hardwicke, *Countess of, see* **Yorke,** Elizabeth.

Hardwicke, Pelham. A bachelor of arts ; comic drama in 2 acts. *In* Lacy. **812 : 1 v12**

Harrington, N. H., *joint author, see* **Yates,** Edmund.

Harrington, R: The pedlar boy, or The old mill ruin ; drama in 1 act. *In* Lacy. **812 : 1 v87**

Harris, Arthur. The avalanche, or The trials of the heart ; romantic drama in 3 acts. *In* Lacy. **812 : 1 v16**
— Doing the "hansom" ; a farce in 1 act. *In* Lacy. **812 : 1 v28**
— The little treasure ; comedy in 2 acts. *In* Lacy. **812 : 1 v23**
— My son, Diana ; a farce in 1 act. *In* Lacy. **812 : 1 v31**
— Ruth Oakley ; a domestic drama in 3 acts. *In* Lacy. **812 : 1 v29**
— Ruthven ; a drama in 4 acts. *In* Lacy. **812 : 1 v41**
— Tom Thrasher ; farce in 1 act. *In* Lacy. **812 : 1 v81**
— Too much of a good thing ; comic drama in 1 act. *In* Lacy. **812 : 1 v22**
— A very serious affair ; a farce in 1 act. *In* Lacy. **812 : 1 v33**
— *joint author, see* **Buckingham,** Leicester.

Harris, A:, *joint author, see* **Williams,** T: J.

Harrison, Wilmot. Margate Sands ; a farce in 1 act. *In* Lacy. **812 : 1 v61**
— "Special" performances ; farce in 1 act. *In* Lacy. **812 : 1 v80**

Harlequin Alfred the great ! or The magic banjo and the mystic raven ! a new and original, grand historical christmas pantomime. *In* Lacy. **812 : 1 v3**

Harlequin and O'Donoghue, or The white horse of Killarney ; an entirely new and original, grand, historical, equestrian christmas pantomime. *In* Lacy. **812 : 1 v3**

Harlequin Blue Beard, the great bashaw, or The good fairy triumphant over the demon of discord ! new, grand, comic christmas pantomime. *In* Lacy. **812 : 1 v17**

Harlequin Hogarth, or The two London 'prentices ; a new grand, comic christmas pantomime. This dish is partly served on Hogarth's "Plates," with extra seasoning to suit the times. *In* Lacy. **812 : 1 v5**

Hartmann, Julius E: Dramatische erstlinge. Leipz. 1850. D. **832 : 41**
   Contents. Theodor Körner.—Der hofnarr.—Der verheissene.—Unsere zeit.—Die testaments-clausel.—Das steildlchein.

Hartmann, Moritz. [Dramatische schriften]. *In his* Gesammelte werke. **830 : 138**
   Contents, see under German literature, Collected works.

Hartopp, W. W. Eclipsing the son ; a comic drama from the french. *In* Lacy. **812 : 1 v54**

Harvey, Frank. Bought ; an original play in 3 acts. *In* French's. **812 : 1 v101**

Hatton, Joseph *and* Arthur **Matthison.** Liz ; a drama in 4 acts, founded upon the novel "That lass o' Lowrie's," by permission of the author [F. H. Burnett.] *In* French's. **812 : 1 v114**
— *joint author, see* **Oxenford,** J:

Hay, F: Caught by the cuff ; an original farce in 1 act. *In* Lacy. **812 : 1 v67**
— The chops of the channel ; original nautical farce in 1 act. *In* Lacy. **812 : 1 v84**
— Cupboard love ; farce in 1 act. *In* Lacy. **812 : 1 v91**
— The french exhibition, or The Noodles in Paris; original farce. *In* Lacy. **812 : 1 v75**
— A lame excuse ; original farce in 1 act. *In* Lacy. **812 : 1 v84**
— Our domestics ; comedy-farce in 2 acts. *In* Lacy. **812 : 1 v76**
— A photographic fix ; an original farce in 1 act. *In* Lacy. **812 : 1 v70**
— A suit of tweeds ; an original farce. *In* Lacy. **812 : 1 v74**
— *and* Westmacott **Chapman.** The deep red rover ; an o'piratic burlesque in 3 scenes. *In* French's. **812 : 1 v111**
— *joint author, see* **Clements,** Arthur.

Hazleton, F: Sweeney Todd, the barber of Fleet street, or The string of pearls ; a drama in 3 acts. *In* French's. **812 : 1 v102**

Hazlewood, Collin H. Ashore and afloat ; a nautical drama in 3 acts. *In* French's. **812 : 1 v106**
— Aurora Floyd, or The dark deed in the wood ; a drama in 3 acts. *In* Lacy. **812 : 1 v58**
— The bitter reckoning ; a drama in 3 acts. *In* French's. **812 : 1 v107**
— The bridal wreath ; a romantic drama in 2 acts. *In* French's. **812 : 1 v107**
— Capitola, or The masked mother and the hidden hand ; a drama in 3 acts. *In* Lacy. **812 : 1 v70**
— For Honor's sake ; an original, romantic, irish drama in 3 acts. *In* French's. **812 : 1 v108**
— Going to Chobham, or The petticoat captains; farce in 1 act. *In* Lacy. **812 : 1 v11**
— The harvest storm ; a domestic drama in 1 act. *In* Lacy. **812 : 1 v55**
— The headless horseman, or The ride of death ; a strange tale of Texas in 2 acts, adapted from Mayne Reid's romance. *In* French's. **812 : 1 v107**
— Hop-pickers and gipsies, or The lost daughter ; original drama in 3 acts. *In* Lacy. **812 : 1 v85**
— Jenny Foster, the sailor's child, or The winter robin ; in 2 acts. *In* Lacy. **812 : 1 v32**

Hazlewood, Collin H.—*Continued.*
— Jessamy's courtship; an original farce in 1 act. *In* French's. 812 : 1 v109
— Jessy Vere, or The return of the wanderer; domestic drama in 2 acts. *In* Lacy. 812 : 1 v25
— Lady Audley's secret; an original version of Miss Braddon's popular novel, in 2 acts. *In* Lacy. 812 : 1 v57
— Lizzie Lyle, or The flower makers of Finsbury; a tale of trials and temptations in 3 acts. *In* Lacy. 812 : 1 v87
— The lost wife, or A husband's confession; domestic drama in 3 acts. *In* Lacy. 812 : 1 v93
— The marble bride, or The elves of the forest; a magical drama in 2 acts, adapted from "Les elves." *In* Lacy. 812 : 1 v32
— Mary Edmonstone; a pathetic and romantic drama. *In* French's. 812 : 1 v103
— The mother's dying child; an original drama in 3 acts. *In* Lacy. 812 : 1 v64
— Poul a Dhoil, or The fairy man; original drama in 3 acts. *In* Lacy. 812 : 1 v77
— The staff of diamonds; a nautical drama in 2 acts. *In* French's. 812 : 1 v104
— The stolen jewess, or Two children of Israel; an original, romantic drama in 3 acts. *In* French's. 812 : 1 v105
— Taking the veil, or The harsh step-father; a drama in 3 acts. *In* French's. 812 : 1 v106
— Waiting for the verdict, or Falsely accused; domestic drama in 3 acts, founded on and embodying the celebrated picture by A. Soloman. *In* Lacy. 812 : 1 v99
— and Arthur **Williams**. "Leave it to me"; farce in 1 act. *In* Lacy. 812 : 1 v96

Hebbel, F: Judith; eine tragödie in 5 acten. Hamburg. 1841. S. 832 : 42
— Julia; ein trauerspiel in drei akten. Nebst einer vorrede und einer abhandlung: Abfertigung eines æsthetischen kannegiessers. Leipz. 1851. S. 832 : 43

Heine, H: Tragödien. *With his* Buch der lieder. 831 : 24
Contents. William Ratcliffe.—Almansor.
— *Same. In his* Sämmtliche werke. 830 : 139 v16

Hell, Theodor, *pseud., see* **Winkler, K:** Gottfried Theodor.

Henry, Re. Fast friends; a comedietta in 1 act. *In* French's. 812 : 1 v120

Herbert, G. C. Our bitterest foe, an incident of 1870; 1 act drama. *In* French's. 812 : 1 v108
— Second thoughts; an original comedietta in 1 act. *In* French's. 812 : 1 v118

Herrmann, B. A. Alles durch die frauen; lustspiel in zwei akten, nach Bayard und Lafont. *n. t.* D. 832 : 45
— Fleck; posse in 2 akten. *n. t.* D. 832 : 47
— Johanna und Hannchen; lustspiel in 2 akten nach Scribe und Varner. *n. t.* D. 832 : 46
— Eine reise nach Spanien; posse in zwei akten, frei nach Gautier. *n. t.* D. 832 : 44

Hertz, H: King René's daughter; a danish lyrical drama. Tr. by Theodore Martin. N. Y. 1867. S. 898.3 : 3
— *Same;* a lyrical drama in 1 act. Rendered into english verse by Edmund Phipps. *In* Lacy. 812 : 1 v36

Hervilly, Marie Ernest d'. From Calais to Dover. *In* Plays for private acting. 812 : 2
— Silence in the ranks. *In the same.* 812 : 2
— The soup tureen. *In the same.* 812 : 2

Higgie, T: A devilish good joke, or A night's frolic; an interlude in 1 act. *In* French's. 812 : 1 v119
— The devil's mount, or The female Blue Beard; romantic drama in 2 acts, adapted from the french. *In* Lacy. 812 : 1 v88
— Laid up in port, or Sharks along shore; a nautical drama in 3 acts. *In* French's. 812 : 1 v105
— Wilful murder; an original farce in 1 act. *In* Lacy. 812 : 1 v32
— *and* T: Hailes **Lacy**. Belphegor, or The mountebank and his wife; romantic drama in 3 acts, adapted from the french. *In* Lacy. 812 : 1 v3
— — The Tower of London, or The death omen and the fate of lady Jane Grey; drama in 3 acts. *In* French's. 812 : 1 v94
— *and* R. **Shepherd.** Watch and wait; a drama in 3 acts. *In* French's. 812 : 1 v106

Hill, Aaron. Alzira; tragedy in 5 acts. *In* British drama. 822.2 : 1 v2
— Zara; tragedy in 5 acts. *In the same.* 822.2 : 1 v2

Hillhouse, James Abraham. Dramas, discourses and other pieces. Bost. 1839. 2 v. S. 822.1 : 10
Contents. V. 1. Demetria.— Hadad.— Percy's masque. 2. The judgment.—Sachem's wood.—Discourses: 1, On the choice of an era in epic and tragic writing; 2, On the relations of literature to a republican government; 3, On the life and services of Lafayette.—The hermit of Warkworth, by bishop Percy.

Hipkins, H. T., *and* Gaston **Murray.** A nice quiet day; a farce in 1 act. *In* Lacy. 812 : 1 v54

His novice; a trifle in 1 act. *In* French's. 812 : 1 v114

Hoadley, B: The suspicious husband; a comedy in 5 acts. *In* French's. 812 : 1 v117
— *Same. In* British drama. 822.2 : 1 v1

Hoare, Prince. No song, no supper; musical entertainment. Musie by Storace. *In* Lacy. 812 : 1 v89
— The spoiled child; farce in 1 act. *In* Lacy. 812 : 1 v85

Hodgson, G. S. Bobby A 1, or A warm reception; farce in 1 act. *In* Lacy. 812 : 1 v100

Holbein, Franz Ignaz v. Die schlittenfahrt, oder Der herr vom hause; original-lustspiel in 4 aufz. *n. t.* D. 832 : 49

Holcroft, T: The road to ruin; a comedy. *In* Lacy. 812 : 1 v2

Holl, H. The forest keeper; a drama in 2 acts. *In* Lacy. 812 : 1 v44
— Grace Huntley; domestic drama in 3 acts. *In* Lacy. 812 : 1 v82

Hollingshead, J: The birthplace of Podgers; an original domestic sketch in 1 act. *In* Lacy. 812 : 1 v35

Home, J: Douglas; tragedy in 5 acts. *In* British drama. 822.2 : 1 v1
— *Same. In* Lacy. 812 : 1 v31

Hood, Tom. Harlequin little Red-Riding-Hood, or The wicked wolf and the wirtuous woodcutter; a juvenile pantomime. *In* Scott, C. W. Drawing-room plays. 822.2 : 14

Horne, F. Lennox. The baronet abroad and the rustic prima donna; an original domestic drama in 1 act. *In* Lacy.　812 : 1 v65

— A tale of a comet; a new and original farce in 1 act. *In* French's.　812 : 1 v111

— Two heads are better than one; a farce in 1 act. *In* Lacy.　812 : 1 v27

Horne, R: H: The death of Marlowe; tragedy in 1 act. *In* Lacy.　812 : 1 v89

Hoskins, Francis Radcliffe. The blossom of Churlington green, or Love, rivalry and revenge; new and entirely original petit burlesque drama in 1 act. *In* Lacy.　812 : 1 v83

Houwald, Christoph Ernst *freiherr* v. Der leuchtthurm; ein trauerspiel in 2 akten. *In* Kürschner, J. Deutsche national-litteratur.　830 : 152 v151

Howe, J. Burdett. Handsome Jack; a melodrama in 3 acts. *In* French's.　812 : 1 v114

— Scarlet Dick, or The king's highwayman; an original drama in 4 acts. *In* French's.　812 : 1 v114

Howells, W: Dean. A counterfeit presentment; a comedy. Bost. 1877. T.　822.1 : 23

— Out of the question; a comedy. Bost. 1877. T.　822.1 : 24

— The register; a farce. Bost. 1884. T.　822.1 : 21

— The sleeping-car; a farce. Bost. 1883. S.　822.1 : 22

Hughes, F. My wife's baby; farce. *In* Lacy.　812 : 1 v97

Hughes, J: The siege of Damascus; tragedy in 5 acts. *In* British drama.　822.2 : 1 v2

Hugo, V: Marie *comte.* Ruy Blas; a romantic drama in 4 acts, adapted from the french. *In* Lacy.　812 : 1 v49

— *and* James Kenney. Hernani, or The pledge of honour; play in 5 acts. *In* Lacy.　812 : 1 v77

— *see also* **Bernard, W:** Bayle. The man of two lives.

Ibsen, H: Brand; dramatisches gedicht in 5 acten. Nach dem norwegischen deutsch bearb. von Alfred freiherr von Wolzogen; den bühnen gegenüber als ms. gedruckt. Wismar. 1877. D.　898.2 : 3

— Der bund der jugend; lustspiel in 5 aufz. Nach dem norwegischen, deutsch von Adolf Strodtmann. Berlin. 1872. D.　898.2 : 4

— The emperor and the galilean; a drama in two parts. Tr. from the norwegian by Catherine Ray. Lond. 1876. D. 898.2 : 11

— Gespenster; ein familiendrama in 3 aufz. Aus dem norwegischen von M. v. Boreh. Leipz. n. d. T.　898.2 : 5

— Die herrin von Oestrot; historisches schauspiel in 5 aufz. Unter mitwirkung von Emma Klingenfeld veranstaltete deutsche originalausg. der Fru Ingerd til Östrot. München. 1877. D.　898.2 : 6

— Die kronprätendenten; historisches schauspiel in 5 akten. Nach dem norwegischen, deutsch von Adolf Strodtmann. Berlin. 1872. D.　898.2 : 7

— Nora; a play. Tr. from the norwegian [Et dukkehjem], by Henrietta Frances Lord. Lond. 1882. S.　898.2 : 2

Ibsen, H:—*Continued.*
— Nordische heerfahrt; trauerspiel in 4 akten. Unter mitwirkung von Emma Klingenfeld veranstaltete deutsche originalausg. der Härmändene paa Helgoland. München. 1876. D.　898.2 : 8

— Peer Gynt; ein dramatisches gedicht. Uebers. von L. Passarge. Leipz. 1881. D. 898.2 : 9

— Stützen der gesellschaft; schauspiel in 4 aufz. Unter mitwirkung von Emma Klingenfeld veranstaltete deutsche originalausg. der Samfundets stötter. München. 1878. D.　898.2 : 10

— Ein volksfeind; schauspiel in 5 aufz. Deutsch von W: Lange, einzige vom verfasser autorisirte deutsche ausg. Leipz. n. d. T. *With his* Gespenster.　898.2 : 5

Iffland, A: W: Theatralische werke in einer auswahl. Leipz. 1844. 10 v. S.　832 : 51
Contents. V. 1. Die jäger.—Reue versöhnt. 2. Die reise nach der stadt.—Herbsttag. 3. Der mann von wort.—Dienstpflicht. 4. Scheinverdienst.—Der spieler.—Der komet. 5. Verbrechen aus ehrsucht.—Leichter sinn.—Die hagestolzen. 6. Die aussteuer.—Das erbtheil des vaters. 7. Die höhen.—Frauenstand. 8. Die advokaten.—Erinnerung.—Albert von Turneisen. 9. Bewusstsein.—Der vormund.—Vaterfreude. 10. Elise von Valberg.—Hausfrieden.—Die mündel.—Nachrichten von Iffland's leben.

Immermann, K: Lebrecht. Die opfer des schweigens; trauersp. in 5 aufz. *n. t.* D.　832 : 52

Inchbald, Elizabeth, *born* Simpson. Every one has his fault; a comedy in 5 acts. *In* French's.　812 : 1 v107

— The midnight hour; a petite comedy in 3 acts. *In* French's.　812 : 1 v122

Irwin, E: King O'Toole's goose, or The legends of Glendalough; an original, national legendary extravaganza. *In* Lacy.　812 : 1 v30

Jackman, I: All the world's a stage; farce in 2 acts. *In* British drama.　822.2 : 1 v2

— Hero and Leander; comic burletta in 2 acts. *In* British drama.　822.2 : 1 v1

James, H:, *jr.* Daisy Miller; a comedy in three acts. Bost. 1883. D.　822.1 : 20

James, Walter, *joint author, see* Stephens, G:

Jameson, Anna Brownell, *born* Murphy. The little gleaner. *In* Follen, E. L. Home dramas.　822.1 : 9

— Much coin, much care. *In the same.* 822.1 : 9

Jerrold, Douglas W: Ambrose Gwinett, a seaside story; melodrama in 3 acts. *In* Lacy.　812 : 1 v86

— Black ey'd Susan, or "All in the Downs"; nautical and domestic drama in 2 acts. *In* Lacy.　812 : 1 v23

— The bride of Ludgate; comic drama in 2 acts. *In* Lacy.　812 : 1 v93

— Comedies. Lond. 1853. D.　822.2 : 22
Contents. Bubbles of the day.—Time works wonders.—The catspaw.—The prisoner of war.—Retired from business.—St. Cupid, or Dorothy's fortune.

— Comedies and dramas. Lond. 1854. D.　822.2 : 23
Contents. The rent day. — Nell Gwynne, or The prologue.—The housekeeper.—The wedding gown.—The school fellows.—Doves in a cage.—The painter of Ghent.—Black-ey'd Susan, or "All in the Downs".

— The devil's ducat, or The gift of Mammon; a romantic drama in 2 acts. *In* French's.　812 : 1 v107

— Doves in a cage; comedy in 2 acts. *In* Lacy.　812 : 1 v99

Jerrold, Douglas W:—*Continued.*
— Gertrude's cherries, or Waterloo in 1835 ; comedy in 2 acts.　*In* Lacy.　　**812 : 1 v88**
— The hazard of the die ; a tragic drama in 2 acts.　*In* French's.　　**812 : 1 v121**
— The housekeeper, or The white rose ; comedy in 2 acts.　*In* Lacy.　　**812 : 1 v29**
— John Overy, the miser of Southwark ferry ; drama in 3 acts.　*In* Lacy.　　**812 : 1 v86**
— Martha Willis, the servant maid ; original domestic drama in 2 acts.　*In* Lacy.　　**812 : 1 v33**
— Nell Gwynne, or The prologue ; comedy in 2 acts.　*In* Lacy.　　**812 : 1 v37**
— The meeting at the Nore ; nautical drama in 2 acts.　*In* Lacy.　　**812 : 1 v78**
— The painter of Ghent ; play in 1 act.　*In* Lacy.　　**812 : 1 v92**
— Paul Pry ; a comedy in 2 acts.　*In* Lacy.　　**812 : 1 v47**
— The prisoner of war ; comedy in 2 acts.　*In* Lacy.　　**812 : 1 v27**
— The rent day ; domestic drama in 2 acts.　*In* Lacy.　　**812 : 1 v15**
— The schoolfellows ; comedy in 2 acts.　*In* Lacy.　　**812 : 1 v35**
— The smoked miser, or The benefit of hanging ; a farce in 1 act.　*In* Lacy.　　**812 : 1 v58**
— Time works wonders ; comedy in 5 acts.　*In* Lacy.　　**812 : 1 v92**
— The tower Lochlain, or The idiot son ; a melodrama in 3 acts.　*In* French's.　　**812 : 1 v110**
— The white milliner ; a comedy in 2 acts.　*In* Lacy.　　**812 : 1 v72**
Jerrold, W: Blanchard. Beau Brummell, the king of Calais ; a drama in 2 acts.　*In* Lacy.　　**812 : 1 v44**
— Cool as a cucumber ; a farce in 1 act.　*In* Lacy.　　**812 : 1 v5**
— Cupid in waiting ; comedy in 3 acts.　*In* Lacy.　　**812 : 1 v94**
Johnson, S: Irene ; a tragedy in 5 acts.　*In his* Works.　　**820.2+13 v1**
Johnstone, J: B. Ben Bolt ; drama in 2 acts.　*In* Lacy.　　**812 : 1 v16**
— The drunkard's children ; drama in 2 acts.　*In* Lacy.　　**812 : 1 v99**
— Gale Breezley, or The tale of a tar ; a drama in 2 acts.　*In* Lacy.　　**812 : 1 v7**
— The gipsy farmer, or Jack and Jack's brother; an original drama in 2 acts.　*In* Lacy.　　**812 : 1 v36**
— Jack Long, or The shot in the eye ; a drama in 2 acts.　*In* Lacy.　　**812 : 1 v119**
— Pedrillo, or A search for two fathers ; drama in 2 acts, adapted from the french.　*In* Lacy.　　**812 : 1 v85**
— The sailor of France, or The republicans of Brest ; drama in 2 acts.　*In* Lacy.　　**812 : 1 v17**
— Tufelhausen, or The lawyer's legend ; an original romantic drama in 2 acts.　*In* Lacy.　　**812 : 1 v27**
Jones, H: The earl of Essex ; tragedy in 5 acts.　*In* British drama.　　**822.2 : 1 v2**
Jones, H: A. A bed of roses ; a comedy in 1 act.　*In* French's.　　**812 : 1 v119**
— Elopement ; a comedy in 2 acts.　*In* French's.　　**812 : 1 v122**
— Harmony ; a domestic drama in 1 act.　*In* French's.　　**812 : 1 v119**

Jones, H: A.—*Continued.*
— Hearts of oak ; a domestic drama in 2 acts.　*In* French's.　　**812 : 1 v122**
— An old master ; a comedy in 1 act.　*In* French's.　　**812 : 1 v119**
Jones, J. S. The carpenter of Rouen, or The revenge for the massacre of St. Bartholomew ; a romantic drama in 3 acts.　*In* Lacy.　　**812 : 1 v4**
Jones, J. W. A first experiment ; a domestic comedietta in 1 act.　*In* French's.　　**812 : 1 v121**
— On an island ; a dramatic sketch in watercolour.　*In* French's.　　**812 : 1 v115**
Jones, T. Percy, *pseud., see* **Aytoun, W:** Edmondstoune.

Jonson, Ben. Works ; with notes, critical and explanatory, and biographical memoir by W. Gifford, in 9 v ; v. 1–7, 9.　Lond. 1816.　8 v. O.　　**822.2 : 6**
　　Contents.　V. 1. Memoirs. — Every man in his humour.　2. Every man out of his humour.　3. Cynthia's revels.—The poetaster.—Sejanus.—The fox.—The silent woman.　4. The alchemist.—Catiline.—Bartholomew fair.　5. The devil is an ass.—The staple of news.—The new inn.　6. The magnetic lady.—A tale of a tub.—The sad shepherd.—The case is altered.—Entertainments.　7. Masques at court.　9. Underwoods.—Translations, etc. — Discoveries.—English grammar.—Jonsonus virbius.
— Every man in his humor ; comedy in 5 acts.　*In* British drama.　　**822.2 : 1 v2**
— *Same.*　*In* Lacy.　　**812 : 1 v91**
Jünger, J: F. Das ehepaar aus der provinz ; ein original-lustspiel.　Leipz. 1792. S.　**832 : 53**
— Die entführung ; ein lustspiel in 3 aufz.　Neue aufl.　Leipz. 1813. S.　　**832 : 54**
— Die geschwister vom lande ; ein lustspiel in 5 aufz.　Leipz. 1794. S.　　**832 : 55**
— Maske für maske ; lustspiel in 3 aufz. nach Marivaux.　Leipz. 1794. S.　　**832 : 56**
— Die unvermuthete wendung ; ein lustspiel in 4 aufz.　Leipz. 1793. S.　　**832 : 57**
Justus Feminis, *pseud.* Ambisexia, das land der entjochten frauen ; lustspiel in 4 aufz.　Leipz. 1848. S.　　**832 : 18**
Kemble, C: Plot and counterplot, or The portrait of Cervantes ; farce in 1 act.　*In* Lacy.　　**812 : 1 v90**
— The point of honour ; a comedy in 3 acts.　*In* French's.　　**812 : 1 v118**
Kemble, Marie Thérèse, *born* DeCamp, *mrs.* **C:** The day after the wedding, or A wife's first lesson ; an interlude in 1 act, adapted from the french.　*In* Lacy.　　**812 : 1 v3**
— Personation, or Fairly taken in ; interlude in 1 act, adapted from the french.　*In* Lacy.　　**812 : 1 v89**
Kenney, James. The blind boy ; a melodrama in 2 acts.　*In* Lacy.　　**812 : 1 v58**
— Fighting by proxy ; a farce in 1 act.　*In* Lacy.　　**812 : 1 v74**
— Love, law and physic ; a farce with an illustration and remarks.　*In* Lacy.　　**812 : 1 v26**
— Raising the wind ; farce in 2 acts.　N. Y. n. d. S.　*With* Talfourd, T: N. Ion.　**822.2 : 3**
— *Same.*　*In* Lacy.　　**812 : 1 v3**
— Spring and autumn, or Married for money ; comic drama in 2 acts.　*In* Lacy.　　**812 : 1 v24**
— Sweethearts and wives ; comedy in 2 acts.　*In* Lacy.　　**812 : 1 v21**

Kenney, James.—Continued.
— and J. V. Millingen. The illustrious stranger, or Married and buried ; a farce in 1 act. In Lacy.   812 : 1 v52
— see also Hugo, V: Marie. Hernani.
Kerr, J: Rip Van Winkle ; a legend of Sleepy Hollow ; a romantic drama in 2 acts, adapted from Washington Irving's Sketch book. In Lacy.   812 : 1 v68
— The wandering boys, or The castle of Olival ; a romantic drama in 2 acts, adapted from "Le pèlerin blanc" of Piexerécourt. In Lacy.   812 : 1 v34
Kimpton, F. He lies like truth ; farce in 1 act, adapted from "Le menteur véridique" [by A. E. Scribe and A. H. J. Duveyrier.] In Lacy.   812 : 1 v75
Kingdom, J: M. The fountain of beauty, or The king, the princess and the geni ; fairy extravaganza in 2 acts. In Lacy.
                                      812 : 1 v12
Klinger, F: Maximilian v. Sturm und drang ; ein schauspiel. In Kürschner, J. Deutsche national-litteratur.   830 : 152 v79
— Die zwillinge ; ein trauerspiel in 5 aufz. In the same.   830 : 152 v79
Klopstock, F: Gottlieb. Dramatische schriften. In his Werke.   831 : 40 v5,6
  Contents. V. 5. Der tod Adams. — Hermanns schlacht.—Salomo. 6. Hermann und die fürsten.—David.—Hermanns tod.
— Hermanns schlacht ; ein bardiet für die schaubühne. In Kürschner, J. Deutsche national-litteratur.   830 : 152 v48
Knowles, James Sheridan. Dramatic works. Lond. 1856. 2 v. D.   822.2 : 24
  Contents. V. 1. Caius Gracchus. — Virginius.— William Tell.—Alfred the great.—The hunchback.—The wife.—The beggar of Bethnal Green.—The daughter. 2. The love-chase.—Woman's wit.—The maid of Mariendorpt.—Love.—John of Procida.—Old maids.—The rose of Arragon.—The secretary.
— Brian Boroihme, or The maid of Erin ; a drama in 3 acts. In French's.
                                      812 : 1 v109
— The bridal ; tragedy in 5 acts, adapted for representation with three original scenes from "The maid's tragedy" of Beaumont and Fletcher. In Sargent, E. Mod. stand. drama.   822.2 : 2 v6
— The hunchback ; a play in 5 acts. In Lacy.
                                      812 : 1 v67
— Love ; a play in 5 acts. In Lacy. 812 : 1 v74
— The love chase ; a comedy in 5 acts. In Lacy.
                                      812 : 1 v68
— The wife ; a tale of Mantua ; a play in 5 acts. In French's.   812 : 1 v109
— William Tell ; a play in 3 acts. In Sargent, E. Mod. stand. drama.   822.2 : 2 v5
— Same. In Lacy.   812 : 1 v83
Kock, H: de, joint author, see Barrière, Théodore.
Koning, V:, joint author, see Clairville, L: François Nicolaie.
Körner, K: Theodor. Dramatische werke. In his Sämmtliche werke.   831 : 41
  Contents. Toni.—Die sühne.—Zriny.—Hedwig.—Rosamunde.—Joseph Heyderich.—Die braut.—Der grüne domino.—Der nachtwächter.—Der vetter aus Bremen.—Die gouvernante.—Das fischermädchen, oder Hass und liebe.—Der vierjährige posten.—Die bergknappen.—Alfred der grosse.—Der kampf mit dem drachen.—Die blumen.
Kotzebue, A: F: Ferdinand v. Adelaide of Wulfingen ; a tragedy in 5 acts. In Thompson, B: Germ. theatre. 832 : 96 v4

Kotzebue, A: F: Ferdinand v.—Continued.
— Count Benyowsky, or The conspiracy of Kamtschatka ; a drama in 5 acts. In the same.   832 : 96 v2
— Deaf and dumb, or The orphan ; an historical drama in 5 acts. In the same. 832 : 96 v2
— False delicacy ; a drama in 5 acts. In the same.   832 : 96 v3
— The indian exiles ; a comedy in 3 acts. In the same.   832 : 96 v3
— Lover's vows, or The natural son ; a drama in 5 acts. In the same.   832 : 96 v3
— The man of forty ; a comedietta in 1 act, adapted for the english stage by W: Poel. In French's.   812 : 1 v119
— Pizarro, or The death of Rolla ; a tragedy in 5 acts. In British drama.
                                      822.2 : 1 v2
— Same. In Lacy.   812 : 1 v27
— Same. In Thompson, B: Germ. theatre.
                                      832 : 96 v1
— Rolla, or The virgin of the sun ; a play in 5 acts. In the same.   832 : 96 v1
— The stranger ; a drama in 5 acts. In the same.   832 : 96 v1
— Same. In Lacy.   812 : 1 v22
— see also Poel, W:
Kröker, Kate Freiligrath. Alice through the looking-glass and other fairy plays for children. N. Y. 1883. S.   x 822.2 : 44
Lacy, Rophino. Cinderella, or The fairy-queen and the glass slipper, in 3 acts. Music by Rossini. In Lacy.   812 : 1 v18
— Doing for the best ; an original domestic drama in 2 acts. In Lacy.   812 : 1 v55
— Doing my uncle ; an original farce in 1 act. In Lacy.   812 : 1 v72
— Robert the devil, or The fiend-father ; a grand romantic opera in 3 acts. The music by Meyerbeer. In Lacy.   812 : 1 v31
Lacy, T: Hailes. The heart of Mid-Lothian ; The sisters of St. Leonard's ; a drama in 3 acts. In Lacy.   812 : 1 v57
— The jewess, or The council of Constance ; a romantic drama in 3 acts, adapted from Scribe's "La juive". In Lacy. 812 : 1 v33
— A silent woman ; a farce in 1 act. In Lacy.
                                      812 : 1 v59
— Winning a wife ; petite comedy in 1 act. In Lacy.   812 : 1 v84
— and J: Courtney. Clarissa Harlowe ; tragic drama in 3 acts, adapted from the french. In Lacy.   812 : 1 v77
— joint author, see Higgie, T: H., also Robertson, T: W:
— publisher. Acting edition of plays, dramas, farces and extravaganzas etc., as performed at the various theatres. Lond. n. d. 122 v. S.   812 : 1
  Note. V. 101-122 are pub. by S: French, but numbered consecutively with Lacy's plays.—The contents of each vol. have been entered in their proper place, under the author's name, and in the title index.
Laferrière, Adolphe, joint author, see Pierron, Eugène.
Lamartine, Alphonse Marie L: de. Toussaint Louverture ; dramatisches gedicht. Aus dem franz. von P. Meyer. Stuttg. 1850. S.
                                      842 : 1
Lamb, C: John Woodvil ; a tragedy. In his Works.   820.2 : 14 v1
— Same. In his Works.   820.2 : 14 v5

Lamb, C:—*Continued.*
— Mr. H— ; a farce in 2 acts. *In his* Works.
   820.2 : 14 v2
— *Same. In his* Works. 820.2 : 14 v4
— The pawnbroker's daughter ; a farce. *In his*
 Eliana. 824.2 : 66
— *Same. In his* Works. 820.2 : 14 v5
— The wife's trial, or The intruding widow ; a
 dramatic poem. *In his* Works.
   820.2 : 14 v1
— *Same. In his* Works. 820.2 : 14 v5
Lambert-Thiboust, *see* **Thiboust,** Lambert.
La Motte Fouqué, F: H: K: *baron* de. Eginhard
 und Emma ; ein schauspiel in 3 aufz. *In*
 his Ausgewählte novellen, *etc.* L 351 v3
Laube, H: Dramatische werke. Leipz. 1845–75.
 13 v. S. 832 : 59
 Contents. V. 1. Monaldeschi, oder Die abenteurer.
 2. Rokoko, oder Die alten herren. 3. Die bernstein-
 hexe. 4. Struensee. 5. Gottsched und Gellert. 6.
 Die Karlsschüler. 7. Prinz Friedrich. 8. Graf Essex.
 9. Montrose, der schwarze markgraf. 10. Der statt-
 halter von Bengalen. 11. Böse zungen. 12. Demetrius, mit benutzung des Schiller'schen fragments.
 13. Cato von eisen. nach Gorostiza.—Nachsicht für
 alle, von Manuel Eduardo de Gorostiza, übersetzt
 von Hedwig Wolf.
Lawrance, F:, *joint author, see* **Halliday,**
 Andrew.
Lawrence, Slingsby, *pseud., see* **Lewes,** G: H:
Lee, Nathaniel. Alexander the great, or The
 rival queens ; tragedy in 5 acts. *In* British
 drama. 822.2 : 1 v2
Legouvé, Joseph Wilfrid Ernest Gabriel. By
 the cradle. *In* Plays for private acting.
   812 : 2
— Medea ; a tragedy in 3 acts. Tr. from the
 french by Matilda Heron. *In* Lacy.
   812 : 1 v53
— *and* Prosper **Mérimée.** The flower of Tlemcen. *In* Plays for private acting. 812 : 2
— *joint author, see* **Goubax,** Prosper Parfait, *also*
 Scribe, Augustin Eugène.
Leisewitz, J: Anton. Julius von Tarent ; ein
 trauerspiel in 5 akten. Hildburgh. 1841. S.
   830 : 9
— *Same. In* **Kürschner,** J. Deutsche national-
 litteratur. 830 : 152 v79
Lemon, Harry. Gertrude's money box ; original
 serio-comic piece in 1 act. *In* Lacy.
   812 : 1 v83
— Go to Putney, or A story of the boat race ;
 original farce in 1 act. *In* Lacy.
   812 : 1 v80
— Wait for an answer ; dramatic sketch. *In*
 Lacy. 812 : 1 v86
— Up for the cattle show ; farce in 1 act. *In*
 Lacy. 812 : 1 v79
Lemon, M: Domestic economy ; a farce in 1 act.
 In Lacy. 812 : 1 v2
— Gwynneth Vaughan ; a drama in 2 acts. *In*
 Lacy. 812 : 1 v29
— Jack in the green, or Hints on etiquette ; an
 original farce in the vulgar tongue. *In*
 Lacy. 812 : 1 v2
— The ladies' club ; comic drama in 2 acts. *In*
 Lacy. 812 : 1 v13
— A moving tale ; farce in 1 act. *In* Lacy.
   812 : 1 v16
— My sister Kate ; a farce in 1 act. *In* Lacy.
   812 : 1 v3
— The railway belle ; farce in 1 act. *In* Lacy.
   812 : 1 v17

Lemon, M:—*Continued.*
— Self accusation, or A brother's love ; drama in
 2 acts. *In* Lacy. 812 : 1 v88
— The slow man ; farce in 1 act. *In* Lacy.
   812 : 1 v24
Lenz, Jacob Michael Reinhold. Der hofmeister,
 oder Vorteile der privaterziehung ; eine
 komödie. *In* **Kürschner,** J. Deutsche
 national-litteratur. 830 : 152 v80
— Die soldaten ; eine komödie. *In the same.*
   830 : 152 v80
Le Ros, Christian. The great gun trick ; magical squib in 1 act. *In* Lacy. 812 : 1 v25
Leslie, H: Adrienne, or The secret of a life ; a
 new and original drama in 3 acts. *In*
 Lacy. 812 : 1 v68
— The mariner's compass ; original drama in a
 prologue and 3 acts. *In* Lacy.
   812 : 1 v83
— The sin and the sorrow ; an entirely original
 drama in a prologue and 3 acts. *In* Lacy.
   812 : 1 v72
— Time and tide, a tale of the Thames ; original
 drama in 3 acts with a prologue. *In* Lacy.
   812 : 1 v81
— *and* N: **Rowe.** The orange girl ; entirely
 original drama in a prologue and 3 acts.
 In Lacy. 812 : 1 v73
Lessing, J: Gotthold Ephraim. Dramatic works.
 Tr. from the german ed. by Ernest Bell,
 with a short memoir by Helen Zimmern.
 Lond. 1878. 2 v. D. 832 : 61
 Contents. V. 1. Memoir. — Tragedies: Miss Sara
 Sampson; Philotas; Emilia Galotti; Nathan the wise.
 2. Preface. — Comedies: Damon, or True friendship; The young scholar; The old maid; The woman-
 hater; The jews; The free thinker; The treasure;
 Minna von Barnhelm.
— Die alte jungfer ; ein lustspiel in 3 aufz. *In*
 Kürschner, J. Deutsche national-littera-
 tur. 830 : 152 v60
— Damon, oder Die wahre freundschaft ; ein
 lustspiel in 1 aufz. *In the same.*
   830 : 152 v60
— Emilia Galotti ; ein trauerspiel in 5 aufz. *In*
 the same. 830 : 152 v59
— *Same. In his* Ausgewählte werke.
   830 : 140 v2
— *Same, eng.* Emilia Galotti ; a tragedy in 5
 acts. *In* **Thompson,** B: German theatre.
   832 : 96 v6
— *Same. With his* Nathan the wise. 832 : 62
— Der freigeist ; ein lustspiel in 5 aufz. *In*
 Kürschner, J. Deutsche national-littera-
 tur. 830 : 152 v59
— Die juden ; ein lustspiel in 1 aufz. *In the*
 same. 830 : 152 v58
— Der junge gelehrte ; ein lustspiel in 3 aufz.
 In the same. 830 : 152 v58
— Minna von Barnhelm, oder Das soldatenglück;
 ein lustspiel in 5 aufz. *In the same.*
   830 : 152 v59
— *Same. In his* Ausgewählte werke.
   830 : 140 v2
— Der misogyn ; ein lustspiel in 3 aufz. *In*
 Kürschner, J. Deutsche national-littera-
 tur. 830 : 152 v59
— Miss Sara Sampson ; ein trauerspiel in 5 aufz.
 In the same. 830 : 152 v59
— *Same. In his* Ausgewählte werke.
   830 : 140 v1
— Nathan der weise ; ein dramatisches gedicht
 in 5 aufz. *In the same.* 830 : 140 v3

Lessing, J: Gotthold Ephraim.—*Continued.*
— *Same. In* **Kürschner, J.** Deutsche national-
litteratur.   830 : 152 v60
— *Same, eng.* Nathan the wise ; a dramatic
poem. **Tr.** by W. Taylor. Leipz. 1868. S.
                                         832 : 62
— Philotas ; ein trauerspiel. *In* **Kürschner, J.**
Deutsche national-litteratur.
                                         830 : 152 v59
— Der schatz ; ein lustspiel in 1 aufz. *In the
same.*   830 : 152 v59
Leuven, Adolphe de, *joint author, see* **St.
Georges,** Jules H: Vernoy de.
Levitschnigg, H: *ritter v.* Löwe und rose. *n. t.*
D.   832 : 63
Lewes, G: H:, (*Slingsby Lawrence*). Buckstone's
adventure with a polish princess ; farce in
1 act. *In* Lacy.   812 : 1 v22
— A cozy couple ; farce in 1 act. *In* Lacy.
                                         812 : 1 v24
— The game of speculation ; a comedy in 3 acts.
In Lacy.   812 : 1 v5
— Give a dog a bad name ; farce in 1 act. *In*
Lacy.   812 : 1 v24
— The lawyers ; comedy in 3 acts   *In* Lacy.
                                         812 : 1 v11
— Sunshine through the clouds ; drama in 1 act,
adapted from "La joie fait peur," by mme.
de Girardin. *In* Lacy.   812 : 1 v15
— *and* C: **Mathews.** A strange history ; drama-
tic tale in 8 chapters. *In* Lacy.
                                         812 : 1 v10
Lewis, Leopold. The bells ; drama in 3 acts,
adapted from "The polish jew", a drama-
tic study by Erckmann - Chatrian. *In*
Lacy.   812 : 1 v97
Lewis, Matthew Gregory. The castle spectre ;
a romantic drama in 3 acts. *In* Lacy.
                                         812 : 1 v30
— One o'clock, or The knight and the wood
demon ; grand operatic romance in 3 acts.
In Lacy.   812 : 1 v90
— Timour the tartar ; romantic drama in 2 acts.
In Lacy.   812 : 1 v79
Liebenau, G. H. Milton's muse ; dramatisches
gedicht in 1 aufz. *n. t.* D.   832 : 64
Lille, Hubert. As like as two peas ; farce in 1
act. *In* Lacy.   812 : 1 v15
Lillo, G: Arden of Feversham ; tragedy in 5
acts. *In* British drama.   822.2 : 1 v1
— Fatal curiosity ; a tragedy in 3 acts. *In the
same.*   822.2 : 1 v1
— George Barnwell, or The London merchant ;
a tragedy in 5 acts. *In the same.*
                                         822.2 : 1 v1
— *Same. In* Lacy.   812 : 1 v79
Linley, G: Law versus love ; a comedietta in 1
act. *In* Lacy.   812 : 1 v57
Lisle, Walter. The love test ; a comedietta in 1
act. *In* French's.   812 : 1 v102
Lockroy, *pseud., see* **Simon,** Joseph Philippe.
Love and rain ; a farce in 1 act, adapted from
the french. *In* Lacy.   812 : 1 v61
Lovell, G: W. Look before you leap, or Woo-
ings and weddings ; comedy in 5 acts. *In*
Sargent, E. Mod. stand. drama.
                                         822.2 : 2 v5
— Love's sacrifice, or The rival merchants ; a
play in 5 acts. *In* Lacy.   812 : 1 v67
— The provost of Bruges ; a tragedy in 5 acts.
In French's.   812 : 1 v112
— The wife's secret ; original play in 5 acts. *In*
Lacy.   812 : 1 v82

Lover, S: MacCarthy More, or Possession nine
points of the law ; a comic drama in 2 acts.
In Lacy.   812 : 1 v51
Love's telegraph ; a comedy in 3 acts. *In* Lacy.
                                         812 : 1 v32
Lowry, James M. Peculiar proposals ; a farce
in 1 act. *In* French's.   812 : 1 v121
Lucas, J. Templeton. Browne, the martyr ;
farce in 1 act. *In* Lacy.   812 : 1 v96
Lucas, W: James. A home of one's own ; farce
in 1 act. *In* Lacy.   812 : 1 v79
— The man with the iron mask ; adapted from
the french, in 4 epochs. *In* Lacy.
                                         812 : 1 v28
— Traitor's gate, or The Tower of London in
1553 ; historical drama in 3 acts. *In* Lacy.
                                         812 : 1 v95
— The white farm, or The widow's vision ; melo-
drama in 2 acts. *In* Lacy.   812 : 1 v28
— Who stole the clock ; an operatic farce in 1
act. Composed by Albert Grisar. *In*
French's.   812 : 1 v106
— The widow bewitched ; a farce in 1 act. *In*
French's.   812 : 1 v116
Lucia di Lammermoor, An english version of ;
grand opera in 3 acts. Music by Donizetti.
In Lacy.   812 : 1 v78
Lunn, Joseph. False and constant ; comedy in
2 acts. *In* Lacy.   812 : 1 v16
— Family jars ; farce in 1 act. *In* Lacy.
                                         812 : 1 v14
— Fish out of water ; farce in 1 act. *In* Lacy.
                                         812 : 1 v16
— Sharp practice, or The "Lear" of Cripplegate ;
a serio-comic drama in 1 act. *In* Lacy.
                                         812 : 1 v55
— The shepherd of Derwentvale ; drama in 2 acts.
In Lacy.   812 : 1 v89
Lynch, T: J. The rose of Ettrick Vale, or The
bridal of the borders ; a drama in 2 acts.
In Lacy.   812 : 1 v7
Lyste, H: P. Only a penny-a-liner ; comedietta
in 1 act. *In* Lacy.   812 : 1 v100
M'Closkey, James. The fatal glass, or The
curse of drink ; a drama in 3 acts. *In*
French's.   812 : 1 v106
Macdonald, *Mrs.* G: Chamber dramas for
children. Lond. 1870. D.   x 822.2 : 36
Contents. Cinderella, or The glass slipper.—Beauty
and the beast.—Snowdrop.—The Tetterbys.
Macfarren, G: Guy Faux, or The gunpowder
conspiracy ; a melodrama in 2 acts. *In*
French's.   812 : 1 v114
Macklin, C: Love à la mode ; afterpiece in 2
acts. *In* British drama.   822.2 : 1 v2
— The man of the world ; a comedy in 5 acts.
In the same.   822.2 : 1 v1
— *Same. In* Lacy.   812 : 1 v71
Macready, W: The irishman in London ; farce
in 1 act, adapted from "The intriguing
footman". *In* Lacy.   812 : 1 v79
Maltby, C. Alfred. Borrowed plumes ; original
farce. *In* Lacy.   812 : 1 v92
— For better or worse ; a farce in 1 act. *In*
French's.   812 : 1 v105
— "I'm not meself at all"; original irish stew.
In Lacy.   812 : 1 v88
— Just my luck ; an entirely original farce. *In*
French's.   812 : 1 v112
— Should this meet the eye ; original farce in 1
act. *In* Lacy.   812 : 1 v97

Maltby, C. Alfred.—*Continued.*
— Two flats and a sharp, original domestic trio ; comedietta in 1 act. *In* Lacy.
812 : 1 v100
— Your vote and your interest ; an electioneering squib. *In* Lacy.
812 : 1 v100
— and Frank **Stainforth.** Sea-gulls ; original farce. *In* Lacy.
812 : 1 v85
Mandarin's daughter, The ; being the simple story of the willow-pattern plate, a chinese tale. *In* Lacy.
812 : 1 v5
Marc-Fournier, *see* **Fournier,** M: J: L:
March, G: Lost and found ; operetta in 1 act. Music by Virginia Gabriel. *In* Lacy.
812 : 1 v89
— One in hand is worth two in the bush ; an original comedietta in 1 act. *In* French's.
812 : 1 v110
— Our friends, "Nos intimes"; comedy drama in 4 acts. *In* French's.
812 : 1 v115
— The shepherd of Cournouailles ; operetta in 1 act. Music by Virginia Gabriel. *In* Lacy.
812 : 1 v96
— Who's the heir ? operetta in 1 act. Music by Virginia Gabriel. *In* Lacy.
812 : 1 v89
Maria Martin, or The murder in the red barn ; a drama in 2 acts. *In* French's. 812 : 1 v108
Marlowe, Christopher. Works ; with some account of the author, and notes by Alexander Dyce. New ed. rev. and corr. Lond. 1876. O.
822.2+38
Contents. Preface to the ed. of 1850.—Some account of Marlowe and his writings.—Tamburlaine the great, 1st pt.— *Same,* 2d pt.— Tragical history of Doctor Faustus, from the quarto of 1604.— *Same,* from the quarto of 1616.—Ballad of Faustus.—The jew of Malta.—Edward II.—The massacre at Paris.—The tragedy of Dido, queen of Carthage.—Hero and Leander.—Ovid's elegies.—Epigrams by J. D.—Ignoto.—The first book of Lucan.—The passionate shepherd to his love.—Fragment.—Dialogue in verse.—In obitum R. Manwood.—App. 1. The atheist's tragedy.—App. 2. Note concerning Marlowe's opinions.—App. 3. Portions of Gager's Dido.—App. 4. Specimens of Petowe's continuation of Hero and Leander.—Index to notes.
— Faustus. With Göthe, J: W. v. Faust.
832 : 97
Marryat, Florence, *see* **Church,** Florence.
Marshall, Francis A. Mad as a hatter ; an original farce in 1 act. *In* Lacy. 812 : 1 v61
— Q. E. D., or All a mistake ; original comedietta in 1 act. *In* French's. 812 : 1 v115
Marston, Westland. Anne Blake ; a play in 5 acts. *In* Lacy. 812 : 1 v49
— A hard struggle ; a domestic drama in 1 act. *In* Lacy. 812 : 1 v48
— A life's ransom ; a play in 3 acts. *In* Lacy.
812 : 1 v54
— The patrician's daughter ; a tragedy in 5 acts. *In* Lacy. 812 : 1 v48
— Pure gold ; a play in 4 acts. *In* Lacy.
812 : 1 v61
— Strathmore, or Love and duty ; a tragic play in 4 acts. *In* Lacy. 812 : 1 v56
— The wife's portrait ; a household picture under two lights. *In* Lacy. 812 : 1 v54
Marthold, Jules de. On the eve of the wedding. *In* Plays for private acting. 812 : 2
Martin, W: D'ye know me now ? an original farce in 1 act. *In* French's. 812 : 1 v105
Massinger, Philip. Plays ; with notes critical and explanatory by W: Gifford. New ed. N. Y. 1857. O.
822.2+7
Contents. Introduction, essays, etc. — The virgin

Massinger, Philip.—*Continued.*
martyr.—The unnatural combat.—The duke of Milan. The bondman.— The renegado.—The parliament of love.—The roman actor.—The great duke of Florence. —The maid of honour.—The picture.—The emperor of the east.—The fatal dowry.—A new way to pay old debts.— The city madam.— The guardian.— A very woman.—The bashful lover.—The old law.—Poems.
— The fatal dowry ; tragedy in 5 acts. *In* Lacy.
812 : 1 v88
— A new way to pay old debts ; comedy in 5 acts. *In* British drama. 822.2 : 1 v1
— *Same. In* Lacy. 812 : 1 v4
— *Same. In* **Sargent,** E. Mod. stand. drama.
822.2 : 2 v5
Mathews, C: The adventures of a love letter ; a comedy in 2 acts. *In* Lacy. 812 : 1 v50
— The dowager ; comedy in 1 act. *In* Lacy.
812 : 1 v22
— His excellency ; a petite comedy in 1 act. *In* Lacy. 812 : 1 v50
— Little Toddlekins ; comic drama in 1 act. *In* Lacy. 812 : 1 v12
— Married for money ; comedy in 3 acts. *In* French's. 812 : 1 v117
— My awful dad ; a comedy in 2 acts. *In* French's.
812 : 1 v117
— My wife's mother ; comic drama in 2 acts. *In* Lacy. 812 : 1 v23
— Patter versus Clatter ; a farce in 1 act. *In* French's. 812 : 1 v118
— Paul Pry married and settled ; a farce in 1 act. *In* Lacy. 812 : 1 v68
— Two in the morning ; comic scene. *In* Lacy.
812 : 1 v20
— Who killed Cock Robin ? farce in 2 acts. *In* Lacy. 812 : 1 v68
— *and others.* Aggravating Sam ; comic drama in 2 acts. *In* Lacy. 812 : 1 v17
— *joint author, see* **Lewes,** G: H:
Matthison, Arthur. A false step ; the prohibited play, freely adapted from "Les lionnes pauvres". *In* French's. 812 : 1 v113
— *joint author, see* **Hatton,** Joseph.
Maurice, Walter. *pseud., see* **Besant,** Walter.
Mayhew, A:, *and* Sutherland **Edwards.** Christmas boxes ; a farce in 1 act. *In* Lacy.
812 : 1 v46
— — The four cousins ; comic drama in 2 acts. *In* Lacy. 812 : 1 v92
— — The goose with the golden eggs ; a farce in 1 act. *In* Lacy. 812 : 1 v44
Mayhew, E:, *and* G. **Smith.** Make your wills ; a farce in 1 act. *In* Lacy. 812 : 1 v59
Mayhew, H: The wandering minstrel ; farce in 1 act. *In* Lacy. 812 : 1 v23
Meadow, A: His own enemy. *In* French's.
812 : 1 v102
Meddlhammer, J: Baptist v., *(Albini).* Die gefährliche tante ; lustspiel in 4 akten mit einem vorspiele. *n. t.* D. 832 : 1
— Die rosen ; ein dramatisches gemälde in 3 abth. und 5 akten. *n. t.* D. 832 : 2
Meilhac, H:, *and* L: **Halévy.** Bluebeard repaired, a worn-out subject done-up anew ; an operatic extravaganza in 1 act, adapted from the french by H: Bellingham. *In* Lacy. 812 : 1 v70
— — Frou-Frou ; play in 5 acts, adapted from the french. *In* Lacy. 812 : 1 v88
— — On bail ; a farcical comedy in 3 acts, adapted from "Le réveillon" by W. S. Gilbert. *In* French's. 812 : 1 v117

Meinhold, Isidor W: Wallenstein und Stralsund ; ein geschichtliches, heroisches schauspiel in 5 aufz. Leipz. 1846. S.
832 : 65

Mélesville, pseud., see Duveyrier, Anne Honoré Joseph baron.

Melville, C:, joint author, see Selby, C:

Mérimée, Prosper. Das theater der Clara Gazul, frei nach dem französischen von K: Hermann. Abth. 1, 2. In his Gesammelte werke.
840 : 1 v4, 5

Contents. V. 4. Die spanier in Dänemark; komödie in 3 aufz.—Ein weib ist ein teufel, oder Die versuchung des heiligen Antonius; komödie. — Ines Mendo, oder Der sieg über das vorurtheil; komödie.—Ines Mendo, oder Der triumph der vorurtheil; komödie in 3 aufz. 5. Afrikanische liebe: komödie.—Die gelegenheit; komödie.—Himmel und hölle; komödie. —Die carosse der heiligen sacrament; zwischenspiel. —Die familie Carvajal; drama.

— joint author, see Legouvé, Joseph Wilfrid Ernest Gabriel.

Meritt, Paul. Chopstick and Spikins ; a farce. In French's.
812 : 1 v109

— Glin Gath, or The man in the cleft ; drama in 4 acts. In Lacy.
812 : 1 v99

— The golden plough ; a new and entirely original melodramatic romance in 4 acts. In French's.
812 : 1 v111

— The word of honour ; a Jersey love story ; an original drama in 3 acts. In French's.
812 : 1 v113

— and H: Pettitt. "British born"; a new and original drama of national and domestic interest in a prologue and 3 acts. In French's.
812 : 1 v109

— joint author, see Conquest, G:

Merivale, Herman C. A husband in clover ; farce in 1 act. In Lacy.
812 : 1 v100

— The lady of Lyons, married and settled ; a vaudeville in 3 scenes. In French's.
812 : 1 v115

— Peacock's holiday ; a farcical comedy in 2 acts, founded on the "Voyage de M. Perrichon." In French's.
812 : 1 v115

— A son of the soil ; romantic play in 3 acts, founded on "Le lion amoreux" of [François] Ponsard. In Lacy.
812 : 1 v97

— The white pilgrim ; a tragedy in 4 acts. The legend by Gilbert A'Beckett. In French's.
812 : 1 v113

— joint author, see Simpson, J. Palgrave.

Metastasio, P: Antonio Domenico Buonaventura Trapassi. Hadrian in Syrien ; oper. Uebers. von Schubart. In Schubart, C. F: D. Gesammelte schriften.
830 : 146 v7

Meurice, François Paul. Fan Fan, the tulip, or A soldier's fortune ; a drama in 2 acts, adapted from the french by W. E. Suter. In Lacy.
812 : 1 v65

Mildenhall, T: The governor's wife ; a comedy in 2 acts. In Lacy.
812 : 1 v31

— The post of honour ; a comic drama in 1 act. In Lacy.
812 : 1 v48

Miller, James. Mahomet, the impostor; tragedy in 5 acts. In British drama.
822.2 : 1 v2

Millett, R. W. F., and R. N. Wilcox. All at C, or The captive, the coffee and the cocoatina ; an original modern musical melodrama. In French's.
812 : 1 v102

Milli ngen, J: Gideon. Ladies at home, or Gentlemen, we can do without you ; female interlude in 1 act. In Lacy.
812 : 1 v10

Millingen, J: Gideon.—Continued.

— Who'll lend me a wife ; a farce in 2 acts. In French's.
812 : 1 v111

— joint author, see Kenney, James.

Milman, H: Hart. Fazio, or The italian wife ; a tragedy. In Lacy.
812 : 1 v66

Milner, H: M. The fair maid of Perth, or The battle of the Inch ; a grand historical, national drama in 3 acts, founded on sir Walter Scott's work. In Lacy.
812 : 1 v71

— Frankenstein, or The man and the monster ; romantic melodrama in 2 acts, founded principally on mrs. Shelley's singular work, "Frankenstein, or The modern Prometheus," and partly on the french piece "Le magicien et le monstre." In Lacy.
812 : 1 v75

— The hut of the red mountain, or Thirty years of a gambler's life ; a drama in 3 acts. In Lacy.
812 : 1 v72

— Mazeppa, or The wild horse of Tartary ; romantic drama in 3 acts, dramatized from lord Byron's poem. In Lacy.
812 : 1 v96

— The veteran of 100 years, or Five generations ; a drama in 1 act, adapted from the french. In Lacy.
812 : 1 v36

Milton, J: Comus ; a masque in 3 acts. In British drama.
822.2 : 1 v2

— Same. In his Poetical works. 821.2+124 v2

Mitford, Mary Russell. Foscari ; tragedy in 5 acts. In Lacy.
812 : 1 v86

— Same. In her Works.
820.2 : 27

— Rienzi ; tragedy in 5 acts. In Lacy.
812 : 1 v90

— Same. In her Works.
820.2 : 27

Molière, J: Baptiste Poquelin called. Works ; french and english. Lond. 1739. 10 v. S.
842 : 3

Contents. V. 1. Memoires sur la vie de Molière; Memoirs of the life of Molière. — L'étourdi; The blunderer.—Le dépit amoureux; The amorous quarrel. 2. [Missing]. 3. L'école des maris; The school for husbands.—L'école des femmes; The school for wives.—La critique de l'école des femmes; The school for wives criticised.—L'impromptu of Versailles; The impromptu of Versailles. 4. Le misantrope; The man-hater. — Le médecin malgré lui; The mock doctor. — Don Juan, ou Le festin de pierre; Don John, or The feast of the statue. 5. L'amour médecin; Love's the best doctor. — Le tartuffe, ou L'imposteur; Tartuffe, or The impostor.—Monsieur Pourceaugnac; Squire Lubberly. 6. Amphitrion; Amphitryon. — Georg Dandin, ou Le mari confudu; George Dandin, or The perplexed husband.—Sganarelle, ou Le cocu imaginaire; Sganarel, or The cuckold in conceit. 7. Le mariage forcé; The forced marriage.—Les amours magnifiques; The magnificent lovers. — Psiché; Psyche. 8. Le bourgeois gentilhomme; The cit turned gentleman.—Les facheux; The impertinents.—Le sicilien, ou L'amour peintre; The sicilian, or Love makes a painter. 9. Les femmes scavantes; The learned ladies.—Les fourberies de Scapin; The cheats of Scapin. — Melicerte; Melicerta. 10. La comtesse d'Escarbagnas; The countess of Escarbagnas. — La princesse d'Elide; The princess of Elis.—Les fêtes de Versailles; The feast of Versailles.—Le malade imaginaire; The hypocondriak.

— Dramatic works ; rendered into english by Henri Van Laun. A new ed. rev., with a prefatory memoir, introductory notices and notes. N. Y. 1880. 3 v. O.
842 : 2

Contents. V. 1. Preface.—Prefatory memoir.—The blunderer. — The love-tiff. — The pretentious young ladies.—Sganarelle.—Don Garcia of Navarre.—The school for husbands.—The bores. — The school for wives.—The school for wives criticised. — The impromptu of Versailles.—The forced marriage. 2. The princess of Elis.—Don Juan.—Love is the best doctor.—The misanthrope.—The physician in spite of himself.—Mellcerte.—A comic pastoral.—The sicilian. —Tartuffe.—Amphitryon.—George Dandin. 3. The miser.— Monsieur de Pourceaugnac.— The magnificent lovers —The citizen who apes the gentleman.— Psyche.—The roguerles of Scapin.—The countess of Escarbagnas. — The learned ladies. — The imaginary invalid.—The jealousy of La Barbouille.—The flying doctor.

Moncrieff, W: T: All at Coventry ; a farce in 1 act. *In* Lacy. 812 : 1 v59
— Eugene Aram, or Saint Robert's cave ; a drama in 3 acts. *In* French's.
  812 : 1 v103
— The mistress of the mill ; comedietta in 1 act, tr. from "La meunière de Marly". *In* Lacy.
  812 : 1 v21
— Monsieur Tonson ; a farce in 2 acts. *In* Lacy.
  812 : 1 v74
— Rochester, or King Charles the second's merry days ; comedy in 2 acts. *In* Lacy.
  812 : 1 v83
— The scamps of London, or The cross roads of life ; drama of the day, adapted from the french, and rearranged by F: Marchant. *In* Lacy. 812 : 1 v81
— The somnambulist. or The phantom of the village ; drama in 2 acts. *In* Lacy.
  812 : 1 v86
— The spectre bridegroom, or A ghost in spite of himself ; a farce in 2 acts. *In* Lacy.
  812 : 1 v35
— Tom and Jerry, or Life in London in 1820 ; drama in 3 acts, from Prince Egan's celebrated work. *In* Lacy. 812 : 1 v88
Monselet, C: A trip through my pockets. *In* Plays for private acting. 812 : 2
Montépin, Xavier Aymon de, *joint author, see* Grangé, P: E. B.
Montgomery, H: W: Handy Andy ; a comic hibernian drama in 1 act, adapted from S: Lover's novel. *In* Lacy. 812 : 1 v74
Monte Cristo ; drama in 5 acts, adapted from Dumas' celebrated novel. *In* Lacy.
  812 : 1 v77
Moore, Arthur, *joint author, see* Hancock, W:
Moore, E: The gamester ; tragedy in 5 acts. *In* British drama. 822.2 : 1 v1
More, Hannah. Percy ; a tragedy in 5 acts. *In* British drama. 822.2 : 1 v1
— *see also her* Works. 820.2 : 28
Moreau, L: Isidore Eugène Lemoine, Paul Siraudin, *and* Alfred Charlemagne Lartigue *called* Delacour. The courier of Lyons, or The attack upon the mail ; drama in 3 acts. Tr. from the french. *In* Lacy. 812 : 1 v15
Morgan, Sidney, *born* Owenson, *lady*. Dramatische scenen aus dem wirklichen leben, übers. von L: Lax. Aachen. 1834. 2 v. S.
  822.2 : 25
  Contents. v. 1. Schloss Sackville. 2. Same, continued.—Die osterferien, oder Die tapisserie-arbeiterinnen.—Das temperament.
Morton, E: The Eton boy ; farce in 1 act. *In* Lacy. 812 : 1 v16
Morton, J: Maddison. The "Alabama" altered from h. m. ship "Spitfire ;" a transatlantic nautical extravaganza. *In* Lacy.
  812 : 1 v62
— Aladdin and the wonderful lamp, or Harlequin and the genie of the ring ; a new comic christmas pantomime. *In* Lacy.
  812 : 1 v29

Morton, J: Maddison.—*Continued.*
— Atchi ! comedietta in 1 act. *In* Lacy.
  812 : 1 v82
— Aunt Charlotte's maid ; a farce in 1 act. *In* Lacy. 812 : 1 v38
— Away with melancholy ; farce in 1 act. *In* Lacy. 812 : 1 v14
— Betsey Baker, or Too attentive by half ; a farce in 1 act. *In* Lacy. 812 : 1 v8
— Box and Cox ; a romance of real life in 1 act. *In* Lacy. 812 : 1 v5
— Brother Ben ; a farce in 1 act. *In* Lacy.
  812 : 1 v34
— A capital match ; a farce in 1 act. *In* Lacy.
  812 : 1 v8
— Catch a weazel ; a farce in 1 act. *In* Lacy.
  812 : 1 v54
— Cousin Lambkin ; an original farce in 1 act. *In* Lacy. 812 : 1 v4
— A day's fishing ; farce in 1 act. *In* Lacy.
  812 : 1 v83
— A desperate game ; comic drama in 1 act. *In* Lacy. 812 : 1 v10
— Done on both sides ; a farce in 1 act. *In* Lacy. 812 : 1 v26
— Don't judge by appearances ; farce in 1 act. *In* Lacy. 812 : 1 v24
— The double-bedded room ; a farce in 1 act. *In* Lacy. 812 : 1 v60
— Drawing rooms, second floor and attics ; farce in 1 act. *In* Lacy. 812 : 1 v62
— Dying for love ; a comedy in 1 act. *In* Lacy.
  812 : 1 v36
— An englishman's house is his castle ; in 1 act. *In* Lacy. 812 : 1 v31
— Fitzsmythe of Fitzsmythe Hall ; a farce in 1 act. *In* Lacy. 812 : 1 v46
— Friend Waggles ; a farce in 1 act. *In* Lacy.
  812 : 1 v33
— From village to court ; comic drama in 2 acts. *In* Lacy. 812 : 1 v15
— A game of romps ; farce in 1 act. *In* Lacy.
  812 : 1 v18
— Going to the Derby ; an original farce in 1 act. *In* Lacy. 812 : 1 v37
— Grimshaw, Bagshaw and Bradshaw ; a farce in 1 act. *In* Lacy. 812 : 1 v4
— The highwayman ; an original farce in 1 act. *In* French's. 812 : 1 v120
— A hopeless passion ; a petite comedy in 1 act. *In* Lacy. 812 : 1 v5
— How stout you're getting ! farce in 1 act. *In* Lacy. 812 : 1 v22
— A husband to order ; a serio-comic drama in 2 acts. *In* Lacy. 812 : 1 v43
— If I had a thousand a year ! farce in 1 act. *In* Lacy. 812 : 1 v79
— The irish tiger ; a farce in 1 act. *In* Lacy.
  812 : 1 v34
— John Dobbs ; a farce in 1 act. *In* Lacy.
  812 : 1 v7
— "The king and I "; a farce in 1 act. *In* Lacy.
  812 : 1 v10
— The lad from the country ; a farce in 1 act. *In* French's. 812 : 1 v116
— Lend me five shillings ; a farce in 1 act. *In* Lacy. 812 : 1 v30
— "Little mother"; a comic piece in 1 act. *In* Lacy. 812 : 1 v91
— The little savage ; a farce in 1 act. *In* Lacy.
  812 : 1 v38
— Love and hunger ; a farce in 1 act. *In* Lacy.
  812 : 1 v42

Morton, J: Maddison.—*Continued.*
— Maggie's situation ; an original comedietta in 1 act. *In* French's. **812 : 1 v120**
— Margery Daw, or The two bumpkins ; a farce in 1 act. *In* Lacy. **812 : 1 v54**
— Master Jones's birthday; farce in 1 act. *In* Lacy. **812 : 1 v81**
— The midnight watch ; an original drama in 1 act. *In* Lacy. **812 : 1 v39**
— The milliner's holiday ; a farce in 1 act. *In* Lacy. **812 : 1 v38**
— A most unwarrantable intrusion ; a comic interlude in 1 act. *In* Lacy. **812 : 1 v7**
— The muleteer of Toledo, or King, queen and knave ; comic drama in 2 acts. *In* Lacy. **812 : 1 v18**
— My first fit of the gout; farce in 1 act. *In* Lacy. **812 : 1 v11**
— My husband's ghost ; farce in 1 act. *In* Lacy. **812 : 1 v93**
— My precious Betsy ! a farce in 1 act. *In* Lacy. **812 : 1 v8**
— My wife's bonnet ; a farce in 1 act. *In* Lacy. **812 : 1 v64**
— My wife's second floor ; an original farce in 1 act. *In* Lacy. **812 : 1 v44**
— Newington Butts ; a farce in 2 scenes, the first by night and the second by day. *In* Lacy. **812 : 1 v73**
— Old Honesty ; a comic drama in 2 acts. *In* Lacy. **812 : 1 v38**
— On the sly ; a farce in 1 act. *In* Lacy. **812 : 1 v63**
— Our wife, or The rose of Amiens ; a comic drama in 2 acts. *In* Lacy. **812 : 1 v28**
— The pacha of Pimlico ; a little eastern farcical extravaganza in 1 act. *In* Lacy. **812 : 1 v51**
— Poor Pillicoddy ; a farce in 1 act. *In* Lacy. **812 : 1 v38**
— Pouter's wedding ; a farce in 1 act. *In* Lacy. **812 : 1 v67**
— A prince for an hour; comic drama in 1 act. *In* Lacy. **812 : 1 v25**
— A regular fix ! a farce in 1 act. *In* Lacy. **812 : 1 v48**
— The rights and wrongs of woman ; a farce in 1 act. *In* Lacy. **812 : 1 v26**
— Sent to the tower ; a farce in 1 act. *In* Lacy. **812 : 1 v28**
— She would and he wouldn't ; a comedy in 2 acts. *In* Lacy. **812 : 1 v56**
— Slasher and Crasher ; an original farce in 1 act. *In* Lacy. **812 : 1v8**
— A slice of luck ; farce in 1 act. *In* Lacy. **812 : 1 v76**
— Slight mistakes ; an original farce in 1 act. *In* French's. **812 : 1 v122**
— Something to do ; a farce in 1 act. *In* French's. **812 : 1 v122**
— The steeple-chase, or In the pigskin ; an original farce in 1 act. *In* Lacy. **812 : 1 v68**
— "Take care of Dowb —"; a farce in 1 act. *In* Lacy. **812 : 1 v34**
— Thirty-three next birthday ; a farce in 1 act. *In* Lacy. **812 : 1 v38**
— The three cuckoos ; a farce in 1 act. *In* Lacy. **812 : 1 v40**
— A thumping legacy ; farce in 1 act. *In* Lacy. **812 : 1 v5**
— Ticklish times ; a farce in 1 act. *In* Lacy. **812 : 1 v35**

Morton, J: Maddison.—*Continued.*
— To Paris and back for five pounds ; an original farce in 1 act. *In* Lacy. **812 : 1 v9**
— Two Bonnycastles ; a farce in 1 act. *In* Lacy. **812 : 1 v5**
— The two Puddifoots ; farce in 1 act. *In* Lacy. **812 : 1 v78**
— Waiting for an omnibus in the lower arcade on a rainy day ; farce in 1 act. *In* Lacy. **812 : 1 v15**
— Where there's a will there's a way ; a comic drama in 1 act. *In* Lacy. **812 : 1 v9**
— The which of the two ? a comedietta in 1 act. *In* Lacy. **812 : 1 v40**
— Whitebait at Greenwich ; farce in 1 act. *In* Lacy. **812 : 1 v12**
— Who do they take me for ? an original farce in 1 act. *In* French's. **812 : 1 v111**
— Who stole the pocket book ? or A dinner for six ; a farce in 1 act. *In* Lacy. **812 : 1 v6**
— Who's my husband ; farce in 1 act. *In* Lacy. **812 : 1 v80**
— The woman I adore ; a farce in 1 act. *In* Lacy. **812 : 1 v8**
— Woodcock's little game ; a comedy-farce in 2 acts. *In* Lacy. **812 : 1 v63**
— Wooing one's wife ; a farce in 1 act. *In* Lacy. **812 : 1 v52**
— Your life's in danger ; farce in 1 act. *In* Lacy. **812 : 1 v29**
— *and* Francis Cowley **Burnand.** Cox and Box ; romance of real life in 1 act. Music by Arthur Sullivan. *In* Lacy. **812 : 1 v99**
— *joint author, see* **Morton, T:**
Morton, T: A cure for the heartache ; a comedy in 3 acts. *In* Lacy. **812 : 1 v34**
— Gotobed Tom ! farce in 1 act. *In* Lacy. **812 : 1 v8**
— A pretty piece of business ; comedy in 1 act. *In* Lacy. **812 : 1 v6**
— A Roland for an Oliver ; comic drama in 2 acts. *In* Lacy. **812 : 1 v75**
— The school of reform, or How to rule a husband ; a comedy in 5 acts. N. Y. *n. d.* S. *With* **Talfourd, T: N.** Ion. **822.2 : 3**
— Sink or swim ! a comedy in 2 acts. *In* Lacy. **812 : 1 v7**
— Speed the plough ; comedy in 5 acts. *In* **Sargent, E.** Mod. stand. drama. **822.2 : 2 v6**
— *Same. In* Lacy. **812 : 1 v51**
— *and* J: Madison **Morton.** All that glitters is not gold ; a comic drama in 2 acts. *In* Lacy. **812 : 1 v3**
— - The writing on the wall ! a melodrama in 3 acts. *In* Lacy. **812 : 1 v7**
Mosen, Julius. Theater. Stuttg. 1842. O. **832 : 66**
Contents. Kaiser Otto III.—Cola Rienzi, der letzte volkstribun der römer.—Die bräute von Florenz.—Wendelin und Helene.
Moss, Hugh. P. U. P., or The dog in the manger ; an original farce in 1 act. *In* French's. **812 : 1 v121**
Mountain sylph ; romantic opera in 2 acts. Music composed by J: Barnett. *In* Lacy. **812 : 1 v22**
— *Same. In* French's. **812 : 1 v120**
Mowatt, Anna Cora, *see* **Ritchie,** Anna Cora.

Müller, F:, called Maler. Golo und Genoveva ; ein schauspiel in 5 aufz. In Kürschner, J. Deutsche national-litteratur.
830 : 152 v81
Müllner, Amandus Gottfried Adolf. Der 29 februar ; trauerspiel in 1 akt. In Kürschner, J. Deutsche national-litteratur.
830 : 152 v151
— Die schuld ; trauerspiel in 4 akten. In the same. 830 : 152 v151
Münch - Bellinghausen, Elegius Franz Josef freiherr v., (Friedrich Halm). Ingomar, the son of the wilderness ; play in 5 acts by Friedrich Halm. Tr. into english verse by W: H: Charlton. In Lacy. 812 : 1 v7
— Same. Ingomar, the barbarian ; play in 5 acts, [tr.] by Maria Lovell. In Lacy.
812 : 1 v75
Murphy, Arthur. The apprentice ; a farce in 2 acts. In British drama. 822.2 : 1 v1
— The grecian daughter ; a tragedy in 5 acts. In the same. 822.2 : 1 v1
— The orphan of China ; tragedy in 5 acts. In the same. 822.2 : 1 v2
— Three weeks after marriage ; farce in 2 acts. In the same. 822.2 : 1 v1
— The way to keep him ; comedy in 5 acts. In the same. 822.2 : 1 v2
Murray, Gaston, joint author, see Hipkins, H. T.
Murray, W: H. Cramond brig, or The gudeman o' Ballangeich ; comic drama in 2 acts. In Lacy. 812 : 1 v21
— Diamond cut diamond ; an interlude in 1 act, altered from " How to die for love." In Lacy. 812 : 1 v7
— Dominique the deserter, or The gentleman in black ; a comic drama in 2 acts, adapted from the french. 812 : 1 v50
— Gilderoy ; a drama in 2 acts. In Lacy.
812 : 1 v9
Murray, W: Mary queen of Scots, or The escape from Loch Leven ; an historical drama in 2 acts. In Lacy. 812 : 1 v4
— "No"! a farce in 1 act, adapted from the french. In Lacy. 812 : 1 v1
— Philippe, or The secret marriage ; a story of the revolution ; domestic drama in 1 act, adapted from the french. In Lacy.
812 : 1 v82
Muskery, W: Atonement ; a romantic drama in 4 acts and 10 tableaux, comprising a prologue, two epochs and an epilogue ; founded on V: Hugo's romance, " Les misérables." In French's. 812 : 1 v104
Musset, L: C: Alfred de. A good little wife ; comedy in 1 act. Tr. and adapted from " Un caprice." In Lacy. 812 : 1 v17
Naek, James. The immortal ; a dramatic romance and other poems ; with a memoir of the author by G: P. Morris. N. Y. 1850. D.
822.1 : 11
Narrey, C: Sophronisba-oh ! In Plays for private acting. 812 : 2
Neville, G: F. The little vixens ; a comedietta in 1 act. In French's. 812 : 1 v112
Night, A, of suspense ; a monologue, as performed by mrs. Stirling. In Lacy.
812 : 1 v89
Normand, Jacques. The invitation to the christening. In Plays for private acting.
812 : 2

Nuitter, C: L: Etienne Truinet, and J. Derley. A cup of tea ; comedietta in 1 act. Tr. from the french. In Lacy. 812 : 1 v83
O'Bryan, C: Lugarto the mulatto ; a drama in 4 acts. In Lacy. 812 : 1 v31
Obstinate family, The ; farce in 1 act. Tr. and adapted from the german. In Lacy.
812 : 1 v10
O'Callaghan, P. P. The married bachelor, or Master and man ; a farce in 1 act. In Lacy. 812 : 1 v4
O'Hara, Kane. Midas ; an english burletta in 2 acts. In British drama. 822.2 : 1 v1
— Same. In Lacy. 812 : 1 v12
— Tom Thumb the great ; burlesque tragedy in 2 acts, altered from Fielding. In Lacy.
812 : 1 v50
— Same. In British drama. 822.2 : 1 v1
Oehlenschläger, Adam Gottlob. Aladdin, or The wonderful lamp ; a dramatic poem in 2 parts. Tr. by Theodore Martin. Edinb. 1863. D. 898.3 : 6
— Correggio ; a tragedy. Tr. with notes by Theodore Martin. Edinb. 1865. D.
898.3 : 7
O'Keeffe, J: The agreeable surprise ; comic opera in 2 acts. In Lacy. 812 : 1 v94
— The poor soldier ; musical farce in 1 act. In Lacy. 812 : 1 v91
— Wild oats, or The strolling gentleman ; comedy in 5 acts. In Lacy. 812 : 1 v88
Omnibus, The, or A convenient distance ; a farce in 1 act, altered from Raymond's farce of " Cherry bounce". In Lacy. 812 : 1 v32
O'Neill, I. R. An optical delusion ; a farce in 1 act. In French's. 812 : 1 v101
Ottmar, F. H. Käthchen von Engen, oder Widerhold auf Hohentwiel, vaterländisches schauspiel. Freiburg. 1836. S. 832 : 67
Otway, T: The orphan, or The unhappy marriage ; tragedy in 5 acts. In British drama.
822.2 : 1 v1
— Venice preserved ; tragedy in 5 acts. In the same. 822.2 : 1 v1
— Same. In Lacy. 812 : 1 v32
Oxberry, W: H: Matteo Falcone, or The brigand and son ; melodrama in 1 act, adapted from the french. In Lacy. 812 : 1 v83
— Norma travestie ; una grandiosa, tragica, comica, seria, domestica, musica, burlesqua burletta in 1 act. Freely rendered (not) from the italian. In Lacy. 812 : 1 v55
Oxenford, J: Adrienne Lecouvreur, the reigning favorite ; a drama in 3 acts. In Lacy.
812 : 1 v1
— Beauty or the beast ; an original farce in 1 act. In Lacy. 812 : 1 v60
— Billing and cooing ; a comedy in 2 acts. In Lacy. 812 : 1 v65
— Bristol diamonds ; a farce in 1 act. In Lacy.
812 : 1 v56
— A cleft stick ; a comedy in 3 acts. In Lacy.
812 : 1 v68
— A day well spent ; a farce in 1 act. In Lacy.
812 : 1 v34
— The dice of death ; a romantic drama in 3 acts. In French's. 812 : 1 v110
— A doubtful victory ; a comedietta in 1 act. In Lacy. 812 : 1 v36
— Down in a balloon ; farce in 1 act. In Lacy.
812 : 1 v92

Oxenford, J:—*Continued.*
— A family failing ; a farce in 1 act. *In* Lacy.
812 : 1 v29
— Five pounds reward ; farce in 1 act. *In* Lacy.
812 : 1 v24
— Der freischütz ; a grand romantic opera in 4 acts. *In* Lacy.   812 : 1 v69
— I couldn't help it ; an original farce in 1 act. *In* Lacy.   812 : 1 v55
— A legal impediment ; a farce in 1 act. *In* Lacy.   812 : 1 v53
— The magic toys ; a ballet farce in 1 act. *In* Lacy.   812 : 1 v42
— My fellow clerk ; a farce in 1 act. *In* Lacy.
812 : 1 v48
— Neighbours ; a new comedy in 2 acts. *In* Lacy.   812 : 1 v73
— Only a half penny ! farce in 1 act. *In* Lacy.
812 : 1 v22
— Please to remember the grotto, or The manageress in a fix ; a metamorphosed, ollapodridical, boy and gal-limaufrical, extravaganzical, pantomimical and entirely nondescriptical rehearsal. *In* Lacy. 812 : 1 v70
— The porter's knot ; a serio-comic drama in 2 acts. *In* Lacy.   812 : 1 v38
— Retained for the defence ; a farce in 1 act. *In* Lacy.   812 : 1 v41
— Sam's arrival ; an absurdity in 1 act. *In* Lacy.
812 : 1 v56
— Twice killed ; farce in 1 act. *In* Lacy.
812 : 1 v24
— The two orphans ; a drama in 8 tableaux divided into 6 acts. *In* French's.
812 : 1 v106
— Uncle Zachary ; a comic drama in 2 acts. *In* Lacy.   812 : 1 v45
— A waltz by Arditi ; a farce in 1 act. *In* French's.   812 : 1 v101
— The world of fashion ; a comedy in 3 acts. *In* Lacy.   812 : 1 v55
— A young lad from the country ; an original farce in 1 act. *In* Lacy.   812 : 1 v64
— *and* C: Shirley **Brooks.** Timour the tartar ! or The iron master of Samarkand-by-Oxus ; an extravaganza. *In* Lacy.   812 : 1 v49
— *and* Joseph **Hatton.** Much too clever, or A friend indeed ; extravagant comedy in 1 act and 3 scenes, adapted from the french. *In* French's.   812 : 1 v114
— *and* Horace **Wigan.** A life chase ; drama in 5 acts. *In* Lacy.   812 : 1 v86
Palmer, T. A. Among the relics ; a comedy drama in 3 acts. *In* French's. 812 : 1 v108
— An appeal to the feelings ; a farce in 1 act. *In* French's.   812 : 1 v112
— A dodge for a dinner ; farce in 1 act. *In* Lacy.
812 : 1 v100
— East Lynne ; a domestic drama in a prologue and 4 acts, adapted from mrs. Wood's novel. *In* French's.   812 : 1 v103
— "Insured at Lloyd's"; drama in 4 acts. *In* French's.   812 : 1 v110
— The last life ; a drama in 3 acts, adapted from one of mrs. S. C. Hall's stories of irish life. *In* French's.   812 : 1 v103
— Rely on my discretion ; an original farce. *In* French's.   812 : 1 v106
— Too late to save, or Doomed to die ; a story of old Paris ; drama in 4 acts. *In* French's.
812 : 1 v112
— Woman's rights ; a comedietta. *In* French's.
812 : 1 v121

Pannasch, Anton. Irrgänge des lebens ; trauerspiel in 5 aufz. *n. t.* D.   832 : 68
Parry, Tom. A cure for love ; comedy in 2 acts. *In* Lacy.   812 : 1 v13
— The lucky horse-shoe, or Woman's trials ; a domestic drama in 3 acts. *In* Lacy.
812 : 1 v26
— P. P., or The man and the tiger ; farce in 1 act. *In* Lacy.   812 : 1 v56
Parselle, J. My son's a daughter ; a comic drama in 2 acts. *In* Lacy.   812 : 1 v56
Paul, J: Howard. A change of system ; a petite comedy in 1 act. *In* Lacy.   812 : 1 v45
— Locked out ; a comic scene illustrative of what may occur after dark in a great metropolis. *In* Lacy.   812 : 1 v27
— A lucky hit ; a petite comedy in 1 act. *In* Lacy.   812 : 1 v35
— The man who follows the ladies ; a piece of impudence in 1 act. *In* Lacy. 812 : 1 v48
— The mob cap, or Love's disguises ; a domestic drama in 2 acts. *In* Lacy.   812 : 1 v11
— Opposite neighbours ; farce in 1 act. *In* Lacy.
812 : 1 v17
— The queen of Arragon ; a petite comedy in 1 act. *In* Lacy.   812 : 1 v30
— Rappings and table movings ; farce in 1 act. *In* Lacy.   812 : 1 v1
— Thrice married ; a personation sketch in 1 act. *In* Lacy.   812 : 1 v45
Pauline ; a drama in 4 acts. *In* Lacy. 812 : 1 v5
Paulton, Joseph *and* **Harry.** The three musketdeers and a little one in ; original military burlesque. *In* Lacy.   812 : 1 v95
Payne, J: Howard. Charles II, or The merry monarch ; a comedy in 2 acts, adapted from " La jeunesse de Henri V." *In* Lacy.
812 : 1 v30
— Clari, the maid of Milan ; musical drama in 2 acts. *In* Lacy.   812 : 1 v95
— Love in humble life ; drama in 1 act, adapted from Scribe and Dupin's "Michel et Christine." *In* Lacy.   812 : 1 v21
— Mrs. Smith, or The wife and the widow ; farce in 1 act. *In* Lacy.   812 : 1 v84
— Peter Smink, or The armistice ; comic drama in 1 act, adapted from the french. *In* Lacy.   812 : 1 v75
— 'Twas I ! a farce in 1 act. *In* Lacy. 812 : 1 v9
— The two galley slaves ; a melodrama in 2 acts, adapted from the french. *In* Lacy.
812 : 1 v72
Peake, R: Brinsley. Comfortable lodgings ; farce. *In* Lacy.   812 : 1 v82
— The evil eye, a legend of the Levant ; a romantic, musical drama in 2 acts. *In* Lacy.
812 : 1 v43
— The haunted inn ; a farce in 2 acts. *In* Lacy.
812 : 1 v1
— Master's rival, or A day at Boulogne ; farce in 2 acts. *In* Lacy.   812 : 1 v94
Peele, G: Dramatic and poetical works ; with memoir of the author and notes by Alexander Dyce. Lond. 1861. O.   822.2+5
Contents. Some account of G: Peele and his writings.—The arraignment of Paris.—Edward I.—A warning piece to England against pride, etc.—The battle of Alcazar.—The old wives' tale.—David and Bethsabe.—Sir Clyomon and sir Clamydes.—Device of the pageant borne before Wolstan Dixie.—Descensus Astrææ.—A farewell to sir J: Norris and sir Francis Drake, etc.—An eclogue gratulatory.—Polyhymnia. —Speeches to queen Elizabeth at Theobalds.—The honour of the order of the garter.—Anglorum feriæ. —Poems.—Peele's merry conceited jests.

Pemberton, T. Edgar. Davenport bros. and co.; a farce in 1 act. *In* French's.
812 : 1 v116
— Freezing a mother-in-law, or A frightful frost; a farce in 1 act. *In* French's.
812 : 1 v116
— A grateful father; a farce in 1 act. *In* French's. 812 : 1 v112
— A happy medium; a farce in 1 act. *In* French's. 812 : 1 v112
— My wife's father's sister; a comedietta in 1 act. *In* French's. 812 : 1 v114
— "Weeds"; a comedietta in 1 act. *In* French's. 812 : 1 v113
Penley, Samson. The sleeping draught; a farce in 1 act. *In* Lacy. 812 : 1 v58
Peter Wilkins, or The flying islanders; melodramatic spectacle in 2 acts, dramatized from R. Paltock. *In* Lacy. 812 : 1 v25
Pettitt, H.; *joint author, see* Meritt, Paul, *also* Conquest, G:
Phillips, *Mrs.* Alfred. Caught in his own trap; an original comedietta in 1 act. *In* French's.
812 : 1 v105
— The master passion; a comedy in 2 acts. *In* Lacy. 812 : 1 v7
— An organic affection; a farce in 1 act. *In* Lacy. 812 : 1 v5
— Uncle Crotchet; farce in 1 act. *In* Lacy.
812 : 1 v10
Phillips, F: A bird in the hand, worth two in the bush; an original play in 3 acts. *In* Lacy. 812 : 1 v29
— Tramp's adventure, or True to the last; a drama in 2 acts. *In* French's. 812 : 1 v105
Phillips, L. Marianne, the vivandiere, or The mystery of twenty years; a serious drama in 3 acts and a prologue. *In* Lacy.
812 : 1 v46
Phillips, Watts. Camilla's husband; an original drama in 3 acts. *In* Lacy. 812 : 1 v59
— The dead heart; historical and original drama in 3 acts and a prologue. *In* Lacy.
812 : 1 v82
— A golden fetter; original drama in 3 acts. *In* Lacy. 812 : 1 v83
— His last victory; an original drama in 2 acts. *In* Lacy. 812 : 1 v59
— The huguenot captain; new and original drama in 3 acts. *In* Lacy. 812 : 1 v75
— A lion at bay; drama in 1 act. *In* Lacy.
812 : 1 v84
— Lost in London; new and original drama in 3 acts. *In* Lacy. 812 : 1 v80
— Maud's peril; play in 4 acts. *In* Lacy.
812 : 1 v80
— Nobody's child; romantic drama in 3 acts. *In* Lacy. 812 : 1 v77
— Not guilty; drama in 4 acts. *In* Lacy.
812 : 1 v84
— Paper wings; original comedy in 3 acts. *In* Lacy. 812 : 1 v83
— Paul's return; an original comedy in 3 acts. *In* Lacy. 812 : 1 v62
— Theodora, actress and empress; an original historical drama in 5 acts. *In* Lacy.
812 : 1 v74
— A ticket-of-leave man; a farce in 1 act. *In* Lacy. 812 : 1 v59
— The white cockade; original drama in 4 acts. *In* Lacy. 812 : 1 v90
— The woman in mauve; sensation drama in 3 acts. *In* Lacy. 812 : 1 v76

Phipps, A. J. My very last proposal; an original farce in 1 act. *In* French's.
812 : 1 v102
— Pretty predicaments; an original farce in 1 act. *In* French's. 812 : 1 v109
Picard, L: Benoit. Nachbar Specht, oder Ihm entgeht nichts; lustsp. in 3 abth. Uebers. von G: Reinbeck. *In* Reinbeck, G: Sämmtliche dramatische werke.
832 : 73 v6
— Der neffe als onkel; lustsp. in 3 aufz. Uebers. von F: v. Schiller. *In* Schiller, J: C. F: v. Sämmtliche werke. 830 : 143 v7
— Der parasit, oder Die kunst sein glück zu machen; ein lustsp. Uebers. von F: v. Schiller. *In the same.* 830 : 143 v7
Pichler, Caroline, *born* v. Greiner. Dramatische dichtungen. Wien. 1822. 3 v. S. 832 : 69
Contents. V. 1. Germanicus.—Wiedersehen.—Das befreyte Deutschland. 2. Heinrich von Hohenstauffen.—Mathilde.—Rudolph von Habsburg. 3. Ferdinand der zweyte.—Amalie von Mannsfeld.
Pierron, Eugène, *and* Adolphe Laferrière. Book the third, chapter the first; comedy in 1 act, adapted and tr. from the french. *In* Lacy.
812 : 1 v7
Pilgrim, James. Paddy Miles, the Limerick boy; a farce in 1 act. *In* Lacy. 812 : 1 v95
Pilon, F: He would be a soldier; comedy in 5 acts. *In* British drama. 822.2 : 1 v2
Pitt, G: Dibdin. The beggar's petition, or A father's love and a mother's care; drama in 3 acts. *In* Lacy. 812 : 1 v87
— The Eddystone elf; a melodrama in 2 acts. *In* Lacy. 812 : 1 v88
— The Jersey girl, or Les rouges voleurs; a melodrama in 2 acts. *In* Lacy. 812 : 1 v26
— Marianne, the child of charity; a domestic drama in 3 acts. *In* French's.
812 : 1 v119
— Simon Lee, or The murder of the Five Fields copse; domestic drama in 3 acts. *In* Lacy. 812 : 1 v78
— Susan Hopley, or The vicissitudes of a servant girl; a domestic drama in 3 acts. *In* Lacy. 812 : 1 v69
— The whistler, or The fate of the lily of St. Leonard's; drama in 3 acts. *In* Lacy.
812 : 1 v97
Planché, Eliza. A handsome husband; comic drama in 1 act. *In* Lacy. 812 : 1 v11
Planché, James Robinson. Beauty and the beast; grand, comic, romantic, operatic, melodramatic fairy extravaganza. *In* Lacy.
812 : 1 v19
— The birds of Aristophanes; dramatic experiment in 1 act; an humble attempt to adapt the said "birds" to this climate by giving them new names, new feathers, new songs and new tales. *In* Lacy. 812 : 1 v20
— The brigand; a romantic drama in 2 acts. *In* Lacy. 812 : 1 v60
— A cabinet question; comic drama in 1 act. *In* Lacy. 812 : 1 v20
— The camp at the Olympic; introductory extravaganza and dramatic review. *In* Lacy.
812 : 1 v12
— The captain of the watch; farce in 1 act. *In* Lacy. 812 : 1 v18

Planché, James Robinson.—*Continued.*
— Charles II; an historical drama in 2 acts. *In* Sargent, E. Mod. stand. drama.
  822.2 : 2 v6
— *Same. In* Lacy.   **812 : 1 v67**
— The child of the wreck; a melodrama in 2 acts. *In* Lacy.   **812 : 1 v39**
— The court beauties; dramatic sketch in 1 act. *In* Lacy.   **812 : 1 v21**
— Cymon and Iphigenia; lyrical, comical pastoral in 1 act, altered from the text of D: Garrick. *In* Lacy.   **812 : 1 v19**
— A daughter to marry; a comedietta in 1 act. *In* Lacy.   **812 : 1 v74**
— A day of reckoning; drama in 3 acts. *In* Lacy.   **812 : 1 v21**
— The discreet princesses, or The three glass distaffs; new and doubly moral, though excessively old melodramatic fairy extravaganza in 1 act. *In* Lacy.   **812 : 1 v24**
— The drama at home, or An evening with Puff; an original, occasional and local extravaganza in 2 acts. *In* Lacy.   **812 : 1 v20**
— Faint heart never won fair lady; comedy in 1 act. *In* Sargent, E. Mod. stand. drama.
  822.2 : 2 v6
— *Same. In* Lacy.   **812 : 1 v35**
— The fair one with golden locks; fairy extravaganza in 1 act. *In* Lacy.   **812 : 1 v19**
— The follies of a night; vaudeville comedy in 2 acts. *With* Talfourd, T: N. Ion. **822.2 : 3**
— *Same. In* Sargent, E. Mod. stand. drama.
  822.2 : 2 v6
— *Same. In* Lacy.   **812 : 1 v14**
— Fortunio and his seven gifted servants; fairy extravaganza in 2 acts. *In* Lacy.
  812 : 1 v19
— The Garrick fever; farce in 1 act. *In* Lacy.
  812 : 1 v22
— The golden branch; fairy extravaganza in 2 acts, founded upon the countess d'Anois' story "Le rameau d'or". *In* Lacy.
  812 : 1 v19
— The golden fleece, or Jason in Colchis and Medea in Corinth; classical extravaganza in 2 pts. *In* Lacy.   **812 : 1 v20**
— The good woman; a new and original fairy extravaganza in 2 acts, founded on mlle. De La Force's fairy tale "La bonne femme". *In* Lacy.   **812 : 1 v9**
— Graciosa and Percinet; fairy extravaganza in 1 act, founded on the nursery tale by countess d'Aulnoy. *In* Lacy. **812 : 1 v20**
— The green-eyed monster; a comedy in 2 acts. *In* French's.   **812 : 1 v101**
— Grist to the mill; comic drama in 2 acts. *In* Lacy.   **812 : 1 v20**
— Hold your tongue; comic drama in 1 act. *In* Lacy.   **812 : 1 v20**
— The invisible prince, or The island of tranquil delights; fairy extravaganza in 1 act, founded on the countess d'Aulnoy's fairy tale of "Prince Lutin". *In* Lacy.
  812 : 1 v19
— The irish post; comic drama in 2 acts. *In* Lacy.   **812 : 1 v20**
— The island of jewels; comic fairy extravaganza in 2 acts, founded on countess d'Aulnoi's story of "Serpentin vert". *In* Lacy.
  812 : 1 v19
— The jacobite; comic drama in 2 acts. *In* Lacy.   **812 : 1 v14**

Planché, James Robinson.—*Continued.*
— The Jenkinses, or Boarded and done for; a farce in 1 act. *In* Lacy.   **812 : 1 v8**
— King Charming, or The blue bird of paradise; comic fairy extravaganza in 2 acts, founded on countess d'Aulnoy's story "L'oiseau bleu". *In* Lacy.   **812 : 1 v19**
— King Christmas; a fancy-full morality. *In* Lacy.   **812 : 1 v95**
— The king of the peacocks; fairy extravaganza in 2 acts, founded upon the countess d'Aulnoy's story "La princesse Rosetta". *In* Lacy.   **812 : 1 v19**
— The knights of the round table; drama in 5 acts. *In* Lacy.   **812 : 1 v15**
— A lady in difficulties; comic drama in 2 acts. *In* Lacy.   **812 : 1 v21**
— The loan of a lover; a vaudeville. *In* Lacy.
  812 : 1 v9
— Love and fortune: a dramatic tableau in Watteau colors. *In* Lacy.   **812 : 1 v42**
— Mr. Buckstone's ascent of Mount Parnassus; panoramic extravaganza in 1 act. *In* Lacy.
  812 : 1 v10
— Mr. Buckstone's voyage round the globe, in Leicester square; a cosmographical, visionary extravaganza and dramatic review in 1 act and four quarters. *In* Lacy.
  812 : 1 v15
— My great aunt, or Relations and friends; comedy in 1 act. *In* Lacy.   **812 : 1 v19**
— My heart's idol, or A desperate remedy; comedy in 2 acts. *In* Lacy.   **812 : 1 v20**
— My lord and my lady, or It might have been worse; a comedy in 5 acts. *In* Lacy.
  812 : 1 v52
— The mysterious lady, or Worth makes the man; a comedy in 2 acts. *In* Lacy.
  812 : 1 v8
— The new Haymarket spring meeting; easter extravaganza in 1 act. *In* Lacy.
  812 : 1 v22
— Norma; a grand, tragic opera in 2 acts, adapted from the italian; the music composed by Bellini. *In* Lacy.   **812 : 1 v32**
— Not a bad judge; a comic drama in 2 acts. *In* Lacy.   **812 : 1 v8**
— Oberon; an opera in 4 acts; the music composed by C: Maria v. Weber, the recitatives and additional pieces selected and arr. from the works of the same composer by Jules Benedict. *In* Lacy.   **812 : 1 v59**
— An old offender; a comic drama in 2 acts. *In* Lacy.   **812 : 1 v41**
— Once upon a time there were two kings; fairy extravaganza in 2 acts, founded on the countess d'Aulnoy's story of "La princesse Carpillon." *In* Lacy.
  812 : 1 v13
— Orpheus in the Haymarket; an opera buffo in 3 tableaux and a last scene, adapted from the french of Hector Crémieux. Music by J. Offenbach. *In* Lacy.
  812 : 1 v68
— The pride of the market; comic drama in 2 acts. *In* Lacy.   **812 : 1 v20**
— Promotion, or A morning at Versailles; vaudeville in 1 act. *In* Lacy.   **812 : 1 v21**
— Queen Mary's bower; comedy in 3 acts. *In* Lacy.   **812 : 1 v20**
— The queen of the frogs; fairy extravaganza in 2 acts. *In* Lacy.   **812 : 1 v19**

Planché, James Robinson.—*Continued.*
— A romantic idea ; comic drama in 1 act. *In* Lacy.   812 : 1 v21
— The seven champions of christendom ; comic fantastic spectacle in 2 acts. *In* Lacy.
812 : 1 v21
— Sleeping beauty in the wood ; comic, romantic, operatic, melodramatic, fairy extravaganza in 3 parts, founded on the nursery tale of the same name. *In* Lacy.
812 : 1 v19
— Somebody else ; farce in 1 act. *In* Lacy.
812 : 1 v11
— Theseus and Ariadne, or The marriage of Bacchus ; classical extravaganza in 2 acts. *In* Lacy.   812 : 1 v19
— The vampire, or The bride of the isles ; a romantic melodrama in 2 acts. *In* French's.
812 : 1 v107
— The white cat ; comic, romantic, operatic, melodramatic, fairy extravaganza in 2 acts. *In* Lacy.   812 : 1 v24
— The yellow dwarf and the king of the gold mines ; fairy extravaganza in 1 act. *In* Lacy.   812 : 1 v17
— Young and handsome ; a new and original fairy extravaganza in 1 act, founded on the countess of Murat's fairy tale of "Jeune et belle." *In* Lacy.   812 : 1 v29
— *and* C: **Dance.** Blue Beard ; grand, musical comi-tragical, melodramatic, burlesque burletta in 1 act. *In* Lacy.   812 : 1 v41
— - The deep, deep sea, or Perseus and Andromeda ; an original, mythological, aquatic, equestrian burletta in 1 act. *In* Lacy.
812 : 1 v41
— - Olympic devils, or Orpheus and Eurydice ; an original, mythological, burlesque burletta in 1 act. *In* Lacy.   812 : 1 v41
— - Olympic revels, or Prometheus and Pandora; a mythological, allegorical burletta in 1 act. Not tr. from the french, but borrowed from the english of G: Colman the younger, the heads being taken from that gentleman's tale of "The sun poker". *In* Lacy.
812 : 1 v41
— The Paphian bower, or Venus and Adonis ; a classical, musical, mythological, astronomical and tragi-comical, burlesque burletta in 1 act. *In* Lacy.   812 : 1 v44
— Telemachus, or The island of Calypso ; a classical and mythological extravaganza. *In* Lacy.   812 : 1 v51
Platen-Hallermünde, A: *graf* v. [Dramatische schriften]. *In his* Gesammelte werke.
830 : 141 v3,4
Contents. V. 3. Die neuen propheten, ein nachspiel. — Mathilde von Valois, drama. — Der gläserne pantoffel, comödie. — Berengar, comödie. — Der schatz des Rhampsinit, lspl. — Der thurm mit sieben pforten, lspl. — Treue um treue, sspl. **4.** Die verhängnissvolle gabel, lspl. — Der romantische Oedipus, lspl. — Die liga von Cambrai, geschichtliches drama.
Plays for private acting. Tr. from the french and italian by members of the Bellevue dramatic club of Newport. (Leisure hour ser.) N. Y. 1878. S.   812 : 2
Contents. **Droz,** G. The registered letter ; The cardinal's illness. — **Sollohub,** W. His hat and cane. — **Legouvé,** E., *and* P. **Mérimée.** The flower of Tlemcen. — **Theuriet,** A. The old homestead. — **Hervilly,** E. d'. The soup tureen ; Silence in the ranks. — **Narrey,** C: Sophronisba, oh ! — He and she. — **Guillemot,** J. The unlucky star. — **Gastineau,** O. Lelia. — **Sollohub,** W. The serenade. — **Goetschy,** G. The professor of elocution. — **Monselet,** C: A trip

through my pockets. — **Cros,** C: A journey to * * *. — **Hervilly,** E. d'. From Calais to Dover. — **Durandeau,** E. Sergeant Bridell's letter. — **Biez,** J. de. The first love-letter. — **Marthold,** J. de. On the eve of the wedding. — **Supersac,** L. The door is locked. — **Normand,** J. The invitation to the christening. — **Legouvé,** E. By the cradle.
Plot and passion ; drama in 3 acts. *In* Lacy.
812 : 1 v13
Plouvier, E., *joint author, see* **Barrière,** T.
Plowman, T: F. Acis and Galatæa, or The beau! the belle!! and the blacksmith!!! a piece of extravagance. *In* Lacy.   812 : 1 v91
Plunkett, H: Grattan. The Minerali, or The dying gift ; a romantic drama in 2 acts. *In* Lacy.   812 : 1 v74
Pocock, I: The maid and the magpie ; drama in 3 acts, adapted from the french. *In* Lacy.   812 : 1 v87
— The miller and his men ; melodrama in 2 acts. *In* Lacy.   812 : 1 v11
— Rob Roy Macgregor, or Auld lang syne ; an operatic drama in 3 acts. *In* Lacy.
812 : 1 v3
— The robber's wife ; a romantic, domestic drama in 2 acts. *In* Lacy.   812 : 1 v69
— Robinson Crusoe, or The bold buccaniers ; romantic drama in 2 acts. *In* Lacy.
812 : 1 v89
Poel, W: Absence of mind, or Wanted £5 ; a comic drama in 1 act. The incidents are taken from one of Kotzebue's farces. *In* French's.   812 : 1 v120
— The wayside cottage ; a comedietta in 1 act, adapted from Kotzebue's farce of "The half-way house". *In* French's.
812 : 1 v120
Polack, Elizabeth. Esther, the royal jewess, or The death of Haman ; an historical drama in 3 acts. *In* French's.   812 : 1 v120
Ponsard, François, *see* **Merivale,** Herman C. A son of the soil.
Poole, J: Hamlet travestie, in 3 acts with annotations by dr. Johnson and G: Steevens, esq. and other commentators. *In* Lacy.
812 : 1 v10
— Intrigue, or The Bath road ; a comic interlude in 1 act. *In* Lacy.   812 : 1 v54
— Lodgings for single gentlemen ; a farce in 1 act. *In* French's.   812 : 1 v115
— Match making ; a petite comedy in 1 act, from the french. *In* Lacy.   812 : 1 v27
— My wife !—what wife ? farce in 1 or 2 acts. *In* Lacy.   812 : 1 v96
— A nabob for an hour ; a farce in 2 acts. *In* French's.   812 : 1 v108
— Past and present, or The hidden treasure ; drama in 3 acts, adapted from the french. *In* Lacy.   812 : 1 v96
— Paul Pry ; comedy in 3 acts. *In* Lacy.
812 : 1 v15
— The scapegoat ; farce in 1 act. *In* Lacy.
812 : 1 v98
— Simpson and co. ; a comedy in 1 act. *In* Lacy.
812 : 1 v74
— Turning the tables ; a farce in 1 act. *In* Lacy.
812 : 1 v40
— 'Twould puzzle a conjuror ! comic drama in 2 acts. *In* Lacy.   812 : 1 v14
Poole, T. Deaf as a post ; farce in 1 act. N. Y. n. d. S. *With* **Talfourd,** T: N. Ion.
822.2 : 3
— *Same.* *In* Lacy.   812 : 1 v14

Power, Tyrone. Born to good luck, or The irishman's fortune ; a farce in 1 act, adapted from "False and true." *In* Lacy.
812 : 1 v2
— Paddy Carey, or The boy of Clogheen ; a farce in 1 act. *In* Lacy.   812 : 1 v26
Prest, T: Peckett. The miser of Shoreditch ; romantic drama in 2 acts. *In* Lacy.
812 : 1 v18
Princesses in the tower, or A match for Lucifer ; a piece of extravagance in 1 act, being a play after Congreve—some 200 years. *In* Lacy.   812 : 1 v2
Procter, Bryan Waller, (*Barry Cornwall*). Dramatic scenes, with other poems. Bost. 1857. D.   822.2 : 26
Prutz, Robert Ernst. Dramatische werke. Leipz. 1847. 4 v. S.   832 : 70
Contents. V. 1. Nach leiden lust. 2. Karl von Bourbon. 3. Erich der bauernkönig. 4. Moritz v. Sachsen.
Pulszky, Terézia. The sleeper awakened. *In* Follen, E. L. Home dramas.   822.1 : 9
Putnam, Mary, *born* Lowell. Tragedy of errors. Bost. 1862. D.   822.1 : 13
Racine, J: The distressed mother ; tragedy in 5 acts. Tr. from the "Andromaque," by Ambrose Philips. *In* British drama.
822.2 : 1 v2
— Phädra ; ein trauerspiel. Uebers. von F: v. Schiller. *In* Schiller, J: C. F: v. Sämmtliche werke.   830 : 143 v7
— *Same. In the same.*   830 : 144 v9
Rae, C: Marsham. "Billy Doo" ; an original farce in 1 act. *In* French's.   812 : 1 v101
— Birds in their little nests agree ; a fanciful conceit in 1 act. *In* French's.
812 : 1 v109
— A fair encounter ; a comedietta in 1 act, from the french. *In* French's.   812 : 1 v104
— Fame ; an original comedy in 3 acts. *In* French's.   812 : 1 v110
— First in the field ; a comedy in 1 act, adapted from the french. *In* French's.
812 : 1 v118
— Follow the leader ; comedy in 1 act. *In* Lacy.
812 : 1 v99
— Love's alarms ; an extravagant comedy in 1 act. *In* French's.   812 : 1 v112
— Poppleton's predicaments ; an original farce in 1 act. *In* French's.   812 : 1 v113
Ramsay, Allan. The gentle shepherd ; a pastoral comedy ; with a life of the author and the opinions of various eminent men on the work. Added, a greatly improved glossary and a catalogue of the scottish poets. N. Y. 1853. D.   822.2 : 27
Rau, Heribert. Der heirathszwang. *In his* Girandolen.   R 454 v2
— Das sträuschen. *In the same.*   R 454 v2
Raymond, R. J. Cherry bounce ; a farce in 1 act. *In* Lacy.   812 : 1 v59
— *Same. See* Omnibus, The.
— Mrs. White ; a farce in 1 act. *In* Lacy.
812 : 1 v55
Rayner, B. F. The dumb man of Manchester ; a melodrama in 2 acts. *In* Lacy.
812 : 1 v26
— Up to town and back again by the "old York highflyer" ; popular entertainment, comprising a variety of tales, anecdotes, recitations, oddities, whims and eccentric portraitures from nature, etc. *In* Lacy.
812 : 1 v71

Reade, C: The ladies' battle, or Un duel en amour ; a comedy in 3 acts. *In* French's.
812 : 1 v108
Rede, W: Leman. An affair of honour ; a farce in 1 act. *In* Lacy.   812 : 1 v78
— Douglas travesty ; a burlesque in 1 act. *In* Lacy.   812 : 1 v46
— His first champagne ; a farce in 1 act. *In* Lacy.   812 : 1 v73
— Our village, or The lost ship ; domestic drama in 3 acts. *In* Lacy.   812 : 1 v88
— The rake's progress ; a drama in 3 acts. *In* Lacy.   812 : 1 v32
Redwitz-Schmölz, Oskar *freiherr v.* Sieglinde ; eine tragödie. Mainz. 1854. T.   832 : 71
— Thomas Morus ; historische tragödie. Mainz. 1857. S.   832 : 72
Reece, Robert. Brown and the brahmins, or Captain Pop and the princess Pretty-eyes ; oriental burlesque, founded on the drama of "The illustrious stranger." *In* Lacy.
812 : 1 v82
— Dora's device ; original comedy in 2 acts. *In* Lacy.   812 : 1 v90
— Green old age ; an original musical improbability in 1 act. *In* French's. 812 : 1 v103
— Ingomar, or The noble savage ; an awful warning in 1 act. *In* Scott, C. W. Drawing-room plays.   822.2 : 14
— The lady of the lake, plaid in a new tartan ; an ephemeral burlesque, founded on sir Walter Scott's immortal poem. *In* Lacy.
812 : 1 v71
— Little Robin Hood, or Quite a new beau ; original anti-historical burlesque. *In* Lacy.
812 : 1 v91
— An old man ; domestic drama. *In* French's.
812 : 1 v108
— Paquita, or Love in a frame ; original comic opera in 2 acts. *In* Lacy. . 812 : 1 v94
— Perfect love ! a spectacular fairy play. *In* Lacy.   812 : 1 v90
— Prometheus, or The man on the rock ; a new and original extravaganza. *In* Lacy.
812 : 1 v68
— Romulus and Remus ; new classical burlesque. *In* Lacy.   812 : 1 v97
— Ruy Blas righted, or The love, the lugger and the lackey ; original burlesque. *In* Lacy.
812 : 1 v100
— The stranger stranger than ever ! piece of extravagance in 1 act. *In* Lacy.
812 : 1 v82
— The very last days of Pompeii ; a new classical burlesque. *In* Lacy.   812 : 1 v95
— Whittington junior and his sensation cat ; original civic burlesque. *In* Lacy.
812 : 1 v89
Reeve, Wybert. The dead witness, or Sin and its shadow ; drama in 3 acts. *In* Lacy.
812 : 1 v99
— "I love you" ; original comedietta in 1 act. *In* Lacy.   812 : 1 v98
— A match for a mother-in-law ; an original comedietta in 1 act. *In* French's.
812 : 1 v118
— Never reckon your chickens etc. ; original farce in 1 act. *In* Lacy.   812 : 1 v95
— Not so bad after all ; original comedy in 3 acts. *In* Lacy.   812 : 1 v88
— Obliging a friend ; original farce in 1 act. *In* Lacy.   812 : 1 v98

Reeve, Wybert.—*Continued.*
— Parted ; an english love story, a comedy
    drama in 4 acts. *In* French's.
                                        812 : 1 v107
— Pike O'Callaghan, or The irish patriot ; orig-
    inal drama in 2 acts. *In* Lacy. 812 : 1 v87
— True as steel ; original comedy in 3 acts. *In*
    Lacy.   812 : 1 v92
— Won at last ; original comedy-drama in 3 acts.
    In Lacy.   812 : 1 v87
Regnard, J: François. The intriguing chamber-
    maid ; farce in 2 acts. From Regnard by
    H: Fielding. *In* British drama.
                                        822.2 : 1 v2
Reinbeck, G: Sämmtliche dramatische werke,
    nebst beiträgen zur theorie der deutschen
    schauspieldichtung und zur kenntniss des
    gegenwärtigen standpunktes der deut-
    schen bühne. Heidelberg und Coblenz.
    1817–22. 6 v. S.   832 : 73
    Contents. V. 1. Vorrede.—Mein dramatischer le-
    benslauf.—Graf Kasowsky.—Der virginier. 2. Ueber
    den werth der schaubühne für die menschheit.—Die
    doppelwette.--Lisinka.—*Anhang:* Ueber das lustspiel
    in b. 1: Der virginier. 3. Briefe über den gegen-
    wärtigen zustand der deutschen bühne.—Die beiden
    wittwen.—Der schuldbrief.—Der quartierzettel. 4.
    Der französische dramaturg über deutsche dramati-
    sche dichtung.—Gordon und Montrose.—Der dichter.
    —Unbesonnenheit und gutes herz. 5. Ueber die
    wahl des schauspielerstandes.—Ein paar worte über
    theaterbeurtheilungen. — Der argwöhnische ehe-
    mann.—Der verführer.—Die rückkehr. 6. Ein paar
    worte über die beurtheilung von schauspieldichtun-
    gen.—Die verschwörung des Fiesko zu Genua, trauer-
    spiel von Schiller; für die bühne neu bearbeitet in
    iamben.—Der westindier, nach dem englischen von
    Cumberland.—Nachbar Specht, nach Picard.
Reitzenstein, K: *freiherr* v.   Count Koenigs-
    mark ; a tragedy in 5 acts. *In* Thompson,
    B: German theatre, v. 6.   832 : 96 v6
Reuter, Fritz. Blücher in Teterow, dramati-
    scher schwank in 1 act. *With his* Der 1.
    april 1856.   832 : 75
— Der 1. april 1856, oder Onkel Jakob und onkel
    Jochen ; lustspiel in 3 acten. Greifswald.
    1857. D.   832 : 75
Reynolds, F: Laugh when you can ; a comedy
    in 5 acts. *In* French's.   812 : 1 v104
Reynolds, G: W. M. Mary Price, or The ad-
    ventures of a servant girl ; a domestic
    drama in 2 acts. *In* Lacy.   812 : 1 v52
Reynoldson, T: H. The brewer of Preston, or
    Malt and hops ; a comic drama in 1 act.
    In French's.   812 : 1 v113
— L'elisir d'amore, or The elixir of love ; an
    opera in 2 acts, adapted from Donizetti.
    In Lacy.   812 : 1 v37
Rhodes, W: Barnes. Bombastes Furioso ; a
    burlesque tragic opera in 1 act. Ill. *In*
    Lacy.   812 : 1 v3
Rice, C: The three musketeers, or The queen,
    the cardinal and the adventurer ; drama
    in 3 acts, founded on Dumas' celebrated
    romance. *In* Lacy.   812 : 1 v17
Rice, James, *joint author, see* **Besant**, Walter.
Riddell, Charlotte Eliza Lawson. *mrs.* J. H., (*F.
    G. Trafford*). George Geith, or Romance
    of a city life ; a drama in 4 acts and a
    tableau founded on [her] novel, by Wybert
    Reeve. *In* French's.   812 : 1 v119
Ritchie, Anna Cora, *born* Ogden, *formerly Mrs.*
    Mowatt. Plays. Bost. 1855. D. 822.1 : 14
    Contents. Armand, or The peer and the peasant.—
    Fashion, or Life in New York.

Ritter, H: L: Possen und lustspiele für die
    deutsche bühne. Heidelberg. 1818. S.
                                        832 : 76
    Contents. Der weibermagistrat zu Klatschhausen.
    —Der betrogene entführer.—Die magnetisirte ver-
    lobung.
Roberts, G: The absent man ; a farcical comedi-
    etta in 1 act. *In* French's.   812 : 1 v10
— Behind the curtain ; drama in 4 acts. *In* Lacy.
                                        812 : 1 v100
— Cousin Tom ; a comedietta in 1 act. *In* Lacy.
                                        812 : 1 v58
— Forty winks ; a comedietta in 1 act. *In* Lacy.
                                        812 : 1 v57
— Idalia. or The adventuress ; drama in 3 acts.
    In Lacy.   812 : 1 v76
— The three furies ; an original comedietta in 1
    act. *In* Lacy.   812 : 1 v66
— Under the rose ; a farce in 1 act. *In* Lacy.
                                        812 : 1 v57
Robertson, T: W: Birds of prey, or A duel in
    the dark ; drama in 3 acts. *In* Lacy.
                                        812 : 1 v93
— David Garrick ; a comedy in 3 acts. Adapted
    from the french of "Sullivan", which was
    founded on a german dramatization of a
    pretended incident in Garrick's life. *In*
    French's.   812 : 1 v117
— The half caste, or The poisoned pearl ; drama
    in 3 acts, adapted from the french. *In*
    Lacy.   812 : 1 v97
— Jocrisse the juggler ; a drama in 3 acts. *In*
    Lacy.   812 : 1 v51
— The ladies' battle ; a comedy in 3 acts, from
    the french of Scribe and Legouvé. *In*
    Lacy.   812 : 1 v4
— Not at all jealous ; farce in 1 act. *In* Lacy.
                                        812 : 1 v91
— Peace at any price ; farce in 1 act, adapted
    from the french. *In* Lacy.   812 : 1 v95
— Society ; a comedy in 3 acts. *In* Lacy.
                                        812 : 1 v71
— The star of the north ; drama in 3 acts, adapt-
    ed from the french. *In* Lacy. 812 : 1 v93
— *and* T: Hailes Lacy. Two gay deceivers, or
    Black, White and Grey ; a farce in 1 act.
    In Lacy.   812 : 1 v33
Robinson, Nugent. Miss Tibbets' back hair ;
    farce in 1 act. *In* Lacy.   812 : 1 v90
— Mr. Joffins' latch-key ; a farce in 1 act. *In*
    French's.   812 : 1 v106
Robson, F: Popocatapetl ; an original piece of
    extravagance in 1 act. *In* French's.
                                        812 : 1 v101
Rodwell, G: Herbert. I'll be your second ; a
    farce in 1 act. *In* Lacy.   812 : 1 v3
— My wife's out ; original farce in 1 act. *In*
    Lacy.   812 : 1 v45
— Teddy the tiler ; farce in 1 act. *In* Lacy.
                                        812 : 1 v81
— Was I to blame ? a farce in 1 act. *In* Lacy.
                                        812 : 1 v82
Rodwell, J. T: G. More blunders than one ; a
    farce in 1 act. *In* Lacy.   812 : 1 v3
— A race for a dinner, or "No dinner yet"; a
    farce in 1 act. *In* French's. 812 : 1 v102
— The young widow ; farce in 1 act. *In* Lacy.
                                        812 : 1 v22
Römer, Dr., *pseud., see* **Deinhardstein**, J: L:
Rose, E:, (*Arthur Sketchley*). The dark cloud ;
    a new and original drama of interest in 2
    acts. *In* Lacy.   812 : 1 v57

Rose, E:—*Continued.*

— Equals ; a comedy in 3 acts, freely adapted from the celebrated "Gendre de M. Poinier" [by Emile Augier and Jules Sandeau.] *In* French's.   **812 : 1 v119**

— How will they get out of it ? an original comedy in 3 acts. *In* Lacy.   **812 : 1 v64**

— Money makes the man ; a drawing - room drama. *In* Scott, C. W. Drawing-room plays.   **822.2 : 14**

— Vice versa ; a lesson for fathers in 2 acts, dramatized from the story by F. Anstey [Guthrie]. *In* French's.   **812 : 1 v121**

— Wild flowers ; a dramatic sketch in 1 act. *In* French's.   **812 : 1 v118**

Rowe, N: Works, in 2 v., consisting of his plays and poems. Lond. 1756. 2 v. S.
     822.2 : 13
Contents. V. 1. The ambitious step-mother.—Tamerlane.—The fair penitent.—Ulysses. 2. The royal convert.—Jane Shore.—Jane Gray.—Poems.

— The fair penitent ; a tragedy in 5 acts. *In* French's.   **812 : 1 v104**

— Same. *In* British drama.   **822.2 : 1 v1**

— Jane Shore ; tragedy in 5 acts. *In the same.*
     822.2 : 1 v1

— Same. *In* Lacy.   **812 : 1 v39**

— Tamerlane ; tragedy in 5 acts. *In* British drama.   **822.2 : 1 v1**

— *joint author, see* Leslie, H:

Rückert, F: Christofero Colombo, oder Die entdeckung der neuen welt ; geschichtsdrama in 3 t. Frankfurt a. M. 1845. 2 v. D.
     832 : 78

Ryan, Desmond L. One too many ; farce in 1 act. *In* Lacy.   **812 : 1 v97**

Ryan, R: Everybody's husband ; farce in 1 act. *In* Lacy.   **812 : 1 v92**

St. Georges, Jules H: Vernoy de, *and* Adolphe *comte* Ribbing *called* **de Leuven.** The jeweller of St. James ; a comedy in 3 acts, adapted by W: E. Suter. *In* Lacy.
     812 : 1 v55

Salmon, J: Old and young, or The four Mowbrays ; farce in 1 act. *In* Lacy.
     812 : 1 v82

Sandeau, Léonard Sylvain Jules, *and* Adrien **Decourcelle,** *see* Clarke, Campbell, Awaking.

Sardou, Victorien, *see* Amcotts, V.

Sargent, Epes, *ed.* The modern standard drama ; a collection of the most popular acting plays, with critical remarks, also the stage business, costumes, etc. V. 5, 6. N. Y. n. d. D.   **822 2 : 2**
Contents. V. 5. Massinger, P. A new way to pay old debts.—Lovell, G: W. Look before you leap.—Shakspere, W: King John.—Bernard, W: B. The nervous man and the man of nerve.—Banim, J: Damon and Pythias.—Coleman, G: The clandestine marriage.—Knowles, J. S. William Tell. 6. Morton, T: Speed the plough.—Shakspere, W: Romeo and Juliet.—White, J. Feudal times.—Planché, J. R. Charles XII.—Knowles, J. S. The bridal.—Planché, J. R. The follies of a night.—Colman, G:, jr. The iron chest.—Planché, J. R. Faint heart never won fair lady.

Savage, J: Sybil ; a tragedy in 5 acts. N. Y. 1865. D.   **822.1 : 15**

Saville, J: Faucit. The miller's maid ; a melodrama in 2 acts. *In* French's. **812 : 1 v105**

Schaad, J: Christian. Nicholas of the flue, the saviour of the Swiss republic ; a dramatic poem in 5 acts. Wash. 1866. D. **822.1 : 16**

Schiller, J: Christoph F: v. Don Carlos, infant of Spain ; a tragedy in 5 acts. *In* Thompson, B: German theatre.   **832 : 96 v2**

— The death of Wallenstein ; a tragedy in 5 acts. Tr. by S: T. Coleridge. *In* Coleridge, S: T. Works.   **820.2 : 7 v7**

— The Piccolomini, or The first part of Wallenstein ; a drama. Tr. from the german by S: T. Coleridge. *In the same.* **820.2 : 7 v7**

— *See also his* Sämmtliche werke.
     830 : 143, 830 : 144
Werke.   **830 : 152 v120,121**
Works.   **830 : 150, 830 : R153**

Schmidt, F: L: Der leichtsinnige lügner ; lustspiel in 3 aufz. Stuttg. 1813. S. **832 : 79**

Schröder, F: L: The ensign ; a comedy in 3 acts. *In* Thompson, B: German theatre.
     832 : 96 v5

Schubar, L: Der günstling, oder Keine jesuiten mehr ! original-lustspiel in 4 acten. Berlin. 1847. D.   **832 : 80**

Scott, Clement W. "The Cape mail" ; a drama in 1 act. *In* French's.   **812 : 1 v119**

— Tears ! idle tears ! ! a 1 act drama. *In* French's.   **812 : 1 v119**

— *comp.* Drawing-room plays and parlour pantomimes. Lond. 1870. D.   **822.2 : 14**
Contents. Blanchard, E. L. An induction.—Simpson, J. P. Two gentlemen at Mivart's.—Gilbert, W. S. A medical man.—Hood, T: Harlequin little Red Riding-Hood, or The wicked wolf and the wirtuous wood-cutter.—Cheltnam, C: S. Fireside diplomacy.—Reece, R. Ingomar, or The noble savage.—Rose, G: Money makes the man.—Thompson. A. The happy dispatch.—Archer, T:, and J. C. Brough. An eligible situation.—Scott, C. W. The pet lamb; The last lily.—Blanchard, E. L. The three temptations.—Sterry, J. A. Katharine and Petruchio, or The shaming of the true.—Daryl, S. His first brief.—B., A. The girls of the period.

Scott, W. S. On the Clyde ; a drama in 3 acts. *In* French's.   **812 : 1 v107**

Scribe, Augustin Eugène. Ein abend vor dem Potsdamer thore. *In* Blum, K: Neue theaterspiele.   **832 : 11 v2**

— Asmodeus, the little demon, or The ——'s share ; a comic drama in 2 acts, adapted from the "Part du diable" by T: Archer. *In* Lacy.   **812 : 1 v46**

— Fesseln ; lustsp. in 5 aufz. Nach dem französischen übers. von K: G. T. Winkler. *n. t.* S.   **832 : 87**

— A glass of water, great events from trifling causes spring ; comedy in 2 acts, freely adapted from the "Verre d'eau" by W. E. Suter. *In* Lacy.   **812 : 1 v79**

— Masaniello, or The dumb girl of Portici ; grand opera in 3 acts. Tr. by James Kenney ; music by Auber. *In* Lacy.
     812 : 1 v93

— Die nachtwandlerin. *In* Blum, K: Neue theaterspiele, v. 1.   **832 : 11 v1**

— Riquet der haarbüschel. *In the same,* v. 2.
     832 : 11 v2

— Der schönste tag des lebens. *In the same,* v. 1.
     832 : 11 v1

— Der sohn Cromwell's, oder Eine restauration ; historisches lustsp. in 5 akten, bearb. von K: G. T. Winkler. *n. t.* S.   **832 : 92**

— The woman that was a cat ; a metamorphosiological sketch in 1 act ; adapted from "La chatte metamorphosée en femme". *In* Lacy.   **812 : 1 v72**

Scribe, Augustin Eugène.—*Continued.*

— *and* Anne Honoré Joseph *baron* **Duveyrier,** (*Mélesville*). Oscar, oder Wie schwer ist's doch seine frau zu betrügen. Uebers. von K: G. T. Winkler. *n. t.* S.   **832 : 90**

— *and* Joseph Wilfrid Ernest Gabriel **Legouvé.** Adrienne Lecouvreur; a play in 5 acts, adapted by H. Herman. *In* French's.   **812 : 1 v119**

— *see also* **Boucicault,** D., The queen of spades; **Lacy,** T: H., The jewess; **Simpson,** J. P., Marco Spada, *and* **Welstead,** B:, Giralda.

Secret, The, or The hole in the wall; a farce in 1 act. *With* **Talfourd,** T: N. Ion. **822.2 : 3**

Séjour, V: The outlaw of the Adriatic, or The female spy and the chief of the ten; a romantic drama in 3 acts, adapted from the french. *In* Lacy.   **812 : 1 v45**

Selby, C: Behind the scenes, or Actors by lamplight; a serio-comic burlesque burletta in 1 act. *In* French's. **812 : 1 v114**

— The bonnie fish wife; an original musical interlude in 1 act. *In* Lacy. **812 : 1 v37**

— The boots at the Swan; an original farce in 1 act. *In* Lacy.   **812 : 1 v34**

— Catching an heiress; a farce in 1 act. *In* Lacy.   **812 : 1 v39**

— Caught by the ears; a farcical extravaganza in 1 act. *In* Lacy.   **812 : 1 v41**

— A day in Paris; a farce in 1 act. *In* Lacy.   **812 : 1 v69**

— The drapery question, or Who's for India? an original apropos sketch in 1 act. *In* Lacy.   **812 : 1 v33**

— " Fearful tragedy in the Seven Dials"; a farcical interlude in 1 act. *In* Lacy.   **812 : 1 v31**

— The fire eater; a farce in 1 act. *In* Lacy. .   **812 : 1 v4**

— Frank Fox Phipps, esq.; farce in 1 act. *In* Lacy.   **812 : 1 v100**

— Frederick of Prussia, or The monarch and the mimic; a burletta in 1 act. *In* Lacy.   **812 : 1 v32**

— Harold Hawk, or The convict's vengeance; an original domestic drama in 2 acts. *In* Lacy.   **812 : 1 v38**

— Hotel charges, or How to cook a biffin! farcical sketch in 1 act. *In* Lacy. **812 : 1 v12**

— An hour at Seville; an original protean interlude. *In* Lacy.   **812 : 1 v53**

— Hunting a turtle; a farce in 1 act. *In* Lacy.   **812 : 1 v40**

— The husband of my heart; a comic drama in 2 acts. *In* Lacy.   **812 : 1 v2**

— Jacques Strop, or A few more passages in the life of the renowned and illustrious Robert Macaire; an original domestic drama in 3 acts. *In* French's.   **812 : 1 v102**

— Kinge Richard ye third, or Ye battel of Bosworth field; being a familiar alteration of the celebrated history by a gentleman from Stratford in Warwickshire; a merrie mysterie in 1 act. *In* Lacy. **812 : 1 v40**

— A lady and a gentleman in a peculiarly perplexing predicament; a farce in 1 act. *In* Lacy.   **812 : 1 v69**

— The last of the pigtails; an original petite comedy in 1 act. *In* Lacy. **812 : 1 v37**

— Little sins and pretty sinners; interlude in 1 act. *In* Lacy.   **812 : 1 v19**

Selby, C:—*Continued.*

— The marble heart, or The sculptor's dream; romance of real life in 5 chapters. *In* Lacy.   **812 : 1 v15**

— The married rake; a farce in 1 act. *In* Lacy.   **812 : 1 v71**

— My aunt's husband; an original comic drama in 1 act. *In* Lacy.   **812 : 1 v37**

— My friend the major; farce in 1 act. *In* Lacy.   **812 : 1 v16**

— My sister from India; a farce in 1 act. *In* French's.   **812 : 1 v108**

— Paris and pleasure, or Home and happiness; a drama fantastique or tale of diablerie in 4 acts. *In* Lacy.   **812 : 1 v49**

— Peggy Green; a comic drama in 1 act. *In* Lacy.   **812 : 1 v42**

— The pet lamb; a comedietta in 1 act. *In* Lacy.   **812 : 1 v47**

— The phantom breakfast; a farce in 1 act. *In* French's.   **812 : 1 v101**

— The pirates of Putney; a nautical extravagance in 1 act. *In* Lacy.   **812 : 1 v60**

— The poor nobleman; a serio-comic drama in 2 acts. *In* Lacy.   **812 : 1 v53**

— The rival pages; a petite comedy in 1 act. *In* Lacy.   **812 : 1 v94**

— Robert Macaire, or The Auberge des Adrêts; a melodrama in 2 acts. *In* Lacy.   **812 : 1 v30**

— The spanish dancers, or Fans and fandangoes; a terpsichorean, semi-burlesque burletta in 1 act. *In* Lacy.   **812 : 1 v49**

— The unfinished gentleman; a farce in 1 act. *In* Lacy.   **812 : 1 v34**

— The widow's victim; a farce in 1 act. *In* Lacy.   **812 : 1 v62**

— The witch of Windermere; original comic drama in 1 act. *In* Lacy.   **812 : 1 v84**

— The young mother; a comic drama in 1 act. *In* Lacy.   **812 : 1 v39**

— *and* C: **Melville.** Barnaby Rudge; a domestic drama in 3 acts. *In* French's.   **812 : 1 v101**

Serle, T: James. Tender precautions, or The romance of marriage; a new and original comedy in 1 act. *In* Lacy.   **812 : 1 v5**

Seume, J: Gottfried. Miltiades. *In his* Poetische und prosaische werke. **830 : 147 v6**

Shakspere, W: Works; ed. by C: **Knight.** Ill. Bost. [1878]. 2 v. Q.   **822.3 : R1**
Contents. V. 1. Preface.—The tempest.—Two gentlemen of Verona.—The merry wives of Windsor.— Measure for measure.—Comedy of errors.—Much ado about nothing.—Love's labour's lost.—A midsummer-night's dream.—The merchant of Venice.— As you like it.—Taming of the shrew.—All's well that ends well.—Twelfth night.—Winter's tale.—King John.—King Richard II.—King Henry IV., pt. 1. *Same,* pt. 2.—King Henry V.—King Henry VI., pt. 1.— *Same,* pt. 2. 2. King Henry VI., pt. 3.—King Richard III.—King Henry VIII.—Roméo and Juliet.— Othello.—King Lear.—Macbeth.—Timon of Athens. —Hamlet.— Troilus and Cressida.— Cymbeline.— Coriolanus.— Julius Cæsar.—Antony and Cleopatra. —Titus Andronicus.—Pericles.—Venus and Adonis.— The rape of Lucrece.—Sonnets.—A lover's complaint. —The passionate pilgrim.—Sonnets to sundry notes of music.—Song.— Verses among the additional poems to Chester's Love's martyr, 1601.—Glossary.

— Works; the plays ed. from the folio of 1623, with various readings from all the editions and all the commentators, notes, introductory remarks, a historical sketch of the text, an account of the rise and progress

Shakspere, W:—_Continued._

of the english drama, a memoir of the poet, and an essay upon his genius by Richard Grant White. Bost. 1875. 12 v. D.

822.3 : 2

Contents. V. 1. Preface. — Supplementary notes and corrections.—Memoirs of Shakespeare.—Shakespeare's will.—Chronological tables of Shakespeare's works.—Notes on the portraits and autograph signatures of Shakespeare.—An account of the rise and progress of the english drama to the time of Shakespeare. — Essay on Shakespeare's genius. — Historical sketch of the text of Shakespeare.—Poems. **2.** Preliminary matter to the folio of 1623.—The tempest.—Two gentlemen of Verona.—Merry wives of Windsor. **3.** Measure for measure.—The comedy of errors.—Much ado about nothing.— Love's labor's lost. **4.** Midsummer-night's dream. — Merchant of Venice.—As you like it.—Taming of the shrew. **5.** All's well that ends well.—Twelfth night, or What you will.—The winter's tale. **6.** King John.—King Richard II.—King Henry IV., pts. 1, 2. **7.** King Henry V.—King Henry VI., pts. 1, 2.—Essay on the authorship of Henry VI. **8.** King Henry VI., pt. 3. — King Richard III.— King Henry VIII. **9.** Troilus and Cressida. — Coriolanus. — Titus Andronicus. **10.** Romeo and Juliet.—Timon of Athens.—Julius Cæsar. —Macbeth. **11.** Hamlet.— King Lear. — Othello. **12.** Antony and Cleopatra.—Cymbeline.—Pericles.—Appendix.—Index.

— Works ; the text carefully restored according to the first editions, with introductions, notes original and selected, and a life of the poet, by H: N. Hudson. Rev. ed. with additional notes, in 6 v. Bost. _n. d._ 6 v. D.

822.3 : 82

Contents. V. 1. The tempest.—The two gentlemen of Verona.—The merry wives of Windsor.—Twelfth night, or What you will.—Measure for measure.—Much ado about nothing.— A midsummer-night's dream.—Love's labour's lost. **2.** The merchant of Venice.—As you like it.—All's well that ends well.—The taming of the shrew.—The winter's tale.—The comedy of errors.—Macbeth.—King John. **3.** King Richard II.—First part of Henry IV.—Second part of Henry IV.—King Henry V.—Antony and Cleopatra.—Othello. **4.** First part of Henry VI.—Second part of Henry VI.—Third part of Henry VI.—King Richard III.—King Henry VIII.—Troilus and Cressida. **5.** Timon of Athens.—Coriolanus.—Julius Cæsar.—Cymbeline.—Titus Andronicus.—Pericles, prince of Tyre.—King Lear. **6.** Romeo and Juliet.—Hamlet.—The life of Shakespeare.—An historical sketch of the english drama before Shakespeare. — Poems. — Sonnets.

— Complete works ; with dr. Johnson's preface, a glossary, and an account of each play and a memoir of the author, by the rev. W: Harness. Lond. _n. d._ 2 v. O.

822.3 + 3

Contents. V. 1. Memoir.—Dr. Johnson's preface.—Glossary.—The tempest.—Two gentlemen of Verona.—Merry wives of Windsor.—Twelfth night, or What you will.—Measure for measure.—Much ado about nothing. — Midsummer-night's dream. — Love's labour's lost.—Merchant of Venice.—As you like it.—All's well that ends well.—Taming of the shrew.—Winter's tale.—Comedy of errors.—Macbeth.—King John.—Richard II.—First part of Henry IV.—Second part of Henry IV.—Henry V.—First part of Henry VI. — Second part of Henry VI. **2.** Third part of Henry VI.—Richard III.—Henry VIII.—Troilus and Cressida.— Timon of Athens. — Coriolanus.—Julius Cæsar.— Antony and Cleopatra.—Cymbeline.— Titus Andronicus. — Pericles, prince of Tyre. — King Lear.— Romeo and Juliet.— Hamlet, prince of Denmark.—Othello.—Venus and Adonis.—The rape of Lucrece.—Sonnets.—Passionate pilgrim.—A lover's complaint.

— Dramatic works of Shakespeare ; the text of the 1st ed. Ill. Edinb. 1883. 8 v. O.

822.3 : R83

Contents. V. 1. The tempest.—The two gentlemen of Verona.—The merry wives of Windsor.—Measure for measure.—The comedie of errors.—Much adoe about nothing. **2.** Love's labour's lost.—A midsommer nights dreame.—The merchant of Venice.—As

Shakspere, W:—_Continued._

you like it.—The taming of the shrew. **3.** All's well that ends well.—Twelfe night, or What you will.— The winters tale.—The life and death of king John.— The life and death of king Richard the second. **4.** The first part of Henry the fourth.—The second part of Henry the fourth.—The life of Henry the fift.— The first part of Henry the sixt. **5.** The second part of Henry the sixt.—The third part of Henry the sixt. —The tragedy of Richard the third.—The life of king Henry the eight. **6.** The tragedie of Troylus and Cressida.—The tragedie of Coriolanus.—The lamentable tragedie of Titus Andronicus.—The tragedie of Romeo and Juliet. **7.** The life of Timon of Athens. — The tragedie of Julius Cæsar. — The tragedie of Macbeth.—The tragedie of Hamlet. **8.** The tragedie of king Lear.—The tragedie of Othello.—The tragedie of Anthonie and Cleopatra.—The tragedie of Cymbeline.

— Dramatische werke, übersetzt von F: Bodenstedt, Nicolaus Delius, O: Gildemeister, G: Herwegh, Paul Heyse, Hermann Kurz, Adolf Wilbrandt ; mit einleitung und anmerkungen herausg. von F: Bodenstedt. 4te aufl. Leipz. 1880. 9 v. D.

822.3 : 47

Contents. V. 1. Ein sommernachtstraum, üb. von F: Bodenstedt.—Das wintermärchen, üb. von O: Gildemeister.—Die lustigen weiber von Windsor, üb. von Hermann Kurz.—Die beiden Veroneser, üb. von G: Herwegh.—Viel lärm um nichts, üb. von Adolf Wilbrandt. **2.** Die komödie der irrungen, üb. von G: Herwegh.—Was ihr wollt, oder Heiliger dreikönigsabend, üb. von O: Gildemeister.—Der sturm, üb. von F: Bodenstedt. — Zähmung einer widerspenstigen, üb. von G: Herwegh.—Verlorene liebesmüh, üb. von O: Gildemeister. **3.** Mass für mass, üb. von F: Bodenstedt.—Perikles, fürst von Tyrus, üb. von Nicolaus Delius.—Der kaufmann von Venedig, üb. von F: Bodenstedt.—Wie es euch gefällt, üb. von G: Herwegh.—Ende gut, alles gut, üb. von G: Herwegh. **4.** König Johann.—König Richard der zweite. —König Heinrich der vierte. 1. theil.—König Heinrich der vierte. 2. theil, üb. von O: Gildemeister. **5.** König Heinrich der fünfte.—König Heinrich der sechste, 1. theil.—König Heinrich der sechste, 2. theil.—König Heinrich der sechste, 3. theil, üb. von O: Gildemeister. **6.** König Richard der dritte.—König Heinrich der achte, üb. von O. Gildemeister.—Hamlet, prinz von Dänemark, üb. von F: Bodenstedt. **7.** Antonius und Kleopatra, üb. von Paul Heyse.—Othello, der mohr von Venedig, üb. von F: Bodenstedt.—Titus Andronicus, üb. von Nicolaus Delius.—Julius Cäsar, üb. von O: Gildemeister. **8.** Romeo und Julia. üb. von F: Bodenstedt. — Cymbelin, üb. von O: Gildemeister.—Timon von Athen, üb. von Paul Heyse.—Coriolanus, üb. von Adolf Wilbrandt. **9.** König Lear, üb. von G: Herwegh.—Troilus und Cressida, üb. von G: Herwegh.—Macbeth, üb. von F: Bodenstedt.—William Shakespeare ; ein rückblick auf sein leben und schaffen.

— Shakespeare, adapted for reading classes and for the family circle, by T: Bulfinch and S. G. Bulfinch. Bost. 1865. S.   **822.3 : 4**

Contents. Midsummer-night's dream.—Romeo and Juliet.—The merchant of Venice.—First part of king Henry IV.—Hamlet.—King Lear.—Macbeth.—The tempest.

— All's well that ends well ; ed. with notes by W: J. Rolfe. Ill. N. Y. 1881. S. **822.3 : 5**

— _Same ;_ a comedy in 5 acts. _In_ French's.

812 : 1 v113

— Anthony and Cleopatra ; ed. with notes by W: J. Rolfe. Ill. N. Y. 1881. S.

822.3 : 49

— _Same ;_ tragedy in 5 acts. _In_ Lacy.

812 : 1 v75

— As you like it ; ed. with notes by W: J. Rolfe. Ill. N. Y. 1878. S. **822.3 : 6**

— _Same ;_ comedy in 5 acts. _In_ Lacy.

812 : 1 v25

— The comedy of errors ; ed. with notes by W: J. Rolfe. Ill. N. Y. 1881. S. **822.3 : 7**

— _Same. In_ Lacy. **812 : 1 v72**

Shakspere, W:—*Continued.*
— Coriolanus ; ed. with notes by W: J. Rolfe.
　Ill. N. Y. 1881. S.　822.3 : 8
— *Same. In* Lacy.　812 : 1 v95
— Cymbeline ; ed. with notes by W: J. Rolfe.
　Ill. N. Y. 1881. S.　822.3 : 9
— *Same. In* Lacy.　812 : 1 v64
— Hamlet, prince of Denmark ; tragedy in 5
　acts. *In* Lacy.　812 : 1 v23
— Julius Cæsar ; ed. with notes by W: J. Rolfe.
　Ill. N. Y. 1878. S.　822.3 : 10
— *Same. In* Lacy.　812 : 1 v40
— Katherine and Petruchio ; a comedy in 3 acts,
　altered by D: Garrick from "The taming
　of the shrew." *In* Lacy.　812 : 1 v62
— King Henr IV., pt. 1 ; ed. with notes by W:
　J. Rolfey Ill. N. Y. 1880. S.　822.3 : 11
— *Same. In* Lacy.　812 : 1 v37
— King Henry IV., pt. 2 ; ed. with notes by W:
　J. Rolfe. Ill. N. Y. 1880. S.　822.3 : 12
— *Same. In* Lacy.　812 : 1 v64
— King Henry V. ; ed. with notes by W: J.
　Rolfe. Ill. N. Y. 1878. S.　822.3 : 13
— *Same. In* Lacy.　812 : 1 v39
— King Henry VI., pt. 1 ; ed. with notes by W:
　J. Rolfe. Ill. N. Y. 1882. S.　822.3 : 57
— King Henry VI., pt. 2. Ill. N. Y. 1882. S.
　822.3 : 58
— King Henry VI., pt. 3. Ill. N. Y. 1882. S.
　822.3 : 59
— King Henry VIII. ; ed. with notes by W: J.
　Rolfe. Ill. N. Y. 1872. S.　822.3 : 14
— *Same. In* Lacy.　812 : 1 v22
— King John ; ed. with notes by W: J. Rolfe.
　Ill. N. Y. 1880. S.　822.3 : 15
— *Same. In* Sargent, E. Mod. stand. drama.
　822.2 : 2 v5
— *Same. In* Lacy.　812 : 1 v38
— King Lear ; ed. with notes by W: J. Rolfe.
　Ill. N. Y. 1880. S.　822.3 : 16
— *Same. In* Lacy.　812 : 1 v31
— King Richard II. ; ed. with notes by W: J.
　Rolfe. Ill. N. Y. 1876. S.　822.3 : 17
— *Same. In* Lacy.　812 : 1 v77
— King Richard III. ; ed. with notes by W: J.
　Rolfe. Ill. N. Y. 1880. S.　822.3 : 18
— *Same. In* Lacy.　812 : 1 v13
— Love's labor's lost ; ed. with notes by W: J.
　Rolfe. Ill. N. Y. 1882. S.　822.3 : 65
— Macbeth ; ed. with notes by W: J. Rolfe. Ill.
　N. Y. 1878. S.　822.3 : 19
— *Same. In* Lacy.　812 : 1 v9
— *Same, germ.* Macbeth ; ein trauersp. Uebers.
　von. F: v. Schiller. *In* Schiller, J: C. F:
　v. Sämmtliche werke.　830 : 143 v6
— *Same. In the same.*　830 : 144 v9
— Measure for measure ; ed. with notes by W:
　J. Rolfe. Ill. N. Y. 1882. S.　822.3 : 61
— The merchant of Venice ; ed. with notes by
　W: J. Rolfe. Ill. N. Y. 1871. S.
　822.3 : 20
— *Same. In* Lacy.　812 : 1 v25
— *Same ;* with introd. and notes, explanatory
　and critical, for use in schools and classes
　by H: N. Hudson. (Classics for children.)
　Bost. 1883. S.　x 822.3 : 75

Shakspere, W:—*Continued:*
— The merry wives of Windsor ; ed. with notes
　by W: J. Rolfe. Ill. N. Y. 1882. S.
　822.3 : 60
— *Same. In* Lacy.　812 : 1 v62
— A midsummer-night's dream ; ed. with notes
　by W: J. Rolfe. N. Y. 1877. S. 822.3 : 21
— *Same. In* Lacy.　812 : 1 v28
— Much ado about nothing ; comedy in 5 acts.
　In Lacy.　812 : 1 v35
— Othello the moor of Venice ; ed. with notes
　by W: J. Rolfe. Ill. N. Y. 1879. S.
　822.3 : 22
— *Same. In* Lacy.　812 : 1 v27
— Pericles, prince of Tyre ; ed. with notes by W:
　J. Rolfe. Ill. N. Y. 1883. S.　822.3 : 66
— *Same, germ.* Pericles, fürst von Tyrus ; ein
　dramatisches mährchen. Uebers. von Adel-
　bert Keller. Stuttg. 1854. S.　822.3 : 27
— Poems, with a memoir by Alexander Dyce.
　Bost. 1854. S.　822.3 : 26
— Romeo and Juliet ; ed. with notes by W: J.
　Rolfe. Ill. N. Y. 1879. S.　822.3 : 23
— *Same. In* Sargent, E. Mod. stand. drama.
　822.2 : 2 v6
— *Same. In* Lacy.　812 : 1 v18
— Sonnets ; ed. with notes by W: J. Rolfe. N. Y.
　1883. S.　822.3 : 70
— *Same, germ.* Sonnette ; in deutscher nachbil-
　dung von F: v. Bodenstedt. Berlin. 1866.
　S.　822.3 : 48
— The taming of the shrew ; ed. with notes by
　W: J. Rolfe. Ill. N. Y. 1881. S. 822.3 : 24
— The tempest ; ed. with notes by W: J. Rolfe.
　Ill. N. Y. 1877. S.　822.3 : 25
— *Same. In* Lacy.　812 : 1 v37
— Timon of Athens ; ed. with notes by W: J.
　Rolfe. N. Y. 1882. S.　822.3 : 63
— Titus Andronicus ; ed. with notes by W: J.
　Rolfe. Ill. N. Y. 1884 [1883]. S.
　822.3 : 76
— Troilus and Cressida ; ed. with notes by W: J.
　Rolfe. N. Y. 1882. S.　822.3 : 62
— Twelfth night, or What you will ; comedy in
　5 acts. *In* Lacy.　812 : 1 v36
— The two gentlemen of Verona ; ed. with notes
　by W: J. Rolfe. N. Y. 1882. S. 822.3 : 64
— Venus and Adonis, Lucrece and other poems ;
　ed. with notes by W: J. Rolfe. N. Y. 1883.
　S.　822.3 : 69
— The winter's tale ; a play in 5 acts. *In* French's.
　812 : 1 v113
— *and* J: Fletcher. The two noble kinsmen ;
　written by the memorable worthies of their
　time... ; ed. with notes by W: J. Rolfe.
　N. Y. 1883. S.　822.3 : 67
Sheil, R: Lalor. Evadne, or The statue ; tragedy
　in 3 acts ; altered from Rivers and Shirley.
　In Lacy.　812 : 1 v24
Shepherd, R., *joint author, see* **Higgie,** T. H.
Sheridan, Richard Brinsley Butler. Dramatic
　works ; with a memoir of his life by G. G.
　S. Lond. 1857. S.　822.2 : 34
　Contents. Memoir.—The rivals.—St. Patrick's day.
　—The duenna.—The school for scandal.—The critic.—
　A trip to Scarborough.—Pizarro.
— Sheridan's comedies, The rivals and The school
　for scandal ; ed. with an introd. and notes
　to each play and a biographical sketch of
　Sheridan by Brander Matthews. Ill. Bost.
　1885 [1884]. O.　822.2†46

Sheridan, Richard Brinsley Butler.—*Continued.*
— The critic, or A tragedy rehearsed ; a drama-
tic piece in 3 acts. *In* British drama.
  822.2 : 1 v2
— *Same. In* Lacy.   812 : 1 v8
— The duenna ; a comic opera in 3 acts. *In*
  British drama.   822.2 : 1 v2
— The rivals ; comedy in 5 acts. *In* British
  drama.   822.2 : 1 v1
— *Same. In* Lacy.   812 : 1 v33
— Saint Patrick's day, or The scheming lieuten-
  ant ; a farce in 1 act. *In* French's.
  812 : 1 v114
— The school for scandal ; comedy in 5 acts.
  In British drama.   822.2 : 1 v2
— *Same. In* Lacy.   812 : 1 v27
— A trip to Scarborough ; a comedy in 3 acts.
  In French's.   812 : 1 v103
Simon, Joseph Philippe, (*Lockroy*), *and* A:
  Arnould. Helene, oder Die verklärungen,
  schausp. in 3 aufz, nach Zschokke's novelle.
  Uebers. von K. G. T. Winkler. *n. t.* S.
  832 : 89
Simpson, J. Palgrave. Appearances ; an origi-
  nal comedy in 2 acts. *In* Lacy.
  812 : 1 v47
— An atrocious criminal ; a farce in 1 act. *In*
  Lacy.   812 : 1 v74
— Broken ties ; domestic drama in 2 acts. *In*
  Lacy.   812 : 1 v96
— Court cards ; a comic drama in 2 acts. *In*
  Lacy.   812 : 1 v53
— Daddy Hardacre ; drama in 2 acts. *In* Lacy.
  812 : 1 v100
— A fair pretender ; an original comic drama in
  2 acts. *In* Lacy.   812 : 1 v66
— First affections ; a comedietta in 1 act. *In*
  Lacy.   812 : 1 v52
— Heads or tails ? comedietta in 1 act. *In* Lacy.
  812 : 1 v15
— Jack in a box ! a comedietta in 1 act. *In*
  Lacy.   812 : 1 v71
— Lady Dedlock's secret ; play in 4 acts, found-
  ed on an episode in C: Dickens' "Bleak
  House ". *In* French's.   812 : 1 v122
— Marco Spada ; drama in 3 acts, altered and
  adapted from the french of Scribe. *In*
  Lacy.   812 : 1 v10
— Matrimonial prospectuses ; comedietta in 1
  act. *In* Lacy.   812 : 1 v6
— Only a clod ; comic drama in 1 act. *In* Lacy.
  812 : 1 v21
— Poor cousin Walter ; a drama in 1 act. *In*
  Lacy.   812 : 1 v2
— A school for coquettes ; a comedietta in 1 act.
  In Lacy.   812 : 1 v41
— A scrap of paper ; a comic drama in 3 acts.
  In Lacy.   812 : 1 v51
— Second love ; an original comic drama in 3
  acts. *In* French's.   812 : 1 v28
— The serpent on the hearth ; romantic drama
  in 3 acts. *In* Lacy.   812 : 1 v85
— Shadows of the past ; comedy drama in 2 acts.
  In Lacy.   812 : 1 v97
— Sybilla, or Step by step ; an original comic
  drama in 3 acts. *In* Lacy.   812 : 1 v64
— Two gentlemen at Mivarts ; a dramatic dia-
  logue in 1 short act. *In* Scott, C. W.
  Drawing-room plays.   822.2 : 14
— Very suspicious ! an original comedietta in 1
  act. *In* Lacy.   812 : 1 v6

Simpson, J. Palgrave.—*Continued.*
— The watch dog of the Walsinghams ; romantic
  drama in 4 acts. *In* Lacy.   812 : 1 v92
— Without incumbrances ; a farce in 1 act. *In*
  Lacy.   812 : 1 v2
— World and stage ; original comedy in 3 acts.
  In Lacy.   812 : 1 v97
— *and* Felix **Dale.** Time and the hour ; original
  romantic drama in 3 acts. *In* Lacy.
  812 : 1 v81
— *and* Herman C. **Merivale.** Alone ; an original
  comedy drama in 3 acts. *In* French's.
  812 : 1 v103
— *and* C: **Wray.** Ranelagh ; comic drama in 2
  acts. *In* Lacy.   812 : 1 v13
— *joint author, see* **Yates,** Edmund.
Siraudin, Paul. Left the stage, or Grassot
  tormented by Ravel ; a personal experiment
  in 1 act. *In* Lacy.   812 : 1 v7
— *joint author, see* Clairville, L: François Nicolaie, *also* Moreau, L: Isidore Eugène
  Lemoine.
Sketchley, Arthur, *pseud., see* **Rose,** G:
Smith, Albert. The Alhambra, or The three
  beautiful princesses ; a new and original
  burlesque extravaganza. *In* Lacy.
  812 : 1 v3
— Blanche Heriot, or The Chertsey curfew ; a
  domestic and historical drama in 2 acts.
  In Lacy.   812 : 1 v73
— The cricket on the hearth ; a fairy tale of home
  in 3 chirps, adapted from C: Dickens. *In*
  Lacy.   812 : 1 v44
— Esmeralda ; an operatico, terpsichorean bur-
  lesque in 2 acts. *In* Lacy.   812 : 1 v2
Smith, G., *joint author, see* Mayhew, E:
Smith, S. Theyre. Cut off with a shilling ; com-
  edietta in 1 act. *In* Lacy.   812 : 1 v7
— A happy pair ; original comedietta in 1 act.
  In Lacy.   812 : 1 v83
— My uncle's will ; a comedietta in 1 act. *In*
  French's.   812 : 1 v110
— Which is which ? comedietta in 1 act. *In*
  Lacy.   812 : 1 v97
Smith, W. H. S. The drunkard ; a moral
  domestic drama of american life, in 4 acts.
  In Lacy.   812 : 1 v7
Soane, G: The innkeeper's daughter, or Mary,
  the maid of the inn ; a melodrama in 2 acts.
  In French's.   812 : 1 v114
— Zarah, the gipsy ; romantic drama in 2 acts.
  In Lacy.   812 : 1 v92
Soane-Roby, Bernard. A deserter in a fix ;
  original farce. *In* French's.   812 : 1 v121
Sollohub, Vladimir Aleksandrovitch, *graf.* His
  hat and cane. *In* Plays for private acting.
  812 : 2
— The serenade. *In the same.*   812 : 2
Somerset, C: A. A day after the fair ; farce in 1
  act. *In* Lacy.   812 : 1 v76
— The mistletoe bough, or The fatal cheat ;
  melodrama in 2 acts. *In* Lacy.
  812 : 1 v100
— The sea ; a nautical drama in 2 acts. *In*
  French's.   812 : 1 v105
— Shakspeare's early days ; drama in 2 acts. *In*
  Lacy.   812 : 1 v93
Sophoklês. Tragedies in english prose. The
  Oxford trans., new ed. rev. according to
  the text of Dindorf. N. Y. 1855. D. 882 : 3
  Contents. Oedipus tyrannus.—Oedipus coloneus.—
  Electra. — Antigone. — Trachiniæ. — Ajax. — Philoc-
  tetes.

Sorrell, W. J. A border marriage; a comic drama in 1 act. *In* Lacy.   812 : 1 v65
— *joint author, see* **French, Sidney.**

Soutar, Robert. Sold again; a farce in 1 act. *In* French's.   812 : 1 v113
— *joint author, see* **Claridge, C. J.**

Southerne, T: Isabella, or The fatal marriage; tragedy in 5 acts. *In* British drama.   822.2 : 1 v1
— *Same. In* Lacy.   812 : 1 v94
— Oroonoko; tragedy in 5 acts. *In* British drama.   822.2 : 1 v1

Speak out boldly; a petite comedy in 1 act. *In* Lacy.   812 : 1 v73

Spencer, G:, *and* Walter **James.** A return ticket; original farce in 1 act. *In* Lacy.   812 : 1 v99

Spindler, C: Hans Waldmann; historisches schauspiel in 5 aufz., nebst einem vorspiel in 1 aufz. Stuttg. 1854. S.   832 : 81

Stainforth, Frank, *joint author, see* **Maltby, C. A.**

Steele, *Sir* R: The tender husband, or The accomplished fools; comedy in 5 acts. *In* British drama.   822.2 : 1 v2

Stephenson, C. H. Tromb-al-ca-zar, or The adventures of an operatic troupe; a musical extravaganza in 1 act, adapted from the french. Music by J. Offenbach. *In* Lacy.   812 : 1 v71

Sterry, J. Ashby. Katharine and Petruchio, or The shaming of the true. *In* Scott, C. W. Drawing-room plays.   822.2 : 14

Stirling, E: Aline the rose of Killarney; drama in 3 acts. *In* Lacy.   812 : 1 v94
— The anchor of hope, or The seaman's star; a drama in 2 acts. *In* French's. 812 : 1 v111
— The blue jackets, or Her majesty's service; a farce in 1 act. *In* French's.   812 : 1 v47
— The bould soger boy; a farce in 1 act. *In* French's.   812 : 1 v111
— By royal command; a comedy drama in 3 acts. *In* French's.   812 : 1 v106
— The cabin boy; a drama in 2 acts. *In* French's.   812 : 1 v104
— Captain Charlotte; a farce in 2 acts. *In* Lacy.   812 : 1 v39
— A cheap excursion; an original farce in 1 act. *In* Lacy.   812 : 1 v4
— Family pictures; a farce in 1 act. *In* French's.   812 : 1 v106
— Grace Darling, or The wreck at sea; a drama in 2 acts. *In* French's.   812 : 1 v104
— Jeannette and Jeannot, or The village pride; a musical drama in 2 acts. *In* French's.   812 : 1 v106
— The jew's daughter; an original drama in 2 acts. *In* Lacy.   812 : 1 v29
— Left in a cab; an original farce in 1 act. *In* Lacy.   812 : 1 v2
— Legacy of honour; an original drama in 2 acts. *In* Lacy.   812 : 1 v50
— The little back parlour; a farce in 1 act. *In* French's.   812 : 1 v111
— The lost diamonds; a drama in 2 acts. *In* French's.   812 : 1 v118
— Margaret Catchpole, the heroine of Suffolk, or The vicissitudes of real life; a drama in 3 acts, adapted from the work of the same title. *In* Lacy.   812 : 1 v35

Stirling, E:—*Continued.*
— The miser's daughter; drama in 3 acts. *In* Lacy.   812 : 1 v99
— The old curiosity shop; drama in 2 acts. *In* Lacy.   812 : 1 v77
— A pair of pigeons; an original domestic sketch in 1 act. *In* Lacy.   812 : 1 v33
— A pet of the public; farce in 1 act. *In* Lacy.   812 : 1 v12
— The ragpicker of Paris and the dressmaker of St. Antoine; drama in 3 acts and a prologue. *In* Lacy.   812 : 1 v81
— The reapers, or Forget and forgive; a drama in 2 acts. *In* Lacy.   812 : 1 v62
— The rifle volunteers; an apropos sketch. *In* Lacy.   812 : 1 v40
— The rose of Corbeil, or The forest of Senart; a melodrama in 2 acts. *In* French's.   812 : 1 v110
— The teacher taught; an original farce in 1 act. *In* Lacy.   812 : 1 v48
— Trapping a tartar; a serio-comic drama in 1 act. *In* Lacy.   812 : 1 v65
— The woodman's spell; a serio-comic drama in 1 act. *In* Lacy.   812 : 1 v2

Stocqueler, J. H. An object of interest; farce in 1 act. *In* Lacy.   812 : 1 v16

Stowe, Harriet Elizabeth, *born* Beecher. Extracts from The christian slave. *In* Follen, E. L. Home dramas.   822.1 : 9
— *see also* **Aikin, G: L.** Uncle Tom's cabin, *and* **Suter, W: E.** Dred.

Straight, Douglas, (*Sidney Daryl*). His first brief; a comedietta. *In* Scott, C. W. Drawing-room plays.   822.2 : 14

Sturgis, Julian Russell. Little comedies. [Appleton's handy-vol. ser.] N. Y. 1880. S.   822.2 : 35
Contents. Apples.—Fireflies.—Picking up the pieces.—Half way to Arcady.—Mabel's holy day.—Heather.

Sullivan, Robert. Elopements in high life; comedy in 5 acts. *In* Lacy.   812 : 1 v10

Supersac, Léon. The door is locked. *In* Plays for private acting.   812 : 2

Suter, W: E. The adventures of Dick Turpin and Tom King; a serio-comic drama in 2 acts. *In* Lacy.   812 : 1 v42
— "Brother Bill and me"; an original farce in 1 act. *In* Lacy.   812 : 1 v52
— Catherine Howard; romantic drama in 3 acts, from the celebrated play by that name by Alexandre Dumas. *In* Lacy. 812 : 1 v37
— The child stealer; a drama in 4 parts, adapted from the french. *In* Lacy. 812 : 1 v70
— Double dealing, or The rifle volunteer; a duologue in 1 act. *In* Lacy. 812 : 1 v47
— Dred; a tale of the Dismal Swamp; a drama in 2 acts, from mrs. Stowe's novel. *In* Lacy.   812 : 1 v57
— The felon's bond; drama in 3 acts. *In* Lacy.   812 : 1 v85
— First love, or The widowed bride; an original drama in 3 acts. *In* Lacy.   812 : 1 v69
— Give me my wife; farce in 1 act. *In* Lacy.   812 : 1 v75
— The highwayman's holiday; a farce in 1 act. *In* Lacy.   812 : 1 v60
— Holly Bush Hall, or The track in the snow; a drama in 2 acts. *In* Lacy.   812 : 1 v44

Suter, W: E.—*Continued.*

— Il trovatore ; a romantic drama in 3 acts, from the popular opera of that name. *In* Lacy.
812 : 1 v56

— Incombatibility of temper ; a farce in 1 act. *In* Lacy. 812 : 1 v73

— Isoline of Bavaria ; drama in 4 acts. *In* Lacy.
812 : 1 v86

— Jack o' the hedge ; original drama in 2 acts. *In* Lacy. 812 : 1 v78

— John Wopps, or "From information I received"; farce in 1 act. *In* Lacy.
812 : 1 v49

— A life's revenge, or Two loves for one heart ; a drama in 3 acts. *In* Lacy.   812 : 1 v39

— Little Annie's birthday ; an original personation farce. *In* Lacy.   812 : 1 v81

— The lost child ; an original farce in 1 act. *In* Lacy.   812 : 1 v62

— More free than welcome ; a farce for three male characters, adapted from the french. *In* Lacy.   812 : 1 v73

— Our new man ; a farce in 1 act. *In* Lacy.
812 : 1 v65

— A quiet family ; an original farce. *In* Lacy.
812 : 1 v30

— The robbers of the Pyrenees ; a drama in 2 acts and a prologue, adapted from the french. *In* Lacy.   812 : 1 v56

— Rocambole, or The knaves of hearts and the companions of crime ; a romantic drama in a prologue and 3 acts. *In* Lacy.
812 : 1 v66

— Sarah's young man ; a farce in 1 act. *In* Lacy.
812 : 1 v31

— The test of truth, or "It's a long lane that has no turning"; comedy in 2 acts. *In* Lacy.
812 : 1 v84

— Two gentlemen in a fix, or How to lose the train ; an interlude. *In* Lacy. 812 : 1 v66

— A very pleasant evening ; farce in 1 act. *In* Lacy.   812 : 1 v80

— Wanted "a young lady" ; a farce in 1 act. *In* Lacy.   812 : 1 v66

— We all have our little faults ; farce in 1 act. *In* Lacy.   812 : 1 v78

— Which shall I marry ? a farce in 1 act. *In* Lacy.   812 : 1 v59

Swinburne, Algernon C: Atalanta in Calydon ; a tragedy. Bost. 1866. S.   822.2 : 28

— Mary Stuart ; a tragedy. N. Y., 1881. D.
822.2 : 40

— The queen mother and Rosamond. Bost. 1866. S.   822.2 : 29

Talfourd, Francis. Abou Hassan, or The hunt after happiness ; a semi-original fairy extravaganza in rhyme in 1 act. *In* Lacy.
812 : 1 v17

— Alcestis, the original strong-minded woman ; classical burlesque in 1 act, being a most shameless misinterpretation of the greek drama of Euripides with an original prologue upon the occasion of its subsequent revival. *In* Lacy.   812 : 1 v21

— Atalanta, or The three golden apples ; an original classical extravaganza in 1 act. *In* Lacy.   812 : 1 v30

— Electra in a new electric light ; an entirely new and original extravaganza in 1 act. *In* Lacy.   812 : 1 v39

— Ganem, the slave of love ; an original extravaganza from "The arabian nights entertainments." *In* Lacy.   812 : 1 v6

Talfourd, Francis.—*Continued.*

— A household fairy ; domestic sketch in 1 act. *In* Lacy.   812 : 1 v44

— King Thrushbeard, or A little pet and the great passion ; preceding the grand christmas comic pantomime of Harlequin Hafiz, and being an entirely new and original fairy and domestic extravaganza. *In* Lacy.
812 : 1 v44

— Macbeth somewhat removed from the text of Shakespeare, in 2 acts. *In* Lacy.
812 : 1 v8

— Pluto and Proserpina, or The belle and the pomegranate ; an entirely new and original mythological extravaganza, or sicilian romance of the (1 ?) 0th century. *In* Lacy.
812 : 1 v36

— The rule of three ; a comedietta in 1 act. *In* Lacy.   812 : 1 v38

— Shylock, or The merchant of Venice preserved ; an entirely new reading of Shakespeare, from an edition hitherto undiscovered by modern authorities, and which it is hoped may be received as the stray leaves of a Jerusalem hearty-joke. 3d ed., rev. and corr. *In* Lacy.   812 : 1 v11

— Tell and the strike of the cantons, or The pair, the meddler and the apple ; an original fairy, romantic and legendary extravaganza. *In* Lacy.   812 : 1 v43

— *and* H: James Byron. The miller and his men ; a burlesque mealy-drama in 1 act. *In* Lacy.   812 : 1 v45

— *and* Alfred **Wigan.** Tit for tat ; comedietta in 2 acts. *In* Lacy.   812 : 1 v17

Talfourd, *Sir* T: Noon. Tragedies. Added, a few sonnets and verses. Bost. 1865. D.
822.2 : 30

Contents. Ion.—The athenian captive.—Glencoe.—Sonnets.—Poems.

— Ion ; a tragedy in 5 acts. N. Y. *n. d.* S.
822.2 : 3

Taming a tiger ; a farce in 1 act, adapted from the french. *In* Lacy.   812 : 1 v72

Tarantula, La, or The spider king ; an extravaganza made up into an english dress from french materials in 2 acts. *In* Lacy.
812 : 1 v3

Taylor, Bayard. Prince Deukalion. Bost. 1878. O.   822.1 : 17

— The prophet ; a tragedy. Bost. 1874. S.
822.1 : 18

Taylor, H: Philip Van Artevelde ; a dramatic romance in 2 parts. Cambridge. 1835. S.
822.2 : 31

Taylor, T: Proclus. "The bottle"; drama in 2 acts, founded upon the graphic illustrations of G: Cruikshank. *In* Lacy.
812 : 1 v17

— The chain of guilt, or The inn on the heath ; a romantic drama in 2 acts. *In* French's.
812 : 1 v110

Taylor, Tom. The babes in the wood ; an original comedy in 3 acts. *In* Lacy.
812 : 1 v50

— A blighted being ; farce in 1 act, adapted from the french vaudeville "Une existence décolorée". *In* Lacy.   812 : 1 v16

— The fool's revenge ; a drama in 3 acts. *In* Lacy.   812 : 1 v43

— Going to the bad ; an original comedy in 2 acts. *In* Lacy.   812 : 1 v37

Taylor, Tom—*Continued.*
— Helping hands ; domestic drama in 2 acts. *In* Lacy. 812 : 1 v22
— Henry Dunbar, or A daughter's trial ; drama in 4 acts, founded on Miss Braddon's novel of the same name. *In* Lacy. 812 : 1 v76
— The house or the home ; a comedy in 2 acts. *In* Lacy. 812 : 1 v42
— A nice firm ; comic drama in 1 act. *In* Lacy. 812 : 1 v13
— Nine points of the law ; an original comedietta in 1 act. *In* Lacy. 812 : 1 v40
— Payable on demand ; an original domestic drama in 2 acts. *In* Lacy. 812 : 1 v41
— Retribution ; a domestic drama in 4 acts. *In* Lacy. 812 : 1 v27
— Sense and sensation, or The seven sisters of Thule ; a new and original morality in a prologue and 7 scenes. *In* Lacy. 812 : 1 v63
— The serf, or Love levels all ; an original drama in 3 acts. *In* Lacy. 812 : 1 v68
— Settling day ; a story of the time in 5 acts. *In* Lacy. 812 : 1 v82
— A sheep in wolf's clothing ; a domestic drama in 1 act. *In* Lacy. 812 : 1 v37
— "Still waters run deep" ; comedy in 3 acts. *In* Lacy. 812 : 1 v22
— A tale of two cities: a drama in 2 acts and a prologue, adapted from C: Dickens. *In* Lacy. 812 : 1 v45
— The ticket-of-leave man ; a drama in 4 acts, founded on a french dramatic tale "Le retour de Melun", included in "Les drames de la vie" by Brisebarre and Nuz. *In* Lacy. 812 : 1 v59
— To oblige Benson ; comedietta in 1 act, adapted from the french vaudeville "Un service à Blanchard" [by Eugène Moreau and Delacour]. *In* Lacy. 812 : 1 v14
— An unequal match ; a comedy in 3 acts. *In* French's. 812 : 1 v118
— Up at the hills ; an original comedy of indian life in 2 acts. *In* Lacy. 812 : 1 v50
— Victims ; an original comedy in 3 acts. *In* Lacy. 812 : 1 v32
— *and* A: W. Dubourg. New men and old acres ; original comedy in 3 acts. *In* Lacy. 812 : 1 v90
— — A sister's penance ; original drama in 3 acts. *In* Lacy. 812 : 1 v75

Tennyson, Alfred, *baron Tennyson.* The falcon and The cup. N. Y. 1884. S. 822.2 : 45
— Harold ; a drama Bost. 1877. S. 822.2 : 32
— Queen Mary ; a drama. Bost. 1875. S. 822.2 : 33

Terentius Afer, Publius. Comedies ; literally trans. into english prose, with notes by H: T: Riley. Lond. 1853. D. 872 : 2
Contents. Andria. or The fair andriän.—Eunuchus. or The eunuch.—Heautout imorumenos, or The self-tormentor.—Adelphi, or The brothers.—Hecyra, the mother-in-law.—Phormio, or The scheming parasite.
— Comedies ; tr. into english prose as near as the propriety of the two languages will admit, together with the original latin from the best editions wherein the words of the latin text are arranged in their grammatical order, the ellipses carefully supplied, the observations of the mos, valuable commentators, both antient and modern, represented, and the beauties of

the original explained in a new and concise manner, with notes pointing out the connecxion of the several scenes and an index critical and phraselogical, adapted to the capacities of youth at school as well as private gentlemen ; by S. Patrick. 3d ed.; prefixed, the life of Terence, with some account of the dramatic poetry of the antients ; v. 1. Lond. 1767. O. 872 : 1

Terry, Daniel. Guy Mannering, or The gipsey's prophecy ; a musical play in 3 acts, adapted from sir Walter Scott. *In* Lacy. 812 : 1 v18

Thetis and Peleus. or The chain of roses ; a mythological love story told in 1 act. *In* Lacy. 812 : 1 v5

Theuriet, André. The old homestead. *In* Plays for private acting. 812 : 2

Thiboust, Lambert, *joint author, see* Grangé, Eugène.

Thomas, C: The queen of hearts ; an operetta in 1 act. Music by Harriet Young. *In* French's. 812 : 1 v115

Thompson, Alfred. The happy dispateh ; a japanese opera-bouffe. Music by Ducenozov. *In* Scott, C. W. Drawing-room plays. 822.2 : 14

Thompson, B:, *of Kingston-upon-Hull,* tr. The german theatre. 4th ed. Lond. 1811. 6 v. S. 832 : 96
Contents. V. 1. Kotzebue, A: F: F. v. The stranger; Rolla; Pizarro. 2. Schiller, J: C. F: v. Don Carlos.—Kotzebue, A: F: F. v. Count Benyowsky. 3. Kotzebue, A: F: F. v. Lovers vows; Deaf and dumb; The indian exiles; False delicacy. 4. Babo, F. M. J: Otto of Wittlesbach; Dagobert, king of the Franks.—Kotzebue, A: F: F. v. Adelaide of Wulfingen. 5. Schiller, J: C. F: v. The robbers.—Kotzebue, A: F: F. v. The happy family.—Iffland, A: W: Conscience. 6. Schröder, F: L: The ensign.—Reitzenstein, K: *freiherr* v. Count Königsmark.—Göthe, J: W. v. Stella.—Lessing, J: G. E. Emilia Galotti.

Thompson, C. Pelham. The dumb savoyard and his monkey ; melodrama in 1 act. *In* Lacy. 812 : 1 v98
— Jack Robinson and his monkey ; a melodrama in 2 acts. *In* Lacy. 812 : 1 v31

Thomson, James. Tancred and Sigismunda ; tragedy in 5 acts. *In* British drama. 822.2 : 1 v1

Tieck, J: L: [Dramatische schriften.] *In his* Schriften. 830 : 148
— *Same. In* Kürschner, J. Deutsche national-litteratur. 830 : 152 v144

Tilbury, W: Harris. Counter attraction, or Strolling and stratagem ; "a trifle light as air". *In* Lacy. 812 : 1 v5

Tobin, J: The honeymoon ; comedy in 5 acts. *In* Lacy. 812 : 1 v16

Toft, P. Out of the frying pan ; a 1 act comedy. Tr. from the danish, adapted for the english stage by A. P. Graves. *In* Lacy. 812 : 1 v96

Tomkins the troubadour ; farce in 1 act. *In* Lacy. 812 : 1 v86

Townley, James. High life below stairs ; farce in 2 acts. *In* British drama. 822.2 : 1 v2
— *Same. In* Lacy. 812 : 1 v3

Townsend, W. Thompson. The bell ringer of St. Paul's. or The huntsman and the spy ; melodrama in 3 acts. *In* French's. 812 : 1 v112
— The blow in the dark ; a comedietta in 1 act. *In* French's. 812 : 1 v106

Townsend, W. Thompson.—*Continued.*
— The gold fiend, or The demon gamester; a drama in 3 acts. *In* Lacy.   **812 : 1 v107**
— The lost ship, or The man of war's man and the privateer; nautical drama in 3 acts. *In* Lacy.   **812 : 1 v20**
— Mary's dream, or Far, far at sea; a melodrama in 3 acts. *In* French's,   **812 : 1 v107**
— Temptation, or The fatal brand; a drama in 2 acts. *In* Lacy. ·   **812 : 1 v52**
— Whitefriars, or The days of Claude Du Val; a drama in 3 acts, from the celebrated romantic novel of the same title. *In* Lacy.   **812 : 1 v40**
Tradesman's son, The; a drama in 2 acts. *In* French's.   **812 : 1 v105**
Trafford, F. G., *pseud., see* **Riddell,** Charlotte Eliza Lawson.
Troughton, Adolphus C: The fly and the web; a comedy in 2 acts: *In* Lacy.   **812 : 1 v69**
— Leading strings; a comedy in 3 acts. *In* Lacy.   **812 : 1 v33**
— Living too fast, or A twelve month's honeymoon; comedietta in 1 act. *In* Lacy.   **812 : 1 v16**
— Shameful · behavior; a comedietta in 2 acts. *In* Lacy.   **812 : 1 v43**
— Short and sweet; a comic drama in 1 act. *In* Lacy.   **812 : 1 v52**
— Unlimited confidence; a comedietta in 1 act. *In* Lacy.   **812 : 1 v61**
— Vandyke Brown; a farce in 1 act. *In* Lacy.   **812 : 1 v39**
— Wooing in jest and loving in earnest; a comedietta in 1 act. *In* Lacy.   **812 : 1 v37**
Twenty minutes with a tiger; farce in 1 act, adapted from the french. *In* Lacy.   **812 : 1 v24**
Valle, Enrico. A family of martyrs; a drama. Tr. from the italian by F. P. Garesché. Cinc. 1864. S.   **852 : 1**
Vanbrugh, *Sir* J: Dramatic works. With **Wycherley,** W:, *and others.* Dramatic works.   **822.2+10**
Contents. The relapse. — The provoked wife. — Aesop.— Same, pt. 2.—The false friend.—The confederacy.—The mistake.—The country house.— A journey to London.
— The city wives' conspiracy; comedy in 5 acts. *In* British drama.   **822.2 : 1 v2**
— Lovers' quarrels, or Like master like man; a farce in 1 act. *In* Lacy.   **812 : 1 v4**
— The provoked husband, or A journey to London; comedy in 5 acts. *In* British drama.   **822.2 : 1 v2**
— The provoked wife; comedy in 5 acts. *In* British drama.   **822.2 : 1 v2**
Vellère, *Dr.* —. King and rebel; historical drama in prologue and 4 acts. *In* Lacy.   **812 : 1 v100**
— Meted out; original modern drama in 4 acts. *In* Lacy.   **812 : 1 v99**
Venable, W. H., *ed.* The amateur actor; a collection of plays for school and home. Cinc. *n. d.* D.   **822 : 1**
Contents. Introd. — Oberon and Titania. — Mrs. Willis's will.—Little Red Ridinghood.—Lady Pentweazel at the artist's.—The discomfited rivals.—The mock doctor.—Sentimentality.—The forest exiles.— Norval.—Matrimonial infelicities.—Country versus city.—The witty servant.—Quackery discovered.— The harvest storm.—Van Dunderman and his servant.—The heartless landlord.—The pedant.—Cara-

Venable, W. H., *ed.*—*Continued.*
tach and Hengo.—A surprised suitor.—The loves of miss Tucker.—The chagrined author.—The father's sacrifice.—Pyramus and Thisbe.
— *ed.* Dramas and dramatic scenes. Cinc. [1874]. D.   **822 : 2**
Contents. Stage terms and directions. — **Shakespeare,** Mercutio. — **Wycherly,** Detraction. — **Farquhar,** Boniface. — **Congreve,** Braggadocio. — **Mitford,** Rienzi. — **Milman,** Ill - gotten gold. — **Shakespeare,** The three caskets. — **O'Keefe,** The positive man. — **Colman,** *the younger,* Pangloss. — **Colman,** *the elder,* Inkle and Yarico. — **Tobin,** The deceived bride.—**Lovell,** The greek girl and the barbarian. — **Dryden,** Ventidius and the emperor.— **Knowles,** William Tell.—**Otway,** Jaffir and Belvidera.—**Sheridan,** The dutiful son.—**Shakespeare,** The pound of flesh.—**Bulwer-Lytton,** The bequest. —**Addison,** The death of Cato.—**Mason,** The forlorn hope of Mona.
Vernon, Leicester. The lancers; drama in 3 acts, adapted from the french. *In* Lacy.   **812 : 1 v13**
Vidocq, the french police spy; a melodrama in 2 acts, adapted for representation from the autobiography of Vidocq. *In* French's.   **812 : 1 v110**
Violet, The; a drama in 2 acts. *In* Lacy.   **812 : 1 v9**
Vogel, W: Christine von Schweden; drama in 3 aufz., nach van der Velde. *n. t.* D.   **832 : 82**
Von Culin, Everett. The dentist's clerk, or Pulling· teeth by steam; a farce in 1 act. *In* French's.   **812 : 1 v113**
Wagner, H: Leopold. Die kindermörderin; ein trauerspiel. *In* Kürschner, J: Deutsche national-litteratur.   **830 : 152 v80**
Wagner, W: R: Der fliegende holländer. *In his* Schriften.   **780 : 20 v1**
— Eine kapitulation; lustspiel in antiker manier. *In the same.*   **780 : 20 v9**
— Lohengrin. *In the same.*   **780 : 20 v2**
— Die meistersinger von Nürnberg. *In the same.*   **780 : 20 v7**
— Das rheingold; vorabend zu dem bühnenfestspiel Der ring des Nibelungen. *In the same.*   **780 : 20 v5**
— Rienzi, der letzte der tribunen; grosse tragische oper in 5 akten, nach Bulwer's gleichnamigem roman. *In the same.*   **780 : 20 v1**
— Der ring des Nibelungen; bühnenfestspiel. *In the same.*   **780 : 20 v6**
Contents. 1er tag. Die walküre. 2ter tag. Siegfried. 3ter tag. Götterdämmerung.
— Siegfried's tod. *In the same.*   **780 : 20 v9**
— Tannhäuser und der sängerkrieg auf Wartburg. *In the same.*   **780 : 20 v2**
— Tristan und Isolde. *In the same.*   **780 : 20 v7**
Wainwright, J: Howard. Rip Van Winkle; an original american opera in 3 acts. Music by G: F. Bristow. *In* Lacy.   **812 : 1 v39**
Walcot, C: M. Nothing to nurse; an original farce in 1 act. *In* Lacy.   **812 : 1 v33**
Waldron, W. R. Lizzie Leigh, or The murder near the old mill; a story of three christmas nights; domestic drama in 3 acts. *In* Lacy.   **812 : 1 v93**
— The will and the way, or The mysteries of Carrow Abbey; a romantic drama in 3 acts, founded on the popular work of the same name by J. F. Smith. *In* Lacy.   **812 : 1 v66**
— Worth a struggle; comedy drama in 4 acts. *In* Lacy.   **812 : 1 v90**

Walker, C. E. The warlock of the glen; a
melodrama in 2 acts. *In* Lacy.
812 : 1 v46
Walker, J: The wild boy of Bohemia, or The
force of nature; a melodrama in 2 acts.
In French's. 812 : 1 v114
Wangenheim, Paul *freiherr* v. Die abtrünni-
gen; drama in 5 acten. Leipz. 1845. D.
832 : 83
Weatherly, F: E:, *and* Alfred W. Moore Weatherly. Champagne; a petite comedy,
adapted from the french. *In* Lacy.
812 : 1 v98
Webster, B: The golden farmer, or The last
crime; melodrama in 2 acts. *In* Lacy.
812 : 1 v76
— Just like Roger! farce in 1 act. *In* Lacy.
812 : 1 v96
— A yule log; a farce in 1 act. *In* Lacy.
812 : 1 v98
Webster, B:, *jr*. Behind time; a farce in 1 act.
In Lacy. 812 : 1 v68
Webster, J: Dramatic works; ed. by W: Hazlitt. Lond. 1857. 4 v. D. 822.2 : 12
Contents. V. 1. Introduction.—The famous history
of sir T: Wyat.—Westward hoe.—Northward hoe. 2.
The white devil.—The duchess of Malfi. 3. The
devil's law-case.—Appius and Virginia.—Monuments
of honor.—A monumental column.—Odes. 4. A cure
for a cuckold.—Induction to The malcontent.—The
thracian wonder.—The weakest goes to the wall.
Weichselbaumer, K: Liebesbotschaften; lustsp.
in 2 akten. *n. t. S.* 832 : 84
Weisse, Christian Felix. Richard der dritte;
ein trauerspiel in 5 aufz. *In* Kürschner,
J. Deutsche national-litteratur.
830 : 152 v72
Welstead, B: Giralda, or The invisible husband;
a comic drama in 3 acts, adapted from
Scribe's opera. *In* Lacy. 812 : 1 v26
Werner, Zacharias. Martin Luther, oder Die
weihe der kraft; eine tragödie. *In* Kürsch-
ner, J. Deutsche national-litteratur.
830 : 152 v151
— Der 24. februar; eine tragödie in 1 akt. *In
the same*. 830 : 152 v151
West, B. Melmoth, the wanderer; a melodram-
atic romance in 3 acts. *In* Lacy.
812 : 1 v85
Where shall I dine? a farcetta in 1 act. *In*
French's. 812 : 1 v114
White, James. Feudal times, or The court of
James III; a scottish historical play. *In*
Sargent, E. Mod. stand. drama.
822.2 : 2 v6
Whitehead, W: The roman father; tragedy in
5 acts. *In* British drama. 822.2 : 1 v2
Whitty, Walter Devereux. My husband's secret;
a farce in 1 act. *In* French's. 812 : 1 v102
Wigan, Alfred. A model of a wife; a farce in 1
act. *In* Lacy. 812 : 1 v61
— *joint author, see* Talfourd, Francis.
Wigan, Horace. Always intended; comedy in
1 act. *In* Lacy. 812 : 1 v77
— The best way; petite comedy in 1 act. *In*
Lacy. 812 : 1 v75
— The charming woman; a comedy in 3 acts.
In Lacy. 812 : 1 v60
— Friends or foes? a comedy in 4 acts. *In* Lacy.
812 : 1 v54
— Observation and flirtation; a comedy in 1 act.
In Lacy. 812 : 1 v47

Wigan, Horace.—*Continued*.
— Real and ideal; a comedy in 1 act. *In* Lacy.
812 : 1 v56
— A southerner just arrived; a farce in 1 act. *In*
Lacy. 812 : 1 v56
— Taming the truant; a comedy in 3 acts. *In*
Lacy. 812 : 1 v58
— *joint author, see* Oxenford, J:
Wilcox, R. N., *joint author, see* Millett, R. W. F.
Wildenbruch, Ernst Adolph v. Harold; tragedy
in 5 acts. Tr. by Marie v. Zglinitzka.
Hanover. 1884. D. 832 : 98
Wilhelmi, Alexander, *pseud., see* Zechmeister,
Alexander V:
Wilkins, J: H. Civilization; play in 5 acts. *In*
Lacy. 812 : 1 v10
— The egyptian; play in 5 acts. *In* Lacy.
812 : 1 v12
Wilks, T: Egerton. Bamboozling; an original
farce in 1 act. *In* Lacy. 812 : 1 v28
— Ben, the boatswain; a nautical drama in 3
acts. *In* Lacy. 812 : 1 v28
— The black domino, or The masked ball; comic
drama in 3 acts. *In* Lacy. 812 : 1 v88
— The captain is not a—miss; a farce in 1 act.
In Lacy. 812 : 1 v29
— Cousin Peter; a comic drama in 1 act. *In*
French's. 812 : 1 v117
— The crown prince, or The buckle of brilliants;
a drama in 2 acts. *In* Lacy. 812 : 1 v26
— The dream spectre; a romantic drama in 3
acts. *In* Lacy. 812 : 1 v40
— Eily O'Connor, or The brides of Garryowen;
a domestic drama in 2 acts. *In* Lacy.
812 : 1 v47
— Halvei, the unknown; an original drama in 3
acts. *In* Lacy. 812 : 1 v41
— How's your uncle? or The ladies of the court;
a farce in 1 act. *In* Lacy. 812 : 1 v41
— The jacket of blue; a comic, original burletta
in 1 act. *In* French's. 812 : 1 v108
— Kennyngton Crosse, or The old house on the
common; a legend of Lambeth; original
romantic drama in 2 acts. *In* Lacy.
812 : 1 v75
— The king's wager, or The camp, the cottage
and the court; a drama in 3 parts. *In*
Lacy. 812 : 1 v62
— Lord Darnley, or The keep of Castle Hill;
original romantic drama in 2 acts. *In* Lacy.
812 : 1 v78
— Michael Erle, the maniac lover, or The fayre
lasse of Lichfield; an original domestic
drama in 2 acts. *In* Lacy. 812 : 1 v33
— The miller of Whetstone, or The cross-bow
letter; an original comic burletta in 1 act.
In Lacy. 812 : 1 v7
— My wife's dentist; an original farce in 1 act.
In Lacy. 812 : 1 v35
— Raffaelle the reprobate, or The secret mission
and the signet ring; drama in 2 acts. *In*
Lacy. 812 : 1 v10
— The railroad station; a farce in 1 act. *In* Lacy.
812 : 1 v47
— Rinaldo Rinaldini, or The brigand and the
blacksmith; a romantic drama in 2 acts.
In French's. 812 : 1 v117
— The roll of the drum; a romantic drama in 3
acts. *In* French's. 812 : 1 v103
— The sergeant's wedding; original comic drama
in 1 act. *In* Lacy. 812 : 1 v91

Wilks, T: Egerton.—*Continued.*
— The seven clerks, or The three thieves and the denouncer; a romantic drama in 2 acts. *In* Lacy.   812 : 1 v40
— Sixteen string Jack, or The knaves of Knave's Acre; a romantic original drama in 2 acts. *In* French's.   812 : 1 v105
— State secrets, or The tailor of Tamworth; a farce in 1 act. *In* Lacy.   812 : 1 v53
— Sudden thoughts; an original farce in 1 act. *In* Lacy.   812 : 1 v33
— Woman's love, or Kate Wynsley, the cottage girl; an original drama in 2 acts. *In* Lacy.   812 : 1 v4
— The Wren boys, or The moment of peril; a drama in 2 acts. *In* Lacy.   812 : 1 v52
Williams, Arthur. Funnibone's fix; a farce in 1 act. *In* French's.   812 : 1 v118
— *joint author, see* **Hazlewood, Colin H.**
Williams, Montagu. A fair exchange; a comedietta in 1 act. *In* Lacy.   812 : 1 v47
— *and* Francis Cowley **Burnand.** " B. B."; an original farce in 1 act. *In* Lacy.
                                                  812 : 1 v45
— – Carte de visite; an original farce, or a piece of light photographical writing. *In* Lacy.
                                                  812 : 1 v57
— – Easy shaving; farce in 1 act. *In* Lacy.
                                                  812 : 1 v60
— – The isle of St. Tropez; a drama in 4 acts. *In* Lacy.   812 : 1 v52
— – The turkish bath; a farce in 1 act. *In* Lacy.
                                                  812 : 1 v51
Williams, T: J. The better half; a comedietta in 1 act. *In* Lacy.   812 : 1 v67
— A charming pair; a farce in 1 act. *In* Lacy.
                                                  812 : 1 v58
— A cure for the fidgets; farce. *In* Lacy.
                                                  812 : 1 v77
— Dandelion's dodges! farce in 1 act. *In* Lacy.
                                                  812 : 1 v78
— Found in a four-wheeler; a farce in 1 act. *In* Lacy.   812 : 1 v70
— I've written to Browne, or A needless stratagem; a comedietta in 1 act. *In* Lacy.
                                                  812 : 1 v40
— " Ici on parle français "; a farce in 1 act. *In* Lacy.   812 : 1 v40
— Jack's delight; a farce in 1 act. *In* Lacy.
                                                  812 : 1 v56
— Keep your eye on her; an original farce in 1 act. *In* Lacy.   812 : 1 v109
— Larkin's love letters; a farce. *In* Lacy.
                                                  812 : 1 v72
— The lion slayer, or Out for a prowl; farce in 1 act. *In* Lacy.   812 : 1 v77
— Little Daisy; a comic drama in 1 act. *In* Lacy.   812 : 1 v60
— The little sentinel; a comedietta in 1 act. *In* Lacy.   812 : 1 v58
— My dress boots; a farce in 1 act. *In* Lacy.
                                                  812 : 1 v63
— My turn next! a farce. *In* Lacy.   812 : 1 v73
— My wife's maid; a farce in 1 act. *In* Lacy.
                                                  812 : 1 v63
— Nursey Chickweed; a farce in 1 act. *In* Lacy.   812 : 1 v43
— On and off; a farce in 1 act. *In* Lacy.
                                                  812 : 1 v51
— One too many for him! farce in 1 act. *In* Lacy.   812 : 1 v80

Williams, T: J.—*Continued.*
— Peace and quiet! farce in 1 act. *In* Lacy.
                                                  812 : 1 v51
— The peep-show man; drama in 2 acts. *In* Lacy.   812 : 1 v80
— Pipkin's rustic retreat! a farce in 1 act. *In* Lacy.   812 : 1 v69
— A race for a widow; a farce in 1 act. *In* Lacy.   812 : 1 v46
— A silent protector; comedietta in 1 act. *In* Lacy.   812 : 1 v80
— The silent system; a farce in 1 act. *In* Lacy.
                                                  812 : 1 v56
— A terrible tinker! farce in 1 act. *In* Lacy.
                                                  812 : 1 v87
— A tourist's ticket; farce. *In* Lacy.
                                                  812 : 1 v96
— The trials of Tompkins; a farce in 1 act. *In* Lacy.   812 : 1 v58
— Turn him out! a farce in 1 act. *In* Lacy.
                                                  812 : 1 v59
— Tweedleton's tail-coat; a farce in 1 act. *In* Lacy.   812 : 1 v73
— An ugly customer; a farce in 1 act. *In* Lacy.   812 : 1 v49
— Up a tree; farce in 1 act. *In* Lacy.
                                                  812 : 1 v98
— The volunteer service, or The little man in green; a farcical extravaganza in 1 act. *In* Lacy.   812 : 1 v80
— Who is who? or All in a fog; farce in 1 act. *In* Lacy.   812 : 1 v96
— Who's to win him? comedietta in 1 act. *In* Lacy.   812 : 1 v79
— *and* A: **Harris.** Cruel to be kind; a farce in 1 act. *In* Lacy.   812 : 1 v46
— – Gossip; a comedy in 2 acts. *In* Lacy.
                                                  812 : 1 v76
Wilson, J. Crawford. Gitanilla, or The children of the zincali; a drama in 3 acts. *In* Lacy.   812 : 1 v48
Winkler, K: Gottfried Theodor, (*Theodor Hell*). Bob, oder Die pulverschwörung; lustspiel in 2 aufz., nach Duport und de Forges bearb. *n. t. S.*   832 : 85
— Die flitterwochen; lustspiel in 2 aufz., nach dem franz. *n. t. S.*   832 : 88
— Die reise nach Russland; lustspiel in 3 aufz., nach dem franz. bearb. *n. t. S.*   832 : 91
Wood, Arthur. A bilious attack; farce in 1 act. *In* Lacy.   812 : 1 v96
— A romantic attachment; comedietta in 1 act. *In* Lacy.   812 : 1 v90
— *joint author, see* **Dixon, Bernard H.**
Wood, G: The irish doctor, or The dumb lady cured; a farce in 1 act, altered from Fielding's trans. of Molière's "Le 'médecin malgré lui." *In* Lacy.   812 : 1 v27
Wooler, J. Plots for petticoats; a farce in 1 act. *In* French's.   812 : 1 v102
Wooler, J. P. Allow me to apologize; a farce in 1 act. *In* French's.   812 : 1 v105
— Did I dream it? an original farce in 1 act. *In* Lacy.   812 : 1 v50
— A faint heart which did win a fair lady; a comedy in 1 act. *In* Lacy.   812 : 1 v57
— Founded on facts; a farce in 1 act. *In* Lacy.
                                                  812 : 1 v45
— The haunted mill; an operetta in 1 act. *In* Lacy.   812 : 1 v72
— A hunt for a husband; a farce in 1 act. *In* Lacy.   812 : 1 v63

Wooler, J. P.—*Continued.*
— I'll write to the "Times"; a farce in 1 act. *In* Lacy.　812 : 1 v28
— Keep your temper; an original farce in 1 act. *In* Lacy.　812 : 1 v55
— Laurence's love suit; an original comedietta in 2 acts. *In* Lacy.　812 : 1 v65
— Marriage at any price; an original farce in 1 act. *In* Lacy.　812 : 1 v55
— A model husband; a farce in 1 act. *In* Lacy.　812 : 1 v47
— Old Phil's birthday; a serio-comic drama in 2 acts. *In* Lacy.　812 : 1 v54
— Orange blossoms; an original comedietta in 1 act. *In* Lacy.　812 : 1 v54
— The ring and the keeper; an operetta. *In* Lacy.　812 : 1 v71
— Sisterly service; a comedietta in 1 act. *In* Lacy.　812 : 1 v44
— A twice told tale; an original farce in 1 act. *In* Lacy.　812 : 1 v37
— A winning hazard; original comedietta in 1 act. *In* Lacy.　812 : 1 v84
Worthington, J. Up in the world; a farce in 1 act. *In* French's.　812 : 1 v109
Wray, C:, *joint author, see* **Simpson,** J. Palgrave.
Wycherley, W:, *and others.* The dramatic works of Wycherley, Congreve, Vanbrugh and Farquhar, with biographical and critical notes by Leigh Hunt. Lond. 1859. O.　822.2+10
　　Contents. Wycherley, W: Biographical and critical notices.—Love in a wood!—The gentleman dancing-master.—The country wife.—The plain dealer.
Y—, H. A. Furnished apartments; comic interlude in 1 act, adapted for private representation. *In* Lacy.　812 : 1 v98
Yates, Edmund, *and* N. H. **Harrington.** Hit him, he has no friends! a farce in 1 act. *In* Lacy.　812 : 1 v47
— — If the cap fits; a comedietta in 1 act. *In* Lacy.　812 : 1 v41
— — My friend from Leatherhead; a farce in 1 act. *In* Lacy.　812 : 1 v30
— — A night at Notting Hill; an original apropos sketch in 1 act. *In* Lacy.　812 : 1 v29
— — Your likeness—one shilling! comic sketch in 1 act. *In* Lacy.　812 : 1 v36
— *and* J. Palgrave **Simpson.** Black sheep; drama in 3 acts, founded on Edmund Yates' novel of the same name. *In* Lacy.　812 : 1 v81

Yonge, Charlotte Mary. Historical dramas. Ill. Lond. *n. d.* S.　x 822.2 : 42
　　Contents. The mice at play.—The apple of discord.—The strayed falcon.
— The mice at play. *n. t.* [Lond]. S.　x 822.2 : 39
Yorke, Elizabeth, *countess of Hardwicke.* The court of Oberon, or The three wishes; dramatic entertainment. *In* Lacy.　812 : 1 v17
Young, Alfred W. A false alarm; a farce in 1 act. *In* French's.　812 : 1 v109
Young, Sir C: Lawrence. The baron's wager; an original comedietta in 1 act. *In* French's.　812 : 1 v121
— Charms; a drama in 4 acts. *In* French's.　812 : 1 v104
— Drifted apart; an original domestic sketch in 1 act. *In* French's.　812 : 1 v121
— For her child's sake; a dramatic episode in 1 act. *In* French's.　812 : 1 v118
— Gilded youth; drama in 4 acts. *In* Lacy.　812 : 1 v99
— The late sir Benjamin; comedy in 1 act, adaptation from the french of E: Romberg. *In* French's.　812 : 1 v121
— Montcalm; romantic drama in 5 acts. *In* Lacy.　812 : 1 v98
— Plot for plot; comedietta in 1 act. *In* French's.　812 : 1 v117
— Shadows; romantic drama in a prologue and 4 acts. *In* Lacy.　812 : 1 v100
— That dreadful doctor; comedietta in 1 act. *In* Lacy.　812 : 1 v117
— *joint author, see* **Church,** Florence.
Young, E: The revenge; tragedy in 5 acts. *In* British drama.　822.2 : 1 v1
— *Same. In* Lacy.　812 : 1 v70
Zechmeister, Alexander V:, (*Alexander Wilhelmi*). One of you must marry; a comic drama in 1 act, adapted from the german. *In* Lacy.　812 : 1 v71
Zimmermann, W: Masaniello, der mann des volkes; trauersp. in 5 aufz. Stuttg. 1833. D.　832 : 94
Zschokke, J: H: Daniel. Abellino; schauspiel in 5 aufz. *In his* Novellen und dichtungen.　Z 302 v15

2. Titles.

Family failing, A. J. Oxenford.   *in* 812 : 1 v29
Family jars. J. Lunn.   *in* 812 : 1 v14
Family legend, The. J. Baillie.   *in* 822.2 : 15 v3
Family of martyrs, A. E. Valle.   852 : 1
Family pictures. E. Stirling.   *in* 812 : 1 v108
Family secret, The. E. Falconer.   *in* 812 : 1 v47
Fan-Fan, the tulip. F. P. Meurice.   *in* 812 : 1 v65
Fancies, chaste and noble, The. J. Ford. *in* 822.2 : 9 v2
Farmer's story, The. W. B. Bernard.   *in* 812 : 1 v44
Fascinating individual, A. H. Danvers.   *in* 812 : 1 v27
Fashion. A. C. Ritchie.   *in* 822.1 : 14
Fast coach, The. C. J. Claridge *and* R. Soutar.
                                           in 812 : 1 v102
Fast friends. R. Henry.   *in* 812 : 1 v120
Fast train, A.   *in* 812 : 1 v10
Fastnachtspiel vom Pater Brey, Ein. J. W. v. Göthe.
                                           in 830 : 137 v22
Fatal curiosity. G. Lillo.   *in* 822.2 : 1 v1
Fatal dowry, The. P. Massinger.   *in* 822.2 : 7
Same.   *in* 812 : 1 v88
Fatal falsehood, The. H. More.   *in* 820.2 : 28 v1
Fatal glass, The. J. M'Closkey.   *in* 812 : 1 v106
Father's sacrifice, The. W. H. Venable.   *in* 822 : 1
Faust. J. W. v. Göthe.   830 : 137 v5,6
Same.   *in* 830 : R 136 v2
Same.   *in* 830 : 152 v93
Same, eng.   832 : 31
Same.   832 : 97
Same.   *in* 830 : 151 v2
Same, prose.   832 : 30
Same.   *in* 830 : 151 v3
Faust and Marguerite. F. C. Burnand.   *in* 812 : 1 v63
Faust and Marguerite. M. Carré.   *in* 812 : 1 v15
Faust and Marguerite. J. Halford.   *in* 812 : 1 v73
Faust, or the fate of Margaret. W. B. Bernard.
                                           in 812 : 1 v83
Faustus. C. Marlowe.   *in* 822.2 : 38
Same.   832 : 97
Fazio. H. H. Milman.   *in* 812 : 1 v66
"Fearful tragedy in the Seven Dials." C. Selby.
                                           in 812 : 1 v31
Fellow-culprits, The. J. W. v. Göthe.   *in* 830 : 151 v4
Felon's bond, The. W. E. Suter.   *in* 812 : 1 v85
Femmes savantes, Les. Molière.   *in* 842 : 3 v9
Ferdinand der zweyte. C. Pichler.   *in* 832 : 69 v3
Fergus Mac Ivor. J. v. Auffenberg.   832 : 4 v6
Fesseln. E. Scribe.   832 : 87
Fêtes de Versailles, Les. Molière.   *in* 842 : 3 v10
Feudal times. J. White.   *in* 822.2 : 2 v6
Field of forty foot steps, The. P. Farren.
                                           in 812 : 1 v16
Field of the cloth of gold, The. W. Brough.
                                           in 812 : 1 v80
Fiesco at Genoa, The conspiracy of. F. v. Schiller.
                                           in 830 : 150 v4
Same.   *in* 830 : R 153 v1
Fiesco zu Genua, Die verschwörung des. F. v. Schiller.
                                           in 830 : 152 v120
Same.   *in* 830 : 143 v2
Same, neu bearb. von G. Reinbeck.   *in* 832 : 73 v8
Fifteen years of labour lost.   *in* 812 : 1 v26
Fighting by proxy. J. Kenney.   *in* 812 : 1 v74
Fille de madame Angot, La. L. F. N. Clairville, P.
       Siraudin *and* V. Koning.   *in* 812 : 1 v103
Fine feathers. H. J. Byron.   *in* 812 : 1 v120
Fire eater, The. C. Selby.   *in* 812 : 1 v4
Fireflies. J. Sturgis.   *in* 822.2 : 35
Fire raiser, The. G. Almar.   *in* 812 : 1 v84
Fireside diplomacy. C. S. Cheltnam.   *in* 822.2 : 14
Firmilian. W. E. Aytoun.   822.2 : 14
First affections. J. P. Simpson.   *in* 812 : 1 v52
First experiment, A. J. W. Jones.   *in* 812 : 1 v121
First floor, The. J. Cobb.   *in* 822.2 : 1 v2
First in the field. C. M. Rae.   *in* 812 : 1 v66
First love. W. E. Suter.   *in* 812 : 1 v69
First love-letter, The. J. de Biez.   *in* 812 : 2
First night, The.   *in* 812 : 1 v13
Fischerin, Die. J. W. v. Göthe.   *in* 830 : 137 v22
                                           in 830 : 152 v88
Fischermädchen, Das. K. T. Körner.   *in* 831 : 41
Fish out of water. J. Lunn.   *in* 812 : 1 v16
Fitzsmythe of Fitzsmythe Hall. J. M. Morton.
                                           in 812 : 1 v46
Five pounds reward. J. Oxenford.   *in* 812 : 1 v24
Fleck. R. A. Herrmann.   832 : 47
Flibustier, Die. J. v. Auffenberg.   *in* 832 : 4 v2
Fliegende holländer, Der. W. R. Wagner.
                                           in 780 : 20 v1
Same.   832 : 5
Flies in the web. J. Brougham.   *in* 812 : 1 v69
Flitterwochen, Die. K. G. T. Winkler.   832 : 88
Floating beacon, The. E. Fitzball.   *in* 812 : 1 v75

Florette. J. L. Deinhardstein.   *in* 832 : 16 v5
Flower of the family, The. G. M. Baker.   *in* 822.1 : 4
Flower of Tiemcen, The. E. Legouvé *and* P. Mérimée.
                                           in 812 : 2
Fly and the web, The. A. C. Troughton.   *in* 812 : 1 v69
Flying doctor, The. Molière.   *in* 842 : 2 v3
Flying dutchman, The. E. Fitzball.   *in* 812 : 1 v71
Follies of a night, The. J. R. Planché.   *in* 822.2 : 3
Same.   *in* 822.2 : 2 v6
Same.   *in* 812 : 1 v14
Follow the leader. C. M. Rae.   *in* 812 : 1 v99
Fool's revenge, The. T. Taylor.   *in* 812 : 1 v43
For better or worse. C. A. Maltby.   *in* 812 : 1 v105
For her child's sake. *Sir* C. L. Young. *in* 812 : 1 v18
For honor's sake. C. H. Hazlewood.   *in* 812 : 1 v108
Forced marriage, The. Molière.   *in* 842 : 2 v1
Forest exiles, The. W. H. Venable.   *in* 822 : 1
Forest keeper, The. H. Holl.   *in* 812 : 1 v44
Fortunat. J. L. Tieck.   *in* 830 : 148 v3
Fortune's frolic. J. T. Allingham.   *in* 822.2 : 1 v1
Same.   *in* 812 : 1 v60
Fortunio. J. R. Planché.   *in* 812 : 1 v19
Forty winks. G. Roberts.   *in* 812 : 1 v57
Foscari. M. R. Mitford.   *in* 812 : 1 v96
Same.   *in* 822.2 : 27
Found in a four-wheeler! T. J. Williams. *in* 812 : 1 v70
Founded on fact. I. P. Wooler.   *in* 812 : 1 v45
Foundling of the forest, The. W. Dimond. *in* 812 : 1 v2
Fountain of beauty, The. J. M. Kingdom.
                                           in 812 : 1 v12
Four cousins, The. A. Mayhew *and* S. Edwardes.
                                           in 812 : 1 v92
Four plays in one. F. Beaumont *and* J. Fletcher.
                                           in 822.2 : 8 v2
Four sisters, The. W. B. Bernard.   *in* 812 : 1 v23
Fourberies de Scapin, Les. Molière.   *in* 842 : 3 v9
Fox, The. B. Jonson.   *in* 822.2 : 6 v3
Fra Diavolo. H. J. Byron.   *in* 812 : 1 v85
Francesca da Rimini. G. H. Boker.   *in* 822.1 : 7 v1
Frank Fox Phipps, esq. C. Selby.   *in* 812 : 1 v100
Frankenstein. H. M. Milner.   *in* 812 : 1 v75
Fraud and its victims. J. S. Coyne.   *in* 812 : 1 v92
Frauenstand. A. W. Iffland.   *in* 832 : 51 v7
Frederick of Prussia. C. Selby.   *in* 812 : 1 v32
Free thinker, The. G. E. Lessing.   *in* 832 : 61 v2
Freezing a mother-in-law. T. E. Pemberton.
                                           in 812 : 1 v116
Freischütz, Der. H. J. Byron.   *in* 812 : 1 v81
Freischütz, Der. J. Oxenford.   *in* 812 : 1 v69
Fremdes glück. K. F. Gutzkow.   *in* 832 : 37 v9
French exhibition, The. F. Hay.   *in* 812 : 1 v75
Frères corses, Les. A. Dumas.   *in* 812 : 1 v88
Friar Bacon and friar Bungay. R. Greene. *in* 822.2 : 5
Friend in need, A. S. French *and* W. J. Sorrell.
                                           in 812 : 1 v46
Friend Waggles. J. M. Morton.   *in* 812 : 1 v33
Friends or foes. H. Wigan.   *in* 812 : 1 v54
From Calais to Dover. E. d'Hervilly.   *in* 812 : 2
From village to court. J. M. Morton.   *in* 812 : 1 v15
Frou-Frou. H. Meilhac *and* L. Halévy.   *in* 812 : 1 v118
Fündling, Der. C. W. Contessa.   *in* 830 : 134 v2
Funnibone's fix. A. Williams.   *in* 812 : 1 v118
Für heimliche beleidigung heimliche rache. P. Calderon
       de la Barca.   *in* 862 : 1 v1
Furies, The. Aischylos.   *in* 882 : 1
Furnished apartments. H. A. Y.   *in* 812 : 1 v98
Fürst und dichter. J. L. Deinhardstein.   *in* 832 : 16 v6

Gale Breezley. J. B. Johnstone.   *in* 812 : 1 v7
Game of romps, A. J. M. Morton.   *in* 812 : 1 v18
Game of speculation, The. G. H. Lewes.   *in* 812 : 1 v5
Gamester, The. E. Moore.   *in* 822.2 : 1 v1
Ganem, the slave of love. F. Talfourd.   *in* 812 : 1 v6
Garibaldi "excursionists". H. J. Byron.   *in* 812 : 1 v48
Garrick fever, The. J. R. Planché.   *in* 812 : 1 v32
Garrick in Bristol. J. L. Deinhardstein. *in* 832 : 16 v7
Gascogner in Paris, Der. G. v. Frank.   832 : 23
Gast, Der. J. L. Deinhardstein.   *in* 832 : 16 v8
Gastfreund, Der. F. Grillparzer.   *in* 832 : 35 v3
Geflehrte tante, Die. J. B. V. Meddlhammer.   832 : 1
Geheime agent, Der. F. W. Hackländer.   832 : 38
Geheime, Der. G. Freytag.   832 : 38
Geliebte dornrose, Die. A. Gryphius.   *in* 830 : 152 v29
Genoveva. J. L. Tieck.   *in* 830 : 148 v2
Gentle shepherd, The. A. Ramsay.   822.2 : 27
Gentleman dancing-master, The. W. Wycherley.
                                           in 822.2 : 10
Gentleman in black, The. W. S. Gilbert.   *in* 812 : 1 v88
Gentlemen of the jury. G. M. Baker.   *in* 822.1 : 2
George-a-Greene. R. Greene.   *in* 822.2 : 5
George Barnwell. G. Lillo.   *in* 822.2 : 1 v1
Same.   *in* 812 : 1 v79
George de Barnwell. H. J. Byron.   *in* 812 : 1 v57

George Dandin. Molière. *in* 842 : 2 v2
Same. *in* 842 : 3 v6
George Geith. C. E. L. Riddell. *in* 812 : 1 v119
Germanicus. C. Pichler. *in* 832 : 69 v1
Gertrude's cherries. D. W. Jerrold. *in* 812 : 1 v88
Gertrude's money box. H. Lemon. *in* 812 : 1 v83
Geschwister, Die. J. W. v. Göthe. *in* 830 : 137 v8
Same. *in* 830 : 152 v87
Geschwister vom lande, Die. J. F. Jünger. 832 : 55
Gespenst auf der brautschau, Das. J. B. v. Zahlhas.
832 ; 93
Gestiefelte kater, Der. J. L. Tieck. *in* 830 : 148 v5
Ghost-seer, The. F. v. Schiller. *in* 830 : 150 v4
Gilded youth. *Sir* C. L. Young. *in* 812 : 1 v99
Gilderoy. W. H. Murray. *in* 812 : 1 v9
Gipsy farmer, The. J. B. Johnstone. *in* 812 : 1 v36
Giralda. H. Welstead. *in* 812 : 1 v26
Girls of the period, The. A. B. *in* 822.2 : 14
Girondisten, Die. W. R. Griepenkerl. 832 : 33
Giselle. H. J. Byron. *in* 812 : 1 v83
Gisippus. G. Griffin. *in* G 2551 v8
Gitanilla. J. C. Wilson. *in* 812 : 1 v48
Give a dog a bad name. G. H. Lewes. *in* 812 : 1 v24
Give me my wife. W. E. Suter. *in* 812 : 1 v75
Gläserne pantoffel, Der. A. v. Platen. *in* 830 : 141 v2
Glass of water, A. E. Scribe. *in* 812 : 1 v79
Gleich und gleich. M. Hartmann. *in* 830 : 138 v10
Glencoe. T. N. Talfourd. *in* 822.2 : 30
Glin Gath. P. Meritt. *in* 812 : 1 v99
Glitter. G. A'Beckett. *in* 812 : 1 v83
Glücksblume, Die. H. C. Andersen. *in* 898.3 : 1
Gnome king, The. W. Brough. *in* 812 : 1 v86
Go to Putney. H. Lemon. *in* 812 : 1 v80
Godiva. *in* 812 : 1 v4
Going to Chobham. C. H. Hazlewood. *in* 812 : 1 v11
Going to the bad. T. Taylor. *in* 812 : 1 v37
Going to the Derby. J. M. Morton. *in* 812 : 1 v37
Going to the dogs! W. Brough *and* A. Halliday.
in 812 : 1 v65
Gold fiend, The. W. T. Townsend. *in* 812 : 1 v107
Golden branch, The. J. R. Planché. *in* 812 : 1 v19
Golden farmer, The. B. Webster. *in* 812 : 1 v76
Golden fetter, A. W. Phillips. *in* 812 : 1 v83
Golden fleece, The. J. R. Planché. *in* 812 : 1 v20
Golden plough, The. P. Meritt. *in* 812 : 1 v11
Goldene boden, Der. K. Arnold. 832 : 3
Goldene vliess, Das. F. Grillparzer. 832 : 35 v3
Golo und Genoveva. F. Müller. *in* 830 : 152 v81
Gönnerschaften, Die. E. Scribe. *in* 832 : 16 v9
Same. *in* 832 : 15 v2
Good for evil. G. V. E. Augier. *in* 812 : 1 v43
Good for nothing. J. B. Buckstone. *in* 812 : 1 v17
Good little wife, A. A. de Musset. *in* 812 : 1 v92
Good-natured man, The. O. Goldsmith. *in* 812 : 1 v109
Good night, signor Pantaloon. *in* 812 : 1 v73
Good run for it, A. I. V. Bridgeman. *in* 812 : 1 v14
Good woman in the wood, The. J. R. Planché.
in 812 : 1 v9
Gordon und Montrose. G. Reinbeck. *in* 832 : 73 v4
Gossip. A. Harris *and* T. J. Williams. *in* 812 : 1 v79
Gotobed Tom. T. Morton. *in* 812 : 1 v8
Götter, helden und Wieland. J. W. v. Göthe.
in 830 : 137 v22
Same. *in* 830 : 152 v87
Götterdämmerung. W. R. Wagner. *in* 780 : 20 v6
Göttergespräche. C. M. Wieland. 830 : 149 v3
Gottsched und Gellert. H. Laube. 832 : 59 v5
Götz von Berlichingen. J. W. v. Göthe.
in 830 : 137 v7
Same, für die bühne bearb. *in* 830 : 137 v31
Same, eng. *in* 830 : 151 v4
Gouvernante, Die. K. T. Körner. *in* 831 : 41
Governor's wife, The. T. Middenhall. *in* 812 : 1 v31
Grace Darling. E. Stirling. *in* 812 : 1 v104
Grace Huntley. H. Holl. *in* 812 : 1 v92
Gracious and Percinet. J. R. Planché. *in* 812 : 1 v20
Graf Essex. H. Laube. 832 : 59 v8
Graf Rasowsky. G. Reinbeck. *in* 832 : 73 v1
Graf Waldemar. G. Freytag. *in* 832 : 95
Grateful father, A. T. E. Pemberton. *in* 812 : 1 v12
Gnue männlein, Das. E. Devrient. *in* 832 : 17 v1
Great duke of Florence, The. P. Massinger. *in* 822.2 : 7
Great elixir, The. G. M. Baker. *in* 822.2 : 1
Great gun trick, The. C. Le Ros. *in* 812 : 1 v25
Grecian bend, A. G. M. Baker. *in* 822.1 : 6
Grecian daughter, The. A. Murphy. *in* 822.2 : 1 v1
Green-eyed monster, The. J. R. Planché.
in 812 : 1 v101
Green old age. R. Reece. *in* 812 : 1 v103
Grimshaw, Bagshaw and Bradshaw. J. M. Morton.
in 812 : 1 v4
"Grin" bushes, The. H. J. Byron. *in* 812 : 1 v64
Grinding organ, The. M. Edgeworth. *in* 822.1 : 9

Grist to the mill. J. R. Planché. *in* 812 : 1 v20
Gross-Kophta, Der. J. W. v. Göthe. *in* 830 : 137 v23
Grossmutter, Die. J. R. Benedix. *in* 832 : 9
Gründung von Santa Fé, Die. J. v. Auffenberg.
832 : 4 v10
Grüne domino, Der. K. T. Körner. *in* 831 : 41
Guardian, The. D. Garrick. *in* 822.2 : 1 v1
Guardian, The. P. Massinger. *in* 822.2 : 7
Guardian angel, The. C. S. Brooks. *in* 812 : 1 v5
Gunst des augenblicks, Die. E. Devrient.
in 832 : 17 v1
Günstling, Der. L. Schubar. 832 : 80
Gustaf Adolf und Ebba Brahe. Gustaf III. *in* 898.1 : 1
Gustaf Wasa. Gustaf III. *in* 898.1 : 1
Gustavus Vasa. H. Brooke. *in* 822.2 : 1
Guy Faux. S. Macfarren. *in* 812 : 1 v114
Guy Mannering. D. Terry. *in* 812 : 1 v92
Gwynneth Vaughan. M. Lemon. *in* 812 : 1 v29

Hadad. J. A. Hillhouse. *in* 822.1 : 10 v1
Hadrian in Syrien. P. Metastasio. *in* 880 : 146 v7
Hagestolzen, Die. A. W. Iffland. *in* 832 : 51 v5
Half caste, The. T. W. Robertson. *in* 812 : 1 v97
Half way to Arcady. J. Sturgis. *in* 822.2 : 35
Halle. L. A. v. Arnim. 832 : 101
Halvei the unknown. T. E. Wilks. *in* 812 : 1 v42
Hamlet. W. Shakspere. *in* 822.3 : R1 v2
Same. *in* 822.3 : 2 v11
Same. *in* 822.3 : 3 v2
Same. *in* 822.3 : 80
Same. *in* 822.3 : R83 v7
Same. -*in* 812 : 1 v23
Same, germ. *in* 822.3 : 47 v6
Hamlet improved. *Col.* Colomb. *in* 812 : 1 v115
Hamlet travestie. J. Poole. *in* 812 : 1 v10
Hand and glove. G. Conquest *and* P. Meritt.
in 812 : 1 v109
Handsome husband, A. E. Planché. *in* 812 : 1 v11
Handsome Jack. J. B. Howe. *in* 812 : 1 v114
Handy Andy. H. W. Montgomery. *in* 812 : 1 v74
Hannibal. C. D. Grabbe. *in* 832 : 32 v3
Hannibal. F. Grillparzer. *in* 832 : 35 v5
Hans Heiling. E. Devrient. *in* 832 : 17 v1
Hans Sachs. J. L. Deinhardstein. *in* 832 : 16 v6
Hans von Stein. S. Fitzball. *in* 812 : 1 v104
Hans Waldmann. C. Spindler. 832 : 81
Happiest day of my life, The. J. B. Buckstone.
in 812 : 1 v80
Happiest man alive, The. W. B. Bernard. *in* 812 : 1 v19
Happy despatch, The. A. Thompson. *in* 822.2 : 14
Happy medium, A. T. E. Pemberton. *in* 812 : 1 v112
Happy pair, A. S. T. Smith. *in* 812 : 1 v83
Hard struggle, A. W. Marston. *in* 812 : 1 v48
Harlequin, Alfred the great! *in* 812 : 1 v3
Harlequin and Mother Goose. T. Dibdin. *in* 812 : 1 v84
Harlequin and O'Donoghue. *in* 812 : 1 v3
Harlequin Blue Beard. *in* 812 : 1 v17
Harlequin, Cherry and Fair Star. G. Ellis. *in* 812 : 1 v9
Harlequin Hogarth. *in* 812 : 1 v5
Harlequin Hudibras! E. L. Blanchard. *in* 812 : 1 v9
Harlequin Little Red Riding-Hood. T. Hood.
in 822.2 : 14
Harlequin novelty. L. Buckingham. *in* 812 : 1 v34
Harmony. H. A. Jones. *in* 812 : 1 v114
Harold. A. Tennyson. 822.2 : 82
Harold. E. A. v. Wildenbruch. 832 : 98
Harold Hawk. C. Selby. *tr.* 812 : 1 v88
Harvest storm, The. C. H. Hazlewood. *in* 812 : 1 v55
Harvest storm, The. W. H. Venable. *in* 822 : 1
Hass und liebe. P. Calderon de la Barca. *in* 862 : 1 v3
Haunted inn, The. R. B. Peake. *in* 812 : 1 v1
Haunted mill, The. J. P. Wooler. *in* 812 : 1 v72
Hausfrieden. A. W. Iffland. *in* 832 : 51 v10
Hazard of the die, The. D. Jerrold. *in* 812 : 1 v121
He and she. 832 : 2
Heautontimorumenos. P. Terentius Afer. *in* 872 : 1
Same. *in* 872 : 2
Hecyra. P. Terentius Afer. *in* 872 : 2
Hedwig. K. T. Körner. *in* 831 : 41
He's a lunatic. F. Dale. *in* 812 : 1 v78
He "lies like truth." F. Kimpton. *in* 812 : 1 v75
He that will not when he may. H. Gardner.
in 812 : 1 v122
He would be a soldier. F. Pilon. *in* 812 : 1 v2
Head of the family, The. W. S. Emden. *in* 812 : 1 v44
Headless horseman, The. C. H. Hazlewood.
in 812 : 1 v107
Heads or tails. J. P. Simpson. *in* 812 : 1 v15
Heart of Mid-Lothian, The. T. H. Lacy. *in* 812 : 1 v57
Heartless landlord, The. W. H. Venable. *in* 822 : 1
Hearts of oak. H. A. Jones. *in* 812 : 1 v122
Heather. J. Sturgis. *in* 822.2 : 35

Thurm mit sieben pforten, Der.　A. v. Platen.
　　　　　　　　　　　　　　　　in 830 : 141 v2
Ticket-of-leave, A.　W. Phillips.　*in* 812 : 1 v59
Ticket-of-leave man, The.　T. Taylor.　*in* 812 : 1 v59
Ticket-of-leave man's wife, The.　C. S. Cheltnam.
　　　　　　　　　　　　　　　　in 812 : 1 v69
Ticklish times.　J. M. Morton.　*in* 812 : 1 v35
Tide of time, The.　W. B. Bernard.　*in* 812 : 1 v38
Time and the hour.　J. P. Simpson *and* F. Dale.
　　　　　　　　　　　　　　　　in 812 : 1 v81
Time and tide.　H. Leslie.　*in* 812 : 1 v81
Time tries all !　J. Courtney.　*by* 812 : 1 v1
Time will tell.　H. Gardner.　*in* 812 : 1 v122
Time works wonders.　D. W. Jerrold.　*in* 822.2 : 22
Same.　　　　　　　　　　　　　*in* 812 : 1 v92
Times, The.　J. Daly.　　　　　　*in* 812 : 1 v11
Timon of Athens.　W. Shakspere.　822.3 : 63
Same.　　　　　　　　　　*in* 822.3 : R1 v2
Same.　　　　　　　　　　*in* 822.3 : 2 v10
Same.　　　　　　　　　　*in* 822.3 : 3 v2
Same.　　　　　　　　　　*in* 822.3 : 82 v5
Same.　　　　　　　　　　*in* 822.3 : R83 v7
Timon von Athen.　W. Shakspere.　*in* 822.3 : 47 v8
Timothy to the rescue.　H. J. Byron.　*in* 812 : 1 v63
Timour the tartar.　M. G. Lewis.　*in* 812 : 1 v79
Timour the tartar !　J. Oxenford *and* C. S. Brooks.
　　　　　　　　　　　　　　　　in 812 : 1 v49
Timur in Tauris.　J. v. Auffenberg.　832 : 4 v22
Tit for tat.　F. Talfourd *and* A. Wigan.　*in* 812 : 1 v17
Titus Andronicus.　W. Shakspere.　822.3 : 76
Same.　　　　　　　　　　*in* 822.3 : R1 v2
Same.　　　　　　　　　　*in* 822.3 : 2 v9
Same.　　　　　　　　　　*in* 822.3 : 3 v2
Same.　　　　　　　　　　*in* 822.3 : 82 v5
Same.　　　　　　　　　　*in* 822.3 : R83 v6
Same, germ.　　　　　　　　*in* 822.3 : 47 v7
To oblige Benson.　T. Taylor.　*in* 812 : 1 v14
"To parents and guardians !", J. S. Coyne.
　　　　　　　　　　　　　　　　in 812 : 1 v13
To Paris and back, for five pounds.　J. M. Morton.
　　　　　　　　　　　　　　　　in 812 : 1 v9
Tod Adams, Der.　F. G. Klopstock.　*in* 831 : 40 v5
Tom and Jerry.　W. T. Moncrieff.　*in* 812 : 1 v88
Tom Bowling.　A. L. V. Campbell.　*in* 812 : 1 v107
Tom Cobb.　W. S. Gilbert.　*in* 812 : 1 v117
Tom Cringle.　E. Fitzball.　*in* 812 : 1 v41
Tom Pinch.　J. J. Dilley *and* L. Clifton.　*in* 812 : 1 v121
Tom Thrasher.　A. Harris.　*in* 812 : 1 v81
Tom Thumb.　K. O'Hara.　*in* 822.2 : 1 v1
Same.　　　　　　　　　　*in* 812 : 1 v50
Tomkins the troubadour.　*in* 812 : 1 v86
Toni.　K. T. Körner.　*in* 831 : 41
Too late for the train.　G. M. Baker.　*in* 822.1 : 6
Too late to save.　T. A. Palmer.　*in* 812 : 1 v112
Too much for good nature !　E. Falconer.　*in* 812 : 1 v42
Too much of a good thing !　A. Harris.　*in* 812 : 1 v22
Torquato Tasso.　J. W. v. Göthe.　*in* 830 : 137 v8
Same, eng.　　　　　　　　*in* 830 : 151 v4
Tourist's ticket, A.　T. J. Williams.　*in* 812 : 1 v96
Toussaint Louverture.　A. M. L. de Lamartine.　842 : 1
Tower of Lochlain, The.　D. Jerrold.　*in* 812 : 1 v110
Tower of London, The.　T. H. Higgie *and* T. H. Lacy.
　　　　　　　　　　　　　　　　in 812 : 1 v94
Tower of Nesle.　T. F. Gaillardet *and* A. Dumas.
　　　　　　　　　　　　　　　　in 812 : 1 v91
Trachiniæ.　Sophoklês.　*in* 882 : 3
Tradesman's son, The.　*in* 812 : 1 v105
Tragedy of errors.　M. Putnam.　822.1 : 13
Traitor's gate.　W. J. Lucas.　*in* 812 : 1 v95
Tramp's adventure.　F. Phillips.　*in* 812 : 1 v105
Trapping a tartar.　E. Stirling.　*in* 812 : 1 v65
Traum, ein leben, Der.　F. Grillparzer.　*in* 832 : 35 v5
Treasure, The.　G. E. Lessing.　*in* 832 : 61 v2
Treue liebe.　E. Devrient.　*in* 832 : 17 v3
Treue um treue.　A. v. Platen.　*in* 830 : 141 v2
Treuer diener seines herrn, ein.　F. Grillparzer.
　　　　　　　　　　　　　　　　in 832 : 35 v4
Trials of Tompkins, The.　T. J. Williams.　*in* 812 : 1 v58
Trip through my pockets, A.　C. Monselet.　*in* 812 : 2
Trip to Scarborough, A.　R. B. Sheridan.　*in* 822.2 : 34
Same.　　　　　　　　　　*in* 812 : 1 v103
Tristan und Isolde.　W. R. Wagner.　*in* 780 : 20 v7
Triumph der empfindsamkeit, Der.　J. W. v. Göthe.
　　　　　　　　　　　　　　　　in 830 : 137 v22
Same.　　　　　　　　　　*in* 830 : 152 v87
Troïlus and Cressida.　W. Shakspere.　822.3 : 62
Same.　　　　　　　　　　*in* 822.3 : R1 v2
Same.　　　　　　　　　　*in* 822.3 : 2 v9
Same.　　　　　　　　　　*in* 822.3 : 3 v2
Same.　　　　　　　　　　*in* 822.3 : 82 v4
Same.　　　　　　　　　　*in* 822.3 : R83 v9
Troïlus und Cressida.　W. Shakspere.　*in* 822.3 : 47 v9
Tromb-al-ca-zar.　C. H. Stephenson.　*in* 812 : 1 v71

Trovatore, Il.　W. E. Suter.　*in* 812 : 1 v56
True as steel.　W. Reeve.　*in* 812 : 1 v92
Trying it on.　W. Brough.　*in* 812 : 1 v11
Tufelhausen.　J. B. Johnstone.　*in* 812 : 1 v27
Turandot, prinzessin von China.　C. Gozzi.
　　　　　　　　　　　　　　　　in 830 : 143 v6
Same.　　　　　　　　　　*in* 830 : 144 v9
Turkish bath, The.　M. Williams *and* F. C. Burnand.
　　　　　　　　　　　　　　　　in 812 : 1 v51
Turn him out.　T. J. Williams.　*in* 812 : 1 v59
Turned head, The.　G. A. A'Beckett.　*in* 812 : 1 v67
Turning the tables.　J. Poole.　*in* 812 : 1 v40
Twas I !　J. H. Payne.　*in* 812 : 1 v9
Tweedleton's tail-coat.　T. J. Williams.　*in* 812 : 1 v73
Twelfth night.　W. Shakspere.　*in* 822.3 : R1 v1
Same.　　　　　　　　　　*in* 822.3 : 2 v5
Same.　　　　　　　　　　*in* 822.3 : 3 v1
Same.　　　　　　　　　　*in* 822.3 : 82 v1
Same.　　　　　　　　　　*in* 812 : 1 v36
Twelve labours of Hercules.　R. B. Brough.
　　　　　　　　　　　　　　　　in 812 : 1 v6
Twenty minutes under an umbrella.　A. W. Dubourg.
　　　　　　　　　　　　　　　　in 812 : 1 v106
Twenty minutes with a tiger.　*in* 812 : 1 v24
Twenty £ a year—all found.　H. J. Byron.
　　　　　　　　　　　　　　　　in 812 : 1 v116
Twice killed.　J. Oxenford.　*in* 812 : 1 v24
Twice told tale, A.　J. P. Wooler.　*in* 812 : 1 v37
Twin rivals, The.　G. Farquhar.　*in* 822.2 : 10
Two blinds, The.　A. Clements.　*in* 812 : 1 v102
Two Bonnycastles.　J. M. Morton.　*in* 812 : 1 v5
Two flats and a sharp.　A. Maltby.　*in* 812 : 1 v100
Two Foscari, The.　G. G. N. *lord* Byron.　*in* 812 : 1 v59
Two galley slaves, The.　J. H. Payne.　*in* 812 : 1 v72
Two gay deceivers.　T. W. Robertson *and* T. H. Lacy.
　　　　　　　　　　　　　　　　in 812 : 1 v83
Two gentlemen at Mivart's.　J. P. Simpson.
　　　　　　　　　　　　　　　　in 822.2 : 14
Two gentlemen in a fix.　W. E. Suter.　*in* 812 : 1 v66
Two gentlemen of Verona, The.　W. Shakspere.
　　　　　　　　　　　　　　　　822.3 : 64
Same.　　　　　　　　　　*in* 822.3 : R1 v1
Same.　　　　　　　　　　*in* 822.3 : 2 v2
Same.　　　　　　　　　　*in* 822.3 : 3 v1
Same.　　　　　　　　　　*in* 822.3 : R83 v1
Two Gregories, The.　T. Dibdin.　*in* 812 : 1 v70
Two heads are better than one.　L. Horne.
　　　　　　　　　　　　　　　　in 812 : 1 v27
Two in the morning.　C. Mathews.　*in* 812 : 1 v20
Two noble kinsmen, The.　F. Beaumont *and* J. Fletcher.
　　　　　　　　　　　　　　　　in 822.3 : 8 v10
Two orphans, The.　J. Oxenford.　*in* 812 : 1 v106
Two photographs.　A. Clements.　*in* 812 : 1 v122
Two Polts, The.　J. Courtney.　*in* 812 : 1 v45
Two Puddifoots, The.　J. M. Morton.　*in* 812 : 1 v78
Two queens, The.　J. B. Buckstone.　*in* 812 : 1 v1
Two roses.　J. Albery.　*in* 812 : 1 v118
Two to one.　A. Clements.　*in* 812 : 1 v98
'Twould puzzle a conjurer.　J. Poole.　*in* 812 : 1 v14

Ugly customer, An.　T. J. Williams.　*in* 812 : 1 v49
Ugolino.　H. W. v. Gerstenberg.　*in* 830 : 152 v48
Ulrich Zwingli's tod.　C. Birch-Pfeiffer.　832 : 10
Ulysses.　N. Rowe.　*in* 822.2 : 13
Ulysses, or The iron-clad warrior.　F. C. Burnand.
　　　　　　　　　　　　　　　　in 812 : 1 v66
Unbesonnenheit und gutes herz.　G. Reinbeck.
　　　　　　　　　　　　　　　　in 832 : 75 v5
"Uncle".　H. J. Byron.　*in* 812 : 1 v120.
Uncle Crotchet.　Mrs. A. Phillips.　*in* 812 : 1 v10
Uncle Tom's cabin.　G. L. Aikin.　*in* 812 : 1 v12
Uncle Zachary.　J. Oxenford.　*in* 812 : 1 v45
Under false colours.　E. A. De Pass.　*in* 812 : 1 v111
Under the gaslight.　A. Daly.　*in* 812 : 1 v81
Under the rose.　G. Roberts.　*in* 812 : 1 v57.
Unequal match, An.　T. Taylor.　*in* 812 : 1 v118
Unfinished gentleman, The.　C. Selby.　*in* 812 : 1 v84
Ungarkönig, Ein.　C. H. Börnstein.　832 : 50
Ungeheuer, Das, und der verzauberte wald.　J. L. Tieck.
　　　　　　　　　　　　　　　　in 830 : 148 v11
Ungleichen hausgenossen, Die.　J. W. v. Göthe.
　　　　　　　　　　　　　　　　in 830 : 135 v22
Same.　　　　　　　　　　*in* 830 : 152 v88

4. Class-list of prose fiction.

(For history, *see* col. 513; for collections of romances, *see* col. 513-515.)

1. Authors.

A. L. O. E., *pseud.*, *see* **Tucker**, Charlotte Maria.

Abbott, E : *The Long Look books* :
1. Long Look house ; a book for boys and girls. Ill. Bost. 1880. D.   **Ax 101**
2. Outdoors at Long Look ; a book for boys and girls. Ill. Bost. 1878. D.   **Ax 102**
3. A trip eastward ; a book for boys and girls. Ill. Bost. 1880. D.   **Ax 103**

Abbott, Jacob. Rollo series. N. Y. *n. d.* 14 v. S.   **Ax 164**
  Contents. 1. Learning to talk. 2. Learning to read. 3. At work. 4. At play. 5. At school. 6. Rollo's vacation. 7. Rollo's experiments. 8. Rollo's museum. 9. Rollo's travels. 10. Rollo's correspondence. 11. Water. 12. Air. 13. Fire. 14. Sky.

About, Edmond François Valentin. Germaine. Aus dem franz. von G. Fink. Stuttg. 1858. T.   **A 101**
— The man with the broken ear. Tr. by H: Holt. (Leisure hour ser.) N. Y. 1867. S.   **A 102**
— The notary's nose. Tr. from the french by H: Holt. (Leisure hour ser.) N. Y. 1874. S.   **A 103**
— The story of an honest man. N. Y. 1880. O.   **A 104**
— Without dowry. *In* **Sargent**, E. The emerald.   **S·551**

Ackermann, Ernst W : Der letzte Montmorency. Leipz. 1851. 2 v. S.   **A 151**

Adam, Juliette, *born* Lamber, *mme.* Edmond. A fascinating woman, (Laide). Phila. [1882.] S.   **A 176**

Adam, Onkel. *pseud.*, *see* **Wetterbergh**, C : A.

Adams, Alicia A., *mrs.* Leith. Madelon Lemoine. Phila. 1879. S.   **A 251**

Adams, F. Colburn, (*Justitia*, *a know-nothing*). Justice in the by-ways ; a tale of life. N. Y. 1857. S.   **A 201**

Adams, H : Cadwallader. Barford Bridge, or Schoolboy trials. Ill. Lond. [1872]. D.   **Ax 202**
— The boy cavaliers, or The siege of Clidesford. Ill. Lond. 1883 [1882]. S.   **Ax 203**
— Friend or foe ; a tale of Sedgmoor. Ill. Lond. 1883. S.   **Ax 206**
— Schoolboy honour ; a tale of Halminster college. Ill. Lond. [1863]. S.   **¹Ax 204**
— The Winborough boys, or Ellerslie Park. Ill. Lond. [1871]. D.   **Ax 205**

Adams, Mary. An honorable surrender. N. Y. 1883. S.   **A 276**

Adams, Nehemiah. The sable cloud ; a southern tale with northern comments. Bost. 1861. S.   **A 301**

Adams, W : H: Davenport, *ed.* Page, squire and knight ; a romance of the days of chivalry. Ill. Bost. 1883 [1882]. D.   **Ax 276**
  Note. A free adaptation of the "Franchise" of Madame Colomb.

Adams, W: Taylor, [*Oliver Optic*]. In doors and out, or Views from the chimney corner. Bost. 1876. D.   **A 326**
— Living too fast, or The confessions of a bank officer. Ill. Bost. 1876. D.   **A 327**
— The way of the world. Bost. 1876. D.   **A 328**

Addison, Joseph. Sir Roger de Coverley, by the Spectator, [with notes]. Bost. 1852. S.   **A 351**

Adee, Alvey A. The life magnet. *In* Stories by american authors.   **S 35 v8**

Adeler, Max, *pseud.*, *see* **Clark**, C : Heber.

Aguilar, Grace. The days of Bruce ; a story from scottish history. N. Y. 1878. 2 v. D.   **A 401**
— Home influence ; a tale for mothers and daughters. N. Y. 1849. D.   **A 402**
— *Same.* N. Y. 1864. D.   **A 402**
— *Same.* N. Y. 1885. Q.   **A 402**
— Home scenes and heart studies. N. Y. 1857. D.   **A 403**
  Contents. The Perez family.—The stone-cutter's boy of Possagno.—Amete and Yafeh.—The fugitive.—The edict ; a tale of 1492.—The escape ; a tale of 1755.—Red Rose villa.—Gonzalvo's daughter.—The authoress.—Helon.—Lucy.—The spirit's entreaty.—Idalie.—Lady Gresham's fête.—The group of sculpture.—The spirit of night.—Recollections of a ramble.—"Cast thy bread upon the waters."—The triumph of love.
— *Same.* N. Y. 1860. S.   **A 403**
— Josephine, or The edict and the escape. Phila. *n. d.* O.   **A 404**
— Die jüdin. Leipzig. 1860. S.   **A 408**
— The mother's recompense ; a sequel to Home influence. N. Y. 1879. D.   **A 405**
— The Vale of Cedars, or The martyrs. N. Y. 1876. D.   **A 406**
— Woman's friendship ; a story of domestic life. N. Y. 1877. D.   **A 407**
— *Same. T. p. w.* S.   **A 407**

Aïdé, Hamilton. Introduced to society. Leipz. 1884. S.   **A 453**
— A nine days' wonder ; a novelette. Bost. 1875. O.   **A 451**
— Poet and peer ; a novel. N. Y. 1880. Q.   **A 452**

Aikin, J:, *and* Anna Lætitia **Barbauld**, *born* Aikin. Evenings at home, or The juvenile budget opened. Lond. 1875. T.   **Ax 401**

Ainslie, Herbert, *pseud.*, *see* **Maitland**, E :

Ainsworth, W: Harrison. Auriol, or The elixir of life. Ill. Lond. 1881. D. **A 551**
— *Same, germ.* Auriol, oder Das lebenselixir ; ein roman. Aus dem englischen übers. von E. Susemihl. Leipz. 1853. S. **A 551**
— Beatrice Tyldesley. Leipz. 1878. 2 v. in 1. S.   **A 552**

x denotes books specially adapted for children.

42

Ainsworth, W: Harrison.—*Continued.*

— Beau Nash, or Bath in the 18th century. Leipz. 1879. 2 v. in 1. S. **A 553**
— *Same.* Ill. Lond. 1880. D. **A 553**
— Boscobel, or The royal oak ; a tale of the year 1651. Ill. Lond. 1879. D. **A 554**
— Cardinal Pole, or The days of Philip and Mary ; an historical novel. Ill. Lond. 1880. D. **A 555**
— The constable de Bourbon. Ill. Lond. 1880. D. **A 564**
— The constable of the Tower ; an historical romance. Ill. Lond. 1880. D. **A 565**
— *Same.* Leipz. 1861. S. **A 565**
— Crichton. Ill. Lond. 1879. D. **A 566**
— *Same.* N. Y. 1864. 2 v. in 1. S. **A 566**
— The flitch of bacon, or the Custom of Dunmow ; a tale of english home. Ill. Lond. 1879. D. **A 567**
— Guy Fawkes, or The gunpowder treason ; an historical romance. Ill. Lond. 1878. D. **A 556**
— *Same, germ.* Guy Fawkes ; ein historischer roman. Aus dem englischen übers. von E. Susemihl. Leipz. 1842. 3 v. S. **A 556**
— Hilary St. Ives. Ill. Lond. 1881. D. **A 568**
— Jack Sheppard ; a romance. Ill. Lond. 1879. D. **A 569**
— John Law, the projector. Ill. Lond. 1881. D. **A 570**
— The Lancashire witches ; a romance of Pendleforest. Ill. Lond. 1878. D. **A 557**
— *Same, germ.* Die hexen von Lancashire ; ein roman aus dem Pendle-walde. Deutsch von A. Kretzschmar. Leipz. 1849. 6 v. T. **A 557**
— The leaguer of Lathom ; a tale of the civil war in Lancashire. Ill. Lond. 1880. D. **A 571**
— The lord mayor of London, or City life in the last century. Ill. Lond. 1880. D. **A 572**
— The Manchester rebels, or The fatal '45. Ill. Lond. 1880. D. **A 573**
— Mervyn Clitheroe. Ill. Lond. 1879. D. **A 574**
— The miser's daughter ; a tale. Ill. Lond. 1879. D. **A 575**
— Myddleton Pomfret. Ill. Lond. 1881. D. **A 576**
— Old Court ; a novel. Ill. Lond. 1880. D. **A 577**
— Old St. Paul's ; a tale of the plague and the fire. Ill. Phila. n. d. O. **A 558**
— *Same.* Lond. 1879. D. **A 558**
— *Same, germ.* Die alte St. Paulskirche ; eine erzählung von der pest und der feuersbrunst. Aus dem englischen übers. von E. Susemihl. Leipz. 1842. 3 v. S. **A 558**
— Ovingdean Grange ; a tale of the South Downs. Ill. Lond. 1879. D. **A 578**
— Preston fight, or The insurrection of 1715 ; a tale. Ill. Lond. 1879. D. **A 579**
— Rookwood ; a romance. Ill. Lond. 1878. D. **A 559**
— *Same, germ.* Rookwood, oder Der bandit der hochstrasse. Aus dem englischen. Stuttg. 1845. 2 v. T. **A 559**
— Saint James, or The court of queen Anne ; an historical romance. Ill. Lond. 1879. D. **A 580**
— Schloss Chiverton. Aus dem englischen von W: A. Lindau. Leipz. 1845. S. **A 560**

Ainsworth, W: Harrison.—*Continued.*

— The spanish match, or Charles Stuart at Madrid. Ill. Lond. 1880. D. **A 581**
— The spendthrift ; a tale. Lond. 1879. D. **A 582**
— The star chamber ; an historical romance. Ill. Lond. 1879. D. **A 561**
— *Same, germ.* Die sternkammer ; ein historischer roman. Aus dem englischen übers. von E. Susemihl. Leipz. 1854. 4 v. T. **A 561**
— The Tower of London ; an historical romance. Ill. Lond. 1878. D. **A 562**
— *Same.* T. p. w. [Phila.] O. **A 562**
— Windsor Castle ; an historical romance. Ill. Lond. 1878. D. **A 563**
— *Same, germ.* Das Windsorschloss ; ein historischer roman. Aus dem englischen übers. von E. Susemihl. Leipz. 1844. 3 v. S. **A 563**

Alarcon, P: Antonio de. Manuel Venegas. Uebers. und eingel. von F. Eyssenhardt. Stuttg. [1882]. S. **A 626**

Alberg, Albert. Fabled stories from the zoo ; tea-time tales for young little folks and young old folks. Ill. Lond. 1880. S. **Ax 451**

Albert, Stanislaus, *pseud., see* **Grabowski,** Stanislaus Stephan Albert *graf* v.

Alcestis. [*Anon.*] (Leisure hour ser.) N. Y. 1874. S. **A 1**

Alcott, Louisa May. Aunt Jo's scrap-bag : 1. My boys, etc. Bost. 1882. S. **Ax 502**
Includes, Tessa's surprises.—Buzz.—The children's joke.—Dandelion.— Madam Cluck and her family.—A curious call.—Tilly's christmas.—My little gentleman.—Back windows.—Little Marie of Lehon.—My may-day among curious birds and beasts.—Our little newsboy.—Patty's patchwork.
— — *Same.* Bost. 1872. S. **Ax 502**
— — 2. Shawl-straps. Bost. 1873. S. **Ax 503**
— — *Same.* Bost. 1882. S. **Ax 503**
— — 3. Cupid and Chow-Chow, etc. Bost. 1882. S. **Ax 504**
Includes, Huckleberry.—Nelly's hospital.—Grandma's team.—Fairy pinafores.—Mamma's plot.—Kate's choice.—The moss people.—What Fanny heard.—A marine merry-making.
— — 4. My girls, etc. Bost. 1881. S. **Ax 505**
Includes, Lost in a London fog.—The boys' joke.—Roses and forget-me-nots.—Old Major. — What the girls did.—Little neighbors.—Marjorie's three gifts.—Patty's place.—The autobiography of an omnibus.—Red tulips.—A happy birthday.
— — 5. Jimmy's cruise in the Pinafore, etc. Bost. 1879. S. **Ax 506**
Includes, Two little travellers.—A jolly fourth.—Seven black cats.—Rosa's tale. — Lunch. — A bright idea.—How they camped out.—My little school-girl.—What a shovel did.—Clams.—Kitty's cattle-show.—What becomes of the pins.
— — 6. An old-fashioned Thanksgiving, etc. Bost. 1882. S. **Ax 507**
Includes, How it all happened.—The doll's journey from Minnesota to Maine.—Morning-glories.—Shadow-children.—Poppy's pranks.—What the swallows did.—Little Gulliver.—The whale's story.—A strange island.—Fancy's friend.
— Eight cousins, or The aunt-hill. Ill. Bost. 1878. S. **Ax 508**
— *Same.* Bost. 1882. S. **Ax 508**
— *Same.* Bost. 1885. S. **Ax 508**
— Hospital sketches, and Camp and fireside stories. Ill. Bost. 1881. S. **A 652**
Includes, The king of clubs and the queen of hearts.—Mrs. Podgers' teapot. — My contraband.—Love and loyalty.—A modern Cinderella.—The blue and the gray.—A hospital christmas.—An hour.

x denotes books specially adapted for children.

Alcott, Louisa May.—*Continued.*
— Jack and Jill; a village story. Ill. Bost. 1880. S. **Ax 510**
— Little men, or Life at Plumfield with Jo's boys. Ill. Bost. 1881. S. **Ax 511**
— *Same.* Bost. 1883. S. **Ax 511**
— *Same.* Bost. 1885. S. **Ax 511**
— Little women, or Meg, Jo, Beth and Amy. Ill. Bost. 1880. O. **Ax 501**
— *Same.* Bost. 1885. S. **Ax 501**
— *Same.* Bost. 1884. D. **Ax 501**
— *Same,* pt. 1. Bost. 1879. S. **Ax 501 v1**
— Moods. Bost. [1864]. D. **A 651**
— *Same.* [New ed.] Bost. 1882. S. **A 651**
— Morning-glories. *T. p. w.* D. **Ax 517**
— An old-fashioned girl. Ill. Bost. 1876. S. **Ax 512**
— *Same.* Bost. 1882. S. **Ax 512**
— Proverb.stories. Bost. 1882. S. **Ax 513**
 Contents. Kitty's class-day.—Aunt Kipp.—Psyche's art.—A country christmas. — On picket duty. — The baron's gloves.—My red cap. — What the bells saw and said.
— [Proverb stories]. Bost. [1868]. S. **Ax 518**
 Contents. Kitty's class-day.—Aunt Kipp.—Psyche's art.
— Rose in bloom ; a sequel to "Eight cousins." Ill. Bost. 1881. S. **Ax 509**
— Silver pitchers, *and* Independence ; a centennial love-story. Bost. 1882. S. **Ax 514**
 Contents. Silver pitchers.—Anna's whim.—Transcendental wild oats.—The romance of a summer day. My rococo watch.—By the river.—Letty's tramp.— Scarlet stockings.—Independence.
— Spinning-wheel stories. Ill. Bost. 1884. S. **Ax 519**
 Contents. Grandma's story.—Tabby's table-cloth.— Eli's education. — Onawandah. — Little things.—The banner of Beaumanoir.—Jerseys, or The girl's ghost. —The little house in the garden.—Daisy's jewel-box and how she filled it. — Corny's catamount. — The cooking-class.—The hare and the tortoise.
— Under the lilacs. Ill. Bost. 1881. S. **Ax 515**
— Work ; a story of experience. Ill. Bost. 1878. S. **Ax 516**
— *Same.* Bost. 1878. S. **Ax 516**
Alden, Isabella M., (Pansy). Ester Ried. *n. d.* D. **A 701**
— Links in Rebecca's life. Bost. [1878]. D. **A 702**
— A new graft on the family tree. Bost. 1880. D. **A 703**
Alden, W: L. The adventures of Jimmy Brown, written by himself. Ill. N. Y. 1885. S. **Ax 554**
— The cruise of the Canoe club. Ill. N. Y. 1883. S. **Ax 553**
— The cruise of the "Ghost." Ill. N. Y. 1882. [1881]. S. **Ax 552**
— The moral pirates. Ill. N. Y. 1881. [1880]. S. **Ax 551**
Aldrich, T: Bailey. Daisy's necklace and what came of it ; a literary episode. N. Y. 1857. D. **A 751**
— Marjorie Daw and other people. Bost. 1873. D. **A 752**
 Includes, A Rivermouth romance. —Quite so.— A young desperado.—Miss Mehetable's son.—A struggle for life.—The friend of my youth.—Mademoiselle Olympe Zabriski.—Père Antoine's date-palm.
— Marjorie Daw, and other people. (Riverside Aldine ser.) Bost. 1885. S. **A 756**
 Includes, Miss Mehetable's son.—Our new neighbors at Ponkapog.—A midnight fantasy. — Mademoiselle Olympe Zabriski. — A struggle for life.— Père Antoine's date - palm. — Quite so.—A Rivermouth romance.—The little violinist.

Aldrich, T: Bailey.—*Continued.*
— Prudence Palfrey. Bost. 1874. D. **A 753**
— The queen of Sheba. Bost. 1877. D. **A 754**
— The Stillwater tragedy. Bost. 1880. D. **A 755**
— The story of a bad boy. Bost. *n. d.* D. **Ax 601**
Aleman, Mateo. The life and adventures of Guzman d'Alfarache, or The spanish rogue. From the french ed. of Le Sage, by J: H: Brady. Ill. Lond. 1881. 2 v. D. *in* **M 2286**
Alexander, Mrs., *pseud.,* see **Hector,** Annie F.
Alexandrowitsch, Leon. Bewegte zeiten ; roman aus dem russisch-türkischen kriege. N. Y. 1881. F. **A 776**
Alexis, Wilibald, *pseud.,* see **Häring,** G: W: H:
Alice, Cousin, *pseud.,* see **Haven,** Emily.
Alland, M., *pseud.,* see **Sauer,** K: M.
Allardyce, Alexander. Edgar Wayne's escape. *In* Tales from Blackwood. **T 177 v7**
— The Pundrapore residency. *In the same.* **T 177 v3**
Alldridge, Lizzie. By love and law ; the story of an honorable woman. Leipz. 1878. 2 v. in 1. S. **A 801**
— The world she awoke in. Leipz. 1879. 2 v. in 1. S. **A 802**
Allston, Washington. Monaldi ; a tale. Bost. 1856. D. **A 851**
Almost a duchess. (No name ser.) Bost. 1884. S. **A 2**
Almquist, C: Jonas L: Drei frauen in Smaland. Aus dem schwedischen. Stuttg. 1884. 2 v. T. **A 901**
— Es geht an ; ein gemälde aus dem leben. Aus dem schwedischen. Stuttg. 1846. T. **A 902**
— Gabriele Mimanso, der letzte mordversuch gegen den könig Ludwig Philipp von Frankreich im herbste 1840 ; roman. Aus dem schwedischen. Leipz. 1842. 5 t. in 1 v. S. **A 904**
— Der königin juwelenschmuck. Aus dem schwedischen fibers. von A. Seubert. Stuttg. 1846. T. **A 903**
— Tintomara ; ereignisse kurz vor, bie und nach der ermordung Gustav III ; roman. Aus dem schwedischen. Leipz. 1842. 4 t. in 1 v. S. **A 905**
Alte von den bergen, Der ; eine erzählung für kinder und kinderfreunde. Neue ill. originalaufl. Regensburg. 1873. S. **A 952**
Alvensleben, K: L: F: W: Gustav v., *(Clodwig, Gustav Sellen.)* Der strafende burggeist, oder Der verfall der Harzbergwerke; geschichtlicher roman aus der zeit kaiser Heinrichs IV, von Clodwig. Meissen. 1880. D. **C 1951**
Ambach, E: Der adler, oder Schuld und sühne ; ein familiengemälde aus den zeiten des 7-jähr. krieges, der reifern jugend gewidmet von dem verf. "Die kinder der wittwe." Ill. Regensb. 1848. S. *With* Der alte von den bergen. **A 952**
— Der feuerreiter, oder Die religion als leitstern ; ein charaktergemälde unserer zeit, der reifern jugend gewidmet von dem verf. "Die kinder der wittwe." Ill. Regensb. 1850. S. *With* Der alte von den bergen. **A 952**

x denotes books specially adapted for children.

Ambach, E:—*Continued.*

— Die johanniter, oder Die einnahme von Rhodus durch Soliman ; charakter- und heldengemälde aus der ersten hälfte des 16. jahrh., der reifern jugend gewidmet von dem verf. "Der kinder der wittwe." Ill. Regensb. 1848. D. *With* Boost, A., *ed.* Sammlung moral. erzähl.　**A 953**

— Die kinder der wittwe, oder Der Herr hilft auf den schuldlos leidenden und demüthigt die sünder bis zur erde ; eine erzählung für die reifere jugend, mit einem vorworte begleitet vom verf. der "Glocke der andacht." 5te verb. aufl. Regensb. 1875. D.　**A 951**

— Der menschenhändler, oder Verstand ohne herz ; charakteristische bilder aus dem republikanischen, sogenannt glücklichen Amerika, der reifern jugend gewidmet. 2te aufl. Ill. Schaffhausen. 1867. D.　**L 2303**

— Der pulverthurm, oder Das gebet als schutzgeist ; ein familiengemälde aus dem letzten drittel des vorigen jahrh., der reifern jugend gewidmet vom verf. "Die kinder der wittwe." Ill. Regensb. 1850. D. *With* Boost, A., *ed.,* Sammlung moral. erzähl.　**A 953**

Améro, Constant, *joint author, see* Tissot, V:

Ames, Fanny B., *comp.* Christmas day and all the year ; "Christian register" stories. Bost. 1880. S.　**Ax 701**

Contents. Coolidge, Susan. On top of the ark.—Axford, G: Resolution first.—Calthrop, S: R. The cats and the clover.—Bartlett, M. C. A game.—Robinson, S. C. Gold-Lisa and king Lazybones.—"Pepsie". The buried treasures.—Stillwell, M. Our life in Naples.—Flint, S. Polly's legacy.—Bartlett, M. C. Step-mothers.—Robinson, S. C. The black box.—Bartlett, M.C. Reconciliation.—MacCauley, C. How Charley Ramsey spent a saturday.—Nugel, L. "Hallowed be thy name."—Lincoln, M. W. "Little sir John."—Bartol, M. Good manners.—Bartlett, M. C. Miss Austin's charge.—Flint, S. Tangles.—Whitney, A. D. T. Trying on bonnets.—Sträszle, F. The bird wedding.—Hall, J. O. Jennie York's holiday.—Preston, A. A. Carrie's visit to the valley of life.—Kipp, C. How Dicky Star served somebody.— Bush, T. D. F. Our Polly's train.—Bartlett, M.C. Joe's evidence. — Andersen, H. C. "Fellow-travellers."

Ames, Mary Clemmer, *see* Hudson, Mary.

Among the chosen. N. Y. 1884. S.　**A 7**
Note. Attributed to Mary S. Emerson.

Amyntor, Gerhard v., *pseud., see* Gerhard, Dagobert v.

Anders, Ferdinand, *see* Stolle, L: Ferdinand.

Andersen, Hans Christian. Aus herz und welt. Leipz. *n. d.* S.　**A 1001**

— The darning-needle, and other stories. Tr. by H. W. Dulcken. Lond. [1870]. S. *With his* The little match girl.　**Ax 754**
Includes, The wicked prince.—Two brothers.—The bell.—By the almshouse window.—Little Tuk.—The flax.—The puppet showman. — A picture from the fortress wall.—In the duck yard.—Soup on a sausage-peg.—The shepherdess and the chimney-sweeper.—A leaf from the sky.—The drop of water.

— The goloshes of fortune, and other stories. Tr. by H. W. Dulcken. Lond. [1870]. S. *With his* The tinder box.　**Ax 759**
Includes, Old street lamp.—The elf-hill.—The loveliest rose in the world.—The swineherd.—Something.—The buckwheat.—The rose-elf.

— Fairy tales. Ill. Phila. *n. d.* D.　**Ax 763**

Andersen, Hans Christian.—*Continued.*

— The hardy tin soldier, and other stories. Tr. by H. W. Dulcken. Lond. [1870]. S. *With his* The marsh king's daughter.　**Ax 755**
Includes, Thumbelina.—The travelling companion.—The naughty boy.—The jewish girl.—The money pig.—What one can invent.—The toad.

— The ice maiden, etc. Tr. by H. W. Dulcken. Lond. [1870.] S. *In his* The old church bell.　**Ax 757**
Contents. The ice maiden.—The bottle-neck.

— The ice-maiden, and other tales. Tr. from the germ. by Fanny Fuller. N. Y. 1863. T.　**Ax 765**
Includes, The butterfly.—The Psyche.—The snail and the rose-tree.

— The improvisatore. From the danish, tr. by Mary Howitt. N. Y. 1863. O.　**A 1002**
— *Same.* Author's ed. Bost. 1880. D.　**A 1002**
— *Same, germ.* Der improvisator. Leipz. *n. d.*　**A 1002**
— *Same.* Nach dem dänischen original neu fibers. und eingel. von Edmund Lobedanz. Stuttg. [1882]. D.　**A 1002**

— In Sweden, and other stories. Tr. by H. W. Dulcken. Ill. Lond. [1870]. S.　**Ax 753**
Contents. In Sweden.—The story of my life.

— The little match girl, and other stories. Tr. by H. W. Dulcken. Lond. [1870]. S.　**Ax 754**
Includes, The flying trunk.—The storks.—The ugly duckling.—Holger Danske.—Days in the Mediterranean.—The grave yard at Scutari.—The Bosphorus.—Athens.—She was good for nothing.—The racers.—In a thousand years.

— Little Rudy, and other stories. Ill. N. Y. *n. d.* S.　**Ax 768**
Includes, The butterfly.—Psyche.—The snail and the rose bush.—Twelve by the mail.—A rose from the grave of Homer.—The racers.

— The marsh king's daughter, and other stories. Tr. by H. W. Dulcken. Lond. [1870]. S.　**Ax 755**
Includes, Twelve by the mail.—The shadow.—The happy family.

— Nur ein geiger. *See below* Only a fiddler.

— The old church bell, and other stories. Tr. by H. W. Dulcken. Lond. [1870]. S.　**Ax 757**
Includes, A story from the sand-dunes.—The last dream of the old oak tree.—The Psyche.—My boots.

— A picture-book without pictures, and other stories. From the danish, tr. by Mary Howitt. N. Y. 1855. T.　**Ax 766**
Contents. Memoir of Hans Christian Andersen.—A picture-book without pictures.—My boots.—Scenes on the Danube.—Pegasus and the post-horses.—The emperor's new clothes.—The swine herd.—The princess.

— O. T. ; a danish romance. N. Y. 1870. D.　**A 1003**
— *Same.* Author's ed. Bost. 1880. D.　**A 1003**
— Only a fiddler ; a danish romance. N. Y. 1870. D.　**A 1004**
— *Same.* Author's ed. Bost. 1881. D.　**A 1004**
— *Same, germ.* Nur ein geiger. Leipz. *n. d.* S.　**A 1004**

— Poultry Meg's family, and other stories. Tr. by H. W. Dulcken. Ill. Lond. [1870]. S. *With his* The will-o'-the wisp.　**Ax 760**
Includes, The dryad.—Charming.

— Put off is not done with, and other stories. Tr. by H. W. Dulcken. Lond. [1870]. S.　**Ax 756**
Includes, The porter's son.—The snowdrop.—Our aunt.—The thistle's experience.—Five out of one shell.

x denotes books specially adapted for children.

Andersen, Hans Christian.—*Continued.*
— The red shoes, and other stories. Tr. by H.
W. Dulcken. Lond. [1870.] S. **Ax 758**
Includes, A great grief.—The jumper.—The shirt
collar.—Old Luk-oie.—Jack the dullard.—The beetle.
—Ole the tower-keeper.—What the old man does is
always right.—Good humour.—Children's prattle.—
"It's quite true!"
— The sand-hills of Jutland. *T. p. w.* S.
Ax 767
Contents. The sand-hills of Jutland.—The mud-
king's daughter.—The quickest runners.—The bell's
hollow.—Soup made of a sausage-stick.—The neck of
a bottle.—The old bachelor's night-cap.—Something.
—The old oak tree's last dream.—Waldemar Daae
and his daughters.—The girl who trod upon bread.—
Olé, the watchman of the tower.—Anne Lisbeth.—
Children's prattle.—A row of pearls.—The pen and
the inkstand.—The child in the grave.—Charming.
— Sein oder nichtsein. Leipz. *n. d.* S. **A 1005**
— The silver shilling, and other stories. Tr. by
H. W. Dulcken. Ill. Lond. [1870]. S. *With
his* The red shoes.
Includes, The snail and the rose-tree.—Little Ida's
flowers.—The emperor's new clothes.—The princess
on the pea.—Little Claus and great Claus.—The pigs.
—Grandmother.—The lovers.—The fir tree.—The last
pearl.—The story of a mother.—The daisy.
— The snow man, and other stories. Tr. by H.
W. Dulcken. Lond. [1870]. S. *With his*
Put off is not done with. **Ax 756**
Includes, There is a difference.—The garden of par-
adise.—The little sea-maid.—The pen and inkstand.—
The swan's nest.—Waldemar Daa and his daughters.
— The snow queen, and other stories. Tr. by H.
W. Dulcken. Lond. [1870]. S. *With his*
In Sweden. **Ax 753**
Includes, The neighbouring families.—The story of
the year.—The phœnix bird.—The thorny road of
honour.—The child in the grave.
— Stories and tales. Ill, Author's ed. Bost.
1880. D. **Ax 752**
— The tinder box, and other stories. Tr. by H.
W. Dulcken. Ill. Lond. [1870]. S.
Ax 759
Includes, The elder tree mother.—Two maidens.—
The old bachelor's nightcap.—The old gravestone.—
The dumb book.—The farm-yard cock and weather
cock.—A rose from the grave of Homer.—The but-
terfly.—The nightingale.—The bond of friendship.
— The two baronesses; a romance. N. Y. 1870.
D. **A 1006**
— *Same.* Author's ed. Bost. 1879. D. **A 1006**
— *Same, germ.* Die zwei baronessèn. Leipz.
n. d. S. **A 1006**
— Under the willow tree, and other stories. Tr.
by H. W. Dulcken. Ill. Lond. [1870]. S.
With his The wild swans. **Ax 761**
Includes, In the uttermost parts of the sea.—The
bishop of Börglum and his warriors.—Anne Lisbeth.
—The bell-deep.—The stone of the wise men.—An
adventure in the catacombs of Rome.
— The wild swans, and other stories. Tr. by H.
W. Dulcken. Ill. Lond. [1870]. S.
Ax 761
Includes, The goblin and the huckster.—The met-
al pig.—The old house.—The girl who trod on the
loaf.—A peasant boy in the Campagna of Rome.
— The will-o'-the wisp, and other stories. Tr.
by H. W. Dulcken. Ill. Lond. [1870.] S.
Ax 760
Includes, The windmill.—In the nursery.—The
golden treasure.—The storm shakes the shield.—The
bird of popular song.—The legend of Nürnberg cas-
tle.—A night in the Apennines.—The carnival in
Rome.—Mahomet's birthday.—My visit to the Bor-
ghese palace.
— Wonder stories told for children. Ill. Author's
ed. Bost. 1880. D. **Ax 751**
— Zwei baronessen. *See above* Two baronesses.

Anderson, Olive San Louie, (*Sola*). An ameri-
can girl and her four years in a boys' col-
lege. N. Y. 1878. D. **A 1051**
Anderson, W: Blanche the huguenot. *T. p. w.*
S. **A 1101**
Andreä, J: G: F: W: Die sturmvögel; cultur-
und sittengeschichtlicher roman aus dem
anfange des 16. jahrhunderts. Jena. 1865.
S. **A 1151**
Andrews, Fanny, (*Elzey Hay*). A family secret.
Phila. 1876. O. **A 1201**
— Prince Hal, or The romance of a rich young
man. Phila. 1882. D. **A 1202**
Andrews, Jane. Each and all, or How the
seven little sisters prove their sisterhood ;
a companion to "The seven little sisters
who live on the round ball that floats in
the air." Bost. 1878. S. **Ax 801**
Angelika Kaufmann ; ein historischer roman.
Frankfurt a. M. 1860. 2 v. D. **A 3**
Angie, Cousin, *pseud.* Worth, not wealth, and
other tales. Bost. *n. d.* D. **Ax 726**
Contents. Worth, not wealth.—Perseverance.—The
bad temper cured.—The school girl's first trial.—
Gleanings from memory's wayside.
Anley, Charlotte. The prisoners of Australia.
[*Anon.*] Lond. 1841. S. **A 1251**
Anneke, Mathilde Franziska. Das geisterhaus
in New York. Jena. 1864. S. **A 1301**
Anson, W. S. W. The three foolish little
gnomes. Lond. *n. d.* Q. **Ax 826**
Anstey, F., *pseud., see* **Guthrie,** F: Anstey.
Anzengruber, L:, (*Ludwig Gruber*). Feldrain
und waldweg ; mit einer einleitung von
Joseph Kürschner. Stuttg. [1882.] D.
A 2251
Contents, see Deutscher katalog, p. 47.
— Hartinger's alte Sixtin. *In* **Vierteljährl. mag.**
V 2 v31
Apeltern, Hermann, *pseud., see* **Engelen,** A. W.
Appeltern, Hermann van, *pseud., see* **Engelen,**
A. W.
Appleton, Elizabeth Haven. A half-life and
half a life. *In* Atlantic tales. **A 1876**
Arabian nights' entertainments, *see* **Thousand**
and one nights.
Arblay, Frances d', *born* Burney. Cecilia, or
Memoirs of an heiress, by the author of
Evelina. 2d amer. ed. Bost. 1803. 3 v. S.
A 1401
— Evelina, or The history of a young lady's in-
troduction to the world. N. Y. 1861. S.
A 1402
— *Same.* N. Y. *n. d.* 2 v. in 1. S. **A 1402**
Arbouville, Sophie d', *born* de Bazancourt. Three
tales: Christine Van Amberg ; Resigna-
tion and The village doctor. Tr. from the
french by Maunsell B. Field. N. Y. 1853.
S. **A 1451**
— The village doctor. *In* Tales from Black-
wood. **T 176 v5**
Archer, E. M. Betwixt my love and me ; a
novel. [*Anon.*] N. Y. 1885. Q. **A 2301**
Arfvedson, C. D. König Karl XI und seine
günstlinge ; geschichtlicher roman in zwei
abth. vom verfasser der Vereinigten
Staaten und Canada, u. s. w. Aus dem
schwedischen übers. von Gottlob Fink.
Stuttg. 1846. 2 v. T. **K 11**
Argles, Margaret, (*The duchess*). Airy, fairy
Lilian ; a novel. Phila. 1883. D. **A 1476**

x denotes books specially adapted for children.

Argles, Margaret, (*The duchess*).—*Continued.*
— Beauty's daughters. Phila. 1880. D.   **A 1477**
— Doris ; a novel. Phila. 1885 [1884]. D. **A 1485**
— Faith and unfaith ; a novel.   Phila. 1882
[1881]. D.   **A 1478**
— In durance vile. *In* Tales from many sources.
T 178 v2
— *Same*, and other stories. Phila. 1885. S.
A 1486
Includes. A week in Killarney.—Moonshine and Marguerites.—Dr. Ball.—A fit of the blues.
— Loÿs lord Beresford, and other tales. Phila.
1883. D.   **A 1483**
Includes, Eric Dering.—Sweet is true love.—Lydia. —Jocelyne.—The witching hour.— The pity of it.— How Snooks got out of it. — Cross purposes.—Her first appearance.—Krin.—Beatrix.—Clarissa's choice. —What a mad world it is, my masters.—The baby.— The dilemma.—That last rehearsal.
— A maiden all forlorn, and other stories. Phila.
1885. D.   **A 1488**
Includes, A rose distill'd.—A passive crime.—Zara. —Barbara.—Nurse Eva.—One new year's eve.—Vivi-enne.
— Mrs. Geoffrey ; a novel. Phila. 1881. D.
A 1479
— Molly Bawn. Phila. 1883. D.   **A 1480**
— O tender Dolores ; a novel. Phila. 1885. D.
A 1487
— Phyllis, by the duchess. Phila. 1877. S.
A 1481
— Portia, or By passions rocked. Phila. 1883. D.
A 1482
— Rossmoyne. Phila. 1884 [1883]. D.   **A 1484**
Argyle, Anna. Olive Lacey ; a tale of the irish
rebellion of 1798. Phila. 1874. D.   **A 1501**
Arlincourt, C: Victor **Le Prevost** *vicomte* d'.
Die fremde. Teutsch von Paul Gauger.
Stuttg. 1838. 2 v. S.   **A 1551**
— Die waise von Unterlachen. Grimma. 1824. 2
v. S.   **A 1552**
Armand, *pseud.*, *see* **Strubberg**, F: A:
Arnim, L: Achim v. Contes bizarres. Tr. de
Théophile Gautier fils, précédée d' une in-
troduction par Théophile Gautier. Nouv.
éd. Paris. 1869. D.   **A 1577**
Contents. Introd. — Isabelle d' Égypte.— Marie Me-luck Blainville.—Les héritiers du majorat.
— Die kronenwächter ; mit einer einleitung von
Johannes Scherr. Stuttg. 1881. D. **A 1576**
Arnold, Birch, *pseud.*, *see* **Bartlett**, A. E. *mrs.*
J. M. D.
Arnold, F: Alfred Leslie ; a story of Glasgow
life. [*Anon.*] Glasgow. 1856. S.   **A 1591**
Arnold, G: Why Thomas was discharged. *In*
Atlantic tales.   **A 1876**
— *Same*. *In* Stories by american authors.
S 35 v5
Arnold, W: Delafield. Oakfield, or Fellowship
in the east. Bost. 1855. D.   **A 1601**
Arnould, A: François, *and* L: P: Narcisse
Fournier. Struensee, oder Günstling und
königin. Nach dem französischen von dr.
Scherr. [*Anon.*] Stuttg. 1845. T.   **S 41**
Arrom, Cecilia Bohl de Faber, (*Fernan Cabal-
lero*). Spanish fairy tales. Tr. by J. H.
Ingram. Phila. 1881. D.   **Ax 851**
Arthalis, *pseud.*, *see* **Steinlein**, Laura.
Arthur, Timothy Shay. The bar-rooms at
Brantly, or The great hotel speculation.
Chicago. [1877]. D.   **A 1751**
— Friends and neighbors, or Two ways of living
in the world. Chicago. 1856. D. **A 1752**

Arthur, Timothy Shay.—*Continued.*
— Heart histories and life-pictures. N. Y. 1853.
S.   **A 1753**
— The lost bride. *T. p. w.* [Phila.] O. **A 1754**
— Making haste to be rich, or The temptation
and fall. N. Y. 1859. T.   **A 1755**
— Retiring from business ; the rich man's error.
N. Y. 1859. T.   **A 1756**
— Ten nights in a bar-room, and what I saw
there. Phila. [1857]. S.   **A 1757**
— The ways of providence, or "He doeth all
things well". Phila. 1864. T.   **A 1758**
— Woman to the rescue ; a story of the new
crusade. Cinc. [1874]. D.   **A 1759**
Arusmont, Frances d', *born* Wright. A few days
in Athens ; being the translation of a greek
manuscript discovered in Herculaneum.
Bost. 1850. D.   **A 1801**
At the red glove ; a novel. Ill. N. Y. 1885. D.
A 81
Atlantic tales. *T. p. w.* [Bost.] D.   **A 1876**
Contents. Hale, E: E. My double, and how he undid me. — O'Brien, F. J. The diamond lens. — Davis, R. B. Life in the iron mills.—Dodge, M. A. The pursuit of knowledge under difficulties. — Lowell, R. T. S. A raft that no man made. — Arnold, G: Why Thomas was discharged.—Chese-bro', C: Victor and Jacqueline. — Nordhoff, C: Elkanah Brewster's temptation.—Hale, L. P. The queen of the red chessmen. — Cooke, R. T. Miss Lucinda.—Whelpley, J. D. The Denslow palace.— Taylor, B. Friend Eli's daughter.—Appleton, E. H. A half-life and half a life.—Hale, E: E. The man without a country.
Auer, Adelheid v., *pseud.*, *see* **Cosel**, Charlotte v.
Auerbach, Berthold. Aloys. Tr. by C: T.
Brooks. (Leisure hour ser.) N. Y. 1877. S.
A 1951
— Auf der höhe ; roman in 8 büchern. 12te aufl.
Stuttg. 1879. 2 v. in 1. S.   **A 1952**
— *Same*, *eng.* On the heights. Tr. by Simon
Adler Stern. N. Y. 1875. D.   **A 1952**
— Barfüssele. Stuttg. 1858. S.   **A 1953**
— *Same*. N. Y. 1881. F.   **A 1953**
— *Same*, *eng.* The little barefoot. Tr. by Eliza
Buckminster Lee. (Leisure hour ser.) N.
Y. 1874. S.   **A 1953**
— Black Forest village stories. *See below* Schwarz-
wälder dorfgeschichten.
— Brigitta ; erzählung. N. Y. 1881. F. **A 1954**
— *Same*, *eng.* Tr. by Clara Bell. (Leisure hour
ser.) N. Y. 1880. S.   **A 1954**
— The convicts and their children. Tr. by C: T.
Brooks. (Leisure hour ser.) N. Y. 1877. S.
A 1955
— Deutsche abende. Stuttg. 1858. S.   **A 1956**
Contents, see Deutscher katalog, p. 47.
— Dichter und kaufmann ; ein lebensgemälde
aus der zeit Moses Mendelssohns. Stuttg.
1858. 2 v. S.   **A 1957**
— Edelweiss. Tr. by Ellen Frothingham. (Leis-
ure hour ser.) N. Y. 1874. S.   **A 1958**
— The foresters. N. Y. 1880. S.   **A 1959**
— Joseph im schnee ; eine erzählung. Stuttg.
1860. S.   **A 1960**
— *Same*, *eng.* Joseph in the snow ; a tale.
(Leisure hour ser.) N. Y. 1874. S. **A 1960**
— Das landhaus am Rhein ; roman. 4te aufl.
Stuttg. 1874. 3 v. in 1. S.   **A 1967**
— *Same*, *eng.* The villa on the Rhine. Tr. by
James Davis, with a portrait of the author,
and a biographical sketch by Bayard
Taylor. (Leisure hour ser.) N. Y. 1874.
2 v. S.   **A 1967**

x denotes books specially adapted for children.

Auerbach, Berthold.—*Continued.*
— Landolin. Tr. by Annie B. Irish. (Leisure hour ser.) N. Y. 1878. S. **A 1961**
— The little barefoot. *See above* Barfüssele.
— Loreley and Reinhard. Tr. by C. T. Brooks. (Leisure hour ser.) N. Y. 1877. S. **A 1962**
— Master Bieland and his workmen. Tr. by E. Hancock. (Leisure hour ser.) N. Y. 1880. S. **A 1970**
— Neues leben ; eine lebensgeschichte in fünf büchern. Stuttg. 1858. 3 v. S. **A 1963**
— On the heights. *See above* Auf der höhe.
— Schatzkästlein des gevattersmanns. Stuttg. 1858. 2 v. S. **A 1964**
— Schwarzwälder dorfgeschichten. Stuttg. 1857. 8 v. S. **A 1965**
  Contents, see Deutscher katalog, p. 47.
— *Same.* N. Y. 1882. F. **A 1965**
— *Same, eng.* Black Forest village stories. Tr. by C: Goepp. Author's ed. Ill. N. Y. 1869. S. **A 1965**
  Contents. The gawk.—The pipe of war.—Manorhouse farmer's Vefela.—Nip-cheeked Toney.—Good government.—The hostile brothers.—Ivo, the gentleman.—Florian and Crescence.—The lauterbacher.
— Spinoza ; ein denkerleben. Stuttg. 1858. 2 v. D. **A 1966**
— *Same.* N. Y. 1882. F. **A 1966**
— *Same, eng.* From the german by E. Nicholson. (Leisure hour ser.) N. Y. 1882. S. **A 1966**
— The villa on the Rhine. *See above* Das land-•haus am Rhein.
— Waldfried. *T. p. w.* [N. Y. 1874]. D. **A 1968**
August, F: L: Die liebe am Rhein ; ein lebensbild aus der gegenwart. Leipz. 1844. S. **A 2001**
Augusti, Bertha, *born* Schöler. Das bildniss ; eine novelle. *In* Vierteljährl. mag. **V 2 v25**
Aulnoy *or* Aunoy, Marie Catherine Junelle de **Berneville**, *comtesse* d'. Fairy tales. New ed., ill. Lond. 1881. D. **Ax 951**
Ausgewiesene, Der. Leipz. 1840. 2 v. D. **A 4**
Austen, Jane. Emma. Bost. 1871. D. **A 2051**
— Mansfield Park. *T. p. w.* [Bost. 1871]. D. **A 2052**
— Northanger Abbey. *With her* Pride and prejudice. **A 2053**
— Persuasion. *With her* Sense and sensibility. **A 2054**
— Pride and prejudice. N. Y. 1880. Q. **A 2053**
— *Same.* Phila. *n. d.* D. **A 2053**
— Sense and sensibility. N. Y. 1879. Q. **A 2054**
— *Same.* Phila. *n. d.* D. **A 2054**
— *See* **Keddie**, Henrietta. Jane Austen and her works. **A 2055**
Austin, Jane Goodwin. The Desmond hundred. (Round-robin ser.) Bost. 1882. S. **A 2104**
— Dora Darling, the daughter of the regiment. Bost. 1884. D. **A 2105**
— Mrs. Beauchamp Brown. (No name ser.) Bost. 1880. S. **A 2101**
— Moonfolk ; a true account of the home of the fairy tales. Ill. N. Y. 1877. D. **Ax 901**
— A nameles nobleman. (Round-robin ser.) Bost. 1881. S. **A 2102**
— Outpost. Bost. 1884. D. **A 2106**
— The shadow of Moloch mountain. N. Y. 1870. O. **A 2103**

Auton, C., *pseud., see* **Hoppin**, A:
Avery, M. A. Shadowed perils. N. Y. 1876. D. **A 2151**
Awdry, Frances, *and others.* The miz-maze, or The Winkworth puzzle, by nine authors. N. Y. 1883. D. **A 2176**
  Note. The other authors are: Mary Bramston, Christabel R. Coleridge, Mary S. Lee, A. E. Mary Anderson Morshead, Frances M. Peard, Eleanor C. Price, Florence Wilford, Charlotte M. Yonge.
Ayguals de Izco, Wenzeslaus. Marie, die spanierin, oder Das schlachtopfer eines mönchs ; historisch-politischer roman, eingeführt von E. Sue. Stuttg. 1847. 2 v. T. **I 451**
Aytoun, W. Edmondstoune. The congress and the Agapedome. *In* Tales from Blackwood. **T 177 v2**
— The emerald studs. *In the same.* **T 176 v6**
— The Glenmutchkin railway. *In the same.* **T 176 v1**
— How I became a yeoman. *In the same.* **T 176 v2**
— How I stood for the Dreepdaily Burghs. *In the same.* **T 176 v4**
— How we got possession of the Tuileries. *In the same.* **T 176 v5**
— The raid of Arnaboll. *In the same.* **T 177 v2**
— Rapping the question. *In the same.* **T 177 v9**
— The surveyor's tale. *In the same.* **T 176 v8**
Azeglio, Giuseppe Maria Gerolamo Raffaele Massimo **Taparelli**, *marchese* d'. Ettore Fieramosca, or The challenge of Barletta ; the struggles of an italian against foreign invaders and foreign protectors. Bost. 1859. D. **A 2202**
— Niccolo di Lapi ; ein roman aus der florentinischen geschichte. Aus dem italienischen. Stuttg. 1845. 2 v. T. **A 2201**

B., M. E. Claudine ; a swiss tale by the author of Always happy. *T. p. w.* [Lond. 1847.] S. **Bx 126**
Bach, Ottilie. Des vaters schuld ; ein roman. *In* Vierteljährl. mag. **V 2 v24**
Baer, *Mrs.* B. F. Irene, or Beach-broken billows. N. Y. 1875. D. **B 101**
Bagger, C: Christian, (*Johan Harring*). Meines bruders leben ; eine erzählung. Aus dem dänischen übertragen von Julius Ruescher. Berlin. 1847. S. **B 126**
Baker, G: M. Running to waste ; the story of a tomboy. Ill. Bost. *n. d.* S. **Bx 101**
Baker, Harriet Newell, *born* Woods, (*Aunt Hattie, Mrs. Madeline Leslie*). Light and shade. Bost. 1864. S. **Bx 150**
— Theology in romance, or The catechism and the Dermott family. Bost. 1859. 2 v. S. **Bx 151**
Baker, *Sir* S: White. Cast up by the sea. Ill. Phila. 1881. D. **Bx 20 1**
— *Same.* N. Y. 1880. Q. **Bx 201**
— True tales for my grandsons. Ill. N. Y. 1883. D. **Bx 202**
Baker, W: Munford, (*George F. Harrington*). Blessed saint Certainty. Bost. 1881. S. **B 151**
— Carter Quarterman. N. Y. 1876. O. **B 152**
— Colonel Dunwoddie, millionaire ; a story of today. [*Anon.*] N. Y. 1878. O. **B 153**
— His majesty myself. (No name ser.) Bost. 1880. S. **B 154**

x denotes books specially adapted for children.

Baker, W: Munford.—*Continued.*
— Inside ; a chronicle of secession, by George F. Harrington. Ill. N. Y. 1866. O.   **B 155**
— The making of a man. [*Anon.*] Bost. 1884. S.   **B 157**
— The new Timothy. N. Y. 1870. D.   **B 156**
— *Same.* N. Y. 1883. Q.   **B 156**
Balch, W: S. A peculiar people, or Reality in romance. Chicago. 1881. D.   **B 176**
Baldamus, Max K: Wahnsinn und liebe. Leipz. 1826. S.   **B 201**
Ballantyne, Robert Michael. The giant of the north, or Pokings round the pole. Ill. Lond. 1882 [1881]. D.   **Bx 251**
— The gorilla hunters ; a tale of the wilds of Africa. Ill. Phila. *n. d.* S.   **Bx 252**
Balzac, Honoré de. The greatness and decline of César Birotteau. From the french, tr. by O. W. Wight and F. B. Goodrich. N. Y. 1860. D.   **B 251**
Banim, J: *and* Michael, (*The O'Hara family*). The bit o' writin'. New ed. with introd. and notes by Michael Banim. N. Y. *n. d.* D.   **B 307**
Contents. The irish lord-lieutenant and his double. —The family of the cold feet.—The barehound and the witch.—The soldiers' bullet.—A peasant girl's love.—The hall of the castle.—The half-brothers.— Twice lost but saved.—The faithful servant.—The roman merchant.— Ill got, ill gone.— The church-yard watch.—The last of the storm.—The rival dream-ers.—The substitute.—The white bristol.—The stolen sheep.—The publican's dream.—The ace of clubs.
— The Boyne water. New ed. with introd. and notes by Michael Banim. N. Y. 1866. D.   **B 301**
— Clough Fionn, or The stone of destiny. N. Y. 1869. D.   **B 302**
— The denounced, or The last baron of Crana. New ed. with notes by Michael Banim, survivor of the "O'Hara family." N. Y. 1866. D.   **B 303**
— The ghost-hunter. N. Y. 1869. D.   **B 304**
— The peep o' day, or John Doe and Crohoore of the billhook. New ed. with introd. and notes by Michael Banim. N. Y. 1875. D.   **B 305**
— Peter of the castle and the fetches. A new ed. with introd. and notes by Michael Banim. N. Y. 1867. D.   **B 306**
— The rival dreamers. *In* Johnson, E. R. Lit-tle classics. Ill. Bost. 1882. D.   **J 926 v12**
Banks, Mary Ross. Bright days in the old plan-tation time. Ill. Bost. 1882. D.   **Bx 1101**
Barbauld, Anna Lætitia, *born* Aikin. Things by their right names and other stories, fables and moral pieces in prose and verse, selected and arranged from [her] writings; with a sketch of her life by S. J. Hale. N. Y. 1854. S.   **Bx 302**
✛ *joint author, see* Aikin, J:
Barham, R: Harris, (*Thomas Ingoldsby*). Jerry Jarvis's wig ; a legend of the weald of Kent. *In* Johnson, E. R. Little classics.   **J 926 v4**
— My cousin Nicholas. *T. p. w.* D.   **B 351**
Barker, Mary Anne *lady, now Mrs.* Napier F. **Broome.** Spring comedies. Lond. 1871. D.   **B 376**
Contents. A wedding story.—A stupid story.—A scotch story.—A man's story.
Barnard, C: Knights of today, or Love and science. N. Y. 1881. D.   **B 401**
Contents. — — — — — [Kate].—A sanitary measure.—Under high pressure.—Applied science.— Love and a lantern.—Put yourself in her place.—The wreck of the Pioneer.

Barnard, Edna A. Maple Range ; a frontier romance. Chicago. 1882. D.   **B 426**
Barnes, Josiah, *sen.* The Green mountain trav-eller's entertainment. N. Y. 1860. D.   **B 451**
Barr, Amelia Edith, *born* Huddleston. Romances and realities ; tales of truth and fancy. N. Y. 1876. D.   **B 501**
Contents. Content. — Wisely, and not too well.— "Sold for naught." — Every cross bears its own inscription.—Seed and fruit.—The God of our idola-try.—The sacrament of poverty.—The law of love.— The weakest goes to the wall.—A faithful woman.— From shore to shore.— Mary's marriage.— Not for gold. — Agnes Stirling. — Little Dime. — Money at interest. — "Your most obedient servant, etc." — A basket of strawberries.—Angling in August.—Scotch songs.—A chime of bells.—W: Wordsworth.—Modern poets as religious teachers.—The story of the english bible.—The book of common prayer.—Touching the vanished hand. — A latent sense. — An autumn rev-erie.—The story of four kings.—Fairies.—A little talk about diet and dress.—Fashions that are always fash-ionable. — Orders for dinner. — A romance of the bread-basket.—A garden of herbs.—The salad bowl.— Oysters and oyster-eaters. — "Cherry ripe." — The honey bee.—Almanacs.—Thus runs the world away.
Barrett, Frank. Honest Davie ; a novel. Lond. 1883. 3 v. in 1. D.   **B 516**
— *Same.* N. Y. 1883. Q.   **B 516**
Barrili, Anton Giulio. The devil's portrait. Tr. from the italian by Evelyn Wodehouse. N. Y. 1885. S.   **B 528**
— The eleventh commandment ; a romance. From the italian by Clara Bell ; rev. and corr. in the U. S. N. Y. 1882. S.   **B 527**
— A whimsical wooing. From the italian by Clara Bell ; rev. and corr. in the U. S. N. Y. 1882. S.   **B 526**
Barthélemy, J: Jacques. Carite and Polydorus. Prefixed, a treatise on morals, with the life of the author. Lond. 1799. S.   **B 4851**
Bartlett, Alice E. *mrs.* J. M. D., (*Birch Arnold*). Until the day break. Phila. 1877. D.   **B 551**
Basil, *pseud.* A coquette's conquest ; a novel. N. Y. 1885. Q.   **B 4653**
— Love the debt ; a novel. N. Y. 1882. Q.   **B 4651**
— *Same.* Lond. 1882. 3 v. in 1. D.   **B 4651**
— The wearing of the green ; a novel. N. Y. 1885. Q.   **B 4652**
Bates, Arlo. The pagans. N. Y. 1884. S.   **B 566**
— Patty's perversities. (Round-robin ser.) Bost. 1881. S.   **B 567**
Bauberger, W: Die Beatushöhle ; eine erzäh-lung für die gesammte edlere lesewelt, besonders für die reifere jugend. Cinc. 1855. S.   **B 576**
— Die irländische hütte ; eine erzählung für die gesammte edlere lesewelt, besonders für die reifere jugend. Cinc. 1855. S.   **B 578**
— Das thal von Almeria ; eine erzählung für die gesammte edlere lesewelt, besonders für die reifere jugend. Neue, ill. originalaufl. Regensburg. 1874. D. *With* Schmid, J. C. v. Mathilde und Wilhelmine.   **S 1467**
— *Same.* Cinc. 1851. S.   **B 577**
— Das wunderweib von Eichbühl ; eine erzäh-lung für die gesammte edlere lesewelt, besonders für die reifere jugend. Cinc. 1856. S.   **B 579**
— *Same.* Cinc. 1862. S.   **B 580**

x denotes books specially adapted for children.

Baudissin, *Graf* Adalbert. Zustände in Amerika. Altona. 1862. O.　**B 601**
Bauer, Clara, (*Karl Detlef*). Auf Capri ; novelle. 2te aufl. Stuttg. 1877. 2 v. in 1. D.　**B 651**
— *Same.* N. Y. 1882. F.　**B 651**
— *Same, eng.* At Capri ; a story of italian life. Tr. from the germ. by M. S. Phila. *n. d.* D.　**B 651**
— Ein dokument ; roman. 2te aufl. Stuttg. 1878. 4 v. in 2. D.　**B 652**
— Die geheimnissvolle sängerin ; novelle. 2te aufl. Stuttg. 1878. D.　**B 653**
— Musste es sein? roman. 2te aufl. Stuttg. 1875. 2 v. in 1. D.　**B 654**
— Nora ; eine charakterstudie aus der deutschen gesellschaft. 3te aufl. Stuttg. 1876. 2 v. in 1. D.　**B 655**
— Novellen. Braunschw. 1874. 2 v. D.　**B 656**
　Contents, see Deutscher katalog, p. 49.
— Russische idyllen; nachgelassene novellen. 2te aufl. Breslau. 1880. D.　**B 657**
　Contents, see Deutscher katalog, p. 49.
— Unlösliche bande ; novelle. 3te aufl. Stuttg. 1877. D.　**B 658**
— Zwischen vater und sohn ; roman. 3te aufl. Stuttg. 1878. 2 v. in 1. D.　**B 659**
— *Same, eng.* Valentine the countess, or Between father and son. Tr. from the german by M. S. Phila. 1874. D.　**B 659**
Bäuerle, Adolf, (*Fels, Otto Horn*). Das eingemauerte mädchen ; Wiener criminalgeschichte aus der neuesten zeit. Pest. 1857. 2 v. in 1. S.　**B 701**
Bayer, K: Robert Emmerich v., (*Robert Byr*). Der heimliche gast, von Robert Byr. N. Y. 1883. F.　**B 726**
— *Same.* Mit einer einleitung von J. Kürschner. Stuttg. [1883]. D.　**B 727**
— Die Spatlauber; novelle. *In* **Vierteljährl.** mag.　**V 2 v21**
Beach, Rebecca G. The puritan and the quaker ; a story of colonial times. N. Y. 1879. D.　**B 751**
Beaconsfield, *Earl of, see* Disraeli, B:
Beale, Anne. The miller's daughter. Lond. 1878. 3 v. in 2. D.　**B 801**
— *Same.* N. Y. 1881. Q.　**B 801**
— The Pennant family. Lond. 1876. 3 v. in 1. D.　**B 802**
— *Same.* N. Y. 1880. Q.　**B 802**
— Rose Mervyn of Whitelake. Lond. 1879. 3 v. in 1. D.　**B 803**
— *Same.* N. Y. 1879. Q.　**B 803**
— Simplicity and fascination. Bost. *n. d.* D.　**B 804**
Beatty, J: The belle o' Becket's Lane. Phila. 1883. D.　**B 816**
Beauvoir, Roger de, *pseud., see* Bully, E: Roger de.
Beazley, S: Der roué. Aus dem englischen von Theodor Ruprecht. [*Anon.*] Leipz. 1853. 4 v. S.　**B 826**
Bechstein, L: Berthold der student, oder Deutschlands erste burschenschaft ; romantisches zeitbild. Halle. 1850. 2 v. S.　**B 851**
— Clarinette ; seitenstück zu den Fahrten eines musikanten. Leipz. 1840. 3 v. S.　**B 852**
— Der dunkelgraf. Frankfurt a. M. 1854. S.　**B 853**

Bechstein, L:—*Continued.*
— Fahrten eines musikanten. Frankfurt a. M. 1855. 2 v. S.　**B 854**
— Der fürstentag ; historisch-romantisches zeitbild aus dem sechzehnten jahrhundert. Frankfurt a. M. 1834. 2 v. D.　**B 855**
— Grimmenthal ; romantisches zeitbild aus dem sechzehnten jahrhundert. Hildburghausen. 1833. D.　**B 856**
— Hainsterne ; berg-, wald- und wandergeschichten. Halle. 1853. 4 v. D.　**B 857**
　Contents, see Deutscher katalog, p. 49.
— Die manuscripte Peter Schlemihls ; kosmologisch-literarische novelle. Berlin. 1851. 2 v. S.　**B 858**
— Novellen und phantasieblüthen. Leipz. 1835. 2 v. S.　**B 859**
　Contents, see Deutscher katalog, p. 49.
— Novellen und phantasiegemälde. Hildburghausen. 1882. 2 v. D.　**B 860**
　Contents, see Deutscher katalog, p. 49.
Bechstein, Reinhold. Altdeutsche märchen, sagen und legenden, treu nacherzählt für jung und alt. 2te aufl. Leipz. 1877. D.　**B 901**
Becker, A: Auf waldwegen. Stuttg. [1881]. D.　**B 955**
— Des rabbi vermächtniss ; roman in 3 abth. 1e abth. Der maler. Berlin. 1866. 2 v. D.　**B 951**
2te abth. Der kabbalist. Berlin. 1866. 2 v. S.　**B 952**
3te abth. Der erbgraf. Berlin. 1867. 2 v. S.　**B 953**
— Vervehmt ; roman aus der gegenwart. Berlin. 1868. 4 v. S.　**B 954**
Becker, L: Theodor, *ed.* Rosen und dornen in erzählungen und scenen aus dem stillen häuslichen leben, in einen kranz gewunden für gute menschen. Nürnberg. *n. d.* 2 v. S.　**B 1001**
　Contents, see Deutscher katalog, p. 49.
Beckford, W: Vathek ; an arabian tale, with a memoir of the author and notes critical and explanatory. Phila. 1854. D.　**B 1051**
— *Same.* [Bayard ser.] Lond. 1875. T.　**B 1051**
Bede, Cuthbert, *pseud., see* Bradley, E:
Beecher, H: Ward. Norwood, or Village life in New England. N. Y. 1868. D.　**B 1101**
Beers, H: A. Split zephyr. *In* Stories by american authors.　**S 35 v8**
Behrens, Bertha, (*W. Heimburg*). Ihr einziger bruder ; novelle. N. Y. 1883. F.　**H 2277**
— Im banne der musen. N. Y. 1883. D.　**H 2278**
— Lottie of the mill. From the german by Katharine S. Dickey. Phila. 1877. D.　**H 2276**
— A penniless girl. From the german by mrs. A. L. Wister. Phila. 1885 [1884]. D.　**H 2279**
Bekenn, M. L. Ursula, a story of the bohemian reformation ; a book for boys and girls. Ill. N. Y. 1880. S.　**Bx 426**
Bela ; erlebnisse eines ungarischen flüchtlings im osten und westen. Aus den papieren des general K——y. N. Y. 1856. T.　**B 1**
Belani, H. E. R., *pseud., see* Häberlin, K: L:
Belcher, *Sir* E: Horatio Howard Brenton ; ein seeroman. Uebers. von E. Buchele. Stuttg. 1856. 3 v. T.　**B 1151**

x denotes books specially adapted for children.

Bell, Acton *and* Ellis, *pseud., see* **Brontë**, Anne *and* Emily.

Bell, Currer, *pseud., see* **Nicholls**, Charlotte, *born* Brontë.

Bell, *Mrs.* Lucia Chase. True blue ; a story of the great northwest. Bost. 1878. D.　　**Bx 501**

Bell, M. M. Seven to seventeen, or Veronica Gordon. Ill. N. Y. 1875. S.　　**Bx 551**

Bell, *Mrs.* Martin, *pseud., see* **Martin**, *Mrs.* Bell.

Bellamy, C: Joseph. The Breton mills. N. Y. 1880. S.　　**B 1251**

Bellamy, E: Lost. *In* Stories by american authors.　　**S 35 v7**

— Miss Ludington's sister ; a romance of immortality. Bost. 1884. S.　　**B 1261**

Bellamy, Elizabeth Whitfield, *born* Croom, (*Kampa Thorpe*). The little Joanna. N. Y. 1876. O.　　**B 1276**

Bellemarre, Eugène L: Gabriel de Ferry de, (*Gabriel Ferry*). Der waldläufer. Aus dem französischen von C. F. Grieb. Stuttg. 1851. 4 v. T.　　**B 1286**

Belot, Adolphe. Die würger von Paris ; eine geschichte von neulich, nach A. Belot von E. Vacano. N. Y. 1881. F.　　**B 4601**

Benedict, Frank Lee. Her friend Laurence. N. Y. 1879. D.　　**B 1301**

— John Worthington's name. N. Y. 1875. O.　　**B 1302**

— Madame. N. Y. 1877. D.　　**B 1303**

— Miss Dorothy's charge. N. Y. 1873. O.　　**B 1304**

— Miss Van Kortland. N. Y. 1875. O.　　**B 1305**

— Mr. Vaughan's heir ; a novel. Lond. 1874. 3 v. in 2. D.　　**B 1306**

— My daughter Elinor. N. Y. 1869. O.　　**B 1307**

— The price she paid ; a novel. Phila. 1883. S.　　**B 1310**

— St. Simon's niece. N. Y. 1875. O.　　**B 1308**

— 'Twixt hammer and anvil ; a novel. N. Y. 1884. D.　　**B 1309**

Benham, G: Chittenden. A year of wreck ; a true story by a victim. [*Anon.*] N. Y. 1880. D.　　**B 1351**

Benjamin, Park. The end of New York. *In* Stories by american authors.　　**S 35 v5**

Bennett, G. J. The empress. Phila. 1836. 2 v. D.　　**B 1401**

Bentzon, Th., *pseud., see* **Blanc**, Marie Thérèse.

Berger, E., *pseud., see* **Sheppard**, Elizabeth Sara.

Berger, W: Das letzte glück ; erzählung. *In* Vierteljährl. mag.　　**V 2 v31**

Bergsöe, W: Jörgen. Die braut von Rörvig ; erzählung. Nach dem dänischen original-manuscript frei bearb. von Adolph Strodtmann. Berlin. 1872. D.　　**B 1451**

— Gespensternovellen. Aus dem dänischen übersetzt von Adolf Strodtmann. Berlin. 1873. D.　　**B 1452**

Contents, see Deutscher katalog, p. 50.

— Pillone. Tr. from the danish by D. G. Hubbard. Bost. [1878]. S.　　**B 1455**

— *Same*, und andere erzählungen. Aus dem dänischen von Adolph Strodtmann. Berlin. 1876. 2 v. in 1. D.　　**B 1453**

Contents, see Deutscher katalog, p. 50.

— Von der Piazza del Popolo ; novellen-cyklus aus Rom. Deutsch von Franz Busch. Bremen. 1871. 3 v. in 1. D.　　**B 1454**

Bernard, C: Bernard Dugrail de la Vilette, *called* C: de. Ausgewählte erzählungen. Aus dem französischen von C. F. Grieb. Stuttg. 1859. 2 v. T.　　**B 1501**

Contents, see Deutscher katalog, p. 50.

— The consultation. From the french. *In* Sargent, E. The emerald.　　**S 551**

Bernays, Isaak, *pseud., see* **Schiff**, Hermann.

Berneck, C: Gustav v., (*Bernd v. Guseck*). Deutschlands ehre ; historischer roman. *T. p. w.* D.　　**B 1526**

— Der erste raub an Deutschland ; historischer roman. Leipz. 1862. 4 v. S.　　**B 1527**

— Der graf von der Liegnitz ; historischer roman. Jena. 1869. 3 v. S.　　**B 1528**

— Im strom der zeit ; roman aus der zeit kaiser Leopold des ersten. Prag. 1860. 4 v. T.　　**B 1529**

— Kaltenborn. Prag. 1855. T.　　**B 1530**

— Karl X Gustav ; historischer roman. Wien. 1862. 2 v. S.　　**B 1531**

— Nach der flut ; historischer roman. Leipz. 1854. 4 v. T.　　**B 1532**

— Salvator. Bremen. 1851. 2 v. S.　　**B 1533**

— Wildfeuer ; novellen. Berlin. 1845. 2 v. S.　　**B 1534**

Contents, see Deutscher katalog, p. 50.

Bernhard, Carl, *pseud., see* **St. Aubain**, Andreas Nicolai.

Bernhardi, L. T. Das fürstenhaus ; ein geschichtliches gemälde aus der mitte des achtzehnten jahrhunderts. Leipz. 1826. 2 v. S.　　**B 1551**

Bernhardt, A: Kinder der zeit. Stuttg. 1858. T.　　**B 1601**

Berquin, Arnold. The looking glass for the mind, or Intellectual mirror. Ill. N. Y. 1860. T.　　**Bx 601**

Berry, Martha E. Celesta ; a girl's book. Bost. *n. d.* S.　　**Bx 651**

— Crooked and straight, or Jotham and Annette at home. Bost. *n. d.* S.　　**Bx 652**

Berthet, Élie Bertrand. Der jüngere sohn aus der Normandie. Aus den neuesten feuilletons des Siècle, übers. von G: Lotz. Hamburg. 1842. S.　　**B 1701**

— The pre-historic world. Tr. from the french by Mary J. Safford. Phila. [1879]. D.　　**B 1702**

— Der wehrwolf. Aus den neuesten feuilletons des journals le Siècle, in's deutsche übers. von G: Lotz. Hamburg. 1843. S.　　**B 1703**

Berthold, Franz, *pseud., see* **Reinbold**, Adelheid.

Bertigny, St. v. Wahnsinnig auf befehl ; novelle. *In* Vierteljährl. mag.　　**V 2 v21**

Besant, Walter, (*Walter Maurice*). All in a garden fair. N. Y. 1883. Q.　　**B 1759**

— All sorts and conditions of men ; an impossible story. New ed. Lond. 1884. D.　　**B 1757**

— *Same*. N. Y. 1882. Q.　　**B 1757**

— Dorothy Forster. Leipz. 1884. 2 v. in 1. S.　　**B 1760**

— In luck at last. N. Y. [1885.] S.　　**B 1771**

— Uncle Jack, and other stories. N. Y. 1885. S.　　**B 1770**

Contents. **Besant**, W. Uncle Jack ; A glorious fortune.—**Besant**, W., *and* W. H. **Pollock**. Sir Jocelyn's cap.

— *and* James Rice. By Celia's arbor ; a tale of Portsmouth town. N. Y. 1878. O. **B 1751**

— — *Same*. New ed. Lond. [1880]. D. **B 1751**

x **denotes books specially adapted for children.**

Besant, Walter, *and* James **Rice**.—*Continued.*
— — The captain's room ; a novel. N. Y. 1882. Q.
 B 1755
— — The case of mr. Lucraft, and other tales.
 New ed. Lond. [1877]. D. **B 1762**
 Contents. From the supernatural: The case of mr.
 Lucraft: The mystery of Joe Morgan; An old, old
 story; Lady Kitty; The old four-poster; My own
 experience.—From fairyland: Titania's farewell.—
 From fact: On the Goodwin: Edelweis; Love finds
 the way; The death of S: Pickwick; When the ship
 comes home.
— — The chaplain of the Fleet. N. Y. 1881. Q.
 B 1752
— — *Same.* New ed. Lond. 1884. D. **B 1752**
— — The golden butterfly ; a novel. New ed.
 Lond. 1877. D. **B 1763**
— — The monks of Thelema ; a novel. New ed.
 Lond. [1880]. D. **B 1764**
— — My little girl. New ed. Lond. [1877]. D.
 B 1765
— — Ready - money Mortiboy ; a matter-of-fact
 story. New ed. Lond. [1877]. D. **B 1761**
— — *Same.* Leipz. 1884. 2 v. in 1. S. **B 1761**
— — The seamy side ; a novel. New ed. Lond.
 [1881]. D. **B 1766**
— — So they were married. N. Y. 1882. Q.
 B 1756
— — Sweet Nelly, my heart's delight. N. Y. 1879.
 Q. **B 1753**
— — The ten years' tenant. *In* **Tales** from many
 sources. **T 178 v4**
— — *Same*, and other stories. New ed. Lond.
 [1882]. D. **B 1767**
 Includes, Sweet Nelly, my heart's delight.—Over
 the sea with a sailor.
— — This son of Vulcan. New ed. Lond. [1878].
 D. **B 1768**
— — 'Twas in Trafalgar's bay, and other stories.
 New ed. Lond. [1880]. D. **B 1769**
 Includes, Shepherds all and maidens fair.—Such a
 good man.—Le chien d'or.
— — With harp and crown. Bost. 1876. O.
 B 1754
— — *Same.* New ed. Lond. [1877]. D. **B 1754**
Betham - Edwards, Matilda Barbara, *see* **Ed-
wards**, Matilda Barbara Betham-.
Bethune, Alexander. The ghost of Gairyburn.
 In **Wilson**, J. M. Tales of the borders.
 W 2202 v11
— The ghost of Howdy Craigs. *In the same.*
 W 2202 v11
— The warning. *In the same.* **W 2202 v15**
— The young laird. *In the same.* **W 2202 v3**
Bethune, G: Washington. The ambassador in
 spite of himself. *In* **Maga** stories. **P 2801**
Bethune, J. The bewildered student. *In* **Wil-
son**, J: M. Tales of the borders.
 W 2203 v3
— *Same. In the same.* **W 2203 v10**
Bethusy-Huc, Valeska *gräfin,* (*Moritz v. Rei-
chenbach*). Die Eichhofs. N. Y. 1881. D.
 R 801
— *Same, eng.* The Eichhofs. From the german
 by mrs. A. L. Wister. Phila. 1881. D.
 R 801
Beyer, Conrad, (*C. Byr*). Arja ; die schönsten
 sagen aus Indien und Iran. Leipz. 1872. D.
 B 1801
 Contents, see Deutscher katalog, p. 50.
Biart, Lucien. Adventures of a young naturalist;
 ed. and adapted by Parker Gillmore. Ill.
 N. Y.. *n. d.* D. **Bx 701**

Bibra, Ernst *freiherr* v. Erlebtes und geträum-
 tes ; novellen und erzählungen. Jena.
 1867. 3 v. in 1. S. **B 1851**
 Contents, see Deutscher katalog, p. 50.
— Reiseskizzen und novellen. Jena. 1864. 4 v.
 in 2. S. **B 1852**
 Contents, see Deutscher katalog, p. 51.
— Tzarogy. Jena. 1865. S. **B 1853**
Biernatzki, J: Christoph. Die hallig, oder Die
 schiffbrüchigen auf dem eiland in der
 nordsee. Mit einer einleitung von H:
 Düntzer. Stuttg. [1881]. D. **B 1901**
— *Same, eng.* The hallig, or The sheepfold in
 the waters ; a tale of humble life on the
 coast of Schleswig. Tr. by mrs. G. P.
 Marsh, with a biog. sketch of the author.
 Bost. 1857. D. **B 1901**
Bigot, Mary, *born* Healy, (*Jeanne Mairet*). A
 mere caprice. Chicago. 1882. T. **B 1926**
Bikelas, D. Loukis Laras ; reminiscences of a
 chiote merchant during the greek war of
 independence. From the greek by J.
 Genadius. N. Y. 1881. S. **B 1951**
Binzer, Emilie v., (*Ernst Ritter*). Charaktere ;
 erzählungen. Prag. 1855. T. **P 1826**
Bird, Robert Montgomery. Calavar ; a ro-
 mance of Mexico. *T. p. w.* D. **B 2001**
— *Same, germ.* Calavar, oder Der ritter der er-
 oberung ; ein roman aus Mexico. Bearb.
 von W: Weber. St. Louis. 1848. D.
 B 2001
— The infidel, or The fall of Mexico. Phila.
 1835. 2 v. in 1. D. **B 2002**
Bischoff, Joseph, (*Konrad von Bolanden*). Kö-
 nigin Bertha ; historischer roman aus dem
 11. jahrhundert. Regensburg. 1860. S.
 B 2051
Bishop, W: H: Choy Susan, and other stories.
 Bost. 1885 [1884]. D. **B 2104**
 Includes, The battle of Bunkerloo. — Deodand.—
 Braxton's new art.—One of the thirty pieces.—Mc-
 Intyre's false face.—Miss Calderon's german.
— Detmold ; a romance. Bost. 1879. T. **B 2101**
— The house of a merchant prince ; a novel of
 New York. Bost. 1883 [1882]. D. **B 2103**
— One of the thirty pieces. *In* **Stories** by ameri-
 can authors. **S 35 v1**
Bitzius, Albert, (*Jeremias Gotthelf*). Wealth and
 welfare. Lond. 1876. 2 v. D. **B 2076**
Björnson, Björnstjerne. Arne. Tr. from the
 norse by Rasmus B. Anderson. Bost. 1881.
 D. **B 2153**
— *Same, germ.* Deutsch von H: Helms. Berlin.
 [1861]. D. **B 2153**
— Bauern - novellen. Aus dem norwegischen
 von Edmund Lobedanz. Leipz. *n. d.* D.
 B 2154
 Contents, see Deutscher katalog, p. 51.
— The bridal march, and other stories. From the
 norse by Rasmus B. Anderson. Author's
 ed. Ill. Bost. 1882. D. **B 2160**
 Includes, Thrond.—A dangerous wooing.—The bear-
 hunter.—The father.—The eagle's nest.—Blakken.—
 Fidelity.—A problem of life.
— Der brautmarsch, und andere erzählungen.
 Uebersetzt und eingeleitet von E. Lobe-
 danz. Stuttg. [1882]. D. **B 2157**
 Includes, Kapitän Mansana.—Eisenbahn und kirch-
 hof.
— Captain Mansana, and other stories. From the
 norse by Rasmus B. Anderson. Author's
 ed. Bost. 1882. D. **B 2159**
 Includes, The railroad and the churchyard.—Dust.

Björnson, Björnstjerne.—*Continued.*
— The fisher maiden ; a norwegian tale. From the author's german ed. by M. E. Niles. (Leisure hour ser.) N. Y. 1874. S. **B 2151**
— *Same.* Tr. from the norse by Rasmus B. Anderson. Author's ed. Bost. 1882. D. **B 2151**
— *Same, germ.* Das fischermädchen ; erzählung aus dem norwegischen leben. Hannover. [1868]. S. **B 2151**
— Giuseppe Mansana ; erzählung, dem norwegischen nacherzählt von Emil J. Jonas. Berlin. 1879. D. **B 2155**
— A happy boy. From the norse by Rasmus B. Anderson. Author's ed. Bost. 1881. D. **B 2158**
— Magnhild. From the norse by Rasmus B. Anderson. Author's ed. Bost. 1883 [1882]. D. **B 2156**
— *Same, germ.* Magnhild ; erzählung, dem norwegischen nacherzählt von Emil J. Jonas. Berlin. [1878]. D. **B 2156**
— Synnöve Solbakken. Tr. from the norse by Rasmus B. Anderson. Author's ed. Bost. 1881. D. **B 2152**
— *Same, germ.* Schön Synnöv. Nach der 4ten aufl. des originals, deutsch von H: Helms. Berlin. [1868]. D. **B 2152**
Black, W: An adventure in Thule ; a story for young people. N. Y. 1882. Q. **Bx 726**
— A daughter of Heth. Leipz. 1871. 2 v. in 1. S. **B 2202**
— The four Macnicols. Ill. N. Y. 1882. S. **Bx 727**
— Green pastures and Piccadilly. Leipz. 1877. 2 v. in 1. S. **B 2203**
— *Same.* N. Y. 1878. O. **B 2203**
— In silk attire. Leipz. 1872. 2 v. in 1. S. **B 2204**
— Judith Shakespeare, her love affairs and other adventures ; a novel. Ill. N. Y. 1884. D. **B 2218**
— *Same.* N. Y. 1884. Q. **B 2218**
— Kilmeny. Leipz. 1874. S. **B 2205**
— Lady Silverdale's sweetheart, and other stories. Leipz. 1876. S. **B 2206**
Includes, The marriage of Moira Fergus.—The man who was like Shakspeare.—The highlands of the city.—The strange house of Loch Suainabahl.
— Macleod of Dare. Leipz. 1878. 2 v. in 1. S. **B 2207**
— *Same.* N. Y. 1879. D. **B 2207**
— Madcap Violet. Leipz. 1877. 2 v. in 1. S. **B 2208**
— *Same.* N. Y. 1877. S. **B 2208**
— The maid of Killena, and other stories. Leipz. 1875. S. **B 2209**
Includes, Queen Tita's wager.—A fight for a wife.— The true legend of a billiard club.—A sequel to the same.
— *Same.* N. Y. 1875. O. **B 2209**
— The monarch of Mincing Lane. Ill. N. Y. 1877. O. **B 2210**
— A princess of Thule. Leipz. 1874. 2 v. in 1. S. **B 2211**
— *Same.* N. Y. 1874. O. **B 2211**
— Queen Tita's wager. *In* Tales from many sources. **T 178 v3**
— Shandon bells ; a novel. N. Y. 1883. D. **B 2216**
— *Same.* N. Y. 1883. Q. **B 2216**

Black, W:—*Continued.*
— The strange adventures of a phaeton. Leipz. 1872. 2 v. in 1. S. **B 2212**
— *Same.* With his A princess of Thule. *in* **B 2211**
— Sunrise ; a story of these times. N. Y. 1881. D. **B 2213**
— *Same.* N. Y. 1881. Q. **B 2213**
— That beautiful wretch ; a Brighton story. N. Y. 1881. D. **B 2201**
— Three feathers. Leipz. 1875. 2 v. in 1. S. **B 2214**
— White wings ; a yachting romance. Ill. N. Y. 1880. D. **B 2215**
— *Same.* Chicago. 1881. D. **B 2215**
— Yolande ; a novel. N. Y. 1883. D. **B 2217**
— *Same.* N. Y. 1883. Q. **B 2217**
Blackburn, W: M. Geneva's shield ; a story of the swiss reformation. N. Y. 1868. D. **B 2236**
Blackburne, E. Owens, *pseud., see* Casey, Elizabeth.
Blackford, M. Arthur Monteith ; a sequel to "The scottish orphans." *With her* The scottish orphans. **Bx 752**
— The Eskdale herd-boy ; a scottish tale for the instruction and amusement of young persons. 1st amer. ed. N. Y. 1828. T. **Bx 751**
— The scottish orphans ; founded on a historical fact. New ed. Phila. 1874. S. **Bx 752**
— The young artist. Lond. 1825. D. **B 2251**
— The young west indian. *With her* The scottish orphans. **Bx 752**
Blackmore, R: Doddridge. Alice Lorraine ; a tale of the South Downs. N. Y. 1875. O. **B 2301**
— *Same.* 6th ed. rev. Lond. 1877. D. **B 2301**
— Christowell ; a Dartmoor tale. N. Y. 1881. Q. **B 2307**
— *Same.* Lond. 1882. D. **B 2307**
— Clara Vaughan ; a novel. N. Y. 1880. Q. **B 2302**
— *Same.* 8th ed. Lond. 1883. D. **B 2302**
— Cradock Nowell ; a tale of the New Forest. N. Y. 1866. O. **B 2303**
— *Same.* Rev. 8th ed. Lond. 1883. D. **B 2303**
— Cripps the carrier ; a woodland tale. 3d ed. Lond. 1877. D. **B 2308**
— Erema, or My father's sin. N. Y. 1877. O. **B 2304**
— *Same.* Ill. Lond. 1880. D. **B 2304**
— Lorna Doone ; a romance of Exmoor. N. Y. n. d. O. **B 2305**
— *Same.* Lond. 1883. D. **B 2305**
— Mary Anerley ; a Yorkshire tale. Leipz. 1880. 3 v. in 1. S. **B 2306**
— *Same.* 4th ed. Lond. 1881. D. **B 2306**
— *Same.* N. Y. 1880. Q. **B 2306**
— The remarkable history of sir Thomas Upmore, bart., M. P., formerly known as "Tommy Upmore." N. Y. 1884. S. **B 2309**
— *Same.* N. Y. 1884. S. **B 2309**
Blake, Lilian Devereux. Fettered for life, or Lord and master ; a story of today. N. Y. 1874. D. **B 2351**
Blanc, Marie Thérèse, (*Th. Bentzon*). Remorse. N. Y. 1878. D. **B 2401**
Blanche, A: The bandit. Tr. from the swedish and ed. by Selma Borg and Marie A. Brown. N. Y. 1872. O. **B 2416**

x denotes books specially adapted for children.

Blanche Seymour, by the author of "Erma's engagement." Phila. 1873. O.   **B 4**

Blaze de Bury, Marie Pauline Rose Stewart *baronin.* Falkenburg ; eine erzählung. Bremen. 1851. 3 v. S.   **B 2426**

Bleiche Toms, Der. Magdeburg. 1837. D.   **B 2**

Blicher, Steen Steensen. Novellen. Aus dem dänischen übertragen von H. Zeise. Altenburg. 1846. 2 v. S.   **B 2451**
Contents, see Deutscher katalog, p. 51.

Blind, Mathilde. Tarantella ; a romance. Bost. 1885. D.   **B 2466**

Bloomfield, J. K. Patient Susie, or Paying the mortgage, by J. K. B. Cinc. 1873. S.   **Bx 776**

Bloss, C. A. Heroines of the crusades. Auburn. [1853]. O.   **B 2476**
Contents. Adela of Blois.—Eleanor of Aquitaine. —Berengaria of Navarre.—Isabella of Angoulême.— Violante of Jerusalem.—Eleanora of Castile.

Blum, Ludoiska v., (*Ernst v. Waldow*). Hildegard ; roman. N. Y. 1881. F.   **W 226**

Blunt, Ellen Key. The Christ-born ; a christmas story. Phila. 1858. S.   **Bx 801**

Blüthgen, V: Ein friedensstörer. N. Y. 1883. F.   **B 726**

Boccaccio, Giovanni. The decameron ; including forty of its hundred novels, with an introd. by H: Morley. N. Y. 1884. D.   **B 2486**

Bodenstedt, F: Martin v. Aus deutschen gauen; erzählungen. 3te aufl. Jena. 1878. 2 v. in 1. S.   **B 2501**
Contents, see Deutscher katalog, p. 51.

— Gräfin Helene. Stuttg. 1880. T.   **B 2503**

— Das herrenhaus im Eschenwalde ; ein roman. 3te aufl. Jena. 1878. 3 v. in 2. D.   **B 2502**

— Die letzten Falkenburger ; erzählung. With Henning, F. Sein guter engel.   **H 2501**

— Vom hofe Elisabeth's und Jakob's ; erzählungen. 3te aufl. Jena. 1878. 2 v in 1. D.   **B 2504**
Contents, see Deutscher katalog, p. 51.

Bohemus, *pseud.,* see Opiz, G: Emanuel.

Böhlau, Helene. Der schöne Valentin ; novelle. *In* Vierteljährl. mag.   **V 2 v35**

Boit, Robert Apthorp. Eustis ; a novel. Bost. 1884. D.   **B 2601**

Bolanden, Konrad v., *pseud.,* see Bischoff, Joseph.

Bölte, Amalia Charlotte Elise Marianne, *known only as* Amely. Das forsthaus. Prag. 1855. T.   **B 2651**

— Frau von Staël ; biographischer roman. Wien. 1861. 3 v. in 2. T.   **B 2652**

— *Same, eng.* Madame de Staël ; an historical novel. Tr. from the german by Theodore Johnson. N. Y. 1869. D.   **B 2652**

— Eine gute versorgung. Hamburg. 1856. 2 v. S.   **B 2653**

— Maria Antonia, oder Dresden vor hundert jahren ; zeitbild. Prag. 1860. 3 v. T.   **B 2654**

Bonner, Sherwood, *pseud.,* see McDowell, Katherine Sherwood.

Boost, A., *ed.* Sammlung moralischer erzählungen für Deutschlands söhne und töchter. Augsburg. n. d. D.   **A 953**
Contents. Bouilly, J: N: Der kleine savoyarde; Ueber die gefahren an den thüren zu lauschen; Das testament. — Der kirschenstrauss.—Die kirschen.— Hungari, A. Heiliger schutz. — Kindlicher liebe

wird immer ihr lohn.—Schubert, H: v. Des vaters segen bauet den kindern häuser.—Ebersberg, J. S. So bin ich reich geworden.—Bouilly, J: N: Schreckliches opfer kindlicher liebe.—Der glücklich gewählte beruf.—Franciskus Xaverius.

Borg, Selma, *and* Marie A. **Brown,** *trans.* Northern lights ; stories from swedish and finnish authors. Ill. Phila. 1873. D.   **Bx 851**

Borrow, G: Lavengro ; the scholar, the gipsy, the priest. N. Y. 1857. O.   **B 2751**

— The Romany rye ; a sequel to "Lavengro". N. N. 1859. O.   **B 2752**

Bothmer, Minny *gräfin* v., *born* Young. Aut Cæsar aut nihil ; a novel. N. Y. 1883. Q.   **B 2776**

— *Same.* Lond. 1883. 3 v. in 1. D.   **B 2776**

Boucicault, Dion, *joint author, see* Reade, C:

Boulger, Dora, *born* Havers, (*Theo Gift*). An innocent maiden ; a story. Lond. 1883. D.   **H 1905**

— Maid Ellice. (Leisure hour ser.) N. Y. 1878. S.   **H 1901**

— A matter-of-fact girl. (Leisure hour ser.) N. Y. 1881. S.   **H 1902**

— Pretty miss Bellew. (Leisure hour ser.) N. Y. 1875. S.   **H 1903**

— Visited on the children. N. Y. 1881. Q.   **H 1904**

Bourdin, H:, *pseud., see* Heyne, C: Traugott.

Bourdin, L:, *pseud., see* Heyne, C: Traugott.

Bourier, F. Frederico und Alfonso, oder Die macht des gewissens ; eine erzählung für die gesammte edlere lesewelt, besonders für die reifere jugend. Cincinnati. 1857. S.   **B 2826**

Boyesen, Hjalmar Hjorth. A daring fiction. *In* Stories by american authors.   **S 35 v10**

— A daughter of the philistines. (No name ser.) Bost. 1883. S.   **B 2857**

— Falconberg. N. Y. 1879. D.   **B 2851**

— Gunnar ; a tale of norse life. N. Y. 1880. D.   **B 2852**

— *Same, germ.* Gunnar ; eine erzählung aus dem norwegischen leben. In autorisirter übersetzung von Paul Jüngling. Breslau. 1880. D.   **B 2852**

— Ilka on the hill-top, and other stories. N. Y. 1881. D.   **B 2853**
Includes, Annunciata.—Under the glacier.—A knight of Dannebrog.—Mabel and I ; a philosophical fairy tale.—How Mr. Storm met his destiny.

— A norseman's pilgrimage. N. Y. 1875. S.   **B 2854**

— Queen Titania. N. Y. 1881. S.   **B 2856**
Includes, The mountain's face.—A dangerous virtue.

— Tales from two hemispheres. N. Y. 1881. S.   **B 2855**
Contents. The man who lost his name.—The story of an outcast.—A good for nothing.—A scientific vagabond. — Truls the nameless. —Asathor's vengeance.

Boyle, F: A good hater ; a novel. N. Y. 1885. Q.   **B 2876**

Boys' and girls' book of enchantment, The. Lond. 1881. O.   **Bx 75**

Boz, *pseud., see* Dickens, C: J: Huffam.

Brachvogel, Albert Emil. Aus dem mittelalter ; historische erinnerungen. Leipz. 1873. D.   **B 2901**
Contents, see Deutscher katalog, p. 52.

— Benoni. Leipz. 1864. 3 v. S.   **B 2902**

— Der deutsche Michael. Berlin. 1868. 4 v. S.   **B 2903**

x denotes books specially adapted for children.

Brachvogel, Albert Emil.—*Continued.*
— Der fliegende holländer. Berlin. 1871. 4 v. in
2. S. **B 2905**
— Hamlet. Breslau. 1867. 3 v. S. **B 2906**
— Historische novellen ; v. 3, 4. Jena. 1864. 2
v. S. **B 2907**
Contents, see Deutscher katalog, p. 52.
— Neue novellen. Breslau. 1867. 2 v. S. **B 2908**
Contents, see Deutscher katalog, p. 52.
— Ein neuer Falstaff. Leipz. 1863. S. **B 2904**
— Schubert und seine zeitgenossen ; historischer
roman. Leipz. 1864. 4 v. S. **B 2909**
— William Hogarth. Berlin. 1866. 3 v. S.
B 2910
Brackel, Ferdinande *freiin* v. Die tochter des
kunstreiters ; roman. 4te aufl. Köln. 1881.
D. **B 2951**
Braddon, Mary Elizabeth, *see* **Maxwell**, Mary
Elizabeth.
Bradley, E:, (*Cuthbert Bede*). Nearer and dearer.
T. p. w. D. **B 3001**
Brahain-Ducange, V: H: Joseph. Schloss Teu-
felslager, oder Isaurine und Jean-Pohl.
Deutsch von L. v. Alvensleben. Altenburg.
1836. 2 v. S. **D 2051**
Bramston, Mary. The thorn fortress ; a tale of
the thirty years' war. Lond. 1879. D.
Bx 876
— *joint author, see* **Awdry**, Frances.
Brandrup, Marie, (*Marie Widdern*). Auf der
Rümmingsburg. N. Y. 1881. F. **W 1701**
— Ebbe und fluth. *With* **Spielhagen**, F: In der
zwölften stunde. **S 4269**
— Prinzessin Schnee ; roman. N. Y. 1882. F.
W 1702
Braun, Isabella. Lebensbilder. Stuttg. 1856. O.
B 3051
Braun, K: J:, *ritter v. Braunthal*, (*Jean Charles*).
Realisten und idealisten ; socialer roman.
Leipz. 1867. 2 v. S. **C 1001**
Braunthal, *Ritter v., see* **Braun**, K: J:
Bread-winners, The ; a social study. N. Y.
1884. S. **B 81**
Note. Now said to be written by Susan D. Nickerson.
Breier, E: Josef Kaiser ; historischer roman aus
den zeiten kaiser Josefs. Berlin. 1861. S.
B 3101
Bremer, Fredrika. Father and daughter ; a por-
traiture from the life. Phila. *n. d.* S.
B 3151
— Geschwisterleben ; roman. Aus dem schwe-
dischen übers. von Gottlob Fink. Stuttg.
1850. T. **B 3161**
— The H—. family ; Trälinnan ; Axel and Anna,
and other tales. Tr. by Mary Howitt. N.
Y. 1875. O. **B 3152**
— *Same, germ.* Die familie H. ; skizze aus dem
alltagsleben. Aus dem schwedischen übers.
von G. Fink. Stuttg. 1843. T. **B 3152**
— Hertha. Tr. by Mary Howitt. N. Y. 1856. D.
B 3153
— *Same, germ.* Hertha, oder Geschichte einer
seele ; skizze aus dem wirklichen leben.
Aus dem schwedischen. Stuttg. 1857. 2 v.
T. **B 3153**
— The home, or Family cares and family joys.
Tr. from the swedish by Mary Howitt. N.
Y. 1859. O. **B 3154**
— *Same.* N. Y. 1873. O. **B 3154**
— *Same, germ.* Das haus, oder Familiensorgen
und familienfreuden. Aus dem schwedi-
schen. Leipz. 1841. 2 v. S. **B 3154**

Bremer, Fredrika.—*Continued.*
— Life in Dalecarlia : The parsonage of Mora.
Tr. by W: Howitt. N. Y. 1873. O.
B 3155
— *Same.* Lond. 1845. S. **B 3155**
— *Same, germ.* In Dalekarlien. Aus dem schwed.
von Gottlob Fink. Stuttg. 1845. T. **B 3155**
— The midnight sun ; a pilgrimage. Tr. from
the unpubl. original by Mary Howitt. N.
Y. 1860. O. **B 3156**
— *Same.* N. Y. 1876. O. **B 3156**
— *Same, germ.* Die johannisreise, eine wallfahrt.
Aus dem schwedischen von Gottlob Fink.
Stuttg. 1849. T. **B 3156**
— *Same, germ.* Sommerreise, eine wallfahrt.
Aus dem schwedischen. Leipz. 1849. S.
B 3156
— The neighbors ; a story of every-day life. Tr.
from the swedish by Mary Howitt. N. Y.
1877. O. **B 3157**
— *Same.* Tr. by Mary Howitt, authorized amer.
ed. with the author's new preface. Phila.
n. d. D. **B 3157**
— *Same, germ.* Die nachbarn. Aus dem schwe-
dischen mit einer vorrede der verfasserin.
Leipz. 1841. 2. v. S. **B 3157**
— New sketches of every-day life : A diary ;
together with Strife and peace. Tr. by
Mary Howitt. N. Y. 1875. O. **B 3158**
— *Same, germ.* Tagebuch. Aus dem schwedi-
schen. Leipz. 1844. T. **B 3158**
— The president's daughters : pt. 1. Tr. by
Mary Howitt. N. Y. 1876. O. **B 3159**
— *Same :* pt. 2, Nina. Tr. by Mary Howitt. N.
Y. 1860. O. **B 3159**
— *Same, germ.* Die töchter des präsidenten ;
erzählung einer gouvernante. Aus dem
schwedischen übers. von G. Fink. Stuttg.
1854. T. **B 3159**
— Strife and peace, or Some scenes in Norway.
With her New sketches of every-day life.
B 3158
— *Same, germ.* Streit und friede, oder Scenen
aus Norwegen. Aus dem schwedischen
übers. von G. Fink. Stuttg. 1855. T.
B 3160
Brenglas, Adolf, *pseud., see* **Glasbrenner**,
Adolf.
Brentano, Clemens. Fairy tales. Told in eng-
lish by Kate Freiligrath Kröker. Ill. Lond.
1885. D. **Bx 1201**
Contents. Dear-my-soul.—The story of sir Skip-and-
a-jump.—The story of Niddy Noddy.—The story of
Wackembhard and his five sons.—Children's page.
Brewster, Anna H. M. Compensation, or Al-
ways a future. Phila. 1860. S. **B 3201**
— St. Martin's summer. Bost. 1866. S. **B 3202**
Briggs, C: F: Elegant Tom Dillar. *In* **Maga**
stories. **P 2801**
Bristed, C: Astor. The upper ten thousand. N.
Y. 1852. D. **B 3251**
Brock, *Mrs.* Carey. Marjory ; a study, by the
author of James Gordon's wife. N. Y. 1882.
Q. **B 3276**
Brökel, Johanna Antonie, (*Antonie Brook*).
Schutzlos aber nicht hülflos ; roman. 3te
aufl. Berlin. [1878]. D. **B 3301**
Brontë, Anne, (*Acton Bell*). Agnes Grey. New
ed., rev., with a biographical sketch of the
author, a selection from her literary re-
mains and a preface by Currer Bell. *With*
Brontë, Emily. Wuthering Heights.
B 3351

x denotes books specially adapted for children.

Bronté, Charlotte, *see* Nicholls, Charlotte.
Bronté, Emily, (*Ellis Bell*). Wuthering Heights.
New ed. rev., with a biographical notice
of the author, a selection from her literary
remains and a preface, by Currer Bell.
Leipz. 1851. 2 v. in 1. S. **B 3351**
Brook, Antonie, *pseud.*, *see* Brökel, Johanna
Antonie.
Brook, Leon. A beautiful woman ; a romance.
Lond. 1878. 2 v. in 1. D. **B 3401**
Brooks, Byron A. Those children and their
teachers ; a story of today. N. Y. 1882. S.
B 4701
Brooks, C: Shirley. The Gordian knot. *T. p. w.*
[N. Y. 186-]. O. **B 3426**
— The silver cord. Leipz. 1862. 2 v. in 1. S.
B 3427
— *Same. germ.* Ernst Adair, oder Des lebens
silberfaden. Aus dem englischen von Marie
Scott. Leipz. 1862. 3 v. S. **B 3427**
— Sooner or later. Leipz. 1868. 3 v. in 2. S.
B 3428
Brooks, Noah. The boy emigrants. Ill. N. Y.
1884. D. **Bx 901**
— The Fairport nine. N. Y. 1880. D. **Bx 902**
— Lost in the fog. *In* Stories by american
authors. **S 35 v4**
— Our baseball club, and how it won the champ-
ionship ; with an introd. by Al. G. Spald-
ing. Ill. N. Y. 1884. O. **Bx 903**
Broome, *Mrs.* Napier F., *see* Barker, Mary Anne
lady.
Brother's watchword, The. N. Y. 1875. S.
Bx 85
Brougham, J: Stories. *In his* Life, stories and
poems. **927.1 : 7**
Contents, *see under* American biography.
Broughton, Rhoda. Cometh up as a flower ; an
autobiography. Leipz. 1867. S. **B 3451**
— "Good-bye, sweetheart !" a novel. N. Y. 1872.
D. **B 3457**
— Joan. Leipz. 1876. 2 v. in 1. S. **B 3452**
— *Same.* N. Y. 1877. O. **B 3452**
— Nancy. Leipz. 1873. 2 v. in 1. S. **B 3453**
— Not wisely, but too well. Leipz. 1867. 2 v. S.
B 3454
— *Same.* N. Y. 1873. O. **B 3454**
— Second thoughts ; a novel. (Appleton's handy-
vol. ser.) N. Y. 1880. 2 v. in 1. S. **B 3455**
— Tales for christmas eve. Leipz. 1872. S.
B 3456
Contents. The truth, the whole truth and nothing
but the truth.—The man with the nose.—Behold, it
was a dream.—Poor pretty Bobby.—Under the cloak.
Brown, C: Brockden. Arthur Mervyn, or Mem-
ories of the year 1793. Phila. 1857. 2 v. in
1. D. **B 3501**
— Jane Talbot. Phila. 1857. D. **B 3502**
— Ormond, or The secret witness. Phila. 1857.
S. **B 3503**
— Wieland, or The transformation ; with a
memoir of the author. Phila. 1857. D.
B 3504
Brown, J: Marjorie Fleming, a sketch ; being
the paper entitled "Pet Marjorie ;" a story
of child-life fifty years ago. Bost. 1864. S.
B 3551
— *Same. In* Johnson, E. R. Little classics.
J 926 v10
— Rab and his friends. *In the same.* **J 926 v4**

Brownson, Orestes A: Charles Elwood, or The
infidel converted. Bost. 1840. D. **B 3601**
— The spirit-rapper ; an autobiography. Bost.
1854. S. **B 3602**
Bruckbräu, F: W: Agnes Bernauer, der engel
von Augsburg ; historisch-romantisches
zeit- und sittengemälde aus dem 15. jahrhundert. Ein deutsches volksbuch. Mün-
chen. 1854. 2 v. S. **B 3651**
Brun, Ida Brunsig *edle* v. (*I. v. Brun-Barnow*).
Falsche wege ; roman. N. Y. 1881. F.
B 3676
Brunius, Louise. Die junge wittwe in Nordland.
Aus dem schwedischen. [*Anon.*] Stuttg.
1844. 2 v. T. **J 2**
Bruno, J., *pseud.*, *see* Mengersen auf Rheder,
Joseph Bruno *graf.*
Brunton, Mary, *born* Balfour. Emmeline, with
some other pieces ; to which is prefixed a
memoir of her life, including some extracts
from her correspondence. Edinb. 1819.
D. **B 3751**
Brush, Christine Chaplin. The colonel's opera
cloak. (No name ser.) Bost. 1879. S.
B 3801
Brush, Mary E. Paul and Persis, or The revo-
lutionary struggle in the Mohawk valley.
Bost. 1883 [1882]. S. **Bx 1151**
Bryant, W: Cullen. Medfield. [*Anon.*] *In* Tales
of Glauber Spa. **T 186**
— The skeleton's cave. [*Anon.*] *In the same.*
T 186
Buchanan, Robert W: Annan water ; a romance.
N. Y. 1883. Q. **B 3854**
— *Same.* Lond. 1883. 3 v. in 1. D. **B 3854**
— A child of nature ; a romance. Lond. 1881.
3 v. in 1. D. **B 3851**
— *Same.* N. Y. 1881. Q. **B 3851**
— God and the man ; a romance. 2d ed. Lond.
3 v. in 2. D. **B 3853**
— *Same.* N. Y. 1882. Q. **B 3853**
— The new Abelard ; a romance. Lond. 1884.
3 v. in 1. D. **B 3855**
— The shadow of the sword ; a romance. N. Y.
1877. O. **B 3852**
Buchholz, Wilhelmine, *pseud.*, *see* Stinde, Julius.
Bührlen, F: L. Die prima donna ; theater-
roman. Stuttg. 1884. 2 v. S. **B 3901**
Bully, E: Roger de, (*Roger de Beauvoir*). Ruysch ;
eine holländische geschichte aus dem sie-
benzehnten jahrhundert. *In* Zitz-Halein,
K. Erzählungen und novellen. **Z 201 v2**
Bulwer-Lytton, E: G: Earle Lytton, *1st baron
Lytton*, (*Pisistratus Caxton*). Alice, or The
mysteries ; a sequel to Ernest Maltravers.
Leipz. 1842. S. **B 4001**
— *Same.* Ernest Maltravers, or The eleusinia,
pt. 2. Lond. *n. d.* D. **B 4001**
— *Same. germ.* Alice, oder Die geheimnisse ;
fortsetzung von Ernest Maltravers. Aus
dem englischen von G. Pfizer. Stuttg.
1858. 2 v. S. **B 4001**
— Arasmenes. *With his* Calderon, der höfling.
B 4002
— Calderon, the courtier. *With his* Leila, or
The siege of Granada. **B 4015**
— *Same, germ.* Calderon, der höfling. Aus dem
englischen von G. Pfizer. Stuttg. 1841.
S. **B 4002**

x denotes books specially adapted for children.

Bulwer-Lytton, E: G: Earle Lytton.—*Continued.*
— The Caxtons ; a family picture. Leipz. 1849. 2 v. in 1. S.   **B 4003**
— *Same, germ.* Die Caxtone ; ein familienge-mälde. Aus dem englischen von K. Kolb. Stuttg. 1860. S.   **B 4003**
— The coming race. Leipz. 1873. S.   **B 4004**
— *Same.* N. Y. 1871. D.   **B 4004**
— Devereux. Lond. *n. d.* S.   **B 4005**
— *Same.* Leipz. 1842. S.   **B 4005**
— *Same.* Phila. 1860. 2 v. D.   **B 4005**
— The disowned. Leipz. 1842. S.   **B 4006**
— Ernest Maltravers. Leipz. 1842. S.   **B 4007**
— *Same, germ.* Ernest Maltravers. Aus dem englischen von G. Pfizer. Stuttg. 1858. 2 v. S.   **B 4007**
  Note. For continuation, *see* Alice.
— Eugene Aram. Leipz. 1842. S.   **B 4008**
— *Same, germ.* Eugen Aram. Aus dem englischen von F. Notter. Stuttg. 1858. 2 v. S.   **B 4008**
— Eva ; a true story of light and darkness.— The ill-omened marriage, other tales and poems,—and The pilgrims of the Rhine. Leipz. 1842. S.   **B 4009**
— Falkland. Phila. *n. d.* O.   **B 4010**
— *Same. With his* Godolphin.   **B 4011**
— *Same, germ.* Falkland ; erzählung. Aus dem englischen von G. Pfizer. *With his* Cal-deron.   **B 4002**
— Godolphin. Leipz. 1842. S.   **B 4011**
— *Same, germ.* Godolphin. Aus dem englischen von G. N. Bärmann. Stuttg. 1859. S.   **B 4011**
— Harold, the last of the saxon kings. Leipz. 1848. 2 v. in 1. S.   **B 4012**
— *Same, germ.* Harold, der letzte sachsen-könig. Aus dem englischen von E. Mauch. Stuttg. 1858. S.   **B 4012**
— The haunters and the haunted, or The house and the brain. *In* Tales from Blackwood. **T 176 v10**
— *Same.* The house and the brain. *In* Johnson, E. R. Little classics.   **J 926 v2**
— Kenelm Chillingly ; his adventures and opin-ions. Leipz. 1873. 4 v. in 2. S.   **B 4013**
— *Same.* N. Y. 1875. O.   **B 4013**
— The last days of Pompeii. Leipz. 1879. S. **B 4014**
— *Same.* Phila. 1860. 2 v. D.   **B 4014**
— *Same, germ.* Die letzten tage Pompejis. Aus dem englischen von F. Notter. Stuttg. 1859. 2 v. S.   **B 4014**
— The last of the barons. Leipz. 1843. 2 v. in 1. S.   **B 4015**
— *Same.* Phila. 1884. D.   **B 4015**
— *Same.* Phila. 1861. 2 v. S.   **B 4015**
— *Same, germ.* Der letzte baron. Aus dem englischen von O. v. Czarnowski. Aachen. 1843. 4 v. S.   **B 4015**
— Leila, or The siege of Granada. Phila. 1860. S.   **B 4016**
— Lucretia, or The children of night. Leipz. 1846. 2 v. in 1. S.   **B 4017**
— *Same, germ.* Lucretia, oder Die kinder der nacht. Aus dem englischen von T. Oel-ckers. Stuttg. 1847. 2 v. T.   **B 4017**
— The maid of Malines. *In* Johnson, E. R. Little classics.   **J 926 v6**

Bulwer-Lytton, E: G: Earle Lytton.—*Continued.*
— My novel, or Varieties in english life. Leipz. 1851. 4 v. in 2. S.   **B 4018**
— *Same, germ.* Meine novelle, oder Wechselfor-men im englischen leben. Aus dem engli-schen von C. Kolb. Stuttg. 1852. 2 v. S.   **B 4018**
— Night and morning Leipz. 1843. S. **B 4019**
— *Same.* Phila. 1862. 2 v. S.   **B 4019**
— *Same, germ.* Nacht und morgen. Aus dem englischen von G. Pfizer. Stuttg. 1858. 2 v. S.   **B 4019**
— The parisians. Leipz. 1873. 4 v. in 2. S. **B 4020**
— *Same.* N. Y. 1874. O.   **B 4020**
— Paul Clifford. Leipz. 1842. S.   **B 4021**
— *Same, germ. T. p. w.* T.   **B 4021**
— Pausanias, the spartan ; an unfinished histori-cal romance, ed. by his son. Leipz. 1876. S.   **B 4022**
— *Same.* Phila. 1876. D.   **B 4022**
— Pelham, or The adventures of a gentleman. Portrait. Leipz. 1842. S.   **B 4023**
— *Same.* Lond. *n. d.* S.   **B 4023**
— *Same, germ.* Pelham, oder Abenteuer eines gentleman. Aus dem englischen. Stuttg. 1858. 2 v. S.   **B 4023**
— The pilgrims of the Rhine. Lond. 1854. D. **B 4024**
— *Same. With his* Eva.   **B 4009**
— Rienzi, the last of the roman tribunes. Leipz. 1842. S.   **B 4025**
— *Same.* Lond. *n. d.* S.   **B 4025**
— *Same, germ.* Rienzi. Aus dem englischen. Aachen. 1836. 3 v. S.   **B 4025**
— A strange story. Leipz. 1861. 2 v. in 1. S.   **B 4026**
— What will he do with it ? *T. p. w.* 2 v. D. **B 4027**
— *Same.* Leipz. 1857. 4 v. in 2. S.   **B 4027**
— Zanoni. Leipz. 1842. S.   **B 4028**
— *Same.* Lond. *n. d.* D.   **B 4028**
— *Same.* Phila. 1862. D.   **B 4028**
— *Same, germ.* Zanoni. Aus dem englischen. Aachen. 1842. 3 v. S.   **B 4028**

Bulwer-Lytton, E: Robert, *1st earl of Lytton,* (*Owen Meredith*). The ring of Amasis, from the papers of a german physician. N. Y. 1863. D.   **B 4051**
Bulwer-Lytton, Rosina Doyle, *born* Wheeler, *lady Lytton.* The budget of the Bubble family. N. Y. 1840. 2 v. D.   **B 4076**
Bunbury, Selina. Sir Guy D'Esterre. Lond. 1858. 2 v. D.   **B 4101**
Bunce, Oliver Bell. The adventures of Timias Terrystone. N. Y. 1885. S.   **B 4116**
Bungener, Laurence L: Felix. The preacher and the king, or Bourdaloue in the court of Louis XIV ; an account of the pulpit eloquence of that distinguished era. Tr. from the french, with an introd. by G: Potts. New ed. rev., with a likeness and a biographical sketch of the author. Bost. 1855. D.   **B 4126**
Bunner, H: C. Love in old cloathes. *In* Stories by american authors.   **S 35 v4**
— A woman of honor. Bost. 1883. S.   **B 4751**
— *joint author, see* **Matthews**, James Brander.
Buntline, Ned, *pseud., see* **Judson**, E: Z. C.

Burdett, C: Never too late. N. Y. 1862. S.
  Bx 951
— The second marriage, or A daughter's trials ;
  a domestic tale of New York. N. Y. 1856.
  S.   **B 4201**
Burnett, Frances, born Hodgson. Dolly; a love
  story. Phila. [1877]. D.   **B 4251**
— A fair barbarian. Bost. 1881. S.   **B 4252**
— Haworths. N. Y. 1879. D.   **B 4253**
— Kathleen ; a love story. Phila. 1878. D.
  B 4254
— Lindsay's luck. N. Y. 1878. S.   **B 4255**
— Louisiana. N. Y. 1880. D.   **B 4256**
— Pretty Polly Pemberton. N. Y. 1878. S.
  B 4257
— A story of the latin quarter. In Stories by
  american authors.   **S 35 v3**
— That lass o' Lowrie's. N. Y. 1877. D. **B 4258**
— Theo ; a love story. Phila. 1877. S. **B 4259**
— Through one administration. Bost. 1883. D.
  B 4260
Burney, Frances, see Arblay, Frances d'.
Burnham, Clara Louise, born Root, (Edith
  Douglas). Dearly bought; a novel. Ill.
  Chicago. 1884. D.   **B 4303**
— "No gentlemen". [Anon.] Chicago. 1881. D.
  B 4301
— A sane lunatic. Chicago. 1882. D.   **B 4302**
— We Von Arldens, by Edith Douglas. Chicago.
  1881. D.   **B 4304**
Burow, Julie, see Pfannenschmidt, Julie.
Bürstenbinder, Elisabeth, (E. Werner). Am
  altar ; roman. N. Y. 1882. F.   **B 4352**
— Same, eng. Bound by his vows, or At the altar.
  From the german, by J. S. L. Phila. [1874].
  S.   **B 4352**
— At a high price. See below Um hohen preis.
— Banned and blessed. See below Gebannt und
  erlöst.
— Frühlingsboten ; roman. N. Y. 1881. F.
  B 4356
— Gartenlaubenblüthen. N. Y. 1881. F. **B 4353**
— Gebannt und erlöst ; roman. N. Y. 1884. F.
  B 4358
— Same, eng. Banned and blessed. After the
  german by mrs. A. L. Wister. Phila. 1884
  [1883]. D.   **B 4358**
— Glück auf ! N. Y. 1881. F.   **B 4354**
— Ein gottesurtheil ; roman. N. Y. 1885. F.
  B 4359
— Um hohen preis ; roman in 2 b. N. Y. 1882. F.
  B 4351
— Same, eng. At a high price. Tr. by Mary
  Stuart Smith. Bost. 1879. S.   **B 4351**
— Vineta ; roman. N. Y. 1881. F.   **B 4355**
— Same, eng. Vineta, the phantom city. Tr.
  by Frances A. Shaw. Bost. 1877. S.
  B 4355
Büsching, J: Gustav, see Roscoe, T: German
  novelists.   **R 2451**
Butler, Mrs. Caroline H. The little messenger
  birds, or The chimes of the silver bells.
  Ill. Bost. 1850. S.   **Bx 1051**
  Contents. A visit to the dominions of Santa Claus.
  —The broken silver spoon.—Fanny's visit to the
  country.—The little birdsnest.—The shell baskets.—
  The little chinese boy.—Pretty Mary Fairlie.—Ber-
  tram and Theodore.—The locket.—Little Belinda.—
  Conclusion.
Butler, W: F. Red Cloud, the solitary Sioux ;
  a story of the great prairies. Bost. 1882.
  D.   **Bx 1076**

Butt, Beatrice May. Delicia. (Leisure hour
  ser.) N. Y. 1879. S.   **B 4401**
— Eugenie. (Leisure hour ser.) N. Y. 1877. S.
  B 4402
— Geraldine Hawthorne. (Leisure hour ser.)
  N. Y. 1883. S.   **B 4404**
— Hester. With Hardy, T: The distracted
  young preacher.   **H 1202**
— Miss Molly. (Leisure hour ser.) N. Y. 1876.
  S.   **B 4403**
Buxton, Bertha H. From the wings ; a novel.
  Lond. 1880. 3 v. in 1. D.   **B 4455**
— Great Grenfell gardens. Leipz. 1879. 2 v. in 1.
  S.   **B 4451**
— Nell, on and off the stage. Leipz. 1880. 2 v.
  in 1. S.   **B 4452**
— Same. Lond. 1879. 3 v. in 2. D.   **B 4452**
— Sceptre and ring. N. Y. 1881. Q.   **B 4454**
— Same. Lond. 1881. 3 v. in 2. D.   **B 4454**
— Won ! Leipz. 1878. 2 v. in 1. S.   **B 4453**
Bynner, Edwin Lassetter. Damen's ghost.
  (Round-robin ser.) Bost. 1881. S.   **B 4501**
Byr, C., pseud., see Beyer, Conrad.
Byr, Robert, pseud., see Bayer, K: Robert Em-
  merich v.
Byrrne, E. Fairfax. Entangled ; a novel. N.
  Y. 1885. Q.   **B 4802**
— A fair country maid ; a novel. N. Y. 1884. Q.
  B 4801

Cable, G: Washington. Dr. Sevier. Bost. 1885
  [1884]. D.   **C 104**
— The Grandissimes ; a story of creole life. N.
  Y. 1880. D.   **C 101**
— Madame Delphine. N. Y. 1881. D.   **C 102**
— Old creole days. N. Y. [1879.] D.   **C 103**
  Contents. Sieur George. — Tite Poulette.— Belles
  Demoiselles plantation.—Jean ah Poquelin.—Madame
  Délicieuse.—Café des exilés.—"Posson Jone."
Caddy, Mrs.—. Adrian Bright ; a novel. N. Y.
  1883. D.   **C 126**
Cadell, H. M. Ida Craven. (Leisure hour ser.)
  N. Y. 1876. S.   **C 151**
Caine, Hall. She's all the world to me ; a novel.
  N. Y. 1885. Q.   **C 166**
Caldwell, Anne Marsh-, see Marsh-Caldwell,
  Anne.
Calm, Marie, (Marie Ruhland). Durch arbeit
  frei. With Henning, F: Sein guter engel.
  H 2501
— Onkel hauptmann ; erzählung. In Viertel-
  jährl. mag.   **V 2 v33**
Cameron, Mrs. H. Lovett. A north country
  maid ; a novel. N. Y. 1884. Q.   **C 176**
Campbell, Alexander. [Tales]. In Wilson, J:
  M. Tales of the borders.   **W 2202**
  Contents. The assassin, v 18.—Autobiography of
  Willie Smith, v. 3.—Chatelard, v. 9.—The countess of
  Cassilis, v. 16.—The countess of Winstonbury, v. 1.—
  The curate of Govan, v. 15.—The curse of Scotland,
  v. 19.—The disasters of Johnny Armstrong, v. 14.—
  Doctor Dobbie, v. 21. — Donald Gorm, v. 2. — The
  dream, v. 13.—Duncan McArthur, v. 8.—The Floshend
  inn, v. 13.—The gipsy, v. 12.—The foundling at sea,
  v. 18.—The good man of Dryfield, v. 8.—Grace Cameron, v. 16.—The Hawick spate, v. 19.—The highland
  boy, v. 5.—A highland tradition, v. 17.—The Katheran,
  v. 4.—Lady Rae, v. 22.—The laird of Lucky's How,
  v. 9. — Leein Jamie Murdieston, v. 8. — The lord of
  Hermitage, v. 19.—The merchant's daughter, v. 21.—
  The monk of St. Anthony, v. 4.—The monks of Dry-
  burg, v. 4.—The mosstrooper, v. 12.—Rattling, roaring Willie, v. 5.—The penny wedding, v. 7.—The recluse, v. 17.—Retribution, v. 14.—The rival night caps,
  v. 3.—The Skean Dhu, v. 14.—The snow storm of 1825,
  v. 6.—The stonebreaker, v. 18.—The surtout, v. 11.—
  The two comrades, v. 11.

x denotes books specially adapted for children.

44

Campbell, Harriette. Self-devotion, or The history of Katherine Randolph ; ed. by J. R. Gleig. N. Y. 1842. O. **C 201**

Campbell, Helen. Under green apple boughs. N. Y. 1882. D. **C 226**
— The what-to-do club ; a story for girls. Bost. 1885. D. **C 227**

Cantacuzène-Altieri, Olga *princesse*. Poverina. Tr. from the french. N. Y. 1881. S. **C 251**
— Sabine's falsehood, (Le mesonge de Sabine) ; a love story. Tr. from the Revue des deux mondes, by Mary Neal Sherwood. Phila. [1881]. S. **C 252**

Canz, Elisabeth. Eritis sicut Deus. [*Anon.*] Hamburg. 1855. S. **C 301**

Capron, Carrie. Helen Lincoln. *T. p. w.* S. **C 351**

Carey, Annie. School-girls, or Life at Montagu Hall. N. Y. [1881]. D. **Cx 101**

Carey, Rosa Nouchette. Nellie's memories ; a novel. Phila. 1880. D. **C 401**
— Not like other girls ; a novel. Phila. 1884. S. **C 404**
— Queenie's whim. Phila. 1881. D. **C 402**
— Robert Ord's atonement ; a novel. Phila. 1885. S. **C 405**
— Wooed and married. *T. p. w.* [Phila. 1876.] D. **C 403**

Carion, Franz, *pseud.*, *see* Lubojatsky, Franz.

Carlén, Emilie Flygare-, *born* Schmidt. Die braut auf dem Omberg. Aus dem schwedischen. Stuttg. 1857. S. **C 501**
— Gustavus Lindorm, or "Lead us not into temptation" ; with a preface to her american readers by the author. From the original swedish by Elbert Perce. N. Y. 1853. D. **C 502**
— *Same, germ.* Gustav Lindorm, oder Führe uns nicht in versuchung ! Aus dem schwedischen. Stuttg. 1857. T. **C 502**
— Ein handelshaus in den scheeren. Aus dem schwedischen von G. Fink. Stuttg. *n. d.* 3 v. S. **C 503**
— Ivar, or The skjuts-boy. From the original swedish by A. L. Krause. N. Y. 1859. O. **C 504**
— *Same, germ.* Der skutsjunge. Aus dem schwedischen. Stuttg. *n. d.* S. **C 504**
— Kammerer Lassman als alter junggeselle und ehemann. Aus dem schwedischen Stuttg. *n. d.* S. **C 505**
— Die kircheinweihung von Hammarby. Aus dem schwedischen. Stuttg. 1857. T. **C 506**
— Der stellvertreter ; ein humoristisches familiengemälde. Aus dem schwedischen. Stuttg. 1844. T. **C 507**
— Waldemar Klein. Aus dem schwedischen. Stuttg. 1857. S. **C 509**

Carleton, *pseud.*, *see* Coffin, C: Carleton.

Carleton, Cousin May, *pseud.*, *see* Fleming, M. A.

Carleton, W: Art Maguire, or The broken pledge. N. Y. 1853. T. **C 551**
— Black prophet ; a tale of irish famine. Belfast. 1847. S. **C 552**
— Neal Malone. *In* Johnson, E. R. Little classics. **J 926 v5**
— The poor scholar, and other tales of irish life. N. Y. 1880. S. **C 555**
Includes, A peasant girl's love.—Talbot and Gaynor, the irish pipers.—Frank Finnegan, the foster brother.
— Redmond count O'Hanlon, the irish rapparee ; an historical tale. Dublin. 1862. T. **C 556**

Carleton, W:—*Continued.*
— Traits and stories of the irish peasantry. Complete ed. Lond. *n. d.* D. **C 554**
Contents. Ned M'Keown.—The three tasks.—Shane Fadh's wedding. — Larry M'Farland's wake. — The battle of the factions.—The party fight and funeral. — The hedge school. — The station. — The midnight mass.—The Donagh.—Phil Purcell, the pig-driver.— The Lianhan Shee.—The geography of an irish oath. —An essay on irish swearing.—The poor scholar. —Wildgoose lodge.—Tubber Derg.—Dennis O'Shaughnessy going to Maynooth.—Phelim O'Toole's courtship.
— Valentine M'Clutchy, the irish agent, or The chronicles of Castle Cumber, together with the pious aspirations, permissions, vouchsafements and other sanctified privileges of Solomon M'Slime, a religious attorney. N. Y. 1854. D. **C 553**

Carlton, Robert, *pseud.*, *see* Hall, Baynard Rust.

Carpenter, Frank De Yeaux. Round about Rio. Chicago. 1884 [1883]. D. **C 576**

Carpenter, W: H. The regicide's daughter ; a tale of two worlds. Phila. 1854. T. **C 601**

Carr, Alice Comyns. Paul Crew's story. N. Y. 1885. S. **C 616**

Carrington, Katie. Aschenbroedel. (No name ser.) Bost. 1882. S. **C 3801**

Caruthers, W: A. The knights of the horse-shoe ; a traditionary tale of the cocked hat gentry in the Old Dominion. N. Y. 1882. Q. **C 626**

Cary, Alice. Clovernook children. Ill. N. Y. *n. d.* D. **Cx 151**
— Snowberries ; a book for young folks. Ill. N. Y. *n. d.* D. **Cx 152**

Casey, Elizabeth, (*E. Owens Blackburne*). The glen of silver birches. N. Y. 1881. Q. **C 651**

Cashel-Hoey, Frances Sarah, *see* Hoey, Frances Sarah Cashel-.

Casseday, D. B. The Hortons, or American life at home. *T. p. w.* S. **C 676**

Castle, Chartley. John Woodburn, royal navy. Lond. 1861. D. **C 701**

Catherwood, Mary Hartwell. Craque-o'-doom ; a story. Phila. 1881. D. **C 726**
— Old caravan days. Ill. Bost. [1884]. D. **Cx 176**

Caustic, Mrs., *pseud.* Matrimony, or Love affairs in our village twenty years ago. *T. p. w.* [N. Y. 1853]. S. **C 751**

Caxton, Pisistratus, *pseud.*, *see* Bulwer-Lytton, E: G: E. L.

Cervantes-Saavedra, Miguel de. Don Quixote de la Mancha. Tr. from the spanish. Phila. 1876. D. **C 801**
— *Same, germ.* Leben und thaten des scharfsinnigen edlen Don Quixote von la Mancha. Uebers. von J: L: Tieck. Berlin. 1860. 2 v. T. **C 801**
— *Same.* The story of Don Quixote and his squire Sancho Panza, by M. Jones. Lond. 1880. D. **Cx 176**
— Moralische novellen. Uebers. von A. v. Keller und F. Notter. Stuttg. 1881. D. **C 802**
Contents, see Deutscher katalog, p. 54.

Chalmers, Alexander. Lesson in biography, or How to write the life of one's friend. *In* Sargent, E. The emerald. **S 551**

Chamberlain, C: The servant-girl of the period, the greatest plague of life ; what mr. and mrs. Honeydew learned of housekeeping. N. Y. 1873. D. **C 851**

x denotes books specially adapted for children.

Chamberlain, Nathan H: The autobiography of a New England farm-house. N. Y. 1865. D.   C 876
Chamberlain, W: Manuela Paredes. (No name ser.) Bost. 1881. S.   C 901
Chambers, Julius. On a margin. [*Anon.*] N. Y. 1884. D.   C 926
Chamisso, L: C: Adelbert v. Peter Schlemihl's wundersame geschichte. *In his* Werke.
                                               830: 133 v2
— *Same, eng.* The wonderful history of Peter Schlemihl. *In* Hedge, F: H: Prose writers of Germany.   830.1 : 8
Champney, Lizzie, *born* Williams. The heartbreak cameo. *In* Stories by american authors.   S 35 v6
Chaney, G: L. F. Grant and co., or Partnerships; a story for the boys who "mean business." Bost. 1875. S.   Cx 201
Chaplin, Heman W., (*C. H. White*). The village convict. *In* Stories by american authors.
                                                S 35 v6
Chapone, Hester, *born* Mulso. The history of Fidelia. *In* Hawkeshurst, J: The adventurer. nos. 77–79.   824.2 : 100
Charles, Elizabeth, *born* Rundle. Against the stream; the story of a heroic age in England. N. Y. 1873. D.   C 951
— The Bertram family. N. Y. *n. d.* D. C 952
— Chronicles of the Schönberg-Cotta family, by two of themselves. N. Y. 1864. S.   C 953
— *Same, germ.* Die familie Schönberg-Cotta; ein charakter- und sittengemälde aus der reformationszeit. Autorisirte übersetzung aus dem englischen von Charlotte Philippi. 7te aufl. Basel. 1880. S.   C 953
— Conquering and to conquer. N. Y. *n. d.* D.
                                                 C 954
— The early dawn, or Sketches of christian life in England in the olden time: with an introd. by H: B. Smith. N. Y. 1865. D.
                                                 C 955
  Contents. Lights and shadows of the early dawn.— Two martyrs of Verulam.— Annals of an anglo-saxon family through three generations: The conversion of Northumbria; Saxon schools and homes; Saxon ministers and missions. — Alfred the truth teller.—Saxon and norman.—A story of the lollards.
— Joan the maid, deliverer of France and England; a story of the 15th century, done into the modern english by the author of "Chronicles of the Schönberg-Cotta family." N. Y. 1879. D.   C 956
— Lapsed, but not lost; a story of roman Carthage. Leipz. 1878. S.   C 957
— The martyrs of Spain and the liberators of Holland. *T. p. w.* S.   C 958
— On both sides of the sea; a story of the commonwealth and the restoration; a sequel to "The Draytons and the Davenants." N. Y. 1868. D.   C 959
— Tales and sketches of christian life in different lands and ages. N. Y. 1865. S. C 960
  Contents. Maia and Cleon; a tale of the egyptian church in the 3rd century.— Sketches from the history of the reformation in Italy.—Extracts from the diary of brother Bartholomew, a monk in the abbey of Marienthal in the Odenwald in the 12th century.— Sketches of the united brethren of Bohemia and Moravia.
— The two vocations, or The sisters of mercy at home; a tale. [*Anon.*] N. Y. 1865. S.
                                                 C 961
— Winifred Bertram, and the world she lived in. N. Y. 1866. D.   C 962

Charles, Jean, *pseud.*, *see* Braun, K: J:, *ritter v.* Braunthal.
Charlesworth, Maria Louisa. Ministering children. N. Y. 1877. D.   Cx 251
— *Same*; a sequel. N. Y. 1877. D.   Cx 252
Charm, The; an illustrated book for boys and girls. Bost. *n. d.* S.   Cx 21
  Contents. Annie Grant's playmates.—"Little children, love one another." — The robins. — Grateful Dick.—Little Lilias.—A narrow escape.—Prince Goldfish and the fishermaid.—Katie Lee; a scotch story.— Tea-kettle's concert. — The tame gemze.—Clara and her brother.—The old wizard and his children.—Gold-Maria and Pitch-Maria.—The unjust judge.—A story for those who never know when to be satisfied. — The witch and the kings's children.
Chateaubriand, René François A: de. Atala. Paris. 1859. D.   C 1051
  Contents. Atala.—René.—Les aventures du dernier Abencerage.—Voyage en Amérique.
Chatterjee, Bankim Chandra. The poison tree; a tale of hindu life in Bengal. Tr. by Miriam S. Knight, with a preface by Edwin Arnold. Lond. 1884. D.   C 1076
Cheadle, Walter B. My hunt of the silver fox. *In* Tales from Blackwood.   T 177 v10
Cheever, G: Barrell. The pilgrim in the shadow of the Jungfrau alp. N. Y. 1846. S. *With* Hall, James. The wilderness and the warpath.   H 701
Cheever, H: T. A reel in a bottle for Jack in the doldrums; the adventures of two of the king's seamen in a voyage to the celestial country, ed. from the manuscripts of an old salt. N. Y. 1852. D.   C 1101
Cheney, Ednah Dean. Sally Williams, the mountain girl. Bost. [1872]. S.   Cx 301
Cherbuliez, V: Count Kostia; a novel. Tr. from the french by O. D. Ashley. (Leisure hour ser.) N. Y. 1873. S.   C 1151
— Jean Têterol's idea. N. Y. 1878. D.   C 1152
— Joseph Noirel's revenge. Tr. from the french by W: F. West. (Leisure hour ser.) N. Y. 1873. S.   C 1153
— Meta Holdenis. N. Y. 1877. D.   C 1154
— Prosper. Tr. from the french by C: Benson. (Leisure hour ser.) N. Y. 1874. S. C 1155
— Saints and sinners, (Noirs et rouges). From the french by Mary Neal Sherwood. N. Y. 1881. O.   C 1155
— Samuel Brohl and company. N. Y. 1878. D.
                                                 C 1156
— A stroke of diplomacy. From the french. N. Y. 1880. S.   C 1157
Chesebro', Caroline. Dream-land by day-light. *T. p. w.* D.   C 1201
— The foe in the household. Bost. 1871. O.
                                                 C 1202
— Isa; a pilgrimage. N. Y. 1852. D.   C 1203
— Victor and Jacqueline. *In* Atlantic tales.
                                                 A 1876
Chesney, G: The battle of Dorking, or Reminiscences of a volunteer, by an eye-witness in 1925. New ed. Ill. Phila. [1885]. D.   C 1226
— *Same. In* Tales from Blackwood.   T 177 v2
— The private secretary; a novel. [*Anon.*] N. Y. 1881. Q.   C 1227
— *Same.* Edinb. 1881. D.   C 1227
Chevalier, H: Émile. Thirty-nine men for one woman; an episode of the colonization of Canada. Tr. from the french by E. I. Sears. N. Y. [1860]. D.   C 1251

x denotes books specially adapted for children.

Child, Lydia Maria, *born* Francis. Autumnal leaves; tales and sketches in prose and rhyme. N. Y. 1857. S.　　　**C 1301**

— Fact and fiction; a collection of stories. N. Y. 1849. D.　　　**C 1302**

— Philothea; a grecian romance. N. Y. 1851. D.　　　**C 1303**

— A romance of the republic. Bost. 1867. D.　　　**C 1304**

Chowanetz, Joseph, (*Julian Chownitz*). Cöle-stine, oder Der eheliche verdacht. Leipz. 1842. 2 v. S.　　　**C 1351**

— Geld und herz. Leipz. 1842. 2 v. S.　　　**C 1352**

— Paolo; eine venezianische liebe aus der neuen zeit. Leipz. 1843. S.　　　**C 1353**

Chownitz, Julian, *pseud., see* **Chowanetz,** Joseph.

Christbaum, Der; taschenbuch zum besten der mission. 7 und 8 jahrg. Stuttg. 1845, 1846. 2 v. T.　　　**C 1**

Church, Alfred J: The chantry priest of Bar-net; a tale of the two roses. Ill. N. Y. 1885. D.　　　**C 1376**

Church, Florence *mrs.* Ross, *born* Marryat, *now mrs.* Francis **Lean.** A broken blossom. Leipz. 1879. 2 v. in 1. S.　　　**C 1401**

— The confessions of Gerald Estcourt. Leipz. 1867. 2 v. in 1. S.　　　**C 1402**

— Fighting the air. Leipz. 1875. 2 v. in 1. S.　　　**C 1403**

— Forever and ever; a drama of life. Leipz. 1866. 2 v. in 1. S.　　　**C 1404**

— *Same.* Bost. *n. d.* O.　　　**C 1404**

— A harvest of wild oats. Leipz. 1877. 2 v. in 1. S.　　　**C 1405**

— Her father's name. Leipz. 1877. 2 v. in 1. S.　　　**C 1406**

— Her lord and master. Leipz. 1871. 2 v. in 1. S.　　　**C 1407**

— Her world against a lie. Leipz. 1879. 2 v. in 1. S.　　　**C 1408**

— A little stepson. Leipz. 1878. S.　　　**C 1409**

— Love's conflict. Leipz. 1865. 2 v. in 1. S.　　　**C 1410**

— A lucky disappointment, and other stories. Leipz. 1876. S.　　　**C 1411**

Includes, The little Gordon.—Sir Marcus's choice.—Meg Hartley's cure.

— Mad Dumaresq. Leipz. 1873. 2 v. in 1. S.　　　**C 1412**

— My own child. Leipz. 1876. 2 v. in 1. S.　　　**C 1413**

— *Same.* N. Y. 1876. O.　　　**C 1413**

— Nelly Brooke; a homely story. Leipz. 1869. 2 v. in 1. S.　　　**C 1414**

— No intentions. Leipz. 1874. 2 v. in 1. S.　　　**C 1415**

— Petronel. Leipz. 1870. 2 v. in 1. S.　　　**C 1416**

— Phyllida; a life drama. Leipz. 1882. 2 v. in 1. S.　　　**C 1423**

— The poison of asps, and other stories. Leipz. 1876. S.　　　**C 1417**

Includes, The bath-chair man's story.—Plucked from the burning.—A happy accident at Brighton.

— The prey of the gods. Leipz. 1872. 2 v. in 1. S.　　　**C 1418**

— The root of all evil. Leipz. 1880. 2 v. in 1. S.　　　**C 1419**

— A star and a heart. Leipz. 1876. S.　　　**C 1420**

— Under the lilies and roses; a novel. Leipz. 1884. 2 v. in 1. S.　　　**C 1424**

Church, Florence, *born* Marryat.—*Continued.*

— An utter impossibility. *With her* A star and a heart.　　　**C 1420**

— Véronique. Leipz. 1869. 2 v. in 1. S.　　　**C 1421**

— With Cupid's eyes; a novel. Leipz. 1881. 2 v. in 1. S.　　　**C 1425**

— Written in the fire. Leipz. 1878. 2 v. in 1. S.　　　**C 1422**

Churton, Henry, *pseud., see* **Tourgée,** Albion Winegar.

Claris de Florian, J: P: Numa Pompilius, second king of Rome. Tr. from the french by J. A. Ferris. Bost. 1850. D.　　　**C 3851**

— *Same.* Lond. 1813. T.　　　**C 3851**

Clark, Alexander. Starting out; a story of the Ohio hills. Phila. 1875. S.　　　**C 1451**

Clark, C: Heber, (*Max Adeler*). The fortunate island, and other stories by Max Adeler. Bost. 1882. D.　　　**C 1476**

Includes, The old fogy.—Major Dunwoody's leg.—Jinnie.

Clark, Charlotte Moore, (*Charles M. Clay*). Baby Rue [her adventures and misadventures, her friends and her enemies]. (No name ser.) Bost. 1881. S.　　　**C 1502**

— How she came into her kingdom. Chicago. 1878. D.　　　**C 1501**

— The modern Hagar; a drama. N. Y. 1882. 2 v. D.　　　**C 1503**

Clark, H. H. Boy life in the U. S. navy Ill. Bost. [1885]. D.　　　**Cx 376**

Clark, *Mrs.* S. R. Graham. Achor. Bost. [1884]. D.　　　**C 1526**

— The triple E. Bost. [1884]. D.　　　**C 1527**

Clarke, James Freeman. The legend of Thomas Didymus, the jewish sceptic. Bost. 1881. D.　　　**249:19**

Clarke, J: A. Gathered fragments. Phila. 1836. D.　　　**C 1601**

Clarke, Mary Cowden, *born* Novello. The girl-hood of Shakespeare's heroines, in a series of tales; 1st and 2d ser. N. Y. 1878. 2 v. O.　　　**C 1651**

Contents. 1st ser. Portia, the heiress of Belmont.—The thane's daughter.—Helena, the physician's orphan.—Desdemona, the magnifico's child.—Meg and Alice, the merry maids of Windsor. 2d ser. Isabella the votaress.—Katharina and Bianca, the shrew and the demure.—Ophelia, the rose of Elsinore.—Rosalind and Celia, the friends.—Juliet, the white dove of Verona.

— *Same.* 2d ser. N. Y. 1857. D.　　　**C 1651 v2**

— A rambling story. Bost. 1875. D.　　　**C 1652**

Clarke, Rebecca Sophia, (*Sophie May*). The Asbury twins. Ill. Bost. *n. d.* D.　　　**Cx 475**

— The doctor's daughter. Ill. Bost. 1872. D.　　　**Cx 478**

— Flaxie Frizzle stories. Ill. Bost. [1876—1884]. 6 v. S.　　　**Cx 469—Cx 474**

Contents. 1. Flaxie Frizzle. 2. Doctor Papa. 3. Little pitchers. 4. The twin cousins. 5. Kittyl.en. 6.' Flaxie growing up.

— Janet; a poor heiress. Ill. Bost. 1883 [1882]. S.　　　**Cx 477**

— Little Prudy series. Ill. Bost. [1863—1865]. 6 v. S.　　　**Cx 451—Cx 456**

Contents. 1. Little Prudy. 2. Sister Susy. 3. Captain Horace. 4. Cousin Grace. 5. Fairy book. 6. Dotty Dimple.

— Little Prudy's Fly-away ser. Bost. [1872, 1873]. 6 v. S.　　　**Cx 463—Cx 468**

Contents. 1. Little folks astray. 2. Prudy keeping house. 3. Aunt Madge's story. 4. Little grand mother. 5. Little grandfather. 6. Miss Thistledown.

x denotes books specially adapted for children.

Clarke, Rebecca Sophia, (*Sophie May*).—*Contin'd.*
— Our Helen. Ill. Bost. *n. d.* S.　　**Cx 479**
— *Same.* Bost. 1875. S.　　**Cx 479**
— Quinnebasset girls. Ill. Bost. 1878. S.　　**Cx 476**
Clarke, W: Three courses and a dessert ; comprising three sets of tales, west country, irish and legal, and a melange. [*Anon.*] Ill. by G: Cruikshank. Lond. 1856. S.　　**C 1676**
Clausberg, Amalie v., *pseud.*, see Donop, Amalie freiin v.
Clavers, Mary, *pseud.*, see Kirkland, Caroline Matilda.
Clay, Charles M., *pseud.*, see Clark, Charlotte Moore.
Clemens, Jeremiah. The rivals ; a tale of the times of Aaron Burr and Alexander Hamilton. Phila. 1860. S.　　**C 1751**
— Tobias Wilson. *T. p. w.* D.　　**C 1752**
Clemens, S: Langhorne, (*Mark Twain*). Adventures of Huckleberry Finn, Tom Sawyer's companion ; scene, the Mississippi valley ; time, forty to fifty years ago. [Ill.] N. Y. 1885. O.　　**Cx 503**
— The adventures of Tom Sawyer. Hartford. 1883. O.　　**Cx 501**
— *Same.* Hartford. 1884. O.　　**Cx 501**
— The prince and the pauper ; a tale for young people of all ages. Ill. Bost. 1882. O.　　**Cx 502**
— The stolen white elephant, etc. Bost. 1882. S.　　**C 1802**
Includes, Some rambling notes of an idle excursion. —The facts about the recent carnival of crime in Connecticut.—About magnanimous-incident literature.—Punch, brothers, punch.—A curious experience.—The great revolution in Pitcairn.—Mrs. McWilliams and the lightning.—On the decay of the art of lying.—The canvasser's tale.—An encounter with an interviewer.—Paris notes.—Speech of the babies.—Legend of Sagenfeld, in Germany.—Rogers.
— *and* C: Dudley **Warner.** The gilded age ; a tale of today. Ill. Hartford. 1874. O.　　**C 1801**
— — *Same.* Hartford. 1882. O.　　**C 1801**
Clement, Clara Erskine, see **Waters,** Clara.
Clemmer, Mary, see **Hudson,** Mary.
Clerke, E. M. A film of gossamer. *In* Tales from many sources.　　**T 178 v3**
Clive, Caroline *mrs.* Archer, *born* Wigley. Why Paul Ferroll killed his wife. N. Y. 1862. D.　　**C 1901**
Clodwig, *pseud.*, see Alvensleben, K: L: F: W: Gustav v.
Cobb, James F. Martin the skipper ; a tale for boys and seafaring folk. Ill. N. Y. [1883]. D.　　**Cx 526**
— The watchers on the Longships; a tale of Cornwall in the last century. N. Y. 1882. D.　　**C 1977**
— Workman and soldier ; a tale of Paris life during the siege and the rule of the commune. Ill. Lond. 1890. D.　　**C 1976**
Cockton, H: George Julian. Lond. 1866. S.　　**C 2001**
— The life and adventures of Valentine Vox the ventriloquist. Lond. *n. d.* S.　　**C 2002**
— Stanley Thorn. Lond. *n. d.* S.　　**C 2003**
Coffin, C: Carleton, (*Carleton*). Caleb Krinkle ; a story of american life. *T. p. w.* D.　　**C 2051**
— Winning his way. Bost. 1881. D.　　**Cx 601**

Coffin, Robert Barry, (*Barry Gray*). Matrimonial infelicities, with an occasional felicity by way of contrast, by an irritable man. Added, as pertinent to the subject, My neighbors and Down in the valley. N. Y. 1865. D.　　**C 2101**
Coffin, Roland T. How old Wiggins wore ship. *In* Stories by american authors.　　**S 35 v9**
Coit, Davida, *pseud.*, see Scudder, Vida D.
Colenfeld, A. v., *pseud.*, see Görling, Adolph.
Coleridge, Christabel Rose, *joint author*, see Awdry, Frances.
Coleridge, Sara, *born* Coleridge. Phantasmion ; a fairy tale ; with an introductory preface by lord Coleridge. Bost. 1874. D.　　**C 2151**
Collier, W: Francis. Tales of english life, or Pictures of the periods. Lond. 1878. D.　　**Cx 626**
Contents. Julius the centurion, [roman].—The weregild of earl Alfgar, [saxon].—How sir Eustace Crispin lost and found his hawk, [norman].—Squire Hazelrig's investment in South Sea stock, [Brunswick].
Collin, Jacques A: Simon, (*Jean de Septchênes*). Jacquemin der freimaurer, oder Die geheimen gesellschaften in Frankreich, ihre tendenzen, politischen und socialen zwecke, historischen überlieferungen, rituale, gebräuche, erkennungszeichen, ausartungen, missbräuche und verbrecherischen umtriebe ; nebst darstellung der französischen arbeiterverbindungen und gesellenschaften. 2te aufl. Grimma. 1852. S.　　**S 2501**
Collingwood, Harry. Under the meteor flag ; the log of a midshipman during the french revolutionary war. Lond. 1884. D.　　**C 2176**
Collins, W: Wilkie. After dark. Leipz. 1856. S.　　**C 2201**
— *Same,* and other stories. Ill. N. Y. 1875. D.　　**C 2228**
Includes, Miss or mrs. ?—The dead alive.—The fatal cradle. otherwise The heartrending story of mr. Heavysides.—"Blow up the brig!"—The frozen deep. —Fatal fortune.
— Antonina, or The fall of Rome ; a romance of the 5th century. Leipz. 1863. 2 v. in 1. S.　　**C 2202**
— *Same.* *T. p. w.* [N. Y. 1868]. O.　　**C 2202**
— Armadale ; a novel. Leipz. 1866. 3 v. in 2. S.　　**C 2203**
— *Same.* Ill. N. Y. *n. d.* D.　　**C 2203**
— Basil. *T. p. w.* D.　　**C 2204**
— *Same.* The crossed path, or Basil ; a story of modern life. Phila. *n. d.* D.　　**C 2204**
— The dead alive. Bost. 1874. S.　　**C 2205**
— The dead secret, and other tales. Leipz. 1857. 2 v. in 1. S.　　**C 2206**
Includes, The murder of the archbishop of Paris.— The new boy at Styles's.—How the old love fared. — Helena Mathewson.—Agnes Lee.—The yellow tiger.—My window.—A queen's revenge.—The Amphlett love match.
— *Same, germ.* Ein tiefes geheimniss. Aus dem englischen von A. Kretzschmar. Leipz. 1862. S.　　**C 2206**
— The fallen leaves. Leipz. 1879. 2 v. in 1. S.　　**C 2207**
— The frozen deep, and other stories ; readings and writings in America. Leipz. 1874. S.　　**C 2208**
Includes, The dream-woman.—John Jago's ghost, or The dead alive.
— The haunted hotel. Leipz. 1878. S.　　**C 2209**

x denotes books specially adapted for children.

Collins, W: Wilkie.—*Continued.*
— Hide and seek. Leipz. 1856. 2 v. in 1. S.
　　　　　　　　　　　　　　　C 2210
— I say no, or The love-letter answered ; a novel.
　N. Y. 1884. Q.　　　　　　　C 2227
— Jezebel's daughter. Leipz. 1880. 2 v. in 1. S.
　　　　　　　　　　　　　　　C 2211
— *Same, germ.* Isabel's tochter ; roman. *In*
　Vierteljährl. mag.　　　　V2 v21
— The law and the lady. Leipz. 1875. 2 v. in 1.
　S.　　　　　　　　　　　　C 2212
— *Same.* N. Y. 1875. D.　　　C 2212
— Man and wife. Leipz. 1870. 3 v. in 2. S.
　　　　　　　　　　　　　　　C 2213
— *Same.* N. Y. 1875. D.　　　C 2213
— *Same.* N. Y. *n. d.* D.　　　C 2213
— Miss or mrs. ? Leipz. 1872. S.　C 2214
— The moonstone. Ill. N. Y. 1871. O. C 2215
— My lady's money. Leipz. 1877. S.　C 2216
— My miscellanies. N. Y. 1874. D.　C 2217
　Note. For contents see The queen's revenge.
— The new Magdalen. Leipz. 1873. 2 v. in 1. S.
　　　　　　　　　　　　　　　C 2218
— No name. Leipz. 1863. 3 v. in 2. S. C 2219
— Percy the prophet. *With his* My lady's money.
　　　　　　　　　　　　　　　C 2216
— A plot in private life, and other tales. Leipz.
　1859. S.　　　　　　　　　　C 2220
　Includes, Mad Monkton.—The black cottage.—The
　family secret.—The biter bit.
— Poor miss Finch. Leipz. 1872. 2 v. in 1. S.
　　　　　　　　　　　　　　　C 2221
— *Same.* Ill. N. Y. 1874. D.　　C 2221
— The queen of hearts. Ill. N. Y. 1874. D.
　　　　　　　　　　　　　　　C 2222
— The queen's revenge, and other stories. Phila.
　n. d. O.　　　　　　　　　　C 2223
　Includes, Talk stoppers.—A journey in search of
　nothing.—A petition to the novel writers.—Laid up
　in lodgings.—A shockingly rude article.—The great
　(forgotten) invasion. —The unknown public. — Give
　us room ! — Portrait of an author, painted by his
　publisher. — My black mirror. — Mrs. Badgery. —
　Memoirs of an adopted son.—The bachelor bed-room.
　—A remarkable revolution.—Douglas Jerrold.—Pray
　employ major Namby!—The poisoned meal.—My
　spinsters.— Dramatic Grub street. "Explored in two
　letters.—To think, or be thought for ?—Save me from
　my friends.—The cauldron of oil.—Bold words by a
　bachelor.—Mrs. Bullwinkle.
— A rogue's life, from his birth to his marriage.
　Y. 1879. S.　　　　　　　　C 2224
— She loves and lies. *In* **Tales** from many
　sources.　　　　　　　　　T 178 v4
— The two destinies. Leipz. 1876. S.　C 2225
— The woman in white. Ill. N. Y. 1875. D.
　　　　　　　　　　　　　　　C 2226
— *Same.* Leipz. 1860. 2 v. in 1. S.　C 2226
— *Same, germ.* Die frau in weiss ; roman. Aus
　dem englischen von Marie Scott. 3te aufl.
　Leipz. 1874. 4 v. in 2. D.　　C 2226
Colombi, La marchesa, *pseud., see* **Torelli-Tor-
　riani, Maria.**
Compton, Frances Snow. Esther ; a novel. N.
　Y. 1884. S.　　　　　　　　C 3951
Conolly, Matthew Forster. Tales of the East
　Neuk of Fife. *In* **Wilson, J** : M. Tales of
　the borders.　　　　　　　W 2202 v10, 17
　Contents. 1. The castle of Crail. 2. The legend of
　the church of Abercrombie. 3. The romance of the
　May. 4. The robbery at Pittenweem. 5. The story of
　Charles Gordon.
Conscience, H: Blind Rosa. *With his* The
　conscript.　　　　　　　　C 2251
— The conscript. Tr. for this ed. Balt. *n. d.*
　D.　　　　　　　　　　　　C 2251

Conscience, H:—*Continued.*
— Count Hugo of Craenhove. Tr. from the
　original flemish. Balt. 1864. D.　C 2252
— *Same, germ.* Graf Hugo von Craenhove und
　sein freund Abulfaragus ; eine erzählung
　für die gesammte edlere lesewelt, besonders
　für die reifere jugend. Cinc. 1856. S. *With*
　Marbach, G. O., *ed.* Geschichte von der
　schönen Magelone.　　　　M 976
— The curse of the village. Balt. 1864. D.
　　　　　　　　　　　　　　　C 2253
— The happiness of being rich. Tr. from the
　original flemish. Balt. 1864. D.　C 2254
— The lion of Flanders, or The battle of the
　golden spurs. New ed. Balt. 1881. S.
　　　　　　　　　　　　　　　C 2262
— The merchant of Antwerp ; a tale. New issue.
　N. Y. 1884. D.　　　　　　　C 2261
— The miser. *With his* The conscript. C 2251
— Mutter Hiob. Aus dem flämischen von K:
　Arenz. Leipz. 1856. S.　　　C 2255
— Off to California ; a tale of the gold country.
　Adapted from the flemish by James F.
　Cobb. Ill. Lond. [1884]. D.　C 2263
— The poor gentleman. Balt. 1864. D. C 2256
— Simon Turchi, oder Die italiener in Antwerpen
　(1550); historische erzählung aus dem sechs-
　zehnten jahrhundert. Aus dem flämischen
　von C. Büchele. Stuttg. 1860. T.　C 2257
— Tales of flemish life. N. Y. 1857. S. C 2258
　Contents. Author's address. — The recruit. — Mine
　host Gansendonck. — Blind Rosa. — The poor noble-
　man.
— The village innkeeper. Balt. 1864. D. C 2259
— Das wunderjahr 1566 ; historischer roman.
　Aus dem flämischen von E. Zeller. Stuttg.
　1846. T.　　　　　　　　　　C 2260
Conway, Hugh, *pseud., see* **Fargus, F: J:**
Cook, Dutton. A prodigal son. Lond. 1863. 3 v.
　D.　　　　　　　　　　　　C 2301
. **Cooke, J:** Esten, (*C. Effingham, esq.*) Bonnybel
　Vane ; embracing the history of Henry St.
　John, gentleman. [New ed. of "Henry
　St. John."] N. Y. 1883. D.　C 2355
— Doctor Vandyke. N. Y. 1873. O.　C 2351
— The Virginia bohemians ; a novel. N. Y. 1880.
　O.　　　　　　　　　　　　C 2352
— The Virginia comedians, or Old days in the
　Old Dominion ; ed. from the mss. of C.
　Effingham, esq. N. Y. 1855. 2 v. D.
　　　　　　　　　　　　　　　C 2353
— The youth of Jefferson ; a chronicle of college
　scrapes at Williamsbury in Virginia, a. d.
　1764. N. Y. 1854. D.　　　　C 2354
Cooke, Rose, *born* Terry. The deacon's week ;
　a story. Ill. N. Y. 1885. D.　C 2402
— Miss Lucinda. *In* Atlantic tales.　A 1876
— Somebody's neighbors. Bost. 1881. D. C 2401
　Contents. Eben Jackson. — Miss Lucinda. — Dely's
　cow.—Squire Paine's confession.—Miss Beulah's bon-
　net. — Cal Culver and the devil. — Amandar. — Polly
　Mariner, tailoress. — Uncle Josh. — Poll Jennings's
　hair.—Freedom Wheeler's controversy with Provi-
　dence.—Mrs. Flint's married experience.
Coolidge, Susan, *pseud., see* **Woolsey,** Sarah
　Chauncey.
Cooper, James Fenimore. Afloat and ashore ; a
　sea tale. Bost. 1878. D.　　C 2451
— *Same, germ.* Miles Wallingford's abenteuer
　zu land und zur see. Stuttg. 1853. T.
　　　　　　　　　　　　　　　C 2451
　Note. For continuation, *see* Miles Wallingford.

x denotes books specially adapted for children.

Cooper, James Fenimore.—*Continued.*
— The bravo. N. Y. 1876. D.   **C 2452**
— *Same, germ.* Der bravo; eine venetianische
   geschichte. Aus dem englischen von G.
   Friedenberg. 3te aufl. Stuttg. 1853. T.
         C 2452
— *Same, germ.* Uebers. von Helene Lobedan.
   Stuttg. [1882]. 2 v. T.   **C 2452**
— The chainbearer, or The Littlepage manu-
   scripts. *T. p. w.* [N. Y. 1852]. D. **C 2453**
— *Same.* Bost. 1879. D.   **C 2453**
— The crater, or Vulcan's Peak; a tale of the
   Pacific. Bost. 1879. D.   **C 2454**
— *Same, germ.* Das Marcus-Riff, oder Der kra-
   ter; eine erzählung aus dem Stillen Meere.
   Aus dem englischen von G. N. Bärmann.
   Stuttg. 1848. 2 v. T.   **C 2454**
— The deer-slayer, or The first war-path; a tale.
   [Leather-stocking tales, no. 1.] Bost. [1883].
   D.   **C 2455**
— *Same.* N. Y. 1878. S.   **C 2455**
— *Same.* Bost. 1879. S.   **C 2455**
— Edward Myers, oder Erinnerungen aus dem
   leben eines seemannes. Deutsch bearb.
   von Erwin v. Moosthal. Stuttg. 1844. T.
         C 2466
— The headsman, or The abbaye des Vignerons.
   N. Y. 1852. D.   **C 2456**
— *Same.* N. Y. 1872. D.   **C 2456**
— The Heidenmauer, or The benedictines; a
   legend of the Rhine. N. Y. 1852. 2 v. in 1.
   D.   **C 2457**
— *Same.* N. Y. 1872. D.   **C 2457**
— Home as found; sequel to "Homeward bound".
   Bost. 1879. D.   **C 2458**
— *Same, germ.* Eva Effingham, oder Die heimath;
   eine fortsetzung der "Heimkehr". Aus
   dem englischen von C. Kolb. 2te aufl.
   Stuttg. 1853. T.   **C 2458**
— Homeward bound, or The chase; a tale of the
   sea. N. Y. 1872. D.   **C 2459**
— *Same.* Bost. 1879. D.   **C 2459**
— *Same.* Phila. 1838. 2 v. S.   **C 2459**
   Note. For continuation, *see* Home as found.
— Jack Tier, or The Florida reef. Bost. 1879. S.
         C 2460
— The last of the Mohicans; a narrative of 1757.
   [Leather-stocking tales, no. 2.] Bost. 1883.
   D.   **C 2461**
— *Same.* N. Y. 1867. D.   **C 2461**
— *Same.* N. Y. 1878. D.   **C 2461**
— *Same.* Bost. 1879. D.   **C 2461**
— Lionel Lincoln, or The leaguer of Boston.
   Bost. 1878. D.   **C 2462**
— *Same, germ.* Lionel Lincoln, oder Die belage-
   rung von Boston. Stuttg. 1853. T. **C 2462**
— Mercedes of Castile, or The voyage to Cathay.
   N. Y. 1876. D.   **C 2463**
— Miles Wallingford; a sequel to "Afloat and
   ashore." N. Y. 1878. D.   **C 2464**
— *Same, germ.* Lucy Hardinge, oder Miles Wall-
   ingford's abenteuer zu land und zur see,
   2ter theil. Aus dem englischen. Stuttg.
   1853. T.   **C 2464**
— The Monikins. N. Y. 1852. 2 v. in 1. D.
         C 2465
— *Same.* N. Y. 1876. D.   **C 2465**
— *Same, germ.* Die Monikins. Uebers. von C.
   F. Meurer. Frankfurt a. M. 1835. 2 v. T.
         C 2465
— The oak openings, or The bee-hunter. Bost.
    1878. S.   **C 2483**

Cooper, James Fenimore:—*Continued.*
— The pathfinder, or The inland sea. [Leather-
   stocking tales, no 3.] Bost. [1883]. D.
         C 2467
— *Same.* N. Y. 1878. D.   **C 2467**
— *Same, germ.* Der pfadfinder, oder Das binnen-
   meer. Aus dem englischen von C. Kolb.
   Stuttg. 1853. S.   **C 2467**
— The pilot; a tale of the sea. Bost. 1879. D.
         C 2468
— *Same.* Bost. 1883. D   **C 2468**
— *Same, germ.* Der lootse; eine erzählung aus
   dem englischen. Stuttg. *n. d.* T.   **C 2468**
— The pioneers, or The sources of the Susque-
   hanna; a descriptive tale. [Leatherstock-
   ing tales, no. 4.] Bost. [1883]. D. **C 2469**
— *Same.* Bost. 1879. D.   **C 2469**
— The prairie; a tale. [Leatherstocking tales,
   no. 5.] Bost. [1883]. D.   **C 2470**
— *Same.* Bost. 1879. D.   **C 2470**
— *Same, germ.* Die prairie. Aus dem englischen
   von G. Friedenberg. Stuttg. 1845. T.
         C 2470
— Precaution. Bost. 1878. D.   **C 2471**
— The red rover. N. Y. 1878. S.   ·**C 2472**
— *Same.* N. Y. 1883. D.   **C 2472**
— The redskins, or Indian and injin; the con-
   clusion of the Littlepage manuscripts.
   Bost. 1878. D.   **C 2473**
— *Same.* Bost. 1872. D.   **C 2473**
— *Same, germ.* Ravensnest, oder Die rothhäute.
   Stuttg. 1853. T.   **C 2473**
— Satanstoe, or The Littlepage manuscripts; a
   tale of the colony. Bost. 1878. D. **C 2474**
— *Same, germ.* Satanstoe, oder Die familie
   Littlepage; eine erzählung aus der colonie.
   Aus dem englischen. Stuttg. 1853. T.
         C 2474
— The sea lions, or The lost sealers. Bost. 1879.
   S.   **C 2475**
— *Same, germ.* Die seelöwen, oder Die verlorene
   robbenjäger. Aus dem englischen übers.
   Stuttg. 1854. S.   **C 2475**
— The spy; a tale of the neutral ground. N. Y.
   1878. D.   **C 2476**
— The two admirals; a tale. Bost. 1878. D.
         C 2477
— *Same, germ.* Die beiden admirale; ein see-
   roman. Aus dem englischen von E. Mauch.
   Stuttg. 1853. T.   **C 2477**
— The Water-witch, or The skimmer of the seas;
   a tale. Bost. 1879. D.   **C 2478**
— *Same.* N. Y. 1883. D.   **C 2478**
— *Same, germ.* Die Wassernixe, oder Der
   streicher durch die meere. Aus dem
   englischen von G. Friedenberg. 3te aufl.
   Stuttg. 1853. S.   **C 2478**
— The ways of the hour. N. Y. 1872. D. **C 2479**
— The wept of the Wish-ton-wish. N. Y. 1877.
   D.   **C 2480**
— *Same.* N. Y. 1854. 2 v. in 1. S.   **C 2480**
— The Wing-and-wing, or Le Feu-follet; a tale.
   Phila. 1842. 2 v. in 1. D.   **C 2481**
— *Same.* Bost. 1879. D.   **C 2481**
— *Same.* N. Y. 1883. D.   **C 2481**
— Wyandotte, or The hutted knoll. N. Y. 1872.
   D.   **C 2482**
— *Same, germ.* Wyandotte, oder Das block-
   haus; eine erzählung aus dem englischen
   von E. Mauch. 2te aufl. Stuttg. 1853. T.
         C 2482

x denotes books specially adapted for children.

Cooper, Katherine, *born* Saunders. The haunted crust. *In* Johnson, E. R. Little classics.
J 926 v5
— The high mills. Leipz. 1874. 2 v. in 1. S.
S 702
— Sebastian. Leipz. 1878. S. S 701
Cooper, T: (*Adam Hornbook*). The family feud. Lond. 1855. S. C 2496
Copley, Esther, *formerly mrs.* Hewlett. Early friendships ; a tale. N. Y. 1857. S. Cx 651
— The poplar grove, or Little Harry and his uncle Benjamin ; a tale for youth. N. Y. 1857. S. Cx 652
Corbett, *Mrs.* E. T. The fairy of the moonbeam, or Karl's queer stories. N. Y. 1885. S.
Cx 686
Corbin, Caroline Elizabeth, *born* Fairfield. Rebecca, or A woman's secret. Chicago. 1877. D. C 2501
Corkran, Alice. Bessie Lang. N. Y. 1877. S.
C 2551
Cornwall, Barry, *pseud.*, *see* Procter, Bryan Waller.
Cornwall, C. M., *pseud.*, *see* Roe, Mary A.
Corvinus, Jakob, *pseud.*, *see* Raabe, W:
Cosel, Charlotte v., (*Adelheid v. Auer*). It is the fashion. From the german, by the translator of "Over yonder," etc. Phila. 1879. S. C 2601
Cottin, Sophie, *born* Ristaud. Elizabeth, or The exiles of Siberia. N. Y. 1867. Tt. C 2651
— *Same, germ.* Elisabeth, oder Die verbannten von Sibirien. Aus dem franz. Jena. 1841. S. C 2651
— Matilda, princess of England ; a romance of the crusades. From the french by Jennie W. Raum, ed. by G: E. Raum. N. Y. 1885. 2 v. S. C 2652
Coulson, J. G. A. Harwood. N. Y. 1875. O.
C 2701
Coulter, *Miss* —. From hay-time to hopping. N. Y. 1861. S. C 2751
Courcillon, Eugène de. Le curé manqué, or Social and religious customs in France. N. Y. 1855. D. C 2801
Courtilz de Sandras, *or* Sandras de Courtilz et de Vergé, Gatien. The french spy, or The memoirs of John Baptist de la Fontaine, lord of Savoy and Fontenai, late brigadier and surveyor of the french king's army, now a prisoner in the Bastile ; containing many secret transactions relating both to England and France. Tr. from the french original printed at Cologn in 1699. Lond. 1700. D. C 2826R
Craddock, Charles Egbert, *pseud.*, *see* Murfree, Mary N.
Craik, Dinah Maria, *born* Mulock. Agatha's husband. Leipz. 1860. S. C 2851
— *Same.* N. Y. 1871. D. C 2851
— Alice Learmont ; a fairy tale. New ed. rev. by the author. Ill. N. Y. 1884. D.
Cx 705
— Alwyn's first wife. *With her* Lord Erlistoun.
C 2862
— A brave lady. N. Y. 1870. D. C 2852
— *Same.* N. Y. *n. d.* D. C 2852
— Bread upon the waters. Leipz. 1865. S.
C 2853
— Christian's mistake. Leipz. 1865. S. C 2854
— *Same.* N. Y. 1870. D. C 2854
— *Same, germ.* Christinen's missgriff. Aus dem

Craik, Dinah Maria, *born* Mulock.—*Continued.*
englischen von Sophie Verena [*pseud. for* Sophie Alberti]. Leipz. 1865. S. C 2854
— Domestic stories. Leipz. 1862. S. C 2855
Contents. The last of the Ruthvens.—The Italian's daughter.—The two homes.—Minor trials.—Philip Armytage, or The blind girl's love.—Adelaide; being fragments from a young wife's diary.—The old mathematician.—The half-caste.—Miss Letty's experiences.—A bride's tragedy.—'Tis useless trying.—The only son.—The doctor's family.—All for the best.
— The double house. *With her* Bread upon the waters. C 2853
— *Same. In* Sargent, E. The emerald. S 551
— The fairy book ; the best popular stories selected and rendered anew. N. Y. *n. d.* D.
Cx 701
— A family in love. *With her* Bread upon the waters. C 2853
— Hannah. Leipz. 1871. 2 v. in 1. S. C 2856
— The head of the family. Leipz. 1858. 2 v. in 1. S. C 2857
— His little mother, and other tales and sketches. N. Y. 1881. D. C 2858
Includes, Poor Prin.—Two little tinkers.—The postman's daughter.—About travelling and travellers.—Save the children.—Sinless sabbath-breaking.—De mortuis.
— *Same.* N. Y. 1881. Q. C 2858
— In a house-boat ; a journal. *With her* Miss Tommy. C 2873
— John Halifax, gentleman. N. Y. 1870. D.
C 2859
— *Same.* Leipz. 1857. 2 v. in 1. S. C 2859
— *Same.* N. Y. *n. d.* D. C 2859
— The last house in C— street. *With her* Lord Erlstoun. C 2862
— The laurel bush ; an old-fashioned love story. Leipz. 1876. S. C 2860
— *Same.* N. Y. 1876. D. C 2860
— A life for a life. N. Y. *n. d.* D. C 2861
— *Same.* Leipz. 1859. 2 v. in 1. S. C 2861
— The little lame prince and his travelling cloak ; a parable for young and old. Ill. Leipz. 1874. S. Cx 702
— Little Sunshine's holiday ; a picture from life. N. Y. 1874. S. Cx 703
— Lord Erlistoun. Leipz. 1864. S. C 2862
— A low marriage. *With her* Bread upon the waters. C 2853
— Miss Tommy ; a mediæval romance. Ill. N. Y. 1884. D. C 2873
— Mistress and maid. Leipz. 1862. S. C 2863
— *Same.* N. Y. 1872. D. C 2863
— My mother and I ; a love story. N. Y. 1874. D. C 2864
— *Same.* Leipz. 1874. S. C 2864
— A noble life. N. Y. *n. d.* D. C 2865
— *Same.* Leipz. 1866. S. C 2865
— The Ogilvies. Leipz. 1863. S. C 2866
— *Same.* N. Y. 1871. D. C 2866
— *Same, germ.* Die Ogilvies, oder Herzenskämpfe ; roman aus dem englischen. Leipz. 1863. 2 v. S. C 2866
— Olive. Leipz. 1866. 2 v. in 1. S. C 2867
— Our year ; a child's book in prose and verse. Ill. N. Y. 1866. S. Cx 704
— Romantic tales. Leipz. 1861. S. Cx 2868
Contents. Avillion, or The happy isles.—The self-seer.—The sculptor of Bruges.—The daughter of Heremon.— King Tolv.—Erotion.—Cleomenes the greek.—The story of Hyas.—The cross on the Snow mountains.—The rosicrucian.—Antonio Melidori.—The story of Elisabetta Sirani.—A life episode.

Craik, Dinah Maria, *born* Mulock.—*Continued.*
— The rosicrucian. *In* Johnson, E. R. Little classics.   J 926 v7
— Two marriages. Leipz. 1867. S.   C 2869
— The two tinkers. *With her* The laurel bush.   C 2860
— The unkind word, and other stories. Leipz. 1869. 2 v. in 1. S.   C 2870

Includes, V. 1· A child's life, sixty years ago.—His young lordship. — Elizabeth and Victoria. — A woman's book.—The age of gold.—On living in perspective.—Sermons.—The house of commons, from the ladies' gallery.—A few words about sorrow.—A hedge-side poet. — The last great exhibition; its beginning.—Same; its end.—To novelists, and a novelist. —Bodies and souls. 2. Blind.—Children of Israel.—Give us air. — In the ring. — A dreadful ghost.—Meadowside House.— In her teens.—Clothes.— The history of a hospital.—Death on the seas.—To parents.—Misery-mongers.—An old scotch love story.—A garden party.—A tale of two walks told to a sick child: My dog and I; The fox hunt.

— The water-cure. *With her* Lord Erlistoun.   C 2862
— The woman's kingdom. Leipz. 1868. 2 v. in 1. S.   C 2871
— *Same;* a love story. N. Y. *n. d.* D.   C 2871
— Young mrs. Jardine. Ill. N. Y. 1880. D.   C 2872
— *and others.* Plucky boys. Ill. Bost. 1884. D.   Cx 706

Craik, Georgiana Marion. Anne Warwick. Leipz. 1877. S.   C 2901
— The cousin from India ; a book for girls. Ill. N. Y. 1871. S.   Cx 726
— Dorcas. Leipz. 1880. 2 v. in 1. S.   C 2902
— Esther Hill's secret. Leipz. 1871. 2 v. in 1. S.   C 2903
— Faith Unwin's ordeal. Leipz. 1866. S.   C 2904
— Fortune's marriage ; a novel. N. Y. 1882. Q.   C 2916
— Godfrey Helstone ; a novel. N. Y. 1884. Q.   C 2917
— Hard to bear. *In* Two tales of married life.   C 2905
— Hero Trevelyan. Leipz. 1872. S.   C 2906
— Leslie Tyrrell. Leipz. 1867. S.   C 2907
— Lost and won. Leipz. 1862. S.   C 2908
— Mark Dennison's charge. Ill. Lond. 1861. D.   Cx 727
— Mildred. Leipz. 1868. S.   C 2910
— Only a butterfly, and other stories. Leipz. 1874. S.   C 2911

Includes, Elspeth Grant.—Lost at sea.—The old lifeboat.—Was Elizabeth right?—Little Barbara.

— Sydney. N. Y. 1881. Q.   C 2915
— Sylvia's choice. Leipz. 1875. 2 v. in 1. S.   C 2918
— Theresa. Leipz. 1875. S. *With her* Sylvia's choice.   C 2918
— Two women. Leipz. 1881. 2 v. in 1. S.   C 2912
— Winifred's wooing, and other tales. Leipz. 1868. S.   C 2913

Includes, A tale of Florence.—Poor Christine.

— Without kith or kin. Leipz. 1872. 2 v. in 1. S.   C 2914

Crane, Anna Moncure, *see* **Seemüller, Anna Moncure.**

Crane, J. L. The two circuits ; a story of Illinois life. Chicago. 1878. D.   C 2951

Craven, Pauline, *born* La Ferronays, *mme.* A: Anne Séverin. N. Y. 1869. D.   C 3001

Craven, Pauline, *born* La Ferronays.—*Continued.*
— Eliane. Tr. from the french by lady Georgiana Fullerton. N. Y. 1882. S.   C 3004
— Fleurange. From the french, tr. by M. M. R. N. Y. 1873. S.   C 3002
— Jettatrice, or The veil withdrawn. Bost. 1875. O.   C 3003

Crawford, Francis Marion. An american politician ; a novel. Bost. 1885 [1884]. D.   C 3030
— Doctor Claudius ; a true story. N. Y. 1883. D.   C 3027
— Mr. Isaacs ; a tale of modern India. N. Y. 1882. D.   C 3026
— A roman singer. Bost. 1884. D.   C 3029
— To leeward. Bost. 1884 [1883]. D.   C 3028
— Zoroaster. N. Y. 1885. D.   C 3031

Crawfurd, Oswald. The world we live in ; a novel. N. Y. 1884. S.   C 3201

Crayon, Geoffrey, *pseud., see* **Irving, Washington.**

Croker, B. M. Pretty Miss Neville. Lond. 1883. 3 v. in 2. D.   C 3901
— Some one else ; a novel. N. Y. 1885. Q.   C 3902

Croly, G: Salathiel ; a story of the past, the present and the future. N. Y. 1833. 2 v. D.   C 3051

Crommelin, May. In the west countrie ; a novel. N. Y. 1884. Q.   C 3102
— Joy, or The light of Coldhome Ford ; a novel. N. Y. 1884. Q.   C 3103
— Orange Lily. N. Y. 1879. Q.   C 3101

Cron, Clara, *pseud., see* **Stock, Clara.**

Cross, Marian, *born* Evans, *formerly mrs.* G: H: Lewes, *(George Eliot).* Adam Bede. Leipz. 1859. 2 v in 1. S.   C 3151
— *Same.* Bost. 1873. D.   C 3151
— *Same.* (Harper's lib. ed.) [Ill.] N. Y. *n. d.* D.   C 3151
— Brother Jacob. *With her* The lifted veil.   C 3154
— Daniel Deronda. Chicago. 1876. 2 v. D.   C 3152
— *Same.* N. Y. 1876. 2 v. D.   C 3152
— *Same.* N. Y. 1876. O.   C 3152
— Felix Holt, the radical. Leipz. 1867. S.   C 3153
— The lifted veil. Leipz. 1878. S.   C 3154
— Middlemarch ; a story of provincial life. N. Y. 1873. 2 v. D.   C 3155
— *Same.* N. Y. 1873. O.   C 3155
— *Same.* (Harper's lib. ed.) [Ill.] N. Y. *n. d.* D.   C 3155
— The mill on the Floss. Leipz. 1860. 2 v. in 1. S.   C 3156
— *Same.* N. Y. 1860. D.   C 3156
— *Same.* N. Y. 1860. O.   C 3156
— *Same.* (Harper's lib. ed.) [Ill.] N. Y. *n. d.* D.   C 3156
— Romola. (Harper's lib. ed.) [Ill.] N. Y. *n. d.* D.   C 3157
— Scenes of clerical life. Leipz. 1859. 2 v. in 1. S.   C 3158

Contents. V. 1. The sad fortunes of the reverend Amos Barton. — Mr. Gilfil's love-story.—2. Janet's repentance.

— Silas Marner, the weaver of Raveloe. Leipz. 1861. S.   C 3159

Crowe, Catherine. The advocate's wedding-day. *In* Johnson, E. R. Little classics.   J 926 v8
— The story of Martha Guinness and her son. *In* Edinburgh tales.   E 426

x denotes books specially adapted for children.

45

Crowquill, Christopher, *pseud.*, *see* Stowe, Harriet Elizabeth.

Crusenstolpe, Magnus Jakob. Carl Johann und die schweden; romantische erzählung. Aus dem schwedischen von G. Fink. Stuttg. 1847. 4 v. T.　　　　C 3251

Cudlip, Annie, *born* Thomas. Allerton Towers; a novel. N. Y. 1882. Q.　　　C 3310
— *Same.* Lond. 1882. 3 v. in 1. D.　　C 3310
— Called to account. Leipz. 1867. 2 v. in 1. S.　　　　C 3301
— *Same.* N. Y. 1875. O.　　　C 3301
— Denis Donne. Leipz. 1864. 2 v. in 1. S.　　　　C 3302
— *Same.* T. p. w. [N. Y. 1865]. O.　　C 3302
— Jenifer; a novel. N. Y. 1883. Q.　　C 3311
— *Same.* Lond. 1883. 3 v. in 1. D.　　C 3311
— A narrow escape. Leipz. 1875. 2 v. in 1. S.　　　　C 3303
— No alternative. Phila. *n. d.* D.　　C 3304
— No medium; a novel. N. Y. 1885. S.　C 3313
— On guard. Leipz. 1861. 2 v. in 1. S.　C 3305
— Only herself. Leipz. 1870. 2 v. in 1. S.　　　　C 3306
— Our set. Lond. 1881. 3 v. in 2. D.　C 3312
　Contents. V. 1. Why not?—The Heywards. 2. *Same, concluded.*—A coloured scrap.—Mrs. Grinling's hampers.—A mystery.—Tested. 3. *Same, concluded.*—Mrs. Allonby.—A ghost in a satin sacque.—Sherringham's wife.—In an apple orchard.—Her last appearance.—Ken Hall.—All over.
— Played out. Leipz. 1867. 2 v. in 1. S. C 3307
— *Same.* N. Y. 1867. O.　　　C 3307
— Theo Leigh. N. Y. 1865. O.　　　C 3308
— Walter Goring. Leipz. 1866. 2 v. in 1. S.　　　　C 3309

Cuffe, W: Ulick O'Connor, *4th earl of Desart.* Kelverdale. N. Y. 1879. Q.　　C 3351
— *Same*; a novel. Lond. 1879. 3 v. in 1. D.　　　　C 3351

Cummings, J. W. Italian legends and sketches. N. Y. 1858. D.　　　C 3401

Cummins, Maria Susanna. El Fureidis. Bost. 1860. S.　　　　C 3451
— The lamplighter. Bost. 1881. D.　　C 3452
— *Same, germ.* Der laternenmann. Aus dem englischen übers. von A. Kretschmar. Leipz. 1854. 4 v. S.　　　C 3452
— Mabel Vaughan. [*Anon.*] New ed. Bost. 1882. D.　　　　C 3453

Cunningham, Allan. The haunted ships. *In* Johnson, E. R. Little classics.　J 926 v8
— The king of the peak. *In the same.* J 926 v7
— Lord Roldan. N. Y. 1860. 2 v. in 1. S.　　　　C 3501

Cunningham, J: W: The velvet cushion. N. Y. 1850. S.　　　　Cx 801

Cunzer, C: Borromäus. Novellen. 1847. 2 v. S.　　　　C 3551
　Contents, see Deutscher katalog, p. 55.

Cupples, G: The "green hand"; a "short" yarn. N. Y. 1879. Q.　　　C 3601
— *Same*; adventures of a naval lieutenant; a sea story for boys. Ill. Lond. 1879. D.　　　　C 3601

Curtis, G: W: My châteaux. *In* Johnson, E. R. Little classics.　　　J 926 v4
— Prue and I. N. Y. 1857. S.　　　C 3651
— Trumps. N. Y. 1873. D.　　　C 3652

Curtis, L. My husband's mother. *In* Maga stories.　　　　P 2801

Custine, Astolphe *marquis* de. Romuald, oder Der beruf. Aus dem franz. Leipz. 1848. 6 v. S.　　　　C 3701

Czajkowski, Michal. Wernyhora, der seher in der Ukraine; historische erzählung aus dem jahr 1768. Aus dem polnischen übers. von G. Diezel. Stuttg. 1843. 2 v. T.　　　　C 3751

D., J. Mit eiserner hand; novelle. *With* Denroth, E. H. Die Baronin.　　　D 701

Dahlgren, Madeleine, *born* Vinton, *formerly mrs.* Goddard. A Washington winter. Bost. 1883. D.　　　　D 126

Dahn, F: Julius Felix. Felicitas; historischer roman aus den volkswanderungen. N. Y. 1883. F.　　　　D 104
— *Same. In* Vierteljährl. mag.　　V 2 v30
— Ein kampf um Rom; historischer roman. N. Y. 1882. 2 v. F.　　　D 103
— *Same.* 10te aufl., mit 2 karten. Leipz. 1884. 4 v. D.　　　　D 103
— *Same, eng.* A struggle for Rome. Tr. from the german by Lily Wolffsohn. Lond. 1878. 3 v. D.　　　　D 103
— Kämpfende herzen; drei erzählungen. 2te aufl. Berlin. 1881. D.　　　D 101
— Die kreuzfahrer; erzählung aus dem 13ten jahrhundert. N. Y. 1885. F.　　D 105
— Odhin's trost; ein nordischer roman aus dem elften jahrhundert. 4te aufl. Leipz. 1880. D.　　　　D 102

Daldorne, Evan. The wooing of the waterwitch; a northern oddity. Ill. by J. Moyr Smith. N. Y. 1880. D.　　　Dx 901

Dame in schwartz, Die. (Hamburger novelle.) Hamburg. 1864. S.　　　H 1

Daniels, W. H. That boy; who shall have him? Cinc. 1878. D.　　　　D 151

D'Arblay, Frances, *see* Arblay, Frances d'.

Darlem, Clary. Elisabeth von Oestreich, königin von Frankreich. Aus dem franz. von W: Schöttlen. Stuttg. 1850. 2 v. T.　　D 251

Dasent, G: Webbe. Lady Sweetapple, or Three to one. Ill. N. Y. 1873. O.　　D 301

Dash, *Comtesse, pseud.*, *see* Saint Mars, Gabrielle Anna *vicomtesse* de.

Dashiell, T. G. A pastor's recollections. N. Y. 1875. D.　　　　D 401

Daudet, Alphonse. L'évangeliste; a parisian novel. Tr. by Mary Neal Sherwood. Phila. [1883]. S.　　　　D 457
— Jack. From the french by Mary Neal Sherwood. Bost. 1877. S.　　　D 451
— The little good-for-nothing, (Le petit Chose.) From the french by Mary Neal Sherwood. Bost. 1878. D.　　　D 452
— The nabob. From the french by Lucy H. Hooper. Bost. 1878. D.　　　D 453
— Numa Roumestan. From the french by Virginia Champlin. Bost. 1882. S.　　D 456
— *Same, germ.* N. Y. 1883. F.　　　D 456
— Prodigious adventures of Tartarin of Tarascon. From the french by Robert S. Minot. Bost. 1880. S.　　　　D 454
— Sidonie. (Fromont jeune et Risler aîné.) From the french. Bost. 1877. D.　D 455
— The siege of Berlin. Tr. from the french. *In* Tales from many sources.　　T 178 v4

Daudet, Ernest. Henriette; fragments from the diary of marquis de Boisgueny, collected and published by Ernest Daudet. N. Y. 1878. Q.　　　　D 476

Daugé, Henri, *pseud.*, *see* Hammond, *Mrs.* E. H.

Daunt, Achilles. Frank Redcliffe, a story of travel and adventure in the forests of Venezuela; a book for boys. Ill. N. Y. 1883. D. **Dx 126**

Davenport, H: E. Rovings on land and sea. Ill. Bost. 1880. D. **Dx 101**

David Armstrong, or Before the dawn. N. Y. 1880. Q. **D 1**
— *Same.* Edinb. 1880. 2 v. in 1. D. **D 1**

Davies, Theodore. Losing to win. N. Y. 1874. D. **D 501**

Davis, L. Clarke. A stranded ship; a story of sea and shore. N. Y. 1880. S. **D 551**

Davis, Rebecca Blaine, *born* Harding. Balacchi brothers. *In* Stories by american authors. **S 35 v1**
— The captain's story. *In* Johnson, E. R. Little classics. **J 926 v2**
— A faded leaf of history. *In the same.* **J 926 v10**
— Life in the iron mills. *In* Atlantic tales. **A 1876**
— Margret Howth; a story of today. Bost. 1862. S. **D 601**

Davis, Robert E., (*Trebor*). As it may happen; a story of american life and character. Phila. [1879]. D. **D 651**

Davis, W: M. Nimrod of the sea, or The american whaleman. N. Y. 1874. D. **Dx 151**

Day, T: The history of Sandford and Merton. N. Y. 1856. S. **Dx 201**
— *Same*, corrected and rev. by Cecil Hartley. [New ed., ill.] N. Y. [1881]. D. **Dx 201**

Deane, Milly. Marjory. . 3d ed. Lond. 1873. D. **D 676**

Decken, Auguste v. der, (*A. v. der Elbe*). Lüneburger geschichten; mit einer einleitung von Hermann Allmers. Stuttg. 1883. D. **D 2651**
Contents. Einleitung.—Gertrude Amburger.—Der stille freund.—Heidabenteuer.

Dedenroth, Eugen Hermann, (*Eugen Hermann, Ernst Pitawall*). Die baronin. Phila. *n. d.* O. **D 701**
— Gabriele, das weib des spielers; criminalnovelle. N. Y. *n. d.* O. **P 1951**
— Louis Napoleon, oder Schicksalskampf und kaiser-krone; historisch-romantische geschichte der zeit und des lebens Napoleon III. Frankfurt a. M. *n. d.* 2 v. D. **P 1952**

Defoe, Daniel. The life and adventures of Robinson Crusoe. Ill. Lond. *n. d.* D. **Dx 251**
— *Same. In his* Novels and miscellaneous works. **820.2 : 8 v7**
— *Same;* ed. for the use of schools by W. H. Lambert. [Classics for children.] Bost. 1883. D. **Dx 252**
— *Same, germ.* Leben und abenteuer des Robinson Crusoe. Aus dem englischen übertragen von K: Altmüller. Hildburgh. 1869. D. **D 726**

DeForest, J: W: The bloody chasm; a novel. N. Y. 1881. S. **D 754**
— The brigade commander. *In* Stories by american authors. **S 35 v8**
— An inspired lobbyist. *In the same.* **S 35 v4**
— The Lauson tragedy. *In* Johnson, E. R. Little classics. **J 926 v3**
— Overland. N. Y. 1871. O. **D 751**
— Playing the mischief. N. Y. 1876. O. **D 752**
— The Wetherell affair. N. Y 1873. O. **D 753**

DeJongh, Anna M. Mossdale; a tale. N. Y. [1870]. S. **D 801**

DeKay, C: Manmath'a. *In* Stories by american authors. **S 35 v10**

DeKoven, James. Dorchester polytechnic academy, dr. Neverasole principal. Milw. 1879. S. **D 776**

DeKroyft, S. Helen, *born* Aldrich. Little Jakey. *In* Johnson, E. R. Little classics. **J 926 v10**

DeMille, James. The "B. O. W. C."; a book for boys. Ill. Bost. 1870. S. **Dx 301**
— The cryptogram. Ill. N. Y. 1874. O. **D 851**
— The Dodge club, or Italy in 1859. Ill. N. Y. 1875. O. **D 852**
— Helena's household; a tale of Rome in the 1st century. N. Y. 1867. D. **D 853**
— The lady of the ice. N. Y. 1876. O. **D 854**

Deming, Philander. Adirondack stories. Bost. 1880. T. **D 901**
Contents. Lost.—Lida Ann.—John's trial.—Joe Baldwin.—Willie.—Benjamin Jacques.—Ike's wife.— An Adirondack neighborhood.
— Tomkins and other folks; stories of the Hudson and Adirondacks. Bost. 1885 [1884]. T. **D 902**
Includes, Rube Jones. — Jacob's insurance. — Mr. Toby's wedding journey.—Hattie's romance.—The court in Schoharie.—An Adirondack home.

Demmler, E: Die tochter des fährmanns; eine rheinische dorfgeschichte. *In* Vierteljährl. mag. **V2 v28**

DeMorgan, Mary. The necklace of princess Fiorimonde, and other stories. Ill. Lond. 1880. D. **Dx 326**
Includes, The wanderings of Arasmon.—The heart of princess Joan.—The peddler's pack.—The bread of discontent.—Three clever kings.—The wise princess.

Dempster, Charlotte Louisa Hawkins. Blue roses, or Helen Malinofska's marriage. Leipz. 1879. 2 v. in 1. S. **D 1001**
— Iseulte. N. Y. 1875. O. **D 1002**
— Within sound of the sea. N. Y. 1879. Q. **D 1003**
— *Same.* Lond. 1879. 2 v. in 1. D. **D 1003**

Denison, Mary, *born* Andrews. His triumph. Bost. 1883. S. **D 1054**
— Like a gentleman. [*Anon.*] Bost. 1882. D. **D 1055**
— A noble sister. Phila. 1868. S. **Dx 351**
— Old Slip warehouse. N. Y. 1878. O. **D 1051**
— Rothmell. Bost. 1878. D. **D 1052**
— That husband of mine. Bost. 1877. S. **D 1053**
— That wife of mine, by the author of "That husband of mine." Bost. 1877. S. **D 1056**

DeQuincey, T: Flight of a tartar tribe. *In his* Narrative and miscellaneous papers. **824.2 : 34 v1**
— *Same. In* Johnson, E. R. Little classics. **J 926 v1**
— Klosterheim, or The masque; with a biographical preface by Shelton Mackenzie. Bost. 1855. D. **D 1101**
— *Same. In his* Memorials. **824.2 : 32 v2**
— Murder considered as one of the fine arts. *In* Johnson, E. R. Little classics. **J 926 v2**
— The vision of sudden death. *In the same.* **J 926 v2**

Desart, Earl of, *see* Cuffe, W: Ulick O'Connor.

Despard, Matilda. Kilrogan cottage. N. Y. 1878. O. **D 1151**

x denotes books specially adapted for children.

Detlef, Karl, *pseud.*, *see* **Bauer, Clara.**

Deutsche schützen-, turner- und liederbrüder, oder Was will das volk? zeitgeschichtlicher roman vom verfasser der romane: "Der ritter der industrie" u. s. w. Jena. 1867. 2 v. S. **D 3**

Dewall, Johannes van, *pseud.*, *see* **Kühne, A:**

De Witt, Henriette, *see* **Witt, Henriette de.**

Diaz, Abby, *born* Morton. Chronicles of the Stimpcett family and others. Ill. Bost. [1882]. O. **Dx 458**

— The Jimmy-Johns, and other stories. Ill. Bost. 1881. D. **Dx 454**

— King Grimalkum and Pussyanita, or The cats' arabian nights. Bost. [1881]. O. **Dx 457**

— Lucy Maria. Ill. Bost. 1874. D. **D 1252**

— Polly Cologne. Bost. [1881]. D. **Dx 456**

— The school master's trunk; containing papers on home-life in Tweenit. Bost. 1874. D. **D 1251**

— A story-book for the children. Ill. Bost. 1881. D. **Dx 455**

— William Henry and his friends. Ill. Bost. 1881. D. **Dx 452**

— The William Henry letters. Ill. Bost. 1881. D. **Dx 451**

Dickens, C: J: Huffam, (*Boz*). Barnaby Rudge. N. Y. 1874. D. **D 1301**

— *Same. In his* Master Humphrey's clock. **D 1311 v2,3**

— Bleak house. Leipz. 1852. 2 v. in 1. S. **D 1302**

— *Same.* N. Y. 1873. D. **D 1302**

— *Same.* Phila. n. d. D. **D 1302**

— A child's dream of a star. *In* Johnson, E. R. Little classics. **J 926 v10**

— The chimes. *In his* Christmas books. **D 1322**

— *Same. With his* Christmas carol in prose. **D 1303**

— *Same, germ.* Die sylvesterglocken, eine koboldgeschichte von glocken die das alte jahr aus-, das neue einläuten. Stuttg. 1845. T. **D 1303 v3**

— Chops, the dwarf. *In* Johnson, E. R. Little classics. **J 926 v2**

— Christmas books. Bost. 1871. D. **D 1322**
Contents. A christmas carol.—The chimes.—The cricket on the hearth.—The battle of life.—The haunted man.

— A christmas carol in prose. Leipz. 1846. S. **D 1303**

— *Same. In* Johnson, E. R. Little classics. **J 926 v5**

— The cricket on the hearth. *In his* Christmas books. **D 1322**

— *Same. With his* Christmas carol in prose. **D 1303**

— *Same, germ.* Das grillchen auf dem heerde; ein feenmärchen aus traulicher häuslichkeit. Frei nach dem englischen von Erwin von Moosthal. Stuttg. 1846. T. **D 1303 v4**

— The personal adventures, experience and observation of David Copperfield the younger, of Blunderstone Rookery, which he never meant to be published on any account. Leipz. 1849. 3 v. in 2. S. **D 1304**

— *Same;* with an introd. by Edwin Percy Whipple. Ill. Bost. n. d. 2 v. D. **D 1304**

— Doctor Marigold. *In* Johnson, E. R. Little classics. **J 926 v18**

Dickens, C: J: Huffam, (*Boz*).—*Continued.*

— Dealings with the firm of Dombey and son, wholesale, retail and for exportation. Leipz. 1847. 3 v. in 2. S. **D 1305**

— *Same.* Bost. n. d. 2 v. D. **D 1305**

— *Same.* N. Y. 1874. D. **D 1305**

— *Same, germ.* Dombey und sohn. Neu aus dem englischen von C. Kolb. Stuttg. 1855. 2 v. T. **D 1305**

— George Silverman's explanation. *With his* Mystery of Edwin Drood. **D 1313**

— Great expectations. N. Y. 1875. D. **D 1306**

— Hard times; for these times. Leipz. 1854. S. **D 1307**

— Holiday romance; in 4 pts. *With his* Mystery of Edwin Drood. **D 1313**

— Hunted down. Leipz. 1860. S. **D 1308**

— Little Dorrit. Ill. Bost. 1871. 2 v. D. **D 1309**

— *Same.* Leipz. 1856. 4 v. in 2. S. **D 1309**

— *Same.* N. Y. 1868. 4 v. in 1. S. **D 1309**

— *Same, germ.* Klein-Dorrit. Aus dem englischen von Edmund Zoller. Stuttg. 1857. 2 v. T. **D 1309**

— The life and adventures of Martin Chuzzlewit, his relatives, friends and neighbors. Leipz. 1844. 2 v. in 1. S. **D 1310**

— *Same, germ.* Leben und schicksale des Martin Chuzzlewit. Neu aus dem englischen von C. Kolb. Stuttg. 1855. 2 v. S. **D 1310**

— Master Humphrey's clock. Leipz. 1846. 3 v. in 2. S. **D 1311**
Contents. V. 1. Master Humphrey's clock.—The old curiosity shop. 2. *Same, continued.*—Barnaby Rudge. 3. *Same, continued.*

— *Same, germ.* Master Humphrey's wanduhr. Neu aus dem englischen von C. Kolb. Stuttg. 1855. 2 v. S. **D 1311**
Note. Contains only Der raritätenladen, Barnaby Rudge not being included.

— Master Humphrey's clock, and other pieces. *In his* Mystery of Edwin Drood. **D 1313**
Note. Does not include either The old curiosity shop or Barnaby Rudge.

— The Mudfog papers, etc. N. Y. 1880. Q. **D 1312**

— *Same.* (Leisure hour ser.) N. Y. 1880. S. **D 1312**
Contents. The public life of mr. Tulrumble.—Full report of the first meeting of the Mudfog association for the advancement of everything.—*Same,* second meeting.—The pantomime of life.—Some particulars concerning a lion.—Mr. Robert Bolton.

— The mystery of Edwin Drood. Leipz. 1870. S. **D 1313**

— *Same.* Phila. n. d. D. **D 1313**

— The life and adventures of Nicholas Nickleby. Leipz. 1843. 2 v. in 1. S. **D 1314**

— *Same.* Bost. 1867. D. **D 1314**

— *Same, germ.* Leben und schicksale des Nicolaus Nickleby und seiner familie. Neu aus dem englischen von C. Kolb. Stuttg. 1855. 3 v. S. **D 1314**

— The old curiosity shop, and reprinted pieces. Phila. n. d. D. **D 1315**

— *Same.* N. Y. 1873. D. **D 1315**

— *Same. In his* Master Humphrey's clock. **D 1311**

— *Same, germ.* Der raritätenladen. *In his* Master Humphrey's wanduhr. **D 1311**

— The adventures of Oliver Twist. Ill. N. Y. 1874. D. **D 1316**

— *Same,* or The parish boy's progress. Leipz. 1843. S. **D 1316**

x denotes books specially adapted for children.

Dickens, C: J: Huffam, (*Boz*).—*Continued.*
— Our mutual friend. N. Y. 1873. 4 v. in 1. S.
        D 1317
— *Same.* Leipz. 1864. 4 v. in 2. S.   **D 1317**
— *Same,* with an introd. by Edwin Percy Whipple. Ill. Bost. *n. d.* D.   **D 1317**
— The posthumous papers of the Pickwick club, containing a faithful record of the perambulations, perils, travels, adventures and sporting transactions of the corresponding members. Portrait. Leipz. 1842. 2 v. in 1. S.   **D 1318**
— The signal-man. *In* Johnson, E. R. Little classics.   **J 926 v8**
— Sketches by Boz ; illustrative of every-day life and every-day people. Ill. Bost. 1871. D.   **D 1319**
— *Same. T. p. w.* [Phila]. O.   **D 1319**
— *Same.* Leipz. 1843. S.   **D 1319**
— *Same. In his* Mystery of Edwin Drood.   **D 1313**
  Contents. Seven sketches from our parish.— Scenes.—Characters.—Tales.
— *Same, germ.* Skizzen aus dem Londoner alltagsleben. Stuttg. 1855. T.   **D 1319**
— A tale of two cities ; with an introd. by Edwin Percy Whipple. Ill. Bost. *n. d.* D.   **D 1320**
— *Same, germ.* Zwei städte. Leipz. 1859. 2 v. S.   **D 1320**
— The uncommercial traveller. N. Y. 1868. D.   **D 1321**
— *Same. With his* Hunted down.   **D 1308**
— *and* W: Wilkie **Collins.** No thoroughfare. Leipz. 1868. S.   **D 1329**
— *and others.* Christmas stories. Leipz. 1862. S.   **D 1323**
  Contents. The haunted house.—A message from the sea.—Tom Tiddler's ground.
— - Doctor Marigold's prescriptions. N. Y. 1866. O.   **D 1324**
— - *Same.* Leipz. 1867. S.   **D 1324**
— - Mrs. Lirriper's legacy. *With his* Somebody's luggage.   **D 1328**
— - Mrs. Lirriper's lodgings. N. Y. 1864. O.   **D 1325**
— - *Same. With his* Somebody's luggage.   **D 1328**
— - Pearl fishing ; choice stories from Dickens' Household words. N. Y. 1854. D. **D 1326**
  Contents. The young advocate.—The last of a long line.—The gentleman beggar.—Evil is wrought by want of thought.—Bed.—The home of Woodruffe the gardener.—The water-drops.— An excellent opportunity.
— - The pic-nic papers. Phila. *n. d.* O. **D 1327**
  Contents. **Dickens, C:** The lamplighter's story.— **Strickland, A.** The knight bannéret.—**F., I.** John Dryden and Jacob Tonson.—**Ritchie, L.** Some account of Marcus Bell, the convict.—**Honan, M. B.** Mustapha, the miser.— The spanish maid, by the author of The provost of Bruges.—**Johns, R:** Allan Skeene.—**Cunningham, A.** Jean Cameron's college.—**Maxwell, W. H.** The expedition of major Ap Owen to the lakes of Killarney.—**Moore, T:** The student of Bagdad.—**Murray, J. E.** Le pas du vent. —An evening in Venice.—The Piaz de Toros of Seville. —Airy Eddie.—The battle of Garscube.—**Ainsworth, W: H.** The old London merchant.—**Strickland, A.** My aunt Honor.—Ripton Rumsey.—**Smith, H.** Esther. —Count Ludwig.
— - Somebody's luggage. Leipz. 1867. S.   **D 1328**
Diethoff, E. Unter der harten hand ; culturhistorisches zeitgemälde, mit einer einleitung von Hans Ziegler. Stuttg. [1884]. D.   **D 2801**

Dietrich, Ewald Christian Victorin, (*G. F. Horvath*). Albrecht der Bär, herzog von Ascanien, markgraf zu Brandenburg, oder Die gründung von Berlin. Meissen. 1830. S.   **D 1351**
— Chitava, Zittaus begründerin, oder Der kampf der deutschen gegen die wenden am wahlenfelde und an der blutmühle bei Teuschnitz im jahre 923 ; historischer roman. Meissen. 1830. S.   **D 1352**
— Des pfarrers tochter in Taubenhayn ; volkssage nach Bürger's ballade. Meissen. 1834. S.   **D 1353**
— Teutobog, oder Der teutonen heereszug gegen die romer im jahre der welt 3900 ; historischer roman. Meissen. 1830. S.   **H 4551**
Dillwyn, E. A. Jill. N. Y. 1885. D.   **D 1376**
Dilthey, Karl, *pseud., see* **Werner,** Julian.
Dincklage-Campe, Amalie Ehrengarte Sophie Wilhelmine *called* Emmy v. Durch die zeitung ; roman. Leipz. 1871. 2 v. in 1. D.   **D 1401**
— Emsland-bilder ; erzählungen aus dem Emslande. Stuttg. [1874]. T.   **D 1402**
  For contents see Deutscher katalog, p. 56.
— Die fünfte frau ; roman. Stuttg. 1873. 2 v. in 1. D.   **D 1403**
— Geschichten aus dem Emslande. Leipz. 1872. 2 v. in 1. D.   **D 1404**
  For contents see Deutscher katalog, p. 56.
— Heimath-geschichten. Paderborn. 1873. D.   **D 1405**
  For contents see Deutscher katalog, p. 56.
— Joseph und seine brüder ; erzählung. *In* Vierteljährl. mag.   **V2 v31**
— Unsere patriarchen ; erzählung aus dem Emslande. *In the same.*   **V2 v30**
Dingelstedt, Franz *freiherr* v. The amazon. Tr. from the german by J. M. Hart. N. Y. 1868. D.   **D 1451**
Dingy house at Kensington, The. N. Y. 1882. S.   **D 19**
Disraeli, B:, *earl of Beaconsfield.* Alroy. Lond. 1858. S.   **D 1501**
— Contarini Fleming. Leipz. 1846. S.   **D 1502**
— Endymion. N. Y. 1880. D.   **D 1503**
— *Same.* N. Y. 1880. Q.   **D 1503**
— Henrietta Temple ; a love story.   **D 1504**
— Lothair. N. Y. 1877. D.   **D 1505**
— The rise of Iskander. *In* Johnson, E. R. Little classics.   **J 926 v6**
— Sybil, or The two nations. Lond. 1858. S.   **D 1506**
— Tancred, or The new crusade. Leipz. 1847. 2 v. in 1. S.   **D 1507**
— Venetia. Leipz. 1858. 2 v. in 1. S.   **D 1508**
— Vivian Grey. Leipz. 1859. 2 v. in 1. S.   **D 1509**
— The young duke. N. Y. 1878. O.   **D 1510**
— *Same.* N. Y. 1878. Q.   **D 1510**
— *Same.* N. Y. 1864. 2 v. in 1. D.   **D 1510**
Dixon, J. Broken columns. *T. p. w.* [N. Y. 1863]. D.   **D 1551**
Dixon, W: Hepworth. Diana, lady Lyle. Leipz. 1877. 2 v. in 1. S.   **D 1601**
Doctor Ben: an episode in the life of a fortunate unfortunate. (Round-robin ser.) Bost. 1882. S.   **D 21**
Dodge, Mary Abigail, (*Gail Hamilton*). Child world, pt. 1. Ill. Bost. 1875. S.   **Dx 501**

x denotes books specially adapted for children.

Dodge, Mary Abigail, (*Gail Hamilton*).—*Contin'd.*
— First love is best ; a sentimental sketch. Bost.
1877. S.   **D 1651**
— Little folk life. N. Y. 1872. S.   **Dx 502**
— The pursuit of knowledge under difficulties.
In **Atlantic** tales.   **A 1876**
— Red-letter days in Applethorpe. Ill. Bost.
1866. S.   **Dx 503**
Dodge, Mary Elizabeth, *born* Mapes. Hans Brin-
ker, or The silver skates ; a story of life in
Holland. Ill. N. Y. 1879. S.   **Dx 551**
— Donald and Dorothy. Ill. Bost. 1883. D.
                                        Dx 552
Dodgson, C: Lutwidge, (*Lewis Carroll*). Alice's
adventures in wonderland. Ill. N. Y. 1880.
D.   **Dx 601**
— Rhyme ? and reason ? Ill. N. Y 1884 [1883].
D.   **Dx 603**
— Through the looking-glass and what Alice
found there. Ill. Lond. 1877. D. **Dx 602**
Doe, C: H. Buffets. Bost. 1875. O.   **D 1701**
Dohm, Hedwig, (*A. Dom*). Der erbe von Mar-
tella ; roman. N. Y. 1882. F.   **D 1726**
Dom, A., *pseud.*, *see* **Dohm**, Hedwig.
Donop, Amalie *freein* v., *born* Weber. (*Amalie
v. Clausberg*). Schloss Bucha. Leipz. 1853.
S.   **C 1701**
Dörle, A. Elisabeth ; eine erzählung für die
gesammte edlere lesewelt, wie auch für
eltern und kinder. Cinc. 1855. S. **D 1751**
— Die zelle der leiden, oder Die Kyburg ; eine
erzählung für die gesammte edlere lese-
welt, besonders für die reifere jugend.
Cinc. 1855. S.   **D 1752**
Doubleday, T: The murderer's last night. *In*
Tales from Blackwood.   **T 176 v7**
Douglas, Amanda Minnie. Claudia. Bost.
[1867]. D.   **D 1801**
— Floyd Grandon's honor. Bost. 1884 [1883]. D.
                                        D 1812
— From hand to mouth. N. Y. 1878. D. **D 1802**
— Home nook, or The crown of duty. Bost.
[1873]. D.   **D 1803**
— Hope mills, or Between friend and sweetheart.
Bost. 1880. D.   **D 1804**
— In trust, or Dr. Bertrand's household. Bost.
[1866]. D.   **D 1805**
— [The Kathie stories.] Bost. 1883. 6 v. S.
                                  Dx 653-Dx 658
   Contents. 1. Kathie's three wishes. 2. Kathie's
aunt Ruth. 3. Kathie's summer at Cedarwood. 4.
Kathie's soldiers. 5. In the ranks. 6. Kathie's har-
vest days.
— Lost in a great city. Bost. 1881. D. **D 1806**
— Nelly Kinnard's kingdom ; [a sequel to Seven
daughters.] Bost. 1876. D.   **Dx 652**
— The old woman who lived in a shoe, or There's
no place like home. New ed. Bost. 1883.
D.   **D 1811**
— Santa Claus land. Ill. Bost. [1883]. D.
                                         D 659
— Seven daughters. Ill. Bost. [1874]. S.
                                        Dx 651
— Stephen Dane. Bost. *n. d.* D.   **D 1807**
— Sydnie Adriance, or Trying the world. Bost.
1868. D.   **D 1808**
— Whom Kathie married. Bost. 1883. D.
                                        D 1810
— With fate against him. N. Y. 1870. D. **D 1809**
Douglas, Christiana Jane. Sir John. [*Anon.*]
N. Y. 1879. Q.   **D 2701**
— *Same.* Lond. 1879. 3 v. in 2. D.   **D 2701**

Douglas, Edith, *pseud.*, *see* **Burnham**, Clara
Louise.
Douglas, *Lady* Gertrude Georgiana.   Mar's
white witch ; a novel. Lond. 1877. 3 v. in
2. D.   **D 2851**
Doyle, A. Conan. Bones. *In* **Tales** from many
sources.   **T 178 v4**
Drayton ; a story of American life. N. Y. 1851.
D.   **D 4**
Drew, Catharine. The lutaniste of St. Jacobi's.
(Leisure hour ser.) N. Y. 1881. S. **D 1826**
Drille, Harton, *pseud.*, *see* **Gray**, Jennie H.
Drobisch, Gustav Theodor. Weisse rosen. Leipz.
1851. D.   **D 1851**
   For contents see Deutscher katalog, p. 57.
Droz, Antoine Gustave. Around a spring. (Leis-
ure hour ser.) N. Y. 1873. S.   **D 1901**
— Babolain ; a novel. Tr. from the french by
M. S. (Leisure hour ser.) N. Y. 1873. S.
                                        D 1902
Drury, Anna Harriet. Deep waters. Bost. 1864.
O.   **D 1951**
— Light and shade, or The young artist. N. Y.
1853. D.   **D 1952**
Duboc, C: E:, (*Robert Waldmüller*). Die Somo-
sierra. N. Y. 1881. F.   **D 2001**
— Unterm krummstab, in zwing und bann ; ro-
man. Leipz. 1858. D.   **D 2002**
— Die verlobte ; roman. N. Y. 1881. F. **D 2003**
Du Boisgobey, Fortuné. The golden tress. From
the french. N. Y. 1881. S.   **D 2102**
— The lost casket. Tr. from "La main coupée"
by S. Lee. N. Y. 1881. S.   **D 2101**
Ducange, V:, *see* **Brahain-Ducange**, V: H:
Joseph.
Duchess, The, *pseud.*, *see* **Argles**, Margaret.
Duchess of Mazarin, The ; a tale of the time of
Lewis XIV. Lond. *n. d.* S.   **D 5**
Dudevant, Amantine Lucile Aurore, *born* Dupin
(*George Sand*). André. Deutsch von L.
Eichler. Leipz. 1843. T.   **D 2151**
— Antonina. Tr. from the french by Virginia
Vaughan. Bost. 1870. S.   **D 2152**
— Der aristokrat und der industrielle. Deutsch
von W. Jordan. Leipz. 1846. 2 v. T.
                                        D 2153
— Bernhard. Deutsch von dr. Scherr. Stuttg.
1848. T.   **D 2154**
— Cesarine Dietrich. N. Y. 1878. O.   **D 2155**
— Consuelo ; a novel. From the french by Fay-
ette Robinson. Phila. [1882]. S. **D 2156**
— *Same, germ.* Consuelo. Deutsch von G. Julius.
Leipz. 1843. 4 v. S.   **D 2156**
   Note. For continuation see Countess of Rudolstadt.
— Der corsar. Deutsch von L. Meyer. Leipz.
1844. S.   **D 2157**
— The countess of Rudolstadt ; a sequel to "Con-
suelo". From the french by Fayette Robin-
son. Phila. [1883]. D.   **D 2161**
— *Same, germ.* Die gräfin von Rudolstadt.
Deutsch von L. Meyer. Leipz. 1844. 4 v.
S.   **D 2161**
— Fanchon, the cricket, or "La petite fadette".
Phila. 1871. D.   **D 2158**
— *Same, germ.* Die kleine fadette, [Die grille] ;
dorfgeschichte. Deutsch von dr. Scherr.
Stuttg. 1850. T.   **D 2158**
— Der geheimsecretär. Deutsch von L. Meyer.
Leipz. 1844. T.   **D 2160**
— Gilberte. Deutsch von dr. Scherr. Stuttg.
1846. 2 v. T.   **D 2159**

    x denotes books specially adapted for children.

Dudevant, Amantine Lucile Aurore, *born* Dupin (*George Sand*).—*Continued.*

— Handsome Lawrence ; a sequel to "A rolling stone". Tr. from the french by Carroll Owen. N. Y. 1878. O.   **D 2162**
— Der handwerker. Deutsch von L. Meyer. Leipz. 1843. 2 v. T.   **D 2163**
— Horace. Deutsch von L. Meyer. Leipz. 1845. S.   **D 2164**
— Indiana. Deutsch von L. Meyer. Leipz. 1843. S.   **D 2165**
— Isidore und Teverino. Deutsch von dr. Scherr. Stuttg. 1846. T.   **D 2166**
— Isolde. Deutsch von dr. Scherr. Stuttg. 1850. 2 v. T.   **D 2167**
— Jacques. Deutsch von L. Meyer. Leipz. 1844. 2 v. T.   **D 2168**
— Johanna. Deutsch von dr. Scherr. Stuttg. 1844. T.   **D 2169**
— Eine landidylle. Deutsch von W. Jordan. Leipz. 1847. T.   **D 2170**
— Ländlicbe erzählungen. Deutsch von A: Cornelius. Hildburgh. 1865. 2 v. in 1. D.   **D 2187**
Contents. Der teufelssumpf.—Franz der champi.
— Lelia. Deutsch von dr. Scherr. Leipz. 1844. 2 v. T.   **D 2171**
— Leone Leoni. Deutsch von L. Eichler. Leipz. 1843. T.   **D 2172**
— Die letzte Aldini. Deutsch von L. Meyer. Leipz. 1843. S.   **D 2173**
— Lucrezia Floriani. Deutsch von dr. Scherr. Stuttg. 1847. T.   **D 2174**
— Marquis de Villemer. Tr. from the french by Ralph Keeler. N. Y. 1878. O.   **D 2175**
— Mauprat. Tr. from the french by Virginia Vaughan. Bost. 1870. D.   **D 2176**
— *Same, germ.* Mauprat. Deutsch von L. Meyer. Leipz. 1844. 2 v. T.   **D 2176**
— Die mosaikarbeiter. Deutsch von L. Meyer. Leipz. 1844. S.   **D 2177**
— Der müller von Angibault. Deutsch von W. Jordan. Leipz. 1845. T.   **D 2178**
— My sister Jeannie. Tr. from the french by S. D. Crocker. Bost. 1874. D.   **D 2179**
— Novellen. Deutsch von dr. Scherr. Stuttg. 1848. 4 v. T.   **D 2180**
For contents see Deutscher katalog, p. 57.
— Pauline. Deutsch von L. Meyer. Leipz. 1843. S.   **D 2181**
— Der Piccinino. Deutsch von dr. Scherr. Stuttg. 1847. 2 v. T.   **D 2182**
— A rolling stone. Tr. from the french by Carroll Owen. N. Y. 1878. O.   **D 2183**
Note. For continuation *see* Handsome Lawrence.
— Das schloss von Oedenweiler. Deutsch von dr. Scherr. Stuttg. 1851. T.   **D 2185**
— Simon. Deutsch von L: Eichler. Leipz. 1843. S.   **D 2184**
— Der teufelssumpf; eine dorfgeschichte. Deutsch von dr. Scherr. *With her* Lucrezia Floriani.   **D 2174**
— The tower of Percemont. N. Y. 1877. S.   **D 2186**

Dufresne, Abel. Stories of Henry and Henrietta. Tr. from the french by H. B. A. Bost. 1860. D.   **Dx 701**
Dumas, Alexandre Davy. Adventures of a marquis. Phila. *n. d.* O.   **D 2251**
— Die beiden Dianen. Aus dem franz. von A: Zoller. Stuttg. 1847. 4 v. T.   **D 2253**

Dumas, Alexandre Davy.—*Continued.*

— Black. Aus dem franz. von G. Fink. Stuttg. 1859. 2 v. T.   **D 2254**
— Bragelonne. *See* The three musketeers.
— Cäsarine. In's deutsche übertragen von L. Fort. Grimma. 1857. S.   **D 2255**
— Catherine Blum. Aus dem franz. von A: Zoller. Stuttg. 1854. T.   **D 2256**
— The corsican brothers. Phila. 1866. O.   **D 2257**
— *Same, germ.* Eine corsische familie. Aus dem franz. von A: Zoller. Stuttg. 1847. T.   **D 2257**
— The count of Monte-Cristo. Ill. Phila. *n. d.* D.   **D 2258**
— Felina de Chambure, or The female fiend. *T. p. w.* [Phila.] O.   **D 2260**
— The forty-five guardsmen. Phila. *n. d.* O.   **D 2261**
— Der frauenkrieg. Aus dem franz. von A: Zoller. Stuttg. 1846. 3 v. T.   **D 2262**
— Gabriel Lambert. *With his* Eine corsische familie.   **D 2257**
— Geschichte eines todten. *With his* Eine corsische familie.   **D 2257**
— Gott und teufel. Aus dem franz. von A: Zoller. Stuttg. 1852. T.   **D 2263**
— Die gräfin von Charny. Aus dem franz. von A: Zoller. Stuttg. 1853. 7 v. T.   **D 2278**
— Der hase meines grossvaters. Aus dem franz. von A: Zoller. Stuttg. 1856. T.   **D 2264**
— Heinrich IV. Aus dem franz. von G. Fink. Stuttg. 1858. T.   **D 2265**
— Das horoscop. Aus dem franz. von G. Fink. Stuttg. 1859. 2 v. T.   **D 2266**
— Ingenue. Aus dem franz. von Ulrich Relsch. Brüssel. 1855. 4 v. S.   **D 2267**
— *Same.* Stuttg. 1855. 3 v. T.   **D 2267**
— The iron hand, or The knight of Mauléon. Phila. *n. d.* O.   **D 2252**
— *Same, germ.* Der bastard von Mauléon. Aus dem franz. von A: Zoller. Stuttg. 1848. 3 v. T.   **D 2252**
— Isaac Lacquedem. Aus dem franz. von A: Zoller. *T. p. w.* [Stuttg. 1853]. T.   **D 2269**
— Isabel of Bavaria, queen of France ; the mysteries of the court of Charles VI. Phila. *n. d.* O.   **D 2270**
— Johanna d'Arc, die jungfrau von Orléans ; historischer roman. Deutsch von F: W: Bruckbräu. Augsburg. 1847. S.   **D 2271**
— Karl der kühne. Aus dem franz. von G. Fink. Stuttg. 1857. 2 v. T.   **D 2272**
— Königin Margot. Aus dem franz. von A: Zoller. Stuttg. 1851. 2 v. T.   **D 2273**
— Meister Adam, der calabrese. Aus dem franz. von C. Büchele. *T. p. w.* [Stuttg.] T.   **D 2274**
— *Memoirs of a physician series.*
  1. The memoirs of a physician, or The secret history of the court of Louis XV. Phila. 1864. O.   **D 2275**
  2. The queen's necklace, or The secret history of the court of Louis XVI. Phila. [1875]. 2 v. in 1. O.   **D 2276**
  3. Six years later, or The taking of the Bastille. Phila. 1875. O.   **D 2277**
  4. The countess of Charny, or The fall of the french monarchy. Phila. [1875]. O.   **D 2278**

x denotes books specially adapted for children.

Dumas, Alexandre Davy.—*Continued.*
5. Andrée de Taverney. Tr. from the french by H: L. Williams, *jr. T. p. w.* [Phila]. O.
D 2279
6. The chevalier ; the 6th series and end of the "Memoirs of a physician." Phila. 1875. O.
D 2280
— *Same, germ.* Denkwürdigkeiten eines arztes.
3. Ange Pitou. Aus dem franz. von A: Zoller. Stuttg. 1851. 3 v. T. **D 2277**
Same. Jena. 1853. 3 v. T. **D 2277**
4. Die gräfin von Charny. Aus dem franz. von A: Zoller. Stuttg. 1853. 7 v. T. **D 2278**
— The Mohicans of Paris. Phila. [1875]. O.
D 2281
— *Same, germ.* Die Mohikaner von Paris. Aus dem franz. von L. v. Alvensleben. Brüssel. 1854. 10 v. S. **D 2281**
Note. For continuation, *see* Salvator.
— Der page des herzogs von Savoyen. Aus dem franz. von L. v. Alvensleben. Brüssel. 1854. 5 v. S. **D 2282**
— *Same.* Stuttg. 1855. 3 v. T. **D 2282**
— Der pechvogel. *T. p. w.* T. **D 2283**
— Der pfarrer von Ashbourn. Aus dem franz. von A: Zoller. Stuttg. 1854. 2 v. T.
D 2284
— El Salteador. Aus dem franz. von A: Zoller. Stuttg. 1854. T. **D 2285**
— Salvator ; fortsetzung der Mohikaner von Paris. Aus dem franz. von A: Zoller. Stuttg. 1856. 8 v. in 6. T. **D 2286**
— Die schwarze tulpe. Aus dem franz. von A: Zoller. Stuttg. 1850. T. **D 2287**
— Spellbound. N. Y. 1879. S. **D 2289**
— Die taube. Aus dem franz. von A: Zoller. Stuttg. 1851. T. **D 2290**
— Tausend und ein gespenst. Aus dem franz. von A: Zoller. Stuttg. 1850. 3 v. T.
D 2291
— *The three guardsmen series:*
1. The three guardsmen. Phila. [1875]. O.
D 2292
2. Twenty years after, [or Milady's son]. Phila. [1875]. O. **D 2293**
3. Bragelonne, the son of Athos. Phila. *n d.* O. **D 2294**
— *Same, germ.* Die drei musketiere.
1. Die drei musketiere. Aus dem franz. Stuttg. 1857. 2 v. T. **D 2292**
2. Zwanzig jahre nachher. Aus dem franz. Stuttg. 1857. 3 v. T. **D 2293**
3. Der graf von Bragelonne, oder Zehn jahre nachher. Aus dem franz. Stuttg. 1857. 7 v. T. **D 2294**
— Der Vesuv, und seine opfer. *With* Berthet, E. B. Der wehrwolf. **B 1703**
— Die wölfinnen von Machecoul ; episode aus dem krieg der Vendée im jahre 1832. Aus dem franz. von dr. Büchele. Stuttg. 1858. 5 v. T. **D 2295**
— Der wolfsführer. Aus dem franz. von G. Fink. Stuttg. 1857. 3 v. T. **D 2296**
Note. A large number of Dumas' works were in reality written by other persons and only revised by him, some not even that ; but all were published under Dumas' name. For particulars, the reader is referred to Quérard's Supercheries littéraires devoilées, v. 1.
Dumas, Alexandre, *fils.* Diana von Lys. Deutsch von C. F. Grieb. Stuttg. 1856. T. **D 2351**
— Drei starke männer ; roman. Deutsch von C. F. Grieb. Stuttg. 1856. T. **D 2355**

Dumas, Alexandre, *fils.*—*Continued.*
— Frauenleben. Deutsch von dr. Grieb. Stuttg. 1856. 2 v. T. **D 2352**
— Sophie Printems. Aus dem franz. von C. F. Grieb. Stuttg. 1857. 2 v. T. **D 2354**
— Tristram der rothe. Aus dem franz. von C. F. Grieb. Stuttg. 1858. T. **D 2353**
Duncan, H: The cottage fireside, or The parish schoolmaster. N. Y. 1843. S. **Dx 751**
— *and others.* Tales of the scottish peasantry. N. Y. 1861. S. **Dx 751**
Contents. Pref.—Maitland Smith.—Jane Morton.—Mary Wilson. — The cotter.—The apprentice.—The benevolent orphan.—The spoiled child.—The friendly farmer.—The honest farmer.—The dishonest farmer.
Dunlap, W: Memoirs of a water drinker. N. Y. 1837. 2 v. in 1. D. **D 2451**
Durand, Alice Marie Céleste Henry, *born* Fleury, (*Henry Gréville*). Ariadne. N. Y. 1878. D. **D 2551**
— Dosia ; a russian story. From the french by Mary Neal Sherwood. Bost. 1877. S.
D 2552
— Dournof ; a russian story. Phila. 1879. S.
D 2553
— Gabrielle, or The house of Maurèze. Tr. from the french. Phila. [1878]. S. **D 2554**
— Markof, the russian violinist. Tr. from the french by Helen Stanley. Phila. [1877]. S. **D 2555**
— Marrying off a daughter, (Marier sa fille). Tr. from the french by Mary Neal Sherwood. Phila. [1878]. S. **D 2556**
— Philomene's marriages ; with a preface to her american readers. Tr. from the french by Helen Stanley. Phila. 1879. S. **D 2557**
— Pretty little countess Zina ; a russian story. Phila. 1878. S. **D 2558**
— The princess Oghérof ; a russian love story. Phila. [1880]. D. **D 2559**
— Sonia ; a russian story. Phila. 1878. S.
D 2560
— Xénie's inheritance, (L'héritage de Xénie) ; a tale of russian life. Tr. from the french by Laura E. Kendall. Phila. [1880]. S.
D 2561
Durden, Dame, *pseud.* Mabel Howard. Bost. 1877. S. **Dx 801**
Düringsfeld, Ida v. **Reinsberg-.** Margarethe von Valois und ihre zeit ; memoiren-roman. Leipz. 1847. 3 v. S. **D 2601**
Dussaud, *Mme.* —, (*Jacques Vincent*). The return of the princess ; a novel. Tr. by Laura E. Kendall. N. Y. 1881. S. **V 751**
Dutheil, Eugénie, (*Mme. la comtesse La Rochère, Mlle. Eugénie La Rochère*). Tebaldo, oder Glaube und vorurtheil. Nach dem franz. von Joseph Borscht. Mainz. 1853. S.
L 626

E., A. L. O., *pseud., see* **Tucker,** Charlotte Maria.
E., D. J. W., *pseud, see* **Strussenfelt,** Ulrika Sophia v.
Early, M. A., *see* **Fleming, M. A.**
Eastman, Mary Henderson. Aunt Phillis's cabin, or Southern life as it is. *T. p. w.* S.
E 201
— Dahcotah, or Life and legends of the Sioux. *T. p. w.* D. **E 202**
Ebers, G: Moritz. Eine ägyptische königstochter ; historischer roman. 9te aufl. Stuttg. 1880. 3 v. in 2. D. **E 251**
— *Same, eng.* An egyptian princess. From the

Ebers, G: Moritz.—*Continued.*
german by Eleanor Grove. Leipz. 1870.
2 v. in 1. S.   **E 251**
— *Same.* N. Y. 1880. 2 v. S.   **E 251**
— The burgomaster's wife, *see below* Die frau
bürgermeisterin.
— An egyptian princess, *see above* Eine ägyptische
königstochter.
— The emperor, *see below* Der kaiser.
— Eine frage; idyll zu einem gemälde seines
freundes Alma Tadema. N. Y. 1881. F.
                                          E 252
— *Same, eng.* A question; the idyl of a picture
by his friend Alma Tadema. From the
· german by Mary J. Safford. N. Y. 1881. S.
                                          E 252
— Die frau bürgermeisterin; romance. 10te aufl.
Stuttg. 1882. D.   **E 257**
— *Same.* N. Y. 1883. F.   **E 257**
— *Same, eng.* The burgomaster's wife; a ro-
mance. From the german by Mary J.
Safford. N. Y. 1882. S.   **E 257**
— Homo sum; roman. 9te aufl. Stuttg. 1881. D.
                                          E 253
— *Same, eng.* Homo sum. Tr. from the german
by Clara Bell. Leipz. 1878. 2 v. in 1. S.
                                          E 253
— *Same.* N. Y. 1880. S.   **E 253**
— Der kaiser; roman. 9te aufl. Stuttg. 1881. 2
v. D.   **E 254**
— *Same.* N. Y. 1881. F.   **E 254**
— *Same, eng.* The emperor. From the german
by Clara Bell. Rev. and corr. in the U. S.
N. Y. 1881. 2 v. S.   **E 254**
— A question, *see above* Eine frage.
— Die schwestern; roman. 12te aufl. Stuttg.
1881. D.   **E 255**
— *Same, eng.* The sisters; a romance. From
the german by Clara Bell. Authorized ed.
N. Y. 1880. S.   **E 255**
— Serapis; historischer roman. N. Y. 1885. F.
                                          E 259
— *Same, eng.* Serapis; a romance. From the
the german; authorized ed., rev. and corr.
in the U. S. N. Y. 1885. S.   **E 259**
— Uarda; roman aus dem alten Aegypten. 9te
aufl. Stuttg. 1881. 3 v. in 1. D.   **E 256**
— *Same.* N. Y. 1882. F.   **E 256**
— *Same, eng.* Uarda; a romance of ancient
Egypt. From the german by Clara Bell.
Leipz. 1877. 2 v. in 1. S.   **E 256**
— Ein wort; roman. 4te aufl. Stuttg. 1883. D.
                                          E 258
— *Same.* N. Y. 1883. F.   **E 258**
— *Same.* *In* Vierteljährl. mag.   **V 2 v30**
— *Same, eng.* A word, only a word; a romance.
From the german by Mary J. Safford. N.
Y. 1883. S.   **E 258**
Ebner v. Eschenbach, Marie *freiin, born gräfin*
Dubsky. Lotti, die uhrmacherin; eine
erzählung. *In* Vierteljährl. mag.
                                          V 2 v24
Eckstein, Ernst. Aus secunda und prima;
humoresken. 19te aufl. Leipz. 1877. D.
                                          E 301
— Der besuch im carcer; humoreske. 49ste aufl.
Leipz. 1881. D.   **E 302**
— Die Claudier; roman aus der römischen kai-
serzeit. N. Y. 1883. F.   **E 308**
— *Same, eng.* Quintus Claudius; a romance of
imperial Rome. From the german by
Clara Bell, rev. and corr. in the U. S. N.
Y. 1882. 2 v. S.   **E 308**

Eckstein, Ernst.—*Continued.*
— Die feuerspritze; humoreske. 2te aufl. Leipz.
1877. D.   **E 304**
— Flatternde blätter; satirische und humoristi-
sche skizzen. Leipz. 1875. D.   **E 305**
— Die mädchen des pensionats; humoreske. 24ste
aufl. Leipz. 1881. D.   **E 303**
— Prusias; a romance of ancient Rome under
the republic. From the german by Clara
Bell. Authorized ed., rev. and corr. in the
U. S. N. Y. 1884. 2 v. S.   **E 309**
— *ed.* Humoristischer hausschatz für's deutsche
volk. Leipz. [1877-8]. 6 v. D.   **E 306**
— — *Same.* Neue folge. Leipz. [1879-81]. 6 v. D.
                                          E 307
Contents, see Deutscher katalog, p. 58.
Eddy, J: A dinner-party. *In* Stories by ameri-
can authors.   **S 35 v2**
Eden, *The hon.* Emily. The semi-detached house;
ed. by lady Theresa Lewis. Bost. 1860. S.
                                          E 851
Edgar, J: G: A boy's adventures in the baron's
wars, or How I won my spurs. Ill. Lond.
n. d. D.   **Ex 126**
Edgeworth, Maria. Tales and novels. 20 v. in
10. N. Y. 1853. D.   **E 401-410**
Contents. V. 1. Castle Rackrent.—Essay on irish
bulls.—Essay on the noble science of self-justification.
2. Forrester.—The prussian vase.—The good aunt.—
3. Angelina.—The good french governess.—Mademoiselle Panache, 2d pt.—The knapsack. **4.** Lame
Jervas.—The will.—The Limerick gloves.—Out of debt,
out of danger.—The lottery.—Rosanna. **5.** Murad,
the unlucky.—The manufactures.—The grateful
negro.—To-morrow. **6.** Ennui.—The dun. **7,8.** *Tales
of fashionable life:* Mancœuvring; Almeria; Vivian.
9, 10. *Tales of fashionable life:* The absentees; Madame de Fleury; Emilie de Coulanges; The modern
Griselda. **11, 12.** Belinda. **13.** Leonora, with letters on various subjects. **14, 15.** Patronage. **16.**
Same, concluded.—*Comic dramas:* Love and law, a
drama in 3 acts; The rose, thistle and shamrock,
drama in 3 acts. **17.** Harrington.—Thoughts on
bores. **18.** Ormond. **19, 20.** Helen.
— Murad, the unlucky. *In* Johnson, E. R. Little
classics.   **J 926 v12**
— Rosamond, with other tales. N. Y. 1859. D.
                                          Ex 601
[Edinburgh tales, The]: The elves, tr. from the
german of Tieck by T: Carlyle, with other
tales and sketches. N. Y. 1859. O.   **E 426**
Contents. Tieck, J: L: The elves.—**Johnstone,** C.
J. The sabbath night's supper.—Fraser, Mrs. The
cousins.—**Nicander,** K: A: The renounced trea-
sure.—**Gore,** C. G. F. The maid of honour.—**Quilli-**
nan, E: The rangers of Connaught.—**Mitford,** M. R.
The fresh-water fisherman.—**Crowe,** C. The story of
Martha Guinness and her son.—**Tytler,** M. Fraser.
The deformed.—**Johnson,** *Col.* The white fawn.—
Howitt, W: Johnny Darbyshire.—**Lauder,** *Sir* T:
D. Story of Farquharson of Inverey.
Eduard von Termont, oder Geschichte eines ver-.
lorenen sohnes. Nach dem franz. 2te aufl.
Schaffhausen. 1868. D. *With* Schmid, J.
C. v. Die kleine lautenspielerin.   **S 1465**
Edwards, Annie. Archie Lovell. N. Y. *n. d.*
O.   **E 451**
— At the eleventh hour. N. Y. 1882. S.   **E 462**
— A blue stocking. N. Y. 1877. D.   **E 452**
— Jet, her face or her fortune. *T. p. w.* [N. Y.
1879.] S.   **E 453**
— Leah; a woman of fashion. Leipz. 1875. 2 v.
in 1. S.   **E 454**
— The ordeal for wives. N. Y. 1872. D.   **E 455**
— Ought we to visit her? N. Y. *n. d.* O. **E 456**
— Philip Earnscliffe, or The morals of May Fair.
T. p. w. O.   **E 457**
— Steven Lawrence, yeoman. Ill. N. Y. *n. d.*
O.   **E 458**

x denotes books specially adapted for children.

Edwardes, Annie.—*Continued.*
— Susan Fielding. N. Y. *n. d.* O.   **E 459**
— A vagabond heroine. N. Y. 1873. D.   **E 460**
— Vivian the beauty. N. Y. 1880. S.   **E 461**
Edwards, Amelia Blandford. Barbara's history. Leipz. 1864. 2 v. in 1. S.   **E 501**
— *Same, germ.* Barbara. Aus dem englischen von Alma v. Metzsch. Leipz. 1865. 2 v. S.   **E 501**
— Debenham's vow. Leipz. 1870. 2 v. 1. S.   **E 502**
— The four-fifteen express. *In* Johnson, E. R. Little classics.   **J 926 v8**
— Hand and glove. N. Y. 1866. O.   **E 503**
— In the days of my youth. Leipz. 1873. 2 v. in 1. S.   **E 504**
— The ladder of life, a heart-history. N. Y. 1865. O.   **E 505**
— *Same.* Lond. *n. d.* S.   **E 505**
— Lord Brackenbury. N. Y. 1880. Q.   **E 506**
— *Same.* Leipz. 1880. 2 v. in 1. S.   **E 506**
— Miss Carew. Leipz. 1865. 2 v. in 1. S.   **E 507**
— Monsieur Maurice. Leipz. 1873. S.   **E 508**
— My brother's wife. N. Y. 1865. O.   **E 509**
— A night on the borders of the Black Forest. Leipz. 1874. S.   **E 510**
   Includes, The story of Salome.—In the confessional. — The tragedy in the palazzo Bordello.—The four-fifteen express. — Sister Johanna's story. — All saints' eve.
Edwards, C: Di Vasari ; a tale of Florence. *In* Tales from Blackwood.   **T 176 v8**
Edwards, Matilda Barbara Betham-. Brother Gabriel. Leipz. 1878. 2 v. in 1. S.   **E 551**
— Disarmed ; a novel. N. Y. 1883. Q.   **E 556**
— Doctor Jacob. Bost. 1869. S.   **E 552**
— Exchange no robbery, or Fated by a jest. N. Y. 1883. Q.   **E 555**
— Felicia. Leipz. 1875. 2 v. in 1. S.   **E 553**
— The flower of doom, and other stories. N. Y. 1885. S.   **E 559**
   Includes, Love and manuscript. — A group of immortals.—The rebuke amid roses.
— Love and mirage, or The waiting on an island ; an out-of-door romance. [*Anon.*] N. Y. 1884. S.   **E 558**
— Pearla, or The world after an island ; a novel. N. Y. 1883. S.   **E 557**
— The Sylvestres. Leipz. 1872. S.   **E 554**
Edwards, Rollin. Twice defeated, or The story of a dark society in two countries. Phila. 1877. D.   **E 601**
Effingham, C., esq. *pseud., see* Cooke, J: Esten.
Eggleston, E: The circuit rider. *T. p. w.* [N. Y. 1874.] D.   **E 651**
— The end of the world ; a love story. Ill. N. Y. [1872.] D.   **E 652**
— The hoosier schoolboy. Ill. N. Y. 1883. D.   **Ex 176**
— The hoosier schoolmaster. Ill. N. Y. 1879. D.   **E 653**
— The mystery of Metropolisville. Ill. N. Y. [1873.] D.   **E 654**
— Queer stories for boys and girls. N. Y. 1884. D.   **Ex 177**
— Roxy. N. Y. [1878]. D.   **E 655**
Eggleston, G: Cary. The big brother ; a story of indian war. N. Y. 1875. D.   **Ex 151**
— Captain Sam, or The boy scouts of 1814. N. Y. 1876. D.   **Ex 152**
— A man of honor. Ill. N. Y. [1873]. D.   **E 701**
— The wreck of the Red Bird ; a story of the Carolina coast. N. Y. 1882. D.   **Ex 154**

Eginhardt, *pseud., see* **Plänckner,** Othello v.
Eichholz, Ehrenreich. Ein mann aus dem volke ; ein buch für das volk. Leipz. 1848. S.   **E 801**
Eikenhorst, L. v. Amsterdams geheimnisse. Aus dem holländischen von Eugen Zoller. Stuttg. 1845. 3 b. T.   **E 851**
Eiloart, Elizabeth, *mrs.* C. J. G. The boy with an idea. *T. p. w.* D.   **Ex 201**
— The curate's discipline. N. Y. 1867. O.   **E 901**
— The dean's wife. N. Y. 1881. Q.   **E 902**
— *Same ;* a novel. Lond. 1880. 3 v. in 2. D.   **E 902**
— The love that lived ; a novel. Lond. 1874. 3 v. in 2. D.   **E 903**
Elbe, A. von der, *pseud., see* **Decken,** Augusta v. der.
Elbon, Barbara, *pseud., see* **Halstead,** Leonora B.
Elder, W: The enchanted beauty and other tales, essays and sketches. Phila. 1860. D.   **E 951**
Eliot, Alice, *pseud., see* **Jewett,** Sarah Orne.
Eliot, George, *pseud., see* **Cross,** Marian.
Elisabeth, Pauline Elisabeth Ottilie Louise *queen of Rumania,* (*Carmen Sylva*). Pilgrim sorrow ; a cycle of tales. Tr. by Helen Zimmern. Portrait. N. Y. 1884. S.   **E 976**
Elizabeth, Charlotte, *pseud., see* **Tonna,** Charlotte Elizabeth.
Ellersberg, Eduard, *pseud., see* **Ziehen,** E: A: Philipp.
Elling, Franz V., *pseud., see* **Müller,** K:
Elliot, Frances. The italians. N. Y. 1875. D.   **E 1001**
Ellis, Sarah Stickney. First impressions, or Hints to those who would make home happy. N. Y. 1857. S.   **Ex 251**
— Home, or The iron rule ; a domestic story. N. Y. 1855. D.   **E 1051**
— Look to the end, or The Bennets abroad. N. Y. 1845. O.   **E 1052**
— The ministers family, or Hints to those who would make home happy. N. Y. 1857. S.   **Ex 252**
— Pictures of private life. Phila. 1833. T.   **E 1053**
   Contents. An apology for fiction.—The hall and the cottage.—Ellen Eskdale.—The curate's wife.—Marriage as it may be.
— Somerville Hall, or Hints to those who would make home happy. N. Y. 1859. S.   **Ex 253**
Elster, Christian. Ein fremder vogel ; erzählung. Aus dem norweg. von J. C. Poestion. *In* Vierteljährl. mag.   **V2 v30**
Elwell, E: H: The boys of thirty-five ; a story of a seaport town. Bost. 1884 [1883]. S.   **Ex 276**
Emery, Sarah A. Three generations. Bost. 1872. O.   **E 1101**
Énault, L: Christine. From the french by Elizabeth W. Pendleton. (Leisure hour scr.) N. Y. 1883. S.   **E 1301**
Enders, M. A. Steevenbord ; novelle. *In* Vierteljährl. mag.   **V2 v22**
— Trautenheim ; novelle. *In the same.*   **V2 v25**
Engel, J: Jakob. Herr Lorenz Stark ; ein charaktergemälde. Mit einer einleitung von Joseph Kürschner. Stuttg. [1882]. D.   **E 1126**
Engelhard, Karoline. Lebensbilder von der verfasserin der Gesammelten briefe von Julie. Leipz. 1824. S.   **E 1151**

Engelen, A. W., (*Herman von Appeltern*). Der Schutzgeist. Frei nach dem holländischen bearb. von J. D. v. Betaz. Stuttg. 1844. 2 v. T.   **A 1351**

Erckmann, Émile, *and* Alexandre **Chatrian.** The blockade, or Episodes of the siege of Phalsbourg. Lond. [187-]. S. **E 1208**

— Brigadier Frederick. N. Y. 1875. O. **E 1201**

— The conscript, or The invasion of France. Tr. by H. W. Dulcken. Lond. [187-]. S.   **E 1209**

Note. For continuation, *see* Waterloo.

— Das forsthaus. Aus dem franz. übers. von H. v. Feltheim. Berlin. 1867. S. **E 1207**

— Friend Fritz ; a tale of the banks of the Lauter. N. Y. 1877. D. **E 1202**

— The invasion of France in 1814 ; comprising the night-march of the russian army past Phalsbourg. N. Y. 1871. D. **E 1206**

— Madame Thérèse, or The volunteers of '92. N. Y. 1869. D. **E 1203**

— The polish jew. From the french by Caroline , A. Merighi. N. Y. [1885]. S. **E 1212**

— The story of a peasant. Lond. *n. d.* 4 v. S.
1. The statesgeneral [1789], or The beginning of the great french revolution. **E 1204 v1**
2. The country in danger [1792], or Episodes of the great french revolution. **E 1204 v2**
3. Year one of the republic [1793]. **E 1204 v3**
4. Citizen Bonaparte, 1794—1815. **E 1204 v4**

— The story of the plébiscite ; told by one of the seven million five hundred thousand who voted "yes". From the french. Lond. 1874. S. **E 1211**

— Strange stories, (Contes fantastiques). From the french. N. Y. 1880. S. **E 1205**

Contents. The mysterious sketch. — The dean's watch.— "Abraham's offering".— The three souls.— The invisible eye.—The wonderful glass.

— Waterloo ; a sequel to "The conscript of 1813". Tr. from the french by H. W. Dulcken. Lond. [187-]. S. **E 1210**

Erma's engagement, by the author of "Blanche Seymour". Phila. 1873. O. **E 1**

Ernesti, Luise, *pseud., see* **Humbracht,** Malvine v.

Erskine, *Mrs.* T: Wyncote. (Leisure hour ser.) N. Y. 1875. S. **E 1251**

Estelle Russell, [by the author of The private life of Galileo]. Leipz. 1870. 2 v. in 1. S. **E 2**

Ettrick shepherd, The, *see* **Hogg,** James.

Evans, Augusta J., *see* **Wilson,** Augusta J.

Evans, Marian, *see* **Cross,** Marian, (*George Eliot*).

Everett, W: Double play, or How Joe Hardy chose his friends. Ill. Bost. 1871. S. **Ex 301**

Ewald, Herman F: The story of Waldemar Krone's youth. Tr. from the danish. Phila. 1868. D. **E 1351**

Ewing, Juliana Horatia, *born* Gatty. The brownies, and other tales. 3d ed. Lond. 1875. D. **Ex 356**

Includes, The land of lost toys.—Three christmas trees.—An idyll of the wood.—Christmas crackers.— Amelia and the dwarfs.

— Jackanapes. Ill. Lond. 1884. O. **Ex 357**

— Jan of the windmill ; a story of the plains. Bost. 1878. S. **Ex 351**

— Mrs. Overtheway's remembrances. Ill. Bost. 1881. S. **Ex 352**

— Six to sixteen ; a story for girls. Ill. Bost. 1880. S. **Ex 353**

— We and the world ; a book for boys. Ill. Bost. 1880. S. **Ex 355**

Eytinge, Margaret. The ball of the vegetables, and other stories in prose and verse. N. Y. 1883. O. **Ex 501**

Fabre, Ferdinand. The abbé Tigrane, candidate for the papal chair. Tr. by the rev. Leonard Woolsey Bacon. N. Y. 1875. D. **F 101**

Fabre d'Olivet, D. Theophrastus Paracelsus, oder Der arzt ; historischer roman aus den zeiten des mittelalters. Nach dem franz. von E: Liber. Magdeb. 1842. 3 v. S. **O 551**

Fadette, *pseud., see* **Rodney,** Minnie Reeves.

Fairfax, Lina R. The misfortunes of bro. Thomas Wheatley. *In* Stories by american authors. **S 35 v6**

Falk, C. Um ein herz ; novelle. N. Y. 1882. F. **F 126**

Famous victory, A. Chicago. 1880. D. **F 1**

Fanchette, by one of her admirers. (Roundrobin ser.) Bost. 1883. S. **F 5**

Fargus, F: J:, (*Hugh Conway*). Bound together ; tales. (Leisure hour ser.) N. Y. 1884. S. **F 2003**

Contents. The secret of the Stradivarius.—Fleurette.— A cabinet secret.—The bandsman's story.— The Blatchford bequest.— My first client.—Our last walk.—Miss River's revenge.—The daughter of the stars.—In one short year.—The truth of it.—A speculative spirit.

— Called back. (Leisure hour ser.) N. Y. 1884. S. **F 2001**

— Carriston's gift, and other tales. (Leisure hour ser.) Portrait and ill. N. Y. 1885. S. **F 2004**

Includes, Chewton-Abbot.— Paul Vargas.— A dead man's face.—Julian Vanneck.—The "bichwa."

— Dark days. (Leisure hour ser.) N. Y. 1884. S. **F 2002**

Farjeon, B: Leopold. Blade-o' grass. N. Y. 1873. O. **F 151**

— Golden grain. N. Y. 1874. O. **F 152**

— Great Porter square ; a mystery. N. Y. 1885. Q. **F 154**

— Grif ; a story of australian life. N. Y. 1872. O. **F 153**

— Love's harvest ; a novel. N. Y. 1885. Q. **F 155**

Farman, Ella, *see* **Pratt,** Ella, *born* Farman.

Farquharson, Martha, *see* **Finley,** Martha.

Farrar, C: A. J. Wild woods life, or A trip to Parmachenee ; a realistic story of life in the woods. Ill. Bost. 1884. S. **Fx 177**

Farrar, Eliza Ware. Young folks' Robinson Crusoe, or The adventures of an englishman who lived alone for five years on an island in the Pacific ocean ; ed. by W: T. Adams. Bost. 1882 [1881]. O. **Fx 101**

Farrar, F: W: Eric, or Little by little ; a tale of Roslyn school. N. Y. 1879. D. **Fx 151**

— Julian Home ; a tale of college life. N. Y. 1878. T. **Fx 152**

— St. Winifred's, or The world of school. N. Y. 1880. T. **Fx 153**

Fawcett, Edgar. The adventures of a widow ; a novel. Bost. 1884. D. **F 205**

— An ambitious woman ; a novel. Bost. 1884 [1883]. D. **F 203**

— A gentleman of leisure. Bost. 1881. T. **F 202**

— A hopeless case. Bost. 1880. T. **F 201**

— Rutherford. N. Y. 1884. D. **F 206**

— Tinkling cymbals ; a novel. Bost. 1884. D. **F 204**

Fels, *pseud., see* **Bäuerle,** Adolf.

Fels, Egon, *pseud., see* **Herbert,** Johanna.

Fénelon, François de **Salignac de La Mothe.** The adventures of Telemachus, the son of Ulysses. From the french by J: Hawkesworth; with a life of the author and remarks on epic poetry and on the excellence of Telemachus. N. Y. 1857. 2 v. in 1. T. **F 301**

Fenn, G: Manville. The clerk of Porthwick. Leipz. 1881. 2 v. in 1. S. **F 352**
— Middy and ensign, or The jungle station; a tale of the Malay peninsula. Ill. N. Y. 1883. D. **Fx 202**
— Off to the wilds; the adventures of two brothers in south Africa. N. Y. 1882. D. **Fx 201**
— The parson o' Dumford. Leipz. 1880. 2 v. in 1. S. **F 351**
— *Same.* N. Y. 1879. Q. **F 351**
— Poverty Corner; a city story. N. Y. 1885. S. **F 353**
— The silver cañon; a tale of the western plains. Ill. N. Y. 1884. D. **Fx 203**
— Sweet Mace; a Sussex legend of the iron times. N. Y. [1885]. D. **F 354**
— The vicar's people. N. Y. 1881. S. **F 355**

Ferdinand * * *. Elise, oder Gesetz und natur; ein roman aus der neuesten zeitgeschichte. Stuttg. 1840. S. **F 401**

Féréal, M. V. de, *pseud., see* **Suberwick,** *Mme.* —.

Ferguson, S: (?) Father Tom and the pope. *In* **Johnson,** E. R. Little classics. **J 926 v9**
— *Same. In* Tales from Blackwood. **T 176 v3**

Fern, Fanny, *pseud., see* **Parton,** Sara Payson.

Ferrier, Susan Edmondstone. Marriage. N. Y. 1860. O. **F 501**

Ferry, Gabriel, *pseud., see* **Bellemarre,** Eugène L: Gabriel de Ferry de.

Fetherstonhaugh, *The hon. mrs.* Maria Georgiana, *born* Carleton. Kingsdene. N. Y. 1878. Q. **F 601**

Feuillet, Octave. Camors, or Life under the new empire. N. Y. 1868. D. **F 651**
— A marriage in high life. From the french by Celia Logan. Phila. [1876]. D. **F 652**

Féval, Paul H: Corentin. Der bucklige. Aus dem franz. Stuttg. 1859. 3 v. T. **F 701**

Fielding, H: The history of the adventures of Joseph Andrews and his friend mr. Abraham Adams; with a short biography by F: Roscoe. Lond. 1876. D. **F 801**
— *Same, germ.* Geschichte und abenteuer von Joseph Andrews und seinem freunde herrn Abraham Adams; geschrieben in nachahmung der manier von Cervantes, verfasser des Don Quixote. Auz dem englischen von O. v. Czarnowski. Braunsch. 1848. 3 v. S. **F 801**
— The history of Tom Jones, a foundling. Leipz. 1844. 2 v. in 1. S. **F 802**
— *Same, germ.* Geschichte des Tom Jones, eines findling. Neu aus dem englischen übertragen von A. Dinzmann. V. 4-6. Braunsch. 1848. 3 v. S. **F 802**

Fields, Annie, *born* Adams, *mrs.* James T. Asphodel. [*Anon.*] Bost. 1866. S. **F 751**

Fieling, C. A., *joint tr., see* **Oxenford,** J:

Fielt, Charlotte. Schloss Grünwald. N. Y. 1882. F. **F 776**

Filibert, *pseud., see* **Kähler,** L: A:

Findlay, Cecilia. Cross purposes. N. Y. 1880. Q. **F 851**

Finley, Martha, *born* Farquharson. Casella, or The children of the valleys. Phila. 1876. D. **F 901**
— *The Elsie series.*
1. Elsie Dinsmore. N. Y. 1877. S. **Fx 252**
2. Holidays at Roselands; with some after scenes in Elsie's life. N. Y. 1877. S. **Fx 253**
3. Elsie's girlhood. N. Y. [1872]. S. **Fx 254**
4. Elsie's womanhood. N. Y. [1875]. S. **Fx 255**
5. Elsie's motherhood. N. Y. 1876. S. **Fx 256**
6. Elsie's children. N. Y. [1877]. S. **Fx 257**

Fischer, J. H: L., (*Paul Hellmuth*). Anselmus, oder Die früchte des wahnes. Leipz. 1831. 2 v. S. **H 235g**
— Augustin. Leipz. 1829. 2 v. S. **H 2351**
— Bilder aus dem leben in erzählungen und novellen. Leipz. 1844. 3 v. S. **H 2354**
Contents, see Deutscher katalog, p. 69.

Fischer, L. V. Am weg zum kloster; eine novelle. *In* **Vierteljährl.** mag. **V 2 v25**
— Zur rechten zeit bankerott; eine novelle. *In the same.* **V 2 v28**

Fischer, W: Eine denkwürdige vorladung. *In* **Vierteljährl.** mag. **V 2 v36**
— Paul; eine erzählung. *In the same.* **V 2 v28**

Fisher, Frances C., (*Christian Reid*). Armine; a story. N. Y. 1884. O. **F 958**
— Bonny Kate. T. p. w. [N. Y. 1878]. O. **F 951**
— A daughter of Bohemia. Ill. N. Y. 1874. O. **F 952**
— Ebb-tide, and other stories. N. Y. 1872. O. **F 953**
Includes, Miss Inglesby's sister-in-law.—The story of a scar.—A doubt.
— A gentle belle. N. Y. 1879. O. **F 954**
— A heart of steel; a novel. N. Y. 1883 [1882]. S. **F 957**
— The land of the sky, or Adventures in mountain by-ways. Ill. N. Y. 1879. O. **F 955**
— Valerie Aylmer. N. Y. 1872. O. **F 956**

Fitzgerald, Percy. Young Cœlebs. Lond. 1881. 3 v. D. **F 976**

Fleming, George, *pseud., see* **Fletcher,** Julia Constance.

Fleming, M. A., *born* Early, (*Cousin May Carleton*). Nathalie Marsh, or Redmon's heiress; a tale of life in Nova Scotia. N. Y. 1865. O. **F 1001**

Flemming, Harford, *pseud., see* **McClellan,** Harriet.

Fletcher, Julia Constance, (*George Fleming*). The head of Medusa. Bost. 1880. S. **F 1051**
— Kismet. (No name ser.) Bost. 1877. S. **F 1052**
— *Same.* Bost. 1883. S. **F 1052**
Note. Also published under the name of A Nile novel.
— Mirage. (No name ser.) Bost. 1878. S. **F 1053**
— Vestigia. Bost. 1884. S. **F 1054**

Fletcher, Miriam. The methodist; incidents and characters from life in the Baltimore conference; with an introd. by W. P. Strickland. N. Y. 1859. 2 v. S. **F 1101**

Florian, J: P: Claris de, *see* **Claris de Florian,** J: P:

Floyd, Cornelia, (*Neil Forrest*). Mice at play; a story for the whole family. Ill. Bost. 1877. S. **F 1201**

x denotes books specially adapted for children.

Floyd, Margaret. Passages from the diary of a social wreck. *In* Stories by american authors. **S 35 v7**

Flygare-Carlén, Emilie, *see* Carlén, Emilie Flygare-.

Following on to know, or Old days at Hethering. N. Y. 1875. S. **F 3**

Foote, Mary, *born* Hallock. Friend Barton's concern. *In* Stories by american authors. **S 35 v4**

— The Led-Horse claim ; a romance of a mining camp. Ill. Bost. 1883. D. **F 1226**

Fornell, Bror E:, (*Jeremias Munter*). Ein funke. Aus dem schwedischen übers. von Gottlieb Fink. Stuttg. 1852. 2 v. T. **M 4701**

Forney, J: Weiss. The new nobility ; a story of Europe and America. N. Y. 1881. D. **F 1251**

Forrest, Neil, *pseud., see* Floyd, Cornelia.

Forrester, Fanny, *pseud., see* Judson, Emily Chubbock.

Forrester, Frank, *pseud., see* Herbert, H: W:

Forstenheim, Anna. Prinz Tantalus ; eine erzählung. *In* Vierteljährl. mag. **V 2 v28**

Foster, Isabella H. (*Faye Huntington*). Echoing and re-echoing. Bost. 1878. D. **Fx 601**

— What Fide remembers. Ill. N. Y. 1884. D. **Fx 602**

Fothergill, Jessie. The first violin. (Leisure hour ser.) N. Y. 1878. S. **F 1401**

— Kith and kin ; a novel. (Leisure hour ser.) N. Y. 1881. S. **F 1405**

— Made or marred. *With her* One of three. **F 1404**

— One of three. (Leisure hour ser.) N. Y. 1881. S. **F 1404**

— Peril ; a novel. (Leisure hour ser.) N. Y. 1881. S. **F 1406**

— Probation. (Leisure hour ser.) N. Y. 1879. S. **F 1402**

— The Wellfields. (Leisure hour ser.) N. Y. 1880. S. **F 1403**

Fouqué, F: H: K: de La Motte, *see* La Motte Fouqué, F: H: K: de.

Fournier, L: P: Narcisse, *joint author, see* Arnould, A: J: François.

Fox, Emily. Gemini. (No name ser.) Bost. 1878. S. **F 1451**

— Will Denbigh, nobleman. (No name ser.) Bost. 1877. S. **F 1452**

Foxton, E. *pseud., see* Palfrey, Sarah Hammond.

Francillon, Robert E: A dog without a tail. *In* Tales from Blackwood. **T 177 v6**

— Face to face ; a fact in seven fables. N. Y. 1884. Q. **F 1506**

— Grace Owen's engagement. *In* Tales from Blackwood. **T 177 v2**

— A great heiress ; a fortune in seven checks. N. Y. 1883. Q. **F 1504**

— Left-handed Elsa. *In* Tales from Blackwood. **T 177 v12**

— Quits at last ; an account in seven items. N. Y. 1882. Q. **F 1503**

— Rare good luck ; a fortune in seven strokes. N. Y. 1877. O. **F 1501**

— A real queen ; a novel. N. Y. 1884. Q. **F 1505**

— *Same;* a romance. Lond. 1884. 3 v. in 1. D. **F 1505**

— A story of Eulenberg. *In* Tales from Blackwood. **T 177 v8**

— Under Slieve-ban ; a yarn in seven knots. (Leisure hour ser.) N. Y. 1881. S. **F 1502**

François, Marie Louise v. Judith die Kluswirtin. Stuttg. *n. d.* D. **F 1527**

— Phosphorus Hollunder. Stuttg. [1881]. D. **F 1526**

— Zu füssen des monarchen. *With her* Phosphorus Hollunder. **F 1526**

Franzos, K: Emil. The jews of Barnow ; stories. From the german by M. W. McDowall. N. Y. 1883. S. **F 1903**
Contents. The Shylock of Barnow. — Chane. — Two saviours of the people. — "The child of the atonement." — Esterka Regina. — "Baron Schmule." — The picture of Christ.—Nameless graves.

— Ein kampf um's recht. N. Y. 1882. F. **F 1902**

— Molchko von Parma ; geschichte eines jüdischen soldaten. N. Y. 1882. F. **F 1901**

— Die reise nach dem schicksal ; erzählung. N. Y. 1885. F. **F 1904**

— *Same. In* Vierteljährl. mag. **V 2 v37**

Fraser, *Mrs.—*. The cousins. *In* Edinburgh tales. **E 426**

Fraser-Tytler, C. C., *see* Liddell, Catherine Christina.

Frazar, Douglas. Perseverance Island, or the Robinson Crusoe of the 19th century. Ill. Bost. 1885 [1884]. D. **F 2051**

Frederick, Bertha, *born* Heyn, (*Golo Raimund, Georg Dannenberg*). Bürgerlich blut ; roman. 2te aufl. Berlin. 1879. D. **D 201**

— Ein hartes herz. Hannover. 1860. 2 v. S. **D 202**

— *Same, eng.* A hard heart. From the german by S. H. Phila. 1884. D. **D 202**

— A new race ; a romance from the german by mrs. A. L. Wister. Phila. 1880. D. **D 203**

— Schloss Elkrath. Hannover. 1866. 3 v. S. **D 204**

— Zwei menschenalter ; roman. 2te aufl. Berlin. 1880. D. **D 205**

— Zweimal vermählt ; roman. 2te aufl. Berlin. [1879]. D. **D 206**

— *Same. n. t.* **D 206**

Frederick, H. Brother Sebastian's friendship. *In* Stories by american authors. **S 35 v6**

Freeland, Carrie J. Bessie Hartwell, or Charity. N. Y. [1873]. S. **Fx 401**

Freese, Arthalis, *pseud., see* Steinlein, Laura.

Freese, Heinrich, *pseud., see* Schiff, Hermann.

French, Alice, (*Octave Thanet*). The bishop's vagabond. *In* Stories by american authors. **S 35 v7**

French, Harry Willard. Nuna, the bramin girl. Bost. 1882 [1881]. S. **F 1951**

French prisoner in Russia, The. Tr. from the french by P. S. N. Y. 1874. S. **F 4**

Frenzel, K: W: Theodor. Ein alter mann. T. *p. w.* O. **F 1551**

— Geld ; novelle. *In* Vierteljährl. mag. **V 2 v36**

— La pucelle. Hannover. 1871. 3 v. D. **F 1553**

— Nach der ersten liebe ; roman. N. Y. 1884. F. **F 1554**

— Papst Ganganelli ; ein historischer roman in 5 büchern. Berlin. 1864. 3 v. D. **F 1552**

Freudenberg, R: Boca del Drago ; ein roman. *In* Vierteljährl. mag. **V 2 v29**

Frey, Jakob. Das erfüllte versprechen. *With* Müller, W: Debora. **M 4436**

Freyer, Gustav, *pseud., see* Lafontaine, A: H: Julius.

Freytag, Gustav. Die ahnen : 1. Ingo und Ingraban ; 2. Das nest der zaunkönige ; 3.

x denotes books specially adapted for children.

Freytag, Gustav.—*Continued.*
　　Die brüder vom deutschen hause ; 4. Marcus König ; 5. Die geschwister ; 6. Aus einer kleinen stadt.
— Aus einer kleinen stadt. Leipz. 1881. D.
　　　　　　　　　　　　　　　　F 1612
— *Same.* N. Y. 1881. F.　　　　　F 1612
— Die brüder vom deutschen hause. Leipz. 1881. D.　　　　　　　　　　　F 1609
— Debit and credit, *see below* Soll und haben.
— *Same.* N. Y. 1881. F.　　　　　F 1609
— Die geschwister. Leipz. 1881. D.　F 1611
— *Same.* N. Y. 1881. F.　　　　　F 1611
— Ingo und Ingraban. Leipz. 1881. D.　F 1607
— *Same.* N. Y. 1881. F.　　　　　F 1607
— *Same, eng.* Ingo ; the first novel of a series entitled "Our forefathers". Tr. from the german by mrs. Malcolm. N. Y. 1873. S.
　　　　　　　　　　　　　　F 1607 v1
— *Same, eng.* Ingraban ; the second novel, *etc.* N. Y. 1873. S.　　　　F 1607 v2
— Karl Mathy ; geschichte seines lebens. 2te aufl. Leipz. 1872. O.　　　　F 1604
— Marcus König. Leipz. 1881. D.　F 1610
— *Same.* N. Y. 1881. F.　　　　　F 1610
— Das nest der zaunkönige. Leipz. 1881. D.
　　　　　　　　　　　　　　　　F 1608
— *Same.* N. Y. 1881. F.　　　　　F 1608
— Soll und haben ; roman in 6 büchern. 25ste aufl. Leipz. 1882. 2 v. O.　　　F 1605
— *Same.* N. Y. 1882. F.　　　　　F 1605
— *Same, eng.* Debit and credit. Tr. from the german by L. C. C., with a preface by C. C. J. Bunsen. N. Y. 1876. D.　　F 1605
— Die verlorene handschrift ; roman in 5 büchern. 11te aufl. Leipz. 1880. 2 v. O.
　　　　　　　　　　　　　　　　F 1606
Frick, Ida. Aus den bergen. Leipz. 1851. S.
　　　　　　　　　　　　　　　　F 1651
— Keine politik. Leipz. 1850. 2 v. S.　F 1652
— Die opfernden götter. Wien. 1862. 2 v. S.
　　　　　　　　　　　　　　　　F 1653
— Sirene. Leipz. 1852. 2 v. S.　　　F 1654
Friedrich, F: Die frau des ministers. Milw. 1871. O.　　　　　　　　　F 1701
Frith, H: On the wings of the wind. Ill. N. Y. 1885 [1884]. D.　　　　　　Fx 651
Fritze, Ernst, *pseud., see* **Reinhardt**, Luise.
Fryer, Alfred C. Book of english fairy-tales from the north-country. Lond. 1884. D.
　　　　　　　　　　　　　　　　Fx 701
Fullerton, Georgiana Charlotte, *born* Leveson-Gower, *lady.* Constance Sherwood ; an autobiography of the 16th century. Leipz. 1865. 2 v. S.　　　　　　F 1801
— Ellen Middleton. Balt. *n. d.* D.　F 1802
— Grantley Manor. Leipz. 1847. 2 v. in 1. S.
　　　　　　　　　　　　　　　　F 1803
— Lady-bird. Leipz. 1863. 2 v. in 1. S.　F 1804
— The lilies of the valley, or "I want it by such a day". Leips. 1879. S.　　F 1805
— Mrs. Gérald's niece. Leipz. 1870. 2 v. in 1. S.
　　　　　　　　　　　　　　　　F 1806
— Rose Leblanc. Leipz. 1880. S.　　F 1807
— Too strange not to be true. *T. p. w.*　F 1808
Fullom, Stephen Watson. The daughter of night ; a story of the present time. N. Y. 1859. O.　　　　　　　　　F 1851

Gaboriau, Émile. The clique of gold. Bost. 1874. O.　　　　　　　　　G 101
— File 113. Bost. [1875]. O.　　　　G 102

Gaboriau, Émile.—*Continued.*
— Other people's money. Bost. [1874]. O.
　　　　　　　　　　　　　　　　G 103
— The widow Lerouge. Bost. 1873. O.　G 104
— Within an inch of his life. Bost. *n. d.* O.
　　　　　　　　　　　　　　　　G 105
Gage, C: S. Mr. Bixby's christmas visitor. *In* Stories by american authors.　S 35 v9
Gagneur, Louise, *born* Mignerot. A nihilist princess. Tr. from the french. Chicago. 1881. D.　　　　　　　　　G 126
Galdós, B. Perez, *see* **Perez Galdós**, Benoit.
Galen, Philippe, *pseud., see* **Lange**, Philipp.
Gall, Luise v., *see* **Schücking**, Luise.
Galt, J: Haddad-Ben-Ahab, the traveller. *In* Johnson, E. R. Little classics.　J 926 v9
— Lawrie Todd, or The settlers in the wood. Lond. 1849. S.　　　　　　G 151
— Sir Andrew Wylie. *T. p. w.* S.　　G 152
— The wearyful woman. *In* Tales from Blackwood.　　　　　　　　　　T 176 v3
Gardiner, Margaret, *born* Power, *formerly mrs.* Farmer, *countess of Blessington.* Marmaduke Herbert, or The fatal error ; a novel founded on fact. Leipz. 1847. 2 v. S.
　　　　　　　　　　　　　　　　G 201
— Memoirs of a femme de chambre. Leipz. 1846. S.　　　　　　　　G 202
Gardonnière, Almire, (*Sir Henry Mortimer*). Die geheimnisse der Bastille. Deutsch von L: Dorn. Leipz. 1846. S.　　M 3851
Garibaldi, Giuseppe. The rule of the monk, or Rome in the 19th century. N. Y. 1870. O.
　　　　　　　　　　　　　　　　G 301
Garrett, Edward, *pseud., see* **Mayo**, Isabella.
Gaskell, Annie. A widow of Windsor. *T. p. w.*
　　　　　　　　　　　　　　　　G 351
Gaskell, Elizabeth Cleghorn, *born* Stevenson. Cousin Phillis. N. Y. 1864. O.　G 401
— Cranford. N. Y. 1860. S.　　　　G 402
— A dark night's work. Lond. 1871. S.　G 403
— Lizzie Leigh, and other tales. New ed., ill. Lond. 1882. D.　　　　　G 411
Includes, A dark night's work.—Round the sofa.—My lady Ludlow.—An accursed race.—The doom of the Griffiths.—Half a life-time ago.—The poor Clare.—The half-brothers.
— Mary Barton ; a tale of Manchester life. Lond. 1872. S.　　　　　　G 404
— *Same.* N. Y. 1883. Q.　　　　　G 404
— *Same, germ.* Mary Barton ; eine erzählung aus Manchester. Aus dem englischen übers. von Gottlob Fink. Stuttg. 1851. 2 v. T.　　　　　　　　　　G 404
— The moorland cottage. N. Y. 1875. S.　G 410
— My lady Ludlow. N. Y. 1858. O.　　G 405
— North and south. New ed., ill. Lond. 1881. D.　　　　　　　　　G 412
— Right at last, and other tales. N. Y. 1860. D.
　　　　　　　　　　　　　　　　G 409
Includes, The Manchester marriage. — Lois the witch.—The crooked branch.
— Ruth. Leipz. 1853. 2 v. in 1. S.　　G 406
— *Same, germ.* Aus dem englischen übers. von C. Buchele. Stuttg. 1853. 2 v. T.　G 406
— Sylvias freier. Aus dem englischen. Leipz. 1864. 2 v. D.　　　　　　G 407
— Wives and daughters ; an everyday story. Leipz. 1866. 3 v. in 2. S.　　G 408
Gaulle, Joséphine Marie, *born* Maillot. Adhemar de Belcastel, or Be not hasty in judging. Tr. from the french by P. S. A. [*Anon.*] N. Y. 1875. D.　　　G 451

x denotes books specially adapted for children.

Gaultier, Bon, *pseud.,* *see* **Martin,** Theodore.
Gautier, Judith. The usurper; an episode in japanese history. From the french by Abby Langdon Alger. Bost. 1884. D.   **G 551**
Gautier, Théophile. Captain Fracasse. From the french by M. M. Ripley. Ill. (Leisure hour ser.) N. Y. 1880. S.   **G 601**
— One of Cleopatra's nights, and other fantastic romances. Tr. by Lafcadio Hearn. N. Y. 1882. O.   **G 604**
    Includes, Clarimonde.—Arria Marcella.—The mummy's foot.—Omphale.—King Candaules.
— The romance of the mummy. From the french by Anne T. Wood, with an introd. by W: C. Prime. N. Y. 1863. D.   **G 602**
— Spirite ; a fantasy. N. Y. 1877. D.   **G 603**
Gayarré, C: E. Arthur. Aubert Dubayet, or The two sister republics. Bost. 1882. D.   **G 626**
Geheime geschichte der lieblinge der fürsten ; aus verschiedenen zeitaltern. Leipz. 1795, 2 v. O.   **G 1**
    Contents, see Deutscher katalog, p. 6¹.
Gerard, E. D., *pseud.* Beggar my neighbor ; a novel. N. Y. 1882. Q.   **G 652**
— My Paris masters. *In* **Tales** from many sources.   **T 178 v2**
— Reata, what's in a name ; a novel. N. Y. 1880. Q.   **G 651**
— The waters of Hercules ; a novel. [*Anon.*] N. Y. 1885. S.   **G 653**
— *Same.* N. Y. 1885. Q.   **G 653**
Gerhardt, Dagobert v., (*Gerhard v. Amyntor*). Drei küsse ; mit einer einleitung von Hans Ziegler. Stuttg. [1883]. D.   **G 676**
Germania ; jahrbuch deutscher belletristik, 1er jahrg. Bremen. 1851. S.   **G 2**
    Contents, see Deutscher katalog, p. 64.
Gerstäcker, F: Das alte haus ; erzählung. Jena. [187-]. S.   **G 701**
— *Same.* Leipz. 1857. S.   **G 701**
— Amerikanische wald- uud strombilder. Leipz. 1856. S.   **G 702**
— Aus dem matrosenleben. Leipz. 1857. S.   **G 703**
— Aus dem waldleben Amerikas. *See* Die regulatoren in Arkansas, *and* Die flusspiraten des Mississippi.
— Aus meinem tagebuch ; gesammelte erzählungen. Leipz. 1863. 2 v. S.   **G 704**
— Aus Nord- und Südamerika ; erzählungen. 3te aufl. *Bound with*
— Aus zwei welttheilen ; gesammelte erzählungen. 2te aufl. Jena. *n. d.* S.   **G 705**
— Die beiden sträflinge ; australischer roman. 3te aufl. Jena. *n. d.* S.   **G 706**
— Blau wasser ; skizzen aus see- und inselleben. 2te aufl. Jena. 1872. S.   **G 707**
— *Same.* Leipz. 1858. S.   **G 707**
— Die blauen und gelben ; venezuelanisches charakterbild aus der letzten revolution. *T. p. w.* O.   **G 708**
— Californische skizzen. Leipz. 1856. S.   **G 709**
— Die colonie ; brazilianisches lebensbild. 2te aufl. Jena. *n. d.* S.   **G 710**
    Note. For continuation, *see* Eine Mutter.
— Der deutschen auswanderer fahrten und schicksale. *With his* Skizzen ans Californien und Südamerika.   **G 723**
— *Same, eng.* The wanderings and fortunes of some german emigrants. Tr. by D: Black. N. Y. 1848. D.   **G 730**
— Die flusspiraten des Mississippi. (Aus dem waldleben Amerikas, 2te abth.) 5te aufl. Jena. 1873. S.   **G 711**

Gerstäcker, F:—*Continued.*
— *Same.* Leipz. 1858. 3 v. S.   **G 711**
— Die franctireurs ; eine erzählung aus dem deutsch-franz. kriege. *With* **Dedenroth,** E. H. Gabrielle.   **P 1951**
— Eine gemsjagd in Tyrol. 2te aufl. *With his* Hell und dunkel.   **G 714**
— General Franco ; lebensbild aus Ecuador. Jena. 1865. 3 v. S.   **G 712**
— Gold ! ; ein californisches lebensbild aus dem jahre 1849. 3te aufl. Jena. *n. d.* S.   **G 713**
— *Same.* Leipz. 1858. 3 v. S.   **G 713**
— Heimliche und unheimliche geschichten ; gesammelte erzählungen. *With his* Das alte haus.   **G 701**
— Hell und dunkel ; gesammelte erzählungen. 2te aufl. Jena. 1873. S.   **G 714**
— Im busch ; australische erzählung. Jena. 1864. 3 v. S.   **G 715**
— Inselwelt ; indische und australische skizzen. 2te aufl. Jena. *n. d.* S.   **G 716**
— *Same.* Leipz. 1860. 2 v. S.   **G 716**
— Der kunstreiter ; erzählung. 2te aufl. Jena. *n. d.* S.   **G 717**
— Mississippi-bilder ; licht- und schattenseiten transatlantischen lebens. 3te aufl. Jena. [187-]. S.   **G 718**
— *Same.* Leipz. 1856. 3 v. S.   **G 718**
— Eine mutter ; roman im anschluss an "Die colonie". N. Y. 1884. F.   **G 729**
— Nach Amerika ; ein volksbuch. 2te aufl. Jena. *n. d.* 2 v. S.   **G 719**
— Pfaire und schule ; eine dorfgeschichte. Leipz. 1849. 3 v. in 1. S.   **G 720**
— Die regulatoren in Arkansas. (Aus dem waldleben Amerikas, 1ste abth.) 5te aufl. Jena. 1873. S.   **G 721**
— Sennor Aguilar ; peruanisches lebensbild. Jena. 1865. 3 v. S.   **G 722**
— Skizzen aus Californien nnd Südamerika ; gesammelte erzählungen. 2te aufl. Jena. *n. d.* S.   **G 723**
— Tahiti ; roman aus der Südsee. 3te aufl. Jena. *n. d.* S.   **G 724**
— Unter dem äquator ; javanisches sittenbild. 2te aufl. Jena. 1872. S.   **G 726**
— Unter den penchuenchen ; chilenischer roman. Jena. 1867. S.   **G 725**
— Unter palmen und buchen ; gesammelte erzählungen. Leipz. 1867. 3 v. S.   **G 727**
— Der wilddieb ; erzählung. N. Y. 1881. F.   **G 728**
Gibbon, C: The braes of Yarrow ; a romance. N. Y. 1881. Q.   **G 802**
— *Same.* Lond. 1881. 3 v. in 2. D.   **G 802**
— By mead and stream ; a novel. N. Y. 1884. Q.   **G 806**
— For lack of gold ; a novel. New ed. Lond. 1881. D.   **G 807**
— For the king ; a novel. New ed. Lond. *n. d.* D.   **G 810**
— The golden shaft ; a novel. N. Y. 1882. Q.   **G 805**
— *Same.* Lond. 1882. 3 v. in 2. D.   **G 805**
— A hard knot ; a novel. N. Y. 1885. S.   **G 812**
— Heart's delight ; a story. N. Y. 1885. Q.   **G 811**
— A heart's problem ; a novel. N. Y. 1882. Q.   **G 803**
— *Same.* Lond. 1881. 2 v. in 1. D.   **G 803**
— In honour bound ; a novel. New ed. Lond. [1881]. D.   **G 808**
— Of high degree ; a story. N. Y. 1882. Q.   **G 804**
— *Same.* Lond. 1883. 3 v. in 2. D.   **G 804**

x denotes books specially adapted for children.

Gibbon, C:—*Continued.*
— The queen of the meadow ; a novel. N. Y. 1880. Q. **G 801**
— *Same.* Lond. 1880. 3 v. in 1. D. **G 801**
— Robin Gray ; a novel. New ed. Lond. [1881]. D. **G 809**
Gift, Theo, *pseud., see* Boulger, Dora.
Gilbert, W: De profundis ; a tale of the social deposits. Lond. 1866. S. **G 851**
— The struggle in Ferrara ; a story of the reformation in Italy. Ill. Phila. 1871. O. **G 852**
Giles, Ella Augusta. Out from the shadows, or Trial and triumph. Madison. 1876. D. **G 901**
Gillespie, T: Gleanings of the covenant. *In* Wilson, J: M. Tales of the borders. **W 2202 v15-23**
Contents. V. **15.** 1. The grandmother's narrative. 2. The covenanters' march. 3. Peden's farewell sermon. 4. The persecution of the M'Michaels. **16.** 5. The rescue at Enterkin. 6. The fatal mistake. 7. Bonny Mary Gibson. 8. The Eskdalemuir story. 9. The Douglas tragedy. **17.** 10. Sergeant Wilson. 11. Helen Palmer. 12. The Cairny cave of Gavin Muir. 13. Porter's Hole. **18.** 14. James Renwick. 15. Old Isbel Kirk. 16. The curlers. **17.** The violated coffin. **19.** 18. Kinaldy. 19. The trials of the rev. S: Austin. **20.** 20. John Goran's narrative. 21. "Old Bluntie ". 22. T: Harkness of Lockerben. 23. The shoes reversed. **21.** 24. The early days of a friend of the covenant. **23.** 25. The last scrap.
— The professor's tales. *In* Wilson, J: M. Tales of the borders. **W 2202 v1-14**
Contents. V. **1.** 1. The mountain storm. 2. The fair maid of Cellardykes. **2.** 3. The convivialists. 4. Phillips Grey. **3.** 5. Pheebe Fortune. **4.** 6. Early recollections of a son of the hills. 7. The suicide's grave. **5.** 8. The last of the pediars. 7. 9. Family incidents. 10. Home and the gipsy maid. 11. The return. 9. 12. The three brethren. 13. The mistake rectified. 14. Dura Den. **10.** 15. Peat-casting time. 16. The medal. **11.** 17. The social man. **12.** 18. The wedding. **13.** 19. The natural history of idiots. **14.** 20. The enthusiasts. 21. Trees and burns. **22.** Kirkyardd.
Gilliat, E. The dragonnades, or Asylum Christi. New ed. Lond. 1881. D **G 926**
Gilman, Caroline, *born* Howard, *mrs.* G: Tales and ballads. N. Y. 1839. D. **G 951**
Girardin, Delphine *born* Gay, *mme.* Émile de, *and others.* The cross of Berny, or Irene's lovers. Phila. 1873. D. **G 1001**
Giseke, H: L: Robert. Moderne titanen ; ein roman der gegenwart. Leipz. 1853. 3 v. S. **G 1051**
Glasbrenner, Adolf, (*Adolf Brennglas*). Aus dem leben eines gespentes. Leipz. 1838. S. **G 1151**
Contents, see Deutscher katalog, p. 65.
Glaser, Adolf, (*Reinald Reimar*). Familie Schaller. Prag. 1857. 2 v. T. **G 1101**
Glaubrecht, Julius. Roland von Rolandseck ; eine geschichtliche erzählung aus den zeiten Carls des grossen, in neuen rahmen gefasst. Ill. Regensb. 1871. S. **H 2783**
Glaubrecht, Otto, *pseud., see* Oeser, Rudolph L:
Gleich, F: Finglash und Maria Stormont, oder Die flüchtlinge. Leipz. 1824. S. **G 1251**
Gleig, G: Robert. Allan Breck. Phila. 1835. 2 v. D. **G 1301**
Glogau, Bertha. Im kopfe der anderen ; novelle. *In* Vierteljährl. mag. **V 2 v25**
— Sitzen geblieben ; eine novelle. *In the same.* **V 2 v25**
Glümer, Claire v. A noble name, or Dönninghausen. From the german by mrs. A. L. Wister. Phila. 1883 [1882]. D. **G 1326**

Godfrey, *Mrs.* G. W. Unspotted from the world; a novel. N. Y. 1883. Q. **G 1351**
— *Same.* Lond. 1883. 3 v. in 1. D. **G 1351**
Godin, Amélie, *pseud., see* Linz, Amélie.
Gödsche, Hermann Ottomar F:, (*Sir John Retcliffe*). Nena Sahib, oder Die empörung in Indien; historisch-politischer roman. N. Y. 1882. 3 v. F. **G 1376**
Contents. V. 1. Die tyrannen der erde. 2. Die böse saat. 3. Der sünden ernte.
Godwin, W: St. Leon ; a tale of the 16th century. Lond. 1850. D. **G 1401**
Gogol, N: Vasilievitch. Altväterische leute, und andere erzählungen. Deutsch von Julius Meixner. Stuttg. [1888]. D. **G 1427**
Contents. Altväterische leute. — Die nase.— Die erzählung von dem streite zwischen Iwan Iwanowitsch und Iwan Nikiforowitsch.—Iwan Theodorowitsch Schponka und seine tante.—Die equipage.— Aufzeichnungen eines wahnsinnigen.
— Russische novellen. Mit einer einleitung von F: Bodenstedt. Stuttg. [1881]. D. **G 1426**
Contents, see Deutscher katalog, p. 65.
Göhren, Caroline v., *pseud., see* Zöllner, Caroline.·
Goldammer, Leo. Schloss Kuckernese. Berlin. 1859. D. **G 1476**
Goldsmith, Oliver. The vicar of Wakefield. Phila. 1869. D. **G 1501**
— *Same. In his* Works. **820.2 : 30 v1**
— *Same. germ.* Der landprediger von Wakefield. Aus dem englischen von A. Dietzmann. Braunschw. 1848. T. **G 1501**
Goodwin, *Mrs.* H. B., *see* Talcot, *Mrs.* Hannah B.
Gore, Catherine Grace Frances, *born* Moody. Cecil, oder Die abenteuer eines stutzers. Aus dem englischen von A. Schraishuon. Stuttg. 1848. 2 v. T. **G 1551**
— The dean's daughter, or The days we live in. Leipz. 1853. 2 v. in 1. S. **G 1561**
— Das erstgeburtsrecht. Deutsch von L: Hauff. Stuttg. 1845. 2 v. T. **G 1552**
— Die frau des gesandten. Deutsch von L: Hauff. Stuttg. 1846. 2 v. T. **G 1553**
— Der geldverleiher. Deutsch bearb. von L: Hauff. Stuttg. 1846. 2 v. T. **G 1554**
— The maid of honor. *In Edinburgh* tales. **E 426**
— Mammon, oder Leiden und freuden des reichthums. Aus dem englischen von O: v. Charnowski. Leipz. 1856. 3 v. S. **G 1555**
— Ormington, oder Cecil als pair. Aus dem englischen von A. Schraishuon. Stuttg. 1848. 2 v. T. **G 1556**
— Progress and prejudice. N. Y. *n. d.* D. **G 1557**
— The queen of Denmark ; an historical novel. N. Y. 1859. O. **G 1558**
— Selbst, vom verfasser von Cecil. Aus dem englischen von A. Schraishuon. Stuttg. 1849. 2 v. T. **G 1560**
— The story of a royal favourite. N. Y. 1864. O. **G 1559**
Görling, Adolph, (*A. v. Oolenfeld*). Die vitalienbrüder, oder Des Störtebeker's leben und ende ; nach historischen quellen. Hannover. 1844. S. **G 1601**
Göthe, J: Wolfgang v. Confessions of a fair saint. *In* Hedge, F: H: Prose writers of Germany. **830.1 : 8**
— Elective affinities. (Leisure hour ser.) N. Y. 1872. S. **G 1651**

x denotes books specially adapted for children.

Göthe, J: Wolfgang v.—*Continued.*
— Novelle. *In* Hedge, F: H: Prose writers of
  Germany. 830.1 : 8
— Novels and tales. Lond. 1873. D. G 1652
  Contents. Elective affinities. — The sorrows of
  young Werther.—The recreations of the german emi-
  grants.—A fairy tale.—The good woman; a tale.
— *Same.* Lond. 1888. D. G 1652
— Wilhelm Meister's apprenticeship and travels.
  From the german by T: Carlyle. Bost.
  1876. 2 v. D. G 1653
— *Same*, extracts. *In* Hedge, F: H: Prose
  writers of Germany. 830.1 : 8
— *See also his collected works, in german*, 830 : R
  136, 830 : 137, *in english*, 830 : 151
Gotthelf, Jeremias, *pseud., see* Bitzius, Albert.
Gottschalck, Caspar F:, *see* Roscoe, W: Ger-
  man novelists. R 2451
Gottschall, K: Rudolf v. Das fräulein von St.
  Amaranthe ; roman. N. Y. 1882. F.
                                        G 1676
Gould, E: S. John Doe and Richard Roe, or
  Episodes of life in New York. N. Y. 1862.
  D. G 1701
Gould, Jeanie T., *see* Lincoln, Jeanie T.
Gozlan, Léon. Aristides Froissart. Deutsch
  von L. Eichler. Leipz. 1844. 2 v. S.
                                        G 1851
— Der arzt. Deutsch von L. Eichler. Leipz.
  1844. 4 v. S. G 1852
Grabowski, Stanislaus Stephan Albert *graf* v.
  (*Stanislaus Albert*). John Paul Jones ;
  biographischer roman. Hannover. 1860. 2
  v. S. G 1901
Graham, Ennis, *pseud., see* Molesworth, Mary
  Louisa.
Grant, James. The cameronians. N. Y. 1881.
  Q. G 1926
— *Same* ; a novel. Lond. 1881. 3 v. D. G 1926
— The royal highlanders, or The black watch in
  Egypt ; a novel. N. Y. 1885. Q. G 1927
Grant, Maria M. Artiste. Lond. 1871. 3 v. in 2.
  D. G 1956
— My heart's in the highlands. Leipz. 1878. 2 v.
  in 1. S. G 1951
— *Same.* N. Y. 1878. Q. G 1951
— One may day, a sketch in summer-time ; a
  novel. N. Y. 1882. Q. G 1954
— *Same.* Lond. 1882. 3 v. in 1. D. G 1954
— Prince Hugo ; a bright episode. N. Y. 1880. Q.
                                        G 1952
— *Same.* Lond. 1880. 3 v. in 1. D. G 1952
— The sun-maid ; a romance. [*Anon.*] Lond. 1876.
  3 v. in 2. D. G 1953
— *Same.* T. p. w. [N. Y. 1877]. O. G 1953
— Victor Lescar. Leipz. 1875. 2 v. in 1. S.
                                        ·G 1955
Grant, Robert. An average man. Bost. 1884.
  D. G 1977
— Confessions of a frivolous girl ; a story of
  fashionable life. Ill. Bost. 1880. D.
                                        G 1976
— *and others.* The king's men ; a tale of to-mor-
  row. N. Y. 1884. D. G 1978
  Note. Written conjointly by Robert Grant, J: Boyle
  O'Reilly, J. S. of Dale and J: T. Wheelwright.
Grattan, T: Colley. Jacqueline of Holland ; a
  historical tale. N. Y. 1831. 2 v. D.
                                        G 2051
Gray, A. M. Adah, the jewish maiden. *T. p. w.*
  [N. Y.] D. G 2101
Gray, Barry, *pseud., see* Coffin, Robert Barry.

Gray, Jennie H., (*Hearton Drille*). Tactics, or
  Cupid in shoulder-straps ; a West Point
  love story, by Hearton Drille. N. Y. 1863.
  S. G 2126
Gray, Robertson, *pseud., see* Raymond, Rossiter
  Worthington.
Grayson, Eldred, esq., *pseud.* Standish, the
  puritan ; a tale of the american revolution.
  N. Y. 1850. D. G 2151
Green, Anna Katherine. Hand and ring. Ill.
  N. Y. 1883. D. G 2205
— The Leavenworth case ; a lawyer's story. N. Y.
  [1878]. S. G 2201
— A strange disappearance. N. Y. 1880. S.
                                        G 2202
— The sword of Damocles ; a story of New York
  life. N. Y. 1881. D. G 2203
— X. Y. Z. ; a detective story. N. Y. 1883. S.
                                        G 2204
Greenough, Sarah Dane, *born* Loring. Ara-
  besques : Monarè, Domitia, Apollyona,
  Ombra. Bost. 1872. D. G 2251
— In extremis. Bost. 1872. D. G 2252
Greenwood, Grace, *pseud., see* Lippincott, Sara
  Jane.
Greenwood, James. A night in a workhouse.
  In Johnson, E. R. Little classics.
                                        J 926 v1
— The adventures of Reuben Davidger ; 17 years
  and 4 months captive among the Dyaks of
  Borneo. Ill. N. Y. 1866. O. G 2266
— *Same.* N. Y. 1879. Q. G 2266
Greg, Percy. Guy Neville's ghost. *In* Tales
  from Blackwood. T 177 v9
— Ivy, cousin and bride. N. Y. 1881. Q. G 2276
— *Same.* Lond. 1881. 3 v. in 1. D. G 2276
Grendel, M. R. Contrasts. N. Y. 1881. D.
                                        G 2301
Gresley, W: Charles Lever, or The man of the
  19th century. N. Y. 1847. D. · G 2351
— Church clavering, or The schoolmaster. Flem-
  ington, N. J. 1844. O. *In* The churchman's
  library. 204 : 16
Gréville, Henry, *pseud., see* Durand, Alice Marie
  Céleste Henry.
Grey, *Mrs.* E. C. Good society, or Contrasts of
  character. *T. p. w.* [N. Y. 1863]. O.
                                        G 2401
— A marriage in high life. Phila. *n. d.* O.
                                        G 2402
Griesinger, K: Theodor. Cagliostriana ; novel-
  lette aus herzog Friedrichs von Württem-
  berg *zeiten.* Stuttg. 1844. S. G 2501
— Friedrich von Zollern ; geschichtliche novelle
  aus dem 13ten jahrhundert. *With his*
  Cagliostriana. G 2501
— Ida, gräfin von Salmandingen ; geschichtliche
  novelle aus dem ende des 12ten jahrhunderts. Stuttg. 1844. S. G 2502
— Lebende bilder aus Amerika. Stuttg. 1858. D.
                                        G 2503
— Die letzten zeiten der Grävenitz ; historische
  novelle aus dem ende der regierungsjahre
  des herzogs Eberhard Ludwig von Würt-
  temberg. Stuttg. 1844. S. G 2504
Griffin, Gerald. Works. N. Y. *n. d.* 10 v. D.
                                        G 2551
  Contents. V. 1. *Tales of the Munster festivals:* The
  collegians; a tale of Garryowen. **2.** *Same:* The
  card-drawer.—The half-sir.— Suil Dhuv, the coiner.
  3. *Same:* "Holland tide."—The Aylmers of Bally-
  Aylmer.—The hand and word.—The barber of Bantry.
  —The brown man.— Owney and Owney-na-peak.—
  The village ruin.—The knight of the sheep.—The
  rock of the candle. **4.** *Same:* The rivals—Tracy's

x denotes books specially adapted for children.

Griffin, Gerald.—*Continued.*
ambition. **5.** Talis qualis, or Tales of the jury-room. **6.** The duke of Monmouth. **7.** Tales of the five senses: christian physiologist.—A night at sea. **8.** Poetical works. — Tragedy of Gisippus. **9.** The invasion. **10.** The life of Gerald Griffin, by his brother [Daniel].
— The duke of Monmouth. N. Y. *n. d.* D.
G 2552
— The invasion. N. Y. *n. d.* D.   G 2553
— Mr. Tibbot O'Leary, the curious. *In* **Johnson**, E. R. Little classics.   **J** 926 v5
— A night at sea. *With his* Tales of the five senses.   G 2554
— The swans of Lir. *In* **Johnson**, E. R. Little classics.   **J** 926 v1
— Tales of the five senses ; christian physiologist. N. Y. *n. d.* D.   G 2554
Contents. Introd.—The mechanism of sight: Uses and government of sight; The kelp-gatherer, a tale. —The mechanism of hearing: Uses of hearing: The day of trial, a tale.—Mechanism and uses of feeling: The voluptuary cured, a tale.—Mechanism and uses of smell; The self-consumed, a tale.—Mechanism and uses of taste; The selfish crotarie, a tale.—Of the intellect; A story of Psyche.
— Tales of the jury-room. *T. p. w.* D.   G 2555
Contents. The jury-room.— Sigismund.—The story teller at fault.—The knight without reproach.—The mistake.—Drink, my brother.—The swans of Lir.— McEneiry, the covetous.—Mr. Tibbot O'Leary, the curious.—The lame tailor of Macel.—Antrim Jack.— The prophecy.—Sir Dowling O'Hartigan.— The raven's nest.
— Tales of the Munster festivals. N. Y. *n. d.* D.
G 2556
Contents. Same as v. 3 of his Works, with sketches illustrative of life and manners in the south of Ireland added.
Griffiths, Arthur. Lola ; a tale of Gibraltar. N. Y. 1877. S.   G 2601
— A wayward woman ; a novel. N. Y. 1880. Q.
G 2602
— *Same.* Lond. 1879. 3 v. D.   G 2602
Grimm, Hermann. Unüberwindliche mächte. Berlin. 1867. 3 v. D.   G 2651
Grimm, Jakob L: *and* W: K: Specimens from the "Kinder und haus märchen." *In* **Roscoe**, W: German novelists.   R 2451
— German popular tales. Phila. *n. d.* D.
Gx 201
Grimmelshausen, Hans Jakob Christoph v. Der abentheuerliche Simplicissimus. *In his* Werke.   830 : 152 v33, 34
Gringo, Harry, *pseud., see* **Wise**, H: A:
Grisebach, E:, *ed. and tr.* Kin-ku-ki-kuan ; neue und alte novellen der chinesischen 1001 nacht. Stuttg. 1880. S.   G 2676
Groose, Julius Waldemar. Ein bürgerlicher Demetrius ; roman. *In* **Vierteljährl.** mag.
V 2 v35
Grossheim, Julie, (*J. E. Mand*). Von schritt zu schritt ; nach einer episode aus dem leben. *In* **Vierteljährl.** mag.   V 2 v25
Grossi, T: Marco Visconte. Tr. from the italian by A. F. D.; the ballads rendered into english verse by C. M. P. Lond. 1881. D.
G 3301
Groth, Klaus. Drei plattdeutsche erzählungen, zum theil erlebtes und erinnerungen von 1848 aus Schleswig-Holstein. Berlin. 1881. D.   G 2686
Contents, see Deutscher katalog, p. 66.
— Erzählungen. Aus ditmarscher mundart übertragen von A. v. Winterfeld. *With his* Quickborn.   831 : 18
— Trina. 2te aufl. Kiel. 1860. S.   G 2687

Grothe, R: Künstlerelend ; skizze. *In* **Vierteljährl.** mag.   V 2 v23
Gruber, F. J. Der mutter- und vatersegen in der geschichte Theodosia und Wunibald, der edelsten kinder hartgeprüfter eltern ; zwei lehrreiche erzählungen für geist und herz. Eine weihnachts- und geburtsgabe für die jugend. Nürnberg. *n. d.* S. G 2701
Gruber, Ludwig, *pseud., see* **Anzengruber**, L:
Guenot, C. *abbé.* Der alpenhirt ; eine erzählung aus der zeit Franz I, königs von Frankreich. Nach dem franz. Ill. Regensb. 1871. S. *With* **Glaubrecht**, J. Roland von Ro-landseck.   H 2783
— The vengeance of a jew. Phila. 1867. S.
G 2751
Guermante, Claire. Robert der waisenknabe, oder Das andenken an die mutter ; eine erzählung für die gesammte edlere lesewelt, besonders für die reifere jugend. Nach dem franz. bearb. von Franz Maria Brug. [*Anon.*] *With* **Bauberger**, W: Das wunderweib von Eichbühl.   B 580
Guernsey, Lucy Ellen. Loveday's history ; a tale of many changes. N. Y. 1885 [1884]. D.
G 2776
— Winifred, or After many days. N. Y. [1869]. D.   G 2777
Guerrazzi, Francesco Domenico. Die belagerung von Florenz ; geschichtlicher roman. Aus dem italiänischen übers. von G. Fink. Stuttg. 1849. 4 v. T.   G 2801
— Isabella Orsini ; [a historical novel of the 15th century]. *T. p. w.* S.   G 2802
— Manfred, or The battle of Benevento. Tr. from the italian by L: Monti. N. Y. 1875. D.
G 2803
— *Same, germ.* Die schlacht von Benevent ; geschichte aus dem 13. jahrhundert. Nach der 15ten aufl. aus dem italiänischen übers. Stuttg. 1853. 2 v. T.   G 2803
Guirey, G: Deacon Crankey, the old sinner. N. Y. [1878]. D.   G 2901
Guischard, Wilhelmine Konstanze. Black Douglas ; ein australischer roman. Leipz. 1882. S.   G 2951
Guise, *Mrs.* Francis. The Cravens of Beach Hall. Lond. 1861. 2 v. D.   G 3001
Guizot, Henriette, *see* **Witt**, Henriette de.
Guizot, Pauline, *see* **Witt**, Pauline de.
Gundling, Julius, (*Lucian Herbert*). 1830 ; roman und geschichte. 2te ausg. Leipz. 1865. 2 v. in 1. S.   G 3051
— Bis zum Rubicon ; roman aus Julius Cäsar's jugendleben. Leipz. 1867. 2 v. S.   G 3052
— Deutsch und slavisch ; roman. N. Y. 1882. F.
G 3057
— Das testament Peter des grossen ; roman und geschichte. N. Y. *n. d.* O.   G 3053
— Die tolte hand ; roman mit anlehnung an das nationale, kirchliche und sociale leben Oesterreichs. Leipz. 1866. 4 v. S.   G 3054
— Zwei kreuzherren ; roman.   G 3056
— Zwischen leben und sterben ; geschichten und skizzen. Leipz. 1866. S.   G 3055
Contents, see Deutscher katalog, p. 66.
Guseck, Bernd v., *pseud., see* **Berneck**, C: Gustav
Gustafsson, R: Alfred. Chit-chat by Puck ; tea-time tales for young little folks and young old folks. Tr. from the swedish by Albert Alberg. Ill. Lond. 1880. D.
Gx 251

Gustafsson, R: Alfred.—*Continued.*
— Märchen. Aus dem schwedischen übers. von Emil J. Jonas. Berlin. 1879. D.   **G 3251**
— Rose-leaves ; tea-time tales for young little folks and young old folks. Tr. from the swedish by Albert Alberg. Ill. Lond. 1880. D.   **Gx 252**
— Woodland notes; tea-time tales for young little folks and young old folks. Tr. from the swedish by Albert Alberg. Ill. Lond. 1880. D.   **Gx 253**
Gustav vom See, *pseud.*, *see* **Struensee,** Gustav v.
Guthrie, F: Anstey, (*F. Anstey*). The black poodle. *In* Tales from many sources.   **T 178 v1**
— *Same,* and other tales. N. Y. 1884. D.   **A 1328**
  Contents. The black poodle.—The story of a sugar prince.—The return of Agamemnon.— The wraith of Barnjum.—A toy tragedy.—An undergraduate's aunt.—The siren.—The curse of the Catafalques.—A farewell apperance.—Accompanied on the flute.
— The giant's robe. N. Y. 1884. S.   **A 1327**
— The tinted Venus ; a farcical romance. N. Y. 1885. D.   **A 1329**
— Vice versá, or A lesson to fathers. N. Y. 1882. D.   **A 1326**
Gutzkow, K: Ferdinand. Blasedow und seine söhne ; ein roman. (Gesammelte werke, b. 7, 8.) Frankfurt a. M. 1845. 2 v. D.   **G 3108**
— Briefe eines narren an eine närrin. Hamburg. 1832. S.   **G 3109**
— Die kleine narrenwelt. Frankfurt a. M. 1856. 3 v. S.   **G 3101**
  Contents, see Deutscher katalog, p. 67.
— Maha Guru ; geschichte eines gottes. (Gesammelte werke, b. 5.) Frankfurt a. M. 1845. D.   **G 3103**
— Ein mädchen aus dem volke. Prag. 1855. T.   **G 3102**
— Novellenbuch. Frankfurt a. M. 1846. D.   **G 1304**
  Contents, see Deutscher katalog, p. 67.
— Die ritter vom geiste ; roman. 6te aufl. Berlin. [1878]. 4 v. in 2. D.   **G 3105**
— Through night to light. From the german by mrs. Faber. Leipz. 1870. S.   **G 3106**
— Ein zauberer von Rom ; roman in 9 büchern. N. Y. 1858. 9 v. S.   **G 3107**
Gwynne, Talbot. Nanette and her lovers. N. Y. 1863. D.   **G 3151**
— The school for fathers ; an old english story. N. Y. 1852. D.   **G 3152**
Gyllembourg - Ehrensvärd, Thomasine Christine, *born* Buntzen. Die novellen des verfassers der "Alltagsgeschichte." Dänisch von J. L. Heiberg ; deutsch von Edmund Zoller. Stuttg. 1852. 3 v. T.   **G 3201**
  Contents, see Deutscher katalog, p. 67.

H., *pseud., see* **Nyblom,** Helène.
H., Dr:, *pseud., see* **Tolderlund,** Hother Hakon Viggo.
H. H., *pseud., see* **Jackson,** Helen Maria.
Haas, G. E. Die passauer in Prag ; historischer roman. Wien. 1862. 2 v. T.   **H 151**
Habberton, J: The Barton experiment. N. Y. 1877. S.   **H 201**
— Helen's babies ; with some account of their ways, innocent, crafty, angelic, impish, witching and repulsive, also a partial record of their doings during ten days of

Habberton, J:—*Continued.*
  their existence ; by their latest victim. Bost. 1876. S.   **H 202**
— The Jericho road. [*Anon.*] *T. p. w.* [Chicago. 1877]. S.   **H 203**
— Other people's children ; containing a veracious account of the management of Helen's babies by a lady who knew just how the children of other people should be trained, also a statement of the exact measure of the success obtained ; by the author of "Helen's babies". N. Y. 1877. S.   **H 204**
— Who was Paul Grayson ? Ill. N. Y. 1881. S.   **Hx 101**
— The worst boy in town. [*Anon.*] N. Y. 1880. S.   **Hx 102**
Häberlin, K:L:, (*H. E. R. Belani, F. Heinemann*). Russische hofgeschichten, von Peter dem grossen bis Katharina II ; historische novellen und lebensbilder. Leipz. 1856. 3 v. S.   **H 251**
  Contents, see Deutscher katalog, p. 67.
— Russische hofgeschichten, neue folge ; von Katharina II bis Nicolaus I. Leipz. 1857. 3 v. S.   **H 252**
  Contents, see Deutscher katalog, p. 67.
Habicht, L: Die poesie der prosa ; novelle. *In* Vierteljährl. mag.   **V 2 v36**
Hackländer, F: W: Behind the counter. *See below* Handel und wandel.
— Eigne und fremde welt. Stuttg. 1868.   **2 v. S. H 301**
  Contents, see Deutscher katalog, p. 67.
— Enchanting and enchanted. From the german by mrs. A. L. Wister. Ill. Phila. 1874. D.   **H 314**
  Contents. The elfin tree.—The dwarf's nest.—The princess Morgana.—Castle Silence.—The fairy tankard.
— Erlebtes. Stuttg. 1861. 2 v. S.   **H 303**
  Contents, see Deutscher katalog, p. 67.
— Eugen Stillfried. Stuttg. 1855. 3 v. T.   **H 302**
— Europäisches sklavenleben. Stuttg. 1856. 5 v. T.   **H 304**
— Forbidden fruit. From the german by Rosalie Kaufman. Bost. *n. d.* S.   **H 305**
— Das geheimniss der stadt. Stuttg. 1868. 3 v. in 1. S.   **H 312**
— Handel und wandel. Stuttg. 1855. 2 v. S.   **H 306**
— *Same, eng.* Behind the counter. From the german by Mary Howitt. Leipz. 1868. S.   **H 306**
— Die kainszeichen ; roman. Phila. *n. d.* 2 v. in 1. O.   **H 307**
— Letzte novellen ; mit seinem ersten literarischen versuch. Stuttg. [1879]. D.   **H 313**
  Contents, see Deutscher katalog, p. 67.
— Märchen. Stuttg. 1855. T.   **H 308**
  Contents. Schloss Schweigern.—Das zwergenest.—Von der prinzessin Morgana.—Das gesicht im mond.—Der zauberkrug.—Weihnachtsmärchen.— Der leibschneider der zwerge.
— Namenlose geschichten. 3te aufl. Stuttg. 1855. 3 v. in 1. S.   **H 309**
— Der pilgerzug nach Mekka. Stuttg. 1855. S.   **H 310**
— Der wechsel des lebens. Stuttg. 1861. 3 v. D.   **H 311**
— Zwei nächte. *With* **Müller,** W: Debora.   **M 4436**
Hadermann, Jeannette R., *see* **Walworth,** Jeannette R.
Hahn, R: Edmund. Schöne frauen ; roman. N. Y. 1883. F.   **H 376**

x denotes books specially adapted for children.

Hahn-Hahn, Ida Marie Louise Sophie Friederike Gustave *gräfin.* Cecil. Berlin. 1844. 2 v. S. **H 401**
— Maria Regina ; eine erzählung aus der gegenwart. Mainz. 1860. 2 v. S. **H 403**
Hainau, K: W. Ein schlimmer augenblick ; novelle. *In* **Vierteljährl.** mag. **V 2 v22**
Hale, E: Everett, (*Col. Frederic Ingham*). The children of the public. *In* **Johnson, E. R.** Little classics. **J 926 v12**
— Christmas in Narragansett. N. Y. 1884. D. **H 463**
— The fortunes of Rachel. N. Y. 1884. D. **H 462**
— His level best, and other stories. Bost. 1873. S. **H 451**
    Includes, The brick moon. — Water talk. — Mouse and lion. — The modern Sinbad. — A tale of a salamander.—The queen of California.—Confidence.
— If, yes and perhaps ; four possibilities and six exaggerations with some bits of fact. Bost. 1868. S. **H 452**
    Contents. The children of the public. — A piece of possible history. — The south american editor. — The old and the new, face to face.—The dot and line alphabet.—The last voyage of the Resolute.—My double, and how he undid me.—The man without a country.—The last of the Florida. — The skeleton in the closet. — Christmas waits in Boston.
— In his name ; a story of the waldenses seven hundred years ago. Bost. 1878. S. **H 453**
— The Ingham papers ; some memorials of the life of capt. F: Ingham, U. S. N., sometime pastor of the 1st sandemanian church in Naguadavick, and major-general by brevet in the patriot service in Italy. Bost. 1869. D. **H 460**
    Contents. Memoir of capt. Ingham. — The good-natured pendulum. — Paul Jones and Denis Duval.—Round the world in a hack.— Friends' meeting. — Did he take the prince to ride ?—How mr. Frye would have preached it.—The rag-man and the rag-woman.—Dinner speaking.—Good society.—Daily bread.
— The man without a country. Bost. 1865. S. **H 454**
— *Same. In* Atlantic tales. **A 1876**
— *Same. In* **Johnson, E. R.** Little classics. **J 926 v1**
— Mrs. Merriam's scholars ; a story of the "original ten". Bost. 1878. S. **H 455**
— My double, and how he undid me. *In* Atlantic tales. **A 1876**
— Our christmas in a palace ; a traveller's story. N. Y. 1882. D. **H 461**
— Our new crusade ; a temperance story. Bost. 1875. T. **H 456**
— Philip Nolan's friends. *T. p. w.* [N. Y. 1877]. D. **H 457**
— The skeleton in the closet, by J. T: Darragh, late C. C. S. *In* **Johnson, E. R.** Little classics. **J 926 v5**
— Ten times one is ten, the possible reformation ; a story in nine chapters by col. Frederic Ingham. Bost. 1878. S. **H 458**
— *Same.* [New ed.] Bost. 1883. S. **H 458**
— Ups and downs ; an every-day novel. Bost. 1873. D. **H 459**
Hale, Lucretia P. The Peterkin papers. Ill. Bost. 1880. D. **Hx 151**
— The queen of the red chessmen. *In* Atlantic tales. **A 1876**
— The spider's eye. *In* **Stories** by american authors. **S 35 v3**
Halévy, Ludovic. Abbé Constantine. From the 20th french ed. by Emily H. Hazen. N. Y. 1882. S. **H 476**

Haliburton, T: Chandler, (*Sam Slick*). Sam Slick, the clockmaker. Ill. Phila. *n. d.* 2 v. in 1. D. **H 501**
Hall, Abraham Oakey. Old Whitey's christmas trot ; a story for the holidays. Ill. N. Y. 1857. S. **Hx 201**
Hall, Anna Maria, *born* Fielding, *mrs.* S: Carter. Leiden der frauen ; moralische erzählungen für die reifere weibliche jugend. Nach dem englischen von Fennimore. Fürth. 1849. 4 v. D. **H 553**
— Midsummer eve ; a fairy tale of love. N. Y. 1863. O. **H 551**
— The white boy ; a story of Ireland in 1822. N. Y. 1861. O. **H 552**
Hall, Baynard Rust. The new purchase, or The seven and a half years in the far west. 2d ed. *T. p. w.* D. **H 602**
— Something for everybody ; gleaned in the old purchase from fields often reaped. N. Y. 1856. D. **H 601**
Hall, C: W. Drifting round the world ; a boy's adventures by sea and land. Ill. Bost. 1881. O. **Hx 251**
— Twice taken ; an historical romance of the maritime british provinces. Bost. 1867. S. **H 651**
Hall, James. The wilderness and the war path. N. Y. 1846. S. **H 701**
    Contents. The black steed of the prairies.—The war belt, a legend of North Bend. — The new moon, a tradition of the Omawhaws. — The red sky of the morning.—The capuchin.—The dark maid of Illinois.—The indian hater.—Pete Featherton.—App.
Hall, *Mrs.* S. C., *see* Hall, Anna Maria.
Hallett, E. V., (*Ferna Vale*). Natalie, or A gem among the seaweeds. *T. p. w.* D. **V 251**
Hallock, Mary, *see* Foote, Mary.
Hallowell, *Mrs.* Sarah Catharine F. Nan, the new fashioned girl. Ill. Bost. 1877. D. **Hx 301**
Halstead, Leonora B., (*Barbara Elbon*). Bethesda ; a novel. N. Y. 1884. D. **H 726**
Hamerling, Robert. Aspasia ; ein künstler- und liebes-roman aus alt-Hellas. N. Y. 1882. F. **H 751**
— *Same, eng.* Aspasia ; a romance of art and and love in ancient Hellas. From the german by Mary J. Safford. N. Y. 1882. S. **H 751**
Hamerton, Eugenie, *mrs.* P. G. The mirror of truth, and other marvellous histories. Ill. Bost. 1875. D. **Hx 361**
Hamerton, Philip Gilbert. Harry Blount ; passages in a boy's life on land and sea. Bost. 1875. S. **Hx 351**
— Marmorne. (No name ser.) Bost. 1878. S. **H 801**
— Wenderholme ; a story of Lancashire and Yorkshire. Bost. 1876. D. **H 802**
Hamilton, C. G. Clear shining after rain. N. Y. 1880. Q. **H 851**
Hamilton, Celia V., *born* Dakin. My bonnie lass. Bost. [1877]. O. **H 902**
— Ropes of sand, and other stories. Bost. 1873. O. **H 903**
    Includes, A woman's story. — Mrs. Gordon's confession.—Every string broken. — A domestic tragedy. — Mr. John.—Drinkers of ashes.
Hamilton, Elizabeth. The cottagers of Glenburnie ; a tale for the farmer's ingle-nook. Phila. 1855. T. **Hx 401**
Hamilton, Gail, *pseud., see* **Dodge**, Mary Abigail.

x denotes books specially adapted for children.

Hamilton, T: The youth and manhood of Cyril Thornton. *T. p. w.* D. **H 951**
— *Same.* N. Y. 1831. 2 v. in 1. D. **H 951**
Hamley, C: The light on the hearth. *In* Tales from Blackwood. **T 177 v5**
— Wassail. *In the same.* **T 177 v6**
Hamley, E: B., (*Alexandre Sue-Sand fils*). The last french hero. *In* Tales from Blackwood. **T 177 v4**
— Lazaro's legacy. *In the same.* **T 176 v2**
— A legend of Gibraltar. *In the same.* **T 176 v1**
— A recent confession of an opium-eater. *In the same.* **T 177 v1**
— Shakespeare's funeral. *In the same.* **T 177 v1**
Hamley, W: G. The house of Lys ; one book of its history. N. Y. 1879. Q. **H 1001**
Hammond, *Mrs.* E. H., (*Henri Daugé*). A fair philosopher. N. Y. 1882. D. **H 1026**
— The georgians. (Round - robin ser.) Bost. 1881. S. **H 1027**
Hammond, M. E. Florence ; a tale. Lond. *n. d.* D. **H 1051**
Hammond, W: Alexander. Doctor Grattan ; a novel. N. Y. 1885 [1884]. D. **H 1077**
— Lal ; a novel. N. Y. 1884. D. **H 1076**
— Mr. Oldmixon ; a novel. N. Y. 1885. D. **H 1078**
— A strong-minded woman, or Two years after ; a sequel to Lal. N. Y. 1885. D. **H 1079**
Hanke, Henriette Wilhelmine, *born* Arndt. Blumen. Hannover. 1841. 2 v. in 1. D. **H 1101**
Contents, *see* Deutscher katalog, p. 68.
— Der brief. Hannover. 1842. D. **H 1102**
— Elfride. Hannover. 1846. 2 v. D. **H 1103**
— Die freundinnen. Hannover. 1842. 2 v. D. **H 1104**
— Perlen. Hannover. 1841. D. **H 1112**
— Der ring. Hannover. 1842. D. **H 1105**
— Der schmuck. Hannover. 1843. 2 v. D. **H 1106**
— Die schwägerinnen. Hannover. 1843. D. **H 1107**
— Die schwester. Hannover. 1842. D. **H 1108**
— Die tochter des pietisten. Hannover. 1847. 2 v. D. **H 1109**
— Wally's garten. Hannover. 1841. D. **H 1110**
— Die wittwen. Hannover. 1842. 2 v. D. **H 1111**
Harder, L: A family feud ; a romance. After the german by mrs. A. L. Wister. Phila. [1877]. D. **H 5351**
Harding, Rebecca Blaine, *see* Davis, Rebecca Blaine.
Hardman, F: Christine ; a dutch story. *In* Tales from Blackwood. **T 176 v6**
— The great unknown. *In the same.* **T 177 v9**
— My english acquaintance. *In the same.* **T 176 v7**
— My friend the dutchman. *In the same.* **T 176 v6**
— *Same.* *In* Sargent, E. The emerald. **S 551**
Hardy, Arthur Sherburne. But yet a woman ; a novel. Bost. 1883. D. **H 1126**
Hardy, Iza Duffus. Friend and lover ; a novel. N. Y. 1880. Q. **H 1151**
— *Same.* Lond. 1880. 3 v. in 1. D. **H 1151**
— Love, honour and obey. Lond. 1881. 3 v. in 1. D. **H 1152**
Hardy, T: Desperate remedies. *T. p. w.* [N. Y. 1874]. S. **H 1201**
— The distracted young preacher. N. Y. 1879. S. **H 1202**

Hardy, T:—*Continued.*
— Far from the madding crowd. (Leisure hour ser.) *T. p. w.* S. **H 1203**
— The hand of Ethelberta ; a comedy in chapters. (Leisure hour ser.) N. Y. 1876. S. **H 1204**
— A laodicean, or The castle of the De Stancy's ; a tale of today. (Leisure hour ser.) N. Y. 1881. S. **H 1209**
— *Same.* N. Y. 1881. Q. **H 1209**
— A pair of blue eyes. (Leisure hour ser.) 1874. S. **H 1205**
— The return of the native. (Leisure hour ser.) N. Y. 1878. S. **H 1206**
— The romantic adventures of a milkmaid ; a novel. N. Y. 1883. Q. **H 1211**
— The three strangers. *In* Tales from many sources. **T 178 v1**
— The trumpet major. (Leisure hour ser.) 1880. S. **H 1207**
— Two on a tower ; a novel. (Leisure hour ser.) N. Y. 1882. S. **H 1210**
— Under the greenwood tree ; a rural painting of the dutch school. N. Y. 1873. S. **H 1208**
Häring, G: W: H:, (*Wilibald Alexis*). Cabanis. Berlin. 1860. 3 v. S. **H 1251**
— Dorothe ; ein roman aus der brandenburgischen geschichte. Berlin. 1856. 3 v. D. **H 1252**
— Das haus Düsterweg ; eine geschichte aus der gegenwart. Leipz. 1835. 2 v. S. **H 1253**
— Die hosen des herrn von Bredow. Berlin. 1860. 2 v. S. **H 1254**
— Isegrimm ; vaterländischer roman. Berlin. 1854. 3 v. D. **H 1255**
— Ja in Neapel. Berlin. 1860. S. **H 1256**
Harland, Marion, *pseud.*, *see* Terhune, Mary Virginia.
Harley, *Dr.* —. The young crusoe, or Adventures of a shipwrecked boy ; a story for boys. Ill. Bost. 1875. D. **Hx 451**
Harring, Johan, *pseud.*, *see* Bagger, C: Christian.
Harrington, George F., *pseud.*, *see* Baker, W: Munford.
Harris, Joel Chandler. Mingo, and other sketches in black and white. Bost. 1884. S. **H 1326**
Contents. Mingo.—At Teague Poteet's.—Blue Dave. —A piece of land.
Harris, Miriam, *born* Cole. Frank Warrington. N. Y. 1871. D. **H 1351**
— Happy-go-lucky. N. Y. 1881. D. **H 1352**
— Louie's last term at St. Mary's. N. Y. 1874. D. **Hx 551**
— A perfect Adonis. N. Y. 1876. D. **H 1353**
— Phœbe ; a novel. Bost. 1884. D. **H 1358**
— Richard Vandermarck ; a novel. N. Y. 1871. D. **H 1354**
— Roundhearts, and other stories. N. Y. 1867. D. **Hx 502**
Contents. Roundhearts.—The christmas sister.— The boy regiment.—Willy Collins.
— Rutledge. N. Y. 1878. D. **H 1355**
— St. Philips. N. Y. 1871. D. **H 1356**
— The Sutherlands. N. Y. 1871. D. **H 1357**
Note. All, except Rutledge, are said to be "by the author of Rutledge".
Harrison, Constance Cary, *mrs.* Burton H. The old-fashioned fairy-book. Ill. N. Y. 1884. S. **Hx 526**
— The story of Helen Troy. [*Anon*]. N. Y. 1881. D. **H 1401**

x denotes books specially adapted for children.

Harrison, *Mrs.* W:, *born* Kingsley, (*Lucas Malet*). Colonel Enderby's wife; a novel. N. Y. 1885. D.   **M 677**
— Mrs. Lorimer ; a sketch in black and white. N. Y. 1883. S.   **M 676**
Harsha, *Judge* —. Ploughed under; the story of an indian chief told by himself, with an introd. by Inshtatheamba (Bright Eyes). [*Anon.*] N. Y. 1881. D.   **H 1426**
Hart, *Mrs.* —. Miss Hitchcock's wedding dress. [*Anon.*] N. Y. 1876. D.   **H 1476**
Hart, Joseph C. Miriam Coffin, or The whale fisherman. N. Y. 1834. 2 v. D.   **H 1451**
Harte, Francis Bret. Aus meinem seeräuberleben, und andere erzählungen. Stuttg. [1878]. S.   **H 1558**
  Contents, see Deutscher katalog, p. 68.
— Baby Sylvester, und andere erzählungen. Stuttg. [1878]. S.   **H 1565**
  Contents, see Deutscher katalog, p. 49.
— By shore and sedge. Bost. 1885. T.   **H 1569**
  Contents. An apostle of the tules.—Sarah Walker. —A ship of '49.
— Drift from two shores. Bost. 1878. T.
                                         H 1551
  Contents. The man on the beach.—Two saints of the foot-hills.—Jinny.—Roger Catron's friend.—Who was my quiet friend?—A ghost of the Sierras.—The hoodlum band ; a condensed novel.—The man whose yoke was not easy.—My friend, the tramp.—The man from Solano.—The office seeker.—A sleeping car experience.—Five o'clock in the morning.— With the entrées.
— Die erbin von Red Dog, und andere erzählungen. Stuttg. [1879]. S.   **H 1559**
  Contents, see Deutscher katalog, p. 68.
— Flip. Bost. 1882. T.   **H 1566**
— Found at Blazing Star. *With his* Flip.
                                         H 1566
— Gabriel Conroy. *T. p. w.* [Hartford. 1876]. O.   **H 1552**
— *Same, germ.* Gabriel Conroy ; roman aus dem englischen. Berlin. [1876]. D.   **H 1552**
— Das geheimniss von Deadwood, und andere erzählungen. Stuttg. [1879]. S.   **H 1560**
  Contents, see Deutscher katalog, p. 68.
— Ein gespenst der Sierras, und andere erzählungen. Deutsch von A. Passow. Stuttg. [1878]. S.   **H 1561**
  Contents, see Dentscher katalog, p. 68.
— Das heidenkind, und andere erzählungen. Stuttg. [1878]. S.   **H 1562**
  Contents, see Deutscher katalog, p. 68.
— In the Carquinez woods. Bost. 1884. S.
                                         H 1567
— *Same, germ.* Im walde von Carquinez ; eine romanze in prosa. Nach dem amerikanischen original; unter einleitung von Eugen Zabel. Stuttg. [1884]. D. **H 1567**
— The luck of Roaring Camp. *In* Johnson, E. R. Little classics.   **J 926 v4**
— *Same,* and other sketches. Bost. 1870. D.
                                         H 1553
  Includes, The outcasts of Poker Flat.— Tennessee's pardner.—The idyl of Red Gulch.—Brown of Calaveras.—High-water mark.—A lonely ride.— The man of no account.—M'liss.—The right eye of the commander.—Notes by flood and field.—Mission Dolores.—John Chinaman.—From a back window.— Boonder.
— Mrs. Skagg's husbands, and other sketches. Bost. 1873. D.   **H 1554**
  Includes, How Santa Claus came to Simpson's Bar. —The princess Bob and her friends.—The Iliad of Sandy Bar.—Mr. Thompson's prodigal.—The romance of Madroño Hollow.—The poet of Sierra Flat.—The christmas gift that came to Rupert.—Urban sketches. —Legends and tales.

Harte, Francis Bret.—*Continued.*
— On the frontier. Bost. 1884. T.   **H 1568**
  Contents. At the mission of San Carmel.—A blue grass Penelope.—Left out on Lone Star mountain.
— The outcasts of Poker Flat. *In* Johnson, E. R. Little classics.   **J 926 v1**
— Roger Catron's freund, und andere erzählungen. Stuttg. [1879]. S.   **H 1563**
  Contents, see Deutscher katalog, p. 68.
— Eine sage aus Sammtstadt, und andere erzählungen. Stuttg. [1879]. S.   **H 1564**
  Contents, see Deutscher katalog, p. 68.
— The story of a mine. Bost. 1878. T.   **H 1555**
— Tales of the Argonauts, and other sketches. Bost. 1876. D.   **H 1556**
  Contents. The rose of Tuolumne.—A passage in the life of Mr. John Oakhurst. — Wan Lee, the pagan. — How old man Plunkett went home.—The fool of Five Forks.—Baby Sylvester.—An episode of Fiddletown. —A Jersey centenarian.
— Thankful Blossom ; a romance of the Jerseys, 1779. Ill. Bost. 1877. T.   **H 1557**
Hartley, May, *born* Laffan. Christy Carew ; a novel. (Leisure hour ser.) N. Y. 1880.
                                         L 251
— Flitters, Tatters and the Counsellor, and other sketches. [*Anon.*] N. Y. 1882. D. **L 253**
  Includes, The game hen.—Baubie Clark.—Weeds.
— Hogan, M. P. New ed. Lond. 1882. D.
                                         L 252
Hartmann, Moritz. The last days of a king ; an historical romance. Tr. from the german by M. E. Niles. Phila. 1867. D.   **H 1601**
Hartner, Eva. Severa ; eine familiengeschichte. N. Y. 1882. F.   **H 1626**
— *Same, eng.* Severa ; a novel from the german by mrs. A. L. Wister. Phila. 1882 [1881]. D.   **H 1626**
Harwood, J: Berwick. One false both fair, or A hard knot ; a novel. N. Y. 1884. Q.
                                         H 1653
— Paul Knox, pitman. N. Y. 1878. Q.   **H 1651**
— *Same.* Lond. 1878. 3 v. in 1. D.   **H 1651**
— Within the clasp ; a story of the Yorkshire jet hunters. N. Y. 1884. Q.   **H 1654**
— Young lord Penrith ; a novel. N. Y. 1880. Q.
                                         H 1652
— *Same.* Lond. 1880. 3 v. in 1. D.   **H 1652**
Hassaurek, F: The secret of the Andes ; a romance. Cincinnati. 1879. D.   **H 1701**
Hatton, Joseph. John Needham's double ; a novel. N. Y. 1885. S.   **H 1753**
— The queen of Bohemia ; a story of english life and manners. N. Y. 1882. Q.   **H 1752**
— Three recruits and the girls they left behind them. N. Y. 1880. Q.   **H 1751**
Hau-kiou-choan, or The pleasing history ; a trans. from the chinese language. Added, The argument or story of a chinese play, A collection of chinese proverbs, Fragments of chinese poetry ; with notes. [Tr. by T. Percy]. Lond. 1861. 4 v. S.   **H 10**
Hauenschild, R: G: Spiller v., (*Max Waldau*). Aus der junkerwelt. Hamburg. 1851. 2 v. S.   **H 1801**
— Nach der natur ; lebende bilder aus der zeit. Hamburg. 1851. 3 v. S.   **H 1802**
Hauff, W: Sämmtliche werke ; mit des dichters leben von Gustav Schwab. Stuttg. 1853. 5 v. S.   **H 1851**
  Contents, see Deutscher katalog, p. 68.
— Arabian days' entertainments. Tr. from the german by Herbert Pelham Curtis. 10th ed. Bost. 1882. D.   **Hx 551**

x denotes books specially adapted for children.

Hauff, W:—*Continued.*

— Die bettlerin vom Pont des Arts. N. Y. 1883. F.   **H 1854**

— *Same, eng.* The beggar girl of the Pont des Arts. *In his* Three tales.   **H 1852**

— Das bild des kaisers. *With his* Die bettlerin.   **H 1854**

— *Same, eng.* The emperor's picture. *In his* Three tales.   **H 1852**

— The cold heart. *In* **Oxenford**, J:, *and* C. A. **Fieling**, Tales from the german. **O 1001**

— *Same. In his* Three tales.   **H 1852**

— The fortunes of Fairylore ; from his Märchen als almanach. *In* **Miniature** romances from the german.   **M 2776**

— Lichtenstein, romantische sage ; mit einer einleitung von Julius Klaiber. Stuttg. [1882]. D.   **H 1853**

— Little Mook, and other fairy tales. Tr. by Percy E. Pinkerton. Ill. N. Y. 1881. D. **Hx 552**

  Contents. Longnose the dwarf. — History of Little Mook.—The caliph turned stork. — The adventures of Said.—The stone-cold heart. — The story of the silver florin.

— Nose the dwarf. *In* **Oxenford**, J:, *and* C. A. **Fieling**, Tales from the german. **O 1001**

— Tales of the caravan, inn and palace. From the german by E: L. Stowell. Ill. Chicago. 1882 [1881]. D.   **Hx 553**

  Contents. The caravan.—The caliph stork.—The amputated hand.—The rescue of Fatima. — Little Muck. — The false prince. — The inn in the Spessart. — The hirsch-gulden.—The marble heart. — Said's adventures.—The cave of Steenfall.—The sheik's palace.— The dwarf Nosey.— Abner the jew. — The young englishman.—The story of Almansor.

— Three tales : The beggar-girl of the Pont des Arts; The emperor's picture; The cold heart. From the german by M. A. Faber. Leipz. 1869. S.   **H 1852**

Hausrath, Adolf, (*George Taylor*). Antinous ; a romance of ancient Rome. From the german by Mary J. Safford. N. Y. 1882. S.   **H 1877**

— Klytia ; historischer roman aus dem 16ten jahrhundert. N. Y. 1884. F.   **H 1876**

— *Same, eng.* Clytia ; a romance of the 16th century. From the german by Mary J. Safford. N. Y. 1884. S.   **H 1878**

Haven, Alice (*originally* Emily) Gordon, *born* Bradley, *formerly mrs.* Neal, (*Cousin Alice, Alice G. Lee*). Contentment better than wealth. Ill. N. Y. 1857. S.   **Hx 601**

— Helen Morton's trial. N. Y. 1849. S. **Hx 602**

  Note. For continuation, *see* Watch and pray.

— Home stories. N. Y. 1869. S.   **Hx 603**

  Contents. Spring winds. — Carriage friends. — Miss Bremer's visit to Cooper's Landing. — Only a familyparty. — The furnished house. — The ordeal, or The spring and mid-summer of a life.—Single lessons, five dollars. —Counsel.—The evil and the good.

— Patient waiting no loss, or The two Christmas days. N. Y. 1861. S.   **Hx 604**

— Watch and pray, or Helen's confirmation ; a sequel to Helen Morton's trial. Ill. N. Y. 1851. S.   **Hx 605**

Havers, Dora, *see* **Boulger, Dora.**

Haweis, Hugh Reginald. Pet, or Pastimes and penalties. Ill. N. Y. 1874. D.   **Hx 651**

Hawthorne, Julian. Archibald Malmaison. N. Y. 1884. D.   **H 2010**

— Beatrix Randolph ; a story. Ill. Bost. 1884. D.   **H 2009**

— Bressant. *T. p. w.* D.   **H 2001**

— Dust ; a novel. N. Y. 1883. D.   **H 2007**

Hawthorne, Julian.—*Continued.*

— Ellice Quentin, and other stories. Lond. 1880. 2 v. D.   **H 2005**

  Includes. V. 1. The countesse's ruby.—A lover in spite of himself. 2. Kildhurm's oak.—The new Endymion.

— Fortune's fool. Bost. 1883. D.   **H 2008**

— Garth. N. Y. 1877. O.   **H 2002**

— Idolatry. Bost. 1874. D.   **H 2003**

— The laughing mill, and other stories. Lond. 1879. D.   **H 2006**

  Includes. Calbot's rival.—Mrs. Gainsborough's diamonds.—The christmas guest; a myth.

— Noble blood. N. Y. 1885 [1884]. S.   **H 2011**

— The pearl-shell necklace, [*same as* The laughing mill.] *With his* Prince Saroni's wife.   **H 2012**

— Prince Saroni's wife. N. Y. 1884. D. **H 2012**

— Sebastian Strome ; a novel. N. Y. 1880. O.   **H 2004**

Hawthorne, Nathaniel. Biographical stories. *With his* Tanglewood tales.   **Hx 704**

  Contents. B: West.—Sir I: Newton.—S: Johnson.— Oliver Cromwell.—B: Franklin.—Queen Christina.

— *Same. With his* True stories.   **Hx 705**

— The birthmark. *In* **Johnson**, E. R. Little classics.   **J 926 v8**

- The Blithedale romance. *With his* The scarlet letter.   **H 2055**

— David Swan ; a fantasy. *In* **Johnson**, E. R. Little classics.   **J 926 v4**

— Doctor Grimshawe's secret ; a romance, ed., with preface and notes, by Julian Hawthorne. Bost. 1883 [1882]. D.   **H 2058**

— The Dolliver romance. *With his* Fanshawe.   **H 2051**

-- Ethan Brand. *In* **Johnson**, E. R. Little classics.   **J 926 v1**

— Fanshawe, The Dolliver romance, and other pieces. Bost. 1876. 2 v. in 1. D. **H 2051**

  Contents. V. 1. Fanshawe.—Biographical sketches: Mrs. Hutchinson; Sir W: Phips; Sir W: Pepperell; T: Green Fessenden; Jonathan Cilley. 2. Scenes from the Dolliver romance.—Sketches from memory.—Fragments from the journal of a solitary man.— My Visit to Niagara.—The antique ring.—Graves and goblins.—Dr. Bullivant.—A book of autographs.—An old woman's tale.—Time's portraiture.—"Browne's folley."

— Grandfather's chair. *With his* Wonder book.   **Hx 703**

— *Same. In his* True stories.   **Hx 705**

— House of seven gables. Bost. 1872. S.   **H 2052**

— *Same,* The snow-image, and other twice-told tales. Bost. 1879. 2 v. in 1. D.   **H 2059**

  Contents. V. 1. The house of seven gables. 2. The snow-image.—The great stone face.—Main street. — Ethan Brand.—A belle's biography.—Sylph Etherege.—The Canterbury pilgrims.—Old news.—The man of adamant. — The devil in manuscript.—John Inglefield's thanksgiving.—Old Ticonderoga.—The wives of the dead.—Little Daffydowndilly.—Major Molineux.

— The marble faun, or The romance of Monte Beni. Bost. 1871. 2 v. in 1. D.   **H 2053**

— *Same.* Bost. 1879. 2 v. in 1. D.   **H 2053**

— *Same, germ.* Miriam, oder Graf und künstlerin. Nach dem englischen "Transformation," deutsch von Clara Marggraff. Leipz. 1862. 3 v. in 2. D.   **H 2053**

— Mosses from an old manse. Bost. 1871. 2 v. D.   **H 2054**

  Contents. 1. The old manse. — The birthmark. — A select party.—Young Goodman Brown.—Rappaccini's daughter.—Mrs. Bullfrog.— Fire worship.—Buds and bird voices. — Monsieur du Miroir.— The hall of fantasy.—The celestial railroad.—The procession of life. — Feathertop ; a moralized legend. 2. The new

Hawthorne, Nathaniel.—*Continued.*

Adam and Eve. — Egotism, or The bosom serpent. — The christmas banquet. — Drowne's wooden image. — The intelligence office.—Roger Malvin's burial.— P.'s correspondence.— Earth's holocaust.— Passages from a relinquished work. — Sketches from memory. — The old apple-dealer. — The artist of the beautiful. — A virtuoso's collection.

— *Same.* Bost. 1878. 2 v. in 1. D.   **H 2054**
— The scarlet letter. N. Y. 1872. D.   **H 2055**
— *Same.* Bost. 1879. D.   **H 2055**
— *Same.* Ill. Bost. 1883. O.   **H 2055P**
— Septimius Felton, or The elixir of life. Bost. 1876. T.   **H 2056**
— *Same.* *With his* Our old home.   **914. 2 : 26**
— The snow-image, and other twice-told tales. *With his* House of seven gables.   **H 2059**
— Tanglewood tales for girls and boys ; a second wonder-book. Bost. 1879. T.   **Hx 702**
Contents. The wayside.—The minotaur.—The pygmies. — The dragon's teeth. — Circe's palace. — The pomegranate seeds.—The golden fleece.

— *Same.* Bost. 1879. D.   **Hx 704**
— The threefold destiny. *In* **Johnson,** E. R. Little classics.   **J 926 v12**
— Tranformation. *Same as* The marble faun.
— True stories from history and biography. Bost. 1876. T.   **Hx 705**
Contents. Grandfather's chair.—Biographical stories: B: West ; Sir I: Newton ; S: Johnson ; Oliver Cromwell ; B: Franklin ; Queen Christina.

— Twice-told tales. Bost. 1872. 2 v. in 1. D.   **H 2057**
Contents. V. 1. Pref.—The gray champion.—Sunday at home.—The wedding knell.—The minister's black veil.—The may-pole of Merry Mount.—The gentle boy. — Mr. Higginbotham's catastrophe. — Little Annie's ramble. — Wakefield. — A rill from the town pump.— The great carbuncle.—The prophetic pictures.—David Swan. — Sights from a steeple. — The hollow of the three hills. — The toll-gatherer's day. — The vision of the fountain. — Fancy's show box. — Dr. Heidegger's experiment. 2. Legends of the Province house : Howe's masquerade ; Edward Randolph's portrait ; Lady Eleanore's mantle ; Old Esther Dudley. — The haunted mind. — The Village uncle. — The ambitious guest. — The sister years. — Snowflakes. — The seven vagabonds.—The white old maid.—Peter Goldthwaite's treasure. — Chippings with a chisel. — The shaker bridal.—Night sketches.—Endicott and the red cross. —The lily's quest. — Foot prints on the sea shore. — Edward Fane's rosebud.—The threefold destiny.

— *Same.* Bost. 1879. 2 v. in 1. D.   **H 2057**
— *Same ;* v. 1. Bost. 1857. D.   **H 2057 v1**
— Wakefield. *In* **Johnson,** E. R. Little classics.   **J 926 v2**
— A wonder-book for girls and boys. Bost. 1879. T.   **Hx 701**
Contents. The gorgon's head.—The golden touch.— The paradise of children.—The three golden apples.— The miraculous pitcher.—The chimæra.

— *Same.* Bost. 1879. D.   **Hx 703**
— *See also his* Works.   **820.1 : 10**
Contents, *see under* English literature, Collected works.

Hay, Elzey, *pseud., see* **Andrews,** Fanny.

Hay, Mary Cecil. Among the ruins, and other stories. N. Y. 1882. Q.   **H 2114**
Includes, One terrible christmas-eve.—Kate's engagement. — Mrs. Duncan's will. — Ploughed by moments. — Mid pleasures. — On and off the line. — Told by a comprador.—Staire Manor.—Co.!

— The Arundel motto. N. Y. *n. d.* O.   **H 2101**
— *Same ;* a novel. Lond. *n. d.* D.   **H 2101**
— At the seaside, and other stories. N. Y. 1881. Q.   **H 2102**
Includes, One winter day.—Penine's choice.—Whereunto is money good.—Athol.—A little aversion.— Upon the waters.—How I met Alphonzo's ghost.— London pride.—After the lessons.

Hay, Mary Cecil.—*Continued.*

— Bid me discourse ; a novel. N. Y. 1883. Q.   **H 2116**
— *Same,* and other tales. Lond. [1884]. D.   **H 2118**
Includes, The sorrow of a secret. — One terrible christmas eve.—Lady Carmichael's will.—On the line. —London pride.—Told in New England. — Ploughed by moments. — Co. — Nellie Dunkayne. — Kate's engagement.—All through Arethusa.—My first offer.— The heir of Rosscairne.—Mrs. Duncan's eccentricity. —A sister's story.—Alphonzo's ghost.—After the lessons.—Kenneth.—Penine's choice.

— Brenda Yorke, and other tales. Lond. [1882].   **H 2119**
Includes, Bart Bannatyne's city home.—One summer month.—A midnight meeting.—Two hallow eves. —A few days.—Well done!—By the night express.— Ricardo's benefit.—What our advertisement brought. —One winter night.—We four.—He stoops to conquer. —Stop thief!—Larry's hut.

— Dorothy's venture ; a novel. N. Y. 1882. Q.   **H 2115**
— *Same.* Lond. 1883. D.   **H 2115**
— For her dear sake ; a novel. N. Y. 1880. Q.   **H 2104**
— *Same.* Lond. [1881]. D.   **H 2104**
— Hidden perils. N. Y. *n. d.* O.   **H 2105**
— *Same ;* a novel. Lond. *n. d.* D.   **H 2105**
— Into the shade, and other stories. N. Y. 1881. Q.   **H 2106**
Includes, Larry's hut. — By and by. A house-keeper's story.—By and by A father's story.— One w ment. — What our advertisement brought. — Sir Rupert's room.—By the night express.—Guy Newton's revenge.—Ricardo's benefit.—Hamilton brothers.—We four.—Bertha's christmas box.—Locked in. —Dolf's big brother.

— Lester's secret ; a novel. N. Y. 1885. Q.   **H 2117**
— Missing. Lond. [1883]. D.   **H 2120**
Includes, Under life's key.—Back to the old home.— A dark inheritance.—A shadow on the threshold.— Dolf's big brother.

— My first offer, and other stories. N. Y. 1881. Q.   **H 2107**
Includes, Kenneth.—Hope deferred.—Lost harmony. —All through Arethusa.—A sister's story.—Cut on a gate.—At last.—Nettie Dunkayne.—The heir of Rosscairne.—Told in New England.—Lettice Vere's last christmas day.

— Nora's love test. N. Y. 1877. O.   **H 2108**
— *Same ;* a novel. Lond. [1878]. D.   **H 2108**
— Old Myddleton's money. N. Y. *n. d.* O.   **H 2109**
— *Same ;* a novel. Lond. *n. d.* D.   **H 2109**
— Reaping the whirlwind. N. Y. 1878. Tt.   **H 2110**
— The squire's legacy. N. Y. *n. d.* O.   **H 2111**
— *Same ;* a novel. Lond. *n. d.* D.   **H 2111**
— Under life's key, and other stories. N. Y. 1881. Q.   **H 2112**
Includes, By a leap.—A few days.—Bart Bannatyne's city house. — Through the breakers. — The end of a fairy tale.—Told in the picture gallery.—My only novel.—In the christmas fire-light.—Notes from a german band.—One summer month.—A midnight meeting.—Two hallow eves.—Well done.

— Under the will. Lond. [1884]. D.   **H 2121**
Includes, Reaping the whirlwind.—My only novel. — By a leap.—In the christmas fire-light.—Notes from a german band.—Through the breakers.—Told in the picture gallery.—The end of a fairy tale.—Guy Newton's revenge. — By-and-by. — The housekeeper's story. — Hamilton brothers. — A father's story. — Bertha's christmas box.—Locked in.—Sir Rupert's room.

— Victor and vanquished. N. Y. *n. d.* O.   **H 2113**
— *Same ;* a novel. Lond. *n. d.* D.   **H 2113**

x denotes books specially adapted for children.

Hayes, A: Allen. The Denver express. *In*
Stories by american authors. **S 35 v6**
Hays, Helen, *mrs.* W. J. The adventures of
prince Lazybones, and other stories. Ill.
N. Y. 1885 [1884]. S. **Hx 729**
*Includes, Phil's fairies. — Florio and Florella. —
Boreas Bluster's christmas present.*
— Castle Comfort ; a story for children. N. Y.
1885 [1884]. D. **Hx 728**
— A domestic heroine ; a story for girls. Ill.
N. Y. 1882. D. **Hx 727**
— The princess Idleways ; a fairy story. N. Y.
1880. S. **Hx 726**
Healy, Mary, *see* **Bigot,** Mary.
Heaton, Ellen Marvin. The octagon club ; a
character study. N. Y. 1880. S. **H 2151**
Heaton, W: The story of Robin Hood. Ill.
4th ed. Lond. *n. d.* S. **Hx 776**
Hector, Annie F., *born* Thomas, (*Mrs. Alexander*).
The admiral's ward ; a novel. (Leisure
hour ser.) N. Y. 1883. S. **H 2209**
— The executor ; a novel. (Leisure hour ser.)
N. Y. 1883. S. **H 2210**
— The Freres ; a novel. (Leisure hour ser.) N.
Y. 1882. S. **H 2207**
— Her dearest foe. (Leisure hour ser.) N. Y.
1876. S. **H 2201**
— The heritage of Langdale. (Leisure hour ser.)
N. Y. 1877. S. **H 2202**
— Look before you leap ; a novel. (Leisure hour
ser.) N. Y. 1882. S. **H 2208**
— Maid, wife or widow ? (Leisure hour ser.)
N. Y. 1879. S. **H 2203**
— Ralph Wilton's weird. (Leisure hour ser.)
N. Y. 1875. S. **H 2204**
— A second life ; a novel. (Leisure hour ser.)
N. Y. 1885. S. **H 2211**
— Which shall it be ? (Leisure hour ser.) N. Y.
1874. S. **H 2205**
— The wooing o't. (Leisure hour ser.) N. Y.
1874. S. **H 2206**
Heege, *Frau* —, (*Penseroso*). Alban und Nanny.
Leipz. 1849. 2 v. S. **H 2228**
— Aristokrat und demokrat. Leipz. 1850. 3 v.
S. **H 2227**
— Manuelitta Dolores. Leipz. 1847. 3 v. S.
H 2228
Heigel, K: Der sangesbruder ; novelle. *In*
Vierteljährl. mag. **V 2 v24**
Heimburg, W:., *pseud.*, *see* **Behrens,** Bertha.
Heinemann, Friedrich, *pseud.*, *see* **Häberlin,**
K: L:
Heinz, Albrecht. Die herrin von Schwarzenhof.
Leipz. 1866. S. **H 2251**
Heller, Isidor. Die alliirten der reaction. Berlin. 1852. 2 v. S. **H 2301**
Heller, W: Robert. Alhambra ; spanische novellen. Altenburg. 1838. S. **H 2326**
— Das erdbeben von Caraccas. Altenburg. 1838.
2 v. S. **H 2327**
— Florian Geyer. Leipz. 1848. 3 v. S. **H 2328**
— Eine neue welt. Altenburg. 1843. 2 v. S.
H 2329
— Novellen aus dem süden. Altenburg. 1841. 3
v. S. **H 2330**
Contents, see Deutscher katalog, p. 69.
— Der prinz von Oranien ; historischer roman.
Leipz. 1843. 6 v. D. **H 2331**
— Das schwarze bret. Altenburg. 1844. 2 v. S.
H 2332
— Sieben winterabende. Leipz. 1847. 2 v. S.
H 2333
Hellmuth, Ernst, *pseud.*, *see* **Schmidt-Weissenfels,** E:

Hellmuth, Paul, *pseud.*, *see* **Fischer,** J. H: L:
Helps, *Sir* Arthur. Casimir Maremma. Bost.
1871. D. **H 2401**
— Ivan de Biron, or The russian court in the
middle of the last century. Bost. 1874. D.
H 2402
— Realmah. Lond. 1876. D. **H 2403**
Hencke, K: L: Daguerreotypen und Chausséegestalten. Leipz. 1841. 2 v. S. **H 2451**
Contents, see Deutscher katalog, p. 69.
Henderson, Frances C. Dunderviksborg, and
other tales ; forming an epitome of modern
european literature. Phila. 1881. D.
H 2476
Contents. **Henderson,** F. C. Priscilla Baker, the
freedwoman.—**Zedritz,** C: E: The double wedding
at Dunderviksborg; tr. from the swedish.—**Kisfaludy,** Károly. Three at once, a farce in 1 act; tr.
from the hungarian. — **Straparola**, *da Caravaggio,*
Giovanni Francesco. Salardo; tr. from the italian.—
Pushkin, Aleksandr Sergeievitch. The snow-storm;
from the russian.—**Palárik,** J: Friendship at the
harvest-feast, a farce in 3 acts; tr. from the slovak.—
Alarcon, P: Antonio de. Black eyes; tr. from the
spanish.—**Doesselaere,** T. S. van. No happiness
without virtue, a drama in 3 acts; tr. from the dutch.
—**Harpiński,** Franciszek. Taxes, a comedy in 3
acts; tr. from the polish.—**Eckstein,** Ernst. Cards
for four; tr. from the german.—**Pfleger,** Gustav.
Revenge; tr. from the czech.—**Stroobant,** Eugeen.
Rue de Pierres, no. 60; tr. from the flemish.—Twelve
portuguese legends, from the Romanceiro portuguez
by V: Eugenio **Harding** and the Epopeas moçarabas
by Teofilo **Braga**.—**Dequet,** Alphonse. Théodore,
conte de la vie littéraire; tr. from the french.—
Milan, N: Amanda, a farce in 1 act; tr. from the
croatian. — **Rask,** Rasmus Kristian. The storm-
bride; tr. from the danish.—**Krypow,** *Dr.* —. Leka,
or Reminiscences of a physician; tr. from the serbian.—**Celestin,** Fr. Roza, a play in 3 acts; tr. from
the slavonian.
Henkel, Friedrika. Die herrin von Ibichstein ;
roman. N. Y. 1885. F. **H 5151**
— *Same, eng.* The mistress of Ibichstein ; a
novel. From the german by S. E. Boggs.
(Leisure hour ser.) N. Y. 1884. S. **H 5151**
Henning, L: F: Sein guter engel ; erzählung
aus der gegenwart. *T. p. w.* O. **H 2501**
Henricus, Bruno. Novellen. Leipz. 1841. S.
H 2551
Henry, Caleb Sprague. Doctor Oldham at Grey-
stones and his talk there. N. Y. 1860. D.
H 2601
Henty, G. A. The boy knight who won his spurs
fighting with king Richard of England ; a
tale of the crusades. Ill. Bost. 1883. D.
Hx 816
Hepworth, G: Hughes. ! ! ! N. Y. 1881. S.
H 2651
Hepworth, *Mrs.* G: Hughes, (*Una Savin*). The
little gentleman in green ; a fairy tale.
Bost. *n. d.* S. **Hx 801**
Her crime. (No name ser.) Bost. 1882. S. **H 41**
Her picture. (No name ser.) Bost. 1882. S.
H 42
Herbert, H: W:, (*Frank Forrester*). Chevaliers
of France from the crusaders to the
maréchals of Louis XIV. N. Y. 1853. D.
H 2701
Contents. Sir Hugues de Coucy; a chivalric legend
of the Low Countries.—Eustache de St. Pierre, or The
surrender of Paris. — The fortunes of the maid of
Arc; a superstitious legend of the english wars in
France.—Hamilton of Bothwelhaugh, or The mas-
sacre of St. Bartholomew; a dark scene in Paris.—
Ahsahgunushk Nunamabtahseng, or The Reed-
shaken-by-the-wind.
— Cromwell ; an historical novel. N. Y. 1838.
2 v. D. **H 2702**

x denotes books specially adapted for children.

Herbert, H: W:, (*Frank Forrester*).—*Continued.*
— The fair puritan ; an historical romance of the
days of witchcraft. Phila. 1875. D. **H 2703**
—- Wager of battle ; a tale of saxon slavery in
Sherwood forest. N. Y. 1855. D. **H 2704**
Herbert, Johanna, (*Egon Fels*). Die rose von
Delhi ; roman aus der zeit des indischen
aufstandes unter Nena Sahib im jahre 1857.
Jena. 1866. 2 v. in 1. S. **H 2751**
— *Same.* N. Y. 1883, 1884. 2 v. F. **H 2751**
— Die weisse frau von Greifenstein ; roman. N.
Y. 1881. F. **H 2752**
Herbert, Lucian, *pseud., see* **Gundling,** Julius.
Herchenbach, W: Bruno und Lucy, oder Die
wege des Herrn sind wunderbar ; eine er-
zählung für volk und jugend. 2te vom ver-
fasser revidirte aufl. Ill. Regensburg.
1869. S. *With* **Glaubrecht, J.** Roland von
Rolandseck. **H 2783**
— Das eiserne halsband ; eine rittergeschichte
für volk und jugend. Ill. Regensburg.
1872. S. **H 2776**
— Der erbe von Sigmundskron ; erzählung für
volk und jugend. Ill. Regensburg. 1874.
S. *With his* Marietta, die römerin. **H 2779**
— Die falschmünzer ; erzählung für volk und
jugend. Ill. Regensburg. 1865. S. *With
his* Der gespensterseher. **H 2777**
— Flambartin, das gestohlene kind ; erzählung
für volk und jugend. Ill. Regensburg.
1865. S. *With his* Der gespensterseher.
H 2777
— Die geheimnisse eines alten koffers ; erzählung
für volk und jugend. Ill. Regensburg.
1872. S. *With his* Verbrechen und strafe.
H 2780
— Der gespensterseher ; erzählung für volk und
jugend. Ill. Regensburg. 1864. S. **H 2777**
— Marietta, die römerin ; erzählung für volk
und jugend. Ill. Regensburg. 1874. S.
H 2779
— Der pächter vom Moorhofe ; erzählung für
volk und jugend. Ill. Regensburg. 1870.
S. *With his* Die wildschützen. **H 2782**
— Die prinzessin vom smaragdengrünen see ;
erzählung für volk und jugend. Ill. Regensburg. 1864. S. *With his* Die wieder-
gefundene tochter. **H 2781**
— Die Schlüsselburg ; erzählung für volk und
jugend. Ill. Regensburg. 1875. S. *With
his* Marietta, die römerin. **H 2779**
— Der sohn vom eisenhammer ; erzählung für
volk und jugend. Ill. Regensburg. 1870.
S. *With his* Die wildschützen. **H 2782**
— Verbrechen und strafe ; eine geheimnissvolle
that ; erzählung für volk und jugend. Ill.
Regensburg. 1864. S. **H 2780**
— Das versunkene schloss ; erzählung für volk
und jugend. Ill. Regensburg. 1869. S.
With his Verbrechen und strafe. **H 2780**
— Die wiedergefundene tochter ; erzählung für
volk und jugend. Ill. Regensburg. 1864.
S. **H 2781**
— Die wildschützen ; erzählung für volk und
jugend. Ill. Regensburg. 1869. S. **H 2782**
Herculano de Carvalho e Aranjo, Alexandro.
Eurich, der priester der gothen. Aus dem
portugiesischen übers. von G. Heiner.
Leipz. 1847. S. **H 2801**
Herlossohn, G: K:, (*originally* K: G: Reginald
Herloss). Arabella, oder Geheimnisse eines
Hoftheaters. Leipz. 1846. 2 v. S. **H 2851**
— *Same.* Leipz. 1872. S. **H 2851**

Herlossohn, G: K:—*Continued.*
— Fahrten und abenteuer des M. Gaudelius
Enzian ; komischer roman. 3te ausg.
Leipz. [1872]. S. **H 2852**
— *Same.* Leipz. 1843. 2 v. S. **H 2852**
— Hahn und henne ; geschichte zweier thiere.
3te ausg. Leipz. [1872]. S. **H 2853**
— Die hussiten, oder Böhmen von 1414—1424 ;
historisch-romantisches gemälde. Tabor.
1851. 5 v. T. **H 2854**
— Mein wanderbuch ; humoristischer roman.
Leipz. 1872. S. **H 2855**
— Mephistopheles; eine politisch-satyrische phan-
tasie. 3te ausg. Leipz. [1872]. S. **H 2856**
— Die mörder Wallensteins ; historischer roman.
Leipz. 1847. 3 v. D. **H 2857**
— Phantasiegemälde ; romantische erzählungen.
Leipz. [1872]. 2 v. in 1. S. **H 2858**
Contents, see Deutscher katalog, p. 70.
— Die sylvesternacht ; novellen und erzählungen.
3te ausg. Leipz. [1872]. S. **H 2859**
Contents, see Deutscher katalog. p. 70.
— Die tochter des Piccolomini ; historisch-ro-
mantisches gemälde. Altenburg. 1846. 3
v. S. **H 2860**
— Der venezianer ; historisch-romantisches ge-
mälde. Leipz. 1846. 3 v. T. **H 2861**
— Waldblumen ; erzählungen, novellen, humo-
resken und phantasiestücke. Altenburg.
1847. 2 v. S. **H 2862**
Contents, see Deutscher katalog, p. 70.
— Eine weihnachtsbescheerung ; roman. 3te
ausg. Leipz. [1872]. S. **H 2863**
Hermann, Eugen, *pseud., see* **Dedenroth,** Eugen
Hermann.
Hesekiel, G: L: Lux et umbra ; ein grosser lie-
beshandel im 16ten jahrhuudert. Aus den
hinterlassenen schriften des magisters Ni-
colaus Longinus und anderen zuverlässigen
mittheilungen. Berlin. 1861. 3 v. D.
H 2901
— Vier junker. Berlin. 1865. 3 v. S. **H 2902**
Hesslein, Bernhard, (*Bernhard Hess*). Unter
dem schleier der nacht ; sittenbild aus Ber-
lins gegenwart. Berlin. 1858. 3 v. S.
H 2951
Hetherington, W: The seer's cave. *In* **Wilson,**
J: M. Tales of the borders. **W 2202 v6**
Heyne, C: Traugott, (*Heinrich Bourdin, Louis
Bourdin*). Fürst Mitternacht ; roman aus
den papieren eines verstorbenen. Leipz.
1848. 2 v. S. **B 2801**
Heyse, Paul J: L: L'arrabiata, and other tales.
From the german by Mary Wilson. Leipz.
1867. S. **H 3001**
Includes, Count Ernest's bome. — Blind. — Walter's
little mother.
— Barbarossa, and other tales. Leipz. 1874. S.
H 3002
Includes, The embroideries of Treviso. — Lottka. —
The lost son.—The fair Kate.—Geoffrey and Garcinde.
— The Dead Lake, and other tales. From the
german by Mary Wilson. Leipz. 1870. S.
H 3003
Contents. A fortnight at the Dead Lake. — Doomed.
Beatrice.—Beginning and end.
— Im Paradiese ; roman in sieben büchern. 7te
aufl. Berlin. 1884. 2 v. S. **H 3004**
— *Same, eng.* In paradise. N. Y. 1879. 2 v. S.
H 3004
— Kinder der welt ; roman in sechs büchern. 7te
aufl. Berlin. 1880. 2 v. D. **H 3005**
— *Same.* N. Y. 1881. F. **H 3005**

x denotes books specially adapted for children.

Heyse, Paul J: L:—*Continued.*
— The lonely one. *With* **John E.,** Magdalena.
    J 908
— Novellen ; 1ste—13te sammlung. Berlin. 1862–
    1881. 13 v. S.   **H 3006–H 3018**
    Contents, see Deutscher katalog, p. 70.
— *Same,* [14te sammlung]. Trobadour-novellen.
    N. Y. 1883. F.   **H 3019**
    Contents. Der lahme engel. — Die rache der vizgrä-
    fin.—Die dichterin von Carcasonne. — Der mönch von
    Montaudon. — Ehre über alles. — Der verkaufte ge-
    sang.
— *Same,* [15te sammlung]. N. Y. 1883. F.
    H 3020
    Contents. Unvergessbare worte. — Die eselin.—Das
    glück von Rothenburg.—Getheiltes herz.
Higginson, T: Wentworth. Malbone; an Oldport
    romance. Bost. 1869. D.   **H 3051**
— Oldport days. Bost. 1873. D.   **H 3052**
High private, A, *pseud., see* **Quincy,** S: Miller
Hilaire, Émile M: (*Marco de Saint-Hilaire*). Der
    kleine hund Josephinens und der papagoy
    Marie Louisens. *With* **Berthet,** E. B. Der
    jüngere sohn aus der Normandie. **B 1701**
Hildebrandt, J: Andreas K: Winter in Spitz-
    bergen ; a tale of the northland. From the
    german by E. Goodrich Smith. N. Y. *n. d.*
    S.   **Hx 826**
Hildreth, R: Der weisse sklave, oder Denkwür-
    digkeiten eines flüchtlings ; eine geschichte
    aus dem sklavenleben in Virginien u. s. w.
    Seitenstück zu Onkel Tom's hütte. Nach
    der 17ten amer. aufl. aus dem englischen.
    Stereotyp-ausg., 2te aufl. Leipz. 1853. S.
    H 3101
Hillern, Wilhelmine v., *born* Birch. Ein arzt der
    seele. N. Y. 1882. Q.   **H 3154**
— *Same, eng.* Only a girl, or A physician for the
    soul ; a romance. From the german by
    mrs. A. L. Wister. Phila. 1877. D.
    H 3154
— Aus eigener kraft ; roman. Leipz. 1872. 3 v.
    in 1. D.   **H 3151**
— *Same.* N. Y. 1882. F.   **H 3151**
— *Same, eng.* By his own might. From the ger-
    man. Phila. 1878. D.   **H 3151**
— Doppelleben ; roman. 2te aufl. Berlin. 1880.
    3 v. in 1. D.   **H 3152**
— *Same, eng.* A twofold life. Phila. 1873. D.
    H 3152
— Friedhofs-blume ; novelle. N. Y. 1884. D.
    H 3155
— Die Geyer-Wally ; eine geschichte aus den ty-
    roler alpen. 4te aufl. Berlin. 1881. D.
— *Same.* N. Y. 1882. F.   **H 3153**
— *Same, eng.* Geier-Wally ; a tale of the Tyrol.
    From the german. N. Y. 1876. S. **H 3153**
— Only a girl. *See above* Ein arzt der seele.
Hinrich, Albertine, *born* Röslein, (*Paul Stein*).
    Aus Andalusien ; erzählungen. 2te ausg.
    Leipz. 1869. 2 v. in 1. S.   **S 4851**
— Handwerk und industrie. Leipz. 1860. 2 v.
    D.   **S 4852**
— Johannes Gutenberg ; kultur-historischer ro-
    man. Leipz. 1861. 3 v. S.   **S 4853**
Hitchcock, Ethan Allan. The story of the red
    book of Appin. *T. p. w.* S.   **Hx 851**
Höcker, Gustav. Geld und frauen. Jena. 1867.
    3 v. in 1. S.   **H 3201**
— Sein und nichtsein. Jena. 1867. S. **H 3202**
Hoey, Frances Sarah Cashel-, *born* Johnston,
    formerly mrs. Stewart. All or nothing. N.
    Y. 1879. Q.   **H 3251**
— *Same.* Lond. 1879. 3 v. in 2. D. **H 3251**

Hoey, Frances Sarah Cashel-.—*Continued.*
— The lover's creed ; a novel. N. Y. 1884. Q.
    H 3253
— The question of Cain ; a novel. N. Y. 1881.
    Q.   **H 3252**
Höfer, Edmund. Das alte fräulein. Berlin. 1866.
    H 3301
— *Same, eng.* The old countess. From the ger-
    man by the tr. of " Over yonder," etc. Phila.
    1870. D.   **H 3301**
— Aus der weiten welt ; geschichten. Stuttg.
    1861. 2 v. S.   **H 3302**
    Contents, see Deutscher katalog, p. 71.
— Aus kriegs- und friedenszeiten ; neue geschich-
    ten. Breslau. 1869. 2 v. in 1. D. **H 3303**
    Contents, see Deutscher katalog. p. 71.
— Bewegtes leben ; geschichten. Stuttg. 1856.
    S.   **H 3304**
    Contents, see Deutscher katalog, p. 71.
— Erzählende schriften ; in 12 b. Stuttg. 1865. 12
    v. in 4. S.   **H 3309**
    Contents, see Deutscher katalog. p. 71.
— Der grosse baron ; eine geschichte. Wien. 1861.
    2 v. T.   **H 3305**
— In sünden ; eine familiengeschichte. Wien.
    1863. 2 v. T.   **H 3306**
— Neue geschichten ; b. 1. Breslau. 1867. D.
    H 3307
    Contents. see Deutscher katalog, p. 71.
— Old countess, The. *See above* Das alte fräulein.
— Pap Kuhn ; 'ne geschicht ut de oll plattdütsch
    tid. Stuttg. 1878. D.   **H 3310**
— Treue siegt ; eine geschichte von der see.
    Stuttg. 1874. S.   **H 3311**
— Unter der fremdherrschaft ; eine geschichte
    von 1812 und 1813. Stuttg. 1863. 3 v. S.
    H 3308
— Von ihr und mir ; eine geschichte. Stuttg.
    1876. S.   **H 3312**
Hoffman, C: Fenno. The man in the reservoir.
    In **Johnson,** E. R. Little classics.
    J 926 v4
— Wild scenes in the forest and prairie, with
    sketches of american life. N. Y. 1843. 2 v.
    in 1. D.   **H 3326**
    Contents. V. 1. The sources of the Hudson. — The
    Sacondaga country: The hunting grounds of the Mo-
    hawks; The flying head; The last arrow; The major's
    story; The ambuscade; The origin of indian corn;
    The hues of autumn; A Sacondaga deer hunt; The
    dead clearing; The stone giants; Rosalie Clare. 2.
    Nights in an indian lodge: The ghost-riders; Nanna-
    bozho; Waw-o-naisa; Petalasharoo; A night on the
    enchanted mountains; The magic gun; The inn of
    Wolfswald; Queen Meg; The twin-doomed; How to
    relish a julep; Old things with new faces; Scenes on
    the Hudson. — The spook-visitor. — The missionary
    bride.
Hoffman, Alexander F: Franz. Buried in the
    snow. Lond. [1879]. S.   **Hx 879**
— The emigrants ; a tale of the last century. Ill.
    [1883]. D.   **Hx 880**
— The inca's treasure. Adapted from the german
    by Jessie Young. Lond. [1879]. S. **Hx 878**
— The iron age of Germany. Tr. from the german
    by Rebecca H. Schively, with a historic
    sketch of the time by C. P. Krauth. Phila.
    1875. S.   **Hx 876**
— Prince Wolfgang ; an historical narrative. Tr.
    from the german by J. F: Smith, with a
    historic sketch. Phila. 1876. S. **Hx 877**
Hoffmann, Ernst Theodor Amadeus (*originally*
    W:). Die elixiere des teufels ; nachgelas-
    sene papiere des bruders Medarus, eines
    capuziners. Berlin. 1872. D.   **H 3351**

x denotes books specially adapted for children.

Hoffmann, Ernst Theodor Amadeus.—*Continued.*
— Erzählungen. Berlin. 1873. 2 v. in 1. D.
                                        H 3352
   Contents, see Deutscher katalog, p. 71.
— The golden pot. *In* **Hedge,** F: H: Prose writers
   of Germany.   **830.1 : 8**
— Klein Zaches, genannt Zinnober ; ein märchen.
   Berlin. 1873. D.   **H 3353**
— Lebens-ansichten des Katers Murr, nebst frag-
   mentarischer biographie des kapellmeisters
   Johannes Kreisler in zufälligen makulatur-
   blättern. Berlin. 1873. 2 v. in 1. D. **H 3354**
— Meister Floh ; ein märchen in sieben abenteu-
   ern zweier freunde. *With his* Seltsame lei-
   den eines theater-direktors.   **H 3357**
— Nachtstücke. Zwei theile in ein. Berlin. 1872.
   D.   **H 3355**
— Phantasiestücke in Callot's manier ; blätter aus
   dem tagebuche eines reisenden enthusiasten,
   mit einer vorrede von Jean Paul. Zwei
   theile in ein. Berlin. 1873. D.   **H 3356**
— Princess Brambilla ; ein capriccio nach Jacob
   Callot. *With his* Klein Zaches.   **H 3353**
— The sandman. *In* **Oxenford,** J:, *and* C. A.
   Fieling, Tales from the german.   **O1001**
— Seltsame leiden eines theater-direktors. Ber-
   lin. 1873. D.   **H 3357**
— Die Serapions-brüder ; gesammelte erzählun-
   gen und märchen. Berlin. 1871. 4 v. in 2.
   D.   **H 3358**
— Weird tales. A new tr. from the german, with
   a biographical memoir by J. T. Bealby.
   Etchings. N. Y. 1885. [1884]. 2 v. D.
                                        H 3359
   Contents. V. 1. The Cremona Violin.—The ferma-
   ta. — Signor Formica. — The sand-man. — The entail.
   2. Arthur's hall. — The doge and dogess. — Master
   Martin the cooper. — Mademoiselle de Scuderi. —
   Gambler's luck.—Master Johannes Wacht.

Hofland, Barbara Wreaks. Decision. Bost.
   1848. S.   **H 3401**
— Iwanowna, or The maid of Moscow. N. Y.
   1816. T.   **H 3402**
— Profession is not principle, or The name of a
   christian is not christianity. Bost. 1824. S.
                                        H 3404
— Reflection. Bost. 1851. S.   **H 3403**
— The young pilgrim, or Alfred Campbell's re-
   turn to the east and his travels in Egypt,
   Palestine, Nubia, Asia Minor, Arabia Pe-
   træa, etc. New ed. Ill. Phila. 1831. T.
                                        Hx 901
Hofmeister, Adolf, (*Wladimir*). Der liebe wonn'
   und weh' ; sagen, novellen und skizzen.
   Altenburg. 1840. S.   **W 2451**
Hogg, James, *the Ettrick shepherd.* Tales and
   sketches, including several pieces not be-
   fore printed. Ill. Edinburgh. *n. d.* 6 v.
   S.   **H 3451**
   Contents. V. 1. The brownie of Bodsbeck.—The
   wool-gatherer.—The surpassing adventures of Allan
   Gordon.—A tale of Pentland.—Ewan M'Gabhar. 2.
   The bridal of Polmood.—Storms.—A shepherd's wedding.—Country dreams and apparitions: The wife
   of Lochmaben; Cousin Mattie; Welldean Hall;
   Tibby Johnston's wraith.—A story of good queen
   Bess. — Sound morality. — Trials of temper. — The
   Fords of Callum.—The Cameronian preacher's tale.
   3. The hunt of Eildon.—The adventures of Basil
   Lee.—Adam Bell. — Duncan Campbell.— An old sol-
   dier's tale.—Katie Cheyne.—The long pack.—A country funeral.—The shepherd's calendar. 4. Shepherd's calendar, *continued.*—The two highlanders.—
   The watchmaker. — A story of the forty-six. — A
   tale of the martyrs.— Adam Scott.— The baron St.
   Gio.—The mysterious bride.—Nature's magic lantern.
   5. Private memoirs and confessions in the life of an
   Edin-   Some remarkable passages in the life of an Edin-

Hogg, James, *the Ettrick shepherd.*—*Continued.*
   burgh bailie.—Julia M'Kenzie. 6. Mary Montgom-
   ery.—The siege of Roxburgh.—The adventures of
   colonel Peter Aston. — Gordon the gipsey. — Wat
   Pringle of the Yair.
— A singular letter from southern Africa. *In*
   Tales from Blackwood.   **T 176 v5**
Holbeach, Henry, *pseud., see* **Rands,** W:
   Brightly.
Holland, C: Aspasia. Phila. 1869. D. **H 3601**
Holland, Josiah Gilbert, (*Timothy Titcomb*).
   Arthur Bonnicastle ; an american novel.
   Ill. N. Y. 1877. D.   **H 3651**
— *Same.* N. Y. 1882. S.   **H 3651**
— The bay path ; a tale of New England colon-
   ial days. N. Y. 1877. D.   **H 3652**
— Miss Gilbert's career ; an american story. N.
   Y. 1860. D.   **H 3653**
— Nicholas Minturn ; a study in a story. N. Y.
   1877. D.   **H 3654**
— Sevenoaks ; a story of today. Ill. N. Y. 1876.
   D.   **H 3655**
Hollister, Gideon Hiram. Kinley Hollow ; a
   novel. (Leisure hour ser.) N. Y. 1882. S.
                                        H 3702
— Mount Hope, or Philip, king of the Wampan-
   sags ; an historical romance. N. Y. 1851.
   D.   **H 3701**
Holm, Saxe, *pseud.* Hetty's strange history.
   (No name ser.) Bost. 1877. S.   **H 3751**
— Mercy Philbrick's choice. (No name ser.)
   Bost. 1876. S.   **H 3752**
— Stories ; 1st and 2d series. N. Y. 1878. 2 v.
   D.   **H 3753**
   Contents. V. 1. Draxy Miller's dowry.—The elder's
   wife.—Whose wife was she?—The one-legged dan-
   cers.—How one woman kept her husband.—Esther
   Wynn's love-letters. 2. A four-leaved clover.—
   Farmer Bassett's romance.—My tourmaline.—Joe
   Hale's red stockings.—Susan Lawton's escape.
Holmes, Oliver Wendell. Elsie Venner ; a ro-
   mance of destiny. Bost. 1878. D. **H 3851**
— The guardian angel. Bost. 1877. D. **H 3852**
— Iris. *In* **Johnson,** E. R. Little classics.
                                        J 926 v7
— *Same. With his* The professor at the break-
   fast table.   **824.1 : 48**
Holt, Emily Sarah. At ye Greene Griffin, or
   Mrs. Treadwell's cook ; a tale of the 15th
   century. Ill. N. Y. 1882. D.   **H 3957**
— Earl Hubert's daughter, or The polishing of
   the pearl ; a tale of the 13th century. New
   ed. Lond. [1880]. D.   **H 3954**
— Joyce Morrell's harvest, or The annals of
   Selwick Hall ; a story of the reign of Eliza-
   beth. Ill. N. Y. [1881]. D.   **H 3952**
— Lady Sybil's choice ; a tale of the crusades.
   N. Y. [1879]. D.   **H 3951**
— Lettice Eden, or The lamps of truth and the
   light of heaven ; a tale of the last days of
   king Henry VIII. N. Y. [1877]. D.
                                        H 3953
— Not for him ; the story of a forgotten hero.
   Ill. N. Y. [1883]. D.   **H 3959**
— Red and white ; a tale of the wars of the roses.
   Ill. N. Y. [1882]. D.   **H 3958**
— Sister Rose, or St. Bartholomew's eve. New
   ed. Lond. [1880]. D.   **H 3955**
— The white rose of Langley ; a story of the
   court of England in the olden time. New
   ed. Lond. [1878]. D.   **H 3956**
Holtei, K: E: v. Haus Treustein ; roman in drei
   theilen. Breslau. 1866. 3 v. D.   **H 4001**
— Noblesse oblige. Prag. 1857. 3 v. T. **H 4002**

   x denotes books specially adapted for children.

Holtei, K: E: v.—_Continued._
— Ein schneider. Breslau. 1858. 3 v. T.
         H 4004
— Ein vornehmer herr, oder Zwei freunde. Prag.
   1855. T.   **H 4003**
Home of Fiesole, The. by the author of "The
   children of Seeligsberg," "Madeleine's
   forgiveness," etc. N. Y. _n. d._ D.   **H 51**
Hood, T: Tales, romances and extravaganzas.
   3d ed. N. Y. 1866. D.   **H 4026**
   Contents. Our family.—Mr. Withering's consump-
   tion and its cure.—The Camberwell beauty.—The con-
   fessions of a phœnix.—Mrs. Burrage.—Mrs. Peck's
   pudding.—The schoolmistress abroad.—The tower of
   Lahneck.—Mrs. Gardiner.—Mr. Chubb.
Hood, Tom. From nowhere to the north pole;
   a Noah's arkæological narrative. Ill.
   Lond. 1875. D.   **Hx 926**
Hook, Theodore E: Births, deaths and mar-
   riages. Phila. 1839. 2 v. D.   **H 4051**
— Gilbert Gurney. _T. p. w._ [Lond.] S.
         H 4052
— Maxwell; rev., corr. and ill. with notes by
   the author. Lond. [1872]. S.   **H 4054**
— Ned Musgrave, or The most unfortunate man
   in the world. Phila. _n. d._ O.   **H 4053**
Hooper, Louisa, _born_ Houghton, _mrs._ W: The
   tsar's window. (No name ser.) Bost. 1881.
   S.   **H 4101**
Hooper, Lucy Hamilton, _born_ Jones. Under the
   tricolor, or The american colony in Paris.
   Phila. 1880. D.   **H 4151**
Hope, Ascott R., _pseud., see_ **Moncrieff,** Robert
   Hope.
Hope, Stanley. A new Godiva. Phila. 1876. D.
         H 4201
Hope, T: Anastasius, or Memoirs of a greek,
   written at the close of the 18th century.
   Lond. 1836. 2 v. S.   **H 4251**
Hopfen, Hans. Brennende liebe; eine wahre
   geschichte aus Südtirol. _In_ **Vierteljährl.**
   mag.   **V 2 v36**
— Mein onkel Don Juan; eine geschichte aus
   dem vorigen jahrhundert. N. Y. 1881. F.
         H 4276
Hopkins, Alonzo A. Sinner and saint; a story
   of the woman's crusade. Bost. 1881. D.
         H 4301
Hopkins, Ellice. Rose Turquand. N. Y. _n. d._
   O.   **H 4351**
Hopkins, S: The youth of the old dominion.
   Bost. 1856. D.   **H 4401**
Hoppin, A:, (_C. Auton_). A fashionable sufferer,
   or Chapters from life's comedy. Ill. Bost.
   1883. D.   **H 4426**
— Recollections of Auton house; a book for
   children by C. Auton. Ill. Bost. 1881. O.
         Hx 951
— Two Compton boys. Ill. Bost. 1885 [1884]. O.
         Hx 952
Hoppus, Mary A. M. A great treason; a story
   of the war of independence. N. Y. 1883.
   D.   **H 4502**
— A story of carnival. (Leisure hour ser.) N.
   Y. 1883. S.   **H 4501**
Horn, G: Count Silvius; a romance. From the
   german by M. J. Safford. N. Y. 1882. D.
         H 4451
Horn, Otto, _pseud., see_ **Bäuerle,** Adolf.
Horn, W. O. v., _pseud., see_ **Oertel,** Philipp F: W:
Hornbook, Adam, _pseud., see_ **Cooper,** T:
Horvath, G. F., _pseud., see_ **Dietrich,** Ewald
   Christian Victorin.

Hosmer, James Kendall. College theatricals.
   _In_ **Tales** from Blackwood.   **T 176 v2**
— The thinking bayonet. Bost. 1865. D.
         H 4601
Howard, Blanche Willis. Aulnay Tower. Bost.
   1885. D.   **H 4654**
— Aunt Serena. Bost. 1881. S.   **H 4652**
— Guenn; a wave on the Breton coast. Ill.
   Bost. 1884 [1883]. O.   **H 4653**
— One summer. [_Anon._] Bost. 1879. T.
         H 4651
— _Same._ Bost. 1884. T.   **H 4651**
Howard, E: Der alte commodore, von Kapitän
   Marryat. Neu auz dem englischen von C:
   Kolb. 2te aufl. Stuttg. 1857. T.   **H 4676**
— Ardent Troughton, oder Abenteuer eines kauf-
   manns, von kapitän Marryat. Neu aus
   dem englischen von C: Kolb. 2te aufl.
   Stuttg. 1857. T.   **H 4677**
— Rattlin the reefer; ed. by captain Marryat.
   [_Anon._] Lond. _n. d._ S.   **H 4678**
Howe, Edgar Watson. The mystery of the locks.
   Bost. 1885. D.   **H 4737**
— The story of a country town. [New issue].
   Bost. 1884. D.   **H 4736**
Howe, Mary A. The merchant mechanic; a
   tale of "New England Athens." N. Y.
   1865. S.   **H 4701**
Howe, Maud. A Newport aquarelle. [_Anon._]
   Bost. 1883. D.   **H 4727**
— The San Rosario ranch. Bost. 1884. S.
         H 4726
Howell, Mrs. Jane L., (_Violet Vane_). Justine's
   lovers. [_Anon._] N. Y. 1878. O.   **V 351**
Howell, J: The sergeant's tales. _In_ **Wilson,**
   J: M. Tales of the borders.
         W 2202 v6-10
   Contents. 1. The palatines. 2. John Square's voy-
   age to India. 3. The beggar's camp. 4. The pack-
   man's journey to London. 5. The imprudent mar-
   riage.
— [Tales.] _In_ **Wilson,** J: M. Tales of the bor-
   ders.   **W 2202**
   Contents. The experimenter, v. 3.—The fortunes of
   W: Wighton, v. 2.—The laird of Darnick tower, v. 7.—
   A legend of Calder Moor, v. 17.—Major Weir's coach,
   v. 5.—The man-of-war's man, v. 16.—The prisoner of
   war, v. 18.—The scottish veteran, v. 12.—The seven
   years death, v. 14.—The slave, v. 4.
Howells, W: Dean. A chance acquaintance.
   Bost. 1877. D.   **H 4751**
— Doctor Breen's practice; a novel. Bost. 1881.
   D.   **H 4759**
— A fearful responsibility, and other stories.
   Bost. 1881. D.   **H 4753**
   Includes, At the sign of the savage. — Tonelli's mar-
   riage.
— A foregone conclusion. Bost. 1877. D.
         H 4754
— The lady of the Aroostook. Bost. 1879. D.
         H 4755
— A modern instance; a novel. Bost. 1882. D.
         H 4761
— The rise of Silas Lapham. Bost. 1885. D.
         H 4756
— A romance of real life. _In_ **Johnson,** E. R.
   Little classics.   **J 926 v4**
— Suburban sketches. New and enl'gd ed. Ill.
   Bost. 1871. D.   **H 4757**
   Contents. Mrs. Johnson. — Doorstep acquaintance.
   — A pedestrian tour. — By horse-car to Boston. — A
   day's pleasure.—A romance of real life.—Scene.—Ju-
   bilee days.—Some lessons from the school of morals.
   — Flitting.
— Their wedding journey. Ill. Bost. 1872. D.
         H 4760

---

x denotes books specially adapted for children.

Howells, W: Dean.—*Continued.*
— The undiscovered country. Bost. 1880. D.
  H 4758
— A woman's reason ; a novel. Bost. 1883. D.
  H 4763
Howitt, Anna Mary, *see* **Watts,** Anna Mary.
Howitt, Mary, *born* Botham. Alice Franklin ; a
  tale ; another part of "Sowing and reaping."
  N. Y. 1855. S.   **Hx 1251**
— *Same.* N. Y. 1859. S.   **Hx 1251**
— The heir of Wast-Wayland. N. Y. 1855. D.
  Hx 1253
— Hope on ! hope ever ! or The boyhood of Felix
  Law. N. Y. 1859. S.   **Hx 1254**
— Little coin, much care, or How poor men live ;
  a tale for young persons. N. Y. 1857. S.
  Hx 1255
  Note. For continuation, *see* Work and wages.
— Love and money ; an every-day tale. N. Y.
  1859. S.   **Hx 2256**
— My own story, or Autobiography of a child.
  N. Y. 1861. S.   **Hx 1257**
— My uncle the clockmaker ; a tale. N. Y. *n. d.*
  Hx 1258
— No sense like common sense, or Some passa-
  ges in the life of C: Middleton, esq. N. Y.
  1862. S.   **Hx 1259**
— Sowing and reaping, or What will come of it.
  N. Y. 1862. S.   **Hx 1260**
  Note. For continuation, *see* Alice Franklin.
— The two apprentices ; a tale for youth. N. Y.
  1861. S.   **Hx 1261**
— Which is the wiser ? or People abroad ; a tale
  for youth. N. Y. 1871. S.   **Hx 1262**
— Who shall be greatest ! N. Y. 1855. S.
  Hx 1263
— *Same.* N. Y. 1862. S.   **Hx 1263**
— Work and wages, or Life in service ; a contin-
  uation of "Little coin, much care." N. Y.
  1859. S.   **Hx 1264**
Howitt, W: The hall and the hamlet, or Scenes
  and characters of country life. Phila. 1847.
  2 v. in 1. D.   **Hx 1202**
— Jack of the mill ; a fireside story. Ill. Lond.
  1870. S.   **Hx 1201**
— Johnny Darbyshire. *In* **Johnson,** E. R. Little
  classics.   **J 926 v9**
— *Same.* *In* **Edinburgh** tales.   **E 426**
— *and* Mary. Stories of english and foreign life.
  Lond. 1853. S.   **H 4801**
  Contents. Margaret von Ehrenberg, the artist wife.
  —The Meldrum family.—Sir Peter and his pigeon.—
  The Woodnook wells, or Neighbors' quarrels.—
  Leaves from the diary of a poor schoolmaster.—The
  Hunnybuns at the sea-side.—Some love-passages in
  the lives of every-day people.—The hunt.—The two
  squires.—The poacher's progress.
Hudson, Mary, *born* Clemmer, *formerly mrs.*
  Ames. His two wives. N. Y. 1875. D.
  C 1851
— *Same.* New ed. Bost. 1883. D.   **C 1851**
Hugessen, E: Hugessen Knatchbull-, *baron*
  Brabourne. The mountain sprite's king-
  dom, and other stories. Lond. 1881.
  D.   **Hx 1001**
  Includes, Black Rolf of Rookstone.—The hermit.—
  The Rhine castle.
— Other stories. Ill. Lond. 1881. D.   **Hx 1005**
  Contents. Prince Marsfiete.—Legend of the St. Dderfel.
  —Kimmelina and the dwarf.—The history of a cat.—
  The grannies of Giddyhorn.
— Puss-cat Mew, and other stories for my child-
  ren. N. Y. *n. d.* D.   **Hx 1003**
— Queer folk ; seven stories. 2d ed. Ill. Lond.
  1874. D.   **Hx 1004**
  Contents. The warlock of Coombe.—The witch of

Hugessen, E: Hugessen Knatchbull-.—*Contin'd.*
  Ballaquolch.—The pig-faced queen.—Little Grub.—
  The barn elves.—The strange city.—The old bachelor
  married.
— Whispers from fairyland. Ill. N. Y. 1875. S.
  Hx 1002
  Contents. The lost prince.—The history of a rook.—
  The silver fairies.—The witches' island.—Harry's
  dream.—The red baron.—The two Etonians.
Hughes, J. The magic lay of the one-horse
  chay. *In* Tales from Blackwood.
  T 176 v4
Hughes, T: School-days at Rugby, by an old
  boy. Bost. 1871. D.   **Hx 1051**
— *Same.* Tom Brown's school-days. Ill. N. Y.
  1882. Q.   **Hx 1051**
— The scouring of the white horse, or The long
  vacation rambles of a London clerk. Ill.
  Cambridge. 1859. D.   **Hx 1053**
— Tom Brown at Oxford. New ed., ill. Lond.
  1879. D.   **Hx 1052**
— *ed.* G. T. T. — Gone to Texas ; letters from
  our boys. N. Y. 1884. D.   **Hx 1054**
Hughes, W. Hastings. A shilling's worth of
  sherry, with three ha'p'orth of love thrown
  in. Cincinnati. 1883 [1882]. S.   **H 4826**
Hugo, V: Marie *comte.* Claude Gueux. N. Y.
  1871. O.   **H 4851**
— The last day of a condemned man. *With
  his* Claude Gueux.   **H 4851**
— The man who laughs. Tr. by W: Young. N.
  Y. 1877. O.   **H 4852**
— *Same, germ.* Der lachende mann. Autorisirte
  übersetzung von G. Büchmann. Berlin.
  1869. 4 v. S.   **H 4852**
— Les misérables. Lond. *n. d.* 5 v. in 3. D.
  H 4853
  Contents. V. 1. Fantine. 2. Cosette. 3. Marius.
  4. St. Denis. 5. Jean Valjean.
— *Same.* Tr. from the original french by C: E.
  Wilbour. N. Y. 1883. 5 v. O.   **H 4853**
— *Same.* N. Y. 1874. O.   **H 4853**
— *Same.* N. Y. 1878. O.   **H 4853**
— *Same, germ.* Die armen und elenden. Deutsch
  von A. Diezmann. Leipz. 1862. 10 v. T.
  H 4853
— Ninety-three. Tr. by Frank Lee Benedict.
  N. Y. 1874. D.   **H 4854**
— *Same, germ.* Dreiundneunzig ; roman in drei
  bänden. Aus dem französischen von L:
  Schneeganz. Wien. 1875. 3 v. in 1. D.
  H 4854
— Notre-Dame, or The bellringer of Paris. Ill.
  Lond. *n. d.* D.   **H 4856**
— The toilers of the sea. N. Y. 1878. O.
  H 4855
— *Same, germ.* Die meer-arbeiter. Einzig recht-
  mässige, authorisirte deutsche überset-
  zung. Berlin. *n. d.* S.   **H 4855**
Hülsen, Helene *gräfin* v., *born* v. Häseler.
  Nemesis. N. Y. 1883. F.   **H 1676**
Humbracht, Malvine v., (*Luise Ernesti*). Die
  aristokratin und der fabrikant. Jena.
  1865. 2 v. S.   **H 4901**
Hundred ministers, A, and how they switched
  off ; some account of the lights and shad-
  ows of ministerial life. Bost. 1874. D.
  H 91
Hunt, E., *mrs.* J: The wards of Plotinus. N.
  Y. 1881. Q.   **H 5001**
Hunt, Margaret, *born* Raine, *mrs.* Alfred W.
  Barrington's fate. (No name ser.) Bost.
  1883. S.   **H 4954**

Hunt, Margaret, mrs. A. W.—Continued.
— Basildon. N. Y. 1879. Q.   H 4951
— Same. Lond. 1879. 2 v. in 1. D.   H 4951
— The leaden casket. (Leisure hour ser.) N. Y.
   1881. S.   H 4952
— The posy ring. N. Y. 1881. Q.   H 4953
— Truth triumphant. In Tales from many
   sources.   T 178 v4
Hunt, Thornton. The foster-brother ; a tale of
   the war of Chiozza, ed. by Leigh Hunt.
   N. Y. 1858. O.   H 5051
Hunter, Hay, and Walter Whyte, pseud. The
   crime of christmas day ; a tale of the
   latin quarter by the author of "My ducats
   and my daughter." [Anon.] N. Y. 1885.
   Q.   M 94
— Same. N. Y. 1885. D.   M 94
— My ducats and my daughter ; a novel. [Anon.]
   N. Y. 1884. Q.   M 93
— Same. New ed. Lond. 1885. D.   M 93
Huntington, Faye, pseud., see Foster, Isabella H.
Huntington, Jedediah Vincent, (John Vincent).
   Alban, or The history of a young puritan.
   N. Y. 1853. 2 v. D.   H 5101
— Blonde and brunette, or The gothamite Ar-
   cady. N. Y. 1858. S.   H 5102
— Lady Alice, or The new Una. T. p. w. [N.
   Y.] O.   H 5183
— The pretty plate. Ill. N. Y. 1862. S.
                                             Hx 1151
Huntington, Lucius Seth. Professor Conant ; a
   story of english and american social and
   political life. N. Y. 1884. D.   H 5201

Illustrirtes familienbuch für winterabende ; erzählungen, novellen, u. s. w. V. 3, 1858.
   T. p. w. S.   I 1
Immermann, K: Lebrecht. Münchhausen ; eine
   geschichte in arabesken. Berlin. 1858. 4
   v. S.   I 101
— Der oberhof. Stuttg. [1881]. D.   I 102
— Wonders in the Spessart. In Oxenford, J:,
   and C. A. Fieling, Tales from the german.
                                             O 1001
Inchbald, Elizabeth. A simple story. N. Y.
   1858. O.   I 151
— Same. Ill. N. Y. 1885 [1884]. D.   I 151
Ingelow, Jean. Don John. (No name ser.)
   Bost. 1881. S.   I 201
— Fated to be free. Bost. 1875. S.   I 202
— Mopso the fairy. Ill. Bost. 1876. S.   Ix 101
— Off the Skelligs. Bost. 1872. S.   I 203
— Poor Matt, or The clouded intellect. Bost.
   1866. S.   Ix 102
— Sarah De Berenger. Bost. 1879. S.   I 204
— Sister's bye-hours. Bost. 1878. S.   Ix 103
   Contents. Prejudice, or The black polyanthus.—
   Laura Richmond.—Poor Matt, or The clouded intel-
   lect.—Widow Maclean, or Lending to the Lord.—Ups
   and downs of life.—Marked.—"Muschachito mio".
— Stories told to a child. [1st and] 2d series.
   Bost. 1872, 1874. 2 v. S.   Ix 104
   Contents. V. 1. The grandmother's shoe.—Two
   ways of telling a story.—Little Rie and the rosebuds.
   —Deborah's book.—The life of mr. J: Smith.—The
   lonely rock.—Can and could.—The suspicious jack-
   daw.—The minnows with silver tails.—I have a right.
   —The moorish gold.—The one-eyed servant.—The
   golden opportunity.—The wild-duck shooter. 2. The
   couphe of the wood.—The middle ages.—The fairy
   who judged her neighbours.—As the crow flies.—
   The bridge.—The prince's dream.—Anselmo.—Night's
   divining glass.—The snowflake.—The water-lily.—
   Nineteen hundred and seventy-two.—Rocking the
   cradle.—A lost wand.

Ingersleben, Emilie v., born v. Loga, (Emmy v.
   Rothenfels). Eleonore. Milw. 1871. O.
                                             I 227
— Same, eng. Eleonore. After the german by
   Frances Elizabeth Bennett. Phila. 1872. D.
                                             I 227
— Haideblume. 2te aufl. Berlin. [1876]. 3 v. in
   1. D.   I 226
Ingersoll, Ernest. The ice queen. Ill. N. Y.
   1885 [1884]. S.   Ix 151
Ingham, Col. Frederic, pseud., see Hale, E:
   Everett.
Inglis, H: D: Rambles in the footsteps of Don
   Quixote. Phila. 1840. D.   I 251
Ingoldsby, Thomas, pseud., see Barham, R:
   Harris.
Ingraham, Joseph Holt. The pillar of fire.
   T. p. w. D.   249 : 20
Irene, the missionary. Bost. 1879. S.   I 71
Irving, Fannie Bell. Six girls ; a home story for
   girls. [New ed.] Ill. Bost. 1885 [1884].
   O.   Ix 301
Irving, J: (John Quad). Harry Harson,
   or The benevolent bachelor. N. Y. n. d. D.
                                             I 351
Irving, Washington, (Geoffrey Crayon, Died-
   rich Knickerbocker). The Alhambra. N. Y.
   1865. S.   I 401
— Same, germ. Die Alhambra, oder Das neue
   skizzenbuch. 2te aufl. Frankfurt. a. M.
   1847. S.   I 401
— Same, mit einer einleitung von L. Pröscholdt.
   Stuttg. [1882]. D.   I 401
— A book of the Hudson, collected from the
   various works of Diedrich Knickerbocker,
   ed. by Geoffrey Crayon. N. Y. 1849. T.
                                             I 402
   Contents. Introd.— Communipaw. — Guests from
   Gibbet Island.— Peter Stuyvesant's voyage up the
   Hudson.—The chronicle of Bearn Island.—The legend
   of Sleepy Hollow.—Dolph Heyliger.—Rip Van Winkle.
   —Wolfert Webber.
— Bracebridge Hall, or The humorists ; a medley
   by Geoffrey Crayon, gent. N. Y. n. d. S.
                                             I 403
— Chronicle of the conquest of Granada, from
   the mss. of fray Antonio Agapida. N. Y.
   1850. D.   I 404
— Same, germ. Die eroberung von Granada. Aus
   dem englischen von Gustav Seelen. Leipz.
   1830. 3 v. S.   I 404
— Wolferts rust ; transatlantische skizzen. Aus
   dem englischen von W. E. Druglein. Leipz.
   1855. S.   I 405
— See also his Works.   820.1 : 11
   Contents, see under English literature, Collected
   works.
Izco, Wenzeslaus Ayguals de, see Ayguals de
   Izco, Wenzeslaus.

Jack in the forecastle, or Incidents in the early
   life of Hawser Martingale. Ill. Bost. 1880.
   D.
Jackson, Helen Maria, born Fiske, formerly mrs.
   Hunt, (H. H.). The hunter cats of Con-
   norloa. Bost. 1884. D.   Jx 104
— Letters from a cat. Ill. Bost. 1880. D.
                                             Jx 103
— Mammy Tittleback and her family ; a true
   story of seventeen cats. Ill. Bost. 1881.
   D.   Jx 101
— Nelly's silver mine ; a story of Colorado life.
   Bost. 1883. S.   Jx 102
— Ramona ; a story. Bost. 1884. S.   J 151

x denotes books specially adapted for children.

Jacob, P. L., *le bibliophile, pseud., see* **Lacroix,** Paul.
Jacobi, Mary Putnam. A martyr to science. *In* Stories by american authors.   **S 35 v2**
Jacquot, C: J: Baptiste, (*Eugène de Mirecourt*). Memoiren der Ninon de L'Enclos. Sondershausen. 1859. 4 v. T.   **M 2801**
Jäger, Hermann. Angelroder dorfgeschichten, oder Die amerikaner in Deutschland ; eine unterhaltende und lehrreiche erzählung für bauern und bauernfreunde. Weimar. 1856. D.   **J 101**
James, G: Payne Rainsford. Agincourt ; a romance. Lond. *n. d.* S.   **J 201**
— *Same, germ.* Agincourt. Aus dem englischen. Stuttg. 1845. 2 v. T.   **J 201**
— Agnes Sorel. N. Y. 1860. O.   **J 202**
— Aims and obstacles. N. Y. 1860. O.   **J 203**
— The ancient régime. *See below* Castelneau.
— Arabella Stuart ; a romance. Lond. *n. d.* S.   **J 205**
— *Same, germ.* Arabella Stuart. Stuttg. 1844. 2 v. T.   **J 205**
— Arrah Neil, or Times of old. N. Y. 1858. O.   **J 206**
— *Same.* Lond. *n. d.* S.   **J 206**
— *Same, germ.* Arrah Neil, oder Alte zeiten. Aus dem englischen. Stuttg. 1844. 2 v. T.   **J 206**
— Attila ; a romance. Lond. *n. d.* S.   **J 207**
— *Same.* N. Y. 1860. 2 v. in 1. S.   **J 207**
— *Same, germ.* Attila. Aus dem englischen. Stuttg. 1846. 2 v. T.   **J 207**
— Beauchamp, or The error. Lond. *n. d.* S.   **J 208**
— *Same.* N. Y. 1860. O.   **J 208**
— *Same, germ.* Beauchamp, oder Der irrthum. Aus dem englischen. Stuttg. 1847. 2 v. T.   **J 208**
— The Black Eagle, or Ticonderoga. New ed. Lond. *n. d.* S.   **J 243**
— *Same. T. p. w.* [N. Y. 1859]. O.   **J 243**
— The bride of Landeck. N. Y. 1878. T.   **J 209**
— The brigand, or Corse de Leon. New ed. N. Y. *n. d.* S.   **J 247**
— Castelneau, or The ancient régime. Lond. *n. d.* S.   **J 204**
— *Same.* N. Y. 1855. 2 v. in 1. D.   **J 204**
— *Same, germ.* Das alte régime. Aus dem englischen. Stuttg. 1843. 2 v. T.   **J 204**
— The castle of Ehrenstein ; a romance. Lond. *n. d.* S.   **J 240**
— *Same, germ.* Schloss Ehrenstein. Aus dem englischen. Stuttg. 1847. 2 v. T.   **J 240**
— Charles Tyrrell, or The bitter blood. Lond. *n. d.* S.   **J 248**
— The convict ; a tale. Lond. *n. d.* D.   **J 245**
— *Same, germ.* Der überwiesene. Aus dem englischen. Stuttg. ·1847·   **J 245**
— Darnley, or The field of the cloth of gold. Lond. *n. d.* S.   **J 210**
— *Same, germ.* Darnley. Aus dem englischen. Stuttg. 1840. 3 v. T.   **J 210**
— Delaware, or The ruined family. Lond. *n. d.* S.   **J 242**
— *Same.* Thirty years since, or The ruined family. N. Y. 1860. S.   **J 242**
— De l'Orme. Lond. *n. d.* S.   **J 211**
— *Same, germ.* De l'Orme. Aus dem englischen. Stuttg. 1846. 2 v. T.   **J 211**
— The desultory man. N. Y. 1855. 2 v. in 1. D.   **J 244**
— *Same, germ.* Der tourist. Stuttg. 1847. 2 v. T.   **J 244**

James, G: Payne Rainsford.—*Continued.*
— The false heir. Lond. *n. d.* S.   **J 212**
— The fate ; a tale of stirring times. N. Y. 1872. O.   **J 255**
— Forest days, or Robin Hood. Lond. *n. d.* S.   **J 214**
— *Same ;* a romance of old times. N. Y. 1860. O.   **J 214**
— The forgery, or Best intentions. Lond. *n. d.* S.   **J 213**
— *Same, germ.* Die fälschung, oder Beste absichten. Stuttg. 1851. T.   **J 213**
— The gentlemen of the old school ; a tale. Lond. *n. d.* S.   **J 215**
— *Same, germ.* Der gentleman von der alten schule. Aus dem englischen. Stuttg. 1846. 2 v. T.   **J 215**
— The gipsy ; a tale. Lond. *n. d.* S.   **J 216**
— *Same.* N. Y. 1864. 2 v. in 1. D.   **J 216**
— Gowrie, or The king's plot. N. Y. 1860. O.   **J 217**
— *Same.* New ed. Lond. *n. d.* S.   **J 217**
— *Same, germ.* Gowrie, oder Des königs komplott. Aus dem englischen. Stuttg. 1852. T.   **J 217**
— Heidelberg. *T. p. w.* [N. Y. 1860]. O.   **J 218**
— *Same.* Lond. *n. d.* S.   **J 218**
— Henry de Ceron, [or The man at arms]. *T. p. w.* [N. Y.] D.   **J 219**
— *Same.* The man at arms, or Henri de Cerons. Lond. *n. d.* S.   **J 219**
— *Same, germ.* Heinrich von Cerons. Aus dem englischen. Stuttg. 1843. 2 v. T.   **J 219**
— Henry Masterton, or the adventures of a young cavalier. N. Y. 1864. 2 v. in 1. D.   **J 220**
— *Same.* Lond. *n. d.* S.   **J 220**
— *Same, germ.* Henry Masterton, oder Die erlebnisse eines jungen kavaliers ; roman. Aus dem englischen. Stuttg. 1844. 2 v. T.   **J 220**
— Henry of Guise, or The state of Blois. Lond. *n. d.* S.   **J 221**
— *Same.* N. Y. 1855. 2 v. in 1. D.   **J 221**
— Henry Smeaton ; a jacobite story of the reign of George I. N. Y. 1860. O.   **J 222**
— *Same, germ.* Henry Smeaton ; eine jakobitengeschichte aus der regierungszeit George I. Aus dem englischen. Stuttg. T.   **J 222**
— The huguenot ; a tale of the french protestants. Lond. *n. d.* S.   **J 223**
— *Same, germ.* Der hugenotte ; eine erzählung von den französischen protestanten. Aus dem englischen. Stuttg. 1839. 2 v. T.   **J 223**
— The jacquerie, or The lady and the page. Lond. *n. d.* S.   **J 224**
— *Same.* N. Y. 1855. 2 v. in 1. D.   **J 224**
— *Same, germ.* La jacquerie, der französische bauernkrieg, oder Das fräulein und der page ; historischer roman. Aus dem englischen. Stuttg. 1842. 4 v. T.   **J 224**
— John Marston Hall, or Little ball o'fire. Lond. *n. d.* S.   **J 226**
— *Same, germ.* Leben und abenteuer John Marston Hall's. Stuttg. 1844. 2 v. T.   **J 226**
— The king's highway ; a novel. Lond. *n. d.* S.   **J 225**
— *Same.* N. Y. 1855. 2 v. in 1. D.   **J 225**
— The last of the fairies ; a christmas tale. N. Y. 1876. S.   **J 227**
— *Same, germ.* Die letzte der feen. Aus dem englischen. Stuttg. 1849. T.   **J 227**

x denotes books specially adapted for children.

James, G: Payne Rainsford.—*Continued.*
— Leonora d'Orco ; a historical romance. Lond.
   n. d. S.   **J 249**
— A life of vicissitudes. N. Y. 1860. O.   **J 228**
— The man at arms. *See above* Henry de Ceron.
— The man in black. Phila. [1860]. O.   **J 229**
— Margaret Graham ; a tale. Lond. *n. d.* S.
                                  J 230
— *Same, germ.* Margarethe Graham. Aus dem
   englischen. Stuttg. 1848. T.   **J 230**
— Mary of Burgundy, or The revolt of Ghent.
   Lond. *n. d.* S.   **J 231**
— *Same.* N. Y. 1855. 2 v. in 1. D.   **J 231**
— *Same, germ.* Maria von Burgund, oder Die em-
   pörung in Gent. Stuttg. 1844. 2 v. T.
                                    J 231
— Morley Ernstein, or The tenants of the heart.
   Lond. *n. d.* D.   **J 232**
— My aunt Pontypool ; a novel. Lond. *n. d.* S.
                                    J 250
— The Old Dominion ; a novel. Lond. *n. d.* S.
                                    J 251
— The old oak chest. N. Y. 1873. O.   **J 233**
— *Same, germ.* Die alte eichenkiste ; erzählung
   aus dem häuslichen leben. Aus dem engli-
   schen. Stuttg. 1853. T.   **J 233**
— One in a thousand ; or The days of Henri
   quatre. Lond. *n. d.* S.   **J 234**
— *Same.* N. Y. 1855. 2 v. in 1. D.   **J 234**
— *Same, germ.* Eine unter tausenden, oder Die
   tage Heinrich des vierten. Aus dem eng-
   lischen. Stuttg. 1845. 2 v. T.   **J 234**
— Philip Augustus, or The brothers in arms.
   Lond. *n. d.* S.   **J 235**
— *Same, germ.* Philipp August, oder Die waffen-
   brüder. Aus dem englischen. Stuttg. 1845.
   2 v. T.   **J 235**
— Richelieu ; a tale of France. Lond. *n. d.* S.
                                    J 236
— *Same, germ.* Richelieu ; eine erzählung aus
   der französischen geschichte. Aus dem
   englischen. Stuttg. 1840. 2 v. T.   **J 236**
— The robber ; a tale. Lond. *n. d.* S.   **J 252**
— Rosa d'Albret ; a romance. Lond. *n. d.* S.
                                    J 237
— *Same, germ.* Rosa d'Albret, oder Stürmische
   zeiten. Aus dem englischen. Stuttg. 1844.
   2 v. T.   **J 252**
— Russell ; a tale of the reign of Charles II. New
   ed. Lond. *n. d.* S.   **J 238**
— *Same, germ.* Russell ; erzählung aus Karls
   II. regierungszeit. Aus dem englischen.
   Stuttg. 1847. 2 v. T.   **J 238**
— Sir Theodore Broughton, or Laurel water.
   N. Y. 1869. O.   **J 239**
— *Same.* Lond. *n. d.* S.   **J 239**
— *Same, germ.* Sir Theodor Broughton, oder
   Der gifttrank. Aus dem englischen.
   Stuttg. 1849. T.   **J 239**
— The smuggler. Lond. *n. d.* S.   **J 241**
— *Same, germ.* Der schmuggler. Stuttg. 1845.
   2 v. T.   **J 241**
— The step-mother. Lond. *n. d.* S.   **J 253**
— The string of pearls. N. Y. *n. d.* D. **J 256**
— Thirty years since. *See above* Delaware.
— A whim and its consequences. Lond. *n. d.* S.
                                  J 254
— The woodman ; an historical romance. Lond.
   n. d. S.   **J 246**
— *Same, germ.* Der waidmann ; erzählung aus
   Richard III. zeiten. Aus dem englischen.
   Stuttg. 1852. T.   **J 246**

James, H:, [*jr.*] The american. Bost. 1877. D.
                                    J 301
— The author of Beltraffio, [and other stories].
   Bost. 1885. D.   **J 314**
   Includes, Pandora.—Georgina's reasons.—The path
   of duty.—Four meetings.
— A bundle of letters. *With his* Diary of a man
   of fifty.
— Confidence. Bost. 1880. D.   **J 302**
— Daisy Miller ; a study, and other stories. N.
   Y. 1883. Q.   **J 311**
   Includes, An international episode.—The diary of a
   man of fifty.—A bundle of letters.
— The diary of a man of fifty. N. Y. 1880. Tt.
                                    J 303
— The europeans. Bost. 1879. D.   **J 304**
— A light man. *In* Stories by american authors.
                                S 35 v5
— The madonna of the future, and other tales.
   New ed. Lond. 1880. D.   **J 309**
   Includes, Longstaff's marriage.— Madame de Mau-
   ves.—Eugene Pickering.—The diary of a man of
   fifty.—Benvolio.
— A passionate pilgrim, and other tales. Bost.
   1875. D.   **J 305**
   Includes, The last of the Valerii.—Eugene Picker-
   ing.—The madonna of the future.—The romance of
   certain old clothes.—Madame de Mauves.
— The pension Beaurepas. *With his* The siege
   of London.   **J 312**
— The point of view. *With same.*   **J 312**
— The portrait of a lady. Bost. 1882. D. **J 310**
— Roderick Hudson. Bost. 1876. D.   **J 308**
— The siege of London. Bost. 1883. D. **J 312**
— Tales of three cities. Bost. 1884. D. **J 313**
   Contents. The impressions of a cousin.—Lady Bar-
   berina.—A New England winter.
— Washington square. N. Y. 1881. S. **J 307**
— Watch and ward. Bost. 1878. T.   **J 308**

Jameson, Anna Brownell, *born* Murphy. [Tales].
   In her Studies, stories and romances.
                              829.2 : 17
   Contents, see under English literature, Miscellany.
Jamieson, Frances. Ashford rectory. *T. p. w.*
   S.   **J 351**
Jansen, Adam. Die sagen Frankens. Würzburg.
   1852. S.   **J 401**
Janson, Kristofer Nagel. The spell-bound fid-
   dler ; a norse romance. Tr. from the origi-
   nal by Auber Forestier [Annie Aubertine
   Woodward]; with introd. by Rasmus B.
   Anderson. Chicago. 1880. D.   **J 451**
Janvier, Margaret, (*Margaret Vandegrift*). The
   absent-minded fairy ; for boys and girls.
   Ill. Phila. [1884]. O.   **Vx 104**
— Clover Beach ; for boys and girls. Ill. Phila.
   1880. O.   **Vx 101**
— Doris and Theodora. Phila. [1885]. D.
                                  Vx 105
— Holidays at home ; for boys and girls. Ill.
   Phila. [1882]. O.   **Vx 102**
— The queen's body guard ; a story of american
   life for girls. Phila. [1883]. D.   **Vx 103**
Janvier, T: A., (*Ivory Black*). Pancha ; a story
   of Monterey. *In* Stories by american
   authors.   **S 35 v10**
Jay, Harriett. Madge Dunraven. [*Anon.*] N.
   Y. 1879. Q.   **J 501**
— *Same;* a tale. Lond. 1873. 3 v. in 1. D. **J 501**
— My Connaught cousins ; a novel. [*Anon.*] N.
   Y. 1883. Q.   **J 502**
— *Same.* 2d ed. Lond. 1883. 3 v. D.   **J 502**
Jay, W. M. L., *pseud., see* **Woodruff,** Julia Louisa
   Matilda.

x denotes books specially adapted for children.

49

Jeaffreson, J: Cordy. Durch's leben überwunden. Aus dem englischen von Marie Scott. Leipz. 1865. 2 v. D. **J 551**
— Olive Blake's good work. N. Y. 1864. O. **J 552**

Jean Paul, *pseud.*, *see* **Richter**, J: Paul F:

Jefferies, R: After London, or Wild England. N. Y. 1885. D. **J 576**
— Wood magic; a fable. Lond. 1881. D. **Jx 151**

Jenkin, *Mrs.* C: Madame de Beaupré. (Leisure hour ser.) N. Y. 1869. S. **J 601**
— A Psyche of to-day. (Leisure hour ser.) N. Y. 1868. S. **J 602**
— Skirmishing. (Leisure hour ser.) N. Y. 1863. D. **J 603**
— Who breaks—pays. *T. p. w.* D. **J 604**
— Within an ace. N. Y. 1875. S. **J 605**

Jenkins, E: The devil's chain. N. Y. 1876. S. **J 651**
— Haverholme, or The apotheosis of Jingo; a satire. N. Y. 1878. Q. **J 652**
— A paladin of finance; contemporary manners. Bost. 1882. S. **J 653**
— A week of passion, or The dilemma of mr. G: Barton, the younger; a novel. N. Y. 1885. Q. **J 654**

Jennings, L: J. The millionaire; a novel. [*Anon.*] N. Y. 1884. Q. **J 676**
— *Same.* N. Y. 1884. S. **J 676**

Jensen, W: Aus Lübeck's alten tagen; novelle. 2te aufl. Berlin. 1878. T. **J 701**
— Die namenlosen; roman. Schwerin i. M. 1873. 3 v. in 1. D. **J 702**
— Neue novellen. Stuttg. 1869. D. **J 703**
    Content, see Deutscher katalog, p. 74.
— Ueber die wolken; roman. N. Y. 1883. F. **J 706**
— Unter heisserer sonne; novelle. Braunschw. 1869. D. **J 704**
— Versunkene welten; historischer roman. N. Y. 1881. F. **J 705**

Jephson, Philippa Prittie. An april day; a novel. N. Y. 1883. Q. **J 726**

Jerrold, Douglas W: St. Giles and St. James. Lond. 1851. D. **J 751**

Jesuiten in New York, Die. Aus dem englischen. N. Y. 1857. T. **J 1**

Jewett, Sarah Orne, (*Alice Eliot*). Country-by-ways. Bost. 1881. S. **J 803**
    Contents. River driftwood. — Andrew's fireside.—An october ride. — From a mournful Villager.—An autumn holiday.—A winter drive.—Good luck.—Miss Becky's pilgrimage.
— A country doctor. Bost. 1884. D. **J 805**
— Deephaven. Bost. 1878. T. **J 801**
— A marsh island. Bost. 1885. D. **J 806**
— The mate of the Daylight and friends ashore. Bost. 1884 [1883]. S. **J 804**
    Includes, A landless farmer.—A new parishioner.—An only son.—Miss Derby's neighbors.—Tom's husband.—The confession of a house-breaker.—A little traveller.
— Old friends and new. Bost. 1879. T. **J 802**
    Contents. A lost lover.—A sorrowful guest.—A late supper.—Mr. Bruce.—Miss Sidney's flowers.—Lady Ferry.—A bit of shore life.
— Play days; a book of stories for children. Bost. 1878. S. **Jx 201**

Jewsbury, Geraldine Herbert. N. Y. 1855. O. **J 851**
— Zoe; the history of two lives. *T. p. w.* [N. Y. 1856]. O. **J 852**

John, Eugenie, (*E. Marlitt*). Amtmanns magd. N. Y. 1881. F. **J 901**
— *Same, eng.* The bailiff's maid. From the german by mrs. A. L. Wister. Phila. 1881. D. **J 901**
— Das geheimniss der alten mamselle. N. Y. 1881. F. **J 903**
— *Same, eng.* The old mamselle's secret. After the german by mrs. A. L. Wister. Phila. 1879. D. **J 903**
— Goldelse. Leipz. *n. d.* D. **J 904**
— *Same*; roman. 17te aufl. Leipz. [188-]. D. **J 904**
— *Same, eng.* Gold Elsie. From the german by mrs. A. L. Wister. Phila. *n. d.* D. **J 904**
— *Same.* Phila. 1883. D. **J 904**
— *Same.* Phila. 1884. D. **J 904**
— Das haideprinzesschen; roman. 5te aufl. Leipz. 1878. 2 v. in 1. D. **J 902**
— *Same.* 6te aufl. Leipz. [1884]. 2 v. D. **J 902**
— *Same.* N. Y. 1882. F. **J 902**
— *Same, eng.* The little moorland princess. Tr. from the german by mrs. A. L. Wister. Phila. 1872. D. **J 902**
— *Same.* Phila. 1876. D. **J 902**
— *Same.* Phila. 1883. D. **J 902**
— Im hause des commerzienrathes; roman. 2te aufl. Leipz. 1877. 2 v. in 1. D. **J 905**
— *Same.* 3te aufl. Leipz. [187-]. 2 v. in 1. D. **J 905**
— *Same.* N. Y. 1882. F. **J 905**
— *Same, eng.* At the councillors, or A nameless history. Tr. from the german by mrs. A. L. Wister. Phila. 1876. D. **J 905**
— *Same.* Phila. 1877. D. **J 905**
— Im Schillingshof; roman. Leipz. [1880]. 2 v. in 1. D. **J 906**
— *Same.* 2te aufl. Leipz. [1880]. 2 v. D. **J 906**
— *Same.* N. Y. 1881. F. **J 906**
— *Same, eng.* In the Schillingscourt. From the german by mrs. A. L. Wister. Phila. 1879. D. **J 906**
— Magdalena. Phila. 1877. O. **J 907**
— Over yonder. Phila. 1877. O. **J 908**
— Die reichsgräfin Gisela. 6te aufl. Leipz. [1880]. 2 v. in 1. D. **J 909**
— *Same.* 7te aufl. Leipz. [188-]. 2 v. D. **J 909**
— *Same.* N. Y. 1881. F. **J 909**
— *Same, eng.* Countess Gisela. From the german by mrs. A. L. Wister. Phila. 1877. D. **J 909**
— *Same.* Phila. 1879. D. **J 909**
— Thüringer erzählungen. 4te aufl. Leipz. 1878. D. **J 911**
    Contents, see Deutscher katalog, p. 74.
— Die zweite frau; roman. 6te aufl. Leipz. [1881]. D. **J 912**
— *Same.* 7te aufl. Leipz. [1884]. 2 v. in 1. D. **J 912**
— *Same.* N. Y. 1882. F. **J 912**
— *Same, eng.* The second wife; a romance. From the german by mrs. A. L. Wister. Phila. 1879. D. **J 912**
— *Same.* Phila. 1880. D. **J 912**
— *Same.* Phila. 1883. D. **J 912**

John Barlow's ward. N. Y. 1881. S. **J 31**

Johnson, *Col.* —. The white fawn; a north american story. *In* **Edinburgh** tales. **E 426**

Johnson, Edwin Rossiter. Phaeton Rogers; a story of boy-life. Ill. N. Y. 1881. D. **Jx 251**

x denotes books specially adapted for children.

Johnson, Edwin Rossiter.—*Continued.*
— *ed.* Little classics. Bost. 1875–81. 18 v. S. **J 926**
Contents. V. 1. *Exile.* **Hawthorne,** N., Ethan Brand.—**Griffin,** G. The swans of Lir.—**Greenwood,** J. A night in the workhouse.—**Harte,** F. B. The outcasts of Poker Flat.—**Hale,** E: E. The man without a country.—**De Quincey,** T. Flight of a tartar tribe.
2. *Intellect.* **Bulwer-Lytton,** E: The house and brain.—**Spofford,** H. P. D'outre mort.—**Poe,** E. A. The fall of the house of Usher.—**Dickens,** C: Chops the dwarf.—**Hawthorne,** N. Wakefield.—**De Quincey,** T: Murder considered as one of the fine arts. —**Davis,** R. H. The captain's story.
3. *Tragedy.* **Poe,** E. A. The murders in the rue Morgue.—**De Forest,** J: W: The Lauson tragedy.—**Mudford,** W: The iron shroud.—**Melville,** H. The bell-tower. — **Judson,** E. C. The kathayan slave. — **Mackenzie,** H: The story of La Roche.—**De Quincey,** T: The vision of sudden death.
4. *Life.* **Brown,** J: Rab and his friends.—**Howells,** W: D. A romance of real life.—**Harte,** F. B. The luck of Roaring Camp.—**Barham,** R: H. Jerry Jarvis's wig.—**Willis,** N. P. Beauty and the beast.—**Hawthorne,** N. David Swan.—**Smith,** A. Dreamthorp.—**Mitchell,** D. G. A bachelor's revery.—**Taylor,** B. F. The grammar of life.—**Curtis,** G: W: My château. — **Lamb,** C: Dream children. — **Hoffman,** C: F. The man in the reservoir.—**Addison,** J. Westminster abbey. — **Macaulay,** T: B. The puritans.—**Lincoln,** A. Gettysburg.
5. *Laughter.* **Dickens,** C: A christmas carol.—**Cooper,** K. The haunted crust. — **Lamb,** C: A dissertation upon roast pig.—**Walker,** K. K. The total depravity of inanimate things. — **Hale,** E: E. The skeleton in the closet.—**Miller,** H. Sandy Wood's sepulchre.—**Holmes,** O. W. A visit to the asylum for aged and decayed punsters.—**Griffin,** G. Mr. Tibbot O'Leary the curious.—**Carleton,** W: Neal Malone.
6. *Love.* **Winthrop,** T. Love and skates. — **Bulwer-Lytton,** E: The maid of Malines.—The story of Ruth, from the Bible.—**Disraeli,** B. The rise of Iskander.
7. *Romance.* **Holmes,** O. W. Iris.—**Craik,** D. M. The rosicrucian.—**Spofford,** H. P. The south breaker.—**Wilson,** J. The snow-storm. — **Cunningham,** A. The king of the peak.
8. *Mystery.* **O'Connor,** W. D. The ghost. — **Edwards,** A. B. The four-fifteen express.—**Dickens,** C: The signal-man.—**Cunningham,** A. The haunted ships.—**Lowell,** R. T. S. A raft that no man made.—**O'Connor,** F. The invisible princess. — **Crowe,** C. The advocate's wedding day.—**Hawthorne,** N. The birthmark.
9. *Comedy.* **Lover,** S: Barney O'Reirdon the navigator.—**Galt,** J: Haddad-Ben-Ahab the traveller.—**Thackeray,** W: M. Bluebeard's ghost. — **Smith,** H. The picnic party. — **Ferguson,** S: Father Tom and the pope. — **Howitt,** W: Johnny Darbyshire. — **Lover,** S: The gridiron.—**Reade,** C: The box tunnel.
10. *Childhood.* **Ramé,** L. de la. A dog of Flanders.—**Ruskin,** J: The king of the Golden River.—**Phelps,** E. S. The lady of Shalott. — **Brown,** J: Marjorie Fleming.—**De Kroyft,** S. H. Little Jakey. — **Kingsley,** H: The lost child.—**Neal,** J: Goody gracious! and the forget-me-not. — **Spofford,** H. P. A faded leaf of history. — **Dickens,** C: A child's dream of a star.
11. *Heroism.* **Ludlow,** F. H. Little Briggs and I. — **Spofford,** H. P. Ray. — **Taylor,** B: F. Three november days. — **Mitford,** A. B. The forty-seven rônins.—**Mayo,** J. A chance child.—**Ramé,** L. de la. A leaf in a storm.
12. *Fortune.* **Poe,** E. A. The gold bug. — **Lover,** S. The fairy finder. — **Edgeworth,** M. Murad the unlucky.—**Hale,** E: E. The children of the public.—**Banim,** J. The rival dreamers. — **Hawthorne,** N. The threefold destiny.
13. *Poems narrative.* **Goldsmith,** O. The deserted village.—**Coleridge,** S: T. The ancient mariner.—**Byron,** G: N. *lord.* The prisoner of Chillon.—**Norton,** C. Bingen on the Rhine. — **Campbell,** T: O'Connor's child. — **Hogg,** J. Kilmeny. — **Hood,** T: The dream of Eugene Aram.—**Smith,** A. Lady Barbara.—**Shelley,** P. B. The sensitive plant.—**Keats,** J: The eve of St. Agnes. — **Moore,** T: Paradise and the peri.—**Poe,** E. A. The raven. — **Longfellow,** H: W. The skeleton in armor.—**Hood,** T: The haunted house. — **Morris,** W: The writing on the image.—**Burns,** R. Tam O'Shanter.—**Ferguson,** S: The forging of the anchor. — **Tennyson,** A. Morte d'Arthur.—**Macaulay,** T: B. Horatius.

14. Poems lyrical.
15. Minor poems.
16. Authors; biographical sketches of the authors represented in the series, with a general index.
17. *Nature.* **Warner,** C: D. A-hunting of the deer. — **Hamerton,** P. G. Dogs.—**Burroughs,** J: In the hemlocks. — **Thoreau,** H: D: A winter walk. **Hawthorne,** N. Buds and bird voices.—**Kingsley,** C: The fens.—**Whymper,** E: Ascent of the Matterhorn.—**King,** C. Ascent of Mount Tyndall.—**Ruskin,** J: The firmament.
18. *Humanity.* **Stoddard,** C: W. Chumming with a savage.—**Dickens,** C: Doctor Marigold.—**Ludlow,** F. H. A brace of boys.—**Thackeray,** W: M. George III.—**Jameson,** A. Juliet.—**Mallock,** W: H. Is life worth living?
Johnson, S: Rasselas, prince of Abyssinia ; with an intr. by the rev. W: West. [Bayard ser]. Lond. 1875. T.   **J 951**
— *Same.* A facsimile reproduction of the 1st ed. publ. in 1759 ; with an introd. by James Macauly and a bibliographical list of editions of Rasselas pub. in England and elsewhere. Lond. 1884. 2 v. D.   **J 952**
— *Same. In his* Works.   **820.2+13 v1**
Johnson, Virginia Wales. An english Daisy Miller. Bost. 1882. D.   **J 1003**
— The Fainalls of Tipton. N. Y. 1884. S. **J 1004**
— The image of St. Donato. *In* Stories by american authors.   **S 35 v7**
— The Neptune vase. N. Y. 1881. Q. **J 1001**
— Two old cats ; a novel. N. Y. 1882. Q. **J 1002**
Johnston, Alma, *born* Calder. Miriam's heritage ; a story of the Delaware river. N. Y. 1878. O.   **J 1051**
Johnston, R: Malcolm, (*Philemon Perch*). Dukesborough tales. N. Y. 1883. Q. **J 1076**
— Old Mark Langston ; a tale of Duke's Creek. N. Y. 1884. S.   **J 1077**
Johnstone, Christina Jane. Clan-Albyn ; a national tale. Lond. 1854. S.   **J 1101**
— Nights of the round-table, or Stories of aunt Jane and her friends. Phila. *n. d.* T.   **J 1102**
— The sabbath night's supper. *In* Edinburgh tales.   **E 426**
Jókai, Mór (*germ.* Maurus). Achtzehn humoristische erzählungen. Aus dem ungarischen übersetzt von einem landsmanne und jugendfreunde des dichters ; mit portrait und biographischer charakteristik *Jókai's.* 2te ausg. Bremen. 1879. 2 v. S.   **J 1152**
Contents, *see* Deutscher katalog, p. 74.
— Die armen reichen ; roman. 3te aufl. Berlin. [1879]. D.   **J 1151**
— Hungarian sketches in peace and war ; with a prefatory notice by Emeric Szabad. Edinburgh. 1854. D.   **J 1154**
Contents. Preface. — Dear relations. — The Bardy family. — Crazy Marcsa. — Comorn. — Mor Ferczel. — Gergely Sonkolyi. — The unlucky weather-cock.—The two brides. — The brewer. — The Szekely mother. — A ball.
— Die komödianten des lebens. 2te aufl. Berlin. [1880]. D.   **J 1153**
— A modern Midas ; a romance. From the german by mrs. Laura Curtis Bullard and Emma Herzog. N. Y. 1884. D. **J 1155**
— Der piraten-könig. *With* **Tenger,** M. Bischof und könig.   **T 546**
— Die sphinx ; eine phantasie. *In* Vierteljährl. mag.   **V2 v21**
Jones, Pascal. My uncle Hobson and I, or Slashes at life with a free broad-axe. N. Y. 1845. D.   **J 1201**
Judson, E: Z. C., (*Ned Buntline*). Norwood, or Life on the prairie. N. Y. *n. d.* O. **J 1251**

x denotes books specially adapted for children.

Judson, Emily, *born* Chubbuck, *(Fanny Forrester)*. Alderbrook, a collection of Fanny Forrester's village sketches, poems etc. Bost. 1848. 2 v. D.　　　　　**J 1301**
— Allen Lucas ; the self-made man. N. Y. 1848. S.　　　　　**Jx 301**
— The kathayan slave. *In* Johnson, E. R. Little classics.　　　　　**J 926 v3**
Juncker, E., *pseud., see* Schmieden, Else.
Junghans, Sophie, *see* Schuhmann, Sophie.
Jüngst, L: Volrad, *(Ludwig Rosen).* Werner Thormann. Breslau. 1859. 3 v. S.　**J 1501**
Just his luck. Bost. 1878. D.　　　**Jx 89**
Justitia, a knownothing, *pseud., see* Adams, F. Colburn.
K., W. v. Laskar Vioresku ; ein moldauisches genrebild. Leipz. 1863. D.　　**K 1601**
Kaiser, Ernst, *pseud., see* König, Ewald A:
Kaler, James Otis, *(James Otis).* Left behind, or Ten days a newsboy. Ill. N. Y. 1885 [1884]. S.　　　　　**Ox 505**
— Mr. Stubbs's brother ; a sequel to Toby Tyler. N. Y. 1883. S.　　　　　**Ox 502**
— Raising the Pearl. N. Y. 1884 [1883]. S.　　　　　**Ox 504**
— Tim and Tip, or The adventures of a boy and a dog. Ill. N. Y. 1883. S.　　**Ox 503**
— Toby Tyler, or Ten weeks with a circus. Ill. N. Y. 1881. S.　　　　　**Ox 501**
Kapper, Siegfried. Vorleben eines künstlers. Prag. 1855. 2 v. T.　　　　　**K 101**
Karl Kiegler, or The fortunes of a foundling. Bost. *n. d.* S.　　　　　**Kx 3**
　Contents. Karl Kiegler.—Don't be too positive, or Frank Shipley and his ducks.
Katsch, Gustav Adolf. Under the stork's nest. From the german by Emily R. Steinestel. Phila. 1875. D.　　　　　**K 151**
　Note. Title-page reads by "A. E. Katsch."
Kauffer, E: Der treu'sten frau ; erzählungen und novellen. Leipz. 1852. D.　　**K 201**
　Contents, see Deutscher katalog, p. 75.
Kaulbach, C. Uriel der teufel ; ein satirischer roman in acht büchern. Stuttg. 1851. 2 v. S.　　　　　**K 251**
Kavanagh, Bridget *and* Julia. The pearl fountain, and other fairy tales. Ill. N. Y. 1876. O.　　　　　**Kx 102**
　Includes, The silver fish.—The golden hen.—Sunbeam and her white rabbit.—Redcap's adventures in fairy land.—Fire and water.—Tipsey's silver bell.—Prince Doran.—Fairie and Brownie.—Batty.—Feather Head.
Kavanagh, Julia. Beatrice. N. Y. 1884. 3 v. in 1. D.　　　　　**K 314**
— Bessie. Leipz. 1872. 2 v. in 1. S.　　**K 301**
— Daisy Burns. *T. p. w.* [N. Y. 1875.] D. **K 302**
— *Same, germ.* Daisy Burns. Aus dem englischen. Stuttg. 1853. T.　　　　**K 302**
— Dora. Leipz. 1868. 2 v. in 1. S.　　**K 303**
— Grace Lee. N. Y. 1881. D.　　　**K 304**
— John Dorrien. N. Y. 1875. D.　　**K 305**
— Madeleine ; a tale of the Auvergne, founded on fact. N. Y. 1873. D.　　　**K 306**
— Nathalie. Leipz. 1851. 2 v. in 1. S. **K 307**
— *Same, germ.* Nathalie. Aus dem englischen von E. Zoller. Stuttg. 1851. 2 v. T.　　　　　**K 307**
— Queen Mab. Leipz. 1863. 2 v. in 1. S. **K 308**
— Rachel Gray ; a tale founded on fact. N. Y. 1873. D.　　　　　**K 309**
— Seven years, and other tales. N. Y. 1872. D.　　　　　**K 310**
　Includes, The conscript.—Gaiety and gloom.—The little dancing master.—A soirée in a porter's lodge.—

Kavanagh, Julia—*Continued.*
　A comedy in a court-yard.—The troubles of a quiet man.—Young France.—Adrien.—The mysterious lodger.—An excellent opportunity.—The experiences of Sylvie Delmare.
— Silvia. Leipz. 1870. 2 v. in 1. S.　**K 311**
— Sybil's second love. N. Y. 1875. D.　**K 312**
— The three paths ; a story for young people. Ill. Lond. 1848. S.　　　　**Kx 101**
— Two Lilies. Leipz. 1877. 2 v. in 1. S.　**K 313**
Keary, Annie. Castle Daly ; the story of an irish home thirty years ago. Leipz. 1875. 2 v. in 1. S.　　　　　**K 351**
— A doubting heart. N. Y. 1879. Q.　**K 352**
— *Same.* Lond. 1879. 3 v. in 2. D.　**K 352**
— Oldbury. Phila. *n. d.* D.　　　**K 353**
— *Same.* Leipz. 1874. 2 v. in 1. D.　**K 353**
— A York and Lancaster Rose. Lond. 1876. D.　　　　　**Kx 116**
Keddie, Henrietta, *(Sarah Tytler).* Beauty and the beast ; a novel. N. Y. 1884. Q.　　　　　**K 1653**
— Citoyenne Jacqueline ; a woman's lot in the great french revolution. Lond. 1881. S.　　　　　**K 1651**
— Jane Austen and her works. Lond. 1880. D.　　　　　**A 2055**
　Contents. Jane Austen.—Jane Austen's novels.—Pride and prejudice.—Northanger Abbey.—Emma.—Sense and sensibility, *and* Mansfield Park.—Persuasion.
— Lady Bell ; a story of last century. [New issue]. Chicago. 1884. D.　　**K 1652**
— The woman with two words. Ill. N. Y. 1885 [1884]. D.　　　　　**Kx 126**
Keenan, H: F. Trojan ; the history of a sentimental young man, with some episodes in the comedy of many lives' errors ; a novel. N. Y. 1885. D.　　　　　**K 1801**
Keene, H. G. Clive's dream before the battle of Plassey. *In* Tales from Blackwood.　　　　　**T 177 v5**
Keeper's travels in search of his master. Worcester. 1847. T.　　　　　**Kx 1**
Keller, Gottfried. Der grüne Heinrich ; roman. Neue ausg. Stuttg. 1879. 4 v. in 2. D.　　　　　**K 376**
— Die leute von Seldwyla ; erzählungen. 3te aufl. Stuttg. 1876. 2 v. in 1. D.　**K 377**
　Contents, see Deutscher katalog, p. 75.
— Romeo und Julia auf dem dorfe ; erzählung. Stuttg. 1876. T.　　　　　**K 378**
— Sieben legenden. 2te aufl. Stuttg. 1872. D.　　　　　**K 379**
　Contents, see Deutscher katalog, p. 75.
— Züricher novellen. 2te aufl. Stuttg. 1879. 2 v. in 1. D.　　　　　**K 380**
　Contents, see Deutscher katalog, p. 75.
Kellogg, Elijah. *Elm Island stories.*
1. Lion Ben of Elm Island. Bost. *n. d.* D.　　　　　**Kx 205**
2. Charlie Bell, the waif of Elm Island. Ill. Bost. *n. d.* D.　　　　　**Kx 206**
3. The ark of Elm Island. Bost. 1875. S.　　　　　**Kx 207**
4. The boy farmers of Elm Island. Bost. 1870. D.　　　　　**Kx 208**
6. The hard scrabble of Elm Island. Bost. 1871. S.　　　　　**Kx 210**
— *The Forest Glen series.*
1. Sowed by the wind, or The poor boy's fortune. Ill. Bost. *n. d.* D.　　**Kx 223**
2. Wolf run, or The boys of the wilderness. Ill. Bost. *n. d.* D.　　　**Kx 224**

x denotes books specially adapted for children.

Kellogg, Elijah.—*Continued.*
4. Black Rifle's mission, or On the trail. Ill. Bost. *n. d.* D. **Kx 226**
— *The good old times series.*
1. Good old times, or Grandfather's struggle for a homestead. Bost. *n. d.* D. **Kx 201**
2. A strong arm and a mother's blessing. Ill. Bost. 1881. D. **Kx 202**
3. The unseen hand, or James Renfrew and his boy helpers. Ill. Bost. 1882 [1881]. D. **Kx 203**
4. The live oak boys, or The adventures of Richard Constable afloat and ashore. Bost. 1883 [1882]. D. **Kx 204**
— *The Pleasant Cove series.*
1. Arthur Brown, the young captain. Ill. Bost. *n. d.* D. **Kx 217**
2. The young deliverers of Pleasant Cove. Ill. Bost. 1871. S. **Kx 218**
— *The whispering pine series.*
1. The spark of genius, or The college life of James Trafton. Ill. Bost. *n. d.* D. **Kx 211**
2. The sophomores of Radcliffe, or James Trafton and his bosom friends. Ill. Bost. *n. d.* D. **Kx 212**
3. The whispering pine, or The graduates of Radcliffe Hall. Ill. Bost. *n. d.* D. **Kx 213**
4. Winning his spurs, or Henry Morton's first trial. Ill. Bost. *n. d.* D. **Kx 214**
5. The turning of the tide, or Radcliffe Rich and his patients. Ill. Bost. *n. d.* D. **Kx 215**
6. A stout heart, or The student from over the sea. Ill. Bost. *n. d.* D. **Kx 216**
Kennedy, J: Pendleton. Horse-shoe Robinson; a tale of tory ascendency. Rev. ed. N. Y. 1881. D. **K 403**
— Quodlibet; containing some annals thereof, with an authentic account of the origin and growth of the borough, and the sayings and doings of sundry of the townspeople; interspersed with sketches of the most remarkable and distinguished characters of that vicinity, by Solomon Secondthoughts, schoolmaster, from original mss. inedited by him, and now made public at the request and under the patronage of the great new-light democratic central committee of Quodlibet. 2d ed. Phila. 1860. D. **K 401**
— Rob of the bowl; a legend of St. Inigoe's. N. Y. 1854. D. **K 402**
Kenney, Minnie E. Gypsie. N. Y. 1882. S. **K 426**
Ker, D: From the Hudson to the Neva. Ill. Bost. [1883]. D. **Kx 376**
— The lost city, or The boy explorers in central Asia. Ill. N. Y. 1885 [1884]. S. **Kx 377**
Kerckhoven, P. F. van. Fernand der seeräuber. Aus dem flämischen von Julius Stern. Augsburg. 1846. S. **K 451**
Kerr, Orpheus C., *pseud., see* Newell, Robert H:
Keyserling, Margarethe, *born* v. Dönniges, *gräfin.* Die sturmhexe; roman. N. Y. 1881. F. **K 476**
Kieffer, Harry M. The recollections of a drummer boy. Ill. Bost. 1883. S. **Kx 601**
Kielland, Alexander L. Arbeiter; roman. Autorisirte übersetzung aus dem norwegischen von C. v. Sarauw. Berlin. 1881. D. **K 1703**

Kielland, Alexander L.—*Continued.*
— Ausgewählte novellen. Aus dem norwegischen von Jos. Cal. Poestion. Wien. 1881. D. **K 1704**
Contents. Grün ist der hoffnung kleid.—Von einem schiffe.—Ein affe.—Der pfarrhof.—Ein diner.—Liebe und ehe.—Torfmoor.—Zwei freunde.—Welke blätter.
— Else; eine weihnachtsgeschichte. Autorisirte übersetzung aus dem norwegischen von C. v. Sarauw. Berlin. 1882. D. **K 1701**
— Garman and Worse; a norwegian novel. Authorized trans. by W. W. Kettlewell. Lond. 1885 [1884]. D. **K 1702**
— *Same, germ.* Garman und Worse. Autorisirte übersetzung aus dem norwegischen von capt. v. Sarauw. Berlin. 1881. D. **K 1702**
— Zwei freunde; novellette. *In* Vierteljährl. mag. **V 2 v23**
Kimball, R: Burleigh. The prince of Kashna. *T. p. w.* D. **K 501**
— Romance of student life abroad. 2d ed. N. Y. 1853. D. **K 504**
— St. Leger. *T. p. w.* D. **K 502**
— Undercurrents of Wall street. N. Y. 1862. S. **K 503**
— *Same. T. p. w.* S. **K 503**
Kincaid, *Sir* J: Random shots from a rifleman. Phila. 1835. D. **K 551**
King, C: The colonel's daughter, or Winning his spurs. Phila. 1883. D. **K 576**
— *Same, germ.* Wer wird sie heimführen? aus dem leben auf kalifornischen grenzstationen. Autorisirte übers. Braunschw. 1885. 2 v. in 1. D. **K 576**
— Kitty's conquest. Phila. 1884. D. **K 577**
King, E: The gentle savage. Bost. 1883. D. **K 626**
King, H. Brown's peccadillo. *In* Tales from Blackwood. **T 177 v12**
King, Katherine. The bubble reputation. N. Y. 1878. Q. **K 601**
— Off the roll. N. Y. 1875. O. **K 602**
— Our detachment. N. Y. 1875. O. **K 603**
Kingsley, C: Alton Locke, tailor and poet. *T. p. w.* D. **K 651**
— *Same,* an autobiography; with prefatory memoir by T: Hughes and portrait. [Works, v. 3.] New ed. Lond. 1882. D. **K 651**
— Hereward the wake, "last of the english". Leipz. 1866. 2 v in 1. S. **K 652**
— *Same.* [Works, v. 11.] Lond. 1881. D. **K 652**
— Hypatia, or New foes with an old face. Leipz. 1857. 2 v. in 1. S. **K 653**
— *Same.* N. Y. 1883. D. **K 653**
— *Same.* Lond. 1883. D. **K 653**
— *Same, germ.* Hypatia, oder Neue feinde mit altem gesicht. In's deutsche übertragen von Sophie von Gilsa; mit einem vorwort von C. K: J. Bunsen. 2te aufl. Leipz. 1878. 2 v. in 1. D. **K 653**
— Two years ago. Lond. 1875. D. **K 654**
— *Same.* [Works, v. 8.] Lond. 1879. D. **K 654**
— The water-babies; a fairy tale for a land baby. Ill. Lond. 1879. D. **Kx 401**
— *Same,* ed. and abridged by J. H. Stickney. [Classics for children. Ill.] Bost. 1884. D. **Kx 402**
— Westward ho! the voyages and adventures of sir Amyas Leigh, knight, of Burrough in the county of Devon, in the reign of her most glorious majesty queen Elizabeth. Bost. 1855. D. **K 655**
— *Same.* [Works, v. 6.] N. Y. 1883. D. **K 655**

x denotes books specially adapted for children.

Kingsley, C:—*Continued.*
— Yeast ; a problem. Lond. 1875. D.   **K 656**
— *Same.* [Works, v. 2.] Lond. 1881. D.   **K 656**
Kingsley, H: The Harveys. Lond. 1872. D.   **K 701**
— The Hillyars and the Burtons ; a story of two families. Leipz. 1865. 2 v. in 1. S.   **K 702**
— Leighton Court ; a country house story. Leipz. 1866. S.   **K 703**
— The lost child. *In* Johnson, E. R. Little classics.   **J 926 v10**
— Ravenshoe. Leipz. 1862. 2 v. in 1. S.   **K 704**
— The recollections of Geoffrey Hamlyn. Leipz. 1864. 2 v. in 1. S.   **K 705**
— Reginald Hetherege. Leipz. 1874. 2. v. in 1. S.   **K 708**
— Silcote of Silcotes. Bost. 1867. O.   **K 706**
— Stretton. *T. p. w.* [Bost.] O.   **K 707**
— *Same.* N. Y. 1869. O.   **K 707**
Kingston, W: H. G. Arctic adventures. Ill. Lond. 1882. D.   **Kx 451**
— Dick Cheveley ; his adventures and misadventures. Ill. Phila. 1884. D.   **Kx 457**
— From powder-monkey to admiral. Ill. N. Y. 1884 [1883]. D.   **Kx 455**
— In the eastern seas, or The regions of the bird of paradise ; a tale for boys. Lond. 1872. ·D.   **Kx 458**
— In the wilds of Florida ; a tale of warfare and hunting. Ill. Lond. 1880. D.   **Kx 452**
— The missing ship, or Notes from the log of the "Ouzel" galley. Ill. Lond. *n. d.* D.   **Kx 459**
— On the banks of the Amazon, or A boy's journal of his adventures in the tropical wilds of South America. N. Y. 1884. D. **Kx 467**
— Peter Trawl, or The adventures of a whaler. Ill. N. Y. 1882. D.   **Kx 453**
— Rob Nixon, the old white trapper ; a tale of central british North America. N. Y. 1866. S.   **Kx 460**
— Roger Willoughby, or The times of Benbow ; a tale of the sea and land. Ill. Lond. 1881. D.   **Kx 454**
— The three admirals, and the adventures of their young followers. Ill. N. Y. *n. d.* D.   **Kx 462**
— The three lieutenants, or Naval life in the 19th century. N. Y. *n. d.* D.   **Kx 463**
— Voyage of the "Steadfast." Bost. *n. d.* D.   **Kx 465**
— Will Weatherhelm ; the yarn of an old sailor about his early life and adventures. Ill. New enl. ed. N. Y. *n. d.* D.   **Kx 466**
Kinkel, J: Gottfried. A family feud. *In* Tales from Blackwood.   **T 177 v11**
Kip, Leonard. Nestlenook ; a tale. N. Y. 1880. S.   **K 801**
— "—mas has come." *In* Stories by american authors.   **S 35 v9**
Kirk, Ellen W., *born* Olney. Clara and Bébé. Phila. 1879. S.   **K 851**
— Fairy gold ; a novel. [*Anon.*] Phila. 1883. O.   **K 855**
— A lesson in love. (Round-robin ser.) Bost. 1881. S.   **K 854**
— Love in idleness ; a summer story. Phila. 1877. O.   **K 852**
— A midsummer madness. Bost. 1884. S.   **K 856**
— Through winding ways. Phila. 1880. O.   **K 853**

Kirkland, Caroline Matilda, (*Mrs. Mary Clavers*). Forest life by the author of "A new home." N. Y. 1842. 2 v. D.   **K 752**
— A new home—who'll follow ? or Glimpses of western life by Mrs. Mary Clavers, an actual settler. 4th ed., rev. by the author. Ill. N. Y. 1850. S.   **K 751**
— Western clearings. N. Y. 1848. D.   **K 753**
Kjelland, A. L., *see* **Kielland.**
Kleinsteuber, Hermann. Ein nordischer Richelieu ; historischer original-roman. Jena. 1867. S.   **K 901**
— Schach dem könig ; historischer roman. Jena. 1867. S.   **K 902**
Kleist, H: v. Michael Kohlhaas. *In* Oxenford, J: Tales from the german.   **O 1001**
Klencke, F: Hermann, (*Hermann v. Maltitz*). Der adept zu Helmstedt ; historischer roman. Leipz. 1851. 4 v. S.   **K 951**
— Swammerdam, oder Die offenbarung der natur ; ein kultur-historischer roman. Leipz. 1864. S.   **K 952**
Knapp, S: Lorenzo. The bachelors and other tales, founded on american incidents and character. N. Y. 1836. D.   **K 1001**
— Tales of the garden of Kosciusko. N. Y. 1834. D.   **K 1002**
Knatchbull-Hugessen, E: H., *see* **Hugessen,** E: H. Knatchbull-.
Knickerbocker, Diedrich, *pseud. see* **Irving,** Washington.
Knorring, *Friherrinnan* Sophia Margaretha, *born* Zelow. The peasant and his landlord. Tr. by Mary Howitt. N. Y. 1855. D.   **K 1051**
— *Same, germ.* Der käthner und seine familie ; schwedische dorfgeschichten. Aus dem schwedischen übers. von C: Stein. Stuttg. 1846. 2 v. T.   **K 1051**
— Skizzen. Aus dem scewedischen von Gottlob Fink. Stuttg. 1847. 2 v. in 1. T.   **K 1052**
Contents, see Deutscher katalog, p. 76.
Knox, T: Wallace. Hunting adventures on land and sea : 1. The young Nimrods in North America ; 2. The young Nimrods around the world ; a book for boys. N. Y. 1881, 1882. 2 v. O.   **Kx 501**
— The voyage of the Vivian to the north pole and beyond ; adventures of two youths in the open polar sea. Ill. and maps. N. Y. 1885. [1884]. O.   **Kx 502**
Kohn, Salomon. Gabriel ; roman. 2te aufl. Jena. 1875. 2 v. in 1. D.   **K 1101**
— Die silberne hochzeit ; roman. N. Y. 1882. F.   **k 1102**
Kompert, Leopold. Böhmische juden. Hamburg. 1866. 2 v. S.   **K 1201**
— *Same.* Prag. 1860. S.   **K 1201**
Contents, see Deutscher katalog, p. 76.
— Geschichten einer gasse ; novellen. Berlin. 1865. 2 v. S.   **K 1202**
Contents, see Deutscher katalog, p. 76.
— Ghetto-geschichten ; novellen. Hamburg. 1866. 2 v. S.   **K 1203**
— *Same.* Neue geschichten aus dem Ghetto. Prag. 1860. 2 v. D.   **K 1203**
Contents, see Deutscher katalog, p. 76.
— Scenes from the ghetto ; studies of jewish life. Tr. from the german. Lond. 1882. D.   **K 1205**
Contents. Schlemiel. — Old Babele. — The Randar's children.—Without authorisation.
— Eine verlorene. N. Y. 1883. F.   **K 1204**

x denotes books specially adapted for children.

König, Ewald A:, (*Ernst Kaiser*). Auf der bahn
des verbrechens ; roman in 4 b. N. Y. 1881.
F.   **K 1252**
— Der goldene schatz aus dem dreissigjährigen
kriege ; roman. N. Y. 1882. F.   **K 1257**
— Das grosse loos ; roman. N. Y. 1881. F.
                                        K 1254
— Die hand der Nemesis. N. Y. 1881. F. **K 1251**
— Das kind Bajazzos. N. Y. 1881. F.   **K 1253**
— Eine million. N. Y. 1881. F.   **K 1256**
— Schuld und sühne ; roman. N. Y. 1882. F.
                                        K 1258
— Um ehre und leben ; roman. N. Y. 1881. F.
                                        K 1255
König, H: Joseph. Marianne, oder um liebe lei-
den. Frankfurt a. M. 1858. 2 v. S. **K 1301**
König, Theodor. Luther und seine zeit. Leipz.
1861. 8 v. S.   **K 1351**
Köstlin, Christian Reinhold, (*C. Reinhold*). Die
karfreitags - christen ; novelle. Bremen.
1848. S.   **K 1376**
— Die kinder der fremde. Bremen. 1847. S.
                                        K 1377
— Real und ideal. Bremen. 1847. S.   **K 1378**
Kouns, Nathan Chapman. Arius the libyan ; an
idyl of the primitive church. [*Anon.*] N.
Y. 1884 [1883]. D.   **K 1752**
— Dorcas, the daughter of Faustina. Ill. N. Y.
1884. D.   **K 1751**
Kronhelm, H., *see* Wilke, H.
Kühne, A:, (*Johannes van Dewall*). Aus meinen
kadettenjahren ; lose blätter. Stuttgart.
1877. D.   **D 1201**
— Don Enrique de Ramiro. Breslau. 1877. D.
                                        D 1202
— Else Hohenthal ; roman. Stuttg. 1878. D.
                                        D 1203
— Far from home. From the german by Kathrine
Hamilton. Bost. [1884]. D.   **D 1210**
— Ein frühlingstraum ; roman. 2te aufl. Stuttg.
1878. D.   **D 1204**
— Der gordische knoten ; roman. 2te aufl.
Stuttg. 1880. D.   **D 1205**
— Graumann ; ein roman aus kleinen kreisen.
2te aufl. Stuttg. 1878. 2 v. in 1. D. **D 1206**
— Eine grosse dame ; novelle. Stuttg. 1875. 2 v.
in 1. D.   **D 1207**
— *Same, eng.* A great lady. From the german
by M. S. Phila. 1874. O.   **D 1207**
— Kadettengeschichten ; erinnerungen aus mei-
nen kadettenjahren. Stuttg. 1878. D.
                                        D 1208
— Der ulan ; roman. N. Y. 1882. F.   **D 1209**
Kühne, F: Gustav. Die freimaurer ; eine fami-
liengeschichte aus dem vorigen jahrhun-
dert. Frankfurt a. M. 1855. S.   **K 1451**
Kürnberger, Ferdinand. Der Amerika-müde ;
amerikanisches kulturbild. Frankfurt a.
M. 1855. S.   **K 1551**
Kürschner, Lola, (*Ossip Schubin*). Our own
set ; a novel. From the german by Clara
Bell, rev. and corr. in the U. S. N. Y.
1884. S.   **K 1476**
— Schneeglöckchen ; eine novellette. *In* Vier-
teljährl. mag.   **V 2 v28**
Kurz, Hermann. Schiller's heimatjahre. Stuttg.
1859. 2 v. S.   **K 1501**
— Der "sonnenwirth" ; schwäbische volksge-
schichte aus dem vorigen jahrhundert.
Frankfurt a. M. 1855. D.   **K 1502**
— Der weihnachtsfund ; ein seelenbild aus dem
schwäbischen volksleben. Frankfurt. a.
M. 1856. T.   **K 1503**

L., A. v. Am hofe von Neapel ; historischer ro-
man aus der gegenwart. Celle. 1861. 3 v.
S.   **L 101**
— Am hofe von Rom ; historischer roman aus der
neuzeit. Leipz. 1866. 3 v. S.   **L 102**
L., L. E., *see* Landon, Lætitia Elizabeth.
La Bédollière, Émile Gigault de. The story of
a cat. Tr. from the french by T: Bailey
Aldrich. Ill. Bost. 1879. O.   **L 1**
Labor and love ; a tale of english life. Bost.
1853. D.   **L 1**
Laboulaye, É: René Lefebvre de. Abdallah, or
The four-leaved shamrock. Tr. by Mary
L. Booth. Lond. 1878. T.   **L 151**
— Fairy tales. Ill. N. Y. 1885 [1884]. O. **Lx 701**
— Last fairy tales. Authorized trans. by Mary
L. Booth. Ill. N. Y. 1885 [1884]. D. **Lx 702**
— More old wives' fables. Ill. N. Y. 1885 [1884].
D.   **Lx 703**
Lacroix, Paul, (*P. L. Jacob, le bibliophile*). Die
beiden hofnarren ; historischer roman.
Deutsch von dr. Scherr. Stuttg. 1848. T.
                                        L 201
— Die katakomben von Rom. Deutsch von dr.
Scherr. Stuttg. 1846. T.   **L 202**
Laffan, May, *see* Hartley, May.
Lakeman, Mary. Ruth Eliot's dream ; a story
for girls. Ill. Bost. 1883 [1882]. S. **Lx 126**
Lamartine, Alphonse Marie L: de. Genevieve,
or The history of a servant girl. Tr. from
the french by A. R. Scoble. Lond. 1850. D.
                                        L 301
— *Same, germ.* Genovefa, die magd ; volkserzäh-
lung. Aus dem französischen. Stuttg. 1850.
T.   **L 301**
— Graziella ; a story of italian love. Tr. from the
french by James B. Runnion. Chicago.
1876. D.   **L 302**
— Raphael ; eine liebesgeschichte. Deutsch von
dr. Scherr. Stuttg. 1849. T.   **L 303**
— *Same.* Gedenkblätter aus dem zwanzigsten
jahre. Uebers. von F. Müller. Stuttg.
1850. S.   **L 303**
— The stone-mason of Saint Point ; a village tale.
Tr. from the french. N. Y. 1859. D.   **L 304**
— *Same, germ.* Der steinhauer von Saint Point ;
ländliche erzählung. Leipz. 1859. S.
                                        L 304
Lamber, Juliette, *see* Adam, Juliette.
La Motte Fouqué, F: H: *baron* de. Ausge-
wählte novellen, erzählungen, schauspiele
und gedichte. Halle. 1841. 4 v. T.   **L 351**
Contents, see Deutscher katalog, p. 77.
— The bottle imp. *In* Popular romances.
                                        P 2126 v1
— *Same, see below* The vial-genie.
— The collier family, or Red-mantle and the
merchant. *In* Miniature romances.
                                        M 2776
— The four seasons. Ill. Lond. 1875. D. **L 358**
Contents. Undine.—The two captains.—Sintram.—
Aslauga's knight.
— *Same.* Undine, and other tales. Tr. by F. E.
Bunnett. Leipz. 1867. S.   **L 358**
— Minstrel love ; a romance. Ill. Lond. 1877. D.
                                        L 356
— Romantic fiction. Ill. Lond. 1876. S. **L 357**
Contents. The eagle and the lion.—The vow.—The
unknown patient.—The Victor's wreath.—Berthold.—
Rose.—Eugenia.—The privy councillor.—The lantern
in the castle-yard.—The prince's sword.—The siege of
Algiers.—Head-master Rhenfried.
— Sintram und seine gefährten. Halle. 1841. T.
                                        L 352

· **x** denotes books specially adapted for children.

La Motte Fouqué, F: H: K: de.—*Continued.*
— Thiodolf, the icelander. From the german.
   N. Y. *n. d.* D.   **L 353**
— *Same.* Lond. 1877. S.   **L 353**
— Undine, eine erzählung. N. Y. 1846. S. **L 354**
— *Same.* Halle. 1841. T.   **L 354**
— *Same, eng. In* Miniature romances. **M 2776**
— *Same, see also above* The four seasons.
— The vial-genie and mad farthing. *In* Minia-
   ture romances.   **M 2776**
— Der zauberring ; ein ritterroman. Braunschw.
   1855. 3 v. T.   **L 355**
— *Same, eng.* The magic ring ; a knightly ro-
   mance. Ill. Lond. 1876. D.   **L 355**
— *see also* **Roscoe, T:** German novelists.
Lander, Meta, *pseud., see* **Lawrence, Margarette**
   Woods.
Lander, *Sir* T: Dick. The story of Farquharson
   of Inverey. *In* Edinburgh tales.   **E 426**
Landor, Walter Savage. Pericles and Aspasia.
   Phila. 1839. 2 v. O.   **L 426**
— *Same. In his* Works.   **820.2 : 15 v5**
Landt, W. H., *ed.* Album der erinnerungen;
   mit beiträgen von Josef Bayer, L: Bowisch,
   und anderen. 2ter jahrg. Prag. 1856. S.
                                                      L 451
Lang, Andrew. The princess Nobody ; a tale of
   fairy-land. Ill. N. Y. [1884]. O. **Lx 601**
Lang, *Mrs.* Andrew. Dissolving views. N. Y.
   1884. S.   **L 401**
Langbein, A: F:, *see* **Roscoe, T:** German novel-
   ists.
Lange, Ernst Philipp, (*Philipp Galen*). Andreas
   Burns und seine familie ; geschichtliches
   lebensbild aus dem deutsch-dänischen
   kriege in den jahren 1848—1850. Leipz.
   1858. 4 v. S.   **L 501**
— Der erbe von Bettys-Ruh. Leipz. 1866. 4 v. S.
                                                      L 502
— Der friedensengel. Berlin. 1870. 3 v. S.
                                                      L 503
— Fritz Stilling ; erinnerungen aus dem leben
   eines arztes. 3te aufl. Leipz. 1858. 4 v. S.
                                                      L 508
— Der inselkönig. Leipz. 1857. 5 v. S. **L 504**
— Der irre von St. James ; aus dem reisetage-
   buche eines arztes. 6te aufl. Leipz. [1878].
   4 v. in 1. S.   **L 507**
— Jane, die jüdin. Berlin. 1867. 3 v. S. **L 505**
— Nach zwanzig jahren. Leipz. 1864. 3 v. S.
                                                      L 506
— Der pechvogel, and andere erzählungen ; mit
   einer einleitung von Hans Ziegler. Stuttg.
   [1883]. D.   **L 509**
   Includes, Onkel Bispink. — Eine partie nach der
   Suleck.
Langer, Anton. Die carbonari in Wien, oder
   Der mann mit der Weissen leber ; charac-
   terbild aus dem Wiener leben. Pesth. 1857.
   2 v. S.   **L 551**
Lankenau, H. v. Ein roman aus der vornehmen
   russischen gesellschaft. N. Y. 1883. F.
                                                      L 2251
Lanza, Clara *marchesa, born* Hammond. Mr.
   Perkins' daughter. N. Y. 1881. S. **L 601**
La Rochère, Mme. la comtesse, *or* Mlle. Eugénie.
   pseud., see **Dutheil,** Eugénie.
Last of the Die Huggermuggers, The ; a giant story.
   Ill. Bost. 1856. O.   **Lx 11**
Lathrop, G: Parsons. Afterglow. (No name
   ser.) Bost. 1877. S.   **L 651**
— An echo of passion. Bost. 1882. D. **L 654**
— In the distance ; a novel. Bost. 1882. S. **L 653**

Lathrop, G: Parsons.—*Continued.*
— Newport. N. Y. 1884. S.   **L 655**
— Somebody else. Bost. 1878. T.   **L 652**
— True, and other stories. N. Y. 1884. D. **L 656**
   Includes. Major Barrington's marriage.—"Bad pep-
   pers."—Three bridges.—In each other's shoes.
— Two purse companions. *In* Stories by ameri-
   can authors.   **S 35 v3**
Latimer, Mary Elizabeth, *born* Wormeley.
   Amabel, or Amor omnia vincit ; a novel.
   N. Y. 1882. Q.   **L 676**
Latter-day saint, A ; being the story of the
   conversion of Ethel Jones, related by
   herself. N. Y. 1884. S.   **L 9**
Lautenschlager, Ottmar. Agathe und Corona,
   oder Die frauen vom guten hirten ; eine
   erzählung für christliche familien, besonders
   für sorgsame eltern, erwachsene töchter,
   lehrerinnen, jugendfreunde, schulbibliothe-
   ken, etc. Ill. Augsburg. 1858. S. *With
   his* Lorenz.   **L 2305**
— Amaranthen ; erzählungen für christliche
   jugend und christliches volk. Ill. Augsburg. 1862. D. *With* Ambach, E. Der
   menschenhändler.   **L 2303**
   Contents. Der christabend.—Das frohnleichnams-
   fest.
— Ehre vater und mutter ; eine erzählung über
   das vierte gebot für christliche jugend und
   christliches volk. Ill. Augsburg. 1858. S.
                                         L 2301
— Die erzählungen des priesters Ottmar für
   christliche jugend und christliches volk ;
   mit einer vorrede von Franz Seraph Hägls-
   perger. Ill. 3te aufl. Augsburg. 1852. S.
   With his Wolfram.   **L 2304**
   Contents. Deodats prüfungen.—Die todtenmesse.—
   Anselm der bettler.
— Lorenz ; die wege der göttlichen liebe und
   gerechtigkeit ; eine erzählung für christliche
   jugend und christliches volk. Ill. Augsburg. 1858. S.   **L 2305**
— Malven ; erzählungen für christliche jugend
   und christliches volk. 2te aufl. Ill.
   Augsburg. 1858. S. *With his* Pfingstrosen.
                                         L 2302
   Contents. Die christnacht.—Die wanderschaft.
— Mathilde ; aus dem leben eines frommen
   kindes ; eine erzählung für christliche jugend und christliches volk. Ill. Augsburg. 1860. S. *With his* Ehre vater und
   mutter.   **L 2301**
— Pfingstrosen ; erzählungen für christliche jugend und christliches volk. 2te aufl. Ill.
   Augsburg. 1855. S.   **L 2302**
   Contents. Die Bibel, oder Der weihnachtsabend.—
   Der rosenkranz, oder Die rettung.—Der acker im
   buchenwalde. — Verachte niemanden. — Der knabe
   Inigo.—Das christkindlein.—Das johannesfest.
— Treue und barmherzigkeit ; eine erzählung für
   christliche jugend und christliches volk.
   3te durchgesehene aufl. Augsburg. 1857.
   D. *With* Ambach, E: Der menschen-
   händler.   **L 2303**
— Violen ; erzählungen für christliche jugend
   und christliches volk. Ill. Augsburg. 1853.
   D. *With* Ambach, E: Der menschenhändler.   **L 2303**
   Contents. Das häubchen.—Rosalie.—Das gericht.—
   Anton und Ferdinand.
— Wolfram, oder Die wunderbare taufpathin,—
   Cassilda, die mohrenfürstin von Toledo ;
   zwei erzählungen für christliche jugend und
   christliches volk ; mit einem empfeh-
   lenden vorwort von Joh. Evang. Stadler.
   2te aufl. Ill. Aubsgurg. 1856. S. **L 2304**

x denotes books specially adapted for children.

Lawless, *The hon.* Emily. A Chelsea householder. [*Anon.*] (Leisure hour ser.) N. Y. 1883. S. **L 2351**
— A millionaire's cousin. (Leisure hour ser.) N. 1885. S. **L 2352**

Lawrence, G: Alfred. Anteros. N. Y. 1874. O. **L 701**
— Barren honour. N. Y. *n. d.* O. **L 702**
— Brakespeare, or The fortunes of a free lance. N. Y. 1877. O. **L 703**
— Breaking a butterfly, or Blance Ellerslie's ending. Ill. Phila. 1875. S. **L 704**
— Guy Livingstone, or "Thorough." N. Y. 1878. Q. **L 705**
— Hagarene. N. Y. 1875. O. **L 706**
— Maurice Dering, or The quadrilateral. N. Y. 1876. O. **L 707**
— Sword and gown. Bost. 1860. S. **L 708**

Lawrence, Margaretta Woods, (*Meta Lander*). Esperance. *T. p. w.* D. **L 751**
Lawrence, Uncle, *pseud.* Young folks' ideas; a story. Ill. Phila. 1885 [1884]. O. **Ux 202**
— Young folks' whys and wherefores; a story. Phila. 1884. [1883]. O. **Ux 201**

Lax, L: Bilder aus den Niederlanden. Aachen. 1838. **L 576**

Lean, *Mrs.* Francis, *see* **Church,** Florence.

Leander, R:, *pseud., see* **Volkmann,** R:

Lebensbilder ; scenen und erzählungen für volk und jugend. Nach dem franz. Ill. Regensb. 1874. S. **T 2451**

Ledyard, Laura W. Very young americans. Ill. Bost. 1873. S. **Lx 151**

Lee, Alice G., *pseud., see* **Haven,** Emily.

Lee, Eliza, *born* Buckminster. Parthenia, or The last days of paganism. Bost. 1858. S. **L 801**

Lee, Hannah F., *born* Sawyer. Elinor Fulton. Bost. 1837. T. **L 826**

Lee, Harriet *and* Sophia. Canterbury tales. N. Y. 1865. 3 v. D. **L 851**
Contents. V. 1. Introd.—**Lee,** H. The landlady's tale: Mary Lawson.—The friend's tale: Stanhope.—The wife's tale: Julia.—The traveller's tale: Montford.—The poet's tale: Arnold.—The old woman's tale: Lothaire, a legend. **2.** The german's tale: Kruitzner.—The scotsman's tale: Claudine.—The frenchman's tale: Constance.—The officer's tale: Cavendish.—**3.** **Lee,** S. The clergyman's tale: Pembroke.—The young lady's tale: The two Emilys.
— *Same,* v. 2. N. Y. 1857. D. **L 851 v2**

Lee, Holme, *pseud., see* **Parr,** Harriet.

Lee, Mary *and* Catherine. Rosamond Fane, or The prisoners of St. James. Ill. Lond. *n. d.* D. **Lx 226**

Lee, Mary Susanna, *joint author, see* **Awdry,** Frances.

Lee, Sarah, *born* Wallis, *formerly* **Bowditch.** The african crusoes, or The adventures of Carlos and Antonio. Bost. *n. d.* D. **Lx 251**
— The australian wanderers, or The adventures of captain Spencer, his horse and dog. Ill. Bost. *n. d.* D. **Lx 252**

Lee, Vernon, *pseud., see* **Paget,** Violet.

Le Fanu, Joseph Sheridan. All in the dark. N. Y. 1866. O. **L 901**
— *Same.* New ed. Lond. *n. d.* D. **L 901**
— The house by the churchyard. N. Y. 1866. 3 v. in 1. D. **L 902**
— The tenants of Malory. *T. p. w.* O. **L 903**

Lefebvre, René, *pseud., see* **Laboulaye,** E: René Lefebvre de.

Leggett, W: The block-house ; a western story. [*Anon.*] *In* Tales of Glauber-Spa. **T 186**

Leighton, Alexander. The burgher's tales. *In* Wilson, J: M. Tales of the borders. **W 2202 v21-23**
Contents. 1. The house in Bell's Wynd. 2. The ancient bureau. 3. The brownie of the West Bow.
— The lawyer's tales. *In the same.* **W 2202 v21, 23**
Contents. 1. The woman with the white mice. 2. Lord Kames's puzzle. 3. The story of Mysie Craig.
— The old chronicler's tales. *In the same.* **W 2202 v14, 15**
Contents. 1. The prince of Scotland. 2. The death of James I. 3. The death of James III.
— The surgeon's tales. *In the same.* **W 2202**
Contents. V. 2. 1. The cured ingrate. 3. 2, The diver and the bell. 5. 3. The conscience stricken. 6. 4. The somnambulist of Redcleugh. 8. 5. The cherry stone. 6. The hen wife. 7. The artist. 11. 8. The suicide. 12. 9. The three letters. 10. The glassback. 15. 11. The case of evidence. 17. 12. The bereaved. 13. The condemned. 18. 14. The monomaniac. 21. 15. The wager.
— [Tales]. *In the same.* **W 2202**
Contents. The abduction, v. 9.—The amateur lawyers, v. 7.—The amateur robbery, v. 22.—The avenger, v. 19.—The barley bannock, v. 20.—The bride of Bell's Tow, v. 21.—The bride of Bramblehaugh, v. 18.—Caleb Crabbin, v. 10.—Christie of the Cleek, v. 9.—The clerical murderer, v. 15.—The contrast of wives, v. 11.—The cradle of Logie, v. 23.—The crooked Comyn, v. 10.—The detective's tale: The chance question, v. 21.—The diamond eyes, v.22.—The dominie of St. Fillan's, v. 20.—The double-bedded room, v. 5.—The droich, v. 7.—Duncan Schulebred's vision of judgement, v. 5.—The faithful wife, v. 23.—Geordie Willison, v. 6.—The girl forger, v. 22.—Gustavus McIver, v. 19.—Harden's revenge, v. 8.—Hogmanay, v. 17.—Hume and the governor of Berwick, v. 17.—Kate Kennedy, v. 1.—Laird Rorieson's will, v. 18.—The legend of fair Kirconnel, v.9.—A legend of Holyrood, v. 14.—The Linton lairds, v. 4.—Lord Durie and Christie's will, v. 2.—The maiden feast of Cairnkibbie, v. 4.—Mike Maxwell, v. 12.—The miser of New-abbey, v. 20.—Mr. S: Ramsey Thriven, v. 16.—Prescription, v. 1.—The romance of the siege of Perth, v. 13.—Rossallan's daughter, v. 13.—The sportsman of Outfieldhaugh, v.19.—The story of Mary Brown, v. 23.—The story of the pelican, v. 23.—The ten of diamonds, v. 2.—The trials of Menie Dempster, v. 13.—The two red slippers, v. 23.

Leïla-Hanoum, *pseud., see* **Piazzi,** Adrienne.

Lennep, Jakob van. Charietto, *und* Das sächsische wesen ; zwei historische novellen. Aus dem holländischen. Aachen. 1840. S. **L 951**
— Die friesen in Rom ; ein historischer roman. Aus dem holländischen. Aachen. 1840. S. **L 952**

Le Sage, Alain René. The adventures of Gil Blas of Santillane. Tr. from the french by T. Smollett ; prefixed, Memoirs of the author. Hartford. 1847 ; Bost. 1865. 3 v. D. **L 1001**
— *Same.* Ill. N. Y. *n. d.* D. **L 1001**
— The bachelor of Salamanca. Tr. from the french by J. Townsend. Phila. 1854. 2 v. S. **L 1002**
— Der hinkende teufel. Aus dem franz. von D. Barrasch. Berlin. 1857. D. **L 1003**
— *Same.* Deutsch von Levin Schücking. Hildburgh. 1866. 2 v. in 1. D. **L 1003**
— *Same.* Mit einer einleitung von Ferdinand Lotheissen. Stuttg. [1881]. D. **L 1003**

Lessmann, Daniel. Das wanderbuch eines schwermüthigen. [2ter t., aus den von Daniel Lessmann hinterlassenen papieren, gesetzt von A: Ellrich.] Berlin. 1831. 2 v. S. **L 1052**

Lever, C: James. Arthur O'Leary, his wanderings and ponderings in many lands, ed. by his friend Harry Lorrequer. Leipz. 1847. 2 v. in 1. S.   **L 1101**
— Barrington. Leipz. 1863. 2 v. in 1. S. **L 1102**
— The Bramleighs of Bishop's Folly. Leipz. 1868. 2 v. in 1. S.   **L 1103**
— Charles O'Malley, the irish dragoon. Leipz. 1848. 3 v. in 2. S.   **L 1104**
— *Same. T. p. w.* O.   **L 1104**
— The confessions of Con Cregan, the irish Gil Blas. Leipz. 1860. 2 v. in 1. S. **L 1105**
— The Daltons, or Three roads in life. Leipz. 1852. 4 v. in 2. S.   **L 1106**
— Davenport Dunn, or The man of the day. Leipz. 1859. 3 v. in 2. S.   **L 1107**
— A day's ride; a life's romance. Leipz. 1864. 2 v. in 1. S.   **L 1108**
— The Dodd family abroad. Leipz. 1854. 3 v. in 2. S.   **L 1109**
— The fortunes of Glencore. Leipz. 1857. 2 v. in 1. S.   **L 1110**
— The confessions of Harry Lorrequer. Leipz. 1847. 2 v. in 1. S.   **L 1111**
— Hero worship and its dangers. *In* Tales from Blackwood.   **T 177 v8**
— Horace Templeton; an autobiography. Phila. *n. d.* O.   **L 1112**
— How Frank Thornton was cured. *In* Tales from Blackwood.   **T 177 v10**
— Jack Hinton, the guardsman. Leipz. 1849. 2 v. in 1. S.   **L 1113**
— The knight of Gwynne; a tale of the time of the union. Leipz. 1847. 3 v. in 2. S. **L 1114**
— Lord Kilgobbin; a tale of Ireland in our own time. Leipz. 1872. 2 v. in 1. S. **L 1115**
— Luttrell of Arran. Leipz. 1865. 2 v. in 1. S.   **L 1116**
— *Same.* Ill. Lond. 1871. O.   **L 1116**
— Maurice Tiernay, the soldier of fortune. Leipz. 1861. 2 v. in 1. S.   **L 1117**
— Die Nevilles von Garretstown; eine erzählung aus dem jahre 1760. Deutsch von G: Fink. Stuttg. 1846. 2 v. T.   **L 1118**
— The O'Donoghue, a tale of Ireland fifty years ago. Leipz. 1845. S.   **L 1119**
— *Same, germ.* O'Donoghue; eine erzählung aus Irland wie es vor fünfzig jahren war. Deutsch von G. Fink. Stuttg. 1846. 2 v. S.   **L 1119**
— One of them. Leipz. 1860. 2 v. in 1. S.   **L 1120**
— Paul Gosselett's confessions in love, law and the civil service. *With his* St. Patrick's eve.   **L 1123**
— A rent in a cloud. Leipz. 1869. S.   **L 1121**
— Roland Cashel. Leipz. 1858. 3 v. in 1. S.   **L 1122**
— St. Patrick's eve. Leipz. 1870. S.   **L 1123**
— *Same, germ.* Der St. Patricks-abend. Deutsch von G. Fink. Stuttg. 1846. T. **L 1123**
— Sir Brook Fosbrooke. Leipz. 1867. 2 v. in 1. S.   **L 1124**
— Sir Jasper Carew, his life and experiences. Leipz. 1861. 2 v. in 1. S.   **L 1125**
— Some one pays. *In* Tales from Blackwood.   **T 177 v12**
— That boy of Norcott's. Leipz. 1869. S. **L 1126**
— *Same.* New ed., ill. Lond. 1872. D.   **L 1126**
— Tom Burke of "ours". Ill. N. Y. *n. d.* D.   **L 1127**
— *Same, germ.* Tom Burke; ein roman aus der

Lever, C: James.—*Continued.*
Napoleon'schen zeit. Aus dem englischen von G. Fink. Stuttg. 1845. 5 v. in 3. T.   **L 1127**
— Tony Butler. Leipz. 1866. 2 v. in 1. S.   **L 1128**
— What I did at Belgrade. *In* Tales from Blackwood.   **T 177 v6**
Lewald, Fanny, *see* **Stahr,** Fanny.
Lewes, G: H: Ranthorpe. Leipz. 1847. T.   **L 1151**
Lewes, Marian, *see* **Cross,** Marian.
Lexow, Rudolph. Der rubin; novelle aus dem New Yorker leben. N. Y. 1872. S. **L 1201**
Liddell, Catharine Christina, *born* Fraser-Tytler. Jonathan. (Leisure hour ser.) N. Y. 1876. S.   **T 2301**
— Margaret. (Leisure hour ser.) N. Y. *n. d.* S.   **T 2302**
— Mistress Judith; a Cambridgeshire story. (Leisure hour ser.) N. Y. 1875. S. **T 2303**
Lie, Jonas Lauritz Edemil. The barque Future, or Life in the far north. Tr. by mrs. Ole Bull. Chicago. 1879. D.   **L 1251**
— Bilder aus Norwegen; drei erzählungen. Aus dem norwegischen von Philipp Schweitzer. Jena. 1878. D.   **L 1252**
   Contents, see Deutscher katalog, p. 79.
— A norse love story; The pilot and his wife. Tr. by mrs. Ole Bull. 2d ed. Chicago. 1877. D.   **L 1253**
Liefde, J. B. de. The maid of Stralsund; a story of the thirty years' war. Lond. 1876. O.   **L 1276**
Lienhart, François de. Der vicomte de Launay; roman aus der zeit der ersten französischen revolution. Frei nach dem franz. von W. Schöttlen. Stuttg. 1846. 3 v. S.   **L 1301**
Lillie, Lucy Cecil. Mildred's bargain, and other stories. Ill. N. Y. 1883. S.   **L 1326**
   Includes, Aunt Ruth's temptation. — Penelope. — Marjorie's new-year's eve.—Miss Holsover's "treasure".—Scrap.
— Nan. Ill. N. Y. 1883. S.   **Lx 302**
— Prudence; a story of æsthetic London. Ill. N. Y. 1882. S.   **L 1326**
Lilliput legends, by the author of "Lilliput levee." Lond. 1872. D.   **Lx 21**
Lincoln, Jeanie T., *born* Gould. Her Washington winter. Bost. 1884. D.   **L 1336**
— Marjorie's quest. Ill. Bost. 1878. D.   **L 1337**
Lindau, H: Gustav Paul. Kleine geschichten. Leipz. 1872. 2 v. in 1. D.   **L 1351**
   Contents, see Deutscher katalog, p. 79.
— Die kranke köchin,—Die liebe im dativ; zwei ernsthafte geschichten. 2te aufl. Stuttg. 1881. D.   **L 1352**
— Mayo; erzählung. N. Y. 1884. T.   **L 1354**
— Wie ein lustspiel entsteht und vergeht. 2te aufl. Berlin. 1877. T.   **L 1353**
Lindau, Rudolph. Erzählungen und novellen. Berlin. *n. d.* 2 v. in 1. D.   **L 1402**
   Contents, see Deutscher katalog, p. 79.
— Gordon Baldwin. N. Y. 1878. S.   **L 1401**
— The philosopher's pendulum. *With his* Gordon Baldwin.   **L 1401**
— *Same. In* Tales from Blackwood. **T 177 v10**
— Robert Ashton; roman. 2te aufl. Stuttg. 1879. 2 v. in 1. D.   **L 1403**
— Stories and novels. Tr. from the german. Chicago. 1885. D.   **L 1404**
   Contents. Hans, the dreamer. — All in vain.—First love.

Linskill, Mary. Between the heather and the northern sea ; a novel. N. Y. 1884. Q.
                                           L 1426
Linton, Eliza Lynn. The atonement of Leam Dumdas. Ill. Phila. 1876. O.   L 1451
— From dreams to waking. N. Y. 1877. O.
                                           L 1452
— Ione. Lond. 1883. 2 v. in 1. D.   L 1459
— Same. Ione Stewart ; a novel. N. Y. 1883. Q.
                                           L 1459
— My love. N. Y. 1881. Q.   L 1453
— Same. Leipz. 1881. 2 v. in 1. S.   L 1453
— Patricia Kemball. Phila. 1875. D.   L 1454
— The rebel of the family. N. Y. 1880. Q.
                                           L 1455
— The true history of Joshua Davidson. Phila. 1873. D.   L 1456
— Under which lord ? Leipz. 1880. 2 v. in 1. S.
                                           L 1457
— The world well lost. Phila. 1878. O.   L 1458
Linz, Amélie, (Amélie Godin). Mutter und sohn. N. Y. 1882. F.   L 1476
Lippard, G: Legenden aus der amerikanischen revolution. Uebers. von A. Strodtmann. Phila. 1858. O.   L 1501
Lippincott, Sara Jane, born Clarke, (Grace Greenwood). History of my pets. Ill. Bost. 1871. S.   Lx 402
— Recollections of my childhood, and other stories. Bost. 1863. S.   Lx 401
— Stories for home-folks, young and old. N. Y. 1884. S.   Lx 403
Lips, Friederich Wilhelm, pseud., see Oertel, Philipp F: W:
Litchfield, Grace Denio. The knight of the Black Forest. Ill. N. Y. 1885. S. L 1226
Little sister. (No name ser.) Bost. 1882. S.
                                           L 31
Lloyd, D: D. Ogla Moga. In Stories by american authors.   S 35 v3
Lobedanz, Edmund Adolph Johannes. Ein neuer glaube ; biographisch-culturhistorischer roman. Frankfurt a. M. 1859. 3 v.
D.   L 1551
Lockhart, J: Gibson. Capt. Paton's lament. Tales from Blackwood.   T 176 v5
— Napoleon. In the same.   T 176 v1
— Reginald Dalton. Edinburgh. 1849. S.
                                           L 1601
— Valerius ; a roman story. Edinburgh. 1856.
D.   L 1602
Lockhart, Lawrence W. M. Mine is thine. Leipz. 1878. 2 v. in 1. S.   L 1651
— A night with the volunteers of Strathnishahan. In Tales from Blackwood.   T 177 v2
— Unlucky Tim Griffin. In the same. T 177 v4
Löffler, K: Valentin Immanuel, (Dr. Tornow, De olle nümärker). Ut 't dörp ; lustige vertellungen van'n oll'n nümärker. Jena. 1868. S.   U 2
Logan, Olive, see Sikes, Olive.
Logan, Walter. Ellen Arundel. In Wilson, J: G. Tales of the borders.   W 2202 v9
— The recluse of the Hebrides. In the same.
                                           W 2202 v9
— The story of Clara Douglas. In the same.
                                           W 2202 v4
Lohmann, Johanna Friderike, born Richter. Sämmtliche erzählungen; v. 1-5, 7-13, 15-18. Leipz. 16 v. S.   L 1751
Contents, see Deutscher katalog, p. 79.
Longfellow, H: Wadsworth. Hyperion ; a romance. Bost. 1855. S.   L 1801

Longfellow, H: Wadsworth.—Continued.
— Kavanagh ; a tale. Bost. 1855. D.   L 1802
— See also his Works.   820.1 : 12
Contents, see under English literature, Collected works.
Longstreet, A: Baldwin. Georgia scenes ; characters, incidents, etc., in the first half century of the republic, by a native georgian. Ill. N. Y. 1884. Q.   G 11
— Same. T. p. w. [N. Y.] D.   G 11
Lorenz, Wilhelmine. Emilie, oder So liebt ein deutsches herz, und Der gefundene schleier; zwei erzählungen. Leipz. 1827. S.   L 1901
— Er kehrt zurück. Leipz. 1835. S.   L 1904
— Eine freundin Napoleons. Leipz. 1882. S.
                                           L 1902
— Friedrich's II. einzige liebe. Leipz. 1846. S.
                                           L 1903
— Olav, der dänenprinz. Leipz. 1843. S. L 1905
— Riesen- und Rosenburg ; ein roman aus dem vierzehnten jahrhundert. Leipz. 1838. 2 v.
S.   L 1906
— Rue de Langlade. Leipz. 1848. S.   L 1907
— Schloss Tornitz ; romantisches gemälde aus dem siebenzehnten jahrhundert. Leipz. 1841. 2 v. S.   L 1908
— Des stammes letzter. Leipz. 1851. 3 v. S.
                                           L 1909
— Der übel grösstes ist die schuld ; wahrheit in romangewande. Leipz. 1839. 2 v. S.
                                           L 1910
— Vor einundfünfzig jahren und heute. Leipz. 1845. 2 v. S.   L 1911
Lorm, Hieronymus, pseud., see Landesmann, H:
Lorrequer, Harry, pseud., see Lever, C: James.
Lothar, pseud., see Roscoe, T: German novellists.
Lothrop, Harriet Mulford, (Margaret Sidney). Five little peppers, and how they grew. Ill. Bost. [1881]. D.   Sx 2001
— A half year at Bronckton. Ill. Bost. [1881]. D.
                                           Sx 2002
— How they went to Europe. Ill. Bost. [1884]. S.   Sx 2005
— The Pettibone name ; a New England story. Bost. 1882. D.   L 1926
— What the seven. did, or The doings of the Wordsworth club. Ill. Bost. [1884]. O.
                                           Sx 2004
— Who told it to me. Ill. Bost. [1883]. O.
                                           Sx 2003
Lottie Eames, or "Do your best and leave the rest." Ill. N. Y. 1873. S.   Lx 41
Lover, S: Barney O'Reirdon, the navigator. In Johnson, E: R. Little classics. J 926 v9
— The fairy finder. In the same.   J 926 v12
— The gridiron. In the same.   J 926 v9
— Handy Andy ; a tale of irish life. Phila. n. d.
D.   L 1951
— He would be a gentleman. N. Y. 1873. D.
                                           L 1952
— Legends and stories of Ireland. N. Y. 1877.
D.   L 1953
Contents. The white horse of the Peppers; a legend of the Boyne. — The Shebeen house. — The curse of Kishogue.—The burial of the tithe.—Paddy the piper. —The priest's ghost.—New potatoes; an irish melody. —Paddy the sport. — National minstrelsy. — Barney O'Reirdon. — King O'Toole and St. Kevin. — Lough Corrib.— Ms. from the cabinet of Mrs.—; a legend of Cong.—The battle of the Berrins. — Father Roach.— The priest's story. — The devil's mill. — The gridiron. —An essay on fools. — The spanish boar and the irish bull. — The fairy finder. — The spanish boar and the irish bull. — Little Fairly.—Judy of Roundwood.
— Rory O'More. N. Y. 1877. D.   L 1954

x denotes books specially adapted for children.

Loves of Manasseh and Nicanzo, The ; a tale of the jews. Lond. [1841]. S. **L 41**

Low, C: R. Cyril Hamilton ; his adventures by sea and land. Ill. N. Y. 1885 [1884]. D.
Lx 451

Lowell, Robert Traill Spence. Antony Brade. Bost. 1874. D. **L 2001**

— The new priest in Conception Bay. Bost. 1878. 2 v. S. **L 2002**

— A raft that no man made. *In* Atlantic tales.
A 1876

— *Same. In* Johnson, E. R. Little classics.
J 926 v8

Lubojatzky, Franz, (*Franz Carion*). Der alte Dessauer ; historischer roman. Leipz. 1867. 2 v. S. **C 451**

— Ein getheiltes herz, oder Karl Theodor und seine zeit ; historischer roman. Leipz. 1858. 3 v. S. **C 452**

— Johann Georg I· von Sachsen ; historischer roman. Leipz. 1865. 2 v. S. **C 453**

— Der letzte deutsche kaiser und seine zeitgenossen ; historischer roman. Leipz. 1850. 4 v. S. **C 454**

— Schloss Stolpen, oder Erinnerungen aus dem leben der gräfin von Cassel ; historischer roman. Dresden. 1853. 3 v. S. **L 2051**

Lucy, H: W. Gideon Fleyce ; a novel. (Leisure hour ser.) N. Y. 1883. S. **L 2026**

Ludlow, Fitz-Hugh. A brace of boys. *In* Johnson, E. R. Little classics. **J 926 v18**

— Little Briggs and I. *In the same.* **J 926 v11**

— Little brother, and other genre pictures. Bost. 1867. D. **L 2101**
Includes, Fleeing to Tarshish.—Little Briggs and I.— A brace of boys.

Ludwig, Julie. Mein grossoheim, und andre erzählungen ; mit einer einleitung von H. v. Bequignolles. Stuttg. [1884]. D. **L 2126**
Includes, Das gericht im walde.—Der schiefe turm.

Ludwig, Otto, *pseud. see* Puttkammer, Emil *freiherr* v.

Lukin, James. The boy engineers, what they did and how they did it ; a book for boys. Ill. N. Y. 1878. D. **Lx 501**

Lyster, Annette. Doctor L'Estrange ; a novel. N. Y. 1881. Q. **L 2201**

— *Same.* Lond. 1882. 3 v. in 1. D. **L 2201**

Lytton, *Lord, see* Bulwer-Lytton, E: G: Earle Lytton, *also* Bulwer-Lytton, E: Robert.

MacCallum, M. C., *born* Stirling. The Grahams of Invermoy. Lond. 1879. 3 v. in 1. D.
S 6052

— The minister's son ; a novel. N. Y. 1882. Q.
S 6051

— A true man. *In* Two tales of married life.
C 2905

McCarthy, Justin. The comet of a season. N. Y. 1881. Q. **M 108**

— *Same.* Lond. 1881. 3 v. in 1. D. **M 108**

— Dear lady Disdain. N. Y. 1876. O. **M 101**

— Donna Quixote. N. Y. 1879. Q. **M 102**

— *Same.* Ill. 2d ed. Lond. 1879. 3 v. in 1. D.
M 102

— A fair saxon. N. Y. *n. d.* D. **M 103**

— Linley Rochford. N. Y. 1874. O. **M 104**

— Maid of Athens ; a novel. N. Y. 1883. Q.
M 109

— *Same.* Lond. 1883. 3 v. in 1. D. **M 109**

— Miss Misanthrope. Leipz. 1878. 2 v. in 1. S.
M 105

— *Same.* N. Y. 1877. O. **M 105**

McCarthy, Justin.—*Continued.*

— My enemy's daughter. N. Y. 1869. O. **M 106**

— *Same.* Lond. 1869. 3 v. in 1. D. **M 106**

— Paul Massie. N. Y. *n. d.* D. **M 107**

— The Waterdale neighbours. Leipz. 1868. 2 v. in 1. S. **M 110**

McClellan, Harriet, *born* Hare, (*Harford Fleming*). A carpet knight ; novel. Bost. 1885. D. **M 152**

— Cupid and the sphinx. N. Y. 1880. D. **M 151**

MacConnel, J: L. Talbot and Vernon. N. Y. 1850. D. **M 201**

McCray, Florine Thayer, *and* Esther Louise **Smith.** Wheels and whims ; an etching. [*Anon.*] Ill. Bost. 1884. S. **M 228**

Macdonald, G: Adela Cathcart. Bost. *n. d.* D.
M 251

— Alec Forbes of Howglen. Leipz. 1865. 2 v. in 1. S. **M 252**

— Annals of a quiet neighbourhood. Leipz. 1867. 2 v. in 1. S. **M 253**

— *Same.* N. Y. 1872. D. **M 253**

— *Same. T. p. w.* D. **M 253**
Note. For continuation, *see* The seabord parish.

— At the back of the north wind. Lond. 1878. D. **Mx 151**

— *Same.* Lond. 1884. D. **Mx 151**

— David Elginbrod. Leipz. 1871. 2 v. in 1 S.
M 254

— Dealings with the fairies. Lond. *n. d.* T.
Mx 152
Contents. The light princess.—The giant's heart.— The shadows.—Cross purposes.—The golden key.

— Donal Grant. Ill. Bost. [1883]. D. **M 270**

— *Same.* N. Y. 1883. Q. **M 270**

— A double story. N. Y. *n. d.* D. **Mx 155**

— *Same.* The wise woman ; a parable. Lond. 1875. D. **Mx 155**

— Guild Court ; a London story. N. Y. 1883. D. **M 271**

— Malcolm. Leipz. 1875. 2 v. in 1. S. **M 255**

— *Same.* Phila. 1875. O. **M 255**

— The marquis of Lossie. Leipz. 1877. 2 v. in 1. S. **M 256**

— Mary Marston. N. Y. 1881. D. **M 257**

— Paul Faber, surgeon. Phila. 1879. O. **M 258**

— Phantastes ; a fairy romance for men and women. Bost. *n. d.* D. **M 259**

— *Same.* N. Y. *n. d.* D. **M 259**

— The portent ; a story of the inner vision of the highlanders, commonly called second sight. Bost. *n. d.* D. **M 260**

— *Same. With his* Phantastes. **M 259**

— The princess and Curdie ; [a sequel to The princess and the goblins]. Lond. 1883 [1882]. D. **Mx 156**

— The princess and the goblins. Lond. 1872. S.
Mx 154

— Ranald Bannerman's boyhood. Lond. *n. d.* S.
Mx 153

— Robert Falconer. Bost. *n. d.* D. **M 261**

— St. George and St. Michael. N. Y. *n. d.* D.
M 262

— *Same.* Leipz. 1876. 2 v. in 1. S. **M 262**

— The seabord parish ; a sequel to "Annals of a quiet neighbourhood ". Lond. 1884. D.
M 263
Note. For continuation, *see* The vicar's daughter.

— Sir Gibbie. Leipz. 1880. 2 v. in 1. S. **M 264**

— *Same.* Phila. 1879. O. **M 264**

— Thomas Wingfold, curate. N. Y. 1876. D.
M 265

x denotes books specially adapted for children.

Macdonald, G:—*Continued.*
— The vicar's daughter, an autobiographical story; a sequel to "Annals of a quiet neighborhood" and "The seaboard parish". Bost. 1872. S.   **M 266**
— *Same.* Leipz. 1872. 2 v. in 1. S.   **M 266**
— Warlock o' Glenwarlock. Bost. [1881]. D.   **M 267**
— *Same.* N. Y. 1881. Q.   **M 267**
— *Same.* *N. t.* [Bost. 1881]. O.   **M 267**
— Weighed and wanting; a novel. Bost. [1883]. D.   **M 269**
— *Same.* N. Y. 1882. Q.   **M 269**
— Wilfrid Cumbermede; an autobiographical story. Toronto. 1872. D.   **M 268**
— The wise woman, *see above* A double story.
Macdonnell, Agnes. Quaker cousins. N. Y. 1879. Q.   **M 301**
— *Same.* Lond. 1879. 3 v. in 1. D.   **M 301**
McDowell, Katherine Sherwood, *born* Bonner, (*Sherwood Bonner*). Dialect tales. N. Y. 1883. O.   **M 326**
Contents. The gentleman of Sarsar.—On the nine-mile. — Hieronymus Pop and the baby. — Sister Weeden's prayer.—Aunt Anniky's teeth.—Dr. Jex's predicament. — In aunt Mely's cabin.—The case of Elizabeth Bleylock.—The bran dance at the Apple settlement. — Lame Jerry.— Jack and the mountain pink.
— Suwanee river tales. Ill. Bost. 1884. S.   **Mx 176**
Macfarlane, C: The romance of history. N. Y. 1832. 2 v. D.   **M 351**
McGloin, Frank. Norodom, king of Cambodia; a romance of the east. N. Y. 1882. D.   **M 376**
McIntosh, Maria Jane. Conquest and self-conquest, or Which makes the hero? N. Y. 1860. S.   **Mx 201**
— The cousins; a tale of early life. N. Y. 1859. S.   **Mx 202**
— Evenings at Donaldson Manor, or The christmas guest. N. Y. 1864. D.   **M 401**
— The lofty and the lowly, or Good in all and none all-good. N. Y. 1881. D.   **M 403**
— Two lives, or To seem and to be. N. Y. 1853. D.   **M 402**
Mackarness, Matilda Anne Planché. The dream chintz. *T. p. w.*   **Mx 251**
McKay, James Thompson. Stella Grayland. *In* Stories by american authors.   **S 35 v7**
Mackenzie, H: The story of La Roche. *In* Johnson, E. R. Little classics.   **J 926 v3**
— *see also his* Miscellaneous works.   **829.2 : 23**
McLean, Sarah Pratt. Cape Cod folks. Bost. 1881. D.   **M 451**
— *Same.* [1st ed.]   **L**
— Some other folks. Bost. 1884. D.   **M 453**
Contents. Santa Maria.—A career.—The singular vote of Aut Tilbox.—Sam Sperry's pension.
— Towhead; the story of a girl. Bost. 1883 [1882]. D.   **M 452**
Macleod, Donald. The bloodstone. N. Y. 1853. D.   **M 551**
— Pynnshurst; his wanderings and ways of thinking. N. Y. 1852. D.   **M 552**
Macleod, Norman. Character sketches. N. Y. 1876. S.   **M 501**
Contents. Billy Buttons.—Our Bob.—Aunt Mary.—T. T. Fitzroy, esq.—Mr. Joseph Walker.—The highland witch.—The old guard.—The water-horse.—A true ghost story.—Job Jacobs and his boxes.—Wee Davie.
— The gold thread; a story for the young. Ill. Lond. 1866. S.   **Mx 276**
— A highland parish. *T. p. w.* S.   **M 502**

Macleod, Norman.—*Continued.*
— The old lieutenant and his son. Toronto. 1876. D.   **M 503**
— The starling. N. Y. *n. d.* S.   **M 504**
Macnish, Robert. The metempsychosis. *In* Tales from Blackwood.   **T 176 v2**
Macquoid, Katherine S. Beside the river. N. Y. 1881. Q.   **M 601**
— *Same.* Leipz. 1881. 2 v. in 1. S.   **M 601**
— Diane. Leipz. 1876. 2 v. in 1. S.   **M 602**
— Elinor Dryden. N. Y. 1878. Q.   **M 603**
— *Same*; new ed. rev. and amended by the author. Lond. 1878. D.   **M 603**
— Esau Runswick. N. Y. 1882. S.   **M 609**
— *Same.* A faithful lover. Leipz. 1882. 2 v. in 1. S.   **M 609**
— Her sailor love. N. Y. 1883. S.   **M 610**
— Louisa; a novel. N. Y. 1885. 2 v. D. **M 611**
— Miriam's marriage. Leipz. 1872. 2 v. in 1. S.   **M 604**
— My story. Leipz. 1875. 2 v. in 1. S. **M 605**
— Patty. Leipz. 1872. 2 v. in 1. S.   **M 606**
— Pictures across the channel. Leipz. 1873. 2 v. in 1. S.   **M 607**
Contents. V. 1. The fisherman of Auge.—"Notre Jean".—The street-sweeper of St. Roque.—The beginning of Mimi's love.—The Calvary of St. Sebastian. 2. "Poor dear Chuquet".—Jeanne Dupont.— The widow Mérand.—Victoire's faith.—Madame Gerder's husband.—The story of Françoise.— The mother of Jacques.
— Too soon; a study of a girl's heart. Leipz. 1874. S.   **M 608**
Macy, W. H. There she blows! or The log of the Arethusa. Bost. *n. d.* D.   **Mx 301**
Madame Lucas. (Round-robin ser.) Bost. 1882. S.   **M 1**
Mädchen von Grenoble, Das; eine erzählung aus der ersten hälfte des neunzehnten jahrhunderts. Nach dem französischen frei umgearbeitet von Julius Glaubrecht. Ill. Regensburg. 1873. S. *With* Herchenbach, W: Die wiedergefundene tochter.   **H 2781**
Madoc, Fayr, *pseud.?* The story of Melicent. N. Y. 1883. Q.   **M 626**
Mag; a story of today. N. Y. 1878. O.   **M 6**
Maga stories. N. Y. 1867. S.   **P 2801**
Contents. **Putnam,** Mary Corinna. Found and lost.—**Perkins,** F: Beecher. My three conversations with miss Chester.—O'Brien, Fitz James. Mrs. Macsimum's bill.—The feast of the cranberries.—Quincy, Josiah Phillips. Toilwotte's ghost *and* Professor Phantillo.—The mormon's wife.—**Stoddard,** R: H: The rich merchant of Cairo.—The legend of Goodman Poverty.—**Perkins,** F: B. The double veil.—Curtis, L. My husband's mother.—**Pratt,** G. The old woman who dried up and blew away.—**Bethune,** G: Wash. The ambassador in spite of himself.—**Briggs,** C: F: Elegant Tom Diller.—**Young,** W: A toss-up for a husband.—Uncle Bernard's story.—How I came to be married.
— *Same.* Found and lost, and other maga stories. N. Y. 1868. S.   **P 2801**
Maginn, W: Tom Burke's duel with ensign Brady. *In* Tales from Blackwood.   **T 176 v3**
Magruder, Julia. Across the chasm. [*Anon.*] N. Y. 1885. D.   **M 5051**
Maidment, James. The cateran of Lochloy. *In* Wilson, J: M. Tales of the borders.   **W 2202 v7**
— The heir of Inshannock. *In the same.*   **W 2202 v12**
— Mortlake. *In the same.*   **W 2203 v3**
— *Same. In the same.*   **W 2202 v8**
Mairet, Jeanne, *pseud., see* **Bigot, Mary.**

x denotes books specially adapted for children.

Maitland, E:, (*Herbert Ainslie*). By and by ; a historical romance of the future. N. Y. 1874. D.   **M 637**
— Higher law ; a romance. N. Y. 1872. D.   **M 638**
— The pilgrim and the shrine, or Passages from the life and correspondence of Herbert Ainslie. Lond. 1871. D.   **M 636**
Majendie, *Lady* Margaret Elizabeth. Giannetto. (Leisure hour ser.) N. Y. 1876. S.   **M 651**
— A railway journey. *In* Tales from Blackwood.   **T 177 v6**
Malet, Lucas, *pseud.*, *see* **Harrison,** *Mrs.* W:
Mallock, W: Hurrell. The new Paul and Virginia, or Positivism on an island. N. Y. 1878. D.   **M 701**
— The new republic, or Culture, faith and philosophy in an english country house. N. Y. 1878. D.   **M 702**
Malory, *Sir* T: Morte d'Arthur ; sir T: Malory's book of king Arthur and of his noble knights of the round table. The original ed. of Caxton rev. for modern use with an introd. by sir E: Strachey. Lond. 1876. D.   **813 : 7**
Malot, Hector H: No relations. From the french by May Laffan. Phila. 1880. S.   **M 801**
Malser, Hans, *pseud.*, *see* **Rosegger,** P. K.
Maltitz, Hermann v., *pseud.*, *see* **Klencke,** F: Hermann.
Mand, J. E., *pseud.*, *see* **Grossheim,** Julie.
Man's a man for a' that, A. N. Y. 1879. S.   **M 7**
Man proposes. Bost. 1880. D.   **M 8**
Mancini-Pierantoni, Grazia, *see* **Pierantoni,** Grazia.
Manning, Anne. The chronicle of Ethelfled. [*Anon.*] Lond. 1861. D.   **M 855**
— Cherry and Violet ; a tale of the great plague. N. Y. 1866. S.   **M 851**
— The household of sir Thomas More. [*Anon.*] 4th ed. with an app. Lond. 1860. S.   **M 853**
— The maiden and married life of Mary Powell, afterwards mistress Milton. N. Y. 1852. S.   **M 852**
— Passages in the life of the faire gospeller mistress Anne Askew, recounted by ye unworthie pen of Nicholas Moldwarp, B. A. N. Y. 1866. D.   **M 854**
Manzoni, Alessandro. I promessi sposi, or The betrothed ; a romance of the 17th century. Baltimore. 1861. S.   **M 901**
— *Same, germ.* Die verlobten ; eine mailändische geschichte aus dem 17. jahrhundert aufgefunden und erneut. Aus dem italienischen übers. von Emilie Schröder ; eingel. von H. Th. Rötscher. Hildburgh. 1867. 2 v. in 1. D.   **M 901**
Maquet, A: Herzensschulden. Aus dem franz. von G. Fink. Stuttg. 1857. T.   **M 3451**
Marana, Giovanni Paolo. The eight volumes of letters writ by a turkish spy, who lived 45 years undiscovered at Paris ; giving an impartial account to the divan at Constantinople of the most remarkable transactions of Europe and discovering several intrigues and secrets of the christian courts, especially that of France, continued from the year 1637 to the year 1682. Written originally in arabick, tr. into italian, from thence into english and now publ. with a

large historical preface and index to illustrate the whole, by the translator of the 1st vol. Lond. 1748. 8 v. S.   **M 951**
Marbach, Gotthard Oswald, *ed.* Geschichte von der schönen Magelone und dem ritter Peter mit den silbernen schlüsseln. N. Y. 1864. S.   **M 976**
March, Walter, *pseud.*, *see* **Willcox,** Orlando B.
March, Wenzeslaus, *pseud.*, *see* **Messenhauser,** Cäsar Wenzel.
Marggraf, Hermann. Fritz Beutel, eine münchhauseniade. Frankfurt. a. M. 1856. D.   **M 1101**
Marguerite's journal ; a story for girls with an editorial introd. by Miriam Harris. N. Y. 1875. D.   **Mx 11**
Maria, *pseud.*, *see* **Brentano,** Clemens.
Marjory Graham ; a novel. N. Y. 1882. S.   **M 5**
Markham, R: Around the yule log ; herein are recorded the doings of five boys and five girls on a visit to the sea at christmastide, together with many stories and ballads for young patriots. Ill. N. Y. 1879. O.   **Mx 352**
— On the edge of winter. N. Y. [1881]. O.   **Mx 353**
Marlin, Josef. Attila. Pesth. 1847. 3 v. S.   **M 1151**
— Jenseits der wälder ; siebenbürgische erzählungen. Pesth. 1850. 2 v. D.   **M 1152**
— Sulamith. Pesth. 1848. 2 v. S.   **M 1153**
Marlitt, E., *pseud.*, *see* **John,** Eugenie.
Married for fun ; a novel. Bost. 1885. S.   **M 10**
Marryat, Florence, *see* **Church,** Florence.
Marryat, F: Der arme Jack. Aus dem englischen von C: Kolb. Stuttg. 1857. T.   **M 1201**
— The children of the New Forest. Leipz. 1848. S.   **M 1202**
— *Same, germ.* Die kinder des Neuwalds. Aus dem englischen übertragen von C: Kolb. Stuttg. 1852. T.   **M 1202**
— Frank Mildmay, der flottenoffizier. Neu aus dem englischen von C: Kolb. Stuttg. 1857. T.   **M 1203**
— Jacob Faithful. Leipz. 1842. S.   **M 1204**
— *Same, germ.* Jacob Erlich. Neu aus dem englischen von C: Kolb. Stuttg. 1843. T.   **M 1204**
— Japhet in search of a father. Leipz. 1843. S.   **M 1205**
— The king's own. N. Y. 1864. D.   **M 1206**
— The mission, or Scenes in Africa ; written for young people. Leipz. 1845. S.   **M 1207**
— *Same, germ.* Die sendung, oder Scenen in Afrika. Neu aus dem englischen von C: Kolb. Stuttg. 1857. T.   **M 1207**
— Mr. midshipman Easy. Leipz. 1869. S.   **M 1208**
— *Same, germ.* Midshipman Easy. Neu aus dem englischen von C: Kolb. Struttg. 1857. T.   **M;1208**
— Narrative of the travels and adventures of monsieur Violet in California, Sonora and western Texas. Leipz. 1843. S.   **M 1209**
— Newton Forster, or The merchant service. N. Y. 1862. D.   **M 1218**
— Der pascha. Neu aus dem englischen von C: Kolb. Stuttg. 1845. T.   **M 1210**
— Percival Keene. Leipz. 1842. S.   **M 1211**
— *Same.* N. Y. 1864. D.   **M 1211**
— *Same, germ.* Percival Keene. Neu aus dem englischen von C: Kolb. Stuttg. 1860. T.   **M 1211**

x denotes books specially adapted for children.

Marryat, F:—*Continued.*
— Peter Simple. Leipz. 1842. S.　　**M 1212**
— *Same, germ.* Peter Simpel. Neu aus dem
　englischen von C: Kolb. Stuttg. 1843. T.
　　　　　　　　　　　　　　M 1212
— The pirate. N. Y. 1884. Q.　　**M 1213**
— *Same, germ.* Der pirat. *T. p. w.* T.　**M 1213**
— The privateersman one hundred years ago.
　Leipz. 1846. S.　　　　　**M 1214**
— *Same, germ.* Der kaperschiffer vor hundert
　jahren. Neu aus dem englischen von C:
　Kolb. Stuttg. 1857. T.　　**M 1214**
— The settlers in Canada; written for young
　people. Leipz. 1844. S.　　**M 1215**
— Snarleyyow, or The dog fiend. N. Y. 1873. D.
　　　　　　　　　　　　　　M 1217
— The three cutters. *With his* The pirate.
　　　　　　　　　　　　　　M 1213
— Valerie, an authobiography. Leipz. 1849. S.
　　　　　　　　　　　　　　M 1216
Marryat, Kapitän, *pseud.,* see **Howard, E:**
Marsh, Mrs.—. Margaret and her bridesmaids.
　[*Anon.*] Bost. *n. d.* D.　　**M 1226**
— The queen of the county. [*Anon.*] Bost.
　[1864]. D.　　　　　　**M 1227**
Marsh, J: Hannah Hawkins; the reformed
　drunkard's daughter. N. Y. 1844. S.
　　　　　　　　　　　　　　Mx 401
Marsh-Caldwell, Anne, *born* Caldwell. Aubrey.
　T. p. w. O.　　　　　**M 1251**
— Castle Avon. Leipz. 1852. 2 v. in 1. S.
　　　　　　　　　　　　　　M 1252
— *Same. T. p. w.* [N. Y. 1862]. O.　**M 1252**
— *Same, germ.* Schloss Avon. Aus dem engli-
　schen von C. Büchele. Stuttg. 1853. S.
　　　　　　　　　　　　　　M 1252
— The deformed. Phila. *n. d.* O.　**M 1253**
— Emilia Wyndham. N. Y. 1863. O.　**M 1255**
— *Same, germ.* Emilie Wyndham. Aus dem eng-
　lischen. Stuttg. 1853. 2 v. S.　**M 1255**
— Evelyn Marston. Leipz. 1856. 2 v. in 1. S.
　　　　　　　　　　　　　　M 1262
— Father Darcy. N. Y. 1863. O.　**M 1256**
— The heiress of Haughton, or The mother's
　secret· Leipz. 1855. 2 v. in 1. S.　**M 1263**
— Lettice Arnold. N. Y. 1867. O.　**M 1257**
— Mordaunt Hall, or A september night; a novel.
　Lond. 1853. S.　　　　　**M 1265**
— Norman's bridge, or The modern Midas. N.
　Y. 1858. O.　　　　　　**M 1258**
— *Same.* N. Y. 1863. O.　　**M 1258**
— Ravenscliffe. Leipz. 1851. 2 v. in 1. S.
　　　　　　　　　　　　　　M 1264
— Time the avenger. N. Y. 1861. O.　**M 1259**
— *Same.* N. Y. 1864. O.　　**M 1259**
— The triumphs of time. N. Y. 1857. O.　**M 1260**
— *Same.* N. Y. 1862. O.　　**M 1260**
— The Wilmingtons. N. Y. 1863. O.　**M 1261**
Marshall, Beatrice. Dolly's charge. Ill. N. Y.
　1880. S.　　　　　　　**Mx 426**
Marshall, Emma, *born* Martin, *mrs.* Hugh Gra-
　ham. Benvenuta, or Rainbow colors. N.
　Y. [1882]. D.　　　　　**M 1307**
— Dayspring; a story of the time of W: Tyndale,
　reformer, scholar and martyr. Ill. N. Y.
　1883. D.　　　　　　　**M 1308**
— Dewdrops and diamonds. Ill. N. Y. [1881].
　D.　　　　　　　　　**Mx 451**
— Dorothy's daughters. Ill. N. Y. 1881. D.
　　　　　　　　　　　　　　M 1306
— In the east country with sir T: Browne, kt.,
　physician and philosopher of the city of
　Norwich. Ill. N. Y. [1884]. D.　**M 1310**

Marshall, Emma, *born* Martin.—*Continued.*
— Lady Alice, or Two sides of a picture. N. Y.
　n. d. D.　　　　　　　**M 1301**
— Life's aftermath; a story of quiet people. N.
　Y. 1876. S.　　　　　　**M 1302**
— Light on the lily, or A flower's message. Ill.
　N. Y. 1880. S.　　　　　**Mx 454**
— Memories of troublous times; being the history
　of dame Alicia Chamberlayne of Ravens-
　holme, Gloucestershire. Lond. 1880. D.
　　　　　　　　　　　　　　M 1305
— Millicent Legh. Phila. 1867. S.　**M 1303**
— Mrs. Willoughby's octave; a tale. Ill. N. Y.
　1884. D.　　　　　　　**M 1309**
— Now-a-days, or King's daughters. N. Y. 1885.
　D.　　　　　　　　　**M 1304**
— Poppies and pansies; a story for children. Ill.
　N. Y. 1883. D.　　　　　**Mx 453**
— Rex and Regina, or The song of the river. Ill.
　N. Y. 1882. D.　　　　　**Mx 452**
— A rose without thorns. Ill. N. Y. 1880. S.
　　　　　　　　　　　　　　Mx 455
Marsham, Clara Catherine, *born* Paley, *the hon.
　mrs.* Robert. Cousin Simon. N. Y. 1880.
　O.　　　　　　　　　**M 1351**
— *Same.* Lond. 1879. D.　　**M 1351**
Martell, W:, *pseud.,* see **Pochhammer,** W: v.
Martin, Mrs. Bell. (*Mrs. Martin Bell*). Julia
　Howard. N. Y. 1859. O.　　**M 1366**
Martin, Effie May, *born* Hand. The alphabet
　club. Ill. Milw. 1884. T.　　**Mx 476**
Martin, Mary E.. *mrs.* Herbert. Beauchamp
　and co. *In* Tales from many sources.
　　　　　　　　　　　　　　T 178 v2
— Bonnie Lesley. N. Y. 1878. Q.　**M 1401**
— For a dream's sake. N. Y. 1879. Q.　**M 1402**
— *Same.* Lond. 1879. 2 v. in 1. D.　**M 1402**
Martin, Kate Byam. Belgian days. Chicago.
　1882. S.　　　　　　　**M 1376**
Martin, Theodore, (*Bon Gaultier*). Bon Gaul-
　tier's tales. *In* **Wilson, J: M.** Tales of the
　borders.　　　　　　　**W 2202 v4, 9**
　Contents. 1. Country quarters. 2. Mrs. Humphrey
　Greenwood's tea party.
Martineau, Harriet. The Crofton boys; a tale.
　N. Y. 1862. S.　　　　　**Mx 551**
— The hour and the man; a historical romance.
　Lond. 1873. S.　　　　　**M 1476**
— Tales for the middle classes. Lond. 1840. T.
　　　　　　　　　　　　　　Mx 552
— Weal and woe in Graveloch; a tale. Bost.
　1833. S.　　　　　　　**Mx 553**
Martineau des Chesnez, Elizabeth, *born* Lair,
　baronne. Lady Green Satin and her maid
　Rosette, or The history of Jean Paul and
　his little white mice. Tr. from the french.
　Phila. *n. d.* D.　　　　　**Mx 526**
Marvel, Ik, *pseud.,* see **Mitchell, Donald Grant.**
Marx, Theodor. Die erben des wahnsinns; ro-
　man. N. Y. 1882. F.　　**M 1426**
Mary, Cousin, *pseud.* Christmas holidays at
　Chestnut Hill. Ill. Bost. *n. d.* S. **Mx 577**
　Contents. Chestnut Hill. — The lost fourpence. —
　Robin red-breast's picnic.—Home scenes.—The after-
　noon with mrs. Pratt.—Perseverance. — Not a genius.
　— "Do as you would be done by." — The adventures
　of a squirrel. — The lonely grave. — Who was Santa-
　Claus?
— Country life, and other stories. Ill. Bost.
　n. d. D.　　　　　　　**Mx 576**
　Includes, Childish wishes.—Autobiography of a pin.
　—The little chip-girl.—Grace and her pets.—The pic-
　nic.—Little Effie and the snow-drop.— The fête of
　flowers.

---

x denotes books specially adapted for children.

Mason, Mary Murdock. Mae Madden ; with an introductory poem by Joaquin Miller. Chicago. 1876. T.   **M 1451**

Mathers, Helen, see Reeves, Helen Buckingham.

Mathews, Albert, (P. Siogvolk). Walter Ashwood ; a love story. N. Y. 1860. D.   **M 1551**

Mathews, Cornelius. Chanticleer ; a thanksgiving story of the Peabody family. Ill. N. Y. [1856]. D.   **M 1601**

Mathews, Joanna H. Fred Bradford's debt. N. Y. [1882]. O.   **Mx 653**
— Harry Bradford's crusade. N. Y. [1883]. O.   **Mx 652**

— Miss Ashton's girls.
1. Fanny's birthday gift. N. Y. n. d. S.   **Mx 654**
2. The new scholars. N. Y. 1883. S.   **Mx 655**
3. Rosalie's pet. N. Y. n. d. S.   **Mx 656**
4. Eleanor's visit. N. Y. n. d. S.   **Mx 657**
5. Mabel Walton's experiment. N. Y. 1882. S.   **Mx 658**
6. Elsie's Santa Claus. N. Y. n. d. S. **Mx 659**

Mathews, Julia A. Bessie Harrington's venture. Bost. 1878. S.   **Mx 701**

Mathews, Margaret Harriet. Dr. Gilbert's daughters ; a story for girls. Ill. Phila. [1881]. D.   **Mx 601**

Mathews, W: The heir of Vallis. Lond. 1854. 3 v. D.   **M 1651**

Matthews, James Brander. Venetian glass. In Stories by american authors.   **S 35 v3**
— and H: C. Bunner. In partnership ; studies in story-telling. N. Y. 1884. S.   **M 1501**
Contents. Matthews, B., and H. C. Bunner. The documents in the case ; The seven conversations of dear Jones and Baby Van Rensselaer.—Matthews, B. Venetian glass ; The rival ghosts ; Playing a part.—Bunner, H. C. The red silk handkerchief ; A letter and a paragraph ; Love in old cloathes.
— - The documents in the case. *In* Stories by american authors.   **S 35 v1**

Maurice, Walter, pseud., see Besant, Walter.

Maxwell, Cecil. A story of three sisters. (Leisure hour ser.) N. Y. 1876. S.   **M 1701**

Maxwell, Mary Elizabeth, born Braddon, mrs. J: Asphodel ; a novel. Lond. 1881. 3 v. in 1. D.   **M 1789**
— Aurora Floyd. Leipz. 1863. 2 v. in 1. S.   **M 1751**
—Same, germ. Aurora Floyd. Aus dem englischen von F. Leybold. Leipz. 1863. 2 v. S.   **M 1751**
— Barbara, or Splendid misery. N. Y. [1880]. Q.   **M 1752**
— Same. The story of Barbara, her splendid misery and her gilded cage ; a novel. Lond. [1880]. 3 v. in 2. D.   **M 1752**
— Birds of prey. T. p. w. [N. Y. 1867]. O.   **M 1753**
— Same; a novel. Lond. 1867. 3 v. in 1. D.   **M 1753**
— Bound to John company, or The adventures and misadventures of Robert Ainsleigh. Ill. N. Y. 1869. O.   **M 1754**
— Charlotte's inheritance ; a novel. Lond. 1868. 3 v. in 1. D.   **M 1755**
— Same. N. Y. 1878. D.   **M 1755**
— The cloven foot. N. Y. 1879. Q.   **M 1756**
— Same; a novel. Lond. [1879]. 3 v. in 1. D.   **M 1756**
— Cut by the county ; a novel. N. Y. 1885. S.   **M 1793**

Maxwell, Mary E., born Braddon.—*Continued.*
— Dead men's shoes. Leipz. 1876. 2 v. in 1. S.   **M 1757**
— Dead Sea fruit. Leipz. 1868. 2 v. in 1. S.   **M 1758**
— The doctor's wife. Leipz. 1864. 2 v. in 1. S.   **M 1759**
— Eleanor's victory. Leipz. 1863. 2 v. in 1. S.   **M 1760**
— Same, eng. Eleanor's sieg. Aus dem englischen von Marie Scott. Leipz. 1853. 2 v. S.   **M 1760**
— Fenton's quest. Leipz. 1871. 2 v. in 1. S.   **M 1761**
— Flower and weed ; a novel. N. Y. 1882. Q.   **M 1785**
— Same, and other tales. Lond. [1884]. D.   **M 1790**
Includes, G: Caulfield's journey.—The clown's quest.—Dr. Carrick.—"If she be not fair to me."—The shadow in the corner.—His secret.—Thou art the man.
— Henry Dunbar, the story of an outcast. Leipz. 1864. 2 v. in 1. S.   **M 1762**
— Hostages to fortune. Leipz. 1875. 2 v. in 1. S.   **M 1763**
— Same. Lond. [1876]. D.   **M 1763**
— In great waters, and other tales. Leipz. 1877. S.   **M 1764**
Includes, Sebastian.—Levison's victim.—Christmas in possession.—John Granger.—Prince Ramji Rowdedow.—Too bright to last.—The scene-painter's wife.—Sir Luke's return.—Her last appearance.—Sir Hanbury's bequest.—A very narrow escape.—My unlucky friend.
— Ishmael ; a novel. N. Y. 1885. Q.   **M 1792**
— John Marchmont's legacy. Leipz. 1864. 2 v. S.   **M 1765**
— Joshua Haggard's daughter. Lond. 1876. 3 v. in 2. D.   **M 1766**
— Same. Leipz. 1877. 2 v. in 1. S.   **M 1766**
— Just as I am. N. Y. 1880. Q.   **M 1767**
— Same. Lond. [1880]. 3 v. in 2. D.   **M 1767**
— Lady Audley's secret. Leipz. 1862. 2 v. in 1. S.   **M 1768**
— Same, germ. Lady Audley's geheimniss. Aus dem englischen. Leipz. 1863. 3 v. S.   **M 1768**
— The lady's mile. Leipz. 1866. 2 v. 1 in 1. S.   **M 1769**
— Lost for love. Leipz. 1874. 2 v. in 1. S.   **M 1770**
— The Lovels of Arden. Leipz. 1871. 2 v. in 1. S.   **M 1771**
— Lucius Davoren, or Publicans and sinners. Leipz. 1873. 3 v. in 2. S.   **M 1772**
— Mount Royal ; a novel. N. Y. 1882. Q.   **M 1784**
— Only a clod. Leipz. 1865. 2 v. in 1. S.   **M 1773**
— Same; a novel. Lond. n. d. D.   **M 1773**
— An open verdict. Leipz. 1873. 3 v. in 2. S.   **M 1774**
— Phantom fortune ; a novel. N. Y. 1883. Q.   **M 1786**
— Run to earth. Leipz. 1869. 2 v. in 1. S.   **M 1775**
— Rupert Godwin. Leipz. 1867. 2 v. in 1. S.   **M 1776**
— Sir Jasper's tenant. Leipz. 1866. 2 v. in 1. S.   **M 1777**
— The story of Barbara, see above Barbara.
— A strange world. N. Y. 1875. O.   **M 1778**
— Same ; a novel. Lond. 1875. 3 v. in 2. D.   **M 1778**

x denotes books specially adapted for children.

Maxwell, Mary E., *born* Braddon.—*Continued.*
— Strangers and pilgrims. Leipz. 1873. 2 v. in 1.
   S.   **M 1779**
— Taken at the flood. Leip. 1874. 3 v. in 2. S.
                                M 1780
— Under the red flag ; a novel. N. Y. [1883]. Q.
                                M 1787
— *Same. T. p. w. O.*   **M 1791**
— Vixen. Lond. 1879. D.   **M 1781**
— *Same.* Leipz. 1879. 2 v. in 1. S.   **M 1781**
— Weavers and weft. Leipz. 1877. S.   **M 1782**
— Wyllard's weird ; a novel. N. Y. 1885. Q.
                                M 1788
— *ed.* The mistletoe bough. N. Y. 1878, 1879,
   1884. 3 v. Q.   **M 1788**
Maxwell, P. The white woman of Tarras. *In*
  Wilson, J: M. Tales of the borders.
                       W 2202 v12
Maxwell, W: Hamilton. Wild sports of the west.
  Phila. *n. d.* O.   **M 1851**
May, Sophie, *pseud.,* see **Clarke,** Rebecca Sophia.
May, T: P. A prince of Breffny. Phila. [1881].
  D.   **M 1876**
Mayhew, A: Horace *and* H: The magic of kind-
  ness, or The wondrous story of the good
  Huan. Ill. N. Y. 1860. S.   **Mx 751**
Mayo, Isabella, *born* Fyvie, (*Edward and Ruth
  Garrett*). At any cost. N. Y. [1884]. S.
                           M 1903
— A chance child. *In* Johnson, E. R. Little
  classics.   **J 926 v11**
— Family fortunes ; a domestic story. Lond.
  1881. D.   **M 1902**
— Gold and dross. N. Y. 1874. D.   **M 1901**
Mayo, W: Starbuck. The Berber, or The moun-
  taineer of the Atlas ; a tale of Morocco.
  N. Y. 1873. D.   **M 1951**
— Kaloolah ; adventures of Jonathan Romer of
  Nantucket. N. Y. 1873. D.   **M 1952**
— Never again. N. Y. 1873. D.   **M 1953**
— Romance dust from the historic placer. N. Y.
  1851. D.   **M 1954**
Meade, L. T. *see* **Smith,** Elizabeth Thomasina.
Mechulle-leut', Die ; ein polizeiroman. Milw.
  1867. O.   **M 11**
Meding, J: Ferdinand Martin Oskar, (*Gregor
  Samarow*). Das haus des fabrikanten ; ein
  roman aus der wirklichkeit. N. Y. 1882. F.
                           M 1980
— Die römerfahrt der Epigonen ; zeit-roman. N.
  Y. 1883. F.   **M 1978**
— Die saxoborussen ; roman. N. Y. 1885. 2 v.
  F.   **M 1981**
— Der todesgruss der legionen ; zeit-roman. N.
  Y. 1882. F.   **M 1976**
— Um den halbmond ; roman. N. Y. 1883. F.
                           M 1979
Meinhold, J: W: Mary Schweidler, the amber
  witch ; the most interesting trial for witch-
  craft ever known ; printed from an imper-
  fect ms. by her father, Abraham Schweid-
  ler, the pastor of Coserow in the island of
  Usedom. Tr. from the german by lady
  Duff Gordon. N. Y. *n. d.* O.   **M 2001**
Meissner, Alfred. Aus der emigration. Berlin.
  1863. 2 v. S.   **M 2051**
— Babel ; roman aus Oesterreich's neuester geschichte. Berlin. 1867. 4 v. S.   **M 2052**
— Die bildhauer von Worms ; eine geschichte aus
  dem vorigen jahrhundert. Berlin. 1875. 2
  v. in 1. D.   **M 2064**

Meissner, Alfred.—*Continued.*
— Charaktermasken. Leipz. 1862. 3 v. in 1. D.
                              M 2067
   Contents, see Deutscher katalog. p. 82.
— Dulder und renegaten. Berlin. 1862. 2 v. S.
                              M 2068
— Der freiherr von Hostiwin. Prag. 1855. 2 v.
  T.   **M 2053**
— Die kinder Roms. Berlin. 1870. 4 v. S. **M 2054**
— Kleine memoiren. Berlin. *n. d.* D.   **M 2065**
   Contents, see Deutscher katalog, p. 82.
— Lemberger und sohn. Berlin. 1865. S.
                              M 2055
— Neuer adel. Leipz. 1861. 3 v. S.   **M 2056**
— Novellen. Leipz. 1865, 1876. 3 v. S.   **M 2057**
   Contents, see Deutscher katalog, p. 82.
— Die opfer der partei. Berlin. 1864. 2 v. S.
                              M 2058
— Oriola. Berlin. 1874. D.   **M 2066**
— Sacro Catino ; historische erzählung. Berlin.
  1868. S.   **M 2059**
— Schwarzgelb ; roman aus Oesterreichs letzten
  12 jahren :
  1. Dulder und renegaten.   **M 2068**
  2. Aus der emigration.   **M 2051**
  3. Væ victis !   **M 2062**
  4. Die opfer der partei.   **M 2058**
— Seltsame geschichten. Prag. 1859. D. **M 2060**
   Contents, see Deutscher katalog, p. 82.
— Die sirene ; erzählung. Berlin. *n. d.* S.
                              M 2061
— Væ victis ! Berlin. 1864. 2 v. S.   **M 2062**
— Zur ehre Gottes ; eine jesuiten - geschichte.
  Leipz. 1860. 2 v. S.   **M 2063**
Meister, F: Der stein des Tiberius ; novelle.
  With **Dahn, F:** J. F. Felicitas.   **D 104**
Mellin, Gustaf H: Die blume auf dem Kinne-
  kulle. Aus dem schwedischen. Stuttg.
  1845. T.   **M 2101**
— Der fremdling von Alsen ; erinnerungen vom
  kriegsschauplatz im jahre 1848. Aus dem
  schwedischen. Stuttg. 1850. T.   **M 2102**
— Eine novelle aus Lappland. Aus dem schwe-
  dischen von H. Helms. Leipz. 1856. S.
                              M 2103
— Die ungesehene gattin. Aus dem schwedischen. Stuttg. 1836. T.   **M 2104**
Melusine, *pseud.* Moy O'Brien. N. Y. 1879. Q.
                              M 2151
Melville, G: J: Whyte-. Black but comely, or
  The adventures of Jane Lee. Leipz. 1879.
  2 v. in 1. S.   **M 2201**
— The Brookes of Bridlemere. Leipz. 1864. 2
  v. in 1. S.   **M 2202**
— Cerise ; a tale of the last century. Lond.
  1866. S.   **M 2203**
— Der dolmetscher ; eine kriegsgeschichte. Aus
  dem englischen von M. Scott. Leipz. 1862.
  2 v. D.   **M 2204**
— Holmby House ; a tale of old Northhampton-
  shire. Leipz. 1860. 2 v. in 1. S.   **M 2205**
— Kate Coventry; an autobiography. Lond. *n. d.*
  S.   **M 2206**
— *Same, germ.* Kate Coventry. Aus dem eng-
  lischen von M. Scott. Leipz. 1863. D.
                              M 2206
— Katerfelto ; a story of Exmoor. Phila. *n. d.*
  D.   **M 2207**
— Die Marien der königin ; ein roman von Holy-
  rood. Aus dem englischen. Leipz. 1865.
  2 v. D.   **M 2208**
— Roy's wife. Leipz. 1878. 2 v. in 1. S. **M 2209**

      x denotes books specially adapted for children.

Melville, G: J: Whyte-.—*Continued.*
— Uncle John. Leipz. 1874. 2 v. in 1. S.
    M 2210
— The white rose. Leipz. 1868. 2 v. in 1. S.
    M 2211
Melville, Herman. The bell-tower. *In* Johnson, E. R. Little classics. **J 926 v3**
— Israel Potter; his fifty years of exile. 3d ed. N. Y. 1855. S. **M 2251**
— Mardi, and a voyage thither. N. Y. 1864. 2 v. D. **M 2257**
— Moby Dick, or The whale. *T. p. w.* D.
    M 2252
— The piazza tales. N. Y. 1856. D.   **M 2253**
  Contents. The piazza.—Bartleby.—Benito Cereno.—The lightning-rod man. — The Encantadas, or Enchanted islands.—The bell-tower.
— Pierre, or The ambiguities. N. Y. 1852. D.
    M 2254
— Typee ; a peep at polynesian life during a four months' residence in a valley of the Marquesas. Rev. ed., with a sequel. N. Y. 1857. D. **M 2255**
— White-Jacket, or The world in a man-of-war. N. Y. 1855. D. **M 2256**
Mendoza, *Don* Diego Hurtado de. The life and adventures of Lazarillo de Tormes. Tr. from the spanish by T: Roscoe. Ill. Lond. 1881. D. **M 2286**
Menger, Rudolph. Ein wahlcampagne; humoreske. *In* Vierteljährl. mag. **V 2 v33**
Mengersen auf Rheder, Joseph Bruno *graf* v., (*J. Bruno*). Irma und Nanka. Leipz. 1842. 2 v. O. **B 3701**
Meredith, G: Diana of the crossways ; a novel. N. Y. 1885. Q. **M 2302**
— The egoist ; a comedy in narrative. N. Y. 1879. Q. **M 2301**
— *Same.* Lond. 1879. 3 v. in 2. D. **M 2301**
Meredith, Owen, *pseud., see* Bulwer-Lytton, E: Robert.
Mérimée, Prosper. Colomba. Tr. from the french. Bost. 1846. D. **M 2351**
Merry Andrew. *T. p. w.* T. **Mx 35**
Mertens, Elisabeth. Zufall oder fügung ? novelle. *In* Vierteljährl. mag. **V 2 v33**
Merx, Eulalie Therese, *born* Hoche. Ein seelengemälde. Königsberg. 1855. 3 v. S.
    M 2401
Méry, Joseph Eugène. Blanka ; eine familiengeschichte. Aus dem franz. von E. O. Schmidt. Weimar. *n. d.* 2 v. S. **M 2451**
— Through thick and thin. Tr. by O. Vibeur. N. Y. 1874. D. **M 2452**
Meshtcherskii, Vladimir *kniaz.* Die realisten der grossen welt ; roman. Aus dem russischen übers. von F. Leoni. *In* Vierteljährl. mag. **V 2 v36**
Messenhauser, Cäsar Wenzel, (*Wenzeslaus March*). Polengräber. Leipz. 1848. S.
    M 1051
— Der rathsherr ; ein nationaler roman. Leipz. 1849. 4 v. S. **M 2501**
Messerer, Theodor. Der alte russländer ; erzählung aus den bayrischen bergen. *T. p. w.* O. **M 2551**
Messner, Josef. Handwerksburschen ; bilder aus dem volksleben. Prag. 1857. T.
    M 2601
— Margarethe Maultasch ; historische erzählung. Prag. 1855. T. **M 2602**
— Waldgeschichten. Prag. 1857. T. **M 2603**

Meyer, Bertha Antoinette Henriette, (*Bertha v. Werder*). Altes lieben, neues hoffen. Leipz. 1847. D. **W 1251**
Meyer, Conrad Ferdinand. Page Leubelfing ; historische novellen. *In* Vierteljährl. mag. **V 2 v29**
Michon, J: Hippolyte, *abbé.* (?) The confessor, (*Le confesseur*). Tr. from the french by J. H: Hager. [*Anon.*] N. Y. 1867. O.
    M 2626
— Under the ban, (Le maudit) ; a tale of the 19th century. N. Y. *n. d.* O. **M 2627**
Millenkovics, Stephan v., (*Stephan v. Milow*). Verlorenes glück ; eine erzählung. Heidelberg. 1866. D. **M 2651**
Miller, Annie, *born* Jenness. Barbara Thayer, her glorious career ; a novel. Bost. 1884. S. **M 2676**
Miller, Emily Huntington. The royal road to fortune. N. Y. *n. d.* S. **Mx 951**
Miller, Cincinnatus Hiner, *called* Joaquin. '49 ; the gold-seeker of the Sierras. N. Y. 1884. D. **M 2703**
— The one fair woman. N. Y. 1876. 3 v. in 1. D.
    M 2701
— Shadows of Shasta. Chicago. 1881. D.
    M 2702
Miller, Hugh. [Tales.] *In* Wilson, J: M. Tales of the borders. **W 2202**
  Contents. Bill Whyte, v. 5.—The lykewake, v. 7.
— Recollections of Burns, v. 2. — Recollections of Ferguson, v. 1.—The salmon fisher of Udoll, v. 4. — The scottish hunters of Hudson's Bay, v. 12. — Thomas of Chartres, v. 18.— Widow of Dunskaith, v. 3.
— Sandy Wood's sepulchre. *In* Johnson, E. R. Little classics. **J 926 v5**
Miller, Joaquin, *see* Miller, Cincinnatus Hiner.
Miller, J: Martin. Siegwart ; eine klostergeschichte. Stuttg. 1844. 3 v. T. **M 2726**
Millet, Frank Davis. "Yatil". *In* Stories by american authors. **S 35 v5**
Milman, E. H. Arthur Conway, or Scenes in the tropics. N. Y. 1859. O. **M 2751**
Milow, Stephan v., *pseud., see* Millenkovics, Stephan v.
Miltenberg, *pseud., see* Lafontaine, A: H: Julius.
Miniature romances from the german, with other prolusions of light literature. Bost. 1841. S. **M 2776**
  Contents. La Motte Fouqué, F: H: K: de. Undine; The vial-genie and mad farthing; The collierfamily, or Red Mantle and the merchant.—Table-talk notices of Phantasmion by Sara Coleridge, including Fortunes of fairy lore by W: Hauff.—The Almadora ravine.— Faithful or false. — The fortieth hour.— Werter's warning.—Maurice, or Away for St. Brandan's.—L'amore an italian trans. of Coleridge's Love.
Mirecourt, Eugène de, *pseud., see* Jacquot, C: J: Baptiste.
Misasi, Nicola. Kalabrische novellen. Uebers. und eingel. von Woldemar Kaden. Autorisierte ausg. Stuttg. [1884]. D. **M 2826**
  Contents. Brigantaggio.—Giovanni.—Cola der wolf. — Marco. — Andrea.— Bruder Thomas der eremit. — Neben dem herdfeuer.—Eine traurige erinnerung.— Die kartause von Serra S. Bruno.— Francesco der almosengänger.
Miss Toosey's mission. Bost. 1884. S. **M 33**
Mr. and mrs. Morton ; a novel. Bost. 1883. D. **M 31**
Mitchell, Bianca, *born* Cogswell. Rigdum Funnidos and Antonia. Milw. 1881. D.
    Mx 1001
Mitchell, Donald Grant, (*Ik Marvel*). A bachelor's revery. *In* Johnson, E. R. Little classics. **J 926 v4**

    x denotes books specially adapted for children.

Mitchell, Donald Grant, (*Ik Marvel*).—*Continued.*
— Doctor Johns ; a narrative of certain events
in the life of an orthodox minister of Con-
necticut. N. Y. 1866. 2 v. S.   **M 2851**
— Dream life ; a fable of the seasons. N. Y.
1868. D.   **M 2852**
— The lorgnette, or Studies of the town by an
opera goer ; v. 2. N. Y. 1853. D.   **M 2853**
— Reveries of a bachelor, or A book of the heart.
N. Y. 1861. S.   **M 2854**
— *Same.* New ed. N. Y. [1863]. D.   **M 2854**
— Seven stories with basement and attic. New
ed. N. Y. 1884 [1883]. D.   ·   **M 2855**
Mitchell, E: P. The ablest man in the world.
In **Stories** by american authors.   **S 35 v10**
— The tachypomp. *In* **Stories** by american
authors.   **S 35 v5**
Mitchell, S: Weir. A draft on the bank of Spain.
With his Hephzibah Guinness.   **M 2901**
— Hephzibah Guinness. Phila. 1880. D. **M 2901**
— In war time. Bost. 1885 [1884]. S.   **M 2902**
— Thee and you. *With his* Hephzibah Guinness.
M 2901
Mitford, A. Bertram. The forty-seven rōnins.
In Johnson, E. R. Little classics.
J 926 v11
Mitford, Mary Russell. The fresh-water fisher-
man. *In* **Edinburgh** tales.   **E 426**
— Our village. Ill. Lond. 1879. Q.   **M 2951P**
— *ed.* Stories of american life by american
writers. Lond. 1830. 3 v. D.   **M 2952**
Contents, v. **1.** Otter-bag, the Oneida chief.—The
french village.—The country cousin.—The sick man
cured.—Mr. de Villecour and his neighbours.—The
Esmeralda.—The tutor.—The indian hater. **2.** Pete
Featherston.—The drunkard.—The marriage blunder.
—A romance of the border.—The ghost.—The seaman's widow.—Unwritten philosophy.—Scenes in
Washington. **3.** The catholic Iroquois.—The pere-
grinations of Petrus Mudd.—Unwritten poetry.—The
captain's lady.—The Isle of Shoals.—The idle man.—
Cacothes scribendi. — The fawn's leap. — Reminis-
cences of New York.—The little dutch sentinel of
the Manhadoes.—The rifle.
— *See also her* Works.   **820.2 : 27**
Contents, see under English literature, Collected
works.
Moir, D: M. The divinity student *In* Wilson,
J: M. Tales of the borders.   **W 2202 v5**
Moldwarp, Nicholas, *pseud., see* **Manning,** Anne.
Molesworth, Mary Louisa, *born* Stewart, (*Ennis
Graham*). Miss Bouverie. N. Y. 1880. Q.
M 3001
— *Same.* Lond. 1880. 3 v. in 1. D.   **M 3001**
Möllhausen, Balduin. Engelid. *With* **Sydow,**
C. v. Spätsommer.   **S 6101**
— Der flüchtling ; erzählung aus Neu-Mexico und
dem angrenzenden Indianergebiet, in an-
schluss an den "Halbindianer." Leipz.
1862. 4 v. S.   **M 3051**
— Der halbindianer ; erzählung aus dem westli-
chen Nordamerika. Leipz. 1861. 4 v. S.
S 3052
— Der leuchtthurm am Michigan, und andere er-
zählungen ; mit einer einleitung von Th.
Fontane. Stuttg. 1882. D.   **M 3053**
Includes, Die auswanderin.— Das squatterindchen.
— Die mandanenwaise ; erzählung aus den Rhein-
landen und dem stromgebiet des Missouri.
Berlin, 1855. 4 v. S.   **M 3056**
— Der mayordomo ; erzählung aus dem südli-
chen Kalifornien und Mexico. Leipz. 1863.
4 v. D.   **M 3053**
— Das mormonenmädchen ; eine erzählung aus
der zeit des kriegszuges der Vereinigten
Staaten gegen die "Heiligen der letzten

Möllhausen, Balduin.—*Continued.*
tage" im jahre 1857-1858. Jena. 1871. 6 v.
in 1. S.   **M 3054**
— Der piratenlieutenant. Berlin. 1870. 4 v. in 2.
D.   **M 3057**
— Reliquien ; erzählungen und schilderungen
aus dem westlichen Nordamerika. Berlin.
1865. 3 v. S.   **M 3055**
— Wildes blut ; erzählung in 2 abth. *In* Vierteljährl. mag.   **V 2 v38**
Contents Abth. **1.** Die braut des schleichhändlers.
2. Dame Freiheit.
Molloy, Joseph Fitzgerald. What hast thou
done ? a novel. N. Y. 1883. Q.   **M 3076**
— *Same.* Lond. 1883. D.   **M 3076**
Moncrieff, Robert Hope, (*Ascott R. Hope.*) Home-
spun stories. N. Y. 1883. S.   **Mx 828**
Contents Introd. — Spinning a story. — Playing the
fool.—My desert island. — The black book. — Crossing
the line. — Caught out. — A scene from history. — The
Guisards.—The secret history. — The secret society.—
At the masthead.—A night in the Black Forest.—Baby
boy.—The banshee.
— The pampas ; a story of adventure in the Ar-
gentine Republic. Ill. Lond. 1878. D.
Mx 827
— Spindle stories ; new yarns spun from old
wool. Ill. Lond. 1880. D.   **Mx 826**
Contents. Four-and-twenty blackbirds. — Humpty-
Dumpty.—Jack and Gill. — Fighting for the crown. —
Baby Bunting.—Boy Blue. — The mouse in the clock.
Monkland, *Mrs.*—. The nabob at home, or the
return to England. N. Y. 1864. O.
M 3101
Montanus, Theodor. König Ottokar der stolze,
oder Der böhmer kreuzzug im Preussen-
lande ; historisches gemälde der vorzeit.
Meissen. 1830. S.   **M 3151**
Montgomery, Florence. Misunderstood. N. Y.
n. d. S.   **M 3201**
— Thwarted, or Duck's eggs in a hen's nest ; a
story. Phila. 1874. D.   **M 3202**
Montgomery, G: Washington. Bernardo del
Carpio ; an historical novel of the 8th cen-
tury. From the spanish of don Jorge
Montgomery. N. Y. 1884. D.   **M 3251**
Monti, L:, (*Samuel Sampleton*). Adventures of
an american consul abroad, by S: Sample-
ton. Bost. 1878. S.   **M 3301**
— Leone. (Round-robin ser). Bost. 1882. S.
M 3302
Montolieu, Jeanne Isabelle Pauline Polier de
Bottens, *dame* de Crousaz, *baronne* de, *joint
author, see* **Wyss,** J: Rudolph.
Moore, Frank Frankfort. Daireen ; a novel. N.
Y. 1880. Q.   **M 3351**
— *Same.* Lond. 1879. 2 v. in 1. D.   **M 3351**
Moore, T: The epicurean. New ed. rev. and
corr. by the author, with notes. N. Y. 1854.
S.   **M 3401**
More, Hannah. Cœlebs in search of a wife.
N. Y. 1861. D.   **M 3501**
— *Same.* N. Y. 1857. D.   **M 3501**
— Domestic tales and allegories illustrating hu-
man life. N. Y. 1862. S.   **Mx 851**
Contents. The shepherd of Salisbury Plain.—Mr.
Fantom.—The two shoemakers.—Giles the poacher.
—The servant turned soldier.—The general jail de-
livery.
— Rural tales. *T. p. w.* S.   **Mx 852**
Contents. The two wealthy farmers. or The his-
tory of Mr. Bragwell.—Parley the porter.—All for
the best.—Tom White, the post boy.—The pilgrims.—
The valley of tears.—The strait gate and the broad
way.

More, Hannah.—*Continued.*
— 'Tis all for the best, The shepherd of Salisbury Plain, and other narratives. Lond. 1861. T.   **Mx 853**
  Contents. Brief sketch of the life of mrs. Hannah More.—'Tis all for the best.—The shepherd of Salisbury Plain.—Parley the porter.—The happy waterman.—History of Mary Wood.—The good mother's legacy.—Honest miller of Gloucestershire.—Turn the carpet.
— *See also her* Works.   **820.2 : 28**
  Contents, see under English literature, Collected works.
Morgan, N. D. George Cardwell, or A month in a country parish. N. Y. 1856. D.
                                                    M 3551
Morgan, *Lady* Sydney, *born* Owenson. Die prinzessin, oder Die beguine. Aus dem englischen von P. Helling. Aachen. 1835. 3 v. S.   **M 3601**
Morgan, *Sir* T: C. *and lady* Sydney. The book without a name. N. Y. 1841. 2 v. D.
                                                    M 3626
Morier, James. The adventures of Hajji Baba in Turkey, Persia and Russia. Phila. 1855. D.   **M 3651**
— Zohrab, the hostage. *T. p. w.* S.   **M 3652**
Mörike, E: Maler Nolten. Stuttg. *n. d.* 2 v. S.
                                                    M 3701
Morley, H: Oberon's horn ; a book of fairy tales. 4th ed., ill. Lond. 1881. D.
                                                    Mx 876
Morley, Susan. Aileen Ferrers. N. Y. 1875. O.
                                                    M 3751
— Margaret Chetwynd. Phila. 1878. D.   **M 3752**
— Throstlethwaite. Phila. 1876. D.   **M 3753**
Morning, Richard, *pseud., see* Zeising, Adolf.
Morse, Clara Frances. Blush roses. N. Y. 1878. O.   **M 3801**
Morshead, A. E. Mary, *joint author, see* Awdry, Frances.
Mortimer, *Sir* Henry, *pseud., see* Gardonnière, Almire.
Morvell, Dr., *pseud., see* Vollmer, W: F. A.
Mosen, Julius, *and* J: L: **Tieck.** Stories translated from the german by G. F. Crossthwaite. Lond. 1842. D.   **M 3951**
  Contents. **Mosen, J.** Ishmael; The italian novel; Helena Valisneria; The picture of the mermaid.—**Tieck, J: L:** Precipitation.
Moser, O: Komische bilder aus dem soldatenleben. Leipz. 1851. S.   **M 4001**
Motley, J: Lothrop. Merry-mount ; a romance of the Massachusetts colony. Bost. 1849. 2 v. D.   **M 4051**
— Morton's hope ; or The memoirs of a provincial. N. Y. 1838. 2 v. D.   **M 4052**
Moulton, Ellen Louise, *born* Chandler. Bedtime stories. *T. p. w.* S.   **Mx 901**
  Contents. Margaret's necklace.—How the girls got rid of Freddy.—Coals of fire.—What Jess Cortrell did.—Sir Harry.—Paying off Jane.—A child's tragedy.—The little mother.—The light in the window.—Mr. Turk and what became of him.—Just a little bit of christmas.—Benjie.—A child's good work.—What Biddie did.—Jamie Leech's angel.—Maud Granger's new dress.
— Firelight stories. Ill. Bost. 1883. S.   **Mx 904**
  Contents. Sol Jones's orphans.—The silver locket.—The bargee's Johnny.—Solomon Girder's customers.—Jenny's baby.— Roger Faithful's invention.—The mortgage on Inglenook.—Edith Bowles's new life.—How Ruth came home. Sister Lucy.—Jenny's valentine.
— More bed-time stories. Ill. Bost. 1878. S.
                                                    Mx 902
  Contents. Against wind and tide.— Blue sky and white clouds.— The cousin from Boston.— Missy.—

Moulton, Ellen Louise.—*Continued.*
  The head boy of Eaglesheight school. — Agatha's lonely days.—Thin ice.—My lost sister.—What came to Olive Haygarth.—Uncle Jack.—Nobody's child.—My little gentleman. — Ruthy's country.—Job Golding's christmas.—My comforter.
— My third book ; a collection of tales. N. Y. 1859. D.   **M 4101**
  Contents. The pride of Moses Grant.— How one woman came to marry. — The tenant of the old brown house.—Uncle Roger's story and mine.—The mist over the valley.—Joseph Thorne, his calling.—Olive Winchester Wight.—My inheritance.—Number 101. — Leona ; a blind man's story.— The mountain road.—The story of a man of business.—The cottage on the hill. —Joanna the actress.—The record of a troubled life.—Four letters from Helen Hamilton.— The phantom face.
— New bed-time stories. Ill. Bost. 1880. S.
                                                    Mx 903
  Contents. "All a-growin' and a-blowin'".—My vagrant.—Helen's temptation.—The surgeon of the doll's hospital.—Pretty miss Kate.—A borrowed rosebud.—Tom's thanksgiving.— Finding Jack.—Her mother's daughter.—My quarrel with Ruth.—Was it her mother ? — The lady from over the way.— His mother's boy.—Dr. Joe's valentine.
— Some women's hearts. Bost. 1874. S. **M 4102**
  Contents. Fleeing from fate. — Brains. — Twelve years of my life.—Little Gibraltar.—Household gods.—The judge's wife.—A letter and what came of it.— Out of Nazareth.
Mountford, W: Thorpe, a quiet english town, and life therein. Bost. 1852. D.   **M 4151**
Mudford, W: First and last. *In* Tales from Blackwood.   **T 176 v4**
— The iron shroud. *In* Johnson, E: R. Little classics.   **J 926 v3**
— *Same. In* Tales from Blackwood.   **T 176 v1**
— *Same. In* Sargent, E. The emerald.   **S 551**
Mügge, Theodor. Afraja ; roman. Frankfurt a. M. 1857. D.   **M 4201**
— *Same, eng.* Afraja, a norwegian and lapland tale, or Life and love in Norway. Tr. from the german by E. Joy Morris. Phila. 1855. D.   **M 4201**
— Alte und neue welt. *Together with* Drei freunde.   **M 4205**
— Am Marlanger Fjord. *With* Behrens, B. Im banne der musen.   **H 2278**
— Arvor Spang. *T. p. w.* 2 v. D.   **M 4202**
— Cosimo Vinci ; historische erzählung. Breslau. 1862. D.   **M 4302**
— Der doppelgänger. Berlin. 1857. D.   **M 4205**
— Drei freunde. Breslau. 1862. D.   **M 4205**
— Erich Randal ; historischer roman aus der zeit der eroberung Finnlands durch die russen im jahre 1808. Frankfurt a. M. 1856. D.
                                                    M 4206
— Leben und lieben in Norwegen ; vier novellen aus dem norwegischen volksleben. Frankfurt a. M. 1858. 2 v. D.   **M 4207**
  Contents, see Deutscher katalog, p. 83.
— Neues leben. Prag. 1856. T.   **M 4208**
— Der pfarrer vom see ; eine lebensgeschichte. Berlin. 1858. D.   **M 4209**
— Der prophet ; historischer roman aus dem bauernkriege. Leipz. 1861. 3 v. D.
                                                    M 4210
— Der propst von Ulensvang, — Vater und sohn ; zwei erzählungen. Breslau. 1862. D.
                                                    M 4211
— Romana ; historische erzählung. Breslau. 1862. D.   **M 4212**
— Vater und sohn. *With* Der propst. *In* **M 4211**
— Verloren und gefunden. Frankfurt a. M. 1859. v. in 1. O.   **M 4213**
— Der voigt von Silt. Berlin. 1858. T.   **M 4214**

Mühlbach, Louise, *pseud.*, *see* Mundt, Clara.
Mühlfeld, Julius, *pseud.*, *see* Rösler, Robert.
Muir, Allan. Lady Beauty, or Charming to her latest day. N. Y. 1882. S. **M 4226**
Muirhead, Findley. Two plots. *In* Tales from many sources. **T 178 v4**
Müller, Adolf, (*Adolf Palm*). Im labyrinth der seele ; zwei novellen. Leipz. 1872. S. **M 4251**
Müller, F: Max. Deutsche liebe ; aus den papieren eines fremdlings herausg., mit einem vorwort begleitet von Max Müller. 5te aufl. Leipz. 1877. O. **M 4351**
— *Same.* With Storm, H. T. W. Hans und Heinz Kirch. **S 5603**
— *Same, eng.* Memories ; a story of german love. Tr. from the german by G: P. Upton. Chicago. 1875. D. **M 4351**
Müller, K:, (*Otfried Mylius, Franz v. Elling*). Am hofe der nordischen Semiramis ; historischer roman. Hannover. 1873. 2 v. in 1. D. **M 4301**
— Drei sinnige erzählungen für alles volk und alle zeit. Stuttg. 1861. S. **M 4302**
   Contents, see Deutscher katalog, p. 84.
— Die frau ökonomierath ; eine geschichte. *With* Müller *von Königswinter*, W. Furioso. **M 4452**
— Die geheimnisse der Bastille; historisch-biographische bilder aus der vergangenheit. Stuttg. 1865. 2 v. S. **M 4303**
— Ein meteor der börse. Leipz. 1872. 3 v. S. **M 4304**
— Die weisse frau ; eine hof- und familiengeschichte aus dem achtzehnten jahrhundert. Milw. 1865. O. **M 4305**
Müller, O: Andrea del Castagno ; erzählungen und charakterbilder. Berlin. 1865. S. **M 4401**
— Aus Petrarca's alten tagen. Berlin. 1862. 2 v. S. **M 4402**
— Charlotte Ackermann; ein Hamburger theaterroman aus dem vorigen jahrhundert. Frankfurt a. M. 1854. D. **M 4403**
— Ekhof und seine schüler. Leipz. 1863. 2 v. S. **M 4404**
— Erzählungen und charakterbilder, v. 3: Der museumsweiler.—Der delikatessenhändler. Berlin. 1865. S. **M 4412**
— Die förstersbraut von Neunkirchen ; erzählung. Stuttg. 1867. D. **M 4405**
— Georg Volker ; ein roman aus dem jahre 1848. Bremen. 1851. 3 v. D. **M 4406**
— Der klosterhof ; ein familienroman. Frankfurt a. M. 1859. 3 v. D. **M 4408**
— Die liebe im grabe. Berlin. 1865. D. **M 4407**
— Der tannenschütz ; weihnachts - novelle für 1851. Bremen. 1852. T. **M 4409**
— Der wildpfarrer ; historischer roman. Berlin. 1866. 3 v. S. **M 4410**
— Die zwei krüglein ; eine erzählung. Braunschweig. 1868. S. **M 4411**
Müller, W: Debora. N. Y. 1884. F. **M 4436**
Müller *von Königswinter*, Wolfgang. Furioso ; novelle. Milw. 1862. O. **M 4452**
— Zum stillen vergnügen ; künstlergeschichten. Leipz. 1865. 2 v. in 1. D. **M 4451**
   Contents, see Deutscher katalog, p. 84.
Mulock, Dinah Maria, *see* Craik, Dinah Maria.
Mund, E. D., *pseud.*, *see* Pechhammer, E.
Mundt, Clara, *born* Müller, (*Louise Mühlbach*).
Der alte Fritz und die neue zeit ; historischer roman. Jena. 1867. 4 v. S. **M 4551**

Mundt, Clara, (*Louise Mühlbach*).—*Continued.*
— *Same, eng.* Old Fritz and the new era. Tr. from the german by P: Langley. Ill. N. Y. 1868. O. **M 4551**
— Andreas Hofer ; an historical novel. N. Y. 1868. O. **M 4552**
— Antonio. Altona. 1860. T. **M 4553**
— Berlin und Sans-Souci ; historischer roman. Leipz. 1858. 2 v. S. **M 4554**
— *Same, eng.* Berlin and Sans-Souci, or Frederick the great and his friends. Tr. from the german by mrs. Chapman Coleman and her daughters. Ill. N. Y. 1879. O. **M 4554**
— Bonners, oder Geschichte eines millionairs. Altona. 1860. 3 v. T. **M 4555**
— *Same, eng.* The story of a millionaire. Tr. from the german by Nathaniel Greene. N. Y. 1872. D. **M 4555**
— The daughter of an empress. Tr. from the german by Nathaniel Greene. N. Y. 1879. O. **M 4556**
— Deutschland gegen Frankreich ; historischer roman. Jena. 1868. 4 v. S. **M 4557**
— Deutschland in sturm und drang:
   1. Der alte Fritz und die neue zeit. **M 4551**
   2. Fürsten und dichter. **M 4566**
   3. Deutschland gegen Frankreich. **M 4557**
   4. Frankreich gegen Deutschland. **M 4562**
— The empress Josephine. *T. p. w.* **M 4558**
— Erzherzog Johann und der herzog von Reichstadt. Berlin. 1862. 3 v. S. **M 4559**
— Erzherzog Johann und Metternich. Berlin. 1860. 3 v. S. **M 4560**
— Frankreich gegen Deutschland ; historischer roman. Jena. 1868. 5 v. S. **M 4562**
— Franz Rákóczy ; ungarisches lebensbild. Wien. 1861. 2 v. T. **M 4563**
— Frau meisterin. Berlin. 1859. 2 v. T. **M 4564**
— Friedrich der grosse und seine geschwister. Berlin. 1859. 4 v. S. **M 4565**
— *Same, eng.* Frederick the great and his family ; an historical novel. Tr. from the german by mrs. Chapman Coleman and her daughters. N. Y. 1878. O. **M 4565**
— Fürsten und dichter ; historischer roman. Jena. 1867. 4 v. S. **M 4566**
— Goethe and Schiller. Tr. from the german by Chapman Coleman. N. Y. 1869. O. **M 4567**
— Graf von Benjowsky ; historischer roman. Jena. 1865. 4 v. S. **M 4568**
— Der grosse kurfürst und seine kinder. Jena. 1866. 4 v. S. **M 4569**
— Der grosse kurfürst und seine zeit:
   1. Der junge kurfürst. **M 4572**
   2. Der grosse kurfürst und sein volk. **M 4570**
   3. Der grosse kurfürst und seine kinder. **M 4569**
— Der grosse kurfürst und sein volk ; historischer roman. Jena. 1865. 4 v. S. **M 4570**
— Henry VIII. *See below* König Heinrich VIII.
— Joseph II and his court. N. Y. 1876. O. **M 4571**
— Der junge kurfürst. Jena. 1865. 3. v. S. **M 4572**
— Kaiserin Claudia, prinzessin von Tirol ; historischer roman. Leipz. 1867. 3 v. S. **M 4573**
— Karl II und sein hof ; historischer roman. Berlin. 1859. 3 v. T. **M 4574**

x denotes books specially adapted for children.

Mundt, Clara, (*Louise Mühlbach*).—*Continued*.
— König Heinrich VIII und sein hof, oder Katharina Parr ; historischer roman. Berlin. 1858. 3 v. T.   **M 4575**
— *Same, eng.* Henry VIII and his court. *T. p. w.*   **M 4575**
— Louisa of Prussia and her times ; an historical novel. Tr. from the german by F. Jordan. Ill. N. Y. 1877. O.   **M 4576**
— Maria Theresia und der pandurenobrist Trenck ; historischer roman. Brünn. 1862. 4 v. S.   **M 4578**
— Marie Antoinette und ihr sohn ; historischer roman. Jena. 1867. 6 v. D.   **M 4577**
— The merchant of Berlin. *T. p. w.* D.   **M 4579**
— Mohammed Ali and his house ; an historical romance. Tr. from the german by Chapman Coleman. Ill. N. Y. 1872. O.   **M 4580**
— Napoleon und königin Louise. Berlin. 1860. 4 v. S.   **M 4581**
— *Same, eng.* Napoleon and the queen of Prussia. N. Y. 1868. O.   **M 4581**
— Napoleon und fürst Blücher. Berlin. 1860. 4 v. S.   **M 4582**
— *Same, eng.* Napoleon and Blücher ; an historical novel. Tr. from the german by F. Jordan. Ill. N. Y. 1876. O.   **M 4582**
— Napoleon und der Wiener congress. 2te aufl. Berlin. 1861. S.   **M 4583**
— Old Fritz, *see above* Der alte Fritz.
— Prinz Eugen und seine zeit.   **M 4584**
  1. Prinz Eugen, der kleine abbé. Berlin. 1864. 4 v. S.   **M 4584 v1-4**
  2. Prinz Eugen, der edle ritter. Berlin. 1864. 4 v. S.   **M 4584 v5-8**
— *Same, eng.* Prince Eugene and his times. Tr. by A. De V. Chaudron. N. Y. 1877. O.   **M 4584**
— Queen Hortense, a life picture of the napoleonic era ; an historical novel. Tr. from the german by Chapman Coleman. N. Y. 1878. O.   **M 4585**
— The story of a millionaire. *See above* Bonners.
— Zwei lebenswege. Altona. 1860. 3 v. T.   **M 4586**
Mundt, Theodor. Cimaletti ; protestantische bilder aus Böhmen. Leipz. 1847. S.   **M 4651**
— Count Mirabeau. *See below* Graf Mirabeau.
— Czar Paul.   **M 4652**
  1. Der grossfürst. Berlin. 1861. 3 v. in 1. D.   **M 4652 v1-3**
  2. Czar Paul und sein volk. Berlin. 1861. 3 v. D.   **M 4652 v4-6**
— Ein deutscher herzog. Leipz. 1855. D.   **M 4653**
— Ein französisches landschloss. Prag. 1855. T.   **M 4654**
— Graf Mirabeau. Berlin. 1860. 4 v. S.   **M 4655**
— *Same, eng.* Count Mirabeau ; an historical novel. Tr. from the german by Thérèse J. Radford. Ill. N. Y. 1868. O.   **M 4655**
— Kleine romane. Berlin. 1857. 2 v. D.   **M 4656**
  Contents, see Deutscher katalog, p. 85.
— Madonna ; unterhaltungen mit einer heiligen. Leipz. 1835. S.   **M 4657**
— Moderne lebenswirren ; briefe und zeitabenteure eines salzschreibers. Leipz. 1834. S.   **M 4658**
— *Same.* Leipz. 1847. S.   **M 4658**
— Robespierre. Milw. 1859. S.   **M 4659**

Munter, Jeremias, *pseud., see* Fornell, Bror E:
Murdoch, D: The dutch dominie of the Catskills, or The times of " Bloody Brandt." N. Y. 1861. D.   **M 4751**
Murfree, Mary Noailles, (*Charles Egbert Craddock*). Down the ravine. Ill. Bost. 1885. S.   **Mx 1051**
— In the Tennessee mountains. Bost. 1884. D.   **M 4776**
  Contents. Drifting down Lost Creek.—A-playin' of old sledge at the settlement.—The star in the valley.—Electioneerin' an Big Injun mounting.—The romanne of Sunrise rock.—The dancin' party at Harrison's Cove.—Over on the other mounting.—The " harnt " that walks Chilhowee.
— Where the battle was fought. Bost. 1884. D.   **M 4777**
Murger, H: Adeline Protat. Aus dem franz. von C. Büchele. Stuttg. 1854. T.   **M 4801**
Murray, C: A: Prärievogel. Uebers. aus dem englischen. Stuttg. 1847. 3 v. T.   **M 4851**
Murray, D: Christie. By the gate of the sea. N. Y. 1883. D.   **M 4879**
— *Same.* N. Y. 1883. Q.   **M 4879**
— Hearts ; a novel. N. Y. 1883. Q.   **M 4880**
— Joseph's coat. N. Y. 1881. S.   **M 4877**
— A life's atonement. N. Y. 1881. Q.   **M 4876**
— Val Strange ; a story of the primrose way. N. Y. 1882. Q.   **M 4878**
— The way of the world ; a novel. N. Y. 1884. Q.   **M 4881**
Murray, Eustace Clare Grenville, (*Trois Etoiles*). Strange tales. Leipz. 1878. S.   **M 4902**
— That artful vicar ; the story of what a clergyman tried to do for others and did for himself. Leipz. 1879. 2 v. in 1. S.   **M 4903**
— *Same.* Lond. 1879. 2 v. in 1. D.   **M 4903**
— Young Brown. Ill. Bost. 1874. O.   **M 4904**
Musäus, J: K: A: Deutsche volksmärchen. Hildburgh. 1842. 3 v. T.   **M 4951**
— *Same.* Volksmärchen der deutschen ; mit einer einleitung und anmerkungen herausg. von Moritz Müller. Leipz. 1868. 3 v. in 1. D.   **M 4951**
  Contents. V. 1. Müller, M., J: K: A: Musäus.—Vorbericht an herrn D: Runkel.—Die bücher der chronika der drei schwestern.—Richilde.—Roland's knappen.—Legenden von Rübezahl.—Die entführung. 2. Die nymphe des brunnens.—Libussa.—Der geraubte schleier.—Stumme liebe. 3. Liebestreue.—Ulrich mit dem bühel.—Dämon Amor.—Melichsala.—Der schatzgräber.
— Dumb love. *In* **Hedge**, F: H: Prose writers of Germany.   **830.1 : 8**
— *Same.* The dumb lover. *In* **Roscoe**, T: German novelists.   **R 2451**
— Libussa. *In* **Oxenford**, J: Tales from the german.   **O 1001**
— The spectre barber. *In* **Popular** tales and romances.   **P 2126 v2**
— The treasure-seeker. *In the same.*   **P 2126 v1**
Musset, Paul Edme de. The wind-spirit and rain-goddess. Tr. from the german [adaptation] of M. Schlimpert. Ill. Bost. 1858. T.   **Mx 1101**
Mützelburg, Adolf. Das attentat ; historische novelle aus der geschichte Portugals. Berlin. 1865. T.   **M 5001**
— Hennig Brabant ; historische novelle aus der stadt Braunschweig. Berlin. 1865. 2 v. T.   **M 5002**
— Die intriganten ; historischer roman aus der zeit der ersten französischen revolution. Berlin. 1867. 5 v. S.   **M 5003**

x denotes books specially adapted for children.

Mützelburg, Adolf.—*Continued.*
— Der konak; eine episode aus dem Kaukasus. Aus den papieren eines amerikaners. Berlin. 1865. T.   **M 5004**
— Luigia Sanfelice.   *T. p. w.* T.   **M 5005**
— Der orang-utang; eine reise-erinnerung. Aus den papieren eines amerikaners. Berlin. 1865. 4 v. T.   **M 5006**
— Robert Clive, der eroberer von Bengalen; historischer roman. Leipz. 1868. 2 v. S.
                                       M 5007
— Das schloss an der Ostsee.   *T. p. w.* S.
                                       M 5008
— Der sohn des kaisers; historische novelle aus der zeit des deutschen bauernkrieges. 2te aufl. Berlin. 1865. 4 v. T.   **M 5009**
My marriage. Bost. 1880. S.   **M 91**
My trivial life and its misfortunes; a gossip with no plot in particular by a plain woman. N. Y. 1883. 2 v. S.   **M 92**
  Contents. V. 1. Spinsterhood. 2. Meum and tuum.
My wife and my wife's sister. (No name ser.) Bost. 1881. S.   **M 90**
Mylius, Otfried, *pseud., see* **Müller,** K:
Mysteries of Heron Dyke, The; a novel of incident by the author of "In the dead of night", "Brought to light," etc. N. Y. 1881. Q.   **M 95**

Nachlese in und ausser mir aus den papieren des verfassers der Selbstbekenntnisse, oder Vierzig jahre aus dem leben eines oftgenannten arztes. Leipz. 1856. 4 v. S.   **N 1**
  Contents, see Deutscher katalog, p. 85.
Nares, E: Thinks - I - to - myself; a serio-ludicro, tragico-comico tale, written by Thinks - I - to - myself who. Phila. 1869. 2 v. 1. S.
                                       Nx 151
Näs, Abraham *and* Josef. Unterhaltungen für die reifere jugend; zweiter jahrgang. St. Gallen. 1842. D.   **N 1051**
Nature's nobleman, by the author of Rachel's secret. N. Y. 1869. O.   **N 5**
Natürliche tochter, Die. Hamburger novelle. Hamburg. 1862. S.   **H 4**
Naubert, Christiane Benedicte Eugenie, *born* Hebenstreit. Volksmärchen der deutschen. 2te aufl. Leipz. 1839. 3 v. S.   **N 101**
Neal, Alice B., *see* **Haven,** Alice.
Neal, J: Goody gracious! and the forget-me-not. *In* Johnson, E. R. Little classics.
                                       J 926 v10
— *Same. In* Sargent, E. The emerald. **S 551**
Neaves, C: *lord.* How to make a pedigree. *In* Tales from Blackwood.   **T 177 v2**
Needell, *Mrs.* J: H. Lucia, Hugh and another; a novel. N. Y. 1884. Q.   **N 176**
Nelk, Theophilus, *pseud., see* **Waibel,** Aloys Adalbert.
Nelly, St., *pseud., see* **Stricker,** Karoline.
Nelson, H: Loomis. John Rantoul. Bost. 1885. [1884]. D.   **N 1101**
Nemmersdorf, Franz v., *pseud., see* **Reitzenstein,** Franziska *freifrau* v.
Neumeister, Theodor. Herzog Hans von Sagan, oder Der hungerthurm zu Priebus; historische original-erzählung. Neusalza. 1857. 4 v. D.   **N 201**
— Verbrechen und strafe, oder So wie die that, so auch der lohn. Pirna. *n. d.* O. **N 202**
Newby, Emma, *mrs.* C. J. Common sense; a novel. Leipz. 1866. 2 v. in 1. S. **N 226**

Newell, C: M. Kaméhaméha, the conquering king; the mystery of his birth, loves and conquests; a romance of Hawaii. Ill. N. Y. 1885. D.   **N 236**
Newell, Robert H:, (*Orpheus C. Kerr*). There was once a man; a story. N. Y. 1884. D.
                                       N 252
— The walking doll, or The asters and disasters of society. N. Y. 1872. D.   **N 251**
Newman, J: H: Callista; a sketch of the 3d century. N. Y. 1859. D.   **N 301**
— Loss and gain, or The story of a convert. Bost. 1855. D.   **N 302**
Newman, *Mrs.* M. W. Jean. N. Y. 1875. O.
                                       N 351
— *Same.* Lond. 1875. D.   **N 351**
— With costs. N. Y. 1881. Q.   **N 352**
— *Same*; a novel. Lond. 1881. 3 v. in 1. D.
                                       N 352
Newton, W: Wilberforce. The priest and the man, or Abelard and Heloisa; a novel. [*Anon.*] Bost. 1883. S.   **N 376**
Nicander, K: A: The renounced treasure. *In* Edinburgh tales.   **E 426**
Nicholls, Charlotte, *born* Brontë, (*Currer Bell*). Jane Eyre; an autobiography. Leipz. 1850. 2 v. in 1. S.   **N 401**
— *Same.* Phila. *n. d.* D.   **N 401**
— *Same, germ.* Aus dem englischen von dr. Grieb. Stuttg. 1850. 2 v. T.   **N 401**
— The professor. Leipz. 1857. S.   **N 402**
— *Same*; a novel. N. Y. 1885. Q.   **N 402**
— Shirley. Leipz. 1849. 2 v. in 1. S. **N 403**
— *Same.* Phila. *n. d.* D.   **N 403**
— *Same, germ.* Aus dem englischen von dr. Grieb. Stuttg. 1851. 2 v. T.   **N 403**
— Villette. Leipz. 1853. 2 v. in 1. S. **N 404**
— *Same, germ.* Aus dem englischen von dr. Grieb. Stuttg. 1853. 2 v. T.   **N 404**
Nicholson, Joseph J. The Blemmertons, or Dottings by the wayside. N. Y. 1856. D.
                                       N 501
Nicolay, *pseud., see* **Scharling,** K: H:
Niemann, A: Bakchen und thyrsosträger; roman. N. Y. 1883. F.   **N 551**
Nieritz, K: Gustav. The young recruit, or The adventures of a drummer boy; a story of the russian campaign. Bost. 1866. S.
                                       Nx 201
Nietschmann, Hermann, (*Armin Stein*). Count Erbach; a story of the reformation. From the german by James I. Helm. N. Y. [1882]. D.   **N 576**
Noble, Annette Lucille. Eunice Lathrop, spinster. N. Y. 1882. S.   **N 602**
— Uncle Jack's executors. N. Y. 1880. S. **N 601**
Noble, Lucretia. A reverend idol; a novel. [*Anon.*] Bost. 1882. D.   **N 626**
Noé, H: A: Der zauberer des hochgebirges; erzählung. Berlin. 1874. D.   **N 651**
Noel, *Lady* Augusta, *born* Keppel. From generation to generation; a novel. N. Y. 1880. Q.   **N 701**
— *Same.* New ed. Lond. 1880. D.   **N 701**
Norden, Marie, *pseud., see* **Wolfhagen,** Friederike.
Nordhoff, C: Cape Cod and all along shore. N. Y. 1880. Q.   **N 801**
  Contents. Captain Tom; a resurrection.—What is best?—A struggle for life.—Elkanah Brewster's temptation.—One pair of blue eyes.—Mehetable Rogers's cranberry swamp.—Maud Elbert's love-match.

x denotes books specially adapted for children.

Nordhoff, C:—*Continued.*
— Elkanah Brewster's temptation. *In* Atlantic tales.   **A 1876**
— Man-of-war life ; a boy's experience in the U. S. navy during a voyage around the world in a ship of the line. Ill. N. Y. *n. d.* D.   **Nx 251**
— *Same. T. p. w.* S.   **Nx 251**
— The merchant vessel ; a sailor boy's voyages to see the world. Ill. N. Y. *n. d.* S.   **Nx 252**
— Stories of the island world. N. Y. 1857. S.   **Nx 254**
— Whaling and fishing. Ill. N. Y. *n. d.* S.   **Nx 253**
Normand, Hugh de. The brigand captive, or The gipsy queen. Auburn. [1854]. S.   **N 851**
Norris, W: E. Adrian Vidal ; a novel. Ill. N. Y. 1885. Q.   **N 908**
— Heaps of money ; a novel. N. Y. 1882. S.   **N 903**
— The hermit of Saint Eugène. *In* Tales from many sources.   **T 178 v1**
— Mademoiselle de Mersac. N. Y. 1880. Q.   **N 901**
— A man of his word, and other stories. N. Y. 1885, Q.   **N 906**
Includes, La bella sorrentina.—The man with the red hair.—Nils Jensen.—The princess Paolini.—Count Waldemar.—The count Adelcrantz.—Miss Van Steen. —The old woman of the sea.
— Matrimony. (Leisure hour ser.) N. Y. 1881. S.   **N 902**
— *Same.* N. Y. 1884. Q.   **N 902**
— No new thing ; a novel. (Leisure hour ser.) N. Y. 1883. S.   **N 904**
— *Same.* N. Y. 1883. Q.   **N 904**
— That terrible man ; a novel. N. Y. 1885. S.   **N 907**
— Thirlby Hall ; a novel. Ill. N. Y. 1884. Q.   **N 905**
North, Christopher, *pseud., see* **Wilson,** J:
Norton, Caroline Elizabeth Sarah, *see* **Stirling-Maxwell,** C. E. S.
Norton, J: N. Rockford parish, or The fortunes of Mr. Mason's successors. N. Y. 1856. D.   **N 951**
Norton Hargrave, and other sketches ; the second series of Shades of character by the author of Charlie Burton, etc. N. Y. 1851. S.   **Nx 61**
Notley, Frances Eliza Millet, *born* Thomas. Love's crosses. N. Y. 1878. Q.   **N 1001**
— *Same;* a novel. Lond. 1878. 3 v. in 1. D.   **N 1001**
— Mildred's wedding. *T. p. w.* O.   **N 1002**
— Olive Varcoe. Bost. *n. d.* O.   **N 1003**
— Red Riding-Hood ; a novel. N. Y. 1884. Q.   **N 1005**
— *Same.* Lond. 1883. 3 v. in 1. D.   **N 1005**
— Time shall try. N. Y. 1878. Q.   **N 1004**
Novellen - kranz, gewunden aus den schönsten blüthen der schön-wissenschaftlichen literatur des in und auslandes. Schwäb. Hall. *n. d.* D.   **N 1051**
Contents, see Deutscher katalog, p. 86.
Nursery governess, The, by the author of "The week." Lond. 1845. T.   **Nx 91**
Nyblom, Helène, *born* Roed, (*H.*). Novellen. Aus dem schwedischen übers. von I. Lorenzen. Bremen. 1879. S.   **H 101**
Contents, see Deutscher katalog, *under* **H.**, p. 67.

Ober, F: Albion. The silver city ; a story of adventure in Mexico. Ill. Bost. [1883]. O.   **Ox 101**
O'Brien, Charlotte G. Light and shade. N. Y. 1878. Q.   **O 101**
— *Same.* Lond. 1878. 2 v. in 1. D.   **O 101**
O'Brien, Fitz James. The diamond lens. *In* Atlantic tales.   **A 1876**
— *Same,* with other stories ; coll. and ed., with a sketch of the author by W: Winter. New ed. N. Y. 1885. D.   **O 126**
Includes, The wondersmith. — Tommatoo.—Mother of Pearl.—The bohemian.—The lost room.—The pot of tulips.—The golden ingot.—My wife's tempter.— What was it?—Duke Humphrey's dinner. — Milly Dove.—The dragon fang.
— Mrs. Macsimum's bill. *In* Maga stories.   **P 2801**
O'Connor, Francis. The invisible princess. *In* Johnson, E. R. Little classics. **J 926 v8**
O'Connor, W: Douglas. The ghost. Ill. N. Y. 1867. S.   **O 151**
— *Same. In* Johnson, E. R. Little classics.   **J 926 v8**
O'Flanagan, James Roderick. The Munster circuit ; tales, trials and traditions. N. Y. 1879. Q.   **O 201**
O'Hanlon, Alice. A costly heritage. N. Y. 1881. Q.   **O 251**
— *Same.* Lond. 1882. 3 v. in 2. D.   **O 251**
— Horace McLean ; a story of a search in a strange place. N. Y. 1880. Q.   **O 252**
— No proof ; a novel. N. Y. 1882. Q.   **O 253**
— Robert Reid, cotton-spinner ; a novel. N. Y. 1883. Q.   **O 254**
— *Same.* Lond. 1883. 3 v. in 2. D.   **O 254**
O'Hara family, *pseud., see* **Banim,** J:
Ohnet, Georges. Lise Fleuron. From the french by lady W: Godolphin Osborne. Lond. 1885. 2 v. D.   **O 276**
O'Itzel, E. Die freunde ; historisch - romantisches gemälde aus dem griechischen befreiungskriege. Leipz. 1834. 2 v. S.   **O 301**
Oelckers, Theodor Hermann. Prinzessin Maria von Oldenhof, oder Der ewige jude. Leipz. 1848. 3 v. S.   **O 351**
Old corner cupboard, The, or The every-day life of every-day people. Cinc. 1856. D.   **O 21**
Oldboy, Oliver, *pseud.* George Bailey ; a tale of New York mercantile life. N. Y. 1880. S.   **O 401**
Oldenburg, Ferdinand A: Janneton und Amalie, oder Nicht das verbrechen sondern die tugend macht glücklich ; eine erzählung für die reifere jugend. Cinc. 1855. S.   **O 426**
— Die wege zum verbrechen ; eine erzählung für die reifere jugend. Cinc. 1851. T. *With* **Schmid,** J. C. v. Fernando.   **S 1459**
Old-fashioned fairy tales. Original ed., ill. Bost. *n. d.* 2 v. S.   **Ox 31**
Oliphant, Laurence. Altiora Peto ; a novel. N. Y. 1883. D.   **O 436**
— *Same.* N. Y. 1883. Q.   **O 436**
— Piccadilly ; a fragment of contemporary biography. N. Y. 1884. S.   **O 437**
— The tender recollections of Irene Macgillicuddy. *In* Tales from Blackwood.   **T 177 v1**
Oliphant, Margaret O., *born* Wilson. Agnes. N. Y. 1866. O.   **O 451**
— *Same.* Leipz. 1865. 2 v. in 1. S.   **O 451**
— At his gates. N. Y. 1873. O.   **O 452**

x denotes books specially adapted for children.

Oliphant, M. O., *born* Wilson.—*Continued.*
— A beleaguered city ; a narrative of certain recent events in the city of Semur, in the department of the Haute Bourgogne ; a story of the seen and the unseen. Lond. 1881. O.   O 492
— Caritá. Leipz. 1877. 2 v. in 1. S.   O 453
— Chronicles of Carlingford.
   1. The perpetual curate.   O 473
   2. Salem chapel.   O 478
   3. Miss Majoribanks.   O 468
   4. The curate in charge.   O 454
   5. Phoebe jr.   O 474
— The curate in charge. Leipz. 1876. S.   O 454
— The days of my life ; an autobiography. N. Y. 1868. D.   O 455
— *Same. T. p. w.* S.   O 455
— The doctor's family. *With her* The rector.
                                      O 476
— For love and life. Leipz. 1874. 2 v. in 1. S.
                                      O 456
— The fugitives. N. Y. 1879. O.   O 457
— The greatest heiress in England. Leipz. 1880. 2 v. in 1. S.   O 458
— *Same.* N. Y. 1880. Q.   O 458
— Harry Joscelyn. N. Y. 1881. Q.   O 459
— *Same.* Lond. 1881. 3 v. in 1. D.   O 459
— He that will not when he may. N. Y. 1880. Q.
                                      O 460
— *Same.* N. Y. 1883. D.   O 460
— Hester ; a story of contemporary life. N. Y. 1883. D.   O 488
— *Same.* Lond. 1883. 3 v. in 1. D.   O 488
— *Same.* N. Y. 1884. Q.   O 488
— Innocent ; a tale of modern life. Leipz. 1873. 2 v. in 1. S.   O 461
— It was a lover and his lass ; a novel. N. Y. 1883. Q.   O 485
— *Same.* 2d ed. Lond. 1883. 3 v. in 1. D.   O 485
— Katie Stewart ; eine einfache geschichte. Leipz. 1885. S.   O 462
— The ladies Lindores ; a novel. N. Y. 1883. Q.
                                      O 486
— *Same.* N. Y. 1883. S.   O 486
— Lady Jane ; a novel. N. Y. 1882. Q.   O 484
— The last of the Mortimers. Leipz. 1862. 2 v. in 1. S.   O 463
— Lucy Crofton. N. Y. 1860. S.   O 464
— Madam ; a novel. N. Y. 1884. Q.   O 490
— *Same.* N. Y. 1885 [1884]. S.   O 490
— Madonna Mary. N. Y. 1866. O.   O 465
— *Same.* Leipz. 1867. 2 v. in 1. S.   O 465
— May. Leipz. 1873. 2 v. in 1. S.   O 466
— The minister's wife. Leipz. 1869. 2 v. in 1. S.
                                      O 467
— Miss Majoribanks. Leipz. 1870. 2 v. in 1. S.
                                      O 468
— Mrs. Arthur. Leipz. 1877. 2 v. in 1. S.   O 469
— An odd couple. Phila. *n. d.* D.   O 470
— Ombra. Leipz. 1872. 2 v. in 1. S.   O 471
— The open door [*and*] The portrait ; two stories of the seen and the unseen. [*Anon.*] Bost. 1885. S.   O 493
— Passages from the life of Mrs. Margaret Maitland of Sunnyside, written by herself. Leipz. 1862. S.   O 472
— The perpetual curate. N. Y. 1865. O.   O 473
— *Same.* Leipz. 1870. 2 v. in 1. S.   O 473
— Phoebe junior ; a last chronicle of Carlingford. Leipz. 1876. 2 v. in 1. S.   O 474
— The primrose path ; a chapter in the annals of the kingdom of Fife. Leipz. 1878. 2 v. in 1. S.   O 475

Oliphant, M. O., *born* Wilson.—*Continued.*
— The rector. Leipz. 1870. S.   O 476
— A rose in june. Leipz. 1874. S.   O 477
— Salem chapel. Leipz. 1870. 2 v. in 1. S.
                                      O 478
— The secret chamber. *In* Tales from Blackwood.   T 177 v1
— Self-sacrifice, by the author of Margaret Maitland. Phila. *n. d.* D.   O 491
— Sir Tom ; a novel. N. Y. 1883. Q.   O 487
— *Same.* Lond. 1884. D.   O 487
— A son of the soil. *T. p. w.* [N. Y. 1865]. O.
                                      O 479
— The story of Valentine and his brother. Leipz. 1875. 2 v. in 1. S.   O 480
— *Same.* Edinb. 1875. 3 v. in 1. D.   O 480
— Whiteladies. Toronto. 1875. D.   O 481
— *Same.* Leipz. 1875. 2 v. in 1. S.   O 481
— Within the precincts. Leipz. 1879. 3 v. in 2. S.   O 482
— *Same.* Lond. 1879. 3 v. in 2. D.   O 482
— The wizard's son ; a novel. N. Y. 1884. Q.
                                      O 489
— Young Musgrave. Leipz. 1878. 2 v. in 1. S.
                                      O 483
— Zaidee ; a romance. Edinb. 1856. 3 v. in 2. D.   O 494
Olivet, Fabre d', *see* Fabre d'Olivet, D.
Olle nümärker, De, *pseud., see* Löffler, K: Valentin Immanuel.
Olney, Ellen W., *see* Kirk, Ellen W.
Oelsner-Monmerqué, Gustave. Die rothen und die blauen, pariser corruptions-skizzen ; ein tendenz-roman. Bremen. 1850. S.
                                      O 602
Onkel Adam, *pseud. see* Wetterbergh, C: A.
Opie, Amelia, *born* Alderson. Works. Lond. 1835–1838. 6 v. in 5. O.   O 653
   Contents. V. 1. The fashionable wife and unfashionable husband.—Madeline's journal.—The mysterious stranger. — Appearance is against her. — The robber.—The brother and sister. 2. Adeline Mowbray. Murder will out. — The revenge. — The orphan. — The soldier's return. — The death-bed. — The black velvet pelisse. 3. Illustrations of lying. — The father and daughter.— The quaker and the young man of the world. — A tale of trials. — The confessions of an odd tempered man. —The ruffian boy.—The welcome home.—The mother and son. 4. Lady Anne and lady Jane. — Austin and his wife.—A woman's love.—A wife's duty. —The two sons.—The opposite neighbor. 5. Love, mystery and superstition.—After the ball.—Happy faces.—Temper. 6. Valentine's eve.
— *Same.* V. 1. Phila. *n. d.* O.   O 653
— White lies. N. Y. 1848. S.   O 652
Opiz, G: Emanuel, (*Bohemus*). Frauengrösse, oder Der blödsinnige. Stuttg. 1835. 2 v. S.
                                      O 701
— Der irrwisch. Stuttg. 1834. S.   O 702
Optic, Oliver. *pseud., see* Adams, W: Taylor.
O'Reilly, Eleanor G., *mrs.* Robert. Our hero. Ill. N. Y. 1885 [1884]. D.   Ox 451
Orford, *Earl of, see* Walpole, Horace.
Ormirod, —. My intimate enemy. Phila. 1878. S.   O 751
Orne, Philip. Simply a love-story. Bost. 1885. D.   O 766
Orr, *Mrs.* Alexander S. The Roseville family ; an historical tale of the 18th century. Lond. 1877. S.   O 776
— The twins of St. Marcel ; a tale of Paris incendié. Lond. 1877. S.   O 777
Orred, Meta. Honor's worth, or The cost of a vow. N. Y. 1878. O.   O 801
— *Same* ; a novel. Lond. 1878. 2 v. D.   O 801

x denotes books specially adapted for children.

Oertel, Philipp F: W:, (*W. O. v. Horn, Friedrich Wilhelm Lips*). Die eroberung von Algier; eine geschichte, der jugend und dem volke erzählt. *With his* Der orkan auf Cuba.   **O 853**
— Friedel; eine geschichte aus dem volksleben. N. Y. 1853. T.   **O 851**
— Gesammelte erzählungen. 2te aufl. Frankfurt a. M. 10 v. D.   **O 852**
   Contents, see Deutscher katalog, p. 87.
— Der orkan auf Cuba; eine geschichte, der deutschen jugend und dem deutschen volke erzählt. 2te aufl. Wiesbaden. *n. d.* T. **O 853**
— Rheinische dorfgeschichten. Frankfurt a. M. 1854. 4 v. T.   **O 854**
   Contents, see Deutscher katalog, p. 87.
— Wie einer ein wallfischfänger wurde, und was er dabei erfuhr und erlebte; eine geschichte, der deutschen jugend und dem deutschen volke erzählt. *With his* Der orkan auf Cuba.   **O 853**
Oeser, Rudolph L:, (*Otto Glaubrecht*). Ein böses jahr; erzählung für das volk. Frankfurt a. M. 1856. S.   **O 1051**
Oswald, E., *pseud., see* **Schulze-Smidt**, Bernhardine.
Other fools and their doings; by one who has seen it. N. Y. 1880. S.   **O 61**
Otis, James, *pseud., see* **Kaler**, James Otis.
Oettinger, E: Maria. Der ring des Nostradamus; historischer roman. Leipz. 1852. T.
                                                   O 901
— Schobri, Ungarn's grösster bandit. Leipz. 1843. S.   **O 902**
— Sophie Arnold. Leipz. 1847. 2 v. S.   **O 903**
Otto, Louise, *see* **Peters**, Louise.
Ouida, *pseud., see* **Ramé**, Louise de la.
Owen, Robert Dale. Village life in the west. Beyond the breakers; a story of the present day. Phila. 1878. O.   **O 951**
Oxenford, J: *and* C. A. Feiling, *trs.* Tales from the german; comprising specimens from the most celebrated authors. N. Y. 1858. O.   **O 1001**
   Contents. **Musäus**, J. H. Libussa. — **Schiller**, J: C. F: v. The criminal from lost honour.—**Hauff**, W: The cold heart.—**Immermann**, K: The wonders in the Spessart. — **Hauff**, W: Nose, the dwarf. — **Velde**, C. A. van der. Axel; a tale of the thirty years war.—**Hoffmann**, E. T. W. The sandman. — **Kleist**, H: v. Michael Kohlhaas.
P. P., *pseud., see* **Rumohr**, Theodor W: Kjerstrup.
P—s, P. Bendegucz, Gyula Kolompos und Pista Kurtaforint; eine donquixottiade nach der neuesten mode. Dichtung und wahrheit. Aus dem magyarischen übers. von L. von Sch. Leipz. 1841. S.   **P 101**
Paalzow, Henriette v., *born* Wach. Godwie-Castle. Aus den papieren der herzogin von Nottingham. Breslau. 1855. 3 v. S.
                                                   P 151
— Jacob van der Nees. Breslau. 1855. 3 v. S.
                                                   P 152
— Ste. Roche. Breslau. 1855. 3 v. S.   **P 153**
— Thomas Thyrnau. Breslau. 1855. 3 v. S.
                                                   P 154
Paddock, Cornelia, *mrs.* A. G. The fate of madame La Tour; a tale of Great Salt Lake. N. Y. 1881. S.   **P 176**
Page, T: Nelson. Marse Chan. *In* Stories by american authors.   **S 35 v9**
Paget, Violet, (*Vernon Lee*). Miss Brown; a novel. N. Y. 1885. Q.   **P 3151**
Palace-prison, A, or The past and the present. N. Y. 1884. S.   **P 5**

Palais Royal, Das; historischer roman von dem verfasser des Heinrichs IV, oder die tage der Ligue. Deutsch bearb. von L: Hauff. Stuttg. 1846. S.   **P 1**
Palfrey, Sarah Hammond, (*E. Foxton*). Herman, or Young knighthood. Bost. 1866. 2 v. D.
                                                   P 201
Palgrave, W: Gifford. Hermann Agha; an eastern narrative. (Leisure hour ser.) N. Y. 1872. S.   **P 251**
Palm, Adolf, *pseud., see* **Müller**, Adolf.
Palmblad, W: F: Aurora Königsmark und ihre verwandten; zeitbilder aus dem siebzehnten und achtzehnten jahrhundert. Aus dem schwedischen. Leipz. 1848. 6 v. in 2. D.   **P 301**
— Die familie Falkenswärd. Aus dem schwedischen übers. von Germanus Metternich. Stuttg. 1845. 2 v. T.   **P 302**
Palmer, H: Vaughan. The younger son. Ill. Lond. *n. d.* O.   **P 351**
Paltock, Robert. The life and adventures of Peter Wilkins; with a preface by A. H. Bullen. Lond. 1884. 2 v. D.   **P 376**
Pansy, *pseud., see* **Alden**, Isabella M.
Pardoe, Julia. A life struggle. *T. p. w.* D. **P 401**
Parr, Harriet, (*Holme Lee*). Against wind and tide. New ed. Lond. 1873. D.   **P 462**
— Annis Warleigh's fortunes. New ed. Lond. 1873. D.   **P 463**
— Basil Godfrey's caprice. Leipz. 1868. 2 v. in 1. S.   **P 461**
— *Same.* New ed. Lond. 1876. D.   **P 461**
— The beautiful miss Barrington. Leipz. 1871. 2 v. in 1. S.   **P 459**
— *Same.* New ed. Lond. 1875. D.   **P 459**
— Ben Milner's wooing. Bost. 1877. S.   **P 451**
— *Same.* New ed. Lond. 1884. D.   **P 451**
— Country stories, old and new, in prose and verse. New ed. Lond. 1875. D.   **P 464**
   Contents. Polly's one offer.—Hawkswell Place.— Coming into a fortune.—By the shore of life.—Lady Seamer's long step.—The grave in the moorland.— Rufus Helstone.—St. Mark's eve.—Under the rose.— Lost on the shore.—Three nights by Ashpool.—The holy well.—Too prudent by half.—The Chetwynds.— The love-test.—Sibyl's disappointment.—May Margaret. — The sighing shade. — The skeleton in the closet.—Sir Ralph and lady Jane.—The sanctuary in the mountains.—An autumn shadow.—Lina Fernie.— Shadows.—Jenny's vocation.—The haunted mere. — A winter wedding in the wolds.
— For richer, for poorer. Leipz. 1870. 2 v. in 1. S.   **P 460**
— Hawksview; a family history of our own times. N. Y. 1860. S.   **P 452**
— Her title of honour. Lond. 1884. D.   **P 470**
— Katherine's trial. New ed. Lond. 1875. D.
                                                   P 465
— Kathie Brand; a fireside history of a quiet life. N. Y. 1857. D.   **P 453**
— *Same.* New ed. Lond. 1873. D.   **P 453**
— Legends from fairy land. Ill. Lond. [1877]. S.   **Px 151**
— Maud Talbot. New ed. Lond. 1873. D.   **P 466**
— Mr. Wynward's ward. New ed. Lond. 1876. D.   **P 467**
— Mrs. Denys of Cote. Leipz. 1880. 2 v. in 1. S.   **P 454**
— Thorney Hall. Aus dem englischen von C: Müller. Stuttg. 1857. T.   **P 457**
— Straightforward. Leipz. 1878. 2 v. in 1. S.
                                                   P 455
— Sylvan Holt's daughter. N. Y. 1860. D. **P 456**
— *Same.* New ed. Lond. 1880. D.   **P 456**
— *Same.* N. Y. 1885. Q.   **P 456**

x denotes books specially adapted for children.

Parr, Harriet, (*Holme Lee*).—*Continued.*
— The vicissitudes of Bessie Fairfax. Phila. *n. d.*
　D. **P 458**
— Warp and woof, or Reminiscences of Doris
　Fletcher. New ed. Lond. 1878. D. **P 468**
— The Wortlebank diary, and some old stories
　from Kathie Brande's portfolio. New ed.
　Lond. 1873. D. **P 469**
　Includes, Kester's evil eye.—The haunted house.—
　Madame Freschon's.—The heir of Hardington.—How
　miss Bootle was photographed.—Stories round the
　yule log: My brother Robert; Poor Dick; A day of
　reckoning; An immortal poem.—At old St. Ann's.—
　From first to last.—The devil's mark.—A sketch from
　my window.—The lady on the Mall.—A governess's
　soliloquy.—Some passages from the diary of mistress
　Margaret Arden. — The poor pensioner. — Ashburn
　rectory.—My blind sister.
Parr, Louisa. Dorothy Fox. Phila. 1876. O.
　P 501
— Robin. (Leisure hour ser.) N. Y. 1882. S.
　P 502
Partington, Mrs., *pseud.*, *see* **Shillaber**, B: Pen-
　hallow.
Parton, Sarah Payson, *born* Willis, *formerly mrs.*
　Etheredge, (*Fanny Fern*). Fern leaves.
　Buffalo. 1853. D. **P 551**
Pastor Arnold, oder Die flucht der waldenser ;
　eine erzählung aus dem siebzehnten jahr-
　hundert. Aus dem englischen. Stuttg.
　1845. 2 v. T.
Patchin, Calista Halsey. Dorothea. (No name
　ser.) Bost. 1882. S.
Patrick, Mary. Christine Brownlee's ordeal. N.
　Y. 1878. Q. **P 601**
— *Same.* Lond. 1878. 3 v. in 1. D. **P 601**
— Marjorie Bruce's lovers. Lond. 1877. 2 v. in 1.
　D. **P 603**
— Mr. Leslie of Underwood ; a story with two
　heroines. N. Y. 1879. Q. **P 602**
— *Same.* Lond. 1879. 3 v. in 1. D. **P 602**
Pauer, F: Neue novellen ; bilder aus der wirk-
　lichen welt. Mannheim. 1832. D. **P 651**
　Contents, see Deutscher katalog, p. 88.
Paul, Jean, *pseud.*, *see* **Richter**, J: Paul F:
Paul, Margaret Agnes. De Cressy. Leipz. 1857.
　S. **P 701**
— Dorothy. Leipz. 1857. S. **P 702**
— Maiden sisters. Leipz. 1859. S. **P 703**
— Martha Brown the heiress. Leipz. 1861. S.
　P 704
— Still waters. Leipz. 1857. S. **P 705**
— Uncle Ralph. Leipz. 1858. S. **P 706**
— Vanessa. Leipz. 1874. S. **P 707**
Paulding, James Kirke. Childe Roeliffe's pil-
　grimage ; a travelling legend. [*Anon.*] *In*
　Tales of Glauber Spa. **T 186**
— The dutchman's fireside. N. Y. 1856. D.
　P 751
— The old continental, or The price of liberty.
　N. Y. 1851. 2 v. in 1. D. **P 752**
— Selim the benefactor of mankind. [*Anon.*] *In*
　Tales of Glauber Spa. **T 186**
— Westward ho ! *T. p. w.* D. **P 753**
Payn, James, (*John S. Sauzade*). At her mercy.
　Leipz. 1874. 2 v. in 1. S. **P 801**
— The best of husbands. Leipz. 1874. 2 v. in 1.
　S. **P 802**
— By proxy. N. Y. 1878. O. **P 803**
— *Same.* Leipz. 1878. 2 v. in 1. S. **P 803**
— The canon's ward ; a novel. N. Y. 1884. Q.
　P 828
— *Same.* Portrait. Lond. 1884. 3 v. in 1. D.
　P 828
— Cecil's tryst. Leipz. 1872. S. **P 804**

Payn, James.—*Continued.*
— A confidential agent ; a novel. N. Y. 1884. Q.
　P 805
— *Same.* New ed. Ill. Lond. 1881. D. **P 805**
— Fallen fortunes. Leipz. 1876. 2 v. in 1. S.
　P 806
— For cash only ; a novel. N. Y. 1882. Q.
　P 824
— *Same.* New ed. Lond. 1883. D. **P 824**
— Found dead. Leipz. 1869. S. **P 807**
— From exile. N. Y. 1881. Q. **P 808**
— *Same.* New ed. Lond. [1881]. D. **P 808**
— Garret Van Horn, or The beggar on horse-
　back, by J: S. Sauzade. N. Y. 1863. D.
　P 826
— A grape from a thorn ; a novel. N. Y. 1881. D.
　P 823
— *Same.* Lond. 1881. 3 v. in 1. D. **P 823**
— Gwendoline's harvest. Leipz. 1870. S. **P 809**
— Halves. Leipz. 1876. 2 v. in 1. S. **P 810**
— High spirits ; being certain stories written in
　them. 1st and 2d series. Leipz. 1879. 2 v.
　S. **P 811**
　Contents. V. 1. A Mayfair mystery.—The confisca-
　ted weeds. —Tasbrook's testimonial. — A mediæval
　mistake.—A chronological error.—An easter holiday.
　—The G. B. C., the tale of a telegram.—Finding his
　level.—An office secret.—An aunt by marriage.—The
　lord of Harpington.—Patient Kitty.—My first record-
　ership. **2.** A change of views.—Simpson of Bussora.
　—Some tales of white elephants.—An adventure in a
　forest.— Capt. Cole's passenger.— An independent
　opinion.—A modern Delilah.—The transfused trans-
　formed ; a tale of blood. — Number forty-seven.—A
　very quiet rubber.—The fatal curiosity.
— *Same.* N. Y. 1879. Q. **P 811**
— In the heart of a hill, and other stories. Leipz.
　1873. S. **P 812**
　Includes, A very bad night. — My financial opera-
　tion.—A treasure of a servant.—A night with the
　fenians.—Charley's bet.—The toll-bar.— Mr. John
　Stott's difficulty.—Hunting extraordinary.—From the
　rank.—On her majesty's service : special. — A paper
　chase.
— Kit, a memory ; a novel. N. Y. 1882. Q.
　P 825
— *Same.* Lond. 1883. 3 v. in 1. D. **P 825**
— Less black than we're painted. Leipz. 1878.
　2 v. in 1. S. **P 813**
— Like father like son. Leipz. 1871. 2 v. in 1. S.
　P 814
— Lost sir Massingberd ; a romance of real life.
　Phila. *n. d.* D. **P 815**
— The luck of the Darrells ; a novel. N. Y.
　1885. S. **P 830**
— Married beneath him. Phila. *n. d.* D. **P 816**
— Murphy's master. Leipz. 1873. S. **P 817**
— Not wooed, but won. Leipz. 1871. 2 v. in 1.
　S. **P 818**
— Patient Kitty. *In* Tales from many sources.
　T 178 v4
— The talk of the town ; a novel. N. Y. 1884.
　Q. **P 829**
— Thicker than water ; a novel. N. Y. 1883. Q.
　P 827
— *Same.* N. Y. 1883. S. **P 827**
— Under one roof ; an episode in a family his-
　tory. N. Y. 1879. Q. **P 819**
— *Same.* New ed. Lond. [1880]. D. **P 819**
— Walter's word. Leipz. 1875. 2 v. in 1. S.
　P 820
— What he cost her. Leipz. 1877. 2 v. in 1. S.
　P 821
— A woman's vengeance. Leipz. 1872. 2 v. in 1.
　S. **P 822**

Peacock, T: Love. Headlong Hall. N. Y. 1845.
D.   **P 851**
— Nightmare Abbey. *With his* Headlong Hall.
                                            P 851
Peard, Francis Mary. Cartouche. Leipz. 1879.
S.   **P 901**
— Castle and town. Phila. 1882. D.   **P 906**
— Contradictions. Leipz. 1883. 2 v. in 1. S.
                                            P 907
— Mother Molly. N. Y. 1880. S.   **P 902**
— One year, or A story of three homes. Leipz.
1869. 2 v. in 1. S.   **P 908**
— The rose-garden. *T. p. w.* D.   **P 903**
— Thorpe Regis. Bost. 1874. D.   **P 904**
— Unawares. Bost. 1872. D.   **P 905**
— *joint author, see* **Awdry**, Frances.
Pearl-fishing ; choice stories from Dickens'
"Household words." Auburn. *n. d.* D.
                                          D, 1326
Contents. The young advocate.—The last of a long
line. — The gentleman beggar. — Evil is wrought by
want of thought.—Bed.—The home of Woodruffe,
the gardener. — The water-drops. — An excellent
opportunity.
Peasant life *;* sketches of the villagers and field
labourers in Glenaldie. 3d ed. Lond. 1871.
D.   **P 11**
Contents. Introd.— Muckle Jock.— Kate Rose and
"her bairns."—The dandy drainer. — The mason's
daughter.—The bourtree.—The red-tiled cottage.—
Conclusion.
Pechammer, E. v. (*E. D. Mund*). Erlebnisse
eines arztes. Leipz. 1866. 2 v. S. **M 4501**
Peck, Ellen, (*Cuyler Pine*). Mary Brandagee ;
an autobiography. N. Y. 1865. D. **P 951**
Pelzeln, Franziska v. Der erbe von Weidenhof.
N. Y. 1885. F.   **P 3201**
Penciller, Harry, *pseud.* Rural life, or prose and
poetry of the woods and fields. Phila.
1859. S.   **P 1051**
Pennot, The rev. Peter, *pseud., see* **Round**, W:
Marshall Fitz.
Penseroso, *pseud., see* **Heege**, *Frau* —.
Perch, Philemon, *pseud., see* **Johnston**, R:
Malcolm.
Perez Galdòs, Benito. Gloria ; a novel. From
the spanish by Clara Bell. Rev. and corr.
in the U. S.   N. Y. 1882. 2 v. S. **P 976**
— Marianela. From the spanish by Clara Bell.
Rev. and corr. in the U. S.   N. Y. 1883. S.
                                            P 977
— Trafalgar ; a tale. From the spanish by Clara
Bell. Rev. and corr. in the U. S.   N. Y.
1884. S.   **P 978**
Perkins, F: Beecher. The double veil. *In*
Maga stories.   **P 2801**
— My three conversations with miss Chester. *In*
the same.   **P 2801**
— *Same.* N. Y. 1877. T.   **P 1151**
Perkins, *Mrs.* Sue Chestnutwood. Honor bright;
a romance. [*Anon.*] Buffalo. 1883. D.
                                            P 1176
Perkins, W: Blair, *ed.* Boys' and girls' annual,
1885 ; illustrated stories for young folks.
Bost. [1885]. O.   **Bx 74**
Perrier, Amelia. A good match. N. Y. 1873. D.
                                            P 1201
Perry, Mary Alice. Esther Pennefather. N. Y.
1878. O.   **P 1251**
Perry, G: B. Corporal Bruce of the Balaklava
"six hundred." Bost. [1878]. S.   **P 1301**
Perry, Nora. A book of love stories. Bost.
1881. S.   **P 1351**
Contents. Dolly.—Dick Halliday's wife.—Laura and
her hero. — Christine. — Mr. and mrs. Meyer. — The

Perry, Nora.—*Continued.*
charmer charmed. — After five years. — John Eccleston's thanksgiving.—An heiress.—Margaret Freyer's
heart.
— The tragedy of the unexpected, and other
stories. Bost. 1880. T.   **P 1352**
Includes, Mrs. Stanhope's last lodger. — A foolish
girl.—Our ice man.—In the red room.—My Nannie O.
— In a street-car.—Mrs. F's waiting-maid.—The ribbon
of honor.
Pestalozzi, J: H: Leonard and Gertrude. Tr.
and abridged by Eva Channing. Bost. 1885.
D.   **P 3251**
— [Erzählungen]. *In his* Sämmtliche werke.
                                            370 : 1
Contents, see Deutscher katalog, p. 14.
Peterkin, Alexander. The parsonage. *In* **Wil-
son**, J: M. Tales of the borders.
                                         W 2203 v3
— *Same.*   **W 2202 v6**
Peters, A:, (*Elfried von Taura*). Zàvis von Ro-
senberg, genannt von Falkenstein ; histori-
scher roman. Prag. 1860. 3 v. T. **P 2851**
Peters, Louise, *born* Otto. Ludwig, der kellner.
Leipz. 1843. 2 v. S.   **P 2901**
— Römisch und deutsch. Leipz. 1847. 4 v. S.
                                            P 2902
— Die schultheisentöchter ; cultur-historischer
roman. Wien. 1861. 3 v. T.   **P 2903**
— Vier geschwister. Dessau. 1852. 2 v. in 1. S.
                                            P 2904
Petersen, Marie. Die irrlichter. 34ste aufl. Ber-
lin. 1881. T. *With her* Prinzessin Ilse.
                                            P 1376
— *Same, eng.* The will-o'-the-wisp. Tr. from the
germ. by Charlotte I. Hart. Ill. Lond.
1883. D.   **Px 401**
— Prinzessin Ilse ; ein märchen aus dem Harz-
gebirge. 20ste aufl. Berlin. 1879. T.
                                            P 1376
Pfannenschmidt, Julie, *born* Burow. Ein bür-
germeister ; geschichtlicher roman. Wien.
1862. 3 v. T.   **P 1401**
— Jonannes Kepler ; historische erzählung. Prag.
1857. 3 v. T.   **P 1402**
— *Same.* Leipz. 1865. S.   **P 1402**
— Ein lebenstraum. Leipz. 1855. T. **P 1303**
Pfeiffer, G. W. Der stadt-hauptmann von Frank-
furt ; eine historische novelle aus Frank-
furts vorzeit. Frankfurt a. M. 1860. S.
                                            P 1001
Phelps, Elizabeth Stuart. Doctor Zay. Bost.
1882. D.   **P 1456**
— *Same, germ.* Doctor Za ; erzählung. *In* Vier-
teljährl. mag.   **V 2 v31**
— Friends ; a duet. Bost. 1881. D.   **P 1451**
— The gates ajar. *T. p. w.* S.   **249 : 21**
— The Gypsy series. N. Y. 1876. 4 v. S.
                                       Px 501-Px 504
Contents. 1. Gypsy Breynton. 2. Gypsy's cousin
Joy. 3. Gypsy's sowing and reaping. 4. Gypsy's
year at the Golden crescent.
— The lady of Shalott. *In* **Johnson**, E. R. Lit-
tle classics.   **J 926 v10**
— An old maid's paradise. Bost. 1885. D.
                                            P 1457
— Sealed orders. Bost. 1879. D.   **P 1453**
Includes, Old mother Goose.—The lady of Shalott.—
The true story of Guenever.—Doherty.—The voyage
of the America.— Wrecked in port. — Running the
risk.—Long, long ago.—Since I died.—A woman's
pulpit.—Number 13.—Two hundred and two.—Cloth
of gold.—Saint Caligula.—Miss Mildred's friend.—
Neblitt.
— The silent partner. 9th ed. Bost. 1884. D.
                                            P 1454

x denotes books specially adapted for children.

Phelps, Elizabeth Stuart.—*Continued.*
— The story of Avis. Bost. 1877. D. **P 1455**
— Tiny. · Bost. 1866. S. **Px 507**
— The Trotty book. Bost. 1875. D. **Px 505**
— Trotty's wedding tour and story book. Ill. Bost. 1874. D. **Px 506**
— Zerviah Hope. *In* **Stories** by american authors. **S 35 v8**
Philleo, Calvin Wheeler. Twice married ; a story of Connecticut life. N. Y. 1855. S. **P 1501**
Phillips, G: Searle, (*January Searle*). The gypsies of Dane's Dike. *T. p. w.* S. **P 1551**
Phillips, S: We're all low people there, and other tales. Lond. 1854. S. **P 1601**
Includes, The banking house.—Elinor Travis.—The freethinker.
Piazzi, Adrienne, (*Leila-hanoum*). A tragedy in the imperial harem at Constantinople. From the french, with notes by R.· E. Colston. N. Y. 1883. S. **L 926**
Pichler, Caroline, *born* v. Greiner. Die belagerung Wiens. Wien. 1824. 3 v. T. **P 1651**
— Elisabeth von Guttenstein ; eine familiengeschichte aus der zeit des östreichischen erbfolgekrieges. Wien. 1835. 3 v. S. **P 1652**
— Friedrich der streitbare. Wien. 1831. 4 v. S. **P 1653**
— Henriette von England ; gemahlin des herzogs von Orleans. Wien. 1832. S. **P 1654**
— Kleine erzählungen ; 2ter *und* 12ter t. Wien. 1823, 1832. 2 v. S. **P 1656**
— Zeitbilder. Wien. 1841. 2 v. S. **P 1657**
Pichler, Louise, *see* **Zeller**, Louise.
Pickering, Ellen. Ellen Wareham ; the single woman of a certain age. *T. p. w.* S. **P 1751**
— The expectant. *T. p. w.* O. **P 1752**
— The grandfather. N. Y. 1861. O. **P 1753**
— The squire. Phila. *n. d.* O. **P 1754**
— Who shall be heir ? Phila. *n. d.* O. **P 1755**
Pierantoni, Grazia, *born* Mancini. Lydia. Aus dem italienischen übers. von Helene Lobedan. Einzige autorisierte deutsche ausg. Stuttg. [1881]. D. **P 2951**
Pigault-Lebrun, Guillaume C: Antoine. Valentins verliebte abenteuer und irrfahrten ; ein komischer roman nach Pigault-Lebrun von Gustav Sellen. Leipz. 1829. 2 v. S. **P 1776**
Pine, Cuyler, *pseud., see* **Peck**, Ellen.
Pinzer, *Frau* v., *see* **Binzer**, Emilie v.
Pipitz, Franz Ernst. Memoiren eines apostaten. Aus dessen papieren herausgegeben. Stuttg. 1842. S. **P 1851**
Pique ; a tale of the english aristocracy. Phila. *n. d.* D. **P 21**
Pirkis, C. L. Lady Lovelace ; a novel. N. Y. 1885. Q. **P 1876**
Pise, C: Constantine. Zenosius, or The pilgrim convert. 3d ed. N. Y. [1845]. D. **P 1901**
Pitawall, Ernst, *pseud., see* **Dedenroth**, Eugen Hermann.
Plänckner, Othello v., (*Eginhardt*). Der erbgraf. Altenburg. 1839. S. **E 751**
— Liebe, rache, reue. Altenburg. 1838. 2 v. S. **E 752**
— Neue abendgenossen. Altenburg. 1842. 2 v. S. **E 753**
Contents, *see* Deutscher katalog, p. 89.
Plympton, A. G. The Mary Jane papers ; a book for girls. Ill. N. Y. 1884. S. **Px 526**

Poe, Edgar Allan. The fall of the house of Usher. *In* **Johnson**, E. R. Little classics. **J 926 v2**
— The gold-bug. *In the same.* **J 926 v12**
— The murders in the rue Morgue. *In the same.* **J 926 v3**
— Seltsame geschichten. Uebers. und eingel. von Alfred Murenberg. Stuttg. [1882]. D. **P 1976**
Contents. Der goldkäfer. — Eine ballonfahrt über den Atlantischen ocean. — Thatsächliches über die magnetisirung des herrn Waldemar. — Eine fahrt in den Mälstrom. — Das verrätherische herz. — Der zweifache mord in der rue Morgue. — Der fall Marie Roget.—Der entwendete brief.
— [Tales]. *In his* Works. **820.1 : 5**
Contents, *see under* English literature, Collected works.
Polko, Elise, *born* Vogel. Flower pictures. Tr. from the german by S. W. Lander. Ill. N. Y. 1861. S. **Px 551**
— Getrennt ; roman. N. Y. 1883. F. **P 2006**
— In der villa Diodati ; aus den erinnerungen eines verstorbenen. Münster. 1878. T. **P 2002**
— Die kleine Marina ; erzählung. *In* Viertel-jährl. mag. **V 2 v31**
— Neue novellen. Zweite folge. Leipz. 1862. D. **P 2003**
Contents, *see* Deutscher katalog, p. 89.
— Phantasien und skizzen. 4te aufl. Leipz. 1859. S. **P 2005**
— Umsonst ; roman. 2te aufl. Breslau. 1880. D. **P 3001**
— Versunkene sterne. Leipz. 1867. D. **P 2004**
Pollok, Robert. Ralph Gemmell ; or the banks of the Irvine ; a tale of the scottish covenanters. N. Y. 1842. S. **Px 601**
Ponsonby, *Lady* Emily Charlotte Mary. Mary Lyndsay. N. Y. 1863. O. **P 2051**
Poole, J: Phineas Quiddy, or Sheer industry. Lond. 1859. S. **P 2101**
Popular tales and romances of the northern nations. Lond. 1823. 3v. D. **P 2126**
Contents. V. 1. **Musäus**, J: K: A: The treasure-seeker.—**La Motte Fouqué**, F: H: K:, baron de. The bottle imp. — The sorcerers.—**Tieck**, J: L: The enchanted castle. — Wake not the dead. — **Tieck**, J: L: Auburn Egbert. 2. **Musäus**, J: K: A: The spectre barber. — The magic dollar.—**La Motte Fouqué**, F: H: K: de. The collier's family.—The victim of priestcraft. —Kibitz. 3. The field of terror.—**Tieck**, J: L: Ellinland.—The tale.—The fatal marksman.—The hoard of the Nibelungen.—The erl king's daughter.
Porter, Ann Emerson. Cousin Polly's gold mine. N. Y. 1878. O. **P 2151**
Porter, D: Dixon. Allan Dare and Robert Le Diable ; a romance. Ill. N. Y. 1885. 2 v. O. **P 2136**
Porter, Jane. The scottish chiefs. Phila. *n. d.* D. **P 2201**
— Sir Edward Seaward's narrative of his shipwreck, and consequent discovery of certain islands in the Caribbean sea ; with details of his residence there, and of various extraordinary and highly interesting events in his life. Ab. and rev. N. Y. 1860. S. **P 2202**
— Thaddeus of Warsaw. Phila. 1873. D. **P 2203**
Porter, Mary W. Five little southerners. Bost. [1880]. D. **Px 651**
— Poor papa. Bost. [1879]. D. **P 2251**
Porter, Rose. The years that are told. N. Y. [1875]. D. **P 2301**
Postl, K:, *see* **Sealsfield**, C:

x denotes books specially adapted for children.

Pouvillon, Émile. Césette; a story of peasant
  life in the south of France. Authorized
  trans. from the french by C: W: Woolsey.
  N. Y. 1882. S.   **P 2326**
Power, Cecil. Philistia; a novel. N. Y. 1884.
  Q.   **P 3101**
Poynter, E. Frances. Among the hills. (Leisure
  hour ser.) N. Y. 1881. S.   **P 2351**
— Ersilia. (Leisure hour ser.) N. Y. 1876. S.
                                          P 2352
— My little lady. (Leisure hour ser.) N. Y. 1873.
  S.   **P 2353**
Prairie crusoe, The, or Adventures in the far
  west; a story for boys. Ill. Bost. n. d. D.
                                          Px 79
Pratt, Ella, born Farman. The cooking club of
  Tu-Whit Hollow. Bost. n. d. S.   **Px 701**
— A little woman; a story for other little women.
  Bost. [1873]. S.   **Px 702**
— Mrs. Hurd's niece; six months of a girl's life.
  Bost. [1876]. S.   **P x703**
— A white hand; a story of noblesse oblige.
  Bost. 1875. D.   **P 2401**
Pratt, G. The old woman who dried up and
  blew away. In Maga stories.   **P 2801**
Pratt, Mary E. Rhoda Thornton's girlhood.
  Ill. Bost. 1874. S.   **Px 751**
Prentiss, Elizabeth, born Payson. Aunt Jane's
  hero. N. Y. [1871]. D.   **P 2451**
— Avis Benson, or Mine and thine, with other
  sketches. N. Y. 1879. D.   **P 2452**
  Includes, Such as I have.—Homeward bound.—
  Taking for granted.—Why Satan trembles.—Having
  nothing, yet having all.—Success and defeat.—On the
  banks of the river of life.—A model servant.—Play-
  ing with sunbeams.—Saved from his friends.
— The flower of the family; a book for girls.
  N. Y. n. d. S.   **Px 801**
— Fred and Maria and me. New ed. Ill. N. Y.
  1883. S.   **P 2456**
— The home at Greylock. N. Y. 1876. D.
                                          P 2453
— Nidworth and his three magic wands. N. Y.
  1869. S.   **Px 802**
— Pemaquid; a story of old times in New Eng-
  land. N. Y. [1877]. D.   **P 2454**
— The Percys. N. Y. 1870. D.   **Px 803**
— Stepping heavenward. N. Y. 1869. D.
                                          P 2455
Preston, Harriet Waters. Is that all ? (No name
  ser.) Bost. 1877. S.   **P 2501**
Price, Miss —. A lost battle. Leipz. 1878. 2 v.
  in 1. S.   **P 2551**
Price, A. Who is Sylvia ? a novel. N. Y. 1883.
  Q.   **P 2576**
— Same. Lond. [1883]. 3 v. in 1. D.   **P 2576**
Price, Eleanor C. Gerald; a novel. N. Y. 1885.
  Q.   **P 2526**
— joint author, see Awdry, Frances.
Price, T: Buchanan. Snap; the ox-train era,
  early troubles of the border trade. N. Y.
  [1881.] D.   **Px 851**
Prime, W: Cowper. Later years. N. Y. 1863.
  D.   **P 2601**
— The old house by the river, by the author of
  the Owl Creek letters. N. Y. 1862. D.
                                          P 2602
Princess Amélie; a fragment of autobiography.
  (No name ser.) Bost. 1883. S.   **P 61**
Prior, H. Expiated, by the author of "Behind
  the veil." Leipz. 1872. 2 v. in 1. S. **P 2626**
Pritchard, H. Baden. George Vanbrugh's mis-
  take; a novel. N. Y. 1883. Q.   **P 3001**

Procter, Bryan Waller, (Barry Cornwall). Essays
  and tales in prose.   **824.2 : 77**
  Contents, see under English literature, Essays.
Professor Büsch. oder Hamburg vor hundert
  \ jahren; Hamburger - novelle. Hamburg.
  1857. S.   **H 5**
Proschko, Franz Isidor. Ein böhmischer stud-
  ent. Wien. 1861. 2 v. T.   **P 2651**
— Ein deutsches schneiderlein. Prag. 1856. T.
                                          P 2652
— Der jesuit; historischer roman aus dem
  schweden-kriege. Prag. 1857. 2. v. T.
                                          P 2653
— Pugačew; geschichtlicher roman. Prag. 1860.
  2 v. T.   **P 2654**
Proschko, Hermine Camille, (C. Wittendorf).
  Der hofkanzler; historische erzählung. In
  Vierteljähel. mag.   **V 2 v21**
— Lorbeer und myrthe; eine historische erzäh-
  lung. In the same.   **V 2 v23**
Pulszky, Ferencz Aurél. Die jacobiner in
  Ungarn; historischer roman. Berlin. 1851.
  2 v. S.   **P 2701**
Pulszky, Teréz. Popular tales and traditions
  of Hungary. N. Y. 1852. D.   **P 2726**
Pushkin, Aleksandr Sergetevitch. Marie; a
  story of russian love. From the russian
  by Marie H. de Zielinska. Chicago. 1877.
  D.   **P 2751**
Putlitz, Gustav H: Ganz herr zu. Das frölen-
  haus; novelle. With Spielhagen, F: Das
  skelet im hause.   In S 4262
— Was nicht der wald erzählt; ein märchen-
  strauss. 40ste aufl. Berlin. 1879. T.   **P 2776**
— Same, eng. Forest voices. Tr. from the german.
  C: A. Smith ed. Albany. 1866. D. P 2776
Putnam, Mary Corinna. Found and lost. In
  Maga stories.   **P 2801**
Putnam, Mary, born Lowell. Fifteen days; an
  extract from Edward Colvil's journal.
  [Anon.] Bost. 1866. D.   **P 3051**
Puttkammer, Emil freiherr v., (Otto Ludwig).
  Zwischen himmel und erde. Berlin. 1862.
  D.   **L 2151**
Pyle, Howard. The merry adventures of Robin
  Hood of great renown in Nottinghamshire.
  Ill. N. Y. 1883. O.   **Px 951**
— Within the capes. N. Y. 1885. D.   **P 3076**
Pyrnelle, Louise Clarke. Diddie, Dumps and
  Tot, or Plantation child-life. N. Y. 1882.
  S.   **Px 1001**
Quad, John, pseud., see Irving, J: Treat.
Quednow, A. Aus der schule des lebens. Stuttg.
  1842. S.   **Q 201**
Quillinan, E: The rangers of Connaught. In
  Edinburgh tales.   **E 426**
Quincy, Josiah Phillips. Professor Phantillo.
  In Maga stories.   **P 2801**
— Tolliwotte's ghost. In the same.   **P 2801**
Quincy, S: Miller. The man who was not a
  colonel, by a high private. [Anon.] Bost.
  [1877]. S.   **Q 201**
Quinton, Abel. The nobleman of '89; an episode
  of the french revolution. Tr. from the
  french by E. Legarde. Baltimore. 1874. D.
                                          Q 151
Quizma. Milw. 1878. S.   **Q 31**
Rachel's share of the road. (Round-robin ser.)
  Bost. 1882. S.   **R 1**
Raabe, W:, (Jakob Corvinus). Abu Telfan, oder
  Die heimkehr vom Mondgebirge; ein ro-
  man in drei theilen. 2te aufl. Stuttg.
  [1870]. D.   **R 101**

x denotes books specially adapted for children.

Raabe, W:, (*Jakob Corvinus*).—*Continued.*
— Alte nester ; zwei bücher lebensgeschichten. Braunschw. 1880. D.   **R 102**
— Christoph Pechlin ; eine internationale liebesgeschichte. Leipz. 1873. 2 v. in 1. D.   **R 103**
— Die chronik der Sperlingsgasse. 2te aufl. Berlin. 1878. D.   **R 104**
— Deutscher adel ; eine erzählung. Braunschw. 1880. D.   **R 105**
— Deutscher mondschein ; vier erzählungen. 2te aufl. Stuttg. 1875. D.   **R 106**
   Contents, see Deutscher katalog, p. 90.
— Drei federn. Berlin. 1865. S.   **R 107**
— Ein frühling. 2te aufl. Berlin. 1872. D.   **R 108**
— Ferne stimmen ; erzählungen. Berlin. 1865. D.   **R 109**
   Contents, see Deutscher katalog, p. 90.
— Der heilige born ; blätter aus dem bilderbuch des sechzehnten jahrhunderts. Wien. 1861. 2 v. in 1. T.   **R 110**
— Horacker, Berlin. 1881. S.   **R 111**
— Der hungerpastor ; ein roman in drei bänden. Berlin. 1864. 3 v. in 1. D.   **R 112**
— Die kinder von Finkenrode. 2te aufl. Stuttg. 1870. S.   **R 113**
— Krähenfelder geschichten. Braunschw. 1879. 3 v. in 1. D.   **R 114**
   Contents, see Deutscher katalog, p. 90.
— Die leute aus dem walde, ihre sterne, wege und schicksale ; ein roman. Braunschw. 1863. D.   **R 115**
— Meister Autor, oder Die geschichte vom versunkenen garten. Leipz. 1874. D.   **R 116**
— Nach dem grossen kriege ; eine geschichte in zwölf briefen. Berlin. 1861. S.   **R 117**
— Der regenbogen ; sieben erzählungen. 2te aufl. Stuttg. [1875]. 2 v. in 1. D.   **R 118**
   Contents, see Deutscher katalog, p. 90.
— Der schüdderump. Braunschw. 1870. 2 v. in 1. D.   **R 119**
— Verworrenes leben ; novellen und skizzen. Glogau. 1862. D.   **R 120**
   Contents, see Deutscher katalog, p. 90.
— Wunnigel ; eine erzählung. Braunschw. 1879. D.   **R 121**
Radcliffe, Anne, *born* Ward. The romance of the forest. Lond. *n. d.* D.   **R 401**
Raimund, Golo, *pseud., see* Frederich, Bertha.
Ramé, Louise de la, (*Ouida*). Bébée, or Two little wooden shoes ; a story. Phila. 1881. D.   **R 151**
— Bimbi ; stories for children. Phila. 1882. D.   **Rx 151**
   Contents. The Nürnberg stove.—The ambitious rosetree.—Moufflow.—Lampblack.—The child of Urbino.—In the apple-country. — Findelkind. — Meleagris gallopavo.—The little earl.
— A dog of Flanders. *In* Johnson, E. R. Little c assics.   **J 926 v10**
— A leaf in a storm. *In the same.*   **J 926 v11**
— *Same,* and other stories. Phila. 1872. O.   **R 156**
   Contents. A Provence rose.— A leaf in a storm.— A dog of Flanders.—A branch of lilacs.
— Mouflou. *In* Tales from many sources.   **T 178 v2**
— Wanda countess von Szalras ; a novel. N. Y. 1883. 2 v. D.   **R 160**
Rand, E: A. The bark-cabin on Kearsarge. Bost. [1880]. D.   **Rx 176**
— Little Brown-Top. Ill. Bost. [1883]. D.   **Rx 178**
— The tent in the notch. Bost. 1881. D.   **Rx 177**

Rand, Mary Abbott. Holly and mistletoe. N. Y. [1881]. O.   **Rx 101**
Randolph, *Mrs.* —. Little Pansy. N. Y. 1881. Q.   **R 251**
— Reseda. N. Y. 1881. Q.   **R 252**
— Wild Hyacinth. Phila. 1876. D.   **R 253**
Rands, W: Brightly, (*Henry Holbeach*). Shoemakers' village. Lond. 1871. 2 v. in 1. D.   **R 301**
Rank, Josef. Achtspännig ; volksroman. Leipz. 1857. 2 v. S.   **R 351**
— Aus dem Böhmerwalde ; bilder und erzählungen aus dem volksleben. Erste gesammtausgabe. Leipz. 1851. 3 v. D.   **R 352**
   Contents, see Deutscher katalog, p. 90.
— Burgei, oder Die drei wünsche. *T. p. w.* S.   **R 353**
— Ein dorfbrutus ; charakterbild. [Nebst einem anhange.] Glogau. 1860. 2 in 1. S.   **R 358**
   Contents, see Deutscher katalog, p. 90.
— Das Hofer-Käthchen ; erzählung. Leipz. 1854. T.   **R 359**
— Johannes Volkh.—Hausmittel der liebe.—Ein guter mensch ; drei erzählungen. Leipz. 1867. S.   **R 354**
— Eine mutter vom lande. Leipz. 1848. S.   **R 355**
— Der seelenfänger ; roman. 2te aufl. Stuttg. 1878. D.   **R 360**
— Sein ideal ; erzählung. Zwickau. 1856. S.   **R 356**
— Waldmeister. Leipz. 1846. 3 v. S.   **R 357**
Rare pale Margaret ; a novel, by the author of "The two miss Flemings." N. Y. 1878. Q.   **R 9**
Raspe, Rudolph Erich. The travels and surprising adventures of baron Munchausen. Ill. N. Y. [1885]. D.   **R 201**
   Note. For summary of evidence as to authorship, which is disputed, *see* Allibone, Dictionary of authors, 820 : R 1 v2.
Rathbone, Hannah Mary. So much of the diary of lady Willoughby as relates to her domestic history and to the eventful period of the reign of Charles I, the protectorate and the restoration. [*Anon.*] Lond. 1873. D.   **R 426**
— Some further portions of [*the same.*] [*Anon.*] Lond. 1848. O.   **R 427**
Rau, Heribert. Alexander von Humboldt ; culturhistorisch-biographischer roman. Leipz. 1860. 7 v. D.   **R 451**
— Beethoven ; historischer roman. Frankfurt a. M. 1859. 4 v. D.   **R 452**
— Garibaldi, Italiens held und schwert ; historisches lebensbild. Berlin. 1864. 3 v. D.   **R 453**
— Girandolen. Stuttg. 1841. 2 v. D.   **R 454**
   Contents, see Deutscher katalog, p. 91.
— Jean Paul ; culturhistorisch - biographischer roman. Leipz. 1861. 4 v. D.   **R 455**
— Mozart ; cultur-historischer roman. Frankfurt a. M. 1858. 6 v. D.   **R 456**
— *Same, eng.* Mozart ; a biographical romance. From the german by E. R. Sill. Bost. 1876. D.   **R 456**
— Der raub Strassburgs im jahre 1681 ; vaterländischer roman. 2te aufl. 3 theile in 1 b. Berlin. [1875]. D.   **R 457**
Raven, Mathilde, *born* Beckmann. Galileo Galilei ; ein geschichtlicher roman. Leipz. 1866. 2 v. S.   **R 501**
— Eine rolle gold. Leipz. 1864. S.   **R 502**

Raymond, Ross. No laggards we. N. Y. 1881.
D.   **R 551**
Raymond, Rossiter Worthington, (*Robertson Gray*). Camp and cabin ; sketches of life and travel in the west. Ill. N. Y. 1880. T.
                                            R 576
Contents. Thanksgiving Joe. — Agamemnon.— Widow Baker.—Wonders of the Yellowstone.—The ice-caves of Washington Territory.—The ascent of Gray's Peak.
Reade, C: Art ; a dramatic tale. *With his* Clouds and sunshine.   **R 603**
— The box tunnel. *In* Johnson, E. R. Little classics.   **J 926 v9**
— Christie Johnstone. Leipz. 1873. S.   **R 601**
— *Same. With his* Peg Woffington.   **R 622**
— The cloister and the hearth ; a tale of the middle ages. Leipz. 1864. 2 v. in 1. S. **R 602**
— Clouds and sunshine. Bost. 1855. S.   **R 603**
— A good fight, and other tales. N. Y. 1859. D.
                                            R 604
Includes, Autobiography of a thief.—Jack of all trades.
— Good stories. Ill. N. Y. 1884. D.   **R 621**
Contents. The history of an acre.—The Knightsbridge mystery.—Singleheart and Doubleface.—Tit for tat.—Rus.—Born to good luck.—There's many a slip 'twixt the cup and the lip.—The picture.—What has become of lord Camelford's body.—*Good stories of man and other animals.* The knight's secret.—A special constable.—Lambert's leap.—Man's life saved by fowls and woman's by a pig.—Reality.—Exchange of animals.—The two Lears.—Doubles.—The jilt; a yarn.—The kindly jest.—An old bachelor's adventure.
— Good stories of man and other animals. N. Y. 1884. Q.   **R 617**
Contents. The knight's secret.—A special constable.—Suspended animation.—Lambert's leap.—Man's life saved by fowls and woman's by a pig.—Reality.—Exchange of animals.—The two Lears.—Doubles.—The jilt; a yarn.—Tit for tat.—Rus.— Born to good luck.—"There's many a slip 'twixt the cup and the lip."—The picture.—What has become of lord Camelford's body ?
— Hard cash ; a matter-of-fact romance. N. Y. n. d. D.   **R 605**
— *Same.* Bost. 1874. D.   **R 605**
— It is never too late to mend ; a matter-of-fact romance. Leipz. 1856. 2 v. in 1. S. **R 606**
— *Same.* Bost. 1856. 2 v. D.   **R 606**
— Jack of all trades ; a matter-of-fact romance ; being a narrative of the famed elephant Djek and her keeper. N. Y. 1884. S.
                                            R 618
— The Knightsbridge mystery. *In* Tales from many sources.   **T 178 v2**
— Love me little, love me long. Leipz. 1859. S.
                                            R 607
— Multum in parvo ; a series of good stories with no waste of words. N. Y. 1882. Q. **R 616**
Contents. The history of an acre.—The Knightsbridge mystery.—Singleheart and Doubleface.
— Peg Woffington. Leipz. 1872. S.   **R 608**
— *Same,* Christie Johnstone, and other stories. N. Y. 1877. D.   **R 622**
Includes, Clouds and sunshine.—Art; a dramatic tale.—Propria quæ maribus.—The box tunnel.—Jack of all trades.
— A perilous secret ; a novel. N. Y. 1884. Q.
                                            R 620
— *Same.* Lond. 1884. 2 v. D.   **R 620**
— The picture. N. Y. 1884. S.   **R 619**
— Put yourself in his place. Leipz. 1870. 2 v. in 1. S.   **R 609**
— *Same.* N. Y. 1871. D.   **R 609**
— A simpleton ; a story of today. Leipz. 1874. 2 v. in 1. S.   **R 610**

Reade, C:—*Continued.*
— A terrible temptation ; a story of today. Leipz. 1872. 2 v. in 1. S.   **R 611**
— *Same.* Bost. 1871. O.   **R 611**
— The wandering heir ; a matter-of-fact romance. Leipz. 1875. S.   **R 612**
— *Same.* Bost. 1873. S.   **R 612**
— White lies. N. Y. 1877. D.   **R 613**
— A woman hater. N. Y. 1877. D.   **R 614**
— *and* Dion **Boucicault.** Foul play. N. Y. 1877. D.   **R 615**
Reade, Compton. Under which king ? a novel. N. Y. 1885. Q.   **R 636**
Reed, Andrew. No fiction, or The test of friendship ; a narrative founded on recent and interesting facts ; with add. Baltimore. 1821. 2 v. S.   **R 651**
Reed, I: G. Erring yet noble ; a tale of and for women. Bost. 1865. D.   **R 701**
Reed, Pamelia M. Converse, *mrs.* Jos. J. The adventures of Olaf Tryggveson, king of Norway ; a tale of the 10th century showing how christianity was introduced into Norway. Bost. 1865. S.   **R 751**
Reeves, Helen Buckingham, *born* Mather, *mrs.* H: As he comes up the stair. Leipz. 1882. S.   **R 3505**
— "Cherry ripe." Leipz. 1878. 2 v. in 1. S.
                                          R 3501
— *Same.* N. Y. 1878. O.   **R 3501**
— *Same.* N. Y. 1881. O.   **R 3501**
— Comin' thro' the Rye. N. Y. 1878. O. **R 3502**
— Eyre's acquittal. Leipz. 1884. 2 v. in 1. S.
                                          R 3506
— Jock O'Hazelgreen. Leipz. 1882. S.   *With her* As he comes up the stair.   **R 3505**
— "Land o' the leal." Leipz. 1879. S. **R 3503**
— My lady Green Sleeves. Leipz. 1879. S.
                                          R 3504
— Sam's sweetheart. Leipz. 1883. 3 v. in 1. S.
                                          R 3507
— "Who maketh the deaf to hear." Leipz. 1882. S. *With her* As he comes up the stair.
                                          R 3505
Rehfues, Philipp Joseph. Die belagerung des castells von Gozzo, oder Der letzte assassine. Von dem verfasser des Scipio Cicala. Leipz. 1834. 2 v. S.   **R 776**
Reichenbach, Moritz v., *pseud., see* Bethusy-Huc, Valeska *gräfin.*
Reid, Christian, *pseud., see* **Fisher,** Frances C.
Reid, Mayne. Afloat in the forest ; or a voyage among the tree-tops. Ill. N. Y. 1882. D.
                                          Rx 401
— The boy hunters, or Adventures in search of a white buffalo. Ill. N. Y. 1882. D. **Rx 402**
— The boy slaves. Ill. N. Y. 1882. D. **Rx 403**
— The boy tar, or The voyage in the dark. Ill. N. Y. 1882. D.   **Rx 404**
— Bruin ; the grand bear hunt. N. Y. 1882. D.
                                          Rx 414
— The bush-boys, or The history and adventures of a Cape farmer and his family in the wild karoos of southern Africa. Ill. N. Y. 1882. D.   **Rx 405**
— The cliff climbers, or The lone home in the Himalayas ; a sequel to the "Plant hunters." Ill. N. Y. 1882. D.   **Rx 406**
— The english family Robinson : The desert home, or The adventures of a lost family in the wilderness. Ill. N. Y. 1882. D.   **Rx 407**

x denotes books specially adapted for children.

Reid, Mayne.—*Continued.*
— The forest exiles, or The perils of a peruvian family amid the wilds of the Amazon. Ill. Bost. 1859. D. **Rx 408**
— *Same.* N. Y. 1882. D. **Rx 408**
— The giraffe-hunters. Ill. N. Y. 1882. D. **Rx 409**
— The ocean waifs ; a story of adventure on land and sea. Ill. N. Y. 1882. D. **Rx 410**
— The plant hunters, or Adventures among the Himalaya mountains. Ill. N. Y. 1882. D. **Rx 411**
  Note. For continuation, *see* The cliff climbers.
— Ran away to sea ; an autobiography for boys. N. Y. 1882. D. **Rx 412**
— The young yägers, or A narrative of hunting adventures in southern Africa. Ill. N. Y. 1882. D. **Rx 413**
Reimar, Reinald, *pseud., see* **Gläser,** Adolf.
Reinbold, Adelheid, (*Franz Berthold*). Irrwisch-Fritze. *With* **Schücking,** L. Die schwester. **S 1831**
Reinhardt, Luise, (*Ernst Fritze*). Caritas ; roman in drei büchern. Prag. 1857. 3 v. T. **R 851**
— Die erben von Wollun ; novelle. Wien. 1861. T. **R 852**
— Erinnerungsblätter ; aus dem leben eines criminalisten. Leipzig. 1857. S. **R 853**
  Contents. see Deutscher katalog, p. 91.
— Die gebrüder Koltrum. Leipz. 1865. S. **R 854**
— Idalium ; novelle. Wien. 1862. 2 v. T. **R 855**
— Im kerker geboren ; ein roman. *In* Vierteljährl. mag. **V 2 v24**
— Schloss Bärenberg ; roman. Leipz. 1867. 3 v. S. **R 856**
Reinhold, C., *pseud., see* **Köstlin,** Christian Reinhold.
Reinow, M. Idealisten ; roman. N. Y. 1882. F. **R 3401**
Reinsberg-Düringsfeld, Ida v., *see* **Düringfeld,** Ida v. **Reinsberg-.**
Reitzenstein, Franziska *freifrau* v., (*Franz von Nemmersdorf*). Allein in der welt ; roman in vier büchern. Berlin. 1868. 3 v. S. **R 876**
— Doge und papst ; historischer roman aus dem siebzehnten jahrhundert in vier büchern. Breslau. 1865. 2 v. D. **R 877**
Rellstab, L.: 1812 ; ein historischer roman. 5te aufl. Leipz. 1860. 4 v. in 2. D. **R 902**
— Drei jahre von dreissigen. N. Y. 1858. 3 v. D. **R 901**
— Neue empfindsame reisen ; post- und seestücke, erzstufen, intermezzo's, etc. Leipz. 1837. 2 v. S. **R 904**
— Sommerblumensträusse den holden jungfrauen gewidmet. Leipz. 1842. 2 v. S. **R 903**
  Contents, see Deutscher katalog, p. 91.
Retcliffe, Sir John, *pseud., see* **Gödsche,** Hermann Ottomar F:
Reuter, Fritz. Sämmtliche werke. N. Y. 1872. 14 v. in 5. D. **R 951**
  Contents, see Deutscher katalog, p. 91.
— An old story of my farming days, (Ut mine stromtid). From the german by M. W. Macdowell. Leipz. 1878. 3 v. in 2. S. **R 953**
— *Same.* Seed-time and harvest, or "During my apprenticeship." Tr. from the "Ut mine stromtid." Phila. 1871. O. **R 953**

Reuter, Fritz.—*Continued.*
— In the year '13 ; a tale of Mecklenburg life. Tr. from the platt-deutsch by C: Lee Lewis. Leipz. 1867. S. **R 952**
Reybaud, Henriette Etiennette Fanny, *born* Arnaud, *mme.* C: Das fräulein von Malepeire. 1855. S. **R 1001**
— Uncle César. N. Y. 1879. S. **R 1002**
— *Same, germ.* Onkel Cäsar. Aus dem franz. von C. Büchele. Stuttg. 1859. T. **R 1002**
Rice, James, *joint author, see* **Besant,** Walter.
Richards, T. Addison. Tallulah and Jocasse, or Romances of southern landscape and other tales. Charleston. 1852. D. **R 1101**
Richardson, James, (*Adam Stwin*). Eyes right ; a bachelor's talks with his boys. Ill. Bost. 1878. O. **Rx 501**
Richardson, J: Hardscrabble, oder Der fall von Chicago ; erzählung aus dem indianerkriege. Leipz. 1857. S. **R 1151**
Richardson, Oliver. [Tales.] *In* Wilson, J: M. Tales of the borders. **W 2202**
  Contents. The angler's tale, v. 16.—The dissolved pledge, v. 19.—The meeting at St. Boswell's, v. 10.—The physiognomist's tales. v. 8.—The restored son, v. 14.—The Rothesay fisherman, v. 6.—The school-fellows, v. 11.—The sea-storm, v. 12.—The story of Tom Bertram, v. 15.—Tom Duncan's yarn, v. 9.—The two sailors, v. 13.
Richardson, S: Clarissa, or The history of a young lady ; comprehending the most important concerns of private life. Lond. 1751. 7 v. D. **R 1201**
— *Same.* Condensed by C. H. Jones. (Leisure hour ser.) N. Y. 1874. S. **R 1202**
— The history of sir C: Grandison in a series of letters. 5th ed. Lond. 1766. 7 v. S. **R 1205**
— *Same.* New and abridged ed. by Mary Howitt. Lond. *n. d.* D. **R 1204**
— Pamela, or Virtue rewarded ; in a series of familiar letters from a beautiful young damsel to her parents, and afterwards in her exalted condition between her and persons of figure and quality, upon the most important and entertaining subjects in genteel life. Publ. in order to cultivate the principles of virtue and religion in the minds of the youth of both sexes. 6th ed., corr. Ill. Lond. 1742. 4 v. D. **R 1203**
Richmond, Legh. Annals of the poor ; containing The dairyman's daughter, The negro servant, and Young cottager, etc. A new ed., enl. and ill., with an introductory sketch of the author by the rev. John Ayre. Bost. 1829. T. **Rx 551**
Richter, J: Paul F:, (*Jean Paul*). Sämmtliche werke. **830 : 142**
  Contents, see Deutscher katalog, p. 21.
— Flower, fruit and thorn pieces, or The married life, death and wedding of the advocate of the poor, Firmian Stanislaus Siebenkäs. Tr. from the german by E: H: Noel, with a memoir of the author by T: Carlyle. Bost. 1863. 2 v. D. **R 1251**
— Hesperus, or Forty-five dog-post days ; a biography from the german, tr. by C: T. Brooks. N. Y. 1877. 2 v. S. **R 1252**
— The invisible lodge. From the german by C: T. Brooks. (Leisure hour ser.) N. Y. 1883. S. **R 1256**
— Titan ; a romance. From the germ., tr. by C: T. Brooks. Bost. 1862. 2 v. D. **R 1253**

x denotes books specially adapted for children.

Richter, J: Paul F:, (Jean Paul).—Continued.
— Walt and Vult, or The twins. From the german, tr. by [E. B. Lee] the author of "Life of Jean Paul." N. Y. 1863. 2 v. D.   R 1254
Richter, Moritz. Die familie Crevecoeur ; historischer roman aus den jahren 1806 und 7. Leipz. 1828. S.   R 1301
Riddell, Charlotte Eliza Lawson, born Cowan, mrs. J. H., (F. G. Trafford). Daisies and and buttercups ; a novel. N. Y. 1882. Q.   R 1353
— Same. Lond. 1882. 3 v. in 1. D.   R 1353
— George Geith of Fen Court. Bost. 1865. D.   R 1351
— The race for wealth ; a novel. Lond. [1876]. D.   R 1356
— The senior partner ; a novel. N. Y. 1882. Q.   R 1352
— Same. Lond. 1881. 3 v. D.   R 1352
— A struggle for fame ; a novel. N. Y. 1883. Q.   R 1354
— Same. Lond. 1883. 3 v. in 1. D.   R 1354
— Susan Drummond ; a novel. N. Y. 1884. Q.   R 1355
— Same. Lond. 1884. 3 v. in 1. D.   R 1355
Ridderstad, C: F: Der fürst. Aus dem schwedischen übers. von Gottlob Fink. Stuttg. 1852. 2 v. T.   R 1401
— Das gewissen, oder Geheimnisse von Stockholm. Aus dem schwedischen übers. von Gottlob Fink. Stuttg. 1852. 6 v. T.   R 1402
— Königin Luise Ulrike und ihr hof. Aus dem schwedischen übers. von Gottlob Fink. Stuttg. 1856. 3 v. T.   R 1403
— Der trabant ; geschichtlicher roman. Aus dem schwedischen übers. von Gottlob Fink. Stuttg. 1852. 4 v. T.   R 1404
— Vater und sohn. Aus dem schwedischen übers. von Gottlob Fink. Stuttg. 1854. 3 v. T.   R 1405
Riddle, Albert Gallatin. Alice Brand ; a romance of the capital. N. Y. 1875. D.   R 1451
Rideing, W: H: Boys coastwise, or All along the shore. Ill. N. Y. [1884]. O.   Rx 602
— Boys in the mountains and on the plains, or The western adventures of Tom Smart, Bob Edge and Peter Small. N. Y. [1882]. O.   Rx 601
— A little upstart ; a novel. Bost. 1885. D.   R 1426
Ridley, Annie E. Better than good ; a story for girls. N. Y. 1881. Q.   R 1501
Riehl, W: H: Culturgeschichtliche novellen. Stuttg. 1856. S.   R 1553
Contents, see Deutscher katalog, p. 92.
— Neues novellenbuch. 2te ausg. Stuttg. 1873. D.   R 1551
Contents, see Deutscher katalog, p. 92.
Ring, Max. Aus dem tagebuche eines Berliner arztes. Leipz. 1870. 2 v. in 1. S.   R 1601
— Die chambregarnisten ; eine stadtgeschichte. Leipz. 1852. T.   R 1602
— Christkind-Agnes ; eine stadtgeschichte. Berlin. 1852. T.   R 1603
— Feine welt ; eine stadtgeschichte. Leipz. 1852. T.   R 1604
— Fürst und musiker. N. Y. 1882. F.   R 1610
— Der geheimrath ; ein lebensbild. Prag. 1857. T.   R 1605
— Das haus Hillel ; historischer roman aus der zeit der zerstörung Jerusalem. N. Y. 1881. F.   R 1606
— Hinter den coulissen : Erinnerungen und bio-

Ring, Max.—Continued.
graphien aus der theaterwelt. Leipz. 1872. 2 v. in 1. S.   R 1607
Contents, see Deutscher katalog, p. 92.
— John Milton und seine zeit ; historischer roman. Leipz. 1871. 4 v. in 1. S.   R 1608
— Same, eng. John Milton and his times ; an historical novel. Tr. from the germ. by F. Jordan. Ill. N. Y. 1868. O.   R 1608
— Die lügner ; roman aus der modernen gesellschaft. 2te aufl. Stuttg. 1880. 3 v. in 1. D.   R 1609
— Verirrt und erlöst ; roman. Leipz. 1870. 3 v. in 1. S.   R 1611
Ritchie, Anna Isabella, born Thackeray. Bluebeard's keys, and other stories. N. Y. 1875. O.   R 1651
Includes, Riquet à la houppe.—Jack and the bean stalk.—The white cat.
— Da capo. N. Y. 1878. T.   R 1658
— Same, and other tales. Leipz. 1880. S.   R 1652
Includes, Fina.—Across the peat-fields.—Miss Morier's visions.
— Miss Angel. N. Y. 1875. O.   R 1653
— Miss Williamson's divagations. N. Y. 1881. Q.   R 1654
Contents, Fina.—Fina's aunt.—Da capo.—A postscript from a stage-box.—Miss Morier's visions.—Across the peat-fields.
— Old Kensington. N. Y. 1873. O.   R 1655
— The story of Elizabeth. N. Y. 1863. S.   R 1656
— The village on the cliff. N. Y. 1867. O.   R 1657
Ritchie, Leitch. Wearyfoot Common. From Chambers' journal. N. Y. 1854. O. R 1701
Ritter, Ernst, pseud., see Binzer, Emilie v.
Ritter Hyneck von Schafgotsch, oder Heldenmuth und edelsinn ; eine erzählung aus den zeiten kaiser Karls IV, könig von Böhmen. Meissen. 1836. 2 v. S.   R 21
Roberts, Margaret. The atelier du lys, or An art student in the reign of terror. [Anon.] Leipz. 1877. 2 v. 1. S.   R 1801
— Same. Noblesse oblige. (Leisure hour ser.) [Anon.] N. Y. 1876. S.   R 1801
— Denise. [Anon.] N. Y. 1864. 2 v. D. F.   R 1802
— In the olden time. [Anon]. (Leisure hour ser.) N. Y. 1883. S.   R 1806
— Madame Fontenoy. [Anon]. Leipz. 1866. S.   R 1803
— Mademoiselle Mori ; a tale of modern Rome. [Anon]. Leipz. 1862. 2 v. in 1. S.   R 1804
— On the edge of the storm. [Anon.] Leipz. 1869. S.   R 1805
Robinson, Agnes Mary Frances. Arden ; a novel. N. Y. 1883. Q.   R 1826
Robinson, F. Mabel. Mr. Butler's ward ; a novel. N. Y. 1885. S.   R 3601
Robinson, F: W: As long as she lived. Lond. 1876. 3 v. in 1. D.   R 1851
— The black speck ; a temperance tale. N. Y. 1881. Q.   R 1852
— The courting of Mary Smith ; a novel. N. Y. 1885. Q.   R 1860
— Coward conscience. Lond. 1879. 3 v. in 1. D.   R 1853
— Same. N. Y. 1879. Q.   R 1853
— A fair maid ; a novel. N. Y. 1884. Q.   R 1857
— The hands of justice ; a novel. N. Y. 1883. Q.   R 1855
— Lazarus in London ; a novel. N. Y. 1885. Q.   R 1859

x denotes books specially adapted for children.

Robinson, F: W:—*Continued.*
— The mau she cared for ; a novel. N. Y. 1884.
 Q.   **R 1856**
— Mattie ; a stray ; N. Y. 1874. O.   **R 1854**
— Women are strange, and other stories. N. Y.
 1884. Q.   **R 1858**
Robinson, Jane. The gold-worshippers, or The
 days we live in ; a future historical novel.
 [*Anon*]. Lond. 1851. 3 v. D.   **R 1901**
— Die jungfrau von Orleans ; historischer roman.
 Aus dem englischen von W. Schöttlen.
 Stuttg. 1850. 3 v. D.   **R 1902**
— Whitefriars, oder Die tage Karls des zweiten ;
 ein historischer roman. Stuttg. 1845. 3 v.
 T.   **R 1903**
Robinson, Therese Albertine Louise, *born* v. Ja-
 cob, (*Talvj*). The exiles. N. Y. 1853. D.
                                       R 1951
Roche, Regina Maria. The children of the abbey.
 Phila. 1876. D.   **R 2001**
Rochefort, V: H: *marquis de Rochefort-Luçay,*
 called H: Mademoiselle Bismarck. From
 the french by Virginia Champlin. N. Y.
 1881. S.   **R 2051**
Rockwell, Reese. A golden inheritance. N. Y.
 1884. D.   **Rx 651**
Rodenberg, Julius. Die neue sündfluth ; ein ro-
 man aus der vorigen jahrhundert. Berlin.
 1865. 4 v. D.   **R 2151**
— Von Gottes gnaden ; ein roman aus Cromwell's
 zeit. 2te aufl. Berlin. 1870. 5 v. in 2. D.
                                       R 2152
Rodney, *Mrs.* Minnie Reeves, (*Fadette*). Inge-
 misco. [*Anon*]. N. Y. 1867. D.   **R 2201**
 Note. Fadette is also supposed to be Marion C. Le-
 gare Reeves.
Rodt-Calkum, —. Echt conservativ ; erzählung.
 In Vierteljährl. mag.   **V 1 v33**
Roe, Azel Stephens. Give me thine heart. N.
 Y. 1880. D.   **R 2251**
— James Montjoy, or I've been thinking. N. Y.
 1884. D.   **R 2253**
— The minister's story. *With his* To love and to
 be loved.   **R 2252**
— To love and to be loved. N. Y. 1871. D.
                                       R 2252
Roe, E: Payson. Barriers burned away. N. Y.
 [1872]. D.   **R 2301**
— A day of fate. N. Y. 1880. D.   **R 2302**
— Driven back to Eden. N. Y. 1885. D. **Rx 676**
— A face illumined. N. Y. [1878]. D.   **R 2303**
— From jest to earnest. N. Y. [1875]. D.
                                       R 2304
— His sombre rivals. N. Y. 1883. D.   **R 2310**
— A knight of the 19th century. N. Y. [1877]. D.
                                       R 2305
— Nature's serial story. Ill. N. Y. 1885 [1884].
 O.   **R 2312**
— Near to nature's heart. N. Y. 1876. D.
                                       R 2306
— The opening of a chestnut burr. N. Y. [1874].
                                       R 2307
— An original belle. N. Y. [1885]. D. **R 2314**
— An unexpected result, and other stories. N. Y.
 [1883]. S.   **R 2313**
 Includes, Christmas-eve in war times. — Three
 thanksgiving kisses.
— What can she do ? N. Y. 1875. D.   **R 2309**
— Without a home. N. Y. 1881. D.   **R 2308**
— A young girl's wooing. N. Y. [1884]. D.
                                       R 2311
Roe, E: Reynolds. Brought to bay ; a novel.
 N. Y. 1882. D.   **R 2326**

Roe, E: Reynolds.—*Continued.*
— The gray and the blue ; a story founded on
 incidents connected with the war for the
 union. Chicago. 1884. D.   **R 2327**
Roe, Mary A., (*C. M. Cornwall*). Free, yet forging their own chains. N. Y. [1876]. D.
                                       R 2351
Roosevelt, Blanche, *see* Tucker - Machetta,
 Blanche.
Ropes, Mary Emily. Finette, the norman maiden
 and her english friends. *T. p. w.* [N. Y.
 1878]. S.   **Rx 701**
Roquette, O: Conrad Hagen's mistake. From
 the german by mrs. S. A. Crozer. Phila.
 1881. D.   **R 2401**
— Heinrich Falk. Breslau. 1858. 3 v. D.
                                       R 2402
— Der kobold ; ein roman. *In* Vierteljährl.
 mag.   **V 2 v37**
— Luginsland ; novellen. N. Y. 1883. F. **R 2405**
 Includes, Lorelei.—Gothenwiek.—Die schneewoche.
 Radüit's buche.—Ich und meine companie.
— Neue erzählungen. Stuttg. 1862. D.   **R 2403**
 Contents, see Deutscher katalog, p. 93.
— Novellen. 2te aufl. Berlin. 1875. D. **R 2404**
 Contents, see Deutscher katalog, p. 93.
— Die schlangen-königin. *With* Schücking,
 Die schwester.   **S 1831**
Roscoe, T: The german novelists. Tr. from the
 originals, with critical and biographical
 notices. (The "Chandos classics"). Lond.
 n. d. D.   **R 2451**
 Contents. The pleasant history of Reynard the fox.
 —How lieglass the merry jester.—Doctor Faustus.—
 Popular traditions. Local popular traditions from the
 south side of the Hartz: The horseshoe on the church
 door; Jacob Nimmernuchtern; Lora the goddess of
 love.—From the Golden Green: The knights' cellar
 in the Kyffhausen; Peter Klaus the goatherd.—
 From the north side of the Hartz: The maiden of
 Conradsburg's tale; Castle Dumburg; The wild hunter of Hackelnberg; The wolf stone.—**Gottschalk,**
 F: The witch-dance on the Brocken; The meadow
 dance; The devil's fight in Goslar cathedral; The
 mouse tower; The castle spectre of Scharzfeld; The
 kingdom of heaven; The monastery; The devil-
 stones; Notburga; Ritter Bodo; The lion fight; The
 unlucky miser of Questenberg; The miraculous fish;
 The prudent princess; The devil's mill.—**Eberhardt,**
 The bet; Treachery its own betrayer.—**Büsching, J:**
 G. History of count Walter and the lady Helgunda;
 Assassination of the empress of Tartary.—**Grimm,**
 J: L: *and* W: K: Specimens from the "Kinder und
 haus märchen".—**Lothar.** The arch-rogue; Castle
 Christburg.—**La Motte Fouqué,** F: H: K: de. The
 field of terror; The mandrake; Head master Rhenfried and his family.—**Popular tales. Musäus,** J: A:
 The dumb lover.—**Schiller,** J: C. F: v. The appari-
 tionist; The sport of destiny; A criminal, or Martyr
 to lost honour; Fraternal magnanimity; A walk
 among the linden trees.—*German novels.* **Tieck,** J:
 L: Love magic some centuries ago; The faithful
 Eckart and the Tannenhäuser; The Tannenhäuser,
 or Lord of the fir woods; Auburn Egbert.—**Langbein,** A: F: Marianne Richards; Seven marriages
 and never a husband; The irreconcilable man; Albert Limbach; An hour's instruction in political
 economy; The lady's palfrey.—**Engel,** M. E. The
 anti-speculator; Toby Witt; Lady Elizabeth Hill.
— The italian novelists. Tr. from the originals
 with critical and biographical notices.
 (The "Chandos classics"). Lond. n. d. D.
                                       R 2452
 Contents. Novelle antiche.—Boccaccio.—Sacchetti.—
 Sir Giovanni Fiorentino.—Masuccio Salernitano.—Sa-
 badino degli Arienti.—Luigi da Porto.—Bernardo Illici-
 ni.—Alessandro Sozzini.—Niccolo Machiavelli.—Agnolo
 Firenzuola.—Pietro Fortini.—Gentile Sermini.—Gio-
 vanni Brevio. — Girolamo Parabosco.—Marco Cade-
 mosto da Lodi.—Giovambattista Giraldi Cinthio.—
 Anton-Francesco Grazzini.—Ortensio Lando.—Giovan-
 Francesco Straparola.—Matteo Bandello.—Francesco
 Sansovino. — Anton - Francesco Doni. — Sebastiano

 x denotes books specially adapted for children.

Roscoe, T:—*Continued.*
Erizzo.—Niccolò Granucci.—Ascanio Mori da Ceno.—Celio Malespini. — Salvuccio Salvucci. — Novela by anonymous authors.—Maiolino Bisaccioni.—Michele Colombo. — Scipioni Bargagli. — Giovanni Bottari.—Albergati Capacelli. — Francesco Soave.—Gianfrancesco Altanesi. — Count Lorenzo Magalotti. —Carlo Lodoli.—Domenico Maria Manni. —Autore Ignoto.—Girolamo Padovani.—Luigi Sanvitale. — Count Carlo Gozzi.—Luigi Bramieri.—Robustiano Gironi.

— The spanish novelists. Tr. from the originals with critical and biographical notices. (The "Chandos classics"). Lond. *n. d.* D. **R 2453**

Contents. **Manuel,** *Don* J: El conde Lucanor.—**Mendoza,** D. H. de. Lazarillo de Tormes. — **Aleman,** M. Guzman d' Alfarache. — **Cervantes Saavedra,** M. de. Riconete and Cortadillo; The pretended aunt; El amante liberal.—**Quevedo Villegas,** *Don* F. Vision of the catchpole possessed; Vision of the last judgment.—Paul, the spanish sharper.—**Montalvan,** *Don* J: Perez de. The test of friendship; The effect of being undeceived.—**Eslava,** A. de. The fountain of truth. — **Zayas y Soto Mayor,** M. de. The miser chastised.—**Reyes,** M. de los. The dumb lover and his physician; The mirror of friends; Love and honour; The king and the minister.—**Lozano,** *Don* C. Soledades de la vida, *etc.;* Jealousy of the dead.—**Guevara,** L: Veliz de. Modern miracles.—**Robles,** I. de. The diamond ring; A prodigious adventure.—**Salorzano,** A. del Castillo. The duchess of Mantua; The mask.

Rosegger, Petri Kettenfeier, (*Hans Malser*). Annonce nummero 99; novelette. *In* Vierteljährl. mag. **V 2 v30**

Rosemary and Rue. (Round - robin ser.) Bost. 1881. S. **R 25**

Rosen, Ludwig, *pseud., see* **Jüngst,** L: Volrad.

Rosenthal-Bonin, Hugo v. Der diamantschleifer. N. Y. 1881. F. **R 2551**
— Das gold des Orion; roman. N. Y. 1883. F. **R 2552**

Roskowska, Marie. Polnische mütter; historische novelle. Prag. 1860. T. **R 2626**

Rösler, Robert, (*Julius Mühlfeld*). Bis zum schaffot; criminal-novelle. Leipz. 1868. S. **R 2626**
— Ehre; roman in sechs büchern. Wien. 1862. **R 2627**
— Gefangen und befreit; vaterländische gemälde aus den jahren 1806—1814. Prag. 1860. T. **R 2628**

Ross, Percy. A misguidit lassie. N. Y. 1883. D. **R 3551**

Rossetti, Christina Georgina. A strange journey, or Pictures from Egypt and the Soudan, by the author of "Common-place". N. Y. 1882. Q. **R 3451**

Rössler, Robert. Mein erster patient; erzählung. *In* Vierteljährl. mag. **V 2 v31**
— Schläs'sche durfgeschichten. 2te aufl. Berlin. 1880. D. **R 2651**
Contents, see Deutscher katalog, p. 93.

Roth, E: Christus judex; a traveller's tale. Phila. 1864. S. **R 2701**

Rothenfels, Emmy v., *pseud., see* **Ingersleben,** Emilie v.

Rotterdam, J: van. Des fischers tochter; geschichte aus den dünen. Aus dem flämischen von A. Kretzschmar. Leipz. 1856. S. **R 2801**

Round, W: Marshall Fitz, (*The rev. Peter Pennot*), Achsah; a New England life study. Bost. 1876. D. **R 2851**
— Child Marion abroad. Ill. Bost. 1878. S. **Rx 901**

Rousselet, L: Ralph, the drummer boy; a story of the days of Washington. Tr. by W. J. Gordon. Ill. N. Y. 1884. D. **Rx 951**

Rowson, Susanna, *born* Haswell. Charlotte Temple; a tale of truth. Cinc. *n. d.* T. **R 2876**

Rudbeck, Thure Gustaf. Stockholms vorzeit; romantisirte schilderungen aus der geschichte Schwedens. Aus dem schwedischen von C. F[risch]. Stuttg. 1847. 8 v. in 2. T. **R 2951**

Rudolphi, J: Die freien schützen. Leipz. 1848. 2 v. S. **R 3001**

Ruffini, Giovanni. Doctor Antonio. Edinb. 1856. S. **R 3051**
— *Same.* Leipz. 1861. S. **R 3051**
— Lorenzo Benoni, or Passages in the life of an italian. N. Y. 1857. D. **R 3052**
— Vincenzo, or Sunken rocks. N. Y. 1863. O. **R 3053**

Ruhland, Marie, *pseud., see* **Calm,** Marie.

Ruinen von Moncaldo, Die, oder Ferrogand und seine genossen; eine abenteuerliche geschichte vom verfasser der Erscheinungen im schlosse der Pyrenäen, etc. Braunschw. 1826. 2 v. S. **R 31

Rumohr, Theodor W: Kjerstrup, (*P. P.*). Nils Juel, der dänische admiral und seine zeit. [*Anon.*] Stuttg. 1848. 3 v. T. **N 11

Runkel, W: M. Wontus, or The corps of observation. Phila. 1874. D. **R 3151**

Ruppius, Otto. Ausgewählte erzählungen. N. Y. 1857. 6 v. D. **R 3201**
Contents, see Deutscher katalog, p. 93.
— Gesammelte werke. Erste gesammt-ausg. Berlin. 1874. 6 v. D. **R 3202**
Contents, see Deutscher katalog, p. 93.

Ruskin, J: The king of the Golden River, or The black brothers; a legend of Stiria. New ed. N. Y. 1882. D. **Rx 1001**
— *Same. In* Johnson, E. R. Little classics. **J 926 v10**

Russell, C: Wells. The fall of Damascus; an historical novel. Bost. 1878. D. **R 3251**

Russell, W: Clarke. Auld lang syne. N. Y. 1878. Q. **R 3301**
— *Same.* Lond. 1878. 2 v. in 1. D. **R 3301**
— Jack's courtship; a sailor's yarn of love and shipwreck. N. Y. 1884. Q. **R 3310**
— *Same.* N. Y. 1885 [1884]. S. **R 3310**
— John Holdsworth, chief mate; a novel. N. Y. 1884. Q. **R 3311**
— The Lady Maud, schooner yacht; from the account of a guest on board. N. Y. 1882. Q. **R 3306**
— Little Loo; a novel. N. Y. 1884. Q. **R 3309**
— My watch below, or Yarns spun when off duty. N. Y. 1882. Q. **R 3305**
— An ocean free lance; from a privateersman's log, 1812. N. Y. 1881. Q. **R 3302**
— On the fo'k'sle head; sea stories. N. Y. 1885. Q. **R 3312**
— Round the galley fire. N. Y. [1883]. Q. **R 3308**
— A sailor's sweetheart; an account of the wreck of the sailing ship "Waldershare", from the narrative of mr. William Lee, second mate. Lond. 1881. 3 v. in 1. D. **R 3303**
— A sea queen; a novel. N. Y. 1883. S. **R 3307**
— *Same.* N. Y. 1883. Q. **R 3307**
— A strange voyage; a novel. N. Y. 1885. Q. **R 3313**
— The wreck of the "Grosvenor"; an account of the mutiny of the crew and the loss of the ship while trying to make the Bermudas. N. Y. [187?-]. D. **R 3304**
— *Same.* N. Y. 1883. Q.- **R 3304**

x denotes books specially adapted for children.

Rydberg, Abraham Viktor. The last athenian. Tr. from the swedish by W: W. Thomas, jr. Phila. [1879]. D.   **R 3351**

S., H. C: Who painted the great Murillo de la Merced. *In* Tales from Blackwood.
   T 177 v3

S., J., of Dale, *pseud., see* Stimson, F: J:

S., M. E. W., *pseud., see* Sherwood, Mary Elizabeth Wilson.

Sacher-Masoch, Leopold *ritter v.* Aus dem tagebuche eines weltmannes; causerien aus der gesellschaft und der bühnenwelt. 2te aufl. Halle. 1872. D.   **S 101**
— Der emissär ; eine galizische geschichte. Bern. 1877. D.   **S 102**
— Galizische geschichten ; novellen. Bern. 1881. D.   **S 103**
   Contents, see Deutscher katalog, p. 93.
— Kaunitz ; kultur-historischer roman. Bern. 1877. 2 v. in 1. D.   **S 104**
— Der letzte könig der magyaren ; historischer roman. 2te ausg. Jena. 1870. 3 v. in 1. S.   **S 105**
— Ein mann wird gesucht ; roman in einem bande. Berlin. 1879. O.   **S 106**
— Der neue Hiob; roman. Stuttg. 1878. D.   **S 107**
— Predigten der frau Ganizka. *In* Vierteljährl. mag.   **V 2 v25**
— Wiener hofgeschichten ; historische novellen. V. 1 : Maria Theresia und die freimaurer. Leipz. 1873. S. — V. 2 : Das rendezvous zu Höchstädt. Bern 1877. 2. v. S.   **S 108**
— Zur ehre Gottes ! ; ein zeitgemälde. Bern. 1877. D.   **S 109**
— *Same.* N. Y. 1881. F.   **S 109**

Sadlier, Mary Anne, *born* Madden. Alice Riordan, the blind man's daughter ; a tale for the young. Bost. 1851. T.   **Sx 101**
— Aunt Honor's keepsake ; a chapter from life. N. Y. *n. d.*   **S 156**
— Confessions of an apostate. N. Y. 1864. S.   **S 151**
— The daughter of Tyrconnell ; a tale of the reign of James I. N. Y. 1863. S.   **S 152**
— The heiress of Kilorgan, or Evenings with the old Geraldines. N. Y. *n. d.* S.   **S 154**
— The hermit of the rock ; a tale of Cashel. N. Y. *n. d.* D.   **S 155**
— The red hand of Ulster. *T. p. w.* T.   **S 153**

Saint-Aubain, Andreas Nicolai, (*Carl Bernhard*). Das glückslude. Deutsch von K. L. Kannegiesser. Leipz. 1850. S.   **S 201**
— König Christian der zweite und seine zeit. Deutsch von K. L. Kannegiesser. Leipz. 1847. 4 v. S.   **S 202**

Saint-Hilaire, Marco de, *pseud., see* Hilaire, Émile Marc.

Saint-Mars, Gabrielle Anna, *born* Cisterne de Courtiras, *vicomtesse* de, (*Comtesse Dash*). Die blutige marquise. Deutsch von dr. Scherr. Stuttg. 1850. T.   **S 251**

Saint Pierre, Jacques H: Bernardin de. The indian cottage. *In his* Works. **840 : 4 v1**
— *Same, germ.* Die indische hütte. *With his* Paul und Virginie.   **S 302**
— Paul and Virginia. Bost. 1879. S.   **S 301**
— *Same. In his* Works.   **840 : 4 v1**
— *Same, germ.* Paul und Virginie ; ein naturgemälde. Nach dem französischen von C. Schüler. Darmstadt. 1851. T.   **S 301**
— *Same.* Uebers. von K: Eitner. Hildburgh. 1866. D.   **S 302**

Saintine, Joseph Xavier Boniface, *called.* Picciola ; the prisoner of Fenestrella, or Captivity captive. Phil. 1848. D.   **S 351**
— Woman's whims, or The female barometer. Tr. from the french by Fayette Robinson. N. Y. 1850. D.   **S 352**

Sala, G: A: The seven sons of Mammon. Bost. 1862. O.   **S 401**
— The two prima donnas ; a novel of real life. Phila. *n. d.* O.   **S 402**

Salkeld, Joseph. The belle, the blue and the bigot, or Three fields for woman's influence. Providence. 1844. T.   **S 451**
— Buds, blossoms and fruit of the church. N. Y. 1843. S.   **S 452**
— Herbert Atherton. *T. p. w.* S.   **S 453**

Salvage. (No name ser.) Bost. 1860. S.   **S 3**

Samarow, Gregor, *pseud., see* Meding, J: Ferdinand Martin Oskar.

Sampleton, Samuel, *pseud., see* Monti, L:

Samuels, Adelaide F. Daisy Travers, or The girls of Hive Hall. Bost. [1876]. S.   **Sx 401**

Sand, George, *pseud., see* Dudevant, Amantine Lucile Aurore.

Sandeau, Léonard Sylvain Jules. The house of Penarvan. *In* Fullerton, *Lady* G. C. The lilies of the valley.   **F 1805**

Sandham, Elizabeth. The twin sisters ; a tale for youth. N. Y. 1859. S.   **Sx 501**

Sands, Robert C: Boyuca. [*Anon.*] *In* Tales of Glauber Spa.   **T 186**
— Mr. Green. *In the same.*   **T 186**
— *See also his* Writings.   **820.1 : 6**

Sangster, Margaret E., *born* Munson. Miss Dewberry's scholars and what they did. N. Y. 1882. D.   **Sx 551**

Sarcey, Francisque. The miseries of Fo Hi, a celestial functionary. From the french by A. R. H. Chicago. 1883. S.   **S 501**

Sargent, Epes, *ed.* The emerald ; a collection of graphic and entertaining tales, brilliant poems and essays gleaned chiefly from the fugitive literature of the 19th century. Bost. 1866. D.   **S 551**
   Contents. **Bernard,** C: de. The consultation.—**Allingham,** W: Invocation.—**Neal,** J: Goody Gracious and the forget-me-not.—**Newton,** C. Wonderland.—Coincidences ; a tale of facts.—**Blood,** H: A. A prayer.—**Smith,** H. The picnic party.—**Kimball,** H. M. The guest.—**Chalmers,** A. Lesson in biography.—**Aiken,** B. Uncrowned kings.—**Scribe,** E. Judith, or The opera-box.—**Townshend,** C. A. Wait.—Evening brings us home.—Revelry in british India.—A few words on social philosophy.—**Townshend,** C. H. Stanzas.—**Mudford,** W: The iron shroud.—**Addey,** H. L. "She is so dear to me."—**Praed,** W. M. Lyrical charades.—How I made my fortune.—The elopement.—**Craik,** D. M. The double house.—**Barbauld,** A. L. Life's second morning.—Fact and fiction.—The youth and the sage.—**Hardman,** F: My friend the dutchman.—**Hunt,** J. H: L. Jenny kissed me.—**About,** E. Without dowry.—**Tennyson,** A. The foolish virgins. — **Chambers,** R. Indoor games. — **Brownell,** H. H. The burial of the dane.

Sargent, G: E. Richard Hunne ; a story of old London. Lond. [1871]. D.   **S 576**
— *joint author, see* Walshe, Elizabeth H.

Sargent, Lucius Manlius. The temperance tales. Bost. 1849. 2 v. in 1. S.   **S 601**

Sartoris, Adelaide, *born* Kemble. Medusa. and other tales. Lond. 1868. O.   **S 626**
   Includes, Madame de Monferrato.—Recollections of the life of Joseph Heywood and of his thoughts about music.—On words best left unsaid.
— A week in a french country-house. Lond. 1867. O.   **S 627**

Sauer, K: Marquard. (*M. Alland*). Monsu Max ;
    roman. *In* **Vierteljährl. mag.**   V 2 v23
Saunders, J : Israel Mort, overman ; a story of
    the mine. N. Y. 1876. O.   S 651
— Martin Pole. N. Y. 1863. O.   S 652
— A noble wife ; a novel. N. Y. 1883. Q. S 654
— The Sherlocks. N. Y. 1879. O.   S 653
Saunders, Katherine, *see* **Cooper**, Katherine.
Sauzade, John S., *pseud.*, *see* **Payn**, James.
Savage, Marmion W.   The bachelor of the
    Albany. N. Y. 1855. D.   S 801
— *Same*.   N. Y. 1878. Q.   S 801
— My uncle the curate.   N. Y. 1860. O.   S 802
— *Same*.   Lond. 1855. S.   S 802
— Reuben Medlicott, or The coming man. N. Y.
    1853. ·D.   S 803
— The woman of business, or The lady and the
    lawyer. N. Y. 1870. O.   S 804
Savage, Minot Judson.   Bluffton ; a story of
    today. Bost. 1878. D.   S 851
Savin, Una, *pseud.*, *see* **Hepworth**, *Mrs*. G:
    Hughes.
Schaick, Cornelis van.   Niederländische dorfge-
    schichten.   Aus dem holländischen, unter
    mitwirkung des verfassers, von E: Wege-
    ner ; mit einer biographischen skizze und
    dem portrait des verfassers. Leipz. 1850.
    4 v. S.   S 951
Scharling, K: H:, (*Nicolay*).   Zur neujahrszeit
    im pastorate zu Nöddeboe ; erzählung von
    Nicolay. Nach der 3ten aufl. des dänischen
    originals, deutsch von W. Reinhardt.   3te
    aufl. Bremen. 1881. S.   S 1001
Schayer, Julia.   The story of two lives. *In*
    Stories by american authors.   S 35 v10
— Tiger Lily, and other stories. N. Y. 1883. D.
            S 106
    Includes, Thirza.—Molly.—A summer's diversion.—
    My friend mrs. Angel.
Schefer, Leopold.   The artist's married life ;
    being that of Albert Dürer. Tr. from the
    german by mrs. J. R. Stodart. Rev. ed.
    with memoir. N. Y. 1862. D.   S 1026
Scheffel, Joseph V: v.   Ekkehard ; eine ge-
    schichte aus dem zehnten jahrhundert.
    Berlin. 1862. S.   S 1051
— *Same*.   N. Y. 1882. F.   S 1051
— *Same*, *eng*.   Ekkehard ; a tale of the 10th cen-
    tury. Tr. from the german by Sofie Delffs.
    Leipz. 1872. 2 v. in 1. S.   S 1051
Schellbach, Emma.   Veronika ; ein roman.
    Neubrandenburg. 1853. S.   S 1851
Scherr, J: Die jesuiten.—Gottlieb Rapfer.—Ra-
    fael Spruhz. — Die rothe dame. — Alles
    schon dagewesen. Leipz. 1874. D.   S 1107
— Michel ; geschichte eines deutschen unserer
    zeit. 4te aufl. Leipz. 1877. 2 v. in 1. D.
            S 1102
— *Same*.   N. Y. *n. d.* 2 v. D.   S 1102
— Nemesis ; novelle. Leipz. 1874. D.   S 1108
— Die pilger der wildniss ; historische novelle.
    2te aufl. Leipz. 1875. 2 v. in 1. D.   S 1109
— Porkeles und Porkelessa ; eine böse geschichte
    .   N. Y. 1883. F.   S 1110
— Der prophet von Florenz ; wahrheit und dich-
    tung. Stuttg. 1845. 3 v. D.   S 1103
— Rosi Zurflüh ; eine geschichte aus den Alpen.
    Prag. 1860. T.   S 1104
— Die tochter der luft. Prag. 1855. 2 v. T.
            S 1105
— Die waise von Wien. Stuttg. 1847. 3 v. S.
            S 1106

Schiff, Hermann, (*Isaak Bernays*). Das koschere
    haus. Hamburg. *n. d.* D.   S 1151
— Das verkaufte skelett. Nebst anhang : Coro-
    larien I, von K: Gutzkow. Hamburg. 1866.
    D.   S 1152
— Die waise von Tamaris ; eine tanznovelle vom
    vefasser des "Schief-Levinche" und der
    "Luftschlösser." Hamburg. 1853. D.
            S 1153
Schiller, J: Christoph F: v.   The criminal from
    lost honour. *In* **Oxenford**, J : Tales from
    the german.   O 1001
— *see also* **Roscoe**, T: German novelists.
            R 2451
— *See also his collected works, in german*, 830 : 143,
    in english, 830 : 150, 830 : R153.
Schilling, Ernst.   Die Ehresburg, oder Der
    sachsen kampf und bekehrung ; histori-
    scher roman aus den zeiten könig Karls
    des grossen und Wittekind, könig der
    sachsen, in den jahren 772 bis 824. Meis-
    sen. 1830. D.   S 1201
Schirmer, Adolf.   Fabrikanten und arbeiter,
    oder Der weg zum irrenhause ; socialer
    roman. Wien. 1862. 3 v. T.   S 1251
Schlägel, Max v.   Die gründer ; roman. 2te
    aufl. Jena. [1880.] D.   S 1303
— Die helden der arbeit ; roman aus der gegen-
    wart. Bielefeld. 1871. D.   S 1304
— Nach uns die sündfluth ! roman aus Frank-
    reichs jüngster vergangenheit. Leipz. 1872.
    4 v. S.   S 1301
— Der rothe fasching ; roman aus Frankreichs
    jüngster vergangenheit. Leipz. 1872. S.
            S 1302
Schmid, Hermann Theodor v. Almenrausch und
    edelweiss ; erzählung aus dem bairischen
    hochgebirge. 2te aufl. Leipz. 1873. S.
            S 1401
— Alte und neue geschichten aus Bayern. 2te
    aufl. Leipz. 1873. 7 v. in 2. S.   S 1402
    Contents, *see* Deutscher katalog, p. 95.
— Am kamin ; novellen und erzählungen. 2te
    aufl. Leipz. [1873]. S.   S 1403
    Contents, *see* Deutscher katalog, p. 95.
— Der bairische Hiesel ; volkserzählung aus
    Bayern. 2te aufl. Leipz. 1873. S.   S 1404
— Der bergwirth ; geschichte aus den bäirischen
    bergen. Leipz. 1874. S.   S 1405
— Erzstufen ; novellen und erzählungen. 2te
    aufl. Leipz. [1873]. S.   S 1406
    Contents, *see* Deutscher katalog, p. 95.
— Friedel und Oswald ; roman aus der tiroler
    geschichte. 2te aufl. Leipz. 1873. 3 v. in
    l. S.   S 1407
— Die gasselbuben ; geschichte aus den bairi-
    schen vorbergen. Leipz. 1873. S. S 1408
— Der habermeister ; ein volksbild aus den bairi-
    schen bergen. Leipz. 1869. S.   S 1409
— *Same*. 2te aufl. Leipz. 1873. S.   S 1409
— Im morgenroth ; eine Münchener geschichte
    aus der zeit Max Joseph's des dritten. 2te
    aufl. Leipz. 1873. 2 v. in l. S.   S 1410
— Der kanzler von Tyrol ; geschichtlicher ro-
    man. 2te aufl. Leipz. 1874. 4 v. in l. S.
            S 1411
— Der loder ; geschichte aus den bairischen ber-
    gen. Leipz. 1874. S.   S 1412
— Mein Eden ; eine Münchener geschichte aus
    den zeiten Karl Theodor's. 2te aufl. Leipz.
    [1873]. S.   S 1413
— Das Münchener kindeln ; erzählung aus |der
    zeit des kurfürsten Ferdinand Maria. Leipz.
    1874. S.   S 1414

x denotes books specially adapted for children.

Schmid, Hermann Theodor v.—*Continued.*
— Mütze und krone ; roman. Leipz. 1869. 5 v.
  S.   **S 1415**
— Das schwalberl ; ein bauernroman aus dem
  oberbaierischen gebirg. 2te aufl. Leipz.
  [1873]. S.   **S 1416**
— Süden und norden ; eine bairische dorfge-
  schichte von 1866. 2te aufl. Leipz. 1873. S.
                                        S 1417
— Tannengrün ; novellen und erzählungen. 2te
  aufl. Leipz. 1872. S.   **S 1418**
— Die türken in München ; roman. Leipz. 1872.
  2 v. S.   **S 1419**
— Die zuwider-wurzen ; geschichte aus den bairischen bergen. Leipz. 1874. S.   **S 1420**
Schmid, J: Christoph v. Angelika. *With* Bauberger, W. Das thal von Almeria. **B 577**
— Das blumenkörbchen ; eine erzählung dem
  blühenden alter gewidmet von dem verfasser der Ostereier. *With his* Der rosenstock.   **S 1455**
— Der blumenkranz ; eine erzählung für kinder
  und kinderfreunde nach dem schauspiele
  gleichen namens. Ill. Regensburg. 1871.
  D. *With his* Der kleine kaminfeger.
                                        S 1462
— Canary bird, The. *See below* Der kanarienvogel.
— Die christliche familie, Das alte raubschloss,
  Das stumme kind ; drei erzählungen für
  kinder und kinderfreunde. Ill. Regens-
  burg. 1864. D.   **S 1458**
— Emma von Finkenstein, oder Gott macht alles
  gut ; eine erzählung für die liebe jugend.
  N. Y. 1858. S. *With* Lautenschlager, O.
  Lorenz.   **L 2305**
— Eustachius ; eine erzählung für die gesammte
  edlere lesewelt, besonders für die reifere
  jugend. Cinc. 1855. S.   !   **S 1456**
— *Same. With* Bauberger, W: Das wunderweib
  vom Eichbühl.   **B 580**
— Fernando, oder Lebensgeschichte eines jungen
  grafen aus Spanien. N. Y. 1855. T. **S 1453**
— *Same.* N. Y. 1864. T.   **S 1459**
— Gottfried der junge einsiedler ; eine erzählung
  für kinder und kinderfreunde. Ill. Regensburg. 1864. D.   **S 1460**
— Gotthold, oder Die wege der vorsehung ; eine
  moralische erzählung für kinder und kin-
  derfreunde. Ill. Regensburg. 1871. D.
  With his Die kleine lautenspielerin. **S 1465**
— Der gute Fridolin und der böse Dietrich ; eine
  erzählung für die gesammte edlere lese-
  welt, besonders für die reifere jugend.
  Cinc. 1855. S.   **S 1457**
— Die hopfenblüthen ; eine begebenheit aus dem
  leben eines armen landschullehrers, er-
  zählt für kinder und kinderfreunde. Ill.
  Regensburg. 1864. D.   **S 1461**
— Das johanniskäferchen. *With his* Der rosen-
  stock.   **S 1455**
— *Same. With his* Der kanarienvogel. **S 1463**
— Der kanarienvogel. *With his* Der rosenstock.
                                        S 1455
— *Same,* Das johanniskäferchen, Die waldka-
  pelle ; drei erzählungen für kinder und
  kinderfreunde. Regensburg. 1869. D.
                                        S 1463
— *Same, eng.* The canary bird, and other tales.
  Tr. by mrs. F. H. Smith. Ill. N. Y. [1883].
  S.   **Sx 626**
  Contents. The canary bird. — Easter eggs. — The
  young count.—The firefly.

Schmid, J: Christoph v.—*Continued.*
— Der kleine kaminfeger ; eine erzählung für
  kinder und kinderfreunde nach dem
  schauspiele gleichen namens. Ill. Regensburg. 1871. D.   **S 1462**
— Die kleine lauterspielerin ; eine erzählung für
  kinder und kinderfreunde nach dem schauspiele gleichen namens. Neue, ill. originalaufl. Regensburg. 1871. D.   **S 1465**
— Das lämmchen ; eine erzählung für kinder
  und kinderfreunde. Neue, ill. originalaufl.
  Regensburg. 1864. D.   **S 1464**
— Ludwig, der kleine auswanderer ; eine erzählung für kinder und kinderfreunde. Neue,
  ill. originalaufl. Regensburg. 1864. D.
                                        S 1466
— Mathilde und Wilhelmine, die ungleichen
  schwestern ; erzählung. Neue, ill. origi-
  nalaufl. Regensburg. 1871. D.   **S 1467**
— Die nachtigall ; eine interessante erzählung.
  With his Heinrich von Eichenfels.   **S 1456**
— Die ostereier ; eine erzählung zum osterge-
  schenke für kinder. *With his* Heinrich von
  Eichenfels.   **S 1456**
— Pauline, die stifterin einer kleinkinderschule ;
  erzählung von dem verfasser der Ostereier.
  Ill. Regensb. 1848. S.   **S 1469**
— Rosa von Tannenburg ; eine geschichte des
  alterthums. N. Y. 1859. S.   **S 1454**
— *Same.* N. Y. 1864. S. *With his* Fernando.
                                        S 1459
— *Same, eng.* Rosa von Tannenburg ; a tale.
  From the german by Lucie Agnes Archer.
  N. Y. 1884 [1883]. D.   **S 1454**
— Der rosenstock ; eine interessante erzählung.
  N. Y. 1857. S.   **S 1455**
— Sieben erzählungen für kinder und kinder-
  freunde. Neue, ill. originalaufl. Regens-
  burg. 1864. D.   **S 1468**
  Contents. Die kirschen.—Die margarethablümchen.
  —Das vergissmeinnicht.—Der kuchen.—Die krebse.—
  Das rothkehlchen.—Das vogelnestchen.
— Timotheus and Philemon ; die geschichte
  christlicher zwillingsbrüder. Neue, ill.
  originalaufl. Regensburg. 1871. D. *With
  his* Der kleine kaminfeger.   **S 1462**
— Die waldkapelle. *With his* Der kanarienvogel.
                                        S 1463
— Der weihnachtsabend ; eine erzählung zum
  weihnachtsgeschenke für kinder. *With*
  Heinrich von Eichenfels.   **S 1456**
— Wie Heinrich von Eichenfels zur erkenntniss
  Gottes kam. N. Y. 1860. D.   **S 1456**
Schmidt, Maximilian. Johannisnacht ; dorfge-
  schichte aus den bayerischen vorbergen.
  N. Y. 1881. F.   **S 1476**
— Glasmacherleut' ; kulturbild aus dem bayri-
  schen walde. Stuttg. [1884]. D.   **S 1478**
— Die Miesenbacher ; ein kulturbild aus dem
  bayrischen hochgebirge, mit einer einleit-
  ung von Joseph Kürschner. Stuttg. [1882].
  D.   **S 1477**
Schmidt - Weissenfels, E:, (*Ernst Hellmuth*).
  Apoll von Byzanz. Wien. 1861. 4 v. T.
                                        H 2346
— Die söhne Barnevelt's ; historischer roman.
  N. Y. *n. d.* O.   **S 1501**
Schmieden, Else, (*E. Juncker*). Margarethe, or
  Life problems ; a romance. From the ger-
  man by mrs. A. L. Wister. Phila. 1878.
                                        J 1401
Schönberg, Henning. Verschlungene wege. *In*
  Vierteljährl. mag.   **V 2 v37**

x denotes books specially adapted for children.

Schoppe, Amalie Emma Sophie, *born* Weise.
Marie, oder Liebe bildet. Leipz. 1832. S.
S 1601

Schrader, A:, *pseud.*, *see* **Simmel**, A:

Schregel, F. Der fürstensohn. Prag. 1860. T.
S 1701

Schröder, W: Hinnerk Swinegel's lebensloop
un enne in'n staate Muffrika ; eene putzige
plattdüdsche historie in dörtein kappitteln.
3te aplage. Berlin. 1871. S.   S 1751
— Kasper Wullkop, de Bremer schippsjung; siene
erlewnisse un abentüer bi de eerste nord-
pohl-eckspeditschoon, van em sülvst ver-
tellt. — Schoolmesters reis' nah'r arvschaft ; eene fahrt mit hindernissen. Berlin. 1872. S.   S 1752
— Snaken un snurren. Berlin. 1872. S. S 1753
— De tambur van Waterloo ; eene dorpgeschicht
van'n hannoverschen jungen unt'r Lüne-
borger haide. Tweete aplage. Berlin.
1871. S.   S 1754

Schubin, Ossip, *pseud.*, *see* **Kürschner**, Lola.

Schücking, Christoph Bernhard Levin Anton
Matthias. Eine actiengesellschaft. Han-
nover. 1863. 3 v. S.   S 1801
— Alte ketten ; roman. N. Y. 1883. F.   S 1830
— Annette von Droste ; ein lebensbild. Hanno-
ver. 1862. D.   S 1802
— Aus alter und neuer zeit ; erzählungen. Leipz.
1865. 2 v. in 1. T.   S 1803
Contents, see Deutscher katalog, p. 96.
— Aus heissen tagen ; geschichten. Stuttg. 1874.
D.   S 1804
Contents, see Deutscher katalog, p. 96.
— Aus den tagen der grossen kaiserin ; histori-
sche novellen. 2te aufl. Prag. 1859. S.
S 1805
Contents, see Deutscher katalog, p. 96.
— Aus der franzosenzeit ; erzählungen. Wien.
1863. T.   S 1806
Contents, see Deutscher katalog, p. 96.
— Bruderpflicht [*und*] Recht und liebe ; zwei
erzählungen. N. Y. 1882. F.   S 1829
— Der doppelgänger ; roman. Stuttg. 1876. D.
S 1808
— *Same.* N. Y. 1881. F.   S 1808
— Eine dunkle that. Leipz. 1846. D.   S 1807
— Der erbe von Hornegg ; roman. Hannover.
1878. 3 v. in 2. D.   S 1809
— Etwas auf dem gewissen ; mit einer einlei-
tung von Joseph Kürschner. Stuttg. [1881].
D.   S 1828
— Filigran. Hannover. 1870, 1872. 2 v. D.
S 1810
Contents, see Deutscher katalog, p. 96.
— Gesammelte erzählungen und novellen. Han-
nover. 1859-1866. 6 v. in 3. D: S 1811
Contents, see Deutscher katalog, p. 96.
— Die heiligen und die ritter ; roman. Hanno-
ver. 1873. 4 v. in 2. D.   S 1812
— Der held der zukunft ; roman. Prag. 1855. 2
v. T.   S 1813
— Herrn Didier's landhaus ; roman. Hannover.
1872. 3 v. in 1. D.   S 1814
— Die königin der nacht. Leipz. 1852. S.
S 1815
— Die malerin aus dem Louvre ; roman. Han-
nover. 1869. 4 v. in 2. D.   S 1816
— Die marketenderin von Köln ; roman. Leipz.
1861. 3 v. D.   S 1817
— Novellen. Pesth. 1846. 2 v. D.   S 1818
Contents, see Deutscher katalog, p. 96.

Schücking, Levin.—*Continued.*
— Novellenbuch. Hannover. 2 v. in 1. S.
S 1819
Contents, see Deutscher katalog, p. 96.
— Paul Bronkhorst, oder Die neuen herren ; ro-
man. 2te aufl. Leipz. 1864. 3 v. in 1. S.
S 1820
— Recht und liebe. *With his* Bruderpflicht.
S 1829
— Die ritterbürtigen. Leipz. 1846. 3 v. S.
S 1821
— Ein schloss am meer ; roman. Leipz. 1843. 2
v. S.   S 1822
— Schloss Dornegge ; roman in 4 büchern. 2te
aufl. Leipz. 1874. 4 v. in 1. S.   S 1823
— Die schwester. N. Y. 1883. F.   S 1831
— Ein sohn des volkes ; roman. Leipz. 1849. 2
v. D.   S 1824
— Ein sohn eines berühmten mannes ; histori-
sche erzählung. Prag. 1856. T.   S 1825
— Die sphinx ; roman. Leipz. 1856. S. S 1826
— Verschlungene wege ; roman. 2te aufl. Leipz.
1874. 3 v. in 1. S.   S 1827
— Zwischen zwei todsünden ; novelle. *In*
Vierteljährl. mag.   V 2 v25

Schulze-Smidt, Bernhardine *frau*, (*E. Oswald*).
Vain forebodings. From the german by
mrs. A. L. Wister. Phila. 1885. D. S 6251

Schumann, Sophie, *born* Junghans. Die erbin
wider willen ; mit einer einleitung von
Joseph Kürschner. Stuttg. [1881]. D.
J 1451
— Hella Jasmund, und andere erzählungen.
Stuttg. [1883]. D.   J 1452
Includes, Onkel Helmar. — Die Howards von
Brereton.

Schultes, C: Maigela ; kulturhistorische novelle
aus mittel-Franken ; mit einer einleitung
von Joseph Kürschner. Stuttg. [1883]. D.
S 1876

Schwartz, Marie Sophie, *born* Birath. Anna's
geheimnis ; roman. Aus dem schwedi-
schen von Emil J. Jonas. Leipz. 1874. 2
v. in 1. D.   S 1910
— Arbeit adelt den mann. Aus dem schwedi-
schen von C. Büchele. N. Y. *n. d.* T.
S 1901
— Gerda, or The children of work. Tr. from
the swedish by Selma Borg and Marie A.
Brown. Phila. 1874. D.   S 1902
— Gold and name. Tr. from the swedish by
Selma Borg and Marie A. Brown. Phila.
1874. O.   S 1903
— *Same, germ.* Gold und name. Aus dem
schwedischen von dr. Otto. N. Y. *n. d.* T.
S 1903
— Guilt and innocence. Tr. from the swedish
by Selma Borg and Marie A. Brown. Phila.
n. d. O.   S 1915
— Little Karin. Tr. from the original swedish
ms. by Selma Borg and Marie A. Brown.
Hartford. 1873. O.   S 1914
— Das mädchen von Korsika ; roman. Aus dem
schwedischen von E. J. Jonas. Leipz.
1876. D.   S 1911
— Der mann von geburt und das weib aus dem
volke ; ein bild aus der wirklichkeit. N. Y.
n. d. 2 v. in 1. T.   S 1913
— Ein opfer der rache ; erzählung. Aus dem
schwedischen von C. Büchele. N. Y. *n. d.*
T.   S 1904

x denotes books specially adapted for children.

Schwartz, Marie Sophie, *born* Birath.—*Continued.*
— The right one. Tr. from the swedish by Selma Borg and Marie A. Brown. Bost. 1871. O. **S 1905**
— *Same, germ.* Der rechte. Aus dem schwedischen von C. Büchele. N. Y. *n. d.* **S 1905**
— Schwedische lebensbilder ; erzählungen. Nach dem original-manuscript frei bearbeitet von J. N. Heynrichs. Berlin. 1868. D. **S 1912**
    Contents, see Deutscher katalog, p. 97.
— The son of the organ-grinder. Tr. from the swedish by Selma Borg and Marie A. Brown. [1883]. D. **S 1906**
— Two family mothers. Tr. from the swedish by Selma Borg and Marie A. Brown. Bost. 1882. O. **S 1907**
— *Same, germ.* Zwei familienmütter. Aus dem schwedischen von dr. Otto. N. Y. *n. d.* T. **S 1907**
— The wife of a vain man. Tr. from the swedish by Selma Borg and Marie A. Brown. Bost. 1873. O. **S 1908**
— Die wittwe und ihre kinder. Aus dem schwedischen von C. Büchele. N. Y. *n. d.* T. **S 1909**
Schwartzkoppen, Klotilde v., *born* v. François. Aquarelle ; mit einer einleitung von Alexander baron v. Roberts. Stuttg. [1884]. D. **S 1926**
    Contents. Einleitung. — Ein osternovellette. — Wie seine grossmutter. — Vier treppen. — Vor thoresschluss.
Schwerin, Alexandrine Franziska *gräfin* v. Das testament des juden. Königsberg. 1852. 3 v. D. **S 1951**
Scott, *Sir* Walter. Novels, abridged and ed. by M. E. Braddon. Lond. [1881]. D. **Sx 651**
    Contents. Waverley.—Guy Mannering.—Rob Roy. —Old Mortality.—The black dwarf.— The bride of Lammermoor.—The heart of Midlothian.—Ivanhoe. —Kenilworth.—The fortunes of Nigel.—Peveril of the Peak.—The talisman.
— The abbot ; being the sequel to The monastery. Bost. 1845. 2 v. in 1. S. **S 2001**
— *Same.* Leipz. 1860. S. **S 2001**
— *Same, germ.* Der abt, fortsetzung des Klosters ; ein historischer roman. Neu übers. von F: Funck. Stuttg. 1851. T. **S 2001**
— Anne of Geierstein. Leipz. 1871. S. **S 2002**
— *Same.* Bost. 1871. D. **S 2002**
— *Same, germ.* Anna von Geierstein, oder Die tochter des nebels. Phila. 1852. T. **S 2002**
— The antiquary. Leipz. 1845. S. **S 2003**
— *Same.* Bost. *n. d.* 2 v. in 1. D. **S 2003**
— *Same.* Bost. 1845. 2 v. in 1. S. **S 2003**
— *Same.* Bost. 1869. 2 v. in 1. D. **S 2003**
— *Same, germ.* Der alterthümler. Phila. 1852. T. **S 2003**
— The betrothed. *T. p. w.* D. **S 2004**
— *Same. In his* Tales of the crusades. **S 2024**
— *Same, germ.* Die verlobten. Phila. 1852. T. **S 2004**
— The black dwarf. *With his* Fortunes of Nigel. **S 2027**
— *Same.* Leipz. 1858. S. **S 2028**
— *Same. In his* Tales of my landlord. **S 2029 v1**
— The bride of Lammermoor. Leipz. 1858. S. **S 2006**
— *Same.* Bost. *n. d.* D. **S 2006**
— *Same.* Bost. 1857. D. **S 2029 v3**
— Castle Dangerous. Bost. 1845. S. **S 2029 v4**
— *Same. With his* The surgeon's daughter. **S 2023**

Scott, *Sir* Walter.—*Continued.*
— Chronicles of the Canongate. 1st and 2d ser. Bost. 1845. *n. d.* 4 v. in 2. D. *and* S. **S 2007**
    Contents. 1st ser. The highland widow.—The two drovers.—The surgeon's daughter. 2d ser. St. Valentine's day.
— Count Robert of Paris. Ill. N. Y. *n. d.* D. **S 2008**
— *Same, germ.* Graf Robert von Paris. Phila. 1852. T. **S 2008**
— The fair maid of Perth. Leipz. 1871. S. **S 2009**
— *Same.* Ill. Bost. 1879. D. **S 2009**
— The fortunes of Nigel. Bost. 1871. 2 v. in 1. D. **S 2010**
— *Same.* Leipz. 1846. S. **S 2010**
— *Same.* Bost. 1879. D. **S 2027**
— *Same, germ.* Nigel's schicksale. Phila. 1852. T. **S 2010**
— Guy Mannering, or The astrologer. Bost. 1869. 2 v. in 1. D. **S 2011**
— *Same.* Leipz. 1846. S. **S 2011**
— *Same.* N. Y. 1873. S. **S 2011**
— *Same, germ.* Guy Mannering, oder Der sterndeuter. Hamburg. 1841. S. **S 2011**
— The heart of Mid-Lothian. Leipz. 1858. 2 v. in 1. S. **S 2012**
— *Same. T. p. w.* D. **S 2012**
— *Same, germ.* Der kerker von Edinburg. Neu übers. von Ernst Susemihl. Stuttg. 1851. T. **S 2012**
— The highland widow. *With his* The betrothed. **S 2004**
— Ivanhoe. Leipz. 1845. S. **S 2013**
— *Same. T. p. w.* D. **S 2013**
— *Same.* (Waverley novels, ill. lib. ed.) Bost. *n. d.* D. **S 2013**
— *Same, germ.* Ivanhoe. Aus dem englischen. Phila. 1852. T. **S 2013**
— Kenilworth. Bost. 1869. 2 v. in 1. D. **S 2014**
— *Same.* Leipz. 1845. S. **S 2014**
— *Same.* (Waverley novels, ill. lib. ed.) Bost. *n. d.* D. **S 2014**
— *Same, germ.* Kenilworth. Phila. 1852. S. **S 2014**
— A legend of Montrose. *With his* Fortunes of Nigel. **S 2027**
— *Same. With his* The black dwarf. **S 2028**
— *Same. With his* The bride of Lammermoor. **S 2029 v3**
— The monastery. Leipz. 1859. S. **S 2015**
— *Same.* Bost. 1869. 2 v. in 1. D. **S 2015**
— *Same.* Bost. *n. d.* 2 v. in 1. D. **S 2015**
— *Same. T. p. w.* S. **S 2015**
— *Same, germ.* Das kloster. Phila. 1852. T. **S 2015**
    Note. For continuation, *see above* The abbot.
— Old Mortality. Leipz. 1846. S. **S 2016**
— *Same.* Bost. 1869. D. **S 2016**
— *Same. With his* The black dwarf. **S 2029 v1**
— Peveril of the Peak. Leipz. 1860. 2 v. in 1. S. **S 2017**
— *Same.* Phila. *n. d.* 2 v. in 1. D. **S 2017**
— *Same. T. p. w.* D. **S 2017**
— *Same, germ.* Peveril vom Gipfel. Phila. 1852. T. **S 2017**
— The pirate. Leipz. 1846. S. **S 2018**
— *Same.* Bost. 1879. D. **S 2018**
— Quentin Durward ; a romance. Bost. 1845. 2 v. in 1. S. **S 2019**
— *Same.* Leipz. 1845. 2 v. in 1. S. **S 2019**
— *Same* ; ed. especially for this series by Charlotte M. Yonge ; with a hist. introd. [Classics for children]. Bost. 1884. S. **Sx 652**

    x denotes books specially adapted for children.

Scott, *Sir* Walter.—*Continued.*
— Redgauntlet. *T. p. w.* D.   **S 2020**
— *Same, germ.* Redgauntlet. Phila. 1852. T.   **S 2020**
— Rob Roy. Bost. 1872. 2 v. in 1. D.   **S 2021**
— *Same.* Leipz. 1846. S.   **S 2021**
— *Same, germ.* Robin der Rothe ; ein historischer roman. Neu übers. von C. Hermann. Stuttg. 1851. T.   **S 2021**
— St. Ronan's well. Bost. 1869. 2 v. in 1. D.   **S 2022**
— *Same.* Bost. 1845. 2 v. in 1. D.   **S 2022**
— *Same.* Bost. *n. d.* 2 v. in 1. D.   **S 2022**
— *Same, germ.* St. Ronansbrunnen. Phila. 1852. T.   **S 2022**
— The surgeon's daughter. *T. p. w.* D.   **S 2023**
    Note. Contains also Castle dangerous *and* Index, glossary, characters introduced and principal incidents of the whole series of Waverley novels.
— Tales of my landlord.
    1. Black dwarf and Old Mortality.
    2. Heart of Midlothian.
    3. Bride of Lammermoor and Legend of Montrose.
    4. Count Robert of Paris and Castle Dangerous.
— Tales of the crusades : The betrothed ; The talisman. *T. p. w.* D.   **S 2024**
— The talisman ; a tale of the crusaders. N. Y. 1879. Q.   **S 2027**
— Waverley, or 'Tis sixty years since. Leipz. 1845. S.   **S 2025**
— *Same, germ.* Waverley, oder Vor sechzig jahren ; ein historischer roman. Neu übers. von C. Hermann. Stuttg. 1851. T.   **S 2025**
— Woodstock. Bost. 1871. 2 v. in 1. D.   **S 2026**
Scribe, Augustin Eugène. Judith, or The opera box. *In* Sargent, E. The emerald. **S 551**
— Moritz ; modernes zeitbild. *T. p. w.* S.   **S 2052**
— Novellen. Deutsch von dr. Scherr. Stuttg. 1847. T.   **S 2051**
Scudder, Horace Elisha. The Bodley books:
    1. Doings of the Bodley family in town and country. Ill. Bost. 1880. O.   **Sx 701**
    2. The Bodleys telling stories. Ill. Bost. 1880. O.   **Sx 702**
    3. The Bodleys afoot. Ill. Bost. 1880. O.   **Sx 703**
    4. Mr. Bodley abroad. Ill. Bost. 1881. O.   **Sx 704**
— Seven little people and their friends. New ed. Bost. 1881. S.   **Sx 705**
— Stories and romances. Bost. 1880. D.   **S 2101**
    Contents. Left over from the last century. — A house of entertainment.—Accidentally overheard.— A hard bargain.—A story of the siege of Boston.— Matthew, Mark, Luke and John.—Do not even the publicans the same.—Nobody's business.
— *ed.* The children's book ; a collection of the best and most famous stories and poems in the english language. Bost. 1881. Q.   **Sx 706**
    Contents. The book of fables.—The book of wonders.—A few songs.—The book of popular tales.— The book of stories in verse. — Stories from Hans Christian Andersen.—Tales from the Arabian nights' entertainments.—The book of ballads.—The book of familiar stories.—A voyage to Lilliput.—Travels of baron Munchausen.—The book of poetry.—The book of ancient stories.
— — *Same.*   **Sx 706R**
Scudder, Moses L., *jr.* Brief honors ; a romance of the great dividable. Chicago. 1877. S.   **S 2151**

Scudder, Vida D., (*Davida Coit*). How the rain sprites were freed. Ill. Bost. [1883]. O.   **Cx 901**
Sea breezes. Ill. N. Y. *n. d.* D.   **Sx 25**
Sealsfield, C: (*originally* K: **Postl**). Das cajütenbuch, oder Nationale charakteristiken. 3te aufl. Stuttg. 1847. 2 v. S.   **S 2201**
— *Same, eng.* The cabin book, or National characteristics. Tr. from the german by Sarah Powell. Lond. 1852. D.   **S 2206**
— Lebensbilder aus der westlichen hemisphäre. 3te aufl. Stuttg. 1846. 5 v. S.   **S 2202**
    Contents, see Deutscher katalog, p. 97.
— *Same, eng.* Life in the new world, or Sketches of american society. Tr. from the german by Gustavus C. Hebbe and James Mackay. N. Y. [1844]. O.   **S 2202**
    Contents. The courtship of G: Howard, esq.—The courtship of Ralph Doughby, esq. — The life of a planter. — Scenes in the southwest. — The squatter chief, or The first american in Texas.
— Der legitime und der republikaner ; eine geschichte aus dem letzten amerikanisch-englischen kriege. 3te aufl. Stuttg. 1845. 3 v. S.   **S 2203**
— Morton, oder Die grosse tour. 3te aufl. Stuttg. 1846. 2 v. S.   **S 2204**
— Der virey und die aristokraten, oder Mexiko im jahre 1812. 3te aufl. Stuttg. 1845. 3 v. S.   **S 2205**
Searle, January, *pseud., see* **Phillips,** G: Searle.
Secondthoughts, Solomon, *pseud., see* **Kennedy,** J: Pendleton.
Sedgwick, Catharine Maria. Hope Leslie, or Early times in the Massachusetts. N. Y. 1872. 2 v. D.   **S 2251**
— Le Bossu. [*Anon.*] *In* Tales of Glauber-Spa.   **T 186**
— The Linwoods, or "Sixty years since" in America. N. Y. 1861. 2 v. S.   **S 2252**
— Live and let live, or Domestic service illustrated. N. Y. 1861. S.   **S 2253**
— Means and ends, or Self-training. N. Y. 1860. S.   **S 2254**
— The poor rich man and the rich poor man. N. Y. 1861. S.   **S 2255**
Sedgwick, Susan Ridley. Walter Thornley, or A peep at the past. N. Y. 1859. S.   **S 2276**
Sedley, H: Dangerfield's rest, or Before the storm. *T. p. w.* D.   **S 2301**
See, Gustav vom, *pseud., see* **Struensee,** Gustav K: O: v.
Seemüller, Anna Moncure, *born* Crane. Emily Chester. Bost. 1874. D.   **S 2351**
Segur, Sophie, *born* Rostopchine, *comtesse.* Fairy tales. Tr. from the french by mrs. Chapman Coleman and her daughters. Phila. [1869]. D.   **Sx 851**
Selchow, *pseud., see* **Lamartine,** A: H: Julius.
Sellen, Gustav, *pseud., see* **Alvensleben,** K: L: F: W. G. v.
Semler, H: Ein banditenstreich ; eine mexikanische erzählung. *In* Vierteljährl. mag.   **V 2 v23**
— Samuels kleiner roman ; eine erzählung. *In* the same.   **V 2 v28**
Septchênes, Jean de, *pseud., see* **Collin,** Jacques A: Simon.
Sergeant, Adeline. Beyond recall ; a novel. (Leisure hour ser.) N. Y. 1883. S.   **S 2516**
Severance, M: Sibley. Hammersmith, his Harvard days. New ed. Bost. 1882. D.   **S 2526**
Severin, Justus, *pseud., see* **Mützelburg,** Adolf.

Sewell, Elizabeth Missing. Cleve Hall. N. Y. 1881. D:　　　　　　　　　　　　S 2559
— The experience of life. N. Y. 1860. S.
　　　　　　　　　　　　　　　　S 2551
— Gertrude ; ed. by W: Sewell. N. Y. 1864. D.
　　　　　　　　　　　　　　　　S 2552
— Hawkstone ; a tale of, and for England in 184—. N. Y. 1848. 2 v. D.　　S 2553
— Ivors. N. Y. 1857. 2 v. D.　　S 2554
— Katharine Ashton. N. Y. 1881. D.　S 2555
— Laneton parsonage. N. Y. 1885. D.　S 2558
— Margaret Percival. N. Y. 1854. D.　S 2556
— Same. N. Y. 1881. D.　　　　　S 2556
— Ursula ; a tale of country life. N. Y. 1859. 2 v. D.　　　　　　　　　　S 2557
Shand, Alexander l. Wrecked off the Riff coast. In Tales from Blackwood.　T 177 v6
Shaw, Flora L. Hector ; a story. Ill. Bost. 1881. S.　　　　　　　　　　　Sx 901
— Phyllis Browne. Bost. 1883 [1882]. S. Sx 902
— A sea change. Bost. 1884. S.　　Sx 903
Shelley, Mary Wollstonecraft, born Godwin. Frankenstein, or The modern Prometheus. Phila. 1833. 2 v. D.　　S 2601
Shelton, F: W: Peeps from a belfry, or The parish sketch book. N. Y. 1855. D. S 2651
— The rector of St.Bardolph's, or Superannuated. N. Y. 1853. D.　　　S 2652
Sheppard, Elizabeth Sara, (E. Berger). Charles Auchester. T. p. w. [N. Y. 1875]. O.
　　　　　　　　　　　　　　　　S 2701
— Counterparts, or The cross of love. Bost. n. d. O.　　　　　　　　　　S 2702
— Rumor. Bost. 1864. O.　　　　S 2703
Sherwood, Mary Elizabeth Wilson, (M. E. W. S.). The sarcasm of destiny, or Nina's experience. N. Y. 1878. D.　　　S 2751
Sherwood, Mary Martha. The history of H: Milner. N. Y. 1858. 2 v. D.　　S 2801
— The lady of the manor ; a series of conversations on the subject of confirmation, intended for the use of the middle and higher ranks of young females. N. Y. 1860. 4 v. D.　　　　　　　　　　　　　S 2802
— Roxobel. N. Y. 1848. 3 v. S.　Sx 951
Shillaber, B: Penhallow, (Mrs. Partington). The double-runner club, or The lively boys of Rivertown. Ill. Bost. 1882 [1881]. S.
　　　　　　　　　　　　　　Sx 1001
Shinn, Milicent Washburn. Young Strong of the "Clarion". In Stories by american authors.　　　　　　　　S 35 v9
Shipley, Mary Elizabeth. Jessie's work, or Faithfulness in little things ; a story for girls. Ill. N. Y. 1873. D.　Sx 1051
Shorthouse, Joseph H: John Inglesant ; a romance. [Anon.] New ed. N. Y. 1881. D.
　　　　　　　　　　　　　　　　S 2826
— The little schoolmaster Mark ; a spiritual romance. N. Y. 1883. D.　　S 2827
— The marquis Jeanne Hyacinth de St. Pelaye. In Tales from many sources.　T 178 v3
Shunsui, Tamenaga. The loyal ronins ; historical romance. Trom the japanese by Shuichiro Saito and E: Greey. Ill. by Kei-Sai-Yei-Sen of Yedo. N. Y. 1880. O.　S 2851
Sidney, Margaret, pseud., see Lothrop, Harriet Mulford.
Sidney, Sir Philip. The countess of Pembroke's Arcadia. [With introductory and biographical essay.] Lond. n. d. D.　S 2876
— Same. 13th ed. With his life and death and

a brief table of the principal heads and some other new add. Lond. 1674. Q.
　　　　　　　　　　　　　　23 : R
Contents. Life and death of sir Philip Sidney.— Epigrams.—The countess of Pembroke's Arcadia.— A sixth book to the countess of Pembroke's Arcadia, by R. Beling.—Sonnets.—The defence of poesie. — Astrophel and Stella.—Supplement to the 3d book of Arcadia by Ja. Johnstoun.—A remedie for love.
Sikes, Olive, born Logan. Chateau Frissac, or Home scenes in France. N. Y. 1865. D.
　　　　　　　　　　　　　　　　S 2901
— Get thee behind me, Satan ! a home-born book of home-truths. N. Y. 1872. D.
　　　　　　　　　　　　　　　　S 2902
Silberstein, A: Dorfschwalben aus Oestreich ; geschichten. München. 1862. D.　S 2951
— Dorfschwalben aus Oesterreich ; frischer flug. Breslau. 1881. 2 v. in 1. D.　S 2952
— Glänzende bahnen. Milw. 1872. O.　S 2953
— Hochlandsgeschichten, mit einer einleitung von Joseph Kürschner. Stuttg. [1882]. D.
　　　　　　　　　　　　　　　　S 2954
Contents of each of the above, see Deutscher katalog, p. 98.
Simcox, Edith. Episodes in the lives of men, women and lovers. 1st amer. from the last Lond. ed. Bost. 1882. S.　　S 2976
Contents. In memoriam.—Consolations.—A diptych. —"Some one has blundered."—Midsummer noon.— At anchor.—Men our brothers.—Looking in the glass. —Love and friendship.—Eclipse.—The shadow of death.—Sat est vixisse.
Sime, W: Boulderstone, or New men and old populations ; a novel. N. Y. 1885. Q.
　　　　　　　　　　　　　　　　S 2988
— Haco the dreamer ; a tale of scotch university life. N. Y. 1884. Q.　　S 2987
— King Capital. N. Y. 1883. S.　S 2986
Simmel, A: (August Schrader.) Mark Sutherland, oder Die wege der vorsehung. Leipz. 1857. S.　　　　　　　　　　S 1651
Simms, W: Gilmore. Beauchampe, or The Kentucky tragedy ; a sequel to Charlemont. New ed. N. Y. 1882. D.　　S 3007
- Same. N. Y. 1856. D.　　　S 3011
— Border beagles ; a tale of the Mississippi. New ed. N. Y. 1882. D.　　　S 3006
— Charlemont, or The pride of the village ; a tale of Kentucky. N. Y. 1882. D. With his Border beagles.　　　　　　S 3006
— Same. N. Y. [1856]. D.　　S 3012
Note. For continuation, see Beauchampe.
— Confession, or The blind heart ; a domestic story. New ed. N. Y. 1882. D. With his Beauchampe.　　　　　　　S 3007
— Eutaw ; a sequel to The forayers, or The raid of the dog-days ; a tale of the revolution. N. Y. 1856. D.　　　　　S 3004
— Same. N. Y. 1882. D.　　　S 3004
— The forayers, or The raid of the dog-days. N. Y. 1882. D. With his Woodcraft. S 3003
Note. For continuation, see Eutaw.
— The golden christmas ; a chronicle of St. Johns, Berkeley, compiled from the notes of a briefless barrister. Charleston. 1852. D.　　　　　　　　　　　　S 3013
— Guy Rivers ; a tale of Georgia. New ed. N. Y. 1882. D.　　　　　　　S 3005
— Katharine Walton, or The rebel of Dorchester. New ed. N. Y. 1882. D.　　S 3002
— Mellichampe ; a legend of the Santee. New ed. N. Y. 1882. D. With his The partisan.
　　　　　　　　　　　　　　　　S 3001
— Same. N. Y. 1853. 2 v. D.　　S 3014

x denotes books specially adapted for children.

Simms, W: Gilmore.—*Continued.*
— The partisan ; a romance of the revolution.
New ed. N. Y. 1882. D. **S 3001**
— *Same.* N. Y. n. d. D. **S 3015**
— Richard Hurdis ; a tale of Alabama. New ed.
N. Y. 1882. D. *With his* Guy Rivers.
S 3005
— The scout, or The black riders of Congaree.
New ed. N. Y. 1882. D. *With his* Kathar-
ine Walton. **S 3002**
— Southward ho ! a spell of sunshine. N. Y.
1882. D. *With his* The Yemasse. **S 3008**
— Vasconselos ; a romance of the new world. N.
Y. 1882. D. **S 3010**
— The wigwam and the cabin. New ed. N. Y.
1882. D. **S 3009**
Contents. Grayling, or Murder will out.—The two
camps, a legend of the old north state.— The last
wager, or The gamester of the Mississippi.— The
arm-chair of the Tustenuggee, a tradition of the
Catawamba.—The snake of the cabin.—Oakatibbe, or
The Choctaw Sampson.—Jocassee, a Cherokee legend.
—The giant's coffin, or The feud of Holt and Hous-
ton.— Sergeant Barnacle, or The raftsman of the
Edisto.—Those old lunes ! or Which is the madman ?
—The lazy crow, a story of the cornfield.—Caloya, or
The loves of the driver.—Lucas de Ayllon.
— Woodcraft, or Hawks about the dove cote ; a
tale of the south at the close of the revolu-
tion. New ed. N. Y. 1882. D. **S 3003**
— The Yemassee ; a romance of Carolina. New
ed. N. Y. 1882. D. **S 3008**
Simon, Emma, *born* Couvely, (*Emma Vely*). Am
strand des Adria ; novellen. Stuttg. 1873.
D. **S 3051**
Contents, see Deutscher katalog, p. 98.
— Schiffbruch ; novelle. *In* **Vierteljährl. mag.**
V 2 v35
Simpson, M. C. M. Geraldine and her suitors ;
a novel. N. Y. 1882. Q. **S 3076**
Sinclair, Catharine. Lord and lady Harcourt,
or Country hospitalities. *T. p. w.* [Phila.
1857.] D. **S 3101**
— Modern accomplishments, or The march of
intellect. *T. p. w.* D. **S 3102**
Siogvolk, P., *pseud., see* **Mathews,** Albert.
Skelton, J: The crookit Meg ; a story of the
year one. Lond. 1880. D. **S 3126**
Slick, Jonathan, *pseud. ?* Das leben in New
York ; in briefen. Stuttg. 1847. T. **S 3151**
Slick, Sam, *pseud., see* **Haliburton,** T: C.
Slip in the fens, A. (Leisure hour ser.) N. Y.
1873. S. **S 21**
Smart, Hawley. Courtship in 1720 and 1860 ;
romances of two centuries. Phila. 1877. S.
S 3201
— From post to finish ; a racing romance. Ill.
N. Y. 1884. Q. **S 3202**
— Tie and trick ; a novel. Ill. N. Y. 1885. Q.
S 3203
Smedley, Frank E. Frank Fairlegh, or Scenes
from the life of a private pupil ; a novel.
N. Y. 1884. Q. **S 3226**
— Lewis Arundel, or The railroad of life. N. Y.
1885. Q. **S 3227**
Smidt, H: Marinebilder ; neue seegeschichten.
Berlin. 1859. D. **S 3251**
Contents, see Deutscher katalog, p. 98.
Smith, Albert. The fortunes of the Scatter-
good family. *T. p. w.* S. **S 3301**
— The Poppleton legacy. *T. p. w.* O. **S 3302**
Smith, Alexander. Alfred Hagart's household.
Bost. 1866. D. **S 3351**
— Dreamthorp. *In* **Johnson,** E. R. Little
classics. **J 926 v4**

Smith, Alexander.—*Continued.*
— Miss Oona McQuarrie ; a sequel to Alfred
Hagart's household. Bost. 1866. D.
S 3352
Smith, Elizabeth Thomasina, *born* Meade, *mrs.*
Toulmin-. Scamp and I ; a story of city
by-ways, by L. T. Meade. Ill. N. Y. n. d.
D. **Mx 801**
Smith, Hannah, (*Hesba Stretton*). Carola. N. Y.
[1884]. S. **S 3405**
— Cobwebs and cables. N. Y. 1881. D. **S 3404**
— The crew of the Dolphin. N. Y. n. d. T.
S 3401
— In prison and out. N. Y. n. d. D. **S 3402**
— Michel Lorio's cross. *In* Tales from many
sources. **T 178 v2**
— Through a needle's eye. N. Y. 1878. D.
S 3403
Smith, Horace. *also called* Horatio. Adam Brown,
the merchant. N. Y. 1858. O. **S 3451**
— Arthur Arundel ; a tale of the english revolu-
tion. N. Y. 1857. O. **S 3452**
— The picnic party. *In* **Johnson,** E. R. Little
classics. **J 926 v9**
— *Same. In* **Sargent,** E. The emerald. **S 551**
— The Tor hill. Cinc. n. d. O. **S 3453**
— *Same, germ.* Der Thurm hill. Nach der zwei-
ten auflage des englischen übers. von
Gustav Sellen. Leipz. 1847. 4 v. S.
S 3453
Smith, J. F: Abtei Carrow. Frei nach dem
englischen von dr. Büchele. Stuttg. 1859.
2 v. T. **S 3501**
— Ebbe und fluth ; roman aus der gegenwart.
Aus dem englischen von C: Kolb. Stuttg.
1860. 6 v. T. **S 3502**
— Das erbe, oder Die lehren des lebens. Frei
nach dem englischen von C. Büchele.
Stuttg. 1858. 4 v. T. **S 3503**
— Der junge prätendent, oder Vor 100 jahren.
Aus dem englischen von A. v. Schraishuon.
Stuttg. 1855. 2 v. T. **S 3504**
— Licht- und schattenseiten des lebens ; volks-
roman. Frei aus dem englischen von A. v.
Schraishuon. Stuttg. 1858. 5 v. T. **S 3505**
— The story of May Darling. *In* **Wilson,** J: M.
Tales of the borders. **W 2202 v10**
Smith, J. Hyatt. Haran the hermit, or The
wonderful lamp. Buffalo. 1860. S.
Sx 1201
Smith, J. Moyr. The prince of Argolis ; a story
of the old greek fairy time. N. Y. 1878. D.
S 3551
Smith, Joseph Emerson. Oakridge ; an old time
story. Bost. 1875. D. **S 3601**
Smith, Julia B. One little rebel. Ill. N. Y.
1884. S. **Sx 1151**
Smith, Mary Prudence, *born* Wells, (*P. Thorne*).
The Browns. Ill. Bost. 1884. S. **Sx 1302**
— The great match, and other matches. (No
name ser.) Bost. 1877. S. **S 3701**
— Jolly good times at school, also some times
not quite so jolly. Bost. 1884. D. **Sx 1301**
Smollett, Tobias G: The expedition of Humph-
rey Clinker. N. Y. 1873. D. **S 3751**
— *Same, germ.* Humphrey Clinker's reisen. Aus
dem englischen übers. von H: Döring.
Braunschw. 1848. 3 v. S. **S 3751**
— *Same.* Aus dem englischen übers. von G.
Fink. Stuttg. 1846. S. **S 3751**
— Ferdinand Fathom ; roman. Aus dem eng-
lischen übers. von G. Fink. Stuttg. 1846. S.
S 3754

x denotes books specially adapted for children.

Smollett, Tobias G:—*Continued.*
— Peregrin Pickle's abenteuer, fahrten und
    schwänke ; ein komischer roman. Nach
    dem englischen von G. N. Bärmann.
    Braunschw. 1848. 6 v. S.   **S 3752**
— *Same.* Aus dem englischen übers. von E.
    Ortlepp. Stuttg. 1846. 2 v. in 1. S.
                                       S 3752
— Abenteuer Roderick Random's. Aus dem
    englischen übers. Braunschw. 1848. 4 v. S.
                                       S 3753
— *Same.* Aus dem englischen übers. von E:
    Keller. Stuttg. 1846. 2 v. in 1. S. **S 3753**
Snieders, A:, *der jüngere.* Bilder aus dem leben.
    Aus dem vlämischen übertragen von K:
    Arenz. Mainz. 1852. S.   **S 3801**
    Contents, *see* Deutscher katalog, p. 99.
Sola, *pseud.,* see **Anderson,** Olive San Louie.
Sommers, W: Die seherin der hochlande. In's
    deutsche übertragen von Leopold Kraft.
    Leipz. 1845. 2 v. T.   **S 3851**
Soulié, Melchior F: Die memoiren des teufels ;
    vorläufer der "Pariser mysterien". Deutsch
    von L: Hauff. Stuttg. 1845. 6 v. T.
                                       S 3901
Southey, Caroline Ann, *born* Bowles. Devereux
    Hall. *In* Tales from Blackwood.
                                       T 176 v2
— La petite Madelaine. *In* Tales from Black-
    wood. ,   **T 176 v3**
Souvestre, Émile. An attic philosopher, or A
    peep at the world from a garret ; being the
    journal of a happy man. N. Y. 1857. D.
                                       S 4051
— *Same.* N. Y. 1859. S.   **S 4051**
— *Same, germ.* Ein philosoph in der dachstube ;
    tagebuch eines glücklichen. Aus dem
    französischen übers. von G: Schmiele.
    Leipz. n. d. T.   **S 4051**
— Der könig der welt, oder Das geld und seine
    macht ; ein roman der vergangenheit und
    gegenwart. Deutsch von A. Kretzschmar.
    Leipz. 1855. 4 v. S.   **S 4052**
— The lake shore, or The slave, The serf and
    The apprentice. Tr. from the french.
    Bost. 1855. S.   **S 4053**
— *Same.* Norva ; a tale of the roman empire,
    and other stories. Tr. from the french.
    Bost. 1857. D.   **S 4053**
    Contents. The slave.—The serf.—The apprentice.
— Leaves from a family journal. From the
    french. N. Y. 1855. D.   **S 4054**
Spanish cavaliers, The ; a tale of the moorish
    wars in Spain. Tr. from the french by
    mrs. J. Sadlier. N. Y. 1861. S.   **S 30**
Sparhawk, Frances Campbell. A lazy man's
    work. (Leisure hour ser.) N. Y. 1881. S.
                                       S 4101
Späth, Charlotte. Die zwillingsschwestern ; eine
    erzählung für herrschaften und dienstbo-
    ten. Stuttg. *n. d.* S.   **S 4151**
Spenden auf dem altar der freundschaft und
    liebe ; ein immortellen-kranz, gewunden
    aus den beliebtesten novellen und erzäh-
    lungen des in- und auslandes. Schwäb.
    Hall. 1848. O.   **S 31**
Spender, Emily. A true marriage. Lond. 1878.
    3 v. in 2. D.   **S 4176**
Spender, Litz, *mrs.* J: Kent. Gabrielle de Bour-
    danie ; a novel. N. Y. 1883. Q.   **S 4203**
— *Same.* Lond. 1882. 3 v. in 1. D.   **S 4203**
— Jocelyn's mistake. Bost. *n. d.* O. **S 4201**
— Mr. Nobody ; a novel. N. Y. 1884. Q. **S 4204**

Spender, Litz, *mrs.* J: Kent.—*Continued.*
— Till death do us part ; a novel. N. Y. 1882. Q.
                                       S 4202
Spielhagen, F: Allzeit voran ; roman. 6te
    aufl. Leipz. 1880. D.   **S 4251**
— Angela. 2te aufl. Leipz. 1880. 2 v. D.
                                       S 4268
— *Same.* N. Y. 1881. F.   **S 4268**
— *Same. In* Vierteljährl. mag.   **V 2 v22**
— Clara Vere ; novelle. 7te aufl. Leipz. 1878. S.
                                       S 4256
— *Same, eng.* Lady Clara de Vere ; a story. N.
    Y. 1882. S.   **S 4256**
— Deutsche pioniere ; eine geschichte aus dem
    vorigen jahrhundert. Berlin 1871. D.
                                       S 4252
— Durch nacht zum licht. *See below* Problema-
    tische naturen.
— Hammer und ambos ; roman. 8te aufl. Leipz.
    1881. 2 v. in 1. D.   **S 4253**
— Hans und Grete ; novelle. N. Y. 1881. F.
                                       S 4266
— Die von Hohenstein. Berlin. 1864. 4 v. D.
                                       S 4254
— *Same.* 5te aufl. Leipz. 1880. D.   **S 4254**
— *Same.* N. Y. 1882. F.   **S 4254**
— In der zwölften stunde ; novelle. N. Y. 1882.
    F.   **S 4269**
— In reih' und glied ; roman. 4te aufl. Leipz.
    1876. 2 v. in 1. D.   **S 4255**
— *Same.* N. Y. 1882. F.   **S 4255**
— Novellen. Leipz. 1880. 2 v. D.   **S 4257**
    Contents, *see* Deutscher katalog, p. 99.
— Platt land ; roman. 3te aufl. Leipz. 1881. D.
                                       S 4258
— Problematische naturen ; in zwei abtheilun-
    gen. [2. abth.: Durch nacht zum licht.]
    9te aufl. Leipz. 1880. 2 v. D.   **S 4259**
— *Same, eng.* [1st pt.] Problematic characters.
    From the germ. by prof. Sebele de Vere.
    N. Y. 1871. S.   **S 4259 v1**
— *Same.* [2d pt.] Through night to light. From
    the german by prof. Schele de Vere. Rev.
    ed. N. Y. 1874. S.   **S 4259 v2**
— Quisisana. N. Y. 1881. F.   **S 4260**
— *Same, eng.* Quisisana, or Rest at last. Lond.
    1881. D.   **S 4260**
— Die schönen amerikanerinnen. N. Y. 1881. F.
                                       S 4267
— Das skelet im hause ; novelle. N. Y. 1882. F.
                                       S 4262
— *Same, eng.* The skeleton in the house. Tr.
    from the german by M. J. Safford. N. Y.
    1881. S.   **S 4262**
— Skizzen, geschichten und gedichte. Leipz.
    1881. D.   **S 4261**
    Contents, *see* Deutscher katalog, p. 99.
— Sturmfluth ; roman. 4te aufl. Leipz. 1878. 2
    v. in 1. D.   **S 4263**
— Through night to light. *See above* Problema-
    tische naturen, pt. 2.
— Uhlenhans ; roman. N. Y. 1884. F. **S 4270**
— Ultimo ; novelle. 5te aufl. Leipz. 1877. D.
                                       S 4264
— *Same. With* Sacher-Masoch, L. Zur ehre
    Gottes.   **S 109**
— Was die schwalbe sang ; roman. 4te aufl.
    Leipz. 1877. D.   **S 4265**
— *Same, eng.* What the swallow sang. N. Y.
    1873. S.   **S 4265**
Spiller v. Hauenschildt, R: G:, *see* **Hauen-
    schildt,** R: G: Spiller v.

Spindler, C: Alte und neue zeit, oder Die reichs-grafen von Schelack; drei geschichten aus dem mund des volkes. Tabor. 1851. T.
S 4301

— Der bastard; eine deutsche sittengeschichte aus dem zeitalter kaiser Rudolph des zweiten. Stuttg. 1854. 4 v. in 2. S.   **S 4302**

— Blümlein wunderhold, oder Abenteuer bei dem grossen freischiessen zu Strassburg im jahre 1576; romantische erzählung. Stuttg. 1854. S.   **S 4303**

— Erzählungen beim licht. Stuttg. 1855. S.
S 4304

— Eugen von Kronstein, oder Des lebens und der liebe masken. 2te aufl. Stuttg. 1834. 2 v. in 1. S.   **S 4327**

— Fridolin Schwertberger; bürgerleben und familienchronik aus einer süddeutschen stadt. Stuttg. 1855. 2 v. S.   **S 4305**

— Für stadt und land. Stuttg. 1855. 2 v. in 1. S.   **S 4306**
Contents, see Deutscher katalog, p. 99.

— Der invalide; historisch-romantische bilder neuerer zeit. Stuttg. 1831. 5 v. in 2. S.
S 4328

— Je länger, je lieber. Stuttg. 1854. S.   **S 4307**

— Der jesuit; charaktergemälde aus dem ersten viertel des achtzehnten jahrhunderts. Stuttg. 1854. S.   **S 4308**

— Der jude; deutsches sittengemälde aus der ersten hälfte des fünfzehnten jahrhunderts. Stuttg. 1839. 4 v. in 2. S.   **S 4309**

— Kettenglieder; gesammelte erzählungen. Stuttg. 1854. 3 v. in 1. S.   **S 4310**
Contents, see Deutscher katalog, p. 100.

— Der könig von Zion; romantisches gemälde aus dem sechszehnten jahrhundert. Stuttg. 1854. 2 v. S.   **S 4311**

— Lesereien; im bade, auf reisen, auf dem lande. Stuttg. 1856. 2 v. in 1. S.   **S 4312**
Contents, see Deutscher katalog, p. 100.

— Lustige geschichten für ernste zeit; weltansichten, historien und wunderliche bekanntschaften vom touristen Theophil Langenstrick, genannt "Grand-Fusil". 3te aufl. Stuttg. 1852. 2 v. in 1. S.   **S 4329**

— Mancherlei. Stuttg. 1855. 2 v. in 1. S. **S 4313**
Contents, see Deutscher katalog, p. 100.

— Meister Kleiderleib; geschichte eines abenteurers während einer sommerzeit in Baden-Baden. Stuttg. 1855. S.   **S 4314**

— Mosaik; erzählungen. Stuttg. 1856. 2 v. in 1. S.   **S 4315**
Contents, see Deutscher katalog, p. 100.

— Muntere lebensbilder. (Die erben des steinernen gastes). Stuttg. 1855. S.   **S 4316**

— Die nonne von Gnadenzell; sittengemälde des fünfzehnten jahrhunderts. Stuttg. 1854. S.   **S 4317**

— Putsch und comp.; 1847-1848-1849. Stuttg. 1856. 2 v. S.   **S 4318**

— Der schwärmer; lebens- und charakterbilder aus vergangener zeit. Stuttg. 1854. S.
S 4319

— Städte und menschen; erinnerungen in bunter reihe. Stuttg. 1856. S.   **S 4320**
Contents, see Deutscher katalog, p. 100.

— Der teufel im bade; aufzeichnungen eines kurgastes in Homburg. Stuttg. 1856. S.
S 4321

— Der vogelhändler von Imst, Tirol vor hundert jahren; volksroman. Stuttg. 1855. 3 v. S.   **S 4322**

Spindler, C:—*Continued.*
— Volksgeschichten. Stuttg. 1855. 2 v. in 1. S.
S 4323
Contents, see Deutscher katalog, p. 100.

— Winterbuch; erzählungen. Stuttg. 1856. 2 v. in 1. S.   **S 4324**
Contents, see Deutscher katalog, p. 100.

— Winterspenden; erzählungen und novellen. Stuttg. 1854. 2 v. in 1. S.   **S 4325**
Contents, see Deutscher katalog, p. 100.

— Winterzeitvertreib; erzählungen. Stuttg. 1855. 2 v. in 1. S.   **S 4326**
Contents, see Deutscher katalog, p. 100.

Spofford, Harriet Elizabeth, *born* Prescott. The amber gods, and other stories. (Leisure hour ser.) N. Y. 1881. S.   **S 4401**
Includes, In a cellar.—Knitting sale-socks.—Circumstance.—Desert sands.—Midsummer and may.—The south breaker.

— Azarian. Bost. 1864. S.   **S 4402**

— *Same.* (Leisure hour ser.) N. Y. 1881. S.
S 4402

— D'outre mort. *In* Johnson, E. R. Little classics.   **J 926 v11**

— Hester Stanley at St. Marks. Bost. 1882. S.
Sx 1351

— The marquis of Carabas. Bost. 1882. S.
S 4404

— A modern Mephistopheles. (No name ser.) Bost. 1877. S.   **S 4403**

— The mount of sorrow. *In* Stories by american authors.   **S 35 v2**

— Ray. *In* Johnson, E. R. Little classics.
J 926 v11

— The south breaker. *In the same.*   **J 926 v7**

Spörlin, Margaretha. Der alte Eli; eine einfache geschichte aus dem elsässischen volksleben. 3te aufl. Basel. 1879. D.
S 4451

Sprague, Mary Aplin. An earnest trifler. [*Anon.*] Bost. 1880. S.   **S 4501**

Spring, Gardiner, *jr.* Giafar al Barmeki; a tale of the court of Haroun al Raschid. N. Y. 1836. 2 v. D.   **S 4551**

Spurr, G: G. The land of gold; a tale of '49, illustrative of early pioneer life in California and founded upon fact. Ill. Bost. 1881. D.   **S 6151**

Spyri, Johanna. Heidi, her years of wandering and learning; a story for children and those who love children. From the german by Louise Brooks. Bost. 1885 [1884]. D.
Sx 2051

Stables, Gordon. The cruise of the Snowbird; a story of arctic adventure. Ill. N. Y. 1884 [1883]. D.   **Sx 1376**

— Wild adventures in wild places. Lond. n. d. Q.   **S 4576**

Staël-Holstein, Anne Louise Germaine, *born* Necker, *baronne* de. Corinne, or Italy. Tr. by Isabel Hill. with metrical versions of the odes by L. E. Landon. Lond. n. d. D.   **S 4601**

— *Same, germ.* Corinna oder Italien. Aus dem franz. von M. Bock; mit einem vorwort von F: Spielhagen. Hildburgh. 1868. D.
S 4601

— Delphine. Aus dem französischen. Leipz. 1847. 3 v. S.   **S 4602**

Stahr, Fanny, *born* Lewald. Adele. Braunschw. 1855. S.   **S 4651**

— Ein armes mädchen. Berlin. 1862. S. **S 4652**

— Auf rother erde. *With her* Clementine.
S 4655

x denotes books specially adapted for children.

Stahr, Fanny, *born* Lewald.—*Continued.*
— Benedikt. Berlin. 1874. 2 v. in 1. D. **S 4653**
— Benvenuto ; ein roman aus der künstlerwelt.
　Berlin. 1876. 2 v. in 1. D. **S 4654**
— *Same.* N. Y. 1882. F. **S 4654**
— Clementine,—Auf rother erde ; zwei erzählun-
　gen. Berlin. 1872. D. **S 4655**
— Deutsche lebensbilder ; erzählungen. 2te ausg.
　Berlin. 1865. 4 v. in 1. S. **S 4658**
　Contents, see Deutscher katalog, p. 100.
— Die dilettanten. Berlin. 1867. S. **S 4656**
— Diogena ; roman von Iduna gräfin H. H. Leipz.
　1847. D. **S 4659**
— Der dritte stand. *T. p. w.* S. **S 4657**
— Dünen- und berggeschichten ; erzählungen.
　Braunschw. 1851. 2 v. in 1. D. **S 4660**
　Contents, see Deutscher katalog, p. 100.
— Emilie. Berlin. 1859. D. **S 4661**
— Die erlöserin ; roman. Berlin. 1873. 3 v. in 2.
　D. **S 4662**
— *Same, germ.* Hulda, or The deliverer ; a ro-
　mance. After the german by mrs. A. L.
　Wister. Phila. 1874. D. **S 4662**
— *Same.* Phila. 1883. D. **S 4662**
— Graf Joachim. Berlin. 1859. D. **S 4663**
— Helmar. Berlin. 1880. O. **S 4664**
— Jasch. Berlin. 1868. S. **S 4665**
— Jenny. Berlin. 1872. D. **S 4666**
— Die kammerjungfer ; roman. Berlin. 1864. 2
　v. in 1. D. **S 4667**
— Eine lebensfrage. Berlin. 1872. D. **S 4668**
— Der letzte seines stammes. Berlin. 1864. D.
　S 4670
— Liebesbriefe aus dem leben eines gefangenen ;
　roman. Braunschw. 1850. D. **S 4669**
— Das mädchen von Hela. Berlin. 1860. 2 v. S.
　S 4671
— Das mädchen von Oyas. *With her* Vornehme
　welt. **S 4682**
— Mamsell Philippinens Philipp. *With her* Der
　letzte seines stammes. **S 4670**
— Nella : eine weihnachtsgeschichte. Berlin.
　1870. D. **S 4672**
— Neue novellen. Berlin. 1877. D. **S 4673**
　Contents, see Deutscher katalog, p. 101.
— Pflegeeltern. *With her* Die unzertrennlichen.
　S 4678
— Prinz Louis Ferdinand ; ein zeitbild. Berlin.
　1859. 3 v. in 1. S. **S 4674**
— Die reisegefährten ; roman. 2te ausg. Berlin.
　1865. 2 v. in 1. D. **S 4675**
— Schloss Tannenburg. Berlin. 1859. D. **S 4677**
— Der seehof. Berlin. 1859. D. **S 4676**
— Stella. From the german by Beatrice Marshall.
　Leipz. 1884. 2 v. in 1. S. **S 4685**
— Die unzertrennlichen,—Pflegeeltern ; zwei er-
　zählungen. Berlin. 1871. D. **S 4678**
— Vater und sohn. N. Y. 1881. F. **S 4679**
— Villa Riunione ; erzählungen eines alten tanz-
　meisters. Berlin. 1869. 2 v. in 1. S.
　S 4680
　Contents, see Deutscher katalog, p. 101.
— Von geschlecht zu geschlecht. Berlin. 1864.
　3 v. S. **S 4681**
— Vornehme welt.—Das mädchen von Oyas.
　Berlin. 1868. S. **S 4682**
— Wandlungen ; roman. 2te ausg. Berlin. 1864.
　4 v. in 2. D. **S 4683**
— Zur weihnachten ; drei erzählungen. Berlin.
　1880. O. **S 4684**
　Contents, see Deutscher katalog, p. 101.
Stanley, H: Morton. My Kalulu, prince, king
　and slave. N. Y. 1874. D. **S 4701**

Stebbins, Sarah Bridges. Annals of a baby ;
　how it was named, how it was nursed, how
　it was a tyrant and how its nose got out of
　joint, also, a few words about its aunties,
　its grandfathers, grandmothers and other
　important relations by one of its slaves.
　[*Anon.*] N. Y. 1877. D. **S 4751**
Steffens, H: Die familien Walseth und Leith ;
　ein cyclus von novellen. 3te aufl. Breslau.
　1837. 5 v. in 3. S. **S 4801**
　Contents, see Deutscher katalog, p. 101.
— Gebirgs - sagen. Als anhang : Die trauung,
　eine sage des nordens. Breslau. 1837. S.
　S 4802
— Malkolm, eine norwegische novelle. 2te aufl.
　Breslau. 1838. 4 v. in 2. S. **S 4803**
— Die vier norweger ; ein cyclus von novellen.
　Breslau. 1837. 6 v. in 2. S. **S 4804**
Stein, A., *pseud., see* Wulff, Margarethe.
Stein, Armin, *pseud., see* Nietschmann, Her-
　mann.
Stein, Paul, *pseud., see* Hinrich, Albertine.
Steinlein, Laura, *born* Freese, (*Arthalis, Artha-
　lis Freese*). Die letzten blüthen. Leipz.
　1851. 2 v. S. **A 1701**
Stengel, Franziska v. Das apulische kind ;
　historischer roman. Leipz. 1843. D.
　S 4901
— Pessimisten ; roman. N. Y. 1882. D. **S 4902**
Stephens, C: Asbury. *The camping-out series :*
　1. Camping out as recorded by "Kit." Ill.
　　Phila. n. d. S. **Sx 1404**
　3. Off to the geysers, or The young yachters in
　　Iceland as recorded by "Wade." Ill. Bost.
　　1875. D. **Sx 1406**
　5. Fox - hunting as recorded by "Raed." Ill.
　　Phila. n. d. S. **Sx 1408**
　6. On the Amazons, or The cruise of the "Ram-
　　bler" as recorded by "Wash." Ill. Bost.
　　1874. D. **Sx 1409**
— Knockabout club along shore ; the adventures
　of a party of young men on a trip from
　Boston to the land of the midnight sun.
　Bost. 1883 [1882]. D. **Sx 1402**
— The knockabout club in the woods ; adven-
　tures of six young men in the wilds of
　Maine and Canada. Ill. Bost. 1882 [1881].
　O. **Sx 1401**
— Young Moll's Peevy. *In* Stories by american
　authors. **S 35 v10**
— The young moose-hunters ; a backwoods boy's
　story. Bost. 1882. D. **Sx 1403**
Stephenson, Eliza, *born* Tabor. Hope Meredith.
　Lond. 1874. 3 v. in 2. D. **T 108**
— Jeanie's quiet life. N. Y. 1868. O. **T 101**
— The last of her line. Lond. 1879. 3 v. in 1. D.
　T 102
— *Same.* N. Y. 1879. Q. **T 102**
— Little miss Primrose. Lond. 1880. 3 v. in 1.
　D. **T 103**
— Meta's faith. N. Y. 1869. O. **T 104**
— Nine years old. New ed. [*Anon.*] Lond.
　1882. D. **Tx 101**
— The senior songman. [*Anon.*] Lond. 1883.
　3 v. in 2. D. **T 107**
— *Same* ; a novel. N. Y. 1883. Q. **T 107**
— When I was a little girl ; stories for children.
　7th ed. [*Anon.*] Lond. 1880. S. **Tx 102**
Sterling, J: The onyx ring ; with a biographi-
　cal preface by C: Hale. Bost. 1856. D.
　S 5001
Stern, Detlef, *pseud., see* Strempel, Dora.
Stern, Otto, *pseud., see* Peters, Louise.

x denotes books specially adapted for children.

Sternberg, Alexander *freiherr* von **Ungern-.**
Die beiden schützen. Bremen. 1849. D.
S 5051
— Elisabeth Charlotte, herzogin von Orleans;
ein biographischer roman. Leipz. 1861. 3
v. D. S 5052
— Fortunat; ein feenmährchen. Leipz. 1838. 2 v.
D. S 5053
— Die gelbe gräfin. Berlin. 1848. 2 v. D.
S 5054
— Die kaiser-wahl. Bremen. 1840. D. S 5055
— Künstlerbilder. Leipz. 1861. 3 v. S. S 5056
Contents, *see* Deutscher katalog, p. 101.
— Novellen. Stuttg. 1834. S. S 5057
Contents, *see* Deutscher katalog, p. 101.
— Peter Paul Rubens; ein biographischer roman.
Leipz. 1862. D. S 5058
— Die ritter von Marienburg. Leipz. 1853. 3 v.
D. S 5059
— Die royalisten. Bremen. 1848. D. S 5060
— Wilhelm. Berlin. 1849. 2 v. S. S 5061
Sterndale, Robert Armitage. The afghan knife.
Lond. 1879. D. S 5101
— *Same.* N. Y. 1879. Q. S 5101
Sterne, Lawrence. A sentimental journey
through France and Italy. *In his* Works.
820.2 : 20 v2
— *Same, germ.* Yoricks empfindsame reise durch
Frankreich und Italien. Aus dem engli-
schen übers. von G. N. Bärmann. Brschw.
1848. S. S 5153
— The story of my uncle Toby, etc., newly ar-
ranged by Percy Fitzgerald. [Bayard
ser.] N. Y. 1871. T. S 5151
— The life and opinions of Tristram Shandy,
gent. *In his* Works. 820.2 : 20 v1, 2
— *Same, germ.* Tristram Shandy's leben und
meinungen. Aus dem englischen von G.
N. Bärmann. Brschw. 1848. 4 v. S.
S 5152
Stevenson, Robert L: , New arabian nights.
(Leisure hour ser.) N. Y. 1882. S. S 5176
Contents. The suicide club.—The rajah's diamond.
—The pavilion on the links.—A lodging for the
night.—The sire de Maletroit's door. —Providence
and the guitar.
— The pavilion on the links. *In* Tales from
many sources. T 178 v1
— Treasure Island. Ill. Bost. 1884. D. Sx 1426
— *and* Fanny van de Grift. More new arabian
nights: The dynamiter. (Leisure hour
ser.) N. Y. 1885. S. S 5177
Stewart, Agnes M. Grace O'Halloran, or Ire-
land and its peasantry; a tale of the past.
Baltimore. 1860. S. Sx 1451
— Justice and mercy, or A tale of all-hallows
e'en. Baltimore. 1864. T. Sx 1452
Stewart, Elizabeth M. Aubrey Conyers, or The
lordship of Allerdale. Lond. 1853. D.
S 5251
— Lady Amabel and the shepherd boy, or The
recluse of Byland Forest. N. Y. 1863. S.
S 5252
Stifter, Adalbert. Bunte steine; ein festge-
schenk. 6te aufl. Leipz. 1881. D. S 5301
Contents, *see* Deutscher katalog, p. 101.
— Der nachsommer. Pesth. 1857. 3 v. D.
S 5302
— Studien. Pesth. 1856. 3 v. S. S 5303
Contents, *see* Deutscher katalog, p. 101.
— Studien. [Neue folge.] Leipz. [1872]. D.
S 5304
Contents, *see* Deutscher katalog, p. 101.

Stimson, F: Jesup, (*J. S. of Dale*). The crime of
Henry Vane; a story with a moral. [*Anon.*]
N. Y. 1884. S. S 5202
— Guerndale; an old story. N. Y. 1882. D.
S 5201
— Mrs. Knollys. *In* Stories by american auth-
ors. S 35 v2
Stinde, Julius, (*Alfred de Valmy, Wilhelmine
Buchholz*). Dreimal zehn jahre; novelle.
In Vierteljährl. mag. V 2 v29
— Die familie Buchholz; aus dem leben der
hauptstadt. 34ste aufl. Berlin. 1885. O.
S 6301
— *Same*; 2ter theil. 26ste aufl. Berlin. 1885. O.
S 6302
— [*Same*; 3ter theil:] Buchholzens in Italien;
reise-abenteuer von Wilhelmine Buchholz.
24ste aufl. Berlin. 1885. O. S 6303
— Prinzess Goldhaar; eine novelle. *In* Viertel-
jährl. mag. V 2 v28
Stirling, A. At daybreak; a novel. Bost. 1884.
S. S 6201
Stirling, M. C., *see* **MacCallum,** M. C.
Stirling - Maxwell, Caroline Elizabeth Sarah
lady, born Sheridan, *formerly mrs.* Norton.
Verloren und gerettet; roman. Aus dem
englischen von F. Seybold. Leipz. 1863. 3
v. In 2. D. S 5326
Stock, Clara, *now frau* Weise, (*Clara Cron*).
Adelaide; ein charakterbild für die frauen-
welt. 2te aufl. Magdeb. [1877]. D.
S 5351
— Auf und ab; gesammelte novellen. Neue
folge. Magdeb. [1874]. D. S 5352
— Regina; ein charakterbild für die frauenwelt.
Magdeb. [1876]. D. S 5353
— Rosen und dornen; gesammelte novellen für
die frauenwelt. Magdeb. [1873]. D.
S 5354
— Schloss Wendsheim; eine erzählung für die
frauenwelt. Magdeb. [1877]. D. S 5355
Note. For contents of the collected stories, *see*
Deutscher katalog, p. 102.
Stockton, Francis R: The floating prince, and
other fairy tales. Ill. N. Y. 1881. O.
Sx 1501
— A jolly fellowship. Ill. N. Y. 1880. D.
Sx 1503
— The lady or the tiger? and other stories. N.
Y. 1884. S. S 5402
Includes, The transferred ghost. — The spectral
mortgage.—Our archery club.—His wife's deceased
sister.— Our story.— The same old 'coon.— Mr. Tol-
man.—On the training of parents.—Our fire-screen.—
A piece of red calico.—Every man his own letter
writer.
— Round-about rambles in lands of fact and
fancy. New ed., ill. N. Y. 1881. O.
Sx 1502
— Rudder Grange. N. Y. 1879. S. S 5401
— The story of Viteau. Ill. N. Y. 1884. D.
Sx 1508
— Tales out of school. Ill. N. Y. 1876. O.
Sx 1505
— *Same.* N. Y. 1881. O. Sx 1505
— Ting-a-ling. Ill. N. Y. 1882. D. Sx 1504
— The transferred ghost. *In* Stories by ameri-
can authors. S 35 v1
— What might have been expected. N. Y. 1874.
S. Sx 1507
Stockton, Louise. Kirby's coals of fire. *In*
Stories by american authors. S 35 v7
Stoddard, C: Warren. Chumming with a sav-
age. *In* Johnson, E. R. Little classics.
J 926 v18

x denotes books specially adapted for children.

Stoddard, Elizabeth Drew, *born* Barstow. The Morgesons. N. Y. 1862. S. **S 5451**
— Osgood's predicament. *In* Stories by american authors. **S 35 v8**
— Two men. *T. p. w.* [N. Y. 1865]. D. **S 5452**
Stoddard, R: H: The rich merchant of Cairo. *In* Maga stories. **P 2801**
Stoddard, W: Osborn. Among the lakes. Ill. N. Y. 1883. D. **Sx 1605**
— Dab Kinzer ; a story of a growing boy. Ill. N. Y. 1881. D. **Sx 1601**
Note. For continuation, *see* The quartet.
— Esau Hardery ; a novel of american life. N. Y. 1881. D. **S 5502**
— The heart of it ; a romance of east and west. N. Y. 1880. S. **S 5501**
— The quartet ; a sequel to "Dab Kinzer". N. Y. 1881. D. **Sx 1602**
— Saltillo boys. N. Y. 1882. D. **Sx 1603**
— The talking leaves ; an indian story. N. Y. 1882. S. **Sx 1604**
— Wrecked? a novel. N. Y. 1883. D. **S 5503**
Stolle, L: Ferdinand, (*originally* L: F. Anders). 1813 ; historischer roman. Leipz. 1858. 3 v. S. **S 5511**
Note. For continuation, *see* Elba und Waterloo.
— Camelien ; novellen und erzählungen. Leipz. 1857, 1858. 2 v. S. **S 5512**
Contents, see Deutscher katalog, p. 102.
— Deutsche Pickwickier ; komischer roman. Leipz. 1859. 3 v. S. **S 5513**
— Elba und Waterloo. Fortsetzung von "1813". Leipz. 1860. 3 v. S. **S 5514**
— Die erbschaft in Kabul ; komischer roman. Leipz. 1858. 2 v. S. **S 5515**
— Je länger, je lieber ; phantasiestücke und erzählungen ; v. 2. 2te aufl. Leipz. 1858. S. **S 5516**
Contents, see Deutscher katalog, p. 102.
— Der könig von Tauharawi ; launiger roman. Prag. 1857. 3 v. T. **S 5517**
— Moosrosen ; novellen und erzählungen ; 2ter t. 2te aufl. Leipz. 1858. S. **S 5518**
Contents, see Deutscher katalog, p. 102.
— Napoleon in Egypten ; historisch-romantisches gemälde. Leipz. 1859. 3 v. S. **S 5519**
— Der neue Cäsar ; ein seitenstück zu "1813" und "Elba und Waterloo." Leipz. 1858. 3 v. S. **S 5520**
— Von Wien nach Vilagos ; historischer roman. Leipz. 1866. 2 v. S. **S 5521**
— Der weltbürger ; historischer roman aus den jahren 1830—1832. Leipz. 1857. 3 v. S. **S 5522**
Storch, L: Der freibeuter. Leipz. 1856. 3 v. S. **S 5551**
— Der freiknecht ; historischer roman. Tabor. 1850. 4 v. T. **S 5552**
— Für stille abende. Leipz. 1857. 2 v. S. **S 5553**
Contents, see Deutscher katalog, p. 102.
— Der galeerensklave. *With his* Orestes. **S 5558**
— Der glockengiesser. Leipz. 1855. S. **S 5554**
— Der heideschenke. Leipz. 1855. 3 v. S. **S 5562**
— Die königsbraut. Leipz. 1856. 2 v. S. **S 5555**
— Kunz von Kauffungen. Leipz. 1855. 3 v. S. **S 5556**
— Madeira. Leipz. 1856. S. **S 5557**
— Orestes. Leipz. 1858. S. **S 5558**
— Der stockfischfang. Leipz. 1856. S. **S 5559**
— Vörwerts-Häns. Leipz. 1855. S. **S 5560**
— Waldmeister. Leipz. 1855. S. **S 5561**

Stories by american authors, no. 1-10. N. Y. 1884, 1885. 10 v. S. **S 35**
Contents. V. 1. **Taylor,** B. Who was she? — **Matthews,** J. B., *and* H: C. **Bunner.** The documents in the case. — **Bishop,** W: H: One of the thirty pieces.—**Davis,** R. H. Balacchi brothers. — **Webster,** A. An operation in money.
2. **Stockton,** F. R. The transferred ghost. — **Jacobi,** M. P. A martyr to science.—**Stimson,** F: J. Mrs. Knollys. — **Eddy,** S: A dinner-party. — **Spofford,** H. P. The mount of sorrow.—**Tincker,** M. A. Sister Silvia.
3. **Hale,** L. P. The spider's eye.—**Burnett,** F. H. A story of the Latin quarter.—**Lathrop,** G: P. Two purse companions.—**Lloyd,** D: D. Ogla Moga.—**Thaxter,** C. A memorable murder.—**Matthews,** J. B. Venetian glass.
4. **Woolson,** C. F. Miss Grief.—**Bunner,** H: C. Love in old cloathes.—**Willis,** N. P. Two buckets in a well.—**Foote,** M. H. Friend Barton's concern.—**DeForest,** J: W: An inspired lobbyist. — **Brooks,** N. Lost in the fog.
5. **James,** H: A light man. — **Millet,** F. D. "Yatil."—**Benjamin,** P. The end of New York.—**Arnold,** G: Why Thomas was discharged.—**Mitchell,** E. P. The tachypomp.
6. **Chaplin,** H. W. The village convict.—**Hayes,** A. A. The Denver express.—**Fairfax,** L. R. The misfortunes of brother Thomas Wheatley.—**Champney,** L. W. The heartbreak cameo.—**Webster,** A. Miss Eunice's glove.—**Frederic,** H. Brother Sebastian's friendship.
7. **Thanet,** O. The bishop's vagabond. — **Bellamy,** E: T. Lost—**Stockton,** L. Kirby's coals of fire. —**Floyd,** M. Passages from the journal of a social wreck.—**McKay,** J. T. Stella Grayland.—**Johnson,** V. W. The image of San Donato.
8. **DeForest,** J: W: The brigade commander. —**Beers,** H: A. Split zephyr.—**Phelps,** E. S. Zerviah Hope. — **Adee,** Alvey A. The life magnet.—**Stoddard,** E. D. B. Osgood's predicament.
9. **Page,** T: N. Marse Chan.—**Gage,** C: S. Mr. Bixby's christmas visitor.—**Chaplin,** H. W. Eli.—**Shinn,** M. W. Young Strong of "The Clarion."—**Coffin,** R. T. How old Wiggins wore ship.—**Kip,** L. —mas has come.
10. **Janvier,** T: A. Pancha. — **Mitchell,** E. P. The ablest man in the world. — **Stephens,** C: A. Young Moll's peevy. —**DeKay,** C: Manmat'ha.—**Boyesen,** H. H. A daring fiction.—**Schayer,** J. The story of two lives.

Stories from the history of Sweden. N. Y. 1854. T. **Sx 85**
Contents. The copper-mine.—The snow king.—The iron king.—Fall of the Hats and Caps.—Perseverance.—The three pictures.

Storm, Hans Theodor Woldsen. Hans und Heinz Kirch. N. Y. 1883. F. **S 5603**
— Immensee, or The old man's reverie. Tr. with the permission of the author from the 8th ed. of the german by H. Clark. Munster. 1863. T. **S 5602**
— Neue novellen. Berlin. 1878, 1880. 2 v. in 1. D. **S 5601**
Contents, see Deutscher katalog, p. 102.

Story, W: Wetmore. A modern magician. *In* Tales from Blackwood. **T 177 v7**
Story library, The, v. 2: The baked head, and other tales. N. Y. 1856. D. **P 2802**
Includes. The wolf in sheep's clothing.—Elkanah Smithers, jr.—Infatuation.— An ordeal.—A royal whim.—A story of Sweden.—Major O'Shaughnessey's adventure on the Duke's Moor.—A cock-fight in Havana.—Angelica Staggers.—The fall of the janissaries.—Leaves from the diary of a law clerk.—The golden guillotine.—Edward Drysdale.—The story of the unfinished picture.

Stowe, Harriet Elizabeth, *born* Beecher, (*Christopher Crowquill*). Agnes of Sorrento. 11th ed. Bost. 1878. D. **S 5651**
— *Same.* 17th ed. Bost. 1884. D. **S 5651**
— A dog's mission, or The story of the old Avery house, and other stories. Ill. N. Y. [1881]. D. **Sx 1701**

x denotes books specially adapted for children.

Stowe, Harriet E., *born* Beecher.—*Continued*.
— Dred. *See below* Nina Gordon.
— Little Pussy Willow. Bost. 1875. D. **Sx 1703**
— The Mayflower, and miscellaneous writings.
  Bost. 1875. D. **S 5652**
— The minister's wooing. Bost. 1879. D.
  S 5653
— My wife and I, or Harry Henderson's history.
  N. Y. 1872. D. **S 5654**
  Note. For continuation, *see* We and our neighbors.
— Nina Gordon ; a tale of the Great Dismal
  Swamp. Bost. 1874. 2 v. in 1. D. **S 5655**
— *Same.* Bost. 1885. D. **S 5655**
— *Same, germ.* Dred ; eine erzählung aus dem
  Grossen Dismal-Sumpfe. Bost. 1856. 2 v.
  S. **S 5655**
— Oldtown folks. Bost. 1869. D. **S 5656**
— Pink and white tyranny ; a society novel.
  Bost. 1874. S. **S 5658**
— Poganuc people, their loves and lives. Ill.
  N. Y. 1878. D. **S 5659**
— Queer little people. [New ed.] N. Y. 1884.
  D. **Sx 1702**
— Sam Lawson's Oldtown fireside stories. Bost.
  1879. S. **S 5660**
  Contents. The ghost in the mill.—The Sullivan look-
  ing glass.—The minister's housekeeper.—The widow's
  bandbox.—Captain Kidd's money.—"Mis' Elderkin's
  pitcher".—The ghost in the cap'n Brown house.—
  Colonel Eph's shoe-buckles.—The bull-fight.—How to
  fight the devil.—Laughin' in meetin'.
— Uncle Tom's cabin, or Life among the lowly.
  Bost. 1874. D. **S 5661**
— *Same.* New ed. with ill., and a bibliography
  of the work by G: Bullen, together with an
  introductory account of the work. Bost.
  1879. D. **S 5661**
— *Same.* Bost. 1884. D. **S 5661**
— *Same, germ.* Sclaverei in dem lande der freiheit, oder Das leben der neger in den skla-
  venstaaten Nord-Amerikas. Nach der 15ten
  aufl. von Onkel Tom's Cabin. Leipz. 1852.
  4 v. S. **S 5661**
— We and our neighbors, or The records of an
  unfashionable street ; sequel to "My wife
  and I". N. Y. [1875]. D. **S 5662**
— *and others.* Six of one by a half a dozen of the
  other. Bost. 1867. S. **S 5663**
  Note. Written conjointly by H. B. Stowe, F. W.
  Loring, A. D. T. Whitney, F. B. Perkins, L. P.
  Hale and E. E. Hale.

Stratford-by-the-sea ; a novel. N. Y. 1884. S.
  S 37

Streckfuss, Adolph. Castle Hohenwald. After
  the german by mrs. A. L. Wister. Phila.
  1879. D. **S 5701**
— *Same.* Phila. 1884. D. **S 5701**
— Quicksands. From the german by mrs. A. L.
  Wister. Phila. 1884. D. **S 5703**
— Too rich. Phila. 1878. D. **S 5702**

Strempel, Dora, (*Detlef Stern*). Hypatia ; roman
  aus dem modernen Konstantinopel. *In*
  Vierteljährl. mag. **V 2 v31**

Stretton, Hesba, *pseud.*, *see* Smith, Hannah.

Stricker, Karoline v., (*St. Nelly*). Blüthen aus
  Tetschens goldenen auen. Leipz. 1843. 3
  v. S. **S 5776**
  Contents, see Deutscher katalog, p. 102.
— Das haus der nichte. Leipz. 1845. 2 v. S.
  S 5777

Strickland, Agnes. Alda the captive. N. Y.
  1841. T. **Sx 1801**

Strubberg, F: A:, (*Armand*). In Mexico. Hannover. 1865. 4 v. S. **S 5801**

Strubberg, F: A:, (*Armand*).—*Continued*.
— Saat und ernte. Leipz. 1866. 5 v. S. **S 5804**
— Sclaverei in Amerika, oder Schwarzes blut.
  Hannover. 1862. 3 v. in 1. S. **S 5802**
  Contents, see Deutscher katalog, p. 102.
— Der sprung vom Niagarafalle. Hannover.
  1864. 4 v. in 2. S. **S 5803**

Struensee, Gustav K: O: v., (*Gustav vom See*).
  Arnstein. Breslau. 1868. 3 v. S. **S 5851**
— Erzählungen eines alten herrn. Breslau. 1860.
  S. **S 5852**
  Contents, see Deutscher katalog, p. 102.
— Gräfin und marquise ; roman. Wien. 1864. 4
  v. in 2. T. **S 5857**
  Note. For continuation, *see* Ost und west.
— Das majorat. Hannover. [1875]. 3 v. in 1. S.
  S 5853
— Neue novellen. Hannover. 1869. S. **S 5854**
— Ost und west ; des romans "Gräfin und mar-
  quise" zweite abtheilung. Breslau. 1865.
  4 v. in 2. T. **S 5855**
— Valerie ; roman. Breslau. 1869. 4 v. S.
  S 5858
— Zwei gnädige frauen. Breslau. 1860. 3 v. D.
  S 5856

Strussenfelt, Ulrika Sophia v. Ein pfarrhaus
  auf dem lande ; ein familiengemälde von
  D. J. W. E. Aus dem schwedischen fibers.
  von G. Fink. Stuttg. 1846. T. **E 101**

Stuart, Esmé. How they were caught in a trap ;
  a tale of France in 1802. Lond. 1880. D.
  Sx 1851

Sturgis, Julian Russell. Dick's wandering. Bost.
  1882. D. **S 5876**
— A disappointing boy. *In* Tales from Black-
  wood. **T 177 v11**
— Lord Richard and I. *In* Tales from many
  sources. **T 178 v1**
— My friends and I. (Leisure hour ser.) N. Y.
  1884. S. **S 5877**
  Contents. Michael and I.—Lord Richard and I.—
  My poor wife.

Stwin, Adam, *pseud.*, *see* Richardson, James.

Suberwick, Mme. —, (*M. V. de Féréal*). Die geheimnisse der inquisition. Aus dem französischen von L. Meyer. Leipz. 1846. 4 v.
  S. **F 451**

Sue, Marie Joseph, *called* Eugène. Der ewige
  jude. Uebers. von A. Diezmann. Leipz.
  1846. 6 v. T. **S 5901**
— *Same, eng.* The wandering jew. Ill. Lond.
  n. d. D. **S 5901**
— Die familie Jouffroy. Aus dem franz. von A:
  Zoller. Stuttg. 1854. 2 v. T. **S 5902**
— Die familiensöhne. Aus dem franz. von A:
  Zoller. Stuttg. 1856. 5 v. T. **S 5903**
— Die fanatiker der Cevennen. Aus dem franz.
  von L. Hauff. Stuttg. 1844. 2 v. T.
  S 5904
— Fernand Duplessis, oder Denkwürdigkeiten
  eines ehemannes. Aus dem franz. von A:
  Zoller. Stuttg. 1851. 4 v. T. **S 5905**
— Gilbert und Gilberte. Aus dem franz. von A:
  Zoller. Stuttg. 1853. 2 v. T. **S 5906**
— Johanne und Louise, oder Die familien der de-
  portirten. Deutsch von Julius Werner.
  Stuttg. 1853. T. **S 5907**
— Die kinder der liebe. Aus dem franz. von A:
  Zoller. Stuttg. 1850. T. **S 5908**
— Martin der findling, oder Denkwürdigkeiten
  eines kammerdieners. Nach dem franz.
  von A: Zoller. Stuttg. 1847. 4 v. T.
  S 5909

Sue, Marie Joseph, *ealled* Eugène.—*Continued.*
— Mathilde ; memoiren einer jungen frau. Deutsch von L. Meyer. Leipz. 1844. 5 v. T. S 5910
— Miss Mary, oder Die erzieherin. Aus dem franz. von A. Zoller. Stuttg. 1851. T. S 5911
— Der teufel als arzt. Aus dem franz. von A. Zoller. Stuttg. 1855. 2 v. T. S 5912
— Therese Dunoyer. Deutsch von dr. Scherr. Stuttg. 1844. T. S 5913
— Die verschwörung, oder Ludwig der XIV und sein hof. Deutsch von dr. Scherr. Stuttg. 1847. 2 v. T. S 5914
Sue-Sand fils, Alexander, *pseud., see* **Hamley,** E: B.
Superior woman, A. (No name ser.) Bost. 1885. S. S 81
Sutro - Schücking, Kathinka. Die erlebnisse einer schutzlosen. N. Y. 1882. F. S 5952
— In beiden hemisphären ; ein lebensbild. N. Y. 1881. F. S 5951
Suttières, S. de, *see* **Sarcey de Suttières,** Francisque.
Swift, A: M. Cupid, M. D.; a story. N. Y. 1882. S. S 5976
Swift, Jonathan. Gulliver's travels into several remote nations of the world ; with a life of the author by J: Mitford and copious notes by W. C. Taylor. Phila. 1880. D. 8x 1901
— *Same. In his* Works. 820.2 : 21 v2
Sydow, Clara v. Spätsommer. N. Y. 1883. F. S 6101
Sylvan queen, A ; a novel by the author of "Rachel's secret." N. Y. 1880. Q. T 106
Synge, W. W. Follett. Tom Singleton, dragoon and dramatist. Lond. 1879. 3 v. in 1 D. S 6001
— *Same* ; a novel. N. Y. 1880. Q. S 6001
Tabor, Eliza, *see* **Stephenson,** Eliza.
Talcot, *Mrs.* Hannah B., *formerly mrs.* Goodwin. Christine's fortune. Bost. 1881. S. T 151
— Dr. Howell's family. Bost. 1881. S. T 152
— One among many. Ill. Bost. 1884. S. T 154
— Sherbrooke. N. Y. 1866. S. T 153
Tales from Blackwood ; [first series.] Edinb. [1860]. 12 v. S. T 176
  Contents. V. 1. **Aytoun,** W: E. The Glenmutchkin railway.—Vanderdecken's message home.—The floating beacon.— Colonna the painter.—**Lockhart,** J: G. Napoleon. — **Hamley,** E. B. A legend of Gibraltar.—**Mudford,** W. The iron shroud.
  2. **Hamley,** E. B. Lazaro's legacy.—A story without a tale.—Faustus and queen Elizabeth.—**Aytoun,** W: E. How I became a yeoman.— **Southey,** C. A. Devereux Hall.—**Macnish,** R. The metempsychosis. — College theatricals.
  3. A reading party in the long vacation.—**Ferguson,** S: Father Tom and the pope.—**Southey,** C. A. La petite Madelaine.—**Maginn,** W: Bob Burke's duel with ensign Brady.—The headsman ; a tale of doom.—**Galt,** J. The wearyful woman.
  4. **Aytoun,** W: E. How I stood for the Dreepdaily Burghs.—**Mudford,** W. First and last.—The duke's dilemma; a chronicle of Neisenstein.— The old gentleman's teetotom.—"Woe to us when we lose the watery wall."—My college friends.—Charles Russell, the gentleman commoner.—**Hughes,** J. The magic lay of the one-horse chay.
  5. Adventures in Texas.—**Aytoun,** W: E. How we got possession of the Tuileries.—**Lockhart,** J: G. Capt. Paton's lament.—**Arbouville,** S. de Bazancourt, *countess* d'. The village doctor.—**Hogg,** J. A singular letter from southern Africa.
  6. **Hardmann,** F: My friend the dutchman.—**Leicester,** H. My college friends, no. 2.—**Aytoun,** W: E. The emerald studs.—**Hardmann,** F: Christine, a dutch story.—The man in the bell.
  7. **Hardmann,** F: My english acquaintance. — **Doubleday,** T. The murderer's last night.—Nar-

Tales from Blackwood.—*Continued.*
ration of certain uncommon things that did formerly happen to me, Herbert Willis, B. D.—The wags.—The wet wooing, a narrative of '98.—**Ben-na-groich.**
  8. **Aytoun,** W: E. The surveyor's tale.—The Forrest-race romance.—**Edwards,** C. Di Vasari; a tale of Florence.—Sigismund Fatello.—The boxes.
  9. Rosaura, a tale of Madrid.—Adventure in the north-west territory.—Harry Bolton's curacy.—The Florida pirate.—The pandour and his princess.— The beauty draught.
  10. Antonio di Carara. — The fatal repast.—The vision of Cagliostro.—The first and last kiss. — The smuggler's leap.—The haunted and the haunters.— The duellists.
  11. The natolian story-teller.—The first and last crime. —John Rintoul.—Major Ross. — The premier and his wife.
  12. Tickler among the thieves.—The bridegroom of Barna.— The involuntary experimentalist. — Lebrun's lawsuit.—The snowing up of Strath Lugas.— A few words on social philosophy.
— *Same* ; new series. Edinb. [1879]. 12 v. S. T 177
  Contents. V. 1. **Oliphant,** L. The tender recollections of Irene Macgillicuddy. —**Walford,** L. B. Nan; a summer scene. — The bells of Botreaux.—**Hamley,** E. B. A recent confession of an opium-eater; Shakespeare's funeral.—**Lockhart,** L. W. M. A night with the volunteers of Strathkinahan.—The philosopher's baby.—**Oliphant,** M. O. The secret chamber.
  2. **Chesney,** G: The battle of Dorking.— Late for the train.—**Aytoun,** W: E. The congress and the Agapedome.—Maga's birthday.—**Francillon,** R. E: Grace Owen's engagement.—**Aytoun,** W: E. The raid of Arnaboll.—**Neaves,** *Lord.* How to make a pedigree.
  3. **S.,** H: C: Who painted the great Murillo de la Merced?—**J.-nes,** Mr. A parochial epic.—A military adventure in the Pyrenees.—**Allardyce,** A. The Pundrapore residency.— Falsely accused. — Witch-Hampton Hall.
  4. The romance of Ladybank.—Metamorphoses.—**Sue-Sands fils,** Alexander. The last french hero.—**Lockhart,** L. W. M. Unlucky Tim Griffin.—**Wilson,** A. The spectre of Milaggio.
  5. The autobiography of a joint stock company [limited].—**Walford,** L. B. Bee or Beatrix.—The night wanderer of an afghan fort.—**Macleod,** N. Ayrshire curling song.—**Hamley,** C: The light on the hearth.—How to boil peas.—**Keene,** H. G. Clive's dream before the battle of Plassey.
  6. **Lever,** C: What I did at Belgrade.—**Shand,** A. I. Wrecked off the Riff coast.—Dollie and the two Smiths.—**Majendie,** *Lady* M. A railway journey.—**Francillon,** R. E: A dog without a tail.—**Hamley,** C: Wassail.
  7. Cousin John's property. — **Story,** W: W. A modern magician.—**Allardyce,** A. Edgar Wayne's escape.—The lost secret of the Cocos group. — The two mrs. Scudamores.—Bates's tour.
  8. The devil's frills.—**Francillon,** R. E: A story of Eulenburg.—The shadow of the door.—**W.,** F. The wreck of the Strathmore.—**Lever,** C: Hero-worship and its dangers.—Annie and her master.—**W.,** H. D. A feuilleton.
  9. **Greg,** P. Guy Neville's ghost.—**Hardmann,** F: The great unknown.—The easter ochlophobists, by one of themselves.—**Aytoun,** W: E. Rapping the question.— My after-dinner adventures with Peter Schlemihl.—Aunt Ann's ghost story.—The blue dragoon.—**Winchelsea,** *Earl* of. Lord Hatton.
  10. The missing title, an unsolved mystery.—**Cheadle,** W. B. My hunt of the silver fox.—Narrative of prince Charlie's escape, by one of his companions.—A fenian alarm.—**Lindau,** R. The philosopher's pendulum.—**Walford,** L. B. Lady Adelaide. —Witcherley ways.— **Lever,** C: How Frank Thornton was cured.—**Walker,** A. L. In life and in death.
  11. The haunted Enghenio. — **Veley,** M. Milly's first love.—Mrs. Beauchamp's vengeance.—**Kinkel,** G. A family feud.—**Sturgis,** J. The disappointing boy.—The cottage by the river.—A ride for life.—A sketch from Babylon.—**R.,** W. J. M. The engine driver to his engine; The coachman of the Skylark.
  12. **Francillon,** R. E. Left-handed Elsa.—The great earthquake at Lisbon. — **Lever,** C: Some one pays.—**H.,** E. B. Tray, an arthurian legend.— Whittlebridge. — Nenuphar, a fancy.—Whist at our club. — My investment in the far west.—**King,** H. Brown's peccadillo.

x denotes books specially adapted for children.

Tales from many sources. N. Y. 1885. 4 v. D.
T 178
Contents. V. 1. **Hardy, T:** The three strangers.
—**Guthrie,** F. A. The black poodle.—**Sturgis,** J.
Lord Richard and I.—**Stevenson,** R. L. The pavil-
ion on the links.—**Norris,** W. E. The hermit of Saint
Eugène.—Mattie.
2. **Gerard,** E. D. My Paris masters.—**Ramé,** L.
de la. Moufiou.—**Martin,** M. E. Beauchamp and
co.—**Reade,** C. The Knightsbridge mystery.—Arch-
deacon Holden's tribulations.—**Smith,** H. Michel
Lorio's cross.—**Argles,** M. In durance vile.
3. The professor and the harpy.—**Shorthouse,** J.
H. The marquis Jeanne Hyacinth de St. Pelaye.—
The rock scorpions.—**Black,** W. Queen Tita's wager.
—King Pepin and sweet Olive.—**Clerke,** E. M. A
film of gossamer.—The lay figure.—The count de
Rochmont.
4. **Besant,** W., *and* J. **Rice.** The ten years' tenant.—**Hunt,** M. Truth triumphant.—**Doyle,** A. C.
Bones.—**Muirhead,** F. Two plots.—**Collins,** W.
She loves and lies.—**Daudet,** A. The siege of Ber-
lin.—**Payn,** J. Patient Kitty.

Tales of Glauber Spa. N. Y. 1856. 2 v. in l. D.
T 186
Contents. V. 1. **Sedgwick,** C. M. Le Bossu.—
Paulding, J. K. Childe Roeliffe's pilgrimage.—
Bryant, W: C. The skeleton's cave; Medfield. 2.
Leggett, W: The block-house.—**Sands,** R. C. Mr.
Green.—**Paulding,** J. K. Selim.—**Sands,** R. C.
Boyuca.

Tallman, G: D., *jr.* Innocents from abroad.
N. Y. 1878. D. **T 201**

Talvj, *pseud., see* **Robinson,** Therese Albertine
Louise, *born* v. Jakob.

Tarnow, Franziska Christiane Johanne Friederike, *called* Fanny. Auswahl aus [ihren]
schriften; v. 1, 3–15. Leipz. 1830. 14 v. S.
T 251
Contents, see Deutscher katalog, p. 103.

Taubert, Emil. Die zwillingsschwester; novelle. *In* **Vierteljährl. mag.** **V 2 v37**

Taura, Elfried v., *pseud., see* **Peters,** A:

Tautphoeus, Jemima, *born* Montgomery, *bar-
onin.* At odds. Phila. 1876. D. **T 351**
— Cyrilla. Leipz. 1853. 2 v. in 1. S. **T 352**
— The initials; a story of modern life. Phila.
n. d. D. **T 353**
— *Same, germ.* Die anfangsbuchstaben. Aus
dem englischen von C: Büchele. Stuttg.
1854. 2 v. S. **T 353**
— Quits; a novel. Phila. 1874. 2 v. in 1. D. **T 354**
— *Same.* Leipz. 1858. 2 v. in 1. S. **T 354**

Tayler, C: B: Arthur and his mother, or The
child of the church; a book for children.
N. Y. 1853. S. **Tx 151**
— Earnestness; the sequel to "Thankfulness."
N. Y. 1858. S. **T 401**
— A fireside book, or The account of a christmas
spent at Old Court. 1st amer. ed. Bost.
1832. S. **Tx 153**
— Lady Mary, or Not of the world. *T. p. w.*
[Phila.] D. **T 402**
— Thankfulness, a narrative; comprising pas-
sages from the diary of the rev. Allan
Temple. N. Y. 1848. S. **T 403**

Taylor, Bayard. Boys of other countries; stories
for american boys. Ill. N. Y. 1877. D.
Tx 201
Contents. The little post boy.—The pasha's son.—
Jon of Iceland.—The two herd boys.—The young
serf.
— Friend Eli's daughter. *In* Atlantic tales.
A 1876
— Hannah Thurston; a story of american life.
N. Y. 1878. D. **T 451**
— John Godfrey's fortunes, related by himself;
a story of american life. N. Y. 1877. D.
T 452

Taylor, Bayard.—*Continued.*
— The story of Kennett. *T. p. w.* D. **T 453**
— Who was she? *In* **Stories** by american
authors. **S 35 v1**

Taylor, B: Franklin. The grammar of life. *In*
Johnson, E. R. Little classics. **J 926 v4**
— Three november days. *In the same.* **J 926 v11**

Taylor, Elizabeth. Blind pits; a story of scottish life. [*Anon.*] N. Y. 1873. D. **T 501**
— Quixstar. [*Anon.*] N. Y. 1873. D. **T 502**

Taylor, George, *pseud., see* **Hausrath,** Adolph.

Taylor, Ida Ashworth. Venus's doves; a novel.
N. Y. 1884. Q. **T 526**

Teetzel, Frances, *born* Grant. The dynamite
cartridge. Bost. 1885. D. **Tx 226**

Telman, Konrad, *pseud., see* **Zitelmann,** E. O. K.

Temme, Jodocus Donatus Hubertus. Adel; ro-
man in drei abth. Glasen. 1860. 2 v. S.
T 551
— Anna Jogszis. Leipz. 1856. 4 v. S. **T 552**
— Damen auf reisen; criminal-geschichte. Ber-
lin. 1863. S. **T 553**
— Der dieb und sein kind; criminal-geschichte.
Berlin. 1864. S. **T 554**
— Die freiherren von Falkenburg; criminal-ge-
schichte. *T. p. w.* [Berlin, 1864.] S. **T 555**
— Gleich und ungleich; roman. Breslau. 1881.
2 v. in 1. D. **T 562**
— Eine kirchmessnacht; criminal - geschichte.
Berlin. 1864. S. **T 556**
— Die klosterruine; criminal-geschichte. Berlin.
1863. S. **T 557**
— Die mühle am Schwarzen Mohr. Berlin. 1864.
S. **T 558**
— Der Pfeifenhannes; criminal-geschichte. Ber-
lin. 1864. S. **T 559**
— Die schwarze Mare; bilder aus Lithauen.
Leipz. 1854. 3 v. D. **T 560**
— Sühnung. *With his* Eine verhaftung. **T 561**
— Eine verhaftung; criminal-geschichte. Berlin.
1861. S. **T 561**

Temple, G: Lancelot Ward, M. P.; a love story.
N. Y. 1884. D. **T 2351**

Tenger, Mariam, *pseud.* Bischof und könig;
historische novelle aus Friedrich des grossen zeit. N. Y. 1881. F. **T 576**

Terhune, Mary Virginia, *born* Hawes, (*Marion
Harland*). Alone. N. Y. 1875. D. **T 601**
— At last. N. Y. 1870. D. **T 602**
— The empty heart, or Husks. N. Y. 1880. D.
T 603
— For better for worse. *With her* The empty
heart. **T 603**
— From my youth up. N. Y. 1875. D. **T 604**
— Handicapped. N. Y. 1881. D. **T 605**
— Husbands and homes. N. Y. 1878. D. **T 606**
— Jessamine. N. Y. 1875. D. **T 607**
— Judith; a chronicle of old Virginia. Ill. N. Y.
1883. D. **T 613**
— Miriam. N. Y. 1880. D. **T 608**
— Moss-side. N. Y. 1857. D. **T 614**
— My little love. N. Y. 1876. D. **T 609**
— Nemesis. N. Y. 1881. D. **T 610**
— *Same.* N. Y. 1884. D. **T 610**
— Ruby's husband. N. Y. 1878. D. **T 611**
— Sunnybank. N. Y. 1870. D. **T 612**

Terry, Rose, *see* **Cooke,** Rose.

Thackeray, Anna Isabella, *see* **Ritchie,** Anna
Isabella.

Thackeray, W: Makepeace, (*Michael Angelo Titmarsh, Samuel Titmarsh*). The adventures
of Philip on his way through the world,
showing who robbed him, who helped him

x denotes books specially adapted for children.

Thackeray, W: Makepeace.—*Continued.*
and who passed him by. Leipz. 1862. 2 v.
in 1. S.   **T 651**
— *Same.* N. Y. 1875. O.   **T 651**
— Bluebeard's ghost. *In* Johnson, E. R. Little
classics.   **J 926 v9**
— Catherine ; a story. Leipz. 1870. S.   **T 652**
— Denis Duval. Leipz. 1867. S.   **T 653**
— The great Hoggarty diamond. N. Y. 1877. O.
                                            T 654
— *Same, germ.* Geschichte von Samuel Titmarsh
und dem grossen Hoggarty'schen diamant.
Stuttg. 1850. T.   **T 654**
— The history of Henry Esmond, esq., colonel in
the service of her majesty queen Anne, writ-
ten by himself. Leipz. 1852. 2 v. in 1. S.
                                            T 655
— *Same, germ.* Geschichte Henry Esmonds, esq.,
obristen in diensten ihrer majestät der
königin Anna, verfasst von ihm selbst.
Deutsch von C. F. Grieb. Stuttg. 1853. 2
v. T.   **T 655**
— The history of Pendennis, his fortunes and
misfortunes, his friends and his greatest
enemy. Leipz. 1849. 3 v. in 2. S.   **T 656**
— *Same.* N. Y. 1850. O.   **T 656**
— *Same.* (Household ed.) N. Y. *n. d.* D. **T 656**
— *Same, germ.* Pendennis. Uebers. von L. Tafel.
Stuttg. 1851. 4 v. T.   **T 656**
— Jeames's diary. N. Y. 1853. S.   **T 657**
— The Kickleburys abroad. N. Y. 1867. T.
                                            T 658
— A legend of the Rhine. *With his* Jeames's
diary.   **T 657**
— *Same. With his* The Kickleburys abroad.
                                            T 658
— Lovel the widower. *T. p. w.* [N. Y. 1860]. O.
                                            T 659
— *Same. With his* The four Georges.
                                        923.21 : 20
— Men's wives. *T. p. w.* S.   **T 660**
— Miscellanies ; prose and verse. Leipz. 1849—
1857. 8 v. in 4. S.   **T 665**
Contents. v. 1. The great Hoggarty diamond.—
The book of snobs. **2.** The Kickleburys abroad.—A
legend of the Rhine.— Rebecca and Rowena.— The
second funeral of Napoleon.—The chronicle of the
drum. **3.** The tremendous adventures of major
Gahagan. — The fatal boots. — Ballads. **4.** The
memoirs of mr. Charles J. Yellowplush.—The diary
of C. Jeames de la Pluche, esq.—Cox's diary. **5.**
Sketches and travels in London.—Novels by eminent
hands. —Character sketches. **6.** The memoirs of
Barry Lyndon, esq. **7.** A little dinner at Timmins's.
— The Bedford Row conspiracy. — The Fitz-Boodle
papers.—A shabby genteel story. **8.** Men's wives:
Mr. and mrs. Frank Berry; Dennis Haggarty's wife;
The Ravenswing.
— The Newcomes ; memoirs of a most respect-
able family, edited by Arthur Pendennis,
esq. (Household ed.) Ill. N. Y. *n. d.* D.
                                            T 661
— *Same.* Leipz. 1855. 4 v. in 2. S.   **T 661**
— *Same, germ.* Die Newcomes ; denkwürdigkei-
ten einer höchst achtungswerthen familie.
Aus dem englischen übers. von O. Büchele.
Stuttg. 1855. 3 v. T.   **T 661**
— *Same.* Stuttg. 1845. 4 v. S.   **T 661**
— Rebecca and Rowena. N. Y. 1853. S. *With
his* Jeames's diary.   **T 657**
— *Same. With his* The Kickleburys abroad.
                                            T 658
— A shabby genteel story, and other tales. N. Y.
1853. S.   **T 662**
Includes, The professor. — The Bedford Row con-
spiracy.—A little dinner at Timmins's.

Thackeray, W: Makepeace.—*Continued.*
— Vanity fair ; a novel without a hero. Ill. by
the author. (Household ed.) N. Y. *n. d.* D.
                                            T 663
— *Same.* Leipz. 1848. 3 v. in 2. S.   **T 663**
— *Same.* Bost. 1870. S.   **T 663**
— *Same, germ.* Der jahrmarkt des lebens.
Stuttg. 1850. 4 v. T.   **T 663**
— The virginians ; a tale of the last century.
Leipz. 1858. 4 v. in 2. S.   **T 664**
Thanet, Octave, *pseud., see* French, Alice.
Thaxter, Celia, *born* Leighton. A memorable
murder. *In* Stories by american authors.
                                            S 35 v3
Therese, *pseud., see* Lützow, Therese v.
Theuriet, André. Gérard's marriage. N. Y.
1877. D.   **T 701**
— The godson of a marquis. N. Y. 1878. D.
                                            T 702
— Young Maugars. N. Y. 1879. D.   **T 703**
Thiusen, Ismar, *pseud.* The Diothas, or A far
look ahead. N. Y. 1883. S.   **T 726**
Thomas, Annie, *see* Cudlip, Annie.
Thomas, Bertha. Ichabod ; a portrait. N. Y.
1885. Q.   **T 2401**
Thomas, M. M. Captain Phil ; a boy's experi-
ence in the western army during the war
of the rebellion. N. Y. 1884. D. **Tx 251**
Thompson, J. W. Der jude von Wien ; eine histo-
rische erzählung aus dem revolutionsjahre
1848 für volk und jugend. Aus dem holländischen übers. von A. Steinbach, autorisirte übersetzung. Ill. Regensburg. 1872.
S.   **T 2451**
Thompson, Daniel Pierce. Centeola, and other
tales. N. Y. 1864. D.   **T 751**
Includes, The starving settlers.—The unfathomable
mystery.—The rustic financiers.—The counterfeiter.
— Locke Amsden, or The schoolmaster ; a tale.
Bost. 1848. D.   **T 752**
Thompson, Maurice. At love's extremes. N. Y.
1885. D.   **T 777**
— His second campaign. (Round-robin ser.)
Bost. 1883. S.   **T 778**
— A Tallahassee girl. (Round-robin ser.) Bost.
1882. S.   **T 776**
Thomson, G. The lost heir of Elphinstone. *In*
Wilson, J : M. Tales of the borders.
                                        W 2202 v20
Thoresen, Anna Magdalene, *born* Kragh. Dorf-
geschichten aus Norwegen. Frei nach dem
norwegischen von Walter Reinmar. Ber-
lin. 1878. 2 v. in 1. D.   **T 901**
Contents, see Deutscher katalog, p. 104.
Thorne, P., *pseud., see* Smith, Mary Prudence.
Thornet, Teresa A. Kate Comerford, or Sketches
of garrison life. Phila. 1881. D.   **T 801**
Thornton, M. Jacqueline. Di Cary. N. Y. 1879.
O.   **T 851**
Thorpe, Kamba, *pseud., see* Bellamy, Elizabeth
Whitfield.
Thousand and one nights, The : The arabian
nights' entertainments. Lond. *n. d.* D. **T 1**
— *Same, germ.* Tausend und eine nacht ; arabi-
sche erzählungen. Deutsch von Alexander
König. Berlin. *n. d.* 7 v. T.   **T 1**
— New arabian nights ; select tales not included
by Galland or Lane. [Tr. and ed. by W.
F. Kirby]. Ill. Phila. 1883 [1882]. D. **T 2**
Tieck, J : L: Auburn Egbert. *In* Popular tales
and romances.   **P 2126 v1**

x denotes books specially adapted for children.

Tieck, J: L:—*Continued.*
— Elfinland. *In the same.*   **P 2126 v3**
— *Same.* The elves. *In* **Hedge,** F; H: Prose
    writers of Germany.   **830. 1 : 8**
— *Same. In* **Edinburgh** tales.   **E 426**
— The enchanted castle. *In* **Popular** tales and
    romances.   **P 2126 v1**
— Gesammelte novellen. Berlin. 1844—1854. 12
    v. D.   **T 951**
    Contents, see Deutscher katalog, p. 104.
— Precipitation. *In* **Stories** from the german.
        M 3951
— *see also his* Schriften **830 : 148** (Deutscher
    katalog, p. 22), *and also* Roscoe, T: German
    novelists, **R 2451.**
Tiernan, *Mrs.* M. F. Homoselle. (Round-robin
    ser.) Bost. 1881. S.   **T 1001**
Tilton, Theodore. Tempest-tossed. N. Y. [1874].
    D.   **T 1051**
Tincker, Mary Agnes. By the Tiber. [*Anon.*]
    Bost. 1881. S.   **T 1101**
— The house of Yorke. N. Y. 1872. O.   **T 1102**
— The jewel in the lotos ; a novel. Ill. Phila.
    1884 [1883]. D.   **T 1104**
— Signor Monaldini's niece. (No name ser.)
    Bost. 1879. S.   **T 1103**
— Sister Silvia. *In* **Stories** by american authors.
        S 35 v2
Tip Cat, by the author of Miss Toosey's mission
    and Laddie. N. Y. 1884. D.   **T 20**
Tissot, V:, *and* Constant Améro. The exiles ; a
    russian story. From the french. by G: D.
    Cox. Phila. [1881]. S.   **T 1126**
Titcomb, Timothy, *pseud., see* **Holland,** Josiah
    Gilbert.
Titmarsh, Michael Angelo, *pseud., see* Thacke-
    ray, W: Makepeace.
Titmarsh, Samuel, *pseud., see* Thackeray, W:
    Makepeace.
Together. N. Y. 1865. D.   **T 41**
Tolstoi, *Graf* Leo Nikolaïevitch. The cossacks ;
    a tale of the Caucasus in 1852. Tr. from the
    russian by E. Schuyler. N. Y. 1878. S.
        T 1151
Tomlinson, Lizzie Joyce. Our laddie. N. Y.
    1880. S.   **Tx 451**
Tommaseo, Nicolo. Der herzog von Athen.
    Aus dem italienischen. Stuttg. 1847. 2 v.
    T.   **T 1201**
— Treue und schönheit. Aus dem italienischen.
    Stuttg. 1845. T.   **T 1202**
Tonna, Charlotte Elizabeth, *born* Brown, (*Char-
    lotte Elizabeth*). Conformity. N. Y. 1860.
    S.   **Tx 501**
— Derry ; a tale of the revolution. New ed.
    Lond. 1882. D.   **T 1226**
— Falsehood and truth. *With her* Conformity.
        Tx 501
— The flower-garden, or Chapters on flowers.
    N. Y. 1864. S.   **Tx 504**
Topelius, Zachris. Snowdrops ; Finland idyls
    for children. Tr. from the swedish by
    Albert Alberg. Lond. 1881. D.   **Tx 601**
— The surgeon's stories :
— — 1. Gustave Adolf and the thirty years' war ;
    an historical novel. Tr. by Selma Borg
    and Marie A. Brown. N. Y. 1872. D.
        T 1251
— — *Same.* Times of Gustaf Adolf. Tr. from
    the original swedish. Chicago. 1883. D.
        T 1251
— — *Same, germ.* Des feldschers erzählungen :
    1er cyclus: Gustav Adolf und der dreissig-

Topelius, Zachris.—*Continued.*
    jährige krieg. Aus dem schwedischen.
    Leipz. 1880. D.   **T 1251**
— — 2. Times of battle and rest. Tr. from the
    original swedish. Chicago. 1883. S.
        T 1252
— — 3. Times of Charles XII. From the origi-
    nal swedish. Chicago. 1884 [1883]. D.
        T 1253
— — 4. Times of Frederick I. From the original
    swedish. Chicago. 1884. D.   **T 1254**
— — 5. Times of Linnæus. From the original
    swedish. Chicago. 1884. D.   **T 1255**
— — 6. Times of alchemy. From the original
    swedish. Chicago. 1884. D.   **T 1256**
— Whisperings in the wood ; Finland idyls for
    children. Tr. from the swedish by Albert
    Alberg. Lond. 1881. D.   **Tx 602**
Töpffer, Rodolphe. Das pfarrhaus. Vollständige
    deutsche ausg. [aus dem französischen].
    Leipz. 1852. 4 v. D.   **T 1301**
— Rosa und Gertrud ; eine Genfer novelle. Aus
    dem französischen übertr. von K: Eitner.
    Hildburgh. 1865. D.   **T 1302**
Torelli-Torriani, Maria, (*La marchesa Colombi*).
    The wane of an ideal ; a novel. From the
    italian by Clara Bell, rev. and corr. in the
    U. S. N. Y. 1885. S.   **C 4001**
Tornow, Dr., *pseud., see* **Löffler,** K: Valentin
    Immanuel.
Toulmin - Smith, Elizabeth Thomasina, *see*
    Smith, Elizabeth Thomasina, *mrs.* Toul-
    min-.
Tourgée, Albion Winegar, (*Henry Churton*).
    Bricks without straw ; a novel. Ill. N. Y.
    [1880]. D.   **T 1351**
— Figs and thistles ; a western story. N. Y.
    [1879]. S.   **T 1352**
— A fool's errand, by one of the fools. N. Y.
    1880. S.   **T 1353**
— Hot plowshares ; a novel. Ill. N. Y. 1888. S.
        T 1356
— John Eax *and* Mamelon, or The south with-
    out the shadow. N. Y. 1882. S.   **T 1355**
— Toinette. N. Y. 1874. D.   **T 1354**
Toussaint, Anna Luize Geertruide, *now mevrouw*
    J : Bosboom. Das haus Lauernesse ; ein
    historischer roman. Stuttg. 1847. 2 v. T.
        T 1401
— Kleine novellen. Nach dem holländische.
    Stuttg. 1847. T.   **T 1402**
    Contents, see Deutscher katalog, p. 105.
Towne, Belle Kellogg. Around the ranche.
    Bost. [1883]. D.   **Tx 626**
Townsend, Virginia Frances. But a philistine.
    Bost. 1884. D.   **T 1456**
— The Deerings of Medbury. Bost. 1871. O.
        T 1451
— Lenox Dare. Bost. 1881. D.   **T 1452**
— The mills of Tuxbury. Bost. [1871]. D.
        T 1453
— One woman's two lovers, or Jacqueline
    Thayne's choice. Phila. 1875. D. **T 1457**
— Only girls. Bost. 1872. S.   **Tx 701**
— Six in all. Bost. [1872]. D.   **T 1454**
— That queer girl. Bost. 1874. S.   **Tx 702**
— A woman's word and how she kept it. Bost.
    1879. D.   **T 1455**
Trafford, F. G., *pseud., see* **Riddell,** Charlotte
    E. L.
Trafton, Adeline. His inheritance. Bost. 1878.
    D.   **T 1501**
— Katherine Earle. Ill. Bost. [1874]. D. **T 1502**

x denotes books specially adapted for children.

Trebor, *pseud.*, *see* Davis, Robert E.

Trois Etoiles, *pseud.*, *see* Murray, Eustace Claire Grenville.

Trolle, H: af. Royalists and republicans, or The victims of the revolution ; a historical novel. Tr. from the swedish by C: G. C. Lagervall. Cleveland. 1883. D.   **T 1552**
— Das testament des königs Gustav III von Schweden ; historisch-romantische zeitbilder. Frei nach dem schwedischen bearb. von Emil J. Jonas. Leipz. 1878. 2 v. in 1. D.   **T 1551**

Trollope, Anthony. The american senator. Leipz. 1877. 3 v. in 1. S.   **T 1601**
— *Same.* N. Y. 1877. O.   **T 1601**
— Ayala's angel. Lond. 1881. 3 v. in 1. D.   **T 1602**
— Barchester Towers. Leipz. 1859. 2 v. in 1. S.   **T 1603**
— The Belton estate. Leipz. 1866. 2 v. in 1. S.   **T 1604**
— The Bertrams ; a novel. New ed. Lond. *n. d.* D.   **T 1605**
— *Same.* Leipz. 1859. 2 v. in 1. S.   **T 1605**
— Can you forgive her ? Leipz. 1865. 3 v. in 2. S.   **T 1606**
— Castle Richmond. Leipz. 1860. 2 v. in 1. S.   **T 1607**
— *Same.* Lond. *n. d.* D.   **T 1607**
— The Claverings. Leipz. 1867. 2 v. in 1. S.   **T 1608**
— *Same.* N. Y. 1875. O.   **T 1608**
— Cousin Henry. Leipz. 1879. S.   **T 1609**
— *Same.* Lond. 1879. D.   **T 1609**
— *Same.* N. Y. 1879. Q.   **T 1609**
— Doctor Thorne. N. Y. 1874. O.   **T 1610**
— *Same.* Leipz. 1858. 2 v. in 1. S.   **T 1610**
— Doctor Wortle's school ; a novel. Lond. 1881. 2 v. D.   **T 1611**
— *Same.* N. Y. 1880. Q.   **T 1611**
— The duke's children ; a novel. Lond. 1880. 3 v. in 2. D.   **T 1612**
— *Same.* N. Y. 1880. Q.   **T 1612**
— The Eustace diamonds. Lond. 1873. 3 v. in 1. D.   **T 1641**
— An eye for an eye. Leipz. 1879. D.   **T 1613**
— *Same.* New ed. Lond. 1879. D.   **T 1613**
— *Same.* N. Y. 1879. D.   **T 1613**
— The fixed period ; a novel. N. Y. 1882. Q.   **T 1636**
— Framley parsonage. Leipz. 1861. 2 v. in 1. S.   **T 1614**
— The Golden Lion of Grandpere. Leipz. 1872. S.   **T 1615**
— Harry Heathcote of Gangoil ; a tale of australian bush life. Leipz. 1874. S.   **T 1616**
— He knew he was right. Leipz. 1869. 3 v. in 2. S.   **T 1617**
— Is he Popenjoy ? a novel. Lond. 1878. 3 v. in 1. D.   **T 1618**
— *Same.* Leipz. 1878. 3 v. in 1. D.   **T 1618**
— John Caldigate. Leipz. 1879. 3 v. in 1. S.   **T 1619**
— *Same.* Lond. 1879. 3 v. D.   **T 1619**
— *Same.* N. Y. 1879. Q.   **T 1619**
— Kept in the dark ; a novel. Lond. 1882. D.   **T 1638**
— *Same.* N. Y. 1882. Q.   **T 1638**
— Lady Anna. Leipz. 1873. 2 v. in 1. S.   **T 1620**
— The last chronicle of Barset. Ill. N. Y. 1867. O.   **T 1621**
— *Same.* Leipz. 1867. 3 v. in 1. S.   **T 1621**

Trollope, Anthony.—*Continued.*
— Marion Fay ; a novel. Lond. 1882. 3 v. in 1. D.   **T 1635**
— *Same.* N. Y. 1882. Q.   **T 1635**
— Miss Mackenzie. 5th ed. Lond. *n. d.* S.   **T 1622**
— *Same.* New ed. Lond. *n. d.* S.   **T 1622**
— Mr. Scarborough's family ; a novel. N. Y. 1883. Q.   **T 1639**
— *Same.* Lond. 1883. 3 v. in 1. D.   **T 1639**
— An old man's love ; a novel. Lond. 1884. 2 v. in 1. D.   **T 1640**
— *Same.* N. Y. 1884. Q.   **T 1640**
— Orley Farm. Aus dem englischen von C. Marggraff. Leipz. 1865. 2 v. S.   **T 1623**
— Phineas Finn, the irish member. Leipz. 1869. 3 v. in 2. S.   **T 1624**
— *Same.* N. Y. 1869. O.   **T 1624**
— Phineas Redux. Ill. N. Y. 1874. O.   **T 1625**
— The prime minister. Leipz. 1876. 4 v. in 2. S.   **T 1626**
— *Same.* N. Y. 1876. O.   **T 1626**
— Rachel Ray. Leipz. 1863. 2 v. in 1. S.   **T 1627**
— Ralph the heir. Leipz. 1871. 2 v. in 1. S.   **T 1628**
— Sir Harry Hotspur of Humblethwaite. Leipz. 1861. S.   **T 1629**
— *Same.* Bost. *n. d.* D.   **T 1629**
— The small house at Allington. Leipz. 1864. 3 v. in 2. S.   **T 1630**
— The struggles of Brown, Jones and Robinson, by one of the firm. N. Y. 1864. O.   **T 1631**
— *Same.* N. Y. 1862. O.   **T 1631**
— The vicar of Bullhampton. Leipz. 1870. 2 v. in 1. S.   **T 1632**
— The warden. N. Y. 1861. S.   **T 1633**
— *Same.* Leipz. 1859. S.   **T 1633**
— The way we live now. Leipz. 1875. 4 v. in 2. S.   **T 1634**
— *Same.* N. Y. 1875. O.   **T 1634**
— Why frau Frohmann raised her prices, and other stories. Lond. 1882. D.   **T 1637**
Includes, The lady of Launay.—Christmas at Thompson Hall.—The telegraph girl.—Alice Dugdale.
— *Same.* N. Y. 1882. Q.   **T 1637**
Note. Several of the political novels are connected in the following series: 1. The warden.—2. Barchester Towers.—3. Doctor Thorne.—4. Framley parsonage.—5. The small house at Arlington.—6. The last chronicle of Barset.—7. Can you forgive her ? 8. Phineas Finn.—9. The Eustace diamonds.—10. Phineas Redux.—11. The prime minister.—12. The duke's children.

Trollope, Frances, *born* Milton. Leben und abenteuer Michael Armstrongs, des fabrikjungen. Nach dem englischen von A. *freiherr* v. T. Stuttg. 1841. 5 v. S.   **T 1701**
— Petticoat government. N. Y. 1862. O.   **T 1702**
— Der vikar von Wrexhill. Aus dem englischen von O. v. Czarnowski. Aachen. 1870. S.   **T 1703**

Trollope, Frances Eleanor, *born* Tiernan. Among aliens. N. Y. 1878. Q.   **T 1751**
— Black spirits and white. N. Y. 1877. O.   **T 1752**
— Like ships upon the sea ; a novel. Lond. 1883. 2 v. in 1. D.   **T 1754**
— *Same.* N. Y. 1883. Q.   **T 1754**
— The sacristan's household ; a story of Lippe-Detmold. N. Y. 1869. O.   **T 1753**

Trollope, T: Adolphus. Diamond cut diamond ; a story of tuscan life. N. Y. 1874. D.   **T 1801**

Trowbridge, J: Townsend. *The Brighthope ser.*:
1. The old battle-ground. N. Y. *n. d.* D.
Tx 815
2. Ironthorpe, the pioneer preacher. N. Y.
n. d. D. Tx 816
3. Father Brighthopes, or An old clergyman's
vacation. N. Y. *n. d.* D. Tx 817
4. Burrcliff, its sunshine and its clouds. N. Y.
n. d. D. Tx 818
5. Hearts and faces, or Home-life unveiled. N.
Y. *n. d.* D. Tx 819
— Coupon bonds, and other stories. Bost. 1884.
D. T 1852
Includes, Madam Waldoborough's carriage. — Fessenden's.—Archibald Blossom, bachelor.—In the ice.
—Nancy Blynn's lovers.—Mr. Blazay's experience.—
Preaching for Selwyn.—The romance for a glove.—
The man who stole a meeting-house.
— Cudjo's cave. Bost. 1884. D. T 1853
— The drummer boy. Bost. 1884. D. T 1854
— Farnell's Folly. Bost. 1885 [1884]. D. T 1858
— *Jack Hazard series*:
1. Jack Hazard and his fortunes. Phila. *n. d.*
S. Tx 805
2. A chance for himself, or Jack Hazard and
his treasure. Phila. *n. d.* S. Tx 806
3. Doing his best. Phila. *n. d.* S. Tx 807
4. Fast friends. Phila. *n. d.* S. Tx 808
5. The young surveyor, or Jack on the prairies.
Phila. *n. d.* S. Tx 809
6. Lawrence's adventures among the ice-cut-
ters, glass-makers, coal-miners, iron-men
and ship-builders. Phila. *n. d.* S. Tx 810
— Martin Merivale his × mark. Bost. 1884. D.
T 1855
— Neighbor Jackwood. Bost. 1884. D. T 1856
— Neighbors' wives. Bost. 1884. D. T 1857
— Phil and his friends. Ill. Bost. 1884 [1883]. S.
Tx 803
— *The silver medal series*:
1. His own master. Ill. Bost. 1882. D.
Tx 811
2. Bound in honor, or A harvest of wild oats.
Bost. *n. d.* D. Tx 812
3. Young Joe, and other boys. Bost. 1880. D.
Tx 813
4. The silver medal. Ill. Bost. 1881. D.
Tx 814
5. The pocket rifle. Bost. 1882 [1881]. S.
Tx 801
6. The Jolly Rover. Bost. 1883 [1882]. S.
Tx 802
— The three scouts. Bost. 1869. D. T 1851
— *Same.* Bost. 1884. D. T 1851
— The Tinkham brothers' tide-mill. Bost. 1884
[1883]. S. Tx 804
Trueba y Cosio, Telesforo de. Der kastilianer.
Aus dem englischen. Leipz. 1829. 3 v. S.
T 1901
Tschabuschnigg, Adolf *ritter* v. Der moderne
eulenspiegel; roman. Pest. 1846. 2 v. in 1.
D. T 1951
Tucker, Charlotte Maria, (*A. L. O. E.*). Exiles
in Babylon, or Children of light. [Ill.]
Lond. 1864. S. Tx 901
— Parliament in the play-room. Lond. 1865. S.
Tx 902
— Rescued from Egypt. N. Y. 1866. S. Tx 903
— The shepherd king, or A sick minister's lec-
tures on the shepherd of Bethlehem and
the blessing that followed them. Ill. Bost.
n. d. S. Tx 904
— True heroism. N. Y. 1863. T. *With her* Walter
Binning. Tx 905

Tucker, Charlotte Maria, (*A. L. O. E.*).—*Contin'd.*
— Walter Binning, the adopted son. *T. p. w.* [N.
Y. 1863]. T. Tx 905
— Wings and stings; a tale for the young. *With
her* Walter Binning. Tx 905
Tucker, Nathaniel Beverly. The partisan leader;
secretly printed in Washington [in 1836] by
Duff Green for circulation in the southern
states, but afterwards suppressed. N. Y.
1861. D. T 2001
Tucker - Machetta, Blanche Roosevelt, *born*
Tucker. Stage-struck, or She *would* be an
opera-singer. N. Y. 1884. D. R 2376
Tugendkranz; erzählungen für die gesammte
edlere lesewelt, besonders für die reifere
jugend. Cinc. 1860. S. *With Marbach,*
G. O., *ed.* Geschichte von der schönen
Magelone. M 976
Contents. Gräfin Itha von Toggenburg. — Schütze
auch den geringsten.—Der kleine spanier.
Tupper, Martin Farquhar. Heart; a social no-
vel. N. Y. 1849. D. *With his* The twins.
T 2051
— The twins; a domestic novel. N. Y. 1849. D.
T 2051
Turgenief, Ivan Sergeïevitch. Annals of a sports-
man. Tr. from the authorized french, ed.
by Franklin Pierce Abbott. (Leisure hour
ser.) N. Y. 1885. S. T 2114
— Annouchka; a tale from the french of the
author's own trans., by Franklin Abbott.
Bost. 1884. D. T 2113
— The diary of a superfluous man. *With his*
Mumu. T 2111
— Dimitri Roudine. Tr. from the french and
german versions. (Leisure hour ser.) N. Y.
1873. S. T 2101
— Erzählungen eines alten mannes. Aus dem
russischen von Adolf Gerstmann. 2te aufl.
Berlin. [1878]. D. T 2108
Contents, see Deutscher katalog, p. 105.
— Fathers and sons. Tr. from the russian with
the approval of the author by Eugene
Schuyler. (Leisure hour ser.) N. Y. 1872.
S. T 2102
— *Same, germ.* Väter und söhne; roman. Aus
dem russischen von Adolf Gerstmann.
Berlin. [1878]. D. T 2102
— *Same.* Uebers. von Claire v. Glümer; mit
einer einleitung von Robert Boxberger.
Stuttg. [1883]. D. T 2102
— A Lear of the steppe. From the french by W:
Hand Browne. *With his* Spring floods.
T 2106
— Liza; a russian novel. Tr. by W. R. S. Ral-
ston. (Leisure hour ser.) N. Y. 1872. S.
T 2103
— Mumu. From the russian by H: Gersoni. N.
Y. 1884. D. T 2111
— Die neue generation; roman. Deutsch von
W: Lange. Berlin. 1877. 2 v. in 1. O.
T 2109
— On the eve. Tr. from the russian by C. E.
Turner. Am. ed. with amendments. (Lei-
sure hour ser.) N. Y. 1873. S. T 2104
— Smoke; a russian novel. Tr. from the auth-
or's french version by W: F. West. (Leis-
ure hour ser.) N. Y. 1872. S. T 2105
— *Same, germ.* Dunst; roman. Aus dem rus-
sischen frei bearb. von H. v. Lankenau.
3te aufl. Berlin. 1878. D. T 2105
— *Same.* Rauch; roman. Uebers. und eingel.
von C. B. Stuttg. [1884]. D. T 2105

x denotes books specially adapted for children.

Turgenief, Ivan Sergeïevitch.—*Continued.*
— Spring floods. Tr. from the russian by Sophie Michell Butts. (Leisure hour ser.) N. Y. 1874. S.   **T 2106**
— Eine unglückliche ; erzählung. Aus dem russischen. 3te aufl. Berlin. [1877]. D.   **T 2110**
— Virgin soil. Tr. with the author's sanction from the french version by T. S. Perry. (Leisure hour ser,) N. Y. 1877. S.   **T 2107**
— *Same, germ.* Neuland ; roman. Aus dem russischen. 3te aufl. Berlin. [1879]. D.   **T 2107**
Turnbull, Charlotte. The Lawrences ; a twenty years' history. N. Y. [1872]. D.   **T 2151**
Turner, Bessie. A woman in the case. N. Y. 1875. D.   **T 2201**
Tuthill, Louisa Caroline, *born* Huggins. Romantic Belinda. *T. p. w.* S.   **Tx 1001**
— A strike for freedom. or Law and order ; a book for boys. 14th ed. Bost. [1850]. S.   **Tx 1002**
Twain, Mark, *pseud., see* Clemens, S: Langhorne.
Twells, Julia Helen. The mills of the gods. Phila. 1875. D.   **T 2251**
Two miss Flemings, The, by the author of "Rare pale Margaret." N. Y. 1879. Q.   **T 81**
Two russian idyls : Marcella ; Esfira. N. Y. 1880. S.   **T 82**
Two tales of married life : Hard to bear, by Georgiana M. Craik ; A true man, by M. C. Stirling. Leipz. 1878. 2 v. in 1. S.   **C 2905**
Tytler, Ann Fraser. Leila in England ; a continuation of "Leila, or The island." Ill. Bost. 1870. S.   **Tx 1202**
— Mary and Florence at sixteen. *T. p. w.* [Bost. 1870]. S.   **Tx 1205**
Tytler, C. C. Fraser, *see* Liddell, Catharine Christina.
Tytler, Margaret Fraser-. The deformed. *In* Edinburgh tales.   **E 426**
Tytler, Sarah, *pseud., see* Keddie, Henrietta.

Uechtritz, F: v. Eleazar ; eine erzählung aus der zeit des grossen jüdischen krieges im ersten jahrhundert nach Christo. Jena. 1867. S.   **U 101**
Ulbach, L: Madame Gosselin. N. Y. 1878. D.   **U 151**
Under the lime-trees, or Grandmamma's stories at Hurst farm by the author of "Aunt Annie's stories", etc. N. Y. 1868. O.   **Ux 51**
Underwood, Francis H: Lord of himself ; a novel. Bost. 1884. S.   **U 301**
Ungern - Sternberg, Alexander *freiherr* v., *see* Sternberg, Alexander *freiherr* v. Ungern-.
Unter dem schleier der nacht ; Hamburger novelle. Hamburg. 1859. S.   **H 6**
Up from the Cape ; a plea for republican simplicity. Ill. Bost. 1883. S.   **U 3**
Urania ; taschenbuch. Neue folge ; 2.—10. jahrg. Leipz. 1840—1848. 9 v. S.   **U 1**
Contents, see Deutscher katalog, p. 106.

V., *Mlle.* Fanny de. Marie, oder Der engel auf erden ; eine erzählung für die gesammte edlere lesewelt, besonders für die reifere jugend. Aus dem französischen von Robert della Torre. Cinc. 1856. S. *With* Marbach, G. O., *ed.* Geschichte von der schönen Magelone.   **M 976**

Vahey, J: W: Julia, or Sister Agnes. Milw. 1875. S.   **V 201**
Vale, Ferna, *pseud., see* Hallett, E. V.
Valmy, Alfred de, *pseud., see* Stinde, Julius.
Vandegrift, Margaret, *pseud., see* Janvier, Margaret.
Van Dyke, Theodore S. Flirtation camp, or The rifle, rod and gun in California, a sporting romance. N. Y. 1881. D.   **V 301**
Vane, Violet, *pseud., see* Howell, *Mrs.* Jane L.
Van Loon, Elizabeth. Under the willows, or The three countesses. Phil. [1879]. D.   **V 401**
Varnbüler, Theodor v. Buchenheim. N. Y. 1881. F.   **V 426**
Varra, Owen. Eddies round the rectory. First issued in America in Littell's living age. N. Y. 1858. O.   **V 451**
Velde, C: Franz van der. Axel ; a tale of the thirty years' war. *In* Oxenford, J: Tales from the german.   **O 1001**
Veley, Margaret. "For Percival". Phila. 1879. O.   **V 501**
— Milly's first love. *In* Tales from Blackwood.   **T 177 v11**
— Mitchelhurst Place ; a novel. N. Y. 1884. Q.   **V 503**
— Rachel's inheritance, or Damocles ; a novel. N. Y. 1882. O.   **V 502**
— *Same.* Damocles. Lond. 1882. 4 v. in 1. D.   **V 502**
Vely, Emma, *pseud., see* Simon, Emma.
Verne, Jules. Adventures in the land of the behemoth. Ill. Bost. 1874. D.   **V 561**
Note. Same as Meridiana below.
— Around the world in eighty days. Tr. by G. M. Towle. Bost. 1874. D.   **V 556**
— *Same, germ.* Reise um die erde in achtzig tagen. N. Y. 1882. Q.   **V 556**
— The blockade runners. *With his* A floating city.   **V 564**
— The child of the cavern, or Strange doings underground. Tr. by W: H: G. Kingston. Lond. 1877. D.   **Vx 303**
— The desert of ice, or The further adventures of captain Hatteras. Tr. from the french. Ill. Phila. *n. d.* D.   **V 559**
— A floating city. Tr. from the french. N. Y. 1875. O.   **V 564**
— From the earth to the moon direct in ninety-seven hours and twenty minutes, and a trip round it. Tr. from the french by L: Mercier and Eleanor E. King. Ill. N. Y. 1874. D.   **V 552**
— *Same, germ.* [1ster t.] Von der erde zum mond. N. Y. 1882. F.   **V 552 v1**
— *Same, germ.* [2ter t.] Reise um den mond. N. Y. 1882.   **V 552 v2**
— The fur country, or Seventy degrees north latitude. Tr. from the french by N. D'Anvers. Ill. N. Y. *n. d.* D.   **V 563**
— The giant raft : 1. Eight hundred leagues on the Amazon. Tr. by W. J. Gordon. N. Y. 1881. D.   **Vx 301 v1**
— — 2. The cryptogram. Tr. by W. J. Gordon. N. Y. 1882. D.   **Vx 301 v2**
— Godfrey Morgan ; a California mystery. Tr. by W. J. Gordon. Ill. N. Y. [1883]. D.   **V 558**
— Hector Servadac. Tr. by Ellen E. Frewer. Ill. N. Y. 1882. O.   **V 555**
— *Same. T. p. w.* [N. Y. 1878]. O.   **V 555**

x denotes books specially adapted for children.

Verne, Jules.—*Continued.*

— A journey to the centre of the earth; containing a complete account of the wonderful and thrilling adventures of the intrepid subterranean explorers, prof. von Hardwigg, his nephew Harry and their icelandic guide Hans Bjelke. Tr. from the french. Ill. N. Y. *n. d.* O.   **V 554**

— *Same, germ.* Reise nach dem mittelpunkt der erde. N. Y. 1882. F.   **V 554**

— Meridiana; the adventures of three englishmen and three russians in South Africa. Tr. from the french. Ill. N. Y. 1874. D.   **V 561**

— *Same.* See Adventures *above.*

— Michael Strogoff, or The courier of the czar. Chicago. *n. d.* S.   **V 551**

— Off on a comet; a journey through planetary space; a sequel to "To the sun." From the french by E: Roth. Ill. Phila. 1878. D.   **V 560**

— The steam house: 1. The demon of Cawnpore. Tr. from the french by A. D. Kingston. Ill. N. Y. 1881. D.   **Vx 304 v1**

— — 2. Tigers and traitors. Tr. from the french by A. D. Kingston. N. Y. 1881. D.   **Vx 304 v2**

— The tribulations of a chinaman in China. From the french by Virginia Champlin. Bost. 1880. S.   **V 562**

— Twenty thousand leagues under the seas, or The marvellous and exciting adventures of Pierre Adronnax, Conseil, his servant, and Ned Land, a canadian harpooner. Ill. N. Y. *n. d.* O.   **V 557**

— *Same, germ.* Zwanzig tausend meilen unter'm meer. N. Y. 1882. Q.   **V 557**

Very young couple, A. N. Y. 1874. S.   **V 6**

Victor, Metta Victoria. Passing the portal, or A girl's struggle; an autobiography. N. Y. 1876. D.   **V 601**

Vierteljährliches magazin der modernen literatur; v. 21-25, 28-31, 33, 35-38. Milw. 1881-85. 14 v. O.   **V 2**

Contents. V. **21.** Protar, F. Beim "wurst"-director; humoreske.—Collins, W: W. Isabel's tochter.—Jókai, M. Die sphinx.—Proschko, H. E. Der hofkanzler.—Bayer, K: R. E. v. Die Spatlauber.—Bertigny, S. v: Wahnsinnig auf befehl. **22.** Glogau, B. Im kopfe der anderen.—Zitelmann, E. O. K. Das jüngste gericht.—Spielhagen, F: Angela.—Wenzel, M. Eine böse nacht.—Hainau, K: W. Ein schlimmer augenblick. **23.** Enders, M. A. Steevenbord.—Proschkow, H. C. Lorbeer und myrthe.—Sauer, K: M. Monsu Max.—Vollmar, A. Mein wille geschehe.—Kjelland, A. L. Zwei freunde.—Wichert, E. Eine vornehme schwester.—Semler, H: Ein banditenstreich.—Winterfeld, A. v. Die diamantknöpfe.—Grothe, R: Künslerelend. **24.** Ebner-Eschenbach, M. v. Lotti, die uhrmacherin.—Bach, O. Des vaters schuld. —Reinhardt, L. Im kerker geboren.—Heigel, K: Der sangesbruder.—Winterfeld, A. v. Das ungethüm. **25.** Augusti, B. Das bildniss.—Wildenbruch, E. v. Vor den schranken.—Enders, M. A. Trautenheim.—Grossheim, J. Von schritt zu schritt.—Schücking, L. Zwischen zwei todsünden.—Fischer, L. V. Am weg zum kloster.—Villamaria, *pseud.* Der pathe Hinkefoot.—Glogau, B. Sitzen geblieben. —Ein ex-pirat; episode aus dem leben.—Wildenbruch, E. v. Mein onkel aus Pommern.—Winterfeld, A. v. Zwei alte freunde.—Sacher-Masoch, L. v. Predigten der frau Ganizka. **28.** Semler, H: Samuels kleiner roman.—Winterfeld, A. v. Der dolmetscher.—Kürschner, L. Schneeglöckchen.—Demmler, E: Die tochter des fährmanns.—Forstenheim, A. Prinz Tantalus.—Stinde, J. Prinzess Goldhaar.—Fischer, L. v. Zur rechten zeit bankerott.—Fischer, W: Paul.

29. Freudenberg, R: Boca del Drago.—Stinde, J. Dreimal zehn jahre.—Winterfeld, A. v. Des königs ordre.—Meyer, C. F. Page Leubelfing. **30.** Ebers, G: M. Ein wort.—Wartenburg, K: F: A. Die dame, die er liebte, nannt' er nicht.—Dahn, F. Felicitas.—Rosegger, P. K. Annonce nummero 99.—Elster, Chr. Ein fremder vogel.—Dincklage-Campe, E. v. Unsere patriarchen. **31.** Strempel, D. Hypatia.—Berger, W: Das letzte glück.—Rössler, R. Mein erster patient.—Phelps, E. S. Doctor Za.—Dincklage-Campe, E. v. Joseph und seine brüder.—Polko, E. Die kleine Marina.—Anzengruber, L: Hartinger's alte Sixtin. **33.** Wachenhusen, H. Magnetische inclination. —Menger, R. Eine wahlcampagne.—Mertens, E. Zufall oder fügung?—Calm, M. Onkel hauptmann. —Villinger, H. Der andere ist's.—Rodt-Calkum. Echt conservativ.—Wachenhusen, H. Sünders kind. **35.** Böhlau, H. Der schöne Valentin.—Wilbrandt, A. Der wille zum leben.—Grosse, J. Ein bürgerlicher Demetrius.—Winterfeld, A. v. Der todte onkel; Der pantoffelheld.—Simon, E. Schiffbruch. **36.** Hopfen, H. Brennende liebe.—Habicht, L: Die poesie der prosa.—Meshtcherskii, V. *kniaz.* Die realisten der grossen welt.—Frenzel, K: Geld. —Fischer, W: Eine denkwürdige vorladung. **37.** Schönberg, H. Verschlungene wege. — Franzos, K: E. Die reise nach dem schicksal.—Wichert, E. Mutter und tochter.—Taubert, E. Die zwillingsschwester.—Roquette, O: Der kobold. **38.** Möllhausen, B. Wildes blut.

Vigny, Alfred V: *comte* de. Cinq-Mars, oder Eine verschwörung gegen Richelieu. Nach der 9. aufl. des originals verdeutscht von dr. Scherr. Stuttg. 1847. 2 v. T.   **V 701**

Villamaria, *pseud.* Der pathe Hinkefoot; eine dorfgeschichte. *In* **Vierteljährl.** mag.   **V2 v25**

Villinger, Hermine, (*H. Willfried*). Der andere ist's; erzählung. *In* **Vierteljährl.** mag.   **V2 v33**

— Die livergnas; roman. N. Y. 1882. F.   **W 1926**

Vincent, Jacques, *pseud., see* **Dussaud,** *Mme.* —.

Vincent, John, *pseud., see* **Huntington,** Jedediah Vincent.

Volckhausen, Ad. v. Why did he not die? or The child from the Ebräergang. After the german by mrs. A. L. Wister. Phila. 1875. D.   **V 801**

Vollmar, Agnes. Mein wille geschehe; erzählung. *In* **Vierteljährl.** mag.   **V2 v23**

Vollmer, W. F. A., (*Dr. Morvell*). Erzählungen und phantasiestücke. Stuttg. 1836. 2 v. S.   **V 901**

Contents, see Deutscher katalog, p. 107.

— Furchtlos und treu; historischer roman aus den zeiten des dreissigjährigen krieges. Stuttg. 1836. 3 v. S.   **V 902**

Voltaire, François Marie Arouet, *called* de. Romances. Tr. from the french; new ed., ill. N. Y. 1885. D.   **V 1051**

Contents. The white bull; a satirical romance.—Zadig, or Fate.—The sage and the atheist.—The princess of Babylon.—The man of forty crowns.—The Huron, or Pulpit of nature.—Micromegas.—The world as it goes.—The black and the white.—Memnon, the philosopher.—André des Touches at Siam.—Bababec.—The study of nature.—A conversation with a chinese.—Plato's dream.—Pleasure in having no pleasure.—An adventure in India.

Vornehmen proletarier, Die; Hamburger novelle. Hamburg. *n. d.* S.   **H 7**

Vosmaer, C: The amazon. Tr. by E. J. Irving; preface by G: Ebers. N. Y. 1884. S.   **V 951**

Voss, R: San Sebastian; mit einer einleitung von Joseph Kürschner. Stuttg. [1883]. D.   **V 1001**

x denotes books specially adapted for children.

W., A. M. Molly Carew ; an autobiography. Ill. N. Y. 1885. S. **W 3051**
W., F. The wreck of the Strathmore. *In* Tales from Blackwood. **T 177 v8**
W., H. D. A feuilleton. *In* Tales from Blackwood. **T 177 v8**
Wachberg, H: Theist und atheist. Wien. 1862. 3 v. T. **W 101**
Wachenhusen, Hans. Die bleiche gräfin ; roman. [2te aufl.] Berlin. 1865. 2 v. in 1. D. **W 151**
— Dame Orange ; roman. N. Y. 1881. F. **W 160**
— Gelebt und gelitten ; roman. Berlin. 1882. 2 v. in 1. D. **W 152**
— Die gräfin von der nadel ; roman. [2te aufl.] Berlin. 1865. D. **W 153**
— Der heiduck ; erzählung aus dem russisch-türkischen kriege. N. Y. 1881. F. **W 159**
— Helene ; roman. N. Y. 1882. F. **W 162**
— Die junge frau ; roman. Berlin. 1877. 3 v. D. **W 158**
— Des königs ballet ; roman. [2te aufl.] Berlin. 1865. 3 v. in 1. D. **W 154**
— Magnetische inclination ; erzählung. *In* Vierteljährl. mag. **V 2 v33**
— Ein neuer Polykrates. Berlin. 1859. 3 v. D. **W 155**
— Rom und Sahara ; roman. [2te aufl.] Berlin. 1865. 4 v. in 2. D. **W 156**
— Rouge et noir. Berlin. 1865. 2 v. in 1. D. **W 157**
— Der schweden-schatz ; roman. N. Y. 1883. F. **W 163**
— Vom armen egyptischen mann ; fellah-leben. N. Y. 1882. F. **W 161**
Wachsmann, C: Adolf v. Denksteine ; historische erzählungen und novellen. Leipz. 1847. 2 v. S. **W 201**
  Contents, see Deutscher katalog, p. 107.
— Epheuranken ; historische erzählungen und novellen. Leipz. 1849. 3 v. S. **W 202**
  Contents, see Deutscher katalog, p. 107.
— Erzählungen und novellen ; dritte folge. Leipz. 1844. 7 v. S. **W 203**
  Contents, see Deutscher katalog, p. 108.
— Erzählungen und novellen ; 4te folge. Leipz. 1846. 4 v. S. **W 204**
  Contents, see Deutscher katalog, p. 108.
— Wieben - Peter ; historische erzählung. *With* Spindler, C: Alte und neue zeit. **S 4301**
Waibel, Aloys Adalbert, (*Theophilus Nelk*). Blumenbeet kleiner lehrreicher geschichten, vorzüglich der jugend gewidmet. Würzburg. 1888. S. **N 126**
Waldau, Max, *pseud., see* Hauenschild, R: G: Spiller v.
Waldmüller, Robert, *pseud., see* Duboc, C: E:
Waldow, Ernst v., *pseud., see* Blum, Ludoiska v.
Walford, Lucy Bethia, *born* Colquhon. The baby's grandmother ; a novel. (Leisure hour ser.) N. Y. 1884. S. **W 256**
— Bee or Beatrix ? *In* Tales from Blackwood. **T 177 v5**
— Cousins. (Leisure hour ser.) N. Y. 1879. S. **W 251**
— Dick Netherby. (Leisure hour ser.) N. Y. 1882 [1881]. S. **W 255**
— Lady Adelaide. *In* Tales from Blackwood. **T 177 v10**
— Mr. Smith ; a part of his life. (Leisure hour ser.) N. Y. 1875. S. **W 252**
— Nan ; a summer scene. *In* Tales from Blackwood. **T 177 v1**

Walford, Lucy B., *born* Colquhon.—*Continued.*
— Pauline. (Leisure hour ser.) *T. p. w.* S. **W 253**
— Troublesome daughters. (Leisure hour ser.) N. Y. 1880. S. **W 254**
Walker, A. L. In life and in death. *In* Tales from Blackwood. **T 177 v10**
Wallace, Lewis. Ben-Hur ; a tale of the Christ. N. Y. 1880. S. **W 301**
— The fair god, or The last of the 'Tzins ; a tale of the conquest of Mexico. 15th ed. Bost. 1884. D. **W 302**
— *Same.* 17th ed. Bost. 1885. D. **W 302**
Wallis, J: Calvin. A prodigious fool. Phila. 1881. D. **W 351**
Walpole, Horace, *4th earl of Orford.* The castle of Otranto ; a gothic story. Phila. 1854. S. **W 401**
Walshe, Elizabeth H., *and* G: E. Sargent. Within sea walls, or How the dutch kept the faith. Lond. [1880]. D. **W 426**
Walter Seyton. *T. p. w.* S. **Wx 15**
  Includes, The shooting festival.
Walworth, Jeannette R., *born* Hadermann, *mrs.* Douglas. Dead men's shoes. Phila. 1872. D. **W 476**
— Forgiven at last. Phila. 1870. D. **W 477**
Walworth, Mansfield Tracy. Delaplaine, or The sacrifice of Irene. N. Y. 1871. D. **W 451**
Warburton, Eliot Bartholomew G: Darien, or The merchant prince ; a historical romance. N. Y. 1862. O. **W 501**
Ward, James. Adolphe Renouard, or Peasant life and political clubs in France. Lond. 1852. S. **W 551**
Ward, Robert Plumer. De Vere, or The man of independence. N. Y. 1881. 2 v. D. **W 601**
Warden, Florence. At the world's mercy. [*Anon.*] N. Y. 1884. D. **W 626**
— Deldee, the ward of Waringham, [or The iron hand] ; a novel. N. Y. 1885. D. **W 628**
— The house on the marsh. [*Anon.*] N. Y. 1884. D. **W 627**
Ware, W: Aurelian, or Rome in the 3d century. N. Y. 1848. 2 v. D. **W 651**
— *Same.* Probus, or Rome in the 3d century ; in letters of Lucius M. Piso from Rome to Fausta, the daughter of Gracchus, at Palmyra. Bost. 1838. 2 v. D. **W 653**
— Julian, or Scenes in Judea. N. Y. 1859. 2 v. in 1. S. **W 652**
— Zenobia, or The fall of Palmyra ; a historical romance in letters of L. Manlius Piso from Palmyra to his friend Marcus Curtius at Rome. N. Y. 1848. 2 v. S. **W 654**
Warfield, Catherine Anne, *born* Ware. A double wedding, or How she was won. Phila. [1875]. D. **W 701**
— The romance of the green seal. N. Y. *n. d.* O. **W 702**
Warner, Anna B. A bag of stories. Ill. N. Y. 1883. S. **Wx 126**
— Dollars and cents. Phila. 1883. D. **W 802**
— Miss Tiller's vegetable garden and the money she made by it. N. Y. [1873]. S. **W 801**
— *joint author, see* Warner, Susan B.
Warner, Beverley Ellison. Troubled waters ; a problem of to-day. Phila. 1885. D. **W 751**
Warner, C: Dudley. Being a boy. Ill. Bost. 1880. S. **Wx 101**
— *joint author, see* Clemens, S: L.

x denotes books specially adapted for children.

Warner, Susan, (*Elizabeth Wetherell*). Daisy. Phila. 1874. D. **W 826**
— Diana. N. Y. 1879. D. **W 827**
— The end of a coil. N. Y. 1880. D. **W 828**
— The hills of the Shatemuc. Phila. 1883. D. **W 829**
— The letter of credit. N. Y. 1882 [1881]. D. **W 835**
— Mr. Rutherford's children. N. Y. 1874. S. **Wx 212**
— My Desire. N. Y. 1879. D. **W 830**
— Nobody. N. Y. 1883 [1882]. D. **W 836**
— The old helmet. N. Y. *n. d.* D. **W 834**
— Pine needles. N. Y. 1881. D. **Wx 207**
— Queechy. Phila. 1868. 2 v. in 1. S. **W 831**
— *Same.* Phila. 1874. 2 v. in 1. S. **W 831**
— *Same.* Phila. 1885. D. **W 831**
— A red wall-flower. N. Y. 1884. D. **W 833**
— *The say and do series:*
1. The little camp on Eagle Hill. N. Y. 1880. S. **Wx 201**
2. Willow Brook. N. Y. 1878. S. **Wx 202**
3. Scepters and crowns. N. Y. 1875. S. **Wx 203**
4. The flag of truce. N. Y. 1878. S. **Wx 204**
5. Bread and oranges. N. Y. 1875. S. **Wx 205**
6. The rapids of Niagara. N. Y. 1880. S. **Wx 206**
— Stephen, M. D. N. Y. 1883. D. **W 837**
— *A story of small beginnings:*
1. What she could. N. Y. 1878. S. **Wx 208**
2. Opportunities. N. Y. 1878. S. **Wx 209**
3. House in town. N. Y. 1876. S. **Wx 210**
4. Trading. N. Y. 1881. S. **Wx 211**
— The wide, wide world. New ed. Phila. 1872. D. **W 832**
— *Same.* Phila. 1885. D. **W 832**
— *Same, germ.* Die weite, weite welt. Aus dem englischen. Leipz. 1856. S. **W 832**
— *and* Anna B. The gold of Chickaree. N. Y. *n. d.* D. **W 876**
— - Say and seal. Phila. 1883. D. **W 877**
— - Wych Hazel. N. Y. 1883. D. **W 878**
Warren, S: Passages from the diary of a late physician. N. Y. *n. d.* 3 v. S. **W 902**
— Ten thousand a year. Phila. *n. d.* D. **W 901**
Warriner, E: A. Victor La Tourette, by a broad churchman. Bost. 1875. D. **W 951**
Wartenburg, K: Die dame, die er liebte. nannt' er nicht; erinnerung. *In* Vierteljährl. mag. **V 2 v30**
— Deutsche opfer. Leipz. 1866. S. **W 1001**
— Neue propheten. Leipz. 1861. 2 v. S. **W 1002**
Waters, Clara, *born* Erskine, *formerly mrs.* Clement. Eleanor Maitland; a novel. Bost. 1881. S. **C 1826**
Watson, H: C. Camp-fires of the revolution, or The war of independence ill. by thrilling events and stories by the old continental soldiers. Ill. N. Y. 1865. O. **W 1026**
— The old bell of independence, or Philadelphia in 1776. Ill. Phila. *n. d.* S. **Wx 301**
— Six nights in a block-house, or Sketches of border life; embracing adventures among the indians, feats of the wild hunters and exploits of Boone, Brady, Kenton, Whetzel, Fleehart, and other border heroes of the west. Ill. Phila. [1851]. D. **Wx 302**
Watts, Anna Mary, *born* Howitt. A school of life. Bost. 1855. D. **W 1051**
Webb, *Mrs.* J. B., *afterwards mrs.* Peploe. Benaiah; a tale of the captivity. Ill. Lond. [1871]. D. **W 1102**

Webb, *Mrs.* J. B.—*Continued.*
— Naomi, or The last days of Jerusalem. Phila. 1871. S. **W 1101**
— Oliver Wyndham; a tale of the great plague. [*Anon.*] Lond. 1881. D. **W 1103**
Webber, C: W. Old Hicks the guide, or Adventures in the Camanche country in search of a gold mine. N. Y. 1868. D. **W 1126**
Weber, Karl, *pseud., see* Mützelburg, Adolf.
Webster, Albert. Miss Eunice's glove. *In* Stories by american authors. **S 35 v6**
— An operation in money. *In the same.* **S 35 v1**
Weed, Ella. A foolish virgin; a novel. N. Y. 1883. Q. **W 2951**
Wegener, Fedor Alexander. Der entscheidende augenblick; sozialer roman. Berlin. 1850. S. **W 1201**
Weill, Alexandre. Sittengemälde aus dem elsässischen volksleben; novellen, mit einem vorwort von H: Heine. 2te aufl. Stuttg. 1847. 2 v. D. **W 1151**
Contents, see Deutscher katalog, p. 108.
Weinzierl, L. A. Die herrin von Orla; eines alten mannes erzählung. *With* Frenzel, K: Ein alter manu. **F 1551**
Wendell, Barrett. The duchess Emilia; a romance. Bost. 1885. S. **W 1376**
Wenzel, Max. Eine böse nacht; eine erzählung aus dem soldatenleben. *In* Vierteljährl. mag. **V 2 v22**
— Humor und ernst aus dem soldatenleben; mit einleitendem vorwort von A. v. Winterfeld. Jena. *n. d.* 2 v. S. **W 1226**
Contents. v. 1. Aus der wachtstube.—Eine tigerjagd in Pommern.—Eine böse nacht. 2. Eine brautwerbung Blücher's.—Verloren.
Werder, Bertha, *pseud., see* Meyer, Bertha Antoinette Henriette.
Werner, E., *pseud., see* Bürstenbinder, Elisabeth.
Werner, Gustav. Die rache; denkwürdigkeiten aus dem leben des ministers Battista Salani. Meissen. 1832. S. **W 1301**
Werner, Julian, (*Karl Dilthey*). Henriette Sontag; blüthen und dornen am baume eines künstlerlebens. N. Y. 1872. S. **W 1351**
Westall, W: The old factory; a Lancashire story. N. Y. 1885. D. **W 1376**
Wetherell, Elizabeth, *pseud., see* Warner, Susan.
Wetterbergh, C: Anton, (*Onkel Adam*). Das altargemälde; ein genrebild. Aus dem schwedischen von Gottlob Fink. Stuttg. 1852. 2 v. T. **W 1401**
— Daheim!; ein genrebild von Onkel Adam. Stuttg. 1859. T. **W 1402**
— Drei genrebilder. Aus dem schwedischen von G. Fink. Stuttg. 1855. T. **W 1403**
Contents, see Deutscher katalog, p. 109.
— Das fideicommiss von Waldemarsburg; episoden, gegenstück zu Simon Sellner's reichthümer. Aus dem schwedischen von Gottlob Fink. Stuttg. 1855. T. **W 1404**
— Gold und arbeit; genrebild. Aus dem schwedischen übers. von Gottlob Fink. Stuttg. 1850. T. **W 1405**
— Genrebilder aus dem alltagsleben, von Onkel Adam. Aus dem schwedischen von C. F. Frisch. Stuttg. 1844. 2 v. T. **W 1406**
Contents, see Deutscher katalog, p. 109.
— Das häuschen am gitterthore bei Nygard. Aus dem schwedischen von C. F. Frisch. Stuttg. 1850. T. **W 1407**

x denotes books specially adapted for children.

Wetterbergh, C: A., (*Onkel Adam*).—*Continued.*
— Herrn Simon Sellner's reichthümer ; episoden
  aus dem alltagsleben. Aus dem schwedi-
  schen übersetzt. Stuttg. 1854. T. **W 1408**
— Der hölzerne löffel ; erzählung von Onkel
  Adam. Aus dem schwedischen von G.
  Fink. Stuttg. 1854. T.   **W 1409**
— Liebe und handel ; genrebild von Onkel Adam.
  Aus dem schwedischen von G. Fink.
  Stuttg. 1854. T.   **W 1410**
— Ein name ; genrebild. Aus dem schwedischen
  von C. F. Stuttg. 1846. T.   **W 1411**
— Neue genrebilder aus dem alltagsleben von
  Onkel Adam. Aus dem schwedischen von
  C. F. Stuttg. 1845. 5 v. T.   **W 1412**
  Contents, see Deutscher katalog, p. 109.
— Olga ; eine erzählung. Aus dem schwedischen
  übersetzt von Gottlob Fink. Stuttg. 1852.
  T.   **W 1413**
— Der pfarradjunkt, genrebild ; ein seitenstück
  der Gouvernante. Aus dem schwedischen
  ˙von C. F. Stuttg. 1846. T.   **W 1410**
Whelpley, James Davenport. The Denslow
  palace. *In* Atlantic tales.   **A 1876**
White, C. H., *pseud., see* **Chaplin,** Heman D.
White, R: Grant. The fate of Mansfield Humph-
  reys ; with the episode of " Mr. Washington
  Adams in England ", and an apology.
  Bost. 1884. D.   **W 1426**
White witch, The ; a novel. N. Y. 1885. Q. **W 9**
Whitney, Adeline Dutton, *born* Train. Boys at
  Chequasset, or " A little leaven." Bost.
  1863. S.   **Wx 601**
— Faith Gartney's girlhood. Bost. 1880. D.
                                  W 1451
— *Same. T. p. w.* D.   **W 1451**
— The Gayworthys ; a story of threads and
  thrums. Bost. [1865]. D.   **W 1452**
— *Same.* Bost. 1880. D.   **W 1452**
— Hitherto. Bost. 1880. D.   **W 1453**
— Odd or even ? Bost. 1880. D.   **W 1454**
— The other girls. Bost. 1880. D. **W 1455**
— Patience Strong's outings. Bost. [1868]. D.
                                  W 1456
— Real folks. Bost. 1879. D.   **W 1457**
— *Same.* Bost. 1884. D.   **W 1457**
— Sights and insights ; Patience Strong's story
  of over the way. Bost. 1876. 2 v. D.
                                  W 1458
— *Same.* 13th ed. Bost. 1884. 2 v. D. **W 1458**
— A summer in Leslie Goldthwaite's life. Ill.
  Bost. 1879. D.   **W 1459**
— *Same.* Bost. 1880. D.   **W 1459**
— We girls ; a home story. Bost. 1874. D.
                                  W 1460
— *Same.* Bost. 1880. D.   **W 1460**
— Zerub Throop's experiment. Bost. 1871. S.
                                  W 1461
  Note. Several of these novels are connected in the
  following series: 1. Leslie Goldthwaite.—2. We girls.
  —3. Real folks.—4. The other girls.
Whittaker, F: The cadet button ; a novel of
  ˙ american army life. N. Y. 1878. D.
                                  W 1501
Whitty, E: Michael. The bohemians of Lon-
  don ; with a notice of the author by R.
  Shelton Mackenzie. Phila. *n. d.* D.
                                  W 1551
Wichert, Ernst Alexander A: G: The green
  gate. Tr. from the german by mrs. A. L.
  Wister. Phila. 1875. D.   **W 1601**
— Ein kleines bild. Jena. 1876. D. **W 1602**
— Mutter und tochter ; eine littauische ge-
  schichte. *In* Vierteljährl. mag. V 2 v37

Wichert, Ernst Alexander A: G:—*Continued.*
— Rauschen ; ein strand-idyll. Leipz. 1881. D.
                                  W 1603
— Schuster Lange. Jena. 1876. D. **W 1604**
— Störungen. *With his* Schuster Lange.
                                  W 1604
— Eine vornehme schwester ; eine erzählung.
  In Vierteljährl. mag.   **V 2 v23**
Wickede, Julius v. Herzog Wallenstein in Meck-
  lenburg ; historischer roman. . Jena. 1865.
  4 v. D.   **W 1651**
— Ein husarenofficier Friedrichs des grossen ;
  nach den eigenhändigen aufzeichnungen
  Hans Leberecht von Bredow's. Jena. 1866.
  3 v. in 2. S.   **W 1653**
— Der lange Isaack ; historischer roman aus
  der zeit des deutschen befreiungskrieges.
  Leipz. 1863. 3 v. D.   **W 1652**
Widdern, Marie, *pseud., see* **Brandrup,** Marie.
Wiederkehr, Die ; eine novelle, herausgegeben
  von dem einsiedler bei St. Johannes. Leipz.
  1843. 3 v. D.   **W 11**
Wikoff, H: My courtship and its consequences.
  N. Y. *n. d.* D.   **W 1751**
Wilbrandt, Adolf. Fridolin's mystical marri-
  age ; a study of an original, founded on
  reminiscences of a friend. From the
  german by Clara Bell, rev. and corr. in the
  U. S. N. Y. 1884. S.   **W 1776**
— Der wille zum leben ; novelle. *In* Viertel-
  jährl. mag.   **V 2 v35**
Wildenbruch, Ernst v. Mein onkel aus Pom-
  mern ; humoreske. *In* Vierteljährl. mag.
                                  V 2 v25
— Vor den schranken ; eine criminal - novelle.
  In the same.   **V 2 v25**
Wildermuth, Ottilie, *born* Rauschütz. Auguste ;
  ein lebensbild. Stuttg. 1858. T. **W 1801**
— Bilder und geschichten aus Schwaben. 3te
  aufl. Stuttg. 1857. 2 v. S.   **W 1802**
  Contents, see Deutscher katalog, p. 110.
— Die heimath der frau. Stuttg. 1859. S.
                                  W 1803
Wilford, Frances, *joint author, see* **Awdry,**
  Frances.
Wilke, H., *born* Kronhelm. Fugaçe, oder Die
  abenteuer im schlosse Saviedro ; eine ro-
  mantische räubergeschichte. Braunschw.
  1827. 2 v. D.   **K 1401**
— Schloss Glenton, oder Die söhne der nacht.
  Braunschw. 1827. 2 v. D.   **K 1402**
Wilkins, W. A. The Cleverdale mystery, or
  The machine and its wheels ; a story of
  american life. N. Y. 1882. D.   **W 1826**
Willcox, Orlando B., (*Walter March*). Shoepac
  recollections ; a wayside glimpse of ameri-
  can life. N. Y. 1856. D.   **W 851**
Wille, Eliza, *born* Sloman. Felicitas ; ein ro-
  man. Leipz. 1850. 2 v. D.   **W 1901**
Willfried, H., *pseud., see* **Villinger,** Hermine.
Williams, G: F. Bullet and shell ; war as the
  soldier saw it, camp, march and picket,
  battle-field and bivouac, prison and hospi-
  tal. Ill. N. Y. 1883. O.   **W 3001**
Williams, H: L. The boys of the Bible. Ill. N.
  Y. 1866. S.   **Wx 951**
Williams, Robert Folkestone. The Luttrells, or
  The two marriages. N. Y. 1855. O.
                                  W 1951
— The secret passion. N. Y. *n. d.* O. **W 1952**
— Shakespeare and his friends, or The golden
  age of merry England. N. Y. *n. d.* O.
                                  W 1953

x denotes books specially adapted for children.

Williams, Robert Folkestone.—*Continued.*
— The youth of Shakespeare. N. Y. *n. d.* O.
W 1954
Willis, Nathaniel Parker. Prose writings; selected by H: A. Beers. N. Y. 1885. D.
W 2004
Contents. The lunatic's skate.—Love in the library. —Trenton Falls.—Tom Fane and I.—F. Smith.—The female ward.—Pasquali, the tailor of Venice.—The gypsy of Sardis.—A log in the Archipelago.—A dinner at lady Blessington's.—A breakfast with C: Lamb.—Wilson, J: M. Midside Maggie.
let of peach-blossoms.—Letters from under a bridge. —Kate Crediford.—The ghost-ball at congress hall.—Ephemera.
— Beauty and the beast. *In* Johnson, E. R. Little classics. J 926 v4
— Inklings of adventure. N. Y. 1836. 2 v. D.
W 2001
Contents. V. 1. Pedlar Karl.—Niagara.—Lake Ontario.—The St. Lawrence.—The Cherokee's threat.—F. Smith.—Edith Linsey.—Scenes of fear: The disturbed vigil; The mad senior; The lunatic's skate.—Incidents on the Hudson. 2. The gipsy of Sardis.—Tom Fane and I.—Larks in vacation.—A log in the Archipelago.—Miscellaneous papers. — The revenge of signor Basil.—Love and diplomacy.—The madhouse of Palermo.—Minute philosophies.
— Life here and there, or Sketches of society and adventures at far apart times and places. N. Y. 1850. D. W 2002
— People I have met, or Pictures of society and people of mark drawn under a thin veil of fiction. N. Y. 1850. D. W 2003
— Two buckets in a well. *In* Stories by american authors. S 35 v4
Willis the pilot, a sequel to the Swiss family Robinson, or Adventures of an emigrant family wrecked on an unknown coast of the Pacific ocean, interspersed with tales, incidents of travel and illustrations of natural history. Bost. *n. d.* D. Wx 41
— *Same.* Ill. Bost. 1875. 2 v. D. Wx 41
Willkomm, Ernst Adolf. Dichter und apostel. Frankfurt a. M. 1859. 2 v. D. W 2051
— Im bann und zauber von leidenschaft und wahn, von ernst und scherz ; licht- und nebelbilder. Leipz. 1862. 3 v. in 1. S.
W 2052
Contents, see Deutscher katalog, p. 110.
— Moderne sünden. Nordhausen. 1861. 3 v. D.
W 2053
— Die töchter des Vatican. Leipz. 1860. 3 v. D.
W 2054
Wilson, Alexander. The spectre of Milaggio. *In* Tales from Blackwood. T 177 v4
Wilson, Augusta J., *born* Evans. Beulah. N. Y. 1883. D. W 2101
— Inez ; a tale of the Alamo. N. Y. 1876. D.
W 2102
— *Same.* N. Y. 1879. D. W 2102
— Infelice. N. Y. 1878. D. W 2103
— *Same.* N. Y. 1879. D. W 2103
— Macaria. N. Y. 1879. D. W 2104
— *Same.* N. Y. 1878. D. W 2104
— St. Elmo ; a novel. N. Y. 1881. D. W 2105
— Vashti, or "Until death do us part." N. Y. 1870. D. W 2106
— *Same.* N. Y. 1878. D. W 2106
Wilson, F. T., (*Saul Wright*). Surf ; a summer pilgrimage. N. Y. [1881]. S. W 2851
Wilson, J:, (*Christopher North*). The Foresters. Edinb. 1852. S. W 2151
— The snow-storm. *In* Johnson, E. R. Little classics. J 926 v7
— The trials of Margaret Lyndsay. Edinb. 1854. S. W 2152

Wilson, J: Mackay, *ed.* Tales of the borders, and of Scotland ; historical, traditionary and imaginative. New ed., rev. by Alexander Leighton. Edinb. [1857]. 24 v. in 12. S. W 2202
Contents. V. 1. **Wilson,** J: M. The vacant chair; The faa's revenge.—**Leighton,** A. Kate Kennedy.—**Miller,** H. Recollections of Ferguson.—**Campbell,** A. The disasters of Johnny Armstrong.—**Gillespie,** T: The professors tales: The mountain storm ; The fair maid of Cellardykes. — **Leighton,** A. Prescription.—**Campbell,** A. The countess of Winstonbury. — **Wilson,** J: M. Midside Maggie.
2. **Wilson,** J: M. A wife or the wuddy.—**Leighton,** A. Lord Durie and Christie's will. — **Miller,** H. Recollections of Burns. — **Gillespie,** T: The professor's tales : The convivialists ; Philips Grey.—**Campbell,** A. Donald Gorm. — **Leighton,** A. The surgeon's tales: The cured ingrate. — **Howell,** J: The fortunes of W: Wighton. — **Wilson,** J: M. My black coat.
3. **Miller,** H. Widow of Dunskaith.—**Wilson,** J: M. The Whitsome tragedy.—**Leighton,** A. The surgeon's tales: The diver and the bell. — **Campbell,** A. Autobiography of Willie Smith. — **Gillespie,** T: The professor's tales: Pheebe Fortune. — **Wilson,** J: M. The royal bridal. — **Leighton,** A. The royal raid.—**Howell,** J: The experimenter.—**Bethune,** A. The young laird. — **Campbell,** A. The rival nightcaps.
4. **Wilson,** J: M. The solitary of the cave. — **Leighton,** A. The maiden feast of Cairnkibble. — **Gillespie,** T: The professor's tales: Early recollections of a son of the hills ; The suicide's grave. — **Miller,** H. The salmon-fisher of Udoll.—**Leighton,** A. The Linton lairds.—**Martin,** T. Bon Gaultier's tales: Country quarters.—**Campbell,** A. The monk of St. Anthony. — **Logan,** W. The story of Clara Douglas. — **Wilson,** J: M. The fair. — **Howell,** J: The slave.—**Campbell,** A. The katheran; The monks of Dryburgh.
5. **Wilson,** J: M. Bill Stanley. — **Leighton,** A. The surgeon's tales: The conscience stricken. — **Campbell,** A. Rattling, roaring Willie.—**Miller,** H. Bill Whyte.— **Gillespie,** T: The professor's tales : The last of the pedlars. — **Leighton,** A. Duncan Schulebred's vision of judgment. — **Wilson,** J: M. Archy Armstrong.—**Logan,** W. The double-bedded room. — **Campbell,** A. The highland boy.—**Howell,** J: Major Wier's coach. — **Moir,** D: M. (*Delta*). The divinity student.
6. **Wilson,** J: M. The guidwife of Coldingham. — **Leighton,** A. The surgeon's tales: The somnambulist of Redcleugh. — **Richardson,** O. The Rothesay fisherman. — **Wilson,** J: M. Leaves from the diary of an aged spinster. — **Leighton,** A. Geordie Willison.—**Campbell,** A. The snow storm of 1825. — Guilty or not guilty. — **Howell,** J: The serjeant's tales: The palatines.—**Peterkin,** A. The parsonage.—**Hetherington,** W: The seer's cave.—**Wilson,** J: M. The laidly worm of Spindleston Heugh ; The sabbath wrecks.
7. **Wilson,** J: M. Judith the egyptian. — **Leighton,** A. The droich. — **Miller,** H. The lykewake. — **Campbell,** A. The penny wedding. — **Leighton,** A. The amateur lawyers. — **Gillespie,** T: The professor's tales : Family incidents ; Home and the gipsy maid ; The return.—**Wilson,** J: M. The poor scholar. — **Howell,** J: The laird of Darnick Tower. — **Wilson,** J. M. The broken heart. — **Maidment,** J. The cateran of Lochloy. — **Howell,** J: The serjeant's tales: John Square's voyage to India.
8. **Wilson,** J: M. The doom of the Soulis. — **Leighton,** A. Harden's revenge. — **Richardson,** O. The physiognomist's tale. — **Campbell,** A. The good man of Dryfield.—**Leighton,** A. The surgeon's tales: The cherry stone ; The hen-wife ; The artist. — **Wilson,** J: M. The bride ; The henpecked man.—**Maidment,** J. Mortlake.—**Howell,** J: The serjeant's camp. — **Campbell,** A. Leein Jamie Murdieston ; Duncan McArthur.
9. **Wilson,** J: M. The cripple. — **Leighton,** A. The legend of fair Helen of Kirconnel.—**Richardson,** O. Tom Duncan's yarn.—**Gillespie,** T: The professor's tales: The three brethren ; The mistako rectified ; Dura Den.—**Campbell,** A. The laird of Lucky's How. — **Leighton,** A. The abduction. — **Wilson,** J: M. Sir Patrick Hume.—**Howell,** J: The serjeant's tales: The packman's journey to London.—**Wilson,** J: M. Charles Lawson.—**Martin,** T. Bon Gaultier's tales : Mrs. Humphrey Greenwood's tea-party. — **Logan,** W. The recluse of the Hebrides ; Ellen

x denotes books specially adapted for children.

Wilson, J: Mackay, *ed.—Continued.*
Arundel.—Campbell, A. Chatelard.—Leighton, A. Christie of the Cleek.
10. **Wilson, J: M.** The first-foot.—**Leighton, A.** The romance of the siege of Perth.— **Gillespie, T:** The professor's tales : Peat-casting time ; The medal.—**Richardson, O.** The meeting of St. Boswell's.—**Smith, J. F.** The story of May Darling.— **Wilson, J: M.** I canna be fashed.—**Conolly, M. F.** Tales of the east neuk of Fife: The castle of Crail; The legend of the church of Abercrombie; The romance of the may.—**Leighton, A.** Caleb Crabbin.—**Howell, J:** The serjeant's tales: The imprudent marriage. **Bethune, J.** The bewildered student.—**Leighton, A.** The crooked Comyn.
11. **Wilson, J: M.** The dominie's class.—**Leighton, A.** The contrast of wives.—**Gillespie, T:** The professor's tales: The social man.—**Campbell, A.** The two comrades; The surtout.—**Leighton, A.** The surgeon's tales: The suicide.—**Bethune, A.** The ghost of Howdy Craigs; The ghost of Gairyburn.—**Wilson, J: M.** The smuggler. — **Richardson, O.** The schoolfellows.—**Wilson, J: M.** The Red Hall.
12. **Miller, H.** The scottish hunters of Hudson's Bay.—**Gillespie, T:** The professor's tales: The wedding.—**Leighton, A.** Mike Maxwell.—**Wilson, J: M.** Reuben Purves.—**Richardson, O.** The sea storm.—**Maidment, J.** The heir of Inshannock.—**Campbell, A.** The moss - trooper; The forger. —**Leighton, A.** The surgeon's tales: The three letters; The glass back.—**Wilson, J: M.** We'll have another.—**Howell, J:** The scottish veteran.—**Maxwell, P.** The white woman of Tarras.
13. **Wilson, J: M.** The unknown. — **Leighton, A.** The trials of Menie Dempster.—**Gillespie, T:** The professor's tales: The natural history of idiots.—**Campbell, A.** The Floshend inn.—**Wilson, J: M.** Lottery Hall. — **Wilson, J.** The dominie and the souter. — **Leighton, A.** Roseallan's daughter.—**Richardson, O.** The two sailors.—**Campbell, A.** The dream.
14. **Wilson, J: M.** The covenanting family. — **Leighton, A.** The old chronicler's tales: The prince of Scotland.—**Campbell, A.** Retribution.—**Gillespie, T:** The professor's tales: The enthusiast; Trees and burns; Kirkyards.—**Wilson, J: M.** Polwarth on the green; The festival.—**Leighton, A.** A legend of Holyrood. — **Richardson, O.** The restored son.—**Campbell, A.** The skean dhu.— **Howell, J:** The seven year's dearth.—**Wilson, J: M.** The order of the garter.
15. **Wilson, J: M.** Recollections of a village patriarch.—**Leighton, A.** The old chronicler's tales: The death of James I.—**Campbell, A.** The curate of Govan.—**Gillespie, T:** Gleanings of the covenant.—**Richardson, O.** The story of Tom Bertram.— The cottar's daughter. — **Leighton, A.** The surgeon's tales: The case of evidence. — **Bethune, A.** The warning. — **Wilson, J: M.** Grizzel Cochrane; Squire Ben.—The battle of Dryffe Sands.—**Leighton, A.** The clerical murderer.
16. **Wilson, J: M.** The leveller.—**Leighton, A.** The old chronicler's tales: The death of James III.—**Gillespie, T:** Gleanings of the covenant.—**Campbell, A.** The countess of Cassilis.—The happy conclusion.—**Leighton, A.** Mr. Samuel Ramsay Thriven.—**Howell, J:** The man-of-war's man.—**Richardson, O.** The angler's tale.—**Wilson, J: M.** Perseverance; The irish reaper.— **Campbell, A.** Grace Cameron.—The mysterious disappearance.
17. **Wilson, J: M.** Roger Goldie's narrative.— **Leighton, A.** Hogmanay.—**Gillespie, T:** Gleanings of the covenant.—**Campbell, A.** The recluse; A highland tradition.—**Leighton, A.** The surgeon's tales: The bereaved; The condemned.—**Wilson, J: M.** The unbidden guest; The simple man is the beggar's brother. — **Conolly, M. F.** Tales of the east neuk of Fife: The robbery at Pittenweem; Story of C: Gordon.—**Howell, J:** A legend of Calder Moor.—**Leighton, A.** Hume and the governor of Berwick.
18. **Miller, H.** Thomas of Chartres.—**Wilson, J: M.** The fugitive.—**Leighton, A.** The bride of Bramblehaugh.—**Gillespie, T:** Gleanings of the covenant.—**Leighton, A.** The surgeon's tales: The monomaniac.—**Campbell, A.** The foundling at sea; The assassin.—**Howell, J:** The prisoner of war.—**Wilson, J: M.** Willie Wastle's account of his wife. —**Campbell, A.** The stone-breaker.—**Leighton, A.** Laird Rorieson's will.
19. **Leighton, A.** Gustavus McIver.—**Wilson, J: M.** The first and second marriage.—**Richardson, O.** The dissolved pledge.—**Campbell, A.** The Hawick spate.—**Leighton, A.** The avenger.—**Campbell, A.**

Wilson, J: Mackay, *ed.—Continued.*
The lord of Hermitage.—**Gillespie, T:** Gleanings of the covenant.—**Campbell, A.** The curse of Scotland. —**Wilson, J: M.** Leaves from the life of Alexander Hamilton.—**Leighton, A.** The sportsman of Outfieldhaugh.—The sea-fight.
20. **Leighton, A.** The dominie of St. Fillan's.— **Wilson, J: M.** Peter Paterson.—**Leighton, A.** The heroine.—**Campbell, A.** The barley bannock.—**Gillespie, T:** Gleanings of the covenant.—**Thomson, G.** The lost heir of Elphinstone. — **Wilson, J: M.** Trials and triumphs.—**Leighton, A.** The miser of Newabbey.—The sea-skirmish.
21. **Leighton, A.** The burgher's tales: The house in Bell's Wynd.—**Wilson, J: M.** The prodigal son.—**Leighton, A.** The lawyer's tales: The woman with the white mice.—**Gillespie, T:** Gleanings of the covenant.—**Leighton, A.** The detective's tales: The chance question. — **Campbell, A.** The merchant's daughter.—**Leighton, A.** The bride of Bell's Tower. —**Campbell, A.** Doctor Dobbie. — **Wilson, J: M.** The seeker. — **Leighton, A.** The surgeon's tales: The wager.
22. **Wilson, J: M.** Ups and downs.—**Leighton, A.** The burgher's tales: The ancient bureau. **Campbell, A.** Lady Rae.—**Leighton, A.** The diamond eyes.—David Lorimer.—The convict.—**Leighton, A.** The amateur robbery.—**Wilson, J: M.** The procrastinator.—**Leighton, A.** The ten of diamonds.
23. **Leighton, A.** The lawyer's tales: Lord Kame's puzzle.— **Wilson, J: M.** The orphan.—**Leighton, A.** The burgher's tales: The brownie of the West Bow.—**Gillespie, T:** Gleanings of the covenant.—**Leighton, A.** The story of Mary Brown.—**Wilson, J: M.** Tibby Fowler.—**Leighton, A.** The cradle of Logie. — **Wilson, J: M.** The death of the chevalier de la Beauté.—**Leighton, A.** The story of the pelican.—**Wilson, J: M.** The widow's son.—**Leighton, A.** The lawyer's tales: The story of Mysie Craig.—**Wilson, J: M.** The twin brothers.—**Leighton, A.** The girl forger; The two red slippers; The faithful wife.
24. *The minstrel's tales:* **Wilson, J: M.** Edmund and Helen. — **Leighton, A.** The romaunt of sir Peregrine and the lady Etheline; The legend of Allerley Hall; The legend of lady Katherine; The legend of the fair Emergilde; The romaunt of St. Mary's Wynde; The legend of Mary Lee; The ballad of age and youth; The legend of Craigullan.—**Wilson, J: M.** The hermit of the hills.—**Leighton, A.** The ballad of the rumbollow; The legend of the burning of mrs. Jamphray; The ballad of Ballogie's daughters; The legend of Dowielee; The ballad of maid Marion; The ballad of Roseallan Castle; The ballad of the tournay; The ballad of golden counsel; The ballad of matrimony; The song of Rosalie; The ballad of the world's vanity.—**Wilson, J. M.** The siege; a dramatic tale.—**G., W.** Farewell to a place on the borders.—Glossary.—General index.

— *Same,* v. 3. *T. p. w. O.* **W 2203**
Contents. The raid of Roxburgh.—Mary Middleton; a tale of the dear years.—The cruise of the Pibroch.—Hume and the governor of Berwick.—Sandy Murray, the legacy-hunter.—The snuff-miller's daughter. —The parsonage.—The simple man is the beggar's brother. —Mike Maxwell of Gretna.—The dream. —The provost of Starvieston.—Recollections of Ferguson.—Red Brie and Lord Delaval.—A chronicle of the death of James III.—The apparition of Flodden field. —The cherry stone. — Christie of the Cleek. — The Eskdalemuir story.—The maiden feast.—Roseallan's daughter.—The lykewake.—The faithful wife.—Roger Goldie's narrative.—The writer's daughter. — Mortlake; a legend of Merton.—Marry for love, and work for money. — The bewildered student. — The freebooter of Coldstream.— Kinaldy.—Donald Gorm.— Leaves from the life of Alexander Hamilton.—Ups and downs, or, David Stuart's account of his pilgrimage. — The festival. — The wife or the wuddy.—The fugitive.—The unknown.—The Whitsome tragedy.—The unbidden guest, or Jedburgh's regal festival.—Trials and triumphs.—Edmund and Helen.—Madeline of Roeclough.—The thriftless heir.—The foundling, or The heiress of Castle Gower.—The fatal secret.—The outlaw, or The maiden of Lednick.—The blacksmith of Plumtrees.—The lord of Hermitage.

— *Same, germ.* Romantische erzählungen aus der geschichte und den überlieferungen des schottischen grenzlandes. Braunschw. n. d. 8. **W 2201**
Contents. Die rothe halle, oder Berwick in 1226.—

x denotes books specially adapted for children.

Grisilde Cochrane.—Des faa-königs rache.—Der ungebetene gast.—Midside Maggy.—Die sabbath-verletzung.—Der hosenband-orden.—Lord Soulis.—Die abtei Coldingham.—Der geplagte wähler.—Das gebrochene herz.—Die covenanter-familie.—Sir Patrick Hume.—Archy Armstrong.

Wilton, T. Mongrels. Lond. 1883. 3 v. in 1. D.
　　　　　　　　　　　　　　　　　　　　W 2276
— *Same.* N. Y. 1883. Q.　　　　　　　　**W 2276**

Winter, J: Strange. Houp-La; novelette. Ill. N. Y. 1885. S.　　　　　　　　　　　**W 2227**
— Mignon, or Bootles's baby; a novelette. Ill. N. Y. 1885. S.　　　　　　　　　　　**W 2226**

Winterfeld, Adolf v. Die diamantknöpfe; skizze. *In Vierteljährl.* mag.　　　　　　**V 2 v23**
— Der dolmetscher; eine soldatengeschichte. *In the same.*　　　　　　　　　　　　**V 2 v28**
— Die ehefabrikanten; komisch-socialer roman. Leipz. 1866. 2 v. D.　　　　　　　**W 2251**
— Der fürst von Montenegro; komischer roman. N. Y. 1882. F.　　　　　　　　　**W 2256**
— Geheimnisse einer kleinen stadt; komischer roman. Jena. [1880]. D.　　　　　**W 2252**
— *Same.* N. Y. 1882. S.　　　　　　　　**W 2252**
— Ein gemeuchelter dichter; komischer roman. N. Y. 1883. F.　　　　　　　　　**W 2259**
— Der könig der luft; komischer roman. N. Y. 1882. F.　　　　　　　　　　　**W 2255**
— Des königs ordre; .eine soldatengeschichte. *In Vierteljährl.* mag.　　　　　　**V 2 v29**
— Modelle. N. Y. 1883. F.　　　　　　　**W 2258**
— Neue garnisongeschichten; soldaten-humor. Jena. *n. d.* 11 v. S.　　　　　　**W 2260**
　Contents. V. 1. Reservist und reservistin.—Der premier-lieutenant von Drenkenberg. 2. Die flöte des grafen Schwülenberg. 3. Die dicke trompete.—Mein vetter aus Stettin. 4. Excellenz will heirathen. 5. Ein geheimnissvoller grenadier. 6. Der alte major Knollen.—Ein eingebildeter lieutenant.—Zu befehl, herr rittmeister. 7. Wie mein freund Dumbart sein examen machte.—Die preussischen farben.—Ein rasender Roland. 8. Ein wettrennen.—Der verwechselte graf.— Der doppelte regiments-commandeur. 9. Der grosse weisse und die kleine braune.—Der marsch gegen den feind.—Zwei perrücken. 10. Das schiefe gesicht.—Die ungarin.—Bratenjäger.—Spleen. 11. Die bremse.—Die letzte ihres stammes.—Invalide im kopf.—Brief des kürassier Heinrich Wollkopf an seine eltern.—Antwort auf den brief des kürassier Heinrich Wollkopf.
— Neue humoristische soldaten - geschichten. Jena. *n. d.* 6 v. S.　　　　　　　**W 2261**
　Contents. V. 1. Das ungethüm.—Der junge vater und der alte sohn.—Ein marsch-quartier.—Der pflaumenschwanzer. — Die blödsichtigen. — Der hut des herrn von Schlawen.—Mourmellieux und Carbonel. 2. Zwei alte freunde.—Die hosen des unterofficiers Bartmann.—Die kegelbahn.—Etwas über pferde.—Die volksversammlung in Loitz.—Theodor's geheimniss.—Eine kadettengeschichte aus alter zeit. 3. Der kleine graf.—Der rittmeister bei den garde-kürassieren.—Des königs ordre. 4. Das examen zur kriegsschule. — Die statue.—Die schlacht bei Schleswig.—Wie ich meine kleine garnison wiedersah.—Der dolmetsch.—Der alte Hannemann.—Flensburg.—Jütland.—Schloss Glücksburg. 5. Drückende verhältnisse.—Der herr oberst.—Eine kleine garnison.—Marsch durch die nacht.—Lauenburg. 6. Der sächsische ordonnanz-officier. — Bivouac bei Satrup.—Mein urgrossvetter.—Die stiefel von Damen.—Die urlaubsreise.—Der überfall und die letzte patrouille.—Eine beschreibung der schlacht bei Waterloo.—Holstein.
— Der pantoffelheld; humoristische novelle. *In Vierteljährl.* mag.　　　　　　　**V 2 v35**
— Das spukehaus; komischer roman. N. Y. 1882. F.　　　　　　　　　　　　**W 2257**
— Der todte onkel; eine soldatengeschichte. *In Vierteljährl.* mag.　　　　　　　**V 2 v35**
— Das ungethüm; eine humoristische soldatengeschichte. *In the same.*　　　　**V 2 v24**

Winterfeld, Adolf v.—*Continued.*
— Die wohnungssucher; komischer roman. N. Y. 1882. F.　　　　　　　　　**W 2254**
— Die zigeunertochter. Nach dem schwedischen original des kammerjunker Kullberg frei bearbeitet. Jena. [1877]. S.　　**W 2253**
— Zwei alte freunde; humoreske. *In Vierteljährl.* mag.　　　　　　　　**V 2 v25**
— *tr.* Unheimliche geschichten in deutscher bearbeitung nach A. B. **Edwards** und Edgar Allan **Poe.** Jena. *n. d.* 4 v. S.　**W 2262**
　Contents. V. 1. Zusammengeschmiedet.—Eine geistergeschichte.—Der spieler.—Auf dem courirzuge.—Brudermord. 2. Unterhaltung mit einer mumie.—Der goldkäfer.—Lebendig begraben.—Merkwürdige wirkungen des mesmerismus, beobachtet an einem sterbenden.—Im malstrom. 3. Zwischen himmel und erde.—Im feurigen ofen.—Die geisterkutsche.—Die fluth.—Zwei neujahrstage.—Die diamantknöpfe. 4. Die morde in der Morgue-strasse.—Hans Pfasls höchst wundersames abenteuer.

Winthrop, Theodore. The canoe and saddle; adventures among the northwestern rivers and forests. (Leisure hour ser.) N. Y. 1876. S.　　　　　　　　　　　　　　**W 2305**
— Cecil Dreeme; with portrait and biog. sketch of the author by G: W: Curtis. (Leisure hour ser.) N. Y. 1876. S.　　**W 2301**
— Edwin Brothertoft. N. Y. 1876. S.　**W 2302**
— Isthmiana. *With his* Canoe and saddle. **W 2305**
— John Brent. *T. p. w.* S.　　　　　**W 2303**
— Love and skates. *In* Johnson, E. R. Little classics.　　　　　　　　　　**J 926 v6**

Wirth, Maximilian. Die flucht von der Harzburg; historische novelle aus dem leben kaiser Heinrichs des vierten. Schwäb. Hall. 1849. D.　　　　　　　　**W 2326**

Wise, H: A:, (Harry Gringo). Captain Brand of the "Centipede"; a pirate of eminence in the West Indies; his loves and exploits, together with some account of the singular manner by which he departed this life. Ill. N. Y. 1883. S.　　　　　　　**W 3001**

Wister, Annis Lee, *born* Furness, *translator of*
Behrens, B., (*W. Heimburg*). A penniless girl.　　　　　　　　　　　　**H 2279**
Bethusy-Huc, v. *gräfin*, (*Moritz v. Reichenbach*). The Eichhofs.　　　　　**R 801**
Bürstenbinder, E., (*E. Werner*). Banned and blessed.　　　　　　　　　**B 4358**
Frederich, B., (*Golo Raimund, Georg Dannenberg*). A new race.　　　　**D 203**
Glümer, C. v. A noble name.　　**G 1326**
Hackländer, F: W: Enchanting and enchanted.　　　　　　　　　**H 314**
Harder, L: A family feud.　　**H 5351**
Hartner, E. Severa.　　　　**H 1626**
Hillern, W. v. Only a girl.　　**H 3154**
John. E., (*E.Marlitt*). At the councillor's. **J 905**
— The bailiff's maid.　　　　　**J 901**
— Countess Gisela.　　　　　　**J 909**
— Gold Elsie.　　　　　　　　**J 904**
— In the Schillingscourt.　　　**J 906**
— The little moorland princess.　**J 902**
— The old mam'selle's secret.　**J 903**
— The second wife.　　　　　**J 912**
Schmieden, E., (*E. Juncker*). Margarethe.　　　　　　　　　　　**J 1401**
Schulze-Smidt, B., (*E. Oswald*). Vain forebodings.　　　　　　　　**S 6251**
Stahr, F., *born* Lewald. Hulda.　**S 4662**
Streckfuss, A. Castle Hohenwald.　**S 5701**
— Quicksands.　　　　　　　**S 5703**
— Too rich.　　　　　　　　**S 5702**
Wichert, E. The green gate.　**W 1601**

　　　x denotes books specially adapted for children.

Witt, Henriette de, *born* Guizot. A french country family. Tr. by Dinah Mulock Craik. N. Y. 1868. D. **Wx 1001**
— Tales of three centuries : 16th, A huguenot family ; 17th, The pilgrim fathers ; 18th, The desert, or The church under the cross. Tr. from the french by Emily Millard and Mary Archer. Bost. 1881. D. **W 2351**
Witt, Pauline de, *born* Guizot. An only sister. Ill. N. Y. 1873. S. **Wx 1002**
Wittendorf, C., *pseud., see* **Proschko,** H. C.
Witzleben, Charlotte v., (*Charlotte Wollmar*). Agnes Felser ; erzählung in briefen. Ellwangen. 1828. S. **W 2501**
Witzleben-Wendelstein, Ferdinand v. Die hofdame der erzherzogin ; roman. N. Y. 1882. F. **W 2401**
Wladimir, *pseud., see* **Hofmeister,** Adolf.
Wolf at the door, The. (No name ser.) Bost. 1877. S. **W 41**
Wolfhagen, Friederike, (*Marie Norden*). Astolfo Vardonnas ; gemälde aus der jüngsten vergangenheit Spaniens. Leipz. 1844. 3 v. S. **N 751**
— Columbus und seine zeit ; historischer roman. Wien. 1861. 4 v. T. **N 752**
— Deutsche lebensbilder. Leipz. 1851. 2 v. S. **N 753**
  Contents, see Deutscher katalog, p. 86, *under* Norden.
— Erzählungen. Leipz. 1848. 2 v. S. **N 754**
— Feldblumen. Leipz. 1847. 2 v. S. **N 755**
— Ilmhorst ; eine skizze aus der vorzeit Hamburgs. Leipz. 1846. 3 v. S. **N 756**
— Paris und Berlin ; roman aus der neuesten zeit. Leipz. 1849. 2 v. S. **N 757**
Wollmar, Charlotte, *pseud., see* **Witzleben,** Charlotte v.
Wolzogen, Friederike Sophie Caroline Auguste v., *born* v. Lengefeld. Agnes von Lilien ; mit einer einleitung von Robert Boxberger. Stuttg. [1884]. D. **W 2527**
— Cordelia. [*Anon.*] Leipz. 1840. 2 v. D. **W 2526**
Wood, C: Buried alone ; a story by a new writer. [*Anon.*] Leipz. 1869. S. **W 2901**
Wood, Ellen, *born* Price, *mrs.* H: Adam Grainger. Leipz. 1876. S. **W 2551**
— Anne Hereford. Leipz. 1869. 2 v. in 1. S. **W 2552**
— Bessy Rane. Leipz. 1870. 2 v. in 1. S. **W 2553**
— The Channings. Leipz. 1862. 2 v. in 1. S. **W 2554**
— *Same, germ.* Die Channings. Aus dem englischen von A. Kretzschmar. Leipz. 1862. 4 v. S. **W 2554**
— Dene Hollow. Leipz. 1871. 2 v. in 1. S. **W 2555**
— East Lynne. Leipz. 1861. 3 v. in 2. S. **W 2556**
— *Same.* Leipz. 1861. 3 v. S. **W 2556**
— *Same.* Chicago. 1883. D. **W 2556**
— *Same.* N. Y. *n. d.* D. **W 2556**
— Edina. Leipz. 1876. 2 v. in 1. S. **W 2557**
— Elster's folly. Leipz. 1866. 2 v. in 1. S. **W 2558**
— The foggy night at Offord. Leipz. 1872. S. **W 2559**
— George Canterbury's will. Leipz. 1870. 2 v. in 1. S. **W 2560**
— Lady Adelaide's oath. Leipz. 1867. 2 v. in 1. S. **W 2561**

Wood, Ellen, *mrs.* H:—*Continued.*
— A life's secret. Leipz. 1867. S. **W 2562**
— A light and a dark christmas. Phila. *n. d.* O. **W 2563**
— Lord Oakburn's daughters. Leipz. 1864. 2 v. in 1. S. **W 2564**
— *Same.* Phila. [1865]. S. **W 2564**
— Martyn Ware's temptation. *With her* The foggy night at Offord. **W 2559**
— Mildred Arkell. Leipz. 1865. 2 v. in 1. S. **W 2565**
— Mrs. Haliburton's troubles. Leipz. 1863. 2 v. in 1. S. **W 2566**
— The night walk over the mill stream. *With her* The foggy night at Offord. Leipz. 1872. S. **W 2559**
— Orville college. Leipz. 1867. S. **W 2567**
— Oswald Cray. Leipz. 1865. 2 v. in 1. S. **W 2568**
— Pomeroy Abbey. Leipz. 1878. 2 v. in 1. S. **W 2569**
— The Red Court farm. Leipz. 1868. 2 v. in 1. S. **W 2570**
— Roland Yorke. Leipz. 1869. 2 v. in 1. S. **W 2571**
— St. Martin's eve. Leipz. 1866. 2 v. in 1. S. **W 2572**
— The shadow of Ashlydyat. Leipz. 1863. 3 v. in 2. S. **W 2573**
— *Same, germ.* Der schatten von Ashlydyat. Aus dem englischen von A. Kretzschmar. Leipz. 1864. 2 v. S. **W 2573**
— Told in the twilight. Leipz. 1875. 3 v. in 1. S. **W 2574**
— Trevlyn Hold ; squire Trevlyn's heir. Leipz. 1864. S. **W 2575**
— Verner's pride. Leipz. 1863. 3 v. in 2. S. **W 2576**
— Within the maze. Leipz. 1872. 2 v. in 1. S. **W 2577**
Wood, G: Future life, or Scenes in another world. N. Y. 1858. S. **W 2601**
  Note. Also published under the title of The gates wide open.
— Modern pilgrims ; showing the improvements in travel and the newest methods of reaching the eternal city. Bost. 1855. 2 v. D. **W 2602**
— Peter Schlemihl in America. Phila. 1848. D. **W 2603**
Wood, *Mrs.* H:, *see* **Wood,** Ellen.
Woodruff, Julia Louisa Matilda, (*W. M. L. Jay*). Holden with cords. N. Y. 1877. D. **W 2651**
— Shiloh, or Without and within. N. Y. 1874. D. **W 2652**
Woolsey, Sarah Chauncey, (*Susan Coolidge*). Cross Patch, and other stories, adapted from the myths of Mother Goose. Ill. Bost. 1881. S. **Wx 1201**
  Includes, Little Tommy Tucker.—Hark, hark ! — Miss Jane.—The old woman who lived in a shoe.— Simple Simon.
— Eyebright ; a story. Ill. Bost. 1879. S. **Wx 1203**
— For summer afternoons. Bost. 1876. T. **W 2701**
  Contents. Lotta's missionary field.—An easter-egg. —Under the sea.— Edson's mother.— Martin.— One may day.—The Gibraltars.— Meta's wedding.— Bayberry Brook.—A camp-meeting idyl.— Blue-board.— An aloe blossom.—Polly's pies.
— A Guernsey Lily, or How the feud was healed ; a story for boys and girls. Bost. 1881. O. **Wx 1204**

x denotes books specially adapted for children.

Woolsey, S. C., (*Susan Coolidge*). —*Continued.*
— Mischief's thanksgiving, and other stories. Ill. Bost. 1879. S. **Wx 1205**
    Includes, Little Roger's night in the church.—The world within the wall.—How the umbrella ran away with Ellie.—Girls of the far north.—Nanny's substitute. — On top of the ark. — Ricket's valentine. — Christie.
— The new-year's bargain. Bost. 1878. S. **Wx 1206**
— A round dozen. Ill. Bost. 1883. S. **Wx 1202**
— What Katy did ; a story. Ill. Bost. 1879. S. **Wx 1207**
— What Katy did at school. Ill. Bost. 1884. D. **Wx 1208**

Woolson, Constance Fenimore. Anne ; a novel. Ill. N. Y. 1882. S. **W 2753**
— Castle Nowhere ; lake-country sketches. Bost. 1875. D. **W 2751**
    Includes, Peter the parson.—Jeannette.—The old agency.—Misery Landing.—Solomon.—Wilhelmina.— St. Clair flats.—The lady of Little Fishing.
— For the major ; a novelette. Ill. N. Y. 1883. S. **W 2754**
— Miss Grief. *In* Stories by american authors. **S 35 v4**
— Rodman the keeper ; southern sketches. N. Y. 1880. D. **W 2752**
    Includes, Sister St. Luke. — Miss Elizabetha.— Old Gardiston.—The south devil.—In the cotton country. — Felipa. — "Bro".— King David. — Up in the Blue Ridge.

Wright, Frances, *see* **Arusmont,** Frances d'.

Wright, Henrietta Christian. Little folk in green ; new fairy stories. Ill. N. Y. 1883. [1882]. D. **Wx 1351**

Wright, J. Hall. Ocean-work, ancient and modern, or Evenings on sea and land. N. Y. 1859. S. **Wx 1301**

Wright, Paul, *pseud.*, *see* **Wilson,** F. T.

Wulff, Margarethe, (*A. Stein*). Little Anna ; a story for pleasant little children. Tr. from the german. Bost. *n. d.* S. **Wx 1451**

Wylde, Katherine. A dreamer. (Leisure hour ser.) N. Y. 1880. S. **W 2801**

Wyss, J: Rudolph, *and* Jeanne Isabelle Pauline **Polier de Bottens** *dame* de Crousaz *baronne* de **Montolieu.** The swiss family Robinson, or Adventures of a father and mother and four sons in a desert island. Ill. Phila. *n. d.* D. **Wx 1501**
— *Same.* Phila. 1878. D. **Wx 1501**
— *Same* ; ed. for the use of schools by J. H. Stickney. [Classics for children.] Bost. 1885. D. **Wx 1502**
    Note. For sequel, *see* **Willis** the pilot.

Yates, Edmund Hodgson. Black sheep. Lond. 1872. D. **Y 101**
— Broken to harness ; a story of english domestic life. Chicago. 1883. D. **Y 108**
— Dr. Wainwright's patient. N. Y. 1873. O. **Y 102**
— Kissing the rod. N. Y. 1866. O. **Y 103**
— Pages in waiting ; a novel. Lond. [1884]. D. **Y 110**
    Contents. Told in the twilight.—Broad awake.— Dreaming.—Two rocks.—From generation to generation.—Aged forty.—Over pipes and palettes.—On relatives and connections. — Summer days. — Lady Greatheart's store.—Amusing "Mossoo".—Our neighborhood.—Invited and declining.—On kicking up one's heels.—Put to the test.—The houseless poor.— The social position of actors.—My convict experiences.—Then, and now.
— A righted wrong. Lond. 1871. D. **Y 104**
— The rock ahead. Lond. 1869. D. **Y 105**

Yates, Edmund Hodgson.—*Continued.*
— Running the gauntlet. Bost. *n. d.* D. **Y 106**
— *Same.* Bost. 1866. D. **Y 106**
— A silent witness. Leipz. 1875. 2 v. in 1. S. **Y 109**
— The yellow flag. Bost. *n. d.* O. **Y 107**

Yelverton, Maria Theresa, *born* Longworth. Zanita ; a tale of the Yosemite. N. Y. 1872. D. **Y 151**

Yesterday ; an american novel. (Leisure hour ser.) N. Y. 1882. S. **Y 11**

Yonge, Charlotte Mary. The armourer's 'prentices ; [a novel of the early Tudor days]. N. Y. 1884. D. **Y 224**
— Beechcroft. N. Y. *n. d.* D. **Y 201**
    Note. For continuation, *see below* The two sides of the shield.
— Ben Sylvester's word. *With her* The little duke. **Yx 303**
— The caged lion. N. Y. 1870. D. **Y 202**
— The castle builders. N. Y. 1855. D. **Y 225**
— The chaplet of pearls, or The white and black Ribaumont. Lond. 1878. D. **Y 203**
— The clever woman of the family. Leipz. 1865. 2 v. in 1. S.. **Y 204**
— The daisy chain, or Aspirations ; a family chronicle. N. Y. 1871. 2 v. D. **Y 205**
— *Same.* N. Y. 1878. 2 v. D. **Y 205**
    Note. For continuation, *see* The trial.
— The Danvers papers. Leipz. 1867. S. **Y 206**
— The dove in the eagle's nest. Leipz. 1866. 2 v. in 1. S. **Y 207**
— *Same. T. p. w.* 2 v. D. **Y 207**
— Dynevor Terrace, or The clue of life. Leipz. 1857. 2 v. S. **Y 208**
— Heartsease, or The brother's wife. Leipz. 1855. 2 v. in 1. S. **Y 209**
— *Same. T. p. w.* 2 v. D. **Y 209**
— The heir of Redclyffe. Leipz. 1855. 2 v. in 1. S. **Y 210**
— *Same.* Lond. 1882. D. **Y 210**
— *Same.* N. Y. 1882. D. **Y 210**
— *Same, germ.* Der erbe von Redcliffe. Nach dem englischen. 2te aufl. Gotha. 1875. 2 v. in 1. S. **Y 210**
— Hopes and fears, or Scenes from the life of a spinster. Leipz. 1861. 2 v. in 1. S. **Y 211**
— Kenneth, or The rear guard of the grand army. N. Y. 1855. D. **Y 212**
— Lady Hester, or Ursula's narrative. Leipz. 1874. S. **Y 214**
— The lances of Lynwood. Ill. N. Y. 1856. S. **Yx 304**
— The little duke, or Richard the fearless. Leipz. 1861. S. **Yx 303**
— Little Lucy's wonderful globe. Ill., new ed. Lond. 1881. S. **Yx 301**
— Love and life ; an old story in 18th century costume. N. Y. 1880. D. **Y 215**
— *Same.* N. Y. 1880. Q. **Y 215**
— Magnum bonum, or Mother Carey's brood. N. Y. 1880. D. **Y 216**
— The mouth of the Leamy. Leipz. 1874. S. **Y 214**
— My young Alcides ; a faded photograph. N. Y. 1876. D. **Y 217**
— Pickle and his page-boy, or Unlooked for ; a story. Ill. N. Y. 1883. D. **Yx 302**
— The pillars of the house, or Under wode, under rode. Ill. Lond. 1882. 2 v. D. **Y 218**
— *Same* ; 2d v. *T. p. w.* **Y 218**
— The prince and the page. *With her* The Danvers papers. **Y 206**

x denotes books specially adapted for children.

Yonge, Charlotte Mary.—*Continued.*
— Stray pearls ; memoirs of Margaret de Ribaumont, viscountess of Bellaise. N. Y. 1883.
D.   **Y 223**
— *Same.* N. Y. 1883. Q.   **Y 223**
— The three brides. Lond. 1882. D.   **Y 219**
— The trial ; more links of " The daisy chain."
Ill. Lond. 1877. D.   **Y 220**
— The two sides of the shield ; [a sequel to Beechcroft]. N. Y. 1885. D.   **Y 226**
— Unknown to history ; story of the captivity
of Mary of Scotland. N. Y. 1883. D.
                                                 Y 222
— *Same.* N. Y. 1883. Q.   **Y 222**
— The young step - mother, or A chronicle of
mistakes. Leipz. 1861. 2 v. in 1. S. **Y 221**
— *joint author, see* **Awdry,** Frances.
Yorke, Stephen. Cleveden. N. Y. 1878. Q.
                                                 Y 251
Young, Betty. Ein vierteljahrhundert ; roman.
N. Y. 1882. F.   **Y 351**
Young, W : A toss up for a husband. *In* **Maga**
stories.   **P 2801**

Zacone, P : Zelle no. 7 ; roman in 3 b. N. Y.
1881. F.   **Z 351**
Zeising, Adolf, (*Richard Morning*). Joppe und
crinoline. Leipz. 1865. D.   **Z 101**
Zeller, Louise, *born* Pichler. Bei lampen- und
sternenschein ; erzählungen. 2te ausg.
Leipz. 1868. 2 v. in 1. S.   **Z 401**
Contents, see Deutscher katalog, p. 111.
— The red mantle. From the german by K. E.
Heyser. Phila. [1884]. S.   **Px 1051**
Ziehen, E : A : Philipp, (*Edward Ellersberg*). Geschichten und bilder aus dem wendischen
volksleben. Hannover. 2 v. in 1. D. **Z 152**
Contents, see Deutscher katalog, p. 111.
— Wendische weiden ; erzählungen aus dem
wendischen volksleben. Frankfurt a. M.
1854. D.   **Z 151**
Contents, see Deutscher katalog, p. 111.
Ziemssen, L : Bartolomäus von Brusehaver,—
Muss ma cussalin ; zwei historische novellen. N. Y. 1883. F.   **Z 177**
— Umwege zum glück ; roman mit einer einleitung von Hans Ziegler. Stuttg. 1883. D.
                                                 Z 176

Zitelmann, Ernst O : Konrad, (*Konrad Telmann*).
Das jüngste gericht ; novelle. *In* Vierteljährl. mag.   **V 2 v22**
Zitz, Kathinka Therese Pauline Modesta, *born*
Halein. Erzählungen und novellen ; fremd
und eigen. Nürnberg. 1845. 2 v. S. **Z 201**
Contents, see Deutscher katalog, p. 111.
Zöllner, Caroline v., *born* Grape, (*Caroline v.
Göhren*). Die brautschau. Berlin. 1856. 2
v. S.   **G 1451**
— Frauenliebe und künstlerberuf. Hamburg.
1856. 2 v. S.   **G 1452**
Zschokke, J : H : Daniel. The goldmakers' village. Tr. from the german. N. Y. 1857. S.
                                                 Z 310
— Grössere novellen. Berlin. [1877]. 3 v. in 1. D.
                                                 Z 309
Note. For contents of this and following collections, see Deutscher katalog, p. 111.
— Historische novellen. Berlin. [1877]. 3 v. in 1.
D.   **Z 306**
— Humoristische novellen. Berlin. [1877]. 3 v.
in 1. D.   **Z 307**
— Incidents of social life amid the european
Alps. Tr. from the german by L : Strack.
N. Y. 1844. S.   **Z 301**
— Kleinere novellen. Berlin. 1877. 3 v. in 1. D.
                                                 Z 308
— Leaves from the journal of a poor vicar in
Wiltshire. *In* Hedge, F : H : Prose writers of Germany.   **830.1 : 8**
— Novellen und dichtungen ; in 17 bändchen.
10te ausg. V. 6-17. Aarau. 1857. 11 v. S.
                                                 Z 302
Contents, see Deutscher katalog, p. 111.
— The princess of Brunswick-Wolfenbüttel, and
other tales. From the german by M. A.
Faber. Leipz. 1867. S.   **Z 303**
Includes, A new-year's eve adventure.—The inn at
Cransac.
— A sylvester night's adventure. Tr. by H. B.
W. Cinc. 1884. D.   **Z 311**
— Der todte gast. *With* Kompert, L. Eine
verlorene.   **K 1204**
— *Same, eng.* The dead guest ; a tale. Tr. from
the german. N. Y. 1840. D.   **Z 312**
— Veronica, or The free court of Aarau. Tr.
from the german by the author of " Giafar
al Barmeki." N. Y. 1858. O.   **Z 305**

2. Titles.

Note. The titles of short stories, forming part of collections which were entered in the german catalogue of 1882,
are not repeated here.

A. Gordon Pym. E. A. Poe.   *in* 820.1 : 5 **v4**
Abbé Constantine. L. Halévy.   **H 476**
Abbé Tigrane, The. F. Fabre.   **F 101**
Abbot, The. *Sir* W. Scott.   **S 2001**
Abdallah. E. de Laboulaye.   **L 151**
Abduction, The. A. Leighton.   *in* W 2202 **v9**
Ablest man in the world, The. E. P. Mitchell.
                                         in S 35 **v10**
About magnanimous incident literature. S. L. Clemens.
                                         in C 1802
Abraham's offering. E. Erckmann *and* A. Chatrian.
                                         in E 1205
Absent-minded fairy, The. M. Janvier.   **Vx 104**
Absentee, The. M. Edgeworth.   *in* E 405
Abstraction, The. T. Hood.   *in* 820.2 : 6
Abt, Der. *Sir* W. Scott.   **S 2001**
Abtei Carrow. J. F. Smith.   **S 3501**
Abu Telfan. W. Raabe.   **R 101**
Accidentally overheard. H. E. Scudder.   *in* S 2101
Accompanied on the flute. F. A. Guthrie. *in* A 1328
Accursed race, An. E. C. Gaskell.   *in* G 411
Ace of clubs, The. J. *and* M. Banim.   *in* B 307
Achor. *Mrs.* S. R. G. Clark.   **C 1526**
Achsah. W. M. F. Round.   **R 2851**
Achtspännig. J. Rank.   **R 351**

Achtzehn humoristische erzählungen. M. Jókai.
                                           J 1152
1812. L. Rellstab.   **R 902**
1813. L. F. Stolle.   **S 5511**
1830. J. Gundling.   **G 3051**
Acker im buchenwalde, Der. O. Lautenschlager.
                                           in L 2302
Across the chasm. J. Magruder.   **M 5051**
Across the peat-fields. A. I. Ritchie.   *in* R 1652
Same.   *in* R 1654
Actiengesellschaft, Eine. L. Schücking.   **S 1801**
Adah. A. M. Gray.   **G 2101**
Adam Bede. M. Cross, (*George Eliot*).   **C 3151**
Adam Bell. J. Hogg.   *in* H 3451 **v3**
Adam Brown. H. Smith.   **S 3451**
Adam Grainger. E. P. Wood.   **W 2551**
Adam Scott. J. Hogg.   *in* H 3451 **v4**
Adel. J. D. H. Temme.   **T 551**
Adela Cathcart. G. Macdonald.   **M 251**
Adelaide. D. M. Craik.   *in* C 2855
Adelaide. C. Stock.   **S 5351**
Adele. F. Stahr.   **S 4651**
Adelina Mowbray. A. Opie.   *in* O 653
Same.   *in* O 653 **v2**
Adeline Protat. H. Murger.   **M 4801**

x denotes books specially adapted for children.

x denotes books specially adapted for children.

x denotes books specially adapted for children.

x denotes books specially adapted for children.

x denotes books specially adapted for children.

x denotes books specially adapted for children.

x denotes books specially adapted for children.

Crooked branch, The. E. C. Gaskell.	*in* G 409
Crooked Comyn, The. A. Leighton.	*in* W 2202 v10
Crookit Meg, The. J. Skelton.	S 3126
Cross of Berny, The. D. de Girardin.	G 1001
Cross on the Snow mountains, The. D. M. Craik.	
	in C 2868
Cross Patch. S. C. Woolsey.	Wx 1201
Cross purposes. M. Argles.	*in* A 1483
Cross purposes. C. Findlay.	F 851
Crossed path, The. W. Collins.	C 2204
Cruelest wrong of all, The.	C 3
Cruise of the Canoe club. W. L. Alden.	Ax 553
Cruise of the Ghost. W. L. Alden.	Ax 552
Cruise of the Pibroch, The.	*in* W 2203 v3
Cruise of the Snowbird, The. G. Stables.	Sx 1376
Cryptogram, The. J. De Mille.	D 851
Cryptogram, The. J. Verne.	Vx 301 v2
Cudjo's cave. J. T. Trowbridge.	T 1853
Culturgeschichtliche novellen. W. H. Riehl.	R 1553
Cupid and Chow-Chow. L. M. Alcott.	Ax 504
Cupid and the sphinx. H. McClellan.	M 151
Cupid, M. D. A. M. Swift.	S 5976
Curate in charge, The. M. O. Oliphant.	O 454
Curate of Govan, The. A. Campbell.	*in* W 2202 v15
Curates' discipline, The. E. Eiloart.	E 901
Cure for melancholy, A. H. More.	*in* 820.2 : 28 v1
Curé manqué, Le. E. de Courcillon.	C 2801
Cured ingrate, The. A. Leighton.	*in* W 2202 v2
Curious experience, A. S. L. Clemens.	*in* C 1802
Curse of Scotland, The. A. Campbell.	*in* W 2202 v19
Curse of the Catafalques, The. F. A. Guthrie.	
	in A 1328
Curse of the village, The. H. Conscience.	C 2253
Cut by the county. M. E. Maxwell.	M 1793
Cut on a gate. M. C. Hay.	*in* H 2107
Cyril Hamilton. C. R. Low.	Lx 451
Cyril Thornton. T. Hamilton.	H 951
Cyrilla. J. M. Tautphœus.	T 352
Czar Paul. T. Mundt.	M 4652
Da capo. A. I. Ritchie.	R 1658
Same.	*in* R 1654
Same.	*in* R 1652
Dab Kinzer. W. O. Stoddard.	Sx 1601
Daguerreotypen. K. L. Hencke.	H 2451
Dahcotah. M. H. Eastman.	E 202
Daheim. C. A. Wetterbergh.	W 1402
Daily bread. E. E. Hale.	*in* H 460
Daireen. F. F. Moore.	M 3351
Daisies and buttercups. C. E. L. Riddell.	R 1363
Daisy. S. Warner.	W 826
Daisy Burns. J. Kavanagh.	K 302
Daisy chain, The. C. M. Yonge.	Y 205
Daisy Miller. H. James, *jr.*	J 211
Daisy Travers. A. F. Samuels.	Sx 401
Daisy's necklace. T. B. Aldrich.	A 751
Daltons, The. C. Lever.	L 1106
Dame, die er liebte, nannt' er nicht, Die. K. F. A. Wartenburg.	*in* V 2 v30
Dame in schwarz, Die.	H 1
Dame Orange. H. Wachenhusen.	W 160
Dame von stande, Eine.	H 2
Damen auf reisen. J. D. H. Temme.	T 553
Damon's ghost. E. L. Bynner.	B 4501
Damocles. M. Veley.	V 502
Dämon Amor. J. K. A. Musäus.	*in* M 4951
Dancin' party at Harrison's Cove, The. M. N. Murfree.	
	in M 4776
Dandy drainer, The.	*in* P 11
Dangerfield's rest. H. Sedley.	S 2301
Dangerous virtue, A. H. H. Boyesen.	*in* B 2856
Dangerous wooing, A. B. Björnson.	*in* B 2160
Daniel Deronda. M. Cross.	C 3152
Danvers papers, The. C. M. Yonge.	Y 206
Darien. E. B. G. Warburton.	W 501
Daring fiction, A. H. H. Boyesen.	*in* S 35 v10
Dark days. F. J. Fargus.	F 2002
Dark inheritance, A. M. C. Hay.	*in* H 2120
Dark maid of Illinois, The. J. Hall.	*in* H 701
Dark night's work, A. E. C. Gaskell.	G 403
Same.	*in* G 411
Darning-needle, The. H. C. Andersen.	*in* Ax 754
Darnley. G. P. R. James.	J 210
Daughter of an empress, The. C. Mundt.	M 4558
Daughter of Bohemia, A. F. C. Fisher.	F 952
Daughter of Heremon, The. D. M. Craik.	*in* C 2868
Daughter of Heth, A. W. Black.	B 2202
Daughter of night, The. S. W. Fullom.	F 1851
Daughter of the Philistines, A. H. H. Boyesen.	B 2857
Daughter of the stars, The. F. J. Fargus.	*in* F 2003
Daughter of Tyrconnell, The. M. A. Sadlier.	S 152
Davenport Dunn. C. Lever.	L 1107
David Armstrong.	D 1

David Copperfield. C. Dickens.	D 1304
David Elginbrod. G. Macdonald.	M 254
David Lorimer.	*in* W 2202 v22
David Swan. N. Hawthorne.	*in* H 2057 v1
Same.	*in* J 926 v4
Day in Venice, A. B. W. Procter.	*in* 824.2 : 77 v1
Day of fate, A. E. P. Roe.	R 2302
Day of reckoning, A. H. Parr.	*in* P 469
Days of Bruce, The. G. Aguilar.	A 401
Days of my life, The. M. O. Oliphant.	O 455
Day's pleasure, A. W. D. Howells.	*in* H 4757
Day's ride, A. C. Lever.	L 1108
Dayspring. E. Marshall.	M 1308
Deacon Crankey. G. Guirey.	G 2901
Deacon's week, The. R. Cooke.	C 2402
Dead alive, The. W. Collins.	C 2205
Same.	*in* C 2208
Same.	*in* C 2228
Dead guest, The. J. H. D. Zschokke.	Z 312
Dead lake, The. P. Heyse.	H 3008
Dead man's face, A. F. J. Fargus.	*in* F 2004
Dead men's shoes. J. R. Walworth.	W 476
Dead men's shoes. M. E. Maxwell.	M 1757
Dead-sea fruit. M. E. Maxwell.	M 1758
Dead secret, The. W. Collins.	C 2206
Dealings with the fairies. G. Macdonald.	Mx 152
Dean's daughter, The. C. G. F. Gore.	G 1561
Dean's watch, The. E. Erckmann *and* A. Chatrian.	
	in E 1205
Dean's wife, The. E. Eiloart.	E 902
Dear lady Disdain. J. McCarthy.	M 101
Dear relations. M. Jókai.	*in* J 1154
Dearly bought. C. L. Burnham.	B 4303
Death-bed, The. A. Opie.	*in* O 653 v2
Same.	*in* O 653 v2
Death of James I. A. Leighton.	*in* W 2202 v15
Death of James III. A. Leighton.	*in* W 2202 v16
Death of Samuel Pickwick, The. W. Besant *and* J. Rice.	
	in B 1762
Debenham's vow. A. B. Edwards.	E 1205
Debit and credit. G. Freytag.	F 1605
Death of the chevalier de la Beauté, The.	
	in W 2202 v23
Debora. W. Müller.	M 4436
Decameron, The. G. Boccaccio.	B 2486
Decision. B. W. Hofland.	H 3401
De Cressy. M. A. Paul.	P 701
Deep waters. A. H. Drury.	D 1951
Deephaven. S. O. Jewett.	J 801
Deer-slayer, The. J. F. Cooper.	C 2455
Deerings of Medbury, The. V. F. Townsend.	T 1451
Deformed, The. A. C. Marsh-Caldwell.	M 1253
Deformed, The. M. F. Tytler.	*in* E 426
Delaphine. M. T. Walworth.	W 451
Deldee. F. Warden.	W 628
Deleware. G. P. R. James.	J 242
Delicia. B. M. Butt.	B 4401
De l'Orme. G. P. R. James.	J 211
Delphine. A. L. G. de Staël-Holstein.	S 4602
Dely's cow. R. T. Cooke.	*in* C 2401
Democracy.	D 2
Demon of Cawnpore, The. J. Verne.	Vx 304 v1
Dene Hollow. E. P. Wood.	W 2555
Denis Donne. A. Cudlip.	C 3302
Denis Duval. W. M. Thackeray.	T 553
Denise. M. Roberts.	R 1802
Denksteine. C. A. v. Wachsmann.	W 201
Denkwürdige vorladung, Eine. W. Fischer.	*in* V2 v36
Dennis Haggarty's wife. W. M. Thackeray.	*in* T 660
Same.	*in* T 665 v6
Dennis O'Shaughnessy. W. Carleton.	*in* C 554
Denounced, The. J. Banim.	B 303
Denslow palace, The. J. D. Whelpley.	*in* A 1876
Denver express, The. A. A. Hayes.	*in* S 35 v6
Deodand. W. H. Bishop.	*in* B 3104
Deodat's prüfungen. O. Lautenschlager.	*in* L 2304
De profundis. W. Gilbert.	G 851
Der mit dem bann belegte. T. G. Rudbeck.	R 2951
Derry. C. E. Tonna.	T 1252
Descent into the maelstrom. E. A. Poe.	*in* 820.1 : 5 v3
Desdemona. M. C. Clarke.	*in* C 1651 v1
Desert, The. H. de Witt.	*in* W 2951
Desert's sands. H. P. Spofford.	V 559
Desert of ice, The. J. Verne.	*in* S 4401
Desmond hundred, The. J. G. Austin.	A 3104
Desperate remedies. T. Hardy.	H 1201
Desultory man, The. G. P. R. James.	J 244
Detective's tale, The. A. Leighton.	*in* W 2222 v21
Detmold. W. H. Bishop.	B 3105
Deutsch und slavisch. J. Gundling.	G 3057
Deutsche abende. B. Auerbach.	A 1956
Deutsche lebensbilder. F. Stahr.	S 4658
Deutsche lebensbilder. F. Wolfhagen.	N 753

x denotes books specially adapted for children.

x denotes books specially adapted for children.

x denotes books specially adapted for children.

Elfinland. J. L. Tieck.	in 830.1:8
Same.	in E 426
Same.	in P 2126 v3
Elfriede. H. W. Hanke.	H 1103
Eli. H. W. Chaplin.	in S 35 v9
Eliane. P. Craven.	C 3004
Elinor Dryden. K. S. Macquoid.	M 603
Elinor Fulton. H. F. Lee.	L 826
Elinor Travis. S. Phillips.	in P 1601
Elisabeth. S. R. Cottin.	C 2651
Elisabeth. A. Dörie.	D 1751
Elisabeth Charlotte. A. v. Sternberg.	S 5052
Elisabeth von Guttenstein. C. Pichler.	P 1652
Elisabeth von Oestreich. C. Doriem.	D 251
Elisabetta Sirani, The story of. D. M. Craik.	in C 2868
Elise. Ferdinand * * *	F 401
Elixiere des teufels, Die. E. T. A. Hoffmann.	H 3351
Elixir of life, The. N. Hawthorne.	H 2056
Elizabeth. S. Cottin.	C 2651
Elizabeth Bleylock, The case of. K. S. McDowell.	in M 326
Elizabeth von Guttenstein. C. Pichler.	P 1652
Elkanah Brewster's temptation. C. Nordhoff.	in N 801
Same.	in A 1876
Elkanah Smithers, jr.	in P 2802
Ellen Arundel. W. Logan.	in W 2202 v9
Ellen Middleton. G. C. Fullerton.	F 1802
Ellen Wareham. E. Pickering.	F 1751
Ellice Quentin. J. Hawthorne.	H 2005
Elm Island stories. E. Kellogg.	Kx 205-Kx 210
Else. A. L. Kielland.	K 1701
Else Hohenthal. A. Kühne.	K 1203
Elsie Dinsmore. M. Finley.	Fx 252
Elsie Venner. O. W. Holmes.	H 3851
Elsie's children. M. Finley.	Fx 257
Elsie's girlhood. M. Finley.	Fx 254
Elsie's motherhood. M. Finley.	Fx 256
Elsie's Santa Claus. J. H. Matthews.	Mx 659
Elsie's womanhood. M. Finley.	Fx 255
Elspeth Grant. G. M. Craik.	in C 2911
Elster's folly. E. P. Wood.	W 2558
Elves, The. J. L. Tieck.	in E 426
Same.	in P 2126 v3
Same.	in 830.1:8
Embroideries of Treviso, The. P. Heyse.	in H 3002
Emerald, The. E. Sargent, ed.	S 551
Emerald studs, The. W. E. Aytoun.	in T 176 v6
Emigrants, The. F. Hoffmann.	Hx 880
Emilia Wyndham. A. C. Marsh-Caldwell.	M 1255
Emilie. W. Lorenz.	L 1901
Emilie. F. Stahr.	S 4661
Emilie De Coulanges. M. Edgeworth.	in E 405
Emilie Wyndham. A. C. Marsh-Caldwell.	M 1255
Emily Chester. A. M. Seemüller.	S 2351
Emissär, Der. L. Sacher-Masoch.	S 102
Emma. J. Austen.	A 2051
Same, [condensed].	A 2055
Emma von Finkenstein. J. C. v. Schmid.	in L 2305
Emmeline. M. Brunton.	B 3751
Emperor, The. G. Ebers.	E 254
Emperor's picture, The. W. Hauff.	in H 1852
Empress, The. G. J. Bennett.	B 1401
Empty heart, The. M. V. Terhune.	T 603
Emsland-bilder. E. A. S. v. Dincklage-Campe.	D 1402
Encantadas, The. H. Melville.	in M 2253
Enchanted beauty, The. W. Elder.	E 951
Enchanted castle, The. J. L. Tieck.	in P 2126 v1
Enchanting and enchanted. F. W. Hackländer.	H 314
Encounter with an interviewer, An. S. L. Clemens.	in C 1802
End of a coil, The. S. Warner.	W 828
End of a fairy tale, The. M. C. Hay.	in H 2112
Same.	in H 2121
End of New York, The. P. Benjamin.	in S 35 v5
End of the world, The. E. Eggleston.	E 652
Endicott and the red cross. N. Hawthorne.	in H 2057 v2
Endymion. B. Disraeli.	D 1503
Engeld. B. Möllhausen.	in S 6101
English Daisy Miller, An. V. W. Johnson.	J 1003
English family Robinson, The. M. Reid.	Rx 407
Ennui. M. Edgeworth.	in E 403
Entail, The. E. T. A. Hoffmann.	in H 3359 v1
Entführung, Die. J. K. A. Musäus.	in M 4951
Enthusiast, The. T. Gillespie.	in W 2202 v14
Entangled. E. F. Byrrne.	B 4802
Entscheidende augenblick, Der. F. A. Wegener.	
Entwendete brief, Der. E. A. Poe.	in P 1978
Epheuranken. C. A. v. Wachsmann.	W 202
Epicurean, The. T. Moore.	M 3401
Episode of Fiddletown, An. F. B. Harte.	in H 1556

Episodes in the lives of men, women and lovers. E. Simcox.	S 2976
Er kehrt zurück. W. Lorenz.	L 1904
Erbe, Das. J. F. Smith.	S 3503
Erbe von Betty's Ruh, Der. P. Lange.	L 509
Erbe von Hornegg, Der. L. Schücking.	S 1809
Erbe von Martella, Der. H. Dohrn.	D 1726
Erbe von Redclyffe, Der. C. M. Yonge.	Y 210
Erbe von Sigmundskron, Der. W. Herchenbach.	in H 2779
Erbe von Weidenhof, Der. F. v. Pelzeln.	P 3201
Erben des steinernen gastes, Die. C. Spindler.	S 4316
Erben des wahnsinns, Die. T. Marx.	M 1426
Erben von Wollun, Die. L. Reinhardt.	R 852
Erbgraf, Der. A. Becker.	B 953
Erbgraf, Der. O. v. Plänckner.	E 751
Erbin von Red Dog, Die. F. B. Harte.	H 1559
Erbin wider willen, Die. S. Schumann.	J 1451
Erbschaft in Kabul, Die. L. F. Stolle.	S 5515
Erdbeben von Caraccas, Das. W. R. Heller.	H 2327
Ereignisss aus dem leben des herrn John Oakhurst. F. B. Harte.	H 1558
Erema. R. D. Blackmore.	B 2304
Erfüllte versprechen, Das. J. Frey.	in M 4436
Eric. F. W. Farrar.	Fx 151
Eric Dering. M. Argles.	in A 1483
Erich Randall. T. Mügge.	M 4206
Erinnerungs-blätter aus dem leben eines criminalisten. L. Reinhardt.	R 853
Eritis sicut Deus. E. Canz.	C 801
Erl-king's daughter, The.	in P 2126 v3
Erlebnisse einer schutzlosen, Die. K. Sutro-Schücking.	S 5952
Erlebnisse eines arztes. E. D. Mund.	M 4501
Erlebtes. F. W. Hackländer.	H 303
Erlebtes und geträumtes. E. v. Bibra.	B 1851
Erlöserin, Die. F. Stahr.	S 4662
Erna's engagement.	E 1
Ernest Maltravers. E. G. E. L. Bulwer-Lytton.	B 4007
Same, pt. 2.	B 4001
Ernst Adair. C. S. Brooks.	B 3427
Ernst Maltravers. E. G. E. L. Bulwer-Lytton.	B 4007
Eroberung von Algier. P. F. W. Oertel.	in O 853
Eroberung von Granada, Die. W. Irving.	I 404
Erotion. D. M. Craik.	in C 2868
Erring, yet noble. I. G. Reed.	R 701
Ersilia. E. F. Poynter.	P 2352
Erste raub an Deutschland, Der. C. G. v. Berneck.	B 1527
Erstgeburtsrecht, Das. C. G. F. Gore.	G 1552
Erzählungen beim licht. C. Spindler.	S 4304
Erzählungen des priesters Ottmar, Die. O. Lautenschlager.	in L 2304
Erzählungen eines alten herrn. G. K. O. v. Struensee.	S 5852
Erzählungen eines alten mannes. I. S. Turgenief.	T 2108
Erzherzog Johann und der herzog von Reichstadt. C. Mundt.	M 4559
Erzherzog Johann und Metternich. C. Mundt.	M 4560
Erzstufen. H. T. v. Schmid.	S 1408
Es geht an. C. J. L. Almquist.	A 902
Esau Hardery. W. O. Stoddard.	S 5502
Esau Runswick. K. S. Macquoid.	M 609
Escape, The. G. Aguilar.	in A 403
Esfira.	T 82
Eskdale herd-boy, The. M. Blackford.	Bx 751
Eskdalemuir story, The.	in W 2203 v3
Esperance. M. W. Lawrence.	L 751
Estelle Russell.	E 2
Ester Ried. I. M. Alden.	A 701
Esterka Regina. K. E. Franzos.	in F 1903
Esther. F. S. Compton.	C 3951
Esther Hill's secret. G. M. Craik.	C 2903
Esther Pennefather. A. Perry.	P 1251 v1
Esther Wynn's love-letters. Saxe Holm.	in H 3753 v1
Ethan Brand. N. Hawthorne.	in J 926 v1
Same.	in H 2059
Ethel Churchill. L. E. Landon.	in 820.2:20
Ettore Fieramosca. Marchea d'Azeglio.	A 2603
Etwas auf dem gewissen. L. Schücking.	S 1828
Etwas über pferde. A. v. Winterfeld.	in W 2261 v2
Eugen Aram. E. G. E. L. Bulwer-Lytton.	B 4008
Eugen Stillfried. F. W. Hackländer.	H 302
Eugen von Kronstein. C. Spindler.	S 4327
Eugene Aram. E. G. E. L. Bulwer-Lytton.	B 4008
Eugene Pickering. H. James, jr.	in J 305
Same.	in J 305
Eugenia. F. H. K. de la Motte Fouqué.	L 357
Eugenie. B. M. Butt.	B 4602
Eunice Lathrop. A. L. Noble.	N 602
Eurich, der priester der gothen. A. Herculano.	H 2801
Europäisches sklavenleben. F. W. Hackländer.	H 304

x denotes books specially adapted for children.

x denotes books specially adapted for children.

x denotes books specially adapted for children.

Found at Blazing Star. F. B. Harte.	*in* **H 1566**
Found dead. J. Payn.	**P 807**
Foundling, The.	*in* **W 2203 v3**
Foundling at sea, The. A. Campbell.	*in* **W 2202 v18**
Fountains, The. S. Johnson.	*in* **820.2:13 v1**
Four-fifteen express, The. A. B. Edwards.	*in* **E 510**
Same.	*in* **J 926 v8**
Four-leaved clover, A. Saxe Holm.	*in* **H 3753 v2**
Four Macnicols. W. Black.	**Bx 727**
Four meetings. H. James, *jr.*	*in* **J 313**
Four seasons, The. F. H. K. de La Motte Fouqué.	**L 358**
Frage, Eine. G. Ebers.	**E 252**
Fox-hunting. C. A. Stephens.	**Sx 1408**
Framley parsonage. A. Trollope.	**T 1614**
Francesca Carrara. L. E. Landon.	*in* **L 401**
Same.	*in* **820.2:26**
Francesco der almosengänger. N. Misasi.	*in* **M 2826**
Franctireurs, Die. F. Gerstäcker.	*in* **P 1951**
Frank Fairlegh. F. E. Smedley.	**S 3226**
Frank Finnegan. W. Carleton.	*in* **C 555**
Frank Mildmay. F. Marryat.	**M 1203**
Frank Redcliffe. A. Daunt.	**Dx 126**
Frank Warrington. M Harris.	**H 1351**
Frankenstein. M. W. Shelley.	**S 2601**
Frankreich gegen Deutschland. C. Mundt.	**M 4562**
Franz Rákóczy. C. Mundt.	**M 4563**
Franz Sternbald's wanderungen. J. L. Tieck.	
	830:148 v16
Franzosen in Hamburg, Die.	**H 5**
Französisches landschloss, Ein. T. Mundt.	**M 4654**
Fraternal magnanimity. F. v. Schiller.	*in* **R 2451**
Frau bürgermeisterin, Die. G. Ebers.	**E 257**
Frau des gesandten, Die. C. G. F. Gore.	**G 1553**
Frau des ministers, Die. F. Friedrich.	**F 1701**
Frau hammerschmiedin, Die. A. Silberstein.	**S 2952**
Frau in weiss, Die. W. Collins.	**C 2226**
Frau meisterin. C. Mundt.	**M 4564**
Frau ökonomierath, Die. F. Elling.	*in* **M 4452**
Frau von Staël. A. Bölte.	**B 2652**
Frauengrosse. G. E. Opiz.	**O 701**
Frauenkrieg, Der. A. Dumas.	**D 2262**
Frauenleben. A. Dumas, *fils.*	**D 2263**
Frauenliebe und künstlerberuf. C. v. Zöllner.	**G 1452**
Frauenraub, Der. T. G. Rudbeck.	**R 2951**
Fräulein von Maalpeire. H. E. F. Reybaud.	**R 1001**
Fräulein v. St. Amaranthe, Das. K. R. v. Gottschall.	
	G 1679
Fred and Maria and me. E. Prentiss.	**P 1456**
Fred Bradford's debt. J. H. Mathews.	**Mx 653**
Frederick the great. C. Mundt.	**M 4554**
Frederico und Alfonso. F. Bourier.	**B 2826**
Free, yet forging their own chains. M. A. Roe.	**R 2351**
Freebooter of Coldstream, The.	*in* **W 2203 v3**
Freedom Wheeler's controversy with Providence. R. T. Cooke.	*in* **W 2401**
Free thinker, The. S. Phillips.	*in* **P 1601**
Freibeuter, Der. . Storch.	**S 5551**
Freien schützen, ILe. J. Rudolphi.	**R 3001**
Freiherr von Hostiwin, Der. A. Meissner.	**M 2053**
Freiherren von Falkenberg, Die. J. D. H. Temme.	
	T 555
Freiknecht, Der. L. Storch.	**S 5552**
Freimaurer, Die. F. G. Kühne.	**K 1451**
Fremde, Die. C. V. Le P. d'Arlincourt.	**A 1551**
Fremder vogel, Ein. C. Elster.	*in* **V 2 v30**
Fremdling von Alsen, Der. G. H. Mellin.	**M 2102**
French country family, A. H. de Witt.	**Wx 1001**
French prisoner in Russia, The.	**F 4**
French spy, The. G. Courtilz de Sandras.	**C 2826R**
Frenchman's tale, The. H. Lee.	*in* **L 851 v2**
Freres, The. A. F. Hector.	**H 2207**
Fresh-water fisherman, The. M. Mitford.	*in* **E 426**
Freude, Die. E. O'Itzel.	**Z 201**
Freundin Napoleons, Eine. W. Lorenz.	**L 1902**
Freundinnen, Die. H. W. Hanke.	**H 1104**
Fridolin. C. Spindler.	**S 4305**
Fridolin's mystical marriage. A. Wilbrandt.	**W 1776**
Friedel. P. F. W. Oertel.	**O 551**
Friedel und Oswald. H. T. v. Schmid.	**S 1407**
Friedensengel, Der. P. Lange.	**L 503**
Friedensstörer, Ein. V. Blüthgen.	**B 726**
Friedhofs-blume. W. v. Hillern.	**H 3155**
Friedrich der grosse und seine geschwister. C. Mundt.	
	M 4565
Friedrich der streitbare. C. Pichler.	**P 1653**
Friedrich von Zollern. C. F. Griesinger.	*in* **G 2501**
Friedrich's II. einzige liebe. W. Lorenz.	**L 1903**
Friend and lover. I. D. Hardy.	**H 1151**
Friend Barton's concern. M. H. Foote.	*in* **S 35 v4**
Friend Eli's daughter. B. Taylor.	*in* **A 1876**
Friend Fritz. E. Erckmann *and* A. Chatrian.	**E 1202**
Friend of my youth, The. T. B. Aldrich.	*in* **A 752**

Friend or foe. H. C. Adams.	**Ax 206**
Friendly farmer, The.	*in* **D 2401**
Friends. E. S. Phelps.	**P 1451**
Friends and neighbors. T. S. Arthur.	**A 1752**
Friends' meeting. E. E. Hale.	*in* **H 460**
Friend's tale, The. H. Lee.	*in* **L 851 v1**
Friesen in Rom. Die. J. van Lennep.	**L 952**
Fritz Beutel. H. Marggraff.	**M 1101**
Fritz Stilling. P. Lange.	**L 508**
Frohnleichnamsfest, Das. O. Lautenschlager.	
	in **L 2303**
Frölenhaus, Das. G. H. G. zu Putlitz.	*in* **S 4262**
From a back window. F. B. Harte.	*in* **H 1553**
From a mournful villager. S. O. Jewett.	*in* **J 903**
From dreams to waking. E. L. Linton.	**L 1452**
From exile. J. Payn.	**P 808**
From first to last. H. Parr.	*in* **P 469**
From generation to generation. E. Yates.	*in* **Y 110**
From generation to generation. *Lady* A. Noel.	**N 701**
From hand to mouth. A. M. Douglas.	**D 1052**
From hay-time to hopping. *Miss* Coulter.	**C 2751**
From jest to earnest. E. P. Roe.	**R 2304**
From my youth up. M. V. Terhune.	**T 604**
From nowhere to the north pole. T. Hood.	**Hx 926**
From post to finish. H. Smart.	**S 3202**
From powder-monkey to admiral. W. H. G. Kingston.	
	Kx 455
From the earth to the moon. J. Verne.	**V 552**
From the Hudson to the Neva. D. Ker.	**Kx 276**
From the rank. J. Payn.	*in* **P 812**
From the wings. B. H. Buxton.	**B 4455**
Frozen deep, The. W. Collins.	**C 2208**
Same.	*in* **C 2228**
Frühlingsboten. E. Bürstenbinder.	**B 4356**
Frühlingstraum, Ein. A. Kühne.	**D 1204**
Fugaçe. H. Wilke.	**K 1401**
Fugitive, The. G. Aguilar.	*in* **A 403**
Fugitive, The. J. M. Wilson.	*in* **W 2202 v18**
Same.	*in* **W 2203 v5**
Fugitives, The. M. O. Oliphant.	**O 457**
Fünfte frau, Die. E. A. S. v. Dincklage-Campe.	**D 1403**
Funke, Ein. B. E. Fornell.	**M 4701**
Fur country, The. J. Verne.	**V 563**
Für stadt und land. C. Spindler.	**S 4306**
Für stille abende. L. Storch.	**S 5553**
Furchtlos und treu. W. F. Vollmer.	**V 902**
Furioso. W. Müller von Königswinter.	**M 4452**
Fürst, Der. C. F. Ridderstad.	**R 1401**
Fürst Mitternacht. C. T. Heyne.	**B 2861**
Fürst und musiker. M. Ring.	**R 1610**
Fürst von Montenegro, Der. A. v. Winterfeld.	**W 2256**
Fürsten und dichter. C. Mundt.	**M 4556**
Fürstenhaus, Das. L. T. Bernhardi.	**B 1551**
Fürstensohn, Der. F. Schregel.	**S 1701**
Fürstentag, Der. L. Bechstein.	**B 355**
Future life. G. Wood.	**W 2601**
G. B. C., The. J. Payn.	*in* **P 811 v1**
G. T. T. T. Hughes. *ed.*	**Hx 1054**
Gabriel. S. Kohn.	**K 1101**
Gabriel Conroy. F. B. Harte.	**H 1552**
Gabriel Lambert. A. Dumas.	*in* **D 2257**
Gabriele Mimanso. C. J. L. Almquist.	**P 1951**
Gabrielle. A. Durand.	**A 904**
Gabrielle de Bourdanie. *Mrs.* J. K. Spender.	**D 2554**
Gaiety and gloom. J. Kavanagh.	**S 4203**
Galeerensklave, Der. L. Storch.	*in* **K 310**
Galileo Galilei. M. Raven.	*in* **S 5558**
Galizische geschichten. L. Sacher-Masoch.	**R 501**
Gambier's luck. E. T. A. Hoffmann.	**H 103**
Game hen, The. M. Hartley.	*in* **H 3359 v2**
Garden party, A. D. M. Craik.	*in* **L 253**
Garibaldi. H. Rau.	*in* **C 2870**
Garman and Worse. A. L. Kielland.	**R 453**
Garman und Worse. A. L. Kielland.	**K 1702**
Gartenlaubenblüthen. E. Bürstenbinder.	**K 1702**
Garret van Horn. J. Payn.	**B 4353**
Garth, The. H. Neele.	**P 826**
Garth. J. Hawthorne.	*in* **820.2:17**
Gasselbuben, Die. H. T. v. Schmid.	**H 2002**
Gates ajar, The. E. S. Phelps.	**S 1408**
Gathered fragments. J. A. Clarke.	**249:21**
Gaudelius Enzian, Fahrten und abenteuer des M. G. K.	**C 1601**
Heriossohn.	**M 2852**
Gawk, The. B. Auerbach.	*in* **A 1965**
Gayworthys, The. A. D. T. Whitney.	**W 1452**
Gebannt und erlöst. E. Bürstenbinder.	**B 4358**
Gebirgs-sagen. H. Steffens.	**B 4358**
Gebrüder Koltrum, Die. L. Reinhardt.	**R 854**
Gedenkblätter aus dem zwanzigsten jahre. A. de La-martine.	**L 303**
Gefangen und befreit. R. Rösler.	**R 2628**

x denotes books specially adapted for children.

x denotes books specially adapted for children.

Hand der Nemesis, Die. E. A. König. K 1251
Hand of Ethelberta, The. T. Hardy. H 1204
Handel und wandel. F. W. Hackländer. H 306
Handelshaus in den scheeren, Ein. E. Carlén. C 503
Handicapped. M. V. Terhune. T 605
Hands of justice, The. F. W. Robinson. R 1855
Handsome Lawrence. A. L. A. Dudevant. D 2162
Handwerk und industrie. P. Stein. S 4852
Handwerker, Der. A. L. A. Dudevant. D 2163
Handwerksburschen. J. Messner. M 2601
Handy Andy. S. Lover. L 1951
Hannah. D. M. Craik. C 2856
Hannah Hawkins. J. March. Mx 401
Hannah Thurston. B. Taylor. T 451
Hans Brinker. M. M. Dodge. Dx 551
Hans Pfaalls höchst wundersame abenteuer. E. A. Poe. *in* W 2262 v4
Hans Pfall, The adventures of one. E. A. Poe. *in* 820.1: 5 v3
Hans the dreamer. R. Lindau. *in* L 1404
Hans und Grete. F. Spielhagen. S 4266
Hanz und Heinz Kirch. H. T. W. Storm. S 5603
Happiest man in England, The. T. Hood. *in* 820.2: 36
Happiness of being rich, The. H. Conscience. C 2254
Happy accident at Brighton, A. F. Church. *in* C 1417
Happy boy, A. B. Björnson. B 2158
Happy conclusion, The. *in* W 2202 v16
Happy faces. A. Opie. *in* O 653
Same. *in* O 653 v3
Happy-go-lucky. M. Harris. H 1352
Haran. J. H. Smith. Sx 1201
Hard bargain, A. H. E. Scudder. *in* S 2101
Hard cash. C. Reade. R 605
Hard heart, A. B. Frederich. D 208
Hard knot, A. C. Gibbon. G 812
Hard scrabble of Elm Island, The. E. Kellogg. Kx 210
Hard times. C. Dickens. D 1307
Hard to bear. G. M. Craik. C 2905
Harden's revenge. A. Leighton. *in* W 2202 v8
Hardscrabble. J. Richardson. R 1151
Hardy tin soldier, The. H. C. Andersen. *in* Ax 755
Harehound and the witch, The. J. *and* M. Banim. *in* B 307
"Harnt" that walks Chilhowee, The. M. N. Murfree. *in* M 4776
Harold. E. G. E. L. Bulwer-Lytton. B 4012
Harrington. M. Edgeworth. *in* E 409
Harry Blount. P. G. Hamerton. Hx 351
Harry Bolton's curacy. *in* T 176 v9
Harry Bradford's crusade. J. H. Mathews. Mx 852
Harry Harson. J. T. Irving. I 351
Harry Heathcote. A. Trollope. T 1616
Harry Joscelyn. M. O. Oliphant. O 459
Harry Lorrequer, Confessions of. C. Lever. L 1111
Hartes herz, Ein. B. Frederich. D 202
Hartinger's alte Sixtin. L. Anzengruber. *in* V 2 v31
Harvest of wild oats, A. F. Church. C 1405
Harveys, The. H. Kingsley. K 701
Harwood. J. G. A. Coulson. C 2701
Hase meines grossvaters, Der. A. Dumas. D 2264
Hattie's romance. P. Deming. *in* D 902
Hau-kiou-choan. H 10
Häubchen, Das. O. Lautenschlager. *in* L 2308
Haunted and the haunter, The. E. G. E. L. Bulwer-Lytton. *in* T 176 v10
Haunted crust, The. K. Cooper. *in* J 926 v5
Haunted Enghenio, The. *in* T 177 v11
Haunted hotel, The. W. Collins. C 2209
Haunted house, The. C. Dickens *and others*. *in* D 1325
Haunted house. H. Parr. T 469
Haunted man, The. C. Dickens. D 1303
Haunted mind, The. N. Hawthorne. *in* H 2057 v2
Haunted ships, The. A. Cunningham. *in* J 926 v8
Haunters and the haunted, The. E. G. E. L. Bulwer-Lytton. *in* T 176 v10
Same. *in* J 926 v2
Haus, Das. F. Bremer. B 3154
Haus der nichte, Das. K. Stricker. S 5777
Haus des fabrikanten, Das. J. F. M. O. Meding. M 1980
Haus Düsterweg, Das. W. Häring. H 1253
Haus Hillel, Das. M. Ring. R 1606
Haus Lauernesse, Das. A. L. G. Toussaint. T 1401
Haus Treustein. K. v. Holtei. H 4001
Häuschen am gitterthore bei Nygard. C. A. Wetterbergh. W 1407
Haverholme. E. Jenkins. J 652
Having nothing, yet having all. E. Prentiss. *in* P 2452
Hawick spate, The. A. Campbell. *in* W 2202 v19
Hawkstone. E. M. Sewell. S 2553
Hawkview. H. Parr. P 453
Haworths. F. H. Burnett. B 4253
He knew he was right. A. Trollope. T 1617

He stoops to conquer. M. C. Hay. *in* H 2106
He that will not when he may. M. O. Oliphant. O 460
He would be a gentleman. S. Lover. L 1952
Head of Medusa, The. J. Fletcher. F 1051
Head of the family, The. D. M. Craik. C 2857
Headlong Hall. T. L. Peacock. P 851
Head-master Rhenfried. F. H. K. de La Motte Fouqué. *in* L 357
Same. *in* R 2451
Head waiter, The. F. W. Robinson. *in* R 1858
Headsman, The. J. F. Cooper. C 2456
Headsman, The; a tale of doom. *in* T 176 v3
Heaps of money. W. E. Norris. N 903
Heart-histories. T. S. Arthur. A 1753
Heart of it, The. W. O. Stoddard. S 5501
Heart of Mid-Lothian, The. *Sir* W. Scott. S 2012
Heart of steel, A. F. C. Fisher. F 957
Heartbreak cameo, The. L. Champney. *in* S 35 v6
Hearts. D. C. Murray. M 4880
Hearts and faces. J. T. Trowbridge. Tx 819
Heart's delight. C. Gibbon. G 811
Heart's problem, A. C. Gibbon. G 803
Heartsease. C. M. Yonge. Y 209
Hector. F. L. Shaw. Sx 901
Hector Servadac. J. Verne. 555
Hedge school, The. W. Carleton. *in* C 554
Heidabenteuer. A. v. d. Decken. *in* D 2651
Heidelberg. G. P. R. James. J 218
Heidenkind, Das. F. B. Harte. H 1562
Heidenmauer, The. J. F. Cooper. C 2457
Heidischenke, Die. L. Storch. S 5561
Heidi. J. Spyri. Sx 2051
Heiduck, Der. H. Wachenhusen. W 159
Heilige born, Der. W. Raabe. R 110
Heiligen und die ritter, Die. L. Schücking. S 1812
Heimath der frau, Die. O. Wildermuth. W 1803
Heimath-geschichten. E. A. S. v. Dincklage-Campe. D 1405
Heimkehr. O. Wildermuth. W 1809
Heimliche gast, Der. K. E. R. Bayer. B 723
Heimliche und unheimliche geschichten. F. Gerstäcker. *in* G 701
Heinrich Falk. O. Roquette. R 2402
Heinrich IV. A. Dumas. D 2265
Heinrich von Cerons. G. P. R. James. J 215
Heinrich von Eichenfels. J. C. v. Schmid. S 1458
Heinrich of Hardington, The. H. Parr. *in* P 469
Heir of Inshannock. J. Maidment. *in* W 2202 v12
Heir of Redclyffe, The. C. M. Yonge. Y 210
Heir of Rosscairne, The. M. C. Hay. *in* H 2107
Same. *in* H 2118
Heir of Vallis, The. W. Mathews. M 1651
Heir of Wast-Wayland, The. M. Howitt. Hx 1253
Heiress, An. N. Perry. *in* P 1351
Heiress of Haughton, The. A. C. Marsh-Caldwell. M 1263
Heiress of Kilorgan, The. M. A. Sadlier. S 154
Held der zukunft, Der. L. Schücking. S 1813
Helden der arbeit, Die. M. v. Schlägel. S 1304
Helen. M. Edgeworth. E 410
Helen Lincoln. C. Capron. C 351
Helen Morton's trial. A. Haven. Hx 602
Heleua. M. C. Clarke. H 1401
Helena Mathewson. W. Collins. *in* C 1651 v1
Helena Vallisneria. J. Mosen. *in* C 2206
Helena's household. J. De Mille. *in* M 3951
Helene. F. Tarnow. D 853
Helene. H. Wachenhusen. T 251
Helen's babies. J. Habberton. W 162
Hell und dunkel. F. Gerstäcker. B 202
Hella Jasmund. S. Schumann. G 714
Helmar. F. Stahr. J 1452
Helon. G. Aguilar. S 4664
Hen-wife, The. A. Leighton. A 403
Henning Brabant. A. Mützelburg. *in* W 2202 v8
Henpecked man, The. J. M. Wilson. M 5002
Henrietta Temple. B. Disraeli. *in* W 2202 v8
Henriette. E. Daudet. D 1504
Henriette Sontag. J. Werner. D 476
Henriette von England. C. Pichler. W 1351
Henry VIII. C. Mundt. P 1654
Henry de Ceron. G. P. R. James. M 4575
Henry Dunbar. M. E. Maxwell. J 219
Henry Esmond. W. M. Thackeray. T 762
Henry Esmond's geschichte. W. M. Thackeray. T 655
Henry Masterton. G. P. R. James. T 655
Henry Milner, The history of. M. M. Sherwood. J 220
Henry of Guise. G. P. R. James. S 2801
Henry St. John. J. E. Cooke. J 221
Henry Smeaton. G. P. R. James. C 2355
Henry Vane. F. J. Stimson. J 222
Hephzibah Guinness. S. W. Mitchell. S 5202
M 2901

x denotes books specially adapted for children.

x denotes books specially adapted for children.

Jocelyn's mistake. *Mrs.* J. K. Spender.	S 4201	Juliet. M. C. Clarke.	*in* C 1651 v2
Jack o'Hazelgreen. H. B. Reeves.	*in* R 3505	Junge frau, Die. H. Wachenhusen.	W 158
Joe Baldwin. P. Deming.	*in* D 901	Junge kurfürst, Der. C. Mundt.	M 4572
Joe Hale's red stockings. Saxe Holm.	*in* H 3753 v2	Junge prätendent, Der. J. F. Smith.	S 3504
Johann Georg L. von Sachsen. F. Lubojatzky.	C 453	Junge vater und der alte sohn, Der. A. v. Winterfeld.	*in* W 2261 v1
Johanna. A. L. A. Dudevant.	D 2169		
Johanna d'Arc. A. Dumas.	D 2271	Junge wittwe in Nordland. L. Brunius.	32
Johanne und Louise. E. Sue.	S 5907	Jüngere sohn, Der. E. B. Berthet.	B 1701
Johannes Gutenberg. P. Stein.	S 4853	Jungfrau von Orleans, Die. J. Robinson.	R 1902
Johannes Kepler. J. Pfannenschmidt.	P 1402	Jüngste gericht, Das. E. O. K. Zitelmann.	*in* V 2 v22
Johannes Volkh. J. Rank.	R 354	Jury room, The. G. Griffin.	*in* G 2555
Johannesfest, Das. O. Lautenschlager.	*in* L 2302	*Same.*	*in* G 2551 v5
Johanniskäferchen, Das. J. C. v. Schmid.	*in* S 1455	Just as I am. M. E. Maxwell.	M 1767
Same.	*in* S 1463	Just his luck.	Jx 89
Johannisnacht. M. Schmidt.	S 1476	Justice and mercy. A. M. Stewart.	S 1452
Johannisreise, Die. F. Bremer.	B 3156	Justice in the by-ways. F. C. Adams.	A 201
Johanniter, Die. E. Ambach.	*in* A 953	Justine's lovers. J. L. Howell.	V 351
John Barlow's ward.	J 31	Jutland. A. v. Winterfeld.	*in* W 2261 v4
John Brent. T. Winthrop.	W 2303		
John Caldigate. A. Trollope.	T 1619	Kabbalist, Der. A. Becker.	B 952
John Chinaman. F. B. Harte.	*in* H 1553	Kadettengeschichte aus alter zeit, Eine. A. v. Winterfeld.	*in* W 2261 v2
John Doe and Croboore of the bill-hook. J. Banim.		Kadettengeschichten. A. Kühne.	D 1208
	B 305	Kainszeichen, Die. F. W. Hackländer.	H 307
John Doe and Richard Roe. E. S. Gould.	G 1701	Kaiser, Der. G. Ebers.	E 254
John Dorrien. J. Kavanagh.	K 305	Kaiser-wahl, Die. A. v. Sternberg.	S 5055
John Eax. A. W. Tourgée.	T 1355	Kaiserin Claudia. C. Mundt.	M 4573
John Eccleston's thanksgiving. N. Perry.	*in* P 1351	Kalabrische novellen. N. Misasi.	M 2826
John Godfrey's fortunes. B. Taylor.	T 452	Kaloolah. W. S. Mayo.	M 1952
John Granger. M. E. Maxwell.	*in* M 1764	Kaltenborn. C. G. v. Berneck.	B 1530
John Halifax. D. M. Craik.	C 2859	Kaméháméha. C. M. Newell.	N 238
John Holdsworth. W. C. Russell.	R 3311	Kammerer Lassman. E. Carlén.	C 505
John Inglefield's thanksgiving. N. Hawthorne.		Kammerjungfer, Die. F. Stahr.	S 4667
	in H 2059	Kampf um Rom, Ein. F. Dahn.	D 103
John Inglesant. J. H. Shorthouse.	S 2826	Kampf um's recht, Ein. K. E. Franzos.	F 1902
John Jago's ghost. W. Collins.	*in* C 2208	Kämpfende herzen. F. Dahn.	D 101
John Law. W. H. Ainsworth.	A 570	Kanarienvogel, Der. J. C. v. Schmid.	*in* S 1455
John Marchmont's legacy. M. E. Maxwell.	M 1765	*Same.*	*in* S 1463
John Marston Hall. G. P. R. James.	J 226	Kanzler von Tyrol, Der. H. T. v. Schmid.	S 1411
John Marston Hall's leben und abenteuer. G. P. R. James.		Kaperschiffer, Der. F. Marryat.	M 1214
	J 226	Karfreitags-christen, Die. C. R. Köstlin.	K 1376
John Milton. M. Ring.	R 1608	Karl der kühne. A. Dumas.	D 2372
John Needham's double. J. Hatton.	H 1753	Karl II und sein hof. C. Mundt.	M 4574
John Oakhurst. F. B. Harte.	*in* H 1556	Karl X Gustav. C. G. v. Berneck.	B 1531
John Paul Jones. S. S. A. Grabowski.	G 1901	Karl Kiegler.	Kx 3
John Rantoul. H. L. Nelson.	N 1101	Karl Mathy. G. Freytag.	F 1604
John Rintoul.	*in* T 176 v11	Kartause von Serra S. Bruno, Die. N. Misasi.	
John Square's voyage to India. J. Howell.			*in* M 2826
	in W 2202 v7	Kasper Wullkop. W. Schröder.	S 1752
John Woodburn. C. Castle.	C 701	Kastilianer, Der. T. de Trueba y Cosio.	T 1901
John Worthington's name. F. L. Benedict.	B 1302	Katakomben von Rom, Die. P. Lacroix.	L 202
Johnny Armstrong, The disasters of.	*in* W 2202 v1	Kate. C. Barnard.	*in* B 401
Johnny Darbyshire. W. Howitt.	*in* J 926 v9	Kate Comerford. T. A. Thornet.	T 901
Same.	*in* E 426	Kate Coventry. G. J. Whyte-Melville.	M 2206
John's trial. P. Deming.	*in* D 901	Kate Crediford. N. P. Willis.	*in* W 2004
Jolly fellowship, A. F. R. Stockton.	Sx 1053	Kate Kennedy. A. Leighton.	*in* W 2202 v1
Jolly good times at school. M. P. W. Smith.	Sx 1301	Kate Rose.	*in* P 11
Jolly rover, The. J. T. Trowbridge.	Tx 802	Katerfelto. G. J. Whyte-Melville.	M 2207
Jonathan. C. C. Liddell.	T 2801	Katers Murr, Lebens-ansichten des. E. T. A. Hoffmann.	
Joppe und crinoline. A. Zeising.	Z 101		H 3354
Josef Kaiser. E. Breier.	B 3101	Kate's engagement. M. C. Hay.	*in* H 2114
Joseph Haywood. A. Sartorius.	*in* S 626	*Same.*	*in* H 2118
Joseph II and his court. C. Mundt.	M 4571	Katharina and Bianca. M. C. Clarke.	*in* C 1651 v2
Joseph Andrews. H. Fielding.	F 801	Katharine Ashton. E. M. Sewell.	S 2555
Joseph im schnee. B. Auerbach.	A 1960	Katharine Walton. W. G. Simms.	S 3002
Joseph in the snow. B. Auerbach.	A 1960	Kathayan slave, The. E. C. Judson.	*in* J 926 v3
Joseph Noirel's revenge. V. Cherbuliez.	C 1153	Katheran, The. A. Campbell.	*in* W 2202 v4
Joseph Thorne. L. C. Moulton.	*in* M 4101	Katherine Earle. A. Trafton.	T 1502
Joseph und seine brüder. E. v. Dincklage-Campe.		Katherine's trial. H. Parr.	P 465
	in V 2 v31	Kathie Brand. H. Parr.	P 453
Josephine. G. Aguilar.	A 404	Kathie stories. A. M. Douglas.	Dx 653-Dx 658
Joseph's coat. D. C. Murray.	M 4877	Kathleen. F. H. Burnett.	B 4254
Joshua Davidson. E. L. Linton.	L 1456	Käthner und seine familie, Der. S. v. Knorring.	
Joshua Haggard's daughter. M. E. Maxwell.	M 1766		K 1051
Journey to the centre of the earth. J. Verne.	V 554	Katie Cheyne. J. Hogg.	*in* H 3451 v3
Joy. M. Crommelin.	C 3103	Katie Stewart. M. O. Oliphant.	O 462
Joyce Morrell's harvest. E. S. Holt.	H 3952	Kaunitz. L. v. Sacher-Masoch.	S 104
Jubilee days. W. D. Howells.	*in* H 4757	Kavanagh. H. W. Longfellow.	L 1802
Jude, Der. C. Spindler.	S 4309	Keeper's travels.	Kx 1
Jude von Wien, Der. J. W. Thompson.	T 2451	Kegelbahn, Die. A. v. Winterfeld.	*in* W 2261 v2
Judge's wife, The. L. C. Moulton.	*in* M 4102	Keine politik. I. Frick.	F 1652
Jüdin, Die. G. Aguilar.	A 408	Kelverdale. W. Cuffe.	C 3351
Judith. E. Scribe.	*in* S 551	Ken Hall. A. Cudlip.	*in* C 3312 v3
Judith. M. V. Terhune.	T 813	Kenelm Chillingly. E. G. E. L. Bulwer-Lytton.	B 4013
Judith Shakespeare. W. Black.	B 2218	Kenilworth. *Sir* W. Scott.	S 2014
Judith, the egyptian. J. M. Wilson.	*in* W 2202 v7	Kenneth. M. C. Hay.	*in* H 2107
Julia. H. Lee.	*in* L 851 v1	*Same.*	*in* H 2118
Julia. J. W. Vahey.	201	Kenneth. C. M. Yonge.	Y 213
Julia de Roubigné. H. Mackenzie.	*in* 829.2:23	Kept in the dark. A. Trollope.	T 1638
Julia Howard. *Mrs.* B. Martin.	B 1201	Kerker von Edinburg, Der. *Sir* W. Scott.	S 2012
Julia McKenzie. J. Hogg.	*in* H 3451 v5	Kester's evil eye. H. Parr.	*in* P 469
Julian. W. Ware.	W 652	Kettenglieder. C. Spindler.	S 4310
Julian Home. F. W. Farrar.	Fx 152	Kibitz.	*in* P 2126 v2
Julian Vanneck. F. J. Fargus.	*in* F 2004		

x denotes books specially adapted for children.

Kickleburys abroad, The. W. M. Thackeray. **T 658**
Same.   *in* **T 665 v2**
Kildhurm's oak. J. Hawthorne.   *in* **H 2005 v2**
Kilmeny. W. Black.   **B 2205**
Kilrogan cottage. M. Despard.   **D 1151**
Kin-ku-ki-kuan. E. Grisebach.   **G 2676**
Kinaldy.   *in* **W 2203 v3**
Kind Bajazzo's, Das. E. A. König.   **K 1253**
Kinder der fremde, Die. C. R. Köstlin.   **K 1377**
Kinder der liebe, Die. E. Sue.   **S 5908**
Kinder der welt. P. Heyse.   **H 3005**
Kinder der wittwe, Die. E. Ambach.   **A 951**
Kinder der zeit. A. Bernhardt.   **B 1601**
Kinder des Neuwalds, Die. F. Marryat.   **M 1202**
Kinder Roms, Die. A. Meissner.   **M 2054**
Kinder von Finkenrode, Die. W. Raabe.   **R 113**
Kindly jest, The. C. Reade.   *in* **R 621**
King Candaules. T. Gautier.   *in* **G 604**
King Capital. W. Sime.   **S 2996**
King David. C. M. Woolson.   *in* **W 2752**
King Grimalkum and Pussyanita. A. M. Diaz. **Dx 457**
King of clubs, The, and the queen of hearts. L. M. Alcott.   *in* **A 652**
King of Hayti, The. T. De Quincey. *in* **330 : 14**
Same.   *in* **J 926 v10**
King of the Golden River, The. J. Ruskin. **Rx 1001**
King of the peak, The. A. Cunningham. *in* **J 926 v7**
King Pepin and sweet Olive.   *in* **T 178 v3**
King Pest. E. A. Poe.   *in* **820.1 : 5 v3**
King Tolv. D. M. Craik.   *in* **C 2868**
King's highway, The. G. P. R. James.   **J 225**
King's men, The. R. Grant *and others.*   **G 1978**
King's own, The. F. Marryat.   **M 1206**
Kingsdene. M. G. Fetherstonhaugh.   **F 601**
Kinley Hollow. G. H. Hollister.   **H 3702**
Kirby's coals of fire. L. Stockton.   *in* **S 35 v7**
Kircheinweihung von Hammarby, Die. E. Carlén.   **C 506**
Kirchmessnacht, Eine. J. D. H. Temme. **T 556**
Kirkyards. T. Gillespie.   *in* **W 2202 v14**
Kismet. J. Fletcher.   **F 1052**
Kissing the rod. E. H. Yates.   **Y 103**
Kit, a memory. J. Payn.   **P 825**
Kit Cobb, the cabman. J. Brougham. *in* **927.1 : 7**
Kith and kin. J. Fothergill.   **F 1405**
Kittyleen. S. S. Clarke.   **Cx 475**
Kitty's class-day. L. M. Alcott.   **Ax 518**
Kitty's conquest. C. King.   **K 577**
Klein Dorrit. C. Dickens.   **D 1309**
Klein Zaches. E. T. A. Hoffmann.   **H 3353**
Kleine erzählungen. C. Pichler.   **P 1656**
Kleine Fadette, Die. A. L. A. Dudevant. *in* **D 2158**
Kleine garnison, Eine. A. v. Winterfeld. *in* **W 2261 v5**
Kleine geschichten. P. Lindau.   **L 1351**
Kleine graf, Der. A. v. Winterfeld. *in* **W 2261 v3**
Kleine hund Josephinens, Der. E. M. Hilaire.   *in* **B 1701**
Kleine kaminfeger, Der. J. C. v. Schmid. **S 1462**
Kleine lautenspielerin, Die. J. C. v. Schmid. **S 1465**
Kleine Marina, Die. E. Polko.   *in* **V 2 v31**
Kleine memoiren. A. Meissner.   **M 2065**
Kleine narrenwelt, Die. K. F. Gutzkow.   **G 3101**
Kleine romane. T. Mundt.   **M 4656**
Kleinere novellen. J. H. D. Zschokke.   **Z 308**
Kleines bild, Ein. E. Wichert.   **W 1602**
Kloster, Das. *Sir* W. Scott.   **S 2015**
Klosterheim. T. De Quincey.   **D 1101**
Same.   *in* **824.2 : 32 v2**
Klosterhof, Der. O. Müller.   **M 4408**
Klosterruine, Die. J. D. H. Temme.   **T 557**
Klytia. A. Hausrath.   **H 1876**
Knabe Inigo, Der. O. Lautenschlager. *in* **L 2302**
Knapsack, The. M. Edgeworth.   *in* **E 402**
Knight of Dannebrog, A. H. H. Boyesen. *in* **B 2853**
Knight of Gwynne, The. C. Lever.   **L 1114**
Knight of the Black Forest, The. G. D. Litchfield.   **L 1226**
Knight of the nineteenth century, A. E. P. Roe.   **R 2305**
Knight of the sheep, The. G. Griffin. *in* **G 2551 v3**
Same.   *in* **G 2556**
Knight without reproach, The. G. Griffin. *in* **G 2555**
Same.   *in* **G 2551 v5**
Knights of the horse-shoe, The. W. A. Caruthers.   **C 626**
Knights of to-day. C. Barnard.   **B 401**
Knight's secret, The. C. Reade.   *in* **R 617**
Same.   *in* **R 621**
Knightsbridge mystery, The. C. Reade. *in* **R 616**
Same.   *in* **R 621**
Same.   *in* **T 178 v2**
Knitting sale socks. H. P. Spofford. *in* **S 4401**
Knockabout club alongshore. C. A. Stephens. **Sx 1402**

Knockabout club in the woods. C. A. Stephens.   **Sx 1401**
Kobold, Der. O. Roquette.   *in* **V 2 v37**
Komet, Der. J. P. F. Richter.   **830 : 142 v28.39**
Komische bilder. O. Moser.   **M 4001**
Komödianten des lebens, Die. M. Jókai.   **J 1153**
Konak, Der. A. Mützelburg.   **M 5004**
König Christian der zweite. A. N. Saint-Aubain. **S 202**
König der luft, Der. A. v. Winterfeld.   **W 2255**
König der welt, Der. E. Souvestre.   **S 4052**
König Heinrich VIII. C. Mundt.   **M 4575**
König Karl XI und seine günstlinge. C. D. Arfvedson.   **K 11**
König Ottokar. T. Montanus.   **M 3151**
König von Tauharawi, Der. L. F. Stolle. **S 5517**
König von Zion, Der. C. Spindler.   **S 4311**
Königin Bertha. J. Bischoff.   **B 2051**
Königin der nacht, Die. L. Schücking.   **S 1815**
Königin juwelenschmuck, Der. C. J. L. Almquist.   **A 903**
Königin Luise Ulrike. C. F. Ridderstad. **R 1403**
Königin Margot. A. Dumas.   **D 2273**
Königs ballet, Des. H. Wachenhusen.   **V 154**
Königs ordre, Des. A. v. Winterfeld. *in* **W 2261 v8**
Same.   *in* **V 2 v29**
Königsbetrug, Der. T. G. Rudbeck.   **R 2951**
Königsbraut, Die. L. Storch.   **S 5555**
Koschere haus, Das. H. Schiff.   **S 1151**
Krähenfelder geschichten. W. Raabe.   **R 114**
Kranke köchin, Die. P. Lindau.   **L 1352**
Kreuzfahrer, Die. F. Dahn.   **D 105**
Kriм. M. Argles.   *in* **A 1483**
Krintzner. H. Lee.   *in* **L 851 v2**
Kronenwächter, Die. L. A. v. Arnim.   **A 1576**
Künstlerbilder. A. v. Sternberg.   **S 5056**
Künstlerelend. R. Grothe.   *in* **V 2 v23**
Kunstreiter, Der. F. Gerstäcker.   **G 717**
Kunz von Kauffungen. L. Storch.   **S 5556**

Labor and love.   **L 1**
Lachende mann, Der. V. Hugo.   **H 4852**
Ladder of life, The. A. B. Edwards.   **E 506**
Ladies Lindores, The. M. O. Oliphant.   **O 486**
Lady Adelaide. L. B. Walford.   *in* **T 177 v10**
Lady Adelaide's oath. E. P. Wood.   **W 2561**
Lady Alice. J. V. Huntington.   **H 5103**
Lady Alice. E. Marshall.   **M 1301**
Lady Amabel. E. M. Stewart.   **S 5252**
Lady Anna. A. Trollope.   **T 1620**
Lady Anne and lady Jane. A. Opie. *in* **O 653 v4**
Lady Audley's geheimniss. M. E. Maxwell. **M 1768**
Lady Audley's secret. M. E. Maxwell.   **M 1768**
Lady Barberina. H. James, *jr.*   *in* **J 313**
Lady Beauty. A. Muir.   **M 4226**
Lady Bell. H. Keddie.   **K 1652**
Lady-bird. G. C. Fullerton.   **F 1304**
Lady Carmichael's will. M. C. Hay.   *in* **H 2118**
Lady Clara De Vere. F. Spielhagen.   **S 4256**
Lady Eleanor's mantle. N. Hawthorne. *in* **H 2057 v2**
Lady Ferry. S. O. Jewett.   *in* **J 802**
Lady Greatheart's store. E. Yates.   *in* **Y 116**
Lady Green Satin. E. Martineau des Chesnez. **Mx 256**
Lady Gresham's fête. G. Aguilar.   *in* **A 403**
Lady Hester. C. M. Yonge.   **Y 214**
Lady Jane. M. O. Oliphant.   **O 484**
Lady Kitty. W. Besant *and* J. Rice.   *in* **B 1762**
Lady Lovelace. C. L. Pirkis.   **P 1876**
Lady Mary. C. B. Tayler.   **T 402**
"Lady Maud," The. W. C. Russell.   **R 3306**
Lady of Launay, The. A. Trollope.   *in* **T 1637**
Lady of Little Fishing, The. C. F. Woolson. *in* **H 2751**
Lady of Shalott, The. E. S. Phelps.   *in* **P 1453**
Same.   *in* **J 926 v10**
Lady of the Aroostook, The. W. D. Howells. **H 4755**
Lady of the ice, The. J. De Mille.   **D 854**
Lady of the manor, The. M. M. Sherwood.   **S 2809**
Lady on the mail. H. Parr.   *in* **P 469**
Lady or the tiger, The. F. R. Stockton. *in* **S 5402**
Lady Rae. A. Campbell.   *in* **W 2202 v22**
Lady Ravelgold. N. P. Willis.   *in* **W 2004**
Lady Seamer's long step. H. Parr.   *in* **P 464**
Lady Silverdale's sweetheart. W. Black.   **B 2061**
Lady Sweetapple. G. W. Dasent.   **D 301**
Lady Sybil's choice. E. S. Holt.   **H 3951**
Lady Willoughby, The diary of. H. M. Rathbone.   **R 426**
Same. Further portions.   **R 427**
Lady's mile, The. M. E. Maxwell.   **M 1769**
Laidley worm of Spindleston Heugh, The. J. M. Wilson.   *in* **W 2202 v6**
Laird of Darnick Tower. The. J. Howell. *in* **W 2202 v7**
Laird of Lucky's How, The. A. Campbell.   *in* **W 2202 v9**

x denotes books specially adapted for children.

Letzte der Abenceragen, Der. R. F. A. de Chateaubri-
  and. *in* C 1051
Letzte der feen, Die. G. P. R. James. J 227
Letzte deutsche kaiser, Der. F. Lubojatzky. C 454
Letzte glück, Das. W. Berger. *in* V 2 v31
Letzte könig der magyaren, Der. L. v. Sacher-Masoch.
  S 105
Letzte Montmorency, Der. E. W. Ackermann. A 151
Letzte novellen. F. W. Hackländer. H 318
Letzte seines stammes, Der. F. Stahr. S 4670
Letzten blüthen, Die. L. Steinlein. A 1701
Letzten tage Pompejis, Die. E. G. E. L. Bulwer-Lytton.
  B 4014
Letzten zeiten der Grävenitz, Die. C. T. Gricsinger.
  G 2504
Leuchtthurm am Michigan, Der. B. Möllhausen.
  M 3058
Leute aus dem walde, Die. W. Raabe. R 115
Leute von Seldwyla, Die. G. Keller. K 377
Leveller, The. J. M. Wilson. *in* W 2202 v16
Levison's victim. M. E. Maxwell. *in* M 1764
Lewis Arundel. F. E. Smedley. S 3227
Lianhau shee, The. W. Carleton. *in* C 554
Libussa. J. K. A. Musäus. *in* O 1001
Same. *in* M 4951
Licht- und schattenseiten des lebens. J. F. Smith.
  S 3505
Lichtenstein. W. Hauff. *in* H 1853
Lida Ann. P. Deming. *in* D 901
Liebe am Rhein, Die. F. L. August. A 2001
Liebe im grabe, Die. O. Müller. M 4407
Liebe, rache, reue. O. v. Plänckner. E 752
Liebe und ehe. A. L. Kielland. *in* K 1704
Liebe und handel. C. A. Wettergergh. W 1410
Liebe wonn' und weh', Der. A. Hofmeister. W 2451
Liebesbriefe aus dem leben eines gefangenen. F. Stahr.
  S 4669
Liebestreue. J. K. A. Musäus. *in* M 4951
Life and adventures of Robinson Crusoe. D. Defoe.
  Dx 252
Same. Dx 251
Same. *in* 820.2: 8 v7
Life episode, A. D. M. Craik. *in* C 2868
Life for a life, A. D. M. Craik. C 2861
Life, here and there. N. P. Willis. W 2002
Life in Dalecarlia. F. Bremer. B 3155
Life in the iron-mills. R. H. Davis. *in* A 1879
Life in the new world. C. Sealsfield. S 2202
Life magnet, The. A. A. Adee. *in* S 35 v8
Life of a planter, The. C. Sealsfield. *in* S 2202
Life of vicissitudes, A. G. P. R. James. J 228
Life struggle. J. Pardoe. P 401
Life's aftermath. E. Marshall. M 1302
Life's atonement, A. D. C. Murray. M 4876
Life's secret, A. E. P. Wood. W 2562
Lifted veil, The. M. Cross, (*George Eliot*). C 3154
Ligeia. E. A. Poe. *in* 820.1: 5 v3
Light and a dark christmas, A. E. P. Wood. W 2563
Light and shade. H. N. W. Baker. Bx 160
Light and shade. A. H. Drury. D 1952
Light and shade. C. G. O'Brien. O 101
Light man, A. H. James, *jr.* *in* S 35 v5
Light on the hearth, The. C. Hamley. *in* T 177 v5
Light on the lily. E. Marshall. Mx 454
Lightning-rod man, The. H. Melville. *in* M 2253
Lights and shadows of the early dawn. E. Charles.
  in C 955
Like a gentleman. M. A. Denison. D 1055
Like father, like son. J. Payn. P 814
Like ships upon the sea. F. E. Trollope. T 1754
Lilliput legends. Lx 21
Lilies of the valley, The. G. C. Fullerton. F 1805
Lily's quest, The. N. Hawthorne. *in* H 2057 v2
Limerick gloves, The. M. Edgeworth. *in* E 402
Lina Fernie. H. Parr. *in* P 464
Lindsay's luck. F. H. Burnett. B 4255
Links in Rebecca's life. I. M. Alden. A 702
Linley Rochford. J. McCarthy. M 104
Linton lairds, The. A. Leighton. *in* W 2202 v4
Linwoods, The. C. M. Sedgwick. S 2252
Lion Ben. E. Kellogg. Kx 205
Lion of Flanders, The. H. Conscience. C 2262
Lionel Lincoln. J. F. Cooper. C 2862
Lionizing. E. A. Poe. *in* 820.1: 5 v3
Little Anna. M. Wulff. Wx 1451
Little Annie's ramble. N. Hawthorne. *in* H 2057 v1
Little aversion, A. M. C. Hay. *in* H 2102
Little Barbara. G. M. Craik. *in* C 2911
Little barefoot, The. B. Auerbach. A 1953
Little brother. F. H. Ludlow. L 2101
Little Briggs and I. F. H. Ludlow. *in* L 2101
Same. *in* J 926 v11
Little Brown-Top. E. A. Rand. Rx 178

Little camp on Eagle Hill, The. S. Warner. Wx 201
Little coin, much care. M. Howitt. Mx 1255
Little Daffydowndilly. N. Hawthorne. *in* H 2059
Little dancing master, The. J. Kavanagh. *in* K 310
Little dinner at Timmins's, A. W. M. Thackeray.
  in T 662
Same. *in* T 665 v7
Little Dorrit. C. Dickens. D 1309
Little duke, The. C. M. Yonge. *in* Yx 303
Little folk in green. H. C. Wright. Wx 1351
Little folk life. M. A. Dodge. Dx 502
Little folks astray. R. S. Clarke. Cx 463 v1
Little gentleman in green. *Mrs.* G. H. Hepworth.
  Hx 801
Little Gibraltar. L. C. Moulton. *in* M 4102
Little good-for-nothing, The. A. Daudet. D 452
Little Gordon, The. F. Church. *in* C 1411
Little grandfather. R. S. Clarke. Cx 467
Little grandmother. R. S. Clarke. Cx 468
Little Jakey. S. H. De Kroyft. *in* J 926 v10
Little Joanna, The. E. W. Bellamy. B 1276
Little Karin. M. S. Schwartz. S 1914
Little lame prince, The. D. M. Craik. Cx 702
Little Loo. W. C. Russell. R 3309
Little Lucy's wonderful globe. C. M. Yonge. Yx 301
Little match girl, The. H. C. Andersen. Ax 754
Little men. L. M. Alcott. Ax 511
Little messenger birds, The. C. H. Butler. Bx 1051
Little miss Primrose. E. Stephenson. T 103
Little Mook. W. Hauff. Hx 552
Little moorland princess, The. E. John. J 902
Little Pansy. *Mrs.* Randolph. R 251
Little pitchers. R. S. Clarke. Cx 471
Little Prudy series. R. S. Clarke. Cx 451-Cx 456
Little Prudy's Fly-away series. R. S. Clarke.
  Cx 463-Cx 468
Little Pussy Willow. H. B. Stowe. Sx 1703
Little Rudy. H. C. Andersen. Ax 768
Little schoolmaster Mark, The. J. H. Shorthouse.
  S 2827
Little sister. L 31
Little stepson, A. F. Church. C 1409
Little Sunshine's holiday. D. M. Craik. Cx 703
Little traveller, A. S. O. Jewett. *in* J 804
Little upstart, A. W. H. Rideing. R 1426
Little violinist, The. T. B. Aldrich. *in* A 756
Little woman, A. E. Pratt. Px 770
Little women. L. M. Alcott. Ax 501
Live and let live. C. M. Sedgwick. S 2253
Live oak boys, The. E. Kellogg. Kx 204
Livergnas, Die. H. Villinger. W 1926
Living too fast. W. T. Adams. A 327
Liza. I. S. Turgenief. T 3103
Lizzie Leigh. E. C. Gaskell. G 411
Locke Amsden. D. P. Thompson. T 752
Locked in. M. C. Hay. *in* H 2106
Same. *in* H 2121
Loder, Der. H. T. v. Schmid. S 1412
Lodging for the night, A. R. L. Stevenson. S 5176
Lofty and the lowly, The. M. J. McIntosh. M 403
Log in the Archipelago, A. N. P. Willis. *in* W 2001 v2
Lola. A. Griffiths. *in* G 409
Lois the witch. E. C. Gaskell. G 2601
Lonely one, The. P. Heyse. *in* J 908
Lonely ride, A. F. B. Harte. *in* H 15
Long, long ago. E. S. Phelps. *in* P 1453
Long look house. E. Abbott. Ax 101
Long pack, The. J. Hogg. *in* H 3451 v3
Longest hour of my life. T. Hood. *in* 820.2: 36
Longstaff's marriage. H. James, *jr.* *in* J 809
Look before you leap. A. F. Hector. H 2208
Look to the end. S. S. Ellis. E 2102
Looking glass for the mind, The. A. Berquin. Bx 601
Looking in the glass. E. Simcox. *in* S 2976
Lookie. Der. J. F. Cooper. C 2468
Lorbeer und myrthe. H. C. Proschko. *in* V 2 v23
Lord and lady Harcourt. C. Sinclair. S 3101
Lord Brackenbury. A. B. Edwards. E 506
Lord Durie and Christie's will. A. Leighton.
  in W 2202 v2
Lord Erlistoun. D. M. Craik. C 2862
Lord Kames's puzzle. A. Leighton. *in* W 2202 v23
Lord Kilgobbin. C. J. Lever. L 1115
Lord mayor of London, The. W. H. Ainsworth. Ax 59
Lord Oakburn's daughters. E. P. Wood. W 2564
Lord of Harpington, The. J. Payn. *in* P 811 v1
Lord of Hermitage, The. A. Campbell. *in* W 2202 v19
Same. *in* W 2203 v3
Lord of himself. F. H. Underwood. U 301
Lord Richard and I. J. Sturgis. *in* S 5877
Same. *in* T 178 v1

x denotes books specially adapted for children.

x denotes books specially adapted for children.

x denotes books specially adapted for children.

x denotes books specially adapted for children.

Mrs. Keith's crime. **M 41**
Mrs. Knollys. F. J. Stimson. *in* **S 35 v2**
Mrs. Lirriper's legacy. C. Dickens *and others. in* **D 1328**
Mrs. Lirriper's lodgings. C. Dickens *and others.* **D 1328**
Mrs. Lorimer. *Mrs.* W. Harrison. **M 676**
Mrs. Macsimum's bill. F. J. O'Brien. *in* **P 2801**
Mrs. McWilliams and the lightning. S. L. Clemens.
in **C 1802**
Mrs. Merriam's scholars. E. E. Hale. **H 455**
Mistress of Ibichstein, The. F. Henkel. **H 5151**
Mrs. Overtheway's remembrances. J. H. Ewing.
Ex 252
Mrs. Peck's pudding. T. Hood. *in* **H 4026**
Same. *in* **820.2 : 36**
Mrs. Podgers' teapot. L. M. Alcott. *in* **A 652**
Mrs. Skaggs's husbands. F. B. Harte. **H 1554**
Mrs. Stanhope's last lodger. N. Perry. *in* **P 1352**
Mrs. Willoughby's octave. E. Marshall. **M 1309**
Misunderstood. F. Montgomery. **M 3201**
Mit eiserner hand. J. D. *in* **D 701**
Mitchelhurst Place. M. Veley. **V 503**
Miz-maze. The. F. Awdry *and others.* **A 2176**
Miss. F. B. Harte. *in* **H 1553**
Moby-Dick. H. Melville. **M 2252**
Model servant, A. A. E. Prentiss. *in* **P 2452**
Modelle. A. v. Winterfeld. **W 2258**
Modern accomplishments. C. Sinclair. **S 3102**
Modern Cinderella, A. L. M. Alcott. *in* **A 652**
Modern Delilah, A. J. Payn. *in* **P 811 v2**
Modern Griselda. The. M. Edgeworth. *in* **E 405**
Modern Hagar, The. C. M. Clark. **C 1503**
Modern instance, A. W. D. Howells. **H 4761**
Modern magician, A. W. W. Story. *in* **T 177 v7**
Modern Mephistopheles, A. H. P. Spofford. **S 4403**
Modern Midas, A. M. Jókai. **J 1155**
Modern pilgrims. G. Wood. **W 2602**
Modern Sinbad, The. E. E. Hale. **H 451**
Moderne Eulenspiegel, Der. A. v. Tschabuschnigg.
T 1951
Moderne lebenswirren. T. Mundt. **M 4658**
Moderne sünden. E. A. Willkomm. **W 2058**
Moderne titanen. H. L. R. Gieske. **G 1051**
Mohammed Ali and his house. C. Mundt. **M 4580**
Mohicans, The. J. F. Cooper. **C 2461**
Mohicans of Paris, The. A. Dumas. **D 2281**
Mohikaner von Paris, Die. A. Dumas. **D 2281**
Molchko von Parma. K. E. Franzos. **F 1901**
Molly. J. Schayer. *in* **S 1016**
Molly Bawn. M. Argles. **A 1480**
Molly Carew. A. M. W. **W 3051**
Monaldi. W. Allston. **A 851**
Monarch of Mincing-Lane, The. W. Black. **B 2210**
Monastery, The. *Sir* W. Scott. **S 2015**
Mongrels. T. Wilton. **W 2276**
Monikins, The. J. F. Cooper. **C 2465**
Same, germ. **C 2465**
Monk of St. Anthony, The. A. Campbell. *in* **W 2202 v4**
Monks of Dryburgh, The. A. Campbell. *in* **W 2202 v4**
Monks of Thelema, The. W. Besant *and* J. Rice.
B 1764
Monomaniac, The. A. Leighton. *in* **W 2202 v18**
Monos and Daimonos. E. G. E. L. Bulwer-Lytton.
in **824.2 : 18 v3**
Monsieur du Miroir. N. Hawthorne. *in* **H 2054 v1**
Monsieur Maurice. A. B. Edwards. **E 508**
Monsieur Violet. F. Marryat. **M 1309**
Monsu Max. K. M. Sauer. *in* **V 2 v23**
Monte-Cristo. The count of. A. Dumas. **D 2258**
Montford. H. Lee. *in* **L 851 v1**
Moods. L. M. Alcott. **A 651**
Moonfolk. J. G. Austin. **Ax 901**
Moonstone, The. W. Collins. **C 2215**
Moosrosen. L. F. Stolle. **S 5518**
Mopsa the fairy. J. Ingelow. **Ix 101**
Mor Perczel. M. Jókai. *in* **J 1154**
Moral pirates, The. W. L. Alden. **Ax 551**
Moralische novellen. M. de Cervantes-Saavedra.
C 802
Mörder Wallenstein's, Die. G. K. Herlossohn. **H 2857**
More bed-time stories. L. C. Moulton. **Mx 902**
More old wives' fables. E. Laboulaye. **Lx 703**
Morella. E. A. Poe. *in* **820.1 : 5 v3**
Morgesons, The. E. D. B. Stoddard. **S 5451**
Moritz. E. Scribe. **S 2052**
Morley Ernstein. G. P. R. James. **J 232**
Mormonenmädchen, Das. B. Möllhausen. **M 3054**
Mormon's wife, The. **M 93**
Morning dream, The. J. Brougham. *in* **927.1 : 7**
Morning-glories. L. M. Alcott. **Ax 517**
Morte d'Arthur. *Sir* T. Malory. **813 : 7**
Mortlake. J. Maidment. *in* **W 2202 v8**
Same. *in* **W 2203 v3**
Morton. C. Sealsfield. **S 2204**

Morton's hope. J. L. Motley. **M 4052**
Mosaik. C. Spindler. **S 4315**
Mosaikarbeiter, Die. A. L. A. Dudevant. **D 2177**
Mossdale. A. M. De Jongh. **D 801**
Mosses from an old manse. N. Hawthorne. **H 2054**
Moss-side. M. V. Terhune. **T 614**
Mosstrooper, The. A. Campbell. *in* **W 2202 v12**
Mother and son, The. A. Opie. *in* **O 653**
Same. *in* **O 653 v8**
Mother Molly. F. M. Peard. **P 903**
Mother of Jacques, The. K. S. Macquoid. *in* **M 807**
Mother of Pearl. F. J. O'Brien. *in* **O 126**
Mother's recompense, The. G. Aguilar. **A 405**
Mouflou. L. de la Ramé. *in* **T 178 v2**
Mount Hope. G. H. Hollister. **H 3701**
Mount of sorrow, The. H. P. Spofford. *in* **S 35 v2**
Mount Royal. M. E. Maxwell. **M 1784**
Mountain road, The. L. C. Moulton. *in* **M 4101**
Mountain sprite's kingdom, The. E. H. Knatchbull-Hugessen. **Hx 1001**
Mountain storm, The. T. Gillespie. *in* **W 2202 v1**
Mountain's face, The. R. H. Boyesen. *in* **B 2856**
Mourmellieux und Carbonel. A. v. Winterfeld.
in **W 2261 v1**
Mouse and lion. E. E. Hale. *in* **H 451**
Mouth of the Leamy, The. C. M. Yonge. **Y 214**
Moy O'Brien. Melusine. **M 2151**
Mozart. H. Rau. **R 456**
Much coin, much care. A. Jameson. *in* **829.2 : 17**
Muckle John. **P 11**
Muddog papers, The. C. Dickens. **D 1312**
Mugby Junction. C. Dickens *and others.* **D 1324**
Mühle am schwarzen moor, Die. J. D. H. Temme.
T 558
Müller von Angibault, Der. A. L. A. Dudevant. **D 2178**
Multum in parvo. C. Reade. **R 616**
Mummy's foot, The. T. Gautier. *in* **G 604**
Mumu. I. S. Turgenief. **T 2111**
Münchener kindeln, Das. H. v. Schmid. **S 1414**
Münchhausen. K. L. Immermann. **I 101**
Munster circuit, The. J. R. O'Flanagan. **O 201**
Muntere lebensbilder. C. Spindler. **S 4316**
Murad, the unlucky. M. Edgeworth. *in* **J 926 v12**
Same. *in* **E 403**
Murder considered as one of the fine arts. T. De Quincey.
in **J 926 v2**
Murder of the archbishop of Paris, The. W. Collins.
in **C 2208**
Murder will out. A. Opie. *in* **O 653**
Same. *in* **O 653 v2**
Murderer's last night, The. T. Doubleday. *in* **T 178 v7**
Murders in the rue Morgue, The. E. A. Poe.
in **J 926 v3**
Same. *in* **820.1 : 5 v3**
Murphy's master. J. Payn. **P 817**
Musikalische märchen, phantasien und skizzen. E. Polko.
P 2005
Muss ma cussalin. L. Ziemssen. **Z 177**
Musste es sein ? C. Bauer. **B 654**
Mutter, Eine. F. Gerstäcker. **G 729**
Mutter Hiob. H. Conscience. **C 2255**
Mutter und sohn. A. Linz. **L 1476**
Mutter und tochter. E. Wichert. *in* **V 2 v37**
Mutter vom lande, Eine. J. Rank. **R 355**
Mütze und krone. H. T. v. Schmid. **S 1415**
My after-dinner adventures with Peter Schlemihl.
in **T 177 v9**
My aunt Pontypool. G. P. R. James. **J 250**
My black cat. J. M. Wilson. *in* **W 2202 v2**
My blind sister. H. Parr. *in* **P 469**
My bonnie lass. C. V. Hamilton. **H 902**
My boys. L. M. Alcott. **Ax 502**
My brother Robert. H. Parr. *in* **P 469**
My brother's wife. A. B. Edwards. **E 509**
My châteaux. G. W. Curtis. *in* **J 926 v4**
My college friends. H. Jay. *in* **J 176 v4,6**
My cnaughtt cousins. H. Jay. **J 502**
My contraband. L. M. Alcott. *in* **A 652**
My courtship and its consequences. H. Wikoff. **W 1751**
My cousin Nicholas. R. H. Barham. **B 351**
My cousin's clients. W. Clarke. *in* **C 1676**
My daughter Elinor. F. L. Benedict. **B 1307**
My Desire. S. Warner. **W 830**
My double and how he undid me. E. E. Hale. *in* **H 452**
Same. *in* **A 1876**
My ducats and my daughter. Hay Hunter *and* Walter Whyte. **M 93**
My enemy's daughter. J. McCarthy. **M 106**
My english acquaintance. F. Hardman. *in* **T 176 v7**
My financial operation. J. Payn. *in* **P 812**
My first client. F. J. Fargus. *in* **F 2003**
My first offer. M. C. Hay. **H 2107**
Same. *in* **H 2118**

x denotes books specially adapted for children.

My first recordership. J. Payn. *in* P 811 v1
My friend, mrs. Angel. J. Schayer. *in* S 1016
My friend the dutchman. F. Hardman. *in* T 176 v6
Same. *in* S 551
My friend the tramp. F. B. Harte. *in* H 1551
My friends and I. J. Sturgis. S 5877
My girls. L. M. Alcott. Ax 505
My heart's in the Highlands. M. M. Grant. G 1951
My hunt of the silver fox. W. B. Cheadle. *in* T 177 v10
My husband's mother. L. Curtis. *in* P 2801
My inheritance. L. C. Moulton. *in* M 4101
My intimate enemy. — Ormirod. O 751
My investment in the far west. *in* T 177 v12
My Kalulu. H. M. Stanley. S 4701
My lady Green Sleeves. H. Reeves. R 3504
My lady Ludlow. E. C. Gaskell. G 405
Same. *in* G 411
My lady's money. W. Collins. C 2216
My little girl. W. Besant *and* J. Rice. B 1765
My little lady. E. F. Poynter. P 2353
My little love. M. V. Terhune. T 609
My love. E. L. Linton. L 1453
My marriage. M 91
My miscellanies. W. Collins. C 2217
My mother and I. D. M. Craik. C 2864
My Nannie O. N. Perry. *in* P 1352
My novel. E. G. E. L. Bulwer-Lytton. B 4018
My only novel. M. C. Hay. *in* H 2112
Same. *in* H 2121
"My own child." F. Church. C 1413
My own experience. W. Besant *and* J. Rice. *in* B 1762
My own story. M. Howitt. Hx 1257
My Paris masters. E. D. Gerard. *in* T 176 v2
My poor wife. J. Sturgis. *in* S 5877
My sister Jeannie. A. L. A. Dudevant. D 2179
My spinsters. W. Collins. *in* C 2217
Same. *in* C 2223
My story. K. S. Macquoid. M 605
My third book. L. C. Moulton. M 4101
My three conversations with miss Chester. F. B. Perkins. P 1151
Same. *in* P 2801
My tourmaline. Saxe Holm. *in* S 3753 v2
My trivial life. M 92
My uncle Hobson and I. P. Jones. J 1201
My uncle, the clockmaker. M. Howitt. Hx 1258
My uncle, the curate. M. W. Savage. S 802
My uncle Toby. L. Sterne. S 5151
My unlucky friend. M. E. Maxwell. *in* M 1764
My watch below. W. C. Russell. R 3305
My wife and I. H. B. Stowe. S 5654
My wife and my wife's sister. M 90
My wife's tempter. F. J. O'Brien. *in* O 126
My window. W. Collins. *in* C 2206
My young Alcides. C. M. Yonge. Y 217
Myddleton Pomfret. W. H. Ainsworth. A 576
Mysie Craig, The story of. A. Leighton. *in* W 2202 v23
Mysteries of Heron Dyke, The. M 95
Mysterious bride, The. J. Hogg. *in* H 3451 v4
Mysterious disappearance, The. *in* W 2202 v10
Mysterious lodger, The. J. Kavanagh. *in* K 310
Mysterious sketch, The. E. Erckmann *and* A. Chatrian. *in* E 1205
Mysterious stranger, The. A. Opie. *in* O 653 v1
Mystery, A. A. Cudlip. *in* C 3312 v2
Mystery of Edwin Drood. C. Dickens. D 1313
Mystery of Joe Morgan, The. W. Besant *and* J. Rice. *in* B 1762
Mystery of Marie Roget, The. E. A. Poe. *in* 820.1: 5 v3
Mystery of Metropolisville, The. E. Eggleston. E 654
Mystery of the locks, The. E. W. Howe. H 4737

Nabob at home, The. *Mrs.* Monkland. M 3101
Nabob, The. F. Daudet. D 453
Nach Amerika. F. Gerstäcker. G 719
Nach dem grossen kriege. W. Raabe. R 117
Nach der ersten liebe. K. Frenzel. F 1554
Nach der flut. C. G. v. Berneck. B 1532
Nach der natur. R. G. S. v. Hauenschild. H 1802
Nach uns die sündfluth. M. v. Schlägel. *t*S 1301
Nach zwanzig jahren. P. Lange. L 506
Nachbarn, Die. F. Bremer. B 3157
Nachlese in und ausser mir. N 1
Nachsommer, Der. A. Stifter. S 5302
Nacht und morgen. E. G. E. L. Bulwer-Lytton. B 4019
Nachtigal, Die. J. C. v. Schmid. *in* S 1456
Nachtstücke. E. T. A. Hoffmann. H 3355
Name, Ein. C. A. Wetterbergh. W 1411
Nameless graves. K. E. Franzos. *in* F 1903
Nameless nobleman, A. J. G. Austin. A 2101
Namenlose geschichten. F. W. Hackländer. H 309

Namenlosen, Die. W. Jensen. J 702
Nan. S. C. F. Hallowell. Hx 301
Nan. L. C. Lillie. Lx 302
Nan. L. B. Walford. *in* T 177 v1
Nancy. R. Broughton. B 3452
Nancy Blynn's lovers. J. T. Trowbridge. *in* T 1852
Nanette and her lovers. T. Gwynne. G 3151
Naomi. *Mrs.* J. B. Webb. W 1101
Napoleon. J. G. Lockhart. *in* T 176 v1
Napoleon and Blücher. C. Mundt. M 4582
Napoleon and the queen of Prussia. C. Mundt. M 4581
Napoleon in Egypten. L. F. Stolle. S 5519
Napoleon und der Wiener congress. C. Mundt.
Napoleon und fürst Blücher. C. Mundt. M 4583
Napoleon und könign Louise. C. Mundt. M 4581
Narration of certain uncommon things that did formerly happen to me, Herbert Willis, B. D. *in* T 176 v7
Narrative of prince Charlie's escape. *in* T 177 v10
Narrow escape, A. A. Cudlip. C 3303
Natalie. E. V. Hallett. V 251
Nathalie. J. Kavanagh. K 307
Nathalie Marsh. M. A. Fleming. F 1501
Natolian story teller, The. *in* T 176 v11
Natural history of idiots, The. T. Gillespie. *in* W 2202 v13
Nature's magic lantern. J. Hogg. *in* H 3451 v3
Nature's nobleman. M 5
Nature's serial story. E. P. Roe. R 2312
Natürliche tochter, Die. H 4
Neal Malone. W. Carleton. *in* J 926 v5
Near to nature's heart. E. P. Roe. R 2305
Nearer and dearer. E. Bradley. B 3001
Neben dem heerdfeuer. N. Misasi. *in* M 2826
Neblitt. E. S. Phelps. *in* P 1453
Necklace of princess Florimonde, The. M. D. Morgan. Dx 326
Ned Geraghty. J. Brougham. *in* 927.1: 7
Ned McKeown. W. Carleton. *in* C 554
Ned Musgrave. T. E. Hook. H 4053
Neighbors, The. F. Bremer. B 3157
Neighbors of an old irish boy. W. Clarke. *in* C 1676
Neighbors' wives. J. T. Trowbridge. T 1857
Nell. B. H. Buxton. B 4452
Nella. F. Stahr. S 4672
Nellie's memories. R. N. Carey. C 401
Nelly Brooks. F. Church. C 1414
Nelly Kinnard's kingdom. A. M. Douglas. Dx 452
Nelly's silver mine. H. M. Jackson. Jx 102
Nemesis. H. v. Hülsen. H 1678
Nemesis. J. Scherr. S 1108
Nemesis. M. V. Terhune. T 610
Nena Sahib. H. O. F. Gödsche. G 1378
Nenuphar, a fancy. *in* T 177 v12
Neptune vase, The. V. W. Johnson. J 1001
Nest der zaunkönige, Das. G. Freytag. F 1608
Nestlenook. L. Kip. K 801
Nettie Dunkayne. M. C. Hay. *in* H 2107
Same. *in* H 2118
Neue abendgenossen. O. v. Plänckner. E 753
Neue Cäsar, Der. L. F. Stolle. S 5520
Neue empfindsame reisen. L. Rellstab. R 604
Neue garnisonsgeschichten. A. v. Winterfeld. W 2260
Neue generation, Die. I. S. Turgenief. T 2109
Neue geschichten. E. Höfer. H 3307
Neue geschichten. L. Kompert. K 1203
Neue Hiob, Der. L. v. Sacher-Masoch. S 107
Neue humoristische soldatengeschichten. A. v. Winterfeld. W 2261
Neue novellen. A. E. Brachvogel. B 2905
Neue novellen. W. Jensen. J 703
Neue propheten. K. Wartenburg. W 1002
Neue sündfluth, Die. J. Rodenberg. R 2151
Neue welt, Eine. W. R. Heller. H 2329
Neuer adel. A. Meissner. M 2056
Neuer Falstaff, Ein. A. E. Brachvogel. B 2904
Neuer glaube, Ein. E. A. J. Lobedanz. L 1551
Neuer Polykrates, Ein. H. Wachenhusen. W 155
Neues leben. B. Auerbach. A 1963
Neues leben. T. Mügge. M 4208
Neues novellenbuch. W. H. Riehl. R 1551
Neuland. I. S. Turgenief. T 2107
Never again. W. S. Mayo. M 1953
Never too late. C. Burdette. Bx 951
Nevilles von Garretstown, Die. C. Lever. L 1118
New Abelard, The. R. Buchanan. B 3555
New Adam and Eve, The. N. Hawthorne. *in* H 2054 v2
New arabian nights. R. L. Stevenson. S 5176
New bed-time stories. L. C. Moulton. Mx 903
New boy at Styles's, The. W. Collins. *in* C 2206
New Endymion, The. J. Hawthorne. *in* H 2005 v2
New England winter, A. H. James. *in* J 313

x denotes books specially adapted for children.

x denotes books specially adapted for children.

x denotes books specially adapted for children.

x denotes books specially adapted for children.

x denotes books specially adapted for children.

x denotes books specially adapted for children.

x denotes books specially adapted for children.

x denotes books specially adapted for children.

x denotes books specially adapted for children.

Schoolfellows, The. O. Richardson.   *in* W 2202 v11
Schoolmesters reis' nah'r arvschaft. W. Schröder.
   S 1752
Schoolmistress abroad, The. T. Hood.   *in* H 4026
  Same.   *in* 820.2 : 36
Schubert und seine zeitgenossen. A. E. Brachvogel.
   B 2909
Schödderump, Der. W. Raabe.   R 119
Schuld und sühne. E. A. König.   K 1258
Schultheissentöchter, Die. L. Peters.   P 2903
Schuster Lange. E. Wichert.   W 1604
Schutzgeist, Der. A. W. Engelen.   A 1351
Schutzlos, aber nicht hülflos. J. A. Brökel.   B 3301
Schwägerinnen, Die. H. W. Hanke.   H 1107
Schwalberl, Das. H. T. v. Schmid.   S 1416
Schwärmer, Der. C. Spindler.   S 4319
Schwarze bret, Das. W. R. Heller.   H 2332
Schwarze Mare, Die. J. D. H. Temme.   T 560
Schwarze tulpe, Die. A. Dumas.   D 2287
Schwarze und weise. G. Oelsner-Monmerqué.   O 602
Schwarzwälder dorfgeschichten. B. Auerbach.   A 1965
Schweden-schatz, Der. H. Wachenhusen.   W 163
Schwedische lebensbilder. M. S. Schwartz.   S 1912
Schwester, Die. H. W. Hanke.   H 1108
Schwester, Die. L. Schücking.   S 1831
Schwestern, Die. G. Ebers.   E 255
Scientific vagabond, A. H. H. Boyesen.   *in* B 2855
Sclaverei in Amerika. F. A. Strubberg.   S 5802
Sclaverei in dem lande der freiheit. H. B. Stowe.
   S 5681
Scotch story, A. M. A. Barker.   *in* B 376
Scotsman's tale, The. H. Lee.   *in* L 851 v2
Scottish chiefs, The. J. Porter.   P 2201
Scottish hunters of Hudson's Bay, The. H. Miller.
   in W 2202 v12
Scottish orphans, The. M. Blackford.   Bx 752
Scottish veteran, The. J. Howell.   *in* W 2202 v12
Scouring of the white horse, The. T. Hughes.   Hx 1053
Scout, The. W. G. Simms.   S 3002
Sculptor of Bruges, The. D. M. Craik.   *in* C 2868
Sea breezes.   Sx 25
Sea change, A. F. L. Shaw.   Sx 903
Sea fight, The.   *in* W 2202 v19
Sea lions, The. J. F. Cooper.   C 2475
Sea queen, A. W. C. Russell.   R 3307
Sea skirmish, The.   *in* W 2202 v20
Sea storm, The. O. Richardson.   *in* W 2202 v12
Sea-totaller, A. T. Hood.   *in* 820.2 : 36
Seaboard parish, The. G. Macdonald.   M 263
Sealed orders. E. S. Phelps.   P 1453
Seamy side, The. W. Besant *and* J. Rice.   B 1766
Seaward's narrative, Sir Edward. J. Porter.   P 2202
Sebastian. M. E. Maxwell.   *in* M 1764
Sebastian. K. Cooper.   S 701
Sebastian Strome. J. Hawthorne.   H 2004
Second life, A. A. F. Hector.   H 2211
Second marriage, The. C. Burdett.   B 4201
Second thoughts. R. Broughton.   B 3455
Second wife, The. E. John.   J 912
Secret chamber, The. M. O. Oliphant.   *in* T 177 v1
Secret of the Andes, The. F. Hassaurek.   H 1701
Secret of the Stradivarius, The. F. J. Fargus.
   in F 2008
Secret passion, The. R. F. Williams.   W 1952
Seed-time and harvest. F. Reuter.   R 953
Seehof, Der. F. Stahr.   S 4676
Seeker, The. J. M. Wilson.   *in* W 2202 v21
Seelenfänger, Der. J. Rank.   R 360
Seelengemälde, Ein. E. T. Merx.   M 2401
Seelöwen, Die. J. F. Cooper.   C 2475
Seer's cave. The. W. Hetherington.   *in* W 2202 v6
Seherin der hochlande, Die. W. Sommers.   S 3851
Sein guter engel. L. F. Henning.   H 2501
Sein ideal. J. Rank.   R 356
Sein oder nichtsein. H. C. Andersen.   A 1005
Sein und nichtsein. G. Höcker.   H 3202
Selbst. C. G. F. Gore.   G 1560
Select party, A. N. Hawthorne.   *in* H 2054 v1
Self-devotion. I. Campbell.   C 201
Self-sacrifice. M. O. Oliphant.   O 491
Self-seer, The. D. M. Craik.   *in* C 2868
Selim. J. K. Paulding.   *in* T 186
Seltsame geschichten. A. Meissner.   M 2060
Seltsame geschichten. E. A. Poe.   P 1976
Seltsame leiden eines theater-direktors. E. T. A. Hoff-
mann.   H 3357
Semi-detached house, The. E. Eden.   E 351
Sendung, Die. F. Marryat.   M 1207
Senior partner, The. C. E. L. Riddell.   R 1352
Senior songman, The. E. Stephenson.   T 107
Sennor Aguilar. F. Gerstäcker.   G 722
Sense and sensibility. J. Austen.   A 2054
  Same, [condensed].   *in* A 2055

Sentimental journey, A. L. Sterne.   *in* 820.2 : 20 v 1, 2
Septimius Felton. N. Hawthorne.   H 2056
  Same.   *in* 914.2 : 26
Serapions-brüder, Die. E. T. A. Hoffmann.   H 3358
Serapis. G. Ebers.   E 259
Serf, The. E. Souvestre.   *in* S 4053
Sergeant Barnacle. W. G. Simms.   *in* S 3009
Serjeant's tales. The. J. Howell.   *in* W 2202
Servant girl of the period. The. C. Chamberlain. C 851
Settlers in Canada, The. F. Marryat.   M 1215
Seven conversations of dear Jones and baby Van Rensse-
laer. B. Matthews *and* H. C. Bunner.   *in* M 1501
Seven daughters. A. M. Douglas.   Dx 651
Seven little people. H. E. Scudder.   Sx 705
Seven marriages. A. F. Langbein.   *in* B 2451
Seven sons of mammon, The. G. A. Sala.   S 401
Seven stories. D. G. Mitchell.   M 2855
Seven to seventeen. M. M. Bell.   B 551
Seven vagabonds. The. N. Hawthorne.   *in* H 2057 v2
Seven years. J. Kavanagh.   K 310
Seven years' dearth, The. J. Howell.   *in* W 2202 v14
Sevenoaks. J. G. Holland.   H 3655
Severa. E. Hartner.   H 1626
Shabby genteel story, A. W. M. Thackeray.   T 662
  Same.   *in* T 665 v7
Shadow in the corner, The. M. E. Maxwell.   *in* M 1790
Shadow of a crime, The. T. H. Caine.   C 167
Shadow of Ashlydyat, The. E. P. Wood.   W 2573
Shadow of death, The. E. Simcox.   *in* S 2976
Shadow of Moloch mountain, The. J. G. Austin.
   A 2103
Shadow of the door, The.   *in* T 177 v8
Shadow of the sword, The. R. Buchanan.   B 3852
Shadow on the threshold, A. M. C. Hay.   *in* H 2130
Shadowed perils. M. A. Avery.   A 2151
Shadows of Shasta. C. H. Miller.   M 2702
Shaker bridal, The. N. Hawthorne.   *in* H 2057 v2
Shakspeare and his friends. R. F. Williams.   W 1953
Shakspeare, The youth of. R. F. Williams.   W 1954
Shakspeare's funeral. E. B. Hamley.   *in* T 177 v1
Shandon bells. W. Black.   B 2216
Shane Fadh's wedding. W. Carleton.   *in* C 554
Shawl-straps. L. M. Alcott.   Ax 503
She'll all the world to me. T. H. Caine.   C 166
She loves and lies. W. Collins.   *in* T 178 v4
Shepherd of Salisbury plain, The. H. More.
   in 820.2 : 28 v1
Shepherd-king, The. C. M. Tucker.   Tx 904
Shepherds all and maidens fair. W. Besant *and* J. Rice.
   in B 1769
Shepherd's calendar. J. Hogg.   *in* H 3451 v3, 4
Shepherd's wedding. A. J. Hogg.   *in* H 3451 v2
Sherbrooke. H. B. Talcot.   T 153
Sherlocks, The. J. Saunders.   S 663
Sherringham's wife. A. Cudlip.   *in* C 3312 v3
Shilling's worth of sherry, A. W. H. Hughes.   H 4826
Ship of '49, A. F. B. Harte.   *in* H 1569
Shirley. C. Nicholls.   N 403
Shoemaker's village. W. B. Rands.   R 301
Shoepac recollections. O. B. Willox.   W 1851
Short mystery, A. B. W. Procter.   *in* 824.2 : 77 v1
Shylock of Barnow, The. K. E. Franzos.   *in* F 1903
Sibyl's disappointment. H. Parr.   *in* F 464
Sidonie. A. Daudet.   D 455
Sieben erzählungen. J. C. v. Schmid.   S 1468
Sieben legenden. G. Keller.   K 379
Sieben winterabende. W. R. Heller.   H 2333
Siege of Algiers, The. F. H. K. de La Motte Fouqué.
   in L 357
Siege of Berlin, The. A. Daudet.   *in* T 178 v4
Siege of London, The. H. James, *jr.*   J 812
Siege of Roxburgh, The. J. Hogg.   *in* H 3451 v6
Siegwart. J. M. Miller.   M 2726
Sieur George. G. W. Cable.   *in* C 103
Sights and insights. A. D. T. Whitney.   W 1458
Sights from a steeple. N. Hawthorne.   *in* H 2057 v1
Sigismund. G. Griffin.   G 2655
Sigismund Fatello.   *in* G 2551 v5
Signal man, The. C. Dickens.   *in* T 176 v8
Signor Formica. E. T. A. Hoffmann.   *in* H 3359 v1
Signor Monaldini's niece. M. A. Tincker.   T 1108
Silas Marner. M. Cross, *(George Eliot).*   C 3159
Silberne hochzeit, Die. S. Kohn.   K 1102
Silcote of Silcotes. H. Kingsley.   K 706
Silent partner, The. E. S. Phelps.   P 1454
Silent witness, A. E. Yates.   Y 106
Silver cañon, The. G. M. Fenn.   Fx 203
Silver city, The. F. A. Ober.   Ox 101
Silver cord, The. C. S. Brooks.   B 3427
Silver medal, The. J. T. Trowbridge.   Tx 814
Silver pitchers. L. M. Alcott.   Ax 514

   x denotes books specially adapted for children.

x denotes books specially adapted for children.

x denotes books specially adapted for children.

x denotes books specially adapted for children.

x denotes books specially adapted for children.

x denotes books specially adapted for children.

· **x** denotes books specially adapted for children.

x denotes books specially adapted for children.

Widow Baker. R. W. Raymond.	*in* R 576
Widow Lerouge, The. E. Gaboriau.	G 104
Widow Mérand, The. K. S. Macquoid.	*in* M 607
Widow of Dunskaith. H. Miller.	*in* W 2202 v3
Widow of Windsor, A. A. Gaskell.	G 351
Widow's ae son, The. J. M. Wilson.	*in* W 2202 v23
Wie ein lustspiel entsteht und vergeht. P. Lindau.	L 1353
Wie einer ein wahlfischfänger wurde. P. F. W. Oertel.	*in* O 853
Wie ich meine kleine garnison wiedersah. A. v. Winterfeld.	*in* W 2261 v1
Wie mein freund Dumbart sein examen machte. A. v. Winterfeld.	*in* W 2260 v7
Wie seine grossmutter. K. v. Schwartzkoppen.	*in* S 1926
Wieben-Peter. C. A. v. Wachsmann.	*in* S 4301
Wiedergefundene tochter, Die. W. Herchenbach.	H 2781
Wiederkehr, Die.	W 11
Wieland. C. B. Brown.	B 3504
Wiener hofgeschichten. L. v. Sacher-Masoch.	S 108
Wife of a vain man, The. M. S. Schwartz.	S 1908
Wife of Lochmaben, The. J. Hogg.	*in* H 3451 v2
Wife or the wuddy, A. J. M. Wilson.	*in* W 2202 v2
Same.	*in* W 2203 v1
Wife's tale. The. H. Lee.	*in* L 851 v1
Wigwam and the cabin, The. W. G. Simms.	S 3009
Wild adventures in wild places. G. Stables.	S 4576
Wild Hyacinth. *Mrs.* Randolph.	R 253
Wild scenes in the forest and prairie. C. F. Hoffmann.	H 3826
Wild sports of the west. W. H. Maxwell.	H 1851
Wild swans, The. H. C. Andersen.	Ax 761
Wild woods life. C. A. J. Farrar.	Fx 177
Wilddieb, Der. F. Gerstäcker.	G 728
Wilderness and warpath. J. Hall.	H 701
Wildes blut. B. Möllhausen.	*in* V 2 38
Wildfeuer. C. G. v. Berneck.	B 1534
Wildpfarrer, Der. O. Müller.	M 4410
Wildschützen, Die. W. Herchenbach.	H 2782
Wilfrid Cumbermede. G. Macdonald.	M 268
Wilhelm. A. v. Sternberg.	S 5061
Wilhelm Meister. J. W. v. Göthe.	G 1653
Wilhelmina. C. M. Woolson.	*in* W 2751
Will, The. M. Edgeworth.	*in* E 402
Will Denbigh, nobleman. E. Fox.	F 1452
Will-o'-the wisp, The. H. C. Andersen.	Ax 760
Will-o'-the wisps, The. M. Petersen.	Px 401
Will Weatherhelm. W. H. G. Kingston.	Kx 466
Wille zum leben, Der. A. Wilbrandt.	*in* V 2 v35
William Henry and his friends. A. M. Diaz.	Dx 452
William Henry letters, The. A. M. Diaz.	Dx 451
William Hogarth. A. E. Brachvogel.	B 2910
William Wighton, The fortunes of.	*in* W 2202 v2
William Wilson. E. A. Poe.	*in* 820.1 : 5 v3
Willie. P. Deming.	*in* D 901
Willie Smith, Autobiography of. A. Campbell.	*in* W 2202 v3
Willie Wastle's account of his wife. J. M. Wilson.	*in* W 2202 v18
Willis the pilot.	Wx 41
Willow Brook. S. Warner.	Wx 202
Wilmingtons, The. A. C. Marsh-Caldwell.	M 1261
Winborough boys, The. H. C. Adams.	Ax 205
Wind-spirit and rain-goddess, The. P. E. de Musset.	Mx 1101
Windsor Castle. W. H. Ainsworth.	A 563
Windsor Schloss. Das. W. H. Ainsworth.	A 563
Wing-and-Wing, The. J. F. Cooper.	C 2481
Wings and things. C. M. Tucker.	*in* Tx 906
Winifred. L. E. Guernsey.	G 2777
Winifred Bertram. E. Charles.	C 962
Winifred's wooing. G. M. Craik.	C 2913
Winning his spurs. E. Kellogg.	Kx 214
Winning his way. S. C. Coffin.	Cx 801
Winter drive, A. S. O. Jewett.	*in* J 803
Winter in Spitzbergen. C. Hildebrandt.	Hx 826
Winter wedding, A. H. Parr.	*in* P 464
Winterbuch. C. Spindler.	S 4324
Winterspenden. C. Spindler.	S 4325
Winterzeitvertreib. C. Spindler.	S 4326
Wise woman, The. G. Macdonald.	Mx 155
Witch Hampton Hall.	*in* T 177 v3
Witcherley ways.	*in* T 177 v10
Witching hour, The. M. Argles.	*in* A 1483
With costs. *Mrs.* M. W. Newman.	N 352
With Cupid's eyes. F. Church.	C 1425
With fate against him. A. M Douglas.	D 1809
With harp and crown. W. Besant *and* J. Rice.	B 1754
With the entrée. F. B. Harte.	*in* H 1551
Within an ace. *Mrs.* C. Jenkin.	J 605
Within an inch of his life. E. Gaboriau.	G 105

Within sea-walls. E. H. Walshe *and* G. E. Sargent.	W 426
Within sound of the sea. C. L. H. Dempster.	D 1003
Within the capes. H. Pyle.	P 3076
Within the clasp. J. B. Harwood.	H 1654
Within the maze. E. P. Wood.	M 2677
Within the precincts. M. O. Oliphant.	O 482
Without a home. E. P. Roe.	R 2808
Without authorisation. L. Kompert.	*in* K 1205
Without dowry. E. About.	*in* S 551
Without kith or kin. G. M. Craik.	C 2914
Wittwe und ihre kinder, Die. M. S. Schwartz.	S 1909
Wittwen, Die. H. W. Hanke.	H 1111
Wives and daughters. E. C. Gaskell.	G 408
Wives of the dead, The. N. Hawthorne.	*in* H 2059
Wizard's son, The. M. O. Oliphant.	O 489
"Woe to us when we lose the watery wall". *in* T 176 v4	
Wohnungsucher, Die. A. v. Winterfeld.	W 2254
Wolf at the door, The.	W 41
Wolf in sheep's clothing, The.	*in* P 2802
Wolf run. E. Kellogg.	Kx 224
Wolfert's Rust. W. Irving.	I 405
Wolfert Webber. W. Irving.	*in* I 402
Wölfinnen von Machecoul, Die. A. Dumas.	D 2295
Wolfram. O. Lautenschlager.	L 2304
Wolfsführer, Der. A. Dumas.	D 2296
Woman-hater, A. C. Reade.	R 814
Woman in the case, A. B. Turner.	T 2201
Woman in white, The. W. Collins.	C 2226
Woman of business, The. M. W. Savage.	S 804
Woman of honor, A. H. C. Bunner.	B 4751
Woman to the rescue. T. S. Arthur.	A 1759
Woman who saved him, The. F. W. Robinson.	*in* R 1858
Woman with the white mice, The. A. Leighton.	*in* W 2202 v21
Woman with two words, The. H. Keddie.	Kx 126
Woman's friendship. G. Aguilar.	A 407
Woman's kingdom, The. D. M. Craik.	C 2871
Woman's love and a wife's duty, A. A. Opie.	*in* O 653 v4
Woman's pulpit, A. E. S. Phelps.	*in* P 1453
Woman's reason, A. W. D. Howells.	H 4763
Woman's story, A. C. V. Hamilton.	*in* H 903
Woman's vengeance, A. J. Payn.	P 822
Woman's whims. J. X. B. Santine.	S 352
Woman's word, A. V. F. Townsend.	T 1456
Women are strange. F. W. Robinson.	R 1859
Won. B. H. Buxton.	B 4453
Wonder-book. N. Hawthorne.	Hx 701
Wonder stories. H. C. Andersen.	Ax 751
Wonderful glass, The. E. Erckmann *and* A. Chatrian.	*in* E 1205
Wonderful history of Peter Schlemihl, The. A. v. Chamisso.	*in* 830.1 : 8
Wonders in the Spessart, The. K. Immermann.	*in* I 1001
Wondersmith, The. F. J. O'Brien.	*in* O 126
Wontus. W. M. Runkel.	R 3151
Wood magic. R. Jefferies.	Jx 151
Woodcraft. W. G. Simms.	S 3003
Woodland notes. R. A. Gustafsson.	Gx 253
Woodman, The. G. P. R. James.	J 246
Woodnook wells, The. M. *and* M. Howitt.	*in* H 4801
Woodstock. *Sir* W. Scott.	S 2026
Wooed and married. R. N. Carey.	C 408
Wooing of the water-witch, The. E. Daldorne.	Dx 901
Wooing o't, The. A. F. Hector.	H 2206
Wool-gatherer, The. J. Hogg.	*in* H 3451 v4
Word, only a word, A. G. Ebers.	E 258
Work. L. M. Alcott.	Ax 516
Work and wages. M. Howitt.	Hx 1264
Workman and soldier. J. F. Cobb.	*in* V 1976
World as it goes, The. Voltaire.	*in* V 1051
World as it is, The. E. G. E. L. Bulwer-Lytton.	*in* 824.2 : 18 v3
World she awoke in, The. L. Alldridge.	A 802
World we live in, The. O. Crawfurd.	C 3201
World well lost, The. E. L. Linton.	L 1458
Worst boy in town, The. J. Habberton.	Hx 102
Wort, Ein. G. Ebers.	*in* V 2 v30
Worth and wealth. Cousin Angie.	Ax 726
Wortlebank diary. The. H. Parr.	P 469
Wraith of Barnjum, The. F. A. Guthrie.	*in* A 1328
Wreck of the "Grosvenor", The. W. C. Russell.	R 3304
Wreck of the Pioneer, The. C. Barnard.	*in* B 401
Wreck of the Red Bird, The. G. C. Eggleston.	Ex 154
Wreck of the Strathmore, The. F. W.	*in* T 177 v8
Wrecked. W. O. Stoddard.	S 5503
Wrecked in port. E. S. Phelps.	*in* P 1458
Wrecked off the Riff const. A. I. Shand.	*in* T 177 v6

x denotes books specially adapted for children.

Writer's daughter, The.	*in* W 2203 v3	Youth of Jefferson, The. J. E. Cooke.	C 2354
Written in the fire. F. Church.	C 1422	Youth of Shakespeare, The. R. F. Williams.	W 1954
Wunderjahr, Das. H. Conscience.	C 2260	Youth of the Old Dominion, The. S. Hopkins.	H 4401
Wunderweib vom Eichbühl, Das. W. Bauberger.	B 579		
Same.	B 580	Zadig. Voltaire.	*in* V 1051
Wunnigel. W. Raabe.	R 121	Zanita. T. Yelverton.	Y 151
Würger von Paris, Die. A. Belot.	B 4601	Zanoni. E. G. E. L. Bulwer-Lytton.	B 4028
Wuthering Heights. E. Brontë.	B 3351	Zara. M. Argles.	*in* A 1488
Wyandotte. J. F. Cooper.	C 2482	Zauberer des hochgebirges, Der. H. A. Noé.	N 651
Wych Hazel. S. and A. B. Warner.	W 878	Zauberer von Rom, Der. K. F. Gutzkow.	G 3107
Wyllard's weird. M. E. Maxwell.	M 1788	Zauberkrug, Der. F. W. Hackländer.	*in* H 308
Wyncote. Mrs. T. Erskine.	E 1251	Zauberring, Der. F. H. K. de La Motte Fouqué.	L 355
		Závis von Rosenberg. A. Peters.	P 2851
X. Y. Z. A. K. Green.	G 2204	Zeitbilder. C. Pichler.	P 1657
Xenie's inheritance. A. Durand.	D 2581	Zelle der leiden, Die. A. Dörle.	D 1752
		Zelle no. 7. P. Zaccone.	Z 351
"Yatil." F. D. Millet.	*in* S 35 v5	Zenobia. W. Ware.	W 654
Year of wreck, A. G. C. Benham.	B 1351	Zenosius. C. C. Pise.	P 1901
Year one of the republic. E. Erckmann and A. Chatrian.		Zerub Throop's experiment. A. D. T. Whitney.	
	E 1204 v3		W 1461
Years that are told, The. R. Porter.	P 2301	Zerviah Hope. E. S. Phelps.	*in* S 35 v8
Yeast. C. Kingsley.	K 656	Zigeunertochter, Die. A. v. Winterfeld.	W 2253
Yellow flag, The. E. H. Yates.	Y 107	Zoe. G. E. Jewsbury.	J 852
Yellow plush papers. W. M. Thackeray.	*in* T 665 v4	Zohrab. J. Morier.	M 3652
Yellow tiger, The. W. Collins.	*in* C 2306	Zu befehl, herr rittmeister. A. v. Winterfeld.	
Yemasse, The. W. G. Simms.	S 3008		*in* W 2260 v6
Yesterday.	Y 11	Zu füssen des monarchen. L. v. François.	*in* F 1526
Yolande. W. Black.	B 2217	Zu weihnachten. F. Stahr.	S 4684
Yoricks empfindsame reise. L. Sterne.	S 5153	Zufall oder fügung? E. Mertens.	M 4451
York and a Lancaster Rose, A. A. Keary.	Kx 116	Zum stillen vergnügen. W. Müller.	M 4451
Young advocate, The.	*in* D 1326	Zur ehre Gottes. A. Meissner.	M 2063
Young artist, The. M. Blackford.	B 2251	Zur ehre Gottes! L. v. Sacher-Masoch.	S 109
Young Brown. E. C. G. Murray.	M 4904	Zur neujahrszeit. K. H. Scharling.	S 1001
Young Cœlebs. P. Fitzgerald.	F 976	Zur rechten zeit bankerott. L. v. Fischer.	*in* V 2 v38
Young crusoe, The. Dr. H.	Hx 451	Zur "wald- und wasserfreude." H. T. W. Storm.	
Young deliverers, The. E. Kellogg.	Hx 218		S 5601
Young desperado, A. T. B. Aldrich.	*in* A 752	Züricher novellen. G. Keller.	K 580
Young duke, The. B. Disraeli.	D 1510	Zustände in Amerika. Graf A. Baudissin.	B 601
Young folks' ideas. Uncle Lawrence.	Ux 202	Zuwider-wurzen, Die. H. T. v. Schmid.	S 1420
Young folks' Robinson Crusoe. E. W. Farrer.	Fx 101	Zwanzig jahre nachher. A. Dumas.	D 2293
Young folks' whys and wherefores. Uncle Lawrence.		Zwanzig tausend meilen unter'm meer. J. Verne.	
	Ux 201		V 557
Young France. J. Kavanagh.	*in* K 310	Zwei alte freunde. A. v. Winterfeld.	*in* W 2281 v2
Young girl's wooing, A. E. P. Roe.	R 2311	Same.	*in* V 2 v25
Young Goodman Brown. N. Hawthorne.		Zwei baronessen, Die. H. C. Andersen.	A 1006
	in H 2054 v1	Zwei familienmütter. M. S. Schwartz.	S 1907
Young Joe. J. T. Trowbridge.	Tx 813	Zwei freunde. A. L. Kielland.	K 1704
Young lady in gray, The. F. W. Robinson.	*in* R 1858	Same.	*in* V 2 v23
Young lady's tale, The. S. Lee.	*in* L 851 v3	Zwei gnädige frauen. G. K. O. v. Struensee.	S 5856
Young laird, The. J. A. Bethune.	*in* W 2202 v3	Zwei kreuzherren. J. Gundling.	G 3056
Young lord Penrith. J. B. Harwood.	H 1652	Zwei kröglein, Die. O. Müller.	M 4411
Young man at Tootle's, The. F. W. Robinson.		Zwei lebenswege. C. Mundt.	M 4586
	in R 1858	Zwei menschenalter. B. Frederich.	D 205
Young Maugars. A. Theuriet.	T 703	Zwei nächte. F. W. Hackländer.	M 4436
Young mrs. Jardine. D. M. Craik.	C 2872	Zwei perrücken. A. v. Winterfeld.	*in* W 2260 v9
Young Moll's peevy. C. A. Stephens.	*in* S 35 v10	Zwei städte. C. Dickens.	D 1320
Young moose-hunters, The. C. A. Stephens.	Sx 1403	Zweimal vermählt. B. Frederich.	D 206
Young Musgrave. M. O. Oliphant.	O 483	Zweite frau, Die. E. John.	J 912
Young nimrods. T. W. Knox.	Kx 901	Zweifache mord in der rue Morgue, Der. E. A. Poe.	
Young pilgrim, The. B. W. Hofland.	Wx 201		*in* P 1976
Young recruit, The. K. G. Nieritz.	Y 221	Zwergenest, Das. F. W. Hackländer.	*in* H 308
Young step-mother. The. C. M. Yonge.	Y 221	Zwillingsschwester, Die. E. Taubert.	*in* V 2 v37
Young Strong. M. W. Shinn.	*in* S 35 v9	Zwillingsschwestern, Die. C. Spath.	S 4151
Young surveyor, The. J. T. Trowbridge.	Tx 809	Zwischen himmel und erde. E. v. Puttkammer.	L 2151
Young west indian, The. M. Blackford.	*in* B 752	Zwischen leben und sterben. J. Gundling.	G 3055
Young yägers, The. M. Reid.	Rx 413	Zwischen vater und sohn. C. Bauer.	B 659
Younger son, The. H. V. Palmer.	P 351	Zwischen zwei todsünden. L. Schücking.	*in* V 2 v25

x denotes books specially adapted for children.

Historical novels. Admirable notes on the various epochs of history, and lists of historical novels relating to each, will be found in the Classlist for english prose fiction in the Lower hall of the Boston public library (3:**L**), and in the following separate publications: Bowen, H. C. Descriptive catalogue of historical novels and tales (16:**L** 823); Allen, W: F. Reader's guide to english history, with supplement on general history (16:**L** and 942:39). The Bulletin of the Mercantile library of Philadelphia for Oct. 1, 1885, contains the beginning of such a list, which promises to be fuller than any heretofore existing.

Select lists of novels will be found in the supplement to the St. Louis public school library bulletin, no. 28 (3:**L**).

Books for the young are described in the last-mentioned place, and in the following publications: Hewins, C. M. Books for the young (16:**L**), continued in the Literary news (805:**M**); Books for young readers in the Buffalo Y. M. library (3:**L**); 28th report of the Sup't of public instruction of Indiana, pp. 89-126 (379:7); Theden, D. Führer durch die jugendliteratur (16:**L**); Rathgeber bei der auswahl von jugendschriften, 1883 (16:**L**).

Classes 814—819.

See col. 515—518.

5. English literature — a, General.

1. History and criticism.

(See also Essays, class 824.)

History— General.

Allibone, S: Austin. A critical dictionary of english literature and british and american authors, living and deceased, from the earliest accounts to the middle of the 19th century; containing 30,000 biographies and literary notices, with 40 indexes of subjects. Phila. 1859–77. 3 v. Q.   **820 : R1**
Contents. V. 1. A–J. 2. K–S. 3. T–Z.—Indexes.

Adams, W: Davenport. Dictionary of english literature; a comprehensive guide to english authors and their works. 3d ed. Lond. 1878. O.   **820 : R2**

Chambers, Robert. History of the english language and literature. Added, a history of american contributors to the english language and literature by Royal Robbins. Hartford. 1837. D.   **820.4 : 32**

Reed, H: Lectures on english literature from Chaucer to Tennyson. 5th ed., rev. Phila. 1866. S.   **820.4 : 10**
Contents. Introductory; Principles of literature.— Application of literary principles. — The english language.— Early english literature.— Literature of the 16th century.— Literature of the 17th century with incidental suggestions on sunday reading. — Literature of the 17th and 18th centuries.—Literature of the 19th century. — Contemporary literature. — Tragic and elegiac poetry.—Literature of wit and humor.—Literature of letter-writing.

Underwood, Francis H: A hand-book of english literature, intended for the use of high schools, as well as a companion and guide for private students, and for general readers : British authors. Bost. 1879. O.   **820.4 : 14**
— *Same.* : American authors. Bost. 1879. O.   **820.4 : 15**

Welsh, Alfred Hix. Development of english literature and language. Chic. 1882. 2 v. O.   **820.4 : 37**

Kellogg, Brainerd. A text-book on english literature, with copious extracts from the leading authors, english and american, with full instructions as to the method in which these are to be studied. N. Y. 1882. D.   **820.4 : 19**

Shaw, T: Budd. Outlines of english literature. New amer. ed., with a sketch of amer. literature by H: T. Tuckerman. N. Y. n. d. D.   **820.4 : 13**
— English and american literature : Shaw's new history of english lit.; together with a history of english literature in America by Truman J. Backus. N. Y. 1884. D.   **820.4 : 38**

Scherr, Johannes. A history of english literature. From the german by M. V. N. Y. 1882. D.   **820.4 : 27**

Engel, E: Geschichte der englischen litteratur von ihren anfängen bis auf die neueste zeit ; mit einem anhange : Die amerikanische litteratur. (Geschichte der weltlitteratur in einzeldarstellungen ; b. 4.) Leipz. [1883]. O.   **820.4 : 35**

History—English authors.

Chambers, Robert, *ed.* Cyclopædia of english literature ; a history, critical and biographical, of british authors. Edinb. 1844. 2 v. Q.   **820.4+1**

Craik, G: Lillie. Sketches of literature and learning in England. [1st ser.] From the norman conquest to the age of Elizabeth, with specimens of the principal writers. Lond. 1844. 2 v. in 1. T. **820.4 : 17 v1,2**
— *Same.* 2d ser. From the accession of Elizabeth to the revolution of 1688. Lond. 1845. 2 v. T.   **820.4 : 17 v3,4**
— *Same.* 3d ser. From the revolution of 1688 to the present day. Lond. 1845. 2 v. in 1. T.   **820.4 : 17 v5,6**
— A compendious history of english literature and of the english language, from the norman conquest ; with numerous specimens. N. Y. 1863. 2 v. O.   **820.4 : 33**

Taine, Hippolyte Adolphe. History of english literature. Tr. by H: Van Laun ; with a pref. prepared expressly for this tr. by the author. N. Y. 1872. 2 v. O.   **820.4 : 4**
Contents. V. 1. Introd.—Book 1, The source: The saxons; The normans; The new tongue.— Book 2, The renaissance: The pagan renaissance: The theatre; Ben Jonson; Shakspeare; The christian renaissance: Milton. — Book 3, The classic age : The restoration. 2. Book 3, *continued:* Dryden; The revolution; Addison; Swift; The novelists: The poets. — Book 4, Modern life: Ideas and productions; Lord Byron; The past and the present. — Book 5, Modern authors: Introd. note; The novel, Dickens, Thackeray; Criticism and history, Macaulay: Philosophy and history, Carlyle: Philosophy, Stuart Mill; Poetry, Tennyson.—Index.

Hart, J: Seely. A manual of english literature ; a text-book for schools and colleges. Phila. [1872]. D.   **820.4 : 7**

Morley, H: A manual of english literature ; thoroughly rev., with an entire re-arrangement of matter, and with numerous retrenchments and additions, by Moses Coit Tyler. N. Y. 1879. O.   **820.4 : 9**

Coppée, H: English literature, considered as an interpreter of english history ; designed as a manual of english literature. 7th ed. Phila. 1881. D.   **820.4 : 5**

Richardson, Abby Sage. Familiar talks on english literature ; a manual, embracing the great epochs of english literature, from the english conquest of Britain, 449, to the death of Walter Scott, 1832. Chicago. 1881. D.   **820.4 : 11**

Buckland, Anna. The story of english literature [to 1850]. N. Y. 1883. D.   **820.4 : 31**

Nicoll, H: J. Landmarks of english literature. N. Y. 1883. D.   **820.4 : 29**
Contents. Introd.—The dawn of eng. lit.—The elizabethan era.—The elizabethan dramatists.—The successors of the elizabethans.—The restauration.—The wits of queen Anne's time.—Our first great novelists. — Dr. Johnson and his contemporaries. — The new era in poetry. — Sir Walter Scott and the prose lit. of the early part of the 19th century.—Our own times.— Periodicals, reviews and encyclopædias.

Brooke, Stopford. English literature [to 1837]. (Literature primer, ed. by J: R: Green). N. Y. 1879. S.   **820.4 : 18**

Chateaubriand, François A: René *vicomte* de. Sketches of english literature, with considerations on the spirit of the times, men and revolutions. 2d ed. Lond. 1837. 2 v. O.   **820.4+3**

Metcalfe, F: Old english literature. *In his* The englishman and the scandinavian. **898 : 3**

Brink, Bernhard ten. Early english literature, to Wiclif, from the german by Horace M. Kennedy, tr. rev. by the author. N. Y. 1883. D.   **820.4 : 26**

Yonge, C: Duke. Three centuries of english literature, [from Shakspere to Dickens; with extracts and specimens]. N. Y. 1879. D.   **820.4 : 16**

Hettner, Hermann. Geschichte der englischen literatur von der wiederherstellung des königthums bis in die zweite hälfte des 18. jahrhunderts, 1660—1770. (Literaturgeschichte des 18. jahrh., 1er theil.) 4te verb. aufl. Brschwg. 1881. O.   **809 : 9 v1**

Perry, T: Sergeant. English literature in the 18th century. N. Y. 1883. D.   **820.4 : 30**

Oliphant, Margaret O., *born* Wilson. The literary history of England in the end of the 18th and beginning of the 19th century. N. Y. 1882. D.   **820.4 : 28**

Brandes, G: Der naturalismus in England. *In his* Hauptströmungen, *etc.*   **809 : 6 v4**
Contents. Die Seeschule.—Byron und seine gruppe.

Morley, H: Of english literature in the reign of Victoria, with a glance at the past. Tauchnitz ed. v. 2000. [Containing facsimiles of the signatures of authors in the Tauchnitz ed., photographed from their correspondence and agreements with baron Tauchnitz.] N. Y. 1882. S.   **820.4 : 20**
Contents. A glance at the past, from the beginning to the reign of Victoria. — Of those who were old at the beginning of the reign ; and of the poets, Woodsworth, Southey, Landor. — Journalists of the elder generation, essayists and poets. — Of women who wrote in the early part of the reign. — Of those by whom cheap literature was made useful; and of the earlier life of T: Babington Macaulay. — Of writers who were between 50 and 60 years old at the beginning of the reign.—Men of the next decade of years.— Of T: Carlyle; and of divines and wits. — Onward battle. — The best vigour of the time; and what remains of it.

Minto, W: A manual of english prose literature, biographical and critical ; designed mainly to show characteristics of style. New ed. Edinb. 1881. D.   **820.4 : 25**
Contents. Introd.: Elements of style : Qualities of style; kinds of composition.—De Quincey, Macaulay, Carlyle.—Prose writers in historical order.

Disraeli, I: Amenities of literature ; consisting of sketches and characters of english literature. 4th ed. N. Y. 1847. 2 v. D.
                                                     820.4 : 6
Contents. V. **1.** The druidical institution.—Britain and the britons.—The name of England and the english.- The anglo-saxons.—Cædmon and Milton.—Beowulf; the hero-life.—The anglo-normans.—The page, the baron and the minstrel.—Gothic romances.—Origin of the vernacular languages of Europe. — Origin of the english language.—Vicissitudes of the english language.—Dialects.—Mandeville, our first traveller.—Chaucer.–Gower.–Piers Ploughman.–Occleve, the scholar of Chaucer. — Lydgate, the monk of Bury. — The invention of printing.—The first english printer. —Early libraries.—Henry VII. — First sources of modern history.—Arnolde's chronicle.—Henry VIII. his literary character.—Books of the people. — The difficulties experienced by a primitive author.—Skelton. —The Ship of fools.—The psychological character of sir T: More. — The earl of Surrey and sir T: Wyatt. — The spoliation of the monasteries.—A crisis and a re-

action; Robert Crowley.—Primitive dramas.—The reformer bishop Bale and the romanist J. Haywood, the court jester.—Roger Ascham. **2.** Public opinion. —Orthography and orthoëpy.—The ancient metres in modern verse.—The origin of rhyme. — Rhyming dictionaries. —The Arte of english poesie.—The Discoverie of witchcraft. — The first jesuits in England. — Hooker. — Sir Philip Sidney. — Spencer.—The Faery queen. — Allegory. — The first tragedy and the first comedy.—The predecessors and the contemporaries of Shakespeare.—Shakespeare. — The "Humors" of Jonson. - Drayton. — The psychological history of Rawleigh.—The occult philosopher, dr. Dee.— The rosacrusian Fludd.—Bacon.—The first founder of a public library.—Early writers, their dread of the press; the transition to authors by profession.—The age of doctrines. — Pamphlets.—The Oceana of Harrington. — The author of The grounds and reasons of monarchy. —Commonwealth.—The True intellectual system of the universe. — Difficulties of the publishers of contemporary memoirs.—The war against books.

Hatton, Joseph. Journalistic London ; a series of sketches of famous pens and papers of the day. Rep., with add. from Harper's magazine. Lond. 1882. O.   **820.4 : 203**

History—American authors.

Duyckinck, Evert A: *and* G: Long. Cyclopædia of american literature ; embracing personal and critical notices of authors and selections from their writings, with portraits, autographs and other ill. N. Y. 1856. 2 v. Q.   **820.4+2**
— *Same.* Supplement, incl. obituaries of authors, continuations of former articles, and notices of earlier and later writings omitted in previous ed. N. Y. 1866. Q.
                                                  820.4+2 v3

Knapp, S: Lorenzo. Lectures on american literature, with remarks on some passages of american history. N. Y. 1829. O.
                                                     820.4 : 24

Hart, J: Seely. A manual of american literature ; a text-book for schools and colleges. Phila. [1872]. D.   **820.4 : 8**

Lawrence, Eugene. A primer of american literature. (Harper's half-hour ser.) N. Y. 1880. T.   **820.4 : 21**

Richardson, C: Francis. A primer of american literature. Bost. 1880. T.   **820.4 : 22**
— *Same.* New and rev. ed. Portr. Bost. 1883. T.   **820.4 : 22**

Nichol, J: American literature ; an historical sketch, 1620—1880. Edinb. 1882. O.
                                                     820.4 : 34

Tyler, Moses Coit. A history of american literature. N. Y. 1878. 2 v. O.   **820.4 : 23**
Contents. v. **1.** 1607—1676. **2.** 1677—1765.

Hudson, F: Journalism in the U. S., from 1690 to 1872. N. Y. 1873. O.   **820.4 : 201**

Warner, C: Dudley. The american newspaper ; an essay read before the social science assoc. at Saratoga Springs, sept. 6, 1881. Bost. 1881. Tt.   **820.4 : 202**

North, S. N. D. History and present condition of the newspaper and periodical press of the U. S.; with a catalogue of the publications of the U. S. Maps. *In* U. S. tenth census, 1880, v. 8.   *in* **317 : D**
Contents. 1st period, 1639—1783.—2d per., 1783—1835. –3d per., 1835—1880.—App. Statistical tables; Catalogue of periodical pub's; Chronological history of the newspaper press of the U. S.; Bound files of amer. newsp. in the possession of the American antiquarian society, Worcester, Mass.—General index.

Criticism and Essays.

Baldwin, James. Introd. to the study of english literature and literary criticism; designed for the use of schools. V. 1, Poetry; v. 2, Prose. Phila. [1882–83]. 2 v. D.
820.5 : 19

Bayne, P: Essays in biography and criticism; 1st and 2d series. Bost. 1857–58. 2 v. D.
820.5 : 1

Contents. V. 1. Thomas De Quincey and his works. —Tennyson and his teachers.—Mrs. Barrett Browning.—Glimpses of recent british art.—Ruskin and his critics.—Hugh Miller.—The modern novel: Dickens; Bulwer; Thackeray.—Currer Bell: Ellis, Acton, Currer. 2. Notice of the author.—C: Kingsley.—T: Babington Macaulay.— Sir Archibald Alison.— S: Taylor Coleridge. — Wellington. — Napoleon Bonaparte.—Plato.—Characteristics of christian civilization.—The modern university.—The pulpit and the press.—"The testimony of the rocks," a defence.

— Lessons from my masters; Carlyle, Tennyson and Ruskin. N. Y. 1879. D. 820.5 : 2

Benton, Joel. Emerson as a poet. [Portrait.] N. Y. 1883. D. 820.5 : 22

Chasles, Victor Euphémion Philarète. Angloamerican literature and manners. From the french. N. Y. 1852. D. 820.5 : 3

Coan, Titus Munson, *ed.* Studies in literature. (Topics of the time, no. 3.) N. Y. 1883. D.
820.5 : 21

Contents. American literature in England.—Leifchild, F. Hamlet, a new reading.—Shorthouse, J. H: The humorous in literature.—Stokes, G: T. The Hollandi?s.—Arnold, M. Isaiah of Jerusalem.—Wright, T: Concerning the unknown public.

DeQuincey, T: Essays on the poets and other english writers. Bost. 1853. D. 820.5 : 24
Contents. The poetry of Wordsworth.—Shelley.—Keats.—Goldsmith.—Pope.— Godwin.—Foster.—Hazlitt.—Landor.

Eminent men and popular books; from "The times." Lond. 1859. S. 820.5 : 4
Contents. G: Stephenson.—Macaulay's History of England.— Sydney Smith. — Westward, ho!— Tom Moore.—Thackeray's miscellanies.—Gainsborough.—Charlotte Brontë.—Dred.—James Boswell.—Herodotus.—Montalembert on England.

Essays from the London times; 2d ser. N. Y. 1852. S. 820.5 : 5
Contents. Captain Peel in the nubian deserts.—Memoirs of lord Langdale.—Alfred Tennyson, the poet of sorrow. — History of spanish literature.—Arctic expeditions.—The life of Sterling by T: Carlyle.—Lord chancellor Clarendon and his friends.—Dickens and Thackeray.—Grote's History of Greece.—Our antipodes. — Lord Holland and his foreign reminiscences. — The autobiography of a chartist [Alton Locke].—Uncle Tom's cabin.—The Blithedale romance.

Fields, James T: Yesterdays with authors. Bost. 1872. D. 820.5 : 6
Contents. Pope.—Thackeray.— Hawthorne.— Dickens.—Wordsworth.—Miss Mitford.

Gilfillan, G: Sketches of modern literature and eminent literary men; a gallery of literary portraits. N. Y. 1846. 2 v. in 1 D.
820.5 : 7
Contents. V. 1. Jeffrey.—Godwin.—Hazlitt.—Hall.—Shelley.—Chalmers.—Carlyle.— De Quincey.—Foster.—Wilson.—Irving and the preachers of the day. 2. Landor.—Campbell.— Brougham.—Coleridge.—Emerson.— Wordsworth.— Pollok.— Lamb and the rural poets.—Elliot.—Keats.—Macaulay.—Aird.— Southey.—Lockhart.

— Modern literature and literary men; a 2d gallery of literary portraits. 4th amer. ed. N. Y. 1860. D. 820.5 : 8
Contents. Milton.— Byron.— Crabbe.— Foster.— Hood.—Macaulay.—Croly.—Bulwer-Lytton.— Emerson.—Dawson.—Tennyson.—Nichol.—Mrs. Hemans.—Mrs. Browning.— Mrs. Shelley. — Cobbett.— Montgomery. — Smith. — Anderson. — Hunt. — Moore. — Taylor.—Longfellow.—Bailey.—Sterling.

Hazeltine, Mayo Williamson. Chats about books; poets and novelists. N. Y. 1883. D.
820.5 : 20

Lowell, James Russell. Among my books. [1st and] 2d series. Bost. 1870, 1876. 2 v. D.
820.5 : 10
Contents. 1st ser. Dryden.—Witchcraft.—Shakespeare once more.—New England two centuries ago. —Lessing. — Rousseau and the sentimentalists. 2d ser. Dante. — Spencer. — Wordsworth. — Milton.—Keats.

— Conversations on some of the old poets. 2d ed. Cambridge. 1846. S. 820.5 : 11
Contents. Chaucer.—The old dramatists: Chapman; Ford.

Ossoli, Sarah Margaret, *marchesa* d', *born* Fuller. Papers on literature and art. N. Y. 1846. 2 v. in 1. D. 820.5 : 23
Contents. V. 1. A short essay on critics.—A dialogue. — The two Herberts. — The prose works of Milton.— Life of sir James Mackintosh. — Modern british poets. — The modern drama. — Dialogue. 2. Poets of the people.—Miss Barrett's poems.—Browning's poems.—Lives of the great composers; Haydn, Mozart, Handel, Bach, Beethoven.— Washington Allston.—American literature.—Swedenborgianism. —Methodism at the fountain.—App.: The tragedy of witchcraft.

Smith, G: Barnett. Poets and novelists; a series of literary studies. N. Y. 1876. D.
820.5 : 12
Contents. W: M. Thackeray.—E. B. Browning.—T: Love Peacock.— N. Hawthorne.— The Brontës.— H: Fielding.—Robert Buchanan.—English fugitive poets.

Stephen, Leslie. Hours in a library; 1st—3d series. N. Y. *and* Lond. 1875–79. 3 v. D.
820.5 : 13
Contents. V. 1. De Foe's novels.—Richardson's novels.—Pope as a moralist.—Mr. Elwin's ed. of Pope. — Some words about sir Walter Scott.—Nathaniel Hawthorne.— Balzac's novels.—De Quincey. 2. Sir T: Browne.—Jonathan Edwards.—W: Law.—Horace Walpole.—Dr. Johnson's writings.—Crabbe's poetry. —W: Hazlitt.—Mr. Disraeli's novels. 3. Massinger. —Fielding's novels.—Cowper and Rousseau.—The first Edinburgh reviewers.—Wordsworth's ethics.—Landor's Imaginary conversations.—Macaulay.—Charlotte Brontë.—C: Kingsley.

Washburn, Emelyn W. Studies in early english literature. N. Y. 1882. D. 820.5 : 18

Whipple, Edwin Percy. Essays and reviews. 3d ed. Bost. 1853. 2 v. S. 820.5 : 14
Contents. V. 1. Macaulay.—Poets and poetry of America: Sprague; Dana; Bryant; Percival; Halleck; Longfellow; Holmes; Whittier; Maria Brooks. — Talfourd. — Words. — James's novels. — Sydney Smith.—Daniel Webster.—Neal's History of the puritans.—Wordsworth. — Byron.—English poets of the 19th century: Shelley; Scott; Coleridge; Southey; Moore; Campbell; Tennyson; Proctor; Keats; Elliott; Miss Barrett [mrs. Browning]; Bailey.—South's sermons.—Coleridge as a philosophical critic. 2. Old english dramatists: Marlowe; Ben Jonson; Decker; Webster; Marston; Heywood; Chapman; Middleton; Tourneur; Beaumont and Fletcher; Massinger; Ford. — Romance of rascality. — The croakers of society and literature.—British critics: Jeffrey; Mackintosh; Sir W: Hamilton; Gifford; Hazlitt; Hunt.—Rufus Choate.—Prescott's histories. Prescott's Conquest of Peru.—Shakspeare's critics: Verplanck; Schlegel; Ulrici; Hudson.—R: Brinsley Sheridan.—H: Fielding.—Dana's poems and prose writings.—App.: T: Hood; Leigh Hunt's poems; T: Carlyle as a politician; Novels of the season.

— The literature of the age of Elizabeth. Bost. 1880. D. 820.5 : 15
Contents. Characteristics of the elizabethan literature. — Marlowe. — Shakespeare. — Ben Jonson. — Minor elizabethan dramatists. — Beaumont and Fletcher, Massinger and Ford. — Spenser. — Minor elizabethan poets.—Sidney and Raleigh.—Bacon.—Hooker.

Wilkinson, W: Cleaver. A free lance in the field of life and letters. N. Y. 1874. D.
　　　　　　　　　　　　　　　　820.5 : 16
Contents. The literary and ethical quality of George Eliot's novels.—Lowell's poetry.—Lowell's " Cathedral."—Lowell's prose.—Bryant's poetry.— Bryant's Iliad.—The christian commission as a part of church history.—The character and the literary influence of Erasmus.

Wilson, J:, (*Christopher North*). Specimens of the british critics. Phila. 1846. D.
　　　　　　　　　　　　　　　　820.5 : 17
Contents. Dryden. — Dryden and Pope. — Dryden on Chaucer.—Supp. to *same.*—MacFlecnoe and the Dunciad.—Supp. to *same.*
Note. See also names of individual writers in the Index of Biography, at the end of the catalogue.

2. Collected works.

Halliwell-Phillipps, James Orchard, *ed.* Contributions to early english literature, derived chiefly from rare books and ancient inedited mss. from the 15th to the 17th century. Lond. 1849. Q.　　**820.2 : R29**
Contents. The suddaine turne of fortune's wheel by J: Taylor, the water poet.—The life of St. Katharine; The tale of the knight and his wife, and an account of the magical manuscript of dr. Caius. — The tale of the smyth and his dame, and the book of Robin Conscience, from the unique black-letter tract in the Bodleian library. — Band, Ruffe and Cuffe, a costume shew.—Newes out of Islington. — A Derbyshire mummer's play.—Ballads and poems respecting Hugh of Lincoln, a boy alleged to have been murdered by the jews in 1255. — The interlude of youth; from the rare black-letter ed., printed by Waley about 1554.

— The literature of the 16th and 17th centuries, illustrated by reprints of very rare tracts. Lond. 1851. Q.　　　　　**820.2 : R31**
Contents. Harry White his humour. — Two italian gentlemen.—Tailors travels from London to the Isle of Wight.—Wyl Bucke his testament.—The booke of meery riddles.—All for money.—Wine, beere, ale and tobacco.—A new booke of new conceits, by T: Johnson.—Loue's garland.

Five centuries of the english language and literature ; vol. 500 of the Tauchnitz ed. with a preface by the ed. Leipz. 1860. S.
　　　　　　　　　　　　　　　　820.2 : 1
Contents. Preface, [missing]. — **Wycliffe,** J: St. John's gospel.—**Chaucer,** G. Canterbury tales: The story of patient Grisilde. — **Hawes,** S. The pastime of pleasure.—**More,** *Sir* T: The descripcion of Richard III.—**Spenser,** E. The faerie queene.—**Jonson,** B. The alchemist. — **Locke,** J. Some thoughts concerning education.—**Gray,** T: Poems.

Beers, H: Augustin, *ed.* A century of american literature, 1776–1876. (Leisure hour ser.) N. Y. 1878. D.　　　　　**820.1 : 1**

　　　　　　　　* 　 * 　 *

Ascham, Roger. English works with notes and observations, and the author's life by James Bennet. Lond. 1761. Q.　　　　**23 : R**
Contents. A report of the affairs of Germany, and the emperor Charles' court. — Toxophilus. — The school-master. — Letters to queen Elizabeth and others.

Bacon, Francis. *baron Verulam and viscount St. Albans.* Works ; with a life of the author by Basil Montagu. Phila. 1857. 3 v. Q.
　　　　　　　　　　　　　　　　820.2+2
Contents. V. 1. Life. — Essays. — Meditationes sacræ.—Of the colours of good and evil.—Miscellaneous tracts upon human philosophy.—Apothegms.—Ornamenta rationalia. — Collection of sentences. — Notes for conversation. — Essay on death. — The advancement of learning. — New Atlantis. — The wisdom of the ancients.—Civil history.—Biography: Queen Elizabeth ; Julius Cæsar ; Augustus Cæsar ; Prince

Henry. — Miscellaneous tracts. **2.** Sylva sylvarum, or A natural history. — Tracts relating to Scotland. — Tracts relating to Ireland.—Tracts relating to Spain. —Tracts relating to England.—Speeches.—Charges.— Papers relating to the earl of Essex.— Theological tracts.—Miscellaneous. — Judicial charges and tracts. —Miscellaneous.—Miscellaneous tracts. tr. from the latin. **3.** Letters from the Cabala. — Letters from the Resuscitatio. — Letters from the Baconiana. — Letters from Stephens.—Letters from Birch.—Letters from the British museum.—Letters from the Lambeth library. — Letters from Mallet. — Letters from Stephens. — Letters from Matthews.—Miscellaneous letters.—Law tracts.—The great instauration. — Miscellaneous tracts. tr. from the latin.

Berkeley, G: Works. Added, an account of his life and several of his letters to T: Prior, dean Garvais, mr. Pope, etc. Lond. 1820. 3 v. O.　　　　　　　**820.2 : 3**
Contents. V. 1. Life. — Letters etc. — Of the principles of human knowledge. — Three dialogues between Hylas and Philonous.—An essay toward a new theory of vision. — Alciphron, or The minute philosopher. **2.** *Same, continued.* — Passive obedience. — Arithmetica absque algebra aut Euclide demonstrata. Miscellanea mathematica. — De motu. — The analyst. **3.** A defence of free-thinking in mathematics.—An app. concerning Walton's vindication of sir I: Newton's principles of fluxions. — Reasons for not replying to Walton's full answer.—Essay toward preventing the ruin of Great Britain.—Discourse addressed to magistrates and men in authority. — A word to the wise.—Letter to the roman catholics of the dioces of Cloyne. — Maxims concerning patriotism. — The querist. — Proposal for the better supplying of churches in our foreign plantations and for converting the savage americans to christianity.—Verses on the prospect of planting arts and learning in America.—Sermon before the Soc. for the propagation of the gospel in foreign parts. — Siris. — Letter on the virtues of tar water.—Further thoughts on tar water. —Second letter on tar water.

Browne, *Sir* T: Works ; incl. his unpub. correspondence and a memoir, ed. by Simon Wilkin. Lond. 1846. 4 v. O.　　**820.2 : 4**
Contents. **1.** Memoirs.—Domestic correspondence, journals, etc. — Miscellaneous correspondence. **2.** Religio medici. — Pseudodoxia epidemica, books 1-4. **3.** Pseudodoxia epidemica, books 4-7.—The garden of Cyrus.—Hydriotaphia.—Brampton urns. **4.** Repertorium. — A letter to a friend. — Christian morals. — Certain miscellany tracts, also miscellanies.—Unpublished papers.—Index.

Bryant, W: Cullen. Prose writings ; ed. by Parke Godwin. N. Y. 1884. 2 v. O.
　　　　　　　　　　　　　　　　820.1.+9
Contents. V. 1. *Literary essays*: Lectures on poetry; Early american verse; On trisyllabic verse in iambic measure ; Nostradamus's Provençal poem; Moriscan romances ; Female troubadours; Oldham's poems; Abraham Cowley; Poets and poetry of the english language. *Narratives*: The whirlwind; The indian spring; The marriage blunder; The skeleton's cave; A story of Cuba. — *Commemorative discourses*: James Fenimore Cooper; Washington Irving; Fitz-Greene Halleck; Gulian Crommelin Verplanck. **2.** *Sketches of travel*: Illinois fifty years ago; A tour in the old south; The early northwest; Glimpses of Europe; Cuba and the cubans; A visit to Mexico.—Occasional addresses.—Editorial comments and criticisms.

Burns, Robert. Works. [ed. with notes by W: Scott Douglas]. Edinb. 1877-79. 6 v. O.
　　　　　　　　　　　　　　　　820.2+P33

Butler, S: General remains in prose and verse, published from the original mss., formerly in the possession of W. Longueville, with notes by R. Thayer. Lond. 1759. 2 v. O.
　　　　　　　　　　　　　　　　820.2 : 5
Contents. V. **1.** Miscellanies in prose and verse. **2.** Characters.—Thoughts on various subjects.

Channing, W: Ellery. Works. 7th ed., with an introd. Bost. 1847. 6 v. D.　　**820.1 : 2**
Contents. V. **1.** Introductory remarks.—Character and writings of Milton.—Life of Napoleon Bonaparte. —Character of the writings of Fenelon.—Moral argument against calvinism.—Remarks on national litera-

ture.— Remarks on associations. — The union. — Remarks on education. 2. Slavery.—The abolitionists. —Annexation of Texas to the U.S.—Letter on catholicism.—Letter on creeds. — Address on temperance. — Address on self culture. 3. Preaching Christ. — War.—Unitarian christianity.—Evidences of revealed religion.—Demands of the age on the ministry.—Unitarian christianity most favorable to piety. — The great purpose of christianity. — Likeness to God. — Christian ministry.—The duties of children. — Honor due to all men.—Evidences of christianity. 4. Character of Christ. — Christianity a rational religion. — Spiritual freedom. — Self denial. — Imitableness of Christ's character.—Evil of sin.—Immortality.—Love to Christ.—The future life. — War. — Ministry for the poor.—Christian worship.—The sunday school. — The philantropist. 5. Remarks on the slavery question. —Lecture on war. — Lectures on the elevation of the laboring portion of the community. — Discourse occasioned by the death of the rev. dr. Follen.—Charge, on preaching the gospel to the poor, at the ordination of C. Barnard and F. T. Gray, as ministers at large.— Charge for the ordination of rev. R. C. Waterston as minister at large. — Charge at the ordination of rev. J. S. Dwight.—Miscellanies.—App. 6. Emancipation. — Discourse on the life and character of the rev. J. Tuckerman.—The present age.—The church.—Duty of the free states. — Address delivered at Lennox, aug. 1st 1842, being the anniversary of emancipation in the british West Indies.

Churchill, C: Works. 5th ed. London. 1774.
4 v. D.   820.2 : 6
Contents. V. 1. The Rosciad. — The apology. — Night. — An epistle to W: Hogarth. — The ghost. 2. *Same, continued.*—The conference.—The author.—The duellist. 3. Gotham. — The candidate. — The farewell.—The times.—Independence.—The journey. 4. Sermons on the Lord's prayer.

Clark, Willis Gaylord. Literary remains, ed. by Lewis Gaylord Clark. 4th ed. N. Y. 1859.
O.   820.1 : 3
Contents. Memoir, by L. G. Clark.—Ollapodiana.— Prose miscellanies.—The spirit of life.— Miscellaneous poems.

Coleridge, S: Taylor. Complete works; with an introd. essay upon his philosophical and theological opinions, ed. by prof. Shedd. N. Y. 1854. 7 v. O.   820.2 : 7
Contents. V. 1. Aids to reflection.— Statesman's manual. 2. The friend. 3. Biographia literaria. 4. Lectures upon Shakspeare and other dramatists. 5. Literary remains. 6. On the constitution of church and state. 7. Poetical and dramatic works.

Dana, R: H: Poems and prose writings. N. Y. 1850. 2 v. D.   820.1 : 4
Contents. V. 1. Poems. — The idle man: Tom Thornton; Edward and Mary; Paul Felton; The son; Kean's acting; Letters from town; Domestic life; Musings. 2. Essays: Old times; The past and the present; Law as suited to man.—Reviews: Allston's Sylphs of the seasons; Edgeworth's Readings on poetry; Hazlitt's Lectures on the english poets; The sketch book; Radcliffe's Gaston de Blondeville; The novels of C: Brockden Brown; Pollok's Course of time; Natural history of enthusiasm; Memoir of H: Martyn.

De Foe, Daniel. Novels and miscellaneous works; with prefaces and notes, incl. those attributed to sir Walter Scott. Lond. 1854–82. 7 v. D.   820.2 : 8
Contents. V. 1. Life, adventures and piracies of captain Singleton; Life of colonel Jack. 2. Memoirs of a cavalier. — Memoirs of captain Carleton. — Dickory Cronke.—Everybody's business is nobody's business. 3. Moll Flanders.—History of the devil.— 4. Roxana.—Mrs. Christian Davies. 5. History of the plague of London.—Historical narrative of the great and terrible fire of London. — The storm. — Poetical essay on the storm.—The true-born english-man. 6. Life and adventures of mr. Duncan Campbell. — A new voyage round the world. — Political tracts relating to the Hanoverian succession. 7. Robinson Crusoe.

Emerson, Ralph Waldo. [Complete works.] New and rev. ed. Bost. 1884 [1883]. 11 v. D.   820.1 : 8
Contents. V. 1. **Nature, addresses and lectures.** Nature.—The american scholar.—Address delivered before the senior class in divinity college, Cambridge. —Literary ethics.—The method of nature.—Man the reformer.—Lecture on the times.—The conservative. —The transcendentalist.—The young american. 2. **Essays,** *1st ser.* History.—Self-reliance.—Compensation. — Spiritual laws. — Love. — Friendship. — Prudence.— Heroism.—The over-soul.— Circles. — Intellect.—Art. 3. **Essays,** *2d ser.* The poet.—Experience. —Character.—Manners.— Gifts.— Nature.— Politics.— Nominalist and realist.—New England reformers.— 4. **Representative men.** Uses of great men.— Plato, or the philosopher.— Plato; new readings.— Swedenborg, or the mystic. — Montaigne, or the skeptic. — Shakespeare, or the poet. — Napoleon, or the man of the world.—Goethe, or the writer. 5. **English traits.** First visit to England.—Voyage to England.—Land.—Race.—Ability.—Manners.— Truth. — Character. — Cockayne.— Wealth. — Aristocracy. — Universities.—Religion.— Literature.—The "Times". —Stonehenge.— Personal.— Result.—Speech at Manchester. 6. **The conduct of life.** Fate.—Power.— Wealth.—Culture.—Behaviour.—Worship.—Considerations by the way.—Beauty.—Illusions. 7. **Society and solitude.** Society and solitude.—Civilization.— Art.—Eloquence.— Domestic life.— Farming.—Work and days.— Books.— Clubs.— Courage. — Success.— Old age. 8. **Letters and social aims.** Poetry and imagination.— Social aims.— Eloquence. — Resources.—The comic.—Quotation and originality.— Progress of culture.— Persian poetry. — Inspiration. — Greatness.— Immortality. 9. **Poems.** 10. **Lectures and biographical sketches.** Demonology. —Aristocracy.—Perpetual forces.—Character.— Education.—The superlative.—The sovereignty of ethics. —The preacher.—The man of letters.—The scholar.— Plutarch.—Historic notes of life and letters in New England. — The Chardon street convention. — Ezra Ripley.— Mary Moody Emerson. — Samuel Hoar.— Thoreau.—Carlyle. 11. **Miscellanies.** The Lord's supper.—Historical discourse in Concord.— Address at the dedication of the soldiers' monument in Concord.—Address on emancipation in the british West Indies.—War.—The fugitive slave law.—The assault upon mr. Sumner.—Speech on affairs in Kansas.— Remarks at a meeting for the relief of John Brown's family.—John Brown.—Theodore Parker.—American civilization.—The emancipation proclamation.—Abraham Lincoln. — Harvard commemoration speech.— Editors' address.—Woman.—Address to Kossuth.

Evelyn, J: Miscellaneous writings, now first collected, with occasional notes by W: Upcott. Lond. 1825. Q.   820.2 : R9
Contents, see Catalogue of the Boston athenæum, v. 2, p. 946.

Gibbon, E: Miscellaneous works, with memoir of his life and writings composed by himself, ill. from his letters, with occasional notes and narrative by John lord Sheffield. Lond. 1796–1815. 3 v. Q.   820.2 : R25

Goldsmith, Oliver. Works, with a life and notes; v. 1, 3, 4. Lond. 1845. 3 v. S.   820.2 : 10
Contents. V. 1. Life.—Poems.— Plays: The good-natured man; She stoops to conquer.—Letters. 2. *Missing.* 3. Citizen of the world. 4. An inquiry into the present state of polite learning.—The bee.— The history of Cyrillo Padovano. — The life of dr. Parnell.—Life of lord Bolingbroke.—Prefaces and introd.—App.

— Works. New ed., containing pieces hitherto uncollected, and a life of the author. with notes from various sources by J. W. M. Gibbs; in 5 v., v. 1–4. Lond. 1884, 1885. 4 v. D.   820.2 : 30
Contents. V. 1. Bohn, H: Life of Goldsmith.— Vicar of Wakefield.—Essays.— Letters. 2. Poems. —Plays.—The bee. — The Cock-lane ghost. 3. The citizen of the world.—Polite learning in Europe. 4. Biographies.—Criticisms.—Later collected essays.

Hallam, Arthur H: Remains in prose and verse; with a preface and a memoir. Bost. 1863. D. **820.2 : 11**
Contents. Pref.—Memoir of Arthur H: Hallam.—Memoir of H: Fitzmaurice Hallam.—Meditative fragments in blank verse. — Timbuctoo. — Sonnets. — Stanzas. — [Various poems]. — Sonnets. — Scene at Rome.—On sympathy.—On the influence of italian works of imagination on the same class of compositions in England.—The philosophical writings of Cicero. — Remarks on prof. Rossetti's Disquisizioni sullo spirito antipapale.—Extract from a review of Tennyson's poems.

Hawthorne, Nathaniel. [Complete works; with introd. notes by G: Parsons Lathrop and ill. with etchings by Blum, Church, Dielman, Gifford, Shirlow and Turner. Riverside ed.] Bost. 1883–85. 12 v. D.
 820.1 : 10
Contents. V. 1. Twice-told tales. 2. Mosses from an old manse. 3. The house of seven gables.—The snow-image, and other twice-told tales. 4. A wonderbook. — Tanglewood tales. — The whole history of grandfather's chair. 5. The scarlet letter. — The Blithedale romance. 6. The marble faun. 7. Our old home.—Passages from the english note-books. 8. Passages from the english note-books, *continued.* 9. Passages from the american note-books. 10. Passages from the french and italian note-books. 11. The Dolliver romance.—Fanshawe.—Septimius Felton.—App.: The ancestral footstep. 12. Tales and sketches.—Biographical stories. — Biographical sketches.—Alice Doane's appeal.—Chiefly about war matters.—Life of Franklin Pierce.—Lathrop, G: P. Biographical sketch of Nathaniel Hawthorne. — Index.

Herbert, W: Works, excepting those on botany and natural history; with additions and corrections by the author. Lond. 1842. 3 v. O. **820.2 : 32**
Contents. V. 1. Horæ scandicæ, or Works relating to old scandinavian literature. — Horæ pierisæ, or Poetry on various subjects. 2. Horæ pedestres, or Prose works, excepting those on botany and natural history. — Attila: Supplement. 3. Attila, or The triumph of christianity; a poem.

Hobbes, T: English works; now first coll. and ed. by sir W: Molesworth. Lond. 1839–45. 11 v. O. **820.2 : 12**
Contents. V. 1. Elements of philosophy: Pt. 1, Logic; pt. 2, The first grounds of philosophy; pt. 3, The proportions of motions and magnitudes; Physics or the phenomena of nature. 2. Philosophical rudiments concerning government and society: Of liberty; Of dominion; Of religion. 3. Leviathan, or The matter, form and power of a commonwealth, ecclesiastical and civil: 1st pt., Of man; 2d pt., Of commonwealth; 3d pt., Of a christian commonwealth; 4th pt., Of the kingdom of darkness. 4. Tripos: Human nature; De corpore politico, or The elements of law; Of liberty and necessity. — An answer to bp. Bramhall's book, called "The catching of the leviathan."—An historical narration concerning heresy and the punishment thereof.—Considerations upon the reputation, loyalty, manners and religion of T: Hobbes.—Answer to sir W: Davenant's preface before "Gondibert."—Letter to E: Howard. 5. The questions concerning liberty, necessity and chance, clearly stated and debated between dr. Bramhall and T: Hobbes. 6. A dialogue between a philosopher and a student of the common laws of England.—Behemoth; the history of the causes of the civil wars of England.—The whole art of rhetoric. —The art of rhetoric, plainly set forth with pertinent examples for the more easy understanding of the same.—The art of sophistry. 7. Seven philosophical problems.—Decameron physiologicum.—Proportion of a straight line to half the arc of a quadrant. —Six lessons to the savilian professors of the mathematics.—Stigmai, or Marks of the absurd geometry, etc., of dr. Wallis. — Extract of a letter from H: Stubbe.—Three papers presented to the Royal society against dr. Wallis.—Consideration on the answer of dr. Wallis.—Letters and other pieces. 8, 9. Thucydides. The history of the grecian war, tr. by T: Hobbes. 10. Homer. The Iliads and Odyssey, tr. by T: Hobbes. 11. Index and plates.

Hood, T: Prose works. Ill. N. Y. 1878. 2 v. in 1. D. **820.2 : 36**
Contents. V. 1. Whims and oddities.—Comic miscellany. — Autobiographical papers. — From Hood's own. — From Hood's magazine. — App.: editorial notes. 2. Up the Rhine.—Romances and extravaganzas.

Irving, Washington. Works; Geoffrey Crayon ed. Ill. N. Y. *n. d.* 27 v. O. **820.1 : P11**
Contents. V. 1. Warner, C: Dudley. Washington Irving; a biographical and critical study.—Knickerbocker's New York. 2. The sketch-book of Geoffrey Crayon, gent. 3. Bracebridge Hall, or The humorist; a medley by Geoffrey Crayon, gent. 4. Tales of a traveller. 5. The Alhambra. 6. Chronicle of the conquest of Granada; from the mss. of fray Antonio Agapida. 7. The Crayon miscellany: A tour on the prairies; Abbotsford; Newstead abbey. 8. The adventures of capt. Bonneville, U. S. A., in the Rocky mountains and the far west; digested from his journal and illustrated from various other sources. 9. Oliver Goldsmith; a biography. 10-12. The life and voyages of Christopher Columbus; added, those of his companions. 13. Astoria, or Anecdotes of an enterprise beyond the Rocky mountains. 14, 15. Mahomet and his successors. 16. Salmagundi, or The whimwhams and opinions of Launcelot Langstaff, esq., and others. 17. Wolfert's Roost.—The birds of spring.—The creole village.— Mountjoy.—The Bermudas.—The widow's ordeal.— The knight of Malta.—"A time of unexampled prosperity." — Sketches in Paris in 1825. — A contented man.—Broek, the dutch paradise.—Guests from Gibbet Island.—The early experiences of Ralph Ringwood.—The Seminoles.—The count van Horn.—Don Juan; a spectral research.—Legend of the engulphed convent.—The phantom island.—Recollections of the Alhambra. 18. Spanish papers: The legend of don Roderick; Legend of the subjugation of Spain; Legend of count Julian and his family; The legend of Pelayo; Abderahman, founder of the dynasty of the Ommiades of Spain; Chronicle of Fernan Gonzales, count of Castile; Chronicle of Fernando the saint; Spanish romance. 19. Letters of Jonathan Oldstyle, gent. — Biographical sketches: Capt. James Lawrence; Lieut. Burrows; Com. Perry; Capt. D: Porter; T: Campbell; Washington Allston; Conversations with Talma; Margaret Miller Davidson.—Reviews and miscellanies: Robert Treat Paine; Edwin C. Holland; Wheaton's History of the northmen; Conquest of Granada; Letter to the editor of "The knickerbocker"; Sleepy Hollow; National nomenclature; Desultory thoughts on criticism; Conspiracy of the cocked hats; Letter from Granada; The Catskill mountains. 20-24. Life of G: Washington. 25-27. The life and letters of Washington Irving, by his nephew, Pierre M. **Irving.**

— [Works.] Chicago. *n. d.* 10 v. D.
 820.1 : 13
Contents. V. 1. The life and voyages of Christopher Columbus. 2. Abbotsford.—Newstead abbey.—The conquest of Granada, gent.—Moorish chronicles. 4. Astoria, or Anecdotes of an enterprise beyond the Rocky mountains.—A tour of the prairies. 5. A history of New York, from the beginning of the world to the end of the dutch dynasty, by Diedrich Knickerbocker. — The Alhambra. 6. The adventures of captain Bonneville.—Spanish voyages of discovery. 7. Bracebridge Hall, or The humorists.—Wolfert's Roost.—Sleepy Hollow.—Birds of spring.—Recollections of the Alhambra.—Abencerrage.—Enchanted island.—Adelantado of the seven cities.—National nomenclature.— Desultory thoughts on criticism.— Spanish romance.—Legend of don Munio Sancho de Hinojosa.—Communipaw.—The Bermudas.—Pelayo and the merchant's daughter.—Knight of Malta.— Legend of the engulphed convent.—Count van Horn. 8. The Crayon papers: Mount Joy; The great Mississippi bubble; Don Juan, a spectral research; Broek, or the dutch paradise; Sketches in Paris, 1825; American researches in Italy; The taking of the veil; The charming Letorières; The early experiences of Ralph Ringwood; The Seminoles; Letter from Granada; Abderahman, founder of the dynasty of the Ommiades in Spain; The widow's ordeal; The creole village; A contented man. 9. Tales of a traveller: Strange stories by a nervous gentleman; Buckthorne and his friends; The italian banditti; The money-diggers. — The life of Oliver Goldsmith. 10. Mahomet and his successors.

Johnson, S: Works; with an essay on his life and genius by Arthur Murphy. 3d amer. ed. N. Y. 1846. 2 v. O.   **820.2+13**
Contents. V. **1.** Life and genius, by A. **Murphy.**—The rambler.—The adventurer.—The idler.—Rasselas. —*Tales of the imagination:* the vision of Theodore the hermit of Teneriffe.—The fountains; a fairy tale.—Letters, selected from the collection of mrs. Piozzi and others.—Irene; a tragedy in 5 acts.—Miscellaneous poems. **2.** Lives of the poets.—Lives of eminent persons: Father Paul Sarpi; Boerhaave; Blake; Sir Francis Drake; Barretier; Morin; Burman; Sydenham; Cheynel; Cave; King of Prussia; Browne; Ascham.—Political tracts.—Philological tracts, etc.—Miscellaneous tracts, etc.—Dedications.—Opinions on questions of law.—Reviews and criticisms.—Journey to the western islands of Scotland.—Prayers and meditations.

Lamb, C: Works; with a sketch of his life and final memorials by sir T: Noon Talfourd. N. Y. 1847, 1857. 2 v. D.   **820.2:14**
Contents. V. **1.** Letters, with a sketch of his life.—Poetical works: Poems; Sonnets; Blank verse; John Woodvil, a tragedy; Miscellaneous poems; Translations; The wife's trial, or The intruding widow, a dramatic poem. **2.** Essays of Elia.—Popular fallacies.—Rosamund Gray.—Recollections of Christ's Hospital.—Essays: On the tragedies of Shakspeare; Characters of dramatic writers contemporary with Shakspeare; Specimens from the writings of Fuller; On the genius and character of Hogarth; On the poetical works of G: Wither. — Letters under assumed signatures. — Curious fragments. — Mr. H—; a farce in 2 acts.—Poetical works.
Note. V. 1 belongs to Harper's ed. of 1847 and v. 2 to Derby and Jackson's ed. of 1857; hence the repetition of the Poetical works at the end of each vol.

— Works. New ed. N. Y. 1883. 5 v. in 3. D.   **820.2:14**
Contents. V. **1, 2.** Letters, with a sketch of his life by sir T: Noon **Talfourd. 3.** Elia.—The last essays of Elia.—Popular fallacies. **4.** Rosamund Gray.—Essays. — Letters under assumed signatures pub. in "The reflector."—Curious fragments extracted from a common-place book which belonged to Robert Burton.—Mr. H—; a farce in 2 acts.—Poems.— Album verses, with a few others. **5.** Essays and sketches.—The pawnbroker's daughter; a farce.— The adventures of Ulysses.— Tales.— Poems.—Letters.

Landon, Lætitia Elizabeth, (*L. E. L.; Mrs. Maclean*). Complete works. Bost. 1856. 2 v. in 1. O.   **820.2:26**
Contents. V. **1.** Romance and reality.—Francesca Carrara.—Traits and trials of early life. **2.** Ethel Churchill.—The book of beauty.—Poetical works.

Landor, Walter Savage. Works and life. Lond. 1876. 8 v. O.   **820.2:15**
Contents. V. **1.** **Forster,** J: Walter Savage Landor; a biography. **2.** Classical dialogues, greek.—*Same,* roman. — Citation and examination of W: Shakespeare for deer-stealing. **3.** Dialogues of sovereigns and statesmen.—The pentameron. **4.** Dialogues of literary men. **5.** *Same, continued.*—Dialogues of famous women.—Pericles and Aspasia. —Minor prose pieces: Opinions on Cæsar, Cromwell, Milton and Buonaparte; Inscription for a statue at S. Ives; Sir Robert Peel and monuments to public men; To Cornelius at Munich; The quarterly review; A story of Santander; The death of Hofer; A vision; The dream of Petrarca; Parable of Asabel; Jeribohaniah. **6.** Miscellaneous dialogues. **7.** Poems: Gebir; Acts and scenes; Hellenics. **8.** Miscellaneous poems. — Criticisms: Idyls of Theocritus; Poems of Catullus; Francesco Petrarca.—Index.

Longfellow, H: Wadsworth. Poetical works. Ill. Bost. [1880]. 2 v. F.   **820.1:R12**
Contents. V. **1.** Voices of the night. — Earlier poems.—Translations.—Ballads and other poems.—The children of the Lord's supper.—Miscellaneous poems.—Translations.—The spanish student.—The belfry of Bruges and other poems.—Evangeline; a tale of Acadie.— The seaside and the fireside.— The blind girl of Castèl Cuillè.—A christmas carol.—The song of Hiawatha.—The courtship of Miles Standish.—Birds of passage.—Tales of a wayside inn. **2.** Tales of a

Longfellow, H: Wadsworth.—*Continued.*
wayside inn, pt. 3, *continued.* — Flower - de - luce. — Christus, a mystery: Pt. 1, The divine tragedy; pt. 2, The golden legend; pt. 3, The New-England tragedies. — Judas Maccabeus. — A handful of translations.—The masque of Pandora.—The hanging of the crane.— Morituri salutamus.—A book of sonnets.—Kéramos.—Birds of passage; flight the fifth.—Translations.— Seven sonnets and a canzone from the italian of Michael Angelo.—Ultima Thule.—Notes.—Index.

— Complete prose works, with his later poems; with a biographical sketch by Octavius B. Frothingham. Ill. Bost. [1883]. F.
   820.1:R12 v3
Contents. In the harbor.—Michael Angelo.—Outremer.—Hyperion; a romance.—Kavanagh; a tale.—Drift-wood. — Frothingham, O. B. H: Wadsworth Longfellow; a sketch.—Notes on the illustrations.

Lyttleton, G:, *1st baron Lyttleton.* Works, formerly printed separately and now first collected, together with some other pieces never before printed, pub. by G: E: Ayscough. 3d ed., with index. Lond. 1776. 3 v. O.   **820.2:16**
Contents. V. **1.** Observations on the life of Cicero. —Observations on the roman history.—Observations on the present state of our affairs at home and abroad.—Letters from a persian in England to his friend at Ispahan.—Two essays from "Common sense." **2.** Observations on the conversion and apostleship of St. Paul.—Dialogues of the dead. **3.** Speeches.—Poems.—Letters.

Mitford, Mary Russell. Works. *T. p. w. O.*
   820.2:27
Contents. Our village; sketches of rural character and scenery.—Belford Regis; sketches of a country town. — Country stories. — Extracts from Finden's Tableaux. — Poetical works: Foscari, a tragedy; Julian, a tragedy; Rienzi, a tragedy.—Charles I; an historical tragedy.

More, Hannah. Works. 1st complete amer. ed. N. Y. 1843. 2 v. O.   **820.2:28**
Contents. V. **1.** [Miscel. poems].—Epitaphs.—Ballads and tales [in verse].—Hymns.—Ballads.—Bible rhymes.—Sacred dramas: The introd.; Moses; David and Goliath; Belshazzar; Daniel. — Reflections of Hezekiah.—Search after happiness.—Ode to charity. —Stories for persons of the middle rank: Mr. Fantom, or The history of the new fashioned philosopher and his man William; The history of mr. Bragwell, or The two wealthy farmers; 'Tis all for the best; A cure for melancholy; The sunday school. — Allegories: The pilgrims; The valley of tears; The strait and the broad way; Parley the porter.—Tales: The shepherd of Salisbury Plain; The two shoemakers; The history of Tom White, the postboy; The history of Hester Wilmot; The grand assizes, or General jail delivery, an allegory; The servant man turned soldier, an allegory; The history of Betty Brown, the St. Giles orange girl; Black Giles the poacher; Tawney Rachel, or The fortune teller.—Thoughts on the manners of the great.—An estimate of the religion of the fashionable world.—Strictures on the modern system of female education.—Practical piety.—Tragedies: Pref.; The inflexible captive; Percy; The fatal falsehood.—Poems. **2.** Hints for forming the character of a young princess.—Christian morals.—An essay on the character and practical writings of St. Paul.—Celebs in search of a wife.—Foreign sketches.—Domestic sketches. — Reflections on prayer.—Spirit of prayer.—Essays on various subjects.—Moriana.

Neele, H: Literary remains; consisting of lectures on english poetry, tales and other miscellaneous pieces in prose and verse. N. Y. 1829. O.   **820.2:17**
Contents. Lectures on english poetry. — Original tales, poems, etc.: The garter, a romance of english history; Blanche of Bourbon, a romance of spanish history; Shakspeare's supernatural characters; A night at the Mermaid; The Trekschuit; Poems. — Miscellaneous prose and poetry.

Perkins, James Handasyd. Memoir and writings; ed. by W: H: Channing. Bost. 1851. 2 v. D.   **820.1 : 7**

Contents. V. 1. Sketches of the life of J. H. Perkins. — Verses. — *Tales.* Melanchthon and Luther. — Lord Ossory.—Dora McCrae.—The hypochondriac.— A week among the "knobs".—The judge's hunt.— The murderer's daughter.—The kindness that kills.— Charity in the counting house and out of it.—Life in Cincinnati in 1840.—The lost child.—The hole in my pocket.—The one true convert. 2. *Historical sketches.* Mohammed.—Gregory VII and his age.—St. Louis of France.—The founder of the jesuits.—Early french travellers in the west.—English discoveries in the Ohio valley. — The pioneers of Kentucky. — Border war of the revolution. — Settlement of the Northwestern Territory.—Fifty years of Ohio.—The french revolution.—A glimpse of Australia.

Poe, Edgar Allan. Works. N. Y. 1876. 4 v. D.   **820.1 : 5**

Contents. V. 1. **Ingram,** J. H. Memoir.—**Lowell,** J. R., and N. P. **Willis.** Notices of his life and genius.—**Moran,** J. J. Memoranda of the death of Poe.—Editorials on his life and character. — Ceremonies of monumental dedication. — Poems and essays. — Poems written in youth. — Eureka. — The rationale of verse.—The philosophy of composition. —Marginalia.—Fifty suggestions. 2. *Autography.*— The literati. 3. *Tales.* The adventures of one Hans Pfall. — The gold bug. — The balloon hoax. — Von Kempelen and his discovery.—Mesmeric revelation.— The facts in the case of M. Valdemar.—The thousand and second tale of Scheherazade.—Ms. found in a bottle.—Descent into the Maelstrom.—The murders of the rue Morgue.—The mystery of Marie Roget.— The purloined letter.—The black cat.—The fall of the house of Usher.—The pit and the pendulum.—The premature burial.—The masque of the red death.— The cask of amontillado.—The imp of the perverse.— The island of the fay.—The oval portrait.—The assignation.— The tell-tale heart.— The domain of Arnheim.— Landor's cottage. — William Wilson. — Berenice.—Eleonora.—Ligeia.—Morella.—Metzengerstein. — A tale of the Ragged mountains.—The spectacles.— The duc de l'Omelette.—The oblong box.—King Pest. —Three sundays in a week.—The devil in the belfrey. —Lionizing. 4. Narrative of A. Gordon Pym.— Miscellanies.

— Works; v. 3, 4. N. Y. 1850, 1856. 2 v. D.   **820.1 : 5** v3,4

Contents. V. 3. Memoir of the author by Rufus Wilmot **Griswold.** — The literati. 4. Narrative of A. Gordon Pym.—Miscellanies.

Pope, Alexander. Works, complete, with his last corrections, additions and improvements . . . ; with the commentaries and notes of mr. Warburton. Lond. 1751. 9 v. O.   **820.2 : 24**

Contents. V. 1. Preface.—Recommendatory poems. —Pastorals.—Messiah.—Windsor forest.—Ode on St. Cecilia's day and other pieces for music.—Essay on criticism.—The rape of the lock.—Elegy.—Prologue to Addison's tragedy of Cato.—Epilogue to Rowe's Jane Shore. 2. *Translations and imitations.* Ovid: Sappho to Phaon; an epistle.—Eloisa to Abelard; an epistle.—The temple of Fame.—Chaucer: January and May; The wife of Bath.—Statius: First book of Thebais.—Ovid: The fable of Dryope; Vertumnus and Pomona.—Imitations. 3. **Brown,** J. Essay on satire.—Essay on man.—*Moral essays.* Of the knowledge and character of men.—Of the characters of women.—Of the use of riches.—To mr. Addison, occasioned by his dialogues on medals. 4. Epistle to dr. Arbuthnot.—Satires and epistles of Horace imitated.—Satires of dr. J: Donne versified.—Epilogue to the satires.—To the lady Frances Shirley. 5. Letter to the publisher.—Prolegomena and illustrations to the Dunciad, with the hypercritics of Aristarchus. —Dunciad, book 1–4.— App. 6. Imitations of Horace.—Epistles.—Epitaphs.—Memoirs of Martinus Scriblerius.—Art of sinking in poetry.—Virgilius restauratus.—Specimen of Scriblerius's reports.—Memoirs of P. P. clerk of this parish.—Of the poet laureate.—Guardians.—Preface to Homer's Iliad.—Preface to the works of Shakespear. 7–9. Letters.

Sands, Robert C: Writings in prose and verse, with a memoir of the author. N. Y. 1834. 2 v. O.   **820.1 : 6**

Contents. V. 1. Memoir.—Historical notice of Her-

nan Cortes.—Domestic literature.—Isaac; a type of the Redeemer. — The Caio-Gracco of Monti. — The garden of Venus.—Yamoyden; a tale of the wars of king Philip. 2. Association.—The german's story.— The man who burned John Rogers.—A simple talc. —Boyuca.—Thoughts on hand-writing.—Mr. De Villecour and his neighbors.—Scenes at Washington, 1, 2. —Ghosts on the stage.—The stranger in Weehawk.— Hoboken.—John Brown.—John Smith.—Police literature.—Letter from Orange county.—Dream of Papantzin.—Poems.

St. John, H:, *viscount Bolingbroke,* (*Humphrey Oldcastle*). Works, with a life prepared for this ed., containing add. information relative to his personal and public character, selected from the best authorities. Phila. 1841. 4 v. O.   **820.2 : 18**

Contents. V. 1. Life.—Letter to sir W: Windham, 1717.—Secret letter from the earl of Stair.—Reflections upon exile.—The occasional writer, no. 1–3.— The first vision of Camilick.—An answer to the London journal of sat., dec. 21, 1728.—An answer to the defence of the inquiry into the reasons of the conduct of Great Britain.—Remarks on the history of England.—A final answer to the Remarks of the craftsmen's vindication.—On luxury.—Remarks on a late-pamphlet entitled " Observations on the conduct of Great Britain," etc., 1729.—On good and bad ministers.—On the policy of the athenians.—On the power of the prince and the freedom of the people. 2. A dissertation upon parties.—Letters on the study and use of history. 3. A letter occasioned by one of archbp. Tillotson's sermons.—Letters or essays addressed to Alex. Pope: Concerning the nature, extent and reality of human knowledge; On the folly and presumption of philosophers; On the rise and progress of monotheism; Concerning authority in matters of religion. 4. Concerning authority in matters of religion, *continued.*—Fragments or minutes of essays.—Index.

Sidney, *Sir* Philip. The countess of Pembroke's Arcadia. 13th ed.; with his life and death, and a brief table of the principal heads and some other new additions. Lond. 1674. Q.   **23 : R**

Contents. Life and death of sir Philip Sidney.— Epigrams on [him]. — The countess of Pembroke's Arcadia.— A sixth book to the countess of Pembroke's Arcadia [by R. Beling].—Sonnets.—The defense of poesie.—Astrophel and Stella.—Supplement to the 3d book of Arcadia by James Johnstoun.—A remedie for love.

Smith, *Capt.* J: Works, 1608–1631 ; ed. by E: Arber. (The english scholar's library.) Birmingham. 1884. D.   **820.2 : 34**

Contents. Preface.—Introd.—Bibliography.—A true relation, etc.—A map of Virginia, etc., pt. 1.—**Simmonds,** W., *Same,* pt. 2.—A description of New England.—New England trials.—The general historie of Virginia.—An introduction for young seamen.—The true travels, etc. — Advertisements for the unexperienced planters of New England, or anywhere, etc.—The last will and the epitaph of J: Smith.

Smith, Sydney. Works. 3 v. in 1. Phila. 1845. O.   **820.2+19**

Contents. Articles originally publ. in the Edinburgh review. Dr. Parr. — Dr. Rennel. — J: Bowles. — Dr. Langford.—Archdeacon Nares.— M. Lewis.—Australia.— Fievée's Letters on England. — Edgeworth on bulls. — Trimmer and Lancaster. — Parnell and Ireland. — Methodism.—Indian missions. — Catholics. — Methodism.—Hannah More.—Professional education. —Female education.— Public schools.— Toleration.— C: Fox. — Mad quakers. — America. — Game laws.— Botany Bay. — Chimney sweepers. — America. — Ireland.—Spring guns.—Prisons.—Persecuting bishops. —Botany Bay.—Game laws.—Cruel treatment of untried prisoners.—America.—Bentham on fallacies.— Waterton.—Man traps and spring guns.—Hamilton's method of teaching languages.—Counsel for prisoners. — Catholics. — Neckar's last views. — Catholics. —Tableau des états danois.—Thoughts on the residence of the clergy.—Travis from Palestine.—Letter on the curates' salary bill.—Proceedings of the Society for the suppression of vice.—Characters of Fox.— Observations on the historical work of C: J. Fox.— Disturbances at Madras.—Bishop of Lincoln's charge. —Mme. d'Epinay.—Poor laws.—Public characters of

1801, 1802.—Anastasius Scarlett's poor bill.—Memoirs of capt. Rock. — Granby. — Island of Ceylon.—Delphine. — Mission to Ashantee. — Wittman's travels. *Speeches.* On the catholic claims.— At the Taunton reform meeting.—At a meeting to celebrate the accession of William IV.— At Taunton in 1831 on the reform bill not being passed.— Respecting the reform bill.— *Miscellaneous.* The ballot.— Letters to archdeacon Singleton.—On the character of sir James Mackintosh. — To lord J: Russell. — Sermon on the duties of the queen. — The lawyer that tempted Christ; a sermon.—The judge that smites contrary to the law; a sermon.—Letter to the electors on the catholic question.—Sermon on the rules of christian charity.—Peter Plymley's letters.

Sterne, Lawrence. Works, with a life of the author written by himself. Lond. 1819. 4 v. O. 820.2 : 20
Contents. V. 1. Memoirs.— Life and opinions of Tristram Shandy, gent. 2. *Same, continued.*— A sentimental journey through France and Italy. 3, 4. Sermons.

Swift, Jonathan. Works; with copious notes and add., and a memoir of the author by T: Roscoe. N. Y. *n. d.* 6 v. D. 820.2 : 21
Contents. V. 1. **Roscoe,** T: Life and poetical works.— Poetical works. 2. Gulliver's travels.— A tale of a tub.—The history of Martin.— The battle of the books.—A discourse concerning the mechanical operations of the spirit.— The Drapier's letters. — Memoirs of capt. J: Creichton. 3. Journal to Stella. —Memoirs relating to that change which happened in queen Anne's ministry in 1710.—A discourse of the contests and dissensions between the nobles and the commons in Rome.—The examiner.—A short character of Thomas earl of Wharton.— Some remarks upon a pamphlet, entitled A letter to the seven lords of the committee appointed to examine Gregg.—A new journey to Paris, with some secret transactions between the french king and an english gentleman. —Some advice humbly offered to the members of the October club. 4, 5. Miscellaneous. 6. A complete

Swift, Jonathan.—*Continued.*
collection of genteel and ingenious conversation.— Directions to servants.—Remarks on the first fifteen psalms of David, tr. into lyric verse.—The address of the house of lords to the queen.—The answer of W: Pulteney to sir Robert Walpole.—Letters.

— *Same* ; v. 3–6. N. Y. 1859. 4 v. D. 820.2 : 21

Taylor, Jane. Writings. Bost. 1832–35. 3 v. O. 820.2 : 22
Contents. V. 1. Memoirs and correspondence.— Poetical remains.—Essays in rhyme on morals and manners. 2. Contributions of Q. Q.: pt. 1, Religious and didactic pieces; pt. 2, Miscellaneous pieces. 3. Correspondence between a mother and her daughter at school, by Mrs. and Jane Taylor.— Original poems for infant minds, by the Taylor family. — Display; a ta'e.

Temple, *Sir* W: Works ; prefixed, the life and character of the author. New ed. Lond. 1757. 4 v. O. 820.2 : 23
Contents. V. 1. Life and character.—Essay upon the origin and nature of government. — Observations upon the United Provinces of the Netherlands. —Letters written by [him] and other ministers of state, containing an account of the most important transactions that passed in christendom from 1665 to 1772. 2. *Same, continued.*—Survey of the constitutions and interests of the empire, Sweden, Denmark, Spain, Holland, France and Flanders, with their relation to England in 1671.—Letter to the duke of Ormond, 1673. — Memoirs from 1672–1679. — Memoirs, 1679, 1680. 3. An essay upon the advancement of trade in Ireland. — Of popular discontents. — An introd. to the history of England.—Of gardening.— An essay upon the cure of gout by moxa.—Of health and long life.— Of heroic virtue. — Of poetry.—An essay upon antient and modern learning.—Thoughts upon reviewing that essay.—Of the excesses of grief. —Of the different conditions of life and fortune.— Heads of an essay on conversation. — Poetry. 4. Letters.—Index.

5. English literature — b, Poetry.

1. History and criticism.

(See also Essays, class 824.)

Warton, T: History of english poetry from the 12th to the close of the 16th century ; with a pref. by R: Price and notes variorum, ed. by W. Carew Hazlitt, with new notes and other add. by sir F: Madden, T: Wright, W. Aldis Wright, Walter W. Skeat, R: Morris, F. J. Furnival and the ed., with indexes of names and subjects. Lond. 1871. 4 v. O. 821.4+1
Contents. V. 1. **Hazlitt,** W: C. Preface to present ed.— Author's preface.— **Price,** R: Preface.— Dissertations: Of the origin of romantic fiction in Europe; On the Lais of Marie de France; On the introd. of learning into England; On the Gesta romanorum; **Wright,** T: On the seven sages. 2. **Sweet,** H: Sketch of the history of anglo-saxon poetry. — Through Chaucer. 3. Through Skelton, 1529. 4. 16th century.

Hazlitt, W: Lectures on the english poets. From the 3d Lond. ed., ed. by his son. N. Y. 1845. D. 821.5 : 2
— *Same.* With *his* Lectures on the english comic writers. *in* 828.5 : 1
Contents. Introductory; On poetry in general.— Chaucer and Spenser.—Shakspeare and Milton.—Dryden and Pope.— Thomson and Cowper. — Swift, Young, Gray, Collins, etc.—On Burns and the old english ballads.—On the living poets. — App.: On Milton's Lycidas.—On the character of Milton's Eve. —On Wordsworth's Excursion. — Pope, lord Byron and mr. Bowles.

Minto, W: Characteristics of english poets from Chaucer to Shirley. Edinb. 1874. D. 821.5 : 10

Reed, H: Lectures on the british poets. Phila. 1858. 2 v. D. 821.5 : 4
Contents. V. 1. On poetry. — Chaucer. — Spenser and the minstrelsy. — Shakspeare. —Milton.—Minor poetry of the 17th century.—The age of the restoration: Dryden.—The age of queen Anne: Pope.— Poets of the latter part of the 18th century: Cowper. 2. Burns, with notices of Johnson's Lives of the poets. — Contemporary literature. — Coleridge. — Southey, with notice of C: Lamb.—Byron.—Wordsworth.—English sonnets.—Poems of Hartley Coleridge.

Stedman, Edmund Clarence. Victorian poets. Bost. 1876. D. 821.5 : 5
Contents. The period.—Landor.—Hood.—Arnold.— Procter. — Mrs. Browning. — Tennyson. — Tennyson and Theocritus.— The general choir. — Browning.— Latter - day singers: Buchanan; Rossetti; Morris; Swinburne.—Index.

Tuckerman, H: Theodore. Thoughts on the poets. N. Y. 1846. S. 821.5 : 7
Contents. Petrarch.—Goldsmith.—Gray.—Collins.— Pope.—Cowper.—Thomson.—Young Alfieri.—Crabbe. —Shelley.—Hunt.—Byron.—Moore.—Rogers.—Burns. — Campbell. — Wordsworth. — Coleridge. — Keats. — Barry Cornwall.—Mrs. Hemans.—Tennyson.— Miss Barrett.—Drake.—Bryant.

Brooke, Stopford A: Theology in english poets ; Cowper, Coleridge, Wordsworth and Burns. N. Y. 1875. D. 821.5 : 1

Holland, F: May. Stories from Robert Browning ; with an introd. by mrs. Sutherland Orr. Lond. 1882. S. 821.5 : 13

Wilson, J: The genius and character of Burns. Phila. 1854. D. 821.5 : 15

Carpenter, Stephen Haskins. English of the 14th century, illustrated by notes, grammatical and philological, on Chaucer's Prologue and Knight's tale ; designed to serve as an introd. to the study of english literature. Bost. 1873. D. 821.5 : 12

Owen, Frances M. John Keats ; a study. Lond. 1880. D. 821.5 : 3

Warton, Joseph. An essay on the genius and writings of Pope. 5th ed. corr. [with] index. Lond. 1806. 2 v. O. 821.5+14

Todhunter, J: A study of Shelley. Lond. 1880. D. 821.5 : 6

Hart, J: Seely. An essay on the life and writings of Edmund Spenser, with a special exposition of the Fairy queen. N. Y. 1847. O. 821.5+8

Hitchcock, Ethan Allen. Spenser's poems, entitled Colin Clouts come home againe, explained, with remarks upon the Amoretti sonnets, and also upon a few of the minor poems of other early english poets. N. Y. 1865. D. 821.5 : 9

Dawson, S. E. A study, with critical and explanatory notes of Alfred Tennyson's poem The princess. Montreal. 1882. S. 821.5 : 11

Hudson, H: Norman. Studies in Wordsworth ; Culture and acquirement, Ethics of tragedy, and other papers. Bost. 1884. D. 821.5 : 16

Contents. Studies in Wordsworth. — Science, culture, acquirement.—Ethics of tragedy.—Parting address.—The church and civil society.

2. Collections.

Durfee, C: A., comp. A concise poetical concordance to the principal poets of the world ; embracing titles, first lines, characters, subjects and quotations. N. Y. 1885. D. 811 : R11

Includes the following english and american poets: Edwin Arnold.—W: E. Aytoun.—Mrs. E. B. Browning.—W: C. Bryant.—Robert Burns.—Lord Byron.—T: Campbell.—G. Chaucer.—S. T. Coleridge.—W: Cowper.—G: Crabbe.—J: Dryden.—George Eliot.—R. W. Emerson.—Oliver Goldsmith.—Mrs. F. D. Hemans.—G: Herbert.—O. W. Holmes.—T: Hood.—Jean Ingelow.—J: Keats.—H: W. Longfellow.—J. R. Lowell.—T. B. Macaulay.—Owen Meredith.—J: Milton.—Ossian.—E. A. Poe.— Alex. Pope.— Adelaide Procter.—S: Rogers.—D. G. Rossetti.—Sir W. Scott.—W: Shakespeare.—P. B. Shelley.—Edmund Spenser.—H: Taylor.—Alfred Tennyson.—James Thomson.—C: Wesley. H: K. White.—J: G. Whittier.—N. P. Willis.—W: Wordsworth.

*　　　*　　　*

Bryant, W: Cullen, ed. A library of poetry and song ; choice selections from the best poets, with an introduction. N. Y. 1873. O. 821 : 1

—— A new library of poetry and song. Ill. N. Y. [1877]. Q. 821 : R19

Dana, C: Anderson, ed. The household book of poetry. N. Y. 1858. O. 821+2
— Same. 11th ed. N. Y. 1882. O. 821+2

Elmo, pseud. Illustrated home book of poetry and song ; choice selections from the poets of all lands and ages. Chicago. [1884]. O. 821+18

Emerson, Ralph Waldo, ed. Parnassus. Bost. 1875. O. 821 : 5

Hervey, T: Kibble, ed. The english Helicon. Lond. 1841. O. 821 : 4

Johnson, Edwin Rossiter, ed. Famous single and fugitive poems. N. Y. 1880. D. 821 : 9

Kirkland, Caroline Matilda, born Stansbury. The school-girl's garland ; a selection of poetry in four parts. N. Y. 1864. 2 v. S. 821 : 11

Linton, W: James, and R: H: Stoddard, eds. English verse. N. Y. 1883. 5 v. D. 821 : 14

Contents. V. 1. Chaucer to Burns. 2. Lyrics of the 19th century. 3. Ballads and romances. 4. Dramatic scenes and characters. 5. Translations.

Sargent, Epes, ed. Harper's cyclopædia of british and american poetry. N. Y. 1881. O. 821 : R13

Whittier, J: Greenleaf, ed. Songs of three centuries. Bost. 1876. D. 821 : 7

Waddington, S:, ed. English sonnets by living writers, selected and arr., with a note on the history of the "sonnet". Lond. 1881. S. 821 : 12

Griswold, Rufus Wilmot. The sacred poets of England and America for three centuries. Ill. N. Y. 1849. O. 821+3

Croke, J. Greenbag, pseud. Lyrics of the law ; a recital of songs and verses pertinent to the law and the legal profession, selected from various sources. San Francisco. 1884. S. 821 : 15

Parton, James, ed. The humorous poetry of the english language, from Chaucer to Saxe. Narratives, satires, enigmas, burlesques, parodies, travesties, epigrams, epitaphs, translations, including the most celebrated comic poems of the Anti-Jacobin, Rejected addresses, the Ingoldsby legends, Blackwoods magazine, Bentley's miscellany, and Punch, with more than 200 epigrams, and the choicest humorous poetry of Wolcott, Cowper, Lamb, Thackeray, Praed, Swift, Scott, Holmes, Aytoun, Gay, Jones, Southey, Saxe, Hood, Prior, Coleridge, Byron, Moore, Lowell, etc., with notes, explanatory and biographical. 12th ed. Bost. 1875. O. 821 : 6

British authors.

Adams, W: Davenport, ed. Songs from the novelists from Elizabeth to Victoria ; with an introd. and notes. Lond. 1885. O. 821.2 : 251

Bethune, G: Washington. The british female poets ; with biographical and critical notices. Phila. [1848]. O. 821.2 : 7

Book of the poets, from Chaucer to Beattie. Lond. 1842. O. 821.2 : 2

Campbell, T:, ed. Specimens of the british poets; with biographical and critical notices and an essay on english poetry. New ed., rev. and with add. notes. Phila. 1855. O. 821.2+4

Farrar, F: W:, comp. With the poets ; a selection of english poetry. N. Y. [1883]. D. 821.2 : 222

Halleck, Fitz Greene. Selections from the british poets. N. Y. 1845. 2 v. S. 821.2 : 9

Hunt, James H: Leigh. Imagination and fancy, or Selections from the english poets, illustrative of those first requisites of their art ; with markings of the best passages, critical notices of the writers, and an essay in answer to the question "What is poetry". N. Y. 1848. D.   **821.2 : 10**

Main, D: M. A treasury of english sonnets, ed. from the original sources with notes and ill. N. Y. 1881. O.   **821.2 : 8**

Motherwell, W: Minstrelsy, ancient and modern, with an historical introd. and notes. Bost. 1846. 2 v. D.   **821.2 : 11**

Palgrave, Francis Turner, *comp.* The golden treasury of the best songs and lyrical poems in the english language, sel. and arr. with notes. Lond. 1881. S. **821.2 : 195**

Select works of the british poets, in a chronological series from Southey to Croly; with biographical and critical notices, designed as a continuation of dr. Aikin's British poets. Phila. 1848. O.   **821.2+5**

Ward, T: Humphrey. The english poets; selected with critical introd. by various writers, with a general introd. by Matthew Arnold. Lond. 1880. 4 v. D.   **821.2 : 6**
Contents. V. **1.** Early poetry; Chaucer to Donne. **2.** The seventeenth century; Ben Jonson to Dryden. **3.** The eighteenth century; Addison to Blake. **4.** The nineteenth century; Wordsworth to Dobell.

Percy, T:, *ed.* Reliques of ancient english poetry; consisting of old heroic ballads, songs, and other pieces of our earlier poets, together with some few of later date, and a copious glossary. Lond. 1859. O.   **821.2+1**

Ellis, G: Specimens of the early english poets; prefixed, an historical sketch of the rise and progress of the english poetry and language. Lond. 1801. 3 v. D.
     821.2 : 253
Contents. V. **1.** Introd. remarks on language.—On the poetry of the anglo-saxons.—Specimens of saxon poetry. — Account of norman poets in England.— Specimens of Wace's Brut.—State of our language and poetry in the reign of Henry II and Richard I, exemplified by an extract from Layamon's trans. of Wace.—Conjectures concerning the period at which the anglo-norman or english language began to be formed.—Early specimens of english poetry from Hickes's Thesaurus.—Various small poems, apparently written during the latter part of the 13th century.—Robert de Brunne. —Edward II to Henry VII. **2.** Henry VIII to Elizabeth. **3.** James I to Charles II.—Conclusion.

— Specimens of early english metrical romances, chiefly written during the early part of the 14th century; prefixed, an historical introd. intended to illustrate the rise and progress of romantic composition in France and England. 2d ed. Lond. 1811. 3 v. D.   **821.2 : 3**
Contents. V. **1.** Introd.—App. **1.** Analysis of the work of Alphonsus De clericali disciplina.—App. **2.** Tr. of the Lays of Marie.—Romances relating to Arthur: Merlin, pt. 1; Merlin, pt. 2; Morte Arthur. **2.** Saxon romances: History of Guy Warwick; History of Sir Bevis. — Anglo-norman romance: History of Richard Cœur de lion.—Romances relating to Charlemagne: Introd.; History of Roland and Ferragus; History of sir Otuel; History of sir Ferumbras. **3.** Romances of oriental origin: History of the seven wise masters.—Miscellaneous romances: Florice and Blauncheflour: Robert of Cysille; Sir Isumbras; Sir Triamour; The lyfe of Ipomydon; Sir Eglamour of Artois; Lay le fraine; Sir Eger, sir Grahame and sir Gray-steel; Sir Degoré; Roswal and Lillian; Amys and Amylion.

— *Same.* New ed., rev. by J. C. Halliwell. Lond. 1848. D.   **821.2 : 3**

Hindley, C:, *ed.* The Roxburghe ballads. Lond. 1873. 2 v. O.   **821.2 : 223**

King, R: J:, *ed.* Selections from the early ballad poetry of England and Scotland. Lond. 1842. S.   **821.2 : 231**

Child, Francis James, *ed.* English and scottish ballads. Bost. 1857. 8 v. S.   **821.2 : 12**

Aytoun, W: Edmondstoune, *ed.* The ballads of Scotland. 2d ed. Edinb. 1859. 2 v. D.
     821.2 : 13

Buchan, P:, *ed.* Ancient ballads and songs of the north of Scotland, hitherto unpublished, with explanatory notes. Repr. from the original ed. of 1828. Edinb. 1875. 2 v. D.
     821.2 : 15

Hayes, E:, *ed.* The ballads of Ireland; coll. and ed. with notes, historical and biographical. 5th ed. Dublin. *n. d.* 2 v. D. **821.2 : 16**

Ritson, Joseph, *ed.* Robin Hood; a collection of poems, songs and ballads, relative to that celebrated english chief. Ill. N. Y. 1884. D.   **821.2 : 235**

Wright, T:, *ed.* Political poems and songs relating to english history, composed during the period from the accession of Edw. III to that of Ric. III; pub. by the authority of the lords commissioners of her majesty's treasury, under the direction of the master of the rolls. Lond. 1859, 1861. 2 v. Q.
     821.2+224

Morley, H:, *ed.* The king and the commons; cavalier and puritan songs sel. and arr. [Bayard ser.] N. Y. 1869. S. **821.2 : 128**

Richardson, Abby, *born* Sage, *formerly mrs.* McFarland. Stories from old english poetry. Bost. 1881. D.   **821.2 : 17**
Contents. **Chaucer**, G. The two noble kinsmen; The pious Constance; The knight's dilemma; Three unknown poets; The story of Candace. — **Spenser**, E. Adventures of the fair Florimel; Campaspe and the painter; Friar Bacon's brass head; Margaret, the fair maid of Fresingfield. — **Shakespeare**, W: The story of Perdita; The story of king Lear and his three daughters; The witty Portia, or The three caskets; The story of Rosalind, or As you like it; Macbeth, king of Scotland; The wonderful adventures of Pericles, prince of Tyre; The tempest.

American authors.

American poems: Longfellow, Whittier, Bryant, Holmes, Lowell, Emerson; with biographical sketches and notes. Bost. 1880. S.   **821.1 : 161**

Bryant, W: Cullen. Selections from the american poets. N. Y. 1860. S.   **821.1 : 6**

Griswold, Rufus Wilmot. The poets and poetry of America, with an historical introd. 8th ed. Ill. Phila. 1847. O.   **821.1+1**

Read, T: Buchanan. The female poets of America; with portraits, biographical notices and specimens of their writings. 6th ed. rev. and enl. Phila. 1855. O. **821.1+212**

Rider, G: T:, *ed.* Lyra americana; or Verses of praise and faith from american poets. N. Y. 1865. D.   **821.1 : 4**

Matthews, James Brander, *comp.* Poems of american patriotism. N. Y. 1882. D.
     821.1 : 186

Spooner, *Mrs.* Z. H., *comp.* Poems of the pilgrims. Bost. 1881. S.   **821.1 : 170**

Moore, Frank, *ed.* Songs and ballads of the american revolution; with notes and ill. N. Y. 1856. D.   **821.1 : 3**

Strodtmann, Adolph, *ed.* Amerikanische anthologie; dichtungen der amerikanischen literatur der gegenwart in den versmassen der originale übers. Hildburgh. 1870. D.
     821.1 : 217

White, R: Grant. Poetry, lyrical, narrative and satirical, of the civil war. N. Y. 1866. D.   **821.1 : 2**

Coggeshall, W : T. The poets and poetry of the west, with biographical and critical notices. Columbus, 1860. O.   **821.1+162**

— *Same.* Columbus. 1861. O.   **821.1+162**

Outcroppings; selections of California verse. San Francisco. 1866. S.   **821.1 : 5**

Masque of poets, A ; incl. Guy Vernon, a novelette in verse. (No name series). Bost. 1878. S.   **821.1 : 7**

For young people.

(Including individual works.)

Johnson, Helen Kendrick. Illustrated poems and songs for young people. Ill. N. Y. [1884]. O.   **x 821 : 16**

Morrison, Mary J., *comp.* Songs and rhymes for the little ones. N. Y. 1884. D. **x 821 : 17**

Patmore, Coventry Kearsey Dighton. The children's garland from the best poets, sel. and arr. Lond. 1882. S.   **x 821.2 : 196**

Stevenson, Robert L: A child's garden of verses. N. Y. 1885. D.   **x 821.2 : 245**

Thaxter, Celia, *born* Leighton. Poems for children. Bost. 1884. [1883]. D.   **x 821.1 : 199**

Whittier, J : Greenleaf. Child life ; a collection of poems, with ill. Bost. [1871]. D.   **x 821 : 8**

Mother Goose's nursery rhymes ; a collection of alphabets, rhymes, tales and jingles. Ill. Lond. *n. d.* O.   **x 821.2 : 191**

Carleton, Will. Young folks' centennial rhymes. Ill. N. Y. 1876. D.   **x 821.1 : 173**

Dodge, Mary Elizabeth, *born* Mapes. Rhymes and jingles. N. Y. 1881. D.   **x 821.1 : 174**

Howitt, Mary, *born* Botham. Songs of animal life ; poems. Ill. Lond. [1880]. S.   **x 821.2 : 197**

— With the birds ; poems. Ill. Lond. [1880]. S.   **x 821.2 : 198**

— With the flowers ; poems. Ill. Lond. [1880]. S.   **x 821.2 : 199**

Lamb, C:, *and* Mary. Poetry for children. Added, Prince Dorus and some uncollected poems by C: Lamb. Ed., prefaced and annotated by R: Herne Shepherd. Lond. 1878. D.   **x 821.2 : 192**

Larcom, Lucy. Childhood songs. Ill. Bost. 1875. D.   **x 821.1 : 175**

Rands, W: Brightly. Lilliput levee ; poems of childhood, child - fancy and child - like moods. [*Anon.*] Lond. 1878. T.   **x 821.2 : 194**

Percy, T: The boy's Percy ; being old ballads of war, adventure and love from T: Percy's "Reliques of ancient english poetry," together with an app. containing two ballads from the original Percy folio ms.; ed. for boys, with an introd. by Sidney Lanier. Ill. N. Y. 1882. O.   **x 821.2 : 14**

Chaucer, Geoffrey. Chaucer for children ; a golden key by mrs. H. R. Haweis. Ill. New ed., rev. N. Y. 1882. Q.   **x 821.2 : 209**

— Canterbury chimes, or Chaucer tales retold for children by Francis Storr and Hawes Turner. Lond. 1878. S.   **x 821.2 : 201**

Contents. Introd.—The knight's tale; Palamon and Arcite.—The man of law's tale; Constance.—Nun's

priest's tale; The cock and the fox.—The squire's tale; Canace.—The franklin's tale; Dorigen.—Chaucer's tale; Gamelyn.

Spenser, Edmund. Spenser for children by M. H. Towry. Ill. Lond. 1878. O.   **x 821.2 : 202**

3. Individual works.

Adams, J: Quincy. Poems of religion and society, with notices of his life and character by J: Davis and T: H. Benton. Auburn. 1853. D.   **821.1 : 8**

Addison, Joseph. Poetical works ; prefixed, an essay on his life and writings by T: Babington Macaulay. N. Y. 1860. D.   **821.2 : 18**

Contents. Editor's preface.—Macaulay, T: B. *lord.* On the life and writings of Addison.—Tickell, T: Preface; To the earl of Warwick.—Translations.—Poems on several occasions.—The campaign.—Miscellaneous poems.—Dramas: Rosamond; The drummer; Cato.—Poemata.

Akenside, M: Poetical works ; ed., with a life, by Alexander Dyce. Bost. 1854. S.   **821.2 : 19**

Alcott, Amos Bronson. Sonnets and canzonets. Bost. 1882. D.   **821.1 : 181**

Aldrich, T: Bailey. Poems. Bost. 1865. T.   **821.1 : 13**

— Poems ; ill. by the Paint and clay club. Bost. 1882. D.   **821.1 : P187**

— The ballad of babie Bell, and other poems. N. Y. 1859. D.   **821.1 : 9**

— Cloth of gold, and other poems. Bost. 1874. D.   **821.1 : 10**

— The course of true love never did run smooth. N. Y. 1858. D.   **821.1 : 11**

— Mercedes, and later lyrics. Bost. 1884 [1883]. O.   **821.1 : 197**

— Pampinea, and other poems. N. Y. 1861. D.   **821.1 : 12**

Allerton, Ellen Palmer, Annabel and other poems. N. Y. 1885. D.   **821.1 : 216**

Allingham, W: Poems. 1st amer. ed. Bost. 1861. T.   **821.2 : 20**

Allston, Washington. Poems. *In his* Lectures on art.   **701 : 4**

Arnold, Edwin. Poems. Bost. 1880. D.   **821.2 : 22**

— The light of Asia, or The great renunciation, Mahâbhinishkramana; the life and teaching of Gautama, prince of India and founder of buddhism, as told in verse by an indian buddhist. Bost. 1879. D.   **821.2 : 21**

— Pearls of the faith, or Islam's rosary; being the ninety-nine beautiful names of Allah, Asmâ-el-husnâ, with comments in verse from various oriental sources, as made by an indian mussulman. Bost. 1883 [1882]. S.   **821.2 : 205**

— The secret of death, from the sanskrit; with some collected poems. Bost. 1885. D.   **821.2 : 241**

Arnold, G: Poems grave and gay. Bost. 1867. S.   **821.1 : 15**

— Drift ; a sea-shore idyl, and other poems. Bost. 1866. S.   **821.1 : 14**

Arnold, Matthew. Poems. Bost. 1856. D.   **821.2 : 24**

— New poems. Bost. 1867. D.   **821.2 : 23**

— Poems. 2 v. N. Y. 1883. D.   **821.2 : 221**

Contents. V. 1. Early poems.—Narrative poems.—Sonnets. 2. Lyric, dramatic and elegiac poems.

Aytoun, W: Edmonstoune. The book of ballads, ed. by Bon Gaultier and ill. 6th ed. Edinb. 1859. D. **821.2 : 25**
— Bothwell ; a poem in six parts. Bost. 1856. D. **821.2 : 26**
Bailey, Philip James. Festus, a poem. 8th amer. ed. Bost. 1849. D. **821.2 : 27**
Banim, J: The celt's paradise, in four duans. N. Y. 1869. D. **821.2 : 28**
Barlow, Joel. The Columbiad, a poem. Lond. 1809. O. **821.2 : 29**
Barnaval de Kerlerec, L: Love poems; ed. with an introd. by C: De Kay. N. Y. 1883. D. **821.1 : 194**
Note. Generally attributed to mr. DeKay himself, the story of Barnaval being considered a myth.
Beach, Elizabeth T. Porter. Pelayo, an epic of the olden moorish time. N. Y. 1864. D. **821.1 : 16**
Beattie, James. Poetical works, with the memoir of the author by Alexander Dyce. Bost. 1854. S. **821.2 : 30**
Beowulf ; an anglo-saxon poem ; [*also*] The fight at Finnsburg. Tr. by James M. Garnett, with fac-simile of the unique ms. in the British museum, Cotton. Vitellius AXV. Bost. 1882. D. **821.2 : 203**
Bickersteth, E: H: Yesterday, to-day, and for ever. N. Y. 1873. D. **821.2 : 31**
Blackie, J: Stuart. Songs of religion and life. N. Y. 1876. S. **821.2 : 32**
Bloede, Gertrude, (*Stuart Sterne*). Giorgio and other poems. Bost. 1881. T. **821.1 : 17**
Bloomfield, Robert. The farmer's boy ; a rural poem. 4th ed. Lond. 1801. S. **821.2 : 33**
Boker, G: H: Poems of the war. Bost. 1864. D. **821.1 : 18**
Booth, Mary H. C. Wayside blossoms among flowers from german gardens. Milw. 1864. T. **821.1 : 19**
Contents. Wayside blossoms.—Flowers from german gardens: L: Uhland; M. F. Anneke; J. G. Fischer; Anastasius Grün; F: Hebbel; H: Heine; G: Herwegh.
Botta, Anne Charlotte, *born* Lynch. Poems. N. Y. 1882. D. **821.1 : 183**
Bowring, J: Matins and vespers ; with hymns and occasional devotional pieces. Bost. 1861. T. **821.2 : 34**
Boyesen, Hjalmar Hjorth. Idyls of Norway, and other poems. N. Y. 1882. S. **821.1 : 179**
Brainard, J: Gardner Calkins. Literary remains, with a sketch of his life by J: G. Whittier. Hartford. [1882]. O. **821.1 : 20**
Brook, C: Timothy. Poems, original and translated ; with a memoir by C: W. Wendte ; sel. and ed. by W. P. Andrews. Portr. Bost. 1885. S. **922.18 : 18**
Brough, Robert B. A cracker bon-bon for christmas parties ; consisting of christmas pieces for private representation, and other seasonable matter in prose and verse. Lond. 1852. S. **821.2 : 185**
Brownell, H: Howard. War-lyrics, and other poems. Bost. 1866. D. **821.1 : 21**
Browning, Elizabeth, *born* Barrett. Poetical works. N. Y. 1858. 2 v. D. **821.2 : 38**
— *Same.* N. Y. 1884. 5 v. D. **821.2 : 38**
— Aurora Leigh. N. Y. [185-]. S. **821.2 : 35**
— Last poems ; with a memorial by Theodore Tilton. N. Y. 1862. T. **821.2 : 36**
— Napoleon III in Italy ; and other poems. N. Y. 1860. D. **821.2 : 37**

Browning, Robert. Poems. Bost. 1856. 2 v. D. **821.2 : 43**
— Aristophanes' apology ; incl. a transcript from Euripides, being the last adventure of Balaustion. Bost. 1875. D. **821.2 : 39**
— Dramatis personæ. Bost. 1864. D. **821.2 : 40**
— Ferishtah's fancies. Bost. 1885 [1884]. S. **821.2 : 237**
— Fifine at the fair, and other poems. Bost. 1872. D. **821.2 : 41**
— The inn album. Bost. 1876. D. **821.2 : 42**
— Jocoseria. Bost. 1883. S. **821.2 : 214**
— Red cotton night-cap country, or Turf and towers. Bost. 1873. D. **821.2 : 44**
— Sordello, Strafford, Christmas-eve and Easter day. Bost. 1864. D. **821.2 : 45**
— **Orr, A.,** *mrs.* Sutherland. A handbook to the works of Robert Browning. Lond. 1885. S. **821.5 : 17**
Bryant, W: Cullen. Poems, coll. and arr. by the author ; in 1 v. Phila. 1849. O. **821.1 : 22**
— Poems, coll. and arr. by the author ; in 3 v. N. Y. 1878. 3 v. D. **821.1 : 23**
— Thirty poems. N. Y. 1864. D. **821.1 : 24**
— **Alden, Joseph.** Studies in Bryant ; a textbook, with an introd. by W: Cullen Bryant. N. Y. 1878. S. **821.1 : 25**
Buchanan, Robert W: Poems. Bost. 1866. S. **821.2 : 48**
— Idyls and legends of Inverburn. Lond. 1865. S. **821.2 : 46**
— London poems. Lond. 1867. D. **821.2 : 47**
— Undertones. Lond. 1863. S. **821.2 : 49**
Buck, James Smith, (*Ichabod*). An address with which Ichabod explains his post-centennial position. **821.1 : Pam**
— Carriers' address, Milwaukee daily news, jan. 1, 1877, 1879. **821.1 : Pam**
Bulwer-Lytton, E: G: Earle Lytton, *1st baron Lytton.* King Arthur. Leipz. 1849. 2 v. in 1 S. **821.2 : 50**
— *Same.* N. Y. 1871. D. **821.2 : 50**
— The lost tales of Miletus. Leipz. 1866. S. **821.2 : 51**
— *Same.* N. Y. 1866. D. **821.2 : 51**
— The new Timon ; a romance of London. 3d ed. Lond. 1846. D. **821.2 : 52**
— *Same, and* St. Stephens ; a poem. Leipz. 1860. S. **821.2 : 52**
Bulwer - Lytton, E: Robert, *1st earl of Lytton,* (*Owen Meredith*). Poetical works. Household ed. Bost. 1875. D. **821.2 : 55**
— Poems, in 2 v. ; v. 2. Bost. 1864. T. **821.2 : 56**
— New poems. Bost. 1868. 2 v. S. **821.2 : 54**
— Lucile, and other poems. Bost. 1879. O. **821.2+53**
— Glenaveril, or The metamorphoses ; a poem in six books. N. Y. 1885. S. **821.2 : 240**
Buntling ball, The ; a græco - american play, being a poetical satire on New York society. Ill. N. Y. 1884. D. **821.1 : 210**
Burns, Robert. Complete poetical works, with an original memoir by W: Gunnyon. Phila. n. d. S. **821.2 : 57**
— Lieder und balladen. Deutsch von K: Bartsch. Hildburgh. 1865. 2 v. in 1. D. **821.2 : 57**
— *See also his* Works. **820.2+P33**
— Rival rhymes in honour of Burns ; with curious illustrative matter, coll. and ed. by Ben Trovato. Lond. 1859. S. **821.2 : 184**

Butler, S: Poetical works. Bost. 1854. 2 v. S.
821.2 : 58
Butler, W: Allen. Nothing to wear ; an episode of city life. From Harper's weekly. Ill. N. Y. 1857. S.   821.1 : 26
— Two millions. N. Y. 1858. D.   821.1 : 27
Byron, G: Gordon Noel, *6th baron Byron.* Poetical works, with copious illustrative notes and a memoir of his life. Phila. *n. d.* ().
821.2 : 59
Contents. Memoir.—Hours of idleness.—Translations and imitations.—Fugitive pieces.—Critique extracted from the Edinburgh review.—English bards and scotch reviewers.—The curse of Minerva.—The prophecy of Dante.—The age of bronze.—The vision of judgment.—Waltz.—The lament of Tasso.—Hebrew melodies.—Miscellaneous poems.—Hints from Horace.—Childe Harold's pilgrimage.—The giaour.—The bride of Abydos.—The corsair.—Lara.—Morgante Maggiore.—The siege of Corinth.—Parisina.—The prisoner of Chillon.—Beppo.—Mazeppa.—The island.—The two Foscari.—Werner.—The deformed transformed.—Cain.—Sardanapalus.—Manfred.—Marino Faliero.—Heaven and earth.—Don Juan.
— Sämmtliche werke. Ins deutsche übers. von mehreren. 3te aufl. gänzlich umgearb., verb. und vervollständigt von Franz Kottenkamp.. Stuttg. 1856. 11 v. in 10. S.
821.2 : 61
Contents, see Deutscher katalog, p. 23.
— Poetry of Byron, chosen and arr. by Matthew Arnold. N. Y. 1881. Q.   821.2 : 60
Cædmon. Exodus and Daniel ; ed. from Grein by Theodore W. Hunt. (Lib. of anglosaxon poetry.) Bost. 1883. D.   821.2 : 225
Calverly, C: Stuart. Fly leaves, with add. from the author's earlier volume of "Verses and translations." 3d ed. with a new poem. N. Y. [1873]. S.   821.2 : 62
Campbell, T: Poetical works. Bost. 1854. S.
821.2 : 63
Carey, Alice. Lyra, and other poems. N. Y. 1852. D.   821.1 : 28
Carleton, Will. City ballads. Ill. N. Y. 1886 [1885]. O.   821.1 : 218
— Farm ballads. N. Y. 1873. O.   821.1+29
— Farm legends. Ill. N. Y. 1876. O. 821.1 : 31
— Farm festivals. Ill. N. Y. 1881. O.
821.1 : 30
Carpenter, Joseph E:, *ed.* Songs ; sacred and devotional. Lond. 1866. S.   821.2 : 64
Caswall, E: Poems. Lond. 1861. S   821.2 : 65
Challen, James. Igdrasil, or The tree of existence. Phila. 1859. D.   821.1 : 32
Chamberlain, *Mrs.* M. H., (*Carrie Carlton*). Wayside flowers. Milw. 1862. D.
821.1 : 33
Chapman, G: W. A tribute to Kane, and other poems. N. Y. 1860. D.   821.1 : 34
Charles, Emily Thornton. Hawthorn blossoms. Phila. 1876. D.   821.1 : 35
Chatterton, Henrietta Georgiana *lady.* Leonore, a tale ; and other poems. Lond. 1864. S.
821.2 : 66
Chatterton, T: Poetical works, with notices of his life, a history of the Rowley controversy, a selection of his letters, notes critical and explanatory and a glossary. Bost. 1857. 2 v. S.   821.2 : 67
Chaucer, Geoffrey. Poetical works, with an essay on his language and versification and an introd. discourse, together with notes and a glossary by T: Tyrwhitt. Lond. 1847. O.
821.2+68
Contents. Preface.—An essay on the language and versification of Chaucer.—An introductory discourse on the Canterbury tales.—The Canterbury tales.—The

Chaucer, Geoffrey.—*Continued.*
romaunt of the rose.—Troilus and Creseide.—The court of love.—The complaint of pity.—Of queen Annelida and the false Arcite.—The assembly of fowles.—The complaint of the black knight.—Chaucer's A. B. C.—The booke of the duchess.—The house of fame.—Chaucer's dream.—The flower and the leaf.—The legend of good women.—The complaint of Mars and Venus.—Of the cuckoo and the nightingale.—Minor poems.—Glossary.
— Poetical works ; appended, poems attributed to Chaucer, ed. by Arthur Gilman. Bost. 1880. 3 v. D.   821.2 : 193
Contents. V. 1. The times and the poet, by the editor.—On reading Chaucer.—Astrological terms and divisions of time.—Biblical reference.—The Canterbury tales. 2. The Canterbury tales.—Minor poems. 3. Minor poems.—Poems attributed to Chaucer.—Index.
— The parlament of foules ; ed. with introd. notes and glossary by T. R. Lounsbury. Bost. 1880. D.   821.2 : 200
— Canterbury geschichten. Uebers. in den versmassen der urschrift und durch einleitung und anmerkungen erläutert von W: Hertzberg. Hildburgh. 1866. D.   821.2 : 193
Churchill, C: Poetical works, with copious notes and a life of the author by W. Tooke. Bost. 1854. 3 v. S.   821.2 : 69
Clough, Arthur Hugh. Poems ; with a memoir by C: Eliot Norton. Bost. 1862. T.
821.2 : 70
Coelebs the younger in search of a wife, or The drawing-room troubles of Moody Robinson, esq. Lond. *n. d.* D.   821.2 : 71
Coleridge, S: Taylor. Christabel and the lyrical and imaginative poems of C., arr. and introd. by Algernon C: Swinburne. Lond. 1875. T.   821.2 : 72
Collins, W: Poetical works. Bost. 1854. S.
821.2 : 73
Colman, G:, *the younger.* Poetical works, now first collected. 1st amer. ed. Phila. 1834. D.   821.2 : 74
Cook, Ebenezer. The sot-weed factor, or A voyage to Maryland ; a satyr in which is described the laws, government, courts and constitutions of the country and also the buildings, feasts, frolicks, entertainments and drunken humours of the inhabitants of that part of America ; in burlesque verse. [Shea's early southern tracts, no. 2.] Lond. 1708 [1865]. O.   821.2 : 75
Cooke, Rose, *born* Terry. Poems. Bost. 1861. D.   821.1 : 36
Cowper, W: Poetical works. Bost. 1854. 3 v. S.   821.2 : 76
Contents. V. 1. Table talk. 2. The task.—Miscellaneous poems. 3. Hymns.—Tr. from the french of madame de la Mothe Guion.—Tr. of the latin and italian poems of Milton.—Tr. from Vincent Bourne.—Minor poems.—Tr. of greek verses.—Epigrams tr. from the latin of Owen.—Tr. from the fables of Gay.
Coxe, Arthur Cleveland. Christian ballads, with corr. and add. 13th ed. Phila. 1864. T.
821.1 : 37
Crabbe, G:, *and others.* Poetical works of Crabbe, Heber and Pollok ; complete in 1 v. Phila. 1857. O.   821.2 : 77
Craik, Dinah Maria, *born* Mulock. Poems. Leipz. 1868. S.   821.2 : 78
Cranch, Christopher Pearse. The bird and the bell, with other poems. Bost. 1875. S.
821.1 : 38
Croly, G: Poetical works, embellished with twenty etchings by Dagley from antique gems. Lond. *n. d.* 2 v. D.   821.2 : 79

Cross, Marian, *born* Evans, *formerly mrs.* G: H: Lewes, (*George Eliot*). Poems. N. Y. 1883. S. **821.2 : 220**
— Poems. Ill. N. Y. [1884]. O. **821.2+236**
— How Lisa loved the king. Bost. 1869. S. **821.2 : 80**
— The legend of Jubal, and other poems, old and new. *With her* Theophrastus Such. **821.2 : 249**
— The spanish gypsy. Bost. 1868. D. **821.2 : 81**
— *Same. With her* Theophrastus Such. **821.2 : 249**

Dagley, R: Takings, or The life of a collegian ; a poem. Ill. [*Also,* Miscellaneous observations on the ludicrous in art.] Lond. 1821. O. **821.2 : 82**

Davidson, Lucretia Maria. Poetical remains, coll. and arr. by her mother ; with a' biography by miss Sedgwick. Bost. 1864. D. *With* **Davidson,** M. M. Biography and poetical remains. *in* **821.1 : 39**

Davidson, Margaret Miller. Biography and poetical remains, by Washington Irving. N. Y. 1864. D. **821.1 : 39**

Davidson, Margaret, *born* Miller. Selections from the writings of the mother of Lucretia Maria and Margaret M. Davidson ; with a pref. by miss C. M. Sedgwick. Phila. 1843. D. **821.1 : 40**

Davis, T: Poems ; [*also* Literary and historical essays], and an introd. by J: Mitchel. N. Y. 1876. D. **821.2 : 83**

DeKay, C: The vision of Nimrod. N. Y. 1881. D. **821.1 : 41**
— The vision of Esther ; a sequel to "The vision of Nimrod ". N. Y. 1882. D. **821.1 : 185**
— *See also* **Barnaval,** L:

DeVere, Aubrey T: Poems. Lond. 1855. S. **821.2 : 85**
— May carols, and hymns and poems. N. Y. 1866. S. **821.2 : 84**

Dobson, Austin H: Vignettes in rhyme, and other verses ; with introd. by E. C. Stedman. N. Y. 1880. D. **821.2 : 254**
— At the sign of the lyre. N. Y. 1885. D. **821.2 : 243**

Donne, J: Poetical works, with a memoir. Bost. 1855. S. **821.2 : 86**

Dorward, Bernard I: Cristofero Colombo. [*Anon.*] *n. t.* [Milw. 1885]. D. **821.1 : 214**
— Wild flowers of Wisconsin ; poems, ed. by his son. Milw. 1872. D. **821.1 : 42**

Doyle, R:. *and* James Robinson Planché. An old fairy tale told anew in pictures and verse. Bost. *n. d.* O. **821.2 : 87**

Drake, Joseph Rodman. The culprit fay. N. Y. 1859. D. **821.1 : 43**

Drummond, W: Poetical works ; ed. by W: B. Turnbull. Lond. 1856. D. **821.2 : 88**

Dryden, J: Works in verse and prose, with a life by J: Mitford. N. Y. 1847. 2 v. O. **821.2+90**
Contents. V. 1. Life.—Poems.—Epistles.— Elegies and epitaphs.—Songs, odes and a masque.—Prologues and epilogues.—Tr. from Theocritus, Lucretius and Horace.—Tales from Chaucer.—Tr. from Boccace.— Tr. from Ovid's Metamorphoses, Epistles, Art of love.—From Juvenal.—From Persius.—From Homer. —Art of poetry.—Hymn for St. John's eve.—On the marriage of mrs. Anastasia Stafford. — To Matilda. 2. Tr. from Virgil: Pastorals, Georgics, Aeneis.— Essay of dramatic poesy.—Heads of an answer to Rymer.—Life of Plutarch.—Dedication of Plutarch's Lives.—Tr. of the History of the league.—Parallel of

Dryden, J:—*Continued.*
poetry and painting.—Observations on the art of painting.—Judgment of C: Alphonse du Fresnoy.— Character of M. St. Evremont.—Character of Polybius.—Life of Lucian.—Dryden's letters.
— Poetical works. Bost. 1854. 4 v. S. **821.2 : 89**
Contents. V. 1. Upon the death of lord Hastings. — To his friend J: Hoddesdon. — Heroic stanzas on the death of Oliver Cromwell. — Astrea redux. — To his sacred majesty. — To the lord chancellor Hyde. — Satire on the dutch.—To her royal highness, the du-. chess.—Annus mirabilis, the year of wonders, 1666.— An essay upon satire. — Absalom and Achitophel, pt. 1. 2. Absalom and Achitophel, pt. 2.—The medal, a satire against sedition. — Religio laici. — Threnodia augustalis.— Verses to J. Northleigh. — The hind and the panther. — MacFlecknoe.— Epistles. 3. Songs, odes and a mask. — Prologues and epilogues. — Translations from Theocritus. Lucretius and Horace. — To his grace the duke of Ormond.—Preface prefixed to the fables.—To her grace the duchess of Ormond. — Palamon and Arcite, bks. 1, 2, 3. — The cock and the fox. 4. The flower and the leaf.—The wife of Bath.—The character of a good parson.—Tr. from Boccace.—Tr. from Ovid's Metamorphoses.

Dudley, Marion Vienna, *born* Churchill. Poems. Milw. 1885. S. **821.1 : R219**

Duganne, Augustine. The mission of intellect ; a poem, delivered at Metropolitan hall, New York, dec. 20, 1852. N. Y. 1853. S. **821.1 : 44**

Dutt, Toru. Ancient ballads and legends of Hindustan ; with an introductory memoir by Edmund W. Gosse. Lond. 1882. S. **821.2 : 217**

Eliot, George, *pseud., see* **Cross,** Marian.

Emerson, Ralph Waldo. Poems. Bost. 1860. D. **821.1 : 46**
— *Same. In his* Works. **820.1 : 8 v9**
— May-day and other pieces. Bost. 1867. D. **821.1 : 45**

Falconer, W: Poetical works, with a life by J: Mitford. Bost. 1854. S. **821.2 : 91**

Ferguson, Robert. Works ; ed. with the life of the author and an essay on his genius and writings by A. B. G. Lond. 1851. D. **821.2 : 92**

Freneau, Philip. Poems relating to the american revolution ; with an introd. memoir and notes by Evert A. Duyckinck. N. Y. 1865. O. **821.1 : 47**

Gascoigne, G: Complete poems ; now first collected and ed. from the early printed copies and from mss., with a memoir and notes by W: Carew Hazlitt. [Roxburghe library.] [Lond.] 1869. 2 v. O. **821.2 : 252**

Gay, J: Poetical works ; with a life of the author by dr. Johnson. Bost. 1854. 2 v. S. **821.2 : 93**
Contents. V. 1. Fables, pt. 1, 2. — Rural sports.— Trivia. 2. The fan. — The shepherd's week. — Acis and Galatea.—Epistles.—Eclogues.—Elegies.—Tales.— Gondibert.—Miscellaneous.

Geraldine, a souvenir of the St. Lawrence. Bost. 1882. S. **821.1 : 177**

Gilbert, W: Schwenck. The "Bab" ballads ; much sound and little sense. Ill. N. Y. [1884]. D. **821.2 : 234**

Gilder, R: Watson. The new day ; a poem in songs and sonnets. N. Y. 1876. D. **821.1 : 48**

Goldsmith, Oliver. Poetical works, ed., with a life, by J: Mitford. Bost. 1853. S. **821.2 : 94**

Goodrich, S: Griswold, (*Peter Parley*). Poems. N. Y. 1851. D. **821.1 : 49**

Grant, Anne, *born* M'Vicar. The highlanders, and other poems. 2nd ed. Lond. 1808. S.
821.2 : 95
Gray, D: Poems; with a memoir of his life. Bost. 1864. D. 821.2 : 96
Gray, T: Poetical works; ed. with a life by J: Mitford. Bost. 1853. D. 821.2 : 227
Green, Anna Katherine. The defence of the bride, and other poems. N. Y. 1882. S.
821.1 : 189
Greene, W: Batchelder. Three vows. N. Y. 1881. S. 821.1 : 163
Griffin, Gerald. Poetical works. N. Y. *n. d.* D.
821.2 : 97
Halleck, Fitz Greene. Poetical works, now first coll. Ill. 2d ed. N. Y. 1848. O.
821.1 : 51
— Fanny, with other poems. N. Y. 1839. D.
821.1 : 50
— Young America; a poem. N. Y. 1865. D.
821.1 : 52
Halpine, C: Graham, (*Miles O'Reilly*). Poetical works, consisting of odes, poems, sonnets, epics and lyrical effusions which have not heretofore been coll. together, ed. by Robert B. Roosevelt. N. Y. 1869. O.
821.1 : 53
Harbaugh, H: Poems. Phila. 1860. D.
821.1 : 54
Hart, *Mrs. —*. Mrs. Jerningham's journal. [*Anon.*] N. Y. 1876. D. 821.2 : 109
— Harry, by the author of "Mrs. Jerningham's journal." [*Anon.*] N. Y. 1877. S.
821.2 : 110
Harte, Francis Bret. Echoes of the foot-hills. Bost. 1875. D. 821.1 : 55
Hay, J: Pike county ballads, and other pieces. Bost. 1871. S. 821.1 : 56
Heber, Reginald. Poetical works. *With* Crabbe, G: Poetical works. *in* 821.2 : 77
Hemans, Felicia Dorothea, *born* Browne. Poetical works, with memoir. Phila. 1840. O.
821.2 : 98
Contents. Pref.—Memoir. -The forest sanctuary.— Lays of many lands.—The siege of Valencia.—The vespers of Palermo.—The league of the Alps. - The restoration of the works of art to Italy.—Tales and historic scenes.—The sceptic.—Stanzas to the memory of the late king.—Modern Greece.—Dartmoor.— Meeting of Wallace and Bruce.—Greek songs.—Songs of the Cid.—Records of woman.—Songs of the affections.—Hymns on the works of nature.—Translations from Camoens and other poets. — Miscellaneous poems.—Scenes and hymns of life.—National lyrics and songs for music.—Miscellaneous poems.
Herbert, G: Poetical works, with a memoir of the author and notes by Robert Avis Willmott. Bost. 1855. S. 821.2 : 99
— The temple; sacred poems and private ejaculations, with The priest to the temple, or The country parson. Halifax. 1860. T.
821.2 : 212
Herrick, Robert. Hesperides, or The works, both humane and divine. Bost. 1856. 2 v. S. 821.2 : 100
Hirst, H: B. Endymion; a tale of Greece. Bost. 1848. D. 821.1 : 57
Hogg, James. Poetical works of the Ettrick shepherd, with an autobiography and illustrative engr., chiefly from original drawings, by D. O. Hill. Glasgow. *n. d.* 5 v. D.
821.2 : 101
Holbrook, Edwin· A. Life-thoughts, poetry and prose. Watertown, N. Y. 1875. O.
821.1 : 58

Holland, Josiah Gilbert, (*Timothy Titcomb*). Bitter-sweet; a poem. 15th ed. N. Y. 1863. D. 821.1 : 59
— *Same.* 30th ed. N. Y. 1877. D. 821.1 : 59
— Kathrina; her life and mine in a poem. N. Y. 1867. D. 821.1 : 60
— *Same* 50th ed. N. Y. *n. d.* D. 821.1 : 60
— The marble prophecy, and other poems. N. Y. 1872. D. 821.1 : 61
— The mistress of the manse. N. Y. 1874. D.
821.1 : 62
— *Same.* 26th thousand. N. Y. 1877. D.
821.1 : 62
— The puritan's guest, and other poems. N. Y. 1881. S. 821.1 : 168
Holmes, Oliver Wendell. Poems. New and enl. ed. Bost. 1849. D. 821.1 : 204
— Poetical works. Bost. 1881. 2 v. T. 821.1 : 64
— The iron gate, and other poems. Bost. 1881. D. 821.1 : 63
— Songs of many seasons, 1862 — 1874. Bost. 1875. S. 821.1 : 65
Hood, T: Poetical works. N. Y. 1879. 2 v. in 1. D. 821.2 : 250
— Poetical works, with some account of the author; v. 2, 4. Bost. 1854, 1856. 2 v. S.
821.2 : 102
— Whims and waifs. N. Y. 1860. D. 821.2 : 103
Hopper, E: The fire on the hearth in Sleepy Hollow; a christmas poem of the olden time. N. Y. 1865. S. 821.1 : 66
Hosmer, W: H: Cuyler. Poetical works. N. Y. 1854. 2 v. D. 821.1 : 67
Houghton, G: Niagara, and other poems. Bost. 1882. T. 821.1 : 182
Howard, H:, *earl of Surrey*. Poetical works, with a memoir. Bost. 1854. S. 821.2 : 104
Howe, Julia, *born* Ward. Later lyrics. Bost. 1866. D. 821.1 : 68
Howells, W: Dean. Poems. *With* Piatt, J: James. Poems. 821.1 : 213
Howitt, Mary, *born* Botham. Ballads and other poems. N. Y. 1854. D. 821.2 : 105
Hoyt, Ralph. Sketches of life and landscape. N. Y. 1862. D. 821.1 : 69
Hudson, Mary, *born* Clemmer, *formerly mrs.* Ames. Poems of life and nature. Bost. 1883 [1882]. D. 821.1 : 180
Hunt, James H: Leigh. Poetical works; finally collected, rev. by himself, and ed. by his son Thornton Hunt. Ill. Lond. *n. d.* D.
821.2 : 230
Huntington, Jedediah Vincent. Poems. N. Y. 1843. D. 821.1 : 70
Hutchinson, Ellen Mackay. Songs and lyrics; with a frontispiece from a painting by G: H. Boughton. Bost. 1881. S. 821.1 : 171
Ingelow, Jean. Poems. Bost. 1864. D.
821.2 : 106
— Poems of the old days and the new. Bost. 1885. S. 821.2 : 247
— The shepherd lady, and other poems. Bost. 1876. O. 821.2 + 107
— A story of doom, and other poems. Bost. 1867. D. 821.2 : 108
John Jerningham's journal. N. Y. 1876. D. *With* Hart, Mrs. —, Mrs. Jerningham's journal. *in* 821.2 : 109
Johnson, Edwin Rossiter. Idler and poet. Bost. 1883 [1882]. D. 821.1 : 178
Joyce, Robert D'wyer. Deirdrè. (No name ser.) Bost. 1876. S. 821.1 : 71

Milnes, R: Monckton, *1st baron Houghton.* Poems of many years. Bost. 1846. D.
    821.2 : 123

Milton, J: Poetical works, with notes and a life of the author. Bost. 1845. 2 v. O.
    821.2 : 124
Contents. V. 1. Life of Milton. — Paradise lost, books I-X. 2. Paradise lost, books XI, XII.—Paradise regained.—Samson Agonistes. — Comus. — Lycidas.—Il penseroso.—L'allegro. — Arcades. — Miscellaneous poems. — Sonnets. — Psalms. — Elegies. — Epigrams.

— Paradise lost; a poem in 12 books. N. Y. *n. d.* S.   **821.2 : 189**

— *Same, germ.* Das verlorene paradies; episches gedicht. Uebers. von K: Eitner. Hildburgh. 1867. D.   **821.2 : 189**

Montgomery, James. Select poetical works. Bost. 1857. D.   **821.2 : 125**

Moore, T: Poetical works, collected by himself, with a memoir. Bost. 1856. 6 v. S.
    821.2 : 127
Contents. V. 1. Memoir.— Odes of Anacreon.— Epigrams from Anthologia.— Juvenile poems. 2. Poems rel. to America.—Corruption and intolerance. —Sceptic.—Two-penny post-bag.—Satirical and humorous poems.—Political and satirical poems.—Fudge family in Paris.— Fables for the holy alliance. 3. Satirical and humorous poems.—Fudges in England. 4. Preface.—Letter to the marchioness dowager of Donegal. — Irish melodies. — National airs. — Sacred songs.—Sets of glees.—Ballads, songs, miscellaneous poems. 5. Evenings in Greece.—Legendary ballads. —Melologue upon national music.—Summer fete. — Songs from the M. P. Misc. poems.—Songs from the greek Anthology.—Unpublished songs.—Rhymes on the road.— Alciphron.— Fragments from the Epicurean. 6. Lalla Rookh.—Loves of the angels.

— Lalla Rookh. Bost. 1855. S.   **821.2 : 126**

— *Same.* N. Y. 1868. D.   **821.2 : 126**

Morris, W: The earthly paradise. Bost. 1871. 3 v. D.   **821.2 : 129**
Contents. V. 1. Prologue: The wanderers. — Pt. 1, *Spring.* March: Atalanta's race ; The man born to be king. — April: The doom of king Acrisius; The proud king. — May: The story of Cupid and Psyche ; The writing on the image. — Pt. 2, *Summer.* June: The love of Alcestis; The lady of the land. — July: The son of Crœsus; The watching of the falcon. — August: Pygmalion and the image; Ogier the dane. 2. Pt. 3, *Autumn.* September: The death of Paris; The land east of the sun and west of the moon. — October : The story of Accontius and Cydippe ; The man who never laughed again. — November: The story of Rhodope; The lovers of Gudrun. 3. Pt. 4, *Winter.* December: The golden apples; The fostering of Aslaug. — January: Bellerophon at Argos; The ring given to Venus.—February: Bellerophon in Lycia; The hill of Venus.—Epilogue.—L'envoi.

— The story of Sigurd the Volsung and the fall of the Niblungs. Bost. 1879. D.
    821.2 : 130

Munby, Arthur Joseph. Dorothy; a country story in elegiac verse. [*Anon.*] Bost. 1882. S.
    821.2 : 206

Newell, Robert H:, (*Orpheus C. Kerr*). The palace beautiful, and other poems. N. Y. 1865. D.   **821.1 : 102**

Nichols, Charlotte, *born* Brontë. Poems. N. Y. 1882. S.   **821.2 : 219**

O'Reilly, J: Boyle. The statues in the block, and other poems. 2d ed. Bost. 1881. S.
    821.1 : 104

O'Sheridan, Mary Grant. Conata ; a collection of poems. Madison. 1881. D. **821.1 : 193**

Ossian. Poems, tr. by James Macpherson; prefixed, a preliminary discourse and dissertation on the æra and poems of Ossian. Bost. 1849. D.   **821.2 : 132**

Palgrave, Francis Turner. The visions of England. Lond. 1881. D.   **821.2 : 190**

Parnell, T: Poetical works ; with a life by Oliver Goldsmith. Bost. 1854. S.   **821.2 : 133**

Parsons, T: W: Poems. Bost. 1854. D.
    821.1 : 105

Patmore, Coventry Kearsey Dighton. The angel in the house: pt. 1, The betrothal; pt. 2, The espousals. Bost. 1856, 1860. 2 v. D.
    821.2 : 134

— Faithful forever. Bost. 1861. D. **821.2 : 135**

— The victories of love. Bost. 1862. D.
    821.2 : 136

Percival, James Gates. Poetical works ; with a biographical sketch. Bost. 1860. 2 v. T.
    821.2 : 137

Peterson, F: Poems and swedish translations. Buffalo. 1883. D.   **821.1 : 196**

Phelps, Elizabeth Stuart. Poetic studies. Bost. 1875. S.   **821.1 : 106**

— Songs of the silent world, and other poems. Portrait. Bost. 1885 [1884]. S. **821.1 : 209**

Piatt, J: James, *and* W: Dean **Howells.** Poems of two friends. Columbus. 1860. D.
    821.1 : 213

Piatt, Sarah Morgan, *born* Bryan. An irish garland. Bost. 1885. D.   **821.1 : 215**

Pierpont, J: Airs of Palestine ; a poem. Balt. 1816. O.   **821.1 : 107**

Pollok, Robert. The course of time ; a poem in ten books. 3d amer. from 3d Edinb. ed. Bost. 1828. D.   **821.2 : 138**

— *Same* ; with enl. index, a memoir of the author and an analysis prefixed to each book. Rev. ed. Bost. 1843. S.   **821.2 : 138**

— *Same. With* Crabbe, G: Poetical works.
    in **821.2 : 77**

Pope, Alexander. Poetical works. Prefixed, the life of the author by dr. Johnson. New ed. Phila. 1847. O.   **821.2 : 229**

— Poetical works ; with a life by Alexander Dyce. Bost. 1854. 3 v. S.   **821.2 : 139**
Contents. V. 1. Memoir.—Plan of an epic poem.— The will of Pope.—Preface.—Pastorals. 2. Essay on criticism.—Essay on man.—Universal prayer.—Moral essays.—Imitations of english poets. 3. Epistle to dr. Arbuthnot, being the prologue to the satires. — Satires, epistles and odes of Horace imitated.— Satires of dr. J: Donne, versified.—Epitaphs.—The Dunciad.

— Poetical works, in 3 v. complete, with his last corr., add. and improvem.; together with all his notes as they were delivered to the ed. a little before his death, together with the commentary and notes of mr. Warburton ; v. 1. Portr. Phila. 1819. D.
    821.2 : 211
Contents. Pref. — Recommendatory poems. — Discourse on pastoral poetry. — Pastorals. — Messiah. — Windsor-forest.—Ode on St. Cecilia's day.—Two choruses to the tragedy of Brutus.—Solitude.—The dying christian to his soul.—Essay on criticism.—The rape of the lock.—Elegy to the memory of an unfortunate lady.—Prologue to mr. Addison's tragedy.—Epilogue to Jane Shore.—Sappho to Phaon.—Eloisa to Abelard. —The temple of fame.—January and May.—The wife of Bath.— The first book of Statius's Thebais.—The fable of Dryope.—Vertumnus and Pomona.

Praed, Winthrop Mackworth. Poetical works. N. Y. 1860. 2 v. D.   **821.2 : 140**

Preston, Margaret, *born* Junkin. Cartoons. Bost. 1875. D.   **821.1 : 108**

Prior, Matthew. Poetical works ; with a life by J: Mitford. Bost. 1854. 2 v. S.
    821.2 : 141

Procter, Bryan Waller, (*Barry Cornwall*). English songs, and other small poems. Bost. 1851. S.   **821.2 : 142**

Proctor, Edna Dean. Poems. N. Y. 1866. S.
821.1 : 109
Quarles, Francis. Emblems, divine and moral, with a sketch of the life and times of the author. Lond. 1859. S. 821.2 : 143
Raymond, G: L. Haydn, and other poems. N. Y. 1870. D. 821.1 : 110
Read, T: Buchanan. The house by the sea; a poem. Phila. 1856. D. 821.1 : 111
— Sylvia, or The last shepherd; an eclogue, and other poems. Phila. 1857. D. 821.1 : 112
— The wagoner of the Alleghanies; a poem of the days of seventy-six. Phila. 1863. D.
821.1 : 113
Richmond, Elizabeth Yates. Poems of the western land. Milw. 1878. O. 821.1 : 114
Richmond, James Cook. Metacomet; a poem of the north american indians. Lond. 1851. S. 821.1 : 115
Rogers, S. Complete poetical works; with a biographical sketch and notes, ed. by Epes Sargent. Bost. 1854. D. 821.2 : 144
Roscoe, W: Poetical works, 1st coll. ed. 1857. S.
821.2 : 145
Rossetti, Dante Gabriel. Poems. New ed. Bost. 1882. S. 821.2 : 204
— Ballads and sonnets. Bost. 1882 [1881]. S.
821.2 : 187
Rossetti, Christina Georgina. Poems. Bost. 1866. D. 821.2 : 146
— A pageant, and other poems. Bost. 1881. S.
821.2 : 188
Ruskin, J: Poems. N. Y. 1882. D.
821.2 : 207
Savage, J: Eva; a goblin romance in 5 parts. N. Y. 1865. D. 821.1 : 117
— Faith and fancy. N. Y. 1864. D. 821.1 : 118
Saxe, J: Godfrey. Poems. 5th ed. Bost. 1854. D. 821.1 : 122
— The flying dutchman, or The wrath of Herr Vonstoppelnoze. Ill. N. Y. 1862. D.
821.1 : 119
— Leisure-day rhymes. Bost. 1875. S.
821.1 : 120
— The masquerade, and other poems. Bost. 1866. S. 821.1 : 121
Scott, Sir Walter. Poetical works, with a memoir of the author. Bost. 1857. 9 v. S.
821.2 : 148
Contents. V. 1. Lay of the last minstrel. 2. Marmion. 3. The lady of the lake. 4. Rokeby.—Vision of don Roderick. 5. Lord of the isles. 6. Imitations of ancient ballads.—Ballads, trans. or imitated from the german.—Songs.—Miscellaneous poems. 7. Misc. poems. — Poems printed in Lockhart's biography. — Lyrical pieces, mottoes etc. from the Waverley novels. 8. Bridal of Triermain.—Harold, the dauntless.—The field of Waterloo.— Halidon Hill. — MacDuff's cross. 9. The doom of Devorgoil. — Auchindrane, or The Ayrshire tragedy. — The house of Aspen. — Goetz of Berlichenden.
— Poetical works. Leipz. 1861. 2 v. in 1. S.
821.2 : 149
Contents. V. 1. The lay of the last minstrel. — Marmion.— The lady of the lake. 2. The vision of don Roderick.— Rokeby.— The lord of the isles.— Songs, Lyrical pieces, Miscellaneous poems, Ballads.
— The lady of the lake. Lond. 1873. T.
821.2 : 147
— Same; ed. with notes by W: J. Rolfe. Ill. Bost. 1883. S. 821.2 : 216
— Same; ed. by Edwin Ginn. [Classics for children]. Bost. 1885. D. x 821.2 : 246
— Same, germ. Das fräulein vom see; romantische dichtung. Uebers. von H: Viehoff. Hildburgh. 1865. D. 821.2 : 147

Scott, Sir Walter.—Continued.
— Marmion; ed. with notes by W: J. Rolfe. Ill. (Students' ser.) Bost. 1885. S.
821.2 : 242
Shea, J: A: Poems collected by his son. N. Y. 1846. D. 821.1 : 123
Shelley, Percy Bysshe. Poetical works; ed. by mrs. Shelley, with a memoir; v. 2, 3. Bost. 1855. S. 821.2 : 150
— Poetical works; ed. with an introd. memoir and ill. by W: B. Scott. Lond. n. d. D.
821.2 : 151
— Ausgewählte dichtungen. Deutsch von Adolf Strodtmann. Hildburgh. 1866. 2 v. in 1. D.
821.2 : 151
Shenstone, W: Poetical works; with life, critical dissertation and explanatory notes, by G: Gilfillan. N. Y. 1854. O. 821.2+152
Sigourney, Lydia Howard, born Huntley. The western home, and other poems. Phila. 1854. D. 821.1 : 124
Simms, W: Gilmore. Atlantis; a story of the sea. Phila. 1848. S. 821.1 : 125
Skelton, J: Poetical works; principa ly according to the ed. of Alexander Dycel Bost. 1856. 3 v. S. 821.2 : 153
Smith, Albert H. Ma-ka-tai-me-she-kia-kiak, or Black Hawk and scenes in the west; a national poem in six cantos, embracing an account of the life and exploits of this celebrated chieftain, the Black Hawk war, a legend of the Illinois tribe of indians, showing the manner in which they became extinct, a succinct description of the Wisconsin and Lake Superior countries and their rich minerals, the massacre of Chicago and other deeply interesting scenes in the west; by a western tourist. N. Y. 1848. D.
821.1 : 211
Smith, Alexander. Poems. Bost. 1854. D.
821.2 : 155
— Edwin of Deira. Bost. 1861. D. 821.2 : 154
Smith, Horace and James. Rejected addresses, or The new theatrum poetarum. Bost. 1851. D. 821.2 : 156
— Same. (Leisure hour ser.) N. Y. 1876. S.
821.2 : 156
Smith, Mary Ann, (Rusco). Teone, or The magic maid. Milw. 1862. S. 821.1 : 116
Smith, Walter Chalmers. Olrig Grange; ed. by Hermann Künst, phlol. professor. [Anon.] Bost. 1872. D. 821.1 : 103
Southey, Robert. Complete poetical works, coll. by himself. A new ed., incl. "Oliver Newman, and other poems," now first pub. Ill. N. Y. 1848. O. 821.2+157
Spenser, Edmund. Works; with observations on his life and writings. New ed. Lond. 1846. O. 821.2+158
— Poetical works; the text carefully rev. and ill. with notes, original and selected, by Francis J. Child. Bost. 1881. 3 v. D.
821.2 : 159
Contents. V. 1, 2. The faerie queen. 3. Miscellanies.—App.
Sperry, H. T. Country love vs. city flirtation, or Ten chapters from the story of a life, reduced to rhyme for convenience sake. N. Y. 1865. D. 821.1 : 126
Spofford, Harriet Elizabeth, born Prescott. Poems. Bost. 1882 [1881]. S. 821.1 : 167
Sprague, C: Poetical and prose writings. New ed. N. Y. 1850. D. 821.1 : 127

Stedman, Edmund Clarence. Poetical works. Bost. 1873. D.   **821.1 : 128**

Stirling - Maxwell, *Lady* Caroline Elizabeth Sarah, *born* Sheridan, *formerly mrs.* Norton. The dream, and other poems. Phila. 1841. D.   **821.2 : 131**

Stoddard, R: H: Poems. Complete ed. N. Y. 1880. O.   **821.1 : 130**

— Abraham Lincoln ; an horatian ode. N. Y. [1865]. O.   **821.1 : 129**

Story, W: Wetmore. He and she, or A poet's portfolio. Bost. 1884 [1883]. S.   **821.1 : 198**

Street, Alfred Billing. Frontenac, or The alotacho of the Iroquois ; a metrical romance. N. Y. 1849. D.   **821.1 : 131**

Swift, Jonathan. Poetical works ; with a life by J: Mitford ; v. 2, 3. Bost. 1854. 2 v. S.   **821.2 : 160**

Swinburne, Algernon C: A century of roundels. N. Y. 1883. D.   **821.2 : 215**

— Tristram of Lyonesse, and other poems. N. Y. 1882. D.   **821.2 : 208**

— A midsummer holiday, and other poems. N. Y. 1885. D.   **821.2 : 244**

Symonds, J: Addington. Vagabunduli libellus. Lond. 1884. D.   **821.2 : 239**

Tannahill, Robert. Poems and songs, chiefly in the scottish dialect ; prefixed, a notice respecting the life and writings of the author. N. Y. 1819. D.   **821.2 : 161**

Taylor, Bayard. Poetical works. Household ed. Bost. 1880. D.   **821.1 : 134**

— Home pastorals, ballads and lyrics. Bost. 1875. S.   **821.1 : 132**

— The picture of St. John. Bost. 1866. S.   **821.1 : 133**

— The poet's journal. Bost. 1863. D.   **821.1 : 135**

Taylor, B: Franklin. Old time pictures and sheaves of rhyme. 2d ed. Chicago. 1874. D.   **821.1 : 136**

Tennyson, Alfred, *baron* Tennyson. Poems ; v. 2. Bost. 1859. D.   **821.2 : 167**

— Poetical works. Bost. 1875. 2 v. O.   **821.2 : 166**

— *Same.* Complete ed. from the author's text. Ill. N. Y. [1885]. O.   **821.2 : R255**

— Ballads and other poems. Bost. 1880. D.   **821.2 : 162**

— Gareth and Lynette. Ill. Bost. 1872. D.   **821.2 : 163**

— The holy grail, and other poems. Bost. 1870. D.   **821.2 : 164**

— Idyls of the king. Bost. 1859. D. **821.2 : 165**

— The princess ; a medley, ed., with notes, by W: J. Rolfe. [Student's ed.] Ill. Bost. 1885. [1884]. S.   **821.2 : 233**

— — [Explanatory study] by S. E. Dawson.   **821.5 : 11**

— Select poems ; ed. with notes, by W: J. Rolfe. Ill. Bost. 1885 [1884]. S.   **821.2 : 232**

— Ausgewählte dichtungen. Deutsch von Adolf Strodtmann. Hildburgh. 1867. D.   **821.2 : 167**

Thackeray, W: Makepeace. Complete poems. N. Y. 1883. S.   **821.2 : 218**

— Ballads. Bost. 1856. D.   **821.2 : 168**

Thomas, Edith M. A new year's masque, and other poems. Bost. 1885 [1884]. D.   **821.1 : 208**

Thompson, Maurice. Songs of fair weather. Bost. 1883. D.   **821.1 : 200**

Thomson, James. Poetical works, [with memoir by sir Harris Nicolas]. Bost. 1854. 2 v. S.   **821.2 : 169**

Tickell, T: Poetical works, with a life by dr. Johnson. Bost. 1854. S. *With* Parnell, T: Poetical works.   **821.2 : 133**

Tilton, Theodore. Swabian stories. N. Y. 1882. D.   **821.1 : 188**

Trench, R: Chenevix. Poems. N. Y. 1862. D.   **821.2 : 170**

— Poems. New ed. Lond. 1885. 2 v. D.   **821.2 : 248**

Trowbridge, J: Townsend. The emigrant's story, and other poems. Bost. 1875. S.   **821.1 : 137**

— A home idyl, and other poems. Bost. 1881. D.   **821.1 : 165**

— The vagabond, and other poems. New ed. Bost. 1881. D.   **821.1 : 166**

Trumbull, J: Poetical works, containing M'Fingal, a modern epic poem, rev. and corr. with copious explanatory notes ; The progress of dulness ; and a collection of poems on various subjects written before and during the revolutionary war. Hartford. 1820. 2 v. in 1. O.   **821.1 : 138**

Tupper, Martin Farquhar. Proverbial philosophy ; a book of thoughts and arguments, originally treated. Two ser. in 1 v. N. Y. 1849. D.   **821.2 : 171**

Vandenhoff, G: Common sense ; a dash at doings of the day, a social satire in verse. Bost. 1858. D.   **821.1 : 139**

Vaughan, H: Sacred poems and private ejaculations ; with a memoir by H. F. Lyte. Bost. 1856. S.   **821.2 : 172**

Very, Jones. Poems ; with an introd. memoir by W: P. Andrews. Bost. 1883. S.   **821.1 : 191**

Wallace, W: Ross. Meditations in America, and other poems. 2d ed. N. Y. 1851. D.   **821.1 : 140**

Ward, T: Englands reformation, from the time of king Henry VIII, to the end of Dates's plot ; a poem in four cantos with large marginal notes, according to the original. Lond. 1716. D.   **821.2 : 173**

Watts, I: Horæ lyricæ and divine songs ; with a memoir by Robert Southey. Bost. 1854. S.   **821.2 : 174**

Weeks, Robert Kelley. Poems. N. Y. 1881. D.   **821.1 : 169**

Wesley, C: Finer and less familiar poems. N. Y. 1867. S.   **821.2 : 175**

White, G: Home ballads ; devotional, sentimental, humorous. Chicago. 1878. D.   **821.1 : 143**

White, H: Kirke. Poetical works ; with a memoir by sir Harris Nicolas. Bost. 1854. S.   **821.2 : 176**

Whitman, Walt. Leaves of grass. Bost. 1881-82. D.   **821.2 : P164**

Whitney, Adeline Dutton, *born* Train. Mother Goose for grown folks. Bost. [1870]. D.   **821.1 : 144**

Whittier, J: Greenleaf. Poetical works. Bost. 1872. 2 v. S.   **821.1 : 153**

— Poetical works. Household ed. Bost. 1874. D.   **821.1 : 152**

— The Bay of Seven Islands, and other poems. Bost. 1883. D.   **821.1 : 201**

— The chapel of the hermits, and other poems. Bost. 1853. D.   **821.1 : 145**

Whittier, J: Greenleaf.—*Continued.*
— Hazel blossoms. Bost. 1875. D.   **821.1 : 146**
— Home ballads and poems. Bost. 1861. D.
    821.1 : 147
— In war time, and other poems. Bost. 1864. D.
    821.1 : 203
— The king's missive, and other poems. Bost.
    1881. D.   **821.1 : 148**
— Mabel Martin ; a harvest idyl. Ill. Bost. 1876.
    S.   **821.1 : 149**
— National lyrics. Bost. 1865. S.   **821.1 : 154**
— The panorama, and other poems. Bost. 1856.
    D.   **821.1 : 150**
— The Pennsylvania pilgrim, and other poems.
    Bost. 1872. D.   **821.1 : 151**
— Snow-bound ; a winter idyl. Bost. 1866. D.
    821.1 : 155
— Songs of labor, and other poems. Bost. 1856.
    D.   **821.1 : 156**
— The tent on the beach, and other poems. Bost.
    1867. D.   **821.1 : 157**
Wilcox, Ella, *born* Wheeler. Maurine. Milw.
    1876. D.   **821.1 : 141**
— Poems of passion. Chicago. 1883. S.
    821.1 : 190
— *Same.*   **821.1 : R190**
— Shells. Milw. 1873. D.   **821.1 : 142**
Wilde, Oscar. Poems. Bost. 1881. D.
    821.2 : 186
Wilkinson, W: Cleaver. Webster ; an ode,
    1782-1852. N. Y. 1882. Q.   **821.1 + 176**
Williams, I: The cathedral, or The catholic
    and apostolic church in England. Oxford.
    1841. S.   **821.2 : 177**
Willis, Nathaniel Parker. Poems, sacred, pas-
    sionate and humorous. N. Y. 1859. S.
    821.1 : 158

Wilson, J: Poetical works. Edinb. 1858. D.
    821.2 : 178
Wilson, W: Poems, ed. by Benson J: Lossing.
    Poughkeepsie. 1869. D.   **821.1 : 159**
Wordsworth, W: Poetical works. Bost. 1854.
    7 v. S.   **821.2 : 180**
    Contents. **V. 1.** Poems written in youth.—Poems
    referring to the period of childhood.—Poems founded
    on the affections. **2.** Poems on the naming of
    places.—Poems of the fancy.—Poems of the imagina-
    tion.—Miscellaneous sonnets. **3.** Memorials of a tour
    in Scotland, 1803.—Memorials of a tour in Scotland,
    1814.—Poems dedicated to national independence and
    liberty.—Memorials of a tour on the continent, 1820.
    —Memorials of a tour in Italy, 1837.—The river Dud-
    don.—Yarrow revisited, and other poems. **4.** The
    white doe of Rylstone. — Ecclesiastical sonnets:
    pt. 1. From the introduction of christianity in-
    to Britain to the consummation of the papal
    dominion; pt. 2, To the close of the troubles in the
    reign of Charles I; pt. 3, From the restoration to
    the present time. — Evening voluntaries. — Poems
    composed or suggested during a tour in the summer
    of 1833.—Poems of sentiment and reflection.—Son-
    nets dedicated to liberty and order.—Sonnets upon
    the punishment of death. **5.** Miscellaneous poems.
    —Inscriptions.—Selections from Chaucer, modern-
    ized.—Poems referring to the period of old age.—
    Epitaphs and elegiac pieces.—App. **6.** The excur-
    sion. **7.** The prelude, or growth of a poet's mind.
    —App.
— Poems. Lond. 1847. O.   **821.2 + 179**
    Contents, see Poetical works, v. 1-6.
Wright, Robert W., (*Quevedo Redivivus jr.*) The
    vision of judgment, or The south church ;
    ecclesiastical councils viewed from celes-
    tial and satanic stand-points, by Quevedo
    Redivivus jr. N. Y. 1867. D.   **821.1 : 160**
Wyatt, *Sir* T: Poetical works ; with a memoir.
    Bost. 1854. S.   **821.2 : 181**

7. English literature — c, Drama.

1. History and criticism.

(*See also* Essays, class 824.)

Ward, Adolphus W: A history of english dra-
    matic literature, to the death of queen
    Anne. Lond. 1875. 2 v. O.   **822.4 : 1**

Hazlitt, W: Lectures on the dramatic literature
    of the age of Elizabeth. Phila. 1848. D.
    822.5 : 1
    Contents. General view of the subject.—On the dra-
    matic writers, contemporary with Shakspeare, Lyly,
    Marlowe, Heywood, Middleton and Rowley.—On Mar-
    ston, Chapman, Decker and Webster.—On Beaumont
    and Fletcher, Ben Jonson, Ford and Massinger.—On
    single plays, poems, etc.. The four P's, the Return
    from Parnassus, Gammer Gurton's needle, etc. — On
    miscellaneous poems, F. Beaumont, P. Fletcher, Dray-
    ton, Daniel, etc., sir P. Sidney's Arcadia and sonnets.
    — Character of lord Bacon's works, compared as to
    style with sir T: Browne and Jeremy Taylor.—On the
    spirit of ancient and modern literature.—On the ger-
    man drama contrasted with the age of Elizabeth.

Symonds, J: Addington. Shakspere's predecess-
    ors in the english drama. Lond. 1884. O.
    822.4 : 2

Coleridge, S: Taylor. Lectures upon Shakspeare
    and other dramatists. *In his* Complete
    works.   **820.2 : 7 v4**
— Lectures and notes on Shakspere and other

english poets ; now first coll. by T. Ashe.
    Lond. 1884. D.   **822.3 : 87**
    Contents. Lectures on Shakspere and Milton. 1811-
    12.—The lectures and notes of 1818: Introd.; Poetry,
    the drama and Shakspere : Order of Shakspere's
    plays; Notes on Shakspere's plays from english his-
    tory; Notes on some other plays of Shakspere; Jon-
    son, Beaumont, Fletcher and Massinger; Notes on
    Ben Jonson; Notes on Beaumont and Fletcher.—Lec-
    tures on Shakspere and Milton at Bristol, 1813-14. —
    App.

Baker, D: Erskine. Biographia dramatica, or
    Companion to the playhouse ; containing
    historical and critical memoirs and original
    anecdotes of british and irish dramatic
    writers from the commencement of our
    theatrical exhibitions, among whom are
    some of the most celebrated actors, also an
    alphabetical account and chronological
    lists of their works, the dates when printed
    and observations on their merits, together
    with an introductory view of the rise and
    progress of the british stage. Originally
    compiled to the end of 1764 by D: Erskine
    Baker, continued thence to 1782 by I:
    Reed and brought down to the end of no-
    vember 1811, with add. and imp., by Stephen
    Jones. Lond. 1812. 4 v. O.   **822.4 : 3**
    Contents. **V. 1.** Introd: A brief view of the rise
    and progress of the english stage. — [Index of
    authors] A–H. **2.** I–Y. **3.** [Index of plays] A–L.
    4. M–Z.—Latin plays by english authors.—Oratorios.
    —App.

2. Shaksperiana.

(For works of Shakspere, *see* col. 594–598; *and see* also references in the Index to biography at the end of the catalogue.)

Shakespeariana, v. 1, 2; nov. 1883—dec. 1885. Phila. [1884–85]. Q.   822.3 : M

Morgan, Horace H. Topical Shakespeariana, or A collection of english shakespeariana, exclusive of editions, arr. under headings, to facilitate reference to special subjects of investigation. St. Louis. 1879. O. 822.3 : 41

Clarke, Mary Cowden-, *born* Novello. The complete concordance to Shakspere; a verbal index to all the passages in the dramatic works of the poet. New and rev. ed. Bost. 1860. Q.   822.3 : R30

Clarke, C: *and* Mary Cowden-. The Shakespeare key; unlocking the treasures of his style, elucidating the peculiarities of his construction, and displaying the beauties of his expression; forming a companion to The complete concordance to Shakespeare. Lond. 1879. O.   822.3 : R31

Arnold, Cecil. An index to Shakespearian thought; a collection of passages from the plays and poems of Shakespeare, classified under appropriate headings and alphabetically arr. Lond. 1880. O.   822.3 : 28

Halliwell-Phillipps, James Orchard. Outlines of the life of Shakespeare. 3d ed. Lond. 1883. O.   822.3 : 71

— An historical account of the New Place, Stratford-upon-Avon, the last residence of Shakespeare. Lond. 1864. F. 822.3 : R72

Norris, J. Parker. The portraits of Shakespeare. [Bibliography, p. xv—xxviii.] Phila. 1885. O.   822.3 : R89

Guizot, François P: Guillaume. Shakspeare and his times. N. Y. 1855. D.   822.3 : 34

Dowden, E: Shakspere. (Literature primer.) N. Y. 1879. S.   822.3 : 32

— Shakspere; a critical study of his mind and art. 5th ed. Lond. 1880. D.   822.3 : 33

Swinburne, Algernon. A study of Shakespeare. N. Y. 1880. D.   822.3 : 44

Hudson, H: Norman. Lectures on Shakespeare. N. Y. 1848. 2 v. D.   822.3 : 38

— Shakespeare, his life, art and characters, with an historical sketch of the origin and growth of the drama in England. 4th ed., rev. Bost. 1882. 2 v. D.   822.3 : 68

White, R: Grant. Studies in Shakespeare. Bost. 1886 [1885]. O.   822.3 : 93

Contents. On reading Shakespeare.—Narrative analysis: The lady Grusch's husband; The case of Hamlet the 'younger; The florentine arithmetician; The tale of the forest of Arden. — Miscellanies: The Bacon-Shakespeare craze; King Lear, the text, plot, and personages; Stage Rosalinds; On the acting of Iago.—Expositors: Glossaries and lexicons; Note on W. S. Walker's Critical examination of the text.

Rümelin, Gustav. Shakespearestudien. 2te aufl. Stuttg. 1874. O.   822.3 : 94

Contents. Die stellung der englischen bühne zu Shakespeares zeit.—Shakespeares stellung zu seinen zeitgenossen.—Die mängel der Shakespearekritik.—Eür wen dichtete Shakespeare?—Shakespeares eigenthümlichkeiten in der charakteristik der personen und in der motivirung der dramatischen handlung.—Die motivirung der handlung in Lear, Mass für mass, Cymbeline, Romeo, Macbeth, Othello, Hamlet.—Zu den englischen historiendramen. — Zu dem dramen über stoffe des classischen alterthums.—Zu den lustspielen.—Shakespeares individualität und bildungsgang.—Shakespeares lebensansichten.—Die deutsche Shakespearecultus und vergleichung Shakespeares mit Schiller und Goethe.

Giles, H: Human life in Shakespeare; with introd. by J: Boyle O'Reilly. New ed. Bost. 1882. S.   822.3 : 55

Jameson, Anna, *born* Murphy. Characteristics of [Shakspere's] women, moral, poetical and historical. Bost. 1859. T.   822.3 : 39

Barr, Amelia E. The young people of Shakespeare's dramas, for youthful readers. N. Y. 1882. D.   x 822.3 : 53

Bucknill, J: C: The mad folk of Shakespeare; psychological essays. 2d ed. rev. Lond. 1867. D.   822.3 : 85

Kellogg, A. O. Shakspeare's delineations of insanity, imbecility and suicide. N. Y. 1866. D.   822.3 : 40

Field, B: Rush. Medical thoughts of Shakespeare. 2d ed., rev. and enl. Easton, Pa. 1885. O.   822.3+90

Campbell, J:, *baron Campbell.* Shakespeare's legal acquirements considered in a letter to J. P. Collier. N.Y. 1859. D. 822.3 : 29

Heard, Franklin Fiske. Shakespeare as a lawyer. Bost. 1883. D.   822.3 : 74

Dyer, T: Firminger Thiselton. Folk-lore of Shakespeare. N. Y. 1884 [1883]. O.   822.3 : 77

Phipson, Emma. The animal-lore of Shakspeare's time, incl. quadrupeds, birds, reptiles, fish and insects. Lond. 1883. D.   822.3 : 78

Wordsworth, C: Shakspeare's knowledge and use of the Bible. 3d ed., with app. containing add. ill. and tercentary sermon. Lond. 1880. D.   822.3 : 46

Rushton, W: Lowes. Shakespeare illustrated by old authors. Lond. 1867. D.   822.3 : 84

— Shakespeare illustrated by the lex scripta, pt. 1. Lond. 1870. D. *With the same.*
                    in 822.3 : 84

— Shakespeare's euphuism. Lond. 1871. D. *With the same.*   *in* 822.3 : 84

— Shakespeare's testamentary language. Lond. 1869. D. *With the same.* *in* 822.3 : 84

Lamb, C: Specimens of english dramatic poets, who lived about the time of Shakspeare, with notes; pts. 1, 2. N. Y. 1845. D.   822.2 : 4

Green, H: Shakespeare and the emblem writers; an exposition of their similarities of thought and expression; preceded by a view of emblem-literature down to a. d. 1616. Ill. Lond. 1870. O.   822.3+81

Collier, J: Payne, *ed.* Shakespeare's library; a collection of the romances, novels, poems and histories used by Shakespeare as the foundation of his dramas, now first coll. and printed from original ed. with introd. notices. Lond. [1843]. 2 v. O.   822.3 : 79

Contents. V. 1. Greene's Pandosto, the story on which is founded the Winter's tale.—Lodge's Rosalynd, the novel on which is founded As you like it.—The historie of Hamblet, on which the tragedy of Hamlet is constructed.—Apollonius, prince of Tyre, from which the incidents of the play Pericles are derived. 2. Romeus and Juliet, a poem by Arthur Brooke.—Rhomeo and Julietta from Paynter's Palace of pleasure.—Giletta of Narbona, on which is founded All's well that ends well, from Paynter's Palace of pleasure.—The story of The two lovers of Pisa, which Shakespeare employed in his Merry wives of Windsor.—The historie of Apollonius and Silla, containing part of the play of Twelfth night, repr. from Rich's Farewell to military profession, 1606.—The historie of Promos and Cassandra, closely resembling the plot of Measure for measure, from

x denotes books specially adapted for children.

Whetstone's Heptameron of civil discourses, 1582.—Novels more or less resembling The merchant of Venice: The adventures of Giannetto, from the Pecorone of sir Giovanni Fiorentino; Of a jew who would for his debt have a pound of the flesh of a christian, from the Orator of Alex. Silvayn. tr. by A. Munday, 1598; The story of the choice of three caskets. from the Gesta romanorum. tr. by Robinson.—The story of a moorish captain, on which is founded the tragedy of Othello, from the Heccatomithi of Cinthio.—Queen Cordila, a poem by J: Higgins, from the Mirror for magistrates, 1587. — The story of The paphlagonian unkind king, on which is founded the episode of Gloster and his sons in King Lear, from sir Philip Sidney's Arcadia, 1591. — The history of Makbeth, from Holinshed's chronicle.—The story of the shepherdess Felismena, from which Shakespeare is said to have taken the plot of the Two gentlemen of Verona. from the Diana of Montemayor. tr. by B. Young, 1598.—The story told by the fishwife of stand on the green, the incidents of which are similar to some of those in Cymbeline, from Westward for smelts, 1620.

Snider, Denton Jaques. System of Shakespeare's dramas. St. Louis. 1877. 2 v. D.
822.3 : 42

Stokes, H: Paine. An attempt to determine the chronological order of Shakespeare's plays. (The Harness essay, 1877). Lond. 1878. S.
822.3 : 43

Gervinus, G: Gottfried. Shakespeare commentaries. Tr. under the author's superintendence by F. E. Bunnètt. New ed., rev. Lond. 1883. O. 822.3 : 80

Hazlitt, W: Characters of Shakespeare's plays. Bost. 1818. D. 822.3 : 36
— *Same.* Phila. 1848. D. *With his* Dramatic literature. *in* 822.5 : 1

Hamilton, N: Esterhazy Stephen Armytage. An inquiry into the genuineness of the manuscript corrections in mr. J. Payne Collier's annotated Shakspere folio, 1632, and of certain Shaksperian documents likewise pub. by mr. Collier. Lond 1860. O.
822.3 : 35

Kemble, Frances Anne. Notes upon some of Shakespeare's p.ays. Lond. 1882. O.
822.3 : 86
Contents. Introd. — Macbeth. — Henry VIII. — The tempest.—Romeo and Juliet.

Leighton, W: The subjection of Hamlet; an essay toward an explanation of the motives of thought and action of Shakespeare's prince of Denmark, with an introd. by Joseph Crosby. Phila. 1882. D. **822.3 : 54**

Vining, E: P. The mystery of Hamlet; an attempt to solve an old problem. Phila. 1881. S. 822.3 : 51

Wilson, Daniel. Caliban; the missing link. Lond. 1873. D. 822.3 : 45

Holmes, Nathaniel. The authorship of Shakespeare. N. Y. 1866. D. 822.3 : 37

Morgan, Appleton. The Shakespearean myth; William Shakespeare and circumstantial evidence. Cinc. 1881. O. 822.3 : 52
— Some Shakespearean commentators. Cinc. 1882. D. 822.3 : 56

Wilkes, G: Shakespeare from an american point of view; incl. an inquiry as to his religious faith and his knowledge of law, with the Baconian theory considered. 3d ed., rev. and corr. N. Y. 1882. O.
822.3 : 73
Note. For illustrations of the similarity between Bacon's expressions and those of Shakspere, see Bacon, F. Promus of formularies, 829.2+44.

*   *   *

Lamb, C: Tales from Shakspeare, designed for the use of young people. Lond. *n. d.* D.
x 822.3 : 50
— *Same.* Ed. for the use of schools. [Classics for children.] Bost. 1885. D.   x 822.3 : 88

Seamer, Mary. Shakespeare's stories simply told. Lond. *n. d.* D.   x 822.3 : 95

x denotes books specially adapted for children.

3. Individual works.

See Class-list of drama, col. 519—614.

8.   English literature — d, Romance.

1. History, Criticism, etc.

(*See also* Essays, class 824.)

Lanier, Sidney. The english novel and the principle of its development. N. Y. 1883. D. 823.2 : 4

Masson, D: British novelists and their styles; a critical sketch of the history of british prose fiction. Bost. 1859. D.   823.2 : 1

Tuckerman, Bayard. History of english prose fiction, from sir T: Malory to George Eliot. N. Y. 1882. D. 823 : 1

Pellew, G: Jane Austen's novels; Bowdoin prize dissertation. Bost. 1883. O.   823.2 : 5

Canning, *The hon.* Albert Stratford G: Philosophy of the Waverley novels. Lond. 1879. D. 823.2 : 2

Pierce, Gilbert A. The Dickens dictionary; a key to the characters and principal incidents in the tales of C: Dickens, with add. by W: A. Wheeler. Ill. Bost. 1879. D. 823.2 : 3

Rogers, May. The Waverley dictionary; an alphabetical arrangement of all the characters in sir Walter Scott's Waverley novels, with a descriptive analysis of each character and illustrative selections from the text. Chicago. 1879. D.   823.2 : 6

Hawthorne, Nathaniel. An analytical index to [his] works, with a sketch of his life. [Libr. ed.] Bost. 1882. D. 823.1 : 1

2. Individual works.

See Class-list of prose fiction, col. 657—902.

9. English literature — e, Essays and Oratory.

(See also Miscellany, class 829, and Political essays and speeches, class 329.)

Dobson, H: Austin. *ed.* Eighteenth century essays, selected and annotated. [Parchment ser.] N. Y. 1882. T.   **824.2 : 96**
Contents. Introd. — Mr. Bickerstaff visits a friend: The trumpet club, by R: **Steele.** — The political upholsterer: Tom Folio; Ned Softly, the poet, by J. **Addison.**—Recollections of childhood, by R: **Steele.** —Adventures of a shilling: Frozen voices: Stage lions; Meditations in Westminster abbey: The exercise of the fan: Will Wimble, by J. **Addison.** — Sir Roger de Coverley's ancestors, by R: **Steele.** —Sir Roger de Coverley hare-hunting, by E. **Budgell.** — The citizen's journal: The fine lady's journal: Sir Roger de Coverley at the play, by J. **Addison.** — A day's ramble in London: Dick Estcourt, by R: **Steele.** —Death of sir Roger de Coverley; The tory foxhunter, by J. **Addison.**—A modern conversation, by lord **Chesterfield.** — The squire in orders, by G: **Colman** *and* B. **Thornton.**—Country congregations, by W: **Cowper.**—Dick Minim, the critic, by S: **Johnson.**—Art-connoisseurs, by sir J. **Reynolds.**—The man in black: Beau Tibbs: Beau Tibbs at home: Beau Tibbs at Vauxhall, by O. **Goldsmith.** — A country dowager, by H: **Mackenzie.**—Ill. notes.

Tatler, The, or Lucubrations of Isaac Bickerstaff, esq., [Sir R: **Steele,** apr. 12, 1709 to jan. 2, 1711]. Lond. 1776. 4 v. D.
        824.2 : 116
— *Same.* With notes and a general index. Lond. 1829. O.   **824.2 : 84**
Note. Numerous essays were contributed by Joseph Addison.

Spectator, The; [march 1. 1711—dec. 6, 1712, and june 18 to dec. 20, 1714]. Lond. 1753. 8 v. S.   **824.2 : 1**
Note. 274 papers are ascribed to Joseph Addison, 240 to sir R: **Steele,** 137 to Eustace Budgell, and 11 to J: **Hughes.** Addison's contributions are signed with a C, L, I, or O, forming the word Clio; v. 8 was pub. two years after the other vols. by Addison alone.

Guardian, The; [march 12 to oct. 1, 1713]. Lond. 1775. 3 v. S.   **824.2 : 115**
— *Same.* With notes and a general index. Lond. 1829. O.   **824.2 : 115**
Note. Written chiefly by sir R: **Steele** and Joseph **Addison.**

Intelligencer, The. Printed at Dublin, repr. at Lond. 1729. D.   **824.2 : 85**
Note. In 19 numbers: 1, 3, 5, 7 and part of 8, 9, 10, 15, 19 were written by Jonathan **Swift,** the rest by T: **Sheridan.**

Rambler, The; a periodical paper, published in 1750, 1751, 1752 by S: **Johnson;** [march 20, 1750 to march 10, 1752]. Lond. 1826. O.
        824.2 : 118
— *Same.* 11th ed. Dublin. 1785. 4 v. S.
Note. No. 30 is by miss Catharine **Talbot;** no. 97 by S: **Richardson;** nos. 44, 100 by Eliz. **Carter.**

Adventurer, The, by J: **Hawkesworth** and others; [nov. 7, 1752 to march 9, 1754]. Lond. 1777. 4 v. S.   **824.2 : 117**
— *Same.* Lond. 1829. O.   **824.2 : 117**
Note. Written by J: Hawkesworth, S: Johnson, T: Warton, D. Bathurst and Hester Chapone.

Connoisseur, The, by Mr. Town, critic and censor general; [jan. 31, 1754 to sept. 23, 1756]. Lond. 1826. O.   **824.2 : 92**
Note. Nos. 14, 17, 33, 40 were by J: **Boyle** *earl of Cork and Orrery;* 119, 134, 138 and probably 111, 115 by W: **Cowper;** 62, 64 by J: **Duncombe,** the remainder by G: **Colman** the elder, and Bonnell **Thornton.**

Idler, The, by S: **Johnson;** [april 15, 1758 to april 6, 1760]. Lond. 1826. O.   **824.2 : 100**
Note. Nos. 33, 93, 96 were by T: **Warton;** nos. 76, 79, 82 by sir Joshua **Reynolds.**

Observer, The; 1785-90. *See* **Cumberland,** R:, *below.*

Papers from the Quarterly review. [*Anon.*] N. Y. 1852. S.   **824.2 : 93**
Contents. **Head,** *Sir* F. B. The printer's devil.— **Hayward,** A. Gastronomy and gastronomers. — **James,** T. The honey-bee.—Music.—Art of dress.

Essays on social subjects, from the Saturday review. Bost. 1865. D.   **824.2 : 105**
Contents. Busy people. — Snubbing. — Ignorance.— Foolish things.—False shame.—Fluency.—Contempt. —Dulness as a sensation.—Mistakes in life.—Scenes. — Acquaintance and friends. — Saying disagreeable things.—On being understood.—Study of character.— Prejudices. — Shirking. — Constancy. — Reserve.—Explanations. — Hugger-mugger. — Attention. — Strong wills.—Talking of self.—Folly.—Time past.—Alloys.— The uses of pathos.—Choice.—One's own way.—Want of money.

About babies, Good looking people, and other "Maga social papers". N. Y. 1867. D.
        824.1 : 96
Contents. **Tomes,** R. Are we a good looking people?— **Brown,** *Mrs.* A. A. The proper sphere of men.—**Storrow,** T. W. The art of eating.—**Osborne,** J. D. The gambling houses of Paris. — **Kirkland,** C. M. Boarding-schools. — The Zay-nis of Yan-ky. — **Mitchell,** A. Natural diplomatists. —The history of a cosmopolite [Vincent Nolte]. — **Higginson,** T: W. African proverbial philosophy.—**Kip,** L. Household skeletons.—**Perkins,** F: B. The compensation office. —**Warner,** C: D. Our new Atlantis. — About babies. —The St. Nicholas and the Five Points. — **Trux,** J. J. Negro minstrelsy, ancient and modern.

Rice, Allan Thorndyke, *ed.* Essays from the North american review. N. Y. 1879. O.
        824.1 : 105
Contents. **Prescott,** W: H. Sir Walter Scott. — **Cushing,** C. Social condition of woman.—**Emerson,** R. W. J: Milton.—**Bancroft,** G: Last moments of eminent men.—**Motley,** J: L. Peter the great.— **Irving,** W. The norsemen.—**Adams,** C: F. The earl of Chesterfield. — **Longfellow,** H: W. Defence of poetry. — **Curtis,** G: W: Nathaniel Hawthorne.— **Parkman,** F. James Fennimore Cooper. — **Lowell,** J. R. Shakespeare once more. — **Holmes,** O. W. Mechanism of vital action.

*   *   *

Alcott, Amos Bronson. Concord days. Bost. 1872. S.   **824.1 : 99**

Alison, *Sir* Archibald. Essays, political, historical and miscellaneous. Edinb. 1850. 2 v. O.   **824.2 : 124**
Contents. V. 1. The reform bill.—Military treason and national guards.—The french revolution of 1830. —The british peerage.—The fall of the constitution. —Negro emancipation.—Ireland.—The commercial crisis of 1837. — Colonial government and the West India question.—Lessons from the past.—Free trade and protection.—Thirty years of liberal legislation.— Fall of the throne of the barricades.—The navigation laws.—The crowning of the column and the crushing of the pedestal.—Crime and transportation. — Free trade at its zenith. 2. Montesquieu.—Homer, Dante and Michael Angelo.—The greek drama.—The roman republic.—Mirabeau.—The french school of painting. —The Tyrol.—Hannibal.—Napoleon.—Partition of the kingdom of the Netherlands.—The athenian democracy.—Robert Bruce.—National monuments.—The crusades.—The carlist struggle in Spain.—The copyright question.—The decline of Turkey.—Lamartine. —The Roman Campagna.—France in 1833.—The earl of Chesterfield. — The afghanistan expedition.—The old scottish parliament.— Ships, colonies and commerce. 3. Chateaubriand.— Virgil, Tasso and Raphael.—Guizot.—The romantic drama.—Wellington.—Humboldt.—The british school of architecture.—Sismondi.—Poland.—The year of revolutions.—British history during the 18th century. —Mme. de Stael. — M. de Tocqueville. — Autobio-

Alison, *Sir* Archibald.—*Continued.*
graphy. — Michelet's France. — The fall of Rome. — Karamsin's Russia.— The historical romance. — The british theatre.— Direct taxation.— Macaulay.—Free-trade reform and finance.—The royal progress.

— Miscellaneous essays. Phila. 1845. O.
                 824.2 : 2
Contents. Chateaubriand. — Napoleon. — Bossuet.— Poland. — Mme. de Staël. — National monuments. — Marshal Ney. — Robert Bruce. — Paris in 1814. — The Louvre in 1814.—Tyrol.—France in 1833.—Italy.—Scott, Campbell and Byron. — The copyright question. — Michelet's France. — Military treason and civic sol-diers.—Arnold's Rome.—Mirabeau.—Bulwer's Athens. —The reign of terror.—The french revolution of 1830. —The fall of Turkey.—The spanish revolution of 1820. —Partition of the kingdom of the Netherlands.—Ka-ramsin's Russia.— Effects of the french revolution of 1830. — Desertion of Portugal. — Carlist struggle in Spain.—Wellington.—The Afghanistaun expedition.— The future.—Guizot.—Homer, Dante and Michael An-gelo.

Arnold, Matthew. Culture and anarchy ; an essay in political and social criticism. N. Y. 1883. D.   **824.2 : 112**
Contents. Introd.—On sweetness and light. — Doing as one likes. — Barbarians, philistines, populace. — Hebraism and hellenism. — Porro unum est necessa-rium.—Our liberal practitioners.—Conclusion.

— Discourses in America. Lond. 1885. D.
               824.2 : 125
Contents. Numbers, or The majority and the rem-nant.—Literature and science.—Emerson.

— Essays in criticism. Bost. 1865. D. **824.2 : 3**
Contents. The function of criticism at the present time.—The literary influence of academies.—Maurice de Guérin.— Eugénie de Guérin. — H : Heine.— Pagan and mediæval religious sentiment. — Joubert. — Spi-noza. — Marcus Aurelius. — On translating Homer.— A french Eton.

— Friendship's garland ; being the conversations, letters and opinions of the late Arminius baron von Thunder-ten-Tronckh, collected and ed., with a dedicatory letter to Adoles-cens Leo, esq., of the "Daily telegraph." *With his* Culture and anarchy.
           in **824.2 : 112**

— Irish essays, and others. Lond. 1882. D.
               824.2 : 110
Contents. The incompatibles.—An unregarded irish grievance. — Ecce, convertimur ad gentes. — The fu-ture of liberalism. — A speech at Eton. — The french play in London.—Copyright.—Prefaces to poems.

— Mixed essays. N. Y. 1879. D.   **824.2 : 4**
Contents. Democracy.— Equality. — Irish catholic-ism and british liberalism.—Porro unum est neces-sarium.—A guide to english literature.—Falkland.— A french critic [Edmond H : Adolphe Scherer] on Mil-ton.—A french critic [Scherer] on Göthe.—George Sand.

Bacon, Francis, *baron Verulam, viscount St. Al-bans.* Essays, or Counsels civil and moral, and the two books of the Proficience and advancement of learning, divine and hu-man. New ed., with memoir and notes by W. C. Taylor. Lond. 1840. D.
               824.2 : 5

Bain, Alexander. Practical essays. N. Y. 1884. D.   **824.2 : 91**
Contents. Common errors on the mind.—Errors of suppressed correlatives.—The civil service examina-tions.—The classical controversy.—Metaphysics and debating societies.— The university ideal, past and present.—The art of study.—Religious tests and sub-scriptions.—Procedure of deliberative bodies.

Baker, G : A., *jr.* The bad habits of good so-ciety. N. Y. 1876. S.   **824.1 : 2**

Ballantyne, T :, *ed.* Essays in mosaic. [Bayard ser.] Lond. 1875. T.   **824.2 : 6**
Contents. The art of reading.—The art of thinking. —The art of conversation.—Gentlemanliness.—Good manners and good breeding. — Concentration and

method. — Statesmanship. — Pococurantelsm, cynic-ism, scepticism.—The uses of adversity.—Solitude and retirement.—Sympathy with nature. — Friendship.— The gospel of labour.—Too much brain-work.—The gospel of rest.

Bancroft, G : Literary and historical miscellan-ies. N. Y. 1855. O.   **824.1+3**
Contents. Essays. The doctrine of temperaments.— Ennui.—The ruling passion in death. *Studies in ger-man literature.* General characteristics.—The revival of german literature.—Men of science and learning. —The age of Schiller and Göthe. — Translations. *Studies in history.* Economy of Athens.—Decline of the roman empire.—Russia.—The wars of Russia and Turkey. *Occasional addresses.* A word on Calvin the reformer.—The office of the people in art, govern-ment and religion.—In memory of W : Ellery Chan-ning.—Oration commemorative of Andrew Jackson. —The necessity, the reality and the promise of the progress of the human race.

Barron, Alfred, (" Q "). Foot notes, or Walking as a fine art. Wallingford, Conn. 1875. D.
               824.1 : 4

Bartol, Cyrus A : The rising faith. Bost. 1874. D.   **824.1 : 5**
Contents. The seeker.—The seer.—The secret power. —Sincerity.—Sex.— Teaching.— Training. — Forms.— Values.—Validity.— Personality.— Prayer.— Unity.— Survival.—Signs.—Ideas.

Birrell, Augustine. Obiter dicta. [*Anon.*] N. Y. 1885. S.   **824.2 : 36**
Contents. Carlyle. — On the alleged obscurity of mr. Browning's poetry.—Truth-hunting.—Actors. — A rogue's memoirs.—The via media.—Falstaff.

Black, Jeremiah Sullivan. Essays and speeches; with a biographical sketch by Chauncey F. Black. N. Y. 1885. O.   **824.1+8**
Contents. Black, C. F. Biogr. sketch.—Miscellan-eous: Address before the agric. soc. of Somerset co.; Religious liberty; Political preaching; Answer to Ingersoll; Legislative oath; A great law-suit and a field fight; The character of mr. Seward; Speech at the centenary of Grattan's declaration of irish in-dependence; Railroad monopoly. — Eulogies: Life and character of Jackson; Death of judge Gibson; Death of senator Carpenter.—Political essays and letters: Observations on territorial sovereignty; Letter to judge Hoar; Letters to H: Wilson; Open letter to gen. Garfield; The great fraud; Letter to mr. Stoughton; The third term; Gen. Grant and strong government; The electoral vote of Louisiana. —Forensic: Ableman vs. Booth; Fossatt vs. the U. S.; Pierce vs. the U. S.; Providence rubber company vs. the Goodyears' executor *et al.*; In defense of the right to trial by jury; U. S. vs. Blyew *et al.*; State of Missouri *ex rel.*; Frank J. Bowman vs. E. A. Lewis *et al.*; The McGarrahan claim; Federal jurisdiction in the territories; The South Carolina case.

Blackwood, *Sir* F : Temple Hamilton-Temple-, *earl of Dufferin.* Speeches and addresses ; ed. by H : Milton. Lond. 1882. O.
               825.2 : 1

Bowen, Francis. Gleanings from a literary life, 1838-1880. N. Y. 1880. O.   **824.1 : 6**
Contents. Education. Prefatory notes.—The con-test between the ancients and the moderns.—Classi-cal and utilitarian studies; App. The abuse of the study of grammar. *Political economy.* A minority report on the silver question.—The perpetuity of na-tional debt.—The financial conduct of the war.—The utility and the limitations of the science of political economy. *Philosophy.* Dualism, materialism or idealism.—The idea of cause. — The latest form of development theory. — Diseases and malformations not hereditable.—The physical effects of etherization. —Buckle's History of civilization.—J : S. Mill's Ex-amination of sir W : Hamilton's philosophy. — The human and the brute mind.—Malthusianism, darwin-ism and pessimism.—Blaise Pascal.—Essays and re-views: the Oxford clergymen's attack on christian-ity. — Restoration of the text of Shakespeare; the battle of the commentators.

Boyd, Andrew Kennedy Hutchinson. The recreations of a country parson. [1st and] 2d series. [*Anon.*] Bost. 1861, 1863. 2 v. D.   **824.2 : 101**

Boyd, Andrew Kennedy Hutchinson.—*Continued.*
— Leisure hours in town. [*Anon.*] Bost. 1862.
D.   **824.2 : 103**
— The everyday philosopher in town and coun-
try, by the author of The recreations of a
country parson. [*Anon.*] Bost. 1863. D.
                                            824.2 : 102
— The autumn holidays of a country parson.
[*Anon.*] Bost. 1865. D.   **824.2 : 104**
Boyle, F: Legends of my bungalow. Lond.
1882. D.   **824.2 : 122**
Brewer, J: Sherren. English studies, or Essays
in english history and literature ; ed., with
a prefatory memoir, by H: Wace. Lond.
1881. O.   **824.2 : 7**
  Contents. Memoir.—List of mr. Brewer's publications.—A sermon.—New sources of english history.—
  Green's Short history of the english people.—Hatfield
  house.—The Stuarts.—Shakspeare.—The study of
  Shakspeare.—The royal supremacy.—Passages from
  the life of Erasmus.— The study of history.—The
  study of english history.—Ancient London.
Brown, J: Spare hours ; 1st and 2d ser. Bost.
1864, 1866. 2 v. D.   **824.2 : 8**
  Contents. 1st ser. Rab and his friends. — "With
  brains, sir."—The mystery of black and tan.— Her
  last half-crown.— Our dogs.— Queen Mary's child-
  garden.— Presence of mind and happy guessing.—
  My father's memoir. — Mystifications. — "Oh, I'm
  Wat, Wat! "—Arthur H. Hallam.—Education through
  the senses.—Vaughan's poems.— Dr. Chalmers.— Dr.
  G: Wilson.—St. Paul's thorn in the flesh.—The Black
  Dwarf's bones.—Notes on art. 2d ser. J: Leech.—
  Marjorie Fleming.—Jeems the door-keeper.—Minch-
  moor.—The Enterkin.—Health.—The duke of Athole.
  —Struan.—Thackeray's death.—Thackeray's literary
  career.—More of our dogs.—Plea for a dog home.—
  "Bibliomania."—" In clear dream and solemn vis-
  ion."—A jacobite family.
Brydges, *Sir* S: Egerton. The ruminator ; containing a series of moral, critical and sen-
timental essays. Lond. 1813. 2 v. S.
                                              824.2 : 9
Buchanan, Robert W: A poet's sketch-book ;
selections from [his] prose writings. Lond.
1883. D.   **824.2 : 13**
  Contents. The poet or seer.—David Gray.— Literary sketches.—Nature sketches.
Buckle, H: T: Essays, with a biographical
sketch of the author. Portrait. N. Y. 1863.
D.   **824.2 : 10**
  Contents. Biog. sketch.—Mill on liberty.—The influence of women on the progress of knowledge.
Bulwer-Lytton, E: G: Earle Lytton, *1st baron
Lytton.* Caxtoniana ; a series of essays on
life, literature and manners. Leipz. 1864.
2 v. in 1. D.   **824.2 : 17**
  Contents. V. 1. Essay 1. On the increased attention to outward nature in the decline of life.—2. On
  the differences between the urban and rural temperament.—3. On monotony in occupation as a source
  of happiness.—4. On the normal clairvoyance of the
  imagination.—5. On intellectual conduct as distinct
  from moral: the "superior man".—6. On shyness.—
  7. On the management of money (addressed chiefly
  to the young).—8. On rhythm in prose, as conducive
  to precision and clearness.—9. On style and diction.
  10. Hints on mental culture.—11. On the moral effect of writers.—12. On the distinction between
  active thought and reverie.—13. On the spirit in
  which new theories should be received. — 14. On
  essay-writing in general, and these essays in particular.—15. The sanguine temperament.—16. The organ
  of weight.—17. The sympathetic temperament.—18.
  Faith and charity, or The union, in practical life, of
  sincerity and conciliation.—19. Upon the efficacy of
  praise, in supp. to the preceeding essay.—20. On self-
  control.—21. The modern misanthrope.   2. Essay 22.
  Motive power.—23. On certain principles of art in
  works of imagination.—24. Posthumous reputation.
  —25. On some authors in whose writings knowledge
  of the world is eminently displayed.—26. Readers
  and writers.— 27. On the spirit of conservatism.—
  L'envoi.

Bulwer-Lytton, E: G: Earle Lytton.—*Continued.*
— Miscellaneous prose works. Leipz. 1868. 4 v.
in 2. S.   **824.2 : 18**
  Contents. V. 1. The reign of terror; its causes
  and results.—Oliver Goldsmith.—C: Lamb and some
  of his companions.—Gray's works.—Sir T: Browne.—
  Pitt and Fox. 2. *Same, continued.* — Pym vs. Falkland.—The life of Schiller. 3. *Essays written in
  youth, or The student.* On the difference between
  authors and the impression of them conveyed by
  their works. — Monos and Daimonos. — On the departure of youth.—The world as it is.—Knebworth.—
  The choice of Phylias.—Lake Leman and its associations.—The true ordeal of love.—On the want of
  sympathy. — Arasmenes, the seeker. — On ill health
  and its consolations.—On satiety.—Chairolas.—On infidelity in love.—Fi-ho-ti, or The pleasures of reputation ; a chinese tale.—The knowledge of the world in
  men and books. 4. The tale of Kosem Kesamim
  the magician.—Many-sidedness and self-completion.
  —Ferdinand Fitzroy, or Too handsome for anything.
  —Juliet's tomb in Verona. —Conversations with an
  ambitious student in his last illness.—The influence
  of love upon literature and real life.
— Der gelehrte ; aus meinen papieren. Aus dem
englischen von L: Lax. Aachen. 1835. 2 v.
S.   **824.2 : 19**
  Contents, see Deutscher katalog, p. 35.
Bunce, Oliver Bell. Bachelor Bluff, his opinions,
sentiments and disputations. N. Y. 1881.
D.   **824.1 : 11**
  Contents. Introducing mr. Bluff.—Domestic bliss.—
  Theory of poetry.—Ideal of a house.—Feminine tact
  and intuitions.— Realism in art. — The country and
  kindred themes.—The privileges of women.—Modern
  fiction— Mr. Bluff's political notions.—As an arithmetician. — Meditations in an art gallery. — On melancholy.—Morals in literature and nudity in art.—
  As a critic on dress.—Sundry topics.—Experiences of
  holidays.
Burritt, Elihu. Ten minute talks on all sorts of
topics ; with autobiography of the author.
Bost. 1874. D.   **824.1 : 12**
  Contents. Autobiography.—Incidents and observations.—Glimpses by the wayside of letters. — Social
  and artistic science.—Industrial and financial questions. — Political questions. — National and international questions.
Burroughs, J: Fresh fields. 2d ed. Bost. 1885
[1884]. S.   **824.1 : 9**
  Contents. Nature in England.—English woods; a
  contrast. — In Carlyle's country. — A hunt for the
  nightingale. — English and american song-birds. —
  Impressions of some english birds.—In Wordsworth's
  country.—A glance at british wild flowers.—British
  fertility.—A sunday in Cheyne Row.—At sea.
— Locusts and wild honey. Bost. 1879. S.
                                             824.1 : 13
  Contents. The pastoral bees.—Sharp eyes.—Straw-
  berries.—Is it going to rain ?—Speckled trout.—Birds
  and birds.—A bed of boughs.—Birds' nesting.—The
  halcyon in Canada.
— Pepacton. Bost. 1881. S.   **824.1 : 14**
  Contents. Pepacton, a summer voyage.—Springs.—
  An idyl of the honey-bee.— Nature and the poets.—
  Notes by the way.—Foot-paths.—A bunch of herbs.—
  Winter pictures.
— Winter sunshine. N. Y. 1876. S.   **824.1 : 15**
  Contents. Winter sunshine. — Exhilarations of the
  road.—The snow-walkers.—The fox.—A march chron-
  icle.—The apple.—An october abroad.
Bushnell, Horace. Literary varieties. N. Y.
1864, 1881. 3 v. D.   **824.1 : 16**
  Contents. V. 1. *Work and play.* Work and play.—
  The true wealth or weal of nations.—The growth of
  law.—The founders great in their unconsciousness.—
  Historical estimate of Connecticut. — Agriculture at
  the east.—Life, or the lives.— City plans.—The doctrine of loyalty.—The age of homespun.—The use of
  roads.—Religious music. 2. *Moral uses of dark things.*
  Of night and sleep.—Of want and waste.—Of bad
  government.—Of oblivion, or dead history.—Of physical pain.—Of physical danger.—Of the conditions of
  solidarity.—Of non-intercourse between worlds.—Of
  winter.— Of things unsightly and disgustful. — Of

plague and pestilence.—Of insanity.—Of the animal infestations.—Of distinctions of color.—Of the mutabilities of life. — Of the sea. **3.** *Building eras in religion.* Building eras in religion.—The new education. — Common schools. — The christian trinity, a practical truth. — Spiritual economy of revivals of religion. — Pulpit talent. — Training for the pulpit manward.—Our gospel a gift to the imagination.—Popular government by divine right. — Our obligations to the dead.—Letter to Gregory XVI.—Christian comprehensiveness.

Carlyle, T: Critical and miscellaneous essays. N. Y. 1876. 4 v. D. **824.2 : 21**
Contents. V. **1.** Richter.—State of german literature. — Life and writings of Werner. — Goethe's Helena.—Goethe.—Burns.—Life of Heyne.—German playwrights.—App. **1.** Pref. and introd. to "German romance"; Musäus; Fouqué; Tieck; Hoffmann; Richter; Goethe. — **2.** Fractions: Tragedy of the night-moth; Cui bono; Four fables; The sower's song; Adieu; The beetle; To-day; Fortuna. **2.** Voltaire. — Novalis.—Signs of the times. — Richter again.—On history.—Luther's psalm.—Schiller.—The Nibelungen-lied.—German literature of the 14th and 15th centuries.—Taylor's Historic survey of german poetry.—App. Richter's review of mme. de Staël's Allemagne. **3.** Characteristics.—Goethe's portrait. —Biography.—Boswell's Life of Johnson.—Death of Goethe. — Goethe's works. — Corn-law rhymes. — On history again.—Diderot.— Count Cagliostro.— Death of Edward Irving.—Novelle.— Schiller, Goethe and mme. de Staël.—The tale. **4.** The diamond necklace. — Mirabeau. — Parliamentary history of the french revolution.—Sir Walter Scott.—Varnhagen v. Ense's memoirs.— Petition on the copyright bill.— On the sinking of the Vengeur.— Baillie the covenanter. — An election to the long parliament.—250 years ago.— The opera.—Project of a national exhibition of scottish portraits.—The Prinzenraub.—Index.

— On heroes and hero-worship, and the heroic in history ; six lectures reported, with emendations and add. N. Y. 1849. D. **824.2 : 22**
Contents. The hero as divinity: Odin; Paganism; Scandinavian mythology. — The hero as prophet: Mahomet; Islam.—The hero as poet: Dante; Shakspeare.—The hero as priest: Luther; Reformation; Knox; Puritanism. — The hero as man of letters: Johnson; Rousseau; Burns. — The hero as king: Cromwell; Napoleon; Modern revolutionism.—Summary and Index.

— *Same.* Lectures on heroes, 1840. *With his Sartor resartus.* *in* **824.2 : 20**

— Latter-day pamphlets. Bost. 1850. D. **824.2 : 23**
Contents. The present time. — Model prisons. — Downing street.—The new Downing street.—Stump orator.—Parliaments.—Hudson's statue.—Jesuitism.

— Past and present. Lond. *n. d.* S. **824.2 : 24**
Contents. Proem.—The ancient monk.—The modern worker.—Horoscope.—Index.

— Sartor resartus, 1831. Lond. 1858. D. **824.2 : 20**

— Ausgewählte schriften. Deutsch von A. Kretzschmar. Leipz. 1855. 6 v. in 3. O. **824.2 : 25**
Contents, see Deutscher katalog, p. 35.

Cleveland, Rose Elizabeth. George Eliot's poetry, and other studies. N. Y. 1885. D. **824.1 : 7**
Includes, Reciprocity.—Altruistic faith.—History.— Studies in the middle ages: Old Rome and new France; Charlemagne; The monastery; Chivalry; Joan of Arc.

Clinton, De Witt. An introductory discourse, delivered before the Literary and philosophical society of New York on 4th may 1814. N. Y. 1815. O. **825.1+1**

Cobbe, Frances Power. Darwinism in morals, and other essays, reprinted from the Theological and Fortnightly reviews, Fraser's and Macmillan's magazines and the Manchester friend. Bost. 1883. D. **824.2 :107**
Contents. Darwinism in morals.—Hereditary piety. — The religion of childhood.— An english broad

Cobbe, Frances Power.—*Continued.*
churchman.— A french theist.— The devil.— A prehistoric religion.— The religions of the world.— The religions of the east.—The religion and literature of India.—Unconscious cerebration.—Dreams, as illustrations of involuntary cerebration.—Auricular confession in the church of England.—The evolution of morals and religion.

— Hours of work and play. Phila. 1867. D. **824.2 : 11**
Contents. Public morality and its teachers. — The indigent class.—The Brahmo samaj.—The fallacies of memory.—The fenian idea.— A day at Adelsberg.— A lady's adventure in the great pyramid. — The diablerets.— The state vault of Christ church.— The shadow of death.—Alured.—The spectral rout.—The humour of various nations.—The fenians of Ballybogmucky.

— Re-echoes. Leipz. 1877. S. **824.2 : 12**

Coleridge, S: Taylor. Miscellanies, æsthetic and literary ; added, The theory of life ; collected and arr. by T. Ashe. Lond. 1885. D. **824.2 : 123**
Contents. Essays on the fine arts. — On the Prometheus of Aeschylus.—Fragments and notes, mainly from the lectures of 1818: The middle ages; Cervantes; Wit and humour; Dante; Mythology, imagination and superstition; Style. — Miscellaneous pieces.—Miscellaneous notes on books and authors.— The theory of life.

Congdon, C: Tabor. Tribune essays; leading articles contributed to the New York tribune from 1857 to 1863, with an introd. by Horace Greeley. N. Y. 1869. D. **824.1 : 18**

Cook, Joseph. Occident, with preludes on current events. (Boston Monday lectures.) Bost. 1884. D. **824.1 :112**
Contents. Advanced thought in England. — Advanced thought in Germany.—Delitzsch on the new criticism of the old testament.— Prof Zöllner's views on spiritualism.—Opponents of Prof. Zöllner's views on spiritualism. — Advanced thought in Italy and Greece.—New departures in and from orthodoxy.— Does death end probation ?—The future of civil service reform.—The vanguards of christian missions.— Amer. and foreign temperance creeds.— Probation at death. — App.: The decline of rationalism in the german universities; Theodore Christlieb and german church life; The new house and its battlement, or The relations of the temperance reform to civil liberty; Reply to prof. Smyth of Andover; A night on the Acropolis.

Cooper, Susan Fenimore. Rural hours by a lady. [*Anon.*] 3d ed. N. Y. 1851. D. **824.1 :17**

Cowley, Abraham. Essays ; with life by the editor, notes and ill. by dr. Hurd and others. [Bayard ser.] Lond. 1868. T. **824.2 : 14**
Contents. Essay introductory and biographical.— Of liberty.—Of solitude.—Of obscurity.—Of agriculture.—The garden.—Of greatness.—Of avarice.—The dangers of an honest man in much company. — The shortness of life and uncertainty of riches.—The danger of procrastination.—Of myself.—A discourse, by way of vision, concerning the government of Oliver Cromwell.—The author's preface to Cutter of Coleman street.—A proposition for the advancement of experimental philosophy.

Cozzens, F: Swartout. The sayings of dr. Bushwhacker and other learned men. N. Y. 1867. D. **824.1 : 19**
Contents. A talk about tea. — Journey around a tapioca pudding.—The radiant dinner castor.—Chocolate and cocoa.—Notables and potables.—A peep into a salad bowl.—Madame Follet.—Old phrases.—Art.— Accidental resemblances. — Sitka.— Phrases and filberts.— Does queen Victoria speak english ?— The noses of eminent men. — Up the Rhine.—The first oyster-eater. — A literary curiosity. — The race between the hare and the hedgehog.—What is the cause of thunder ?— A french breakfast.—Dainty hints for epicurean smokers.—Was champagne known to the ancients ? — German wines and a wine cellar. — A christmas piece.—Oxyporian wine.

Emerson, Ralph Waldo. Miscellanies; embracing Nature, Addresses and lectures. Bost. 1857. D.   **824.1 : 22**
Contents. Nature. — The american scholar. — An address to the senior class in Divinity college, Cambridge.— Literary ethics.— The method of nature.— Man the reformer. — Introductory lecture on the times.— The conservative.— The transcendentalist.— The young american.
— *Same.* New rev. ed. Bost. 1884. D. *In his* Works.   **820.1 : 8 v1**
— Essays ; 1st and 2d ser. Bost. 1854, 1858. 2 v. D.   **824.1 : 24**
Contents. V. 1. History.—Self-reliance.—Compensation.— Spiritual laws.— Love.— Friendship.— Prudence.—Heroism.—The over-soul.—Circles.—Intellect. — Art. 2. The poet. — Experience. — Character. — Manners. — Gifts. — Nature. — Politics. — Nominalist and realist.—New England reformers.
— *Same.* New rev. ed. Bost. 1879. 2 v. T.   **824.1 : 24**
— *Same.* Bost. 1884. D. *In his* Works.   **820.1 : 8 v2,3**
— Fortune of the republic ; lecture del. at the Old south church, march 30, 1878. Bost. 1879. S.   **824.1 : 25**
— Letters and social aims. Bost. 1876. D.   **824.1 : 26**
Contents. Poetry and imagination.—Social aims.— Eloquence.—Resources.—The comic.—Quotation and originality.—Progress of culture.— Persian poetry.— Inspiration.—Greatness.—Immortality.
— *Same.* New rev. ed. Bost. 1884. D. *In his* Works.   **820.1 : 8 v8**
— Society and solitude ; twelve chapters. Bost. 1879. T.   **824.1 : 27**
Contents. Society and solitude.—Civilization.—Art. —Eloquence.— Domestic life.— Farming.—Work and days.—Books.—Clubs.—Courage.—Success.— Old age.
— *Same.* New rev. ed. Bost. 1884. D. *In his* Works.   **820.1 : 8 v7**
Everett, E: The Mount Vernon papers. N. Y. 1860. D.   **824.1 : 28**
Contents. [Introductory].—Christmas.— The house of Franklin.—A safe answer.—The comet.—An incursion into the Empire State.— The parable against persecution. — Washington's diary. — Robertson's miniatures of gen. and mrs. Washington.—Washington's diary, pt. 2.— Louis Napoleon.— Washington's diary.—Abbotsford visited and re-visited.—The 4th of march, 1789.—Abbotsford visited and re-visited, pt. 2. —The court of France, 1818.— Lord Erskine's testimony to Washington.—The financial distress of 1857. —Travelling in former times.—Travel in Europe.— Havre and Rouen.—Will there be a war in Europe ?— Another vol. of Washington's diary.—Washington's southern tour.— Adams' express and the express system of the U. S.—At Paris in 1818.—The illustrious dead of 1859: Prescott; Bond; Hallam; v. Humboldt. — Italian nationality.—The light-house.—Prince Metternich.—Seven critical occasions and incidents in the life of Washington.—Fontainebleau, Burgundy, Autun.—Talleyrand.—Lyons.— From Lyons to Geneva. —Excursion from Geneva to Chamouni, Mont Blanc. —The Montauvert, the Sea of Ice, and the Green Garden.— Geneva, Ferney, Lausanne.— From Lausanne to Freyburg. — Berne.— 19th of april 1775.— From Berne to Sachseln.— Stanz, Lucerne, Tell.— Goldau, Aloys Reding, Grutli, the Tellensprung.— Altorf, the valley of the Reuss, the Valais.—Daniel Boon.—The New York ledger.

— Orations and speeches on various occasions. Bost. 1853–79. 4 v. O.   **825.1+2**
Contents. V. 1. (3d ed.) The circumstances favorable to the progress of literature in America.—The first settlement of New England.—The first battles of the revolutionary war.—The principle of the amer. constitutions.—Adams and Jefferson.—The history of liberty.—Monument to Harvard.— Speech at Nashville.—Speech at Lexington, Ky.—Speech at the Yellow Springs in Ohio.—The settlement of Mass.—Importance of scientific knowledge to practical men and the encouragement to its pursuit.—The workingmen's party.—Advantage of scientific knowledge to workingmen. — Colonization and civilization of

Africa. — Education in the western states. — The Bunker Hill monument.—Temperance.—The seven years' war, the school of the revolution.—The education of mankind.—Agriculture. — Eulogy on Lafayette.—The battle of Lexington.—The youth of Washington.—Education favorable to liberty, morals and knowledge.—The battle of Bloody Brook. 2. (2d ed.) The boyhood and youth of Franklin.— Fourth of july at Lowell. — American manufactures. — Anecdotes of early local history.—The western railroad.— Anniversary of the settlement of Springfield.—The importance of the militia. — The 17th of june at Charlestown. — Harvard centennial anniversary. — The settlement of Dedham.—The cattle show at Danvers.—The Irish charitable society.—Improvements in prison discipline.—Superior and popular education.—The Boston schools.—The importance of the mechanic arts.—Reception of the Sauks and Foxes. —Dr. Bowditch.—4th of july, 1838. — Education the nurture of the mind.—Festival at Exeter.—Accumulation, property, capital, credit.—Importance of education in a republic.—The settlement of Barnstable. —Normal schools.—Opening of the railroad to Springfield.—The Scots' charitable society.—J: Lowell, jr., founder of the Lowell institute. — Dr. Robinson's medal.— British association at Manchester.—University of Cambridge.—The Royal agricultural society at Bristol.—Agricultural society at Waltham.—York minster.—Lord mayor's day.—The Geological society of London.—The Royal academy of art.—Royal literary fund.—The Agricultural society at Derby.—Reception at Hereford.—Saffron Walden agricultural society.— Scientific association at Cambridge.— The pilgrim fathers. — University education.— The new medical college.—The famine in Ireland.—Aid to the colleges.—Eulogy on J: Quincy Adams.—The Cambridge high school.—Second speech on aid to colleges.—American scientific association.—The departure of the pilgrims.—Cattle show at Dedham.—The 19th of april at Concord.—The Bible. 3. Battle of Bunker Hill.—Opening of the Brattle house.—Cambridge high school.—The Ottoman empire.—The birthday of Washington.—Conditions of a good school.— Beneficial influence of railroads.—The husbandman, mechanic and manufacturer.—Treatment of animals. —Effects of immigration.—Festival of the alumni of Harvard.—Education and civilization.—Dinner to T: Baring.—Progress of agriculture.—The death of Daniel Webster. — The colonization of Africa.— Abdul Rahaman. — Discovery of America. — Stability and progress.—The pilgrim fathers.—New Hampshire.— Vice-president King. — P: Chardon Brooks.— Dorchester in 1630, 1776 and 1855.—Boston school festival. — Launch of the Defender. — Abbott Lawrence.— Obituary notice of Abbott Lawrence.—Vegetable and mineral gold.—Daniel Webster as a man. — Reception at Philadelphia.—Mr. Dowse's library.—The uses of astronomy.—G: Peabody.— Obituary notice of mr. Dowse.—Memorial of the Franklin family.—Academical education.—The statue of Warren.—The importance of agriculture. — Charitable institutions and charity.— Dedication of the public library.— Dedication of Crawford's Washington.— Presentation of the cane of Washington.—Recollections of Turkey.—Washington abroad and at home.—The 4th of july. 4. The character of Washington. — Cattle show at Springfield.—The New York state inebriate asylum.—Agricultural society at Danvers.—Minot's Ledge light-house.—Eulogy on T: Dowse.— Franklin the Boston boy.—W: Hickling Prescott.—H: Hallam. —Latin school prize declamation.—Powers's statue of Webster.— Alex. v. Humboldt.—Rufus Choate.— Daniel Webster union meeting in Faneuil hall.— Washington Irving.— Birthday of Washington Irving.—Eliot school-house.—H: D. Gilpin. — American expedition to the Arctic sea.—Sanitary convention. —Vindication of american institutions.—Inauguration of president Felton.— Everett school-house.— Flag-raising in Chester square.— The call to arms.— Daniel Drury Barnard.— The questions of the day. —"E pluribus unum."—Nathan Appleton.—50th anniversary of graduation—12th Mass. regiment.—Agriculture as affected by the war.— Dinner to prince Napoleon.—The causes and conduct of the civil war. — Cornelius Conway Felton. — The army of the Potomac.—Opportunities of Harvard students.—Female education.—The duty of crushing the rebellion. —The demand for reinforcements.—The Irish regiments.—Nathan Hale.—Inauguration of the Union club.—U. S. naval academy.—Harvard college in the war.—The education of the poor.—National cemetery at Gettysburg.—Aid to east Tennessee.—The navy in the war.—Russia and the U. S.—Josiah Quincy.—The

Everett, E:—*Continued.*
administration of president Quincy. — The duty of supporting the government.—The sailors' home.—Reception of capt. Winslow.—President Lincoln.—Mass. electoral college of 1864.—The relief of Savannah.
Note. For special index, alphabetical arrangement, *see* Catalogue of the Brooklyn library, p. 451.

— The great issue now before the country ; an oration del. at the New York academy of music, july 4, 1861. N. Y. 1861. D.
    825.1 : 4

Fay, Theodore Sedgwick. Dreams and reveries of a quiet man ; consisting of The little genius and other essays, by one of the eds. of the New York mirror. N. Y. 1832. 2 v. D.
    824.1 : 29

Fields, James T: Underbrush. Bost. 1877. T.
    824.1 : 30
Contents. My friend's library.—A peculiar case.—Familiar letter to house-breakers.—Our village dog-matist.—A watch that "wanted cleaning."—Bother-some people.—Pleasant ghosts.—The Pettibone lineage.—Getting home again.—How to rough it. — An old-time scholar.—Diamonds and pearls.—The author of "Paul and Virginia."—If I were a boy again.

Fiske, J: Darwinism, and other essays. Lond. 1879. D.
    824.1 : 31
Contents. Darwinism verified.—Mr. Mivart on darwinism.—Dr. Bateman on darwinism.— Dr. Büchner on darwinism.—A crumb for the modern symposium.—Chauncey Wright.—What is inspiration?—Dr. Hammond and the table-tippers.—Mr. Buckle's fallacies. — Postscript on mr. Buckle. — The races of the Danube.—A librarian's work.

— Excursions of an evolutionist. Bost. 1884. D.
    824.1 : 107
Contents. Europe before the arrival of man.—The arrival of man in Europe.—Our aryan forefathers.—What we learn from old aryan words.—Was there a primeval mother tongue ? — Sociology and hero-worship.—Heroes of industry.—The causes of perse-cution.— The origins of protestantism. — Evolution and religion.—The meaning of infancy.—A universe of mind-stuff.—In memoriam C: Darwin.

— The unseen world, and other essays. Bost. 1876. D.
    824.1 : 32
Contents. The unseen world.—"The tomorrow of death."—The Jesus of history.—The Christ of dogma.—A .word about miracles.—Draper on science and religion.—Nathan the wise.—Historical difficulties.—The famine of 1770 in Bengal.—Spain and the Nether-lands.—Longfellow's Dante. — Paine's "St Peter."—A philosophy of art.—Athenian and american life.—Index.

Flagg, Wilson. Studies in the field and forest. Bost. 1857. O.
    824.1 : 33
— Halcyon days. Bost. 1881. D.
    824.1 : 102

Foster, J: Biographical, literary and philoso-phical essays ; contributed to the Eclectic review. N. Y. 1844. D.
    824.2 : 39
Contents. Chalmers' astronomical discourses.—J: Horne Tooke.—Coleridge's Friend.—Fox's James II. — Edgeworth's Professional education. — British statesmen.— Lord Kames.— Defence of the stage.— H: Franklin.— James Beattie.— Fashionable life.— Hugh Blair.—D: Hume.—Philosophy of nature.—Ire-land.—Epic poetry.—Superstitions of the highland-ers. — Ecclesiastical biography. — Spain. — Modern egyptians.

— Essays, in a series of letters. 5th amer. ed. Bost. 1833. S.
    824.2 : 41
Contents. On a man's writing memoirs of himself. On decision of character.—On the application of the epithet romantic.—On some of the causes by which evangelical religion has been rendered unacceptable to persons of cultured taste.

Froude, James Anthony. Historical and other sketches ; ed. with an introd. by D: H. Wheeler. N. Y. [1883]. D.
    824.2 : 113
Contents. A siding at a railway station.—The Nor-way fjords.—A Cagliostro of the 2d century.—Social condition of England in the 16th century.—Corona-

Froude, James Anthony.—*Continued.*
tion of Anne Boleyn.—J: Bunyan.—Leaves from a south african journal.—A day's fishing at Cheneys.—T: Carlyle and his wife.—Political economy of the 18th century.—Reynard the fox.

— Short studies on great subjects. N. Y. *n. d.* 4 v. D.
    824.2 : 42
Contents. V. 1. The science of history. — Times of Erasmus and Luther.—The influence of the reforma-tion on the scottish character. — The philosophy of catholicism. — A plea for the free discussion of theo-logical difficulties.—Criticism and the gospel history. — The book of Job.—Spinoza.—The dissolution of the monasteries.—England's forgotten worthies.—Homer. — The lives of the saints. — Representative men. — Reynard the fox. — The cat's pilgrimage. — Fables. — Parable of the bread-fruit tree. — Compensation. — **2.** Calvinism.—A bishop of the 12th century.—Father Newman on "The grammar of assent." — Condition and prospects of protestantism. — England and her colonies. — A fortnight in Kerry, pt. 1. — Reciprocal duties of state and subject. — The merchant and his wife.—On progress.—The colonies once more.— Edu-cation.—A fortnight in Kerry, pt. 2.—England's war. — The eastern question. — Scientific method applied to history. **3.** Annals of an english abbey.—Revival of romanism. — Sea studies. — Society in Italy in the last days of the roman republic. — Lucian. — Divus Cæsar.—On the uses of a landed gentry.—Party poli-tics.—Leaves from a south african journal. **4.** Life and times of Thomas Becket. — The Oxford counter-reformation. — Origen and Celsus. — A Cagliostro of the 2d century.—Cheneys and the house of Russell.—A siding at a railway station.

Gibbons, Phebe Earle. "Pennsylvania dutch," and other essays. 3d ed. rev. and enl. Phila. 1882. D.
    824.1 : 101
Contents. Pennsylvania dutch.—An Amish meeting.—Swiss exiles.—The dunker love-feast.— Ephrata.—Bethlehem and the moravians. — Schwenkfelders.—A friend.—Cousin Jemima.—The miners of Scranton. — Irish farmers.—English.—App.

Giles, H: Illustrations of genius in some of its relations to culture and society. Bost. 1854. D.
    824.1 : 35
Contents. Cervantes.— Don Quixote. — The scarlet letter.—Fiction.— Public opinion. — The philantropic sentiment.—Music. — The cost of a cultivated man.— Conversation.—Wordsworth.—Robert Burns.—T: De Quincey.

Gleig, G: Robert. Essays, biographical, histor-ical and miscellaneous ; contributed chiefly to the Edinburgh and Quarterly reviews, Lond. 1858. 2 v. O.
    824.2 : 43
Contents. V. 1. Dr. Chalmers.—Our defensive ar-mament.—Natural theology.—Military bridges.—The war of the Punjaub. **2.** The puritans. — General Miller. — India and its army. — The Mädchenstein.—Military education.

Goodale, Elaine. Journal of a farmer's daughter. N. Y. 1881. S.
    824.1 : 36

Greene, G: Washington. Biographical studies. N. Y. 1860. D.
    824.1 : 37
Contents. Cooper.— Personal recollections of Coo-per. — Cole.— Crawford.— Irving's works. — Irving's Washington.

— Historical studies. N. Y. 1850. D. **824.1 : 38**
Contents. Petrarch.—Machiavelli.—Reformation in Italy. — Italian literature in the first half of the 19th century.—Manzoni.—The hopes of Italy. — Historical romance in Italy.—Libraries.—Verrazzano.—Charles Edward.—Supplement to The hopes of Italy.—Contri-butions for the popes.

Hall, Granville Stanley. Aspects of german cul-ture. Bost. 1881. D.
    824.1 : 39
Contents. Religious opinion.—The vivisection ques-tion. — The passion play. — Some recent pessimistic theories.—The new cultus war.—Ferdinand Lassalle.—The graphic method.—The Leipzig "messe."—A pom-eranian watering place.—Emperor Wilhelm's return. —Hermann Lotze.—Is æsthetics a science ?— *The* ger-man science.—Are the german universities declining?—Fowler's Locke and german psychology.—Spiritual-ism in Germany. — Recent studies on hypnotism.—Popular science in Germany. — A note on Hegel, his followers and critics. — Hartmann's new system of

pessimistic ethics — The latest german philosophical literature.—Democritus and Heraclitus.—The muscular perception of space. — Laura Bridgeman. — The perception of color.—A note on the present condition of philosophy.—First impressions on returning from Germany.

Halpine, C: Graham. Baked meats of the funeral ; a collection of essays, poems, speeches, histories and banquets by private Miles O'Reilly. N. Y. 1866. D.   **824.1 : 40**

Hamerton, Philip Gilbert. Human intercourse. Bost. 1884. D.   **824.2 : 120**

— The intellectual life ; with a portr. of Leonardo da Vinci etched by Leopold Flameng. Bost. 1877. D.   **824.2 : 44**

Contents. — The physical basis. — The moral basis. — Of education.—The power of time.—The influences of money.—Custom and tradition. — Women and marriage.—Aristocracy and democracy.— Society and solitude.—Intellectual hygienics. — Trades and professions.—Surroundings.

Hayward, Abraham. Sketches of eminent statesmen and writers, with other essays ; reprinted from the Quarterly review, with add. and corr. Lond. 1880. 2 v. O. **824.2 : 45**

Contents. V. 1. Thiers. — Bismarck. — Cavour. — Metternich.—Charles comte de Montalembert.—Lord Melbourne.—The marquess Wellesley. 2. Mme. de Sévigné. — Saint-Simon. — Mme. Du Deffand and her correspondents.— Holland House. — Strawberry Hill. —Byron and Tennyson.—The republic of Venice ; its rise, decline and fall.

— Selected essays. N. Y. 1879. 2 v. D. **824.2:46**

Contents. V. 1. The rev. Sidney Smith; his life, character and writings.— S: Rogers. — F: v. Gentz.— Maria Edgeworth; her life and writings. — The countess Hahn-Hahn.—De Stendhal, H: Beyle.—Alexander Dumas. 2. The british parliament, its history and eloquence.—The pearls and mock pearls of history.— Vicissitudes of families, english, scotch, irish and continental nobility.—England and France ; their national qualities, manners, morals and society. — Lady Palmerston. — Lord Landsdowne. — Lord Dalling and Bulwer.—Whist and whist-players.

Hazlitt, W: The round table. [Bayard ser]. Lond. 1869. T.   **824.2 : 47**

Contents. The love of life. — Classical education. — The Tatler.—Modern comedy. — Posthumous fame. — Hogarth's marriage à-la-mode. — Milton's versification. — Manner. — The tendency of sects. — Causes of methodism. — The Midsummer night's dream. — The Beggar's opera.—Patriotism.—Beauty. — Imitation.— Gusto.—Pedantry. — Character of Rousseau. — Different sorts of fame. — Character of John Bull. — Goodnature.—Character of Milton's Eve.—Observations on mr. Wordsworth's poem: The excursion. — A day by the fire. — Religious hypocrisy. — The literary character.—Common-place critics.—Actors and acting.

— The spirit of the age, or Contemporary portraits. 1st amer. ed. Phila. 1848. D.   **824.2 : 48**

Contents. Bentham.—Godwin.— Coleridge. — E: Irving. — Horne Tooke. — Scott. — Byron. — Southey.— Wordsworth. — Mackintosh. — Malthus. — Gifford.— Jeffrey.—Brougham. — Sir F. Burdett.—Lord Eldon.— Mr. Wilberforce.— Cobbett. — Campbell. — Crabbe.— Moore.—Hunt.—Elia.—Geoffrey Crayon.

— Table talk; opinions on books, men and things. [1st and] 2d series. Phila. 1848. 2 v. D.   **824.2 : 49**

Contents. V. 1, pt. 1. On the pleasure of painting. On the past and future. — On people with one idea. — On the ignorance of the learned. — On will-making.— On a landscape of Nicolas Poussin.—On going a journey. — Why distant objects please. — On corporate bodies. — On the knowledge of character. — On the fear of death. — On application to study. — On the old age of artists. — On egotism.—On the regal character. Pt. 2: On the look of a gentleman. — On reading old books.—On personal character.—On vulgarity and affectation.—On antiquity.—On the conduct of life, or Advise to a school-boy.—The Indian jugglers.—On the prose-style of poets. — On the conversation of authors.—My first acquaintance with poets.—Of persons one would wish to have seen. — Shyness of scholars.

— On old english writers and speakers. 2, pt. 1. On the feeling of immortality in youth.—On the want of money.—On sitting for one's picture.—Whether genius is conscious of its powers. — On londoners and country people.—On living to one's self. — On genius and common sense.—Hot and cold.—On thought and action.—Portrait by Vandyke.—On dreams.—On envy; a dialogue. — On the difference between writing and speaking.—On inconsistencies in sir Joshua Reynold's discourses. — On qualifications necessary to success in life. — Madame Pasta and mademoiselle Mars. — Sir Walter Scott, Racine, and Shakespeare. Pt. 2. On the spirit of monarchy. — The Vatican. — On Milton's sonnets.— On coffee-house politicians. — On the aristocracy of letters. — On criticism. — On great and little things. — On familiar style. — On effeminacy of character.—Whether actors ought to sit in the boxes. — On the disadvantages of intellectual superiority. — On patronage and puffing. — On the picturesque and ideal. — The main chance. — On reason and imagination.—On respectable people. — On novelty and familiarity.

Head, *Sir* Francis Bond. Descriptive essays, contributed to the Quarterly review. Lond. 1857. 2 v. O.   **824.2 : 50**

Contents. V. 1. Cornish miners in America.—English charity.—Locomotion by steam. — British policy. — The printer's devil.—The red man. 2. The air we live in. — Memorandum on the battle of Waterloo. — The London and northwestern railway.—The electric telegraph.—The Britannia bridge. — The London post office.

Helps, *Sir* Arthur. Essays, written in the intervals of business ; added, an essay on organization in daily life. Bost. 1871. D.   **824.2 : 51**

Contents. On practical wisdom. — Aids to contentment.—On self-discipline.—On our judgments of other men. — On the exercise of benevolence. — Domestic rule.—Advice.—Secrecy.—On the education of a man of business.—On the transaction of business.—On the choice and management of agents.—On the treatment of suitors. — Interviews. — Of councils, commissions and, in general, of bodies of men called together to counsel or to direct. — Party-spirit.—An essay on organization of daily life.

Higginson, T: Wentworth. Out-door papers. Bost. 1863. D.   **824.1 : 41**

Contents. Saints and their bodies. — Physical courage.— A letter to a dyspeptic. —The murder of the innocents.—Barbarism and civilization.—Gymnastics. — A new counterblast. — The health of our girls. — April days.—My out-door study.—Water-lilies. — The life of birds.—The procession of the flowers. — Snow.

Holland, Josiah Gilbert, (*Timothy Titcomb*). Every-day topics ; a book of briefs. N. Y. 1876. D.   **824.1 : 42**

Contents. Culture.—Literature and literary men.— Criticism.—The popular lecture. — Personal dangers. — Personal development.—Preachers and preaching. —Christianity and science. — Revivals and reforms.— Christian practice.—The church of the future. — The common moralities.—Woman and home.— Amusements. — The temperance question. — Social intercourse.—Town and country.—The rich and the poor.—Politics and political men.—American life and manners.

— *Same.* 2d ser. N. Y. 1882. S.   **824.1 : 42**

— Lessons in life ; a series of familiar essays, by Timothy Titcomb. 15th ed. N. Y. 1874. D.   **824.1 : 43**

Contents. Moods and frames of mind.—Bodily imperfections and impediments. — Animal content. — Reproduction in kind. — Truth and truthfulness. — Mistakes of penance.—The rights of woman.—American public education.—Perverseness.—Undeveloped resources. — Greatness in littleness. — Rural life. — Repose.—The ways of charity.—Men of one idea.— Shying people.—Faith in humanity.—Sore spots and sensitive spots.—The influence of praise.—Unnecessary burdens.—Proper people and perfect people.— The poetic test. — The food of life. — Half-finished work.

— Plain talks on familiar subjects ; a series of popular lectures. N. Y. 1866. D.   **824.1 : 45**

Contents. Self-help.— Fashion.— Work and play.—

Holland, Josiah Gilbert.—*Continued.*
Working and shirking.—High life and low life.—The national heart.— Cost and compensation.— Art and life.—The popular lecture.
— *Same.* N. Y. 1873. S.   **824.1 : 45**
— Titcomb's letters to young people, single and married. N. Y. 1874. S.   **824.1 : 44**

Holmes, Oliver Wendell. The autocrat of the breakfast-table ; every man his own Boswell. [*Anon.*] Bost. 1871. D.   **824.1 : 46**
— The poet at the breakfast-table ; his talks with his fellow-boarders and the reader. [*Anon.*] Bost. 1872. D.   **824.1 : 47**
— The professor at the breakfast-table. [*Anon.*] Bost. 1879. D.   **824.1 : 48**
— Pages from an old volume of life ; a collection of essays, 1857—1881. Bost. 1883. O.
        824.1 : 104
Contents. Bread and the newspaper.—My hunt after "the captain".—The inevitable trial.—The physiology of walking.—The seasons.—The human body and its management.—Cinders from the ashes.—Mechanism in thought and morals.—The physiology of versification.—Crime and automatism.—Jonathan Edwards.—The pulpit and the pew.
— Soundings from the Atlantic. Bost. 1864. D.
        824.1 : 49
Contents. Bread and the newspaper.— My hunt after "the captain".— The stereoscope and the stereograph.—Sun-painting and sun-sculpture; with a stereoscopic trip across the Atlantic.— Doings of the sunbeam.— The human wheel, its spokes and fellows.—A visit to the autocrat's land-lady.—A visit to the asylum for aged and decayed punsters.—The great instrument.—The inevitable trial.

Howells, W: Dean. Three villages. Bost. 1884. S.   **824.1 : 111**
Contents. Lexington: [a typical New England village].—Shirley: [the Shaker community].—Gnadenhütten; [Moravian village].

Howitt, Mary, *born* Botham, *ed.* Pictorial calendar of the seasons; exhibiting the pleasures, pursuits and characteristics of country life for every month in the year, and embodying the whole of Aikin's Calendar of nature. Ill. Lond. 1854. D.
        824.2 : 52

Howitt, W: The rural life of England. From the 3d Lond. ed. corr. and rev. Phila. 1854. 2 v. D.   **824.2 : 53**

Hudson, Mary, *born* Clemmer, *formerly mrs.* Ames. Outlines of men, women and things. N. Y. 1873. D.   **824.1 : 1**
Contents. Arlington in may. — Northern Vermont in august.—Newport in september.—Indian summer in Virginia.—Charles Sumner's home.—Grand duke Alexis in New York.—A rainy morning in the country.—Margaret Fuller Ossoli.—A french journalist.—Fanny Fern.— Horace Greeley and Edwin Forrest.— Lola Montez. — Things gone by.—The fallen man.—Physical basis of statesmanship.—Instinctive philosophers and statesmen.— Pin-money.— Breadmaking.— Our kitchens.—Caste in sex.—Woman suffrage.—Una and her paupers.—Let us live.

Hueffer, Francis. Italian and other studies. Lond. 1883. O.   **824.2 : 121**
Contents. The poets of young Italy. — A literary friendship of the 14th century [Boccaccio and Petrarch].—The renaissance in Italy.—Exhibitions of Rossetti's pictures.—Troubadours, ancient and modern.—Music and musicians.—The literary aspect of Schopenhauer's work. — Musical criticism. — Mr. Pepys, the musician.

Hunt, James H: Leigh. A day by the fire, and other papers hitherto uncollected. Bost. 1870. D.   **824.2 : 54**
Contents. A day by the fire.— On common place people.—A popular view of the heathen mythology. — On the genii of the greeks and romans.— On the genii of antiquity and the poets.—Fairies.—Genii and fairies of the east, the Arabian nights, etc.—The satyr

Hunt, James H: Leigh.—*Continued.*
of mythology and the poets.—Tritons and men of the sea.—On giants, ogres and cyclops.—Gog and Magog, and the wall of Dhoulkarnein.— Aeronautics, real and fabulous.—On the talking of nonsense.—A rainy day.—The true enjoyment of splendor.—Retrospective review.—The murdered pump.—Christmas eve and christmas day.—New year's gifts.— Sale of the late mr. West's pictures. — Translation from Milton into welsh.—The bull-fight.—Love and will.
— Men, women and books ; a selection of sketches, essays and critical memoirs from his uncollected prose writings. N. Y. 1847. 2 v. D.   **824.2 : 55**
Contents. V. 1. Fiction and matter of fact.—The inside of an omnibus.—The day of disasters of Carfington Blundell, esq. — A visit to the zoological gardens. — A man introduced to his ancestors.— A novel party.—Beds and bedrooms.—The world of books.—Jack Abbott's breakfast.—On seeing a pigeon make love.—The month of may.—The Giuli tre.—A few remarks on the rare vice called lying.—Criticism on female beauty.—Of statesmen who have written verses.—Female sovereigns. 2. Social morality.—Pope in some lights, in which he is not usually regarded.—Garth, physicians and love letters.—Cowley and Thomson.—Bookstalls and "Galateo".—Bookbinding and "Heliodorus".—Ver-Vert, or The parrot of the nuns. — Specimens of british poetesses. — Duchess of St. Albans and marriages from the stage. —Lady Mary Wortley Montague.—Life and african visit of Pepys.—Life and letters of mme. de Sévigné.
— The seer, or Common-places refreshed. Bost. 1856. 2 v. D.   **824.2 : 56**

Jameson, Anna, *born* Murphy. Memoirs and essays, illustrative of art, literature and social morals. N. Y. 1846. D.   **824.2 : 57**
Contents. The house of Titian. — Adelaide Kemble and the lyrical drama. — The xanthian marbles. — Washington Allston. — "Woman's mission" and woman's position.—On the relative social position of mothers and governesses.
— Sketches of art, literature and character. Bost. 1859. T.   **824.2 : 58**
Contents. Pt. 1, in three dialogues: 1. A scene in a steamboat.— A singular character. — Gallery at Ghent.—The prince of Orange's pictures.—A female gambler.—Cologne; the Medusa.— Prof. Wallraf.—Schlegel and mme. de Staël.—Story of archbp. Gerard. —Heidelberg; Elizabeth Stuart. 2. Frankfort.—The theatre; Mme. Haitsinger.—The versorgung-haus.— The Städel museum.—Dannecker, memoir of his life and works. — German sculpture; Rauch, Tieck, Schwanthaler. 3. Goethe and his daughter-in-law.—The german women.—German authoresses.—German domestic life and manners.—German coquetterie and german romance. — The story of a devoted sister. Pt. 2. Memoranda at Munich, Nuremberg and Dresden.

Jefferies, R: The life of the fields. Lond. 1884. D.   **824.2 : 59**
Contents. The field-play.—Bits of oak bark.—The pageant of summer. — Meadow thoughts.—Clematis lane.—Nature near Brighton.—Sea, sky and down.—January in the Sussex woods. — By the Exe.—The water-colley.—Notes on landscape painting.— Village miners.—Mind under water.— Sport and science.—Nature and the gamekeeper.—The sacrifice to trout. —The hovering of the kestrel.—Birds climbing the air. — Country literature.— Sunlight on a London square.—Venice in the East end.—The pigeons at the British museum.—The plainest city in Europe.
— Round about a great estate. Bost. 1880. S.
        824.2 : 60
— The story of my heart ; my autobiography. Bost. 1883. S.   **824.2 : 111**
— Wild life in a southern county. [*Anon.*] Bost. 1879. S.   **824.2 : 61**

Jenyns, Soame. Disquisitions on several subjects. Lond. 1822. S.   **824.2 : 99**
Contents. On the chain of universal being. — On cruelty to inferior animals.—On a pre-existent state. —On the nature of time.—On the analogy between things material and intellectual.—On rational christianity.—On government and civil liberty.—On religious establishments.

King, T: Starr. Patriotism, and other papers; with a biographical sketch by R: Frothingham. Bost. 1864. D.   **824.1 : 50**
Contents. Patriotism.—Washington, or Greatness.—Beauty and religion.—Great principles and small duties.—Plato's views of immortality.—Thought and things.—True greatness.—Indirect influences.—Life more than meat.—Inward resources.—Natural and spiritual providence.—Philosophy and theology.—Natural and revealed religion.—The idea of God and the truths of christianity.—The harmony of opposite qualities in the Saviour's character and teachings.—The chief appeal of religion.

Kingsley, C: Literary and general lectures and essays. [Works, v. 20]. Lond. 1880. D.
824.2 : 62
Contents. The stage as it was once.—Thoughts on Shelley and Byron.—Alexander Smith and Alexander Pope.—Tennyson.—Burns and his school.—The poetry of sacred and legendary art.—On english composition.—On english literature.— Grots and groves. — Hours with the mystics.— F: Denison Maurice, in memoriam.—Phaethon, or Loose thoughts for loose thinkers.

— Prose idylls, new and old. [Works, v. 15]. Lond. 1882. D.   **824.2 : 63**
Contents. A charm of birds.—Chalk-stream studies.—The fens.—My winter-garden.—From ocean to sea.

— North Devon.

— New miscellanies. Bost. 1860. D.   **824.2 : 64**
Contents. "A mad world, my masters."—Chalk-stream studies.— Alex. Smith and Alex. Pope.—Thoughts on Shelley and Byron.—Mansfield's Paraguay, Brazil and the Plate.—The agricultural crisis.—The water supply of London.—Speech in behalf of the Ladies' sanitary association, 1859.—Great cities and their influence for good and evil.—On the study of natural history.—Thoughts in a gravel pit.—J: Tauler.—H: Brooke and the Fool of quality.—Pilgrim's progress, ill.

— Sir Walter Raleigh and his time, with other papers. Bost. 1859. D.   **824.2 : 65**
Contents. Sir Walter Raleigh and his time.—Plays and puritans.— Burns and his school.—Hours with the mystics.—Tennyson.—The poetry of sacred and legendary art.—North Devon. — Phaethon. — Alexandria and her schools.—My winter-garden.—England from Wolsey to Elizabeth.

Kirkland, Caroline Matilda, (*Mary Clavers*). The evening book, or Fireside talk on morals and manners, with sketches of western life. N. Y. 1853. D.   **824.1 : 51**
Contents. Hospitality.—Conversation.—The household.—The toilet.—The log school house.— Courting by proxy.—The country funeral.

Lackland, T: Homespun, or Five and twenty years ago. N. Y. 1867. D.   **824.1 : 52**

Lamb, C: Eliana : hitherto uncollected writings. N. Y. 1865. D.   **824.2 : 66**
Contents. Essays and sketches.—The pawnbroker's daughter. — The adventures of Ulysses. — Tales. — Poems.—Letters.

Lanman, C: Essays for summer hours. 3d ed., rev. N. Y. 1853. S.   **824.1 : 53**
Contents. Summer morning.— Night musings.— Old Louis Olmstead. — The poet's pilgrimage. — An evening in the city.— Lilly Larnard.— Afternoon in the woodlands. — Sabbath evening reflections. — The unhappy strangers.—Something about bells.—The return. — The primeval forests.— A music rhapsody. — The early called. — The old academy. — Wilderness poetry.— Mirth and sadness. — Summer evening twilight. — Thoughts on literature. — The dying year. — A song of memory.

Leland, C: Godfrey. Sunshine in thought. N. Y. 1863. S.   **824.1 : 54**

Lowell, James Russell. My study windows. Bost. 1879. D.   **824.1 : 55**
Contents. My garden acquaintance.— A good word for winter.—On a certain condescension in foreigners. — A great public character. — Carlyle. — Abraham Lincoln.— The life and letters of James Gates Percival.—Thoreau.— Swinburne's tragedies.— Chaucer.— Library of old authors. — Emerson, the lecturer. — Pope.

Macaulay, T: Babington, *baron Macaulay.* Critical and miscellaneous essays. N. Y. 1880. 7 v. in 5. D.   **824.2 : 67**
Contents. **V. 1.** Milton. — Machiavelli.—Dryden.—History.—Hallam's Constitutional history. **2.** Croker's ed. of Boswell's Life of Johnson.—Lord Nugent's Memorials of Hampden. — Nares's Memoires of lord Burghley. — Dumont's Recollections of Mirabeau. — Lord Mahon's War of the succession.—Walpole's Letters to sir Horace Mann.—Thackeray's History of the earl of Chatham. — Lord Bacon. **3.** Mackintosh's History of the revolution in England in 1688. — Sir John Malcolm's Life of lord Clive. — Life and writings of sir W: Temple.—Church and state. — Ranke's History of the popes.—Cowley and Milton. — On Mitford's History of Greece.—On the athenian orators. **4.** Comic dramatists of the restauration.— The late lord Holland; — Warren Hastings. — Frederick the great. **5.** Mme. D'Arblay. — Life and writings of Addison.— Barère's memoirs. — Mr. Rob. Montgomery's poems.—Civil disabilities of the jews.—Mill's Essay on government. — Bentham's Defence of Mill.—Utilitarian theory of government. — The earl of Chatham. — Speech on his installation as lord rector of the university at Glasgow. — Speech on retiring from political life. **6.** Biographical and historical sketches. — App. Pompeii ; The battle of Ivry. **7.** Fragments of a roman tale. —On the Royal society of literature. — Scenes from "Athenian revels." — Criticism on the principal italian writers.—Some account of the great law suit between the parishes of St.Dennis and St. George-in-the-water. — Conversation between mr. Abraham Cowley and mr. John Milton touching the great civil war.—A prophetic account of a grand national epic poem, to be entitled "The Wellingtoniad," and to be published a. d. 2824.—Sadler's Law of population. — Sadler's refutation refuted. — Mirabeau.—William Pitt.—Miscellaneous poems, inscriptions, etc.

— Same ; v. 1, 2, 4–6. N. Y. 1857. D. **824.2 : 67**
Contents same as above except that v. 4 has, in addition, The lays of ancient Rome.

Macdonald, G: The imagination, and other essays. Bost. [1883]. D.   **824.2 : 98**
Contents. The imagination ; its functions and its culture. — A sketch of individual development. — St. George's day, 1564 [Shakspere].—The art of Shakspere as revealed by himself. — The elder Hamlet. — On polish. — Browning's "Christmas eve." — "Essays on some of the forms of literature." — "The history and heroes of medicine."—Wordsworth's poetry.-Shelley. —A sermon.—True greatness.

Mathews, W: Getting on in the world, or Hints on success in life. Chicago. 1879. D.
824.1 : 106
Contents. Success and failure.—Good and bad luck. — Choice of a profession. — Physical culture. — Concentration or oneness of aim.—Self-reliance.—Originality in aims and methods. — Attention to details. — Practical talent. — Decision. — Manner. — Business habits.—Self-advertising.—The will and the way.—Reserved power. — Economy of time. — Money, its use and abuse.— Mercantile failures. —Overwork and under-rest.—True and false success.—Index.

— The great conversers, and other essays. 7th ed. Chicago. 1877. D.   **824.1 : 57**
Contents. The great conversers. — Literary clubs.—Epigrams.—Popular fallacies.— Faces. — Compulsory morality.—The power of trifles.—A peep into literary workshops.—French traits.—Pleasantry in literature. —Our dull lives.—Merry saints.—One book. — Pulpit oratory.—Originality in literature.— Is literature ill-paid ? — Curiosities of criticism. — Timidity in public speaking. — Noses. — The battle of Waterloo (with map).—Index.

— Hours with men and books. Chicago. 1878. D.
824.1 : 56
Contents. T: De Quincey. — Robert South. — C: H. Spurgeon.— Recollections of judge Story. — Moral Grahamism. — Strength and health. — Professorships of books and reading. — The morality of good living. — The illusions of history. — Homilies on early rising. — Literary triflers. — Waiting for the press. — The magic of modern languages.—Working by rule.—Too much speaking.—A forgotten wit.—Are we anglo-saxon ?— A day at Oxford. — An hour at Christ's hospital.—Book-buying.—A pinch of snuff.

Mathews, W:—*Continued.*
— Literary style, and other essays. Chicago. 1881. D. **824.1 : 58**
Contents. Literary style.—The duty of praise.—Periodical literature.—"The blues" and their remedy.—The modesty of genius.—Sensitiveness to criticism.—The ideal and the real.—Fat vs. lean.—Memory and its marvels.—Fools.—Angling.—Intellectual playfulness.—A plea for the erring.—The secret of longevity.—The season of travel.—Hot-house education.—Originality.—The art of listening.—Who are gentlemen?—Office-seeking.—Americanisms.—Index.

Mathias, G. H. D. En avant, messieurs! a tutor's counsel to his pupils. Phila. 1867. S. **824.2 : 69**

Mill, J: Stuart. Dissertations and discussions; political, philosophical and historical. Bost. 1865. 4 v. D. **824.2 : 70**
Contents. V. 1. The contest in America.—The right and wrong of state interference with corporation and church property.—The currency juggle.—A few observations on the french revolution.—Thoughts on poetry and its varieties. — Prof. Sedgwick's discourse on the studies of the university of Cambridge.—Civilization.—Aphorisms; a fragment.—Armand Carrel.—A prophecy.—Writings of Alfred de Vigny.—Bentham.—App. 2. Coleridge.—De Tocqueville on Democracy in America.—Bailey on Berkeley's Theory of vision.—Michelet's History of France.—The claims of labor.—Guizot's essays and lectures on history.—Early grecian history and legend. 3. Vindication of the french revolution of febr. 1848.—Enfranchisement of women.— Dr. Whewell on moral philosophy. — Grote's History of Greece. — A few words on non-intervention. — The slave power.—Utilitarianism. 4. Thoughts on parliamentary reform.—Recent writers on reform.—Bain's Psychology.—A few words on non-intervention.—The contest in America.— Austin on jurisprudence. — Plato. — Inaugural address.

Miller, Hugh. Essays; historical and biographical, political, social, literary and scientific, ed., with a preface, by P: Bayne. Bost. 1865. D. **824.2 : 71**
Contents. Historical and biographical. The new year.—Royal progresses, recent and remote.— The infant prince.—Remains of Napoleon.—Jean d'Acre.—The Cromwell controversy.—The third french revolution.— The duke of Wellington.—Earl Grey.—Lord Jeffrey.—Fire at the Tower of London.—The centenary of "the forty-five".—The half century.—The echoes of the world.—Glen tilt tabooed.—Edinburgh an age ago. — The Burns festival and hero worship. *Political and social.* Our working classes.—Peasant properties.—The franchise.—A five-pound qualification. — The strikes. — The cottages of our hinds. — The bothy system.—The Highlands. — The scotch poor-law.—Pauperism.—Pauper labor.—The crime-making laws.—Is game property?—The felons of the country.—The legislative court.—The peace meetings.—Literature of the people. *Literary and scientific.* Parting impressions of the great exhibition.—Criticism for the uninitiated.— Geology vs. astronomy.—The spaces and the periods.—Unity of the human races. — Norway and its glaciers.—The amenities of literature.—A strange story, but true.—The idealistic school.— The poesy of intellect and fancy.—The untaught poets.—Our novel literature.—Eugene Sue.—The Abbotsford baronetcy.

Mitchell, Donald Grant, (*Ik Marvel*). Bound together; a sheaf of papers. N. Y. 1884. D. **824.1 : 109**
Contents. Washington Irving.— Titian and his times.—Procession of the months.—Beginnings of an old town.—Two college talks.—In-doors and out of doors.

— Wet days at Edgewood with old farmers, old gardeners and old pastorals. [*Anon.*] N. Y. 1865. D. **824.1 : 59**

Mivart, St. G: Contemporary evolution; an essay on some recent social changes. N. Y. 1876. D. **824.2 : 72**
Contents. Introductory. — Political evolution. — Three ideals. — Scientific evolution. — Philosophic evolution.—Aesthetic evolution.

Mogridge, G: Old Humphrey's observations. [*Anon.*] 3d ed. N. Y. 1841. S. **824.2 : 73**

Montez, Marie Dolores Eliza Rosanna Porris y, *born Gilbert, countess of Landsfeld, called* Lola Montez. Lectures of Lola Montez, countess of Landsfeld, including her autobiography. N. Y. 1858. D. **824.1 : 60**

Müller, F: Max. Chips from a german workshop. N. Y. 1876-81. 5 v. D. **824.2 : 74**
Contents. V. 1. **Essays on the science of religion.** Lecture on the Vedas, or the sacred books of the brahmans, 1865.—Christ and other masters, 1858.—The Veda and Zend-Avesta, 1853. — The Aitareya-Brâhmana, 1864.—On the study of the Zend-Avesta in India, 1862.—Progress of Zend scholarship, 1865.—Genesis and the Zend-Avesta, 1864. — The modern Parsis, 1862. — Buddhism, 1862. — Buddhist pilgrims, 1857.—The meaning of Nirvâna, 1857.—Chinese translations of sanscrit texts, 1861.—The works of Confucius, 1861.—Popol Vuh, 1862.—Semitic monotheism, 1860.
2. **Essays on mythology, traditions and customs.** Comparative mythology, 1856. — Greek mythology, 1858.—Greek legends, 1867.—Bellerophon, 1855. — The norsemen in Iceland, 1858. — Folk-lore, 1863.—Zulu nursery tales, 1867.—Popular tales from the norse, 1859.—Tales of the west Highlands, 1861.—On manners and costums, 1865.—Our figures, 1863.—Caste. 1858.—Index.
3. **Essays on literature, biography and antiquities.** German literature, 1858. — Old german love-songs, 1858.—Ye schyppe of fooles, 1858.—Life of Schiller, 1859.—W: Müller, 1858.—On the language and poetry of Schleswig-Holstein, 1864.—Joinville, 1866.—The Journal des savants and the Journal de Trévoux, 1866.— Chasot, 1856. — Shakespeare, 1864. — Bacon in Germany, 1857.—A german traveller in England, a. d. 1598, 1857.—Cornish antiquities, 1867.—Are there jews in Cornwall? 1867.—The insulation of St. Michael's Mount, 1867.—Bunsen, 1868.—Letters from Bunsen to Max Müller in 1848-59.
4. **Essays, chiefly on the science of language.** Inaugural lecture: On the value of comparative philology as a branch of academic study, 1868. — Rede lecture, pt. 1, On the stratification of language, 1868; pt. 2, On Curtius' chronology of the indo-germanic languages, 1875.—Lecture on the migration of fables, 1870. — Lectures on the results of the science of language, 1872.—Lecture on missions, 1873.—Address on the importance of oriental studies, 1874.—Life of Colebrooke, 1872. — Reply to mr. Darwin, 1875. — In self-defense.—Index to v. 3, 4.
5. **Miscellaneous later essays.** On freedom, 1879.—The philosophy of mythology, 1871.—On false analogies in comparative theology, 1870. — On spelling, 1876.—On sanskrit texts discovered in Japan, 1880.

Nadal, Ehrman Syme. Essays at home and elsewhere. N. Y. 1882. D. **824.1 : 61**
Contents. The old Boston road.—Artemus Ward.—Byron.—Thackeray's relation to english society.—The conditions of dandyism.—Mr. Matthew Arnold.—A day or two in Sussex.—Two poems of Collins.—W: Cullen Bryant.—A trip to a political convention.—A recollection of the south. — Journalism as exemplified by Walter Bagehot.—Newspaper literary criticism.

Newman, J: H: Historical sketches. Lond. 1876-81. 3 v. D. **824.2 : 75**
Contents. V. 1. [4th ed.] The turks in their relation to Europe.—Marcus Tullius Cicero.—Apollonius of Tyana.—Primitive christianity. 2. The church of the fathers.—St. Chrysostom.—Theodoret.—Mission of St. Benedict.—Benedictine schools. 3. Rise and progress of universities.—Northmen and normans in England and Ireland.—Medieval Oxford.—Convocation of Canterbury.

— *Same*; v. 1. 3d ed. Lond. 1876. D.
824.2 : 75 v1

Norton, James. Australian essays on subjects political, moral and religious. Lond. 1857. O. **824.2 : 76**
Contents. 1st pt. England and her colonies.—Port Jackson and the city of Sydney.— The genius of Australia.—The press of Australia.—The new constitution.—Railways and telegraphic dispatch.—Rail communication in Australia.—Prospects of Ireland.

—The memory.—Beauty. — Vestiges of creation.—A history of failures. 2d pt. Bishop Broughton.— Charity.—The shortness of human life. — Time.— Eternity.—The physical sufferings of Christ. — The agency of the devil.—The definition of mysteries.— Baptism.—The burial service.— Apostolical succession.—Repentance of necessity progressive. — Idle words.—Prisoners of hope.—The resurrection of the body.—Further observations on the resurrection.— The redemption, a vision.—The after-state of the wicked, a vision.—The joy of the righteous, a vision.

Osgood, S: Mile stones in our life journey. N. Y. 1860. D.   824.1 : 62

Ossoli, Sarah Margaret, *born* Fuller, *marchesa* d'. Life without and life within, or Reviews, narratives, essays and poems; ed. by her brother, Arthur B. Fuller. Bost. 1860. D.   824.1 : 63

Contents. Reviews: Menzel's view of Goethe; Goethe; T: Hood; Letters from a landscape painter; Beethoven; Brown's novels; Edgar A. Poe; Alfieri and Cellini; Italy; Cary's Dante; American facts; Napoleon and his marshals; Physical education; F: Douglass; Philip van Artevelde; U. S. exploring expedition; Story books for the hot weather; Shelley's poems; Festus; French novelists of the day; The new science, or The philosophy of mesmerism or animal magnetism; Deutsche schnellpost; Oliver Cromwell; Emerson's essays; Capital punishment.— Miscellaneous: First of january; New year's day; St. Valentine's day; Fourth of july; First of august; Thanksgiving; Christmas; Moriana; Sunday meditations; Appeal for an asylum for discharged female convicts; The rich man; The poor man; The celestial empire; Klopstock and Meta; What fits a man to be a voter; Discoveries; Politeness too great a luxury to be given to the poor; Cassius M. Clay; The magnolia of Lake Ponchartrain; Consecration of Grace church; Late aspirations; Fragmentary thoughts; Farewell to New York.—Poems.

Parker, Theodore. Critical and miscellaneous writings. 2d ed. Bost. 1856. D.   824.1 : 65

Contents. A lesson for the day.—German literature.—The life of St. Bernard of Clairvaux.—Truth against the world.—Thoughts on labor.—A discourse on the transient and permanent in christianity.— The pharisees. — On the education of the laboring class.—How to move the world. — Primitive christianity.—Strauss's Life of Jesus.—Thoughts on theology.

Parr, Harriet, (*Holme Lee*). In the silver age; essays, "that is, dispersed meditations." New ed. Lond. 1877. D.   824.2 : 68

Contents. Round about home in the spring-time.— Village life, quiet life. — Old familiar places, old familiar faces.—From day to day.—Summer holidays. —River scenery.—In the workaday world.—In harvest time.—In the fall of the leaf.—By the fireside.— Within and without.

Peabody, Elizabeth Palmer, *ed.* Aesthetic papers. Bost. 1849. O.   824.1 : 64

Contents. **Ward,** S. G. Criticism.—**Dwight,** J. S. Music.—**Emerson,** R. W. War.—**Godwin,** P. Organization.—**Reed,** S. Genius.—**Peabody,** E. P. The dorian measure, with a modern application.—**Wilkinson,** J. J. G. Correspondence.—**Hawthorne,** N. Main-street.—**Perkins,** S. H. Abuse of representative government. — **Thoreau,** H. D. Resistance to civil government. — **Peabody,** E. P. Language.— Vegetation about Salem, Mass., by an english resident. *Poetry:* **Peabody,** E. P. Crawford's Orpheus. —A spirit's reply.—Hymn of a spirit shrouded.—Meditations of a widow.—The twofold being. — The favorite.

Phillips, Wendell. Speeches, lectures and letters. Bost. 1880. D.   825.1 : 3

Contents. The murder of Lovejoy. — Woman's rights.—Public opinion.—Surrender of Sims.— Sims' anniversary.—Philosophy of the abolition movement. —Removal of judge Loring.—The Boston mob.—The pilgrims. — Letter to judge Shaw and president Walker.—Idols.—Harper's Ferry.—Burial of John Brown.—Lincoln's election. — Mobs and education.— Disunion.—Progress.—Under the flag.—The war for the union.—The cabinet.— Letter to the Tribune.— Toussaint L'Ouverture.—A metropolitan police.—The state of the country.

Phillips, Wendell.—*Continued.*
— *Same.* With a biographical sketch. Bost. 1884. D.   825.1 : 3
— The scholar in a republic; address at the centennial anniversary of the Phi Beta Kappa of Harvard college, june 30, 1881. Bost. 1881. O.   824.1 : 100

Prescott, W: Hickling. Biographical and critical miscellanies. N. Y. 1845. O.   824.1+66

Contents. C: Brockden Brown.— Asylum for the blind.—Irving's Conquest of Granada.—Cervantes.— Sir Walter Scott. — Chateaubriand's English literature.—Bancroft's United States.—Mme. Calderon's Life in Mexico.—Molière.—Italian narrative poetry. —Poetry and romance of the italians.—Scottish song. Da Ponte's observations.

Procter, Bryan Waller, (*Barry Cornwall*). Essays and tales in prose, by Barry Cornwall. Bost. 1853. D.   824.2 : 77

Contents. V. 1. Memoir and essay on the genius of Shakspere.—The death of friends.—The spanish student. — A short mystery.—The portrait on my uncle's snuff box.—A day in Venice.—The Stauntons. —A chapter on portraits.—The prison-breaker.—The planter.—Vicissitudes in a lawyer's life.—The manhunter.—The two soldiers. **2.** The story of the back-room window.—A chapter of fragments.—The usher.—M. de Bearn.—The happy day.—On english tragedy.—On english poetry.—A defence of poetry.— Four dramatic scenes.

Putnam, E. The bridle of vanity, or Knowledge, progress, liberty and equality considered in their verity and their fallacy. Bost. 1862. D.   824.1 : 67

Contents. Of knowledge, or Charlemagne, his scholarship.—The tyranny of progress.—The fact of liberty.—The limitations of equality.—The consent of the governed.

Quincy, Josiah Phillips. The protection of majorities, or Considerations relating to electoral reform; with other papers. Bost. 1876. D.   824.1 : 68

Contents. Introductory.—The protection of majorities.—Coercion in the later stages of education.— The function of town libraries.—The abuse of reading.—The better samaritan.

Rands, W: Brightly. Lilliput lectures by the author of "Lilliput levee." Lond. 1871. D.   x 824.2 : 97

Contents. Introd.—The world.—The sky.—Cities.— Science and philosophy.—Art and artists.—Trade.— The family.—Thoughts of God.—Government.—Character.—Justice, mercy, charity.—In church.

Russell, Addison Peale. Characteristics; sketches and essays. Bost. 1884 [1883]. D.   824:1 : 113

Contents. The conversation of Coleridge.— Sarah Siddons.—Dr. Johnson.— Lord Macaulay.— Lamb.— Burns.—The christianity of Woolman.—J: Randolph and J: Brown.—The audacity of Foote.—Habit.—The habit of detraction.—The art of living.
— Library notes. N. Y. 1875. D.   824.1 : 69
Contents. Insufficiency.—Extremes. — Disguises.— Standards.—Rewards.—Limits.—Incongruity.—Mutations.—Paradoxes.

Ruskin, J: Sesame and lilies; three lectures. Rev. and enl. ed. N. Y. 1875. O.   824.2 : 78

Contents. Of kings' treasuries.—Of queens' gardens.—Of the mystery of life.
— The true and the beautiful in nature, art, morals and religion, selected from [his] works with a notice of the author by mrs. L. C. Tuthill. N. Y. 1859. D.   842.2 : 79

Sargent, Lucius Manlius. Dealings with the dead, by a sexton of the old school. Bost. 1856. 2 v. O.   824.1 : 71

x denotes books specially adapted for children.

Sargent, M. E., *mrs.* J: T., *ed.* Sketches and reminiscences of the Radical club of Chestnut street. Bost. 1880. D. 824.1 : 70

Savage, Minot Judson. The modern sphinx and some of her riddles. Bost. 1883. D. 824.1 : 103
Contents. Pref. — The modern sphinx. — The chief end of man.—What is business for ?—What are brains for ?—The newspaper; its good and its evil. — A true republic. — Progress and poverty. — Religious transition.—The reign of the dead.

Shedd, W: Greenough Thayer. Literary essays. N. Y. [1878]. D. 824.1 : 73
Contents. The true nature of the beautiful and its relation to culture. — The influence and method of english studies. — The ethical theory of rhetoric and eloquence.—The characteristics and importance of a natural rhetoric.—The relation of language and style to thought. — Scientific and popular education. — Intellectual temperance.—The puritan character.—The african nature.—Coleridge as a philosopher and theologian.—The confessions of Augustine.

Smith, Alexander. Dreamthorp ; a book of essays written in the country. Bost. 1864. D. 824.2 : 106
Contents. Dreamthorp. — On the writing of essays. — Of death and the fear of dying. — W: Dunbar. — A lark's flight.—Christmas.—Men of letters.—On the importance of a man to himself. — A shelf in my bookcase.— Geoffrey Chaucer. — Books and gardens. — On vagabonds.

Smith, Goldwin. Lectures and essays. N. Y. 1881. O. 824.2+94
Contents. The greatness of the romans.—The greatness of England.—The great duel of the 17th century. — The lamps of fiction. — An address to the Oxford school of science and art. — The ascent of man.— The proposed substitutes for religion.—The labour movement.—What is culpable luxury ?— A true captain of industry.—A wirepuller of kings.—The early years of the conqueror of Quebec.— Falkland and the puritans.—The early years of Abraham Lincoln. — Alfredus rex fundator. — The last republicans of Rome. — Austen.—Leigh's memoir of Jane Austen.—Pattison's Milton.—Coleridge's Life of Keble.

Smith, Sidney. Essays. Authorized ed. Lond. *n. d.* D. 824.2 : 88
Contents, see Works, col. 1018, "Articles from the Edinburgh review."

Southey, Robert. The doctor, etc.; ed. by his son-in-law, J: Wood Warter. Lond. 1848. O. 824.2 : 80

Spalding, Martin J: Miscellanea; comprising reviews, lectures and essays on historical, theological and miscellaneous subjects. 3d ed. Louisville. 1858. O. 824.1+75
Contents. Introductory address. — Church history: The early ages ; The middle ages ; Since the reformation. — Literature and arts in the middle ages. — Literature and the catholic clergy; Libraries. — Schools and universities in the "dark" ages. — Influence of catholicity on civil liberty. — Age of pope Gregory VII; The deposing power. — The great schism of the west ; Rome and Avignon.—John Huss and the hussites ; The council of Constance. — The spanish inquisition ; Prescott's review.— The reformation in Switzerland ; Bernese intrigues. — Prescott's Conquest of Mexico ; Character of the conqueror's ; The religious point of view of the conquest. — Early catholic missions in the northwest: Bancroft's account ; The Huron mission; Fathers De Brebeuf and Lallement. — Webster's Bunker Hill speech.—Our colonial blue laws: Union of church and state ; Heretics, quakers and witches.—The spirit of the age. — The charge of idolatry. — The catholic doctrine of satisfaction.—The confessional.—Catholic and protestant countries. — England and France; Holland and Belgium ; Germany and Italy; England as she is and was ; Ireland and the irish ; Italian society : Brazil and the brazilians. — The oriental churches. — Rome. — The papal government. — The Philadelphia riots.—A chapter on mobs.

Spencer, Herbert. Essays, moral, political and æsthetic. N. Y. 1865. D. 824.2 : 81
Contents. The philosophy of style. — Over-legisla-

Spencer, Herbert.—*Continued.*
tion. — The morals of trade. — Personal beauty. — Representative government. — Prison-ethics. — Railway morals and railway policy. — Gracefulness. — State-tamperings with money and banks. — Parliamentary reform ; the dangers and safeguards.

— Illustrations of universal progress ; a series of discussions. N. Y. 1864. D. 824.2 : 82
Contents. Progress; its law and cause. — Manners and fashion.—The genesis of science. — The physiology of laughter.—The origin and function of music.— The nebular hypothesis. — Bain on The emotions and The will.—Illogical geology.—The development hypothesis.—The social organism. — Use and beauty.—The sources of architectural types. — The use of anthropomorphism.

— Recent discussions in science, philosophy and morals. N. Y. 1871. D. 824.2 : 83
Contents. Morals and moral sentiments.—Origin of animal worship. — The classification of the sciences. —Postscript replying to criticisms. — Reasons for dissenting from the philosophy of Comte. — Of laws in nature, and the order of their discovery.—The genesis of science.

Stevenson, Robert L: Familiar studies of men and books. Lond. 1882. D. 824.2 : 108
Contents. Pref. — Victor Hugo's romances. — Some aspects of Robert Burns. — Walt Whitman. — H: D: Thoreau; his character and opinions. — Yoshida-Torajiro.—François Villon, student, poet and housebreaker.—Charles of Orleans.—Pepys. — J: Knox and women.

— Virginibus puerisque, and other papers. Lond. 1881. D. 824.2 : 109
Contents. Virginibus puerisque.— Crabbed age and youth.—An apology for idlers.—Ordered south. — Æs triplex. — El Dorado. — The english admirals. — Some portraits by Raeburn.—Child's play.—Walking tours—Pan's pipes.—A plea for gas lamps.

Storrs, R: Salter. Manliness in the scholar. N. Y. [1883]. S. 824.1 : 108

Story, Joseph. Miscellaneous writings ; literary, critical, juridical and political, now first coll. Bost. 1835. O. 824.1+77
Contents. Literary discourses.—Biographical sketches: S: Dexter ; J: Marshall ; R. Trumble ; B. Washington; I: Parker; W: Pinkney; T: A. Emmet.—Reviews.—Juridical discourses and arguments.—Political papers.

Swing, D: Club essays. 2d ed. Chicago. 1881. S. 824.1 : 76
Contents. Augustine and his mother. — A roman home. — Parlez-vous français ? — The history of love. — The greatest of the fine arts.

Symonds, J: Addington. Sketches and studies in southern Europe. N. Y. 1880. 2 v. D. 824.2 : 86
Contents. V. 1. The Cornice.—Ajaccio. — Florence and the Medici.—The debt of english to italian literature. — Popular italian poetry of the renaissance. — The Orfeo of Poliziano.—Siena. — Perugia. — Popular songs of Tuscany. — Orvieto. — Thoughts in Rome about christmas.— Antinous. — Lucretius. — Amalfi, Pæstum, Capri. 2. Palermo.—Syracuse and Girgenti. —Aetna.—Athens.—Rimini. — Ravenna. — Canossa. — Parma.— Fornovo. — Two dramatists of the last century [Goldoni and Alfieri]. — Crema and the crucifix. — Bergamo and Bartolommeo Colleoni. — Como and Il Medeghino.- Lombard vignettes.—Monte Generoso —Love of the alps. — Old towns of Provence. — App.: Blank verse ; Note on the Orfeo ; Eight sonnets of Petrarch.

Talfourd, T: Noon. Critical and miscellaneous writings. 2d amer. ed. with add. articles. Phila. 1846. O. 824.2+87
Contents. On british novels and romances.—Mackenzie.—The author of Waverley.—Godwin.—Maturin.— Rymer on tragedy. — Colley Cibber's Apology for his life.—John Dennis's works.—Modern periodical literature.—On the genius and writings of Wordsworth.—North's Life of lord Guilford.—Hazlitt's Lectures on the drama.—Wallace's Prospects of mankind, nature and providence. — On pulpit oratory. — Recollections of Lisbon.—Lloyd's poems. — Mr. Oldaker on modern improvements.—A chapter on "time." — On the pro-

fession of the bar.—The wine cellar. — Destruction of the Brunswick theatre by fire. — First appearance of miss Fanny Kemble. — The melodramas against gambling. — On the intellectual character of the late W: Hazlitt.—The late dowager lady Holland.—Address of the anniversary of the Manchester athenæum. — Lord Eldon and lord Stowell. — Speech for the defendant in the prosecution of the queen vs. Moxon for the publication of Shelley's works. — Speeches on copyright.—The Westminster play.

Taylor, Bayard. Critical essays and literary notes. N. Y. 1880. D.   **824.1 : 78**
    Contents. Tennyson.—Hugo. — The german Burns. — F: Rückert. — The author of "Saul."—Thackeray.—Autumn days in Weimar. — Weimar in june. — Notes on books and events.

Thompson, Maurice. By-ways and bird notes. N. Y. 1885. D.   **824.1 : 117**
    Contents. In the haunts of the mocking-bird.—A red-headed family.—Tangle-leaf papers.—The threshold of the gods.—Browsing and nibbling.—Out-door influences in literature.—A fortnight in a palace of reeds. — Cuckoo notes. — Some minor song-birds.—Birds of the rocks.

Thoreau, H: D: Early spring in Massachusetts, from [his] journal. Bost. 1881. D.
                                      824.1 : 79
— Excursions. Bost. 1863. D.   **824.1 : 80**
    Contents. Biog. sketch.—Natural history of Massachusetts.—A walk to Wachusett. — The landlord.—A winter walk.—The succession of forest trees.—Walking. — Autumnal tints. — Wild apples. — Night and moonlight.

— Summer ; from [his] journal, ed. by H. G. O. Blake. Map. Bost. 1884. D.   **824.1 : 110**
— Walden, or Life in the woods. Bost. 1854. D.
                                      824.1 : 81
    Contents. Economy. — Where I lived, and what I lived for.—Reading.—Sounds. — Solitude.—Visitors.—The bean-field. — The village. — The ponds. — Baker farm. — Higher laws. — Brute neighbors. — Housewarming. — Former inhabitants; and winter visitors. — Winter animals. — The pond in winter. — Spring. — Conclusion.

— A week on the Concord and Merrimac rivers. Bost. 1862. D.   **824.1 : 82**

Tuckerman, H: Theodore. The criterion, or The test of talk about familiar things ; a series of essays. N. Y. 1866. D. **824.1 : 83**
    Contents. Inns.—Authors. — Pictures. — Doctors. — Holidays. — Lawyers. — Sepulchres. — Actors.—Newspapers.—Preachers.—Statues.—Bridges.

— Essays, biographical and critical, or Studies of character. Bost. 1857. O.   **824.1 : 84**
    Contents. Washington, the patriot. — Chesterfield, the man of the world.—Boone, the pioneer.—Southey, the man of letters.—Digby, the modern knight. — Lafitte, the financier. — Kean, the actor. — Körner, the youthful hero.—Fulton, the mechanician.—Constable, the landscape painter. — Chateaubriand, the poet of the old regime.—Jeffrey, the reviewer.—Williams, the tolerant colonist.—Savage, the literary adventurer.—Clinton, the national economist. — Jenny Lind, the vocalist.—Berkeley, the christian philosopher. — Leopardi, the sceptical genius. — De Foe, the writer for the people. — Audubon, the ornithologist. — Sterne, the sentimentalist. — D'Azeglio, the literary statesman. — Smith, the genial churchman. — Brown, the supernaturalist.—Wilkie, the painter of character.—Addison, the lay preacher. — Morris, the american statesman. — Pellico, the italian martyr. — Campbell, the popular poet. — Franklin, the american philosopher.

— The optimist. N. Y. 1850. D.   **824.1 : 85**
    Contents. New England philosophy. — Travel.—Music.—Conversation.—Art and artists.—Lyric poetry.—Social life. — Costume. — Walking. — A chapter on hands. — The New York colonists. — Eye-language. — Humor. — The gold fever. — The profession of literature. — Hair. — A presidential inauguration. — The weather.—Manner.—Flowers.—Broad views.—The rationale of love.

Wallace, Horace Binney. Literary criticism, and other papers. Phila. 1856. D.
                                      824.1 : 86
    Contents. Literary criticisms: The prose writers of America by R. W. Griswold ; Forest leaves and other poems, by Lydia Pearson ; Memoir of Philip Syng Physic, by J. Randolph ; Poems of Fitz-Greene Halleck ; Memoirs of the administrations of Washington and Adams, by Oliver Wolcott ; Washington Irving, his works, genius and character ; The female poets of America, by R. W. Griswold ; Letters on the study and use of history, by lord Bolingbroke ; The authorship of "The doctor;" Von Raumer on America ; The prose works of J: Milton ; Memoirs of George III, by H. Walpole ; Letters of the earl of Chesterfield ; Spence's Anecdotes of books and men ; Dr. Arnold's Lectures on modern history ; Wiley and Putnam's Lib. of choice reading ; S: Warren, Law studies; Life of Blanco White ; Sydney Smith's Sermons; Carlyle's essays; Gilfillan's Literary portraits; M. F. Tupper; Rubio's Rambles in the U. S; Undine; The rosicrucian philosophy; Legal rights of woman; Fanny Forrester ; Nourse's Legacies of the past. — *Literary portraits;* G: P. Morris ; R. W. Griswold. — Fragmental literary disquisitions. — Miscellaneous pieces.—Dramatic criticisms.

Warner, C: Dudley. Backlog studies. Ill. Bost. 1873. S.   **824.1 : 87**
— Baddeck and that sort of a thing. Bost. 1874. T.   **824.1 : 88**
— Calvin ; a study of character. *With his* My summer in a garden.   **824.1 : 90**
— In the wilderness. Bost. 1878. T. **824.1 : 89**
    Contents. In the wilderness: How I killed a bear ; Lost in the woods ; A fight with a trout; A-hunting of the deer; A character study; Camping out.—How spring came in New England.

— My summer in a garden. Bost. 1872. D.
                                      824.1 : 90
— *Same.* [2d ed.] Bost. 1885. S.   **824.1 : 90**

Webster, Noah. A collection of papers on political, literary and moral subjects. N. Y. 1843. O.   **824.1+98**
    Contents. Revolution in France.—The rights of neutral nations.—On the supposed change of temperature in modern winters.—Origin of the first bank in the U. S.—Letter from Washington respecting the last campaign in the revolution. — Correspondence with mr. Madison respecting the origin of the present constitution.—Origin of the copy-right laws of the U. S.—Vindication of the treaty with Great Britain in 1795.—Origin of Amherst college.—Address on agriculture.—Letter to Daniel Webster.—Answer of the house of rep. of Mass. to the governor's message.—Letter to S: Lee.—Reply to a letter of D: McClure.—Letter to a young gentleman commencing his education.—Form of association for young men. — Modes of teaching the english language.—Origin of the Hartford convention in 1814.—Brief history of political parties.—State of english philology.

Wells, Kate Gannett. About people. Bost. 1885 [1884]. T.   **824.1 : 114**
    Contents. Average people. — Individuality.—Striving.—Loyalty and liberality.—Transitional woman.—Personal influence.—Who's who.—Caste in american society.

Wheeler, D: Hilton. By-ways of literature, or Essays on old things and new in the customs, education, character, literature and language of the english-speaking people. N. Y. [1883]. D.   **824.1 : 116**
    Contents. A 14th century book for women.—English girls and boys in the old times.—Old education and modern.—The Robin Hood ballads.—The legends of king Arthur.—The founders' age in our literature. — Shakespeare on greatness. — Englishmen, their language and countries.—A grammatical revolution.—Our spoken english.

Whipple, Edwin Percy. Character and characteristic men. Bost. 1866. D. **824.1 : 91**
    Contents. Character. — Eccentric character. — Intellectual character.—Heroic character.—The american mind.—The english mind.—Thackeray.—Nathan-

Whipple, Edwin Percy.—*Continued.*
iel Hawthorne.—E: Everett.—T: Starr King.—Agassiz.—Washington and the principles of the revolution.
— Success and its conditions. Bost. 1879. D.
824.1 : 92
Contents. Young men in history.—The ethics of popularity.—Grit.—The vital and the mechanical.—The economy of invective.—The sale of souls.—The tricks of imagination.—Cheerfulness. — Mental and moral pauperism.—The genius of Dickens.—Shoddy.—J: A. Andrew.
— Literature and life. Enl. ed. Bost. 1883.
824.1 : 93
Contents. Authors in their relations to life.—Novels and novelists; C: Dickens. — Wit and humor.—The ludicrous side of life.—Genius.—Intellectual health and disease.— Use and misuse of words. — Wordsworth.—Bryant.—Stupid conservatism and malignant reform.

Willis, Nathaniel Parker. Rural letters and other records of thought at leisure, written in the intervals of more hurried literary labor. N. Y. 1853. D.   824.1 : 97
Contents. Letters from under a bridge.—The four rivers.—Letter to the unknown purchaser and next occupant of Glenmary.—Glenmary poems.—Open-air musings in the city.—Invalid rambles in Germany.—Letters from watering-places.—A plain man's love.

Willmott, Robert Aris. A journal of summertime in the country. N. Y. 1852. S.
824.2 : 89

Wilson, J:, (*Christopher North*). The recreations of Christopher North. Phila. 1845. O.
824.2 : 90
Contents. Christopher in his sporting jacket.—A tale of expiation.—Morning monologue.—The field of flowers.—Cottages.—An hour's talk about poetry.—Inch-Cruin.—A day at Windermere.—The moors.—Highland snow-storm.—The holy child.—Our parish.— May-day. — Sacred poetry. — Christopher in his aviary.—Dr. Kitchener.—Soliloquy on the seasons.—A few words on Thomson.—The snowball bicker of Pedmount.—Christmas dreams.—Our winter quarters.—Stroll to Grassmere.—L'envoy.

Wirt, W: The letters of the british spy. 10th ed., rev. and corr.; prefixed, a biographical sketch of the author. N. Y. 1848. D.
824.1 : 94

Woolson, Abba Goold. Browsing among books, and other essays. Bost. 1881. S.
824.1 : 95
Contents. Browsing among books. — Cats. — The humdrum aspect of life.—Smoking. — The morality of amusements.—Duds.—Boston common on a september afternoon.—The selection of gifts.—Goodwill towards men.—Old-fashioned flowers.—College commencements.—Luxuries. — Small-talk as one of the fine arts.—Our modern winters.—Spring, as seen from a city window.—Taking a turkish bath.—Our minor rights.—The trials of visiting.—An evening's adventure at the Deacon house.

10. English literature — f, Letters.

(*Note.* For collections of letters illustrating special subjects, periods of history or lives of individuals, *see* History, Biography, and other classes.)

Scoones, W. Baptiste, *ed.* Four centuries of english letters; selections from the correspondence of 150 writers from the period of the Paston letters to the present day. N. Y. 1880. O.   826.2 : 10

Richardson, Abby, *born* Sage, *formerly mrs.* McFarland, *ed.* Old love letters, or Letters of sentiment, written by persons eminent in English literature and history. Bost. 1883 [1882]. T.   826 : 2

Parker, Matthew. Correspondence, comprising letters written by and to him from a. d. 1535 to his death, a. d. 1575; ed. for the Parker society by J: Bruce and T: Thomason Perowne. Cambridge. 1853. O.
826.2 : 17

Mary Stuart, *queen of Scots.* Lettres, instructions et mémoires; publiés sur les originaux et les manuscrits du State paper office de Londres et des principales archives et bibliothèques de l'Europe et accompagnés d'un résumé chronologique par le prince Alexandre Labanoff. Lond. 1845. 7 v. O.
826.2 : 32
— Letters, now first pub. from the originals, coll. from various sources, private as well as public, with an introd. and notes by Agnes Strickland. New ed. Lond. 1844. 2 v. D.   826.2 : 25

Howel, James. Epistolæ Ho-Elianæ; familiar letters, domestic and forren, divided into 4 books, partly historical, partial, philosophicall, upon emergent occasions. Lond. 1678. D.   826.2 : 30

Williams, Roger. Letters, 1632—1682; now first coll., ed. by J: Russell Bartlett. Providence. 1874. O.   826.1+10

Cromwell, Oliver. Letters and speeches, incl. the supp. to the 1st ed.; with elucidations by T: Carlyle. N. Y. 1856. 2 v. D.
826.2 : 20

Montagu, *Lady* Mary Wortley-, *born* Pierrepont. Letters and works, ed. by her great grandson, lord Wharncliffe. Paris. 1837. 3 v. O.
826.2 : 7
Contents. V. 1. Memoir, by J. Dallaway.—Introductory anecdotes.—Account of the court of George I at his accession.—On the state of party at the accession of George I, by mr. Wortley.—Letters, written before 1717.—The enchiridion of Epictetus.—Letters during mr. Wortley's embassy.—To the countess of Mar.—To lady Pomfret. 2. Letters to mr. Wortley during her second residence abroad, 1739-61.—During residence abroad, 1746-57.—To mrs. Hewet.—To Henrietta, countess of Oxford and Mortimer.—To sir James and lady Frances Steuart.—Essays.—Poems.—App.—Index.

Russell, *Lady* Rachel, *born* Wriothesley, *formerly lady* Vaughan. Letters. Phila. 1854. D.
826.2 : 21

Atterbury, Francis. Private correspondence of dr. Francis Atterbury and his friends in 1725, never before pub., printed in the year 1768. *With* Brown, J: Dissertation on poetry and music.   *in* 23 : R

Russell, J:, *4th duke of Bedford.* Correspondence, sel. from the originals at Woburn Abbey with an introd. by lord J: Russell. Lond. 1842-46. 3 v. O.   826.2 : 14

Stanhope, Philip Dormer, *4th earl of Chesterfield.* Works, incl. his letters to his son, etc. Prefixed, an original life of the author. 1st amer. ed. N. Y. 1859. O.   826.2+12
Contents. Life.—Speech of the stage licensing bill.—Speeches on the gin act.—Letters to his son, with several other pieces on various subjects.

Warburton, W: Letters from a late eminent prelate to one of his friends. 2d ed. Lond. 1809. O.   **826.2 : 15**

Carter, Elizabeth, and Catherine Talbot. A series of letters, 1741—1770 ; added, letters from mrs. Carter to mrs. Vesey, 1763—1787, pub. from the original mss. in the possession of Montagu Pennington. Lond. 1809. 4 v. D.   **826.2 : 1**

Junius. [Letters] ; including letters by the same writer under other signatures ; added, his confidential correspondence with mr. Wilkes, and his private letters to mr. H. S. Woodfall ; a new and enl. ed., with new evidence as to the authorship, and extracts from an analysis by sir Harris Nicolas, by J: Wade. Lond. 1850, 1881. 2 v. D.   **826.2 : 4**

— **Griffin, F:** Junius discovered. Bost. 1854. D.   **826.5 : 1**

Note. A full review of the evidence as to the authorship of these letters, by Albert R. Frey, will be found in **Cushing, W:** Initials and pseudonyms, (14 : L), pp. 145–156.

George III. Correspondence with lord North, from 1768 to 1783 ; ed. from the originals at Windsor, with an introd. by W. Bodham Donne. Pub. by permission of the queen. Lond. 1867. 2 v. O.   **826.2 : 29**

Walpole, Horace, *4th earl of Orford.* Letters ; incl. numerous letters now first pub. from the original mss. Phila. 1842. 4 v. O.   **826.2+13**

— Letters to the earl of Hertford during his lordship's embassy in Paris, to which are added mr. Walpole's letters to the rev. H: Zouch. Lond. 1825. Q.   **826.2 : R19**

Grant, Anne, *born* Macvicar. Letters from the mountains ; the real correspondence of a lady between 1773 and 1807. 5th ed. Lond. 1813. 3 v. D.   **826.2 : 3**

Adams, J: Letters, addressed to his wife ; ed. by his grandson C: Francis Adams. Bost. 1841. 2 v. D.   **826.1 : 1**

— *and* Abigail. Familiar letters, during the revolution ; with a memoir of mrs. Adams by C: Francis Adams. N. Y. 1876. D.   **826.1 : 2**

Adams, Abigail, *born* Smith. Letters ; with an introd. memoir by her grandson C: Francis Adams. 4th ed., rev. and enl. with an app. containing letters addressed by J: Q. Adams to his son, on the study of the Bible. Bost. 1848. D.   **826.1 : 3**

Smith, Abigail, *born* Adams. Correspondence ; ed. by her daughter [mrs. C. A. De Windt]. *T. p. w.* D.   **826.1 : 4**

Washington, G: Official letters to the honorable american congress, written during the war between the United Colonies and Great Britain. Bost. 1795. 2 v. D.   **826.1 : 11**

— Reprint of the original letters from Washington to Joseph Reed during the american revolution, referred to in the pamphlets of lord Mahon and mr. Sparks. by W: B. Reed. Phila. 1852. O.   **826.1 : 5**

— **Butterfield, Consul Willshire,** *ed.* The Washington-Crawford letters ; the correspondence between G: Washington and W: Crawford, from 1767 to 1781, concerning western lands ; with an app. containing later letters of Washington on the same subject, and letters from Valentine Crawford to Washington, written in 1774 and

Washington, G:—Continued.

1775, chronologically arr. and carefully annotated. Cinc. 1877. O.   **826.1+7**

— — The Washington-Irvine correspondence ; the official letters which passed between Washington and brig.-gen. W: Irvine and between Irvine and others, concerning military affairs in the west from 1781 to 1783, arr. and annotated, with an introd. containing an outline of events occuring previously in the trans-Alleghany country. Ill. Madison, Wis. 1882. O.   **826.1+6**

Cowper, W: Private correspondence with several of his most intimate friends now first pub. from the originals in the possession of his kinsman J: Johnson. 1st amer. ed. Phila. 1824. O.   **826.2 : 16**

Burns, Robert. The correspondence between Burns and Clarinda ; with a memoir of mrs. M'Lehose (Clarinda). arr. and ed. by her grandson, W. C. M'Lehose. Edinb. 1843. D.   **826.2 : 26**

— [Letters]. *In his* Works.   **820.2+P33**

Napier, Macvey. Selection from [his] correspondence ; ed. by his son, Macvey Napier. Lond. 1879. O.   **826.2 : 8**

Austen, Jane. Letters ; ed. with an introd. and critical remarks by Edward, lord Brabourne. Lond. 1884. 2 v. O.   **826.2 : 33**

More, Hannah. Letters to Zachary Macaulay containing notices of lord Macaulay's youth, now first pub.; ed. and arr. by Arthur Roberts. N. Y. 1860. S. **826.2 : 24**

Keats, J: Letters to Fanny Brawne, written in 1819 and 1820 and now given from the original mss., with introd. and notes by Harry Buxton Forman. N. Y. 1878. D. **826.2 : 5**

Lamb, C: Literary sketches and letters, being the final memorials of C: Lamb, never before pub., by T: Noon Talfourd. 2d ed. N. Y. 1849. D.   **826.2 : 23**

Hunt, James H: Leigh. Correspondence ; ed. by his eldest son. Portr. Lond. 1862. 2 v. D.   **826.2 : 31**

Southey, Robert, *and* Caroline Anne Southey, *born* Bowles. Correspondence ; added, correspondence with Shelley and Southey's Dreams ; ed. with an introd. by E: Dowden. Dublin. 1881. O.   **826.2 : 34**

Scott, *Sir* Walter. Paul's letters to his kinsfolk. [*Anon.*] Edinb. 1816. O.   **826.2 : 11**

Lockhart, J: Gibson, (*Peter Morris*). Peter's letters to his kinsfolk. 1st amer. ed. N. Y. 1820. O.   **826.2 : 6**

Channing, W: Ellery, *and* Lucy Aikin. Correspondence, from 1826 to 1842 ; ed. by Anna Letitia Le Breton. Bost. 1874. D.   **826 : 1**

L'Estrange, Alfred Guy Kingham, *ed.* Friendships of Mary Russell Mitford, as recorded in letters from her literary correspondents. N. Y. 1882. D.   **826.2 : 18**

— *Same* N. Y. 1882. Q.   **826.2+18**

Webster, Daniel. Private correspondence ; ed. by Fletcher Webster. Bost. 1857. 2 v. O.   **826.1+8**

Disraeli, B:, *earl of Beaconsfield.* Home letters, written in 1830 and 1831. Ill. N. Y. 1885. S: **826.2 : 36**

Note. Written from Gibraltar, Spain, Malta, the Ionian Islands, Egypt, etc.

Dickens, C: J: Huffam. Letters; ed. by his sister-in-law [Georgina Hogarth] and his eldest daughter [Mamie Dickens]. N. Y. 1879–1881. 3 v. D. **826.2 : 2**
Contents. V. 1. 1833–1856. 2. 1857–1870. 3. 1836–1870.

Carlyle, Jane, *born* Welsh. Letters and memorials; prepared for publication by T: Carlyle. ed. by James Anthony Froude. Authorized ed. N. Y. 1883. 2 v. in 1. D. **826.2 : 27**
— *Same.* N. Y. 1883. Q. **826.2+27**

Carlyle, T:, *and* Ralph Waldo **Emerson**. Correspondence, 1834–1872. Bost. 1883. 2 v. D. **826 : 3**

Ruskin, J: Arrows of the chace; a collection of scattered letters, pub. chiefly in the daily newspapers, 1840–1880, and now ed. by an Oxford pupil, with pref. by the author. N. Y. 1881. 2 v. in 1. O. **826.2 : 9**
Contents. V. 1. Letters on art and science. Letters on art: Art criticism and art education; Public institutions and the national gallery; Pre-raphaelitism; Turner; Pictures and artists; Architecture and restoration.—Letters on science: Geological; Miscellaneous. 2. Letters on politics, economy and miscellaneous matters. On politics and war.—On political economy.—Miscellaneous letters: The management of railways; Servants and houses; Roman inundations; Education for rich and poor; Women, their work and dress; Literary criticism.—App.—Epilogue.—Chronological list of letters in both vols.—Index.

Thirlwall, Connop. Letters to a friend; ed. by Arthur Penrhyn Stanley. Bost. 1883. D. **826.2 : 28**

Child, Lydia Maria, *born* Francis. Letters; with a biographical introd. by J: G. Whittier and an app. by Wendell Phillips. Bost. 1883 [1882]. S. **826.1 : 9**

Rogers, H: The Greyson letters; selections from the correspondence of R. E. H. Greyson, [pseud. for Rogers himself]. Bost. 1857. D. **826.2 : 22**

Gordon, C: G: Letters from the Crimea, the Danube and Armenia, aug. 18, 1854 to nov. 17, 1858; ed. by Demetrius C. Boulger. Lond. 1884. D. **826.2 : 35**

11. English literature — g, Satire and Humor.

1. Satire and parodies.

Hamilton, Walter. Parodies of the works of english and american authors collected and annotated, v. 1, 2. Lond. 1884–85. O. **827 : 1**
Contents. V. 1. Alfred lord Tennyson.—H: Wadsworth Longfellow. — Bret Harte. — T: Hood. — C. Wolfe. 2. Alfred lord Tennyson.—H: Wadsworth Longfellow.—Bret Harte.—T: Hood. — Edgar Allan Poe.—Ann Taylor.—Shakespeare's plays.—I: Watts.—J: Milton.—Matthew Arnold.—J: Dryden.

Ashton, J: English caricature and satire on Napoleon 1. Ill. N. Y. 1884. 2 v. O. **827.2 : 5**

Bates, Arlo. Mr. Jacobs; a tale of the drummer, the reporter and the prestidigitateur. [*Anon.*] Bost. 1883. T. **827.1 : 10**
Note. A parody on Mr. Isaacs by F. M. Crawford.

Buck, James Smith. The chronicles of the land of Columbia, commonly called America, from the landing of the pilgrim fathers to the second reign of Ulysses I, a period of 252 years, by the prophet James. Milw. 1876. O. **827.1 : 1**

Cooke, C: Wallwyn Radcliffe, (*Angelina Gushington*). Thoughts on men and things. N. Y. 1872. D. **827.2 : 2**

Coverdale, *Sir* Henry Standish, *pseud.* The fall of the great republic, 1886–88. Bost. 1885. S. **827.2 : 6**

Curtis, G: W: The Potiphar papers. N. Y. 1858. D. **827.1 : 7**

Harte, Francis Bret. Condensed novels. Ill. Bost. 1871. D. **827.1 : 2**
Contents. Handsome is as handsome does, by Ch-s R-de. — Lothaw, by Mr. Benjamins. — Muck-a-Muck, after Cooper. — Terence Denville, by Ch-l-s L-v-r. — Selina Sedilia, by miss M. E. B-dd-n and mrs. H-n-y W-d.—The ninety-nine guardsmen, by Al-x-d-r D-m-s. — The dweller of the threshold, by sir Ed-d L-tt-n B-lw-r.—The haunted man, by Ch-r-s D-ck-ns. —Miss Mix, by Ch-l-tte Br-nte.—Guy Heavystone, by the author of "Sword and gun." — Mr. Midshipman Breezy, by Captain M-rry-t, R. N.—John Jenkins, by T. S. A-th-r.

Jenkins, E: Ginx's baby, his birth and other misfortunes; a satire. [*Anon.*] N. Y. 1872. D. **827.2 : 1**
— Lord Bantam; a satire by the author of "Ginx's baby." N. Y. 187-. D. **827.2 : 7**

Locke, D: Ross, (*Petroleum Vesuvius Nasby*). Nasby; divers opinions and prophecies of yoors trooly Petroleum V. Nasby. Ill. 6th ed. Cinc. 1867. D. **827.1 : 5**
— "Swingin round the cirkle" by Petroleum V. Nasby, late pastor of the church of the new dispensation, chaplain to his excellency the president and P. M. at Confederate × roads, Kentucky; his ideas of men, politics and things as set forth in his letters to the public press during the year 1866. Ill. Bost. 1867. D. **827.1 : 12**
— Ekkoes from Kentucky by Petroleum V. Nasby; bein a perfect record uv de ups, downs, and experiences uv the democrisy, doorin the eventful year 1867, ez seen by a naturalized kentuckian. Ill. by T. Nast. Bost. 1868. D. **827.1 : 6**

Mahan, Milo. The comedy of canonization; in four scenes. [*Anon.*] 3d thous. N. Y. 1868. D. **827.1 : R4**

Marshall, T: W: M. The comedy of convocation in the English church, in two scenes; ed. by archdeacon Chasuble. N. Y. 1868. D. **827.1 : 3**

Peace parliament, The, or The reconstruction creed of christendom. Bost. [1879]. S. **827.2 : 3**

Reed, S: Rockwell. The war of 1886 between the U. S. and Great Britain; the surprising experience, the military and financial situation of our beloved country, capture of the lake, seaboard and Mississippi river cities and the capital, the british terms of peace, the military and financial reconstruction. 2d ed. Cinc. 1882. D. **827.1 : 8**

Strong, G: A. (*Marc Anthony Henderson*.) The song of Milkanwatha; tr. from the original Feejee. Ill. by Frank Beard. 3d ed. Albany. 1883. S. **827.1 : 11**

Swift, Jonathan. Gulliver's travels into several remote nations of the world ; with introd. and explan. notes by Robert Mackenzie. Facsimiles of the original maps etc. of the work and ill. Lond. 1883. D.   827.2 : 4
— Same. In his Works.   820.2 : 21 v2

2. Wit and humor.

Hazlitt, W: Lectures on the English comic writers. Phila. 1848. D.   828.5 : 1
Contents. Introductory; On wit and humour. — Shakspeare and Ben Johnson. — Cowley, Butler, Suckling, Etheredge, etc. — Wycherley, Congreve, Vanbrugh and Farquhar.—The periodical essayists.— The english novelists. — The works of Hogarth.—The comic writers of the last century.

Hazlitt, W: Carew, ed. Shakespeare jest-books ; reprints of the early and very rare jest-books supposed to have been used by Shakespeare, ed. with introd. and notes. Lond. 1864. 3 v. D.   828.2 : P20
Contents. V. 1. A hundred mery talys; from the only known copy.—Mery tales and quicke answeres from the rare ed. of 1567. 2. Merie tales of Skelton.— Jests of Scogin. — Sackfull of newes. — Tarleton's jests. — Merrie conceited jests of George Peele.— Jacke of Dover. 3. Merie tales of the mad men of Gotham.—XII mery jests of the widow Edyth.—Pasquils jests, with mother Bunches merriments.—The pleasant conceits of old Hobson. — Certayne conceits and jeasts.—Taylors wit and mirth.—Conceits, clinches, flashes and whimsies.

Ashton, J:, comp. Humor, wit and satire of the 17th century ; collected and ill. N. Y. 1884 [1883]. D.   828.2 : 19
Adams, W: Davenport, ed. Quips and quiddities ; a quintessence of quirks, quaint, quizzable and quotable. Lond. 1881. S.   828 : 2
Burton, W: Evans. The cyclopædia of wit and humor ; containing choice and characteristic selections from the writings of the most eminent humorists of America, Ireland, Scotland and England. Ill. N. Y. 1875. O.   828+1
— Same. N. Y. 1858. 2 v. in 4. Q.   828 : R1
Sanborn, Kate, ed. The wit of women. N. Y. 1885. D.   828 : 3
Enchiridion, The, of wit ; the best specimens of english conversational wit. Phila. 1884. O.   828.2 : 21
Comic almanack, The ; an ephemeris in jest and earnest, containing merry tales, humorous poetry, quips and oddities by Thackeray, Albert Smith, Gilbert A'Beckett, the brothers Mayhew. Ill. by G: Cruikshank and other artists. 1st ser. 1835—1843 ; 2d ser. 1844—1853. Lond. n. d. 2 v. D.   828.2 : 18

*   *   *

Anstey, J:, (John Surrebutter, esq.) The pleader's guide, a didactic poem, containing the conduct of a suit at law, with the arguments of counsellor Bother'um and counsellor Bore'um, in an action betwixt John-a-Gull and John-a-Gudgeon, for assault and battery. Amer. ed. by James L. High, with notes. Chicago. 1871. D. With Beckett, G. A. À', Comic Blackstone.   in 828.2 : 1
Arbuthnot, J: Miscellaneous works ; with an account of the author's life. Lond. 1770. 2 v. S.   828.2 : 2
Contents, see Catalogue of the Boston athenaeum, v. 1, p. 124.

Beckett, Gilbert Abbott À'. The comic Blackstone. Ill. Chicago. 1871. D.   828.2 : 1
Browne, C: Farrar, (Artemus Ward). Artemus Ward his travels : pt. 1, Miscellaneous ; pt. 2, Among the mormons. Ill. N. Y. 1865. D.   828.1 : 3
— Artemus Ward in London, and other papers. Ill. N. Y. 1867. D.   828.1 : 2
Burnand, Francis Cowley. Happy - thought Hall. Ill. Bost. 1872. D.   828.2 : 4
— Happy thoughts. Bost. 1878. S.   828.2 : 3
Carleton, G: W. Our artist in Peru, 50 drawings on wood ; leaves from the sketch-book of a traveller during the winter of 1865-6. N. Y. 1866. D.   828.1 : 33
Clemens, S: Langhorne, (Mark Twain). Mark Twain's sketches, new and old. Hartford. 1875. O.   828.1 : 19
— Roughing it. Ill. Hartford, Conn. 1878. O.   828.1 : 29
Cozzens, F: Swartout. The Sparrowgrass papers, or Living in the country. N. Y. 1856. D.   828.1 : 4
Derby, G: Horatio, (John Phœnix). Phœnixiana, or Sketches and burlesques by John Phœnix. 12th ed. N. Y. 1863. D.   828.1 : 5
Halpine, C: Graham, (Private Miles O' Reilly). The life and adventures, songs, services and speeches of private Miles O'Reilly. Ill. N. Y. 1864. D.   828.1 : 6
Harris, Joel Chandler. Uncle Remus, his songs and his sayings ; the folk-lore of the old plantation. Ill. N. Y. 1884. D. 828.1 : 7
— Nights with Uncle Remus ; myths and legends of the old plantation. Bost. 1883. D.   828.1 : 8
Holley, Marietta. My opinions and Betsey Bobbet's ; designed as a beacon light to guide women to life, liberty and the pursuit of happiness, but which may be read by members of the sterner sex without injury to themselves or the book. [Anon.] Hartford. 1883. O.   828.1 : 31
Hood, T: [Our family, and other writings.] T. p. w. D.   828.2 : 6
Contents. Our family.—Comic miscellany. — Autobiographical poems.
— Whimsicalities. Ill. N. Y. 1852. D. 828.2 : 7
Irving, Washington. A history of New York from the beginning of the world to the end of the Dutch dynasty . . . , by Diedrich Knickerbocker. Author's rev. ed. N. Y. 1856. S.   828.1 : 9
"Containing, among many surprising and curious matters, the unutterable ponderings of Walter the doubter, the disastrous projects of William the testy, and the chivalrous achievements of Peter the headstrong, the three dutch governors of New Amsterdam, being the only authentic history of the times that ever hath been or ever will be published."
— Same. In his Works.
820.1 : 13 v5, 820.1 : P11 v1
Jerrold, Douglas W: Cakes and ale. T. p. w. [Lond. 1852]. S.   828.2 : 8
— Fireside saints. Mr. Caudle's breakfast talk, and other papers ; now first coll. Bost. 1873. S.   828.2 : 9
— Men of character. Lond. 1851. D. 828.2 : 10
— Punch's letters to his son. Lond. 1853. S.   828.2 : 11
— Punch's complete letter writer. With his Punch's letters to his son.   in 828.2 : 11
— Sketches of the english. With his Punch's letters to his son.   in 828.2 : 11

Kingsbury, J: H. Kingsbury sketches; a truthful and succinct account of the doings and misdoings of the inhabitants of Pine Grove, their private trials and public tribulations. N. Y. 1875. D.   **828.1 : 10**

Landon, Melville D., *(Eli Perkins).* Saratoga in 1901, by Eli Perkins. Ill. N. Y. 1872. O.   **828.1 : 11**

Leland, H: Perry. The grey-bay mare, and humorous american sketches. Ill. Phila. 1861. D.   **828.1 : 12**

Lewis, C: B., *(M. Quad, the Detroit free press man).* Quad's odds; anecdote, humor and pathos and other things, a book never offered to the public before. Ill. Detroit. 1875. O.   **828.1 : 34**

Locke, D: Ross, *(Petroleum Vesuvius Nasby.)* Eastern fruit on western dishes: The morals of Abou Ben Adhem. Bost. 1875. D.   **828.1 : 13**

Meadows, Kenny. Heads of the people, or Portraits of the english, drawn by Kenny Meadows, with original essays by Douglas Jerrold, W: Thackeray, Laman Blanchard, S: Lover, Leman Rede, Leigh Hunt, mrs. Gore, mrs. S. C. Hall, W: Howitt and others. Lond. 1864. 2 v. O.   **828.2 : 12**

Mitchell, Donald Grant, *(Ik Marvel.)* Fudge doings; being Tom Fudge's record of the same in forty chapters, by Ik Marvel. N. Y. 1855. 2 v. D.   **828.1 : 14**

Morford, H: Sprees and splashes, or Droll recollections of town and country; a book for railroad rides and odd half-hours. N. Y. 1863. D.   **828.1 : 15**

Morris, James W., *(Jacques Maurice).* K. N. pepper and other condiments, put up for general use. N. Y. 1859. D.   **828.1 : 16**

Neal, Joseph Clay. Charcoal sketches, or Scenes in a metropolis. Ill. Phila. [1843]. D.   **828.1 : 32**

Newell, Robert H: *(Orpheus C. Kerr).* The Orpheus C. Kerr papers; a complete contemporaneous military history of the Mackerel brigade, a series of unparalleled strategetical exploits on land and water, and unprecedented struggles for the union and its presidency, in the war with the southern confederacy. N. Y. 1871. 2 v. in 1 D.   **828.1 : 17**

Peck, G: Wilbur. Peck's fun; extracts from the La-Crosse sun, and Peck's sun, Milwaukee ...; comp. by V. W. Richardson. Chicago. 1880. D.   **828.1 : 30**

Prentice, G: Denison. Prenticeana, or Wit and humor in paragraphs, by the editor of the Louisville journal. N. Y. 1860. D.   **828.1 : 20**

Riley, H. H. The Puddleford papers, or Humors of the west. Ill. Bost. 1882. D. **828.1 : 27**

Russell, M. C. Uncle Dudley's odd hours; the vagaries of a country editor. Also, as an app., J. Proctor Knott's famous speech on Duluth. Duluth, Minn. 1882. D.   **828.1 : 28**

Sherwood, J: D. The comic history of the U. S. New ed. Boston. 1881. D.   **828.1 : 25**

Shillaber, B: Penhallow, *(Mrs. Partington).* Partingtonian patchwork. Bost. 1873. D.   **828.1 : 21**
Contents. Blifkins the martyr; the domestic trials of a model husband. — The modern syntax; dr. Spooner's experiences in search of the delectable. — Partington papers; strippings of the warm milk of human kindness. — New and old dips from an unambitious inkstand.

Smith, C: H., *(Bill Arp).* Bill Arp's peace papers. Ill. N. Y. 1873. D.   **828.1 : 18**

Smith, Horace, *(Paul Chatfield, M. D.)* The tin trumpet, or Heads and tales for the wise and waggish. New amer. ed. with alterations and add. N. Y. 1859. D.   **828.2 : 5**

Thackeray, W: Makepeace. Mr. Brown's letters to a man about town, with The proser and other papers. N. Y. 1853. S.   **828.2 : 14**
Contents. Mr. Brown's letters to a young man about town: Introductory; On tailoring and toilettes in general; The influence of lovely woman upon society; Some more words about the ladies; On friendship; Mr. Brown the elder takes mr. Brown the younger to a club; A word about balls in season; A word about dinners; On some old customs at the dinner table; Great and little dinners; On love, marriage, men and women; On friendship; Out of town. — The proser: On a lady in an opera box; On the pleasures of being a fogy; On the benefits of being a fogy.—Miscellanies: Child's parties; The story of Koompanee Jehan; Science at Cambridge; A dream of Whitefriars; Mr. Punch's address to the great city of Castlebar; Irish gems; The Charles II ball; The Georges; Death of the earl of Robinson.

— *Same.* [Bound with the following]. **828.2 : 15**

— Punch's prize novelists, The fat contributor, and Travels in London. N. Y. 1853. S. *With his* Mr. Brown's letters. *in* **828.2 : 15**
Contents. Punch's prize novelists: G: De Barnwell; Phil. Fogarty; Barbazure; Lords and liveries; Codlingsby.—The fat contributor: Brighton; Meditations over Brighton; A Brighton night entertainment; Brighton in 1847; Travelling notes; Punch in the east.—Travels in London: The curate's walk; A dinner in the city; A club in an uproar; Waiting at the station; A night's pleasure. — Going to see a man hanged.

— Sketches and travels in London; Novels by eminent hands; Character sketches. *T. p. w.*   **828.2 : 16**
Contents. Same as Mr. Brown's letters *and* Punch's prize novelists, with character sketches; Captain Rook and Mr. Pigeon; The fashionable authoress; The artists.

— Thackerayana, notes and anecdotes; depicting humorous incidents in his school life and favourite scenes and characters in the books of his every-day reading. New ed. Ill. Lond. *n. d.* D.   **828.2 : 17**

Thompson, Mortimer N., *(Q. K. Philander Doesticks, P. B.)* Plu-ri-bus-tah, a song that's by no author, a deed without a name perpetrated by Q. K. Philander Doesticks. N. Y. 1856. D.   **828.1 : 22**

— The witches of New York as encountered by Q. K. Philander Doesticks, P. B. N. Y. 1859. S.   **828.1 : 23**

Whitcher, Frances Miriam, *born* Berry. The widow Bedott papers; with an introd. by A. B. Neal. New add. N. Y. 1883. D.   **828.1 : 26**

12. English literature — h, Miscellany.

1. Collections.

Waller, J: Francis. Pictures from english litera-
ture. Ill. Lond. *n. d.* O.   **829.2+27**
Contents. **Chaucer,** G. Griseld. — **Spenser,** E.
Una.—**Shakespeare,** W: Falstaff.—**Milton,** J: The
lady in Comus.—**Addison.** J. Sir Roger de Coverley.
—**Fielding,** H: Sophia Western.—**Sterne,** L. The
Shandies. — **Sheridan,** R. S. The rivals. — **Gold-
smith,** O. The vicar of Wakefield.— **Cowper,** W:
John Gilpin.—**Burns,** R. Tam O'Shanter.—**Colman,**
G:, *jr.* The heir-at-law. — **Scott,** *Sir* W. Jeanie
Deans.— **Coleridge,** S: T. The ancient mariner. —
Campbell, T: Gertrude of Wyoming. — **Byron,**
Lord. Haidée.—**Lytton,** *Lord.* Nydia.—**Thackeray,**
W: M. Colonel Newcome.—**Dickens,** C: Pecksniff.
—**Tennyson,** A. Dora.

Hunt, James H: Leigh, *ed.* A book for a corner,
or Selections in prose and verse from
authors the best suited to that mode of
enjoyment, with comments on each and a
general introd. 2 ser. in 1. N. Y. 1852. D.
                                        829.2 : 16
Contents, see Catalogue of the Boston athenæum,
v. 2, p. 1474.
— *Same.* 2d ser. N. Y. 1852. D. **829.2 : 16 v2**

Jerrold, W: Blanchard, *ed.* The best of all good
company. 1st series : C: Dickens, Walter
Scott, W. M. Thackeray, Douglas Jerrold.
Ill. Boston. 1875. O.   **829.2 : 67**

Ashton, J: Chap-books of the 18th century,
with fac-similes, notes and introd. Lond.
1882. D.   **829.2 : 50**

Small books on great subjects ; v. 1–3. [*Anon.*]
Phila. 1847. S.   **829.2 : 48**
Contents. V. 1. **Cornwallis,** C. F. Philosophical
inquiries and philosophical experience by a pariah.—
Barlow, J: The connection between physiology and
intellectual philosophy. — **Barlow,** J: On man's
power over himself to prevent or control insanity.—
Cornwallis, C. F. An introduction to practical
organic chemistry. 2. **Cornwallis,** C. F. A brief
view of greek philosophy up to the age of Pericles.—
Cornwallis, C. F. A brief view of greek philosophy
from the age of Socrates to the coming of Christ.—
Cornwallis, C. F. Christian doctrine and practice
in the 2d century. — **Cornwallis,** C. F., (*Thomas
Brown redivivus*). An exposition of vulgar and common errors adapted to 1845. 3. An introduction to
vegetable physiology with references to De Candolle,
Lindley, etc.—On the principles of criminal law. —
Cornwallis, C. F. Christian sects in the 19th century.—**Cornwallis,** C. F. The general principles of
grammar.

Aikin, J:, *and* Anna Lætitia **Barbauld.** Evenings at home, or The juvenile budget
opened. Rev. ed. from the 15th Lond. ed.
Ill. N. Y. 1855. D.   **x829.2 : 65**

Chambers, W: *and* Robert, *eds.* Miscellany of
instructive and entertaining tracts. New
and rev. ed. Edinb. 1869–72. 20 v. D.
                                        829.2 : 4
Contents. V. **1.** Life of G: Stephenson.—Maurice
and Genevieve. — Picciola, or The prison flower.—
Abyssinia and Theodore.— Cases of circumstantial
evidence.—The last earl of Derwentwater.—Home
plants, water animals, and the aquarium. — Anecdotes of dogs.—The heroine of Siberia.—Poems of
the domestic affections.
2. Lord Dundonald.—Journal of a poor vicar.—
Blanche Raymond.—Romance of geology.—Laroche-
jaquelein and the war in La Vendée.—Anecdotes of
the horse.—Story of Peter Williamson.—Curiosities
of vegetation.—Children of the wilds.—Select poems
on love for flowers.
3. Life of Nelson. — The goldmakers' village. —
Story of the indian mutiny.—Story of Silvio Pellico.
—William Tell and Switzerland.— The herring and

x denotes books specially adapted for children.

the whale.—Scottish traditionary stories.—Selections
from american poetry.
4. Wallace and Bruce. — The village mayor. —
Anecdotes of ants.—Shipwreck of the Medusa.—History of Poland.—Arctic explorations.— Flora Macdonald.—It's only a drop.—Select poems from Cowper.
5. Louis Napoleon, emperor of the french.—Love
is power.— Anecdotes of spiders. — Adventures of
Robert Drury.—Account of the borders.—The plague
in London.—Mutiny of the Bounty.—Select poetry of
Scott.
6. Captain Cook.—Earthquakes and volcanos.—A
tale of Norfolk island.—The two beggar boys.—The
widow's son.—Anecdotes of the deaf, dumb, and
blind.—Story of R: Falconer.—Byron's narrative of
the loss of the Wager.—History of the mormons.—
The scottish adventurers.—Walter Ruysdael.—Poems
on kindness to animals.
7. Joan of Arc, maid of Orleans.—Annals of the
poor.—Gold and gold-diggers.—Traditionary tales of
Tweeddale. — There is no hurry ! — Abby's year in
Lowell.—Anecdotes of elephants.—The russian campaign.—The ancient mariner, and other poems.
8. Life of Washington.—Hinduism. — Intelligent
negroes.—Visit to Shetland.—Story of Lavalette.—
Religious impostors.—Wonders and curiosities of
architecture.—Time enough.—Chevy chase.
9. William, prince of Orange.—Anecdotes of the
cat and the rat.—The sun.—Story of Colbert.—Happy
families of animals.—The story of Valentine Duval.
—The moors in Spain.—The man with the iron mask.
—Visit to Vesuvius and Pompeii.—The hermit of
Warkworth, etc.
10. Life of sir Walter Scott.—Wonders and curiosities of civil engineering.—Life assurance.—Passion
and principle.—The ancient cave-men of Devonshire.
—Life of a sailor boy.—Madame Roland.— The norman conquest.—Selections from Shakspeare.
11. Life of Peter the great.—The stranger's visit
to Edinburg.— Wonders of the microscope.—The
story of De la Tude.—Mrs. Macclarty.—The persecutions in Scotland.—The christmas holiday.—Be just
before you are generous.—The heir of Linne, and
other ballads.
12. Life of Columbus.—Stories of aims and ends.
—A lord provost's holiday.—Story of a french prisoner of war in England.—H: Arnaud and the waldenses.—Heroism in humble life.— Prince Le Boo.—
Sir Stamford Raffles and the Malayan Archipelago.—
Poems by G: Crabbe.
13. Life of Henry IV of France.—Anecdotes of
serpents. — Story of Alexander Andrayne. — Helen
Gray.—France; its revolutions and misfortunes.—
The Montyon prizes.— Three ways of living.—The
childe of Elle, and other ballads.
14. Life of Howard.— Names of persons. —The
magic flute.—Why the sea is salt.—Account of the
gipsies.—Elizabeth Stuart and the palatinate.—The
Camisards.—Women's trials in humble life.—Selections from french and german poetry.
15. Life of W: Hutton.— The deserters. — Pearls
and pearl fisheries. — Moral tales from the french.—
Gustavus Adolphus and the thirty years' war.—The
sister of Rembrandt.—Eminent astronomers.—Poems
on birds.
16. Life of W: Penn.—Do you think I'd inform?—
The schoolmaster's dream. — The crusades. — Anecdotes of shoemakers. — Monuments of unrecorded
ages.—Speculative manias.—Valerie Duclos. — Selections from Byron.
17. Life of James Watt. — The little captive king.
— The pilgrim fathers. — History of the Bastille. —
Anecdotes of the early painters. — Life of Alexander
Selkirk.—The wooden spoon.—The Tintoretto. — History of William Jones.
18. Sir W: Jones, etc. — Excursion to the Oregon.
—The friendly arrest, a tale. — The british conquest
of India.—The old witchcrafts.—Conquest of Mexico.
—The stranger's visit to London.—Poems on insects.
19. Life of Oberlin. — Scenes from peasant life in
Norway.—Quintin Matsys.—Life and travels of Burckhardt. — Leon Gondy; a legend of Ghent. — Rob Roy
and the clan McGregor.—Toussaint L'Ouverture and
Hayti.—Jim Cronin.— Songs of home and fatherland.
20. Count Rumford. — The guerilla. — History of
the jews in England. — Arnold and André.— African
discovery. — The hope of Leascombe. — Spectral illusions.—Selections from the Elizabethan poets.

Chambers, W:, *ed.* Miscellany of useful and entertaining knowledge ; v. 1—4, 6—8, 10. Bost. *n. d.* 8 v. S.   **829.2 : 5**

Contents. V. 1. The life of Louis Philippe, king of the french.—A tale of Norfolk Island. — Story of Colbert.—Happy family of animals. — The employer and employed.—Time enough; a tale by mrs. S. C. Hall.—My native bay. — Manual for infant management. — Picciola, or The prison flower. — Life in the bush. — William Tell and Switzerland.—The two beggar boys. The widow's son, by Mrs. Stone.—Select poems of the domestic affections. — Life of Grace Darling, etc. — Volney Beckner.—James Maxwell.—Story of Maurice and Genevieve.—Religious impostors.—Anecdotes of dogs.—La Rochejaquelein and the war in La Vendée. —Journal of a poor vicar.—Blanche Raymond; a parisian story.—The romance of geology.—History of the slave trade. — Story of Walter Ruysdale, the watchmaker.—Chevy Chase.—Beggar's daughter of Bethnal Green.
2. Life of Lord Nelson. — The temperance movement.—Story of P: Williamson. — Joan of Arc, maid of Orleans. — Annals of the poor. — Slavery in America.— A visit to Vesuvius. Pompeii and Herculaneum.—Story of Baptiste Lulli, the boy musician.— Select poems of kindness to animals. — William Wallace and Robert Bruce. — Cases of circumstantial evidence.— Story of R. Falconer. — Byron's narrative of the loss of the *Wager*.—The goldmaker's village.—The last earl of Derwentwater.—The heroine of Siberia.— Domestic flour culture.—Insurrections in Lyons.—The hermit of Warkworth, and other ballads.
3. Life of capt. James Cook.—Anecdotes of the horse. — William of Orange and the Netherlands. — Passion and principle; a tale from the french.—Life insurance, a familiar dialogue.—Excursion to the Oregon.—Mrs. Macclarty; scenes from the "Cottagers of Glenburnie."—The little captive king.— Children of the wilds. —Select poems on love for flowers. — Life of Flora McDonald.—Cleanliness, bathing, ventilation.—Anecdotes of the deaf, dumb and blind. — Sir Stamford Raffles and the Spice Islands. — The sister of Rembrandt; a flemish story.—Anecdotes of the cat. — It's only a drop; an irish tale by mrs. S. C. Hall. — Toussaint L'Ouverture and the republic of Hayti.—Curiosities of vegetation.—The ancient mariner, and other poems by Coleridge.
4. Life of Washington. — Anecdotes of elephants. — The story of Lavalette. — Intelligent negroes. — A visit to Madeira and Teneriffe. — The life of a sailor boy.—Hindoo superstitions.—The story of Valentine Duval. — The history of Will and Jean; a ballad. — Life of W: Hutton. — Spectral illusions. — Prince Le Boo.—The Tintoretto.—History of Poland.—The scottish adventurers. — A visit to Shetland. — Story of baron Trenck. — The heir of Linne, and other ballads.
6. Life of Christopher Columbus. — Narrative of the russian campaign. — Love is power. — The story of Alexander Andrayne. — Anecdotes of spiders.—The village mayor by Zschokke.—The story of Fritz Körner. — The bird catcher and his canary.— An account of the borders.—Select poetical pieces of W: Cowper. — Life of Peter the great. — The story of De la Tude. — The moors of Spain. — The Montyon prizes. — Curiosities of art, 1: Architecture. — The persecutions in Scotland.— The three ways of living. — The child of Elle, and other ballads.
7. Life of J: Howard, the philanthropist. — Curiosities of art, 2: Mechanics, Manufactures. — The Camisards. — Anecdotes of shoemakers. — Story of a french prisoner of war in England.—Rob Roy and the clan MacGregor.—There is no hurry; a tale of life assurance, by mrs. S. C. Hall. — Abby's year in Lowell; a tale of self-denial. — Selections from american poets.—Gustavus Adolphus and the thirty years' war. —The stranger's visit to Edinburgh. — Narrative of the mutiny of the *Bounty*. — The Ettrick shepherd. — History of the plague in London. — Schools of industry.—Quintin Matsys, the blacksmith of Antwerp. —Selections from Shakspeare.
8. Life of W: Penn.—"Do you think I'd inform ?" by mrs. S. C. Hall. — The schoolmaster's dream, by mrs. S. C. Hall.—Treasures of the earth, 1: Minerals.—The man with the iron mask.—The norman conquest. — Life and travels of Burckhardt.—The christmas holiday. — Be just before you are generous. — Selections from french and german poetry.—Life of James Watt. — Pictures of war. — Stories of alms and ends. — Account of the gipsies. — Life of Alexander Selkirk. — Account of the Highlands. — African discovery.—Select poems on insects.

10. Life of count Rumford. — The crusades. — Women's trials in humble life.—Overland journey to India.—Moral tales, from the french.—History of the Bastille.—Pearls and pearl fisheries.—Selections from Byron.— Eminent astronomers. — Hints to workmen. —The guerilla; a story of the peninsular war. — Speculative manias.— Four months in Cape Colony. — A selection of english and scotch proverbs. — Wonders of the telescope.—Jim Cronin; an irish tale, by mrs. Hoare.—Songs of home and fatherland.

Dickens, C: J: Huffam, *ed.* Household words ; [reprinted]. Leipz. 1851-56. 36 v. in 18. S.   **829.2 : 62**

Timbs, J: Things not generally known, familiarly explained ; a book for old and young. Lond. 1880. 12 v. S.   **829.2 : 64**

Contents. 1st series. Marvels of the heavens.—The earth, its surface and interior. — The sea.— The atmosphere.—Sight and sound. — Geographical discovery.—Life and death.—Animal kingdom. — Trees and plants. — Natural magic. — Domestic manners. — The calendar. — Laws and customs. — Church and state.— Parliament.—Nationalities.— Dignities.—Science, the arts and manufactures.—Money.— Art-terms.— Language and books.
2d series. Old english manners, ceremonies and customs.— Olden meals and house-wifery. — Punch and Judy, old plays, pageants and music. — English laws, legal customs, privileges and dignities.—Money, weights and measures. — Olden herbs and fruit. — Phenomena and life. — Funeral customs and ceremonies. — Home proverbs, sayings and phrases. — Weather-wisdom. — Pictures and the care of them. — Inventions and discoveries.
[3d series]. Curiosities of science; v. 1. Introd. Physical phenomena. — Sound and light. — Astronomy. — Geology and paleontology. — Meteorological phenomena. — Physical geography of the sea. — Phenomena of heat. — Magnetism and electricity. — The electric telegraph.—Miscellanea.
[4th series]. Curiosities of science ; v. 2. Alchemy and chemistry. — Modern chemistry. — Chemistry of metals. — Poisons. — Hippocrates. — Physiological chemistry. — Chemistry of food. — The laboratory. — Chemical manufactures. — General science.—A chapter on chloroform.—App.
[5th series]. Curiosities of history. The sacred story. — Greece and Rome, Babylon and Carthage, etc. — Legendary and fabulous. — Voyages, travels and adventures. — Modern history. — British history. — The seven wonders of the world. — Historic sayings and origins. — Ensigns, laws and government. — Historic doubts. — Miscellanea.
[6th series]. Popular errors explained. Errors respecting the economy of man. — Erroneous views of natural phenomena. — Errors in the progress of society. — Errors in science, art and invention. — Erroneous and traditional history.—Errors in natural history. — Fabulous animals. — Superstition and credulity. — Erroneous laws and customs. — Errors in domestic history.—Miscellanea.
[7th series]. Notable things of our own time. Introd. — Marvels of the universe. — Geological progress. — Seas, lakes and rivers.—Antiquity of man. — Study of man and his monuments. — New countries. — Animal life.— Trees and plants. — Science applied to the arts. — Mining and working in metals. — The railway. — The electric telegraph. — Operations of war.—Diamonds. — Life, health and death. — Historic jottings.—Great exhibition.—Miscellaneous.
[8th series]. Things to be remembered in daily life. Time. — Life and length of days. — The school of life. — Business life. — Home traits. — The spirit of the age.—World knowledge.—Conclusion.
[9th series]. Something for everybody. A garland for the year. Pall Mall; the game and the street.—Whitehall. — Personal recollections of Brambletye. — Domestic arts and customs. — Glories of a garden. — Early gardeners and writers on gardening. —Lord Bacon, J: Evelyn and sir W: Temple. — A day at Hatfield.—London gardens.—Pope at Twickenham. —Celebrated gardens.—Curiosities of bees. — Prompt remedies and small services.
[10th series]. Knowledge for the time. Historico-political information. — Progress of civilization. — Dignities and distinctions. — Changes in laws.— Measure and value. — Progress of science.—Life and health.—Religious thought.
[11th series]. Mysteries of life, death and futurity. Life and time.— Nature of the soul.— Spiritual life. — Mental operations.—Belief and scepticism.

— What is superstition ? — Premature interment. — Phenomena of death. — Sin and punishment. — The crucifixion of our Lord. — The end of the world foretold. — Man after death. — The intermediate state.— The christian resurrection. — The future states.—The recognition of each other by the blessed. — Adversaria. — The pilgrim's progress.—App.— Literary history of madmen.
[12th series]. **Predictions realized.** Days and numbers.—Prophesying almanacs. — Omens.—Historical predictions. — Predictions of the french revolution. — The Bonaparte family. — Discoveries and inventions anticipated.—Scriptural prophecies.—Miscellaneous.

Gifts of genius ; a miscellany of prose and poetry by american authors. N. Y. [1859]. D.
829.1 : 17

Stauffer, F. H. The queer, the quaint, the quizzical ; a cabinet for the curious. N. Y. 1883. O.
829.1 : 55

Harper's christmas, 1882. N. Y. 1882. F.
829.1 : R50
Note. A remarkable specimen of modern wood-engraving, with descriptive letter-press.

American nights' entertainments ; consisting of numerous stories, tales, adventures, biographies and papers in natural history, geography, astronomy, etc. by Julian Hawthorne and others. Ill. N. Y. *n. d.* O.
x 829.1 : 64

Worthington's annual ; a series of interesting stories, biographies, papers on natural history for the young. Ill. N. Y. [1883, 1884]. 2 v. O.
x 829.1 : 62

Appleton's summer book, for the seaside, the forest, the camp, the train, the steamboat, the arbor and the watering-place. N. Y. 1880. O.
829.2+1
Contents. **Bunce,** O. B. Our summer pleasure-places.—Wonders of the shore.—Trout-fishing.—Bird-shooting on the coast of New Jersey.—Air-painting. — Cooper, G: The hunter's return. — A miniature marine aquarium.—How to make an herbarium.— **Phillips,** B. About fishing.—**Jones,** C. H. A trip up the Hudson.—**Englishman,** An. The Thousand Isles. —**Ingersoll,** E. The birds of the brookside.—**Rideing,** W.H. Vacations in Colorado.—**Stedman,** E. C. The strawberry-pickers.—How to preserve autumn leaves.—**Ferris,** G: T. New Haven sketches. — **F.,** E. T. Witch-hazel. — Mountain-climbing. — **Bunce,** O. B. Summer pictures. — **Montgommery,** G: E. The skies.—**Bowker,** R. R. Camping out.—**Rückert,** F: Alone by the sea.—**McKay,** J. T. Blake's Ferry. —**Street,** A. B. The pine-root fence.—**Rideing,** W. H. Holidays off the beaten path. — **Robinson,** N. How I dined on the Boulevard des Italiens.—**Craddock,** C: E. Taking the blue ribbon at the county fair.—**Jones,** C. H. A western adventure.—Life on a California ranch.—**Lady,** A. Dogs I have known and loved.—Fifth avenue on an august night.—New York at the seaside.

2. Individual authors.

Addison, Joseph. Miscellaneous works in verse and prose ; consisting of such as were never before printed in twelves, with some account of the life and writings of the author by mr. Tickell. Lond. 1746. 3 v. 8.
829.2 : 61
Contents. V. 1. **Tickell,** T: Preface.—Poems on several occasions.—Rossmond; an opera.—Poems on several occasions. 2. Cato; a tragedy.—To sir Godfrey Kneller. — Poemata. — The drummer, or The haunted house; a comedy.—The trial and conviction of count Tariff.—The whig-examiner. 3. Dialogues upon the usefulness of ancient medals.—The present state of the war.—Of the christian religion.

Albert, Francis C: A: Albert Emmanuel von Sachsen-Coburg-Gotha, *prince consort of England.* Prince Albert's golden precepts,

or The opinions and maxims of his royal highness the prince consort, selected from his addresses, etc., some now for the first time coll. and carefully arr., with an index. New ed. [Bayard ser.] Lond. 1873. T.
829.2 : 1

Allen, C: Grant. Colin Clout's calendar ; the record of a summer, april—october. N. Y. 1883. D.
829.2 : 56

Bacon, Francis, *baron Verulam and viscount St. Albans.* The Promus of formularies and elegancies, being private notes circa 1594, hitherto unpub.; ill. and elucidated by passages from Shakespeare by mrs. H: Pott, with a pref. by E. A. Abbott. Bost. 1883. O.
829.2+44

Barham, R: Harris, (*Thomas Ingoldsby*). The Ingoldsby legends, or Mirth and marvels by T: Ingoldsby ; with a memoir of the author. Ill. Phila. 1860. 2 v. D.
829.2 : 63

Beecher, H: Ward. Eyes and ears. Bost. 1862. D.
829.1 : 2
— Star papers, or Experiences of art and nature. N. Y. 1858. D.
829.1 : 3

Blackwell, Robert. Original acrostics on 'all the states and presidents of the U. S., and various other subjects, religious, political and personal. Ill. Nashville, Tenn. 1861. O.
829.1 : R4

Blanchard, Laman. Sketches from life ; ed. with a memoir of the author by sir E: Bulwer-Lytton. N. Y. 1846. 2 v. in 1. D.
829.2 : 2
Contents. V. 1. Memoir.—A quarrel with some old acquaintances. — Suggestion for the celebration of Shakespeare's birthday.—Anonymous.— Quotations. —£. s. d.—The last book.—Public dinners.—Content or not content.—Some account of the inconsolable society.—The blunders of the remarkably skilful.— Eccentricities of affectation.— Speech-making after dinner. 2. Keeping secrets. — Advice gratis. — Et-cetera.—April fool's day all the year round.—How to make a long day.—" Faults on both sides."—On considering oneself horsewhipped. — Confessions of a keyhole.—Just going out.—My christmas dinner.— The flower-stealers.

Bowles, T: Gibson. Flotsam and jetsam ; a yachtsman's experiences at sea and ashore. N. Y. [1883]. D.
829.2 : 57

Buckle, H: T: Miscellaneous and posthumous works ; ed. with a biographical notice by Helen Taylor. Lond. 1872. 3 v. O.
829.2 : 3
Contents. V. 1. Biographical notice. — Introd.— Miscellaneous works: The influence of women on the progress of knowledge: Mill on Liberty; Letter respecting Pooley's case.—Posthumous works: The reign of Elizabeth: Fragments. 2. Common place books. 3. *Same, continued.*—16th century.—Manners in the 17th century. — Notes for english history.— Indexes to v. 2, 3.

Burritt, Elihu. Thoughts and things at home and abroad ; with a memoir by Mary Howitt. Bost. 1856. D.
829.1 : 5

Child, Lydia Maria, *born* Francis. The freedmen's book. Bost. 1865. D.
829.1 : 6
— Looking toward sunset ; from sources old and new, original and selected. Bost. 1865. D.
829.1 : 7

Clark, Lewis Gaylord. Knick-knacks from an editor's table. *T. p. w.* [N. Y. 1852]. D.
829.1 : 8

Colton, C: Caleb. Lacon, or Many things in few words, addressed to those who think. Rev. ed., with a life of the author. N. Y. 1860. D.
829.2 : 6

Colton, Walter. The sea and the sailor, Notes on France and Italy, and other literary remains; with a memoir by H: T. Cheever. N. Y. 1854. D.   829.1 : 54.
Contents. The sea and the sailor.—A tale of the sea; a poem.—Notes on France and Italy.—Rodieker's youth; a poem.—Aphorisms, maxims and laconics.— An unfinished satire.—Selections from editorials.— In the pulpit.—Memoir.

Cooper, Anthony Ashley, *3d earl of Shaftesbury.* Characteristicks of men, manners, opinions, times. 4th ed. 1727. 3 v. D.   829.2 : 47
Contents. V. 1. A letter concerning enthusiasm.— Sensus communis; an essay on the freedom of wit and humour.—Soliloquy, or Advice to an author. 2. An inquiry into virtue and merit.—The moralists; a philosophical rhapsody. 3. Miscellaneous reflections.—A notion of the tablature, or Judgment of Hercules.

Cornish, T. H. The volume of the affections, or Bridal offering. Lond. 1836. D.   829.2 : 53

Croly, Jennie, *born* Cunningham, *(Jennie June).* Jennie Juniana; talks on woman's topics. Bost. 1864. D.   829.1 : 10

Cross, Marian, *born* Evans, *formerly mrs.* G: H: Lewes, *(George Eliot).* Wit and wisdom of George Eliot. Bost. 1878. T.   829.2 : 7
— Character readings from George Eliot; selected and arr. by Nathan Sheppard. N. Y. 1883. Q.   829.2+45

Disraeli, B:, *earl of Beaconsfield.* Wit and wisdom of B: Disraeli, earl of Beaconsfield; coll. from his writings and speeches [by H: G: Calcraft]. N. Y. 1881. D. 829.2 : 42

Dodge, Mary Abigail, *(Gail Hamilton).* A battle of the books, recorded by an unknown writer for the use of authors and publishers; to the first for doctrine, to the second for reproof, to both for correction and instruction in righteousness. Cambridge. 1870. D.   829.1 : 12
— Country living and country thinking. Bost. 1863. S.   829.1 : 13
Contents. Moving.—The bank.—My garden.—Men and women.—My birds.—Tommy.—Boston and home again.—Brown-bread cakes.—A complaint of friends. —Dog-days. — Summer gone. — Winter.— My flower-bed.—Lights among the shadows of our civil war.
— Gala-days. Bost. 1863. S.   829.1 : 14
Contents. Gala-days.—A call to my countrywomen. —A spasm of sense.—Camilla's concert.—Cheri.—Side glances at Harvard class-day. — Success in life.— Happiest days.
— Summer rest. Bost. 1866. D.   829.1 : 15
Contents. Orchard talk.—A prose Henriade.—Larva lessons.—Fancy farming.—A council about a council. — Gilfillan's Sabbath. — The kingdom coming.— King James the first.—Well done.
— Twelve miles from a lemon. N. Y. 1874. D.   829.1 : 16
Contents. Twelve miles from a lemon. — Lemon-drops.—Hemlock poison.—The wonders and wisdom of carpentry.—Science pure and practical.—American inventions.—The pleasures of poverty.—To Tudiz by railroad.—The higher laws of railroads.—Holidays. —Conference wrong side out.—Country character.— Autumn voices. — On social formula and social freedom. — The fashions. — Sleep and sickness.— Dinners.

Forbes, Archibald. Glimpses through the cannon-smoke; a series of sketches. Bost. 1881. D.   829.2 : 8
Contents. Matrimony among the bomb-shells.—An evening party among the navvies.—The parade of the commissionaires.—Christmas night in very common lodgings.— How I "saved France".— The Inverness character fair.—Miss Priest's bridecake.— The Cawnpore of today.—Christmas presents by post. —On the line of march.—George Martell's bundobust. Reverencing the golden feet.—Christmas day on a

Forbes, Archibald.—*Continued.*
"growler".—The Lucknow of today.—Railway Lizz.— A hill story.
— Soldiering and scribbling; a series of sketches. Leipz. 1872. S.   829.2 : 9
Contents. A penny a day.—At the christmas cattle-market. — Soldiers' wives. — In a military prison.— German war prayers.—Flogged. — A sunday afternoon at Guy's.—Butcher Jack's story.—Bummarees. —A deserter's story.—Lions and lion taming.—Cat's-meat.—Army crimes and punishment.—Christmas in the forecastle.—The story of the Megara.—A march on Brighton.—Furs.—Christmas in a cavalry regiment.—Christmas in the foreposts, 1870.—Workhouse and christmas depravity, 1871.—Christmas among the beggars.
— Souvenirs of some continents. N. Y. 1885. S.   829.2 : 66
Contents. Skobeleff. — How I became a war correspondent.—The emperor and his marshal.—Social Australia.—Macpahan, the american war correspondent.—Where was Villiers?—Wolseley, a character sketch. — The american gentleman with the moist eye.— Interviewed by an emperor. — Some society aspects of America.—Doughton scrip.—A poet waif. —Christmastide in Khyber Pass.
— *Same.* Lond. 1885. D.   829.2 : 66

Foster, J: John Foster; his life and thoughts by W. W. Everts. N. Y. 1883. D.   829.2 : 58

Garfield, James Abram. Garfield's words; suggestive passages from [his] public and private writings, comp. by W: Ralston Balch. Bost. 1881. T.   829.1 : 48

Gestrin, C: E: H. Vacation labors, by C: E. H. G. Montpelier, Vt. 1879. D.   829.1 : 65
Contents. Glimpses of the old world and the new: 1. The immigrant; 2, Old country education and free country education.—Kan't be kured. — A swedish country minister and his house 100 years ago.

Greenwood, James, *(The amateur casual).* In strange company; the experiences of a roving correspondent. 2d ed., with much add. matter. Portr. Lond. 1883. D.   829.2 : 49

Hare, Julius C: *and* A: W: Guesses at truth by two brothers. From the 5th Lond. ed. Bost. 1861. D.   829.2 : 10

Hawes, W: Post, *(J. Cypress, jr.).* Sporting scenes and sundry sketches; the miscellaneous writings of J. Cypress, jr., ed. by Frank Forrester. N. Y. 1842. 2 v. D.   829.1 : 11

Helps, *Sir* Arthur. Brevia; short essays and aphorisms, by the author of "Friends in council", [with index]. Bost. 1871. D.   829.2 : 11
— Companions of my solitude, [with index]. Bost. 1878. D.   829.2 : 12
— Friends in council; a series of readings and discourse thereon. [*Anon.*] N. Y. 1885. 2 v. in 1. D.   829.2 : 13 v1
Contents. V. 1. Truth. — Conformity. — Despair.— Recreation. — Greatness. — Fiction.—On the art of living with others. — Education. — Unreasonable claims in social affections and relations.—Public improvements. — History. — Reading.—On giving and taking criticism.—On the art of living. 2. Improvement of the condition of the rural poor.— Government.—Slavery.
— *Same.* V. 1. Bost. 1853. S.   829.2 : 13 v1
— *Same;* New series. New ed. N. Y. 1885. 2 v. in 1. D.   829.2 : 13 v2
Contents. V. 1. Address to the reader.—Introd.— Worry.—War.—A love story.—Criticism.—Biography. —Proverbs.—On the arts of self-advancement. 2. Ellesmere's plan for a new essay.—On the miseries of human life.—Life not so miserable after all.—On pleasantness.—Conversation on pleasantness.—Lovers' quarrels. — Rowing down the river Moselle.— On government.— Despotism. — The farm-yard.— Chiefly showing the need for tolerance.
— Social pressure. Bost. 1875. D.   829.2 : 14

Howe, W. W. The Pasha papers; epistles of Mohammed Pasha, rear admiral of the turkish navy, written from New York to his friend Abel Ben Hassen; tr. into anglo-american from the original mss. Added, sundry other letters, critical and explanatory, laudatory and objurgatory, from gratified or injured individuals in various parts of the planet. N. Y. 1859. D.
829.1 : 58

Hunt, James H: Leigh. Mirror of the months. Lond. 1826. D. **829.2 : 59**

— Table-talk. Added, Imaginary conversations of Pope and Swift. New ed. Lond. 1882. S. **829.2 : 60**

Irving, Washington. The Crayon miscellany. Author's rev. ed. N. Y. 1849. D.
829.1 : 18
Contents. A tour on the prairies.—Abbotsford.—Newstead abbey.

— Spanish papers, and other miscellanies, hitherto unpub. or uncoll.; arr. and ed. by Pierre M. Irving. N. Y. 1866. 2 v. D. **829.1 : 19**
Contents. V. 1. The legend of Don Roderick.— Legend of the subjugation of Spain.— Legend of count Julian and his family.— Abderahman, the founder of the dynasty of the Ommiades in Spain.— Chronicle of Fernan Gonzalez, count of Castile.— Chronicle of Fernando the saint.—Spanish romance. 2. Letters of Jonathan Oldstyle, gent.—*Biographical sketches:* Capt. James Lawrence; Lieut. Burrows; Commodore Perry; Capt. D: Porter; T: Campbell; Washington Allston; Conversations with Talma; Margaret Miller Davidson.—*Reviews and miscellanies:* Robert Treat Paine; Edwin C. Holland; Wheaton's History of the northmen; Conquest of Granada; Letter to the ed. of "The knickerbocker"; Sleepy Hollow; National nomenclature; Desultory thoughts on criticism; Communipaw; Conspiracy of the Cocked Hats; Letter from Granada; The Catskill mountains.

— The sketch-book of Geoffrey Crayon, gent. (Stratford ed.) N. Y. *n. d.* D. **829.1 : 20**
Contents. The author's account of himself.—The voyage.— Roscoe.—The wife.— Rip Van Winkle.—English writers on America.—Rural life in England.—The broken heart.— The art of book-making.—A royal poet.—The country church.—The widow and her son.—A sunday in London.—The Boar's Head tavern, Eastcheap.— The mutability of literature.— Rural funerals.— The inn kitchen.— The spectre bridegroom.—Westminster abbey.—Christmas.—The stage coach.—Christmas eve.—Christmas day.— The christmas dinner.—London antiques.—Little Britain.—Stratford-on-Avon.— Traits of indian character.— Philip of Pokanoket.—John Bull.—The pride of the village.—The angler.—The legend of Sleepy Hollow.—L'envoy.—App.

— Christmas in England; papers from the "Sketch-book." Ill. N. Y. 1867. O.
829.1+22
— *See also his* Works. 820.1 : 13, 820.1 : P11
Contents, see col. 1014.

Jackson, Helen Maria. *born* Fiske, *formerly mrs.* Hunt, *(H. H.)* Bits of talk, in verse and prose, for young folks by H. H. Bost. 1879. T. **x 829.1 : 49**
Contents. The parable of St. Christopher.—A christmas-tree for cats.—The legend of St. Nicholas.—My ant's cow.—St. Martin's cloak.— Runna Rig.— The palace of Gondoforus.—The ant's monday dinner.—The nest.—The festival of San Eustachio in Rome.— Colorado snow-birds.—The water-works of Heilbrun.— Morning-glory.—Children's preaching in the church of Ara Cœli in Rome.—"The penny ye meant to gie".—A parable.—My broken-winged bird.—Cheery people. — A short catechism. — The expression of rooms.—By stage to Boston.—Good temper.—Lizzy of La Bourget.—Kicking against pricks.— My first voyage round the world.—"A good time".

x denotes books specially adapted for children.

Jameson, Anna, *born* Murphy. Studies, stories and memoirs. Bost. 1869. T. **829.2 : 17**
Contents. **Studies.** The tragedy of Correggio.—German actresses.—Goethe's Tasso, Iphigenia, and Clavigo.—Music and musicians.—On the female character.—Goethe and Ekermann.—Goethe's last love.—Goethe's table-talk.—Goethe's ideas on the position of woman.—Lord Byron.—Schiller.—Historical skepticism.—The supernatural.—Ghost stories.—Detached thoughts.— Hoffmann.— Rückert.— Grillparzer's Sappho and Medea. — Sternberg's novels. — Don Carlos. **Tales.** The false one.—Halloran the peddler.—The indian mother.— Much coin, much care. **Memoirs illustrative of art.** The house of Titian.—Washington Allston.—Adelaide Kemble.

— *Same.* Bost. 1875. T. **829.2 : 17**

Keddie, Henrietta, *(Sarah Tytler).* Papers for thoughtful girls; with sketches of some girls' lives. Ill. 6th ed. Lond. 1865. S.
829.2 : 43

Ker, J: Bellenden. An essay on the archæology of our popular phrases and nursery rhymes. New ed. Lond. 1837. 2 v. S. ` 829 : 2

King, W: Political and literary anecdotes of his own times. Bost. 1819. D. **829.2 : 19**

Landor, Walter Savage. Selections from [his] writings; ed. by G: Stillman Hillard. Bost. 1856. D. **829.2 : 20**

Lippincott, Sarah Jane, *born* Clarke, *(Grace Greenwood).* Records of five years. Bost. 1867. D. **829.1 : 21**
Contents. In peace. The baby in the bath-tub.—The baby in the prison. — Our little daughter's cab. — Words spoken in prison.— Pictures of town and country. *In war.* The northern uprising.— A few plain words, addressed to certain english friends.— Lights of the war cloud.—A taste of camp life.—Bon voyage.

Macaulay, T: Babington, *baron Macaulay.* Selections from [his] writings; ed. with occasional notes by G: O: Trevelyan. N. Y. 1877. O. **829.2 : 21**
Contents. **Historical scenes.** The battle of Sedgemore, and the fate of Monmouth.—Landing of the Prince of Orange.—The siege of Londonderry.—Killiecrankie.—The battle of the Boyne.—The battle of La Hogue.—The battle of Landen.—The black hole of Calcutta, and the battle of Plassey.—The impeachment of Warren Hastings. **Historical portraits.** Charles II.— William or Orange.— Judge Jeffreys.— The junto.— Sir W: Temple.—Lord Chatham's eloquence.— S: Johnson.— Frederic the great.— Horace Walpole. **Historical sketches.** The church of Rome.—The puritans.—Unpopularity of the puritans after the restoration.—The jesuits.—The revolution.—Death of queen Mary.—Fire at Whitehall, and visit of Peter the great to England.—Montague's unpopularity.—The advantages of the alternations of party government.—Death of William III.—Lord Chatham as a war minister. **Literary criticism.** Milton's poetry.—The Pilgrim's progress.—The controversy about the epistles of Phalaris.—Addison's poem of the campaign.—The Spectator.— Horace Walpole's writings.—Lord Byron.—The historian.—Lord Macaulay's feelings with regard to great authors. **Miscellaneous.** Manners of the 17th century.—Traveling in the 17th century.—The country gentleman of the 17th century.—The towns of England in the reign of Charles II.—Civilization and its effect on the mass of the people.—The highlands of Scotland.—State of the currency in the 17th century.—Jeremy Collier and the english stage.—The court life of miss Burney.—The duty of the state with regard to education. **Poetry.** The battle of Moncontour.—The armada.—Ivry.—Epitaph on a jacobite.—Virginia.

Mackay, C: The gouty philosopher, or The friends, acquaintances, opinions, whims and eccentricities of John Wagstaffe, esq., of Wilbye Grange, J. P. and ex M. P. 2d ed. Lond. 1864. D. **829.2 : 22**

Mackenzie, H: Miscellaneous works. 3d ed. N. Y. 1847. D. **829.2 : 23**
Contents. Memoir, by sir W. Scott.—Man of feeling.—Papers from the Lounger.—Man of the world.—Julia de Roubigné.—Papers from the Mirror.

Mackenzie, Robert Shelton. Bits of blarney. N. Y. [1854]. D.   829.2 : 55
Contents. Legends: Blarney Castle; Con O'Keefe and the golden cup; Legends of Finn MacCoul.—Irish stories: The petrified piper; The Geraldine; Captain Rock; A night with the Whiteboys; Buck English.—Eccentric characters: The bard O'Kelly; Father Prout; Father Prout's sermon; Irish dancing masters; Charley Crofts.—Irish publicists: H: Grattan; Daniel O'Connell.

Maginn, W: Fraserian papers, annotated, with a life of the author, by R. Shelton Mackenzie. N. Y. 1857. D.   829.2 : 24
— The Odoherty papers, annotated by Shelton Mackenzie. N. Y. 1855. 2 v. D.
829.2 : 25

Milburn, W: H: The pioneer preacher, or Rifle, axe and saddle-bags, and other lectures; with an introd. by J. McClintock. N. Y. 1860. D.   829.1 : 23

Milner, G: Country pleasures; the chronicle of a year, chiefly in a garden. Bost. 1881. S.   829.2 : 41

More, *Sir* T: A selection from his works, as well in prose as in verse, forming a sequel to "Life and times of sir T: More" by W. Jos. Walter. Baltimore. *n. d.* S.   829.2 : 26
Contents. Utopia; a political romance.—History of Richard III.—Apology.—Controversial writings: The supplication of souls; The refutation of Tindal and Barnes; On general councils; Treatise on those words of scripture, "Remember thy latter end and thou shall never sin."—Devotional.—Letters.—Apothegms, etc.—Poetry.—Postscript.

Murdoch, James E: Patriotism in poetry and prose; selected passages from lectures and patriotic readings, also poems by T: Buchanan Reed, G: H. Boker, Francis De Haes Janvier and other american authors, commemorative of the gallant deeds of our noble defenders on land and sea. Phila. 1865. D.   829.1 : 24

Osgood, S: American leaves; familiar notes of thought and life. N. Y. 1867. D.
829.1 : 25
Contents. Little children. — Our old pew. — School influences.—American boys. — American girls.—Fortune.—The flag at home.—Learning statesmanship.—Off-hand speaking.—Art among the people.— American nerves.—The ethics of love.—Garden philosophy.—Easter flowers.—Toward sunset.

Overbury, *Sir* T: Miscellaneous works in prose and verse, now first coll.; ed. with notes and a biographical account of the author by E: F. Rimbault. Lond. 1856. S.
829.2 : 52
Contents. Introd.—Life.—The wife.—Characters.—The first and second part of the Remedy of love. — Observations upon the 17 provinces as they stood a. d. 1609.—Crumms fal'n from king James table.

Parton, Sara Payson, *born* Willis, *formerly mrs.* Eldridge, *(Fanny Fern).* Ginger-snaps by Fanny Fern. N. Y. 1871. D.   829.1 : 26

Prime, S: Irenæus. Under the trees. N. Y. 1874. O.   829.1 : 27

Prime, W: Cowper. I go a-fishing. N. Y. 1873. O.   829.1 : 28

Rands, W: Brightly, *(Henry Holbeach).* Henry Holbeach, student in life and philosophy; a narrative and a discussion. [*Anon.*] London. 1865. 2 v. D.   829.2 : 15
Contents. V. 1. First words by the editor.—*Studies in life, literature and philosophy.* A study of an obscure puritan colony.—The puzzles of a puritan boy. — The profitableness of unprofitable servants.—Cavaliers and roundheads.—The game of tradition.—The weighing of the pig.—Self-love.—Truth and honour. — The mountains and their shadows. — The terrors of the Lord. — To one who feels that a principle may be

pushed too far.—Women's movements. — To a young lady about to write a novel. —To a young man about to become a critic.—Intermediate words by the editor.
2. *Controversial letters.* To J: Stuart Mill; The sphere of law.—To the rev. F. D. Maurice; The sphere of love. — To T: Carlyle; Mights and rights. — To the rev. H: L. Mansel; Reason and faith. — To the rev. J: H: Newman; Authoritative truth. — To G: H: Lewes; Science and philosophy. — To Alex. Bain; The study of character.—To Arthur Helps; A man's property in himself.—To Matthew Arnold; Application of ideals.—Last words from the editor.—App.

Rice, Harvey. Nature and culture. Bost. 1875. D.   829.1 : 29
Contents. Nature and her lessons.—Woman and her sphere.—Education and its errors.—America and her future. — Life and its aspirations. — Mission monument and its dedication.

Richmond, James Cook, *(Admonish Crime, anagram).* A midsummer's day dream libellous, or A little book of the vision of Shawmut, by Admonish Crime. Milw. 1859. S.   829.1 : R30

Rogers, S: Recollections of [his] table talk. Added, Porsoniana. N. Y. 1856. D.
829.2 : 54

Rush, R: Occasional productions, political, diplomatic and miscellaneous; including a glance at the court and government of Louis Philippe and the french revolution of 1848; ed. by his executors, with an index. Phila. 1860. O.   829.1+57

Sala, G: A: Breakfast in bed, or Philosophy between the sheets; a series of indigestible discourses. Bost. 1863. D.   829.2 : 29
— Living London; being "Echoes" re-echoed. Lond. 1883. O.   829.2 : 51
Note. A collection of the "Echoes," that appeared in the *London illustrated news* during the year 1882.
— Looking at life, or Thoughts and things. Lond. 1860. D.   829.2 : 30

Saunders, F: Pastime papers. [*Anon.*] N. Y. 1885. D.   829.1 : 67
Contents. The apology.—Notes on names.—Letters and letter-writing.—The old masters.—Touching tailors.—Genius in jail.—The marvels of memory.—Concerning cobblers.—Coffee and tea.—Printers of the olden time.
— Salad for the social. [*Anon.*] N. Y. 1856. D.   829.1 : 31
Contents. Introductory. — Bookcraft.—The modern Moloch.—The toilet and its devotees. — The mysteries of medicine.—The cycle of the seasons.—The humors of law.—The mute creation. — Pulpit peculiarities. — The larcenies of literature.—A stray leaf.
— Salad for the solitary, by an epicure. N. Y. 1856. D.   829.1 : 32
Contents. Dietetics. — The talkative and the taciturn.—Facts and fancies about flowers. — A monologue on matrimony. — Curious and costly books. — Something about nothing. — Pastimes and sports. — Dying words of distinguished men. — The poetry of plants. — Infelicities of the intellectual. — Citations from the cemeteries. — The shrines of genius. — The selfish and the social. — Pleasures of the pen. — Sleep and its mysteries.

Selden, J: Table talk; being [his] discourses, or his sense of various matters of weight and high consequence, relating especially to religion and state. New ed. Lond. 1777. S.   829.2 : 31

Smith, Horace. Gaieties and gravities. N. Y. 1852. D.   829.2 : 32

Smith, Sidney. Wit and wisdom; selections from his writings and passages of his letters and table-talk; with a biographical memoir and notes by Evert A. Duyckinck. N. Y. 1856. D.   829.2 : 33
— *Same;* a selection of the most memorable passages in his writings and conversation. New ed. Lond. *n. d.* D.   829.2 : 33

Soane, G: New curiosities of literature, and book of the months. 2d ed. Lond. 1849. 2 v. O.   **829.2 : 35**

Stanhope, Philip Dormer, *4th earl of Chesterfield.* Letters, sentences and maxims ; with a critical essay by C: A. Sainte Beuve. 4th ed. [Bayard ser.] Lond. 1878. T.   **829.2 : 34**

Stowe, Harriet Elizabeth, *born* Beecher, (*Christopher Crowfield*). The chimney corner, by Christopher Crowfield. Bost. 1868. D.   **829.1 : 33**
Contents. What will you do with her, or The woman question. — Woman's sphere. — A family talk on reconstruction. — Is woman a worker? — The transition.—Bodily religion, a sermon on good health. —How shall we entertain our company? — How shall we be amused? — Dress, or who makes the fashions? What are the sources of beauty in dress. — The cathedral.— The new year. — The noble army of martyrs.

Taylor, Bayard. The echo club, and other literary diversions. Bost. 1876. T.   **829.1 : 61**
Contents. The echo club. — The battle of the bards. — A review.—Paradise discovered.

Taylor, B: Franklin. January and june. N. Y. 1864. D.   **829.1 : 34**

Taylor, Lute A. Chip basket ; choice selections from [his] lectures, essays, addresses, editorials and public and social correspondence ; comp. and ed. by H. A. Taylor. Hudson, Wis. 1874. S.   **829.1 : 35**

Thackeray, W: Makepeace. Early and late papers, hitherto uncollected. Bost. 1867. D.   **829.2 : 36**
Contents. Memorials of gormandizing.— Men and coats. — Bluebeard's ghost. — Dickens in France.— John Leech's pictures of life and character.—Little travels and road-side sketches.—On men and pictures.—Picture gossip.—The anonymous in periodical literature.—Goethe.—A leaf out of a sketch-book.— The last sketch.—"Strange to say, on club paper."— Autour de mon chapeau.—On a peal of bells.—On some carp at Sans Souci.—Dessein's.—On a pear tree. —On a medal of George IV.—On alexandrines.—The notch on the axe.—De finibus.

— Roundabout papers. [Reprinted from the Cornhill magazine.] Leipz. 1869. 2 v. in 1. D.   **829.2 : 37**
Contents. V. 1. On a lazy idle boy.—On two children in black.—On ribbons.—On some late great victories.—Thorns in the cushion.—On screens in dining-rooms. — Tunbridge toys.—De juventute.—On a joke I once heard from the late T: Hood.—Roundabout the christmas tree.—On a chalk-mark on the door.— On being found out. — On a hundred years hence. — Small-beer chronicle. — Ogres. — On two Roundabout papers which I intended to write.—A Mississippi bubble.—On Letts's diary. 2. Notes of a week's holiday.—Nil nisi bonum.—On half a loaf.— The notch on the axe ; a story à la mode.—De finibus. —On a peal of bells.—On a pear-tree.— Dessein's.— On some carp at Sans Souci.—Autour de mon chapeau.—On alexandrines.—On a medal of George IV.— "Strange to say, on club paper."—The last sketch.

— *Same.* Ill. N. Y. 1863. D.   **829.2 : 37 v1**
Contents, same as v. 1, above.

— Stray moments with Thackeray, his humor, satire and characters ; selections from his writings, prefaced with a few biographical notes by W: H. Rideing. N. Y. 1880. S.   **829.2 : 28**

Tilton, Warren, *and* W: A. Crafts. Trifleton papers, by Trifle and the editor. Bost. 1856. D.   **829.1 : 9**

Townsend, F: Clouds and sunshine. [*Anon.*] N. Y. 1853. D.   **829.1 : 42**

— Fancies of a whimsical man. [*Anon.*] 4th ed. N. Y. 1859. D.   **829.1 : 36**

— Fun and earnest. [*Anon.*] N. Y. 1853. D.   **829.1 : 37**

Townsend, F:—*Continued.*
— Ghostly colloquies. [*Anon.*] N. Y. 1856. D.   **829.1 : 38**
Contents. Cadmus-Columbus. — Sophocles-Gray.— Salvator Rosa- Byron. — Hortensius - Beckford. — Jason-Raleigh. — Tacitus-Gibbon. — Apicius - Vattel. —Sejanus-Richard III.—Marcus Brutus-J: Adams.— Praxiteles-Canova. — Petronius-D'Orsay. — Germanicus-Rienzi.

— Glimpses of Nineveh, b. c. 960. [*Anon.*] N. Y. 1857. D.   **829.1 : 39**

— Letters from Rome, a. d. 138. [*Anon.*] N. Y. 1854. D.   **829.1 : 40**

— Musings of an invalid. 2d ed. [*Anon.*] N. Y. 1852. D.   **829.1 : 41**

— Spiritual visitors. [*Anon.*] N. Y. 1854. D.   **829.1 : 43**
Contents. Alcibiades - Sheridan. — H: Dandolo- P: Stuyvesant. — Rubens-Cole. — Pindar-Drake. — Diogenes-Rabelais.—Aristides-Jay. — Chrysostom-Channing.—Amphion-Bellini. — Roscius-Kemble.— Archimedes-Fulton. — Aurelius- Howard. — Corinna-Lady Jane Grey. — Ben Jonson-Sam Johnson. — Julius Cæsar-Zachary Taylor. — Timon-Swift. — J: Smith-Sidney Smith.—Lucian-Lamb. — Father Nile-Father Mississippi.—Pericles-Hamilton.—Phidias-Raphael.

Watterson, H:, *ed.* Oddities in southern life and character. Ill. Bost. 1883 [1882]. S.   **829.1 : 51**

Webb, C: H:, (*John Paul*). Sea-weed and what we seed ; my vacation at Long Branch and Saratoga. N. Y. 1876. D.   **829.1 : 59**

Wellesley, Arthur, *1st duke of Wellington.* The words of Wellington ; collected from his despatches, letters and speeches, with anecdotes, etc., compiled by Edith Walford. [Bayard ser.] Lond. 1869. T.   **829.2 : 38**

Whitman, Walt. Specimen days and Collect. Phila. 1883. D.   **829.1 : 52**

Whittier, J: Greenleaf. Literary recreations and miscellanies. Bost. 1854. D. **829.1 : 60**
Contents. Utopian schemes and political theorists. —Peculiar institutions of Massachusetts.—T: Carlyle on the slave question. — England under the last Stuart.—The two processions.—Evangeline.—A chapter of history.—Fame and glory.—Fanaticism.—The border war of 1708.—The great Ipswich fright.—Lord Ashley and the thieves.—Mirth and medicine.—Pope night.—The better land.—The poetry of the north.— The boy captives.—The black men in the revolution and war of 1812.—My summer with dr. Singletary.— Charms and fairy faith.—Magicians and witchfolk. —The agency of evil.—The little iron soldier.—The city of a day.—Patucket falls.—Hamlet among the graves.—Yankee gypsies.—The world's end.—Swedenborg.—First day in Lowell.—Taking comfort.—The beautiful.—The lighting up.—The scottish reformers. —The training.

Willis, Nathaniel Parker. The convalescent. N. Y. 1859. D.   **829.1 : 44**

— Hurry-graphs, or Sketches of scenery, celebrities and society taken from life. 2d ed. N. Y. 1851. D.   **829.1 : 45**

— Out-doors at Idlewild, or The shaping of a home on the banks of the Hudson. N. Y. 1855. D.   **829.1 : 46**

— The rag-bag ; a collection of ephemera. N. Y. 1855. D.   **829.1 : 47**

Wilson, J:, (*Christopher North*). Dies borealis, or Christopher under canvas. Phila. 1850. D.   **829.2 : 39**

— The Noctes ambrosianæ of "Blackwood." Phila. 1843. 4 v. D.   **829.2 : 40**

Winthrop, Theodore. Life in the open air, and other papers. (Leisure hour ser.) N. Y. 1876. S.   **829.1 : 63**
Contents. Life in the open air; Katahdin and the Penobscot.—Love and skates.—New York 7th regiment; Our march to Washington.—Washington as a camp.—Fortress Monroe.—Brightly's orphan.—"The heart of the Andes."

13. German literature — a, General.

1. History and criticism.

(See also Essays and Miscellany, cl. 834, 839.)

In general.

Stern, Adolf. Lexikon der deutschen national-literatur ; die deutschen dichter und pro-saiker aller zeiten, mit berücksichtigung der hervorragendsten dichterisch behandelten stoffe und motive. Leipz. 1882. D.
830.1 : R6

König, Robert. Deutsche literaturgeschichte. 8te aufl. Bielefeld. 1880. O. **830.1+2**

Kurz, H: Geschichte der deutschen literatur, mit ausgewählten stücken aus den werken der vorzüglichsten schriftsteller. 7te aufl. Ill. and portr. Leipz. 1874–76. 4 v. Q.
830.1+1

Contents. V. 1–3. Von den ältesten zeiten bis zu Göthe's tod, 1832.—Register. **4.** Die neueste literatur, von 1830 bis auf die gegenwart [1866].—Register.

— and F: Christian **Paldamus.** Deutsche dichter und prosaisten, nach ihrem leben und wirken geschildert. Neue ausg. Portr. Leipz. 1867. 4 v. S. **830.1 : 16**

Contents. V. 1. Niklas von Wyle.—H: Steinhöwel.—Albrecht von Eyb.—J: Geiler von Kaisersberg.—Sebastian Brant.—T: Murner.—Johannes Aventinus.—Ulrich von Hutten.—Martin Luther.—Burkard Waldis.— Sebastian Franck.— Aegidius Tschudi.— Hans Sachs.—Johannes Fischart.—F: Spee.—Martin Opitz.—J: Valentin Andreä.—J: Lauremberg.—F: v. Logau.— Paul Fleming.— Andreas Gryphius.— Hans Jakob Christoffel v. Grimmelshausen. **2.** Klopstock.—Michael Denis.—K: F: Kretschmann.—H: W: v. Gerstenberg.—Christian F: Daniel Schubart.—Salomon Gessner.—Christoph Martin Wieland.—J: Baptist v. Alxinger.—Aloys Blumauer.—Gottfried A: Bürger.—J: H: Voss.—L: H: Christoph Hölty.—J: Martin Miller.—H: Christian Boje.—F: Leopold graf v. Stolberg.—Matthias Claudius.—F: W: Gotter.—Leopold F: Günther v. Göckingk.—Gotthold Ephraim Lessing.—Justus Möser.—J: Joachim Winkelmann.—Christian Gottlob Heyne. **3.** J: Gottfried v. Herder.—J: G: Hamann.—J: H: Jung, genannt Stilling.—J: Wolfgang v. Göthe. — G: Forster. — F: Maximilian Klinger. — Albrecht Haller. — G: Zimmermann. — J: H: Merck.—Johannes Müller.—F: v. Schiller.—J: Caspar Lavater.—Immanuel Kant.—A: W: Iffland. **4.** Christian Fürchtegott Gellert. — Gottlieb W: Rabener. — J: Elias Schlegel. — Abraham Gotthelf Kästner.—Ewald Christian v. Kleist.—Christian Felix Weisse.—J: L: W: Gleim.—J: P: Uz.—Anna Louise Karschin.—Just F: W: Zachariä.—K: W: Ramler.— Moses Mendelssohn.—Christoph F: Nicolai.—Jacob Michael Reinhold Lenz.—Theodor Gottlieb v. Hippel.—J: Jacob W: Heinse.—Moritz A: v. Thümmel.— A: F: Ferdinand v. Kotzebue.—J: Paul F: Richter.

Hosmer, James Kendall. Short history of german literature. St. Louis. 1879. O.
830.1 : 9

Koberstein, A: K: Grundriss der geschichte der deutschen nationalliteratur. V. 1, 6te ; v. 2–5, 5te umgearb. aufl. von K: Bartsch. Leipz. 1872–84. 5 v. O. **830.1+15**

Contents. V. 1. Bis zum ende des 16ten jahrhunderts. **2.** Bis zum zweiten viertel des 18ten jahrhunderts. **3–5.** Bis zu Göthe's tod, 1832.—General-register.

Vilmar, A: F: Christian. Geschichte der deutschen national-literatur [bis 1852]. 19te aufl. Marburg. 1879. O. **830.1+3**

Menzel, Wolfgang. German literature. Tr. from the german by C. C. Felton. (Specimens of foreign standard literature, ed. by G: Ripley, v. 7–9.) Bost. 1840. 3 v. D.
830.1 : 10

Moschzisker, Franz Adolph. A guide to german literature, or Manual to facilitate an acquaintance with the german classic authors. Lond. 1850. 2 v. S. **830.1 : 11**

Note. Contains extracts and specimens in the original, with biographical and literary notes and commentaries in english.

Hirsch, Franz W: Geschichte der deutschen litteratur von ihren anfängen bis auf die neueste zeit ; b. 1, 2. (Geschichte der weltlitteratur in einzeldarstellungen, b. 5, 6.) Leipz. [1884–85]. 2 v. O. **830.1 : 14**

Contents. V. 1. Das mittelalter. 2. Von Luther bis Lessing.

Solling, Gustav. A review of the literary history of Germany, from the earliest period to the beginning of the 19th century. Lond. 1859, O. **830.1 : 12**

Perry, T: Sergeant. From Opitz to Lessing ; a study of pseudo-classicism in literature. Bost. 1885 [1884]. D. **830.2 : 6**

Schmidt, Julian. Geschichte des geistigen lebens in Deutschland, von Leibnitz bis auf Lessing's tod. Leipz. 1862–64. 2 v. O.
830.1 : 19

Contents. V. 1. Von Leibnitz bis auf Klopstock, 1681—1750. 2. Von Klopstock bis auf Lessing's tod, 1750—1781.

— Geschichte der deutschen literatur seit Lessing's tod. 5te durchweg umgearb. und verm. aufl. Leipz. 1866, 1867. 3 v. O.
830.1 : 5

Contents. V. 1. Das classische zeitalter, 1781—1797. **2.** Die romantik, 1797—1813. **3.** Die gegenwart, 1814—1867.

Hettner, Hermann. Geschichte der deutschen literatur im 18. jahrhundert [1648–1832]. 3te umgearb. aufl. (Literaturgeschichte des 18. jahrh., 3ter theil.) Brschwg. 1879. 3 v. in 4. O. **809 : 9 v3–6**

Contents. **[3.]** 1es buch. Vom westfälischen frieden bis zur thronbesteigung Friedrichs des grossen, 1648–1740. **[4.]** 2es buch. Das zeitalter Friedrichs des grossen. **[5.]** 3es buch. Das klassische zeitalter der deutschen literatur: 1e abth., Die sturm- und drangperiode. **[6.]** 2e abth., Das ideal der humanität.

Hillebrand, Joseph. Die deutsche nationalliteratur im 18. und 19. jahrhundert historisch und ästhetisch - kritisch dargestellt ; 3te aufl., durchgesehen und vervollständigt vom sohne des verfassers. Gotha. 1875. 3 v. O. **830.1 : 17**

Contents. V. 1. Die deutsche nationalliteratur im 18. jahrhundert bis auf Göthe und Schiller: Zustand der deutschen nationalliteratur in der ersten hälfte des 18. jahrh. bis auf Lessing; Die nationalliterarische reformation unter Lessing; Die nationalliteratur in der sturm- und drangperiode. 2. Die deutsche nationalliteratur im letzten viertel des 18. jahrh.: Göthe und Schiller; Die deutsche nationalliteratur um die blüthezeit Göthe's und Schiller's. **3.** Die deutsche nationalliteratur im 19. jahrh.: Die neue romantik; Die nationalliteratur in dem zweiten und dritten viertel des 19. jahrh.

Hillebrand, K: German thought, from the seven years' war to Goethe's death ; six lectures del. at the Royal institution of Great Britain, may and june 1879. N. Y. 1880. D.
830.2 : 4

Haym, Rudolph. Die romantische schule ; ein beitrag zur geschichte des deutschen geistes. Berlin. 1870. Q. **830.1+18**

Heine, H: The romantic school. Tr. by S. L. Fleishman. N. Y. 1882. D.   **830.1 : 7**
Includes, The suabian mirror.—Introduction to an édition de luxe of Don Quixote.

Brandes, G: Die romantische schule in Deutschland. *In his* Hauptströmungen der literatur des 19. jahrh.   **809 : 6 v1,2**

Gottschall, K: Rudolf v. Die deutsche nationallitteratur des 19. jahrhunderts; litterarhistorisch und kritisch dargestellt. 5te verm. und verb. aufl. Breslau. 1881. 4 v. O.   **830.1 : 20**
Contents. V. 1. Die klassiker.— Die romantiker. 2. Die modernen: 1, Deutsche originalgeister und die jungdeutsche sturm- und drangperiode.—2, Die moderne philosophie. — 3, Litteratur, wissenschaft und leben. 3. Die modernen: 4, Die moderne zeit. —5, Das moderne drama. 4. *Same, continued.*—6, Der moderne roman.

Salomon, L: Geschichte der deutschen nationalliteratur des neunzehnten jahrhunderts. Portr. Stuttg. 1881. O.   **830.1+4**

Taylor, Bayard. Studies in german literature; with an introd. by G: H. Boker. N. Y. 1879. D.   **830.2 : 5**
Contents. Introd.— Earliest german literature.— The minne-singers.—The mediæval epic.—The Nibelungenlied.—The literature of the reformation.—The literature of the 17th century.—Lessing.—Klopstock, Wieland and Herder.—Schiller.— Goethe.—Goethe's Faust.—Richter.

Lindau, H: Gustav Paul. Gesammelte aufsätze; beiträge zur literatur-geschichte der gegenwart. Berlin. 1875. D.   **830.2 : 2**

Goltz, Bogumil. Zur geschichte und characteristik des deutschen genius; eine ethnographische studie. 2te aufl. von "Die deutschen". Berlin. 1864. 2 v. in 1. D.   **830.2 : 3**

Special classes.

Hedge, F: H: Prose writers of Germany. Portr. Phila. 1848. O.   **830.1+8**
Contents. **Luther,** M. On education ; Concerning God the Father ; Concerning angels ; How to pray ; Prayer at the diet of Worms; Selections from letters. — **Boehme,** J: E. Extracts from the "Compendious view of the grounds of the teutonic philosophy": Concerning the supersensual life; Extract from "The threefold life of man"; Extract from "The way to Christ." — *Abraham a Sancta Clara.* On envy. — **Möser, J.** Letter from an old married woman to a sensitive young lady; The moral advantages of public calamities.—**Kant,** J. [Introductory remarks, by J. E. Cabot]; From the "Critique of the judgment"; From the "Plan for an everlasting peace"; Supposed beginning of the history of man.—**Lessing,** J: G. E. From "Laocoon"; From "The education of the human race"; Fables. — **Mendelssohn,** M. Letter to J. C. Lavater; On the sublime and naïve in polite literature.—**Hamann,** J: G: The merchant. — **Wieland,** C. M. Philosophy as the art of life and the healing art of the soul; Letter to a young poet; On the relation of the agreeable and the beautiful to the useful; From the Dialogues of the gods.— **Musäus,** J: C: A: Dumb love.— **Claudius,** M. Dedication to friend Hain; Advertisement for subscribers; Speculations on new year's day; The sorrows of young Werther; On prayer; A correspondence; On Klopstock's odes. — **Lavater,** J. C. On the nature of man, which is the foundation of the science of physiognomy.— **Jacobi,** F: H: From the "Flying leaves"; Learned societies, their spirit and aim. — **Herder,** J: G. v. Love and self; Tithon and Aurora; Metempsychosis. — **Goethe,** J: W. v. The vicar of Wakefield; From "Elective affinities"; From Wilhelm Meister, The confessions of a fair saint, Indenture, The exequies of Mignon; From Wilhelm Meister's travels; Novelle; The tale.—**Schiller,** J: C. F: v. Upon naïve and sentimental poetry.— **Fichte,** J: G. The destination of man.—**Richter,** J: P. F: Rome, from "The titan"; From "Flower, fruit and thorn pieces"; From "Quintus Fixlein"; Thoughts.— **Schlegel,** A: W: v. Lectures on dramatic literature.— **Schleiermacher,**

F: E. D. Discourse IV, on the social element in religion.—**Hegel,** G: W: F: Introd. to the philosophy of history; Who thinks abstractly ?— **Zschokke,** J: H: D. Leaves from the journal of a poor vicar in Wiltshire.—**Schlegel,** F: v. Lectures on the philosophy of history.— **Hardenberg,** F. v., *(Novalis).* From Heinrich von Ofterdingen; From the Fragments.—**Tieck,** J: L: The elves.— **Schelling,** F: W: J. v. On the relation of the plastic arts to nature. — **Hoffmann,** E. T. A. The golden pot. — **Chamisso,** L: C: A. v. The wonderful history of Peter Schlemihl.

Gödeke, K: Grundrisz zur geschichte der deutschen dichtung, aus den quellen. Hanover. 1859–81. 3 v. in 4. O.   **830.1 : L**
Contents. V. 1. Buch 1–4. Von der ältesten zeit bis zum 30jähr. kriege. 2. Buch 5–6: Vom 30jähr. kriege bis zum weltkriege. — Register. 3, *in 2 pts.* Buch 7: Zeit des weltkrieges.—Buch 8: Vom weltfrieden bis auf die gegenwart, 1er abschnitt: Vom kriege bis zur franz. revolution 1830.—Register.

— *Same.* 1er band: Das mittelalter. 2te ganz neu bearb. aufl. Dresden. 1884. O.   **830.1 : L v1**

Gervinus, G: Gottfried. Geschichte der deutschen dichtung. 5te völlig umgearb. aufl. Leipz. 1871–74. 4 v. O.   **830.1 : 13**
Note. V. 3–5 ed. by K: Bartsch; V. 5 contains a general index. Ends with Schiller and Goethe, and a short review of the romantic school.

Uhland, L: Schriften zur geschichte der dichtung und sage. Stuttg. 1865–73. 8 v. O.   **830.1 : 21**
Contents. V. 1, 2. Geschichte der altdeutschen poesie [bis zu dem 16. jahrh.] 3. Alte hoch- und niederdeutsche volkslieder, mit abbandlung und anmerkungen: Abhandlung. 4. *Same:* Anmerkungen.—Ueber das altfranzösische epos. 5. Walther von der Vogelweide.—Der minnesang.— Ueber die aufgabe einer gesellschaft für deutsche sprache.— Zur geschichte der freisch=lessen.— Ueber die sage vom herzog Ernst. 6. Sagenforschungen: Der mythus von Thôr, nach nordischen quellen; Odin. 7. Sagengeschichte der germanischen und romanischen völker. 8. Schwäbische sagenkunde, 1er b.: Suevisch-alamannische vorzeit.—Abhandlungen aus Pfeiffers Germania.—Nachträge.

Wilken, E. Geschichte der geistlichen spiele in Deutschland. Göttingen. 1872. O.   **832.1 : 3**

Köstlin, Christian Reinhold, *(C. Reinhold).* Die dramatische literatur und das theater der deutschen im 19. jahrh., nach ihren historischen voraussetzungen betrachtet. *T. p. w.* D.   **832.1 : 1**

Börne, L: Dramaturgische blätter. N. Y. 1858. 2 v. D.   **832.1 : 2**

Genée, Rudolph. Das deutsche theater und die reform-frage. *In* Deutsche zeit- und streitfragen.   **304 : 15 v7**

Minckwitz, Johannes. Die entwicklung eines neuen dramatischen styls in Deutschland. *In* Deutsche zeit- und streit-fragen.   **304 : 15 v13**

Special authors.

(See also names of individual authors in the Index to biography, at the end of the catalogue.)

Biedermann, Gustav Woldemar *freiherr* v. Goetheforschungen. Frankfurt a. M. 1879. O.   **830.2 : 7**
Contents. Zwei gedichte Goethe's.— Quellen und anlässe Goethe'scher dramen.—Dramatische entwürfe Goethe's.—Goethe mit zeitgenossen.—Vermischtes.—Berichtigungen und nachträge.

Reichlin-Meldegg, K: Alexander *freiherr* v. Faust ; an exposition of Goethe's Faust. From the german by R: H. Chittenden. N. Y. [1864]. D.   **832.2 : 1**

Vischer, F: Theodor. Goethe's Faust ; neue beiträge zur kritik des gedichts. Stuttg. 1875.
O.   **831 : 115**
Note. For a defense of the author's views, *see his* Altes und neues, 834:17 v2.

Lasswitz, Emil. Goethe's Faust-tragödie. Milw. 1877. O.   **832.2 : Pam**

Gottsched, J: Christoph. Gottsched und seine zeit ; auszüge aus seinem briefwechsel zusammengestellt und erläutert von Theodor W: Danzel. Anhang: Daniel W: Trillers anmerkungen zu Klopstocks Gelehrtenrepublik. 2te ausg. Leipz. 1855. O.   **830.1 : 22**

Jung, Jakob F: Alexander. Briefe über Gutzkow's Ritter vom geiste. Leipz. 1856. S.   **830.2 : 1**

Frey, Adolf. Albrecht von Haller und seine bedeutung für die deutsche literatur. Leipz. 1879. O.   **830.1 : 24**

Köpke, Rudolph. Die älteste deutsche dichterin [Hrosuitha]; kulturgeschichtliches bild aus dem zehnten jahrhundert. Berlin. 1869. D.   **830.1 : 23**

2. Collected works.

Kürschner, Joseph, *ed.* Deutsche national-litteratur ; historisch kritische ausgabe, unter mitwirkung von [mehreren gelehrten] herausgegeben. 111. Berlin und Stuttg. [1882–85]. 57 v. D.   **830 : 152**
Contents of volumes published:
1. Die älteste deutsche litteratur bis um das jahr 1060 ; bearb. von Paul Piper, [mit wörterverzeichnis]. **6.** Kudrun ; herausg. vcn K: Bartsch, [mit glossar].
11. Narrenbuch, herausg. und erläutert von Felix Bobertag. Der pfarrer vom Kalenberg.—Peter Leu. —Neithart Fuchs.— Salomon und Markolf.— Bruder Rausch.
13. Deutsches leben im volkslied um 1530, herausg. von Rochus *freiherrn* v. Liliencron. Einleitung [über die volkspoesie].—Volkslieder, mit musik.
20, 21. Sachs, Hans. Werke, herausg. von [Bernhard] Arnold. **1.** Einleitung.—Chronologische übersicht der spruchgedichte. — Disputation zwischen einem chorherren und schuchmacher. — Strophische gedichte.—Einfache spriche. **2.** Dramatische spriche.—Wortregister.
26. Albertinus, Aegidius. Lucifers königreich und seelengejaidt; herausg. von Rochus *freiherrn* v. Liliencron.
28. Fleming, Paul. Poetische wälder; Oden; Sonette.—Logau, F: v. Sinngedichte.—Olearius [*originally* Oelschläger], Adam. Neue orientalische reisebeschreibung. Herausg. von [H.] Oesterley.
29. *Erste schlesische schule,* 4: Gryphius, Andreas. Werke, herausg. von Hermann Palm. Einleitung.— Leo Armenius, trspl.—Cardenio und Celinde, oder Unglücklich verliebte; trspl.—Absurda Comica, oder Herr Peter Squentz; schimpfspiel.—Horribilicribrifax, deutsch; scherz-spiel.—Die gelibte Dornrose; scherz-spiel.—Gedichte.
30. *Erste schlesische schule,* 5: Dach, Simon, seine freunde [Robert Robertin, H: Albert, Christoph Kaldenbach, Andreas Adersbach], und J: Röling; herausg. von H. Oesterley. Gedichte.
32. Moscherosch, Hans Michael. Gesichte Philanders von Sittewald; herausg. von Felix Bobertag.
33–35. Grimmelshausen, Hans Jacob Christoffel v. Werke, herausg. von Felix Bobertag. 1, 2. Einleitung: Ueber den deutschen roman vor Grimmelshausen.—Der abentheurliche Simplicius Simplicissimus. **3.** Simplicianische schriften: Trutz Simplex, oder . . . Die ertzbetrügerin und landstörtzerin Courrasche; Aus dem Seltsamen Springinsfeld; Das wunderbarliche vogel-nest; Das rathstübel Plutonis; Aus dem Ratio status.
37. *Zweite schlesische schule,* 2: Zigler und Kliphausen, H: Anselm v. Asiatische Banise; nebst proben aus der romanprosa des 17. und 18. jahrh., herausg. von Felix Bobertag.
38, 39. Die gegner der zweiten schlesischen schule, herausg. von L: Fulda: **1.** Günther, J:

Christian. Gedichte. **2.** Weise, Christian. Bäurischer Machiavellus; Comödie von der bösen Catharine.—**Brockes,** Barthold, H: Gedichte.—Canitz, F: Rudolf L: *freiherr* v. Gedichte.— **Neukirch,** B: Gedichte.—**Wernike,** Christian. Epigramme.
40. Abraham *a S. Clara,* [Ulrich Megerle]. Judas der ertzschelm, auswahl; herausg. von Felix Bobertag.
41, *in 2 abt.,* herausg. von Adolf Frey: **1.** Gessner, Salomon. Werke, auswahl: Die nacht; Daphnis; Idyllen, 1ste folge; Der Tod Abels; Vermischte gedichte; Der erste schiffer; Idyllen, 2te folge; Brief über die landschaftsmalerei. **2.** Haller, Albrecht v. Versuch schweizerischer gedichte; Usong, les buch.— Salis-Seewis, J: Gaudenz v. Gedichte; Anhang.— Wortregister.
42. Gottsched, J: Christoph, und die schweizer J: Jakob Bodmer und J: Jakob Breitinger; herausg. von Johannes Crüger. Einleitung, [mit der geschichte und bedeutung ihres streites].—Bodmer und Breitinger's Discourse der mahlern.—Gottsched's Sterbender Cato, trspl.—Bodmer's Gottsched, trspl in versen, oder Der parodirte Cato.—Ein kapitel aus Breitinger's kritischer dichtkunst.—Bodmer's Rache der schwester; die erste neuhochdeutsche umarheitung der Nibelungen.—Abschnitt aus Bodmer's Homerübersetzung.—Gottsched, Luise Adelgunde Victorine, *born* Kulm. Das testament, lspl.
46 *(in 2 pts.)-***48.** Klopstock, F: Gottlieb. Werke; herausg. von R: Hamel. **1.** Einleitung.—Der Messias; 1-7 gesang. **2.** Der Messias; 8-20 gesang. **3.** Oden. — Geistliche lieder. — Epigramme. **4.** Hermanns schlacht; ein bardiet. — Anhang: Das bardengesang des 18. jahrh. : Denis, J: Nepomuk Cosmas Michael, gedichte; Gerstenberg, H: W: v. Ugolino. Gedichte, Ariadne auf Naxos, Der skalde; Kretschmann, K: F:. Gedichte: Der gesang Rhingulphs des Barden.—Wörterverzeichnis.
52–54. Wieland, Christoph Martin. Werke, 2er-4er teil; herausg. von H: Pröhle. **2.** Oberon.— Verschiedene erzählungen und märchen in versen: Geron der adelige; Das wintermärchen; Das sommermärchen; Hann und Gulpenheh; Pervonte; Die wasserkufe; Der vogelgesang; Gandalin; Schach Lolo. **3.** Geschichte der abderiten. **4.** Aristipp; 1es und 2es buch.
58-60 *(pt. 1),* **64** *(in 2 pts.).* Lessing, J: Gotthold Ephraim. Werke; herausg. von R. Boxberger. **1.** Lieder.—Oden.—Gereimte fabeln und erzählungen.— Sinngedichte.—Epigrammata; mit übers. des herausg. — Fragmente. — Fabeln in prosa.— Jugenddramen, [1ste abt.] : Der junge gelehrte, lspl in 3 aufz.; Die juden, lspl in 1 aufz.— Register zu den Gedichten und Fabeln. **2.** Jugenddramen, 2te abt.: Der freigeist, lspl in 5 aufz.; Der schatz, lspl in 1 aufz.; Der misogyn, lspl in 3 aufz.; Miss Sara Sampson, trspl in 5 aufz.; Philotas, trspl. — Dramatische meisterwerke, 1ste abt.: Minna von Barnhelm, oder Das soldatenglück, lspl in 5 aufz.; Emilia Galotti, trspl in 5 aufz. **3.** 1ste abt. Dramatische meisterwerke, 2te abt.: Nathan der weise, dramatisches gedicht in 5 aufz. — Anhang; Jugenddramen, die Lessing in seine schriften nicht aufgenommen: Damon, oder Die wahre freundschaft, lspl in 1 aufz.; Die alte jungfer, lspl in 3 aufz. **4.** 1ste abt. Recensionen und anderes aus zeitschriften; 1747-1751. 2te abt.: Das neueste aus dem reiche des witzes, als eine beilage zu den Berlinischen staats- und gelehrten zeitungen, apr.-dez. 1751.—Dramaturgische zeitschriften. **1,** Beiträge zur historie und aufnahme des theaters: Abhandlung von dem leben und den werken des Marcus Accius Plautus; Die gefangenen, ein lspl aus dem latein. des Plautus übers.; Kritik über "Die gefangenen."
72. Weisses jugendfreunde, herausg. von Jacob Minor. Weisse, Christian Felix. Richard III, trspl in 5 aufz.; Die verwandelten weiber, oder Der teufel ist los, komische oper in 3 aufz. — Cronegk, J: F: v. Olint und Sophronia, trspl: Roschmann's fortsetzung. — Brawe, Joachim W: v. Brutus, trspl in 5 aufz.— Nicolai, Christoph F: Abhandlung vom trauerspiele: Freuden des jungen Werthers, Leiden und freuden Werthers des mannes, ein gespräch.
73. Fabeldichter, satiriker und popularphilosophen des 18. jahrh., herausg. von Jacob Minor. Lichtwer, Magnus Gottfried. Aesopische fabeln.— Pfeffel, Gottlieb Konrad. Fabeln. — Kästner, Abraham Gotthelf. Sinngedichte. — Göckingk, Leopold F: Günther. Episteln. — Aus den liedern zweier liebenden.—Mendelssohn, Moses. Phädon, oder Ueber die unsterblichkeit der seele.—Zimmermann, J: G: Ueber die einsamkeit.—Wortregister.
75. Herder, J: Gottfried v. Werke, 2er teil; herausg. von Hans Lambel. **2.** Der Cid: Einleitung; Ge-

schichte des don Ruy Diaz, grafen von Bivar, nach spanischen romanzen. — Paramythien. — Blätter der vorzeit, und Jüdische parabeln.—Legenden.—Admetus haus, der tausch des schicksals; drama mit gesängen.—Gedichte.

78. Bürger, Gottfried A: Gedichte, herausg. von A: Sauer. [mit biogr. und litterarhistorischer einleitung und register].

79-81. Stürmer und dränger; herausg. von A: Sauer. **1.** Die sturm- und drangperiode. — **Klinger,** F: Maximilian v. Die zwillinge, trspl in 5 aufz.; Sturm und drang, sspl; Der verbannte götter-sohn, eine unterhaltung; Gedichte; Fausts leben, thaten und höllenfahrt.—**Leisewitz,** J: Anton. Julius von Tarent, trspl. **2. Lenz,** Jacob Michael Reinhold. Der hofmeister, oder Vorteile der privaterziehung, komödie; Die soldaten, komödie; Pandaemonium germanicum, skizze; Leopold Wagner, matinée; Tantalus, dramolett; Der waldbruder [ein pendant zu Werther's leiden]; Gedichte.—**Wagner,** H: Leopold. Die kindermörderin, trspl; Prometheus, Deukalion und seine recensenten. **3. Müller,** F: called Maler. Golo und Genoveva, sspl in 5 aufz.; Situation aus Fausts leben; Der faun, idylle; Der erschlagene Abel, skizze; Die schaaf-schur, pfälzische idylle; Das Heidelberger schloss; Kreuznach; Gedichte. — **Schubert,** Christian F: Daniel. Gedichte.

82, 83, 86-88, 93, 114. Göthe, J: Wolfgang v. Werke. **1, 2, 5.** Gedichte, herausg. von H: Düntzer; Lieder; Gesellige lieder; Balladen; Elegieen; Episteln; Epigramme; Weissagungen des Bakis; Vier jahreszeiten. — Sonette; Kantaten; Vermischte gedichte; Aus Wilhelm Meister; Antiker form sich nähernd; Parabolisch; Gott, gemüt und welt; Sprichwörtlich; Epigrammatisch.—Hermann und Dorothea; Achilles; Der ewige jude; Reineke Fuchs. **6, 7.** Dramen, herausg. von K.J. Schröer: B. **1,** Übersicht und anordnung.—Bekenntnisse: Die laune des verliebten, schäferspiel in 1 akte; Die mitschuldigen, lspl in 3 akt.; Stella, trspl in 5 akt.; Die geschwister, trspl in 1 akt. — Puppenspiele und fastnachtspiele: Neueröffnetes moralisch-politisches puppenspiel, Künstlers erdewallen, Des künstlers vergötterung, Künstlers apotheose, Das jahrmarktsfest zu Plundersweilen; Das neueste von Plundersweilen; Ein fastnachtspiel von Pater Brey; Satyros, oder Der vergötterte waldteufel; Hanswursts hochzeit, oder Der lauf der welt.—Satiren: Prolog zu den Neuesten offenbarungen gottes verdeutscht durch dr. K: F: Bahrdt; Götter, helden und Wieland; Der triumph der empfindsamkeit; Die vögel, nach den Aristophanes.—**B. 2.** Singspiele: Erwin und Elmire. — Claudine von Villa Bella.—Lila.—Jery und Bätely.—Die fischerin—Scherz, list und rache.—Die unglelchen hausgenossen. — Der zauberflöte zweiter teil. **12.** Faust, herausg. von H: Düntzer. **33.** Naturwissenschaftliche schriften, 1er band, herausg. von Rudolf Steiner, mit einem vorworte von K.J. Schröer. Vorwort. —Uebersicht und anordnung.—Einleitung: Die entstehung der metamorphosenlehre; Die entstehung von Goethes gedanken über die bildung der tiere; Ueber wesen und bedeutung von Goethes schriften über organische bildung; Ueber die morphologischen hefte. — Bildung und umbildung organischer naturen: Zur morphologie; Verfolg; Anhang. —Register.

120, 121, 124. Schiller, J: Christoph F: v. Werke: **3, 4,** 7 teil, herausg. von R. Boxberger. **3.** Die räuber; sspl in 5 akt.—Same [theater-ausgabe].—Die verschwörung des Fiesco zu Genua; republikanisches trspl in 5 akt. — Same [theater-ausgabe]. **4.** Einleitung [mit übers. von abbé César Vischard de St.-Réals "Don Carlos, nouvelle historique"].—Kabale und liebe; bürgerl. trspl. —Don Karlos, infant von Spanien; dramatisches gedicht.—Same; erster druck aus der Thalia.—Same; trspl in 5 aufz., [bühnen-bearbeitung]. **7.** Uebersetzungen und bearbeitungen fremder lustspiele: Turandot, prinzessin von China, tragikomisches märchen nach [C:] Gozzi; Der parasit, oder die kunst sein glück zu machen, lspl nach dem franz., [Méldiore et rampant von L: B. Picard]; Der neffe als onkel, lspl in 3 aufz. aus dem franz., [Encore des Ménechmes] des Picard. —Bühnenbearbeitungen fremder stücke: Goethes Egmont; Lessings Nathan der weise; Shakespeares Othello, [fragment].

130. Richter, J: Paul F: Jean Pauls werke, herausgeg. von Paul Nerrlich. **1.** Einleitung: Biographie und charakteristik; Verzeichnis der werke.—Kleine schriften zur philosophie und religion.—Satiren und idyllen: 1, Mein aufenthalt in der Nepomukskirche während der belagerung der reichsfestung

Ziebingen; 2, Des amts-vogts Josuah Freudel klaglibell gegen seinen verfluchten dämon; 3, Des feldpredigers Schmelzle reise nach Flätz mit fortlaufenden noten, nebst der Beichte des teufels bei einem staatsmanne; 4, Des rektors Florian Fälbels und seiner primaner reise nach dem Fichtelberg; 5, Die wenig erwogene gefahr, die beiden herrschaften Walchern und Lilzelberg in der verlosung am 3t. juni dieses jahrs zu gewinnen, in einem briefwechsel zwischen dem rektor Seemaus und mir; 6, Leben des vergnügten schulmeisterleins Maria Wuz in Auenthal.

140. Kortum, C: Arnold. Die Jobsiade, ein komisches heldengedicht; herausg. von F. Bobertag.

142 (in 2 pts.). **Hebel,** J: P: Werke, herausg. von O. Behaghel. **1er t.** Einleitung, mit bibliographie.— Allemannische gedichte. **2er t.** Schatzkästlein des Rheinischen hausfreundes.

144, 1e abt. **Tieck,** J: L: Werke, 1er t.; herausg. von Jacob Minor. — Wundersame liebesgeschichte der schönen Magelone und des grafen Peter aus der Provence.— Leben und tod der heiligen Genoveva, trspl.

149, 2e abt. **Kleist,** H: v. Sämmtliche werke, 2ter t.; herausg. von Theophil Zolling. Der zerbrochene krug, lspl. — Fragment aus dem trspl Robert Guiskard, herzog der normänner.—Amphitryon; lspl nach Molière.—Penthesilea. trspl.

51. Das schicksalsdrama, herausg. von Jacob Minor. **Werner,** Zacharias. Martin Luther, oder Die weihe der kraft, tragödie; Die weihe der unkraft, ein ergänzungsblatt zur Deutschen haustafel; Der vierundzwanzigste februar, tragödie in 1 akt.—**Müllner,** Adolf. Der neunundzwanzigste februar, trspl in 1 akt; Die schuld, trspl in 4 akten. — **Houwald,** Christoph Ernst freiherr v. Der leuchtturm, trspl in 2 akten.—Register.

Familien-bibliothek der deutschen classiker; eine anthologie in 100 bänden und 30 supplement. [*a large number of which are missing*]. Hildburghausen. 1841-46. 65 v. S.   **830 : 8-130**

Contents of the volumes on hand:

8. Hölty, L: H: Christoph. Gedichte; mit biogr. und portr.—**Starke,** Gotthelf W: Christopher. Ausgewählte gedichte und erzählungen.

9. Leisewitz, J: Anton. Julius von Tarent; ein trauerspiel in 5 akten.—Classische gedichte von vergessenen; aus den Göttinger Musenalmanachen von 1775—1784.

13-15. Seume, J: Gottfried. Selbstbiographie *und* Spaziergang nach Syrakus. 3 v.

18. Hebel, J: P: Zwei kränze aus [seinen] schriften: ler kranz.

19. Haller, Albrecht v. Sämmtliche gedichte; mit der biogr. des dichters.

21, 22. Sturz, Helfrich P: Beste schriften; mit lebensbeschreibung und portr. des verf. 2 v.

24, 27. Musäus, J: K: A: Deutsche volksmährchen; mit der biogr. und portr. des verf., b. 1, 4.—**28.** Ausgewählte werke.

30. Lichtwer, Magnus Gottfried. Fabeln.

31, 32. Claudius, Mathias. (*Der Wandsbecker Bote*). Auswahl des besten und schönsten aus Claudius' schriften. 2 v.

33. Kleist, H: v. Käthchen von Hellbronn, ritterschauspiel; mit der biogr. des dichters.

43, 44. Klopstock, F: Gottlieb. Briefwechsel. 2 v.

52. Neuffer, Christian L: Gedichte; mit der biogr. und dem portr. des verf.

60-63. Epigrammen-dichter: b. 3-6.

66, 67. Richter, J: Paul F: Anthologie; mit biogr. vorwort. 2 v.

68. Collin, H: Joseph edler v. Anthologie aus [seinen] werken.— **69.** Regulus; eine tragödie in 5 aufz.

74. Kosegarten, L: Theobul. Anthologie aus [seinen] gedichten.

75. Mathisson, F: v. Anthologie aus [seinen] gedichten.—**Salis-Seewis,** J: Gaudenz freiherr v. Gedichte; anthologie.

76, 77. Rotteck, C: v. Geist aus [seinen] sämmtlichen werken; mit biogr. und portr. 2 v.

78. Eberhard, A: Gottlieb. Geist aus [seinen] sämmtlichen werken.

79. Voss, J: H: Anthologie aus [seinen] schriften; mit biogr. und portr.—Deutsche freiheitslieder von Voss und andern.

82, 83. Zschokke, J: H: Daniel. Anthologie aus [seinen] werken. 2 v.

84. Stolberg, F: Leopold *and* Christian *grafen* zu. Anthologie aus den gedichten von den gebrüdern grafen zu Stolberg; mit biogr. und portr.

85. Lichtenberg, G: Christoph. Ideen; mit biogr. und portr.

86, 87. Gleim, J: W: L: Anthologie aus [seinen] sämmtlichen werken; mit biogr. 2 v.

89. Schlegel, A: W: *and* K: W: F: v. Anthologie aus [ihren] werken; mit biographien und A: W: [v.] Schlegel's portr.

93. Garve, Christian. Anthologie aus [seinen] sämmtlichen werken.

94. Baggesen, Jens, *and* Adam Gottlob **Oehlenschläger.** Anthologie aus [ihren] gedichten; mit biogr. und Baggesen's portr.

95. Pichler, Caroline, *born* Greiner. Anthologie aus [ihren] sämmtlichen werken; mit biogr. und portr.

96. Hagedorn, F: v. Anthologie aus [seinen] gedichten; mit biogr. und portr.

99. Kind, J: F: Anthologie aus [seinen] gedichten; mit biogr. und portr.

102. Müller, Johannes v. Anthologie aus [seinen] werken; mit biogr. und portr.

103. Conz, C: Philipp. Anthologie aus [seinen] gedichten.

105. Göckingk, Leopold F: Günther v. Anthologie aus [seinen] gedichten; mit biogr. und portr.

106. Horn, Franz Christoph. Geist aus [seinen] sämmtlichen werken.

108. Kleist, Ewald Christian v. Anthologie aus [seinen] gedichten.—**Krug v. Nidda,** F: Ausgewählte poetisch-prosaische schriften.

109. Möser, Justus. Patriotische phantasien, im auszuge: mit portr. und biogr.—Anhang: **Zachariä,** Justus F: W: Ausgewählte gedichte.

111. Manso, J: Kasper F: Anthologie aus [seinen] schriften; mit biogr. und portr.—**Hubert,** L: Ferdinand. Ausgewählte erzählungen.

112. Winkler, K: Gottfried Theodor, (*Theodor Hell*). Ausgewählte gedichte; mit portr. und biogr.—**Clepp,** Ernst. Ausgewählte gedichte.

113. Wessenberg, Ignatz H: K: *freiherr* v. Anthologie aus [seinen] gedichten.

115. Wagner, J: Ernst. Genius [aus seinen werken].

117. Aus den ältern deutschen dichtern, von den zeiten der minnesänger bis auf Gryphius; mit Luther's portr.

119. Haug, F:, *and* F: **Rückert.** Anthologie aus [ihren] gedichten.

120. Dusch, J: Jakob. Moralische briefe.—**Kästner,** Abraham Gottelf. Epigramme; mit portr.—**Uz,** J: P: Ausgewählte gedichte.

121. Weissbar, C: Biographische spittelfreuden des abgesetzten privatschreibers Jeremias Kätzlein; eine erzählung.—**Gotter,** F: W: Ausgewählte gedichte.

124. Ramler, K: W:, Max v. **Schenkendorf** *and* Valerius W: **Neubeck.** Anthologie aus [ihren] werken.

125. Benzel-Sternau, Christian Ernst *graf* v. Geist aus [seinen] werken; mit portr. und biogr.

127. Schulze, Ernst Konrad F: Anthologie aus [seinen] werken.

128. Cramer, J: Andreas, *and* K: H: **Heidenreich.** Anthologie aus [ihren] gedichten.

129. Brachmann, Karoline Marie Louise, *and* Gotthelf A: *freiherr* v. **Maltitz.** Anthologie aus [ihren] gedichten.

130. Klinger, F: Max v. Anthologie aus [seinen] werken.
Contents, see Deutscher katalog, p. 20.

Börne, L: Gesammelte schriften. Milw. 1858. 5 v. D.   **830 : 131**
Contents, see Deutscher katalog, p. 19.

Büchner, G: Nachgelassene schriften. *T. p. w.* S.   **830 : 132**
Contents, see Deutscher katalog, p. 19.

Campe, Joachim H: Kinderbibliothek; durchgesehen und herausg. von C. Michael. 13te rechtmässige ausg. Braunschw. 1881. 6 t. in 1 v. S.   **x 830 : 157**

Chamisso, A: C: Adelbert v. Werke. 6te aufl. Berlin. 1874. 4 v. in 2. S.   **830 : 133**
Contents, see Deutscher katalog, p. 19.

x denotes books specially adapted for children.

Contessa, C: W: *Salice-*. Schriften; herausg. von E. v. Houwald; b. 2–5, 7–9. Leipz. 1826. 7 v. D.   **830 : 134**
Contents, see Deutscher katalog, p. 19.

Gaudy, Franz Bernhard H: W: *freiherr* v. Poetische und prosaische werke; herausg. von Arthur Müller. Berlin. 1853, 1854. 8 v. in 2. S.   **830 : 135**
Contents, see Deutscher katalog, p. 19.

Göthe, J: Wolfgang v. Sämmtliche werke. Vollständige ausg. Stuttg. 1854, 1855. 6 v. O.   **830 : R136**

— Werke. Erste ill. ausg. mit erläuternden einleitungen [von G. Wendt und E. Hermann]. 9te aufl. Berlin. 1876–81. 34 v. in 17. D.   **830 : 137**
Contents, see Deutscher katalog, p. 20.

— [Works.] Cambridge ed., ed. and rev. by F. H. Hedge and L. Noa. Bost. 1882. 10 v. O.   **830 : 151**
Contents. V. 1. Poems, tr. in the original metres by E. A. Bowring, W. E. Aytoun, Theodore Martin, G. H. Lewes, E: Chawner, Leopold Noa. T: Carlyle, J. S. Dwight, A. J. W. Morrison, H. W. Longfellow, C: J. Sprague, H: Dale. 2. Faust: pt. 1, ed. and annotated by F. H. Hedge; metrical version by miss Swanwick; pt. 2, tr. by miss Swanwick. 3. Faust: a prose translation by A. Hayward.—Clavigo.—Egmont.—The wayward lover. 4. Iphigenia in Tauris, tr. by A. Swanwick.—Torquato Tasso, tr. by A. Swanwick.—Goetz von Berlichingen, tr. by sir W. Scott.—The fellow culprits, tr. by E. A. Bowring. 5. Sorrows of Werther.—Elective affinities.—A tale. 6. Wilhelm Meister's apprenticeship, tr. by T: Carlyle. 7. Same, continued.—Meister's travels, or The renunciate.—The recreations of the german emigrants. 8. Letters from Switzerland.—Travels in Italy, tr. by A. J. W. Morrison. 9, 10. Autobiography, tr. by J: Oxenford.

Hartmann, Moritz. Gesammelte werke; mit portr. Stuttg. 1873, 1874. 10 v. D.   **830 : 138**
Contents, see Deutscher katalog, p. 20.

Heine, H: Sämmtliche werke. Hamburg. 1876. 18 v. in 9. S.   **830 : 139**
Contents, see Deutscher katalog, p. 20.

Herder, J: Gottfried v. Werke; nach den besten quellen revidirte ausgabe, herausg. und mit anmerkungen begleitet von H: Düntzer, [b. 4, 5, von Anton Edmund Wollheim da Fonseca]. Berlin. [1879]. 24 v. in 13. S.   **830 : 154**
Contents. V. 1. Gedichte; nebst einer biographie des dichters. 2. Legenden. — Dramatische stücke und reden: Admetus' haus, der tausch des schicksais; Ariadne-Libera, melodrama; Der entfesselte Prometheus, scenen; Aeon und Aeonis, allegorie; Philoktet, scenen; Brutus, drama; Psyche.—Prosaische dichtungen: Paramythien; Ob malerei oder tonkunst eine grössere wirkung gewähre; Voraussicht und zurücksicht; Verstand und herz; Das fest der grazien; Kalligenia; Mandeville's Bienenfabel. 3. Terpsichore [nach Jakob Balde].—Uebersetzungen aus Campanella, Sarbievius, Faustina Zappi, Swift und Young. 4. Der Cid; nach spanischen romanzen. 5. Stimmen der völker in liedern: Vorrede: Lieder aus dem hohen nord; Aus dem süd; Nordwestliche lieder; Nordische lieder; Deutsche lieder; Lieder der wilden.—Anhang: Ueber Ossian und die lieder alter völker; Von ähnlichkeit der mittlern englischen und deutschen dichtkunst. 6. Morgenländische literatur.—Griechische literatur. 7. Römische literatur, mit anhang: Bemühungen des vergangenen jahrh. in der kritik; Herculanum, Winckelmann's Geschichte der kunst. 9–12. Ideen zur philosophie der geschichte der menschheit. 13. Briefe zur beförderung der humanität. 14. Adrastea: Begebenheiten und charaktere des vergangenen jahrh.; Früchte aus den sogenannten goldnen zeiten des 18. jahrh.; Wissenschaften, ereignisse und charaktere des vergangenen jahrh. zur beförderung eines geistigen reiches; Nachlese. 15. Zerstreute blätter. Die seelenwanderung.—Liebe und selbstheit.—G. E. Les-

sing.— Bild, dichtung und fabel.— Persepolis.— Die menschliche unsterblichkeit.—Denkmale der vorwelt. —Tithon und Aurora.—Parabeln und Einige vaterländische gespräche [von J: Valentin Andreä].—Andenken an einige ältere deutsche dichter.— Cäcilia. — Denkmal Ulrich's von Hutten.—Das land der seelen. — Palingenesie. — Wissen und nichtwissen der zukunft.—Wissen, ahnen, wünschen, hoffen und glauben. 16. Schulreden: nebst hodegetischen vorträgen und pädagogischen aufsätzen. 17. Gesammelte abhandlungen, aufsätze, beurtheilungen und vorreden aus der Weimarer zeit. Wirkung der dichtkunst auf die sitten der völker in alten und neuen zeiten.—Einfluss der regierung auf die wissenschaften und der wissenschaften auf die regierung.—Einfluss der schönen in die höhern wissenschaften.— Erkennen und empfinden der menschlichen seele; bemerkungen und träume.— Plastik; einige wahrnehmungen über form und gestalt aus Pygmalion's bildendem traume.—Aus dem "Teutschen merkur", 1776–82.—Aus Schiller's "Horen", 1795–96.—Aus der "Neuen deutschen monatsschrift", 1795.—Aus Herder's nachlass: Zu K: v. Dalberg's Betrachtungen über das universum: Eine muthmassung über die sündfluth: Persepolitanische briefe. — Entwürfe zu abhandlungen.—Recensionen.—Vorreden. 18. Gott; einige gespräche über Spinoza's system; nebst Shaftesbury's Naturhymnus.—Metakritik zur kritik der reinen vernunft.—Kalligone: Vom angenehmen und schönen; Von kunst und kunstrichterei; Vom erhabnen und vom ideal. 19. Fragmente über die neuere deutsche litteratur, 1, Vorrede; Einleitung; Fragmente von abhandlungen; Beschluss.—2, Vorläufiger discurs: Einleitung: Vergleichung unserer orientalischen dichtkunst mit ihren originalen; Von der griechischen litteratur in Deutschland; Nachschrift.—3, Aussicht über die neuere römische litteratur; Vom neuern gebrauch der mythologie; Von einigen nachbildungen der römer; Nachschrift. — Abänderungen und zusätze. 20. Kritische wälder: Ueber Lessing's Laokoon; Ueber einige Klotzische schriften; Ueber Riedel's Theorie der schönen künste.—Ueber T: Abbt's schriften. 21. Kleinere schriften aus der vor-Weimarer zeit. Haben wir noch jetzt das publicum und vaterland der alten?— Ueber den ursprung der sprache.—Auch eine philosophie der geschichte zur bildung der menschheit.— Ursachen des gesunkenen geschmacks bei den verschiedenen völkern, da er geblüht. 22, 23. Aus zeitschriften und sammelwerken vor der Weimarer zeit: 1, Aus den Königsbergschen gelehrten und politischen zeitungen; recensionen; Aus den Rigischen gelehrten beiträgen.—2, Aus Nicolai's Allgemeiner deutscher bibliothek, recensionen; Aus dem Wandsbecker boten; Aus den Frankfurter gelehrten anzeigen; Aus der sammlung von deutscher art und kunst. Shakespeare; Aus der Lemgoer Auserlesenen bibliothek der neuesten deutschen litteratur. 24. Nachlass der vor-Weimarer zeit: Königsberg und Riga; Während des aufenthaltes in Frankreich; Bückeburg.—Nachträge.

Lessing, J: Gotthold Ephraim. Werke; nebst biographie des dichters. Berlin. [1868–1877]. 20 v. in 12. S. 830 : 155
  Contents. V 1. Gotthold Ephraim Lessing; eine biographische skizze. — Gedichte und fabeln. 2. Minna von Barnhelm.—Miss Sara Sampson.—Philotas. 3. Emilia Galotti.—Nathan der weise. 4. Der junge gelehrte.—Die juden.—Der misogyn. 5. Der freigeist.—Der schatz.—Damon.—Die alte jungfer. 6. Laokoon. 7. Hamburgische dramaturgie.—Namenund sachregister zu *derselben*, nebst litteraturgeschichtlichen ergänzungen von G: Zimmermann. 8. Das neueste aus dem reiche des witzes, *und* Die kritischen briefe von 1753; herausg. und mit anm. begleitet von Robert Pilger. — Namen- und sachregister. 9. Briefe, die neueste litteratur betreffend; herausg. und mit anm. begl. von C: Christian Redlich.—Register. 10. Abhandlungen über die fabel *und* Anmerkungen über das epigramm; herausg. und mit anm. begl. von C: C. Redlich. 11 (*in 2 abth.*). Kleinere schriften zur dramatischen poesie: 1, Beiträge zur historie und aufnahme des theaters; Theatralische bibliothek; Vorrede zu Thomson; Sophokles; 2, Das theater des herrn Diderot; Dramatische entwürfe, pläne und fragmente aus Lessing's nachlass. — Kleinere schriften zur fabel.—Alphabetische übersicht. 12. Kleinere schriften zur modernen litteratur und sprache; herausg. und mit anm. begl. von C: C. Redlich.—Alphabet. übersicht. 13. Classische litteratur; herausg. und mit anm. begl. von Emil Grosse. — Bildende künste; herausg.

Lessing, J: Gotthold Ephraim.—*Continued.*
  und mit anm. begl. von Alfred Schöne.—Register. 14. 17. Theologische schriften; herausg. und mit anm. begl. von Christian Gross. 18. Philosophische schriften; herausg. und mit anm. begl. von Chr. Gross.— Register zu 14–18. 19, herausg. und mit anm. begl. von C: Chr. Redlich. Zur geschichte und gelehrtengeschichte. — Vermischtes. — Nachträge. — Lessingbibliothek [bibliographie]. — Register zu 1–19. 20, herausg. und mit anm. begl. von C: Chr. Redlich; *1ste abth.*, Briefe von Lessing; *2te abth.*, Briefe an Lessing.
— **Ausgewählte werke. Leipz. 1867. 6 v. S.**
  830 : 140
  Contents, see Deutscher katalog, p. 20, 21.
Platen-Hallermünde, A: *graf* v. Gesammelte werke. Stuttg. 1853. 5 v. S. 830 : 141
  Contents, see Deutscher katalog, p. 21.
Richter, J: Paul F:. (*Jean Paul*). Sämmtliche werke. 3te aufl. Berlin. 1860–62. 34 v. in 16. S. 830 : 142
  Contents, see Deutscher katalog, p. 21.
— **Sämmtliche werke; b. 54, 55. Berlin. 1828. 2 v. in 1. D. 830 : 142 v54,55**
  Contents. V. 54. Leben Fibel's, des verfassers der Bienrodischen fibel. 55. Ueber die deutschen doppelwörter.
Schiller, J: Christoph F: Sämmtliche werke. Leipz. *n. d.* 12 v. in 4. S. 830 : 143
— **Sämmtliche werke. Neue, mit gedichten und einer umfassenden biogr. vermehrte, nach den ersten drucken verb. aufl.; b. 2, 5, 7–9. 11–18. Stuttg. 1837. S. 830 : 144**
  Contents, see Deutscher katalog, p. 21.
— **Works. Tr. from the german. Lond. 1853–80. 6 v. D. 830 : 150**
  Contents. V. 1. History of the thirty years' war. tr. by A. J. W. Morrison.—History of the revolt of the Netherlands, to the confederacy of the Gueux, tr. by A. J. W. Morrison. 2. History of the revolt of the Netherlands, *continued.*—Trials of counts Egmont and Horn.—Siege of Antwerp.—Wallenstein's camp, tr. by James Churchill.—The Piccolomini; Death of Wallenstein, tr. by S: T. Coleridge.—Wilhelm Tell, tr. by Theodore Martin. 3. Don Carlos, tr. by R. D. Boylan.—Mary Stuart, tr. by Joseph Mellish.— The maid of Orleans, tr. by Anna Swanwick.—The bride of Messina, tr. by A. Lodge. 4. tr. by H: G: Bohn. The robbers.—Fiesco.—Love and intrigue.— Demetrius. — The ghost-seer.—The sport of destiny. 5. Poems, tr. by E. A. Bowring. 6. Essays, aesthetical and philosophical, including the dissertation on the "Connexion between the animal and spiritual in man".
— **The works of Schiller; with a biographical introd. by Hjalmar H. Boyesen. *Special ed.* Ill. Phila. 1884, 1885. 3 v. Q. 830 : R153**
  Contents. V. 1. Poems.—Semele.—The robbers; a tragedy.—The conspiracy of Fiesco at Genoa; a republican tragedy.—Love and intrigue; a tragedy. 2. Don Carlos; a dramatic history.—The misanthrope; a fragment.—Wallenstein. A dramatic history: Wallenstein's camp; Piccolomini; The death of Wallenstein.—Mary Stuart; a tragedy.—The maid of Orleans; a romantic tragedy. 3. The bride of Messina; a tragedy with chorus.—William Tell; a play.—Fragments: Warbeck; The maltese; The children of the house; Demetrius. Prosaic writings. The criminal from lost honor.—The sport of destiny; a fragment of true history.—The ghost-seer.—The revolt of the United Netherlands.—The thirty years' war.
Schlegel, A: W: v. Sämmtliche werke, herausg. von E: Böcking. Leipz. 1846, 1847. 12 v. S. 830 : 145
  Contents, see Deutscher katalog, p. 21, 22.
Schubart, Christian F: Daniel. Gesammelte schriften und schicksale. Stuttg. 1839–40. 8 v. in 4. S. 830 : 146
  Contents, see Deutscher katalog, p. 22.
Seume, J: Gottfried. Prosaische und poetische werke. Berlin. *n. d.* 10 v. in 4. S.
  830 : 147
  Contents, see Deutscher katalog, p. 22.

Tieck, J: L: Schriften. Berlin. 1828–43. 16 v.
830 : 148
Contents, see Deutscher katalog. p. 22.
— Werke ; mit einer einleitung von L. H. Fischer.
V. 1. Berlin. [1885]. D. 830 : 156
Contents. V. 1. Das fest zu Kenelworth.—Dichter-
leben.

Wagner, W: R: Gesammelte schriften und dich-
tungen. Leipz. 1871–73. 8 v. O. 780 : 20
Contents, see under Music, Collected works, col. 491.
Wieland, Christoph Martin. Werke, herausg.
von H: Kurz. Kritisch durchgesehene ausg.
Leipz. n. d. 3 v. S. 830 : 149
Contents, see Deutscher katalog, p. 22.

14. German literature — b, Poetry.

1. Collections.

(See also Romance, col. 514—515.)

Durfee, C: A. Poetical concordance. 811 : R11
Note. For full title, see col. 1021.—Includes references to the poems of Goethe and Schiller.
Schwab, Gustav, *ed.* Fünf bücher deutscher lieder und gedichte, von A. v. Haller bis auf
die neueste zeit ; eine mustersammlung.
5te neu verm. aufl., besorgt von Michael
Bernays. Leipz. 1871. D. 831 : 69
Taylor, W: Historic survey of german poetry ;
with various translations. Lond. 1830. 3
v. O. 831 : 117
Baskerville, Alfred. The poetry of Germany ;
selections from upwards of seventy of the
most celebrated poets tr. into english verse,
with the orig. text on the opposite page.
12th ed. Phila. 1882. D. 831 : 97
Brooks, C: Timothy, *ed.* Songs and ballads, tr.
from Uhland, Körner, Bürger and other
german lyric poets, with notes. (Specimens
of foreign standard literature, ed. by G:
Ripley ; v. 14.) Bost. 1842. D. 831 : 110
Includes Hölty, Schiller, Goethe, Rückert, Klopstock,
Follen, Arndt, Herder, Richter, Pfeffel, Stolberg,
Claudius, Gleim, Schmidt, Langbein, Gellert, Kerner,
Mahlmann, Tieck, Brunn, Kosegarten, Krummacher,
Novalis, and miscellaneous writers collected under
the divisions of Songs of life, Songs of nature, Home
and liberty.
— *tr.* German lyrics. Bost. 1853. D. 831 : 90
Contains translations from Anastasius Grün, Rück-
ert, Uhland, Freiligrath, W: Müller, Langbein, Cha-
misso, Gellert, Seidl, Kerner, Nathusius, Geibel,
Platen, Lenau, Würkert, Claudius and miscellaneous
writers.
Campbell, J: James, *tr.* The song of the bell,
and other poems from the german of
Goethe, Schiller, Bürger, Matthisson and
Salis. Edinb. 1836. S. 831 : 91
Winkworth, Catherine, *tr.* Lyra germanica ;
2d ser., The christian life. Tr. from the
germ. N. Y. 1863. S. 831 : 112
Dulcken, H. W., *ed.* The golden harp ; hymns,
rhymes and songs for the young, adapted
[from the works of german poets]. Ill.
Lond. 1864. D. 831 : 92

*   *   *

Simrock, K: Joseph, *tr.* Das heldenbuch. Stuttg.
1863–78. 6 v. O. 831 : 71
Contents. V. 1. Gudrun. übersetzt. 10te aufl. 1877.
2. Das Nibelungenlied. übers. 37ste aufl. 1878. 3.
Das kleine heldenbuch. übers. 3te aufl. 1874. Walter
und Hildegunde.—Alphart.—Der hornerne Siegfried.
—Der rosengarten. — Das Hildebrandslied.—Ortnit.—
Hugdietrich und Wolfdietrich. 4-6. Das Amelun-
genlied von Simrock. 2te aufl. In 3 t.: 1. Wieland,
der schmied. — Wittich Wielands sohn. — Ecken-aus-
fahrt. 2. Dietlieb. — Sibichs verrath. 3. Die beiden
Dietriche.—Die rabenschlacht.—Die heimkehr.
— - Heliand ; Christi leben und lehre. Nach dem
altsächsischen. Elberfeld. 1856. S.
831 : 73

Simrock, K: Joseph.—*Continued.*
— *ed.* Rheinsagen aus dem munde des volks und
deutscher dichter ; für schule, haus und
wanderschaft. 8te aufl. Bonn. 1870. O.
831 : 74
Dippold, G: Theodore. The great epics of mediæval Germany ; an outline of their contents and history. Bost. 1882. S. 831 : 99
Kudrun ; herausg. und erklärt von Ernst Martin.
Halle. 1872. O. 831 : 101
The original text.
— *Same* ; herausg. von K: Bartsch. *In* Kürschner, J., *ed.* Deutsche national - litteratur.
830 : 152 v6
— *Same.* Gudrun ; eine erzählung aus der deut-
schen heldenzeit für jung und alt. 6te aufl.
Ill. Kreuznach. [1884]. S. 831 : 126
Nibelungenlied, Das, übersetzt von K: Simrock.
39ste aufl. Stuttg. 1880. O. 831 : 72
— *Same* ; übersetzung der handschrift A, Hohe-
nems, München, nebst vorwort und histo-
risch-ästhetische einleitung von Werner
Hahn. Stuttg. [1885]. D. 831 : 123
— *Same.* Nibelungen, Die ; eine heldendichtung
für jung und alt, erzählt von Ferdinand
Schmidt. 8te aufl. Ill. Kreuznach. [1884].
S. 831 : 125
Echoes from mist-land, or the Nibelungen lay
revealed to lovers of romance and chivalry
by Auber Forestier [*pseud. for* A. A. Wood-
ward]. Chicago. 1877. D. 831 : 89
Reinecke Fuchs, aus dem niederdeutschen von
K: Simrock. Frankfurt a. M. [1877]. S.
831 : 58
Hagen, F: H: v. der. Minnesinger ; deutsche
liederdichter des 12ten, 13ten und 14ten
jahrhunderts, aus allen bekannten handschriften und früheren drucken gesammelt
und berichtigt ; mit den lesarten derselben,
geschichte des lebens der dichter und ihrer
werke, sangweisen der lieder, reimver-
zeichnis der anfänge und abbildung sämmtlicher handschriften. Leipz. 1838. 4 v. in 3.
Q. 831+P100
Contents. V, 1, 2: Manessische sammlung aus der
Pariser urschrift, nach G. W. Rassmanns vergleichung, ergänzt und hergestellt. 3. 1er b. Aus den
Jenaer, Heidelberger und Weingarter sammlungen
und den übrigen handschriften und früheren drucken
ergänzt und hergestellt. — 2er b. Verzeichniss der
namhaften 162 dichter in den vorigen drei theilen ;
Anfangszeilen der strophen, kehrreime und leich-
sätze nach den reimen ; Lesarten aller verglichenen
urkunden, mit nachweisung aller darin enthaltenen
lieder der einzelnen dichter ; Druckfehler der früheren ausgaben. 4. Geschichte der dichter und ihrer
werke.—Abbildungen der handschriften. — Sangweisen der Jenaer hs. ; des Nithart in Hagens hs.—Fischer, E. Ueber die musik der minnesinger. — Alte
zeugnisse von den altdeutschen liederdichtern. —
Handschriften, abdrücke, ausgaben, erläuterungen
und erneuungen der minnesinger. — Uebersicht der
dichter nach der zeitfolge. — Verzeichnisse der personen und ortsnamen. — Sangweisen der Nürnberger
meistersänger nach den tönen der minnesinger.

Uhland, L:, ed. Alte hoch- und niederdeutsche volkslieder, mit abhandluug und anmerkungen. 2te unverändete aufl. B. 1: Liedersammlung. Stuttg. 1881. O. **831:121**
Note. B. 2, 3, containing the Abhandlung and Annerkungen respectively, form v. 3 and 4 of Uhland's Schriften zur geschichte der dichtung und sage, 830.1:21 v3, 4, which see.

2. Individual works.

Auersperg, Anton Alexander graf v.,(Anastasius Grün). Gesammelte werke; herausg. vou L. A: Frankl. Berlin. 1877. 5 v. D. **831:1**
Contents, see Deutscher katalog, p. 22.
— The last knight; a romance garland. Tr. with notes by J: O. Sargent. N. Y. 1871. O.
831:113
Balde, Jakob. [Gedichte, nachgebildet von J: G. v. Herder]. See Herder, J: G. v., Terpsichore; in his Werke. 830:154 v3
Bodenstedt, F: Martin v. Alte und neue gedichte. Berlin. 1867, 1868. 3 v. in 1. S.
831:2
— Aus morgenland und abendland, neue gedichte und sprüche. Leipz. 1882. D. **831:94**
— Epische dichtungen. Berlin. 1862. T. **831:3**
Contents, see Deutscher katalog, p. 22.
— Die lieder des Mirza Schaffy, mit einem prolog. 70ste aufl. Berlin. 1877. S. **831:4**
— Same, eng. The songs of Mirza Schaffy, with a prologue. Tr. approved by the poet, from the 84th german ed. by E. d'Esterre. Hamburg. 1880. D. **831:4**
Brennglas, A., pseud., see Glasbrenner, Adolf.
Dilg, W:, (Henricus vom See). Gedichte. Milw. 1866. D. **831:5**
Dingelstedt, Franz. Lyrische dichtungen. Berlin. 1877. 2 v. D. **831:6**
Duboc, C: E:, (Robert Waldmüller). Dorf-idyllen. Stuttg. 1860. T. **831:7**
Eckstein, Ernst. Die gespenster von Varzin; groteskes nachtstück. 3te aufl. Leipz. 1878. S. **831:8**
— Schach der königin! humoristisches epos. 3te aufl. Stuttg. 1879. S. **831:9**
— Venus Urania; humoristisches epos. 2te aufl. Leipz. 1877. S. **831:10**
Ekkehard der erste. Das Waltarilied, verdeutscht von J. V. Scheffel. Ill. Stuttg. [1875.] F.
831:R11
— Same. In Scheffel, J. V. v. Ekkehard.
S 1051
Ende, Henrich [v.]. Mississippi und Rhein; centennial-phantasie. Milw. 1876. D.
831:86
Eschenbach, Wolfram v., see Wolfram.
Freiligrath, Ferdinand v. Sämmtliche werke. N. Y. 1858–59. 6 v. D. **831:12**
Contents, see Deutscher katalog, p. 24.
Fröhlich, Abraham Emanuel. Reimsprüche aus staat, kirche, schule. Zürich. 1850. S.
831:13
Geibel, Emanuel. Gesammelte werke. Stuttg. 1883. 8 v. in 4. D. **831:118**
Contents. V. 1. Jugendgedichte.—Zeitstimmen.—Sonette. 2. Juniuslieder.—Julian. 3. Neue gedichte. —Gedichte und gedenkblätter. 4. Spätherbstblätter. —Heroldsrufe. 5. Judas Ischarioth.—Die blutrache. —Dichtungen in antiker form.—Classisches liederbuch, griechen und römer in deutscher nachbildung: Griechische lyriker; Römische elegien und verwandtes. 6. Brunhild; eine tragödie aus der Nibelungensage.—Die Loreley. 7. Echtes gold wird klar im feuer; ein sprichwort. Sophonisbe; tragödie in 5 aufz.— Meister Andrea; lustspiel in 2 aufz.—Die jagd von

Geibel, Emanuel.—Continued.
Bezier; vorspiel einer albigensertragödie. 8. Gelegenheitsgedichte. — Uebersetzungen französischer lyrik vom zeitalter der revolution bis auf unsere tage.—Drei gedichte lord Byrons.—Spanische romanzen: Romanzen von kaiser Karl und der Paladinen; Romanzen aus der geschichte und sage der pyrenäischen halbinsel; Vermischte romanzen.
— Gedichte. Stuttg. 1883–1885. 3 v. D.
831:120
Contents. V. 1. Erste periode; 103te aufl. 2. Zweite periode; 27ste aufl. 3. Dritte periode; 18te aufl.
Gerok, K: Palm leaves. Tr. from the germ. by J. E. A. Brown. Lond. 1869. S. **831:98**
Gessner, Salomon. The death of Abel. Tr. from the germ., with original notes, by F: Shoberl. Added: Death, a vision. or The solemn departure of saints and sinners; under the similitude of a dream, by J: Macgowan. Lond. 1813. O. **831:93**
Note. Written in poetic prose, and intended as a biblical epos.
Glasbrenner, Adolf, (A. Brennglas). Neuer Reinecke Fuchs. 2te aufl. Frankfurt. M. 1854. S. **831:14**
— Die verkehrte welt; ein komisches gedicht. 2te aufl. Frankfurt a. M. 1856. S.
831:15
Glück, Elisabeth, (Betty Paoli). Romancero. Leipz. 1845. O. **831:16**
Göthe, J: Wolfgang v. Poems and ballads. T. p. w. S. **831:104**
Grimme, W: Gedichte. Münster. 1855. T.
831:17
Groth, Klaus. Quickborn; gedichte aus dem volksleben. Aus Ditmarscher mundart übertr. von A. v. Winterfeld. Berlin. 1856. S. **831:18**
Grün, Anastasius, pseud., see Auersperg, Anton Alex. graf v.
Güll, F: Kinderheimath in liedern. Gütersloh. 1875. D. **x 831:127**
Günther, J: Christian. Aushwahl aus [seinen] dichten. In Roquette, O: Leben und dichten Günthers. **928.3:52**
Gutzkow, K: Ferdinand. Gedichte.—Nero, eine tragödie. — Hamlet in Wittenberg; dramatische phantasie.—Xenien und Epigramme. (Gesammelte werke, b. 1). Frankfurt a. M. 1845. D. **831:19**
Hamerling, Robert. Ahasver in Rom; eine dichtung in sechs gesängen, mit einem epilog an die kritiker. 12te aufl. Hamb. 1877. D. **831:20**
— Amor und Psyche; eine dichtung in sechs gesängen. Ill. von Paul Thumann. 3te aufl. Leipz. n.-d. Q. **831:R103**
— Der könig von Sion; epische dichtung in zehn gesängen. 7te aufl. Hamb. 1876. O.
831:21
— Sinnen und minnen; ein jugendleben in liedern. 6te aufl. Hamb. 1877. D. 831:22
Hebel, J: P: Allemanische gedichte für freunde ländlicher natur und sitten. Ins hochdeutsche übertr. von R. Reinick, mit bildern nach zeichnungen von L: Richter. 6te aufl. Leipz. 1876. S. **831:23**
Heine, H: Buch der lieder.—Neue lieder.—Tragödien. 2te aufl. Phila. 1856. D. **831:24**
— Höllenfahrt. 2te aufl. Hannover. 1856. D.
831:25
— Poems and ballads. Tr. by Emma Lazarus; prefixed, a biographical sketch of Heine. N. Y. 1881. D. **831:105**

x denotes books specially adapted for children.

Herlossohn, G: K:, (*originally* K: G: Reginald
Herloss). Buch der lieder. 3te ausg.
Leipz. [1872]. S. **831 : 26**
— Reliquien in liedern ; herausg. von Adolf
Böttger. 3te ausg. *With his* Buch der
lieder. **831 : 26**
Contents, see Deutscher katalog, p. 24.
Hertz, W: Heinrich von Schwaben ; eine
deutsche kaisersage. Leips. 1867. T.
831 : 27
Herwegh, G: Gedichte eines lebendigen. 10te
aufl. Stuttg. 1877. D. **831 : 28**
— Neue gedichte ; herausg. nach seinem tode.
Milw. 1877. D. **831 : 29**
Hoffmann v. Fallersleben, A: H: Gedichte.
Berlin. 1874. D. **831 : 30**
— Unpolitische lieder ; 2ter t. Hamb. 1841. S.
831 : 31
Hölderlin, J: Christian F: Ausgewählte werke,
herausg. von Christoph Theodor Schwab.
Stuttg. 1874. S. **831 : 32**
Jocundus, Frater, *pseud., see* **Müller,** W:
Keller, Gottfried. Gedichte. Heidelb. 1846. T.
831 : 33
Kerner, Justinus Andreas Christian. Der letzte
blüthenstrauss. Stuttg. 1852. T. **831 : 34**
— Lyrische gedichte. 5te aufl. Stuttg. 1854. T.
831 : 35
— Winterblüthen. Stuttg. 1859. T. **831 : 36**
Kinkel, J: Gottfried. Gedichte. 7te aufl. Stuttg.
1868–72. 2 v. D. **831 : 37**
— Der grobschmied von Antwerpen, in sieben
historien. 2te aufl. Stuttg. 1872. T.
831 : 38
— Otto der schütz ; eine rheinische geschichte in
zwölf abenteuern. 55ste aufl. Stuttg. 1881.
S. **831 : 39**
Klopstock, F: Gottlieb. Werke, mit einer bio-
graphie Klopstock's und zumm theil mit
erklärenden anmerkungen, herausg. von
A. L. Back. Stuttg. 1876. 6 v. S. **831 : 40**
Contents, see Deutscher katalog, p. 24.
— The messiah. A new tr. from the germ.; the
five last books prepared for the press by
T: Raffles. Lond. 1814. 3 v. S. **831 : 106**
Körner, K: Theodor. Sämmtliche werke, im
auftrage der mutter des dichters herausg.
und mit einem vorwort begleitet von K:
Streckfuss. Berlin. 1879. D. **831 : 41**
Contents, see Deutscher katalog, p. 24.
Kortum, C: Arnold. Die Jobsiade ; ein komi-
sches heldengedicht in 3 t.; mit einleitung
und anmerk. herausg. von F: W. Ebeling.
Leipz. 1868. D. **831 : 42**
— *Same* ; herausg. von F. Bobertag. *In* Kürsch-
ner, J., *ed.* Deutsche national-litteratur.
830 : 152 v140
— *Same,* The Jobsiad ; a grotesco-comico-
heroic poem. From the germ. by C: T.
Brooks. Phila. 1863. D. **831 : 107**
Krez, Konrad. Aus Wiskonsin ; gedichte. N.
Y. 1875. S. **831 : 116**
La Motte Fouqué, F: H: K: *baron* de. Der held
des nordens ; in 3 t. Halle. 1841. 3 v. S.
831 : 43
Langbein, A: F: Ausgewählte gedichte. *T. p.
w.* [Hildburghausen]. S. **831 : 44**
Lenau, Nikolaus, *pseud., see* Niembsch v. Strehlenau, N: F.
Levitschnigg, H: *ritter* v. Ein märchen. Pesth.
1847. D. **831 : 51**
Märklin, Edmund. Familienbilder ; ein poeti-
scher blumenstrauss für die deutsch-amer.
frauen. Milw. 1877. S. **831 : 85**

Müller von der Werra, F: Konrad. Das buch
der lieder. 2te aufl. Potsdam. 1873. D.
831 : 46
Müller, W: Griechenlieder. Neue ausg. Leipz.
1844. S. **831 : 47**
Müller, W:, (*Frater Jocundus*). Schabiade ;
leben und thaten des Fritz Schäbig ; eine
erbauliche historie in lustigen reimen von
Frater Jocundus. Milw. 1877. T. **831 : 88**
Müller von Königswinter, Wolfgang. Johann
von Werth ; eine deutsche rittergeschichte.
Köln. 1858. S. **831 : 48**
Niembsch v. Strehlenau, N: Franz, (*Nikolaus
Lenau*). Sämmtliche werke, herausg. von
Anastasius Grün. Stuttg. 1880. 2 v. in 1.
D. **831 : 49**
— Faust, ein gedicht. 2te aufl. Stuttg. 1840. S.
831 : 50
Paoli, Betty, *pseud., see* **Glück,** Elisabeth.
Pape, Joseph. Josephine ; romanzen. Münster.
1854. S. **831 : 51**
Pfizer, Gustav. Gedichte. Stuttg. 1831, 1835.
2 v. S. **831 : 52**
Pichler, Caroline. Gedichte. Neue aufl. Wien.
1822. S. **831 : 53**
— Idyllen. Neue aufl. Wien. 1822. S. **831 : 54**
Puchner, Rudolph. Klänge aus dem westen.
Milw. 1879. D. **831 : 87**
Pyrker v. Felsö-Eör, J: Ladislas. Sämmtliche
werke. Neue ausg. Stuttg. 1845. 3 v. T.
831 : 56
Contents, see Deutscher katalog, p. 25.
— Perlen der heiligen vorzeit. Stuttg. 1841. D.
831 : 55
Roquette, O: Waldmeisters brautfahrt ; ein
Rhein-, wein- und wandermärchen. 50ste
aufl. Stuttg. 1880. S. **831 : 59**
Rückert, F: Gesammelte poetische werke. Neue
ausg. Frankfurt a. M. 1882. 12 v. in 9. D.
831 : 122
Contents. V. 1. Lyrische gedichte, 1–3. Vaterland:
Geharnischte sonette; Zeitgedichte, 1814–17; Kriege-
rische spott- und ehrenlieder; Nach dem freiheitsjah-
ren.—Amaryllis.—Agnes.—Liebesfrühling. 2. Lyrische gedichte, 4. Haus und jahr: Eigner herd; Fest-
und trauerklänge; Des dorfamtmannsohnes kinder-
jahre; Lenz; Sommer; Herbst; Winter. 3. Erzählungen, 1. Heimath.—Winterträume.—Brahmanische
erzählungen. 4. Erzählungen, 2. Morgenländische
sagen und geschichten. 5. Wanderung, 1. Italienische gedichte.—Lieder und sprüche der minnesänger.
— Ghaselen. —Oestliche rosen. 6. Wanderung, 2.
Erbauliches und beschauliches aus dem morgenlande.
—Schi-king; chinesisches liederbuch. 7. Pantheon,
1. Kritik. — Selbstschau. — Kirchenjahr. — Mikrokos-
mus.—Zahme xenien. 8. Pantheon, 2. Weisheit des
brahmanen, ein lehrgedicht. 9. Dramatische gedichte, 1. Saul und David; ein drama der heiligen geschichte.—Herodes der grosse, in 2 stücken: Herodes
und Mariamne; Herodes und seine söhne. 10. Dramatische gedichte, 2. Kaiser Heinrich IV, drama:
Des kaisers krönung; Des kaisers begräbniss. — Cristofero Colombo, geschichtsdrama in 3 theilen. 11.
Epische gedichte, 1. Leben Jesu; evangelien-harmo-
nie in gereimter rede. — Die verwandlungen des
Abu Said von Serug, oder Die makamen des Hariri.
12. Epische gedichte, 2. Nal und Damajanti; indische geschichte. — Rostem und Suhrab; eine helden-
geschichte.—Hidimba; eine brahmanische erzählung.
—Sawitri.—Der räthselmann; abfälle von Hariri's
Räthselmakamen. — Der blinde. — Herr Malegis. — Kind
Horn; eine altenglische erzählung. — Rodach; ein
denkmal der gastfreundschaft. —Anhang: Nachrich-
ten von F: Rückerts leben.
— Gedichte ; auswahl des verfassers. 20ste aufl.
Frankfurt a. M. 1879. D. **831 : 60**
— Wisdom of the brahmin ; a didactic poem.
From the germ. by C: T. Brooks. Books
1–6. Bost. 1882. S. **831 : 95**

Schack, Adolf F: *graf* v. Gesammelte werke.
2te verb. und verm. aufl. Portr. Stuttgart.
1884–85. 6 v. D.   **831 : 119**
    Contents. V. 1. Nächte des orients, oder Die welt-
    alter.—Episoden, erzählende dichtungen: Fiordispina;
    Lais; Ubaldo Lapo; Heinrich Dandolo; Der flücht-
    ling von Damascus; Rosa; Der regenbogenprinz;
    Glycera; Stefano; Giorgione.—Nachwort. 2. Weih-
    gesänge.—Gedichte: Liebesgedichte und lieder; Aus
    allen zonen; Romanzen und balladen; Vermischte
    gedichte. — Lotosblätter: Vermischte gedichte; Aus
    fremden ländern: Verwehte blätter; Kampf und
    sieg.—Nachwort. 3. Die plejaden. — Lothar. — Tag-
    und nachtstücke: Camoens in Cintra; Ein maler;
    Antar; Sarpedon: Die neapolitanische nonne; Aure-
    lia und Alciphron; Otmar; Achilles; Antonio; Ly-
    kambes; Swammerdam; Kassandra; Der räuber von
    Ronda; Der gefangene von Valladolid; Ardavast;
    Satinig; Die vision Karls IX; Berenice; In den kata-
    komben; König Cheops.—Nachwort. 4. Drei erzäh-
    lungen: Drei mädchen; Elsbeth und Reinhold; An-
    dreas und Leila.—Durch alle wetter; roman in versen.
    —Ebenbürtig; roman in versen. 5. Die pisaner, trspl
    in 5 act. — Gaston; trspl in 5 act. und vorspiel. — Ti-
    mandra; trspl in 5 act. — Atlantis; trspl in 5 act. —
    Nachwort. 6. Heliodor; dramatisches gedichte. —
    Kaiser Balduin; trspl in 5 act. — Der kaiserbote: ko-
    mödie in 5 act.—Cancan; komödie in 5 act.

Schaffy, Mirza, *pseud., see* **Bodenstedt,** F:
M. v.

Scheffel, Joseph Viktor v. Bergpsalmen ; dichtung. Bilder von Anton v. Werner. 3te
aufl. Stuttg. 1878. S.   **831 : 61**
— Frau Aventiure ; lieder aus Heinrich von Ofterdingen's zeit. 10te aufl Stuttg. 1878. S.
                                    831 : 62
— Gaudeamus ! lieder aus dem engeren und
weiteren. 20ste aufl. Stuttg. 1878. S.
                                    831 : 63
— Juniperus ; geschichte eines kreuzfahrers.
3te aufl. Stuttg. 1878. S.   **831 : 64**
— Der trompeter von Säkkingen ; ein sang vom
Oberrhein. 71ste aufl. Stuttg. 1878. S.
                                    831 : 65
— *Same, eng.* The trumpeter of Säkkingen ; a
song from the upper Rhein. Tr. from the
germ. by mrs. Francis Brünnow, tr. author-
ized by the poet. Lond. 1877. D. **831 : 65**
Schenkendorf, F: Ferdinand Gottfried Max
Schenk v. Gedichte ; mit einem lebens-
abriss und erläuterungen, herausg. von A:
Hagen. 5te aufl. 1878. S.   **831 : 66**

Schiller, J: Christoph F: v. Poems and ballads.
Tr. by sir E: Bulwer-Lytton, with a brief
sketch of the author's life. Leipz. 1844. S.
                                    831 : 109
Schröder, W: Riemels un döntjes ; spassige ge-
schichten un klöönkram. Berlin. 1872. S.
                                    831 : 67
Schulze, Ernst Konrad F: Cäcilie ; ein roman-
tisches gedicht in 20 gesängen. Leipz. 1822.
2 v. D.   **831 : 68**
See, Henricus vom, *pseud., see* **Dilg,** W:
Soubron, W: O: Soubron's souvenir ; gedichte,
gewidmet seinen freunden vom verfasser.
Milw. 1878. S.   **831 : 75**
Stolle, L: Ferdinand, (*originally* L: F. Anders).
Lieder und gedichte, nebst lebensgeschicht-
lichen umrissen. 2te aufl. Leipz. 1858. S.
                                    831 : 76
Strodtmann, Adolf H: Lothar ; zeitarabesken.
Phila. 1853. T.   **831 : 77**
Tiedge, Christoph A: Urania. Neue aufl.
Halle. 1833. S.   **831 : 78**
Uhland, L: Gedichte. 62ste aufl. Stuttg. 1879.
S.   **831 : 79**
Voss, J: H: Luise ; ein ländliches gedicht in
drei idyllen. Berlin. 1867. S.   **831 : 80**
→ *Same, eng.* Louisa. From the germ. by
James Cochrane. Edinb. 1852. D.   **831 : 80**
Waldmüller, Robert, *pseud., see* **Duboc,** C: E:
Walther *von der Vogelweide.* Gedichte, über-
setzt von K: Simrock. 6te aufl. Leipz.
1876. T.   **831 : 81**
Wieland, Christoph Martin. Oberon ; a poem.
From the germ. by W: Sotheby. Lond.
1798. 2 v. D.   **831 : 114**
Wolff, Julius. Der wilde jäger ; eine waid-
mannsmär. 11te aufl. Berlin. 1881. S.
                                    831 : 82
Wolfram von Eschenbach. Leben und dichten ;
herausg. von San-Marte. Magdeburg. 1836.
2 v. O.   **831 : 124**
    Contents. V. 1. Vorrede. — Einleitung.—Parcival;
    rittergedicht. 2. Lieder. — Wilhelm von Orange. —
    Titurel. — Leben und dichten Wolfram's von Eschen-
    bach.—Der heilige gral.
Zedlitz, J: Christian F: v. Altnordische bilder.
Stuttg. 1850. D.   **831 : 83**
— Gedichte. 2te aufl. Stuttg. 1839. D. **831 : 84**

German literature — Drama.
Class 832.
See **Class-List of Drama, col. 519.**

German literature — Romance.
Class 833.
See **Class-List of Prose fiction, col. 657.**

15. German literature — e, Miscellaneous.

1. Essays.

Auerbach, Berthold. Schrift und volk ; grundzüge der volksthümlichen literatur, ange-
schlossen an eine charakteristik J. P. Hebel's. Stuttg. 1858. S.   **834 : 1**
Bodenstedt, F: Martin v. Aus ost und west ;
sieben vorlesungen. Berlin. 1869. S.
                                    834 : 2
    Contents, see Deutscher katalog, p. 34, 35.

Börne, L: Briefe aus Paris ; nebst einer cha-
rakteristik seines lebens und wirkens. N.
Y. 1858. 2 v. D.   **834 : 3**
Eckstein, Ernst. Beiträge zur geschichte des
feuilletons. Leipz. 1876. 2 v. in l. D.
                                    834 : 4
— Leichte waare ; skizzenblätter. 2te aufl.
Leipz. 1879. D.   **834 : 5**

Goltz, Bogumil. Buch der kindheit. 4te aufl. Berlin. [1877]. S.   **834 : 6**
— Vorlesungen. Berlin. [1869]. 2 v. in 1. S.   **834 : 7**

Griesinger, K: Theodor. Skizzenbuch. Stuttg. 1844. S.   **834 : 8**

Grimm, Hermann. Essays. Hannover. 1859. D.   **834 : 24**

Contents. Altieri und die Ristori. — Die Venus von Milo.—Lord Byron and Leigh Hunt. — Die erwartung des jüngsten gerichtes von Cornelius. — Die bearbeitung von Shakespeare's Sturm durch Dryden und Davenant. — Deutsches theater im 18. jahrhundert: Das Luzerner neujahrspiel und der Henno des Reuchlin; Das theater des herzogs Heinrich Julius von Braunschweig zu Wolfenbüttel. — Rafael und Michelangelo — Friedrich der grosse und Macaulay. — Schiller und Goethe.

Hartmann, K: Robert E: v. Gesammelte studien und aufsätze gemeinverständlichen inhalts. Berlin. 1876. O.   **834+19**

Contents. Aufsätze vermischten inhalts. Mein entwickelungsgang.— Ueber wissenschaftliche polemik. —Leibniz als praktischer optimist.—Der kampf zwischen kirche und staat.—Die geographisch-politische lage Deutschlands. — Princip und zukunft des völkerrechts. — Ist der pessimismus trostlos? — Ein chinesischer classiker.— Symptome des verfalls im künstler- und gelehrtenthum. — Das gefängniss der zukunft. — Dichters schönstes denkmal. *Aesthetische studien.* Zur ästhetik des dramas.—Das problem des tragischen.— Ueber ältere und moderne tragödienstoffe. — Aus einer dichterwerkstatt.—Shakespeare's Romeo und Julia. — Der ideengehalt in Goethe's Faust. — Schiller's gedichte. — Zur geschichte der ästhetik. *Beiträge zur naturphilosophie.* Naturwissenschaft und philosophie. — Anfänge naturwissenschaftlicher selbsterkenntniss. — Ernst Häckel als vorkämpfer der abstammungslehre in Deutschland. —Ueber die lebenskraft.—Das wesen des gesammtgeistes. — Schopenhauer und die farbenlehre. — *Dynamismus und atomismus. Das philosophische dreigestirn des 19ten jahrhunderts.* Zur orientirung in der philosophie der letzten hundert jahre.—Schelling's identätsphilosophie. — Hegel's panlogismus.— Schopenhauer's pantheismus.— Schelling's positive philosophie.—Schlusswort.

Hillebrand, K: Zeiten, völker und menschen. Berlin. 1875-82. 6 v. O.   **834 : 22**

Contents. V. 1. Frankreich und die franzosen in der zweiten hälfte des 19. jahr.; eindrücke und erfahrungen. 3te aufl.
2. **Wälsches und deutsches.** Zur renaissance: Petrarca; Lorenzo de Medici; Die Borgia.—Zeitgenössisches aus Italien: Alessandro Manzoni; Guerrazzi; Niccolò Tommaseo; Giosuè Carducci's neueste gedichte; Bei gelegenheit einer italienischen "Faust"-übersetzung.—Französisches: Ueber einige revolutionäre gemeinplätze; Jules Michelet; Prosper Mérimée und die unbekannte; E. d'Alton; Delirium tremens; Styl- und gedankenmoden.—Aus den zukünftigen schriftthum Deutschlands: G. G. Gervinus; Einiges über den verfall der deutschen sprache und der deutschen gesinnung; Ueber historisches wissen und historischen sinn; Ueber sprachvermengung.—Aus dem unzünftigen schriftthum Deutschlands: Schopenhauer und das deutsche publikum; Zur neuesten deutschen memorien-literatur; Der verstorbene; Rahel, Varnhagen und ihre zeit.
3. **Aus und über England.** Briefe aus England. —Französisches studien englischer zeitgenossen: Pariser zustände im lichte des englischen romans; Englische beobachtungen über französisches familienleben; J. Morley's studien über das 18. jahrh. in Frankreich. —Zur literatur- und sittengeschichte des 18. jahrh.: Fielding's Tom Jones; Lawrence Sterne.
4. **Profile.** X. Doudan.—H. de Balzac.— Gräfin d'Agoult (Daniel Stern).—M. Buloz.—M. Thiers.—E. Renan als philosoph.—H. Taine als historiker.—Die gefürsteten Medicäer.—Ein fürstlicher reformer.— Gino Capponi. — N. Macchiavelli.—F. Rabelais.—T. Tasso.—! Milton.
5. **Aus dem jahrhundert der revolution.** Montesquieu.—England im 18. jahrh.—Fr. Albergati. —Katharina II und Grimm. — 1789. — H: Costa de Beauregard.—Mme. de Rémusat und Napoléon Bonaparte.—Metternich.—Nach einer lecture.
6. **Zeitgenossen und zeitgenössisches.** Zur charakteristik Sainte-Beuve's. — Guizot im privat-

leben. — Philaréte Chasles. — Ernest Bersot. — Graf Circourt.—Eine ostindische laufbahn.—Ein englischer journalist.—Antonio Panizzi.—L: Settembrini's denkwürdigkeiten.—Giuseppe Pasolini.—Das belgische experiment.—Deutsche stimmungen und verstimmungen.—Halbbildung und gymnasialreform.

Jung, Jakob F: Alexander. Charaktere, charakteristiken und vermischte schriften. Königsberg. 1848. 2 v. D.   **834 : 9**
Contents. see Deutscher katalog, p. 35.

Koberstein, K: A: Vermischte aufsätze zur literaturgeschichte und ästhetik. Leipz. 1858. O.   **834 : 23**

Contents. Ueber das gemüthliche naturgefühl der deutschen und dessen behandlung im liebesliede, mit besonderer beziehung auf Goethe.—Ueber die in sage und dichtung gangbare vorstellung von dem fortleben abgeschiedener menschlicher seelen in der pflanzenwelt.—Zu und über Goethe's gedicht, Hans Sachsen's poetische sendung.—Ueber das neudeutsche gelegenheitsgedicht, mit besonderer beziehung auf Goethe's elegie "Euphrosyne."—Inwiefern darf Goethe's Iphigenie als ein, sowohl dem geist und der ganzen innern behandlung als der äussern form nach, durchaus deutsches kunstwerk angesehen werden?—Shakspeare's allmähliges bekanntwerden in Deutschland und urtheile über ihn bis zum jahre 1773. — Ueber das verhältniss Thüringens und Hessens zur deutschen literatur und über einige überbleibsel der ältesten und bekannten vaterländischen poesie, die zu diesen gegenden in einem sehr nahen bezuge stehen. — Andeutungen über das besondern erfolgreichen antheil Preussens an der neugestaltung der deutschen literatur seit dem ausgange des 17. jahrh.

Lindau, H: Gustav Paul. Aus Paris. Beiträge zur charakteristik des gegenwärtigen Frankreichs. Stuttg. 1865. D.   **834 : 10**
— Literarische rücksichtslosigkeiten; feuilletonistische und polemische aufsätze. 3te aufl. Leipz. 1871. D.   **834 : 12**
— Ueberflüssige briefe an eine freundin; gesammelte feuilletons. 3te aufl. Breslau. 1878. D.   **834 : 13**

Schmidt, Julian. Bilder aus dem geistigen leben unserer zeit. Leipz. 1870-73. 3 v. O.   **834 : 20**

Contents. V. 1. Die neue generation: Die europäische literatur in ihrem gegenwärtigen standpunkt; Die wendung des jahres 1848.—Der einfluss des preussischen staats auf die deutsche literatur.—Ueber über die romantische schule: Aus Schelling's leben in briefen; Göthe und Suleika; Heinrich v. Kleist's Prinz vom Homburg; Hegel im licht der gegenwart. —Walter Scott.—Sainte Beuve und die französische romantik.—E: Bulwer.—George Eliot.—Paul Heyse. — Iwan Turgenjew.— Erkmann-Chatrian. 2. *Neue folge.* C: Dickens.— Fernan Caballero und alt-Spanien. — Lamartine. — Pariser moralische velleitäten: Wider den cancan; Dumas fils; Moral und ästhetik; V: Hugo; Prosper Mérimée; Dumas der ältere.—H: Heine.—Berliner plaudereien: Der berliner; Deutsche kleinstaaterei; Der parlamentarismus; Graf Bismarck; Waldeck; K: Twesten; Der realismus in der kunst.—Hans Makart; R: Wagner; K: Gutzkow. —Der krieg gegen Frankreich. 3. *Neue bilder.* Fragmente über Shakespeare. — Willibald Alexis. — Fritz Reuter.—F: Spielhagen.—Herman Grimm.—G: Gervinus.—Plaudereien: Die ideale; Die philosophie und das kathede; Lebrecht Uhlich; Jacob Kaufmann.
— Portraits aus dem 19ten jahrhundert. Berlin. 1878. O.   **834 : 21**

Contents. Lord Byron.—Fürst Pückler.—T: Carlyle. —L: Feuerbach.—George Sand.—C: Dickens.—Thackeray.—C: Kingsley.—R: Wagner.—Gustave Flaubert. Emile Zola. — Alphonse Daudet. — Emil Erkmann.— Julius Wolf.—Alwina v. M.—Rudolf Reichenau.

Schopenhauer, Arthur. Select essays. Tr. by Garritt Droppers and C. A. P. Dachsel. Milw. 1881. D.   **834 : 18**
Contents. Biogr. sketch. — The misery of life. — Metaphysics of love.—Genius.—Aesthetics of poetry. —Education.

Steub, L: Altbayerische culturbilder. Leipz. 1869. D.   **834 : 16**

Vischer, F: Theodor. Altes und neues. Stuttg. 1881–82. ·3 v. in 2. O. **834 : 17**
Contents. V. 1. Aus einer griechischen reise. — Satyrische zeichnung.—Ein malerischer stoff.—Nachruf an Eduard Mörike's grab, 6. juni 1875, und Rede bei der einweihung seines denkmales, 4. juni 1880.— Der traum, eine studie zu der schrift: Die traumphantasie von dr. Joh. Volkelt. 2. Zur vertheidigung meiner schrift: Göthe's Faust. — Gottfried Keller.—Ein italienisches bad.—Noch ein wort über thiermissbandlung in Italien. 3. Alfred Rethel.— L: Weisser.— Ein internationaler gruss (Benelli).— Voltaire (Strauss).— Oberschwäbische zeitbilder (K. Planck und H. Günthert). — Publizistisches.— K. G. Reuschle.—Philosophie und naturwissenschaft.—Zur erinnerung an Fr. Strauss.—Mein lebensgang.
— Kritische gänge ; 2tes—6tes heft. Stuttg. 1861 –1873. 3 v. O. **834 : 25**
Contents. 2tes heft. Shakspeare in seinem verhältniss zur deutschen poesie, insbesondere zur politischen.—Shakspeare's Hamlet. 3tes heft. F. Strauss als biograph.—Vernünftige gedanken über bie jetzige mode.—Zum zweiten theile von Goethe's Faust. 4tes heft. Ein schützengang. — Pro domo. — L: Uhland. 5tes heft. Kritik meiner ästhetik.—An herrn staatsrath Hehn in Petersburg. — Ein gang am strande. 6tes heft. Kritik meiner ästhetik, *forts. und schlus.* — Eine schrift über Jean Paul. — Die Rottmann-fresken in München.—Offener brief an den redakteur des feuilletons der "Deutschen zeitung", dr. Speidel.— Der alte und neue glaube; ein bekenntniss von D. Fr. Strauss.

2. Letters.

(See note under English letters, col. 1078.)

Beethoven, L: van. Letters, 1790—1826, from the collection of dr. L: Nohl; also his letters to the archduke Rudolph, from the collection of dr. L: Ritter von Köchel. Tr. by lady Wallace. Portr. and fac-simile. N. Y. 1867. 2 v. D. **836 : 4**
Bürger, Gottfried A: Briefe von und an Gottfried A: Bürger ; ein beitrag zur literaturgeschichte seiner zeit. Aus dem nachlasse Bürger's und andern, meist handschriftlichen quellen herausg. von Adolf Strodtmann. Berlin. 1874. 4 v. O. **836+15**
Contents. V. I. Briefe von 1767—1776. 2. 1777– 1779. 3. 1780—1789. 4. 1790—1794.—Nachtrag.—Register.
Fichte, J: Gottlieb. Literarischer briefwechsel. *In* Fichte, J. H. J: G. Fichte's leben. **921.3 : 6 v2**
Friedrich II, *of Prussia.* Friedrich der grosse ; ein lebensbild in seinen briefen, von E: Schröder. Stuttg. *n. d.* D. **836 : 14**
Göthe, Catharine Elisabeth, *born* Textor. Goethe's mother : Correspondence of Catharine Elizabeth Goethe with Goethe, Lavater, Wieland, duchess Anna Amalia of Saxe-Weimar, F: v. Stein and others. Tr. from the germ., with the add. of biogr. sketches and notes by Alfred S. Gibbs ; introd. note by Clarence Cook. N. Y. [1880]. O. **836 : 5**
Göthe, J: Wolfgang v. Der junge Goethe ; seine briefe und dichtungen von 1764—1776, mit einer einleitung von Michael Bernays. Leipz. 1875. 3 v. D. **836 : 17**
Contents. V. 1. Einleitung.—Frankfurt und Leipzig 1764-68, Frankfurt 1768-70: Briefe; Dichtungen; Die laune des verliebten; Judenpredigt; Die mitschuldigen. — Strassburg 1770-71: Briefe; Dichtungen; Aus Ossian. Frankfurt 1771-72, Wetzlar 1772, Frankfurt 1772-73: Briefe. 2. *Same:* Dichtungen; Zum Schäkespears tag; Geschichte Gottfriedens von Berlichingen mit der eisernen hand, dramatisirt; Concerto dramatico; Vom deutscher baukunst; Brief des pastors zu *** an den neuen pastor zu ***; Zwo wichtige bisher unerörtete biblische fragen; Götz von Berlichingen, ein schauspiel; Prolog zu den neusten offenbarungen Gottes; Götter, helden und Wie-

Göthe, J: Wolfgang v.—*Continued.*
land; Recensionen. 3. Frankfurt 1774-75, Weimar 1775-76: Briefe; Dichtungen; Neu eröfnetes moralisch - politisches puppenspiel; Des künstlers erdewallen; Jahrmarktsfest zu Plundersweilen; Ein fastnachtsspiel vom pater Brey; Die leiden des jungen Werthers; Clavigo; Der ewige jude; Prometheus; Satyros; Hanswursts hochzeit; Salomons güldne worte; Erwin und Elmire; Anekdoten zu den Freuden d. j. Werthers; Claudine von Villa Bella; Stella.
— Early and miscellaneous letters, incl. letters to his mother ; with notes and a short biography by E: Bell. Phila. 1884. D. **836 : 13**
— Briefwechsel des grossherzogs Carl August von Sachsen-Weimar-Eisenach mit Goethe in den jahren von 1775 bis 1828. Portraits. Wien. 1873. 2 v. O. **836 : 10**
— Briefwechsel mit Schiller. *See* **Schiller**, *below.*
— Goethe's correspondence with a child [Bettina v. Arnim]. Bost. 1859. D. **836 : 6**
Günderode, Karoline v., *and* Elisabeth v. Arnim. Correspondence. Bost. 1861. D. **836 : 7**
Humboldt, C: W: *freiherr* v. Briefe an eine freundin ; mit einer einleitung von L: Geiger; b. 1, 2. Stuttg. [1884-85]. D. **836 : 8**
— *Same, eng.* Letters to a lady. From the german, with an introd. by C: Godfrey Leland. Phila. 1864. S. **836 : 8**
Humboldt, F: H: Alexander *freiherr* v. Briefe an Varnhagen von Ense aus 1827 bis 1858 ; nebst auszügen aus Varnhagens tagebüchern, und briefen von Varnhagen und andern an Humboldt. 3te aufl. Leipz. 1860. O. **836 : 1**
— *Same, eng.* Letters to Varnhagen von Ense, from 1827 to 1858 ; with extracts from Varnhagen's diaries and letters of Varnhagen and others to Humboldt. Tr. from the 2d germ. ed. by F: Kapp. N. Y. 1860. D. **836 : 1**
Mendelssohn-Bartholdy, Jakob L: Felix. Letters, 1833—1847 ; ed. by Paul and C: Mendelssohn-Bartholdy, with a catalogue of all his musical compositions, comp. by Julius Rietz. Tr. by lady Wallace. Phila. 1864. S. **836 : 10**
— Letters from Italy and Switzerland. Tr. from the germ. by lady Wallace ; with a biogr. notice by Julie de Marguerittes. 3d ed. Phila. 1865. S. **836 : 9**
Mozart, Wolfgang Amadeus. Letters, 1769— 1791. Tr. from the collection of L: Nohl by lady Wallace. Portr. and fac-simile. N. Y. 1866. 2 v. D. **836 : 11**
Schiller, J: Christoph F: v. Briefwechsel mit Körner, von 1784 bis zum tode Schillers. 2te ausg. Leipz. 1859. 4 v. S. **836 : 2**
— Briefwechsel zwischen Schiller und Goethe in den jahren 1794 bis 1805 ; eingel. und revidirt von R. Boxberger. Stuttg. [1882]. 2 v. D. **836 : 3**
— *Same, eng.* Correspondence between Schiller and Goethe from 1794 to 1805. Tr. by G: Calvert. V. 1. N. Y. 1845. D. **836 : 3**
— Letters, selected from his private correspondence prior to his marriage. Tr. by J. L. Weisse. Bost. 1841. D. **836 : 12**
Schubart, Christian F: Daniel. [Sein] leben in seinen briefen ; gesammelt, bearb. und herausg. von D: F: Strauss ; mit einem vorworte von E: Zeller. 2te aufl. Bonn. 1878. 2 v. in 1. O. **836 : 16**

3. Satire and Humor.

Buch zum lachen, enthaltend: Anecdoten und kurzweiligkeiten, wie man sie auf der reise — auch zu hause — gern liest. Leipz. 1855. T.　　　　**838 : 1**

Eulenspiegel. The marvellous adventures, and rare conceits of master Tyll Owlglass, newly collected, chronicled and set forth in our english tongue by Kenneth R. H. Mackenzie. Ill. Bost. 1860. D.　**838 : 12**

Falck, Robert, *ed.* Wohlgefülltes schatzkästlein deutschen scherzes und humors; zu nutz und frommen lachlustiger leser aus den schachten deutscher litteratur ans licht befördert, mit einer einleitung. Stuttg. [1884]. D.　　　　**838 : 11**

Gubitz, F: W: Lachender ernst und stacheln der laune; gesammelte blättchen des humors. Berlin. 1855. S.　**838 : 2**

Hoffmann, H: Humoristische studien. Frankfurt a. M. 1847. S.　　　　**838 : 3**
Contents, see Deutscher katalog, p. 35.

Illustrirte mannsperson, Die; humor, satire und wahrheit; ein gegenstück zum "Illustrirten frauenzimmer", von einer dame. Leipz. 1852. T.　　　　**838 : 8**

Moll, F. E. Museum komischer vorträge für das haus und die ganze welt; sammlung der besten, kernigsten vorträge, poesie und prosa, welche in den letzten 10 jahren überhaupt bekannt geworden sind. 3te aufl. Berlin. *n. d.* T.　　　　**838 : 5**

— **and others.** Illustrirter Berliner vocativus, neu in bunter menge bietend scherzegedichte, spässe, schwänke, puffs und jokus aller art. Berlin. 1857. 2 v. T.　**838 : 4**

Olschen, M. B. v., *ed.* Humoristisches vergissmeinnicht für 1848, 1849. Leipz. 1848, 1849. 2 v. S.　　　　**838 : 6**

Saphir, Moritz Gottlieb. Schriften; gesammtausg. Brünn. [1880]. 26 v. in 9. S.　**838 : 7**
Contents, see Deutscher katalog, p. 36.

Seyppel, C. M. Schlau, schläuer, am schläusten; ægyptische humoreske, niedergeschrieben und abgemalt 1315 jahre vor Christi geburt von C. M. Seyppel, hofmaler und poët seiner majestät des königs Rhampsinit III. Memphis, Mumienstrasse, no. 35, 3 etage, 4 × klingeln. [Düsseldorf. 1882]. Q.　　　　**838 : R10**

— **He, she, it;** egyptian court chronicle, b. c. 1302, a veracious and truthful version preserved and transcribed for general use by the peerless poet laureate of his late majesty Rhampsinnit III. Memphis, Pyramid row, no. 36, fifth floor. close on saturdays 2 p. m. [Düsseldorf. 1883.] Q.　**838 : R9**

4. Miscellany.

Collections.

Büchmann, G: Geflügelte worte; der citatenschatz des deutschen volks. 11te aufl. Berlin. 1879. D.　　　　**839 : 1**

Simrock, K: Joseph, *ed.* Die deutschen sprichwörter. Frankfurt a. M. 1863. S. **839 : 1 : 2**

Wächter, Oskar, *comp.* Altes gold in deutschen sprüchwörtern. Stuttg. [1883]. D.
　　　　839 : 14

Dörflinger, C:, *ed.* Onkel Karl; eine gabe für die deutsch-amer. jugend aller altersstufen,

aus originalarbeiten und ausgewähltem zusammengestellt. 2te aufl. Milw. 1881. O.
　　　　839 : 12

Masius, Hermann, *ed.* Der jugend lust und lehre; album für das reifere jugendalter. V. 4-8. Glogau. [1861–65]. 5 v. O.
　　　　x 839 : 20

Wagner, Hermann, *ed.* Hausschatz für die deutsche jugend; fortsetzung von "Der jugend lust und lehre". Ill. Glogau. [1866–73]. 8 v.　　　　**x 839 : 21**

Schober, Thekla v., *born* v. Gumbert, *ed.* Töchter-album; unterhaltungen im häuslichen kreise zur bildung des verstandes und gemüthes der heranwachsenden weiblichen jugend; mit beiträgen von gymnasial-lehrer Albani, Tante Amanda, *etc.* Ill. Glogau. [1855–85]. 31 v. O.　**x 839 : 19**

Oertel, Philipp F: W:, (*W. O. v. Horn*), *ed.* Die spinnstube; ein volksbuch für 1858–1886. Frankfurt a. M. [1858–1874], Wiesbaden. [1875–1886]. 29 v. in 16. S.　**839 : 26**
Note. Since 1871 "Im vereine mit namhaften volksschriftstellern fortgeführt von H. Oertel".

Individual authors.

Börne, L: Fragmente und aphorismen. N. Y. *n. d.* D.　　　　**839 : 1**

— **Menzel, der franzosenfresser,** — Schilderungen aus Paris. N. Y. 1858. D.　**839 : 2**

— **Vermischte aufsätze, erzählungen, reisen.** N. Y. *n. d.* 2 v. D.　　**839 : 3**

Diesterweg, F: Adolf W: Lichtstrahlen aus seinen schriften; mit einer biographischen einleitung von E: Langenberg. Leipz. 1875. S.　　　　**839 : 22**
Contents. Langenberg, E: Vorwort: Leben Diesterweg's.—Lichtstrahlen: Religion und sittlichkeit; Zur psychologie; Philosophisches; Erziehung.

Göthe, J: Wolfgang v. The wisdom of Goethe; with a list of citations prepared especially for this ed. with references to the text of the more important works by J: Stuart Blackie. N. Y. 1883 S.　**839 : 16**

Heine, H: Sämmtliche werke; b. 3: Salon. Phila. 1855. D.　　　　**839 : 5**

— **Prose miscellanies.** Tr. by S. L. Fleishman. Phila. 1876. D.　　　　**839 : 6**
Contents. Introductory sketch, biogr. and critical. —"The salon," the exhibition of paintings in Paris, 1831.—The memoirs of Herr von Schnabelewopski.—On the history of religion and philosophy in Germany.—The romantic school.—The suabian school.—The gods in exile.—Confessions.

— **Wit, wisdom and pathos from [his] prose,** with a few pieces from the "Book of songs"; selected and tr. by J. Snodgrass. Lond. 1879. D.　　　　**839 : 10**

Hey, W: Fünfzig fabeln für kinder; in bildern gezeichnet nach O: Speckter; nebst einem ernsthaften anhange. Gotha. [1879]. O.
　　　　x 839+23

— **Same, eng.** Picture fables drawn by O: Speckter, with rhymes tr. from the german of F. [*sic*] Hey, by H: W. Dulcken. N. Y. 1858. D.　　　　**x 839 : 13**

— **Same.** Lond. *n. d.* D.　　**x 839 : 13**

Horn, Franz Christofer. Psyche; aus Franz Horn's nachlasse, ausgewählt von Gustav Schwab und F: Förster. Leipz. 1841. 3 v. S.　　　　**839 : 7**
Contents, see Deutscher katalog, p. 35.

---

x denotes books specially adapted for children.

Lessmann, Daniel. Nachlass. Berlin. 1837. 3 v. S.   **839 : 8**

Lohmeyer, Julius. Komische thiere ; ein lustiges bilderbuch. Ill. Glogau. [1880]. F.   **x 839+25**

Müller, J: F:, *called* Maler. Mittheilungen aus seinem nachlass. *In* Seuffert, B. Maler Müller.   **928.3+56**

Pietsch, L: Aus welt und kunst ; studien und bilder. Jena. 1867. 2 v. in 1. S.   **839 : 9**
Contents, see Deutscher katalog, p. 36.

Pückler-Muskau, Hermann L: H: *fürst v.* Tuttifrutti, by the author of "The tour of a german prince". N. Y. 1834. D.   **839 : 11**
Contents. Biogr. sketch of the author, by Edmund Spencer. — The wanderer's return. — A visit to the establishment of Herrnhuters. — The album of an active mind. — Extracts from my note-book. — Scenes and sketches of a tour in the Riesengebirge. — The

modern Alcibiades. — A dialogue, between doctor Alcibiades and the arabian emyr Abdoulach, upon religion and true philosophy. — A letter from Berlin.

Richter, J: Paul F:, *(Jean Paul).* The Campaner Thal, and other writings. From the german. Bost. 1864. D.   **839 : 15**
Contents. The Campaner Thal, or Discourses on the immortality of the soul, tr. by Juliette Bauer. — Life of Quintus Fixlein, tr. by T: Carlyle. — Army-chaplain Schmelzle's journey to Flätz, tr. by T: Carlyle. — Analects from Richter, tr. by T: De Quincey. — Miscellaneous pieces.

— Wit, wisdom, and philosophy ; ed. by Giles P. Hawley. N. Y. 1884. D.   **839 : 17**

Sturm, Julius K: Reinhold. Das buch für meine kinder ; märchen und lieder. Ill. 2te verm. aufl. Leipz. 1880. Q.   **x 839+27**

— Neues fabelbuch. Ill. Leipz. 1881. O.   **x 839+24**

x denotes books specially adapted for children.

16. Romanic literatures.

For Dramas, *see* Class-List of Drama, col. 519.
For Romances, *see* Class-List of Prose fiction, col. 657.

1. In general.

Simonde de Sismondi, J: C: Léonard. Historical view of the literature of the south of Europe [to 1813]. Tr. from the original, with notes and a life of the author, by T: Roscoe ; from the last Lond. ed., with all the notes from the last Paris ed. N. Y. 1871. 2 v. D.   **850.1 : 1**
Contents. V. 1. Life. — Introd.: Corruption of the latin, and formation of the romance languages. — On the literature of the arabians. — On the literature of the troubadours. — On the literature of the trouvères. — On the literature of the italians. 2. *Same, continued.* — On the literature of the spaniards. — On the literature of the portuguese. — Index.

2. French.

History.

Laun, H: van. History of french literature. N. Y. 1876–77. 3 v. O.   **840.1 : 1**
Contents. V. 1. From its origin to the renaissance. 2. From the classical renaissance to 1715. 3. 1715–1848.

Saintsbury, G: Warner. Short history of french literature. [Clarendon press ser.] N. Y. 1882. D.   **840.1 : 2**

Bridge, Christiana. History of french literature ; adapted from the french of [Jacques Claude] Demogeot. New ed. [Hist. handbooks]. Lond. 1884. S.   **840.1 : 3**

Engel, E: Geschichte der französischen litteratur von ihren anfängen bis auf die neueste zeit. (Geschichte der weltlitteratur in einzeldarstellungen, 1). Leipz. [1883]. O.   **840.1 : 7**

Ampère, J: Jacques Antoine. Histoire littéraire de la France avant Charlemagne. 3e éd. Paris. 1870. 2 v. D.   **840.1 : 4**

— Histoire littéraire de la France sous Charlemagne et durant les 10e et 11e siècles. 3e éd. Paris. 1870. D.   **840.1 : 5**

Tilley, Arthur. The literature of the french renaissance ; an introductory essay. Cambridge. 1885. D.   **840.1 : 8**

Hettner, Hermann. Geschichte der französischen literatur in 18. jahrh. (Literaturgeschichte des 18. jahrh ; 2er theil). 4te verb. aufl. Brschwg. 1881. O.   **809 : 9 v2**
Contents. ies buch. Der ursprung der französischen aufklärungsliteratur: Die letzten jahre Ludwig's XIV: Die regentschaft des herzogs von Orleans und das ministerium des cardinal Fleury. — 2es buch. Die blüthe der franz. aukiärungsliteratur: Literatur unter Ludwig XV; Voltaire und Montesquieu; Diderot und die encyklopädisten; Rousseau und die demokratie. — 3es buch. Die macht der franz. aufklärungsliteratur.

Schmidt, Julian. Geschichte der französischen literatur seit Ludwig XVI, 1774. 2te vollständig umgearb. aufl. Leipz. 1873, 1874. 2 v. O.   **840.1+6**

Brandes, G: Die emigrantenliteratur. *In his* Hauptströmungen der literatur des 19. jahrh.   **809 : 6 v1**

— Die reaktion in Frankreich. *In the same.*   **809 : 6 v3**

— Die romantische schule in Frankreich. *In the same.*   **809 : 6 v5**

Véricour, L. Raymond de. Modern french literature ; rev. with notes alluding particularly to writers prominent in late political events in Paris, by W: Staughton Chase. Bost. 1848. D.   **840.1 : 9**

Matthews, James Brander. French dramatists of the 19th century. N. Y. 1881. O.   **842.2 : 1**
Contents. Preface. — A brief chronology of the french drama in the 19th century. — The romantic movement. — Victor Hugo. — Alexandre Dumas. — Eugène Scribe. — Émile Augier. — Alexandre Dumas, *fils.* — Victorien Sardou. — Octave Feuillet. — Eugène Labiche. — Meilhac und Halévy. — Émile Zola and the present tendencies of french drama. — Notes. — Index.
Note. See also names of individual writers in the Index to biography, at the end of the catalogue.

Collected works.

Mérimée, Prosper. Gesammelte werke, übersetzt von H: Elsner. Stuttg. 1845. 7 v. S.   **840 : 1**
Contents, see Deutscher katalog, p. 21.

Montaigne, Michel **Eyquem** de. Works, comprising his essays, journey into Italy, and letters ; with notes from all the commentators, biogr. and bibliogr. notices, etc., by W. Hazlitt. New and rev. ed., ed. by O. W. Wight. N. Y. 1859. 4 v. D.   **840 : 2**
Contents. V. 1-3. Life of Montaigne. — Essays.— App.: Bibliographical notice of the editions of the essays; Portraits of M.; Index to authors quoted. 4. St. John, Percy Bayle. Biography of M.—Diary of a journey through Switzerland and Germany into Italy.—Letters of M.—App.: References to the principal opinions which have been passed upon M. and his writings.—General index.

Saint Évremond, C: **Marguetel de Saint Denis** *seigneur* de. Works ; made english from the french original, with the life of the author by mr. [P:] Des Maizeaux. Added, The memoirs of the dutchess of Mazarin, etc. 2d ed., corr. and enl. Lond. 1728. 3 v. D.   **840 : 3**

Saint-Pierre, Jacques H: Bernardin de. Works ; with memoir of the author and explanatory notes by E. Clarke. Lond. 1846. 2 v. D.   **840 : 4**
Contents. V. 1. Paul and Virginia. — The indian cottage.—Studies of nature. 2. Studies of nature.

Poetry.

Béranger, P: J: de. Two hundred lyrical poems. Done into english verse by W: Young. New ed. N. Y. 1857. D.   **841 : 1**

Chanson de Roland, La. Tr. from the 7th ed. of Léon Gautier by Leonce Rabillon. N. Y. 1885. S.   **841 : 4**

Mistral, F: Mirèio ; a provençal poem. Tr. by Harriet W. Preston. Bost. 1874. S.   **841 : 2**

Voltaire, François Marie Arouet *called* de. The Henriade; with The battle of Fontenoy, Dissertations on man, Law of nature, Destruction of Lisbon. Temple of taste and Temple of friendship. From the french. with notes from all the commentators, ed. by O. W. Wight. N. Y. 1859. D.   **841 : 3**

Essays.

Chasles, Victor Euphémion Philarète. Notabilities in France and England ; with an autobiography. N. Y. 1853. D.   **844 : 3**
Contents. Autobiography.—Residence in England. —English society in 1817.—A visit to South Stack.— Scenes of a life in Ireland.—Thoughts upon Ireland. —Sea-shore scenes.—An hour on board the "Swallow."—Thoughts upon french society.

Chateaubriand, François A: René *vicomte* de. Recollections of Italy, England and America, with essays on various subjects in morals and literature. Phila. 1816. O.   **844 : 1**

Sainte-Beuve, C: A: Monday-chats ; selected and tr. from the "Causeries du lundi", with an introd. essay on the life and writings of Sainte-Beuve by W: Mathews. Chicago. 1877. D.   **844 : 2**
Contents. The life and writings of Sainte-Beuve.— Lewis XIV.—Fénelon.—Bossuet.—Massillon.—Pascal. Rousseau.—Mme. Geoffrin.—Joubert.—Guizot.—The abbé Gallaui.—Frederic the great.—Index.

Letters.

(See note under English letters, col. 1078).

Calvin *or* Cauvin, J: Letters, compiled from the original mss. and ed. with historical notes by Jules Bonnet. Tr. from the original latin and french. Phila. *n. d.* 4 v. O.   **846+5**

Sévigné, Marie de Rabutin-Chantal *marquise* de. Letters to her daughter and friends ; ed. by Sarah J. Hale. N. Y. 1859. D.   **846 : 3**

Elisabeth Charlotte *of Bavaria, duchesse d' Orléans, princesse* Palatine. Briefe der Elisabeth Charlotte von Orléans, 1673 bis 1715 ; ausgewählt, mit einl. und anmerk. versehen von L: Geiger. Stuttg. [1884]. D.   **846 : 11**

Maintenon, Françoise d'Aubigné, *mme.* Scarron, *afterward marquise* de. The letters of madam de Maintenon and other eminent persons in the age of Lewis XIV. Added, some characters. Tr. from the french. Dublin, 1853. S.   **846 : 9**

Simon, É: Étienne, (*Edouard Lockroy*). The great french revolution, 1785—1793 ; narrated in the letters of madame J—— of the jacobin party, ed. by her grandson, Edouard Lockroy. From the french by miss Martin and an american collaborateur. Lond. 1881. D.   **846 : 10**

Napoléon I, *emperor of the french.* Confidential correspondence with his brother Joseph ; selected and tr., with explanatory notes, from the "Mémoires du roi Joseph". N. Y. 1856. 2 v. D.   **846 : 7**

— A selection from the letters and despatches of the first Napoleon ; with explanatory notes by the hon. D. A. Bingham. Lond. 1884. 3 v. O.   **846 : 13**

Rémusat, Claire Elisabeth Jeanne Gravier de Vergennes *comtesse* de. Selection from the letters of madame de Rémusat to her husband and her son, from 1804 to 1813. From the french by mrs. Cashel Hoey and J: Lillie. N. Y. 1881. D.   **846 : 1**

— *Same.* N. Y. 1881. Q.   **846+1**

Talleyrand-Périgord, Maurice, *prince de Bénévent.* Correspondence of prince Talleyrand and king Louis XVIII during the congress of Vienna, hitherto unpub.; from the mss. preserved in the archives of the ministry of foreign affairs at Paris ; with a pref., observations and notes by M. G. Pallain. N. Y. 1881. O.   **846 : 4**

Guérin, Eugénie de. Letters ; ed. by G. S. Trébutein. N. Y. 1866. D.   **846 : 6**

Mérimée, Prosper. Letters to Panizzi ; ed. by L: Fagan. Lond. 1881. 2 v. O.   **846 : 8**

Balzac, Honoré de. Correspondence ; with a memoir by his sister, madame de Surville. Tr. by C: Lamb Kenney. Portr. and facsimile of the handwriting of Balzac. Lond. 1878. 2 v. O.   **846 : 12**

Bacourt, Adolphe *chevalier* de. Souvenirs of a diplomat; private letters from America during the administrations of presidents Van Buren, Harrison and Tyler ; with a memoir of the author by the comtesse de Mirabeau. Tr. from the french. N. Y. 1885. D.   **846 : 14**

Miscellany.

Gasparin, Valérie Boissier *comtesse* de. Vesper, Tr. from the 3d french ed. by Mary L. Booth. N. Y. 1863. D.   **849 : 1**

La Fontaine, J: de. Fables. Tr. from the french by Elizur Wright, jr. 4th ed. Bost. 1856. 2 v. in 1. S.   **849 : 2**

Napoléon I, *emperor of the french.* Table talk and opinions. 4th ed. [Bayard ser.] Lond. 1875. T.   **849 : 3**

Maistre, Xavier de. A journey round my room. Tr. from the french, with a notice of the author's life, by H: Atwell. Lond. 1883. S.
849 : 4

Karr, J: Baptiste Alphonse. A tour round my garden. Tr. from the french, rev. and ed. by J. G. Wood. New ed., ill. Lond. 1859. S.
849 : 5

Rabelais, François. Readings in Rabelais by Walter Besant. Edinburgh. 1883. D.
848 : 1

2. Italian.

History.

Sauer, K: Marquard. Geschichte der italienischen litteratur von ihren anfängen bis auf die neueste zeit. (Geschichte der weltlitteratur in einzeldarstellungen, 3.) Leipz. [1884]. O.
850.1 : 3

Barbacovi, Francesco Virgilio conte. Compendium of the literary history of Italy until the formation of the modern italian language. Tr. from the italian. Edinb. 1835. D.
850.1 : 4

Symonds, J: Addington. Renaissance in Italy; italian literature, in 2 pts. Lond. 1881. 2 v. O.
850.1 : 2

— [Studies in italian literature]. *In his* Sketches and studies. **824.2 : 86**
Contents, see English literature, Essays, col. 1074.

Hueffer, Francis. Italian studies. *in* 824.2 : 121
Contents, see English literature, Essays, col. 1065.

Greene, G: Washington. Historical [and literary] studies. **824.1 : 38**
Contents, see English literature, Essays, col. 1062.
Note. See also names of individual authors in the Index to biography, at the end of the catalogue.

Poetry.

Hunt, James H: Leigh. Stories from the italian poets ; a summary in prose of the poems of Dante, Pulci, Boiardo, Ariosto and Tasso, with comments throughout, occasional passages versified and critical notices of the lives and genius of the authors. N. Y. 1846. D.
851 : 8
Contents. Dante: The italian pilgrim's progress.— Pulci: Humours of giants; The battle of Roncesvalles.—Boiardo: The adventures of Angelica; The death of Agrican; The saracen friends. — Seeing and believing.— Ariosto: The adventures of Angelica; Astolfo's journey to the moon; Ariodante and Ginevra; Suspicion; Isabella. — Tasso: Olindo and Sophronia; Tancred and Clorinda; Rinaldo and Armida. — App.: The story of Paulo and Francesca; Accounts given by different writers of the circumstances relating to Paulo and Francesca, concluding with the only facts ascertained; Story of Ugolino; Picture of Florence in the time of Dante's ancestors; The death of Agrican: Angelica and Medoro; The jealousy of Orlando; The death of Clorinda; Tancred in the enchanted forest.

Ariosto, L: The Orlando Furioso. Tr. into english verse, with notes by W: Stewart Rose. New ed., ill. Lond. 1858. 2 v. D.
851 : 6

— Paladin and saracen ; stories from Ariosto by H. C. Hollway-Calthrop. Ill. Lond. 1882. D.
x 851 : 10
Contents. Introd.—The adventures of Roger and Bradamante.—The journeys and madness of Roland.—Astulf.—The siege of Paris. — Biserta.—Last adventures of Roger and Bradamante.

Ariosto, L:—*Continued.*
— Tales from Ariosto, retold for children by a lady. Ill. Lond. 1879. S.
x 851 : 9
Contents. The story of the princess Angelica.—The story of Ginevra. — The story of Ruggiero and Bradamante.

Buonarroti, Michelangelo. Selected poems; with translations from various sources ; ed. by Ednah D. Cheney. Bost. 1885. D.
851 : 12

Dante Alighieri. The divine comedy. Tr. by H: Wadsworth Longfellow. Bost. 1872, 1873. 3 v. D.
851 : 1
Contents. v. 1. Inferno. 2. Purgatorio. 3. Paradiso.

— *Same.* Bost. 1867. 2 v. O.
851+1
Contents. V. 1. Inferno. 2. Purgatorio.

— *Same.* Dante's Divine comedy: The inferno ; a literal prose trans., with the text of the original, collated from the best ed., and explan. notes by J: A. Carlyle. 2d ed. 1867. Lond. 1882. D.
851 : 11

— *Same, germ.* Göttliche komödie. Ins deutsche übers. von K: Gustav v. Berneck. 2te aufl. Stuttg. 1856. S.
851 : 1

— Lyrische gedichte. Uebers. und erklärt von K: L: Kannegiesser und K: Wittwe. 2te aufl. Leipz. 1842. v. S.
851 : 2

— Das neue leben. Aus dem ital. übers. und erläutert von K: Förster. Leipz. 1841. S.
851 : 3
Note. References to Dante are included in Durfee's Poetical concordance, 811 : R11; see col. 1021.

Leopardi, Giacomo conte. Gedichte. Verdeutscht in den versmassen des originals von Robert Hamerling. Hildburgh. 1866. D.
851 : 13

Tasso, Torquato. Jerusalem delivered. Tr. into english spenserian verse, with a life of the author, by J. H. Wiffin. New ed. ill. Lond. 1881. D.
851 : 7

— *Same.* N. Y. 1849. D.
851 : 7

— Auserlesene lyrische gedichte. Aus dem italien. übers. von K: Förster ; mit einer einleitung : Ueber Torquato Tasso als lyrischen dichter. 2te aufl. Leipz. 1844. 2 v. in 1. S.
851 : 4

Tassoni, Alessandro. Der geraubte eimer. Aus dem italien. übers. von P. L. Kritz. Leipz. 1842. D.
851 : 5

Miscellany.

Amicis, Edmondo de. Studies of Paris. Tr. from the italian by W. W. C. N. Y. 1879. D.
854 : 1
Contents. The first day in Paris.—A glance at the exposition.—Victor Hugo.—Emile Zola.—Paris.

Boccaccio, Giovanni. The decameron, or Ten days' entertainment. Tr. from the italian ; prefixed, remarks on the life and writings of Boccaccio. Hartford. 1848. 2 v. in 1. S.
853 : R
Note. An ed. for general reading will be found in the Fiction class-list, col. 681.

Leopardi, Giacomo conte. Essays and dialogues. Tr. by C: Edwardes, with a biographical sketch. [Eng. and for. phil. lib.] Lond. 1882. O.
854 : 2
Contents. Biogr. sketch.—History of the human race.—Dialogue between Hercules and Atlas.—Dialogue between fashion and death.—Prize competition of the academy of sillographs.—Dialogue between a goblin and a gnome. — Dialogue between Malambruno and Farfarello.—Dialogue between nature and a soul.—Dialogue between the earth and the

x denotes books specially adapted for children.

moon.— The wager of Prometheus. — Dialogue between a natural philosopher and a metaphysician.— Dialogue between Tasso and his familiar spirit.—Dialogue between nature and an Icelander.—Parini on glory.—Dialogue between Ruysch and his mummies. —Remarkable sayings of Philip Ottonieri.—Dialogue between Columbus and Gutierrez. — Panegyric of birds.—The song of the wild cock.—Dialogue between Timandro and Eleandro.—Copernicus.—Dialogue between an almanac seller and a passer-by.—Dialogue between Plotinus and Porphyrus.— Comparison of the last words of Brutus and Theophrastus. — Dialogue between Tristano and a friend.

Machiavelli, Niccolo. Historical, political and diplomatic writings. Tr. from the italian by Christian E. Detmold. Bost. 1882. 4 v. O. **850+1**

Contents. V. 1. Pref.—Life.—History of Florence. 2. The prince.—Discourse on the first ten books of Titus Livius.—Thoughts of a statesman. 3. Missions. 4. Missions.—Miscellaneous papers.—Index.

3. Spanish.

Ticknor, G: History of spanish literature. N. Y. 1849. 3 v. O. **860.1+1**

Contents. V. 1. 1st period. The literature that existed in Spain between the first appearance of the present written language and the early part of the reign of the emperor Charles V, or from the end of the 12th century to the beginning of the 16th.—2d period. From the accession of the austrian family to its extinction, or from the begining of the 16th century to the end of the 17th. 2. Same, continued. 3. Same, concluded. 3d period. Between the accession of the Bourbon family and the invasion of Bonaparte, or from the beginning of the 18th century to the early part of the 19th.—App. Origin of the spanish language; The romances; Fernan Gomez de Cibdareal and the Ceuton epistolario; The Buscapié; Editions, translations and imitations of the Don Quixote; Early collections of old spanish plays; On the origin of the cultismo.—Inedita: Poema de José el Patriarca; La danza general de la muerte; El libro del rabi Santob.—Index.

Lockhart, J: Gibson, tr. Ancient spanish ballads; historical and romantic. A new rev. ed. with a biogr. notice. Bost. 1856. D. **861:4**

Kennedy, James. Modern poets and poetry of Spain. Lond. 1852. O. **861+3**

Vingut, Gertrude Fairfield de, ed. Selections from the best spanish poets. N. Y. 1856. D. **861:5**

Yriarte, T: Literary fables. Tr. from the spanish by G: H. Devereux. Bost. 1855. D. **861:6**

Cervantes-Saavedra, Miguel de. Wit and wisdom of Don Quixote. Bost. 1882. T. **869:1**

4. Portuguese.

Camoens, L: de. The Lusiad, or The discovery of India; an epic poem. Tr. from the portuguese with an historical introd. and notes by W: Julius Mickle. New ed. Lond. 1807. 3 v. S. **861:1**

— Same, germ. Die Lusiaden; heroisch-episches gedicht. Aus dem portugiesischen in iamben übers. von K: Eitner. Hildburgh. 1869. D. **861:1**

— Poems. From the portuguese, with remarks on his life and writings, notes, etc., by lord viscount Strangford. New ed. Lond. 1824. D. **861:2**

— The lyricks, sonnets, canzons, odes and sextines, englished by R: F. Burton. Lond. 1884. 2 v. S. **861:8**

Burton, R: Francis. Camoens; his life and his Lusiads, a commentary. Lond. 1881. 2 v. S. **861.2:1**

17. Classical literatures.

1. In general.

White, C. A. Classic literature, principally sanskrit, greek and roman, with some account of the persian, chinese and japanese, in the form of sketches of the authors and specimens from translations of their works. N. Y. 1877. D. **880.1:1**

Creuzer, F: Zur geschichte der griechischen und römischen literatur; besorgt von Julius Kayser. Leipz. 1847. O. **880.1:3**

Jennings, G. H., and W. S. Johnstone. Half-hours with greek and latin authors; from various english trans. with biogr. notices. N. Y. 1882 [1881]. D. **870:1**

Elton, C: Abraham. Specimens of the greek and roman classic poets, in a chronological series from Homer to Tryphiodorus, trans. into english verse and ill. with biogr. and critical notices. Phila. 1860. 3 v. D. **871:1**

Savage, J: A select collection of letters of the antients, whereby is discovered the morality, gallantry, wit, humour, manner of arguing and in a word the genius of both greeks and romans. Lond. 1703. D. **876:3**

2. Roman.

History and Collections.

Bähr, J: Christian Felix. Geschichte der römischen literatur. 4te verb. und verm. aufl. Carlsruhe. 1868-72. 4 v. O. **870.1:5**

Contents. V. 1. Allgemeiner theil. — Die poesie. 2, 3. Die prosa. 4. Die christlichen dichter und geschichtschreiber Roms.

Teuffel, W: Siegmund. A history of roman literature. Tr. with the author's sanction, by W: Wagner. Lond. 1873. 2 v. O. **870.1+4**

Cruttwell, C: T: A history of roman literature from the earliest period to the death of Marcus Aurelius; with chronological tables, etc., for the use of students. N. Y. n. d. O. **870.1:3**

Browne, Robert W: A history of roman classical literature. T. p. w. O. **870.1:1**

Simcox, G: A: History of latin literature from Ennius to Boethius. N. Y. 1883. 2 v. D. **870.1:2**

Sellar, W. Y. The roman poets of the republic. New ed., rev. and enl. Oxford. 1881. O. **871:2**

Herder, J: Gottfried v. Römische literatur. In his Werke. **830:154 v8**

Contents. Aus Horaz.—Briefe über das lesen des Horaz.—Aus Persius.—Aus Phädrus.

Note. See also names of individual writers in the Index to biography, at the end of the catalogue.

Individual authors.

Cæsar, Caius Julius. Commentaries. **937:10**
See under Ancient roman history.

Cæsar, Caius Julius.—*Continued.*
— **Trollope**, Anthony. The commentaries of
Cæsar. [Ancient classics for eng. readers.]
Phila. 1875. S.   **879 : 4**
Catullus, Caius Valerius. **Davies**, James.
Catullus. Tibullus and Propertius. [Ancient
classics for eng. readers.] Phila. 1877. S.
   874 : 4
Cicero, Marcus Tullius. [Works.] N. Y. 1867–
70. 3 v. S.   **875 : 1**
   Contents. V. 1. Biogr. sketch.—The orations. tr.
   by prof. Duncan. 2. *Same, continued.* 3. The offices,
   tr. by T: Cockman.—Cato, or An essay on old age;
   Lælius, or An essay on friendship, tr. by dr. Melmoth.
— Orationes quaedam selectæ. notis anglicis
illustratæ cura et studio Thomæ Dugdale,
jr. Quibus præfigitur vita Ciceronis, per
annos consulares digesta ; huic ed. acc.
dialogi De senectute et De amicitia. Phila.
1815. O.   **875 : 4**
— The three dialogues on the orator. Tr. into
eng. by W. Guthrie, rev. and corr. with
notes. 2d amer. ed. N. Y. 1860. S.
   875 : 2
— **Collins**, W: Lucas. Cicero. [Ancient classics
for eng. readers.] Phila. 1875. S.   **875 : 3**
Horatius Flaccus, Quintus, (*eng.* Horace). A
poetical translation of the works of Horace,
with the original text and critical notes,
collected from his best latin and french
commentators, by Philip Francis. 5th ed.
rev. and corr. Lond. 1853. 4 v. O.   **871 : 4**
   Contents. V. 1, 2. Odes.—Epodes.—The secular
   poem. 3. Satires. 4. Epistles.—Art of poetry.
— Odes and epodes of Horace ; a metrical trans.
into english, with introd. and commentaries
by lord Lytton, with latin text. Leipz. 1869.
2 v. in 1. S.   **874 : 2**
— Works. Tr. literally into english prose, for
the use of those who are desirous of acquiring or recovering a competent knowledge of the latin language, by C. Smart ;
in 2 v. Edinb. 1801. V. 1. T.   **874 : 6**
   Contents. 1–5th book of odes.
— **Martin**, *Sir* Theodore. Horace. [Ancient
classics for eng. readers.] Phila. 1877. S.
   871 : 3
Juvenalis, Decimus Junius. **Walford**, E: Juvenal. [Ancient classics for eng. readers].
Phila. 1878. S.   **877 : 2**
Livius Patavinus, Titus, (*eng.* Livy). History of
Rome. 4 v.   **937 : 6**
   See under Ancient roman history.
— **Capes**, W. Wolfe. Livy. (Classical writers).
N. Y. 1880. S.   **879 : 1**
— **Collins**, W: Lucas. Livy. [Ancient classics
for eng. readers]. Phila. 1876. S.   **879 : 2**
Lucretius Carus, Titus. Lucretius on the nature
of things ; a philosophical poem in six
books. Literally tr. into english prose by
J: Selby Watson. Adjoined, the poetical
version of J: Mason Good. Lond. 1851. D.
   871 : 5
— **Mallock**, W: Hurrell. Lucretius. [Ancient
classics for eng. readers]. Phila. 1878. S.
   874 : 5
Ovidius Naso, Publius, (*eng.* Ovid). Metamorphoseon libri 15 ; interpretatione et notis
illustravit Daniel Chrispinus Helvetius in
usum serenissimi Delphini. In hac ed. nona
notarum pars expungitur, quarum loco
adjiciuntur aliæ, et interpretatio passim

Ovidius Naso, Publius, (*eng.* Ovid).—*Continued.*
emendatur ; hanc ed. recensuit et emenda-
vit T: S. Joy. Novi-Eboraci. 1823. O.
   874 : 7
— The heroïdes, or Epistles of the heroines,—
The amours. — Art of love. — Remedy of
love, and minor works of Ovid. Literally
tr. into english prose, with copious notes
by H: T. Riley. Lond. 1852. D.   **871 : 6**
— **Church**, Alfred J: Ovid. [Ancient classics
for eng. readers]. Phila. 1876. S.   **874 : 3**
Plautus, Titus Maccius. **Collins**, W: Lucas.
Plautus and Terence. [Ancient classics for
eng. readers]. Phila. 1875. S.   **872 : 3**
Plinius Secundus *major*, Caius, (*eng.* Pliny). Natural history. 6 v.   **500 : 6**
   See under Natural science, col. 281.
Plinius Cæcilus Secundus *junior*, Caius. The
letters of Pliny the consul, with occasional
remarks by W: Melmoth. 4th ed. Lond.
1757. 2 v. O.   **876 : 1**
— **Church**, Alfred J:, *and* W. J. **Brodribb**. Pli-
ny's letters. [Ancient classics for eng.
readers]. · Phila. 1879. S.   **876 : 2**
Propertius, Sextus Aurelius. *See* **Catullus**, *above.*
Sallustius Crispus, Caius, (*eng.* Sallust). [Histor-
ical works].   **937 : 7**
   See under Ancient roman history.
Seneca, Lucius Annæus. Morals.   **171 : 10**
   See under Ethics, col. 62.
Tacitus, Caius Cornelius. Works. 2 v.   **937 : 38**
   Contents. see under Ancient roman history.
— **Donne**, W: Bodham. Tacitus. [Ancient clas-
sics for eng. readers]. Phila. 1875. S.
   879 : 3
Terentius Afer, Publius, (*eng.* Terence). Com-
edies.   **872 : 2**
   See Class-list of drama, col. 605.
— *See* **Plautus**, *above.*
Tibullus, Albius. *See* **Catullus**, *above.*
Vergilius Maro, Publius, (*eng.* Virgil). The
Georgics of Vergil. Tr. into english verse
by Harriet Waters Preston. Bost. 1881. T.
   874 : 1
— **Collins**, W: Lucas. Virgil. [Ancient classics
for eng. readers]. Phila. 1878. S.   **873 : 3**
   Note. References to Virgil are included in Dur-
   fee's Poetical concordance, 811:R11; *see* col. 1021.
— **Nettleship**, H. Vergil. (Classical writers).
N. Y. 1880. S.   **873 : 2**
— Stories from Virgil by Alfred J. Church. Ill.
N. Y. 1879. D.   **873 : 1**

3. Greek.

History and criticism.

Mahaffy, J: Peytland. A history of classical
greek literature. N. Y. 1880. 2 v. D.
   880.1 : 2
   Contents. V. 1. The poets; with an app. on Homer
   by prof. Sayce. 2. The prose writers; with an index
   to both vols.
Müller, K: Ottfried, *and* J: W: **Donaldson**. A
history of the literature of ancient Greece.
Lond. 1858 3 v. O.   **880.1 : 4**
Mure, W: A critical history of the language
and literature of ancient Greece. Lond.
1850. 5 v. O.   **880.1 : 5**
Jebb, R: Claverhouse. Greek literature. (Literature primer.) N. Y. 1878. S.   **880.1 : 6**
Mills, Abraham. The poets and poetry of the
ancient greeks ; with an historical introd.
and a brief view of grecian philosophers,
orators and historians. Bost. 1854. O.
   881.1+4

Coleridge, H: Nelson. Introductions to the study of the greek classic poets ; designed principally for the use of young persons at school and college. Bost. 1842. D.
　　　　　　　　　　　　　　　　　　881.2 : 1
　Contents. Gen. introd.—History of the origin and preservation of the Iliad.—Odyssey.—Margites.—Batrachomyomachia.—Hymns.—Epigrams.—Fragments.—Conclusion.

Symonds, J: Addington. Studies of the greek poets. N. Y. 1880. 2 v. S.　**881.2 : 3**
　Contents. V. 1. The periods of greek literature.—Mythology.—Achilles.—The women of Homer.—Hesiod.—Parmenides.—Empedocles.—The gnomic poets.—The satirists.—The lyric poets.—Pindar.—Aeschylus.—Sophocles. 2. Greek tragedy and Euripides.—The fragments of Aeschylus, Sophocles, Euripides.—The fragments of the lost tragic poets.—Ancient and modern tragedy.—Aristophanes.—The comic fragments.—The idyllists.—The anthology.—Hero and Leander.—The genius of greek art.—Conclusion.

Felton, Cornelius Conway. The greek language and poetry. *In his* Greece, ancient and modern.　　　　　　　　　　**938 : 19**

Gladstone, W: Ewart. Studies on Homer and the Homeric age. Oxford. 1858. 3 v. O.
　　　　　　　　　　　　　　　　　　883.2 : 4
　Contents. V. 1. Prolegomena.—Achæis, or The ethnology of the greek races. 2. Olympus, or The religion of the Homeric age. 3. Agorè; politics of the Homeric age.—Ilios; trojans and greeks compared.—Thalassa; the outer geography.—Aoidos; some points of the poetry of Homer.
—— Homer. (Literature primer.) N. Y. 1878. S.
　　　　　　　　　　　　　　　　　　883.2 : 2

Geddes, W: Duguid. The problem of the Homeric poems. Lond. 1878. O.　**883.2 : 3**

Bonitz, Hermann. The origin of the Homeric poems ; a lecture. Tr. from the 4th german ed. by Lewis R. Packard. N. Y. 1880. S.　　　　　　　　　　　　　　　**883.2 : 1**

Donaldson, J: W. The theatre of the greeks ; a treatise on the history and exhibition of the greek drama with various supplements. 7th ed. rev., enl. and in part remodelled. Ill. Lond. 1860. O.　　　**882 : 10**

De Quincey, T: Theory of greek tragedy. *In his* Letters to a young man.　**824.2 : 31**
　Note. See also names of individual writers in the Index to biography, at the end of the catalogue.

Collections.

Herder, J: Gottfried v. Griechische literatur. *In his* Werke.　　　　　**830 : 154 v7**
　Contents. Blumen aus der griechischen Anthologie.—Anmerkungen über die Anthologie der griechen, besonders über die griechische epigramm.—Hyle kleiner griechischer gedichte.—Siegesgesänge von Pindar.—Homer, ein günstling der zeit.—Homer und das epos.—Pindar, ein bote der götter.—Nemesis, ein lehrendes sinnbild.—Wie die alten den tod gebildet; ein nachtrag zu Lessing's abhandlung.

Neaves, C: *lord.* The greek anthology. [Ancient classics for eng. readers]. Phila. 1875. S.
　　　　　　　　　　　　　　　　　　884 : 1

Phalaris. Epistles. Tr. from the greek ; added, some select epistles of the most eminent greek writers, by T: Francklin. Lond. 1849. D.　　　　　　　　　　　　　**886 : 1**

Brandes, Gustav. Ein griechisches liederbuch ; verdeutschungen aus griechischen dichtern. Hannover. 1881. D.　　　　　**884 : 5**

Menzies, Louisa. Lives of the greek heroines. Lond. 1880. D.　　　　　**881 : 1**
　Contents. Niobe.—Alcestis.—Atalanta.—Antigone.—Klytemnaestra.—Helene.—Penelope.—Iphigenia.—Kassandra.—Laodameia.—Notes.

72

Church, Alfred J: Stories from the greek tragedians. Ill. Lond. 1880. D.　**882 : 9**
　Contents. The love of Alcestis.—The vengeance of Medea.—The death of Hercules.—The seven chiefs against Thebes.—Antigone.—Iphigenia in Aulis.—Philoctetes, or The bow of Hercules.—The death of Agamemnon.—Electra, or The return of Orestes.—The furies, or The loosing of Orestes.—Iphigenia among the Taurians.—The persians, or The battle of Salamis.—Ion.
—— Heroes and kings ; stories from the greek. Ill. N. Y. 1883. T.　　　**883 : 11**
　Contents. The story of the ship Argo.—The meeting of Glaucus and Diomed.—The embassy to Achilles.—The battle of the gods.—The funeral games of Patroclus.—The visit of Ulysses to the dead.—The triumph of Ulysses.—The story of Periander of Corinth.—The story of Polycrates of Samos.

Schmidt, Ferdinand. Oedipus und sein geschlecht ; erzählungen aus der griechischen heroenzeit. 3te aufl. Ill. Kreuznach. [1885]. S.　　　　　　　　　　　　　**882 : 12**

Individual authors.

Aischylos, *(lat.* Æschylus). Tragedies.　**882 : 1**
　See Class-list of drama, col. 519.
—— Copleston, Reginald Stephen. Æschylus. [Ancient classics for eng. readers]. Phila. 1879. S.　　　　　　　　　　**882 : 4**

Aisôpos, *(lat.* Æsopus, *eng.* Aesop). Fables; with a life of the author. Ill. N. Y. 1868. O.
　　　　　　　　　　　　　　　　　　887 : 3
—— *and others.* Fables. Tr. into english, with instructive applications and ill. by S: Croxall. N. Y. 1853. T.　　　　　**887 : 1**

Aristophanês. Collins, W: Lucas. Aristophanes. [Ancient classics for eng. readers]. Phila. 1879. S.　　　　　　　　**882 : 5**

Aristotelês, *(eng.* Aristotle). Grant, *Sir* Alexander. Aristotle. [Ancient classics for eng. readers]. Phila. 1877. S.　**888 : 1**

Arrianos, *(eng.* Arrian). Expedition of Alexander the great.　　　**in 938+41**
　See under Ancient greek history.

Dêmosthenês. Orations. Tr. by T: Leland. N. Y. *n. d.* 2 v. S.　　　**885 : 1**
—— Brodribb, W: J. Demosthenes. [Ancient classics for eng. readers]. Phila. 1877. S.
　　　　　　　　　　　　　　　　　　885 : 2
—— Butcher, S: H. Demosthenes. (Classical writers.) N. Y. 1882. S.　**885 : 3**

Epiktêtos, *(lat.* Epictetus). Morals.　**171 : 8**
　See under Ethics, col. 60.

Euripidês. Medea.　　　　　　**882 : 2**
　See Class-list of drama, col. 547.
—— Donne, W: Bodham. Euripides. [Ancient classics for eng. readers]. Phila. 1875. S.
　　　　　　　　　　　　　　　　　　882 : 6

Hêrodotos, *(lat.* Herodotus). History. 4 v.
　　　　　　　　　　　　　　　　　930+2
　See under Ancient greek history, General.
—— Swayne, G: C. Herodotus. [Ancient classics for eng. readers]. Phila. 1879. S.　**889 : 1**

Hêsiodos, *(eng.* Hesiod). The works of Hesiod, Callimachus and Theognis. Literally tr. into english prose with copious notes by J. Banks ; appended, the metrical trans. of Elton, Tytler and Frere. Lond. 1876. D.
　　　　　　　　　　　　　　　　　　881 : 2
—— Davies, James. Hesiod and Theognis. [Ancient classics for eng. readers]. Phila. 1875. S.　　　　　　　　　　**884 : 2**

Homêros, *(lat.* Homerus, *eng.* Homer). Homeric ballads. Tr. by the late W: Maginn, annotated by Shelton Mackenzie. N. Y. 1856. D.　　　　　　　　　　　　　**884 : 3**

Homêros.—*Continued.*

— The Iliads and Odysses. Tr. out of greek into english by T: Hobbes, with a large pref. concerning the virtues of an heroic poem written by the tr. *In* Hobbes, T: English works.   820.2 : 12 v10

— The Iliad of Homer. Tr. into english blank verse by W: Cullen Bryant. Bost. 1876. 2 v. S.   883 : 1

— The Iliad of Homer, rendered into english blank verse by Edward earl of Derby ; with a biogr. sketch by R. Shelton Mackenzie. 5th ed. from the 9th rev. eng. ed. Phila. *n. d.* 2 v. in 1. D.   883 : 2

— The Iliad. Tr. by Alexander Pope ; with notes by Theodore Alois Buckley and Flaxman's designs. Lond. *n. d.* D.   883 : 13

— The Iliad, done into english prose by Andrew Lang, Walter Leaf and Ernest Myers. Bost. 1883. D.   883 : 12

— Homer's Ilias, [übersetzt] von J: H: Voss. Stuttg. 1878. S.   883 : 5

— Homer's Iliade, erzählt von Ferdinand Schmidt. Ill. 7te aufl. Leipz. 1883. S.   x 883 : 16

— Collins, W: Lucas. Homer: the Iliad. [Ancient classics for eng. readers]. Phila. 1878. S.   883 : 3

— The Odyssey of Homer. Tr. into english blank verse by W: Cullen Bryant. Bost. 1873. 2 v. D.   883 : 4

— The Odyssey. Tr. by Alexander Pope ; with notes by Theodore Alois Buckley and Flaxman's designs. Lond. *n. d.* D.   883 : 14

— The Odyssey, books 1—12; the text and an english version in rhythmic prose by G: Herbert Palmer. Bost. 1884. O.   883 : 15

— Homer's Odyssee, [übersetzt] von J: H: Voss. Stuttg. 1878. S.   883 : 6

— Homer's Odyssee, erzählt von Ferdinand Schmidt. Ill. 7te aufl. Leipz. 1883. S.   x 883 : 17

— Witt, C. The wanderings of Ulysses. Tr. by Frances Younghusband. N. Y. 1885. D.   883 : 18

— Collins, W: Lucas. Homer: the Odyssey. [Ancient classics for eng. readers]. Phila. 1879. S.   883 : 8

— Stories from Homer by Alfred J. Church. Ill. N. Y. 1878. D.   883 : 9

— Homer's stories simply told by C: H: Hanson. Ill. N. Y. 1882. S.   x 883 : 10

— Arnold, Matthew. On translating Homer. *With his* On the study of celtic literature.   896 : 4

Note. References to Homer are included in Durfee's Poetical concordance, 811 : R11; *see* col. 1021.

Julianus *Apostata*, *Flavius Claudius, emperor.* Select works ; and some pieces of the sophist Libanius. Tr. from the greek, with notes from Petau, La Bleterie, Gibbon, etc. Added, the history of the emperor Jovian, from the french of the abbé de La Bleterie by J: Duncombe. Lond. 1784. 2 v. O.   880 : 1

Contents. V. 1. Pref.—Annals and pedigree of Julian.—Gallus Cæsar to his brother Julian.—Epistle to Themistius. — A consolatory oration on the departure of Sallust.—Epistle to the emperor Constantius.—Epistle to the senate and people of Athens.— An allegorical fable, from orat. 7.—The duties of a priest, from the fragment. — The Cæsars. — The Misopogon, or The antiochian.—Epistles of Libanius

to Julian. 2. Epistles of Julian.—**Fabricius.** The life of Libanius.—**Libanius:** Monody on Nicomedia, destroyed by an earthquake; Monody on the Daphnæan temple of Apollo, destroyed by fire.—**Bleterie,** J: P. R. de la. History of the emperor Jovian; Abstract of an essay.—Additional notes.

Kallimachos, *(lat.* Callimachus). *See* **Hêsiodos,** *above.*

Libanios. *See* **Julianus,** *above.*

Lukianos, *lat.* Lucianus *Samosatensis, (eng.* Lucian). Comedies, tr. by W: Maginn, annotated by Shelton Mackenzie. *With* Homeric ballads.   *in* 884 : 3

Contents. Timon, or The misanthrope.—Charon, or The lookers-on. — Menippus, or The necyomantia. — Menippus and Chiron.

— A traveller's true tale. After the greek of Lucian of Samosata by Alfred J. Church. Ill. Lond. 1880. D.   887 : 2

— Collins, W: Lucas. Lucian. [Ancient classics for eng. readers]. Phila. 1875. S.   887 : 4

Pindaros, *(eng.* Pindar). Odes. Literally tr. into english prose by Dawson W. Turner ; adjoined, a metrical version by Abraham Moore. Lond. 1852. D.   881 : 3

— Morice, F. D. Pindar. [Ancient classics for eng. readers]. Phila. 1879. S.   884 : 4

Platôn, *(lat.* Plato). Works. 6 v.   184 : 12

Contents, see under Ancient philosophies, col. 46.

— Plato's best thoughts ; compiled from prof. Jowett's tr. of the Dialogues of Plato. New ed. N. Y. 1883. D.   888 : 3

— Collins, Clifton Wilbraham. Plato. [Ancient classics for eng. readers]. Phila. 1879. S.   888 : 2

Plutarchos, *(eng.* Plutarch). Lives of the ancient greeks and romans.   923.6 : 16

See under Biography of statesmen, Ancient.

— Morals. Tr. from the greek by several hands, corr. and rev. by W: W. Goodwin ; with an introd. by Ralph Waldo Emerson. Bost. 1874. 5 v. O.   880 : 3

Contents. V. 1. **Goodwin,** W: W. Pref.—**Emerson,** R. W. Introd.—A discourse touching the training of children. — Concerning the cure of anger. — Of bashfulness. — That virtue may be taught. — The account of the laws and customs of the lacedaemonians.—Concerning music. — On the tranquillity of the mind.—Of superstition, or indiscreet devotion. — The apophthegms or remarkable sayings of kings and great commanders. — Rules for the preservation of health.— How a man may receive advantage and profit from his enemies. — Consolation to Appolonius. — Concerning the virtues of women.—Of hearing. — Of large acquaintance. — Concerning the fortune or virtue of Alexander the great. 2. The banquet of the seven wise men.— How a young man ought to hear poems.—Of envy and hatred.— How to know a flatterer from a friend. — That it is not possible to live pleasurably according to the doctrine of Epicurus.— Roman questions.—Greek questions. — Of the love of wealth.—How a man may inoffensively express himself without being liable to envy. — Concerning the procreation of the soul as discoursed in Timæus. — That a philosopher ought chiefly to converse with great men. — A discourse concerning Socrates's daemon.— Of curiosity.—How a man may be sensible of his progress in virtue. — Of fortune. — Of virtue and vice. — Conjugal precepts. 3. Whether 'twere rightly said, live concealed. — An abstract of a comparison between witt Aristophanes and Menander. — Of banishment. —Of brotherly love.—Wherefore the pythian priestess now ceases to deliver her oracles in verse.—Of those sentiments concerning nature with which philosophers were delighted.— A breviate of a discourse showing that the stoics speak greater improbabilities than the poets. — Symposiacs.— Of moral virtue.—Natural questions. 4. Why the oracles cease to give answers. —Of Isis and Osiris. — Concerning such whom God is slow to punish. — Of natural affection towards one's offspring. — Concerning the fortune of the romans.— Of garrulity or talkativeness.—Of love.— Five tragical histories of love. — A discourse to an unlearned prince. — Of Herodotus's malice. — Of common conceptions against the stoics. — The contradictions of the stoics. — Of the word *ei* engraved over the gate of Appollo's temple at Delphi.—Whether vice is sufficient to render a man unhappy. — Whether the passions of the soul or diseases of the body are worse. **5.** Of eating of flesh. — Lives of the ten orators. — Whether an aged man ought to meddle in state affairs. —Political precepts.—Which are the most crafty, water-animals or those creatures that breed upon the land.—That brute beasts make use of reason.—Of the face appearing within the orb of the moon.—Of fate.— Concerning the first principle of cold. — Whether water or fire be most useful. — Against Colotes, the disciple and favorite of Epicurus. — Plutarch's consolatory letter to his wife.—Of the three sorts of government, monarchy, democracy and oligarchy.—Whether the athenians were more renowned for their warlike achievements or their learning.— Against running in debt or taking up money by usury. — Platonic questions. — Parallels, or A comparison between the greek and roman histories. — Of the names of rivers and mountains and of such things as are to be found therein.—Index.

Polybios, (*lat.* Polybius). General history. 2 v.   **930 : 27**
    See under Ancient history, General.

Sophoklês, (*lat.* Sophocles). Tragedies. **882 : 3**
    See Class-list of drama, col. 600.

— **Collins,** Clifton Wilbraham. Sophocles. [Ancient classics for eng. readers]. Phila. 1875. S.   **882 : 7**

Sophoklês.—*Continued.*

— **Campbell,** Lewis. Sophocles. (Classical writers). N. Y. 1880. S.   **882 : 8**

Theognis. *See* **Hêsiodos,** *above.*

Thukydidês, (*lat.* Thucydides]. History of the peloponnesian war. 2 v.   **938 : 23**
    See under Ancient greek history.

— **Collins,** W: Lucas. Thucydides. [Ancient classics for eng. readers]. Phila. 1878.   **889 : 2**

Xenophôn. Whole works. Tr. by Ashley Cooper, Spelman, Smith, Fielding and others. N. Y. 1858. O.   **880 : 2**
    Contents. The institution of Cyrus.—The expedition of Cyrus.—The affairs of Greece.—The defence of Socrates. — Memoirs of Socrates. — The banquet of Xenophon. — Hiero; on the condition of royalty. — The science of good husbandry. — Revenue of the state of Athens.— On the athenian republic. — On the lacedemonian republic.—On horsemanship.—Epistles.

— The Cyropædia.   **935 : 1**
    See under Ancient persian history.

— Expedition of Cyrus.   **938+41**
    See under Ancient greek history,

— **Grant,** *Sir* Alexander. Xenophon. [Ancient classics for eng. readers]. Phila. 1878. S.   **889 : 3**

18. Minor european literatures.

For **Dramas,** *see* **Class-List of Drama, col. 519.**
For **Romances,** *see* **Class-List of Prose fiction, col. 657.**

1. Scandinavian.

(*See also* Mythology, col. 136-137; *and* Folk-lore, col. 142.)

Horn, F: Winkel. Geschichte der literatur des skandinavischen nordens von den ältesten zeiten bis auf die gegenwart. Leipz. 1880. O.   **898 : 5**
— *Same, eng.* History of the literature of the scandinavian north, from the most ancient times to the present. Rev. by the author and tr. by Rasmus B. Anderson. [*Also*] A bibliography of the most important books in the english language, relating to the scandinavian countries, prepared for the tr. by Thorvald Solberg. Chicago. 1884 [1883]. O.   **898 : 5**

Howitt, W: *and* Mary. The literature and romance of northern Europe; constituting a complete history of the literature of Sweden, Norway and Iceland, with copious specimens of the most celebrated histories, romances, popular legends and tales, old chivalrous ballads, tragic and comic dramas, national and favorite songs, novels and scenes from the life of the present day. Lond. 1852. 2 v. D. **898 : 4**

Gosse, Edmund W: Studies in the literature of northern Europe.   **804 : 2**
    Contents, see col. 508.

Metcalfe, F: The englishman and the scandinavian, or A comparison of anglo-saxon and old norse literature. Bost. [1880]. O.   **898 : 3**

Herbert, W: Horæ scandicæ, or Works relating to old scandinavian literature. *In his* Works.   **820.2 : 32 v1**
    Contents. Hedin. — Helga. — Song of Vala. — Brynhilda.— Sir Ebba.— Select icelandic poetry, tr. from

the originals, with notes; rev., with 3 add. pieces from Sæmund's Edda.

Vigfusson, Gudbrand *and* F: York Powell. Corpus poeticum boreale; the poetry of the old northern tongue, from the earliest times to the 13th century, ed. classified and tr. with introd., excursus and notes. Oxford. 1883. 2 v. O.   **898 : 6**
    Contents. V. 1. **Eddic poetry.** Introd. — Oldest northern poetry.— Earliest western poems. — Early western epics.— Early historic poems. — The latest epics.—Scholia.—Appendix.—Excursus: Beliefs and worship of the ancient northmen; On the northern and old teutonic metres.—Notes.
    2. **Court poetry.** Heathen poetry in court metre. —Christian court poetry.—Epigonic poetry.—Medieval and book poetry.—Excursus: On the figures and metaphors of old northern poetry, with some reference to the ancient life, thought and belief, as embodied therein; A chronology; Trace of old heroic teutonic songs to be found in the Islendinga sogur and in other tales; The creation myth and the northern genealogies in Hyndla's lay.—Appendix.— Notes.—Indexes: Mythical; Historical; Subjects.

Edda. Die Edda, die ältere und jüngere, nebst den mythischen erzählungen der Skalda, übersetzt und mit erläuterungen begleitet von K:[Joseph] Simrock. 7te aufl. Stuttg. 1878. O.   **831 : 70**
    Contents. Die ältere Edda: Göttersage; Heldensage.—Die jüngere Edda.—Erläuterungen: Einleitung; Anmerkungen; Heldensage; Register.
— Die Edda; nebst einer einleitung über nordische poesie und mythologie und einem anhang über die historische literatur der isländer von F: Rühs. Berlin. 1812. O.   **898 : 7**

Anderson, Rasmus B., *and* Jón Bjarnason, *trs.* Viking tales of the north; the sagas of Thorstein Viking's son and Fridthjof the bold. Tr. from the icelandic. Chicago. 1877. D.   **898 : 2**

Buchanan, Robert W: Ballad stories of the affections. From the scandinavian. [Bayard ser.] N. Y. 1869. T.   **898 : 1**

Swedish.

Runeberg, J: L: Lyrical songs and epigrams. Done into english by Eirikr Magnusson and E. H. Palmer. Lond. 1878. S.   **898.1 : 9**
— Hanna; episches gedicht in drei gesängen. Aus dem schwed. von A: Kluge. Dessau. 1877. D.   **898.1 : 4**
— König Fjalar; epos aus der nordischen vorzeit, in fünf gesängen. Deutsch von Ida Merves, geb. Lappe. Leipz. 1877. D.   **898.1 : 3**
— Nadeschda; a poem in nine cantos. Tr. from the swedish by Marie A. Brown. Bost. 1879. O.   **898.1 : 2**
— *Same. In* Hoffman, W. Leisure hours in Russia.   **914.7 : 41**
— *Same, germ.* Nadeschda; neun gesänge. Aus dem schwed. von Selma Mohnike. 2te aufl. Halle. 1879. T.   **898.1 : 2**
— Die sagen des fähnrich Stahl. Aus dem schwed. von C. F. N. Helsingfors. 1882. D.   **898.1 : 11**
Sjöberg, Erik, (*Vitalis*). Gedichte. Aus dem schwed. übers. von K: L: Kannegiesser. Leipz. 1843. D.   **898.1 : 5**
Tegnér, Esaias. Axel. From the swedish by R. G. Latham. Lond. 1838. O.   **898.1 : 6**
— *Same, germ.* Axel; romanze. Deutsch von Max Vogel. Leipz. 1877. S.   **898.1 : 6**
— Frithiof's saga. From the swedish by W: Lewery Blackley. 1st amer. ed., ed. by Bayard Taylor. N. Y. 1867. D.   **898.1 : 8**
— *Same.* Fridthjof's saga; a norse romance. Tr. from the swedish by T: A. E. Holcomb and Martha A. Lyon Holcomb. 2d ed. Chicago. 1883. D.   **898.1 : 8**
— *Same.* Fridthjof's saga. Tr. into english by G: Stephens. *With* Anderson, R. B., *and* J. Bjarnason. Viking tales of the north.   **898 : 2**
— *Same, germ.* Die Frithiofs-sage; mit den Abendmahlskindern. Uebers. von K: Simrock. 3te aufl. Stuttg. 1875. S.   **898.1 : 8**
— *Same.* Die Frithjofs-sage. Nach dem schwed. original in den versmassen desselben neu übers. von Edmund Lobedanz. Stuttg. [1882]. D.   **898.1 : 10**
— Die Frithiof - sage; erzählt von Ferdinand Schmidt. 5te aufl. Ill. Kreuznach. [1883]. S.   **898.1 : 12**
— Kleinere gedichte, in einer auswahl. Aus dem schwed. übertr. von Gustav Zeller. Stuttg. [1862]. T.   **898.1 : 7**

Danish and Norwegian.

Nyerup, Rasmus, *and* Jens E. Kraft. Almindeligt litteraturlexicon for Danmark, Norge og Island [til 1814].   **15 : L**
See col. 20.
Erslew, T: Hansen. Almindeligt forfatterlexicon for Danmark med tilhörende bilande fra 1814 til 1840.   **15 : L**
— Supplement, 1840—1853.   **15 : L**
See col. 20.
Halvorsen, J. B. Norsk forfatter-lexikon, 1814—1880; v. 1, A–B.   **15 : L**
See col. 20.

Feldborg, Andreas Andersen, *comp.* Poems from the danish; selected and ill. with historical notes. Tr. into english verse by W: Sidney Walker. Lond. 1815. S.   **898.3 : 5**
Andersen, Hans Christian. Dramatische schriften und gedichte. Leipz. *n. d.* S.   **898.3 : 1**
Contents, see Deutscher katalog, p. 26.
Baggesen, Jens. Anthologie aus [seinen] gedichten; mit biogr. und portr. Hildbgh. 1844. S.   **830 : 94**
Holberg, *Baron* L: v. Nicolai Klimii iter subterraneum, novam telluris theoriam ac historiam quintæ monarchiæ adhuc nobis incognitæ exhibens. E bibliotheca B. Abellini, ed. secunda auctior et emendatior. Hafniæ et Lipsiæ. 1745. S.   **898.3 : 2**
— *Same, germ.* Niels Klim's wallfahrt in die unterwelt. Aus dem latein. übers. von Ernst Gottlob Wolf. 2te aufl. Leipz. 1847. S.   **898.3 : 2**
Oehlenschläger, Adam Gottlob. Anthologie aus [seinen] gedichten. *With* Baggesen, Jens. Anthologie.   **830 : 94**
Paludan-Müller, F: Adam Homo; ein roman in versen; mit einer vorrede von G: Brandes. N. Y. 1883. F.   **898.3 + 4**
Steffens, H: Nachgelassene schriften; mit einem vorworte von Schelling. Berlin. 1846. S.   **898.2 : 1**
Contents, see Deutscher katalog, p. 36.

2. Keltic.

(See also Folk-lore, col. 141.)

Arnold, Matthew. On the study of celtic literature. N. Y. 1883. D.   **896 : 4**
Williams, Alfred Mason. The poets and poetry of Ireland; with historical and critical essays and notes. Bost. 1881. D.   **896 : 2**
Rodenberg, Julius. Die harfe von Erin; märchen und dichtung in Irland. 2te ausg. Leipz. 1864. S.   **896 : 1**
O'Kearney, N:, *ed.* The prophecies of SS. Columbkille. Maeltamlacht, Ultan, Seadhua, Coireall, Bearcan, Malachy, etc.; together with the prophetic collectanea, or gleanings of several writers who have preserved portions of the now lost prophecies of our saints, with literal tr. and notes. N. Y. 1866. S.   **896 : 3**
Evans, Evan, *ed.* Some specimens of the poetry of the ancient welsh bards. Tr. into english, with explanatory notes on the historical passages and a short account of men and places mentioned by the bards. Repr. from Dodsley's ed. of 1764. Llanidloes. *n. d.* O.   **896 : 5**
Mabinogion, The.   *in* **813 : 12, x 813 : 4**
See col. 514.

3. Slavic.

(See also Folk-lore, col. 142.)

Robinson, Therese Albertine Louise, *born* v. Jakob, (*Talvj*). Historical view of the languages and literature of the slavic nations, with a sketch of their popular poetry by Talvi. Pref. by E: Robinson. N. Y. 1850. D.   **897 : 2**
Contents. Introd.—Pt. 1: Old or church slavic language and lit.—Pt. 2, Eastern slavi: Russian lang. and lit.; Illyrico-servian lang. and lit.; Lang. of the bulgarians.—Pt. 3, Western slavi: Czekho-slovakian branch; Polish lang. and lit.; Sorabian-vendes in

Lusatia and other vendish tribes now extinct. Pt. 4: Sketch of the popular poetry of the slavic nations.—Index of authors.

Morfill, W: R. [Early] slavonic literature. (The dawn of european literature.) Lond. 1883. S. **897:9**
Contents. Classification *and* Nomenclature of the slavonic races. — Russian lit. — Malo - russian *and* White-russian lit.—Bulgarian lit.—Serbs, croats and slovenes.—Poland.—Bohemia.—Wends in Saxony and Prussia.—Polabes.

*   *   *

Nitschmann, H: Geschichte der polnischen litteratur. (Geschichte der weltlitteratur in einzeldarstellungen, 2). Leipz. [1883]. O. **897:10**

Soboleski, Paul. Poets and poetry of Poland; a collection of polish verse, incl. a short account of the history of polish poetry, with 60 biogr. sketches of Poland's poets and specimens of their composition, tr. into the english language. Chicago. 1881. O. **897:3**

Krasinski, *Hrabia* Zygmunt Napoleon. The undivine comedy, and other poems by the anonymous poet of Poland; his polish annotators, Adam and Ladislas Mickiewicz; Polish poetry in the 19th century by Julian **Klaczko,** *and* a short biogr. of the poet. Tr. by Martha Walker Cook. Phila. 1875. D. **897:5**

*   *   *

Otto, F: The history of russian literature; with a lexicon of russian authors. Tr. from the german, under the superintendence of the author, by G: Cox. Oxford. 1839. O. **897:12**

Turner, C: E: Studies in russian literature. Lond. 1882. D. **897:7**
Contents. Lomonosoff.—Kantemier.— Catherine II. —Sumarokoff.—Von Viezin. — Derzhavin. — Karamsin.—Jukovsky.—Kriloff.—Life and genius of Gogol. —The works of Gogol.—Life and genius of Pushkin. —The poems of Poushkin.— Evjenie Onegin.—The dramas of Poushkin. — Poushkin's later works. — Lermontoff. — Genius and works of Lermontoff.— Nekrasoff.

Bodenstedt, F: Martin v. Russische dichter. Deutsch von F: Bodenstedt. Berlin. 1866. 4 v. in 2. S. **897:1**
Contents, see Deutscher katalog, p. 23.

Pushkin, Aleksandr Sergeïevitch. Eugene Onéguine; romance of russian life in verse. From the russian, with short biogr. notice, by lieut.-col. Spalding. N. Y. 1881. O. **897:6**

— Dichtungen. Deutsch von Ferdinand Löwe. Hildburgh. 1869. D. **897:14**

Turgenief, Ivan Sergeïevitch. Poems in prose. Portr. Bost. 1883. S. **897:8**

Krilof, Ivan Andreïevitch. Original fables. Tr. by I. Henry Harrison. Lond. 1883. D. **897:13**

Svetchin, Anna Sofiya, *born* Soimonof. Writings; ed by [Alfred P:] count de Falloux. Tr. by W. H. Preston. Bost. 1869. O. **897:15**
Contents. Airelles. — Thoughts. — On old age.—On resignation.

*   *   *

Bowring, J: Wýbor z básnictwi českého: Cheskian anthology; a history of the poetical literature of Bohemia, with translated specimens. Lond. 1832. S. **897:4**

4. Hungarian and Finnish.

Loew, W: N. Gems from Petöfi and other hungarian poets, trans.; with a memoir of the former and review of Hungary's poetical literature. N. Y. 1881. O. **899+3**

Petöfi, *originally* Petrovics, Sándor. Der held János; ein bauernmärchen. Aus dem ungarischen übers. durch Kertbeny. Stuttg. 1850. T. **899:1**

— Wolken; lyrischer cyklus. Zum ersten male ins deutsche übers., nebst einer biographie des dichters aus bisher unbenutzten quellen von Hugo Meltzl von Lomnitz. Lübeck. [1884]. S. **899:4**

Kalevala. Selections from the Kalevala; tr. from a german version by J: A. Porter, with an introd. and analysis of the poem. N. Y. 1873. S. **899:2**

— *See also in* **Hoffmann,** W. Leisure hours in Russia. **914.7:41**

19. Oriental literatures.

1. In general.

White, C. A. [Sanskrit literature, with some account of the persian, chinese and japanese.] *in* **880.1:1**
See under Classical literature, col.

Herder, J: Gottfried v. Morgenländische literatur. *In his* Werke. **830:2 v6**
Contents. Blätter der vorzeit; dichtungen aus der morgenländischen sage. — Blumen aus morgenländischen dichtern. — Spruch und bild, insonderheit bei den morgenländern.— Der fliegende wagen; ein morgenländischer erzählungen. — Gedanken einiger brasnen.—Ueber ein morgenländisches drama.—Das buch der gerechten mitte.—Exempel der tage.

Meier, Ernst, *tr.* Morgenländische anthologie; eine auswahl klassischer dichtungen aus der sinesischen, indischen, persischen und hebräischen literatur. Hildburgh. 1869. D. **890:2**

Alger, W: Rounseville. The poetry of the east. Bost. 1856. D. **890:1**
Contents. Introd.: Historical dissertation on orien-

tal poetry. — Metrical specimens of the thought, sentiment and fancy of the east.—Index.

2. Hebrew and Arabic.

(*See also* The Bible, col. 88-88; Judaism, col. 139; Mohammedanism, col. 140.)

Taylor, I: The spirit of hebrew poetry; with a sketch of the life of the author and a catalogue of his writings. N. Y. 1862. D. **893:5**

Gilfillan, G: The poets and poetry of the Bible. Auburn. 1854. D. **893:1**

Murray, T: Chalmers. Lectures on the origin and growth of the psalms. N. Y. 1880. D. **893:3**

Heilprin, Michael. The historical poetry of the ancient hebrews translated and critically examined. N. Y. 1879. 2 v. O. **893:2**

Sekles, S. The poetry of the Talmud. N. Y. 1880. O. **893:4**

Hebrew tales; sel. and tr. from the writings of the ancient hebrew sages. Bost. 1845. S. **893:7**

Deutsch, Emanuel Oscar Menahem. Literary remains, with a brief memoir. N. Y. 1874. O.   **893+6**
Contents. Memoir.—The Talmud.—Islam.—Notes of a lecture on the Talmud. — A lecture del. at the Midland institute, Birmingham. — Notes of a lecture on Semitic palæography. — Notes of three lectures on Semitic culture.—Egypt, ancient and modern. — Hermes Trismegistus.—Judæo-arabic metaphysics. — Les apôtres. — Five letters on the œcumenical council. — Apostolicæ sedis. — The roman passion drama. — On semitic languages.—On the targums.—On the samaritan pentateuch.—The book of Jasher. — Early arabic poetry.—Arabic poetry in Spain and Sicily.

Clouston, W. A., *ed.* Arabian poetry for english readers, ed. with introd. and notes. Glasgow. 1881. D.   **893 : 8**

Book of the thousand nights and one night, The ; now first completely done into english prose and verse from the original arabic by J: Payne. In 9 v.; v. 1, 2. Ill. N. Y. 1884. 2 v. O.   **893 : R9**
Note. Versions for general reading will be found in the class-list of prose fiction, col. 874, *under* Thousand and one nights.

Hariri, Al Kâsem. Makamen, oder die verwandlungen des Abu Said von Serug. *In* Rückert, F: Gesammelte poetische werke.   **831:122 v11**

3. Indian and Persian.
(See also Brahmanism and buddhism, col. 137; *and* Parseeism, col. 139.)

Whitney, W: Dwight. Oriental and linguistic studies : The Veda ; the Avesta ; the Science of language. N. Y. 1873. D.   **894 : 3**
Contents. The Veda. — The vedic doctrine of a future life.— Müller's History of vedic literature.—The translation of the Veda. — Müller's Rig-Veda translation. — The Avesta. — Indo-european philology and ethnology.—Müller's lecture on language. — Present state of the question as to the origin of language.— Bleek and Simious theory of language—Schleicher and the physical theory of language.—Steinthal and the psychological theory of language. — Language and education.—Index.

Poor, Laura Elizabeth. Sanskrit and its kindred literatures ; studies in comparative mythology. Bost. 1880. D.   **894 : 2**
Contents. The origin of literature.—Brahmanism and the Mahabharata. — Buddhism and the Ramayana. — Sanskrit philosophy, fable and drama. — The persian literature, aryan and semitic.—Comparative mythol. of the greek poetry and drama. — Greek philosophy and history. — Compar. mythol. of the latin and keltic literatures.—Compar. mythol. of the teutonic literature: Scandinavian families; Anglo-saxon and german families.—Mediæval hymns, and compar. mythol. of the mediæval ballads.—Compar. mythol. of slavonic literature.—The modern poetry of Europe.—Partial list of books consulted.—Index.

Indian.

Höfer, Albert, *tr.* Indische gedichte in deutschen nachbildungen. Leipz. 1844. 2 v. D.   **894 : 1**

Rückert, F: [Uebersetzungen aus der indischen literatur]. *In his* Gesammelte poetische werke.   **831 : 122 v12**
Contents, see under German literature, Poetry, col. 1118.

Arnold, Edwin. Indian idylls ; from the sanskrit of the Mahâbhârata. Bost. 1883. D.   **894 : 6**

Bhâgvât-Gîîtâ, The, or Dialogues of Krĕĕshnă and Ärjŏŏn. Tr. by C: Wilkins. N. Y. 1867. O.   **894 : 5**

Dasakumacharitam, The. Hindoo tales, or The adventures of ten princes. Freely tr. from the sanscrit by P. W. Jacob. Lond. 1873. D.   **894 : 7**

Milman, H: Hart, *tr. and ed.* Nala and Damayanti, and other poems. Tr. from the sanscrit into english verse, with mythological and critical notes. Oxford. 1835. Q.   **894 : 8**

Schmidt, Ferdinand, *tr.* Nal und Damajanti, — Sakuntala ; zwei erzählungen aus dem indischen. 4te aufl. Ill. Kreuznach. [1883]. S.   **894 : 10**

Kâlidasâ. Śakoontalá, or The lost ring ; an indian drama. Tr. into english prose and verse from the sanskrit by Monier Williams. N. Y. 1885. O.   **894 : 9**
— *Same, germ.* Sakuntala ; ein indisches schauspiel. Aus dem sanskrit und prakrit metrisch übers. von Ernst Meier. Hildburgh. 1867. D.   **894 : 9**

Bidpai *or* Pilpay. The fables of Pilpay. Rev. ed. N. Y. 1872. D.   **894 : 4**

Persian.

Firdausî *or* Firdusi, Abû'l-Kâsim-Mansûr *called.* The epic of kings ; stories retold from Firdusi by Helen Zimmern. With two etchings by L. Alma Tadema and a prefatory poem by Edmund W. Gosse. N. Y. 1883. D.   **895 : 3**

Jâmî, Nûr-ed-din Abd-er-Rahmân *called.* Yûsuf and Zulaikha ; a poem by Jâmî. Tr. from the persian in english verse by Ralph T. H. Griffith. Lond. 1882. O.   **895 : 4**

Omar Khayyâm, Ghiyâth ed-din Abulfath 'Omar bin Ibrâhim al-Khayyâmî *called.* Rubáiyát of Omar Khayyam, the astronomer-poet of Persia, rendered into english verse. 1st amer. from the 3d Lond. ed. Bost. 1878. S.   **895 : 2**

Sâdi, Muslih-ed-din *called.* The Gulistan or rose garden. Tr. from the original by Francis Gladwin, with an essay on Saadi's life and genius by James Ross and a preface by R. W. Emerson. Bost. 1865. D.   **895 : 1**
— *Same, germ.* Rosengarten. Nach dem texte und dem arabischen commentar Sururi's, aus dem persischen übers. mit anmerk. und zugaben von K: H: Graf. Leipz. 1846. S.   **895 : 1**

4. Chinese and Japanese.
(See also Chinese religions, col. 139.)

Giles, Herbert A., *ed.* Gems of chinese literature. Lond. 1884. D.   **891 : 1**
Note. Short extracts from the works of the most famous writers of all ages from b. c. 550 to a. d. 1650, with biographical and dynastic notices.

Hau-kiou-choan.   **H 10**
See Class-list of prose fiction, col. 748.

Kin-ku-ki-kuan.   **G 2676**
See **Grisebach,** E:, *ed.,* in Class-list of prose fiction, col. 739.

Schi-king ; chinesisches liederbuch, gesammelt von Confucius. *In* Rückert, F: Gesammelte poetische werke.   **831 : 122 v6**

Moule, Arthur E., *ed. and tr.* Chinese stories for boys and girls ; and chinese wisdom for old and young. Ill. Lond. 1880. S.   **x 915.1 : 33**

Shunsui, Tamenaga. The loyal ronins. **S 2851**
See Class-list of prose fiction, col. 853.

Mitford, A. Bertram, *tr.* The forty-seven rônins. *In* Johnson, E. R., *ed.* Little classics.   **J 926 v11**

x denotes books specially adapted for children.

X. HISTORY AND GEOGRAPHY.

1. History in general.

(See also History of civilization, cl. 309, col. 150–152.)

1. Philosophy and study.

Droysen, J: Gustav. Grundriss der historik. 3te umgearb. aufl. Leipz. 1882. O. **901 : 5**

Herder, J: Gottfried v. Ideen zur philosophie der geschichte der menschheit. 4 v. in 1. *In his* Werke. **830 : 154 v9-12**

Schlegel, K: W: F: v. The philosophy of history, in a course of lectures del. at Vienna. Tr. from the germ., with a memoir of the author, by James Burton Robertson. 7th ed. rev. Lond. 1873. D. **901 : 2**

Hegel, G: W: F: Lectures on the philosophy of history. Tr. from the 3d germ. ed. by J. Sibree. Lond. 1872. D. **901 : 4**

— *Same.* Lond. 1881. D. **901 : 4**

Gutzkow, K: F: Philosophie der that und des ereignisses. Frankfurt a. M. 1845. D. **901 : 1**

Flint, Robert. The philosophy of history in France and Germany. Edinb. 1874. O. **901 : 3**

Atkinson, W: P. On history and the study of history ; three lectures. Bost. 1884. S. **900 : 1**

St. John, H:, *viscount Bolingbroke.* Letters on the study and use of history. *In his* Works. **820.2 : 18 v2**

Freeman, E: A: The office of the historical professor ; an inaugural lecture read in the Museum at Oxford, oct. 15, 1884. Lond. 1884. S. **907 : 3**

Adams, Herbert B. Methods of historical study. *In* Johns Hopkins university studies. **904+32 v2**

Adams, C: Kendall. A manual of historical literature ; comprising brief descriptions of the most important histories in english, french and german, together with practical suggestions as to methods and courses of historical study, for the use of students, general readers and collectors of books. N. Y. 1882. D. **907 : 1**

— *Same.* **16 : L**

Allen, W: Francis. History topics for the use of high schools and colleges. Bost. 1883. S. **907 : 2**

2. Dictionaries and charts.

Herbst, W:, [*and* Alfred Schulz], *eds.* Encyklopädie der neueren geschichte ; in verbindung mit namhaften deutschen und ausserdeutschen historikern herausg.; v. 1, 2. Gotha. 1880-84. 2 v. O. **903 : R7**
Contents. V. 1. A-D. 2. E-K. The original editor superintended the work to and including the letter G.

Hermann, K. Lexikon der allgemeinen weltgeschichte ; die historischen begebenheiten und personen aller zeiten und völker, geschichte aller reiche, mit besonderer berücksichtigung der neuzeit. Leipz. 1882. D. **909 : R28**

Heilprin, L: The historical reference-book ; comprising a chronolog. table of universal history, a chronolog. dictionary of universal history, a biogr. dictionary, with geogr. notes, for the use of students, teachers and readers. N. Y. 1884. O. **903 : 9**

Putnam, G: Palmer, *ed.* Ten years of the world's progress ; a supplement to the work of that title, embracing a comprehensive record of facts in the annals of nations and progress of the arts from 1850 to 1861, with corr. and add. N. Y. 1861. D. **902 : 4**

— Handbook of chronology and history ; the world's progress, a dictionary of dates, with tabular views of general history and a historical chart. 6th ed. [Putnam's home encyclopedias]. N. Y. 1873. D. **902 : 3**

— The world's progress ; a dictionary of dates, being a chronological and alphabetical record of all essential facts in the progress of society from the creation of the world, with a chart. Rev. and continued to august 1877, by F: B. Perkins. 21st ed. N. Y. 1878. O. **902 : R2**

Hayden, Joseph. Dictionary of dates and universal information, relating to all ages and nations. 16th ed., containing the history of the world to the autumn of 1878 by B: Vincent. Lond. 1878. O. **902 : R1**

— *Same.* 17th ed., to the autumn of 1881. N. Y. 1882. O. **902 : R1**

Haskel, Daniel. A chronological view of the world ; exhibiting the leading events of universal history, the origin and progress of the arts and sciences, the obituary of distinguished men, and the periods in which they ·flourished, together with an account of the appearance of comets, and a complete view of the fall of meteoric stones in all ages; from the article "chronology" in the New Edinb. encyclopædia, ed. by sir D: Brewster, with an enl. view of important events, particularly in regard to american history, and a continuation to the present time, collected from authentic sources. N. Y. 1848. D. **902 : 5**

Nichol, J: Tables of ancient literature and history, b. c. 1500—a. d. 200. Glasgow. 1877. Q. **902 : R8**

Nichol, J:—*Continued.*
— Tables of european history, literature and art, a. d. 200 to 1882, and of american history, literature and art. 3d ed. rev. and enl. Glasgow. 1884. Q.   **902 : R7**

Lyman, Azel S. Historical chart; containing the prominent events of the civil, religious and literary history of the world from the earliest times to the present day. Rev., enl. and imp. Cinc. 1874. F.   **908 : R1**
— Questions designed for the use of those engaged in the study of Lyman's Historical chart, with a key to the names mentioned in the chart and a list of geographical names of ancient and middle history, with their corresponding modern names. Rev. enl. and imp. Cinc. 1874. S.   **908 : R1 v2**

Chambers, Robert, *ed.* The book of days; a miscellany of popular antiquities in connection with the calendar, incl. anecdote, biography and history, curiosities of literature and oddities of human life and character. Edinb. 1863. 2 v. O.   **903+2**
— *Same.* Edinb. *n. d.* 2 v. Q.   **903 : R1**

Perce, Elbert. The battle roll; an encyclopedia, containing descriptions of the most famous and memorable land battles and sieges in all ages, arr. alphab. and chronolog. Ill. N. Y. 1858. Q.   **903+3**

3. Universal histories.

Freeman, E: A: General sketch of history, adapted for amer. students. New ed., rev. with chronological table, maps and index. [Freeman's historical course for schools]. N. Y. [1876]. S.   **902 : 6**

Plötz, C: Epitome of ancient, mediæval and modern history. Tr. with extensive add. by W: H. Tillinghast. Bost. 1884. D.   **909 : 13**

Weber, G: Outlines of universal history from the creation of the world to the present time. Tr. from the germ. by M. Behr; rev. and corr. with the addition of a history of the United States of America by Francis Bowen. Bost. *n. d.* O.   **909 : 10**

Cottinger, H. M. Elements of universal history for higher institutes in republics and for self-instruction. Milw. 1884. O.   **909 : 24**

Wheeler, C: Gardner. The course of empires; outlines of the chief political changes in the history of the world, arr. by centuries, with variorum illustrations. Maps. Bost. 1883. O.   **909 : 9**

Schmidt, Ferdinand. Die weltgeschichte in übersichtlicher darstellung erzählt. Ill. Berlin. 1882. O.   **909 : 27**
Contents. Das alterthum. — Das mittelalter. — Die neuzeit.

Grube, A: W:, *ed.* Charakterbilder aus der geschichte und sage für einen propädeutischen geschichtsunterricht. 24ste aufl. Leipz. 1882, 1883. 3 v. O.   **909+15**
Contents. V. 1. Die vorchristliche zeit. 2. Das mittelalter. 3. Die neue zeit.

Voltaire, François Marie Arouet *called* de. An essay on universal history, the manners and spirit of nations, from the reign of Charlemaign to the age of Lewis XIV, with a supplement carrying down the history to the peace of Versailles. Written in french, and tr. into eng., with add. notes

and chronol. tables, by mr. Nugent. New ed. rev. Edinb. 1777. 4 v. S.   **909 : 7**

Universal history, An, from the earliest accounts to the present time; compiled from original authors. Ill. with charts, maps, notes, etc., and a general index to the whole. [Antient pt.] Lond. 1779. 18 v. O.   **909 : 11**
Contents. V. 1. From the creation to the flood.—From the deluge to the birth of Abraham.—History of Egypt to the time of Alexander the great. — History of the Moabites, Ammonites, Amalekites, Cannanites and Philistines.—History of the ancient Syrians. 2. History of the Phoenicians.—Jews to the babylonish captivity. 3. Jews to the destruction of Jerusalem.—Assyria.—The Babylonians.—Ancient Phrygians, Trojans, Lycians, Lydians, etc. 4. Medes. —Persians.—Mysians.—Lydians.—Lycians. 5. The fabulous and heroic times.—Athenians.—Sparta to union with the Achæans. 6. Thebes.—The Achæan league. — Grecian states in Asia minor. — Sicily.—Syracuse to b. c. 265. 7. Syracuse.—Rhodes.—Crete.—Cyprus.—Samos.—Other greek islands.—Macedonians, to b. c. 306. 8. Macedonians from b. c. 306 to the conquest by the romans. — The Seleucidæ in Syria.—Egypt.—Armenians.—Kingdom of Pontus. 9. Cappadocians.—Pergamus. — Thrace. — Epirus.—Bithynia.—Colchis, Iberia, Albania, Bosporus, Media, Bactria, Edessa, Emesa, Adiabene, Characene, Elymais, Comagene, Chalcydene.—Parthians.—Persians. Ancient state of Italy to the building of Rome. — Roman history to the commonwealth. 10-14. Roman history to the death of Justinian. 15. Constantinopolitan history to the taking of Constantinople by the turks.—The Carthaginians. 16. Carthage to its destruction by Aemilianus.—Numidians.—Mauritanians.—Gaetulians.—Melanogœtuli.—Libyans of Marmarica, Cyrenaica, Regio Syrtica. — Ethiopians.—Arabs to Mohammed.—Empires of Nice and Trapezon.—Spain, to the expulsion of the carthaginians and briefly to Ferdinand and Isabella.—Ancient state of the Gauls. 17. Ancient Germans.—Ancient state and history of Britain.— Northern nations.—The Ostrogoths in Italy, the exarchs of Ravenna and the Lombards in Italy. 18. Turks, Tartars and Moguls.—Indians.—Opinions with respect to the creation.—History of the Etruscans.

Universal history, An ; modern part from the earliest accounts to the present time, compiled from original authors by the authors of the ancient part. Lond. 1780. 42 v. O.   **909 : 12**
Contents. V. 1. Life of Mohammed.—Arabs to 685. 2. 685—1041. 3. 1041—1058.—Turks to destruction of their empire in Tartary.—Seljukians of Irán to 1151. 4. Seljukians of Irán from 1151.—Moguls and Tartars from the time of Jenghiz Khán to reign of Timúr Bek, 1396. 5. Mogul empire to 1505.—Shahs reigning in Persia.— Arab kings of Ormús. — Turkmans and Usbeks.—Kingdom of Karazm.—Hindústán, or the empire of the Great Mogol. 6. Countries in the Hither peninsula of India.—Religion of the Hindús.—Countries in the Farther peninsula of India. 7. Eastern Tartars. — Empire of China. — Empire of Japan.—History of commerce to, and settlements in the East Indies by european nations: Methods of communication before the discovery of the Cape of Good Hope. 8. History of commerce to, and settlements in the East Indies by various european nations: English East India company.—Conquests, settlements and discoveries of the Dutch in the East Indies. 9. *Same, continued.*—Danes and French in the East Indies.—Ostend East India company.—East India company estab. in Sweden.—Othman empire to 1481. 10. *Same,* to 1687.—The history of the dispersion of the jews, to 7th century. 11. *Same,* to 18th century.—History of Africa and of all the principal nations and states which inhabit it. — Modern Egypt.—African islands. 12. *Same, continued.*—Abyssinia.—Kingdoms adjacent to Abyssinia.—Coast of Zanguebar. — Hottentots. 13. West coast of Africa. — Western Ethiopia. — Angola or Dongo. — Loango.—Benin.—Gold Coast. 14. *Same, continued.*—Ivory Coast.—Grain or Malaguetta Coast. — Sierra Leone.—Interior countries of Africa.—Modern Barbary.— Morocco and Fez.—Algiers. 15. *Same, continued.*—Tunis.— Tripoli.— Barca.— Island and order of the knights of Malta. 16, 17. Spain to 1621. 18. Spain to 1713.—Portugal to 1667. 19. Portugal to

1713.—Navarro.—France to 1180. **20.** 1180—1574. **21.** 1574—1715. **22.** Italy to 1428. **23.** 1291—1517.—Venice to 1381. **24.** Venice to 1700.—Naples to 1269. **25.** Naples to 1713.—Genoa to 1684.—Germany, 887—1152. **26.** 1152—1526. **27.** 1526—1714.— United provinces, or republic of Holland to 1602. **28.** Republic of Holland to 1697.—Denmark to 1182. **29.** Denmark to 1730.— Sweden to 1520. **30.** Sweden to 1721.—Poland to 1668. **31.** Poland to 1715.—Prussia.—Russia to 1699. **32.** Russia to 1725.—Hungary.—The modern empire.— The imperial cities.— Republic of the Swiss.—Republic of Geneva.—Bohemia.—Saxony.— Bavaria.— Palatine electorate.— Archduchy of Austria. — Hanover. — Brunswick - Wolfenbuttel. — Brandenburg.—Mecklenburg to 1592. **33.** Mecklenburg to Adolphus Frederick IV.—Tuscan states.— Milan to 1822. **34.** Milan to 1706.—House of Savoy.—America to 1548. **35.** America.—Establishment and progress of the british settlements: Newfoundland; Nova Scotia; New England; New Jersey; Canada. **36.** *Same, continued*; Louisiana; Carolina; Maryland; Pennsylvania; Hudson's Bay.— British and other islands in the American West Indies.—*Conclusion of the modern history.* Asia: Asia Minor; Syria; Arabia; Eastern Asiatic Turkey; Turks. **37.** *Conclusion of the modern history.* Asia: Persia; Great Tartary and Asiatic Russia; China and Japan; India and the oriental islands. — Africa. — Europe. **38.** America. **39.** History of England to 1558. **40.** England to 1762. **41.** History of Scotland to the union of the two kingdoms. **42.** History of Ireland to 1691.

Mavor, W: Universal history, ancient and modern, from the earliest records of time to the general peace of 1801. Lond. 1802-08. 25 v. S.   **909 : 8**
Contents. V. 1. Preliminary View, with a history of the antediluvians, ancient Egypt and the neighbouring nations. 2. The Canaanites, Philistines and Jews.— Assyrian and Babylonian empires. 3, 4. Greece. 5-7. Rome. 8. Medes, Persians, Phoenicians, Ancient Syrians, Seleucidæ in Syria, Phrygians, Trojans, Mysians, Lydians. Lycians, Ancient Cilicians, Celtes, Scythians, Armenians, Cappadocians, Pergamians, Thracians, Bithynians.– 9. Pontus, Epirus.–Colchis, Iberia, Albania, etc.—Parthia.—Numidians, Mauritanians, Gætulians, Melanogætuli. — Lybians and Greeks.—Ethiopians, Ancient Arabs. — Empires of Nice and Trapezond.—Ancient Spaniards, Gauls, Germans and Britons.— Northern nations.— Ostrogotha, Lombards, Turks, Tartars and Moguls, Chinese. —Index to ancient history. 10. Arabs, incl. a life of Mohammed. 11. Mogul empire, parts of Tartary and China, Hindostan. 12. India. the Ottoman empire, Korea, Japan and Jedso. 13. The dispersion of the jews, modern Egypt and other african nations. 14. Various modern african nations. 15. Portugal and Spain. 16. Italy, Venice and the Italian states. 17. Empire of Germany, electorates of Saxony, Bavaria, palatinate of Hanover and Brunswick - Wolfenbuttel. 18. Hungary, Holland and Switzerland. 19, 20. England. 21. Scotland and Ireland. 22. Russia, Poland, Sweden, Denmark, Prussia. 23. France and Navarre. 24. North and South America and the West Indies. 25. Chronological index to modern history, [v. 11-25].—General index [to same].

Tytler, Alexander Fraser, *and* E: **Nares.** Universal history from the creation of the world to the decease of George III, 1820 ; ed. by an american. [Harper's family library]. N. Y. 1845. 6 v. S.   **909 : 6**
Contents. V. 1. Greece to 168. 2. Greece, 168.—Rome to 30 b. c. 3. 30 b. c.—1066 a. d. 4. 1066—1763. 5. 1513—1724. 6. 1715—1820.

Turner, Sharon. The sacred history of the world, attempted to be philosophically considered in a series of letters to his son. N. Y. 1846. 3 v. S.   **909 : 5**

Müller, Johannes v. Vierundzwanzig bücher allgemeiner geschichten, besonders der europäischen menschheit. Stuttg. 1861. 4 v. in 2. S.   **909 : 3**

Struve, Gustav. Weltgeschichte in neun büchern. Coburg. 1864, 1865. 8 v. O.   **909+18**
Contents. V. 1. Alte geschichte. 2. Geschichte

[3]

des mittelalters, a. d. 476 — 1291. **3.** Geschichte des mittelalters, a. d. 1291—1517. **4.** Geschichte der neuzeit, 1517—1648. **5.** Geschichte der neu-zeit, 1648—1789. **6.** Revolutions-zeitalter, 1789 bis 1815. **7.** Revolutions-zeitalter, 1815—1848. [**8**]. Die zeit von 1848 bis 1863.—Die zeit von 1863 bis 1866.

— *Same.* Geschichte der neuzeit. N. Y. 1860. O.   **909+18 v6, 7**

Schlosser, F: Christoph. Weltgeschichte für das deutsche volk. 2te ausg., mit der fortsetzung bis auf die gegenwart ; mit zugrundelegung der bearb. von G. L. Kriegk besorgt von Oscar Jäger und Th. Creizenach. 17te ster.-abdruck. Berlin. 1876. 19 v. O.   **909 : 2**
Contains V. 1-3. Geschichte der alten welt. 4-8. Geschichte des mittelalters. 9-15. Geschichte der neueren zeit. 16-18. Jäger, Oscar. 1815—1871 ; geschichte der neuesten zeit vom Wiener congress bis zum Frankfurter frieden. 19. **Treutler,** J. Vollständiges namen- und sachregister.

Becker, K: F: Weltgeschichte. 8te neu bearb. bis auf die gegenwart fortgeführte ausg. ; herausg. von Adolf Schmidt, mit der fortsetzung von E: Arnd. Supplement-band 1 und 2 : Geschichte der jahre 1871-1877 von Constantin Bulle. Leipz. 1876-78. 24 v. in 14. O.   **909 : 1**
Contents. V. 1-4. Alte geschichte. 5-8. Mittlere geschichte. 9-13. Neuere geschichte. 14-22. **Arnd,** E: Geschichte der neuesten zeit, 1789—1871. 23, 24. **Bulle,** Constantin. Geschichte der jahre 1871-77.

Schmidt, Ferdinand. Weltgeschichte. 1ster b. 3te aufl. ; 2er—3er b. 2te aufl. Ill. Berlin. 1878, 1882. 4 v. O.   **909 : 26**
Contents. V. 1. Geschichte des alterthums: Die ägypter; Die chinesen in älterer zeit; Die inder; Die phönicier; Die babylonier und die perser; Die israeliten: Die griechen; Die römer. 2. Geschichte des mittelalters: Von eintritt des christenthums bis zum untergange des weströmischen reiches bis zum vertrage von Verdun und bis zum verfall des chalifats: Von Heinrich I. bis zu den Hohenstaufen ; Die Hohenstaufen; Vom untergange der Hohenstaufen bis Maximilian I ; Andere europäischen staaten: Geschichtstafel. 3. Geschichte der neueren zeit: Die reformation; Gegen-reformation; Der dreissigjährige krieg ; Die englische thronumwälzung; Vorginge in anderen staaten in der zeit bis gegen ende des 17. jahrh. ; Bis zur mitte des 18. jahrh. 4. Geschichte der neuesten zeit: Die zweite hälfte des 18. jahrb. bis zur französischen revolution; Friedrich des grossen staatsverwaltung und privatleben; Umblick; Die französische revolution; Napoleon Bonaparte's machtherrschaft; Der deutsche befreiungskampf; Umblick: Das julikönigthum; Kriege Deutschlands seit 1863.

Weber, G: Allgemeine weltgeschichte. 2te aufl., unter mitwirkung von fachgelehrten revidirt und überarbeitet ; b. 1-9 *und* Register 2 b. Leipz. 1882-85. 11 v. O.   **909+17**
Contents. V. 1. Geschichte des morgenlandes: Vorrede; Einleitung; Chinesen und Aegypter; Arier und Iranier; Semitische völker. 2. Geschichte des Hellenischen volkes: Das land der Griechen; Griechenlands mythenwelt und das homerische zeitalter; Die herrschaft der edeln; Gesetzgebung und colonisation; Die zeit der perserkriege; Athens vorherrschaft und das perikleische zeitalter; Die zeiten des peloponnesischen krieges; Spartas zweite vorherrschaft bis zum frieden des Antalkidas; Spartas überhebung und fall und Thebens vorherrschaft; Griechenlands fall und Makedoniens emporkommen. 3. Römische geschichte bis zu ende der republik und geschichte der alexandrinisch - hellenischen welt: Widmung und vorrede; Roms ursprünge; Die alexandrinisch-hellenische welt; Roms wachsthum und grösse; Rom während der socialen und politischen partelkämpfe. 4. Geschichte des römischen kaiserreichs der völkerwanderung und der neuen staatenbildungen: Cäsar Octavianus Augustus und seine zeit; Die römische kaiserzeit bis zu Vespasian; Die Flavier; Trajan und Hadrian; Die Antoninen; Cultur und geistesleben im kaiserlichen Rom; Die vollen-

dete militärherrschaft; Das römische reich im vierten jahrh.; Das getheilte reich bis zum falle Roms; Die neuen staatenbildungen im 5ten und 6ten jahrh.; Der orient vor dem islam.—Register, b. 1-4.
5. Geschichte des mittelalters, 1ster t.: Die mohamedanische welt; Das zeitalter der Karolinger und das oströmische reich. 6. Geschichte des mittelalters, 2ter t.: Die vorherrschaft des deutschen reichs; Das zeitalter der kreuzzüge und der Hohenstaufen. 7. Geschichte des mittelalters, 3ter t.: Das zeitalter her kreuzzüge etc., zweite abt.; Verfall der lehnsmonarchie und des pontifikats und herausbildung ständischer verfassungen. 8. Geschichte des mittelalters, 4ter t.: Verfall der lehnsmonarchie etc., zweite abt.; Sieg des monarchischen prinzips über den feodalismus. Ausgang des mittelalters.—Register, b. 5-8.
9. Geschichte der völker und staaten im übergang vom mittelalter zur neuzeit: Sieg des monarchischen princips etc., zweite abt.; Das zeitalter der entdeckungen.

Ranke, Franz Leopold v. Weltgeschichte. 3te aufl. Leipz. 1882-84. O. 909:24
Contents. V. 1. Die älteste historische völkergruppe und die griechen. 2. Die römische republik und ihre weltherrschaft. 3. Das altrömische kaiserthum.—Analekten, kritische erörterungen zur alten geschichte: Zur alttestamentlichen literatur; Diodorus Siculus und seine berichte über Alexander den grossen; Ueber die Römischen alterthümer des Dionysius von Halicarnass; Analyse der traditionen über die eroberung Roms durch die gallier; Erörterung über einige zweifelhaft erscheinende nachrichten bei Polybius; Appian und der werth seiner quellen; Dio-Zonaras; Vellejus Paterculus; die Varusschlacht; Würdigung und kritik der geschichtschreibung des Cornelius Tacitus; Zur kaisergeschichte. 4. Das kaiserthum in Constantinopel und der ursprung romanisch-germanischer königreiche.—Analekte: Eusebius über das leben Constantins; Zosimus; Procopius; Jordanes; Gregor von Tours. 5. Die arabische weltherrschaft und das reich Karls des grossen.—Analekte: Zur geschichte der eroberung von Syrien und Jerusalem; Amru in Aegypten; Zwei lateinische chronisten in Spanien unter den Omajjaden; Zur analyse der Annales Mettenses.

— Same, eng. Universal history: The oldest historical group of nations and the greeks; ed. by G. W. Prothero. N. Y. 1884. O. 909:24 v1

Oncken, W:, ed. Allgemeine geschichte in einzeldarstellungen: 1ste hauptabth., [Alte zeit]. Berlin 1879. 2 v. O. 909+19
Contents. V. 5. Hertzberg, G. F: Geschichte von Hellas und Rom, [in 2 v.].
— Same: 2te hauptabth., [Mittelalter]. Berlin. 1880-85. 8 v. O. 909+20
Contents. V. 1. Hertzberg, G. F: Geschichte des römischen kaiserreichs. 2. Dahn, F: J. F. Urgeschichte der germanischen und romanischen völker, [in 2 v.]. 4. Müller, A: Der islam im morgen- und abendland; b. 1. 5. Kugler, B. Geschichte der kreuzzüge. 7. Hertzberg, G. F: Geschichte der Byzantiner und des Osmanischen reiches bis gegen ende des 16. jahrb. 8. Geiger, L: Renaissance und humanismus in Italien und Deutschland. 9. Ruge, S. Geschichte des zeitalters der entdeckungen.
— Same: 3te hauptabth., [Neue zeit.] Ill. Berlin. 1879-84. 8 v. O. 909+21
Contents. V. 2. Philippson, M. Westeuropa im zeitalter vom Philipp II. Elisabeth und Heinrich IV. 4. Stern, A. Geschichte der revolution in England. 5. Philippson, M. Das zeitalter Ludwigs XIV. 6. Brückner, A. Peter der grosse. 8. Oncken, W: Das zeitalter Friedrichs des grossen, [in 2 v.]. 9. Wolf, A., and H: v. Zwiedineck-Südenhorst. Oesterreich unter Maria Theresia, Josef II und Leopold II, 1740—1792. 10. Brückner, A. Katharina II.
— Same: 4te hauptabth., [Neueste zeit.] Ill. Berlin. 1883. O. 909+22
Contents. V. 2. Flathe, Theodor. Das zeitalter der restauration und revolution, 1815—1851.

Bulle, Constantin. Geschichte der neuesten zeit, 1815—1871. Leipz. 1876. 2 v. O. 909:14
— Same. In Becker, K: F: Weltgeschichte. 909:1 v23, 24

Corvin-Wiersbitzki, O: Julius Bernhard v. 1848—1871; geschichte der neuzeit von Corvin. Leipz. [1882]. 3 v. O. 909:16

Historical geography.

Labberton, Robert H. An historical atlas; comprising 141 maps; added, besides an explanatory text on the period delineated in each map, a carefully selected bibliography of the english books and magazine articles bearing on that period. 8th ed. N. Y. 1885. Q. 911+7

Freeman, E: A: The historical geography of Europe: v. 1, Text, v. 2, Maps. Lond. 1881. 2 v. O. 911:1

Spruner v. Mertz, K: Atlas antiquus. [3e aufl. neu bearb. von Theodor Menke.] Gothæ. 1865. F. 911:R3
— Hand-atlas für die geschichte des mittelalters und der neueren zeit. 3te aufl. neu bearb. von Th. Menke. Gotha. 1880. F. 911:R4
— Hand-atlas zur geschichte Asiens, Afrika's Amerika's und Australiens. 2e aufl. Gotha. 1855. F. 911:R5

Köppen, Adolphus L: Historico-geographical atlas of the middle ages; containing a series of 6 general maps, delineating the migrations of the northern and eastern nations, together with the states arising from the ancient Roman empire in Europe, western Asia and northern Africa from the close of the 4th to the middle of the 15th century. Repub. from the historico-geographical hand-atlas of Spruner with concise explanatory description. N. Y. 1855. F. 912:R5

4. Collected works, Essays.

(See also Political essays, cl. 304, col. 146; English essays, cl. 824, col. 1050.)

Mackintosh, Sir James. Miscellaneous works. N. Y. 1878. 3 v. in 1. O. 904+28
Contents. On the philosophical genius of lord Bacon and mr. Locke.—A discourse on the law of nature and of nations.—Life of sir T: Moore.—A refutation of the claim on behalf of Charles I to the authorship of the Eikōn basilikē.—On the progress of ethical philosophy chiefly during the 17th and 18th centuries.—An account of the partition of Poland.—Sketch of the administration and fall of Struensee.—Statement of the case of donna Maria da Gloria.—Character of Charles, 1st marquis Cornwallis. — Character of G: Canning.—Preface to a reprint of the Edinburgh review of 1755.—On the writings of Machiavel.—Review of mr. Godwin's Lives of E: and J: Philips.—Review of Rogers' poems.—Review of Mme. de Stael's De l'Allemagne.—Review of the causes of the revolution of 1688.— Memoir of the affairs of Holland, 1667—1686.—Discourse read at the opening of the Literary society of Bombay.—Vindiciæ gallicæ.—Reasons against the french war of 1793. — On the state of France in 1815.— On the right of parliamentary suffrage. — Speeches.

Ranke, Franz Leopold v. Sämmtliche werke. Leipz. 1867-81. 48 v. in 41. O. 904:36
Contents. V. 1-6. Deutsche geschichte im zeitalter der reformation. 7. Zur deutschen geschichte vom religionsfrieden bis zum dreissigjährigen krieg. 8-13. Französische geschichte, vornehmlich im 16. und 17. jahrh. 14-22. Englische geschichte, vornehmlich im 17. jahrh. 23. Geschichte Wallensteins. 24. Abhandlungen und versuche. Die grossen mächte. — Zur kritik preussischer memoiren. — Ueber den fall des brandenburgischen ministers von Danckelmann. — Ueber die erste bearbeitung der geschichte der schlesischen kriege von könig Friedrich II.—Ueber den briefwechsel Friedrich des grossen.—Zur geschichte der politischen theorien.—Anhang.

25-29. Zwölf bücher preussischer geschichte. 30. Zur geschichte von Oesterreich und Preussen, 1748—1763. 31, 32. Die deutschen mächte und der fürstenbund, 1780 bis 1790. 33, 34. Geschichten der romanischen und germanischen völker von 1494 bis 1514.— Zur kritik neuerer geschichtschreiber. 35, 36. Die osmanen und die spanische monarchie im 16. und 17. jahr. 37-39. Die römischen päpste in den letzten vier jahrh. 40, 41. *Historisch-biographische studien.* Cardinal Consalvi und seine staatsverwaltung unter dem pontificat Pius VII.—Savonarola und die florentinische republik gegen ende des 15. jahrh.—Filippo Strozzi und Cosimo Medici, der erste grossherzog von Toscana. — Don Carlos, prinz von Asturien, sohn könig Philipps II von Spanien. 42. Zur venetianischen geschichte. 43, 44. Serbien und die Türkei im 19. jahrh. 45. Ursprung und beginn der revolutionskriege 1791 und 1792. 46-48. Hardenberg und die geschichte des preussischen staates, 1793—1813.

*   *   *

Archer, T: Decisive events in history. Ill. Lond. [1879]. O.   **904 : 6**
Contents. The battle of Marathon.—The defeat of the carthaginians at Zama.—The fall of Jerusalem.— The dedication of Constantinople.—The foundation of Venice.—The landing of St. Augustine in Britain. —The defeat of the saracens at Tours.—The norman conquest.—The emperor Henry IV at Canossa.—The first crusade.—The signing of Magna charta.—The dawn of the reformation.—The defeat of the spanish armada. — The maintenance of the "Petition of right."—The surrender of Napoleon Bonaparte.—The restoration of the german empire.

Creasy, *Sir* E: Shepherd. The fifteen decisive battles of the world, from Marathon to Waterloo. N. Y. 1859. D.   **904 : 7**
Contents. The battle of Marathon.—Defeat of the athenians at Syracuse.—The battle of Arbela.—The battle of the Metaurus.—Victory of Arminius over the roman legions under Varus.—The battle of Châlons.—The battle of Tours.—The battle of Hastings. —Joan of Arc's victory over the english at Orleans.— The defeat of the spanish armada. — The battle of Blenheim.—The battle of Pultowa.—Victory of the americans over Burgoyne at Saratoga.—The battle of Valmy.—The battle of Waterloo.

King, C: Famous and decisive battles of the world, or History from the battlefield. [Ill.] Phila. 1884. O.   **904+33**
Contents. Marathon. — Thermopylæ. — Platæa. — Mantinea.—Arbela.—Cannæ.—Zama.—Cynoscephalæ. —Magnesia.— Pydna.— Pharsalia. — Philippi. — Chalons.—Tours.—Hastings.—Jerusalem.—Acre.—Cressy. — Orleans. — Constantinople. — Leipsic. — Lützen.— Vienna.—Narva.—Pultowa. — Blenheim.—Ramilies.— Oudenarde. —Leuthen.—Kunersdorf.— Torgau.—Saratoga.—Marengo. — Austerlitz.—Jena.—Auerstadt.— Waterloo.—Balaclava.— Manassas.— Gettysburg.— Nashville.—Five Forks and Lee's surrender.—Gravelotte.—Plevna.

Davenport, R: Alfred. Perilous adventures, or Remarkable instances of travel, perseverance and suffering. N. Y. 1844. S. **904 : 8**
Contents. Wanderings of prince Charles Edward.— Escape of J. J. Casanova from the state prison of Venice.—Attempt of Charles II to recover the english crown, his defeat at Worcester and his wanderings until his escape from England.—Escape of the earl of Nithsdale.—Perils of Stanislaus Leczinski, king of Poland.—Expulsion of Cortez from Mexico, and his reconquest of that city.

James, G: Payne Rainsford. Dark scenes of history. Lond. *n. d.* S.   **904 : 29**
Contents. France: Amboise. — England: Arthur; Perkin Warbeck.— Last days of the templars.— France: The albigenses.— Venice: The conspiracy of Cueva.—Wallenstein.—Herod the great.

Lea, H: C: Superstition and force; essays on the wager of law, the wager of battle, the ordeal and torture. 3d ed., rev. Phila. 1878. O.   **904 : 27**

Timbs, J: Curiosities of history. *In his* Things not generally known: **829.2 : 64 v5**
Contents, see under English literature, Miscellany, col. 1090.

Gervinus, G: Gottfried. Introd. to the history of the 19th century. From the german, with a brief notice of the author by the transl. Lond. 1853. D.   **904 : 11**

Arnold, T: Introductory lectures on modern history, del. in lent term 1842, with the inaugural lecture del. in dec. 1841 ; ed. from the 2d Lond. ed. with pref. and notes by H: Reed. N. Y. 1847. D.   **904 : 1**

*   *   *

Anderson, W:, *ed.* Treasury of history and biography for the young. Lond. *n. d.* S.   **x 904 : 18**

Bisset, Andrew. Essays on historical truth. Lond. 1871. O.   **904 : 34**
Contents. Is there a science of government?— Hobbes.— James Mill.— Hume.—Sir Walter Scott.— The government of the commonwealth and the government of Cromwell.—Prince Henry.—Sir T: Overbury.

Coan, Titus Munson, *ed.* Historical studies. (Topics of the time, no. 4.) N. Y. 1883. S.   **904 : 24**
Contents. **Jessopp,** A: Village life in Norfolk 600 years ago.— **Cappar,** S: J. Siena.— **Harrison,** F: O. France and England in 1793.—General Chanzy.

Dutt, Shoshee Chunder. Historical studies and recreations. Lond. 1879. 2 v. O. **904 : 19**
Contents. V. 1. The world's history retold in two parts: I. *The ancient world:* Prefatory remarks.— China.—India. — Persia.—Assyria, Media, Lydia and Tartary. — Phœnicia, Syria, Palestine and Arabia.— Egypt.—Greece.—Rome.—Résumé.—Index. II. *The modern world:* Prefatory remarks.—Great Britain.— The dependencies of the british empire.—The United States of America.—France, or The grande nation. —Germany.—Russia.—The minor states of Europe.— The independent states of Asia, Africa and America. —Résumé. 2. I. Bengal, an account of the country from the earliest times. II. The great wars of India. III. The ruins of the old world, read as milestones of civilization.

Fox-Vassall, H: R:, *3d baron Holland.* Foreign reminiscences ; ed. by his son H: E: lord Holland. N. Y. 1851. S.   **904 : 14**

Freeman, E: A: Historical essays; 1st–3d series. Lond. 1875–80. 3 v. O.   **904 : 9**
Contents. 1st ser. The mythical and romantic elements in early english history.—The continuity of english history.—The relations between the crowns of England and Scotland.—Saint Thomas of Canterbury and his biographers.—The reign of Edward III. —The holy roman empire.— The franks and the gauls.—The early sieges of Paris.—Frederick I, king of Italy.—The emperor Frederick II.—Charles the bold.—Presidential government.
2d ser. Ancient Greece and mediæval Italy.—Mr. Gladstone's Homer and the homeric age.—The historians of Athens.—The athenian democracy.—Alexander the great.— Greece during the macedonian period.—The primeval archæology of Rome.—Mommsen's History of Rome. — Lucius Cornelius Sulla.— The Flavian cæsars.
3d ser. First impressions of Rome.—The illyrian emperors and their land; app: Diocletian's place in architectural history. — Augusta Trevirorum; app: The panegyrists of the fourth century.—The goths at Ravenna.—Race and language; app: The jews in Europe.—The Byzantine empire. — First impressions of Athens.—Mediæval and modern Greece.— The southern slaves.—Sicilian cycles.—The normans at Palermo.

— Select historical essays. Leipz. 1873. S. **904 : 10**
Contents. The holy roman empire.—The franks and the gauls.—The early sieges of Paris. — Frederick I, king of Italy.—The emperor Frederick II.—Charles the bold.—Presidential government.

— Lectures to american audiences; The english people in its three homes ; The practical bearings of general european' history. Phila. [1883]. O.   **904 : 20**

x denotes books specially adapted for children.

Gilman, Arthur. Kings, queens and barbarians, or Talks about seven historic ages. New ed., enl. Bost. [1881]. S.   **x 904 : 12**

Contents. The golden age of Greece: Pericles; Simon.—*The golden age of Rome* : The punic wars; The three-man power; The emperor Augustus.—*The dark ages:* Three barbarians (Alaric, Attila, Genseric); Three kings (Charlemagne, Egbert, Alfred); Two more kings (Canute, William the conqueror); A hermit and a pilgrimage; The crusades; Just before dawn; The morning star (Wiclif).—*The age of Leo X:* Sunrise; A great church; A greate reformation.—*The golden age of England:* Queen Mary; Good queen Bess; Mary, the beautiful queen of Scots; The puritans.—*The golden age of France:* Louis XIV.—A general talk.—A shut up people (Chinese).—The gorgeous east (India).—The further east.—The land of the pharaohs.—One hundred dates.

Heeren, Arnold Hermann L: Three historical treatises. *With his* Ancient Greece.
    938 : 30

Contents. Political consequences of the reformation.—The rise, progress and practical influence of political theories.—The rise and growth of the continental interests of Great Britain.

Hillebrand, K: Zeiten, völker und menschen.
    834 : 22

Contents, see under German literature, Essays, col. 1121.

Historical selections from the London Rambler and other catholic periodicals. St. Louis. 1860. O.   **904 : 13**

Contents. The church and the people. — Schools of the benedictines.—St. Ursula and the 11,000 virgins.—Hofer and the tyrolese war of independence.— Maitland on the reformation.— Ancient irish dominican schools.—Oliver Cromwell.—Masters and workmen in the middle ages. — King William III. — A chapter in the reformation in Ireland. — The chancellors in England. — The Maronites and the Druses. — The russian and anglican hierarchies. — The anglican priesthood. —Anthony, earl of Shaftesbury.

Kingsley, C: Historical lectures and essays. [Works, v. 17]. Lond. 1880. D.   **904 : 23**

Contents. Alexandria and her schools.—The ancien régime. — The first discovery of America. — Cyrus servant of the Lord.—Ancient civilisation.—Rondelet. —Vesalius.—Paracelsus.—Buchanan.

— Plays and puritans, and other historical essays. [Works, v. 16]. Lond. 1880. D.
    904 : 22

Includes, Sir Walter Raleigh and his time.—Froude's History of England.

Lieber, Francis, *ed.* Great events, described by distinguished historians, chroniclers and other writers. N. Y. 1862. D.   **904 : 15**

Contents. **Herodotus.** The battle of Thermopylae.—**Plato.** The death of Socrates.—**Livy.** The surrender of the roman army at the defile near Caudium; Impeachment of Publius Cornelius Scipio, surnamed Africanus and Lucius Cornelius Scipio, surnamed Asiaticus.—**Tschudi,** A. Delivery of the four swiss forest districts. — **Müller,** J: v. The battle of Sempach.—**Theobald,** Z. The death of Huss. — **Gibbon,** E: The conquest of Constantinople.— **Marheinecke,** P. Martin Luther's appearance before the diet at Worms. — **Vertot d'Aubeuf,** R. A. *abbé* de. The siege and surrender of Rhodes. — **Bonaparte,** J. The sack of Rome.—**Cavendish,** G: Henry VIII and Catharine of Aragon before the legatine court.—**Bentivoglio,** G. The sieges of Leyden and Ostend. — **Stowe,** J: The destruction of the invincible armada.—*Southey,* R., *and Sir* W: F. P. **Napier.** The siege of Zaragoza.—Glossary.—Index.

Lodge, H: Cabot. Studies in history. Bost. 1884. D.   **904 : 35**

Contents. The puritans and the restoration. — A puritan pepys.—The early days of Fox.—W: Cobbett. —Alex. Hamilton.—Timothy Pickering.—Caleb Strong. —Albert Gallatin.— Daniel Webster. — Colonialism in the U. S. — French opinions in the U. S., 1840–1881.

x denotes books specially adapted for children.

Lord, J: Beacon lights of history. N. Y. 1884–85. 5 v. O.   **904 : 31**

Contents. **V. 1. Antiquity.** Moses; jewish jurisprudence. — Socrates; greek philosophy. — Phidias; ancient art. — Julius Cæsar; imperialism. — Cicero; roman literature. — Marcus Aurelius; the glory of Rome. — Constantine the great; christianity enthroned. — Chrysostom; sacred eloquence. — St. Ambrose; episcopal authority.—St. Augustine; christian theology.—Theodosius the great; latter days of Rome. —Leo the great; foundation of the papacy.

2. The middle ages. Mohammed; saracenic conquests.—Charlemagne; revival of western empire. —Alfred the great; the saxons in England. — Hildebrand; the papal empire.—St. Bernard; monastic institutions.—St. Anselm; mediæval theology.—Thomas Aquinas; the scholastic philosophy. — Thomas Becket; prelatical power.—The feudal system. — The crusades.—William of Wykeham; gothic architecture. —John Wycliffe; dawn of the reformation.

3. Renaissance and reformation. Dante; rise of modern poetry. — Chaucer; english life in the 14th century.—Columbus; maritime discoveries.—Savonarola; unsuccessful reforms. — Michael Angelo; the revival of art. — Luther; the protestant reformation. —Cranmer; the english reformation. — Loyola; rise and influence of the jesuits. — Calvin; protestant theology.— Henry of Navarre; the hugenots. — Lord Bacon; the new philosophy. — Galileo; astronomical discoveries.

4. Warriors and statesmen. Gustavus Adolphus; thirty years war.—Cardinal Richelieu; absolutism.— Oliver Cromwell; english revolution. — Louis XIV; the french monarchy. — Louis XV; remote causes of revolution. — Peter the great; his services to Russia.—Frederick the great; The prussian power. —Edmund Burke; political morality.—Mirabeau; the french revolution. — Alexander Hamilton; american constitution. — Napoleon Bonaparte; the french empire.—Daniel Webster; the american union.

5. Great women. Cleopatra; the woman of paganism.—Paula; woman as friend.—Héloïse; love.— Joan of Arc; heroic women.—Saint Theresa; religious enthusiasm. — Queen Elizabeth; woman as a sovereign. — Mme. de Maintenon; the political woman. — Sarah, duchess of Marlborough; the woman of the world.—Mme. Récamier; woman in society.—Mme. de Staël; literary women.—Hannah More; education of women.—George Eliot; woman as novelist.

Parton, James. Triumphs of enterprise, ingenuity and public spirit. Ill. N. Y. 1873. O.
    904 : 26

Contents. Introd., autobiographical. — The Cooper institute and its founder. —The wonderful growth of Chicago. — C: Dickens as a citizen. — The founder of the Vassar college.—The beginnings of science in the U. S. — Origin of the electric telegraph. — Career of Jared Sparks.—History of the sewing machine. — Invention of circulating libraries, [B: Franklin].—Some of the marvels and curiosities of Pittsburgh.—Origin of the cotton-weaving machinery. — J: Fillmore and his victory over the pirates.—Painting without hands, [J: Carter]. — T: Hood. — The first bostonian and the first new-yorker.—Irving, Cooper, Bryant.— E. A. Poe and Artemus Ward; how they lived, and why they died so young.—Josiah Quincy.—The piano among us, and the history of the instrument from the remotest times. — Anecdotes of Faraday. — T: Nast. — David Crockett.—Oil paintings by machinery.—The founder of the Rothschilds.—A millionaire in the ranks [Elias Howe, jr.]. — How the amer. people learned to nominate presidents. — The founder of the internal improvement system of the U. S. — Pocahontas and her husband. — Invention of the compass, and who first used it. — Discovery of the island of Madeira. — The real merits of Columbus. — The naming of the new world. — Marcus Aurelius and some of his thoughts. —Aristotle. — Invention of the daguerreotype. — J: Macadam. — W: Ged, the first stereotyper. — P: A. Berryer.—J: Eliot, the apostle to the indians. — Life, trial and execution of Algernon Sidney.—The city of St. Louis.—What sort of a man is Bismarck?—Painless surgery by ether. — B: Thompson, *alias* count Rumford.

Perkins, James Handasyd. Historical sketches. *In his* Memoir and writings.   **820.1 : 7 v2**

Contents, see under English literature, Collected works, col. 1017.

Robertson, James Burton. Public lectures, del. before the catholic university of Ireland, on some subjects of ancient and modern history, in 1856–1858. Lond. 1859. S.
    904 : 16
Contents. Geography considered in its relations to history.—The geography and history of Phœnicia.—The colonies of Phœnicia, and especially Carthage.—The geography, institutions, trade, arts, and sciences of ancient Egypt.—Theory of the christian monarchy.—Theory and history of the british constitution of 1688.—Moral and Political causes of the french revol. of 1789.—App.

Scherr, Johannes. Menschliche tragikomödie; gesammelte studien und bilder. Leipz. 1874. 3 v. D.   **904 : 2**
Contents, see Deutscher katalog, p. 40.

— Drei hofgeschichten. 3te aufl. Leipz. 1875. D.
    904 : 3
Contents. Katharina die zweite, carin von Russland.—Mathilde, königin von Dänemark.—Karolina, königin von England.

Schiller, J: Christoph F: v. Kleinere historische schriften. *In his* Sämmtliche werke.
    830 : 143 v11, 12
Contents, see Deutscher katalog, p. 21.

Skelton, J:, (*Shirley*). Essays in history and biography, incl. the defence of Mary Stuart. Edinb. 1883. O.   **904 : 25**
Contents. Some last words, by way of preface.—The defence of Mary Stuart.—William the silent.—The roses of Kilravock.—Chester in 1488.—The marquis of Montrose.—Claverhouse.—John Dryden.—The great lord Bolingbroke.—From Chatham to Canning.—Disraeli.—W: Blake.—Lacordaire.—C: James Napier.—Lord Macaulay.—J: Wilson.—James F: Ferrier.—W. M. Thackeray.—Charlotte Brontë.—Robertson of Ellon.—Robert Lee.—W: Edmonstoune Aytoun.—Lord Neaves.—J: Hill Burton.

Smith, Goldwin. Lectures on modern history, del. in Oxford 1859–61. Oxford. 1861. O.
    904 : 17
Contents. An inaugural lecture.—On the study of history.—On some supposed consequences of the doctrine of historical progress.—On the foundation of the american colonies.

— *Same.* Lectures on the study of history; added, a lecture on the university of Oxford. N. Y. 1866. D.   **904 : 17**

Thierry, Jacques N: Augustin. Historical essays; pub. under the title of "Dix ans d'études historiques", with an autobiogr. pref. Phila. 1845. O.   **904+37**
Contents. Revolutions of England.—On the character of the great men of the revolution of 1640.—Life of col. Hutchinson.—Restoration of 1660.—The revolution of 1688.—The national spirit of the irish.—The conquest of England by the normans.—The life of Anne Boleyn.—The history of Scotland and the

national character of the scotch.—The history of the english constitution.—M. Daunou's historical course at the Collége de France.—The roman empire.—The primitive meaning and extent of the title king.—The real constitution of the Ottoman empire.—Local and municipal freedom.—The ancient and modern spirit of french lawyers.—The philosophy of the 18th and that of the 19th century.—On the antipathy of race which divides the french nation.—The true history of Jacques Bonhomme.—On some errors of our modern historians.—First letter on the history of France.—The classification of the history of France by royal races.—The character and policy of the franks.—The enfranchisement of the communes.—A glance at the history of Spain.—An episode of the history of Brittany.

Treitschke, H: v. Historische aufsätze. **304 : 3**
Contents, see col. 150.

Williams, W: R. Eras and characters of history. N. Y. 1882. D.   **904 : 21**
Contents. Nero and Paul.—The emperor Titus and the apostle John.—Monasticism.—Augustine and Chrysostom.—Buddhism.—Wycliffe, Savonarola and Huss.—Mohammedanism.—The crusades.—Luther and his times.—J: Calvin.—J: Knox.—The puritan and mystic.

Yonge, Charlotte Maria. A book of golden deeds of all times and all lands, gathered and narrated by the author of the "Heir of Redclyffe". Cambridge. 1865. S.
    x 904 : 30

5. Periodicals.

(*See also* Statistics, Yearbooks, cl. 310, col. 156.)

Annual register, The; a review of public events at home and abroad; v. 1–126, 1758–1884. Lond. 1758–1885. O.   **905 : P1**
Note. Vol. 105 for 1863 commences a New series.—The arrangement of each vol. is as follows: English history; Foreign history; Chronicle of events; Retrospect of literature, science and art; Obituary of eminent persons; Remarkable trials; Public documents and state papers.

Household narrative of current events, The; for 1850—1855; a monthly supplement to Household words, conducted by C: Dickens. Lond. 1850–55. 6 v. in 2. Q.   **905+4**

History of the year, The; a narrative of the chief events of interest; oct. 1, 1881 to sept. 30, 1883. Lond. 1882, 1883. 2 v. D.
    905 : 3

American annual cyclopædia and register of important events.   **31 : R**
Note. For full title and other particulars, see col. 31. For periodicals, devoted to the history and antiquities of special countries, see under the name of each country.

x denotes books specially adapted for children.

2. Ancient world — a, General and Oriental.

1. In general.

Geography.

Spruner v. Mertz, K: Atlas antiquus. Gothæ. 1865. F.   **911 : R3**

Strabo. Geography. Tr. with notes, the first six books by H. C. Hamilton, the remainder by W. Falconer. Lond. 1854. 3 v. O.   **912 : 3**

Niebuhr, Barthold G: Lectures on ancient ethnography and geography, comprising Greece and her colonies, Epirus, Macedonia, Illyricum, Italy, Gaul, Spain, Britain, the north of Africa, etc. Tr. from the

german ed. of dr. Isler by Leonhard Schmitz, with add. and corr. from his own ms. notes. Lond. 1853. 2 v. O.   **912 : 2**

Bunbury, E: Herbert. A history of ancient geography among the greeks and romans from the earliest ages till the fall of the roman empire; with 20 maps. Lond. 1879. 2 v. O.   **911 : 2**

Tozer, H: Fanshawe. Classical geography. (Literature primers.) N. Y. 1878. S.
    912 : 4

Comparative view of antient and modern geography. *In* Zosimus, History. *in* **938+41**

History and antiquities.

(For accounts of excavations and antiquarian researches, see the various localities in modern geography.)

Peter, H: Lexikon der geschichte des altertums und dem alten geographie; die historischen personen, völker, länder und stätten aus der orientalischen, griechischen und römischen geschichte bis zur zeit der völkerwanderung. Leipz. 1882. D.
930 : R35

Kanngiesser, P: F: Grundriss der alterthumswissenschaft. Halle. 1815. O.   930 : 28

Mahaffy, J: Peytland. Prolegomena to ancient history, containing: pt. 1, The interpretation of legends and inscriptions; pt. 2, A survey of old egyptian literature. Lond. 1871. O.   930 : 25

Birch, S:, ed. Records of the past; english translations of the assyrian and egyptian monuments, pub. under the sanction of the Society of biblical archæology. Lond. [1874–81]. 12 v. D.   930 : 26
Contents. V. 1, 3, 5, 7, 9, 11. Assyrian texts.— 2, 4, 6, 8, 10, 12. Egyptian texts.—V. 12 has a general index.

Cooper, W. R. A dictionary, from the egyptian, assyrian and etruscan monuments and papyri, biographical, historical and mythological. Lond. 1882. O.   903 : R6

Hêrodotos. History; a new eng. version, ed., with copious notes and app., ill. the history and geography of Herodotus, from the most recent sources of information, and embodying the chief results, historical and ethnogr., which have been obtained in the progress of cuneiform and hieroglyphical discovery, by G: Rawlinson, assisted by sir H: Rawlinson and sir J. G. Wilkinson. Maps and ill. N. Y. 1860–62. 4 v. O.
930+2

— The boys' and girls' Herodotus; being parts of the history of Herodotus, ed. for boys and girls with an introd. by J: S. White. Ill. N. Y. 1884. O.   x 930 : 30

— Stories of the east from Herodotus, by Alfred J. Church; with ill. from ancient frescoes and sculptures. Lond. 1881. D.   x 930 : 3

— The story of the persian war, from Herodotus, by Alfred J: Church; with ill. from the antique. Lond. 1882. D.   x 930 : 5

Polybios. General history. Tr. from the greek by mr. Hampton. 5th ed. Oxford. 1823. 2 v. O.   930 : 27

Rawlinson, G: The origin of nations, in two parts: pt. 1, On early civilizations, pt. 2, On ethnic affinities. N. Y. 1878. D.
930 : 6

Ralegh, *Sir* Walter. The history of the world in 5 books. Lond. 1667. F.   23 : R
, *Contents.* Book 1. Intreating of the beginning and first ages of the same from the creation unto Abraham. Book 2. Of the times from the birth of Abraham to the destruction of the temple of Salomen. Book 3. From the destruction of Jerusalem to the time of Philip of Macedon. Book 4. From the reign of Philip of Macedon to the establishing of that kingdom in the race of Antigonus. Book 5. From the settled rule of Alexander's successors in the east, until the romans, prevailing over all, made conquest of Asia and Macedon.

---

x denotes books specially adapted for children.

Rollin, C: Histoire ancienne des égyptiens, des carthaginois, des assyriens, des babyloniens, des medes et des perses, des macédoniens, des grecs. Nouvelle éd. Paris. 1740–48. 10 v. S.   930 : 7

— *Same, eng.* The ancient history of the egyptians, carthaginians, assyrians, babylonians, medes and persians, grecians and macedonians, incl. a history of the arts and sciences of the ancients; with a life of the author by James Bell. 1st complete amer. ed. N. Y. 1845. 2 v. O.   930+7

Heeren, Arnold Hermann L: Historical researches into the politics, intercourse and trade of the carthaginians, ethiopians and egyptians. Tr. from the german; 2d ed. corr.; added, an index, a life of the author, new app. and other add. Oxford. 1838. 2 v. O.   930 : 21
Contents. V. 1. Biogr. sketch by himself.—General introd. to the Historical researches on the nations of antiquity. — Carthaginians. — Ethiopians. — App. 2. Egyptians.—App.

— Historical researches into the politics, intercourse and trade of the principal nations of antiquity. Tr. from the german. Lond. 1846. 2 v. O.   930 : 20
Contents. V. 1. Persians, Phœnicians, Babylonians. 2. Scythians, Indians.—App.

— A manual of ancient history, particularly with regard to the constitutions, the commerce and the colonies of the states of antiquity. Tr. from the german. Lond. 1847. O.
930 : 22

Taylor, W: Cooke. A manual of ancient history; containing the po itica history, geographical position and social state of the principal nations of antiquity, carefully rev. from the ancient writers. Rev. by C. S. Henry, with questions adapted for schools and colleges. N. Y. 1847. O.   930 : 12

Shuckford, S: The sacred and profane history of the world connected, from the creation of the world to the dissolution of the assyrian empire at the death of Sardanapalus, and to the declension of the kingdoms of Judah and Israel, under the reigns of Ahaz and Pekah. New ed. rev. with notes and analyses by J. Talboys Wheeler. Lond. 1858. 2 v. O.   930 : 10

Russell, Michael. A connection of sacred and profane history, from the death of Joshua to the decline of the kingdoms of Israel and Judah. Intended to complete the works of Shuckford and Prideaux. New ed., rev. with notes and analyses by J. Talboys Wheeler. Lond. 1865. 2 v. O.
930 : 9

Prideaux, Humphrey. The old and new testament connected in the history of the jews, and neighboring nations, from the declension of the kingdoms of Israel and Judah to the time of Christ. 15th amer. from the 20th Lond. ed. Prefixed, the life of the author, containing some letters which he wrote in defence and ill. of certain parts of his connexions. Maps and plates. N. Y. 1860. 2 v. O.   930+8

Niebuhr, Barthold G: Lectures on ancient history, from the earliest times to the taking of Alexandria by Octavianus; comprising the history of the asiatic nations, the egyptians, greeks, macedonians ·and carthaginians. Tr. from the germ. ed. of Marcus

Niebuhr by Leonhard Schmitz, with add. and corr. from his own ms. notes. Phila. 1852. 3 v. O.   **930 : 32**

Thalheimer, Mary Elsie. A manual of ancient history. Cinc. *n. d.* O.   **930 : 29**

Rawlinson, G: A manual of ancient history, from the earliest times to the fall of the western empire ; comprising the history of Chaldea, Assyria, Media, Babylonia, Lydia, Phœnicia, Syria, Judæa, Egypt, Carthage, Persia, Greece, Macedonia, Parthia and Rome. N. Y. 1884. D.   **930 : 23**

Smith, Philip. A history of the world, from the earliest records to the present time. N. Y. 1865–82. 3 v. O.   **930+11**
Contents. V. 1. **Ancient history:** From the creation to b. c. 360. 2. B. c. 359—129. 3. B. c. 133—n. d. 476.

— The ancient history of the east, from the earliest times to the conquest by Alexander the great ; incl. Egypt, Assyria, Babylonia, Media, Persia, Asia Minor and Phœnicia. Ill. (The students ancient history). N. Y. 1882. D.   **930 : 24**

Keary, Annie. The nations around [Palestine]. Lond. 1875. D.   **930 : 17**

Lenormant, François. The beginnings of history, according to the Bible and the traditions of oriental peoples, from the creation of man to the deluge. From the 2nd french ed., with an introd. by Francis Bowen. N. Y. 1882. D.   **930 : 19**

— *and* E. **Chevallier.** The student's manual of oriental history ; a manual of the ancient history of the east to the commencement of the median wars. New ed. Phila. 1871. 2 v. D.   **930 : 4**
Contents. V. 1. Israelites.—Egyptians.—Assyrians. — Babylonians. 2. Medes and Persians.— Phœnicians.—Arabians.

Duncker, Max Wolfgang. Geschichte des alterthums. 5te aufl. Leipz. 1875–78. 4 v. O.   **930 : 1**
Contents. V. 1. Die ägypter. — Die semiten. 2. Die gründung der macht Assyriens und die staaten und städte der syrer. — Die machthöhe Assyriens, die wiedererhebung Aegyptens und Babyloniens. 3. Die arier am Indus und Ganges.—Buddhismus und brahmanenthum. 4. Die arier Ostirans.—Die herrschaft der meder und das reich der perser.

— *Same, eng.* The history of antiquity. From the german by Evelyn Abbott. Lond. 1877. 6 v. O.   **930 : 1**
Contents. V. 1. Egypt. — The semitic nations. 2. Assyria, Phœnicia, Israel. 3. Assyria, Israel, Egypt, Babylon, Lydia. 4. The arians on the Indus and the Ganges.—Buddhists and brahmans. 5. The arians of eastern Iran.—The empire of the medes and persians. 6. *Same, continued.*

Sayce, Archibald H: The ancient empires of the east. N. Y. 1884. D.   **930 : 31**

— Fresh light from the ancient monuments ; a sketch of the most striking confirmations of the Bible from recent discoveries in Egypt, Assyria, Palestine, Babylonia, Asia Minor. 2d ed. (By-paths of Bible knowledge, no. 3). Lond. 1884. D.   **930 : 33**

Schmidt, Ferdinand. Völkerbilder ; für schule und haus gesammelt und bearb. Ill. Hamburg. 1868. 2 v. Q.   **930+34**
Contents. V. 1. Heroenzeitalter der griechen. — Aus der geschichte der aegyptier.— Chinesen, mongolen, tataren. — Aus der geschichte der israeliten. — Meder und perser. — Aus der geschichte der griechen vor den perserkriegen.— Die perserkriege. — Athens blüthezeit. — Die zeit der inneren kämpfe, oder vom

peloponnesischen kriege bis zur macedonischen herrschaft. — Dichter, künstler und weise der letzten zeit Griechenlands.—Die macedonischen reiche. 2. Rom.

Yonge, Charlotte Maria. Landmarks of history: Ancient history ; from the earliest times to the mahometan conquest. 1st amer. from the 5th eng. ed. [ed. by Edith L. Chase]. Phila. 1865. S.   **x 930 : 13**
— *Same.* 5th ed. rev. N. Y. *n. d.* D.   **x 930 : 13**

True stories from ancient history ; chron. arr., from the creation of the world to the death of Charlemagne, by a mother, author of Always happy, etc. Phila. *n. d.* S.   **x 930 : 18**

Bucke, C: Ruins of ancient cities ; with general and particular accounts of their rise, fall and present condition. [Harpers family lib.] N. Y. 1845. 2 v. S.   **930 : 14**

Buckley, Theodore Alois. The great cities of the ancient world in their glory and their desolation. New ed. ill. Lond. [1856]. D.   **930 : 15**
Contents. Introd. — Babylon.—Nineveh.—Thebes.— Memphis and Heliopolis. — Persepolis.—Damascus.— Baalbek or Baalgad.—Palmyra.—Tyre.—Petra. — The rock-hewn cities of India. — Peking. — Jerusalem. — Smyrna.—Ephesus.— Sardis. — The ruins of american civilization. — Athens. — Corinth. — Elis.—Mycenæ.— Veii.—Rome.—Scandinavia.

— The seven wonders of the world, with their associations in art and history. Ill. Lond. [1869]. D.   **930 : 16**
Contents. Pyramids. — The temple, walls and hanging gardens of Babylon.—Statue of Jupiter.—Temple to Diana at Ephesus.—The mausoleum. — The Pharos at Alexandria.—The colossus of Rhodes.

2. Egypt.

Wilkinson, Sir J: Gardner. The manners and customs of the ancient egyptians. New ed. rev. and corr. by S: Birch. Ill. Lond. 1878. 3 v. O.   **932+P9**

— A popular account of the ancient egyptians, rev. and abr. from his larger work. Ill. N. Y. 1854. 2 v. D.   **932 : 4**

Oppel, K: Das alte wunderland der pyramiden ; geographische, geschichtliche und kulturhistorische bilder aus der vorzeit, der periode der blüte sowie des verfalls des alten Aegyptens. 4te umgearb. und verm. aufl. Ill. Leipz. 1881. O.   **932 : 13**

Sharp, S: The history of Egypt, from the earliest times till the conquest by the arabs, a. d. 640. 6th ed. Lond. 1876. 2 v. D.   **932 : 5**

Rawlinson, G: History of ancient Egypt. Lond. 1881. 2 v. O.   **932 : 3**

Brugsch-*Bey,* H: A history of Egypt under the pharaohs, derived entirely from the monuments. Tr. from the german by H: Danby Seymour, completed and ed. by Philip Smith. Added, a memoir on the exodus of the israelites and the egyptian monuments. Lond. 1879. 2 v. O.   **932 : P1**

— The true story of the exodus of Israel ; together with a brief view of the history of monumental Egypt ; ed. with an introd. by Francis H. Underwood. Bost. 1880. D.   **932 : 2**

Birch, S: Egypt to b. c. 300. (Ancient history from the monuments.) N. Y. 1875. D.   **932 : 6**

Harkness, M. E. Egyptian life and history according to the monuments. (By-paths of Bible knowledge, no. 6.) Lond. 1884. D.
932 : 11

Osborn, H: S. Ancient Egypt in the light of modern discoveries. Map. Cinc. 1883. D.
932 : 8

Poole, Reginald Stuart. The cities of Egypt. Lond. 1882. D. 932 : 7

Pickering, C: On the Gliddon mummy case in the museum of the Smithsonian institution. *In* Smithsonian contributions.
506 : R3 v16

King, James. Cleopatra's needle; a history of the London obelisk with an exposition of the hieroglyphics. 2d ed. (By-paths of Bible knowledge, no. 1.) Lond. 1884. D.
932 : 10

Note. For further descriptions of the obelisks and pyramids *see also* Modern Egypt, cl. 916.2.

Rawlinson, G: Egypt and Babylon, from sacred and profane sources. N. Y. 1885. D.
932 : 12

Palmer, H: Spencer. Sinai from the 4th egyptian dynasty to the present day. (Ancient history from the monuments.) Lond. *n. d.* S. 939 : 4

3. Israel, (incl. modern history).

(*See also* the Bible, col. 83-88, *and* Judaism, col. 139.)

Josephus, Flavius. Flavii Josephi vom Krieg I der Juden und der Zerstörung Hieru- | salem Siben Bücher nach den Griechiscen | Exemplaren restituiert und gebessert | im jar M. D. **XXXV**. | Sampt einer Vorred in welcher die History diser bücher | aufts kürtzest verstendig und hell begriffen ist, und Teütschland ab frembden schaden | gewarnet wird | Im Jar M. D. XXXV [1535]. [Strassburg, Balthasar Beck]. F.
23 : R

— Josephi des hoch- | berümpten und fast nützlich- | en bistori beschreibers. | Zwentzig bücher von den alten geschichten | nach den alten Exemplaren fleissig corrigiert und gebessert. | Siben bücher von dem Jüdischen krieg und der zerstörung Hierusalem, | nach dem Griechischen Exemplaren besichtigt und verstendiger gemacht. | Zwey bücher wider Appionem Grammaticum durch zusatz eticher blet- | ter auss Griechischen büchern gemeert und gebessert. | Von meisterschafft der vernunfft, oder von den Machabeern ein buch | durch den Hochgelerten D. Erasmum vom Roterodam im Latein wider | besichtigt. | Zum Leser. | Hie findextu über erzölten inhalt fast nützlichen vorrede yeder bücher dar | zu Scholien und erklerungen eticher schurren capitel, yetz newlich hinzu- | truckt sampt dem entscheyd viler sententz Chaldaischer, Hebreischer und | Griechischer etc. wörter, dem leser hoch dienstlich. Auch die jarzal durch | die geburten vo anfang der welt biss auf Christum mit erzölung | der regenten Hörtzogen, Richter, Künig in Israel Juda | uñ Ben Jamin, frembder Künig, viler Heroden, Rö | mischer landpfleger von den Keysern in Judeam | gesant. Item das leben F. Josephi vo Euse- | bio Hieronimo Suida vñ Volaterans verzeychnet unnd diser ding

Josephus, Flavius.—*Continued.*

al- | ler zwey reiche und rich- | tige Register. Strassburg. M. D. XXXIX [1589]. F. 23 : R

— **Works**. Tr. from the original greek, according to Havercamp's ed., with notes and observ. by W: Whiston. Phila. 1847. 2 v. O. 933 : 3

Contents. V. 1. Jewish antiquities. 2. Seven books of the jewish war.—The life of Josephus.—Three dissertations.—Josephus against Apion.

— Our young folks' Josephus ; the antiquities of the jews and the jewish wars, simplified by W: Shepard. Ill. Phila. 1884. O.
x 933 : 14

— The story of the last days of Jerusalem, from Josephus, by Alfred J: Church. Lond. 1881. D. x 933 : 2

Lewis, T: Origines hebrææ, the antiquities of the hebrew republick. Lond. 1774, 1775. 4 v. D.
Contents. V. 1. The origin of the hebrews.—Their civil government.—The constitution of the Sanhedrim.— Forms of trial in courts of justice. 2. The ecclesiastical government. 3. Places of worship. 4. The religion of the hebrews.

Mills, Abraham. The ancient hebrews ; with an introd. essay concerning the world before the flood. N. Y. 1856. D. 933 : 6

Alexander, Archibald. History of the israelitish nation, from their origin to the destruction of Jerusalem by the romans. Phila. 1853. O. 933+1

Conder, Claude Reignier. Judas Maccabeus, and the jewish war of independence. [The new Plutarch]. N. Y. 1879. D. 933 : 4

Wise, I: M. History of the hebrews' second commonwealth, with special reference to its literature, culture, and the origin of rabbinism and christianity. Cinc. 1880. D.
933 : 10

Delitzsch, Franz. Jewish artisan life in the time of Jesus, according to the oldest sources. Tr. from the 3d rev. ed. by B. Pick. N. Y. [1883]. D. 933 : 11

Tonna, Charlotte Elizabeth, *born* Brown. (*Charlotte Elizabeth*). Judæa capta. N. Y. 1864. S. x 933 : 12

Note. Is a history of the capture and destruction of Jerusalem.

Ewald, H: G: A: The history of Israel. Tr. from the german. Lond. 1883-85. 7 v. O.
933 : 9
Contents. V. 1. Introd. and preliminary history, ed. by Russell Martineau; 4th ed. rev. and corr. 2. History of Moses and the theocracy, ed. by Russell Martineau; 4th ed. rev. and corr. 3. The rise and splendour of the hebrew monarchy, ed. by J. Estlin Carpenter; 2d ed. 4. From the disruption of the monarchy to its fall, ed. by J. Estlin Carpenter; 2d ed. 5. The history of Ezra and of the hagiocracy in Israel to the time of Christ, ed. by J. Estlin Carpenter; 2d ed. 6. The life and times of Christ. Tr. by J. F: Smith. 7. The apostolic age. Tr. by J. F: Smith.

Milman, H: Hart. The history of the jews, from the earliest period to the present time. Ill. [Harper's family lib.] N. Y. 1843. 3 v. S. 933 : 7

— *Same.* Repr. from the newly rev. and corr. Lond. N. Y. 1881. 3 v. in 2. D. 933 : 8

Grätz, H: Geschichte der juden von den ältesten zeiten bis auf die gegenwart ; aus den quellen bearb. Leipz. 1871-1882. 11 v. O.
933 : 16
Contents. V. 1. Vorwort. — Einleitung. — Die vorexilische biblische zeit, 1500—977: 1ste epoche, Die an-

x denotes books specially adapted for children.

fänge; 2te epoche, Die blüthezeit. **2.** Vom tode königs Salomo, bis zum babylonischen exile, 586. — Vom babylonischen exile, bis zum tode des Juda Makkabi, 160. **3.** Von dem tode Juda Makkabi's, bis zum untergange des jüdischen staates, a. d. 70. **4.** Vom untergange des jüdischen staates bis zum abschluss des Talmud, 500. **5.** Vom abschluss des Talmud, bis zum aufblühen der jüdisch-spanischen cultur, 1027. **6.** Vom aufblühen der jüdisch-spanischen cultur, bis Maimuni's tod, 1205. **7, 8.** Von Maimuni's tod bis zur verbannung der juden aus Spanien und Portugal, 1496. **9.** Von der verbannung der juden aus Spanien und Portugal, bis zur dauernden ansiedlung der Marranen in Holland, 1618. **10.** Von der dauernden ansiedlung der Marranen in Holland, bis zum beginne der Mendelssohn'schen zeit, 1750. **11.** Vom beginn der Mendelssohn'schen zeit bis in die neueste zeit, 1848.

Hudson, Elizabeth Harriot. A history of the jews in Rome, b. c. 160—a. d. 604. Lond. 1882. O.   **933 : 15**

*   *   *

Wright, W: The empire of the Hittites ; with decipherment of Hittite inscriptions by A. H. Sayce, a Hittite map by sir C: Wilson and capt. Conder, and a complete set of Hittite inscriptions, rev. by W. H. Rylands. N. Y. 1884. O.   **933+13**

4. Other asiatic nations.

(For Troy and the greek colonies in Asia Minor, see Ancient greek history.)

Rawlinson, G: The five great monarchies of the ancient eastern world, or The history, geography and antiquities of Chaldæa, Assyria, Babylon, Media and Persia, coll. and ill. from ancient and modern sources. 2d ed. Maps and ill. N. Y. 1873. 3 v. O.   **935 : 2**

Contents. V. 1. Chaldæa. — Assyria. 2. Assyria, *concluded.* — Media. — Babylonia. 3. Babylonia, *concluded.* — Persia.

— The sixth great oriental monarchy, or The geography, history and antiquities of Parthia, coll. and ill. from ancient and modern sources. N. Y. 1882. O.   **935 : 3**

— The seventh great oriental monarchy, or The geography, history and antiquities of the Sassanian or New persian empire. Lond. 1876. O.   **935 : 4**

Brown, Francis. Assyriology ; its use and abuse in Old testament study. N. Y. 1885. D.   **935 : 9**

Smith, G: Assyria, from the earliest times to the fall of Nineveh. (Ancient history from the monuments.) N. Y. 1876. D.   **935 : 5**

— The history of Babylonia ; ed. by A. H. Sayce. (Ancient history from the monuments.) Lond. *n. d.* S.   **935 : 7**

Budge, Ernest A. Wallis. Babylonian life and history. (By-paths of Bible knowledge, no. 5.) Lond. 1884. D.   **935 : 8**

Vaux, W: Sandys W. Persia, to the arab conquest. (Ancient history from the monuments.) N. Y. 1876. D.   **935 : 6**

Xenophon. The Cyropædia, or Institution of Cyrus. Tr. from the greek by the hon. Maurice Ashly Cooper. [Harper's family library]. N. Y. 1842. S.   **935 : 1**

Geiger, W: Civilization of the eastern iránians in ancient times ; with an introd. on the Avesta religion. Tr. from the german, with a pref., notes and a biogr. of the author by Dárâb Dastur Peshotan Sanjânâ. Lond. 1885. O.   **935 : 10**

Contents. V. 1. Ethnography and social life.

Mitra, Rájendralála. Indo - aryans ; contributions towards the elucidation of their ancient and mediæval history. Lond. 1881. 2 v. O.   **934 : 1**

Contents. V. 1. Origin of indian architecture. — Principles of indian temple architecture. — Indian sculpture.—Dress and ornament in ancient India.—Furniture, domestic utensils, musical instruments, arms, horses and cars in ancient India. — Beef in ancient India.—Spirituous drinks in ancient India.—A picnic in ancient India.
2. An imperial coronation.—On human sacrifices.—Funeral ceremony.—On the supposed identity of the greeks with the yavanas of the sanskrit writers. —On the Páía and the Sena dynasties of Bengal.—On the peculiarities of the gáthá dialect.—On the Kishya of the Aitareya bráhmana. — On the origin of the hindi language, and its relation to the urdu dialect.—Vestiges of the kings of Gwalior.—Bobja rája of Dhár and his homonyms.—Early life of Asóka.—The primitive aryans.—Origin of the sanskrit alphabet.—App.: On human sacrifice among the athenians; On the indian Styx and its ferriage.

See also in the Index to biography **Artaxerxês—Dareios—Kyros—Xerxês.**

---

3. Ancient world — b, Classical.

1. In general.

(See also Mythology, col. 135; *and* History of civilization, col. 151, 152*).*

Smith, W:, *ed.* Dictionary of greek and roman antiquities. Ill. 3d amer. ed. rev. and containing numerous articles relative to the botany, mineralogy and zoology of the ancients. N. Y. 1847. O.   **903 : R4**

— — A new classical dictionary of greek and roman biography, mythology and geography, partly based upon the Dictionary of greek and roman biography and mythology. Rev. with corr. and add. by C: Anthon. N. Y. 1857. O.   **903 : R5**

Rich, Anthony. A dictionary of roman and greek antiquities, with nearly 2000 engr. on wood from ancient originals, ill. of the industrial arts and social life of the greeks and romans. 3d ed., rev. and impr. N. Y. 1881. O.   **938 : 21**

Seyffert, Oskar. Lexikon der klassischen altertumskunde ; kulturgeschichte der griechen und römer, mythologie und religion, litteratur. kunst und altertümer des staats- und privatlebens. Ill. Leipz. 1882. D.   **903 : R8**

Salkeld, Joseph. Classical antiquities, or A compendium of roman and grecian antiquities, with a sketch of ancient mythology. N. Y. 1844. S.   **937 : 34**

Bojesen, Ernst F: Christian. A manual of grecian and roman antiquities. Tr. from the german ; ed., with occasional notes and a complete series of questions, by T: Kercheaver Arnold. Rev., with add. and corr. 2d ed. N. Y. 1848. D.   **937 : 52**

Fustel de Coulanges, Numa Denis. The ancient city ; a study on the religion, laws and institutions of Greece and Rome. Tr. from the latest french ed. by Willard Small. Bost. 1874. O.   **937 : 23**

Guhl, Ernst, *and* W: Koner. Das leben der griechen und römer; nach antiken bildwerken dargestellt. 4te aufl. Berlin. 1876. O. **938 : 1**
— - *Same, eng.* The life of the greeks and romans; described from antique monuments. Tr. from the 3d german ed. by F. Hüffer. Ill. N. Y. 1876. O. **938 : 1**
Falke, Jakob v. Greece and Rome; their life and art. Tr. by W: Hand Browne. N. Y. 1882 [1881]. F. **938 : R29**
Göll, Hermann. Kulturbilder aus Hellas und Rom. 3te berichtigte und verm. aufl. Leipz. 1880. 2 v. O. **938 : 39**
Weisser, L: Lebensbilder aus dem klassischen alterthum, mit erläut. text von Hermann Kurz. Stuttg. 1864. Plates, 1 v. F.; Text, 1 v. O. **938 : P2**

*   *   *

Hertzberg, Gustav F: Geschichte von Hellas und Rom. (Oncken, W:, *ed.* Allgemeine geschichte in einzeldarstellungen; 1ste hauptabth., 5ter th.) Ill. und karten. Berlin. 1879. 2 v. O. **909+19 v5**
Contents. V. 1. Hellas. 2. Rome, bis zum untergang der republik, b. c. 29.

2. Greece.

Antiquities.

(For excavations and antiquarian researches, see Modern Greece, cl. 914.93.)

Felton, Cornelius Conway. Greece, ancient and modern; lectures del. before the Lowell institute. Bost. 1879. 2 v. in 1. O. **938 : 19**
Contents. V. 1. The greek language and poetry.—The life of Greece. 2. Constitutions and orators of Greece.—Modern Greece.
Schönmann, G: F: The antiquities of Greece. Tr. from the german by E. G. Hardy and J. S. Mann. [V. 1,] The state. Lond. 1880. O. **938 : 22**
Hermann, C: F: A manual of the political antiquities of Greece, historically considered. From the german. Oxford. 1836. O. **938+45**
Heeren, Arnold Hermann L: Ancient Greece. Tr. from the german by G: Bancroft. New and impr. ed. Lond. 1847. O. **938 : 30**
Contents. Geographical View.—Earliest condition of the nation; and its branches.—Original sources of the culture of the greeks.—The heroic age; the trojan war.—The period following the heroic age; migrations; origin of republican forms of government and their character.—Homer; the epic poets.—Means of preserving the national character.—The persian wars and their consequences. — Constitutions of the grecian states. — The political economy of the greeks. — The judicial institutions.—The army and navy.— Statesmen and orators.—The sciences *and* Poetry and the arts in connexion with the state.—Causes of the fall of Greece.
Wägner, W: Hellas; das land und volk der alten griechen, bearb. für freunde des klassischen alterthums, insbesondere für die deutsche jugend. 4te aufl. Leipz. 1877. 2 v. O. **938 : 3**
St. John, James A: The hellenes; the history of the manners [and customs] of the ancient greeks. New ed. Lond. 1844. 3 v. in 1. O. **938 : 33**
Timayenis, T. T. Greece in the times of Homer; an account of the life, customs and habits of the greeks during the homeric period. N. Y. 1885. S. **938 : 43**

Mahaffy, J: Peytland. Old greek life. [History primers: classical antiquities, 1]. N. Y. 1879. S. **938 : 25**
— Social life in Greece from Homer to Menander. 4th ed., rev. Lond. 1879. D. **938 : 31**
Becker, W: Adolph. Charikles; bilder altgriechischer sitte, zur genaueren kenntniss des griechischen privatlebens, neu bearb. von Hermann Göll. Berlin. 1877, 1878. 3 v. D. **938 : 4**
— *Same, eng.* Charicles, or Illustrations of the private life of the ancient greeks; with notes and excursuses. From the germ., tr. by F: Metcalfe. 5th ed. Lond. 1880. D. **938 : 4**
Note. A novel in form, embodying the conclusions of modern critical research in the social condition of the ancient world.
Barthélemy, J: Jacques *abbé.* Travels of Anacharsis the younger in Greece, during the middle of the 4th century before the christian æra. Tr. from the french. 2d ed. Lond. 1794. Text, 7 v. O. Atlas, 1 v. Q. **938 : 49**
Note. Fictitious incidents, but presents a vivid and truthful picture of the condition of Greece, its antiquities, manners, customs, religious ceremonies, laws, arts and literature, at the period of its greatest splendor, immediately before the macedonian conquest.
Jannet, Claudio. Les institutions sociales et le droit civil à Sparte. 2e éd., rev. et augm. Paris. 1880. O. **938 : 37**
Stuart, James, *and* N: Revett. The antiquities of Athens and other monuments of Greece. Plates. 3d ed. Lond. 1881. D. **938 : 36**
Archæological institute of America; American school of classical studies at Athens. Papers; v. 1, 1882—1883. [Ill.] Bost. 1885. O. **906+15**
Contents. Sterrett, J. R. S., *ed.* Inscriptions of Assos; Inscriptions of Tralleis.—Wheeler, J. R. The theatre of Dionysius.—Bevier, L: The Olympieion at Athens.—Fowler, H. N. The Erechtheion at Athens.—Goodwin; W: W. The battle of Salamis.

History.

(See also Modern Greece, cl. 949.3.)

In general.

Cox, *Sir* G: W: A general history of Greece, from the earliest period to the death of Alexander the great, with a sketch of the subsequent history to the present time. N. Y. 1876. D. **938 : 10**
Timayenis, T. T. A history of Greece, from the earliest times to the present. Maps and ill. N. Y. 1881. 2 v. O. **938 : 18**
Contents. V. 1. The mythological age.—The dawn of history.—The persian wars.—Athenian supremacy. —The peloponnesian war.—Hegemony of Sparta. 2. Theban supremacy. — Macedonian hellenism. — The successors.—The roman supremacy.—Byzantine hellenism.—Modern hellenism.—Index.
Schmitz, Leonhard. A history of Greece for junior classes; with an app., giving a sketch of the history from the roman conquest to the present day, by A. Grennadios. N. Y. [1874]. S. **x 938 : 28**
Yonge, Charlotte Mary. Young folks' history of Greece [to the present time]. Bost. [1878]. S. **x 938 : 24**
Bonner, J: A child's history of Greece. Ill. N. Y. 1878. 2 v. S. **x 938 : 26**
Contents. V. 1. Greece, b. .c. 500.—Stories and legends.—History, to b. c. 449. 2. History, to the present time.

x denotes books specially adapted for children.

Willson, Marcius, *and* Robert Pierpont **Willson.**
Mosaics of grecian history; the historical
narrative, with numerous illustrations, poetic and prose selections; a popular course
of reading in grecian history and literature. N. Y. 1883. D.   **938 : 32**
Note. Continued to the present time.

*   *   *

Curtius, Ernst. The history of Greece. Tr. by
Adolphus W: Ward. N. Y. [1876]. 5 v. D.
    938 : 5
Contents. V. 1. The greeks before the dorian migration.—From the dorian migration to the persian
wars. 2. *Same, continued.*—From the termination of
the ionian revolt to the outbreak of the peloponnesian war. 3. The peloponnesian war. 4. Sparta
supreme in Greece.—Thebes the great power of
Greece. 5. Macedonia and Greece [to b. c. 337].—
General index.

Grote, G: History of Greece. N. Y. 1861. 12 v.
D.   **938 : 6**
Contents. V. 1. Legendary Greece. 2. *Same, con-
tinued.*—General geography and limits of Greece.—
Peloponnesus. 3. Corinth, Sikyon and Megara.—
Age of the despots.—Ionic portion of Hellas.—Athens
before Solon. — Solonian laws and constitution.—
Eubœa. — Cyclades. — Asiatic colonies. — Lydians.—
Medes.—Cimmerians. — Scythians. — Phenicians.—As-
syrians.—Babylon.—Egyptians.—Decline of the phen-
icians.— Carthage. — Western colonies of Greece.—
Epirus. — Akarnians. — Epirots. 4. Illyrians, Macedonians, Pæonians. — Thracians. — Kyrene, Barka,
Hesperides.—Pan-Hellenic festivals.— Lyric poetry.
—The seven wise men.— Peisistratus and his sons.—
Establishment of democracy at Athens.— Rise and
growth of the persian empire.—Demokedes.—Darius
invades Scythia.—Ionic revolt.—From the ionic revolt to the battle of Marathon.—Ionic philosophers.
5. 490—445 b. c.— Constitutional and judicial changes
at Athens under Perikles. 6. 445—421 b. c. 7. 421–
413 b. c. 8. 413—404 b. c —The drama.—Rhetoric and
dialectics.—The sophists.— Sokrates. 9. Retreat of
the ten thousand.—404—387 b. c. 10. 387—359 b. c.—
Sicilian affairs, 413—394 b. c. 11. 359—336 b. c. 12.
Alexander the great.—Grecian affairs to b. c. 294.—
Sicilian and italian greeks.— Agathokles.—Outlying
hellenic cities: In Gaul and Spain; On the Euxine.—
Index.

Smith, W: A history of Greece, from the earliest times to the roman conquest; with
supp. chapters on the history of literature
and art. Rev., with an app., by G: W.
Greene. Ill. N. Y. 1861. D.   **938 : 9**

Mitford, W: The history of Greece [to the
death of Alexander], with his final add.
and corr.; prefixed by a brief memoir of
the author by his brother, lord Redesdale,
rev. by W: King. Lond. 1838. 8 v. O.
    938 : 7
— *Same.* V. 2–8. Bost. 1823. 7 v. O.   **938 : 7**

Thirlwall, Connop. A history of Greece. N. Y.
1845. 2 v. O.   **938+8**
Contents. V. 1. To b. c. 387. 2. To b. c. 146.

Keightley, T: The history of Greece [to the
roman conquest]; added, a chronol. table
of contemporary history by Joshua Toulmin Smith. Bost. 1839. O.   **938+27**

Fyffe, C: Alan. History of Greece. [History
primers]. N. Y. 1878. S.   **938 : 17**

Harrison, James Albert. The story of Greece.
(The story of the nations.) [Ill.] N. Y.
1885. D.   **x 938 : 44**
Note. Ends with the death of Alexander.

Stacke, L: Christian. Erzählungen aus der
griechischen geschichte in biographischer
form. Karte. 22ste aufl. Oldenb. 1885. D.
    938 : 46

---

x denotes books specially adapted for children.

By periods.

Cox, *Sir* G: W: A history of Greece. New ed.
Lond. 1878. 2 v. O.   **938 : 34**
Contents. V. 1. To the end of the persian war. 2.
From the formation of the confederacy of Delos to
the close of the peloponnesian war.

Duncker, Max Wolfgang. History of Greece,
from the earliest times to the end of the
persian war. Tr. from the germ. by S. F.
Alleyne. V. 1. Lond. 1883. O.   **938 : 11**
Contents. V. 1. The greeks in ancient times. —
Conquests and migrations.—Index.

Vaux, W: Sandys W. Greek cities and islands
of Asia Minor. (Ancient history from the
monuments.) Lond. 1877. S.   **939 : 3**

Benjamin, S: Green Wheeler. Troy; its legend,
history and literature, with a sketch of the
topography of the Troad in the light of
recent investigation. (Epochs of ancient
history.) N. Y. (1880). S.   **938 : 12**

Müller, C: Ottfried. The history and antiquities
of the doric race. Tr. from the german by
H: Tufnell and G: Cornewall Lewis. Maps.
Oxford. 1830. 2 v. O.   **938 : 40**
Contents. V. 1. Introd.—History from the earliest
times to the end of the peloponnesian war.—Religion
and mythology.—App. 2. Political institutions.—
Domestic institutions, arts and literature.—App.

Hertzberg, Gustav F: Die geschichte der mes-
senischen kriege, nach Pausanias erzählt.
3te durchgesehene aufl. Halle. 1875. D.
    938 : 48
— Die geschichte der perserkriege, nach den
quellen erzählt. Halle. 1877. D.   **938 : 47**

Cox, *Sir* G: W: The greeks and the persians.
2d ed. (Epochs of ancient history.) Lond.
1877. S.   **938 : 14**
— The athenian empire. 2d ed. (Epochs of
ancient history.) Lond. 1877. S. **938 : 15**

Bulwer-Lytton, E: G: Earle Lytton, *1st baron
Lytton.* Athens; its rise and fall, with
Views of the literature, philosophy and
social life of the athenian people. N. Y.
1847. 2 v. D.   **938 : 20**
— *Same.* [Tauchnitz ed.] Leipz. 1843. 2 v. in
1. S.   **938 : 20**

Lloyd, W: Watkiss. The age of Pericles; a
history of the politics and arts of Greece,
from the persian to the peloponnesian war.
Lond. 1875. 2 v. O.   **938 : 35**

Thukydidês, (*lat.* Thucydides). History of the
peloponnesian war. A new and literal
version from the text of Arnold, collated
with Bekker, Göller and Poppo, by H:
Dale. Lond. 1853, 1855. 2 v. D. **938 : 23**
— The history of the grecian war, tr. by T:
Hobbes. *In* Hobbes, T: English works.
    820.2 : 12 v8,9

Xenophôn. The expedition of Cyrus into Persia
and the retreat of the ten thousand greeks.
Tr. from the original greek by E: Spelman.
Lond. 1812. O.   **938+41**

Ainsworth, W: Francis. Travels in the track of
the ten thousand greeks; a geographical
and descriptive account of the expedition
of Cyrus and the retreat of the ten thousand
greeks, as related by Xenophon. Lond.
1844. O.   **911 : 6**

Sankey, C: The spartan and theban supremacies. (Epochs of ancient history.) Lond.
1877. S.   **938 : 13**

Curteis, Arthur M. Rise of the Macedonian
empire. (Epochs of ancient history.) N.
Y. [1880]. S.   **938 : 16**

Arrianos. History of the expedition of Alexander the great and conquest of Persia. Tr.
from the original greek by mr. Rooke and
now corr. and enl. with add. Lond. 1812.
O.   *in* 938+41
Droysen, J: Gustav. Geschichte des hellen-
ismus. Gotha. 1877, 1878. 3 v. O.
                                        938 : 38
   Contents. V. 1. Geschichte Alexanders des grossen.
   2. Geschichte der Diadochen. 3. Geschichte der
   Epigonen.—Anhang: Ueber die hellenischen städte-
   gründungen.
Freeman, E: A: History of the greek federa-
tions, from the foundation of the Achaian
League. *In his* History of federal govern-
ment.   324 : 1 v1
   See also in the Index to biography **Agêsilaos —
   Agis—Alexandros—Alkibiadês—Aratos—Aris-
   tagoras—Aristeidês—Dêmêtrios—Demosthenes
   —Dîôn — Eumenês—Gelôn—Kimôn — Kleome-
   nês—Lykurgos—Lysandros — Miltiadês — Ni-
   kias—Pausanias — Peisistratos — Pelopidas —
   Periklês—Philopoimen—Polykratês — Pyrrhos
   —Solôn—Themistoklês—Thêseus—Thukydidês
   —Timoleôn.**

3. Rome.

A n t i q u i t i e s .

(For excavations and antiquarian researches, see Modern
Italy, cl. 914.5.)

Thierry, Amédée Simon Dominique. Tableau
de l'empire romain, depuis la fondation de
Rome jusqu'à la fin du gouvernement impérial en occident. 6e éd. Paris 1872. O.
                                        937 : 43
   Contents. Introd.—Formation de la société romaine.
   — Marche du monde romain vers l'unité politique et
   administrative. — Marche du monde romain vers
   l'unité par les idées sociales; par le droit; par la religion.—Du monde barbare.
Becker, W: Adolph, *and* Joachim **Marquardt.**
Handbuch der römischen alterthümer;
nach den quellen bearb. Leipz. 1843. 5 v.
in 9. O.   937 : 45
   Contents. **Becker,** W: A. V. 1. Die quellen.—Topographie der stadt; mit vergleichendem plane der stadt
   und vier anderen tafeln. 2. 1ste abth. Die stadtverfas-
   sung.—2te abth. Die republik. **Marquardt,** J. 3te
   abth. Die republik, *fortsetzung;* Die volksversamm-
   lungen. 3. 1ste abth. Italien und die provinzen. —
   2te abth. Der staatshaushalt. 4. Der gottesdienst.
   5. Römische privatalterthümer.
Marquardt, Joachim, *and* Theodor **Mommsen.**
Handbuch der römischen alterthümer; b.
1, 2, 4–7. 2te aufl. Leipz. 1876–85. 6 v. O.
                                        937 : 46
   Contents. V. 1, 2. **Mommsen,** T. Römisches staats-
   recht: b. 1, Die magistratur; 2, 1e abth., Die einzelnen magistraten. 4–6. **Marquardt,** J. Römische
   staatsverwaltung.: b. 1, Organisation des römischen
   reichs; 2, besorgt von H. Dessau und A. v. Doma-
   zewski, Das finanzwesen, Das militärwesen; 3, besorgt
   von G: Wissowa, Das sacralwesen. 7. **Marquardt,**
   J. Das privatleben der römer: b. 1, Die familie.
Lange, L: Römische alterthümer. B. 1, 3te ; b.
2–3, 2te aufl. 1867–76. Berlin. 3 v. O. 937 : 1
   Contents. V. 1. Einleitung. — Der staatsalterthümer 1er theil. 2. Der staatsalterthümer
   2er theil. 3. Der staatsalterthümer 3er theil, 1e
   abth. [bis zur befestigung der alleinherrschaft des
   Octavianus]. — Register. — **Mendelssohn,** L: Register, b. 1–3, *(bound at the end of v. 2).*
Wilkins, A: S: Roman antiquities. [History
primers : Classical antiquities, 2]. Ill. N.
Y. 1878. S.   937 : 28
Creuzer, F: Zur römischen geschichte und al-
terthumskunde. Leipz. 1836. O. 937 : 41
   Contents. Blicke auf die sklaverei im alten Rom;
   mit erklärung einiger unedirten inschriften.—Galie-
   nus und Salonina; zur kritik der römischen kaisergeschichte.

Buschmann, H. Bilder aus dem alten Rom.
Leipz. 1883. O.   937 : 48
Herbermann, C: G. Business life in ancient
Rome. [Harper's half hour ser]. N. Y.
1880. T.   937 : 24
Church, Alfred J: Roman life in the days of Cicero ; sketches drawn from his letters and
speeches. Ill. Lond. 1884. D.   937 : 40
Becker, W: Adolph. Gallus, or Roman scenes
of the time of Augustus, with notes and excursuses, ill. of the manners and customs
of the romans. Tr. by F: Metcalfe. 5th ed.
Lond. 1876. D.   937 : 20
   See note under his Charicles, col. 1172.
Dyer, T: H: A history of the city of Rome, its
structures and monuments, from its foundation to the end of the middle ages. Lond.
1865. O.   937 : 22

H i s t o r y

In general.

Duruy, V: History of Rome and of the roman
people from its origin to the establishment
of the christian empire. Tr. by M. M.
Ripley and W. J. Clarke, ed. by J. P. Mahaffy. [*Edition de luxe*]. V. 1–4. Bost. 1884,
1885. 4 v. in 8. F.   937 : R50
   Contents. V. 1. Introd., The pre-roman epoch. —
   Rome under the kings, 753—510 b. c.; formation of
   the roman people. — Rome under the patrician consuls, 509 — 367 b. c.; struggles within, weakness without. — War of italian independence, or conquest of
   Italy, 343—265 b. c.—The punic wars, 264—201 b c. 2.
   Same, continued.—Conquest of the world, 201—133 b. c.
   —The Gracchi, Marius and Sylla, 133—79 b. c.; efforts
   at reform. 3. *Same, continued.* — The triumvirates
   and the revolution, 79—30 b. c. 4. *Same, continued.*—
   Augustus, or the foundation of the empire, 30 b. c. —
   14 a. d. — The Caesars and the Flavii, 14—96 a. d.; conspiracies and civil wars.
Keightley, T: The history of Rome ; added, a
chronol. table of contemporary history by
Joshua Toulmin Smith. N. Y. *n. d.* D.
                                        937 : 33
— History of the Roman Empire, from the accession of Augustus to the end of the empire
of the west; a continuation of The history
of Rome, ed. by Joshua Toulmin Smith.
With his History of Rome.   937 : 33
Merivale, C: A general history of Rome from
the foundation of the city to the fall of
Augustulus, b. c. 753—a. d. 476. (The student's Merivale). N. Y. 1883. D.   937 : 39
Leighton, R. F. A history of Rome. Maps,
plans and ill. (Anderson's hist. ser.) N.Y.
1883. D.   937 : 36
Wägner, W: Rom ; anfang, fortgang, ausbreitung und verfall des weltreiches der
römer, für freunde des klassischen alterthums, insbesondere für die deutsche
jugend bearb. 3te aufl. Leipz. 1876, 1877.
3 v. O.   937 : 4
Creighton, Mandell. History of Rome. [History
primers]. N. Y. 1878. S.   937 : 27
Shepard, W: Our young folks' history of the
roman empire. Ill. Phila. 1886 [1885]. O.
                                        x 937 : 11
Bonner, J: A child's history of Rome. N. Y.
1880. 2 v. S.   x 937 : 32
   Contents. V. 1. Rome, b. c. 282.—Stories and legends.—The republic. 2. The civil wars.—The emperors.—Index.

x denotes books specially adapted for children.

Yonge, Charlotte Maria.   Aunt Charlotte's stories of roman history for the little ones. Lond. 1877. S.   **x 937 : 26**

Stacke, L: Christian.   Erzählungen aus der römischen geschichte in biographischer form. 19te aufl. Karten. Oldenb. 1884. D.
937 : 12

Vertot d'Aubeuf, Réne Aubert *abbé* de.   The history of the revolutions that happened in the government of the roman republic. Written in french, english'd by mr. Ozell from the original, newly printed at Paris, with amendments and add. by the author. 2d ed. Lond. 1721. 2 v. D.   **937 : 19**
Note. Extends from the beginning of Rome to the reign of Augustus.

Regal and republican Rome.

Donaldson, J: W: Varronianus ; a critical and historical introd. to the ethnography of ancient Italy.... 3d ed., rev. and enl. Lond. 1860. O.   **470 : 1**

Lewis, *Sir* G: Cornewall.   An inquiry into the credibility of early roman history. Lond. 1855. 2 v. O.   **937 : 49**
Contents. V. 1. Introd.—On the sources of roman history during the last two centuries of the republic. —On the sources and oral traditions of roman history, the public records and memorials of the roman state, the private memorials and historical poems of Rome, for the period before the war with Pyrrhus.— On the treatment of the early roman history by the extant historians of antiquity.—On the primitive history of the nations of Italy.—Æneas in Italy.—The Alban kingdom and the foundation of Rome. 2. History of Rome, from the expulsion of the kings to the burning of the city by the gauls.—History of Rome, from the rebuilding of the city to the landing of Pyrrhus in Italy.—General results of the preceding inquiry; Comparison with the corresponding period of greek history.

Livius *Patavinus*, Titus.   The romane historie written by T. Livius of Padva ; also the breviaries of L. Florus, with a chronologie to the whole historie and the topographie of Rome in old time. Tr. out of the latine into english by Philemon Holland. Lond. 1600. F.   **937 : R51**
— The history of Rome ; literally tr. with notes and ill. Lond. 1850–54. 4 v. D.   **937 : 6**
Contents. V. 1. Books 1-8, tr. by D. Spillan. 2. Books 9-26, tr. by D. Spillan and Cyrus Edmonds. 3. Books 27-36, tr. by Cyrus Edmonds. 4. Books 37 to the end, with the epitomes and fragments of the lost books, tr. by W: A. M'Devitte.
— Stories from Livy, by Alfred J: Church. Lond. 1883. D.   **x 937 : 35**

Machiavelli, Niccolo.   Discourse on the first ten books of Titus Livius. *In his* Writings.
850+1 v2

Niebuhr, Barthold G: Römische geschichte [bis zum ersten punischen kriege]. Neue ausg. von M. Isler, [mit einem ausführlichen register]. Berlin. 1873, 1874. 3 v. D.
937 : 3
Note. V. 3 was issued after the author's death, from his papers, by J. Classen.
— *Same, eng.* The history of Rome. V. 1, 2 tr. by Julius C: Hare and Connop Thirlwall ; v. 3 tr. by W: Smith and Leonhard Schmitz. New ed. Lond. 1851. 3 v. O.   **937 : 2**

Arnold, T: The history of Rome. N. Y. 1846. 3 v. in 2. O.   **937 : 8**
Contents. V. 1. 1 (*of London ed.*), Early history to the burning of Rome by the Gauls.—2, From the end of the gaulish invasion to the end of the first punic war, [to a. u. c. 450]. 2. *Same, continued.*—3, From

the end of the first to the end of the second punic war.

Mommsen, Theodor.   Römische geschichte. 6te aufl. Berlin. 1874, 1875. 3 v. O.   **937 : 2**
Contents. V. 1. Bis zur schlacht von Pydna, b. c. 168. 2. Bis auf Sulla's tod, b. c. 68. 3. Bis zur schlacht von Thapsus, b. c. 46.—Index, 1-3.
— *Same, eng.* The history of Rome. Tr., with the author's sanction and add. by W: P. Dickson, with a pref. by Leonhard Schmitz. New ed. N. Y. [1868]. 4 v. D.   **937 : 2**
Contents. V. 1. To the union of Italy. 2. To the battle of Pydna. 3. To the death of Sulla. 4. To the battle of Thapsus.—Index.

Ihne, W: The history of Rome. English ed. Lond. 1871–82. 5 v. O.   **937 : 5**
Contents. V. 1. The regal period. — The early history of the republic. — Conquest of Italy. 2. Struggle for the ascendancy in the west, to 201 b. c. 3. The wars for the supremacy in the west, to 133 b. c. 4. The constitution, laws, religion and magistrates of the roman people. — Expansion of the republic into an empire, [to the death of C. Gracchus]. 5. *Same, continued* [to the death of Sulla, 78 b. c.].— General index.
— Early Rome, from the foundation of the city to its destruction by the gauls. 2d ed. (Epochs of ancient history.) Lond. 1877. S.
937 : 13

Schwegler, Albert F: K: Franz.   Römische geschichte. Tübingen. 1867. 3 v. O. **937 : 44**
Contents. V. 1. Im zeitalter der könige. 2. Im zeitalter des kampfs der stände: Von der gründung der republik bis zum decemvirat. 3. Im zeitalter des kampfs der stände: Vom ersten decemvirat bis zu den licinischen gesetzen; nach des verf. tod herausg. von F. F. Baur. 4. Clason, Octavius. *Fortsetzung:* Seit der verwüstung Roms durch die gallier [bis zum ersten samniterkriege].

Newman, Francis W: Regal Rome ; an introd. to roman history. N. Y. 1852. D. **937 : 25**

Laing, *Mrs.* C. H. B.   The seven kings of the seven hills. Phila. [1872]. S.   **x 937 : 29**
— The heroes of the seven hills. Phila. [1870]. S.
x 937 : 30
— The conquests of the seven hills. Phila. [1875]. S.   **x 937 : 31**

Smith, Reginald Bosworth.   Carthage and the carthaginians. Lond. 1878. D.   **939 : 2**
— Rome and Carthage ; the punic wars. (Epochs of ancient history.) N. Y. [1881]. S.
937 : 14

Beesly, A: H: The Gracchi, Marius and Sulla. (Epochs of ancient history.) Lond. 1877. S.   **937 : 16**

Sallustius Crispus, Caius.   C. Crispi Salustii de L. Sergii Catilinae coniuratione, ac bello Iugurthino historiæ. Ex castigatione Ioan. Riuij Atthendoriensis, cum annotationib. marginialib. D. Philip. Melanth. Adiecimus nunc primum in omnia Sallustij, quae hodie extant fragmenta, Henrici Glareani Heluetij poëtæ laureati annotationes ; Cum quibusdam alijs in Catilin. & Iugurth. Salust. Iacobi Bononiensis annotatiunculis. Coloniae. 1544. S.   **23 : R**
— Sallust, Florus and Velleius Paterculus ; literally tr., with copious notes and a general index, by J: Selby Watson. N. Y. 1877. D.
937 : 7
Contents. **Sallust.** Conspiracy of Catiline.—The Jugurthine war.— Fragments of the history of Sallust. — Two epistles to Julius Cæsar on the government of the state, ascribed to Sallust.—A declamation against Sallust, falsely attributed to Cicero.—**Lucius Annæus Florus.** Epitome of roman history.—**Velleius Paterculus.** Remains of his compendium of the history of Rome.

x denotes books specially adapted for children.

Cæsar, Caius Julius. Commentaries on the gallic and civil wars ; with the supp. books attributed to Hirtius, incl. the alexandrian, african and spanish wars. Literally tr. with notes and index. Lond. 1882. D.
937 : 10

Merivale, C: The roman triumvirates 2d ed. (Epochs of ancient history.) Lond. 1877. S.
937 : 15

— The fall of the roman republic ; a short history of the last century of the commonwealth [b. c. 137–29]. New ed. Lond. 1874. D.
937 : 47

Imperial Rome, and the barbaric invasion.

Merivale, C: History of the romans under the empire. [New ed.] Lond. 1862. 7 v. O.
937+9
Contents. V. 1, 2. From the first triumvirate to the fall of Julius Cæsar, b. c. 88—44. 3. To the establishment of the monarchy by Augustus, b. c. 44—27. 4, 5. From Augustus to Claudius, b. c. 27—a. d. 54. 6. From the reign of Nero to the destruction of Jerusalem, a. d. 54—70. 7. The Flavian era, to the death of Antoninus, a. d. 180.

Zosimus, *Comes.* The history of count Zosimus. Tr. from the original greek, with the notes of the Oxford ed. Lond. 1814. O.
in 938+41
Note. Comprises a history of the decline of Rome, from the beginning of the empire to a. d. 410.

Hertzberg, Gustav F: Geschichte des römischen kaiserreiches. (Oncken, W:, ed. Allgemeine geschichte in einzeldarstellungen ; 2te hauptabth., 1er th.) Berlin. 1880. O.
909+20 v1

De Quincey, T: The cæsars [from Augustus to Dioclesian]. Bost. 1851. D.   937 : 21

Tacitus, Caius Cornelius. Works. Oxford tr., rev. with notes. N. Y. 1881, 1883. 2 v. D.
937 : 38
Contents. V. 1. The annals [from the death of Augustus to within two years of Nero's death, except Caligula and the first five years of Claudius]. 2. The history, a. d. 68—70. — A treatise on the manners of the germans. — Life of Cnæus Julius Agricola. — Dialogue concerning oratory, or The causes of corrupt eloquence.—Index.

Capes, W: Wolfe. Roman history ; the early empire, from the assassination of Julius Cæsar to that of Domitian. Maps. (Epochs of ancient history.) N. Y. *n. d.* S. 937 : 37

— The roman empire of the 2nd century, or The age of the Antonines. (Epochs of ancient history.) Lond. 1876. S.   937 : 18

Ammianus Marcellinus. Roman history, during the reigns of the emperors Constantius, Julian, Jovianus, Valentinian and Valens. Tr. by C. D. Yonge. Lond. 1862. D.
937 : 42

Simonde de Sismondi, J: C: Léonard. History of the fall of the Roman Empire, comprising a view of the invasion and settlement of the barbarians. Phila. 1835. O.
Note. A general history of the nations concerned in the dissolution of the roman empire, both in Europe and Asia, from the fourth century to the year 1000.

Montesquieu, C: de Secondat, *baron* de la **Brède et de.** Grandeur and decline of the Roman Empire. *In his* Complete works.
340 : 6 v3

Gibbon, E: The history of the decline and fall of the Roman Empire ; with notes by H. H. Milman. Maps. N. Y. 1847. 4 v. O.
937.1 : 1

— The history of the decline and fall of the Roman Empire ; with notes of Milman, Guizot and W: Smith. N. Y. 1880. 6 v. O.
937.1 : 4
Note. "The period embraced extends from the middle of the second century of our era to the fall of Constantinople, in 1453. The author did not pursue a strict chronological order, but massed his materials and arranged them in accordance with their moral and political significance. The completed work, therefore, has somewhat the appearance of a succession of monographs, each one of which is perfect, or nearly perfect, in itself." It comprises the political and religious history of all the peoples and kingdoms more or less intimately connected with the roman world during this long and turbulent period.

— The student's Gibbon : The history of the decline and fall of the Roman Empire, abridged, incorporating the researches of recent commentators, by W: Smith. N. Y. 1862. D.   937.1 : 2

Hodgkin, T: Italy and her invaders, 376—476. Oxford. 1880. 2 v. O.   937.1 : 6
Contents. V. 1. The visigothic invasion. 2. The hunnish invasion.—The vandal invasion and the herulean mutiny.—Causes of the fall of the western empire.—Index.

Kingsley, C: The roman and the teuton ; a series of lectures del. before the university of Cambridge. New ed. with pref. by F: Max Müller. [Works, v. 10]. Lond. 1881. D.
937.1 : 5
Contents. Preface.—The forest children.—The dying empire.—The human deluge. — The gothic civilizer.—Dietrich's end. — The nemesis of the goths. — Paulus Diaconus.—The clergy and the heathen.—The monk a civilizer. — The lombard laws. — The popes and the lombards.—The strategy of providence. — App. The limits of exact science, as applied to history.

Sheppard, J: G. The fall of Rome and the rise of the new nationalities ; a series of lectures on the connection between ancient and modern history, [to the death of Charlemagne]. Lond. 1861. D.   937.1 : 7

Curteis, Arthur M. History of the Roman Empire from the death of Theodosius the great to the coronation of Charles the great, a. d. 395—800. Maps. [Hist. handbooks]. Lond. 1875. S.   937.1 : 8

— *Same.* Phila. 1875. S.   937.1 : 8

Bryce, James. The holy roman empire [to its end in 1806]. 7th ed. Lond. 1884. D.
937.1 : 9
See also in the Index to biography Agrippina—Antoninus—Antonius—Attila—Brutus—Cæsar—Camillus— Cato— Cicero — Coriolanus — Crassus—Fabius—Flamininus—Galba—Gracchus—Hannibal—Jovianus—Lucullus—Marcellus—Marius—Nero—Numa—Otho—Paulus—Pompeius—Publicola—Romulus—Scipio—Sertorius—Sulla—Theodosius.

4. Modern geography in general.

(For General modern history, see Universal history, cl. 900-909, col. 1151-1156.)

1. Geography, proper.

(See also Physical geogr., cl. 551, col. 323; Ethnology, cl. 572, col. 350; Statistics, cl. 310, col. 155.)

Dictionaries.

Williams, Edwin. The new universal gazetteer, or Geographical dictionary, derived from the latest and best authorities; pt. 2 of The treasury of knowledge and library of reference. N. Y. 1832. S.   **910 : 8**

Murray, Hugh, *and others*. The encyclopædia of geography, comprising a complete description of the earth, physical, statistical, civil and political, exhibiting its relation to the heavenly bodies, its physical structure, the natural history of each country, and the industry, commerce, political institutions and civil and social state of all nations. Ill., with maps. Rev. with add. by T: G. Bradford. Phila. 1847. 3 v. O.   **910 : R7**

McCulloch, J: Ramsay. Universal gazetteer; a dictionary, geographical, statistical and historical, of the various countries, places and principal natural objects in the world; the articles relating to the U. S. multiplied, extended and adapted by Daniel Haskell. N. Y. 1852. 2 v. O.   **910 : R8**

Thomas, Joseph, *and* T: **Baldwin**, *eds.* Lippincott's pronouncing gazetteer or geographical dictionary of the world. Phila. 1856.   **910 +5**
— *Same.* Rev. ed. with app., containing 10,000 new notices and the census of 1870. Phila. 1878. O.   **910 : 5**
— *Same.* New ed., thoroughly rewritten, rev. and greatly enl. Phila. 1880. Q. **910 : R5**
— *Same.* Supplementary tables of population; a complement to Lippincott's pronouncing gazetteer of the world. Phila. 1883 [1882].   **910 : R5**

Hoffmann, S: F: W:, *ed.* Encyklopädie der erd-, völker- und staatenkunde; eine geographisch-statistische darstellung der erdtheile, länder, meere, inseln, gebirge, berge, vorgebirge, buchten, häfen, flüsse, seen, völker, staaten, städte, flecken, dörfer, bäder, berg- und hüttenwerke, leuchtthürme, kanäle, eisenbahnen u. s. w., nebst den geographisch-astronomischen bestimmungen der lage der orte. Leipz. 1864-69. 3 v. Q.   **913 : R3**

Jung, K: Emil. Lexikon der handelsgeographie; handels- und industrieverhältnisse aller staaten, mit den neuesten ausweisen über aus- und einfuhr, produktion, verkehr und zahlreichen statistischen tabellen; mit einer karte des weltverkehrs. Leipz. 1882. D.   **913 : R14**

Treatises and essays.

Malte-Brun, *originally* Malthe Conrad **Bruun**, *known as* Conrad. Universal geography, or A description of all parts of the world on a new plan, according to the great natural divisions of the globe; accompanied with analytical, synoptical and elementary tables, improved by the add. of the most recent information, derived from various sources. Phila. 1827-32. 6 v. O. **910 +12**

Mitchell, S: A: Accompaniment to Mitchell's map of the world on Mercator's projection. Phila. 1838. O.   **913 : 5**

Van Waters, G: The poetical geography; made to accompany any of the common school atlases. Milw. 1848. D.   **910 : 14**

Morse, Jedidiah. The american universal geography, or A view of the present state of all the kingdoms, states and colonies in the known world. Added, an abridgement of the last census of the U. S., a chronol. table of remarkable events from the creation to this time, a list of ancient and modern learned and eminent men and an index. 6th ed. Bost. 1812. 2 v. O. **913 : 10**

Stein, Christian Gottfried Daniel, *and* Ferdinand **Hörschelmann**. Handbuch der geographie und statistik für die gebildeten stände; neu bearbeitet, unter mitwirkung mehrerer gelehrten, von J: E: Wappäus. 7te aufl. Leipz. 1855-71. 9 v. O.   **910 : 15**

Contents. [V. 1.] *1r b., 1e u. 2e abth.* **Wappäus**, J: E: Allgemeine geographie und statistik; Nordamerika. 1855. [2.] *1r b., 3e abth.* **Wappäus**, J: E: Das ehemalige spanische Mittel- und Süd-Amerika, nebst den europäischen besitzungen [und Patagonien]. 1863-70. [3.] *1r b., 4e abth.* **Wappäus**, J: E: Das kaiserreich Brasilien. 1871.—**Delitsch**, O: Westindien und die Südpolar-länder. 1871. [4.] *2r b., 1e u. 2e abth.* **Gumprecht**, Thaddäus E: Afrika. mit nachträgen und ergänzungen von O: Delitsch.—**Meinicke**, C: E: Australien. 1886. [5.] *2e b., 3e abth.* **Brauer**, J: Hartwig, *and* J: H: **Plath**. Asien. 1864. [6.] *3r b., 1e abth.* **Wappäus**, J: E: Allgemeine übersicht von Europa.—Ost- und Nord-Europa: **Possart**, Fedor. Das Russische reich; **Brachelli**, Hugo Franz. Das Osmanische reich nebst den drei Donaufürstenthümern, Das fürstenthum Montenegro, Das königreich Griechenland, und Die republik der Ionischen inseln; **Frisch**, C: F:. Das königreich Dänemark, Die königreiche Schweden und Norwegen; **Ravenstein**, Ernst G:, Das Britische reich; **Baumhauer**, M. M. v., Das königreich der Niederlande.—Nachträge und verbesserungen. 1858-63. [7.] *3r b., 2e abth.* West- und Süd-Europa: **Willkomm**, H: Moritz, Das pyrenäische halbinselland; **Block**, Maurice, Das kaiserthum Frankreich; **Heuschling**, Philippe François Xavier Théodose, Das königreich Belgien; **Brachelli**, Hugo Franz, Die Schweizerische Eidgenossenschaft, Die italienische halbinsel.—Nachträge zu Spanien, Portugal, Frankreich und Belgien. 1862-71. [8.] *4r b., 1e abth.* **Brachelli**, Hugo Franz, Der deutsche bund im allgemeinen; Das kaiserthum Oesterreich. 1867. — Oesterreichisch-ungarische monarchie, 1871. [9.] *4r b., 2e abth.* **Brachelli**, Hugo Franz, Das königreich Preussen und die deutschen mittel- und klein-staaten; mit einer statistischen skizze des Nord-deutschen bundes, der Süd-deutschen staaten, des grossherzogthums Luxemburg und des deutschen zoll- und handelsvereins, 1868. 1864-68.

Hoffmann, K: F: Vollrath. Die erde und ihre bewohner; ein hand- und lesebuch für alle stände: 1, Allgemeiner theil, bearbeit. von H: Berghaus und Daniel Völter; 2, Specieller theil, bearb. von Daniel Völter. Stuttg. 1867. 2 v. O.   **913 +2**

Daniel, Hermann Adalbert. Handbuch der geographie. 4te aufl. Leipz. 1874. 4 v. O.
913 : 1

Contents. V. 1. Allgemeine geographie.— Die aussereuropäischen erdtheile. 2. Die europäischen länder ausser Deutschland. 3. Deutschland, physische geographie. 4. Deutschland, politische geographie.

Ungewitter, Franz H: Neueste erdbeschreibung und staatenkunde, oder Geographischstatistisch-historisches handbuch; mit besonderer berücksichtigung der neuesten gestaltung Deutschlands. 5te aufl. 3te ausg., durch einen ausführlichen nachtrag bis auf die neueste zeit vervollständigt und berichtigt; unter benutzung amtlicher quellen und der sonst zuverlässigsten unterlagen bearb. von G: W: Hopf. Dresden. 1879. 2 v. O.
913+4

Reclus, J: Jacques Elisée. The earth and its inhabitants. Ill. and maps. N. Y. 1882–85. 9 v. O.
913 : R11

Contents. Europe, 5 v. V. 1. Greece, Turkey in Europe, Rumania, Servia, Montenegro, Italy, Spain and Portugal. 2. France and Switzerland. 3. Austria, Hungary, Germany, Belgium and the Netherlands. 4. The British Isles. 5. The north-east Atlantic, Islands of the north Atlantic, Scandinavia, European islands of the Arctic ocean, Russia in Europe.

    Asia, 4 v. ed. by E. G. Ravenstein and A. H. Keane. V. 1. Asiatic Russia: Caucasia, Aralo-caspian basin, Siberia. 2. East Asia: Chinese empire, Corea and Japan. 3. India and Indo-China. 4. South-western Asia: General survey; Afghanistan; Balauchistan; Persia; Asiatic Turkey; Lower Kurdistan, Mesopotamia. Irak-Arabi; Asia Minor; Cyprus; Syria, Palestine, Sinai; Arabia; Statistical tables; Index.

Grube, A: W:, *ed.* Geographische charakterbilder in abgerundeten gemälden aus der länder und völkerkunde; nach musterdarstellungen der deutschen und ausländischen litteratur für die obere stufe des geographischen unterrichts in schulen, sowie zu einer bildenden lektüre für freunde der erdkunde überhaupt. Leipz. 1881. 3 v. O.
913+12

Grove, G: Geography. [History primers]. N. Y. 1877. S.
910 : 9

Mortimer, *Mrs.* T: Far off: pt. 1, Asia described; pt. 2, Oceanica, Africa and America described; with anecdotes and ill. New ed. rev. [by L. C. Meyer] and enl. Lond. 1881, 1882. 2 v. S.
913 : 8

Colange, Leo de, *ed.* The picturesque world, or scenes in many lands; picturesque views from all parts of the world, comprising mountain, lake and river scenery, parks, palaces, cathedrals, churches, castles, abbeys and other views selected from the most noted and interesting parts of the world, with original and authentic descriptions by the best authors. Bost. 1879. 2 v. Q.
913 : R12

Contents. V. 1. Rome.— Tivoli.— Paris and its environs.—St. Petersburg and its environs.—Novgorod. — Moscow. — Siberia. — Chateaux and churches of France.—Belgium.—Meissen.—Treves. — Zeeland and Holland. — Strasburg, the Black Forest and Heidelberg.—Wurtemburg.— Bavaria.— Down the Danube. — Transylvania and the turkish principalities. — Mount Athos and Athens. — Sicily and the Lipari Islands.— The temples of Præstum.— Siena. — Vintimiglia.—Spain. 2. Northern provinces of Portugal. — Northern Africa. — The Nile. — Eastern Africa. Mauritius.—Constantinople and Asiatic Turkey.—Niniveh and Babylon. — Persia.—India. — Indo-China.— Australia.—China.—Japan.—Sandwich Islands.—California and the Rocky Mountains.—Mexico.— Cuba.—

Guiana and Brazil. — Peru. — Norway.— Denmark.— Poland. — The German Empire. — Down the Rhine.— Great Britain.—The United States.

Brown, Robert. The countries of the world; a popular description of the various continents, islands, rivers, seas and peoples of the globe. Lond. [1877–80]. 5 v. Q. **913+7**

Contents. V. 1. Introd.—The arctic regions in general.—The fur countries of North America. — The Dominion of Canada. — The commerce of the forest. — The United States. 2. *Same, continued.*—Mexico. — The West Indies. 3. Central America.—South America. 4. Oceania.—New Zealand. — Tasmania. — Australia.—The Malay Archipelago. — The Japanese empire. 5. Siberia.—The Chinese empire. — Burmah. — Siam.—Cambodia.—Anam. — Cochin-China. — India.— Afghan Turkestan, and the other central asiatic states.—Russian Central Asia.—Persia. 6. The Turkish empire.—Africa.—Oceanic islands.—Europe, [except Great Britain).—General index.

Hodder, Edwin. Cities of the world; their origin, progress and present aspect. Ill. Lond. 1882–[1884]. 3 v. Q. **913.1+60**

Contents. V 1. Introd.—Constantinople.—**Sweetser,** M: F. New York.— Alexandria. — Venice.—Amsterdam.—Melbourne and the great towns of Victoria. —Paris. — Rotterdam. — **Sweetser,** M. F. Boston.— Vienna. 2. **Sweetser,** M. F. San Francisco. — Rouen.—Madrid.—Cairo.—**Sweetser,** M. F. Toronto and Quebec.— Marseilles. — Calcutta and the cities of the Ganges. — Munich and Nuremberg. — St. Petersburg.—Pekin. — Lyons.—**Sweetser,** M. F. Chicago. 3. Jerusalem.—Brussels and the cities of Belgium.— Athens.—**Sweetser,** M. F. Philadelphia.—Moscow.— Rome.—Berlin.—The cities of New Zealand.—Geneva. Scandinavian cities.—Florence.

Whymper, F: The sea; its thrilling story of adventure, peril and heroism. Ill. Lond. 1878–80. 4 v. Q. **910+10**

Contents. V. 1. Men-of-war.— Men of peace.—The men of the sea.—Perils of the sailor's life.—Round the world on a man-of-war. — The service; Officers' life on board.—The reverse of the picture; Mutiny.—The history of ships and shipping interests. 2. *Same, continued.* — The lighthouse and its history. — The breakwater. — The greatest storm in english history. "Man the life-boat!"—"Wrecking" as a profession.— "Hovelling" vs. wrecking. — Ships that "pass by on the other side." — The ship on fire!, Swamped at sea. —Early steamship wrecks and their lessons. 3. The pirates and bucaniers. — The pirates of the 18th century. — Paul Jones and De Soto. — Our arctic expeditions.— Cruise of the Pandora. — The Albert and Discovery.—The first arctic voyages.—Early arctic expeditions.—The voyages of Barents. — Voyages of Hudson and his successors. — Expeditions in the 18th century.—The expeditions of Ross and Parry.—The magnetic pole; A land journey to the polar sea.—Voyage of the Terror.—Franklin's last voyage.—The Franklin search. — Kane's expedition. — Hayes' expedition. — Swedish expeditions.—The second german polar expedition. — Hall's expedition; The austro-hungarian expedition; Nordenskjöld. — The Antarctic regions.— Decisive voyages in history: Diaz; Columbus; Vasco da Gama. — The companions and followers of Columbus. 4. The great Atlantic ferry. — Ocean to ocean; the connecting link.—The Pacific ferry. — Woman at sea.—Davy Jones's locker and its treasures, and those who dive into it. — The ocean and some of its phenomena.—Submarine cables. — The ocean and its living wonders. — Ocean life; the harvest of the sea. — Monsters of the deep.— By the sea-shore. — Sketches of [the english] coasts.—The art of swimming: Feats of natation; Life savers. — The haven at last; home in the Thames. — What poets have sung of the sea; the sailor and the ship.—General index.

Bastian, Adolf. Geographische und ethnologische bilder. Jena. 1873. O. **910 : 1**
Contents, see Deutscher katalog, p. 36.

Peschel, Oscar Ferdinand. Abhandlungen zur erd- und völkerkunde; herausg. von J. Löwenberg. Leipz. 1877, 1878. 2 v. O.
910.2

Contents, see Deutscher katalog, p. 37.

Deming, Clarence. By-ways of nature and life. N. Y. 1885. S. **913.1 : 66**
Contents. The flowery of London.— Curiosities of zoology. — A british election-day. — England's gun-foundry.—London in a fog.—Waterloo to-day. — The giant tides of Fundy. — Newfoundland and the cod-fishers.—Seal-hunting on the ice-fields.—Heart's Content and the ocean cables. — Deep fishing in tropic seas.—Shadows in Cuba.—The Bahama sponge-fishers. — Down in a coal-mine. — The buried forests of New Jersey. — Petrolia and its marvels. — A yankee town-meeting.—On black ice.—The old college ball-ground. —An historic meeting-house.—Oddities of fishcraft.—Among the maniacs. — Silver spring. — Catching the grayling.—A yankee coon-hunt.—Logging in Michigan wilds. — The father of waters. — The shoestring district.—The southern planter.—The negro of the Mississippi bends. — Negro rites and worship. — Negro songs and hymns.

Reid, Mayne. The man-eaters and other odd people ; a popular description of singular races of man. Ill. N. Y. 1882. D. **913 : 6**
Contents. Man-eaters of the Feegee islands.—Mundrucus or beheaders. — The centaurs of the "Gran Chaco." — Bosjesmen or Bushmen. — The amazonian indians.—The water-dwellers of Maracaibo. — The Esquimaux.—The Tongans or Friendly islanders. — The Turcomans.—The Ottomacs or dirt-eaters.—The Comanches or prairie indians. — The Pehuenches or Pampas indians. — The Yamparicos or root-diggers.—The Guaranos or palm-dwellers. — The Laplanders.— The Andamaners, or mud-bedaubers. — The Patagonian giants. — The Fuegian dwarfs.

— *Same.* Odd people. N. Y. 1860. S. **913.1 : 6**

Children of all nations ; their homes, their schools, their playgrounds. Ill. N. Y. [1884]. O. **x 913 : 15**

Atlases and Periodicals.

Colton, G: Woolworth. General atlas of the world, accompanied by geographical, statistical and historical letter-press descriptions. N. Y. 1878. F. **910 : R4**

Black, Adam *and* C: General atlas of the world. Amer. ed., embracing the latest discoveries, new boundaries and other changes, accompanied by introd. letter-press and index. Edinb. 1879. F. **910 : R3**

Stieler, Adolf. Hand-atlas über alle theile der erde und über das weltgebäude. 95 karten. [Neu bearb. von A: Petermann, Hermann Berghaus und C: Vogel]. Gotha. [1884]. F. **913 : R13**

Rand, McNally *and* co. Indexed atlas of the world ; containing large scale maps of every country and civil division upon the face of the globe, together with historical, statistical and descriptive matter relative to each. Chicago. 1884. F. **910 : R12**

Petermann's, Dr. A., mittheilungen aus Justus Perthes' geographischer anstalt ; herausg. von E. Behm ; v. 27–31. Gotha. [1881–85]. Q. **905.1 : M**
Note. From oct. 1884 ed. by A. Supan.

— *Same.* Ergänzungsband 14–17. Gotha. 1881–85. Q. *in* **905.1 : M**
Contents. 14, 1880–81. Rivoli, J. Die Serra da Estrella.—Behm, E., *and* H. Wagner. Die bevölkerung der erde, pt. 6.—Mohn, H: Die norwegische Nordmeer-expedition.—Fischer, T. Die dattelpalme. —Berlepsch, H. A. Die Gotthard-bahn. 15, 1881–82. Schreiber, P. Die bedeutung der windrosen.— Blumentritt, F. Ethnographie der Philippinen.— Berndt, G. Das Val d'Anniviers und das Bassin de Sierre.—Behm, E., *and* H. Wagner. Die bevölkerung der erde, pt. 7.—Bayberger, F. Der Inngletscher von Kufstein bis Haag. 16, 1883–84. Stein,

F. v. Die russischen kosakenheere.—Schuver, J: M. Reisen im oberen Nilgebiet.—Schumann, C: Kritische untersuchungen über die Zimtländer.—Drude, O. Die florenreiche der erde.— Lendenfeld, R. v. Der Tasman-gletscher. 17, 1884–85. Regel, Fritz. Die entwickelung der ortschaften im Thüringerwald. —Stolze, F., *and* F. C. Andreas. Die handelsverhältnisse Persiens.—Fritsche, H. Ein beitrag zur geographie und lehre vom erdmagnetismus Asiens und Europas.—Mohn, H: Die strömungen des europäischen nordmeeres.—Boas, Franz. Baffin-Land ; geographische ergebnisse einer in 1883 und 1884 ausgeführten forschungsreise.

Ocean highways; the geographical review, ed. by Clements R. Markham. New ser., v. 1. Ill. Lond. 1874. Q. **905.1 : M**

Geographical magazine, The, ed. by Clements R. Markham ; v. 1–5. apr. 1874—nov. 1878. Ill. Lond. 1874–78. Q. **905.1 : M**

Royal geographical society. Proceedings and monthly record of geography ; pub. under the authority of the council and ed. by the assistant sec. New monthly ser., v. 1–6. Lond. 1879–84. O. **906.1 : R1**

2. Collected travels.

Knox, T: Wallace. How to travel; hints, advice and suggestions to travellers by land and sea all over the globe. N. Y. 1881. T. **913.1 : 3**

Embacher, F: Lexikon der reisen und entdeckungen, in 2 abth.: 1, Die forschungsreisenden aller zeiten und länder ; 2, Entdeckungsgeschichte der einzelnen erdteile. Leipz. 1882. D. **910 : R11**

Harris, J: Navigantium atque itinerantium bibliotheca, or A complete collection of voyages and travels ; consisting of above 600 of the most authentic writers, beginning with Hackluit, Purchass, etc., in english, Ramusio, Alamandini, Carreri, etc., in italian, Thevenot, Renaudot, Labat, etc., in french, De Brye, Grynæus, Masseus, etc., in latin, Herrera, Ovideo, Coreal, etc., in spanish, and the voyages under the direction of the East India company in Holland, in dutch, together with such other histories, voyages, travels, or discoveries as are in general esteem, whether pub. in english, latin, french, italian, spanish, portuguese, high and low dutch, or in any other european language; containing whatever has been observed worthy of notice in Europe, Asia, Africa and America in respect to the extent and situation of empires, kingdoms, provinces, etc., the climate, soil and produce, whether animal, vegetable or mineral of each country, likewise the religion, manners and customs of the several inhabitants, their government, arts, sciences, publick buildings, mountains, rivers, harbours, etc., ill. by proper charts, maps and cuts; to which is prefixed a copious introd., comprehending the rise and progress of the art of navigation and its successive improvements, together with the invention and use of the load stone and its variation ; carefully rev., with add., incl. particular accounts of the manufactures and commerce of each country. Lond. 1744. 2 v. F. **23 : R**
Contents, see Catalogue of the library of the Boston athenæum, v. 2, p. 1343.

Pinkerton, J: A general collection of the best and most interesting voyages and travels in all parts of the world; many of which are now first tr. into english, digested on a new plan. Ill. Lond. 1808. 17 v. Q. 913.1 : R53

Historical account, An, of the circumnavigation of the globe and of the progress of discovery in the Pacific ocean from the voyage of Magellan to the death of Cook. Ill. [Harper's family lib.] N. Y. 1845. S. 913.1 : 13

Kippis, Andrew. Cook's three voyages around the world; comprising a complete account of the great expeditions of this illustrious navigator, with his life during the previous and intervening periods. Phila. *n. d.* 2 v. in 1. S. 913.1 : 49

Voyages round the world from the death of capt. Cook; incl. remarks on the social condition of the inhabitants in the recently discovered countries, their progress in the arts, and more especially their advancement in religious knowledge. [Harper's fam. lib.] N. Y. 1844. S. 913.1 : 38

ern shores of America.—Voyages of d'Entrecasteaux, Marchand and Vancouver.—Edwards, Wilson, Fanning and Turnbull.—Baudin, Freycinet, Duperrey, d'Urville, Bougainville and La Place.—Krusenstern, Kotzebue and Lutké.—Hall, Ruschenberger and Fitzroy.—Meyen, Wilson, Belcher and Ross.

Kingsley, H: Tales of old travel re-narrated. New ed., ill. Lond. 1882. D.   **913.1 : 46**
Contents. Marco Polo.—The shipwreck of Felsart. —The wonderful adventures of Andrew Battel. — The wanderings of a capuchin.—P: Carder. — The preservation of the "Terra Nova."—Spitzbergen.— D'Ermenonville's acclimatization adventure. — The old slave trade.—Miles Philips. — The sufferings of Robert Everard.—J: Fox.—Alvaro Nunez.—The foundation of an empire.

Bell, N. R. E., (*N. D'Anvers*). The story of early exploration. Ill. and maps. (Science ladders, no. 2.) N. Y. 1884. S.
     x 913.1 : 56

Verne, Jules. Exploration of the world. From the french. Ill. N. Y. 1879–81. 3 v. O.
     913.1 : 5
Contents. V. **1.** Famous travels and travelers. **2.** Great navigators of the 18th century. **3.** Great explorers of the 19th century.

Cleveland, R: J. A narrative of voyages and commercial enterprises. Cambridge. 1842. 2 v. D.   **913.1 : 14**
— *Same.* 3d ed. Ill. Bost. 1850. D. **913.1 : 14**

Payne, E. J., *ed.* Voyages of the Elizabethan seamen to America ; thirteen original narratives from the collection of Hakluyt, sel. and ed. with historical notices. Lond. 1880. D.   **913.1 : 39**
Contents. Hawkins' 1st, 2d and 3d voyages.—Frobisher's 1st, 2d and 3d voyages.—Drake's famous voyage.—Gilbert's voyage.—Amada's and Barlow's voyage.—Drake's 2d great voyage.—Cavendish's 1st and last voyage.—Raleigh's voyage to Guiana.

Taylor, Bayard, *comp.* Cyclopædia of modern travel ; a record of adventure, exploration and discovery for the last 50 years, comprising narratives of the most distinguished travelers since the beginning of this century. Cinc. 1856. O.   **913.1┼4**
Contents. Life and travels of Alexander v. Humboldt.— Mungo Park's travels in western Africa.— Lewis and Clark's journey to the Pacific ocean.— Burkhart's travels in Syria, Africa and Arabia.—Belzoni's explorations in Egypt.—Cailliand's journey to the Libyan oases, Ethiopia and Senaar.—Franklin's overland journey to the Polar sea. — Meyendorff's journey to Bokhara. — Timkovski's journey from Siberia to Pekin. — Cochrane's pedestrian journey through Siberia.—Golownin's captivity in Japan.— De Lascaris's and Clapperton's expedition to central Africa.—Clapperton's second journey to Sackatoo.— Explorations of the Niger.—Moffat's life in southern Africa.—Sturt's explorations in Australia.— Back's Arctic land expedition.—Wellsted's travels in Oman. —Explorations of the White Nile.—Major Harris's mission to Shoa.— Parkyns's life in Abyssinia.— Wood's journey to the Oxus.—Fremont's explorations of the Rocky mountains and California.—Huc's travels in Tartary, Thibet and China.— Fortune's journeys to the tea-countries of China.—Recent explorations in Australia.—Lynch's exploration of the Dead Sea. — Layard's explorations at Nineveh and Babylon.—Travels of Ida Pfeiffer.—Explorations of the Amazon river. — Richardson's travels in the Sahara.—Richardson and Barth's expedition to central Africa.—Burton's pilgrimage to Mecca. — Expedition to Loo-Choo.

Remarkable voyages and travels ; consisting of Anson's Voyages round the world, Stephens' Incidents of travel in Greece, Turkey, Russia and Poland, and Kämpfer's Account of Japan. Ill. Lond. *n. d.* O.
     913.1┼45

Hodder, Edwin, *ed.* All the world over. Maps and ill. Lond. 1875. 2 v. D.   **913.1 : 61**
Note. Originally published as a monthly magazine by the famous firm of Thos. Cook & son.

Over seas, or Here, there and everywhere, by popular authors. Bost. [1881]. D.
     x 913.1 : 44

Maga excursion papers. (Putnam's railway classics.) N. Y. 1867. D.   **913.1 : 27**
Contents. Newport in winter. — From Venice to Vienna. — Sketches in a Parisian café. — Robinson Crusoe's island.—The midnight sun.—A few days in Vienna.—Experiences in Mt. Lebanon.—Acadie and the birthplace of Evangeline. — Adventures on a drift-log.—The ghost of a city.—Hayti and the haitians.—A glimpse of Munich.—How they live in Havana.—Wood-notes.—Forty days in a western hotel.

3.   Extensive individual journeys.

(*See also* Scientific travels, cl. 508, col. 295.)

R o u n d   t h e   w o r l d.

Ballou, Maturin Murray. Due west, or Round the world in ten months. Bost. 1884. D.
     913.1 : 54

Brassey, Anna, *born* Allnutt, *lady.* Around the world in the yacht Sunbeam ; our home on the ocean for eleven months. Ill. N. Y. 1878. O.   **913.1 : 8**

Brooks, James. A seven months' run, up, down and around the world ; written in letters to the N. Y. Evening express. N. Y. 1872. D.   **913.1 : 9**

Carnegie, Andrew. Round the world. N. Y. 1884. O.   **913.1 : 57**

Carr, Addis Emmet. All the way round, or What a boy saw and heard on his way round the world ; a book for young people and older ones with young hearts. [*Anon.*] Lond. *n. d.* D.   **x 913.1 : 48**

Carlisle, A. D. Round the world in 1870 ; an account of a brief tour made through India, China, Japan, California and South America. Lond. 1872. O.   **913.1 : 12**

Coffin, C: Carleton. Our new way round the world. Bost. 1881. O.   **913.1 : 51**

Coggeshall, G: Thirty-six voyages to various parts of the world, made between 1799 and 1841 ; selected from his ms. journal of 80 voyages. 3d ed., ill., rev., corr. and enl., with add. notes and explan. N. Y. 1858. O.   **913.1 : 15**

Field, H: Martyn. [Journey round the world]. From the lakes of Killarney to the Golden Horn ; From Egypt to Japan. N. Y. *n. d.* 2 v. D.   **913.1 : 18**

Gerstäcker, F: Reisen um die welt ; ein familienbuch. Leipz. 1856. 6 v. S.   **913.1 : 1**
— Reisen, 2te aufl. Jena. 1873. 2 v. D.
     913.1 : 2
Contents. Vol. **1.** Südamerika.— Californien.— Die Südseeinseln. **2.** *Same, continued.*—Australien.
— *Same, eng.* Narrative of a journey round the world ; comprising a winter-passage across the Andes to Chili, with a visit to the gold regions of California and Australia, the South sea islands, Java, etc. N. Y. 1854. D.   **913.1 : 2**

Morrell, B: Four voyages to the South sea, north and south Pacific ocean, Chinese sea, Ethiopic and southern Atlantic ocean, Indian and Antarctic ocean, from 1822 to 1831 ;

x denotes books specially adapted for children.

comprising critical surveys of coasts and islands, with sailing directions and an account of some new and valuable discoveries, includ. the Massacre islands, where 13 of the author's crew were massacred and eaten by the cannibals. Prefixed, a brief sketch of the author's early life. N. Y. 1832. O.
913.1 : 20

Pfeiffer, Ida Laura, *born* Reyer. A lady's voyage round the world ; a selected tr. from the german by mrs. Percy Sinnett. N. Y. 1852. D.
913.1 : 23

— A lady's second journey round the world ; from London to the cape of Good Hope, Borneo, Java, Sumatra, Celebes, Ceram, the Moluccas, etc., California, Panama, Peru, Ecuador and the United States. N. Y. 1856. D.
913.1 : 24

— Last travels, incl. of a visit to Madagascar, with an autobiogr. memoir of the author. Tr. by H. W. Dulcken. N. Y. 1861. D.
913.1 : 25

— Round the world ; a story of travel, compiled from the narrative of Ida Pfeiffer by D. Murray Smith. Ill. Lond. 1881. S.
x 913.1 : 47

Prime, E: Dorr Griffin. Around the world ; sketches of travel through many lands and over many seas. Ill. N. Y. 1876. D.
913.1 : 26

Pumpelly, Raphael. Across America and Asia ; notes of a five years' journey around the world and of residence in Arizona, Japan and China. [Map and ill.] N. Y. 1870. O.
913.1 : 64

Seward, W: H: Travels round the world ; ed. by Olive Risley Seward. N. Y. 1873. O.
913.1 + 42

Simpson, *Sir* G: An overland journey round the world, during 1841 and 1842. Phila. 1847. O.
913.1 : 29

Smiles, S:, *jr.* Round the world ; incl. a residence in Victoria and a journey by rail across North America, by a boy ; ed. by S: Smiles. Ill. N. Y. 1875. D.
913.1 : 30

Smith, *Capt.* J: The true travels, adventures and observations of captaine John Smith in Europe, Asia, Africke and America, 1593—1629, [with Generall historie of Virginia, New-England and the Summer Isles, etc.]. From the funtal. ed. of 1629. Richmond. 1819. 2 v. O.
913.1 : P31
Note. The "Generall historie" has a separate title page in v. 1. The title page of v. 2 reads "Generall historie, etc., v. 2".

— The adventures and discoveries of captain John Smith, some time president of Virginia and admiral of New England, newly ordered by John Ashton ; with ill. taken by him from orig. sources. N. Y. 1884. D.
913.1 : 55

Spalding, J. Willett. The Japan expedition : Japan and around the world ; an account of three visits to the Japanese empire, with sketches of Madeira, St. Helena, Cape of Good Hope, Mauritius, Ceylon, Singapore, China and Loo-Choo. Ill. N. Y. 1855.
915.2 : 4

Train, G: Francis. An american merchant in Europe, Asia and Australia ; a series of letters from Java, Singapore, China, Bengal, Egypt, the Holy Land, the Crimea and

its battle grounds, England, Melbourne, Sidney, etc.; with an introd. by Freeman Hunt. N. Y. 1857. D.
913.1 : 36

Cruises.

Stewart, C: S: A visit to the south seas, in the U. S. ship Vincennes, during 1829 and 1830; incl. notices of Brazil, Peru, Manilla, the Cape of Good Hope and St. Helena. N. Y. 1833. 2 v. D.
919.6 : 6

Reynolds, J: N. Voyage of the U. S. frigate Potomac, under the command of commodore John Downes, during the circumnavigation of the globe in 1831—1834 ; incl. a particular account of the engagement at Quallah-Battoo on the coast of Sumatra, with all the official documents. Ill. N. Y. 1835. O.
913.1 : 28

Wood, W: Maxwell. Wandering sketches of people and things in South America, Polynesia and California, and other places visited during a cruise on board of the U. S. ships Levant, Portsmouth and Savannah. Phila. 1849. D.
913.1 : 43

Coppinger, R: W. Cruise of the Alert ; four years in Patagonian, Polynesian and Mascarene waters, 1878—1882. Ill. Lond. 1883. Q.
913.1 + 44

Beehler, W: H. The cruise of the Brooklyn ; a journal of the principal events of a three years cruise in the U. S. flag-ship Brooklyn in the South Atlantic station, extending south of the equator from Cape Horn east to the limits in the Indian ocean of the 70th mer. of east long., descriptions of places in South America, Africa and Madagascar, with details of the peculiar customs and industries of their inhabitants, [incl.] the cruises of the other vessels of the american squadron from nov. 1881 to nov. 1884. Ill. Phila. 1885. O. **913.1 + 65**

Visits to several continents.

Aiton, J: The lands of the Messiah, Mahomet and the pope, as visited in 1851. 3d ed. Lond. 1854. D.
913.1 : 6

Bandmann, Daniel E. An actor's tour ; or Seventy thousand miles with Shakespeare ; ed. by Barnard Gisby. Portr. Bost. 1885. D.
913.1 : 59

Baynes, C. R. Notes and reflections during a ramble in the east, an overland journey from India, visit to Athens, etc. Lond. 1843. D.
913.1 : 7

Bisani, Alessandro. A picturesque tour through part of Europe, Asia and Africa ; containing many new remarks on the present state of society, remains of ancient edifices etc., with plates after designs by James Stuart, written by an italian gentleman. Lond. 1793. O.
913.1 : 32

Butler, W: Francis. Far out ; rovings retold. Lond. 1880. D.
913.1 : 10
Contents. Introd. chapter.—A dog and his doings. —A journey of a dog and a man from Cariboo to California.—The Yosemite valley.—Afghanistan and the afghans.—The zulus.—South Africa.—A plea for the peasant.—A trip to Cyprus.

Carpenter, Stephen Cullen, (*Donald Campbell*). A narrative of [his] extraordinary adventures and sufferings by shipwreck and imprisonment, with the singular humours of his tartar guide, Hassan Artaz ; compris-

---

x denotes books specially adapted for children.

ing the occurrences of four years and five days in an overland journey to India, in a series of letters to his son. 2d amer. ed. N. Y. 1798. S.   **913.1 : 11**

Coote, Walter. Wanderings, south and east. Maps and ill. Lond. 1882. O.   **913.1 : 63**
Contents. The australasian colonies.—The Pacific islands.—The far east.—Spanish America.

Day, H: A lawyer abroad ; what to see and how to see. N. Y. 1874. D.   **913.1 : 16**

Dilke, *Sir* C: Wentworth. Greater Britain ; a record of travel in english-speaking countries, during 1866 and 1867. Maps and ill. N. Y. 1869. D.   **913.1 : 17**

Eddy, Daniel Clarke, (*Rupert Van Wert*). Rip Van Winkle's travels in Asia and Africa. N. Y. [1882]. O.   **x 913.1 : 50**

Govea de Vittoria, P: Joannis Bisselii, è societate Jesu, Argonauticon americanorum, sive Historiae periculorum Petri de Victoria ac sociorum eïus libri XV. Monachii. 1647. T.   **23 : R**

Lowell, James Russell. Fireside travels. Bost. 1864. S.   **913.1 : 19**
Contents. Cambridge thirty years ago.—A Moosehead journal.—Leaves from my journal in Italy and elsewhere: At sea; In the Mediterranean; Italy; A few bits of roman mosaic.

MacMichael, Morton, *3d.* A landlubber's log of his voyage around Cape Horn ; a journal during a four months' voyage on an american merchantman, bound from Phila. to San Francisco. Phila. 1883 [1882]. D.   **913.1 : 52**

Maundevile, *Sir* J: The voiage and travaile of sir John Maundevile ; which treateth of the way to Hierusalem and of marvayles of Inde, with other ilands and countryes. Reprinted from the ed. of a. d. 1725, with an introd., add. notes and a glossary by J. O. Halliwell. Lond. 1883. O.   **913.1 : 58**

Minturn, Robert B., *jr.* From New York to Delhi, by way of Rio de Janeiro, Australia and China. N. Y. 1858. D.   **915.4 : 8**

Mitford, E: Ledwich. A land march from England to Ceylon forty years ago ; through Dalmatia, Montenegro, Turkey, Asia Minor, Syria, Palestine, Assyria, Persia, Afghanistan, Scinde, and India, of which 7000 miles on horseback. Ill. Lond. 1884. 2 v. O.   **913.1 : 62**

Oliphant, Laurence. Patriots and filibusters, or Incidents of political and exploratory travel. Edinb. 1860. D.   **913.1 : 21**
Contents. Patriots: [Travels in Circassia]; Progress and policy of Russia in central Asia.—Filibusters; [travels in the southern U. S. and Central America].

Ossoli, Sarah Margaret, *born* Fuller, *marchesa* d'. At home and abroad, or Things and thoughts in America and Europe; ed. by her brother, Arthur B. Fuller. 2d ed. Bost. 1856. D.   **913.1 : 22**

Pfeiffer, Emily. Flying leaves from east and west, 1885. Lond. [1885]. D.   **913.1 : 67**

Rand, E: A. All aboard for sunrise lands ; a trip through California, across the Pacific to Japan, China and Australia. Bost. [1881]. O.   **x 915 : 17**

Taylor, Bayard. At home and abroad ; a sketchbook of life, scenery and men. N. Y. 1885. D.   **913.1 : 34 v1**
Contents. The first journey I ever made.—A night walk.—First difficulties with foreign tongues.—A

x denotes books specially adapted for children.

Taylor, Bayard.—*Continued.*
young author's life in London. — The Atlantic. — Rambles in Warwickshire.—A walk from Heidelberg to Nuremberg.—Panorama of the upper Danube.— The road from Vienna to Trieste.—Smyrna and the grecian Archipelago.—A walk through the Thüringian forest.—My supernatural experiences.—More of the supernatural.—A november trip northwards.— The Mammoth cave.—Mackinaw and the lakes.—A telegraphic trip to Newfoundland.—Holidays in Switzerland and Italy. — A german home. — Life in the Thüringian forest.—Interviews with german authors. — Alexander v. Humboldt. — Summer gossip from England.—The castles of the Gleichen.—Weimar and its dead.—A german idyl.—The 300th anniversary of the university of Jena.—Some english celebrities.— Scenes at a target-schooting.—Aspects of german society.—A true story.—The landscapes of the world. —Preferences after seeing the world.

— *Same.* 2d series. N. Y. 1862. D. **913.1 : 34 v2**
Contents. A country home in America. — New pictures from California.—A home in the Thüringian forest.—A walk through the Franconian Switzerland. —Travels at home: The Hudson and the Catskills; Berkshire and Boston; The Saco valley; The ascent of Mt. Washington; Montreal and Quebec; Up the Saguenay; Niagara and its visitors; Trenton falls and Saratoga.—Personal sketches: The Leslies; The Brownings; The writers for "Punch"; Leigh Hunt; Hans Christian Andersen. — The confessions of a medium.—The haunted shanty.

— Egypt and Iceland in 1874. N. Y. 1874. D.   **913.1 : 33**

Thackeray, W: Makepeace. Notes of a journey from Cornhill to Grand Cairo, by way of Lisbon, Athens, Constantinople and Jerusalem by mr. M. A. Titmarsh. N. Y. 1848. D.   **913.1 : 35**

— *Same.* N. Y. 1846. D. *With* **Head,** *Sir* F. B. Bubbles.   **914.3 : 41**

Upham, T: Cogswell. Letters, æsthetic, social and moral, written from Europe, Egypt and Palestine. Phila. 1857. O. **913.1 : 37**

Vincent, Frank, *jr.* Through and through the tropics ; 30,000 miles of travel in Oceanica, Australasia and India. N. Y. 1876. D.   **915.4 : 23**

Wiggs, A. R. Hal's travels in Europe, Egypt and the Holy Land ; a twelve months tour during which he saw many wonderful things and a vast deal of fun. Nashville. 1861. D.   **913.1 : 40**

Mediterranean and the Orient.

Walpole, Robert, *ed.* Memoirs relating to european and asiatic Turkey and other countries of the east ; ed. from manuscript journals. 2d ed. Lond. 1818. Q.   **914.9 : R1**
Contents, see Catalogue of the Boston athenæum, v. 5, p. 3245.

— Travels in various countries of the east ; a continuation of Memoirs relating to european and asiatic Turkey, etc. Lond. 1820. Q.   **914.9 : R2**
Contents. **Hawkins,** J: On the tar springs of Zante. — **Sibthorp,** J. Voyage in the grecian seas. —**Whittington,** —. Discovery of the remains of the Acropolis of Patmos.—**Sibthorp,** J. Second voyage in the grecian seas. — **Hunt,** P. Lemnos. — **Sibthorp,** J. Continuation of journal. — *Same,* rel. to ancient Elis, Arcadia, Argolis, Laconia, Messenia and the islands on the western shores of Greece. — **Browne,** W: G. Journey from Constantinople through Asia Minor.—Biogr. memoir of mr. Browne. —**Leake,** W: M. Journey through some provinces of Asia Minor. — **Hawkins,** J: Some particulars respecting the police of Constantinople.—*Same.* An account of the discovery of a very ancient temple on mount Ocha. Eubœa. — **Squire,** J. Travels through part of the antient Coele Syria, and Syria Salutaria.— **Clarke,** E: D. Letter on a remarkable egyptian

bass-relief.—**Fazakerley**, J. Journey from Cairo to Mount Sinai, and return to Cairo. — **Hawkins**, J: On a law of custom which is peculiar to the islands of the archipelago.—**Cockerell**, C: R. The labyrinth of Crete. — **Wilkins**, W: On the sculptures of the Parthenon.—**Walpole**, R. Notice of some remarkable antiquities found among the ruins of Susa in Persia. — Figures on a supposed head of Isis. — **Sibthorp**, J. Natural history. — **Bilzoni**, G. B. Tr. of the arabic inscription found in the interior of the pyramid of Cephreues.—**Whittington**,-. Account of a journey through part of Little Tartary and some of the armenian, greek and tartar settlements in that portion of the Russian empire. — **Hawkins**, J: On the site of Dodona. — **Gordon**, G. H., *earl of Aberdeen*. Letter on the authenticity of the inscriptions of Fourmont. — **Leake**, W: M. Inscriptions copied in various parts of Greece. — **Walpole**, R. Remarks on the preceding. — **Cockerell**, C: R. Letters concerning inscriptions engraved in annexed plate. — **Walpole**, R. Remarks on the inscriptions discovered in Asia Minor by col. Leake and mr. Cockerell.— Inscriptions copied in different parts in Asia Minor, Greece and Egypt with remarks by the ed.—App.

Chateaubriand, François A: René *vicomte* de. Travels in Greece, Palestine, Egypt and Barbary during 1806, 1807. Tr. from the french by F. Shoberl. Map and ill. N. Y. 1814. O.   **915.6 : 15**

Turner, W: Journal of a tour in the Levant. Ill. Lond. 1820. 3 v. O.   **914.94 : 17**
Contents. V. 1. Cadiz, Gibraltar, Sicily, Malta, Milo and Constantinople.—Zante, Albania and Greece.— App. 2. Rhodes. Cyprus and Barout.—Mount Lebanon, Sidon, Tyre, Acre, Nazareth and the sea of Galilee, through Samaria to Jerusalem, Jaffa, Damietta, Rosetta, Cairo, Suez, Mount Sinai. and return to Alexandria and Cyprus.—App. 3. From Cyprus to Rhodes, Symi, Cos and Boudroun.—Melasso, Yassus, Miletus.—Patmos, Samos, and Scala Nova.— Ephesus, Smyrna, Brusa, and Constantinople. — Home through Brusa, Troad, Pergamus, Smyrna, Mitylen, Zante, Trieste, Venice, Milan and Paris.— Customs, etc., of the turks, arabs and greeks.

Emerson, James. Letters from the Ægean. N. Y. 1829. O.   **915.6 : 66**

Napier, Hungerford Delavan Elers. Excursions along the shores of the Mediterranean, [1837-38]. Lond. 1862. 2 v. O.   **914 : 62**

Schroeder, Francis. Shores of the Mediterranean. with sketches of travel. Ill. N. Y. 1846. 2 v. O.   **914 : 64**
Note. A record of the cruise of the U. S. squadron in 1843-45.

Pfeiffer, Ida Laura, *born* Reyer. Visit to the Holy Land, Egypt and Italy. Tr. from the germ. by H. W. Dulcken. Ill. 2d ed. Lond. 1853. D.   **915.6 : 35**

Browne, J: Ross. Yusef, or The journey of the Frangi ; a crusade in the east. Ill. Lond. 1853. O.   **915.6 : 12**
Contents. A gira through Sicily.—A crusade in the east.

Willis, Nathaniel Parker. Summer cruise in the Mediterranean on board an american frigate. N. Y. 1853. D.   **914 : 78**

Taylor, Bayard. The lands of the saracen, or Pictures of Palestine, Asia Minor. Sicily and Spain. N. Y. 1855. D.   **915.6 : 60**

Hackländer, F: W: Reise in den orient. Stuttg. 1855. 2 v. S.   **915.6 : 4**

Bremer, Fredrika. [Tagebuch im orient.]
    in **914 : 3 v7-16**
Contents, see under General european travel.

Wise, H: A:. (*Harry Gringo*). Scampavias from Gibel Tarek [*i. e.* Gibraltar] to Stamboul, by Harry Gringo. N. Y. 1857. D. **914 : 38**

Cox, S: Sullivan. Search for winter sunbeams in the Riviera, Corsica, Algiers and Spain. Ill. N. Y. 1870. O.   **914 : 28**

Warner, C: Dudley. In the Levant. Bost. 1877. D.   **915.6 : 8**

Moore, Joseph, *jr.* [The nearer orient.] *In his* Outlying Europe.   **914 : 59**

Cox, S: Sullivan. Orient sunbeans, or From the Porte to the pyramids by way of Palestine. N. Y. 1882. D.   **914.94 : 26**
Note. A continuation of his Arctic sunbeams.

Harriman, Walter. Travels and observations in the orient, and a hasty flight in the countries of Europe. Bost. 1883. D. **915.6 : 68**

De La Warr, Constance Mary Elizabeth, *born* Cochrane - Baillie, *countess*. An eastern cruise in the "Edeline". Edinb. 1877. S.   **914.9 : 5**

Wallace, Susan E. The storied sea, [the Mediterranean]. Bost. 1883. S.   **914 : 102**

4. Adventure.

Frost, J: The panorama of nations, comprising the characteristics of courage, perseverance, enterprise, cunning, shrewdness, vivacity, ingenuity, contempt of danger and of death. exhibited by people of the principal nations of the world, as ill. in narratives of peril and adventure. Auburn. *n. d.* D.   **913.2 : 7**

Headley, Joel Tyler, *ed.* Mountain adventures in various parts of the world ; sel. from the narratives of celebrated travellers, with an introd. and add. Ill. [Ill. lib. of wonders.] N. Y. 1872. D.   **913.2 : 6**

Mountains and mountain-climbing ; records of adventure and enterprise among the famous mountains of the world by the author of "The Mediterranean illustrated". Ill. N. Y. 1883. D.   **913.2 : 20**

Heroic adventure ; chapters in recent exploration and discovery. N. Y. [1882]. D.   **x 913.2 : 15**
Contents. Schweinfurth and the heart of Africa.— Prejevalsky in eastern Asia. — Commander Markham's whaling trip.—Vambéry's dervish disguise.— Markham's Arctic sledging experiences.—Maj. Serpa-Pinto's journey across Africa.—Nordenskiöld and the northeast passage.

Hale, E: Everett, *ed.* Stories of adventure, told by adventurers. Bost. 1881. S. **x 913.2 : 5**
Contents. Marco Polo.—Sir J: Mandeville and the crusades. — Bertrandon in Palestine. — Geoffrey of Vinsauf. — Hernando Cortes's Letters. — Fra Marco and Coronado.—The jesuit relations.—Northern discoveries.—Humboldt's travels.—A young man's voyage.— The northwest.—Siberia and Kamtschatka.— Index.

— — Stories of discovery told by discoverers. Bost. 1883 [1882]. S.   **x 913.2 : 13**
Contents. Introd.—Da Gama and the east.—Magalhaens and the Pacific. — Sir Francis Drake. — The Atlantic coast.—Voyages in the Pacific.—The northwest passage.—The source of the Nile.—The mouth of the Niger.—West of the Mississippi.—The Antarctic continent.

— — Stories of the sea, told by sailors. Bost. 1880. S.   **x 913.2 : 4**
Contents. Columbus's return from his first voyage.—The Chancellor voyage.—The spanish armada. The battle of Lepanto.—Sir R: Grenville.—Alexander Selkirk.—The buccaneers.—Paul Jones and R: Pearson.—Nelson and Trafalgar.—The english navy. — Pitcairn's island.—Naval battles.—Shipwrecks.

Book of the ocean, The, and life on the sea ; containing thrilling narratives and adventures of ocean life in all countries, from the earliest period. Ill. Auburn. *n. d.* 2 v. in 1. D.   **913.2 : 1**

x denotes books specially adapted for children,

Goodrich, Frank Boott. Man upon the sea, or A history of maritime adventure, exploration and discovery from the earliest ages to the present time; comprising a detailed account of remarkable voyages, ancient as well as modern. Ill. Phila. 1858. O.
913.2 : 2

Mariner's chronicle, The ; containing narratives of the most remarkable disasters at sea, such as shipwrecks, storms, fires and famines, also, naval engagements, piratical adventures, incidents of discovery and other extraordinary and interesting occurrences. New Haven. 1834. D   913.2 : 3

Senior, W:, (*Uncle Hardy*). Notable shipwrecks ; being tales of disaster and heroism at sea, re-told by Uncle Hardy. Lond. *n. d.* D.
x 913.2 : 9

Saxby, Mrs. —. Breakers ahead, or Uncle Jack's stories of great shipwrecks of recent times, 1869 to 1880. N. Y. 1882. D.
x 913.2 : 14

Payn, James. In peril and privation ; stories of marine disaster retold. Ill. N. Y. 1885. S.
x 913.2 : 24
Contents. The wreck of the "Grosvenor".—The loss of the "Royal George".—On the keys of Honduras.—The loss of the "Halsewell".—Wager island.—The trials of Philip Austin.—The wreck of the Juno.—A castaway ambassador.—The burning of the "New Horn".—In sight of home.—Arctic travel.—The undiscovered island.—The raft of the "Medusa".—The

burning of "Le prince".—The romance of M. de Belleisle.—Slavery.—The last extremity.

Dana, R: H:, *jr.* Two years before the mast ; a personal narrative of life at sea. [New issue.] N. Y. [1885]. D.   913.2 : 23

Dixon, Robert B. Fore and aft ; a story of actual sea life. Bost. 1883. D. x 913.2 : 16

Keane, J: F. On blue water ; some narratives of sport and adventure in the modern merchant service. Lond. 1883. O.
913.2 : 17

Richardson, Robert. Adventurous boat voyages. N. Y. 1884. S.   913.2 : 21

Andrews, W: A. A daring voyage across the Atlantic ocean, by two americans, the brothers Andrews : The log of the voyage by capt. W: A. Andrews, with introd. and notes by dr. Macaulay. Lond. 1880. D.
913.2 : 10

Friswell, James Hain. Out and about ; a boy's adventures written for adventurous boys. Ill. Lond. 1881. D.   x 913.2 : 11

Spooner, Walter W. The back-woodsmen, or Tales of the borders ; a collection of historical and authentic accounts of early adventure among the indians, with an introd. by Florus B. Plimpton. Ill. Cinc. 1883. O.
913.2+19

Keim, De B. Randolph. Sheridan's troopers on the borders ; a winter campaign on the plains. Ill. Phila. 1870. D.   913.2 : 8

For Classes 930-939, see col. 1161-1180.

5. Europe — a, In general.

1. History.

General.

Freeman, E: A: History of Europe. [History primers]. N. Y. 1877. S.   940 : 26

White, James. Eighteen christian centuries ; with a copious index. From the 2d Edinb. ed. N. Y. 1879. D.   940 : 5

Russell, W: The history of modern Europe ; a view of the progress of society from the rise of the modern kingdoms to the peace of Paris, in 1763 ; and a continuation to the present time, by W: Jones, with annotations by an american. N. Y. 1859. 1869. 3 v. O.   940+20
Contents. V. 1. From the rise of the modern kingdoms [a. d. 476], to the peace of Westphalia in 1648. 2. From the peace of Westphalia in 1648, to the peace of Paris in 1763. 3. From the peace of Paris in 1763, to the treaty of Amiens in 1802.

Thalheimer, Mary Elsie. A manual of medieval and modern history. Cinc. [1874]. O.
940 : 63

Stacke, L: Christian. Erzählungen aus der mittleren, neuen und neuesten geschichte. Oldenb. 1880–1885. 3 v. D.   940 : 64
Contents. V. 1. 13te aufl. 375–1437. 2. 11te aufl. Geschichte der entdeckungen. — Das zeitalter der reformation. — Das zeitalter Ludwigs XIV. — Die zeit Peters des grossen. — Das zeitalter Friedrichs des grossen.—Die französische revolution. 3. Die zeit vom Wiener kongress bis zur julirevolution, 1815 — 1830. — Von der julirevolution bis zur februarrevolution in Frankreich, 1830—1848.—Von der februarrevolution bis zum tode Friedrichs VII von Dänemark, 1848—1863. — Vom tode Friedrichs VII von Dänemark bis zum Frankfurter frieden, 1863—1871.

Pufendorf, *or* Puffendorf, S: *freiherr v.* An introd. to the history of the principal states of Europe, continued by mr. de La Martinière, improved by Joseph Sayer. New ed. rev. and corr. Lond. 1764. 2 v. O.
940 : 48

Smyth, W: Lectures on modern history ; from the irruption of the northern nations to the close of the american revolution. New ed. Lond. 1854. 2 v. D.   940 : 28
Contents. V. 1. List of books recommended. — Introd. lecture.—Barbarians and romans.—Laws of the barbarians.—Mahomet; progress of society, etc. — The dark ages.— England.— France.— Spain, Germany, Italy, Switzerland.—Reformation.—France; civil and religious wars.—Henry IV and the Low Countries. — Thirty years' war. — Henry VIII, Elizabeth, James I, Charles I.— Charles I.— Civil war. — Cromwell, Monk, regicides. — Charles II. 2. Charles II.— James II, revolution.— East and West Indies.—William III.—Anne.— Union of England and Scotland.—Sir Robert Walpole.— Law; Mississippi scheme, South Sea bubble, etc. — George II, Pelham, Rebellion of 1745. — Prussia and Maria Theresa.—George III.—American war.

Schlegel, K: W: F: v. A course of lectures on modern history [from the beginning of the middle ages to the revolution]; added, historical essays On the beginning of our history, and on Cæsar and Alexander. Tr. by Lyndsey Purcell and R. H. Whitelock. Lond. 1849. D.   940 : 27

Edgar, J: G: History for boys, or Annals of the nations of modern Europe. N. Y. *n. d.* S.
x 940 : 31

True stories from modern history ; chronol. arr. from the death of Charlemagne to the

x denotes books specially adapted for children.

battle of Waterloo, by the author of·True
stories from ancient history, Always happy,
etc. Revised and amended. Phila. *n. d.*
S.   x 940 : 30
Goodrich, S: Griswold, (*Peter Parley*). Lights
and shadows of european history. [Youth's
lib. of history]. Bost. [1844]. S.   x 940 : 37
Pryde, D: Great men of european history from
the beginning of the christian era [to a. d.
1864]. N. Y. [1869]. S.   x 940 : 40
— *Same.* Edinb. 1881. S.   x 940 : 40
Fischer, J. H. L. Schlachtengemälde aus Europa's vorzeit für freunde der geschichte, sowie überhaupt für gebildete leser. Leipz.
1839. D.   940 : 21
    Contents. Chalons, 451.—Taginas und Sarnus, 552.—
    Tours. 732.—Hastings, 1066.—Legnano, 1176.—Tiberias,
    1187.—Tolosa, 1212.—Bornhövet 1227.—Liegnitz, 1241.—
    Skurkola, 1268.—Morgarten, 1315; Laupen, 1339; Sem-
    pach, 1386; Granson, Murten, 1476; Nancy, 1477. —
    Tannenberg. 1410.—Alcazar, 1578. — Fehrbellin, 1675.—
    Pultawa, 1709.—Belgrad, 1717.

Medieval.

(For the beginning of the middle ages, see also Roman
history, cl. 937, col. 1180; and for the crusades,
see also cl. 274, col. 121).

Gibbon, E: [History of the middle ages to 1453].
In his Decline and fall of the Roman Em-
pire.   937.1 : 4
Duruy, V: Histoire du moyen âge, depuis la
chute de l'empire d'occident jusqu'au milieu
du 15e siècle. 11e éd. Paris. 1882. D.
    940 : 54
Dunham, S: Astley. A history of Europe during
the middle ages. [Lardner's cabinet cycl.].
Lond. 1833, 1834. 4 v. D.   940 : 61
Chambers, W: *and* Robert, eds. Mediæval history. [Chambers educational course].
Lond. 1855. S.   940 : 13
Grube, A: W: Heroes of history and legend ; [v.
2, The middle ages]. Tr. from the german
by J: Lancelot Shadwell. Lond. 1880. D.
    909 : 15 v2
Yonge, Charlotte Mary. Landmarks of history,
in 3 pts: pt. 2, Mediæval history from the
mahomedan invasion to the reformation ;
with alterations and amendments by Edith
L. Chase. 3d amer. ed., rev. N. Y. *n. d.* D.
    x 940 : 32
Smith, S: Francis, ed. Knights and sea-kings,
or The middle ages. Bost. *n. d.* D. 940 : 34
Hallam, H: View of the state of Europe during
the middle ages. N. Y. 1877. 3 v. D. 940 : 4
    Contents. V. 1. The history of France, from its
    conquest by Clovis to the invasion of Naples by
    Charles VIII. — Of the feudal system, especially in
    France.—The history of Italy, from the extinction of
    the Carlovingian emperors to the invasion of Naples
    by Charles VIII. 2. History of Spain, to the con-
    quest of Granada. — History of Germany, to the diet
    of Worms in 1495. — History of the greeks and sara-
    cens. — History of ecclesiastical power during the
    middle ages.—The constitutional history of England;
    The anglo-saxon constitution; The anglo-norman
    constitution. 3. *Same:* The english constitution. —
    On the state of society in Europe during the middle
    ages.—Index.
Stillé, C: J. Studies in mediæval history. Phila.
1882. D.   940 : 41
    Contents. General characteristics of the mediæval
    era.—The barbarians and their invasions.—The frank-
    ish conquests and Charlemagne.—Mohammed and his
    system. — Mediæval France. — Germany, feudal and
    imperial. — Saxon and danish England. — England,
    after the norman conquest.—The papacy to the reign
    of Charlemagne.—The papacy and the empire. — The

x denotes books, especially adapted for children.

struggle for italian nationality. — Monasticism, chivalry and the crusades. — Scholastic philosophy, the
schoolmen, universities.—The laboring classes in the
middle age.—Mediæval commerce. — The era of secu-
larization.—App.—Index.

Adams, G: Burton. Mediæval civilization. N.
Y. 1883. T.   309 : 21
Lacroix, Paul, (*Le bibliophile Jacob*). Manners,
customs and dress during the middle ages
and during the renaissance period. Ill.
Lond. 1876. Q.   392 : R1
    Contents, see col. 259.
— Military and religious life in the middle ages,
and at the period of the renaissance. Ill.
Lond. 1874. Q.   940 : R10
    Contents. Feudalism. — War and armies. — Naval
    matters.—The crusades.—Chivalry, duels and tourna-
    ments.—Military orders. — Liturgy and ceremonies.—
    The popes. — The secular clergy. — The religious
    orders.—Charitable institutions.—Pilgrimages.—Here-
    sies.—The inquisition. — Burials and funeral ceremo-
    nies.
Buckley, Theodore Alois. The great cities of
the middle ages, or The landmarks of european civilization ; historical sketches.
New ed. Ill. Lond. [1862]. S.   940 : 12
    Contents. Introd. — Aix-la-Chapelle. — Basle.— Up-
    sala and Stockholm. — Julin and Wisby. — Venice. —
    Florence.—Pisa and Genoa.— Rouen. — Paris. — Lon-
    don.—York.—Winchester.—Oxford.—Toledo.—Yuste.
    —Granada.— Cologne. — Nuremberg. — Hamburgh.—
    Malta.—Bagdad.

By periods.

Dahn, F: Julius Felix. Urgeschichte der germanischen und romanischen völker. (Oncken,
W:, *ed.* Allgemeine geschichte in einzeldarstellungen; 2te hauptabth., 2ter th.) Ill.
und karten. Berlin. 1881. 2 v. O.
    909 : 20 v2
Church, R: W: The beginning of the middle
ages. (Epochs of modern history). N. Y.
[1877]. S.   940 : 15
Ozanam, Antoine F: History of civilization in
the 5th century. Tr., by permission, from
the french by Ashley C. Glyn. Phila. 1867.
2 v. D.   940 : 56
Johnson, Arthur H: The normans in europe.
(Epochs of modern history). Maps. Bost.
1877. S.   940 : 17
    Note. A history of the scandinavian exodus from
    abt. 800 to 1066.
Sybel, H: v. The history and literature of the
crusades. From the german, ed. by lady
Duff Gordon. Lond. 1861. D.   940 : 59
Saint Maurice, C: R. E. de. Die geschichte der
kreuzzüge. Nach dem franz. von J. H. G.
Heusinger. (Allg. historische taschenbi-
bliothek, 7ter th.) Dresden. 1826. 3 v. in 1.
S.   940 : 62
Michaud, Joseph François. The history of the
crusades. Tr. by. W: Robson ; new ed.,
with pref. and supp. chapter by Hamilton
W. Mabie. N. Y. 1881. 3 v. D.   940 : 9
Proctor, G: History of the crusades ; their rise,
progress and results. Ill. Phila. 1860. O.
    940 : 6
Cox, *Sir* G: W: The crusades. (Epochs of mod-
ern history). N. Y. 1874. S.   940 : 16
Kugler, Bernhard. Geschichte der kreuzzüge.
(Oncken, W:, *ed.* Allgemeine geschichte
in einzeldarstellungen ; 2te hauptabth, 5ter
th.) Ill. und karten. Berlin. 1880. O.
    909+20 v5
Pears, Edwin. The fall of Constantinople ; the
story of the 4th crusade. N. Y. 1886 [1885].
O.   940 : 65

Sutherland, Alexander. Achievements of the knights of Malta. Phila. 1846. 2 v. in 1. D.
　　　　　　　　　　　　　　　　940 : 7

James, G: Payne Rainsford. The history of chivalry. [Harper's family lib.] N. Y. 1845. S.
　　　　　　　　　　　　　　　　940 : 11

Mills, C: The history of chivalry, or Knighthood and its times. Phila. 1844. O. *With his* History of the crusades.　　**274 : 1**

Doran, J: Knights and their days.　**824.2 : 37**
　Contents, see under English literature, Essays, col. 1058.

Bohn, H: G:, *ed.* Chronicles of the crusades; contemporary narratives of the crusade of Richard Cœur de Lion, by Richard of Devizes and Geoffrey de Vinsauf, and of the crusade of St. Louis by lord J: de Joinville; with ill. notes and index. Lond. 1848. D.　　　　　　　　　**940 : 14**

Froissart, *Sir* J: Chronicles of England, France, Spain and the adjoining countries, from the latter part of the reign of Edward II to the coronation of Henry IV. Tr. from the french, with variations and add. from many celebrated mss. by T: Johnes. Prefixed, life of the author, an essay on his works, and a criticism on his history with an original introd. essay on the character and society of the middle ages by J: Lord. N. Y. 1860. O.　　　　　**940 : 1**

— The boys' Froissart; being sir John Froissart's Chronicles of adventure, battle and custom in England, France, Spain, etc., ed. for boys with an introd. by Sidney Lanier. Ill. N. Y. 1879. O.　　　　**x 940 : 2**

Monstrelet, Enguerrand de. Chronicles; containing an account of the cruel civil wars between the houses of Orleans and Burgundy, of the possession of Paris and Normandy by the english, their expulsion thence and of other memorable events that happened in the kingdom of France, as well as in other countries; a history of fair example and of great profit to the french, beginning at the year 1400, where that of sir J: Froissart finishes, and ending at the year 1467, and continued by others to the year 1516. Tr. by T: Johnes. Lond. 1867. 2 v. O.　　　　**940 + 3**
　Contents. V. 1. Dacier, M. The life of Monstrelet, with an essay on his chronicles.—Observations on the chronicle by M. Foncamagne.— 1380—1435. 2. 1435—1516.

Jones, Meredith. Stories of the olden time, from De Joinville and Froissart. Lond. [1880]. D.　　　　　　**x 940 : 38**

S., E. L. Belt and spur; stories of the knights of the middle ages from the old chronicles. Ill. Lond. 1883. D.　　　**x 940 : 50**

Modern.

(For the period of the reformation, see also cl. 274, col. 121-124.)

Dyer, T: H: Modern Europe, from the fall of Constantinople to the establishment of the german empire, 1453—1871. 2d ed. rev. and continued. Lond. 1877. 5 v. O.
　　　　　　　　　　　　　　　　940 : 53
　Contents. V. 1. 1453—1530. 2. 1521—1598. 3. 1598—1721. 4. 1714—1796. 5. 1794—1871.

Duruy, V: Histoire des temps modernes, depuis 1453 jusqu'à 1789. 9e éd. Paris. 1881. D.
　　　　　　　　　　　　　　　　940 : 55

Michelet, Jules. Modern history [1453—1789]. From the french, with an introd. by A. Potter. [Harper's family lib.] N. Y. 1846. S.
　　　　　　　　　　　　　　　　940 : 8

Yonge, C: Duke. Three centuries of modern history, [1494-1821]. N. Y. 1878. D.
　　　　　　　　　　　　　　　　940 : 36

Yonge, Charlotte Mary. Landmarks of history; in 3 pts.: Pt. 3, Modern history from the beginning of the reformation to our times. 4th amer. ed., rev. and enl. N. Y. *n. d.* D.
　　　　　　　　　　　　　　x 940 : 33

Ranke, Franz Leopold v. Geschichten der romanischen und germanischen völker von 1494 bis 1514. 2te aufl. Leipz. 1874. 2 v. in 1. O.　　　　　**904 : 36 v33,34**

Raumer, F: L: G: v. Geschichte Europas seit dem ende des 15ten jahrh. Leipz. 1882-50. 8 v. O.　　　　　　　　**940 : 44**
　Contents. V. 1. Italien, Portugal, Spanien und Deutschland bis zum tode Karls V, 1494—1558. 2, Dänemark, Norwegen, Schweden, Frankreich und England bis zum tode Christians III, 1559, Gustavs I, 1550, Heinrichs IV, 1610, und Elisabeths, 1603. 3. Die Niederlande, Dänemark, Schweden und Deutschland vom tode Karls V, bis zum Westphälischen frieden, 1648. 4. Frankreich, 1610—1661. und England, 1603—1660. 5. *Same, continued.* — Schweden und Dänemark, 1632—1660.—Die vereinigten Niederlande, 1621—1661.—Spanien und Portugal während der regierungen Philipps III und Philipps IV. 6. Das südwestliche Europa, 1661—1715. 7. Das nördliche Europa von 1660 bis 1740, und das südwestliche Europa vom Utrechter frieden bis 1740. 8. Geschichte Frankreichs und der französischen revolution, 1740—1795.

Heeren, Arnold Hermann L: A manual of the history of the political system of Europe and its colonies, from its formation at the close of the 15th century to its re-establishment upon the fall of Napoleon. Tr. from the 5th german ed. Lond. 1846. O.
　　　　　　　　　　　　　　　　940 : 45

By periods.

Seebohm, F: The era of the protestant revolution. 2d ed., with notes on books in english relating to the reformation by G: P. Fisher. (Epochs of modern history.) N. Y. 1875. S.　　　　　**940 : 18**

Häusser, L: The period of the reformation; ed. by W: Oncken. Tr. by mrs. G. Sturge. New ed. N. Y. [1884]. D.　　**940 : 49**

Fischer, K: Geschichte der auswärtigen politik und diplomatie im reformations-zeitalter, 1485—1556. Gotha. 1874. O.　**940 : 57**

Maxwell, *Sir* W: Stirling-. Don John of Austria, or Passages from the history of the 16th century, 1547—1578. Ill. Lond. 1883. 2 v. Q.　　　　　　　　　　**940 + 51**

Philippson, Martin. Westeuropa im zeitalter von Philipp II, Elisabeth und Heinrich IV. (Oncken, W:, *ed.* Allgemeine geschichte in einzeldarstellungen; 3te hauptabth., 2ter th.) Portr., ill. und karten. Berlin. 1882. O.
　　　　　　　　　　　　　909 + 21 v2

Tillotson, J: Stories of the wars, 1574—1658, from the rise of the Dutch Republic to the death of Oliver Cromwell. Ill. Lond. [1865]. D.　　　　　**x 940 : 35**

Praet, Jules van. Essays on the political history of the 15th, 16th and 17th centuries; ed. by sir Edmund Head. Lond. 1868. O.
　　　　　　　　　　　　　　　　940 : 60
　Contents. Introd.—Charles V.—Philip II and William the silent.—Cardinal Richelieu,—The first English reformation.—William III.

x denotes books specially adapted for children.

Noorden, C: v. Europäische geschichte im 18ten jahrhundert, 1te abth: Der spanische erbfolgekrieg. Leipz. 1870–82. 3 v. O.   **940+58**

Gerard, James W. The peace of Utrecht; a historical review of the great treaty of 1713–14 and of the principal events of the war of the spanish succession. N. Y. 1885. O.   **940 : 66**

Russell, J:, *1st earl Russell.* Memoirs of the affairs of Europe, from the peace of Utrecht. Lond. 1824. 2 v. Q.   **940+P46**

Schlosser, F: Christoph. History of the 18th century and of the 19th, till the overthrow of the french empire, with particular reference to mental cultivation and progress. Tr. with a pref. and notes by D. Davidson. Lond. 1843. 8 v. O.   **940 : 52**

Alison, *Sir* Archibald. History of Europe from the commencement of the french revolution in 1789 to the restoration of the Bourbons in 1815. N. Y. 1847. 4 v. O.   **940+22**

— History of Europe from the fall of Napoleon in 1815 to the accession of Louis Napoleon in 1852. Edinb. 1854–59. 9 v. O.   **940+23**

Fyffe, C: Alan. A history of modern Europe, v. 1 ; From the outbreak of the revolutionary war in 1792 to the accession of Louis XVIII in 1814. Maps. N. Y. 1881. O.   **940 : 24**

Vane, C: W: Stewart, *1st earl Vane and 3d marquis of Londonderry.* Narrative of the war in Germany and France in 1813 and 1814. Phila. 1831. D.   **940 : 29**

Müller, W: Politische geschichte der neuesten zeit, 1816–1875, mit besonderer berücksichtigung Deutschlands. 3te aufl. Stuttg. 1875. O.   **940 : 42**

— *Same, eng.* Political history of recent times, 1816–1875, with special reference to Germany ; rev., and enl. by the author. Tr., with an app. covering the period from 1876 to 1881, by J: P. Peters. N. Y. 1882. D.   **940 : 42**

Mackenzie, Robert. The 19th century ; a history. N. Y. 1880. Q.   **940+25**

Present state of Europe, The ; explaining the interests, connections, political and commercial views of its several powers, comprehending also a clear and concise history of each country, so as to show the nature of their present constitutions. 6th ed. rev., corr. and continued by the author. Lond. 1861. O.   **940 : 19**

2. Description.

Geography.

Rudler, F. W., *and* G: G. Chisholm. Europe; ed. by Sir Andrew C. Ramsay, with ethnological app. by A. H. Keane. (Stanford's compendium of geography and travel, based on Hellwald's "Die erde und ihre völker".) Maps and ill. Lond. 1885. O.   **914 : 114**

Kohl, J: G: Die völker Europa's; cultur- und charakterskizzen der europäischen völker. 2te aufl. Hamburg. 1872. O.   **914+5**

Taylor, Bayard, *ed.* Picturesque Europe ; a delineation by pen and pencil of the natural features and the picturesque and historical places of Great Britain and the continent. Ill. N. Y. [1875–79]. 3 v. Q.   **914 : R116**
Contents. V. 1. Windsor.—Eaton.—North Wales.—Warwick and Stratford. — The south coast from Mar-

gate to Portsmouth. — The forest scenery of Great Britain. — The dales of Derbyshire. — Edinburgh and the south lowlands. — Ireland. — Scenery of the Thames. — The south coast from Portsmouth to the Lizard.—English abbeys and churches. — The Land's End.—Old english homes.—The west coast of Ireland. —Border castles and counties.—Cathedral cities.—The Grampians. — Oxford. — Scotland from Loch Ness to Loch Eil.—The west coast of Wales. — The lake country.
2. Cambridge.—The south coast of Devonshire.— South Wales. — North Devon. — The Isle of Wight.— Normandy and Brittany.— The italian lakes. — The passes of the Alps.—The Cornice road.—The forest of Fontainebleau.—The Rhine.— Venice. — The Channel islands. — The Pyrenees. — Rome and its environs. — The Tyrol.—Gibraltar and Ronda. — Dresden and the Saxon Switzerland.— Eastern Switzerland.—Constantinople.—Belgium.—The high Alps.—Granada and the east coast of Spain.—Russia.—The Jura.—Athens and its environs.—Holland.—The Danube.
3. Norway.—Spain, New Castile and Estremadura. —The Lake of Geneva.—The frontiers of France, east and south.—North Italy. — Norway, the Sogne Fjord, Nord Fjord, Ramsdal. — Spain, Cordova, Seville and Cadiz. — The frontiers of France, west and north. — Calabria and Sicily. — The Black Forest. — Sweden.— The Bernese Oberland.—The Rhine, from Boppart to the Drachenfels.– Spain, the north and Old Castile.— Auvergne and Dauphiné. — Old german towns. — Naples.

Fetridge, W. Pembroke, *ed.* Harper's handbook for travellers in Europe and the east ; a guide through Great Britain and Ireland, France, Belgium, Holland, Germany, Italy, Egypt, Syria, Turkey, Greece, Switzerland, Tyrol, Spain, Russia, Denmark, Norway, Sweden, United States and Canada. 22d year. Maps and plans. N. Y. 1883. 3 v. D.   **914 : 98**

Loomis, Lafayette C. The index guide to travel and art-study in Europe ; compendium of geographical, historical and artistic information for the use of americans, alphab. arr.; with plans and catalogues of the chief art galleries, tables of routes, maps and ill. N. Y. 1882. S.   **914 : 95**

Mortimer, E., *mrs.* T: Near home, or The countries of Europe described ; with anecdotes and numerous ill. [*Anon.*] N. Y. 1882. S.   **x914 : 81**

Travels.

In general.

Hunnewell, James F. The lands of Scott. Bost. 1880. D.   **914 : 47**
Note. Contains descriptions of and visits to the places in Scotland, England, France, Spain, Belgium, the valley of the Rhine, Switzerland and the east, in which the scenes of Scott's writings are laid, and also incidents of Scott's life and work.

Heine, H: Reisebilder. *In his* Sämmtliche werke.   **830 : 139 v1, 2**
Contents, *see* Deutscher katalog, p. 20.

— Englische fragmente. *In the same.*   **830 : 139 v3**

— *Same, eng.* Pictures of travel. Tr. from the german by C: Godfrey Leland. 9th rev. ed. Phila. 1882. D.   **914 : 119**
Contents. The homeward journey, 1823–24. — The Hartz journey, 1824.—The North Sea, 1825–26. — Ideas. —A new spring.— Italy, 1828. — English fragments, 1828.

Longfellow, H: Wadsworth. Outre-mer ; a pilgrimage beyond the sea [1833]. 7th ed. Bost. 1855. D.   **914 : 53**

— *Same. In his* Works.   **820.1 : R12 v3**

x denotes books specially adapted for children.

Vane, C: W: Stewart, *1st earl Vane and 3d marquis of Londonderry.* A steam voyage to Constantinople by the Rhine and Danube, in 1840–41, and to Portugal, Spain, etc., in 1839. Annexed, the author's correspondence with prince Metternich, lords Ponsonby, Palmer ston, etc. Lond. 1842. 2 v. O.   **914 : 75**

Andersen, Hans Christian. A poet's bazaar ; a picturesque tour in Germany, Italy, Greece, and the orient, [1840–41]. Author's ed. Bost. 1879. D.   **914 : 1**

— Pictures of travel, in Sweden, among the Hartz mountains and in Switzerland, with a visit to C: Dickens' house, [1849–51]. Author's ed. Bost. 1880. D.   **914 : 82**

Channing, Walter. A physician's vacation in Europe, [1852]. Bost. 1856. O.   **914 : 21**

Bremer, Fredrika. Life in the old world, or Two years in Switzerland and Italy, [1856–58]. Tr. by Mary Howitt. Phila. [1860]. 2 v. D.   **914 : 117**

— Leben in der alten welt ; tagebuch während eines vierjährigen aufenthalts im süden und im orient. Aus dem schwed. Leipz. 1861. 16 v. S.   **914 : 3**
Contents. V. 1-6. Die Schweiz und Italien. 7-11. Die Türkei und Palästina. 12-16. Griechenland und dessen inseln.—Venedig und Mailand.—In Deutschland.—In Schweden.

Hackländer, F: W: Tagebuch-blätter. Stuttg. 1861. 2 v. S.   **914 : 4**
Contents. V. 1. Venedig, Paris, 1851. 2. London, 1851.—Ungarn in 1857.—Die feste in Russland in 1846.

Hartmann, Moritz. Reisebriefe. *In his* Sämmtliche werke.   **830 : 138 v3**
Contents. Briefe aus Dublin, 1850. — Tagebuch aus Languedoc und Provence, 1851.—Wanderungen durch celtisches land.—Bilder aus Dänemark, 1859.

Taylor, Bayard. By-ways of Europe, [about 1862]. Household ed. N. Y. 1878. D.   **914 : 69**
Contents. A familiar letter to the reader.—A cruise on Lake Ladoga. — Between Europe and Asia. — Winter-life in St. Petersburg. — The little land of Appenzell.— From Perpignan to Montserrat. — Balearic days.—Catalonian bridle-roads. — The republic of the Pyrenees.— The Grande Chartreuse. — The Kyffehäuser and its legends. — A week on Capri. — A trip to Ischia.—The land of Paoli.—The island of Maddalena, with a distant view of Caprera. — In the Teutoberger forest.

Macgregor, J: A thousand miles in the Rob Roy canoe on rivers and lakes of Europe, [1805]. Ill. and map. 7th ed. Bost. 1871. S.   **914 : 56**

— The voyage alone in the yawl Rob Roy, from London to Paris, and by Ha₊re across the channel to the Isle of Wight, south coast, etc. [1867]. 4th ed. Lond. 1880. S.   **914 : 55**

Clemens, S: Langhorne, *(Mark Twain).* The innocents abroad, or The new pilgrims' progress ; being some account of the steamship Quaker City's pleasure excursion to Europe and the Holy Land ; with descriptions of countries, nations, incidents and adventures, as they appeared to the author. Ill. Hartford, Conn. 1878. O.   **914 : 23**

— *Same.* Hartford. 1884. O.   **914 : 23**

— A tramp abroad. Ill. Hartford. 1880. O.   **914 : 24**

Moore, Joseph, *jr.* Outlying Europe and the nearer orient ; a narrative of recent travel. Phila. 1880. O.   **914 : 59**
Contents. Pt. 1. A winter in the south. — Pt. 2. A summer in the north.

On the Rhine, and other sketches of european travel. Phila. 1881. O.   **914 + 44**
Contents. **Murphy,** *Lady* B. Down the Rhine.— **Trollope,** T. A. Baden and Allerheiligen.—**Wister,** S. B. Why do we like Paris?—**Catlin,** G: L. Among the biscayans.—**Lejeune,** L. Trouville.—**McLeod,** R. A. The italian lakes.—**R.,** W. D. Easter on the Riviera.—**Bacon,** A. T. A month in Sicily.—**Harrison,** J. A. Glimpses of Sweden. — **Sikes,** O. Try Norway.—**King,** E: Hungarian types and austrian pictures; Old corners of Austria; Along the Danube.

Seguin, L. G. A picturesque tour in picturesque lands ; France, Spain, Germany, Switzerland, Holland, Belgium, Tyrol, Italy, Scandinavia. Lond. 1882. F. **914 : R113**

Stoddard, J: L. Red-letter days abroad. Ill. Bost. 1884 [1883]. O.   **914 : 103**
Contents. Travels in sunny Spain.—The passion play at Ober-Ammergau in 1880.—The cities of the czar: St. Petersburg; Moscow.

Pitman, Marie J., *born* Davis, *(Margery Deane).* European breezes. Bost. 1882. S. **914 : 120**
Contents. North Germany, Austria, Hungary, Switzerland.

Aldrich, T: Bailey. From Ponkapog to Pesth. Bost. 1883. D.   **914 : 99**

Eddy, Daniel Clarke, *(Rupert Van Wert).* Rip Van Winkle's travels in foreign lands. N. Y. [1881]. O.   **x 914 : 76**

Hale, E: Everett *and* Susan. A family flight through France, Germany, Norway and Switzerland. Bost. [1881]. O. **x 914 : 40**

Butterworth, Hezekiah. Zigzag journeys in classic lands, or Tommy Toby's trip to Mount Parnassus. Bost. 1881. O.   **x 914 : 15**

— Zigzag journeys in Europe ; vacation rambles in historic lands. [Ill.] Bost. 1881. O.   **x 914 : 14**

— Zigzag journeys in the orient, the Adriatic to the Baltic ; a journey of the Zigzag club from Vienna to the Golden Horn, the Euxine, Moscow and St. Petersburg. Ill. Bost. 1882 [1881]. O.   **x 914 : 16**

— Zigzag journeys in northern lands ; the Rhine to the Arctic ; a summer trip of the Zigzag club through Holland, Germany, Denmark, Norway and Sweden. Ill. Bost. 1884 [1883]. O.   **x 914 : 101**

Abbott, Jacob. Rollo's tour in Europe. N. Y. [1858]. 10 v. S.   **x 914 : 83–x 914 : 92**
Contents. V. 1. On the Atlantic. x 914: 83. 2. In Paris. x 914: 84. 3. In Switzerland. x 914: 85. 4. In London. x 914: 86. 5. On the Rhine. x 914 :87. 6. In Scotland. x 914: 88. 7. In Geneva. x 914: 89. 8. In Holland. x 914: 90. 9. In Naples. x 914: 91. 10. In Rome. x 914: 92.

-- Florence's return. (The Florence stories.) N. Y. 1864. S.   **x 914 : 110**

West and south.

Burnet, Gilbert. Some letters containing an account of what seem'd most remarkable travelling thro' Switzerland, Italy, some parts of Germany, etc., in 1685 and 1686. Added, an app. containing some remarks on Switzerland and Italy, by a person of quality and communicated to the author. Lond. 1724. D.   **914 : 13**

Moore, J: A view of society and manners in France, Switzerland and Germany ; with anecdotes relating to some eminent characters. 7th ed. Lond. 1789. 2 v. O.   **914 : 60**

---

x denotes books specially adapted for children.

Göthe, J: Wolfgang v. Reisen. *In his* Werke. **830 : 137 v25**
Contents. Campagne in Frankreich, 1792. — Belagerung von Mainz, 1793. — Aus einer reise in die Schweiz, 1797.

Berrian, W: Travels in France and Italy in 1817 and 1818. N. Y. 1821. O. **914.5 : 4**

Carter, Nathaniel Hazeltine. Letters from Europe ; comprising the journal of a tour through Ireland, England, Scotland, France, Italy and Switzerland in 1825–1827. N. Y. 1827. 2 v. O. **914+19**

Pückler-Muskau, Hermann L: H: *fürst* v. Tour in England, Ireland and France, in 1826–1829 ; with remarks on the manners and customs of the inhabitants and anecdotes of distinguished public characters, in a series of letters by a german prince. [*Anon.*] Phila. 1833. O. **914 : 63**

Willis, Nathaniel Parker. Pencillings by the way, 1832–34. *T. p. w.* S. **914 : 79**

Dewey, Orville. The old world and the new, or A journal of reflections and observations made on a tour in Europe, [1833–34]. N. Y. 1836. 2 v. D. **914 : 31**

Humphrey, Heman. Great Britain, France and Belgium ; a short tour in 1835. Amherst. 1838. 2 v. D. **914 : 46**

Bechstein, L: Die reisetage ; aus meinem leben. Mannheim. 1836. 2 v. S. **914 : 2**
Contents, see Deutscher katalog, p. 37.

Breckinridge, Robert Jefferson. Memoranda of foreign travel ; containing notices of a pilgrimage through some of the principal states of western Europe, [1836–37]. Balt. 1845. 2 v. D. **914 : 10**

Fisk, Wilbur. Travels on the continent of Europe ; in England, Ireland, Scotland, France. Italy, Switzerland, Germany and the Netherlands. Ill. N. Y. 1838. O. **914 : 36**

Sedgwick, Catharine Maria. Letters from abroad to kindred at home, [1839–40]. N. Y. 1845. 2 v. D. **914 : 65**
Contents. V. 1. London, Belgium, the Rhine, Switzerland. 2. Italy.

Hall, Basil. Patchwork. Phila. 1841. 2 v. D. **914 : 41**
Contents. V. 1. Switzerland, France, Italy. 2. Italy. — On the improvements which have been introduced into the arts of seamanship and navigation of late years.

Catlin, G: Notes of eight years travels [from 1839] and residence in Europe with his north american indian collection ; with anecdotes and incidents of the travels and adventures of three different parties of american indians whom he introduced to the courts of England, France and Belgium. Ill. 2d ed. Lond. 1848. 2 v. O. **914 : 20**

Durbin, J: Price. Observations in Europe, principally in France and Great Britain, [1842]. 9th ed. N. Y. 1848. 2 v. D. **914 : 32**

Colman, H: European life and manners ; in familiar letters to friends, [1843–48]. Bost. 1850. 2 v. D. **914 : 25**
Contents. V. 1. Great Britain. 2. Great Britain, France, Italy, Up the Rhine.

Taylor, Bayard. Views a-foot, or Europe seen with knapsack and staff, [1841–46]. Household ed., rev. N. Y. 1879. D. **914 : 70**
— *Same.* Kennett ed., rev. Ill. N. Y. 1884. O. **914 : 70**

Corson, J: W. Loiterings in Europe, or Sketches of travel in France, Belgium, Switzerland, Italy, Austria, Prussia, Great Britain and Ireland ; with an app. containing observations on european charities and medical institutions, [1846]. 2d ed. N. Y. 1848. D. **914 : 18**

Mitchell, Donald Grant, (*Ik Marvel*). Fresh gleanings, or A new sheaf from the old fields of continental Europe, by Ik Marvel. N. Y. 1847. D. **914 : 58**
Contents. First step toward the continent [to Paris]. —The country towns and inns of France.—A gallop through southern Austria.—A pipe with the dutchmen.

Lee, Edwin. Continental travel ; with an app. on the influence of climate, the remedial advantages of travelling, etc. Lond. 1848. O. **914 : 54**

Stahr, Fanny, *born* Lewald. Erinnerungen aus dem jahre 1848. Brschw. 1852. 2 v. in 1. D. **914 : 7**
Contents, see Deutscher katalog, p. 39.

Kirkland, Caroline Matilda. Holidays abroad, or Europe from the west. N. Y. 1849. 2 v. D. **914 : 50**

Calvert, G: H: Scenes and thoughts in Europe ; 1st and 2d series. [1840–43, 1850]. New ed. Bost. 1863. 2 v. D. **914 : 17**

Clarke, James Freeman. Eleven weeks in Europe and what may be seen in that time, [1849]. Bost. 1852. D. **914 : 22**

Bullard, *Mrs.* Anna T. Jones. Sights and scenes in Europe ; a series of letters from England, France, Germany, Switzerland and Italy, in 1850. St. Louis. 1852. D. **914 : 12**

Copway, G:, *or* Kah-ge-ga-gah-bowh. Running sketches of men and places in England, France, Germany, Belgium and Scotland. Ill. N. Y. 1851. D. **914 : 26**

Silliman, B: A visit to Europe, in 1851. N. Y. 1854. 2 v. D. **914 : 66**

Murray, N:, (*Kirwan*). Men and things as I saw them in Europe [1851], by Kirwan. N. Y. 1854. D. **914 : 61**

Greeley, Horace. Glances at Europe in a series of letters from Great Britain, France, Italy, Switzerland, etc., during the summer of 1851 ; incl. notices of the great exhibition or world's fair. N. Y. 1851. D. **914 : 37**

Tappan, H: Philip. A step from the new world to the old and back again ; with thoughts on the good and evil in both. N. Y. 1852. 2 v. D. **914 : 68**
Contents. V. 1. England, Scotland, Holland. 2. The Rhine, Switzerland, Belgium, France.

Cox, S: Sullivan. A buckeye abroad, or Wanderings in Europe and in the orient. N. Y. 1852. D. **914 : 27**

Le Vert, Octavia, *born* Walton. Souvenirs of travel, [1852–55]. N. Y. 1857. 2 v. S. **914 : 52**

Tripp, Alonzo. Crests from the ocean-world, or Experiences in a voyage to Europe, principally in France, Belgium and England, [1853] ; comprising sketches in the miniature worlds, Paris, Brussels and London, by a traveller and teacher. Bost. 1864. D. **914 : 73**

Felton, Cornelius Conway. Familiar letters from Europe, [1853–54]. Bost. 1865. D. **914 : 35**

Stowe, Harriet Elizabeth, *born* Beecher. Sunny memories of foreign lands. Ill. Bost. 1854. 2 v. D. **914 : 97**

Haskins, G: Foxcroft. Travels in England, France, Italy and Ireland, [1854]. Bost. 1856. D.   **914 : 43**

Leland, C: Godfrey. Meister Karl's sketch book. Phila. 1855. D.   **914 : 51**

De Forest, J: W: European acquaintance; being sketches of people in Europe. N. Y. 1858. O.   **914 : 30**

Bryant, W: Cullen. Letters of a traveller; 2d series. N. Y. 1859. D.   **914 : 11**

Fairbanks, C: Bullard. Aguecheek. [*Anon*]. Bost. 1859. D.   **914 : 33**
Contents. Sketches of foreign travel. — Essays: Street life; Hard up in Paris; The old corner; Sacred to the memory of Theatre alley; The old cathedral; The philosophy of suffering; Boyhood and boys; Girlhood and girls; Shakespeare and his commentators; Memorials of mrs. Grundy; The philosophy of life; Behind the scenes; The philosophy of cant.

Field, H: Martyn. Summer pictures from Copenhagen to Venice. N. Y. 1859. D.   **914 : 34**

Hale, E: Everett. Ninety days' worth of Europe, [1859]. Bost. 1861. D.   **914 : 39**

Hawthorne, Nathaniel. Passages from the french and italian note-books, [1858—1862]. Bost. 1879. 2 v. in 1. D.   **914.5 : 17**

Rodenberg, Julius. Verschollene inseln; sandund seebilder. Berlin. 1861. D. **914.96 : 1**
Contents. Die matrosen von St. Pauli in Hamburg. —Die düne von Helgoland.—Stilleben auf Sylt.—Die insel Thanet.—Jersey und Guernsey.—Schlusswort.

Haven, Gilbert. The pilgrim's wallet, or Scraps of travel, gathered in England, France and Germany. N. Y. 1866. D.   **914 : 96**

Meissner, Alfred. Unterwegs; reisebilder. Leipz. 1867. D.   **914 : 6**
Contents. From Bregenz to Scotland over Belgium.

Bellows, H: Whitney. The old world in its new face; impressions of Europe in 1867—1868; v. 1. N. Y. 1868. D.   **914 : 8**
Note. Contains principally Switzerland and Germany.

Urbino, Lavinia Buoncore. An american woman in Europe; the journal of two years and a half sojourn in Germany, Switzerland, France and Italy. Bost. 1869. D. **914 : 74**

Jackson, Helen Maria, *born* Fiske, *formerly mrs.* Hunt, (*H. H.*). Bits of travel. Bost. 1872. T.   **914 : 48**

Wallace, *Mrs.* E. D. A woman's experiences in Europe, incl. England, France, Germany and Switzerland. N. Y. 1872. D. **914 : 77**

Warner, C: Dudley. Saunterings. Bost. 1872. T.   **914 : 104**
Contents. Misapprehensions corrected. — Paris and London.—The low countries and Rhineland.— Alpine notes.—Bavaria.— Looking for warm weather. — Ravenna.—A high day in Rome. — Vesuvius. — Sorrento days.

Holiday rambles in ordinary places, by a wife with her husband. Repr. from the "Spectator". Lond. 1880. D.   **914 : 45**
Contents. A wife on her travels, 1867: The Engadin; The Bernese Alps. — Rambles of a working man in search of rest, 1868: The Jura, *etc.* — Letters of an english woman in difficulties, 1870: The Ammergau play; The Oetzthal and Hochjoch; The war.— A holiday in Yorkshire, 1874.—A summer driving-tour, 1875: Winchester; The New Forest; Stonehenge. — A drive in Devonshire, 1876: Lyme Regis and Dartmoor.

Moulton, Ellen Louise, *born* Chandler. Random rambles. Bost. 1881. T.   **914 : 118**

James, H: Portraits of places. Bost. 1884. D.   **914 : 112**
Contains chapters on Venice.—Turin.—Genoa.—Florence.—Paris.—Rheims.—Chartres.—Rouen.—Etretat. — Normandy.— English life. — Saratoga, Newport,

James, H:—*Continued.*
Quebec, Niagara, in 1871. — All except Venice, are among the author's earlier efforts, publ. in various periodicals.

— Transatlantic sketches. Bost. 1875. D.   **914 : 49**
Contents. Chester.—Lichfield and Warwick.—North Devon.— Wells and Salisbury. — Swiss notes. — From Chambéry to Milan. — From Venice to Strasburg. — The Parisian stage. — A roman holiday. — Roman brides.—Roman neighborhoods.—The after-season in Rome.—From a roman note-book. — A chain of cities. —The St. Gothard.—Siena.—The autumn in Florence. —Florentine notes.—Tuscan cities. — Ravenna.—The Splägen.—Homburg reformed. — Darmstadt.—In Holland.—In Belgium.

Trafton, Adeline. An american girl abroad. Ill. Bost. 1875. D.   **914 : 72**

Hamerton, Philip Gilbert. A painter's camp. Bost. 1876. D.   **914 : 42**
England.—Scotland.—France.

Terhune, Mary Virginia, *born* Hawes, (*Marion Harland*). Loiterings in pleasant paths. N. Y. 1880. D.   **914 : 71**

Warner, C: Dudley. A roundabout journey. Bost. 1884 [1883]. O.   **914 : 111**
Contents. France, Spain, Italy, 1881.

Croffut, W: A. A midsummer lark. (Leisure hour ser.) N. Y. 1883. S.   **914 : 100**
Note. A story of travel in rhymed prose.

Champney, Lizzie, *born* Williams. Three Vassar girls abroad; rambles of three college girls on a vacation trip through France and Spain for amusement and instruction, with their haps and mishaps. Ill. Bost. 1883 [1882]. D.   **914 : 93**

North and east.

Wraxall, *Sir* Nathaniel W: A tour through some of the northern parts of Europe, particularly Copenhagen, Stockholm and Petersburgh, in a series of letters. 2d ed., corr. Lond. 1775. O.   **914 : 80**

Coxe, W: Travels in Poland, Russia, Sweden and Denmark, [1784—85]. Ill. with charts and engr. 5th ed. Lond. 1802. 5 v. O.   **914 : 29**
Contents. V. 1. Poland—Russia. 2. Russia, *continued.*—App. 3. Russia, *continued.*—App. 4. Sweden.—App. 5. Norway.—Sweden.—Denmark.—App. —Index.

Grosvenor, Elizabeth Mary, *marchioness of Westminster.* Diary of a tour in Sweden, Norway and Russia, in 1827, with letters. Lond. 1879. O.   **914.8 : 29**

Tietz, F: St. Petersburgh, Constantinople and Napoli di Romania, in 1833 and 1834; a characteristic picture, drawn during a residence there. N. Y. 1836. D. **914.7 : 15**

Stephens, J: Lloyd. Incidents of travel in Greece, Turkey, Russia, and Poland. [1835]. [*Anon.*] Map and ill. 7th ed. N. Y. 1845. 2 v. D.   **914 : 67**

Maxwell, J: S. The czar, his court and people; incl. a tour in Norway and Sweden. N. Y. 1848. D.   **914.7 : 6**

Taylor, Bayard. Travels in Greece and Russia; with an excursion to Crete, [1857-58]. N. Y. 1868. D.   **914.93 : 11**

Macgregor, J: The Rob Roy on the Baltic; a canoe cruise through Norway, Sweden, Denmark, Sleswig Holstein, the North Sea and the Baltic, [1866]. Ill., maps and music. 3d ed. Bost. *n. d.* S.   **914 : 57**

Atkinson, J. Beavington. An art tour to northern capitals of Europe, [1870]. Lond. 1873. O.   **914 : 115**
Contents. Copenhagen.—Thorwaldsen.—Christiania.—Stockholm. — Åbo, Helsingfors and Wiborg. — St. Petersburg: The Hermitage; The picture galleries in the Hermitage; The Kertch antiquities and the miscellaneous collections in the Hermitage.—Russian artists.— The imperial manufactory of mosaics at St. Petersburg. — Landscape painting in Russia.—Moscow.—Art-education in Moscow.—Kief, the city of pilgrimage.—Relation between the religious arts, the russian church and the russian people.—App.—Index.

Brassey, Anna, *born* Allnutt, *lady.* Sunshine and storm in the east, or Cruises to Cyprus and Constantinople. Ill. N. Y. 1880. O.   **914 : 9**
Contents. Constantinople, Ionian Islands, 1874. — Cyprus, Constantinople, 1878.—App.—Index.

Cox, S: Sullivan. Arctic sunbeams, or From Broadway to the Bosphorus by way of the North Cape. N. Y. 1882. D.   **914 : 94**
Note. For continuation, see his Orient sunbeams.

Mediterranean countries.
(See also col. 1194-1196.)

Beckford, W: Italy, Spain and Portugal, with an excursion to the monasteries of Alcobaça and Batalha. N. Y. 1845. 2 v. in 1. D.   **914.5 : 3**

Dix, J: Adams. A winter in Madeira, and a summer in Spain and Florence. 4th ed. N. Y. 1851. D.   **914.6 : 28**

Colton, Walter. Ship and shore in Madeira, Lisbon and the Mediterranean. Rev. from the "Journal of a cruise in the frigate Constellation", by H: T. Cheever. N. Y. 1860. D.   **914.6 : 9**

Miller, W: Wintering in the Riviera with notes of travel in Italy and France, and practical hints to travellers. Ill. Lond. 1879. O.   **914.5 : 25**

Black, C. B. The Riviera, or The coast from Marseilles to Leghorn, incl. Carrara, Lucca, Pisa, Pistoja and Florence. Maps and plans. Edinb. 1884. S.   **914.5 : 71**

6. Europe — b, Great Britain and Ireland.

1. Irish history.
(See also British domestic relations, col. 172.)

O'Grady, Standish. History of Ireland, critical and philosophical; v. 1. Lond. 1881. O.   **941 : 18**
Contents. V. 1. Pre-historic Ireland; testimony of rock and cave.—Classical references to Ireland. — Introduction to the bardic history of Ireland.—Predecessors and progenitors of the irish gods.—Classic gods of ethnic Ireland.—Natural mythology of the irish. — Pre-historic kings of Ireland, being chief persons of ancient heroic cycles.—Approach of the great Red Branch cycle.—Tara and her kings.—Ossian and the ossianic heroes.—Irish military predominance.—Verification of the irish bardic history; how far reliable, doubtful and mythical.

Mac-Geoghegan, Jacques. The history of Ireland ancient and modern, taken from the most authentic records; with a continuation from the treaty of Limerick to the present time, by J: Mitchel. N. Y. [1868]. Q.   **941+16**

McCarthy, Justin Huntly. An outline of irish history from the earliest times to the present day. N. Y. 1883. Q.   **941+29**
— *Same.* Baltimore. 1883. D.   **941 : 29**
Contents. The legends.—Christianity.—The norman conquest.—Elizabeth.—The Cromwellian settlement. The restoration; William of Orange.—The eighteenth century. — Emmet ; O'Connell. — Young Ireland ; Fenianism. — The land question; Home rule; The land league.

Giraldus de Barri *Cambrensis.* Historical works; containing the Topography of Ireland, and the History of the conquest of Ireland, tr. by T: Forester; the Itinerary through Wales, and the Description of Wales, tr. by sir R: Colt Hoare. Rev. and ed. with add. notes by T: Wright. Lond. 1863. D.   **941 : 1**

Moore, T: The history of Ireland, commencing with its earliest period, to the great expedition against Scotland in 1545. Phila. 1843. 2 v. O.   **941+17**

Walpole, C: G: A short history of the kingdom of Ireland, from the earliest times to the union with Great Britain. N. Y. 1882. D.   **941 : 26**
— *Same.* N. Y. 1882. Q.   **941+26**

Taylor, W: Cooke. History of Ireland from the anglo-norman invasion till the union of the country with Great Britain ; with add. by W: Sampson. [Harper's family lib.] N. Y. 1847. 2 v. S.   **941 : 20**
Contents. V. 1. 1169–1649. 2. 1649–1801.

McGee, T: D'Arcy. A popular history of Ireland, from the earliest period to the emancipation of the catholics, [1829]. N. Y. 1864. 2 v. D.   **941 : 15**

Bagwell, R: Ireland under the Tudors; with a succinct account of the earlier history. [Maps.] Lond. 1885. 2 v. O.   **941 : 45**

Froude, James Anthony. The english in Ireland in the 18th century. N. Y. 1873-75. 3 v. D.   **941 : 25**
Contents. V. 1. Preliminary. — Insurrection of 1641.—The revolution. — Opening of the penal era.—First attempt at union.—Protestant administration. Irish ideas. — The smugglers. — Efforts of the irish parliament.—Progress of anarchy. 2. The revival of the celts. — Lord Townshend's administration. — Lord Harcourt and colonel Blaquiere.—The beginnings of retribution.—The constitution of 1782.—The convention. — Whiteboys, high and low. 3. The united irishmen.—The Fitzwilliam crisis.—The french at Bantry.—The succession of the opposition.—The eve of '98.—The rebellion.—Lord Cornwallis and the union.

Savage, J: '98 and '48 ; the modern revolutionary history and literature of Ireland. N. Y. 1856. D.   **941 : 19**

Duffy, *Sir* C: Gavan. Young Ireland ; a fragment of irish history, 1840—1850. N. Y. 1881. D.   **941 : 23**
— Four years of irish history ; 1845—1849. N. Y. [1883]. O.   **941 : 30**

Witherow, T: The Boyne and the Aghrim, or The story of some famous battlefields in Ireland. Lond. 1879. D.   **941 : 21**

Flatley, P. J. Ireland and the land league; key to the irish question, with an introd. by Wendell Phillips. Bost. 1881. S.   **941 : 24**

King, D: Bennett. The irish question. N. Y. 1882. D.   **941.1 : 3**

Carey, Matthew. Vindiciæ hibernicæ, or Ireland vindicated; an attempt to develop and expose a few of the multifarious errors and falsehoods respecting Ireland in the histories of May, Temple, Whitelock, Borlase, Rushworth, Clarendon, Cox, Carte, Leland, Warner, Macaulay, Hume and others, particularly in the legendary tales of the conspiracy and pretended massacre of 1641. Phila. 1819. O.   **941 : R33**

Cudmore, P. The irish republic ; a historical memoir on Ireland and her oppressors. St. Paul. 1871. O.   **941 : 22**

Bagenal, Philip H. The american irish, and their influence on irish politics. Author's ed. Bost. 1882. S.   **941 : 28**

See also in the Index to biography **Burke—Emmet —Flood—Grattan—O'Connell.**

2. Scottish history.

Sinclair, Sir J: Analysis of the statistical account of Scotland ; with a general view of the history of that country and discussions on some important branches of political economy. Edinb. 1831. 2 pts. in 1 v. O.   **941 : 12**

Halsey, Leroy W. Scotland's influence on civilization. Phila. [1885]. D.   **941 : 44**

Mackintosh, J: The history of civilization in Scotland. Lond. 1878. 2 v. O.   **941 : 38**

Ramsay, E: Bannerman. Reminiscences of scottish life and character. From the 7th Edinb. ed. Bost. 1861. D.   **941 : 8**
— Same. 2d ser. Edinb. 1861. D.   **941 : 8 v2**
— Same. From the 7th Edinb. ed. N. Y. 1880. D.   **941 : 8 v2**

Maclagan, Robert Craig. Scottish myths ; notes on scottish history and tradition. Edinb. 1882. O.   **941+34**

Historians of Scotland, The. [Maps]. Edinb. 1871—1880. 10 v. O.   **941 : P43**

Letter from the nobility, barons and commons of Scotland, in the year 1320, yet extant under all the seals of the nobility, directed to pope John. Tr. from the original in latine, as it is insert by sir G: Mackenzie of Rosebaugh in his Observations on precedency, etc. Edinb.; repr. in the year 1689. N. Y. 1861. D.   **941 : R27**

Burton, J: Hill. The history of Scotland from Agricola's invasion to the extinction of the last jacobite insurrection, [84—1745]. New ed. rev. Edinb. n. d. 9 v. D.   **941 : 39**

Taylor, James, and others. The pictorial history of Scotland from the roman invasion to the close of the jacobite rebellion, a. d. 79—1746. Ill. N. Y. n. d. 2 v. Q.   **941+35**

Scott, Sir Walter. The history of Scotland [to 1603]. [Harper's family lib.] N. Y. 1845. 2 v. S.   **941 : 11**
— History of Scotland [to 1746]: Tales of a grandfather, with notes; 1st-3d ser. (Ill. lib. ed.) Bost. 1870. 6 v. in 3. D.   **941 : 6**
— Same. Tales of a grandfather ; stories taken from scottish history; 2d ser. [1603—1707]. Parker's ed. Bost. 1845. 2 v. S.   **941 : 6 v3, 4**
— Same. 3d ser. [1707—1746]. Bost. n. d. 2 v. in 1. D.   **941 : 6 v5, 6**
— Tales of a grandfather ; the history of Scotland from the earliest period to the close of the reign of James the fifth ; abr. and ed. by Edwin Ginn. [Classics for children]. V. 1. Boston. 1885. D.   **x 941 : 42**

Macarthur, Margaret. History of Scotland [to 1843] ; ed. by E: A: Freeman. Ed. adapted for amer. students. [Freeman's historical course]. N. Y. 1874. S.   **941 : 5**

Lindau, W: Adolf. Die geschichte Schottlands. 2te verb. aufl. (Allg. historische taschenbibliothek, 3er th.) Dresden. 1827. 4 v. in 1. S.   **941 : 40**

Buchanan, G: The history of Scotland. Tr. from the latin, with notes and a continuation to the union in the reign of queen Anne, by James Aikman. Glasgow. 1827. 4 v. O.   **941 : 3**

Tytler, Patrick Fraser. The history of Scotland, from the accession of Alexander III. to the union. Edinb. 1864. 4 v. D.   **941 : 14**

Robertson, W: The history of Scotland during the reigns of queen Mary and of king James VI, till his accession to the crown of England, with a review of the scottish history previous to that period, and an app. containing original letters. N. Y. 1844. O.   **941 : 10**

Ross, J: Merry. Scottish history and literature to the period of the reformation ; ed. with a biographical sketch by James Brown. Glasgow. 1884. O.   **941+41**

Chambers, Robert. Domestic annals of Scotland from the reformation to the revolution. 2d ed. Edinb. 1859. 2 v. O.   **941 : 4**

Burnet, Gilbert. The memoires of the lives and actions of James and William, dukes of Hamilton and Castleherald, etc.; in which an account is given of the rise and progress of the civil wars in Scotland, with other great transactions, both in England and Germany, from the year 1625 to the year 1652, together with many letters, instruc-

x denotes books specially adapted for children.

tions and other papers written by king
Charles I, never before pub., all drawn
out of or copied from the originals. In 7
books. Lond. 1677. F.   **23 : R**

Lippincott, Sara Jane, *born* Clarke, (*Grace
Greenwood*). Bonnie Scotland ; tales of her
history, heroes, and poets. Ill. Bost. 1865.
S.   **x 941 : 37**

Historical tales of the wars of Scotland, and of
the border raids, forays and conflicts ; v.
1, 3, 4. Edinb. *n. d.* 3 v. S.   **941 : 7**

Browne, James. A history of the Highlands
and of the Highland clans ; with an extensive selection from the hitherto inedited
Stuart papers. New ed. Ill. Edinb. 1852-
55. 4 v. O.   **941+P2**
Contents. V. 1. Pref. *and* Dissertation.—Catalogue
of gaelic and irish mss. — History of the Highlands to
1646. 2. 1646—1745. — App. 3. 1745—1788. — App. 4.
App.— Military service of the Highland regiments. —
History of the Highland clans.

Macleay, K. Historical memoirs of Rob Roy
and the clan Macgregor ; incl. original notices of lady Grange ; with an introd.
sketch ill. of the condition of the Highlands
prior to 1745. Edinb. 1881. D.   **941 : 36**

Logan, James. The scottish gaël, or Celtic manners as preserved amongthe highlanders ;
being an historical and descriptive account
of the inhabitants, antiquities and national
peculiarities of Scotland, more particularly
of the northern or gaëlic parts of the country, where the singular habits of the original celts are most tenaciously retained.
Lond. 1831. 2 v. D.   **941 : 9**

History of the abbey and palace of Holyrood.
Edinb. *n. d.* S.   **941 : 31**

History and antiquities of Melrose, old Melrose
and Dryburgh abbeys, with a description
ot Abbotsford, Eildon Hills, etc. Melrose,
1869. S.   **941 : 32**
See also in the Index to biography Campbell —
James—Magdalene—Margaret—Robert Bruce.

3. English history.

(*See also* History of the English constitution and politics,
col. 161—163.)

General.

Allen, W: Francis. The reader's guide to english history. [*with* supplement]. Bost. 1882,
1883. *Obl.* T.   **942 : 39**
Contents of supp. Ancient history; modern history
of Europe; American history.

— *Same.*   **16 : L**

Low, Sidney J., *and* F. S. **Pulling**, *eds.* The
dictionary of english history. N. Y. 1884.
O.   **942 : R56**

Gardiner, S: Rawson, *and* James Bass **Mullinger**.
Introduction to the study of english history.
Lond. 1881. O.   **942 : 13**
Contents. Pt. 1. **Gardiner**, S: R. Introd. to english
history [from the earliest times to 1881].—Pt. 2. **Mullinger**, J. B. [Lists and critidal estimates of] authorities.—Index.

Bodin, Felix. Die geschichte Englands. 2te
aufs neue durchgesehene und erweiterte
aufl. von J. H. G. Heusinger. (Allg. historische taschenbibliothek, 2ter th.) Dresden. 1827. 2 v. in 1. S.   **942 : 53**

Bright, James Franck. A history of England.
Maps and plans. Lond. 1880. 3 v. S.
                                    942 : 48
Contents. V. 1. Mediæval monarchy, 449—1485. 2.
Personal monarchy, 1485 — 1688. 3. Constitutional
monarchy, 1689—1837. Each vol. has an index.

Chambers, W: *and* Robert, *eds.* History and
present state of the British empire. Edinb.
1856. S.   **942 : 25**

Gardiner, S: Rawson. English history for
young folks, b. c. 55—a. d. 1880. Rev. ed.
for amer. students. N. Y. 1881. S.
                                    x 942 : 12

Green, J: R: History of the english people.
Maps. N. Y. 1878-80. 4 v. O.   **942 : 4**
Contents. V. 1. Early England, 449—1071.—England
under foreign kings, 1071—1214.—The charter, 1204—
1291.—The parliament, 1307—1461. 2. The monarchy,
1461—1540.—The reformation, 1540—1603. 3. Puritan
England, 1603—1660.—The revolution, 1660—1688. 4.
The revolution, 1683—1760.—Modern England, 1760—
1815.

— A short history of the english people. N. Y.
1877. O.   **942 : 3**

Guest, M. J. Lectures on the history of England. Lond. 1879. D.   **942 : 16**
Note. A continuous history from the earliest
times to the battle of Waterloo.

Guizot, François P: Guillaume. A popular history of England from the earliest times to
the accession of Victoria. [*Added*]: From
the accession of Victoria 1837—1874, ed. by
madame Guizot De Witt, from notes and
documents by M. Guizot. Tr. by M. M.
Ripley. Ill. Bost. 1877-81. 5 v. O.
                                    942+5
Contents. V. 1. Roman dominion to Henry V, b. c.
55—1422. 2. Henry VI to Charles I and his government, 1422—1642. 3. Charles I and his government to
William and Mary, 1642—1694. 4. William III to William IV, 1694—1837. 5. The reign of Victoria, 1837—
1874.—Index.

Hume, D: The students' Hume: A history of
England from the earliest times to the
revolution in 1688 ; based on the history of
D: Hume, incorporating the corr. and researches of recent historians ; continued to
the treaty of Berlin in 1878. New ed. rev.
and corr. by J. S. Brewer, with an app. by
an amer. ed. Ill. N. Y. 1880. D. **942 : 1**

Keightley, T: The history of England, from
the earliest period to 1839. From the 2d
Lond. ed., with notes by the amer. ed.
[Harper's family lib.] N. Y. 1845. 5 v. S.
                                    942 : 6
Contents. V. 1. 55 b. c.—1377 a. d. 2. 1377—1558. 3.
1558—1644. 4. 1644—1685. 5. 1685—1837.

Knight, C: The popular history of England.
1st amer. ed. N. Y. 1878. 8 v. D. **942 : 7**
Contents. V. 1. From the invasion of Cæsar to the
end of the reign of Henry IV. 2. From the reign of
Henry V to the reign of Mary. 3. From the reign
of Elizabeth to the commonwealth. 4. From the
commonwealth to the reign of William and Mary.
5. From the reign of William III to George II. 6.
From the defence of the country by foreign troops,
1756, to the assassination of Marat by Charlotte
Corday, 1793. 7. From the war of 1793 to the material
progress of British India, 1826. 8. From the administration of lord Goderich, 1827, to the final extinction
of the corn-laws, feb. 1849.—App. of annals, 1849—1867.
—Index.

Knox, Isa, *born* Craig, *mrs.* J: The little folks'
history of England. Ill. 7th ed. Lond.
[1874]. S.   **x 942 : 34**

x denotes books specially adapted for children.

Rapin de Thoyras, Paul. The history of England from the earliest periods ; newly tr., corr. and rev. and continued to the present time, with illustrative annotations, historical, political and statistical, from private collections and from public records deposited in the British museum, the Tower of London, etc., presenting a luminous exposition of every political, military and commercial event relating to the British empire and its colonial possessions in the East and West Indies and on the continents of Africa and America, a general view of the french revolution and its consequent wars throughout Europe, accounts of voyages and discoveries, and of the progress of literature, science and the polite arts, and biogr. sketches of the most distinguished british legislators, warriors, poets, divines and others who have rendered themselves conspicuous in the history of their country, by H: Robertson. Lond. 1813, 1816. 2 v. F.　　　　**23 : R**

Thompson, Edith. History of England, ed. by E: A: Freeman. [Freeman's historical course for schools]. N. Y. 1880. S.　　　　　　　　　　　　**x 942 : 22**

Yonge, Charlotte Mary. Young folks' history of England. Bost. [1879]. D.　　**x 942 : 29**

Long periods.

Hume, D: The history of England from the invasion of Julius Cæsar to the revolution in 1688. Phila. 1836. 2 v. O.　　**942 : 2**
— *Same.* New ed., with the author's last corr. and impr.; prefixed, a short account of his life, written by himself ; v. 2-4. Phila. 1821, 1822. 3 v. O.　　　**942 : 2**

Smollett, Tobias G: The history of England, from the revolution in 1688 to the death of George II ; designed as a continuation of mr. Hume's history. New ed., with the author's last corr. and impr. Phila. 1822. 2 v. O.　　　　　　　**942.5 : 6**
— *Same.* Phila. 1836. O.　　　**942.5 : 6**

Miller, J. R. The history of Great Britain from the death of George II to the coronation of George IV; designed as a continuation of Hume and Smollett. Phila. 1836. O.
　　　　　　　　　　　　942.5+7

Mackintosh, *Sir* James, W: Wallace *and* Robert Bell. The history of England. (Lardner's cabinet cyc.) Lond. 1830-40. 10 v. D.
　　　　　　　　　　　　　942 : 58
Contents. **Mackintosh,** *Sir* J. V. 1. British and roman period to Henry VI. 2. Henry VI, *continued,* to Mary, 1422—1558. 3. Accession of Elizabeth, 1558—1588. **Wallace,** W: 4. 1588—1624. 5. 1625—1645. 6. 1645—1661. 7. 1661—1684. 8. 1685—1689. 9. 1690—1713. **Bell,** R. 10. 1714—1760.—Index.
— *Same.* V. 1-3. N. Y. 1856. S. **942 : 58 v1-3**

Lingard, J: The history of England from the first invasion of the romans to the accession of William and Mary in 1688. 6th ed. rev. and enl. Dublin. 1874. 10 v. D.
　　　　　　　　　　　　　942 : 9
Contents. V. 1. 55 b. c.—1100 a. d. 2. 1100—1307. 3. 1307—1422. 4. 1422—1532. 5. 1532—1555. 6. 1555—1603. 7. 1603—1642. 8. 1642—1660. 9. 1660—1680. 10. 1680—1689.
— *Same.* 5th ed., in 8 v.; v. 1, 3-6, 8. Paris. 1840. 6 v. O.　　　　　　　　　　　**942 : 8**

Dickens, C: J: Huffam. A child's history of England [to 1688]. Phila. *n. d.* D.
　　　　　　　　　　　　　x 942 : 11
— *Same. Also* A holiday romance, and other pieces. Bost. 1871. D.　　**x 942 : 11**
Contents. A child's history of England. — Holiday romance. — George Silverman's explanation. — Sketches of young couples. — New uncommercial samples.

Raumer, F: L: G: v. The political history of England during the 16th, 17th and 18th centuries. Lond. 1837. 2 v. O.　**942 : 51**
Contents. V. 1. From the accession of Henry VII, 1528, to the troubles in Scotland, 1637. 2. From the breaking out of the scotch troubles to the restoration of Charles II, 1637—1660.

Ranke, Franz Leopold v. Englische geschichte, vornehmlich im 17. jahrhundert. 3te aufl. Leipz. 1870-72. 9 v. O.　**904 : 36 v14-22**
Contents. [V. 14] 1. Welthistorische momente der früheren geschichte von England.—Versuche einer abgesonderten consolidation des königreichs in weltlicher und geistlicher beziehung.—Königin Elisabeth; verwickelung englischer und schottischer ereignisse. [15] 2. 1603—1640. [16] 3. 1640—1649. [17] 4. 1649—1664. [18] 5. 1664—1685. [19] 6. 1685—1690. [20] 7. 1690—1702. [21] 8. Die ersten sechs decennien des 18. jahrh.—Analecten: Urkundliche erläuterungen einzelner momente; Zur kritik der historiker, Clarendon. Burnet. und autobiogr. aufzeichnungen Jacobs II; Fuchs und Bentink. [22] 9. Analecten: Zur geschichte des krieges in Irland; Aus den berichten F: Bonnets an den brandenburgischen hof; Aus dem briefwechsel Wilhelms III.—Register, 1-9.
— *Same, eng.* A history of England, principally in the 17th century. Oxford. 1875. 6 v. O.
　　　　　　　　　　　　　942.4 : 17
Cntents. V. 1. To 1629. 2. 1629—1649. 3. 1649—1674. 4. 1675—1691. 5. 1690—1760.—App. 1st section. 6. App. 2d—5th sections.—Index.

From the earliest times to 1485.

Lappenberg, J: Martin, *and* Reinhold Pauli. Geschichte von England. [Geschichte der europäischen staaten, herausg. von A. H. L. Heeren und F. A. Ukert.] Hamburg *and* Gotha. 1834-58. 5 v. O.　　**942 : 52**
Contents. **Lappenberg,** J: M. V. 1. Literarische einleitung.—Geschichte bis 1066.— Innere zustände der angelsachsen. 2. Aeltere geschichte der Normandie.—Englische geschichte, 1066—1154.—Von den quellen der älteren geschichte der Normandie.—Zusätze und berichtigungen. **Pauli,** R. 3. Vorwort von Lappenberg.—Geschichte, 1154—1272.—Die quellen zur geschichte der vier ersten Plantagenets.—Abdruck der Magna charta, und proclamation von 1258. 4. Geschichte, 1272—1399.—Quellen. 5. 1399—1509.—Die quellen zur geschichte des 15. jahrh.

Green, J: R: The making of England [to 830]. Maps. N. Y. 1882. O.　　**942.1 : 4**
— *Same.* N. Y. 1882. Q.　　　**942.1+4**
— The conquest of England [758—1071]. Portr. and maps. N. Y. 1884. O.　**942.1 : 16**

Gairdner, James. Early chroniclers of England. Lond. *n. d.* D.　　**942.1 : 9**

Freeman, E: A: Old-english history [to 1066]. New ed. Maps. Lond. 1881. S. **942.1 : 7**

Armitage, Ella S. The childhood of the english nation, or The beginnings of english history [to 1200]. N. Y. 1877. S.　**942.1 : 13**

Geldart, H. R., *Mrs.* T: A popular history of England [to 1087]. N. Y. 1860. D.
　　　　　　　　　　　　　x 942.1 : 5

Longman, W: Lectures on the history of England ; from the earliest times to the death of Edward II [1327]. Maps and ill. Lond. 1863. O.　　　　　　　　　**942 : 47**

Pearson, C: H.   History of England during the early and middle ages.   Lond. 1867.   2 v.   O.
942.1 : 15
Contents. V. 1. To 1199. 2. 1199—1307.

Wright, T: Essays on subjects connected with the literature, popular superstitions and history of England in the middle ages.   Lond. 1846.   2 v.   O.   942 : 50
Contents. V. 1. Anglo - saxon poetry. — Anglo-norman poetry.—Historical romances of the middle ages. — On proverbs and popular sayings. — On the anglo-latin poets of the 12th century.—Abelard and the scholastic philosophy.—On dr. Grimm's German mythology. — On the national fairy mythology of England.—On the popular superstitions of modern Greece. 2. On friar Rush and the frolicsome elves. —Observations on Dunlop's History of fiction.—On the history and transmission of popular stories.—On the poetry of history.—Adventures of Hereward the saxon.—The story of Eustace the monk.—The history of Fulke Fitz Warine.—On the popular cycle of the Robin Hood ballads.—The conquest of Ireland by the anglo-normans.—On old english political songs.—On the scottish poet Dunbar.

Nicholas, T: The pedigree of the english people ; an argument, historical and scientific, on the formation and growth of the nation, tracing race-admixture in Britain from the earliest times, with especial reference to the incorporation of the celtic aborigines.   5th ed.   Lond. 1878.   O.   942 : 23

Norman people, The, and their existing descendants in the british dominions and the U. S. of America.   Lond. 1874.   O.   942 : 10
Contents. Discovery of the descendants of the norman nobility, *and* commonalty, in England. — Criticism of family history.—National character of the norman settlement in England.—The danish settlement in England.— Gothic origin of the normans, danes, and anglo-saxons; Present diffusion and numbers of the gothic race.—Alphabetical series of existing norman names and families, taken from the London post office directory.—App.—Index.

Edgar, J: G: Danes, saxons and normans, or Stories of our ancestors.   Lond. 1863.   O.
x 942.2 : 15

Rhys, J.   Early Britain: Celtic Britain.   Maps and ill.   Lond. 1882.   S.   942.1 : 10

Scarth, H: Mengden.   Early Britain : Roman Britain.   Map.   Lond. *n. d.*   S.   942.1 : 11

Haigh, Daniel H.   The conquest of Britain by the saxons ; a harmony of the "Historia britonum," the writings of Gildas, the " Brut " and the Saxon chronicle, with reference to the events of the 5th and 6th centuries.   Lond. 1861.   O.   942.1 : 19

Allen, C: Grant.   Early Britain: Anglo-saxon Britain.   Lond. *n. d.*   S.   942.1 : 12

Turner, Sharon.   The history of the anglo-saxons, from the earliest period to the norman conquest.   Paris. 1840.   3 v.   O.   942.1 : P3
Contents. V. 1. To the death of Alfred, 900. 2. The character of Alfred. — 900-1066. — App. Language: Money; History of the laws; Agriculture and landed property. 3. Manners of the a.-s. after their occupation of England.—Government and constitution. — Poetry, literature, arts and sciences. — Religion.—A vindication of the genuineness of the ancient british poems.

Lappenberg, J: Martin.   A history of England under the anglo-saxon kings.   Tr. from the german by B: Thorpe.   New ed. rev. by E. C. Otté.   Lond. 1881.   2 v.   D.   942.1 : 14
Contents. V. 1. Pref. — Literary introduction. — Britain under the romans, b. c. 54-a. d. 449.— From the landing of Hengest and Horsa to the accession of Ecgberht, a. d. 449-800.—Notes; Genealogical tables.—Index. 2. From the union of the anglo-saxon states under the supremacy of Wessex to the accession of Cnut, a. d. 800-1016.—The danish dynasty, a. d. 1016—

1042.—Restoration and end of the anglo-saxon dynasty, 1042-1066.—The social state of the anglo-saxons. —Genealogical tables.—Index.
Note. The original german work will be found in 942:51 v1.

Kemble, J: Mitchell.   The saxons in England ; a history of the english commonwealth till the period of the norman conquest.   New ed. rev. by Walter DeGray Birch.   Lond. 1876.   2 v.   O.   942.1 : 8
Contents. V. 1. The original settlement of the anglo-saxon commonwealth.—App. 2. The principles and progress of the change in England.—App.

Worsaae, Jens Jacob Asmussen.   An account of the danes and norwegians in England, Scotland and Ireland.   Ill.   Lond. 1852.   D.
942.1 : 17

Streatfeild, G: Sydney.   Lincolnshire and the danes.   Lond. 1884.   D.   942.1 : 18

From the norman conquest.

Thierry, Jacques N: Augustin.   History of the conquest of England by the normans, its causes and consequences in England, Scotland, Ireland and on the continent.   Tr. from the 7th Paris ed. by W: Hazlitt.   Lond. 1847.   2 v.   D.   942.2 : 5
Contents. V. 1. 55 b. c.—1137 a. d. 2. 1137—1196.—Conclusion.—App.

Freeman, E: A: The history of the norman conquest of England ; its causes and its results.   Rev. amer. ed.   N. Y. 1873-79.   6 v.   O.   942.2 : 4
Contents. V. 1. The preliminary history to the election of Eadward the confessor. 2. The reign of Eadward the confessor. 3. The reign of Harold and the interregnum. 4. The reign of William the conqueror. 5. The effects of the norman conquest. 6. Index.

— A short history of the norman conquest of England.   2d ed.   Oxford. 1880.   S.
x 942.2 : 13

— The reign of William Rufus and the accession of Henry I.   Oxford. 1882.   2 v.   O.
942.2 : 16

Palgrave, *Sir* Francis.   History of...England [from the norman conquest in 1066 to the death of Rufus in 1101].   *in* 944 : 5 v3, 4

Cobbe, T: History of the norman kings of England ; from a new collation of the contemporary chronicles.   Lond. 1869.   O.
942.2 : 21
Contents. Pref.— Introd.— Genealogical tables. — William I.—William II Rufus.—Henry I.—Stephen.

Ingulphus.   Chronicles of the abbey of Croyland, with the continuations by Peter of Blois and anonymous writers.   Tr. from the latin, with notes, by H: T. Riley.   Lond. 1854.   D.   942.2 : 1
Note. Covers, with varying degrees of fulness, the period from 704 to 1486.

Gulielmus *Malmesburiensis.*   Chronicle of the kings of England, from the earliest period to the reign of king Stephen ; with notes and ill. by J. A. Giles.   Lond. 1847.   D.
942.2 : 3

Florentius *Wigoriensis,* (eng. Florence *of Worcester).*   Chronicle, with the two continuations, comprising annals of english history from the departure of the romans to the reign of Edward I.   Tr. from the latin, with notes and ill., by T: Forester.   Lond. 1854.   D.   942.1 : 1

x denotes books specially adapted for children.

Rogerus *de Wendover*. Flowers of history; comprising the history of England from the descent of the saxons to a. d. 1235, formerly ascribed to Matthew Paris. Tr. from the latin by J. A. Giles. Lond. 1849. 2 v. D.
942.1 : 2

Matthæus *Paris*. English history, from the year 1235 to 1273. Tr. from the latin by J. A. Giles. Lond. 1852–54. 3 v. D.
942.2 : 2

Stubbs, W: The early Plantagenets, [1135—1327]. (Epochs of modern history.) Maps. Bost. 1876. S.
942.2 : 6

Warburton, W. Edward III. (Epochs of modern history.) 2d ed. Maps. Lond. 1876. S.
942.2 : 7

Pearson, C: H. English history in the 14th century. [Hist. handbooks.] Lond. 1876. S.
942.2 : 19

Longman, W: The history of the life and times of Edward III. Maps and ill. Lond. 1869. 2 v. O.
942.2 : 20

Dunster, H: P: True stories of the times of Richard II; illustrating the history, manners and customs of that king's reign. Lond. *n. d.* D.
942.2 : 14

Gairdner, James. The houses of Lancaster and York, with the conquest and loss of France. (Epochs of modern history.) Maps. N. Y. 1875. S.
942.2 : 8

Edgar, J: G: The wars of the roses, or Stories of the struggle of York and Lancaster. Ill. N. Y. [1860]. S.
942.2 : 9

Brougham, H:, *baron Brougham and Vaux*. History of England and France under the house of Lancaster, with an introd. view of the early reformation. New ed. Lond. 1861. O.
942.2 : 17

Towle, G: Makepeace. The history of Henry V, king of England, lord of Ireland, and heir of France. N. Y. 1866. O.
942.2+12

Fenn, Sir J:, *ed.* Paston letters; original letters written during the reigns of Henry VI, Edward IV, and Richard III, by various persons of rank or consequence, containing many curious anecdotes relative to that turbulent and bloody, but hitherto dark, period of our history and elucidating not only public matters of state, but likewise the private manners of the age; with notes histor. and explan. and authenticated by engr. of autographs and seals. New ed., digested in chronol. order, with add. notes by A. Ramsay. Lond. 1859. 2 v. in 1. D.
942.2 : 10

— The Paston letters, 1422—1509 a. d. New ed., containing upwards of 400 letters, etc., hitherto unpub., ed. by James Gairdner. Lond. 1872–75. 3 v. S.
942.2 : 11
Contents. V. 1. Henry VI, 1422—1461. 2. Edward IV, 1461—1471. 3. Edward IV—Henry VII, 1471—1509.

Warner, W: Albions England; a continued history of the same kingdome from the originals of the first inhabitants thereof unto the raigne of queen Elizabeth; rev. and newly enl. by the same author, whereunto is also newly added an epitome of the whole historie of England. *T. p. w.* [Lond. 1602 ?] S.
23 : R
Added, before the Epitome, A continuance of Albions England by the first author, W. W. Lond. 1606; *and* An addition in proese to the second booke of Albions England, contayning a Breulate of the true historie of Æneas.

From 1485 to 1688.

Brewer, J: Sherren. The reign of Henry VIII, from his accession to the death of Wolsey, reviewed and ill. from original documents; ed. by J. Gairdner. Portr. Lond. 1884. 2 v. O.
942.3 : 8

Froude, James Anthony. History of England from the fall of Woolsey to the death of Elizabeth, [1530—1603]. N. Y. 1865–70. 12 v. D.
942.3 : 1

Hopkins, S: The puritans, or The church, court and parliament of England during the reigns of Edward VI and queen Elizabeth. Bost. 1859–61. 3 v. O.
942.3 : 2
Contents. V. 1. 1549—1575. 2. 1575—1585. 3. 1585—1601.—Index.

Nichols, J: Gough, *ed.* The chronicle of queen Jane and of two years of queen Mary, and especially of the rebellion of sir T: Wyatt, written by a resident in the Tower of London; with illustrative documents and notes. [Camden society, no. 48. Lond]. *n. d.* O.
942.3 : 4

Creighton, Mandell. The age of Elizabeth. (Epochs of modern history). Maps and tables. N. Y. 1876. S.
942.3 : 6

Hayward, Sir J: Annals of the first four years of queen Elizabeth, ed. from a ms. in the Harleian collection by J: Bruce. [Camden soc. pub., no. 7]. Lond. 1840. O.
942.3 : 3

Aikin, Lucy. Memoirs of the court of queen Elizabeth. 2d ed. Lond. 1818. 2 v. O.
942.3 : 5

Gardiner, S: Rawson. History of England from the accession of James I to the outbreak of the civil war, 1603—1642. Lond. 1883. 10 v. D.
942.4 : 16
Contents. V. 1. 1603—1607. 2. 1607—1616. 3. 1616—1621. 4. 1621—1623. 5. 1623—1625. 6. 1625—1629. 7. 1629—1635. 8. 1635—1639. 9. 1639—1641. 10. 1641—1643.

— The first two Stuarts and the puritan revolution, 1603—1660. (Epochs of modern history.) Maps. Bost. 1876. S.
942.4 : 11

Guizot, François P: Guillaume. History of the english revolution from the accession of Charles I. Tr. from the french by Louise H. R. Couter. Oxford. 1838. 2 v. O.
942.4 : 23
Contents. V. 1. 1625—1643. 2. 1643—1649.

— History of Oliver Cromwell and the english commonwealth, from the execution of Charles I to the death of Cromwell. Tr. by Andrew R. Scoble. Phila. 1854. 2 v. D.
942.4 : 25
Contents. V. 1. 1649—1653. 2. 1653—1658.

— History of Richard Cromwell and the restoration of Charles II. Tr. by Andrew R. Scoble. Lond. 1856. 2 v. O.
942.4 : 26
Contents. V. 1. 1658—1659. 2. 1659—1660.

— Memoirs of G: Monk.
923.22 : 64

Bayne, P: The chief actors in the puritan revolution. Lond. 1878. O.
942.4 : 18
Contents. Three centuries ago. — The transition period: James I. — The anglo-catholic reaction: Archb. Laud. — Henrietta Maria. — Charles I. — The covenanters, Charles II and Argyle. — Montrose. — Milton.—Sir H: Vane.—Oliver Cromwell.—Clarendon.

Adams, W: H: Davenport. The great civil war, from the accession of Charles I to the dissolution of the long parliament, [1625—1653]. Lond. 1880. S.
x 942.4 : 14

x denotes books specially adapted for children.

Stern, Alfred. Geschichte der revolution in England, [1625–1660]. **(Oncken, W:,** *ed.* Allgemeine geschichte in einzeldarstellungen ; 3te hauptabth., 4ter th. Portr., ill. und karten. Berlin. 1881. O.   **909+21 v4**

Burnet, Gilbert. History of his own time ; from the restoration of Charles II to the conclusion of the treaty of peace at Utrecht, in the reign of queen Anne ; prefixed a summary recapitulation of affairs in church and state, from king James I to the restoration in 1660, together with the author's life by the ed. and some explanatory notes; the whole rev. and corr. by him. Lond. 1753. 4 v. O.   **942.4 : 2**

Cary, H: Memorials of the great civil war in England from 1646 to 1652 ; ed. from original letters in the Bodleian library of Charles I, Charles II, queen Henrietta, prince Rupert, prince Maurice, prince Charles Ludovic, duke of York, Hyde earl of Clarendon, archb. Sancroft, marquis of Worcester, earl of Derby, Oliver Cromwell, sir T: Fairfax, sir Walter Strickland, sir Arthur Haslerig, maj.-gen. Monk, maj.-gen. Poyntz, maj.-gen. Skippon, col. Ireton, col. Hammond, admiral Deane, admiral Blake, and of numerous other eminent persons. Lond. 1842. 2 v. O.   **942.4 : 3**

Hyde, E:, *1st earl of Clarendon.* The history of the rebellion and civil wars in England, begun in the year 1641, with the precedent passages and actions, that contributed thereunto, and the happy end and conclusion thereof by the king's blessed restoration and return, upon the 29th of may 1660. Oxford. 1732. 6 v. O.   **942.4 : 4**

Jesse, J: Heneage. Memoirs of the court of England during the reign of the Stuarts, incl. the protectorate. New ed., ill. Lond. 1857. 3 v. D.   **942.4 : 27**

Contents. V. 1. James I.— Anne of Denmark.— Henry, prince of Wales.— Elizabeth, queen of Bohemia.— Lady Arabella Stuart.— Lodowick Stuart.— Frances Howard, duchess of Richmond.— Mary Villiers, countess of Buckingham.— T: Sackville, earl of Dorset.— Robert Cecil, earl of Salisbury.— Robert Carr, earl of Somerset.— Francis Howard, countess of Somerset.— H: Howard, earl of Northampton.— Mary, countess of Pembroke.— W: Herbert, earl of Pembroke.— Philip Herbert, earl of Pembroke and Montgomery.—James Hay, earl of Carlisle.—Francis, lord Bacon.— Edward, lord Herbert of Cherbury.— Archee, the court fool.—Charles I. 2. Henrietta Maria.—Henry, duke of Gloucester.— Mary, princess of Orange.— Elizabeth, daughter of Charles I.— Anne, daughter of Charles I.— Elizabeth, daughter of Charles I.— G: Villiers, duke of Buckingham.— T: Wentworth, earl of Strafford.— W: Laud, archbp. of Canterbury.—H: Rich, earl of Holland.—Lucius Cary, viscount Falkland.— Lucy, countess of Carlisle.— Sir Kenelm Digby.— Sir J: Suckling.— Sir Jeffcrey Hudson.— Oliver Cromwell.— Elizabeth Cromwell.— R: Cromwell.— H: Cromwell.— Bridget Cromwell, Mrs. Ireton.— Elizabeth Cromwell, Mrs. Claypole.— Mary Cromwell, countess of Falconberg.— Frances Cromwell, Mrs. Rich.—Charles II. 3. Catherine, queen of Charles II.—Prince Rupert.—G: Monk, duke of Albermarle.— G: Villiers, second duke of Buckingham.— James, duke of Monmouth.—Mary Villiers, duchess of Richmond.—Mary Fairfax, duchess of Buckingham.— Barbara Villiers, duchess of Cleveland.— Louise du Quéroualle, duchess of Portsmouth.—Hortensia Mancini, duchess of Mazarin.— Frances Stewart, duchess of Richmond.— Frances Jennings, duchess of Tyrconnel.—C: Sackville, earl of Dorset.—J: Wilmot, earl of Rochester.— H: Jermyn, lord Dover.— Elizabeth Butler, countess of Chesterfield.— Elizabeth Bagot, countess of Falmouth and Dorset.— Elizabeth Hamilton, countess of Grammont.— Anne, countess of Southesk.—Susan, lady Bellasyse.—Isabella, lady Robarts.—Anne Temple, lady Lyttleton.— Miss Brooke,

Jesse, J: Heneage.—*Continued.*
lady Denham.—Sir G: Etherege.— Sir C: Sedley.— T: Killegrew.—W: Chiffinch.—H: Brounker.—T: Thynne.—Lucy Walters.— Nell Gwynn.— Mary Davis.— Mrs. Middleton.—James II.—Anne Hyde, duchess of York.—Mary of Modena.— James Fitz-James, duke of Berwick.— Catherine Sedley, countess of Dorchester.— Arabella Churchill.

— Memoirs of the pretenders and their adherents. Phila. 1846. 2 v. S.   **942.4 : 28**

Contents. V. 1. James F: E: Stuart.—Clementina Maria Sobieski.—James Radcliffe, earl of Derwentwater.—Simon, lord Lovat.— W: Gordon, viscount Kenmure.— Charles Edward. 2. *Same, continued.*—Louisa, countess of Albany.—H: Stuart, cardinal York.—A. Elphinstone, lord Balmerino.—W: Boyd, earl of Kilmarnock.—G: Mackenzie, earl of Cromartie.—Lord G: Murray.—Flora Macdonald.

Aikin, Lucy. Memoirs of the court of king James I. Lond. 1822. 2 v. O.   **942.4 : 6**
— Memoirs of the court of king Charles I. 1833. 2 v. O.   **942.4 : 5**

Bisset, Andrew. The history of the struggle for parliamentary government in England, [during the reign of Charles I]. Lond. 1877. 2 v. O.   **942.4 : 10**

Verney, *Sir* Ralph. Verney papers ; notes of proceedings in the long parliament, temp. Charles I, printed from the original pencil memoranda taken in the house, now in the possession of sir Harry Verney ; ed. by J: Bruce. [Camden soc. pub., no. 31]. Lond. 1845. O.   **942.4 : 8**

Forster, J: The arrest of the five members by Charles I; a chapter of english history rewritten. Lond. 1860. O.   **942.4 : 19**

De Foe, Daniel. The history of the plague of London ; together with Religious courtship. Complete in 1 v. N. Y. 1857. D.   **942.4 : 13**

Adams, W: H: Davenport. The merry monarch, or England under Charles II ; its art, literature and society. Lond. 1885. 2 v. O.   **942.4 : 24**

Contents. V. 1. The diarists.— The musicians.— The dramatic authors.—The duchesses.—J: Dryden.— App.: The siege of Rhodes; The man of mode; On chapter III. 2. The actors of the restoration.—The actresses.— The poets.—A couple of courtiers.—The prose writers.

Sidney, H:, *1st earl of Romney.* Diary of the times of Charles II; incl. his correspondence with the countess of Sunderland, and other distinguished persons at the english court. Added, letters illustrative of the times of James II and William III, ed. with notes, by R. W. Blencoe. Lond. 1843. 2 v. O.   **942.4 : 7**

Hale, E: The fall of the Stuarts, and western Europe from 1678 to 1697. (Epochs of modern history). Maps and plans. Bost. 1876. S.   **942.4 : 9**

Yonge, C: Duke. History of the english revolution of 1688. Lond. 1874. D.   **942.4 : 9**

Dalrymple, *Sir* J: Memoirs of Great Britain and Ireland ; from the dissolution of the last parliament of Charles II till the capture of the french and spanish fleets at Vigo, [1702]. A new ed., in three vols.; with the app. complete : consisting chiefly of letters from the french ambassadors in England to their court; and from Charles II, James II, king William, and queen Mary, and the ministers and generals of those princes. Taken from the Depôt des affaires étrangères at Versailles, and king William's private cabinet at Kensington ; interspersed with

historical relations, necessary to connect the papers together. Lond. 1790. 3 v. O.
942.4 : 21

Macaulay, T: Babington, *1st baron Macaulay.* The history of England from the accession of James II. N. Y. 1856. 5 v. D. 942.4 : 1
— *Same.* N. Y. 1849–61. 5 v. O. *and* D.
942.4+1
Contents. V. 1. Introd. to 1685. 2. 1685–1688. 3. 1689–1690. 4. 1691–1697. 5, ed. by his sister, lady Trevelyan, 1697–1702.—Index.

Paget, J: The new "examen," or An inquiry into the evidence relating to certain passages in lord Macaulay's history concerning 1, The duke of Marlborough. 2, The massacre of Glencoe, 3, The Highlands of Scotland, 4. The viscount of Dundee, 5, W: Penn. Edinb. 1861. D. 942.4 : 20

From 1688 to the present.

Jesse, J: Heneage. Memoirs of the court of England from the revolution in 1688 to the death of George II. Lond. 1843. 3 v. O.
942.5 : 13

Vernon, James. Letters illustrative of the reign of William III, from 1696 to 1708, addressed to the duke of Shrewsbury. Now first pub. from the originals, ed. by G: P. R. James. [Portr.] Lond. 1841. 3 v. O. 942.5+16

Lecky, W: E: Hartpole. A history of England in the 18th century. N. Y. 1878–82. 4 v. O.
942.5 : 1

Morris, E: E. The age of Anne. (Epochs of modern history). Maps and plans. Bost. 1877. S. 942.5 : 4

Burton, J: Hill. A history of the reign of queen Anne. Edinb. 1880. 3 v. O. 942.5 : 5

Stanhope, Philip H:, *5th earl Stanhope, viscount Mahon.* History of England, comprising the reign of queen Anne until the peace of Utrecht ; 1701–1713. 4th ed. Lond. 1872. 2 v. D. 942.5 : 2
— History of England from the peace of Utrecht to the peace of Versailles ; 1713—1783. 4th ed. Lond. 1853, 1854. 7 v. O. 942.5 : 3

McCarthy, Justin. A history of the four Georges, in 4 v. ; v. 1. N. Y. 1884. Q. 942.5+17
Contents. V. 1. 1714–1733.

Thackeray, W: Makepeace. The four Georges ; sketches of manners, morals, court and town life. Leipz. 1861. S. 923.21 : 20

Molloy, J. Fitzgerald. Court life below stairs. Lond. 1882, 1883. 4 v. D. 942.5 : 18
Contents. V. 1, 2. London under the first Georges, 1714–1760. 3, 4. London under the last Georges, 1760–1830.

Ashton, J: Old times ; a picture of social life at the end of the 18th century, collected and ill. from the satirical and other sketches of the day. Ill. N. Y. 1885. O. 942.4 : 22

Hervey, J:, *lord Hervey of Ickworth.* Memoirs of the reign of George II, from his accession to the death of queen Caroline ; ed. from the original ms. at Ickworth by J: Wilson Croker. Phila. 1848. 2 v. D.
942.5 : 9

Bissett, Robert. The history of the reign of George III ; prefixed, a view of the progressive improvement of England, in prosperity and strength, to the accession of his majesty. New ed. brought down to the death of the king. Phila. 1822. 3 v. O.
942.5 : 10

Grenville, R: Plantagenet Temple Nugent Brydges Chandos, *2d duke of Buckingham and Chandos.* Memoirs of the court and cabinets of George III, from original family documents. 2d ed. rev. Lond. 1853. 2 v. O.
942.5 : 11

Walpole, Horace, *4th earl of Orford.* Memoirs of the reign of king George III. Now first pub. from the original mss., ed. with notes by sir Denis le Marchant. Phila. 1845. 2 v.
942.5+12

Wraxall, *Sir* Nathaniel W: Historical memoirs of my own time, [1772—1784]. Phila. 1845. O. 942.5+14
— Posthumous memoirs of his own time, [1784—1789]. From the 2d Lond. ed. Phila. 1845. O. 942.5+15

Bury, *Lady* Charlotte Susanna Maria Campbell. Continuation of the diary illustrative of the times of George IV, interspersed with original letters from the late queen Caroline, the princess Charlotte, and from various distinguished persons. [*Anon.*] Ed. by J: Galt. Phila. 1839. 2 v. D. 942.6 : 2

Greville, C: Cavendish Fulke. The Greville memoirs ; a journal of the reigns of king George IV and king William IV ; ed. by H: Reeve. N. Y. 1875. 2 v. D. 942.6 : 7
— *Same,* [abridged and ed. by R: H: Stoddard]. (Bric-a-brac ser.) N. Y. 1875. S. 942.6 : 8

Greville, H: W: Leaves from [his] diary ; ed. by [Alice Harriet Fredrica] viscountess Enfield. Lond. 1883. 2 v. O. 942.6 : 11
Contents. V. 1. 1832–1852. 2. 1852–1856.

Cory, W: A guide to modern english history. Pt. 1, 1815—1830 ; pt. 2, 1830—1835. N. Y. 1880, 1882. 2 v. O. 942.6 : 1

Walpole, Spencer. A history of England from the conclusion of the great war in 1815. 2d ed. Lond. 1879, 1880. 3 v. O. 942.6 : 10

Martineau, Harriet. History of the peace ; a history of England from 1816 to 1854, with an introd., 1800—1815. Bost. 1864–66, 4 v. O. 942.6 : 5
— Introd. to the history of the peace, 1800 to 1815. Lond. 1851. Q. 942.6+5 v1

McCarthy, Justin. The epoch of reform ; 1830—1850. (Epochs of modern history.) N. Y. [1882]. S. 942.6 : 3

Molesworth, W: Nassau. The history of England, 1830—1874. Lond. 1877. 3 v. D.
942.6 : 6

McCarthy, Justin. A history of our own times, from the accession of queen Victoria to the general election of 1880. N. Y. 1880. 2 v. D. 942.6 : 4
— *Same.* N. Y. 1880. 2 v. Q. 942.6+4
— A short history of our own times, from the accession of Victoria to the general election of 1880. N. Y. 1884. Q. 942.6 : 9
— *Same.* N. Y. 1884. Q. 942.6+9

McCarthy, Justin Huntly. England under Gladstone, 1880—1885. 2d ed., rev. and enl. N. Y. 1886. Q. 942.6+12

See also Kings and rulers *in* Biography, *and in the* Index *to* biography Adelicia — Albany — Albert — Alfred — Anne — Berengaria — Boadicea — Brougham—Campbell, C.—Canning—Caroline — Cary, L.—Catharine—Cecil—Charles—Charlotte —Churchill—Clive—Cromwell—Devereux—Disraeli—Dodington—Drake—Dudley, Jane—Edward — Eleanor — Elizabeth — Fox — George — Gladstone—Grenville—Greville—Grey—Harold — Hastings — Havelock — Henrietta — Henry — Hyde—Isabella—James—Jane—Jervis—Joanna

—Katherine—Lamb—Lawrence—Margaret—Mary—Matilda—Monk—Montfort—Nelson—Peel—Philippa—Pitt—Ralegh—Richard—Rupert—Sophia—Temple—Victoria—Wellesley—Wentworth—William—Wolsey.

Selections, incidents, topics.

Knight, C:, *ed.* Half hours of english history, from the roman period to the death of Elizabeth. Lond. 1868. O.   **942 : 17**

Valentine, *Mrs.* R:, *ed.* Half hours of english history; selected and ed. by mrs. Valentine : [Pt. 1], From James I to William and Mary; [Pt. 2], Anne to Victoria. Lond. [1881]. 2 v. D.   **942 : 18**

Green, J: R:, *ed.* Readings from english history, selected and ed. 3 pts. in 1 v. N. Y. 1879. D.   **942 : 36**
Contents. Pt. 1. From Hengest to Cressy. 2. From Cressy to Cromwell. 3. From Cromwell to Balaclava.

Yonge, Charlotte Mary. Cameos from english history : 1st—5th ser. [*Anon.*] N. Y. 1869; Lond. 1880–83. 5 v. D.   **x 942 : 28**
Contents. V. 1. Rollo-Edward II. 2. The wars in France. 3. The wars of the roses. 4. Reformation times. 5. England and Spain.

Selby, C: Events to be remembered in the history of England, forming a series of interesting narratives of the most remarkable occurences in each reign, with reviews of the manners, domestic habits, amusements, costumes, etc., of the people. 13th ed. Lond. *n. d.* S.   **942 : 26**

Sargent, G: E. Stories of old England. Lond. [1869, 1871]. 2 v. D.   **x 942 : 35**

Neele, H: The romance of history : England. Ill. Lond. *n. d.* D.   **942 : 30**

Hood, Edwin Paxton. Old England ; historic pictures of life in old castles, forests, abbeys and cities, etc. 2d ed. Lond. 1852. S.   **942 : 16**

Lippincott, Sara Jane, *born* Clarke, (*Grace Greenwood*). Merrie England ; travels, descriptions, tales and historical sketches. Ill. Bost. 1866. S.   **x 942 : 45**

Reed, H: Lectures on english history and tragic poetry, as ill. by Shakespeare. Lond. 1865. D.   **942 : 21**
Contents. On the study of history.—The legendary period of Britain: King Lear.—The roman and saxon periods: Cymbeline and Macbeth.—The reign of king John.—The reign of Richard II.—The reign of Henry IV.—The character and reign of Henry V.—The reign of Henry VI.—The wars of the roses.—Richard III; Henry VIII.—Lectures on tragic poetry: King Lear; Macbeth; Hamlet; Othello.

Seeley, J: Robert. The expansion of England ; two courses of lectures. Bost. 1883. D.   **942 : 43**
Contents. Tendency in eng. history.—England in the 18th century.—The empire.—The old colonial system.—Effect of the new world on the old.—Commerce and war.—Phases of expansion.—Schism in greater Britain.—History and politics.—The Indian empire.—How we conquered India.—How we govern India.—Mutual influence of England and India.—Phases in the conquest of India.—Internal and external dangers.—Recapitulation.

Vaughan, Robert. Revolutions in english history. Lond. 1859. 3 v. O.   **942+49**
Contents. V. 1. **Revolutions of race.** Celts and romans.—Saxons and danes.—Normans and english.—English and normans.—Lancaster and York. 2. **Revolutions in religion.** Nationalists and romanists.—Protestants and nationalists.— Romanists and protestants.—Anglicans and romanists.— Anglicans and puritans.—England under Elizabeth. 3. **Gov-**

x denotes books specially adapted for children.

Vaughan, Robert.—*Continued.*
ernment. Parliamentarians and royalists.—Republicans and royalists.—Court and country.—National progress since 1688.
— *Same* ; v. 1. N. Y. 1860. O.   **942 : 49 v1**

Ewald, Alexander C: Stories from the state papers. Bost. 1882. D.   **942 : 38**
Contents. Our waste paper office.—The youth of Henry V.—The captive of Castile.—A love match.—The sweating sickness.—A holy mission.—A princess of the period.—The invincible armada.—The earl of Essex's rebellion.—The gun powder plot.—A perished kernel.—The massacre of Amboyna.—The gathering of the storm.—The Lancashire witches.—The great fire of London.—A national scare.

State trials.   *cl.* **345.2**
See col. 223.

Davidson, J. Morrison. The new book of kings. Bost. 1884. S.   **942 : 54**

Camden society. Miscellany ; v. 1. [Lond.] 1847. O.   **942 : 24**
Contents. **Ellis,** *Sir* H:, *ed.* Register and chronicle of the abbey of Aberconway.—**Nichols,** J: G., *ed.* Chronicle of the rebellion in Lincolnshire, 1470.—**Collier,** J. P. Bull of pope Innocent VIII, on the marriage of Henry VII with Elizabeth of York.—**Coningsby,** *Sir* T: Journal of the siege of Rouen, 1591, ed. by J: Gough Nichols.—**Egerton,** *Sir* P. de M. G., *ed.* Letter from G: Fleetwood to his father, giving an account of the battle of Lutzen and the death of Gustavus Adolphus.

Battles on land and sea.

(See also The army and navy, col. 233–234.)

Grant, James. British battles on land and sea. Ill. Lond. *n. d.* 3 v. Q.   **942+37**
Contents. V. 1. 1066—1743. 2. 1744—1826. 3. 1827—1874.—Chronological résumé.—Index.
— Recent british battles on land and sea. Ill. Lond. [1885]. Q.   **942+37 v4**

Adams, W: H: Davenport. Memorable battles in english history, with lives of the commanders. New ed., rev. and enl. Lond. 1879. 2 v. D.   **942 : 32**
Contents. V. 1. The battle of Hastings, and Harold.—The battle of Lewes, and Simon de Montfort.—The battle of Cressy, and Edward the black prince.—The battle of Agincourt, and Henry V.—Oliver Cromwell and the great battles of the civil war. 2. The battle of Blenheim, and the duke of Marlborough.—The battle of Plassey, and lord Clive.—The Heights of Abraham, and gen. Wolfe.—The battle of Waterloo, and Arthur duke of Wellington.—The battle of Inkermann, and the seige of Delhi.

MacFarlane, C: Great battles of the british army. New ed., incl. the russian war. [*Anon.*] Ill. Lond. 1860. D.   **942 : 19**

Allen, Joseph. Battles of the british navy. New ed., rev. and enl. Lond. 1864. 2 v. D.   **942 : 27**

Southey, Robert. The early naval history of England. Phila. 1835. S.   **942.2 : 18**
Note. From the roman invasion to 1395.

Local history and antiquities.

Edmunds, Flavell. Traces of history in the names of places ; with a vocabulary of the roots out of which names of places in England and Wales are formed. New ed. Lond. 1872. D.   **911 : 8**

Doran, J: Memories of our great towns, with anecdotic gleanings concerning their worthies and their oddities. Lond. 1878 [1860–77]. O.   **942 : 44**
— *Same.* New ed., with ill. Lond. 1882. D.   **942 : 44**

Freeman, E: A: English towns and districts ; a series of addresses and sketches. Ill. and map. Lond. 1883. O.   **942 : 40**
Contents. South Wales : Cardiff and Glamorgan; Llanthony; Anglia Transwalliana; South Pembrokeshire castles.—Wessex: The place of Wessex in english history; Glastonbury, british and english: The shire and the gå; Bradford-on-Avon; Devizes; Wareham and Corfe castle; Silchester; Christchurch; Twinham; Carisbrooke; Merton priory. — Mercia: Lindum Colonia; York and Lincoln minsters; Chester; Pre-academic Cambridge; Pre-academic Oxford; Saint Alban's abbey.—Northumberland: Points in early Northumberland history; Kirkstall; Selby; Notes in the North Riding; The Percy castles; Bamburgh and Dunstanburgh.—Sussex: The case of the collegiate church of Arundel, App.; Cowdray; Chichester.—Colonia Camulodunum.—Carlisle: The place of Carlisle in english history.

Marshall, Emma. Stories of the cathedral cities of England. N. Y. 1880. D.   **x 942 : 21**
Contents. Canterbury. — York. — London. — Westminster.—Winchester.—Durham.—Carlisle.—Chester.

Hunt, James H: Leigh. The town [London]; its memorable characters and events. Ill. New ed. Lond. 1878. S.   **942 : 46**

Crosland, Camilla, born Toulmin. Stories of the city of London, retold for youthful readers. Ill. Lond. 1881. D.   **x 942 : 31**
Contents. London bridge. — The temple church.—The royal exchange.—The Tower.—The great plague.—The great fire. — The Gordon riots. — The Thames tunnel.

Rideing, W: H: Young folks' history of London. Bost. 1884. D.   **x 942 : 55**

Stanley, Arthur Penrhyn. Historical memorials of Westminster abbey. 5th ed., with the author's final revisions. Ill. Lond. 1882. O.   **942 : 41**

Dixon, W: Hepworth. Her majesty's Tower. Leipz. 1869-71. 4 v. in 2. S.   **942 : 14**
— Royal Windsor. 3d ed. Lond. 1879, 1880. 4 v. O.   **942 : 42**

Hutton, Barbara. Castles and their heroes. Ill. Lond. n. d. D.   **x 942 : 33**
Contents. Conway castle.—Castle of Willesmieswick. — Corfe castle. — Chepstow castle. — Raglan castle.—Carisbrooke castle.—Warwick castle.—Ludlow castle.—Montgomery castle.

Timbs, J: Abbeys, castles, and ancient halls of England and Wales ; their legendary lore and popular history ; re-ed., rev. and enl. by Alex. Gunn. Ill. Lond. [1885]. 3 v. O.   **942 : 57**
Contents. V. I. South. 2. Midland. 3. North.

Antiquary, The ; a magazine devoted to the study of the past, ed. by E: Walford ; v. 1—12, jan. 1880—dec. 1885. Lond. 1880-85. Q.   **905 : LM**

*   *   *

Martin, Robert Montgomery. History of the british possessions in the Mediterranean ; comprising Gibraltar, Malta, Gozo and the Ionian Islands. [British col. lib. v. 7.] Lond. 1837. S.   **940 : 47**

4. Description.

General.

Chamberlayne, J: Magnæ Britaniæ notitia, or The present state of Great Britain, with diverse remarks upon the ancient state thereof. 36th ed. of the south part, called England, and the 15th of the north part, called Scotland. Added, a compleat list

of their R. H. the prince and princess of Wale's household, as also those of their R. H. the duke of Cumberland, the princess Amelia, and the princess Caroline. Lond. 1745. D.   **914.2 : 8**

Camden, W: Britannia, or A chorographical description of Great Britain and Ireland, together with the adjacent islands ; written in latin and tr. into english, with add. and impr., rev., digested and pub. with large add., by Edmund Gibson. 3d ed., ill. with maps of all the counties and prints of the british, roman and saxon coins. Lond. 1753. 2 v. F.   **23 : R**

Wheaton, Nathaniel Sheldon. A journal of a residence of several months in London, incl. excursions through various parts of England, and a short tour in France and Scotland in 1823 and 1824. Hartford. 1830. O.   **914.2 : 47**

Colton, Calvin. Four years in Great Britain. 1831—1835. N. Y. 1835. 2 v. D. **914.2 : 12**

Haussez, C: Lemercher de Longpré, baron d'. Great Britain in 1833. Phila. 1833. 2 v. D.   **914.2 : 22**

Carus, C: Gustav. The king of Saxony's journey through England and Scotland in 1844. Tr. by S. C. Davidson. Lond. 1846. O.   **914.2 : 9**

Willis, Nathaniel Parker. Famous persons and places. N. Y. n. d. D.   **914.2 : 49**
Contents. Scotland and the border.—Second visit to England, 1839.—The Eglinton tournament.—Talks over travel: London, Isle of Wight. etc. — Letters from England and the continent, 1845-46.—Nature criticised by art.

Floyd, M. Travels in France and the British Islands, [1855]. Phila. 1859. D. **914.2 : 17**

Harcourt, R. Rambles through the British Isles, or Where I went and what I saw in England, Ireland and Scotland. N. Y. [1869]. D.   **914.2 : 20**

Carnegie, Andrew. An american four-in-hand in Britain. N. Y. 1883. O.   **914.2 : 66**

Silloway, T: W., and Lee L. Powers. The cathedral towns and intervening places of England, Ireland and Scotland ; description of cities, cathedrals, lakes, mountains, rivers and watering-places. Bost. 1883. D.   **914.2 : 70**

Ingram, J: H. The haunted homes and family traditions of Great Britain. [1st and] 2d series. Lond. 1884. 2 v. D.   **133 : 30**

Ireland.

Hall, S: Carter and Anna Maria. Ireland ; its scenery, character, etc. New ed. Ill. N. Y. n. d. 3 v. Q.   **914.1 : R11**

Shaw's tourists' picturesque guide to Killarney and Cork. Map of the lakes, the south-west of Ireland and plan of Cork. Ill. Lond. n. d. S.   **914.1 : 12**

Thackeray, W: Makepeace. The irish sketch-book ; ill. by the author, [pub. 1843]. 3d ed. Lond. 1860. D.   **914.1 : 5**
— Same. Leipz. 1872. 2 v. S.   **914.1 : 5**

Carlyle, T: Reminiscences of my irish journey in 1849. N. Y. 1882. Q.   **914.1+2**

Rodenberg, (originally Levy), Julius. Die insel der heiligen ; eine pilgerfahrt durch Irland. Berlin. 1860. 2 v. D.   **914.1 : 1**

Trench, W. Steuart. Realities of irish life, [1821-68]. Bost. 1880. S.   **914.1 : 6**

· **x** denotes books specially adapted for children.

McGrath, Terence. Pictures from Ireland. (Leisure hour ser.) N. Y. 1881. S.
914.1 : 4

Becker, Bernard H: Disturbed Ireland ; the letters written during the winter of 1880–81. Maps. Lond. 1881. D.   914.1 : 17

Scotland.

Forsyth, Robert. The beauties of Scotland ; containing a clear and full account of the agriculture, commerce, mines and manufactures of the population, cities, towns, villages, etc., of each county. Ill. Edinb. 1805—1808. 5 v. O.   914.1 : 16
Contents. V. 1. Midlothian. — East Lothian.—Berwick. 2. Berwick, continued.—Roxburgh.—Selkirk.—Tweeddale.— Dumfries.— Galloway.— Kirkcudbright. — Wighton. — Air. 3. Renfrew. — Lanark. — Glasgow.—Dunbarton. — Stirling. — Linlithgow. — Clackmannan. 4. Clackmannan, continued. — Kinross.—Fife.—Perth.—Angus, or Forfarshire.—Kincardine.—Aberdeen.— Banff.—Moray. — Nairn. — Cromarty,—Caithness. 5. Caithness, continued.—Orkney Islands.—Shetland Islands.—Sutherland.— Ross.— Inverness, and islands.—Argyle, and islands.—Conclusion.

Turnbull, Robert. The genius of Scotland, or Sketches of scottish scenery, literature and religion. 5th ed., ill. N. Y. 1850. S.
914.1 : 19

Hood, Edwin Paxton. Scottish characteristics. N. Y. [1883]. D.   914.1 : 13
Contents. The old scottish minister.—Characteristics of scottish humor. — The humors of scottish character.—Some varieties of scottish superstition.—The scot abroad.—The humors of scottish dialect.—The old scottish lawyers and the law courts.—Old Edinburgh.—The old scottish lady.—Scottish proverbial philosophy. — The old scottish sabbath. — Northern lights.

Sinclair, Catherine. Scotland and the scotch, or The western circuit. N. Y. 1840. D.
914.1 : 8

Victoria, Alexandrina, queen of England. Leaves from the journal of her life in the Highlands, from 1848 to 1861 ; prefixed and added, extracts from the same journal giving an account of earlier visits to Scotland, and tours in England and Ireland and yachting excursions ; ed. by Arthur Helps. N. Y. 1868. D.   914.1 : 10 v1
— More leaves from the journal of a life in the Highlands, from 1862 to 1882. N. Y. 1884. D.   914.1 : 10 v2
— Same. N. Y. 1884. Q.   914.1+10 v2

Stewart, Alexander. Nether Lochaber ; the natural history, legends and folk-lore of the west Highlands. Edinb. 1888. O.
914.1 : 14

Cumming, Constance Frederica Gordon-. In the Hebrides. New ed., ill. Lond. 1883. D.
914.1 : 15

Smith, Alexander. A summer in Skye. Bost. 1865. D.   914.1 : 9

Grant, James. Cassell's old and new Edinburgh ; its history, its people and places. Ill. Lond. [1884, 1885]. 3 v. Q.   914.1+18

England.

In general.

Brayley, E: Wedlake, J: Britton and others. Beauties of England and Wales, or Delineations, topographical, historical and descriptive, of each county. Lond. 1801-15. 18 v. in 25. O.   914.2 : 78
Contents. Brayley, E: W., and J: Britton. V. 1. Bedfordshire. — Berkshire. — Buckinghamshire. 2.

Cambridgeshire.—Cheshire.—Cornwall. 3. Cumberland.— Isle of Man.— Derbyshire. 4. Devonshire.—Dorsetshire. 5. Durham.—Essex,—Gloucestershire, 6. Hampshire.— Isle of Wight.— Herefordshire. 7. **Brayley**, E: W. Hertfordshire. — Kent. 8. Kent, continued. 9. **Britton**, J: Lancashire.—Leicestershire.—Lincolnshire. 10. London and Middlesex, or An historical, commercial and descriptive survey of the metropolis of Great Britain, incl. sketches of its environs and a topographical account of the most remarkable places in the above county : v. 1, 2 by E: W. **Brayley**, v. 3 [in 2 pts.] by J. **Nightingale**; v. 4 by J. N. **Brewer**. 11. **Evans**, J., and J: Britton. Monmouthshire. — Norfolk. — Northamptonshire. 12, pt. 1. **Hodgson**, J., and F. C. **Laird**, Northumberland, Nottinghamshire; pt. 2, **Brewer**, J. N., Oxfordshire, Rutlandshire. 13. **Nightingale**, J., pt. 1, Shropshire, Somersetshire; pt. 2, Staffordshire. 14. **Shoberl**, F: Suffolk.—Surrey.—Sussex. 15, pt. 1. Wiltshire by J: Britton, Warwickshire by J. N. **Brewer**; pt. 2, Westmoreland by J. **Hodgson**, Worcestershire by F. C. **Laird**. 16. **Bigland**, J: Yorkshire. 17. **Evans**, J. North Wales. 18. **Rees**, T: South Wales.

Cook, Joel. England, picturesque and descriptive ; a reminiscence of foreign travel. Ill. Phila. [1882]. Q.   914.2+90

Hall, S: Carter. The baronial halls and ancient picturesque edifices of England ; from drawings by J. D. Harding, G. Cattermole, S. Prout, W. Muller, J. Holland and other artists, col'd lithotints. Lond. 1881. 2 v. F.   914.2 : R91

Escott, T: Hay Sweet. England, her people, polity and pursuits. N. Y. 1880. O.
914.2 : 5

Bulwer-Lytton, E: G: Earle Lytton, 1st baron Lytton. England and the english. N. Y. 1857. 2 v. in 1. D.   914.2 : 1
Contents. V. 1. View of the eng. character. — Society and manners.—Survey of the state of education, aristocratic and popular, and of the general influences of morality and religion. 2. View of the intellectual spirit of the times. — A view of our political state.—App.
— Same, germ. England und die engländer. Aus dem engl. von F: Notter. Stuttg. 1836. 6 v. in 2. T.   914.2 : 1

Rodenberg, (originally Levy), Julius. England, literary and social, from a german point of view. Lond. 1875. O.   914.2 : 6
Contents. Author's pref.—Tr.'s preface.—Kent and the Canterbury tales. — Shakspeare's England. — Coffee-houses and clubs of London.—The jews in England.—Pictures of english highroads.— Autumn on the english lakes.

Daryl, Philippe. Public life in England. Tr. by H: Frith and rev. by the author. N. Y. [1884]. D.   914.2 : 80
Contents. Pt. 1. Literature. — Journalism.— The theatre. — Poetry and science. Pt. 2. Parliament and municipal corporations. Pt. 3. The queen.—The army.—The navy.—The law courts and the police courts.

Blouet, Paul, (Max O'Rell). John Bull and his island. Tr. from the french under the supervision of the author. N. Y. 1884 [1883]. D.   914.2 : 74

Isham, Warren. The mud cabin, or The character and tendency of british institutions, as ill. in their effect upon human character and destiny. 2d ed. N. Y. 1853. D.
914.2 : 30

Heath, Francis. The english peasantry. Lond. 1874. O.   914.2 : 23

Greenwood, James. Low-life deeps ; an account of the strange fish to be found there. New ed. [The wanderer's lib.] Lond. 1881. D.
914.2 : 54

Groome, Francis Hindes. In gipsy tents. 2d ed. Edinb. 1881. D.   914.2 : 19

Morwood, Vernon S. Our gipsies in city, tent and van ; an account of their origin and strange life, fortune-telling practices, etc., specimens of their dialect and amusing anecdotes of gipsy kings, queens and other gipsy notabilities. Ill. Lond. 1885. O.
914.2 : 89

Howitt, W: Visits to remarkable places, old halls, battle fields and scenes, illustrative of striking passages in english history and poetry. 1st and 2d series. Phila. 1842. 2 v. O.
914.2+29

Contents. 1st ser. Penshurst in Kent. — Culloden. — Stratford-on-Avon and the haunts of Shakespeare. — Combe Abbey; Warwickshire. — Lindisfarne, Flodden Field and other scenery of Marmion. — Bolton Priory.—Hampton Court. — Compton-Wingates, Warwickshire. — A day-dream at Tintagel. — Staffa and Iona. — Edge-Hill. — Great Jesuits' college at Stonyhurst in Lancashire. — Winchester. — Wotton Hall. Staffordshire. — Sacrament sunday at Kilmorac. 2d ser. Durham.—Houghton-le-Spring.— Sherburn hospital, Wilton-Gilbert, Beaurepaire and Finchall Priory.—Lumley Castle.—Lambton Castle.—Jarrow.—Hilton Castle.—Castles of Brancepeth and Raby.—Darlington and Sockburn.— Newcastle-on-Tyne. — Birthplace and tomb of Bewick. — Seaton-Delaval. — Morpeth and Mitford. — Warkworth,— Alnwick Castle.— Bamborough Castle and the Farn Isles. — Berwick-upon-Tweed.—A stroll along the borders.—Hermitage Castle.—Annual border games. — Keeldar Castle.— Dilston Hall.

Hassell, J. Beauties of antiquity, or Remnants of feudal splendor and monastic times. Lond. 1807. O.
914.2 : R21

Roberts, Mary. Ruins and old trees, associated with remarkable events in english history. Lond. *n. d.* D.
914.2 : 52

English forests and forest trees : historical, legendary and descriptive. Ill. Lond. 1853. O.
914.2 : 51

Howitt, W: Homes and haunts of the most eminent british poets. N. Y. 1851. 2 v. D.
914.2 : 28

Contents. V. 1. Chaucer.—Spenser.—Shakespeare. —Cowley. — Milton.— Butler.—Dryden.— Addison.— Gay.—Pope.—Swift.—Thomson.—Shenstone. — Chatterton.—Gray.—Goldsmith.—Burns.—Cowper.— Mrs. Tighe.—Keats.—Shelley.—Byron. 2. Crabbe.—Hogg. —Coleridge.—Mrs. Hemans.—L. E. L.— Scott.—Campbell.—Southey.—Baillie.—Wordsworth. — Montgomery. — Landor. — Leigh Hunt. — Rogers. — Moore.— Elliott.—Wilson.—Procter.—Tennyson.

Daniel, G: Merrie England in the olden time. New ed., ill. [The wanderer's lib.]. Lond. 1881. D.
914.2 : 53

Thornbury, G: Walter. Shakspere's England, or Sketches of our social history in the reign of Elizabeth. Lond. 1856. 2 v. D.
914.2 : 63

Goadby, Edwin. The England of Shakespeare. Lond. 1881. D.
914.2 : 61

Ashton, J: Social life in the reign of queen Anne ; taken from original sources. New ed. ill. N. Y. 1883. D.
914.2 : 65

See also Manners and customs in Great Britain, under Sociology, col. 261.

General travels.

Voltaire, François Marie Arouet *called* de. Letters concerning the english nation. New ed. Lond. 1767. S.
914.2 : 81

Sinclair, Catherine. Hill and valley, or Hours in England and Wales, [1833]. N. Y. 1838. D.
914.2 : 41

Willard, Emma. Letters from Great Britain, 1833.
in 914.4 : 28

Thorburn, Grant. Men and manners in Britain, or A bone to gnaw for the Trollopes, Fid-

lers, etc.; notes from a journal on sea and on land in 1833-4. N. Y. 1834. D.
914.2 : 43

Raumer, F: L: G: v. England in 1835 ; a series of letters written to friends in Germany, during a residence in London and excursions into the provinces. Tr. from the german by Sarah Austin and H. E. Lloyd. Phila. 1836. O.
914.2+38

Cooper, James Fenimore. Gleanings in Europe: England, by an american. [*Anon.*] Phila. 1837. 2 v. D.
914.2 : 13

Sigourney, Lydia Howard, *born* Huntly. Pleasant memories of pleasant lands, [1840-41]. 2d ed. Bost. 1844. D.
914.2 : 40

Lester, C: Edwards. The glory and the shame of England. N. Y. 1841. 2 v. D. 914.2 : 32

Tyng, Stephen Higginson. Recollections of England, [1842]. Lond. 1848. D.
914.2 : 45

Palmer, Francis Paul, *and* Alfred H: Forrester, (*A. Crowquill*). The wanderings of a pen and pencil. Lond. 1846. O.
914.2+36

Wayland, Jane. Recollections of real life in England ; with an introd. by Francis Wayland. N. Y. 1848. S.
914.2 : 46

Emerson, Ralph Waldo. English traits, [1847-48]. 7th thous. Bost. 1857. D. 914.2 : 15

Coxe, Arthur Cleveland. Impressions of England, or Sketches of english scenery and society, [1851]. N. Y. 1856. D. 914.2 : 14

Tuckerman, H: Theodore. A month in England. N. Y. 1853. D.
914.2 : 44

Hawthorne, Nathaniel. Passages from [his] english note - books, [1853-58]. (Libr. ed.) Bost. 1879. 2 v. in 1. D. 914.2 : 24

— Our old home ; a series of english sketches. Bost. 1863. S.
914.2 : 25

— *Same.* (Ill. lib. ed.) Bost. 1878. D. 914.2 : 26

Hawthorne, Sophia, *born* Peabody, *mrs.* Nathaniel. Notes in England, [Scotland] and Italy, [1857]. N. Y. 1878. D. 914.2 : 64

Miller, Hugh. First impressions of England and its people. Bost. 1859. S. 914.2 : 33

Hoppin, James Mason. Old England ; its scenery, art and people. N. Y. 1867. S.
914.2 : 27

Taine, Hippolyte Adolphe. Notes on England. Tr. with an introd. chapter by W. F. Rae. Portr. N. Y. 1876. O. 914.2 : 42

Chandler, Alfred D. A bicycle tour in England and Wales, made in 1879 by the president, Alfred D. Chandler, and capt. J : C. Sharp, jr., of the Suffolk bicycle club of Boston, Mass.; with an app. on the use of the bicycle, both in Europe and the U. S. Maps and ill. Bost. 1881. S. 914.2 : 10

White, R: Grant. England without and within, [from observations during a journey in 1876]. Bost. 1881. D. 914.2 : 48

Winter, W: The trip to England [in 1877]. 2d ed., rev. and enl. Ill. by Joseph Jefferson. Bost. 1881. D.
914.2 : 50

— English rambles, and other fugitive pieces in prose and verse. Bost. 1884 [1883]. D.
914.2 : 75

Contents. English rambles, 1882.— In memory of Longfellow.—Wanderers; poems.

Champney, Lizzie, *born* Williams. Three Vassar girls in England ; a holiday excursion of three college girls through the mother country. Ill. Bost. 1884 [1883]. O.
914.2 : 67

Scudder, Horace Elisha. The english Bodley family. Bost. 1884 [1883]. O.   x 914.2 : 68

Pennell, Joseph *and* **Elizabeth Robins.** A Canterbury pilgrimage ; ridden, written and ill. by [the authors]. N. Y. 1885. O.   914.2 : 88

Hassard, J: R. G. A Pickwickian pilgrimage. Bost. 1881. T.   914.2 : 60
Includes also A boat-voyage on the Wye.

Rimmer, Alfred. About England with Dickens. Ill. Lond. 1883. D.   914.2 : 73

London.

Knight, C:, ed. London. Ill. Lond. 1841–44. 6 v. Q.   914.2+37
Note. A collection of papers by C: Knight, G. L. Craik, J. Saunders, W. Weir, J. C. Platt and others.

Thornbury, Walter, *and* **E: Walford.** Old and new London ; a narrative of its history, its people and its places. Ill. Lond. *n. d.* 7 v. Q.   914.2+79
Contents. V. 1, 2. Thornbury, W. East of Temple Bar. 3, 4. Walford, E: Westminster and the western suburbs. 5. Walford, E: The western and northern suburbs. 6. Walford, E: The southern suburbs.—Index. 7. Maps.

Walford, E: Greater London ; a narrative of its history, its people and its places ; v. 1, 2. Ill. N. Y. [1884]. 2 v. Q.   914.2+82
Note. The district included extends about 15 miles in all directions from Charing Cross.

Thornbury, Walter. Haunted London ; ed. by E: Walford. Ill. by F. W. Fairholt. Lond. 1880. D.   914.2 : 59
"Deals less with the London of the ghost-stories, than with the London consecrated by manifold traditions."—*Preface.*

Grant, James. The great metropolis, by the author of "Random recollections of the lords and commons." 2d ed. N. Y. 1837. 2 v. in 1. D.   914.2 : 18

Coghlan, Francis. Pocket picture of London and its environs, alphabetically arr. New ed., rev., corr. and enl. by Alexander Cooper Lee. Lond. 1847. T: 914.2 : 31

Grillparzer, Franz. London, 1836.
in 832 : 35 v10

Kalisch, L: Paris und London ; v. 2 : London. Frankfurt a. M. 1851. S.   914.2 : 2

Saunders, F: Memoirs of the great metropolis. or London from the Tower to the Crystal palace. N. Y. 1852. D.   914.2 : 39

Rodenberg *(originally* Levy*),* **Julius.** Alltagsleben in London ; ein skizzebuch. Berlin. 1860. D.   914.2 : 3

London, Reduced ordnance map ; index, showing the new postal divisions, railway stations, etc., containing references to 16,000 streets, squares, postal districts, cab fares,. etc., and a list of the principal exhibitions and places of amusement. Lond. *n. d.* S.   914.2 : 76

Nadal, Ehrman Syme. Impressions of London social life ; with other papers suggested by an english residence. N. Y. 1875. D.   914.2 : 35
Contents. Impressions of London social life.— English sundays and London churches.—Two visits to Oxford.—The british upper class in fiction.—Presumption.— English court festivities.—English tradition and the english future.—Childhood and english scenery.—New York and London winters.—The evening call.— Our latest notions of republics.—English conservative temper.—English and american newspaper-writing.— Americans abroad.— Society in New York and fiction.

Hare, A: J: Cuthbert. Walks in London. N. Y. 1876. 2 v. in 1. D.   914.2 : 7

Amicis, Edmondo de. Jottings about London. From the italian by Robert S. Minot. Bost. 1883. D.   914.2 : 69

Society in London, by a foreign resident. N. Y. 1885. S.   914.2 : 86

Vasili, *Count* Paul, *pseud.* The world of London, (La société de Londres) ; [expurgated]. N. Y. 1885. S.   914.2 : 87
See note under Berlin society, col. 1247.

Mayhew, H: London labour and London poor, a cyclopædia of the condition and earnings of those that will work, those that cannot work and those that will not work ; the London street folk, comprising street sellers, street buyers, street finders, street performers, street artizans, street labourers. Ill. Lond. 1861. 3 v. O.   914.2 : 58

— London characters ;. ill. of the humour, pathos and peculiarities of London life. Lond. 1874. D.   914.2 : 57

— *Same.* New ed., ill. [The wanderer's lib.]. Lond. 1881. D.   914.2 : 57

Greenwood, James. The wilds of London. New ed. [The wanderer's lib.] Lond. 1881. D.   914.2 : 55

Sadler, L. R., *(Jacob Larwood).* The story of the London parks, by Jacob Larwood. New ed., with ill. [The wanderer's lib.]. Lond. 1881. D.   914.2 : 56

Tower of London, Sketch of, as a fortress, a prison and a palace ; also a guide to the armories. Ill. Lond. *n. d.* D.   914.2 : 71

— The, its armouries and regalia, a hand-book guide for visitors. [Ill.]. Lond. *n. d.* D.   *in* 914.2 : 71

Westminster abbey, A historical description of ; its monuments and curiosities. Lond. *n. d.* S.   914.2 : 72

Other localities.

Irving, Washington. Abbotsford. — Newstead abbey. *In his* Works.
820.1 : 13 v2 ; 820.1 : P11 v7

— *Same,* germ. *In his* Alhambra.   I 401

Davies, G. Christopher. Norfolk broads and rivers, or The water-ways, lagoons, and decoys of East Anglia. New ed. Ill. Edinb. 1884. D.   914.2 : 85

Hicklin, J: Guide to Eaton Hall, near Chester. Chester. *n. d.* D.   914.2 : 77

Isle of Wight, The ; its history, topography, and antiquities. New and rev. ed., with maps and plans. N. Y. 1882. D.   914.2 : 82

Wise, J: R. The New Forest ; its history and its scenery. 3d ed. Ill. Lond. 1880. O.   914.2 : 62

Collins, W: Wilkie. Sights a-foot [through Cornwall, in 1850]. Phila. *n. d.* O.   914.2:11

Craik, Dinah Maria, *born* Mulock. An unsentimental journey through Cornwall. Ill. N. Y. 1884. Q.   914.2+84

Evans, T: Walks through north and south Wales ; containing a topographical and statistical description of the principality ; prefixed, a travelling guide exhibiting the direct and principal cross roads, inns, distances of stages and noblemen's and gentlemen's seats. 4th ed. Maps and ill. Lond. *n. d.* Q.   914.2 : 16

Rodenberg *(originally* Levy*),* **Julius.** Ein herbst in Wales ; land und leute, märchen und lieder. Hannover. 1858. D.   914.2 : 4

7. Europe — c, Germany and Austria.

1. General history.

(See also Constitutional history, col. 213.)

Brosien, Hermann. Lexikon der deutschen geschichte; die völker, länder, historischen personen und stätten Deutschlands, mit einschluss der germanischen stämme Oesterreichs, Burgunds, der Niederlande und der Schweiz bis zu ihrer abtrennung. Leipz. 1882. D.   **943 : R78**

Dunham, S: Astley. A history of the germanic empire. [Lardner's cabinet cycl.] Lond. 1834, 1835. 3 v. D.   **943 : 62**
Contents. V. 1. Political and civil history during the middle ages, 752—1272. 2. *Same, continued,* 1273—1437.— Religious and intellectual history of the germanic church during the middle ages, 752—1493.— Modern history, political, civil and religious, 1437—1519. 3. *Same, continued,* 1519—1792.

Pfister, J: Christian. Geschichte der teutschen; nach den quellen. [Geschichte der europ. staaten, herausg. von A. H. L. Heeren und F. A. Ukert.] Hamburg. 1829—1836. 6 v.   **943 : 65**
Contents. V. 1. Von den ältesten zeiten bis zum abgange der Karolinger. 2. Von der wahl Konrads I bis nach dem untergange der Hohenstaufen. 3. Von der herstellung des reiches nach den Hohenstaufen bis zu kaiser Maximilians I tod. 4. Von der kirchenreformation bis zum westphälischen frieden. 5. Vom westphälischen frieden bis zur auflösung des reiches [1806]. [6.] **Möller,** J. H. Register.

Bülau, F: Geschichte Deutschlands von 1806—1830; zugleich als fortsetzung von Pfisters Geschichte der teutschen. [Geschichte der europ. staaten, herausg. von A. H. L. Heeren und F. A. Ukert.] Hamburg. 1842. O.   **943 : 66**

Menzel, Wolfgang. The history of Germany, from the earliest period to the present time. Tr. from the 4th german ed. by mrs. G: Horrocks. Lond. 1849—82. 3 v. D.   **943 : 16**
Contents. V. 1. To 1250. 2. To 1710. 3. To 1842.

Kohlrausch, H: F: Theodor. A history of Germany from the earliest period to the present time. Tr. from the last german ed. by James D. Haas. Index. N. Y. 1847. O.   **943+14**

Sime, James. History of Germany; ed. by E: A. Freeman. [Freeman's historical course]. N. Y. 1875. S.   **943 : 17**

Taylor, Bayard. A school history of Germany, from the earliest period to the establishment of the German Empire in 1871. Ill. and maps. N. Y. 1882. D.   **943 : 35**

Zimmermann, W: Illustrirte geschichte des deutschen volkes. Stuttg. 1873. 3 v. Q.   **943+3**
Contents. V. 1. Von der heidnischen urzeit bis 911. 2. 911—1273. 3. 1273—1871.

— *Same, eng.* A popular history of Germany from the earliest period to the present day. Tr. by Hugh Craig. N. Y. [1878]. 4 v. Q.   **943+3**
Contents. V. 1. To 768. 2. 768—1024. 3. 1024—1516. 4. 1516—1871.

Stacke, L: Christian. Deutsche geschichte; in verbindung mit anderen von L. Stacke. Leipz. 1880, 1881. 2 v. O.   **943+**
Contents. V. 1. Von der älteren zeit bis zu Maximilian I. 2. Von Maximilian I bis zur neuesten zeit [1871].

Lewis, Charlton T. A history of Germany, from the earliest times; founded on D: Müller's "History of the german people". N. Y. 1874. O.   **943 : 15**

Yonge, Charlotte Mary. Young folks' history of Germany. Bost. [1878]. D.   **x 943 : 18**

Brewer, Ebenezer Cobham. The political, social and literary history of Germany, from the commencement to the present day. Lond. 1881. D.   **943 : 13**
Note. Has numerous dynastic tables, a table of the imperial wives, and one of men of mark from the earliest time to the present.

By periods.

Dahn, F: Julius Felix. Geschichte der deutschen urzeit; 1ste hälfte bis a. 476. [Geschichte der europ. staaten, herausg. von A. H. L. Heeren, F. A. Ukert und W. v. Giesebrecht.] Gotha. 1883. O.   **943 : 71**

Arnold, W: Deutsche geschichte. Gotha. 1881. O.   **943 : 57 v2**
ontents. V. 2. Fränkische zeit, erste hälfte; 481—81C.

Lindner, Theodor. Geschichte des Deutschen reiches vom ende des 14ten jahrb. bis zur reformation; 1ste abth.: Geschichte des Deutschen reiches unter könig Wenzel, [1378—1400]. Brschw. 1875. 2 v. in 1. O.   **943+44**

Geiger, L: Renaissance und humanismus ... in Deutschland.   *in* **909+20 v8**

Ranke, Franz Leopold v. Deutsche geschichte im zeitalter der reformation. 4te aufl. Leipz. 1867—68. 6 v. O.   **904 : 36 v1-6**
Contents. V. 1. Einleitung : Ansicht der früheren deutschen geschichte.—1486—1521.—Beilage. 2. 1521—1528. — Beilagen. 3. 1528—1535. 4. 1535—1547. 5. 1547—1558. — Beilagen. 6. Analekten : Urkunden, auszüge und kritische bemerkungen.—Register, 1-6.

— Zur deutschen geschichte; vom religionsfrieden [zu Augsburg, 1555] bis zum 30jährigen krieg. Leipz. 1868. O.   **904 : 36 v7**

Schiller, J: Christoph F: v. Geschichte des dreissigjährigen krieges. *In his* Sämmtliche werke.   **830 : 144 v14, 15 ; 830 : 143 v9**

— *Same, eng.* History of the thirty years' war. Tr. from the german, by A. J. W. Morrison. N. Y. 1846. D.   **943 : 21**

— *Same. In his* Works.   **830 : 150 v1**

— *Same.* The thirty years' war. *In his* Works.   **830 : R153 v3**

Gardiner, S: Rawson. The thirty years' war, 1618—1648. (Epochs of* modern history). N. Y. 1875. S.   **943 : 23**

Gindely, Anton. History of the thirty years' war. Tr. by Andrew Ten Brook, with an introductory and a concluding chapter by the tr. Maps and ill. N. Y. 1884. 2 v. D.   **943 : 41**
Contents. V. 1. 1618—1629. 2. 1630—1648.

— Geschichte des dreissigjährigen krieges. 1869—80. 4 v. O.   **943 : 39**
Contents V. 1—3. *Erste abth.* Geschichte des böhmischen aufstandes von 1618. 4. *Zweite abth.* Die stratdekrete Ferdinands II, und der pfälzische krieg. 1621—1623.

x denotes books specially adapted for children.

Naylor, Francis Hare. The civil and military history of Germany, from the landing of Gustavus to the conclusion of the treaty of Westphalia. In 2 v.; v. 1 [to the death of Gustavus Adolphus]. Lond. 1816. 1 v. in 2. O.   943 : 76

Biedermann, F: K: Deutschland im achtzehnten jahrhundert. Leipz. 1880. 4 v. O.
943 : 43
Contents. V. 1. Politische, materielle und sociale zustände, 2te aufl. 2.-4. Geistige, sittliche und gesellige zustände.—Generalregister.

Ranke, Franz Leopold v. Die deutschen mächte und der fürstenbund ; deutsche geschichte von 1780 bis 1790. 2te ausg. Leipz. 1875. 2 v. in 1. O.   904 : 36 v31, 32

Häusser, L: Deutsche geschichte vom tode Friedrichs des grossen bis zur gründung des Deutschen bundes. 4te aufl. Berlin. 1869. 4 v. O.   943 : 37
Contents. V. 1. Einleitung; von dem westfälischen frieden bis zum tode Friedrichs des grossen. — 1786–1795. 2. 1795–1806. 3. 1807–1812. 4. 1813–1815.

Treitschke, H: Gotthard v. Deutsche geschichte im 19ten jahrhundert. 3te aufl. [Staatengeschichte der neuesten zeit]. Leipz. 1882. 2 v. O.   943+60
Contents. V. 1. Bis zum zweiten Pariser frieden, 1815. 2. Bis zu den Karlsbader beschlüssen, 1819. — Beilagen.

Droysen, J: Gustav. Carl August und die deutsche politik, ein festgruss zum 3. sept. 1857. Jena. 1857. O.   943 : 81

Klüpfel, K: Geschichte der deutschen einheitsbestrebungen bis zu ihrer erfüllung, 1848–1871. Berlin, 1872, 1873. 2 v. O.   943 : 50
Contents. V. 1. 1848–1865. 2. 1865–1871.

Schmidt, Ferdinand. Deutsche kriege 1864, 1866, 1870–71. Kreuznach. [1883]. 2 v. S.
943 : 85

Hozier, H: M. The seven weeks' war ; its antecedents and its incidents, based upon letters reprinted from "The times." Phila. 1867. 2 v. O.   943 : 38

Blumé, W: Campaign 1870—1871. The operations of the german armies in France from Sedan to the end of the war, from the journals of the head-quarters staff. Tr. by E. M. Jones ; with maps and appd. Lond. 1872. O.   355.3 : 2
Note. For other works on the franco-prussian war. *see* History of France, cl. 944.6; *and* Military science, col. 232.

By topics.

Tacitus, Caius Cornelius. Germanische alterthümer ; mit text, übers. und erklärung von Tacitus Germania von Adolf Holtzmann, herausg. von Alfred Holder. Leipz. 1873. O.   943 : 4

— Same. A treatise on the manners of the germans. *In his* Works.   937 : 38

Arnold, W: Ansiedelungen und wanderungen deutscher stämme; zumeist nach hessischen ortsnamen. 2te unveränderte ausg. Marburg. 1881. O.   943+56

Freytag, Gustav. Bilder aus der deutschen vergangenheit. 11te aufl. Leipz. 1877–79. 4 v. in 5. D.   943 : 1
Contents. V. 1. Aus dem mittelalter. 2. 1ste abth. Vom mittelalter zur neuzeit. — 2te abth. Aus dem jahrhundert der reformation. 3. Aus dem jahrhundert des grossen krieges. 4. Aus neuer zeit.

— Pictures of german life in the 18th and 19th

centuries ; 2d series. Tr. from the original by mrs. Malcolm. Lond. 1863. 2 v. in 1. D.
943 : 61

Scherr, Johannes. Germania ; zwei jahrtausende deutschen lebens, kulturgeschichtlich geschildert. Ill. Phila. [1883]. O.
943+P34

— Deutsche kultur- und sittengeschichte. 309 : 2

Wessely, J. E. Deutschlands lehrjahre.
309 : 20

Kriegk, G: L: Deutsches bürgerthum im mittelalter ; nach urkundlichen forschungen und mit besonderer beziehung auf Frankfurt a. M. Frankfurt a. M. 1868, 1871. 2 v. O.
943 : 49

Balcke, Theodor. Bilder aus der geschichte der deutschen landwirthschaft. Berlin. 1876, 1877. 3 v. in 2. D.   943 : 53
Contents. V. 1. Von den ältesten zeiten bis zum ende des bauernkrieges. 2. Von der kirchlichen bis zur wirthschaftlichen reformation. 3. Aus dem alten in das neue reich.

Vehse, K: E: Geschichte der deutschen höfe seit der reformation. Hamburg. 1851–60. 48 v. in 45. S.   943 : 5
Contents. V. 1-6. 1te abth. Geschichte des preussischen hofs und adels der preussischen diplomatie. 7-17. 2e abth. Geschichte des östreichischen hofs und adels und der österreichischen diplomatie. 18-22. 3e abth. Geschichte der höfe des hauses Braunschweig. Deutschland und England ; die hofhaltungen zu Hannover, London und Braunschweig. 23-27. 4e abth. Geschichte der höfe der häuser Baiern, Würtemberg, Baden und Hessen. 28-34. 5e abth. Geschichte der höfe des hauses Sachsen. 35-48. 6e abth. Geschichte der kleinen deutschen höfe.

Malleson, G: Bruce. The battle fields of Germany, from the outbreak of the thirty years' war to the battle of Blenheim, [1631—1704]. Maps and plan. Lond. 1884. O.   943 : 80

Schlosser, L: W: Gottlob. Erlebnisse eines sächsischen landpredigers in den kriegsjahren von 1806 bis 1815. Leipz. *n. d.* S.   943 : 9

Mändler, F: Erinnerungen aus meinen feldzügen in Oesterreich, Tyrol, Russland, Sachsen und Frankreich, 1809—1815, und episoden aus meinem garnisonsleben. Nach dessen tode herausg. von Franz Joseph Adolph Schneidawind. Nürnberg. 1854. S.
943 : 8

Krasiński, *Hrabia* Waleryi. Panslavism and germanism. Lond. 1848. D.   943 : 82

Treitschke, H: Gotthard v. Zehn jahre deutscher kämpfe ; schriften zur tagespolitik. 2te aufl., fortg. bis zum jahre 1879. Berlin. 1879. O.   304 : 20
Contents. 1865. Die lösung der schleswigholsteinischen frage.— Herr Biedermann und die annexion. —Die parteien und die herzogthümer.— Herr v. Beust und die Preussischen jahrbücher. 1866. Der krieg und die bundesreform. — Politische correspondenz.— Die zukunft der norddeutschen mittelstaaten.—Reinhold Pauli und minister Golther. 1867. Zum jahresanfang.— Die verfassung des Norddeutschen bundes. — Die schöne gleichheit der franzosen. 1868. Altpreussen und die deutsch-russischen Ostsee-provinzen. 1869. Zum jahreswechsel. 1870. Badens eintritt in den bund. — Das strafgesetzbuch vor dem reichstage. — An den briefschreiber der Weser-zeitung. — Ein lied vom schwarzen adler. — Die feuerprobe des Norddeutschen bundes. — Was fordern wir von Frankreich ?—Friedenshoffnungen.—Luxemburg und das Deutsche Reich. — Die verträge mit den südstaaten. 1871. Oesterreich und das Deutsche Reich. 1872. Das aufgaben des neuen cultusministers. 1873. Das zweikammersystem und den herrenhaus. —Die letzte scholle welfischer erde. — Die maigesetze und ihre folgen. 1874. Das reichs-militärgesetz. — Der socialismus und seine gönner.—Bund und Reich. —Ein wort über russische kirchenpolitik. 1875. Die

gerechte vertheilung der güter. — Libera chiesa in libero stato, 1. **1876**. *Same*, 2, 3. — Die Türkei und die grossmächte.—Deutschland und die orientalische frage. **1877**. Das ergebniss der letzten wahlen. — Noch ein wort zur arbeiterfrage. — Die europäische lage am jahresschlusse. **1878**. Zum jahresanfang. —Zur lage. — Der socialismus und der meuchelmord. **1879**. Zur lage. — Der reichstag und die finanzreform.—Unsere ansichten.

Gould, Sabine Baring-. Germany, present and past. Lond. 1879. 2 v. D. **943 : 12**
Contents. V. 1. The upper nobility. — The lower nobility.—The laws of succession. — Peasant proprietors.—Marriage.—Women.— Forest royalty. — Education.—The universities.—The army. **2**. The stage. — Music.—The kulturkampf. — Protestantism. — The labour question.—Social democracy.— Culture.—Architecture.—The stove.—App. [bibliography].—Index.

White, Andrew Dickson. Neu - Deutschland. Aus dem engl. von. W: Ruprecht. Göttingen. 1883. O. **943 : 32**

2. History of special states.

Austria, and the old German empire.

Bryce, James. The holy roman empire [from Augustus to Francis II]. 7th ed. Lond. 1884. D. **937.1 : 9**

Giesebrecht, W: v. Geschichte der deutschen kaiserzeit ; mit einer übersichtskarte von H. Kiepert. Braunschweig. 1875-81. 5 v. O. **943+51**
Contents. V. 1. Gründung des kaiserthums. 5te aufl. **2**. Blüthe des kaiserthums. 4te aufl. **3**. Das kaiserthum im kampfe mit dem papstthum. 4te aufl. **4**. Staufer und Welfen. 2te bearb. **5**. Die zeit kaiser Friedrichs des Rothbarts.

Raumer, F: L: G: v. Geschichte der Hohenstaufen und ihrer zeit. 5te aufl. Leipz. 1878. 6 v. O. **943 : 59**
Contents. V. 1. 395—1152. **2**. 1152—1209. **3**. 1209—1241. **4**. 1241—1270. **5**. Alterthümer des staats- und privatrechts.— Landwirthschaft, gewerbe, handel.— Münzwesen, mass und gewicht. — Abgaben, zöllen und regalien.—Kriegs- und seewesen. **6**. Kirchliche alterthümer.— Wissenschaft und kunst.— Häusliche verhältnisse, sitten, gebräuche. — Verzeichniss der quellen.—Register.

Schmidt, Ferdinand. Die Hohenstaufen und ihre zeit. Berlin. [1885]. 2 v. in 1 S. **943 : 88**

Abbott, J: Stevens Cabot. The empire of Austria ; its rise and present power, [1232—1792]. (The monarchies of continental Europe). 3d ed. N. Y. 1859. O. **943 : 79**

Mailáth Székhelyi, J: Nepomuk József *gróf*. Geschichte des östreichischen kaiserstaates. [Geschichte der europ. staaten, herausg. von A. H. L. Heeren und F. A. Ukert.] Hamburg. 1834-50. 5 v. O. **943 : 67**
Contents. V. 1. 1218—1526. **2**. 1527—1619. **3**. 1619—1648. **4**. 1648—1740. **5**. 1740—1849.— Möller, J. H. Register.

Coxe, W: History of the house of Austria, from the foundation of the monarchy by Rhodolph of Hapsburgh, to the death of Leopold II, 1218 to 1792. 3d ed. Lond. 1847. 3 v. D. **943 : 28**

Kelly, Walter Keating. History of the house of Austria, from the accession of Francis I to the revolution of 1848, in continuation of the history written by archdeacon Coxe. Added, Genesis, or Details of the late austrian revolution by an officer of state, [Franz *graf* v. **Hartig**], tr. from the german. Lond. 1853. D. **943 : 28 v4**

Robertson, W: The history of the reign of the emperor Charles V. New ed. Glasgow. 1817. 4 v. D. **943 : 10**
Contents. V. 1. A view of the progress of society in Europe, from the subversion of the roman empire to the beginning of the 16th century.—Proofs and illustrations.—Index. **2**. Charles V, to 1527. **3**. 1527—1548. **4**. 1549—1556.—Index, v. 2-4.

— *Same* ; with A view of the progress of society in Europe to the beginning of the 16th century. Added, questions for the examinations of students by J. Frost. N. Y. 1843. O. **943 : 10**

— *Same*. Abridged ed. [School dist. lib.] N. Y. 1844. S. **943 : 10**

— *Same* ; with an account of the emperor's life after his abdication by W: H. Prescott. Phila. 1869. 3 v. O. **943 : 11**
Contents. V. 1. A view, *etc.*—1502—1520. **2**. 1520—1549. **3**. 1549—1558.—Index.

Malden, H: Elliot. Vienna, 1683 ; the history and consequences of the defeat of the turks before Vienna, sept. 12, 1683, by John Sobieski, king of Poland, and Charles Leopold, duke of Lorraine. Lond. 1883. D. **943 : 33**

Arneth, Alfred *ritter* v. Geschichte Maria Theresias. Wien. 1863-79. 10 v. O. **943+42**
Contents. V. 1-3. Maria Theresias erste regierungsjahre. **4**. Maria Theresia nach dem erbfolgekriege. **5, 6**. Maria Theresia und der siebenjährige krieg. **7-10**. Maria Theresia's letzte regierungszeit.

Wolf, Adam, *and* Hans v. **Zwiedineck-Südenhorst**. Oesterreich unter Maria Theresia, Josef II und Leopold II, 1740 — 1792. (Oncken, W:, *ed.* Allgemeine geschichte in einzeldarstellungen ; 3te hauptabth., 9ter th.) Ill. und portr. Berlin. 1884. O. **909+21 v9**

Adair, *Sir* Robert. Historical memoir of a mission to the court of Vienna in 1806, with a selection from his despatches. Lond. 1844. O. **943 : 30**

Beer, Adolf. Zehn jahre österreichischer politik, 1801—1810. Leipz. 1877. O. **943 : 52**

Springer, Anton. Geschichte Oesterreichs seit dem Wiener frieden, 1809. [Staatengeschichte der neuesten zeit.] Leipz. 1863, 1865. 2 v. O. **943+48**
Contents. V. 1. Der verfall des alten reiches. **2**. Die österreichische revolution.

Füster, Anton. Memoiren vom märz 1848 bis juli 1849 ; beiträge zur geschichte der Wiener revolution. Frankfurt a. M. 1850. 2 v. S. **943 : 6**

Klapka, György. Memoirs of the war of independence in Hungary. Tr. from the original ms. by O: Wenckstern. Lond. 1850. 2 v. O. **943 : 53**

Levitschnigg, H: *ritter* v. Kossuth und seine bannerschaft ; silhouetten aus dem nachmärz in Ungarn. Pesth. 1850. 2 v. S. **943 : 7**

Kossuth, L: Memories of my exile. Tr. from the original hungarian by Ferencz Jausz. N. Y. 1880. O. **943 : 27**

Schröer, K: Julius. Die deutschen in Oesterreich-Ungarn und ihre bedeutung für die monarchie ; vortrag gehalten im Deutschen verein in Wien, den 16. jan. 1879. *In* Deutsche zeit- und streit-fragen. **304 : 15 v8**

Milner, Emanuel. · Schwäbische kolonisten in Ungarn ; vortrag gehalten am 7. feb. 1879 im museum zu Tübingen. *In* Deutsche zeit- und streit-fragen.   **304 : 15 v9**

Peabody, Elizabeth Palmer, *ed.* Crimes of the house of Austria against mankind ; collected from accredited history. N. Y. 1852. D.   **943 : 29**

Schneller, Julius Franz. Geschichte von Böhmen. (Allg. historische taschenbibliothek, 18ter th.) Dresden. 1827. 2 v. in 1. S.   **943 : 75**

See also in the Index *to biography* **Eugène—Franz Josef — Friedrich — Heinrich — Joseph — Karl— Latour—Leopold—Maria Theresia— Metternich —Otto—Rudolf—Waldstein.**

P r u s s i a , a n d   t h e   n e w   G e r m a n   e m p i r e .

Pölitz, K: H: L: Die geschichte Preussens. (Allg. historische taschenbibliothek, 14ter th.) Dresden. 1827. 4 v. in 1. S.   **943 : 73**

Heinel, E: F: R: Geschichte Preussens ; bearb. und vom jahre 1867-71 fortgeführt von C. F. **Laudien.** 7te aufl. Karte. Königsberg. 1876. O.   **943 : 45**

Eberty, Felix. Geschichte des preussischen staats. Breslau. 1867-73. 7 v. in 6. D.   **943 : 55**
Contents. V. **1.** 1411—1688. **2.** 1688—1740. **3.** 1740—1756. **4.** 1756—1763. **5.** 1763—1806. **6.** 1806—1815. **7.** 1815—1871.

Abbott, J: Stevens Cabot. The history of Prussia ; with an app. by another hand, continuing the history to date. N. Y. [1882]. O.   **943 : 31**

Wyatt, Walter J. The history of Prussia, from the earliest times to the· present day ; tracing the origin and development of her military organization. Lond. 1876. 2 v. O.   **943 : 77**
Contents. V. **1.** 700—1390. **2.** 1390—1525.—Pedigree of the house of Hohenzollern, till the accession of Frederick VI, burgrave of Nuremberg, to the rank of kurfürst of Brandenburg.— The early history of Nuremberg and other leading imperial cities of Germany.

Tuttle, Herbert. History of Prussia to the accession of Frederick the great, 1134—1740. Map. Bost.·1884 [1883]. D.   **943 : 36**

Ranke, Franz Leopold v. Zwölf bücher preussischer geschichte. Leipz. 1874. 5 v. in 3. O.   **904 : 36 v25-29**
Contents. [V. **25, 26**] 1, 2. Genesis des preussischen staates [bis 1715].— Analekten. [**27, 28**] 3, 4. 1715—1742.—Analekten. [**29**] 5. 1742—1755.—Register, 1—5, (bound with vol. 30).

— *Same, eng.* Memoirs of the house of Brandenburg and history of Prussia during the 17th and 18th centuries. Tr. from the german by sir Alexander and lady Duff Gordon. Lond. 1849. 3 v. O.   **943 : 63**
Note. This is a translation of the first ed. of the german work, pub. in 1847 and entitled "Neun bücher preussischer geschichte." In the new german ed., the "first book" has been extended to four under the collective title of "Genesis des preussischen staates."

Stenzel, Gustav Adolf Harald. Geschichte des preussischen staats. [Geschichte der europäischen staaten, herausg. von A. H. L. Heeren und F. A. Ukert]. Hamburg. 1830-51. Gotha. 1854. 5 v. O.   **943 : 68**
Contents. V. **1.** Von den ältesten zeiten bis 1640. **2.** 1640—1688. **3.** 1688—1739. **4.** 1739—1756. **5.** 1756—1763.—**Möller,** J. H. Register.

Schmidt, Ferdinand. Oranienburg und Fehrbellin ; ein historisches gemälde aus der regierungszeit des grossen kurfürsten. 5te aufl. Ill. Kreuznach. [1882]. S.   **943 : 84**

Duncker, Max Wolfgang. Aus der zeit Friedrichs des grossen und Friedrich Wilhelms III ; abhandlungen zur preussischen geschichte. Leipz. 1876. O.   **943 : 47**

Oncken, W: Das zeitalter Friedrichs des grossen. (Oncken, W:, *ed.* Allgemeine geschichte in einzeldarstellungen ; 8te hauptabth., 8ter th.) Portr., ill. und karten. Berlin. 1881, 1882. 2 v. O.   **909+21 v8**

Frederick the great, his court and times ; with an introd. by T: Campbell. 2d ed. Lond. 1845. 2 v. D.   **943 : 19**

Friedrich II *the great, king of Prussia.* [Posthumous works]. Tr. from the french by T: Holcroft. Dublin. 1791. 4 v. in 2. O.   **943 : 20**
Contents. V. **1.** History of my own time. **2, 3.** The history of the seven years' war. **4.** Memoirs. from the peace of Hubertsburg to the partition of Poland, and of the bavarian war.

Broglie, Jacques Victor Albert *duc* de. Frederick II and Maria Theresa ; from hitherto unpub. documents, 1740 — 1742. From the french by mrs. Cashel Hoey and J: Lillie. N. Y. 1883. Q.   **943+25**

Ranke, Franz Leopold v. Zur geschichte von Oesterreich und Preussen zwischen den friedensschlüssen zu Aachen [1748] und Hubertsburg [1763]. Leipz. 1875. O.   **904 : 36 v30**
Contents. Maria Theresia, ihr staat und ihr hof im jahre 1755 ; aus den papieren des grosskanzlers Fürst.—Der ursprung des siebenjähr. krieges.— Analekten.—Ansicht des siebenjähr. krieges.

Longman, F: W. Frederick the great and the seven years' war. (Epochs of modern history.) N. Y. [1881]. S.   **943 : 24**

Schäfer, Arnold. Geschichte des siebenjährigen kriegs. Berlin. 1867-74. 2 v. in 3. O.   **943 : 46**
Contents. V. **1.** Der ursprung und die ersten zeiten des krieges bis zur schlacht bei Leuthen. **2.** Von anfange des krieges bis zur eröffnung des feldzuges von 1760. **3.** Die drei letzten kriegsjahre und die friedensschlüsse.—Register.

Ranke, Franz Leopold v. Hardenberg und die geschichte des preussischen staates von 1793—1813. 2te aufl. der in dem werke "Denkwürdigkeiten des staatskanzlers fürsten von Hardenberg" den eigenhändigen memoiren Hardenberg's beigegebenen historischen darstellung des herausgebers. Leipz. 1879-81. 3 v. O.   **904 : 36 v46-48**
Contents. [V. **46**] 1. [K: A: *fürst* v.] Hardenberg bis zu seinem eintritt in den preussischen dienst.— 1793-1795.—1796-1806, 1er abschnitt. [**47**] 2. *Same,* 2er abschnitt.— 1806-1813.—Notiz über die memoiren des grafen von Haugwitz. [**48**] 3. 1806-1813.—Denkschrift Hardenberg's: Ueber die reorganisation des preussischen staates, 1807.

Oncken, W: Das Deutsche Reich im jahre 1872 ; zeitgeschichtliche skizzen, 1, 2. *In* Deutsche zeit- und streitfragen.   **304 : 15 v2**
Contents. **1.** Die krone Preussen im Deutschen reich. — Die rettung der deutschen volksschule in Preussen.—Die neugründung der universität Strassburg—Die jesuitendebatte. **2.** Der innere ausbau des reichs.—Das verbot des jesuitenordens und der episcopat.—Die dreikaiser-zusammenkunft und das verhältniss zu Frankreich.—Die neue kreisordnung in Preussen und das herrenhaus.

Martin, Theodor. Verfassung und grundgesetze des Deutschen Reiches ; zum praktischen gebrauch für richter, anwälte, bürger-

meister und polizeibeamte zusammenge-
ste]]t nach authentischen quellen. Mit an-
hang : Die verfassungsurkunde für das
Deutsche Reich. 2te ausg. Jena. 1872. O.
         342 : 9
See also in the Index to biography **Bismarck —
Blücher — Dörfling — Friedrica — Friedrich —
Gneisenau—Hohenlohe—Moltke— Scharnhorst
—Stein—Wilhelm—York.**

Other states.

Sartorius, G: F: Christoph, *freiherr von Waltershausen.* Geschichte des Hanseatischen bundes. Göttingen. 1802–8. 3 v. O. **943 : 40**
 Contents. V. 1. Einleitung.—Von der entstehung
der deutschen Hanse im 13. jahrh. bis zum frieden
mit Woldemar III, 1370.—Beylagen: Quellen; Verzeichniss der urkunden und acten-stücke. 2. Von
dem frieden mit Dänemark, 1370, bis zu dem allgemeinen deutschen landfrieden, 1495.— Beylagen:
Quellen; Ueber die zu dem bunde gehörigen com-
munen; Urkunden. 3. Von dem allgemeinen deutschen landfrieden bis nach dem 30jährigen kriege.—
Beylage: Verzeichniss der urkunden.
Schäfer, Dietrich. Die Hansestädte und könig
 Waldemar von Dänemark ; hansische geschichte bis 1376. Jena. 1879. O. **943+54**
Francke, W: Die nachfolge in Braunschweig
 als frage des rechts ; mit 4 stammtafeln.
 In Deutsche zeit- und streitfragen.
        304 : 15 v13
Böttiger, C: W:, *and* Th. Flathe. Geschichte
 des kurstaates und königreiches Sachsen.
 [Geschichte der europ. staaten, herausg.
 von A. H. L. Heeren und F. A. Ukert.]
 Hamburg. 1830, 1831. Gotha. 1873. 4 v. O.
         943 : 69
 Contents. V. 1. Böttiger, C: W: Von den frühern
zeiten bis zur mitte des 16. jahrh. 2. 1553–1831. 3.
Flathe, Th. 1806–1866. [4.] Möller, J. H. Register.
Pölitz, K: H: L: Die geschichte des königreiches
 Sachsen. (Allg.-historische taschenbiblio-
 thek, 10ter th.) Dresden. 1826. 2 v. in 1. S.
         943 : 72
— Die geschichte der staaten des Ernestinischen
 hauses Sachsen ; des grossherzogthums
 Weimar-Eisenach, und der herzogthümer
 Altenburg, Meiningen - Hildburghausen -
 Saalfeld, und Coburg-Gotha. (Allg. histo-
 rische taschenbibliothek, 17ter th.) Dres-
 den. 1827. S.   **943 : 74**
Regel, Fritz. Die entwickelung der ortschaften
 im Thüringer wald, nordwestliches und zen-
 trales gebiet ; ein beitrag zur siedelungs-
 lehre Thüringens. Karte. Gotha. 1884. Q.
 In Petermann's mittheilungen, Ergän-
 zungsb. 17.   **905.1 : M**
Riezler, Sigmund. Geschichte Baierns. [Ge-
 schichte der europ. staaten, herausg. von
 A. H. L. Heeren, F. A. Ukert und W. v.
 Giesebrecht.] Gotha. 1878, 1880. 2 v. O.
         943 : 64
 Contents. V. 1. Bis 1180. 2. Bis 1347.
Stälin, Paul F: Geschichte Württembergs ; 1ster
 b., 1ste hälfte, bis 1268. [Geschichte der
 europ. staaten, herausg. von A. H. L. Hee-
 ren, F. A. Ukert und W. v. Giesebrecht.]
 Gotha. 1882. O.   • **943 : 70**
Schmidt, Ferdinand. Bilder aus dem Elsass ;
 mit der ansicht des Strassburger münsters.
 Bremen. [1876]. 2 v. in 1. S. **943 : 87**
 Contents. V. 1. Von der ältesten zeit bis zum mit-
telalter. 2. Vom mittelalter bis zur neueren zeit.
— Bilder aus der geschichte Lothringens ; mit
 der ansicht der Metzer kathedrale. Bremen. [1876]. S. *With his* Bilder aus dem
 Elsass.   **943 : 87**

2. Description.

General.

Daniel, Herrmann Adalbert. Deutschland, nach
 seinen physischen und politischen verhältnissen geschildert. 5te aufl. Leipz. 1878.
 2 v. O.   **914.3 : 1**
— *Same. In his* Handbuch der geographie.
         913 : 1 v3,4
 Contents. V. 1. Physische geographie. 2. Politische geographie.
Neumann, Gustav. Geographisches lexikon
 des Deutschen Reichs ; mit Ravensteins
 spezialatlas von Deutschland, vielen städte-
 plänen, statistischen karten, tabellen und
 mehreren hundert abbildungen deutscher
 staaten- und städtewappen. Leipz. 1883.
 O.   **914.3 : R53**
Ravenstein, L: Atlas des Deutschen Reichs ;
 im masstab 1 : 850,000, mit
 vollständigem register aller auf der karte
 enthaltenen namen, nebst drei statistischen
 karten der bevölkerungsdichtigkeit, kon-
 fessionen und gewerbthätigkeit in Deutschland. und 16 produktionskärtchen über
 bodenkultur, tierzucht, und nutzbare
 mineralien, mit ausführlichen statistischen
 übersichtstabellen. Leipz. [1883]. F.
         914.3 : R54
Gäbler, E: Special-atlas der grössten städte
 des Deutschen Reichs, nebst ihren umgebungen ; 26 karten in gleichen massstabe
 von 1 : 25000 der natürlichen länge. Leipz.-
 Neustadt. [1885]. O.   **914.3 : R58**
Gould, Sabine Baring-. Germany. [Foreign
 countries and british colonies]. Ill. Lond.
 1883. S.   **914.3 : 45**
Staël-Holstein, Anne Louise Germaine, *born*
 Necker, *baronne* de. Germany ; with notes
 and app. by O. W. Wight. N. Y. 1859. 2 v.
 D.   **914.3 : 47**
 Contents. V. 1. Fref.—Of Germany and the manners of the germans.—On literature and the arts.
2. *Same, continued.*—Philosophy and ethics.—Religion and enthusiasm.—App.: **Müller,** Max, General
survey of germ. literature to the close of the 18th
century; Hegel and recent germ. philosophy; Recent
germ. theology.
Johnson, Anna C. Peasant life in Germany.
 N. Y. 1858. D.   **914.3 : 25**
Schwarz, Agnes Sophie, *born* Becker. Vor hundert jahren ; Elise von der Reckes reisen
 durch Deutschland, 1784–86, nach dem
 tagebuche ihrer begleiterin Sophie Becker,
 herausg. und eingel. von G. Karo und M.
 Geyer. Stuttg. [1884]. D. **914.3 : 51**
Spencer, Edmund. Sketches of Germany and
 the germans, with a glance at Poland,
 Hungary and Switzerland, 1834—1836, by
 an englishman resident in Germany. 2d
 ed. In 2 v. ; v. 1. Lond. 1836. O.
         914.3 : 28
Shelley, Mary Wolstonecraft, *born* Godwin.
 Rambles in Germany and Italy, in 1840,
 1842 and 1843. Lond. 1844. 2 v. S.
         914.3 : 27
König, H: Stationen. Frankfurt a. M. 1846. S.
         914.3 : 9
 Contents, see Deutscher katalog, p. 38.
Strickland, H: Travel thoughts and travel
 fancies. Lond. 1854. D. **914.3 : 29**
Calvert, G: H: First years in Europe. Bost.
 1866. D.   **914.3 : 21**
 Note. Antwerp, Göttingen, Weimar and Edinburgh.

Browne, J: Ross. An american family in Germany. Ill. N. Y. [1866]. D. **914.3 : 55**
Braun, K: An den grenzen des Deutschen Reiches. *In his* Aus der mappe.
304 : 2 v1
Contents, see Deutscher katalog, p. 14.
Lindau, H: Gustav Paul. Vergnügungsreisen; gelegentliche aufzeichnungen. Stuttg. 1876. S. **914.3 : 11**
Contents, see Deutscher katalog, p. 38.
Howard, Blanche Willis. One year abroad, by the author of "One summer." Bost. 1878. S. **914.3 : 24**
Chetwynd, Julia Bosville, *born* Davidson, *the hon mrs.* H: Weyland. Life in a german village. 2d ed. Edinb. 1880. D.
914.3 : 49
Ruggles, H: Germany seen without spectacles, or Random sketches of various subjects, penned from different standpoints in the empire. Bost. 1883. O. **914.3 : 42**

North Germany.

Tolderlund, Hother Hakon Viggo, (*Dr. H.*) Ein sommer in Schleswig; skizzen und bilder von dr. H. Aus dem dänischen von H. Helms. Leipz. 1855. S. **914.3 : 6**
Rodenberg (*originally* Levy), Julius. Stillleben auf Sylt. 3 aufl. Berlin. 1876. D. **914.3 : 13**
Heinemann, O. v. Das königreich Hannover und das herzogthum Braunschweig, dargestellt in malerischen originalansichten ihrer interessantesten gegenden, merkwürdigsten städte, badeorte, kirchen, burgen und sonstigen baudenkmäler alter und neuer zeit. Ill. Darmstadt. 1853. O.
914.3+19
Lander, Sarah W. Berlin. (Spectacles for young eyes, no. 6). N. Y. *n. d.* S. **914.3 : 48**
Vizetelly, H: Berlin under the new empire; its institutions, inhabitants, industry, monuments, museums, social life, manners and amusements. Ill. Lond. 1879. 2 v. O.
914.3 : 30
Vasili, *Graf* Paul, *pseud.* Die Berliner gesellschaft. N. Y. 1884. O. **914.3+56**
— *Same, eng.* Berlin society. From the french by J. Loder. N. Y. 1884. D. **914.3 : 56**
Note. "The original author was the German empress's former french reader, Gérard, who used to write regularly to Gambetta. These letters were found among Gambetta's papers by his literary executor, mme. Edmond Adam. For effect, certain personal sketches made by an alsatian named Weiss were worked in, while the editor, with the aid of a former secretary of legation, Otto von Loë, harmonized the parts and gave the whole literary finish."—*Nation.*
Mayhew, H: German life and manners as seen in Saxony at the present day; with an account of village life, town life, fashionable life, school and university life, etc., of Germany at the present day. Ill. with songs and pictures of the student customs at the university of Jena. Lond. 1862. 2 v. O.
914.3 : 26
Hawthorne, Julian. Saxon studies. Bost. 1876. D. **914.3 : 22**
Contents. Dresden environs. — Of Gambrinus. — Sidewalks and roadways.—Stone and plaster. — Dresden diversions.—Types, civil and uncivil.—Mountaineering in miniature.
White, Walter. A july holiday in Saxony, Bohemia and Silesia. Lond. 1857. D.
914.3 : 31

Diezmann, A: Leipzig; skizzen aus der vergangenheit und gegenwart. Leipz. 1856. S.
914.3 : 2

The Rhine.

Hugo, V: Marie *comte.* The Rhine. N. Y. 1845. S.
914.3 : 3
Oertel, Philipp F: W:, (*W. O. von Horn*). Der Rhein; geschichte und sagen seiner burgen, abteien, klöster und städte. 2te aufl. Ill. Wiesbaden. 1875. O. **914.3 : 12**
Stieler, K:, Hans Wachenhusen *and* F: W: **Hackländer.** The Rhine from its source to the sea. Tr. by G. T. C. Bartley. Ill. Lond. [1877]. F. **914.3 : R43**
Göthe, J: Wolfgang v. Aus einer reise am Rhein, Main und Neckar in 1814 und 1815. *In his* Werke. **830 : 137 v26**
Cooper, James Fenimore. Excursion up the Rhine, 1832. *in* **914.4 : 5**
Murphy, *Lady* Blanche Elizabeth Mary Annunciata, *born* Noel. Down the Rhine. *With* **Whymper, E:** Scrambles amongst the Alps. **914.92 : 11**
— *Same. In* On the Rhine. **914 : 44**
Hill, Lucy A. Rhine roamings. Ill. Bost. 1880. O. **914.3 : 23**
Kinkel, J: Gottfried. Die Ahr; landschaft, geschichte und volksleben; zugleich ein führer für Ahrreisende. Ill. Leipz. 1846. S.
914.3 : 8
Head, *Sir* Francis Bond. Bubbles from the brunnen of Nassau, by an old man. N. Y. 1845. D. **914.3 : 41**
— *Same.* Bubbles from some brunnens of Germany, by an old englishman. N. Y. 1848. T. **914.3 : 20**
Heyner, C. Erinnerungen an Frankfurt; führer durch Frankfurt a. M. und seine umgebungen; nebst kurzem wegweiser zu ausflügen in den Taunus und die Bergstrasse für fremde und einheimische. 5te aufl., ill. Frankfurt a. M. [187-]. Tt. **914.3 : 52**
Kühne, F. Gustav. Von Cöln bis Worms und Speyer; rheinische städte und landschaften. Leipz. 1856. S. **914.3 : 10**
Riehl, W: H: Die pfälzer; ein rheinisches volksbild. 2te aufl. Stuttg. 1858. O. **914.3 : 18**
Waring, G: Edwin, *jr.* The bride of the Rhine; 200 miles in a Mosel row-boat. Added, a paper on the latin poet Ausonius and his poem "Mosella" by C: T. Brooks. Repr. with add., from Scribner's monthly. Bost. 1878. S. **914.3 : 40**

South Germany.

Lee, Katharine. In the alsatian mountains; a narrative of a tour in the Vosges. Ill. Lond. 1883. D. **914.3 : 50**
Wood, C: W. In the Black Forest. [Ill.] Lond. 1882. D. **914.3 : 44**
Griesinger, K: Theodor. Humoristische bilder aus Schwaben. Stuttg. 1844. S. **914.3 : 5**
— Silhouetten aus Schwaben. Stuttg. 1843. S.
914.3 : 4
Watts, Anna Mary, *born* Howitt. An art-student in Munich. 2d ed. Lond. 1880. 2 v. D.
914.3 : 32
Steub, L: Aus dem bayrischen hochlande. München. 1850. D. **914.3 : 17**
Seguin, L. G. The country of the passionplay; the highlands and highlanders of Bavaria. Lond. [1880]. D. **914.3 : 38**

Austria-Hungary.

Kay, D: Austria-Hungary. Maps and ill. [Foreign countries and british colonies]. Lond. 1880. S. **914.3:33**

White, Walter. On foot through Tyrol, in the summer of 1855. Lond. 1856. D. **914.3:39**

Rasch, Gustav. Hochlandsfahrten. Berlin. 1861. S. **914.3:14**
Note. Tyrol, the Satzkammergut, etc.

Edwards, Amelia Blandford. Untrodden peaks and unfrequented valleys; a midsummer ramble in the Dolomites. Leipz. 1873. S. **914.3:36**

Busk, *Miss* B. H. The valleys of Tirol, their traditions and customs, and how to visit them. Ill. and maps. Lond. 1874. D. **914.3:59**

Grohman, W: A. Baillie-. Gaddings with a primitive people; a series of sketches of tyrolese life and customs. (Leisure hour ser.) N. Y. 1878. S. **914.3:37**

Häring, W:, (*Wilibald Alexis*). Wiener bilder. Leipz. 1833. 2 v. S. **914.3:7**

Schlögl, F: "Wiener blut"; kleine culturbilder aus dem volksleben der alten kaiserstadt an der Donau. 4te aufl. Wien. 1875. O. **914.3:15**

Schlögl, F:—*Continued.*
— "Wiener luft"; kleine culturbilder aus dem volksleben der alten kaiserstadt an der Donau. Neue folge von "Wiener blut." 2te aufl. Wien. 1876. O. **914.3:16**

Quin, Michael Joseph. A steam voyage down the Danube; with sketches of Hungary, Wallachia, Servia, Turkey, etc. 1st amer. from 3d Lond. ed. N. Y. 1836. O. **914.3:34**

Pardoe, Julia. The city of the magyar, or Hungary and her institutions in 1839-40. Portr. Lond. 1840. 3 v. O. **914.3:57**

Brace, C: Loring. Hungary in 1851; with an experience of the austrian police. N. Y. 1852. D. **914.3:35**

"**Magyarland**"; the narrative of our travels through the highlands and lowlands of Hungary, by a fellow of the Carpathian society. Ill. Lond. 1881. 2 v. in 1. O. **914.3+46**
Note. The author is a lady.

Paton, Andrew Archibald. [Hungary, Transylvania, Dalmatia and Croatia.] *In his* Researches on the Danube. **914.94:27**

8. Europe — d, France.

1. History.

(*See also* Constitutional history, col. 212-213.)

In general.

Dareste de la Chavanne, Antoine Elisabeth Cleophas. Histoire de France, depuis les origines jusqu'à nos jours, 2e éd. Paris 1874. 9 v. O. **944+21**
Contents. V. 1. Depuis les origines jusqu'aux croisades. 2. Depuis les croisades jusqu'à Charles VI. 3. Depuis Charles VI jusqu'à François I. 4. Depuis François I jusqu'à Henry IV. 5. Louis XIII et Louis XIV, jusqu'à la paix de Ryswick. 6. Depuis la paix de Ryswick jusqu'à Louis XVI. 7. Louis XVI et la révolution, jusqu'à la paix de Bâle en 1795. 8. Directoire, consulat et empire. 9. La restauration.—Les gouvernements depuis 1830.

Duruy, V: Histoire de France. Nouvelle éd., ill. Paris. 1883. 2 v. D. **944:22**
Contents. V. 1. Introd.: Description géographique de la France.—1600 b. c.-1559 a. d. 2. 1559-1815. Résumé des événements de 1815 à 1883.

Martin, Bon L: H: Histoire de France depuis les temps les plus reculés jusqu'en 1789. 4e éd. Paris 1878. 17 v. O. **944+19**
Contents. V. 1. Origines, jusqu'en, 511. 2. *Same,* 511-843. — Féodalite, 843-987. 3. 987-1206. 4. 1206-1328. 5. 1328-1415. 6. 1415-1465. 7. 1465-1522. 8. 1522-1559. 9. 1559-1585. 10. 1585-1610. 11. 1610-1643. 12. Mouvement intellectuel et morale.—1643-1661. 13. 1661-1683. 14. 1683-1715. 15. 1715-1763. 16. Les philosophes.—1763-1789. 17. Table analytique.
Note. For an english translation of v. 13-16, *see* 944.4+1.

— Histoire de France depuis 1789 jusqu'à nos jours. 2e éd. Paris. 1878. 6 v. O. **944+20**
Contents. V. 1. 1789-1793. 2. 1793-1797. 3. 1797-1812. 4. 1812-1831. 5. 1831-1849. 6. 1849-1869.
Note. For an english translation, see 944+3.

Guizot, François P: Guillaume. A popular history of France, from the earliest times [to 1789]. Tr. by Robert Black. Ill. Bost. 1876. 6 v. O. **944+2**
Contents. V. 1. To 1099. 2. 1099-1380. 3. 1380-1515. 4. 1515-1589. 5. 1589-1711. 6. 1711-1789.

— Outlines of the history of France, from the earliest times to the outbreak of the revolution; an abridgement of [his] Popular history of France, with chronological index, historical and genealogical tables, portr., etc., by Gustave Masson. Bost. [1881]. D. **944:4**

— *and* Henriette de **Witt**, *born* Guizot. The history of France from the earliest times to 1848. Tr. by Robert Black. Ill. N. Y. 1885. 8 v. O. **944:6**
Contents. V. 1. To 1270.—The kingship in France. 2. The communes and the third estate. — 1328-1514. 3. 1515-1610. 4. 1610-1715. 5. 1715-1789. 6. 1789-1799. 7. 1799-1812. 8. 1813-1848.—Index.

Bodin, Felix. Die geschichte Frankreichs. 2te aufs neue durchgesehene und erweiterte aufl. von A. L. Herrmann. (Allg. historische taschenbibliothek, 1ster th.) Dresden. 1827. 2 v. in 1. S. **944:26**

Schmidt, Ernst Alexander. Geschichte von Frankreich. [Geschichte der europ. staaten, herausg. von A. H. L. Heeren und F. A. Ukert.] Hamburg. 1835-48. 4 v. O. **944:25**
Contents. V. 1. Bis 1328. 2. 1328-1559. 3. 1559-1643. 4. 1643-1774.—**Möller**, J. H. Register.

Wachsmuth, Ernst W: Gottlieb. Geschichte Frankreichs im revolutionszeitalter. [Geschichte der europ. staaten, herausg. von A. H. L. Heeren und F. A. Ukert.] Hamburg. 1840-44. 4 v. O. **944.5:29**
Contents. V. 1. 1774-1792. 2. 1792-1798. 3. 1798-1812. 4. 1810-1830.—**Möller**, J. H. Register.

Hillebrand, K: Geschichte Frankreichs von der thronbesteigung Louis Philipps bis zum falle Napoleon's III. Gotha. 1877, 1879. 2 v. O.　　**944.6 : 21**
Contents. V. **1.** 1830-1837. **2.** 1830-1848.

Crowe, Eyre Evans. History of France. Phila. 1835. 3 v. S.　　**944 : 27**
— *Same.* N. Y. 1844. 3 v. S.　　**944 : 27**
Contents. V. **1.** To 1610. **2.** 1610-1792. **3.** 1792-1814.—Index.

White, James. History of France to 1848. Edinb. 1875. D.　　**944 : 18**

Jervis, H. W. The student's France; a history of France from the earliest times to the establishment of the 2d empire in 1852. [*Anon.*] Ill. N. Y. 1879. D.　　**944 : 8**

Stephen, Caroline Emilia, (*Sarah Brook*). French history for english children. Maps. Lond. 1881. D.　　**x 944 : 13**
— *Same.* Rev. and ed. by G: Cary Eggleston. Ill. and maps. N. Y. 1882. S.　　**x 944 : 13**

Yonge, Charlotte Mary. History of France; ed. by E: A: Freeman. [Freeman's historical course.] N. Y. 1879. S.　　**x 944 : 12**
— Aunt Charlotte's stories of french history for the little ones. Lond. 1877. S.　　**x 944 : 14**
— *Same.* Young folks' history of France [to 1871]. Bost. [1879]. D.　　**x 944 : 14**

Lacombe, Paul. The growth of a people; a short study in french history. A tr. of the Petite histoire du peuple français by L: A. Stimson. N. Y. 1883. S.　　**944 : 16**

Laurent, François. Études sur l'histoire de l'humanité.　　**309 : 22**
Contents, see col. 151.

Bonnemère, Eugène. Histoire des paysans depuis la fin du moyen âge jusqu'à nos jours, 1200—1850; précédée d'une introd., an 50 avant J. C.—1200 après J. C. Paris. 1856. 2 v. O.　　**944 : 23**
Contents. V. **1.** Introd.—13e-16e siècle. **2.** 17e-19e siècle.

Stephen, *Sir* James. Lectures on the history of France. N. Y. [1851]. O.　　**944+11**
Contents. Decline and fall of the romano-gallic province. — Decline and fall of the Merovingian dynasty.—Character and influence of Charlemagne.— Decline and fall of the Carlovingian dynasty.—Anti-feudal influence of the municipalities of France; of the eastern crusades; of the albigeosian crusades.— Influence of the judicial on the monarchical system of France.—Influence of the privileged orders on the monarchy of France.—States-general of the 14th, 15th and 16th century.—Sources and management of the revenues of France. — Power of the purse in France.—The reformation and the wars of religion.— Power of the pen in France.—Absolute monarchy, as administered by Henry IV and by Richelieu; during the minority of Louis XIV; by Colbert and Louvois; by Louis XIV in person.—Growth of the french and the english monarchies compared.

Reeve, H: Royal and republican France; a series of essays, repr. from the Edinburgh, Quarterly and British and foreign reviews. Lond. 1872. 2 v. O.　　**944 : 24**
Contents. V. **1.** Louis XIV.—Saint-Simon.—Mirabeau. — Marie Antoinette. — Beugnot.— Mollien. **2.** Chateaubriand.—Louis Philippe.—Alexis de Tocqueville.— Agricultural France.— France in 1870.—Communal France.—Epilogue.

Jackson, Catherine Charlotte *lady*. Old Paris; its court and literary salons, [1610—1715]. N. Y. 1880. D.　　**944.4 : 4**
— The old régime; court, salons and theatres, [1715—1774]. Lond. 1880. 2 v. O.
　　944.4 : 5

---

x denotes books specially adapted for children.

Jackson, Catherine Charlotte *lady.—Continued.*
— The french court and society; reign of Louis XVI and the first empire, [1774—1815]. Lond. 1881. 2 v. O.　　**944.4 : 6**
— The court of the Tuileries, from the restoration to the flight of Louis Philippe, [1815—1848]. Lond. 1883. 2 v. O.　　**944.6 : 20**
— *Same.* N. Y. 1884. Q.　　**944.6+20**

Davenport, R: Alfred. The history of the Bastile and of its principal captives. Phila. 1846. S.　　**944 : 9**

Ritchie, Leitch. The romance of history: France. Ill. Lond. *n. d.* D.　　**944 : 15**

To the revolution of 1789.

Michelet, Jules. History of France. Tr. by G. H. Smith. N. Y. 1847, 1848. 2 v. O.
　　944+1
Contents. V. **1.** To 1380. **2.** 1380—1483.

Daniel, Gabriel. The history of France. from the time the french monarchy was establish'd in Gaul, to the death of Lewis XIV. Written originally in french, and now tr. into eng. Lond. 1726. 5 v. D.　**944 : 7**
Contents. V. **1.** An historical preface. — 486-1270. **2.** 1270—1461. **3.** 1461—1560. **4.** 1560—1610. **5.** An historical journal of the reign of Lewis XIII, and Lewis XIV, 1610—1715.

Scott, *Sir* Walter. Tales of a grandfather, 4th ser.: Stories taken from the history of France, [to 1413]. Parker's ed., in 2 v. Bost. 1845. 2 v. in 1. D.　　**944 : 10**
— *Same.* Bost. *n. d.* 2 v. in 1. D.　　**944 : 10**

Godwin, Parke. The history of France. V. 1: Ancient Gaul, [to 843]. N. Y. 1860. O.
　　944.1+1

Fustel de Coulanges, Numa Denis. Histoire des institutions politiques de l'ancienne France, 1e partie: L'empire romain; Les germains; La royauté mérovingienne. 2e éd. Paris. 1877. O.　　**944.1 : 3**

Thierry, Amédée Simon Dominique. Histoire des gaulois depuis les temps les plus reculés jusqu'à l'entière soumission de la Gaule à la domination romaine. 10e éd. Paris. 1881. 2 v. O.　　**944.1 : 4**

Masson, Gustave. Early chroniclers of Europe: France. Lond. *n. d.* D.　　**944.1 : 2**

Thierry, Jacques N: Augustin. Narratives of the Merovingian era, or Scenes of the 6th century, [a. d. 561—583]. *With his* Historical essays.　　*in* **904+37**

Palgrave, *Sir* Francis. The history of Normandy and of England. Lond. 1857-78. 4 v. O.　　**944 : 5**
Contents. V. **1.** Introd.: General relations of medieval history.—Carlovingian Normandy; 741—912. **2.** *Same, continued.* The three first dukes of Normandy: Rollo, Guillaume-Longue-Epée, and Richard-Sans-Peur.—The Carlovingian line supplanted by the Capets. **3.** Richard Sans-Peur. — Richard Le-Bon.— Richard III. — Robert Le-Diable. — William the Conqueror. **4.** William Rufus. — Accession of Henry Beauclerc.

Guizot, François P: Guillaume. Charlemagne and the Carlovingians; ed. from Guizot's History of France, with notes and genealogical, historical and other tables by Gustave Masson. (Episodes of french history, 1.) Lond. 1880. S.　　**944.2 : 2**
— St. Louis and the 13th century; ed. from Guizot's History of France, with notes and genealogical, historical and other tables by Gustave Masson. (Episodes of french history, 2.) Lond. 1880. S.　　**944.2 : 3**

Wallon, H: Alexandre. Saint Louis et son temps. 2e éd. Paris. 1876. 2 v. O.
　　　　　　　　　　　　　　　　944.2 : 5
Willert, Paul Ferdinand. The reign of Louis XI. Map. [Hist. handbooks]. Lond. 1876. S.　　　　　　　　　　　　**944.2 : 4**
Comines, Philippe de, *sieur d'Argenton.* Memoirs ; containing the histories of Louis XI and Charles VIII, kings of France, and of Charles the bold, duke of Burgundy. Added, The scandalous chronicle, or secret history of Louis XI by J: de Troyes. Ed. with life and notes, by Andrew R. Scoble. Lond. 1855, 1856. 2 v. D.　　**944.2 : 1**
Guizot, François P: Guillaume. Francis I and the 16th century ; ed. from Guizot's History of France, with notes and genealogical, historical and other tables, by Gustave Masson. (Episodes of french history, 3.) Lond. 1881. 2 v. S.　**944.3 : 2**
　Contents. V. 1. Francis I and the emperor Charles V. 2. Francis I and the renaissance.
Mignet, François A: Alexis. Rivalité de François I et de Charles V. 2e éd. Paris. 1876. 2 v. D.　　　　　　　　　　　　　　**944.3 : 5**
White, H: The massacre of St. Bartholomew, preceded by a history of the religious wars in the reign of Charles IX. Ill. N. Y. 1868. O.　　　　　　　　　　　　　**944.3 : 4**
Ranke, Franz Leopold v. Französische geschichte, vornehmlich im 16. und 17. jahrhundert. Leipz. 1868–70. 6 v. O.
　　　　　　　　　　　　904 : 36 v8-13
　Contents. [V. 8] 1. Frühere epochen der franz. geschichte. — Politik und krieg in der zweiten hälfte des 15. und der ersten des 16. jahrh. — Emporkommen kirchlicher reformbestrebungen. — 1562–1594. [9] 2. 1594–1642. [10] 3. 1643–1686. [11] 4. 1687–*abt.* 1756. [12] 5, umgearb. und vermehrt. Analecten: Ueber Davila's Geschichte der franz. bürgerkriege; Venetianische relationen vom ausgang des 15. bis gegen ende des 16. jahrh.; Mittheilungen aus franz. hss. und kritische bemerkungen ; Aus den spätern venetianischen relationen; Ueber die versammlung der franz. notabeln, 1787. [13] 6. Aus den briefen der herzogin von Orleans, Elisabeth Charlotte, an die kurfürstin Sophie von Hannover. — Register, 1–6.
　― Civil wars and monarchy in France, in the 16th and 17th centuries; a history of France, principally during that period. Tr. by M. A. Garvey. N. Y. 1853. D.　**944.3 : 3**
　Contents. The earlier epochs of french history.—Politics and war from 1450—1550. — Appearance of efforts for ecclesiastical reform in France. — Fifteen years of religious civil war. — Henry III and the League. — Henry IV in contest with the League, to 1594.
Davila, Enrico *or* Arrigo Cattarino. The history of the civil wars of France, [1559—1598]. Written in italian, tr. out of the original. 2d impression, whereunto is added a table. Lond. 1678. F.　**23 : R**
Sully, Maximilien de Bethune, *duc* de. Memoirs ; annexed, the trial of Francis Ravaillac for the murder of Henry the great. Tr. from the french. New ed. Lond. 1812. 5 v. D.　　　　　　　　**944.3 : 1**
　Contents. V. 1. Memoirs, 1570—1594. 2. 1594—1601. 3. 1602—1605. 4. 1605—1610. 5. 1610—1611.—Discussion of the political scheme commonly called the grand design of Henry IV.—Supp. to the life of the duke of Sully, after his retreat. — Trial of Ravaillac.—Index.
Chéruel, P: Adolphe. Histoire de France pendant la minorité de Louis XIV. Paris. 1879–80. 4 v. O.　　　　　　**944.4 : 11**
　Contents. V. 1. Introd.—1642—1644.—App. 2. 1644—1648. 3. 1648—1650.—App. 4. 1650—1651.—Conclusion:

Fin de la Fronde, 1651–53; Retour de Mazarin, son administration intérieure, 1653–61; Politique extérieure de Mazarin, 1653–61.
Martin, Bon L: H: History of France from the most remote period to 1789. Tr. from the 4th Paris ed. by Mary L. Booth. V. 13–16. Bost. 1865, 1866. 4 v. O.　**944.4+1**
　Contents. V. 13, 14. The age of Louis XIV. 15, 16. Decline of the monarchy. *No more translated.*— The original work will be found in **944+19.**
Philippson, Martin. Das zeitalter Ludwigs XIV. (Oncken, W:, *ed.* Allgemeine geschichte in einzeldarstellungen: 3te hauptabth., 5ter th.) Ill. and portr. Berlin. 1879. O.　　　　　　　**909+21 v5**
Pardoe, Julia. Louis XIV, and the court of France in the 17th century. N. Y. 1848. 2 v. D.　　　　　　　　　**944.4 : 8**
　Contents. V. 1. 1615—1658. 2. 1659—1715.
Lacroix, Paul, (*Le bibliophile Jacob*). The 18th century ; its institutions, customs and costumes: France, 1700—1789. Ill. Lond. 1876. Q.　　　　　　　　　　　**944.4 : R2**
Poole, Reginald Lane. A history of the huguenots of the dispersion at the recall of the edict of Nantes. Lond. 1880. D.
　　　　　　　　　　　　　944.4 : 10
Broglie, Jacques Victor Albert *duc* de. The king's secret ; the secret correspondence of Louis XV with his diplomatic agents, from 1752 to 1774. Lond. *n. d.* 2 v. O. **944.4 : 3**
　Contents. V. 1. Origin of the secret diplomacy.— Change of the system of the political alliances of France; the rôle of secret diplomacy subsequent to that change.—The secret diplomacy opposed to the russian army in Poland, 1756–58.—The secret diplomacy with the army, 1758–62. 2. The secret diplomacy in exile, 1762–63.—The secret diplomacy in England; the chevalier d'Eon, 1764–66.—The polish succession, 1764–70.— The partition of Poland, 1771–73. — Secret diplomacy in the Bastille, 1773–74.—Conclusion, 1774–1881.
Vizetelly, H: The story of the diamond necklace told in detail for the first time, by the aid of contemporary memoirs, original letters, and official and other documents, and comprising a sketch of the life of the countess de La Motte, pretended confidant of the Marie-Antoinette, with particulars of the careers of the other actors in this remarkable drama. 3d ed., rev. Lond. 1881. O.　　　　　　　　　　　　　　**944.4 : 9**
Collier, *Sir* G: France on the eve of the great revolution: France, Holland and the Netherlands a century ago; ed. by his granddaughter, mrs. C: Tennant. Lond. 1865. O.　　　　　　　　　　**944.5 : 27**

From 1789 to the present time.

Martin, Bon L: H: A popular history of France, from the first revolution to the present time ; with concl. chapters by F: Martin. Tr. by Mary L. Booth and A. L. Alger. Ill. Bost. 1876, 1882. 3 v. O.　**944+3**
　Contents. V. 1. 1789—1795. 2. 1795—1832. 3. 1832—1861.—Martin, F: 1861—1881.
　Note. The original work will be found in **944+20.**
Laun, H: van. The french revolutionary epoch; a history of France from the beginning of the first french revolution to the end of the second empire. Lond. [1878]. 2 v. O.　　　　　　　　　　　　　**944.5 : 28**
　Contents. V. 1. 1789—1804. 2. 1804—1870.
Adams, C: Kendall. Democracy and monarchy in France, from the inception of the great

revolution to the overthrow of the second empire. N. Y. 1874. O.   **944 : 17**
Contents. Introd.—The philosophers of the revolution.—The politics of the revolution.—The rise of napoleonism.—The restoration.—The ministry of Guizot.—The revolution of 1848.—From the second republic to the second empire.—Universal suffrage under the second empire.—The decline and fall.—Index.

Doniol, J: H: Antoine. La révolution française et la féodalité. 3e éd. Paris. 1883. O.   **944.5 : 22**
Contents. Préf.—L'abolition en France.—L'abolition dans les autres états du continent.—L'abolition en Angleterre.

The revolution and first empire.

Tocqueville, Alexis C: H: Clérel de. The old regime and the revolution. Tr. by J: Bonner. N. Y. 1856. D.   **944.5 : 6**
Blanc, J: Joseph L: History of the french revolution of 1789. Tr. from the french. V. 1. Phila. 1848. D.   **944.5 : 8**
Contents. Origin and causes of the revolution.—The two revolutions, [to aug. 1789].

Taine, Hippolyte Adolphe. The origins of contemporary France, tr. by J: Durand. [Pt. 1,] The ancient régime. N. Y. 1876. O. [Pt. 2,] The french revolution. N. Y. 1876–81. 3 v. O.   **944.5 : 5**
Contents. V. 1. The structure of society.—Habits and characters.—The spirit and the doctrine.—The propagation of the doctrine.—The people.—Index. 2. Spontaneous anarchy.—The constituent assembly, and the result of its labours.—The application of the constitution. 3. The jacobin conquest. 4. Establishment of the revolutionary government.—The jacobin programme.—The governors.—The governed.—The end of the revolutionary government.—Index, v. 2-4.

Sybel, H: K: Ludolf v. History of the french revolution, [1785–1799]. Tr. from the 3d ed. of the original german work by Walter C. Perry. Lond. 1867. 4 v. O. **944.5 : 21**
Contents. V. 1. Breaking out of the revolution.—First effects of the revolution on Europe.—Abolition of royalty in France. 2. Campaign in Champagne.—Commencement of the war between England and France.—Second partition of Poland. 3. Interruption of the coalition war.—Reign of terror in France.—Victories of the french republic. 4. Third partition of Poland.—Treaty of Basle.—End of the french national convention.

Abbott, J: Stevens Cabot. The french revolution of 1789 [to 1799], as viewed in the light of republican institutions. N. Y. 1859. O.   **944.5+7**

Häusser, L: Geschichte der französischen revolution, 1789—1799; herausg. von W: Oncken. 2te aufl. Berlin. 1877. O.   **944.5 : 1**
Carlyle, T: The french revolution; a history. N. Y. 1871. 2 v. D.   **944.5 : 9**
Contents. V. 1. Death of Louis XV.—The paper age.—The parlement of Paris.—States-general.—The third estate.—Consolidation.—The insurrection of women.—The feast of pikes.—Nanci.—The Tuileries.—Varennes. 2. Parliament first.—The marseillese.—September.—Regicide.—The girondins.—Terror.—Terror the order of the day.—Thermidor.—Vendemaire.

Geschichte der französischen revolution von 1789; zusammengestellt aus den werken von [François. A: Alexis] Mignet, [Jules Abel] Hugo, [T:] Carlyle. 2te aufl. Chicago. 1858. D.   **944.5 : 2**
Staël-Holstein, Anne Louise Germaine *baronne* de. Considerations on the principal events of the french revolution; posthumous work of the baroness de Staël, ed. by the duke de Broglie and the baron de Staël,

Tr. from the original ms. N. Y. 1818. 2 v. O.   **944.5 : 13**
Contents. V. 1. 1774—1799. 2. 1799—1815.—Considerations on the history and character of the english.—Index.

Smyth, W: Lectures on the history of the french revolution. New ed., with the author's last corr. and an add. lecture. Lond. 1855. 2 v. D.   **944.5 : 12**
Contents. V. 1. Louis XIV to june 20, 1792. 2. June 20, 1792, to the fall of Robespierre.—Supp. lectures: Dumont; Prelim. lectures, 1833, 1835; America; General summary.—Index.

Michelet, Jules. Histoire de la révolution française. Paris. 1876. 6 v. O.   **944.5 : 30**
Contents. V. 1. Introd.: De la religion du moyen âge; De l'ancienne monarchie.—Avril 1789–14 juillet 1790. 2. Juillet 1790–sept. 1791. 3. Oct. 1791–sept. 1792. 4. Sept. 1792–avril 1793. 5. Avril–déc. 1793. 6. Déc. 1793–29 juillet 1794.

Croker, J: Wilson. Essays on the early period of the french revolution; reprinted from the "Quarterly review", with add. and corr. Lond. 1857. O.   **944.5 : 26**
Contents. Thiers' histories.—Louis XVI and Marie Antoinette.—The journey to Varennes and Brussels, june 1791.—On the 20th june and 10th august 1792.—The captivity in the Temple.—Robespierre.—The revolutionary tribunals.—The guillotine.

Ranke, Franz Leopold v. Ursprung und beginn der revolutionskriege, 1791 und 1792. 2te aufl. Leipz. 1879. O.   **904 : 36 v45**

Lamartine, Alphonse Marie L: de. History of the girondists, or Personal memoirs of the patriots of the french revolution from unpublished sources, with a biogr. sketch of the author. Tr. by H: T. Ryde. N. Y. 1847–49. 3 v. D.   **944.5 : 19**
Contents. V. 1. April 1791–july 1792. 2. Aug. 1792—may 27, 1793. 3. Memoir of Lamartine.—May 28, 1793–july 28, 1794.—Index.

Berriat Saint-Prix, C: La justice révolutionnaire, août 1792 — prairial an III [mai 1795] ; d'après des documents originaux, la plupart inédits. 2e éd. Paris. 1870. O.   **944.5+23**

Mignet, François A: Alexis. History of the french revolution, from 1789 to 1814. Lond. 1846. D.   **944.5 : 10**

Thiers, L: Adolphe. The history of the french revolution. Tr. with notes and ill. from the most authentic sources by F: Shoberl. New ed. Lond. *n. d.* 5 v. D.   **944.5 : 3**
Contents. V. 1. To aug. 1792. 2. Sept. 1792–may 1793. 3. June 1793–july 1794. 4. Aug. 1794–feb. 1797. 5. Feb. 1797–nov. 1799.—Index.

— *Same.* 3d amer. ed. in 4 v.; v. 3, 4, [apr. 1794–nov. 1799]. Auburn, N. Y. 1846. 2 v. O.   **944.5 : 3**

— *Same* : Atlas; dressé par Th. Duvotenay. Paris. *n. d.* Q.   **944.5+3**

— History of the consulate and the empire of France under Napoleon ; a sequel to The history of the french revolution. Tr. from the french by D. Forbes Campbell and H. W. Herbert. Phila. 1855–63. 5 v. O.   **944.5+4**
Contents. V. 1. Nov. 1799–aug. 1805. 2. Aug. 1805–july 1808. 3. May 1808–may 1811. 4. March 1811–nov. 1813. 5. Nov. 1813–1821.

— *Same, germ.* Geschichte des consulats und kaiserreichs. Deutsch von W: Jordan. Leipz. 1845. 24 v. in 6. T.   **944.5 : 4**
Contents. V. 1. Die verfassung des jahres VIII.—Innere verwaltung.—Ulm und Genua.—Marengo. 2. Heliopolis.—Waffenstillstand.—Hohenlinden.—Höllenmaschine.—Die neutralen.—Räumung Aegyptens. 3. Allgemeiner friede.—Konkordat.—Das

Thiers, L: Adolphe.—*Continued.*
tribunat.—Lebenslängliches konsulat.—Die säkulari-
sationen. **4.** Bruch des friedens von Amiens. —
Rüstungen.—Die royalistenverschwörung.—Das kaiserthum. **5.** Die krönung.—Dritte koalition.—Ulm
und Trafalgar. **6.** Austerlitz.— Der Rheinbund.—
Jena.—Eylau, bis 1809.
— *Same.* Atlas, dressé et dessiné sous la direc-
tion de M. Thiers par A. Dufour et [Th.]
Duvotenay. Paris. 1875. Q.　**944.5+4**
Barni, Jules. Napoléon et son historien, M.
Thiers. Paris. *n. d.* D.　　**944.5 : 24**
Morris, W: O'Connor. The french revolution
and first empire; an historical sketch,
with an app. upon the bibliography of the
subject and a course of study by Andrew
D. White. (Epochs of modern history.)
N. Y. [1875]. S.　　　**944.5 : 11**
Pardoe, Julia. Episodes of french history during the consulate and first empire. N. Y.
1859. D.　　　　**944.5 : 17**
Headley, Joel Tyler. The imperial guard of
Napoleon from Marengo to Waterloo. N.
Y. 1861. D.　　　**944.5 : 18**
Williams, Helen Maria. A narrative of the
events which have taken place in France,
from the landing of Napoleon Bonaparte,
on the 1st of march 1815, till the restora-
tion of Louis XVIII, with an account of
the present state of society and public
opinion. Lond. 1815. O.　**944.6 : 19**
Siborne, W: History of the war in France and
Belgium in 1815; containing minute de-
tails of the battles of Quatre-Bras, Ligny,
Wavre and Waterloo. 1st amer. ed. Phila.
1845. O.　　　　**944.5 : 14**
Gardner, Dorsey. Quatre Bras, Ligny and
Waterloo; narrative of the campaign in
Belgium 1815. Bost. 1882. O.　**944.5 : 20**
Gleig, G: Robert. Story of the battle of Water-
loo. N. Y. 1860. D.　　**944.5 : 15**
Jomini, Antoine H: *baron* de. The political and
military history of the campaign of Water-
loo. Tr. from the french by S. V. Benét.
N. Y. 1860. D.　　　**944.5 : 16**
Simpson, James. A visit to Flanders and the
field of Waterloo, in 1815.　*in* **914.4 : 36**

From the restoration.

Browning, Oscar. Modern France, 1814—1879.
[Harper's half-hour ser.]　N. Y. 1880. T.
　　　　　　944.6 : 13
Lamartine, Alfonse Marie L: de. The history
of the restoration of monarchy in France.
N. Y. 1851-53. 4 v. D.　　**944.6 : 1**
Contents. V. **1.** 1813—1815. **2.** 1814—1815. **3.** 1815—
1821. **4.** 1821—1830.
— *Same, germ.* Geschichte der restauration.
Aus dem franz. von Theodor Roth. Stuttg.
1851-53. 8 v. S.　　　**944.6 : 1**
Blanc, J: Joseph L: The history of ten years.
1830—1840. Lond. 1844. 2 v. O.　**944.6 : 6**
Contents. V. **1.** 1830—1832. **2.** 1832—1840.
Cass, Lewis. France; its king, court and gov-
ernment, by an american. N. Y. 1840. O.
　　　　　　914.4 : 3
Heine, H: Französische zustände, 1832—1848.
In his Sämmtliche werke.　　**830 : 139 v8-10**
Lamartine, Alfonse Marie L: de. History of the
french revolution of 1848. Tr. by Francis
A. Durivage and W: S. Chase. 1st amer.
ed. Bost. 1860. 2 v. in 1. D.　**944.6 : 4**

Lamartine, Alfonse Marie L: de.—*Continued.*
— The past, present and future of the republic
[of 1848]. Tr. from the french. N. Y. 1850.
D.　　　　　**944.6 : 2**
— *Same, germ.* Die vergangenheit, gegenwart
und zukunft der französischen republik.
Aus dem franz. von P. Meyer. Stuttg. 1850.
S.　　　　　**944.6 : 2**
St. John, Percy Bolingbroke. French revolu-
tion in 1848 : The three days of february
1848 ; with sketches of Lamartine, Guizot,
etc. N. Y. 1848. S.　　**944.6 . 8**
Phipps, Constantine H:, *1st marquis of Nor-
manby.* A year of revolution ; from a jour-
nal kept in Paris in 1848. Lond. 1857. 2 v.
O.　　　　　**944.6 : 25**
Mitchell, Donald Grant, (*Ik Marvel*). The battle
summer ; transcript from personal obser-
vation in Paris, during 1848, by Ik Mar-
vel. N. Y. 1850. D.　　**944.6 : 7**
Meissner, Alfred. Revolutionäre studien aus
Paris, [1849]. Frankfurt a. M. 1849. 2 v. in
1. D.　　　　**944.6 : 3**
Senior, Nassau W: Journals kept in France and
Italy from 1848 to 1852, with a sketch of
the revolution of 1848 ; ed. by his daughter,
M. C. M. Simpson. Lond. 1871. 2 v. O.
　　　　　　944.6 : 15
Contents. V. **1.** Sketch of the revolution of 1848.—
Journal in France, 1848—oct. 1850. **2.** Journal in
Italy, dec. 1850—apr. 1851; in Paris, may 1851—jan. 1852.
— Conversations with M. Thiers, M. Guizot and
other distinguished persons during the
second empire ; ed. by his daughter, M. C.
M. Simpson. Lond. 1878. 2 v. O.
　　　　　　944.6 : 16
Contents. V. **1.** 1852—1854. **2.** 1855—1860.
— Conversations with distinguished persons dur-
ing the second empire, from 1860 to 1863 ;
ed. by his daughter, M. C. M. Simpson.
Lond. 1880. 2 v. O.　　**944.6 : 17**
Contents. V. **1.** 1860—1861. **2.** 1861—1863.
Ténot, P: Eugène. Paris in december 1851,
or The coup d'état of Napoleon III. Tr.
from the 13th french ed., with many original notes, by S. W. Adams and A. H. Bran-
don. N. Y. 1870. D.　　**944.6 : 10**
Maupas, Charlemagne Émile de. The story of
the coup d'état. Freely tr. with notes by
Albert D. Vandam. N. Y. 1884. D.
　　　　　　944.6 : 19
Hugo, V: Marie *comte.* The history of a crime ;
the testimony of an eye-witness. Ill. N. Y.
1878. O.　　　　**944.6 : 9**
Note. The story of the coup d'état of Napoleon in
1851.
Delord, Texile. Histoire du second empire.
Paris. 1869-76. 6 v. O.　　**944.6 : 18**
Contents. V. **1.** Introd.: Comment l'empire s'est
fait.—1853—1856. **2.** 1856—1859. **3.** 1860—1864. **4.** 1865
—1866. **5.** 1867—1869. **6.** 1870.—Conclusion.
Deutsch-französische krieg, Der, 1870–71 ; redigirt von der kriegsgeschichtlichen abtheilung des Grossen generalstabes : 1er t., Geschichte des krieges bis zum sturz des kaiserreichs ; 2ter t., Geschichte des krieges
gegen die republik. Berlin. 1874–81. 5 v.
text ; 3 v. maps. O:　　**944.6+22**
Contents. V. **1.** Vom beginn der feindseligkeiten
bis zur schlacht von Grave'otte. **2.** Von der schlacht
bei Gravelotte bis zum sturz des kaiserreichs. **3.**
Von der einschliessung von Paris bis zur wiederbe-
setzung von Orléans durch die deutschen. **4.** Die ereignisse im norden Frankreichs von ende november,
im nordwesten von anfang dezember und die belagerung von Paris von anfang dezember bis zum waffen-

stillstand.—Die operationen im südosten von mitte november bis mitte januar. **5.** Die ereignisse im südosten Frankreichs von mitte januar bis zur beendigung der feindseligkeiten. — Rückwärtige verbindungen.—Der waffenstillstand. — Rückmarsch und okkupation.—Rückblicke. **6-8.** Maps.

Ollier, Edmund. Cassell's history of the war between France and Germany, 1870—1871. London. 1871, 1872. 2 v. Q.   **944.6+11**

Forbes, Archibald. My experiences of the war between France and Germany. Leipz. 1871. 2 v. in 1. S.   **944.6 : 14**

Vizetelly, H:, *ed.* Paris in peril. Lond. 1882. 2 v. O.   **944.6 : 23**
Note. Comprises a history of life in Paris, during the siege of 1870-71.

Simon, Jules, *originally* Jules François Simon Suisse. The government of M. Thiers, from 8th february 1871 to 24th may 1873. From the french. N. Y. 1879. 2 v. O.   **944.6 : 12**

Jerrold, W: Blanchard. At home in Paris. Lond. 1884. 2 v. D.   **944.6 : 24**
Contents. V. 1. The gavroche party; literary estimates of the fall of the second empire, 1868—1870.—The observations of monsieur Chose.—The Montreux goat-herd. — Goodman Misery. — Supping men of Roger de Beauvoir's time. — His excellency M. Rougon. — Citizen Gugusse at play. **2.** The art of alms in France.—App.
See also in the Index to biography Alton-Shée —Anne—Bayard — Bonaparte—Bourbon—Broglie — Charles — Chevreuse — Coligny — Condé—Corday — Danton — Darc — Eugénie — Ferry — Henri — Hortense—Joseph Bonaparte—Joséphine — LaFayette — Lamballe — Louis — Mac Mahon—Maintenon—Marie Antoinette—Mirabeau — Napoléon — Ney— Orléans — Rémusat—Retz—Richelieu—Robespierre—Roland—Saint-Simon—Soult—Talleyrand—Thiers—Turenne.

2. Description.

In general.

Roberts, Margaret. France, by the author of "The atelier du lys" etc. [Foreign countries and british colonies]. Lond. 1881. S.   **914.4 : 29**

Bulwer, *Sir* H: Lytton Earle, *baron Dalling and Bulwer.* France, social, literary, political. N. Y. 1857. 2 v. in 1. D.   **914.4 : 21**

Hillebrand, K: France and the french in the 2d half of the 19th century. Tr. from the 3d germ. ed. Lond. 1881. O.   **914.4 : 30**

Marshall, F: French home life. Repr. from Blackwood's mag. [*Anon.*] N. Y. 1874. D.   **914.4 : 9**
Contents. Servants.—Children.—Furniture.—Food.—Manners.—Language.—Dress.—Marriage.

Field, *Mrs.* H: Martyn. Home sketches in France, and other papers ; with some notices of her life and character. N. Y. 1875. D.   **914.4 : 8**
Contents. The last illness. — Kind words spoken of the dead.—Home sketches in France.—The author of Adam Bede in her own home. — The author of the Schönberg-Cotta family.—The advantages of country life for women. — The dignity of labor for woman. — Training-school for nurses.

Hamerton, Philip Gilbert. Round my house ; notes of rural life in France in peace and war. Bost. 1876. D.   **914.4 : 11**

Blouet, Paul, (*Max O'Rell*). The dear neighbours! Lond. [1885]. D.   **914.4 : 55**

Young, Arthur. Travels during 1787, 1788 and 1789 ; undertaken more particularly with a view of ascertaining the cultivation, wealth,

resources and national prosperity of the kingdom of France. 2d ed. Lond. 1794. 2 v. Q.   **914.4+38**

Bray, Anna Eliza, *born* Kempe, *formerly mrs.* C: Stothard. Letters written during a tour through Normandy and Brittany and other parts of France, in 1818 ; incl. local and historical descriptions, with remarks on the manners and character of the people, by mrs. C: Stothard. Ill. Lond. 1820. Q.   **914.4 : R25**

Willard, Emma. Journal and letters from France and Great Britain. Troy. 1833. D.   **914.4 : 28**

Cooper, James Fenimore. Residence in France ; with an excursion up the Rhine and a second visit to Switzerland. Paris. 1836. O.   **914.4 : 5**

Allies, T: W: Journal in France in 1845 and 1848 ; with letters from Italy in 1847, of things and persons concerning the church and education. Brussels. 1850. T.   **914.4 : 1**

Barrell, G:, *jr.* The pedestrian in France and Switzerland. N. Y. 1853. D.   **914.4 : 2**

Floyd, M. Travels in France, 1855.   *in* **914.2 : 17**

Gundling, Julius, (*Lucian Herbert*). Aus Frankreich ; federzeichnungen aus dem Frankreich Napoleon's III. Leipz. 1861. S.   **914.4 : 13**

Jerrold, W: Blanchard. On the boulevards, or Memorable men and things drawn on the spot, 1853 — 1866 ; together with trips through Normany and Brittanny. Lond. 1867. 2 v. D.   **914.4 : 35**
Note. The greater part of v. 2 contains Through Normandy and Brittany.

Craik, Dinah Maria, *born* Mulock. Fair France ; impressions of a traveller, by the author of "John Halifax, gentleman." Leipz. 1872. S.   **914.4 : 6**

Paris.

Galignâni's new Paris guide, for 1873. Paris. [1873]. S.   **914.4 : 49**

Logerot, A:, *ed.* Paris actuel en 20 arrondisements, dans un rayon de 7 kilomètres. Paris. 1868. S.   **914.4 : 48**

Hamerton, Philip Gilbert. Paris in old and present times ; with especial reference to changes in its architecture and topography. Ill. Bost. 1885. O.   **914.4 : 53**

Simpson, James. Paris after Waterloo ; notes taken at the time and hitherto unpub., incl. a rev. ed., 10th, of A visit to Flanders and the field. Edinb. 1853. D.   **914.4 : 36**
Contents. Visit to Waterloo, 1815. — Reflections written in 1815; in 1852.—Paris in 1815.—App.

Grillparzer, Franz. Tagebuch aus dem jahre 1836: Paris und London. *In his* Sämmtliche werke.   **832 : 35 v10**

Thackeray, W: Makepeace. The Paris sketch-book. [Pub. in 1840]. N. Y. 1858. 2 v. in 1. S.   **914.4 : 43**
— *Same.* With portr. Leipz. 1873. 2 v. in 1. S.   **914.4 : 43**

Janin, Jules Gabriel. The american in Paris, or Heath's picturesque annual for 1843. Ill. Lond. 1843. O.   **914.4 : 20**
— *Same, french.* Un hiver à Paris. 2e éd. Paris. 1844. Q.   **914.4 : R20**

Gutzkow, K: Ferdinand. Briefe aus Paris, 1842.
—Pariser eindrücke, 1846. Frankfurt a. M.
1846. D.   **914.4 : 12**
   Contents, see Deutscher katalog, p. 37.

Gardner, A: Kingsley. Old wine in new bottles,
or Spare hours of a student in Paris. N. Y.
1848. D.   **914.4 : 10**

Kalisch, L: Paris und London: Paris. Frankfurt a. M. 1851. D.   **914.4 : 14**

Goodrich, Frank Boott. Tricolored sketches in
Paris, during 1851—1853. N. Y. 1855. D.
                         914.4 : 34

St. John, Bayle. Purple tints of Paris ; character and manners in the new empire. N.
Y. 1854. 2 v. in 1. D.   **914.4 : 40**

Marguerrites, Julie de. The ins and outs of
Paris, or Paris by day and night. Phila.
1855. S.   **914.4 : 39**

Wachenhusen, Hans. Das neue Paris. Leipz.
1855. S.   **914.4 : 18**

Piatt, Louisa Kirby. Bell Smith abroad. Ill.
N. Y. 1859. S.   **914.4 : 22**

Rodenberg (*originally* Levy), Julius. Pariser
bilderbuch. Brschw. 1856. S. **914.4 : 16**
   Contents. Album-blätter. — Studien. — Farbenskiz-
zen.—Lyrische stücke.
— *ed.* Paris bei sonnenschein und lampenlicht ;
ein skizzenbuch zur weltausstellung. 2te
aufl. Leipz. 1867. D.   **914.4 : 15**
   Contents, see Deutscher katalog, p. 38.

Tuckerman, H: Theodore. Maga papers about
Paris. N. Y. 1867. D.   **914.4 : 37**
   Contents. Across the Channel. — Tints and tones of
Paris life.—Art.— History. — A ball at the Tuileries.—
Character.—App. The great exposition of 1867.

Taine, Hippolyte Adolphe. Notes on Paris.
with notes by J: Austin Stevens. N. Y.
1875. O.   **914.4 : 42**

Sala, G: A: Paris herself again in 1878–9. 3d
ed. Ill. Lond. 1879. 2 v. O. **914.4 : 41**

Amicis, Edmondo de. Studies of Paris. Tr.
from the italian by W. W. C. N. Y. 1879.
D.   **854 : 1**
   Contents see under Italian literature, col. 1132.

Zolling, Theophil. Reise um die Pariser welt.
Stuttg. [1881]. 2 v. D.   **914.4 : 19**
   Contents, see Deutscher katalog, p. 39.

Houssaye, Arsène. Life in Paris ; letters on art,
literature and society. N. Y. 1881. D.
                         914.4 : 46

Bacon, H: A parisian year. Ill. by the author.
Bost. 1882. S.   **914.4 : 45**

The provinces.

Collins, C: Allston. A cruise upon wheels ; the
chronicle of some autumn wanderings
among the deserted postroads of France.
2d ed. Lond. 1863. D.   **914.4 : 4**

James, H: A little tour in France. Bost. 1885
[1884]. D.   **914.4 : 51**

Stevenson, Robert L: Travels with a donkey in
the Cévennes. Bost. 1879. S.   **914.4 : 24**

Tomes, Robert. The champagne country. N.
Y. 1867. D.   **914.4 : 27**

Blackburn, H: Normandy picturesque. 1st
amer. from 2d Lond. ed. Ill. Bost. 1873.
T.   **914.4 : 54**

Macquoid, Katharine S. Through Normandy.
Ill. 2d ed. N. Y. n. d. D.   **914.4 : 32**

Macquoid, T: *and* Katharine S. Pictures and legends from Normandy and Brittany. N.
Y. 1881. D.   **914.4 : 33**

Blackburn, H: Breton folk, an artistic tour in
Brittany. Ill. by R. Caldecott. Bost. 1881.
S.   **914.4 : 31**

Dumas, Alexandre Davy. Pictures of travel in
the south of France. Ill. Lond. n. d. D.
                         914.4 : 7

Venedy, Jakob. Das südliche Frankreich.
Frankfurt a. M. 1846. 2 v. O.   **914.4 : 17**

Taine, Hippolyte Adolphe. A tour through the
Pyrenees. Tr. by J. Safford Fiske. N. Y.
1874. O.   **914.4 : 26**

Vincent, Marvin Richardson. In the shadow
of the Pyrenees ; from Basque-land to Car-
casonne. Maps and ill. N. Y. 1883. D.
                         914.4 : 47

Monte Carlo and public opinion ; ed. by a visitor
to the Riviera. Ill. Lond. 1884. D.
                         914.4 : 52
   Note. For the Riviera, *see also* col. 1212.

9.   Europe — e, Italy.

1. History.

General.

Sforzosi, L. A compendious history of Italy.
Tr. from the original italian by Nathaniel
Greene. [Harper's family lib.] N. Y.
1842. S.   **945 : 4**
   Note. From the foundation of Rome to 1831 a. d.

Spalding, W: Italy and the italian islands.
from the earliest ages to the present time.
Ill. [Harper's family lib.] N. Y. 1843. 3 v.
S.   **945 : 6**
   Contents. V. 1. Ancient Italy to a. d. 476: Political history ; Literature, art and character ; Topography. **2.** *Same, continued*: Character, literature,
art and topography of early christianity.—Italy in
the dark and middle ages.—Modern Italy: Political
history to 1789; Literature and art in the 16th, 17th
and 18th centuries. **3.** *Same*: Political history to
1840; Topography of modern italian cities: Literature
and art in the 19th century; National character and
habits ; Natural history, resources and industry;
Statistics of the 19th century.

Hunt, W: History of Italy, [476—1870]; ed. by
E: A: Freeman. Ed. adapted for amer.
students. [Freeman's historical course].
N. Y. 1875. S.   **945 : 5**

Bosco, Giovanni. A compendium of italian history from the fall of the roman empire.
Tr. from the italian and completed to the
present time by J. D. Morell. Lond. 1881.
Q.   **945+34**

Leo, H: Geschichte der italienischen staaten.
[Geschichte der europ. staaten, herausg
von A. H. L. Heeren und F. A. Ukert].
Hamburg. 1829–32. 6 v. O.   **945 : 37**
   Contents. V. 1. 568—1125. **2.** 1125—1268. **3, 4.** 1268
—1492. **5.** 1492–1830. [**6.**] **Möller**, J. H. Register.

Macfarlane, C. The romance of history: Italy.
Lond. n. d. D.   **945 : 20**

Balzani, Ugo. Early chroniclers of Europe:
Italy. Lond. 1883. D.   **945 : 21**

Simonde de Sismondi, J: C: Léonard. A history of the italian republics ; being a view

of the rise, progress and fall of italian freedom. New ed. N. Y. 1847. S.
945 : 19

Geiger, L: Renaissance und humanismus in Italien und Deutschland. (**Oncken,** W:, cd. Allgemeine geschichte in einzeldarstellungen ; 2te hauptabth., 8ter th.) Ill. und facsimile-beilagen. Berlin. 1882. O.
909+20 v8

Symonds, J: Addington. Renaissance in Italy: [pt. 1]. The age of the despots ; [pt. 2.] The revival of learning. N. Y. 1881. 2 v. O.
945 : 7

— — [Pt. 3]. The fine arts.   **709 : 5**

— — [Pts. 4, 5]. Italian literature.   **850.1 : 2**

Wrightson, R: Heber. A history of modern Italy, from the first french revolution to 1850. Lond. 1855. O.   **945 : 32**

Botta, C: Guiseppe Guglielmo. History of Italy during the consulate and empire of Napoleon Buonaparte. Tr. from the italian by the author of " The life of Joanna, queen of Naples." Lond. 1828. 2 v. O. **945+41**

Pacca, Bartolommeo. Historical memoirs, [1808—1814]. Tr. from the italian by sir G: Head. Lond. 1850. 2 v. O.   **945 : 9**

Probyn, J: Webb. Italy ; from the fall of Napoleon I in 1815 to the death of Victor Emmanuel in 1878. N. Y. 1884. O.
945 : 40

Reuchlin, Hermann. Geschichte Italiens von der gründung der regierenden dynastien bis zur gegenwart. [Staatengeschichte der neuesten zeit]. Leipz. 1859-70. 3 v. in 2. O.
945+30

Contents. V. 1. Bis zum jahr 1848. **2.** Vom jan. 1848 bis zum tode Karl Alberts. **3.** Die reaktionszeit und die nationale erhebung Italiens von der bekämpfung der römischen republik im frühjahr 1849 bis zum letzten ministerium Cavours im jan. 1860.

Whiteside, James. Italy in the nineteenth century, contrasted with its past condition. Lond. 1848. 3 v. O.   **945 : 39**
Contents. V. 1. Tuscany. **2.** Rome. **3.** Naples and Rome.

Hackländer, F: W: Bilder aus dem soldatenleben im kriege. Stuttg. 1860. 2 v. S.
945 : 3
Note. Pictures of the austrian campaign of 1849 in Italy.

Arthur, W: Italy in transition ; public scenes and private opinions in the spring of 1860, ill. by official documents from the papal archives of the revolted legations. N. Y. 1860. D.   **945 : 14**

Abbott, J: Stevens Cabot. Italy and the war for italian independence ; containing a brief narrative of all the most interesting events in the past history of the kingdom, and an account of the causes and results of the recent struggle for italian unity, incl. a biograph. sketch of pope Pius IX, and a recital of the political complications with which the cabinets of Europe are now agitated. Bost. 1871. O.   **945 : 12**

Gallenga, Antonio. The pope and the king ; the war between the church and state in Italy. Lond. 1879. 2 v. O.   **945 : 17**

Löher, Franz v. Das neue Italien. *In* Deutsche zeit- und streit-fragen.   **304 : 15 v11**

See also in the index *to biography* **Alberoni— Alessandro — Cavour — Clemens XIV — Francesco — Garibaldi — Giovanno — Leo — Machiavelli—Medici—Pasolini— Pépé— Pius — Rienzi— Vittorio Emanuele.**

Venice, Genoa, etc.

Yriarte, C: Émile. Venice ; its history, art, industries and modern life. Tr. from the french by F. J. Sitwell. Ill. Lond. 1880. F.   **945 : R22**

Hazlitt, W: Carew. History of the Venetian republic ; her rise, her greatness and her civilization. [Maps and ill.] Lond, 1860. 4 v. O.   **945 : 10**
Contents. V. 1. 409–1201. **2.** 1202–1309. **3.** 1310–1413. **4.** 1414–1457.

Smedley, E: Sketches from venetian history. [*Anon.*] [Harper's family libr.] N. Y. 1846. S.   **945 : 11**

Ruskin, J: St. Mark's rest ; the history of Venice, written for the help of the few travellers who still care for her monuments. N. Y. 1884. D.   **945 : 27**

S., E. L. The city in the sea ; stories of the deeds of the old venetians from the chronicles, by the author of "Belt and spur". Ill. Lond. 1884. D.   **945 : 24**

Ranke, Franz Leopold v. Zur venezianischen geschichte. Leipz. 1878. O. **904 : 36 v42**
Contents. Venedig im 16. jahrh. und im anfang des 17.— Die verschwörung gegen Venedig, 1618.— Die venezianer in Morea.

Hasse, F: Christian A: Die geschichte der Lombardei. (Allg. historische taschenbibliothek, 12ter th.) Dresden. 1826. 2 v. in 1. S.   **945 : 38**

Bent, J. Theodore. Genoa ; how the republic rose and fell. Ill. Lond. 1881. O. **945 : 8**

Florence and Tuscany.

Napier, H: E: Florentine history to the accession of Ferdinand III, grand duke of Tuscany. Lond. 1846. 6 v. D.   **945 : 25**
Contents. V. 1. 17–1336. **2.** 1336–1402. **3.** 1402–1500. **4.** 1500–1532. **5.** 1532–1737. **6.** 1737–1815.

Perrens, François Tommy. Histoire de Florence depuis sés origines jusqu'à la domination des Médicis. Paris. 1883. 6 v. O. **945 : 26**
Contents. V. 1. Jusqu'en 1260. **2.** 1261–1300. **3.** 1300–1319.—Les arts et métiers ; les conditions sociales. —La vie privée.—Les belles-lettres.—Les beaux-arts. **4.** 1313–1358. **5.** 1358–1382.— Les belles-lettres.— Les beaux-arts. **6.** 1382–1435.—La régime économique au 14. et au 15. siècle.

Machiavelli, N: The history of Florence and of the affairs of Italy, from the earliest times to the death of Lorenzo the magnificent [1492] ; together with The prince and various historical tracts. New tr. Lond. 1854. D.   **945 : 1**
— *Same. In his* Writings.   **850+1 v1**
— *Same, germ.* Florentinische geschichten, übers. von Alfred Reumont. Leipz. 1846. 2 v. S.
945 : 1
Contents. V. 1. Bis 1435. **2.** 1435–1492.

Trollope, T: Adolphus. A history of the commonwealth of Florence from the earliest independence of the commune to the fall of the republic in 1531. Lond. 1865. 4 v. O.   **945 : 33**
Contents. V. 1. 1107–1328. **2.** 1328–1428. **3.** 1428–1492. **4.** 1492–1531.—App.—Index.

Capponi, Gino *marchese.* Geschichte der Florentinischen republik. Aus dem italienischen übers. von Hans Dütschke. Leipz. 1876. 2 v. in 1. O.   **945 : 29**
Contents. V. 1. Ursprung von Florenz.—1050–1434. **2.** 1434–1532.

Reumont, Alfred v. Geschichte Toscana's seit dem ende des Florentinischen freistaats. [Geschichte der europ. staaten, herausg. von A. H. L. Heeren, F. A. Ukert und W. v. Giesebrecht.] Gotha. 1876, 1877. 2 v. O.
         945 : 36
Contents. V. 1. Die Medici, 1530-1737. 2. Haus Lothringen-Habsburg, 1737-1859.

Yriarte, C: Émile. Florence, its history ; the Medici, the humanists, letters, arts. Tr. by C. B. Pitman. Ill. Lond. 1882. F.
         945 : R23

Scheffer-Boichorst, Paul. Florentiner studien. Leipz. 1874. O.   **945 : 28**
Contents. Die geschichte der Malespini eine fälschung.—Die chronik des Dino Compagni eine fälschung.—Gesta florentinorum.

Oliphant, Margaret O., *born* Wilson. Makers of Florence.   **920.5+P1**

Papal states, Rome.

Brosch, Moritz. Geschichte des Kirchenstaates. [Geschichte der europ. staaten, herausg. von A. H. L. Heeren, F. A. Ukert und W: v. Giesebrecht.] Gotha. 1880, 1882. 2 v. O.
         945 : 35
Contents. V. 1. Das 16. und 17. jahrhundert. 2. 1700-1870.—Register.

Gregorovius, Ferdinand Adolf. Geschichte der stadt Rom im mittelalter vom 5ten bis zum 16ten jahrh. 3te verb. aufl. Stuttg. 1875-81. 8 v. O.   **945 : 31**
Contents. V. 1. Vom anfange des 5. jahrh. bis zur einrichtung des exarchats in Ravenna, 568. 2. 568-800. 3. Von der kaiserkrönung Carl's bis zum ende des 10. jahrh. 4. Das 11. und 12. jahrh. 5. Das 13. jahrh. bis 1305. 6. 1305-1420. 7. Das 15. jahrh. 8. Die ersten drei decennien des 16. jahrh.

Wiseman, N: Patrice Stephen. A vindication of Italy and the papal states. From the Dublin review for oct. 1856. [*Anon.*] Cinc. n. d. S.   **945 : 16**

Maguire, J: Francis. Rome ; its ruler and its institutions. N. Y. 1858. D.   **945 : 18**

About, Edmond François Valentin. The roman question. Tr. from the french by mrs. Annie T. Wood ; ed., with an introd., by E. N. Kirk. Bost. 1859. D.   **945 : 13**

British and amer. archæol. society, *Rome.* Proceedings, season 1875-6. Rome. 1876. O.
         906 : Pam

Naples.

Coletta, P: History of the kingdom of Naples, 1734—1825. Tr. from the italian by S. Horner ; with a supp. chapter 1825—1856. Edinb. 1857. 2 v. O.   **945 : 2**
— *Same,* germ. Geschichte des königreichs Neapel. 2te aufl. Cassel. 1854. 3 v. T. **945 : 2**

Platen-Hallermünde, A: *graf* v. Geschichten des königreichs Neapel, 1130—1448. *In his* Gesammelte werke.   **830 : 141 v5**

Oertel, Philipp F: W:, (*W. O. v. Horn*). Zwei ausbrüche des Vesuv's, dargestellt für die jugend und das volk. 2te aufl. Ill. Wiesbaden. 1876. S.   **945 : 42**

2. Description.

In general.

Italy ; from the Alps to Mount Etna. Ill. Lond. n. d. F.   **914.5 : R70**
Contents. **Stieler,** K: From the Alps to the Arno. — **Paulus,** E: From the Arno to the Tiber.—**Kaden,** Woldemar. From the Tiber to Etna.

Bädeker, K: Italy ; handbook for travellers. 3d ed. rev. and augm. Coblenz. 1870-72. 3 v. S.   **914.5 : 65**
Contents. V. 1. Northern Italy and Corsica. 2. Central Italy and Rome. 3. Southern Italy, Sicily and excursions to the Lipari Islands, Tunis, Sardinia, Malta and Athens.

Moore, J: A view of society and manners in Italy, with anecdotes relating to some eminent characters. 5th ed., corr. London. 1790. 2 v. O.   **914.5 : 27**

Göthe, J: Wolfgang v. Italienische reise, 1786 -87. *In his* Werke. **830 : 137 v15, 16**
— *Same,* eng. Travels in Italy. *In his* Works.
         830 : 151 v8

Seume, J: Gottlieb. Spaziergang nach Syrakus in 1802. *In his* Werke. **830 : 147 v4**
— *Same.* With *his* Selbstbiographie.
         830 : 13-15

Forsyth, Joseph. Remarks on antiquities, arts and letters, during an excursion in Italy in 1802 and 1803. 4th ed. Lond. 1835. D.
         914.5 : 15

Cooper, James Fenimore. Excursions in Italy. Paris. 1838. O.   **914.5 : 12**

Gaudy, Franz Bernhard H: W: *freiherr* v. Mein römerzug. *In his* Werke.
         830 : 135 v2, 3
— Portogalli ; reise- und lebensbilder aus Italien, 1838. *In the same.* **830 : 135 v7**

Raumer, F: L: G: v. Italy and the italians. Lond. 1840. 2 v. O.   **924.5 : 29**

Shelley, Mary Wolstonecraft. Rambles in . . . Italy, 1840-43. *in* **914.3 : 27**

Hahn-Hahn, Ida Marie Louise Sophie Friederike Gustave *gräfin.* Jenseits der berge. 2te aufl. Leipz. 1845. 2 v. S.   **914.5 : 7**
Contents, see Deutscher katalog, p. 38.

Heeringen, Gustav v. Mein sommer. Leipz. 1844. 2 v. S.   **914.5 : 8**
Contents. V. 1. Genf.—Lausanne.—Lyon.—Marseille.—Genua.—Livorno.—Civita Vecchia. 2. Neapel.—Rom.

Dickens, C: J: Huffam. Pictures from Italy, [1844—45]. With *his* Great expectations.
         in **D1306**
— *Same.* In Cruisings and adventures.
         914.5 : 14

Gould, W: M. Zephyrs from Italy and Sicily, 1846. N. Y. 1852. D.   **914.5 : 34**

Allies, T: W: Letters from Italy in 1847.
         in **914.4 : 1**

Kemble, Frances Anne, *formerly mrs.* Butler. A year of consolation, by Mrs. Butler. N. Y. 1847. 2 v. in 1. D.   **914.5 : 5**

Hillard, G: Stillman. Six months in Italy, [1847—48]. 4th ed. Bost. 1854. 2 v. D.
         914.5 : 18

Townsend, G: Journal of a tour in Italy in 1850 ; with an account of an interview with the pope at the Vatican. Lond. 1850. O.
         914.5 : 30

Lester, C: Edwards. My consulship. N. Y. 1853. 2 v. D.   **914.5 : 24**
Note. At the end of v. 2, is an examination of the consular system.

Düringsfeld, Ida *freiin* v. **Reinsberg-.** Aus Italien. Bremen. 1851. S.   **914.5 : 6**

Honan, Michael Burke. The personal adventures of "our own correspondent" in Italy. N. Y. 1852. D.   **914.5 : 16**
Contents. Lisbon.—At sea; Gibraltar.—The gulf of Lyons. — Italia, Italia ! — Milan. — Turin. — Genoa. — Milan: the revolution. — The war. — Valeggio. — The war.—The retreat.—Milan.—The austrians at Milan.—Turin.—Leghorn.—Florence.

Norton, C: Eliot. Notes of travel and study in Italy, [1855]. Bost. 1860. D.   **914.5 : 28**

Hawthorne, Sophia, *born* Peabody. Notes in Italy, 1857.   **914.2 : 64**

Jameson, Anna, *born* Murphy. The diary of an ennuyée. Bost. 1860. T.   **914.5 : 22**

Mundt, Theodor. Italienische zustände. Berlin. 1859. 4 v. D.   **914.5 : 10**
Contents. V. 1. Skizzen aus Piemont und Rom. 2. Rom und Pius IX. 3, 4. Rom und Neapel.

Taine, Hippolyte Adolphe. Italy [1863]: Rome and Naples. From the french, by J. Durand. 4th ed. with corr. and an index. N. Y. 1877. O.   **914.5 : 42**
Contents. The route and the arrival. — Naples. — Rome.—Villas, palaces and churches.—Society.

— - Florence and Venice. From the french, by J. Durand. 4th ed. N. Y. 1877. O.
    914.5 : 41
Contents. Perugia and Assisi.—Florence. — The florentine school of art. — From Florence to Venice. — Venice.—Venetian art.—Lombardy.

Alford, H: Letters from abroad, [1861]. 2d ed. Lond. 1865. D.   **914.5 : 1**

Arnold, Howard Payson. European mosaic. Bost. 1864. D.   **914.5 : 2**

Howells, W: Dean. Italian journeys. N. Y. 1872. D.   **914.5 : 20**

Castelar y Rissoll, Emilio. Old Rome and new Italy, (Recuerdos de Italia). Tr. by mrs. Arthur Arnold. N. Y. 1873. D.
    914.5 : 43
Contents. Arrival in Rome.—The great ruin.—The roman catacombs.—The Sistine chapel.—The Campo Santo of Pisa.—Venice.— On the lagunes.—The god of the Vatican.—The ghetto.—The great city.—Parthenope.

Amicis, Edmondo de. Military life in Italy; sketches. Tr. by Wilhelmina W. Cady. N. Y. 1882. D.   **914.5 : 56**
Contents. A midsummer march. — The orderly.—The officer of the guard.—The wounded sentinel.—The mother.—The son of the regiment.—The conscript.—A bunch of flowers.—A nocturnal march.—Carmela.—That day.—The sentinel.—The camp.—The disabled soldier.—A medal.—An original orderly.—At twenty.—Departure and return; reminiscences of 1866.—Dead on the field of battle.—The italian army during the cholera of 1867.

Benson, Eugene. Art and nature in Italy. Bost. 1882. S.   **914.5 : 57**

Symonds, J: Addington. [Sketches in Italy]. *In his* Sketches and studies.   **824.2 : 86**
Contents, see under English literature, Essays, col. 1074.

— Italian by-ways. N. Y. 1883. D.   **914.5 : 61**

Jarves, James Jackson. Italian rambles; studies of life and manners in new and old Italy. N. Y. 1883. S.   **914.5 : 60**

Bianciardi, *Mrs.* E. D. R. At home in Italy. Bost. 1884. D.   **914.5 : 67**
Contents. Italy as a residence.— The city of the winds.—A mountain excursion in the province of Siena.—Summer days in Perugia.—An italian watering-place.—A week in northern Italy.—An april day on the Consuma pass.—A florentine family in the 15th century.—Camaldoli.—Vallombrosa.

Sala, G: A: A journey due south; travels in search of sunshine. Ill. Lond. 1885. O.
    914.5 : 74

Champney, Lizzie, *born* Williams. Three Vassar girls in Italy; a holiday excursion of three college girls through the classic lands. Ill. Bost. 1886 [1885]. O.
    914.5 : 73

Channing, Barbara H. Sunny skies, or Adventures in Italy. Bost. *n. d.* S. x **914.5 : 54**

x denotes books specially adapted for children.

Northern and central.
(*For the Riviera, see* col. 1212.)

Hare, A: J: Cuthbert. Cities of northern and central Italy. N. Y. 1876. 3 v. D.
    914.5 : 44
Contents. V. 1. On the Rivieras and in Lombardy and Piedmont. 2. In Venetia, Parma, the Emilia, the Marche and northern Tuscany. 3. Florence, Siena and other towns of Tuscany and Umbria.

— Venice. Ill. and map. N. Y. [1884]. D.
    914.5 : 69

Howells, W: Dean. Venetian life, [1866]. New and enl. ed. Bost. 1874. D.   **914.5 : 21**

Brown, Horatio F. Life on the lagoons. Lond. 1884. D.   **914.5 : 72**

Freeman, E: A: Sketches from the subject and neighbor lands of Venice. N. Y. 1881. D.
    914.5 : 40
Contents. The Lombard Austria.—Trieste to Spalato.—Spalato and its neighbours.—Spalato to Cattaro.—Venice in the footsteps of the normans.

Young, Arthur. Lombardy in 1789. *In his* Travels.   **914.4+38 v2**

Crawford, Mabel Sharman. Life in Tuscany. N. Y. 1859. D.   **914.5 : 13**

Janin, Jules Gabriel. Sketches of Genoa, Pisa and Florence, with a description of the cathedral of Milan. Tr. from the french by mrs. M. Harrison Robinson. Phila. 1854. T.   **914.5 : 23**

Story, W: Wetmore. Vallombrosa. Edinb. 1881. D.   **914.5 : 31**

Hare, A: J: Cuthbert. Florence. Ill. and map. N. Y. [1884]. D.   **914.5 : 68**

Howells, W: Dean. Tuscan cities. Ill. Bost. [1885]. O.   **914.5+77**

Rome.

Lumisden, Andrew. Remarks on the antiquities of Rome and its environs; a classical and topographical survey of the ruins of that celebrated city. Ill. 2d ed. Lond. 1812. Q.   **914.5 : R50**

Eaton, Charlotte A. Rome in the 19th century; containing an account of the ruins of the ancient city, the remains of the middle ages and the monuments of modern times, with remarks on the fine arts, the museums of sculpture and painting, the manners, customs and religious ceremonies of the modern romans. 5th ed. Lond. 1852. 2 v. D.   **914.5 : 47**

Parker, J: H: The archæology of Rome. Pts. 1, 4–12. Oxford. 1876–79. 9 v. O.
    914.5 : 63
Contents. [V. 1] Pt. 1, The primitive fortifications, 2d ed. [4] Pt. 4, The egyptian obelisks. [5] Pt. 5, Forum romanum et magnum. [6] Pt. 6, The via sacra, 2d ed.—Excavations in Rome, 1438-1882. [7] Pt. 7, The Flavian amphitheatre commonly called the Colosseum. [8] Pt. 8, The aqueducts. [9] Pt. 9, Tombs in and near Rome.—Pt. 10, Sculptures. [10] Pt. 11, Church and altar decorations and mosaic pictures. [11] Pt. 12, The catacombs.

Burn, Robert. Rome and the Campagna; an historical and topographical description of the site, buildings and neighbourhood of ancient Rome. App. and add. plan, illustrating recent excavations. Lond. 1876. Q.
    914.5 : R66

Hare, A: J: Cuthbert. Walks in Rome. 3d amer. ed. N. Y. 1873. D.   **914.5 : 46**

Story, W: Wetmore. Roba di Roma. 7th ed. [Portr.] Lond. 1875. D.   **914.5 : 53**
— Castle St. Angelo, *and* The evil eye; being additional chapters to "Roba di Roma". [Ill.] Lond. 1877. O.   **914.5 : 62**
Rydberg, Abraham V: Roman days. From the swedish by Alfred Corning Clark; with a sketch of Rydberg by H. A. W. Lindehn. Authorized tr. Ill. N. Y. 1879. D.
          914.5 : 52
<small>*Contents.* Biogr. sketch of V. Rydberg.—The roman emperors in marble: Julius Cæsar and Augustus; Tiberius; Caligula; Claudius; Nero.—Antique statues: The Aphrodite of Melos; Antinous.—Roman traditions of Peter and Paul: Paul in Naples; Paul in Rome; The ascension of Simon the sorcerer; Prisca and Pudentiana; Nero and his love; Lord, whither goest thou? The death of the apostles.—Pencil sketches in Rome: Ecclesiastical Rome and italian; The carnival; The Colosseum; La Campagna di Roma; The beggars in Rome.</small>
Butler, Clement Moore. Inner Rome; political, religious and social. Phila. 1866. D.
          914.5 : 58
Grillparzer, Franz. Reise - erinnerungen an Rom und Neapel in 1819. *In his* Sämmtliche werke.   **832 : 35 v10**
Schücking, Christoph Bernhard Levin Anton Matthias. Eine römerfahrt. Coblenz. 1848. D.   **914.5 : 11**
Kip, W: Ingraham. The christmas holydays in Rome. N. Y. 1856. D.   **914.5 : 48**
Neligan, W: H. Rome, its churches, its charities and its schools. N. Y. 1858. D.
          914.5 : 51
Leland, H: Perry. Americans in Rome. N. Y. 1863. D.   **914.5 : 49**
Lander, Sarah W. Rome. (Spectacles for young eyes.) N. Y. *n. d.* S.   **914.5 : 64**
Hare, A: J: Cuthbert. Days near Rome. Ill. Phila. 1875. 2 v. in 1. D.   **914.5 : 45**
Davies, W: The pilgrimage of the Tiber from its mouth to its source; with some account of its tributaries. 2d ed. rev. Lond. 1875. O.   **914.5 : 75**

Naples and Sicily.

Hare, A: J: Cuthbert. Cities of southern Italy and Sicily. Ill. N. Y. [1883]. D.
          914.5 : 59
Stamer, W: J: Alexander. Dolce Napoli; Naples, its streets, people, fêtes, pilgrimages, environs, etc. Lond. 1878. O.   **914.5 : 76**
Dyer, T: H:, *ed.* Pompeii, its history, buildings and antiquities; an account of the destruction of the city, with a full description of the remains, and of the recent excavations,

and also an itinerary for visitors. Ill. New ed., rev. and enl. Lond. 1875. D.
          914.5 : 37
Gell, *Sir* W:, *and* J: P. **Gandy.** Pompeiana; the topography, edifices and ornaments of Pompeii. 3d ed. Lond. 1852. O.
          914.5 : 38
Monnier, M: The wonders of Pompeii. Tr. from the original french. [Ill. lib. of wonders.] N. Y. 1870. D.   **914.5 : 39**
Adams, W: H: Davenport. Pompeii and Herculaneum, the buried cities of Campania; their history, their destruction and their remains. Ill. Lond. 1881. D. **914.5 : 55**
Pompeii illustrated. N. Y. [1885]. D. **914.5 : 78**
Hoare, *Sir* R: Colt. A classical tour through Italy and Sicily, tending to illustrate some districts, which have not been described by mr. Eustace in his Classical tour. 2d ed. Lond. 1819. 2 v. O.   **914.5 : 19**
<small>*Contents.* V. 1. From Siena to Rome and Naples. 2. Sicily and Malta in 1790.</small>
Moens, W. J. C. English travellers and italian brigands; a narrative of capture and captivity. Map and ill. N. Y. 1866. D.
          914.5 : 26
Spielhagen, F: Von Neapel bis Syrakus. *In his* Skizzen.   **S 4261**
Gregorovius, Ferdinand Adolf. The island of Capri. Tr. from the germ., by the author's permission, by Lilian Clarke. Bost. 1879. S.
          914.5 : 36
Brydone, Patrick. A tour through Sicily and Malta; in a series of letters to W: Beckford. N. Y. 1813. D.   **914.5 : 33**
Tuckerman, H: Theodore. Sicily; a pilgrimage. N. Y. 1852. D.   **914.5 : 35**
Holst, Hans Peter. Sicilianische novellen und skizzen. Deutsch von Henrik Helms. Leipz. 1855. S.   **914.5 : 9**

Other islands.

Forrester, T: Rambles in the islands of Corsica and Sardinia; with notices of their history, antiquities and present condition. 2d ed. Lond. 1861. O.   **914.95+4**
Gregorovius, Ferdinand Adolf. Corsica, picturesque, historical and social; with a sketch of the early life of Napoleon, and an account of the Bonaparte, Paoli, Pozzo di Borgo, and other principal families, suggested by a tour in 1852. Tr. from the germ. by E: Joy Morris. Phila. 1855. D.
          914.95 : 5

10. Europe, — f, Spain and Portugal.

1. History.

Dunham, S: Astley. History of Spain and Portugal. [*Anon.*] [School dist. lib.] N. Y. 1840. 5 v. S.   **946 : 1**
<small>*Contents.* V. 1. Introd. — Under the romans, 218 b. c.—409 a. d.—Under the goths, 409—711.—Mohammedan Spain, 711—1030. 2. *Same,* 1031—1492.— Christian Spain: The Asturias, Leon and Castile, 1516—1516. 3. *Same:* Navarre, 885—1512; Counts of Barcelona, 801—1162; Aragon, 1035—1516; Portugal, 1095—1521. 4. Political, civil and religious state of the peninsula during the domination of the mohammedans: Moham-</small>

<small>medan Spain; Christian Spain. 5. The Spanish monarchy, 1516—1788.—The Portuguese monarchy, 1521—1788.— Glance at the decline of the spanish monarchy under the house of Austria, and its restoration under the house of Bourbon.—Index.</small>
Bollaert, W: The wars of succession of Portugal and Spain, from 1826 to 1840; with résume of the political history of Portugal and Spain to the present time. Maps and ill. Lond. 1870. 2 v. O.   **946 : 20**
<small>*Contents.* V. 1. Portugal; with accounts of the siege of Oporto, 1832-3. 2. Spain; with account of the flight of Isabella II, in sept. 1868.</small>

Spain.

Harrison, James Albert. Spain. [Lothrop's library of entertaining history, ed. by Arthur Gilman.] Ill. Bost. [1881]. D. **946 : 2**

Abbott, J: Stevens Cabot. The romance of spanish history. Ill. N. Y. 1869. D. **946 : 14**

Trueba y Cosio, Joaquin Telesforo de. The romance of history: Spain. Ill. Lond. *n. d.* D. **946 : 15**

Rabbe, Alphonse. Die geschichte Spaniens. Frei bearb. von Belmont. (Allg. historische taschenbibliothek, 6ter th.) Dresden. 1826. 3 v. in 1. S. **946 : 23**

Lembke, F: W:, *and* H: **Schäfer.** Geschichte von Spanien. [Geschichte der europäischen staaten, herausg. von A. H. L. Heeren und F. A. Ukert]. Hamburg. 1831–44 ; Gotha. 1861–81. 4 v. O. **946 : 22**
Contents. V. 1. **Lembke,** F: W: Die zeiten von der vollständigen eroberung durch die römer bis gegen die mitte des 9ten jahrh. 2. **Schäfer,** H: Von den ersten jahrzehnten des 9ten jahrh. bis zum anfange des 12ten. 3. Geschichte des südöstlichen Spaniens, insbesondere seiner inneren zustände, im mittelalter. 4. Geschichte Castiliens im 12. und 13. jahrh.

Condé, José Antonio. History of the dominion of the arabs in Spain. Tr. from the spanish by mrs. Jonathan Foster. Lond. 1854, 1855. 3 v. D. **946 : 3**
Contents. V. 1. To 983. 2. 983—1160. 3. 1160—1492. — Index.

Coppée, H: History of the conquest of Spain by the arab-moors ; with a sketch of the civilization which they achieved and imparted to Europe. Bost. 1881. 2 v. D. **946 : 4**
Contents. V. 1. To 731. 2. 732—1492.—Arabian civilization in Spain.

Yonge, Charlotte Mary. The story of the christians and moors of Spain. Lond. 1879. S. **946 : 6**

Southey, Robert. Chronicle of the Cid, from the spanish. 1st amer. ed. Lowell. 1846. O. **946+7**
Note. "Is wholly translation, but it is not the translation of any single work. The three following have been used: Chronica del famoso cavallero Cid Ruydiez Campeador, 1593; Las quatro partes enteras de la Cronica de España, que mando componer el serenissimo rey Don Alonso; Poema del Cid."—*Preface.*
— The chronicle of the Cid, [condensed from Southey's work]; ed. with an introd. and app. by R: Markham. Ill. N. Y. 1883. O. **946 : 25**

Herder, J: Gottfried v. Der Cid ; geschichte des don Ruy Diaz, grafen von Bivar, nach spanischen romanzen. *In his* Werke. **830 : 152 v75**
— *Same. In his* Werke. **830 : 154 v4**

Jaime I, *king of Aragon.* The chronicle of James I, king of Aragon, surnamed the conqueror, written by himself. Tr. from the catalan by J: Forster ; with an histor. introd., notes, app., glossary and general index, by Pascual de Gayangos. Lond. 1883. 2 v. O. **946+17**

Prescott, W: Hickling. History of the reign of Ferdinand and Isabella the catholic. 10th ed. N. Y. 1848. 3 v. O. **946+8**

Ranke, Franz Leopold v. Die Osmanen und die Spanische monarchie im 16. und 17. jahrhundert. 4te, erweiterte aufl. des werkes :

Fürsten und völker von Süd-Europa. Leipz. 1877. 2 v. in 1. O. **904:36 v35, 36**
Contents. Osmanen. — Die spanische monarchie. — Carl V, Philipp II, Philipp III. — Zur geschichte der weltstellung der spanischen monarchie. — Analecten.

Prescott, W: Hickling. History of the reign of PhilipII, king of Spain. Bost. 1856. 3 v. O. **946+9**

Gayarré, C: E. Arthur. Philip II, of Spain ; with an introd. letter by G: Bancroft. N. Y. 1866. O. **946 : 10**

Watson, Robert. The history of the reign of Philip II, king of Spain. 5th ed. Lond. 1794. 3 v. O. **946 : 11**
— *and* W: **Thomson.** The history of the reign of Philip III. 3d ed. Lond. 1793. 2 v. O. **946 : 12**

Dunlop, J: Memoirs of Spain, during the reigns of Philip IV and Charles II, from 1621 to 1700. Edinb. 1834. 2 v. O. **946 : 19**

Baumgarten, Hermann. Geschichte Spaniens vom ausbruch der französischen revolution bis auf unsere tage. [Staatengeschichte der neuesten zeit]. Leipz. 1865–71. 3 v. O. **946+18**
Contents. V. 1. 1788—1814. 2. 1814—1825. 3. 1825—1840.

Napier, *Sir* W: Francis Patrick. History of the war in the Peninsula and in the south of France from 1807—1814. Ill. N. Y. 1882. 5 v. D. **946 : 16**
Contents. V. 1. 1807—1809. 2. 1809—1810. 3. 1810—1812. 4. 1812—1813. 5. 1813—1814. — Controversial pieces.—Index.

Southey, Robert. History of the peninsular war. Lond. 1823–32. 3 v. Q. **946 : R13**

Irving, Washington. Spanish papers. **829.1 : 19 v1**
Contents, see under English literature, miscellany, col. 1095.
See also in the Index to biography **Castelar—Cid —Felipe—Gonsalvo—Isabella.**

Portugal.

Münch, Ernst. Die geschichte von Portugal. (Allg. historische taschenbibliothek, 16ter th.) Dresden. 1827. 3 v. in 1. S. **946 : 24**

Schäfer, H: Geschichte von Portugal. [Geschichte der europ. staaten, herausg. von A. H. L. Heeren und F. A. Ukert]. Hamburg. 1836–52. Gotha. 1854. 5 v. O. **946 : 21**
Contents. V. 1. Von der entstehung des staates bis zum erlöschen der echten burgundischen linie, 1383. 2. Vom erlöschen der echten burgundischen linie bis zum schlusse des mittelalters, 1495. 3. Vom regierungsantritt des königs Manuel bis zur vereinigung mit Spanien, 1580. 4. Von der vereinigung Portugals mit Spanien bis zur absetzung des königs Affonso VI, 1667. 5. Von der absetzung Affonso's VI bis zum ausbruch der revolution, 1820.—**Möller,** J. H. Register.
See also in the Index to biography, **Almeida.**

2. Description.

Twiss, R: Travels through Portugal and Spain in 1772 and 1773. Plates and app. Lond. 1775. O. **914.6 : 23**

March, C: W. Sketches and adventures in Madeira, Portugal and the Andalusias of Spain, by the author of "Daniel Webster and his contemporaries." N. Y. 1856. D. **914.6 : 29**

Andersen, Hans Christian. In Spain and a visit to Portugal, [1866]. Author's ed. Bost. 1879. D. **914.6 : 12**

Gallenga, Antonio. Iberian reminiscences ; fifteen years' travelling impressions of Spain and Portugal. Lond. 1883. 2 v. O.
914.6 : 39
Contents. V. 1. Queen Isabella, 1865-66. — Don Juan Prim, 1868 - 69. — Don Carlos, 1874 - 75. 2. King Alfonso, 1874 - 75.—A spanish tour, 1879 - 82.

Spain.

Davillier, J: C: *baron.* Spain ; ill. by Gustave Doré. Tr. by J. Thomson. Lond. 1881. F.
914.6 : R34
Young, Arthur. Spain in 1789. *In his* Travels.
914.4+38 v2
Mérimée, Prosper. Reisebriefe aus Spanien, 1831. *In his* Gesammelte werke.
840 : 1 v6
Cushing, Caleb. Reminiscences of Spain, its country, its people, history and monuments. Bost. 1833. 2 v. D.   914.6 : 10
Mackenzie, Alexander Slidell. A year in Spain. 5th ed. N. Y. 1847. 3 v. D.   914.6 : 17
— Spain revisited, by the author of a "Year in Spain." N. Y. 1836. 2 v. D.   914.6 : 18
Rosen, Gustav v. Bilder aus Spanien und der fremdenlegion ; nebst einem anhang, enthaltend: Die unternehmung Muñagorris. Kiel. 1843, 1844. 2 v. D. 914.6 : 8
Poco Mas, *pseud.* Scenes and adventures in Spain, from 1835 to 1840. Phila. 1846. S.
914.6 : 21
Borrow, G: The Bible in Spain, or The journeys, adventures and imprisonments of an englishman in an attempt to circulate the scriptures in the peninsula. 13th ed. N. Y. 1847. O.   914.6 : 3
— The zincali, or An account of the gypsies of Spain ; with an original collection of their songs and poetry. N. Y. 1847. O. *With his* The Bible in Spain.   914.6 : 3
Ford, R: The spaniards and their country. N. Y. 1847. 2 pts. in 1 v. D.   914.6 : 9
Ozanam, Alphonse Frédéric. A pilgrimage to the land of the Cid, [1852]. Tr. from the french by P. S. N. Y. 1875. S. 914.6 : 20
Gautier, Theophile. Wanderings in Spain. Ill. Lond. 1853. D.   914.6 : 13
Wallis, Severn Teackle. Spain, her institutions, politics and public men ; a sketch. Bost. 1853. D.   914.6 : 22
Kenyon, Arthur. Letters from Spain, to his nephews at home. Lond. 1853. S.
x 914.6 : 38
Mackie, J: Milton. Cosas de España, or Going to Madrid via Barcelona. [*Anon.*] N. Y. 1855. D.   914.6 : 19
Calderon de la Barca, *Mme.* Frances Erskine Inglis. The attaché in Madrid, or Sketches of the court of Isabella II. Tr. from the german. [*Anon.*] N. Y. 1856. D.
914.6 : 6
Bryant, W: Cullen. Letters of a traveller ; 2d series, [Spain, 1857]. N. Y. 1860. D.
914.6 : 4
Hackländer, F: W: Ein winter in Spanien. Stuttg. 1860. 3 v. S.   914.6 : 7
Byrne, *Mrs.* W: Pitt. Cosas de España, illustrative of Spain and the spaniards, as they are. Lond. 1866. 2 v. D.   914.6 : 5

* x denotes books specially adapted for children.

Hay, J: Castilian days. Bost. 1872. D.
914.6 : 15
Hare, A: J: Cuthbert. Wanderings in Spain. 3d ed. Lond. 1873. D.   914.6 : 32
— *Same.* N. Y. [1885]. S.   914.6 : 32
Baxley, H: Willis. Spain, art-remains and art-realities, painters, priests and princes ; notes of things seen and of opinions formed, during nearly three years' residence and travels in that country. N. Y. 1875. 2 v. D.   914.6 : 2
Harrison, James Albert. Spain in profile ; a summer among the olives and aloes. Bost. 1879. S.   914.6 : 14
Amicis, Edmondo de. Spain. Tr. from the italian by Wilhelmina W. Cady. N. Y. 1881. D.   914.6 : 1
Edwardes, E. C. Hope-. Azahar ; extracts from a journal in Spain in 1881-82. Lond. 1883. D.   914.6 : 35
Lathrop, G: Parsons. Spanish vistas. Ill. N. Y. 1883. D.   914.6+30
Day, H: From the Pyrenees to the pillars of Hercules ; observations on Spain, its history and its people. Ill. N. Y. 1883. D.
914.6 : 31
Downes, W: Howe. Spanish ways and by-ways ; with a glimpse of the Pyrenees. Ill. Bost. 1883. O.   914.6 : 37
Hale, E: Everett. Seven spanish cities and the way to them. Bost. 1883. S.   914.6 : 33
Hale, Susan. A family flight through Spain. Bost. [1883]. O.   914.6 : 36
Patch, Olive, *pseud?* Sunny Spain, its people and places ; with glimpses of its history. [Ill.] Lond. 1884. O.   914.6+42
Irving, Washington. The Alhambra.   I 401
See col. 766.

Portugal and the Azores.

Murphy, James. Travels in Portugal, through the provinces of Entre Douro e Minho, Beira, Estremadura and Alem - Tejo, in 1789 and 1790 ; consisting of observations on the manners, customs, trade, public buildings, arts, antiquities, etc., of that kingdom. Ill. Lond. 1795. Q.
914.6 : R24
Jackson, Catherine Charlotte *lady.* Fair Lusitania. Ill. Lond. 1874. O.   914.6+P43
Crawford, Oswald J : F:, (*John Latouche*). Travels in Portugal. 3d ed. Map and ill. Lond. [1878]. D.   914.6 : 40
— Portugal, old and new. Maps and ill. N. Y. 1880. O.   914.6 : 27
Weeks, Lyman H. Among the Azores. Bost. 1882. S.   914.6 : 25
Baker, Charlotte Alice. A summer in the Azores ; with a glimpse of Madeira. Bost. 1882. T.   914.6 : 26
Benjamin, S: Green Wheeler. [The Azores and Madeira]. *In his* Atlantic islands.
552.2 : 1

11.   Europe — g, Russia and Poland.

(*See also* Russia in Asia, cl. 915.7.)

1. Russian history.

In general.

Strahl, Philipp, *and* Ernst **Herrmann.** Geschichte des russischen staates. [Geschichte der europ. staaten, herausg. von A. H. L. Heeren und F. A. Ukert]. Hamburg. 1832–53. Gotha. 1860–66. 7 v. O.   **947 : 19**
Contents. **Strahl,** P. V. 1. Zum jahre 1224. 2. 1224 – 1505. **Herrmann,** E. 3. 1505 – 1682. 4. 1682 - 1741. 5. 1742 - 1775. 6. 1775 - 1792. [7.] *Ergänzungs- band.* Diplomatische correspondenzen aus der revolutionszeit, 1791 - 1797.

Herrmann, A: L. Die geschichte Russlands. (Allg. historische taschenbibliothek, 9ter th.) Dresden. 1826. 4 v. in 1. S.   **947 : 20**

Bernhardi, Theodor v. Geschichte Russlands und der europäischen politik in den jahren 1814 bis 1831. [Staatengeschichte der neuesten zeit.] Leipz. 1863–77. 3 v. O. **947+18**
Contents. V. 1. Vom Wiener congress bis zum zweiten Pariser frieden. 2. Einleitung. [Geschichte Russlands bis zum Wiener congress.] 3. Vom zweiten Pariser frieden bis zu dem congress zu Aachen.

Tyrrell, H: History of the Russian empire ; from its foundation by Ruric the pirate, to the accession of the emperor Alexander II. Ill. Lond. *n. d.* Q.   **947+21**

Kelly, Walter Keating, *comp.* The history of Russia, from the earliest period to the present time ; compiled from the most authentic sources, incl. the works of Karamsin, Tooke and Ségur. Lond. 1854. 2 v. D.   **947 : 2**
Contents. V. 1. To 1762. 2. 1762 - 1854.—Index.

Abbott, J: Stevens Cabot. The monarchies of continental Europe : The empire of Russia, from the remotest periods to the present time. [1855.] N. Y. 1860. D.   **947 : 3**

Rambaud, Alfred. The history of Russia, from the earliest times to 1877. Tr. by Leonora B. Lang. Ill. Lond. 1879. 2 v. O. **947+1**
Contents. V. 1. To 1700. 2. 1700 - 1877.—Bibliographical notes.—Index.

— *Same* ; from the earliest times to 1880 ; incl. a history of the turko-russian war of 1877–78, from the best authorities by the ed. Ill. Bost. 1879–82. 3 v. O.   **947+1**
Contents. V. 1. To 1682. 2. 1682 - 1825. 3. 1825 - 1881.—Index.

Dole, Nathan Haskell. Young folks' history of Russia. Bost. 1881. D.   **x 947 : 4**

Bodenstedt, F: Martin v. Der Kreml in Moskau, als träger und mittelpunkt der russischen geschichte.—Peter der grosse. *In his* Aus ost und west.   **834 : 2**

By periods.

Grahame, F. R. The archer and the steppe, or The empires of Scythia ; a history of Russia and Tartary, from the earliest ages till the fall of the Mongul power in Europe in the middle of the 16th century. Lond. *n. d.* D.   **947 : 5**
Contents. From the earliest authentic history of

x denotes books specially adapted for children.

Scythia to the conquests of the mongul tartars.— From the conquests of the monguls to the rise of Timur.—The history of Timur and his successors. — Continuation of the history of Russia to the final extinction of the mongul power in Europe.

Russell, Frank Shirley. Russian wars with Turkey. Maps. Lond. 1877. D.   **947 : 13**

Brückner, Alexander. Peter der grosse. (**Oncken,** W:, *ed.* Allgemeine geschichte in einzeldarstellungen ; 3te hauptabth., 6ter th.) Portr. Berlin. 1879. O.   **909+21 v6**

Manstein, Christoph Hermann v. Contemporary memoirs of Russia, from the year 1727 to 1744. First ed. in eng. by D: Hume, and now re-ed., compared with the original french, and ill. with brief notes by a Hertfordshire incumbent. Lond. 1856. D.   **947 : 12**

Brückner, Alexander. Katharina II. (**Oncken,** W:, *ed.* Allgemeine geschichte in einzeldarstellungen ; 3te hauptabth., 10ter th.) Portr. und ill. Berlin. 1883. O.   **909+21 v10**

Ségur, Philippe Paul *comte* de. History of the expedition to Russia, undertaken by the emperor Napoleon in 1812. [Harper's family lib.] N. Y. 1845. 2 v. S.   **947 : 7**

Porter, *Sir* Robert Ker. A narrative of the campaign in Russia, during the year 1812. Added, a narrative of the events which followed Buonaparte's campaign in Russia to the period of his dethronement, by W: Dunlap. Hartford. 1815. O.   **947 : 6**

Oertel, Philipp F: W:, (*W. O. v. Horn*). Der brand von Moskau ; ein geschichtsbild, dargestellt für die deutsche jugend und das volk. 5te aufl. Wiesbaden. *n. d.* S.   **947 : 23**

Russell, W: Howard. The british expedition to the Crimea. A rev. ed. with numerous emend. and add. Ill. Lond. 1858. O.   **947 : 9**

Kinglake, Alexander W: The invasion of the Crimea ; its origin and an account of its progress down to the death of lord Raglan. V. 1–3, N. Y. 1868–75. D. V. 4. [v. 6 of eng. ed.], Edinb. 1880. 4 v. O.   **947 : 8**
Contents. V. 1. Transactions which brought on the war.—Invasion of the Crimea to the battle of Alma. 2. *Same, continued,* to the battle of Balaclava. 3. Battle of Inkerman. 4. The winter troubles.

Maynard, Félix, *ed.* Recollections of a zouave before Sebastopol. Tr. from the french by mrs. M. Harrison Robinson. Phila. 1856. D.   **947 : 10**

Cler, *Gen.*—. Reminiscences of an officer of zouaves. Tr. from the french. [*Anon*]. N. Y. 1860. D.   **947 : 11**

Greene, Francis Vinton. The russian army and its campaigns in Turkey, in 1877–1878. N. Y. 1879. 2 v. O.   **947+14**
Note. For other accounts of the war see Turkish history, cl. 949.3.

— Sketches of army life in Russia. N. Y. 1880. D.   **914.7 : 24**
Contents. The tsar. — The russian soldier. — Shipka pass.—Plevna.—The winter campaign.—Russian generals.—War correspondents. — Constantinople. — St. Petersburg.—The eastern question.

Noble, Edmund. The russian revolt ; its causes, condition and prospects. Bost. 1885. D.
           947 : 22
Contents. Nomadic survivals.—Apolism.—Environment.—Old russian life. — Byzantinism and the three unities.—Domestic slavery. —The religious protest.— Western enlightenment. — First fruits. — Mysticism and pessimism. — The dynamic period. — Personal characteristics.—Modern irritations.—Europe and the revolt, the future.

Seume, J: Gottfried. Historische aufsätze. *In his* Werke.   **830 : 147 v9**
Contents, see Deutscher katalog, p. 42.

See also in the Index *to* biography **Aleksandr— Menshikof—Nikolai—Piotr—Shamyl—Skobelef —Suvorof.**

2. Polish history.

Dunham, S: Astley. The history of Poland, [560 — 1830]. [Lardner's cabinet cycl.] Lond. 1831. D.   **949.5 : 8**
Fletcher, James. The history of Poland, from the earliest period to the present time ; with a narrative of the recent events, obtained from a polish patriot nobleman. [Harper's family lib.] N. Y. 1846. S.
           949.5 : 2
Oppeln-Bronikowski, Alexander A: Ferdinand v. Die geschichte Polens. (Allg. historische taschenbibliothek, 13ter th). Dresden. 1827. 4 v. in 1. S.   **949.5 : 10**
Röpell, R:, *and* Jacob **Caro.** Geschichte Polens. [Geschichte der europ. staaten, herausg. von A. H. L. Heeren und F. A. Ukert]. Hamburg. 1840. Gotha. 1863-75. 4 v. O.
           949.5 : 9
Contents. Röpell, R: V. 1. Einleitung.—Die monarchie der Piasten, 850—1138. — Der kampf um die monarchie und deren gänzliche auflösung, 1140—1300. Caro, J. 2. 1300—1386. 3. 1386—1430. 4. 1430—1455.
Röpell, R: Polen um die mitte des 18. jahrhunderts. Gotha. 1876. O.   **949.5 : 6**
Beer, Adolf. Die erste theilung Polens. Wien. 1873. 2 v. O.   **949.5+4**
— *ed. Same :* Documente. Wien. 1873. O.
           949.5+4 v3
Brüggen, Ernst *freiherr* v. der. Polens auflösung ; kulturgeschichtliche skizzen aus den letzten jahrzehnten der polnischen selbständigkeit. Leipz. 1878. O.   **949.5 : 5**
Moltke, Helmuth C: Bernhard *graf* v. Poland ; an historical sketch. Authorized tr., with a biogr. notice by Emma S. Buchenheim. Lond. 1885. D.   **949.5 : 11**
Note. Originally pub. in 1832.
Hordynski, Jozef. History of the late polish revolution, and the events of the campaign. 2d ed. Bost. 1833. O.   **949.5+1**
Allen, Julian. Autocrasy in Poland and Russia, or A description of russian misrule in Poland, and an account of the surveillance of russian spies at home and abroad, incl. the experience of an exile. N. Y. 1854. O.
           947 : 15
Day, W. A. The russian government in Poland; with a narrative of the polish insurrection of 1863. Lond. 1867. O.   **949.5 : 7**
See also in the Index *to* biography **Jan Sobieski —Kosciuszko—Pulaski.**

3. Description.

Custine, Astolphe *marquis* de. La Russie en 1839. 3e éd. rev., corr. et augm. Paris. 1846. 4 v. D.   **914.7 : 47**

Lacroix, F: Geheimnisse von Russland; ein politisches sittengemälde des russischen reichs. Aus dem franz. [*Anon.*] 2te ausg. Regensburg. 1848. 2 v. D.   **914.7 : 9**
Contents. V. 1. Der despotismus.—Der kaiser und seine familie. — Die geheimen gesellschaften und die verschwörung im jahre 1825. — Porträt und character der russen.—Sitten und gebräuche; St. Petersburg.— Religion und geistlichkeit. 2. Politische organisation; Regierung, verwaltung, polizei. — Gesetzgebung; Justiz; Gefängnisse; Sibirien.—Der adel; der mittelstand und die leibeigenen.—Das heer.—Die marine.—Nationalreichthum. — Russlands politik gegen besiegte und unterjochte völker.—Schluss.
Kohl, J: G: Russia, St. Petersburg, Moscow, Kharkoff, Riga, Odessa, the german provinces on the Baltic, the steppes, the Crimea, and the interior of the empire. Lond. 1844. O.   **914.7 : 7**
Gurowski, Adam *comte* de. Russia as it is. 3d ed. N. Y. 1854. D.   **914.7 : 5**
Lagny, Germain de. The knout and the russians, or The muscovite empire, the czar and his people. Tr. from the french by J: Bridgeman. N. Y. 1854. D.   **914.7 : 17**
Dixon, W: Hepworth. Free Russia. Leipz. 1872. 2 v. in 1. S.   **914.7 : 4**
Celestin, F: J. Russland seit aufhebung der leibeigenschaft. Laibach. 1875. O.
           914.7 : 35
Wallace, Donald Mackenzie. Russia. N. Y. 1877. O.   **914.7 : 1**
Murray, Eustace Clare Grenville. The russians of to-day. Leipz. 1878. S.   **914.7 : 25**
Edwards, H. Sutherland. The russians at home and the russians abroad ; sketches, unpolitical and political of russian life under Alexander II. Lond. 1879. 2 v. D.
           914.7 : 27
Contents. V. 1. Russians at home; unpolitical sketches. 2. Russians abroad. The reform period in Russia. — Serf-emancipation and self-government. —Some practical effects of serf-emancipation. — Nihilism. — A nihilist conspiracy. — An unpolitical secret society. — Panslavonianism. — A panslavonian agent in eastern Galicia. — The russians in Poland. — The russians in central Asia. — Russian expeditions toward India.—App.—Index.
Morfill, W: R. Russia. Ill. [Foreign countries and british colonies]. Lond. 1880. S.
           914.7 : 3
Geddie, J: The Russian empire ; historical and descriptive. N. Y. 1882. D.   **914.7 : 18**
Lankenau, H:, *and* L. v. d. **Oelsnitz,** *ed.* Das heutige Russland : bilder und schilderungen aus allen theilen des europäischen zarenreichs. 2e wohlf. ausg. [Ill. bibliothek der länder- und völkerkunde]. Leipz. 1881. O.   **914.7 : 20**
— *Same, eng.* Russia past and present. Adapted from the german by Henrietta M. Chester. N. Y. 1882. D.   **914.7 : 19**
Eckardt, Julius. Modern Russia. Lond. 1870. O.   **914.7 : 37**
Contents. Russia under Alexander II. — Russian communism.—The greek orthodox church and its sects.—The Baltic provinces of Russia.
— Von Nicolaus I zu Alexander III; St. Petersburger beiträge zur neuesten russischen geschichte. Leipz. 1881. D.   **914.7 : 38**
Contents. Aus der "Dritten abtheilung." — Die Petraschewskische verschwörung, 1848—1849. — Die russische emigration in London, 1852 bis 1864. — Feldmarschall Paskewitsch und M. D. Gortschakow.—Eine russische geheime denkschrift von 1864.—*Same.* 1868, 69.— Zwei neue aktenstücke zur geschichte des polnischen aufstandes von 1868. — Der ausgang Alexanders II.— Nach dem 1—13. märz.

Eckardt, Julius.—*Continued.*
— Russland vor und nach dem kriege ; auch "Aus der Petersburger gesellschaft." [*Anon.*] 2te aufl. Leipz. 1879. O. **914.7 : 23**
— Aus der Petersburger gesellschaft. [*Anon.*] Leipz. 1880, 1881. 2 v. D.   **914.7 : 36**
Contents. V. 1. 5te verm. bis auf die gegenwart fortg. aufl. Aus den tagen des kaisers Nikolaus.— Die grossfürstin Helene.—Graf P. Schuwalow.— Die gräfin Antoinette Bludow.— Die grafen Adlerberg.— Die brüder Miljutin.—Die drei Turgenjew.—Graf Pro-tassow.— P. A. Walujew.— Unsere unterrichtsmini-ster.— Fürst Gortschakow. — Schriftsteller und jour-nalisten.—General Ignatjew. 2, *Neue folge.* 3te verm. bis auf die gegenwart fortg. aufl. Die nationalitä-ten.—Kaiserliche brüder und söhne.—Fürst Bismarck in St. Petersburg. — Literatur und presse unter dem kaiser Nikolaus. — Puschkin und Dantes. — Wassily Ostrow und die Akademie der wissenschaften. — Das höhere beamtenthum. — Die umgebung kaiser Alex-ander's II.

Stepniak, S., *pseud.* Underground Russia ; re-volutionary profiles and sketches from life ; with a preface by P: Lavroff. Tr. from the italian. N. Y. 1883. D.   **914.7 : 26**
— Russia under the tzars. Rendered into eng. by W: Westall. N. Y. 1885. Q. **914.7+39**
— *Same.* Authorized ed. N. Y. 1885. D.   **914.7 : 39**
Note. Attributed to Mikhaïl Dragomanoff, ap-parently contradicted, however, by the pref.

Tissot, V: Russes et allemands. 8e éd. Paris. 1884. D.   **914.7 : 34**
Contents. Les pères du nihilisme.—De l'éducation des femmes en Russie.—Les universités russes.—La décadence des mœurs.—Qu'est-ce que la Russie ?— L'armée russe.— La nouvelle Allemagne et la nou-velle Russie.—Les allemands en Russie.—Le social-isme allemand et l'état moral de Russie.

Hare, A: J: Cuthbert. Studies in Russia. Ill. N. Y. [1885]. D.   **914.7 : 42**
Contents. Introd.— St. Petersburg.— Excursions round St. Petersburg.—Novogorod the great.—Mos-cow. — The monasteries near Moscow. — The new Jerusalem.—Kieff.—A glimpse of Poland.—Index.

Colange, Leo de. Picturesque Russia and Greece. Ill. Troy. 1886. Q.   **914.7 : R45**

General travels.

Ritchie, Leitch. Russia and the russians, or A journey to St. Petersburg and Moscow through Courland and Livonia ; with char-acteristic sketches of the people. Phila. 1836. D.   **914.7 : 8**

McCormick, R: C. A visit to the camp before Sevastopol. 4th thous. N. Y. 1855. D.   **914.7 : 16**

Poole, Sophia Lane-. The englishwoman in Russia ; impressions of the society and manners of the russians at home, by a lady ten years resident in that country. Ill. N. Y. 1856. D.   **914.7 : 11**

Sala, G: A: A journey due north ; notes of a residence in Russia. Bost. 1858. S.   **914.7 : 14**

Moltke, Helmuth C: Bernhard *graf* v. Briefe aus Russland, [1856]. 2te aufl. Berlin. 1877. O.   **914.7 : 44**

Proctor, Edna Dean. A russian journey. Bost. 1872. D.   **914.7 : 12**

Gautier, Théophile. A winter in Russia. N. Y. 1874. D.   **914.7 : 13**

Gallenga, Antonio. A summer tour in Russia. Lond. 1882. O.   **914.7 : 33**

Special localities.

Jerrmann, E: Pictures from St. Petersburg. Tr. from the original german by F: Hard-man. N. Y. 1852. D.   **914.7 : 22**

Lander, Sarah W. St. Petersburg. (Spectacles for young eyes, no. 2.) N. Y. *n. d.* S.   **x 914.7 : 30**
— Moscow. (Spectacles for young eyes, no. 4.) N. Y. *n. d.* S.   **x 914.7 : 31**

Hoffman, Wickham. Leisure hours in Russia. Lond. 1883. D.   **914.7 : 41**
Contents. St. Petersburg.—Russian superstitions.— **Runeberg,** J: L. Nadeschda.—Finland.—The Kale-vala.— Runeberg, J: L. Döbeln at Jutas ; Lieut. Zieden ; The cloud's brother ; "Our land".

Lindemann, Moritz v. Finnland und seine be-wohner ; eine historisch - geographische skizze, mit einem vorwort von K: Andree. Leipz. 1855. S.   **914.7 : 10**

Brown, J: Croumbie. Finland ; its forest and forest management. Edinb. 1883. D.   **914.7 : 32**
Note. For travels in Finland and Lapland, *see also* Sweden and Norway, cl. 914.8.

Tromholt, Sophus. Under the rays of the aurora borealis ; in the land of the lapps and kvaens ; ed. by C: Siewers. Map, ill., portr., diagrams, etc. Bost. 1885. 2 v. O.   **914.7 : 43**

Rae, E: The land of the north wind, or Travels among the laplanders and the samoyedes. Lond. 1875. D.   **914.7 : 29**
— The White Sea peninsula ; a journey in russian Lapland and Karelia. Maps and ill. Lond. 1881. O.   **914.7 : 28**

Seebohm, H: Siberia in Europe ; a visit to the valley of the Petchora, in north-east Russia, with descriptions of the natural history, migration of birds, etc. Map and ill. Lond. 1880. O.   **914.7 : 2**

Hamel, Josef. Early english voyages to north-ern Russia ; comprising the voyages of John Tradescant the elder, sir Hugh Wil-loughby, R: Chancellor Nelson and others. Tr. by J: Studdy Leigh. Lond. 1857. O.   **914.7+46**

Browne, J: Ross. A visit to the salt-mines of Wieliczka.   *in* **914.3 : 55**

Koch, K: H: Emanuel. The Crimea, from Kertch to Perekop, with a visit to Odessa ; incl. a chapter on the climate, soil and vegetation of the Crimean south coast and southern Russia. Ill. Lond. 1855. S.   **914.7 : 21**

Marvin, C: The region of the eternal fire ; an account of a journey to the petroleum region of the Caspian in 1883. Lond. 1884. O.   **914.7 : 40**

Wanderer, *pseud.* Notes on the Caucasus. Lond. 1883. O.   **915.7 : 9**
Contents. Introd.— Caucasian mountaineers.— De-scription of Tiflis.—Rambles in Georgia.—The tartars and the Karyas steppe.—Kutaïs.—Batoum.—Imeritia. —Mingrelia.—Sport in Circassia and the Caucasus in general.—Russian character, civil and military.

x denotes books specially adapted for children.

12. Europe — h, Scandinavia.

1. History.

In general.

Mallet, Paul H: Northern antiquities, or An historical account of the manners, customs, religion and laws, maritime expeditions and discoveries, language and literature of the ancient scandinavians, (danes, swedes, norwegians and icelanders), with incidental notices respecting our saxon ancestors. Tr. from the french by bishop Percy. New ed., rev. and enl., with a tr. of the prose Edda from the original old norse text, and notes critical and explanatory, by I. A. Blackwell; added, an abstract of the Eyrbyggja saga by sir Walter Scott. Lond. 1847. D.   **948 : 1**

Crichton, Andrew, *and* H: **Wheaton.** Scandinavia, ancient and modern ; a history of Denmark, Sweden and Norway, comprehending a description of these countries, an account of the mythology, government, laws, manners and institutions of the early inhabitants and of the present state of society, religion, literature, arts and commerce, with ill. of their natural history. Ill. [Harper's family lib.] N. Y. 1846. 2 v. S.   **948 : 3**
Contents. V. 1. To 1523. **2.** 1523 - 1837.

Dunham, S: Astley. Denmark, Sweden and Norway. [Lardner's cabinet cycl.] Lond. 1839-40. 3 v. D.   **948 : 6**
Contents. V. 1. Introd.—Denmark, b. c. 40 - a. d. 1014.—Sweden, b. c. 70 - a. d. 1001.—Norway, about 70 b. c. - a. d. 1030.—Maritime expeditions of the northmen during the pagan age: England, France and Ireland. **2.** *Same:* The Orkneys, Hebrides, Iceland, Greenland, North America, Russia, etc., 795 - 1026.—Cosmogony and religion of Scandinavia.—Introduction of christianity into Denmark and Sweden.—Denmark, 1014 - 1387.—Norway, 1030 - 1387.—Sweden, 1001 - 1389.—App.: St. Canute. **3.** The three scandinavian kingdoms, 1387 - 1523.—Denmark and Norway, 1523 - 1699.—Sweden, 1523 - 1697.—Denmark, Norway and Sweden, 1697 - 1814.

Sinding, Poul Christian. History of Scandinavia, from the early times of the northmen and vikings to the present day, [1852]. 5th ed. Pittsburgh. 1862. D.   **948 : 5**
Note. Is, properly speaking, a history of Denmark.

Otté, Emily C. Scandinavian history. Lond. 1874. D.   **948 : 4**

Sweden and Norway.

Geijer, Eric Gustaf. The history of the swedes. Tr. from the swedish, with an introd. and notes by J. H. Turner. The first portion, comprising the first 3 v. of the original, from the earliest period to the accession of Charles X. Lond. *n. d.* O.   **948.1 : 1**
Note. V. 1-3 of the following is the same work in german.

— *and* F: Ferdinand **Carlson.** Geschichte Schwedens, [v. 1-3] aus der schwed. hs. des verf. übers. von Swen P. Leffler ; [v. 4, 5] aus dem schwed. hs. des verf. übers. von J. E. Petersen. [Geschichte der europ. staaten, herausg. von A. H. L. Heeren und

F. A. Ukert.] Hamburg. 1832-36. Gotha. 1855, 1875. 5 v. O.   **948.1 : 2**
Contents. **Geijer,** E. G. V. 1. Bis 1520. **2.** 1520 - 1611. **3.** 1611 - 1654. **Carlson,** F: F. **4.** 1654 - 1680. **5.** 1680 - 1697.

Starbäck, C: G: Små berättelser ur svenska historien för barn. 7de uppl. Stockholm. 1874. D.   **x 948.1 : 5**

Vertot d'Aubeuf, René Aubert *abbé* de. The history of the revolution in Sweden, occasioned by the changes of religion and alteration of the government in that kingdom, [1350 - 1560]. Tr. from the french. Glasgow. 1750. S.   **948.1 : 3**

Alberg, Albert. Gustavus Vasa and his stirring times ; scenes from history told for youthful readers. Lond. *n. d.* D.   **x 948.1 : 4**

Snorri Sturluson. The heimskringla, or Chronicle of the kings of Norway. Tr. from the icelandic, with a preliminary dissertation by S: Laing. Lond. 1844. 3 v. O.   **948.2 : P2**

Carlyle, T: The early kings of Norway ; also an essay on the portraits of John Knox. N. Y. 1875. D.   **948.2 : 1**
See also in the Index to biography **Christina — Gustaf — Harald — Karl — Olaf.**

Denmark and Iceland.

Dahlmann, F: Christoph. Geschichte von Dännemark. [Geschichte der europ. staaten, herausg. von A. H. L. Heeren und F. A. Ukert.] Hamburg. 1840-43. 3 v. O.   **948.3 : 2**
Contents. V. 1. Von den anfängen der staatsbildung bis auf den grossen Waldemar.—Das zeitalter der Waldemare, 1134 - 1360. **2.** Die union der drei nordischen kronen: 1361 - 1400: Blick auf die geschichte Norwegens, Islands anfänge, bis 1000; Norwegen, 1000 - 1263; Island, gerichtswesen, dichtkunst, etc.; Grundzüge der verfassung und verwaltung von Norwegen, bis auf Magnus den gesetzbesserer; Norwegen, 1263 - 1397. **3.** *Same, continued:* Adel und bauern in Dännemark; Geschichte, 1397 - 1523.—Anlagen.

Gosch, C: A: Denmark and Germany since 1815. Maps. Lond. 1862. O.   **948.3 : 3**

Nicoll, James. An historical and descriptive account of Iceland, Greenland and the Faroe islands. [*Anon.*] [Harper's family lib.] N. Y. 1846. S.   **948.3 : 1**

Maurer, Konrad. Island, von seiner ersten entdeckung bis zum untergange des freistaats. München. 1874. O.   **948.3 + 2**

2. Description.

In general.

Baird, Robert. Visit to northern Europe, or Sketches descriptive, historical, political and moral, of Denmark, Norway, Sweden and Finland, and the free cities of Hamburg and Lubeck ; containing notices of the manners and customs, commerce, manufactures, arts and sciences, education, literature and religion of those countries and cities. Map and ill. N. Y. 1841. 2 v. D.   **914.8 : 3**

x denotes books specially adapted for children.

Taylor, Bayard. Northern travel ; summer and winter pictures, Sweden, Denmark and Lapland, [1857]. N. Y. 1881. D.
914.8 : 14
— *Same.* N. Y. 1880. D.   914.8 : 14
Mügge, Theodor. Nordisches bilderbuch ; reise-bilder. Frankfurt a. M. 1857. S.
914.8 : 12
Browne, J : Ross. The land of Thor. Ill. N. Y. 1867. D.   914.8 : 4
Note. Russia, Sweden, Norway, Iceland.
Vincent, Frank, *jr.* Norsk, lapp and finn, or Travel tracings from the far north of Europe. Map and ill. N. Y. 1881. D.
914.8 : 7
Note. Includes also Denmark and Sweden.
Tyler, Katharine E. The story of a scandinavian summer. N. Y. 1881. D.   914.8 : 13
Note. Principally Norway.
Hare, A: J: Cuthbert. Sketches in . . . Scandinavia.   *in* 914.91 : 14
Stone, *Mrs.* Mary Amelia. A summer in Scandinavia. [Ill.] N. Y. [1885]. D.
914.8 : 28
Scudder, Horace Elisha. The viking Bodleys ; an excursion into Norway and Denmark. Ill. Bost. 1885 [1884]. O.   x 914.8 : 25

Sweden and Norway.

(For Lapland, *see also under Russia,* col. 1289.)

Woods, Francis H. Sweden and Norway. Ill. [Foreign countries and british colonies]. Lond. 1882. S.   914.8 : 22
Contents. Geogr. description. — Fauna and flora, geology, etc. — Origin of the scandinavian kingdoms. —Histor. sketch of Sweden and Norway.—Language, literature and art. — Occupations, industries, etc. — Religion, government, institutions, etc. — Habits, characters, etc.—Towns, etc.—Lapps and finns.—App. —Index.
Acerbi, Joseph. Travels through Sweden, Finland and Lapland to the North cape in 1798 and 1799. Ill. Lond. 1802. 2 v. Q.
914.8+26
Contents. V. 1. Sweden.—Finland. 2. Lapland.
Pfeiffer, Ida Laura, *born* Reyer. A journey to Iceland, and travels in Sweden and Norway, [1845]. Tr. from the germ. by Charlotte Fenimore Cooper. N. Y. 1852. D.
914.8 : 10
Kent, S. H. Within the arctic circle ; experiences of travel through Norway to the North cape, Sweden and Lapland. Lond. 1877. 2 v. D.   914.8 : 5
Du Chaillu, Paul Belloni. The land of the midnight sun ; summer and winter journeys through Sweden, Norway, Lapland and

x denotes books specially adapted for children.

northern Finland. N. Y. 1882 [1881]. 2 v. O.   914.8 : 1
* * *
Laing, S: A tour in Sweden in 1838; comprising observations on the moral, political and economical state of the swedish nation. Lond. 1839. O.   914.8 : 16
Colton, Robert, (*Sylvanus*). Rambles in Sweden and Gottland, with etchings by the wayside. Lond. 1847. O.   914.8 : 6
Marryat, Horace. One year in Sweden ; incl. a visit to the isle of Götland (*sic*). Map and ill. Lond, 1862. 2 v. D.   914.8 : 23
Lloyd, Llewellyn. Peasant life in Sweden. Ill. Lond. 1870. O.   914.8 : 2
Wood, C: W. Round about Norway. Ill. Lond. 1880. O.   914.8 : 17
Three in Norway, by two of them ; with a map and numerous ill., engr. on wood by G. H. Ford, from original sketches. Phila. [1882]. D.   914.8 : 15

Denmark and Iceland.

Gould, Sabine Baring-. Iceland ; its scenes and sagas. Ill. and map. Lond. 1863. Q.
914.8:P24
Contents of app. Newton, A. Ornithology of Iceland.—R., J. W. Advice to sportsmen. — List of icelandic plants.—List of icelandic published sagas.—Expenses of tour.
Burton, R: Francis. Ultima Thule or A summer in Iceland ; with historical introd., maps and ill. Lond. 1875. 2 v. O.   914.8 : 19
Contents. V. 1. Of Thule.—Physical geogr.— Historical notes.—Political geogr.—Anthropology. — Education and professions.—Zoological notes, etc. — Taxation, etc. — Catalogue of modern travels. — Travels. 2. Travels, *continued.* — App. on sulphur in Iceland and elsewhere.—Index.
Headley, Phineas Camp. The island of fire, or A thousand years of the old northmen's home, 874—1874. Bost. 1875. D. 914.8 : 8
Miles, Pliny. Eine nordfahrt ; streifzüge in Island. Aus dem engl. von W. E. Drugulin. Leipz. 1855. S.   914.8 : 11
Paijkull, K: Vilhelm. A summer in Iceland. Tr. by M. R. Barnard. Ill. Lond. 1868. O.
914.8 : 27
Taylor, Bayard. Iceland, in 1874. *in* 913.1 : 33
Watts, W: Lord. Snioland, or Iceland, its jökulls and fjälls. Lond. 1875. D.
914.8 : 20
— Across the Vatnajökull, or Scenes in Iceland ; a description of hitherto unknown regions. Lond. 1876. D.   914.8 : 21
De Fonblanque, C. A. Five weeks in Iceland. Lond. 1880. D.   914.8 : 9
Oswald, E. J. By fell and fjord, or Scenes and studies in Iceland. Ill. Edinb. 1882. O.
914.8 : 18

13. Europe — i, The Netherlands.

1. History.

Young, Alexander. History of the Netherlands, Holland and Belgium. Ill. Bost. 1884. O.
949.1 : 14
Note. To 1688, with an outline of the later history.
Grattan, T: Colley. The history of the Netherlands, [b. c. 50—a. d. 1815]. N. Y. 1843. S.
949.1 : 6

Kampen, N: Godfried v. Geschichte der Niederlande. [Geschichte der europ. staaten herausg. von A. H. L. Heeren und F. A. Ukert.] Hamburg. 1831, 1833. 3 v. O.
949.1 : 12
Contents. V. 1. Von den ältesten zeiten bis zum jahre 1609. 2. 1609 - 1815. [3.] Möller, J. H. Register.
Wenzelburger, K. Th. Geschichte der Niederlande, b. 1. [Geschichte der europ. staa-

ten, herausg. von A. H. L. Heeren, F. A. Ukert und W. v. Giesebrecht.] Gotha. 1879. O.   949.1 : 13
Contents. V. 1. Die römer und franken in den Niederlanden.—Holland unter den grafen aus dem holländischen, hennegauischen und baierischen hause.— Flandern und Brabant; Johann von Lüttich und Jacoba von Baiern; Das haus Burgund und seine politik.—Geldern. Friesland und Groningen.—Utrecht. —Die Niederlande unter Karl V.

Ashley, W : J. James and Philip van Artevelde. (Lothian prize essay for 1882). N. Y. 1883. D.   949.1 : 9

Hutton, James. James and Philip Van Arteveld ; two episodes in the history of the 14th century. N. Y. 1883. Q.   949.1+8

Schiller, J : Christoph F: v. Geschichte des abfalls der vereingten Niederlande von der spanischen regierung. In his Sämmtliche werke.   830 : 143 v8; 830 : 144 v12, 13
Contents. Einleitung.—Frühere geschichte der Niederlande bis zum 16ten jahrh.—Geschichte bis 1567.— Beilagen: Process und hinrichtung der grafen v. Egmont und v. Hoorn; Belagerung von Antwerpen durch den prinzen von Parma in 1584 und 1585.

— Same, eng. History of the revolt of the Netherlands to the confederacy of the Gueux. In his Works.   830 : 150 v1, 2
— Same. The revolt of the United Netherlands. In his Works.   830 : R153 v3

Motley, J : Lothrop. The rise of the Dutch Republic ; a history. N. Y. 1856-75. 3 v. O.
                                        949.1+1
Contents. V. 1. Histor. introd. — Philip II in the Netherlands, 1555 — 1559. — Administration of the duchess Margaret, 1559—1566. 2. Same, continued, 1566—1567.—Alva, 1567—1573. — Administration of the grand commander, 1573 — 1574. 3. Same, continued, 1574—1576. — Don John of Austria, 1576—1578. — Alexander of Parma, 1578—1584.—Index.

— History of the United Netherlands, from the death of William the silent to the synod of Dort ; with a full view of the english-dutch struggle against Spain, and the origin and destruction of the spanish armada. N. Y. 1861-71. 4 v. O.   949.1+2
Contents. V. 1. 1584 — 1586. 2. 1586 — 1590. 3. 1590 – 1600. 4. 1600 – 1609.—Index.

— The life and death of John of Barneveld, advocate of Holland ; with a view of the primary causes and movements of the thirty years' war. N. Y. 1874. 2 v. O.
                                        949.1+3
Contents. V. 1. 1609 – 1614. 2. 1614 – 1623.

Albert, Mary. Holland and her heroes to the year 1585 ; an adaptation of Motley's "Rise of the Dutch Republic." Lond. 1878. S.   x 949.1 : 4

Nutting, Mary O., (Mary Barrett). The story of William the silent and the Netherland war, 1555—1584. Bost. [1869]. S. x 949.1 : 7

Geddes, James. History of the administration of John De Witt, grand pensionary of Holland ; v. 1, 1623—1654. N. Y. 1880. O.
                                        949.1 : 5
See also in the Index to biography Arteveld — Evertsen—Ruyter—Tromp—Willem — de Witte.

Belgium.

Juste, Théodore. Histoire de Belgique depuis les temps primitifs jusqu'à la fin du règne

Juste, Théodore.—Continued. de Léopold I. Ill. Bruxelles. 1868. 3 v. Q.
                                        949.1+10
Contents. V. 1. 7e siècle av. J. C.—1383. 2. 1384 - 1715. 3. 1715 - 1865.

— La révolution belge de 1830, d'après des documents inédits. Bruxelles. 1872. 2 v. O.
                                        949.1 : 11

2. Description.

Holland.

Lax, L: Bilder aus den Niederlanden ; v. 2 : Briefe. Aachen. 1838. S.   914.91 : 4

Havard, H: The heart of Holland. Tr. by mrs. Cashel Hoey. N. Y. 1880. Q. 914.91+2

Amicis, Edmondo de. Holland and its people. Tr. from the italian by Caroline Tilton. N. Y. 1881. D.   914.91 : 1
— Same. Holland. Tr. from the italian by Maurice Saltire. Lond. 1883. 2 v. D.
                                        914.91 : 13

Bird, F: Spencer. The land of dykes and windmills, or Life in Holland ; with anecdotes of noted persons and historical incidents in connection with England. Lond. 1882. D.   914.91 : 11

Hare, A: J: Cuthbert. Sketches in Holland and Scandinavia. [Ill.] N. Y. [1885]. S.
                                        914.91 : 14

Broughton, G: H: Sketching rambles in Holland. Ill. by the author and E. A. Abbey. N. Y. 1885 [1884]. O.   914.91 : 12

Scudder, Horace Elisha. The Bodley grandchildren and their journey in Holland. Bost. 1882. O.   x 914.91 : 9

Belgium.

Ferrier de Tourettes, Alexandre. Belgium, historical and picturesque. From the french by H. R. Addison. Lond. [1838]. O.
                                        914.91 : 8

Tennent, Sir James Emerson. Belgium. Lond. 1841. 2 v. O.   914.91 : 6

Trollope, W: Belgium since the revolution of 1830 ; comprising a topographical and antiquarian description of the country, and a review of its political, commercial, literary, religious and social relations, as affecting its present condition and future prospects. Lond. 1842. O.   914.91 : 7

König, H: Eine fahrt nach Ostende. Frankfurt a. M. 1845. S.   914.91 : 3

Stevenson, Robert L: An inland voyage. Bost. 1883. S.   914.91 : 10

Macquoid, Katharine S. In the Ardennes. Ill. Lond. 1881. D.   914.91 : 5

Gantier, V: Das heutige Belgien. In Deutsche zeit- und streit-fragen.   304 : 15 v9

Jagemann, Eugen v. Die stellung der niederdeutschen, vlaamen, in Belgien. In Deutsche zeit- und streit-fragen.   304 : 15 v5

x denotes books specially adapted for children.

14. Europe — j, Switzerland.

1. History.

Wilson, J: The history of Switzerland from b. c. 110 to a. d. 1830. [*Anon*]. New ed. N. Y. 1840. S.   **949.2 : 2**

Zschokke, J: H: Daniel. The history of Switzerland. Tr. by Francis G. Shaw. N. Y. 1875. D.   **949.2 : 3**
Contents. Zschokke, H: 100 b. c.—1833 a. d. — Zschokke, Emil. 1834—1848.

Mackenzie, Harriet D. S. Switzerland. [Lothrop's library of entertaining history, ed. by Arthur Gilman]. Bost. [1881]. D.   **949.2 : 1**

Baumgarten-Crusius, Detlef K: W: Die geschichte der Schweiz. (Allg. historische taschenbibliothek, 5ter th.) Dresden. 1826. 2 v. in 1. S.   **949.2 : 7**

Daguet, Alexandre. Histoire de la Confédération suisse. 7e éd. refondue et augmentée. Genève. 1879. 2 v. O.   **949.2+5**
Contents. V. 1. Depuis un temps immémorial jusqu'en 1520. 2. De 1520 à 1874.

Morin, Antoine. Précis de l'histoire politique de la Suisse, depuis l'origine de la confédération jusqu'à nos jours. Genève. 1856-75. 5 v. D.   **949.2 : 4**
Contents. V. 1. Jusqu'en 1803. 2. 1803—1856. — Pièces justificatives. 3. App. Question de Neuchâtel.—Table chronologique et analytique. 4. Introd.— La question de Savoie.—Traités et modifications constitutionelles, 1866-72. — La Suisse pendant la guerre d'Autriche et la guerre franco-allemande; Développement intérieur. — Suite de la révision constitutionelle, 1872-74. 5. Les cantons de 1857 à 1874. — La question religieuse et confessionelle à Genève et dans la Confédération. — App. La répresentation proportionelle.

Rochholz, Ernst L: Tell und Gessler in sage und geschichte, nach urkundlichen quellen. Heilbronn. 1877. O.   **949.2 : 6**

2. Description.

Kaden, Woldemar. Switzerland, its mountains and valleys. Ill. Lond. 1878. F.   **914.92 : R12**

Byers, S: Hawkins Marshall. Switzerland, by an american resident. [*Anon*. Ill.] Zürich. 1875. O.   **914.92 : 18**

Dixon, W: Hepworth. The switzers. 3d ed. Lond. 1872. O.   **914.92 : 15**

Göthe, J: Wolfgang v. Briefe aus der Schweiz. *In his* Werke.   **830 : 137 v14**
— *Same, eng.* Letters from Switzerland. *In his* Works.   **830 : 151 v8**

Cooper, James Fenimore. Second visit to Switzerland. 1832.   *in* **914.4 : 5**

Düringsfeld, Ida *freiin* v. **Reinsberg**-. Aus der Schweiz. Bremen. 1850. S.   **914.92 : 2**

Barrell, G:, *jr*. The pedestrian in . . . Switzerland, 1851.   *in* **914.4 : 2**

Johnson, Anna C. The cottages of the Alps, or Life and manners in Switzerland, by the author of "Peasant life in Germany." N Y. 1860. D.   **914.92 : 7**

Prime, S: Irenæus. Letters from Switzerland. N. Y. 1860. D.   **914.92 : 8**

Ring, Max. In der Schweiz; reisebilder und novellen. Leipz. 1870. 2 v. in 1. D.   **914.92 : 3**

Havergal, Frances Ridley. Swiss letters and Alpine poems, ed. by J. Miriam Crane. N. Y. 1882. D.   **914.92 : 5**

Berlepsch, Herrmann Alexander [v.]. Die Alpen in natur- und lebensbildern. Jena. 1871. O.   **914.92 : 1**

Tyndall, J: Hours of exercise in the Alps. N. Y. 1871. D.   **914.92 : 10**

Whymper, E: Scrambles amongst the Alps. Ill. Phila. [1883.] O.   **914.92+11**

Burnaby, Elizabeth A. F., *born* Hawkins-Whitshed, *mrs*. Fred. The high Alps in winter, or Mountaineering in search of health. Lond. 1883. D.   **914.92 : 13**

Smith, Albert. The story of Mont Blanc. N. Y. 1853. D.   **914.92 : 9**

Cheever, G: Barrell. Wanderings of a pilgrim in the shadow of Mont Blanc. N. Y. 1846. D.   **914.92 : 6**

— The pilgrim in the shadow of the Jungfrau Alp. N. Y. 1846. D. *With his* Wanderings of a pilgrim.   **914.92 : 6**

Butler, S: Alps and sanctuaries of Piedmont and the canton Ticino; (op. 6). Ill. Lond. 1882. O.   **914.92 : 16**

Stahr, Fanny, *born* Lewald. Sommer und winter am Genfersee ; ein tagebuch. Berlin. 1872. D.   **914.92 : 4**

Lander, Sarah W. Zurich. (Spectacles for young eyes, no. 5.) N. Y. *n. d.* S.   **914.92 : 14**

15. Europe — k, Modern Greece.

1. History.

(*See also* Ancient Greece, col. 1172—1173.)

Finlay, G: A history of Greece from its conquest by the romans to the present time, b. c. 146—a. d. 1864. New ed. rev. and in part re-written, with considerable add. by the author, ed. by H. F. Tozer. Oxf. 1877. 7 v. O.   **949.3 : 1**
Contents. V. 1. Greece under the romans, b. c. 146—a. d. 716. 2. The Byzantine empire; pt. 1. 716—1057. 3. Same; pt. 2, 1057—1453. 4. Mediæval Greece and the empire of Trebizond, 1204—1461. 5. Greece under othoman and venetian domination, 1453—1821.

6. The greek revolution, 1821—1827. 7. Establishment of the greek kingdom, 1827—1843. — Supplementary, 1844—1864.—Index.

Lüdemann, G: W: v. Geschichte Griechenlands und der Türkei. (Allg. historische taschenbibliothek, 15ter th.) Dresden. 1827. 4 v. in 1. S.   **949.3 : 6**
Contents. V. 1. Die alte geschichte von Griechenland. 2. Geschichte des Byzantinischen reiches. 3. Geschichte des Osmanischen reiches bis 1774. 4. Geschichte der osmanen und griechen, 1774—1827.

Hertzberg, Gustav F: Geschichte Griechenlands seit dem absterben des antiken lebens bis zur gegenwart. [Geschichte der

europ. staaten, herausg. von A. H. L. Heeren, F. A. Ukert und W. v. Giesebrecht]. Gotha. 1876–79. 4 v. O.   **949.3 : 5**
Contents. V. 1. Von kaiser Arcadius bis zum lateinischen kreuzzuge. 395—1204. **2.** 1204—1470. **3.** 1470—1821. **4.** 1821—1878.—Register.

Comstock, J : L. History of the greek revolution; compiled from official documents of the greek government, Sketches of the war in Greece by Philip James Green, and the recent publications by mr. Blaquiere, mr. Humphrey, mr. Emerson, count Pecchio, col. Stanhope, The modern traveller and other authentic sources. Map and ill. N. Y. 1828. D.   **949.3 : 3**

Stanhope, Leicester. Greece in 1823 and 1824 ; a series of letters and other documents on the greek revolution, written during a visit to that country. Ill. with facsimiles ; added, the life of Mustapha Ali. Lond. 1824. O.   **949.3 : 4**

Strong, F : Greece as a kingdom, or A statistical description of that country, from the arrival of king Otho, in 1833, to the present time ; drawn from official documents and other authentic sources. Lond. 1842. D.   **949.3 : 2**

Clark, Edson L. The modern greeks. *In his* Races of european Turkey.   **949.4 : 2**

2. Description.

(*See also* The orient, col. 1194—1196.)

Sergeant, Lewis. Greece. Ill. [Foreign countries and english colonies]. Lond. 1880. S.   **914.93 : 10**

Wordsworth, Christopher. Greece, pictorial, descriptive and historical, with engr., ill. of the scenery, architecture, costume and fine arts of that country and a history of the characteristics of greek art by G: Scharf. New ed. rev., with notices of recent discoveries, by H. F. Tozer. Lond. 1882. Q.   **914.93 : R16**

Colange, Leo de. Picturesque . . . Greece.   *in* **914.7 : R45**

Gell, *Sir* W: The itinerary of Greece, containing one hundred routes in Attica, Bœotia, Phocis, Locris and Thessaly. Lond. 1819. O.   **914.93 : 5**
— Itinerary of the Morea ; a description of the routes of that peninsula. Lond. 1817. D.   **914.93 : 6**

Bulwer, *Sir* H : Lytton Earle, *baron Dalling and Bulwer.* An autumn in Greece; comprising sketches of the character, customs and scenery of the country, with a view of the present critical state, in letters addressed to C. B. Sheridan. Subjoined, Greece to the close of 1825 by a resident with the greeks. Lond. 1826. O.   **914.93 : 4**

Pericardis, G. A. The Greece of the greeks. N. Y. 1845. 2 v. D.   **914.93 : 8**
Contents. V. 1. Continental Greece and the islands. **2.** Morea.

Baird, H: Martyn. Modern Greece ; a narrative of a residence and travels in that country, with observations on its antiquities, literature, language, politics and religion. Ill. N. Y. 1856. D.   **914.93 : 2**

About, Edmond François Valentin. Greece and the greeks of the present day. N. Y. 1857. D.   **914.93 : 1**

Tuckerman, C: K. The greeks of to-day. 2d ed. rev. and corr. N. Y. 1878. D.   **914.93 : 12**

Mahaffy, J : Peytland. Rambles and studies in Greece. 2d ed. rev. and enl. Lond. 1878. D.   **914.93 : 15**

Jebb, R: Claverhouse. Modern Greece ; two lectures del. before the Philosophical institution of Edinburgh, with papers on "The progress of Greece" and "Byron in Greece." Lond. 1880. D.   **914.93 : 7**

Snider, Denton Jaques. A walk in Hellas, or The old in the new. Bost. 1883. O.   **914.93 : 13**

Colton, Walter. [Athens]. *In his* Land and lee.   **914.94 : 5**

Eddy, Daniel Clarke. Walter in Athens. (Walter's tour in the east, v. 6). N. Y. *n. d.* D.   **x 914.93 : 14**

Schliemann, H: Mycenæ ; a narrative of researches and discoveries at Mycenæ and Tiryns. Preface by W. E. Gladstone. Maps, plans and other ill. N. Y. 1878. Q.   **914.93+P9**
— Tiryns : The prehistoric palace of the kings of Tiryns ; the results of the latest excavations ; the pref. by F. Adler and contributions by W: Dörpfeld. Map, plans and ill. N. Y. 1885. Q.   **914.93+P17**

x denotes books specially adapted for children.

16. Europe — 1, Turkey and the Danubian states.

1. History.

Zinkeisen, J: W: Geschichte des Osmanischen reiches in Europa. [Geschichte der europ. staaten, herausg. von A. H. L. Heeren und F. A. Ukert]. Hamburg. 1840–63. 7 v. O.   **949.4 : 12**
Contents. V. 1. Urgeschichte und wachsthum des reiches bis zum jahre 1453. **2.** 1453 – 1574. **3.** Das innere leben und angehender verfall des reiches bis zum jahre 1623. **4.** Zunehmender verfall und neuer aufschwung des reiches bis zum frieden von Vasvar und dem falle von Candia in 1664 und 1669. **5.** 1669 – 1774. **6.** 1774 – 1802. **7.** 1802 – 1812. — Möller, J. H. Register.

Hammer-Purgstall, Joseph *freiherr* v. Geschichte des Osmanischen reiches, gröss-

tentheils aus bisher unbenützten handschriften und archiven. Pest. 1827. 10 v. O.   **949.4 : 11**
Contents. V. 1. 1300 – 1453. **2.** 1453 – 1520. **3.** 1520 – 1574. **4.** 1574 – 1623. **5.** 1623 – 1656. **6.** 1656 – 1699. **7.** 1699 – 1739. **8.** 1739 – 1774. **9.** Schlussrede und übersichten. **10.** Verzeichnisse, hauptregister und anhang.

Creasy, *Sir* E: Shepherd. History of the ottoman turks ; from the beginning of their empire to the present time ; chiefly founded on von Hammer. Lond. 1856. 2 v. O.   **949.4 : 3**
Contents. V. 1. 1250 –1640. **2.** 1640 –1839. — App.— Index.

Hertzberg, Gustav F: Geschichte der Byzantiner und des Osmanischen reiches bis gegen ende des 16ten jahrh. (Oncken, W:, *ed.* Allgemeine geschichte in einzeldarstellungen ; 2te hauptabth., 7ter th.) Ill. Berlin. 1883. O. **909+20 v7**

Neale, F: Arthur. Islamism ; its rise and progress, or The present and past condition of the turks. Lond. 1854. 2 v. O.
949.4 : 7

Freeman, E: A: The history and conquests of the saracens ; six lectures del. before the Edinburgh philosophical institution. 3d ed., with new pref. Lond. 1876. D.
949.4 : 6
Contents. The world at the coming of Mahomet.—Mahomet and his creed.—The undivided caliphate.—The saracens in the east. — The saracens in the west.—The later dynasties of Persia and India.

— The ottoman power in Europe ; its nature, its growth and its decline. Maps. Lond. 1877. D. **949.4 : 5**

Loper, F. K. Die türken im kampfe mit dem christlichen Europa ; in historischen gemälden vorgestellt. Meissen. 1829. 2 v. D.
949.4 : 4

Schmidt, Ferdinand. Die türken vor Wien ; ein historisches gemälde, für jung und alt erzählt. 6te aufl. Ill. Kreuznach. [1882]. S. **949.4 : 13**

Chesney, Francis Rawdon. The russo-turkish campaigns of 1828 and 1829 ; with a view of the present state of affairs in the east, [and] an app. containing the diplomatic corresp. between the four powers and the secret corresp. between the russian and english governments. N. Y. 1854. D.
949.4 : 8

Sandwith, Humphrey. Geschichte der belagerung von Kars und des sechsmonatlichen widerstandes der türkischen garnison unter general Williams gegen die russische armee ; nebst einer beschreibung von reisen und abenteuern in Armenien und Lazistan, mit bemerkungen über den gegenwärtigen zustand der Türkei. Aus dem eng. von Reinhard Otto. Braunsch. 1856. D. **956 : 4**

Ollier, Edmund. Cassell's illustrated history of the russo-turkish war. Lond. [1879, 1880]. 2 v. Q. **949.4 : 14**
Contents. V. 1. To the fall of Plevna, incl. an historical sketch of the Russian and Turkish empire. 2. From dec. 1878 to the ratification of peace, incl. a history of Cyprus, and of the Afghan war.

War correspondence of the Daily news, 1877 ; with a connecting narrative, forming a continuous history of the war between Russia and Turkey to the fall of Kars, incl. the letters of A. Forbes, J. A. MacGahan and many other special correspondents in Europe and Asia. Leipz. 1878. 3 v. in 2. S.
949.4 : 10

Baker-*pacha*, Valentine. War in Bulgaria ; a narrative of personal experiences. Lond. 1879. 2 v. O. **949.4 : 9**

Williams, C: The armenian campaign ; a diary of the campaign of 1877, in Armenia and Koordistan. Lond. 1878. D. **956 : 5**
Note. See also The eastern question, col. 172.

Servia, Rumania, etc.

Clark, Edson L. The races of european Turkey, their history, condition and prospects ;

Clark, Edson L.—*Continued.*
in three parts : pt. 1, The Byzantine empire ; pt. 2, The modern greeks and the albanians ; pt. 3, The turkish slavonians, the wallachians, and the gypsies. N. Y. 1878. O. **949.4 : 2**
— *Same.* N. Y. [1878]. O. **949.4 : 2**

Ranke, Franz Leopold v. Serbien und die Türkei im 19. jahrhundert. Leipz. 1879. 2 v. in 1. O. **904 : 36 v43, 44**
Contents. Geschichte Serbiens bis 1842 ; 3te aufl.—Bosnien in seinem verhältniss zu den reformen des sultans Mahmud II. 1820 - 1832. — Verflechtung der orientalischen und der occidentalischen angelegenheiten, 1839 - 1841.—Das fürstenthum Serbien unter der einwirkung der europäischen mächte seit 1842 [bis 1868].—Analecten : Zur ältern geschichte und geographie von Serbien ; Ueber die allmähliche abnahme der christlichen bevölkerung in der Türkei ; Zur orientalischen politik des fürsten Metternich.

— A history of Servia and the servian revolution ; from the original mss. and documents. Tr. from the german by mrs. Alexander Kerr. Lond. 1847. O. **949.5 : 3**
Note. A tr. of the 1st ed. of the original.

Samuelson, James. Roumania, past and present. Maps, portraits and ill. Lond. 1882. O. **914.9 : 3**
Contents. Roumania to-day.—History, about 335 b. c. - 1881 a. d.—App.—Index.

2. Description.
(See also Turkey in Asia, cl. 915.6.)

General geography and travels.

Bessé, Alfred v. The turkish empire ; its historical, statistical and religious condition, also its manners, customs, etc. Tr., rev. and enl. from the 4th germ. ed., with memoirs of the reigning sultan, Omer Pacha, the turkish cabinet, etc., by E: Joy Morris. Phila. 1854. D. **949.4 : 1**

Smith, Jerome Van Crowninshield. Turkey and the turks. Bost. 1854. D. **914.94 : 14**

Oscanyan, Christopher. The sultan and his people. Ill. N. Y. 1857. D. **914.94 : 13**

Aristarchi *bey,* (*Charikles*). Türkische skizzen in briefen an eine freundin, 1876. *In* Deutsche zeit- und streit-fragen. **304 : 15 v6**

Baker, James. Turkey. [Maps]. N. Y. 1877. O. **914.94 : 3**
Contents. The voyage out.—The bulgarians.—The Bosphorus and Black Sea.—Ottoman-greek subjects.—En voyage.—From Burgas to Yanboli.—The turks.—Turkish government.—The fall of the Byzantine empire.—Modern turkish history.—En route again.—Across the Balkan.—Ottoman slaves.—Turkey's army and navy. — Turkey as a military power. — From Troyan to Samakov.—The albanians.—From Rilo to Salonica.—The Macedonian plains.—A second visit to Turkey.—Taxation, etc.—Agriculture.—Turkey as a field for emigration.—The crimean tartars.—App.

Hellwald, F: v., *and* L. C. Beck. Die heutige Türkei ; schilderung von land und leuten des Osmanischen reiches in Europa, vor und nach dem kriege von 1877–1878. 2te aufl. Leipz. 1878. O. **914.94 : 1**
Contents. Hellwald, F: v. Einleitung: Geogr. übersicht ; Ethnographie und geschichte ; Türkische zustände. — Beck, L. C. Rumänien, Serbien und Montenegro.—Hellwald, F: v. Bulgarien.—Beck, L. C. Bosnien und die Herzegowina.—Beck, L. C. Die europäische Türkei: Albanien ; Thessalien und Makedonien ; Thrakien.—Beck, L. C. Der krieg und seine folgen.

Blunt, *Mrs.* J: Elijah. The people of Turkey ; twenty years' residence among bulgarians, greeks, albanians, turks, and armenians, by a consul's daughter and wife, ed. by Stanley Lane Poole. [*Anon.*] Lond. 1878. 2 v. O.   914.94 : 26
— *Same.* N. Y. 1878. Q.   914.94+26

*   *   *

Sutherland, D: A tour up the straits from Gibraltar to Constantinople, with the leading events in the present war between the austrians, russians and the turks, to the commencement of the year 1789. Lond. 1790. O.   914.94 : 16

MacFarlane, C: Constantinople in 1828 ; a residence of 16 months in the turkish capital and provinces with an account of the present state of the naval and military power and of the resources of the Ottoman empire. 2d ed.; added an app. containing remarks and observations to the autumn of 1829. Lond. 1829. 2 v. O.   914.94+19

DeKay, James E. Sketches of Turkey, in 1831 and 1832, by an american. N. Y. 1833. O.
914.94 : 6

Moltke, Helmuth C: Bernhard *graf* v. Briefe über zustände und begebenheiten in der Türkei aus den jahren 1835 bis 1839. 4te aufl. Portr. Berlin. 1882. O.   914.94 : 30

MacFarlane, C: Turkey and its destiny ; the result of journeys made in 1847 and 1848 to examine into the state of that country. Phila. 1850. 2 v. D.   914.94 : 4
— Kismet, or The doom of Turkey. Lond. 1853. D.   914.94 : 9

Smyth, Warington Wilkinson. A year with the turks, or Sketches of travel in the european and asiatic dominions of the sultan. N. Y. 1854. D.   914.94 : 15

Colton, Walter. Land and lee in the Bosphorus and Ægean, or Views of Constantinople and Athens ; ed. from the notes and ms. of the author by H: T. Cheever. N. Y. 1860. O.   914.94 : 5

Prime, E: Dorr Griffin. Forty years in the turkish empire ; a memoir of W: Goodell by his son-in-law. N. Y. 1876. O.
914.94 : 8

Dwight, H: O. Turkish life in war time. N. Y. 1881. D.   914.94 : 7

Constantinople.

Hornby, Emelia Bythinia *lady.* In and around Stamboul. Phila. *n. d.* D.   914.94 : 23
— Constantinople, during the crimean war. Ill. Lond. 1863. Q.   914.94+20

Gautier, Théophile. Constantinople. From the french by Robert Howe Gould. Amer. ed. rev. N. Y. 1875. D.   914.94 : 22

Amicis, Edmondo de. Constantinople. Tr. from the 7th italian ed. by Caroline Tilton. N. Y. 1878. O.   914.94 : 21

Eddy, Daniel Clarke. Walter in Constantinople. (Walter's tour in the east, v. 5.) N. Y. *n. d.* D.   914.94 : 29

Rumania, Servia, etc.

Urquhart, D: The spirit of the east, ill. in a journal of travels through Roumeli during an eventful period. Phila. 1839. 2 v. D.
914.94 : 18

O'Brien, Patrick. Journal of a residence in the Danubian principalities, in the autumn and winter of 1853. Lond. 1854. O.
914.94 : 12

Wachenhusen, Hans. Von Widdin nach Stambul ; streifzüge durch Bulgarien und Rumelien. Leipz. 1855. S.   914.94 : 2

Noyes, James O. Roumania, the border land of the christian and the turk ; adventures of travel in eastern Europe and western Asia. N. Y. 1858. S.   914.94 : 11

Paton, Andrew Archibald. Researches on the Danube and the Adriatic, or contributions to the modern history of Hungary and Transylvania, Dalmatia and Croatia, Servia and Bulgaria. Leipz. 1861. 2 v. in 1. D.   914.94 : 27
Contents. V. 1. Servia.—Highlands and islands of the Adriatic. 2. The goth and the hun. — The bulgarian, the turk and the german.—App.

More, Robert Jasper. Under the Balkans ; notes of a visit to the district of Philippopolis in 1876. Map and ill. Lond. 1877. D.
914.94 : 10

Sebright, Georgina Mary *lady, born* Muir-Mackenzie, *and* A. P. **Irby.** Travels in the slavonic provinces of Turkey-in-Europe, by G. Muir-Mackenzie and A. P. Irby ; with a pref. by the right hon. W. E. Gladstone. 2d ed. rev. Lond. 1877. 2 v. O.
914.94 : 25

Evans, Arthur J. Through Bosnia and the Herzegovina on foot, during the insurrection aug. and sept. 1875, with an historical review of Bosnia ; rev. and enl., and a glimpse at croats. slavonians and the ancient republic of Ragusa. Map and ill. 2d ed. Lond. 1877. O.   914.9+6

Wright, Alfred. Adventures in Servia, or The experiences of a medical free lance among the bashi-bazouks, etc.; ed. by A. G. Farquhar-Bernard. Ill. Lond. 1884. O.
914.9 : 4

Chirol, Valentine. Twixt greek and turk, or Jottings during a journey through Thessaly, Macedonia and Epirus, in the autumn of 1880. Frontispiece and map. Edinb. 1881. O.   914.94 : 24

The islands.

Mariti, Giovanni. Travels through Cyprus.
915.6 : 28 v1

Löher, Franz v. Cyprus ; historical and descriptive from the earliest times to the present day. Adapted from the germ., with much add. matter by mrs. A. Batson Joyner. Maps and ill. N. Y. 1878. O.   914.95 : 3

Cesnola, L: Palma Di. Cyprus, its ancient cities, tombs and temples ; a narrative of researches and excavations during ten years' residence in that island. Maps and ill. 2d ed. N. Y. 1878. O.   914.95+2

Dixon, W: Hepworth. British Cyprus. Lond. 1879. O.   914.95 : 1

17. Dispersed nationalities.

1. The jews.

See under Ancient history of Israel, col. 1168—1169.

2. The gipsies.

Leland, C: Godfrey. The gypsies. Bost. 1882. D.   **949 : 1**
Contents. Introd.—Russian gypsies.—Austrian gypsies.—Welsh gypsies.—American gypsies.—Gypsies in the east.—Gypsy names and family characteristics.—Gypsy stories in romany, with translation. — The origin of the gypsies.—A gypsy magic spell.—Shelta, the tinkers' talk.

Simson, Walter. A history of the gipsies, with specimens of the gipsy language ; ed. with preface, introd. and notes and a disquisition on the past, present and future of gipsydom by James Simson. N. Y. 1866. D.   **949 : 2**
Contents. Pref. — Introd. — Continental gipsies. — English gipsies.—Scottish gipsies down to 1715. — Linlithgowshire gipsies. — Fife and Stirlingshire gipsies. — Tweed-dale and Clydesdale gipsies. — Border gipsies.—Marriage and divorce ceremonies.—Language. — Present condition and number of the gipsies in Scotland.—Disquisition.—Index.

Morwood, Vernon S. Our gipsies in city, tent and van ; an account of their origin and strange life, fortune-telling practices, etc., specimens of their dialect, and anecdotes of gipsy kings, queens and other notabilities. Ill. Lond. 1885. O.   **914.2 : 89**

Groome, Francis Hindes. In gipsy tents. 2d ed. Edinb. 1881. D.   **914.2 : 19**

English gipsy-songs ; in rommany with metrical english, by C: G. Leland, E. H. Palmer and Janet Tuckey. Phila. 1875. S.   **821.2 : 115**

Borrow, G: The zincali. or an account of the gypsies of Spain ; with an original collection of their songs and poetry. N. Y. 1847. O.   *in* **914.6 : 3**
Contents. The gypsies.—The zincali.—Poetry of the gitanos.—On the language of the gitanos.—On robber language. — Vocabulary of the language of the zincali.

Clark, Edson L. [The gypsies]. *In his* Races of European Turkey.   **949.4 : 2**

18. Asia — a, General and Eastern.

1. General.

Keane, A: H. Asia, with ethnological appendix ; ed. by sir R: Temple. (Stanford's compendium of geography and travel, based on Hellwald's "Die erde und ihre völker".) Maps and ill. Lond. 1882. O.   **915 : 21**

Goodrich, S: Griswold. Lights and shadows of asiatic history. [Youth's library of history.] Bost. [1844]. S.   **x 950 : 1**

Miller, Olive Thorne. Little people of Asia. N. Y. 1883 [1882]. O.   **x 915 : 18**

Polo, Marco. Travels ; emended and enl. from early mss. recently pub. by the french society of geography and in Italy by count Baldelli Boni, with notes, ill. the routes and observations of the author and comparing them with those of more recent travellers, by Hugh Murray. Maps. N. Y. 1845. T.   **915 : 10**

Towle, G: Makepeace. Marco Polo, his travels and adventures. (Young folks' heroes of history.) Bost. 1880. D.   **x 915 : 11**

Knox, T: Wallace. The travels of Marco Polo for boys and girls ; with explanatory notes and comments. Ill. N. Y. 1885. O.   **x 915+26**

Travels of the jesuits into various parts of the world, particularly China and the East-Indies, intermix'd with an account of the manners, government, civil and religious ceremonies, natural history and curiosities of the several nations visited by those fathers. Tr. from the celebrated "Lettres édifiantes et curieuses, écrites des missions étrangères, par les missionaires de la Compagnie de Jésus". Ill. Prefixed, an account of the spanish settlements in America, with a general index to the whole work by [J:] Lockman. 2d ed. corr. Lond. 1762. 2 v. D.   **915 : 9**

Buchanan, C: Christian researches in Asia ; with notices of the tr. of the scriptures into the oriental languages. Added, Melville Horne's sermon, preached in London, june 4, 1811. Bost. 1811. D.   **915 : 6**

Taylor, Bayard. A visit to India, China and Japan, in 1853. N. Y. 1855. D.   **915 : 13**

Scherzer, K: v., *ed.* Die k. u. k. österreichisch-ungarische expedition nach Indien, China, Siam und Japan, 1868—1871, zur erforschung der handels- und verkehrsverhältnisse dieser länder, mit besonderer rücksicht auf den österreichischen handel. 2te aufl. Stuttg. 1873. O.   **915+2**

Knox, T: Wallace. The boy travellers in the far east ; adventures of two youths in a journey to Japan and China. N. Y. 1880 [1879]. O.   **x 915 : 14**

— *Same,* pt. 2 : Adventures of two youths in a journey to Siam and Java with descriptions of Cochin-China, Cambodia, Sumatra and the Malay archipelago. Ill. N. Y. 1881. O.   **x 915 : 15**

— *Same,* pt. 3 : Adventures of two youths in a journey to Ceylon and India ; with descriptions of Borneo, the Philippine Islands and Burmah. N. Y. 1882 [1881]. O. **x 915 : 16**

— *Same,* pt. 4 : Adventures of two youths in a journey to Egypt and the Holy Land. N. Y. 1883 [1882]. O.   **x 915 : 19**

x denotes books specially adapted for children.

Myers, Philip Van Ness. Remains of lost empires; sketches of the ruins of Palmyra, Nineveh, Babylon and Persepolis, with some notices on India and the Cashmerian Himalayas. Ill. N. Y. 1875. O.　**915 : 20**

* * *

Thomson, J: The straits of Malacca, Indo-China and China, or Ten years' travels, adventures and residence abroad. Ill. N. Y. 1875. O.　**915.1+14**

Johnston, James D. China and Japan; a narrative of the cruise of the U. S. steamfrigate Powhattan in 1857—1860, incl. an account of the japanese embassy to the U. S. Ill. Phila. 1861. D.　**915.1 : 9**

United States. *Exploring expedition to the China seas and Japan.* Narrative of the expedition of an american squadron to the China seas and Japan, 1852—1854, under commodore M. C. **Perry,** by order of the govt. of the U. S. Ill. Wash. 1856. 3 v. Q.　**915.2 : D**

Note. V. 1 contains the general report and was compiled from the original notes and journals of com. Perry and his officers, by Francis L. **Hawks.** V. 2 contains special reports on explorations, agriculture and products of various countries visited, by D. S. Green and others; papers on natural history by J: Cassin, Asa Gray and others; facsimile and trans. of the treaty with Japan, etc., with maps and ill. V. 3 has separate title: **Jones,** G: Observations on the zodiacal light, with conclusions thus obtained.

2. China.

History.

Boulger, Demetrius C: History of China. Lond. 1881–84. 3 v. O.　**951 : 1**
Contents. V. 1. From the earliest ages to the decline of the mongols, about 1350. 2. From the expulsion of the mongols to the end of Keen Lung's reign, 1796. 3. From the reign of Kiaking to 1881.—Chronological table.—App.—Index.

Douglas, Robert K. China; [ed. by Arthur Gilman]. Ill. Bost. [1885]. D.　**951 : 8**

Gray, J: H: China; a history of the laws, manners and customs of the people; ed. by W: Gow Gregor. Lond. 1878. 2 v. O.　**951 : 7**

Du Halde, J: Baptiste. The general history of China, containing a geographical, historical, chronological, political and physical description of the empire of China, Chinese Tartary, Corea and Thibet, incl. an exact and particular account of their customs, manners, ceremonies, religion, arts and sciences. Maps and plates. 3d ed. corr. Lond. 1741. 4 v. D.　**951 : 3**

Gutzlaff, C: F: A: A sketch of chinese history, ancient and modern, comprising a retrospect of the foreign intercourse and trade with China. N. Y. 1834. 2 v. D.　**951 : 4**

Davis, J: Francis. The chinese; a general description of the empire of China and its inhabitants. Ill. [Harper's family lib.] N. Y. 1845. 2 v. S.　**951 : 2**

MacFarlane, C: The chinese revolution; with details of the habits, manners and customs of China and the chinese. Lond. 1853. S.　**951 : 5**

Callery, J. M., *and* Melchior **Yvan.** History of the insurrection in China; with notices of the christianity, creed and proclamations of the insurgents. Tr. from the french, with a supp. chapter, narrating the most recent events, by J: Oxenford. N. Y. 1853. D.　**951 : 6**

Scott, James G:, (*Shway Yoe*). France and Tongking; a narrative of the campaign of 1884 and the occupation of Further India. Map and plans. Lond. 1885. O.　**951 : 9**
See also in the Index to biography **Jinghiz-khan** —**Tai-ping-wang.**

Description.

Williams, S: Wells. The middle kingdom; a survey of the geography, government, education, social life, arts, religion, etc., of the Chinese empire and its inhabitants. 2d ed. N. Y. 1848. 2 v. D.　**915.1 : 15**

— The middle kingdom; a survey of the geography, government, literature, social life, arts and history of the Chinese empire and its inhabitants. Rev. ed., with ill. and a new map. N. Y. 1883. 2 v. O.　**915.1+23**

Richthofen, Ferdinand Paul W: Dieprand *freiherr v.* China; ergebnisse eigener reisen und darauf gegründeter studien. Ill. and maps. Berlin. 1877. 2 v. Q.　**915.1 : R29**
Contents. V. 1. Einleitender theil. Vorerläuterungen.—China und Central-Asien.— Entwickelung der kentaiss von China. — Index. 2. Das nördliche China.

Tcheng-Ki-Tong. The chinese painted by themselves. Tr. from the french by James Millington. Lond. [1885]. D.　**915.1 : 32**

Martin, Robert Montgomery. China, political, commercial and social; in an official report to her majesty's government. Lond. 1847. 2 v. O.　**915.1 : 18**

Martin, W: A. P. The chinese; their education, philosophy and letters. N. Y. 1881. D.　**915.1 : 11**

Doolittle, Justus. Social life of the chinese; with some account of their religious, governmental, educational and business customs and opinions, with special, but not exclusive, reference to Fuhchau. Ill. N. Y. 1865. 2 v. D.　**915.1 : 5**

Bridgman, Eliza J. Gillett. Daughters of China, or Sketches of domestic life in the celestial empire. N. Y. 1853. S.　**915.1 : 4**

Moule, Arthur E., *ed. and tr.* Chinese stories for boys and girls, and chinese wisdom for old and young. Ill. Lond. 1880. D.　**x 915.1 : 33**
Contents. A letter of introd.—Chinese children at home.—Chinese stories for young and old.—Chinese proverbs, grave and gay.—The story of a chinese girl.

* * *

Barrow, *Sir* J: Travels in China; containing descriptions, observations and comparisons made and collected in the course of a short residence at the imperial palace of Yuen-Min-Yuen, and on a subsequent journey through the country from Pekin to Canton, in which it is attempted to appreciate the rank that this extraordinary empire may be considered to hold in the scale of civilized nations. Ill. Lond. 1804. Q.　**915.1 : R3**

Gutzlaff, C: F: A: Journal of three voyages along the coast of China in 1831—1833, with notices of Siam, Corea and the Loo-Choo islands. Prefixed, an introd. essay on the policy, religion, etc., of China by W. Ellis. 2d ed. Lond. 1834. O.　**915.1 : 7**

x denotes books specially adapted for children.

Abeel, D: Journal of a residence in China and the neighboring countries ; with a prelim. essay on the commencement and progress of missions in the world. 2d ed. N. Y. 1836. D.   **915.1 : 1**

Ball, B. L. Rambles in eastern Asia, incl. China and Manilla, during several years' residence ; with notes of the voyage to China, excursions in Manilla, Hong-Kong, Canton, Shanghai, Ningpoo, Amoy, Fouchow and Macao. Bost. 1855. D. **915.1 : 2**

Huc, Évariste Régis. Recollections of a journey through Tartary, Thibet and China, during 1844—1846. N. Y. 1852. 2 v. S.
    915.1 : 28
— A journey through the Chinese empire. N. Y. 1855. 2 v. D.   **915.1 : 8**

Milne, W: C. Life in China. Maps. Lond. 1857. D.   **915.1 : 12**

Nevius, Helen S. C. Our life in China. N. Y. 1869. S.   **915.1 : 21**

Wheeler, Lucius N. The foreigner in China ; with introd. by W. C. Sawyer. Chicago. 1881. D.   **915.1 : 13**

French, Harry Willard. Our boys in China ; the thrilling story of two young americans, Scott and Paul Clayton, wrecked in the China sea, on their return from India, and their strange adventures in China. Ill. Bost. 1883. O.   **x 915.1 : 24**

Lander, Sarah W. Pekin. (Spectacles for young eyes). N. Y. n. d. S.   **x 915.1 : 26**

Gray, Mrs. J: H: Fourteen months in Canton. Ill. Lond. 1880. D.   **915.1 : 6**

Colquhoun, Archibald Ross. Across Chrysê ; the narrative of a journey of exploration through the south China border lands from Canton to Mandalay. Maps and ill. N. Y. 1883. 2 v. O.   **915.1 : 20**

Gill, W: J: The river of golden sand ; the narrative of a journey through China and eastern Thibet to Burmah ; condensed by E: Colborne Baber, ed. with a memoir and introd. essay by col. H: Yule. Portr., map and ill. Lond. 1883. D.   **915.1 : 30**

Shaw, Robert. Visits to High Tartary, Yârkand and Kâshgar, formerly Chinese Tartary and return journey over the Karakoram pass. Map and ill. Lond. 1871. O.
    915.1+22

Piassetskii, P. Russian travellers in Mongolia and China, [1874]. Tr. by J. Gordon-Cumming. Lond. 1884. 2 v. D.   **915.1 : 27**

Gilmour, James. Among the mongols. Map and ill. N. Y. [1883]. D.   **915.1 : 25**

3. Corea.

McLeod, J: Narrative of a voyage in h. m. s. Alceste to the Yellow Sea, along the coast of Corea and through its numerous hitherto undiscovered islands to the island of Lewchew, with an account of her shipwreck in the straits of Gaspar. Phila. 1818. O.   **915.1 : 10**

Hall, Basil. Account of a voyage of discovery to the west coast of Corea and the great Loo-Choo island ; with an app., containing charts and various hydrographical and scientific notes, and a vocabulary of the Loo-Choo language by H. J. Clifford. Lond. 1818. Q.   **915.1 : R16**

x denotes books specially adapted for children.

Oppert, Ernest. A forbidden land ; voyages to the Corea ; with an account of its geography, history, productions and commercial capabilities, etc. Charts and ill. N. Y. 1880. O.   **915.1 : 17**

Griffis, W: Elliot. Corea, the hermit nation : 1, Ancient and mediæval history ; 2, Political and social Corea ; 3, Modern and recent history. N. Y. 1882. O.   **915.1 : 19**
— Corea without and within ; chapters on corean history, manners and religion, with Hendrik Hamel's Narrative of captivity and travels in Corea, annotated. [Ill., map]. Phila. [1885]. S.   **915.1 : 31**

4. Japan.

Reed, Sir E: James. japan ; its history, traditions and religions. Map and ill. Lond. 1880. 2 v. O.   **915.2 : 11**
Contents. V. 1. Introd. — The land and its inhabitants. — Religions. — History. 2. Description of travels.

Griffis, W: Elliot. The mikado's empire. N. Y. 1876. O.   **915.2 : 1**
Contents. Book 1. History of Japan. b. c. 660—a. d. 1872. — Book 2. Personal experiences, observations and studies in Japan, 1870—1874.

Manners and customs of the japanese in the 19th century, from the account of recent dutch residents in Japan, and from the german work of Ph. Fr. v. Siebold. [Harper's family lib.] N. Y. 1841. S.   **915.2 : 3**

Hildreth, R: Japan, as it was and is. Bost. 1855. D.   **952 : 3**

Alcock, Sir Rutherford. The capital of the tycoon ; narrative of a three years residence in Japan. Map and ill. N. Y. 1863. 2 v. D.   **915.2 : 7**

Taylor, Bayard, ed. Japan in our day. (Ill. library of travel.) N. Y. 1872. D.   **915.2 : 7**
— Same. N. Y. 1881. D.   **915.2 : 7**

Mossman, S: Japan. Ill. [Foreign countries and english colonies]. Lond. 1880. S.
    915.2 : 6

Black, J: R. Young Japan. Yokohama and Yeddo ; a narrative of the settlement and the city from the signing of the treaties in 1858, to the close of the year 1879, with a glance at the progress of Japan during a period of 21 years. Yokohama. 1880. 2 v. O.   **952+1**

Wernich, Agathon. Ueber ausbreitung und bedeutung der neuen culturbestrebungen in Japan. In Deutsche zeit- und streit-fragen.   **304 : 15 v6**

House, E: H. Japanese episodes. Bost. 1881. T.   **915.2 : 9**

Bishop, Isabella L., born Bird. Unbeaten tracks in Japan ; an account of travels on horseback in the interior, incl. visits to the aborigines of Yezo and the shrines of Nikkô and Isé. Map and ill. N. Y. 1881. 2 v. O.   **915.2 : 5**

Dixon, W: Gray. The land of the morning, an account of Japan and its people, based on a four years' residence in that country, incl. travels into the remotest parts of the interior. Map and ill. Edinb. 1882. D.   **915.2 : 15**

Crow, Arthur H. Highways and byways in Japan ; the experiences of two pedestrian tourists. Lond. 1883. D.   **915.2 : 12**

Rein, Johannes Justus. Travels and researches undertaken at the cost of the prussian government. From the german. 2d ed. Maps and ill. N. Y. 1884. O.   915.2 : R14
Contents. The physiography of Japan. — The japanese people: History: Ethnography: Topography.

Dresser, Christopher. Japan; its architecture, art and art manufactures. Lond. 1882. O.   748+16

Greey, E: Young americans in Japan, or The adventures of the Jewett family and their

Greey, E:—Continued.
friend, Oto Nambo. Bost. 1882 [1881]. O.   x 915.2 : 8
— The wonderful city of Tokio, or Further adventures of the Jewett family and their friend Oto Nambo. Bost. 1883 [1882]. O.   x 915.2 : 10
— The bear-worshippers of Yezo and the island of Karafuto (Saghalin), or The adventures of the Jewett family and their friend Oto Nambo. Bost. 1884 [1883]. O. x 915.2 : 13

x denotes books specially adapted for children.

19.   Asia — b, Southern.

1.   Hither India.

History.

Wheeler, J: Talboys. A short history of India and of the frontier states of Afghanistan, Nipal and Burma. Maps and tables. Lond. 1880. D.   954 : 10
Trotter, Lionel James. History of India; from the earliest times to the present day. Lond. [1874]. D.   954 : 2
Feudge, Fannie Roper. India; [ed. by Arthur Gilman]. Bost. 1880. D.   954 : 1
Wheeler, J: Talboys. The history of India from the earliest ages. Lond. 1847–81. 4 v. in 5. O.   954 : R15
Contents. V. 1. The Vedic period and the Mahá Bhárata: Introd.; The Mahá Bhárata; Episodes in the Mahá Bhárata: Index. 2. The Rámáyana. — The brahmanic period.—Index. 3. Hindú, buddhist and brahmanical: Retrospect of Vedic India: Retrospect of brahmanic India; Life and teachings of Gótama Buddha, b. c. 623–543; Greek and roman India; Buddhist India, b. c. 300 to a. d. 645; The hindú drama; The Rajpoots; The brahmanical revival, a. d. 600—1600; Portuguese india, a. d. 1500–1600.—App.—Index. 4. Musselman rule: Pt. 1, Islam before the conquest of India, a. d. 570 to 977; Sunni conquest of the Punjab and Hindustan, a. d. 1001 to 1526; Shiah revolt in the Dekhan, a. d. 1347 to 1565; The Moghul empire, 1505—1558. — Pt. 2, Moghul empire under Aurangzeb, a. d. 1658 to 1707; Decline and fall, a. d. 1707 to 1761; Civilisation, a. d. 1600 to 1764; Provincial history, Bengal, a. d. 1700 to 1756. — App. The Sháh námeh of Firdusi: Hindú annals compiled from the Mackenzie mss. —Index.
Mill, James. The history of British India. 5th ed., with notes and a continuation, by Horace Hayman Wilson. Lond. 1858. 6 v. D.   954 : 13
Contents. Mill, J. V. 1. Pref.—Glossary. — From the commencement of the british intercourse with India to 1708.—Of the hindus. 2. Same, continued.—The mohammedans. 3. 1708—1774. 4. 1775—1784. 5. 1785—1793. 6. 1793—1805. Wilson, H. H. 7. 1805—1812. 8. 1813—1823. 9. 1823—1833. 10. Index, 1-6.—Index, 7-9.
Martin, Robert Montgomery. History of the possessions of the honorable East India company. [British col. lib., v. 8, 9]. Lond. 1837. 2 v. S.   954 : 12
Caunter, Horace. The romance of history: India. Ill. Lond. n. d. D.   954 : 9
Robertson, W: An historical disquisition concerning the knowledge which the ancients had of India, and the progress of trade with that country, prior to the discovery of the passage to it by the Cape of Good Hope, with an app. containing observations on the civil policy, the laws and judicial proceedings, the arts, the sciences and re-

ligious institutions of the indians. N. Y. 1844. O. With his History of Scotland.   941 : 10
Erskine, W: A history of India under the two first sovereigns of the house of Taimur, Báber aud Humáyun, [1519—1556]. Lond. 1854. 2 v. O.   954 : 3
Murray, Hugh, and others. Historical and descriptive account of British India, from the most remote period to the present time; incl. a narrative of the early portuguese and english voyages, the revolutions in the Mogul empire and the origin, progress and establishment of the british power, with ill. of the zoology, botany, climate, geology, and mineralogy, also medical observations, an account of the hindoo astronomy, the trigonometrical surveys and the navigation of the Indian seas. Ill. [Harper's family lib.] N. Y. 1844. 3 v. S.   954 : 4
Capper, J: The three presidencies of India; a history of the rise and progress of the british indian possessions, from the earliest records to the present time, with an account of their government, religion, manners, customs, education, etc. Ill. Lond. 1853. O.   954 : 5
Malleson, G: Bruce. The founders of the indian empire, Clive, Warren Hastings and Wellesly: Clive. Portr. and maps. Lond. 1882. O.   954 : 11
Malcolm, Sir J: The political history of India from 1784 to 1823. Lond. 1826. 2 v. O.   954 : 14
Contents. V 1. The history, 1784—1823. 2. India Company's progress to political power.—Observations and reflections on the general administration of the Indian government in England. — Local government of India.—App.
Dodd, G: The history of the Indian revolt and of the expeditions to Persia, China and Japan, 1856—1858. Ill. [Anon.] Lond. [1859]. O.   954+7
Valbezen, Eugène de, (Major Fridolin). The english and India; new sketches. Tr. from the french, with the author's permission by a diplomate. Lond. 1883. O.   954 : 6
Bellew, H: Walther, (?) Invasions of India from central Asia. Lond. 1879. O.   954 : 8
Contents. Pref. — The turkish invasion of India under sultan Baber, in 1525. — The persian invasion of India under Nadir Shah, in 1739.—The english invasion of Kabul, in 1839.—App.
Edwards, H: Sutherland. Russian projects against India, from the czar Peter to general Skobeleff. Map. Lond. 1885. O.   954 : 16

Martin, Robert Montgomery. History of the british possessions in the Indian and Atlantic oceans ; comprising Ceylon, Penang, Malacca, Sincapore, the Falkland islands, St. Helena, Ascension, Sierra Leone, the Gambia, Cape Coast Castle, etc. [Brit. col. lib., v. 10]. Lond. 1837. S.   **959 : 4**

Description.

Heber, Reginald. Narrative of a journey through the upper provinces of India, from Calcutta to Bombay, 1824, 1825 ; with notes upon Ceylon, an account of a journey to Madras and the southern provinces, 1825, and letters written in India. Phila. 1829. 2 v. D.
915.4 : 4

Roberts, Emma. Scenes and characters of Hindostan ; with sketches of anglo-indian society. Phila. 1836. 2 v. D.   915.4 : 13

Tucker, S. South indian sketches ; containing a short account of some of the missionary stations, connected with the church missionary society in southern India, in letters to a young friend. Pt. 1, Madras and Mayaveram. 2d ed. Lond. 1842. S.
915.4 : 14

Ward, Ferdinand DeWard. India and the hindoos ; a popular view of the geography, history, government, manners, customs, literature and religion of that ancient people, with an account of christian missions among them. N. Y. 1850. D.
915.4 : 15

Russell, W: Howard. My diary in India, in 1858-9. Ill. Lond. 1860. 2 v. D.
915.4 : 28

Humphrey, *Mrs.* E. J. Six years in India, or Sketches of India and its people, as seen by a lady missionary ; given in a series of letters to her mother. Ill. N. Y. [1866]. S.
915.4 : 5

Cumming, W: Gordon. Wild men and wild beasts, or Scenes in camp and jungle. (Ill. lib. of travel.) N. Y. 1872. D. 915.4 : 29

Williams, Monier. Modern India and the indians ; a series of impressions, notes and essays. 2d ed. Lond. 1878. O.   915.4 : 3

Kennedy, James. Life and work in Benares and Kumaon, 1839—1877 ; with an introd. note by sir W: Muir. Ill. Lond. 1884. D.
915.4 : 33

Dutt, Shoshee Chunder. India, past and present ; with minor essays on cognate subjects. Lond. 1880. O.   915.4 : 1
Contents. India past and present.—Minor essays: Taxation in India; The indian statute book; British opium policy and its results. — Half - hours with nature: Introd.; The foot-prints of the deity; The attributes of the deity; Human life; Our duties; The intermediate future; Good and evil; Futurity, heaven and hell.

Temple, *Sir* R: India in 1880. Lond. 1880. O.
915.4 : 2

— Men and events of my time in India, [1847—1881]. Lond. 1882. O.   915.4 : 35

Baxter, W: E: Winter in India. Map. N. Y. [1883]. D.   915.4 : 31

French, Harry Willard. Our boys in India ; the wanderings of two young americans in Hindustan, with their adventures on the sacred rivers and wild mountains, etc. Bost. 1883 [1882]. O.   **x** 915.4 : 25

x denotes books specially adapted for children.

Bradbury, James. India, its condition, religion and missions. Lond. 1884. D. 915.4 : 34

Cumming, Constance Frederica Gordon-. In the Himalayas and on the indian plains. Ill. Lond. 1884. O.   915.4 : 38

Leonowens, Anna Harriette. Life and travel in India ; recollections of a journey before the days of railroads. [Ill.] Phila. [1885]. D.
915.4 : 37

Hornaday, W: T. Two years in the jungle ; the experiences of a hunter and naturalist in India, Ceylon, the Malay peninsula and Borneo. Map and ill. N. Y. 1885. O.
915.4 : 42

Robinson, Philip. Under the sun ; with a pref. by Edwin Arnold. Bost. 1882. D.
915.4 : 24
Contents. Indian sketches: In my indian garden; Visitors in feathers; Visitors in fur and others.—The indian seasons.—Unnatural history: Monkeys and metaphysics; Hunting of the soko: Elephants: The elephants' fellow-countrymen; Cats and sparrows; Bears, wolves, dogs, rats; Some sea-folk.—Idle hours under the punkah: The man-eating tree; Eastern smells and western noses; Gamins; On tailors; The hara-kiri; My wife's birds; The legend of the blameless priest.

Williams, Arthur Lukyn. Famines in India ; their causes and possible prevention ; the Cambridge university Le Bas prize essay, 1875. Lond. 1876. D.   915.4 : 16

Himalayan regions.

Schlagintweit-Sakünlünski, Hermann v. Reisen in Indien und Hochasien ; eine darstellung der landschaft, der cultur und sitten der bewohner, in verbindung mit klimatischen und geologischen verhältnissen. Basirt auf die resultate der wissenschaftlichen mission von Hermann, Adolph und Robert von Schlagintweit, ausgeführt in 1854—1858. Ill. und karten. Jena. 1869-80. 4 v. O.   915 : 3
Contents. V. 1. Indien.—Register. 2. Hochasien: 1, Der Himalaya von Bhutan bis Kashmir. 3. Same: 2, Tibet, zwischen der Himalaya- und der Karakorumkette. 4. Same: 3, Oest-Turkistan und umgebungen; nebst wissenschaftlichen zusammenstellungen über die höhengebiete und über die thermischen verhältnisse.

Wilson, Andrew. The abode of snow ; observations on a tour from Chinese Tibet to the Indian Caucasus, through the upper valleys of the Himalaya. N. Y. 1875. D.
915.4 : 17

Lambert, Cowley. A trip to Cashmere and Ladâk. Ill. Lond. 1877. D.   915.4 : 7

Aynsley, Harriett Georgina Maria Murray-, *born* Sutton. Our visit to Hindostan, Kashmir and Ladakh. Lond. 1879. O.
915.4 : 32

Inglis, James, *(Maori).* Sport and work on the Nepaul frontier, or Twelve years' sporting reminiscences of an indigo-planter by "Maori". N. Y. 1879. Q.   915.4+8

Oliphant, Laurence. A journey to Katmandu, the capital of Nepaul, with the camp of Jung Bahadoor, incl. a sketch of the nepaulese ambassador at home. N. Y. 1852. S.   915.4 : 12

Cooper, T. T. The Mishmee hills ; an account of a journey made in an attempt to penetrate Thibet from Assam to open new routes for commerce. Ill. Lond. 1873. D.
915.4 : 11

Taylor, Bayard, *ed.* Central Asia; travels in Cashmere, Little Tibet and Central Asia. (Ill. lib. of travel). N. Y. 1881. D.
　　　　　　　　　　　　　　　915 : 12

Ceylon.

Baker, *Sir* S: White. Eight years' wanderings in Ceylon. Ill. Phila. 1877. D. **915.4 : 9**
— The rifle and the bound in Ceylon. Ill. Phila. 1877. D. **915.4 : 10**
Häckel, Ernst H: A visit to Ceylon. Tr. by Clara Bell. Bost. 1883. D. **915.4 : 30**

2. Farther India.

(*For the* Malayan archipelago, *see* Oceanica, cl. 991, 992, and 919.1, 919.2.)

In general.

Raynal, Guillaume T: François *abbé.* History of the settlements... of the europeans in the East... Indies. **382 : 3**
　See col. 256.
Vincent, Frank, *jr.* The land of the white elephant; sights and scenes in southeastern Asia; a personal narrative of travel and adventure in Farther India, embracing the countries of Burma, Siam, Cambodia, and Cochin-China, 1871-2. Maps, plans and ill. N. Y. 1874. O. **915.4 : 22**
Hellwald, F: v. Hinterindische länder und völker; reisen in den flussgebieten des Irrawaddy und Mekong, in Birma, Annam, Kambodscha und Siam, unter besonderer berücksichtigung der neuesten zustände in Birma bearbeitet. 2e vermehrte aufl. [Ill. bibliothek der länder- und völkerkunde.] Leipz. 1880. O. **915.4 : 27**
Colquhon, Archibald Ross. Amongst the shans; with an historical sketch of the shans by Holt S. Hallett, preceded by an introd. on the Cradle of the shan race by Terrien de Lacouperie. N. Y. 1885. O. **915 : 8**
　See also his Across Chrysê, **915.1 : 20.**

Burma.

Palmer, J: Williamson. The golden dagon, or Up and down the Irrawaddi; passages of adventure in the Burman empire, by an american. N. Y. 1856. D. **915.4 : 21**
— *Same.* New ed. N. Y. 1859. D. **915.4 : 21**
Fytche, Albert. Burma, past and present, with personal reminiscences of the country. Ill. Lond. 1878. 2 v. O. **915.4 : 19**
Scott, James George. (*Shway Yoe, subject of the great queen*). The burman; his life and notions. Lond. 1882. 2 v. D. **915.4 : 26**

Siam.

Neale, F: Arthur. Narrative of a residence in Siam. Lond. 1852. D. **915.4 : 20**
Leonowens, Anna Harriette. The english governess at the siamese court; recollections of six years in the royal palace at Bangkok. Ill. Bost. 1871. O. **915.4 : 41**
— The romance of the harem. Ill. Bost. 1873. O. **915.4 : 39**
Bacon, G: B., *ed.* Siam, the land of the white elephant, as it was and is. (Ill. lib. of travel). N. Y. 1878. D. **915.4 : 18**

Bock, C: Temples and elephants; the narrative of a journey of exploration through upper Siam and Lao. Map and ill. Lond. 1884. O. **915.4 : 36**

Malay peninsula.

McNair, F: Perak and the Malays: Sârong and Kris. Ill. Lond. 1878. O. **915.9 : 6**
Bishop, Isabella L., *born* Bird. The Golden Chersonese and the way thither. Ill. N. Y. 1883. D. **915.9 : 8**
　Note. Travels in Sungei Ujong, Selângor and Pêrak.
Lowe, J. Eleanor. Ten days in the jungle [of Pêrak], by J. E. L. Bost. 1885 [1884]. D.
　　　　　　　　　　　　　　　915.9 : 9
Loftus, Arthur J: Notes of a journey across the isthmus of Krâ, made with the french government survey expedition, jan.—april 1883; with explanatory map and sections, and app. containing reprint of report to the indian government by captains Fraser and Forlong, in 1863. Lond. 1883. O.
　　　　　　　　　　　　　　　915.4 : 40

3. Persia.

History.

(*See also* Ancient Persia, col. 1169—1170).

Fraser, James Baillie. Historical and descriptive account of Persia from the earliest ages to the present time; with a detailed view of its resources, government, population, natural history, and the character of its inhabitants, particularly of the wandering tribes, incl. a description of Afghanistan and Beloochistan. Ill. [Harper's family lib.] N. Y. 1845. S. **955 : 1**
Piggot, J: Persia, ancient and modern. Lond. 1874. D. **955 : 3**
　See also in the Index to biography Nâdir.
Karaka, Dosabhai Framji. History of the parsis, incl. their manners, customs, religion and present position. Ill. Lond. 1884. 2 v. O. **955 : 2**
　Contents. V. 1. Historical sketch. — The zoroastrians in Persia.—The zoroastrians in India; their manners and customs.—Internal government and laws.—Education. 2. Distinguished parsis of Gujarat; of Bombay.—Zoroaster.—The parsi creed.—Monotheism and fire-reverence.—Progress and present position.—App.

Description.

Wagner, Moriz F: Reise nach Persien und dem lande der kurden. Leipz. 1852. 2 v. D.
　　　　　　　　　　　　　　　915.5 : 1
　Contents. V. 1. Vorläufer: Denkwürdigkeiten von der Donau und vom Bosporus.—Von Trapezunt nach Erzerum und dem türkisch-persischen hochlande. 2. Persisch-Kurdistan.—Schlussbetrachtungen [über die central-asiatische frage].—Anhang: Beiträge zur ethnographie des orients; zur naturgeschichte Vorderasiens.
Shepherd, W: Ashton. From Bombay to Bushire and Bussora, incl. an account of the present state of Persia and notes on the persian war. Lond. 1857. D. **915.5 : 3**
Ballantine, H: Midnight marches through Persia; with an introd. by J. H. Seelye. Maps and ill. Bost. 1876. O. **915.5 : 5**
Arnold, Arthur. Through Persia by caravan. N. Y. 1877. D. **915.5 : 2**

Stack, E: Six months in Persia. N. Y. 1882. 2 v. D.   **915.5 : 4**

Willis, C: J. In the land of the lion and sun, or Modern Persia; experiences of life in Persia during a residence of 15 years in various parts of that country, from 1866 to 1881. N. Y. 1883. O.   **915.5 : 6**

Blunt, *Lady* Anne Isabella Noel. Our persian campaign. *In her* Pilgrimage to Nejd.   **915.3 : 11 v2**

Stolze, F., *and* F. C. **Andreas.** Die handels-verhältnisse Persiens; mit besonderer berücksichtigung der deutschen interessen. Karte. *In* Petermann's mitteilungen, Ergänzungsb. 17.   **905.1 : M**

4. Arabia.

History.

(*See also under* Turkey, col. 1289—1291.)

Crichton, Andrew. The history of Arabia, ancient and modern. Ill. [Harper's family lib.] N. Y. 1842. 2 v. S.   **953 : 1**
Contents. V. 1. Introd. View of arabian history.—Description of Arabia. — Primitive inhabitants.— Ancient kings.—Character, manners and customs of the ancient arabs. — Life of Mohammed. — The Koran. — Conquest of the saracens. — Wars of the caliphs. — Conquest of Africa and Spain. 2. The Abassides, or caliphs of Bagdad. — Caliphs of Africa, Egypt and Spain. — Literature of the arabs. — Civil history and government of Arabia. — Hejaz, or holy land of the moslem. — The mohammedan pilgrimage. — History of the wahabees.—Social state of the arabs.—Natural history of Arabia.

Müller, A: Der islam im morgen- und abendland; b. 1, Die araber. (**Oncken,** W:, *ed.* Allgemeine geschichte in einzeldarstellungen; 2te hauptabth., 4ter th.) Ill. und karten. Berlin. 1885. O.   **909+20 v4**

Ockley, Simon. The history of the saracens; comprising lives of Mohammed and his successors to the death of Abdalmelik, the eleventh caliph [705], with an account of their most remarkable battles, sieges, revolts, etc., coll. from authentic sources, especially arabic mss. 4th ed., rev. and enl. Lond. 1847. D.   **953 : 4**

Muir, *Sir* W: The life of Mahomet, from original sources. New ed., abr. from the 1st ed. in 4 v., with an index. Lond. 1878. O.   **953 : 2**

— Annals of the early caliphate, from original sources, [632—680]. Map. Lond. 1883. O.   **953 : 3**

Kremer, Alfred v. Culturgeschichte des orients unter den chalifen. Wien. 1875, 1877. 2 v. O.   **953+5**

Hutton, Barbara. Tales of the saracens. Ill. Lond. 1871. D.   **x 953 : 6**
See also in the Index to biography **Harûn—Muhammad.**

Description.

Lane, E: W: Arabian society in the middle ages; studies from the Thousand and one nights, ed. by his grand-nephew Stanley Lane-Poole. Lond. 1883. D.   **915.3 : 10**

Taylor, Bayard, *comp.* Travels in Arabia. (Ill. lib. of travel.) N. Y. 1872. D.   **915.3 : 5**

Burton, R: Francis, (*Shaykh Hajj Abdallah.*) Personal narrative of a pilgrimage to El-Medinah and Meccah; with introd. by Bayard Taylor. Map and ill. 1st amer. ed. N. Y. 1856. D.   **915.3 : 1**

— The gold mines of Midian and the ruined midianite cities; a fortnight's tour in north-western Arabia. Lond. 1878. O.   **915.3 : 2**

Keane, J: F., (*Hajj Mohammed Amin*). Six months in Meccah; an account of the mohammedan pilgrimage to Meccah, recently accomplished by an englishman, professing mohammedanism. Lond. 1881. O.   **915.3 : 6**

— My journey to Medinah; describing a pilgrimage to Medinah, performed by the author disguised as a mohammedan. Lond. 1881. O.   **915.3 : 7**

Blunt, *Lady* Anne Isabella Noel, *born* King-Noel. A pilgrimage to Nejd, the cradle of the arab race,—A visit to the court of the arab emir,—and "Our persian campaign." Map, portr. and ill., 2d ed. Lond. 1881. 2 v. O.   **915.3 : 11**
Contents of app. in v. 2: Notes of the physical geography of northern Arabia.—Historical sketch of the rise and decline of wahbabism in Arabia. — Mem. on the Euphrates valley railway, and its kindred schemes of railway communication between the Mediterranean and the Persian Gulf.

Fogg, W: Perry. Land of the Arabian nights, being travels through Egypt, Arabia and Persia to Bagdad with an introd. by Bayard Taylor. [New rev. ed.] N. Y. 1882. D.   **915.3 : 8**

Wise, Daniel. Boy travellers in Arabia, or From Boston to Bagdad; incl. pictures, sketches and anecdotes of the wandering arabs and of the city "of good Haroun Alraschid." Ill. N. Y. 1885. D.   **x 915.3 : 12**

x denotes books specially adapted for children.

20. Asia — c, Turkish empire.

(*For* Cyprus, *see* Turkey in Europe, col. 1294.)

1. General and Eastern.

Beck, L. C. Die heutige Türkei; schilderung von land und leuten des Osmanischen reiches in Asien vor und nach dem krieg von 1877-78, mit berücksichtigung der arabischen halbinsel. Leipz. 1879. O. **915.6 : 1**

Smith, Eli. Researches of E. Smith and H. G. O. Dwight in Armenia, incl. a journey through Asia Minor, and into Georgia and Persia with a visit to the nestorian and chaldean christians of Oormiah and Salmas. Bost. 1833. 2 v. D.   **915.6 : 57**

Skinner, T: Adventures during a journey overland to India, by way of Egypt, Syria and the Holy Land, in 2 v.; v. 2. Lond. 1836. D.   **915.6 : 63**
Contains the journey from Damascus to India.

Durbin, J: Price. Observations in the east, chiefly in Egypt, Palestine, Syria and Asia Minor. 9th ed. N. Y. 1847. 2 v. D.   **915.6 : 18**

Kinglake, Alexander W: Eôthen, or Traces of travel, brought home from the east. N. Y. 1846. D.   **915.6 : 24**

El-Mukattem. Lands of the moslem ; a narrative of oriental travel. N. Y. 1851. O.   **915.6 : 19**

Bodenstedt, F: Martin v. Tausend und ein tag im orient. Berlin. 1865. 3 v. in 1. S.   **915.6 : 2**

Burnaby, F: Gustavus. On horseback through Asia Minor. Portr. and maps. 2d ed. Lond. 1877. 2 v. O.   **915.6 : 50**

Geary, Grattan. Through Asiatic Turkey ; narrative of a journey from Bombay to the Bosphorus. Map and ill. Lond. 1878. 2 v. D.   **915.6 : 62**

Cameron, Verney Lovett. Our future highway to India. [Ill.] Lond. 1880. 2 v. D.   **915 : 22**

Note. A record of travels along the route of the proposed Euphrates valley railway, through Cyprus, Syria, Mesopotamia and, by way of the Persian Gulf, to India.

A r m e n i a .

Parrot, F: Journey to Ararat. Map and ill. Tr. by W. D. Cooley. N. Y. 1846. D.   **915.6 : 56**

Wagner, Moriz F: Reise nach dem Ararat und dem hochland Armenien ; mit einem anhange : Beiträge zur naturgeschichte des hochlandes Armenien. Stuttg. 1848. O.   **915.6 : 5**

Curzon, Robert. Armenia ; a year at Erzeroom and on the frontiers of Russia. Turkey and Persia. Map and ill. N. Y. 1854. O.   **915.6 : 51**

Thielmann, Max *freiherr* v. Journey in the Caucasus, Persia and Turkey in Asia. Tr. by C: Heneage. Map and ill. Lond. 1875. 2 v. D.   **915 : 24**

Creagh, James. Armenians, koords and turks. Lond. 1880. 2 v. O.   **915.6 : 79**

Tozer, H: Fanshawe. Turkish Armenia and eastern Asia Minor. Lond. 1881. O.   **915.6 : 61**

M e s o p o t a m i a .

Fraser, James Baillie. Mesopotamia and Assyria, from the earliest ages to the present time ; with ill. of their natural history. [Harper's family lib.] N. Y. 1845. S.   **959 : 3**

Southgate, Horatio. Narrative of a visit to the syrian (jacobite) church of Mesopotamia, with statements and reflections upon the present state of christianity in Turkey, and the character and prospects of the eastern churches. N. Y. 1844. D.   **915.6 : 59**

Blunt, *Lady* Anne Isabella Noel, *born* King-Noel. Bedouin tribes of the Euphrates ; ed., with a pref. and some account of the arabs and their horses, by W[illis] S. B[lunt]. Map and ill. N. Y. 1879. O.   **915.6 : 49**

Wheeler, C: H. Letters from Eden ; reminiscences of missionary life in the east. N. Y. n. d. S.   **915.6 : 65**

E x p l o r a t i o n s .

Layard, Austen H: Nineveh and its remains ; with an account of a visit to the chaldean christians of Kurdistan and the yezidis or

Layard, Austen H:—*Continued.*
devil-worshippers, and an inquiry into the manners and arts of the ancient assyrians. N. Y. 1849. 2 v. O.   **915.6+53**

— Discoveries among the ruins of Nineveh and Babylon ; with travels in Armenia, Kurdistan and the desert, the result of a 2d expedition undertaken for the trustees of the British museum. Maps, plans and ill. N. Y. 1853. O.   **915.6 : 52**

Buried city of the east, The; Nineveh. Ill. Lond. [1851]. D.   **915.6 : 55**

Loftus, W: Kennett. Travels and researches in Chaldæa and Susiana ; with an account of excavations at Warka, the "Erech" of Nimrod, and Shush, "Shushan the palace" of Esther, in 1849--1852, under the orders of maj.-gen. sir W. F. Williams and also of the Assyrian excavation fund in 1853—1854. N. Y. 1857. O.   **915.6 : 54**

Smith, G: Assyrian discoveries ; an account of explorations and discoveries on the site of Nineveh, during 1873 and 1874. Ill. N. Y. 1875. O.   **915.6+58**

De Hass, Frank S. Buried cities recovered, or Explorations in bible lands ; giving the results of recent researches in the orient and recovery of many places in sacred and profane history long considered lost. 10th ed., with app., containing a full account of Egypt and the egyptians, rise and fall of empires in the light of prophecy and wonderful confirmation of revelation by late discoveries. Map and ill. Phila. 1884. O.   **915.6 : 82**

Schliemann, H: Troy and its remains ; a narrative of researches and discoveries made on the site of Ilium and the Trojan plain. Tr. with the author's sanction ; ed. by Philip Smith. Maps, plans and ill. N. Y. 1876. O.   **915.6 : 7**

— Ilios, the city and country of the trojans ; the results of researches and discoveries on the site of Troy and throughout the Troad in 1871—1873, 1878, 1879, incl. an autobiogr. of the author. With a pref., apps. and notes by Rudolf Virchow, Max Müller, A. H. Sayce, J. P. Mahaffy, H. Brugsch-bey, P. Ascherson, M. A. Postolaccas, M. E. Burnouf, F. Calvert and A. J. Duffield. Maps, plans and ill. N. Y. 1881. Q.   **915.6+P6**

— Troja ; results of the latest researches and discoveries on the site of Homer's Troy, and in the heroic tumuli and other sites, made in 1882, a narrative of a journey in the Troad in 1881. Preface by A. H. Sayce. Ill., map and plans. N. Y. 1884. O.   **915.6+75**

2. Syria and Palestine.

(*See also* Mediterranean travels, col. 1194–1196.)

H i s t o r y a n d g e o g r a p h y .

Russell, Michael. Palestine, or The Holy Land, from the earliest period to the present time. [Harper's family lib.] N. Y. 1846. S.   **956 : 2**

Kitto, J: The history of Palestine, from the patriarchal age to the present time ; with introd. chapters on the geography and natural history of the country and on the

Kitto, J:—*Continued.*
customs and institutions of the hebrews.
Ill. Bost. 1860. D.   **956:1**
— Scripture lands; described in a series of
historical, geographical and topographical
sketches. Lond. 1850. D.   **915.6:25**

Henderson, Archibald. Palestine; its historical
geography, with topographical index, and
maps.   **915.6:77**

Osborn, H: S. Palestine, past and present, with
biblical, literary and scientific notes. Ill.
Phila. 1859. O.   **915.6+34**

Newman, J: P. "From Dan to Beersheba," or
The land of promise as it now appears,
incl. a description of the boundaries, topography, agriculture, antiquities, cities and
present inhabitants of that wonderful land,
with ill. of the remarkable accuracy of
the sacred writers in their allusions to
their native country. Ill. N. Y. 1864. D.
     915.6:33

Dixon, W: Hepworth. The Holy Land. Ill.
Lond. 1865. 2 v. O.   **915.6:17**

Stanley, Arthur Penrhyn. Sinai and Palestine,
in connection with their history. New ed.,
with maps and plans. N. Y. 1865. O.
     915.6:39

Thomson, W: McClure. The land and the book,
or Biblical illustrations drawn from the
manners and customs, the scenes and scenery of the Holy Land: [v. 1], Southern
Palestine and Jerusalem; [v. 2], Central
Palestine and Phœnicia; [v. 3], Lebanon,
Damascus and beyond Jordan. N. Y. 1880-
85. 3 v. O.   **915.6:40**
— *Same.* N. Y. 1860. 2 v. D.   **915.6:41**

McGarvey, J. W. Lands of the Bible; a geographical and topographical description
of Palestine, with letters of travel in Egypt,
Syria, Asia Minor and Greece. Phila. 1882
[1881]. O.   **915.6:42**

Headley, Joel Tyler. The sacred mountains.
Ill. N. Y. 1862 [1846]. D.   **915.6:20**
Contents. Ararat.—Moriah.—Sinai.— Hor.— Pisgah.
—Horeb.—Carmel.—Lebanon.—Zion.—Tabor.—Mount
of Olives.—Calvary.—Mount of God.
— The sacred plains. Buffalo. 1856. D.
     915.6:21
Contents. Sbinar.—Jordan.—Mamre.— Moab.—Jer-
icho.—Sharon.— Shiloh.— Moreh.—Dura.—Esdraelon.
—Damascus.— Galilee.

Barclay, James T. The city of the great king,
or Jerusalem as it was, as it is, and as it is
to be. Phila. 1858. O.   **915.6:10**

Fergusson, James. An essay on the ancient
topography of Jerusalem, with restored
plans of the temple, etc., and plans, sections and details of the church built by
Constantine the great over the holy sepulchre, now known as the mosque of Omar,
and other ill. Lond. 1847. Q.   **915.6+80**

King, James. Recent discoveries on the temple
hill at Jerusalem. Maps, plans and ill.
(By-paths of bible knowledge, no. 4.) Lond.
1884. D.   **915.6:76**

Travels.

Wright, T: *ed.* Early travels in Palestine; comprising the narratives of Arculf, Willibald,
Bernard, Sæwulf, Sigurd, Benjamin of
Tudela, sir John Maundeville, De la Broc-
quière and Maundrell, with notes. Lond.
1848. D.   **915.6:44**

Mariti, Giovanni. Travels through Cyprus,
Syria and Palestine, with a general history
of the Levant. Tr. from the italian. Lond.
1791. 3 v. O.   **915.6:28**
Contents. V. 1. Cyprus. 2. Syria.—Palestine. 3.
Palestine, *continued.*—History of the city of Jerusalem.

Chateaubriand, René François Auguste de.
Travels to Jerusalem and the Holy
Land through Egypt. Tr. from the french
by F: Shoberl. 3d ed. Lond. 1835. 2 v. O.
     915.6:15
Contents. V. 1. Introd.—Greece.—The Archipelago,
Anatolia and Constantinople.—Rhodes, Jaffa, Bethle-
hem and the Dead Sea. 2. Jerusalem. — Egypt. —
Tunis and return to France.—App.

Lamartine, Alphonse Marie de. A pilgrimage
to the Holy Land, comprising recollections,
sketches and reflections made during a
tour in the east, [1832–33]. N. Y. 1848. 2 v.
D.   **915.6:26**

Stephens, J: Lloyd. Incidents of travel in
Egypt, Arabia Petræa and the Holy Land,
[1835–36], by an american. Map and ill.
10th ed., with add. N. Y. 1844. D.
     915.6:30

Lindsay, Alexander W: Crawford, *25th earl of
Crawford and 8th earl of Balcarres.* Letters from Egypt, Edom and the Holy
Land, [1836–37]. 5th ed., with add. pref.
and notes. Ill. Lond. 1858. D. **915.6:31**

Addison, C: G. Damascus and Palmyra; a journey to the east, with a sketch of the state
and prospects of Syria under Ibrahim
Pasha. Phila. 1838. 2 v. D.   **915.6:47**

Olin, Stephen. Travels in Egypt, Arabia Petræa
and the Holy Land, [1839–40]. Ill. N. Y.
1860. 2 v. D.   **915.6:32**

Damoiseau, L: Hippologische wanderungen in
Syrien und der wüste. Aus dem franz.
übers. von Amadeus Theodor Heinze.
Leipz. 1842. 2 v. S.   **915.6:3**

Millard, D: A journal of travels in Egypt,
Arabia Petræa and the Holy Land during
1841-2. 3d ed. N. Y. 1847. D. **915.6:29**

Lowthian, J: Narrative of a recent visit to
Jerusalem and several parts of Palestine,
in 1843–44. 3d thous. Lond. *n. d.* S.
     915.6:27

Willan, Robert. A narrative of journeyings in
the land of Israel, [1847–48]. Lond. *n. d.*
D.   **915.6:43**

Lynch, W: F. Report to the sec. of the navy of
an examination of the Dead Sea in 1848.
Maps. (U. S. 30th cong. 2 sess. Sen. ex.
doc. v. 4, no. 34). Wash. *n. d.* O.
     in **915.6:D**
Contents. Report.— **Cassin,** J: Ornithological re-
port.—Botanical report.—Latitudes and longitudes.—
Meteorol. observ.
— Narrative of the U. S. expedition to the river
Jordan and the Dead Sea. Maps and ill.
7th ed. rev. Phila. 1850. O.   **915.6:67**

Saulcy, L: Félicien Joseph **Caignart** de. Narrative of a journey round the Dead Sea and
in bible lands in 1850 and 1851; incl. an
account of the discovery of the sites of
Sodom and Gomorrah; ed. by count E: de
Warren. New ed. Phila. 1854. 2 v. D.
     915.6:38

Curtis, G: W: The Howadji in Syria. N. Y.
1852. D.   **915.6:16**
Contents. The desert.—Jerusalem.—Damascus.

Robinson, E: Later biblical researches in Palestine and in the adjacent regions ; a journal of travels in 1852, by E. Robinson, E. Smith and others, drawn from the original diaries, with historical ill. Maps and plans. Bost. 1856. O.   **915.6+37**

Johnson, Sarah Barclay. Hadji in Syria, or Three years in Jerusalem. Phila. [1858]. S.   **915.6 : 23**

Bovet, Félix. Egypt, Palestine and Phoenicia ; a visit to sacred lands, [1858]. Tr. by W. H. Lyttleton. with a biogr. sketch of the author by F. Godet. N. Y. 1883. D.   **915.6 : 69**

Prime, W: Cowper. Tent life in the Holy Land. N. Y. 1859. D.   **915.6 : 36**
    Note. A continuation of his Boat-life in Egypt and Nubia, **916.2 : 9.**

Charles, Elizabeth, *born* Rundle. Wanderings over bible lands and seas, by the author of the "Schönberg-Cotta family." N. Y. 1866. S.   **915.6 : 14**

Porter, Josias Leslie. The giant cities of Bashan and Syria's holy places. N. Y. 1866. D.   **915.6 : 48**

Burton, Isabel. The inner life of Syria, Palestine and the Holy Land, from my private journal. Map and ill. Lond. 1875. 2 v. O.   **915.6 : 13**

Macgregor, J: The Rob Roy on the Jordan, Nile, Red Sea and Gennesareth. etc. ; a canoe cruise in Palestine and Egypt and the waters of Damascus. Maps and ill. N. Y. 1875. O.   **915.6 : 64**

Appleton, T: Gold. Syrian sunshine, [1875]. Bost. 1877. S.   **915.6 : 9**

Hunt, *Mrs.* W: Holman. Children at Jerusalem; a sketch of modern life in Syria.. Lond. n. d. D.   **915.6 : 22**

Field, H: Martyn. Among the holy hills. Map. N. Y. 1884 [1883]. D.   **915.6 : 73**

Eddy, Daniel Clarke. Walter in Jerusalem. (Walter's tour in the east, v. 2). N. Y. n. d. D.   **915.6 : 70**

Eddy, Daniel Clarke.—*Continued.*
— Walter in Samaria. (Walter's tour in the east, v. 3). N. Y. n. d. D.   **915.6 : 71**
— Walter in Damascus. (Walter's tour in the east, v. 4). N. Y. n. d. D.   **915.6 : 72**

*   *   *

Tristram, H: Baker. The land of Moab ; travels and discoveries on the east side of the Dead Sea and the Jordan ; with a chapter on the persian palace of Mashita by Jas. Fergusson. Map and ill. N. Y. 1873. O. **915.6 : 81**

Oliphant, Laurence. The land of Gilead. with excursions in the Lebanon. N. Y. 1881. O.   **915.6 : 45**

Merrill, Selah. East of the Jordan ; a record of travel and observation in the countries of Moab, Gilead and Bashan, during the years 1875—1877 ; with introd. by Roswell D. Hitchcock. N. Y. 1881. O.   **915.6 : 46**

Palmer, E: H: The desert of the exodus ; journeys on foot in the wilderness of the forty years' wanderings, undertaken in connection with the ordnance survey of Sinai and the Palestine exploration fund. Maps and ill. N. Y. 1872. O.   **915.3 : 4**

Bartlett, S: Colcord. From Egypt to Palestine through Sinai, the wilderness and the south country ; observations of a journey made with special reference to the history of the israelites. Maps and ill. N. Y. 1879. O.   **915.6 : 11**

Trumbull, H: Clay. Kadesh-Barnea ; its importance and probable site, with the story of a hunt for it, incl. studies of the route of the exodus and the southern boundary of the Holy Land. Ill. and maps. N. Y. 1884. [1883]. O.   **915.6+74**

Field, H: Martyn. On the desert ; with a brief review of recent events in Egypt. Map. N. Y. 1883. O.   **915.3 : 9**

Ebers, G: Durch Gosen zum Sinai ; aus dem wanderbuche und der bibliothek. Leipz. 1872. O.   **916.2 : 14**

21. Asia — d, Russian and Central.

1. Siberia.

Coxe, W: Account of the russian discoveries between Asia and America ; added, the conquest of Siberia and the history of the transactions and commerce between Russia and China. 4th ed. ed. Lond. 1803. O.   **957 : 1**

Lankenau, H. v.. *and* L. v. d. **Oelsnitz,** *eds.* Das heutige Russland ; bilder und schilderungen aus allen theilen des zarenreichs in Asien. 2te wohlf. ausg. [Ill. bibliothek der länder- und völkerkunde]. Leipz. 1881. O.   **915.7 : 2**

Kohn, Albin, *and* R: **Andree.** Sibirien und das Amurgebiet ; geschichte und reisen, landschaft und völker zwischen Aral und Beringsstrasse. Leipz. 1876. 2 v. O. **915.7 : 1**
    Contents. V. 1. Kohn, A. Sibirien. 2. Andree, R. Das Amurgebiet.

Atkinson, T: Witlam. Oriental and western Siberia ; a narrative of seven years' explorations and adventures in Siberia, Mongolia, the Kirghis steppes, Chinese Tartary and

Atkinson, T: Witlam.—*Continued.*
    part of central Asia. Map and ill. N. Y. 1858. O.   **915.7+3**
— Travels in the regions of the upper and lower Amoor and the russian acquisitions on the confines of India and China ; with adventures among the mountain kirghis, and the manjours, manyargs, toungous, toungous, goldi and gelyaks, the hunting and pastoral tribes. Map and ill. N. Y. 1860. O.   **915.7 : 4**

Collins, Perry McDonough. A voyage down the Amoor, with a land journey through Siberia and incidental notices of Manchooria, Kamschatka and Japan. N. Y. 1860. D.   **915 : 7**
— *Same.* Overland explorations in Siberia, northern Asia and the great Amoor river country ; incidental notices of Manchooria, Mongolia, Kamschatka and Japan, with map and plan of an overland telegraph around the world, via Behring's strait and asiatic Russia to Europe. N. Y. 1864. D.   **915 : 7**

Eden, C: H. Frozen Asia ; a sketch of modern Siberia, together with an account of the native tribes inhabiting that region. Lond. [1879]. D.   **915.7 : 6**

Kennan, G: Tent life in Siberia and adventures among the koraks and other tribes in Kamtchatka. Map. N. Y. 1877. D.   **915.7 : 7**

Landsell, H: Through Siberia. New ed. in 1 v. Map and ill. Bost. 1882. O.   **915.7 : 8**

Dostoyefskii, Fiodor Mikhailovitch. Buried alive, or Ten years of penal servitude in Siberia. Tr. from the russian by Marie v. Thilo. N. Y. 1881. D.   **915.7 : 5**

2. Central Asia.

(For Cashmere, Ladák and Yárkand, see col. 1304.)

Marvin, C: Reconnoitering central Asia ; pioneering adventures in the region lying between Russia and India. [Ill. and maps]. Lond. 1884. O.   **915 : 27**
Contents. Arminius Vámbéry's journey in disguise to the khanates of central Asia.—Captain Marsh's ride from the Caspian to India.—Col. Valentine Baker's visit to the perso-turcoman frontier.—J. A. MacGahan's chase of gen. Kaufmann's army.—Capt. Napier's secret mission.—Col. C. M. Macgregor's survey of Khorassan.—Capt. Burnaby's ride to Khiva.—Gen. Petrusevitch and the turcomans.—Capt. Butler, the secret english agent.—Pashino, the secret russian agent.—Grodekoff's ride to Herat.—O'Donovan's dash to Merv.—Col. Stewart's watch over Skobeleff's army.—Lieut. Alikhanoff's journey with a russian caravan to Merv.—Lessar's discovery of the easy road to India.—The past and future of pioneering in central Asia.

Wood, J: A personal narrative of a journey to the source of the river Oxus, by the route of the Indus, Kabul and Badakshan, performed under the sanction of the supreme government of India, in 1836—1838. Lond. 1841. O.   **915.9 : 3**

Wolff, Joseph. Narrative of a mission to Bokhara in 1843—1845, to ascertain the fate of col. Stoddart and capt. Conolly. N. Y. 1845. O.   **915.9+5**

Vámbéry, Armin. Travels in central Asia ; account of a journey from Teheran across the Turkoman desert on the eastern shore of the Caspian to Khiva, Bokhara and Samarcand, performed in 1863. N. Y. 1865. O.   **915+4**

— History of Bokhara from the earliest period down to the present; composed for the first time after oriental known and unknown mss. 2d ed. Lond. 1873. O.   **959 : 1**

MacGahan, J: A. Campaigning on the Oxus and the fall of Khiva. Map and ill. N. Y. 1874. O.   **915.9 : 2**

Schuyler, Eugene. Turkistan ; notes of a journey in russian Turkistan, Khokand, Bukhara and Kuldja. Maps and ill. N. Y. 1877. 2 v. O.   **915.9 : 4**
Contents of appendices: V. 1. A sketch of the history of Khokand in recent times. — **Grigorief,** V. Review of Vámbéry's History of Bukhara.—Mediæval travellers in central Asia. 2. **Grigorief,** V. The russian policy regarding central Asia; an historical sketch.—Russia and Khiva.—Index.

Burnaby, F: Gustavus. A ride to Khiva ; travels and adventures in central Asia. Maps and app.; containing among other information, a series of march-routes from a russian work. N. Y. 1878. D.   **915.9 : 1**

Hellwald, F: v. The russians in central Asia ; a critical examination down to the present time of the geography and history of central Asia. Tr. from the german by Theodore Wirgman. Lond. 1874. O.   **959 : 2**

— Centralasien ; landschaften und völker in Kaschgar, Turkestan, Kaschmir und Tibet ; mit besonderer berücksichtigung auf Russlands bestrebungen und seinen kulturberuf. [Ill. bibliothek der länder- und völkerkunde]. Leipz. 1875. O.   **915 : 1**

— *Same* ; unter berücksichtigung der jüngsten ereignisse in Afghanistan und von Russlands bestrebungen und kulturberuf. 2te verm. und verb. ausgabe. Leipz. 1880. Q.   **915 : 1**

Lansdell, H: Russian central Asia ; including Kuldja, Bokhara, Khiva and Merv [with app. on the fauna and flora of russian Turkistan, and on the bibliography of the region]. Map and ill. Bost. 1885. 2 v. O.   **915.7 : 10**

O'Donovan, Edmond. The Merv oasis ; travels and adventures east of the Caspian during the years 1879—1881. incl. five months' residence among the tekkés of Merv. Portr., maps and facsimiles of state documents. N. Y. 1883 [1882]. 2 v. O.   **915.9 : 7**

Marvin, C: Merv, the queen of the world, and the scourge of the man-stealing turcomans; with an exposition of the Khorassan question. Maps. Lond. 1881. O.   **915.9 : 10**

— The russian advance towards India ; conversations with Skobeleff, Ignatief and other distinguished russian generals and statesmen on the central-asian question. Lond. 1882. O.   **957 : 3**

— The russians at Merv and Herat, and their power of invading India. Lond. 1883. O.   **957 : 2**

— The russians at the gates of Herat. Maps and portr. N. Y. 1885. D.   **957 : 4**

— *Same.* Maps and ill. N. Y. 1885. Q.   **957+4**

Vámbéry, Armin. The coming struggle for India ; an account of the encroachments of Russia in central Asia, and of the difficulties sure to arise therefrom to England. Lond. 1885. D.   **957 : 5**

Boulger, Demetrius C: Central asian questions ; essays on Afghanistan, China and central Asia. Portr. and maps. Lond. 1885. O.   **915 : 25**
Contents. Russia's empire in central Asia.—Peter the great and the policy of Russia.—England's policy toward Afghanistan.—Ought we to hold Candahar.—Herat and the turcomans.—Why Candabar should be retained. — Lord Lawrence and masterly inactivity. —Subsidising the ameer.—Merv! what next?—The future of China.—The mongols.—The chinese in central Asia.—Russia and China.—The french in Anam and Tonquin.—China and foreign powers.—France and China.—Foreigners in China.—Tibet and the way thither.—Tso Tsung Tang.—The late Yakoob Beg of Kashgar.—The history of the opium traffic.—Three chinese generals.—The chinese art of war.—Reflections on chinese history with reference to the present situation of affairs.—The russian railway east of the Caspian.—Index of subjects.

3. Afghanistan.

Fraser, James Baillie. [Description of Afghanistan and Beloochistan]. *In his* Persia.   **955 : 1**

Bellew, H: Walther. Afghanistan and the afghans; a brief review of the history of the country, and account of its people, with a special reference to the present crisis and war with the amir Sher Ali Khan. Lond. 1879. D.   **958 : 1**
Ashe, Waller, *ed.* Personal records of the Kandahar campaign by officers engaged

therein ; ed. and annotated, with an introd. Lond. 1881. O.   **958 : 2**
Rodenbough, Theophilus F. Afghanistan and the anglo-russian dispute. Maps and ill. N. Y. 1885. D.   **958 : 3**
Malleson, G: Bruce. Herat, the granary and garden of central Asia ; with an index and map. Lond. 1880. O.   **915.8 : 1**

22. Africa.

1. In general.

Goodrich, S: Griswold. Lights and shadows of african history. [Youth's lib. of history]. Bost. 1844. S.   **x 960 : 1**
Johnston, Alexander Keith, *ed.* Africa. (Stanford's compendium of geography and travel, based on Hellwald's Die erde und ihre völker) ; ed. and extended by Keith Johnston, with ethnological app. by A. H. Keane. Maps and ill. Lond. 1878. O.   **916:1**
Jameson, Robert, *and others.* Narrative of discovery and adventure in Africa from the earliest ages, with ill. of the geology, mineralogy and zoology. Map and ill. [Harper's fam. lib.] N. Y. 1846. S.   **916 : 3**
Jones, C: H. Africa ; the history of exploration and adventure as given in the leading authorities from Herodotus to Livingstone. Ill. N. Y. 1875. O.   **916:2**
Ingersoll, L. D., *ed.* Explorations in Africa by dr. D: Livingstone and others ; an account of the Stanley-Livingstone expedition of search under the patronage of the New York herald, as furnished by dr. Livingstone and mr. Stanley ; with a biogr. sketch of dr. Livingstone, mr. Stanley and others connected with the discoveries in Africa, and an epitome of historical and geographical information in regard to the continent inhabited by the black man. Maps and ill. Chicago. 1872. O.   **916:4**
Reade, W: Winwood. Savage Africa ; being the narrative of a tour in equatorial, southwestern and northwestern Africa, with notes on the habits of the gorilla, on the existence of unicorns and tailed men, on the slave trade, on the origin, character and capabilities of the negro, and on the future civilization of western Africa. Ill. and map. N. Y. 1864. O.   **916:5**
Knox, T: Wallace. The boy travellers in the far east, pt. 5: Adventures of two youths in a journey through Africa. Ill. N. Y. 1884 [1883]. O.   **x 916 : 6**
McCabe, James D. Our young folks in Africa ; the adventures of a party of young americans in Algeria and in south central Africa. Phila. 1883 [1882]. O.   **x 916 : 7**

2. Barbary and Sahara.

General and western.

Russell, Michael. History and present condition of the Barbary states ; comprehending a view of their civil institutions, antiquities, arts, religion, literature, commerce,

x denotes books specially adapted for children.

agriculture, and natural productions. Ill. [Harper's family lib.] N. Y. 1842. S.   **961 : 1**
Paddock, Judah. A narrative of the shipwreck of the ship Oswego on the coast of south Barbary, and of the sufferings of the master and the crew while in bondage among the arabs ; interspersed with remarks upon the country and its inhabitants and concerning the peculiar perils of that coast. N. Y. 1818. O.   **916.1 : 1**
Riley, James. Narrative of the loss of the american brig Commerce, wrecked on the western coast of Africa, aug. 1815, with an account of the sufferings of the surviving officers and crew, who were enslaved by the wandering arabs on the african desert or Zahahrah, and observations historical, geographical, etc., made during the travels of the author, while a slave to the arabs, in the empire of Morocco. Preceded by a brief sketch of the author's life, and containing a description of the famous city Tombuctoo, and of another larger city, far south of it, on the same river, called Wassanah, narrated to the author at Mogadore by Sidi Hamet, the arabian merchant. Rev., and life continued by the author in jan. 1828. N. Y. 1839. O.   **916.1 : 2**
— *Same.* N. Y. 1859. S.   **916.1 : 2**
Robbins, Archibald. A journal comprising an account of the loss of the brig Commerce of Hartford, Conn., James Riley, master, upon the western coast of Africa, aug. 28th 1815, also of the slavery and sufferings of the author and the rest of the crew, upon the desert of Zahara, in 1815—1817, with accounts of the manners, customs and habits of the wandering arabs, also a brief historical and geographical view of the continent of Africa. Hartford. 1851. D.   **916.1 : 3**
Campbell, T: Letters from the south, written during a journey to Algiers, etc. Phila. 1836. D.   **916.1 : 4**
Rohlfs, Gerhard. Adventures in Morocco, and journeys through the oases of Draa and Tafilet. With an introd. by Winwood Reade. Lond. 1874. O.   **916.1 : 5**
Amicis, Edmondo de. Morocco ; its people and places. Tr. by C. Rollin Tilton. [1879]. Q.   **916.1+P6**
Richardson, James. Travels in the great desert of Sahara, in 1845 and 1846 ; containing a narrative of personal adventures during a tour of nine months through the desert, amongst the touaricks and other tribes of saharan people ; incl. a description of the oases and cities of Ghat, Ghadames and Mourzuk. Lond. 1848. 2 v. O.   **916.1 : 7**

Mackenzie, Donald. The flooding of the Sahara; an account of the proposed plan for opening central Africa to commerce and civilization from the north-west coast, with a description of Soudan and western Sahara, and notes on ancient mss. Lond. 1877. D.
    916.1 : 8

Eastern.

Prus, *Mme.* —. A residence in Algeria. Lond. 1852. O. **916.1 : 9**

Cooke, G: Wingrove. Conquest and colonisation in north Africa ; the substance of a series of letters from Algeria, pub. in the "Times", with introd. and supp., containing the most recent french and other information on Morocco. Edinb. 1860. D.
    916.1 : 10

Ditson, G: L. Adventures and observations on the north coast of Africa, or The crescent and the french crusaders. N. Y. 1860. D.
    916.1 : 11

— *Same.* The crescent and the french crusaders. N. Y. 1859. D. **916.1 : 11**

Cruisings and adventures in Italy and Africa. N. Y. *n. d.* D. **914.5 : 14**
Contents. **Dickens**, C: Pictures from Italy.—[The french in Algiers:] **Lamping**, Clemens, The soldier of the foreign legion; **France**, A. de. The prisoners of Abd-el-Kader, or Five months' captivity among the arabs.

Browne, J: Ross. A whirl through Algeria.
    in **914.3 : 55**

Blackburn, H: Artists and arabs, or Sketching in sunshine. Ill. Bost. 1874. T.
    916.1 : 12

Dumergue, E: The chotts of Tunis, or The great inland sea of north Africa in ancient times. Lond. 1883. D. **916.1 : 13**

Rae, E: The country of the moors, a journey from Tripoli in Barbary to the city of Kairwân. Map and ill. Lond. 1877. D.
    916.1 : 14

Hesse-Wartegg, Ernst v. Tunis, the land and the people. Ill. Lond. 1882. O. **916.1 : 15**

Boddy, Alexander A. To Kairwân the holy; scenes in muhammedan Africa. Ill. Lond. 1885. D. **916.1 : 16**

Davis, Nathan. Carthage and her remains ; an account of the excavations and researches on the site of the phœnician metropolis in Africa and other adjacent places, conducted under the auspices of her majesty's government. Lond. 1861. O. **916.1+17**

3. Egypt and Abyssinia.

Egypt.

(*See also* Ancient history, col. 1166—1167.)

Buckingham, James Silk. Notes on the Buckingham lectures ; embracing sketches of the geography, antiquities and present condition of Egypt and Palestine, compiled from [his] oral discourses, together with a sketch of his life by James Hildreth. N. Y. 1838. S. **916.2 : 3**

Lane, E: W: An account of the manners and customs of the modern egyptians ; written in Egypt during 1833-35, partly from notes made during a former visit to that country in 1825-28. 5th ed. with add. and imp. from

Lane, E: W:—*Continued.*
a copy annotated by the author, ed. by his nephew E: Stanley Poole. Lond. 1871. 2 v. D. **916.2 : 13**

— *Same, germ.* Sitten und gebräuche der heutigen egypter. Aus dem eng. übers. von Julius Theodor Zenker. 2te ausg. Leipz. *n. d.* 3 v. T. **916.2 : 13**

Russell, Michael. View of ancient and modern Egypt ; with an outline of its natural history. Ill. [Harper's family lib.] N. Y. 1842. S. **962 : 2**

Poole, Stanley Lane-. Egypt. Ill. [Foreign countries and english colonies.] Lond. 1881. S.
    916.2 : 8

Ebers, G: Moritz. Egypt ; descriptive, historical and picturesque. From the german by Clara Bell, with introd. and notes by S. Birch. N. Y. [1882]. 2 v. Q. **916.2 : R2**

McCoan, James Carlile. Egypt as it is. Map. 2d ed. N. Y. [1882]. O. **916.2 : 29**

Waters, Clara, *born* Erskine, *formerly mrs.* Clement. Egypt. [Lothrop's library of entertaining history, ed. by Arthur Gilman.] Bost. [1880]. D. **962 : 1**

De Leon, Edwin. Egypt under its khedives, or The old house of bondage under new masters. Ill. N. Y. 1882. Q. **916.2+21**

Wallace, Donald Mackenzie. Egypt and the egyptian question. Lond. 1883. O.
    916.2 : 32

Loring, W: W. A confederate soldier in Egypt. Portr. and ill. N. Y. [1884]. O. **916.2 : 33**
Contents. Pt. 1. Egypt.— Pt. 2. Military experiences in Abyssinia.

Towle, G: Makepeace. England in Egypt. (Timely topics.) Maps. Bost. 1886 [1885]. S. **962 : 5**

Broadley, A. M. How we defended Arábi and his friends ; a story of Egypt and the egyptians. Ill. Lond. 1884. O. **962 : 4**

Long, C: Chaillé. The three prophets ; Chinese Gordon, Mohammed-Ahmed el Maahdi, Arabi Pasha ; events before and after the bombardment of Alexandria. N. Y. 1884. S. **962 : 3**

Burleigh, Bennet. Desert warfare ; the chronicle of the eastern Soudan campaign. Maps. Lond. 1884. O. **963 : 2**

Buchta, R: The true history of the rebellion in the Soudan, by one who knows the Mahdi personally. Tr. from the german by mrs. R. W. Felkin. Map. Lond. *n. d.* O.
    963 : 3

See also British foreign relations, col. 172.

Paul, Ewald. Egypten in handelspolitischer hinsicht. *In* Deutsche zeit- und streitfragen. **304 : 15 v12**

Travels.

(*See also* Palestine, col. 1310—1313.)

Denon, Dominique Vivant. Voyages dans la basse et la haute Egypte, pendant les campagnes de Bonaparte en 1798 et 1799. Ed. ornée de 109 planches en tailledouce. Londres. 1807. Text, 2 v. Q. Plates, 1 v. F. **916.2 : R1**

Minutoli, Wolfardine Auguste Louise Menu *freiherrin* v. Recollections of Egypt. Phila. 1827. O. **916.2 : 6**

Atkins, Sarah. Fruits of enterprize, exhibited in the adventures of [Giovanni Battista] Belzoni in Egypt and Nubia; with an account of his discoveries in the pyramids, among the ruins of cities and in the ancient tombs. New ed., rev., with add. N.Y. 1842. S.   916.2:24

Poole, Sophia, *born* Lane. The english-woman in Egypt, letters from Cairo during a residence there in 1842—1844 with E. W. Lane, by his sister. Phila. 1845. S.   916.2:5

Warburton, Eliot Bartholomew G: The crescent and the cross, or Romances and realities of eastern travel. New ed. N. Y. 1848. D.   916.2:17

Goltz, Bogumil. Ein kleinstädter in Aegypten; reise, [1849–50]. 3te aufl. Berlin. [1877]. S.   916.2:11

St. John, Bayle. Two years' residence in a levantine family. Lond. 1850. D. 916.2:15
— Village life in Egypt; with sketches of the Saïd. Bost. 1853. 2 v. D.   916.2:16

Smith, Jerome Van Crowninshield. A pilgrimage to Egypt; embracing a diary of exploration on the Nile, with observations of the manners, customs and institutions of the people and of the present condition of the antiquities and ruins. Ill. Bost. 1852. D.   916.2:10

Prime, W: Cowper. Boat life in Egypt and Nubia, [1855–56.]. N. Y. 1877. D. 916.2:9
Note. For continuation of the journey, *see his* Tent life in the Holy Land, **915.6:36.**

Paine, Caroline. Tent and harem; notes of an oriental trip. N. Y. 1859. D.   916.2:7

Warner, C: Dudley. My winter on the Nile, [1875]. New ed., rev. Bost. 1881. D.   916.2:18
Note. For continuation of the journey, *see his* In the Levant, **915.6:8.**

Edwards, Amelia Blandford. A thousand miles up the Nile. Leipz. 1878. 2 v. in 1. S.   916.2:4

Loftie, W. J. A ride in Egypt, from Sioot to Luxor, in 1879; with notes of the present state and ancient history of the Nile valley, and some account of the various ways of making the voyage out and home. Lond. 1879. D.   916.2:35

Edwardes, E. C. Hope-. Eau-de-Nil; a chronicle. Lond. 1882. O.   916.2:30

Warren, W: Wilkins. Life on the Nile in a dahabééh and excursions on shore between Cairo and Assouan; also a tour in Syria and Palestine in 1866–67. 3d ed. Bost. 1883. S.   916.2:25

Oliphant, Laurence. The land of Khemi; up and down the middle Nile. Ill. 2d ed. Edinb. 1882. D.   916.2:31
Contents. The arsinoïte home. — The labyrinth and the lakes.—Old and new.—Society in the provinces.— Excavations at Isembheb.

Stuart, Villiers. Egypt after the war; being the narrative of a tour of inspection, undertaken last autumn, incl. experiences among the natives, with descriptions of their homes and habits, in which are embodied notices of the latest archæological discoveries, and a revised account of the funeral canopy of an egyptian queen, with interesting add. Ill. Lond. 1883. Q.   916.2+38

Cumming, Constance Frederica Gordon-. Via Cornwall to Egypt. Lond. 1885. O.   916.2:39

Eddy, Daniel Clarke. Walter in Egypt. (Walter's tour in the east, v. 1.) N. Y. *n. d.* D.   916.2:28

Whately, Mary L. Letters from Egypt. Ill. N. Y. *n. d.* S.   x 916.2:22

Hale, E: Everett *and* Susan. A family flight over Egypt and Syria. Bost. [1882]. O.   x 916.2:23

Butterworth, Hezekiah. Zigzag journeys in the Levant, with a talmudist story-teller; a spring trip of the Zigzag through Egypt to the Holy Land. Ill. Bost. 1886 [1885]. O.   x 916.2:41

Pyramids and obelisks.

Hawks, Francis Lister. The monuments of Egypt, or Egypt a witness for the Bible. Ill. 2d ed. rev. and enl. N. Y. 1850. O.   916.2+19

Seiss, Joseph A: A miracle in stone. or The great pyramid of Egypt. 2d ed. Phila. [1878]. D.   916.2:27

Proctor, R: Anthony. The great pyramid, observatory, tomb and temple. N. Y. 1883. D.   916.2:26
Contents. The great pyramid. — The origin of the week. — Saturn and the sabbath of the jews. — Astronomy and the jewish festival. — The history of sunday.—Astrology.

Smyth, C. Piazzi. Our inheritance in the great pyramid, 4th ed., incl. all the most important discoveries up to the time of publication. With 25 explan. plates, giving maps, plans, elevations and sections of all crucial parts of the structure. Lond. 1880. O.   916.2:20

Totten, C: A. L. An important question in metrology, based upon recent and original discoveries; a challenge to the metric system, and an earnest word with the english-speaking people on their ancient weights and measures. Diagrams. N. Y. 1884. O.   916.2+36

Barnard, F: A: Porter. The imaginary metrological system of the great pyramid of Gizeh; from the proceedings of the Amer. metrological society, presented to the society dec. 9, 1883. Repr. from the School of mines quarterly of jan., march and may 1884. Ill. N. Y. 1884. O.   916.2:34

Gorringe, H: H. Egyptian obelisks. Ill. N. Y. [1882]. F.   916.2:R37

Nubia, Abyssinia.

(See also Upper Nile region, col. 1325.)

Russell, Michael. Nubia and Abyssinia; comprehending their civil history, antiquities, arts, religion, literature and natural history. Ill. [Harper's family lib.]. N. Y. 1843. S.   963:1

Harris, *Sir* W: Cornwallis. Adventures in Africa, during a tour of two years through that country. *T. p. w.* [Phila.] O.   916.3:6
— *Same.* The highlands of Ethiopia. From 1st Lond ed. N. Y. *n. d.* O.   916.3:6
Note. A record of an embassy to Abyssinia, in 1841–43, by way of Aden and the Red Sea.

Pallme, Hynek (*lat.* Ignatius). Travels in Kordofan; embracing a description of that province of Egypt and some of the bordering

x denotes books specially adapted for children.

countries, with a review of the present state of the commerce in those countries, of the habits and customs of the inhabitants, as also an account of the slave-hunts taking place under the government of Mehemed Ali ; from notes coll. during a residence of nearly two years in Kordofan. Lond. 1844. O.   916.2 : 40

Gobat, S: Journal of three years' residence in Abyssinia. Preceded by an introd., geographical and historical, on Abyssinia, tr. from the french by Sereno D. Clark, accompanied with a biogr. sketch of bishop Gobat by Robert Baird. N. Y. 1850. D.
                            916.3 : 2

Taylor, Bayard. A journey to central Africa, or Life and landscapes from Egypt to the negro kingdoms of the White Nile. Map and ill. N. Y. 1854. D.   916.3 : 7
— Same. N. Y. 1878. D.   916.3 : 7

Parkyns, Mansfield. Life in Abyssinia ; notes coll. during three years' residence and travels in that country. Ill. N. Y. 1854. 2 v. O.   916.3 : 4

Baker, Sir S: White. The Nile tributaries of Abyssinia, and the sword hunters of the Hamran arabs. 5th ed. Phila. 1869. D.
                            916.3 : 1

Jonveaux, Émile. Two years in east Africa ; adventures in Abyssinia and Nubia, with a journey to the sources of the Nile. Maps and ill. Lond. 1875. D.   916.3 : 3

Klunzinger, C: B: Bilder aus Oberägypten, der wüste und dem Rothen Meere ; mit einem vorwort von G: Schweinfurth. 2te aufl. Stuttg. 1878. O.   916.2 : 12

James, Frank L. The wild tribes of the Soudan ; account of travel and sport, chiefly in the Basé country, personal experiences and adventures during three winters spent in the Soudan. Maps and ill. N. Y. [1883]. O.   916.3 + 8

Winstanley, W. A visit to Abyssinia ; an account of travel in modern Ethiopia. Lond. 1881. 2 v. D.   916.3 : 5

Schuver, Juan Maria. Reisen im oberen Nilgebiet ; erlebnisse und beobachtungen auf der wasserscheide zwischen Blauem und Weissem Nil, und in den ägyptisch-abessinischen grenzländern 1881 und 1882. Karte. Gotha. 1883. In Petermann's mitteilungen, Ergänzungsb. 16.   905.1 : M

4. Western Soudan and Guinea.

Bridge, Horatio. Journal of an african cruiser ; comprising sketches of the Canaries, the Cape de Verds, Liberia, Madeira, Sierra Leone and other places of interest on the west coast of Africa, by an officer of the U. S. navy, ed. by Nathaniel Hawthorne. N. Y. 1848. D.   916.5 : 1

Carnes, J. A. Journal of a voyage from Boston to the west coast of Africa, with a full description of the manner of trading with the natives of the coast. Bost. 1852. D.
                            916.5 : 2

Foote, Andrew Hull. Africa and the american flag. N. Y. 1854. D.   916.5 : 3

Hale, Sarah Josepha, ed. Liberia, or Mr. Peyton's experiment. N. Y. 1853. D. 916.5 : 4

Park, Mungo, Life and travels of ; with supp. chapter, detailing the results of recent discovery. Edinb. 1864. D.·   916.5 : 5

Steger, F:, ed. Mungo Park's reisen in Afrika von der westküste zum Niger. Leipz. 1856. D.   916.5 : 6

Lander, J: and R: Journal of an expedition to explore the course and termination of the Niger, with a narrative of a voyage down that river to its termination, [1830–31]. Maps and ill. [Harper's fam. lib.] N. Y. 1858. 2 v. S.   916.5 : 7

Allen, W:, and T: R: Heywood **Thomson.** Narrative of the expedition sent by her majesty's government to the river Niger in 1841 under the command of capt. H. D. Trotter. Pub. with the sanction of the colonial office and the admiralty. Lond. 1848. 2 v. O.   916.5 : 8

Barth, H: Travels and discoveries in north and central Africa ; being a journal of an expedition undertaken under the auspices of H. B. M.'s government in 1849—1855. N. Y. 1857-59. 3 v. O.   916.5 + 9

Richardson, James. Narrative of a mission to central Africa performed in 1850–51, under the orders and at the expense of her majesty's government. Lond. 1853. 2 v. D.
                            916.5 : 10

Campbell, Robert. A pilgrimage to my motherland ; an account of a journey among the egbas and yorubas of central Africa, in 1859–60. N. Y. 1861. D.   916.5 : 11

Rohlfs, Gerhard. Quer durch Afrika ; reise vom Mittelmeer nach dem Tschad-see und zum Golf vom Guinea, [1865–67]. Leipz. 1874. 2 v. in 1. O.   916.5 : 12

Stanley, H: Morton. Coomassie and Magdala ; the story of two british campaigns in Africa. Ill. N. Y. 1874. O.   966 + 1

Burton, R: Francis, and Verney Lovett **Cameron.** To the Gold Coast for gold ; a personal narrative. Lond. 1883. 2 v. O.   916.5 : 13
    Contents. V. 1. Lisbon to Sierra Leone, by way of Madeira and Grand Canary. 2. Sá Leone to Axim and the gold mines.—App.: The Ashanti scare; The labour-question in western Africa; Gold-digging in n. w. Africa; Lists of birds and plants collected.—Index.

Oberländer, R:, ed. Westafrika vom Senegal bis Benguela ; reisen und schilderungen aus Senegambien, Ober- und Niederguinea, mit besonderer rücksicht auf die deutsche expedition an die Loangoküste und deren ausgang. 3te ergänzte aufl. [Ill. bibliothek der länder- und völkerkunde]. Leipz. 1878. O.   916.6 : 13

Du Chaillu, Paul Belloni. Explorations and adventures in equatorial Africa ; with accounts of the manners and customs of the people and of the chace of the gorilla, crocodile, leopard, elephant, hippopotamus and other animals. Map and ill. Lond. 1861. O.   916.7 : 1
— A journey to Ashango-land and further penetration into equatorial Africa. Map and ill. N. Y. 1871. O.   916.7 + 7
— Stories of the gorilla country, narrated for young people. Ill. N. Y. 1867. D.
                            x 916.7 : 2
— Wild life under the equator, narrated for young people. Ill. N. Y. [1868]. D.
                            x 916.7 : 3

x denotes books specially adapted for children.

Du Chaillu, Paul Belloni.—*Continued.*
— Lost in the jungle, narrated for young people.
Ill. N. Y. [1869]. D.   x 916.7:4
— My Apingi kingdom, with life in the great
Sahars, and sketches of the chase of the
ostrich, hyena, etc. Ill. N. Y. [1870]. D.
          x 916.7:5
— The country of the dwarfs. Ill. N. Y. [1871].
D.   x 916.7:6

5. Upper Nile region.

(See also Nubia and Abyssinia, col. 1322.)

Geddie, J: The lake regions of central Africa;
a record of modern discovery. N. Y. 1881.
D.   916.4:1
Contents. Introductory and historical.—The Nile.—
The Congo.—The Zambesi.

Taylor, Bayard, *ed.* The lake regions of central
Africa; comp. and arr. Map and ill. (Ill.
lib. of travel). N. Y. 1881. D.   916.4:2
Note. Comprises the travels of Burton, Speke and
Baker.

Krapf, J: L: Travels, researches and missionary labors during an eighteen years residence in eastern Africa, together with journeys to Jagga, Usambara, Ukambani, Shoa,
Abessinia and Khartum and a coasting
voyage from Mombaz to Cape Delgado.
With an app. respecting the snow-capped
mountains of eastern Africa, the sources of
the Nile, the languages and literature of
Abessinia and eastern Africa, etc., and an
account of geographical researches in eastern Africa up to the discovery of the Uyen-
yesi by dr. Livingstone, by E. J. Ravenstein. Bost. 1860. O.   916.4:3

Burton, R: Francis. The lake regions of central
Africa; a picture of exploration. N. Y.
1860. O.   916.4:4

Speke, J: Hanning. Journal of the discovery of
the source of the Nile. Map, portr. and ill.
N. Y. 1864. O.   916.4:5

Baker, *Sir* S: White. The Albert Nyanza, great
basin of the Nile and explorations of the
Nile sources. Maps, ill. and portr. Lond.
1866. O.   916.4:6
— Ismailïa, a narrative of the expedition to central Africa for the suppression of the slave
trade, organized by Ismail, khedive of
Egypt. Maps, portr. and ill. N. Y. 1875.
O.   916.4+7

Schweinfurth, G: A: The heart of Africa; three
years' travels and adventures in the unex-
plored regions of central Africa from 1868
to 1871. Tr. by Ellen E. Frewer; with an
introd. by Winwood Reade. Maps and ill.
N. Y. 1874. 2 v. O.   916.4+8

Hill, G: Birbeck, *ed.* Colonel Gordon in central
Africa, 1874—1879; with a portr. and map
of the country, prep. under col. Gordon's
supervision. From original letters and documents. Lond. 1881. O.   916.4:9

Wilson, C: T., *and* R. W. **Felkin.** Uganda and
the Egyptian Soudan. Lond. 1882. 2 v. D.
          916.4:10
Contents. V. 1. Wilson, C: T. Narrative.—Felkin, R. W. Narrative. — App.: Wilson, C: T. On
trade, List of plants, Itinerary, Vocabularies. — Ravenstein, E. G. Wilson *and* Felkin's meteorological
and hypsometrical observ.—Index. 2. Felkin, R. W.
Narrative, *continued.*—App.: Felkin, R. W. Authro-
pological notes and measurements, Itinerary; Caspari, R. Analysis of iron ore from Madi and Dar-

four; **Gerrard,** A. W. Report on water from hot
springs, Busi.—Index.—Maps.

Long, C: Chaillé. Central Africa, naked truths
of naked people; an account of the expeditions to the lake Victoria Nyanza and
the Makraka-Niam-Niam, west of the Bahr-
el-Abiad (White Nile). Ill. N. Y. 1877. O.
          916.4:11

Thomson, Joseph. To the central african lakes
and back; the narrative of the Royal geographical society's East central african expedition, 1878–80; with a short biogr. notice
of Keith Johnston. Portr. and map. 2d ed.
Bost. 1881. 2 v. D.   916.4:12
— Through Masäi land; a journey of exploration among the snow-clad volcanic mountains and strange tribes of eastern equatorial Africa, the narrative of the Royal geographical society's expedition to Mount
Kenia and lake Victoria Nyanza, 1883–1884.
4th ed. Bost. 1885. O.   916.4:13

Cameron, Verney Lovett. Across Africa. Leipz.
1877. 2 v. in 1. S.   916.4:14

6. South central region.

Livingstone, D: Missionary travels and researches in south Africa, incl. a sketch of
16 years' residence in the interior of Africa
and a journey from the Cape of Good Hope
to Loanda on the west coast, thence across
the continent down the river Zambesi to
the eastern ocean. Portr., maps and ill.
25 ed., with index. N. Y. 1870. O.
          916.6:1
— *Same.* N. Y. 1858. O.   916.6:1
— *and* C: Narrative of an expedition to the
Zambesi and its tributaries and of the discovery of the lakes Shirwa and Nyassa,
1858—1864. Map and ill. N. Y. 1866. O.
          916.6:2
— Last journals in central Africa from 1865 to his
death; continued by a narrative of his last
moments and sufferings obtained from his
faithful servants Chuma and Susi, by Horace Waller. Portr., maps and ill. N. Y.
1875. O.   916.6+3

Barth, Hermann v. David Livingstone, der
Afrikareisende: Ostafrika vom Limpopo
bis zum Somalilande; erforschungsreisen
im osten Afrika's, mit besonderer rücksicht
auf leben, reisen und tod von David Livingstone; auf grund des neuesten standpunk-
tes der ostafrikanischen völkerkunde bearb. An stelle der vierten aufl. von "Livingstone, der missionär"; 2te ausg. vermehrt durch einen auszug aus D: Livingstone's hinterlassenen tagebüchern. Leipz.
1876. O.   916.6+4

Stanley, H: Morton. How I found Livingstone;
travels, adventures and discoveries in central Africa; incl. four months residence
with dr. Livingstone. Ill. and maps. 2d ed.
Lond. 1872. O.   916.6:5
— Through the dark continent, or The sources of
the Nile around the great lakes of equatorial Africa and down the Livingstone river
to the Atlantic ocean. Maps and ill. N. Y.
1878. 2 v. O.   916.6:6

Roth, R: Stanleys reise durch den dunkeln
welttheil; für die jugend bearb. Karte und
ill. Stuttg. *n. d.* S.   x 916.6:7

x denotes books specially adapted for children.

Chambliss, J. E., *comp.* The lives and travels of Livingstone and Stanley, covering their entire career in southern and central Africa. Ill. and maps. Phila. [1881]. O. **916 : 6+8**

Young, E: D. Nyassa; a journal of adventures whilst exploring lake Nyassa, central Africa, and establishing the settlement of "Livingstonia," rev. by Horace Waller. 2d ed. Maps. Lond. 1877. D. **916.6 : 9**

Elton, James F: Travels and researches among the lakes and mountains of eastern and central Africa; ed. by H. B. Cotterill. Maps and ill. Lond. 1879. O. **916.6 : 10**

Serpa Pinto, Alexandre Alberto da Rocha. How I crossed Africa from the Atlantic to the Indian ocean, through unknown countries, discovery of the great Zambesi affluents, etc. Tr. from the author's ms. by Alfred Elwes. Maps and ill. Phila. 1881. 2 v. O. **916.6 : 11**
Contents. V. 1. The king's rifle. 2. The Coillard family.

Monteiro, Joachim J: Angola and the river Congo. Map and ill. N. Y. 1876. D. **916.7 : 9**

Capello, Hermenigildo C: de **Brito-**, *and* Roberto **Ivens**. From Benguella to the territory of Yacca; description of a journey into central and west Africa, comprising narratives, adventures and important surveys of the sources of the rivers Cunene, Cubango, Luando, Cuanza and Cuango, and of great part of the course of the two latter, together with the discovery of the rivers Hamba, Cauali, Sussa and Cugho and a detailed account of the territories of Quiteca, N'bungo, Sosso, Futa and Yacca. Expedition organized in 1877—1880. Tr. by Alfred Elwes. Maps and ill. Lond. 1882. 2 v. O. **916.6 : 12**

Johnston, H. H. The river Congo, from its mouth to Bóbóbó; with a general description of the natural history and anthropology of its western basin. Ill. 2d ed. Lond. 1884. O. **916.7 : 8**

Stanley, H: Morton. The Congo and the founding of its free state; a story of work and exploration. Maps and ill. N. Y. 1885. 2 v. O. **916.7 : 10**

7. South Africa.

History.

Martin, Robert Montgomery. History of southern Africa; comprising the Cape of Good Hope, Mauritius, Seychelles, etc. 2d ed. [British colonial lib., v. 3]. Lond. 1843. S. **968 : 3**

Greswell, W: Our south african empire. [Map.] Lond. 1885. 2 v. O. **968 : 6**
Contents. V. 1. Introd.—The dutch occupation.—The english occupation.—Native races: The bushmen and hottentots; The kafirs.—Kafir wars.—The dutch republics: The Free State; The Transvaal.—South African Confederation.—The Frere administration. 2. *Same, continued.*—The late sir Bartle Frere; review of his work and life.—Basutoland.—Forms of government in south Africa.—The Afrikaner Bond. —A colonial question; the germans in south Africa. —Imperial federation. — Some social blots in Cape life.—Education at the Cape.—The education of the south african tribes.

Lucas, T: J. The zulus and the british frontiers. Lond. 1879. O. **968 : 2**

Vijn, Cornelius. Cetshwayo's dutchman; the private journal of a white trader in Zululand during the british invasion. Tr. from the dutch and ed. with a' pref. by J. W. Colenso. Portr. of Cetshwayo. Lond. 1880. D. **968 : 4**

Colenso, Frances Ellen. History of the zulu war and its origin, [the author] assisted in those portions of the work which touch upon military matters by lieut.-col. E: **Durnford**. Lond. 1880. O. **968 : 1**
— *Same.* 2d ed. Lond. 1881. D. **968 : 1**
— The ruin of Zululand; an account of british doings in Zululand since the invasion of 1879; a sequel to The history of the zulu war by Frances Ellen Colenso and lieut.-col. E: Durnford. Portr. of bp. Colenso and Cetshwayo. Lond. 1884, 1885. 2 v. O. **968 : 5**

Nixon, J: The complete story of the Transvaal; from the "great trek" to the convention of London; with app. comprising ministerial declarations of policy and official documents. Lond. 1885. O. **968 : 7**

Description and travels.

Taylor, Bayard, *comp.* Travels in south Africa. (Ill. lib. of travel.) N. Y. 1872. D. **916.8 : 18**
Note. Principally Livingstone's and Andersson's journeys.

Steedman, Andrew. Wanderings and adventures in the interior of southern Africa. Ill. Lond. 1835. 2 v. O. **916.8 : 17**

Moffat, Robert. Missionary labours and scenes in southern Africa. 3d ed. N. Y. 1843. D. **916.8 : 20**

Hatfield, Edwin F. St. Helena and the Cape of Good Hope, or Incidents in the missionary life of James McGregor Bertram; with an introd. by G: B. Cheever. N. Y. 1852. D. **916.8 : 11**

Fleming, Francis. Southern Africa; a geography and natural history of the country, colonies and inhabitants from the Cape of Good Hope to Angola, with notices of their origins, manners, habits, customs, traditions, superstitions, religious usages, languages, past and present conditions, manufactures, weapons, etc. Lond. 1856. D. **916.8 : 8**

Andersson, C: J: Lake Ngami, or Explorations and discoveries during eight years wanderings in the wilds of south western Africa; with an introd. letter by J: C: Frémont. Ill. N. Y. 1857. O. **916.8 : 3**
— The Okavango river; a narrative of travel, exploration and adventure. Ill. and map. N. Y. 1861. O. **916.8 : 4**
— Notes of travel in south-western Africa. N. Y. 1875. D. **916.8 : 2**

Cumming, Roualeyn Gordon. Five years of a hunter's life in the far interior of south Africa; with notices of the native tribes and anecdotes of the chase of the lion, elephant, hippopotamus, giraffe, rhinoceros, etc. N. Y. 1874. 2 v. D. **916.8 : 7**

Cunynghame, *Sir* Arthur Thurlow. My command in south Africa, 1874—1878; comprising experiences of travel in the colonies of south Africa and the independent states. Maps. 2d thous. Lond. 1879. O. **916.8 : 6**

Trollope, Anthony. South Africa. Leipz. 1878. 2 v. in 1. S.   **916.8 : 19**
Contents. V. 1. South Africa; history.—The Cape Colony. — Natal. 2. The Transvaal. — Griqualand West.—The Orange Free State.—Native territories.—Conclusion.

Nixon, J: Among the boers, or Notes of a trip to south Africa in search of health, [1877-78]. Ill. Lond. 1880. O.   **916.8 : 22**

Aylward, Alfred. The Transvaal of to-day; war, witchcraft, sport and spoils in south Africa. Edinb. 1878. O.   **916.8 : 5**

Hutchinson, *Mrs.* Louisa. In tents in the Transvaal. Lond. 1879. O.   **916.8 : 13**

Montague, W: E. Campaigning in south Africa; reminiscences of an officer in 1879. Edinb. 1880. O.   **916.8 : 21**

Gillmore, Parker, (*Ubique*). The great thirst land; a ride through Natal, Orange Free State, Transvaal and Kalahri desert. Ill. Lond. *n. d.* O.   **916.8 : 9**

— A ride through hostile Africa, with adventures among the boers. Ill., new ed. Lond. 1881. O.   **916.8 : 23**

Holub, Emil. Seven years in south Africa; travels, researches and hunting adventures, between the diamond-fields and the Zambesi, 1872 — 1879. Tr. by Ellen E. Frewer. Ill. and map. Bost. 1881. 2 v. O.   **916.8 : 12**

Grout, Lewis. Zulu-land, or Life among the zulu-kafirs of Natal and Zulu-land, south Africa. Map and ill. Phila. [1864]. D.   **916.8 : 10**

Barker, Mary Anne *lady, now mrs.* F: Napier **Broome.** A year's housekeeping in south Africa. Leipz. 1877. S.   **916.8 : 1**
Note. Zululand and Natal.

8. Madagascar.

Ellis, W: Three visits to Madagascar, during the years 1853—1854—1856; incl. a journey to the capital, with notices of the natural history of the country and the present civilization of the people. Ill. N. Y. 1859. O.   **916.9+1**

Little, H: W: Madagascar, its history and people. Map. Edinb. 1884. O.   **916.9 : 2**

Shaw, G: A. Madagascar and France; with some account of the island, its people, its resources and development. Ill. and map. Lond. 1885. O.   **969 : 2**

Oliver, S: Pasfield. The true story of the french dispute in Madagascar. Map. Lond. 1885. O.   **969 : 1**

23. North America — a, In general.

1. Discovery and History.

History in general.

Winsor, Justin, *ed.* Narrative and critical history of America; v. 2 - 4. Bost. 1885. Q.   **970+R22**
Contents. V. 2. Spanish explorations and settlements in America, from the 15th to 17th century. **Winsor,** J. Documentary sources of early spanish-amer. history; Columbus and his discoveries, with critical essay and notes; The earliest maps of the spanish and portuguese discoveries. — **Gay,** Sidney Howard. Amerigo Vespucci.—**Winsor,** J. Notes on Vespucius and the naming of America; Bibliography of Pomponius Mela, Solinus, Vadianus and Apianus. —**Channing,** E: The companions of Columbus, with critical essay. — **Winsor,** J. The early cartography of the Gulf of Mexico and adjacent parts. — **Shea,** J: G. Ancient Florida, with critical essay on the indians, with critical essay and editorial note.—**Winsor,** J. Cortés and his companions, with critical essay and notes; Discoveries of the Pacific coast of North Amer.—**Haynes,** H: W. Early explorations of New Mexico, with critical essay and editorial note. — **Markham,** Clements R. Pizarro, and the conquest and settlement of Peru and Chili, with editorial notes. — **Winsor,** J. The Amazon and Eldorado. — **Hale,** E: E. Magellan's discovery, with critical essay. —Index.

3. English explorations and settlements in North America, 1497 - 1689. Editor's note.—**Deane,** C: The voyages of the Cabots, with critical essay.—**Hale,** E: E. Hawkins and Drake, with critical essay on Drake's Bay.—**Winsor,** J. Notes on the sources of information. — **Smith,** C: C. Explorations to the north-west, with critical essay.—**Winsor,** J. The Zeno influence on early cartography; Frobisher's and Hudson's voyages.—**Henry,** W: Wirt. Sir Walter Ralegh; Settlements at Roanoke and voyages to Guiana, with critical essay.—**Brock,** Robert A. Virginia, 1606 - 1689, with critical essay. — **Winsor,** J. Notes on the maps of Virginia, etc.—**De Costa,** B: F. Norumbega and its english explorers, with critical essay.—**Winsor,** J. Earliest english publications

on America and other notes.—**Ellis,** G: E. The religious element in the settlement of New England; puritans and separatists in England, with critical essay. — **Dexter,** Franklin B. The pilgrim church and Plymouth colony, with critical essay. — **Deane,** C: New England, with critical essay.—**Winsor,** J. Bibliographical notes; early maps of New England. —**Stevens,** J: Austin. The english in New York, with critical essay.—**Winsor,** J. Notes. — **Whitehead,** W: A. The english in east and west Jersey, 1664 - 1689, with critical essay.—**Winsor,** J. Note.— **Keen,** Gregory B. Note on New Albion.—**Stone,** F: D. The founding of Pennsylvania, with critical essay. — **Brantly,** W: T. The english in Maryland, 1632 - 1691, with critical essay.—Index.

4. French explorations and settlements in North America, and those of the portuguese, dutch and swedes, 1500-1700. **Shaler,** Nathaniel S. Physiography of North America.—**Dexter,** G: Cortereal, Verrazano, Gomez, Thevet, with critical essay.—**Winsor,** J. Maps of the eastern coast of North America, 1500-1535.—**De Costa,** B: F. Jacques Cartier and his successors, with critical essay.—**Winsor,** J. Cartography of the northeast coast of North America, 1535-1600.—**Slafter,** Edmund F. Champlain, with critical essay.—**Smith,** C: C. Acadia, with critical essay.—**Winsor,** J. Joliet, Marquette and La Salle; Father L: Hennepin; Baron La Hontan.—**Shea,** J: G. The jesuits, recollects, and the indians, with critical essay.—**Winsor,** J. Their jesuit relations.—**Stewart,** G:, jr. Frontenac and his times, with critical essay and editorial notes.—**Winsor,** J. General atlases and charts of the 16th and 17th centuries; Maps of the 17th century showing Canada.—**Fernow,** Berthold. New Netherland, or The dutch in North America, with critical essay and editorial notes.—**Keen,** Gregory B. The swedes on the Delaware, with critical essay.—Index.

Note. The contents of the other volumes, when completed, will be as follows: 1, America before Columbus. 5, The french and english in North America, from the english revolution to the peace of Paris, 1689—1763. 6, The american revolution, 1763—1783. 7, The U. S., 1783—1850. 8, Canada and the american outgrowths of continental Europe, dependent and independent, in the 18th and 19th centuries.

Robertson, W: The history of America. Lond. 1824. 3 v. D. **970 : 12**
Contents. V. 1. Catalogue of spanish books and mss.—Review of navigation and discovery before Columbus.—Voyages and discoveries of Columbus.—Discoveries of the immediate successors of Columbus.—View of America, when first discovered, and of the manners and policy of its uncivilized inhabitants. 2. *Same, continued.*—History of the conquest of New Spain by Cortes.—History of the conquest of Peru by Pizarro. 3. View of the institutions and manners of the mexicans and peruvians.—View of the interior government, commerce, etc., of the spanish colonies.—History of Virginia to 1688.—History of New England to 1652.—Index.

— *Same* ; with an account of his life and writings. Added, questions for the examination of students. N. Y. 1843. O. **970 : 12**

— *Same*, abridged ; with a memoir of the author from that by Dugald Stewart. [Harper's family lib.] N. Y. 1844. S. **970 : 23**

Holmes, Abiel. The annals of America, from the discovery by Columbus, in 1492, to 1826. 2d ed. Cambridge. 1829. 2 v. O.
Contents. V. 1. European discoveries and settlements, 1492-1607.—British american colonies, 1607-1732. 2. *Same*, 1732-1776.—The U. S. of Amer., 1776-1826.—Index.

Mackenzie, Robert. America ; a history [to the present time]. N. Y. 1882 [1881]. D. **970 : 6**

— *Same.* N. Y. 1882. Q. **970+6**
Contents. United States.—Dominion of Canada.—South America, etc.—Index.

Goodrich, S: Griswold. Lights and shadows of american history. [Youth's lib. of history.] Bost. [1844]. S. **x 970 : 9**

Yonge, Charlotte Mary, *and* **Horatio Hastings Weld.** Aunt Charlotte's stories of american history. Ill. N. Y. [1883]. S. **x 970 : 13**

Wright, Henrietta Christian. Children's stories in american history. Ill. N. Y. 1885. D. **x 970 : 21**

Discovery.

(See also History of the U. S. and of Mexico.)

Leland, C: Godfrey. Fusang, or The discovery of America by chinese priests in the 5th century. Lond. 1875. D. **970 : 1**
Contents. The narrative of Hoei-Shin, with comments by C: F: Neumann.—Remarks on the text of prof. Neumann.—Letter from col. Barclay Kennon on the navigation of the north Pacific ocean.—American antiquities, with their relation to the old world.—The advocates and opponents of the narrative of Hoei-Shin.—The latest discussion of Fusang.

Vining, E: P. An inglorious Columbus, or Evidence that Hwui Shân and a party of buddhist monks from Afghanistan discovered America in the fifth century. N. Y. 1885. O. **x 970 : 14**

Copenhagen. *Kongelige nordiske oldskrift-selskab.* Antiquitates americanae sive scriptores septentrionales rerum ante-Columbianorum in America: Samling af de i nordens oldskrifter indeholdte efterretninger om de gamle nordboers opdagelsesreiser til America fra det 10de til det 14de aarhundrede; edidit Societas regia antiquariorum septentrionalium [by C: Christian Rafn]. Hafniae. 1837. F. **970 : R19**
Contents. Prefatio.—Conspectus codicum membranearum in quibus terrarum americarum mentio fit.—America discovered by scandinavians in the 10th century.—Narrationes de Eiriko Rufo et Greenlandis.—Historia Thorfinni Karlsefnii et Snórrii Thor-

brandi filii.—De inhabitatione Grœnlandiæ.—De Ario Maris filio.—De Björne Breidvikensium athleta.—De Gudleivo Gudlœgi filio. — Excerpta ex annalibus islandorum.—De mansione grœnlandorum in locis borealibus.—Excerpta e geographicis scriptis veterum islandorum. — Carmen Færöicum in quo Vinlandiæ mentio fit.—Adami Bremensis relatio de Vinlandia.—Monumenta europæa in oris Grönlandiæ. — Monumentum vetustum in Massachusetts.—Monumenta vetusta in Rhode Island. — Annotationes geographicæ.

Smith, Joshua Toulmin. The discovery of America by the northmen in the 10th century ; comprising translations of all the most important original narratives of this event, together with a critical examination of their authenticity ; added, an examination of the comparative merits of the northmen and Columbus. 2d ed. Maps and plates. Lond. 1842. D. **970 : 18**

Anderson, Rasmus B. America not discovered by Columbus ; an historical sketch of the discovery of America by the norsemen in the 10th century ; with an app. on the historical, linguistic, literary and scientific value of the scandinavian languages. New ed. Chicago. 1877. D. **970 : 10**

Weise, Arthur James. The discoveries of America to 1525. N. Y. 1884. O. **970+20**

Campe, Joachim H: Die entdeckung von Amerika ; ein unterhaltungsbuch für kinder und junge leute. Brschw. 1852. 3 v. T. **x 970 : 7**
Contents. V. 1. Kolumbus. 2. Kortes. 3. Pizarro.

Bell, N. R. E., (*N. D' Anvers*). Heroes of american discovery. Ill. Lond. 1884. D. **970 : 15**
Note. Comprises the voyages and expeditions from Columbus, to the U. S. and Canada boundary commission, continued to 1880.

Fox, G. V. An attempt to solve the problem of the first landing place of Columbus in the new world. Maps. *In* U. S. coast survey rep. 1880. *in* 622 : D

Kohl, J: G: History of discovery and exploration on the coasts of the U. S. *In* U. S. Coast survey report, 1884. *in* 622 : D
Contents. Atlantic coast.—Gulf of Mexico.—Pacific coast.

See also in the Index to biography Colombo — Cortés—Pizarro—Ralegh—Vespucci.

New France.

(See also Louisiana, cl. 974.6; Canada, cl. 976.)

Charlevoix, P: François Xavier de. History and general description of New France. Tr., with notes by J: Gilmary Shea. N. Y. 1866. 6 v. Q. **970+F2**
Contents. V. 1. Preface.—Chronological tables of the new world, and of the colonies planted there by europeans. — Critical list of authors. — Canada and Florida, 1504-1614. 2. Quebec and New France, 1609-1656. 3. *Same*, 1657-1688. 4. *Same*, incl. La Salle's expedition to the Mississippi, 1688-1696.—App.—Life and death of some indian christians. 5. New France, 1696-1725. 6. Louysiana, 1720-1736.—Index.

Le Clercq, Chrétien. First establishment of the faith in New France. Now first tr., with notes by J: Gilmary Shea. [Mississippi ser., no. 2.] N. Y. 1881. 2 v. O. **917 : P10**
Contents. V. 1. Sketch of father Le Clercq.—From the first discoveries of New France to abt. 1660. 2. From abt. 1660 to 1690.—Index.

Hennepin, L: A description of Louisiana. Tr. from the ed. of 1683 and compared with the Nouvelle découvert, the La Salle documents

x denotes books specially adapted for children.

and other contemporaneous papers, by J:
Gilmary Shea. [Mississippi series, no. 1].
N. Y. 1880. O.   **917.1 : P45**

Freytas, Nicolas de. The expedition of don
Diego Dionisio de Peñalosa, governor of
New Mexico, from Santa Fe to the river
Mischipi and Quivira in 1662; with an account of Peñalosa's projects to aid the
french to conquer the mining country in
northern Mexico; and his connection with
Cavelier de La Salle. [Mississippi ser. no.
3.] N. Y. 1882. O.   **917.1+P46**

Parkman, Francis, *jr.* France and England in
North America; a series of historical narratives. Bost. 1880–84. 7 v. D. *and* O.
                            970 : 4
Contents. Pt. **1.** Pioneers of France in the new
world. 17th ed. **2.** The jesuits in North America in
the 17th century. 14th ed. **3.** La Salle and the discovery of the great west. 12th ed., rev. **4.** The old
régime in Canada. 8th ed. **5.** Count Frontenac and
New France under Louis XIV. 7th ed. **6.** *not pub.*
7. Montcalm and Wolfe. 2 v.

— *Same.* Pts. 1, 3. Bost. 1865, 1879. 2 v. O.
                            970 : 4

— History of the conspiracy of Pontiac and the
wars of the north amer. tribes against the
english colonies after the conquest of
Canada. Bost. 1851. O.   **970+5**

— *Same.* 9th ed., with add. Bost. 1880. 2 v. D.
                            970 : 5

— Historic handbook of the northern tour : Lakes
George and Champlain, Niagara, Montreal,
Quebec. [Maps and ill.] Bost. 1885. D.
                         970 : 16

Baird, C: W. History of the huguenot emigration
to America. N. Y. [1885]. 2 v. O.
                        970+14
Contents. V. **1.** Pref. — Attempted settlements in
Brazil and Florida. — Under the edict: Acadia and
Canada.—New Netherland.—The Antilles.—Approach
of the revocation. — The revocation: Flight from La
Rochelle and Aunis. — App. **2.** The revocation:
Flight from Saintonge, Poitou, Touraine, the north-
ern provinces, the eastern and southern provinces.
— The refuge: England. — The emigration: On the
high seas. — The settlement: Boston; Oxford; Rhode
Island; Connecticut.—App.—Index.

See also in the Index to biography **Champlain—LaSalle.**

New Spain.

See Mexico, cl. 977; Central America, cl. 978; West Indies,
cl. 979; South America, cl. 980–989.

Archeology, essays and periodi-cals.

(*See also* Prehistoric America, col. 348–349.)

Haven, S: Foster. Archæology of the U. S., or
Sketches, historical and bibliographical, of
the progress of information and opinion
respecting vestiges of antiquity in the U. S.
In Smithsonian contributions.
                      506 : R3 v8

Archæological institute of America. American
series; Papers. Bost. 1881. O. **906+13**
Contents. **1. Bandelier,** A. F. Historical introd.
to studies among the sedentary indians of New
Mexico. **2. Bandelier,** A. F. Report on the ruins
of the pueblo of Pecos.

American antiquarian and oriental journal,
The; ed. by Stephen D. Peet; v. 1 – 7, april
1878—dec. 1885. Chicago. 1878–85. O.
                            905 : M
Note. Title-page of v. 1, 2 reads "a quarterly journal devoted to early american history, ethnology and
archæology."

Magazine of american history, The, with notes
and queries; v. 5–14, july 1880– dec. 1885.
Ill. N. Y. 1880—85. O.   **905 : M**

Magazine of western history, ill.; ed. by W:
W. Williams; v. 1, 2, nov. 1884—oct. 1885.
Cleveland. 1885. O.   **905 : M**

American historical association. Papers. N.
Y. 1885. O.   **906+10**
Contents. V. **1. Adams,** H. B. Report of the organization and proceedings, Saratoga, sept. 9, 10, 1884.
—**White,** A. D. On studies in general history and the
history of civilization.—**Knight,** G: W. History and
management of land grants for education in the
Northwest Territory (Ohio, Indiana, Illinois, Michigan, Wisconsin).—**Robertson,** C. F. The Louisiana
purchase in its influence upon the american system.

Johns Hopkins university. Studies in historical and political science; Herbert B. Adams,
ed. Balt. 1882–85. 3 v. O. **904+32**
Contents. V. **1.** *1st series: Local institutions.* **1.**
Freeman, E: A: An introduction to american institutional history. **2. Adams,** H. B. The germanic
origin of New England towns; read before the Harvard hist. soc., may 9, 1881, *and* Notes on cooperation
in university work. **3. Shaw,** A. Local government
in Illinois; repr. from the Fortnightly review. —
Gould, E. R. L. Local government in Pennsylvania;
read before the Pennsylvania hist. soc., may 1, 1882.
4. Adams, H. B. Saxon tithing-men in America;
read before the Amer. antiqu. soc., oct. 21, 1881. **5.**
Bemis, E: W. Local government in Michigan and
the northwest; read before the Amer. social science
assoc., sept. 7, 1882. **6. Ingle,** E: Parish institutions
of Maryland, with ill. from parish records. **7. Johnson,** J: Old Maryland manors, with the records of
a court leet and a court baron. **8. Adams,** H. B.
Norman constables in America, read before the New
England hist. geneal soc., feb. 1, 1882. **9-10. Adams,**
H. B. Village communities of Cape Anne and Salem,
from the hist. collections of the Essex institute. **11.**
Johnston, A. The genesis of a New England state,
Connecticut; read before the Histor. and polit. science assoc. april 13, 1883. **12. Ramage,** B. J. Local
government and free schools in South Carolina, 1st
pt., read before the Hist. Soc. of S. C., dec. 15, 1882.
2. *2d series: Institutions and economics.* **1. 2.**
Adams, H. B. Methods of historical study. **3. Ely,**
R: T. The past and present of political economy. **4.**
Hosmer, J. K. S: Adams, the man of the town-
meeting. **5, 6. Adams,** H: C. Taxation in the U. S.
1789–1816. **7. Macy,** J. Institutional beginnings in a
western state. **8, 9. Weeden,** W: B. Indian money
as a factor in New England civilization. **10. Channing,** E: Town and county government in the english colonies of North America. **11. Johnson,** J:
Rudimentary society among boys. **12. Shinn,** C: H.
Land laws of mining districts.
3. *3d series: Maryland, Virginia and Washington.*
1. Adams, H. B. Maryland's influence upon land
cessions to the U. S., with minor papers on G: Washington's interest in western lands, the Potomac company and a national university. **2, 3. Ingle,** E:
Local institutions of Virginia. **4. Ely,** R: T. Recent
american socialism. **5-7. Wilhelm,** L: W. Local
institutions of Maryland. **8. Scott,** A. The influence of the proprietors in founding the state of New
Jersey. **9, 10. Davis,** H. American constitutions;
the relations of the three departments as adjusted
by a century. **11, 12. Porter,** J: Addison. The city
of Washington; its origin and administration.

2. The aborigines.

(*See also* Folk-lore, col. 143–144; Indian biography, class
920.1; *and* The United States, *particularly*
The far west, in cl. 975.)

Drake, Francis S: Indian history for young
folks. Ill. and map. N. Y. 1885 [1884]. O.
                    x 970.1+20

Frost, J: Indian wars of the U. S.; from the
earliest period to the present time. Ill. N.
Y. 1860. O.   **970.1 : 19**

Drake, S: Gardner. Tragedies of the wilderness, or Narratives of captives, who have

x denotes books specially adapted for children.

been carried away by the indians from the various frontier settlements of the U. S., from the earliest to the present time. Bost. 1846. D.   **970:8**

Walker, Francis Amasa. The indian question. Bost. 1874. D.   **970.1:9**

Manypenny, G: W. Our indian wards. Cinc. 1880. O.   **970.1+8**

Jackson, Helen Maria, *born Fiske, formerly mrs.* Hunt. (*H. H.*) A century of dishonor ; a sketch of the U. S. government's dealings with some of the indian tribes. N. Y. 1881. D.   **327.1:4**

— *Same.* New ed., enlarged by the add. of the report of the needs of the mission indians of Cal. Bost. 1886. D.   **327.1:10**

See also American state papers, col. 174–175.

* * *

Goodrich, S: Griswold. The manners, customs and antiquities of the indians of North and South America. [Youth's library of history]. Bost. [1843]. S.   **x 970.1:12**

— History of the indians of North and South America. [Youth's library of history]. Bost. [1844]. S.   **x 970.1:13**

Ellis, G: E. The red man and the white man in North America, from its discovery to the present time. Bost. 1882. O.   **970.1:16**

Carlier, A: Histoire ... [des] rapports avec les indiens ... jusqu' en 1776. Paris. **971.1:16**

Schoolcraft, H: Rowe. The red race of America. N. Y. 1848. O.   **970.1:4**

Contents. Personal reminiscences.—Scenes and adventures in the Ozark mountains, 1818 and 1819.—Personal incidents and impressions of the indian race.—Tales of a wigwam. — Mythology, religion, manners and customs. — Ethnology, alphab. arr. ; Letter A. — Language, 3 (1 and 2 will be found in 917.5:42). — Picture writing.—Antiquities of the western country.—Settlement of Detroit.—Cartier's voyages.—Influence of ardent spirits on the condition of the north amer. indians. — Indian policy of the government. — Nursery, cradle and war songs.

— Algic researches.   **299:9**
See col. 143.

— Personal memoirs of thirty years with the indian tribes.   **917.5:43**

— Information respecting the history, condition and prospects of the indian tribes of the the U. S., collected and prepared under the direction of the Bureau of indian affairs, per act of congress of march 3d 1847. Ill. Pub. by authority of congress. Phila. 1853–56. 5 v. Q.   **970.1:R3**

Contents. **General history:** V. 1. Earliest traditions of the indians respecting their origin and the cosmogony of the earth.—Summary of the beliefs of the various tribes. 2. First interview with the tribes of Va., N. Y. and N. E., at the close of the 16th and commencement of the 16th century.—General ethnography. 3. Spanish discoveries in Fla., Ala., La., Miss., Tenn., Mo. and Ark.—Expeditions of D'Allyon, Narvaez and De Soto.—Discovery of the Miss. river. 4. Discoveries on the Gila, Colorado and Rio del Norte.— Expedition of Coronado in 1542, and conquest and founding of New Mexico.—First excursions into the present area of western Texas and Ark. 5. Origin of the indian race, and summary view of the indian character.—Effect on the indian of the contiguous civilization of the white man.—App. Cusic, D: Sketches of the ancient history of the six nations; Sketch of the earliest explorations of the french in Canada and the valley of the Mississippi. 6. (*See* at the end of the contents.) **Manners and customs:** V. 2. Generic view.—The constitution of the indian family.—Forest teachings.—Art of hunting.—Sugar-making.—War and its incidents.—The wigwam and its mates.—Birth and its incidents. — Death and its incidents.—Games of

Schoolcraft, H: Rowe.— *Continued.*
chance.—The indian on his hunting-ground.—Miscel. traits. 3. Generic traits of mind.—Traces of foreign origin. — Distinctive phases of the hunter state.— Costume. — Accoutrements. 4. Social state of the indians. — Manners and customs: Winnebagoes; Dacotahs; Moqui and Navajo tribes of New Mexico. —Hunting the buffalo on the western prairies. 5. Resumé and examination of the manners, customs, rites and religion of the indian tribes, to determine whether they are of foreign origin.—Generic conclusions. — App. **Kern**, E: M. Indian customs of Cal.; **Irvin**, S. M. A scene on the prairies; **Alvord**, B: Manners and customs of the indians of Oregon. **Antiquities:** V. 1. General archæology. — Antique skill in fortification.—Erection of tumuli, or altars of sacrifice.—Evidences of fixed cultivation at an antique period.—The state of arts and miscellaneous fabrics.—Attempts in mining and metallurgy.—Ossuaries.—Archæological evidences of the continent having been visited by a people having letters, prior to the era of Columbus. 2. Floridian teocalli or elevated platform residences of the native rulers and priests.—Antiquities of Lake Erie.—Archæological relics from S. C. and western N. Y. — Aboriginal embankments and excavations at lake Vieux Desert on the boundary of Wis. and Mich. 3. **Schoolcraft**, H. R. Pictographic inscription on the banks of the Hudson; Pottery from minor mounds on the coasts of Fla. and Ga.; Colored earthenware from the Rio Gila, N. M.; Erie inscription of the Kekeewin; Metallic plates exhibited in annual dances among the Muscogees. 4. Sketch of the antiquities of the U. S. —Essay on the Congaree indians of S. C.—New elementary facts in the current discovery of amer. archæology. 5. Considerations of the mound-period of the Miss. valley, and on the general state of indian art prior to the discovery.—Traits and comparison of american antiquities. — App. **Gilliss**, G. M. Peruvian antiquities; **Loughridge**, R. M. Antique Muscogee brass plates; **Locke**, J: Ruins of an ancient fortress in Ohio; **Gibbs**, G: No antiquities in Oregon; **Woods**, J: Antique copper implements from the Miami valley; **Maxwell**, T: Aboriginal antiquities and history of western N. Y. **Physical geography:** V. 1. Geographical memoranda respecting the discovery of the Mississippi river.—Gold deposits of California. — Mineralogical and geographical notices, denoting the value of aboriginal territory.—Existing geological action of the american lakes.—Antique osteology of the monster period. — The Oneida stone. — Minnesota. 2. **Nicollet**, N. J. Natural caves in the Sioux country, on the left bank of the upper Miss. river.—**Whipple**, A. W. Physical data, respecting the southern part of Cal. included in the line of boundary between San Diego and the mouth of the river Gila; with incidental notices of Diegunos and Yuma indian tribes. 3. Indian territories of the U. S.— Series of saline strata in Onondaga county. — **Gibbs**, G: Journal of the expedition of col. Redick M'Kee, U. S. indian agt., through northwestern California, in 1851. 4. Area of the U. S. still possessed by the indian tribes and its ultimate division into states and territories.—Sectional view of the great lake basin, being the ancient seats of the Algonquin and Iroquois power, and their striking position between the Atlantic and Miss. valley tribes.—The sources of the Miss. a suitable position as a refuge for the Chippewas. 5. Present geographical position of the indian tribes of the U. S. **Tribal organization, history and government:** V. 1. Prelim. remarks.—Shoshonee or Snake nation. — **Wyeth**, N. J. Tribes of Oregon, etc. — **Burnet**, D. G. Comanches and other tribes of Texas.—**Bent**, C: Tribes of New Mexico.—**Williamson**, T: S. Dacotas of the Mississippi.—The smallpox a scourge to the aborigines.—Tribes on the Santa Fé trail and at the foot of the Rocky mountains.—History of the Creeks or Muskogees.—Massachusetts indians.— Former indian population of Kentucky.— History of the Menomonies and Chippewas.—Miscothis and Assignuaigs.—Origin and history of the Chickasaws. 2. The Nabni or Comanches of Texas. — Oral traditions resp. the history of the Ojibwa nation.—**Prescott**, P. Contributions to the history, customs and opinions of the Dacota tribes. 3. **Schoolcraft**, H. R. History of the Iroquois republic; Origin of the Mandan tribe, and its stock of affiliation; Migrations of the Iowas; Hochungara family of the Dacotah group; Ancient Eries; History, language and archeology of the Pimos of the river Gila, N. M.; Moqui tribe of New Mexico.—Em-

---

x denotes books specially adapted for children.

Schoolcraft, H: Rowe.—*Continued.*

mons, G. F. Indian tribes of Oregon and Cal.—Prescott, P. Dacotah tribes, *continued*: Sioux or Dacotah proper.—Irvin, S. M., *and* W: Hamilton. History of the Iowa or Sac tribes.—Fletcher, J. E. Winnebagoes.—Carolina ms. respecting the origin of the Catawbas. **4. Schoolcraft,** H. R. Sketch of the ancient Eries, *continued*.—Shea, J: G. Inquiries respecting the lost neutral nations; Brief researches in the missionary authors, respecting the Mascoutins of the french era.—Backus, E. Account of the Navajoes of N. M.—Eaton, J. H. Description of the true state and character of the N. M. tribes.—Johnston, A. Manners, customs and history of the Root-diggers and other Cal. tribes. — Fletcher, J. E. Origin, history, and traits of the Winnebagoes, *continued*. **5.** Tribal influence and general character: Alleghans, Delawares, Chippewas, Oneidas, Ononda-gas, Kenistenos, Athapascas, Blackfeet, Pillagers or Mukkundwas, Michigamies, Utahs, Apachees, California tribes, Pennacooks.—App. Perley, G. H. Indians of New Brunswick; M. Moravians in Dutchess co., N. Y., during the early part of the 18th cent.; Parker, W: B. Indians of s. w. Texas; Mitchell, D. D. Blackfeet Indians; Henry, T. C. Apachees; Origin and history.

Intellectual capacity and character: V. 1. Mythology and oral traditions.—Indian pictography or symbolic writing. **2.** Numeration.—Art of pictography. — Aboriginal alphabetical notation. — Oral imaginative legends. **3.** Oral fictions. — Poetic development of the indian mind. **4.** Indian pictography.— Oral traditions and fictions from the wig-wam.—Indian shrewdness and business talent in public speaking. **5.** The indian mind.

Topical history: V. 2. Mandans.—Pontiac ms.; journal of the events of the siege of Detroit by the confederated indians in 1763.—Anacoana, queen of the Caribs. **3. Madison,** James. Upper posts of Canada in 1778.—Brantz, Lewis. Western America beyond the Alleghanies in 1785; memoranda of a journey.—Perrault, J: Baptiste. Indian life in the n.-w. regions of the U. S. in 1783; voyages and adventures of a merchant voyager. **4. Duane,** W. Diary of Matthew Clarkson, west of the Alleghanies, in 1766.—**Schoolcraft,** H. R. Passages of a tour in the country of the Osages in Miss., Mo. and Ark., traversed by De Soto in 1542.—Wiser, Conrad. Narrative of a journey from Tolpehocken in Pa. to Ouondaga, in 1737.—Franklin, B. Remarks concerning the savages of North Amer.—Tyler, A. Traditions of the Senecas respecting the battle of Oriskany and the massacre of Wyoming; Brant exonerated. **5. Swan,** C. Position and state of manners and arts in the Creek nation, in 1791.

Ethnology: V. 1. Generic views of the mental type of the indian race. **4.** Prelim. remarks to Some considerations on the geographical position occupied by the various stocks of tribes in the present area of the U. S., at the close of the 15th century, and their subsequent migrations.

Physical type: V. 2. Morton, S: G: Physical characteristics.—Phillips, J. S. Admeasurements of crania of the principal groups of indians of the U. S. **3.** Unity of the human race. — Browne, P: A. Examination and description of the hair of the head of the north-amer. indians, and its comparison with that of other varieties of men. **4.** Remarks on the means of obtaining information.—Forrey, S: Considerations of the distinctive characteristics of the amer. aborig. tribes. **5.** The aboriginal features and physiognomy.

Language: V. 1. Vocabularies: Natic or Massachusetts; Shoshonee; Yuma. **2. Schoolcraft,** H. R. Indian languages of the U. S.—Lieber, Francis. Plan of thought of the amer. languages.—Schoolcraft, H. R. Essay on the grammatical structure of the Algonquin lang.—Worcester, S. N. Remarks on the principles of the Cherokee lang.—Vocabularies: Algonquin group: Iroquois group; Miscellaneous. **3.** Classification of the indian languages.—Principles of the indian languages: Analysis of the pronominal and verbal forms; Gibbs, G. Observ. on some of the indian dialects of northern Cal.; New vocabularies of various dialects and languages. **4.** Observ. on the manner of compounding words in the indian lang.—Hurlbut, T: Memoir of the inflections of the Chippewa tongue.—Remarks on the Iowa lang.—Johnson, Adam. Languages of California; with vocabularies. **5.** Chippewa language: Conjugation. —App. Lane, W: C. Letter on the affinities of dialects in

Schoolcraft, H: Rowe.—*Continued.*

N. M.; Kidder, F: Examples of Passamaquoddy lang.; Rand, S. T. Milicite numerals.

State of indian art: V. 1. Ancient art. **2.** Modern art: Existing handicraft skill. **3.** *Same:* Handicraft skill in arts of first necessity. **4.** *Same:* Earthenware of the pueblo indians of N. M.; Domestic handicraft of Moqui and Navajo tribes; Making blankets: Spinning and weaving of the Navajoes.—Antique indian art: Its generic type of architecture; Arts at the era of the discovery of Amer. **5.** Synoptical sketch of indian art.—App. Swan, C. Arts and mfrs. of Creek indians in 1791.—S. Embalming by the Oregon indians.

Religion and mythology: V. 1. Medaism or indian priestcraft. **4. Schoolcraft,** H. R. Aboriginal idea of religion.—Pond, G. H. Power and influence of Dacota medicine-men. **5.** The indian elysium.—The mythology of the Vesperic tribes, and its influences on their social state.

Dæmonology, magic and witchcraft: V. 1. Exhibition of magic in indian life. **3. Schoolcraft,** H. R. Introd. remarks: Magical dances of the Ontonagons; Invulnerability and invisibility from magic influences; Genii worship. — Eastman, S. Gods of the Dacotahs; The giant's feast and dance.—Magical pictographs from Utah. **4. Schoolcraft,** H. R. Evidences of the unity of belief in the necromancy and demon worship of the ancient pop. of Asia and the present indian tribes in North Amer.—Eastman, S. Demoniacal observances of the tribes of the Dacotahs, upper Mississippi. **5.** Remarks on the practice of sorcery and medical magic by the indian priesthood.

Medical knowledge: V. 1. Remarks on the medical and surgical knowledge of the Dacotahs. **3.** Practice of medicine among the Winnebagoes. **4.** Prelim. remarks on the indian notions of anatomy and medicine.—Pitcher, Z. Medicine, or Some account of the remedies used by the amer. indians in the cure of diseases, and treatment of injuries to which they are liable, and their methods of administering and applying them. **5.** The indian as a physician.

Condition and prospects: V. 1. Tables of inquiries. **2. Schoolcraft,** H. R. Importance of the pastoral state on races of men.—Johnston, J: Means of melioration.—Lowry, D. Moral questions relative to practical plans for educating and civilizing the aborig. — Angel, W. P. Present geogr. position, number and means of the Iroquois. **3.** Lowry, D. Education, christianity and the arts. **4. Schoolcraft,** H. R. Plan of colonization, and present condition of the tribes; Discouragements to education arising from hunter habits; Necessity of a government of some fixed form. **5.** Summary sketch of the policy of the U. S. respecting the indians.—App. Hartley, A. J. Pleasing prospects of the Chickasaws; Henry, T. C. Hopeless prospects of the Apachees; Riggs, R. Education among the Dakotahs; Native churches.

Statistics and population: V. 1. General remarks.—Census returns of the indian tribes of the U. S., with their vital and industrial statistics. — Tables of the tribes within the newly acquired states and territories. **2.** Period of 1850.—Period of 1820.—Lands purchased from the indians. **3.** Comparison of the number of fighting men in the northern and western tribes in the U. S. and Canada, as estimated at various periods from 1736 to 1812.—Boquet, Col. Indians in the english colonies in 1764.—Madison, J. Indian force on the breaking out of the amer. rev. in 1778.—Pike, Z. M. Indian pop. of the upper Miss. in 1806.—Lewis *and* Clark. Indian pop. of the Columbia valley in 1806.—Monroe, James. Plan of indian colonization west of the Miss. in 1825; with a statement of the different tribes then within the U. S. and land claimed by them.—Porter, P: B. Names and situations of indian tribes in 1829.—Position and pop. of the indian tribes on lakes Huron and Superior and the upper Miss. in 1832.—Cass, Lewis. Tribes west of the Miss. under treaty stipulations, and also those with whom the U. S. have no relations. — Official estimates of the indian pop. of the U. S. in 1836.—Sioux pop. in 1836.—Indian pop. of Mich. in 1840.—Census and statistics in 1846.—Estimate of the indian pop. of the Missouri valley in 1850.—Dart, Anson. Indian pop. of western Oregon in 1851.—Calhoun, J. S. Pop. of the pueblos of N. M.—M'Kee, R. Indian pop. of n.-w. Cal.—Stem, Jesse. Indian pop. of Texas in 1851. **4.** Miscel. statistics as to expenditures for the indians, and the census of different tribes at

Schoolcraft, H: Rowe.—*Continued.*
various periods; incl. Population of the Iroquois confederacy, from 1778 to 1852. **5.** Synopsis of statistics; progress of the census, and means recommended for its completion.—App. Statistics of indians in Oreg., W. T., etc.
Biography: **V. 4.** Logan, Cayuga. **5.** Skenandoah, Oneida.—Occum, Mahican.—Adario, Wyandot. — Waub Ojeeg, Chippewa. — Peshkewah, Miami. — Waubunsce, Pottawattamie.
Literature of the indian languages, by H. R. Schoolcraft. V. 3. Plan of a system of geographical names for the U. S., derived from the aborig. lang.—Indian nomenclature; a critical dictionary of indian names in the history, geography and mythology of the U. S.: Letter A. **4.** Bibliographical catalogue of books, translations of the scriptures and other publications into the indian tongues of the U. S.—Indian nomenclature: Letter B. **5.** List of anglo-indian words incorporated into the eng. lang.—Philosophy of utterance.—Comparisons of the lang. of the ancient Pampticos and Waccoas of N. Carolina with the Algonquin and Catawba.—Original words of indian songs, literally transl.—A lexicon of of the Algonquin lang.: Pt. 1, Chippewa, letter A.— Indian nomenclature: Letter C. — Vocabularies of the Apachee and the Micmac.—The Lord's prayer in several Algonquin dialects. — Indian etymology. — Some data resp. the principles of the Chippewa and Mahican lang., in a series of letters, written 1822-1827. —Names based on the indian vocabularies, suggested for new subdivisions of the public domain—App. **Bonneville,** B. L. E. Etymology of the word Oregon; **Marcy,** R. B. Specimens of the Caddo and Witchita lang.; **S.** Indian numerals.

— *Same.* Pt. 6: History of the indian tribes of the U. S.; their present condition and prospects, and a sketch of their ancient status. Pub. by order of congress, under the dir. of the dep. of the interior, Indian bureau. Ill. Phila. 1857. Q.   **970.1 : R3 v6**
Contents. V. **6.** Pref.—A condensed view of the post-columbian or modern indian history: Introd. considerations; First european acquaintance with the indian tribes; Contention of France and Spain for the occupation of Florida; The english element of civilization in Amer.; The littoral tribes of the north Atlantic, within whose terr. the colonies were planted; Synopsis of the history of the N. E. tribes; Indian tribes of Md.; Occupancy of N. Y. by the english, and sequel to the indian wars of N. E.; Lenno Lenapi of Pa., and Chicora tribes of the Carolinas; Progressive intercourse with the tribes during 1700 - 1750; Momentous period of indian history, preceding the conquest of Canada; From the conquest of Canada to the commencement of the amer. revolution; History of the indian tribes during the amer. revolution; Events from the definitive treaty of peace in 1783 to the close of Washington's administration; Perturbed state of the tribes and their political relations during the growth and expansion of the Union westward, 1800 - 1825; Effects of the expansion of the population westward and of the creation of new states out of the exhausted indian huntinggrounds of the Mississippi valley; The political culmination of the indian history; The first decade of the colonization plan, 1831 - 1841; Hostile attitude of the southern tribes, previous to their final removal; Consummation of the gov. policy of removal; Principles contended for by the indians during three centuries; Present condition and prospects of the tribes.—Economy and statistics, capacity of industrial and social development and national position, ill. by some notices of the mental character of the hunter race and their ancient status and archæology: Causes of decline of the indian tribes: Indicia from their ancient status and archæol., from manners and customs, from mythology and religion, from language; Statistics, tribal and general. — Index to v. 6.

Drake, S: Gardner. The aboriginal races of America; comprising biographical sketches of eminent individuals, and an historical account of the different tribes, from the first discovery of the continent to the present period, with a dissertation on their origin, antiquities, manners and customs, illustrative narratives and index. 15th ed.,

rev. with add. by J. W. O'Neill. Phila. 1859. O.   **970.1+6**
Catlin, G: Illustrations of the manners, customs and condition of the north american indians ; with letters and notes, written during eight years of travel and adventure among the wildest and most remarkable tribes now existing. Ill. Lond. 1876. 2 v. Q.
    970.1+2
— *Same.* 8th ed.; v. 2. Lond. 1851. O. **970.1 : 2**
— Life among the indians. Lond. *n. d.* S.
    970.1 : 15
— Last rambles among the indians of the Rocky mountains and the Andes. Ill. Lond. *n. d.* S.   **970.1 : 14**
Drake, Francis S:, *ed.* The indian tribes of the U. S.; their history, antiquities, customs, religion, arts, language, traditions, oral legends and myths. Phila. 1884. 2 v. Q.
    970.1 : R18
Note. A compilation of that part of Schoolcraft's work which is of general interest, with add. to the present time.
Contents. V. 1. Introd.—Origin, traditions, physical and mental type.—Language, literature and pictography. — Indian art, industry and medical knowledge.—Antiquities. — Religion and magic. — Manners and customs. — The tribes; ethnological distribution, organization, government. 2. European discovery and exploration.—Early european settlements.—War of races; early colonial history.—France and England contend for the possession of the Ohio valley. — The amer. revolution.—Post-revolutionary. — Removal of the tribes west of the Mississippi. — Indian affairs since the acquisition of New Mexico and California.

Smithsonian institution. *Bureau of ethnology.* 1st—3d annual reports to the secretary of the Smithsonian institution, by J. W. Powell ; 1879-82. Wash. 1881-84. 3 v. Q.
    970.1 : D
Contents. V. 1. **Powell,** J. W. Report of the director; On the evolution of language ; Sketch of the mythology of the north amer. indians; Wyandot government; On limitations to the use of anthropologic data. — **Yarrow,** H. C. A further contribution to the study of the mortuary customs of north amer. indians. — **Holden,** E: S. Studies in central amer. picture writing.—**Royce,** C. C. Cessions of land by indian tribes to the U. S. — **Mallory,** G. Sign language among north amer. indians. — **Pilling,** J. C. Catalogue of linguistic mss. in the library of the Bureau of ethnology.—Illustration of the method of recording indian languages, from the mss. of J. O. Dorsey, A. S. Gatschet and S. R. Riggs.
2. **Powell,** J. W. Report of the director.—**Cushing,** F. H. Zuñi fetiches. — **Smith,** E. A. Myths of the Iroquois.—**Henshaw,** H: W. Animal carvings from the mounds of the Mississippi valley. — **Matthews,** W. Navajo silversmiths. — **Holmes,** W: H. Art in shell of the ancient americans. — **Stevenson,** J. Ill. catalogue of the collections obtained from the indians of New Mexico and Arizona in 1879, 1880.
3. **Powell,** J. W. Report of the director. — **Thomas,** C. Notes on certain Maya and mexican mss. —**Dall,** W. H. On masks, labrets and certain aboriginal customs.— **Dorsey,** J. O. Omaha sociology.— **Matthews,** W. Navajo weavers. — **Holmes,** W. H. Prehistoric textile fabrics of the U. S., derived from impressions of pottery; Ill. catalogue of a portion of the collections made during the field season of 1881.— **Stevenson,** J. Ill. catalogue of the collections obtained from the pueblos of New Mexico and Arizona in 1881.

— — [Unclassified publications]. Wash. 1880. 3 v. Q.   **970.1 : D**
Contents. 1. **Powell,** J. W. Introd. to the study of indian languages, with words and phrases to be collected. 2d ed. with charts. — **2. Yarrow,** H. C. Introd. to the study of mortuary customs among the north amer. indians. 3. **Mallory,** G. Introd. to the study of sign language among the north amer. indians as ill. the gesture speech of mankind.

Abbott, C: Conrad. Primitive industry, or Illustrations of the handiwork in stone, bone

and clay, of the native races of the northern Atlantic seaboard of America. Salem. Mass. 1881. O.   **970.1+5**
Schoolcraft, H: Rowe. Notes on the Iroquois, or Contributions to american history, antiquities and general ethnology. Albany. 1847. O.   **970.1+21**
Morgan, Lewis H: League of the Ho-de'-no-saunee, or Iroquois. Rochester. 1851. O.
                                         970.1+P7
Wilson, Daniel. The Huron-Iroquois of Canada; a typical race of american aborigines. *In* Transactions of the Royal soc. of Canada, v. 2.   **61 : R**
Vetromile, Eugene. The Abnakis and their history, or Historical notices on the aborigines of Acadia. N. Y. 1866. D.   **970.1 : 10**
Copway, G:, Kah-ge-gah-bowh, *chief of the Ojibway nation.* The traditional history of the Ojibway nation. Ill. Bost. 1851. D.
                                         970.1 : 17
Lapham, Increase Allen, Levi Blossom *and* **G:** G. Dousman, a committee of the Old settlers' club of Milwaukee county. A paper on the number, locality and times of removal of the indians of Wisconsin ; with an app. containing a complete chronology of Wis., from the earliest times down to the adoption of the state constitution in 1848. Milw. 1870. O.   **970.1 : Pam**
Domenech, Emmanuel *abbé.* Seven years' residence in the great deserts of North America. Ill. and maps. Lond. 1860. 2 v. O.
                                         970.1 : 22
Contents. V. 1. Ancient emigrations.—American origins.— Descriptions.— Antiquities. 2. Origin of the americans.— Character of the indians.—Indian languages.—Festivals and industry.—Customs of the indians.—Indian religions.
Dodge, R: Irving. Our wild indians ; 33 years' personal experience among the red men of the great west, a popular account of their social life, religion, habits, traits, customs, exploits, etc., with thrilling adventures and experiences on the great plains and in the mountains of our wide frontier ; with an introd. by gen. Sherman. Ill. Hartford. 1882. O.   **970.1 : 11**
Jackson, W. H. Descriptive catalogue of the photographs of the U. S. geol. survey of the territories from 1869 to 1875 incl. 2d ed. Ill. (U. S. geol. survey of the terr., Hayden; Miscel. pub., no. 5). Wash. 1875. O.
                                         in **557.5 : D**
— Descriptive catalogue of photographs of north american indians. (U. S. geol. survey of the terr., Hayden; Miscel. pub., no. 9). Wash. 1877. O.   *in* **557.5 : D**
Whipple, A. W., T:Ewbank *and* **W: W. Turner.** The indian tribes near the 35th parallel of north lat., from the Mississippi river to the Pacific ocean ; with vocabularies of north american languages. *In* Report of the U. S. Pacific r. r. surveys, v. 3.   *in* **625 : D**
Putnam, F: W., *and others.* Reports upon archæological and ethnological collections from vicinity of Santa Barbara, California and from ruined pueblos of Arizona and New Mexico and certain interior tribes ; app. of indian vocabularies, rev. and prepared by Albert S. Gatschet. In 2 pts. with two app. Ill. (U. S. geogr. surveys west of the 100th meridian, Wheeler ; [Final] reports, v. 7).   *in* **557.5 : D**

Holmes, W. H., *and others.* Ancient ruins in Colorado, Arizona and Utah. *In* U. S. geol. survey of the terr., Hayden ; Bulletin, v. 2.   *in* **557.5 : D**
Matthews, Washington. Ethnography and philology of the Hidatsa indians. (U. S. geol. survey of the terr., Hayden ; Miscel. pub., no. 7). Wash. 1877. O.   *in* **557.5 : D**
United States. *Geological and geographical survey of the Rocky mountain region,* J : W. Powell, *geologist in charge.* Contributions to north american ethnology ; v. 1, 3–5. Ill. Wash. 1877–82. 4 v. O.   **970.1 : D**
Contents. V. 1. **Dall, W:** Healy. On the distribution and nomenclature of the native tribes of Alaska and the adjacent territory, with a map: On succession in the shell-heaps of the Aleutian islands; Remarks on the origin of the Innuit; App. Linguistics. **Gibbs, G:** Tribes of western Washington and northwestern Oregon, with map; App. Linguistics. 3. **Powers,** Stephen. Tribes of California. 4. **Morgan,** Lewis H. Houses and house-life of the american aborigines. 5. **Rau, C:** Observations on cup-shaped and other lapidarian sculpture in the old world and in America. — **Fletcher,** Robert. On prehistoric trephining and cranial amulets. — **Thomas,** Cyrus. A study of the manuscript Troano; with an introd. by D. G. Brinton.
Bancroft, Hubert Howe. The native races of the Pacific states of North America. N. Y. 1875. 5 v. O.   **970.1+1**
Contents. V. I. Wild tribes. 2. Civilized nations. 3. Myths and languages. 4. Antiquities. 5. Primitive history.
Swan, James G. The Haidah indians of Queen Charlotte's Island. *In* Smithsonian contributions.   **506 : R3 v21**
— Indians at Cape Flattery, Washington Territory. *In the same.*   **506 : R3 v16**
Brinton, Daniel Garrison. Brinton's library of aboriginal american literature, no. 1–6. Phila. 1882–85. 6 v. O.   **970+11**
Contents. No. 1. The Maya chronicle. 2. The Iroquois book of rites, ed. by Horatio Hale. 3. The Güegüence; a comedy ballet in the Nahuatal-spanish dialect of Nicaragua. 4. A migration legend of the Creek indians; with a linguistic, historic and ethnographic introd. by Alfred S. Gatschet, v. 1. 5. The Lenápé and their legends; with the complete text and symbols of the Walam Olum, a new tr. and an inquiry into its authenticity by D. G. Brinton. 6. The annals of the Cakchiquels; the original text with a tr., note and introd. by D. G. Brinton.
See also in the Index to biography Philip—Pocahontas—Sa-go-ye-wat-ha—Tecumseh—Thayandenega—Uncas—Weathersford.

3. Description.

Hayden, Ferdinand Vandeveer, *and* **Alfred R. C. Selwyn,** *eds.* North America. (Stanford's compendium of geography and travel, based on Hellwald's "Die erde und ihre völker.") Maps and ill. Lond. 1883. O.   **917 : 15**
Fetridge, W: Pembroke, *ed.* Harper's handbook for travellers in . . . United States and Canada. N. Y. 1883.   *in* **914 : 98 v3**
Sears, E: S. Faxon's illustrated handbook of travel to Saratoga, Lakes George and Champlain, the Adirondacks, Niagara falls, Montreal, Quebec, the Saguenay river, the White mountains, Lakes Memphremagog and Winnepiseogee. [*Anon.*] Rev. ed., 1874. Bost. *n. d.* S.   **917 : 17**
Kingston, W: H: G. The western world ; picturesque sketches of nature and natural history in northern and central America. N. Y. 1884. D.   **917 : 17**

Eden, R:, *tr.* The first three english books on America [?1511]—1555 a. d.; being chiefly translations, compilations, etc., from the writings, maps, etc., of Pietro Martire of Anghiera (1455—1526), Sebastian Münster, the cosmographer (1489—1552), Sebastian Cabot of Bristol (1474—1557), with extracts, etc., from the works of other spanish, italian and german writers of the time, ed. by E: Archer. Birmingham. 1885. O.
917+19

Carver, Jonathan. Three years' travels [1766—1769] through the interior parts of North America, for more than 5,000 miles; containing an account of the great lakes and all the lakes, islands and rivers, cataracts, mountains, minerals, soil and vegetable productions of the northwest region of that vast continent, with a description of the birds, beasts, reptiles, insects and fishes peculiar to the country, together with a history of the genius, manners and customs of the indians inhabiting the lands that lie adjacent to the heads and to the westward of the great river Mississippi, and an app. describing the uncultivated parts of America that are most proper for forming settlements. Phila. 1796. O.
917:2

— *Same.* Travels in Wisconsin; [added, some account of the author and an index]. From the 3d Lond. ed.   N. Y. 1838. O.   **917:2**

Chateaubriand, René François A: de. Voyage en Amerique, [1791—92]. *With his* Atala.
C 1051

Coke, E: T: A subaltern's furlough; descriptive of scenes in various parts of the U. S., Upper and Lower Canada. New Brunswick and Nova Scotia, in the summer and autumn of 1832.   N. Y. 1833. 2 v. D.
917.1:13

Montgomery, Cora. Eagle Pass, or Life on the border.   N. Y. 1852. D.   *With* **Osborn,** Sherard. Stray leaves from an arctic journal.   **919.8:29**

Lanman, C: Haw-ho-noo, or Records of a tourist.   Phila. 1850. D.   **917:4**

Bartlett, J: Russell. Personal narrative of explorations and incidents in Texas, New Mexico, California, Sonora and Chihuahua, connected with the U. S. and Mexican

boundary commission, during 1850—1853. Map and ill.   N. Y. 1854. 2 v. O.   **917:1**

Murray, *The hon.* Amelia Matilda. Letters from the U. S., Cuba and Canada.   N. Y. 1856. 2 v. in 1. D.   **917.1:27**

Mowry, Sylvester. Arizona and Sonora; the geography, history and resources of the silver region of North America. 3d ed. rev. and enl.   N. Y. 1864. D.   **917:5**

Ellet, Elizabeth Fries, *born* Lummis. Rambles about the country.   N. Y. 1868. S.
x 917:12

Price, *Sir* Rose Lambart. The two Americas.
in **918:6**

Rae, W: Fraser. Westward by rail; a journey to San Francisco and back, and a visit to the mormons. 2d ed., with a new introd. chapter.   Lond. 1871. O.   **917:7**

— Columbia and Canada; notes on the great republic and the new dominion. A supp. to Westward by rail.   Lond. 1877. O.   **917:8**

Biart, Lucien. My rambles in the new world, [from Labrador to Mexico]. Tr. by Mary de Hauteville.   Lond. 1877. O.   **917:13**

Hardy, Mary, *born* McDowell, *lady* T: Duffus. Through cities and prairie lands; sketch of an american tour.   N. Y. 1881. O.
917:6

Hatton, Joseph. To-day in America; studies for the old world and the new.   Lond. 1881. 2 v. O.   **917:16**

— *Same.*   N. Y. 1881. Q.   **917+16**

Russell, W: Howard. Hesperothen; notes from the west; a record of a ramble in the U. S. and Canada in the spring and summer of 1881.   N. Y. 1882. Q.   **917:9**

Barneby, W: H: Life and labour in the far, far west; notes of a tour in the western states, British Columbia, Manitoba and the Northwest Territory. Map.   Lond. 1884. O.
917:18

United States. *Dept. of state.* Reports upon the survey of the boundary between the territory of the U. S. and the possessions of Great Britain from the Lake of the Woods to the summit of the Rocky mountains, authorized by an act of congress approved march 19, 1872. Archibald **Campbell,** comr., W. J. **Twining,** chief astronomer.   Wash. 1878. Q.   **917:D**

x denotes books specially adapted for children.

24.   North America — b, United States, In general.

1. General history.

(See also History of politics, col. 164—168; Slavery, col. 169-170; Constitutional history, col. 210—212.)

Lossing, Benson J: Harper's popular cyclopædia of the U. S. history, from the aboriginal period to 1876; containing brief sketches of important events and conspicuous actors. Ill.   N. Y. 1881. 2 v. O.   **971:R1**

Bryant, W: Cullen. *and* Sidney Howard **Gay.** A popular history of the U. S., from the first discovery of the western hemisphere by the northmen, to the end of the first century of the union of the states; preceded by a sketch of the pre-historic period and

the age of the mound builders.   N. Y. 1876—81. 4 v. Q.   **971+P3**

Contents. V. **1.** Pref. — Pre-historic man. — The mound-builders. — The northmen in America. — Pre-Columbian voyages westward.—Discovery and colonization to abt. 1636.—Index. **2.** English, dutch, french and spanish colonies to the latter part of the 17th century.—Index. **3.** The colonies, and the revolution to 1779.—Index. **4.** The United States, 1779—1865.—Index, v. 1-4.

Bonner, J: A child's history of the U. S.   N. Y. 1866-76. 3 v. S.   **x 971:31**

Butterworth, Hezekiah, *ed.* Young folks' history of America. Ill.   Bost. 1881. D.
x 971:5

x denotes books specially adapted for children.

Doyle, J: Andrew. History of the U. S.; with maps, illustrative of the acquisition of territory and the increase of population, by Francis A. Walker. [Freeman's historical course]. N. Y. [1876]. S.   971 : 4

Gilman, Arthur. A history of the american people. Bost. [1883]. O.   971 : 37

Goodrich, S: Griswold. A pictorial history of the U. S., with notices of other portions of America, North and South. Phila. 1864. D.   971 : 27

Higginson, T: Wentworth. Young folks' history of the U. S. Ill. Bost. 1882. S.   x 971 : 28

— Same. Bost. 1884. S.   x 971 : 28

Johnston, Alexander. History of amer. politics. [Handbooks for students and general readers]. N. Y. 1879. S.   324.1 : 22

— A history of the U. S. for schools ; with an introd. history of the discovery and english colonization of North America. Maps, plans, ill. and questions. N. Y. 1885. D.   x 971 : 50

Lossing, Benson, J: A history of the U. S., for families and libraries. Ill. Hartford. 1874. Q.   971+45

— Centennial history of the U. S., from the discovery of the amer. continent to the end of the first century of the republic. Balt. 1875. O.   971 : 16

Monroe, Mrs. Lewis B. The story of our country. Bost. 1881. D.   x 971 : 30

S., J. D. A brief history of the U. S. (Barnes' historical ser.) N. Y. 1885. O.   971 : 48

Scudder, Horace Elisha. A history of the U. S. of America ; preceded by a narrative of the discovery and settlement of North America and of the events. which led to the independence of the thirteen english colonies, for the use of schools and academies. Maps and ill. Phila. [1885]. D.   x 971 : 51

Spencer, Jesse Ames. A complete history of the U. S. of America ; continued by Benson J: Lossing. Ill. Phila. [1878]. 4 v. in 2. Q.   971+17
Contents. V. 1. 1492—1778. 2. 1778—1801. 3. 1801—1861. 4. 1861—1876.—Index.

— Geschichte der Vereinigten Staaten, von den frühesten zeiten bis zur administration von James Buchanan. [Uebers. von F: Kapp.] N. Y. 1858. 3 v. Q.   971+18
Contents. V. 1. 1492—1778. 2. 1778—1801. 3. 1801—1857.

Thousand questions on american history, A; an outline of the history of the U. S. in the form of questions and answers. Syracuse. 1884. S.   971 : 44

Including several periods.

Force, P:, ed. American archives; consisting of a collection of authentick records, state papers, debates and letters and other notices of publick affairs, the whole forming a documentary history of the origin and progress of the north american colonies, of the causes and accomplishment of the american revolution and of the constitution of government for the U. S., to the final ratification thereof ; in 6 series. 4th ser. v. 1-6 ; 5th ser. v. 1-3. Wash. 1837-53. 9 v. F.   971 : D
Contents. 4th ser. Documentary history of the

x denotes books specially adapted for children.

85

english colonies in North Amer. from the king's message to parliament of march 7, 1774 to the declaration of independence by the U. S.; v. 1-6. **5th ser.** Documentary history of the U. S. of Amer. from the declaration of independence. july 4, 1776, to the definitive treaty of peace with Great Britain, sept. 3, 1783 ; v. 1-3 [to the end of 1776].
Note. This is all that has been published so far, although the whole coll. was bought by the U. S. government for the purpose of publication.

Smith, J: Jay, and J: F. **Watson,** eds. American historical and literary curiosities ; consisting of fac-similes of original documents, relating to the events of the revolution, etc., with a variety of reliques, antiquities and modern autographs. 4th ed. with add. N. Y. 1852. Q.   971 : R46

Bancroft, G: History of the U. S., from the discovery of the american continent. 13th ed. Bost. 1846-74. 10 v. O.   971+2
Contents. V. 1. History of the colonization of the U. S., 1492—1660. 2. Same, 1660—1688. 3. Same, 1688—1748. — Index, v. 1-3. 4. The amer. revolution, 1st epoch: The overthrow of the european colonial system, 1748—1763. 5. Same, 2d epoch: How Great Britain estranged Amer., 1763 — 1766. 6. Same, continued, 1766—1774. 7. Same, 3d epoch: Amer. declares itself independent, 1774 — june 17, 1775. 8. Same, continued, june 18, 1775—july 4, 1776. 9. Same, 4th epoch: The independence of America is acknowledged, july 1776-1778. 10. Same, continued, 1778-1782.

— History of the formation of the constitution of the U. S. of America. N. Y. 1882. 2 v. O.   342.1+21
Contents. V. 1. Book 1, The confederation, 1683-1783.—Book 2, On the way to a federal convention, 1783 - 1787. App. Letters and papers. 2. Book 3, The federal convention, 1787.—Book 4, The people of the states in judgment on the constitution, 1787-1788.—Book 5, The federal government, june 1787.—App. Letters and papers.

— History of the U. S. of America, from the discovery of the continent. Author's last rev. N. Y. 1883, 1884. 6 v. O.   971 : 36
Contents. V. 1, 1492-1688. The english people found a nation in America.—The colonies obtain geographical unity. 2, 1688—1763. The colonization of the west and of Georgia. — The american revolution in five epochs: 1st epoch, Britain overthrows the european colonial system. 3. 2d epoch, Britain estranges America, 1763-1776. 4. 3d epoch, America takes up arms for self-defence and arrives at independence, 1774-1776. 5. America in alliance with France.—The people of America take their equal station among the powers of the earth, july 1776—nov. 1783. 6. The formation of the amer. constitution: The confederation, with retrospect. 1643-1783; On the way to a federal convention, 1783-1787; The federal convention, with retrospect on the constitution, sept. 18, 1787—june 25, 1788; The federal government, june 1787—may 5, 1789.—Index, v. 1-6.

Hildreth, R: The history of the U. S. of America, [1st ser.] from the discovery of the continent to the organization of government under the federal constitution. N. Y. 1849. 3 v. O.   971+13
Contents. V. 1. Discovery and settlement, 1492—abt. 1688. 2. Progress of settlement and colonial wars, abt. 1650-1773. 3. Revolutionary epoch, 1773—1789.—Authorities.—Index.

— Same. [2d ser.], from the adoption of the federal constitution to the end of the 16th congress. N. Y. 1852. 3 v. O.   971+14
Contents. V. 1. Administration of Washington, 1789-1797. 2. John Adams and Jefferson, 1797-1807. 3. Madison and Monroe, 1807-1821. — Authorities. — Index.

Hale, Salma. History of the U. S. from their first settlement as colonies, to the close of the administration of mr. Monroe in 1817. [Harper's family lib.] N. Y. 1840. 2 v. S.   971 : 11
Contents. V. 1. To 1776. 2. 1776 - 1817.—App.

M'Conkey, Rebecca. True stories of the american fathers [to 1783], for the girls and boys all over the land. Ill. Lond. [1874]. D.   **x 971 : 32**

Frothingham, R: The rise of the republic of the U. S., [1643—1790]. 2d ed. Bost. 1873. O.   **324.1 : 59**

Philippi, K: Ferdinand. Geschichte der Vereinigten Freistaaten von Nordamerika. 2te verb. aufl. (Allg. historische taschenbibliothek, 4ter th.) Dresden. 1827. 3 v. in 1. S.   **971 : 42**

Hinton, J: Howard. The history and topography of the U. S. of North America, from the earliest period to the present time; comprising political and biographical history, geography, geology, mineralogy, zoology and botany, agriculture, manufacture and commerce, laws, manners, customs and religion, with a topographical description of the cities, towns, sea-ports, public edifices, canals, etc.; ed. by J: Howard Hinton, assisted by several literary gentlemen in England and America. New ed. with add. and corr. by S: L. Knapp. Ill. Bost. 1834. 2 v. in 1. Q.   **971+24**

Higginson, T: Wentworth. A larger history of the U. S. of America to the close of president Jackson's administration. Maps, plans, portr. and ill. N. Y. 1886 [1885]. O.   **971+49**

Tucker, G: The history of the U. S. from their colonization to the end of the 26th congress, in 1841, in 4 v.: v. 1 [to 1797]. Phila. 1856. O.   **971 : 21**

Willard, Emma. History of the U. S., or Republic of America [to 1826]; designed for schools and private libraries. 5th ed., rev. N. Y. 1837. O.   **971+23**
— Same ; continued to the close of the mexican war. N. Y. 1849. O.   **971 : 47**
— Last leaves of american history ; comprising a separate history of California. N. Y. 1853. D.   **971 : 22**
Contents. Pt. 1. General U. S. history, 1841 – 1848.— Pt. 2. History of California, 1534 - 1849.—Pt. 3. General U. S. history, 1847 - 1853.

Howitt, Mary. A popular history of the U. S. of America, from the discovery of the amer. continent to the present time. Ill. N. Y. 1860. 2 v. D.   **971 : 29**

Neumann, K: F: Geschichte der Vereinigten Staaten von Amerika. Berlin. 1863–65. 3 v. O.   **971 : 41**
Contents. V. 1. Die gründung der kolonien bis zur präsidentschaft des T: Jefferson. 2. Von der ersten präsidentschaft des T: Jefferson bis zum ende der zweiten präsidentschaft des Andrew Jackson. 3. Von der präsidentschaft des Martin Van Buren bis zur inauguration des Abraham Lincoln.

Hamilton, J: Church. History of the republic of the U. S. of America, as traced in the writings of Alexander Hamilton and his contemporaries. 2d ed. Phila. 1864, 1865. 7 v. O.   **971+12**
Contents. V. 1. Introd.—1774 – 1779. 2. 1780 – 1783. 3. 1783 – 1789. 4. 1789 – 1792. 5. 1792 – 1794. 6. 1794 – 1797. 7. 1797 – 1804.—Index.

McMaster, J: Bach. A history of the people of the U. S., from the revolution to the civil war, in 5 v.; v. 1, 2. N. Y. 1883, 1885. 2 v. O.   **971 : 6**
Contents. V. 1. 1784 - 1790.—Index. 2. 1790 - 1803.—Index.

Coffin, C: Carleton. Building the nation ; events in the history of the U. S. from the revolution to the beginning of the war between the states. N. Y. 1883 [1882]. O.   **x 971 : 33**

Schouler, James. History of the U. S. of America under the constitution. Wash. 1880— 1885. 3 v. D.   **971 : 26**
Contents. V. 1. 1783-1801. 2. 1801-1817. 3. 1817-1831.

First century of the republic, The ; a review of american progress. N. Y. 1876. O.   **971+9**
Contents. Lawrence, E. Introd.; Colonial progress. — Knight, E: H. Mechanical progress.— Wells, D: A. Progress in manufacture. — Brewer, W: H. Agricultural progress.—Hunt, T. S. The development of our mineral resources.—Atkinson, E: Commercial development. — Walker, F. A. Growth and distribution of population.—Sumner, W: G. Monetary development. — Woolsey, T. D. The experiment of the union, with its preparations. —Lawrence, E. Educational progress.—Barnard, F: A: P. Scientific progress; The exact sciences.— Gill, T. Scientific progress; Natural science.—Whipple, E. P. A century of american literature.— Conant, S. S. Progress of the fine arts.—Flint, A. Medical and sanitary progress. — Abbott, B: V. American jurisprudence.—Brace, C: L. Humanitarian progress.—Hurst, J: F. Religious development.

Wilson, H: History of the rise and fall of the slave power in America. Bost. 1875-77. 3 v. O.   **326+26**
Contents. V. 1. 4th ed. To 1845. 2. 2d ed. 1845-1860. 3. 1860-1875.

The army and the navy.

(See also col. 233—234.)

Cooper, James Fenimore. The history of the navy of the U. S. of America. Paris. 1839. 2 v. O.   **971 : 38**
Contents. V. 1. To 1802. 2. 1803 - 1815.
— Same. T. p. w. O.   **971 : 38**

Peterson, C: J. The american navy ; being an authentic history of the U. S. navy and biogr. sketches of amer. naval heroes, from the formation of the navy to the close of the mexican war. Ill. Phila. 1859. O.   **971 : 25**

Lossing, Benson J: The story of the U. S. navy, for boys. Ill. N. Y. 1881. D.   **x 971 : 7**

Aldrich, Moses Almy. History of the U. S. marine corps, [1775—1875]. From official reports and other documents, compiled by capt. R: S. Collum. Bost. 1875. O.   **971+8**
Note. For the history of the flag of the U. S., see Heraldry, cl. 929.

Special nationalities.

McGee, T: D'Arcy. A history of the irish settlers in North America, from the earliest period to the census of 1850. 6th ed. Bost. 1855. D.   **971 : 19**
— The catholic history of North America, five discourses ; added, two discourses on the relations of Ireland and America. Bost. 1855. D.   **971 : 20**

Seidensticker, Oswald. Die erste deutsche einwanderung in Amerika und die gründung von Germantown im jahre 1683 ; festschrift zum deutsch - amerikanischen pionier-jubiläum am 6 oct. 1883. Phila. 1883. O.   **971+35**
— Same. In his Bilder aus der deutsch-pennsylv. geschichte.   **973.3 : 6**

x denotes books specially adapted for children.

Körner, Gustav. Das deutsche element in den Vereinigten Staaten von Nordamerika, 1818—1848. Cinc. 1880. O.   **917.1 : 8**

Rosengarten, J. G. The german soldier in the wars of the U. S.; an address read before the Pionier-verein at the hall of the German society. Repr. from the United service magazine. Phila. 1886. O.   **971+52**

Eickhoff, Anton, *ed.* In der neuen heimath ; geschichtliche mittheilungen über die deutschen einwanderer in allen theilen der Union. N. Y. 1884. O.   **971+43**

Anhang; Die Deutsche gesellschaft der stadt New York, 1784 - 1883.

2. Colonial period.

(See also New France, col. 1332; and New England, cl. 972.)

Graham, James. The history of the U. S. of North America, from the plantation of the british colonies till their assumption of national independence. 2d ed., enl. and amended. Phila. 1856. 2 v. O.   **971.1+2**

Higginson, T: Wentworth. A book of american explorers, [985—1631]. (Young folks' ser.) Bost. 1877. S.   **x 971.1 : 5**

Moncrieff, Robert Hope, *(Ascott R. Hope).* The heroes of young America. Maps and ill. Lond. 1877. D.   **971.1 : 8**

Contents. The american argonauts.—The first english planters.—John Smith.—The pilgrim fathers.—The early settlers of New England.—The american colonies.

Gilman, Arthur. Tales of the pathfinders. Bost. 1884. D.   **x 971.1 : 18**

Lodge, H: Cabot. A short history of the english colonies in America. N. Y. 1881. O.   **971.1 : 3**

Coffin, C: Carleton. Old times in the colonies. Ill. N. Y. 1881. O.   **x 971.1 : 11**

Banvard, Joseph. Plymouth and the pilgrims, or Incidents of adventure in the history of the first settlers. New ed., rev. and enl. Bost. 1874. S.   **x 971.1 : 10**

Neill, E: Duffield. The english colonization of America during the 17th century. Lond. 1871. O.   **971.1 : 17**

Doyle, J: Andrew. The american colonies previous to the declaration of independence ; the Arnold prize essay, read in the theatre at Oxford, june 9, 1869. Lond. 1869. O.   **971.1 : 14**

— English colonies in America ; Virginia, Maryland and the Carolinas. Map. N. Y. 1880. O.   **971.1 : 13**

Irving, Theodore. The conquest of Florida by Hernando de Soto. N. Y. 1857. D.   **971.1 : 7**

Shipp, Bernard. History of Hernando de Soto and Florida, or Record of the events of 56 years, from 1512 to 1568. Phila. 1881. O.   **971.1+1**

Schele de Vere, Maximilian. The romance of american history ; early annals. N. Y. 1872. D.   **971.1 : 6**

Contents. Lo the poor indian !—The hidden river.—Our first romance.—A few town-names.—Kaisers, kings and knights.—Lost towns.—Lost lands.

Brucker, Joseph. Vorträge über die entwicklungs-geschichte des volkes der Vereinigten Staaten von Nord-Amerika ; 1er-3er vortr. Milw. 1878-79. O.   **- 971.1 : Pam**

Note. Only to new year's 1776.

Carlier, A: Histoire du peuple américain, États-Unis, et de ses rapports avec les indiens depuis la fondation des colonies anglaises jusqu'à la révolution de 1776. Paris. 1864. 2 v. O.   **971.1 : 16**

Contents. V. 1. Préf.—Race blanche.—Race rouge.—Races blanche et rouge après l'occupation anglaise; La Virginie et La Nouvelle Angleterre. 2. *Suite:* Les autres colonies anglaises. — Race blanche ; considérations générales sur l'ensemble des colonies. — App. Race rouge; considérations générales sur l'origine des indiens et leur aptitude à la civilisation.

Moncrieff, Robert Hope, *(Ascott R. Hope).* The men of the backwoods ; true stories and sketches of the indians and the indian fighters. Ill. Lond. 1880. D.   **971.1 : 9**

Markham, R: A narrative history of king Philip's war, and the indian troubles in New England. Map. (Minor wars of the U. S.) N. Y. [1883]. D.   **x 971.1 : 15**

Johnson, Edwin Rossiter. History of the french war, ending in the conquest of Canada ; with a prelim. account of the early attempts at colonization and struggles for the possession of the country. (Minor wars of the U. S.) N. Y. [1882]. D.   **x 971.1 : 12**

Putnam, Rufus. Journal of gen. Rufus Putnam kept in northern N. Y. during the four campaigns of the old french and indian war, 1757-1760 ; copiously ill. with notes and preceded by a biogr. sketch of gen. Putnam by E. C. Dawes. Albany, N. Y. 1886. O.   **971.1 : 20**

See also in the Index to biography **Montgomery—Philip.**

3. The revolution and the confederation.

Gordon, W: The history of the rise, progress and establishment of the independence of the U. S. of America ; incl. an account of the late war and of the thirteen colonies from their origin to that period. N. Y. 1789. 3 v. O.   **971.2 : 21**

Botta, C: Guiseppe Guglielmo. History of the war of independence of the U. S. of America. Tr. from the italian by G: Alexander Otis. 8th ed. New Haven. 1838. 2 v. O.   **971.2 : 2**

Greene, G: Washington. Historical view of the american revolution. Bost. 1865. D.   **971.2 : 8**

Ludlow, J: Malcolm. The war of American independence, 1775—1783. Maps. (Epochs of modern history.) Bost. 1876. S.   **917.2 : 10**

Lossing, Benson J: The pictorial field-book of the revolution, or Illustrations by pen and pencil of the history, biography, scenery, relics and traditions of the war for independence. Ill. N. Y. 1860. 2 v. O.   **971.2+9**

Coffin, C: Carleton. The boys of '76 ; a history of the battles of the revolution. Ill. N. Y. 1878. O.   **x 971.2 : 1**

Peterson, C: J. The military heroes of the revolution ; with a narrative of the war of independence. Phila. 1860. O.   **971.2+12**

Rhoads, T: Y. The battle-fields of the revolution ; comprising descriptions of the principal battles, sieges and other events of the war of independence, interspersed with characteristic anecdotes. Phila. 1858. D.   **971.2 : 13**

x denotes books specially adapted for children.

Thacher, James. Military journal during the amer. revolutionary war, from 1775 to 1783; describing the events and transactions of this period, with numerous historical facts and anecdotes ; added, an app., containing biogr. sketches of several general officers. Hartford. 1854. O.   **971.2 : 16**

Carrington, H: Beebe. Battles of the amer. revolution, 1775—1781; historical and military criticism, with topographical ill. N. Y. [1876]. O.   **971.2+3**

Ellis, G: E: History of the battle of Bunker's (Breed's) Hill, on june 17, 1775 ; from authentic sources in print and ms. Map. Bost. 1875. O.   **971.2+24**

Jones, C: H: History of the campaign for the conquest of Canada in 1776, from the death of Montgomery to the retreat of the british army under sir Guy Carleton. Phila. 1881. O.   **971.2+20**

Riedesel, Friederike Charlotte Louise, *born* v. Massow, *freiin* v. Letters and journals relating to the war of the amer. revolution and capture of the german troops at Saratoga. Albany. 1867. O.   **971.2 : 14**

Draper, Lyman C. King's Mountain and its heroes ; history of the battle of King's mountain, Oct. 7th 1780, and the events which led to it. Ill. Cinc. 1881. O.   **971.2+5**

Deux-Ponts, Guillaume *comte* de. My campaigns in America ; a journal, 1780—1781. Tr. from the french ms., with an introd. and notes by S: Abbott Green. Bost. 1868. O.   **971.2+22**

Johnston, H: P. The Yorktown campaign and the surrender of Cornwallis, 1781. Ill. N. Y. 1881. O.   **971.2 : 6**

Stone, W: Leete. Border wars of the american revolution. [Harper's family lib.] N. Y. 1846. 2 v. S.   **971.2 : 19**

Moore, Frank, *ed.* Diary of the amer. revolution, from newspapers and original documents. N. Y. 1863. 2 v. O.   **971.2+11**
Contents. V. 1. 1775—1777. 2. 1778—oct. 1781.—Index.

Greene, G: Washington. The german element in the war of american independence. N. Y. 1876. D.   **971.2 : 18**

Lowell, E: J. The hessians and the other german auxiliaries of Great Britain in the revolutionary war. Maps and plans. N. Y. 1884. D.   **971.2 : 23**

Ellet, Elizabeth Fries, *born* Lummis. Domestic history of the american revolution. N. Y. 1850. D.   **971.2 : 7**

Smith, T. Marshall. Legends of the war of independence, and of the earlier settlements in the west. Louisville. 1855. O.   **971.2 : 15**

Sparks, Jared, *ed.* Correspondence of the amer. revolution ; letters of eminent men to G: Washington, from the time of his taking command of the army to the end of his presidency. Bost. 1853. 4 v. O.   **971.2+4**
Contents. V. 1. Pref.—July 12, 1775—oct. 8, 1777.—App. Operations in Canada. 2. Oct. 9, 1777—june 20, 1780.—App. Operations in Va. and S. C.; of the northern army against Burgoyne; on Hudson's river. 3. June 22, 1780—feb. 27, 1783. 4. March 12, 1783—feb. 6, 1797.—Indexes.

Scudder, Horace Elisha, *ed.* Sans-souci series : Men and manners in America one hundred years ago. N. Y. 1876. S.   **971.2 : 17**
Contents. New England.—New York and the Jerseys.—Pennsylvania.—The southern colonies.

Abbott, E: Revolutionary times ; sketches of our country, its people and their ways one hundred years ago. Bost. 1876. T.   **917.1 : 47**

Boardman, Timothy. Log-book, kept on board the privateer Oliver Cromwell, during a cruise from New London, Ct., to Charleston, S. C., and return in 1778 ; also a biogr. sketch of the author by S: W. Boardman. Issued under the auspices of the Rutland co. hist. soc. Albany. 1885. O.   **971.2 : 26**

Butterfield, Consul Willshire, *ed.* Journal of capt. Jonathan Heart on the march with his company from Connecticut to Fort Pitt in Pittsburgh, Pa., from the 7th of sept. to the 12th of oct. 1785 incl. Added, the Dickinson-Harmar corresp. of 1784-5 ; the whole ill. with notes and preceded by a biogr. sketch of captain Heart. Albany. N. Y. 1885. O.   **971.2 : 25**
See also in the Index to biography **Adams,** S:—**Allen,** E.—**André**—**Arnold**—**Franklin**—**Greene**—**Hull**—**Jay**—**Jones**—**Kalb**—**La Fayette**—**Marion**—**Morgan**—**Morris**—**Mosby**—**Otis**—**Pickering**—**Pulaski**—**Putnam**—**Reed**—**Saint Clair**—**Schuyler**—**Steuben**—**Warren**—**Washington**—**Wayne.**

4.   The federal union, to the rebellion.

Griswold, Rufus Wilmot. The republican court, or american society in the days of Washington. New ed. N. Y. 1867. O.   **971.3+1**

Wood, J: The suppressed history of the administration of J: Adams, from 1797 to 1801, as printed and suppressed in 1802. Now repub. with notes and an app. by J: H: Sherburne. Phila. 1846. D.   **971.3 : 15**

Ingersoll, C: Jared. Historical sketch of the second war between the U. S. of America and Great Britain, declared by act of cong. june 15th 1812 and concluded by peace feb. 15th 1815 ; v. 1, comprising the events of 1812-13. Phila. 1845. O.   **971.3+10**

— *Same.* 2d series, embracing the events of 1814 —15. Phila. 1852. 2 v. O.   **971.3+17**
Contents. V. 1. Naval hostilities ; privateers ; Dartmoor prison.—History of war law.—The french consular republic, 1799—1804.—French republican empire, 1804—1815—1844. 2. Negociations at Ghent ; treaty and peace.—Invasion of Louisiana.—Last session of war congress.—War with the Barbary powers.

Johnson, Edwin Rossiter. History of the war of 1812-15 between the U. S. and Great Britain. (Minor wars of the U. S.) N. Y. [1882]. D.   **x 971.3 : 11**

Lossing, Benson J: The pictorial field-book of of the war of 1812, or Illustrations by pen and pencil of the history, biography, scenery. relics and traditions of the last war for american independence. Ill. N. Y. 1869. Q.   **971.3+10**

Clarke, James Freeman. History of the campaign of 1812, and the surrender of the fort of Detroit.   *in* **923.15 : 16**

Ingraham, E: D. A sketch of the events which preceded the capture of Washington by the british, aug. 24, 1814. [*Anon.*] Phila. 1849. O.   **971.3 : 7**

Roosevelt, Theodore. The naval war of 1812, or The history of the U. S. navy during the last war with Great Britain. N. Y. 1882. O.   **971.3 : 9**

x denotes books specially adapted for children

Sargent, Nathan, (*Oliver Oldschool*). Public men and events from the commencement of mr. Monroe's administration in 1817, to the close of mr. Fillmore's administration in 1853. Phila. 1875. 2 v. O.   971.3 : 8

Mansfield, E: Deering. The mexican war; a history of its origin, and a detailed account of the victories which terminated in the surrender of the capital, with the official despatches of the generals; added, the treaty of peace and tables of the strength and losses of the U. S. army. 7th ed. N. Y. 1848. D.   971.3 : 4

Jenkins, J: S. History of the war between the U. S. and Mexico, from the commencement of hostilities to the ratification of the treaty of peace. Phila. [1881]. D.   971.3 : 5

Ladd, Horatio O. History of the war with Mexico. Ill. and map. (Minor wars of the U. S.) N. Y. [1883]. D.   x 971.3 : 14

Henry, W: S. Campaign sketches of the war with Mexico. Ill. N. Y. 1848. D.   971.3 +2

Jay, W: A review of the causes and consequences of the mexican war. 4th ed. Bost. 1849. D.   971.3 : 13

Livermore, Abiel Abbot. The war with Mexico reviewed. Bost. 1850. D.   971.3 : 12

Giddings, Joshua Reed. The exiles of Florida, or The crimes committed by our government against the maroons, who fled from South Carolina and other slave states, seeking protection under spanish laws. Columbus, O. 1858. D.   971.3 : 6

Kip, Lawrence. Army life on the Pacific; a journal of the expedition against the northern indians, the tribes of the Cœur D'Alenes, Spokans and Pelouzes in the summer of 1858. N. Y. 1859. D.   971.3 : 3

See also in the Index to biography **Adams,** J:— **Adams,** J: Q.—**Ames**—**Blennerhasset**—**Bowles**— **Buchanan** — **Burr** — **Cabot** — **Calhoun** — **Cass** — **Choate** — **Clay** — **Clinton** — **Corwin** — **Dale** — **Decatur**—**Gallatin**—**Garrison**—**Giddings**—**Hamilton**—**Henry**—**Jackson,** A.—**Jefferson**—**Madison** —**Monroe**—**Perry**—**Pierce**—**Polk**—**Quincy**—**Quitman**—**Randolph**—**Scott**—**Stevens**—**Webster.**

5. The civil war, and since.

(*See also* Slavery, col. 169-170; U. S. domestic relations, col. 171; Army and navy history, col. 233-234.)

General history.

United States. *War dep't.* The war of the rebellion; a compilation of the official records of the union and confederate armies, prepared under the direction of the sec. of war by Robert N. Scott, and pub. pursuant to act of congress appr. june 16, 1880. Ser. 1, v. 1–14. Wash. 1880–85. 23 v. O.
                in 971.4 : D
Contents. V. 1. Operations in Charleston harbor, S. C., dec. 20, 1860—apr. 14, 1861.—Secession of Ga., jan. 3-26, 1861.—Secession of Ala. and Miss., jan. 4-20, 1861. —Oper. in Fla., jan. 6—aug. 31, 1861. — Secession of N. C., jan. 9—may 20, 1861.—Secession of La., jan. 10— feb. 19, 1861.—Oper. in Tex. and N. M., feb. 1—june 11, 1861.—Oper. in Ark., I. T., and Mo., feb. 7—may 9, 1861. **2.** Oper. in Md., Pa., Va., and W. Va., apr. 16—july 31, 1861. **3.** Oper. in Mo., Ark., Ks., and I. T. may 10— nov. 19, 1861. **4.** Oper. in Tex., N.M., and Ariz., june 11, 1861—feb. 1, 1862.—Oper. in Ky., and Tenn., july 1— nov. 19, 1861.—Oper. in N. C., and s. e. Va., aug. 1, 1861 —jan. 11, 1862. **5.** Oper. in Md., n. Va., and W. Va., aug. 1, 1861—mar. 17, 1862. **6.** Oper. on the coasts of S. C., Ga., and middle and east Fla., aug. 21, 1861—apr.

United States. *War dep't.—Continued.*
11, 1862.—Oper. in w. Fla., s. Ala., s. Miss., and La., sept. 1, 1861—may 12, 1862. **7.** Oper. in Ky., Tenn., n. Ala., and s. w. Va., nov. 19, 1861—mar. 4, 1862. **8.** Oper. in Mo., Ark., Ks., and I. T., nov. 19, 1861—apr. 10, 1862. **9.** Oper. in s. e. Va., jan. 11—mar. 17, 1862.—Oper. in N. C., jan. 11—aug. 20, 1862.—Oper. in Tex., N. M., and Ariz., feb. 1—sept. 20, 1862. **10.** Oper. in Ky., Tenn., n. Miss., n. Ala., and s. w. Va., mar. 4—june 10, 1862: Pt. 1, Reports; pt. 2, Correspondence. **11.** The peninsular campaign, Va., mar. 17—sept. 2, 1862: Pt. 1, Reports mar. 17—june 24; pt. 2, Reports june 25— sept. 2; pt. 3, Correspondence. **12.** Oper. in n. Va., W. Va., and Md., mar. 17—sept. 2, 1862: Pt. 1, Reports mar. 17—june 25; pt. 2, Reports june 26—sept. 2; pt. 3, Correspondence. **13.** Oper. in Mo., Ark., Ks., I. T., and the dep't of the northwest, apr. 10—nov. 20, 1862. **14.** Oper. on the coast of S. C., Ga., and middle and east Fla., apr. 12, 1862—june 11, 1863.

— *Congress.* Report of the joint committee on the conduct of the war. (37th cong. 3d sess.; Senate rep. no. 108.) Wash. 1863. 3 v. O.   *in* 328.1 : D
Contents. V. 1. Army of the Potomac. **2.** Bull Run and Ball's Bluff. **3.** Dep't of the west or Missouri.— Miscellaneous.

— — *Same.* (38th cong. 2d sess.; Sen. rep. no. 142.) Wash. 1865. 3 v. O.   *in* 328.1 : D
Contents. V. 1. Army of the Potomac.—Battle of Petersburg. **2.** Red River expedition.—Fort Fisher expedition.—Heavy ordnance. **3.** Sherman-Johnston.—Light-draft monitors.—Massacre of the Cheyenne Indians. — Ice contracts. — Rosecrans's campaigns.—Miscellaneous.

— — *Same,* Supp. (39th cong. 1st sess.) Wash. 1866. 2 v. O.   *in* 328.1 : D
Contents. V. 1. Reports of W. T. Sherman, G: H. Thomas. **2.** Reports of J: Pope. J. S. Foster, A. Pleasanton, E. A. Hitchcock, P. H. Sheridan, J. B. Ricketts.—Communication and memorial of Norman Wiard.

Guernsey, Alfred H., *and* H: Mills **Alden.** Harper's pictorial history of the great rebellion. Ill. Chicago. [1868]. 2 v. F.
                971.4 : R103

Pictorial battles of the civil war, The. Ill. N. Y. 1884-85. 2 v. F.   971.4 : R108
Contents. V. 1. Government.—Our national government.—The confederation.—Confederation of the original 13 states.—The seat of government at different periods. — Declaration of independence. — Names of the signers.—Articles of confederation and perpetual union between the states.—Names of the signers.—Constitution of the U. S.—Names of the signers.—Amendments to the constitution.—Dates of ratification. — **La Bree,** B:, *ed.* History of the civil war.—The emancipation proclamation.—Corps badges of the U. S. army.—Battles of the civil war alphab. arr.—Naval battles of the civil war alphab. arr. **2.** Most important battles of the civil war.— Chronological history of the civil war.—Number of men called for by the president, and number furnished by each state, territory and District of Columbia from april 15, 1861, to close of war.—Organizations mustered into the service of the U. S.—Military division of the U. S. forces.—Principal armies of the U. S., 1861-1865.—Strength of the army at various dates. —Honors conferred by the congress of the U. S. in public acts. — Statement of the casualties in the military forces of the U. S.—National cemeteries, total interments, etc. — Union military prisons.— Losses in killed, wounded and missing.—Cost of the civil war.—Principal battles of the revolution; Indian wars; War of 1812; Mexican war.—Length and cost of american wars.—Federal prisons at Andersonville, Ga.—Chief commanders of the army.—Naval history of the U. S.—Map and roster of all the union and confederate corps, divisions, brigades, and regiments of infantry, cavalry and artillery engaged, and officers killed in the battle of Gettysburg. — **Porter,** D: D. The use of a navy.—General officers U. S. army and their record during the civil war, 1861-1865.—**Wright,** Marcus J. Roster of the general officers of the confederate army, 1861-1865.—Officers of the U. S. navy, 1861-1865.—Casualties of the U. S. navy.—Officers of the Confederate States navy.—List of vessels of the U. S. navy, 1861-1865.—List of vessels of the U. S. navy, 1885.—List of vessels of the Con-

federate States navy and their commanders, 1861-1865. —The confederate government. — **Sheridan**, P. H. The last days of the rebellion.—Organizations of the union and confederate armies.—Songs of the soldiers. — Presidents of the continental congress and congress of the confederation, 1774-1788. — Presidents and vice-presidents of the U. S.—Cabinet officers of the administrations.—First and last events of the civil war.—**Beath**, R. B. Historical sketch of the G. A. R. — Confederate veterans' assoc. — General Grant, his battles and victories in war and peace.

Union side.

Abbott, J: Stevens Cabot. The history of the civil war in America; comprising a full and impartial account of the origin and progress of the rebellion, of the various naval and military engagements, of the heroic deeds performed by armies and individuals, and of touching scenes in the field, the camp, the hospital and the cabin. Ill. N. Y. 1866, 1873. 2 v. O.   **971.4+1**
— *Same, germ.* Geschichte des bürgerkrieges in Amerika. *T. p. w.* 2 v. O.   **971.4+1**

Boynton, C: B. History of the navy during the rebellion. Ill. N. Y. 1868. 2 v. O.
   971.4:18

Champlin, J: Denison, *jr.* Young folks' history of the war for the Union. Ill. N. Y. 1881. O.   **x 971.4:14**

Cheney, C. Emma. Young folks' history of the civil war. Bost. 1884 [1883]. D.
   x 971.4:97

Dodge, Theodore Ayrault. A bird's-eye view of our civil war. Maps and charts. Bost. 1883. O.   **971.4+93**

Draper, J: W: History of the american civil war. N. Y. 1867-76. 3 v. O.   **971.4+7**
Contents. V. 1. The causes of the war and the events preparatory to it up to the close of president Buchanan's administration. 2. The events from the inauguration of president Lincoln to the proclamation of emancipation of the slaves. 3. To the end of the war.

Duyckinck, Evert A: Geschichte des krieges für die Union, politisch und militärisch nach offiziellen und andern authentischen dokumenten beschrieben. Deutsch bearb. von F: Kapp. Ill. N. Y. *n. d.* Q.
   971.4+2

Giddings, Joshua Reed. History of the rebellion; its authors and causes. N. Y. 1864. O.   **971.4+9**

Greeley, Horace. The amer. conflict; a history of the great rebellion in the U. S. of America, 1860-64. its causes, incidents and results, intended to exhibit especially its moral and political phases, with the drift and progress of amer. opinion respecting human slavery from 1776 to the close of the war for the union. Hartford. 1865, 1866. 2 v. O.   **971.4+13**

Lossing, Benson J: Pictorial history of the civil war in the U. S. of America., Phila. 1866-68. 3 v. O.   **971.4+4**

Moore, Frank, *ed.* The rebellion record; a diary of american events, with documents, narratives, illustrative incidents, poetry, etc., with an introd. address on the causes of the struggle and the great issues before the country. N. Y. 1861-68. 11 v. O.
   971.4:R5

Paris, L: Philippe Albert d'Orléans *comte* de. History of the civil war in America; v. 1-3.

Tr. by L: F. Tasistro. Maps and ill. Phila. 1875-[83]. 3 v. O.   **971.4:6**
Contents. V. 1. The american army.—Secossion.— The first conflict. — The first autumn. — The first winter. 2. Richmond.—The naval war.—Maryland. —Kentucky. — Tennessee. — Virginia. — Politics. 3. The war on the Rapidan.—The Mississippi.—Pennsylvania.—The third winter.—App.

Thayer, W: Makepeace. A youth's history of the rebellion, from the battle of Murfreesboro' to the massacre at Fort Pillow. Bost. 1865. S.   **x 971.4:12**

Tomes, Robert, *and* B: G. **Smith**. The great civil war; a history of the late rebellion, with biogr. sketches of leading statesmen and distinguished naval and military commanders, etc. N. Y. [1876]. 3 v. O.
   971.4+68

*   *   *

Moore, Frank, *ed.* Anecdotes, poetry and incidents of the war, north and south; 1860-65. N. Y. 1882. O.   **971.4+94**

Townsend, E: Davis. Anecdotes of the civil war in the U. S. N. Y. 1884 [1883]. D.
   971.4:95

Porter, D: Dixon. Incidents and anecdotes of the civil war. N. Y. 1885. D. **971.4:111**

Davis, Washington. Camp-fire chats of the civil war; the incident, adventure and wayside exploit of the bivouac and battle field, as related by members of the Grand army of the republic; embracing the tragedy, romance, comedy, humor and pathos in the varied experience of army life. Containing a history and other information for members of the G. A. R. Fond du Lac. 1884. D.   **971.4:100**

Fry, James B. New York and the conscription of 1863; a chapter in the history of the civil war. N. Y. 1885. D.   **971.4:105**

Frémont, Jessie, *born* Benton. The story of the guard. Bost. 1863. D.   **971.4:30**
Note. The guard was a cavalry corps, known as "Frémont's body-guard", dissolved in nov. 1861.

Confederate side.

Davis, Jefferson. The rise and fall of the confederate government. N. Y. 1881. 2 v. O.
   971.4+8
Contents. V. 1. Introd.·—The constitution.—Secession and confederation. — The war. — App. 2. The war, *continued.*

Foote, H: Stuart. War of the rebellion, or Scylla and Charybdis; consisting of observations upon the causes, course and consequences of the late civil war in the U.S. N. Y. 1866. D.   **971.4:29**

Pollard, E: A. Southern history of the war; first, second, third. year. N. Y. 1863-65. 3 v. O.   **971.4:11**
App. v. 3: Jail-journal in Fort Warren.

Campaigns and battles.

(See also articles in the Century, beginning nov. 1884.)

Union side.

Campaigns of the civil war:
1. **Nicolay**, J: G. The outbreak of rebellion. N. Y. 1881. D.   **971.4:70**
2. **Force**, Manning F. From Fort Henry to Corinth. N. Y. 1881. D. **971.4:71**
3. **Webb**, Alexander S. The peninsula; McClellan's campaign of 1862. N. Y. 1881. D.
   971.4:72

x denotes books specially adapted for children.

Campaigns of the civil war.—*Continued.*
4. **Ropes,** J: Codman. The army under Pope. N. Y. 1881. D.   **971.4:73**
5. **Palfrey,** Francis Winthrop. The Antietam and Fredericksburg. N. Y. 1882. D.
     971.4:74
6. **Doubleday,** Abner. Chancellorsville and Gettysburg. N. Y. 1882. D. **971.4:75**
7. **Cist,** H: Martyn. The army of the Cumberland. N. Y. 1882. D.   **971.4:76**
8. **Greene,** Francis Vinton. The Mississippi. N. Y. 1882. D.   **971.4:77**
9. **Cox,** Jacob D. Atlanta. N. Y. 1882. D.
     971.4:78
10. **Cox,** Jacob D. The march to the sea; Franklin and Nashville. N. Y. 1882. D.
     971.4:79
11. **Pond,** G: E: The Shenandoah valley in 1864. N. Y. 1883. D.   **971.4:80**
12. **Humphreys,** Andrew Atkinson. The Virginia campaign of 1864 and '65; the army of the Potomac and the army of the James. N. Y. 1883. D.   **971.4:81**
Supp.: **Phisterer,** F: Statistical record of the armies of the U. S. N. Y. 1883. D.
     355.1:4

Navy in the civil war, The:
1. **Soley,** James Russell. The blockade and the cruisers. N. Y. 1883. D. **971.4:82**
2. **Ammen,** Daniel. The Atlantic coast. N. Y. 1883. D.   **971.4:83**
3. **Mahan,** Alfred Thayer. The gulf and inland waters. N. Y. 1883. D. **971.4:84**

Swinton, W: The twelve decisive battles of the war; a history of the eastern and western campaigns, in relation to the actions that decided their issue. N. Y. *n. d.* O.
     971.4:66
Contents. Bull Run.—Donelson.—Shiloh.—Antietam.—Murfreesborough.—The monitor and the Merrimac.—Vicksburg.—Gettysburg.— Wilderness.—Atlanta.—Nashville.—Five Forks.

Glazier, Willard. Battles for the union; comprising descriptions of many of the most stubbornly contested battles in the war of the great rebellion, together with incidents and reminiscences of the camp, the march and the skirmish line, embracing a record of the privations, heroic deeds, and glorious triumphs of the soldiers of the republic. Hartford. 1878. D.   **971.4:31**

*   *   *

Doubleday, Abner. Reminiscences of Forts Sumter and Moultrie in 1860–61. N. Y. 1876. D.   **971.4:26**
Anderson, T: M. The political conspiracies preceding the rebellion, or True stories of Sumter and Pickens. N. Y. 1882. O.
     971.4:86
Parton, James. Gen. Butler in New Orleans; history of the administration of the department of the Gulf in the year 1862, with an account of the capture of New Orleans and a sketch of the previous career of the general, civil and military. Bost. 1871. O.
     971.4:69
Swinton, W: Campaigns of the army of the Potomac; a critical history of operations in Virginia, Maryland and Pennsylvania, from the commencement to the close of the war, 1861–5. N. Y. 1866. O.
     971.4+52

Military hist. society of Mass. [Publications:] The peninsular campaigns of gen. McClellan in 1862; papers read before the society in 1876, 1877, 1878 and 1879. Bost. 1881. O.
     971.4+44
Contents. **Ropes,** J: C., Gen. McClellan's plans for the campaign of 1862, and the alleged interference of the government with them. — **Palfrey,** J: C., The siege of Yorktown. — **Palfrey,** F. W., The period which elapsed between the fall of Yorktown and the seven days battles; The seven days battles to Malvern Hills; The battle of Malvern Hill. — **Whittier,** C: A., Comments on the peninsular campaign.

McClellan, G: Brinton. Report on the organization and campaigns of the army of the Potomac; added, an account of the campaign in western Virginia, with plans of battlefields. N. Y. 1864. O. **971.4+62**
Joinville, François Ferdinand Philippe L: Marie d'Orléans *prince* de. The army of the Potomac; its organization, its commander and its campaign. Tr. from the french, with notes, by W: H: Hurlburt. N. Y. 1862. O.   **971.4:40**
Gordon, G: H. Brook Farm to Cedar Mountain in the war of the great rebellion, 1861–62. Maps. Bost. 1883. D.   **971.4:92**
— History of the campaign of the army of Virginia, under John Pope, from Cedar Mountain to Alexandria, 1862. Bost. 1880. O.
     971.4+58
Cox, Jacob D. The second battle of Bull Run, as connected with the Fitz-John Porter case; paper read before the Society of ex-army and navy officers of Cinc., feb. 28, 1882. Cinc. 1882. D.   **971.4:87**
Gillmore, Quincy A. Official report of the siege and reduction of Fort Pulaski, Ga., 1862.
     in **623:D**
Rosecrans, W: Starke. Report on the battle of Murfreesboro', Tenn. Map. (U. S. 37th cong. spec. sess. Sen. ex. doc. no. 2). Wash. 1863. O.   *in* **971.4:D**
Stevenson, Alexander F. The battle of Stone's river, near Murfreesboro, Tenn., dec. 30, 1862 to jan. 3, 1863. Maps and plans. Bost. 1884. O.   **971.4+104**
Military hist. society of Mass. [Publications:] The campaign of Chancellorsville, by Theodore A. Dodge. Bost. 1881. O.
     971.4+45
Huey, Pennock. A true history of the charge of the Eighth Pennsylvania cavalry, at Chancellorsville. Phil. 1883. D. **971.4:98**
Van Horne, T: B. History of the army of the Cumberland, its organization, campaigns and battles, written at the request of maj.-gen. G: H. Thomas, chiefly from his private military journal and official and other documents, furnished by him. Maps, comp. by E: Ruger. 2 v. and atlas. Cinc. 1875. 3 v. O.   **971.4+89**
Reed, S: Rockwell. The Vicksburg campaign and the battles about Chattanooga under the command of gen. U. S. Grant in 1862–63; an historical review. Cinc. 1882. O.
     971.4:88
Humphreys, Andrew Atkinson. From Gettysburg to the Rapidan; the army of the Potomac, july 1863 to april 1864. Maps. N. Y. 1883. D.   **971.4:91**
Note. Intended as an introd. to vol. 12 of the Campaigns of the civil war, **971.4:81**.

Conyngham, D: P. Sherman's march through the south, with sketches and incidents of the campaign. N. Y. 1865. D.   971.4:24

Nichols, G: Ward. The story of the great march, from the diary of a staff officer. Ill. 6th ed. N. Y. 1865. D.   971.4:47

Grant, Ulysses Simpson. Report of the armies of the U. S., 1864–65. N. Y. 1866. O.
971.4 63

Confederate side.

Battlefields of the south, from Bull Run to Fredricksburgh; with sketches of confederate commanders, and gossip of the camps. N. Y. 1864. O.   971.4+16

Owen, W: Miller. In camp and battle with the Washington artillery of New Orleans; a narrative of events during the late civil war from Bull Run to Appomatox and Spanish Fort, comp. by the adjutant from his diary and from authentic documents and orders. Ill. Bost. 1885. O. 971.4:110

Allan, W: History of the campaign of gen. T. J. (Stonewall) Jackson in the Shenandoah valley of Virginia, from nov. 4, 1861, to june 17, 1862. Maps. Phila. 1880. O.
971.4:57

Johnston, Joseph Eccleston. Narrative of military operations directed, during the late war between the states, by [him]. N. Y. 1874. O.   971.4+10

Early, Jubal A. A memoir of the last year of the war for independence in the Confederate States of America, containing an account of the operations of his commands in 1864, 1865. New Orleans. 1867. O.
971.4:27

Personal war narratives.

Union side.

Hale, E: Everett, *ed.* Stories of war, told by soldiers. Bost. 1880. S.   x 971.4:35
Contents. Introd.—Life at Little Crastis.—The first Bull Run.— Fort Henry and Fort Donelson.— Gen. Mc Clellan and the Peninsula. — West Virginia.— Antietam. — Pittsburgh Landing. — Vicksburg. — Gettysburg. — Chickamauga and Chattanooga.— Grant's advance on Richmond. — The Wilderness. —Sheridan's ride.— Sherman's great march.—Nashville.–Siege of Richmond.–The last week.–The end.

Beatty, J: The citizen soldier, or Memoirs of a volunteer. Cinc. 1879. D.   971.4:17

Bradley, G: S. The star corps, or Notes of an army chaplain, during Sherman's famous march to the sea. Milw. 1865. D.
971.4:19

Brownlow, W: Gannaway. Sketches of the rise, progress and decline of secession; with a narrative of personal adventures among the rebels. Phila. 1862. D.   971.4:20

Castleman, Alfred L. The army of the Potomac behind the scenes; a diary of unwritten history, from the organization of the army by gen. G: B. McClellan, to the close of the campaign in Va. about the first day of jan., 1863. Milw. 1863. D.
971.4:21

Coffin, C: Carleton, (*Carleton*). The boys of '61, or Four years of fighting; record of personal observations with the army and navy from the first battle of Bull Run to the fall of Richmond. [New issue]. Bost. 1881. O.   x 971.4:61

x denotes books specially adapted for children.

Coffin, C: Carleton, (*Carleton*).—*Continued.*
— Following the flag from aug. 1861 to nov. 1862, with the army of the Potomac. [Ill.] Bost. 1865. S.   971.4:22

— My days and nights on the battlefield. Bost. 1881. D.   971.4:23

Glazier, Willard. Three years in the federal cavalry. Ill. N. Y. 1872. D.   971.4:33

Gordon, G: H. A war-diary of events in the war of the great rebellion, 1863–1865. Bost. 1882. D.   971.4:85

Gurowski, Adam *comte* de. Diary from march 4, 1861 to oct. 18, 1863. Bost. 1862, 1864. 2 v. D.   971.4:34

Hazen, W: Babcock. A narrative of military service. Bost. 1885. O.   971.4:109

Hepworth, G: Hughes. The whip, hoe and sword, or The Gulf-department in '63. Bost. 1864. D.   971.4:37

Higginson, T: Wentworth. Army life in a black regiment. Bost. 1882. D.   971.4:65

Hosmer, James Kendall. The color-guard; a corporal's notes of military service in the 19th army corps. Bost. 1864. D.
971.4:39

Kennedy, J: Pendleton. Mr. Ambrose's letters on the rebellion. N. Y. 1865. S. 971.4:41

Nott, C: C. Sketches of the war; a series of letters to the North Moore street school of New York. 4th ed. N. Y. 1865. D.
971.4:48

Noyes, G: F. The bivouac and the battlefield, or Campaign sketches. N. Y. 1863. D.
971.4:59

Pittenger, W: Capturing a locomotive; a history of secret service in the late war. Phila. 1882. D.   971.4:50

Taylor, B: Franklin. Pictures of life in camp and field. Chicago. 1875. D.   971.4:53

Townsend, G: Alfred. Campaigns of a noncombatant, and his romaunt abroad during the war. N. Y. 1866. D.   971.4:56

Confederate side.

Bullock, James D. The secret service of the Confederate States in Europe, or How the confederate cruisers were equipped. N. Y. 1883. 2 v. O.   971.4:96

Estvàn, B. War pictures from the south. N. Y. 1864. D.   971.4:28

Gilmor, Harry. Four years in the saddle. N. Y. 1866. D.   971.4:64

Hood, J: Bell. Advance and retreat; personal experiences in the U. S. and confederate armies. New Orleans. 1880. O. 971.4:38

Lady, A. My cave life in Vicksburg; with letters of trial and travel. N. Y. 1864. D.
971.4:46

Putnam, Sarah A., *born* Brock. Richmond during the war; four years of personal observation by a Richmond lady. *T. p. w.* [N. Y. 1867]. D.   971.4:60

Taylor, R: Destruction and reconstruction; personal experiences of the late war. N. Y. 1879. O.   971.4:54

Figg, R. W. Where men only dare to go, or The story of a boy company, C. S. A., by an ex-boy. [Portraits]. Richmond, Va. 1885. D.   971.4:106

Prison narratives.

Union side.

Abbott, A. O. Prison life in the south at Richmond, Macon, Savannah, Charleston, Columbia, Charlotte, Raleigh, Goldsborough and Andersonville during 1864 and 1865. Ill. N. Y. 1865. S. **971.4 : 15**

Arnold, Joseph. Belle Island. *In* **Domschcke, B.** Zwanzig monate, *etc.* **971.4 : 3**

Davidson, H. M. Fourteen months in southern prisons; a narrative of the treatment of federal prisoners of war in the rebel military prisons... Milw. 1865. D. **971.4 : 25**

Domschcke, Bernhard. Zwanzig monate in kriegsgefangenschaft, erinnerungen; nebst einem anhang. Milw. 1865. D. **971.4 : 3**

Drake, J. Madison. Fast and loose in Dixie; unprejudiced narrative of personal experience as a prisoner of war at Libby, Macon, Savannah and Charleston. N. Y. [1880]. D. **971.4 : 67**

Harris, W: C. Prison-life in the tobacco warehouse at Richmond, by a Ball's Bluff prisoner. Phila. 1862. D. **971.4 : 36**

Hobart, Harrison Carroll. Capture, imprisonment and escape. *With* **Beatty, J:** The citizen soldier. **971.4 : 17**

McElroy, J: Andersonville; a story of rebel military prisons, fifteen months a guest of the so-called southern confederacy; a private soldier's experience in Richmond, Andersonville, Savannah, Millen, Blackshear and Florence. Toledo. 1879. O. **971.4 : 99**

Spencer, Ambrose. A narrative of Andersonville, drawn from the evidence elicited on the trial of Henry Wirz, the jailer, with the argument of col. N. P. Chipman, judge advocate. N. Y. 1866. D. **971.4 : 51**

Wallber, Albert. Die flucht aus dem Libbygefängniss. *In* **Domschcke, B.** Zwanzig monate, *etc.* **971.4 : 3**

Confederate side.

Lawrence, G: Alfred. Border and bastille, by the author of "Guy Livingstone." N. Y. 1863. D. **971.4 : 42**

Mahony, D. A. The prisoner of state. N. Y. 1863. D. **971.4 : 43**

Medical and hospital service.

H—, *Mrs.* Three years in field hospitals of the army of the Potomac. Phila. 1867. D. **971.4 : 55**

U. S. sanitary commission. **361 : 5**
See col. 235.

Boynton, C: B. History of the great western sanitary fair. **361 : 6**
See col. 235.

Medical and surgical history of the war. *in* **610 : D**
See col. 393.

Political history; Reconstruction, etc.

(See col. 167, 171.)

Blankenburg, H: Die innern kämpfe der nordamerikanischen Union bis zur präsidentenwahl von 1868. Leipz. 1869. O. **324.1 : 58**
Contents. Die ursachen des innern conflicts und dessen entwickelung bis zum abfall der südstaaten.—

Der secessionskrieg.—Die politischen kämpfe nach beendigung des secessionskriegs.—Anhang: Verfassung der V. S.

Barnes, W: H. History of the 39th congress of the U. S. Portr. N. Y. 1868. O. **324.1+56**

Blaine, James Gillespie. Twenty years of congress, from Lincoln to Garfield; with a review of the events which led to the political revolution of 1860; v. 1. Norwich, Ct. 1884. O. **324.1+57**
Contents. V. 1. Review, etc. — 1860-1864. — Appendices of tables and statistics.—Map.

* * *

King, C: The 5th cavalry in the Sioux war of 1876: Campaigning with Crook. Milw. 1880. O. **971.5 : 2**
See also in the Index to biography Brown, J: — Burnside — Cleveland — Custer — Dahlgren — Davis — Dix—Ericsson—Farragut —Frémont—Garfield—Grant—Greeley — Hancock—Hayes—Jackson, T: J. — Lee—Lincoln—Logan—McClellan—Seward—Sheridan—Sherman— Stephens—Sumner—Thomas—Wheeler—Wilson.

6. General description.

(See also Statistics, col. 157—158.)

Gazetteers, guides, etc.

Darby, W:. and Theodore **Dwight,** *jr.* A new gazetteer of the U. S. of America; containing a copious description of the states, territories, counties, etc., commerce, manufactures. agriculture and the arts generally, of the U. S.; with the population of 1830. Rev. ed. Hartford. 1836. O. **917.1 : R1**

Sears, Robert, *ed.* A new and popular pictorial description of the U. S.; containing an account of the topography, settlement, history, revolutionary and other interesting events. statistics, progress in agriculture, manufactures and population, etc., of each state in the union. Ill. 2d ed. N. Y. 1848. O. **917.1+34**

Colange, Leo de, *ed.* The national gazetteer; a geographical dictionary of the U. S., compiled from the latest official authorities and original sources, embracing a comprehensive account of every state, territory, county, city, town and village throughout the union, with populations from the last national census, information pertaining to railroads, navigation, lakes, rivers, canals, mountains, valleys, as well as the physical and statistical geography of the country. Phila. [1884]. O. **917.1 : R69**

Tenner, Armin, *ed.* Amerika: der heutige standpunkt der kultur in den Vereinigten Staaten; monographieen aus der feder hervorragender deutsch-amerikanischer schriftsteller gesammelt und herausg. Anhang: **Tenners** Deutsch-amerikanisches vademecum; kurzgefasste erläuterungen amerikanischer eigenthümlichkeiten in sprache und leben. N. Y. 1884. O. **917.1 : 85**
Contents. Vorwort.—**Güterbock,** Bernhard. Der hafen von New York.—**Klemm, L: R:** Das schulwesen in den Vereinigten Staaten. — **Müller, W:** Die bühne in den Vereinigten Staaten.—**Douai, K:** Daniel Adolf. Die lage der lohnarbeiter in Amerika.—**Brachvogel,** Udo. Die deutsche presse in den Vereinigten Staaten.—**Rothe,** Emil. Das deutsche element in Amerika. — **Jüngst, W:** Die landwirthschaftlichen und industriellen verhältnisse in den Vereinigten Staaten. — **Liebhart, H.** Der amerikanische sonntag und die temperenzfrage.— **Rümelin,**

C: Das eisenbahnwesen in den Vereinigten Staaten;
Das postwesen in den Vereinigten Staaten. — Nachträge und berichtigungen. — Alphabetisches namen-
und sachregister.

Bryant, W: Cullen, *ed.* Picturesque America,
or The land we live in ; a delineation by
pen and pencil of the mountains, rivers,
lakes, forests, water-falls, shores, cañons,
valleys, cities and other picturesque fea-
tures of our country. Ill. N. Y. *n. d.* 2 v.
Q.   **917.1 : R12**
Contents. V. 1. Bunce, O. B. On the coast of
Maine.—Thorpe, T. B. St. John's and Ocklawaha ri-
vers, Florida. — Runkle, L. J. G. Up and down the
Columbia.—Bunce, O. B. Lookout mountain and the
Tennessee. — Thompson, J. R. Richmond, scenic
and historic.—Cooke, J: E. Natural bridge, Virginia.
— Ringwalt, J. E. Delaware water-gap. — Bunce,
O. B. Mauch-Chunk. — Thompson, W. V. On the
Savannah.—Fontaine, F. G. de. The French Broad.
—Carter, S. N. The White mountains. — Bunce, O.
B. Neversink highlands. — Carter, R. St. Augus-
tine, Florida.—Bunce, O. B. Charleston and its sub-
urbs. — Brock, S. A. Weyer's Cave, Virginia. —
Bunce, O. B. Scenes on the Brandywine. — Fon-
taine, F. G. de. Cumberland gap. — Bunce, O. B.
Watkins glen ; Scenes in eastern Long Island. —
Thorpe, T. B. The lower Mississippi. — Woolson, C.
F. Mackinac. — Bunce, O. B. Our great national
park. — Carpenter, J. C. Harper's Ferry.— Bagby,
G. W. Scenes in Virginia.—Clarke, T. M. Newport.—
Strother, D. H. West Virginia. — Woolson, C. F.
Lake Superior.—Garczynski, R. E. Northern Cali-
fornia; Niagara; Trenton falls.—Smilley, J. D. The
Yosemite falls. — Clarke, T. M. Providence and vi-
cinity. — Woolson, C. F. South shore of Lake Erie.
— Garczynski, R. E. On the coast of California.
2. Burlingame, E. L. Highlands and palisades of
the Hudson. — Gardette, C. D. Philadelphia and its
suburbs. — Williams, W. F. Northern New Jersey.
— Richards, W. C. Valley of the Connecticut. —
Carpenter, J. C. Baltimore and environs.—Brown,
H: A. The Catskills.—Garczynski, R. E. The Jua-
nita.—Woolson, C. F. On the Ohio. — Burlingame,
E. L. The plains and the Sierras.—Garczynski,R.E.
The Susquehanna.—Towle, G. M. Boston.—Bunce,
O. B. Lake George and Lake Champlain.—Johnson,
R. Mount Mansfield. — Richards, W. C. Valley of
the Housatonic.—Garczynski, R. E. The upper Mis-
sissippi. — Ward, W. S. Valley of the Gennesee. —
Rideing, W. H. St. Lawrence and the Saguenay. —
Towle, G. M. Eastern shore. — Carter, R. The
Adirondack region.—Richards, W. C. The Connec-
ticut shore of the Sound.—Rideing, W. H. Lake
Memphremagog.—Garczynski, R. E. The Mohawk,
Albany and Troy.—Rideing, W. H. The upper Dela-
ware; Water-falls at Cayuga lake; The Rocky moun-
tains.—Colburn, J. E. The cañons of the Colorado.
—Bunce, O. B. Chicago and Milwaukee.—Rideing,
W. H. A glance at the northwest; The Mammoth
cave. — Bunce, O. B. New York and Brooklyn. —
Towle, G. M. Washington.

Flint, Timothy. The history and geography of
the Mississippi valley ; appended, a condensed physical geography of the Atlantic
U. S., and the whole amer. continent. 2d
ed. Cinc. 1832. 2 v. in 1. O.   **917.1 : 2**

Young, J. H. Mitchell's travellers' guide through
the U. S.; a map of the roads, distances,
steam boat and canal routes, etc. Phila.
1833. T.   **917.1 : 55**

Phelps's travellers' guide through the U. S. N.
Y. 1847. T.   **917.1 : 64**

Appletons' general guide to the U. S. and Canada ; rev. each year to date of issue. Ill.,
maps, plans and tables. N. Y. 1885. S.
                                   917.1 : 84

Disturnell, J: The great lakes or inland seas
of America ; embracing a full description
of Lakes Superior, Huron, Michigan, Erie,
and Ontario ; Rivers St. Mary, St. Clair,
Detroit, Niagara, and St. Lawrence ; commerce of the lakes, etc.; together with a
guide to the upper Mississippi river, giv-

ing a description of cities, towns, etc., forming altogether a guide for the pleasure
traveler and emigrant. Maps and ill. N. Y.
1868. S.   **917.1 : 16**

Sweet, O. P. Amusement directory and travelers' guide from the Atlantic to the Pacific.
Rochester. 1870-71. O.   **917.1-‡49**

Glazier, Willard. Peculiarities of amer. cities.
Ill. Phila. 1884. D.   **917.1 : 65**

Maps, atlases, etc.

United States. *Census office.* Statistical atlas of
the U. S. based on the results of the 9th
census, 1870 ; with contributions from many
eminent men of science and several departments of the government, compiled under
authority of congress by Francis A. Walker.
n. p. 1874. F.   **317 : R2**
Contents. Memoirs and discussions. Walker, F. A.
Preface and introd. — Whitney, J. D. The physical
features of the U. S. — Brewer, W: H. The woodlands and forest systems of the U. S. — Hitchcock,
C: H., *and* W: P. Blake. Geological map of the U. S.
and territories. — Raymond, R. W. The gold and
silver mines of the west. — Hitchcock, C: H. The
coal measures of the U. S. — Stocking, S. W. The
political divisions of the U. S. — Galpin, S. A. The
minor political divisions of the U. S. — Walker, F. A.
The progress of the nation.—Elliott, E. B. Population 1780 - 1880; An approximate life table for the U. S.
— Walker, F. A. Relations of race and nationality
to mortality in the U. S. *Maps and charts.* Pt. 1.
Physical features of the U. S.: River systems; Woodlands; Rain-fall; Storm centres; Temperature; Iso-
bars; Hypsometric sketch; Coal measures; Geological formations.— Pt. 2, Population, social and industrial statistics: Area and political divisions; Density of population; Constituent elements of population; Colored population; Foreign population; Illiteracy; Church accommodations; Occupations of the
people; Wealth; Debt, state and local; Taxation,
state and local; Fiscal chart; Crops; Pacific coast
maps. — Pt. 3, Vital statistics: Predominating sex;
Age and sex; Birth rate; Deaths; The afflicted
c asses.

Hewes, Fletcher W., *and* H: **Gannett.** Scribner's statistical atlas of the U. S.; showing
by graphic methods their present condition
and their political, social and industrial
development. N. Y. [1883]. F.   **317 : R3**
Contents. Physical geography.—Political history.—
Progress.—Population.—Mortality. — Education.—Religion. — Occupations. — Finance and commerce. —
Agriculture. — Live stock and products. — Manufactures.—Miscellaneous.—General index.

Rand, McNally and co.'s new indexed business
atlas and shippers' guide ; containing large
scale maps of the Dominion of Canada,
old Mexico, Central America, Cuba and the
several states and territories of the U. S.,
with a reference map of the world, accompanied by a new and original compilation
and ready reference index of 175,000 places,
showing in detail the entire railroad system
of North America, the express company
doing business over each road and locating
all cities, towns, post offices, railroad stations, villages, counties, parishes, islands,
lakes, rivers, mountains, etc., on the continent. The special features of this ed. are
naming the nearest mailing point' of all
local places in the U. S. and the full census
returns of 1880. Chicago. 1881. F. **917 : R3**

United States. *Coast survey.* List of geographical positions determined. *In* Report 1851,
53, 55, 57, 59, 64, 65,68.   *in* **622 : D**

— Geographical positions of prominent places in
the U. S., determined astronomically or
geodetically. *In* Report 1874. *in* **622 : D**

Smiley, C: W. List of 1817 of the principal lakes of the U. S., with a designation of their locations, *and* List of the principal rivers of the U. S., which empty into the Atlantic ocean, Pacific ocean and Gulf of Mexico, with their tributaries. *In* U. S. fish com. report, v. 10.   *in* 639 : D

Travels, etc.

Tuckerman, H: Theodore. America and her commentators; with a critical sketch of travel in the U. S. N. Y. 1864. O.
                                          917.1 : 3
Contents. Introd.—Early discoverers and explorers.—French missionary explorations.— French travellers and writers.—British travellers and writers.—English abuse of America.—Northern european writers.— Italian travellers.—American travellers and writers.—Conclusion.—Index.

Chastellux, François J: de. Voyages dans l' Amérique septentrionale dans 1780—1782. Paris. 1786. 2 v. D.   917.1 : 87
— *Same, eng.* Travels in North America in 1780—1782. Tr. from the french by an english gentleman who resided in America at that period, with notes by the tr. Lond. 1787. 2 v. O.   917.1 : 87

Atwater, Caleb. Remarks made on a tour to Prairie du Chien, thence to Washington city, in 1829. Columbus, O. 1831. S.
                                          917.1 : P57

Hamilton, T: Men and manners in America, by the author of Cyril Thornton, etc. Edinb. 1833. 2 v. D.   917.1 : 56

Power, Tyrone. Impressions of America during 1833—1835. 2d amer. ed. Phila. 1836. 2 v. D.   917.1 : 29

Kemble, Frances Anne. Journal [in America]. Phila. 1835. 2 v. in 1. D.   917.1 : 11

Reed, Andrew, *and* James Matheson. A narrative of the visit to the amer. churches by the deputation from the Congregational union of England and Wales. Lond. 1835. 2 v. O.   917.1+32

Martineau, Harriet. Society in America. N. Y. 1837. 2 v. D.   917.1 : 25
Contents. V. 1. Introd.—Politics.— Economy. 2. *Same, continued.*—Civilization.—Religion.—App.
— Retrospect of western travel. N. Y. 1838. 2 v. D.   917.1 : 26

Gilman, Caroline. The poetry of travelling in the U. S.; with add. sketches by a few friends, and A week among autographs by S. Gilman. N. Y. 1838. D.   917.1 : 18

Marryat, F: Diary in America; with remarks on its institutions; 1st and 2d series. Phila. 1840. 2 v. D.   917.1 : 24

Dickens, C: J: Huffam. American notes. *T. p. w.* [Pub. 1842]. O.   917.1 : 15
— *Same. With his* Great expectations.
                                          in D 1306

Hawthorne, Nathaniel. Passages from [his] amer. note-books, [1835–43]. (Lib. ed.) Bost. 1878. D.   917.1 : 44

Silliman, A: E. A gallop among amer. scenery, or Sketches of amer. scenes and military adventure. N. Y. 1843. D.   917.1 : 35

Gerstäcker, F: Streif- und jagdzüge durch die Vereinigten Staaten Nord-Amerikas, mit einem vorworte von Tr. Bromme. Dresden. 1844. 2 v. S.   917.1 : 6
— *Same.* 2te aufl. Leipz. 1856. 2 v. S.
                                          917.1 : 6
— *Same.* 3te aufl. Jena. *n. d.* S.   917.1 : 6

Lyell, *Sir* C: Travels in North America, in 1841-2, with geological observations on the U. S., Canada and Nova Scotia. N. Y. 1845. 2 v. in 1. D.   917.1 : 21
— A second visit to the U. S. of North America, [1845–46]. N. Y. 1849. 2 v. D.   917.1 : 22

Raumer, F: L: G: v. America and the amer. people. Tr. from the germ. by W: W. Turner. N. Y. 1846. O.   917.1 : 31
Note. Contains a review of the history, and the political, social, educational, religious and economical condition of the U. S., with short extracts from letters describing personal incidents of travel.

Sigourney, Lydia Howard, *born* Huntley. Scenes in my native land. Bost. 1845. D.
                                          917.1 : 88
Note. Sketches and poems of various places in the east.

Wortley, *Lady* Emmeline Stuart. Travels in the U. S., etc., during 1849 and 1850. N. Y. 1851. D.   917.1 : 37

Cooper, James Fenimore. The travelling bachelor, or Notions of the americans. New ed. N. Y. 1852. 2 v. in 1. D.   917.1 : 14

Bunn, Alfred. Old England and New England, in a series of views taken on the spot. Phila. 1853. 2 v. in 1. D.   917.1 : 10

Pulszky, Ferencz Aurél *and* Teréz. White, red and black; sketches of amer. society in the U. S. during the visit of their guests. N. Y. 1853. 2 v. D.   917.1 : 30

Bremer, Fredrika. The homes of the new world; impressions of America. N. Y. 1854. 2 v. D.   917.1 : 5
— *Same, germ.* Die heimat in der neuen welt; ein tagebuch in briefen, geschrie en während zweijähr. reisen in Nordamérika und auf Cuba. Aus dem schwed. Leipz. 1854. 9 v. S.   917.1 : 5

Hohbach, F: W., *ed.* Aus Amerika, gesammelt von [ihm]. Leipz. 1856. S.   917.1 : 7

Beauvallet, Léon. Rachel and the new world; a trip to the U. S. and Cuba. Tr. from the french. N. Y. 1856. D.   917.1 : 9

Mackay, C: Life and liberty in America, or Sketches of a tour in the U. S. and Canada, in 1857-8. Ill. Lond. 1859. 2 v. D.
                                          917.1 : 23

Trollope, Anthony. North America. N. Y. 1862. D.   917.1 : 36

Laboulaye, E: René Lefebvre. Paris in America by René Lefebvre. Tr. by Mary L. Booth. N. Y. 1863. D.   917.1 : 20

Russell, W: Howard. My diary, north and south, [march 1861—apr. 1862]. N. Y. 1863. O.   917.1+33

Dodge, Mary Abigail. Wool-gathering, by Gail Hamilton. Bost. 1867. D.   917.1 : 17
Note. Journeys west and south.

Dixon, W: Hepworth. New America. Ill. Phila. 1867. D.   917.1 : 89
Note. Descriptions of the indians of the west. Utah and mormonism, position of woman in America, shaker communities, perfectionists of Oneida, characteristics of "young America," etc.
— White conquest. Leipz. 1876. 2 v. in 1. D.   917.1 : 90
Note. V. 1 contains descriptions of jesuit missionaries and indians in the west, polygamy, communism, indian wars, condition of the Indian Territory, Texas and its feuds of races, Louisiana and its political complications in 1875. V. 2 continues the history of the Kellogg government in New Orleans, discusses Georgia and the negro question, Washington, Philadelphia, the chinese question in America, temperance, illiteracy and education.

Kirchhoff, Theodor. Reisebilder und skizzen aus Amerika. Altona. 1875, 1876. 2 v. D.
917.1 : 83
Contents. V. 1. Vorwort.—1500 meilen in der stagekutsche. — Eine fahrt mit dem "hotelzuge" der Pacificbahn.—Bilder aus dem goldland.—Bilder aus dem süden, 1866 - 1870. 2. Nach Oregon.—Streifzüge im nordwesten.

Ratzel, F: Städte- und culturbilder aus Nordamerika. Leipz. 1876. 2 v. in 1. D.
917.1 : 82
Contents. V. 1. Neuyork.—Der Hudson.—Saratoga. —Boston.—Cambridge.— Philadelphia.— Washington. 2. Südliche städte.—Richmond.—Charleston.—Columbia. — Savannah. — Ansiedelungen und curorte in Florida.—Durch Georgia und Alabama.—Neuorleans. —Mississippi und Ohio.—Die drei hauptstädte des westens: Cincinnati, Saint-Louis, Chicago.—Denver. — Reise auf der Pacificbahn. — San - Francisco. — Ruinen.

Bishop, Nathaniel Holmes. Voyage of the paper canoe ; a geographical journey of 2500 miles, from Quebec to the Gulf of Mexico, during 1874-5. Bost. 1878. O.   917.1 : 39
— Four months in a sneak-box ; a boat journey of 2600 miles down the Ohio and Mississippi rivers and along the Gulf of Mexico. Bost. 1879. O.   917.1 : 38

Saunders, W: Through the light continent, or The U. S. in 1877-8. 2d ed. Lond. 1879. O.
917.1 : 41

Campbell, *Sir* G: White and black ; the outcome of a visit to the U. S. N. Y. 1879. O.
917.1 : 40
Contents. A bird's-eye view of the U. S.—The management of coloured races.—Black and white in the southern states.—Some of the contents of my journal.—State constitutions.

Marshall, W. G. Through America, or Nine months in the U. S. Lond. 1881. O.
917.1 : 42
Note. Principally Utah and California.

Holyoake, G: Jacob. Among the americans, and A stranger in America. Chicago. 1881. D.   917.1 : 43
Contents. Sea ways and sea society.—Courtesies of N. Y.—The republican convention at Saratoga. — Propagandist uses of interviewing.—Men of action in Boston.—City of Holyoke.— Wanderings in five great cities.—American orators.—Famous preachers. —Co-operation in the new world.—State socialism in America.—Co-operative emigration. — Wayside incidents.— Manners and opinions in America. — Emigrant education.—A stranger in America.

Bodenstedt, F: Martin v. Vom Atlantischen zum Stillen ocean. Leipz. 1882. O.   917.1 : 48

Sala, G: A: America revisited ; from the bay of New York to the Gulf of Mexico, and from Lake Michigan to the Pacific. Ill. Lond. 1882. 2 v. O.   917.1 : 80

Freeman, E: A: Some impressions of the U. S. N. Y. 1883. O.   917.1 : 52

Blake, Mary E., (*M. E. B.*) On the wing ; rambling notes of a trip to the Pacific. Bost. 1883. S.   917.1 : 53

Robinson, Philip. Sinners and saints ; a tour across the states and around them, with three months among the mormons. Bost. 1883. D.   917.1 : 54

Faithfull, Emily. Three visits to America. N. Y. [1884]. D.   917.1 : 67
Note. Throughout my three visits I had one object specially before me, namely, to supplement the experience gained during twenty years of practical work in England, in regard to the changed position of women in the nineteenth century, by ascertaining how America is trying to solve the most delicate and difficult problem presented by modern civilization.— Preface.

Hardy, Iza Duffus. Between two oceans, or Sketches of american travel. Lond. 1884. O.   917.1 : 70

Griffin, *Sir* Lepel H: The great republic. Lond. 1884. D.   917.1 : 79
Note. An arraignment of american institutions and society.

Schönhof, Jacob. Deutsche urtheile über Amerika. *In* Deutsche zeit- und streit-fragen.
304 : 15 v10

Oberländer, R: Von ozean zu ozean ; kulturbilder und naturschilderungen aus dem fernen westen von Amerika, nach eigenen beobachtungen und reisestudien. Ill. Leipz. 1885. O.   917.1 : 68
Contents. Zur see. — New York. — Eisenbahnen in den V. S.— Der grosse nordwesten. — Der pacifische nordwesten. — Kalifornien. — Der neue südwesten.— Register.

Neide, C: A. The canoe Aurora ; a cruise from the Adirondacks to the Gulf. N. Y. 1885. D.   917.1 : 81

Butterworth, Hezekiah. Zigzag journeys in the occident, the Atlantic to the Pacific ; a summer trip of the Zigzag club from Boston to the Golden Gate. Bost. 1888 [1882]. D.   x 917.1 : 50

Bromfield, E: T., *ed.* Picturesque journeys in America of the Junior united tourist club. N. Y. 1883 [1882]. O.   x 917.1 : 51

Hale, E: Everett *and* Susan. A family flight around home. Ill. Bost. [1884]. O.
x 917.1 : 66

Abbott, Jacob. Marco Paul's voyages and travels :
— In New York. Ill. N. Y. *n. d.* S.   x 917.1 : 58
— On the Erie Canal. Ill. N. Y. *n. d.* S.
x 917.1 : 59
— In the forests of Maine. Ill. N. Y. *n. d.* S.
x 917.1 : 60
— In Vermont. Ill. N. Y. *n. d.* S.   x 917.1 : 61
— At the Springfield armory. Ill. N. Y. *n. d.* S.
x 917.1 : 63

American adventure by land and sea ; remarkable instances of enterprise and fortitude among americans, shipwrecks, adventures at home and abroad, indian captivities, etc., in 2 v.; v. 2. N. Y. 1843. T.
913.2 : 25

x denotes books specially adapted for children.

25.   North America — c, U. S., East and South.

1. New England.

In general.

Palfrey, J: Gorham. History of New England. Bost. 1858-82. 4 v. O.   972+3

Elliott, C: Wyllys. The New England history, from the discovery of the continent by the northmen, a. d. 986, to the period when the colonies declared their independence, a. d. 1776. N. Y. 1857. 2 v. O. 972 : 1

Contents. V. 1. To 1691. 2. 1691-1776.—App. Westminster Shorter catechism; Body of liberties; Articles of confederation; Mass. slave laws; Census; Signers of declaration of independence; Chronology.

Winthrop, J: The history of New England from 1630 to 1649, from his original mss.; with notes to illustrate the civil and ecclesiastical concerns, the geography, settlement and institutions of the country, and the lives and manners of the principal planters by James Savage. New ed. Bost. 1853. 2 2. O. 972+4

Josselyn, J: An account of two voyages to New-England, made during the years 1638, 1663. Bost. 1865. O. 917.2 : 22

— New England's rarities discovered in birds, beasts, fishes, serpents and plants of that country; with an introd. and notes by E: Tuckerman. Bost. 1865. O. 917.2 : 23

Caverly, Robert Boodey. History of the indian wars of New England, with Eliot the apostle in the midst of them. Bost. 1882. 2 v. in 1. D. 972 : 5

Note. V. 2 has a separate title as follows: Life and labors of John Eliot, the apostle among the indian nations of New England; together with an account of the Eliots in New England. Bost. 1882.

Whitefield, Edwin. The homes of our forefathers ; a selection of the oldest and most interesting buildings, historical houses and noted places in Massachusetts, from original drawings made on the spot. 3d ed. Bost. 1880. O. 917.2 : R1 v1

— *Same.* 2d series : Rhode Island and Connecticut. Bost. 1882. O. 917.2 : R1 v2

Carter, Robert. A summer cruise on the coast of New England. Bost. 1864. D. 917.2 : 3

Rollins, Ellen Chapman, *born* Hobbs, (*E. H. Arr*). New England bygones. Phila. 1880. D. 917.2 : 5

— Old-time child-life. Phila. 1881. D. 917.2 : 6

Jackson, Helen Maria, *born* Fiske, *formerly mrs.* Hunt, (*H. H.*). New England. *in* 917.5 : 28

Drake, S: Adams. Nooks and corners of the New England coast. Ill. N. Y. 1875. O. 917.2 : 4

— New England legends and folk-lore, in prose and poetry. Ill. Bost. 1883. O. 972 : 6

Gibson, W: Hamilton. Pastoral days, or Memories of a New England year. N. Y. 1881 [1880]. Q. 917.2 : R2

Fellows, H: Parker. Boating trips on New England rivers. Ill. and map. Bost. 1884. D. 917.2 : 24

Pidgeon, Daniel. Old-world questions and new-world answers. Lond. 1884. D. 917.2 : 25

— *Same.* N. Y. 1885. S. 917.2 : 25

Contents. Americans and americans. — New England; Ansonia.—Clockland.—Winsted; A temperance town. — Among the Berkshire hills; Great Barrington.—Common schools; A town meeting.—Pittsfield; Dalton; An industrial pioneer. — A shaker village; Communism. — North Adams; An industrial battle; Williamstown.—The Hoosac tunnel; Deerfield; Holyoke. — The regicide judges; Birds and traps; The higher education of women. — Hartford; Silk; A creamery.—The Willimantic thread company; Benevolent mill-owning.—Lowell, past and present.—The factory system. — Labour, wages and the tariff. — Boston. — The Hudson river. — Lakes George and Champlain.—Canada, present and past.

Maine.

Maine historical society. Collections. V. 1-6, 8, Portland. 1831—1881 ; v. 7, Bath. 1876. 8 v. O. 906+P6

Contents. V. 1-7. See Catalogue of the library of the Boston athenæum, pt. 3, p. 1841. 8. **Washburn,** Israel, *jr.* The north-eastern boundary.—**Goold,** W: Col. Arthur Noble of Georgetown.—**Champlin,** J. T. Educational institutions in Maine while a district of Massachusetts.—**Richardson,** H. W. The Pemaquid country under the Stuarts.—**Goold,** W: Fort Halifax, its projectors, builders and garrison; Col. Vaughan of Matinicus and Damariscotta. — **Godfrey,** J : E. Norambega. *Memoirs and biogr. sketches.* **Poor,** J: A., Reuel Williams.—**Smith,** E. B., E: Emerson Bourne. —**Washburn,** Israel, Ether Shepley.—**Talbot,** G: F., G: T. Davis.—**Godfrey,** J: E., E: Kent.—**Everett,** C: C., Leonard Woods.

— [Collections, 2d ser.] Documentary history of the state of Maine ; [v. 1, 2] ed. by W: Willis. Portland. 1869, 1884 ; Cambridge. 1877. 3 v. O. 906 : P7

Contents. V. 1. **Kohl,** J: G: History of the discovery of Maine; with an app. on the voyages of the Cabots by M. d'Avezac. 2. **Hakluyt,** R: A discourse on western planting written in 1584; with a pref. and introd. by Leonard Woods, ed. with notes in the app. by C: Deane. 3. The Trelawney papers; ed. and ill. with historical notes by James Phinney Baxter.

New Sweden, *Maine.* Celebration of the decennial anniversary of the founding of New Sweden, july 23, 1880. [Portland]. 1881. O. 972.1 : 1

Ballard, E: Geographical names on the coast of Maine. *In* U. S. coast survey rep. 1868. *in* 622 : D

Boardman, S: L. The climate, soil, physical resources and agricultural capabilities of the state of Maine, with special reference to the occupation of its new lands. (U. S. dep. of agr. Miscel. special rep. no. 4.) Wash. 1884. O. *in* 630 : D

Martin, *Mrs.* Clara Barnes. Mount Desert on the coast of Maine. Map. and ill. 5th ed. Portland. 1880. D. 917.2 : 17

Hubbard, Lucius L. Woods and lakes of Maine; a trip from Moosehead lake to New Brunswick in a birch-bark canoe ; added, some indian place-names and their meanings, now first pub. Ill. Bost. 1884. D. 917.2 : 20

Springer, J: S. Forest life and forest trees ; comprising winter camp-life among the loggers, and wild-wood adventure, with descriptions of lumbering operations on the various rivers of Maine and New Brunswick. N. Y. 1856. D. 917.2 : 12

Thoreau, H: D: The Maine woods. Bost. 1864. D. 917.2 : 8

Contents. Ktaadn. — Chesuncook. — The Allegash and East branch.—App.

Steele, T: Sedgwick. Canoe and camera ; a two hundred mile tour through the Maine forests. [New ed.] Bost. 1882. D. 917.2 : 14

— Paddle and portage from Moosehead lake to the Aroostook river, Maine. Bost. 1882. D. 917.2 : 15

Bishop, W: H: Fish and men in the Maine islands. Ill. N. Y. 1885. S. 917.2 : 26

New Hampshire and Vermont.

Belknap, Jeremy. The history of New Hampshire. Bost. 1784-92. 3 v. D. 972.2 : 1

Contents. V. 1. Comprehending the events of one complete century from the discovery of the river

Piscataqua. 2. 1715-1790. 3. Geographical description of the state; with sketches of its natural history, productions, improvements and present state of society and manners, laws and government.

Williams, S: The natural and civil history of Vermont. 2d ed., enl. and corr. Burlington. 1809. 2 v. O.   972.3 : 1

Farmer, J:, and Jacob Bailey Moore. A gazetteer of the state of New Hampshire. Ill. Concord. 1823. D.   917.2 : 10

Drake, S: Adams. The heart of the White Mountains ; their legend and scenery, with ill. by W: Hamilton Gibson. Tourist's ed. N. Y. 1882. O.   917.2+16

Massachusetts.

(See also Witchcraft delusion, col. 54-55.)

Barry, J: Stetson. The history of Massachusetts. Bost. 1855-57. 3 v. O.   972.4 : 11
Contents. V. I. The colonial period. 2. The provincial period. 3. The commonwealth period.

Hutchinson, T: The history of Massachusetts, from the first settlement thereof in 1628 until 1750. 3d ed., with add. notes and corr. Bost. 1795. 2 v. O. — V. 3. History of the province of Massachusetts Bay from 1750 until june 1774. Lond. 1828. O.   972.4 : 8

Minot, G: Richards. Continuation of the history of the province of Massachusetts Bay from 1748 ; with an introd. sketch of events from its original settlement. Pub. according to act of congress. Bost. 1798, 1803. 2 v. O.   972.4 : 13

Bradford, Alden. History of Massachusetts from 1764 to july 1775, when gen. Washington took command of the amer. army. Bost. 1822. O.   972.4+1
— History of Massachusetts from july 1775, when gen. Washington took command of the amer. army at Cambridge, to 1789 incl., when the federal government was estab. under the present constitution. Bost. 1825. O.   972.4+12

Oliver, P: The puritan commonwealth ; an historical review of the puritan government in Massachusetts, in its civil and ecclesiastical relations, from its rise to the abrogation of the first charter, together with some general reflections on the english colonial policy, and on the character of puritanism. Bost. 1856. O.   972+2

Bradford, W: History of Plymouth plantation. Now first printed from the original ms. for the Mass. historical society ; pub. at the charge of the Appleton fund. Bost. 1856. O.   972.4+15

Young, Alexander. Chronicles of the first planters of the colony of Massachusetts Bay, from 1623 to 1636 ; now first coll. from original records and contemporaneous mss., and ill. with notes. Bost. 1846. O.   972.4+14

Massachusetts *state.* Records of the colony of New Plymouth in New England ; printed by order of the legislature of the commonwealth of Massachusetts, [v. 1-8, ed. by Nathaniel B. Shurtleff, v. 9-12 ed. by D: Pulsifer.] Bost. 1855-61. 12 v. in 10. Q.   972.4 : R17
Contents. V. I. Court orders, 1633-1640. 2. *Same,* 1641-1651. 3. *Same,* 1651-1661. 4. *Same,* 1661-1668. 5. *Same,* 1668-1678. 6. *Same,* 1678-1691. 7. Judicial

acts, 1636-1692. 8. Miscellaneous records. 1633-1689. 9. Acts of the commissioners of the United Colonies of New England, v. 1, 1643-1651. 10. *Same,* v. 2, 1653-1679. 11. Laws, 1623-1682. 12. Deeds, etc., v. 1, 1620-1651.—Book of Indian records for their lands.

Walcott, C: H. Concord in the colonial period ; a history of the town of Concord, Mass., from the earliest settlement to the overthrow of the Andros government. 1635-1689. Map. Bost. 1884. O.   972.4+16

Hallowell, R: Price. The quaker invasion of Massachusetts. Bost. 1883. D. 972.4 : 10

Spofford, Jeremiah. A gazetteer of Massachusetts ; containing a general view of the state, with an historical sketch of the principal events from its settlement to the present time, and notices of the several towns, alphab. arr. Newburyport. 1828. D.   917.2 : 11

Holland, Josiah Gilbert. History of western Massachusetts ; the counties of Hampden, Hampshire, Franklin and Berkshire, embracing an outline or general history of the section, an account of its scientific aspects and leading interests, and separate histories of its 100 towns. Springfield. 1855. 2 v. D.   972.4 : 9

Massachusetts historical society. Collections : 5th series, v. 2, 3. Bost. 1877. 2 v. O.   906+9
Contents. V. 2. Officers of the society, elected april 1876. — Members. — Corresp. between Jeremy Belknap and Ebenezer Hazard, pt. 1. 3. *Same,* pt. 2.— Letters and documents relating to slavery in Mass.

Old colony historical society. Collections ; papers read before the society. Taunton. 1879-85. O.   906+4
Contents. No. 1. Emery, S. H. Historical sketch. — Alger, A. M. Biographical sketch. — Tarbox, I. N. Pilgrims and puritans.—Sproat, T: C. Value of a historical society. 2. Reed, C: A. The province of Massachusetts Bay in the 17th century with a sketch of capt. T: Coram, founder of the Foundling hospital in London. — Williams, H: Was Elizabeth Pool the first purchaser of the territory and now dress of Taunton ? 3. Fuller, W: E. Obituary paper. — Blake, M. Taunton north purchase. — Brigham, C: H. Historical sketch of Taunton, England. — Leland, P. W. Algonquin or Indian terms as applied to places and things. — Brigham, C: H. Description of the ms. dictionary of the Bible in the Indian language.—Peirce, E. W. The original owners and early settlers of Freetown and Assonet. — Hall, J. W. D. Ancient iron works in Taunton.

Weymouth historical society. (No. 1:) The original journal of gen. Solomon Lovell, kept during the Penobscot expedition, 1779, with a sketch of his life by Gilbert Nash ; together with the proceedings of the society for 1879-80. Weymouth, Mass. 1881. O.   906+5

Thoreau, H: D: Cape Cod. Bost. 1865. S.   917.2 : 7

Boston.

Winsor, Justin, *ed.* The memorial history of Boston, incl. Suffolk county, Mass., 1630-1880. Bost. 1880-82. 4 v. Q.   972.4 : R2
Contents. V. 1. The colonial period. 2. The provincial period. 3. The revolutionary period. — The last hundred years, pt. 1. 4. The last hundred years. pt. 2.—Special topics.—General index.

Quincy, Josiah. A municipal history of the town and city of Boston, during two centuries, from sept. 17, 1630 to sept. 17, 1830. Bost. 1852. O.   972.4+3

Wheildon, W: W. Curiosities of history: Boston, sept. 17th 1630—1880. Bost. 1880. D.
972.4 : 4
Contents. Topography of Boston. — The public ferries.—The Boston cornfields.—Puritan government. — Narragansett indians. — Names of places, streets, etc. — Persecution of the quakers. — First newspaper in America.—Curious Boston lectures. — Remarkable proclamations.—Popular puritan literature.—Revolutionary proclamations.—Curiosities of the market.

Drake, S: Adams. Old landmarks and historic personages of Boston. Ill. Bost. 1875. D.
917.2 : 19
— Around the Hub ; a boys' book about Boston. Bost. 1881. D.   x 972.4 : 6

Butterworth, Hezekiah. Young folks' history of Boston. Ill. Bost. 1881. D. x 972.4 : 5

Scudder, Horace Elisha. Boston town. Bost. 1881. O.   x 972.4 : 7

Lander, Sarah W. Boston. (Spectacles for young eyes, no. 1.) N. Y. *n. d.* S.
x 917.2 : 18

Bostonian society. Proceedings at the annual meeting, jan. 8, 1884. Bost. 1884. O.
906 : Pam
— *Same ;* jan. 13, 1885. Bost. 1885. O.
906 : Pam
See also in the Index to biography **Bellingham**—Bradford—Bradstreet—Carver—Dudley—Endicott — Haynes — Hinckley — Hutchinson—Leverett—Prince—Standish—Strong—Vane—Winslow—Winthrop.

Rhode Island.

Arnold, S: Greene. History of the state of Rhode Island and Providence plantations. N. Y. 1859, 1860. 2 v. O.   972.5+1
Contents. V. 1. 1636—1700.—Index, 2. 1700—1790.—Index.

Greene, G: Washington. A short history of Rhode Island. Providence. 1877. O.
972.5 : 2

Mason, G: Champlin. Reminiscences of Newport. Ill. Newport, R. I. 1884. O.
972.5 : 3

Newport, *Rhode Island.* Map of Newport and vicinity. N. Y. *n. d.* T.   917.2 : 21

Austin, Jane Goodwin. Nantucket scraps; being experiences of an off-islander, in season and out of season, among a passing people. Bost. 1883 [1882]. S.   917.2 : 13
See also in the Index to biography **Williams.**

Connecticut.

Peters, S: General history of Connecticut, from its first settlement under George Fenwick to its latest period of amity with Great Britain prior to the revolution, incl. a description of the country and many curious and interesting anecdotes ; with an app. pointing out the causes of the rebellion in America, together with the particular part taken by the people of Conn. in its promotion. By a gentleman of the province. London. 1781. Added, additions to app., notes and extracts from letters, verifying many important statements made by the author by S: Jarvis McCormick. N. Y. 1877. D.   972.6 : 2

Trumbull, B: A history of Connecticut, civil and ecclesiastical, from the emigration of its first planters from England in 1630 to 1764, and to the close of the indian wars. New Haven. 1818. 2 v. O.   972.6 : 3
App. V. 1 : The original patent of New England.

Dwight, Theodore, *jr.* The history of Connecticut, from the first settlement to the present time. [Harper's family lib.] N. Y. 1845. S.
972.6 : 1
See also in the Index to biography **Trumbull.**

2. Middle States.

New York.

New York *state.* The documentary history of the state of New York, arr. under dir. of the hon. Christopher Morgan by E. B. O'Callaghan. Albany. 1850-51. 4 v. Q. 973.1 : R1
Contents. V. 1. Iroquois and other indian tribes.—First settlement at Onandaga and the discovery of the salt springs at Salina. — De Courcelles and De Tracy's exped. against the Mohawk indians, 1665-66. — Reports on the province of N. Y., 1669-78. — De la Barre's exped. to Hungry Bay. — Gov. Dongan's report on the state of the province, 1687.— Denonville's exped. to the Genessee country and Niagara, 1687.— Names of the male inhabitants of Ulster co., 1689. — Invasion of N. Y. and the burning of Schenectady by the french, 1690. — Civil list of the province of N. Y., 1693. — Frontenac's exped. against the Onondagoes, 1696.— N. Y. army list, 1700.—Census of the counties of Orange, Dutchess and Albany, 1702, 1714, 1720. — Cadwallader Colden on the lands of N. Y. 1732. — Susquehanna river, 1683—1757.—Ogdensburgh, 1749.—Oswego. —The Oneida country and Mohawk valley, 1756, 1757. —French seigniories on Lake Champlain.— Boundary line between the whites and the indians, 1765. — City of N. Y. — Long Island.—Statistics of population, 1647 —1774. — Statistics of revenue, imports, exports, etc., 1691—1768.—Trade and manufactures, 1705—1757. — Report of gov. Tryon on the state of the province, 1774. 2. Papers relating to lt. gov. Liesler's administration.—Early rate lists of Long Island.—M⁹s. of sir W: Johnson.— Early steam navigation. — Western New York. 3. Champlain's expeditions to northern and western N. Y., 1609, 1615. — First settlement of N. Y. by the dutch. — Restoration of N. Y. to the english and the charges against capt. Manning for its previous surrender to the dutch, 1674, 1675. — State of religion in the province, 1657—1712. — King's county, L. I. —Churches in Queen's county.—Suffolk county.—City of N. Y.— The palatines.— Manor of Livingston, including the first settlement of Schoharie, 1680—1795.— Census of slaves, 1755. — Albany and adjacent places. — Westchester county. — Ulster and Dutchess counties. — Quakers and moravians. — Rev. Gideon Hawley's journey to Oghquaga, Broome county, 1753. — State of the anglo-american church in 1776.—Prices of land in the state of N. Y., 1791.— Report of a com. appointed to explore the western waters in the state of N. Y., 1792.—Journal of rev. J: Taylor's missionary tour through the Mohawk and Black river countries in 1802.—Rectors of St. Peter's church, Albany.—App. —Medals and coins.—Miscellany. 4. Journal of New Netherland, 1641—1646. —Joguès, I: Description of New Netherland. — Tienhoven, C. van. Information for taking up land in New Netherland, 1650.—Kregier, M. Journal of the second Esopus war, 1663.—Extracts from the Breeden raedt, 1649. — Montanus, A. Description of New Netherland, 1671.—Trial for witchcraft in N. Y. 1665.— Assessment roll of the five dutch towns on L. I., 1675. —State of the province of N. Y. in 1738. — Reasons in support of triennial elections in the province of N. Y. — Journal of sir W: Johnson's scouts, 1755, 1756. — Papers relating to the six nations. — The erection of Fort Stanwix, 1758. — The difficulties between N. Y. and N. H.—Memoir of James Delancey. lieut. gov. of the prov. of N. Y. — Miscellanies. — Memoir of hon. James Duane.—Proclamation of the last royal governors of N. Y.—Inglis, C: Memorial concerning the Iroquois.

— Documents relative to the colonial history of the state of New York, procured in Holland, England and France, by J: Romeyn Brodhead, agent, under and by virtue of an act of leg., may 2, 1839, pub. under and

x denotes books specially adapted for children.

by virtue of an act of leg. march 30, 1849, and an act, passed april 12, 1856; ed. by E. B. O'Callaghan, with a general introd. by the agent. Albany. 1853–61. 11 v. Q.

973.1:R3

Contents. V. 1. General introd.—Holland documents, 1603–1656. 2. *Same*, 1657–1678. 3. London documents, 1614–1692. 4. *Same*, 1693–1706. 5. *Same*, 1707–1733. 6. *Same*, 1734–1755. 7. *Same*, 1756–1767. 8. *Same*, 1768–1782. 9. Paris documents, 1631–1744. 10. *Same*, 1745–1774. [11]. General index.

New York historical society. Collections; 2d series, v. 3, pt. 1. N. Y. 1857. O. **906+3**
Contents. Vries, D. P. de. Voyages from Holland to America. a. d. 1632 to 1644; tr. by H: C. Murphy.— Short sketch of the Mohawk indians, by J. Megapolensis, jr.— The Jogues paper.—Extract from Castell's Discoverie of America, 1644.—Broad advice to the United Netherland provinces.— Extract from Wagenaar's Beschryving van Amsterdam, relating to New Amstel.—The seven articles from the church of Leyden.— Negotiations between New England and Canada, 1648 - 1651.—Proceedings of the first assembly of Virginia, 1619.

Brodhead, J: Romeyn. History of the state of New York; 1st period, 1609—1664. 2d ed. N. Y. 1859. O. **973.1+3**

O'Callaghan, Edmund Burke. History of New Netherland, or New York under the dutch. N. Y. 1846, 1848. 2 v. O. **973.1+6**
Contents. V. 1. 1492 - 1846.—App.—Index. 2. 1846 - 1664.—App.—Index.
See also in the Index to biography **Stuyvesant.**

Miller, J: A description of the province and city of New York; with plans of the city and several forts, as they existed in the year 1695. New ed., with an introd. and historical notes by J: Gilmary Shea. [Gowan's Bibliotheca amer., 3.] N. Y. 1862. O. **973.1+4**

Wooley, C: A two years' journal in New York and part of its territories in America, [1701]. A new ed. with an introd. and historical notes by E. B. O'Callaghan. [Gowan's Bibliotheca amer., 2.] N. Y. 1860. O. **973.1+13**

Barber, J: Warner. Pictorial history of the state of New York; a general collection of the most interesting facts, biogr. sketches, varied descriptions, etc., relating to the past and present, with geogr. descriptions of the counties, cities and principal villages throughout the state. Cooperstown, N. Y. 1846. O. **973.1:5**

Hammond, Jabez D. The history of political parties in the state of New York to 1840. 4th ed. corr. and enl., with add. notes by gen. Root. Syracuse. 1852. 2 v. O. **973.1:9**
Contents. V. 1. 1783 - 1821. 2. 1821 - 1840.
— *Same*; v. 3, jan. 1841—jan. 1847; incl. the life of Silas Wright. Syracuse. 1848. O. **973.1:9 v3**

Kapp, F: Die deutschen im staate New York während des 18ten jahrh. (Geschichtsblätter, hrsg. von C: Schurz, 1er b.) N. Y. 1884. O. **973.1:12**

Booth, Mary L. History of the city of New York. Ill. N. Y. 1880. O. **973.1+10**

New York Mercantile library association. New York city during the revolution; a collection of original papers, now first pub. from the mss. in possession of the M. L. A. of New York city. N. Y. 1861. Q. **973.1:R7**
Contents. Introd.: New York city in 1767.— The stamp act riot.—New York in 1770.— Col. Marinus Willett's narrative.— The Hickey plot.— New York

correspondence. — The battle of Harlem plains. — New York loyalists of 1776.—Preparations for evacuation.—Statement of W: Butler, esq.—Sir Harry Clinton's defence.

Lamb, Martha Joan Reade, *born* Nash. Wall street in history. Ill. N. Y. 1883. O. **973.1+11**

Francis, J: Wakefield. Old New York, or Reminiscences of the past sixty years; with a memoir of the author by H: T. Tuckerman. N. Y. 1866. O. **973.1:8**

Dayton, Abram C. Last days of knickerbocker life in New York. N. Y. 1882. S. **917.3:7**
Note. Descriptions of life in N. Y. about 1830.

Mayo, Amory Dwight. Symbols of the capital, or Civilization in New York. N. Y. 1859. D. **917.3:5**

Lander, Sarah W. New York. (Spectacles for young eyes, no. 8). N. Y. *n. d.* S. **x 917.3:13**

*   *   *

Letters about the Hudson river and its vicinity, written in 1835—1837. 3d ed., ill. N. Y. 1837. S. **917.3:4**

Curtis, G: W: Lotus-eating; a summer book. Ill. N. Y. 1852. D. **917.3:1**
Contents. The Hudson and the Rhine.—Catskill.— Trenton.— Niagara. — Saratoga.—Lake George.—Nahant.—Newport.

Wise, Daniel. Summer days on the Hudson; the story of a pleasure tour from Sandy Hook to the Saranac lakes, incl. incidents of travel, legends, historical anecdotes, sketches of scenery, etc. Ill. N. Y. 1876. D. **917.3:6**

Searing, A. E. P. The land of Rip Van Winkle; a tour through the romantic parts of the Catskills; its legends and traditions. Ill. N. Y. 1884. Q. **917.3:R14**

Nelson's guide to Lake George and Lake Champlain. Ill. Lond. 1866. T. **917.3:10**

Headley, Joel Tyler. The Adirondack, or Life in the woods. N. Y. 1849. S. **917.3:3**

Murray, W: H: Harrison. Adventures in the wilderness, or Camp-life in the Adirondacks. Ill. Bost. *n. d.* S. **917.3:9**

Hammond, S: H. Hills, lakes and forest streams, or A tramp in the Chateaugay woods. N. Y. 1854. D. **917.3:2**

Kurtz, D. Morris. Ithaca and its resources; an historical and descriptive sketch of the Forest city ..., Cornell university and the principal manuf. and commercial interests. Ill. Ithaca, N. Y. 1883. O. **917.3:Pam**

Allen, H. T. Tunis' illustrated guide to Niagara, rev. Niagara Falls. 1877. S. **917.3:11**

New Jersey.

Smith, S: The history of the colony of Nova-Cæsaria, or New Jersey; containing an account of its first settlement, progressive improvements, the original and present constitution and other events to 1721, with some particulars since and a short view of its present state. Burlington. 1765. [Trenton. 1877]. O. **973.2:2**

New Jersey historical society. Documents relating to the colonial history of the state of New Jersey; ed. by W: A. Whitehead; v. 1-8. Newark. 1880–85. 8 v. O. **973.2:1**
Contents. V. 1. 1631 - 1687. 2. 1687 - 1703. 3. 1703 - 1709. 4. 1709 - 1720. 5. 1720 - 1737. 6. 1738 - 1747. 7. 1746 - 1751. 8. 1751 - 1757.

Pennsylvania and Delaware.

Watson, J: Fanning. Annals of Philadelphia and Pennsylvania in the olden time; a collection of memoirs, anecdotes and incidents of the city and its inhabitants, and of the earliest settlements of the inland part of Pennsylvania, from the days of the founders. Phila. 1850. 2 v. O.   **973.3+1**

Philadelphia and its environs. Phila. 1876. O.   **917.3+8**

Campbell, Helen, *and others*. A sylvan city, or Quaint corners in Philadelphia. (Our continent lib.) Ill. N. Y. 1883. D.   **917.3 : 12**

Peck, G: Wyoming; its history, stirring incidents and romantic adventures. Ill. 3d ed. N. Y. *n. d.* D.   **973.3 : 4**
— *Same.* N. Y. 1872. D.   **973.3 : 4**

Stone, W: Leete. The poetry and history of Wyoming; containing Campbell's Gertrude of Wyoming. *T. p. w.* D.   **973.3 : 2**

Wyoming, The valley of; the romance of its history and its poetry, also specimens of indian eloquence, compiled by a native of the valley. N. Y. 1866. D.   **973.3 : 3**

Pennsylvania historical society. [Memoirs, vol. 11.] A history of New Sweden or the settlements on the river Delaware by Israel **Acrelius**. Tr. from the swedish with an introd. and notes by W: M. Reynolds. Phila. 1876. O.   **973.3+5**

Seidensticker, Oswald. Bilder aus der deutsch-pennsylvanischen geschichte. (Geschichts-blätter, hrsg. von C: Schurz, 2er b.) N. Y. 1885. D.   **973.3 : 6**

See also in the Index to biography **Penn**.

3. Southern states.

In general.

Featherstonhaugh, G: W: Excursion through the slave states, from Washington on the Potomac to the frontier of Mexico, with sketches of popular manners and geological notices. Lond. 1844. 2 v. O.   **917.4 : 10**

Abbott, J: Stevens Cabot. South and north, or Impressions received during a trip to Cuba and the south. N. Y. 1860. D.   **917.4 : 19**

Olmsted, F: Law. A journey in the sea-board slave states [1856]; with remarks on their economy. [Our slave states, 1.] N. Y. 1861. D.   **917.4 : 7**

Olmsted, F: Law.—*Continued.*
— A journey through Texas, or A saddle-trip on the southwestern frontier; with a statistical app. [Our slave states, 2.] N. Y. 1857. D.   **917.4 : 8**
— A journey in the back country. [Our slave states, 3.] N. Y. 1860. D.   **917.4 : 9**

Mackie, J: Milton. From Cape Cod to Dixie and the tropics. *T. p. w.* [N. Y. 1864.] D.   **917.4 : 1**

Note. Sketches, written before the war.

Gilmore, James Roberts, (*Edmund Kirke*). Down in Tennessee and back by way of Richmond, by Edmund Kirke. N. Y. 1864. D: **917.4 : 5**

Trowbridge, J: Townsend. A picture of the desolated states and the work of restoration, 1865-1868. Hartford. 1868. O.   **917.4 : 15**

Somers, Robert. The southern states since the war, 1870-1. Map. Lond. 1871. O.   **917.4 : 33**

King, E: The great south ; a record of journeys in Louisiana, Texas, the Indian Territory, Missouri, Arkansas, Mississippi, Alabama, Georgia, Florida, South Carolina, North Carolina, Kentucky, Tennessee, Virginia, West Virginia and Maryland. Ill. Hartford. 1875. Q.   **917.4 : 32**

Nordhoff, C: The cotton states, in the spring and summer of 1875. N. Y. 1876. O.   **327.1+6**

Brown, W: Wells. My southern home, or The south and its people. Bost. 1880. D.   **917.4 : 2**

Hardy, Mary, *born* McDowell, *lady* T: Duffus. Down south. Lond. 1883. O.   **917.4 : 30**

Maryland.

Scharf, J. T: History of Maryland, from the earliest period to the present day. Balt. 1879. 3 v. O.   **974.1+3**

Bozman, J: Leeds. The history of Maryland, from its first settlement in 1633 to the restoration in 1660; with introd. and notes and ill. Balt. 1837. 2 v. in 1. O. **974.1+4**

Browne, W: Hand. Maryland; the history of a palatinate [to 1783]. (Amer. commonwealths.) Map. Bost. 1884. D. **974.1 : 5**

McSherry, James. A history of Maryland, from its settlement in 1634 to 1848; with an account of its first discovery and the various explorations of Chesapeake bay anterior to its settlement; added, a copious app. for the use schools. Balt. 1852. D. **974.1 : 2**

Maryland historical society. Fund publication no. 18. The foundation of Maryland, and the origin of the act concerning religion of april 21, 1649; prep. and partly read by Bradley T. **Johnson**. Balt. 1883. O.   **906+8**

Shea, J: Gilmary. Early southern tracts. [Lond.] Repr. Balt. 1865. O. **974.1 : 1**
Contents. V. 1. A relation of the successfull beginnings of the lord Baltemore's plantation in Maryland; being an extract of certaine letters written from thence by some of the adventurers to their friends in England, anno domini 1634.

Rothrock, Joseph Trumbull. Vacation cruising in Chesapeake and Delaware bays. Phila. 1884. D. **917.4 : 25**
See also in the Index to biography Calvert, lord *Baltimore.*

Washington city.

Staples, O. G. A descriptive sketch and guide book to all points of interest in Washington. Wash. *n. d.* S. **917.4 : 29**

Hudson, Mary, *born* Clemmer. *formerly mrs.* Ames. Ten years in Washington; life and scenes in the national capital, as a woman sees them. Ill. Hartford. 1873. O. **917.4 : 13**

Gemmill, Jane Wilson. Notes on Washington, or Six years at the national capital. Phila. 1884. D. **917.4 : 24**

Virginia.

Cooke, J: Esten. Virginia; a history of the people. Maps. (Amer. commonwealths.) Bost. 1883. S. **974.2 : 3**

Howison, Robert R. A history of Virginia from its discovery and settlement by europeans to the present time. Phila. 1846, 1848. 2 v. O. **974.2+4**
Contents. V. 1. History of the colony, to the peace of Paris in 1763. **2.** History of the colony and of the state from 1763 to the retrocession of Alexandria in 1847, with a review of the present condition.—Index.

Campbell, C: History of the colony and ancient dominion of Virginia [to the surrender of Cornwallis, 1781]. Phila. 1860. O. **974.2 : 1**

Cooke, J: Esten. Stories of the Old Dominion, from the settlement to the end of the revolution. N. Y. 1879. D. **x 974.2 : 2**
Contents. The adventures of captain John Smith.— Why Virginia was called the "Old Dominion."—The great rebellion in Virginia.—The Knights of the golden horseshoe.—George Washington, the young surveyor.—Washington in the wilderness. — Braddock and his sash.—Point Pleasant and the death of Cornstalk.—Patrick Henry, "the man of the people."— T: Jefferson, "the pen of the revolution."—A ball at the capitol.—Lord Dunmore and the gunpowder.— Elizabeth Zane, the story of a brave girl.—The fate of col. Rogers.—The capture of Vincennes.— John Marshall, the chief justice. — John Randolph of Roanoke.—Rosewell, and Selim the algerine.—Morgan, "the thunderbolt of the revolution." — Cornwallis and "the boy" Lafayette.—The surrender at Yorktown.

Grigsby, Hugh Blair. The Virginia convention of 1776; a discourse del. before the Virginia Alpha of the Phi beta kappa society in the chapel of William and Mary college, Williamsburg, july 3d 1855. Richmond. 1855. O. **342.14+201**

Jefferson, T: Notes on the state of Virginia; ill. with a map, incl. the states of Virginia, Maryland, Delaware and Pennsylvania. New ed. prepared by the author, containing notes and plates never before pub. Richmond. 1853. O. **917.4+34**

Howe, H: Historical collections of Virginia; a collection of the most interesting facts,

x denotes books specially adapted for children.

traditions, biographical sketches, anecdotes, etc., relating to its history and antiquities, with geographical and statistical descriptions. Appended, An historical and descriptive sketch of the District of Columbia. Ill. Charleston. 1849. O. **974.2+5**

Virginia historical register and literary advertiser, The; ed. by W: Maxwell. V. 1-6, jan. 1848—oct. 1853. Richmond. 1848-53. 6 v. in 3. D. **905 : M**
Note. Title-page of v. 3, 4 altered by substitution of "note book" for "advertiser"; v. 5, 6 substitutes "companion" for "note book."

Strother, D: H:, (*Porte Crayon*). Virginia illustrated; containing a visit to the Virginia canaan, and the adventures of Porte Crayon and his cousins. N. Y. 1857. O. **917.4+11**

New virginians, The; by the author of Junia, Estelle Russell. The private life of Galileo, etc. Edinb. 1880. 2 v. O. **917.4 : 27**
See also in the Index to biography **Dale—Gates— Lee—Smith—West,** lord **Delawarr—Yeardley.**

Carolinas and Georgia.

Wheeler, J: H. Historical sketches of North Carolina, from 1584 to 1851; compiled from original records, official documents and traditional statements, with biogr. sketches of her distinguished statesmen, jurists. lawyers, soldiers, divines, etc. Ill. Phila. 1851. 2 v. in 1. O. **974.3 : 5**
Contents. V. 1. The colony.—The state. **2.** Separate counties.—Index.

Hawks, Francis Lister. History of North Carolina. 3d ed. Maps and ill. Fayetteville, N. C. 1859. 2 v. O. **974.3+4**
Contents. V. 1. Early colonization, 1584 - 1591. **2.** Proprietary government, 1663 - 1729.

Simms, W: Gilmore. The history of South Carolina from its first european discovery to its erection into a republic; with a supp. book, bringing the narrative down to the present time. New and rev. ed. N. Y. 1860. D. **974.3 : 3**
— *Same.* N. Y. 1866. D. **974.3 : 3**

Ramsay, D: History of South Carolina, from its first settlement in 1670 to 1808. Newberry, S. C. 1858. O. **974.3 : 2**

Rivers, W: James. A sketch of the history of South Carolina to the close of the proprietary government by the revolution of 1719; with an app. containing many valuable records, hitherto unpub. Charleston. 1856. O. **974.3 : 1**

Stevens, W: Bacon. A history of Georgia, from its first discovery by europeans to the adoption of the present constitution in 1798. N. Y. 1847. 2 v. O. **974.4 : 1**
Contents. V. 1. To 1760. **2.** 1760-1798.—Index.

* * *

Kemble, Frances Anne. Journal of a residence on a Georgia plantation, in 1838-1839. N. Y. 1863. D. **917.4 : 3**

Andrews, Sidney. The south since the war, as shown by fourteen weeks of travel and observation in Georgia and the Carolinas. Bost. 1866. D. **917.4 : 14**

Carpet-bagger, A. Recollections of the inhabitants, localities, superstitions and Ku-klux outrages of the Carolinas, by a carpet-bagger who was born and lived there. [Cleveland, O.] 1880. O. **917.4 : 20**

Leigh, · Frances, *born* Butler,' *the hon. mrs.* James Wentworth. Ten years on a Georgia plantation since the war. Lond. 1883. O. **917.4 : 21**

Florida.

Lanier, Sidney. Florida, its scenery, climate and history ; with an account of Charleston, Savannah, Augusta and Aiken, a chapter for consumptives, various papers on fruit-culture and a complete hand-book and guide. Ill. Phila. 1876. D. **917.4 : 16**

Barbour, G: M. Florida for tourists, invalids and settlers ; containing practical information regarding climate, soil, productions ; cities, towns and people ; the culture of the orange and other tropical fruits ; farming and gardening ; scenery and resorts ; sports ; routes of travel, etc. N. Y. 1882 [1881]. D. **917.4 : 18**

Carse, G: B. Florida ; its climate, soil, productions and agricultural capabilities. Wash. 1882. O. *In* U. S. dep. of agr. ; [Special rep., v. 9.] *in* **630 : D**

Saunders, W: Observations on the soils and products of Florida. (U. S. dep. of agr. ; Special rep., no. 62.) Wash. 1883. O. *in* **630 : D**

Drew, C. New map of the state of Florida showing the progress of the U. S. surveys, the completed and projected railroads, the different railroad stations and growing railroad towns, the new towns on the rivers and interior and the new counties up to the year 1870. Jacksonville. 1870. T. **917.4 : 22**

Stowe, Harriet Elizabeth, *born* Beecher. Palmetto-leaves. Ill. Bost. 1873. S. **917.4 : 17**

Henshall, James A. Camping and cruising in Florida. Ill. and map. Cinc. 1884. D. **917.4 : 26**

Dewhurst, W: W. The history of Saint Augustine, Florida ; with an introd. account of the early spanish and french attempts at exploration and settlement in the territory of Florida, together with sketches of events and objects of interest connected with the oldest town in the U. S. Added, a short description of the climate and advantages of Saint Augustine, as a health resort. N. Y. 1881. D. **974.5 : 1**

Reynolds, C: B. Old Saint Augustine ; a story of three centuries. [Ill.] St. Augustine, Fla. 1885. D. **974.5 : 2**

St. Augustine, Florida ; sketches of its history, objects of interest and advantages as a resort for health and recreation, by an english visitor ; with notes for northern tourists on St. John's river, etc. N. Y. 1869. S. **917.4 : 23**

Bloomfield's illustrated historical guide, embracing an account of the antiquities of St. Augustine, Florida, with map. Added, A condensed guide of the St. John's, Ocklawaha, Halifax and Indian rivers, distance tables to points on the above-

mentioned rivers and principal cities, north, east and west. St. Augustine. 1883. D. **917.4 : 28**

Middle Gulf states.

Hurt, A. B. Mississippi ; its climate, soil, productions, and agricultural capabilities. (U. S. dep. of agr. Miscel. Special rep. no. 3). Wash. 1883. O. *in* **630 : D**

Louisiana, old and new.

French, B: Franklin, *ed.* Historical collections of Louisiana ; embracing many rare and valuable documents relating to the natural, civil and political history of that state ; compiled, with historical and biographical notes and an introd. N. Y. 1846—1852. 4 v. O. **974.6+P2**

 Contents. V. 1. **Bullard,** H: A. Discourse, del. before the Historical society of Louisiana, jan. 13, 1836.—Memoir of Robert Cavelier de La Salle, on the necessity of fitting out an expedition to take possession of Louisiana.—Letters patent to the sieur de La Salle.—Memoir of the sieur de La Salle, reporting to M. de Seignelay the discoveries made by him.—Account (procès verbal) of the taking possession of Louisiana by M. de La Salle.—Will of M. de La Salle.—Memoir sent in 1693, on the discovery of the Mississippi and the neighboring nations by M. de La Salle from 1678 to the time of his death, and by the sieur de Tonty to 1691.—Chevalier Tonty's petition to the king.—Chevalier de Tonty's account of the route from the Illinois by the river Mississippi to the Gulf of Mexico.—Joutel's historical journal of M. de La Salle's last voyage to discover the river Mississippi.—Account of the discovery of the river Mississippi and the adjacent country by father L: Hennepin.—Account of M. de La Salle's undertaking to discover the river Mississippi by way of the Gulf of Mexico.

 2. An account of the Louisiana historical society. —Bullard, H: A. Life, writings and character of François Xavier Martin.—Forstall, E. J. An analytical index of the whole of the public documents relative to Louisiana deposited in the archives of the department "De la marine et des colonies" et "Bibliothèque du roi" at Paris.—A translation of the original letter of Hernando de Soto on the conquest of Florida.—A translation of a recently discovered ms. journal of the expedition of Hernando de Soto into Florida by Luis Hernandez de Biedma.—A narrative of the expedition of Hernando de Soto into Florida by a gentleman of Elvas, pub. at Evora 1557; tr. from the portuguese by R: Hackluyt, London 1609.—Coxe, Daniel. A description of the english province of Carolana, by the spaniards called Florida and by the french La Louisiane, as also of the great and famous river Meschacebe or Mississippi, the vast navigable lakes of fresh water and the parts adjacent, with an account of the commodities of the growth and production of the said province.— An account of the discovery of some new countries and nations in North America in 1673 by père Marquette and sieur Joliet: tr. from the french.

 3. Memoir of H: A. Bullard.—La Harpe, Benard de. Historical journal of the establishment of the french in Louisiana; tr. from the french.—Charlevoix, P: François Xavier de. Historical journal in letters addressed to the dutchess of Lesdeguieres; tr. from the french—Coppie d'vne lettre venant de la Floride, enuoyee a Rouen et depuis au seigneur d'Eueron; ensemble le pian et portraict du fort que les françois y ont faict. 1564.—Histoire mémorable du dernier voyage aux Indes. lieu appele la Floride, Nouuelle France, fait par le capitaine Iean Ribault, 1565.—Journal historique de l'établissement des français à la Louisiane par M. de Sauvole.—Mémoire de M. de Richebourg sur la première guerre des Natchez.—The New Orleans free library.

 [4]. Shea, J: Gilmary. Discovery and exploration of the Mississippi valley; with the original narratives of Marquette, Allouez, Membré, Hennepin and Anastace Douay: with a facsimile of the newly-discovered map of Marquette.

— [*Same*, v. 5.] Historical memoirs of Louisiana from the first settlement of the colony to

French, B: Franklin, *ed.—Continued.*

the departure of governor O'Reilly in 1770 ; with historical and biographical notes. N. Y. 1853. O.   **974.6+P2 v5**

Contents. **Butel-Dumont**, G: Marie. History of Louisiana; tr. from [his] historical memoirs.—**Champigny**, J: *chevalier* de. Memoir of the present state of Louisiana; tr. from the french.—App. of historical documents and elucidations.

— [*Same*, v. 6, 7.] Historical collections of Louisiana and Florida ; incl. translations of original mss. relating to their discovery and settlement, with numerous historical and biographical notes. N. Y. 1869, 1875. 2 v. O.   **974.6+P2 v6,7**

Contents. V. 6. New series. Rémonville, *M.* de. Memoir addressed to count de Pontchartrain on the importance of establishing a colony in Louisiana.— Le Moyne d'Iberville, P: Narrative of the voyage made in 1698 to take possession of Louisiana.— Penicaut, *M.* Annals of Louisiana, from the establishment of the first colony under M. d'Iberville to the departure of the author to France in 1722; incl. an account of the manners, customs and religion of the numerous indian tribes of that country. — Laudonnière, René Goulaine de. History of the first attempt of the french (the huguenots) to colonize the newly discovered country of Florida; History of Jean Ribault's first voyage to Florida.
7. Introd.—La Salle, Robert Cavalier *sieur* de. Memoir addressed to M. de Seignelay of the discoveries made by him.—Narrative of the expedition of M. Cavalier de La Salle to explore the (Mississippi) Colbert river and take possession of Louisiana under the orders and letters patent of Louis XIV in 1682.— Historical journal or narrative of the expeditions made by order of Louis XIV to colonize Louisiana under the command of M. P: Le Moyne d'Iberville; incl. an account of his explorations of the Colbert or Mississippi river from its mouth to the Natchez nation, of the physical features of the country, and of the manners and customs of the numerous indian tribes he visited.—Memoir sent by the king to M. de Denonville, explanatory of the french possessions in North America, especially the south part of Acadia from Pantagouet to the Kennebeck river, of the Iroquois and Hudson's Bay, done at Versailles, 8th march 1688. — Historical collections relating to the first discovery and settlement of Florida; with historical and critical notes: Introd.; Proclamation of Pamfilo de Narvaez to the inhabitants of the countries and provinces from Rio de Palmas to the Cape of Florida, 1527; Narrative of the first voyage of J: de Ribault, made in the reign of Charles IX of France under the orders and instructions of Gaspard de Coligny, to make discoveries and found a colony of french protestants, huguenots, in Florida, 1562; Mendoza Grajales, Francisco Lopez de, Memoir of the happy result and prosperous voyage of the fleet commanded by P: Menendez de Aviles, which sailed from Cadiz on the morning of thursday, june 28th for the coast of Florida and arrived there on the 28th of august 1565; Escalante Fontanedo, Hernando d', Memoir of the country and ancient indian tribes of Florida.—App.: La reprinse de la Floride par le cappitaine Gourgues; Memoria de J: de la Vandera en que se hace relacion de los lugares y tierra de la Florida por donde el capitan Juan Pardo entró á descubrir camino para Nueva España por los años de 1566, 1567; Carta en que se da noticia de un viaje hecho a la bahia de Espirito Santo, Tejas (Texas), y de la poblacion que tenian ahi los franceses, 1689; Historical notice of works pub. on the indian languages of Florida and Texas.

Shea, J: Gilmary. Discovery and exploration of the Mississippi valley ; with the original narratives of Marquette, Allouez, Membré, Hennepin and Anastase Douay. N. Y. 1852. O.   **975+7**

Contents. History of the discovery of the Mississippi valley. — Life of father Marquette. — Notice on the sieur Jolliet. — Dablon, Claudius. Relation of the voyages, discoveries and death of father James Marquette and the subsequent voyages of father Claudius Allouez. — Bibliographical notice of the "Etablissement de la foi" by father Christian Le Clercq.—Narrative of the first attempt by M. Cavalier de La Salle to explore the Mississippi, drawn up from

Shea, J: Gilmary.—*Continued.*

the mss. of father Zenobius Membré by father Chrétien Leclercq.—Bibliographical notes of the works of father L: Hennepin. — Hennepin, L: Narrative of the voyage to the Upper Mississippi; from his "Description de la Louisiane." — Membré, Zenobius. Narrative of the adventures of La Salle's party at Fort Crevecœur, in Illinois, from feb. 1680 to june 1681; Narrative of La Salle's voyage down the Mississippi.—Le Clercq, Christian. Account of La Salle's attempt to reach the Mississippi by sea and of the establishment of a french colony in St. Louis Bay.— Douay, Anastasius. Narrative of La Salle's attempt to ascend the Mississippi in 1687. — Recit des voyages et des decouvertes du P. Jacques Marquette en l'anné 1673 et aux suivantes. — Unfinished letter of father Marquette to father Claude Dablon, containing a journal of his last visit to the Ilinois. — La Salle's patent of nobility."

— *Same.* N. Y. 1852. O. *In* French, B. F. Historical collections of Louisiana.   **974.6+P2 v4**

Monette, J: W. History of the discovery and settlement of the valley of the Mississippi, by the three great european powers, Spain, France and Great Britain, and the subsequent occupation, settlement and extension of civil government by the U. S. until 1846. N. Y. 1846. 2 v. O.   **975+5**

Contents. V. 1. Early explorations of the spaniards.—France, 1608—1764.—Great Britain, 1757—1782.— Spain, 1763—1804. 2. United States, 1770—1846.

Bunner, E. History of Louisiana, from its first discovery and settlement to the present time. [Harper's family lib.] N. Y. 1842. S.   **974 : 1**

Gayarré, C: E. Arthur. History of Louisiana. N. Y. 1854–66. 3 v. O.   **974+3**

Contents. [Pt. 1.] The french domination, 1539— 1769. 2 v. in 1. [2.] The spanish domination, 1769 — 1803. [3.] The american domination, 1803—1861.

— *Same.* [Pt. 1, v. 1:] Louisiana ; its colonial history and romance. N. Y. 1851. O.   **974+2**

Cable, G: Washington. The creoles of Louisiana. Ill. N. Y. 1884. O.   **974.6 : 1**

Marcy, Randolph B., *assisted by* G: B. McClellan. Exploration of the Red River of Louisiana in 1852. Maps and ill. (U. S. 32d cong. 2d sess. Sen. ex. doc. no. 54). Wash. 1854. O.   *in* **917.4 : D**

Contents. Report.—Meteorol. observations.—Tables of courses and distances. — Shepard, C: Upham. Mineralogy.—Geology. — Palæontology. — Zoology.— Botany. — Ethnology: Vocabulary of the Comanches and Witchitas, by R. B. Marcy. (The principal scientific reports have been entered in their proper places in this catalogue).

Milburn, W: H: The pioneers, preachers and people of the Mississippi valley. N. Y. 1860. D.   **975 : 3**

Clemens, S: Langhorne, (*Mark Twain*). Life on the Mississippi, by Mark Twain. Ill. Bost. 1883. O.   **917.5 : 84**

Hall, Abraham Oakey. The manhattaner in New Orleans, or Phases of "Crescent city" life. N. Y. 1851. D.   **917.4 : 4**

Willis, Nathaniel Parker. [New Orleans in 1852]. *In his* Health trip.   **917.9 : 5**

Texas.

Yoakum, H. History of Texas, from its first settlement in 1685 to its annexation to the U. S. in 1846. N. Y. 1856. 2 v. O.   **974.9 : 2**

Contents. V. 1. 1685—1835. — App. 2. 1835—1846. App.—Index.

Green, T: J. Journal of the texian expedition against Mier ; subsequent imprisonment of the author, his sufferings and final escape from the castle of Perote, with reflections upon the present political and probable future relations of Texas, Mexico and the U. S. Ill. N. Y. 1845. O.   **974.9+1**

Vielé, Theresa. "Following the drum"; a glimpse of frontier life [in Texas]. N. Y. 1858. D.   **917.4 : 12**

Interior states.

Shaler, Nathaniel Southgate. Kentucky ; a pioneer commonwealth. Bost. 1885 [1884]. S.   **974.7 : 2**

Hall, James. Events in the early history of Kentucky. *In his* Sketches.   **975 : 4**

Willis, Nathaniel Parker. [Travels in Kentucky and description of Mammoth cave, 1852]. *In his* Health trip.   **917.9 : 5**
    See also in the Index to biography, **Boone.**

Ramsey, J. G. M. The annals of Tennessee to the end of the 18th century ; comprising its settlement as the Watauga association from 1769 to 1777, a part of North Carolina from 1777 to 1784, the state of Franklin from 1784 to 1788, a part of North Carolina from 1788 to 1790, the Territory of the U. S. south of Ohio from 1790 to 1796, the state of Tennessee from 1796 to 1800. Charleston. 1853. O.   **974.7+1**

Hughes, T: Rugby, Tennessee ; some account of the settlement founded on the Cumberland plateau by the Board of aid to land ownership, limited, a company incorp. in England and authorised to hold and deal in land by act of the legislature of Tennessee ; with a report on the soils of the plateau by F. W. Killebrew. N. Y. 1881. D.   **917.4 : 6**

Davis, Walter Bickford, *and* Daniel S. **Durrie.** An illustrated history of Missouri, comprising its early record, and civil, political and military history from the first exploration to the present time. St. Louis. 1876. O.   **974.8+1**

Waterhouse, Sylvester. The resources of Missouri. St. Louis. 1867. O.   **917.4 : Pam**

26. North America — d, U. S., West.

1. The northwest.

In general.

(*See also* Louisiana, col. 1382.) ·

Tuttle, C: R., *and* A. C. **Pennock.** The centennial northwest ; an ill. history of the northwest, being a civil, political and military history of this great section of the U. S. from its earliest settlement to the present time ; comprising a general and condensed history of Ohio, Indiana, Michigan, Illinois, Wisconsin, Minnesota, Iowa, etc., includ. Kansas and Nebraska, the whole forming a complete encyclopædia of the great northwest. Madison, Wis. 1876. O.   **975+6**

Burnet, Jacob. Notes on the early settlement of the Northwestern Territory. N. Y. 1847. O.   **975+2**

Butterfield, Consul Willshire. History of the discovery of the northwest by J: Nicolet in 1634 ; with a sketch of his life. Cinc. 1881. D.   **975 : 10**

Blanchard, Rufus. Discovery and conquests of the north-west, with the history of Chicago. Wheaton. 1881. O.   **975+1**

Hall, James. Letters from the west ; containing sketches of scenery, manners and customs, and anecdotes, connected with the first settlement of the western sections of the U. S. Lond. 1828. O.   **917.5 : 23**
    Note. Pittsburgh and down the Ohio river.

— Sketches of history, life and manners in the west. Phila. 1835. 2 v. in 1. S.   **975 : 4**
    Contents. V. 1. Introd.—Intercourse of the amer. people with the indians. — History of the french settlements.—Events in the early history of Ky.— 2. *Same, continued.* V. 1. Military operations in the Northwestern Terr.—Civil institutions of the territories and new states.—App.

Hoffman, C: Fenno. A winter in the west, by a New Yorker. N. Y. 1835. 2 v. D.   **917.5 : 33**
    Note. Pennsylvania, Ohio, Indiana, Illinois, Michigan, Wisconsin, the Mississippi to St. Louis, the Ohio, Kentucky, Virginia.

McConnel, J: L. Western characters, or Types of border life in the western states. Ill. N. Y. 1853. D.   **917.5 : 71**
    Contents. Introd. — The indian. — The voyageur.—The pioneer. — The ranger. — The regulator. — The justice of the peace. — The peddler. — The schoolmaster.—The schoolmistress.—The politician.

Strickland, W: P. The pioneers of the west, or Life in the woods. Ill. N. Y. 1868. D.   **975 : 9**

Kinzie, Juliette A., *mrs.* J: H. Wau-bun, the "early day" in the north west, [1830—1833]. 2d ed., ill. Chicago. 1857. O.   **975 : 8**

Schoolcraft, H: Rowe. Narrative of an expedition through the upper Mississippi to Itasca lake, the actual source of this river ; embracing An exploratory trip through the St. Croix and Burntwood or Broule rivers in 1832. [Maps]. N. Y. 1834. O. **917.5+42**
    Contents. Narrative, *etc.* — Exploratory trip, *etc.* — App. 1. Natural history. — App. 2. Indian language: Lectures on the Chippewa substantive; A vocabulary of words and phrases in the Chippewa language, A-B.—App. 3. Official reports.

— Personal memoirs of a residence of thirty years with the indian tribes on the american frontiers, with brief notices of passing events, facts and opinions, 1812—1842. Phila. 1851. O.   **917.5 : 43**

Ossoli, Sarah Margaret, *born* Fuller, *marchesa* d'. Summer on the lakes in 1843. [Ill.] Bost. 1844. D.   **917.5 : 20**

Bradford, W: J. Alden. Notes on the north west, or valley of the upper Mississippi. N. Y. 1846. D.   **917.5 : 70**
    Contents. Introd.— Physical geogr. — History.—Population, political gov., topography, *etc.* — Society, laws, public lands, *etc.* — Indians; monuments.—App.

Lanman, C: A summer in the wilderness ; embracing a canoe voyage up the Mississippi and around Lake Superior. N. Y. 1847. D.   **917.5 : 20**

Featherstonhaugh, G: W: A canoe voyage up the Minnay Sotor ; with an account of the lead and copper deposits in Wisconsin, of the gold region in the Cherokee country and sketches of popular manners, etc. Lond. 1847. 2 v. O.   917.5:18

Foster, J: Wells. The Mississippi valley; its physical geography, incl. sketches of the topography, botany, climate, geology and mineral resources; and of the progress of development in population and material wealth. Maps and sections. Chicago. 1869. O.   917.5+2

Ohio and Indiana.

Rice, Harvey. Pioneers of the Western Reserve. Bost. 1883. D.   975.1:3

Kilbourn, J: The Ohio gazetteer, or Topographical dictionary. describing the several counties, towns, villages, canals, roads, rivers, lakes, springs, mines, etc. in the state of Ohio. 10th ed., rev., enlarged and corr. Columbus. 1831. S.   917.5:29

Young, J. H. The tourist's pocket map of the state of Ohio, exhibiting its internal improvements, roads, distances etc. Phila. 1843. T.   917.5:R78

Reid, Whitelaw. Ohio in the war; her statesmen, her generals and soldiers. [Ill.] Cinc. 1868. 2 v. Q.   975.1+7
Contents. V. **1.** History of the state during the war.—Lives of her generals. **2.** History of her regiments and other military organizations.

Studer, Jacob H. Columbus, Ohio; its history, resources and progress, with ill. Columbus. 1873. D.   917.5:30
See also in the Index to biography **Calvert, L.**

Illinois.

Blanchard, Rufus. History of Illinois, to accompany an historical map of the state. Chicago. 1883. O.   975.1:6

Breese, Sidney. The early history of Illinois, from its discovery by the french in 1673 until its cession to Great Britain in 1763, incl. the narrative of Marquette's discovery of the Mississippi, with a biogr. memoir by Melville W. Fuller, ed. by T: Hoyne. Chicago. 1884. O.   975.1+5

Matson, N. Pioneers of Illinois; containing a series of sketches relating to events that occurred previous to 1813, also narratives of many thrilling incidents connected with the early settlement of the west, drawn from history, tradition and personal reminiscences. Chicago. 1882. D.   975.1:2

Ford, T: A history of Illinois, from its commencement as a state in 1818 to 1847; containing a full account of the Black Hawk war, the rise, progress and fall of mormonism, the Alton and Lovejoy riots, and other events. Chicago. 1854. O. 975.1+1

Fergus historical series; nos. 1—24 in 4 v. Chicago. 1876—1884. 4 v. O.   975.1:4
Contents. V. **1. Balestier**, Joseph N. Annals of Chicago; a lecture before the Chicago lyceum, jan. 21, 1840. Repub. from the original ed. of 1840, with an introd. written by the author in 1876; and also a review of the lecture, pub. in the *Chicago tribune* in 1872. **2. Fergus**, Robert. *comp.* Fergus' directory of the city of Chicago, 1839; with city and county officers, churches, public buildings, hotels, etc.; also lists of sheriffs of Cook county and mayors of the city since their organization, together with the poll-list of the first city election, (may 2, 1837); Lists of purchasers of lots in Fort Dearborn addition, the no. of the lots

and the prices paid, etc. **3. Caton**, J: Dean. The last of the Illinois, and a sketch of the Pottawatomies; read before the Chicago hist. soc., dec. 13, 1870; *and* Origin of the prairies, read before the Ottawa academy of natural science, dec. 30, 1869. **4. Brown**, W: H. An historical sketch of the early movement in Illinois for the legalization of slavery; read before the Chicago hist. soc., dec. 5, 1864. **5. Bushnell**, W: H. Biographical sketches of early settlers of Chicago, pt. **1**: S. Lisle Smith, G: Davis, Dr. Philip Maxwell, J: J. Brown, R: L. Wilson, Col. Lewis C. Kerchival, U. P. Harris, H: B. Clarke and sheriff S: J. Lowe. **6.** *Same*, pt. **2**: W: H. Brown, B: W. Raymond, J: Young Scammon, C: Walker, T: Church. **7. Wentworth**, J: Early Chicago; a lecture at McCormick's hall, may 7, 1876, with supplemental notes. (2d lecture). **8. Wentworth**, J: Early Chicago; a lecture at McCormick's hall, april 11, 1875, with supplemental notes. (1st lecture). **9. Brown**, H: Present and future prospects of Chicago; an address before the Chicago lyceum, jan. 20, 1846. — **Marshall**, J. A. Rise and progress of Chicago; an address before the Centennial library asso., march 21, 1876. — **Martineau**, Harriet. Chicago in 1836; "strange early days." **10.** Addresses read before Chicago hist. soc., by J. Young Scammon, I: N. Arnold, W: Hickling, col. G. S. Hubbard and Hiram W. Beckwith; sketches of col. J: H. Kenzie, by his wife, Juliette A. Kenzie; Judge G: Manierre, Luther Haven, and other early settlers; *also* Billy Caldwell and Shabonee, and the "Winnebago scare," july 1827, by Hiram W. Beckwith, and other matter connected with "Early Chicago." **11. Hyde**, James Nevins. Early medical Chicago; an historical sketch of the first practitioners of medicine, with the present faculties and graduates since their organization of the medical colleges of Chicago. **12. Mason**, E: G. Illinois in the 18th century: Kaskaskia and its parish records; read before the Chicago hist. soc., dec. 16, 1879; *and* Old Fort Chartres; read before the Chicago hist. soc., june 16, 1880; *and* Col. John Todd's record-book; read before the Chicago hist. soc., feb. 15, 1881. **13. Gillespie**, Joseph. Recollections of early Illinois and her noted men; read before the Chicago hist. soc., march 16, 1880; with portraits. **14. Porter**, Jeremiah. The earliest religious history of Chicago; read before the Chicago hist. soc. in 1859.— **Brown**, W: H. Early history of Illinois; a lecture before the Chicago lyceum, dec. 8, 1840—**Patterson**, Robert W. Early society in southern Illinois; an address before the Chicago hist. soc., oct. 19, 1880.— **Arnold**, I: N. Reminiscences of the Illinois bar forty years ago: Lincoln and Douglas as orators and lawyers; read before the Illinois bar assoc. Springfield, jan. 7, 1881.—The first murder trial in Iroquois county for the first murder in Cook county. **15. Arnold**, I: N. Abraham Lincoln; read before the Royal hist. soc., London, june 16, 1881.—**Sheahan**, J. W. Stephen Arnold Douglas; an eulogy, del. before the Chicago university, Bryan hall, july 3, 1861. **16. Wentworth**, J: Early Chicago: Fort Dearbon; an address read at the unveiling of a tablet on the Fort site, under the auspices of the Chicago hist. soc., may 21, 1881; (3d paper). Portr. and indexes to nr. Wentworth's 1st and 2d lectures, and "Calumet club reception." **17. Arnold**, I: N. William B. Ogden and early days in Chicago; read before the Chicago hist. soc., dec. 20, 1881.—**Scammon**, J. Y. Sketches of William B. Ogden. **18. Fergus** R., *comp.* Chicago river-and-harbor convention, july 5, 6 and 7, 1847; an account of its origin and proceedings, by W: Mosley Hall.—Wentworth, S: Lisle Smith. Horace Greeley, Thurlow Weed; list of delegates, together with statistics concerning Chicago, by Jesse B. Thomas and James L. Barton. **19. Cleaver**, C: Reminiscences of early Chicago (1833). **20. Hoffman**, C: Fenno. A winter in the west, [printed in] London, 1835; reprint, with add. notes. **21. Fergus**, Robert. Biographical sketch of John Dean Caton. **22. Arnold**, I: N. Recollections of early Chicago and the Illinois bar; read june 10, 1880.—**Conkling**, James C. Recollections of the bench and bar of central Illinois; read jan. 12, 1881.—**Hoyne**, T: The lawyer as a pioneer; read at Fairbank hall, feb. 10, 1881. **23. Ackerman**, W: K. Early Illinois railroads; a paper read before the Chicago hist. soc., feb. 20, 1883; notes by J: Wentworth, also an app. with the Breese-Douglas corresp. **24. Wentworth**, J: Congressional reminiscences; sketches of J: Quincy Adams, T: H. Benton, J: C. Calhoun, H: Clay and Daniel Webster; an address read before the Chicago hist. soc., at Central music hall, march 16, 1882; with app. and index.

Blanchard, Rufus. History of Chicago.
　　　　　　　　　　　　　in 975+1
Land, Jno. E. Chicago, the future metropolis
of the new world; her trade, commerce
and industries, mfg. advantages, business
and transportation facilities, together with
sketches of the leading business houses
and mfg. concerns in the "Garden city";
historical and descriptive review. Chicago.
1883. F.　　　　　　　　917.5+88
Marquis's hand-book of Chicago; a complete
history, reference book and guide to the
city. Ill. Chicago. 1885. D.　917.5 : 103
See also in the Index to biography Coles.

Michigan.

Cooley, T: McIntyre. Michigan; a history of
governments. (Amer. commonwealths).
Bost. 1885. D.　　　　　　975.2 : 6
Lanman, James H. History of Michigan, from
its earliest colonization to the present time.
[Harper's fam. lib.] N. Y. 1843. S.
　　　　　　　　　　　　　975.2 : 1
Campbell, James V. Outlines of the political
history of Michigan. Detroit. 1876. O.
　　　　　　　　　　　　　975.2+2
Farmer, Silas. The history of Detroit and Michigan, or The metropolis illustrated; a
chronological cyclopædia of the past and
present, incl. a full record of territorial
days in Michigan and the annals of Wayne
county. [Ill.] Detroit. 1884. Q. 975.2+4
Hamlin, Marie Caroline Watson. Legends of
le Détroit. Ill. Detroit. 1884. D.
　　　　　　　　　　　　　975.2 : 3
Everett, Franklin. Memorials of the Grand
river valley. Chicago. 1878. O. 975.2+5
Strickland, W: P. Old Mackinaw, or The fortress of the lakes and its surroundings.
Phila. 1860. D.　　　　　　917.5 : 69
King, J: Lyle. Trouting on the Brulé river, or
Lawyers' summer-wayfaring in the northern wilderness. Chicago. 1879. D.
　　　　　　　　　　　　　917.5 : 97
Morley, F: Michigan and its resources; sketches
of the growth of the state, its industries,
agricultural productions, institutions, and
means of transportation, descriptions of
its soil, climate, timber, financial condition
and the situation of its unoccupied lands,
and a review of its general characteristics
as a home. Compiled under authority of
the state, by the comm. of immigration.
2d ed. Lansing. 1882. O.　917.5+74

Wisconsin.

General history.

Tuttle, C: R. An ill. history of the state of Wisconsin; a complete civil, political and military history of the state from its first exploration down to 1875; incl. a cyclopædia
of legislation during the administration of
each governor; from the organization of
the territorial government down to governor Taylor, with historical and descriptive sketches of each county in the state
separately, embracing interesting narratives of pioneer life, incl. an account of the
commercial, agricultural and educational
growth of Wisconsin. Bost. 1875. O.
　　　　　　　　　　　　　975.3 : 2

Smith, W: Rudolph. The history of Wisconsin,
in three parts, historical, documentary and
descriptive; compiled by direction of the
legislature of the state; v. 1, 3. Madison.
1854. 2 v. O.　　　　　　　975.3+1
Contents. Pt. 1, Historical, v. 1 : From the earliest
discoveries in the Mississippi valley to april 1836;
with notes. 2, *not published.* Pt. 2, Documentary,
v. 3 : Jesuit relations.—Black Hawk war.—Capture
of the Halls.—Battle of Pecatonica.— Release of the
Halls.—Battle of Wisconsin Heights.—Battle of Bad
Axe.—Memorial of the miners of the lead region.—
Earth works. — Carver's grant; examination of its
validity. — Indian deed, from Green Bay records.—
Annals of the legislature.—First convention; members.—Second convention; members.— Siege of Detroit in 1712.—Early adventure: W: Farnsworth, W:
S. Hamilton. — Early mail carriers, J: Halpin.—Lead
trade with the Indians.—Attack at Rock Island, 1812.
— Red Bird's disturbances.— Indian lead furnaces. —
Milwaukee and Rock river canal; its history.
Strong, Moses McCure. History of the territory
of Wisconsin from 1836 to 1848; preceded by
an account of some events during the
period in which it was under the dominion
of kings, states or other territories. pre i-
ous to 1836. Madison. 1885. O. 975.3 r7
Sketches of the west, or The home of the badg-
ers; comprising an early history of Wisconsin, with, a series of familiar letters
and remarks on territorial character and
characteristics, etc. Milw. 1847. O.
　　　　　　　　　　　　　975.3+P6
Love, W: DeLoss. Wisconsin in the war of the
rebellion; a history of all regiments and
battalions the state has sent to the field,
and deeds of her citizens, governors and
other military officers and state and national legislators to suppress the rebellion.
Chicago. 1866. O.　　　　　975.3+4
Quiner, E. B. The military history of Wisconsin; a record of the civil and military
patriotism of the state in the war for the
union, with a history of the campaigns in
which Wisconsin soldiers have been conspicuous, regimental histories, sketches of
distinguished officers, the roll of the illustrious dead, movements of the legislature
and state officers, etc. Ill. Chicago. 1866.
O.　　　　　　　　　　　　975.3 : 5
Note. For report of the adjutant-general, see
col. 233.
Wisconsin state historical society. The charter
and revised statutes relating to [the so-
ciety], *also* The constitution and by-laws
of the society. Madison. 1884. O.
　　　　　　　　　　　　　906 : Pam
— Annual reports [1st–28th] and collections.
Madison. 1854-82. 9 v. D.　　906 : R1
Contents. V. 1. Whittlesey, C: Green Bay in
1726.—Gorrell, J: Journal in Green Bay.—Biddle,
J. W: Recollections of Green Bay in 1816-17.—Whit-
tlesey, C: Recollections of a tour through Wis. in
1832.—Haskins, R. W: Legend of the Winnebagoes.
—Tenney, H. A. Early times in Wis.—Cammuck,
T: Sketch of Calumet county.—Brunson, A. Wis.
geographical names.—Hathaway, J. Indian names.
—Calkins, H. Indian nomenclature of northern
Wis.; with a sketch of the manners and customs of
the Chippewas. — Pratt, A. F. Reminiscences of
Wis.—Objects of coll. desired by the society.
2. Eulogies on Wright, McLane and Sully. —
Baird, H. S. Early history and condition of Wis.
—Lockwood, J. H. Early times and events in
Wis.—Shaw, J. Personal narrative.—Brunson, A.
Memoir of T: P. Burnett.—Parkison, D. M. Pio-
neer life in Wis.—Bracken, C:, *and* P: Parkison. *fr.*
Pekatonica battle controversy.—Parkison, P: Stric-
tures upon gov. Ford's History of the Black Hawk
war. — Bracken, C: Further strictures on Ford's
History of the Black Hawk war.—Ellis, A. G. Some

Wisconsin state hist. soc.—*Continued.*

account of the advent of N. Y. indians into Wis.—**Lothrop**, J. A sketch of the early history of Kenosha co. and of the Western emigration company.—**Taylor**, S. Wisconsin, its rise and progress; with notices of Mineral Point and Richland co.—**Robinson**, C: D. Legend of the Red Banks.—**Edwards**, T. O. Progress, condition and prospects of Wis.
3. Introd. — **Calkins**, E. A., *and* H. **Rublee**. Eulogies on J. G. Percival.—Notices of W: A. White.—**Law**, J. Jesuit missionaries in the northwest.—**Shea**, J: G. The indian tribes of Wis.—The Cass manuscripts, tr. by C: Whittlesey. — **Brunson**, A. Ancient mounds or tumuli in Crawford co.—**Barry**, W: Antiquities of Wis.—**Grignon**, A. Seventy-two years' recollections of Wis. —**Witherell**, B. F. H. Reminiscences of the north-west.—**Morse**, R: E. The Chippewas of Lake Superior.—**Frank**, M. Early history of Kenosha.—**Mygatt**, W: Some account of the first settlement of Kenosha.—**Stewart**, J. W. Early history of Green co.—**Leonard**, J. A. Sketch of Whitewater.—**Ellis**, A. G. The upper Wisconsin country.—**Gibbs**, O., *jr*, *and* C: E. **Young**. Sketch of Prescott and Pierce co.—**Hall**, T. D. Hudson and its tributary region.—**Lawson**, A. J. New London, and surrounding country. — **Quiner**, E. B. Resources of north-eastern Wis.—Wis. and her internal navigation.—**McBride**, D. The Lemonweir river.—The Baraboo valley, a dairy region.—**Cruzat**, F. Message to the Sauks and Foxes.—**Draper**, L. C. Statistics of Wis. public libraries.
4. Introd.—**Smith**, J. Y. Origin of the amer. indians. — **Childs**, E. Recollections of Wis. since 1820.—**Baird**, H: S. Recollections of the early history of northern Wis.—**Brunson**, A. Early history of Wis.—**Holton**, E: D., *and others*. Commercial history of Milwaukee.—**Commuck**, T: Sketch of the Brothertown indians.—**Marsh**, C. The Stockbridges.—**Konkapot**, L., *jr*. The last of the Mohicans.—Death of J: W. Quinney.—**Quinney**, J: W. Speech on Stockbridge traditionary history, *and* Memorial to congress.—**Rublee**, H. Early times in Sheboygan co.—**Chapman**, C. B. Early events in the Four Lake country. — **Vinton**, S: F. North-eastern boundary of Wis.—**Lapham**, I. A. On the public land surveys, *and* The latitude and longitude of places in Wis.; On the man - shaped mounds of Wis. — **Brunson**, A. Death of Tecumseh.—**Kingston**, J: T. Death of Tecumseh.—**Ballou**, D. W., *jr*. First grave in the city of Watertown.—**McMillan**, M. Early settlement of La Crosse and Monroe co.—**Graham**, J. D. On the latitude and longitude of Milwaukee, Prairie du Chien, Racine and Madison, Wis.
5. **Carr**, E. S. *and* J. P. **Atwood**. Eulogies on J. W. Hunt.—**Atwood**, D: Eulogy on L: P. Harvey.—Canadian documents. — **Snelling**, W: J. Early days at Prairie du Chien.—Indian honor.—**Cass**, L. On the Winnebago outbreak.—**Dodge**, *Gen*. H. Letter to gen. H. Atkinson.—**Edwards**, A. A western reminiscence.—**Pinney**, S. U. Eulogy on gen. H: Dodge.—**McKenney**, T: L. The Winnebago war of 1827.—**Fonda**, J: H. Early reminiscences of Wis.—Reminiscences of Black-Hawk and the Black-Hawk war.—**Whitford**, W. C. Early history of education in Wis. *and* History of school supervision in Wis.—**Ellis**, Q. G. Life and public services of J. D. Doty.—**Clark**, J. T., *and others*. Reminiscences of Hole-in-the-day.—Gen. Cass at St. Marie in 1820.
6. Introd.—**Atwood**, D: Life and services of B: F. Hopkins.—**Hastings**, S. D. Memoir of G. De W. Elwood.—**Hunter**, E: M. The civil life, services and character of W: A. Barstow.—**Calkins**, E. A. Sketch of W: A. Barstow's military services.—**Frank**, M. Events in the life of C: Durkee.—**Draper**, L. C. *and* H. A. **Tenney**. Life, services and character of G: Hyer.—**Storrow**, S: A. The north-west in 1817.—**Forsyth**, T: Journal of a voyage from St. Louis to the falls of St. Anthony, in 1819.—**Durrie**, D. S. Captain Jonathan Carver and "Carver's grant."—**Meeker**, Moses. Early history of the lead region of Wis. — **Palmer**, S. M. Western Wis. in 1836. — Smith, J: Y. Eleazer Williams and the lost prince.—Reminiscences of the first house and first resident family of Madison.—Naming of Madison and Dane county, and the location of the capital. — Michel St. Cyr. — **Salisbury**, A. Green co. pioneers. — **Smith**, I: T. Early settlement of Rock co.—**Janes**, H: F. Early reminiscences of Janesville.—Neyon de Villiers.
7. Introd. — **Butler**, J. D. Pre-historic Wis.; Westphalian medal, 1648.—**Shea**, J: G. The discov-

ery of the Mississippi.—**Tasse**, J. Memoir of C: de Langlade.—**Draper**, L. C. Notice of Match-e-ke-wis.—**Doty**, J. D. Northern Wis. in 1820.—**Ellis**, A. G. Fifty-four years' recollections of men and events in Wis.—The fur trade and factory system at Green Bay, 1816 - 21. — E: D. Beouchard's vindication. — **Kingston**, J: T. Early western days.—**La Ronde**, J: T. de. Personal narrative.—**Merrill**, H: Pioneer life in Wis.—Sketch of officers at Fort Winnebago in 1834, and subsequently.—**De Peyster**, A. S. Langlade's movements in 1777.—**Noonan**, J. A. Recollections of Wis. in feb. 1837.—**Trowbridge**, C. C. Note on Eleazer Williams.—**Matson**, N. Sketch of Shaube-na.—**Durrie**, D. S. Memoir of G: Gale.—**Ellis**, E. H. Memoir of H: S. Baird.—**Braley**, A. B. Memoir of J: Catlin.—**Durrie**, D. S. Sketch of the life and services of J: Y. Smith.—**Draper**, L. C. Wisconsin necrology, 1874–75.
8. Introd.—In memoriam, S. H. Carpenter. — In memoriam, G: B. Smith.—**Houghton**, J. Ancient copper mines of Lake Superior. — **Slafter**, E. F. Pre-historic copper implements. — **Draper**, L. C. *and others*. Ancient copper implements, how fabricated.—**Brown**, E: Pictured cave of La Crosse valley.—**Rice**, J. A. Add. notes on the La Crosse cave.—**Sulte**, B: Notes on J: Nicolet.—**Butler**, J. D. Early historic relics of the north-west.—Tradition of the Fox indians, 1730.—**Langlade** papers, 1737 - 1800. — **Schoolcraft**, H. R. Incident of Chegoimegon, 1760.—**Porlier**, L. J. Capture of Mackinaw, 1763.—**Moran**, E., *and others*. Green Bay and the frontiers, 1763-65.—**Strong**, M. M. Indian wars of Wis.—**Tanner**, E: Wis. in 1818.—**Bristol**, *Mrs*. M. A. B. Reminiscences of the northwest. — **Clark**, S. Early times at Fort Winnebago.—**Ellis**, A. G. Recollections of Eleazer Williams.—**Draper**, L. C. Add. notes on Eleazer Williams.—**Kingston**, J: T. Early exploration and settlement of Juneau co.—**Luchsinger**, J: The swiss colony of New Glarus. — **Tschudy**, J. J. Add. notes on New Glarus.—**Draper**, L. C. Wis. necrology, 1876–78.
9. **Peet**, S. D. Emblematic mounds in Wis.—**Dean**, C. K. A mound near Boscobel.—**Butler**, J. D. Portraits of Columbus; Early historic relics of the north-west.—Lake Sakaegan; its identity.—**Anderson**, T: G. Personal narrative: Journal, 1814.—Prairie du Chien documents, 1814-15.—Traditions and recollections of Prairie du Chien, as related by B. W. Brisbois and noted down by Lyman C. Draper.—**Baird**, *Mrs*. H. S. Indian customs and early recollections. — In memoriam, hon. C. C. Washburn. — **Draper**, L. C. Sketch of C. H. Larrabee.—**Thomas**, J. E. Pioneer settlement of Sheboygan co.—**Martin**, M. L. Sketch of W: Farnsworth; Sketch of Moses Hardwick.—**Fifield**, S. S. Sketch of H. D. Barron.—**Hastings**, S. D. Sketch of C. H. Purple.—**Calkins**, E. A. Two men of note: W: Hull and Sat Clark.—**Braley**, A. B. Character of L. B. Vilas.—**Draper**, L. C. Necrology of Wis. 1878-81.

— 29th–31st annual reports, submitted at the annual meetings, jan. 2d 1883, 1884, 1885.
    906 : Pam

Thomas, G: Francis, (*George Francis*). Legends of the land of lakes, or History, traditions and mysteries gleaned from years of experience among the pioneers, voyageurs and indians; with descriptive accounts of the many natural curiosities met with from Lake Huron to the Columbia river, and the meaning and derivation of names of rivers, lakes, towns, etc. of the northwest. Chicago. 1884. O.   **917.5 : 93**
  Contents. [Pt. 1]. Lake Superior and surroundings.—[Pt. 2]. Wisconsin.

Tenney, H. A., *and* D: **Atwood**. Fathers of Wisconsin.   **920.1 : 9**
  See under Biography.

General description.

Carver, Jonathan. Travels in Wisconsin.
    917 : 2
  See col. 1343.

Smith, W: Rudolph. Observations on the Wisconsin territory ; chiefly on that part called the Wisconsin land district, with a map exhibiting the settled parts of the territory, as laid off in counties by act of the leg. in 1837. Phila. 1838. D.   **917.51 : 3**

Plumbe, J:, *jr.* Sketches of Iowa and Wisconsin, taken during a residence of three years in those territories. St. Louis. 1839. D.   **917.51 : 2**

Lapham, Increase Allen. A geographical and topographical description of Wisconsin, with brief sketches of its history, geology, mineralogy, natural history, population, soil, productions, government, antiquities, etc. Milw. 1844. 8.   **917.51 : 6**

— Wisconsin, its geography and topography, history, geology and mineralogy, together with brief sketches of its antiquities, natural history, soil, production, population and government. 2d ed. Milw. 1846. D.   **917.51 : 6**

Wisconsin; a sectional map, with the most recent surveys by I. A. Lapham, 1849. Milw. T.   **917.51 : R11**

Hunt, J: Warren. Wisconsin gazetteer, containing the names, location and advantages of the counties, cities, towns, villages, post-offices and settlements, together with a description of the lakes, watercourses, prairies and public localities, alphab. arr. Madison. 1853. O. **917.51 : 1**

Chapman, Silas. Hand book of Wisconsin. 2d ed. enl. and improved. Milw. 1855. T.   **917.51 : 4**

Gregory, J: Industrial resources of Wisconsin. Milw. 1855. S.   **917.51 : 5**

Ritchie, James S. Wisconsin and its resources ; with Lake Superior, its commerce and navigation, incl. a trip up the Mississippi and a canoe voyage on the St. Croix and Brulé rivers to Lake Superior; appended, the constitution of the state, with the routes of the principal railroads, lists of post-offices, etc. Ill. 3d rev. ed. Phila. 1858. D.   **917.51 : 8**

State of Wisconsin, The ; embracing brief sketches of its history, position, resources and industries, and a catalogue of its exhibits at the centennial at Phila. 1876. Madison, Wis. 1876. O.   **917.51 : 9**

Wisconsin state gazetteer and business directory ; v. 1-5, 1876-1886. Milw. *and* Chicago. 1876-86. 5 v. O.   **917.51+R10**

Snyder, Van Vechten and co. Historical atlas of Wisconsin ; embracing complete state and county maps, city and village plats, with separate state and county histories ; also, special articles on the geology, education, agriculture and other important interests of the state. Ill. Milw. 1878. F.   **917.51 : R13**

Milwaukee county.

Buck, James Smith. [History of Milwaukee.] Milw. 1876-84. 3 v. O.   **975.32+1**
    Contents. V. 1. Pioneer history, from the first american settlement in 1833 to 1841, with a topographical description as it appeared in a state of nature, ill. with a map. 2. *Same,* 1840-1846. 3. Milwaukee under the charter, from 1847 to 1853 incl.

— *Same.*   **975.32 : R1**

Wheeler, Andrew C. The chronicles of Milwaukee ; being a narrative history of the town from its earliest period to the present. Milw. 1861. D.   **975.32 : 2**

Western historical society. History of Milwaukee, Wisconsin, from pre-historic times to the present date, embracing a summary sketch of the native tribes and an exhaustive record of men and events for the past century, describing the city as it now is, its commercial, religious, educational and benevolent institutions, its government, courts, press and public affairs, its musical, dramatic, literary, scientific and social societies, its patriotism during the late war, its development and future possibilities, and incl. biogr. sketches of pioneers and citizens. Ill. Chicago. 1881. Q.   **975.32 : R3**

Koss, Rudolph Alexander. Milwaukee. Milw. 1871. O.   **975.32 : 4**
    Contents. Die zeit der sage. — Die alte zeit. bis 1843. — Die alten deutschen, 1844 - 1848. — Deutsch-Athen, 1848 - 1854.—Personal-index.

Bleyer, Julius *and* Herman. Burning of the Newhall house. [Milw.] 1883. D.   **975.32 : 5**

Dupré, Julius V: Quarter-sectional atlas of the city of Milwaukee, drawn and compiled from the records of Milwaukee co. 2d and rev. ed., 1884. Milw. 1884. F. **917.52 : R4**

Harger, C: B., *comp.* Milwaukee and its prominent points of interest. Ill. [Milw. 1877]. O.   **917.52 : Pam**

Chapman, Silas, *pub.* In and around Milwaukee in 1880, arr. alphab.; with a map. Milw. 1880. S.   **917.52 : Pam**

Milwaukee city. Directory of the city of Milwaukee for the years 1847-48 ; containing an epitomized history, *etc.*, by Julius P. Bolivar MacCabe. Milw. 1847. *Repr. in* Edwards' Directory for 1865. **917.52 : R1**

— *Same,* for 1848-49. 2d year. Milw. 1848. O.   **917.52 : R1**

— Milwaukee city directory and business advertiser, … J. M. Van Slyck, pub.; 1854-55, 1856-57. Milw. 1854, 1856. 2 v. D.   **917.52 : R1**

— Erving, Burdick & co.'s Milwaukee city directory for 1857-58. V. 1, new ser. Milw. [1857]. O.   **917.52 : R1**

— Milwaukee city directory … comp. by Smith, DuMoulin & co. Milw. 1858. O.   **917.52 : R1**

— *Same,* for 1859-60, comp. by Franklin E. Town. Milw. [1859]. O.   **917.52 : R1**

— Directory of the city of Milwaukee … pub. annually [by Starr & son]. 1860-61. Milw. 1860. O.   **917.52 : R1**

— Milwaukee city directory for 1862, 1863, comp. by A. Bailey. Milw. 1862, 1863. 2 v. O.   **917.52 : R1**

— [R:] Edwards' annual directory to the … city of Milwaukee for 1865, 1866. Milw. 1865, 1866. 2 v. O.   **917.52 : R1**

— Milwaukee city directory for 1868-69, 1869-70, 1870-71, 1871-72, 1872-73, 1873-74, 1875-76… comp. and pub. by J: Thickens. Milw. 1868-74. 7 v. O.   **917.52 : R1**

— *Same,* v. 8-18, for 1875-76, 1876-77, 1877-78, 1878, 1879, 1880, 1881, 1882, 1883, 1884, 1885. Milw. 1875-85. 11 v. O.   **917.52 : R1**

Bailey's, A., Milwaukee almanac and business directory for 1862. Milw. 1862. O.   **917.52 : R2**

Bailey, A.—*Continued.*
— Milwaukee business directory, city guide and almanac for 1867 ... Milw. 1867. O.
917.52 : R2

Other localities.

Western historical society. The history of Columbia county, Wisconsin; containing an account of its settlement, growth, development and resources, etc. Ill. Chicago. 1880. O.   975.31+2
— The history of Fond du Lac county; its early settlement, growth, development, resources, etc.; a sketch of its cities, their improvements, industries, manufactories, churches, schools, societies, etc., war record, biogr. sketches, portr. of prominent men and early settlers, etc.; also history of Wisconsin, constitution of the U. S. and of Wis., condensed abstract of laws of Wis., miscellaneous, etc. Ill. Chicago. 1880. O.   975.31+1
Durrie, Daniel Steele. A history of Madison, the capital of Wisconsin; incl. the Four Lake country to july 1874, with an app. of notes on Dane county and its towns. Madison, Wis. 1874. D.   975.33+1
Madison city directory and business mirror, The; containing the names of the citizens, a business directory, state and city record and an app. Milw. 1858. D.   917.51 : 7
Randall, T: E. History of the Chippewa valley; a faithful record of all prominent events, incidents and circumstances that have transpired in the valley of the Chippewa, from its earliest settlement by white people, indian treaties, organization of the territory and state; also of the counties embracing the valley, senatorial, assembly and congressional districts, etc., also a brief biogr. sketch of the most prominent persons in the settlement of the valley. Eau Claire, Wis. 1875. O.   975.3 : 3

Minnesota and Dakota.

Neill, E: Duffield. The history of Minnesota from the earliest french explorations to the present time. Phila. 1858. O.   975.5 : 1
Minnesota historical society. Collections, v. 1; a repub. of the original parts issued in 1850–53, 56. St. Paul. 1872. O.   906+2
Contents. Preface.—Sketch of the society.—Charter.—Officers and committees.—Objects of coll. desired.—**Neill, E: D.** The french voyageurs to Minn. during the 17th century.—**Sibley,** H. H. Description of Minn., 1850.—**Ramsey,** A. Our field of historical research.—Organization of Minn. territory.—**Sibley,** H. H. Speech.—**Goodrich,** A. A. Early courts of Minn.—**Baker,** D. A. J. Early schools of Minn.—**Hobart,** C. Religious movements in Minn.—**Riggs,** S. R. The Dakota language.—**Schoolcraft,** H: R. History and physical geography of Minn.—**Mather,** W. W. Letter.—**Neill,** E: D. Letter of Mesnard.—**Fullerton,** T. M. The St. Louis river.—**Pond,** G. H. Iowa indians and mounds.—**Aiton,** J. F. Stone heaps of Red Wing.—**Riggs,** S. R. Mounds of Minn. valley.—**Boutwell,** W. T. Schoolcraft's exploring tour of 1832.—**Neill,** E: D. Battle of Lake Pokeguma.—**Sibley,** H. H. Memoir of Jean N. Nicollet.—**Neill,** E: D. A sketch of Joseph Renville.—**Belcourt,** G. A. Department of Hudson's Bay.—**Neill,** E: D. Obituary of James M. Goodhue; Dakota land and Dakota life.—**Williamson,** T. S. Who where the first men?—Louis Hennepin, the franciscan.—Sieur Du Luth.—Le Sueur.—D'Iberville.—The Fox and Ojibway war.—Capt. Jonathan Carver and his explor.—Pike's explor. in Minn.—**Morrison,** W: Who discovered Itaska

Lake.—Early days at Fort Snelling.—**Snelling,** W: J. Running the gauntlet. — **Sibley,** H. H. Reminiscences, historical and personal.
Keating, W: H. Narrative of an expedition to the source of St. Peter's River, Lake Winnepeek, Lake of the Woods, etc. in 1823, under command of Stephen H. Long; comp. from the notes of major Long; messrs. Say, Keating and Colhoun. Phila. 1824. 2 v. O.   917.5+98
Note. This is major Long's 2d exped.; for his 1st exped., see col. 1397, under **James.**
Contents of app. in v. 2. **Long,** S. H. General description of the country traversed by the expedition, designed as a topographical report to the war dep't.—**Say,** T: Zoology.—**Schweinitz,** L: D. de. Botany.—**Colhoun,** J. E: Astronomical obs. and calculations.—**Lovell,** Joseph. Meteorol. register for 1822.—Vocabularies of indian languages.
McClung, J. W. Minnesota as it is in 1870; its general resources and attractions for immigrants, invalids, tourists, capitalists and business men, principally from official authorities, with special descriptions of all its counties and towns, their topography, population, nationalities, products, business, wealth, social advantages and inducements to those in quest of homes, health or pleasure. [St. Paul.] 1870. D.
917.5 : 35
Custer, *Mrs.* Elizabeth B. Boots and saddles, or Life in Dakota with general Custer. N. Y. 1885. D.   917.5 : 100
Rowbotham, Francis Jameson. A trip to prairieland; a glance at the shady side of emigration. In 2 pts.: pt. 1, The life on the prairie; pt. 2, The farming prospects of northern Dakota. Lond. 1885. D.
917.5 : 105

Iowa, Kansas, Nebraska.

Parker, Nathan Howe. Iowa as it is in 1855; a gazetteer for citizens and a handbook for immigrants, embracing a full description of the state of Iowa. Chicago. 1855. D.
917.5 : 39
Hale, E: Everett. Kansas and Nebraska; the history, geographical and physical characteristics, and political position of those territories, an account of the emigrant aid companies, and directions to emigrants. Bost. 1854. D.   917.5 : 73
Spring, Leverett W. Kansas; the prelude to the war for the union. (Amer. commonwealths.) Bost. 1885. D.   975.6 : 1
Brewerton, G: Douglas. The war in Kansas; a rough trip to the border among new homes and a strange people. N. Y. 1856. D.
917.5 : 7

2. The far west in general.

(*See also* Geology, col. 338-343; Pacific railroad surveys, col. 422-423.)

Biddle, N: History of the expedition under the command of Lewis and Clarke to the sources of the Missouri, thence across the Rocky mountains and down the river Columbia to the Pacific ocean, performed during 1804–1806, by order of the gov. of the U. S. Prepared for the press by Paul Allen; rev. and abr., with introd. and notes by Archibald McVickar. [Harper's family lib.] N. Y. 1847. 2 v. S. 917.5 : 3

Coues, Elliott. An account of the various publications relating to the travels of Lewis and Clarke, with a commentary on the zoological results of their expedition. *In* U. S. geol. survey of the terr., Hayden; Bulletin, v. 1. *in* 557.5 : D

Pike, Zebulon Montgomery. An account of expeditions to the sources of the Mississippi and through the western parts of Louisiana, to the sources of the Arkansaw, Kans, La Platte and Pierre Jaun rivers ; performed by order of the government of the U. S., during 1805–1807, and a tour through the interior parts of New Spain, when conducted through the provinces by order of the capt.-gen., in 1807. Maps and charts. Phila. 1810. O. 917.1 : 28

James, Edwin. Account of an expedition from Pittsburgh to the Rocky Mountains in 1819, 1820, under maj. S. H. Long ; comp. from the notes of major Long, T: Say and other gentlemen of the party. Lond. 1823. 3 v. O. 917.5 : 99

Note. For major Long's 2d exped. see col. 1396, under **Keating**.

Irving, Washington. [Captain] Bonneville's adventures, [1831–1835]. N. Y. 1856. S. 917.5 : 27

— *Same. In his* Works. 820.1 : 13 v6

— *Same.* The adventures of capt. Bonneville, U. S. A., in the Rocky mountains and the far west ; digested from his journal and ill. from various other sources. *In his* Works. 820.1 : P11 v8

Frémont, J: C: Report of the exploring expedition to the Rocky mountains in 1842, and to Oregon and north California in 1843–44. Maps and ill. (U. S. 28th cong. 2d sess. House ex. doc. no. 166.) Wash. 1845. O. *in* 917.5 : D

Contents. Report on an exploration of the country lying between the Missouri river and the Rocky mountains on the line of the Kansas and Great Platte rivers.—Catalogue of plants collected.—Report of the exploring expedition to Oregon and north California. — Geological formations. — Organic remains.—Note concerning plants collected.—Astron. observations.—Meteorol. observ. made during the exped. of 1843-44.—Astron. observ. made during the exped. to the Rocky mountains in 1842.—Meteorol. observ.

— Narrative of the exploring expedition to the Rocky mountains, in 1842, and to Oregon and north California in 1843-44. Rep. from the official copy. Syracuse. 1846. D. 917.5 : 19

Carvalho, S. N. Incidents of travel and adventure in the far west, with Fremont's last expedition across the Rocky mountains, incl. three months' residence in Utah and a perilous trip across the great amer. desert to the Pacific. N. Y. 1860. D. 917.5 : 9

Emory, W: Helmsley. Notes of a military reconnoissance from Ft. Leavenworth in Missouri to San Diego in California, incl. part of the Arkansas, Del Norte and Gila rivers; made in 1846-47 with the advanced guard of the army of the west. Maps and ill. (U. S. 30th cong. 1 sess. House ex. doc. no. 41.) Wash. 1848. O. *in* 917.5 : D

Contents. **Emory**, W. H. Notes *etc.*—App. [Ethnological and botanical notes]; Meteorol. and astron. observ.; **Abert**, J. W. Report on natural history.— **Abert**, J. W. Report of his examination of New

Mexico, in 1846-47.—**Cooke**, P. St. G: Report of his march from Santa Fé, N. M., to San Diego, upper Cal.—**Johnston**, *capt.* A. R. Journal.

Parkman, Francis. The Oregon trail ; sketches of prairie and Rocky mountain life [in 1846]. 7th ed., rev. Bost. 1880. D. 917.5 : 65

Bryant, Edwin. What I saw in California; journal of a tour by the emigrant route and South pass of the Rocky mountains across North America, the great desert basin and through California, in 1846, 1847. 7th ed., with an app., containing accounts of the gold mines, various routes, outfit, etc. N. Y. 1849. D. 917.5 : 55

Heap, Gwinn Harris. Central route to the Pacific. from the valley of the Mississippi to California ; journal of the expedition of E. F. Beale and Gwinn Harris Heap from Missouri to California, in 1853. Phila. 1854. O. 917.5 : 25

Domenech, Emmanuel *abbé.* Seven years' residence in the great deserts of North America. 970.1 : 22

Contents, see col. 1341.

Froebel, Julius. Travel in . . . the far west of the U. S. *in* 917.8 : 3

Möllhausen, Balduin. Diary of a journey from the Mississippi to the coasts of the Pacific with a U. S. gov. expedition; with an introd. by Alexander v. Humboldt. Tr. by mrs. Percy Sinnett. Ill. Lond. 1858. 2 v. O. 917.5 : 106

Note. This expedition was the one under command of -lieut. A. W. Whipple, for the exploration of a Pacific r. r. route, in 1853-54.

Hall, E: H. The great west ; emigrants', settlers' and travellers' guide and hand-book to the states of California and Oregon and the territories of Nebraska, Utah, Colorado, Idaho, Montana, Nevada, and Washington; with an account of their climate, soil, resources, and products, accompanied by a map showing the several routes to the gold fields, and a complete table of distances. N. Y. 1864. S. 917.5 : 24

Greeley, Horace. An overland journey from New York to San Francisco in the summer of 1859. N. Y. 1860. D. 917.5 : 22

Marcy, Randolph B. Thirty years of army life on the border ; comprising descriptions of the indian nomads of the plains, explorations of new territory, a trip across the Rocky mountains in the winter, descriptions of the habits of different animals found in the west and the methods of hunting them, with incidents in the life of different frontier men. Ill. N. Y. 1866. O. 917.5 : 36

Burton, R: Francis. The city of the saints, and across the Rocky mountains to California. Ill. N. Y. 1862. O. 917.5.+8

Bowles, S: Across the continent ; a summer's journey to the Rocky mountains, the mormons and the Pacific states, with speaker Colfax. Springfield, Mass. 1865. D. 917.5 : 5

Seymour, Silas. Incidents of a trip through the Great Platte valley to the Rocky mountains and Laramie plains, in the fall of 1866, with a synoptical statement of the various Pacific railroads and an account of the great Union Pacific excursion to the 100th meridian. N. Y. 1867. D. 917.5 : 44

Van Tramp, J: C. Prairie and Rocky mountain adventures, or Life in the west; added, a view of the states and territorial regions of our western empire, embracing history, statistics and geography, and descriptions of the chief cities of the west. Columbus. O. 1870. 1 v. in 2 pts. O.   **917.5 : 47**

Rusling, James F. Across America, or The great west and the Pacific coast. N. Y. 1874. D.   **917.5 : 41**

Dodge, R: Irving. The plains of the great west and their inhabitants; a description of the plains, game, indians, etc., of the great north amer. desert; with an introd. by W: Blackmore. Ill. N. Y. 1877. O.   **917.5 : 81**

Jackson, Helen Maria, *born* Fiske, *formerly mrs.* Hunt, (*H. H.*). Bits of travel at home, by H. H. Bost. 1878. S.   **917.5 : 28**
Contents. California.—New England.—Colorado.

Codman, J: The round trip by way of Panama, through California, Oregon, Nevada, Utah, Idaho and Colorado; with notes on railroads, commerce, agriculture, mining, scenery and people. N. Y. 1879. D.   **917.5 : 11**

Holton, E: Dwight. Travels with jottings, from midland to the Pacific; letters written for, and publ. chiefly as souvenirs to personal acquaintances and friends. Portr. Milw. 1880. O.   **917.5+26**

Dall, Caroline, *born* Healey. My first holiday, or Letters home from Colorado, Utah and California. Bost. 1881. D.   **917.5 : 13**

Rupert, A. E. D. de. Californians and mormons. N. Y. 1881. D.   **917.5 : 86**

Gleed, C: S. From river to sea; a tourists' and miners' guide from the Missouri river to the Pacific ocean, via Kansas, Colorado, New Mexico, Arizona and California. Chicago. 1882. D.   **917.5 : 85**

Aldridge, Reginald. Life on a ranch; notes in Kansas, Colorado, the Indian Territory and northern Texas. Ill. N. Y. 1884. S.   **917.5 : 96**

3. Rocky mountain region.

Northern.

Quin, *Sir* Windham T: Wyndham-, *4th earl of Dunraven.* The great divide; travels in the upper Yellowstone in the summer of 1874. Ill. Lond. 1876. O.   **917.5 : 17**

Murphy, J: Mortimer. Rambles in north-western America from the Pacific ocean to the Rocky mountains; a description of the physical geography, climate, soil, productions, industrial and commercial resources, scenery, population, educational institutions, arboreal botany, and game animals of Oregon, Washington territory, Idaho, Montana, Utah and Wyoming. Lond. 1879. O.   **917.5 : 38**

Richardson, James, *ed.* Wonders of the Yellowstone. New ed., with map and ill. [Ill. lib. of travel]. N. Y. 1882. D.   **917.5 : 75**
Note. For full descriptions of the Yellowstone national park, see 12th annual report of the U. S. geol. survey of the territories, col. 340.

Middle.

Sitgreaves, Lorenzo. Report of an expedition down the Zuñi and Colorado rivers. Maps and ill. (U. S. 32d cong. 2d sess.; Sen. ex. doc. no. 59.) Wash. 1854. O.   *in* **917.5 : D**
Contents. Report.—Tables of distances, geographical positions and meteorol. observ.—Rep. on natural history.—**Woodhouse**, S. W. Medical report. (The scientific reports have been entered in their proper places in this catalogue).

Stansbury, Howard. An expedition to the valley of the Great Salt Lake of Utah; incl. a description of its geography, natural history and minerals, and an analysis of its waters, with an authentic account of the mormon settlement, also a reconnoissance of a new route through the Rocky mountains. Maps and ill. (U. S. 32d cong. spec. sess.; Sen. ex. doc. no. 3.) Phila. 1855. O.   *in* **917.5 : D**
Contents. Report.—App.; Measured distances, geographical positions, etc.; Zoology; Botany; Geology and palæontology; **Gale**, L. D. Chemical analysis of the mineral waters and other specimens collected; Meteorol. observations. (The scientific papers have been entered in their proper places in this catalogue.)

Simpson, James H. Report of explorations across the great basin of the territory of Utah, for a direct wagon-route from Camp Floyd to Genoa in Carson valley, in 1859. Maps and ill. (Engineer dept., U. S. army.) Wash. 1876. Q.   *in* **917.5 : D**
Contents. Introd.: History of the explorations within the great basin from 1776, and a general description of the country.—Report and journal.—Itineraries of wagon-routes. — Astron. observ. and geographical positions.—**Engelmann**, H: Astron. and meteorol. observ., and computation of altitude therefrom.—Table of distances, altitudes and grades. — Magnetic observ. and results. — Railroad routes from the Atlantic to the Pacific ocean.—**Engelmann**, H: Geology of the country between Fort Leavenworth, Ks., and the Sierra Nevada, near Carson valley.—**Meek**, F. B. Report on the palæontological collections.—**Baird**, Spencer F. Ornithology; a list of birds collected on the exped. by C: S. McCarthy. — **Gill**, Theodore. Report on the ichthyology of the exped.—**Engelmann**, G: Report on the botany of the exped.—**Hurt**, Garland. Population and resources of the terr. of Utah; Indians of Utah.—**Collins**, C. R. Languages of the different tribes of indians, inhabiting the terr. of Utah.—**Kern**, E: M. Journal of an explor. of Mary's or Humboldt river, Carson lake, and Owens river and lake, in 1845.—**Harry**, Philip. Journeyings of father Escalante from Santa Fé to Utah lake and the Moqui villages in 1776; with map.

Ives, Joseph Christmas. Report upon the Colorado river of the west, explored in 1857-8 under the direction of the office of explorations and surveys, by order of the sec. of war. Maps and ill. Wash. 1861. Q.   *in* **917.5 : D**
Contents. General rep.—Hydrographic rep.—**Newberry**, J. S. Geological rep.—**Gray**, A., *and others.* Botany. — **Baird**, S. F. Zoology. — App. Astron., barometric and meteorol. observations, *etc.*

Powell, John Wesley. Report of the exploration of the Colorado river of the west and its tributaries, explored in 1869-72, under the dir. of the sec. of the Smithsonian institution. Map and ill. Wash. 1875. Q.   *in* **917.5 : D**
Contents. Pt. 1. History of the exploration of the cañons of the Colorado. — Pt. 2. On the physical features of the valley of the Colorado.—Pt. 3. **Coues**, E. Zoology.

Bishop, Isabella L., *born* Bird. A lady's life in the Rocky mountains. Ill. N. Y. 1879-80. D.   **917.5 : 4**

King, Clarence. Mountaineering in the Sierra Nevada. 6th ed., with maps and add. Bost. 1879. D.   **917.5 : 77**

Grohman, W: A. Baillie-. Camps in the Rockies; being a narrative of life on the frontier and sport in the Rocky mountains, with an account of the cattle ranches of the west. Map. N. Y. 1882. D. **917.5 : 76**

Ingersoll, Ernest. Knocking round the Rockies. N. Y. 1883 [1882]. O. **917.5 : 79**

— The crest of the continent; a record of a summer's ramble in the Rocky mountains and beyond. [Map and ill.] Chic. 1885. O. **917.5 : 104**

Hayes, A: Allen, jr. New Colorado and the Santa Fe trail. Ill. N. Y. 1880. O. **917.5+52**

Fossett, Frank. Colorado, its gold and silver mines, farms and stock ranges and health and pleasure resorts; tourist's guide to the Rocky mountains. 2d ed. N. Y. 1880. D. **917.5 : 51**

Pabor, W: E. Colorado, as an agricultural state; its farms. fields and garden lands. N. Y. 1883 [1882]. O. **917.5 : 80**

The southwest.

Gregg, Josiah. Commerce of the prairies, or The journal of a Santa Fé trader during eight expeditions across the great western prairies and a residence of nearly nine years in northern Mexico. Maps and ill. N. Y. 1844. 2 v. D. **917.5 : 1**

— Same, germ. Wanderungen durch die prärien und das nördliche Mexiko. Aus dem eng. übertr. von Gottlob Fink. 2te ausg. Stuttg. 1851. 2 v. S. **917.5 : 1**

Anderson, Alexander D. The silver country, or The great south-west; a review of the mineral and other wealth, the attractions and material development of the former kingdom of New Spain, comprising Mexico and the mexican cessions to the U. S. in 1848 and 1853. N. Y. 1877. O. **917.5 : 49**

Davis, W: Watts Hart. El gringo, or New Mexico and her people. N. Y. 1857. D. **917.5 : 57**

Cozzens, S: Woodworth. The marvellous country, or Three years in Arizona and New Mexico, the Apaches' home; comprising a description of this wonderful country, its immense mineral wealth, its magnificent mountain scenery, its towns and cities found therein, with a history of the Apache tribe and a description of the authors guide, Cochise, the great Apache war chief, the whole interspersed with strange events and adventures. Ill. Bost. 1873. O. **917.5 : 50**

Bishop, W: H: [Journey in southern California and Arizona.] in **917.7 : 15**

Roberts, Edwards. With the invader; glimpses of the southwest. [Ill.] San Francisco. 1885. S. **917.5 : 102**

Bourke, J: G. The snake-dance of the Moquis of Arizona; a narrative of a journey from Santa Fé, New Mexico, to the villages of the Moqui indians of Arizona; with a description of the manners and customs of this peculiar people, and especially of the revolting religious rite, the snake-dance; added, a brief dissertation upon serpent-worship in general, with an account of the tablet dance of the pueblo of Santo Domingo, New Mexico, etc. N. Y. 1884. O. **917.5 : 95**

4. Pacific states.

History.

Greenhow, Robert. The history of Oregon and California, and other territories on the north-west coast of North America; accompanied by a geographical view and map of those countries and a number of documents as proofs and ill. of the history. 3d ed. N. Y. 1845. O. **975.8+1**

Soulé, Frank, J: H. **Gihon** and James **Nisbet.** The annals of San Francisco; containing a summary of the history of the first discovery, settlement, progress and present condition of California, and a complete history of all the important events connected with its great city; added, biogr. memoirs of some prominent citizens. N. Y. 1855. O. **975.8 : 2**

Norman, Lucia. A popular history of California from the earliest period of its discovery to the present time. 2d ed. rev. and enl. by T. E. Ill. San Francisco. 1883. S. **975.8 : 7**

Bancroft, Hubert Howe. History of the Pacific states of North America: California, v. 1–3. San Francisco. 1884–85. 3 v. O. **975.8+4**
Contents. V. 1. 1542 - 1800. 2. 1801 - 1824. 3. 1825 - 1840.

— - The northwest coast, v. 1, 2. San Francisco. 1884. 2 v. O. **975.8+5**
Contents. V. 1. 1543 - 1800. 2. 1800 - 1846.

Leonard, H. L. W. Oregon territory; containing a brief but authentic account of spanish, english, russian and american discoveries on the northwest coast of America, also the different treaty stipulations confirming the claim of the U. S. and overland expeditions to the Columbia river, with incidents of peril and adventure connected with their history, etc. Cleveland. 1846. D. **975.8 : 6**

Barrows, W: Oregon; the struggle for possession. Maps. (Amer. commonwealths). Bost. 1884 [1883]. S. **975.8 : 3**

Description.

Davidson, G: Directory for the Pacific coast of the U. S. In U. S. coast survey rep. 1858. in **622 : D**

— Same. Revised ed. In the same, 1862. in **622 : D**

California.

Colton, Walter. Three years in California. Ill. N. Y. 1850. D. **917.5 : 56**

Revere, Joseph Warren. A tour of duty in California; incl. a description of the gold region and an account of the voyage around Cape Horn. with notices of Lower California, the Gulf and Pacific coasts, and the principal events attending the conquest of the Californias; ed. by Joseph N. Balestier. Maps and ill. N. Y. 1849. D. **917.5 : 62**

Taylor, Bayard. Eldorado, or Adventures in the path of empire, comprising a voyage to California, via Panama, life in San Francisco and Monterey, pictures of the gold region and experiences of mexican travel, [1849]. 4th ed. N. Y. 1854. 2 v. in 1. D. **917.5 : 66**

Borthwick, J. D. Three years in California, [1851—1854]. Ill. Edinb. 1857. O.
917.5 : 54

Marryat, Frank. Mountains and molehills, or Recollections of a burnt journal. Ill. N. Y. 1855. D. 917.5 : 37

Farnham, Eliza W., *born* Burhaus. California, in-doors and out, or How we farm, mine and live generally in the golden state. N. Y. 1856. D. 917.5 : 58

Palmer, J: Williamson. New and old, or California and India in romantic aspects. *T. p. w.* [N. Y. 1859]. D. 917.5 : 60

Browne, J: Ross. Sketches of adventure in California and Washoe. *With his* Crusoe's island. 919.7 : 5
Contents. A dangerous journey, 1849.—Observations in office: My official experiences; The great Port Townsend controversy; The Indians of California.— A peep at Washoe, 1860.

Brace, C: Loring. The new west, or California in 1867—1868. N. Y. 1869. D. 917.5 : 6

Taylor, B: Franklin. Between the gates. Ill. Chicago. 1878. D. 917.5 : 46

Nordhoff, C: California for health, pleasure and residence; a book for travellers and settlers. N. Y. 1873. O. 917.5 : 53
— *Same.* New ed., thoroughly rev., giving detailed accounts of the culture of the wine and raisin grape, the orange, lemon, olive and other semi-tropical fruits, colony settlements, methods of irrigation, etc. N. Y. 1882. O. 917.5 : 53

Stevenson, Robert L: The Silverado squatters. Ill. Bost. 1884. D. 917.5 : 90

All about Santa Barbara, Cal., the sanitarium of the Pacific coast. Santa Barbara. 1878. O.
917.5 : 72

Oregon, Washington Terr.

Irving, Washington. Astoria, or Notes of an enterprise beyond the Rocky mountains. Author's rev. ed. N. Y. 1883. S.
917.5 : 31
— *Same. In his* Works. 820.1 : 13 v4
— *Same. In his* Works. 820.1 : P11 v13

Franchère, Gabriel. Narrative of a voyage to the northwest coast of America in 1811—1814, or The first american settlement on the Pacific. Tr. and ed. by J. V. Huntington. N. Y. 1854. D. 917.5 : 59

Bulfinch, T: Oregon and Eldorado, or Romance of the rivers. Bost. 1866. D. 917.5 : 63
Note. Pt. 1, Oregon, is principally a relation of Lewis and Clarke's expedition along the Columbia river; pt. 2, Eldorado, is a narrative of explorations on the Amazons.

Cox, Ross. Adventures on the Columbia river; incl. the narrative of a residence of six years on the western side of the Rocky mountains among various tribes of indians hitherto unknown, together with a journey across the american continent. N. Y. 1832. O. 917.5 : 12
— *Same.* The Columbia river, or Scenes and adventures during a residence of six years. etc. 2d ed. Lond. 1832. 2 v. O. 917.5 : 12

Parker, S: Journal of an exploring tour beyond the Rocky mountains, under the direction of the A. B. C. F. M. in 1835—1837; containing a description of the geography, geology, climate, productions of the country, and the numbers, manners and customs of the natives. Map of Oregon. 3d ed. Ithaca. 1842. D. 917.5 : 40

Hines, Gustavus. Life on the plains of the Pacific: Oregon; its history, condition and prospects, containing a description of the geography, climate and productions, with personal adventures among the indians during a residence of the author on the plains bordering the Pacific, while connected with the Oregon mission, embracing extended notes of a voyage around the world. Buffalo. 1851. D. 917.5 : 64

Swan, James G. The northwest coast, or Three years' residence in Washington territory. Ill. N. Y. 1857. D. 917.5 : 45

Nordhoff, C: Northern California, Oregon and the Sandwich Islands. N. Y. 1874. O.
917.5 : 61

Symons, T: W. Report of an examination of the upper Columbia river and the territory in its vicinity, in sept. and oct. 1881, to determine its navigability and adaptability to steamboat transportation; made by dir. of the commanding general of the dep. of the Columbia. Ill. (U. S. 47th cong. 1 sess. Sen. ex. doc. no. 186). Wash. 1882. Q. *in* 917.5 : D

Nash, Wallis. Two years in Oregon. N. Y. 1882. D. 917.5 : 83

Leighton, Caroline C. Life at Puget Sound; with sketches of travel in Washington territory, British Columbia, Oregon and California, 1865—1881. Bost. 1884. D.
917.5 : 91

5. Alaska.

Bancroft, Hubert Howe. History of the Pacific states of North America: Alaska, 1730—1885. San Francisco. 1886. O. 975.9+1

Davidson, G: Report relative to the resources and the coast features of Alaska territory. *In* U. S. coast survey rep. 1867. *in* 622 : D
Contents. General report.—Directory of the coast. —List of geographical positions.—Aids to navigation.—Blake, Theodore A. Geology.—Harford, W. G. W. Zoology. — Vocabularies of the Kadiak, Unalaska, Kenai and Sitka languages.—Meteorology.— Kellogg, Albert. Botany. — Comparative alaskan vocabulary.

Whymper, F: Travel and adventure in the territory of Alaska, formerly Russian America, now ceded to the U. S., and in various parts of the north Pacific. Map and ill. N. Y. 1869. O. 917.5 : 68

Morris, W: Gouverneur. Report upon the customs district, public service and resources of Alaska territory. Wash. 1879. O.
917.5+82
— *Same.* (45th cong. 3d sess.; Sen. doc. 59). Wash. 1879. O. *in* 328.1 : D

Jackson, Sheldon. Alaska, and missions on the north Pacific coast. Ill. N. Y. [1880]. D.
917.5 : 67

Petroff, Ivan. Report on the population, industries and resources of Alaska. Maps and ill. *In* U. S. tenth census, 1880, v. 8.
in 317 : D
Contents. Statistical view by geographical divisions. — Resources. — Geography and topography.— Historical sketch.—Notes on alaskan ethnology.

Elliott, H: W. Report on the seal islands of Alaska. Ill. *In* U. S. tenth census, 1880, v. 8. *in* 317 : D

Wright, Julia McNair. Among the alaskans. Map and ill. Phila. [1883]. S. **917.5 : 89**

Pierrepont, E: Fifth avenue to Alaska. Maps by Leonard Forbes Beckwith. N. Y. 1884. D. **917.5 : 92**

Wardman, G: A trip to Alaska ; a narrative of what was seen and heard during a summer cruise in Alaska waters. Bost. 1884. D. **917.5 : 94**

Scidmore, *Miss* Eliza Ruhamah. Alaska ; its southern coast and the Sitkan archipelago. Maps and ill. Bost. [1885]. D. **917.5 : 101**

27.　North America — e, British and Mexican.

1. British America.

In general.

Murray, Hugh. An historical and descriptive account of British America, comprehending Canada, Upper and Lower, Nova Scotia, New Brunswick, Newfoundland, Prince Edward Island, the Bermudas and the fur countries, their history from the earliest settlement, their statistics, topography, commerce, fisheries, etc., their social and political condition, and also an account of the manners and present state of the aboriginal tribes. [Harper's family lib.] N. Y. 1845. 2 v. S. **976 : 1**

Buckingham, James Silk. Canada, Nova Scotia, New Brunswick and the other british provinces in North America ; with a plan of national colonization. Lond. [1843]. O. **917.6 : 1**

Mackenzie, *Sir* Alexander. Voyage from Montreal on the river St. Lawrence, through the continent of North America, to the Frozen and Pacific oceans, in the years 1789 and 1793 ; with a prelim. account of the rise, progress and present state of the fur trade of that country. Ill. with maps. Lond. 1801. Q. **917.6 : R6**

Rae, W: Fraser. Newfoundland to Manitoba, through Canada's maritime, mining and prairie provinces. N. Y. 1881. D. **917.6 : 18**

East and north.

Martin, Robert Montgomery. History of Nova Scotia, Cape Breton, the Sable Islands, New Brunswick, Prince Edward Island, the Bermudas, Newfoundland, etc. [British col. lib., v. 4.] Lond. 1844. S. **976 : 6**

Hepworth, G: Hughes. Starboard and port ; the "Nettie" along shore. N. Y. 1876. D. **917.6 : 19**

Benjamin, S: Green Wheeler. The cruise of the Alice May in the Gulf of St. Lawrence and adjacent waters. Repr. from the Century magazine. Ill. N. Y. 1885 [1884]. O. **917.6 : 31**

Norton, C: Ledyard, *and* J: Habberton. Canoeing in Kanuckia, or Haps and mishaps afloat and ashore of the statesman, the editor, the artist and the scribbler, recorded by the commodore and the cook. Ill. N. Y. 1878. D. **917.6 : 10**

Butterworth, Hezekiah. Zigzag journeys in Acadia and New France ; a summer's journey of the Zigzag club through the historic fields of the early french settlements of America. Ill. Bost. 1885 [1884]. O. **x 917.6 : 29**

——— **x** denotes books specially adapted for children.

Haliburton, T: Chandler, (*Sam Slick*). Historical and statistical account of Nova Scotia. Map and ill. Halifax. 1829. 2 v. O. **976 : 3**

Contents. V. 1. History. 2. Statistical account.

Smith, Philip H. Acadia ; a lost chapter in american history. Ill. Pauling, N. Y. [1884]. O. **976 : 7**

Cozzens, F: Swartwout. Acadia, or A month with the blue noses. N. Y. 1859. D. **917.6 : 2**

Chase, Eliza Brown. Over the border ; Acadia, the home of Evangeline, by E. B. C. Ill. Bost. 1884. O. **917.6 : 26**

Lyell, *Sir* C: Travels and observations in Nova Scotia. *in* **917.1 : 21**

Hatton, Joseph, *and* M. Harvey. Newfoundland ; its history, its present condition and its prospects in the future. Rep. from the eng. ed., rev., corr. and enl. Ill. Bost. 1883. O. **917.6 : 24**

Mullaly, J: A trip to Newfoundland, its scenery and fisheries ; with an account of the laying of the submarine telegraph cable. Ill. N. Y. 1855. D. **917.6 : 8**

Noble, L: L. After icebergs with a painter ; a summer voyage to Labrador and around Newfoundland. N. Y. 1861. D. **917.6 : 9**

Stearns, Winfrid Allen. Labrador ; a sketch of its peoples, its industries and its natural history. Bost. 1884. D. **917.6 : 30**

Robinson, H: M. The great fur land, or Sketches of life in the Hudson's Bay territory. Ill. N. Y. 1879. D. **917.6 : 11**

Ballantyne, Robert Michael. Hudson Bay, or Everyday life in the wilds of North America, during six years' residence in the territories of the hon. Hudson Bay company. Ill. Lond. 1882. D. **917.6 : 20**

Butler, W: Francis. The wild north land ; being the story of a winter journey, with dogs, across northern North America. Ill. and route map. 8th ed. Lond. 1881. D. **917.6 : 22**

Tytler, Patrick Fraser. Historical view of the progress of discovery on the more northern coasts of America, from the earliest period ; with descriptive sketches of the natural history of north american regions, by James Wilson. Add. an app., containing remarks on a late memoir of Sebastian Cabot, with a vindication of R: Hakluyt. Map and ill. [Harper's fam. lib.] N. Y. 1846. S. **917.6 : 17**

The Canadas.

(*See also* New France, col. 1332.)

Martin, Robert Montgomery. History, statistics and geography of Upper and Lower Canada. [British col. lib., v. 1.] 2d ed. Lond. 1838. S. **976 : 5**

Garneau, François Xavier. History of Canada, from the time of its discovery till the union, 1840-41. Tr. from L'histoire du Canada, and accompanied with ill. notes, etc., by Andrew Bell. 3d ed., rev. Montreal. 1866. 2 v. O.   **976 : 2**
Contents. V. 1. 1492 - 1758. 2. 1759 - 1841.

Warburton, G: The conquest of Canada, by the author of "Hochelaga." N. Y. 1855. 2 v. D.   **976 : 4**

Scadding, H:, and J: C: Dent. Toronto; past and present, historical and descriptive; a memorial volume for the semi-centennial of 1884. Pub. by authority of the Citizens' semi-centennial committee. Toronto. 1884. F.   **976+8**

    *   *   *

Campbell, J: G: E: H: Douglas Sutherland, *marquess of Lorne.* Canadian pictures, drawn with pen and pencil. Ill. N. Y. [1884]. Q.   **917.6+28**

Moore's handbook of Canada; with a tariff of rates and the hours of arrival and departure of the railway trains and steamers, rates of postage, coinage and other useful information. 2d ed. Montreal. 1860. T.   **917.6 : 25**

Sansom, Joseph. Sketches of Lower Canada, historical and descriptive; with the author's recollections of the soil and aspect, habits and religious institutions of that isolated country during a tour to Quebec in july 1817. N. Y. 1817. D.   **917.6 : 13**

Silliman, B: Remarks on a short tour made between Hartford and Quebec in the autumn of 1819, by the author of A journal of travels in England, Holland and Scotland. N. Y. 1820. D.   **917.6 : 14**

Talbot, E: Allen. Five years' residence in the Canadas, incl. a tour through part of the U. S. of America in 1823. Lond. 1824. 2 v. O.   **917.6 : 15**

Jameson, Anna, *born* Murphy. Winter studies and summer rambles in Canada. N. Y. 1839. 2 v. D.   **917.6 : 4**

Lanman, C: A tour to the river Saguenay in Lower Canada. Phila. 1848. D. **917.6 : 5**

Moodie, Susanna, *born* Strickland. Roughing it in the bush, or Life in Canada. N. Y. 1852. 2 v. D.   **917.6 : 7**

Russell, W: Howard. Canada, its defences, condition and resources; a second and concl. vol. of "My diary, north and south" [917.1+33]. Bost. 1865. D.   **917.6 : 12**

Thoreau, H: D: A yankee in Canada, with anti-slavery and reform papers. Bost. 1866. D.   **917.6 : 16**
Contents. A yankee in Canada.—Anti-slavery and reform papers: Slavery in Mass.; Prayers; Civil disobedience; A plea for capt. J: Brown; Paradise, to be regained; Herald of freedom; T: Carlyle and his works; Life without principle; Wendell Phillips before the Concord lyceum; The last days of John Brown.

Geikie, Cunningham. The backwoods of Canada. 4th ed. Lond. 1881. D. **917.6 : 21**

Fleming, Sandford. England and Canada; a summer tour between old and new Westminster, with historical notes. Montreal. 1884. D.   **917.6 : 27**

Ritchie, James Ewing. To Canada with emigrants; a record of actual experiences. Ill. Lond. 1885. D.   **917.6 : 32**

The west.

Hind, H: Youle. Narrative of the canadian Red river exploring expedition of 1857 and of the Assinniboine and Saskatchewan exploring expedition of 1858. Ill. Lond. 1860. 2 v. O.   **917.6 : 3**
Contents. V. 1. The Canadian Red river explor. exped. — Assiniboine and Saskatchewan explor. exped. 2, *Same, continued.*—Geology of the basin of Lake Winnipeg.—Climate of the southern part of Rupert's Land.—App.

Fitzgibbon, Mary. A trip to Manitoba. Lond. 1880. O.   **917.6 : 23**

2. Mexico.

History.

Bancroft, Hubert Howe. History of the Pacific states of North America: History of Mexico, vols. 1-5. San Francisco. 1883-85. 5 v. O.   **977+12**
Contents. V. 1. 1516-1521. 2. 1521-1600. 3. 1600-1803. 4. 1804-1824. 5. 1824-1861.

— — North Mexican states, v. 1, 1531—1800. San Francisco. 1883. O.   **977+13**

Ober, F: Albion. Young folks' history of Mexico. (Young folks' history ser.) Bost. 1883 [1882]. S.   **977 : 11**

Witter, Marina, (*Th. Armin*). Das alte Mexiko und die eroberung Neuspaniens durch Ferdinand Cortez; nach W: [H.] Prescott und Bernal Diaz, sowie unter benutzung der schriften von Alexander v. Humboldt, des abbé Brasseur, des abt F. X. Clavigero und anderen. Leipz. 1865. O.   **977 : 1**

— Das heutige Mexiko; land und volk unter Spaniens herrschaft, sowie nach erlangter selbstständigkeit bis zum tode des kaisers Maximilian; unter benutzung der neuesten und zuverlässigsten quellen herausg. 2te aufl. Leipz. 1868. O.   **977 : 2**

Mayer, Brantz. Mexico, aztec, spanish and republican; a historical, geographical, political, statistical and social account of that country from the period of the invasion by the spaniards to the present time; with a view of the ancient Aztec empire and civilization, a historical sketch of the late war, and notices of New Mexico and California. Hartford. 1853. 2 v. O.   **977+7**
Contents. V. 1. History to 1850. 2. Description: In general; The mexican states and territories; The territory of New Mexico and the state of California, as parts of the U. S.

Frost, J: Pictorial history of Mexico and the mexican war; comprising an account of the ancient Aztec empire, the conquest by Cortes, Mexico under the spaniards, the mexican revolution, the republic, the texan war, and the recent war with the U. S. Phila. 1856. O.   **977 : 4**

Solis y Rivadeneira, Antonio de. The history of the conquest of Mexico by the spaniards. Done into eng. from the original spanish by T: Townsend. Ill. Dublin. 1727. 2 v. S.   **977 : 9**

Prescott, W: Hickling. History of the conquest of Mexico, with a prelim. view of the ancient mexican civilization and the life of the conqueror, Hernando Cortés. 8th ed. N. Y. 1847. 3 v. O.   **977 : 8**
Contents. V. 1. Introd.: View of the aztec civilisation. — Discovery of Mexico. — March to Mexico.

Prescott, W: Hickling.—*Continued.*
2. *Same, continued.* — Residence in Mexico. — Expulsion from Mexico. 3. Siege and surrender of Mexico.—Conclusion; Subsequent career of Cortés.—App.: Origin of the mexican civilization, analogies with the old world; Original documents.—Index.
— *Same.* [New popular ed.] ; ed. by J: Foster Kirk. Phila. *n. d.* 3 v. D.   **977 : 8**
Helps, *Sir* Arthur. [Conquest of Mexico.] *In his* The spanish conquest in America.
       977 : 5
Contents, see under South and Central America.
Oertel, Philipp F: W:, (*W. O. v. Horn*). Die eroberung von Mexiko durch Hernando Cortez ; der deutschen jugend und dem volke erzählt. 2te aufl. Ill. Wiesbaden. 1874. S.
       977 : 14
Cortés, Hernando. Despatches to Charles V, during the conquest. Tr. with introd. and notes by G. Folsom. *T. p. w.* [N. Y. 1843.] D.   **977 : 3**
Eloin, Paula, *born gräfin* Kollonitz. The court of Mexico. Tr. by J. E. Ollivant. 4th ed. Lond. 1868. O.   **977 : 6**
Mayer, Brantz. Observations on mexican history and archæology, with a special notice of Zapotec remains as delineated in mr. J. G. Sawkin's drawings of Mitla. *In* Smithsonian contributions.   **506 : R3 v9**
Archaeological institute of America. Papers : American series, 2. Report of an archaeological tour in Mexico in 1881. 2d ed. Bost. 1885. O.   **906+13**
Contents. From Tampico to the City of Mexico.—Notes about the City of Mexico. — Studies about Cholula and its vicinity.—An excursion to Mitla.
See also in the Index to biography **Cortés— Juarez Maximilian—Montezuma.**

Description.

Humboldt, F: H: Alexander *freiherr* v. Political essay on the kingdom of New Spain. Tr. from the original french by J: Black. N. Y. 1811. 2 v. O.   **917.7 : 3**
Containing Researches relative to the geography of Mexico, the extent of its surface and its political division into intendancies, the physical aspect of the country, the population, the state of agriculture and manufacturing and commercial interests, the canals projected between the South Sea and Atlantic ocean, the crown revenues, the quantity of the precious metals which have flowed from Mexico into Europe and Asia since the discovery of the new continent, and the military defence of New Spain ; with physical sections and maps, founded on astronomical observations, and trigonometrical and barometrical measurements.—*Title-page.*
Modern traveller, The ; a popular description, geographical, historical and topographical, of the various countries of the globe : [v. 25, 26.] Mexico and Guatimala. Lond. 1825. 2 v. T.   **917.7 : 5**
Emory, W: Helmsley. Report on the U. S. and Mexican boundary survey, made under the dir. of the sec. of the interior. (U. S. 34th cong. 1 sess.; House ex. doc., no. 135.) Maps and ill. Wash. 1857–59. 2 v. in 3. Q.
       917.7 : D
Contents. V. 1. General report. **2,** pt. 1. Botany of the boundary; pt. 2. Zoology of the boundary.—*Note.* The contents of v. 2 have been entered in their proper places, in this catalogue.
García Cubas, Antonio. The republic of Mexico in 1876 ; a political and ethnographical account of the population, character, habits, costumes and vocations of its inhabitants.

García Cubas, Antonio.—*Continued.*
Written in spanish, tr. by G: F. Henderson. Ill. Mexico. 1876. O.   **917.7+12**
— Cuadro geográfico, estadístico, descriptivo é histórico de lós Estados Unidos Mexicanos. [Ill.] México. 1884. O.   **917.7 : 18**
Brocklehurst, T: Unett. Mexico to-day ; a country with a great future, and a glance at the prehistoric remains and antiquities of the Montezumas. Ill. N. Y. 1883. O.
       917.7+11
Ober, F: Albion. Mexican resources ; a guide to and through Mexico. Map. Ill. Bost. 1884. O.   **917.7+17**
Ramirez, Santiago. Noticia histórica de la riqueza minera de México y de su actual estado de explotacion ; escrita por disposicion de la Secretaría de fomento. México. 1884. O.   **628 : 41**
Conkling, Alfred R. Appleton's guide to Mexico; incl. a chapter on Guatemala and a complete english-spanish vocabulary. N. Y. 1884 [1883].   **917.7 : 16**

         *   *   *

Latrobe, C: Joseph. The rambler in Mexico, 1834. N. Y. 1836. D.   **917.7 : 4**
Ferry, Gabriel. Vagabond life in Mexico. N. Y. 1856. D.   **917.7 : 1**
Wise, H: A: Los gringos, or An inside view of Mexico and California, with wanderings in Peru, Chili and Polynesia. N. Y. 1857. D.
       917.7 : 10
Haven, Gilbert. Our next-door neighbor ; a winter in Mexico. N. Y. 1875. O. **917.7 : 2**
Oswald, Felix Leopold. Summerland sketches, or Rambles in the backwoods of Mexico and Central America. Ill. Phila. 1880. O.
       917.7 : 7
Conkling, Howard. Mexico and the mexicans, or Notes of travel in the winter and spring of 1883. N. Y. 1883. D.   **917.7 : 14**
Bishop, W: H: Old Mexico and her lost provinces ; a journey in Mexico, southern California and Arizona, by way of Cuba. N. Y. 1883. D.   **917.7 : 15**
Stephens, C: Asbury. The Knockabout club in the tropics ; the adventures of a party of young men in New Mexico, Mexico and Central America. Ill. Bost. 1884 [1883]. O.   **x 917.7 : 13**

Yucatan.
(See also Central America.)

Fancourt, C: St. J: The history of Yucatan, from its discovery to the close of the 17th century. Lond. 1854. O.   **977 : 10**
Norman, B: Moore. Rambles in Yucatan, or Notes of travel through the peninsula, incl. a visit to the remarkable ruins of Chi-Chen, Kabah, Zayi and Uxmal. Ill. N. Y. 1843. O.   **917.7+6**
Stephens, J: Lloyd. Incidents of travel in Yucatan. N. Y. 1848. 2 v. O.   **917.7+8**
Tempsky, Gustav Ferdinand v. Mitla ; a narrative of incidents and personal adventures on a journey in Mexico, Guatemala and Salvador in 1853 to 1855, with observations on the modes of life in those countries ; ed. by J. S. Bell. Lond. 1858. O.   **917.7 : 9**

x denotes books specially adapted for children.

28.   Central and South America, West Indies.

1. In general.

Helps, *Sir* Arthur.   The spanish conquest in America, and its relation to the history of slavery and the government of colonies. N. Y. 1856.   3 v.   D.   **977 : 5**
Contents. **V. 1.** Prince Henry of Portugal. — Columbus. — Ovando. — The dominicans. — Ojeda and Nicuesa. — Vasco Nuñez de Balboa. — Cuba. — Las Casas as a colonist and a reformer. **2.** Las Casas. — Hernando Cortez. — The siege of Mexico. **3.** The administration of Cortez. — Nicaragua. — Encomiendas. — Guatemala. — The conquest of Peru.

Bates, H: Walter, *ed.*   Central America, the West Indies and South America ; with ethnological app. by A. H. Keane. (Stanford's compendium of geography and travel, based on Hellwald's "Die erde und ihre völker".) Maps and ill. Lond. 1878. O.   **918 : 1**

Wilkes, C: U. S. exploring expedition.   *in* **919 : D**
Contents, see under Oceanica.

Trollope, Anthony.   The West Indies and the Spanish Main.   Leipz. 1860.   S.   **917.9 : 12**
Contents. Introd. — Jamaica. — Cuba. — British Guiana. — Barbados. — Trinidad. — St. Thomas. — New Granada and the Isthmus of Panamá. — Central America. — The Bermudas. — Conclusion.

Baxley, H: Willis.   What I saw on the west coast of South and North America and the Hawaiian Islands.   N. Y. 1865.   O.   **918 + 2**

2. Central America.

(See also Mexico, col. 1406; and Canals, col. 423-424.)

Bancroft, Hubert Howe.   History of the Pacific states of North America : Central America ; v. 1, 2.   San Francisco. 1883.   2 v.   O.   **978 + 2**
Contents. **V. 1.** 1501-1530. **2.** 1530-1800.

Stephens, J: Lloyd.   Incidents of travel in Central America, Chiapas and Yucatan. 12th ed.   Ill.   N. Y. 1863.   2 v. O.   **917.8 + 6**

Froebel, Julius.   Seven years' travel in Central America, northern Mexico and the far west of the U. S.   Ill.   Lond. 1859.   O.   **917.8 : 3**

Pictures of travel in far-off lands ; a companion to the study of geography : Central America.   Ill.   Lond. 1881.   S.   **x 917.8 : 1**

Habel, Simeon.   The sculptures of Santa Lucia Cosumalwhuapa in Guatemala ; with an account of travels in Central America and on the western coast of South America.   *In* Smithsonian contributions.   **506 : R3 v22**

Gibbs, Archibald Robertson.   British Honduras ; an historical and descriptive account of the colony from its settlement, 1670.   Comp. from original and authentic sources.   Lond. 1883.   D.   **978 : 3**

Soltera, Maria, *pseud.*   A lady's ride across spanish Honduras.   Ill.   Edinb. 1884.   O.   **917.8 : 10**

Wells, W: Vincent.   Explorations and adventures in Honduras, comprising sketches of travel in the gold regions of Olancho, and

---

a review of the history and general resources of Central America.   Maps and ill. N. Y. 1857.   O.   **917.8 + 8**

Scherzer, C: v.   Wanderungen durch die mittel-amerikanischen freistaaten Nicaragua, Honduras und San Salvador ; mit hinblick auf deutsche emigration und deutschen handel.   Maps.   Brschw. 1857.   O.   **917.8 : 12**

Squier, Ephraim G: Notes on Central America, particularly the states of Honduras and San Salvador ; their geography, topography, climate, population, resources, productions, etc., and the proposed Honduras inter-oceanic railway.   Maps and ill.   N. Y. 1855.   O.   **917.8 + 5**

— Nicaragua ; its people, scenery, monuments and the proposed inter-oceanic canal.   Maps and ill.   N. Y. 1852.   2 v.   O.   **917.8 + 4**
Contents. **V. 1.** Introd.: Central America; Nicaragua. — Narrative. **2.** *Same, continued.* — Interoceanic canal. — Aborigines of Nicaragua. — Outline of political history.

Wells, W: Vincent.   Walker's expedition to Nicaragua ; a history of the central-american war and the Sonora and Kinney expeditions, incl. all the recent diplomatic corresp.   Map and portr. of Walker.   N. Y. 1856.   D.   **917.8 : 7**

Walker, W: The war in Nicaragua.   Map.   N. Y. 1860.   D.   **978 : 1**

Belt, T: The naturalist in Nicaragua ; a narrative of a residence at the gold mines of Chontales, journeys in the savannahs and forests, with observations on animals and plants, in reference to the theory of evolution of living forms.   Map and ill.   Lond. 1874.   D.   **917.8 : 9**

Squier, Ephraim G:, *(Samuel A. Bard)*.   Waikna, or Adventures on the Mosquito Shore, by Samuel A. Bard.   Ill.   N. Y. 1855.   D.   **917.8 : 2**

Headley, Joel Tyler.   Darien exploring expedition under command of lieut. I: C. Strain ; repr. from Harper's magazine.   N. Y. 1885. Q.   **917.8 + 11**

3. West Indies.

In general.

Raynal, Guillaume T: François *abbé.* History of the settlements . . . of the europeans in the . . . West Indies.   **382 : 3**
See col. 256.

Eden, C: H.   The West Indies. [English colonies and foreign countries.]   Lond. 1880.   S.   **917.9 : 1**

Willis, Nathaniel Parker.   Health trip to the tropics.   N. Y. 1854.   D.   **917.9 : 5**
App.: Coronation of Soulouque as emperor of Hayti.

Kingsley, C: At last ; a christmas in the West Indies.   Ill.   [Works, v. 14.]   Lond. 1883. D.   **917.9 : 13**

Brassey, Anna, *born* Allnutt, *lady.*   In the trades, the tropics and the roaring forties. [Ill.]   N. Y. 1885 [1884].   O.   **917.9 : 16**
Contents. England to Madeira. — Madeira. — Trinidad. — Venezuela. — Jamaica. — Bahamas. — Bermuda. — Azores. — App. — Index.

---

x denotes books specially adapted for children.

Drysdale, W: In sunny lands; out-door life in Nassau and Cuba. Ill. N. Y. 1885. Q. 917.9+18

Cuba.

Turnbull, D: Travels in the west: Cuba; with notices of Porto Rico and the slave trade. Lond. 1840. O. 917.9:10

Humboldt, F: H: Alexander *freiherr* v. The island of Cuba. Tr. from the spanish, with notes and a prelim. essay by J:S. Thrasher. N. Y. 1856. D. 917.9:9

Dana, R: H: To Cuba and back; a vacation voyage. Bost. 1859. D. 917.9:6

Howe, Julia Ward. A trip to Cuba. Bost. 1860. D. 917.9:7

Gibbes, Robert Wilson. Cuba for invalids. N. Y. 1860. D. 552.2:7

Gallenga, Antonio. The pearl of the Antilles. Lond. 1873. O. 917.9:14

O'Kelly, James J. The Mambi-land, or Adventures of a Herald correspondent in Cuba. Phila. 1874. D. 917.9:8

Steele, James W. Cuban sketches. N. Y. 1881. D. 917.9:11

Ballou, Maturin Murray. Due south, or Cuba, past and present. Bost. 1885. D. 917.9:20

Hayti.

Philippi, K: Ferdinand. Geschichte des freistaats von St. Domingo, Hayti. (Allg. historische taschenbibliothek, 11ter th.) Dresden. 1826. 3 v. in 1. S. 979:2

Fabens, Joseph Warren. In the tropics, by a settler in Santo Domingo; with an introd. notice by R: B. Kimball. [*Anon.*] 5th ed. N. Y. 1863. D. 917.9:3

United States. Dominican republic: report of the commission of inquiry to Santo Domingo, with the introd. message of the pres., special reports made to the commission, state papers furnished by the Dominican government and the statements of over 70 witnesses. Commissioners B. F. Wade, A. D. White, S. G. Howe; A. A. Burton, sec., F. Douglass, ass't. Wash. 1871. O. *in* 917.9:D

Hazard, S: Santo Domingo, past and present; with a glance at Hayti. Maps and ill. N. Y. 1873. D. 917.9:19

Bird, M. B. The republic of Hayti and its struggles; from historical notes, issued under the auspices of the Haytian government. Lond. *n. d.* D. 979:3

St. John, *Sir* Spenser. Hayti, or The black republic. Lond. 1884. O. 917.9:17

Other islands.

Martin, Robert Montgomery. History of the West Indies. [British col. lib., v. 5, 6]. Lond. 1836-37. 2 v. S. 979:1
Contents. V. 1. Jamaica.—Honduras.—Trinidad.— Tobago.—Grenada.—The Bahamas.—The Virgin Isles. 2. British Guiana.—Barbadoes.—St. Vincent's.—St. Lucia. — Dominica.— Montserrat. — Antigua. — St. Christopher's or St. Kitt's, Nevis, Anguilla.—Conclusion.

Ives, C: The isles of summer, or Nassau and the Bahamas. Ill. ed. New Haven. 1880. D. 917.9:2

Dorr, Julia Caroline, *born* Ripley. Bermuda; an idyl of the summer islands. Maps. N. Y. 1884. S. 917.9:15

Ober, F: Albion. Camps in the Caribbees; adventures of a naturalist in the Lesser Antilles. Bost. 1880. O. 917.9:4

4. South America.

In general.

Juan y Santacilia, Jorge, *and* Antonio de **Ulloa**. A voyage to South America, describing at large the spanish cities, towns, provinces, etc., on that extensive continent; interspersed throughout with reflexions on whatever is peculiar in the religion and civil policy, in the genius, customs, manners, dress, etc., of the several inhabitants, whether natives, spaniards, creoles, indians, mulattoes or negroes; together with the natural, as well as commercial history of the country, and an account of their gold and silver mines, undertaken by command of the king of Spain. Tr. from the spanish. Ill. Lond. 1760. 2 v. O. 918:7

Humboldt, F: H: Alexander *freiherr* v. Travels in the equinoctial regions of America, during 1799—1804. 508:1
For full title, see col. 295.

Gerstäcker, F: Achtzehn monate in Süd-Amerika und dessen deutschen colonien; 1er th. Leipz. 1863. 3 v. S. 918:10
Contents. V. 1. Ausfahrt.—Ecuador.—Peru. 2. *Same, continued.*—Chile. 3. *Same, continued.*—Uruguay and La Plata.—Brasilien.

— *Same, and* Aus meinem tagebuch; gesammelte erzählungen. 2te aufl. Jena. *n. d.* 2 v. S. 918:10
Contents, same as the preceding; v. 2 begins with Uruguay.

Tschudi, J: Jakob v. Reisen durch Südamerika. Ill. und karten. Leipz. 1866-69. 5 v. O. 918:11
Contents. V. 1. Von Hamburg nach Rio de Janeiro. —Rio de Janeiro.—Petropolis.—Von Petropolis nach Ouro-Preto. 2. Von Ouro-Preto nach Diamantina.— Diamantina.—Von Diamantina nach den urwäldern des Mucury.—Aufenthalt in Philadelphia.—Rückreise nach Rio de Janeiro. 3. Nach der provinz Espiritu Santo.—Durch die provinz Rio de Janeiro.—Besuch der parcerie colonien in der provinz São Paolo.—Besuch der colonien in der provinz Santa Catharina. 4. Besuch der provinz Rio Grande do Sul.—Küstenreise von Rio de Janeiro nach São Pedro do Rio Grande.— Von Rio Grande do Sul nach Rosario.—Von Rosario nach Catamarca. 5. Von Catamarca über die Cordillera und durch die wüste von Atacama nach Cobija.—Von Cobija nach Tacna.—Von Tacna nach Arequipa.—Von Arequipa nach Southampton.

Dahlgren, Madeleine. *born* Vinton, *formerly mrs.* Goddard. South sea sketches; a narrative. Bost. 1881. D. 918:8
Note. Travels along the western coast, from Callao to Valparaiso, in 1867.

Orton, James. The Andes and the Amazon, or Across the continent of South America. Map and ill. N. Y. 1870. D. 918:5

Bishop, Nathaniel Holmes. The pampas and Andes: A thousand miles' walk across South America; with an introd. by E: A. Samuels. 3d ed. Ill. Bost. *n. d.* D. 918:3

— *Same.* Bost. 1875. S. 918:3

Price, *Sir* Rose Lambart. The two Americas; an account of sport and travel, with notes of men and manners, in North and South America. Ill. Phila. 1877. O. 918:6

Gallenga, Antonio. South America. Lond.
1880. O.　　　　　　　　　　918 : 13
　Contents. Introd.—The isthmus.—Peru.—Bolivia.—
　Chili.—The strait.—Region of the Plate.—Paraguay.
　—Brazil.
Mulhall, Marion. Between the Amazon and
the Andes, or Ten years of a lady's travels
in the pampas, Gran Chaco. Paraguay and
Matto Grosso. Maps and ill. Lond. 1881.
O.　　　　　　　　　　　　　918 : 9
Pictures of travel in far-off lands ; a companion
to the study of geography: South America. Ill. Lond. 1881. S.　　x 918 : 12
Champney, Lizzie, *born* Williams. Three Vassar
girls in South America ; a holiday trip of
three college girls through the southern
continent, up the Amazon, down the Madeira, across the Andes and up the Pacific
coast to Panama. Ill. Bost. 1885 [1884]. O.
　　　　　　　　　　　　　918 : 14
Knox, T: Wallace. The boy travellers in South
America ; adventures of two youths in a
journey through Equador, Peru, Bolivia,
Brazil, Paraguay, Argentine Republic and
Chili, with descriptions of Patagonia and
Tierra del Fuego and voyages upon the
Amazon and La Plata rivers. Ill. N. Y.
1886 [1885]. O.　　　　　　x 918 : 15

The Amazons and Brazil.

Bulfinch, T: Eldorado. *In his* Oregon, *etc.*
　　　　　　　　　　　　　917.5 : 63
　Contents. Discovery of the Amazon. — Orellana's
　adventure.—Sir Walter Raleigh. — The french phil-
　osophers.—Madame Godin's voyage.—Herndon's ex-
　pedition.—Latest explorations.—The naturalist on
　the Amazon.—Animated nature.
Herndon, W: Lewis, *and* Lardner Gibbon. Exploration of the valley of the Amazon,
made under the direction of the navy dep't.
Ill. (U. S. 32d cong. 2d sess.; Sen. ex.
doc., no. 36). Maps. Wash. 1853, 1854. 2 v.
O.　　　　　　　　　　*in* 918.1 : D
　Contents. v. 1. Report of Herndon, with maps.
　2. Report of Gibbon, with maps.
Warren, J: Esaias. Para, or Scenes and adventures on the banks of the Amazon. N.
Y. 1851. D.　　　　　　　918.1 : 6
Ewbank, T: Life in Brazil, or A journal of a
visit to the land of the cocoa and the palm ;
with an app. containing ill. of ancient
south amer. arts in recently discovered
implements and products of domestic industry and works in stone, pottery, gold,
silver, bronze, etc. Ill. N. Y. 1856. O.
　　　　　　　　　　　　　918.1 : 3
Codman, J: Ten months in Brazil ; with incidents of voyages and travels, descriptions
of scenery and character, notices of commerce and productions, etc. Bost. 1867. D.
　　　　　　　　　　　　　918.1 : 2
Agassiz, L: J: Rudolphe, *and* Elizabeth Cabot,
born Cary. A journey in Brazil, [1865–66.
9th ed.] Bost. 1875. O.　　　918.1 : 1
　App.: The Gulf stream; Flying fishes; Resolutions
　passed on board the Colorado; Dom Pedro Segundo
　railroad; Permanence of characteristics in different
　human species; Sketches of separate journeys under-
　taken by different members of the expedition.
Bates, H: Walter. The naturalist on the river
Amazons ; a record of adventures, habits of
animals, sketches of brazilian and indian
life, and aspects of nature under the equa-

x denotes books specially adapted for children.

tor, during eleven years of travel. 4th ed.
Ill. Lond. 1875. D.　　　　　508 : 4
Fletcher, James Cooley, *and* Daniel Parrish Kid-
der. Brazil and the brazilians, portrayed
in historical and descriptive sketches. Ill.
9th ed. rev. and brought down to date.
Bost. 1879. O.　　　　　　918.1 : 4
Brown, C: Barrington, *and* W: Lidstone. Fif-
teen thousand miles on the Amazon and
its tributaries. Map and ill. Lond. 1878.
O.　　　　　　　　　　　918.1 : 8
Smith, Herbert H. Brazil: The Amazons and
the coast. Ill. N. Y. 1879. O.　918.1 : 5
　App.: Geology and physical geography of the
　Amazons valley.
Wither, T: P. Bigg-. Pioneering in South Brazil ; three years of forest and prairie life in
the province of Parana. Maps and ill.
Lond. 1878. 2 v. O.　　　　918.1 : 7

La Plata states.

Page, T: Jefferson. La Plata, the Argentine
Confederation and Paraguay ; being a narrative of the exploration of the tributaries
of the river La Plata and adjacent countries during 1853—1856, under the orders of
the U. S. government. Map and ill. N. Y.
1859. O.　　　　　　　　918.2+2
Washburn, C: A. The history of Paraguay ;
with notes of personal observations and
reminiscences of diplomacy under difficulties. Bost. 1871. 2 v. O.　　989+1
Uruguay, South America, The republic of ; its
geography, history, rural industries, commerce and general statistics. Issued by
authority of the consulate - general of
Uruguay. Maps. Lond. 1883. O. 918.9 : 5
King, J. Anthony. Twenty-four years in the
Argentine Republic ; embracing its civil
and military history and an account of its
political condition before and during the
administration of gov. Rosas ; his course of
policy, the causes and character of his interference with the government of Monte-
video, and the circumstances which led to
the interference of England and France.
N. Y. 1846. D.　　　　　　982 : 1
Napp, R:, *and others.* The Argentine Republic.
Written in germ., for the central Argentine
commission on the centenary exhibition at
Philadelphia. Maps. Buenos Aires. 1876.
O.　　　　　　　　　　　918.2 : 1

Patagonia.

Bourne, B: Franklin. The captive in Patagonia,
or Life among the giants ; a personal narrative. Ill. Bost. 1874. D.　　918.9 : 1
Beerbohm, Julius. Wanderings in Patagonia,
or Life among the ostrich-hunters. (Leisure hour ser.) N. Y. 1879. S.　918.9 : 2
Coan, Titus. Adventures in Patagonia ; with an
introd. by H: M. Field. N. Y. 1880. D.
　　　　　　　　　　　　　918.9 : 3
Dixie, *Lady* Florence Caroline, *born* Douglas.
Across Patagonia. Ill. N. Y. 1881. O.
　　　　　　　　　　　　　918.9 : 4

Chili and Peru.

Wise, H: A: Wanderings in Peru and Chili. *In
his* Los gringos.　　　　　917.7 : 10

Gilliss, James Melville. Chile ; its geography, climate, earthquakes, government, social condition, mineral and agricultural resources, commerce, etc. Maps and ill. (U. S. naval astron. exped. report, v. 1). Wash. 1855. Q.   *in* 508 : D

Smith, Edmond Reuel. The Araucanians, or Notes of a tour among the indian tribes of southern Chili. N. Y. 1855. D.   985 : 5

Rivero, Mariano E: de, *and* J: Jakob v. Tschudi. Peruvian antiquities. N. Y. 1855. D.
                    985 : 5

Reiss, W:, *and* Alphons Stübel. Peruvian antiquities : The necropolis of Ancon in Peru ; a series of ill. of the civilisation and industry of the empire of the Incas ; the results of excavations made on the spot. With the aid of the gen. administration of the Royal museums of Berlin. Berlin. [1881–85]. 13 pts. F.   985 : R3

Prescott, W: Hickling. History of the conquest of Peru ; with a prelim. view of the civilization of the Incas. N. Y. 1847, 1848. 2 v. O.
                    985+1

— *Same,* ed. by J: Foster Kirk. Phila. 2 v. D.
                    985 : 1

Contents. V. 1. Introd.; view of the civilization of the Incas.—Discovery of Peru.—Conquest of Peru. 2. *Same, continued.*—Civil wars of the conquerors.—Settlement of the country.—App.: Original documents.

Trueba y Cosio, Telesforo de. History of the conquest of Peru by the spaniards. Phila. 1846. D.   985 : 2

Adams, W: H: Davenport. The land of the Incas and the city of the sun ; the story of Francisco Pizarro and the conquest of Peru. Ill. Bost. 1885 [1884]. O.   985 : 4

Markham, Clements Robert. The war between Peru and Chili, 1879–82. N. Y. 1883. D.
                    983 : 1

— Peru. [English colonies and foreign countries]. Ill. Lond. 1880. S.   918.5 : 2

Tschudi, J: Jakob v. Travels in Peru ; on the coast, in the Sierra, across the Cordilleras and the Andes, into the primeval forests. Tr. from the germ. by Thomasina Ross. New ed. N. Y. 1854. D.   918.5 : 4

Squier, Ephraim G: Peru ; incidents of travel and exploration in the land of the Incas. Ill. N. Y. 1877. O.   918.5+3

Cole, G: Ralph Fitz-Roy. The peruvians at home. Lond. 1884. D.   918.5 : 5

Northern states.

Hassaurek, F: Four years among spanish americans [of Ecuador, 1861 — 1865]. 3d ed. Cinc. 1881. D   918.6 : 1

Spence, James Mudie. The land of Bolivar, or War, peace and adventure in the republic of Venezuela, [1871—1872]. 2d ed. Maps and ill. Lond. 1878. 2 v. O.   918.7 : 1

Contents of app., v. 2: Ancient history of Venezuela.—**Ernst,** A. List of plants obs. in Los Roques.—**Sclater,** P. L., *and* O. **Salvin.** On some venezuelan birds, coll. by J. M. Spence.—**Ernst,** A. Sertulum naiguatense; notes on a coll. of alpine plants from the summit of Naiguatá.—**Plant,** J: Description of minerals and ores.—Exhibition of curiosities from Venezuela, Manchester.—**Ernst,** A. Orchideæ venezuelanæ.—Letter on the ascent of the Naiguatá.—**Axon,** W: E. A. The spanish poetry of S. Amer.—**Cajigal,** J: M. Ascent of the Silla de Carácas.—First venezuelan fine arts exhibition.—Decree constituting the islands of the republic into a territory.—Working of the coal mines of the Naricual.—Extraction of mineral phosphates.—List of public works in progress in Venezuela, dec. 1873.—Select list of books, pamphlets, maps and mss. relating to Venezuela.—**Plant,** J: Neolithic stone implements.—The church of Rome in Venezuela.—Index.

Whetham, J: Whetham Boddam-. Roraima and British Guiana ; with a glance at Bermuda, the West Indies and the Spanish Main. Lond. 1879. O.   918.8 : 1

Thurn, Everard F. im. Among the indians of Guiana ; being sketches, chiefly anthropologic, from the interior of British Guiana. Map and ill. Lond. 1883. O.   918.8 : 2

29. Oceanica.

1. In general.

Wilkes, C: Narrative of the U. S. exploring expedition during 1838—1842. Maps and ill. Phila. 1845. 5 v. and Atlas. Q.   919 : D

Contents. V. 1. Introd.—Madeira.—Rio Janeiro.—Political state of Brazil. — Rio Negro. — Terra del Fuego. — Southern cruise. — Chili-Peru. — Paumotu group.—App. 2. Tahiti.—Eimeo.—Samoan Islands. —New South Wales.—Antarctic cruise.—New Zealand. —App. 3. Hapai or Friendly Isles.—Feejee group.— Honolulu.—App. 4. Hawaiian Islands.—Cruise of the "Porpoise" to the Paumotu group and Penrhyn island.—Nisqually and Columbia river.—Willamette valley.—Wallawalla.—Puget Sound and Okanagan.— Indian tribes of the interior of Oregon.—De Fuca's Straits and loss of the "Peacock".—App. 5. Bowditch Island.—Ellice's and Kingsmill group.—Columbia river.—California.—Southern Oregon.—San Francisco to Manilla.—Manilla.—Sooloo.—Singpore.—Cape of Good Hope.—Currents and whaling.—App.—General index. [6]. Atlas.

— *Same.* Phila. 1845. 5 v. O.   919 : 4
— *See* **Jenkins,** J: S., *below.*

Reynolds, J: N. Pacific and Indian oceans, or The South sea surveying expedition, its inception, progress and objects. N. Y. 1841. O.   919 : 2

Jenkins, J: S. U. S. exploring expeditions : Voyage of the U. S. exploring squadron, commanded by capt. C: Wilkes in 1838— 1842 ; together with explorations and discoveries made by admiral d'Urville, capt. Ross and other navigators and travellers, and an account of the expedition to the Dead Sea under lieut. Lynch. Ill. Auburn. 1850. O.   919 : 3

Wallace, Alfred Russel, *ed.* Australasia ; with ethnological app. by A. H. Keane. (Stanford's compendium of geography and travel, based on Hellwald's "Die erde und ihre völker".) Maps and ill. Lond. 1879. O.
                    919 : 1

Contents. Australasia. — Australia. — The Malay archipelago. — Melanesia. — Mikronesia. — New Zealand.—App.

2. Malaysia.

Earl, G: Windsor. The eastern seas, or Voyages and adventures in the Indian archipelago in 1832—1834 ; comprising a tour of the island of Java, visits to Borneo, the Malay peninsula, Siam, etc., also an account of the present state of Singapore, with observations on the commercial resources of the archipelago. Lond. 1837. O. **919.1 : 2**

Gibson, Walter M. The prison of Weltevreden, and a glance at the East Indian archipelago. Ill. N. Y. 1855. D. **919.1 : 3**

Wallace, Alfred Russel. The Malay archipelago, the land of the orang-utan and the bird of paradise ; a narrative of travel, with studies of man and nature. N. Y. 1869. O. **919.1 : 4**
Contents. Physical geogr. — Indo-Malay islands. — The Timor group.—The Celebes group.—The Moluccas.—App. on crania and languages.—Index.

Adams, W: H: Davenport. The eastern archipelago ; description of the scenery, animal and vegetable life, people and physical wonders of the islands in the eastern seas. [Anon.] N. Y. 1880. D. **919.1 : 1**
Contents. Introd.; General view. — The Asiatic-Malay islands. — The Australo-Malay islands. — The Philippine islands.

Forbes, H: O. A naturalist's wanderings in the eastern archipelago ; a narrative of travel and exploration from 1878 to 1883 ; with ill. from the author's sketches and descriptions by J: B. Gibbs. Maps and ill. N. Y. 1885. O. **919.1 : 5**
Contents. In the Cocos-Keeling islands.—In Java.—In Sumatra.—In the Moluccas and in Timor-Laut.—In the island of Buru.—In Timor.—App., Language and natural history.—Index.

Keppel, H: The expedition to Borneo of h. m. s. Dido for the suppression of piracy, with extracts from the journal of James Brooke. N. Y. 1846. D. **919.2 : 2**

Burbidge, F: W. The gardens of the sun, or A naturalist's journal on the mountains and in the forests and swamps of Borneo and the Sulu archipelago, [with app. on the ferns and avifauna of the region]. Ill. Lond. 1880. O. **919.2 : 1**

Bock, C: Alfred. The head-hunters of Borneo ; a narrative of travel up the Mahakkam and down the Barito ; also journeyings in Sumatra, [with app. on language and natural history]. Ill. Lond. 1881. O. **919.2+P3**

Hornaday, W: T. [Travels in Borneo.] In his Two years in the jungle. **915.4 : 42**

3. Australasia.

Martin, Robert Montgomery. History of Austral-Asia ; comprising New South Wales, Van Diemen's island, Swan river, South Australia, etc. 2d ed. [British colonial lib. v. 2]. Lond. 1839. S. **993 : 1**

Fitzgerald, J: Foster Vesey. Australia. Ill. and map. [Foreign countries and british colonies.] Lond. 1881. S. **919.4 : 5**

Oberländer, R:, ed. Australien ; geschichte der entdeckung und kolonisation, bilder aus dem leben der ansiedler in busch und stadt, ursprünglich herausg. von Fr. Christmann. 2te aufl., unter berücksichtigung der neuesten gewerbe- und verkehrsverhältnisse bearb. [Ill. bibliothek der länder- und völkerkunde.] Leipz. 1880. O. **919.4 : 8**

Eden, C: H. Australia's heroes ; a slight sketch of the most prominent amongst the band of gallant men who devoted their lives and energies to the cause of science and the development of the fifth continent. 4th ed. rev. Lond. 1882. D. **919.4 : 7**

Pridden, W: Australia, its history and present condition ; containing an account both of the bush and of the colonies with their respective inhabitants. 2d ed. Lond. 1845. S. **994 : 1**

Sidney, S: The three colonies of Australia : New South Wales, Victoria, South Australia ; their pastures, copper mines and gold fields. Ill. Lond. 1852. O. **919.4 : 3**

Peck, G: W. Melbourne and the Chincha islands, with sketches of Lima and a voyage round the world. N. Y. 1854. D. **919.4 : 9**

Eldershaw, F. Australia, as it really is in its life, scenery and adventure ; with the habits and customs of its aboriginal inhabitants, and the prospects and extent of its gold fields. Lond. 1854. S. **919.4 : 1**

Howitt, W: Land, labor and gold, or Two years in Victoria ; with visits to Sydney and Van Diemen's Land. Bost. 1855. 2 v. D. **919.4 : 2**

Warburton, P: Egerton. Journey across the western interior of Australia ; with an introd. and add. by C: H. Eden, ed. by H. W. Bates. Ill. and map. Lond. 1875. O. **919.4 : 6**

Reid, G. H. An essay on New South Wales, the mother colony of the Australias. Sydney. 1876. O. **919.4+10**

Trollope, Anthony. Australia and New Zealand. Leipz. 1873. 3 v. in 2. S. **919.4 : 4**
Contents. V. 1. Introd.—Queensland.—New South Wales. — App. 2. Victoria.— Tasmania. — Western Australia.— App. 3. South Australia.— Australian institutions.—New Zealand.—App.

Barker, Mary Anne lady. Station life in New Zealand. Leipz. 1876. S. **919.3 : 1**

Nicholls, James H: Kerry-. The King country, or Explorations in New Zealand ; a narrative of 600 miles of travel through Maoriland. Ill. and map. N. Y. 1884. O. **919.3 : 4**

Albertis, L: Maria d'. New Guinea ; what I did and what I saw. 2d ed. Bost. 1881. 2 v. O. **919.5+P1**
Contents. V. 1. My voyage of 1871-72-73.—A voyage to Yule island in 1875.—Notes and summary of observations. — Catalogue of birds coll. in 1872. 2. First exploration of the Fly river, 1875.—Second exploration, 1876; 1st voyage of the "Neva".—Third exploration, 1877; 2d voyage of the "Neva".—Summary of observations. — Vocabularies. — Plants and birds collected.

Stone, Octavius C. A few months in New Guinea. N. Y. 1879. Q. **919.5+2**

Powell, Wilfrid. Wanderings in a wild country, or Three years among the cannibals of New Britain. Ill. Lond. 1884. D. **919.3 : 3**

4. Polynesia.

In general.

Russell, Michael. Polynesia, or An historical account of the principal islands in the South sea, incl. New Zealand ; the introd. of christianity, and the actual condition of the inhabitants in regard to civilization, commerce, and the arts of social life. [Harper's family lib.] N. Y. 1845. S. **996 : 1**

Christmann, F:, and R: Oberländer. Ozeanien, die inseln der südsee ; ältere und ne uere erforschungsreisen im gebiete der insel-gruppen des Stillen ozeans, mit besonderer rücksicht auf leben, sprache und sitten der aussterbenden naturvölker jener eilande. [Ill. bibliothek der länder- und völker-kunde.] Leipz: 1873. O. **919.6 : 10**

Fornander, Abraham. An account of the poly-nesian race. **572 : 12**
See col. 351.

Montgomery, James. Journal of the voyages and travels by Daniel Tyerman and G: Bennet, deputed from the London mis-sionary society, to visit their various sta-tions in the South sea islands, China, India, etc., between 1821 and 1829, comp. from original documents. From the 1st Lond. ed., rev. by an amer. ed. Bost. 1832. 3 v. D. **919.6 : 4**

Ellis, W: Polynesian researches, during a resi-dence of nearly eight years in the Society and Sandwich Islands. N. Y. 1833. 4 v. D. **919.6 : 2**

Wise, H: A: Wanderings in Polynesia, 1846–48. *In his* Los gringos. **917.7 : 10**
Note. Sandwich, Marquesas and Society Islands.

Perkins, E: T. Na Motu, or Reef-rovings in the South seas; a narrative of adventures at the Hawaiian, Georgian and Society Islands. Maps, ill. and app. relating to the resources of Polynesia. N. Y. 1854. O. **919.6 : 5**

South Pacific.

Coote, Walter. The western Pacific; a descrip-tion of the groups of islands to the north and east of the australian continent. Map and ill. Lond. 1883. S. **919.6 : 13**

Barrow, *Sir* J: A description of Pitcairn's Island and its inhabitants, with an authen-tic account of the mutiny of the ship Bounty, and of the subsequent fortunes of the mutineers. [*Anon.*] [Harper's family lib.] N. Y. 1840. S. **919.7 : 4**

Belcher, Diana *lady*. The mutineers of the Bounty and their descendants in Pitcairn and Norfolk Islands. Map and ill. N. Y. 1871. D. **997 : 2**

Wallis, *Mrs.* M. D. Life in Feejee, or Five years among the cannibals, by a lady. Bost. 1851. S. **919.6 : 8**

Williams, T:, *and* James Calvert. Fiji and the fijians; ed. by G: Stringer Rowe. N. Y. 1859. O. **919.6+9**

Cumming, Constance Frederica Gordon-. At home in Fiji. Map and ill. 2d ed. Edinb. 1881. 2 v. O. **919.6 : 7**

Cumming, C. F. Gordon-.—*Continued.*
— A lady's cruise in a french man-of-war. Map and ill. Edinb. 1882. 2 v. O. **919.6 : 11**
Contents. V. 1. Tonga.—Samoa.—Tahiti. 2. Tahiti; with sketches of the Marquesas and Paumotus.

Brassey, Anna, *born* Allnutt, *lady*. Tahiti; a series of photographs taken by col. Stuart Wortley, with letterpress by lady Brassey. Lond. 1882. O. **919.6 : 12**

Browne, J: Ross. Crusoe's island, a ramble in the footsteps of Alexander Selkirk [in 1849]; with sketches of adventure in Cali-fornia and Washoe. N. Y. 1875. D. **919.7 : 5**

North Pacific.

Jarves, James Jackson. History of the Hawa-iian or Sandwich Islands; embracing their antiquities, mythology, legends, discovery by europeans in the 16th century, re-dis-covery by Cook, with their civil, religious and political history, from the earliest traditionary period to the present time. 2d ed. Bost. 1844. D. **997 : 1**

Stewart, C: S: A residence in the Sandwich Islands. 5th ed., enl.; incl. an introd. and notes by W: Ellis. Bost. 1839. D. **919.7 : 3**

Cheever, H: Theodore. The island world of the Pacific; the personal narrative and results of travel through the Sandwich or Hawaiian Islands, and other parts of Polynesia. Ill. N. Y. 1851. D. **919.6 : 1**

Bates, G: W. Sandwich Island notes, by a Häolé. N. Y. 1854. D. **919.7 : 2**

Anderson, Rufus. The Hawaiian Islands; their progress and condition under missionary labors. Bost. 1864. D. **919.7 : 6**

Nordhoff, C: [The Sandwich Islands] *in* **917.5 : 61**

Bishop, Isabella L., *born* Bird. The Hawaiian archipelago; six months among the palm groves, coral reefs and volcanoes of the Sandwich Islands. 2d ed. Ill. Lond. 1876. D. **919.7 : 1**

Cumming, Constance Frederica Gordon-. Fire fountains; the kingdom of Hawaii, its vol-canoes and the history of its missions. Ill. and maps. Edinb. 1883. 2 v. O. **919.7 : 7**

Fornander, Abraham. Ancient history of the hawaiian people to the times of Kameha-meha I. *in* **572 : 12**
See col. 351.

30. Polar regions.

1. In general.

Hartwig, G: The polar world; a popular de-scription of man and nature in the arctic and antarctic regions of the globe. 2d ed. Ill. Lond. 1874. O. **919.8 : 3**

Royal society of London. Manual of the natural history, geology and physics of Greenland and the neighbouring regions; prepared for the use of the arctic expedition of 1875, under the dir. of the Arctic committee of the Royal society, and ed. by T. Rupert Jones; together with instructions sug-gested by the Arctic committee of the

Royal society, for the use of the expedition. Pub. by the authority of the lords com-missioners of the admiralty. Lond. 1875. O. **919.8 : 25**

Howgate, H: W. Polar colonization; memorial to congress and action of scientific and commercial associations. Wash. *n. d.* O. **919.8 : 9**

Barrow, *Sir* J:, *ed.* Voyages of discovery and research within the arctic regions, from 1818 to the present time; under the com-mand of the several naval officers em-ployed, by sea and land, in search of a northwest passage from the Atlantic to the Pacific, with two attempts to reach the north pole, abr. and arr. from the official narratives with occasional remarks. N. Y. 1846. D.   **919.8:2**

Leslie, *Sir J:, and others.* Narrative of discovery and adventure in the polar seas and regions, with ill. of their climate, geology and natural history, with an account of the whale-fishery. N. Y. 1843. S.   **919.8:28**

Tillotson, J: Adventures in the ice; a comprehensive summary of arctic exploration, discovery and adventure; incl. experiences of captain Penny, the veteran whaler, now first pub. Ill. Lond. [1865]. D.
                                                x **919.8:38**

Sargent, Epes, *ed.* Arctic adventure by sea and land from the earliest date to the last expeditions in search of sir John Franklin. Map and ill. Bost. 1867. D.   **919.8:42**

Adams, W: H: Davenport. Recent polar voyages; a record of discovery and adventure, from the search after Franklin to the British polar expedition. 1875–1876. [*Anon.*] Lond. 1880. D.   **919.8:39**

Nourse, Joseph E., *ed.* American explorations in the ice zones; prepared chiefly from official sources. Maps and ill. Bost. [1884]. O.   **919.8:45**

2. Special voyages.

Northwest.

Ellis, H: A voyage to Hudson's Bay by the Dobbs galley and California in 1746 and 1747, for discovering a northwest passage; with an accurate survey of the coast and a short natural history of the country, with a fair view of the facts and arguments from which the future finding of such a passage is rendered probable. Prefixed, an historical account of the attempts hitherto made for the finding of a passage that way to the East Indies. Chart and ill. Lond. 1748. D.   **919.8:6**

Parry, W: E: Journals of the 1st, 2d and 3d voyages for the discovery of a northwest passage from the Atlantic to the Pacific, in 1819–1825, in his majesty's ships Hecla, Griper and Fury. Plates. Lond. 1828. 5 v. in 3. T.   **919.8:30**

— *Same.* Three voyages for the discovery of a northwest passage from the Atlantic to the Pacific, and narrative of an attempt to reach the north pole. N. Y. 1845. 2 v. S.
                                              919.8:30

Franklin, *Sir* J: Narrative of a journey to the shores of the Polar sea in 1819–1822. 2d ed. Lond. 1824. 2 v. O.   **919.8:10**

Ross, *Sir* J: Narrative of a second voyage in search of a northwest passage and of a residence in the arctic regions during 1829–1833; incl. the reports of capt. James Clark Ross and the discovery of the northern magnetic pole. Lond. 1835. Q.
                                              919.8:R33

— *Same.* Paris. 1835. O.   **919.8:33**

Back, *Sir* G: Narrative of the arctic land expedition to the mouth of the Great Fish river and along the shores of the Arctic ocean, in 1833–1835. Map. Phila. 1836. O.
                                              919.8:1

x denotes books specially adapted for children.

Simpson, T: Narrative of the discoveries on the north coast of America; effected by the officers of the Hudson's Bay company during 1836–1839. Lond. 1843. O.   **919.8:34**

Richardson, *Sir* J: Arctic searching expedition; a journal of a boat-voyage through Rupert's Land and the Arctic sea, in search of the discovery ships under the command of sir J: Franklin; with an app. on the physical geography of North America. N. Y. 1852. D.   **919.8:11**

Osborn, Sherard. Stray leaves from an arctic journal, or Eighteen months in the polar regions, in search of sir John Franklin's expedition, in 1850-51. N. Y. 1850. D.
                                              919.8:29

Kane, Elisha Kent. Grinnell expedition in search of sir John Franklin. Ill. *T. p. w.* [N. Y. 1854]. O.   **919.8+12**

— Arctic explorations; the second and last U. S. Grinnell expedition in search of sir John Franklin; with a biogr. sketch of the author by C: W. Shields. Ill. Hartford. 1871. O.   **919.8:14**

— *Same, germ.* Kane, der nordpolfahrer; arktische fahrten und entdeckungen der zweiten Grinnell-expedition zur aussuchung sir John Franklins. 1853, 1854 und 1855, unter Elisha Kent Kane, beschrieben von ihm selbst. 6te aufl. Leipz. 1879. D.
                                              919.8:14

   Contents of Einleitung: Die entdeckungsreisen im norden.—Die nordwestliche durchfahrt.—Die natur und der mensch im nordpolarkreise. — Dr. Elisha Kent Kane.

— Die Grinnell-expedition nach dem Arctischen ocean, 1853, 1854 und 1855, zur aussuchung des sir John Franklin unter dem commando des dr. Elisha Kent Kane, von der Ver. Staaten navy. Phila. 1857. O.
                                              919.8:13

Hayes, I: Israel. An arctic boat journey, in the autumn of 1854. Bost. 1860. D.   **919.8:7**

McClintock, *Sir* Francis Leopold. The voyage of the Fox in the arctic seas; a narrative of the discovery of the fate of sir John Franklin and his companions. Maps and ill. Bost. 1860. D.   **919.8:15**

— *Same.* 4th ed. Lond. 1875. D.   **919.8:15**

Hall, C: Francis. Arctic researches and life among the esquimaux; the narrative of an expedition in search of sir John Franklin in 1860–1862. Maps and ill. N. Y. 1865. O.   **919.8:17**

Nourse, Joseph E. Narrative of the 2d arctic expedition made by C: Francis Hall; his voyage to Repulse Bay, sledge journeys to the straits of Fury and Hecla and King William's Land, and residence among the eskimos during 1864–69; ed. under the orders of the sec. of the navy. Maps and ill. (U. S. naval observatory.) Wash. 1879. Q.   *in* **919.8:D**

Hayes, I: Israel. The open polar sea; a narrative of a voyage of discovery towards the north pole in the schooner United States. N. Y. 1867. O.   **919.8:43**

Davis, C: H: Narrative of the north polar expedition, U. S. ship Polaris, capt. C: Francis Hall commanding; ed. under the dir. of G. M. Robeson, sec. of the navy. (U. S. naval observatory.) Wash. 1876. O.
                                              in **919.8:D**

Blake, E. Vale, *ed.* Arctic experiences ; containing capt. G: E. Tyson's wonderful drift on the ice-floe, a history of the Polaris expedition, of the cruise of the Tigress and the rescue of the Polaris survivors ; added, a general arctic chronology. N. Y. 1874. O.   **919.8+37**

MacGahan, J : A. Under the northern lights. Ill. Lond. 1876. O.   **919.8 : 48**
Note. A record of the expedition down Peel Strait in 1875, under capt. Allen Young.

Nares, *Sir* G: Strong. Narrative of a voyage to the Polar sea during 1875–6 in h. m. ships Alert and Discovery ; with notes on the natural history, ed. by H. W. Feilden. 4th ed. Lond. 1878. 2 v. O.   **919.8 : 21**

Gilder, W : H: Schwatka's search ; sledging in the Arctic in quest of the Franklin records. N. Y. 1881. O.   **919.8+24**

Boas, Franz. Baffin-Land ; geographische ergebnisse einer in 1883 und 1884 ausgeführten forschungsreise. Karten. *In* Petermann's mitteilungen, ergänzungsb. 17.   **905.1 : M**

United States. *Treasury dep't.* Cruise of the revenue-steamer Corwin in Alaska and the n. w. Arctic ocean in 1881 ; notes and memoranda, medical and anthropological, botanical, ornithological. Ill. Wash. 1883. Q.   *in* **919.8 : D**
Contents. **Rosse,** Irving C. Medical and anthropological notes on Alaska.—**Muir,** J: Botanical notes on Alaska.—**Nelson,** E. W. Birds of Bering sea and the Arctic ocean.—**Bean,** Tarleton H. List of fishes known to exist in the Arctic ocean north of Bering Strait.

Greenland.

Cranz, D: The history of Greenland ; containing a description of the country and its inhabitants, and particularly a relation of the mission carried on for above these 30 years by the unitas fratrum at New Herrnhuth and Lichtenfels in that country. Tr. from the high-dutch and ill. with maps and other copper-plates. Lond. 1767. 2 v. O. **998 : 1**

Rink, H: Johannes. Danish Greenland ; its people and its products ; ed. by Robert Brown. Ill. by the Eskimo and map. Lond. 1877. D.   **919.8 : 26**

Hayes, I: Israel. The land of desolation ; being a personal narrative of observation and adventure in Greenland. Ill. N. Y. 1872. D.   **919.8 : 36**

— Pictures of arctic travel : Greenland. N. Y. 1881. D.   **919.8 : 8**

Northeast.

Wrangell *or* Wrangel, *Baron* Ferdinand Petrovitch. Narrative of an expedition to the Polar sea, in 1820—1823 ; [ed. in german from his mss. and notes by G. Engelhardt, prep. for press by C. Ritter. Eng. ed. edited by E: Sabine.] [Harper's fam. lib.] N. Y. 1845. S.   **919.8 : 35**

Blackwood, *Sir* F: Temple Hamilton-Temple-, *earl of Dufferin.* A yacht voyage : Letters from high latitudes ; some account of a voyage in the schooner yacht "Foam" 85 O. M. to Iceland, Jan Mayen and Spitzbergen, in 1856. Bost. 1859. D.   **919.8 : 5**

Lamont, James. Seasons with the sea-horses, or Sporting adventures in the northern seas [round Spitzbergen]. N. Y. 1861. O.   **919.8+27**

Recent expeditions to eastern polar seas ; voyage of the Hansa and Germania, voyage of the Tegethoff. Ill. and maps. Lond. 1882. D.   **919.8 : 46**

Koldewey, K: The german arctic expedition of 1869–70 and narrative of the wreck of the Hansa in the ice. Ill., maps and portr. Tr. and abr. by L. Mercier, and ed. by H. W. Bates. Lond. 1874. O.   **919.8+P19**

Payer, Julius. New lands within the arctic circle ; narrative of the discoveries of the austrian ship Tegetthoff, 1872—1874. Tr. from the german with the author's approbation. Maps and ill. N. Y. 1877. O.   **919.8 : 31**

Leslie, Alexander. The arctic voyages of Adolf Erik Nordenskiöld, 1858—1879. Ill. and maps. Lond. 1879. O.   **919.8+22**

Nordenskiöld, *Friherre* Nils Adolf Erik. The voyage of the Vega round Asia and Europe ; with a historical review of previous journeys along the north coast of the old world. Tr. by Alexander Leslie. maps and ill. Lond. 1881. 2 v. O.   **919.8 : 23**

Hovgaard, Andre. Nordenskiöld's voyage round Asia and Europe ; a popular account of the northeast passage of the Vega, 1878–80. Tr. from the danish by H. L. Brækstad. Maps. Ill. Lond. 1882. O.   **919.8 : 49**

Loll, E: Von Schweden nach Japan : Die nordpolfahrten Adolf Erich von Nordenskjöld's. Ill. Wien. *n. d.* S.   **919.8 : 50**

Markham, Albert H. A polar reconnaissance ; the voyage of the Isbjörn to Novaya Zemlya in 1879. Maps and ill. Lond. 1881. O.   **919.8 : 20**

De Long, G: W. The voyage of the Jeannette ; the ship and ice journals of lieut.-commander G: W. DeLong, ed. by his wife Emma DeLong. Portr. and maps. Bost. 1882. 2 v. O.   **919.8+44**

Danenhower, J: Wilson. Narrative of the Jeannette. Bost. 1882. D.   **919.8 : 40**

Gilder, W: H: Ice-pack and tundra ; an account of the search for the Jeannette, and a sledge journey through Siberia. N. Y. 1883. O.   **919.8+41**

Harber, Giles B. Report of his search for the missing people of the Jeannette expedition, and the transportation of lieut.-com. De-Long and companions to the U. S. Ill. (U. S. 48th cong. 1st sess.; House ex. doc. no. 163). Wash. 1884. O.   **919.8 : Pam**

Melville, G: W. In the Lena delta ; a narrative of the search for lieut.-commander De-Long, followed by an account of the Greely relief expedition and a proposed method of reaching the north pole ; ed. by Melville Philips. Maps and ill. Bost. 1885 [1884]. O.   **919.8 : 47**

XI. BIOGRAPHY.

1. In general.

1. Universal dictionaries.

Oettinger, E: Marie. Bibliographie biographique universelle ; dictionnaire des ouvrages relatifs à l'histoire de la vie publique et privée des personnages célèbres de tous les temps et de toutes les nations, depuis le commencement du monde jusqu'à nos jours. Paris. 1866. 2 v. Q.   **16 : L**
Contenant, 1° La désignation chronologique de toutes les monographies biographiques, 2° L'énumeration de leurs diverses éditions, réimpressions et traductions, 3° Les dates exactes de la naissance et de la mort des personnages mentionnés, 4° La date de l'avénement des souverains et celle du mariage des reines et des princesses, 5° L'indication des portraits joints aux ouvrages cités, 6° Des reseignements sur les bibliothèques publiques où se trouvent les biographies indiquées, 7° Des notes historiques et littéraires sur les auteurs et les écrits curieux, sur les ouvrages condamnés au feu, mis à l'Index ou saisis par la police, ainsi que sur les écrits couronnés par les académies et les sociétés savantes, et sur les pamphlets, libelles, satires, pasquilles etc., enrichi du répertoire des bio-bibliographies générales, nationales et speciales.—Title-page.

Phillips, Lawrence B. The dictionary of biographical reference ; containing 100,000 names, together with a classed index of the biographical literature of Europe and America. Lond. 1871. O.   **920 : R3**
— *Same.* 2d ed., with an app. continuing the work by an addenda of necrology of eminent persons for the last ten years. Phila. 1881. O.   **920 : L**

Bayle, P: A general dictionary, historical and critical ; in which a new and accurate translation of that of mr. Bayle is included, the whole containing the history of the most illustrious persons of all ages and nations, particularly those of Great Britain and Ireland, distinguished by their rank, actions, learning and other accomplishments, with reflections on those passages of mr. Bayle which seem to favour scepticism and the manichee system by J: P: Bernard, T: Birch, J: Lockman and other hands. Lond. 1734. 10 v. F.   **920 : R56**

Gorton, J: A general biographical dictionary. New ed.; in 3 v.; v. 2, 3. Lond. 1841. O.   **920 : R6**

Hawks, Francis Lister, *ed.* Appleton's cyclopædia of biography ; embracing a series of original memoirs of the most distinguished persons of all times, written for this work by sir Archibald Alison and others. Ill. N. Y. 1863. Q.   **920 : R4**

Hoefer, J: Chrétien Ferdinand, *ed.* Nouvelle biographie universelle depuis les temps les plus reculés jusqu'à nos jours ; avec les renseignements bibliographiques et l'indication des sources à consulter. Paris. 1852–67. 46 v. in 23. O.   **920 : R1**

Godwin, Parke. The cyclopædia of biography ; a record of the lives of eminent persons, with a supp., brought down to aug. 1877. N. Y. 1878. O.   **920 : R5**

Oettinger, E: Maria. Moniteur des dates: Biographisch-genealogisch - historisches weltregister, enthaltend die personal-akten der menschheit, d. h. den heimaths- und geburts-schein, den heirathsakt und todestag von mehr als 100,000 geschichtlichen persönlichkeiten aller zeiten und nationen von erschaffung der welt bis auf den heutigen tag ; mit zahlreich eingestreuten noten aus allen zweigen der curiosität. Leipz. 1869–82. 9 v. in 3. F.   **920 : R58**
Contents. V. 1. A—C. 2. D—Holmes. 3. Holmgrén—Meal. 4. Méan—R. 5. S—Wiebeking. 6. Wiebel—Z. — Moniteur des faits. 7. Supplément, éd. par Hugo Schramm - Macdonald. A—L. 8. M—Witzs. 9. Witzt—Z. — Anhang, A—Z.

Thomas, Joseph. Universal pronouncing dictionary of biography and mythology. Phila. 1878. Q.   **920 : L2**
— *Same.* new ed., thoroughly rev. and enl. Phila. 1886 [1885]. Q.   **920 : R2**

Vapereau, L: Gustave. Dictionnaire universel des contemporains, contenant toutes les personnes notables de la France et des pays étrangers...redigé et tenu à jour avec le concours d'écrivains de tous les pays. 5e éd.; entièrement refondue et considérablement augm. Paris. 1880. Q.   **920 : R7**

Men of the time, The, or Sketches of living notables, authors, architects, artists, composers, demagogues, divines, dramatists, engineers, journalists, ministers, monarchs, novelists, philanthropists, poets, politicians, preachers, savans, statesmen, travellers, voyagers, warriors. N. Y. 1852. D.   **920 : 34**

Cooper, Thompson, *ed.* Men of the time ; a dictionary of contemporaries, containing biogr. notices of eminent characters of both sexes. 10th ed., rev. Lond. 1879. D.   **920 : R8**
— *Same.* 11th ed., rev. Lond. 1884. D.   **920 : R8**

2. Collections.

General.

Duyckinck, Evert A: Portrait gallery of eminent men and women of Europe and Amer-

ica ; embracing history, statesmanship, naval and military life, philosophy, the drama, science, literature and art, with biographies. Ill. N. Y. [1872]. 2 v. Q.
                   920 : R54

Great men and great women of history ; their portr. from the rare and authentic collection in the Munich pinakothek, with biogr. sketches. Authorized ed. N. Y. [1885]. F.
                   920 : R70

Wood, Wallace, *ed.* The hundred greatest men ; portraits of the one hundred greatest men of history, reprod. from steel-engr. Ill. N. Y. 1884. O.   **920+63**

Coan, Titus Munson, *ed.* Studies in biography. (Topics of the time, no. 2). N. Y. 1883. D.
                   920 : 53
    Contents. **Harrison,** F: Leon Gambetta.—Jonathan Swift.—**Christie,** M. E. Miss Burney's own story.—**Dasent,** *Sir* G. W. Samuel Wilberforce.—**Traill,** H. D. Lord Westbury and bishop Wilberforce; a Lucianic dialogue. — Correspondence de Georges Sand.—Literary bohemians.

Cooke, Frances E. Three great lives. Ill. Lond. 1884. D.   **920 : 65**
    Contents. Savonarola.—Sir T: Moore.—Latimer.

Distinguished men of modern times. N. Y. 1845. 2 v. T.   **920 : 33**
    Contents. V. 1. Dante.—Wiclif. — Chaucer.—Erasmus. — Copernicus. — Cortez. — Loyola.—Tasso.—Cervantes. — Shakspeare. — Raleigh. — Bacon.—Kepler.— Coke.—Gustavus Adolphus.—Galileo.— Hampden. — Grotius. — Descartes. — Harvey. — Pascal. — De Witt. —Milton.—Hale. **2.** Sobieski.—Bossuet. — Locke.— Fenelon.—Penn.—Newton.—Defoe. — Handel.—Chatham. — Linnæus. — Euler. — Buffon. — De L'Epée.— Mozart.—Sir W. Jones.—Burke.— Schwartz.—Cowper. —Pitt.—Fox.—Kosciusko.—Jenner.— Cuvier.—Walter Scott.—Wilberforce.

Drake, S: Adams, *ed.* Our great benefactors ; short biographies of the men and women most eminent in literature, science, philanthropy, art, etc. Portr. Bost. 1884. O.
                   920 : 62

Emerson, Ralph Waldo. Representative men ; twelve lectures. New rev. ed. Bost. 1883. T.   **920 : 12**
    Contents. Uses of great men.—Plato, or The philosopher.—Swedenborg, or The mystic.—Montaigne, or The sceptic. — Shakespeare, or The poet. — Napoleon, or The man of the world.—Goethe, or The writer.
— *Same. In his* Complete works.   **820.1 : 8 v4**

Entertaining biography ; from Chambers's repository. Lond. 1855. S.   **920 : 46**
    Contents. Sir J: Sinclair.—Mme. de Sévigné; her life and letters.—Arnold and André.—H: Arnaud and the waldenses.—Elizabeth Stuart and the Palatinate. Cap. J: Smith.—M. de Cervantes.—Louisa, queen of Prussia.—W: Cobbett.—Mme. de Staël-Holstein; her life and works.—C: J. Fox. — Christina, queen of Sweden. — Lord Clive. — Field-marshal Suvorov. — The moravian brethren: Count Zinzendorf.—Story of the dauphin, commonly called Louis XVII.

Friswell, James Hain. Footsteps to fame ; a book to open other books. New ed. Ill. Lond. 1881. D.   **920 : 43**

Gottschall, K: Rudolph v., *ed.* Der neue Plutarch ; biographien hervorragender charaktere der geschichte, literatur und kunst. Leipz. 1874–85. 11 v. D.   **920 : 78**
    Contents. V. 1. **Rückert,** H:, Martin Luther. — **Pauli,** Reinhold. Oliver Cromwell. — **Philippson,** Martin. König Heinrich IV von Frankreich. — **Rosenkranz,** K:, Voltaire.
    2. Gottschall, K: Rudolph v. Maximilian Robespierre.—**Beer,** Adolf. Maria Theresia.—**Speyer,** O:, Camillo graf v. Cavour.
    3. Philippson, Martin. König Philipp II von Spanien.—**Althaus,** F: C:, James Fox.—**Gottschall,** K: Rudolf v. F: v. Schiller.

4. Prutz, Hans. Ulrich v. Hutten.—**Uhde,** Hermann. Konrad Ekhof.—**Gottschall,** K: Rudolf v. Lord Byron.
    5. Kogge, Walter. Prinz Eugen von Savoyen.— **Brockerhoff,** Ferdinand. J: Jacques Rousseau.— **Beer,** Adolf. Fürst Clemens Metternich.
    6. Erdmannsdörffer, Bernhard. Der grosse kurfürst.—**Pauli,** Reinhold. Arthur herzog v. Wellington.—**Bärenbach,** F: v. J: Gottfried v. Herder. —**Althaus,** F:, Graf J: Russell.
    7. Kleinschmidt, Arthur. Napoleon I.— **Carrière,** Moriz. P: Cornelius.
    8. Prutz, Hans. Franz von Sickingen.—**Althaus,** F:, Admiral Nelson.—**Reissmann,** A:, Wolfgang Amadeus Mozart.
    9. Prutz, Hans. Moritz v. Sachsen. — **Beer,** Adolf. Joseph II.—**Althaus,** F:, B: D'Israeli, lord Beaconsfield.
    10. Kugler, Bernhard. Wallenstein.—**Speyer,** O:, Torquato Tasso. —**Gottschall,** K: Rudolf v. Napoleon III.
    11. Philippson, Martin. Friedrich II, könig von Preussen. — **Schmidt,** Julian. Gotthold Ephraim Lessing.

Grube, A: W: Biographische miniaturbilder ; zur bildenden lektüre für die reifere jugend verfasst. 6te verm. und verb. aufl. Ill. Leipz. 1884. 2 v. in 1. O.   **920+79**
    Contents. V. 1. Raphael Santi.—P: Paul Rubens.— Galileo Galilei.—I: Newton. — Paskal. — Fénélon.— Boerhave.—Linné. — Cuvier.— Franz Arago.— Abraham Gottlob Werner.—Fraunhofer.—James Watt.— G: Stephenson.—Garrik. — K: Seydelmann.—Christian Gottlob Heyne.—Der alte Heim.—Bertel Thorwaldsen. — Christian Rauch. — L: van Beethoven.— Felix Mendelssohn - Bartholdy. — N: Lenau. — L: Uhland.—Lord Byron.—Walter Scott. **2.** Johannes Kepler.—Immanuel Kant.—J: Jakob v. Moser.—Justus Möser.—Philipp Jakob Spener.—J: Kaspar Lavater.— W: Penn.— B: Franklin. — Washington. — W: Pitt.—Nelson.—Wellington.—Talleyrand.—Palafox.— Romana. —Joachim Nettelbeck.—F: Perthes.— Ferdinand v. Schill. — Andreas Hofer. — Joseph Speckbacher.—Joachim Haspinger. — Erzherzog Karl.—K: Theodor Körner.—Freiherr v. Stein.

Lamartine, Alphonse Marie Louise de. Memoirs of celebrated characters. N. Y. 1854, 1856. 3 v. D.   **920 : 19**
    Contents. V. 1. Introd.—Nelson.—Heloise.—Christopher Columbus.—Bernard de Palissy, the potter— Rooram. — Marcus Tullius Cicero. **2.** Socrates. — Jacquard.— Joan of Arc.—Cromwell.—Homer.—Gutenberg. — Fénelon. **3.** William Tell.— Madame de Sévigné.—Milton.—Antar.—Bossuet.

Maccall, W: Foreign biographies. Lond. 1873. 2 v. O.   **920 : 59**
    Contents. V. 1. Joseph de Maistre.—S: Vincent.— Vincent de Paul.—Paul L: Courier.—Vauvenargues. —The abbé de Saint-Pierre.—St. Francis of Assisi.— Ulrich v. Hutten.—Benedict Spinoza. **2.** Godfrey W: Leibnitz.—L: Claude de Saint-Martin.—Giordano Bruno.—Vasco Nunez de Balboa.— Alexander of Russia.—P: d'Aubusson.—Martin Behaim.—Cardinal Alberoni.—President Boyer.— Francis d'Almeida.— G: Cadoudal.—Lazarus Carnot.

Mott, A., *comp.* Biogr. sketches and interesting anecdotes of persons of color ; added, a selection of pieces in poetry. N. Y. [1889]. D.   **920 : 21**

Parton, James. Illustrious men and their achievements, or The people's book of biography ; containing sketches of the most interesting persons of all ages and countries and containing sketches of the lives and deeds of the most eminent philanthropists, inventors, authors, poets, discoverers, soldiers, adventurers, travellers, politicians and rulers that have ever lived. N. Y. n. d. O.
                   920+55

Pictures of heroes and lessons from their lives. Phila. n. d. D.   **920+64**
    Contents. An imperial convert [Constantine].—The moslem's dream, or The crescent on the Loire [Charles Martel].—King Alfred, or A thousand years ago.—Frederic Barbarossa, or The "Red-beard" of

the Rhine.— Brother John of Vicenza. — Northern lights [Gustaf Vasa]. —The "snow-king" [Gustaf Adolf].—Scenes in the life of William the silent.— The polish wizard [Jan Sobieski].— Innsbrück and its echoes, or The rescue, the run, the bribe and the ruin.

Pursuit of knowledge under difficulties; its pleasures and rewards, illustrated by memoirs of eminent men. N. Y. 1847. 2 v. S.
920 : 35

Q., *pseud.* You have heard of them. N. Y. 1854. D. 920 : 24
Contents. Horace Vernet.— Fanny Cerito.— Mendelssohn.—Lady Bulwer.—T: Moore.—Giulia Grisi.— Hector Berlioz.—H: Clay.— B: Disraeli.—Hans Christian Andersen. — Lablache. — G: P. Morris. — Lola Montez.—Ronconi.— Berryer.—J: Oxenford.— Catherine Hayes.—B: Haydon.—Carlotta Grisi.—W: Vincent Wallace.—Ary Scheffer.—C: Kean.—Jules Janin. —Gaetano Donizetti.—Edwin Landseer.—Dion Boucicault.—Jenny Lind.— Bayard Taylor.—M. W. Balfe.— Mark Lemon.—Vidocq.—Charlotte Cushman.—Emanuel Geibel.—Lady Blessington.— Gudin.— L: Jullien. —Mrs. Trollope.— Gavarni. — Leopold der Meyer.— Walter Savage Landor.—T: Hood.— Guizot.—Vivier. —Kenny.

Smiles, S: Brief biographies. Portr. Bost. 1861. D. 920 : 26
Contents. J. Watt.—R. Stephenson.—Dr. Arnold.— H. Miller. — R: Cobden. — Sir E: Bulwer Lytton.—F. Jeffrey.— E. Elliott.— G: Borrow.—J: J. Audubon.— W: Magillivray.—Lord J: Russell.—B: Disraeli.—W: E. Gladstone.—N. Hawthorne.—T: Carlyle.—J: Sterling.—Leigh Hunt.—H. Coleridge.— Dr. Kitto.—E. A. Poe.— T. Hook.— Dr. A. Combe.—R. Browning.— E. Chadwick.— R. Nicoll.— S: Bamford.—J: Clare.— G. Massey.—E. B. Browning.—F. Brown.—S. M. Fuller.— S. Martin.—H. Martineau.—Mrs. Chisholm.

Spamer, J: Gottlieb Christian Franz O:, (*Franz Otto*), *ed.* Wohlthäter der menschheit ; vorbilder des hochsinns, der duldung und menschenliebe, herausg. in verbindung mit Th. Armin, E: Grosse, C. F. Lankhard, K. L. F. Mezger, K. Roth, M. Schlimpert, und in neuer aufl. der jugend und dem volke vorgeführt von Franz Otto. 2te verb. aufl., ill. Leipz. 1876. O. 920 : 74
Contents. **Grosse**, E: Der edle bischof Las Casas. —**Stötzner**, H. E., F: v. Spee und Christian Thomasius.—**Grosse**, E:, A: Hermann Francke.—**Stötzner**, H. E. Abbé de l'Epée, S: Heinicke und Valentin Hauy.—**Grosse**, E:, J: H: Pestalozzi und Christian Gotthilf Salzmann. — **Schlimpert**, M:, Christian Fürchtegott Gellert. — **Mezger**, K. L. F., Ernst L: Heim.—**Schuhmann**, B., W: Wilberforce.—**Spamer**, O:, *and* W: **Roth.** F: W: A: Fröbel; F: Adolf W: Diesterweg.—**Spamer**, O:, Gottlob Nathusius; Sir Deschamsidtschi Dschischibhoy. — **Stötzner**, H. E. G: Peabody; Gustav Werner.—**Armin**, Th., *and* E. **Stötzner.** Elisabeth Fry, Sarah Martin, Miss Carpenter, Amalie Sieveking, Florence Nightingale.

Whittier, J: Greenleaf. Old portraits and modern sketches. Bost. 1850. D. 920 : 30
Contents. J: Bunyan.—T: Ellwood.—James Nayler. — Andrew Marvell.— J: Roberts. — S: Hopkins. — R: Baxter.—W: Leggett.—Nathaniel P. Rogers.—Robert Dinsmore.

Special periods.

Houssaye, Arsène. Men and women of the 18th century. N. Y. 1852. 2 v. D. 920 : 15
Contents. V. 1. Introd.—Dufresny.—Fontenelle.— Marivaux.—Piron.—The abbé Prevost.—Gentil-Bernard.—Florian.—Boufflers.—Rivarol.—Chevalier de la Clos.—Gretry.—Diderot.—Boucher.—Lantara.— Louis XV.—Mlle. de Camargo.—Mlle. Guimard, a goddess of the opera. — Sophie Arnould. — Marie-Antoinette. 2. Crebillon, the tragic. — Crebillon, the gay. — La Motte, an innovator of the 18th century.— Buffon. — Cardinal de Bernis.— Vadé.— Dorat.—Abbé Trublet, one of the forty.—Debïe, a philosopher.—Watteau and Lancret.—The Vanloos.—Greuze.—Madame de Pompadour.—Three pages from the life of Dancourt. — Mme. de la Popelinière. — Mlle. Clairon.—A promenade in the Palais-royal.

Houssaye, Arsène.—*Continued.*
— Philosophers and actresses. N. Y. 1853. 2 v. D. 920 : 16
Contents. V. 1. The house of Scarron.—Voltaire.— Voltaire and mlle. de Livry.—The republic of Plato.— Mademoiselle Gaussin.— Jacques Callot.— Raoul and Gabrielle.—The hundred and one pictures of Tardif, the friend of Gillot.—Mademoiselle de Marivaux.— La Tour.—The whims of the marchioness.— A romance of the banks of the Lignon. 2. Chamfort.— Three pages from the life of madame de Parabère.— Abelard and Heloise.—The death of André Chenier.— The marquis of Sainte-Aulaire.—Colle.—The daughter of Sedaine. — Prudhon.— Blangini.— An unknown sculptor.— Vandyck.—A lost poet. — Hands full of roses, full of gold and full of blood.—The mistress of knowledge. — Marie de Joysel. — The tree of knowledge.

Brougham, H:, *baron Brougham and Vaux.* Lives of men of letters and science, who flourished in the time of George III. [1st series.] Paris. 1845. O. 2d series. 1846. D. 920 : 45
Contents. 1st series. Voltaire.—Rousseau.—Hume. Robertson.—Black.— Watt.—Priestley.— Cavendish.— Davy.—Simson. 2d series. Johnson.—Adam Smith. — Lavoisier.— Gibbon.— Sir Joseph Banks.— D'Alembert.—Add. note on sir Joseph Banks.—Note on the lives of Cavendish, Watt and Black.

Goodrich, S: Griswold, (*Peter Parley*). Famous men of modern times, by the author of P: Parley's tales. Bost. 1844. S. 920 : 41
Contents. Sir W. Scott.— Lord Byron. — Napoleon Bonaparte.—Goethe.—Robert Burns.—Edmund Burke. — S: Johnson. — J: Milton. — W: Shakspere. — Lord Bacon.—Cervantes.

Field, Maunsell Bradhurst. Memories of many men and some women ; personal recollections of emperors, kings, queens, princes, presidents, statesmen, authors, and artists, at home and abroad, during the last thirty years. N. Y. 1874. D. 920 : 13

Boyd, M: Reminiscences of fifty years. N. Y. 1871. D. 920 : 48

Gutzkow, K: Ferdinand. Oeffentliche charaktere. Frankfurt. a. M. 1845. D. 920 : 18
Contents, see Deutscher katalog, p. 43.

Sprague, W: Buell. Visits to european celebrities. Bost. 1855. D. 920 : 27

Pressensé, Edmond Marcellin Déhault de. Contemporary portraits. Tr. by Annie Harwood Holmden. N. Y. 1880. D. 920 : 23
Contents. Thiers.—The antecedents of the Vatican council.—Strauss and Voltaire.—The culturkampf in Germany.—Arnaud de l'Arïege.—Dupanloup, bishop of Orleans. — Adolph Monod. — Emile Augier.— Verny and Robertson.

Parton, James, *ed.* Some noted princes, authors and statesmen of our time, by canon Farrar, James T. Fields, Archibald Forbes, E. P. Whipple, James Parton, Louise Chandler Moulton and others. N. Y. 1885. O. 920+71

Müller, F: Max. Biographical essays. N. Y. 1884. D. 920 : 60
Contents. Rájah Rámmohun Roy, 1774-1883.—Keshub Chunder Sen, 1838-1884. — Dayánanda Sarasvati, 1827-1883.—Bunyin Nanjio, 1849.—Kenjiu Kasawara, 1851-1883.—Julius Mohl, 1800-1876.—Kingsley, 1820-1875.

Morais, H: S: Eminent israelites of the 19th century ; a series of biogr. sketches. Phila. 1880. O. 920 : 20

Women.

Hale, Sarah Josepha, *born* Buell. Woman's record, or Sketches of all distinguished women, from the creation to a. d. 1868, arr. in four eras, with selections from authoresses of each era. Ill. 3d ed. rev. N. Y. 1874. Q. 920 : R9

James, G: Payne Rainsford, *ed.* Memoirs of celebrated women. Ill. Lond. 1876. D.
                                            923 : 7
Contents. Joan of Arc.—Margaret of Anjou.—Lady Jane Grey. — Anna Comnena.—France d'Aubigné, marchioness de Maintenon. — Queen Elizabeth. — Donna Maria Pacheco.

Jenkins, J: Stilwell. The heroines of history. Auburn. [1851]. D.   923 : 9
Contents. Cleopatra.—Isabella of Castile.—Joan of Arc.—Maria Theresa.—Josephine.—Elizabeth of England.— Mary of Scotland.— Catherine of Russia. — Marie Antoinette.—Madame Roland.

Hewitt, Mary Elizabeth, *ed.* Heroines of history. Ill. N. Y. 1859. D.   923 : 6
Contents. Semiramis. — Nictoris [*sic*, Nitocris]. — Zenobia.— Boadicea.— Berengaria.— Laura.—Joan of Arc. — Isabella of Castile. — Beatrice Cenci. — Ann Boleyn.—Lady Jane Grey.—Leonora d'Este.—Catherine Alexiewna.—Maria Theresa.—Charlotte Corday.—Josephine.
Note. Principally taken from mrs. Jameson's Memoirs of celebrated female sovereigns.

Watson, H: C. Heroic women of history, comprising some of the most remarkable examples of female courage, disinterestedness and self-sacrifice of ancient and modern times. Phila. *n. d.* D.   923 : 20

Higgins, Sophia Elizabeth, *born* Bernard. *mrs.* Joseph Napier. Women of Europe in the 15th and 16th centuries. Lond. 1885. 2 v. O.   923 : 32
Contents. V. 1. Denmark, Norway, Sweden, etc.: Margaret of Denmark; Elizabeth of Holstein; Ingegerd, Canute's daughter; Elizabeth of Brunswick; Philippa of Lancaster; Katherine of Saxony; Ingerborg of Holstein; Katharine, Charles's daughter. —Russia, Lithuania, Hungary, Poland, etc.: Eudoxia of Suzdal; Anna of Masovia; Juliana of Olszany; Sophia of Lithuania; Daughters of Louis the great, king of Hungary and Poland; Mary of Hungary, Hedwig of Hungary; Anna of Poland; Hedwig of Poland; Elizabeth of Pilcza; Sophia of Olszany; Alexandra of Lithuania. **2.** Germany and Hungary: Sophia of Bavaria; Barbara of Cilly; Elizabeth of Luxemburg.— Germany: Elizabeth of Nuremberg; Blanche of Lancaster; Margaret of Bavaria; Maud of Savoy; Henrietta of Montbéliard; Anna of Wirtemberg; Margaret of Berg; Anna of Schwarzburg; Katharine of Brunswick; Margaret of Schwangau; Sabina Jäger; Anna of Brunswick; Agnes Bernauer.

Parton, James. Noted women of Europe and America, authors, artists, reformers and heroines, queens, princesses and women of society, women eccentric and peculiar, from the most recent and authentic sources. Hartford. 1883. D.   920 : 31

Eminent women of the age ; narratives of the lives and deeds of the most prominent women of the present generation, by James Parton, etc. Ill. Hartford. 1868. O.
                                            920 : 50
Contents. Florence Nightingale, by James Parton. — Lydia Maria Child, by T: W. Higginson.— Fanny Fern, Mrs. Parton, by Grace Greenwood.—Lydia H. Sigourney, by E. B. Huntington.— Frances Anne Kemble, by James Parton.—Eugenie, empress of the french, by J: S. C. Abbott.—Grace Greenwood, Mrs. Lippincott, by Joseph B. Lyman.—Alice and Phebe Cary, by Horace Greeley.— M. F. Ossoli, by T: W. Higginson.— Gail Hamilton, Miss Dodge, by Fanny Fern.—E. B. Browning, by E: Y. Hincks.—Jenny Lind Goldschmidt, by James Parton.— Our pioneer educators, Mrs. Emma Willard, Mrs. Marianne P. Dascomb.—H. B. Stowe, by E. P. Parker.—Mrs. E. C. Stanton, by Theodore Tilton.—The women's rights movement and its champions in the U. S., by E. C. Stanton: Sarah and Angelina Grimke; Abby Kelley; Mary Grew; Anne Greene Phillips; Lucretia Mott; Caroline M. Severance; Frances D. Gage; Abby Hutchinson; Antoinette Brown; Lucy Stone; Mrs. C. H. Dall; Mrs. C. I. H. Nichols; Susan B. Anthony; Olympia Brown. — Victoria, queen of England, by James Parton.— Eminent women of the drama, by

W; Winter: Adelaide Ristori; Euphrosyne Parepa Rosa; Ellen Tree, mrs. C: Kean; Clara Louisa Kellogg; Kate Bateman, mrs. G: Crowe; Helen Faucit, mrs. Theodore Martin.—Anna E. Dickinson, by E. C. Stanton. — Woman as a physician, by H. B. Elliot: Mrs. C. S. Lozier; Elizabeth Blackwell; Harriot K. Hunt; Mrs. Hannah E. Longshore; Ann Preston.— Camilla Urso, by M. A. Betts.—Harriet G. Hosmer, by R. B. Thurston. — Rosa Bonheur, by James M. Hoppin.— Mrs. Julia Ward Howe, by Mrs. Lucia Gilbert Calhoun.

Hays, Frances. Women of the day ; a biogr. dictionary of notable contemporaries. Phila. 1885. D.   920 : R68

Crosland, Camilla, *born* Toulmin. Memorable women ; the story of their lives. Ill. Bost. 1857. D.   920 : 52
Contents. Rachel Wriothesly, lady Russell. — Madame d'Arblay and Mrs. Piozzi.—Mary L. Ware.— Mrs. Hutchinson and Lady Fanshawe. — Margaret Fuller, marchesa Ossoli.—Lady Sale.

Starling, Elizabeth. Noble deeds of woman, or Examples of female courage and virtue. 9th ed., ill. Lond. 1879. D.   920 : 42

Gray, E. Conder. Wise words and loving deeds ; a book of biographies for girls. N. Y. 1881. D.   920 : 14
Contents. Mary Somerville.—Lady Duff Gordon.— Sarah Martin.— Ann Taylor. — Charlotte Elliott.— Madame Feller.—Baroness Bunsen.— Amelia Sieveking. — Mary Carpenter. — Catherine Tait. — Maria Louisa Charlesworth.

Belloc, Bessie Rayner Parkes. Vignettes ; twelve biogr. sketches. Lond. 1866. D.   920 : 22
Contents. Mme. Swetchine.— La sœur Rosalie. — Mme. Pape-Carpantier.—Mme. de Lamartine.—Mme. Luce of Algiers. — Gov. Winthrop's wife.—Cornelia Knight.—Bianca Milesi Mojon.—Mrs. Delany.—Harriot K. Hunt.—Miss Bosanquet.—Mrs. Jameson.

Holloway, Laura Carter. The mothers of great men and women, and some wives of great men. Ill. N. Y. 1883. O.   920+57

Child, Lydia Maria, *born* Francis. Biographies of good wives. 6th ed., rev. N. Y. 1855. D.   920 : 49
Contents. Mme.Lavater.—Mrs. Lucy Hutchinson.— Lady Biron.—Mrs. Fletcher.—Lady Fanshawe.—Mrs. Flaxman.—Mrs. Blake.— Mme. Luther.— Mme. Oberlin.— Mme. Grotius.— Mrs. Howard.— Gertrude von der Wart.—Panthea.— Chelonis.— Calphurnia.—Mme. Klopstock.— Mme. Wieland.— Mme. Huber.— Queen Mary.— Queen Anne.— Countess of Dorset.— Selina, countess of Huntingdon.—Mrs. Rose.—Lady Harriet Ackland.— Baroness Riedesel.—Mrs. Judson.—Mrs. Experience West. — Lady Arabella Johnson.— Mrs. Winthrop.— Mme. Reiske.— Arria.— Eponina.— Mme. Lafayette.— Countess Segur. — Mme. Lavalette.— Countess of Nithsdale.— Mme. Spurzheim. — Lady Collingwood.—Mme. Schiller.

Self-made men.

Seymour, C: C. B. Self-made men. N. Y. *n. d.* D.   920 : 25
Contents. Andrew Jackson.—Jacob Leisler.—Daniel Webster. — Elihu Burritt. — Alexander Murray.— Matthew F. Maury. — Christian Gottlob Heyne.— Robert Burns. — G: Fox.— Amos Lawrence.— Hans Christian Andersen.—Anthony Wayne.— Immanuel Kant.—J: Gottlieb Fichte.—D: Rittenhouse.—Carsten Niebuhr.—H: Clay.—J: Ledyard.—Stephen Girard.— Sir W: Phipps.—Daniel Boone.—Joseph Bramah.— James Hargreaves or Hargreeves.—Alexander Wilson. —Edmund Cartwright.—B: Thompson, count Rumford.— T: Posey.— Israel Putnam.—J: Prideaux.— Roger Williams.— W: Hutton.—J: Paul Jones.— W: Falconer.— Sir Humphrey Davy.—Robert Dodsley.— Antonio Canova. Philip Vayringe.—Nathaniel Bowditch.—Valentine Jamerai Duval.—C: Dickens.—Sir T: Lawrence.— W: Gifford.—B: West.—J: Fitch.— Patrick Henry.—Eli Whitney.—B: Franklin.—Oliver Evans.— Roger Sherman.— Robert Fulton.— Sir W: Jones.—Capt. J: Smith.—James Brindley.— T: Holcroft.—Robert Bloomfield.—B: Arkwright.—B: Kirke White.—James Watt.— W: Cobbett.— Amos Whittemore.—Capt. James Cook.—G: Stephenson.

Cobb, James F. Stories of success, as ill. by the lives of humble men, who have made themselves great. Lond. [1872]. D. **x 920 : 44**
Contents. Alexander Menschikoff. — J: Anton Knecht. — St. Vincent de Paule. — J: Bart. — Franz Pistek.—Corporal Weltsch.—Sebastian de Carvalho.— Antoine Drouot.—Antonin Caréme.—Guiseppe Mezzofanti. — G: Huebner.— Bertel Thorwaldsen. — Gaspard Deguerry.

Parton, James. Captains of industry, or Men of business who did something beside making money; a book for young americans. Portr. Bost. 1884. D. **920 : 61**

Spamer, J: Gottlieb Christian Franz O:, (Franz Otto). Helden der arbeit: Männer eigener kraft; lebensbilder durch hochsinn, thatkraft und selbsthülfe gehobener männer, hervorragender künstler, dichter, werkleute, kriegshelden, etc., der jugend und dem volke in verbindung mit gleichgesinnten zur aneiferung vorgeführt von Franz Otto. 2te verb. und verm. aufl., ill. Leipz. 1881. O. **920 : 76**
Contents. Einführung. — Joseph Haydn. — Robert Burns.—Albert Bartholomäus (Bertel) Thorwaldsen. —Robert Bloomfield und T: Edward.—H: Zschokke.— Prinz Heinrich von Preussen.—Graf A: Neithardt v. Gneisenau. — Sir H: Havelock.— W: Kaulbach.— Joseph Ressel.—James Nasmyth.—Sir James Brook.

— Männer eigener kraft : "Hilf dir selbst!" lebensbilder durch selbsthülfe und thatkraft emporgekommener männer, gelehrte und forscher, erfinder, techniker, werkleute; der jugend und dem volke in verbindung mit gleichgesinnten zur aneiferung vorgeführt von Franz Otto. 2te verm. und verb. aufl., ill. Leipz. 1881. O. **920 : 77**
Contents. J: Walter.— F: König und Andreas F: Bauer. — Alois Senefelder. — K: v. Linné. — Franz Arago.— Sir Humphrey Davy.— Michael Faraday.— R: Arkwright. — G: Stephenson. — Sir Isambert Maurice Brunel.— Elias Howe.— Matthias Näf.— W: Sattler.—R: Hartmann.—Elihu Burritt.

Of and for children.

Goodrich, S: Griswold, (Peter Parley). Lives of benefactors. [Youth's library of biogr.] Bost. [1844]. S. **x 920 : 39**
Contents. Washington.—Jay.—Henry.—Franklin.— La Fayette.—Kosciusko.— W: Tell.—Howard.—Jenner. — Oberlin. — Guttenberg. — Hargraves. — Arkwright.—Whitney.—Fulton.—Copernicus.—Galileo.— Linnæus.—Bowditch.—Huber.—Herschel.—Davy.

— Lives of celebrated women. [Youth's library of biogr.] Bost. [1845]. S. **x 923 : 25**
Contents. Lucretia and Margaret Davidson.—Mrs. Adams.—Mrs. Washington.—Madame de Staël.—Lady Hester Stanhope.—Hannah More.—Mrs. Barbauld.— Madame de Genlis.—Josephine.—Marie Antoinette.— Madame Roland.—Madame de Sévigné.—Mary, queen of Scots.—Elizabeth, queen of England.—Isabella of Spain.—Joan of Arc.

— Curiosities of human nature. [Youth's library of biogr.] Bost. [1845]. S. **x 920 : 40**

Japp, Alexander Hay, (H. A. Page). Leaders of men; a book of biographies, specially written for youth by H. A. Page. N. Y. 1881. D. **x 920 : 17**
Contents. The prince consort.—Robert Dick, baker and geologist.—Commodore Goodenough.—G: Moore. —J: Duncan, weaver and botanist.—S: Greg.—Dr. J: Wilson.—Dr. Andrew Reed.—Lord Lawrence.

Edgar, J: G: Footprints of famous men; designed as incitements to intellectual industry. Ill. N. Y. 1878. S. **x 920 : 11**
Contents. Men of action: Washington; Burke; Necker; Pitt; Lord Erskine; Lord Collingwood; Lord Teignmouth.—Men of letters: Dean Milner; D:

Edgar, J: G:—Continued.
Hume; Southey; Moore.—Artists: Sir Joshua Reynolds; Sir Francis Chantrey; Sir Christopher Wren.— Men of science: Dr. W: Hunter; Black; Brindley; Watt; Adam Smith.

— The boyhood of great men, intended as an example to youth. N. Y. [1853]. S. **x 920 : 10**
Contents. Sir Walter Scott.—Pope.—Gibbon. — Sir James Mackintosh.— Dr. Johnson.— Lord Jeffrey.— Canning.—Webster.—Lord Mansfield.—Lord Eldon.— Wilberforce. — Sir T: Fowell Buxton. — Galileo.— Ferguson.— Sir I: Newton.— Gassendi.— Franklin.— Pascal.— D'Alembert. — Cavendish.— Sir Humphrey Davy.—Lord St. Vincent.— Nelson.— Duke of Marlborough.— Bonaparte.— Handel.— Mozart. — Sir T. Lawrence.—Sir D: Wilkie.—Canova.—Thorwaldsen.— Sir W: Jones.—Dr. Arnold.—Bishop Ken.—Dr. Parr.— Dr. Chalmers.—J: Hunter.—Sir Astley Cooper.—Sir Joseph Banks.—Audubon.

Famous boys and famous men. Ill. N. Y. 1878. **x 920 : 32**
Contents. D. Webster.—S: Drew.—B: Franklin.—R. Burns.—E. K. Kane.—H: Clay.—J: Leyden.—J. Montgomery.— N. Bowditch.— H: Havelock.— D: Livingstone.— O. Evans.— S: T. Coleridge.—R. Fulton.—J: Kitto.— H. Davy. — A. Lawrence.— S. Girard.— S: Crompton.—T: Chalmers.—J. Laffitte.—J: J. Audubon.—W: Jay.—R. Sherman.

Brooks, Elbridge S. Historic boys; their endeavors, their achievements and their times. N. Y. 1885. O. **x 920 : 72**
Contents. Marcus of Rome.—Brian of Munster.— Olaf of Norway.—William of Normandy.—Baldwin of Jerusalem.—Frederick of Hohenstaufen.—Harry of Monmouth.— Giovanni of Florence.—Ixtlil of Texcuco.—Louis of Bourbon.—Charles of Sweden.—Van Rensselaer of Rensselaerswyck.

Bolton, Sarah, born Knowles. Lives of poor boys who became famous. Portr. N. Y. [1885]. D. **920 : 73**
Contents. G: Peabody.—Bayard Taylor.—James B. Eads.—James Watt. — Sir Josiah Mason. — Bernard Palissy.— Bertel Thorwaldsen.— Wolfgang Mozart.— S: Johnson.—Oliver Goldsmith.—Michael Faraday.— Sir H: Bessemer.— Sir Titus Salt.— Joseph Marie Jacquard.— Horace Greeley. — W: Lloyd Garrison.— J: Paul Richter.— Leon Gambetta.— D: G. Farragut.—Lieut.-gen. Sheridan.—T: Cole.—Ole Bull. Meissonier. — G: W. Childs. — Dwight L. Moody. — Abraham Lincoln.

Russell, W: Extraordinary men; their boyhood and early life. Lond. n. d. D. **920 : 37**
Contents. Michael Angelo.—Martin Luther.—Shakspere.— Oliver Cromwell.— Molière.— Blaise Pascal.— Duke of Marlborough.—Peter the great.—Franklin.— Mirabeau.— Mozart. — Sir S: Romilly. — Nelson.— Robert Burns.—Sir T: Lawrence.—Wilkie.—Napoleon Bonaparte.—Lord Byron.—Duke of Wellington.—Sir William.— W: Cobbett.—Sheridan.—J: Paul Richter.

— Extraordinary women; their girlhood and early life. Lond. n. d. D. **920 : 38**
Contents. The maid of Orleans. — Mrs. Fry. — The empress Josephine. — Madame Roland. — Christina, queen of Sweden. — Elizabeth Woodville. — Mrs. Hutchinson.—Queen Elizabeth.—Madame de Sévigné. —Isabella of Castile. — Anne Boleyn. — Lady Jane Grey.— Mary, queen of Scots.— Lady Mary Wortley Montague.—Marie-Antoinette.—Mrs. Siddons.—Mme. de Staël-Holstein.— Charlotte Corday.— Madame Récamier.—Margaret Fuller.—Lady Hester Stanhope.— Mme. de Genlis.—Catherine II, empress of Russia.— Mrs. Opie.—Maria Theresa.

Adams, W: H: Davenport. Child-life and girlhood of remarkable women; a series of chapters from female biogr. Lond. 1883. D. **920 : 66**

Spamer, J: Gottlieb Christian Franz O:, (Franz Otto), ed. Das buch merkwürdiger kinder; lebensbilder aus der jugendzeit und den entwickelungsjahren denkwürdiger men-

x denotes books specially adapted for children.

schen, herausg. in verbindung mit M.
Schlimpert, B. Schuhmann, W. Wägner u. a.
5te verb. aufl., ill. Leipz. 1884. O.

                       920 : 75

Contents. Konradin von Hohenstaufen.—R: Whittington.—Jeanne d'Arc. — Die sachsische prinzenraub.—Die söhne könig Eduards IV von England.—
Alexander Menschikoff. — Valentine Duval. — Der
kleine Heineken.—Raphael Mengs.—J: M. Georg.—
J: G. Seume.—G. Mezzofanti.—Der sohn Ludwigs
XVI von Frankreich.—Cäsar Ducornet.—Der könig
von Rom.—Kaspar Hauser.

Masson, A: Michel Benoit **Gaudichot-,** *known as*
Michel. Celebrated children of all ages
and nations. Tr. from the french by mrs.
L. Burke. Ill. Lond. 1867. D. **x 920 : 36**

Contents. Royal children. The children of Edward
IV.—Eudocia, empress of the east.—Lady Jane Grey.
—Ivan VI, emperor of Russia.—Joash, king of Israel.
—Louis XVII.—Napoleon II.—Edward VI, the last of
the Tudors. *Martyr children.* N: Ferry.—Nicolette
de Foix.—Gaspar Hauser.—The Maccabees.—Marcelli,
called the man with the iron mask.—H: of Nemours.
—The sons of Ugolino. *Children celebrated for their
filial affection.* Appius.—Elizabeth Cazotte.—Fi-ken.
Hal-mehi.—Prascovia Lopouloff, or The exiles of
Siberia. *Laborious children.* Valentine Jameray
Duval.—P: Laramée, or Ramus.—C: Linnæus.—Mich-
ael Verino. *Courageous children.* Silvina d'Auben-
court.—Ambrose de Boufflers. — David. — Matthew
Goffin.—Joan of Arc. — Frances Mariette.—Volney
Bekner. *Poet children.* Frances de Beauchateau.—
Milton.—Lucretia Davidson.—Metastasio.—Lucius
Valerius. *Learned children.* James Crichton.—Gio-
vanni Pico della Mirandola. —Vincenzio Viviani.
Artist children. Adrian Brauwer.—Antonio Canova.
—The two Lazzaroni.—Lesueur.—J: Baptiste Lulli.—
Marcilla Euphrosine.—Peter of Cortona.—The Raisin
family.—J: Philippe Rameau.

3. National biographies.

American.

Allen, W: The american biographical dictionary ; containing an account of the lives,
characters and writings of the most eminent persons deceased in North America
from its first settlement. Bost. 1857. Q.
                       920.1 : R1

Drake, Francis S: Dictionary of american biography, incl. men of the time ; containing
nearly 10,000 notices of persons of both
sexes, of native and foreign birth, who have
been remarkable, or prominently connected with the arts, sciences, literature,
politics or history of the amer. continent ;
giving also the pronunciation of many of
the foreign and peculiar amer. names, a
key to the assumed names of writers, and
a supp. Bost. 1872. O.   **920.1 : R2**

Duyckinck, Evert A: National portrait gallery
of eminent americans ; incl. orators, statesmen, naval and military heroes, jurists,
authors, etc., from original paintings by
Alonzo Chappel, with biogr. and historical narratives. N. Y. [1862]. 2 v. O.
                       920.1 : R3

Sparks, Jared. The library of american biography. [1st series]. N. Y. 1845–1848. 10
v. S.   **923.1 : 21**

Contents. V. **1. Everett,** E:, J: **Stark.—Prescott,**
W: H., C: Brockden **Brown.—Armstrong,** J:, R:
Montgomery.—Sparks, J., Ethan Allen. **2. Pea-
body,** W: B. O., Alexander **Brown.—Hillard,** G: S.,
Capt. J: Smith. **3. Sparks,** J., Benedict Arnold.—
4. Armstrong, J:, Anthony **Wayne.—Upham,** C:
W., Sir H: Vane. **5. Francis,** C., J: Eliot. **6.
Wheaton,** H:, W: **Pinkney. — Channing,** E: T.,
W: **Eller.y—Peabody,** W: B. O., Cotton Mather.

x denotes books specially adapted for children.

Sparks, Jared.—*Continued.*
7. Bowen, F., Sir W: **Phips.—Peabody,** O. W. B.,
Israel **Putnam.—Sedgwick,** C. M., L. M. Davidson.
— **Renwick,** J., D: Rittenhouse. **8. Miller,** S:,
Jonathan **Edwards.—Peabody,** W: B. O., D: Brain-
erd. **9. Bowen,** F., Baron **Steuben.—Hayward,**
C: *jr.*, Sebastian **Cabot.—Felton,** C. C., W: Eaton.
10. Renwick, J., Robert **Fulton.—Everett,** A. H.,
Joseph H. Warren.—**Cleveland,** H: R., H: Hudson.
—**Sparks,** J., Father Marquette.—List of lives.—In-
dex to the 10 v.

— - 2d series. Bost. 1844–48. 15 v. S. **923.1 : 22**

Contents. V. **1. Sparks,** J., Robert Cavelier de La
Salle.—Everett, A. H., Patrick Henry. **2. Bowen,**
F., James **Otis.—Peabody,** W: B. O., James Ogle-
thorpe. **3. Peabody,** O. W. B., J: **Sullivan.—Hoff-
man,** C: F., Administration of Jacob Leisler.—
Ware, W:, Nathaniel **Bacon. — Ellis,** G: E., J:
Maron. **4. Gammell,** W:, Roger Williams. —
Sprague, W: B., Timothy **Dwight. — Sparks,** J.,
Count **Pulaski. 5. Renwick,** J., Count Rumford.—
Whiting, H:, Zebulon Montgomery **Pike.—Mackie,**
J: M., S: Gorton. **6. Kingsley,** J. L., Ezra Stiles.
—**Whittlesey,** C:, J: **Fitch.—Ellis,** G: E., Anne
Hutchinson. **7. Sparks,** J., J: Ribault.—**Francis,**
C:, Sebastian Rale.—**Palfrey** J: G., W: Palfrey.
8. Sparks, J., C: **Lee.—Reed,** H:, Joseph Reed.
9. Burnap, G: W., Leonard **Calvert.—Gammell,**
W:, S: **Ward. — Hall,** J., T: Posey. **10. Greene,**
G: W., Nathaniel Greene. **11. Mackenzie,** A. S.,
Stephen Decatur. **12. Sabine,** L., E: Preble.—
Ellis, G: E., W: Penn. **13. Peck,** J: M., Daniel
Boone.—**Bowen,** F., B: Lincoln. **14. Sparks,** J.,
J: Ledyard. **15. Hubbard,** F. M., W: Richardson.
—**Lothrop,** S: K., S: Kirkland.

New England historic genealogical society.
Memorial biographies: Towne memorial
fund. Bost. 1880–1883. 3 v. O.
                       923.1 : R16

Muzzey, Artemas B. Reminiscences and memorials of men of the revolution and their
families. Portr. and ill. Bost. 1883. O.
                       920.1 : 8

Ellet, Elizabeth Fries, *born* Lummis. The women of the amer. revolution. 5th ed. N.
Y. 1852, 1853. 3 v. D.   **920.1 : 11**

Carroll, Howard. Twelve americans ; their lives
and times. N. Y. 1883. D.   **920.1 : 10**

Contents. Horatio Seymour.— C: F. Adams.— P:
Cooper.—Hannibal Hamlin.—J: Gilbert.—Robert C:
Schenck.—F: Douglass.—W: Allen.—Allen G. Thur-
man.—Joseph Jefferson.—E. B. Washburne.—A. H.
Stephens.

Parton, James. Famous americans of recent
times. Bost. 1881. O.   **920.1 : 6**

Contents. H: Clay.— Daniel Webster. — J: C. Cal-
houn.—J: Randolph.—Stephen Girard, and his college.
—James Gordon Bennett, and the New York herald.
—C: Goodyear.—H: Ward Beecher and his church.—
Commodore Vanderbilt.—Theodosia Burr.—J: Jacob
Astor.

Bolton, Sarah, *born* Knowles. How success is
won. Portr. Bost. [1885]. S. **920.1 : 13**

Contents. P: Cooper.—J: B. Gough.—J: G. Whittier.—J: Wanamaker.—H: M. Stanley.—Johns Hopkins.—W: M. Hunt.—Elias Howe, *jr.*—Alexander H.
Stephens.—T: A. Edison.—W: G. T. Morton.—J: H.
Vincent.

Holloway, Laura Carter. Famous american
fortunes and the men who have made them;
a series of sketches of many of the notable
merchants, manufacturers, capitalists, railroad presidents, bonanza and cattle kings
of the country. Portr. Phila. 1884. O.
                       920.1+14

Bonney, Catharina, *born* Van Rensselaer. A
legacy of historical g eanings, compiled
and arr. by mrs. C. V. R. Bonney. Ill. and
autographs. Albany. 1875. 2 v. O.
                       920.1+7

Anthony, H: Bowen. Memorial addresses on
several occasions del. in the senate of the
U. S. Providence. 1875. Q.   **920.1+12**

Ellet, Elizabeth Fries, *born* Lummis. Pioneer women of the west. N. Y. 1852. D. **920.1 : 4**

Frost, J: Heroic women of the west; comprising narratives of the pioneer mothers of the western country. *T. p. w.* [Phila. 1854]. S.   **920.1 : 5**

Tenney, Horace A., *and* D: Atwood. Memorial record of the fathers of Wisconsin; sketches of the lives and career of the members of the constitutional conventions of 1846 and 1847-8, with a history of early settlement in Wisconsin. Madison. 1880. O. **920.1 : 9**

American biogr. pub. company. The U. S. biographical dictionary and portrait gallery of eminent and self-made men : Wisconsin volume. Chicago. 1877. Q.
920.1 : R15

American indians.

Thatcher, B: Bussey. Indian biography, an historical account of those individuals who have been distinguished among the north american natives as orators, warriors, statesmen and other remarkable characters. N. Y. 1845. 2 v. S.   **920.1 : 102**

Goodrich, S: Griswold. Celebrated american indians. [Youths' library of biogr.] Bost. [1844]. S.   **x 920.1 : 101**
Contents. Manco Capac.—Mayta Capac. — Huayna Capac.—Atahualpa.—Caupolican.—Ychoalay.—Tupac Amaru. — Quetzalcoatl. — Xolotl. — Acamapitzin. — Montezuma I. — Donna Marina. — Montezuma II.— Cofachiqui.—Tascaluza.— Vitachuco.— Pocahontas.— Philip.—Pontiac.—Logan.

Abbott, J: Stevens Cabot. History of king Philip, incl. the early history of the settlers of New England. Ill. N. Y. *n. d.* S.
920.1 : 112

Eggleston, G: Cary. Red Eagle and the wars with the Creek indians of Alabama. (Famous amer. indians). N. Y. 1878. D.
920.1 : 111

— *and* Lillie Eggleston Seelye. Montezuma, and the conquest of Mexico. (Famous amer. indians). N. Y. 1880. D.   **920.1 : 109**

— - Pocahontas ; incl. an account of the early settlement of Virginia, and of the adventures of capt. J: Smith. (Famous amer. indians). N. Y. [1879]. D.   **920.1 : 110**

— - Brant and Red Jacket ; incl. an account of the early wars of the six nations and the border warfare of the revolution. (Famous amer. indians). N. Y. 1879. D.
920.1 : 105

Stone, W: Leete. Life of Joseph Brant, incl. the border wars of the amer. revolution, and sketches of the indian campaigns of gens. Harmar, St. Clair and Wayne, and other matters connected with the indian relations of the U. S. and Great Britain, from the peace of 1783 to the indian peace of 1790. Cooperstown. 1846. 2 v. O.
920.1 : 104

— Life and times of Red Jacket ; with a memoir of the author by his son. Albany. 1866. O.
920.1 : 106

— Uncas and Miantonomoh ; a historical discourse, del. at Norwich, Conn., on the 4th of july 1842, on the occasion of the erection of a monument to the memory of Uncas. N. Y. 1842. S.   **920.1 : 113**

Hubbard, J. Niles. An account of Sa-go-ye-wat-ha, or Red Jacket and his people, 1750—1830. Albany. 1886. O.   **920.1 : 116**

Drake, B: Life of Tecumseh and his brother the prophet, with a historical sketch of the Shawanoe indians. Cinc. 1841. D.
920.1 : 107

Eggleston, E:, *and* Lillie Eggleston Seelye. Tecumseh and the Shawnee prophet ; incl. sketches of G: Rogers Clark, Simon Kenton, W: H: Harrison, Cornstalk, Blackhoof, Bluejacket, the Shawnee Logan, and others famous in the wars of Tecumseh's time. (Famous amer. indians). N. Y. [1878]. D.   **x 920.1 : 114**

Copway, G: Kah-ge-ga-gah-bowh. Life, letters and speeches. N. Y. 1850. D.
920.1 : 115

Beckwourth, James P. Life and adventures, written from his own dictation by T. D. Bonner. N. Y. 1856. D.   **920.1 : 103**

Howard, Oliver O. Nez Percé Joseph ; an account of his ancestors, his lands, his confederates, his enemies, his.murders, his war, his pursuit and capture. Bost. 1881. O.
920.1 : 108

Great Britain and Ireland.

Biographia britannica, or The lives of the most eminent persons who have flourished in Great Britain and Ireland from the earliest ages down to the present times ; collected from the best authorities, both printed and ms., and digested in the manner of mr. Bayle's historical and critical dictionary. Lond. 1747—1766. 6 v. F.
920.2 : R2

Stephen, Leslie, *ed.* Dictionary of national biography. N. Y. 1885-86. 5 v. O.
920.2 : R15
Contents. V. 1. A—Anne.   2. Annesley— Baird. 3. Baker—Beadon.   4. Beal—Biber.   5. Bicheno—Bottisham.

Ward, T: Humphrey, *ed.* Men of the reign ; a biographical dictionary of eminent persons of british and colonial birth who have died during the reign of queen Victoria. Lond. 1885. D.   **920.2 : R19**

Lodge, Edmund. Portraits of illustrious personages of Great Britain, with biogr. and historical memoirs of their lives and actions. Lond. 1849, 1850. 8 v. D.
923.2 : 1
Contents. V. 1. Elizabeth of York.—T: Stanley, earl of Derby.—Margaret of Lancaster, mother of Henry VII.—Cardinal Wolsey.—W: Warham, archbp. of Canterbury. — Sir J: More. — Sir T: More. — Anne Bullen.—Jane Seymour.—Sir N: Carew.— T: Cromwell, earl of Essex.—Margaret Tudor.—C: Brandon, duke of Suffolk.—Cardinal Beatoun.—H: Howard, earl of Surrey.—Henry VIII.—Catharine Parr.—T: lord Seymour of Sudeley. — Sir Anthony Denny.— E: Seymour, duke of Somerset.—Edward VI.— J: Dudley, duke of Northumberland.—T: Howard, duke of Norfolk.—Lady Jane Grey.—H: Grey, duke of Suffolk.—J: Russell, 1st earl of Bedford.—N: Ridley, bishop of London.—T: Cranmer, archbp. of Canterbury.—E: Courtenay, earl of Devonshire.—Cardinal Pole.
2. Mary, queen of England.—W: 1st lord Paget.— E: 1st lord North.—H: Stuart. lord Darnley.—James Stuart, earl of Murray.—J: Knox.—T: Howard, 4th duke of Norfolk.—W: Powlett, marquis of Winchester.— Sir W: Maitland.— James Hamilton, earl of Arran.—Matthew Parker, archbp. of Canterbury.— Walter Devereux, earl of Essex.--Sir N: Bacon.--Sir

x denotes books specially adapted for children.

T: Gresham.—H: Fitzalan, earl of Arundel.—James Douglas, earl of Morton. — T: Radclyffe, earl of Sussex. — E: Clinton, earl of Lincoln. — Sir Philip Sidney.—Mary Stuart.—Robert Dudley, earl of Leicester.—Ambrose Dudley, earl of Warwick.—Sir Francis Walsingham. — Sir Christopher Hatton. — Cardinal Allen.— Sir Francis Drake.— Philip Howard, earl of Arundel. — J: 1st lord Maitland. — W: Cecil, lord Burghley.—Robert Devereux, earl of Essex.

3. Elizabeth.—John, 1st marquis of Hamilton.—G: Clifford, earl of Cumberland. — C: Blount, baron Montjoy and earl of Devonshire.—T: Sackville, earl of Dorset. — Sir T: Bodley.—Robert Cecil, earl of Salisbury.— Henry, prince of Wales. — H: Howard, earl of Northhampton.— Lady Arabella Stuart.— T: Egerton, viscount Brackley.— Sir Walter Raleigh.— Mary Sydney, countess of Pembroke.—T: Cecil, 1st earl of Exeter.—H: Wriothesley, earl of Southhampton.—James, 2d marquis of Hamilton.—C: Howard of Effingham, earl of Nottingham. — Lodowick Stuart, duke of Richmond. — Francis Bacon. — T: Howard, earl of Suffolk.— E: Somerset, earl of Worcester.— Lucy Harington, countess of Bedford.—G: Villiers, duke of Buckingham.—Fulke Greville, lord Brooke.— G: Carew, earl of Totnes.—W: Herbert, earl of Pembroke.— Sir Hugh Middleton. — H: Percy, earl of Northumberland.—G: Abbot, archbp. of Canterbury. —R: Weston, earl of Portland.

4. Walter, 1st lord Aston.— Frances Howard, duchess of Richmond. — Sir H: Wotton. — Thomas, lord keeper Coventry.—Francis Russell, earl of Bedford. — T: Wentworth, earl of Strafford. — Robert Bertie, earl of Lindsey. — Robert Greville, lord Brooke.—Spencer Compton, earl of Northhampton. —Robert Dormer, earl of Caernarvon.—W: Villiers, viscount Grandison.—W: Fielding, earl of Denbigh.— H: Spencer, earl of Sunderland.—Lucius Carey, viscount Falkland.— H: Danvers, earl of Danby.— W: Laud, archbp. of Canterbury.—Lionel Cranfield, earl of Middlesex.—H: Somerset, 1st marquis of Worcester. — T: Howard, earl of Arundel and Surrey.— Robert Devereux, earl of Essex.— Arthur, lord Capel.— Charles I.— Edward, lord Herbert of Cherbury.— James, 1st duke of Hamilton.— Blanch Somerset, baroness Arundell of Wardour.— H: Rich, earl of Holland.—G: Gordon, marquis of Huntley.—George, lord Goring.—James Graham, marquis of Montrose. Philip Herbert, earl of Pembroke and Montgomery.

5. William, 2d duke of Hamilton.—James Stanley, earl of Derby.— Francis. lord Cottington.— Ralph, lord Hopton.— E: Sackville, 4th earl of Dorset.— J: Selden.—James Stuart, duke of Richmond.—Robert Rich, earl of Warwick.—Oliver Cromwell.—Dorothy Percy, countess of Leicester.—W: Seymour, marquis of Hertford.— Lucy Percy, countess of Carlisle.— Archibald Campbell, marquis of Argyll.—Elizabeth, queen of Bohemia. — Charlotte de La Trémoüille, countess of Derby.—Sir Kenelm Digby.— Montague Bertie, earl of Lindsey.—E: Somerset, 2d marquis of Worcester.—T: Wriothesley, earl of Southhampton.— Algernon Percy, earl of Northumberland.—Henrietta Maria.—G: Monk, duke of Albemarle.—E: Montagu, earl of Manchester.—Anne Hyde, duchess of York.— E: Montagu, earl of Sandwich.— Thomas, lord Clifford of Chudleigh.— E: Hyde, earl of Clarendon.— J: Powlett, marquis of Winchester. — Anne Clifford, countess of Dorset, Pembroke and Montgomery.— W: Kerr, earl of Lothian.

6. W: Cavendish, duke of Newcastle.—Sir Matthew Hale.—G: Digby, earl of Bristol.— W: Howard, viscount Stafford.—J: Leslie, duke of Rothes.—Prince Rupert.—J: Maitland, duke of Lauderdale.—Heneage Finch, earl of Nottingham. — D: Leslie, 1st lord Newark.—Dorothy Sidney, countess of Sunderland.— W:, lord Russell.—Algernon Sidney.—Anne Carre, countess of Bedford.—King Charles II.—James Scot, duke of Monmouth.—H: Bennet, earl of Arlington.— Francis North, lord Guildford.—Archibald Campbell, earl of Argyll.—James Butler, duke of Ormond.—J: Graham, viscount of Dundee.— Elizabeth Cecil, countess of Devonshire.—The hon. Rober Boyle.—J: Tillotson.—W:, 1st earl of Craven.—W: Russell, duke of Bedford.—Robert Spencer, earl of Sunderland.— Frances Theresa Stewart, duchess of Richmond.— Archibald Campbell, 1st duke of Argyll.—J: Locke.— Catherine of Braganza.

7. W: Cavendish, 1st duke of Devonshire.—Sidney Godolphin, earl of Godolphin.—T: Osborne, 1st duke of Leeds.—Queen Anne.—Gilbert Burnet.—John, 1st lord Somers.— C: Talbot, duke of Shrewsbury. — J: Churchill, duke of Marlborough.—Rachel Wriothesley, lady Russell.—Robert Harley, earl of Oxford.—

Sir I: Newton.—Francis Atterbury.—C: Mordaunt, 3d earl of Peterborough. — J: Campbell, 2d duke of Argyll.—Sarah Jennings, duchess of Marlborough.— James Butler, 2d duke of Ormond.—Robert Walpole, 1st earl of Orford.—C: Seymour, 6th duke of Somerset.—J: Montagu, 2d duke of Montagu.—H: St. John, 1st viscount Bolingbroke.—R: Boyle, earl of Burlington.—Horatio, 1st lord Walpole.— W: Pulteney, earl of Bath.— Philip Yorke, 1st earl of Hardwicke.— T: Pelham Holles, duke of Newcastle. — J: Manners, marquis of Granby.—J: Russell, duke of Bedford.— H: Fox, 1st lord Holland.— Robert, lord Clive.— W: Pitt, 1st earl of Chatham.

8. Admiral lord Hawke.—C: Watson Wentworth, 2d marquis of Rockingham.—Admiral viscount Keppel.—G: A: Elliott, lord Heathfield.—Admiral lord Rodney.—F: North, lord Guildford.—J: Stuart, earl of Bute.—Lord chief justice Mansfield.—Lord Chancellor Camden.—Sir W: Jones.—Horace Walpole, earl of Orford.—Jeffrey, 1st lord Amherst.—Admiral earl Howe.— Sir Ralph Abercromby.— Francis' Russell, duke of Bedford.—Admiral viscount Duncan.— Admiral viscount Nelson.—C:, 1st marquis Cornwallis.— William, 1st marquis of Lansdowne. — W: Pitt.— C: James Fox.—Admiral viscount Bridport.— Admiral viscount Hood. — Princess Charlotte.— Sir Joseph Banks.— Admiral the earl of St. Vincent. — Robert Bank Jenkinson, earl of Liverpool.—Sir Walter Scott. — Admiral viscount Exmouth. — Arthur Wellesley, duke of Wellington.

Walford, E: Tales of our great families. Lond. 1877. 2 v. D.   **920.2 : 17**
— *Same.* 2d series. Lond. 1880. 2 v. D.   **920.2 : 18**

Nicoll, H: J. Great movements and those who achieved them. N. Y. 1882. D. **920.2 : 11**
Contents. Prison reform: J: Howard.—The abolition of the slave-trade: W: Wilberforce.—The amelioration of the criminal code: Sir S: Romilly.—Popular education: Lord Brougham.—Cheap literature: Constable, Chambers, Knight and Cassell.—Penny postage: Sir Rowland Hill.—The repeal of the corn-laws: R: Cobden, J: Bright and C. P. Villiers.—The repeal of the fiscal restrictions upon literature and the press: T: Milner Gibson and others.—The introduction of gas: Murdoch, Winsor, Clegg and others.— The steam-engine and its application to locomotion by land and water: Watt, Stephenson, Fulton and Bell.—The electric telegraph: Cooke, Wheatstone and others.—Index.

Lives of Englishmen in past days; v. 1. Lond. [1845]. S.   **920.2 : 9**
Contents. Alfred the great.—Sir T: More.—J: Evelyn.—J: Kettlewell.—H. Hammond.—Bp. Wilson.— W. Mompesson.—J. Bold.

Gardiner, S: Rawson. Historical biographies. (English history reading books.) Lond. 1884. S.   **x 923.2 : 7**
Contents. Simon de Montfort.—The black prince.— Sir T: More.—Sir Francis Drake.—Oliver Cromwell.— William III.

Adams, W: H: Davenport. Lives of old english worthies before the conquest. Ill. Lond. 1877. D.   **x 920.2 : 3**
Contents. Alfred the great.—Dunstan.—Harold.— Stigand.

— Warrior, priest and statesman, or English heroes in the 13th century. Edinb. 1873. D.   **x 920.2 : 5**
Contents. Thomas A'Becket.—Stephen Langton.— Simon de Montfort.

— Sword and pen, or English worthies in the reign of Elizabeth. Lond. 1877. D.   **x 920.2 : 4**
Contents. Raleigh.—Hawkins.—Gilbert.—T: Cavendish.—Drake.—Sidney.—Shakespeare.

Gillow, Joseph. A literary and biographical history, or Bibliographical dictionary of the english catholics, from the breach with Rome in 1534 to the present time ; v. 1, A–C. Lond. [1885]. O.   **16 : L**

x denotes books specially adapted for children.

Georgian era, The ; memoirs of the most eminent persons who have flourished in Great Britain from [1714 to 1828]. Lond. 1833, 1834. 4 v. D. **920.2 : 7**
Contents. V. 1. The royal family.—The pretenders and their adherents. — Churchmen. — Dissenters. — Statesmen. 2. Military and naval commanders.— Judges and barristers.— Physicians and surgeons.— 3. Voyages and travellers.—Philosophers and men of science.—Authors. 4. Political and rural economists.—Painters, sculptors, architects and engravers.—Composers.—Vocal, instrumental and dramatic performers.

Taylor, W: Cooke. The modern british Plutarch, or Lives of men distinguished in the recent history of England for their talents, virtues or achievements. N. Y. 1846. D. **920.2 : 8**
Contents. R: Arkwright.—Edmund Burke.—Robert Burns. — Lord Byron. — G: Canning.— Earl of Chatham.—Adam Clarke.— Lord Clive.— Capt. Cook.— W: Cowper.— G: Grabbe.— Sir Humphrey Davy.— Lord Eldon.—Lord Erskine.—C: James Fox.— B: Franklin. —Oliver Goldsmith.—H: Grattan.—Earl Grey.— Warren Hastings.—Bishop Heber.—J: Howard.—Dr. Jenner.— Sir W: Jones. — Sir James Mackintosh. — H: Martyn.— Sir J: Moore.— Lord Nelson.— W: Pitt.— Sir S: Romilly.—Sir Walter Scott.—R: Brinsley Sheridan. — J: Smeaton.— James Watt.—Marquis of Wellesley.— W: Wilberforce.— Sir D: Wilkie.— Duke of Wellington.

Stewart, Dugald. Biographical memoirs of Adam Smith, W: Robertson, T: Reid ; ed. by sir W: Hamilton. Prefixed, A memoir of Dugald Stewart, with sel. from his correspondence by J: Veitch. Edinb. 1877. O. **191+8 v10**

Bagehot, Walter. Biographical studies ; ed. by R: Holt Hutton. Lond. 1881. O. **920.2 : 1**
Contents. The character of sir Robert Peel.—Lord Brougham.— Mr. Gladstone.—W: Pitt.—Bolingbroke as a statesman. —Sir G: Cornewall Lewis.—Adam Smith as a person.—Lord Althorp and the reform act of 1832.—Addenda: The prince consort; What Lord Lyndhurst really was; The tribute at Hereford to sir G: C. Lewis; Mr. Cobden; Lord Palmerston; The earl of Clarendon; Mr. Lowe as chancellor of the exchequer; M. Guizot; Prof. Cairnes; Mr. Disraeli as a member of the house of commons.

Rogers, S: Recollections. Bost. 1859. D. **920.2 : 6**
Contents. C: James Fox. — Edmund Burke. — H: Grattan.—R: Porson.—J: Horne Tooke.—Prince Talleyrand.—T: Erskine.—Sir Walter Scott.—Lord Grenville.–Duke of Wellington.

Paul, C: Kegan. Biographical sketches. Lond. 1883. D. **920.2 : 12**
Contents. E: Irving.— J: Keble. — Maria Hare.— Rowland Williams.— C: Kingsley.— George Eliot. — J: H: Newman.

Adams, W: H: Davenport. Women of fashion and representative women in letters and society ; a series of biogr. and critical studies. Lond. 1878. 2 v. D. **920.2 : 14**
Contents. V. 1. Lady Mary Wortley Montague.— The duchess of Marlborough.— Lady Morgan.— Miss Berry. 2. Madame d'Arblay.—Mrs. Elizabeth Inchbald.— The countess of Blessington. — Charlotte Brontë.—Harriet Martineau.

Fortunes made in business ; a series of original sketches, biographical and anecdotic from the recent history of industry and commerce, by various writers. Lond. 1884. 2 v. O. **920.2 : 16**
Contents. V. 1. The story of I: Holden.—Mr. S. C. Lister and the story of "silk waste."—The Low Moor company.—Sir Josiah Mason. —The romance of invention: Sir H: Bessemer.—Sir J: Brown.—The Salts, and the discovery of alpaca.—The Peases of Darlington.—The Elsons and Forsters of Burley-in-Wharfedale.—The Fieldens of Todmorden. 2. The Fosters of Queensbury.—Hornby castle.—The fortunes of the Gladstone family.—The fortunes of the Bright family.—The Fairbairns of Manchester and Leeds.—

The revolutions of industry; W. H. Perkin. — The Cunard steamship company. — Messrs. T: Wilson, sons and co., the Hull shipowners.—Messrs. Bass and the Burton breweries.

*   *   *

Irving, Joseph, comp. The book of scotsmen eminent for achievements in arms and arts, church and state, law, legislation and literature, commerce, science, travel and philanthropy. Paisley. 1881. O. **920.2 : R13**

Webb, Alfred. A compendium of irish biography ; comprising sketches of distinguished irishmen and of eminent persons, connected with Ireland by office or by their writings. Dublin. 1878. O. **920.2 : R10**

Other modern.

München. Königliche akademie der wissenschaften ; historische commission. Allgemeine deutsche biographie ; [Rochus freiherr v. Liliencron and Franz Xaver Wegele, eds.] Leipz. 1875-85. 22 v. O. **920.3 : R1**
Note. V. 22 ends with Münchhausen.

Spamer, J: Gottlieb Christian Franz O:, (Franz Otto). Deutsche dichter, denker und wissensfürsten im 18. und 18. jahrh.; in lebensbildern für jugend und volk, in verbindung mit O: Banck, H. Birnbaum, G. Höcker, K: Müller von Halle, K. Schröder, A: Werner, in 2ter sehr verm. aufl. herausg. von Franz Otto. Ill. Leipz. 1877. O. **920.3 : 2**
Contents. Heroen des deutschen schriftthums: Banck, O:, Winckelmann, Lessing; Werner, A:, Klopstock, Herder; Höcker, G., Wieland: Spamer, O:, Goethe, Schiller.— Die alt- und grossmeister der philosophie: Werner, A:, Leibnitz, Kant, Fichte.— Deutsche wissensfürsten im 18. und 19. jahrh.: Müller von Halle, K:, Albrecht v. Haller; Mohl, M. O., Alexander v. Humboldt: Steinhard, S., Leopold v. Buch; Birnbaum, H., K: Ritter.

*   *   *

Loménie, L: Léonard de. Sketches of conspicuous living characters of France. Tr. by R. M. Walsh. Phila. 1841. D. **920.4 : 2**
Contents. Preface. — Thiers. — Chateaubriand.— Lafitte.—Guizot.—Lamartine.–Soult.— Berryer.—De la Mennais.— Victor Hugo. — Dupin.— Béranger.— Odillon Barrot.—Arago. — George Sand.—The duke de Broglie.

Hamerton, Philip Gilbert. Modern frenchmen ; five biographies. Bost. 1878. D. **920.4 : 1**
Contents. Victor Jacquemont. — H: Perreyve. — François Rude.—J: Jacques Ampère.–H: Regnault.

Daudet, Ernest, and others. French celebrities as seen by their contemporaries ; a series of brief biographies of the foremost frenchmen of our day. Tr. by Francis W. Potter. N. Y. 1883. 2 v. D. **920.4 : 3**
Contents. 1st ser. Daudet, E., Marshal de MacMahon. — Depasse, H., Léon Gambetta. — Delabrosse, L., Jules Grévy.–Edmond, C:, L: Blanc.— Depasse, H., C: de Freycinet.–Claretie, J., Victor Hugo.–Pinard, A., Ferdinand de Lesseps. 2d ser. Sylvin, E:, Jules Ferry.–Pelletin, C., G: Clémenceau.— Bourget, P., Ernest Renan. — Bazire, E., H: Rochefort.— Depasse, H., Challemel-Lacour.— Daudet, E., Jules Simon.–Claretie, J., Erckmann-Chatrian.—Depasse, H., Paul Bert.–Claretie, J., Alphonse Daudet.

*   *   *

Oliphant, Margaret O., born Wilson. The makers of Florence ; Dante, Giotto, Savonarola and their city. Portr. of Savonarola and ill. Lond. 1877. O. **920.5+P1**

Aa, Abraham Jacob van der, K. J. R. van **Harderwijk,** G. J. D. **Schotel,** *and others.* Biographisch woordenboek der Nederlanden ; bevattende levensbeschrijvingen van zoodanige personen die zich op eenigerlei wijze in ons vaderland hebben vermaard gemaakt. Haarlem. 1852-78. 21 v. in 20. O.   **920.5 : R4**

*   *   *

Macedo, Joaquim Manoel de. Brazilian biographical annual. Rio de Janeiro. 1876. 3 v. O.   **920.5 : 2**

*   *   *

Lanman, C: Leading men of Japan ; with an historical summary of the empire. Bost. [1883]. D.   **920.5 : 3**

Ancient.

Smith, W:, *ed.* Dictionary of greek and roman biography and mythology. Bost. 1859. 3 v. O.   **R1**
Göll, Hermann. Die weisen und gelehrten des alterthums ; leben und wirken der hervorragendsten forscher und entdecker auf dem gebiete der wissenschaft bei den griechen und römern. Leipz. 1876. O.   **920.6 : 3**
Plutarchos. Plutarch's lives ; the translation called Dryden's, corr. from the greek and rev. by A. H. Clough. Bost. 1885. 5 v. O.   **923.6 : 31**
     Contents. V. 1. Pref. and life of Plutarch.—Theseus.—Romulus.— Lycurgus.— Numa Pompilius.—Solon.—Poplicola.— Themistocles.— Camillus.—Pericles.—Fabius.— App. 2. Alcibiades.— Coriolanus.—Timoleon.—Aemilius Paulus.—Pelopidas.—Marcellus.—Aristides.— Cato the elder.— Philopœmen.—Flam-

Plutarchos.—*Continued.*
     ininus.—App. **3.** Pyrrhus. — Marius. — Lysander.— Sylla.—Cimon.—Lucullus.— Nicias.— Crassus.—Sertorius.—Eumenes.— App. **4.** Agesilaus. — Pompey.—Alexander.—Cæsar.—Phocion.— Cato the younger.—Agis. — Cleomenes. — Tiberius Gracchus. — Caius Gracchus.—App. **5.** Demosthenes.— Cicero.—Demetrius.—Antony.—Dion.—Marcus Brutus.—Aratus.—Artaxerxes.—Galba.—Otho.—App. —Index of proper names.—Pronunciation of proper names.
— *Same.* Tr., with notes and a life of the author, by J: and W: Langhorne. *T. p. w.* [N. Y. *n. d.*] O.   **923.6 : 16**
     Contents, same as above, with the add. of Tables of coins, weights, measures, etc., *and* Chronological table.
— Our young folks' Plutarch ; ed. by Rosalie Kaufman. Ill. Phila. 1883. O.   **x 923.6 : 29**
— The boys' and girls' Plutarch ; parts of the "Lives of Plutarch " ed. for boys and girls, with an introd. by J: S. White. Ill. N. Y. 1883. O.   **x 923.6 : 30**
Lives of illustrious greeks ; for schools and families. Lond. [1849]. D.   **923.6 : 17**
     Contents. Theseus.—Lycurgus.—Solon.—Aristeides.—Themistocles.— Cimon.— Pericles.— Nicias.— Alcibiades.—Lysander.— Agesilaus. — Pelopidas.— Timoleon.—Demosthenes.— Phocion.— Eumenes.—Aratus.—Agis.—Cleomenes.—Philopœmen.
Goodrich, S: Griswold. Famous men of ancient times. [Youths' library of biogr.] Bost. [1844]. S.   **x 920.6 : 4**
     Contents. Mohammed.—Belisarius.— Attila.—Nero.—Seneca.—Virgil.—Cicero.—Julius Cæsar.—Hannibal.—Alexander.— Aristotle.— Demosthenes.—Apelles.—Diogenes.— Plato.— Socrates.— Alcibiades.— Democritus.—Pericles.
Thayer, W: Makepeace. Soldiers of the Bible. *T. p. w.* S.   **x 920.6 : 7**

x denotes books specially adapted for children.

2. Philosophy and Religion.

1. Philosophy.

Collective biogr.

Fénelon, François de **Salignac de la Mothe.** Lives of the ancient philosophers. Tr. from the french, with notes and a life of the author by J: Cormack. N. Y. 1846. S.   **921.6 : 1**
Denslow, Van Buren. Modern thinkers, principally upon social science ; what they think and why, with an introd. by Robert G. Ingersoll. Chicago. 1880. D.   **921 : 1**
     Contents. Pref. — Introd. — Sketch of the life of Swedenborg.—Emanuel Swedenborg and the origin of the christian ideas of heaven, hell and virtue.—Sketch of the life of Adam Smith.—Adam Smith, founder of the school of the economists.—Sketch of the life of Jeremy Bentham.—Jeremy Bentham, the apostle of law reform, and of utilitarianism in morals.—Sketch of the life of T: Paine.—T: Paine, the apostle of chronic revolution, in his relations to the declaration of independence and democracy in America. — Sketch of the life of Fourier.—C: Fourier, the philosopher of passional harmony and co-operative association.—Sketch of the life of Spencer.—Herbert Spencer, a review of his theories of evolution and of morals. — Sketch of the life of Haeckel. — Ernst Haeckel, the demonstrator of the doctrine of evolution.—Auguste Comte, founder of the positive philosophy and pontiff of the religion of humanity, includ. a sketch of his life.—The authorship of Junius, a sequel to the critique on T: Paine.—Wealth, a sequel to the critique on Adam Smith.

Morris, G: S. British thought and thinkers ; introd. studies, critical, biogr. and philosophical. Chicago. 1880. D.   **921.2 : 1**
     Contents. General philosophical attitude of the english mind.—Mediæval anticipations of the modern english mind: John of Salisbury; Roger Bacon; Duns Scotus; William of Occam.—Englishmen of the renaissance: Edmund Spenser; Sir J: Davies; R: Hooker.—W: Shakespeare. — Francis Bacon. — T: Hobbes.—J: Locke.—G: Berkeley.—D: Hume. — Sir W: Hamilton.—J: Stuart Mill.—Herbert Spencer.

Individual biogr.

Fraser, Alexander Campbell. B e r k e l e y . [Phil. classics for eng. readers]. Phila. 1881. S.   **921.2 : 2**
Mill, J: Stuart. Berkeley's life and writings. *With his* Three essays on religion. **204 : 30**
Collins, W: Lucas. B u t l e r . [Phil. classics for eng. readers]. Phila. 1881. S.   **921.2 : 3**
Mahaffy, J: Peytland. D e s c a r t e s . [Phil. classics for eng. readers]. Phila. 1881. S.   **921.4 : 1**
Conway, Moncure Daniel. E m e r s o n at home and abroad. Bost. 1882. D.   **921.1 : 2**
Cooke, G: Willis. Ralph Waldo Emerson ; his i e, writings and philosophy. Bost. 1881. D   **921.1 : 1**

Guernsey, Alfred H. Ralph Waldo Emerson, philosopher and poet. [Appleton's new handy vol. ser.] N. Y. 1881. S. 921.1 : 4
Holmes, Oliver Wendell. Ralph Waldo Emerson. (Amer. men of letters.) Portr. Bost. 1885 [1884]. S. 921.1 : 6
Ireland, Alexander. Ralph Waldo Emerson; his life, genius and writings, a biogr. sketch ; added, personal recollections of his visits to England, extracts from unpub. letters and miscellaneous characteristic records. 2d ed. augm. Portr. Lond. 1882. D. 921.1 : 3
Sanborn, Franklin B:, ed. The genius and character of Emerson ; lectures at the Concord school of philosophy. Portr. and ill. Bost. 1885 [1884]. D. 921.1 : 5
Adamson, Robert. F i c h t e. [Phil. classics for eng. readers]. Phila. 1881. S. 921.3 : 1
Fichte, Immanuel Hermann. J: Gottlieb Fichte's leben und briefwechsel von seinem sohne. 2te sehr verm. und verb. aufl. Portr. Leipz. 1862. 2 v. O. 921.3+6
Schmidt, Ferdinand. J: Gottlieb Fichte ; ein lebensbild für jung und alt. 4te aufl., ill. Kreuznach. [1883]. S. 921.3 : 9
Huxley, T: H: H u m e. [Eng. men of letters]. N. Y. [1879]. D. 921.2 : 4
Wallace, W: K a n t. [Phil. classics for eng. readers]. Phila. 1882. D. 921.3 : 3
Brandes, G: Morris Cohen. Sören K i e r k e - g a a r d ; ein literarisches charakterbild. Autorisierte deutsche ausg. Leipz. 1879· D. 921.5 : 1
Merz, J: Theodore. L e i b n i z. [Phil. classics for eng. readers]. Portr. Phila. 1884. D. 921.3 : 5
Mackie, J: Milton. Life of Godfrey W: v. Leibnitz ; on the basis of the germ. work of G[ottschalk] [Eduard] Guhrauer. Bost. 1845. D. 921.3 : 2
Bourne, H. R. Fox. Life of J: L o c k e. N. Y. 1876. 2 v. O. 921.2 : 5
Fowler, T: Locke. [Eng. men of letters]. N. Y. 1880. D. 921.2 : 6
King, P:, 7th baron King. Life and letters of J: Locke ; with extracts from his journals and common-place books. New ed., with index. Lond. 1858. D. 921.2 : 7
Bain, Alexander. James M i l l ; a biography. N. Y. 1882. D. 921.2 : 10
Mill, J: Stuart. Autobiography. N. Y. 1875. O. 921.2 : 8
Bain, Alexander. John Stuart M i l l ; a criticism, with personal recollections. N. Y. 1882. D. 921.2 : 9
Heath, R: Edgar Q u i n e t ; his early life and writings. [Eng. and foreign phil. classics]. Bost. 1881. O. 921.4 : 2
Gwinner, W: S c h o p e n h a u e r ' s leben ; 2te umgearb. und vielfach verm. aufl. der schrift : Arthur Schopenhauer, aus persönlichem umgange dargestellt. Portr. Leipz. 1878. O. 921.3 : 7
— Schopenhauer und seine freunde ; zur beleuchtung der Frauenstädt-Lindner'schen vertheidigung Schopenhauer's, sowie zur erganzung der schrift : Arthur Schopenhauer, aus persönlichem umgange dargestellt. Leipz. 1863. O. 921.3 : 8
Xenophōn. Memoirs of S o c r a t e s for english readers ; a new tr. from Xenophon's

Memorabilia, with ill. notes by E: Levien. [Bayard ser.] Lond. 1872. S. 921.6 : 2
Martineau, James. A study of S p i n o z a. 2d ed., rev. Portr. Lond. 1883. D. 921.5 : 2
Knight, W:, ed. Spinoza ; four essays by Land, Kuno Fischer, J. van Vloten and Ernst Renan. Lond. 1882. O. 921.3 : 4
Contents. Land, J. In memory of Spinoza; a lecture del. on the occasion of the bicentenary of Spinoza to the class of philosophy at Leyden, feb. 24th 1877. Tr. by Allan Menzies. — Fisher, Ernst Kuno Bertold. The life and character of Baruch Spinoza: a lecture. Tr. by Frida Schmidt. — Vloten, J. van. Spinoza, the glad herald to mankind of the good news of its majority; an oration del. on the occasion of the unveiling of the statue at the Hague, sept. 18th, 1880. Tr. by Allan Menzies. — Renan, Joseph Ernest. Spinoza, 1677 and 1877; address at the unveiling of the monument at the Hague on the 21st of feb. 1877.
Hamley, E: B. V o l t a i r e. [Foreign classics for eng. readers]. Phila. 1878. S. 921.4 : 4
Morley, J: Voltaire. N. Y. 1878. O. 921.4 : 5
Parton, James. Life of Voltaire. Bost. 1881. 2 v. O. 921.4 : 3
Strauss, D: F: Voltaire ; sechs vorträge. 4te aufl. Bonn. 1877. O. 921.4 : 6

2. Collective religious biogr.

Foxe or Fox, J: History of the lives, sufferings and triumphant deaths of the primitive as well as the protestant martyrs from the commencement of christianity to the latest periods of pagan and popish persecution ; originally composed by J: Fox. Added, an account of the inquisition, the Bartholomew massacre, the massacre in France and general persecution under Louis XIV, the massacres of the irish rebellion in 1641, and the recent persecutions of protestants in the south of France. Ill. ed. Bost. 1848. D. 922 : 1
Note. This is an abbreviation of the "Acts and monuments," 272+6, for which see col. 119.
Baillie, J: Life studies, or How to live ; illustrated in the biogr. of Bunyan, Tersteegen, Montgomery, Perthes and mrs. Winslow. N. Y. 1857. S. 922 : 2
Favourite passages in modern christian biography. Lond. n. d. D. 922 : 3
Contents. R: Cecil.—Andrew Fuller.—Adolphe Monod.—F: W: Krummacher.—Robert Hall.—J: Foster.—T: Arnold.—W: Archer Butler.—T: Chalmers.—H: Martyn.—J: Williams.—Robert Murray M'Cheyne.—J: Mackintosh.—H: Havelock.—Hedley Vicars.—James Wilson.—Patrick Frazer Tytler.
Portraits of the principal reformers of the 16th century; with a narrative of the reformation of religion. N. Y. 1836. S. 922 : 5
Tulloch, J: Leaders of the reformation : Luther, Calvin, Latimer, Knox ; the representative men of Germany, France, England and Scotland. Bost. 1860. D. 922 : 7
Wittenmyer, Mrs. Annie. The women of the reformation ; with an introduction by mrs. Kate Brownlee Sherwood. [Ill.] N.Y. 1885. D. 922 : 12
Contents. Joan, mother of Richard II of England.—Anne of Bohemia, queen of Richard II.—The reformation in Bohemia.—Marguerite of Valois.—Renée, duchess of Ferrara.—Jeanne d'Albret.—Duchess de Bourbon, princess of Orange.—Louise de Coligny, princess of Orange.—The reformation in England.—Anne Boleyn.—Catherine Parr.—Lady Jane Grey.—Catherine Willoughby, duchess of Suffolk.—Queen Elizabeth.—Princess Elizabeth, electress of Brandenburg.—Elizabeth, duchess of Brunswick-Calenberg.

—Elizabeth Knox, wife of J: Welsh.—Lady Anne Hamilton, marchioness of Hamilton.—Lady Margaret Douglas, marchioness of Argyll.—Lady Anne, duchess of Hamilton.—Barbara Cunningham, lady Caldwell.—Lady Anne Lindsay, countess of Rothes.—Lady Anne Mackenzie, countess of Balcarres, afterward countess of Argyll, and her daughters lady Sophia and lady Henrietta Campbell.—Lady Grisell Hume.—Lady Baillie of Jerviswood.

Chapman, W: Notable women of the reformation ; their lives and times. Lond. 1884. D. 922 : 13

Contents. Ursula Cotta—Katharine v. Bora.—Elizabeth of Brandenberg.—The princess of Henneberg.—Sibylla of Cleves.—The princess of Schwartzburg.—The electress Palatine.—Anna Reinhard and Idelette Calvin.—Marguerite, queen of Navarre.—Renée, duchess of Ferrara.—Leanor de Cisneros.—Maria de Bohorques.

Weld, Horatio Hastings, *ed.* The women of the scriptures. Phila. [1848]. O. 922+9

Kavanagh, Julia. Women of christianity, exemplary for acts of piety and charity. N. Y. 1852. D. 922 : 4

Darton, J. M. The heroism of christian women of our own time. N. Y. 1882 [1881]. D. 923.2 : 3

Contents. Princess Louise.—Agnes Elizabeth Jones.—Lady Hope.—Mary Carpenter.—Mrs. Lucas.—Mrs. Daniell.—Miss Weston.—Mrs. Ranyard.—Mrs. Reed.—Catherine Tait.—Francis Ridley Havergal.—Sister Dora.—Mrs. Fisher.—Mrs. Wakefield.—Christine R. Alsop.— Anne Mackenzie. — Charlotte Elizabeth Tonna.

Charles, Elizabeth. Sketches of the women of christendom. N. Y. [1880]. D. 922 : 10

Contents. Introd.—The first woman: Eve. — The women of the gospels: Mary, the mother of our Lord; Mary Magdalene; The story of the two alabaster boxes.—The women of the Acts of the apostles: Lois and Eunice; Lydia: Aquila and Priscilla.—The women of the early church: The story of Blandina; Perpetua and Felicitas; Monica, the mother of St. Augustine.—The christian women of the middle ages: The abbess Hilda; Joan of Arc.—Christian women of modern times: Prascovia Lopouloff; Lady Rachel Russell; Madame Elizabeth of France; The mother of the Wesleys ; Catherine Tait.—The women of the army of succor: Mademoiselle Legras; Hannah More; Sarah Martin; Mrs. Fry.—Conclusion.

Waterbury, Jared Bell. Sketches of eloquent preachers. N. Y. [1864]. D. 922 : 8

Contents. J: M. Mason. — Archibald Alexander.—J: Summerfield.—Sylvester Larned.—Asahel Nettleton.—Lyman Beecher.—H: B. Bascom.—E: Payson.—E: Dorr Griffin. — Robert Hall. — T: Chalmers.—R: Melvill.—Rowland Hill.— Legh Richmond.—Timothy Dwight. — Jonathan Edwards.—G: Whitefield. — R: Baxter.—J: Bunyan.—James Saurin.—J: Baptist Massillon.—Martin Luther.—Apostle Paul.

Steel, Robert. Burning and shining lights, or Memoirs of eminent ministers of Christ. Lond. 1864. D. 922 : 6

Contents. Patrick Hamilton.—Joseph Alleine.—Jonathan Edwards.—Francis Asbury. — W: Tennent.—Asahel Nettleton.— Robert M'Cheyne.—E: Bickersteth.—J: Brown.—T: Chalmers. — Daniel Baker. — J: Angell James.—Dr. Coke.—J: Kennedy.—J: Morison. Dr. Burns.—James Allan.

Yonge, Charlotte Mary. Pioneers and founders, or Recent workers in the mission field. Lond. *n. d.* D. 922 : 11

Contents. J: Eliot, the apostle of the red indians.—D: Brainerd, the enthusiast. — Christian F: Schwartz, councillor of Tanjore.—H: Martyn, the scholar-missionary.—W: Carey and Joshua Marshman, the Serampore missionaries.—The Judson family.—The bishopric of Calcutta: T: Middleton, Reginald Heber, Daniel Wilson.—S: Marsden, the australian chaplain and friend of the Maori.—J: Williams, the martyr of Erromango.—Allen Gardiner, the sailor martyr.—C: F: Mackenzie, the martyr of the Zambesi.

3. American religious biogr.

Collective.

Headley, Joel Tyler. The chaplains and clergy of the revolution. N. Y. 1864. D. 922.1 : 2

Contents. Religious element of the revolution. — Systematic influence of the clergy.—Election sermons preached after the assembling of the continental congress and organization of colonial government.—Sermons during the war.—Personal influence of the clergy.—Jonas Clark.—Jacob Duché.— S: Spring. — Ebenezer Prime.—S: Eaton.— W: Tennent.— P: Gabriel Muhlenberg.—T: Allen.—J: Rossburg.— Abner Benedict.—W: White.—Timothy Dwight.— Naphthali Dagget.—Ezra Styles.—Joel Barlow.—James Caldwell.—H: Trumbull.—S: Kirkland.—James Hall.—J: Gano.—C: Cummings.—Daniel McCalla.—J: Witherspoon.—D: Avery.—Israel Evans.— Cotton Mather Smith.—Judah Champion.—Alex. McWhorter.—Moses Allen.—B: Pomeroy.—J: Rogers.—G: Duffield.—D: Sandford.—Nathan Ker.—W: McKay Tennent.—Mr. Boardman.—Mr. Magoon.—T: Coombs.— A roman catholic chaplain.—A chaplain at Brandywine.

Sprague, W: Buell. Annals of the american pulpit, or Commemorative notices of distinguished amer. clergymen of various denominations, from the early settlement of the country to the close of the year 1855, with historical introd. N. Y. 1857–61. 7 v. O. 922.1+4

Contents. V. 1, 2. Trinitarian congregational. 3, 4. Presbyterian. 5. Episcopalian. 6. Baptist. 7. Methodist.

— Annals of the american unitarian pulpit, or Commemorative notices of distinguished clergymen of the unitarian denomination in the U. S., from its commencement to the close of the year 1855 ; with an historical introd. N. Y. 1865. O. 922.1+5

Alexander, Archibald, *ed.* Biographical sketches of the founder and principal alumni of the Log college ; together with an account of the revivals of religion, under their ministry. Princeton. 1845. D. 922.1 : 1

Contents. The log college.— W: Tennent, *sen.*—Gilbert Tennent.—The New London school.—J: Tennent.—W: Tennent's letter.—W: Tennent, *jr.*—Remarks.—Anecdotes of W: Tennent.—C: Tennent.—S: Blair.—J: Blair.—S: Finley.—W: Robinson.—J: Rowland.—C: Beatty.

Roman-catholic.

Bayley, James Roosevelt. Memoirs of Simon W: Gabriel B r u t é ; with sketches, describing his recollections of scenes connected with the french revolution, and extracts from his journal. New ed. N. Y. 1865. D. 922.12 : 4

Hassard, J: R. G. Life of J: H u g h e s ; with extracts from his private correspondence. N. Y. 1866. O. 922.12+1

Losa, Francisco. The life of Gregory L o p e z , a hermit in America. [*Anon.*] N. Y. 1841. S. 922.12 : 2

White, C: I. Life of Eliza A. S e t o n ; with copious extracts from her writings, and an historical sketch of the sisterhood from its foundation to the time of her death. 5th rev. ed. Balt. 1865. D. 922.12 : 3

Protestant-episcopal.

Brown, J. W., *ed.* Memorial of Lewis P. B a y a r d ; containing a memoir of his life, extracts from his journals and corresp., notices of his tour through Europe and the

Holy Land, selections from his sermons and the discourse preached on the occasion of his decease by H: U. Onderdonk. N. Y. 1841. D.   **922.13 : 1**

Tyng, Stephen Higginson. Memoir of Gregory T. Bedell. 2d ed. enl. and impr. N. Y. 1854. D.   **922.13 : 2**

Chase, Philander. Reminiscences; an autobiography. 2d ed., comprising a history of the principal events in the author's life to a. d. 1847. Portr. and ill. Bost. 1848. 2 v. O.   **922.13+3**

Croswell, Harry. Memoir of W: Croswell, by his father. N. Y. 1853. O.   **922.13+4**

Cummins, Alexandrine Macomb, *born* Balch. Memoir of G: D: Cummins, by his wife. N. Y. [1878]. O.   **922.13 : 13**

Gadsden, Christopher Edwards. An essay on the life of Theodore Dehon. Charleston. 1833. O.   **922.13 : 5**

Stone, J: Seely. Memoir of the life of Alexander Viets Griswold, with an app.; added, a sermon, charge and pastoral letter of the late bishop. Phila. 1844. O.   **922.13 : 6**

McVickar, J: Early years of the late bishop Hobart. N. Y. 1834. D.   **922.13 : 7**
— Professional years of J: H: Hobart; a sequel to his "Early years". N. Y. 1836. D.   **922.13 : 8**

Cummins, G: D: Life of Virginia Hale Hoffman. Phila. 1859. D.   **922.13 : 9**

Stone, J: Seely. Memoir of the life of James Milnor; abr. by the author. N. Y. [1849]. D.   **922.13 : 10**

Ayres, Anne. Life and work of W: A: Muhlenberg. N. Y. 1880. O.   **922.13 : 14**

Hanson, J: H. The lost prince; facts tending to prove the identity of Louis XVII of France and rev. E. Williams. N. Y. 1854. D.   **922.13 : 11**

Bronson, W: White. Memorial of Bird Wilson. Phila. 1864. D.   **922.13 : 12**

Presbyterian.

Baird, H: Martyn. Life of Robert Baird, by his son. N. Y. 1866. D.   **922.14 : 7**

Barnes, Albert. Life at three-score; a sermon del. in the 1st presb. church, Phila., nov. 28, 1858. 3d ed. Phila. 1859. D. **922.14 : 1**

Beecher, Lyman. Autobiography, correspondence, etc.; ed. by C: Beecher. N. Y. 1864. 2 v. D.   **922.14 : 2**

Hodge, Archibald Alexander. Life of C: Hodge by his son. N. Y. [1880]. O.   **922.14 : 8**

Prime, S: Irenæus. Memoirs of N: Murray. N. Y. 1862. D.   **922.14 : 3**

Miller, S: Memoir of C: Nisbet. N. Y. 1840. D.   **922.14 : 4**

Spring, Gardiner. Personal reminiscences of [his] life and times. N. Y. 1866. D.   **922.14 : 5**

Walker, James B. Experiences of pioneer life in the early settlements and cities of the west. Chicago. 1881. D.   **922.14 : 6**

Puritan and Congregational.

Abbott, Lyman. Henry Ward Beecher, a sketch of his career, with analyses of his power as a preacher, lecturer, orator and journalist, and incidents and reminiscences

of his life; commemorative of his entrance upon his 70th year. Portr. and ill. N. Y. 1883. O.   **922.15+14**

Edwards, Jonathan. Memoirs of D: Brainerd; chiefly taken from his own diary, incl. his journal, now for the first time incorporated with the rest of his diary in a regular chronol. series by Sereno Edwards Dwight. New Haven. 1822. O.   **922.15 : 1**

Steele, Ashbel. Chief of the pilgrims, or The life and time of W: Brewster. Ill. Phila. 1857. O.   **922.15 : 2**

Lee, Eliza, *born* Buckminster. Memoirs of Joseph Buckminster and Joseph Stevens Buckminster. Bost. 1851. D.   **922.15 : 10**

Cheney, Mary, *born* Bushnell, *ed.* Life and letters of Horace Bushnell. N. Y. 1880. O.   **922.15 : 3**

Hallock, W: A. "Light and love"; a sketch of the life and labors of Justin Edwards. N. Y. [1855]. D.   **922.15 : 4**

Laurie, T: Dr. Grant and the mountain nestorians. Portr., map and ill. 3d ed. rev. Bost. 1856. D.   **922.15 : 5**

Thompson, Joseph Parrish. Memoir of D: Hale; with selections from his miscellaneous writings. 2d ed. Hartford. 1850. O.   **922.15+6**

Contents. Memoir.— Letters on the theater.—Permanent funds.— Slavery; colonization; abolition.— Church polity and ecclesiastical questions.—Romanism and collateral subjects.—Miscellaneous topics.

Lawrence, Margarette Woods, (*Meta Lander*). Light on the dark river, or Memorials of Henrietta A. L. Hamlin. Bost. 1863. D.   **922.15 : 7**

Cooley, Timothy Mather. Sketches of the life and character of Lemuel Haynes; with some introd. remarks by W: B. Sprague. N. Y. 1844. D.   **922.15 : 8**

Helmer, Susan R., *born* Bonnell, *ed.* C: D. Helmer; an earnest life of faith by grace. N. Y. 1880. O.   **922.15 : 9**

Marsh, J: Temperance recollections, labors, defeats, triumphs; an autobiogr. N. Y. 1866. D.   **922.15 : 11**

Scudder, Horace Elisha. Life and letters of D: Coit Scudder. N. Y. 1864. D.   **922.15 : 12**

Todd, J: The story of his life, told mainly by himself; comp. and ed. by J: E. Todd. N. Y. 1876. D.   **922.15 : 13**

Baptist.

Cone, E: W. *and* Spencer W. Some account of the life of Spencer Houghton Cone, a baptist preacher in America. [*Anon.*] N. Y. 1856. D.   **922.16 : 1**

Randolph, E. A. The life of rev. J: Jasper, pastor of 6th Mt. Zion baptist church, Richmond, Va., from his birth to the present time, with his theory of the rotation of the sun. Richmond. 1884. D.   **922.16 : 8**

Conant, Hannah Chaplin. The earnest man; a sketch of the character and labors of Adoniram Judson. Bost. 1856. D.   **922.16 : 3**

Wayland, Francis. Memoir of the life and labors of Adoniram Judson. Bost. 1853. 2 v. D.   **922.16 : 2**

Knowles, James Davis. Memoir of Ann H. Judson. Bost. 1855. S.   **922.16 : 4**

Kendrick, Asahel C. The life and letters of mrs. Emily C. J u d s o n. N. Y. 1862. D.   **922.16:6**

Judson, Emily, *born* Chubbuck. Memoir of Sarah B. J u d s o n of the Amer. mission to Burmah. New rev. ed., with notes by the author. N. Y. 1855. S.   **922.16:5**

Guild, Reuben Aldrich. Life, times and correspondence of James M a n n i n g and the early history of Brown university. Bost. 1864. D.   **922.16:7**

Methodist.

Stevens, Abel. Life and times of N. B a n g s. N. Y. [1863]. D.   **922.17:1**

Manship, Andrew. Thirteen years' experience in the itinerancy. 5th ed. Phila. 1856. D.   **922.17:2**

Milburn, W: H: Ten years of preacher-life; chapters from an autobiogr. N. Y. 1860. D.   **922.17:3**

Olin, Stephen. Life and letters. N. Y. 1853. 2 v. D.   **922.17:4**

Pierson, Hamilton W. In the brush, or Old-time social, political and religious life in the south-west. Ill. N. Y. 1881. D.   **922.17:5**

Ingraham, Sarah R. Walks of usefulness, or Reminiscences of mrs. Margaret P r i o r. 3d ed. N. Y. 1844. S.   **922.17:6**

Unitarian.

Brooks, C: Timothy. W: Ellery C h a n n i n g; a centennial memory. Ill. Bost. 1880. D.   **922.18:1**

Channing, W: H. Memoir of W: Ellery Channing; with extracts from his corresp. and mss. 6th ed. Bost. 1854. 3 v. D. **922.18:1**

— *Same.* Centenary memorial ed. Bost. 1880. O.   **922.18:3**

Peabody, Elizabeth Palmer. Reminiscences of W: Ellery Channing. Bost. 1880. D.   **922.18:2**

Frothingham, R: Tribute to T: Starr K i n g. Bost. 1865. D.   **922.18:4**

Cooke, Frances E. Story of Theodore P a r k e r; with an introd. by Grace A. Oliver. [Lives of the great and good]. Bost. 1883. D.   **922.18:16**

Weiss, J: Life and correspondence of Theodore Parker. N. Y. 1864. 2 v. O.   **922.18+6**

Parker, Theodore. Experience as a minister, with some account of his early life and education for the ministry; contained in a letter to the members of the 28th congreg. society of Boston. Bost. 1859. D.   **922.18:5**

Ware, J: Memoir of H: W a r e, jr. Bost. 1854. D.   **922.18:7**

Hall, E: B. Memoir of Mary L. W a r e. Bost. 1854. D.   **922.18:8**

Other.

Ellis, Sumner. Life of Edwin H. C h a p i n. Portr. and ill. Bost. 1882. O. **922.18:14**

Janney, S. N. Memoirs, written by himself. 3d ed. Phila. 1862. D.   **922.18:12**

Hallowell, Anna Davis, *ed.* James and Lucretia M o t t; life and letters ed. by their grand-daughter. Portr. Bost. 1884. D.   **922.18:17**

Bates, Joseph. Autobiography; embracing a long life on ship-board, with sketches of voyages on the Atlantic and Pacific oceans, the Baltic and Mediterranean seas, also impressment and service on board british war ships, long confinement in Dartmoor prison, early experience in reformatory movements, travels in various parts of the world and a brief account of the great advent movement of 1840–44. Battle Creek, Mich. 1868. S.   **922.18:10**

— Early life and late experience and labors, ed. by elder James White. Battle Creek, Mich, 1878. D.   **922.18:11**

White, James. Life sketches; ancestry, early life, christian experience and extensive labors of elder James White and his wife Ellen G. White. Battle Creek, Mich. 1880. D.   **922.18:15**

Home, Daniel Douglas. Incidents in my life; with an introd. by judge [J. W.] Edmonds. N. Y. 1863. D.   **922.18:13**

Stone, W: Leete. Matthias and his impostures, or, The progress of fanaticism. ill. in the extraordinary case of Robert M a t t h e w s and some of his forerunners and disciples. N. Y. 1835. S.   **922.18:9**

Cohen, Mrs. S. J. Henry Luria, or The little jewish convert, being contained in [her] memoir. N. Y. 1864. D.   **922.19:1**

4. British religious biogr.

Collective.

Bayne, P: The christian life, social and individual. Bost. 1859. D.   **922.2:2**
Contents. Pt. 1. *Statement:* The individual life; The social life. Pt. 2. *Exposition and illustration:* Book 1, Christianity the basis of social life: First principles; Howard and the rise of philanthropy; Wilberforce and the development of philanthropy; Budgett, the christian freeman; The social problem of the age, and one or two hints toward its solution. —Book 2, Christianity the basis of individual character: Introductory, a few words on modern doubt: J: Foster; T: Arnold; T: Chalmers. —Outlook: The positive philosophy; Pantheistic spiritualism.—General conclusion.

Adams, W: H: Davenport. The home library: Great english churchmen, or Famous names in english church history and literature; a series of biogr. studies, intended to illustrate the annals, character, teaching and influence of the church of England. Lond. 1879. D.   **922.2:3**
Contents. Statesmen: S. Anselm; T: Becket; Stephen Langton; W: Laud.—Poets and divines: G: Herbert; Jeremy Taylor.—Martyrs and confessors: W: Tyndale; Hugh Latimer; Bp. Ken.

Tulloch, J: English puritanism and its leaders; Cromwell, Milton, Baxter, Bunyan. Edinb. 1861. D.   **922.2:6**

Lives, The, of dr. E: Pocock, the celebrated orientalist, by dr. Twells; of dr. Zachary Pearce, bishop of Rochester and of dr. T: Newton, bishop of Bristol, by themselves; and of the rev. Philip Skelton by mr. Burdy. Lond. 1816. 2 v. O.   **922.2:8**

Grant, James. The metropolitan pulpit, or Sketches of the most popular preachers in London. Lond. 1839. 2 v. O.   **922.2+5**
Contents. V. 1. Miscellaneous observations. — Lately-deceased ministers: Dr. Waugh; Matthew Wilks; W: Howels; Rowland Hill; E: Irving.—The episcopal clergy-ministers of churches: T: Snow; J. T. Robinson; T: Dale; J: Harding; Dr. Croly.—The

episcopal clergy-assistants or lecturers: J. F. Denham; Hobart Seymour; Watts Wilkinson.—The episcopal clergy-ministers of chapels: Sanderson Robins; Dr. Dillon; H. H. Beamish. **2.** The episcopal clergy-ministers of chapels: H: Melvill; T. J. Judkin; Baptist W. Noel; T: Mortimer; James Hambleton.—Ministers of the scotch church: Dr. Brown; J: Cumming; Dr. Crombie.—Ministers of the scotch secession church: Robert Redpath; T: Archer; J: Young; Alex. Fletcher.—Independent ministers: Dr. Morison; Dr. Leifchild; Dr. Collyer; Caleb Morris; James Sherman; J: Burnet; J: Blackburn; Dr. Bennett; J: Clayton; T: Binney; Andrew Reed; J. Fletcher.—Baptist ministers: J: Stevens; G: Coomb; W: Overbury; James Harrington Evans; E: Steane; J: Howard Hinton; C. Stovel; F. A. Cox.—Ministers of various denominations: Jabez Bunting; T: Jackson; J. Dorman; G: Abrahams; Robert Aitken.—Concluding remarks.

Walton, I: The lives of dr. John Donne, sir Henry Wotton, Richard Hooker, George Herbert and dr. Robert Sanderson ; with some account of the author and his writings by T: Zouch. New ed. with ill. notes. Bost. 1860. D.   **922.2 : 7**

Anderson, James. The ladies of the covenant; memoirs of distinguished scottish female characters, embracing the period of the covenant and the persecution. N. Y. 1851. D.   **922.2 : 1**
Contents. Introd.—Lady Anne Cunningham, marchioness of Hamilton.— Lady Boyd.— Elizabeth Melvill, lady Culross.—Lady Jane Campbell, viscountess of Kenmure.—Lady Margaret Douglas, marchioness of Argyll.—Mrs. James Guthrie.—Mrs. James Durham. —Mrs. J: Carstairs.—Lady Anne, duchess of Hamilton.— Mrs. W: Veitch.— Mrs. J: Livingstone.— Lady Anne Lindsay, duchess of Rothes.—Lady Mary Johnston, countess of Crawford.—Barbara Cunningham, lady Caldwell.— Lady Colvill.— Catherine Rigg, lady Cavers.— Isabel Alison.— Marion Harvey.— Helen Johnston, lady Graden.— Lilias Dunbar, mrs. Campbell.—Margaret M'Lauchlan and Margaret Wilson.— Lady Anne Mackenzie, countess of Balcarres, afterward countess of Argyll.—Henrietta Lindsay, lady Campbell of Auchinbreck. — Grisell Hume, lady Baillie of Jerviswood.— Lady Catharine Hamilton, duchess of Atholl.—App.

Roman-catholic.

[Instructive biography.] Lond. 1842. S.   **922.22 : 5**
Contents. William of Wykeham, by J: Chandler.— Histories of the bishops of the ancient church.— Stories from Bede, with a sketch of his life.—Life of G: Herbert.

Milman, H: Hart. Life of Thomas à Becket. N. Y. 1860. S.   **922.22 : 4**

Pius *a Sp. Sancto, Father.* Life of father Ignatius of St. Paul, passionist; comp. chiefly from his autobiogr., journal and letters. Dublin. 1866. D.   **922.22 : 3**

Maguire, J: Francis. Father Mathew ; a biography. N. Y. 1864. D.   **922.22 : 1**

Newman, J: H: Apologia pro vita sua ; a reply to a pamphlet entitled "What, then, does dr. Newman mean?" 3d ed. N. Y. 1865. O.   **922.22 : 2**

Protestant-episcopal.

Stanley, Arthur Penrhyn. Life and correspondence of T: Arnold. 3d amer. ed. Bost. 1860. 2 v. D.   **922.23 : 1**

Worboise, Emma Jane. Life of T: Arnold. 2d ed. Lond. 1865. S.   **922.23 : 2**

Atterbury, Francis. Memoirs and correspondence ; with notices of his distinguished contemporaries, comp., chiefly from the Atterbury and Stuart papers by Folkestone Williams. Lond. 1869. 2 v. in 1. O.   **922.23 : 29**

Southey, Robert *and* C: Cuthbert. Life of dr. Bell; comprising the history of the rise and progress of the system of mutual tuition. Lond. 1844. 3 v. O.   **922.23 : 3**

Bickersteth, J: Lang. Memoir ; with a pref. by J. Bickersteth. Lond. *n. d.* T.   **922.23 : 4**

Brett, Robert. The doctrine of the cross, as exhibited in the faith and patience of a humble follower of Christ. [*Anon.*] Lond. 1843. S.   **922.23 : 5**

Cartwright, T: Diary, aug. 1686 to oct. 1687; now first printed from the original ms. in the possession of Joseph Hunter. [Camden soc. pub. no. 22.] Lond. 1843. O.   **922.23 : 26**

Fuller, Morris. The "life, times and writings" of Thomas Fuller, the church historian, 1608-1661. Lond. 1884. 2 v. D.   **922.23 : 31**

Gobat, S: S: Gobat, of Jerusalem, his life and work ; a biogr. sketch drawn chiefly from his own journals ; pref. by the earl of Shaftesbury. Portr. and ill. N. Y. 1885. D.   **922.23 : 33**

Haslam, W: From death unto life, or Twenty years of my ministry. N. Y. 1880. D.   **922.23 : 6**

Robinson, T: Last days of bishop Heber. N. Y. 1831. D.   **922.23 : 7**

Hodgson, James T. Memoir of the rev. Francis Hodgson, scholar, poet, and divine ; with numerous letters from lord Byron and others, by his son. Lond. 1878. 2 v. D.   **922.23 : 8**

Housman, Robert Fletcher. Life and remains of Robert Housman ; slightly abr. N. Y. 1846. D.   **922.23 : 9**

Morton, J: N: Life of archbishop Laud. Bost. 1864. D.   **922.23 : 10**

Caswall, H: The martyr of the Pongas ; a memoir of Hamble James Leacock. N. Y. 1857. D.   **922.23 : 11**

Bell, C: Dent. Henry Martyn. [Heroes of christian history.] N. Y. 1881. D.   **922.23 : 28**

Sargent, J: Memoir of H: Martyn. From the 10th Lond. ed. Phila. 1831. D.   **922.23 : 12**

Maurice, F:, *ed.* The life of F: Denison Maurice, chiefly told in his own letters, ed. by his son. N. Y. 1884. 2 v. D.   **922.23 : 27**

Mozley, T: Reminiscences, chiefly of Oriel college and the Oxford movement. Bost. 1882. 2 v. D.   **922.23 : 13**

Pattison, M: Memoirs. Lond. 1885. D.   **922.23 : 34**

Cornell, W: Mason. Life of Robert Raikes. Bost. *n. d.* T.   **922.23 : 23**

Reed, Andrew. Martha ; a memorial of an only and beloved sister. N. Y. 1835. D.   **922.23 : 14**

Grimshawe, T. S. Memoir of Leigh Richmond; abr. by W: Patton. N. Y. 1829. D.   **922.23 : 15**

Ridley, Glocester. The life of Nicholas Ridley, sometime bp. of London ; showing the plan and progress of the reformation, in which he was a principal instrument and suffered martyrdom for it in the reign of queen Mary. Lond. 1763. Q.   **922.23 : R19**

Brooke, Stopford A: Life and letters of F: W. R o b e r t s o n. Bost. 1865. 2 v. D.
                922.23 : 16

Holland, Saba, *born* Smith, *lady*. A memoir of Sydney S m i t h by his daughter; with a selection from his letters, ed. by mrs. Austin. N. Y. 1855. 2 v. D.   **922.23 : 17**
— *Same.* Lond. *n. d.* D.   **922.23 : 17**
— *Same.* N. Y. 1880. Q.   **922.23+17**

Reid, Stuart J. A sketch of the life and times of Sydney Smith; based on family documents and recollections of personal friends. Portr. and ill. N. Y. 1885 [1884]. O.   **922.23 : 30**

Bradley, G: Granville. Recollections of Arthur Penrhyn S t a n l e y, late dean of Westminster; three lectures del. in Edinb. nov. 1882. N. Y. 1883. D.   **922.23 : 24**

Oliver, Grace Atkinson, *born* Little, *formerly mrs.* Ellis. Arthur Penrhyn Stanley; his life, work and teachings. Portr. Bost. 1885. D.   **922.23 : 32**

Heber, Reginald. Life of Jeremy T a y l o r; with a critical examination of his writings. Hartford. 1832. D.   **922.23 : 18**

Douglas, *Mrs.* Stair. The life, and selections from the correspondence of W: W h e w e l l, late master of Trinity college, Cambridge. Portr. Lond. 1881. O.   **922.23 : 20**

Ashwell, A. R., *and* Reginald G. **Wilberforce.** Life of Samuel W i l b e r f o r c e, lord bp. of Oxford, and afterward of Winchester; with selections from his diaries and correspondence, abr. from the eng. ed. Ill. N. Y. 1883. O.   **922.23 : 25**

Stoughton, J: William W i l b e r f o r c e. (Heroes of christian history). N. Y. 1880. D.
                922.23 : 21

Bateman, Josiah. The life of Daniel W i l s o n, bp. of Calcutta. Ill. Bost. 1860. O.
                922.23+22

Presbyterian.

Boyle, G: D: Richard B a x t e r. (Heroes of christian history). N. Y. 1884. D.
                922.24 : 17

Carlyle, Alexander. Autobiography; containing memorials of the men and events of his time. Bost. 1861. D.   **922.24 : 1**

Anderson, J: Reminiscences of T: C h a l m e r s. Edinb. 1851. D.   **922.24 : 2**

Fraser, Donald. T: Chalmers. (Heroes of christian history). N. Y. 1882. D.
                922.24 : 3

Hanna, W: Memoirs of the life and writings of T: Chalmers by his son-in-law. N. Y. 1855. 3 v. D.   **922.24 : 4**

Harsha, D: Addison. Life of Philip D o d d r i d g e; with notices of some of his contemporaries and specimens of his style. Albany. 1865. O.   **922.24 : 5**

Stanford, C: Philip Doddridge. (Heroes of christian history). N. Y. 1880. D.
                922.24 : 6

Lundie, *Mrs.* —. Memoir of Mary Lundie D u n c a n; recollections of a daughter by her mother, abr. N. Y. *n. d.* S.   **922.24 : 7**

Oliphant, Margaret O., *born* Wilson. The life of Edward I r v i n g, minister of the national scotch church, London; ill. by his journals and corresp. N. Y. 1862. O.
                922.24+8

Henry, Philip. Diaries and letters; ed. by Matthew H: Lee. Lond. 1882. D.
                922.24 : 21

McCrie, T: Life of J: K n o x, containing illustrations of the history of the reformation in Scotland; with biogr. notices of the principal reformers, and sketches of the progress of literature in Scotland during a great part of the 16th century; subjoined, an app., consisting of letters and other papers hitherto unpub. 2d ed., corr. and enl. Edinb. 1813. 2 v. O.   **922.24 : 9**

Little, J: Conversion and death-bed experience of mrs. Jessie L i t t l e. N. Y. *n. d.* S.
                922.24 : 10

Macleod, Norman. The earnest student; memorials of J: M a c k i n t o s h. Lond. 1863. D.   **922.24 : 11**

Macleod, Donald. Memoir of Norman M a c l e o d. N. Y. 1877. 2 v. in 1. O.
                922.24 : 12

Scott, J: Life of T: S c o t t; incl. a narrative drawn up by himself and copious extracts of his letters. Phila. 1823. O. **922.24 : 13**

Taylor, I: Memoirs and corresp. of Jane T a y l o r. N. Y. 1847. S.   **922.24 : 14**

Buddensieg, Rudolf. John W i c l i f, patriot and reformer; life and writings. Quincentenary ed. Lond. 1884. T.   **922.24 : 18**

Burrows, Montagu. Wiclif's place in history; three lectures del. before the university of Oxford in 1881. New and rev. ed. Lond. 1884. D.   **922.24 : 20**

Coxe, Margaret. Life of Wycliffe. Columbus, Ohio. 1840. S.   **922.24 : 16**

LeBas, C: Webb. Life of Wyclif. N. Y. 1832. S.   **922.24 : 15**

Loserth, J: Wiclif and Hus. From the german, tr. by M. J. Evans. Lond. 1884. O.
                922.24 : 19

Wilson, J: Laird. J: Wycliffe, patriot and reformer, "the morning star of the reformation"; a biogr. N. Y. 1884. D.
                922.24 : 23

Baptist.

Froude, James Anthony. B u n y a n. [Eng. men of letters]. N. Y. 1880. D. **922.26 : 1**

Carey, Eustace. Memoir of W: C a r e y; with an introd. essay by Francis Wayland. Bost. 1836. D.   **922.26 : 2**

Culross, James. W: Carey. (Heroes of christian history). N. Y. 1882. D. **922.26 : 8**

Phillips, D: Memoir of the life, labors and extensive usefulness of Christmas E v a n s; extracted from the Welsh memoir. N. Y. 1843. D.   **922.26 : 3**

Ryland, Jonathan E:, *ed.* Life and corresp. of J: F o s t e r; with notices of mr. Foster as a preacher and a companion by J: Sheppard. Bost. 1860. 2 v. in 1. D. **922.26 : 4**

Morris, J: Williams. Memoirs of the life and writings of Andrew F u l l e r. 1st amer. ed., ed. by Rufus Babcock, jr. Bost. 1830. O.   **922.26 : 5**

Hood, Edwin Paxton. Robert H a l l. (Heroes of christian history). N. Y. 1881. D.
                922.26 : 6

Sketch of the life and ministry of C: H. S p u r g e o n; from original documents, incl. anecdotes and incidents of travel, biogr. notices of former pastors, historical sketch

of Park-st. chapel and an outline of mr.
Spurgeon's articles of faith. N. Y. 1858. D.
                                      922.26:7

Methodist.

Knight, Helen C., *comp.* Lady Huntington and
her friends, or The revival of the work of
God in the days of Wesley, Whitefield, Romaine, Venn and others in the last century. N. Y. [1853]. D.   **922.27:2**
Clarke, Adam. An account of the infancy, religious and literary life of Adam C l a r k e,
written by one who was intimately acquainted with him from his boyhood to
the 60th year of his age [by himself]; ed.
by J. B. B. Clarke. N. Y. 1833. 2 v. D.
                                      922.27:1
Adams, C: The poet preacher [C: W e s l e y];
a brief memorial. Ill. N. Y. *n. d.* S.
                                      922.27:4
Southey, Robert. The life of W e s l e y and rise
and progress of methodism; notes by S:
T. Coleridge and remarks on the life and
character of J: Wesley by Alexander Knox.
Ed. by C: Cuthbert Southey. 2d amer. ed.,
with notes, etc., by Daniel Curry. N. Y.
1858. 2 v. D.   **922.27:5**
Taylor, I: Wesley and methodism. N. Y. 1852.
D.   **922.27:7**
Watson, R: Life of J: Wesley. N. Y. 1831. D.
                                      922.27:6
Whitehead, J: Life of J: Wesley; collected
from his private papers and printed works,
and written at the request of his executors.
Prefixed, some account of his ancestors
and relations, with the life of C: Wesley.
collected from his private journal and
never before pub. The whole forming a
history of methodism in which the principles and economy of the methodists are
unfolded. Auburn. *n. d.* D.   **922.27:8**
Wesley, J: Journal. Lond. 1827. 4 v. in 2. O.
                                      922.27:3
Kirk, J: The mother of the Wesleys; a biogr.
Cinc. 1865. D.   **922.27:9**
Gillies, J: Memoirs and sermons of G: W h i t e ·
f i e l d. Rev. and corr. with add. and
impr., with an introd. by C. E. Stowe.
Phila. 1854. O.   **922.27+11**
Philip, Robert. Life and times of G: Whitefield.
N. Y. 1838. D.   **922.27:12**
Whitefield, G: Continuation of [his] journal
from his arrival at London to his depart-
ure from thence on his way to Georgia.
3d ed. Lond. 1739. O.   **922.27:10**

Quaker.

Bickley, A. C. G: Fox and the early quakers.
Lond. 1884. D.   **922.28:4**
Janney, S: M. The life of G: Fox; with disser-
tations on his views concerning the doc-
trines, testimonies and discipline of the
christian church. Phila. 1878. D.
                                      922.28:1
Account, An, of the life, ministry and travels of
that ancient servant of Jesus Christ, John
Richardson. Phila. 1867. D.   **922.28:2**
Woolman, J: Journal; with an introd. by J:
G. Whittier. Bost. 1882. D.   **922.28:3**

5. Other modern religious biogr.

German and Swiss.

Sister Augustine, an old catholic, superior of
the sisters of charity in St. Johannis hospital at Bonn. Authorized tr. from the
german Memorials of Amalie v. Lasaulx.
N. Y. 1881. D.   **922.3:1**
Montalembert, C: Forbes de Tryon, *comte* de.
Life of St. E l i z a b e t h of Hungary. Tr.
by Mary Hackett; introd. tr. by mrs. J.
Sadlier. N. Y. 1863. D.   **922.3:2**
Gillett, Ezra Hall. Life and times of J: H u s s,
or The bohemian reformation of the 15th
century. 2d ed. rev. Bost. 1864. 2 v. O.
                                      922.3:3
Mears, J: W. Heroes of Bohemia; Huss,
Jerome and Zisca. Phila. [1879]. D.
                                      922.3:4
Jung-Stilling, J: H: Autobiography. Tr. from
the german by S. Jackson. N. Y. 1844. O.
                                      922.3:11
Kettlewell, S: T h o m a s à K e m p i s and the
brothers of common life. N. Y. 1882. 2 v.
O.   **922.3:12**
Bunsen, Christian C: Josias *freiherr* v. Life of
Martin L u t h e r; with an estimate of
Luther's character and genius by T: Car-
lyle and an app. by sir W: Hamilton. N.
Y. 1861. T.   **922.3:5**
Froude, James Anthony. Luther; a short bio-
graphy. Repr. from the Contemporary re-
view. N. Y. 1884. D.   **922.3:17**
Köstlin, Julius. Life of Luther. From the
germ. N. Y. 1883. O.   **922.3:13**
Michelet, Jules. Life of Martin Luther, gath-
ered from his own writings. Tr. by G. H.
Smith. N. Y. 1846. D.   **922.3:6**
Rae, J: Martin Luther; student, monk, reformer. Ill. Lond. 1884. O. **922.3:19**
Rein, W: The life of Martin Luther. N. Y.
[1883]. D.   **922.3:19**
Schmidt, Ferdinand. Martin Luther; ein le-
bensbild. Neue ausg. Berlin. [1880]. S.
                                      922.3:23
Seiss, Joseph A: Luther and the reformation;
the life-springs of our liberties. Phila.
[1884]. D.   **922.3:16**
Tischer, J: F: W: Life of Martin Luther. Added
a selection from the most celebrated sermons of Luther. [Phila.] 1841. O.
                                      922.3:7
Treadwell, J: H. Martin Luther and his work.
[New Plutarch ser.] N. Y. 1881. S.
                                      922.3:8
Whately, E. Jane. *ed.* The story of Martin
Luther. N. Y. 1867. S.   **922.3:9**
Mayhew, H: The boyhood of Martin Luther,
or The sufferings of the heroic little beggar-
boy who afterwards became the great
german reformer. Ill. N. Y. 1864. S.
                                    x 922.3:14
Ledderhose, C: F: Life of Philip M e l a n c h-
t h o n. Tr. from the germ. by G. F. Krotel.
Phila. 1855. D.   **922.3:10**
Schmidt, C: W: Adolf. Philipp Melanchthon;
leben und ausgewählte schriften. Elberfeld. 1861. O.   **922.3+22**

x denotes books specially adapted for children.

Bost, J: Augustin. Letters and biography of Felix Neff. Tr. from the french by Margaret Anne Wyatt. Lond. 1843. D.   **922.5 : 16**

Gilly, W: Stephen. Memoir of Felix Neff. Bost. 1832. D.   **922.5 : 13**

Schenkel, Daniel. F: Schleiermacher, ein lebens- und charakterbild; zur erinnerung an den 21. nov. 1768 für das deutsche volk bearb. Elberfeld. 1868. O.   **922.3+21**

Zeisberger, D: Diary among the indians of Ohio. Tr. from the original german and ed. by Eugene F. Bliss. Cinc. 1885. 2 v. O.   **922.3+20**

Grob, J: The life of Ulric Zwingli. From the germ. N. Y. 1883. D.   **922.5 : 22**

Swedish.

Worcester, B: The life and mission of Emanuel Swedenborg. Bost. 1883. D. **922.5 : 19**

French.

Wight, Orlando Williams. Lives and letters of Abelard and Heloise. N. Y. 1861. S.   **922.4 : 1**

Richardson, Abby, *born* Sage, *formerly mrs.* McFarland, *ed.* Abelard and Heloise, a mediæval romance; with the letters of Heloise. Bost. 1884 [1883]. S. **922.4 : 11**

Ratisbonne, Marie Théodore. Life and times of St. Bernard. Tr. from the french; with a pref. by H: E: Manning. N. Y. 1863. D.   **922.4 : 2**

James, J: Angell. Memoir of Clementine Cuvier [by M: Wilks], with reflections by J: A. James. N. Y. *n. d.* S.   **922.4 : 3**

Digby, Kenelm H: The chapel of St. John. or A life of faith in the 19th century [Jane Mary Digby]. Lond. 1861. D. **922.4 : 4**

Bausset, L: François de. Life of Fénelon. Tr. from the french by W: Mudford. Lond. 1810. 2 v. O.   **922.4 : 5**

Butler, C: Life of Fénelon. Balt. 1811. S.   **922.4 : 6**

Upham, T: C. Life and religious opinions and experience of mme. Guyon; with some account of the personal history and religious opinions of Fenelon. N. Y. 1849. 2 v. D.   **922.4 : 7**

Lear, H. L. Sidney. Henri Dominique Lacordaire; a biogr. sketch. Lond. 1883. D.   **922.4 : 9**

Montalembert, C: Forbes de Tryon, *comte de.* Memoir of the abbé Lacordaire. Authorized tr. Lond. 1863. O.   **922.4 : 8**

Marteilhe, J: The huguenot galley-slave; the autobiogr. of a french protestant condemned to the galleys for the sake of his religion. Tr. from the french. N. Y. 1867. D.   **922.4 : 10**

Monod, Sarah. Life and letters of Adolphe Monod, by one of his daughters. [*Anon.*] Authorised tr. abr. from the original. Lond. 1885. D.   **922.4 : 12**

Italian and spanish.

Artaud de Montor, Alexis François. The lives and times of the roman pontiffs from St. Peter to Pius IX. Tr. from the french and ed. by dr. Neligan. N. Y. [1865]. O.   **922.5+2**

Villemain, Abel François. Life of Gregory VII; preceded by a sketch of the papacy to the 11th century. Tr. by James Baber Brockley. Lond. 1874. 2 v. O.   **922.5 : 21**

Roscoe, W: Life and pontificate of Leo X. 5th ed. rev. by T: Roscoe. Lond. 1846. 2 v. D.   **922.5 : 9**

Hübner, Joseph Alexander *freiherr* v. The life and times of Sixtus V; from unpub. diplomatic corresp. in the state archives of Vatican, Simancas, Venice, Paris, Vienna and Florence. Tr. from the original french by Hubert E. H. Jerningham. Lond. 1872. 2 v. O.   **922.5 : 1**

Clement XIV. Interesting letters. Prefixed, anecdotes of his life. Tr. from the french ed. 5th ed. Lond. 1781. 2 v. S. **922.5 : 6**

Wiseman, N: Patrice Stephen. Recollections of the last four popes and of Rome in their times. Bost. 1858. D.   **922.5 : 3**
Contents. Pius VII. — Leo XII. — Pius VIII. — Gregory XVI.

Hassard, J: R. G. Life of Pius IX. N. Y. 1878. S.   **922.5 : 14**

Legge, Alfred Owen. Pius IX; the story of his life to the restoration in 1850; with glimpses at the national movement in Italy. Lond. 1875. 2 v. O.   **922.5 : 23**

Hahn-Hahn, Ida Marie Louise Sophie Friederike Gustave *gräfin.* Vier lebensbilder: ein papst, ein bishof, ein priester, ein jesuit. Mainz. 1861. D.   **922.2 : 5**
Contents, see Deutscher katalog, p. 48.

Upham, T: Cogswell. Life of mme. Catherine Adorna; incl. some leading facts and traits in her religious experience, together with explanations and remarks tending to ill. the doctrine of holiness. 2d ed. Bost. 1847. S.   **922.5 : 4**

Fullerton, Georgiana Charlotte *lady.* Life of St. Frances of Rome, [also] Of blessed Lucy of Narni, of Dominica of Paradiso, and of Anne de Montmorency; with an introd. essay on the miraculous life of the saints, by J. M. Capes. N. Y. *n. d.* D.   **922.5 : 7**

Bartoli, Daniel. History of the life and institute of St. Ignatius de Loyola. Tr. by the author of Life in Mexico. N. Y. 1856. 2 v. D.   **922.5 : 8**

Helps, *Sir* Arthur. The life of Las Casas, the apostle of the Indies. 3d ed. Lond. 1873. D.   **922.5 : 17**

Ripa, Matteo. Memoirs during 13 years' residence at the court of Peking in the service of the emperor of China; with an account of the foundation of the college for the education of young chinese at Naples. Selected and tr. from the italian by Fortunato Prandi. N. Y. 1846. D.   **922.5 : 15**

Alexander, Frances, (*Francesca*). The story of Ida; epitaph on an etrurian tomb, ed. with a pref. by J: Ruskin. Portr. N. Y. 1883. D.   **922.5 : 20**

Bigelow, J: Molinos, the quietist. N. Y. 1882. D.   **922.5 : 18**

Mohammedan.

Bush, G: Life of Mohammed. N. Y. 1847. S.   **922.5 : 10**

Gibbon, E: Life of Mohammed. With notes by H: Hart Milman and W: Smith. [Biogr. series.] Bost. 1881. T.   **922.5 : 12**

Muir, *Sir* W: Mahomet and islam; a sketch of the prophet's life from original sources and a brief outline of his religion. Map and ill. Lond. [1885]. D.   **922.5 : 25**

Irving, Washington. Mahomet and his successors. N. Y. 1850. 2 v. D.   **922.5 : 11**
— *Same. In his* Works.   **820.1 : 13 v10**
— *Same. In his* Works.   **820.1 : P11 v14,15**

6. Ancient religious biogr.

Spring, Gardiner. The contrast between good and bad men, illustrated by the biography and truths of the Bible. N. Y. 1855. 2 v. D.   **922.6 : 17**

Old testament.

Blunt, H: Lectures on the history of Abraham, Jacob and Elisha. Phila. 1851. D.   **922.6 : 1**

Cumming, J: The last of the patriarchs, or Lessons chiefly from the life of Joseph. Phila. 1856. D.   **922.6 : 4**

Schupp, Ottokar. Joseph in Ägypten; ein lebensbild der deutschen jugend und dem volke dargestellt. Wiesbaden. 1883. S.   **922.6 : 23**

Taylor, W. Mackergo. Moses, the law-giver. N. Y. 1879. D.   **922.6 : 5**
— David, king of Israel; his life and its lessons. N. Y. 1883. Q.   **922.6+20**

Gallaudet, T: H. Scripture biography for the young; with critical ill. and practical remarks: David, incl. the life of Joseph. N. Y. *n. d.* S.   **922.6 : 21**

Krummacher, F: W: Elijah the Tishbite. Tr. from the germ. N. Y. [1838]. S.   **922.6 : 2**
— Elisha. Tr. from the germ. Phila. 1840. D.   **922.6 : 3**

New testament.

(For the life of Christ, see col. 93-94.)

Adams, Nehemiah. The friends of Christ in the New testament. Bost. 1864. D.   **922.6 : 9**

Baldwin, G: C. Representative men of the New testament. N. Y. 1860. D.   **922.6 : 10**
Contents. John the Baptist. — Herod. — Peter. — Judas.—John.—Thomas.—Nicodemus.—Ananias.— Stephen.—The nameless moral young man.—Agrippa. —The jailor.—Paul.

Chapin, Edwin Hubbell. Characters in the gospels, illustrating phases of character at the present day. N. Y. 1852. D.   **922.6 : 12**

Charles, Elizabeth. Mary, the handmaid of the Lord. [*Anon.*] N. Y. 1865. D. **922.6 : 18**

Renan, Joseph Ernest. The apostles. Tr. from the original french. [Origins of christianity, 2.] N. Y. 1866. D.   **922.6 : 13**
— Saint Paul. Tr. from the original french by Ingersoll Lockwood. [Origins of christianity, 3.] N. Y. 1869. D.   **922.6 : 7**

Conybeare, W: J:. *and* J: Saul **Howson.** The life and epistles of St. Paul. 7th ed. N. Y. 1864. 2 v. O.   **922.6+6**

Farrar, F: W: The life and work of St. Paul. N. Y. 1880. O.   **922.6 : 22**

Blunt, H: Lectures on the history of St. Paul and St. Peter. 3d amer. from the 7th Lond. ed. Phila. 1851. D.   **922.6 : 8**

Early christians.

Cave, W: Biographia ecclesiastica, or The lives of the most eminent fathers of the christian church, who flourished in the first four centuries, and part of the fifth; with a discourse concerning the state of religion during those ages. [*Anon.*] Portr. Lond. 1704. 2 v. in 1. D.   **922.6 : 11**
Contents. V. 1. S. Stephen.—Philip.—Timothy.— Titus.– Dionysius.—Clement.—Simeon.—Ignatius.— Polycarp.—Quadratus.—Justin.—Melito.—Theophilus.—Irenæus.—Pantæus.—Clemens.—Tertullian. —Origen.—Babylas.—Cyprian.—Gregory.—Dionysius. —Eusebius.—S. Athanasius. 2. Hilary.—Basil.— Gregory Nazianzen.—Ambrose.—Epiphanius.— Chrysostom.—Jerom.—Augustin.—State of religion during the first ages of christianity.

Wilson, W: The popular preachers of the ancient church; their lives, their manner and their work. Ill. Lond. [1859]. S.   **922.6 : 16**
Contents. The christian philanthropist. Cyprian of Carthage.—The faithful minister, Ambrose of Milan. —The homely preacher, Augustine of Hippo.—The fearless bishop, Basil the great.—The genial theologian, Gregory Nazianzen.—The "golden mouthed" orator, Chrysostom of Byzantium.

Kingsley, C: The hermits. Ill. [Works, v. 12.] N. Y. 1882. D.   **922.6 : 19**

Augustinus, Aurelius, *St.* St. Augustin's confessions, or Praises of God, in 10 books. Newly tr. from the original latin. N. Y. *n. d.* S.   **922.6 : 14**

Schaff, Philip. Life and labors of St. Augustine. Tr. from the germ. by T. C. Porter. N. Y. 1854. D.   **922.6 : 15**

3. Sociology — a, Government.

1. Presidents of the U. S.

Collective biogr.

Abbott, J: Stevens Cabot. Lives of the presidents of the U. S. of America; a narrative of events in the career of each president; added, the centennial jubilee, showing the hundred years' progress of the republic. Ill. Bost. 1876. O.   **923.11 : 1**

Fiske, J: The presidents of America; a series of original steel engr. taken from paintings and photographs by distinguished artists in the possession of relatives and family friends, by H. W. Smith; with biogr. sketches and an introductory essay by J: Fiske. Bost. 1879. F.   **923.11 : R 61**

Individual biogr.

Abbott, J: Stevens Cabot. G: Washington, or Life in America 100 years ago. [Amer. pioneers and patriots.] N. Y. *n. d.* D.   **923.11 : 4**

Bancroft, Aaron. Life of Washington. Bost. 1860. 2 v. in 1. O.   **923.11 : 5**

Brown, E. E. Young folks' life of Washington. Ill. and portr. Bost. [1883]. D.
x **923.11 : 62**

Everett, E: Life of G: Washington. N. Y. 1860. D.
923.11 : 6

Girault, A. N. Vie de George Washington. Phila. 1836. S.   x **923.11 : 63**

Guizot, François P: Guillaume. Essay on the character and influence of Washington in the revolution of the U. S. of America. Tr. from the french. 2d ed. Bost. 1851. D.
923.11 : 7

Habberton, J: George Washington, 1732–1799. (Lives of amer. worthies.) N. Y. 1884. S.
923.11 : 64

Hyde, Anna M. The american boy's life of Washington. N. Y. *n. d.* D. x **923.11 : 51**

Irving, Washington. Life of George Washington. [Knickerbocker ed.] N. Y. *n. d.* 5 v. D.   **923.11 : 8**
— *Same.* N. Y. 1855–57. 4 v. O.   **923.11 : 8**
— *Same. In his* Works.   **820.1 : P11 v20–24**
— *Same, condensed.* Ill. N. Y. *n. d.* D.
923.11 : 57

Kirkland, Caroline Matilda, *(Mary Clavers).* Memoirs of Washington. Ill. N. Y. 1857. D.   **923.11 : 9**

Marshall, J: Life of G: Washington ; compiled under the inspection of the hon. Bushrod Washington, from original papers bequeathed to him by his deceased relative. 2d ed. rev. and corr. by the author. Phila. 1846. 2 v. O.   **923.11 : 10**

Oertel, Philip F: W:, *(W. O. v. Horn).* Der lebensgang George Washingtons, des begründers der freiheit der Vereinigten Staaten Nordamerika's ; der jugend und dem volke erzählt. 2te aufl., ill. Wiesbaden. 1871. S.   **923.11 : 72**

Paulding, James Kirke. A life of Washington. N. Y. 1845. 2 v. S.   **923.11 : 11**

Sparks, Jared. The life of G: Washington. Bost. 1843. O.   **923.11+12**

Washington, G: Diary from 1789 to 1791 ; embracing the opening of the first congress and his tours through New England, Long Island and the Southern states, together with his journal of a tour to the Ohio in 1753 ; ed. by Benson J. Lossing. N. Y. 1860. D.   **923.11 : 2**
— Political legacies ; annexed, an app. containing an account of his illness, death and the national tributes of respect paid to his memory, with a biogr. outline of his life and character. Phila. 1800. O. **923.11 : 3**
Contents, see Catalogue of the Boston athenæum, pt. 5, p. 3259.

Conkling, Margaret C. Memoirs of the mother and wife of Washington. 2d ed. rev. and enl. Auburn. 1850. S.   **923.11 : 15**

Morse, J: Torrey, *jr.* John Adams. (Amer. statesmen.) Bost. 1885 [1884]. S.
923.11 : 67
— Thomas Jefferson. (Amer. statesmen.) Bost. 1883. S.   **923.11 : 55**

Parton, James. Life of T: Jefferson. 1880. O.
923.11 : 16

Pierson, Hamilton Wilcox. Jefferson at Monticello ; private life from entirely new materials. N. Y. 1862. O   **923.11+17**

Randall, H: Stephens. Life of T: Jefferson. N. Y. 1858. 3 v. O.   **923.11 : 18**

x denotes books specially adapted for children.

Randolph, Sarah Nicholas. Domestic life of T: Jefferson ; comp. from family letters and reminiscences by his great granddaughter. N. Y. 1871. D.   **923.11 : 19**

Tucker, G: Life of T: Jefferson : with parts of his corresp. never before pub. and notices of his opinions on questions of civil government, national policy and constitutional law. Phila. 1837. 2 v. O.   **923.11+20**

Gay, Sydney Howard. James Madison. (Amer. statesmen.) Bost. 1884. S.   **923.11 : 65**

Rives, W: Cabell. History of the life and times of James Madison. Bost. 1859, 1866. 2 v. O.   **923.11+21**

Gilman, Daniel Coit. James Monroe in his relations to the public service during half a century, 1776–1826. (Amer. statesmen.) Bost. 1883. S.   **923.11 : 56**

Adams, J: Quincy. Memoirs, comprising portions of his diary from 1795 to 1848 ; ed. by C: Francis Adams. Phila. 1874–77. 12 v. O.   **923.11+22**

Morse, J: Torrey, *jr* John Quincy Adams. (Amer. statesmen.) Bost. 1882. D.
923.11 : 49

Quincy, Josiah. Memoir of the life of J: Quincy Adams. Bost. 1859. O.   **923.11+23**

Seward, W: H: Life and public services of J: Quincy Adams ; with the eulogy del. before the legislature of N. Y. Auburn. 1849. D.
923.11 : 24

Cobbett, W: Life of Andrew Jackson. N. Y. 1834. S.   **923.11 : 25**

Frost, J: Pictorial life of Andrew Jackson. Hartford. 1847. O.   **923.11 : 26**

Goodwin, Philo A. Biography of Andrew Jackson. Hartford. 1832. D.   **923.11 : 27**

Parton, James. Life of Andrew Jackson. N. Y. 1861. 3 v. O.   **923.11 : 28**

Sumner, W: Graham. Andrew Jackson, as a public man ; what he was, what chances he had and what he did with them. (Amer. statesmen.) Bost. 1882. D. **923.11 : 54**

Jenkins, J: Stilwell. James Knox Polk, and a history of his administration, embracing the annexation of Texas, the difficulties with Mexico, the settlement of the Oregon question, and other important events. Auburn. [1850]. D.   **923.11 : 29**

Hawthorne, Nathaniel. Life of Franklin Pierce. Bost. 1852. D.   **923.11 : 30**

Curtis, G: Ticknor. Life of James Buchanan. [Portr.] N. Y. 1883. 2 v. O. **923.11 : 59**

Arnold, I: Newton. History of Abraham Lincoln, and the overthrow of slavery. Chicago. 1866. O.   **923.11+31**
— The life of Abraham Lincoln. 3d ed. Portr. Chicago. 1885. O   **923.11 : 69**

Bartlett, D: W. Life and public services of Abraham Lincoln ; added, a biogr. sketch of Hannibal Hamlin. Portr. N. Y. 1860. D.   **923.11 : 32**

Foster, Ernest. Abraham Lincoln. (The world's workers.) [Portr.] Lond. 1885. D.
923.11 : 71

Hanaford, Phebe A. Abraham Lincoln ; his life and public services. [Famous americans, 2d ser.] Bost. [1881]. D.   **923.11 : 33**

Holland, Josiah Gilbert. Life of Abraham Lincoln. Springfield, Mass. 1866. O.
923.11 : 52

Leland, C: Godfrey. Abraham Lincoln and the abolition of slavery in the U. S. [New Plutarch.] N. Y. 1879. D.   **923.11 : 34**

Mudge, Zachariah A. The forest boy ; a sketch of the life of Abraham Lincoln for young people. Ill. N. Y. *n. d.* S.   **x 923.11 : 50**

Raymond, H: Jarvis. Life and public services of Abraham Lincoln ; together with his state papers, incl. his speeches, addresses, messages, letters and proclamations, and the closing scenes connected with his life and death. Added, anecdotes and personal reminiscences of pres. Lincoln by Frank B. Carpenter. Portr. and ill. N. Y. 1865. O.   **923.11+35**

Stoddard, W: Osborn. Abraham Lincoln ; the true story of a great life, showing the inner growth, special training and peculiar fitness of the man for his work. Portr. and ill. N. Y. 1884. O.   **923.11 : 66**

Sumner, C: The promises of the declaration of independence ; eulogy on Abraham Lincoln, del. before the municipal authorities of the city of Boston, june 1, 1865. Bost. 1865. O.   **923.11+36**

Morris, B. F., *comp.* Memorial record of the nation's tribute to Abraham Lincoln. Wash. 1865. O.   **923.11+37**

Grant, Ulysses Simpson. Personal memoirs ; v. 1. N. Y. 1885. O.   **923.11+70**

Badeau, Adam. Military history of Ulysses S. Grant, from april 1861 to april 1865. N. Y. 1868-81. 3 v. O.   **923.11+38**

Coppée, H: Grant and his campaigns; a military biography. N. Y. 1866. O.   **923.11 : 39**

Headley, Joel Tyler. Life and travels of gen. Grant. Ill. Springfield, Mass. 1879. O.   **923.11 : 40**

Headley, Phineas Camp. Fight it out on this line ; the life and deeds of gen. U. S. Grant. [Heroes of the rebellion.] Bost. 1883 [1882]. D.   **x 923.11 : 53**

Larke, Julian K. Gen. Grant and his campaigns. Portr. and ill. N. Y. 1864. D.   **923.11 : 41**

Howells, W: Dean. Sketch of the life and character of Rutherford B. Hayes. N. Y. 1876. D.   **923.11 : 42**

Balch, W: Ralston. The life of James Abram Garfield, late pres. of the U. S. Hartford. [1881]. D.   **923.11 : 43**

Blaine, James Gillespie. James A. Garfield ; memorial address pronounced in the hall of representatives, feb. 27, 1882, before the departments of the gov. of the U. S., in response to an invitation from the two houses of congress. Wash. 1882. Q.   **923.11+60**

Bundy, J. M. The life of gen. James A. Garfield. N. Y. 1880. S.   **923.11+44**

— The nation's hero: In memoriam; life of James Abram Garfield, 20th president of the U. S; with an account of the president's death and funeral obsequies. N. Y. 1881. D.   **923.11 : 45**

Gilmore, James R., (*Edmund Kirke*). The life of James A. Garfield ; with extracts from his speeches by Edmund Kirke. N. Y. 1880. Q.   **923.11+46**

Hinsdale, Burt A. President Garfield and education ; Hiram college memorial. Bost. 1882 [1881]. D.   **923.11 : 47**

Hoar, G: F. Eulogy upon the life, character and public services of James Abram Garfield ; del. at the invitation of the city council of Worcester, Mass., in Mechanics' hall. dec. 30, 1881. Worcester. 1881. O.   **923.11 : 58**

Thayer, W: Makepeace. From log-cabin to the White House ; life of James A. Garfield, boyhood, youth, manhood, assassination, death, funeral. Bost. 1881. D.   **x 923.11 : 48**

King, Pendleton. Life and public services of Grover Cleveland. Portr. N. Y. 1884. S.   **923.12 : 101**

2. Royalty in general.

Lamb, *Lady* —. Warrior kings, from Charlemagne to Frederick the great. Ill. N. Y. 1883 [1882]. D.   **923 : 27**
Contents. Charlemagne.—William the conqueror.—Frederick Barbarossa.—Richard Coeur de Lion.—Edward I. — Robert Bruce.—Henry V. — Francis I.—Henry IV. — Gustavus Adolphus. — Charles XII of Sweden. — Frederic the great.

Jameson, Anna, *born* Murphy. Memoirs of celebrated female sovereigns. N. Y. 1845. 2 v. S.   **923 : 8**
Contents. V. 1. Semiramis.—Cleopatra.—Zenobia.—Joanna I. — Joanna II. — Isabella of Castile.—Mary, queen of Scots.—Elizabeth. 2. Christina.—Anne.—Maria Theresa.—Catherine.

Ingram, J: H. Claimants to royalty. Lond. 1882. O.   **923 : 5**
Contents. Introd.—The false Smerdis of Persia.—The false Antiochus of Syria.—The false Alexander Balas of Syria.—The false Philip of Macedon.—The false Alexander of Jerusalem.—The false Nero of Rome.—The false Clotaire II of France.—The false Clovis III of France.—The false Suatocoplus of Moravia.—The false Henry V of Germany.—The false Alexis, emperor of the east.—The false Baldwin of Flanders.—The false Frederick II of Germany. — The The false Voldemar II of Brandenburg. — The false Richard II of England.—The false Mustapha of Turkey. — The false Edward VI of England. — The false Richard IV of England. — The false Mustapha II of Turkey.—The false Sebastian of Portugal.—The false Demetrius of Russia. — The false Demetrius the younger of Russia.—The false Zaga Christ of Abyssinia.—The false Ibrahim of Turkey.—The false Mahomet Bey of Turkey.—The false Hercules D'Este of Modena.—The false Charlotte of Russia.— The false Peter III of Russia.—The false herditary prince of Baden.—The false Dauphins.—The false princess of Cumberland.—The false counts of Albany.

Doran, J: Monarchs retired from business. N. Y. 1857. 2 v. D.   **923 : 26**
Contents. V. 1. The king. — Of some scripture kings and eastern monarchs.—Of some sovereigns of the olden time.—The canonized ex-kings.—*Britain*: Dethroned british and saxon kings; Deposed kings from the conquest to James II; James II at St. Germains; Deposed monarchs of Scotland; Ireland; Wales and Mann.— *France*: The Merovingian race and the "lazy kings"; The Carlovingians and Charles the fat; The house of Capet and Louis the saint; King John in the Savoy; The Bourbons and Charles X; Louis Philippe.—*Corsica*: Theodore of Corsica; A family of kings. — *Holland*: William Frederick, or all for love.—*The German empire*: Charles the fat; Henry IV; Charles V; Ferdinand I of Austria.—*Bohemia*: The winter king.—*Hungary*: The four deposed kings of Hungary.—*Bavaria*: Ludwig the lover.—*Poland*: The early abdications; John Casimir V; Stanislaus Leczinski; Stanislaus Poniatowski. 2. *Rome*: Incidents in the lives of retired monarchs down to the death of Valerian; Diocletian; Maximian to Romulus Augustus.— *The eastern empire*: Grave or cloister; The Byzantine cesars of the iconoclastic period; The Basilian dynasty; Monarchs among the monks; The Comneni; More tenants for Studion; The Baldwins; The most christian king; The papal dynasty.—The three Pii.—*Russia*: The czars; Ivan VI.—*Sardinia*: Victor Amadeus I;

---

x denotes books specially adapted for children.

Three crownless kings. — *Scandinavia*: Denmark, Eric IX; Christian II; Sweden, The story of Eric XIV, Christina, Gustavus IV.—*Spain*: Preliminary remarks; Philip V; Charles IV.—*Portugal*: Historic sketch; Sancho II; Alphonso VI.—*Turkey*: Historic sketch; The two Bajazets.—Conclusion.

Stern, Adolf. Vier titularkönige im 18. jahrhundert. Dresden. 1860. D.   **923:18**
Contents, see Deutscher katalog, p. 44.

3. Great Britain.

Kings and "protectors".

Yonge, Charlotte Mary. Kings of England; a history for young children. [*Anon.*] Lond. 1882. T.   **x 923.21:43**
Strickland, Agnes. Lives of the bachelor kings of England. Lond. 1861. D.   **923.21:55**
Contents. William Rufus. — Edward V. — Edward VI.—App.
Abbott, Jacob. History of Alfred of England. Ill. N. Y. *n. d.* S.   **923.21:1**
Hughes, T: Alfred the great. New ed. Lond. 1874. D.   **923.21:2**
Pauli, G: Reinhold. The life of Alfred the great. Tr. from the german; appended, Alfred's anglo-saxon version of Orosius, with a literal eng. tr. and an anglo-saxon alphabet and glossary by B. Thorpe. Lond. 1853. D.   **923.21:59**
Abbott, Jacob. History of William the conqueror. Ill. N. Y. *n. d.* S.   **923.21:3**
Roscoe, T: Life of William the conqueror. Now first pub. from official records and other authentic documents. Phila. 1846. D.   **923.21:4**
Abbott, Jacob. History of king Richard I of England. Ill. N. Y. *n. d.* S.   **923.21:5**
James, G: Payne Rainsford. History of the life of Richard Coeur-de-lion. New ed. Lond. 1854. 2 v. D.   **923.21:6**
Abbott, Jacob. History of king Richard II of England. Ill. N. Y. 1877. S.   **923.21:7**
— History of king Richard III of England. Ill. N. Y. *n. d.* S.   **923.21:8**
Halsted, Caroline Amelia. Richard III, as duke of Gloucester and king of England. Phila. 1844. O.   **923.21:9**
Abbott, Jacob. History of king Charles I of England. Ill. N. Y. *n. d.* S.   **923.21:12**
Hawks, Francis Lister. Life of Oliver Cromwell. *T. p. w.* [N. Y. 1857]. S.   **923.21:15**
Headley, Joel Tyler. Life of Oliver Cromwell. N. Y. 1848. D.   **923.21:16**
Hood, Edwin Paxton. Oliver Cromwell; his life, times, battlefields and contemporaries. N. Y. 1883. D.   **923.21:49**
Lamartine, Alfonse Marie L: de. Life of Oliver Cromwell. [Biogr. series]. Bost. *n. d.* T.   **923.21:42**
Merle d'Aubigné, J: H: The protector, a vindication. N. Y. 1850. D.   **923.21:13**
Picton, James Allanson. Oliver Cromwell; the man and his mission. Portr. N. Y. [1883]. O.   **923.21:50**
Russell, Michael. Life of Oliver Cromwell. N. Y. 1844. 2 v. S.   **923.21:17**
Abbott, Jacob. History of king Charles II of England. Ill. N. Y. *n. d.* S. **923.21:19**
Barker, C: Character and anecdotes of Charles II. Lond. 1853. S. *With* **Cavendish, G:** Cardinal Wolsey.   *in* **923.22:51**

Croly, G: Life and times of George IV; with anecdotes of distinguished persons of the last fifty years. New ed. N. Y. 1846. S.   **923.21:21**
Fitzgerald, Percy. Life of George IV; incl. his letters and opinions, with a view of the men, manners, and politics of his reign. Ill. N. Y. 1881. O.   **923.21:22**
— *Same.* N. Y. 1881. Q.   **923.21+22**

Queens.

Hall, *Mrs.* Matthew. Lives of the queens of England before the norman conquest. Bost. 1859. O.   **923.21:25**
Contents. Cartismandua, queen of Cymbeline. — Boadicea. ' the warlike", queen of Arviragus. — Gwenissa the fair, second queen of Arviragus. — Julia "domina." empress of Severus.— Victoria, Viturgia and Humila, empresses of Bonosus and Proculus.—St. Helena, queen of Constantius Chlorus. —Cartandis, queen of Eugenius I.—Helena ap Eudda, empress of Maximus.— Rowena, second queen of Vortigern—Guenever I, II, III, queens of Arthur.— Bertha, queen of Etelbert.—Ethelburga "the silent." and Enfleda, queens of Edwin "the great" and Oswy.— St. Ebba, Quenburga surnamed "Bebba," and Saxburga, queens of Cwichelme, Kynigil and Cenwalch.—Ostrida and Werburga, queens of Ethelred and Ceolred.—Quenburga, Quenswitha and Alfleda, queens of Alfred, Penda and Peada.—Hereswytha, Sexburga, Etheldreda, Ermenberga and Ermenilda, queens of Anna, Ercombert, Egfrid and Wulphere.—Domneva, queen of Merowald.— Ethelburga and Fridogitha, queens of Ina and Ethelard.— Quendrida-Petronilla, queen of Offa "the proud." —Eadburga, Elfleda, queens of Bertric and Wimond. —Quendrida II.—Osburga and Ethelswrytha, queens of Ethelwulf and Burhred. — Judith of France, second queen of Ethelwulf.— Elswitha, queen of Alfred the great and Ethelfleda, "lady of Mercia."— Egwina, Elfleda, Edgifa and Elfgifa, queens of Edward "the elder" and Edmund "the pious."—Ethelgiva, queen of Edwy "the fair."—Elfrida, queen of Edgar "the peaceable."—Emma of Normandy, surnamed "the pearl," queen of Ethred "the unready" and Canute "the great."—Editha the "good," queen of Edward "the confessor." — Editha "the fair," queen of Harold II.

Strickland, Agnes. Lives of the queens of England, from the norman conquest. New ed. Lond. 1872–80. 6 v. D.   **923.21:26**
Contents. V. 1. Introd.— Matilda of Flanders.— Matilda of Scotland.—Adelicia of Louvaine.—Matilda of Boulogne.—Eleanora of Aquitaine.— Berengaria of Navarre.—Isabella of Angouleme.— Eleanor of Provence.— Eleanora of Castile. — Marguerite of France.—Isabella of France.—Philippa of Hainault.— Anne of Bohemia.—Isabella of Valois.—Joanna of Navarre.—Katherine of Valois.—Margaret of Anjou. 2. Elizabeth Woodville.—Anne of Warwick.—Elizabeth of York.—Katherine of Arragon.—Anne Boleyn.—Jane Seymour.—Anne of Cleves.—Katherine Howard.—Catherine Parr.—Mary. 3. Elizabeth. 4. Anne of Denmark.—Henrietta Maria.—Catharine of Braganza.— Mary Beatrice of Modena. 5. *Same, continued.*—Mary II. 6. *Same, continued.*—Anne.
— *Same.* Abridged by the author; rev. and ed. by Caroline G. Parker. [Students' historical series.] N. Y. 1873. D.   **923.21:27**
— The queens of England; abridged, adapted and continued by Rosalie Kaufman. (Young folks' history.) Ill. Bost. 1883 [1882]—1884. 3 v. S.   **x 923.21:48**
Contents. V. 1. Matilda of Flanders to Katherine Parr. 2. Mary I to Anne. 3. Sophia Dorothea of Zell to Victoria.
— Lives of the queens of Scotland and english princesses connected with the regal succession of Great Britain. N. Y. 1851–59. 8 v. D.   **923.21:35**
Contents. V. 1. Introd. pref.— Margaret Tudor, queen of James IV.—Magdalene of France, 1st queen

of James V.—Mary of Lorraine, 2d queen of James V. **2.** *Same, continued.* — Lady Margaret Douglas, countess of Lennox. **3-7.** Mary Stuart. **8.** Elizabeth Stuart, 1st princess royal of Great Britain. — Sophia, electress of Hanover.

Smith, J. P. Romantic incidents in the lives of the queens of England. [1st series.] N. Y. 1853. D.   **923.21 : 28**
Contents. Elizabeth Woodville.—Eleanora of Aquitaine.—Matilda of Flanders. —Matilda Atheling.

Doran, J: Lives of the queens of England of the house of Hanover. N. Y. 1865. 2 v. O.   **923.21 : 33**
Contents. V. 1. Sophia Dorothea of Zell, wife of George I.—Caroline Wilhelmina Dorothea, wife of George II. 2. Charlotte Sophia, wife of George III. —Caroline of Brunswick.

Abbott, Jacob. History of Margaret of Anjou. Ill. N. Y. n. d. S.   **923.21 : 29**

Hookham, Mary Ann. The life and times of Margaret of Anjou, queen of England and France, and of her father, René "the good", king of Sicily, Naples and Jerusalem ; with memoirs of the houses of Anjou. Portr. and ill. Lond. 1872. 2 v.   **923.21 : 58**

Dixon, W: Hepworth. History of two queens ; Catharine of Aragon ; Anne Boleyn. Leipz. 1873, 1874. 6 v. in 4. D.   **923.21 : 30**

Du Boys, Albert. Catharine of Aragon and the sources of the english reformation ; ed. from the french, with notes by Charlotte M. Yonge. Lond. 1881. 2 v. D.   **923.21 : 31**

Benger, Elizabeth Ogilvy. Memoirs of the life of Anne Boleyn. From the 3d Lond. ed., with a memoir of the author by miss Aikin. Phila. n. d. D.   **923.21 : 32**

Friedmann, Paul. Anne Boleyn ; a chapter of english history, 1527-36. Lond. 1884. 2 v. O.   **923.21 : 60**

Abbott, Jacob. History of queen Elizabeth. Ill. N. Y. 1878. S.   **923.21 : 10**

Townsend, Virginia Frances. Elizabeth Tudor ; the queen and the woman. Ill. N. Y. 1878. S.   **x 923.21 : 39**

Abbott, Jacob. History of Mary, queen of scots. Ill. N. Y. n. d. S.   **923.21 : 36**

Bell, H: Glassford. Life of Mary, queen of scots. N. Y. 1846. 2 v. S.   **923.21 : 37**

Headley, Phineas Camp. Life of Mary, queen of scots. Bost. n. d. D.   **923.21 : 40**

Lamartine, Alfonse Marie L. de. Life of Mary Stuart, queen of scots. [Biogr. series.] Bost. n. d. T.   **923.21 : 41**

Nau, Claude. The history of Mary Stewart, from the murder of Riccio until her flight into England ; now first printed from the original mss. with ill. papers from the secret archives of the Vatican and other collections in Rome, ed. with historical pref. by Joseph Stevenson. Edinb. 1883. D.   **923.21 : 51**

Tytler, W:, (*Lucretius*). An inquiry, historical and critical, into the evidence against Mary, queen of scots, and an examination of the histories of dr. Robertson and mr. Hume, with respect to that evidence. 3d ed. with add. and a postscript. Edinb. 1772. O.   **923.21 : 38**

Lippincott, Sarah Jane, *born* Clarke, (*Grace Greenwood*). Queen Victoria, her girlhood and womanhood. (Exemplary women ser.) Ill. N. Y. 1883. D.   **x 923.21 : 53**

Oliphant, Margaret O., *born* Wilson. The queen, [Victoria]. N. Y. 1880. Q.   **923.21+23**

Princes and princesses.

Green, Mary Ann Everett, *born* Wood. Lives of the princesses of England, from the norman conquest. Lond. 1850-55. 6 v. D.   **923.21 : 47**
Contents. V. 1. Daughters of William the conqueror: Cæcilia; Adeliza; Matilda; Constance; Adela; Gundred, supposed daughter. — Matilda, daughter of Henry I. — Matilda, daughter of king Stephen.— Mary, daughter of king Stephen. — Daughters of Henry II: Matilda; Eleanora; Joanna. —Daughters of king John: Joanna. **2.** *Same, continued:* Isabella; Eleanora.—Daughters of Henry III: Margaret; Beatrice; Katherine. — Daughters of Edward I: Eleanora; Joanna; Margaret; Berengaria; Mary. **3.** *Same, continued:* Elizabeth; Eleanora.— Daughters of Edward II: Eleanora; Joanna. — Daughters of Edward III: Isabella; Joanna; Blanche; Mary; Margaret.—Daughters of Henry IV: Blanche; Philippa.—Daughters of Edward IV: Mary; Cecilia; Margaret. **4.** *Same, continued:* Anne; Catherine; Bridget.—Daughters of Henry VII: Margaret; Elizabeth. **5.** *Same, continued:* Mary; Catherine. — Daughters of James I: Elizabeth. **6.** *Same, continued:* Elizabeth, *continued;* Sophia.—Daughters of Charles I: Mary; Elizabeth; Anne; Catherine; Henrietta Anne.

Strickland, Agnes. Lives of the Tudor princesses, incl. lady Jane Gray and her sisters. Lond. 1868. O.   **923.21 : 56**
Contents. Princess Mary Tudor, queen of France, duchess of Suffolk.— Lady Jane Gray, wife of lord Guildford Dudley.— Lady Katharine Gray, countess of Hertford. — Lady Mary Gray, wife of Thomas Keyes.—Lady Eleanor Brandon, countess of Cumberland.—Lady Margaret Clifford, countess of Derby and queen in Man.— Lady Arabella Stuart, wife of W: Seymour.

Alice, Maud Mary, *grand duchess of Hesse, princess of Great Britain and Ireland.* Biographical sketch and letters. Portr. N. Y. 1884. O.   **923.21 : 57**

Creighton, Louise. Life of Edward the black prince. Maps and plans. [Hist. biogr.] Lond. 1877. S.   **923.21 : 44**

Jones, Meredith. The story of Edward the black prince ; a book for boys. Ill. Lond. 1881.   **x 923.21 : 46**

Ewald, Alexander C: The life and times of prince Charles Stuart, count of Albany, commonly called the young pretender, from the state papers and other sources. New ed. Lond. 1883. D.   **923.22 : 59**

Fitzgerald, Percy. The royal dukes and princesses of the family of George III ; a view of court life and manners for seventy years, 1760—1830. Lond. 1882. 2 v. O.   **923.22 : 61**

Neale, Erskine. Life of Edward, duke of Kent, with extracts from his correspondence and original letters never before pub. 2d ed. with corr. and add. Lond. 1850. O.   **923.21 : 45**

Martin, *Sir* Theodore. The life of the prince consort. Portr. and views. N. Y. 1875-80. 5 v. O.   **923.21 : 52**

Grey, *The hon.* C: The early years of the prince consort, compiled under the direction of her majesty the queen. N. Y. 1867. D.   **923.21 : 24**

4. Germany and Austria.

Eginhard. Life of Charlemagne. Tr. from the text of the "Monumenta germanica" by S: Epes Turner; with notes and a map. N. Y. 1880. Tt.   **923.3 : 64**

Oertel, Hugo. Karl der grosse, der begründer des deutschen kaiserthums; der deutschen jugend und dem deutschen volke geschildert. Ill. Wiesbaden. 1875. S.   **923.3 : 65**

Schmidt, Ferdinand. Karl der grosse; ein lebensbild. Wittenberg. 1878. D. **923.3 : 66**

Oertel, Hugo. Heinrich I; ein fürstenbild aus deutscher vorzeit, für die deutsche jugend und das deutsche volk gezeichnet. Ill. Wiesbaden. 1877. S.   **923.3 : 37**

— Otto I, der grosse; ein kaiserbild aus deutscher vorzeit, für die deutsche jugend und das deutsche volk gezeichnet. Ill. Wiesbaden. 1877. S.   **923.3 : 38**

— Otto II; ein kaiserbild aus Deutschlands grosser vorzeit, für die deutsche jugend und das deutsche volk gezeichnet. Ill. Wiesbaden. 1877. S.   **923.3 : 39**

— Otto III; ein lebensbild aus Deutschlands grosser vorzeit, für die deutsche jugend und das deutsche volk gezeichnet. Ill. Wiesbaden. 1878. S.   **923.3 : 40**

— Friedrich I Barbarossa; ein kaiserbild aus deutscher vergangenheit, für die jugend und das volk gezeichnet. Ill. Wiesbaden. 1875. S.   **923.3 : 57**

— Friedrich II; ein lebensbild aus Deutschlands grosser kaiserzeit, für die deutsche jugend und das deutsche volk gezeichnet. Ill. Wiesbaden. 1879. S.   **923.3 : 58**

— Rudolph von Habsburg; ein fürstenbild aus Deutschlands vorzeit, für die deutsche jugend und das deutsche volk dargestellt. Ill. Wiesbaden. 1879. S.   **923.3 : 36**

Karl V of Germany. Correspondence of the emperor Charles V and his ambassadors at the courts of England and France; from the original letters in the imperial family archives at Vienna; with a connecting narrative and biogr. notices of the emperor and of some of the most distinguished officers of his army and household, together with the emperor's itinerary from 1519–1551; ed. by W: Bradford. Lond. 1850. O.   **923.3 : 17**

Oertel, Philip F: W:, (W. O. v. Horn). Das leben der kurfürstin Dorothea von Brandenburg, genannt die liebe Dorel, und der frommen landgräfin Elizabeth von Thüringen. 3te aufl. Wiesbaden. [1877]. S. **923.3 : 49**

— Ernst der fromme, herzog von Gotha; ein lebensbild aus den zeiten des dreissigjährigen krieges, der jugend und dem volk erzählt. Ill. Wiesbaden. [1875]. S.   **923.3 : 35**

Schmidt, Ferdinand. Aus der jugendzeit des grossen kurfürsten; ein historisches gemälde. 5te aufl., ill. Kreuznach. [1883]. S.   **923.3 : 60**

Schupp, Ottokar. Friedrich Wilhelm, der grosse kurfürst, der bahnbrecher für Preussens und Deutschlands grösse; ein lebensbild, der jugend und dem volke dargestellt. Ill. Wiesbaden. 1873. S.   **923.3 : 41**

— Friedrich Wilhelm I, könig von Preussen; ein lebensbild, für die jugend und das volk bearb. Ill. Wiesbaden. 1874. S.   **923.3 : 33**

Abbott, J: Stevens Cabot. History of Frederick the great. Ill. N. Y. 1871. Q.   **923.3+18**

Brackenbury, C: Booth. Frederick the great. [New Plutarch.] N. Y. 1884. S. **923.3 : 20**

Carlyle, T: History of Friederich II. N. Y. 1859–68. 6 v. D.   **923.3 : 1**

— Same, germ. Geschichte Friedrichs des zweiten, königs von Preussen, genannt Friedrich der grosse. Deutsch von I. Neuberg. Berlin. 1858–69. 6 v. O.   **923.3 : 1**

Ellis, G: James Welbore Agar. 2d viscount Clifton. Life of Frederick II of Prussia, by lord Dover. N. Y. 1844. 2 v. S. **923.3 : 3**

Macaulay, T: Babington baron. Life of Frederick the great. N. Y. 1859. T.   **923.3 : 2**

Oertel, Philip F: W:, (W. O. v. Horn). Der alte Fritz, der held und liebling des deutschen volkes; für die jugend und das volk dargestellt. 3te aufl., ill. Wiesbaden. 1877. S.   **923.3 : 55**

Schmidt, Ferdinand. Friedrich der grosse bis zu seiner thronbesteigung; ein historisches gemälde. 7te aufl., ill. Kreuznach. [1882]. S.   **923.3 : 45**

Thiébault, Paul C: François Adrien H: Dieudonné. Original anecdotes of Frederick the great, king of Prussia, and of his family, his court, his ministers, his academies and his literary friends, collected during a familiar intercourse of twenty years with that prince. Tr. from the french. Phila. 1806. 2 v. O. **923.3 : 23**

Frederica Sophia Wilhelmina, markgräfin von Baireuth. Autobiography: Memoirs; with an essay by W: D. Howells. Bost. 1877. 2 v. S.   **923.3 : 6**

Oertel, Philip F: W:, (W. O. v. Horn). Die kaiserin Maria Theresia; ein lebensbild, der jugend und dem volke dargestellt. 2te aufl., ill. Wiesbaden. 1875. S. **923.3 : 56**

Schmidt, Ferdinand. Kaiser Joseph II; ein lebensbild. 3te aufl., ill. Kreuznach. [1883]. S.   **923.3 : 67**

— Königin Luise; ein lebensbild. Ill. Glogau. [1877]. D.   **923.3 : 42**

Kluckhorn, A: Louise, queen of Prussia; a memorial. Tr. from the german by Elizabeth H. Denio. Cambridge. 1881. D.   **923.3 : 16**

Schupp, Ottokar. Louise, königin von Preussen; ein lebensbild für die jugend und das volk bearb. Ill. 2te aufl. Wiesbaden. 1878. S.   **923.3 : 62**

Müller, W: Kaiser Wilhelm, 1797–1877. 3te aufl. Portr. Berlin. 1877. O. **923.3 : 29**

Schmidt, Ferdinand. Kaiser Wilhelm; ein buch für schule und haus. Portr. Leipz. [1882]. S.   **923.3 : 44**

5. France.

White, G: Queens and princesses of France. Balt. 1861. T.   **923.4 : 5**

Joinville, J: sire de. Saint Louis, king of France. Tr. by James Hutton. 2d ed. [Bayard ser.] Lond. 1869. T. **923.4 : 49**

Kirk, J: Forster. History of Charles the bold, duke of Burgundy. Phila. 1864, 1868. 3 v. O.   **923.4+40**

Weitzel, Sophie Winthrop. Renée of France, duchess of Ferrara. N. Y. [1883]. D.   **923.4 : 75**

Aumale, H: Eugène Philippe L: d'**Orléans,** *duc* d'. History of the princes de Condé in the 16th and 17th centuries. Tr. from the french by Robert Brown Borthwick. Lond. 1872. 2 v. O.　　**923.4 : 80**

Stanhope, Philip H:, *5th earl Stanhope.* Life of Louis, prince of Condé. N. Y. 1845. 2 v. in 1. D.　　**923.4 : 54**

Abbott, J: Stevens Cabot. History of Henry IV of France. Ill. N. Y. *n. d.* S.　　**923.4 : 45**

James, G: Payne Rainsford. Life of Henry IV of France. N. Y. 1847. 2 v. D.
　　923.4 : 46

Abbott, J: Stevens Cabot. History of Louis XIV. N. Y. 1871. S.　　**923.4 : 50**

James, G: Payne Rainsford. Life and times of Louis XIV. New ed. Lond. 1851. 2 v. D.
　　923.4 : 52

Abbott, J: Stevens Cabot. History of Marie Antoinette. Ill. N. Y. *n. d.* S.　**923.4 : 57**

Keddie, Henrietta, *(Sarah Tytler).* Marie Antoinette. [The new Plutarch.] N. Y. 1883. S.　　**923.4 : 73**

Yonge, C: Duke. Life of Marie Antoinette. N. Y. 1876. O.　　**923.4 : 58**

Campan, Jeanne Louise Henriette. The private life of Marie Antoinette, queen of France and Navarre ; with sketches and anecdotes of the court of Louis XIV, XV, and XVI. 2d rev. ed. Ill. N. Y. 1884. 2 v. O.
　　923.4 : 82

Lamballe, Marie Thérèse Louise de Savoie-Carignan, *princesse* de. Secret memoirs of the royal family of France during the revolution ; with original and authentic anecdotes of contemporary sovereigns and other distinguished personages of that eventful period, now first publ. from the journal, letters and conversations of the princess Lamballe by a lady of rank in [her] confidential service. Portr. and cipher of the secret corresp. of Marie Antoinette. Lond. 1826. 2 v. in 1. D. **923.4 : 3**

Beauchesne, Alcide Hyacinthe du Bois de. Louis XVII ; his life, his suffering, his death ; the captivity of the royal family in the Temple. Tr. and ed. by W. Hazlitt. Ill. N. Y. 1853. 2 v. O.　　**923.4 : 55**

— The Bourbon prince ; the history of the royal dauphin, Louis XVII of France. [Abridged.] N. Y. 1853. S.　　**923.4 : 56**

Abbott, J: Stevens Cabot. The history of Napoleon Bonaparte. Maps and ill. N. Y. *n. d.* 2 v. O.　　**923.4+8**

— *Same* ; v. 2. N. Y. 1870. O.　**923.4+8 v2**

Hazlitt, W: Life of Napoleon Buonaparte. 2d ed. rev. by his son. Lond. 1852. 4 v. D.
　　923.4 : 10

Headley, Phineas Camp. Life of Napoleon Bonaparte. *T. p. w.* D.　**923.4 : 11**

Horne, R: H: The history of Napoleon Bonaparte ; new ed. thoroughly rev., with add. by S. R. Townshend Mayer. Ill. Lond. [1885]. O.　　**923.4+87**

Lanfrey, P: The history of Napoleon I. Lond. 1871-79. 4 v. O.　　**923.4 : 7**
Contents. v. 1. 1768-1800. 2. 1800-1806. 3. 1806-1810. 4. 1810-1811.—Index. The author died nov. 16, 1877, leaving his work unfinished.

Lockhart, J: Gibson. History of Napoleon Buonaparte. Repr. from the Family library ; with an app. Ill. Lond. 1867. D.
　　923.4 : 12

— *Same.* N. Y. 1875. 2 v. S.　　**923.4 : 12**

Scott, *Sir* Walter. Life of Napoleon Bonaparte. N. Y. 1857. O.　　**923.4 : 13**

Strahlheim, C., *ed.* Napoleon Bonaparte's vollständige lebensbeschreibung ; nach den zuverlässigsten quellen bearb. Frankfurt a. M. 1839. 4 v. O.　　**923.4 : 25**

Forsyth, W: History of the captivity of Napoleon at St. Helena, from the letters and journals of lieut.-gen. sir Hudson Lowe and official documents not before made public. N. Y. 1855. 2 v. D.　**923.4 : 15**

Las Cases, Emmanuel Augustin Dieudonné Marin Joseph *marquis* de. Memorial de Sainte Hélène ; journal of the private life and conversations of the emperor Napoleon at St. Helena. Phila. 1823. 8 v. in 4. D.　　**923.4 : 16**

Montholon-Sémonville, C: Tristan *marquis* de. History of the captivity of Napoleon at St. Helena. N. Y. 1846. O.　　**923.4+17**

O'Meara, Barry E: Napoleon in exile, or A voice from St. Helena ; the opinions and reflections of Napoleon on the most important events in his life and government, in his own words. N. Y. 1854. 2 v. D. **923.4 : 18**

Napoleon gallery ; illustrations of his life and times. *T. p. w.* [Lond. 1846]. D.
　　923.4 : R72

Abrantès, Laure Junot, *born* Permon, *duchesse* d'. Memoirs of Napoleon, his court and family. N. Y. 1854. 2 v. O.　　**923.4 : 14**

— *Same* ; v. 1. N. Y. 1832. ·O.　**923.4 : 14 v1**

Fauvelet de Bourrienne, L: Antoine. Private memoirs of Napoleon Bonaparte, during the periods of the directory, the consulate and the empire. Phila. 1831. 2 v. O.
　　923.4 : 9

— Memoirs of Napoleon Bonaparte ; added, an account of the important events of the hundred days, of Napoleon's surrender to the british, and of his residence and death at St. Helena, with anecdotes and illustrative extracts from all the most authentic sources ; ed. by R. W. Phipps. New and rev. ed., with numerous ill. N. Y. 1885. 3 v. O.　　**923.4 : 84**

Lester, C: Edwards, *and* Edwin **Williams,** *(The Berkeley men).* The Napoleon dynasty, or The history of the Bonaparte family, brought down to the present time, by the Berkeley men. Ill. N. Y. 1860. O.
　　923.4 : 6

Bingham, *The hon.* Dennis Arthur. The marriages of the Bonapartes. 2d ed. Lond. 1882. 2 v. D.　　**923.4 : 24**

— *Same.* N. Y. 1882. Q.　　**923.4+24**

Abbott, J: Stevens Cabot. History of Josephine. Ill. N. Y. *n. d.* S.　　**923.4 : 29**

Headley, Phineas Camp. Life of the empress Josephine. N. Y. *n. d.* D.　**923.4 : 30**

Memes, J: S. Memoirs of the empress Josephine. N. Y. 1847. S.　　**923.4 : 31**

Le Normand, Marie Anne Adélaide. Historical and secret memoirs of the empress Josephine. Tr. from the french by Jacob M. Howard. Phila. 1852. 2 v. D. **923.4 : 32**

Abbott, J: Stevens Cabot. History of Joseph Bonaparte. N. Y. 1869. S.　**923.4 : 28**

Bonaparte, Lucien, *prince de Canino.* Memoirs written by himself. Tr. from the original ms., under the immediate superintendence of the author. Pt. 1. N. Y. 1836. D.
　　923.4 : 27

Woodward, E. M. Bonaparte's Park and the Murats. Trenton, N. J. 1879. O.
923.4+26

Abbott, J: Stevens Cabot. History of Louis Philippe. Ill. N. Y. 1871. S. 923.4+53
— History of Hortense. Ill. N. Y. *n. d.* S.
923.4 : 35

Lagarde, A: de **Messence,** *comte* de. Memoirs of queen Hortense. [*Anon.*] Phila. 1833. S.
923.4 : 33

Abbott, J: Stevens Cabot. History of Napoleon III ; incl. a brief narrative of all the most important events which have occurred in Europe since the fall of Napoleon I, until the overthrow of the second empire and the death of Napoleon III. Ill. Bost. 1873. O.
923.4+20

Jerrold, W: Blanchard. Life of Napoleon III ; derived from state records, from unpub. family correspondence, and from personal testimony. Portr., facsimiles of letters, etc. Lond. 1877-82. 4 v. O. 923.4 : 21
Contents. V. 1. Birth, youth and education.—The italian insurrection.—Arenenberg.—App. 2. Between Strasburg and Boulogne.—Ham.—The revolution of 1848.—App. 3. The presidency.—The coup d'état.—Establishment of the empire.—App. 4. The crimean war.—Italian independence.—Home policy.—Home affairs.—1870.—App.—Index.

Smucker, S: Mosheim. Public and private history of Napoleon III ; with biogr. notices of his most distinguished generals, relatives and favorites, and various details descriptive of France under the second empire. Phila. 1858. D. 923.4 : 22

Wikoff, H: Napoleon L: Bonaparte ; biographical and personal sketches, incl. a visit to the prince at the castle of Ham. N. Y. 1849. D. 923.4 : 23

6.　Other modern countries.

Italy.

Dennistoun, James. Memoirs of the dukes of Urbino, illustrating the arms, arts and literature of Italy, from 1440 to 1630. Lond. 1851. 3 v. O. 923.5 : 2

Life and times of Rienzi. Phila. 1836. O.
923.5 : 5

Urquhart, W: Pollard. Life and times of Francesco Sforza ; with a prelim. sketch of the history of Italy. Edinb. 1852. 2 v. O.
923.5 : 7

Reumont, Alfred v. Lorenzo de' Medici the magnificent. Tr. from the german by Robert Harrison. Lond. 1876. 2 v. O.
923.5 : 1

Roscoe, W: Life of Lorenzo de' Medici. 9th ed.; rev. by T: Roscoe. Lond. 1847. D.
923.5 : 4

Trollope, T: Adolphus. The life of Vittoria Colonna. [Biogr. ser.] N. Y. 1877. T.
923.5 : 17

Dicey, E: Victor Emmanuel. [New Plutarch]. N. Y. 1882. S. 923.5 : 16

Godkin, G. S. Life of Victor Emmanuel II. Lond. 1879. 2 v. D. 923.5 : 14

Spain.

Coxe, W: Memoirs of the kings of Spain of the house of Bourbon from the accession of Philip V to the death of Charles III, 1700

to 1788 ; drawn from original and unpub. documents. Lond. 1815. 5 v. O.
923.5 : 53
Contents. V. 1. Historical introd., or A sketch of spanish history from the union of Castile and Aragon to the extinction of the Austrian line.—Philip V, 1709. 2. Philip V, 1710—1720. 3. Philip V, 1720—1724.—Louis, 1724—1725.—Philip V, 1725—1746. 4. Ferdinand VI, 1746—1759.—Charles III, 1759—1773. 5. Charles VI, 1774—1788.—Administration of Florida Blanca.—Statistical account of Spain.

George, Anita. Annals of the queens of Spain. N. Y. 1850. 2 v. D. 923.5 : 3
Contents. V. 1. Gothic queens, 415—714.—Queens of Oviedo and Leon, 718—1037.—Queens of Aragon, 1034—1468.—Queens of Castile, 1034—1475. 2. Isabel the catholic, 1474—1504.

Russia.

Abbott, Jacob. History of Peter the great. Ill. N. Y. *n. d.* S. 923.5 : 19

Cobb, James F. The story of the great czar ; a sketch of the life of Peter of Russia. Lond. [1874]. S. x 923.5 : 44

Motley, J: Lothrop. Peter the great. [Harper's half-hour ser.] N. Y. *n. d.* Tt.
923.5 : 20

Schuyler, Eugene. Peter the great, emperor of Russia ; a study of historical biography. Ill., portr. and maps. N. Y. 1884. 2 v. O.
923.5+51

Wight, Orlando Williams, *ed.* Life of Peter the great. [Biogr. series]. Bost. 1882. 2 v. S.
923.5 : 18

Yekaterina II. Memoirs of the empress Catherine II, written by herself ; with a pref. by A. Herzen. Tr. from the french. New issue. Lond. 1863. D. 923.5 : 54

Beaumont - Vassy, E: Ferdinand *vicomte* de. Geschichte des kaisers Nikolaus I ; nach dem franz., fortgesetzt bis zum tode des kaisers. Leipz. 1855. S. 923.5 : 21

Smucker, S: Mosheim. Life and reign of Nicholas 1 ; with descriptions of russian society and government, a complete history of the war in the east, and sketches of Schamyl, the circassian chief, and other distinguished characters. Phila. 1860. D. 923.5 : 22

Sweden and Denmark.

History of Gustavus Vasa, king of Sweden ; with extracts from his corresp. Lond. 1852. O. 923.5 : 49

Chapman, B. The history of Gustavus Adolphus and of the thirty years war, up to the king's death ; with some account of its conclusion by the peace of Westphalia, anno 1648. Ill. with plans of the battles of Leipsig and Lützen and a rough project of the imperialists' order of battle at Lützen, from a plan drawn out in Wallenstein's own hand. Lond. 1856. O.
923.5 : 28

Droysen, J: Gustav. Gustaf Adolf. Leipz. 1869, 1870. 2 v. in 1. O. 923.5 : 52

Harte, Walter. The history of the life of Gustavus Adolphus. 2d ed. corr., with alterations and enlargements. Lond. 1767. 2 v. O. 923.5 : 65

Stevens, J: Lloyd. History of Gustavus Adolphus. Portr. N. Y. 1884. O. 923.5 : 55

x denotes books specially adapted for children.

Oscar II Fredrik, *king of Sweden and Norway.* Charles XII by Oscar Fredrik. Tr. from the original swedish, with the sanction of the author, by G: F. Apgeorge. Lond. 1879. O.   **923.5+29**

Voltaire, François Marie **Arouet** *called* de. The history of Charles XII, king of Sweden. New tr. Hartford. 1825. D.   **923.5 : 30**

— *Same.* Tr. from the french by Smollett. N. Y. 1847. S.   **923.5 : 30**

Ulfeldt, *Grevinde* Leonora Christina. Memoirs of Leonora Christina, daughter of Christian IV of Denmark, written during her imprisonment in the Blue tower at Copenhagen, 1663—1685. Tr. by F. E. Bunnètt. 2d ed. Lond. 1872. O.   **923.5 : 47**

Netherlands.

Merriman, T. M. William, prince of Orange, or The king and his hostage. Bost. [1874]. D.   **923.5 : 32**

Schupp, Ottokar. Wilhelm von Oranien, der begründer der niederländischen freiheit; ein lebensbild, der deutschen jugend und dem volke dargestellt. Ill. Wiesbaden. 1875. S.   **923.5 : 66**

The orient.

Palmer, E: H: The caliph Haroun Alraschid and saracen civilization. [New Plutarch]. N. Y. 1881. S.   **923.5 : 37**

Abbott, Jacob. History of Genghis khan. N. Y. 1860. S.   **923.5 : 36**

Fraser, James. The history of Nadir shah, formerly called Thamas Kuli khan, the present emperor of Persia. Prefixed, a short history of the Moghol emperors; [added], a catalogue of about 200 mss. in the persic and other oriental languages, collected in the east. 2d ed. Lond. 1742. D.   **923.5 : 34**

Africa and America, *exclusive of U. S.*

Khedives and pashas; sketches of contemporary egyptian rulers and statesmen, by one who knows them well. Lond. 1884. D.   **923.5 : 57**

Contents. The ex-khedive Ismail.—The khedive.—Arabi.—Riaz pasha.—Nubar pasha.—Chérif pasha.—The Chérif ministry.—Some consuls-general. — Conclusion.

Whiting, W: B. Andamana, the first queen of Canary, ancestress of the family of Eugenie, late empress of the french, and her

remarkable and successful coup d'etat; [*also an essay on* Woman]. N. Y. 1875. S.   **923.5 : R46**

Beard, J: R. Life of Toussaint L' Ouverture, the negro patriot of Hayti; comprising an account of the struggle for liberty in the island and a sketch of its history to the present period. Ill. Lond. 1853. D.   **923.5 : 38**

Hall, F: Life of Maximilian I, with a sketch of the empress Carlotta. N. Y. 1868. D.   **923.3 : 7**

Salm-Salm, Agnes, *born* Leclerq, *afterward mrs.* Heneage. *prinzessin* v. Ten years of my life, by the princess Felix Salm-Salm. N. Y. 1877. D.   **923.3 : 12**

7. Ancient world.

Tugnot de Lanoye, Ferdinand. Rameses the great, or Egypt 3000 years ago. Tr. from the french. [Ill. lib. of wonders]. N. Y. 1875. D.   **923.6 : 1**

Abbott, Jacob. History of Cleopatra. Ill. N. Y. *n. d.* S.   **923.6 : 2**

— History of Cyrus the great. Ill. N. Y. *n. d.* S.   **923.6 : 3**

— History of Darius the great. N. Y. 1878. S.   **923.6 : 5**

— History of Xerxes the great. Ill. N. Y. 1878. S.   **923.6 : 4**

— History of Alexander the great. Ill. N. Y. 1876. S.   **923.6 : 19**

Curtius Rufus, Quintus. The life of Alexander the great. Written in latin and tr. into english by several gentlemen in the university of Cambridge. Lond. 1687. D.   **923.6 : 20**

Williams, J: Life and actions of Alexander the great. N. Y. 1843. S.   **923.6 : 21**

Abbott, Jacob. History of Pyrrhus. N. Y. 1878. S.   **923.6 : 23**

— History of Romulus. Ill. N. Y. *n. d.* S.   **923.6 : 7**

Suetonius Tranquillus, Caius. The lives of the twelve Cæsars. Added, his Lives of the grammarians, rhetoricians and poets. The trans. of Alexander Thomson, rev. and corr. by T. Forester. Lond. 1881. D.   **923.6 : 25**

Abbott, Jacob. History of Nero. N. Y. 1878. S.   **923.6 : 14**

Watson, Paul Barron. Marcus Aurelius Antoninus. Portr. N. Y. 1884. O.   **923.6 : 27**

Neander, J: A: W: The emperor Julian and his generation; an historical picture. Tr. by G. V. Cox. N. Y. 1850. D.   **923.6 : 15**

4. Sociology — b, Statesmanship and politics.

1. In general.

Stephen, Caroline Emilia, (*Sarah Brook*). Three 16th century sketches. Lond. [1884]. D.   **923 : 30**

Contents. William of Orange. — Coligny.—The regent Murray.

Brougham, H:, *baron Brougham and Vaux.* Historical sketches of statesmen who flourished in the time of George III.

Added, remarks on party and an app. New ed. Phila. 1842-44. 3 v. D.   **923 : 2**

Contents. V. 1. Introd.—George III.—Lord Chatham. — Lord North. — Lord Loughborough. — Lord Thurlow.—Lord Mansfield.—Lord chief justice Gibbs.—Sir W: Grant.—Mr. Burke.—Mr. Fox.—Mr. Pitt.—Mr. Sheridan.—Mr. Windham.—Mr. Dundas.—Mr. Erskine.—Mr. Perceval.—Lord Grenville.—Mr. Grattan.—Mr. Wilberforce.—Mr. Canning.—Sir S: Romilly.—Effects of party.—Franklin.—Frederic II.—Gustavus III.—The emperor Joseph.— The empress Catherine. 2. Introd.—George IV, includ. Sir J: Leach and others.

Brougham, H:—*Continued.*

—Lord Eldon.—Sir W: Scott, lord Stowell.—Dr. Laurence.—Sir Philip Francis.—Mr. Horne Tooke.—Lord Castlereagh.—Lord Liverpool.—Mr. Tierney. — Lord St. Vincent.—Lord Nelson.—Mr. Horner.—Lord King. —Mr. Ricardo and the currency question.—Note on mr. Curran.—C: Carrol.—Neckar.—Madame de Staël. —Mirabeau family. — Carnot. — Lafayette. — Prince Talleyrand.—Napoleon.—Washington. **3.** The french revolution. — Robespierre.—Danton. — Camille Desmoulins.—St. Just.—Sieyès.—Fouché, afterwards duke of Otranto.—J: fourth duke of Bedford.—Earl Camden. — J: Wilkes.—Demagogue arts. — Lord Ellenborough.—Lord chief justice Bushe.—T: Jefferson.— American democracy.—Marquess Wellesley.— Lord Holland.—J: Allen.—Walpole.—Bolingbroke.

— Historical sketches of statesmen who flourished in the time of George III, together with remarks on the french revolution ; v. 2. Phila. 1854. D.   **923 : 2 v2**

Contents. V. 2. 2d series, continued. *Same as v. 2 above, from* Lord King.—3d series. *Same as v. 3 above.*

Bulwer, *Sir* H: Lytton Earle, *lord Dalling and Bulwer.* Historical characters : Talleyrand, Cobbett, Mackintosh, Canning. Leipz. 1868. 2 v. in 1. D.   **923 : 3**

Smith, G: Barnett. Half-hours with some famous ambassadors. Lond. *n. d.* D.
     923 : 28

Contents. Sir R. M. Keith and queen Carolina Matilda of Denmark.—Talleyrand, prince of diplomatists.— Gondomar and the spanish marriage. — The story of the chevalier D'Eon.—Metternich, Napoleon and Maria Louisa.—Harley and the court of queen Anne. — Alberoni, cardinal and adventurer. — Lord Malmesbury and queen Caroline.

Menzies, Sutherland. Political women. Lond. 1873. 2 v. O.   **923 : 29**

Contents. V. 1. The duchess de Longueville.—The duchess de Chevreuse. — Anne of Austria. — The duchess de Montbazon.—The princess Palatine.—The princess de Condé. — The duchess de Châtillon. **2.** Mlle. de Montpensier. — The duchess of Portsmouth. —Princess des Ursins.—The duchess of Marlborough.

Towle, G: Makepeace. Certain men of mark ; studies of living celebrities. Bost. 1880. D.
     923 : 10

Contents. Gladstone. — Bismarck. — Gambetta. — Beaconsfield.—Castelar.—Victor Hugo.—J: Bright.— Three emperors.

2. United States.

C o l l e c t i v e   b i o g r.

Belknap, Jeremy. American biography ; with add. and notes by F. M. Hubbard. N. Y. 1859. 3 v. S.   **923.1 : 8**

Contents. V. 1. Prel. dissertation.—Chronological detail.—Biron.—Madoc.—Zeno. — Columbus.—Cartier. — De Soto. — Gilbert. — Raleigh and Grenville. **2.** De Fuca.—De Monts, Poutrincourt and Champlain. — Gorges and J: Mason. — The Virginia colony. — Lord Delaware, Sir T: Gates, Sir G: Somers, Sir Newport, Sir T: Dale, Sir F. Wainman. — Sir S: Argal, Sir G: Yeardley.—Sir F. Wyat.—Bartholomew Gosnold, Martin Pring, Bartholomew Gilbert, G: Weymouth. — J: Robinson.—J: Carver. **3.** W: Bradford.—W: Brewster. — R. Cushman. — E: Winslow.— Miles Standish. — J: Winthrop.—J. Winthrop, *jr.*—G: Calvert, Cecilius Calvert, lords Baltimore, Leonard Calvert. — W: Penn.— App.—Index.

Lossing, Benson J: Eminent americans ; brief biographies of 330 distinguished persons. Ill. N. Y. 1857. O.   **923.1 : 12**

Moore, Jacob Bailey. Lives of the governors of New Plymouth and Massachusetts Bay, from the landing of the pilgrims at Plymouth in 1620 to the union of the two colonies in 1692. Boston. 1851. O.   **923.1 : 15**

Contents. Pt. 1, *Governors of New Plymouth :* J: Carver.—W: Bradford.—E: Winslow.—T: Prince.—Josias

---

Winslow. — T: Hinckley. Pt. 2. *Governors of Massachusetts Bay :* J: Winthrop.—T: Dudley.—J: Haynes.— H: Vane.—R: Bellingham.—J: Endecott.—J: Leverett. —Simon Bradstreet. — Joseph Dudley. — Edmund Andros.

Lossing, Benson J: Biographical sketches of the declaration of amer. independence ; the declaration, historically considered, and a sketch of the leading events connected with the adoption of the articles of confederation and of the federal constitution. Ill. N. Y. [1848]. D.   **923.1 : 11**

Dwight, Nathaniel. The lives of the signers of the declaration of independence. New ed. N. Y. 1889. D.   **923.1 : 3**

Sullivan, W: The public men of the revolution, incl. events from the peace of 1783 to the peace of 1815 in a series of letters ; with a biogr. sketch of the author, and add. notes and reference by his son, J: T. S. Sullivan. Phila. 1847. O.   **923.1 : 23**

Watson, Elkanah. Men and times of the revolution, or Memoirs of Elkanah Watson ; incl. journals of travels in Europe and America from 1777 to 1842, with his corresp. with public men and reminiscences and incidents of the revolution ; ed. by his son, Winslow C. Watson. N. Y. 1856. O.   **923.1 : 24**

Woodman, C: H. The boys and girls of the revolution. Phila. 1877. D.   **x 923.1 : 25**

Contents. The youth of '76.—The first martyr.—Boys in the Boston massacre.—The son of Stark. — The young west indian. — Little Burr. — The volunteer against Quebec. — The beautiful spy. — The angel of the house. — The dove's nest in the lion's den. — The little black-eyed rebel.—How the cattle were saved.— A heroine in pinafores.—The maids of Fort Griswold. —Anecdotes.

Sabine, Lorenzo. The american loyalists, or Biographical sketches of adherents to the british crown in the war of the revolution, alphab. arr., with a prelim. historical essay. Bost. 1847. O.   **923.1 : 18**

Magoon, Elijah Lyman. Orators of the american revolution. 5th ed. N. Y. 1859. D.
     923.1 : 13

Contents. The battle-fields of early american eloquence.—James Otis. — S: Adams. — Josiah Quincy.— J: Hancock.—Joseph Warren.—J: Adams.—Patriotic piety of '76.—Patrick Henry.—R: H: Lee.—Alexander Hamilton.—Fisher Ames.—W: Pinckney.—W: Wirt. —T: Addis Emmet.—J: Randolph.

— Living orators of America. N. Y. 1860. D.
     923.1 : 14

Contents. Daniel Webster.—E: Everett.—H: Clay.— J: C. Calhoun.—G: McDuffie.—Lewis Cass.—T: H. Benton.—W: C. Preston.—T: Corwin.

Loring, James Spear. The hundred Boston orators, appointed by the municipal authorities and other public bodies, from 1770 to 1852 ; comprising historical gleanings, ill. the principles and progress of our republican institutions. Bost. 1852. O. **923.1+10**

Parker, Theodore. Historic americans. Bost. 1878. D.   **923.1 : 27**

Contents. Franklin.—Washington. — J: Adams.—T: Jefferson.

Baldwin, Joseph G. Party leaders ; sketches of T: Jefferson, Alexander Hamilton, Andrew Jackson, H: Clay, J: Randolph of Roanoke, incl. notices of many other distinguished amer. statesmen. N. Y. 1864. D. **923.1 : 1**

x denotes books specially adapted for children,

Bogart, W: H., (*Sentinel*). Who goes there? or Men and events by "Sentinel". N. Y. 1866. D.   **923.1 : 2**
Contents. Washington.— Lafayette. — From Hamilton to E. C. Genet. — From Eleazer Williams to H. R. Storrs. — From Erastus Root to J: Randolph. — From Josiah Quincy to T: Moore. — E: Everett. — From Daniel Webster to Zachary Taylor.

Campbell, J: W. Biographical sketches, with other literary remains, compiled by his widow. Columbus, O. 1838. O.   **923.1 : 4**
Contents. Biogr. sketches: J: W. Campbell, by a friend; Rufus Putnam; W: A. Trimble; Paul Fearing; Return J. Meigs; G: W. Burnet. — Miscellaneous papers. — Epistolary fragments. — Poetical effusions.— Congressional speeches.—Addenda.

Savage, J: Our living representative men ; from official and original sources. Phila. 1860. D.   **923.1 : 20**
Contents. N. P. Banks.—E: Bates.— J: Bell. — J: M. Botts. — J: C. Breckenridge. — A. G. Brown. — S. Cameron.—S. P. Chase.—H. Cobb.—J: J. Crittenden.— C. Cushing.— G: M. Dallas.—J. Davis. — W: L. Dayton. —D. S. Dickinson.— S. A. Douglas. — E: Everett.— M. Fillmore.—J: C. Frémont.—J. Guthrie. — J. M. Hammond.—S: Houston.— R. M. T. Hunter.— A. Johnson. —J. Lane. — J: McLean.— J. L. Orr.—J. M. Read.—W: H: Seward.—H. Seymour.—J: Slidell.—A. H. Stephens. —H: A. Wise.—J: E. Wool.

Forney, J: Weiss. Anecdotes of public men ; originally pub. in the Washington Sunday chronicle and Philadelphia press. N. Y. 1873, 1878. 2 v. D.   **923.1 : 6**

Perry, B: Franklin. Reminiscences of public men ; prefaced by a life of the author by Hext M. Perry. Portr. Phila. 1883. D.   **923.1 : 28**

Quincy, Josiah. Figures of the past ; from the leaves of old journals. Bost. 1883. D.   **923.1 : 26**

Birney, Catherine H. The Grimké sisters : Sarah and Angelina Grimké, the first american women advocates of abolition and woman's rights. Bost. 1885. D.   **923.1 : 30**

Homes of american statesmen, with anecdotical, personal and descriptive sketches by various writers. Ill. N. Y. 1854. O.   **923.12 : 66**
Contents. **Kirkland,** C. M., Washington.—**Briggs,** C. F., Franklin.—**Godwin,** P., Jefferson.—**Hildreth,** R:, Hancock. — **Cook,** C., J: Adams. — **Johnston,** E: W., Patrick Henry; Madison. — **Thayer,** W: S., Jay. —Carter, J. C., Hamilton. — **Griswold,** R. W., Marshall. — **Thayer,** J. B., Ames. — Child, D. L., J: Q. Adams.—**Godwin,** P., Jackson. — **King,** C:, Rufus King.—**Greeley,** H., Clay.— **Godwin,** P., Calhoun. **Becks,** T. R., Clinton. — **Howland,** F., Story. — Wheaton.

Civil government.

Peterson, C: Dictionary of the U. S. congress, containing biogr. sketches of its members from the foundation of the government ; with an app. compiled as a manual of reference for the legislator and statesman. Phila. 1859. O.   **923.1 : R9**

Lanman, C: Biographical annals of the civil government of the U. S. during its first century ; from original and official sources. Wash. 1876. Q.   **923.1 : R29**

Poore, B: Perley. The political register and congressional directory ; a statistical record of the federal officials, legislative, executive and judicial, of the U. S. of America, 1776 – 1878. Bost. 1878. Q.   **923.1 : R17**

Headley, Phineas Camp, *and another.* Public men of to-day ; biographies of the president and vice-president of the U. S., each member of the cabinet, the U. S. senators

and the members of the house of representatives of the 47th congress, the chief justice and the justices of the supreme court of the U. S., and of the governors of the several states. Portr. Hartford. 1883. Q.   **923.1 : 19**

Individual biogr.

Hosmer, James Kendall. Samuel Adams. (Amer. statesmen.) Bost. 1885. S.   **923.12 : 103**

Wells, W: Vincent. Life and public services of S: Adams ; a narrative of his acts and opinions, and of his agency in producing and forwarding the amer. revolution, with extracts from his corresp., state papers and political essays. Bost. 1865. 3 v. O.   **923.12 : 1**

Spencer, E: An outline of the public life and services of Thomas F. Bayard, 1869—1880, with extracts from his speeches and the debates of congress. N. Y. 1880. D.   **923.12 : 85**

Biddle, C: Autobiography, 1745—1821. Privately printed. Phila. 1883. O.   **923.12 : 90**

Balestier, C: Wolcott. James G. Blaine ; a sketch of his life ; with a brief record of the life of J: A. Logan. Portr. N. Y. 1884. D.   **913.12 : 98**

Buel, J. W., *and* W. E. S. **Whitman.** The authorized pictorial lives of James Gillespie Blaine and J: Alexander Logan. Ill. N. Y. 1884. D.   **923.12 : 99**

Safford, W: H. Life of Harmon Blennerhasset ; authentic narrative of the Burr expedition, and containing many add. facts not heretofore pub. Chillicothe, O. 1850. D.   **923.12 : 2**

Brown, G: W. The truth at last ; history corrected : Reminiscenses of old J: Brown ; thrilling incidents of border life in Kansas, with an app., containing statements and full details of the Pottawotomie massacre, by gov. Crawford, col. Blood, Jas. Townsley, col. Walker and others. Added, a review by Eli Thayer. Rockford, Ill. 1880. O.   **923.12 : 3**

Redpath, James. Public life of J: Brown ; with an autobiography of his childhood and youth. Lond. 1860. D.   **923.12 : 4**
— *Same.* Bost. 1860. D.   **923.12 : 4**

Sanborn, Franklin B:, *ed.* The life and letters of J: Brown, liberator of Kansas and martyr of Virginia. Bost. 1885. O.   **923.12 : 105**

Davis, Matthew L. Memoirs of Aaron Burr, with miscel. selections from his corresp. N. Y. 1838. 2 v. O.   **923.12 : 6**

Parton, James. Life and times of Aaron Burr. Enl. ed., with app., containing new and interesting information. Bost. 1881. 2 v. O.   **923.12 : 7**

Burr, Aaron. Private journal during his four years residence in Europe, with selections from his corresp. ; ed. by Matthew L. Davis. N. Y. 1858. 2 v. O.   **923.12+5**

Lodge, H: Cabot. Life and letters of George Cabot. Bost. 1878. O.   **923.12 : 92**

Holst, H: von. John C. Calhoun. (Amer. statesmen.) Bost. 1882. D.   **923.12 : 78**

Jenkins, J: Stilwell. Life of J: C. Calhoun. Auburn. [1850]. D.   **923.12 : 8**

Memorial addresses on the life and character of Matthew Hale C a r p e n t e r, del. in the senate and house of rep., 47th cong., 1st sess., jan. 26, 1882 ; with the funeral of the deceased. Wash. 1882. Q.   **923.12+75**

Smith, W: L. G. Fifty years of public life ; life and times of Lewis C a s s. Portr. N. Y. 1856. O.   **923.12+9**

Young, W: T. Sketch of the life and public services of Lewis Cass ; with the pamphlet on the Right of search, and some of his speeches on the great political questions of the day. 2d ed. Detroit. 1852. O.   **923.12 : 10**

Memorial addresses on the life and character of Zachariah C h a n d l e r, a senator from Michigan ; del. in the senate and house of rep., 46th congress, 2d session, jan. 28, 1880. Wash. 1880. Q.   **923.12+11**

Memorial addresses on the life and character of Rush C l a r k, a representative from Iowa, del. in the house of rep. and in the senate, 46th congress, 2d session, [jan. 31, 1880]. Wash. 1881. Q.   **923.12+12**

Colton, Calvin. The last seven years of the life of H: C l a y. N. Y. 1856. O.   **923.12 : 13**

Washburn, Elihu B: Sketch of Edward C o l e s, second gov. of Illinois, and of the slavery struggle of 1823–4 ; prep. for the Chicago historical soc. Chicago. 1882 [1881]. O.   **923.12 : 14**

Russell, Addison Peale. Thomas C o r w i n ; a sketch. Cinc. 1881. D.   **923.12 : 15**

Curtis, B: Robbins, ed. Memoir, with some of his professional and miscellaneous writings ; ed. by his son. Bost. 1879. 2 v. O.   **923.12 : 16**

Curwen, S: Journal and letters ; with an app. of biogr. sketches, by G: Atkinson Ward. 4th ed. Bost. 1864. O.   **923.12+17**

Creswell, J: A. J. Oration on the life and character of H: Winter D a v i s. Wash. 1866. O.   **923.12 : 18**

Craven, J: J. Prison life of Jefferson D a v i s. N. Y. 1866. D.   **923.12 : 19**

King, Daniel. Life and times of T: Wilson D o r r, with outlines of political history of Rhode Island. Bost. 1859. D. **923.12 : 20**

Douglass, F: Life and times, written by himself, his early life as a slave, his escape from bondage and his complete history to the present time ; with an introd. by G: L. Ruffin. Hartford. 1881. D.   **923.12 : 68**

Weld, Horatio Hastings. B: F r a n k l i n; his autobiography, with a narrative of his public life and services. Ill. N. Y. 1856. O.   **923.12+23**

Franklin, B: Memoirs, written by himself ; with his most interesting essays, letters and miscell. writings, familiar, moral, political, economical and philosophical. N. Y. 1847. 2 v. S.   **923.12 : 21**

— Autobiography ; ed. from his ms., with notes and an introd. by J: Bigelow. Phila. 1868. O.   **923.12 : 22**

— Life, written by himself ; now first ed. from original mss. and from his printed corresp. and other writings by J: Bigelow. 2d ed., rev. and corr. Phila. 1879. 3 v. D.   **923.12 : 88**

Abbott, J: Stevens Cabot. B: Franklin ; a picture of our infant nation 100 years ago. [Amer. pioneers and patriots.] Ill. N. Y. n. d. D.   **923.12 : 24**

Hill, G: C. Benjamin Franklin ; a biography. [Amer. biogr.] Phila. 1869. S.   **x 923.12 : 70**

Mayhew, H: Young Benjamin Franklin, or The right road through life ; a story to show how young Benjamin learned the principles which raised him from a printer's boy to the first ambassador of the amer. republic ; a boy's book on a boy's own subject. Ill. N. Y. n. d. S.   **x 923.12 : 69**

Mignet, François A: Marie. B: Franklin ; eine biographie. Aus dem franz. von E: Burckhardt. Leipz. 1855. S.   **923.12 : 71**

Oertel, Philipp F: W:, (W. O. v. Horn). Benjamin Franklin ; lebensbild eines ehrenmannes aus Amerika, der jugend und dem volke erzählt. 3te aufl., ill. Wiesbaden. n. d. S.   **923.12 : 108**

Parton, James. Life and times of B: Franklin. N. Y. 1864. 2 v. O.   **923.12 : 25**

Schmidt, Ferdinand. B: Franklin ; ein lebensbild für jung und alt. 3te aufl., ill. Kreuznach. [1883]. S.   **923.12 : 107**

Sparks, Jared. Life of B: Franklin ; containing the autobiography, with notes and a continuation. Bost. 1853. O.   **923.12+26**

Tomkinson, E. M. B: Franklin. (The world's workers.) [Portr.] Lond. 1885. D.   **923.12 : 106**

Adams, H: Life of Albert G a l l a t i n. Phila. 1879. O.   **923.12 : 27**

Stevens, J: Austin. Albert Gallatin. (Amer. statesmen.) Bost. 1884 [1883]. D.   **923.12 : 86**

Garrison, Wendell Phillips and Francis Jackson. William Lloyd G a r r i s o n, 1805 — 1879 ; the story of his life, told by his children. N. Y. 1885. 2 v. O.   **923.12+104**

Johnson, Oliver. W: Lloyd Garrison and his times, or Sketches of the anti-slavery movement in America, and of the man who was its founder and moral leader ; with an introd. by J: G. Whittier. Bost. 1880. D.   **923.12 : 28**

Graydon, Alexander. Memoirs of his own time, with reminiscences of the men and events of the revolution ; ed. by J: Stockton Littell. Phila. 1846. O.   **923.12+29**

Buell, Walter. Joshua R. G i d d i n g s ; a sketch. Cleveland. 1882. D. **923.12 : 81**

Lodge, H: Cabot. Alexander H a m i l t o n. (Amer. statesmen.) Bost. 1882. S.   **923.12 : 77**

Morse, J: Torrey, jr. The life of Alexander Hamilton. 3d ed. Bost. 1882. 2 v. D.   **923.12 : 87**

Smucker, S: Mosheim. Life and times of Alexander Hamilton. Phila. 1860. D.   **923.12 : 30**

Shea, G: Life and epoch of Alexander Hamilton ; a historical study. Bost. 1879. O.   **923.12+31**

Memorial addresses on the life and character of Julian H a r t r i d g e, a representative from Georgia, del. in the house of rep. and in the senate, 45th congress, 3d session. Wash. 1879. Q.   **923.12+32**

---

x denotes books specially adapted for children.

Arnold, S: G. Life of Patrick Henry. N. Y. 1857. S. **923.12 : 34**

Wirt, W: Sketches of the life and character of Patrick Henry. 10th ed., corr. Hartford. 1848. O. **923.12 : 33**

Child, Lydia Maria, *born* Francis. I: T. Hopper; a true life. Bost. 1854. D. **923.12 : 35**

Renwick, H: B. Life of J: Jay; ed. by James Renwick. N. Y. 1840. S. **923.12 : 36**

Hutchinson, P: Orlando, *comp.* The diary and letters of his excellency, T: Hutchinson, esq., captain-general and governor-in-chief of his late majesty's province of Massachusetts Bay in North America, compiled from the original documents still remaining in the possession of his descendants. Portr. and facsimiles. Bost. 1884. O. **923.12 : 97**

Obituary addresses on the occasion of the death of W: R. King, del. in the senate and house of rep., and in the supreme court of the U. S., 8th and 9th dec. 1853. Wash. 1854. O. **923.12 : 73**

Hawkins, W: G. Lunsford Lane, or Another helper from North Carolina. Bost. 1863. D. **923.12 : 37**

Memorial addresses on the life, and character of J: Edwards Leonard, a representative from Louisiana, del. in the house of rep. April 18, 1878, 45th congress, 2d session. Wash. 1879. Q. **923.12+102**

Hunt, C: Havens. Life of E: Livingston; with an introd. by G: Bancroft. N. Y. 1864. O. **923.12 : 38**

Sedgwick, Theodore, *jr.* Memoir of the life of W: Livingston; with extracts from his correspondence, and notices of various members of his family. N. Y. 1833. O. **923.12+39**

Sparks, Jared. The life of Gouverneur Morris, with selections from his corresp. and miscel. papers; detailing events in the american revolution, the french revolution and in the political history of the U. S. Bost. 1832. 3 v. O. **923.12 : 91**
Contents. V. 1. Life. 2. Corresp., official and private, respecting a negociation with the british ministry.—Corresp., official and private, concerning the french revolution and the affairs of France.—Letters and miscel. papers relating to french affairs. 3. Miscel. corresp. during the residence of mr. Morris in Europe. — Corresp. after the return of mr. Morris from Europe on private and political affairs in the U. S.—Speeches del. in the senate of the U. S.—Address to the assembly of Pa. on the abolition of the laws of North America.—Observations on the finances of the U. S., in 1789.—Notes on a form of a constitution for France.

Dixon, W: Hepworth. W: Penn; an historical biography founded on family and state papers. New ed. with a new pref. in reply to the accusations of mr. Macaulay. Lond. 1856. S. **923.12 : 40**

Clarkson, T: Memoirs of the public and private life of W: Penn. New ed. with a pref. in reply to the charges against his character made by mr. Macaulay in his History of England, by W. E. Foster. Lond. 1849. D. **923.12 : 41**

Janney, S: M. The life of W: Penn; with selections from his corresp. and autobiogr. 4th ed. rev., with index. Phila. 1878. D. **923.12 : 42**

Oertel, Hugo. William Penn, der begründer des nordamerikanischen staates Pennsylvanien; ein lebensbild, für die jugend und das volk gezeichnet. Ill. Wiesbaden. 1882. S. **923.12 : 109**

Burdette, Robert J., (*The Burlington Hawkeye man*). William Penn, 1644—1718. (Amer. worthies.) N. Y. 1882. S. **923.12 : 76**

Grayson, W: J. Biographical sketch of James L. Petigru. N. Y. 1866. D. **923.12 : 43**

Shields, Joseph D. The life and times of Sergeant Smith Prentiss. Phila. 1884. O. **923.12 : 95**

Prentiss, Seargent Smith. Memoirs; ed. by his brother. N. Y. 1860. 2 v. D. **923.12 : 44**

Curtis, G: W: Wendell Phillips; a eulogy, del. before the municipal authorities of Boston, Mass., april 18, 1884. N. Y. 1884. O. **923.12 : 96**

Quincy, Edmund. Life of Josiah Quincy, by his son. Bost. 1867. O. **923.12 : 45**

Claiborne, J: F. H. Life and corresp. of J: A. Quitman. N. Y. 1860. 2 v. D. **923.12 : 46**

Adams, H: John Randolph. (Amer. statesmen.) Bost. 1882. S. **923.12 : 79**

Garland, H. A. Life of J: Randolph. N. Y. 1853. O. **923.12 : 47**

Reed, W: Bradford. Life and corresp. of Joseph Reed, by his grandson. Phila. 1847. 2 v. O. **923.12+48**

Rush, R: Memoranda of a residence at the court of London, comprising incidents, official and personal, from 1819 to 1825; incl. negotiations on the Oregon question, and other unsettled questions between the U. S. and Great Britain. Phila. 1845. O. **923.12+80**

Grant, Anne. Memoirs of an american lady, [Catherine Schuyler]; with sketches of manners and scenery in America, as they existed previous to the revolution. N. Y. 1846. 2 v. in 1. D. **923.12 : 49**

Baker, G: E., *ed.* Life of W: H. Seward; with selections from his works. New ed. with add. brought down to date. N. Y. 1860. D. **923.12 : 50**

Seward, W: H: Autobiography, from 1801 to 1834; with a memoir of his life and selections from his letters from 1831 to 1836, by F: W. Seward. N. Y. 1877. O. **923.12+72**

Seward memorial, The; the ceremonies at the unveiling of the statue in Madison square, New York, sept. 17, 1876, with description of the statue and list of subscribers. N. Y. *n. d.* Q. **923.12+94**

Frothingham, Octavius Brooks. Gerrit Smith; a biography. 2d ed. N. Y. 1879. O. **923.12 : 51**

Cleveland, H: Alexander H. Stephens, in public and private, with letters and speeches, before, during and since the war. Phila. 1866. O. **923.12 : 52**

Johnston, R: Malcolm, *and* W: Hand Browne. Life of Alexander H. Stephens. New and rev. ed. Phila. 1884. O. **923.12 : 93**

Callender, E: B. Thaddeus Stevens, commoner. Bost. 1882. D. **923.12 : 82**

Memorial addresses on the life and character of Thaddeus Stevens, del. in the house of representatives. Wash. 1869. O. **923.12 : 53**

Abbott, J: Stevens Cabot. Peter Stuyvesant, the last dutch governor of New Amsterdam. [Amer. pioneers and patriots.] Ill. N. Y. 1877. D. **923.12 : 54**

Pierce, E: Lillie. Memoirs and letters of C: S u m n e r. Bost. 1878. 2 v. O.
           923.12 : 55

Memorial addresses on the life and character of C: Sumner, del. in the senate and house of representatives, 43d congress, 1st session, april 27, 1874, with other congressional tributes of respect. Wash. 1874. Q.
           923.12+56

Stuart, I: W: Life of Jonathan T r u m b u l l, sr. 2d ed. Bost. 1859. O.   **923.12+57**

Frothingham, R: Life and times of Joseph W a r r e n. Bost. 1865. O.   **923.12+58**

Banvard, Joseph. The american statesman, or Illustrations of the life and character of Daniel W e b s t e r, designed for amer. youth. Bost. 1859. S.   **923.12 : 74**

Curtis, G: Ticknor. Life of Daniel Webster. 4th ed. N. Y. 1872. 2 v. O.   **923.12 : 89**

Lodge, H: Cabot. Daniel Webster. (Amer. statesmen.) Bost. 1883. S.   **923.12 : 83**

Lanman, C: The private life of Daniel Webster. N. Y. 1852. D.   **923.12 : 59**

Harvey, P: Reminiscences and anecdotes of Daniel Webster. Bost. 1878. O.
           923.12 : 60

Weed, Harriet A., *and* Thurlow Weed **Barnes.** The life of Thurlow W e e d ; incl. his autobiography, ed. by his daughter and a memoir by his grandson. Ill. and portr. Bost. 1883. O.   **923.12+84**

Wikoff, H: The adventures of a roving diplomatist. N. Y. 1857. D.   **923.12 : 61**

Memorial addresses on the life and character of Alpheus S. W i l l i a m s, a representative from Michigan, del. in the house of rep. and in the senate, 45th congress, 3d session. Wash. 1880. Q.   **923.12+100**

Nason, Elias, *and* T: **Russell.** Life and public services of H: W i l s o n. Bost. 1876. D.
           923.12 : 62

Winthrop, Robert C: Life and letters of J: W i n t h r o p. Bost. 1864. O. **923.12+63**

Kennedy, J: Pendleton. Memoirs of the life of W: W i r t. New and rev. ed. Phila. 1850. 2 v. D.   **923.12 : 64**

Jenkins, J: Stilwell. Life of Silas W r i g h t ; with an app. containing a selection from his speeches in the senate of the U. S. and his address read before the N. Y. state agr. soc. Auburn. 1847. D.   **923.12 : 65**

Waite, Catharine V. The mormon prophet and his harem, or A history of Brigham Y o u n g; his numerous wives and children. Cambridge. 1866. D.   **923.12 : 67**

3. Great Britain and Ireland,

(including courtiers).

C o l l e c t i v e   b i o g r.

Forster, J:, T: Peregrine **Courtenay,** *and others.* Lives of eminent british statesmen. [Lardner's cab. cycl.] Lond. [1831-39]. 7 v. S.
           923.22 : 2
Contents. V. 1. Sir T: More. [by sir James Mackintosh].—Cardinal Wolsey.—Archbp. Cranmer.—W: Cecil, lord Burleigh. 2, by J: **Forster.** Sir J: Eliot. —T: Wentworth, earl of Strafford. 3, by J: **Forster.** J: Pym.—J: Hampden. 4, by J: **Forster.** Sir H: Vane.—H: Marten. 5, by T: P. **Courtenay.** Robert Cecil, earl of Salisbury.—T: Osborne, earl of Danby. 6, 7, by J: **Forster.** Oliver Cromwell.

Forster, J: The statesmen of the commonwealth of England ; with a treatise on the popular progress in english history. Lond. 1853. 5 v. S.   **923.22 : 3**
Contents. V. 1. Sir J: Eliot.—T: Wentworth, earl of Strafford. 2. J: Pym.—J: Hampden. 3. Sir H: Vane.—H: Marten. 4, 5. Oliver Cromwell.
Note. A republication of Forster's share of the preceding work.

Smith, Goldwin. Three english statesmen ; a course of lectures on the political history of England. N. Y. 1867. D.   **923.22 : 8**
Contents. Pym.—Cromwell.—Pitt.

Lewis, *Lady* Maria Theresa, *born* Lister Villiers. Lives of the friends and contemporaries of lord chancellor Clarendon ; illustrative of portraits in his gallery. Ill. Lond. 1852. 3 v. O.   **923.22 : 6**
Contents. V. 1. Introd. Pt. 1, The Clarendon gallery ; Pt. 2, The Clarendon mss. — Life of lord Falkland.—Life of lord Capell. 2. *Same, continued.*—Life of marquis of Hertford. 3. *Same, continued.*—App.—Account of the origin of the collection of portr. in the gallery and a descriptive catalogue of the pictures.

Rae, W: Fraser. Wilkes, Sheridan, Fox ; the opposition under George III. N. Y. 1874. D.   **923.22 : 49**

Francis, G: H: Orators of the age ; comprising portraits, critical, biographical and descriptive. N. Y. 1847. S.   **923.22 : 4**
Contents. Sir Robert Peel.—Lord J: Russell.—T: B. Macaulay.—Lord Stanley.—Lord Palmerston.—Lord Lyndhurst.— Earl Grey.— Sir James Graham.—Lord Morpeth.— The duke of Buckingham.—Earl of Radnor.— The duke of Richmond. — Mr. Bright. — Mr. Sheil.—Lord G: Beutinck.—Mr. Villiers.—Mr. T. Milner Gibson.—Mr. Wakley.—Dr. Bowring.—Mr. T. S. Duncombe.—Mr. Wyse.— Mr. Hawse.—Mr. Ward.— Mr. Roebuck.—Sir T: Wilde.—Lord Sandon.—Rev. Hugh M'Neile.

Higginson, T: Wentworth. Brief biographies : English statesmen. N. Y. 1875. D.
           923.22 : 5
Contents. Mr. Gladstone.—Mr. Disraeli.—Mr. Bright. -Earl Russell.—Earl Granville.—The duke of Argyll.—Mr. Disraeli's ministry: Lord Cairns; The duke of Richmond; The earl of Derby; The marquis of Salisbury; Sir Stafford Northcote; Mr. Gathorne Hardy.—Candidates for the liberal leadership: The marquis of Hartington; Mr. Forster; Mr. Lowe; Sir W: Harcourt; Mr. Goschen; Mr. Childers.

Hinton, R: J. Brief biographies : English radical leaders. N. Y. 1877. D.   **923.22 : 6**
Contents. The independent members: Sir C: W. Dilke; P: A. Taylor; Sir J: Lubbock; Joseph Cowen; R. M. Carter.—The labor agitation and its friends: T: Hughes; A. J. Mundella; Alex. Macdonald; T: Brassey; S: Morley.— Parliamentary agitators: S: Plimsoll; Sir W. Lawson; E: Miall; H: Richards.—Popular leaders: G: J. Holyoake; Joseph Arch; C: Bradlaugh; G: Odger; J. Chamberlain.

Davidson, J. Morrison. Eminent english liberals in and out of parliament. Bost. 1880. D.
           923.22 : 1
Contents. Eminent liberals in parliament. W: E. Gladstone. —J: Bright. — P: A. Taylor. — Sir C: W. Dilke.—Joseph Cowen.—Sir W. Lawson.—H: Fawcett. — Joseph Chamberlain. — T: Burt. — H: Richard. — Leonard H: Courtney.—A. J: Mundella.—C: Bradlaugh. *Eminent liberals out of parliament.* J: Morley. R. W: Dale.—J. Arch.—E: S. Beesly.—C: H. Spurgeon. —J. Beal.— M. D. Conway.— J. A. Picton.— F: A: Maxse.—The hon. A. Herbert.—E: A: Freeman.

       ✻   ✻   ✻

Thomson, Katherine, *born* Byerley. Memoirs of the jacobites of 1715 and 1745. [Portr.] Lond. 1845, 1846. 3 v. O.   **923.22+77**
Contents. V. 1. Introd.—J: Erskine, earl of Mar.—James Radcliffe, earl of Derwentwater.—The master of Sinclair.—Cameron of Lochiel. 2. W: Maxwell earl of Nithisdale.— W: Gordon, viscount Kenmure.

—W: Murray, marquis of Tullibardine.—Sir J: Maclean.—Rob Roy Macgregor Campbell.—Simon Fraser, lord Lovat. 8. Lord G: Murray.—James Drummond, duke of Perth.—Flora Macdonald.—W: Boyd, earl of Kilmarnock.—C: Radcliffe.

Fitzpatrick, W: J: The sham squire and the informers of 1798, with a view of their contemporaries ; added, jottings about Ireland 70 years ago. Bost. 1866. S.   **923.22 : 9**

Lecky, W: E: Hartpole. The leaders of public opinion in Ireland ; Swift, Flood, Grattan, O'Connell. N. Y. 1872. D.   **923.22 : 7**

Individual biogr.

McCrie, T: Memoirs of sir Andrew Agnew. 2d ed. Edinb. 1852. O.   **923.22 : 11**

Paget, Violet, (*Vernon Lee*). The countess of Albany. (Famous women ser.) Bost. 1884. S.   **923.22 : 71**

Eden, W:, *1st baron Auckland*. Journal and correspondence, with a pref. and introd. by [Robert J: Eden, lord Auckland]. Lond. 1861. 2 v. O.   **923.22 : 12**

Barrington, *Sir* Jonah. Personal sketches of his own times. N. Y. 1854. D.   **923.22 : 13**

Brandes, G: Morris Cohen. Lord Beaconsfield ; a study. Authorized tr. by mrs. G: Sturge. N. Y. 1880. D.   **923.22 : 19**

Hitchman, Francis. Public life of the rt. hon. the earl of Beaconsfield. 2d and rev. ed. Lond. 1881. D.   **923.22 : 20**

O'Connor, T. P. Lord Beaconsfield, a biography. 2d ed. Lond. 1879. D.   923.22 : 21
For 2d v., see **Foggo**, A. Benjamin Disraeli.

Foggo, Algernon. Benjamin Disraeli, earl of Beaconsfield, v. 2. Lond. [1881]. D.   **923.22 : 22**
For v. 1, see O'Connor, T. P. Lord Beaconsfield.

Towle, G: Makepeace. Beaconsfield. [Appleton's new handy-vol. ser.] N. Y. 1879. S.   **923.22 : 23**

Life, The, of the right hon. B: Disraeli, earl of Beaconsfield. N. Y. 1878. Q. **923.22+25**

Political adventures of lord Beaconsfield. N. Y. 1878. S.   **923.22 : 24**

Bloomfield, Georgiana, *born* Liddell, *baroness*. Reminiscences of court and diplomatic life. [Ill.] Lond. 1883. 2 v. O.   **923.22 : 73**

Robertson, W: Life and times of the right hon. J: Bright. N. Y. [1884]. O. **923.22 : 63**

Smith, G: Barnett. Life and speeches of the rt. hon. John Bright. N. Y. 1881. 2 v. in 1. O.   **923.22 : 14**

Burke, P: Public and domestic life of Edmund Burke. Lond. 1853. D.   **923.22 : 16**

Morley, J: Burke. [Eng. men of letters.] N. Y. 1879. D.   **923.22 : 17**

Prior, James. Memoir of the life and character of the rt. hon. Edmund Burke ; with specimens of his poetry and letters, and an estimate of his genius and talents, compared with those of his great contemporaries. 3d ed. Lond. 1839. O. **923.22 : 15**

Bell, Robert. Life of G: Canning. N. Y. 1846. S.   **923.22 : 54**

Hyde, E:, *1st earl of Clarendon*. Life, containing, I, An account of the chancellor's life from his birth to the restoration in 1660 ; II. A continuation of the same and of his history of the grand rebellion, from the restoration to his banishment in 1667, written by himself. Printed from his orig.

mss. given to the university of Oxford by the heirs. Oxford. 1760. 2 v. O.   **923.22 : 26**

Lister, T: H: Life and corresp. of lord Clarendon ; with original corresp. and authentic papers never before pub. Lond. 1837, 1838. 3 v. O.   **923.22 : 27**

Waters, Robert. How to get on in the world as demonstrated by the life and language of W: Cobbett. Portr. N. Y. 1883. D.   **923.23 : 4**

Gowing, R: R: Cobden. (The world's workers.) [Portr.] Lond. 1885. D.   **923.23 : 5**

McGilchrist, J: R: Cobden, his political career and public services ; a biography. N. Y. 1865. S.   **923.23 : 1**

Morley, J: The life of Richard Cobden. Bost. 1881. O.   **923.23 : 2**

Davies, *Lady* Lucy Clementina, *born* Drummond. Recollections of society in France and England. Lond. 1872. 2 v. D.   **923.22 : 67**

D'Ewes, *Sir* Simonds. Autobiography and corresp. during the reigns of James I and Charles I ; ed. by James Orchard Halliwell. Lond. 1845. 2 v. O.   **923.22 : 60**

Dodington, G: Bubb, *baron Melcombe*. Diary ; from march 8, 1749 to feb. 6, 1761 ; with an app., containing some curious and interesting papers which are either referred or alluded to in the diary. New ed. by H: Penruddocke Wyndham. Salisbury. 1784. O.   **923.22 : 70**

Forster, J: Sir John Eliot ; a biography, 1592-1632. 2d ed. Lond. 1872. D.   **923.22 : 62**

Teale, W: H: The life of Lucius Cary, viscount Falkland. Flemington, N. J. 1844. O. *In* The churchman's library.   **204 : 16**

Fanshawe, Anne, *born* Harrison, *lady*. Memoirs, written by herself ; with extracts from the corresp. of sir R: Fanshawe. New ed. Lond. 1830. O.   **923.22 : 28**

Fox, C: James. Memorials and corresp.; ed. by lord J: Russell. Phila. 1853. 2 v. D.   **923.22 : 30**

Trevelyan, G: O: Early history of C: James Fox. N. Y. 1880. O.   **923.22 : 29**

Jones, C: H. Short life of W: E. Gladstone; with extracts from his speeches and writings. [Appleton's new handy-vol. ser.] N. Y. 1880. S.   **923.22 : 31**

Ritchie, James Ewing. The life of W: Ewart Gladstone. Ill. Lond. [1884]. D.   **923.22 : 74**

Evelyn, J: Life of Mrs. Godolphin. Now first pub. and ed. by Samuel, lord bishop of Oxford. N. Y. 1847. D.   **923.22 : 32**

Grenville, G: Nugent Temple, *baron Nugent*. Memorials of J: Hampden, his party and his times. 4th ed., with a memoir of the writer and index. Ill. Lond. 1860. D.   **923.22 : 33**

Hill, *Sir* Rowland *and* G: Birbeck. The life of sir Rowland Hill, and the history of penny postage by sir Rowland Hill and his nephew, G: Birbeck Hill. Lond. 1880. 2 v. O.   **923.22 : 34**

Horner, Francis. Memoirs ; with selections from his corresp. Edinb. 1849. D.   **923.22 : 35**

Keith, *Sir* Robert Murray. Memoirs and corresp. official and familiar; with a memoir of queen Caroline Matilda of Denmark, and an account of the revolution there in 1772; ed. by mrs. Gillespie Smyth. Lond. 1849. 2 v. O.   923.22:36

Knighton, Dorothea, *born* Hawkes, *lady*. Memoirs of sir W: K n i g h t o n; including his corresp. Lond. 1838. 2 v. O.   923.22+37

Thiers, L: Adolphe. The Mississippi bubble; a memoir of J: L a w. Added, authentic accounts of the Darien expedition [from the Encyclopædia britannica] and the South sea scheme [from Mackay's Memoirs of extraordinary delusions]. Tr. by F. S. Fiske. *T. p. w.* [N. Y. 1859]. D. 923.23:3

Smith, Reginald Bosworth. Life of lord L a w - r e n c e. N. Y. 1883. 2 v. O.   923.22:58

Martin, *Sir* Theodore. A life of lord L y n d - h u r s t; from letters and papers in possession of his family. Lond. 1883. O.
923.22:65

Mackintosh, *Sir* James. Memoirs; ed. by his son, Robert James M a c k i n t o s h. From the 2d Lond. ed. Bost. 1853. 2 v. O.
923.22+38

Harris, *Sir* James Howard, *3d earl of M a l m e s - b u r y*. Memoirs of an ex-minister. New ed. Lond. 1885. D.   923.22:72

Thomson, Katherine, *born* Byerley. Memoirs of Sarah, duchess of M a r l b o r o u g h, and the court of queen Anne. Lond. 1839. 2 v. O.   923.22:18

Torrens, W: Torrens McCullagh. Memoirs of the right hon. William, second viscount M e l - b o u r n e. Portr. 2d ed. Lond. 1878. 2 v. O.   923.22:69

Guizot, François P: Guillaume. Memoirs of George M o n k, duke of Albemarle. From the french, tr. and ed. with add. notes and ill. by J. Stuart Wortley. Lond. 1838. O.   923.22:64

Creighton, Louise. Life of Simon de M o n t - f o r t. Maps. [Hist. biogr]. Lond. 1877. S.   923.22:55

Cusack, Mary Frances, (*The nun of Kenmare*). Daniel O'C o n n e l l, the liberator; his life and times, political and social. (Kenmare publ.) N. Y. 1872. O.   923.22:56
— *Same*. [Lond.] *n. d.* 2 v. O.   923.22+56

Vale, G. Life of T: P a i n e, with critical and explan. observ. on his writings; with an app. containing his letters to Washington, suppressed in his works at present pub. in this country. N. Y. 1853. O.   923.22:39

Bulwer, *Sir* H: Lytton Earle, *baron Dalling and Bulwer*. Life of H: J: Temple, viscount P a l m e r s t o n, with selections from his diaries and corresp. Leipz. 1871. 3 v. in 2. D.   923.22:46

Smith, G: Barnett. Sir Robert P e e l. [Eng. political leaders]. Lond. 1881. D.
923.22:40

Pepys, S: Life, journals and correspondence; incl. a narrative of his voyage to Tangier, deciphered from the shorthand mss. in the Bodleian library by the rev. J: Smith. Now first pub. from the originals. Lond. 1841. 2 v. O.   923.22:42
— Diary and correspondence in the reigns of Charles II and James II; the diary deciphered by the rev. J. Smith, from the original shorthand mss. in the Pepysian library,

Pepys, S:—*Continued.*
with a life and notes by R: lord Braybrooke. 1st amer. from the 5th Lond. ed. Phila. 1855. 4 v. O.   923.22:41
— Diary and correspondence; from his ms. cypher in the Pepysian library, with a life and notes by Richard lord Braybrooke, deciphered with add. notes by Mynors Bright. Portr. from the collection in the Pepysian library, printed in permanent woodbury type. Lond. 1875. 6 v. O.   923.22:R41

Wheatley, H: B. S: P e p y s and the world he lived in. 2d ed. Lond. 1880. D.   923.22:81

Wilson, James Grant, (*Allan Grant*). Mr. secretary Pepys, with extracts from his diary. N. Y. 1867. S.   923.22:43

Walpole, Spencer. The life of the rt. hon. Spencer P e r c e v a l, incl. his corresp. with numerous distinguished persons, by his grandson. Lond. 1874. 2 v. O.
923.22:66

Macaulay, T: Babington, *baron Macaulay*. Life of W: P i t t. [Biogr. series]. Bost. 1881. T.   923.22:53
— Same. N. Y. *n. d.* T.   923.22:53

Reresby, *Sir* J: Memoirs and travels, the former containing anecdotes and secret history of the courts of Charles II and James II, the latter, now first pub., exhibiting a view of the governments and society in the principal states and courts of Europe during the time of Cromwell's usurpation. Lond. 1813. Q.   923.22+52

Rossa, O'Donovan. Irish rebels in english prisons; a record of prison life. N. Y. 1882. O.   923.22:57

Pulling, F. S. The life and speeches of the marquis of S a l i s b u r y. Lond. 1885. 2 v. D.
923.22:76

Crossley, James. Sir Philip S i d n e y and the Arcadia. Lond. 1853. S. *With* Cavendish, G: Cardinal Wolsey.   923.22:51

Madden, R: Robert. Memoirs of the lady Hester S t a n h o p e, as related by herself in conversation with her physician; comprising her opinions and anecdotes of some of the most remarkable persons of her time. [*Anon.*] Lond. 1846. 3 v. D. 923.22:78
— Travels of lady Hester Stanhope, narrated by her physician. [*Anon.*] Lond. 1846. 3 v. D.   923.22:79

Thomson, Katherine, *born* Byerley. Memoirs of the court and times of king George II and his consort, queen Caroline; incl. numerous private letters of the most celebrated persons of the time, addressed to viscountess S u n d o n, mistress of the robes to the queen, and her confidential adviser; exhibiting much of the secret, political, religious and literary history and a variety of particulars not mentioned by our historians, now first pub. from the originals. Portr. Lond. 1850. 2 v. D.   923.22:80

Walpole, Horace, *4th earl of Orford*. Memoirs of Horace W a l p o l e and his contemporaries; incl. numerous original letters chiefly from Strawberry Hill, ed. by Eliot Warburton. Lond. 1852. 2 v. D.
923.22:47
— Horace Walpole and his world; select passages from his letters, ed. by L. B. Seeley. Ill. after sir Joshua Reynolds and sir T: Lawrence.   923.22:44

Cooper, Elizabeth. The life of Thomas W e n t-w o r t h, earl of Strafford and lord-lieutenant of Ireland. Lond. 1874. 2 v. O.
923.22 : 68

Besant, Walter, *and* James **Rice.** Sir R: W h i t t i n g t o n, lord mayor of London. N. Y. 1881. S.　923.22 : 48

Galt, J: Life of Cardinal W o l s e y. 3d ed. with ill. Lond. 1846. D.　923.22 : 50

Cavendish, G: Cardinal Wolsey; his rise and fall. Lond. 1855. S.　923.22 : 51

4. Other modern countries.

G e r m a n y.

Tuttle, Herbert. Brief biographies: German political leaders. N. Y. 1876. D.
923.3 : 15

Contents. The chancellor: Prince Bismarck. — Ministers: Dr. Falk; President Delbrück; Herr Camphausen.—The diplomatic service: Prince Hohenlohe; Count v. Arnim. — The parliamentarians: Herr v. Bennigsen; Dr. Simson. — The party leaders: Herr Lasker; Herr Windthorst; Dr. Löwe; Herr Schulze-Delitzsch; Herr Jacoby; Herr Hasselmann; Herr Sonnemann.—The scholars in politics: Prof. Gneist; Prof. Virchow; Prof. Treitschke; Prof. v. Sybel.

Hesekiel, G: L: Life of B i s m a r c k, private and political; with descriptive notices of his ancestry. Tr. and ed. with an introd., explan. notes and app. by Kenneth R. H. Mackenzie., Ill. N. Y. 1870. O.　923.3+5

Busch, Moritz. Our chancellor; sketches for a historical picture. From the german by W: Beatty-Kingston. N. Y. 1884. D.
923.3 : 21

— Bismarck in the franco-german war, 1870—1871. Authorized tr. from the german. N. Y. [1879]. 2 v. D.　923.3 : 4

Schmidt, Ferdinand. Fürst Bismarck; ein lebensbild. Ill. Glogau. 1878. S. 923.3 : 61

Holtzendorff, Joachim W: Franz Philipp v. J. C. B l u n t s c h l i und seine verdienste um die staatswissenschaften; mit dem bildniss B's. *In* Deutsche zeit- und streit-fragen.　304.15 : v11

Corvin-Wiersbitzki, O: Julius Bernhardt v. Aus dem leben eines volkskämpfers. Amsterdam. 1861. 3 v. D.　923.3 : 9

Brandes, G: Morris Cohen. Ferdinand L a s-s a l l e; ein literarisches charakterbild. Aus dem dänischen autorisirte übers. Berlin. 1877. D.　923.3 : 7

Freytag, Gustav. K: M a t h y; geschichte seines lebens. 2te aufl. Leipz. 1872. O.
923.3 : 28

Metternich-Winneburg, Clemens Wenzel Nepomuk Lothar *reichsfürst* v. Memoirs; ed. by prince R: M e t t e r n i c h, the papers classified and arr. by M. A. de Klinkowström. Tr. by mrs. Alexander Napier. N. Y. 1880. 5 v. O.　923.3 : 8

Nettelbeck, Joachim Christian, bürger zu Colberg; eine lebensbeschreibung von ihm selbst aufgezeichnet, mit einer einleitung von K. Koberstein. Berlin. [1885]. 2 v. D.
923.3 : 63

Arndt, Ernst Moritz. Meine wanderungen und wandelungen mit dem reichsfreiherrn H: K: F: v. S t e i n. 3er abdruck. Berlin. 1869. D.　923.3 : 30

Pertz, G: H: Das leben des ministers freiherr vom Stein. Berlin. 1849—1855. 6 v. in 7. O.　923.3 : 26

Contents. V. 1. 1757—1807. 2. 1807—1812. 3. 1812—1814. 4. 1814, 1815. 5. 1815—1823. 6, *in* 2. 1823—1831.

Schupp, Ottokar. Der freiherr vom Stein, des rechtes grundstein, des unrechtes eckstein, des deutschen volkes edelstein; der jugend und dem volke erzählt. 2te aufl., ill. Wiesbaden. *n. d.* S.　923.3 : 47

Seeley, J: Robert. Life and times of Stein, or Germany and Prussia in the Napoleonic age. Bost. 1879. 2 v. O.　923.3 : 13

Stockmar, Ernst Alfred Christian *freiherr* v. Memoirs of baron S t o c k m a r, by his son. Tr. from the german by G. A. M.; ed. by F. Max Müller. Lond. 1873. 2 v. D.
923.3 : 46

Oertel, Philipp F: W:, (*W. O. v. Horn.*) Der alte V i n c k e; ein lebensbild für das volk und die jugend dargestellt. 2te aufl., ill. Wiesbaden. 1877. S.　923.3 : 51

F r a n c e.

King, T: Brief biographies: French political leaders. N. Y. 1875. D.　923.4 : 2

Contents. V. M. Hugo.—L: A. Thiers. — Léon Gambetta.—Jules Simon. — Marshal MacMahon. — M. Dupanloup. — Jules Grévy. — E: Laboulaye. — Eugène Rouher. — E. R. Duval. — The duc de Broglie. — L: J. Buffet. — The duc d'Audifret-Pasquier. — J. A. S. Dufaure. — E. Ollivier. — Jules Favre. — The comte de Chambord.—The duc d'Aumale.—The comte de Paris. —Ernest Picard. — H: Rochefort. — Casimir Périer. — Jules Ferry.

Cormenin, L: Marie **La Haye,** *vicomte* de, (*Timon*). The orators of France by Timon. Tr. by a member of the N. Y. bar from the 14th Paris ed.; with an essay on the rise of french revolutionary eloquence and the orators of the girondists by J. T. **Headley.** Ed. by G. H. Colton, with notes and biogr. addenda. Ill. N. Y. 1847. S.
923.4 : 1

Contents. Constituent assembly: Mirabeau. — The convention: Danton. — The empire: Napoleon Bonaparte. — The restoration: De Serre; Gen. Foy; B: Constant; Royer-Collard; Manuel. — Revolution of July: Garnier-Pages; Casimir-Perier; Sauzet; Lafayette; Odilion-Barrot; Dupin; Berryer; Lamartine; Guizot; Thiers; O'Connell. — Biogr. addenda: Mirabeau; Danton; B: Constant; Royer-Collard; Lamartine; Guizot; Thiers.

Cousin, V: Secret history of the french court under Richelieu and Mazarin, or Life and times of madame de C h e v r e u s e. Tr. by Mary L. Booth. N. Y. 1859. D.
923.4 : 41

Hamilton, Antoine *comte.* Memoirs of count G r a m m o n t; ed., with notes by sir Walter Scott. New ed. with portr. Lond. 1876. O.　923.4 : 74

Guizot, François P: Guillaume. Memoirs to illustrate the history of my time. Lond. 1858—61. 4 v. O.　923.4 : 79

Witt, Henriette de, *born* Guizot. Monsieur Guizot in private life; 1787—1874, by his daughter. Tr. by M. C. M. Simpson. Bost. 1881. O.　923.4 : 44

Harcourt, Césarine Charlotte Laure Sidonie, *born* de Choiseul-Praslin, *duchesse* d'. Memoir of the duchess of Orleans, by the marques de H—; with biogr. souvenirs and original letters. coll. by G. H. de Schubert. Tr. from the french. N. Y. 1860. D. 923.4:61

Cousin, V: The youth of madame de L o n g u e-v i l l e, or New revelations of court and convent in the 17th century. From the french by F. W. Ricord. N. Y. 1854. D.
923.4 : 48

Miot, André François, *comte de Melito.* Memoirs; ed. by general Fleischman. From the french by mrs. Cashel Hoey and J: Lillie; with notes and an index, prepared especially for the amer. ed. N. Y. 1881. O.
923.4 : 60

Oliphant, Margaret O., *born* Wilson. Memoir of count de M o n t a l e m b e r t; a chapter of recent french history. Leipz. 1872. 2 v. in 1. S.
923.4 : 59

Pompadour, Jeanne Antoinette Poisson, *marquise* de. Secret memoirs; col. and arr. by Jules Beaujoint. Lond. 1885. O.
923.4 : 91

Rémusat, Claire Élisabeth Jeanne de, *born* Gravier de Vergennes. Memoirs, 1802–1808; with a pref. and notes by her grandson, Paul de Rémusat. N. Y. 1880. 3 v. O.
923.4 : 37

Retz, J: François Paul de **Gondi,** *cardinal* de. Memoirs; containing the particulars of his own life, with the most secret transactions of the french court and the civil wars. Tr. from the french. Phila. 1817. 3 v. O.
923.4 : 62

Robson, W: Life of R i c h e l i e u. Ill. Lond. *n. d.* S.
923.4 : 77

Lewes, G: H: Life of R o b e s p i e r r e. *T. p. w.* D.
923.4 : 63

Abbott, J: Stevens Cabot. History of madame R o l a n d. Ill. N. Y. *n. d.* S. 923.4 : 64

Saint-Simon, L: de **Rouvroy,** *duc* de. The memoirs of the duke of S a i n t S i m o n on the reign of Louis XIV and the regency. Tr. from the french by Bayle St. John. Lond. *n. d.* 1876. 3 v. O.
923.4 : 66

Collins, Clifton Wilbraham. Saint Simon. [Foreign classics for eng. readers]. Phila. 1880. S.
923.4 : 65

McHarg, C: K. Life of prince T a l l e y r a n d; with extracts from his speeches and writings. N. Y. 1857. D.
923.4 : 67

Le Goff, François. Life of L: Adolphe T h i e r s. Tr. from the unpub. ms. by Theodore Stanton. N. Y. 1879. D.
923.4 : 68

Italy   and   Spain.

Mazade, C: de. Life of count C a v o u r. From the french. N. Y. 1877. O.
923.5 : 8

Villari, Pasquale. Niccolò M a c h i a v e l l i and his times. Tr. by Linda Villari. Lond. 1878. 4 v. D.
923.5 : 50

Orsi, *Conte* Giuseppe. Recollections of the last half century. Lond. 1881. D.
923.5 : 15

Pasolini, P: Desiderio. Memoir of count Giuseppe P a s o l i n i, late president of the senate of Italy, b. 1815, d. 1876, compiled by his son. Tr. and abridged by the dowa-ger countess of Dalhousie. Portr. Lond. 1885. O.
923.5 : 60

Pépé, Guglielmo. Memoirs; comprising the principal military and political events of modern Italy, written by himself. Lond. 1846. O.
923.5 : 62

Miraflores, *Don* Manuel Pando Fernandez de Pinedo Alava y Davila *marques* de. Denkwürdigkeiten. Deutsch von L. Starkhof. 2te ausg. Leipz. 1851. 2 v. S. 923.5 : 12

Ponte, Lorenzo da. Memoiren; von ihm selbst in New York herausg. Aus dem italien. Stuttg. 1847. 2 v. T.
923.5 : 13

Russia and Denmark.

Pietzker, M. A., *tr.* From peasant to prince; the life of Alexander Menschikoff, freely tr. from the russian. Ill. Lond. *n. d.* S.
x 923.5 : 43

Münter, Balthasar. A faithful narrative of the conversion and death of count Struensee, late prime minister of Denmark; with letters of his parents to him and also a letter of his own wherein he relates how he came to alter his sentiments of religion. Added, [**Hee,** Jörgen,] The history of count Enevold Brandt from the time of his imprisonment to his death; with two anonymous letters found in his pocket-book, wherein he was forewarned of what happened to him four months after, and likewise an exact copy of his sentence. The whole tr. from the original german [by F: A: Wendeborn]. Portr. Lond. 1773. D. 923.5 : 59

Hindustan.

Lutfu'lláh. Autobiography of Lutfullah, a mohamedan gentleman, and his transactions with his fellow-creatures; interspersed with remarks on the habits, customs and character of the people with whom he had to deal; ed. by E: B. Eastwick. 3d ed. Lond. 1858. D.
923.5 : 33

5. Ancient world.

Cox, *Sir* G: W: Lives of greek statesmen; So-lon—Themistokles. N. Y. 1885. S.
923.6 : 28

Schäfer, Arnold. Demosthenes und seine zeit. Leipz. 1856–58. 3 v. O. 923.6 : 26

Brédif, L. Political eloquence in Greece: Demosthenes; with extracts from his orations and a critical discussion of the "Trial on the crown." Tr. by M. J. MacMahon. Chicago. 1881. O.
923.6 : 18

Cicero, Marcus Tullius. Life and letters. Lond. 1854. O.
923.6+11
Contents. Life, by Conyers **Middleton.**—Cicero's letters to several of his friends, tr. by W: Melmoth.— Cicero's letters to Atticus, tr. by dr. Heberden.

Trollope, Anthony. Life of Cicero. N. Y. 1881. 2 v. D.
923.6 : 12

Hamilton, Elizabeth. Memoirs of the life of Agrippina, the wife of Germanicus. 2d ed. Lond. 1811. 2 v. O.
923.6 : 13

x denotes books specially adapted for children.

5. Sociology — c, Army and navy.

1. In general.

Wilson, James Grant. Sketches of illustrious soldiers. N. Y. 1880. D.   **923 : 19**
Contents. Gonsalvo of Cordova. — The chevalier Bayard.—The constable Bourbon.—Prince of Orange. —Duke of Parma.—Prince Wallenstein. — Gustavus Adolphus.—Oliver Cromwell. — Marshal Turenne.— The great Condé.—Duke of Marlborough.— Prince Eugene.—Charles XII.—Marshal Saxe.—Frederick the great.—Marshal Suwarrow.—General Washington.— Duke of Wellington.— Napoleon Bonaparte.— General Scott.—Lord Clyde.—Marshal Moltke.—General Lee.—General Sherman.—General Grant.

Adams, W: H: Davenport. Eminent soldiers ; a series of biographical sketches of great military commanders, english and foreign. Lond. *n. d.* D.   **x 923 : 1**
Contents. Wallenstein, duke of Friedland. —Marshall Turenne. — John Churchill, duke of Marlborough.—Arthur, duke of Wellington.—Napoleon, emperor of the french.—General sir Charles Napier. —General Grant.—Field-marshal count Moltke.

Guizot, François P: Guillaume. Monk and Washington ; historical studies. Lond. 1851. S.   **923 : 4**

Edgar, J: G: Sea-kings and naval heroes ; a book for boys. Ill. N. Y. 1868. S.   **x 923.25 : 3**
Contents. Rollo the norman. — Hasting. — Sweyn, king of Denmark.—Harold Hardrada. — Sir Robert Morley.—The earl of Pembroke.—The duke of Bedford.—Sir Andrew Wood.—Sir Francis Drake. — Sir Walter Raleigh.—The earl of Cumberland.—Admiral Drake.—Prince Rupert.—Sir Cloudesley Shovel.—Admiral Benbow.—Lord Rodney.—Earl Howe.—Earl St. Vincent.— Lord Duncan. — Lord Nelson.—Lord Collingwood.

2. United States.

Collective biogr.

Glazier, Willard. Heroes of three wars ; comprising a series of biogr. sketches of the most distinguished soldiers of the war of the revolution, the war with Mexico, and the war for the union, who have contributed by their valor to establish and perpetuate the republic of the U. S. Phila. 1880. D.   **923.15 : 2**

Griswold, Rufus Wilmot. Washington and the generals of the american revolution. Ill. Phila. 1847. 2 v. D.   **923.15 : 69**
Contents. V. 1. Washington.—Greene.—Wayne.— Putnam.— Gates.— W: earl of Stirling.— Schuyler. —Sullivan.—Mercer.—Armstrong.—Knox.—Arnold.— Smallwood.— DeHaas.—St. Clair.—Elbert.—Irvine.— Weedon.— Varnum. — Woodford.— Williams. — Moylan.—McDougall.—Glover.—McIntosh.—Thompson.— Nixon.—Gist.—Wooster.—Spencer.—Poor.—Moore.— Patterson.—Reed.— Pomroy.—Sumner. 2. Stark.— Moultrie.—Reed.—Greaton.—Morgan.—Marion.—Lee. --Mifflin.—Parsons. — Lincoln.—Montgomery.—Whitcomb.—Cadwalader.— Heath.— Thomas.—G: Clinton. — Ja. Clinton. — Larned. — Lafayette. — Deborre. — Count Pulaski.— Russell.—Ducoudray.—De la Neuville.—Baron Steuben. — Baron De Woedtke.— Kosciusko.— Tuffin. — Duportail. — Roche de Fermoy.— Conway. — Baron de Kalb. — Gadsden. — Hogan. — Huger.— Hazen. — Wilkinson. — Sumter. — Scott. — Pinckney.—Howe.—Frye. — Ward. — Rufus Putnam. —Nash.—Stephen.—Dayton.—Hand. — Muhlenberg.— Lewis.—Huntington.—Maxwell.

---

x denotes books specially adapted for children.

Headley, Joel Tyler. Washington and his generals. N. Y. 1861. 2 v. D.   **923.15 : 70**
Contents. V. 1. Washington.—Putnam.—Montgomery.—Arnold.—Stark.—Schuyler.—Gates.—Steuben.— Wayne. — Conway and Mifflin. — Ward and Heath. 2. Greene.—Moultrie.—Knox.—Lincoln.— Lee.—Clinton.—Sullivan.— St. Clair. — Marion. — Stirling.—Lafayette.— DeKalb.—Thomas and McDougall.—Wooster, Howe and Parsons.—Commodore Paul Jones.— The brigadier generals.—Morgan.

Peterson, C: J. The military heroes of the war of 1812, with a narrative of the war. 10th ed. Phila. *n. d.* O.   **923.15+3**
Contents. The war of 1812.—The heroes of the war of 1812: W: Hull; James Winchester; Zebulon Montgomery Pike; H: Dearborn; James Wilkinson; J: Armstrong; G: Croban; W: H: Harrison; R: M. Johnson; I: Shelby; Jacob Brown; Eleazer W. Ripley; James Miller; Nathan Towson; T: S. Jessup; Edmund Pendleton Gaines; P: B. Porter; Alexander Macomb; S: Smith; Andrew Jackson.

— The military heroes of the war with Mexico ; with a narrative of the war. 10th ed. Phila. *n. d.* O.   **923.15+1**
Contents. The war with Mexico.—The heroes of the war with Mexico: Zachary Taylor; S: Ringgold; C: May; W: O. Butler; W: J. Worth; J: E. Wool; Stephen W. Kearney; J: C. Fremont; A. W. Doniphan; S: H. Walker; Winfield Scott; D: E. Twiggs; Joseph G. Totten; Robert Patterson; Persifer F. Smith; James Shields; James Duncan; Bennett Riley; J: A. Quitman; Joseph Lane; Gideon J. Pillow; G: Cadwalader; W: S. Harney; Franklin Pierce; Roger Jones.

Shea, J: Gilmary, *ed.* The fallen brave ; a biographical memorial of the amer. officers who have given their lives for the preservation of the union. N. Y. 1861. Q.   **923.15 : R4**
Contents. Col. E. E. Ellsworth.—Lieut. J. T. Greble. —Capt. S. A. Ward.—Col. N. L. Farnham.—Col. J. Cameron.— Col. J. S. Slocum. — Lieut.-col. H. Haggarty.—Brig.-gen. N. Lyon.—Lieuts. L. L. Jones *and* C. S. Pratt.—Lieut. W. Shipley.—Capt. H. H. Alden.— Maj. J. S. Gavitt.—Curtis, G: W: Maj. T. Winthrop. — Maj. S. Ballou.—Capt. L. Tower.—Bates, A. J. Capt. E. W. Jones.—Tillinghast, J. S. Capt. O. H. Tillinghast. — Craig, J. N. Lieut. P. O. Craig.— McCook, D. Capt. C. McCook.—Lowe, T. O. Col. J. W. Lowe. — Wilkes, G. Col. E. D. Baker. — Clarke, J. F. Lieut. W. L. Putnam. — Cutter, E. Lieut. J. W. Grant.

Headley, Joel Tyler. Farragut and our naval commanders. N. Y. 1867. O. **923.15+48**
Contents. Farragut. — Wilkes. — Stringham.— Dupont. — Foote. — Boggs. — Goldsborough. — Ellet. — Bailey.—Davis.—Blake.—Winslow.— Porter.—Rowan. —Lee.—Jenkins. — Thatcher.— Porter. — Dahlgren.— Paulding.— Palmer. — Worden.—Bell.—Smith. — Rogers.—Craven.— Bell. — Pearson. — Godon.—Lander.— Gregory Radford.—Walke.—Alden.—Drayton.

Moore, Frank. Women of the war ; their heroism and self-sacrifice. Ill. Hartford. 1866. O.   **923.15 : 59**

Hamersly, Lewis R. The records of living officers of the U. S. navy and marine corps, compiled from official sources. 3d ed., with add. Phila. 1878. O.   **923.15 : R61**

Individual biogr.

DePuy, H: Walter. Ethan Allan and the Green-Mountain heroes of '76. N. Y. 1860. D.   **923.15 : 46**
— *Same.* N. Y. 1872. D.   **923.15 : 46**

Arnold, I: Newton. The life of Benedict Arnold; his patriotism and his treason. Chicago. 1880. O.   **923.15 : 5**

Hill, G: Canning. Benedict Arnold; a biography. [Amer. biogr.] Phila. 1875. S.   **x 923.15 : 45**

Poore, B: Perley. The life and public services of Ambrose E. B u r n s i d e, soldier, citizen, statesman; with an introd. by H: B. Anthony. Maps and ill. Providence. 1882. O.   **923.15 : 58**

Memorial addresses on the life and character of Ambrose C. Burnside, del. in the senate and house of rep., 47th cong., 1st sess., jan. 23, 1882; with the proceedings connected with the funeral of the deceased. Wash. 1882. Q.   **923.15+57**

Renwick, James. Life of DeWitt C l i n t o n. N. Y. 1845. S.   **923.15 : 6**

Cheever, H: Theodore. The autobiography and memorials of capt. Obadiah C o n g a r. N. Y. 1851. S.   **923.15 : 7**

Whittaker, F: A popular life of gen. G. A. C u s t e r. N. Y. [1876]. O.   **923.15 : 49**

Dahlgren, Madeleine, *born* Vinton, *formerly* *mrs.* Goddard. Memoir of J: A. D a h l - g r e n, rear-admiral U. S. N., by his widow. Portr. and ill. Bost. 1882. O.   **923.15+55**

Claiborne, J: F. H. Life and times of S: D a l e. Ill. N. Y. 1860. D.   **923.15 : 8**

Dix, Morgan. Memoirs of J: Adams D i x; compiled by his son. Ill. N. Y. 1883. 2 v. O.   **923.15 : 60**

Farragut, Loyall. Life of D: Glasgow F a r r a - g u t, embodying his journal and letters, by his son. Portr., maps and ill. N. Y. 1879. O.   **923.15+9**

Headley, Phineas Camp. Old Salamander; life and naval career of David Glascoe Farragut. [Heroes of the rebellion.] Bost. 1883 [1882]. D.   **x 923.15 : 52**

Upham, C: Wentworth. Life, explorations and public services of J: C: F r é m o n t. Bost. 1856. S.   **923.15 : 10**

Owens, J: Algernon. Sword and pen; ventures and adventures of Willard G l a z i e r. Phila. 1880. D.   **923.15 : 11**

Greene, G: Washington. The life of Nathaniel G r e e n e. N. Y. 1871. 3 v. O. **923.15 : 65**

Simms, W: Gilmore, *ed.* Life of Nathaniel Greene. N. Y. 1861. D.   **923.15 : 12**

Caldwell, C: Memoirs of the life and campaigns of Nathaniel Greene. Phila. 1819. O.   **923.15+13**

Junkin, D. X., *and* **Frank H. Norton.** Life of Winfield Scott H a n c o c k; personal, military and political. N. Y. 1880. D.   **923.15 : 14**

Southworth, Alvan S. Life of Winfield Scott Hancock; with an introd. by T: F. Bayard, embracing also original contributions from C: Francis Adams, Wade Hampton, Abram S. Hewitt, Roger A. Pryor, D: Davis, D: Dudley Field, Algernon S. Sullivan, J: Kelly. Authorized ed. N. Y. 1880. S.   **923.15 : 15**

Campbell, Maria, *born* Hull. Revolutionary services and civil life of gen. W: H u l l; prepared from his mss. by his daughter; together with the history of the campaign of 1812, and the surrender of the post of

Detroit, by his grandson James Freeman Clarke. N. Y. 1848. O.   **923.15+16**

Addey, Markinfield. Stonewall J a c k s o n; life and military career. Portr. N. Y. 1863. D.   **923.15 : 19**

Cooke, J: Esten. Stonewall Jackson; a military biography. Portr. and maps. N. Y. 1866. O.   **923.15 : 17**

Randolph, Sarah Nicholas. Life of T: J. Jackson. Ill. Phila. 1876. O.   **923.15 : 18**

Abbott, J: Stevens Cabot. The life and adventures of rear-admiral John Paul J o n e s, commonly called Paul Jones. (Amer. pioneers and patriots.) Ill. N. Y n. d. D..   **923.15 : 21**

Sherburne, J: Paul. Life and character of Paul Jones. Wash. 1825. O.   **923.15 : 20**

Kapp, F: The life of John K a l b, major-general in the revolutionary army. N. Y. 1884. D.   **923.15 : 66**

Keyes, Erasmus D. Fifty years' observation of men and events, civil and military. N. Y. 1884. D.   **923.15 : 67**

Abbott, J: Stevens Cabot. Captain W: K i d d, and others of the pirates or buccaneers who ravaged the seas, the islands and the continents of America two hundred years ago. (Amer. pioneers and patriots). Ill. N. Y. 1876. D.   **923.15 : 31**

Leake, I: Q. Memoirs of the life and times of gen. J: L a m b and his corresp. with Washington, Clinton, Patrick Henry and other distinguished men of his time. Albany. 1850. O.   **923.15+22**

Cooke, J: Esten. Life of Robert E. Lee. N. Y. 1871. O.   **923.15 : 24**

Taylor, Walter H. Four years with gen. Lee; a summary of the more important events touching [his] career in the war between the states, together with an authoritative statement of the strength of the army which he commanded in the field. N. Y. 1858. O.   **923.15+25**

Hartley, Cecil B. Lives of H: Lee and T: Sumter. Ill. Phila. 1859. D.   **923.15 : 23**

Hillard, G: Stillman. Life and campaigns of G: B. M c C l e l l a n. Phila. 1864. D.   **923.15 : 26**

Hartley, Cecil B. The life of gen. Francis M a - r i o n; also lives of gens. Moultrie and Pickens, and gov. Rutledge, with sketches of other distinguished heroes and patriots who served in the revolutionary war in the southern states. Ill. Phila. [1867]. D.   **923.15 : 47**

Headley, Phineas Camp. Old stars; life and military career of maj.-gen. Ormsby M. M i t c h e l. [Heroes of the rebellion]. Bost. 1883. [1882]. D.   **x 923.15 : 54**

Graham, James. Life of gen. Daniel M o r g a n, with portions of his correspondence; compiled from authentic sources. N. Y. 1859. D.   **923.15 : 27**

Crawford, J: Marshall. Mosby and his men; a record of the adventures of J: S. M o s b y, incl. the exploits of Smith, Chapman, Richards, Montjoy, Turner, Russell, Glasscock, and the men under them. N. Y. 1867. D.   **923.15 : 28**

Parker, W: Harwar. Recollections of a naval officer, 1841–1865. N. Y. 1883. D.   **923.15 : 63**

x denotes books specially adapted for children.

Mackenzie, Alexander Slidell. Life of Oliver Hazard Perry. N. Y. 1845. 2 v. S.
923.15 : 29

Pickering, Octavius, *and* C: Wentworth **Upham.** The life of Timothy Pickering. Bost. 1867–73. 4 v. O.   923.15+64

Cutter, W: Life of Israel Putnam; compiled from the best authorities. 3d ed. N. Y. 1847. D.   923.15 : 30

Hill, G: Canning. Gen. Israel Putnam, "Old Put"; a biography. [Amer. biogr]. Phila. 1875. S.   x 923.15 : 44

Lossing, Benson J: The life and times of Philip Schuyler. N. Y. 1883. 2 v. D.
923.15 : 62

— *Same.* Vol. 1. N. Y. [1860]. D.   923.15 : 62

Headley, Joel Tyler. Life of Winfield Scott. N. Y. 1861. D.   923.15 : 32

Mansfield, E: Deering. Life of Winfield Scott. N. Y. 1846. O.   923.15 : 33

Scott, Winfield. Memoirs, written by himself. N. Y. 1864. 2 v. D.   923.15 : 34

Headley, Phineas Camp. Fighting Phil; the life and military career of lieut.-gen. Philip H: Sheridan. [Heroes of the rebellion]. Bost. 1880 [1882]. D.
x 923.15 : 51

— Facing the enemy; the life and military career of gen. W: Tecumseh Sherman. [Heroes of the rebellion]. Bost. 1883 [1882]. D.   x 923.15 : 50

Sherman, W: Tecumseh. Memoirs, by himself. N. Y. 1875. 2 v. O.   923.15 : 35

Armstrong, W. C. Life and adventures of capt. J: Smith; comprising the account of his travels in Europe, Asia, Africa and America, also the early history of Virginia and New England, incl. sketches of Pocahontas, Powhatan, Opechancanough and other distinguished characters. Principally compiled from his own work. Hartford. 1865. D.   923.15 : 37

Hill, G: Canning. Capt. John Smith; a biography. [Amer. biogr.] Phila. 1875. S.
x 923.15 : 43

Simms, W: Gilmore. Life of capt. J: Smith. 3d ed. N. Y. *n. d.* D.   923.15 : 36

Warner, C: Dudley. Capt. John Smith, 1579–1631, sometime governor of Virginia and admiral of New England; a study of his life and writings. [Lives of amer. worthies]. N. Y. 1881. S.   923.15 : 38

Abbott, J: Stevens Cabot. Miles Standish, the puritan captain. Ill. [Amer. pioneers and patriots]. N. Y. 1873. D. 923.15 : 39

Kapp, F: Life of F: W: v. Steuben; with an introd. by G: Bancroft. 2d ed. N. Y. 1859. D.   923.15 : 40

Johnson, R: W. Memoir of general G: H. Thomas. Phila. 1881. O.   923.15 : 41

Van Horne, T: B. The life of maj.-gen. G: H. Thomas. N. Y. 1882. O.   923.15 : 56

Michie, P. S. The life and letters of Emory Upton, colonel of the fourth reg. of artillery, and brev. maj.-gen. U. S. army; with an introd. by James Harrison Wilson. N. Y. 1885. D.   923.15 : 68

Moore, H. N. Life and services of gen. Anthony Wayne; founded on documentary and other evidence furnished by his son, I: Wayne. Ill. Phila. *n. d.* S.
923.15 : 42

3. Great Britain.

Collective biogr.

Phillips, E. C. Sir H: Havelock and Colin Campbell, lord Clyde. (The world's workers.) [Portr.] Lond. 1885. D. 923.25 : 37

Bartlett, D: The heroes of the indian rebellion. Columbus, Ohio. 1859. D.   923.25 : 2
Contents. Pref.—Capt. Hodson.—Havelock.—Rev. mr. Polehampton.—A lady's escape from Gwalior.—The story of Cawnpore.—The chaplain's narrative of the siege of Delhi.—The adventures of judge Edwards in Rohilcund, Futtehghur and Oude.—Sir H: Lawrence and the defence of Lucknow.—Greathed and Campbell after the fall of Delhi.

Adams, W: H: Davenport. Eminent sailors; a series of biographies of great naval commanders; incl. an historical sketch of the british navy from Drake to Collingwood. N. Y. 1882 [1881]. D.   x 923.25 : 1

Mackenzie, C: Naval biography; comprising memoirs of the most distinguished commanders of Great Britain. Lond. 1846. T.
923.25 : 4

Lives and voyages of Drake, Cavendish and Dampier; incl. an introductory view of the earlier discoveries in the South sea, and the history of the buccaniers. Portr. N. Y. 1846. S.   923.25 : 5

Individual biogr.

Sargent, Winthrop. Life and career of major John André. Bost. 1861. D.   923.25 : 6

Dixon, W: Hepworth. Robert Blake, admiral and general at sea; based on family and state papers. Lond. 1852. O.   923.25 : 7

Ware, J. Redding, *and* R. K. **Mann.** The life and times of colonel Fred. Burnaby. Lond. [1885]. D.   923.25 : 36

Towle, G: Makepeace. Drake; the sea-king of Devon. Ill. Bost. 1883 [1882]. S.
x 923.25 : 30

Oertel, Philipp F: W:, (*W. O. v. Horn*). Franz Drake, der mann der uns die kartoffeln gebracht hat; der jugend und dem volke dargestellt. Anhang, cap. 5: Geschichte der einführung der kartoffeln in Europa. 3te aufl. Wiesbaden. [1878]. S. 923.25 : 38

Allen, Joseph. Life of T: Cochrane, earl of Dundonald. Lond. 1861. S.
923.25 : 10

Cochrane, T:, *10th earl of Dundonald.* The autobiography of a seaman. 2d ed. Lond. 1860. 2 v. O.   923.25 : 11

Gleig, G: Robert. Der leichte dragoner. Aus dem engl. Stuttg. 1845. T.   923.25 : 12

Forbes, Archibald. Chinese Gordon; a succinct record of his life. Ill. and map. N. Y. 1884. Q.   923.25+32

— *Same.* N. Y. 1884. S.   923.25 : 32

Hake, A. Egmont. The story of Chinese Gordon. Portr. and maps. N. Y. 1884. O.
923.25 : 31

Mossman, S: General Gordon in China; the story of the "ever victorious army". Ill. Lond. [1875]. D.   923.25 : 33

Gordon, C: G: Journals at Kartoum; printed from the original mss., introd. and notes by A. Egmont Hake. Portr., maps and ill. Bost. 1885. D.   923.25 : 34

x denotes books specially adapted for children.

Headley, Joel Tyler. The life of gen. H. Have-lock. Ill. N. Y. 1859. D.   **923.25 : 13**

Hodson, W: Stephen Raikes. Twelve years of a soldier's life in India; extracts from [his] letters, incl. a personal narrative of the siege of Delhi and capture of the king and princes, ed. by his brother G: H. Hodson. From 3d and enl. eng. ed. Bost. 1860. D.   **923.25 : 14**

Hutchinson, Lucy, *born* Apsley. Memoirs of the life of colonel.Hutchinson, with original anecdotes of many of the most distinguished of his contemporaries and a summary review of public affairs, written by his widow. From the original ms. by the rev. Julius Hutchinson; prefixed, the life of mrs. Hutchinson written by herself. 5th ed., added, an account of the siege of Lathom House, defended by the countess of Derby against sir T: Fairfax. Lond. 1846. D.   **923.25 : 15**

— *Same.* Memoirs of the life of colonel Hutchin-son by his widow; ed. from the original ms. by the rev. Julius Hutchinson; added, the letters of col. Hutchinson and other papers, rev., with add. notes by C. H. Firth. Portr. N. Y. 1885. 2 v. O.   **923.25 : 35**

Stone, W: Leete. Life and times of sir W: Johnson. Albany. 1865. 2 v. O.   **923.25+16**

Alison, *Sir* Archibald. Military life of John duke of Marlborough. N. Y. 1848. D.   **923.25 : 9**

Coxe, W: Memoirs of the duke of Marlborough; with his original corresp., coll. from the family records at Blenheim and other authentic sources. New ed. rev. by J: Wade. Lond. 1847, 1848. 3 v. D.   **923.25 : 8**

Creighton, Louise. Life of John Churchill, duke of Marlborough. Portr., maps and plans. [Hist. biogr.] N. Y. 1879. S.   **923.25 : 28**

Gleig, G: Robert. Life of sir T: Munro; with extracts from his corresp. and private papers. Lond. 1830. 3 v. O.   **923.25 : 17**

Southey, Robert. The life of Nelson; with biographical notice of the author. N. Y. 1843. S.   **923.25 : 18**

— *Same.* [New issue.] Phila. 1883. D.   **923.25 : 18**

Creighton, Louise. Life of sir Walter Raleigh. [Hist. biogr.] Lond. 1877. S.   **923.25 : 27**

Thomson, Katherine, *born* Byerley. Memoirs of the life of sir Walter Ralegh; with some account of the period in which he lived. Phila. 1831. D.   **923.25 : 20**

Towle, G: Makepeace. Ralegh, his exploits and voyages. [Young folks' heroes of history.] Bost. 1882 [1881]. S.   **923.25 : 21**

Warburton, Eliot Bartholomew G: Memoirs of prince Rupert and the cavaliers, incl. their private correspondence; now first pub. from the original mss. Portr. Lond. 1849. 3 v. O.   **923.3 : 31**

Marsh, Catherine. Memorials of captain Hedley Vicars, by the author of "The victory won". N. Y. 1856. D.   **923.25 : 22**

Paterson, James. Wallace, the hero of Scot-land. Edinb. 1881. D.   **923.25 : 29**

Bonar, Andrew R. Life of the duke of Wel-lington. Halifax. 1847. Tt. **923.25 : 23**

McFarlane, C: Memoir of the duke of Welling-ton; in 4 books, with a concl. chapter by T. A. Buckley. Lond. 1858. S. **923.25 : 24**

Wilson, J: Marius. A memoir of field-marshal the duke of Wellington; with interspersed notices of his principal associates in council and companions and opponents in arms. Lond. *n. d.* 2 v. O.   **923.25+25**

Waite, Rosamond. Life of the duke of Welling-ton. Portr., map and plans. [Hist. biogr.] N. Y. 1879. S.   **923.25 : 26**

4. Other countries.

Germany.

Scherr, Johannes. Blücher, seine zeit und sein leben. 3te ausg. Leipz. 1882. 3 v. O.   **923.3 : 25**
Contents. V. 1. Die revolution, 1740-1790. 2. 1800-1812. 3. 1813-1819.

Oertel, Philipp F: W:, (*W. O. v. Horn*). Das büchlein von dem feldmarschall Blücher; für die deutsche jugend und das deutsche volk. 5te aufl., ill. Wiesbaden. *n. d.* S.   **923.5 : 48**

— Das leben des feldmarschalls Derfflinger; der deutschen jugend und dem deutschen volke erzählt. 4te aufl., ill. Wiesbaden. 1876. S.   **923.3 : 34**

Eickemeyer, Rudolph. Denkwürdigkeiten des generals Eickemeyer, ehem. kurmainz. ingenieur - oberstlieutenant, sodann im dienste der französischen republik, her-ausg. von H: König. Frankfurt a. M. 1845. S.   **923.3 : 10**

Oertel, Philipp F: W:, (*W. O. v. Horn*). Prinz Eugenius, der edle ritter; eine ge-schichte, der deutschen jugend und dem deutschen volke erzählt. 6te aufl., ill. Wiesbaden. 1877. S.   **923.5 : 67**

Oertel, Hugo. Georg von Frundsberg, "der frommen landsknechte liber vater"; ein lebensbild, für die deutsche jugend und das deutsche volk erzählt. Ill. Wiesbaden. 1882. S.   **923.3 : 59**

Schupp, Ottokar. Der feldmarschall graf Neit-hardt v. Gneisenau, der kriegmeister deutscher freiheit; für die jugend und das volk. Ill. Wiesbaden. 1870. S.   **923.3 : 32**

Klippel, G: H: Das leben des generals v. Scharnhorst; nach grösstentheils bis-her unbenutzten quellen dargestellt. Portr. Leipz. 1869-71. 3 v. in 2. O.   **923.3+54**
Contents. V. 1. 1755-1793. 2. 1793-1801. 3. 1801-1813.

Oertel, Philipp F: W:, (*W. O. v. Horn*). Scharn-horst; ein lebensbild aus den zeiten schwe-ren druckes und lebensfrischer erhebung gegen fremde gewalt, der jugend und dem volke dargestellt. 2te aufl., ill. Wiesba-den. 1879. S.   **923.3 : 53**

Schmidt - Weissenfels, E: Scharnhorst; eine biographie. Leipz. 1859. D.   **923.3 : 11**

Oertel, Philipp F: W:, (*W. O. v. Horn*). Von dem frischen und muthigen Seydlitz; ein lebensbild, für das volk und die jugend dargestellt. 3te aufl., ill. Wiesbaden. 1873. S.   **923.3 : 53**

Ranke, Franz Leopold v. Geschichte Wallen-steins. 3te aufl. Leipz. 1872. O.   **904 : 36 v23**

Droysen, J: Gustav. Das leben des feldmarschalls grafen York von Wartenburg. 9te aufl. Portr. and maps. Leipz. 1884. 2 v. in 1. O.   **923.3+27**

Oertel, Philipp F: W:, (*W. O. v. Horn*). Das leben und thaten Hans Joachim v. Zietens; der jugend und dem volke erzählt. 3te aufl., ill. Wiesbaden. 1877. S.   **923.3 : 50**

France.

Headley, Joel Tyler. Napoleon and his marshals. Ill. N. Y. 1883. 2 v. in 1. D.   **923.4 : 19**

Contents. V. **1.** Napoleon.—Berthier.—Augereau.—Davoust.—St. Cyr.—Lannes.—Moncey.—Macdonald.—Mortier.—Soult. **2.** Murat.—Lefebvre.—Massena.—Marmont.— Victor.— Brune.— Oudinot.— Bessieres.—Jourdan. — Bernadotte. — Suchet. — Poniatowski. —Grouchy.—Ney.

— *Same* ; v. 1. *T. p. w.* [N. Y. 1848]. D.   **923.4 : 19 v1**

Kindersley, E: Cockburn. The very joyous, pleasant and refreshing history of the good knight without fear and without reproach, the gentle lord de Bayard, set forth in english. N. Y. 1884. O.   **x 923.4+83**

[Mailles, Jacques de.] History of Bayard, the good chevalier sans peur et sans reproche, compiled by the loyal serviteur. Tr. into english · from the french of Loredan Larchey. Ill. Lond. 1883. Q. **923.4 : P76**

— Spotless and fearless ; the story of the chevalier Bayard from the french of the loyal servant, M. de Berville and others ; with notes and introd. by the ed. 5th ed. [Bayard ser.] Lond. 1875. T.   **923.4 : 38**

Ideville, H: *comte d'*. Memoirs of marshal Bugeaud from his private corresp. and original documents, 1784—1849. Ed. from the french by Charlotte M. Yonge. Lond. 1884. 2 v. O.   **923.4 : 81**

Besant, Walter. Gaspard de Coligny. [New Plutarch.] N. Y. 1879. S.   **923.4 : 42**

Bersier, Eugène. Coligny ; the earlier life of the great huguenot. Tr. by Annie Harwood Holmden. Lond. 1884. O.   **923.4 : 85**

Doisy de Villargennes, Adelbert J. Reminiscences of army life under Napoleon Bonaparte. Cinc. 1884. D.   **923.5 : 56**

Michelet, Jules. Joan of Arc, or The maid of Orleans ; from [his] history of France. [Biogr. series.] Bost. 1882. T. **923.4 : 70**

Tuckey, Janet. Joan of Arc, "the maid". [New Plutarch.] N. Y. 1880. S.   **923.4 : 47**

Wallon, H: Alexandre. Jeanne d'Arc. 5e éd. Paris. 1879. 2 v. D.   **923.4 : 78**

Headley, Phineas Camp. The life of gen. Lafayette. Bost. *n. d.* D. **923.4 : 69**

Ward, Robert D., *comp.* An account of general La Fayette's visit to Virginia in the years 1824–25. Portr. Richmond, Va. 1881. O.   **923.4 : 71**

Italy.

Garibaldi, Giuseppe. Life, written by himself ; with sketches of his companions in arms. Tr. [and continued] by T. Dwight, jr. *T. p. w.* [N. Y. 1859.] D.   **923.5 : 9**

Garibaldi, G.— *Continued.*

— *Same, ger.* Garibaldi's denkwürdigkeiten ; nach handschriftlichen aufzeichnungen desselben, und nach authentischen quellen bearb. und herausg. von Elpis Melena [*pseud. for* Esperance v. Schwarz]. Hamburg. 1861. 2 v. in 1. D.   **923.5 : 9**

Bent, J. Theodore. The life of Giuseppe Garibaldi. Portr. Lond. 1881. D. **923.5 : 10**

— *Same.* N. Y. 1881. Q.   **923.5+10**

Russia.

Novikoff, Olga, *born* Kireef, (*O. K.*). Skobeleff and the slavonic cause by O. K. Lond. 1883. O.   **923.5 : 48**

Nemirovitch-Dantchenko, V. I. Personal reminiscences of general Skobeleff. Tr. from the russian by E. A. Brayley Hodgetts. Portr. Lond. 1884. O.   **923.5+58**

Mackie, J: Milton. Life of Schamyl, the circassian chief, and narrative of the circassian war of independence against Russia. Bost. 1856. D.   **923.5 : 35**

Holland.

Liefde, Jacob de. The great dutch admirals. 4th ed., ill. Lond. [1880]. D. **x 923.5 : 42**

Contents. Jacob van Heemskerk. — Piet Hein. — Marten Harperts Tromp.—Witte Cornelis de With.— Michiel Adrianszoon de Ruyter.—Johan Evertsen.— Cornelis Tromp.

Oertel, Philipp F: W:, (*W. O. v. Horn*). Der admiral de Ruiter ; lebensbild eines seehelden, für die jugend und das volk dargestellt. 2te aufl., ill. Wiesbaden. 1875. S.   **923.5 : 63**

China.

Mackie, J: Milton. The rebel chief, or The chinese insurrection. N. Y. 1860. D.   **923.5 : 45**

Ancient.

Herbert, H: W: The captains of the roman republic, as compared with the great modern strategists ; their campaigns, character, and conduct from the punic wars to the death of Cæsar. N. Y. 1854. D. **923.6 : 6**

Contents. Publius Cornelius Scipio, Africanus. — Titus Quinctius Flaminius.—Lucius Æmilius Paullus. — Caius Marius, of Arpinum. — Lucius Cornelius Sylla.—Caius Julius Cæsar.

Abbott, Jacob. History of Julius Cæsar. N. Y. 1878. S.   **923.6 : 8**

Froude, James Anthony. Cæsar, a sketch. N. Y. 1879. O.   **923.6 : 9**

— *Same.* N. Y. 1881. Q.   **923.6+9**

Napoléon III. History of Julius Cæsar. N. Y. 1865. 2 v. O.   **923.6+10**

Abbott, Jacob. History of Hannibal. Ill. N. Y. *n. d.* S.   **923.6 : 22**

Arnold, T: Life of Hannibal. [Biogr. ser.] Bost. 1881. T.   **923.6 : 24**

x denotes books specially adapted for children.

6. Sociology — d, Miscellaneous classes.

1. The law.

United States.

Flanders, H: The lives and times of the chief justices of the supreme court of the U. S. Phila. 1855, 1858. 2 v. O.   **923.14+2**
Contents. V. I. *1st series.* J: Jay. — J: Rutledge.
2. *2d series.* W: Cushing. — Oliver Ellsworth. — J: Marshall.

Van Santvoord, G: Sketches of the lives and judicial services of the chief justices of the supreme court of the U. S. N. Y. 1856. O.   **923.14:3**
Contents. J: Jay.—J: Rutledge.— Oliver Ellsworth. —J: Marshall.—Roger B. Taney.

Reed, Parker McCobb. The bench and bar of Wisconsin ; history and biography. Portr. Milw. 1882. O.   **923.14+9**

Flower, Frank A. Life of Matthew Hale Carpenter ; a view of the honors and achievements that, in the american republic, are the fruits of well-directed ambition and persistent industry. Madison. 1883. O.
923.14+11

Cowley, C: Leaves from a lawyer's life ashort and ashore. Lowell, Mass. 1879. D.
923.14:12

United States. Exercises at the ceremony of unveiling the statue of J: Marshall, chief justice of the U. S., in front of the capitol, Washington, may 10, 1884 ; with the address of mr. chief justice Waite and the oration of W: H: Rawle ; with the proceedings of the Philadelphia bar relating to the monument to chief justice Marshall. Wash. 1884. Q.   **923.14+13**

Parsons, Theophilus, *jr.* Memoir of Theophilus Parsons ; with notices of some of his contemporaries, by his son. Bost. 1859. D.
923.14:4

Waddell, James D., *ed.* Biographical sketch of Linton Stephens, containing a sel. of his letters, speeches, state papers, etc. Atlanta, Ga. 1877. O.   **923.14:5**

Story, W: Wetmore, *ed.* Life and letters of Joseph Story ; ed. by his son. Bost. 1851. 2 v. O.   **923.14+6**

Tyler, S: Memoir of Roger Brooke Taney. 2d rev. and enl. ed. Baltimore. 1876. O.
923.14+10

Memorial, A, of James A. Van Dyke, pub. by the fire department of the city of Detroit. For private circulation. Detroit. 1856. O.
923.14:7

*   *   *

Ross, Christian K. The father's story of Charley Ross, the kidnapped child. *T. p. w.* [Phila. 1876]. D.   **923.14:8**

Great Britain.

Campbell, J:, *baron Campbell.* The lives of the lord chancellors and keepers of the great seal of England from the earliest times till the reign of king George IV. Phila. 1847, 1848. 7 v. D.
Contents. V. 1-3. *1st ser. to 1688.* (V. 1), Introd. on the origin, functions and jurisdiction of the office

Campbell, J:, *baron Campbell.—Continued.*
of lord chancellor in England.— Under the anglo-saxon kings. — From the conquest to Henry II. — Thomas á Becket. — Till the appointment of queen Eleanor as keeper of the great seal.—Queen Eleanor. — Through the reign of Richard III. — From the accession of Henry VII to the appointment of archbp. Warham.—Life of archbp. Warham.—Wolsey.—Sir T: More.— Audley.— Wriothesley. (2), Life of sir W: Paulet.—Rich.—Goodrich.—Stephen Gardyner.—Heath.—Sir N: Bacon. — Sir T: Bromley.—Sir Cph. Hatton.—Sir J: Puckering.—Lord Ellesmere.— Lord Bacon.—Ld. keeper Williams.—Ld. keeper Coventry.—Ld. keeper Finch.—Ld. keeper Littleton.— Ld. keeper Lane. (3), Under the commonwealth.— Ld. keeper Herbert.—Clarendon.—Ld. keeper Bridgeman.—Shaftesbury.—Nottingham.—Ld. keeper Guilford.—Jeffreys. 4, 5. *2d ser. to 1806.* (4), Lord commissioners of the great seal on the accession of William and Mary.—Life of ld. commissioner Maynard.—Ld. com. Trevor.—Lord Somers.—Ld. keeper Wright. —Lord Cowper. — Lord Harcourt. — Lord Macclesfield.—King.—Lord Talbot. (5), Lord Hardwicke. — Lord Northington. — Lord Camden. — C: Yorke.— Lord Bathurst. — Lord Thurlow. 6, 7. *3d ser. to the reign of George IV.* (6), Lord Loughborough. — Lord Erskine. (7), Lord Eldon.—Postscript. — Chronological and alphabetical tables of chancellors.

— The lives of the chief justices of England, from the Norman conquest till the death of lord Mansfield [v. 3 to the death of lord Tenterden]. 2d amer. ed. Phila. 1853, 1857. 3 v. O.   **923.24:2**
Contents. V. 1. Odo. — W: Fitz-Osborne. — W: de Warrenne and R: de Benefacta.—W: de Carilefo.—Flambard.—Roger, bp. of Salisbury.—Ralph Basset.—Prince Henry.—R: de Luci.—Robert, earl of Leicester.—Ranulfus de Glanville. — Hugh Pusar, bp. of Durham.—W: Longchamp.—Walter Hubert, archbp. of Canterbury.—Geoffrey Fitzpeter.—P: de Rupibus.—Hubert de Burgh.— Stephen le Segrave. — Hugh Bigod.—Hugh le Despencer.—Philip Basset.—H: de Bracton.—Robert de Bruce.—Ralph de Hengham.— De Wayland.—De Thornton.—Roger le Brabazon.— H: le Scrope.—H: de Staunton. — Sir Robert Parnyng.—Sir W: de Thorpe.— Sir W: Shareshall.—Sir H: Green.—Sir J: Knyvet.—Sir J: de Cavendish.— Sir Robert Tresilian.—Sir Robert Belknappe.—Sir W: Thirnynge.—Sir W: Gascoigne.—Sir W: Hankford.— Sir J: Fortescue.—Sir J: Markham.—Sir T: Billing.— Sir J: Hussey.—Sir J: Fineux.—Sir J: Fitzjames.—Sir E: Montagu.—Sir James Dyer.—Sir Robert Catlyne.— Sir Christopher Wray.—Sir J: Popham.—Sir T: Fleming.—Sir E: Coke.—Sir H: Montagu.—Sir James Ley.—Sir Randolf Crewe.—Sir N: Hyde.—Sir T: Richardson.—Sir J: Brampston.—Sir Robert Heath.—Rolle.—Glyn.—Newdigate.—Oliver St. John. — Bradshaw.— Sir Robert Foster.—Sir Robert Hyde.—Sir J: Kelynge. —Sir Matthew Hale. 2. Sir R: Raynsford.—Scroggs. —Sir Francis Pemberton.—Sir Edmund Saunders.— Jeffreys.—Sir E: Herbert.—Sir Robert Wright.—Sir J: Holt.—Sir T: Parker.—Sir J: Pratt.—Ld. Raymond. — Lee.—Hardwicke.—Sir W: Lee.—Sir Dudley Ryder.— Sir J: Willes.—Ld. Marshfield. 3. Ld. Kenyon.—Ld. Ellenborough.—Ld. Tenterden.—Index.

Arnould, *Sir* Joseph. Memoir of Thomas, first lord Denman, formerly lord chief justice of England. Lond. 1873. 2 v. O.
923.24:14

Campbell, J:, *baron Campbell.* Atrocius judges ; lives of judges infamous as tools of tyrants and instruments of oppression, compiled from [his] judicial biographies, with an app. containing the case of Passmore Williamson ; ed. with an introd. and notes by R: Hildreth. N. Y. 1856. D.   **923.24:4**
Contents. Introd.—Roger le Brabancon. — Robert Tresiliad.—T: Billing.—J: Fitzjames.—T: Fleming.— N: Hyde.—J: Brampston.—Robert Heath. — Robert

Foster.—Robert Hyde.—J: Kelynge.—W: Scroggs.—
Francis North.—Edmund Saunders.—G: Jeffreys.—
Robert Wright.

Foss, E: Memories of Westminster hall; a collection of interesting incidents, anecdotes and historical sketches relating to Westminster hall, its famous judges and lawyers and its great trials, with an historical introd. V. 1. Bost. 1874. O.   **923.24 : 3**

Roscoe, H: Lives of eminent british lawyers. Phila. 1841. 2 v. D.   **923.24 : 8**
Contents. V. 1. Sir E: Coke.—J: Selden.—Sir Matthew Hale.—Lord Guildford.— Lord Jeffries.—Lord Somers. — Lord Mansfield. 2. Sir J. E. Wilmot.— Sir W. Blackstone.—Lord Ashburton. — Lord Thurlow.—Sir W. Jones.— Lord Erskine.—Sir S: Romilly.

Sheil, R: Lalor. Sketches of the irish bar; with memoir and notes by R. Shelton Mackenzie. N. Y. *n. d.* 2 v. D.   **923.24 : 5**

O'Flanagan, J. Roderick. The irish bar; comprising anecdotes, bon-mots and biogr. sketches of the bench and bar of Ireland. N. Y. 1878. Q.   **923.24+6**

*   *   *

Ballantine, W: Some experiences of a barrister's life. New rev. ed. from the 6th London ed., with add., corr. and a new pref., written by the author in America. Phila. 1883. D.   **923.24 : 20**

Cockburn, H: T: Memorials of his time. N. Y. 1856. D.   **923.24 : 11**

Curran, W: H: Life of J: Philpot Curran; with add. and notes by R. Shelton Mackenzie. N. Y. 1855. D.   **923.24 : 12**

Phillips, C: Curran and his contemporaries. N. Y. 1851. D.   **923.24 : 13**

Twiss, Horace. Public and private life of lord Eldon; with selections from his corresp. Phila. 1844. 2 v. O.   **923.24 : 15**

Madden, R: Robert. Life and times of Robert Emmet; with notes and add. N. Y. 1868. D.   **923.24 : 16**

Hughes, T: Memoir of a brother. Bost. 1875. D.   **923.24 : 17**

Woolrych, Humphrey W. Life of judge Jeffreys. Buffalo. 1856. D.   **923.24 : 18**

Robinson, H: Crabb. Diary, reminiscences and corresp.; sel. and ed. by T: Sadler. Bost. 1869. 2 v. D.   **923.24 : 19**

*   *   *

Campbell, W: W. An historical sketch of Robin Hood and captain Kidd. N. Y. 1853. D.   **923.24 : 10**

Other countries.

Trenck, F: *freiherr* v. der. Merkwürdige lebensgeschichte, von ihm selbst als ein lehrbuch für menschen, die wirklich unglücklich sind, nicht gute vorbilder für alle fälle zur nachfolge bedürfen; mit einer einleitung von O: Henne am Rhyn. Stuttg. [1883]. D.   **923.3 : 14**

— *Same, eng.* Life [by himself]; containing his adventures and cruel and excessive sufferings during an imprisonment of 10 years, in the fortress of Magdeburg. Phila. 1848. S.   **923.3 : 14**

Sanson, H:, *ed.* Seven generations of executioners; memoirs of the Sansons, 1688-1847. New ed. Lond. 1881. D.   **923.4 : 51**

— *Same, germ.* Mysterien vom schaffot; denkwürdigkeiten der scharfrichter-familie Sanson. Aus dem franz. von C. Büchele. N. Y. *n. d.* 2 v. T.   **923.4 : 51**

Galotti, Antonio. Memoiren von Anton Galotti, drei mal zum tode verurteiltem italienischen offizier. In franz. sprache herausg. und mit historischen aktenstücken belegt durch S. Vecchiarelli. Aus dem franz. übers. Meissen. 1832. 2 v. S.   **923.5 : 11**

2. Philanthropy.

Blaikie, W: Garden. Leaders in modern philanthropy. Portr. N. Y. [1885]. D.   **923.26 : 10**
Contents. Introd.—J: Howard.—W: Wilberforce.— Elizabeth Fry.—T: Chalmers.—Zachary Macaulay.— Stephen Grellet.—Joseph Sturge.—Andrew Reed.—T: Guthrie.—D: Livingstone.—W: Burns.—J: Patterson. —Titus Salt.—G: Moore.—Agnes Jones.

Kirton, J: W: Dr. Guthrie, Father Matthew, Elihu Burritt, Joseph Livesey. (The world's workers). [Portr.] Lond. 1885. D.   **923.26 : 11**

Alldridge, Lizzie. Florence Nightingale, Frances Ridley Havergal, Catherine Marsh, Mrs. Ranyard ("L. N. R."). (The world's workers). [Portr.] Lond. 1885. D.   **923.26 : 12**

Pitman, Emma Raymond. G: Müller and Andrew Reed. (The world's workers). [Portr.] Lond. 1885. D.   **923.26 : 13**

— Elizabeth F r y. (Famous women ser.) Bost. 1884. S.   **923.26 : 6**

Ryder, E:, *comp.* Elizabeth Fry; life and labors of the eminent philanthropist, preacher and prison reformer, comp. from her journals and other sources. Portr. N. Y. 1883. O.   **923.26 : 5**

Gough, J: B. Autobiography. Bost. 1877. S.   **923.16 : 2**

— Sunlight and shadow, or Gleanings from my life work; comprising personal experiences and opinions, anecdotes, incidents and reminiscences gathered from 37 years' experience on the platform and among the people at home and abroad. Ill. Hartford, Ct. 1881. O.   **923.16 : 1**

Aikin, J: View of the character and public services of J: H o w a r d . Lond. 1792. D.   **923.26 : 1**

Dixon, W: Hepworth. J: Howard, and the prison world of Europe; from original and authentic documents. N. Y. 1869. S.   **923.26 : 2**

Stoughton, J: Howard, the philanthropist, and his friends. Lond. 1884. O.   **923.26 : 8**

Weston, James. Sir Moses M o n t e f i o r e; the story of his life. Lond. [1885]. S.   **923.26 : 9**

Wolf, Lucien. Sir Moses Montefiore; a centennial biography, with selections from his letters and journals. N. Y. 1884. Q.   **923.26+7**

Oertel, Philipp F: W:, (*W. O. v. Horn*). Graf Auget de M o n t y o n, einer der edelsten söhne Frankreichs; der jugend und dem volke erzählt. Ill. Wiesbaden. [1876]. D.   **923.4 : 89**

More, Martha. Mendip annals, or A narrative of the charitable labours of Hannah and Martha M o r e in their neighborhood; being the journal of Martha More, ed. with add. matter by Arthur Roberts. N. Y. 1859. S.   **923.26 : 3**

Packard, F: Adolphus. Life of Robert O w e n .
[*Anon.*] Phila. 1866. D.   923.26 : 4
Hanaford, Phebe A. The life of George P e a -
b o d y ; . . . with an introd. by Joseph H.
Hanaford. Bost. [1882]. D.   923.16 : 3
Oertel, Hugo. William W i l b e r f o r c e , der
sklavenfreund ; ein lebensbild, für die
deutsche jugend und das deutsche volk
gezeichnet. Ill. Wiesbaden. 1885. S.
                                                     923.26 : 14

*   *   *

Hendrickson, H: Out from the darkness ; an
autobiography, unfolding the life-story and
singular vicissitudes of a scandinavian
Bartimeus. Chicago. 1879. D. 923.5 : 31

3. Education.

Sedgwick, Catharine Maria. Memoir of Joseph
C u r t i s , a model man. N. Y. 1858. S.
                                                     923.17 : 1
Lange, Wichard, *ed.* Aus F r ö b e l ' s leben und
erstem streben ; autobiographie und
kleinere schriften, herausg. Portr. Ber-
lin. 1862. O.   923.3 : 43
Shirreff, Emily. A sketch of· the life of F:
Fröbel ; together with a notice of madame
v. Marenholtz Bülow's "Personal recollections of F. Fröbel". Pub. for the Fröbel
society. Lond. 1877. D.   923.3 : 22
Hitchcock, E:, *and others.* The power of christian benevolence, as ill. in the life and
labors of Mary L y o n . 12th ed. Northhampton. 1860. D.   923.17 : 2
Thayer, W: Makepeace. The good girl and
true woman, or Elements of success,
drawn from the life of Mary Lyon and
other similar characters. N. Y. *n. d.* S.
                                                 x 923.17 : 5
Mann, Mary, *born* Peabody. Life of Horace
M a n n , by his wife. Bost. 1865. O.
                                                     923.17 : 3
Krüsi, Hermann. P e s t a l o z z i ; his life, work
and influence. Cinc. 1875. O. 923.5 : 40
Schmidt, Ferdinand. H: Pestalozzi ; ein lebensbild für jung und alt. 3te aufl., ill.
Kreuznach. [1883]. S.   923.5 : 64
Seyffarth, L. W. J: H: Pestalozzi ; nach seinem
leben und seinen schriften dargestellt.
4te aufl. Leipz. 1873. D.   923.5 : 61
Pestalozzi, H: Sein leben und wirken einfach
und getreu erzählt für das volk, herausg.
von der Zürcherischen schulsynode zum
hundertsten geburtstage Pestalozzi's. 2te
aufl. Zürich. 1846. D.   923.5 : 41
Platter, T: Leben ; herausg. von H: Düntzer.
Stuttg. [1882]. D.   923.3 : 24
Lloyd, Harriet, *born* Raymond, *ed.* Life and
letters of J: Howard R a y m o n d . N. Y.
1881. O.   923.17 : 4

4. Commerce.

A m e r i c a n   m e r c h a n t s .

Hunt, Freeman, *ed.* Lives of american mer-
chants. N. Y. 1856, 1858. 2 v. O.
                                                     923.18 : 1
Contents. V. 1. Introd. essay by G: R. Russell.
—T: Handasyd Perkins, by T: G. Cary.—T: Pym
Cope, by Joseph R. Chandler.—P: Chardon Brooks,
by E: **Everett.**—James Gore King, by C: **King.**—
N: Brown.—Stephen Girard.—S: Ward, by C: **King.**—

Mathew Carey.—T: Eddy.—Jonathan Goodhue.—Joseph Peabody, by G: Atkinson **Ward.**—Jacob Lorill-
ard, by W: **Berrian.**—Gideon Lee, by C: M. Leupp.
—Walter Restored Jones, by W: A. **Jones.**—S: Appleton, by Ephraim **Peabody.**—Joseph May.—S: Slater,
by J: L. **Blake.**—Alexander Henry, by S. Austin
Allibone.—Jonas Chickering, by J: L. **Blake.**—Asa
Clapp.—Patrick Tracy Jackson, by J: A. **Lowell.** 2.
Elias Hasket Derby, by E. H. **Derby.**—Sir W: Pep-
perell, by Usher **Parsons.**—Stephen Allen, by W:
M. **Allen.**—Maj. S: Shaw, by Amos **Lawrence.**—Ab-
bott Lawrence, by Nathan **Appleton.**—W: Lawrence,
by S: Kirkland **Lothrop.**—J: Jacob Astor, by D:
Ralph **Jaques.**—Judah Touro, by Alexander **Walk-
er.**—J: Bromfield, by Josiah **Quincy.**—Harry R. W.
Hill, by W. R. **King.**—James Brown, by G: Stillman
Hillard.—J: Hancock, by G. **Mountfort.**—Robert
Morris.

Scoville, Joseph A., (*Walter Barrett*). The old
merchants of New York city by Walter
Barrett, clerk. 1st, 3d-4th series. N. Y.
1863–66. 3 v. D.   923.18 : 7
Parton, James. Life of J. J. A s t o r ; append-
ed, a copy of his last will. N. Y. 1865. D.
                                                     923.18 : 2
Oertel, Philipp F: W: (*W. O. v. Horn*). Johan
Jacob Astor ; ein lebensbild aus dem volke,
für das volk und die jugend bearb 2te
aufl. Wiesbaden. 1877. S.   923.18 : 10
Bristed, C: Astor. A Letter to the hon. Horace
Mann. 2d ed. N. Y. 1850. S. 923.18 : 3
Note. A criticism of Mann's opinion of J: Jacob
Astor, expressed in his "Thoughts for a young man."
Ingram, H: Atlee. The life and character of
Stephen G i r a r d of Philadelphia in the
commonwealth of Pennsylvania, mariner
and merchant ; with app. descriptive of
the Girard college at Phila. Ill. Phila.
1884. D.   923.18 : 8
Hoyne, T: In memoriam: Sketch of the life
and character of T: H o y n e ; with the
proceedings of public bodies on the occasion of his death and memorial addresses.
[Chicago. 1886]. O.   923.18+11
Lawrence, W: R., *ed.* Extracts from the diary
and corresp. of Amos L a w r e n c e ; with
a brief account of some incidents in his
life, ed. by his son. Bost. 1856. D.
                                                     923.18 : 4
Hill, Hamilton Andrews. Memoir of Abbott
Lawrence ; with an app. 2d ed. Bost.
1884. O.   923.18+6
Thayer, W: Makepeace. The poor boy and
merchant prince, or Elements of success,
drawn from the life of Amos Lawrence
and other similar characters. N. Y. *n. d.*
S.   x 923.18 : 5

E n g l i s h   m e r c h a n t s .

Bourne, H. R. Fox. Famous London merchants;
a book for boys. Ill. N. Y. 1869. S.
                                                 x 923.28 : 5
Contents. Sir R: Whittington, 1353–1423. — Sir T:
Gresham, 1519–1579.—Sir E: Osborne, 1530–1591.—Sir W:
Herrick, 1557–1653.—Sir T: Smythe, 1560–1625.—Sir H:
Garway, 1570–1645.—Sir Dudley North, 1641–1691.—T:
Guy, 1644–1724.—W: Beckford, 1708–1770.—H: Thornton,
1762–1815.— Nathan Meyer Rothschild, 1776–1836. — S:
Gurney, 1786–1856.—G: Peabody.
Burnley, James. Sir Titus Salt and G: Moore.
(The world's workers). [Portr.] Lond.
1885. D.   923.28 : 4
Lackington, James. Memoirs of the first 45
years of [his] life, written by himself in a
series of letters to a friend. Lond. *n. d.*
O.   923.28 : 1

x denotes books specially adapted for children.

Smiles, S: The successful merchant ; the story of the life of G: Moore, merchant and philanthropist. Lond. *n. d.* D.   **923.28 : 3**
Somerville, Alexander. Life of Roger Mowbray. Lond. 1853. S.   **923.28 : 2**

5. Exploration and travel.

Collective biogr.

Verne, Jules. The exploration of the world. Ill. and maps. N. Y. 1879—1881. 3 v. O.   **913.1 : 5**
Contents. V. 1. **Famous travels and travellers.** Celebrated travellers before the christian era. — From the 1st to the 9th centuries. — Between the 10th and 13th centuries : Benjamin of Tudela; Pion de Carpin or Carpini; Rubruquis.—Marco Polo, 1253-1324.—Jean de Béthencourt, 1339-1425. — Christopher Columbus, 1436-1506.—The conquest of India and of the spice countries. — The conquerors of Central America.—The first voyage round the world.—The polar expeditions and the search for the north-west passage. — Voyages of adventure and privateering warfare : Drake; Cavendish; De Noort; Walter Raleigh.—Missionaries and settlers.—Merchants and tourists.—The great corsair; W: Dampier.—The pole and America. 2. **The great navigators of the 18th century.** Astronomers and cartographers. — Voyages in the 18th century.—Captain Cook's predecessors.—Cook's 1st-3d voyages. — French navigators. — African explorers.—Asia and its inhabitants.—The two Americas. 3. **The great explorers of the 19th century.** The dawn of a century of discovery.—The exploration and colonization of Africa.—The oriental scientific movement and american discoveries.—Voyages round the world and polar expeditions. — French circumnavigators. — Polar expeditions. — The north pole.

St. John, James A: The lives of celebrated travellers. N. Y. 1844. 3 v. S.   **923 : 11**
Contents. V. 1. W: de Rubruquis.—Marco Polo.—Ibn Batúta.—Leo Africanus.—P: della Valle.—J: B. Tavernier.—F. Bernier.—Sir J: Chardin.—E. Kämpfer.—H: Maundrell. 2. J. P. de Tournefort.—T: Shaw.—F: Hasselquist.—Lady Wortley Montague.—R: Pococke.—J: Bell.—J: Ledyard.—G: Forster.—J. Bruce.—J. Hanway.—Antonio de Ulloa. 3. Mungo Park.—P: S. Pallas.—C. Niebuhr. —Choiseul-Gouffier. — J: L. Burckhardt.—Volney.—E: D. Clarke.—F. Le Vaillant.—Belzoni.—D. V. Denon.—R. Heber.

Adams, W: H: Davenport. Some heroes of travel, or Chapters from the history of geographical discovery and enterprise. Map. Lond. 1880. D.   **923 : 12**
Contents. Sir Marco Polo, the venetian, and his Travels in Asia.—G: F. Ruxton, and his Adventures in Mexico and the Rocky mountains.—Dr. Barth and Central Africa. — T: Witlam Atkinson, and his Adventures in Siberia and Central Asia.—Alexina Tinné, and her Wanderings in the Soudan.—J. A. MacGahan, and Campaigning on the Oxus.—Egerton Warburton, and Exploration in west Australia.—Major Burnaby, and A ride to Khiva.—Sir S: Baker, and The sources of the Nile.

Mossman, S: Heroes of discovery : Livingstone, Park, Franklin, Cook, Magellan. New ed. Edinb. 1877. D.   **923 : 13**

Markham, Clements Robert. The sea fathers ; a series of lives of great navigators of former times. N. Y. 1884. D.   **923 : 31**
Contents. Prince Henry, the navigator.—Columbus.— Sebastian del Cano. — The dutch navigators. — Sebastian Cabota and Sir Francis Drake.—Rise of the East India company.—Hudson and Baffin.—W: Dampier.—Cook, Scoresby and Dance.

Adams, W: H: Davenport. Shore and sea, or Stories of great vikings and sea captains. Lond. 1883. D.   **x 923 : 14**
Contents. The northmen in America: Erik the red; Biarni Leifr the lucky; Thorwald; Karlsefni. — The norse sea-kings: Harald Haarfagr; Hakon the good; St. Olaf; Harald Hardrada; Olaf the tranquil; Sigurd the crusader.—An early english discoverer; Sebastian Cabot.—A spanish sea-king; How de Soto conquered Florida.—The early colonizers of Virginia: Raleigh; Amadas and Barlow; J: White.—Sir Francis Drake, a new biography.—The story of H: Hudson, his deeds and sufferings.—Sir H: Morgan, the last of the great buccaneers.

Monarchs of ocean : Columbus and Cook ; two narratives of maritime discovery. Edinb. *n. d.* S.   **923 : 15**
Frost, T: Modern explorers. 2d ed. Ill. N. Y. 1883. O.   **x 923 : 16**
Oberländer, R:, *ed.* Berühmte reisende, geographen und landentdecker im 19ten jahrh.; lebensbilder. Ill. Leipz. 1880. D.   **923 : 17**
Contents. K: Ritter, der vater der neueren erdkunde. — H: Barth. Deutschlands grösster entdeckungsreisender. — Elisha Kent Kane, der weltfahrer. — D: Livingstone, der missionär und landentdecker. — Stanley, der Bismarck der Afrikaforschung.

Adams, W: H: Davenport. Celebrated women travellers of the 19th century. Lond. 1883. D.   **923 : 22**
Contents. Countess Dora D'Istria.—The princess Beliojoso.—Mme. Hommaire de Hell.—Mme. Léonie d'Aunet. — Miss Fredrika Bremer. — Mlle. Alexina Tinné.— Mme. Ida Pfeiffer.—Mme. de Bourboulon.— Lady Hester Stanhope. — Lady Brassey. — Lady Morgan.—Mrs. Trollope.—Miss Harriet Martineau.— Miss Isabella Bird. — Lady Florence Dixie. — Miss Gordon Cumming.—Florence and Rosamond Hill.— Lady Barker.—"Magyarland".

Bourne, C. E. The heroes of african discovery and adventure. Lond. *n. d.* 2 v. D.   **923 : 23**
Contents. V. 1. To the death of Livingstone. 2. From the death of Livingstone to 1882.

Manning, Anne. Heroes of the desert ; the story of the lives and labours of Moffat and Livingstone, by the author of "Mary Powell". Lond. 1880. D.   **923 : 3**

Individual biogr.

Head, *Sir* Francis Bond. The life and adventures of [James] Bruce. N. Y. 1846. S.   **923.29 : 4**
Buckingham, James Silk. Autobiography; incl. his voyages, travels, adventures, speculations, successes and failures, interspersed with characteristic sketches of public men, with whom he had intercourse during more than fifty years. Portr. Lond. 1855. 2 v. O.   **923.29 : 1**
Müller, K:, *ed.* C o o k, der weltumsegler: Leben, reisen und ende des kapitän James Cook, seinem einem blick auf die heutige zustände der Südsee-inselwelt ; ursprünglich herausg. von K: Müller, in den späteren auflagen bearb. von der "Redaktion des Buchs der reisen." 3te verm. aufl. Ill. Leipz. 1882. O.   **923.29 : 2**
Oertel, Philipp F: W:, (*W. O. v. Horn*). James Cook ; leben und thaten des weltberühmten seefahrers und erdumseglers, der jugend und dem volke erzählt. 2te aufl. Ill. Wiesbaden. 1875. S.   **923.29 : 5**
Beesly, A: H. Sir J: F r a n k l i n. [The new Plutarch.] [Maps.] N. Y. 1881. D.   **923.29 : 6**
Hall, Basil. Aus dem seeleben ; [selbstbiographie]. Aus dem engl. von W. E. Drugulin. Leipz. 1855. S.   **923.29 : 7**

Towle, G: Makepeace. The voyages and adventures of Vasco da G a m a . (Young folks' heroes of history). Bost. [1878]. D.
　　　　　　　　　　　　　　　x 923.5 :23
Elder, W: Biography of Elisha Kent K a n e . Phila. 1858. O.　　　　　**923.19 : 4**
Love life of dr. Kane, The ; containing the corresp. and a history of the acquaintance, engagement and secret marriage between Elisha K. Kane and Margaret Fox. Facsimilies of letters and her portr. N. Y. 1866. D.　　　　　　　**923.19 : 5**
Adams, H. G. David L i v i n g s t o n e ; the weaver boy who became a missionary. Lond. 1881. D.　　　　　**923.29 : 8**
Blaikie, W: Garden. The personal life of D: Livingstone ; chiefly from his unpublished journal and correspondence in the possession of his family. Portr. and map. N. Y. 1881. O.　　　　　　　**923.29+9**
Roberts, J : S. The life and explorations of D: Livingstone ; incl. extracts from Livingstone's Last journal by E. A. Manning. Bost. [1881]. D.　　　　　**923.29 : 10**
Towle, G : Makepeace. M a g e l l a n , or The first voyage around the world. (Young folks' heroes of history.) Bost. 1880. D.
　　　　　　　　　　　　　　　x 923.5 : 39
Life and travels of Mungo P a r k , The ; the accounts of his death from the journal of Isaaco, the substance of later discoveries relative to his lamented fate, and the termination of the Niger. N. Y. 1847. S.
　　　　　　　　　　　　　　　916.5 : 14
　See also col. 1334.
Mc Ilraith, J : Life of Sir John R i c h a r d s o n . Lond. 1868. D.　　　　　**923.29 : 11**
Simpson, Alexander. The life and travels of T: S i m p s o n , the arctic discoverer. by his brother. [Portr. and maps]. Lond. 1845. O.　　　　　　　　　**923.29 : 12**
Rowlands, Cadwalader. Henry M. S t a n l e y ; the story of his life, from his birth in 1841 to his discovery of Livingstone, 1871. Ill. Lond. [1872]. D.　　　　　**923.19 : 11**
Wells, W: The heroine of the White Nile, or What a woman did and dared ; a sketch of the remarkable travels and experiences of miss Alexandrine T i n n é . Ill. N. Y. 1881. S.　　　　　　　**x 923.5 : 69**
Vámbéry, Armin. Arminius V a m b é r y ; his life and adventures, written by himself. Popular ed., portr. and ill. N. Y. [1884]. D.　　　　　　　　　　**923.3 : 68**

American discoverers.

Abbott, J : Stevens Cabot. Life of Christopher C o l u m b u s . (Amer. pioneers and patriots.) Ill. N. Y. 1875. D.　　**923.5 : 70**
Alden, W: L. Christopher Columbus, 1440–1506; the first american citizen, by adoption. (Lives of amer. worthies). N. Y. 1881. S.
　　　　　　　　　　　　　　　923.5 : 71
Cubitt, G: Columbus, or The discovery of America. [Discoverers and conquerors.] Bost. 1881. D.　　　　　**923.5 : 72**
Helps, *Sir* Arthur. The life of Columbus, the discoverer of America. 7th ed. Lond. 1881. D.　　　　　　**923.5 : 73**
Irving, Washington. A history of the life and voyages of Christopher Columbus. N. Y. 1828. 3 v. O.　　　　　**923.5 : 74**

Irving, Washington.—*Continued.*
— The life and voyages of Christopher Columbus ; added, those of his companions. Author's rev. ed. N. Y. 1849. 3 v. D.
　　　　　　　　　　　　　　　923.5 : 74
— *Same. In his* Works.　　**820.1 : 13 v1**
— *Same. In his* Works.　　**820.1 : P11 v10-12**
Lamartine, Alfonse Marie L: de. Life of Columbus. [Biogr. series.] Bost. 1881. T.
　　　　　　　　　　　　　　　923.5 : 75
Oertel, Philipp F: W:, (*W. O. v. Horn*). Von dem manne, der uns den weg nach Amerika gewiesen hat ; ein büchlein für die jugend und das volk geschrieben. 4te aufl., ill. Wiesbaden. [1878]. S.　**923.5 : 76**
Abbott, J : Stevens Cabot. History of Hernando C o r t e z . Ill. N. Y. n. d. S.　**923.5 : 24**
Allen, Fred H., *ed.* Cortes, or The discovery and conquest of Mexico. [Discoverers and conquerors]. Bost. [1881]. D.　**923.5 : 25**
Abbott, J : Stevens Cabot. Adventures of the chevalier de L a S a l l e and his companions in their explorations of the prairies, forests, lakes, and rivers of the new world and their interviews with the savage tribes 200 years ago. (Amer. pioneers and patriots). Ill. N. Y. n. d. D.　**923.4 : 43**
Allen, Fred H., *ed.* P i z a r r o , or The discovery and conquest of Peru. [Discoverers and conquerors]. Bost. [1881]. D.
　　　　　　　　　　　　　　　923.5 : 26
Helps, *Sir* Arthur. The life of Pizarro ; with some account of his associates in the conquest of Peru. 2d ed. Lond. 1869. D.
　　　　　　　　　　　　　　　923.5 : 27
Towle, G : Makepeace. Pizarro ; his adventures and conquests. [Young folks' heroes of history]. Bost. 1879. D.　　**x 923.5 : 77**
Abbott, J : Stevens Cabot. Ferdinand de S o t o ; the discoverer of the Mississippi. Ill. N. Y. n. d. D.　　　　　**923.5 : 78**
Lester, C: Edwards, *and* Andrew Foster. The life and voyages of Americus V e s p u c i u s ; with illustrations concerning the navigation and discovery of the new world. N. Y. 1846. O.　　　　　　**923.5 : 79**
Santarem, Manoel Francisco de Barros y Souza, *visconde* de. Researches respecting Americus Vespucius and his voyages. Tr. by E. V. Childe. Bost. 1850. D.　**923.5 : 6**

American pioneers.

Abbott, J : Stevens Cabot. Daniel B o o n e, the pioneer of Kentucky. Ill. (Amer. pioneers and patriots). Ill. N. Y. n. d. D.
　　　　　　　　　　　　　　　923.19 : 1
Hill, G: Canning. Daniel Boone, the pioneer of Kentucky ; a biography. [Amer. biogr.] Phila. 1873. S.　　　**x 923.19 : 2**
Burnett, P: Hardeman. Recollections and opinions of an old pioneer. N. Y. 1880. D.
　　　　　　　　　　　　　　　923.19 : 6
Abbott, J : Stevens Cabot. Christopher C a r s o n, familiarly known as Kit Carson. (Amer. pioneers and patriots). Ill. N. Y. n. d. D.　　　　　　　**923.19 : 9**
Peters, Dewitt C. Pioneer life and frontier adventures ; an authentic record of the romantic life and daring exploits of Kit Carson and his companions, from his own narrative. Bost. 1881. O.　**923.19 : 3**

x denotes books specially adapted for children.

Abbott, J: Stevens Cabot. David C r o c k e t t; his life and adventures. Ill. (Amer. pioneers and patriots). N. Y. *n. d.* D.
                  923.19 : 8

Crockett, D: Life [by himself]; his early history, his bear hunting and other adventures, his services in the Creek war, his electioneering speeches and career in congress, with his triumphal tour through the northern states and services in ·the texan war. Added, an account of his glorious death at the Alamo while fighting in defence of texan independence. Ill. Phila. *n. d.* D.·
                  923.19 : 10

Leith, J: L e i t h ' s narrative; a short biography, with a brief account of his life among the indians. A reprint with ill. notes by C. W. Butterfield. Cinc. 1883. O.
                  923.19+7

6. Society.

Ellet, Ellen Fries, *born* Lummis. The queens of american society. 3d ed. N. Y. 1868. O.
                  923.1 : 5

Holloway, Laura Carter. The ladies of the White House, or In the home of the presidents; a complete history of the social and domestic lives of the presidents from Washington to Hayes, 1789—1880. Ill. Phila. 1881. O.   **923.1 : 7**

Thomson, Katherine, *born* Byerley, *and* J: Cockburn **Thomson,** (*Grace and Philip Wharton*). The queens of society. N. Y. 1861. D.   **920 : 28**
Contents. Sarah duchess of Marlborough.—Mme. Roland.—Lady Mary Wortley Montagu.—Georgiana,

Thomson, K. *and* J: C.—*Continued.*
duchess of Devonshire.—Letitia Elizabeth Landon.—Mme. de Sévigné. — Sidney lady Morgan.—Jane duchess of Gordon.—Mme. Récamier.—Lady Hervey.—Mme. de Staël.—Mrs. Thrale-Piozzi.—Lady Caroline Lamb. — Anne Seymour Damer. — La marquise du Deffand.—Mrs. Elizabeth Montagu.—Mary countess of Pembroke.—La marquise de Maintenon.

— – The wits and beaux of society. Ill. N. Y. 1861. D.   **920 : 29**
Contents. G: Villiers, 2d duke of Buckingham.—Count de Grammont, St. Evremond and lord Rochester.—Beau Fielding.—On certain clubs and club-wits under Anne.—W: Congreve.—Beau Nash. — Philip, duke of Wharton.—Lord Hervey. — Philip Dormer Stanhope, 4th earl of Chesterfield.—The Abbé Scarron.—François duc de la Rochefoucault and the duc de Saint-Simon.—G: Selwyn.—R: Brinsley Sheridan. — Beau Brummell. — Theodore E: Hook. — Sidney Smith.—G: Bubb Dodington, lord Melcombe.

Jameson, Anna, *born* Murphy. Memoirs of the beauties of the court of Charles II. *T. p. w.* D.   **923.2 : 4**
Contents. Catherine of Braganza.—Barbara duchess of Cleveland.—La belle Hamilton, countess de Grammont.—Emilia countess of Ossory.—Lady Denham.—Nell Gwynn.—Elizabeth duchess of Somerset.—Frances duchess of Richmond. — Mrs. Lawson. — Elizabeth countess of Chesterfield. — Henrietta countess of Rochester. — Miss Bagot.—Mrs. Nott.—Anne countess of Southesk.—Susan lady Bellasys.—The countess of Sunderland.—Mrs. Middleton.—The countess of Northumberland. — The duchess of Portsmouth. — The duchess of Devonshire. — Mrs. Jennings.

Jesse, W: The life of G: Brummell, esq., commonly called beau Brummell. Rev. and annotated ed. from the author's own interleaved copy. Portr. N. Y. 1886 [1885]. 2 v. O.   **923.2 : 8**

7. Philology and Science.

1. Philology.

Pökel, W. Philologisches schriftsteller-lexikon. Leipz. 1882. O.   **924 : R1**

Scudder, Horace Elisha. Noah Webster. [Amer. men of letters]. Bost. 1882. D.   **924.1 : 1**

Haym, Rudolph. W: v. Humboldt; lebensbild und characteristik. Berlin. 1856. O.
                  924.3 : 1

Scherer, W: Jacob Grimm; zwei artikel der Preussischen jahrbücher, aus deren 14., 15. und 16. bande besonders abgedruckt. Berlin. 1865. O.   **924.3+2**

2. Natural science.

In general.

Arago, Dominique François J: Gedächtnissreden und biographieen. *In his* Sämmtliche werke.   **500 : 3 v1-3**
Contents, see Deutscher katalog. p. 15.

— *Same, eng.* Biographies of distinguished scientific men. Tr. by W. H. Smyth, Baden Powell and Robert Grant. 1st and 2d series. Bost. 1859. 2 v. D.   **925 : 1**
Contents. 1st ser. The history of my youth; autobiography.— Bailly.— Herschel.— Laplace.— Fourier. 2d ser. Carnot. — Malus. — Fresnel. — T: Young.—Watt.

Arago, Dominique François J:—*Continued.*
— Biographieen der bedeutendsten astronomen [von Hipparch bis Laplace]. *In his* Sämmtliche werke.   **500 : 3 v3**

Brewster, *Sir* D: The martyrs of science, or The lives of Galileo, Tycho Brahe and Kepler. N. Y. 1844. S.   **925 : 2**

Duncan, P: Martin. Heroes of science : botanists, zoologists and geologists. Lond. 1882. D.   **925 : 4**
Contents. The infancy of the knowledge of the science of plants.—The rise of the science of plants : J: Ray; Joseph de Tournefort.—Linnæus.—Consolidation of the science of plants : De Candolle; The natural system.—Heroes of zoology.— Buffon, Pennant and Lamarck.—Cuvier.—Heroes of geology.—Hutton.—W: Smith.—Murchison.—Lyell.

Morton, E: J. C. Heroes of science : astronomers. N. Y. 1883. D.   **925 : 5**
Contents. Ancient astronomy.—Copernik and his system.—Tycho Brahé and his observations.—Kepler and his laws.—Galileo and the laws of motion.—Newton and the discovery of the law of gravitation.—Newton's 'Principia'.—Newton and his followers.—Lagrange and the distribution of the stars.—Modern astronomy.

Muir, Matthew M. Pattison. Heroes of science : chemists. Lond. 1883. D.   **925 : 6**

Brightwell, Cecilia L. Romantic incidents in the lives of naturalists and celebrated travellers. Lond. 1861. D.   **925 : 3**

American.

Agassiz, Elizabeth Cabot, *born* Cary, *ed.* Louis A g a s s i z ; his life and corresp. [Portr.] Bost. 1886 [1885]. 2 v. O.   **925.1 : 8**

Audubon, Lucy, *ed.* Life of J : J. A u d u b o n ; ed. by his widow, with an introd. by James Grant Wilson. N. Y. 1869. D.   **925.1 : 2**

St. John, *Mrs.* Horace Roscoe. Audubon, the naturalist of the new world ; his adventures and discoveries. N. Y. 1856. S.   **925.1 : 1**

Northend, C:, *ed.* Elihu B u r r i t t ; a memorial vol., containing a sketch of his life and labors, with sel. from his writings and lectures, and extracts from his private journals in Europe and America. N. Y. [1879]. D.   **925.1 : 7**

Memorial of Joseph H e n r y. Wash. 1880. Q.   **925.1+6**

Sherman, S: S. Increase Allen L a p h a m ; a biogr. sketch read before the Old settlers' club, Milwaukee, dec. 11, 1875. Mil. 1876. O.   **925.1+4**

Memorial of S: Finley Breese M o r s e, incl. appropriate ceremonies of respect at the national capitol and elsewhere. Pub. by order of cong. Wash. 1875. Q.   **925.1+3**

Fisher, G: Park. Life of B: S i l l i m a n ; chiefly from his ms. reminiscences, diaries, and corresp. N. Y. 1866. 2 v. D.   **925.1 : 5**

British.

Bompas, G: C. Life of Frank B u c k l a n d, by his brother-in-law. Portr. Phila. 1885. O.   **925.2 : 21**

Otter, W: Life and remains of E: Daniel C l a r k e. N. Y. 1827. O.   **925.2 : 1**

Charles D a r w i n ; memorial notices, reprinted from "Nature". (Nature ser.) Lond. 1882. D.   **925.2 : 20**

Krause, Ernst L:, (*Carus Sterne*). Erasmus D a r w i n. Tr. from the german by W. S. Dallas ; with a prelim. notice by C: Darwin. Portr. and ill. N. Y. 1880. D.   **925.2 : 2**

Mayhew, H: The wonders of science, or Young Humphrey D a v y, the cornish apothecary's boy, who taught himself natural philosophy and eventually became president of the Royal society ; the life of a wonderful boy written for boys. N. Y. *n. d.* S.   **x 925.2 : 17**

Smiles, S: Robert D i c k, baker of Thurso, geologist and botanist ; with portr. and ill. N. Y. 1879. D.   **925.2 : 3**

Peirce, Bradford Kinney. The young shetlander [T: E d m o n d s t o n], and his home. Ill. N. Y. [1871]. S.   **x 925.2 : 16**

Smiles, S: Life of a scotch naturalist, [T: E d w a r d] ; associate of the Linnean society. Portr. and ill. N. Y. 1877. D.   **925.2 : 4**

Gladstone, J: H. Michael F a r a d a y. N. Y. 1872. S.   **925.2 : 5**

Tyndall, J: Faraday as a discoverer. N. Y. 1868. D.   **925.2 : 6**

Mayhew, H: The story of the peasant-boy philosopher, or "A child gathering pebbles on the sea-shore" ; founded on the early life of F e r g u s o n, the shepherd-boy astronomer, and intended to show how a poor lad

became acquainted with the principles of natural science. Ill. N. Y. 1855. D.   **x 925.2 : 19**

Herschel, *Mrs.* J: Memoir and corresp. of Caroline H e r s c h e l. Portr. N. Y. 1876. D.   **925.2 : 7**

Holden, E: Singleton. Sir W: H e r s c h e l ; his life and works. N. Y. 1881. D.   **925.2 : 8**

Lyell, *Mrs.* —, *ed.* Life, letters and journals of sir Charles L y e l l, bart., edited by his sister-in-law, mrs. Lyell. Portr. Lond. 1881. 2 v. O.   **925.2 : 12**

Campbell, Lewis, *and* W: **Garnett**. The life of James Clerk M a x w e l l, with a selection from his corresp. and occasional writings, and a sketch of his contributions to science. Portr. and ill. Lond. 1882. O.   **925.2 : 18**

Bayne, P: Life and letters of Hugh M i l l e r. Lond. 1871. 2 v. O.   **925.2 : 11**

Brown, T: N. Life and times of Hugh Miller. N. Y. 1858. D.   **925.2 : 10**

Miller, Hugh. Autobiography : my schools and schoolmasters, or The story of my education. Bost. 1859. D.   **925.2 : 9**

Brewster, *Sir* D: The life of sir I: N e w t o n. N. Y. 1845. S.   **925.2 : 14**

— Memoirs of the life, writings and discoveries of sir I: Newton. Edinb. 1855. 2 v. O.   **925.2+13**

Odling, Elizabeth Mary, *born* Smee. Memoir of the late Alfred S m e e, by his daughter ; with a selection from his miscel. writings. Lond. 1878. O.   **925.2 : 15**

German and other.

Oertel, Philipp F: W:, (*W. O. v. Horn*). Hanns Conrad E s c h e r von der Linth ; lebensbild eines braven schweizers, dargestellt für die jugend und das volk. 2te aufl., ill. Wiesbaden. 1880. S.   **925.5 : 2**

Bauer, Juliette. Lives of the brothers H u m b o l d t. Tr. and arr. from the german of Klencke and Schlesier. Portr. N. Y. 1854. D.   **925.3 : 3**

Bruhns, K:, *ed.* Alexander v. Humboldt ; eine wissenschaftliche biographie, im verein mit R. Avé-Lallemant, J. V. Carus, A. Dove, H. W. Dove, J. W. Ewald, A. H. R. Grisebach, J. Löwenberg, O. Peschel, G. H. Weidemann, W. Wundt bearb. und herausg. Portr. Leipz. 1872. 3 v. O.   **925.3+5**

Klencke, Philipp F: Hermann. Alexander v. Humboldt's leben und wirken, reisen und wissen ; ein biographisches denkmal. fortgesetzt, vielfach erweitert und theilweise umgearb. von H. Th. Kühne und Ed. Hintze. 7e aufl. [Ill. bibliothek der länder- und völkerkunde.] Leipz. 1882. O.   **925.3 : 2**

Schmidt, Ferdinand. Alexander v. Humboldt ; ein lebensbild für jung und alt. 4te aufl., ill. Kreuznach. [1883]. S.   **925.3 : 6**

Thompson, Silvanus P. Philipp R e i s, inventor of the telephone ; a biogr. sketch, with documentary testimony, translations of the original papers of the inventor and contemporary publications. Lond. 1883. O.   **925.3 : 4**

Gage, W: Leonard. Life of C: R i t t e r. N. Y. 1867. D.   **925.3 : 1**

x denotes books specially adapted for children.

Radot, Valery. Louis Paste u r; his life and labours, by his son-in-law. From the french by lady Claud Hamilton; [introd. by J: Tyndall]. [*Anon.*] N. Y. 1885. D.
925.4 : 1

Gebler, K: v. Galileo G a l i l e i and the roman curia; from authentic sources. Tr., with the sanction of the author, by mrs. G: Sturge. Lond. 1879. O.   925.5 : 1

3. Practical science and arts.

Physicians and nurses.

Hirsch, A:, *ed.* Biographisches lexikon der hervorragenden ärzte aller zeiten und völker; unter mitwirkung [zahlreicher gelehrten in den verschiedenen ländern] und unter special-redaction von A[gathon] Wernich [A–F], E[rnst Julius] Gurlt [von G an]; v. 1–3. Wien. 1884–86. 3 v. O. 926 : R15
Contents. V. 1. Aaskow—Chavasse. 2. Chavet— Gwinne. 3. Haab—Lindsley.

Francis, S: W. Biographical sketches of distinguished living New York physicians. N. Y. 1867. O.   926.1 : 2
Contents. Martyn Paine.—J: W. Draper.—J: H. Griscom.—Fordyce Barker.—C. E. Brown-Séquard.— James Anderson.—F. Campbell Stewart.—A. K. Gardner.—I: E. Taylor.—I: Wood.—E: Delafield.— J: C: Beales.—W: A. Hammond.—Horace Green.

Macilwain, G: Memoirs of J: A b e r n e t h y; with a view of his lectures, writings and character. N. Y. 1853. D.   926.2 : 2

Holland, *Sir* H: Recollections of past life. N. Y. 1872. D.   926.2 : 7

Hunt, Harriot Kesia. Glances and glimpses, or Fifty years social, incl. twenty years professional life. Bost. 1856. D.   926.1 : 5

Francis, S: W. Memoir of the life and character of Valentine M o t t. N. Y. 1865. O.
926.1 : 6

Ward, T: Humphry. Humphry S a n d w i t h, a memoir; compiled from autobiographical notes by his nephew. Portr. N. Y. 1884. O.   926.2 : 27

Sims, James Marion. The story of my life; edited by his son, H. Marion - S i m s. N. Y. 1884. D.   926.1 : 3

Tomes, Robert. My college days. N. Y. 1880. S.   926.1 : 8

Zakrzewska, Marie E. A practical illustration of "Woman's right to labor"; a letter, ed. by Caroline H. Dall. Bost. 1860. D.
926.1 : 9

Lonsdale, Margaret. Sister D o r a; a biography. Bost. 1880. S.   926.2 : 11

Inventors, mechanics and artisans.

Collective biogr.

Smiles, S: Men of invention and industry. N. Y. 1885 [1884]. D.   926 : 14

Brightwell, Cecelia Lucy. Heroes of the laboratory and workshop. Lond. *n. d.* S.
x 926 : 7
Contents. R: Arkwright.—C. L: Bertbollet.—J. Brindley.—W: Caxton.—Benvenuto Cellini.—Sir H. Davy.—S. Erard and C. Montal.—Graham and Breguet.—L. Ghiberti and Q. Matsys.—J. Jacquard and his loom.—R: Lenoir.—Oberkampf and calico printing in France.—B. Palissy.—J: Rennie.—J. Roubo.—A. Sennefelder.—G: Stephenson.—Vaucan-

son.—The steam-engine: The marquis of Worcester; S. de Caus; Newcomen; Watt.—J. Wedgwood.— Rennequin; Laurens; Harrison; Gobelin and others. —Bezaleel, Hiram and Paul.

Hale, E: Everett, *ed.* Stories of invention, told by inventors and their friends. Bost. 1885. S.   x 926 : 17
Contents. Introd.—Archimedes.—Friar Bacon.— Benvenuto Cellini.—Bernard Palissy.—B. Franklin.— Theorists of the 18th century.—James Watt.—Robert Fulton.—G: Stephenson and the locomotive.—Eli Whitney.—James Nasmyth.—Sir H: Bessemer.—The last meeting.

Lewis, T. C. Heroes of science: mechanicians. Lond. 1884. D.   926.2 : 25
Contents. Introd.—The first steam-engines.—James Watt.—G: Stephenson.—Sir R. Arkwright.—S: Crompton.—H: Maudsley.—Joseph Clement.—James Nasmyth.—Sir Joseph Whitworth.—C: Babbage.

Triumphs of steam, The; stories from the lives of Watt, Arkwright and Stephenson, by the author of "Might not right", etc. Ill. Lond. *n. d.* D.   x 926.2 : 17

Smiles, S: Industrial biography: iron-workers and tool-makers. Bost. 1864. D. 926.2 : 1
Contents. Iron and civilization.—Beginnings of the iron manufacture in Britain.—Iron-smelting by pit coal.—Dud Dudley.—Andrew Yarranton.—Coalbrookdale iron-works.—The Darbys and the Reynoldses.— Invention of cast steel.—B: Huntsman.—The inventions of H: Cort.—The scotch iron manufacture.— Dr. Roebuck.—D: Mushet.—Invention of the hot-blast.—James Beaumont Neilson.—Mechanical institutions and inventors.—Joseph Bramah.—H: Maudsley.—Joseph Clement.—Fox of Derby.—Murray of Leeds.—Roberts and Whitworth of Manchester. —James Nasmyth.—W: Fairbairn.

Jeans, W: T. The creators of the age of steel. N. Y. 1884. D.   926.2 : 23
Contents. Sir H: Bessemer.—Sir W: Siemens.—Sir Joseph Whitworth.—Sir J: Brown.—S. G. Thomas.— G. F. Snelus.

Foucaud, E: The book of illustrious mechanics of Europe and America. Tr. from the french. New ed., with a supp. chapter on amer. mechanics and their inventions; ed. by J: Frost. Hartford. *n. d.* D. 926 : 1

Howe, H: Memoirs of the most eminent american mechanics, also lives of distinguished european mechanics; together with a coll. of anecdotes, descriptions, etc., relating to the mechanic arts. Ill. N. Y. 1858. D.
926 : 2
Contents. J: Fitch.—B: Franklin.—Oliver Evans.— S: Slater.—Eli Whitney.—D: Bushnell.—Amos Whittemore.—Robert Fulton.—Jacob Perkins.—T: Blanchard.—H: Eckford.

Lives of distinguished shoemakers. Portland. 1849. D.   926 : 3
Contents. St. Crispin.—J. Lackington.—T. Bennett. R. Sherman.—W: Carey.—R: Bloomfield.—S. Antoine. —Hans Sachs.—W: Gifford.—T: Holcroft.—T: Hardy. —Cloudesley Shovel.—G: Fox.—J. Woodhouse.—J. Behmen.—N. Worcester.—J: Pounds.

Winks, W: E: Lives of illustrious shoemakers. Portr. N. Y. [1883]. D.   926 : 13

Individual biogr.

Helps, *Sir* Arthur. Life and labours of T: B r a s s e y, 1805–1870; with a pref. to the amer. ed. by the author. Bost. 1874. O.
926.2 : 3

Blades, W: Biography and typography of W: C a x t o n, England's first printer. 2d ed. Lond. 1882. D.   926.2 : 4

Smith, J. E. A. Pioneer paper-making in Berkshire; life, life work and influence of Zenas C r a n e. *N. p.* [1885]. O.   926.1+13

x denotes books specially adapted for children.

Headley, Phineas Camp. The miner boy and his Monitor, or The career and achievements of John E r i c s s o n, the engineer. N. Y. 1865. S.   x 926.1 : 12
— *Same*. [Heroes of the rebellion.] Bost. 1883 [1882]. D.   x 926.1 : 12

Westcott, Thompson. Life of J : F i t c h. Phila. 1857. D.   926.1 : 4

Peirce, Bradford Kinney. Trials of an inventor; life and discoveries of Charles G o o d - y e a r. N. Y. *n. d.* S.   926.1 : 10

Oertel, Hugo. Johann G u t e n b e r g, der erfinder der buchdruckerkunst; zur dankbaren erinnerung, der deutschen jugend und dem deutschen volke geschildert. Ill. Wiesbaden. 1880. S.   926.3 : 2

Fulton, Justin D. Sam H o b a r t, the locomotive engineer; a workingman's solution of the labor problem. Portr. N. Y. [1883]. D.   926.1 : 11

Nasmyth, James : an autobiography, ed. by S: Smiles. N. Y. 1883. Q.   926.2+22
— *Same*. Ill. N. Y. 1883. D.   926.2 : 22

White, G: Savage. Memoir of S: S l a t e r ; connected with a history of the rise and progress of the cotton manufacture in England and America, with remarks on the moral

influence of manufactories in the U. S. 2d ed. Phila. 1836. O.   926.1+7

Smiles, S: Life of G: S t e p h e n s o n. Bost. 1860. D.   926.2 : 13

Clarke, F. L. G: Stephenson; his life and career. Lond. 1884 [1883]. D.   x 926.2 : 26

Matéaux, C. L. G: and Robert Stephenson. (The world's workers.) [Portr.] Lond. 1885. D.   926.2 : 28

Oertel, Philipp F: W:, (*W. O. v. Horn*). George Stephenson, der mann der eisenbahnen und der lokomotiven; ein lebensbild für die deutsche jugend und das volk. 2te aufl., ill. Wiesbaden. 1876. S.   926.2 : 29

Muirhead, James Patrick. Life of James W a t t; with selections from his corresp. N. Y. 1859. D.   926.2 : 14

Oertel, Philipp F: W:, (*W. O. v. Horn*). James Watt, der erfinder; ein lebensbild für die deutsche jugend und das volk. 2te aufl., ill. Wiesbaden. 1876. S.   926.2 : 30

Working-man's way in the world, The; the autobiography of a journey man printer. N. Y. 1854. D.   926.2 : 15

Green, W: The life and adventures of a cheap Jack, by one of the fraternity; ed. by C: Hindley, new ed. [The wanderer's lib.] Lond. 1881. D.   926.2 : 6

x denotes books specially adapted for children.

8. Fine arts.

1. Architects, sculptors, painters and engravers.

In general.

Müller, Herrmann Alexander. Biographisches künstler-lexikon der gegenwart; die bekanntesten zeitgenossen auf dem gesammtgebiet der bildenden künste aller länder, mit angabe ihrer werke. Leipz. 1882. D.   927 : R25

Pilkington, Matthew. The gentleman's and connoisseur's dictionary of painters. Lond. 1770. Q.   927 : R27
Containing, A complete collection and account of the most distinguished artists who have flourished in the art of painting in Italy, Holland, Flanders, England, Germany or France from 1250 to 1767; added, a catalogue of the disciples of the most famous masters, and a catalogue of painters who have imitated the works of the eminent masters.— *Title-page.*

Bryan, Michael. A biographical and critical dictionary of painters and engravers; with a list of ciphers, monograms and marks. New ed., comprising above 1000 add. memoirs and new plates of ciphers and monograms. Lond. 1878. Q.   927 : R1

Ottley, H: A biographical and critical dictionary of recent living painters and engravers; forming a suppl. to Bryan's Dictionary of painters and engravers, as ed. by G: Stanley. Lond. 1877. Q.   927 : R2

Daryl, Philippe. A dictionary of painters and handbook for picture amateurs; incl. an explanation of the different methods of painting, instructions for cleaning, relining and restoring oil-paintings, a glossary of terms, an historical sketch of the principal schools of painting. With notes

on the copyists and imitators of each master. [Weale's ser.] Lond. [1883]. D.   927 : 17

Waters, Clara Erskine, *formerly mrs.* Clement. Painters, sculptors, architects, engravers and their works; a handbook. Ill. and monograms. 5th ed. Bost. 1879. D.   927 : 3
— *and* Lawrence **Hutton**. Artists of the 19th century and their works; a handbook containing 2050 biogr. sketches. Bost. 1879. 2 v. D.   927 : 4
— *Same*. 3d ed. rev. Bost. 1885. 2 v. in 1. D.   927 : R4

Keddie, Henrietta, (*Sarah Tytler*). The old masters and their pictures; for the use of schools and learners in art by Sarah Tytler. Bost. 1880. D.   927 : 10
Contents. Early italian art.—Early flemish art.—In early schools of italian art.—Leonardo da Vinci.—Michael Angelo.—Raphael.—Titian. — German art; Albrecht Dürer.—Later italian art.—Carracci.—Guido Reni.—Domenichino.—Salvator Rosa.—Later flemish art.—Spanish art.—French art. — Foreign artists in England.
— Modern painters and their paintings; for the use of schools and learners in art, by Sarah Tytler. Bost. 1880. D.   927 : 11
Contents. English art.—Later french art.—Modern german art.—Later english art.—Contemporary english art.—Modern continental painters. — American painters.

Viardot, L:, *and others*. An illustrated history of painters of all schools. Lond. 1877. Q.   927 : R16

Eastlake, Elizabeth, *born* Rigby, *lady*. Five great painters; essays reprinted from the Edinburgh and Quarterly reviews. Lond. 1883. 2 v. D.   927.5 : 47
Contents. V. 1. Leonardo da Vinci.—Michael Angelo. — Titian, pt. 1. 2. Titian, pt. 2.—Raphael.—Albert Dürer.

Dohme, Robert, *ed.* The early teutonic, italian and french masters. Tr. and ed. from the Dohme series by A. H. Keane. Ill. Lond. 1880. Q.   **927 : R24**

Contents. The early german masters. Dohme, R., Einhart.—**Schultz,** A., Tustilo of St. Gall; St. Bernward; The german minster builders.—**Schmidt,** W., Martin Schongauer; Albert Dürer.—**Rosenberg,** A., The german little masters.—**Woltmann,** A., Matthias Grunewald; Hans Baldung Grien; Hans Burckmair. *The early flemish and dutch masters.* **Eisenmann,** O., The brothers van Eyck.—**Rosenberg,** A., Lucas van Leyden. — **Eisenmann,** O., Quentin Matsys.—**Lemcke,** K:, Gerhard Terborch. *The early italian masters.* **Woermann,** K:, Masaccio; Fra Filippo Lippi; Filippino Lippi; Sandro Botticelli; Domenico Ghirlandajo.—**Woltmann,** A., Andrea Mantegna.—**Lucke,** H., Fra Bartolommeo.—**Janitschek,** D. H., Andrea del Sarto.—**Vischer,** R., Luca Signorelli; Giovanni Antonio de'Bazzi. *The early french masters.* **Regnet,** C. A., N: Poussin; C: Lebrun; P: Mignard; Claude Lorraine.

Meynell, Wilfrid, *ed.* Some modern artists and their work. Ill. N. Y. 1883. Q.   **927 : R19**

Contents. Sir F: Leighton.—Sir J: Gilbert. — G. H. Boughton.— Vicat Cole.—Joseph Edgar Boehm.—J: L: Ernest Meissonier.—Sir Joseph Noel Paton. — H: Stacy Marks.—Mrs. Butler.—Laurens Alma-Tadema.—Hamo Thornycroft.—Luke Fields.—Rosa Bonheur.—W: F: Yeames.—G: Dunlop Leslie.—Michael Munkacsy. — Briton Riviere.—Erskine Nicol. — Eastman Johnson.—James Clarke Hook.—Frank Holl.—Prof. Legros.—Haynes Williams.—W: H. Beard.—J: Pettie.—Louise Jopling.—Marcus Stone. — R. Ansdell.—G: F: Watts.— Philip Hermogenes Calderon.—Joseph Flüggen.

Ellet, Elizabeth Fries, *born* Lummis. Women artists in all ages and countries. N. Y. 1859. D.   **927 : 9**

American.

Tuckerman, H: Theodore. Artist - life, or Sketches of american painters. N. Y. 1847. D.   **927.1 : 16**

Contents. B: West.—Copley.—Stuart.— Trumbull.—Allston.—Malbone.—Vanderlyn. — Morse.—Durand.—W. E. West.—Sully. — Inman.— Cole.—Leslie.—Weir.—Chapman.—Edmonds.—Freeman. — Leutze.—Huntington.—Deas.—Flagg.—G. L. Brown.

— Book of the artists: American artist life, comprising biographical and critical sketches of amer. artists ; preceded by an historical account of the rise and progress of art in America, with an app. containing an account of notable pictures and private collections. N. Y. 1867. O.   **927.1 : R1**

Benjamin, S: Green Wheeler. Our american artists. Portr. and ill. Bost. [1880]. O.   **x 927.1+P3**

Contents. W: H. Beard.—Albert F. Bellows.—Robert Swain Gifford.—W: M. Chase.—Sanford R. Gifford. — Walter Shirlaw. — J: J. Enneking. — T: W. Wood. — S: Colman. — Wordsworth Thompson.— G: Loring Brown.—D: Neal.

— *Same,* 2d series: Painters, sculptors, engravers and architects. Ill. Bost. [1881]. O.   **x 927.1+P4**

Contents. J: Lafarge.— Arthur Quartley. — Daniel Huntington.—T: Hill.—Edwin Lord Weeks.—James Wells Champney.—G: Inness.—J. S. Hartley.—C: S. Reinhart. — Lady illustrators.—A. V. S. Anthony.—Architecture.

Sheldon, G. W. American painters ; with examples of their work engr. on wood. N. Y. 1880. Q.   **927.1 : R2**

Sweetser, Moses Foster. Artist - biographies : Allston. Bost. 1879. T.   **927.1 : 17**

Amory, Martha Babcock. The domestic and artistic life of J: Singleton Copley, R. A.;

with notices of his works and reminiscences of his son lord Lyndhurst, lord high chancellor of Great Britain, by his granddaughter. Bost. 1882. O.   **927.1 : 22**

British.

Collective biogr.

Redgrave, S: A dictionary of artists of the english school ; painters, sculptors, architects, engravers and ornamentists, with notices of their lives and work. New ed. rev. to date. Lond. 1878. O.   **927.2 : R34**

Cunningham, Allan. The lives of the most eminent british painters and sculptors. N. Y. 1859. 5 v. S.   **927.2 : 1**

Contents. V. 1. The early painters.—W: Hogarth.—R: Wilson. — Sir J. Reynolds. — T: Gainsborough. 2. R: West.—Ja. Barry.—W: Blake. — J: Opie.—G: Morland.—E: Bird.—H: Fuseli. 3. G. Gibbons. — C. G. Cibber.—L: F. Roubillac.—J. Wilton.—T: Banks.—J. Nollekens.—J: Bacon. — Anne Damer.—J: Flaxman. 4. Jameson.—Ramsey.—Romney.—Runciman.—Copley.—Mortimer.— Raeburn.— Hoppner.— Owen. — Harlow. — Bonington. 5. Cosway. — D: Allan.—Northcote. — Beaumont. — Lawrence. — Jackson. — Liverseege.—Burnet.

British painters ; with examples of their work engr. on wood. N. Y. 1881 [1880]. O.   **927.2 : R2**

Walpole, Horace, *4th earl of Orford.* Anecdotes of painting in England, with some account of the principal artists ; with add. by James Dallaway and Vertue's catalogue of engravers who have been born or resided in England. New ed. rev. with notes. Lond. *n. d.* 3 v. O.   **927.2 : P35**

Clayton, Ellen Creathorne. English female artists. Lond. 1876. 2 v. O.   **927.2 : 44**

Contents. V. 1. Susannah Hornebolt. — Lavinia Teerlinck.—Anne Carlisle.—Artemisia Gentileschi.—The sisters Cleyn.—Anna Maria Carew.— Elizabeth Neale. — Mary More.—Mrs. Boardman. — Elizabeth Creed.—Mary Beale.— Susan Penelope Rose.—Anne Killegrew. — Maria Varelot.— Anne, princess of Orange.—Princess Caroline.— Agatha Vandermijn.—Sarah Hoadley.—Elizabeth Blackwell.—Mary Delany.—Frances Reynolds. — Maria Anna Angelika Catherine Kauffman.—Mary Moser.—Mary Cecilia Louisa Cosway.—Amateurs: temp. George III.—The close of the 18th century.—The earlier years of the 19th century.—Mary Harrison.—Anna Maria Charretie.—Adelaide A. Maguire. 2. Figure painters. — Landscape painters. — Portrait and miniature painters, painters on enamel, etc.—Painters of flowers, fruit and still life.—Animal painters.—Humorous designers.—Decorative artists.—Amateurs.—Index.

Gower, *Lord* Ronald C: Romney and Lawrence. [Ill. biogr. of the great artists]. N. Y. 1882. D.   **927.2 : 29**

Individual biogr.

Dobson, H: Austin. T: B e w i c k and his pupils. Portr. and ill. Bost. 1884. D.   **927.2 : 38**

Thomson, D: Croal. Life and labours of Hablôt Knight B r o w n e, "Phiz". Ill. Lond. 1884. Q.   **927.2 : R40**

Jerrold, W: Blanchard. The life of G: C r u i k - s h a n k, in two epochs. Ill. N. Y. 1882. 2 v. D.   **927.2 : 30**

Arnold, G: Moss Brock-. G a i n s b o r o u g h. [Ill. biogr. of the great artists]. Lond. 1881. D.   **927.2 : 3**

Gower, *Lord* Ronald C: My reminiscences. Lond. 1883. 2 v. O.   **927.2 : 32**

---

x denotes books specially adapted for children.

Haydon, B: Robert. Correspondence and table-talk ; with a memoir by his son, F: Wordsworth Haydon. Ill. Bost. 1877. 2 v. Q.   **927.2+45**
— **Stoddard**, R: H:. *ed.* The life, letters and table-talk of B: Robert Haydon. (Sans-souci ser.) N. Y. 1876. S.   **927.2 : 5**
— **Taylor**, T:, *ed.* Life of B: Robert Haydon ; from his autobiogr. and journals. N. Y. 1859. 2 v. D.   **927.2 : 6**
Dobson, H: Austin. H o g a r t h. [Ill. biogr. of the great artists]. Lond. 1879. D.   **927.2 : 7**
Stephens, F: G. Sir Edwin L a n d s e e r. [Ill. biogr. of the great artists]. Lond. 1880. D.   **927.2 : 9**
Sweetser, Moses Foster. Artist-biographies : Landseer. Bost. 1879. T.   **927.2 : 8**
Leslie, C: Robert. Autobiographical recollections ; ed. with a pref. essay on L e s l i e as an artist, and selections from his corresp., by Tom Taylor. Portr. Bost. 1860. D.   **927.2 : 10**
Ferry, B: Recollections of A. N. Welby P u g i n and his father A: Pugin, with some notices of their works ; with an app. by E. Sheridan Purcell. Lond. 1861. O.   **927.2 : 27**
Pulling, F. S. Sir Joshua R e y n o l d s. [Ill. biogr. of the great artists]. Lond. 1880. D.   **927.2 : 11**
Sweetser, Moses Foster. Artist-biographies : Sir Joshua Reynolds. Bost. 1878. T.   **927.2 : 12**
Hamerton, Philip Gilbert. Life of J. M. W. T u r n e r. Bost. 1879. D.   **927.2 : 13**
Monkhouse, W. Cosmo. Turner. [Ill. biogr. of the great artists]. Lond. 1879. D.   **927.2 : 14**
Sweetser, Moses Foster. Artist-biographies : Turner. Bost. 1878. T.   **927.2 : 15**
Mollett, J: W. Sir D: W i l k i e. [Ill. biogr. of the great artists]. Lond. 1881. D.   **927.2 : 16**
Phillimore, Lucy. Sir Christopher W r e n, his family and his times ; with original letters and a discourse on architecture, hitherto unpub., 1585—1723. Lond. 1881. O.   **927.2 : 28**
—— *Same.* N. Y. 1881. O.   **927.2+28**

G e r m a n , d u t c h , f l e m i s h , d a n i s h .

Fromentin, Eugène. The old masters of Belgium and Holland, (Les maitres d'autrefois). Tr. by Mary C. Robbins. Boston. 1882. D.   **927.5 : 40**
Gower, *Lord* Ronald C: The figure painters of Holland. [Ill. biogr. of the great artists]. Lond. 1880. D.   **927.5 : 27**
<small>Contents. Introd.—Gerard van Hanthorst.—Adrian Brouwer. — Gerard Ter-Borch. — Adrian Jansz van Ostade. — Ferdinand Bol. — Bartholomeus van der Helst. — Gerard Dou. — Philips Wouverman. — Isack Jansz van Ostade.—Jan Steen.—Gabriel Metsu. — Nicolaas Maes.—Jan ver Meer, of Delft.—Peter de Hoch.—Frans van Mieris.— Caspar Netscher. — List of the principal paintings of the dutch figure painters. — Bibliography.—Index.</small>
Scott, W: Bell. The little masters. [Ill. biogr. of the great artists]. Lond. 1879. D.   **927.3 : 1**
<small>Contents. Albrecht Altdorfer.—Hans Sebald Beham.—Barthel Beham.—H: Aldegrever.—G: Pencz.—Jacob Bink.—Hans Brosamer.</small>

Stöhr, Hans Adam, *ed.* Deutscher künstler-kalender auf das jahr 1884. 3ter jahrg. Berlin. [1884]. T.   **927.3 : R26**
Heath, R: Ford. Albrecht D ü r e r. [Ill. biogr. of the great artists]. Lond. 1881. D.   **927.3 : 2**
Sweetser, Moses Foster. Artist biographies : Dürer. Bost. 1878. T.   **927.3 : 3**
Thausing, Moriz. Albert Dürer ; his life and his works. Tr. from the german, ed. by Fred. A. Eaton. Portr. and ill. Lond. 1882. 2 v. O.   **927.3+4**
Cundall, Joseph. Hans H o l b e i n ; from Holbein und seine zeit by dr. Alfred Woltmann. [Ill. biogr. of the great artists]. Lond. 1879. D.   **927.3 : 39**
Woltmann, Alfred. Holbein und seine zeit ; des künstlers familie, leben und schaffen. 2te umgearb. aufl. Ill. Leipz. 1874. O.   **927.3+38**
Eggers, Hartwig K: F:, *and* K: F: P: **Eggers.** Christian Daniel R a u c h. Portr. Berlin. 1873, 1878. 2 v. O.   **927.3+33**
Mollett, J: W. R e m b r a n d t. [Ill. biogr. of the great artists]. Lond. 1879. D.   **927.5 : 29**
Sweetser, Moses Foster. Artist-biographies : Rembrandt. Bost. 1878. T.   **927.5 : 30**
Kett, C: W. R u b e n s. [Ill. biogr. of the great artists]. Lond. 1879. D.   **927.5 : 31**
Holland, Hyacinth. Moritz v. S c h w i n d ; sein leben und seine werke, aus des künstlers eigenen briefen und dem erinnerungen seiner freunde zusammengestellt. Stuttg. 1873. O.   **927.3 : 42**
Plon, Eugene. T h o r v a l d s e n ; his life and works. Tr. from the french by I. M. Luyster. Ill. 2d amer. ed. Bost. 1884. O.   **927.5 : 33**
Head, Percy Rendell. V a n D y c k. [Ill. biogr. of the great artists]. Lond. 1879. D.   **927.5 : 32**
Justi, K: W i n c k e l m a n n ; sein leben, seine werke und seine zeitgenossen ; [mit skizzen zur kunst- und gelehrtengeschichte des 18ten jahrh., nach gedruckten und handschriftlichen quellen dargestellt]. Leipz. 1866—72. 2 v. in 3. O.   **927.3 : 43**
<small>Contents. V. 1. Winckelmann in Preussen.—Winckelmann in Sachsen. 2. 1ste abth. Römische lehrjahre, 1755—1763. — 2te abth. Römische meisterjahre, 1763—1768.</small>

F r e n c h .

Sweetser, Moses Foster. Artist biographies : C l a u d e Lorraine. Bost. 1878. T.   **927.4 : 1**
Tucker-Machetta, Blanche Roosevelt, *born* Tucker. Life and reminiscences of Gustave D o r é ; compiled from material supplied by Doré's relations and friends and from personal recollection ; with many original unpub. sketches and selections from Doré's best publ. illustrations, by Blanche Roosevelt. Lond. 1885. O.   **927.4+14**
Gonse, L: Eugène F r o m e n t i n, painter and writer. Tr. by Mary Caroline Robbins. Bost. 1883. O.   **927.4 : 13**
Le Brun, Marie Louise Elisabeth, *born* Vigée. Souvenirs. Portr. N. Y. 1879. O.   **927.4 : 6**
Mollett, J: W. M e i s s o n i e r. [Ill. biogr. of the great artists]. Lond. 1882. D.   **927.4 : 2**

Sensier, Alfred. Jean-François M i l l e t, peasant and painter. Tr. by Helena de Kay from the french. Bost. 1881. O.   **927.4:3**

Rees, J. Ruutz-. Horace V e r n e t. [Ill. biogr. of the great artists]. N. Y. 1880. D.
927.4:5

Mollett, J: W. W a t t e a u. [Ill. biogr. of the great artists]. N. Y. 1883. D.   **927.4:12**

Italian and Spanish.

Collective biogr.

Vasari, G: Lives of the most eminent painters, sculptors and architects. Tr. from the italian, with notes and ill., chiefly selected from various commentators by mrs. Jonathan Foster. Lond. 1850-52. 5 v. D.
927.5:1
Contents, see Catalogue of the Boston athenæum, v. 5, p. 3184.

— Stories of the italian artists, from Vasari, by the author of "Belt and spur," etc. Ill. N. Y. 1885 [1884]. D.   **927.5:46**

Jameson, Anna, *born* Murphy. Memoirs of the early italian painters. Bost. 1878. S.
927.5:3
Contents. Giovanni Cimabue. — Giotto. — Lorenzo Ghiberti.—Masaccio. — Filippo Lippi and Angelico da Fiesole. — Benozzo Gozzoli. — Andrea Castagno and Luca Signorelli. — Domenico Dal Ghirlandajo. — Andrea Mantegna. — The Bellini. — Pietro Perugino. — Francesco Raibolini.—Fra Bartolomeo.—Lionardo da Vinci.—Michael Angelo.—Andrea del Sarto.—Raphael Sanzio d'Urbino.—The scholars of Raphael.—Corregio and Giorgione and their scholars. — Parmigiano. — Giorgione. — Titian. — Tintoretto.—Paul Veronese.—Jacopo Bassano.

Boyhood of great painters. From the french. 1st and 2d ser. N. Y. [1856]. 2 v. S.
x 927.5:2

Cartwright, Julia. Mantegna and Francia. [Ill. biogr. of the great artists]. Lond. 1881. D.   **927.5:12**

Perkins, C: Callahan. Raphael and Michelangelo ; a critical and biogr. essay. Bost. 1878. O.   **927.5:18**

Baxter, Lucy E., (*Leader Scott*). Ghiberti and Donatello, with other early italian sculptors. [Ill. biogr. of the great artists]. N. Y. 1882. D.   **927.5:41**

— Luca della Robbia, with other italian sculptors. [Ill. biogr. of the great artists]. Lond. 1883. D.   **927.5:43**

Individual biogr.

Phillimore, Catherine Mary. Fra A n g e l i c o : [Ill. biogr. of the great artists]. Lond. 1881. D.   **927.5:4**

Sweetser, Moses Foster. Artist-biographies. Fra Angelico. Bost. 1879. T.   **927.5:5**

Baxter, Lucy E., (*Leader Scott*). Fra B a r t o l o m e o. [Ill. biogr. of the great artists]. Lond. 1881. D.   **927.5:6**

Cellini, Benvenuto. Memoirs, written by himself ; containing a variety of information respecting the arts and history of the 16th century, with the notes and observations of G. P. Carpani. Tr. by T: Roscoe. N. Y. 1845. 2 v. D.   **927.5:7**

Heaton, M. Compton. C o r r e g g i o. [Ill. biogr. of the great artists]. N. Y. 1882. D.   **927.5:42**

---

x denotes books specially adapted for children.

Davillier, J: C: *baron.* Life of F o r t u n y ; with his works and corresp. From the french ; with notes and reminiscences by a friend. Phila. 1885. D.   **927.5:48**

Quilter, Harry. G i o t t o. [Ill. biogr. of the great artists]. Lond. 1881. D.   **927.5:8**

Sweetser, Moses Foster. Artist-biographies : G u i d o Reni. Bost. 1878. T.   **927.5:9**

Richter, J: Paul. L e o n a r d o. [Ill. biogr. of the great artists]. N. Y. 1880. D.
927.5:11

Sweetser, Moses Foster. Artist-biographies : Leonardo da Vinci. Bost. [1879]. T.
927.5:10

Black, C: Christopher. M i c h a e l A n g e l o Buonarroti, sculptor, painter, architect ; the story of his life and labours. Lond. 1875. O.   **927.5+P13**

Clément, C: Michelangelo. [Ill. biogr. of the great artists]. Lond. 1880. D.   **927.5:14**

Grimm, Herman. Life of Michael Angelo. Tr. with the author's sanction by Fanny Elizabeth Bunnett. 4th ed. Bost. 1866. 2 v. D.   **927.5:15**

Harford, J: Scandrett. Life of Michael Angelo Buonarroti ; with tr. of many of his poems and letters, also memoirs of Savonarola, Raphael and Vittoria Colonna. Lond. 1857. 2 v. O.   **927.5:16**

Sweetser, Moses Foster. Artist-biographies : Michael Angelo. Bost. 1878. T.   **927.5:17**

Minor, Ellen F. M u r i l l o. [Ill. biogr. of the great artists]. Lond. 1882. D.   **927.5:25**

Sweetser, Moses Foster. Artist-biographies : Murillo. Bost. 1878. T.   **927.5:24**

Bell, N. R. E., (*N. D'Anvers*). R a p h a e l. [Ill. biogr. of the great artists]. Lond. 1880. D.   **927.5:19**

Crowe, Joseph Archer, *and* Giovanni Battista Cavalcaselle. Raphael ; his life and works, with particular reference to recently discovered records and an exhaustive study of extant drawings and pictures. Lond. 1885. 2 v. O.   **927.5:50**

Sweetser, Moses Foster. Artist-biographies : Raphael. Bost. 1877. T.   **927.5:20**

Vasari, G: Das leben Rapbaels von Urbino ; italiänischer text von Vasari, übersetzung und commentar von Herman Grimm. Berlin. 1872. O.   **927.5:51**

Morgan, Sydney, *born* Owenson, *lady.* The life and times of Salvator Rosa. New ed. Lond. 1885. D.   **927.5:36**

Osler, W: Roscoe. T i n t o r e t t o. [Ill. biogr. of the great artists]. Lond. 1879. D.
927.5:21

Crowe, Joseph Archer, *and* Giovanni Battista Cavalcaselle. The life and times of T i t i a n ; with some account of his family. 2d ed. with portr. and ill. Lond. 1881. 2 v. O.   **927.5:49**

Heath, R: Ford. Titian. 2d ed. [Ill. biogr. of the great artists]. Lond. 1879. D.
927.5:22

Sweetser, Moses Foster. Artist-biographies : Titian. Bost. 1878. T.   **927.5:23**

Stowe, Edwin. V e l a z q u e z. [Ill. biogr. of the great artists]. Lond. 1881. D.
927.5:26

2. Musicians and singers.

Collective biogr.

Baptie, D:, *ed.* A handbook of musical biography. Lond. [1883]. D.   **927 : R20**

Keddie, Henrietta, *(Sarah Tytler)*. Musical composers and their works ; for the use of schools and students of music. Bost. 1881. D.   **927 : 12**

Contents. Rise of cultivated music.—Dunstable.—Palestrina.—Orlando Gibbons.—Bull.—Purcell.—Scarlatti, father and son.—Stradella.—Bach.—Handel.—Gluck.—Haydn.—Mozart.—Beethoven.—Weber.—Mendelssohn.—Cherubini.— Spontini,— Rossini.—Bellini.—Donizetti.—Croft.—Arne.—Bishop.—Clementi.—Cramer.—Woelfl.— Balfe.— Macfarren.—Spohr.— Hummel.—Schubert.—Schumann.— Chopin.—Moscheles.—Auber.— Halévy.— Meyerbeer.— Verdi, Gounod, Thomas, Flotow.—Berlioz.—David.—Hiller.—Ernst.—Heller.—Liszt.—Brahms.—Von Bülow.—Rietz.—Reinecke.—Benedict, Costa, Randegger.—Sterndale Bennett, Sullivan, etc.—R: Wagner.—Index.

Urbino, Lavinia Buoncore. Biographical sketches of eminent musical composers, arr. in chronological order. Bost. 1876. S.   **927 : 23**

Ferris, G: T. The great italian and french composers. [Appleton's new handy-vol. ser.] N. Y. 1879. S.   **927.5 : 34**

Contents. Palestrina.—Piccini, Paisiello and Cimarosa.—Rossini.—Donizetti and Bellini.—Verdi.—Cherubini and his predecessors.—Méhul, Spontini and Halévy.—Boïeldieu and Auber.—Meyerbeer.—Gounod.

— The great german composers. [Appleton's handy-vol. ser]. [*Anon.*] N. Y. 1879. S.   **927.3 : 5**

Contents. Bach. — Handel. — Gluck.— Haydn.—Mozart. — Beethoven. — Schubert, Schumann and Franz.—Chopin.—Weber.—Mendelssohn.—Wagner.

Barrett, W: Alexander. English church composers. (The great musicians). Lond. 1882. D.   **927.2 : 33**

Crowest, F. The great tone-poets ; short memoirs of the greater musical composers. Cinc. 1877. O.   **927 : 18**

Contents. Bach. — Handel. — Gluck. — Haydn.—Mozart.—Beethoven. — Weber. — Rossini. — Schubert.—Mendelssohn.—Schumann.

Barnard, C:, *(Jane Kingsford)*. The tone masters ; a musical series for young people. Bost. [1876]. 3 v. S.   **x 927:13-15**

Contents. V. 1. Mozart and Mendelssohn. 2. Händel and Haydn. 3. Bach and Beethoven.

Butterworth, Hezekiah. The great composers. (Little biogr.) Ill. Bost. [1884]. S.   **x 927 : 22**

Rimbault, E: Francis. Gallery of great composers ; a portraits engr. on steel from oil paintings by C: Jäger, reproduced by the heliotype process, with biogr. and critical notices. Bost. 1881. Q.   **927 : R21**

Contents. Bach. — Handel. — Gluck.— Haydn.—Mozart.—Beethoven.—Schubert.—Weber.—Mendelssohn.—Schumann.—Meyerbeer.—Wagner.

Celebrated musicians of all nations ; a collection of portraits, with short biogr. notices. Tr. from the german, with an app. for England, by M. F. S. Hervey. Lond. [1883]. F.   **927 : R26**

Ferris, G: T. The great violinists. [Appleton's new handy-vol. ser.] N. Y. 1881. S.   **927 : 7**

Contents. The violinists and pianists.—Viotti.—L: Spohr. — Nicolo Paganini.— De Bériot.—Ole Bull.—Muzio Clementi.—Moscheles.— The Schumanns and Chopin.—Thalberg and Gottschalk.—Franz Liszt.

x denotes books specially adapted to children.

Clayton, Ellen Creathorne. Queens of song ; memoirs of some of the most celebrated female vocalists who have performed on the lyric stage from the earliest days of opera to the present time. Added, a chronol. list of all the operas that have been performed in Europe. N. Y. 1865. O.   **927 : 5**

Contents. Katherine Tofts and Margarita de L'Epine.—Anastasia Robinson (countess of Peterborough).—Lavinia Fenton (duchess of Bolton).—Early french singers ; Marthe le Rochois; La Maupin.—Rival queens: Francesca Cuzzoni and Faustina Bordoni.—Caterina Mingotti. — Caterina Gabrielli. — Sophie Arnould.—Antoinette Cécile Clavel St. Huberty.—Gertrude Elizabeth Mara.—Anna Maria Crouch.—Anna Selina Storace.—Elizabeth Billington.—Giuseppa Grassini.—Angelica Catalani.—Josephine Mainville Fodor.—Laure Cinthie Damoreau.—Violante Camporese.—Rosamunda Pisaroni.—Giuditta Pasta.—Catharine Stephens.—Mary Anne Paton.—Wilhelmina Schröder Devrient.—Henrietta Sontag.—Julia Dorus Gras.—Cornélie Falcon.—Maria Felicita Malibran.—Giulia Grisi.—Clara Anastasia Novello.—Paulina Viardot Garcia.— Fanny Persiani.— Catherine Hayes.—Marietta Alboni.—Angiolina Bosio.—Jenny Lind Goldschmidt.—Sophie Cruvelli.—Marietta Piccolomini.—Louisa Pyne.—Teresa Tietjens.—Chronological list of operas.—Index.

Ferris, G: T. Great singers; Faustina Bordoni to Henrietta Sontag. [Appleton's handy-vol. ser.] N. Y. 1880, 1881. 2 v. S.   **927 : 6**

Contents. 1st ser. Faustina Bordoni. — Catarina Gabrielli.—Elizabeth Billington and Gertrude Mara.—Angelica Catalani.—Giuditta Pasta.—Henrietta Sontag. 2d ser. Maria Felicia Malibran.— Wilhelmina Schröder Devrient. — Giulia Grisi.— Pauline Viardot.—Fanny Persiani.—Marietta Alboni. — Jenny Lind. — Sophie Cruvelli. — Theresa Tietiens.

Individual biogr.

Poole, Reginald Lane. Sebastian B a c h . (The great musicians). N. Y. 1882. S.   **927.3 : 18**

Spitta, Julius A: Philipp. J: Sebastian Bach. Leipz. 1873, 1880. 2 v. O.   **927.3+40**

Kenney, C: Lamb. A memoir of Michael W: Balfe. Portr. Lond. 1875. O. **927.2+39**

Nohl, L: Life of Beethoven. Tr. from the german, by J: J. Lalor. [Biogr. of musicians.] Chicago. 1881. D.   **937.3 : 6**

Berlioz, L: Hector. Selections from his letters and æsthetic, humerous and satirical writings. Tr. and preceded by a biogr. sketch of the author by W: F. Apthorp. [Amateur ser.] N. Y. 1879. D.   **927.4 : 10**

Bull, Sara C., *born* Thorpe. Ole B u l l ; a memoir, with Ole Bull's " Violin notes" and dr. A. B. Crosby's "Anatomy of the violinist". Bost. 1883 [1882]. O.   **927.5 : 39**

Karasowski, Moritz. Frederic C h o p i n , his life, works and letters ; with the portr. of Chopin and fac simile of the original ms. of his e-minor prelude op. 28, no. 4. Cinc. 1880. 2 v. O.   **927.5 : 44**

Liszt, Franz. Life of Chopin. Tr. from the french by Martha Walker Cook. 2d rev. ed. Phila. 1863. S.   **927. 5 : 38**

Gottschalk, L: Moreau. Notes of a pianist during his professional tours in the U. S., Canada, the Antilles and South America ; preceded by a short biogr. sketch, with contemporaneous criticisms, ed. by his sister, Clara Gottschalk. From the french by R. E. Peterson. Phila. 1881. O.   **927.1 : 12**

Marshall, Florence A., *born* Thomas, *mrs.* Julian. H a n d e l. (The great musicians.) N. Y. 1883. S.   **927.3 : 20**

Reissmann, A: G: F: Händel; sein leben und seine werke dargestellt. Berlin. 1882. O.   **927.3 : 35**

Rockstro, W: S.   Life of G: F: Handel; with an introd. notice by G: Grove. Portr. N. Y. 1883. D.   **927.3 : 22**

Schölcher, V: Life of Handel. N. Y. 1857. D.   **927.3 : 8**

Nohl, L: Life of H a y d n. From the german by G: P. Upton. [Biogr. of musicians.] Chicago. 1883 [1882]. D.   **927.3 : 7**

Seeburg, Franz v., *originally* Franz Hacker. Joseph Haydn; the story of his life. Tr. from the german by J. M. Toohey. Notre Dame, Ind. 1884. D.   **927.3 : 24**

Townsend, Pauline D. Joseph Haydn. (The great musicians.) N. Y. 1884. D.   **927.3 : 31**

Willis, Nathaniel Parker. Memoranda of the life of Jenny L i n d. Phila. 1851. S.   **927.5 : 37**

Nohl, L: Life of L i s z t. From the german by G: P. Upton. Portr. Chicago. 1884. D.   **927.3 : 27**

Hiller, Ferdinand. M e n d e l s s o h n; letters and recollections. Tr., with the consent and revision of the author, by M. E. v. Glehn. Lond. 1874. O.   **927.3 : 9**

Lampadius, W: A: Life of Mendelssohn; sketches by Julius Benedict, H: F. Chorley, L: Rellstab, Bayard Taylor, R. S. Willis and J. S. Dwight; ed. and tr. by W: Leonhard Gage. N. Y. 1865. S.   **927.3 : 10**

Reissmann, A: Felix Mendelssohn-Bartholdy; sein leben und seine werke. 2te stark verm. und verb. aufl. Portr. Berlin. 1872. O.   **927.3 : 36**

Rockstro, W: S. Mendelssohn. (The great musicians.) N. Y. 1884. D.   **927.3 : 25**

Hensel, Sebastian. The Mendelssohn family [1729–1847], from letters and journals; with portr. from drawings by W: Hensel. 2d rev. ed. Tr. by C: Klingemann and an amer. collaborator; with a notice by G: Grove. N. Y. 1882 [1881]. 2 v. O.   **927.3 : 11**

Moscheles, Ignaz. Recent music and musicians as described in [his] diaries and corresp.; ed. by his wife and adapted from the original german by A. D. Coleridge. [Amateur ser.] N. Y. 1875. D.   **927.3 : 12**

Gehring, Franz. M o z a r t. (The great musicians.) N. Y. 1883. S.   **927.3 : 20**

Holmes, E: Life of Mozart, incl. his corresp. N. Y. 1845. S.   **927.3 : 14**

Jahn, O: W. A. Mozart. 2te durchaus umgearb. aufl. Portr. Leipz. 1867. 2 v. O.   **927.3 : 30**

— *Same, eng.* Life of Mozart. Tr. from the german by Pauline D. Townsend; with a pref. by G: Grove. Lond. 1882. 3 v. O.   **927.3 : 30**

Nohl, L: Life of Mozart. Tr. from the german by J: J. Lalor. [Biogr. of musicians]. Chicago. 1880. D.   **927.3 : 13**

Waterston, Anna Morton, *born* Quincy, *mrs* R. C. Adelaide P h i l l i p p s; a record. Bost. 1883. D.   **927.1 : 23**

Cummings, W: H. P u r c e l l. (The great musicians). Lond. 1881. D.   **927.2 : 4**

Edwards, H: Sutherland. R o s s i n i and his school. (The great musicians). Lond. 1881. D.   **927.5 : 35**

Frost, H. F. S c h u b e r t. (The great musicians). Lond. 1881. D.   **927.3 : 15**

Kreissle von Heilborn, H: Franz Schubert. Wien. 1865. O.   **927.3 : 41**

— *Same, eng.* The life of Franz Schubert. Tr. from the german by Arthur Duke Coleridge, with an app. by G: Grove. Lond. 1869. 2 v. D.   **927.3 : 29**

Maitland, J. A. Fuller. S c h u m a n n. (The great musicians). N. Y. 1884. D.   **927.3 : 28**

Wasielewski, W: Joseph v. Robert Schumann; eine biographie. 3te verm. aufl. Portr. Bonn. 1880. O.   **927.3 : 37**

Barnard, C: Camilla, a tale of a violin; being the artist life of Camilla U r s o. Bost. [1874]. S.   **927.4 : 7**

Gautier, Judith. Richard W a g n e r and his poetical works, from Rienzi to Parsifal; tr. by L. S. J. Bost. 1883. D.   **927.3 : 19**

Glasenapp, C: F: R: Wagner's leben und werken, in 6 büchern dargestellt; neue verm. ausg., mit einem namen- und sachregister. Leipz. 1882. 2 v. O.   **927.3 : 34**

Hueffer, Francis. Richard Wagner. (The great musicians). N. Y. 1881. D.   **927.3 : 16**

Nohl, L: Life of Wagner. From the german by G: P. Upton. Chicago. 1884 [1883]. D.   **927.3 : 23**

Benedict, *Sir* Julius. W e b e r . (The great musicians). Lond. 1881. D.   **927.3 : 17**

3. Actors, conjurers, etc.

A m e r i c a n   a n d   B r i t i s h .

Cook, Dutton. Hours with the players. Lond. 1881. 2 v. D.   **927 : 8**

    Contents. V. 1. Will Mountford and lord Mohun.— Mistress Woffington. — Poor Perdita. — "Sir Peter Teazle". — "Lady Teazle". — "Joseph Surface". — "Charles Surface". — "Sir Benjamin Backbite". — "Mr. Crabtree". — "Mrs. Candour". — "Sir Oliver Surface". 2. Mr. and Mrs. Baddeley. — "Married beneath her". — "A gentleman of the name of Booth". — Miss Smithson. — "Old Farren". — Mrs. Glover. — Sir Charles Coldstream. — Charlotte Cushman. — Rachel Felix. — Charles Kean. — A note on Fechter.

A m e r i c a n .

Farrar, J. M. Mary A n d e r s o n; the story of her life and professional career. Portr. Lond. 1884. Q.   **927.1+24**

Barnum, Phineas Taylor. Struggles and triumphs, or Forty years' recollections, written by himself, to 1872. Buffalo. 1872. D.   **927.1 : 14**

Clarke, Asia, *born* Booth. The elder and the younger B o o t h. [Amer. actor ser.] Bost. 1882. D.   **927.1 : 6**

— Booth memorials; passages, incidents and anecdotes in the life of Junius Brutus Booth by his daughter. N. Y. 1866. D.   **927.1 : 5**

Brougham, J: Life, stories and poems; ed. by W: Winter. Bost. 1881. D.   **927.1 : 7**

    Contents. Autobiography; a fragment. — Supp. memoir, by the ed.—Brougham in his club life, by Noah Brooks. **Selected writings.** Terry Magra's Leprechaun.—O'Bryan's luck.—Romance and reality.—Kit Cobb, the cabman.—The morning dream.—The test of blood.—Fatality.—The Blarney stone.—Ned Geraghty.—The fairies' warning.—O'Dearmid's ride.—Jasper Leech.—A night with the spirits.—Poems.

Stebbins, Emma, *ed.* Charlotte Cushman; her letters and memories of her life. Bost. 1879. O.   **927.1 : 8**

Waters, Clara, *born* Erskine, *formerly mrs.* Clement. Charlotte Cushman. [Amer. actor ser.] Ill. Bost. 1882. D. **927.1 : 15**

Ireland, Joseph N. Mrs. Duff. [Amer. actor ser.] Bost. 1882. D.   **927.1 : 19**

Field, Kate. C: Albert Fechter. [Amer. actor ser.] Ill. Bost. 1882. D. **927.1 : 18**

Barrett, Lawrence. Edwin Forrest. [Amer. actor ser.] Bost. 1881. D. **927.1 : 9**

Winter, W: The Jeffersons. [Amer. actor ser.] Bost. 1881. D. **927.1 : 10**

Ritchie, Anna Cora, *born* Ogden, *afterward mrs.* Mowatt. Autobiography, or Eight years on the stage. Bost. 1854. S. **927.1 : 11**

Gustafson, Zadel, *born* Barnes. Genevieve Ward; a biogr. sketch from original material, derived from her family and friends. Bost. 1882 [1881]. S. **927.1 : 21**

Wood, W: B. Personal recollections of the stage; embracing notices of actors, authors and auditors, during a period of forty years. Portr. Phila. 1855. D. **927.1 : 20**

British.

Lewes, G: H: On actors and the art of acting. [Amateur ser.] N. Y. 1878. D. **927.2 : 19**

Baker, H: Barton. English actors from Shakespeare to Macready. [Amateur ser] N. Y. 1879. 2 v. D.   **927.2 : 18**

Stoddard, R: H:, *ed.* Bric-a-brac series: Personal reminiscences by O'Keeffe, Kelly and Taylor. N. Y. 1876. S. **927.2 : 17**

Pascoe, C: Eyre, *ed.* Our actors and actresses: The dramatic list; a record of the performances of living actors and actresses of the british stage. 2d ed., rev. and enl. Lond. 1880. D.   **927.2 : 43**

*   *   *

Austin, L:, *(Frederic Daly).* Henry Irving in England and America, 1838–84. Portr. N. Y. 1884. D.   **927.2 : 37**

Irving, H: A short account of his public life. Portr. N. Y. 1883. D. **927.2 : 31**

Hatton, Joseph H: Irving's impressions of America; narrated in a series of sketches, chronicles and conversations. Bost. 1884. D.   **927.2 : 36**

Winter, W: Henry Irving. N. Y. 1885. S. **927.2 : 42**

Cole, J: W: Life and theatrical times of C: Kean; incl. a summary of the english stage for the last fifty years, and a detailed account of the management of the Princess's theatre from 1850 to 1859. Lond. 1859. 2 v. D.   **927.2 : 20**

Procter, Bryan Waller, *(Barry Cornwall).* Life of Edmund Kean. [*Anon.*] N. Y. 1835. D.   **927.2 : 22**

Kemble, Frances Ann, *formerly mrs.* Butler. Records of a girlhood. 2d ed. N. Y. 1879. D.   **927.2 : 23**

— Records of later life. N. Y. 1882. O. **927.2 : 24**

Macready, W: C: Reminiscences and selections from his diary and letters; ed. by sir F: Pollock. Portr. *T. p. w.* [N. Y.] O. **927.2 : 21**

— *Same.* Lond. 1875. 2 v. O. **927.2 : 21**

Mathews, Anne, *born* Jackson. Memoirs of Charles Mathews. Lond. 1839. 4 v. O. **927.2+25**

Molloy, J. Fitzgerald. The life and adventures of Peg Woffington, with pictures of the period in which she lived. Lond. 1884. 2 v. D.   **927.2 : 41**

Young, Julian C: Memoir of C: Mayne Young, with extracts from his son's journal. Portr. and sketches. Lond. 1871. D. **927.2 : 26**

Other.

Bauer, Karoline. Caroline Bauer and the Coburgs. Tr. and ed. from [her] Nachgelassene memoiren by C: Nisbet. Lond. 1885. D.   **927.3 : 32**

Houdin, Robert J: Eugène. Memoirs, written by himself; ed. by R. Shelton Mackenzie. Phila. 1860. D.   **927.4 : 9**

Allen, G: The life of Philidor, musician and chess-player; with a supp. essay on Philidor as chess-author and chess-player, by Tassilo v. Heydebrand und der Lasa. Phila. 1863. O.   **927.4 : 4**

Altemus, Jameson Torr. Helena Modjeska. Portr. N. Y. [1883]. D. **927.5 : 45**

Memoirs of Rachel by mme. de B—. N. Y. 1858. D.   **927.4 : 8**

9. Literature.

1. In general.

Bornmüller, Franz, *ed.* Biographisches schriftsteller-lexikon der gegenwart; die bekanntesten zeitgenossen auf dem gebiet der nationallitteratur aller völker, mit angabe ihrer werke. Leipz. 1882. D. **928 : R1**

DeQuincey, T: Biographical essays. Bost. 1851. D.   **928 : 2**
Contents. Shakspeare. — Pope.—C: Lamb.—Goethe. —Schiller.

Harris, Amanda B. Pleasant authors for young folks. Ill. Bost. [1884]. D. **x 928 : 4**

Hatfield, Edwin F. The poets of the church; a series of biogr. sketches of hymn-writers,

with notes on their hymns. N. Y. [1884]. O.   **928+5**

Bates, W: The Maclise portrait - gallery of "illustrious literary characters"; with memoirs, biogr., critical, bibliogr. and anecdotal ill. of the literature of the former half of the present century. Portr. Lond. 1882. D.   **928 : 6**

Jameson, Anna, *born* Murphy. Memoirs of the lives of the poets; biogr. sketches of women celebrated in ancient and modern poetry. Bost. 1857. T. **928 : 3**

Allibone, S: Austin. A critical dictionary of ... british and american authors. **820 : R1**
See col. 1003.

x denotes books specially adapted for children.

2. American authors.

Collective biogr.

Adams, Oscar Fay. A brief handbook of american authors. Bost. 1884. D. **928.1 : R66**
— *Same.* **928.1 : 66**

Homes of american authors; comprising anecdotical, personal and descriptive sketches by various writers. Ill. N. Y. 1853. O. **928.1 : 64**
Contents. Audubon.—Paulding.—Irving. — Bryant. —Bancroft. — Dana. — Prescott. — Miss Sedgwick. — Cooper.—Everett.—Emerson.—Simms. — Longfellow. —Hawthorne.—Webster.—Kennedy.—Lowell.

Homes and haunts of our elder poets, The. Portr. and ill. N. Y. [1881]. Q. **928.1+P1**
Contents. **Powers,** H. N., W: Cullen Bryant. — **Sanborn,** F. B:, Ralph Waldo Emerson.—**Stoddard,** R: H:, H: Wadsworth Longfellow; J: Greenleaf Whittier.—**Sanborn,** F. B:, Oliver Wendell Holmes; James Russell Lowell.

Powell, T: The living authors of America. 1st series. N. Y. 1850. D. **928.1 : 3**
Contents. Cooper.—Emerson.—Willis.—Poe.—Longfellow. — Prescott. — Bryant. — Halleck. — Dana. — Frances Osgood.— S. M. Fuller.—Mrs. Kirkland.— Sparks.

Wilson, James Grant. Bryant and his friends; some reminiscences of the Knickerbocker writers. [Portr. and facsimiles]. N. Y. 1886 [1885]. D. **928.1 : 78**
Contents. W: Cullen Bryant.—James K. Paulding. —Washington Irving.— R: H: Dana.— James Fenimore Cooper.— Fitz-Greene Halleck.— Joseph Rodman Drake. — Nathaniel Parker Willis. — Edgar A. Poe.—Bayard Taylor.— Knickerbocker literature.— Index.

Haweis, Hugh Reginald. American humorists. N. Y. [1883]. D. **928.1 : 56**
Contents. Washington Irving.—O. W. Holmes.—J. R. Lowell.— Artemus Ward. — Mark Twain.— Bret Harte.

Clemens, Will M. Famous funny fellows; brief biogr. sketches of amer. humorists. Cleveland. 1882. D. **928.1 : 2**

Griswold, W: Maccrillis. A directory of writers for the literary press in the U. S. Bangor, Me. 1884. O. **928.1 : R77**

Individual biogr.

Hale, Susan, *ed.* Life and letters of T: Gold Appleton. Portr. N. Y. 1885. D. **928.1 : 76**

Memoirs of James Gordon Bennett and his times, by a journalist. N. Y. 1855. D. **928.1 : 4**

Didier, Eugene Lemoine. The life and letters of madame Bonaparte. N. Y. 1879. D. **928.1 : 5**

Merriam, G: S. The life and times of S: Bowles. N. Y. 1885. 2 v. O. **928.1 : 79**

Hingston, E: P. The genial showman; reminiscences of the life of Artemus Ward [C: F. Browne], and pictures of a showman's career in the western world. N. Y. 1870. O. **928.1 : 20**

Godwin, Parke. A biography of William Cullen Bryant, with extracts from his private corresp. Portr. N. Y. 1883. 2 v. O. **928.1+55**

Hill, D: J. American authors: W: Cullen Bryant. Portr. N. Y. 1879. S. **928.1 : 6**

Symington, Andrew James. W: Cullen Bryant; a biogr. sketch, with sel. from his poems and other writings. N. Y. 1880. S. **928.1 : 7**

Curtis, G: W: Life, character and writings of W: Cullen Bryant; a commemorative address, del. before the N. Y. historical society. N. Y. [1879]. D. **928.1 : 8**

Century, The, *New York.* Bryant memorial meeting of the Century, tuesday evening, nov. 12th 1878. N. Y. [1878]. O. **928.1+63**
Contents. Introductory.—Catalogue of pictures.— Program.— **Taylor,** B. Epicedium.— **Bigelow,** J: Oration.—**Stoddard,** R: H: The dead master.—**Stedman,** E. C. The death of Bryant.

Hudson, Mary, *born* Clemmer, *formerly mrs.* Ames. A memorial of Alice and Phœbe Cary; with some of their later poems. Portr. N. Y. 1873. D. **928.1 : 9**

Lounsbury, T: R. James Fenimore Cooper. (Amer. men of letters.) Bost. 1888 [1882]. S. **928.1 : 48**

Derby, James C. Fifty years among authors, books and publishers. Portr. N. Y. 1884. O. **928.1+72**

Farrar, Eliza Ware, *born* Rotch. Recollections of seventy years. Bost. 1866. S. **928.1 : 10**

Fields, James T: Biographical notes and personal sketches; with unpub. fragments and tributes from men and women of letters. Bost. 1881. O. **928.1 : 11**

Emerson, Ralph Waldo, W: H: Channing *and* James Freeman Clarke. Memoirs of Margaret Fuller Ossoli. Bost. 1852. 2 v. D. **928.1 : 29**
— *Same.* [New ed.] Portr. and app. Bost. 1884. 2 v. in 1. D. **928.1 : 29**
Contents of app. I: Fuller and his descendants.— Memorial of mrs. Margaret Fuller.—Poetical tributes.

Higginson, T: Wentworth. Margaret Fuller Ossoli. (Amer. men of letters.) Bost. 1884. S. **928.1 : 67**

Howe, Julia Ward. Margaret Fuller, marchesa Ossoli. (Famous women.) Bost. 1883. S. **928.1 : 61**

Goodrich, S: Griswold. (*Peter Parley*.) Recollections of a lifetime, or Men and things I have seen, in a series of familiar letters to a friend; historical, biographical, anecdotal and descriptive. N. Y. 1857. 2 v. O. **928.1 : 12**

Cornell, W: Mason. Life and public career of the hon. Horace Greeley. Bost. [1882]. D. **928.1 : 45**

Parton, James. Life of Horace Greeley. N. Y. 1855. D. **928.1 : 14**
— *Same.* From his birth to the present time. [New ed.] Portr. and ill. Bost. 1872. D. **928.1 : 15**

Greeley, Horace. Recollections of a busy life, incl. reminiscences of amer. politics and politicians, from the opening of the Missouri contest to the downfall of slavery; added, miscellanies: "Literature as a vocation"; "Poets and poetry"; "Reforms and reformers"; "A defence of protection", etc., also a discussion with Robert Dale Owen on the law of divorce. N. Y. 1868. O. **928.1 : 13**

Cleveland, Cecilia. The story of a summer or Journal leaves from Chappaqua [relating to Horace Greeley]. N. Y. 1874. T. **928.1 : 16**

Wilson, James Grant. Life and letters of Fitz-Greene H a l l e c k. N. Y. 1869. D.
928.1 : 17

Cousin, Alice ; a memoir of Alice B. H a v e n. N. Y. 1865. D. 928.1 : 44

Hawthorne, Julian. Nathaniel H a w t h o r n e and his wife ; a biography. Portr. Bost. 1885 [1884]. 2 v. D. 928.1 : 71

James, H:, jr. Hawthorne. [Eng. men of letters]. N. Y. 1880. D. 928.1 : 18

Lathrop, G: Parsons. A study of Hawthorne. Bost. 1876. T. 928.1 : 19

Brown, E. E. Life of Oliver Wendell H o l m e s. Portr. Bost. [1884]. D. 928.1 : 68

Kennedy, W: Sloane. Oliver Wendell Holmes; poet, litterateur, scientist. Bost. 1883. D.
928.1 : 58

Bryant, W: Cullen. Discourse on the life, character and genius of Washington I r v i n g. N. Y. 1860. D. 928.1 : 26

Hill, D: J. American authors : Washington Irving. Portr. N. Y. 1879. S. 928.1 : 22

Irving, Pierre M. Life and letters of Washington Irving, by his nephew. N. Y. 1862–1864. 4 v. D. 928.1 : 24

— Same. In Irving, W. Works.
820.1 : P11 v25–27

Warner, C: Dudley. Washington Irving. (Amer. men of letters). Bost. 1881. S. 928.1 : 21

— and others. Studies of Irving. N. Y. 1880. O. 928.1 : 25

Irvinginana ; a memorial. N. Y. 1860. O.
928.1+23

Contents. Memoranda of [his] literary career, by E. A. Duyckinck.—Funeral, by W. F. Williams.—Proceedings of the New York board of aldermen and councilmen.—Resolutions of the Athenæum club.—Proceedings of the New York historical society.—Proceedings of the Massachusetts historical society.—Sunnyside; a poem, by H: T. Tuckerman.—An editorial of the Evening post.—An editorial of the Richmond (L. I.) Gazette.—Mr. Irving's religious character, by rev. dr. Creighton.—Passage from a discourse by the rev. J: A. Todd.—The rev. dr. Chapin's remarks.—Posthumous influence, by the rev. dr. W: F. Morgan.—Goldsmith and Irving, by G: W. Greene.—Irving described in verse by J. R. Lowell.—Visits to Sunnyside, by N. P. Willis.—Half an hour at Sunnyside, by T. Tilton.—A day at Sunnyside, by O: Tiffany.—Anecdote.—Washington Irving, by G: W: Curtis.—Same, by F: S. Cozzens.—Table-talk by J. G. Wilson. Anecdotes by F. Saunders.—Icha bod Crane, from a letter by Irving.—Cockloft Hall, a reminiscence.—Irving portraits.—Mr. Irving's objection to public dinners.—Anecdote, from the Spirit of the times.—Two poems, by Irving.—American literary commissions in London in 1822, a letter by Irving.—Life and letters of Irving.

Keese, W: Linn. John K e e s e, wit and littérateur ; a biogr. memoir. Portr. N. Y. 1883. O. 928.1 : 59

Austin, G: Lowell. Henry Wadsworth L o n g-f e l l o w ; his life, his works, his friendships. Ill. Bost. 1883. O. 928.1 : 69

Kennedy, W: Sloane. Henry W. Longfellow ; biography, anecdote, letters, criticism. Cambridge. 1882. O. 928.1 : 52

Longfellow, S:, ed. Life of Henry Wadsworth Longfellow ; with extracts from his journals and corresp. Ill. Bost. 1886. 2 v. O.
928.1 : 80

Stoddard, R: H: Henry Wadsworth Longfellow; a medley in prose and verse. N. Y. 1882. O. 928.1 : 57

Underwood, Francis H: Henry Wadsworth Longfellow : a biogr. sketch. Bost. 1882. D. 928.1 : 53

Underwood, Francis H:—*Continued.*
— James Russell L o w e l l ; a biogr. sketch. Bost. 1882. O. 928.1 : 46

Mansfield, E: Deering. Personal memoirs ; social, political and literary, with sketches of many noted people, 1803–1843. Cinc. 1879. D. 928.1 : 27

Holmes, Oliver Wendell. J: Lothrop M o t l e y ; a memoir. Bost. 1879. S. 928.1 : 28

Owen, Robert Dale. Twenty-seven years of autobiography : Threading my way. N. Y. 1874. D. 928.1 : 30

Paine, Martyn and Mary Ann, born Weeks. Memoir of Robert Troup P a i n e by his parents. Printed for private distribution, especially for the class-mates of the youth. N. Y. 1852. Q. 928.1 : R31

Harrison, Gabriel. John Howard P a y n e, dramatist, poet, actor and author of "Home, sweet home"; his life and writings. Rev. ed. Ill. Phila. 1884. O.
928.1+73

Ward, Julius H. Life and letters of James Gates P e r c i v a l. Bost. 1866. D. 928.1 : 32

Gill, W: Fearing. Life of Edgar Allan P o e. 5th ed., rev. and enl. Ill. N. Y. 1880. D.
928.1 : 34

Ingram, J: H. Edgar Allan Poe ; his life, letters and opinions. Portr. Lond. 1880. 2 v. D. 928.1 : 33

Woodberry, G: E: Edgar Allan Poe. (Amer. men of letters.) Bost. 1885. S. 928.1 : 74

Brinley, Francis. Life of W: T. P o r t e r. N. Y. 1860. D. 928.1 : 35

Prentiss, G: L. Life and letters of Elizabeth P r e n t i s s. N. Y. [1882]. O. 928.1 : 54

Ticknor, G: Life of W: Hickling P r e s c o t t. Bost. 1864. Q. 928.1+36

Frothingham, Octavius Brooks. George R i p-l e y. (Amer. men of letters.) Bost. 1882. S. 928.1 : 51

Sigourney, Lydia Howard, born Huntley. Letters of life. N. Y. 1866. D. 928.1 : 37

Swisshelm, Jane Grey, born Cannon. Half a century. 2d ed. Chicago. 1880. D.
928.1 : 47

Conwell, Russell H. The life, travels and literary career of Bayard T a y l o r. Bost. [1881]. D. 928.1 : 38

Taylor, Marie, born Hansen, and Horace Elisha Scudder, eds. Life and letters of Bayard Taylor. Portr. Bost. 1884. 2 v. D.
928.1 : 70

Thorburn, Grant. Forty years' residence in America, or The doctrine of a particular providence, exemplified in his life; written by himself. Bost. 1834. D. 928.1 : 40

Channing, W: Ellery. T h o r e a u, the poet-naturalist ; with memorial verses. Bost. 1873. D. 928.1 : 39

Sanborn, Franklin B: Henry D. Thoreau. Bost. 1882. D. 928.1 : 50

Hillard, G: Stillman, ed. Life, letters and journals of G: T i c k n o r. Ill. Bost. 1876. 2 v. O. 928.1 : 41

Wheaton, Robert. Memoir, with selections from his writings. Bost. 1854. D. 928.1 : 42

Contents. Memoir. — *Selections from his writings:* The sources of the Divina commedia; Jasmin, the barber poet; Coquerel's Experimental christianity; The revolution in Prussia; The revolution of 1848 in Sicily; Schmidt's History of the Albigenses; Thiers' History of the consulate and the empire; Memoir of the late dr. Wheaton.

Bucke, R: Maurice. Walt Whitman. Portr.
Phila. 1883. D.   **928.1 : 60**
Kennedy, W: Sloane. John Greenleaf Whittier; his life, genius and writings. Bost.
1882. O.   **928.1 : 49**
Underwood, Francis H: John Greenleaf Whittier; a biography. Ill. and portr. Bost.
1883. D.   **928.1 : 62**
Wikoff, H: Reminiscences of an idler. N. Y.
1880. O.   **928.1 : 43**
Beers, H: Augustin. Nathaniel Parker Willis.
(Amer. men of letters.) Portr. Bost. 1885.
S.   **928.1 : 75**
Life and poems of Theodore Winthrop, The ;
ed. by his sister. Portr. N. Y. 1884. D.
928.1 : 65

3. British authors.

(*For* Shakspere, *see* cl. 822.3, col. 1045.)

Collective biogr.

Adams, Oscar Fay. A brief hand-book of english authors. Bost. 1884 [1883]. D.
928.2 : R189
— *Same.*   **928.2 : 189**
Wright, T: Biographia britannica literaria, or
Biography of literary characters of Great
Britain and Ireland, arr. in chronological
order. Lond. 1842, 1846.   2 v. O.
928.2 : 187
Contents. V. 1. Anglo-saxon period. 2. Anglonorman period.
Mason, E: T., *ed.* Personal traits of british
authors. Portr. N. Y. 1885.   4 v. D.
928.2 : 215
Contents. V. 1. Wordsworth.—Coleridge.—Lamb.—
Hazlitt.—Leigh Hunt.—Procter. 2. Scott.—Hogg.—
Campbell.—Chalmers.—Wilson.—De Quincey.—Jeffrey. 3. Byron.—Shelley.—Moore.—Rogers.—Keats.
Southey.—Landor. 4. Hood.—Macaulay.—Sydney
Smith. — Jerrold. — Dickens. — Charlotte Brontë. —
Thackeray.
Stoddard, R: H:, *ed.* Bric-a-brac series: Personal reminiscences by Chorley, Planché
and Young. N. Y. 1874. S.   **928.2 : 42**
— *Same :* Anecdote biographies of Thackeray
and Dickens. N. Y. 1874. S.   **928.2 : 137**
— *Same :* Personal reminiscences by Moore and
Jerdan. N. Y. 1875. D.   **928.2 : 106**
— *Same :* Personal reminiscences by Cornelia
Knight and Thomas Raikes. N. Y. 1875. S.
928.2 : 152
— *Same :* Personal reminiscences by Constable
and Gillies. N. Y. 1876. S.   **928.2 : 46**
— *Same :* Personal reminiscences by Barham,
Harness and Hodder. N. Y. 1876. S.
928.2 : 6
— *Same :* Personal reminiscences of Lamb,
Hazlitt and others. N. Y. 1878. S.
928.2 : 7
Contents. C: Lamb.—W: Hazlitt.—T: Campbell.—
Countess of Blessington.
Clarke, C:, *and* Mary Virginia, *born* Novello,
Cowden-. Recollections of writers; with
letters of C: Lamb, Leigh Hunt, Douglas
Jerrold and C: Dickens, and a pref. by
Mary Cowden Clarke. N. Y. [1878]. O.
928.2 : 47
Contents. Preface.— General recollections.—Recollections of J: Keats.—C: Lamb and his letters.—Mary
Lamb.—Leigh Hunt and his letters.—Douglas Jerrold
and his letters.—C: Dickens and his letters.—Index.

Johnson, S: The lives of the most eminent
english poets, with critical observations on
their works. New ed., corr. Lond. 1794.
4 v. O.   **928.2 : 4**
Contents. V. 1. Cowley.—Denham. — Milton.—Butler.—Rochester. — Roscommon. — Otway. — Waller.—
Pomfret. — Dorset. — Stepney. — J. Philips.—Walsh.
2. Dryden.—Smith.—Duke.— King.—Sprat.—Halifax.
—Parnell. — Garth. — Rowe. — Addison. — Hughes.—
Sheffield, duke of Buckinghamshire. 3. Prior. —
Congreve.— Blackmore. — Fenton.—Gay.—Granville.
—Yalden.—Tickell.— Hammond. — Somerville.—Savage.—Swift.—Broome. 4. Pope.—Pitt.—Thomson.—
Watts.—A. Philips.— West. — Collins. — Dyer.—Shenstone. —Young. — Mallet. — Akenside. — Gray.—Lyttelton.
— *Same.* Aberdeen. 1847.   4 v. in 1. S.
928.2 : 4
Cary, H: Francis. Lives of the english poets
from Johnson to Kirke White, designed as
a continuation of Johnson's Lives. Lond.
1846. S.   **928.2 : 2**
Contents. S: Johnson.—J: Armstrong.—R: Jago.—
R: O. Cambridge. — Tobias Smollett.—T: Warton.—
Joseph Warton. — Christopher Anstey.—W: Mason.
— Oliver Goldsmith. — Erasmus Darwin. — W: J.
Mickle.—James Beattie.—W: Hayley.—Sir W: Jones.
—T: Chatterton.—H: Kirke White.
Rossetti, W: Michael. Lives of famous poets;
a companion volume to the series Moxon's
popular poets. Lond. 1878. D.   **928.2 : 5**
Contents. Chaucer.—Spenser. — Shakespeare.—Milton.—Butler. — Dryden.—Pope. — Thomson.—Gray.—
Goldsmith.—Cowper.—Burns. — Wordsworth.—Scott.
—Coleridge.—Campbell.—Moore.— Byron.—Shelley.—
Mrs. Hemans.—Keats.—Hood.—Longfellow.
Dennis, J: Heroes of literature : English
poets ; a book for young readers. Lond.
1883. D.   **928.2 : 192**
Robertson, Eric S. English poetesses ; a series
of critical biographies with illustrative
extracts. Lond. 1883. D.   **928.2 : 196**
Gosse, Edmund W: Seventeenth-century studies ; a contribution to the history of english
poetry. Lond. 1883. O.   **928.2 : 213**
Contents. T: Lodge.—J: Webster.—S: Rowlands.—
Capt. Dover's Cotswold games.—Robert Herrick.—R:
Crashaw.—Abraham Cowley.—The matchless Orinda.
—Sir G: Etheredge.—T: Otway.
Howitt, W: Homes and haunts of the most
eminent british poets. Ill. N. Y. 1851. 2
v. D.   **914.2 : 28**
Contents, see col. 1233.
Baker, D: Erskine. Biographia dramatica, or
Companion to the playhouse, *etc.*
822.4 : 3
See col. 1044.
Campbell, T:, *and others.* Lives of the british
dramatists. Phila. 1846. 2 v. in 1. S.
928.2 : 1
Contents. V. 1. **Campbell,** T: Remarks on the
life and writings of W: Shakspeare.—**Gifford,** W:
Memoirs of Ben Jonson. 2. **Darley,** G: Lives of
Beaumont and Fletcher.—**Coleridge,** H. Lives of
Massinger and Ford.—**Hunt,** J. H: L. Biographical
and critical notices of Wycherley, Congreve, Vanbrugh and Farquhar.
Archer, W: English dramatists of today.
Lond. 1882. D.   **928.2 : 183**
Contents. Introd. — Playwrights of yesterday.—J.
Albery.—F. W. Broughton.—F. C. Burnand. —H: J.
Byron.—W. S. Gilbert.—S. Grundy. — B. Howard.—
H. A. Jones.—P. Meritt.—H. C. Merivale. — A. W.
Pinero.—R. Reece.—G: R. Sims.—S. T. Smith.—Tennyson.—W. G. Wills.
Ritchie, Anna Isabella, *born* Thackeray. A
book of sibyls: Mrs. Barbauld, miss Edgeworth, mrs. Opie, miss Austen. Lond.
1883. O.   **928.2 : 175**
— *Same.* N. Y. 1883. Q.   **928.2+175**

Anton, P: England's essayists; Addison, Bacon, DeQuincey, Lamb. Lond. [1884]. D.
         928.2 : 208

Thackeray, W: Makepeace. The english humourists of the 18th century; a series of lectures, del. in England, Scotland and the U. S. of America. Leipz. 1853. S.
         928.2 : 8
   Contents. Swift.—Congreve and Addison.— Steele.—Prior, Gay and Pope.—Hogarth, Smollett and Fielding.—Sterne and Goldsmith.—Charity and humour.
— *Same. T. p. w.* [N. Y. 1860]. D. **928.2 : 8**

Adams, W: H: Davenport. Celebrated englishwomen of the victorian era. Lond. 1884. D.
         928.2 : 212
   Contents. Queen Victoria. — Harriet Martineau.—Charlotte Brontë. — Mary Russell Mitford. — Mary Somerville. — Sara Coleridge. — Mary Carpenter. — Adelaide Anne Procter.—George Eliot.—Jane Welsh Carlyle.

Curwen, H: A history of booksellers; the old and the new. Portr. and ill. Lond. *n. d.* D.   **928.2 : 144**
   Contents. The booksellers of olden times. — The Longman family.—Constable, Cadell and Black. — J: Murray.— W: Blackwood. — Chambers, Knight and Cassell.—H: Colburn.—The Rivingtons, the Parkers and James Nisbet.—Butterworth and Churchill.—E: Moxon.—Kelly and Virtue.—T: Tegg.—T: Nelson.—Simpkin, Marshall and co. — C: E: Mudie.—W. H. Smith and son.—Provincial booksellers.

Individual biogr.

Aikin, Lucy. Life of Joseph A d d i s o n. Phila. 1846. D.   **928.2 : 12**

Courthope, W: J: Addison. [Eng. men of letters]. N. Y. 1884. D.   **928.2 : 194**

Aikin, Lucy. Memoir of John A i k i n; with a selection of his miscellaneous pieces, biographical, moral and critical. Phila. 1824. O.   **928.2 : 13**
   Contents. Memoir. — Critical essays on english poets: Account of the life and works of Spencer [sic]; On the poetry of Milton; On the heroic poem of Gondibert; Critical remarks on Dryden's fables; Observations on Pope's Essay on man; Plan and character of Thomson's Seasons; Comparison between Thomson and Cowper as descriptive poets; On dr. Armstrong's Art of preserving health; On the poems of Green; On Somerville's Poem of the chase; On the poetry of Goldsmith.—Miscellaneous pieces: Aphorisms on mind and manners; What man is made for; On the touch for the king's evil; Literary prophecies for 1797; Remarks on the charge of jacobism; On the probable melioration in the state of mankind; On toleration in Russia; Military piety; Inquiry into the nature of family pride; Apology for the demolition of ruins; Inquiry into the essential character of man; Thoughts on the formation of character; On self-biographers; On the attachment to Mary, queen of scots; On the imitative principle; Historical relations of poisonings; A word for philosophy; On cant; On mottoes.—App.: Descriptions of vegetables from the roman poets; Biogr. account of the rev. dr. Enfield; Description of the country about Dorking; Biogr. account of R: Pulteney; Memoir of Gilbert Wakefield; Memoir of Joseph Priestley; Memoir of James Currie; Memoir of rev. G: Walker.

Arblay, Frances, *born* Burney, *mme.* d'. Diary and letters; ed. by her niece [Charlotte Barrett]. Lond. 1854. 7 v. S. **928.2 : 14**

Abbott, Edwin Abbott. Francis B a c o n; an account of his life and works. Lond. 1885. O.   **928.2 + 217**

Church, R: W: Bacon. [Eng. men of letters.] N. Y. 1884. D.   **928.2 : 197**

Dixon, W: Hepworth. Personal history of lord Bacon; from unpub. papers. Bost. 1861. D.   **928.2 : 15**

Oliver, Grace Atkinson, *born* Little, *formerly mrs.* Ellis. [Memoir, letters and a selection from the poems and prose writings of Anna Lætitia B a r b a u l d.] Bost. 1874. 2 v. D.
         928.2 : 16
   Contents. V. 1. Memoir, with many of her letters. 2. Poems. *Prose works.* Miscellaneous: The hill of science; On romances; An inquiry into those kinds of distress which excite agreeable sensations, with a tale; The curé of the banks of the Rhone; On evil; On monastic institutions; Against inconsistency in our expectations; On education; On prejudice; On female studies; On the classics; Selama; Letter on watering-places; Dialogue in the shades; Knowledge and her daughter. — Legacy for young ladies: True magicians; The pine and the olive; On riddles; Enigma, to the ladies; The king in his castle; The misses, addressed to a careless girl; The four sisters; Letter of a young king; On the uses of history; Fashion, a vision; Description of two sisters; On friendship; Confidence and modesty, a fable; Picnic; Letter from Grimalkin to Selima; Allegory on sleep; Expense, a dialogue.

Barton, Lucy. Memoir, letters and poems of Bernard B a r t o n; ed. by his daughter. Phila. 1850. D.   **928.2 : 17**

Beloe, W: The sexagenarian, or The recollections of a literary life. 2d ed. Lond. 1818. 2 v. O.   **928.2 : 200**

Jebb, R: Claverhouse. B e n t l e y. [Eng. men on letters]. N. Y. 1882. D.   **928.2 : 159**

Madden, R: Robert. Literary life and corresp. of the countess of B l e s s i n g t o n. N. Y. 1855. 2 v. D.   **928.2 : 18**

Waller, J: Francis. B o s w e l l. *in* **928.2 : 85**

Gaskell, Elizabeth Cleghorn, *born* Stevenson. Life of Charlotte B r o n t ë. N. Y. 1864. 2 v. in 1. D.   **928.2 : 20**

Holloway, Laura Carter. An hour with Charlotte Brontë, or Flowers from a Yorkshire moor. N. Y. [1883]. D.   **928.2 : 193**

Reid, T. Wemyss. Charlotte Brontë; a monograph. Ill. N. Y. 1877. D.   **928.2 : 19**

Robinson, A. Mary F. Emily B r o n t ë. (Famous women.) Bost. 1883. S. **928.2 : 171**

Huth, Alfred H: Life and writings of H: T: B u c k l e. N. Y. 1880. O. **928.2 : 21**

Bulwer-Lytton, *Sir* E: G: Earle Lytton, *1st baron Lytton.* The life, letters and literary remains of E: B u l w e r lord Lytton, by his son; v. 1, containing v. 1 and 2 of the eng. ed. N. Y. 1884 [1883]. D.   **928.2 : 191**
— *Same.* 2 pts. N. Y. 1884 [1883]. Q.
         928.2 + 191
   Contents. V. 1, Pt. 1. Autobiography, 1803–1825. — Pt. 2. Biography, 1825–1832.

Hare, A: J: Cuthbert. Life and letters of baroness B u n s e n. N. Y. 1879. 2 v. D.
         928.2 : 22

Carlyle, T: Life of Robert B u r n s. N. Y. 1860. S.   **928.2 : 24**
— *Same.* [Biogr. series]. N. Y. 1877. T.
         928.2 : 24

Sharp, J: Campbell. Robert Burns. [Eng. men of letters]. N. Y. 1879. D. **928.2 : 25**
— *Same.* N. Y. 1879. S.   *in* **928.2 + 9**

Burns club, *Milwaukee.* The centennial anniversary of the birthday of Robert Burns, as commemorated by his countrymen in the city of Milw., Wis., jan. 25th 1859; reported for the Burn's club by G: W: Featherstonhaugh. Milw. 1859. D. **928.2 : 149**

Burns club, *New York.* The centennial birthday of Robert Burns, as celebrated by the Burns club of the city of N. Y., tuesday jan. 25th 1859, by J. Cunningham. N. Y. 1860. O.   **928.2 : 150**

Butler, C: Reminiscenses; with a letter to a lady on ancient and modern music. 2d amer. ed. N. Y. 1825. D.   **928.2 : 26**

Castelar y Rissoll, Emilio. The life of lord B y r o n , and other sketches. N. Y. 1876. D.   **928.2 : 28**
Contents. Life of lord Byron.—Victor Hugo.—Alexander Dumas.— Emile Girardin. — Daniel Manin. — Adolphe Thiers.

Elze, F: K: Lord Byron. 2te verm. ausg. Berlin. 1881. O.   **928.2 : 220**

Galt, J: Life of lord Byron. N. Y. 1845. S.   **928.2 : 29**

Jeaffreson, J: Cordy. The real lord Byron; new views of the poet's life. Bost. 1883. D.   **928.2 : 169**

— Same. N. Y. 1883. Q.   **928.2+169**

Moore, T: Life of lord Byron ; with his letters and journals. Phila. 1846. 2 v. D.   **928.2 : 30**

Nichol, J: Byron. [Eng. men of letters]. N. Y. 1880. D.   **928.2 : 33**

Trelawney, E: J: Records of Byron.
in **928.2 : 125**

Boissy, Teresa Gamba *marquise* de, *formerly contessa* Guiccioli. My recollections of lord Byron and those of eye-witnesses of his life. N. Y. 1869. D.   **928.2 : 32**

Gardiner, Margaret, *born* Power, *formerly mrs.* Farmer, *countess of Blessington*. A journal of conversations with lord Byron; with a sketch of the life of the author. Bost. 1859. D.   **928.2 : 31**

Medwin, T: Conversations with lord Byron, noted during a residence with his lordship at Pisa, in 1821 and 1822. New ed. Lond. 1824. O.   **928.2 : 27**

Beattie, W:, *ed.* Life and letters of T: C a m p - b e l l . N. Y. 1850. 2 v. D.   **928.2 : 34**

Carlyle, T: Reminiscences; ed. by James Anthony Froude. N. Y. 1881. O.   **928.2 : 35**

Conway, Moncure Daniel. T: C a r l y l e . N. Y. 1881. D.   **928.2 : 37**

Froude, James Anthony. T: Carlyle. Ill. and portr. N. Y. 1882, 1884. 2 v. D.· **928.2 : 40**
Contents. V. 1. A history of the first forty years of his life, 1795-1835. 2. A history of his life in London, 1834-1881.

— Same. N. Y. 1882, 1884. 4 v. Q. **928.2+40**

Masson, D: Carlyle, personally and in his writings; two Edinburgh lectures. N. Y. 1885. D.   **928.2 : 214**

Shepherd, R: Herne, *and* C: Norris Williamson, *eds.* Memoirs of the life and writings of Thomas Carlyle, with personal reminiscences and selections from his private letters. Lond. 1881. 2 v. D.   **928.2 : 38**

Wylie, W: Howie. Thomas Carlyle, the man and his books; ill. by personal reminiscences, table-talk and anecdotes of himself and his friends. 2d ed. Lond. 1881. D.   **928.2 : 39**

Pennington, Montagu. Memoirs of the life of Elizabeth C a r t e r ; with a new ed. of her poems, incl. some which have never appeared before. Added, some miscell. essays in prose, together with her notes on the Bible and answers to objections concerning the christian religion. 2d ed. Lond. 1808. 2 v. O.   **928.2 : 145**

Chambers, W: Story of a long and busy life. Lond. 1882. S.   **928.2 : 161**

Ward, Adolphus W: C h a u c e r . [Eng. men of letters]. N. Y. 1880. D.   **928.2 : 41**

Chorley, H: Fothergill. Recent art and society as described in [his] autobiogr. and memoirs ; compiled from the ed. of H: G. Hewlett by C. H. Jones. [Amateur ser.] N. Y. 1874. D.   **928.2 : 43**

Waddington, S: Arthur Hugh Cl o u g h ; a monograph. Lond. 1883. D. **928.2 : 181**

Traill, H. D. C o l e r i d g e [Eng. men of letters]. N. Y. 1884. D.   **928.2 : 202**

Cottle, Joseph. Reminiscences of S: Taylor Coleridge and Robert Southey. N. Y. 1848. D.   **928.2 : 44**

Coleridge, Sara, *born* C o l e r i d g e . Memoir and letters ; ed. by her daughter. N. Y. 1874. O.   **928.2 : 45**

Hayley, W: Life and posthumous writings of W: C o w p e r ; with an introd. letter to the right hon. earl Cowper. N. Y. 1803. 2 v. in 1. O.   **928.2 : 50**

Smith, Goldwin. Cowper, [Eng. men of letters]. N. Y. 1880. D.   **928.2 : 48**

— Same. N. Y. 1882. Q.   in **928.2+11**

Southey, Robert. Life of W: Cowper. Bost. 1843. 2 v. D.   **928.2 : 49**

Taylor, T: Life of W: Cowper ; compiled from his corresp. and other authentic sources of information ; containing remarks on his writings and on the peculiarities of his interesting character never before pub. 2d amer. ed. Phila. 1834. D.   **928.2 : 51**

Crabbe, G: Life of G: C r a b b e ; with his letters and journals, by his son. Phila. 1835. D.   **928.2 : 146**

Croker, J: Wilson. The C r o k e r papers, the corresp. and diaries of J: Wilson Croker, secretary of the admiralty, from 1809 to 1830 ; ed. by L: J. Jennings. Portr. N. Y. 1884. 2 v. O.   **928.2 : 204**

Cumberland, R: Memoirs, written by himself ; containing an account of his life and writings, interspersed with anecdotes and characters of several of the most distinguished persons of his time with whom he had intercourse and connection, with ill. notes by H: Flanders. Phila. 1856. O.   **928.2 : 52**

Chadwick, W: The life and times of Daniel D e F o e ; with remarks, digressive and discursive. Lond. 1859. O.   **928.2 : 54**

Minto, W: Daniel Defoe. [Eng. men of letters]. N. Y. 1879. D.   **928.2 : 53**

Delaney, Mary, *born* Granville, *formerly mrs.* Pendarves. Autobiography and corresp.; rev. from lady Llanover's ed. and ed. by Sarah Chauncey Woolsey. Bost. 1880. 2 v. D.   **928.2 : 155**

De Quincey, T: Confessions of an english opium-eater, *and* Suspiria de profundis. Bost. 1850. D.   **928.2 : 55**

— Autobiographic sketches. Bost. 1853. D.   **928.2 : 56**

Japp, Alexander Hay, (*H. A. Page*). T: D e Q u i n c e y ; his life and writings from unpub. corresp., by H. A. Page. N. Y. 1877. 2 v. D.   **928.2 : 57**

Masson, D: De Quincey. [Eng. men of letters.] N. Y. 1882 [1881]. D.   **928.2 : 58**

Forster, J: Life of C: D i c k e n s . Phila. 1874. 3 v. D.   **928.2 : 60**

Hanaford, Phebe A. The life and writings of C: Dickens. Bost. 1882. D.   **928.2 : 168**

Jones, C: H. Short life of C: Dickens; with selections from his letters. [Appletons' new handy-vol. ser.] N. Y. 1880. S. **928.2 : 59**

Ward, Adolphus W: Dickens. [Eng. men of letters.] N. Y. 1882. D. **928.2 : 158**

Saintsbury, G: Warner. D r y d e n. [Eng. men of letters.] N. Y. 1881. D. **928.2 : 61**

Oliver, Grace Atkinson. *born* Little, *formerly mrs.* Ellis. A study of Maria E d g e w o r t h; with notices of her father and friends. Portr. and ill. Bost. 1882. D. **928.2 : 173**

Zimmern, Helen. Maria Edgeworth. (Famous women.) Bost. 1883. S. **928.2 : 190**

Blind, Mathilde. G e o r g e E l i o t. (Famous women.) Bost. 1883. S. **928.2 : 172**

Cooke, G: Willis. George Eliot; a critical study of her life, writings, and philosophy. Bost. 1883. D. **928.2 : 188**

Cross, J: W. George Eliot's life as related in her letters and journals; arr. and ed. by her husband. Ill. and portr. N. Y. 1885. 3 v. D. **928.2 : 205**

— *Same.* N. Y. 1885. 3 v. Q. **928.2+205**

Ames, C: G. George Eliot's two marriages; an essay. 3d ed. Phila. 1885. S. **928.2 : 221**

Evelyn, J: Diary; to which are added a selection from his familiar letters and the private corresp. between king Charles I and sir E: Nicholas, and between sir E: Hyde, afterwards earl of Clarendon, and sir R: Browne, ed. from the original mss. by W: Bray. A new ed. in 4 v., with a life of the author by H: B. Wheatley. Portr. Lond. 1879. 4 v. O. **928.2 : R195**

Dobson, H: Austin. F i e l d i n g. [Eng. men of letters.] N. Y. 1883. D. **928.2 : 170**

Fletcher, Elizabeth, *born* Dawson. Autobiography, with letters and other family memorials; ed. by the survivor of her family [lady Mary Richardson]. Bost. 1876. D. **928.2 : 62**

Fox, Caroline. Memories of old friends; extracts from the journals and letters of Caroline F o x, of Penjerrick, Cornwall, from 1835 to 1871, ed. by Horace N. Pym. 2d ed.; added, 14 original letters from J: Stuart Mill, never before pub. [Large paper ed. ill.] Phila. 1882. O. **928.2+P63**

— *Same.* Phila. 1883. D. **928.2 : 63**

— *Same.* N. Y. 1882. D. **928.2+63**

Frost, T: Forty years' recollections; literary and political. Lond. 1880. D. **928.2 : 198**

Galt, J: Autobiography. Phila. 1833. 2 v. D. **928.2 : 64**

Morison, James Cotter. G i b b o n. [Eng. men of letters.] N. Y. 1879. D. **928.2 : 65**

Paul, C: Kegan. William G o d w i n; his friends and contemporaries. Portr. and ill. Lond. 1876. 2 v. O. **928.2 : 151**

Black, W: G o l d s m i t h. [Eng. men of letters.] N. Y. 1879. D. **928.2 : 68**

— *Same.* N. Y. 1879. Q. *in* **928.2+9**

Forster, J: Life and times of Oliver Goldsmith. 2d ed. Lond. 1854. 2 v. O. **928.2 : 67**

Irving, Washington. Life of Oliver Goldsmith; with selections from his writings. N. Y. 1847. 2 v. S. **928.2 : 70**

Contents. V. 1. Biogr. sketch.—Poetical extracts. —Miscellaneous essays.— From the Bee.—From the Citizen of the world. 2. *Same, continued.*—Miscellaneous.

— Oliver Goldsmith; a biography. N. Y. 1849. D. **928.2 : 69**

Prior, *Sir* James. Life of Oliver Goldsmith; from a variety of original sources. Lond. 1837. 2 v. O. **928.2 : 66**

Gosse, Edmund W: G r a y. [Eng. men of letters.] N. Y. 1882. D. **928.2 : 160**

Griffin, Daniel. Life of Gerald G r i f f i n, by his brother. N. Y. *n. d.* D. **928.2 : 71**

— *Same.* **G 2551 v10**

Hall, S: Carter. Retrospect of a long life from 1815 to 1883. N. Y. 1883. O. **928.2 : 174**

Hare, A: J: Cuthbert. Records of a quiet life [Maria H a r e]; rev. for amer. readers by W: L. Gage. Bost. 1873. D. **928.2 : 72**

Chorley, H: Fothergill. Memorials of mrs. H e m a n s; with ill. of her literary character from her private corresp. Phila. 1836. D. **928.2 : 73**

Owen, Harriet Mary, *born* Browne. Memoir of the life and writings of Felicia Hemans, by her sister. [*Anon.*] With an essay on her genius by mrs. Sigourney. N. Y. 1845. S. **928.2 : 74**

Herbert, E:, *1st baron Herbert of Cherbury.* Autobiography; with an essay by W: D. Howells. Bost. 1877. S. **928.2 : 154**

Broderipp, Frances Freeling, *born* Hood. Memorial of T: H o o d; coll., arr. and ed. by his daughter, with a preface and notes by his son [T: Hood]. Ill. Bost. 1860. 2 v. D. **928.2 : 75**

Hunt, James H: Leigh. Autobiography; with reminiscences of friends and contemporaries. N. Y. 1860. 2 v. D. **928.2 : 76**

Macpherson, Gerardine, *born* Bate. Memoirs of the life of Anna J a m e s o n, by her niece. Portr. Lond. 1878. O. **928.2 : 180**

Cockburn, H: T: *lord.* Life of lord J e f f r e y; with a selection from his corresp. Phila. 1852. 2 v. O. **928.2 : 77**

Jerrold, W: Blanchard. Life and remains of Douglas J e r r o l d, by his son. Bost. 1859. D. **928.2 : 78**

Boswell, James. Life of S: J o h n s o n, incl. a journal of a tour to the Hebrides. New ed., with add. and notes by J: Wilson Croker. N. Y. 1846. 2 v. O. **928.2+79**

Page, W: P., *ed.* Life and writings of S: Johnson. N. Y. 1847. 2 v. S. **928.2 : 81**

Russell, J: Fuller. Life of S: Johnson. Lond. 1847. S. **928.2 : 82**

Stephen, Leslie. Samuel Johnson. [Eng. men of letters.] N. Y. 1878. D. **928.2 : 80**

— *Same.* N. Y. 1878. Q. *in* **928.2+10**

Croker, J: Wilson, *ed.* Johnsoniana, or Supplement to Boswell; anecdotes and sayings of dr. Johnson. Phila. 1842. D. **928.2 : 84**

Mason, E. T., *ed.* S: Johnson, his words and his ways; what he said, what he did and what men thought and spoke concerning him. N. Y. 1879. D. **928.2 : 83**

Waller, J: Francis. Boswell and Johnson; their companions and contemporaries. Lond. [1881]. S. **928.2 : 85**

Keary, Eliza. Memoir of Annie K e a r y, by her sister. Lond. 1882. D. **928.2 : 165**

Milnes, R: Monckton, *1st baron Houghton.* Life, letters and literary remains of J: K e a t s. N. Y. 1848. D. **928.2 : 86**

Kingsley, Fanny E., *born* Grenfell, *ed.* C: K i n g s l e y; his letters and memoirs of his life, ed. by his wife. Abr. from the Lond. ed. N. Y. 1877. O. **928.2 : 87**

Ainger, Alfred. Charles Lamb. [Eng. men of letters]. N. Y. 1882. D.　**928.2 : 157**

Procter, Bryan Waller, (*Barry Cornwall*). Charles Lamb ; a memoir by Barry Cornwall. Bost. 1866. D.　**928.2 : 88**

Gilchrist, Anne. Mary Lamb. (Famous women). Bost. 1881. S.　**928.2 : 179**

Lamb, Mary *and* C: Poems, letters and remains, now first collected ; with reminiscences and notes by W: Carew Hazlitt. Lond. 1874. D.　**928.2 : 89**

Colvin, Sidney. Landor. [Eng. men of letters]. N. Y. 1881. D.　**928.2 : 90**

Mackay, C:, *ed.* Medora Leigh ; a history and an autobiogr., with an introd. and a commentary on the charges brought against lord Byron by mrs. Beecher Stowe. N. Y. 1870. O.　**928.2 : 91**

Fitzpatrick, W: J: The life of Charles Lever. N. Y. 1879. Q.　**928.2+92**

Wilson, Margaret Cornwall Baron. The life and corresp. of M. G. Lewis ; with many pieces in prose and verse, never before pub. [*Anon.*] Lond. 1839. 2 v. O.　**928.2 : 93**

Symington, Andrew James. S: Lover ; a biogr. sketch, with selections from his writings and corresp. N. Y. 1880. D.　**928.2 : 94**

Canning, *The hon.* Albert Stratford G: Lord Macaulay, essayist and historian. Lond. 1882. D.　**928.2 : 184**

Jones, C: H. Lord Macaulay ; his life, his writings. [Appleton's new handy-vol. ser.] N. Y. 1880. S.　**928.2 : 95**

Morison, James Cotter. Macaulay. [Eng. men of letters]. N. Y. 1883 [1882]. D.　**928.2 : 164**

Trevelyan, G: O: Life and letters of Macaulay, by his nephew. N. Y. 1876. 2 v. O.　**928.2 : 96**

Hughes, T: Memoir of Daniel Macmillan. N. Y. 1882. D.　**928.2 : 166**

Lean, Florence, *born* Marryat, *afterward mrs.* Ross Church. Life and letters of capt. Marryat. Leipz. 1872. S.　**928.2 : 97**

Craik, Dinah Maria, *born* Mulock. A legacy ; being the life and remains of J: Martin, schoolmaster and poet. Leipz. 1878. 2 v. in 1. S.　**928.2 : 98**

Martin, Mary E., *mrs.* Herbert, *ed.* Memories of seventy years by one of a literary family. Lond. 1882. D.　**928.2 : 209**

Martineau, Harriet. Autobiography ; ed. by Maria Weston Chapman. Bost. 1877. 2 v. O.　**928.2 : 99**

Miller, *Mrs.* Florence Fenwick, *wife of* F: A. Ford. Harriet Martineau. (Famous women). Bost. 1885. S.　**928.2 : 216**

Masson, D: Life of J: Milton ; narrated in connexion with the political, ecclesiastical and literary history of his time. Lond. 1871–81. 6 v. O.　**928.2 : 100**

— Life of Milton ; with an estimate of his genius and character by lord Macaulay. N. Y. 1860. S.　**928.2 : 156**

Pattison, M: Milton. [Eng. men of letters]. N. Y. 1880. D.　**928.2 : 101**

— *Same.* N. Y. 1882. Q.　*in* **928.2+11**

Mitford, Mary Russell. Recollections of a literary life, or Books, places and people. N. Y. 1858. D.　**928.2 : 102**

— Life, related in a selection from her letters to her friends ; ed. by A. G. L'Estrange. Lond. 1870. 3 v. D.　**928.2 : 182**

Doran, J: A lady of the last century ; mrs. Elizabeth Montagu, ill. in her unpub. letters, coll. and arr. with a biogr. sketch and a chapter on blue stockings. 2d ed. Lond. 1873. O.　**928.2 : 186**

Knight, Helen C. Life of James Montgomery. Bost. 1857. D.　**928.2 : 103**

Symington, Andrew James. T: Moore, the poet ; his life and works. N. Y. 1880. S.　**928.2 : 105**

Moore, T: Memoirs, journal and corresp., ed. by the right hon. lord J: Russell. N. Y. 1857. 2 v. O.　**928.2+104**

— Notes from [his] letters to his music publisher, James Power, the publication of which was suppressed in London ; with an introd. letter from T: Crofton Croker. N. Y. *n. d.* D.　**928.2 : 107**

Roberts, W: Memoirs of the life and corresp. of Hannah More. N. Y. 1845. 2 v. D.　**928.2 : 108**

Morgan, Sydney, *born* Owenson, *lady.* Passages from my autobiography. N. Y. 1859. D.　**928.2 : 109**

Besant, Walter. The life and achievements of E: H: Palmer. Portr. N. Y. 1883. D.　**928.2 : 177**

Fagan, L: Life and corresp. of sir Anthony Panizzi. Bost. 1881. 2 v. O.　**928.2 : 110**

Payn, James. Some literary recollections. Portr. N. Y. 1884. D.　**928.2 : 203**

Piozzi, Hester Lynch, *born* Salusbury, *formerly mrs.* Thrale. Autobiography, letters and literary remains ; ed. with notes and an introd. account of her life and writings by A. Hayward. Bost. 1861. D.　**928.2 : 111**

Stephen, Leslie. Alexander Pope. [Eng. men of letters]. N. Y. 1880. D.　**928.2 : 112**

— *Same.* N. Y. 1882. Q.　*in* **928.2+11**

Richardson, S: Correspondence, sel. from the original mss., bequeathed by him to his family ; prefixed, a biogr. account of that author, and observations on his writings by Anna Lætitia Barbauld. Lond. 1804. O.　**928.2 : 113**

Caine, T. Hall. Recollections of Dante Gabriel Rossetti. Lond. 1882. O.　**928.2 : 185**

Sharp, W: Dante Gabriel Rossetti ; a record and study. N. Y. 1882. D.　**928.2 : 167**

Allan, G: Life of sir Walter Scott ; with critical notices of his writings. Phila. 1835. O.　**928.2+119**

Cunningham, Allan. Some account of the life and works of sir Walter Scott. Bost. 1832. S.　**928.2 : 120**

Hutton, R: Holt. Sir Walter Scott. [Eng. men of letters]. N. Y. 1879. D.　**928.2 : 115**

— *Same.* N. Y. 1879. Q.　*in* **928.2+10**

Lockhart, J: Gibson. Memoirs of the life of sir Walter Scott. Phila. 1837, 1838. 7 v. D.　**928.2 : 116**

Macleod, Xavier Donald. Life of sir Walter Scott. N. Y. 1856. D.　**928.2 : 118**

Hogg, James. Familiar anecdotes of sir Walter Scott ; with a sketch of the life of the [Ettrick] shepherd by S. Dewitt Bloodgood. N. Y. 1834. D.　**928.2 : 117**

Jeaffreson, J: Cordy. The real S h e l l e y ; new views of the poet's life. Lond. 1885. 2 v. O.   **928.2 : 219**

Smith, G: Barnett. Shelley; a critical biography. Edinb. 1877. D.   **928.2 : 124**

Symonds, J: Addington. Shelley. [Eng. men of letters]. N. Y. 1881. D.   **928.2 : 121**

Shelley, Jane, *born* Gibson, *formerly mrs.* St. John, *lady*. Shelley memorials ; from authentic sources ; added, an essay on christianity by Percy Bysshe Shelley, now first printed. Bost. 1859. D.   **928.2 : 123**

Trelawney, E: J: Recollections of the last days of Shelley and Byron. Bost. 1858. D.   **928.2 : 122**

— Records of Shelley, Byron and the author. Lond. 1878. 2 v. D.   **928.2 : 125**

Moore, T: Memoirs of the life of R: Brinsley S h e r i d a n. Phila. 1826. 2 v. in 1. S.   **928.2 : 126**

Oliphant, Margaret O., *born* Wilson. [Eng. men of letters.] N. Y. 1883. D.   **928.2 : 178**

Sherwood, Mary Martha, *born* Butt. Life, chiefly autobiographical, with extracts from mr. S h e r w o o d 's journal during his imprisonment in France and residence in India ; ed. by her daughter, Sophia Kelly. Lond. 1857. O.   **928.2 : 127**

Davis, *Mrs.* S. M. Life and times of sir Philip S i d n e y . [*Anon.*] 3d ed. Bost. 1859. D.   **928.2 : 128**

Furnivall, F: J. Teena Rochfort-S m i t h ; a memoir with three woodbury-types of her, one each of Robert Browning and F. J. Furnivall, and memorial lines by Mary Grace Walker. *n. p.* 1883. O. **928.2 : 199**

Browne, C: T. Memoirs of Robert S o u t h e y , poet-laureate. New ed. Lond. *n. d.* S.   **928.2 : 131**

Dowden, E: Southey. [Eng. men of letters]. N. Y. 1880. D.   **928.2 : 129**

Southey, C: Cuthbert, *ed.* The life and corresp. of Robert Southey ; ed. by his son. N. Y. 1851. O.   **928.2+130**

Cottle, Joseph. Reminiscences of Robert Southey.   *in* **928.2 : 44**

Church, R: W: S p e n s e r . [Eng. men of letters]. N. Y. 1879. D.   **928.2 : 132**

Carlyle, T: Life of J: S t e r l i n g. 2d ed. Bost. 1832. D.   **928.2 : 133**

Traill, H: D. S t e r n e . [Eng. men of letters]. N. Y. 1882. D.   **928.2 : 163**

Stephen, Leslie. S w i f t . [Eng. men of letters]. N. Y. 1882. D.   **928.2 : 162**

Taylor, *Sir* H: Autobiography. Portr. N. Y. 1885. 2 v. D.   **928.2 : 218**

Taylor, J: Records of my life. N. Y. 1833. O.   **928.2+134**

Jennings, H: J. Lord T e n n y s o n ; a biogr. sketch. Portr. Lond. 1884. D. **928.2 : 207**

Wace, Walter E. Alfred Tennyson ; his life and works. Edinb. 1881. D.   **928.2 : 210**

Hotten, J: Camden, (*Theodore Taylor*). T h a c k e r a y , the humorist and man of letters ; the story of his life and literary labors, incl. a selection from his characteristic speeches now for the first time gathered together by Theodore Taylor. Added, In memoriam by C: Dickens, and a sketch by Anthony Trollope. Portr. and ill. N. Y. 1864. D.   **928.2 : 135**

Trollope, Anthony. Thackeray. [Eng. men of letters.] N. Y. 1879. D.   **928.2 : 136**

— *Same.* N. Y. 1879. Q.   *in* **928.2+10**

Tonna, Lewis Hypolytus Joseph. Life of Charlotte Elizabeth [T o n n a], as contained in her personal recollections ; with explanatory notes and a memoir, embracing the period from the close of personal recollections to her death. N. Y. 1864. S.   **928.2 : 138**

Some account of the life and writings of mrs. T r i m m e r ; with original letters, and meditations and prayers, selected from her journal. 2d ed. Lond. 1816. 2 v. O.   **928.2 : 147**

Trollope, Anthony. Autobiography. N. Y. 1883. D.   **928.2 : 176**

— *Same.* N. Y. 1883. Q.   **928.2+176**

Watts, Alaric Alfred. Alaric W a t t s ; a narrative of his life, by his son. Portr. Lond. 1884. 2 v. D.   **928.2 : 211**

Gordon, Mary, *born* Wilson. Christopher North; a memoir of J: W i l s o n , compiled from family papers and other sources by his daughter, with an introd. by R. Shelton Mackenzie. N. Y. 1863. O.   **928.2 : 139**

Pennell, Elizabeth Robins. Life of Mary W o l l s t o n e c r a f t . (Famous women). Bost. 1884. S.   **928.2 : 206**

Myers, F: W: H: W o r d s w o r t h . [Eng. men of letters]. N. Y. 1881. D.   **928.2 : 141**

Phillips, G: Searle, (*January Searle*). Memoirs of W: Wordsworth ; compiled from authentic sources, with numerous quotations from his poems, ill. of his life and character. Lond. 1852. D.   **928.2 : 142**

Symington, Andrew James. William Wordsworth ; biogr. sketch, with selections from his writings in poetry and prose. Bost. [1881]. 2 v. S.   **928.2 : 143**

Wordsworth, Christopher. Memoirs of W: Wordsworth ; ed. by H: Reed. Bost. 1851. 2 v. D.   **928.2 : 140**

Yates, Edmund Hodgson. Fifty years of London life ; memoirs of a man of the world. N. Y. 1884. 2 v. Q.   **928.2+201**

4. German authors.

Collective biography.

Kürschner, Joseph, *ed.* Deutscher litteratur-kalender, 1884, 1885, 1886. 6ter-8ter jahrg. Berlin. [1884—1886]. 3 v. T.   **928.3 : R47**

Kurz, H:, *and* F: Christian **Paldamus**. Deutsche dichter und prosaisten.   **830.1 : 16**
Contents, see col. 1101.

Brümmer, Franz. Deutsche dichter-lexikon ; biographische und bibliographische mittheilungen über deutsche dichter aller zeiten, unter besonderer berücksichtigung der gegenwart für freunde der literatur zusammengestellt. Eichstädt. 1876. 2 v. O.   **928.3 : R42**

Gross, H: Deutschlands dichterinnen und schriftstellerinnen ; eine literarhistorische skizze. 2te ausg. Wien. 1882. O.   **928.3+43**

Gostwick, Joseph. German poets; a series of memoirs and translations. Portr. by C. Jäger. N. Y. n. d. O. . . **928.3 : R41**
Contents. The poets of the Hohenstaufen time. — The master-singers and their times. — Klopstock. — Wieland. — Lessing. — Herder. — Goethe.— Schiller.— Jean Paul.—Körner. — Chamisso.— Rückert.—Uhland. —Heine.

Japp, Alexander Hay. German life and literature, in a series of biographical studies. Lond. [1880]. O. **928.3 : 8**
Contents. Introd. — Lessing.—Winckelmann.—Moses Mendelssohn.—Herder. — Goethe. — L: Tieck.—F: v. Hardenberg (Novalis). — The romantic element in german lit. — German philosophy and political life.— App.: Christian Tobias Damm ; Hamann; F:v. Logau.

Schröder, Hans. Lexikon der hamburgischen schriftsteller bis zur gegenwart ; im auftrage des Vereins für hamburgische geschichte ausg. Hamburg. 1851–83. 8 v. in 7. O. **928.3 : R49**
Contents. V. 1. A—Daffovius. 2. Daffovius—Günther 3. Günther—Kleye. 4. Cropp, F: A: and C: R. W: Klose. Klincker —Lyser. 5. Klose, C: R. W:, Maack—Pauli.. 6. Klose, C: R. W:, Pauli—Schoff. 7. Kellinghusen, A. H., Scholvin—Westphalen. 8. Kellinghusen, A. H., Westphalen—Zyllus.

Gleim, J: W: L: Lessing, Wieland, Heinse ; nach den handschriftlichen quellen in Gleims nachlasse dargestellt von H: Pröhle. 2te ausg. Berlin. 1879. O. **928.3 : 74**

Boyesen, Hjalmar Hjorth. Goethe and Schiller ; their lives and works, incl. a commentary on Goethe's Faust. N. Y. 1879. D. **928.3 : 10**

Individual biogr.

Langenberg, E. Ernst Moritz Arndt; sein leben und seine schriften. Neue wohlfeile ausg. Bonn. 1869. D. **928.3 : 90**

Schmidt, Ferdinand. Ernst Moritz Arndt; ein lebensbild. 6te aufl., ill. Kreuznach. [1885]. S. **928.3 : 96**

Schupp, Ottokar. Das büchlein vom vater Arndt, dem sänger deutscher freiheit und dem propheten deutscher grösse und einheit ; der jugend und dem volke gewidmet. Ill. Wiesbaden. 1872. S. **928.3 : 1**
[Biographische skizze von] E: v. Bauernfeld. Cassel. n. d. T. **928.3 : 1**

Gutzkow, K: Ferdinand. Börne's leben ; aus Börne's ungedrucktem nachlasse reich vermehrt. Frankfurt a. M. 1845. S. **928.3 : 6**

Pröhle, H: Christoph Ferdinand. Gottfried A: Bürger; sein leben und seine dichtungen. Leipz. 1856. O. **928.3 : 68**

Fulda, K: Chamisso und seine zeit. Portr. Leipz. 1881. D. **928.3 : 79**

Mönckeberg, C: Matthias Claudius; ein beitrag zur kirchen- und litteraturgeschichte seiner zeit, mit einem facsimile. Hamburg. 1869. O. **928.3 : 63**

Oertel, Hugo. Matthias Claudius, der Wandsbecker Bote ; ein lebensbild, für die deutsche jugend und das deutsche volk gezeichnet. Ill. Wiesbaden. 1884. S. **928.3 : 105**

Creuzer, F: Aus dem leben eines alten professors ; mit literarischen beilagen und dem porträt des verf. Leipz. 1848. O. *With his* Zur römischen geschichte. *in* **937 : 41**

Buchner, W: Ferdinand Freiligrath; ein dichterleben in briefen. Lahr. 1882. 2 v. O. **928.3 : 51**
[Biographische skizze von] Franz freiherr Gaudy. Cassel. 1853. T. **928.3 : 2**

Leimbach, C: L. Emanuel Geibel; des dichters leben, werke und bedeutung für das deutsche volk. Wolfenbüttel. 1877. S. **928.3 : 94**
[Biographische skizze von] Emanuel Geibel. Cassel. 1852. T. **928.3 : 3**

Oertel, Philipp F: W:, (W. O. v. Horn). Christian Fürchtegott Gellert; ein lebensbild für Deutschlands jugend und volk. 3te aufl. Wiesbaden. 1875. S. **928.3 : 103**

Schmidt, Ferdinand. Gellert; ein lebensbild. 5te aufl. Ill. Kreuznach. n. d. S. **928.5 : 95**

Körte, W: J:W:L: Gleims leben; aus seinen briefen und schriften. Halberstadt. 1811. D. **928.3 : 101**

Düntzer, J: H: Joseph. Göthe's leben. 2te durchgesehene, mit neuen abbildungen und einem register verm. aufl. Ill. Leipz. 1885. D. **928.3 : 46**
— Same, eng. Life of Goethe. Tr. by T: W: Lyster. Ill. Lond. 1883. 2 v. D. **928.3 : 46**

Falk, J: Daniel, called Johannes, (Johannes von der Ostsee). Goethe aus näherm persönlichen umgange dargestellt ; ein nachgelassenes werk. 3te aufl. Leipz. 1856. D. **928.3 : 53**

Göthe, J: Wolfgang v. Aus meinem leben : wahrheit und dichtung. In his Werke. **830 : 137 v17-19**
— Same, eng. Truth and poetry from my own life, or The autobiography of Goethe ; ed. by Parke Godwin. N. Y. 1850. 2 v. D. **928.3 : 9**

Grimm, Herman. Goethe ; vorlesungen gehalten an der Kgl. universität zu Berlin. 3te durchg. aufl. Berlin. 1882. O. **928.3 : 11**
— Same, eng. Life and times of Goethe. Tr. by Sarah Holland Adams. Bost. 1880. O. **928.3 : 11**

Hayward, Abraham. Goethe. [Foreign classics for eng. readers]. Phila. 1878. S. **928.3 : 12**

Lewes, G: H: Life and works of Goethe ; with sketches of his age and contemporaries, from pub. and unpub. sources. Bost. 1856. 2 v. D. **928.3 : 14**
— The story of Goethe's life. Abridged from his Life and works of Goethe. Bost. 1879. D. **928.3 : 7**
— Same, germ. Goethe's leben. Autorisirte deutsche ausg., übers. von J: v. Sydow. 2te aufl. Berlin. 1878. D. **928.3 : 7**

Riemer, F: W: Mittheilungen über Goethe; aus mündlichen und schriftlichen, gedruckten und ungedruckten quellen. Berlin. 1841. 2 v. O. **928.3 : 75**
Contents. V. 1. Einleitung.—Johannes Falk.—Bettine Brentano.—Persönlichkeit.— Gesundheit.—Character.— Gesinnung.—Thätigkeit.— Totalität.— Eigenheiten. — Fehler. — Häuslicher zustand. — Reisen. — Fremde.—Juden.—Freunde.—Umgebung.— Ruhm.— Publikum. 2. Weimarische zustände. — Goethe's leben und wirken.—Goethe's reise nach Italien.—Goethe nach seiner rückkunft 1788 und 1789.—Goethe's verhältniss zu Schiller.—Goethe's und Schiller's briefwechsel.—Goethe's schriften.—Goethe's urtheile über dichter; künstler; kunstkenner; naturforscher; philosophen; regenten und staatsmänner.—Goethe's tischreden.

Schäfer, J: W: Goethe's leben. 3te aufl. Portr. Leipz. 1877. 2 v. in 1. O.   **928.3 : 80**

Schmidt, Ferdinand. Goethe's jugend- und jünglingszeit; ein lebensbild für jung und alt. 4te aufl. Ill. Kreuznach. [1882]. S.   **928.3 : 93**

Viehoff, H: Goethe's leben, geistentwickelung und werke. 4te umgearb. aufl. Stuttg. 1877. 4 v. in 2. D.   **928.3 : 84**

Eckermann, J: P: Gespräche mit Goethe in den letzten jahren seines lebens. 6te aufl. mit einleitenden abhandlungen und anmerkungen von H: Düntzer; nebst neuem register. Leipz. 1885. 3 v. D.   **928.3 : 54**

— *eng.* Conversations with Goethe in the last years of his life. Tr. from [the 2 first v. of] the german by S. M. Fuller, marchesa Ossoli. New ed. Bost. 1852. D.   **928.3 : 15**

Franke, L: A: Zur biographie Franz Grillparzer's. 2te verm. aufl., mit portr. Wien. 1884. D.   **928.3 : 78**

Roquette, O: Leben und dichten Joh. Christ. Günther's. Stuttg. 1860. O.   **928.3 : 52**

Friedrich Halm; [biographische skizze]. Cassel. 1853. T.   **928.3 : 4**

Längin, G: J: P: Hebel; ein lebensbild. Portr. Karlsruhe. 1875. O.   **928.3 : 89**

Arnold, Matthew. Heinrich Heine. Phila. 1863. S.   **928.3 : 16**

Heine, H: Memoirs and some newly discovered fragments of his writings; with an introd. essay by T: W. Evans. Lond. 1884. D.   **928.3 : 28**

Meissner, Alfred. Erinnerungen an H: Heine. Hamburg. 1856. D.   **928.3 : 17**

Stigand, W: Life, works and opinions of H: Heine. N. Y. 1880. 2 v. O.   **928.3 : 18**

Strodtmann, Adolf H: H. Heine's leben und werke. 3te aufl. Hamburg. 1884. 2 v. S.   **928.3 : 82**

Selden, Camille. The last days of H: Heine. Tr. into english by Clare Brune. Lond. 1884. D.   **928.3 : 50**

Schober, J: N. J: Jakob W: Heinse, sein leben und seine werke; ein kultur- und literaturbild. Portr. Leipz. 1882. D.   **928.3 : 85**

Haym, Rudolph. Herder, nach seinem leben und seinen werken dargestellt. Berlin. 1880. 1885. 2 v. O.   **928.3 : 83**

Schmidt, Ferdinand. Herder, als knabe und jüngling; für jung und alt erzählt. 9te aufl. ill. Kreuznach. [1883]. S.   **928.3 : 98**

Strauss, D: F: Ulrich v. Hutten. Als anhang: Vorrede zu "Gespräche von Ulrich v. Hutten, übers und erläutert von D: F: Strauss. Leipz. 1860". 4te aufl. Bonn. 1878. D.   **928.3 : 77**

— *Same, eng.* Ulrich v. Hutten; his life and times. Tr. with the author's permission from the 2d german ed. by mrs. G. Sturge. Lond. 1874. O.   **928.3 : 77**

Euler, C: F: L: Jahn; sein leben und wirken. Portr. Stuttg. 1881. O.   **928.3 : 59**

Wilbrandt, Adolf. H: v. Kleist. Nördlingen. 1863. O.   **928.3 : 69**

Rieger, Max. Klinger, in -der sturm- und drangperiode dargestellt; mit vielen briefen. Darmstadt. 1880. O.   **928.3 : 65**

Strauss, D: F: Klopstock's jugendgeschichte, und Klopstock und der markgraf Karl Friedrich von Baden; bruchstücke einer Klopstockbiographie. Bonn. 1878. O.   **928.3 : 73**

Oertel, Hugo. Karl Theodor Körner; ein lebensbild aus der zeit des deutschen freiheitskampfes, für die deutsche jugend und das deutsche volk gezeichnet. Ill. Wiesbaden. 1880. S.   **928.3 : 107**

[**Biographische** skizze von] K: Theodor Körner. Cassell. 1853. T.   **928.3 : 5**

Danzel, Theodor W:, *and* Gottschalck E: **Guhrauer**. Gotthold Ephraim Lessing; sein leben und seine werke. 2te berichtigte und verm. aufl. herausg. von W. v. Maltzahn und R. Boxberger. Berlin. 1880, 1881. 2 v. O.   **928.3 : 61**

Düntzer, J: H: Joseph. Lessings leben. Ill. Leipz. 1882. O.   **928.3 : 58**

Schmidt, Ferdinand. Gotthold Fphraim Lessing; ein lebensbild. 3te aufl., ill. Kreuznach. [1883]. S.   **928.3 : 92**

Sime, James. Lessing. Portr. [Eng. and foreign phil. library]. Lond. 1879. 2 v. O.   **928.3 : 19**

Thiele, R: Eva Lessing; ein lebensbild. Portr. Halle a. S. 1881. O.   **928.3 : 62**

Stahr, Fanny, *born* Lewald. Meine lebensgeschichte: 1te abth., Im vaterhaus; 2te abth., Leidensjahre; 3te abth., Befreiung und wanderleben. Berlin. 1861, 1862. 6 v. S.   **928.3 : 37**

Meding, J: Ferdinand Martin Oskar, (*Gregor Samarow*). Memoiren zur zeitgeschichte. Leipz. 1881. 3 v. D.   **928.3 : 86**

Contents. V. 1. Vor dem sturm. 2. Das jahr 1866. 3. Im exil.

Schmidt, Ferdinand. Moses Mendelssohn; ein lebensbild. 2te aufl., ill. Kreuznach. [1883]. S.   **928.3 : 100**

Seuffert, Bernhard. Maler Müller. Anhang: Mittheilungen aus Müller's nachlass. Berlin. 1877. O.   **928.3 + 56**

Classen, Johannes. Barthold G: Niebuhr; eine gedächtnisschrift zu seinem hundertjährigen geburtstage den 27. aug. 1876. Portr. Gotha. 1876. O.   **928.3 : 76**

Life and letters of Barthold G: Niebuhr, The; with essays on his character and influence by the chevalier Bunsen and profs. Brandis and Lorbell [*sic*, Loebell]. N. Y. 1852. D.   **928.3 : 27**

Note. Tr. and abridged by Susan Winkworth from the Lebensnachrichten über Niebuhr, ed. by *frau* Dora Hensler, *born* Behrens.

Weinhold, K: Martin Opitz von Boberfeld; ein vortrag in der Harmonie zu Kiel am 15. feb. 1862 gehalten. Kiel. 1862. O.   **928.3 : 72**

W. O. von Horn (Wilhelm Oertel), ein wahrer freund des volkes; ein lebensbild für das deutsche volk gezeichnet von einem, der ihn lieb gehabt hat. Ill. Wiesbaden. 1860. S.   **928.3 : 104**

Pichler, Caroline, *born* Greiner. Denkwürdigkeiten aus meinem leben. Wien. 1844. 4 v. S.   **928.3 : 21**

Rellstab, L: Aus meinem leben. Berlin. 1861. 2 v. D.   **928.3 : 22**

Ebert, Hermann. Fritz Reuter; sein leben und seine werke. Güstrow. 1874. D.   **928.3 : 81**

Richter, J: Paul F:, (*Jean Paul*). Life, compiled from various sources, together with his autobiography. Tr. by Eliza Buckminster Lee. N. Y. 1850. D.   **928.3 : 20**

Nerrlich, Paul. Jean Paul und seine zeitgenossen. Berlin. 1876. O.   **928.3 + 66**

Kramer, Gustav. Carl Ritter; ein lebensbild nach seinem handschriftlichen nachlass dargestellt. 2te durchgesehene und mit einigen reisebriefeu verm. ausg. Portr. Halle. 1875. 2 v. in 1. O.   **928.3 : 97**

Beyer, Conrad. F: Rückert, ein biographisches denkmal; mit vielen bis jetzt ungedruckten und unbekannten aktenstücken, briefen und poesieen F: Rückert's. Frankfurt a. M. 1868. O.   **928.3 : 70**

Oertel, Hugo. Hans Sachs; ein lebensbild aus dem handwerkerstande. Ill. Wiesbaden. 1881. S.   **928.3 : 106**

[Biographische skizze von] F: v. Sallet. Cassel. 1852. T.   **928.3 : 23**

Döring, J: Michael H: F: v. Schiller's biographie. Jena. 1853. S.   **928.3 : 25**

Düntzer, H: Life of Schiller. Tr. by Percy E. Pinkerton. Ill. and facsimiles. N. Y. 1883. D.   **928.3 : 45**

Scherr, Johannes. Schiller und seine zeit. N. Y. n. d. 2 v. D.   **928.3 : 24**

— *Same, eng.* Schiller and his times. From the german by Elisabeth McClellan. Phila. 1880. D.   **928.3 : 24**

Schmidt, Ferdinand. Schiller; ein lebensbild für jung und alt. 7te aufl., ill. Kreuznach. [1883]. S.   **928.3 : 99**

Sime, James. Schiller. [Foreign classics for eng. readers.] Phila. [1882]. S. **928.3 : 26**

Viehoff, H: Schiller's leben, geistesentwickelung und werke; auf der grundlage der Karl Hoffmeister'schen schriften neu bearb. Stuttg. 1874. 3 v. in 1 D.   **928.3 : 88**

[Biographische skizze von] Gustav Schwab. Cassel. 1852. T.   **928.3 : 36**

Düntzer, J: H: Joseph. Charlotte v. Stein, Göthe's freundin; ein lebensbild, mit benutzung der familienpapiere entworfen. Portr. Stuttg. 1874. 2 v. O.   **928.3 : 67**

Jung-Stilling, J: H: Heinrich Stillings jugend, jünglingsjahre, wanderschaft; mit einer einleitung von Robert Boxberger. Stuttg. [1883]. D.   **928.3 : 44**

Zeller, E: D: F: Strauss, in seinem leben und seinen schriften geschildert. 2te aufl. Bonn. 1874. O.   **928.3 : 48**

Friesen, Hermann *freiherr* v. L: Tieck; erinnerungen eines alten freundes aus den jahren 1825–1842. Portr. Wien. 1871. 2 v. D.   **928.3 : 60**

Mayer, K: F: Hartmann. L: Uhland, seine freunde und zeitgenossen; erinnerungen. Stuttg. 1867. 2 v. in 1. O.   **928.3 : 57**

[Biographische skizze von] J: Nepomuk Vogl. Cassel. 1853. T.   **928.3 : 38**

Herbst, W: J: H: Voss. Leipz. 1872–76. 2 v. in 3. O.   **928.3 : 91**
Contents. V. 1. 1751-1782. 2. 1ste abth. 1782-1802; 2te abth. 1802-1805.

Wilmanns, W: Franz. Leben und dichten Walthers von der Vogelweide. Bonn. 1882. O.   **928.3 : 71**

Ofterdinger, L. F. Christoph Martin Wielands leben und wirken in Schwaben und in der Schweiz. Heilbronn. 1877. D.   **928.3 : 87**

Zschokke, J: H: Daniel. Eine biographie; herausg. von W: Neumann. Cassel. 1853. T.   **928.3 : 39**

— Eine selbstschau : 1er t. Das schicksal und der mensch; 2er t. Welt- und gottanschauung. 2te ausg. Aarau. 1859. 2 v. S.   **928.3 : 40**

— *Same, eng.* Autobiography. Lond. 1845. O.   **928.3 : 40**

5. French authors.

Collective biogr.

Shelley, Mary Wollstonecraft, *and others.* Lives of the most eminent french writers. 1877. Phila. 1840. 2 v. in 1. D.   **928.4 : 45**
Contents. V. 1. Montaigne.—Rabelais. — Corneille. Rochefoucauld. — Molière. — La Fontaine. — Pascal.— Mme. de Sévigné. — Boileau. — Racine. — Fénélon. 2. Voltaire.—Rousseau.— Condorcet.—Mirabeau.—Mme. Roland.—Mme. de Staël.

Gautier, Theophile, Eugène C: J: Baptiste Jacquot, (*Eugène de Mirecourt*), *and others.* Famous french authors; biographical portraits of distinguished french writers. N. Y. 1879. D.   **928.4 : 38**
Contents. **Sainte-Beuve,** C: A:, Theophile Gautier.— **Jacquot,** E. C: J: B., Sainte-Beuve.— Pontmartin, A. de. Mme. Swetchine.—Imbert de Saint-Amand, A. L., Mme. de Girardin. — **Jacquot,** E. C: J: B., Arsène Houssaye; George Sand.— **Musset,** P. E. de, Alfred de Musset.—**Jacquot,** E. C: J: B., Victor Hugo.—**Gautier,** T., Paul de Kock; Alphonse de Lamartine; Gavarni; C: Baudelaire; Honoré de Balzac; Béranger.— **Jacquot,** E. C: J: B., Brizeux; H: Monnier. — **Fitzgerald,** P., Alexandre Dumas.— **Arnold,** M., Maurice de Guérin.—**Morley,** J:, Denis Diderot.—Jean de La Fontaine.

Mauris, Maurice, *marchese di Calenzano.* French men of letters. [Appleton's new handy-vol. ser.] N. Y. 1880. S.   **928.4 : 2**
Contents. Victor Hugo.—Alfred de Musset.—Théophile Gautier.—H: Murger.—Sainte-Beuve.—Gérard de Nerval.— A. Dumas, *fils.* — Émile Augier. — Octave Feuillet. — Victorien Sardou. — Alphonse Daudet.— Emile Zola.

James, H:, *jr.* French poets and novelists. Lond. 1878. D.   **928.4 : 1**
Contents. Alfred de Musset. — Theophile Gautier.— C: Baudelaire.—Honoré de Balzac.—Balzac's letters. — G: Sand. — C: de Bernard and Gustave Flaubert.— Ivan Turgenieff. — The two Ampères. — Mme. de Sabran.—Mérimée's letters.—The Théâtre français.

Castelar y Rissoll, Emilio. [Sketches of french authors]. *In his* Life of lord Byron.   **928.2 : 28**
Contents, see col. 1547.

Sainte-Beuve, C: A: Portraits of celebrated women. Tr. from the french by H. W. Preston. Bost. 1868. D.   **928.4 : 3**
Contents. Mme. de Sévigné.—Mme. de La Fayette.— Mme. de Souza.—Mme. Roland.— Mme. de Staël.— Mme. de Duras.— Mme. de Rémusat.—Mme. de Krudener.— Mme. Guizot.

Stoddard, R: H:, *ed.* Bric-a-brac series : Prosper Mérimée's letters to an incognita, with recollections by Lamartine and George Sand. N. Y. 1874. S.   **928.4 : 4**
Contents. Preface.—Prosper Mérimée, Letters to an incognita. — Alphonse de Lamartine, Twenty-five years of my life.—George Sand, Recollections.

Trollope, H: M. Corneille and Racine. [Foreign classics for eng. readers]. Phila. 1881. S.   **928.4 : 13**

Individual biogr.

Saltus, Edgar Evertson. B a l z a c. Portr. Bost. 1884. D.   **928.4 : 39**

Loménie, L: Léonard de. B e a u m a r c h a i s and his times ; sketches of french society in the 18th century from unpub. documents. Tr. by H: S. Edwards. N. Y. 1857. D.   **928.4 : 5**

Guizot, François P: Guillaume. C o r n e i l l e and his times. N. Y. 1855. D. **928.4 : 6**

Sainte-Beuve, C: A: Memoirs of Mme. D e s - b o r d e s - V a l m o r e ; with a selection from her poems. Tr. by Harriet W. Preston. Bost. 1873. D.   **928.4 : 7**

Morley, J: D i d e r o t and the encyclopædists. New ed. N. Y. 1878. O.   **928.4 : 8**

Borel, T: Count Agénor de G a s p a r i n. Tr. from the french by O. O. Howard. N. Y. 1881. D.   **928.4 : 9**

Guérin, Eugénie de. Journal ; ed. by G. S. Trébutien. Lond. 1865. D.   **928.4 : 14**

Barbou, Alfred. Great citizens of France : Victor H u g o ; his life and his works. From the french by Frances A. Shaw. Chicago. 1881. S.   **928.4 : 15**

— Victor Hugo and his time. Tr. from the french by Ellen E. Frewer. Ill. Lond. 1882. Q.   **928.4+40**

— *Same.* N. Y. 1885. Q.   **928.4+40**

Hugo, J. Adèle, *born* Foucher. Victor Hugo, by a witness of his life. Tr. from the original french by C: Edwin Wilbour. N. Y. 1864. O.   **928.4+16**

Smith, G: Barnett. Victor Hugo ; his life and work. Portr. Lond. 1885. D. **928.4 : 42**

Collins, W: Lucas. L a F o n t a i n e and other french fabulists. [Foreign classics for eng. readers]. Phila. [1882]. S.   **928.4 : 35**

Lacretelle, H: de. L a m a r t i n e and his friends. Tr. from the french by Maria E. Odell. N. Y. 1880. D.   **928.4 : 10**

Lamartine, Alfonse Marie L: de Memoirs of my youth. N. Y. 1860. O.   **928.4 : 11**

— *Same, germ.* Enthüllungen. Aus dem franz. von P. Meyer. Stuttg. 1850. 2 v. S.   **928.4 : 11**

Dumont, P: Étienne L: Recollections of M i r a - b e a u and of the first two legislative assemblies of France. 2d ed., rev. Lond. 1832. O.   **928.4 : 17**

Smith, J: Stores. Mirabeau ; a life-history. Phila. 1848. D.   **928.4 : 18**

Mahrenholtz, R: M o l i è r e ' s leben und werke, vom standpunkt der heutigen forschung. Heilbronn. 1881. O.   **928.4 : 43**

Oliphant, Margaret O. *born* Wilson, *and* F. **Tarver.** Molière. [Foreign classics for eng. readers]. Phila. 1878. S. **928.4 : 19**

Collins, W: Lucas. M o n t a i g n e. [Foreign classics for eng. readers]. Phila. [1879]. S.   **928.4 : 20**

Musset, Paul Edme de. Biography of Alfred de M u s s e t. Tr. from the french by Harriet W. Preston. Bost. 1877. D. **928.4 : 34**

Haussonville, Gabriel Paul Othenin de Cléron, *vicomte* d'. The salon of madame N e c k e r. Tr. from the french by H: M. Trollope. N. Y. 1885. Q. **928.4 : 41**

Brightwell, Cecelia Lucy. P a l i s s y the potter, or The huguenot, artist and martyr, a true narrative. N. Y. *n. d.* S. **x 928.4 : 21**

Morley, H: Palissy the potter ; [his] life, with an outline of his philosophical doctrines and a tr. of illustrative selections from his works. Bost. 1853. 2 v. D. **928.4 : 22**

Tulloch, J: P a s c a l. [Foreign classics for eng. readers]. Phila. [1878]. S. **928.4 : 23**

Jacqueline P a s c a l, or A glimpse of convent life at Port Royal. From the french of Victor Cousin, Prosper Faugère. M. Vinet and other sources, tr. by H. N.; with an introd. by W. R. Williams. N. Y. 1860. D.   **928.4 : 24**

Besant, Walter. R a b e l a i s. [Foreign classics for eng. readers]. Phila. [1880]. S.   **928.4 : 25**

Récamier, Jeanne Françoise Julie Adélaïde, *born* Bernard. Memoirs and corresp. Tr. from the french and ed. by Isaphene M. Luyster. 5th ed. Bost. 1867. S. **928.4 : 26**

Rénan, Joseph Ernest. Recollections of my youth. Tr. by C. B. Pitman. N. Y. 1883. S.   **928.4 : 37**

Brockerhoff, F. J: Jacques R o u s s e a u ; sein leben und seine werke. Leipz. 1863-74. 3 v. in 2. O.   **928.4 : 44**

Contents. V. 1. Genf-Paris, 1712 - 1741. — Paris, 1741 - 1756. 2. La Chevrette, 1756 - 1757. — Montmorency, 1757 - 1762. 3. Montmorency, 1757 - 1762, *schluss.* —Schweiz-England, 1762 - 1767.—Frankreich, in der provinz.—Paris-Eremonville, 1768 - 1778.

Graham, H: Grey. Rousseau. [Foreign classics for eng. readers]. Phila. 1883. S.   **928.4 : 33**

Morley, J: Rousseau. Lond. 1873. 2 v. O.   **928.4+27**

Rousseau, J: Jacques. Bekenntnisse. Leipz. 1854. 4 v. T.   **928.4 : 12**

Thomas, Bertha. George S a n d. (Famous women). Bost. 1883. S. **928.4 : 36**

Ritchie, Anna Isabella, *born* Thackeray. Madame de S é v i g n é. [Foreign classics for eng. readers]. Phila. [1881]. S.   **928.4 : 28**

Stevens, Abel. Madame de S t a ë l ; a study of her life and times, the first revolution and the first empire. N. Y. [1880]. 2 v. D.   **928.4 : 30**

Child, Lydia Maria. Memoirs of mme. de Staël and mme. Roland. New ed. rev. and enl. N. Y. 1854. S.   **928.4 : 29**

Tocqueville, Alexis C: H: Clérel de. Memoirs, letters and remains. Tr. from the french by the tr. of Napoleon's corresp. with king Joseph ; with add. Bost. 1862. 2 v. D.   **928.4 : 31**

6. Other literatures.

Italian.

Shelley, Mary Wollstonecraft, *and others.* Lives of eminent literary and scientific men of Italy. Phila. 1841. 2 v. D.   **928.5 : 24**
Contents. V. 1. Dante.—Petrarch.—Boccaccio.—Lorenzo de' Medici.—Bojardo.—Berni.—Ariosto.—Machiavelli. **2.** Galileo.—Guicciardini.—Vittoria Colonna.—Guarini.—Tasso.—Chiabrera.—Tassoni.—Marini.—Filicaja.—Metastasio.—Goldoni.—Alfieri.—Monti.—Ugo Foscolo.

Stebbing, H: Lives of the italian poets. 2d ed., with add. Lond. 1882. 3 v. D.   **928.5 : 2**
Contents. V. 1. Dante.—Petrarch.—Boccaccio.—Lorenzo de' Medici.—Angiolo Poliziano.—The Pulci.—Burchiello.—Girolamo Benivieni.—Serafino Aquilano.—Antonio Tibaldeo.—Giusto de' Conti.—Antonio Fulgoso.—Antonio Cornazzani dal Borzetti.—Gasparo Visconti.—Francesco Cieco. **2.** Boiardo.—Sannazzaro.—Ariosto.—Bembo.—Vittoria Colonna. Pietro Aretino.—Bernardo Tasso.—Giovan-Giorgio Trissino.—Francesco Berni.—Luigi Alamanni.—Battista Guarini.—Marco Girolamo Vida.—Girolamo Fracastoro.—Jacopo Sadoleto. **3.** Torquato Tasso.—Chiabrera.—Tassoni.—Giambattista Marini.—Marini and Murtola.—Marini and Stigliani.—Achillini and Preti.—Fulvio Testi.—Metastasio.—Apostolo Zeno.—Filicaja.—Alexander Guidi.—Frugoni.—Giuseppe Parini.—Vittorio Alfieri.—Melchior Cesarotti.—Ippolito Pindemonte.—Vincenzo Monti.—Ugo Foscolo.

Alfieri, V: *conte.* Autobiography; with an essay by W: D. Howells. Bost. 1877. S.   **928.5 : 3**

Azeglio, Giuseppe Maria Gerolamo Raffaele Massimo **Taparelli,** *marchese* d'. Recollections. Tr. with notes and an introd. by count Maffei. Lond. 1868. 2 v. D.   **928.5 : 18**

Trollope, T: Adolphus. Life of Vittoria Colonna. [Biogr. ser.] N. Y. 1877. T.   **928.5 : 16**

Balbo, Cesare. Life and times of Dante Alighieri. Tr. from the italian by F. J. Bunbury. Lond. 1852. 2 v. D.   **928.5 : 4**

Church, R: W: Dante; an essay. Added, a trans. of De monarchia by F. J. Church. Lond. 1879. D.   **928.5 : 5**

Oliphant, Margaret O., *born* Wilson. Dante. [Foreign classics for eng. readers]. Phila. [1878]. S.   **928.5 : 6**

Wegele, Franz Xaver. Dante Alighieri's leben und werke in zusammenhange dargestellt. 3te theilweise veränderte und verm. aufl. Ill. Jena. 1879. O.   **928.5+22**

Gallenga, Antonio, (*Luigi Mariotti*). Episodes of my second life; american and english experiences. Phila. 1885 [1884]. D.   **928.5 : 21**

Goldoni, C: Autobiography: Memoirs, tr. from the original french by J: Black; with an essay by W: D. Howells. Bost. 1877. S.   **928.5 : 7**

Pellico, Silvio. Le mie prigioni; memorie: My imprisonments; memoirs. Tr. from the italian by T: Roscoe. [In ital. and eng.] Parigi. 1837. O.   **928.5 : 8**

Campbell, T: Life of Petrarch. Phila. 1841. O.   **928.5+9**

Reeve, H: Petrarch. [Foreign classics for eng. readers.] Phila. [1878]. S.   **928.5 : 10**

Körting, Gustav. Petrarca's leben und werke. Leipz. 1878. O.   **928.5 : 23**

Benson, Eugene. Gaspara Stampa; with a selection from her sonnets, tr. by G: Fleming [Miss Julia Fletcher]. Bost. 1881. S.   **928.5 : 11**

Hasell, E. J. Tasso. [Foreign classics for eng. readers]. Phila. [1882]. S.   **928.5 : 17**

Spanish.

Hasell, E. J. Calderon. [Foreign classics for eng. readers]. Phila. 1880. S.   **928.5 : 19**

Trench, R: Chenevix. Calderon; his life and genius, with specimens of his plays. N. Y. 1856. D.   **928.5 : 12**

Oliphant, Margaret O., *born* Wilson. Cervantes. [Foreign classics for eng. readers]. Phila. [1881]. S.   **928.5 : 14**

Fox-Vassall, H: R:, *3d baron Holland.* Some account of the life and writings of Felix Lope da Vega. Lond. 1806. O.   **928.5 : 13**

Scandinavian and Dutch.

Nyerup, Rasmus, *and* Jens E. **Kraft.** Almindeligt litteratur-lexicon for Danmark, Norge og Island.   **15 : L**
See col. 20.

Halvorsen, J. B. Norsk forfatter-lexikon, 1814–1880.   **15 : L**
See col. 20.

Erslew, T: Hansen. Almindeligt forfatter-lexicon for kongeriget Danmark, 1814–1853.   **1[5] : L**
See col. 20.

Andersen, Hans Christian. The story of my life. Now first tr. into eng., and containing chapters add. to those pub. in the danish ed., bringing the narrative down to the Odense festival of 1867. Author's ed. Bost. 1880. D.   **928.5 : 25**

— *Same. With his* In Sweden.   **Ax 753**

— Reiseskizzen. Leipz. *n. d.* S.   **928.5 : 1**
Contents. Reiseschatten.—In Schweden.—Das märchen meines lebens.

Bremer, Fredrika. Life, letters, and posthumous works, ed. by her sister, Charlotte Bremer. Tr. from the swedish by F: Milow; [some of] the poetry tr. by Emily Nonnen. N. Y. 1880. D.   **928.5 : 20**

Butler, C: Life of Hugo Grotius, with brief minutes of the civil, ecclesiastical and literary history of the Netherlands. Lond. 1826. O.   **928.5 : 15**

10.　Genealogy and heraldry.

1.　Onomatology.

Arthur, W: An etymological dictionary of family and christian names, with an essay on their derivation and import. N. Y. 1857. D.　　　　　　　　　　**929 : 2**

Yonge, Charlotte Mary. History of christian names. New ed., rev. N. Y. 1885. D.　　　　　　　　　　**929 : 6**

Wilkinson, W: Francis. Personal names in the Bible, [interpreted and ill.] Lond. 1866. D.　　　　　　　　　**929.6 : 1**

Lower, M: Anthony. English surnames; an essay on family nomenclature; historical, etymological and humorous, with several illustrative app. 3d ed. enl. Lond. 1849. 2 v. O.　　　　　　　　　**929.2 : 8**

Bardsley, C: Wareing. English surnames; their sources and significations. 2d ed., rev. and enl. Lond. 1875. D.　　　　　**929.2 : 7**

— Curiosities of puritan nomenclature. N. Y. 1880. D.　　　　　　　　　　**929.2 : 6**

[**Norman** names, Lists and derivations of.] *In* The norman people.　　　　**942 : 10**

2.　Heraldry and insignia.

Barrington, Archibald. A familiar introduction to heraldry; explaining, in a series of lectures, the principles of the science, and showing its application to the study of history and architecture. Ill. Lond. 1848. S.　　　　　　　　　　**929 : 3**

Whitmore, W: H: The elements of heraldry; containing an explanation of the principles of the science and a glossary of the technical terms employed; with an essay upon the use of coat-armor in the U. S. N. Y. 1866. O.　　　　　　　　**929+4**

Jones, W: ·Crowns and coronations; a history of regalia. Ill. Lond. 1883. D.　**929 : 5**

Orden, wappen und flaggen, Die, aller regenten und staaten in originalgetreuen abbildungen. Leipz. 1880. Q.　　　　**929 : R1**

Macgeorge, A. Flags; some account of their history and uses. [Ill.] Lond. 1881. O.　　　　　　　　　　**929 : 7**

United States. *Bureau of navigation.* Flags of maritime nations; from the most authentic sources, prepared by order of the sec. of the navy. 5th ed. (U. S. 47th cong. 1 sess. House misc. doc. no. 48.) Wash. 1882. Q.　　　　　　　　　　*in* **929 : D**

Preble, G: H: History of the flag of the U. S. of America, and of the naval and yacht-club signals, seals and arms and principal national songs of the U. S., with a chronicle of the symbols, standards, banners, and flags of ancient and modern nations. 2d rev. ed. Ill. Bost. 1880. O.　**929.1+P2**

Hamilton, Schuyler. History of the national flag of the U. S. of America. Phila. 1852. D.　　　　　　　　　　**929.1 : 1**

3.　Special countries.

United States.

Hotten, J: Camden, *ed.* The original lists of persons of quality, emigrants, religious exiles, political rebels, serving men sold for a term of years, apprentices, children stolen, maidens pressed, and others who went from Great Britain to the american plantations, 1600—1700; with their ages, the localities where they formerly lived in the mother country; the names of the ships in which they embarked, and other interesting particulars. From mss. preserved in the state paper department of her majesty's public record office, England. Lond. 1874. Q.　　　　　**929.1 : R3**

Farmer, J: A genealogical register of the first settlers of New England; containing an alphabetical list of the governours, deputy-governours, assistants or counsellors, and ministers of the gospel in the several colonies from 1620 to 1692, representatives of the general court of Massachusetts from 1634 to 1692, graduates of Harvard college to 1662, members of the ancient and honorable artillery company to 1662, freemen admitted to the Massachusetts colony from 1630 to 1662, with many other of the early inhabitants of New England and Long Island, N. Y., from 1620 to 1675. Added, various genealogical and biographical notes collected from ancient records, manuscripts and printed works. Lancaster, Mass. 1829. O.　　**929.1 : R5**

Savage, James. A genealogical dictionary of the first settlers of New England, showing three generations of those, who came before may 1692, on the basis of Farmer's Register. Bost. 1860–62. 4 v. Q. **929.1 : R4**

Durrie, Daniel Steele. Bibliographia genealogica americana; an alphabetical index to american genealogies and pedigrees, contained in state, county and town histories, printed genealogies and kindred works. 2d ed., rev. and enl. Albany. 1878. O. **929.1 : 11**

Slocum, C: Elihu. A short history of the Slocums, Slocumbs and Slocombs of America, genealogical and biographical; embracing eleven generations of the first-named family from 1637 to 1881, with their alliances and the descendants in the female lines so far as ascertained, also the etymology of those surnames, an account of some researches in England concerning their ancestors who bore the parent surname, Slocombe, etc. Syracuse. 1882. O.　　　　　　　　　　**929.1+12**

Tenney, Horace A. Genealogy of the Tenney family, more particularly of the family of Daniel Tenney and Sylvia Kent, his wife, from 1634 and 1638 to 1875. Madison. 1875. O.　　　　　　　　　　**929.1+10**

Great Britain.

Dodd, C: Roger. A manual of dignities, privilege and precedence, incl. lists of the great public functionaries from the revolution to the present time. Lond. 1843. S. **929.2 : 5**

Burke, *Sir* J: Bernard. The general armory of England, Scotland, Ireland and Wales; comprising a registry of armorial bearings from the earliest to the present time; with a supp. Lond. 1883. Q.   **929.2 : R12**

Fairbairn, James. Crests of the families of Great Britain and Ireland, compiled from the best authorities, rev. by Lawrence Butters. Edinb. *n. d.* 2 v. O.   **929.2 : R10**

Burke, *Sir* J: Bernard. A genealogical and heraldic dictionary of the peerage and baronetage of the British empire. Lond. 1857. Q.   **929.2 : R1**

— *Same*; together with memoirs of the privy counsellors and knights. 41st ed. Lond. 1879. Q.   **929.2 : R1**

— *Same*. 46th ed. Lond. 1884. Q. **929.2 : R1**

Burke, *Sir* J: Bernard.—*Continued.*

— A genealogical history of the dormant, abeyant, forfeited and extinct peerages of the British empire. New ed. Lond. 1883. Q.   **929.2 : R4**

— A genealogical and heraldic history of the landed gentry of Great Britian and Ireland. 6th ed., with supp. Lond. 1882. 2 v. Q.   **929.2 : R3**

— Vicissitudes of families. New ed. Lond. 1883. 2 v. D.   **929.2 : 11**

Scott, *Sir* Walter. Description of the regalia of Scotland. Edinb. 1877. D.   **929.2 : 9**

Germany.

Gothaisches genealogisches taschenbuch der gräflichen häuser. Gotha. 1883. T. **929.3 : 1**

Gothaisches genealogisches taschenbuch der freiherrlichen häuser, 1882, 1883. Gotha. 1882, 1883. 2 v. T.   **929.3 : 2**

Almanach de Gotha.   **310 : 13**
    See col. 156.

XII. INDEX TO BIOGRAPHY.

SYNOPSIS OF CLASSIFICATION

AND

SUBJECT INDEX.

The system of classification in use in this library is mainly the one, devised by Mr. Melvil Dewey for the Amherst College library and described in his "Classification and Subject Index", published in 1875, and subsequently introduced, with slight modifications and amplifications, in the library of the Young Men's Association of Buffalo in 1878. The distinguishing feature of this scheme is the arrangement of a library, on the decimal basis, in nine great groups or classes, each group partitioned into nine divisions, and each division into nine sections, the whole being preceded by a group for books of a general character. The series of 999 classes thus formed, following each other in the usual numerical order, and in which each figure has a distinct meaning, the Sections being represented by units, the Divisions by tens, and the Groups by hundreds, is almost identical with the original scheme of Mr. Dewey. The only variation consists in a more or less complete rearrangement of the distribution of subjects in the divisions "Political Science", "Law", "Sermons", "Africa", and "North America", as well as changing a single section or its name here and there, and adding a division for "Libraries". In adopting the system for use, however, it was found desirable to further subdivide a large number of the original classes, by the addition of a fourth and occasionally a fifth figure. These subsections, including all of those already employed at Buffalo, but for which the author of the system is not responsible, have been added wherever it was considered expedient and in conformity with the general plan ; and the figures denoting them have in all cases been treated as decimal fractions of the original class. All these changes and additions are in no way intended as an improvement or amendment of Mr. Dewey's system of classification, but simply as an attempt to adapt it to the particular needs of this library. Since the printing of this catalogue began, our modifications have been rendered unnecessary by a minute elaboration and partial reconstruction of the "Decimal Classification " by the author himself, published in 1885, and it is a matter of regret that the thus completed system was not available for use in this library, if for no other reason, for the manifest advantages arising from a uniformity of classification in a large number of libraries. As it is, the fact must be emphasized, that the class-numbers, as employed in this library, frequently have a different meaning from those of the Dewey Decimal Classification.

For a detailed description and explanation of the principles underlying this scheme of classification, the reader is referred to either of the publications mentioned above.

Synopsis of Classification and Subject-Index.

CLASSIFICATION.

General Works.

0 Libraries.
1 Theory and scope.
2 Manuals.
3 Catalogues.
4 *Private libraries.*
5 Periodicals.
6 Societies.
7
8 Reports.
9 History.
10 Bibliography.
11 General bibliographies.
12 Special forms.
13 *Manuscripts.*
14 *Anonyms, pseudonyms, etc.*
15 Special countries.
16 Special subjects.
17 Subject catalogues.
18 Author catalogues.
19 Publishers' and antiquarian catalogues.
20 Book Rarities.
21 Manuscripts.
22 Block books.
23 Early printing.
24 Rare printing.
25 Rare binding.
26 Rare illustrations or materials.
27 Ownership.
28 Prohibited books..
29 Other rarities, curiosa
30 General Cyclopedias.
31 American.
32 English.

33 German.
34 French.
35 Italian.
36 Spanish.
37 Slavic.
38 Scandinavian.
39 Other.

40 Polygraphy.
41 American.
42 English.
43 German.
44 French.
45 Italian.
46 Spanish.
47 Slavic.
48 Scandinavian.
49 Other.

50 General Periodicals.
51 Indexes.
52 English language.
53 German "
54 French "
55 Italian "
56 Spanish "
57 Slavic languages.
58 Scandinavian "
59 Other "

.60 General Societies.
61 American.
62 English.
63 German.
64 French.
65 Italian.
66 Spanish.
67 Slavic.
68 Scandinavian.

69 Other.
70—90 (Vacant.)

Philosophy.

100 Philosophy.
101 Utility.
102 Compends.
103 Dictionaries and cyclopedias.
104 Essays, miscellany.
105 Periodicals.
106 Societies.
107 Education.
108
109 History.
110 Metaphysics.
111 Ontology.
112 Methodology.
113 Cosmology.
114—129 (Vacant.)
130 Mind and Body.
131 Mental physiology and hygiene.
132 Mental derangements.
133 Delusions, witchcraft, magic.
134 Mesmerism.
135 Sleep, dreams, somnambulism.
136 Sexes.
137 Temperaments.
138 Physiognomy.
139 Phrenology.
140 Philosophical systems.
141 Idealistic school.
142 Critical "
143 Intuitive "

(3)

144	Empirical school,		196	Spanish.		232	Christ.
145	Sensational "		197	Slavic.		233	Man.
146	Materialistic "		198	Scandinavian.		234	Salvation.
147	Pantheistic "		199	Other modern.		235	Angels.
148	Electic "					236	Death, resurrection.
149	Other. "			**Religion.**		237	*Future state.*

150 Mental Faculties.
151 Intellect.
152 Sense.
153 Understanding.
154 Memory.
155 Reason.
156 Imagination.
157 Sensibility, emotions.
158 Instincts.
159 Will.

160 Logic.
161 Inductive.
162 Deductive.
163 Assent.
164—169 (Vacant.)

170 Ethics.
171 Theoretical.
172 State.
173 Family.
174 Business.
175 Amusements.
176 Sexual.
177 Social.
178 Temperance.
179 Other topics.

180 Ancient Philosophers.
181 Oriental.
182 Early greek.
183 Sophistic, Socratic.
184 Platonic.
185 Aristotelian.
186 Pyrrhonist, New Platonist.
187 Epicurean.
188 Stoic.
189 Early christian, arabian.

190 Modern Philosophers.
191 Scotch and American.
192 English.
193 German.
194 French.
195 Italian.

200 Religion.
201 Philosophy.
202 Compends.
203 Dictionaries and cyclopedias.
204 Essays, miscellany.
205 Periodicals.
206 Societies.
207 Education.
208
209 History of theology.

210 Natural Theology.
211 Theism, atheism.
212 Pantheism.
213 Creation.
214 Providence.
215 Religion and science.
216 Evil.
217 Prayer.
218 Future life.
219

220 Bible.
.1 *Original texts and latin versions.*
.2 *English versions.*
.3 *Other versions.*
.4 *Concordances.*
.5 *Commentaries.*
.6 *Dictionaries and cyclopedias.*
.7 *Antiquities.*
.8 *Other biblical aids.*
.9 *History.*
(The same sub-sections for all the several sections of Bible.)
221 Old Testament.
222 *Historical books.*
223 *Poetical "*
224 *Prophetical "*
225 New Testament.
226 *Gospels and acts.*
227 *Epistles.*
228 *Apocalypse.*
229 Apocrypha.

230 Doctrinal.
231 God.

232 Christ.
233 Man.
234 Salvation.
235 Angels.
236 Death, resurrection.
237 *Future state.*
238 Inspiration.
239 Apologetics, Analogies.

240 Practical and Devotional.
241 Didactic.
242 Meditative.
243 Hortatory.
244 Ritual.
245 Hymnology.
246 Public worship.
247 Social "
248 Private "
249 Religious fiction and anecdote.

250 Homiletic and Pastoral.
251 Homiletics.
252 Sermons in English.
253 " German.
254 " French.
255 " Italian.
256 " Spanish.
257 " Slavic.
258 " Scandinavian.
259 " other languages.

260 Institutions and Church work.
261 Church.
262 *Ecclesiastical polity.*
263 Sabbath.
264 Baptism.
265 Lord's supper.
266 Missions.
267 *Foreign.*
268 Sunday schools.
269 Revivals.

270 Ecclesiastical History.
271 Religious orders.
272 Persecutions.
273 Doctrines.
274 Europe. .
.1 *Scotland and Ireland.*

274.2	*England and Wales.*
.3	*Germany, Austria.*
.4	*France.*
.5	*Italy.*
.6	*Spain and Portugal.*
.7	*Russia.*
.8	*Scandinavia.*
.9	*Other countries.*
275	Asia.
276	Africa.
277	North America.
.1	*United States.*
.2	*New England.*
.3	*Middle states.*
.4	*Southern states.*
.5	*Western and Pacific states.*
.6	*British America.*
.7	*Mexico.*
.8	*Central America.*
.9	*West Indies and other.*
278	South America.
279	Oceanica.
280	**Christian Churches and Sects.**
281	Oriental.
282	Roman catholic.
283	Protestant episcopal.
284	Presbyterian.
285	Congregational, Puritan.
286	Baptist.
287	Methodist.
288	Unitarian, Universalist.
289	Other christian sects.
.1	*Swedenborgians.*
290	**Non-Christian Religions.**
291	Mythology, general and comparative.
292	*Greek and Roman.*
293	*Teutonic, Northern.*
.1	*Folk-lore.*
294	Brahmanism, Buddhism.
295	Parseeism.
296	Judaism.
297	Mohammedanism.
298	Mormonism.
299	Other religious systems.

Sociology.

300	**Sociology.**
301	Philosophy.
302	Compends.
303	Dictionaries and cyclopedias.
304	Essays, miscellany.
305	Periodicals.
.1	*Statistics.*
.2	*Political science.*
.3	*Sociology.*
.4	*Law.*
.5	*Administration.*
.6	*Associations and Institutions.*
.7	*Education.*
.8	*Commerce and communication.*
.9	*Customs and Costumes.*
306	Societies.
307	Woman question.
308	
309	History of civilization.
310	**Statistics.**
311	Theory and methods.
312	Population.
313	Special topics.
314	Europe.
315	Asia.
316	Africa.
317	North America.
318	South America.
319	Oceanica.
320	**Political Science.**
321	Patriarchal institutions.
322	Feudal institutions.
323	Monarchy, constitutional.
.2	*Great Britain and dependencies.*
.3	*Other countries.*
324	Republican institutions.
.1	*United States.*
.2	*Great Britain and dependencies.*
.3	*Other countries.*
325	Colonies, emigration.
326	Slavery.
327	Foreign and domestic relations.
.1	*United States.*

327.2	*Great Britain and dependencies.*
.3	*Other countries.*
328	Legislative bodies and annals.
.1	*United States.*
.2	*Great Britain and dependencies.*
.3	*Other countries.*
329	Political essays, speeches, etc.
.1	*United States.*
.2	*Great Britain and dependencies.*
.3	*Other countries.*
330	**Political Economy.**
331	Capital and labor, co-operation.
332	Banks and money.
333	Land and stocks.
334	Credit and interest.
335	Socialism and communism.
336	Public funds and taxation.
337	Protection, free trade.
338	Production.
339	Pauperism, charity.
340	**Law.**
341	International.
342	Constitutional.
.1	*United States.*
.2	*Great Britain and dependencies.*
.3	*Other countries.*
343	Statute and Common.
.1	*United States.*
.2	*Great Britain and dependencies.*
.3	*Other countries.*
344	Equity.
345	Criminal.
.1	*United States.*
.2	*Great Britain and dependencies.*
.3	*Other countries.*
346	Maritime, martial.
347	Civil and canon.
348	Administrative.
.1	*United States.*
.2	*Great Britain and dependencies.*
.3	*Other countries.*
349	Evidence, forms of practice.

350 Administration.	
.1	*United States.*
.2	*Great Britain and dependencies.*
.3	*Other countries.*
(Same sub-sections for all the sections 351-355, 359.)	
351	Civil service.
352	*Treasury.*
353	*Interior.*
354	*Police.*
355	Army.
356	*Infantry.*
357	*Cavalry.*
358	*Artillery.*
359	Navy.
360 Associations and Institutions.	
361	Charitable.
362	Religious.
363	Political.
364	Reformatory and sanitary.
365	Prisons.
366	Secret societies.
367	Trades unions.
368	Insurance.
.1	*Fire.*
.2	*Life.*
369	Other associations.
370 Education.	
371	Teachers, methods, discipline.
372	Elementary.
.1	*Kindergartens.*
373	Higher.
374	Self-education.
375	Classical and real.
376	Of women.
377	Religious and secular.
378	Schools, universities.
379	Reports.
380 Commerce, Communication.	
.1	*United States.*
.2	*Great Britain and dependencies.*
.3	*Other countries.*
(Same sub-sections for first five sections of Commerce.)	
381	Domestic trade.
382	Foreign trade.
383	Post office.

384	Telegraph.
385	Railroad and express.
386	Canal transportation.
387	River and ocean-transportation.
388	City transit.
389	Weights, measures.
390 Customs and Costumes.	
391	Ancient.
392	Medieval.
393	Modern.
.1	*Etiquette.*
394	*Europe.*
395	*Asia.*
396	*Africa.*
397	*North America.*
398	*South America.*
399	*Oceanica.*

Philology.

400 Philology.	
401	Philosophy.
402	Compends.
403	Dictionaries and cyclopedias.
404	Essays, miscellany.
405	Periodicals.
406	Societies.
407	Education.
408	Universal language.
409	History.
410 Comparative.	
411	Orthography.
412	Etymology.
413	Dictionaries.
414	Phonology.
415	Grammar.
416	Prosody.
417	Inscriptions.
418	Texts.
419	Hieroglyphics.
420 English Language.	
421	Orthography.
422	Etymology.
423	Dictionaries.
424	Synonyms.
425	Grammar.
426	Prosody.
427	Dialects.
428	School texts.
429	Anglo-Saxon.

430 German Language.	
431	Orthography.
432	Etymology.
433	Dictionaries.
434	Synonyms.
435	Grammar.
436	Prosody.
437	Dialects.
438	School texts.
439	Dutch and Low German.
440 French Language.	
441	Orthography.
442	Etymology.
443	Dictionaries.
444	Synonyms.
445	Grammar.
446	Prosody.
447	Dialects.
448	School texts.
449	Provençal.
450 Italian Language	
451	Orthography.
452	Etymology.
453	Dictionaries.
454	Synonyms.
455	Grammar.
456	Prosody.
457	Dialects.
458	School texts.
459	Rumansh and Wallachian.
460 Spanish Language.	
461	Orthography.
462	Etymology.
463	Dictionaries.
464	Synonyms.
465	Grammar.
466	Prosody.
467	Dialects.
468	School texts.
469	Portuguese.
470 Latin Language.	
471	Orthography.
472	Etymology.
473	Dictionaries.
474	Synonyms.
475	Grammar.
476	Prosody.
477	Dialects.
478	School texts.
479	Minor Italic.

480	**Greek Language.**	515	Conic sections.	554.6	*Spain, Portugal.*
481	Orthography.	516	Analytical geometry.	.7	*Russia.*
482	Etymology.	517	Calculus.	.8	*Scandinavia.*
483	Dictionaries.	518	Quaternions.	.9	*Other countries.*
484	Synonyms.	519	Special applications.	555	Asia.
485	Grammar.	**520**	**Astronomy.**	.1	*China.*
486	Prosody.	521	Theoretical.	.2	*Japan.*
487	Dialects.	522	Practical.	.3	*Arabia.*
488	School texts.	523	Descriptive.	.4	*India.*
489	Modern Greek.	524	Maps.	.5	*Persia.*
490	**Other Languages.**	525	Observations.	.6	*Asiatic Turkey.*
491	Chinese, Japanese.	526	Figure of the earth.	.7	*Asiatic Russia.*
492	Egyptian.	527	Navigation.	.8	*Afghanistan.*
493	Semitic.	528	Almanacs.	.9	*Other countries.*
494	Indian.	529	Chronology.	556	Africa.
495	Iranian.	**530**	**Physics.**	557	North America.
496	Keltic.	531	Mechanics.	.1	*United States.*
497	Slavic.	532	Hydrostatics.	.2	*Eastern states.*
498	Scandinavian.	533	Pneumatics.	.3	*Middle states.*
.1	*Swedish.*	534	Acoustics.	.4	*Southern states.*
.2	*Norwegian.*	535	Optics.	.5	*Western and Pa-*
.3	*Danish.*	536	Heat.		*cific states.*
499	Other languages.	537	Electricity.	.6	*British America.*
		538	Magnetism.	.7	*Mexico.*
	Natural Science.	539	Molecular physics.	.8	*Central America.*
500	**Natural Science.**	**540**	**Chemistry.**	.9	*West Indies.*
501	Philosophy.	541	Theoretical.	558	South America.
502	Compends.	542	Practical and experi-	559	Oceanica.
503	Dictionaries and cy-		mental.	**560**	**Paleontology.**
	clopedias.	543	Analysis.	561	Plants.
504	Essays, miscellany.	544	*Qualitative.*	562	Invertebrates.
505	Periodicals.	545	*Quantitative.*	563	*Protozoa, radiates.*
.1	*Mathematics.*	546	Inorganic.	564	*Mollusca.*
.2	*Astronomy.*	547	Organic.	565	*Articulates.*
.3	*Physics.*	548	Crystallography.	566	Vertebrates.
.4	*Chemistry.*	549	Mineralogy.	567	*Fishes, Reptiles.*
.5	*Geology.*	**550**	**Geology.**	.1	*Reptiles, amphib-*
.6	*Paleontology.*	551	Physical geography.		*ians.*
.7	*Biology.*	.1	*Land.*	568	*Birds.*
.8	*Botany.*	.2	*Ocean.*	569	*Mammals.*
.9	*Zoology.*	552	Meteorology.	**570**	**Biology, Anthro-**
506	Societies.	.1	*Reports.*		**pology.**
	(Same sub-sections as under 505.)	.2	*Medical climatology.*	571	Prehistoric arche-
507	Education.	553	Dynamical geology.		ology.
508	Scientific expeditions.	554	Europe.	572	Ethnology.
509	History of science.	.1	*Scotland, Ireland.*	573	Natural history of
510	**Mathematics.**	.2	*England and Wales.*		man.
511	Arithmetic.	.3	*Germany, Austria.*	574	Homologies.
512	Algebra.	.4	*France.*	575	Evolution.
513	Geometry.	.5	*Italy.*	576	Embryology.
514	Trigonometry.			577	Spontaneous genera-
					tion.
				578	Microscopy.

(7)

, 579   Collectors' manuals.

580 Botany.
581   Physiological.
582   Systematic.
583   Geographical distribution.
584   Europe.
585   Asia.
586   Africa.
587   North America.
588   South America.
589   Oceanica.

590 Zoology.
591   Comparative anatomy.
592   Invertebrates.
593   *Protozoa, radiates.*
594   *Mollusca.*
595   *Articulates.*
596   Vertebrates.
597   *Fishes, Reptiles.*
 .1   *Reptiles, amphibians.*
598   *Birds.*
599   *Mammals.*

Useful Arts.

600 Useful Arts.
601   Philosophy.
602   Compends.
603   Dictionaries and cyclopedias.
604   Essays, miscellany.
605   Periodicals.
 .1   *Medicine.*
 .2   *Engineering.*
 .3   *Agriculture.*
 .4   *Domestic economy.*
 .5   *Communication.*
 .6   *Chemical technology.*
 .7   *Manufactures.*
 .8   *Mechanic trades.*
 .9   *Building.*
606   Societies, exhibitions.
(Same sub-sections as under 605.)
607   Education.
608   Patents.
609   History of inventions.

610 Medicine.
611   Anatomy.
612   Physiology.
613   Hygiene, gymnastics.
614   Public health.
615   Materia medica, therapeutics.
616   Pathology, theory and practice.
617   Surgery, dentistry.
618   Obstetrics, sexual science.
619   Veterinary medicine.

620 Engineering.
621   Mechanical.
622   Topographical.
623   Military.
624   Bridge.
625   Road and railroad.
626   Canal.
627   River and harbor.
628   Hydraulic, mining.
629   Instruments and field books.

630 Agriculture.
631   Soil and preparation.
632   Pests and hindrances.
633   Productions of the soil.
 .1   *Forestry.*
634   Fruits, orchards.
635   Garden.
 .1   *Flower-culture.*
 .2   *Kitchen-gardening.*
636   Domestic animals.
 .1   *Horses.*
 .2   *Cattle, sheep, swine.*
 .3   *Poultry.*
 .4   *Dogs.*
 .5   *Other.*
637   Dairy.
638   Bees, silkworms.
639   Fishing, trapping.

640 Domestic Economy.
641   Cookery.
642   Confectionery.
643   Food and dining.
644   Fuel and lights.
645   Furniture.
646   Clothing and toilet.
647   Servants.
648   Laundry.
649   Nursery and sickroom.

650 Communication, Commerce.
651   Writing.
652   *Penmanship.*
653   *Short-hand.*
654   Telegraphy, telephony.
655   Printing, publishing.
656   Sailing, railroading.
657   Book-keeping.
658   Business manuals.
659   Other topics.

660 Chemical Technology.
661   Chemicals.
662   Pyrotechnics, explosives.
663   Wines, liquors, ales.
664   Sugar, salt, starch.
665   Lights, gas, oil, etc.
666   Glass.
667   Dyeing and bleaching, inks.
668   Assaying.
669   Metallurgy.

670 Manufactures.
671   Metal working.
672   *Iron and steel.*
673   Stone and clay.
674   Wood and lumber.
675   Leather and rubber.
676   Paper, celluloid.
677   Textile fabrics.
678   *Cotton.*
679   Flour and other.

680 Mechanic Trades.
681   Watch and instrument making.
682   Blacksmithing.
683   Lock and gun-making.
684   Carriage and cabinet-making.
685   Saddlery, shoe-making.
686   Book-binding.
687   Clothes-making.
688   Toy-making.
689   Other trades.

690 Building.
691   Materials.
692   Plans, specifications.
693   Masonry.

694	Carpentry.	737	Numismatics.	782	Dramatic.
695	Slating and tiling.	738	Pottery and metals.	783	Church.
696	Plumbing, gas and steam fitting.	739	Collections of sculptures.	784	Vocal.
697	Warming and ventilation.	**740**	**Drawing and Design.**	785	Instrumental.
				786	*Piano and organ.*
698	Painting, glazing, paper-hanging.	741	Free-hand.	787	*String instruments·*
		742	Perspective.	788	*Wind instruments.*
699	Car and Ship-building.	743	Art anatomy.	789	Associations and institutions.
		744	Mathematical drawing.	**790**	**Amusements.**
	Fine Arts.	745	Ornamentation.	791	Entertainments.
700	**Fine Arts.**	746	*Ancient.*	792	*Theater.*
701	Philosophy, æsthetics.	747	*Medieval.*	.1	*Amateur theatricals.*
702	Compends.	748	*Modern.*	793	In-door amusements.
703	Dictionaries and cyclopedias.	749 ·	Collections of drawings.	794	*Chess.*
704	Essays, miscellany.	**750**	**Painting.**	795	*Other games.*
705	Periodicals.	751	Materials, methods.	796	Out-door sports.
706	Societies.	752	Color.	797	*Boating, ball.*
707	Education.	753	Flemish and Dutch schools.	798	*Horsemanship, racing.*
708	Galleries.	754	French schools.	799	*Field sports.*
709	History.	755	Italian schools.	.1	*Fishing.*
710	**Landscape gardening.**	756	Other schools.	.2	*Hunting.*
711	Public parks.	757	Portrait.	.3	*Shooting.*
712	Private grounds.	758	Landscape, marine.		
713	Walks and drives.	759	Collections of paintings.		**Literature.**
714	Water, fountains.	**760**	**Engraving.**	**800**	**Literature.**
715	Trees and hedges.	761	Wood.	801	Philosophy.
716	Plants and flowers.	762	Steel, copper.	802	Compends.
717	Arbors.	763	Lithography.	803	Dictionaries and cyclopedias.
718	Monuments.	764 ·	Chromolithography.	804	Essays, miscellany.
719	Cemeteries.	765	Line, stipple.	805	Periodicals.
720	**Architecture.**	766	Mezzotint, aquatint.	806	Societies.
721	Architectural construction.	767	Etching.	807	Courses of reading.
		768	Bank note, machine.	808	
722	Ancient and Oriental.	769 ·	Collections of engravings.	809	History.
723	Medieval, Gothic.	**770**	**Photography.**	**810**	**Treatises and Collections.**
724	Modern.	771	Materials, chemistry.	811	Poetry.
725	Public buildings.	772	Silver processes.	.1	*History.*
726	Church.	773	Gelatine and pigment processes.	.2	*Criticism.*
727	School.	774	Heliotype, etc.	(Same sub-sections for all sections 812–819.)	
728	Domestic and rural.	775	Photolithography.	812	Drama.
729	Of special countries.	776	Photozincography.	813	Romance.
730	**Plastic arts.**	777	Photo-engraving.	814	Essays.
731	Materials and methods.	778	Special applications.	815	Rhetoric and oratory.
		779	Collections of photographs.	816	Letters.
732	Ancient sculpture.	**780**	**Music.** ·	817	Satire.
733	*Greek and Roman.*	781	Theory. .	818	Humor.
734	Medieval sculpture.			819	Miscellany.
735	Modern sculpture.				
736	Carving, gems, seals.				

(9) ;

820	**English Literature.**	853	Italian Romance.	**890**	**Minor Literatures.**
.1	*American authors.*	854	" Essays.	891	Chinese, Japanese.
.2	*British authors.*	855	" Oratory.	892	Egyptian.
.4	*History.*	856	" Letters.	893	Semitic.
.5	*Criticism.*	857	" Satire.	894	Indian.

820 **English Literature.**
.1 *American authors.*
.2 *British authors.*
.4 *History.*
.5 *Criticism.*
(Same sub-sections for all sections of English literature.)
821 English Poetry.
822 " Drama.
.3 *Shakspere.*
823 " Romance.
824 " Essays.
825 " Oratory.
826 " Letters.
827 " Satire.
828 " Humor.
829 " Miscellany.
.3 *Quotations.*
830 **German Literature.**
.1 *History.*
.2 *Criticism.*
(Same sub-sections for all the sections 831-838.)
831 German Poetry.
832 " Drama.
833 " Romance.
834 " Essays.
835 " Oratory.
836 " Letters.
837 " Satire.
838 " Humor.
839 " Miscellany.
.1 *Quotations.*
840 **French Literature.**
.1 *History.*
.2 *Criticism.*
(Same sub-sections for all the sections 841-848.)
841 French Poetry.
842 " Drama.
843 " Romance.
844 " Essays.
845 " Oratory.
846 " Letters.
847 " Satire.
848 " Humor.
849 " Miscellany.
.1 *Quotations.*
850 **Italian Literature.**
.1 *History.*
.2 *Criticism.*
(Same sub-sections for all the sections 851-858.)
851 Italian Poetry.
852 " Drama.

853 Italian Romance.
854 " Essays.
855 " Oratory.
856 " Letters.
857 " Satire.
858 " Humor.
859 " Miscellany.
.1 *Quotations.*
860 **Spanish, Portuguese Literatures.**
.1 *History.*
.2 *Criticism.*
(Same sub-sections for all the sections 861-868.)
861 Spanish Poetry.
862 " Drama.
863 " Romance.
864 " Essays.
865 " Oratory.
866 " Letters.
867 " Satire.
868 " Humor.
869 " Miscellany.
.1 *Quotations.*
870 **Latin Literature.**
.1 *History.*
.2 *Criticism.*
(Same sub-sections for all sections of Latin literature.)
871 Latin Poetry.
872 *Dramatic.*
873 *Epic.*
874 *Lyric and other.*
875 " Oratory.
876 " Letters.
877 " Satire.
878 " Philosophy.
879 " History.
880 **Greek Literature.**
.1 *History.*
.2 *Criticism.*
(Same sub-sections for all sections of Greek literature.)
881 Greek Poetry.
882 *Dramatic.*
883 *Epic.*
884 *Lyric and other.*
885 " Oratory.
886 " Letters.
887 " Humor and miscellany.
888 " Philosophy.
889 " History.

890 **Minor Literatures.**
891 Chinese, Japanese.
892 Egyptian.
893 Semitic.
894 Indian.
895 Iranian.
896 Keltic.
897 Slavic.
898 Scandinavian.
.1 *Swedish.*
.2 *Norwegian.*
.3 *Danish.*
899 Other languages.
.1 *Dutch, Flemish.*

History.

900 **History.**
901 Philosophy.
902 Compends, chronology.
903 Dictionaries and cyclopedias.
904 Essays, miscellany.
905 Periodicals.
.1 *Geography.*
.2 *Biography.*
.3 *Ancient history.*
.4 *Europe.*
.5 *Asia.*
.6 *Africa.*
.7 *North America.*
.8 *South America.*
.9 *Oceanica and Polar regions.*
906 Societies.
.1 *Geography.*
.2 *History.*
907 Education.
908 Charts.
909 Universal histories.
910 **Geography and Description.**
911 Historical.
912 Ancient, medieval.
913 Modern.
.1 *General travels.*
.2 *Adventures.*
914 Europe.
.1 *Scotland, Ireland.*
.2 *England and Wales.*
.3 *Germany, Austria.*
.4 *France.*

914.5	*Italy.*	918.7	*Venezuela.*	929.29	*Non-christian.*
.6	*Spain, Portugal.*	.8	*Guiana.*	.3	*German.*
.7	*Russia.*	.9	*Other countries.*	.4	*French.*
.8	*Scandinavia.*	919	Oceanica.	.5	*Other modern.*
.9	*Minor countries.*	.1	*Malaysia.*	.6	*Ancient.*
.91	*Holland, Belgium.*	.2	*Sunda, Borneo, Celebes.*	923	Of sociology.
.92	*Switzerland.*			.1	*American.*
.93	*Greece.*	.3	*Australasia.*	.11	*Presidents.*
.94	*European Turkey.*	.4	*Australia.*	.12	*Statesmen, politicians, etc.*
.95	*Southern islands.*	.5	*New Guinea, New Zealand.*		
.96	*Northern islands.*			.13	*Bankers, capitalists, financiers.*
915	Asia.	.6	*Polynesia.*		
.1	*China.*	.7	*Isolated islands.*	.14	*Lawyers, judges, criminals.*
.2	*Japan.*	.8	**Polar regions.**		
.3	*Arabia.*	.9	*Antarctic regions.*	.15	*Soldiers, sailors.*
.4	*India.*	**920**	**Biography.**	.16	*Philanthropists.*
.5	*Persia.*	.1	*American.*	.17	*Educators.*
.6	*Asiatic Turkey.*	.2	*British.*	.18	*Merchants, R. R. officials.*
.7	*Asiatic Russia.*	.3	*German.*		
.8	*Afghanistan, Beloochistan.*	.4	*French.*	.19	*Travelers, society.*
		.5	*Other modern.*	.2	*British.*
.9	*Other countries.*	.6	*Ancient.*	.21	*Kings, queens, rulers.*
916	Africa.	921	Of philosophy.		
.1	*Barbary.*	.1	*American.*	.22	*Nobles, statesmen, politicians.*
.2	*Egypt.*	.2	*British.*		
.3	*Nubia and Abyssinia.*	.3	*German.*	.23	*Bankers, capitalists, financiers.*
		.4	*French.*		
.4	*Nile sources.*	.5	*Other modern.*	.24	*Lawyers, judges, criminals.*
.5	*Niger region.*	.6	*Ancient.*		
.6	*South central.*	922	Of theology.	.25	*Soldiers, sailors.*
.7	*Congo.*	.1	*American.*	.26	*Philanthropists.*
.8	*South Africa.*	.11	*Oriental.*	.27	*Educators.*
.9	*Islands.*	.12	*Roman catholic.*	.28	*Merchants, R. R. officials.*
917	North America.	.13	*Protestant episcopal.*		
.1	*United States.*			.29	*Travelers, society.*
.2	*Eastern states.*	.14	*Presbyterian.*	.3	*German.*
.3	*Middle states.*	.15	*Puritan, Congregational.*	.4	*French.*
.4	*Southern states.*			.5	*Other modern.*
.5	*Western and Pacific states.*	.16	*Baptist.*	.6	*Ancient.*
		.17	*Methodist.*	924	Of philology.
.51	*Wisconsin.*	.18	*Unitarian, Universalist and other.*	.1	*American.*
.52	*Milwaukee.*			.2	*British.*
.6	*British America.*	.19	*Non-christian.*	.3	*German.*
.7	*Mexico.*	.20	*British.*	.4	*French.*
.8	*Central America.*	.21	*Oriental.*	.5	*Other modern.*
.9	*West Indies.*	.22	*Roman catholic.*	.6	*Ancient.*
918	South America.	.23	*Anglican church.*	(Same sub-sections for all succeeding sections of Biography.)
.1	*Brazil.*	.24	*Presbyterian.*	
.2	*Argentine Republic.*	.25	*Puritan, Congregational.*	925	Of science.
.3	*Chili.*			926	Of useful arts.
.4	*Bolivia.*	.26	*Baptist.*	927	Of fine arts.
.5	*Peru.*	.27	*Methodist.*	928	Of literature.
.6	*Ecuador. Colombia.*	.28	*Unitarian, Universalist and other.*	929	**Genealogy, Heraldry.**

(11)

930 Ancient History.

931	Chinese.
932	Egyptian.
933	Jewish.
934	Indian.
935	Persian.
936	Keltic.
937.	Roman.
.1	*Barbaric invasions.*
938	Greek.
939	Minor countries.

940 Europe.

941	Scotland and Ireland.
942	England and Wales.
.1	*1st period, to 1066.*
.2	*2d period, 1066–1485.*
.3	*3d period, 1485–1603.*
.4	*4th period, 1603–1688.*
.5	*5th period, 1688–1820.*
.6	*6th period, 1820—.*
943	Germany, Austria.
944	France.
.1	*1st period, to 752.*
.2	*2d period, 752–1498.*
.3	*3d period, 1498–1610.*
.4	*4th period, 1610–1789.*
.5	*5th period, 1789–1815.*
.6	*6th period, 1815—.*
945	Italy.
946	Spain and Portugal.
947	Russia.
948	Scandinavia.
.1	*Sweden.*
.2	*Norway.*
.3	*Denmark.*
949	Minor European states.
.1	*Holland, Belgium.*
.2	*Switzerland.*
.3	*Byzantine Empire, Modern Greece.*
.4	*European Turkey.*
.5	*Other countries.*

950 Asia.

951	China.
952	Japan.
953	Arabia.
954	India.
955	Persia.
956	Asiatic Turkey.
957	Asiatic Russia.
958	Afghanistan, Beloochistan.
959	Other countries.

960 Africa.

961	Barbary states.
962	Egypt.
963	Nubia, Abyssinia.
964	Nile sources.
965	Niger region.
966	South central.
967	*Congo country.*
968	South Africa.
969	Islands.

970 North America.

.1	*American indians.*
971	United States.
.1	*1st period, to 1776.*
.2	*2d period, 1776–1789.*
.3	*3d period, 1789–1860.*
.4	*4th period, 1860–1865.*
.5	*5th period, 1865—.*
972	Eastern states.
.1	*Maine.*
.2	*New Hampshire.*
.3	*Vermont.*
.4	*Massachusetts.*
.5	*Rhode Island.*
.6	*Connecticut.*
973	Middle states.
.1	*New York.*
.2	*New Jersey.*
.3	*Pennsylvania.*
.4	*Delaware.*
974	Southern states.
.1	*Maryland.*
.2	*Virginia, West Virginia.*
.3	*North and South Carolina.*
.4	*Georgia.*
.5	*Florida.*
.6	*Alabama, Mississippi, Louisiana.*
.7	*Kentucky, Tennessee.*
974.8	*Missouri, Arkansas.*
.9	*Texas, Indian Territory.*
975	Western and Pacific states and territories.
.1	*Ohio, Indiana, Illinois.*
.2	*Michigan.*
.3	*Wisconsin.*
.31	*Separate counties.*
.32	*Milwaukee.*
.33	*Other cities.*
.4	*Iowa.*
.5	*Minnesota.*
.6	*Missouri valley states and territories.*
.7	*Rocky mountain states and territories.*
.8	*Pacific coast states and territories.*
.9	*Alaska.*
976	British America.
977	Mexico.
978	Central America.
979	West Indies and other.

980 South America.

981	Brazil.
982	Argentine Republic.
983	Chili.
984	Bolivia.
985	Peru.
986	Ecuador, Colombia.
987	Venezuela.
988	Guiana.
989	Other countries.

990 Oceanica.

991	Malaysia.
992	*Sunda, Borneo, Celebes.*
993	Australasia.
994	*Australia.*
995	*New Guinea, New Zealand.*
996	Polynesia.
997	Isolated islands.
998	Polar regions.
999	*Antarctic regions.*

SUBJECT-INDEX.

The numbers refer to classes.

(13)

The numbers refer to classes.

The numbers refer to classes.

The numbers refer to classes.

The numbers refer to classes.

The numbers refer to classes.

(21)

The numbers refer to classes.

The numbers refer to classes.

The numbers refer to classes.

The numbers refer to classes.

The numbers refer to classes.

The numbers refer to classes.

The numbers refer to classes.

The numbers refer to classes.

The numbers refer to classes.

ERRATA.

Col.	123,	line 31,	for	Fisher	read	Fischer.
"	166,	" 29,	"	Greely	"	Greeley.
"	523,	" 65,	"	James Fletcher	"	John.
"	549,	" 27,	"	" "	"	"
"	783.	" 18,	"	Lander	"	Lauder.
"	891,	" 55,	"	Wilson, Alexander	"	Andrew.
"	1010,	" 74,	"	General	"	Genuine.
"	1095,	" 4.	"	Abel	"	Abu.
"	1171,	" 37,	"	Schönmann	"	Schömann.
"	1286,	" 29,	"	Broughton	"	Boughton.
"	1307,	" 3,	"	Willis	"	Wills.
"	1315,	" 9,	"	Landsell	"	Lansdell.
"	1437,	" 72,	"	Alex. Brown	"	Alex. Wilson.
"	1438,	" 19,	"	Maron	"	Mason.
"	1444,	" 27,	"	18. und 18.	"	18. und 19.
"	1456,	" 40,	"	Morton	"	Norton.
"	1538,	" 58,	"	lives	"	loves.
"	1541,	" 32,	"	Irvinginana	"	Irvingiana.
"	1546,	" 64,	"	Sharp	"	Shairp.

Col. 784 after line 14, *add:* Lauder, *see* **Lander**, *misprint.*
" 1127 after line 2, *add:* Contents, *see* Deutscher katalog, p. 35.
" 1301 under **Rein**, *read* Japan; travels *etc.*
" 1482 after line 6, *add:* the signers of.

Col. 508. 1168, 1176, W: **Shepard** *is a pseud. for* W: Shepard **Walsh.**
" 1434, E. Conder **Gray** *is a pseud. for* Alexander Hay **Japp.**